Contents

KU-504-504

2018/19

THE DIRECTORY OF GRANT MAKING TRUSTS

WEST DUNBARTONSHIRE LIBRARIES

25th edition

Ian Pembridge, Mairéad Bailie, Rachel Cain, Denise Lillya, Jennifer Reynolds and Judith Turner

Additional research by Rhiannon Doherty, Anthony Robson and Joanne Sarginson

Published by the Directory of Social Change (Registered Charity no. 800517 in England and Wales)
Head office: Resource for London, 352 Holloway Rd, London N7 6PA
Northern office: Suite 103, 1 Old Hall Street, Liverpool L3 9HG
Tel: 020 7697 4200

Visit www.dsc.org.uk to find out more about our books, subscription funding website and training events. You can also sign up for e-newsletters so that you're always the first to hear about what's new.

The publisher welcomes suggestions and comments that will help to inform and improve future versions of this and all of our titles. Please give us your feedback by emailing publications@dsc.org.uk.

It should be understood that this publication is intended for guidance only and is not a substitute for professional or legal advice. No responsibility for loss occasioned as a result of any person acting or refraining from acting can be accepted by the authors or publisher.

First published by Charities Aid Foundation 1968
Second edition 1971
Third edition 1974
Fourth edition 1975
Fifth edition 1977
Sixth edition 1978
Seventh edition 1981
Eighth edition 1983
Ninth edition 1985
Tenth edition 1987
Eleventh edition 1989
Twelfth edition 1991
Thirteenth edition 1993
Fourteenth edition 1995
Fifteenth edition 1997
Sixteenth edition 1999
Seventeenth edition published by Directory of Social Change 2001
Eighteenth edition 2003
Nineteenth edition 2005
Twentieth edition 2007
Twenty-first edition 2010
Twenty-second edition 2012
Twenty-third edition 2014
Twenty-fourth edition 2015
Twenty-fifth edition 2017

Copyright © Directory of Social Change 2001, 2003, 2005, 2007, 2010, 2012, 2014, 2015, 2017

All rights reserved. **No part of this book may be stored in a retrieval system or reproduced in any form whatsoever without prior permission in writing from the publisher.** This book is sold subject to the condition that it shall not, by way of trade or otherwise, be lent, re-sold, hired out or otherwise circulated without the publisher's prior permission in any form of binding or cover other than that in which it is published, and without a similar condition including this condition being imposed on the subsequent purchaser.

The publisher and author have made every effort to contact copyright holders. If anyone believes that their copyright material has not been correctly acknowledged, please contact the publisher **who will be pleased to rectify the omission.**

The moral right of the author has been asserted in accordance with the Copyrights, Designs and Patents Act 1988.

ISBN 978 1 78482 042 8

British Library Cataloguing in Publication Data
A catalogue record for this book is available from the British

Cover design by Kate Griffith
Text designed by Eugenie Dodd Typographics, London
Typeset by Marlinzo Services, Frome
Printed and bound in Great Britain by CPI Group, Croydon

WEST DUNBARTONSHIRE LIBRARIES TITLE

C 03 0271275

Askews & Holts	28-Sep-2017
361.7630941	£145.00
WESDU	Basement

Foreword

Congratulations on your wise investment in this excellent publication, which will provide invaluable orientation to the diversity of funding offered by the UK's grant-making foundations.

Grants are an increasingly vital source of support for civil society. Foundation grant-making in the UK is now at a record £2.7 billion, according to our 2016 report *Giving Trends: Top 300 Foundation Grant-makers*, which makes grant-making foundations the biggest single source of grant funding to the voluntary sector. At the same time, grants from government are waning as it increasingly shifts its funding priorities towards contracts. This matters, because grants represent a unique social currency that enables charities to be innovative, resilient, and responsive in pursuit of their mission. So while funding from grant-making foundations cannot be expected to replace the loss of government grants, their sustained commitment to maintaining their level of grant spend should be celebrated.

The nature of the grants is as important as the amount. The UK has nearly 13,000 grant-making foundations (according to NCVO's *UK Civil Society Almanac 2017*), and these organisations bring pluralism and creativity to civil society, backing unpopular causes, preserving what works and challenging what does not. They need not be driven by short-term political or economic cycles and can weather history's storms in a way that other sources of funding cannot. They come in all shapes and sizes, offering support to causes ranging from research on the human genome to repairing village halls – a variety of provision that reflects the vibrant diversity of UK society. So the good news is that whatever cause you are fundraising for, you are likely to find a good potential match within the pages of this volume.

In order to make grants effectively, grant-making foundations increasingly rely on good data to inform decision-making and help them make the most of their resources. Equally, in this tough climate for fundraisers, data on who is funding what, where, and how can make all the difference.

The Directory of Grant Making Trusts is an invaluable source of quality data connecting fundraisers with grant-making foundations. By providing such data, the directory saves fundraisers and grant-makers alike an enormous amount of time, effort and, ultimately, precious resources. Most importantly, the directory opens up new opportunities for grant-making foundations to build partnerships with grantees. After all, it is these relationships that enable funders to achieve their charitable objectives, preserving social good when it is under threat and catalysing it where it is absent.

Carol Mack
Chief Executive, Association of Charitable Foundations (ACF)

About the Directory of Social Change

The Directory of Social Change (DSC) has a vision of an independent voluntary sector at the heart of social change. We believe that the activities of independent charities, voluntary organisations and community groups are fundamental to achieve social change. We exist to support these organisations in achieving their goals.

We do this by:

- Providing practical tools that organisations and activists need, including online and printed publications, training courses, and conferences on a huge range of topics
- Acting as a 'concerned citizen' in public policy debates, often on behalf of smaller charities, voluntary organisations and community groups
- Leading campaigns and stimulating debate on key policy issues that affect those groups
- Carrying out research and providing information to influence policymakers, as well as offering bespoke research for the voluntary sector

DSC is the leading provider of information and training for the voluntary sector and publishes an extensive range of guides and handbooks covering subjects such as fundraising, management, communication, finance and law. Our subscription-based website contains a wealth of information on funding from grant-making charities, companies and government sources. We run more than 300 training courses each year, including bespoke in-house training provided at the client's location. DSC conferences and fairs, which take place throughout the year, also provide training on a wide range of topics and offer a welcome opportunity for networking.

For details of all our activities, and to order publications and book courses, go to www.dsc.org.uk, call 020 7697 4200 or email cs@dsc.org.uk.

Introduction

After 25 editions, *The Directory of Grant Making Trusts* (DGMT) is still a staple of charity bookshelves throughout the country. This is a reflection of your repeated success. As we celebrate the book's silver anniversary we are also celebrating the charities listed in this guide and the thousands that benefit from their grant-giving. From the outset we have strived to match you with the funding you need and the focus of our Research Team today is still helping you to help others. As you dip into this special edition we hope that the information inside allows you to continue achieving your organisation's goals.

The Charities Aid Foundation published the first edition of DGMT in 1968 and it has been researched and published by DSC since 2001. Over this time the title has gained a notable reputation as a comprehensive guide to UK grant-making charities and their funding policies. It is designed to provide a bridge between the grant-makers and fundraising communities in the UK. Today, as the directory approaches a landmark 50th year in print, it is hard to imagine the difficulties which must have been encountered and the amount of time spent trying to obtain funds from these charities before DGMT brought together so many of them in one place.

DGMT remains a key source of information with each entry reflecting, where possible, the trustees' own view of policies, priorities and exclusions. DSC's other guides include independent, sometimes critical, comment on and analysis of funders' activities. DGMT does not. Rather, it is a concise and to-the-point guide to grant-making charities.

This edition covers just over 2,000 of the largest UK-based grant-making charities that give grants to UK organisations and includes over 200 which are completely new to DGMT. In the course of our research we scrutinised their annual reports and accounts mainly for years 2015 and 2015/16. We also examined the content of other resources, such as charities' websites and application guidelines in order to provide the most relevant information for our readers. In some cases we also made direct contact with the funders themselves. We have included grant-makers giving from around £40,000 per year in grants to a staggering £751 million awarded by The Wellcome Trust in 2015/16.

Each of the entries gives a figure for the annual grant total distributed by the charity and the amount awarded to organisations only. In the majority of cases the two figures will match because the grant-maker only gives to organisations; however, where support is given to both organisations and individuals you will be able to see there are two separate totals. In some cases we were unable to determine the breakdown and both fields will show the same figure to reflect the charity's potential to give. In other instances full accounts were not available to view and we had to estimate the grant total based on the charity's spending or previous grant-making.

The combined giving of all the grant-makers in this edition totalled almost £5.4 billion, of which nearly £5.2 billion was given to organisations. This marks an increase of almost £1.1 billion from the last edition of the guide. The increase can be explained by two main factors. Firstly, there are over 200 grant-makers completely new to this edition, including the Heritage Lottery Fund which funds many projects that are community assets and will be of interest to readers. Many of the funders which have not been featured in previous editions of DGMT give significant amounts of grants each year. Secondly, there has been an overall increase in grants made by the other grant-makers, including a £158 million increase in grants by The Wellcome Trust. If we look at those charities which appear in both this edition and the previous one there has been an overall increase in giving of £355 million or 9%. Furthermore, almost 60% of these grant-makers have increased the total amount given in grants compared with the previous edition.

In the previous edition we noted a general improvement in the financial situation of the charities listed in the book and the research conducted for this edition seems to suggest this is a continuing trend. As well as the increase in grant totals noted above, for grant-makers for which we have comparable information, from the previous edition there was a 9.9% increase in the total assets held. Despite the seemingly improved finances, we noted many grant-makers commenting that because of the high amount of requests received they are having to turn down a lot of applications from deserving charities which are well aligned with their aims. Other common concerns expressed in charities' annual reports and accounts revolved around the stability of financial markets and uncertainty attached to Brexit. The full impact of Brexit on grant-making charities may not be known for many years to come and we will be monitoring this closely through our continued research into the sector.

We value the opinions of our readers on all aspects of our work including this directory. We are always looking to improve the guide and would welcome any feedback – positive or negative – which could be useful for future editions. Please contact us at: Research Team, Directory of Social Change, Suite 103, 1 Old Hall Street, Liverpool L3 9HG, telephone 0151 708 0136 or email us at: research@dsc.org.uk with any comments you would like to make.

The grant-making charities we have listed

This directory aims to include the majority of UK-based grant-makers that are capable of giving at least around £40,000 a year to organisations. Many of their trustees and/or staff are extremely helpful and we have been able to access comprehensive information on current policies via their websites, published material or direct communication. However, not all are so open. Where we have found this to be the case and information is not readily available, the funder's details have been updated, where possible, using the information on the appropriate regulator's website. Grant-makers have been included in the index under the appropriate headings according to their own published guidelines/grant-making practices/annual reports. We have placed those for which we do not have such information under what we believe to be the most suitable categories based on the information available.

Some trustees have stated their wish for their charity not to be included in this book. However, we believe that our guides provide an invaluable bridge between the charitable community and the rest of the voluntary sector, and that charities in receipt of public funds through tax relief should not attempt to draw a veil of secrecy over their activities, barring the most exceptional cases. Furthermore, we believe it is in the interests of the charitable sector to have information in the public domain about the activities of grant-makers as a group. Consequently, we have declined requests from grant-makers to be excluded from this directory. We are happy to explain the reasons why the organisation may not be awarding grants or accepting applications, and we think this is more helpful than letting the charity remain an obscure name in the sea of funders.

In general we have included:

- charities with a grant-making capacity of at least about £40,000 per year which make grants to charities and voluntary organisations. This includes Big Lottery Fund and its programme Awards for All (which operate like grant-making charities). Please note that while grant totals of some of the funders listed here could be below £40,000 in the given year, their grant-making activities either have the potential to exceed this amount or vary significantly each year.

We have excluded:

- grant-makers which fund individuals only;
- grant-makers which fund one organisation exclusively;
- grant-makers which generally have a grant-making capacity of less than £40,000 (smaller grant-making charities are included on our funding website; for more information visit: dsc.org.uk);
- grant-makers which have ceased to exist or are being wound up with any remaining funds fully committed.

We continue to include grant-making charities which state that they do not respond to unsolicited applications. We believe that their inclusion benefits fundraisers by giving a broader overview of the grant-making community, and that the information could be important in building relationships with funders. We feel it benefits the grant-makers in helping them to communicate that they do not wish to receive applications, which fundraisers might not know if they identified that particular grant-maker through other avenues. This also reduces the number of ineligible applications that are submitted to very busy and often over-stretched grant-making charities. As outlined in DSC's Responsible Giving policy principle, clear and accessible information is essential for both funders and applicants and ensures effective use of time and charitable resources (please visit www.dsc.org.uk for more information).

Acknowledgements

We would like to thank Carol Mack, Chief Executive of ACF, for contributing the foreword to this edition.

We would also like to thank all those trustees and staff of grant-making charities who strive to make their information openly available, and all those who help our research by responding to our communications and providing helpful comments.

How to use DGMT

The directory starts with three indexes:

- grant-makers by geographical area;
- grant-makers by field of interest and type of beneficiary;
- grant-makers by grant type.

There is a listing of the top 150 grant-makers by grant total on page xxiii. All of these are in alphabetical order.

Using these indexes, readers should end up with a shortlist of grant-makers whose funding policies match their needs.

Grant-makers by geographical area

This index enables you to see which grant-makers will consider applications from a charity or project in a particular geographical area. It contains two separate listings:

LIST OF GEOGRAPHICAL AREA HEADINGS

This is a complete list of all the geographical area headings used in DGMT.

LIST OF GRANT-MAKERS BY GEOGRAPHICAL AREA

These pages list grant-makers under the geographical areas where they will consider funding.

Grant-makers by field of interest and type of beneficiary

This index enables you to see which grant-makers are likely to fund projects doing a particular type of work to benefit a particular type of person. It lists grant-makers according to:

- the type of activity or work they are willing to fund – their fields of interest;
- who they want to benefit – their preferred beneficiaries.

These pages contain two separate listings:

CATEGORISATION OF FIELDS OF INTEREST AND TYPES OF BENEFICIARY

This lists all of the headings used in DGMT to categorise fields of interest and types of beneficiary. This listing should help you match your project with one – or more – of the categories used. The page numbers relate to the second listing.

LIST OF GRANT-MAKERS BY FIELD OF INTEREST AND TYPE OF BENEFICIARY

These pages list grant-makers under the fields of interest and types of beneficiary they have indicated they have a preference for or that our research suggests they might be willing to support.

The index is structured hierarchically. This means that the general heading comes first, followed by more specific subject areas. For example, under 'Beneficial groups' you can find 'Social or economic circumstances' category which is then split into further sub-headings, including 'People who are homeless', 'Prisoners and their families' and 'Victims of disasters'.

So, if your project falls under a specific heading such as 'Victims of disasters', it is also worth looking at the grant-makers which have expressed a general interest in funding 'Social or economic circumstances'. Grant-makers might be interested in funding your project even if they have not specifically expressed a preference for a particular field as long as it falls within the broad area they are supporting.

Grant-makers by type of grant

This index enables you to see which grant-makers can consider making the types of grant you are looking for. Grant-makers are listed under the types of grant that our research suggests they are willing or are likely to make. These pages contain two separate listings:

LIST OF GRANT TYPES

This lists all of the headings used in DGMT to categorise grant types. Page numbers relate to the second listing.

LIST OF GRANT-MAKERS BY GRANT TYPE

These pages list grant-makers under the types of grant that they are willing or likely to make.

The largest grant-makers

On page xxiii we have listed the largest 150 grant-makers by grant total in alphabetical order. Between them they account for around £4.5 billion, or about 83% of the funds available in the book. *Please do not* use this simply as a mailing list: these grant-makers cover a wide range of specialist interests and many of them will never fund your work.

We strongly recommend that you read each entry carefully and compile your own list of major grant-makers relevant to you. You can then set this list alongside the other lists generated from the other indexes in the directory. We believe this list should only be used as an effective way of ensuring that you do not omit any major grant-makers.

How to use DGMT
Key steps

STEP 1

Define the project, programme or work for which you are seeking funding.

STEP 2

Geographical area: find the area most local to your requirements. Note down the names of the grant-makers listed here.

STEP 3

Field of interest and type of beneficiary: identify the categories that match your project. Note down the names of the grant-makers listed here.

STEP 4

Type of grant: identify the type of grant you are looking for. Note down the names of the grant-makers listed here.

STEP 5

Compare the three lists of grant-makers to produce a list of those whose funding policies most closely match the characteristics of the project for which you are seeking funding.

STEP 6

If your list is too short you could include grant-makers that have a general interest in funding your area – while these may not define a specific field as a priority or preference they will consider applications as long as they fall within the broad category.

STEP 7

Look up entries for the grant-makers identified, study their details carefully and pay close attention to 'What is funded', 'What is not funded' and note the preferred method of communication or where further details may be found.

STEP 8

Look at the list of the top 150 grant-makers to make sure you do not miss any major funders. Look up entries for the grant-makers identified, study their details carefully and again pay particularly close attention to 'What is funded' and 'What is not funded'. Remember that these funders are likely to be more well-known and consequently over-subscribed.

Checklist

STEP 1 The following checklist will help you assemble the information you need.

- What is the geographical location of the people who will benefit from any funding received?
- What charitable activities, facilities or services will the funding provide?
- What are the characteristics which best describe the people who will benefit from any funding received?
- What type of grant are you looking for?

EXAMPLE *Funding is being sought for a project in North Wales to improve a community care centre for women in poverty*

- The geographical location is: United Kingdom → Wales → North Wales
- The service to be provided is: Community care
- The key characteristic of the people to benefit is that they are: Poor or on low incomes
- The type of grant being sought is: Development funding

STEP 2 Look up the area where your project is based in the list of geographical area headings on page 2.

- Turn to the relevant pages in the list of grant-makers by geographical area and note down the names of the grant-makers which have stated that they will consider funding projects in your area.

EXAMPLE Look up the area most local to your requirements (North Wales) in the list of geographical area headings. Then turn to the relevant page in the list of grant-makers by geographical area and look up the names of the grant-makers listed under North Wales. You may want to look at the grant-makers listed under the broader region (Wales) as well. Note down the names so that they can be compared with the lists through the indexes by type of grant and by field of interest and type of beneficiary.

It is also worth looking at grant-makers listed under United Kingdom because a grant-maker listed under a more general heading may be just as willing to fund activity in a specific region as another which states that it has a specific interest in that region.

STEP 3 Using the 'Field of interest and type of beneficiary' category on page 38, identify all the categories that match the project, programme or work for which you are seeking funding.

Turn to the relevant pages in the list of grant-makers by field of interest and type of beneficiary and look up the headings identified.

Note down the names of the grant-makers that appear under these headings so that you can compare them with the names identified through the indexes by geographical area and by type of grant.

EXAMPLE With a project to develop a community care centre, you will probably look first under the main heading 'Social welfare'. Under this heading you will find the sub-headings 'Community care services' and 'Services for women'. Note down the page numbers beside 'Community care services' and 'Services for women'. Grant-makers that have expressed an interest in funding services for women may represent your best prospects, but grant-makers with a more general interest in funding community care services might be as worth approaching – particularly if they like to fund projects in your area.

If you look under 'Beneficial groups' you will find 'People who are poor, on low incomes', which is under 'Social and economic circumstances', and 'Women', which is under 'Gender and relationships'. Note down these page numbers too.

STEP 4 Look up the type of grant that you are seeking in 'Grant-makers by type of grant' on page 164.

Turn to the relevant pages in the list of grant-makers by type of grant and note down the names of the grant-makers which can consider giving the type of grant that you are seeking. Compare these names with those that you identified through the indexes by geographical area and by field of interest and type of beneficiary.

EXAMPLE Look up the type of grant you are seeking in the list of grant types (in this case 'Development funding'). Then turn to the relevant page of the list of grant-makers by type of grant and look at the names of the grant-makers listed under 'Development funding'. Note down the names of all these grant-makers.

STEP 5 Compare the lists of charity names produced via steps 2, 3 and 4, and make a list of all the grant-makers which appear on more than one list. This will produce a list of grant-makers whose funding policies most closely match the characteristics of the project for which you are seeking funding.

STEP 6 If the list turns out to be too short it can easily be adjusted.

EXAMPLE You will end up with a list of grant-makers most accurately matching your project criteria.

By going back to step 3, you could include the grant-makers which come under 'Social welfare', or, by going back to step 2, you could include grant-makers which will consider funding projects in Wales.

STEP 7 Look up the entries for the grant-makers identified and study their details carefully, paying particular attention to 'Where funding can be given', 'What is funded' and 'What is not funded'.

If you feel that there is a good match between the characteristics of the project for which you require support and the funding policies of the grant-making charity identified, you could submit an application, making sure you choose appropriate means of doing so.

STEP 8 Look at the list of the top 150 grant-makers.

Check that you have not missed any of the major funders because you have made your search too specific. Some of the largest foundations give to a wide range of organisations and projects, and they tend to give the largest grants. They are also the most over-subscribed.

Look up the entries for each grant-maker and study their details carefully, paying particular attention to 'Where funding can be given', 'What is funded' and 'What is not funded'. If you feel that there is a good match between the characteristics of the project for which you require support and the funding policies of the charity identified, you could submit an application.

Most importantly, make sure that there is a good reason for writing to any grant-maker that you select: do not just send off indiscriminate applications to the whole list!

A typical grant-making charity entry

A complete entry should contain information under the headings listed below. An explanation of the information which should appear in these fields is given alongside.

CC NO
Charity registration number

WHERE FUNDING CAN BE GIVEN
The village, town, borough, parish or other geographical area the trust is prepared to fund

WHAT IS FUNDED
Details of the types of project or activity the trust plans to fund and groups it intends to ultimately benefit

WHAT IS NOT FUNDED
The types of projects or causes the trust does not fund, e.g. expeditions, scholarships

SAMPLE GRANTS
Examples of grants previously awarded by the trust

TRUSTEES
Names of the trustees

WHO TO APPLY TO
The name and address of the person to whom applications should be sent

■ The Fictitious Trust

CC NO 123456 **ESTABLISHED** 1993

WHERE FUNDING CAN BE GIVEN UK.

WHO CAN BENEFIT Registered charities.

WHAT IS FUNDED Education and training.

WHAT IS NOT FUNDED Individuals.

TYPE OF GRANT One-off; capital; running costs.

RANGE OF GRANTS £250 to £5,000.

SAMPLE GRANTS A school (£5,000); a university (£1,000); a school library (£800); a school (£600); a grammar school, a further education college and for classroom equipment (£500 each); a university appeal (£400); a wheelchair ramp (£250).

FINANCES *Year* 2015/16 *Income* £55,000 *Grants* £50,000 *Grants to organisations* £40,000 *Assets* £800,000

TRUSTEES Ernestine Papadopoulos, Chair; Samuel Akintola; Mary Brown; Alistair Johnson; Dr Angelique Kidjo; Prof. Miriam Masekela.

OTHER INFORMATION This grant-making charity recently merged with the Fictional Trust.

HOW TO APPLY Apply in writing to the address below. An sae should be enclosed if an acknowledgement is required.

WHO TO APPLY TO A. Grant, Secretary, The Old Barn, Main Street, New Town ZC48 2QQ *Tel.* 020 7123 4567 *Fax* 020 7123 4567 *Email* grantsteam@fictitioustrust.co.uk *Website* www.fictitioustrust.co.uk

ESTABLISHED
Year the trust was established

WHO CAN BENEFIT
The types of organisations that can be supported

TYPE OF GRANT
The types of grant or loan the trust is prepared to give, e.g. one-off, core costs, project costs

RANGE OF GRANTS
The smallest, largest and typical size of grant normally given

FINANCES
The most recent financial information available, including the total amount given in grants during the year

OTHER INFORMATION
Any other information which might be useful to grant-seekers

HOW TO APPLY
Useful information to those preparing their grant application

The top 150 grant-makers by grant total

This is a list of the largest 150 grant-makers by grant total in alphabetical order. Between them they account for around £4.5 billion, or about 83% of the funds available in the book. *Please do not* use this simply as a mailing list: these grant-makers cover a wide range of specialist interests and many of them will never fund your work.

We recommend that you read each entry carefully and compile your own list of major grant-makers relevant to you. You can use this list alongside the other lists generated from the indexes in the directory. We believe this is the most effective way of ensuring that you do not omit any major grant-makers.

The A. B. Charitable Trust
The Aberdeen Foundation
ABF The Soldiers' Charity
Achisomoch Aid Company Ltd
Age UK
Aid to the Church in Need (UK)
AKO Foundation
Allchurches Trust Ltd
Alzheimer's Research UK
Alzheimer's Society
Arcadia Charitable Trust
Arthritis Research UK
Arts Council England
Arts Council of Northern Ireland
Arts Council of Wales (also known as Cyngor Celfyddydau Cymru)
The Asda Foundation
The Associated Board of The Royal Schools of Music
Backstage Trust
Bauer Radio's Cash for Kids Charities
BBC Children in Need
Benesco Charity Ltd
BHP Billiton Sustainable Communities
The Big Lottery Fund
Asser Bishvil Foundation
Bloodwise
The Liz and Terry Bramall Foundation
Breast Cancer Now
The British Academy for the Promotion of Historical Philosophical and Philological Studies (The British Academy)
British Gas Energy Trust
British Heart Foundation (BHF)
The Barrow Cadbury Trust
CAFOD (Catholic Agency for Overseas Development)
Children with Cancer UK
Christian Aid
Church Urban Fund
The City Bridge Trust (Bridge House Estates)
The Clore Duffield Foundation
The Clothworkers' Foundation
Comic Relief
Creative Scotland
England and Wales Cricket Trust
Cumbria Community Foundation
Dawat-E-Hadiyah Trust (United Kingdom)
Diabetes UK
The Dunhill Medical Trust
Echoes of Service
The John Ellerman Foundation
Esmée Fairbairn Foundation
The Fidelity UK Foundation
The Football Foundation
The Foyle Foundation
The Gatsby Charitable Foundation
Goldman Sachs Gives (UK)
The Gosling Foundation Ltd
Greenham Common Community Trust Ltd
M. and R. Gross Charities Ltd
Hadras Kodesh Trust
Paul Hamlyn Foundation
The Headley Trust
The Health Foundation
The Helping Foundation
Heritage Lottery Fund
The Hintze Family Charity Foundation
The Sir Joseph Hotung Charitable Settlement
Impetus – The Private Equity Foundation (Impetus – PEF)
International Fund for Animal Welfare (IFAW)
The Jerusalem Trust
The Elton John AIDS Foundation (EJAF)
Keren Association Ltd
Kidney Research UK
Maurice and Hilda Laing Charitable Trust
The Kirby Laing Foundation
The LankellyChase Foundation

Leeds Community Foundation (LCF)
The Legal Education Foundation
The Leverhulme Trust
The Linbury Trust
Lloyds Bank Foundation for England and Wales
Lloyd's Register Foundation
The Lolev Charitable Trust
The London Community Foundation (LCF)
Trust for London
John Lyons Charity
The Marcela Trust
Maudsley Charity
Mayfair Charities Ltd
Medical Research Foundation
The Mercers' Charitable Foundation
The Monument Trust
Moondance Foundation
Motor Neurone Disease Association
Multiple Sclerosis Society
Muslim Hands
National Arts Collections Fund
The Nuffield Foundation
Old Possum's Practical Trust
Oxfam (GB)
Parkinson's Disease Society of The United Kingdom
The Pears Family Charitable Foundation
People's Health Trust
The Jack Petchey Foundation
Power to Change Trust
The Prince of Wales's Charitable Foundation
The Professional Footballers' Association Charity
Prostate Cancer UK
The Queen's Trust
Rachel Charitable Trust
The Rank Foundation Ltd
The Sigrid Rausing Trust
Responsible Gambling Trust (GambleAware)
The Robertson Trust
The Joseph Rowntree Charitable Trust
The Joseph Rowntree Foundation
The Royal British Legion
The Royal Navy and Royal Marines Charity
Royal Society of Wildlife Trusts
The Dr Mortimer and Theresa Sackler Foundation
The Sackler Trust
The Save the Children Fund
Foundation Scotland
ShareGift (The Orr Mackintosh Foundation)
The Shetland Charitable Trust
Shulem B. Association Ltd
The Henry Smith Charity
The Sobell Foundation
The Souter Charitable Trust
St James's Place Foundation
Stewards' Company Ltd
The Stoller Charitable Trust
Tearfund
The Thompson Family Charitable Trust
Tropical Health and Education Trust
The Tudor Trust
Community Foundation serving Tyne and Wear and Northumberland
The Michael Uren Foundation
The Veolia Environmental Trust
The Nigel Vinson Charitable Trust
The Virgin Foundation (Virgin Unite)
Viridor Credits Environmental Company
The Vodafone Foundation
Voluntary Action Fund (VAF)
Wales Council for Voluntary Action
The Waterloo Foundation
The Wellcome Trust
The Westminster Foundation
The Garfield Weston Foundation
The Charles Wolfson Charitable Trust
The Wolfson Foundation
The Wood Foundation
Youth Music
The Zochonis Charitable Trust

Other publications and resources

The following publications and resources may also be of interest to readers of DGMT. They are all available directly from DSC by ringing 020 7697 4200 or visiting our website at www.dsc.org.uk.

Publications

The Guide to Grants for Individuals in Need

This best-selling funding guide gives details of a wide range of funds and other support available for the relief of individual poverty and hardship. It remains a key reference book for social workers, as well as the individuals themselves and those concerned with their welfare. It contains:

- Details on national and local charitable grant-makers which collectively give around £268 million a year towards the relief of individual poverty and hardship.
- Essential advice on applications for each source: eligibility; types of grants given; annual grant total; contact details.
- An example of how to make an effective application, and advice on finding the right sources to apply to.

The Guide to Educational Grants

This popular guide gives details on a wide range of funds and other support available to schoolchildren and students in need, up to and including first degree level. It is a key reference book for educational social workers, student welfare officers, teachers and advice agencies, and the individuals themselves and their families. It includes:

- Sources of funding for children and students up to and including first degree level from grant-makers that collectively give over £55.6 million each year.
- Essential advice and information on applications for each source including eligibility, types of grants given, annual grant total and contact details.
- An example of how to make an effective application, and advice on finding the right sources to apply to.

The Guide to UK Company Giving

This invaluable guide includes details of over 400 companies in the UK that give a combined total of around £420 million in community contributions to voluntary and community organisations. It contains:

- Essential information on whom to contact within each company.
- Detailed information on cash and in-kind donations, employee-led support, sponsorship, Charity of the Year partnerships and details of CSR programmes.
- A section containing essential details on 132 corporate charities.

The Guide to the Major Trusts

The in-depth research and independent comment that this flagship title offers has made it an essential reference guide for all fundraisers. This guide is the only source of independent critical analysis of grant-makers in practice. It includes:

- Essential information on the 1,000 largest grant makers which together give a total of around £5.62 billion.
- Clear descriptions of charities' policies and practices, as well as details of grant programmes, contact details, eligibility criteria and information on how to apply.

DSC funding website

The DSC funding website provides information on:

Grant-making charities

- Information on more than 4,500 UK grant-making charities that collectively give about £5.7 billion each year.
- Search by geographical area, name of grant-maker, type of grant or by keyword.
- Choose to receive notification when information on a particular grant-maker is updated.
- Receive monthly bulletins that keep you informed of news and updates.

Grants for individuals

- Details on around 3,500 charities that give to individuals for educational and welfare purposes. Collectively they give over £332 million each year.
- Search by name of the grant-maker, type of grant or by keyword.
- Choose to receive notification when information on a particular grant-maker is updated.

Companies

- Information on 544 companies, including those featured in *The Guide to UK Company Giving*. Entries contain full details on the various giving methods (cash donations, in-kind support, employee-led support, sponsorship, commercially led support and Charity of the Year partnerships), and describe both what the company is prepared to fund and the organisations it has supported in the past.
- Search by geographical area, name of company, type of grant or by keyword.
- Choose to receive notification when information on a particular company or companies is updated.

Government funding	■ Details on over £2.3 billion of funding from local, regional, national and European sources. ■ Receive notification of funding rounds when they open. ■ Search by type of grant, for example small grants, loans and contracts.

DSC offers a wide range of specialist guides for fundraisers, providing essential tailored reference points for work in specific areas. For more details see our website www.dsc.org.uk.

Grant-makers by geographical area

This index contains two separate listings:

Geographical area headings: This lists all of the geographical area headings used in DGMT.

Grant-makers by geographical area: This lists the funders appearing in DGMT under the geographical area for which they have expressed a funding preference. Asterisks mark funders which have not been featured in DGMT before.

Grant-makers by geographical area

The index contains two separate listings:

Geographical area headings
This lists all of the geographical area headings used in DGMT.

Grant-makers by geographical area
This lists the funders appearing in DGMT under the geographical areas for which they have expressed a funding preference

Worldwide

The 3Ts Charitable Trust*
Aberdeen Asset Management Charitable Foundation
The Aberdeen Foundation
ABF The Soldiers' Charity
The Accenture Foundation
Achisomoch Aid Company Ltd
The ACT Foundation
Adenfirst Ltd
Age UK
Ajahma Charitable Trust
The Alborada Trust
The Alchemy Foundation
Al-Fayed Charitable Foundation
The Derrill Allatt Foundation
Allchurches Trust Ltd
AM Charitable Trust
The Amalur Foundation Ltd
The Anchor Foundation
The Andrew Anderson Trust
Arcadia Charitable Trust*
The Ove Arup Foundation
The Ashden Trust
The Ashworth Charitable Trust
The Associated Board of the Royal Schools of Music*
The Barham Charitable Trust
The Batchworth Trust
Bay Charitable Trust
The Bay Tree Charitable Trust
Beauland Ltd
The Becht Family Charitable Trust*
The Becker Family Charitable Trust
The John Beckwith Charitable Trust
The Ruth Berkowitz Charitable Trust
BHP Billiton Sustainable Communities*
Miss Jeanne Bisgood's Charitable Trust
The Michael Bishop Foundation
The Blandford Lake Trust
The Sir Victor Blank Charitable Settlement
Bloom Foundation
The Boltini Trust
Salo Bordon Charitable Trust
The Borrows Charitable Trust*
P. G. and N. J. Boulton Trust
Friends of Boyan Trust
The British and Foreign School Society
The British Academy for the Promotion of Historical Philosophical and Philological Studies (The British Academy)*
The British and Foreign Bible Society*
British Council for Prevention of Blindness (Save Eyes Everywhere)
The Bromley Trust
The Rory and Elizabeth Brooks Foundation
Brushmill Ltd
Buckingham Trust
The Clara E. Burgess Charity
The Arnold Burton 1998 Charitable Trust
The Derek Butler Trust
CAFOD (Catholic Agency for Overseas Development)
The Casey Trust
The Elizabeth Casson Trust
The Thomas Sivewright Catto Charitable Settlement
The CBD Charitable Trust
The Charter 600 Charity
Christadelphian Samaritan Fund
Chrysalis Trust
The Hilda and Alice Clark Charitable Trust
Denise Coates Foundation
The Cobalt Trust
The John S. Cohen Foundation
The R. and S. Cohen Foundation
The Coltstaple Trust
Comic Relief
Michael Cornish Charitable Trust
The Evan Cornish Foundation
Criffel Charitable Trust
The Cross Trust
The Cuby Charitable Trust
The Cumber Family Charitable Trust
Oizer Dalim Trust
The Biss Davies Charitable Trust*
The Crispin Davis Family Trust
Dawat-E-Hadiyah Trust (United Kingdom)*
The Dawe Charitable Trust
The De La Rue Charitable Trust*
The Delius Trust
The Desmond Foundation
The Laduma Dhamecha Charitable Trust
The Diageo Foundation
The Dorfman Foundation*
The Double 'O' Charity Ltd
The Royal Foundation of the Duke and Duchess of Cambridge and Prince Harry
The Mildred Duveen Charitable Trust
Echoes Of Service
The Gilbert and Eileen Edgar Foundation
Edupoor Ltd
Ellador Ltd
The Eranda Rothschild Foundation
The Ericson Trust
The Esfandi Charitable Foundation
Joseph Ettedgui Charitable Foundation
Euro Charity Trust
The Fairstead Trust
The Farthing Trust
Allan and Nesta Ferguson Charitable Settlement
Fisherbeck Charitable Trust
The Follett Trust
Forest Hill Charitable Trust
Donald Forrester Trust
The Anna Rosa Forster Charitable Trust
The Forte Charitable Trust
The Michael and Clara Freeman Charitable Trust
The Freshfield Foundation
The Raphael Freshwater Memorial Association*
The Adrian and Jane Frost Charitable Trust
Mejer and Gertrude Miriam Frydman Foundation
The G. D. Charitable Trust
The Galanthus Trust
The Jacqueline and Michael Gee Charitable Trust
The Generations Foundation
The Gibbs Charitable Trust
The G. C. Gibson Charitable Trust
The Gloag Foundation
The Golden Bottle Trust
The Goldman Sachs Charitable Gift Fund (UK)
Goldman Sachs Gives (UK)
The Goodman Foundation
The Goshen Trust
The Hemraj Goyal Foundation
Grace Charitable Trust
Graff Foundation
The Green Hall Foundation
The Walter Guinness Charitable Trust
The Gunter Charitable Trust
H. C. D. Memorial Fund
Hadras Kodesh Trust
The Happold Foundation*
The Haramead Trust
Harbinson Charitable Trust
The Charlotte Heber-Percy Charitable Trust
The Michael Heller Charitable Foundation
Henderson Firstfruits*
Philip Henman Trust
Highcroft Charitable Trust
The Hillier Trust
R. G. Hills Charitable Trust
The Hinduja Foundation
The Hiscox Foundation

The Hollick Family Charitable Trust
Sir Harold Hood's Charitable Trust
The Hope Trust
The Horizon Foundation
Hospice UK
Howman Charitable Trust*
The Hunting Horn General Charitable Trust
The Hutchinson Charitable Trust
The Hutton Foundation
The Innocent Foundation
International Bible Students Association*
The J. A. R. Charitable Trust
Nick Jenkins Foundation
The Jephcott Charitable Trust
The Christopher and Kirsty Johnston Charitable Trust
The Muriel Jones Foundation
The Joron Charitable Trust
The Cyril and Eve Jumbo Charitable Trust
The Jusaca Charitable Trust
Kahal Chassidim Bobov
Karaviotis Foundation
E. and E. Kernkraut Charities Ltd
Laura Kinsella Foundation
The Ernest Kleinwort Charitable Trust
Kollel and Co. Ltd
The K. P. Ladd Charitable Trust
Maurice and Hilda Laing Charitable Trust
The David Laing Foundation
The Kirby Laing Foundation
The Martin Laing Foundation
The Beatrice Laing Trust
The Lancashire Foundation*
Mrs F. B. Laurence Charitable Trust
The Law Society Charity
The Leigh Trust
The Lidbury Family Trust*
Lifeline 4 Kids (Handicapped Children's Aid Committee)
The Light Fund Company*
The Limbourne Trust
The Linbury Trust
The Ruth and Stuart Lipton Charitable Trust
Lloyd's Register Foundation*
The Joyce Lomax Bullock Charitable Trust
The Loseley and Guildway Charitable Trust
The Lower Green Foundation
The Henry Lumley Charitable Trust
Paul Lunn-Rockliffe Charitable Trust
The Madeline Mabey Trust
The Mackintosh Foundation
The Mactaggart Third Fund
The Mallinckrodt Foundation
R. W. Mann Trust
The Manoukian Charitable Foundation
The Marchig Animal Welfare Trust
Mariapolis Ltd
The Michael Marks Charitable Trust
Marmot Charitable Trust
The Master Charitable Trust*
The Mayfield Valley Arts Trust
Mazars Charitable Trust
Medical Research Foundation*
The Brian Mercer Charitable Trust
Mercury Phoenix Trust
T. and J. Meyer Family Foundation Ltd
The Millward Charitable Trust
The James Milner Foundation*
The Henry Moore Foundation
The Diana and Allan Morgenthau Charitable Trust
Vyoel Moshe Charitable Trust
The Edwina Mountbatten and Leonora Children's Foundation
The Frederick Mulder Foundation
MW (GK) Foundation
MW (HO) Foundation
MW (RH) Foundation
National Committee of the Women's World Day of Prayer for England and Wales and Northern Ireland
The NDL Foundation
Network for Social Change Charitable Trust
Alice Noakes Memorial Charitable Trust
Nominet Charitable Foundation
The Norton Rose Fulbright Charitable Foundation
The Sir Peter O'Sullevan Charitable Trust
The Oakdale Trust
The Ogle Christian Trust
The Onaway Trust*
Open Gate
The Doris Pacey Charitable Foundation
The Paget Charitable Trust
Palmtree Memorial Trust*
The Paphitis Charitable Trust
The Paragon Trust
The Park House Charitable Trust
Susanna Peake Charitable Trust
The Pears Family Charitable Foundation
The Persson Charitable Trust
The Pharsalia Charitable Trust
Pilkington Charities Fund
Edith and Ferdinand Porjes Charitable Trust
The Porta Pia 2012 Foundation
The W. L. Pratt Charitable Trust
Premishlaner Charitable Trust
The Puebla Charitable Trust
Quercus Foundation*
The Bishop Radford Trust
The Rainford Trust
The Rambourg Foundation
The Joseph and Lena Randall Charitable Trust
The Ranworth Trust
The Eleanor Rathbone Charitable Trust
The Sigrid Rausing Trust
The Roger Raymond Charitable Trust
Reed Family Foundation
Reuben Foundation
The Rhododendron Trust
RJM Charity Trust
Robyn Charitable Trust
The Roddick Foundation
The Sir James Roll Charitable Trust
The Gerald Ronson Family Foundation
The Rubin Foundation Charitable Trust
The Rufford Foundation
S. F. Foundation
The Michael Sacher Charitable Trust
Erach and Roshan Sadri Foundation
The Saga Charitable Trust
The Alan and Babette Sainsbury Charitable Fund
The M. J. Samuel Charitable Trust
The Sandhu Charitable Foundation
The Sands Family Trust
The Save the Children Fund*
The Annie Schiff Charitable Trust
The Schmidt-Bodner Charitable Trust
Schroder Charity Trust
Seafarers UK (King George's Fund for Sailors)
The Seedfield Trust
The Shanley Charitable Trust
Ruth Smart Foundation
The SMB Trust
The Stanley Smith UK Horticultural Trust
Spears-Stutz Charitable Trust
The Squires Foundation
St James's Place Foundation

*Standard Life Foundation**
C. E. K. Stern Charitable Trust
The Sigmund Sternberg Charitable Foundation
Stewards' Company Ltd
The Andy Stewart Charitable Foundation
Sir Halley Stewart Trust
The Stone Family Foundation
Sylvia Waddilove Foundation UK
Tabeel Trust
The Gay and Keith Talbot Trust
Tearfund
The Thornton Trust
The Three Oaks Trust
The Tinsley Foundation
The Tory Family Foundation
The Toye Foundation
*The Trysil Charitable Trust**
The Udlington Trust
Ulting Overseas Trust
The Ulverscroft Foundation
The David Uri Memorial Trust
*The Utley Family Charitable Trust**
The Albert Van Den Bergh Charitable Trust
Roger Vere Foundation
Virgin Atlantic Foundation
The Virgin Foundation (Virgin Unite)
The Barbara Ward Children's Foundation
The Waterloo Foundation
The Weinstein Foundation
The Wellcome Trust
The Westcroft Trust
Dame Violet Wills Charitable Trust
Woodlands Green Ltd
Wychdale Ltd
Wychville Ltd
*The Wyfold Charitable Trust**
Yankov Charitable Trust
Zephyr Charitable Trust

Europe

Bridgepoint Charitable Trust
The Catholic Charitable Trust
*Credit Suisse EMEA Foundation**
eaga Charitable Trust
The Goldman Sachs Charitable Gift Fund (UK)
IBM United Kingdom Trust
The Elton John Aids Foundation (EJAF)
*Mitsubishi Corporation Fund for Europe and Africa**
Morgan Stanley International Foundation
Vyoel Moshe Charitable Trust
The Nuffield Foundation
*QBE European Operations Foundation**
Rachel Charitable Trust
*Rothschild Foundation (Hanadiv) Europe**

Central Europe

The Apax Foundation
The Andrew Balint Charitable Trust
The Maurice Hatter Foundation
The Headley Trust
The Father O'Mahoney Memorial Trust
The Norman Whiteley Trust

Eastern Europe

Aid to the Church in Need (UK)
The William A. Cadbury Charitable Trust
Global Care
The Headley Trust
Jewish Childs Day (JCD)
The Father O'Mahoney Memorial Trust
Oxfam (GB)
Saint Sarkis Charity Trust

Northern Europe

*AKO Foundation**

Southern Europe

The Apax Foundation
The Ecology Trust
Kusuma Trust UK
Merchant Navy Welfare Board
The Father O'Mahoney Memorial Trust
Oxfam (GB)

Western Europe exluding Republic of Ireland

The Derrill Allatt Foundation
The Apax Foundation
The CIBC World Markets Children's Miracle Foundation
The Martin Laing Foundation
The Rambourg Foundation
*Sofronie Foundation**
R. H. Southern Trust

Republic of Ireland

The Animal Defence Trust
Arts Council of Northern Ireland
*Breast Cancer Now**
The William A. Cadbury Charitable Trust
Calouste Gulbenkian Foundation – UK Branch
Celtic Charity Fund
Church of Ireland Priorities Fund
*The Eighty Eight Foundation**
The Edith Maud Ellis 1985 Charitable Trust
EMI Music Sound Foundation
Marc Fitch Fund
The Haramead Trust
The Charles Hayward Foundation
The Hospital Saturday Fund
The Reta Lila Howard Foundation
The Ireland Fund of Great Britain
Ladbrokes in the Community Charitable Trust
The Community Foundation for Northern Ireland
The Ouseley Church Music Trust
The Joseph Rank Trust
Sodexo Stop Hunger Foundation
C. B. and H. H. Taylor 1984 Trust
*DM Thomas Foundation for Young People**

Asia

4 Charity Foundation
A. W. Charitable Trust
The Acacia Charitable Trust
Aid to the Church in Need (UK)
The Derrill Allatt Foundation
*The Allen & Overy Foundation**
The Alliance Family Foundation
Anglo American Group Foundation
The Apax Foundation
The Arah Foundation
The Ardwick Trust
*The Asfari Foundation**
The Ashmore Foundation
The Associated Country Women of the World (ACWW)
The Bagri Foundation
*Bairdwatson Charitable Trust**
The Andrew Balint Charitable Trust
The Bestway Foundation
The Bertie Black Foundation

The Bluston Charitable Settlement
The Bonamy Charitable Trust
The Breadsticks Foundation
The Burberry Foundation*
The William A. Cadbury Charitable Trust
The CH (1980) Charitable Trust
Charitworth Ltd
Christian Aid
J. A. Clark Charitable Trust
Closehelm Ltd
The Vivienne and Samuel Cohen Charitable Trust
Col-Reno Ltd
The Craps Charitable Trust
Credit Suisse EMEA Foundation*
Itzchok Meyer Cymerman Trust Ltd
The Daiwa Anglo-Japanese Foundation
The Davis Foundation
Debmar Benevolent Trust Ltd
Diageo Foundation
The Djanogly Foundation
The DM Charitable Trust
The Dollond Charitable Trust
The Doughty Charity Trust
Dushinsky Trust Ltd
The Ecology Trust
The Economist Charitable Trust
Entindale Ltd
Euro Charity Trust
The Exilarch's Foundation
Extonglen Ltd
Famos Foundation Trust
The Isaac and Freda Frankel Memorial Charitable Trust
Friends of Biala Ltd
The G. R. P. Charitable Trust
Global Care
The Gould Charitable Trust
The Great Britain Sasakawa Foundation
N. and R. Grunbaum Charitable Trust
Paul Hamlyn Foundation
The Helen Hamlyn Trust
The Harbour Charitable Trust
The Harrison-Frank Family Foundation (UK) Ltd
The Hathaway Trust
The Maurice Hatter Foundation
The Heathside Charitable Trust
The Daniel Howard Trust
The Humanitarian Trust
The Huntingdon Foundation Ltd
IBM United Kingdom Trust
IGO Foundation Ltd
Investream Charitable Trust
The Elton John Aids Foundation (EJAF)
J. E. Joseph Charitable Fund
The Bernard Kahn Charitable Trust
The Stanley Kalms Foundation
The Kasner Charitable Trust
Keren Association Ltd
Kupath Gemach Chaim Bechesed Viznitz Trust
Kusuma Trust UK
The Lambert Charitable Trust
The Lancashire Foundation*
Largsmount Ltd
The Lauffer Family Charitable Foundation
The Kennedy Leigh Charitable Trust
David and Ruth Lewis Family Charitable Trust
Jack Livingstone Charitable Trust
Lloyds TSB Foundation for Scotland
The Locker Foundation
The Sir Jack Lyons Charitable Trust
Marbeh Torah Trust
The Hilda and Samuel Marks Foundation
The Marr-Munning Trust
Mayfair Charities Ltd
Melodor Ltd
Mercaz Torah Vechesed Ltd
The Mittal Foundation
Morgan Stanley International Foundation
Ner Foundation
NJD Charitable Trust
The Father O'Mahoney Memorial Trust
Oxfam (GB)
Open Gate
The Polonsky Foundation
The Puri Foundation
The Queen Anne's Gate Foundation
The Rayne Trust
Rhodi Charitable Trust*
Rowanville Ltd
The Ruzin Sadagora Trust
Sam and Bella Sebba Charitable Trust
The Archie Sherman Cardiff Foundation
The Archie Sherman Charitable Trust
Shlomo Memorial Fund Ltd
The Shoe Zone Trust
The Sino-British Fellowship Trust
The Sobell Foundation
Solev Co. Ltd
The Solo Charitable Settlement
Songdale Ltd
The E. C. Sosnow Charitable Trust
R. H. Southern Trust
Rosalyn and Nicholas Springer Charitable Trust
The Steinberg Family Charitable Trust
The Adrienne and Leslie Sussman Charitable Trust
The Tajtelbaum Charitable Trust
The David Tannen Charitable Trust
Tegham Ltd
Tropical Health and Education Trust*
TVML Foundation
Tzedakah
Ulting Overseas Trust
The Vail Foundation
The Williams Family Charitable Trust
The Witzenfeld Foundation
The Maurice Wohl Charitable Foundation
The Wolfson Family Charitable Trust
The Wolfson Foundation

Far East

Anglo American Group Foundation
The Apax Foundation
The Burberry Foundation*
The Daiwa Anglo-Japanese Foundation
The Goldman Sachs Charitable Gift Fund (UK)
The Great Britain Sasakawa Foundation
The Sino-British Fellowship Trust

Middle East excluding Israel

The Derrill Allatt Foundation
The Allen & Overy Foundation*
The Arah Foundation
The Asfari Foundation*
The Ashmore Foundation
Credit Suisse EMEA Foundation*
The Exilarch's Foundation
IBM United Kingdom Trust
Morgan Stanley International Foundation

Israel

4 Charity Foundation
A. W. Charitable Trust
The Acacia Charitable Trust
The Alliance Family Foundation
The Ardwick Trust

The Andrew Balint Charitable Trust
The Bertie Black Foundation
The Bluston Charitable Settlement
The Bonamy Charitable Trust
The CH (1980) Charitable Trust
Charitworth Ltd
Closehelm Ltd
The Vivienne and Samuel Cohen Charitable Trust
Col-Reno Ltd
The Craps Charitable Trust
Itzchok Meyer Cymerman Trust Ltd
The Davis Foundation
Debmar Benevolent Trust Ltd
The Djanogly Foundation
The DM Charitable Trust
The Dollond Charitable Trust
The Doughty Charity Trust
Dushinsky Trust Ltd
Entindale Ltd
The Exilarch's Foundation
Extonglen Ltd
Famos Foundation Trust
The Isaac and Freda Frankel Memorial Charitable Trust
Friends of Biala Ltd
The G. R. P. Charitable Trust
The Gould Charitable Trust
N. and R. Grunbaum Charitable Trust
The Harbour Charitable Trust
The Harrison-Frank Family Foundation (UK) Ltd
The Hathaway Trust
The Maurice Hatter Foundation
The Heathside Charitable Trust
The Daniel Howard Trust
The Humanitarian Trust
The Huntingdon Foundation Ltd
IGO Foundation Ltd
Investream Charitable Trust
Jewish Childs Day (JCD)
J. E. Joseph Charitable Fund
The Bernard Kahn Charitable Trust
The Stanley Kalms Foundation
The Kasner Charitable Trust
Keren Association Ltd
Kupath Gemach Chaim Bechesed Viznitz Trust
The Lambert Charitable Trust
Largsmount Ltd
The Lauffer Family Charitable Foundation
The Kennedy Leigh Charitable Trust
David and Ruth Lewis Family Charitable Trust
Jack Livingstone Charitable Trust
The Locker Foundation
The Sir Jack Lyons Charitable Trust
Marbeh Torah Trust
The Hilda and Samuel Marks Foundation
Mayfair Charities Ltd
Melodor Ltd
Mercaz Torah Vechesed Ltd
Vyoel Moshe Charitable Trust
The Mutual Trust Group
Ner Foundation
Newpier Charity Ltd
NJD Charitable Trust
The Polonsky Foundation
The Rayne Trust
Reuben Foundation
Rokach Family Charitable Trust
Rowanville Ltd
Michael Sacher Charitable Trust
The Ruzin Sadagora Trust
Sam and Bella Sebba Charitable Trust
Sellata Ltd
The Archie Sherman Cardiff Foundation
The Archie Sherman Charitable Trust
Shlomo Memorial Fund Ltd
The Sobell Foundation
Solev Co. Ltd
The Solo Charitable Settlement
Songdale Ltd
The E. C. Sosnow Charitable Trust
Rosalyn and Nicholas Springer Charitable Trust
The Steinberg Family Charitable Trust
C. E. K. Stern Charitable Trust
The Adrienne and Leslie Sussman Charitable Trust
The Tajtelbaum Charitable Trust
The David Tannen Charitable Trust
Tegham Ltd
Trumros Ltd
TVML Foundation
Tzedakah
The Vail Foundation
The Williams Family Charitable Trust
The Witzenfeld Foundation
The Maurice Wohl Charitable Foundation
The Wolfson Family Charitable Trust
The Wolfson Foundation

South Asia

The Allen & Overy Foundation*
Anglo American Group Foundation
The Apax Foundation
The Bagri Foundation
Bairdwatson Charitable Trust*
Paul Hamlyn Foundation
The Helen Hamlyn Trust
J. E. Joseph Charitable Fund
Kusuma Trust UK
The Lauffer Family Charitable Foundation
Lloyds TSB Foundation for Scotland
The Marr-Munning Trust
The Mittal Foundation
The Puri Foundation
Rhodi Charitable Trust*
R. H. Southern Trust

South East Asia

The Ashmore Foundation
The Ecology Trust
The Martin Laing Foundation
The Marr-Munning Trust
The Shoe Zone Trust

Africa

Aid to the Church in Need (UK)
The Derrill Allatt Foundation
The Apax Foundation
The Associated Country Women of the World (ACWW)
The Breadsticks Foundation
The William A. Cadbury Charitable Trust
Christian Aid
J. A. Clark Charitable Trust
Credit Suisse EMEA Foundation*
Diageo Foundation
Didymus
The Economist Charitable Trust
The Expat Foundation
Global Care
The Charles Hayward Foundation
The Headley Trust
The Hunter Foundation
IBM United Kingdom Trust
The Indigo Trust
The Elton John Aids Foundation (EJAF)
Lancaster Foundation
The Marr-Munning Trust
Medical Research Foundation*
Mitsubishi Corporation Fund for Europe and Africa*
Morgan Stanley International Foundation
The Miles Morland Foundation
The Father O'Mahoney Memorial Trust
Open Gate

Oxfam (GB)
The Rambourg Foundation
The Samworth Foundation
Mrs R. P. Tindall's Charitable Trust
*Tropical Health and Education Trust**
The True Colours Trust
The Tudor Trust
Ulting Overseas Trust
The Wood Foundation

Central Africa

The Dulverton Trust
Joffe Charitable Trust

East Africa

*The Allen & Overy Foundation**
The Consuelo and Anthony Brooke Charitable Trust
The Noel Buxton Trust
The Dulverton Trust
The John Ellerman Foundation
The Gatsby Charitable Foundation
*Heb Ffin (Without Frontier)**
The Hunter Foundation
Joffe Charitable Trust
The Lauffer Family Charitable Foundation
Lloyds TSB Foundation for Scotland
The Nuffield Foundation
*The Watson Family Charitable Trust**

Southern Africa

*AKO Foundation**
Anglo American Group Foundation
The Noel Buxton Trust
The Childwick Trust
The John Ellerman Foundation
Euro Charity Trust
The Estelle Trust
Philip and Judith Green Trust
The Maurice Hatter Foundation
Joffe Charitable Trust
The Lauffer Family Charitable Foundation
Lloyds TSB Foundation for Scotland
Lord and Lady Lurgan Trust
The Monument Trust
The Nuffield Foundation
David and Elaine Potter Foundation
The Scurrah Wainwright Charity

West Africa

*C. H. Dixon Charitable Trust**
Joffe Charitable Trust
The Tudor Trust

America and the West Indies

The Economist Charitable Trust

Caribbean, West Indies

The Derrill Allatt Foundation
The Arah Foundation
Christian Aid
*The Lancashire Foundation**
The Lauffer Family Charitable Foundation
The Father O'Mahoney Memorial Trust
Oxfam (GB)

Central America

The Derrill Allatt Foundation
Christian Aid
Diageo Foundation
Global Care
The Father O'Mahoney Memorial Trust
Open Gate
Oxfam (GB)
Ulting Overseas Trust
G. R. Waters Charitable Trust 2000

North America

The Aberdeen Foundation
*AKO Foundation**
The Apax Foundation
The Ashmore Foundation
The Linda and Gordon Bonnyman Charitable Trust
*The Burberry Foundation**
The G. W. Cadbury Charitable Trust
The Catholic Charitable Trust
The Ecology Trust
The Goldman Sachs Charitable Gift Fund (UK)
The Hathaway Trust
The Maurice Hatter Foundation
The Christina Mary Hendrie Trust for Scottish and Canadian Charities
IGO Foundation Ltd
Kupath Gemach Chaim Bechesed Viznitz Trust
*The Lancashire Foundation**
The Lauffer Family Charitable Foundation
Littlefield Foundation (UK) Ltd
The Monument Trust
Vyoel Moshe Charitable Trust
The Mutual Trust Group
The Polonsky Foundation
Reuben Foundation
The Dr Mortimer and Theresa Sackler Foundation
SEM Charitable Trust
Shlomo Memorial Fund Ltd
Ruth Smart Foundation
The ScottishPower Energy People
TVML Foundation
G. R. Waters Charitable Trust 2000
*The Worwin UK Foundation**

South America

The Aberdeen Foundation
Aid to the Church in Need (UK)
The Derrill Allatt Foundation
Anglo American Group Foundation
The Apax Foundation
The Ashmore Foundation
*The Burberry Foundation**
The William A. Cadbury Charitable Trust
Diageo Foundation
Didymus
Jewish Childs Day (JCD)
The Father O'Mahoney Memorial Trust
Oxfam (GB)
TVML Foundation
Ulting Overseas Trust

Australasia

The Lauffer Family Charitable Foundation

United Kingdom

The 1970 Trust
The 29th May 1961 Charitable Trust
4 Charity Foundation
The A. B. Charitable Trust
The A. S. Charitable Trust
The Acacia Charitable Trust
Action Medical Research
The Adint Charitable Trust
The AIM Foundation
The Sylvia Aitken Charitable Trust
All Saints Educational Trust
The H. B. Allen Charitable Trust
The Alliance Family Foundation
*Alzheimer's Research UK**
Sir John and Lady Amory's Charitable Trust
The Ampelos Trust
Andor Charitable Trust
The André Christian Trust
The Mary Andrew Charitable Trust
Andrews Charitable Trust
Anglo American Group Foundation
The Animal Defence Trust
The Annandale Charitable Trust
The Anson Charitable Trust
The Apax Foundation
The John Apthorp Charity
The Archer Trust
The Ardeola Charitable Trust
The Ardwick Trust
The Argus Appeal
The Armourers' and Brasiers' Gauntlet Trust
The Arsenal Foundation Ltd
The Artemis Charitable Trust
Arthritis Research UK
Arts Council of Northern Ireland
Ove Arup Partnership Charitable Trust
ASCB Charitable Fund
*The Asfari Foundation**
The Ashburnham Thanksgiving Trust
The Ian Askew Charitable Trust
The Association of Colleges Charitable Trust
Asthma UK
The Astor Foundation
The Atlas Fund
The Aurelius Charitable Trust
Awards for All (see also the Big Lottery Fund)
The Bacit Foundation
The Harry Bacon Foundation
The Bagri Foundation
The Baily Thomas Charitable Fund
The Baker Charitable Trust
The Balcombe Charitable Trust
The Balfour Beatty Charitable Trust
The Andrew Balint Charitable Trust
The Baltic Charitable Fund
The Bamford Charitable Foundation
The Band Trust
The Barclay Foundation
The Baring Foundation
Lord Barnby's Foundation
*The Barrack Charitable Trust**
Misses Barrie Charitable Trust
The Paul Bassham Charitable Trust
BC Partners Foundation
Beefy's Charity Foundation
The David and Ruth Behrend Fund
*The Behrens Foundation**
Belljoe Tzedoko Ltd
*Benesco Charity Ltd**
The Benham Charitable Settlement
The Bestway Foundation
The Big Lottery Fund (see also Awards for All)
Percy Bilton Charity
The Sydney Black Charitable Trust
The Bertie Black Foundation
The Morgan Blake Charitable Trust
Bloodwise
*The Bloomfield Charitable Trust**
The Bluston Charitable Settlement
The Bonamy Charitable Trust
The Charlotte Bonham-Carter Charitable Trust
The Linda and Gordon Bonnyman Charitable Trust
BOOST Charitable Trust
The Oliver Borthwick Memorial Trust
The Bothwell Charitable Trust
Sir Clive Bourne Family Trust
Bourneheights Ltd
The Bowerman Charitable Trust
The William Brake Charitable Trust
The Tony Bramall Charitable Trust
The Liz and Terry Bramall Foundation
The Breadsticks Foundation
*Breast Cancer Now**
The Breast Cancer Research Trust (BCRT)
Bridgepoint Charitable Trust
The British Dietetic Association General and Education Trust Fund
*British Eye Research Foundation (Fight for Sight)**
British Heart Foundation (BHF)
British Humane Association
British Record Industry Trust
The Britten-Pears Foundation (The Britten Pears Library)
The Consuelo and Anthony Brooke Charitable Trust
Bill Brown 1989 Charitable Trust
R. S. Brownless Charitable Trust
The T. B. H. Brunner's Charitable Settlement
The Buffini Chao Foundation
BUPA UK Foundation
*The Burberry Foundation**
The Burden Trust
The Burdett Trust for Nursing
The Burry Charitable Trust
The Noel Buxton Trust
The Christopher Cadbury Charitable Trust
The G. W. Cadbury Charitable Trust
The William A. Cadbury Charitable Trust
The Cadbury Foundation
The Barrow Cadbury Trust
The George Cadbury Trust
The Cadogan Charity
Calleva Foundation
Calouste Gulbenkian Foundation – UK Branch
*Canary Wharf Contractors Fund**
Cardy Beaver Foundation
The Richard Carne Trust
The Carpenters' Company Charitable Trust
The Carrington Charitable Trust
*Sir Ernest Cassel Educational Trust**
The Castang Foundation
The Wilfrid and Constance Cave Foundation
The Cayo Foundation
The B. G. S. Cayzer Charitable Trust
The Cazenove Charitable Trust
Celtic Charity Fund
CEO Sleepout
The CH (1980) Charitable Trust
The Amelia Chadwick Trust
Champneys Charitable Foundation
The Chapman Charitable Trust
Charitworth Ltd
Chartered Accountants' Livery Charity (CALC)
The Cheruby Trust
Chesterhill Charitable Trust

Children's Liver Disease Foundation
CHK Charities Ltd
The Chownes Foundation
Christian Aid
The CIBC World Markets Children's Miracle Foundation
The City Educational Trust Fund
Stephen Clark 1957 Charitable Trust
J. A. Clark Charitable Trust
*The Clark Foundation**
The Cleopatra Trust
The Clore Duffield Foundation
Closehelm Ltd
The Clothworkers' Foundation
The Clover Trust
The Robert Clutterbuck Charitable Trust
Clydpride Ltd
The Francis Coales Charitable Foundation
The John Coates Charitable Trust
The Vivienne and Samuel Cohen Charitable Trust
Col-Reno Ltd
The Colt Foundation
Colwinston Charitable Trust
The Comino Foundation
The Congregational and General Charitable Trust
*The Thomas Cook Chidlren's Charity**
The Ernest Cook Trust
The Cooks Charity
The Catherine Cookson Charitable Trust
Mabel Cooper Charity
The Alice Ellen Cooper Dean Charitable Foundation
The Worshipful Company of Cordwainers Charitable Trusts (Minges Gift and the Pooled Trusts)
The Gershon Coren Charitable Foundation (also known as The Muriel and Gus Coren Charitable Foundation)
*The Corporation of Trinity House of Deptford Strond**
The Costa Family Charitable Trust
The Cotton Industry War Memorial Trust
The Cotton Trust
The Augustine Courtauld Trust
Dudley and Geoffrey Cox Charitable Trust
The Craignish Trust
The Craps Charitable Trust
The Crescent Trust
The Violet and Milo Cripps Charitable Trust
The Ronald Cruickshanks Foundation
*CSIS Charity Fund**
Cullum Family Trust
Itzchok Meyer Cymerman Trust Ltd
The D. G. Charitable Settlement
The D'Oyly Carte Charitable Trust
Roald Dahl's Marvellous Children's Charity
The Daiwa Anglo-Japanese Foundation
The Davidson Family Charitable Trust
Michael Davies Charitable Settlement
The De Brye Charitable Trust
Peter De Haan Charitable Trust
The De Laszlo Foundation
William Dean Countryside and Educational Trust
Debenhams Foundation
Debmar Benevolent Trust Ltd
The Dellal Foundation
The Demigryphon Trust
Dentons UKMEA LLP Charitable Trust
The J. N. Derbyshire Trust
The Duke of Devonshire's Charitable Trust
The Sandy Dewhirst Charitable Trust
Diabetes UK
Alan and Sheila Diamond Charitable Trust
Dinwoodie Charitable Company
The Djanogly Foundation
The DLM Charitable Trust
The DM Charitable Trust
The Dollond Charitable Trust
The Dorcas Trust
The Dorus Trust
Douglas Arter Foundation
The Drapers' Charitable Fund
Dromintee Trust
The Dulverton Trust
Dunard Fund 2016
The Dunhill Medical Trust
The Dunn Family Charitable Trust
The Charles Dunstone Charitable Trust
The Dyers' Company Charitable Trust
The James Dyson Foundation
eaga Charitable Trust
Audrey Earle Charitable Trust
The Sir John Eastwood Foundation
The EBM Charitable Trust
*The ECHO Trust**
The Ecology Trust
The Economist Charitable Trust
EDF Energy Trust (EDFET)
*Edge Foundation**
The W. G. Edwards Charitable Foundation
*The Eighty Eight Foundation**
*Elanore Ltd**
The George Elias Charitable Trust
The John Ellerman Foundation
The Edith Maud Ellis 1985 Charitable Trust
The Emerton-Christie Charity
EMI Music Sound Foundation
Entindale Ltd
The Epigoni Trust
Epilepsy Research UK
The Estelle Trust
The Alan Evans Memorial Trust
The Exilarch's Foundation
The Expat Foundation
Extonglen Ltd
The F. P. Ltd Charitable Trust
Esmée Fairbairn Foundation
Famos Foundation Trust
The Lord Faringdon Charitable Trust
The February Foundation
Elizabeth Ferguson Charitable Trust Fund
The Fidelity UK Foundation
The Doris Field Charitable Trust
Dixie Rose Findlay Charitable Trust
Marc Fitch Fund
The Earl Fitzwilliam Charitable Trust
The Football Association National Sports Centre Trust
The Forbes Charitable Foundation
The Oliver Ford Charitable Trust
Fordeve Ltd
*The Fore Trust**
The Lord Forte Foundation
The Foyle Foundation
The Isaac and Freda Frankel Memorial Charitable Trust
The Elizabeth Frankland Moore and Star Foundation
The Gordon Fraser Charitable Trust
The Hugh Fraser Foundation
The Louis and Valerie Freedman Charitable Settlement
Friends of Biala Ltd
Friends Provident Charitable Foundation
The Frognal Trust
The Patrick and Helena Frost Foundation

The G. R. P. Charitable Trust
The Gatsby Charitable Foundation
The Simon Gibson Charitable Trust
Gilchrist Educational Trust*
The Glass-House Trust
Global Charities
Worshipful Company of Glovers of London Charitable Trust
The Golsoncott Foundation
Nicholas and Judith Goodison's Charitable Settlement
The Mike Gooley Trailfinders Charity
The Gosling Foundation Ltd
The Gould Charitable Trust
Gowling WLG (UK) Charitable Trust
A. and S. Graham Charitable Trust
The Graham Trust*
The Great Britain Sasakawa Foundation
Philip and Judith Green Trust
Mrs H. R. Greene Charitable Settlement
Greys Charitable Trust
The Grocers' Charity
N. and R. Grunbaum Charitable Trust
The Hadley Trust
Paul Hamlyn Foundation
The Helen Hamlyn Trust
The Harbour Charitable Trust
The Harebell Centenary Fund
The Harrison-Frank Family Foundation (UK) Ltd
The Hasluck Charitable Trust
The Hathaway Trust
The Maurice Hatter Foundation
The Charles Hayward Foundation
The Headley Trust
May Hearnshaw Charitable Trust (May Hearnshaw's Charity)
Heart Research UK
The Heathside Charitable Trust
Heb Ffin (Without Frontier)*
Hedley Foundation Ltd (The Hedley Foundation)
Help the Homeless Ltd
P. and C. Hickinbotham Charitable Trust
The Hilden Charitable Fund
Hinchley Charitable Trust
Hockerill Educational Foundation
The Jane Hodge Foundation
The Holden Charitable Trust
The Holliday Foundation
P. H. Holt Foundation
The Homelands Charitable Trust
The Homestead Charitable Trust
The Mary Homfray Charitable Trust
The Hoover Foundation
The Antony Hornby Charitable Trust
The Thomas J. Horne Memorial Trust
Horwich Shotter Charitable Trust*
The Hospital Saturday Fund
The Reta Lila Howard Foundation
The Daniel Howard Trust
The Humanitarian Trust
The Hunter Foundation
The Huntingdon Foundation Ltd
IBM United Kingdom Trust
ICE Futures Charitable Trust*
IGO Foundation Ltd
Impetus – The Private Equity Foundation (Impetus – PEF)
The Worshipful Company of Information Technologists*
The Ingram Trust
The Inlight Trust
The Inman Charity
The International Bankers Charitable Trust (The Worshipful Company of Interntional Bankers)
Interserve Employee Foundation Ltd
The Inverforth Charitable Trust
Investream Charitable Trust
The Ireland Fund of Great Britain
The Ironmongers' Company
The JRSST Charitable Trust
The Ruth and Lionel Jacobson Trust (Second Fund) No. 2
Rees Jeffreys Road Fund
The Jenour Foundation
The Jerwood Charitable Foundation
The Jewish Youth Fund (JYF)
Joffe Charitable Trust
The Elton John Aids Foundation (EJAF)
Lillie Johnson Charitable Trust
The Joicey Trust
Anton Jurgens Charitable Trust
The Bernard Kahn Charitable Trust
The Stanley Kalms Foundation
The Kasner Charitable Trust
C. S. Kaufman Charitable Trust
The Kelly Family Charitable Trust
The Kay Kendall Leukaemia Fund
The Kennel Club Charitable Trust
The Nancy Kenyon Charitable Trust
Keren Association Ltd
Kidney Research UK
The Robert Kiln Charitable Trust
The King/Cullimore Charitable Trust
The Mary Kinross Charitable Trust
The Graham Kirkham Foundation*
The Richard Kirkman Trust
The Kirschel Foundation
The Kobler Trust
The Kohn Foundation
Kreditor Charitable Trust
The Kreitman Foundation
The Neil Kreitman Foundation
Kupath Gemach Chaim Bechesed Viznitz Trust
The Kyte Charitable Trust
Ladbrokes in the Community Charitable Trust
John Laing Charitable Trust
Christopher Laing Foundation
The Lambert Charitable Trust
Lancaster Foundation
LandAid Charitable Trust (Land Aid)
The Allen Lane Foundation
Langdale Trust
The LankellyChase Foundation
Largsmount Ltd
The Lauffer Family Charitable Foundation
The Kathleen Laurence Trust
The Edgar E. Lawley Foundation
Lawson Beckman Charitable Trust
The Raymond and Blanche Lawson Charitable Trust
The Leathersellers' Company Charitable Fund
The Leche Trust
The Arnold Lee Charitable Trust
Leeds Building Society Charitable Foundation
The Legal Education Foundation*
The Kennedy Leigh Charitable Trust
P. Leigh-Bramwell Trust 'E'
The Lennox Hannay Charitable Trust
The Mark Leonard Trust
The Leverhulme Trade Charities Trust
The Leverhulme Trust
Lord Leverhulme's Charitable Trust

*The Maisie and Raphael Lewis Charitable Trust**
David and Ruth Lewis Family Charitable Trust
The Sir Edward Lewis Foundation
John Lewis Partnership General Community Fund
Liberum Foundation
Limoges Charitable Trust
The Lind Trust
The Linden Charitable Trust
The Enid Linder Foundation
The Lister Charitable Trust
The Frank Litchfield Charitable Trust
Littlefield Foundation (UK) Ltd
The Charles Littlewood Hill Trust
The Second Joseph Aaron Littman Foundation
The George John and Sheilah Livanos Charitable Trust
Jack Livingstone Charitable Trust
The Elaine and Angus Lloyd Charitable Trust
The Andrew Lloyd Webber Foundation
Lloyd's Charities Trust
Localtrent Ltd
The Locker Foundation
Loftus Charitable Trust
The William and Katherine Longman Trust
The Lord's Taverners
*P. and M. Lovell Charitable Settlement**
The C. L. Loyd Charitable Trust
LPW Ltd
Robert Luff Foundation Ltd
C. F. Lunoe Trust Fund
The Lyndhurst Trust
The Lynn Foundation
The Sir Jack Lyons Charitable Trust
M. and C. Trust
*M. B. Foundation**
The M. K. Charitable Trust
The E. M. MacAndrew Trust
The Macdonald-Buchanan Charitable Trust
The Mackay and Brewer Charitable Trust
The MacRobert Trust
The Ian Mactaggart Trust (The Mactaggart Second Fund)
The Magen Charitable Trust
The Makers of Playing Cards Charity
Man Group PLC Charitable Trust
The Manackerman Charitable Trust
The Manifold Charitable Trust
Marbeh Torah Trust
The Marcela Trust
The Stella and Alexander Margulies Charitable Trust
The Hilda and Samuel Marks Foundation
The J. P. Marland Charitable Trust
The Marsh Christian Trust
Charlotte Marshall Charitable Trust
Sir George Martin Trust
The Dan Maskell Tennis Trust
The Mason Porter Charitable Trust
The Matliwala Family Charitable Trust
Mayfair Charities Ltd
*Maypride Ltd**
The Robert McAlpine Foundation
McGreevy No. 5 Settlement
D. D. McPhail Charitable Settlement
The Medlock Charitable Trust
The Mercers' Charitable Foundation
Merchant Navy Welfare Board
The Merchant Taylors' Company Charities Fund
The Mickel Fund
The Mickleham Trust
Middlesex Sports Foundation
The Ronald Miller Foundation
The Millfield Trust
The Millichope Foundation
*Mills and Reeve Charitable Trust**
The Edgar Milward Charity
The Mirianog Trust
The Laurence Misener Charitable Trust
The Mishcon Family Charitable Trust
The Brian Mitchell Charitable Settlement
*Mitsubishi Corporation Fund for Europe and Africa**
The Mittal Foundation
Keren Mitzvah Trust
The Mizpah Trust
Mole Charitable Trust
The Monatrea Charitable Trust
The Monument Trust
The Morel Charitable Trust
The Morgan Charitable Foundation
The Miles Morland Foundation
The Morris Charitable Trust
The Willie and Mabel Morris Charitable Trust
G. M. Morrison Charitable Trust
The Moshal Charitable Trust
The Mosselson Charitable Trust
Motor Neurone Disease Association
British Motor Sports Training Trust
J. P. Moulton Charitable Foundation
The Mulberry Trust
The Edith Murphy Foundation
Murphy-Neumann Charity Company Ltd
The John R. Murray Charitable Trust
The Mutual Trust Group
The Janet Nash Charitable Settlement
National Art Collections Fund
The National Churches Trust
*The National Gardens Scheme**
The National Manuscripts Conservation Trust
The Nationwide Foundation
Ner Foundation
Nesswall Ltd
*Nesta**
Newby Trust Ltd
The Frances and Augustus Newman Foundation
Newpier Charity Ltd
The NFU Mutual Charitable Trust
NJD Charitable Trust
Normanby Charitable Trust
The Northmoor Trust
*The Northwick Trust**
The Norton Foundation
The Nuffield Foundation
The Father O'Mahoney Memorial Trust
The Oakley Charitable Trust
Odin Charitable Trust
The Ofenheim Charitable Trust
Oizer Charitable Trust
Old Possum's Practical Trust
The John Oldacre Foundation
The Olga Charitable Trust
OneFamily Foundation
The Ormsby Charitable Trust
The Owen Family Trust
Oxfam (GB)
P. F. Charitable Trust
*Parkinson's Disease Society of the United Kingdom**
Peacock Charitable Trust
The Dowager Countess Eleanor Peel Trust
The Pell Charitable Trust
The Pennycress Trust
The Performing Right Society Foundation
B. E. Perl Charitable Trust
The Persula Foundation
Petplan Charitable Trust
The Phillips and Rubens Charitable Trust
The Phillips Charitable Trust

The Phillips Family Charitable Trust
The Austin and Hope Pilkington Trust
Miss A. M. Pilkington's Charitable Trust
The DLA Piper Charitable Trust
Polden-Puckham Charitable Foundation
*The Institute for Policy Research**
The George and Esme Pollitzer Charitable Settlement
Pollywally Charitable Trust
The Polonsky Foundation
The Portrack Charitable Trust
David and Elaine Potter Foundation
The Primrose Trust
The Prince of Wales's Charitable Foundation
The Princess Anne's Charities
Prison Service Charity Fund
The Privy Purse Charitable Trust
*The Professional Footballers' Association Charity**
*Prostate Cancer UK**
The Puri Foundation
Mr and Mrs J. A. Pye's Charitable Settlement
*QBE European Operations Foundation**
The Queen Anne's Gate Foundation
Queen Mary's Roehampton Trust
The Queen's Trust
R. S. Charitable Trust
The Monica Rabagliati Charitable Trust
Rachel Charitable Trust
The Radcliffe Trust
*The Edward Ramsden Charitable Trust**
The Rank Foundation Ltd
The Joseph Rank Trust
Rashbass Family Trust
The Ratcliff Foundation
Elizabeth Rathbone Charity
The Rayne Foundation
The Rayne Trust
The John Rayner Charitable Trust
The Sir James Reckitt Charity
C. A. Redfern Charitable Foundation
The Rest Harrow Trust
*Rhodi Charitable Trust**
*Riada Trust**
Daisie Rich Trust
The Clive and Sylvia Richards Charity Ltd
Ridgesave Ltd
The Sir John Ritblat Family Foundation
The River Farm Foundation
The River Trust
Rivers Foundation
*Riverside Charitable Trust Ltd**
The Rix-Thompson-Rothenberg Foundation
The Rofeh Trust
The Richard Rogers Charitable Settlement
Rokach Family Charitable Trust
The Helen Roll Charity
*Mrs L. D. Rope's Second Charitable Settlement**
Mrs L. D. Rope's Third Charitable Settlement
*The Cissie Rosefield Charitable Trust**
The Cecil Rosen Foundation
*The David Ross Foundation**
*Rothschild Foundation (Hanadiv) Europe**
Rowanville Ltd
The Rowlands Trust
The Joseph Rowntree Charitable Trust
The Joseph Rowntree Foundation
The RVW Trust
The Dr Mortimer and Theresa Sackler Foundation
The Ruzin Sadagora Trust
The Saddlers' Company Charitable Fund
The Jean Sainsbury Animal Welfare Trust
The Sainsbury Family Charitable Trusts
Saint Sarkis Charity Trust
The Saintbury Trust
The Saints and Sinners Trust Ltd
The Salamander Charitable Trust
*The Salisbury New Pool Settlement**
Salters' Charitable Foundation
The Andrew Salvesen Charitable Trust
Coral Samuel Charitable Trust
The Samworth Foundation
The Sandra Charitable Trust
Santander UK Foundation Ltd
The Scarfe Charitable Trust
The Schapira Charitable Trust
The Schreib Trust
The Schreiber Charitable Trust
The Schroder Foundation
The Scotshill Trust
Sir Samuel Scott of Yews Trust
The ScottishPower Foundation
The Scouloudi Foundation
The SDL Foundation
Seafarers Hospital Society
The Searchlight Electric Charitable Trust
Sam and Bella Sebba Charitable Trust
Leslie Sell Charitable Trust
Sellata Ltd
SEM Charitable Trust
The Seven Fifty Trust
The Cyril Shack Trust
The Jean Shanks Foundation
The Shanti Charitable Trust
ShareGift (The Orr Mackintosh Foundation)
The Linley Shaw Foundation
The Shears Foundation
The Sheepdrove Trust
The Sheldon Trust
The Patricia and Donald Shepherd Charitable Trust
*Sherling Charitable Trust**
The Archie Sherman Cardiff Foundation
The Archie Sherman Charitable Trust
The Bassil Shippam and Alsford Trust
The Shipwrights' Company Charitable Fund
The Shirley Foundation
*The Florence Shute Millennium Trust**
David and Jennifer Sieff Charitable Trust
Silver Family Charitable Trust
The Huntly and Margery Sinclair Charitable Trust
The Sino-British Fellowship Trust
The Charles Skey Charitable Trust
Skipton Building Society Charitable Foundation
The John Slater Foundation
Sloane Robinson Foundation
Rita and David Slowe Charitable Trust
The N. Smith Charitable Settlement
The Smith Charitable Trust
The Henry Smith Charity
The Leslie Smith Foundation
*The Martin Smith Foundation**
The WH Smith Group Charitable Trust
Philip Smith's Charitable Trust
Sodexo Stop Hunger Foundation
*Sofronie Foundation**
Solev Co. Ltd
The Solo Charitable Settlement
David Solomons Charitable Trust
Songdale Ltd
The E. C. Sosnow Charitable Trust
The Souter Charitable Trust
The South Square Trust

The W. F. Southall Trust
Spar Charitable Fund
Sparks Charity (Sport Aiding Medical Research for Kids)
The Spear Charitable Trust
The Worshipful Company of Spectacle Makers' Charity
The Jessie Spencer Trust
The Spielman Charitable Trust
Rosalyn and Nicholas Springer Charitable Trust
The Spurrell Charitable Trust
The Geoff and Fiona Squire Foundation
The St James's Trust Settlement
St Luke's College Foundation
The Stafford Trust
The Stanley Charitable Trust*
The Stanley Foundation Ltd
The Staples Trust
The Peter Stebbings Memorial Charity
The Steel Charitable Trust
The Steinberg Family Charitable Trust
Stervon Ltd
Stevenson Family's Charitable Trust
The Stewards' Charitable Trust
The Stewarts Law Foundation
The Stobart Newlands Charitable Trust
The Stoller Charitable Trust
M. J. C. Stone Charitable Trust
The Samuel Storey Family Charitable Trust
Peter Stormonth Darling Charitable Trust
Peter Storrs Trust
The Strawberry Charitable Trust
The W. O. Street Charitable Foundation
The Sudborough Foundation
Sueberry Ltd
The Alan Sugar Foundation
Support Adoption For Pets*
The Adrienne and Leslie Sussman Charitable Trust
The Sutasoma Trust
Swan Mountain Trust
The John Swire (1989) Charitable Trust
The Adrian Swire Charitable Trust
The Swire Charitable Trust
The Hugh and Ruby Sykes Charitable Trust
The Charles and Elsie Sykes Trust
T. and S. Trust Fund
The Tajtelbaum Charitable Trust
Talteg Ltd
The Lady Tangye Charitable Trust Ltd
The David Tannen Charitable Trust
The Tanner Trust
The Lili Tapper Charitable Foundation
The Taurus Foundation
The Tay Charitable Trust
Khoo Teck Puat UK Foundation*
The Tedworth Charitable Trust
Tegham Ltd
The C. Paul Thackray General Charitable Trust
The Thistle Trust
The David Thomas Charitable Trust
DM Thomas Foundation for Young People*
The Thompson Family Charitable Trust
The Sir Jules Thorn Charitable Trust
The Thornton Foundation
The Thousandth Man- Richard Burns Charitable Trust
The Three Guineas Trust
The Thriplow Charitable Trust
The John Raymond Tijou Charitable Trust
Tilney Charitable Trust
Mrs R. P. Tindall's Charitable Trust
The Tisbury Telegraph Trust
The Tolkien Trust
The Tompkins Foundation
Toras Chesed (London) Trust
The Toy Trust
Toyota Manufacturing UK Charitable Trust
Annie Tranmer Charitable Trust
The Constance Travis Charitable Trust
The Treeside Trust
The Trefoil Trust
The True Colours Trust
Truedene Co. Ltd
The Truemark Trust
Truemart Ltd
Trumros Ltd
The Trusthouse Charitable Foundation
The James Tudor Foundation
The Tudor Trust
The Tufton Charitable Trust
The Tuixen Foundation
The Florence Turner Trust
TVML Foundation
Tzedakah
The Underwood Trust
The Union of Orthodox Hebrew Congregations
UnLtd (Foundation for Social Entrepreneurs)
The Michael Uren Foundation
The Vail Foundation
The Valiant Charitable Trust
The Van Neste Foundation
Mrs Maud Van Norden's Charitable Foundation
The Vandervell Foundation
The Vardy Foundation
Variety The Children's Charity (Variety Club)
The Veolia Environmental Trust*
The Nigel Vinson Charitable Trust
The Virgin Money Foundation
Vivdale Ltd
The Bruce Wake Charity*
The Wakefield Trust*
The Wakeham Trust
Sir Siegmund Warburg's Voluntary Settlement
The Ward Blenkinsop Trust
Mrs N. E. M. Warren's Charitable Trust*
Mrs Waterhouse Charitable Trust
G. R. Waters Charitable Trust 2000
The Watson Family Charitable Trust*
The Weavers' Company Benevolent Fund
Webb Memorial Trust
The David Webster Charitable Trust
The James Weir Foundation
The Welton Foundation
The Wessex Youth Trust
The Westfield Health Charitable Trust
The Garfield Weston Foundation
The Barbara Whatmore Charitable Trust
The Whitaker Charitable Trust
Colonel W. H. Whitbread Charitable Trust
The Whitecourt Charitable Trust
The Whitley Animal Protection Trust
The Lionel Wigram Memorial Trust
The Will Charitable Trust
The Kay Williams Charitable Foundation
The Williams Charitable Trust
The Williams Family Charitable Trust
Williams Serendipity Trust
The HDH Wills 1965 Charitable Trust
The Wilmcote Charitrust
Sumner Wilson Charitable Trust
The Wimbledon Foundation*

The W. Wing Yip and Brothers Foundation
The Harold Hyam Wingate Foundation
Winton Philanthropies
The Witzenfeld Foundation
The Michael and Anna Wix Charitable Trust
The Wixamtree Trust
The Maurice Wohl Charitable Foundation
The Charles Wolfson Charitable Trust
The Wolfson Family Charitable Trust
The Wolfson Foundation
The Wood Foundation
Woodroffe Benton Foundation
The A. and R. Woolf Charitable Trust
The Worwin UK Foundation*
The Diana Edgson Wright Charitable Trust
The Wyndham Charitable Trust
The Wyseliot Rose Charitable Trust
Yorkshire and Clydesdale Bank Foundation
Yorkshire Building Society Charitable Foundation
The William Allen Young Charitable Trust
The John Kirkhope Young Endowment Fund
The Z. Foundation
Elizabeth and Prince Zaiger Trust*
The Marjorie and Arnold Ziff Charitable Foundation
Stephen Zimmerman Charitable Trust
The Zochonis Charitable Trust
Zurich Community Trust (UK) Ltd

England

The Neville Abraham Foundation*
Access Sport CIO
The Sylvia Adams Charitable Trust
AF Trust Company
AKO Foundation*
D. C. R. Allen Charitable Trust
AO Smile Foundation*
The Arah Foundation
The John Armitage Charitable Trust
Arts Council England
The Asda Foundation
The Ashley Family Foundation
Barchester Healthcare Foundation
The Berkeley Charitable Foundation
Birthday House Trust
Blakemore Foundation
The Boodle & Dunthorne Charitable Trust
The Boshier-Hinton Foundation
The Bridging Fund Charitable Trust
British Gas (Scottish Gas) Energy Trust
The Butters Foundation (UK) Ltd*
The Catholic Trust for England and Wales
Chalfords Ltd
Church Urban Fund
The Marjorie Coote Animal Charity Trust
Country Houses Foundation
England and Wales Cricket Trust*
The Peter Cruddas Foundation
The Davis Foundation
The Henry and Suzanne Davis Foundation
Didymus
C. H. Dixon Charitable Trust*
The DM Charitable Trust
The Doughty Charity Trust
The Elephant Trust
Esher House Charitable Trust
Matthew Eyton Animal Welfare Trust
The Football Foundation
Gwyneth Forrester Trust
The Fort Foundation
The Joseph Strong Frazer Trust
The General Nursing Council for England and Wales Trust
The Girdlers' Company Charitable Trust
Grand Charitable Trust of the Order of Women Freemasons
Gordon Gray Trust
H. and T. Clients Charitable Trust
The Haley Family Charitable Trust
The Peter and Teresa Harris Charitable Trust
HC Foundation*
Ernest Hecht Charitable Foundation
The Hintze Family Charity Foundation
The J. Isaacs Charitable Trust
The J. and J. Benevolent Foundation
The KPMG Foundation
The Leonard Laity Stoate Charitable Trust
Bernard Lewis Family Charitable Trust*
The Lindley Foundation (TLF)
Lloyds Bank Foundation for England and Wales
The Lockwood Charitable Foundation*
Lord and Lady Lurgan Trust
The Marks Family Foundation
Charity of John Marshall
Masonic Charitable Foundation*
The Moss Family Charitable Trust
Moto in the Community
The Norwood and Newton Settlement
The Ouseley Church Music Trust
Parabola Foundation*
The Pargiter Trust*
People's Health Trust
People's Postcode Trust
Postcode Community Trust*
Postcode Dream Trust – Dream Fund
Power to Change Trust*
Princes Gate Trust*
Rigby Foundation*
Rosetrees Trust
The Royal British Legion
Rugby Football Foundation
The Dr Mortimer and Theresa Sackler Foundation
The Sackler Trust
The Savoy Educational Trust*
O. and G. Schreiber Charitable Trust
The ScottishPower Energy People Trust
SHINE (Support and Help in Education)
Shulem B. Association Ltd*
The DS Smith Charitable Foundation
The Sobell Foundation
R. H. Southern Trust
Sparquote Ltd
Springrule Ltd

*The Stoneygate Trust**
*The Street Foundation**
The Bernard Sunley Charitable Foundation
*The Transform Foundation**
*Viridor Credits Environmental Company**
Robert and Felicity Waley-Cohen Charitable Trust
*The Watson Family Charitable Trust**
*The Wheeler Family Charitable Trust**
*The Wigoder Family Foundation**
The Francis Winham Foundation
*The Woodstock Family Charitable Foundation**
The Yapp Charitable Trust
Youth Music

Greater London

A. W. Charitable Trust
*A2BD Foundation UK Ltd**
The Addleshaw Goddard Charitable Trust
Aldgate and All Hallows' Foundation
*The Allen & Overy Foundation**
Amabrill Ltd
The Arah Foundation
Anglo American Group Foundation
Anpride Ltd
The Armourers' and Brasiers' Gauntlet Trust
The Arsenal Foundation
Autonomous Research Charitable Trust (ARCT)
The Barbers' Company General Charities
*The Battersea Power Station Foundation**
Bauer Radio's Cash for Kids Charities
Bergqvist Charitable Trust
*Asser Bishvil Foundation**
*Sir William Boreman's Foundation**
The Consuelo and Anthony Brooke Charitable Trust
The Cadogan Charity
The Ellis Campbell Foundation
The Campden Charities Trustee
*Canary Wharf Contractors Fund**
The Carpenters' Company Charitable Trust
The Carr-Gregory Trust
Sir John Cass's Foundation
The Chapman Charitable Trust
The Childhood Trust
The Childwick Trust
The City Bridge Trust (Bridge House Estates)
J. A. Clark Charitable Trust
Richard Cloudesley's Charity
Dudley and Geoffrey Cox Charitable Trust
Cripplegate Foundation
The Croydon Relief in Need Charities
Dentons UKMEA LLP Charitable Trust
Dischma Charitable Trust
East End Community Foundation
Dr Edwards Bishop King's Fulham Charity
The Vernon N. Ely Charitable Trust
The Fidelity UK Foundation
Fishmongers' Company's Charitable Trust
Ford Britain Trust
The Charles S. French Charitable Trust
Friends of Essex Churches Trust
Friends of Wiznitz Ltd
Gardeners of London
The Garrard Family Foundation
The Gertner Charitable Trust
The Gibbs Charitable Trust
The Girdlers' Company Charitable Trust
The B. and P. Glasser Charitable Trust
Worshipful Company of Gold and Silver Wyre Drawers Charitable Trust Fund
The Goldsmiths' Company Charity
Grahame Charitable Foundation Ltd
The Greggs Foundation
The Gretna Charitable Trust
M. and R. Gross Charities Ltd
The Gur Trust
Hackney Parochial Charities
*Hammersmith United Charities**
The Hampstead Wells and Campden Trust
Hampton Fuel Allotment Charity
The Harbour Foundation
The Alfred and Peggy Harvey Charitable Trust
The Maurice Hatter Foundation
The Health Foundation
Heathrow Community Fund (LHR Airport Communities Trust)
The Simon Heller Charitable Settlement
The Helping Foundation
The Hillingdon Community Trust
The Worshipful Company of Horners' Charitable Trusts
The Sir Joseph Hotung Charitable Settlement
The Huntingdon Foundation Ltd
Hurdale Charity Ltd
The P. Y. N. and B. Hyams Trust
Hyde Charitable Trust (Youth Plus)
Hyde Park Place Estate Charity
*ICE Futures Charitable Trust**
The Worshipful Company of Insurers Charitable Trust Fund
The International Bankers Charitable Trust
*International Fund for Animal Welfare (IFAW)**
The ITF Seafarers' Trust
The Ironmongers' Company
The J. J. Charitable Trust
Jewish Childs Day (JCD)
J. E. Joseph Charitable Fund
William Kendall's Charity (Wax Chandlers' Company)
Robert Kitchin (Saddlers' Company)
The Kreditor Charitable Trust
The Leathersellers' Company Charitable Fund
Liberum Foundation
The Ruth and Stuart Lipton Charitable Trust
Lloyd's Charities Trust
The Lolev Charitable Trust
London Catalyst
The London Community Foundation (LCF)
London Housing Foundation Ltd (LHF)
London Legal Support Trust (LLST)
Inner London Magistrates Court's Poor Box and Feeder Charity
The London Marathon Charitable Trust Ltd
Trust for London
Lord and Lady Lurgan Trust
John Lyons Charity
The M. Y. A. Charitable Trust
Man Group PLC Charitable Trust
*Maudsley Charity**
The Mercers' Charitable Foundation
The Merchant Taylors' Company Charities Fund
Merchant Taylors' Consolidated Charities for the Infirm
The Metropolitan Masonic Charity

The Masonic Province of Middlesex Charitable Trust (Middlesex Masonic Charity)
The Peter Minet Trust
Morgan Stanley International Foundation
The Music Sales Charitable Trust
The Worshipful Company of Needlemakers' Charitable Fund
Nemoral Ltd
The Newcomen Collett Foundation
*North London Charities Ltd**
*The Paddington Charitable Estate Educational Fund**
Peacock Charitable Trust
The Jack Petchey Foundation
Richard Reeve's Foundation
Richmond Parish Lands Charity
The Rose Foundation
Royal Docks Trust (London)
The Royal Victoria Hall Foundation
*S. and R. Charitable Trust**
The Basil Samuel Charitable Trust
The Shanly Foundation
SHINE (Support and Help in Education)
The Simmons & Simmons Charitable Foundation
The Slaughter and May Charitable Trust
The Leslie Smith Foundation
The Mrs Smith and Mount Trust
Sir Walter St John's Educational Charity
*St Marylebone Educational Foundation**
St Olave's and St Saviour's Schools Foundation – Foundation Fund
The Peter Stebbings Memorial Charity
T. and S. Trust Fund
Tallow Chandlers Benevolent Fund No. 2
*The Talmud Torah Machzikei Hadass Trust**
Humphrey Richardson Taylor Charitable Trust
The Taylor Family Foundation
The Thousandth Man- Richard Burns Charitable Trust
The Tobacco Pipe Makers and Tobacco Trade Benevolent Fund
Tottenham Grammar School Foundation
The Tower Hill Trust
The Vintners' Company Charitable Foundation
The Wakefield and Tetley Trust
Walcot Educational Foundation
The Wates Foundation
Westminster Amalgamated Charity
The Westminster Foundation
Westway Trust
The Lionel Wigram Memorial Trust
Williams Serendipity Trust

■ Barking and Dagenham

Ford Britain Trust
The Charles S. French Charitable Trust
Friends of Essex Churches Trust

■ Barnet

Amabrill Ltd
The Consuelo and Anthony Brooke Charitable Trust
Jewish Child's Day (JCD)
John Lyon's Charity
Mercaz Torah Vechesed Ltd
*North London Charities Ltd**
Rashbass Family Trust

■ Bexley

Ford Britain Trust
The Alfred And Peggy Harvey Charitable Trust
William Kendall's Charity (Wax Chandlers' Company)

■ Brent

Amabrill Ltd
The Huntingdon Foundation Ltd
Hyde Charitable Trust (Youth Plus)
John Lyon's Charity

■ Bromley

The Alfred And Peggy Harvey Charitable Trust

■ Camden

The Consuelo and Anthony Brooke Charitable Trust
Sir John Cass's Foundation
Fishmongers' Company's Charitable Trust
Grahame Charitable Foundation Ltd
The Hampstead Wells and Campden Trust
The Huntingdon Foundation Ltd
John Lyon's Charity
*North London Charities Ltd**
Richard Reeve's Foundation

■ City of London

*A2BD Foundation UK Ltd**
Aldgate and All Hallows' Foundation
The Barbers' Company General Charities
Baltic Charitable Fund
Sir John Cass's Foundation
The Worshipful Company of Cordwainers Charitable Trusts (Minges Gift and the Pooled Trusts)
The Drapers' Charitable Fund
East End Community Foundation
Fishmongers' Company's Charitable Trust
The Charles S. French Charitable Trust
The B. and P. Glasser Charitable Trust
Worshipful Company of Glovers of London Charitable Trust
Worshipful Company of Gold and Silver Wyre Drawers Charitable Trust Fund
The Sir Joseph Hotung Charitable Settlement
*The Worshipful Company of Insurers – First Charitable Trust Fund**
John Lyon's Charity
The Makers of Playing Cards Charity
The Worshipful Company of Needlemakers' Charitable Fund
Richard Reeve's Foundation
The Simmons & Simmons Charitable Foundation
Tallow Chandlers Benevolent Fund No. 2
The Tobacco Pipe Makers and Tobacco Trade Benevolent Fund
The Wakefield and Tetley Trust

■ City of Westminster

Anglo American Group Foundation
The Consuelo and Anthony Brooke Charitable Trust
Sir John Cass's Foundation
The Dischma Charitable Trust

Fishmongers' Company's Charitable Trust
The Garrard Family Foundation
The Gertner Charitable Trust
M. and R. Gross Charities Ltd
The Health Foundation
The Simon Heller Charitable Settlement
The P. Y. N. and B. Hyams Trust
*The Hyde Park Place Estate Charity – civil trustees**
The J. J. Charitable Trust
John Lyon's Charity
Nemoral Ltd
*The Paddington Charitable Estate Educational Fund**
The Basil Samuel Charitable Trust
*St Marylebone Educational Foundation**
*The Westminster Amalgamated Charity**
The Westminster Foundation

■ Croydon

The Croydon Relief in Need Charities
Hyde Charitable Trust (Youth Plus)
*Maudsley Charity**

■ Ealing

Amabrill Ltd
Heathrow Community Fund (LHR Airport Communities Trust)
John Lyon's Charity

■ Enfield

*North London Charities Ltd**

■ Greenwich

*Sir William Boreman's Foundation**
Sir John Cass's Foundation
Ford Britain Trust
The Alfred And Peggy Harvey Charitable Trust
Hyde Charitable Trust (Youth Plus)

■ Hackney

Sir John Cass's Foundation
East End Community Foundation
Fishmongers' Company's Charitable Trust
Friends of Wiznitz Ltd
The Gur Trust
Hackney Parochial Charities
The Harbour Foundation
Hurdale Charity Ltd
The Lolev Charitable Trust
The M. Y. A. Charitable Trust
Mercaz Torah Vechesed Ltd
The Merchant Taylors' Company Charities Fund
Merchant Taylors' Consolidated Charities for the Infirm
*The Talmud Torah Machzikei Hadass Trust**

■ Hammersmith and Fulham

Sir John Cass's Foundation
Dr Edwards Bishop King's Fulham Endowment Fund
*Hammersmith United Charities**
John Lyon's Charity

■ Haringey

North London Charities Ltd North London Charities Ltd
Tottenham Grammar School Foundation Tottenham Grammar School Foundation

■ Harrow

Amabrill Ltd
John Lyon's Charity

■ Havening

Ford Britain Trust
The Charles S. French Charitable Trust
Friends of Essex Churches Trust

■ Hillingdon

Amabrill Ltd
Heathrow Community Fund (LHR Airport Communities Trust)
The Hillingdon Community Trust

■ Hounslow

Heathrow Community Fund (LHR Airport Communities Trust)

■ Islington

Sir John Cass's Foundation
Richard Cloudesley's Charity
Cripplegate Foundation
Fishmongers' Company's Charitable Trust
Hyde Charitable Trust (Youth Plus)
The Morris Charitable Trust
*North London Charities Ltd**
Richard Reeve's Foundation
The Slaughter and May Charitable Trust

■ Kensington and Chelsea

The Consuelo and Anthony Brooke Charitable Trust
The Campden Charities Trustee
Sir John Cass's Foundation
John Lyon's Charity
Westway Trust

■ Lambeth

Anglo American Group Foundation
*The Battersea Power Station Foundation**
Sir John Cass's Foundation
Fishmongers' Company's Charitable Trust
Hyde Charitable Trust (Youth Plus)
*International Fund for Animal Welfare (IFAW)**
*Maudsley Charity**
Sir Walter St John's Educational Charity
The Walcot Foundation

■ Lewisham

*Sir William Boreman's Foundation**
Sir John Cass's Foundation
The Alfred And Peggy Harvey Charitable Trust
Hyde Charitable Trust (Youth Plus)
*Maudsley Charity**
The Merchant Taylors' Company Charities Fund
Merchant Taylors' Consolidated Charities for the Infirm

■ Merton

The Vernon N. Ely Charitable Trust
The Generations Foundation

Newham

Sir John Cass's Foundation
East End Community Foundation
Ford Britain Trust
The Charles S. French Charitable Trust
Friends of Essex Churches Trust
Royal Docks Trust (London)

Redbridge

Ford Britain Trust
The Charles S. French Charitable Trust
Friends of Essex Churches Trust

Richmond upon Thames

The Greggs Foundation
Hampton Fuel Allotment Charity
Heathrow Community Fund (LHR Airport Communities Trust)
Richmond Parish Lands Charity

Southwark

Anglo American Group Foundation
Sir John Cass's Foundation
Fishmongers' Company's Charitable Trust
The Alfred And Peggy Harvey Charitable Trust
The Hintze Family Charity Foundation
Hyde Charitable Trust (Youth Plus)
The ITF Seafarers' Trust
*Maudsley Charity**
The Merchant Taylors' Company Charities Fund
Merchant Taylors' Consolidated Charities for the Infirm
The Newcomen Collett Foundation
The Norton Rose Fulbright Charitable Foundation
St Olave's and St Saviour's Schools Foundation – Foundation Fund
The Wakefield and Tetley Trust

Sutton

Humphrey Richardson Taylor Charitable Trust

Tower Hamlets

Aldgate and All Hallows' Foundation
Sir John Cass's Foundation
East End Community Foundation
Fishmongers' Company's Charitable Trust
The Charles S. French Charitable Trust
The Merchant Taylors' Company Charities Fund
Merchant Taylors' Consolidated Charities for the Infirm
Morgan Stanley International Foundation
The Simmons & Simmons Charitable Foundation
The Tower Hill Trust
The Wakefield and Tetley Trust

Waltham Forest

The Charles S. French Charitable Trust
Friends of Essex Churches Trust

Wandsworth

*The Battersea Power Station Foundation**
Sir John Cass's Foundation
Sir Walter St John's Educational Charity
The Wates Foundation

South Eastern England

The Ammco Trust
The Banbury Charities
The Barker-Mill Foundation
The Barnsbury Charitable Trust
The Bartlett Taylor Charitable Trust
Bauer Radio's Cash for Kids Charities
*The Rowan Bentall Charitable Trust**
Bergqvist Charitable Trust
The Berkshire Community Foundation
The Billmeir Charitable Trust
Isabel Blackman Foundation
The Blagrave Trust
The Bordon Liphook Haslemere Charity
The Frank Brake Charitable Trust
John Bristow and Thomas Mason Trust
The Consuelo and Anthony Brooke Charitable Trust
Buckinghamshire Community Foundation
The Buckinghamshire Historic Churches Trust
The Ellis Campbell Charitable Foundation
The Chapman Charitable Trust
The Childwick Trust
The Coalfields Regeneration Trust
The John Coates Charitable Trust
The Cobtree Charity Trust Ltd
John Coldman Charitable Trust
The Cole Charitable Trust
The Colefax Charitable Trust
John and Freda Coleman Charitable Trust
The Sir Jeremiah Colman Gift Trust
Colyer-Fergusson Charitable Trust
Coventry Building Society Charitable Foundation
The John Cowan Foundation
*The Roger De Haan Charitable Trust**
Disability Aid Fund (The Roger and Jean Jefcoate Trust)
Dischma Charitable Trust
The Derek and Eileen Dodgson Foundation
The Dulverton Trust
The Earley Charity
The Gerald Palmer Eling Trust Company
The Englefield Charitable Trust
Ford Britain Trust
The Friends of Kent Churches
Gatwick Airport Community Trust
The Gibbons Family Trust
The Godinton Charitable Trust
Greenham Common Community Trust Ltd
The Bishop of Guildford's Foundation
The Hampshire and Islands Historic Churches Trust
Hampshire and Isle of Wight Community Foundation
William Harding's Charity
The Peter Harrison Foundation
The Alfred And Peggy Harvey Charitable Trust
Heathrow Community Fund (LHR Airport Communities Trust)
Henley Educational Trust
The Hollands-Warren Fund
Hyde Charitable Trust (Youth Plus)
The Iliffe Family Charitable Trust

Johnson Wax Ltd Charitable Trust
Anton Jurgens Charitable Trust
Kent Community Foundation
The David Laing Foundation
The Elaine and Angus Lloyd Charitable Trust
London Legal Support Trust (LLST)
The London Marathon Charitable Trust Ltd
The Magdalen and Lasher Charity (General Fund)
The Gerald Micklem Charitable Trust
The Masonic Province of Middlesex Charitable Trust (Middlesex Masonic Charity)
Milton Keynes Community Foundation Ltd
Mobbs Memorial Trust Ltd
Oxfordshire Community Foundation
*Oxfordshire Historic Churches Trust**
Paradigm Foundation
Peacock Charitable Trust
*The Polehampton Charity**
*The Prince Philip Trust Fund**
Richard Radcliffe Trust
Red Hill Charitable Trust
*Robertson Hall Trust**
The Rugby Group Benevolent Fund Ltd
The Sants Charitable Trust
The Shanly Foundation
The Mrs Smith and Mount Trust
The Southover Manor General Education Trust
The Spoore, Merry and Rixman Foundation
The Alan Sugar Foundation
*Sunninghill Fuel Allotment Trust**
Community Foundation for Surrey
The Sussex Community Foundation
Humphrey Richardson Taylor Charitable Trust
The Taylor Family Foundation
Walton on Thames Charity
The Wates Foundation
The F. Glenister Woodger Trust
Zurich Community Trust (UK) Ltd

■ Berkshire

The Louis Baylis (Maidenhead Advertiser) Charitable Trust
Bergqvist Charitable Trust
The Berkshire Community Foundation
The Blagrave Trust
Cardy Beaver Foundation
The Wilfrid and Constance Cave Foundation
The Childwick Trust
The Colefax Charitable Trust
The Cumber Family Charitable Trust
The Earley Charity
The Gerald Palmer Eling Trust Company
The Englefield Charitable Trust
Greenham Common Community Trust Ltd
Heathrow Community Fund (LHR Airport Communities Trust)
Henley Educational Trust
The Iliffe Family Charitable Trust
The Edgar Milward Charity
*The Polehampton Charity**
*The Prince Philip Trust Fund**
The Shanly Foundation
The Spoore, Merry and Rixman Foundation
*Sunninghill Fuel Allotment Trust**
The Tompkins Foundation

■ Buckinghamshire

Bergqvist Charitable Trust
Buckinghamshire Community Foundation
The Buckinghamshire Historic Churches Trust
The Carrington Charitable Trust
The Childwick Trust
The Francis Coales Charitable Foundation
Coventry Building Society Charitable Foundation
Dentons UKMEA LLP Charitable Trust
The Eranda Rothschild Foundation
The Louis and Valerie Freedman Charitable Settlement
William Harding's Charity
Heathrow Community Fund (LHR Airport Communities Trust)
London Legal Support Trust (LLST)
The London Marathon Charitable Trust Ltd
Milton Keynes Community Foundation Ltd
Mobbs Memorial Trust Ltd
The Pennycress Trust
The Shanly Foundation
Roger Vere Foundation

■ East Sussex

The Ian Askew Charitable Trust
Isabel Blackman Foundation
The Blagrave Trust
The Consuelo and Anthony Brooke Charitable Trust
The Childwick Trust
The Chownes Foundation
The Duke of Devonshire's Charitable Trust
The Derek and Eileen Dodgson Foundation
Gatwick Airport Community Trust
Hyde Charitable Trust (Youth Plus)
The Ernest Kleinwort Charitable Trust
The Raymond and Blanche Lawson Charitable Trust
The Magdalen and Lasher Charity (General Fund)
The Ofenheim Charitable Trust
The River Trust
*Robertson Hall Trust**
The Rugby Group Benevolent Fund Ltd
The Henry Smith Charity
The Southover Manor General Education Trust
The Sussex Community Foundation
Zurich Community Trust (UK) Ltd

■ Hampshire

The Barker-Mill Foundation
Bauer Radio's Cash for Kids Charities
The Blagrave Trust
The Charlotte Bonham-Carter Charitable Trust
The Bordon Liphook Haslemere Charity
The Burry Charitable Trust
The Ellis Campbell Charitable Foundation
The Wilfrid and Constance Cave Foundation
The Childwick Trust
The Colefax Charitable Trust
John and Freda Coleman Charitable Trust
The Sir Jeremiah Colman Gift Trust
The Alice Ellen Cooper Dean Charitable Foundation
Ford Britain Trust
Greenham Common Community Trust Ltd
The Hampshire and Islands Historic Churches Trust
Hampshire and Isle of Wight Community Foundation

The Richard Kirkman Trust
Paul Lunn-Rockliffe Charitable Trust
The Gerald Micklem Charitable Trust
Thomas Roberts Trust
The Shanly Foundation
The Henry Smith Charity

■ Isle of Wight

Hampshire and Isle of Wight Community Foundation
Daisie Rich Trust

■ Kent

The Frank Brake Charitable Trust
The Childwick Trust
The Coalfields Regeneration Trust
The Cobtree Charity Trust Ltd
John Coldman Charitable Trust
The Cole Charitable Trust
Colyer-Fergusson Charitable Trust
The Ronald Cruickshanks Foundation
*The Roger De Haan Charitable Trust**
The Fidelity UK Foundation
The Friends of Kent Churches
Gatwick Airport Community Trust
The Gibbons Family Trust
The Godinton Charitable Trust
The Alfred And Peggy Harvey Charitable Trust
R. G. Hills Charitable Trust
The Hollands-Warren Fund
Hyde Charitable Trust (Youth Plus)
Kent Community Foundation
The Raymond and Blanche Lawson Charitable Trust
The Elaine and Angus Lloyd Charitable Trust
London Legal Support Trust (LLST)
The Sir James Roll Charitable Trust
The Rugby Group Benevolent Fund Ltd
The Shanly Foundation
The Henry Smith Charity
The John Swire (1989) Charitable Trust
The Tory Family Foundation
The Diana Edgson Wright Charitable Trust

■ Oxfordshire

The Ammco Trust
The Banbury Charities
The Barnsbury Charitable Trust
The Bartlett Taylor Charitable Trust
Bergqvist Charitable Trust
The T. B. H. Brunner's Charitable Settlement
The Wilfrid and Constance Cave Foundation
The Childwick Trust
The Cumber Family Charitable Trust
The Faringdon Charitable Trust
The Doris Field Charitable Trust
Greys Charitable Trust
Henley Educational Trust
The C. L. Loyd Charitable Trust
McGreevy No. 5 Settlement
Oxfordshire Community Foundation
*Oxfordshire Historic Churches Trust**
P. F. Charitable Trust
The Pharsalia Charitable Trust
The Rugby Group Benevolent Fund Ltd
The Sants Charitable Trust
The Shanly Foundation
*The Martin Smith Foundation**
The Tolkien Trust
Robert and Felicity Waley-Cohen Charitable Trust

■ Surrey

The Billmeir Charitable Trust
The Boltini Trust
John Bristow and Thomas Mason Trust
The Childwick Trust
John and Freda Coleman Charitable Trust
The John Cowan Foundation
The Fidelity UK Foundation
Gatwick Airport Community Trust
The Bishop of Guildford's Foundation
Hamamelis Trust
The Alfred And Peggy Harvey Charitable Trust
Heathrow Community Fund (LHR Airport Communities Trust)
The Ingram Trust
Johnson Wax Ltd Charitable Trust
The Sir Edward Lewis Foundation
The Elaine and Angus Lloyd Charitable Trust
London Legal Support Trust (LLST)
The London Marathon Charitable Trust Ltd
The Loseley and Guildway Charitable Trust
The Masonic Province of Middlesex Charitable Trust (Middlesex Masonic Charity)
The Henry Smith Charity
Community Foundation for Surrey
Humphrey Richardson Taylor Charitable Trust
Walton on Thames Charity

■ West Sussex

The Ian Askew Charitable Trust
The Blagrave Trust
The Boltini Trust
The Consuelo and Anthony Brooke Charitable Trust
The Childwick Trust
The Chownes Foundation
The Derek and Eileen Dodgson Foundation
Friarsgate Trust
Gatwick Airport Community Trust
Heathrow Community Fund (LHR Airport Communities Trust)
Hyde Charitable Trust (Youth Plus)
The Ernest Kleinwort Charitable Trust
The Raymond and Blanche Lawson Charitable Trust
The Gerald Micklem Charitable Trust
The River Trust
The Southover Manor General Education Trust
The Bassil Shippam and Alsford Trust
The Henry Smith Charity
The Sussex Community Foundation
The Three Oaks Trust
The Tompkins Foundation
The F. Glenister Woodger Trust

South Western England

D. G. Albright Charitable Trust
Viscount Amory's Charitable Trust
Sir John and Lady Amory's Charitable Trust
The Avon and Somerset Police Community Trust
Barnwood Trust

The Battens Charitable Trust
The Rowan Bentall Charitable Trust*
The Blagrave Trust
Bridge Trust
Bristol Archdeaconry Charity
Bristol Charities
The J. and M. Britton Charitable Trust
The Carr-Gregory Trust
The Childwick Trust
The John Coates Charitable Trust
Community First (Landfill Communities Fund)
Cornwall Community Foundation
The Duke of Cornwall's Benevolent Fund
The Cornwell Charitable Trust
Coventry Building Society Charitable Foundation
J. A. Clark Charitable Trust
The Dr and Mrs A. Darlington Charitable Trust
The Denman Charitable Trust
Devon Community Foundation
The Devon Historic Churches Trust
Dorset Community Foundation
The Dorset Historic Churches Trust
Duchy Health Charity Ltd
The Dulverton Trust
Samuel William Farmer Trust
The Joyce Fletcher Charitable Trust
The Galanthus Trust
The Gerrick Rose Animal Trust*
The Gibbons Family Trust
The David Gibbons Foundation
Gloucestershire Community Foundation
The Gloucestershire Historic Churches Trust
The Peter Harrison Foundation
The Heathcoat Trust
The Nani Huyu Charitable Trust
The Charles Irving Charitable Trust
John James Bristol Foundation
The Marjorie and Geoffrey Jones Charitable Trust
The Michael and Ilse Katz Foundation
The David Laing Foundation
The Leonard Laity Stoate Charitable Trust
The Jack Lane Charitable Trust
The Langtree Trust
The Elaine and Angus Lloyd Charitable Trust
Sylvanus Lysons Charity
The Merchant Venturers' Charity
The Clare Milne Trust
The Norman Family Charitable Trust
The Notgrove Trust
The Oldham Foundation
The Patrick Trust
Peacock Charitable Trust
The Portishead Nautical Trust
Quartet Community Foundation
Sarum St Michael Educational Charity*
The Severn Trent Water Charitable Trust Fund
SITA Cornwall Trust Ltd
Somerset Community Foundation*
St Monica Trust
The Summerfield Charitable Trust
The Talbot Village Trust
The Valentine Charitable Trust
The Wates Foundation
The West Looe Town Trust*
The Dame Violet Wills Will Trust
Wiltshire Community Foundation
Elizabeth and Prince Zaiger Trust*

Avon

The Avon and Somerset Police Community Trust
Bristol Archdeaconry Charity
Bristol Charities
The J. and M. Britton Charitable Trust
The Burden Trust
The Carr-Gregory Trust
Coventry Building Society Charitable Foundation
The Denman Charitable Trust
Douglas Arter Foundation
The Gibbs Charitable Trust
The Gloucestershire Historic Churches Trust
The Nani Huyu Charitable Trust
John James Bristol Foundation
The Merchant Venturers' Charity
The Portishead Nautical Trust
Quartet Community Foundation
The Dame Violet Wills Will Trust

Cornwall and the Scilly Isles

The Wilfrid and Constance Cave Foundation
Cornwall Community Foundation
The Duke of Cornwall's Benevolent Fund
The Cornwell Charitable Trust
Duchy Health Charity Ltd
The Gerrick Rose Animal Trust*
The Heathcoat Trust
The Michael and Ilse Katz Foundation
The Clare Milne Trust
The Patrick Trust
SITA Cornwall Trust Ltd
The West Looe Town Trust*

Devon

Viscount Amory's Charitable Trust
The Ashworth Charitable Trust
Bridge Trust
The Wilfrid and Constance Cave Foundation
Mabel Cooper Charity
The Dr and Mrs A. Darlington Charitable Trust
Devon Community Foundation
The Devon Historic Churches Trust
The Gerrick Rose Animal Trust*
The Gibbons Family Trust
The David Gibbons Foundation
The Heathcoat Trust
The Clare Milne Trust
St Luke's College Foundation
The Wakefield Trust*

Dorset

The Battens Charitable Trust
The Bisgood Charitable Trust
The Burry Charitable Trust
The Wilfrid and Constance Cave Foundation
The Clover Trust
The Alice Ellen Cooper Dean Charitable Foundation
Dorset Community Foundation
The Dorset Historic Churches Trust
The Dorothy Holmes Charitable Trust
Sarum St Michael Educational Charity*
The Leslie Smith Foundation
The Talbot Village Trust
Mrs R. P. Tindall's Charitable Trust
The Valentine Charitable Trust
Elizabeth and Prince Zaiger Trust*

Gloucestershire

D. G. Albright Charitable Trust
Barnwood Trust
The Childwick Trust

Douglas Arter Foundation
Gloucestershire Community Foundation
The Gloucestershire Historic Churches Trust
Gordon Gray Trust
*M. V. Hillhouse Trust**
The Charles Irving Charitable Trust
The Jack Lane Charitable Trust
The Langtree Trust
Sylvanus Lysons Charity
The Notgrove Trust
Susanna Peake Charitable Trust
Quartet Community Foundation
The Saintbury Trust
The Severn Trent Water Charitable Trust Fund
*The Florence Shute Millennium Trust**
The Henry Smith Charity
Philip Smith's Charitable Trust
St Monica Trust
The Summerfield Charitable Trust
The David Thomas Charitable Trust
The Dame Violet Wills Will Trust

■ Somerset

The Avon and Somerset Police Community Trust
The Battens Charitable Trust
The Wilfrid and Constance Cave Foundation
Stephen Clark 1957 Charitable Trust
The Roger and Sarah Bancroft Clark Charitable Trust
Coventry Building Society Charitable Foundation
Douglas Arter Foundation
Quartet Community Foundation
*Somerset Community Foundation**
St Monica Trust
*Mrs N. E. M. Warren's Charitable Trust**
The Dame Violet Wills Will Trust
*Elizabeth and Prince Zaiger Trust**

■ Wiltshire

The Bailey-Williams Charitable Trust
The Battens Charitable Trust
The Bellinger Donnay Trust
The Blagrave Trust
The Wilfrid and Constance Cave Foundation
The Sidney George Chamberlain Goodwill Trust
The Childwick Trust
The Chippenham Borough Lands Charity
Community First (Landfill Communities Fund)
Coventry Building Society Charitable Foundation
The Wallace Curzon Charitable Trust
The James Dyson Foundation
Samuel William Farmer Trust
The Fulmer Charitable Trust
The Thomas Freke and Lady Norton Charity
The Walter Guinness Charitable Trust
Haine and Smith Charitable Trust
The Jack Lane Charitable Trust
The Malmesbury Community Trust
The Lord Margadale Charitable Trust
The John Rayner Charitable Trust
*Sarum St Michael Educational Charity**
The Leslie Smith Foundation
St Monica Trust
Mrs R. P. Tindall's Charitable Trust
The Underwood Trust
The Wayland Estates
Wessex Cancer Trust
Wiltshire Community Foundation
The Wiltshire Gardens Trust

West Midlands Region

The Lord Austin Trust
The Aylesford Family Charitable Trust
Bauer Radio's Cash for Kids Charities
The James Beattie Charitable Trust
The Birmingham District Nursing Charitable Trust
Birmingham International Airport Community Trust Fund
The Lord Mayor of Birmingham's Charity
The Michael Bishop Foundation
The Bransford Trust
The Charles Brotherton Trust
The Bruntwood Charity
The E. F. Bulmer Benevolent Fund
Consolidated Charity of Burton upon Trent
The George Cadbury Trust
The Christopher Cadbury Charitable Trust
The Edward Cadbury Charitable Trust
The William A. Cadbury Charitable Trust
The Edward and Dorothy Cadbury Trust
CHK Charities Ltd
The Coalfields Regeneration Trust
The Cole Charitable Trust
General Charity of Coventry
Coventry Building Society Charitable Foundation
Baron Davenport's Charity
The Dulverton Trust
The Dumbreck Charity
The Wilfred and Elsie Elkes Charity Fund
The Elmley Foundation
The Eveson Charitable Trust
The John Feeney Charitable Bequest
The George Fentham Birmingham Charity
The Lady Forester Trust
The Grantham Yorke Trust
The Greggs Foundation
The Grimmitt Trust
The Alfred Haines Charitable Trust
The Peter Harrison Foundation
Heart of England Community Foundation
Herefordshire Community Foundation
The Herefordshire Historic Churches Trust
The Alan Edward Higgs Charity
Hopmarket Charity
The Huntingdon Foundation Ltd
The Sir Barry Jackson County Fund (incorporating the Hornton Fund)
The Jabbs Foundation
The Jarman Charitable Trust
Lillie Johnson Charitable Trust
Johnnie Johnson Trust
*The Kildare Trust**
The King Henry VIII Endowed Trust – Warwick
Laslett's (Hinton) Charity
*Michael Lowe's and Associated Charities**
The Michael Marsh Charitable Trust
John Martin's Charity
The Mercers' Charitable Foundation
The Oakley Charitable Trust
The Owen Family Trust

The Patrick Trust
The Bernard Piggott Charitable Trust
Quothquan Trust
The Ratcliff Foundation
The Roughley Charitable Trust
The Rugby Group Benevolent Fund Ltd
The Severn Trent Water Charitable Trust Fund
The Sheldon Trust
The Shropshire Historic Churches Trust*
St Peter's Saltley Trust
Staffordshire Community Foundation*
Stratford upon Avon Town Trust
Sutton Coldfield Charitable Trust
C. B. and H. H. Taylor 1984 Trust
The Connie and Albert Taylor Charitable Trust
The Roger and Douglas Turner Charitable Trust
The G. J. W. Turner Trust
The Walker Trust
Warwick Relief in Need Charity*
The Wates Foundation
Worcester Municipal Charities (CIO)

Herefordshire

The E. F. Bulmer Benevolent Fund
The Elmley Foundation
The Eveson Charitable Trust
Herefordshire Community Foundation
The Herefordshire Historic Churches Trust
The Huntingdon Foundation Ltd
The Jordan Charitable Foundation
The Saintbury Trust
St Peter's Saltley Trust

Shropshire

The Bamford Charitable Foundation
The Lady Forester Trust
Mrs H. R. Greene Charitable Settlement
The Millichope Foundation
The Shropshire Historic Churches Trust*
The Walker Trust
The Westcroft Trust

Staffordshire

Consolidated Charity of Burton upon Trent
The Evan Cornish Foundation
Coventry Building Society Charitable Foundation
William Dean Countryside and Educational Trust
The Wilfred and Elsie Elkes Charity Fund
Michael Lowe's and Associated Charities*
The Michael Marsh Charitable Trust
St Peter's Saltley Trust
Staffordshire Community Foundation*
Consolidated Charity of Burton upon Trent
Coventry Building Society Charitable Foundation
The Wilfred and Elsie Elkes Charity Fund
Michael Lowe's and Associated Charities*
The Michael Marsh Charitable Trust
St Peter's Saltley Trust
Staffordshire Community Foundation*

Warwickshire

The Aylesford Family Charitable Trust
Birmingham International Airport Community Trust Fund
The Wilfrid and Constance Cave Foundation
Coventry Building Society Charitable Foundation
The Elizabeth Creak Charitable Trust*
The Dumbreck Charity
Heart of England Community Foundation
The Alan Edward Higgs Charity
The King Henry VIII Endowed Trust – Warwick
The Michael Marsh Charitable Trust
The Park House Charitable Trust
The Patrick Trust
Rigby Foundation*
The Rugby Group Benevolent Fund Ltd
Stratford upon Avon Town Trust
Robert and Felicity Waley-Cohen Charitable Trust
Warwick Relief in Need Charity*

West Midlands

The Lord Austin Trust
The Aylesford Family Charitable Trust
Bauer Radio's Cash for Kids Charities
The James Beattie Charitable Trust
The Birmingham District Nursing Charitable Trust
Birmingham International Airport Community Trust Fund
The Lord Mayor of Birmingham's Charity
The Charles Brotherton Trust
The Bruntwood Charity
The Cole Charitable Trust
The Keith Coombs Trust
The Evan Cornish Foundation
General Charity of Coventry
Coventry Building Society Charitable Foundation
The Dumbreck Charity
The Eveson Charitable Trust
The John Feeney Charitable Bequest
The George Fentham Birmingham Charity
G. M. C. Trust
The Grantham Yorke Trust
The Greggs Foundation
The Grimmitt Trust
The Alfred Haines Charitable Trust
Heart of England Community Foundation
The Alan Edward Higgs Charity
The Sir Barry Jackson County Fund (incorporating the Hornton Fund)
Langdale Trust
The Edgar E. Lawley Foundation
Liberum Foundation
The Michael Marsh Charitable Trust
The Millichope Foundation
The Patrick Trust
The Bernard Piggott Charitable Trust
Quothquan Trust
The Roughley Charitable Trust
The Saintbury Trust
St Peter's Saltley Trust
Sutton Coldfield Charitable Trust
The Lady Tangye Trust Ltd
C. B. and H. H. Taylor 1984 Trust
The Thousandth Man- Richard Burns Charitable Trust
The Roger and Douglas Turner Charitable Trust

Worcestershire

The Bransford Trust
The Dumbreck Charity
The Elmley Foundation
The Eveson Charitable Trust
Gordon Gray Trust
Hopmarket Charity
The Kildare Trust*
Laslett's (Hinton) Charity
The Michael Marsh Charitable Trust
John Martin's Charity
The Patrick Trust
The Saintbury Trust
St Peter's Saltley Trust
The Roger and Douglas Turner Charitable Trust
Worcester Municipal Charities (CIO)

East Midlands

Bauer Radio's Cash for Kids Charities
Bergqvist Charitable Trust
The Bingham Trust
The Michael Bishop Foundation
Boots Charitable Trust
The Christopher Cadbury Charitable Trust
The Edward Cadbury Charitable Trust
The Frederick and Phyllis Cann Trust
The Childwick Trust
The Coalfields Regeneration Trust
The Douglas Compton James Charitable Trust
The Helen Jean Cope Trust
The J. Reginald Corah Foundation Fund
Coventry Building Society Charitable Foundation
Foundation Derbyshire
Provincial Grand Charity of the Province of Derbyshire
The Dulverton Trust
The Maud Elkington Charitable Trust
The Everard Foundation
The Thomas Farr Charity
The Fifty Fund
Ford Britain Trust
The Gordon Trust*
The Gray Trust
The Peter Harrison Foundation
The Hartley Charitable Trust
Help for Health
The Hesslewood Children's Trust (Hull Seamen's and General Orphanage)
Johnnie Johnson Trust
The Jones 1986 Charitable Trust
The David Laing Foundation
Leicester and Leicestershire Historic Churches Preservation Trust (Leicestershire Historic Churches Trust)
Leicestershire and Rutland Masonic Charity Association*
Leicestershire, Leicester and Rutland Community Foundation
Lincolnshire Community Foundation
The London Marathon Charitable Trust Ltd
The Edith Murphy Foundation
Alderman Newton's Educational Foundation
Provincial Grand Charity of Northamptonshire and Huntingdonshire*
Northamptonshire Community Foundation
Nottinghamshire Community Foundation
The Nottinghamshire Historic Churches Trust
The Jack Patston Charitable Trust
The Mary Potter Convent Hospital Trust
The Puri Foundation
The Ratcliff Foundation
The Rugby Group Benevolent Fund Ltd
The Samworth Foundation
The Severn Trent Water Charitable Trust Fund
The Shoe Zone Trust
The Skerritt Trust*
The Jessie Spencer Trust
The Lady Tangye Trust Ltd
The G. J. W. Turner Trust
Waynflete Charitable Trust
The Whitaker Charitable Trust
The Wilson Foundation

Derbyshire

The Bingham Trust
The Evan Cornish Foundation
William Dean Countryside and Educational Trust
Foundation Derbyshire
Provincial Grand Charity of the Province of Derbyshire
The Duke of Devonshire's Charitable Trust
The Gordon Trust*
Open Gate
The Samworth Foundation
The Hugh and Ruby Sykes Charitable Trust
Toyota Manufacturing UK Charitable Trust

Leicestershire

The J. Reginald Corah Foundation Fund
Coventry Building Society Charitable Foundation
The Maud Elkington Charitable Trust
The Everard Foundation
The Gordon Trust*
Leicester and Leicestershire Historic Churches Preservation Trust (Leicestershire Historic Churches Trust)
Leicestershire and Rutland Masonic Charity Association*
Leicestershire, Leicester and Rutland Community Foundation
The Edith Murphy Foundation
Alderman Newton's Educational Foundation
The Paget Charitable Trust
The Jack Patston Charitable Trust
The Samworth Foundation
The Shoe Zone Trust
The Henry Smith Charity
The Florence Turner Trust

Lincolnshire

The Ancaster Trust*
Michael Cornish Charitable Trust
The Evan Cornish Foundation
Help for Health
The Hesslewood Children's Trust (Hull Seamen's and General Orphanage)
Lincolnshire Community Foundation
The Rugby Group Benevolent Fund Ltd
Waynflete Charitable Trust

Northamptonshire

The Benham Charitable Settlement
Bergqvist Charitable Trust
The Frederick and Phyllis Cann Trust
The Childwick Trust
The Francis Coales Charitable Foundation
The Douglas Compton James Charitable Trust
Coventry Building Society Charitable Foundation

The Maud Elkington Charitable Trust
Ford Britain Trust
The Gordon Trust*
The London Marathon Charitable Trust Ltd
The Macdonald-Buchanan Charitable Trust
Provincial Grand Charity of Northamptonshire and Huntingdonshire*
Northamptonshire Community Foundation
The Phillips Charitable Trust
The Constance Travis Charitable Trust
The Florence Turner Trust
The Wilson Foundation

■ Nottinghamshire

Bauer Radio's Cash for Kids Charities
Boots Charitable Trust
The Evan Cornish Foundation
Coventry Building Society Charitable Foundation
The Dunn Family Charitable Trust
The Sir John Eastwood Foundation
The Thomas Farr Charity
The Fifty Fund
The Forman Hardy Charitable Trust
The Gordon Trust*
The Gray Trust
The Hartley Charitable Trust
The Jones 1986 Charitable Trust
The Charles Littlewood Hill Trust
Open Gate
Nottinghamshire Community Foundation
The Nottinghamshire Historic Churches Trust
The Mary Potter Convent Hospital Trust
The Puri Foundation
The Samworth Foundation
The Skerritt Trust*

Eastern England

The Adnams Community Trust
Anguish's Educational Foundation
The Bedfordshire and Hertfordshire Historic Churches Trust
The Bedfordshire and Luton Community Foundation
The Rowan Bentall Charitable Trust*
Bergqvist Charitable Trust
The Morgan Blake Charitable Trust
The Britten-Pears Foundation
The Cambridgeshire Community Foundation
The Leslie Mary Carter Charitable Trust
The Childwick Trust
The Clan Trust Ltd*
The Colchester Catalyst Charity
The Cole Charitable Trust
The Lord Cozens-Hardy Trust
The Harry Cureton Charitable Trust
The Dulverton Trust
Earls Colne and Halstead Educational Charity
Eastern Counties Educational Trust Ltd
The Essex and Southend Sports Trust
Essex Community Foundation
The Essex Heritage Trust
The Essex Youth Trust
Ford Britain Trust
The Charles S. French Charitable Trust
The Anne French Memorial Trust
Friends of Essex Churches Trust
The Ganzoni Charitable Trust
The Harpur Trust
The Peter Harrison Foundation
Hertfordshire Community Foundation
House of Industry Estate
The Hudson Foundation
The Huntingdon Foundation Ltd
Huntingdon Freemen's Trust
Ibbett Trust*
Kirkley Poor's Land Estate
London Legal Support Trust (LLST)
The Masonic Province of Middlesex Charitable Trust (Middlesex Masonic Charity)
The Mills Charity
The Norfolk Churches Trust Ltd*
Norfolk Community Foundation
Educational Foundation of Alderman John Norman
Provincial Grand Charity of Northamptonshire and Huntingdonshire*
Norwich Town Close Estate Charity
The Jack Patston Charitable Trust
The Jack Petchey Foundation
The Pye Foundation*
Richard Radcliffe Trust
Red Hill Charitable Trust
Rosca Trust
The Rugby Group Benevolent Fund Ltd
The Shanly Foundation
The R. C. Snelling Charitable Trust
The Stevenage Community Trust
The Strangward Trust
Suffolk Community Foundation
The Suffolk Historic Churches Trust
The Wates Foundation
The Geoffrey Watling Charity*
The Alfred Williams Charitable Trust*

■ Bedfordshire

The Bedfordshire and Hertfordshire Historic Churches Trust
The Bedfordshire and Luton Community Foundation
Bergqvist Charitable Trust
The Francis Coales Charitable Foundation
The Eranda Rothschild Foundation
The Gale Family Charity Trust
The Harpur Trust
House of Industry Estate
Ibbett Trust*
The Robert Kiln Charitable Trust
The Panacea Charitable Trust
The Rugby Group Benevolent Fund Ltd
The Steel Charitable Trust
The Wixamtree Trust

■ Cambridgeshire

The Cambridgeshire Community Foundation
The Cole Charitable Trust
The Harry Cureton Charitable Trust
The Dawe Charitable Trust
Eastern Counties Educational Trust Ltd
The Earl Fitzwilliam Charitable Trust
The Simon Gibson Charitable Trust
The Hudson Foundation
Huntingdon Freemen's Trust
The Hutchinson Charitable Trust
D. G. Marshall of Cambridge Trust

Provincial Grand Charity of Northamptonshire and Huntingdonshire*
The Jack Patston Charitable Trust
The Pye Foundation*
The Rugby Group Benevolent Fund Ltd

■ Essex

The Leslie Mary Carter Charitable Trust
The Colchester Catalyst Charity
The Augustine Courtauld Trust
Earls Colne and Halstead Educational Charity
Eastern Counties Educational Trust Ltd
The Essex and Southend Sports Trust
Essex Community Foundation
The Essex Heritage Trust
The Essex Youth Trust
Ford Britain Trust
The Charles S. French Charitable Trust
Friends of Essex Churches Trust
Hockerill Educational Foundation
The Huntingdon Foundation Ltd
London Legal Support Trust (LLST)
The Mulberry Trust
The Jack Petchey Foundation
Rosca Trust
The Rugby Group Benevolent Fund Ltd
Tabeel Trust
The Witzenfeld Foundation

■ Hertfordshire

The John Apthorp Charity
The Bedfordshire and Hertfordshire Historic Churches Trust
Bergqvist Charitable Trust
The Robert Clutterbuck Charitable Trust
The Francis Coales Charitable Foundation
Eastern Counties Educational Trust Ltd
The Follett Trust
The Simon Gibson Charitable Trust
The Gretna Charitable Trust
Hertfordshire Community Foundation
Hockerill Educational Foundation
The Robert Kiln Charitable Trust
Christopher Laing Foundation
London Legal Support Trust (LLST)
The Masonic Province of Middlesex Charitable Trust (Middlesex Masonic Charity)
The Clive and Sylvia Richards Charity
The Shanly Foundation
The Stevenage Community Trust
The A. and R. Woolf Charitable Trust

■ Norfolk

Anguish's Educational Foundation
The Paul Bassham Charitable Trust
The Leslie Mary Carter Charitable Trust
The Clan Trust Ltd*
The Lord Cozens-Hardy Trust
Eastern Counties Educational Trust Ltd
The Anne French Memorial Trust
The Simon Gibson Charitable Trust
Mrs H. R. Greene Charitable Settlement
The Lind Trust
The Charles Littlewood Hill Trust
The Mickleham Trust
The Norfolk Churches Trust Ltd*
Norfolk Community Foundation
Educational Foundation of Alderman John Norman
Norwich Town Close Estate Charity
The Pennycress Trust
The Ranworth Trust
The Leslie Smith Foundation
The R. C. Snelling Charitable Trust
The Spurrell Charitable Trust
The Geoffrey Watling Charity*

■ Suffolk

The Adnams Community Trust
The Britten-Pears Foundation
The Leslie Mary Carter Charitable Trust
Eastern Counties Educational Trust Ltd
The Ganzoni Charitable Trust
The Simon Gibson Charitable Trust
Kirkley Poor's Land Estate
The Mills Charity
The Music Sales Charitable Trust
Mrs L. D. Rope's Second Charitable Settlement*
Mrs L. D. Rope's Third Charitable Settlement
The Scarfe Charitable Trust
The Henry Smith Charity
Suffolk Community Foundation
The Suffolk Historic Churches Trust
Annie Tranmer Charitable Trust
The Geoffrey Watling Charity*
The Alfred Williams Charitable Trust*

North West

A. W. Charitable Trust
The Addleshaw Goddard Charitable Trust
The Anne Duchess of Westminster's Charity*
The Philip Barker Charity*
Bauer Radio's Cash for Kids Charities
BCH Trust
Asser Bishvil Foundation*
The Marjory Boddy Charitable Trust
The Bonamy Charitable Trust
The Booth Charities
The Bowland Charitable Trust
The Harold and Alice Bridges Charity
The Charles Brotherton Trust
The Bruntwood Charity
The Chadwick Educational Foundation*
Cheshire Community Foundation Ltd*
Cheshire Freemason's Charity
The Coalfields Regeneration Trust
The Lord Cozens-Hardy Trust
Cumbria Community Foundation
The Hamilton Davies Trust
The John Grant Davies Trust*
The Dulverton Trust
Esh Foundation
The Eventhall Family Charitable Trust
Forever Manchester
Jill Franklin Trust
The Granada Foundation
The Greggs Foundation
The Hadfield Charitable Trust
The W. A. Handley Charity Trust
The Harris Charity
The Peter Harrison Foundation
The Helping Foundation
The Hemby Charitable Trust

The Edward Holt Trust
Hulme Trust Estates (Educational)
The Johnson Foundation
J. E. Joseph Charitable Fund
Kelsick's Educational Foundation
The Peter Kershaw Trust
The Ursula Keyes Trust
Community Foundations for Lancashire and Merseyside
Lancashire Environmental Fund Ltd
Duchy of Lancaster Benevolent Fund
The Herd Lawson and Muriel Lawson Charitable Trust
Liverpool Charity and Voluntary Services (LCVS)
The W. M. and B. W. Lloyd Trust*
Manchester Airport Community Trust Fund
The Manchester Guardian Society Charitable Trust
Lord Mayor of Manchester's Charity Appeal Trust
The Ann and David Marks Foundation
John Moores Foundation
The Steve Morgan Foundation
North West Cancer Research (incorporating Clatterbridge Cancer Research)
Oglesby Charitable Trust
The Oldham Foundation
The Ravensdale Trust
Samjo Ltd*
The Francis C. Scott Charitable Trust
The Frieda Scott Charitable Trust
The Sellafield Charity Trust Fund*
The Patricia and Donald Shepherd Charitable Trust
The Skelton Bounty
The John Slater Foundation
The Steinberg Family Charitable Trust
The W. O. Street Charitable Foundation
UKH Foundation*
United Utilities Trust Fund
The Warrington Church of England Educational Trust*
Mrs Waterhouse Charitable Trust
West Derby Waste Lands Charity
The Westminster Foundation
The Norman Whiteley Trust
The Williams Family Foundation*
Brian Wilson Charitable Trust*

Cheshire

The Anne Duchess of Westminster's Charity*
The Philip Barker Charity*
The Marjory Boddy Charitable Trust
Cheshire Community Foundation Ltd*
Cheshire Freemason's Charity
The Robert Clutterbuck Charitable Trust
The Evan Cornish Foundation
The Hamilton Davies Trust
William Dean Countryside and Educational Trust
The Ursula Keyes Trust
Lord Leverhulme's Charitable Trust
Manchester Airport Community Trust Fund
John Moores Foundation
The Pennycress Trust
The Sellafield Charity Trust Fund*
The Warrington Church of England Educational Trust*
The Westminster Foundation
The Williams Family Foundation*
Brian Wilson Charitable Trust*

Cumbria

The Harold and Alice Bridges Charity
The Evan Cornish Foundation
Cumbria Community Foundation
Esh Foundation
The Sir John Fisher Foundation
The Hadfield Charitable Trust
The W. A. Handley Charity Trust
Kelsick's Educational Foundation
The Herd Lawson and Muriel Lawson Charitable Trust
The Frieda Scott Charitable Trust
The Sellafield Charity Trust Fund*
The Squires Foundation
The Norman Whiteley Trust

Greater Manchester

A. W. Charitable Trust
The Addleshaw Goddard Charitable Trust
BCH Trust
Beauland Ltd
Asser Bishvil Foundation*
The Booth Charities
The Bruntwood Charity
The Chadwick Educational Foundation*
Cheshire Freemason's Charity
The Hamilton Davies Trust
The John Grant Davies Trust*
Forever Manchester
The F. P. Ltd Charitable Trust
The Greggs Foundation
The Hathaway Trust
The Helping Foundation
The Holden Charitable Trust
The Edward Holt Trust
The Hoover Foundation
Hulme Trust Estates (Educational)
J. E. Joseph Charitable Fund
The Peter Kershaw Trust
Duchy of Lancaster Benevolent Fund
Jack Livingstone Charitable Trust
Localtrent Ltd
M. B. Foundation*
Manchester Airport Community Trust Fund
The Manchester Guardian Society Charitable Trust
Lord Mayor of Manchester's Charity Appeal Trust
The Ann and David Marks Foundation
Mole Charitable Trust
Oizer Charitable Trust
Samjo Ltd*
The Searchlight Electric Charitable Trust
SHINE (Support and Help in Education)
The Skelton Bounty
The Stoller Charitable Trust
The Strawberry Charitable Trust
T. and S. Trust Fund
The Thousandth Man- Richard Burns Charitable Trust

Lancashire

The Harold and Alice Bridges Charity
The Chadwick Educational Foundation*
The Evan Cornish Foundation
The Sir John Fisher Foundation
The Fort Foundation
The Harris Charity
Community Foundations for Lancashire and Merseyside
Lancashire Environmental Fund Ltd
Duchy of Lancaster Benevolent Fund
Lancaster Foundation
Lord Leverhulme's Charitable Trust

*The W. M. and B. W. Lloyd Trust**
John Moores Foundation
The Dowager Countess Eleanor Peel Trust
*Rhodi Charitable Trust**
*Riverside Charitable Trust Ltd**
The Francis C. Scott Charitable Trust
The Skelton Bounty
Mrs Waterhouse Charitable Trust
The Westminster Foundation

Merseyside

*The Anne Duchess of Westminster's Charity**
The Baring Foundation
The David and Ruth Behrend Fund
The Marjory Boddy Charitable Trust
The Charles Brotherton Trust
The Bruntwood Charity
The Amelia Chadwick Trust
Cheshire Freemason's Charity
The Evan Cornish Foundation
The Lord Cozens-Hardy Trust
William Dean Countryside and Educational Trust
The Steven Gerrard Foundation
The Hemby Charitable Trust
The Johnson Foundation
Community Foundations for Lancashire and Merseyside
Duchy of Lancaster Benevolent Fund
Lord Leverhulme's Charitable Trust
Liverpool Charity and Voluntary Services (LCVS)
John Moores Foundation
Pilkington Charities Fund
The Ravensdale Trust
The Rainford Trust
The Eleanor Rathbone Charitable Trust
Elizabeth Rathbone Charity
The John Rayner Charitable Trust
The Skelton Bounty
The Ward Blenkinsop Trust
West Derby Waste Lands Charity

Yorkshire and the Humber

The Addleshaw Goddard Charitable Trust
Bauer Radio's Cash for Kids Charities
The Bearder Charity
The Harry Bottom Charitable Trust
The Tony Bramall Charitable Trust
The Liz and Terry Bramall Foundation
*The Brelms Trust CIO**
The Charles Brotherton Trust
The Jack Brunton Charitable Trust
The Bruntwood Charity
The Arnold Burton 1998 Charitable Trust
Community Foundation for Calderdale
The Joseph and Annie Cattle Trust
The Church Burgesses Educational Foundation
Church Burgesses Trust
The Coalfields Regeneration Trust
The Marjorie Coote Old People's Charity
The Evan Cornish Foundation
*The Coulthurst Trust**
Coventry Building Society Charitable Foundation
The Crerar Hotels Trust
The Dulverton Trust
*The Emerald Foundation**
Esh Foundation
The Earl Fitzwilliam Charitable Trust
The Freshgate Trust Foundation
The J. G. Graves Charitable Trust
The Greggs Foundation
The Peter Harrison Foundation
The Hartley Charitable Trust
Help for Health
The Hesslewood Children's Trust (Hull Seamen's and General Orphanage)
The Hull and East Riding Charitable Trust
Incommunities Foundation
Duchy of Lancaster Benevolent Fund
Leeds Community Foundation (LCF)
The George A. Moore Foundation
The James Neill Trust Fund
*One Community Foundation Ltd**
*Parish Estate of the Church of St Michael Spurriergate York**
Sir John Priestman Charity Trust
The J. S. and E. C. Rymer Charitable Trust
The Sheffield Town Trust
The Talbot Trusts
The C. Paul Thackray General Charitable Trust
Two Ridings Community Foundation
Wade's Charity
The Scurrah Wainwright Charity
Waynflete Charitable Trust
*York Children's Trust**
*Yorkshire Cancer Research**
The South Yorkshire Community Foundation
The Yorkshire Historic Churches Trust
The Marjorie and Arnold Ziff Charitable Foundation

Humberside, East Riding

*The Brelms Trust CIO**
The Joseph and Annie Cattle Trust
The Sandy Dewhirst Charitable Trust
Help for Health
The Hesslewood Children's Trust (Hull Seamen's and General Orphanage)
The Hull and East Riding Charitable Trust
The J. S. and E. C. Rymer Charitable Trust
Waynflete Charitable Trust

North Yorkshire

*The Brelms Trust CIO**
The Charles Brotherton Trust
The Jack Brunton Charitable Trust
*The Coulthurst Trust**
The Sandy Dewhirst Charitable Trust
The Duke of Devonshire's Charitable Trust
Esh Foundation
The A. M. Fenton Trust
The Normanby Charitable Trust
*Parish Estate of the Church of St Michael Spurriergate York**
The W. L. Pratt Charitable Trust
Sir John Priestman Charity Trust
The Sylvia and Colin Shepherd Charitable Trust
The C. Paul Thackray General Charitable Trust
Two Ridings Community Foundation
*York Children's Trust**

South Yorkshire

The Harry Bottom Charitable Trust
*The Brelms Trust CIO**
The Church Burgesses Educational Foundation
Church Burgesses Trust
The Marjorie Coote Old People's Charity
Coventry Building Society Charitable Foundation
The Freshgate Trust Foundation
The J. G. Graves Charitable Trust
The James Neill Trust Fund
The Sheffield Town Trust
The Swann-Morton Foundation
The Talbot Trusts
The Westfield Health Charitable Trust
The Whitecourt Charitable Trust
The South Yorkshire Community Foundation
The Zochonis Charitable Trust

West Yorkshire

The Addleshaw Goddard Charitable Trust
The Bearder Charity
*The Brelms Trust CIO**
The Charles Brotherton Trust
The Bruntwood Charity
Community Foundation for Calderdale
The Crerar Hotels Trust
*The Emerald Foundation**
The Greggs Foundation
Incommunities Foundation
Duchy of Lancaster Benevolent Fund
Leeds Community Foundation (LCF)
The Linden Charitable trust
*One Community Foundation Ltd**
The Shanti Charitable Trust
The Squires Foundation
The Thousandth Man- Richard Burns Charitable Trust
Wade's Charity

North East

The 1989 Willan Charitable Trust
The Roy and Pixie Baker Charitable Trust
The Ballinger Charitable Trust
The Barbour Foundation
Bauer Radio's Cash for Kids Charities
Chrysalis Trust
J. A. Clark Charitable Trust
The Coalfields Regeneration Trust
The Catherine Cookson Charitable Trust
The Sir Tom Cowie Charitable Trust
The Gillian Dickinson Trust
The Dulverton Trust
County Durham Community Foundation
The Ellinson Foundation Ltd
Esh Foundation
Jill Franklin Trust
The Goshen Trust
E. C. Graham Belford Charitable Settlement
The Greggs Foundation
The Hadrian Trust
The W. A. Handley Charity Trust
The Peter Harrison Foundation
The Hospital of God at Greatham
The Ruth and Lionel Jacobson Trust (Second Fund) No. 2
The Sir James Knott Trust
The Kreditor Charitable Trust
The William Leech Charity
The Lyndhurst Trust
R. W. Mann Trust
The Millfield House Foundation (1)
*North East Area Miners Welfare Trust Fund**
The Northumberland Village Homes Trust
The Normanby Charitable Trust
The Northumbria Historic Churches Trust
*The JGW Patterson Foundation**
Sir John Priestman Charity Trust
The Rothley Trust
The Patricia and Donald Shepherd Charitable Trust
*Sherburn House Charity**
The Henry Smith Charity
The St Hilda's Trust
The Squires Foundation
Tees Valley Community Foundation
Community Foundation serving Tyne and Wear and Northumberland
The Vardy Foundation
The Nigel Vinson Charitable Trust
The Virgin Money Foundation
The William Webster Charitable Trust

Cleveland

The Hospital of God at Greatham
The Sir James Knott Trust
The Northumbria Historic Churches Trust
*Sherburn House Charity**
Tees Valley Community Foundation

Durham

The Evan Cornish Foundation
The Sir Tom Cowie Charitable Trust
The Gillian Dickinson Trust
County Durham Community Foundation
Esh Foundation
The Hospital of God at Greatham
The Sir James Knott Trust
The William Leech Charity
The Northumbria Historic Churches Trust
Sir John Priestman Charity Trust
*Sherburn House Charity**
Tees Valley Community Foundation

Northumberland

The Evan Cornish Foundation
The Gillian Dickinson Trust
Esh Foundation
E. C. Graham Belford Charitable Settlement
The Percy Hedley 1990 Charitable Trust
The Hospital of God at Greatham
The Joicey Trust
The Sir James Knott Trust
The William Leech Charity
The Northumbria Historic Churches Trust
*Sherburn House Charity**
The St Hilda's Trust
Community Foundation serving Tyne and Wear and Northumberland

Tyne and Wear

A. W. Charitable Trust
The Sir Tom Cowie Charitable Trust
The Gillian Dickinson Trust
The Ellinson Foundation Ltd
The Percy Hedley 1990 Charitable Trust
The Hospital of God at Greatham

The Joicey Trust
The Sir James Knott Trust
The William Leech Charity
The Northumbria Historic Churches Trust
Sir John Priestman Charity Trust
Sherburn House Charity*
The St Hilda's Trust
T. and S. Trust Fund
Community Foundation serving Tyne and Wear and Northumberland

Northern Ireland

The Allen & Overy Foundation*
Bauer Radio's Cash for Kids Charities
Church of Ireland Priorities Fund
The Marjorie Coote Animal Charity Trust
The Drapers' Charitable Fund
The Enkalon Foundation
Halifax Foundation for Northern Ireland
The Peter Harrison Foundation
Integrated Education Fund*
Lord and Lady Lurgan Trust
John Moores Foundation
The Community Foundation for Northern Ireland
The Royal British Legion
The Sackler Trust
R. H. Southern Trust
Ulster Garden Villages Ltd
Viridor Credits Environmental Company*

Scotland

The Aberbrothock Skea Trust
The AEB Charitable Trust*
Age Scotland
The Sylvia Aitken Charitable Trust
The AMW Charitable Trust
The Mary Andrew Charitable Trust
The Anne Duchess of Westminster's Charity*
The Baird Trust
Bairdwatson Charitable Trust*
The Bank of Scotland Foundation
The Barcapel Foundation
Barchester Healthcare Foundation
The Bellahouston Bequest Fund
The Blair Foundation
British Gas (Scottish Gas) Energy Trust
The Cadogan Charity
Callander Charitable Trust
The Ellis Campbell Charitable Foundation
The W. A. Cargill Charitable Trust*
David William Traill Cargill Fund
The Carnegie Dunfermline Trust
The Carnegie Trust for the Universities of Scotland
The Castansa Trust*
The Cattanach Charitable Trust
Celtic Charity Fund
Chest Heart and Stroke Scotland
John Christie Trust*
The Coalfields Regeneration Trust
Martin Connell Charitable Trust
The Marjorie Coote Animal Charity Trust
The Craignish Trust
The Cray Trust
Creative Scotland
The Crerar Hotels Trust
The Cross Trust
Cruden Foundation Ltd
The Cunningham Trust
The Davidson (Nairn) Charitable Trust
The Dulverton Trust
Dunard Fund 2016
Edinburgh Children's Holiday Fund
The Erskine Cunningham Hill Trust
Elizabeth Ferguson Charitable Trust Fund
The Gordon Fraser Charitable Trust

The Hugh Fraser Foundation
The Gannochy Trust
The Greggs Foundation
Guildry Incorporation of Perth
Dr Guthrie's Association
The Peter Harrison Foundation
Heathrow Community Fund (LHR Airport Communities Trust)
The Christina Mary Hendrie Trust for Scottish and Canadian Charities
*M. V. Hillhouse Trust**
The Holywood Trust
The Hope Trust
Miss Agnes H. Hunter's Trust
Lady Eda Jardine Charitable Trust
The Kelly Family Charitable Trust
The KPMG Foundation
The R. J. Larg Family Charitable Trust
*Leng Charitable Trust**
*The Lethendy Charitable Trust**
*Life Changes Trust**
Lloyds TSB Foundation for Scotland
The MacRobert Trust
The R. S. Macdonald Charitable Trust
The Ian Mactaggart Trust (The Mactaggart Second Fund)
The W. M. Mann Foundation
*The Martin Charitable Trust**
The Nancie Massey Charitable Trust
The Mathew Trust
*Medical Research Scotland**
The Mickel Fund
Hugh and Mary Miller Bequest Trust
The Ronald Miller Foundation
Morgan Stanley International Foundation
*The Morton Charitable Trust**
The Mugdock Children's Trust
Northwood Charitable Trust
P. F. Charitable Trust
People's Health Trust
People's Postcode Trust
The Ponton House Trust
*Postcode Community Trust**
Postcode Dream Trust – Dream Fund
The Robertson Trust
Rosetrees Trust
Mrs Gladys Row Fogo Charitable Trust
The Royal British Legion
*Rozelle Trust**
The Sackler Trust
Foundation Scotland
*The John Scott Trust Fund**
The ScottishPower Energy People Trust
The Shetland Charitable Trust
The Souter Charitable Trust
R. H. Southern Trust
The Stafford Trust
The Hugh Stenhouse Foundation
Talteg Ltd
The Tay Charitable Trust
The Templeton Goodwill Trust
*Tenovus Scotland**
The Arthur and Margaret Thompson Charitable Trust
*The Trades House of Glasgow**
The Turtleton Charitable Trust
The Underwood Trust
*Viridor Credits Environmental Company**
Volant Charitable Trust
Voluntary Action Fund (VAF)
*Walton Foundation**
John Watson's Trust
*The Weir Charitable Trust**
The Westminster Foundation
The Whitaker Charitable Trust
J. and J. R. Wilson Trust
The James Wood Bequest Fund
The Wood Foundation

Central

Mrs Gladys Row Fogo Charitable Trust
The James Wood Bequest Fund

Grampian

The Aberbrothock Skea Trust
Heathrow Community Fund (LHR Airport Communities Trust)

Highlands and Islands

*The Anne Duchess of Westminster's Charity**
The Davidson (Nairn) Charitable Trust
The Jordan Charitable Foundation
The Shetland Charitable Trust
The Westminster Foundation

Lothians Region

*The AEB Charitable Trust**
Edinburgh Children's Holiday Fund
The Nancie Massey Charitable Trust
The Ponton House Trust
Mrs Gladys Row Fogo Charitable Trust
John Watson's Trust

Southern Scotland

*The AEB Charitable Trust**
The Holywood Trust
The Joicey Trust

Strathclyde

*Bairdwatson Charitable Trust**
The Bellahouston Bequest Fund
*The W. A. Cargill Fund**
The Greggs Foundation
Heathrow Community Fund (LHR Airport Communities Trust)
The Hoover Foundation
*The Martin Charitable Trust**
Morgan Stanley International Foundation
The Schroder Foundation
John Scott Trust Fund
The Templeton Goodwill Trust
*The Trades House of Glasgow**
*Walton Foundation**
The James Weir Foundation
The James Wood Bequest Fund

Tayside and Fife

The Aberbrothock Skea Trust
The Ellis Campbell Charitable Foundation
The Carnegie Dunfermline Trust
Guildry Incorporation of Perth
*The Lethendy Charitable Trust**
Northwood Charitable Trust
The Tay Charitable Trust
The Arthur and Margaret Thompson Charitable Trust

Wales

*A2BD Foundation UK Ltd**
*The Neville Abraham Foundation**
Access Sport CIO
The Sylvia Adams Charitable Trust
D. C. R. Allen Charitable Trust
*The Anne Duchess of Westminster's Charity**
*AO Smile Foundation**
The Arah Foundation
The John Armitage Charitable Trust
Arts Council of Wales (also known as Cyngor Celfyddydau Cymru)
The Asda Foundation
The Ashley Family Foundation
Barchester Healthcare Foundation
The Berkeley Charitable Foundation
Birthday House Trust
Blakemore Foundation
The Marjory Boddy Charitable Trust
The Boodle & Dunthorne Charitable Trust
The Boshier-Hinton Foundation
The Bridging Fund Charitable Trust
British Gas (Scottish Gas) Energy Trust
*The Butters Foundation (UK) Ltd**
The Catholic Trust for England and Wales
Chalfords Ltd
The Coalfields Regeneration Trust
Colwinston Charitable Trust
Country Houses Foundation
The County Council of Dyfed Welsh Curch Fund
Coventry Building Society Charitable Foundation
*England and Wales Cricket Trust**
The Peter Cruddas Foundation
Margaret Davies Charity
The Henry and Suzanne Davis Foundation
Didymus
The DM Charitable Trust
The Dulverton Trust
The Elephant Trust
Esher House Charitable Trust
Matthew Eyton Animal Welfare Trust
Ford Britain Trust
Gwyneth Forrester Trust
The Fort Foundation
Jill Franklin Trust
The Joseph Strong Frazer Trust
The General Nursing Council for England and Wales Trust
The Simon Gibson Charitable Trust
The Girdlers' Company Charitable Trust
Grand Charitable Trust of the Order of Women Freemasons
The Greggs Foundation
H. and T. Clients Charitable Trust
The Haley Family Charitable Trust
The Peter and Teresa Harris Charitable Trust
The Peter Harrison Foundation
*Heb Ffin (Without Frontier)**
Ernest Hecht Charitable Foundation
The Hintze Family Charity Foundation
The Jane Hodge Foundation
The Mary Homfray Charitable Trust
The J. Isaacs Charitable Trust
The Isle of Anglesey Charitable Trust
The Jenour Foundation
The Dezna Robins Jones Charitable Foundation
The KPMG Foundation
The Leonard Laity Stoate Charitable Trust
*Bernard Lewis Family Charitable Trust**
The Lindley Foundation (TLF)
Lloyds Bank Foundation for England and Wales
*The Lockwood Charitable Foundation**
Lord and Lady Lurgan Trust
Charity of John Marshall
*Masonic Charitable Foundation**
Millennium Stadium Charitable Trust (Ymddiriedolaeth Elusennol Stadiwm Y. Mileniwm)
The Monmouthshire County Council Welsh Church Act Fund
The Steve Morgan Foundation
The Moss Family Charitable Trust
Moto in the Community
North West Cancer Research (incorporating Clatterbridge Cancer Research)
The Norwood and Newton Settlement
The Oakdale Trust
The Ouseley Church Music Trust
The James Pantyfedwen Foundation
People's Health Trust
People's Postcode Trust
The Bernard Piggott Charitable Trust
*Postcode Community Trust**
Postcode Dream Trust – Dream Fund
*Powys Welsh Church Fund**
*Princes Gate Trust**
Rhondda Cynon Taff Welsh Church Acts Fund
Rosetrees Trust
The Royal British Legion
The Dr Mortimer and Theresa Sackler Foundation
The Sackler Trust
*The Savoy Educational Trust**
O. and G. Schreiber Charitable Trust
The ScottishPower Energy People Trust
The Severn Trent Water Charitable Trust Fund
The DS Smith Charitable Foundation
The Sobell Foundation
R. H. Southern Trust
Sparquote Ltd
Springrule Ltd
*The Stoneygate Trust**
*The Street Foundation**
The Bernard Sunley Charitable Foundation
*The Transform Foundation**
Vale of Glamorgan Welsh Church Fund
*Viridor Credits Environmental Company**
The Community Foundation in Wales
Wales Council for Voluntary Action
Robert and Felicity Waley-Cohen Charitable Trust
The Waterloo Foundation
*The Watson Family Charitable Trust**
*The Wheeler Family Charitable Trust**
*The Wigoder Family Foundation**
*The Williams Family Foundation**
*The Woodstock Family Charitable Foundation**
The Yapp Charitable Trust

North Wales

*The Anne Duchess of Westminster's Charity**
The Marjory Boddy Charitable Trust
The Chapman Charitable Trust

The Earl Fitzwilliam Charitable Trust
The Isle of Anglesey Charitable Trust
The Steve Morgan Foundation
North West Cancer Research (incorporating Clatterbridge Cancer Research)
The Bernard Piggott Charitable Trust
The Ratcliff Foundation
Toyota Manufacturing UK Charitable Trust
*The Williams Family Foundation**

Mid and West Wales

*The Anne Duchess of Westminster's Charity**
The Isle of Anglesey Charitable Trust
The Steve Morgan Foundation
North West Cancer Research (incorporating Clatterbridge Cancer Research)
The Bernard Piggott Charitable Trust
*The Williams Family Foundation**

South Wales

Ford Britain Trust
The Gibbs Charitable Trust
*Heb Ffin (Without Frontier)**
The Hoover Foundation
The Dezna Robins Jones Charitable Foundation
The Monmouthshire County Council Welsh Church Act Fund
Rhondda Cynon Taff Welsh Church Acts Fund
*The Florence Shute Millennium Trust**
Vale of Glamorgan Welsh Church Fund

Channel Islands

The Hampshire and Islands Historic Churches Trust
Lloyds Bank Foundation for the Channel Islands
Lord and Lady Lurgan Trust
The National Churches Trust
The Oakley Charitable Trust
The W. O. Street Charitable Foundation

Isle of Man

Lord and Lady Lurgan Trust
The George A. Moore Foundation
The National Churches Trust

Grant-makers by field of interest and type of beneficiary

This index contains two separate listings:

Categorisation of fields of interest and type of beneficiary: This lists all of the headings used in DGMT to categorise fields of interest and types of beneficiary. Note that 'Overseas aid/projects' category includes support in financially developing countries. Funding for research into specific medical conditions has been included under appropriate headings in the 'Beneficial groups' category.

Grant-makers by field of interest and type of beneficiary: This lists funders under the fields of interest and types of beneficiary for which they have expressed a funding preference. Asterisks mark funders which have not been featured in DGMT before.

Grant-makers by field of interest and type of beneficiary

These pages contain two separate listings:

Categorisation of fields of interest and type of beneficiary
This lists all of the headings used in DGMT to categorise fields of interest and types of beneficiary

Grant-makers by field of interest and type of beneficiary
This lists funders under the fields of interest and types of beneficiary for which they have expressed a funding preference

Arts, culture, sport and recreation

The 29th May 1961 Charitable Trust
The Ammco Trust
The Astor Foundation
The Roy and Pixie Baker Charitable Trust
The Berkshire Community Foundation
The Bingham Trust
*The Brelms Trust CIO**
The Charles Brotherton Trust
The Arnold Burton 1998 Charitable Trust
The George Cadbury Trust
The B. G. S. Cayzer Charitable Trust
The Amelia Chadwick Trust
The Chapman Charitable Trust
*The Clark Foundation**
The John Coates Charitable Trust
The Vivienne and Samuel Cohen Charitable Trust
The Sir Jeremiah Colman Gift Trust
The Craps Charitable Trust
Dorset Community Foundation
The Dorus Trust
County Durham Community Foundation
The Gilbert and Eileen Edgar Foundation
The Epigoni Trust
The Doris Field Charitable Trust
Donald Forrester Trust
The Golden Bottle Trust
Greenham Common Community Trust Ltd
The Greggs Foundation
Hampshire and Isle of Wight Community Foundation
The Kathleen Hannay Memorial Charity
William Harding's Charity
The Harrison-Frank Family Foundation (UK) Ltd
The Hawthorne Charitable Trust
Heart of England Community Foundation
The Charlotte Heber-Percy Charitable Trust
The Percy Hedley 1990 Charitable Trust
The Hemby Charitable Trust
The Hillier Trust
The Hillingdon Community Trust
The Hobson Charity Ltd
The Hollick Family Charitable Trust
P. H. Holt Foundation
The Mary Homfray Charitable Trust
Incommunities Foundation
Irish Youth Foundation (UK) Ltd (incorporating The Lawlor Foundation)
The Isle of Anglesey Charitable Trust
The Jewish Youth Fund (JYF)
Johnson Wax Ltd Charitable Trust
The Joicey Trust
The Marjorie and Geoffrey Jones Charitable Trust
*The Graham Kirkham Foundation**
The Sir James Knott Trust
The David Laing Foundation
The Lambert Charitable Trust
Duchy of Lancaster Benevolent Fund
The Jack Lane Charitable Trust
The R. J. Larg Family Charitable Trust
The Edgar E. Lawley Foundation
Lawson Beckman Charitable Trust
Leicestershire, Leicester and Rutland Community Foundation
The Lennox Hannay Charitable Trust
John Lewis Partnership General Community Fund
Liberum Foundation
Lincolnshire Community Foundation
The Lindley Foundation (TLF)
The Lister Charitable Trust
The Elaine and Angus Lloyd Charitable Trust
Lloyd's Charities Trust
The London Community Foundation (LCF)
The C. L. Loyd Charitable Trust
The Lynn Foundation
The E. M. MacAndrew Trust
*Mace Foundation**
The Mactaggart Third Fund
The W. M. Mann Foundation
R. W. Mann Trust
The Manoukian Charitable Foundation
The Marks Family Foundation
The J. P. Marland Charitable Trust
The Merchant Taylors' Company Charities Fund
The Metropolitan Masonic Charity
The Mickel Fund
The Ronald Miller Foundation
The Millichope Foundation
Milton Keynes Community Foundation Ltd
The Monmouthshire County Council Welsh Church Act Fund
*Moondance Foundation**
The George A. Moore Foundation
The Morris Charitable Trust
The NDL Foundation
The Norton Foundation
The Oldham Foundation
P. F. Charitable Trust
The Portrack Charitable Trust
Rhondda Cynon Taff Welsh Church Acts Fund
*Rigby Foundation**
Rivers Foundation
The Saintbury Trust
The Salamander Charitable Trust
The M. J. Samuel Charitable Trust
The Sandhu Charitable Foundation
The Scotshill Trust
The ScottishPower Foundation
The Scouloudi Foundation
St James's Place Foundation
The Sussex Community Foundation
Sutton Coldfield Charitable Trust
The Tompkins Foundation
Two Ridings Community Foundation
Community Foundation serving Tyne and Wear and Northumberland
The Nigel Vinson Charitable Trust
Wade's Charity
Wales Council for Voluntary Action
The Barbara Ward Children's Foundation
*The Weir Charitable Trust**
The Garfield Weston Foundation
*The Williams Family Foundation**
Williams Serendipity Trust
The Maurice Wohl Charitable Foundation
Yorkshire and Clydesdale Bank Foundation

Arts and culture

The Acacia Charitable Trust
*The AEB Charitable Trust**
The Sylvia Aitken Charitable Trust
*AKO Foundation**
Aldgate and All Hallows' Foundation
The Derrill Allatt Foundation
Andor Charitable Trust
The Arah Foundation
The John Armitage Charitable Trust
Arts Council England
Arts Council of Northern Ireland

Arts Council of Wales (also known as Cyngor Celfyddydau Cymru)
The Ashley Family Foundation
The Aurelius Charitable Trust
Backstage Trust
The Ballinger Charitable Trust
The Band Trust
The Barbour Foundation
The Baring Foundation
*The Barrack Charitable Trust**
BC Partners Foundation
The John Beckwith Charitable Trust
*The Behrens Foundation**
The Benham Charitable Settlement
Bennett Lowell Ltd
The Boltini Trust
The Bowerman Charitable Trust
The Liz and Terry Bramall Foundation
The Bransford Trust
The Consuelo and Anthony Brooke Charitable Trust
The Rory and Elizabeth Brooks Foundation
The T. B. H. Brunner's Charitable Settlement
The Edward Cadbury Charitable Trust
The G. W. Cadbury Charitable Trust
The William A. Cadbury Charitable Trust
The Edward and Dorothy Cadbury Trust
David William Traill Cargill Fund
*The W. A. Cargill Fund**
The Carnegie Dunfermline Trust
*The Castansa Trust**
The Charter 600 Charity
CHK Charities Ltd
The City Educational Trust Fund
Denise Coates Foundation
The Denise Cohen Charitable Trust
The R. and S. Cohen Foundation
The Catherine Cookson Charitable Trust
The Keith Coombs Trust
The Duke of Cornwall's Benevolent Fund
Creative Scotland
The Cross Trust
Cruden Foundation Ltd
The D'Oyly Carte Charitable Trust
The Davidson (Nairn) Charitable Trust
The Davidson Family Charitable Trust
Michael Davies Charitable Settlement
Margaret Davies Charity
The Davis Foundation
The Henry and Suzanne Davis Foundation
Peter De Haan Charitable Trust
*The Roger De Haan Charitable Trust**
Devon Community Foundation
The Gillian Dickinson Trust
Didymus
The Dischma Charitable Trust
The Djanogly Foundation
The Drapers' Charitable Fund
The Charles Dunstone Charitable Trust
The Dyers' Company Charitable Trust
The Earley Charity
The John Ellerman Foundation
The Emerton-Christie Charity
The Englefield Charitable Trust
The Eranda Rothschild Foundation
The Estelle Trust
G. F. Eyre Charitable Trust
Esmée Fairbairn Foundation
The Lord Faringdon Charitable Trust
The John Feeney Charitable Bequest
The Sir John Fisher Foundation
The Earl Fitzwilliam Charitable Trust
The Follett Trust
The Forman Hardy Charitable Trust
The Fort Foundation
The Foyle Foundation
The Elizabeth Frankland Moore and Star Foundation
The Freshgate Trust Foundation
The Adrian and Jane Frost Charitable Trust
The Gatsby Charitable Foundation
Gatwick Airport Community Trust
The Jacqueline and Michael Gee Charitable Trust
The Gibbs Charitable Trust
The G. C. Gibson Charitable Trust
The Simon Gibson Charitable Trust
The Glass-House Trust
The Godinton Charitable Trust
Goldman Sachs Gives (UK)
The Goldsmiths' Company Charity
The Golsoncott Foundation
Nicholas and Judith Goodison's Charitable Settlement
A. and S. Graham Charitable Trust
*The Graham Trust**
The Granada Foundation
The Kenneth and Susan Green Charitable Foundation
Greys Charitable Trust
The Grimmitt Trust
The Grocers' Charity
Guildry Incorporation of Perth
The Hadfield Charitable Trust
The Hadrian Trust
Paul Hamlyn Foundation
Hampton Fuel Allotment Charity
The W. A. Handley Charity Trust
The Harbour Charitable Trust
The Harbour Foundation
The Headley Trust
The Heathside Charitable Trust
Ernest Hecht Charitable Foundation
The Alan Edward Higgs Charity
The Derek Hill Foundation
*M. V. Hillhouse Trust**
R. G. Hills Charitable Trust
The Hinduja Foundation
The Hintze Family Charity Foundation
The Hiscox Foundation
The Henry C. Hoare Charitable Trust
The Holywood Trust
The Homestead Charitable Trust
The Hoover Foundation
The Antony Hornby Charitable Trust
The Sir Joseph Hotung Charitable Settlement
The Daniel Howard Trust
The Hull and East Riding Charitable Trust
Huntingdon Freemen's Trust
The Idlewild Trust
The Ingram Trust
The Inverforth Charitable Trust
The Ireland Fund of Great Britain
The Jabbs Foundation
John Jarrold Trust Ltd
The Jenour Foundation
The Jerwood Charitable Foundation
The Cyril and Eve Jumbo Charitable Trust
The Jusaca Charitable Trust
The Stanley Kalms Foundation
Karaviotis Foundation
Laura Kinsella Foundation
The Kobler Trust
The Neil Kreitman Foundation
Christopher Laing Foundation
The Martin Laing Foundation
The Leonard Laity Stoate Charitable Trust

Community Foundations for Lancashire and Merseyside
The Lauffer Family Charitable Foundation
The Leathersellers' Company Charitable Fund
The Kennedy Leigh Charitable Trust
*Leng Charitable Trust**
The Leverhulme Trust
Lord Leverhulme's Charitable Trust
The Limbourne Trust
Limoges Charitable Trust
The Linbury Trust
The Linden Charitable Trust
The Enid Linder Foundation
The Ruth and Stuart Lipton Charitable Trust
The Charles Littlewood Hill Trust
The Andrew Lloyd Webber Foundation
The William and Katherine Longman Trust
*P. and M. Lovell Charitable Settlement**
Lord and Lady Lurgan Trust
John Lyon's Charity
The Sir Jack Lyons Charitable Trust
The Ian Mactaggart Trust (The Mactaggart Second Fund)
The Manchester Guardian Society Charitable Trust
The Michael Marks Charitable Trust
The Marsh Christian Trust
John Martin's Charity
The Nancie Massey Charitable Trust
*The Master Charitable Trust**
The Mercers' Charitable Foundation
The Merchant Venturers' Charity
The Brian Mitchell Charitable Settlement
The Monument Trust
The Diana and Allan Morgenthau Charitable Trust
The Music Sales Charitable Trust
*Nesta**
Network for Social Change Charitable Trust
Normanby Charitable Trust
Northwood Charitable Trust
The Notgrove Trust
The Oakley Charitable Trust
Odin Charitable Trust
The Ofenheim Charitable Trust
Oglesby Charitable Trust
Old Possum's Practical Trust
The Owen Family Trust
Oxfordshire Community Foundation
The Doris Pacey Charitable Foundation
*Parabola Foundation**
The Patrick Trust
The Phillips and Rubens Charitable Trust
The George and Esme Pollitzer Charitable Settlement
The Polonsky Foundation
The J. E. Posnansky Charitable Trust
Postcode Dream Trust – Dream Fund
*Powys Welsh Church Fund**
The Prince of Wales's Charitable Foundation
Mr and Mrs J. A. Pye's Charitable Settlement
Quartet Community Foundation
The Ranworth Trust
The Ravensdale Trust
The Rayne Foundation
The Rhododendron Trust
Daisie Rich Trust
The Clive and Sylvia Richards Charity Ltd
The Sir John Ritblat Family Foundation
The River Farm Foundation
The Roddick Foundation
The Richard Rogers Charitable Settlement
The Helen Roll Charity
*The David Ross Foundation**
The Rothermere Foundation
The Roughley Charitable Trust
Royal Docks Trust (London)
The Michael and Nicola Sacher Charitable Trust
The Michael Sacher Charitable Trust
The Dr Mortimer and Theresa Sackler Foundation
The Sackler Trust
The Alan and Babette Sainsbury Charitable Fund
The Andrew Salvesen Charitable Trust
Coral Samuel Charitable Trust
The Basil Samuel Charitable Trust
The Scarfe Charitable Trust
Schroder Charity Trust
The Frieda Scott Charitable Trust
The Shears Foundation
The Sheepdrove Trust
The Archie Sherman Charitable Trust
The Shetland Charitable Trust
The Bassil Shippam and Alsford Trust
David and Jennifer Sieff Charitable Trust
The E. C. Sosnow Charitable Trust
The Spielman Charitable Trust
Rosalyn and Nicholas Springer Charitable Trust
The Stanley Foundation Ltd
The Steel Charitable Trust
The Stevenage Community Trust
Stevenson Family's Charitable Trust
The Summerfield Charitable Trust
Sylvia Waddilove Foundation UK
C. B. and H. H. Taylor 1984 Trust
The Taylor Family Foundation
*Khoo Teck Puat UK Foundation**
The Tedworth Charitable Trust
The Thistle Trust
The Tolkien Trust
The Trefoil Trust
The Trusthouse Charitable Foundation
The Roger and Douglas Turner Charitable Trust
The Turtleton Charitable Trust
Ulster Garden Villages Ltd
The Underwood Trust
The Albert Van Den Bergh Charitable Trust
The Vardy Foundation
*The Wakefield Trust**
The Community Foundation in Wales
Robert and Felicity Waley-Cohen Charitable Trust
Sir Siegmund Warburg's Voluntary Settlement
*The Geoffrey Watling Charity**
Blyth Watson Charitable Trust
The Weinstock Fund
The Welton Foundation
The Wessex Youth Trust
*The West Looe Town Trust**
Westway Trust
The Barbara Whatmore Charitable Trust
The Kay Williams Charitable Foundation
The Williams Charitable Trust
The Harold Hyam Wingate Foundation
The Wolfson Family Charitable Trust
The Wolfson Foundation
*The Worwin UK Foundation**
The Wyseliot Rose Charitable Trust
*York Children's Trust**
The Marjorie and Arnold Ziff Charitable Foundation

Access to the arts

The Ashden Trust
Calouste Gulbenkian Foundation – UK Branch
The Ericson Trust

Joseph Ettedgui Charitable Foundation
The Joyce Fletcher Charitable Trust
Herefordshire Community Foundation
The Allen Lane Foundation
Sir George Martin Trust
Millennium Stadium Charitable Trust (Ymddiriedolaeth Elusennol Stadiwm Y. Mileniwm)
The Morel Charitable Trust
The Community Foundation for Northern Ireland
The Oakdale Trust
The James Pantyfedwen Foundation
The St James's Trust Settlement
Suffolk Community Foundation
Youth Music

Amateur and community arts

The Ashden Trust
Calouste Gulbenkian Foundation – UK Branch
The Ericson Trust
Joseph Ettedgui Charitable Foundation
The Joyce Fletcher Charitable Trust
Herefordshire Community Foundation
The Allen Lane Foundation
Sir George Martin Trust
Millennium Stadium Charitable Trust (Ymddiriedolaeth Elusennol Stadiwm Y. Mileniwm)
The Morel Charitable Trust
The Community Foundation for Northern Ireland
The Oakdale Trust
The James Pantyfedwen Foundation
The St James's Trust Settlement
Suffolk Community Foundation
Youth Music

Art and culture of specific countries

*Arcadia Charitable Trust**
The Bagri Foundation
The Daiwa Anglo-Japanese Foundation
The Great Britain Sasakawa Foundation
*Heritage Lottery Fund**
IGO Foundation Ltd
The Allen Lane Foundation
*The Onaway Trust**
Youth Music

Arts management, policy and planning

The De Laszlo Foundation
Youth Music

Combined arts

The Elmley Foundation
The Joyce Fletcher Charitable Trust
Youth Music

Crafts

The Carpenters' Company Charitable Trust
The Ernest Cook Trust
The Worshipful Company of Cordwainers Charitable Trusts (Minges Gift and the Pooled Trusts)
The Elmley Foundation
The Girdlers' Company Charitable Trust
Worshipful Company of Glovers of London Charitable Trust
Worshipful Company of Gold and Silver Wyre Drawers Charitable Trust Fund
The Community Foundation for Northern Ireland
The Radcliffe Trust
The Weavers' Company Benevolent Fund

Art for people with disabilities

Barchester Healthcare Foundation
Barnwood Trust
The Joyce Fletcher Charitable Trust
The Rix-Thompson-Rothenberg Foundation
Variety The Children's Charity (Variety Club)
*The Bruce Wake Charity**
Youth Music

Libraries

The Big Lottery Fund (see also Awards for All)
Elizabeth Cayzer Charitable Trust
Colwinston Charitable Trust
*Heritage Lottery Fund**
The John R. Murray Charitable Trust
The Pilgrim Trust
*Rothschild Foundation (Hanadiv) Europe**

Literature

The Clore Duffield Foundation
The Elmley Foundation
The Garrick Charitable Trust
The Miles Morland Foundation
The John R. Murray Charitable Trust
*The Prince Philip Trust Fund**

Museums and galleries

The H. B. Allen Charitable Trust
Elizabeth Cayzer Charitable Trust
The Clore Duffield Foundation
The John S. Cohen Foundation
Colwinston Charitable Trust
The Crescent Trust
The De Laszlo Foundation
The Essex Heritage Trust
The Fidelity UK Foundation
Fishmongers' Company's Charitable Trust
Marc Fitch Fund
The Gordon Fraser Charitable Trust
The Girdlers' Company Charitable Trust
The Charles Hayward Foundation
*Heritage Lottery Fund**
The Robert Kiln Charitable Trust
The Leche Trust
Jack Livingstone Charitable Trust
The Manifold Charitable Trust
Sir George Martin Trust
The Laurence Misener Charitable Trust
The Henry Moore Foundation
The John R. Murray Charitable Trust
National Art Collections Fund
The National Manuscripts Conservation Trust
The Pilgrim Trust
The Radcliffe Trust
*Rothschild Foundation (Hanadiv) Europe**
Peter Stormonth Darling Charitable Trust
Suffolk Community Foundation

Performing arts

*The Neville Abraham Foundation**
Calouste Gulbenkian Foundation – UK Branch
The Richard Carne Trust
The Carr-Gregory Trust
The Cayo Foundation
The Clore Duffield Foundation
The John S. Cohen Foundation
The Elmley Foundation
*The Emerald Foundation**
*The Fidelio Charitable Trust**
The Fidelity UK Foundation
The Joyce Fletcher Charitable Trust
The Gordon Fraser Charitable Trust
The Garrick Charitable Trust
The Harding Trust
Henley Educational Trust
The Boris Karloff Charitable Foundation
The Kohn Foundation
Millennium Stadium Charitable Trust (Ymddiriedolaeth Elusennol Stadiwm Y. Mileniwm)
The Millward Charitable Trust
The Peter Minet Trust
The Morel Charitable Trust
The Pell Charitable Trust
Reed Family Foundation
The Sands Family Trust
*The Martin Smith Foundation**
The Vandervell Foundation
*The Alfred Williams Charitable Trust**

Music

*The Associated Board of the Royal Schools of Music**
British Record Industry Trust
The Britten-Pears Foundation (The Britten Pears Library)
The Derek Butler Trust
Colwinston Charitable Trust
The Delius Trust
Dunard Fund 2016
The Hugh Fraser Foundation
The Hinrichsen Foundation
The Michael and Ilse Katz Foundation
The Leche Trust
Sylvanus Lysons Charity
The Mackintosh Foundation
Sir George Martin Trust
The Mayfield Valley Arts Trust
The Oakdale Trust
The Ouseley Church Music Trust
The Performing Right Society Foundation
The Radcliffe Trust
The Rowlands Trust
The RVW Trust
Humphrey Richardson Taylor Charitable Trust
Mrs R. P. Tindall's Charitable Trust
The Whitaker Charitable Trust
Youth Music

Theatre

The Hugh Fraser Foundation
The Sir Barry Jackson County Fund (incorporating the Hornton Fund)
The Leche Trust
The Mackintosh Foundation
The Miles Morland Foundation
Royal Victoria Hall Foundation

Opera

Colwinston Charitable Trust

Dance

The Girdlers' Company Charitable Trust

Visual arts

Colwinston Charitable Trust
The De Laszlo Foundation
Dunard Fund 2016
The Elephant Trust
The Elmley Foundation
The Fidelity UK Foundation
The Gordon Fraser Charitable Trust
The Hugh Fraser Foundation
The David Lean Foundation
The Brian Mercer Charitable Trust
Millennium Stadium Charitable Trust (Ymddiriedolaeth Elusennol Stadiwm Y. Mileniwm)
The Peter Minet Trust

Fine arts

The Henry Moore Foundation
National Art Collections Fund
*The Prince Philip Trust Fund**

Public art and sculpture

The David Lean Foundation
The Henry Moore Foundation

Heritage and the built environment

Allchurches Trust Ltd
The H. B. Allen Charitable Trust
The Ian Askew Charitable Trust
The Barbour Foundation
The Barcapel Foundation
Bennett Lowell Ltd
The Consuelo and Anthony Brooke Charitable Trust
The Ellis Campbell Charitable Foundation
David William Traill Cargill Fund
*The W. A. Cargill Fund**
The John S. Cohen Foundation
Community First (Landfill Communities Fund)
The Keith Coombs Trust
The Duke of Cornwall's Benevolent Fund
Country Houses Foundation
Cruden Foundation Ltd
*The Roger De Haan Charitable Trust**
The Demigryphon Trust
The Dischma Charitable Trust
The Drapers' Charitable Fund
The Gerald Palmer Eling Trust Company
The Englefield Charitable Trust
The February Foundation
Fisherbeck Charitable Trust
Marc Fitch Fund
The Gordon Fraser Charitable Trust
The Freshgate Trust Foundation
The Frognal Trust
The Simon Gibson Charitable Trust
The Godinton Charitable Trust
*The Graham Trust**
The Grocers' Charity
The Helen Hamlyn Trust
The Charles Hayward Foundation
The Headley Trust
*Heritage Lottery Fund**
The Hiscox Foundation
The Daniel Howard Trust
The Idlewild Trust
The Jerusalem Trust
The Robert Kiln Charitable Trust
Laura Kinsella Foundation
The Kirby Laing Foundation
Mrs F. B. Laurence Charitable Trust
The Raymond and Blanche Lawson Charitable Trust
The Leathersellers' Company Charitable Fund
The Kennedy Leigh Charitable Trust
Limoges Charitable Trust

The Charles Littlewood Hill Trust
The Andrew Lloyd Webber Foundation
P. and M. Lovell Charitable Settlement*
The Macdonald-Buchanan Charitable Trust
The Michael Marks Charitable Trust
The Marsh Christian Trust
The Master Charitable Trust*
The Mercers' Charitable Foundation
Northwood Charitable Trust
Postcode Dream Trust – Dream Fund
Mr and Mrs J. A. Pye's Charitable Settlement
The Sir John Ritblat Family Foundation
The River Farm Foundation
The David Ross Foundation*
The Roughley Charitable Trust
The Rowlands Trust
The J. S. and E. C. Rymer Charitable Trust
The Salisbury New Pool Settlement*
Schroder Charity Trust
SITA Cornwall Trust Ltd
The Steel Charitable Trust
Stevenson Family's Charitable Trust
The Summerfield Charitable Trust
The Tanner Trust
The Roger and Douglas Turner Charitable Trust
The Turtleton Charitable Trust
The Wakefield Trust*
The Geoffrey Watling Charity*
Waynflete Charitable Trust
The Barbara Whatmore Charitable Trust
Colonel W. H. Whitbread Charitable Trust
The Wolfson Family Charitable Trust

Arts and the environment

The Architectural Heritage Fund
Elizabeth Cayzer Charitable Trust
The Clore Duffield Foundation
The Crescent Trust
The Leche Trust
The Monument Trust
Nesta*

Architecture

Dunard Fund 2016
The Happold Foundation*
Old Possum's Practical Trust

Landscape

Manchester Airport Community Trust Fund
The National Gardens Scheme*
The Stanley Smith UK Horticultural Trust
The Marjorie and Arnold Ziff Charitable Foundation

Heritage

The Adnams Community Trust
The Architectural Heritage Fund
Birmingham International Airport Community Trust Fund
The T. B. H. Brunner's Charitable Settlement
Elizabeth Cayzer Charitable Trust
The Francis Coales Charitable Foundation
The Henry and Suzanne Davis Foundation
The Elephant Trust
The Ericson Trust
The Essex Heritage Trust
The Alan Evans Memorial Trust
G. F. Eyre Charitable Trust
The John Feeney Charitable Bequest
The Fidelity UK Foundation
Fishmongers' Company's Charitable Trust
The Gosling Foundation Ltd
GrantScape
The J. G. Graves Charitable Trust
The W. A. Handley Charity Trust
The Maurice Hatter Foundation
The Inverforth Charitable Trust
The Ironmongers' Company
The Langtree Trust
The Leche Trust
The Linbury Trust
GPS Macpherson Charitable Settlement*
The Manifold Charitable Trust
Charity of John Marshall
Sir George Martin Trust
The Laurence Misener Charitable Trust
The Monument Trust
The John R. Murray Charitable Trust
Normanby Charitable Trust
Old Possum's Practical Trust
The Owen Family Trust
The Pilgrim Trust
The Radcliffe Trust
The Clive and Sylvia Richards Charity Ltd
Mrs L. D. Rope's Third Charitable Settlement
The Rose Foundation
Rothschild Foundation (Hanadiv) Europe*
Peter Stormonth Darling Charitable Trust
The Swire Charitable Trust
The Connie and Albert Taylor Charitable Trust
The Trusthouse Charitable Foundation
Ulster Garden Villages Ltd
Mrs Waterhouse Charitable Trust
The Alfred Williams Charitable Trust*
The Wolfson Foundation

Maintenance and preservation of buildings

The Architectural Heritage Fund
The City Educational Trust Fund
The Dr and Mrs A. Darlington Charitable Trust
The Dulverton Trust
Dunard Fund 2016
The Essex Heritage Trust
The Alan Evans Memorial Trust
The Earl Fitzwilliam Charitable Trust
GrantScape
Greys Charitable Trust
Leicester and Leicestershire Historic Churches Preservation Trust (Leicestershire Historic Churches Trust)
The Owen Family Trust
Parish Estate of the Church of St Michael Spurriergate York*
Powys Welsh Church Fund*
The Rose Foundation
Royal Docks Trust (London)
The Connie and Albert Taylor Charitable Trust
The Michael Uren Foundation

Religious buildings

The Baird Trust
The Bedfordshire and Hertfordshire Historic Churches Trust
The Bellahouston Bequest Fund

The Buckinghamshire Historic Churches Trust
The Francis Coales Charitable Foundation
The Congregational and General Charitable Trust
The County Council of Dyfed Welsh Curch Fund
The Devon Historic Churches Trust
The Dorset Historic Churches Trust
Jill Franklin Trust
Friends of Essex Churches Trust
The Friends of Kent Churches
The Girdlers' Company Charitable Trust
The Gloucestershire Historic Churches Trust
The Hampshire and Islands Historic Churches Trust
The Herefordshire Historic Churches Trust
Laslett's (Hinton) Charity
Manchester Airport Community Trust Fund
The Manifold Charitable Trust
Charity of John Marshall
*The Norfolk Churches Trust Ltd**
The Northumbria Historic Churches Trust
The Nottinghamshire Historic Churches Trust
*Oxfordshire Historic Churches Trust**
The James Pantyfedwen Foundation
The Jack Patston Charitable Trust
The Pilgrim Trust
The Prince of Wales's Charitable Foundation
*The Shropshire Historic Churches Trust**
The Suffolk Historic Churches Trust
The Yorkshire Historic Churches Trust

Restoration and maintenance of inland waterways

The Pilgrim Trust

Built environment – education and research

The Architectural Heritage Fund
The Ove Arup Foundation
The Frederick and Phyllis Cann Trust
The Ernest Cook Trust
The Glass-House Trust
The Ironmongers' Company
*Nesta**

Humanities

The Aurelius Charitable Trust
*The British Academy for the Promotion of Historical Philosophical and Philological Studies (The British Academy)**
The Denise Cohen Charitable Trust
Laura Kinsella Foundation
The Neil Kreitman Foundation
The Linbury Trust
The Michael Marks Charitable Trust
The Wolfson Family Charitable Trust

Archaeology

Marc Fitch Fund
The Robert Kiln Charitable Trust

History

The Francis Coales Charitable Foundation
Marc Fitch Fund
IGO Foundation Ltd

International understanding

The Daiwa Anglo-Japanese Foundation
The Great Britain Sasakawa Foundation
*The Onaway Trust**
The Pears Family Charitable Foundation
The Rayne Trust
The Tinsley Foundation
The Westcroft Trust
The W. Wing Yip and Brothers Foundation
*York Children's Trust**

Philosophy and ethics

The Inlight Trust
Mariapolis Ltd
*The Onaway Trust**
Polden-Puckham Charitable Foundation
The Joseph Rowntree Charitable Trust

Media and communications

The Elmley Foundation
The David Lean Foundation
The Miles Morland Foundation
The Roddick Foundation
Suffolk Community Foundation
The Transform Foundation*

Recreation and sport

The Arsenal Foundation Ltd
ASCB Charitable Fund
The Asda Foundation
The Balfour Beatty Charitable Trust
BBC Children in Need
The Big Lottery Fund (see also Awards for All)
Birmingham International Airport Community Trust Fund
Isabel Blackman Foundation
BOOST Charitable Trust
The Booth Charities
The Cadbury Foundation
The Charter 600 Charity
Cheshire Community Foundation Ltd*
The Robert Clutterbuck Charitable Trust
The Coalfields Regeneration Trust
The Keith Coombs Trust
Michael Cornish Charitable Trust
England and Wales Cricket Trust*
The Hamilton Davies Trust
The Roger De Haan Charitable Trust*
The Englefield Charitable Trust
The Essex and Southend Sports Trust
The Lord Faringdon Charitable Trust
The Joseph Strong Frazer Trust
The Freshgate Trust Foundation
Gatwick Airport Community Trust
The Girdlers' Company Charitable Trust
Gowling WLG (UK) Charitable Trust
The Grantham Yorke Trust
The J. G. Graves Charitable Trust
Dr Guthrie's Association
The Hadrian Trust
The Harpur Trust
The Harris Charity
Hedley Foundation Ltd (The Hedley Foundation)
M. V. Hillhouse Trust*
The Holywood Trust
The Hoover Foundation
Huntingdon Freemen's Trust
Johnnie Johnson Trust
The Leathersellers' Company Charitable Fund
The William Leech Charity
John Lyon's Charity
Sir George Martin Trust
The Master Charitable Trust*
Middlesex Sports Foundation
Millennium Stadium Charitable Trust (Ymddiriedolaeth Elusennol Stadiwm Y. Mileniwm)
The James Milner Foundation*
The Morton Charitable Trust*
The National Express Foundation
One Community Foundation Ltd*
Oxfordshire Community Foundation
The Paphitis Charitable Trust
People's Postcode Trust
Postcode Community Trust*
The Prince Philip Trust Fund*
The Professional Footballers' Association Charity*
The Puri Foundation
Quartet Community Foundation
Reed Family Foundation
The David Ross Foundation*
The Rothermere Foundation
Royal Docks Trust (London)
The Shanly Foundation
The Martin Smith Foundation*
St Olave's and St Saviour's Schools Foundation – Foundation Fund
The Stevenage Community Trust
The Summerfield Charitable Trust
The Connie and Albert Taylor Charitable Trust
The Taylor Family Foundation
The Tower Hill Trust
Variety The Children's Charity (Variety Club)
Wates Family Enterprise Trust
The Geoffrey Watling Charity*
The Wessex Youth Trust
The West Looe Town Trust*
Westway Trust
The Wimbledon Foundation*
The Wixamtree Trust
The William Allen Young Charitable Trust

Parks and open spaces

The John Feeney Charitable Bequest
Lancashire Environmental Fund Ltd
The John Spedan Lewis Foundation
Manchester Airport Community Trust Fund
The Merchant Venturers' Charity
The National Gardens Scheme*
SITA Cornwall Trust Ltd
The Tanner Trust

*Viridor Credits Environmental Company**

Recreation facilities

*The Barrack Charitable Trust**
The Carnegie Dunfermline Trust
Church Burgesses Trust
The Essex Youth Trust
The Football Association National Sports Centre Trust
The Gibbons Family Trust
The Granada Foundation
Hampton Fuel Allotment Charity
The Peter Harrison Foundation
Henley Educational Trust
Lancashire Environmental Fund Ltd
The Community Foundation for Northern Ireland
Richmond Parish Lands Charity
SITA Cornwall Trust Ltd
*Sunninghill Fuel Allotment Trust**
*Viridor Credits Environmental Company**
*The Bruce Wake Charity**
Wooden Spoon Society

Sports for people with a disability

Barnwood Trust
The Football Association National Sports Centre Trust
Get Kids Going
The Peter Harrison Foundation
Henley Educational Trust
The London Marathon Charitable Trust Ltd
The Lord's Taverners
The Dan Maskell Tennis Trust
The Brian Mercer Charitable Trust
The Community Foundation for Northern Ireland
The Frieda Scott Charitable Trust
*The Bruce Wake Charity**
Wooden Spoon Society

Sports

Access Sport CIO
*The Anne Duchess of Westminster's Charity**
The John Beckwith Charitable Trust
The Benham Charitable Settlement
The Clover Trust
*The John Grant Davies Trust**
The Vernon N. Ely Charitable Trust
*The Emerald Foundation**
The Essex Youth Trust
The Football Association National Sports Centre Trust
The Football Foundation
The Fort Foundation
The Adrian and Jane Frost Charitable Trust
The Golf Foundation Ltd
The Great Britain Sasakawa Foundation
The Peter Harrison Foundation
Henley Educational Trust
The Boris Karloff Charitable Foundation
The Kyte Charitable Trust
The London Marathon Charitable Trust Ltd
The Lord's Taverners
The Dan Maskell Tennis Trust
British Motor Sports Training Trust
The Racing Foundation
Rugby Football Foundation
The Saddlers' Company Charitable Fund
The Frieda Scott Charitable Trust
The Shipwrights' Company Charitable Fund
The Huntly and Margery Sinclair Charitable Trust
The Stewards' Charitable Trust
Peter Stormonth Darling Charitable Trust
The Tennis Foundation
The Valiant Charitable Trust
Colonel W. H. Whitbread Charitable Trust
Wooden Spoon Society
*York Children's Trust**

Development, housing and employment

ABF The Soldiers' Charity
Ajahma Charitable Trust
The Ashden Trust
The Associated Country Women of the World
The Berkeley Charitable Foundation
The Berkshire Community Foundation
The Big Lottery Fund (see also Awards for All)
R. S. Brownless Charitable Trust
CAFOD (Catholic Agency for Overseas Development)
Chrysalis Trust
Dorset Community Foundation
The Dorus Trust
The Dyers' Company Charitable Trust
EDF Energy Trust (EDFET)
The Epigoni Trust
Donald Forrester Trust
The G. D. Charitable Trust
The Greggs Foundation
William Harding's Charity
The Hasluck Charitable Trust
The Hemby Charitable Trust
*M. V. Hillhouse Trust**
The Hobson Charity Ltd
The Hollick Family Charitable Trust
The Mary Homfray Charitable Trust
The Ireland Fund of Great Britain
John Jarrold Trust Ltd
The Joicey Trust
Kent Community Foundation
Duchy of Lancaster Benevolent Fund
The Jack Lane Charitable Trust
Mrs F. B. Laurence Charitable Trust
Lawson Beckman Charitable Trust
Leicestershire, Leicester and Rutland Community Foundation
Lincolnshire Community Foundation
Lloyd's Charities Trust
Manchester Airport Community Trust Fund
R. W. Mann Trust
The Medlock Charitable Trust
The Steve Morgan Foundation
Muslim Hands
Norfolk Community Foundation
Nottinghamshire Community Foundation
The Porta Pia 2012 Foundation

The Sandhu Charitable Foundation
The Sants Charitable Trust
The SDL Foundation
The Mrs Smith and Mount Trust
Mrs Maud Van Norden's Charitable Foundation
The Nigel Vinson Charitable Trust
The Virgin Money Foundation
The Waterloo Foundation
The Wixamtree Trust
The Wood Foundation
Zurich Community Trust (UK) Ltd

Community and economic development

The 1989 Willan Charitable Trust
Aberdeen Asset Management Charitable Foundation
The Accenture Foundation
The AIM Foundation
Anglo American Group Foundation
The Anne Duchess of Westminster's Charity*
The Apax Foundation
Ove Arup Partnership Charitable Trust
The Asda Foundation
The Ashley Family Foundation
The Ashmore Foundation
Autonomous Research Charitable Trust (ARCT)
Awards for All (see also the Big Lottery Fund)
Bairdwatson Charitable Trust*
The Bank of Scotland Foundation
The Philip Barker Charity*
Barnwood Trust
The Barrack Charitable Trust*
The Battersea Power Station Foundation*
BC Partners Foundation
The Bedfordshire and Luton Community Foundation
The Ruth Berkowitz Charitable Trust
The Bestway Foundation
The Bingham Trust
Birmingham International Airport Community Trust Fund
The Lord Mayor of Birmingham's Charity
The Blagrave Trust
Boots Charitable Trust
The Liz and Terry Bramall Foundation
The Bransford Trust
The Brelms Trust CIO*
The Harold and Alice Bridges Charity
John Bristow and Thomas Mason Trust
The Consuelo and Anthony Brooke Charitable Trust
Buckinghamshire Community Foundation
The Noel Buxton Trust
The Edward Cadbury Charitable Trust
The Cadbury Foundation
Community Foundation for Calderdale
Calouste Gulbenkian Foundation – UK Branch
The Ellis Campbell Charitable Foundation
The Carnegie Dunfermline Trust
The Castansa Trust*
The Chapman Charitable Trust
The Charter 600 Charity
Cheshire Community Foundation Ltd*
CHK Charities Ltd
Christian Aid
Church Urban Fund
The Coalfields Regeneration Trust
The Cole Charitable Trust
Colyer-Fergusson Charitable Trust
Comic Relief
Community First (Landfill Communities Fund)
Michael Cornish Charitable Trust
Coventry Building Society Charitable Foundation
The Peter Cruddas Foundation
Cumbria Community Foundation
The Hamilton Davies Trust
The John Grant Davies Trust*
The Roger De Haan Charitable Trust*
Debenhams Foundation
The Delves Charitable Trust
Foundation Derbyshire
The Diageo Foundation
The Dulverton Trust
County Durham Community Foundation
East End Community Foundation
The Ecology Trust
The Economist Charitable Trust
The Edith Maud Ellis 1985 Charitable Trust
The Englefield Charitable Trust
The Enkalon Foundation
Esh Foundation
Essex Community Foundation
The Expat Foundation
Esmée Fairbairn Foundation
Allan and Nesta Ferguson Charitable Settlement
The Fidelity UK Foundation
The Follett Trust
The Football Association National Sports Centre Trust
The Football Foundation
Ford Britain Trust
Forever Manchester
The Fort Foundation
Jill Franklin Trust
The Charles S. French Charitable Trust
Friends Provident Charitable Foundation
The Adrian and Jane Frost Charitable Trust
The Gannochy Trust
Gatwick Airport Community Trust
The Genesis Charitable Trust*
The G. C. Gibson Charitable Trust
Global Care
Gloucestershire Community Foundation
The Golden Bottle Trust
The Goldman Sachs Charitable Gift Fund (UK)
Goldman Sachs Gives (UK)
The Grantham Yorke Trust
GrantScape
The J. G. Graves Charitable Trust
Greenham Common Community Trust Ltd
The Grimmitt Trust
The Bishop of Guildford's Foundation
Dr Guthrie's Association
H. C. D. Memorial Fund
The Hadfield Charitable Trust
The Hadrian Trust
The Alfred Haines Charitable Trust
Halifax Foundation for Northern Ireland (previously known as Lloyds Bank Foundation for Northern Ireland)
Hammersmith United Charities*
Hampshire and Isle of Wight Community Foundation
The W. A. Handley Charity Trust
The Kathleen Hannay Memorial Charity
The Charles Hayward Foundation
Heart of England Community Foundation
Heathrow Community Fund (LHR Airport Communities Trust)
Heb Ffin (Without Frontier)*
Help the Homeless Ltd

Philip Henman Trust
Herefordshire Community Foundation
Hertfordshire Community Foundation
The Alan Edward Higgs Charity
The Hilden Charitable Fund
The Hillingdon Community Trust
R. G. Hills Charitable Trust
The Hiscox Foundation
The Henry C. Hoare Charitable Trust
Human Relief Foundation
The Hunter Foundation
Miss Agnes H. Hunter's Trust
Hyde Charitable Trust (Youth Plus)
Imagine Foundation
Impetus – The Private Equity Foundation (Impetus – PEF)
Incommunities Foundation
The Innocent Foundation
The International Bankers Charitable Trust (The Worshipful Company of Interntional Bankers)
Investream Charitable Trust
The Charles Irving Charitable Trust
The Isle of Anglesey Charitable Trust
Rees Jeffreys Road Fund
Joffe Charitable Trust
The Johnson Foundation
Johnson Wax Ltd Charitable Trust
The Joron Charitable Trust
The Cyril and Eve Jumbo Charitable Trust
The Mary Kinross Charitable Trust
Robert Kitchin (Saddlers' Company)
The KPMG Foundation
Kusuma Trust UK
Ladbrokes in the Community Charitable Trust
John Laing Charitable Trust
Community Foundations for Lancashire and Merseyside
Lancaster Foundation
LandAid Charitable Trust (Land Aid)
The Allen Lane Foundation
The R. J. Larg Family Charitable Trust
The William Leech Charity
Leeds Building Society Charitable Foundation
Leeds Community Foundation (LCF)
The Lennox Hannay Charitable Trust
The Mark Leonard Trust
David and Ruth Lewis Family Charitable Trust
John Lewis Partnership General Community Fund
Liberum Foundation
The Linden Charitable Trust
The Charles Littlewood Hill Trust
*The W. M. and B. W. Lloyd Trust**
Lloyds Bank Foundation for England and Wales
Lloyds Bank Foundation for the Channel Islands
Lloyds TSB Foundation for Scotland
Trust for London
The London Community Foundation (LCF)
John Lyon's Charity
*Mace Foundation**
The Mactaggart Third Fund
Lord Mayor of Manchester's Charity Appeal Trust
The W. M. Mann Foundation
The Hilda and Samuel Marks Foundation
The J. P. Marland Charitable Trust
D. G. Marshall of Cambridge Trust
*The Master Charitable Trust**
The Mathew Trust
The Matliwala Family Charitable Trust
The Merchant Venturers' Charity
T. and J. Meyer Family Foundation Ltd
The Mickleham Trust
Millennium Stadium Charitable Trust (Ymddiriedolaeth Elusennol Stadiwm Y. Mileniwm)
The Millfield House Foundation (1)
Milton Keynes Community Foundation Ltd
The Peter Minet Trust
The MITIE Foundation
The Monmouthshire County Council Welsh Church Act Fund
The George A. Moore Foundation
John Moores Foundation
The Morris Charitable Trust
Vyoel Moshe Charitable Trust
The MSE Charity
The Nationwide Foundation
The NFU Mutual Charitable Trust
Nominet Charitable Foundation
The Community Foundation for Northern Ireland
Norwich Town Close Estate Charity
The Oakdale Trust
*The Onaway Trust**
Oxfam (GB)
Oxfordshire Community Foundation
The Paphitis Charitable Trust
Paradigm Foundation
People's Health Trust
People's Postcode Trust
Pilkington Charities Fund
The George and Esme Pollitzer Charitable Settlement
*Postcode Community Trust**
*Power to Change Trust**
*Powys Welsh Church Fund**
The Puebla Charitable Trust
The Ranworth Trust
Elizabeth Rathbone Charity
The Sigrid Rausing Trust
Daisie Rich Trust
Richmond Parish Lands Charity
Rivers Foundation
The Robertson Trust
*The David Ross Foundation**
The Rothley Trust
The Joseph Rowntree Charitable Trust
Royal Docks Trust (London)
*Royal Society Of Wildlife Trusts**
The Saga Charitable Trust
The Alan and Babette Sainsbury Charitable Fund
*The Salisbury New Pool Settlement**
Santander UK Foundation Ltd
*The Save the Children Fund**
Foundation Scotland
The ScottishPower Foundation
*The Sellafield Charity Trust Fund**
The Shanti Charitable Trust
The Shears Foundation
The Sheldon Trust
*Sherburn House Charity**
The Simmons & Simmons Charitable Foundation
SITA Cornwall Trust Ltd
The Henry Smith Charity
*Social Investment Business Foundation**
Sodexo Stop Hunger Foundation
*Somerset Community Foundation**
The Squires Foundation
The Stafford Trust
The Stanley Foundation Ltd
The Peter Stebbings Memorial Charity
The Stevenage Community Trust
Sir Halley Stewart Trust
Suffolk Community Foundation
The Summerfield Charitable Trust
The Bernard Sunley Charitable Foundation
Community Foundation for Surrey

The Sussex Community Foundation
Sutton Coldfield Charitable Trust
The Talbot Village Trust
The Tanner Trust
C. B. and H. H. Taylor 1984 Trust
Tees Valley Community Foundation
The Tolkien Trust
The Tower Hill Trust
The Truemark Trust
The Trusthouse Charitable Foundation
The Tudor Trust
The Roger and Douglas Turner Charitable Trust
Community Foundation serving Tyne and Wear and Northumberland
The Veolia Environmental Trust*
The Virgin Foundation (Virgin Unite)
Viridor Credits Environmental Company*
The Vodafone Foundation
Volant Charitable Trust
Voluntary Action Fund (VAF)
The Scurrah Wainwright Charity
The Wakefield and Tetley Trust
The Wakefield Trust*
The Wakeham Trust
The Community Foundation in Wales
Wales Council for Voluntary Action
Wates Family Enterprise Trust
The Wates Foundation
Waynflete Charitable Trust
The Welton Foundation
The Westminster Amalgamated Charity*
The Westminster Foundation
Westway Trust
White Stuff Foundation
The Willmott Dixon Foundation*
Wiltshire Community Foundation
Worcester Municipal Charities (CIO)
Yorkshire and Clydesdale Bank Foundation
The South Yorkshire Community Foundation
Zephyr Charitable Trust

Housing

The Anne Duchess of Westminster's Charity*
The Barbour Foundation
Barnwood Trust
The Oliver Borthwick Memorial Trust
CEO Sleepout
Cheshire Community Foundation Ltd*
The Cole Charitable Trust
The Coltstaple Trust
Mabel Cooper Charity
Crisis UK*
Baron Davenport's Charity
County Durham Community Foundation
The Eveson Charitable Trust
Fisherbeck Charitable Trust
The Oliver Ford Charitable Trust
The Elizabeth Frankland Moore and Star Foundation
The Girdlers' Company Charitable Trust
The Gordon Trust*
The Green Hall Foundation
The Hadrian Trust
The Alfred Haines Charitable Trust
Hampton Fuel Allotment Charity
The W. A. Handley Charity Trust
The Haramead Trust
The Harbour Foundation
The Harrison-Frank Family Foundation (UK) Ltd
The Alfred And Peggy Harvey Charitable Trust
May Hearnshaw Charitable Trust (May Hearnshaw's Charity)
Help the Homeless Ltd
The Hilden Charitable Fund
The Edward Holt Trust
The Thomas J. Horne Memorial Trust
The Hospital of God at Greatham
The Albert Hunt Trust
The Nani Huyu Charitable Trust
Irish Youth Foundation (UK) Ltd (incorporating The Lawlor Foundation)
The Charles Irving Charitable Trust
The Jusaca Charitable Trust
The Sir James Knott Trust
The Beatrice Laing Trust
The Lambert Charitable Trust
LandAid Charitable Trust (Land Aid)
Laslett's (Hinton) Charity
The Raymond and Blanche Lawson Charitable Trust
Leeds Building Society Charitable Foundation
The Mark Leonard Trust
The Charles Littlewood Hill Trust
Trust for London
The London Community Foundation (LCF)
London Housing Foundation Ltd (LHF)
John Lyon's Charity
Merchant Navy Welfare Board
The Mickleham Trust
The Mills Charity
The Monument Trust
The Morgan Charitable Foundation
The Nationwide Foundation
The Norton Foundation
The Phillips and Rubens Charitable Trust
The Pilgrim Trust
Mrs L. D. Rope's Third Charitable Settlement
The Royal British Legion
Erach and Roshan Sadri Foundation
The Henry Smith Charity
St James's Place Foundation
St Monica Trust
Sylvia Waddilove Foundation UK
The Tudor Trust
Community Foundation serving Tyne and Wear and Northumberland
Walton on Thames Charity

Specific industries

The Worshipful Company of Cordwainers Charitable Trusts (Minges Gift and the Pooled Trusts)
The Cotton Industry War Memorial Trust
The Drapers' Charitable Fund
The Sir John Fisher Foundation
The Happold Foundation*
The Worshipful Company of Horners' Charitable Trusts
The Leathersellers' Company Charitable Fund
The Mark Leonard Trust
C. F. Lunoe Trust Fund
The Worshipful Company of Needlemakers' Charitable Fund
North East Area Miners Welfare Trust Fund*
The Phillips Charitable Trust
The Saddlers' Company Charitable Fund

Education and training

The 1989 Willan Charitable Trust
The 29th May 1961 Charitable Trust
A2BD Foundation UK Ltd*
Aberdeen Asset Management Charitable Foundation
The Aberdeen Foundation
ABF The Soldiers' Charity
The Neville Abraham Foundation*
The Acacia Charitable Trust
The Accenture Foundation
The Addleshaw Goddard Charitable Trust
The Adnams Community Trust
AKO Foundation*
The Alborada Trust
Aldgate and All Hallows' Foundation
Al-Fayed Charitable Foundation
The Derrill Allatt Foundation
Allchurches Trust Ltd
The Allen & Overy Foundation*
Viscount Amory's Charitable Trust
Andor Charitable Trust
Anglo American Group Foundation
Anguish's Educational Foundation
The Anne Duchess of Westminster's Charity*
The Apax Foundation
The John Apthorp Charity
The Arah Foundation
The Arbib Foundation
The Ardwick Trust
The John Armitage Charitable Trust
The Armourers' and Brasiers' Gauntlet Trust
The Arsenal Foundation Ltd
Ove Arup Partnership Charitable Trust
The Asfari Foundation*
The Ashmore Foundation
The Ian Askew Charitable Trust
The Associated Country Women of the World
Autonomous Research Charitable Trust (ARCT)
The Bagri Foundation
The Roy and Pixie Baker Charitable Trust
The Balcombe Charitable Trust
The Balfour Beatty Charitable Trust
The Baltic Charitable Fund
The Bamford Charitable Foundation
The Banbury Charities
The Band Trust
The Barbers' Company General Charities
The Barbour Foundation
The Philip Barker Charity*
BC Partners Foundation
BCH Trust
The Becht Family Charitable Trust*
The John Beckwith Charitable Trust
The Bellahouston Bequest Fund
Benesco Charity Ltd*
The Benham Charitable Settlement
Bergqvist Charitable Trust
The Ruth Berkowitz Charitable Trust
The Berkshire Community Foundation
The Bestway Foundation
Asser Bishvil Foundation*
The Sydney Black Charitable Trust
Isabel Blackman Foundation
Bloom Foundation
The Booth Charities
Sir William Boreman's Foundation*
The Bowerman Charitable Trust
The Bowland Charitable Trust
The Liz and Terry Bramall Foundation
The Bransford Trust
The Breadsticks Foundation
The Brelms Trust CIO*
Bridgepoint Charitable Trust
John Bristow and Thomas Mason Trust
The British and Foreign School Society
The J. and M. Britton Charitable Trust
The Consuelo and Anthony Brooke Charitable Trust
The Charles Brotherton Trust
The Buffini Chao Foundation
The Burberry Foundation*
The Clara E. Burgess Charity
The Burry Charitable Trust
The Arnold Burton 1998 Charitable Trust
The Butters Foundation (UK) Ltd*
The Edward Cadbury Charitable Trust
The G. W. Cadbury Charitable Trust
The William A. Cadbury Charitable Trust
The Edward and Dorothy Cadbury Trust
The Cadogan Charity
CAFOD (Catholic Agency for Overseas Development)
Calleva Foundation
The Ellis Campbell Charitable Foundation
The Campden Charities Trustee
Canary Wharf Contractors Fund*
The Frederick and Phyllis Cann Trust
The W. A. Cargill Fund*
The Carpenters' Company Charitable Trust
Sir John Cass's Foundation
The Castansa Trust*
The B. G. S. Cayzer Charitable Trust
Celtic Charity Fund
The Amelia Chadwick Trust
Charitworth Ltd
The Charter 600 Charity
Chartered Accountants' Livery Charity (CALC)
The Cheruby Trust
Cheshire Community Foundation Ltd*
Chesterhill Charitable Trust
The Childhood Trust
The Childwick Trust
CHK Charities Ltd
Chrysalis Trust
The Church Burgesses Educational Foundation
Church Burgesses Trust
J. A. Clark Charitable Trust
The Roger and Sarah Bancroft Clark Charitable Trust
The Clark Foundation*
The Clothworkers' Foundation
The Robert Clutterbuck Charitable Trust
The Coalfields Regeneration Trust
The John Coates Charitable Trust
The Denise Cohen Charitable Trust
The Vivienne and Samuel Cohen Charitable Trust
The R. and S. Cohen Foundation
John Coldman Charitable Trust
The Sir Jeremiah Colman Gift Trust
Colyer-Fergusson Charitable Trust
Comic Relief
The Comino Foundation
The Douglas Compton James Charitable Trust
The Thomas Cook Chidlren's Charity*
The Cooks Charity
The Catherine Cookson Charitable Trust
The Keith Coombs Trust
The J. Reginald Corah Foundation Fund
The Worshipful Company of Cordwainers Charitable Trusts (Minges Gift and the Pooled Trusts)

Heart of England Community Foundation
The Heathcoat Trust
The Heathside Charitable Trust
*Heb Ffin (Without Frontier)**
The Charlotte Heber-Percy Charitable Trust
The Percy Hedley 1990 Charitable Trust
Hedley Foundation Ltd (The Hedley Foundation)
The Helping Foundation
The Hemby Charitable Trust
Philip Henman Trust
Herefordshire Community Foundation
Hertfordshire Community Foundation
P. and C. Hickinbotham Charitable Trust
The Alan Edward Higgs Charity
Highcroft Charitable Trust
The Hilden Charitable Fund
*M. V. Hillhouse Trust**
The Hillier Trust
R. G. Hills Charitable Trust
The Hinduja Foundation
The Hintze Family Charity Foundation
The Hiscox Foundation
The Henry C. Hoare Charitable Trust
The Hobson Charity Ltd
The Jane Hodge Foundation
The Holden Charitable Trust
The Hollick Family Charitable Trust
The Holliday Foundation
P. H. Holt Foundation
The Mary Homfray Charitable Trust
The Hoover Foundation
The Horizon Foundation
The Antony Hornby Charitable Trust
The Worshipful Company of Horners' Charitable Trusts
*Horwich Shotter Charitable Trust**
Hospice UK
The Sir Joseph Hotung Charitable Settlement
House of Industry Estate
The Reta Lila Howard Foundation
The Daniel Howard Trust
Human Relief Foundation
The Humanitarian Trust
The Hunter Foundation
Miss Agnes H. Hunter's Trust
The Huntingdon Foundation Ltd
Huntingdon Freemen's Trust
Hurdale Charity Ltd
The Hutchinson Charitable Trust
*The Hyde Park Place Estate Charity – civil trustees**
Ibrahim Foundation Ltd
*ICE Futures Charitable Trust**
The Iliffe Family Charitable Trust
Impetus – The Private Equity Foundation (Impetus – PEF)
Incommunities Foundation
*The Worshipful Company of Insurers – First Charitable Trust Fund**
Interserve Employee Foundation Ltd
The Inverforth Charitable Trust
Investream Charitable Trust
The Ireland Fund of Great Britain
Irish Youth Foundation (UK) Ltd (incorporating The Lawlor Foundation)
The Ironmongers' Company
The J. Isaacs Charitable Trust
The Isle of Anglesey Charitable Trust
The J. and J. Benevolent Foundation
The J. A. R. Charitable Trust
The Jabbs Foundation
C. Richard Jackson Charitable Trust
The Ruth and Lionel Jacobson Trust (Second Fund) No. 2
John James Bristol Foundation
John Jarrold Trust Ltd
The Jephcott Charitable Trust
The Jewish Youth Fund (JYF)
The Johnson Foundation
Johnson Wax Ltd Charitable Trust
The Joicey Trust
The Dezna Robins Jones Charitable Foundation
The Marjorie and Geoffrey Jones Charitable Trust
The Joron Charitable Trust
J. E. Joseph Charitable Fund
The Cyril and Eve Jumbo Charitable Trust
Anton Jurgens Charitable Trust
The Jusaca Charitable Trust
The Bernard Kahn Charitable Trust
The Stanley Kalms Foundation
C. S. Kaufman Charitable Trust
Kelsick's Educational Foundation
Keren Association Ltd
E. and E. Kernkraut Charities Ltd
The Mary Kinross Charitable Trust
*The Graham Kirkham Foundation**
Kirkley Poor's Land Estate
The Kirschel Foundation
Robert Kitchin (Saddlers' Company)
The Sir James Knott Trust
The Kobler Trust
The Kohn Foundation
The KPMG Foundation
Kreditor Charitable Trust
The Kreitman Foundation
The Neil Kreitman Foundation
Kusuma Trust UK
The Kyte Charitable Trust
Ladbrokes in the Community Charitable Trust
John Laing Charitable Trust
The David Laing Foundation
The Kirby Laing Foundation
The Beatrice Laing Trust
The Lambert Charitable Trust
Community Foundations for Lancashire and Merseyside
*The Lancashire Foundation**
Duchy of Lancaster Benevolent Fund
LandAid Charitable Trust (Land Aid)
The Jack Lane Charitable Trust
Langdale Trust
The R. J. Larg Family Charitable Trust
The Lauffer Family Charitable Foundation
Mrs F. B. Laurence Charitable Trust
The Edgar E. Lawley Foundation
Lawson Beckman Charitable Trust
The David Lean Foundation
The Leathersellers' Company Charitable Fund
The Arnold Lee Charitable Trust
Leicestershire, Leicester and Rutland Community Foundation
The Kennedy Leigh Charitable Trust
The Leigh Trust
P. Leigh-Bramwell Trust 'E'
*Leng Charitable Trust**
The Lennox Hannay Charitable Trust
The Leverhulme Trust
Lord Leverhulme's Charitable Trust
*Bernard Lewis Family Charitable Trust**
David and Ruth Lewis Family Charitable Trust
The John Spedan Lewis Foundation
John Lewis Partnership General Community Fund
Liberum Foundation
The Limbourne Trust
Limoges Charitable Trust
The Linbury Trust
Lincolnshire Community Foundation
Lindale Educational Foundation

The Linden Charitable Trust
The Lindley Foundation (TLF)
The Ruth and Stuart Lipton Charitable Trust
The Lister Charitable Trust
The Second Joseph Aaron Littman Foundation
The Elaine and Angus Lloyd Charitable Trust
The W. M. and B. W. Lloyd Trust*
Lloyd's Charities Trust
Lloyds Bank Foundation for England and Wales
Lloyds TSB Foundation for Scotland
Localtrent Ltd
Loftus Charitable Trust
The London Community Foundation (LCF)
The William and Katherine Longman Trust
The C. L. Loyd Charitable Trust
The Henry Lumley Charitable Trust
Lord and Lady Lurgan Trust
The Lynn Foundation
John Lyon's Charity
M. and C. Trust
The M. K. Charitable Trust
The Madeline Mabey Trust
The E. M. MacAndrew Trust
The Macdonald-Buchanan Charitable Trust
Mace Foundation*
The Mackintosh Foundation
GPS Macpherson Charitable Settlement*
The MacRobert Trust
The Ian Mactaggart Trust (The Mactaggart Second Fund)
The Magen Charitable Trust
The Makers of Playing Cards Charity
The Manackerman Charitable Trust
The Manchester Guardian Society Charitable Trust
The Manifold Charitable Trust
The W. M. Mann Foundation
R. W. Mann Trust
The Manoukian Charitable Foundation
The Stella and Alexander Margulies Charitable Trust
Mariapolis Ltd
The Ann and David Marks Foundation
The Hilda and Samuel Marks Foundation
The J. P. Marland Charitable Trust
The Michael Marsh Charitable Trust
The Marsh Christian Trust
Charlotte Marshall Charitable Trust
D. G. Marshall of Cambridge Trust
John Martin's Charity
Masonic Charitable Foundation*
The Nancie Massey Charitable Trust
The Master Charitable Trust*
The Matliwala Family Charitable Trust
The Robert McAlpine Foundation
The Medlock Charitable Trust
Melodor Ltd
The Mercers' Charitable Foundation
The Merchant Taylors' Company Charities Fund
The Merchant Venturers' Charity
The Metropolitan Masonic Charity
T. and J. Meyer Family Foundation Ltd
The Mickel Fund
The Mickleham Trust
The Ronald Miller Foundation
The Millfield Trust
The James Milner Foundation*
The Edgar Milward Charity
The Peter Minet Trust
The Laurence Misener Charitable Trust
The Brian Mitchell Charitable Settlement
The MITIE Foundation
Keren Mitzvah Trust
The Mizpah Trust
Mole Charitable Trust
The Monmouthshire County Council Welsh Church Act Fund
Moondance Foundation*
The George A. Moore Foundation
The Steve Morgan Foundation
Morgan Stanley International Foundation
The Diana and Allan Morgenthau Charitable Trust
The Morris Charitable Trust
G. M. Morrison Charitable Trust
The Morton Charitable Trust*
The Moshal Charitable Trust
Vyoel Moshe Charitable Trust
The Mosselson Charitable Trust
Moto in the Community
J. P. Moulton Charitable Foundation
The Edith Murphy Foundation
The Music Sales Charitable Trust
Muslim Hands
The Mutual Trust Group
MW (CL) Foundation
MW (GK) Foundation
MW (HO) Foundation
MW (RH) Foundation
The National Express Foundation
The NDL Foundation
The Worshipful Company of Needlemakers' Charitable Fund
Ner Foundation
Nesta*
Newby Trust Ltd
Newpier Charity Ltd
Alderman Newton's Educational Foundation
The NFU Mutual Charitable Trust
Nominet Charitable Foundation
Norfolk Community Foundation
Educational Foundation of Alderman John Norman
Normanby Charitable Trust
Northamptonshire Community Foundation
The Northumberland Village Homes Trust
The Norton Foundation
The Norton Rose Fulbright Charitable Foundation
Norwich Town Close Estate Charity
The Notgrove Trust
The Nuffield Foundation
The Father O'Mahoney Memorial Trust
The Oakley Charitable Trust
Oglesby Charitable Trust
Oizer Charitable Trust
The John Oldacre Foundation
Open Gate
The O'Sullivan Family Charitable Trust
The Doris Pacey Charitable Foundation
The Paget Charitable Trust
Palmtree Memorial Trust*
The Paphitis Charitable Trust
Parabola Foundation*
Paradigm Foundation
The Park House Charitable Trust
Susanna Peake Charitable Trust
The Dowager Countess Eleanor Peel Trust
Personal Assurance Charitable Trust
The Phillips and Rubens Charitable Trust
The Austin and Hope Pilkington Trust
The Polehampton Charity*
The George and Esme Pollitzer Charitable Settlement
Pollywally Charitable Trust
The Ponton House Trust
The Portishead Nautical Trust

Community Foundation serving Tyne and Wear and Northumberland
The Underwood Trust
The Michael Uren Foundation
The Utley Family Charitable Trust*
Mrs Maud Van Norden's Charitable Foundation
The Vandervell Foundation
The Vardy Foundation
Roger Vere Foundation
The Nigel Vinson Charitable Trust
The Vintners' Foundation
The Virgin Money Foundation
The Vodafone Foundation
Voluntary Action Fund (VAF)
The Wakefield Trust*
The Wakeham Trust
The Walcot Foundation
The Community Foundation in Wales
Wales Council for Voluntary Action
The Walker Trust
Walton Foundation*
The Barbara Ward Children's Foundation
The Waterloo Foundation
Wates Family Enterprise Trust
The Wates Foundation
The Geoffrey Watling Charity*
John Watson's Trust
The Weavers' Company Benevolent Fund
The James Weir Foundation
The Welton Foundation
The Wessex Youth Trust
The West Looe Town Trust*
The Garfield Weston Foundation
Westway Trust
The Barbara Whatmore Charitable Trust
The Wheeler Family Charitable Trust*
The Whitaker Charitable Trust
The Williams Charitable Trust
Williams Serendipity Trust
The Wilson Foundation
The W. Wing Yip and Brothers Foundation
The Harold Hyam Wingate Foundation
The Michael and Anna Wix Charitable Trust
The Wixamtree Trust
The Maurice Wohl Charitable Foundation
The Charles Wolfson Charitable Trust
The Wolfson Family Charitable Trust
The Wolfson Foundation
The Wood Foundation
Woodroffe Benton Foundation
Worcester Municipal Charities (CIO)
The Worwin UK Foundation*
Wychville Ltd
The Yapp Charitable Trust
York Children's Trust*
Yorkshire and Clydesdale Bank Foundation
Yorkshire Building Society Charitable Foundation
Elizabeth and Prince Zaiger Trust*
The Marjorie and Arnold Ziff Charitable Foundation
The Zochonis Charitable Trust

Higher education and universities

The 29th May 1961 Charitable Trust
The 3Ts Charitable Trust*
A. W. Charitable Trust
Action Medical Research
AF Trust Company
Age UK
AKO Foundation*
The Alborada Trust
All Saints Educational Trust
The H. B. Allen Charitable Trust
The Alliance Family Foundation
Alzheimer's Research UK*
Alzheimer's Society*
Viscount Amory's Charitable Trust
The Ancaster Trust*
The Arbib Foundation
Arcadia Charitable Trust*
The Ardeola Charitable Trust
The Ardwick Trust
The Armourers' and Brasiers' Gauntlet Trust
The Artemis Charitable Trust
Arthritis Research UK
The Ove Arup Foundation
The Asfari Foundation*
The Ashley Family Foundation
The Associated Board of the Royal Schools of Music*
The Association of Colleges Charitable Trust
Asthma UK
The Astor Foundation
The Atlas Fund
The Aurelius Charitable Trust
Awards for All (see also the Big Lottery Fund)
The Aylesford Family Charitable Trust
The Baily Thomas Charitable Fund
The Baily Thomas Charitable Trust
The Barclay Foundation
The Barham Charitable Trust
The Paul Bassham Charitable Trust
The Batchworth Trust
The Becht Family Charitable Trust*
Beefy's Charity Foundation
Benesco Charity Ltd*
The Ruth Berkowitz Charitable Trust
The Bestway Foundation
The Big Lottery Fund (see also Awards for All)
Blakemore Foundation
The Sir Victor Blank Charitable Settlement
Bloodwise
The Bluston Charitable Settlement
Sir William Boreman's Foundation*
The Harry Bottom Charitable Trust
The Tony Bramall Charitable Trust
The Liz and Terry Bramall Foundation
Breast Cancer Now*
The Breast Cancer Research Trust (BCRT)
The British Academy for the Promotion of Historical Philosophical and Philological Studies (The British Academy)*
The British and Foreign Bible Society*
British Council for Prevention of Blindness (Save Eyes Everywhere)
British Eye Research Foundation (Fight for Sight)*
British Heart Foundation (BHF)
British Record Industry Trust
The J. and M. Britton Charitable Trust
The Rory and Elizabeth Brooks Foundation
The Charles Brotherton Trust
The Burberry Foundation*
The Burdett Trust for Nursing
The Derek Butler Trust
The Edward Cadbury Charitable Trust
The Barrow Cadbury Trust
CAFOD (Catholic Agency for Overseas Development)
Callander Charitable Trust
Calleva Foundation
The W. A. Cargill Charitable Trust*
The W. A. Cargill Fund*
The Richard Carne Trust
The Carnegie Trust for the Universities of Scotland
The Carr-Gregory Trust
Sir John Cass's Foundation

Sir Ernest Cassel Educational Trust*
The Elizabeth Casson Trust
The Castang Foundation
The Chadwick Educational Foundation*
The Chapman Charitable Trust
Chest Heart and Stroke Scotland
Children with Cancer UK
Children's Liver Disease Foundation
The Church Burgesses Educational Foundation
The City Educational Trust Fund
The Clothworkers' Foundation
The Robert Clutterbuck Charitable Trust
Denise Coates Foundation
The Vivienne and Samuel Cohen Charitable Trust
The John S. Cohen Foundation
The Colchester Catalyst Charity
The Colt Foundation
The Comino Foundation
The Marjorie Coote Old People's Charity
The Worshipful Company of Cordwainers Charitable Trusts (Minges Gift and the Pooled Trusts)
The Gershon Coren Charitable Foundation (also known as The Muriel and Gus Coren Charitable Foundation)
Country Houses Foundation
The Sir Tom Cowie Charitable Trust
Dudley and Geoffrey Cox Charitable Trust
The Craps Charitable Trust
The Elizabeth Creak Charitable Trust*
The Crerar Hotels Trust
The Crescent Trust
The Cross Trust
The Peter Cruddas Foundation
Cullum Family Trust
The Cunningham Trust
The D. G. Charitable Settlement
The Daiwa Anglo-Japanese Foundation
Michael Davies Charitable Settlement
The Biss Davies Charitable Trust*
Margaret Davies Charity
The Hamilton Davies Trust
The Davis Foundation
The De Laszlo Foundation
The Demigryphon Trust
Diabetes UK
Dinwoodie Charitable Company
Disability Aid Fund (The Roger and Jean Jefcoate Trust)
Dischma Charitable Trust
The Djanogly Foundation
The Dorfman Foundation*
The Drapers' Charitable Fund
The Dunhill Medical Trust
The James Dyson Foundation
Eaga Charitable Trust
Eastern Counties Educational Trust Ltd
Echoes Of Service
The Gilbert and Eileen Edgar Foundation
Edge Foundation*
Edinburgh Children's Holiday Fund
The Elephant Trust
The Gerald Palmer Eling Trust Company
The Maud Elkington Charitable Trust
The John Ellerman Foundation
The Elmley Foundation
Entindale Ltd
Epilepsy Research UK
The Eranda Rothschild Foundation
Joseph Ettedgui Charitable Foundation
The Everard Foundation
The Eveson Charitable Trust
The Exilarch's Foundation
Esmée Fairbairn Foundation
The Fairstead Trust
The Lord Faringdon Charitable Trust
The Thomas Farr Charity
The February Foundation
Allan and Nesta Ferguson Charitable Settlement
Elizabeth Ferguson Charitable Trust Fund
The Fidelio Charitable Trust*
The Doris Field Charitable Trust
The Fifty Fund
The Sir John Fisher Foundation
Fishmongers' Company's Charitable Trust
Marc Fitch Fund
The Football Association National Sports Centre Trust
The Football Foundation
The Forman Hardy Charitable Trust
The Fort Foundation
The Lord Forte Foundation
The Foyle Foundation
The Hugh Fraser Foundation
The Freshgate Trust Foundation
The Raphael Freshwater Memorial Association*
Friends Provident Charitable Foundation
The Frognal Trust
The Patrick and Helena Frost Foundation
G. M. C. Trust
The G. R. P. Charitable Trust
The Garrard Family Foundation
The Gatsby Charitable Foundation
The Robert Gavron Charitable Trust
The Jacqueline and Michael Gee Charitable Trust
The General Nursing Council for England and Wales Trust
Gilchrist Educational Trust*
Worshipful Company of Glovers of London Charitable Trust
Worshipful Company of Gold and Silver Wyre Drawers Charitable Trust Fund
The Goldman Sachs Charitable Gift Fund (UK)
Goldman Sachs Gives (UK)
The Golsoncott Foundation
Nicholas and Judith Goodison's Charitable Settlement
The Mike Gooley Trailfinders Charity
The Granada Foundation
The Gray Trust
The Great Britain Sasakawa Foundation
The Grocers' Charity
The Hadrian Trust
Paul Hamlyn Foundation
The Helen Hamlyn Trust
The Kathleen Hannay Memorial Charity
The Happold Foundation*
The Haramead Trust
The Harbour Foundation
The Harpur Trust
The Peter and Teresa Harris Charitable Trust
The Harris Charity
The Peter Harrison Foundation
The Maurice Hatter Foundation
The Headley Trust
The Health Foundation
Heart Research UK
The Heathside Charitable Trust
The Charlotte Heber-Percy Charitable Trust
The Michael Heller Charitable Foundation
The Simon Heller Charitable Settlement
Help for Health
The Helping Foundation
Henley Educational Trust
Heritage Lottery Fund*
The Hesslewood Children's Trust (Hull Seamen's and General Orphanage)
The Hesslewood Children's Trust (Hull Seamen's and General Orphanage)

P. and C. Hickinbotham Charitable Trust
The Hilden Charitable Fund
M. V. Hillhouse Trust*
The Hillingdon Community Trust
The Hintze Family Charity Foundation
The Hobson Charity Ltd
Hockerill Educational Foundation
The Jane Hodge Foundation
The Holden Charitable Trust
The Hollick Family Charitable Trust
P. H. Holt Foundation
The Holywood Trust
The Homelands Charitable Trust
The Homestead Charitable Trust
The Hope Trust
The Horizon Foundation
The Antony Hornby Charitable Trust
The Sir Joseph Hotung Charitable Settlement
Howman Charitable Trust*
The Hull and East Riding Charitable Trust
Hulme Trust Estates (Educational)
The Humanitarian Trust
The Hunter Foundation
IBM United Kingdom Trust
Ibrahim Foundation Ltd
Impetus – The Private Equity Foundation (Impetus – PEF)
The Worshipful Company of Information Technologists*
The Worshipful Company of Insurers – First Charitable Trust Fund*
The International Bankers Charitable Trust (The Worshipful Company of International Bankers)
The International Bankers Charitable Trust (The Worshipful Company of Interntional Bankers)
The Ireland Fund of Great Britain
Irish Youth Foundation (UK) Ltd (incorporating The Lawlor Foundation)
The Ironmongers' Company
The JRSST Charitable Trust
The Jabbs Foundation
The Ruth and Lionel Jacobson Trust (Second Fund) No. 2
John James Bristol Foundation
The Susan and Stephen James Charitable Settlement
Lady Eda Jardine Charitable Trust
John Jarrold Trust Ltd
Rees Jeffreys Road Fund
Nick Jenkins Foundation
The Jerusalem Trust
Joffe Charitable Trust
The Johnson Foundation
The Dezna Robins Jones Charitable Foundation
J. E. Joseph Charitable Fund
The Stanley Kalms Foundation
The Kasner Charitable Trust
The Michael and Ilse Katz Foundation
C. S. Kaufman Charitable Trust
The Kay Kendall Leukaemia Fund
The Kennel Club Charitable Trust
Kidney Research UK
The Robert Kiln Charitable Trust
The Mary Kinross Charitable Trust
Robert Kitchin (Saddlers' Company)
The Sir James Knott Trust
The Kohn Foundation
Kollel and Co. Ltd
The KPMG Foundation
The Kreitman Foundation
The Neil Kreitman Foundation
Kusuma Trust UK
The Kirby Laing Foundation
Duchy of Lancaster Benevolent Fund
The R. J. Larg Family Charitable Trust
The Lauffer Family Charitable Foundation
The Kathleen Laurence Trust
The Law Society Charity
The Edgar E. Lawley Foundation
The David Lean Foundation
The Leathersellers' Company Charitable Fund
The Leche Trust
The Legal Education Foundation*
Leicestershire and Rutland Masonic Charity Association*
The Kennedy Leigh Charitable Trust
P. Leigh-Bramwell Trust 'E'
The Lennox Hannay Charitable Trust
The Mark Leonard Trust
The Leverhulme Trade Charities Trust
The Leverhulme Trust
Lord Leverhulme's Charitable Trust
David and Ruth Lewis Family Charitable Trust
The John Spedan Lewis Foundation
Limoges Charitable Trust
The Linbury Trust
Lindale Educational Foundation
The Enid Linder Foundation
The Frank Litchfield Charitable Trust
The Charles Littlewood Hill Trust
The Second Joseph Aaron Littman Foundation
The George John and Sheilah Livanos Charitable Trust
Lloyd's Register Foundation*
Loftus Charitable Trust
The Lower Green Foundation
The Henry Lumley Charitable Trust
C. F. Lunoe Trust Fund
Lord and Lady Lurgan Trust
The Sir Jack Lyons Charitable Trust
The R. S. Macdonald Charitable Trust
GPS Macpherson Charitable Settlement*
The MacRobert Trust
The Mactaggart Third Fund
The Ian Mactaggart Trust (The Mactaggart Second Fund)
The Magen Charitable Trust
The Mallinckrodt Foundation
The W. M. Mann Foundation
R. W. Mann Trust
Marbeh Torah Trust
The Marcela Trust
The Marchig Animal Welfare Trust
The Michael Marks Charitable Trust
Sir George Martin Trust
The Nancie Massey Charitable Trust
The Master Charitable Trust*
The Mathew Trust
Mayfair Charities Ltd
D. D. McPhail Charitable Settlement
Medical Research Foundation*
Medical Research Scotland*
The Medlock Charitable Trust
Melodor Ltd
The Brian Mercer Charitable Trust
The Mercers' Charitable Foundation
The Merchant Venturers' Charity
The Merchant Venturers' Charity
T. and J. Meyer Family Foundation Ltd
The Mickel Fund
The Masonic Province of Middlesex Charitable Trust (Middlesex Masonic Charity)
The Millfield House Foundation (1)

The Millichope Foundation
*Mills and Reeve Charitable Trust**
The Millward Charitable Trust
The Edgar Milward Charity
The Mishcon Family Charitable Trust
*Mitsubishi Corporation Fund for Europe and Africa**
Mole Charitable Trust
The Henry Moore Foundation
The Morel Charitable Trust
The Morel Charitable Trust (The Morel Trust) Morel Charitable Trust
The Morgan Charitable Foundation
Morgan Stanley International Foundation
The Morris Charitable Trust
G. M. Morrison Charitable Trust
The Moshal Charitable Trust
Motor Neurone Disease Association
J. P. Moulton Charitable Foundation
*Multiple Sclerosis Society**
The Edith Murphy Foundation
The John R. Murray Charitable Trust
The National Express Foundation
*The National Gardens Scheme**
The National Manuscripts Conservation Trust
*Nesta**
Network for Social Change Charitable Trust
Newby Trust Ltd
The Frances and Augustus Newman Foundation
The NFU Mutual Charitable Trust
Alice Noakes Memorial Charitable Trust
Nominet Charitable Foundation
The Norman Family Charitable Trust
North West Cancer Research (incorporating Clatterbridge Cancer Research)
Northwood Charitable Trust
Norwich Town Close Estate Charity
The Nuffield Foundation
The Oakdale Trust
Oglesby Charitable Trust
The John Oldacre Foundation
The O'Sullivan Family Charitable Trust
The Ouseley Church Music Trust
The Owen Family Trust
P. F. Charitable Trust
The Panacea Charitable Trust
The James Pantyfedwen Foundation
*Parkinson's Disease Society of the United Kingdom**
*The JGW Patterson Foundation**
The Pears Family Charitable Foundation
The Dowager Countess Eleanor Peel Trust
The Pell Charitable Trust
B. E. Perl Charitable Trust
Petplan Charitable Trust
The Phillips and Rubens Charitable Trust
The Phillips Family Charitable Trust
The Pilgrim Trust
*The Institute for Policy Research**
The Polonsky Foundation
Postcode Dream Trust – Dream Fund
David and Elaine Potter Foundation
*Prostate Cancer UK**
Mr and Mrs J. A. Pye's Charitable Settlement
The Queen Anne's Gate Foundation
The Queen's Trust
The Racing Foundation
The Radcliffe Trust
The Joseph and Lena Randall Charitable Trust
The Joseph Rank Trust
The Sigrid Rausing Trust
The Ravensdale Trust
The Sir James Reckitt Charity
Red Hill Charitable Trust
Richard Reeve's Foundation
Responsible Gambling Trust (GambleAware)
Reuben Foundation
The Clive and Sylvia Richards Charity Ltd
The Helen Roll Charity
The Rose Foundation
*The Cissie Rosefield Charitable Trust**
Rosetrees Trust
*The David Ross Foundation**
The Rothermere Foundation
*Rothschild Foundation (Hanadiv) Europe**
Rowanville Ltd
The Joseph Rowntree Foundation
The Rubin Foundation
The Rubin Foundation Charitable Trust
Michael Sacher Charitable Trust
The Michael and Nicola Sacher Trust
The Dr Mortimer and Theresa Sackler Foundation
The Sackler Trust
The Saintbury Trust
Coral Samuel Charitable Trust
The Sandhu Charitable Foundation
The Sants Charitable Trust
*Sarum St Michael Educational Charity**
*The Save the Children Fund**
*The Savoy Educational Trust**
Sir Samuel Scott of Yews Trust
The ScottishPower Foundation
The Scouloudi Foundation
The Jean Shanks Foundation
The Sheepdrove Trust
The Sylvia and Colin Shepherd Charitable Trust
The Shipwrights' Company Charitable Fund
The Shirley Foundation
David and Jennifer Sieff Charitable Trust
The Sino-British Fellowship Trust
Sloane Robinson Foundation
The WH Smith Group Charitable Trust
The Stanley Smith UK Horticultural Trust
*Sofronie Foundation**
Solev Co. Ltd
The South Square Trust
Sparks Charity (Sport Aiding Medical Research for Kids)
The Spear Charitable Trust
Rosalyn and Nicholas Springer Charitable Trust
Sir Walter St John's Educational Charity
St Luke's College Foundation
*St Marylebone Educational Foundation**
St Peter's Saltley Trust
The Staples Trust
The Steel Charitable Trust
The Sigmund Sternberg Charitable Foundation
Stewards' Company Ltd
Sir Halley Stewart Trust
The Stone Family Foundation
*The Stoneygate Trust**
The Samuel Storey Family Charitable Trust
Peter Stormonth Darling Charitable Trust
Stratford upon Avon Town Trust
The Sudborough Foundation
*Surgo Foundation UK Ltd**
The Sutasoma Trust
The John Swire (1989) Charitable Trust
The Swire Charitable Trust
The Charles and Elsie Sykes Trust
The Talbot Village Trust
Tallow Chandlers Benevolent Fund No. 2

C. B. and H. H. Taylor 1984 Trust
Humphrey Richardson Taylor Charitable Trust
The Tennis Foundation
*Tenovus Scotland**
*DM Thomas Foundation for Young People**
The Thompson Family Charitable Trust
The Sir Jules Thorn Charitable Trust
The Thornton Trust
The Thriplow Charitable Trust
The Tolkien Trust
*The Trades House of Glasgow**
The Constance Travis Charitable Trust
The Treeside Trust
*Tropical Health and Education Trust**
The James Tudor Foundation
The Tuixen Foundation
Ulting Overseas Trust
The Ulverscroft Foundation
The Vandervell Foundation
The Nigel Vinson Charitable Trust
Wade's Charity
The Walker Trust
The Waterloo Foundation
Wates Family Enterprise Trust
The Weavers' Company Benevolent Fund
Webb Memorial Trust
The Wellcome Trust
The Welton Foundation
The Westminster Foundation
The Garfield Weston Foundation
The Whitaker Charitable Trust
Williams Serendipity Trust
Dame Violet Wills Charitable Trust
The W. Wing Yip and Brothers Foundation
The Harold Hyam Wingate Foundation
Winton Philanthropies
The Michael and Anna Wix Charitable Trust
The Wixamtree Trust
The Maurice Wohl Charitable Foundation
The Charles Wolfson Charitable Trust
The Wolfson Family Charitable Trust
The Wolfson Foundation
The Wood Foundation
Woodroffe Benton Foundation
*Yorkshire Cancer Research**
The John Kirkhope Young Endowment Fund
The Zochonis Charitable Trust
The Nigel Vinson Charitable Trust
Wade's Charity
The Walker Trust
The Waterloo Foundation
Wates Family Enterprise Trust
The Weavers' Company Benevolent Fund
Webb Memorial Trust
The Wellcome Trust
The Welton Foundation
The Westminster Foundation
The Garfield Weston Foundation
The Whitaker Charitable Trust
Williams Serendipity Trust
Dame Violet Wills Charitable Trust
The W. Wing Yip and Brothers Foundation
The Harold Hyam Wingate Foundation
Winton Philanthropies
The Michael and Anna Wix Charitable Trust
The Wixamtree Trust
The Maurice Wohl Charitable Foundation
The Charles Wolfson Charitable Trust
The Wolfson Family Charitable Trust
The Wolfson Foundation
The Wood Foundation
Woodroffe Benton Foundation
*Yorkshire Cancer Research**
The John Kirkhope Young Endowment Fund
The Zochonis Charitable Trust

Informal, continuing and adult education

The Association of Colleges Charitable Trust
*Bairdwatson Charitable Trust**
The Big Lottery Fund (see also Awards for All)
The Blagrave Trust
Boots Charitable Trust
The Cadbury Foundation
*Sir Ernest Cassel Educational Trust**
John and Freda Coleman Charitable Trust
Devon Community Foundation
The Royal Foundation of the Duke and Duchess of Cambridge and Prince Harry
The February Foundation
The Gannochy Trust
The Girdlers' Company Charitable Trust
The Harris Charity
The Hillingdon Community Trust
The Nani Huyu Charitable Trust
The Allen Lane Foundation
Lloyds Bank Foundation for the Channel Islands
Trust for London
The Lower Green Foundation
The Marr-Munning Trust
The Mathew Trust
The Millichope Foundation
John Moores Foundation
*The National Gardens Scheme**
The Community Foundation for Northern Ireland
OneFamily Foundation
Richard Reeve's Foundation
Responsible Gambling Trust (GambleAware)
The Royal British Legion
Seafarers UK (King George's Fund for Sailors)
The Shipwrights' Company Charitable Fund

Adult and community education

*Sir Ernest Cassel Educational Trust**
Trust for London
Responsible Gambling Trust (GambleAware)

Vocational education and training

John and Freda Coleman Charitable Trust
The Girdlers' Company Charitable Trust
The Harris Charity
The Allen Lane Foundation
The Lower Green Foundation
*The National Gardens Scheme**
Seafarers UK (King George's Fund for Sailors)
The Shipwrights' Company Charitable Fund

Integrated education

The February Foundation
*Integrated Education Fund**
The Lord's Taverners
Variety The Children's Charity (Variety Club)

Management of schools

Calouste Gulbenkian Foundation – UK Branch
The February Foundation
St Marylebone Educational Foundation*

Arts education and training

Arts Council of Wales (also known as Cyngor Celfyddydau Cymru)
The Associated Board of the Royal Schools of Music*
The British Academy for the Promotion of Historical Philosophical and Philological Studies (The British Academy)*
British Record Industry Trust
The Britten-Pears Foundation (The Britten Pears Library)
The Derek Butler Trust
Calouste Gulbenkian Foundation – UK Branch
The Richard Carne Trust
The Clore Duffield Foundation
The De Laszlo Foundation
The James Dyson Foundation
EMI Music Sound Foundation
The Golsoncott Foundation
Nicholas and Judith Goodison's Charitable Settlement
Paul Hamlyn Foundation
The Happold Foundation*
The Derek Hill Foundation
The Hinrichsen Foundation
The Idlewild Trust
The Robert Kiln Charitable Trust
The Mayfield Valley Arts Trust
The Henry Moore Foundation
The Ouseley Church Music Trust
The Performing Right Society Foundation
The Radcliffe Trust
Richard Reeve's Foundation
Royal Victoria Hall Foundation
The Dr Mortimer and Theresa Sackler Foundation
The Alan and Babette Sainsbury Charitable Fund
The South Square Trust
Humphrey Richardson Taylor Charitable Trust
Youth Music

Business education

The De Laszlo Foundation
The International Bankers Charitable Trust (The Worshipful Company of Interntional Bankers)
The MSE Charity

Citizenship, personal and social education

The Big Lottery Fund (see also Awards for All)

Construction industry education

The Happold Foundation*
C. F. Lunoe Trust Fund

Home economics and life skills education

All Saints Educational Trust
The Girdlers' Company Charitable Trust
Sodexo Stop Hunger Foundation

Hospitality and leisure industry education

The Lord Forte Foundation
The Savoy Educational Trust*

Language and literacy education

The City Bridge Trust (Bridge House Estates)
The J. J. Charitable Trust
Man Group PLC Charitable Trust
Old Possum's Practical Trust
Richard Reeve's Foundation
The Sino-British Fellowship Trust

Legal education

The Edwina Mountbatten and Leonora Children's Foundation
The Law Society Charity
The Legal Education Foundation*

Religious education

All Saints Educational Trust
Brushmill Ltd
Clydpride Ltd
Dushinsky Trust Ltd
Famos Foundation Trust
Friends of Biala Ltd
Friends of Wiznitz Ltd
The Girdlers' Company Charitable Trust
The Gur Trust
H. P. Charitable Trust
Hadras Kodesh Trust
Hockerill Educational Foundation
The Hope Trust
The Jerusalem Trust
Kollel and Co. Ltd
Kupath Gemach Chaim Bechesed Viznitz Trust
Largsmount Ltd
The Lyndhurst Trust
M. B. Foundation*
Marbeh Torah Trust
The Panacea Charitable Trust
B. E. Perl Charitable Trust
Sir John Priestman Charity Trust
Quothquan Trust
The River Trust
Rothschild Foundation (Hanadiv) Europe*
Sarum St Michael Educational Charity*
The Spalding Trust*
St Luke's College Foundation
St Peter's Saltley Trust
Ulting Overseas Trust
The Norman Whiteley Trust

Science education

The Ernest Cook Trust
The Elizabeth Creak Charitable Trust*
The De Laszlo Foundation
Lloyd's Register Foundation*
The Racing Foundation
Richard Reeve's Foundation
The Dr Mortimer and Theresa Sackler Foundation
Salters' Charitable Foundation
Winton Philanthropies

Sports education

The Essex Youth Trust
The Girdlers' Company Charitable Trust
Johnnie Johnson Trust

The Lord's Taverners
The Professional Footballers' Association Charity*

Technology, engineering and computer education

The James Dyson Foundation
IBM United Kingdom Trust
The Worshipful Company of Information Technologists*
The Sir James Roll Charitable Trust

Pre-school education

BBC Children in Need
The February Foundation
The Football Association National Sports Centre Trust
Hampton Fuel Allotment Charity
Henley Educational Trust
The Hesslewood Children's Trust (Hull Seamen's and General Orphanage)
Richard Reeve's Foundation
Variety The Children's Charity (Variety Club)

Primary and secondary school education

The Ammco Trust
The Baily Thomas Charitable Fund
BBC Children in Need
The Harry Bottom Charitable Trust
Bristol Charities
The Cadbury Foundation
Calouste Gulbenkian Foundation – UK Branch
The Chadwick Educational Foundation*
Eastern Counties Educational Trust Ltd
Esmée Fairbairn Foundation
The Joyce Fletcher Charitable Trust
The Football Association National Sports Centre Trust
The Girdlers' Company Charitable Trust
The J. G. Graves Charitable Trust
Hadras Kodesh Trust
Hampton Fuel Allotment Charity
The Harris Charity
Heathrow Community Fund (LHR Airport Communities Trust)
Henley Educational Trust
The Hesslewood Children's Trust (Hull Seamen's and General Orphanage)
Hulme Trust Estates (Educational)
Integrated Education Fund*
The J. J. Charitable Trust
The Peter Kershaw Trust
The Leche Trust
The Mark Leonard Trust
The Charles Littlewood Hill Trust
The Lord's Taverners
The Marr-Munning Trust
The Newcomen Collett Foundation
The Owen Family Trust
The Paddington Charitable Estate Educational Fund*
The Jack Petchey Foundation
Richard Reeve's Foundation
The Rix-Thompson-Rothenberg Foundation
Sarum St Michael Educational Charity*
The Leslie Smith Foundation
The South Square Trust
St Marylebone Educational Foundation*
Variety The Children's Charity (Variety Club)
The Warrington Church of England Educational Trust*
Colonel W. H. Whitbread Charitable Trust

Faith schools

Hadras Kodesh Trust
The Owen Family Trust
Sarum St Michael Educational Charity*
The Warrington Church of England Educational Trust*

Public and independent schools

Integrated Education Fund*
The Leche Trust
The Owen Family Trust

Special needs schools

The Ammco Trust
The Baily Thomas Charitable Fund
Eastern Counties Educational Trust Ltd
The Joyce Fletcher Charitable Trust
The Girdlers' Company Charitable Trust
The J. G. Graves Charitable Trust
The Lord's Taverners
The Rix-Thompson-Rothenberg Foundation

State schools

Aberdeen Asset Management Charitable Foundation
The Aberdeen Foundation
The Acacia Charitable Trust
The Accenture Foundation
The ACT Foundation
The Sylvia Adams Charitable Trust
The Adnams Community Trust
Age Scotland
Aid to the Church in Need (UK)
Aldgate and All Hallows' Foundation
Al-Fayed Charitable Foundation
Allchurches Trust Ltd
Viscount Amory's Charitable Trust
Anguish's Educational Foundation
The Anne Duchess of Westminster's Charity*
The Arbib Foundation
The Ardwick Trust
The John Armitage Charitable Trust
The Armourers' and Brasiers' Gauntlet Trust
The Asfari Foundation*
The Ashley Family Foundation
The Ian Askew Charitable Trust
The Associated Board of the Royal Schools of Music*
The Associated Country Women of the World
The Association of Colleges Charitable Trust
The Atlas Fund
The Avon and Somerset Police Community Trust
Awards for All (see also the Big Lottery Fund)
Backstage Trust
The Baily Thomas Charitable Fund
The Banbury Charities
The Barham Charitable Trust
The Barker-Mill Foundation

Lord Barnby's Foundation
The Paul Bassham Charitable Trust
Bauer Radio's Cash for Kids Charities
Bay Charitable Trust
The James Beattie Charitable Trust
Beauland Ltd
The John Beckwith Charitable Trust
*Benesco Charity Ltd**
The Bestway Foundation
The Big Lottery Fund (see also Awards for All)
Percy Bilton Charity
The Bingham Trust
Birmingham International Airport Community Trust Fund
Birthday House Trust
Isabel Blackman Foundation
Blakemore Foundation
Bloom Foundation
The Booth Charities
*Sir William Boreman's Foundation**
The Boshier-Hinton Foundation
The Harry Bottom Charitable Trust
The Bowland Charitable Trust
The Bransford Trust
The Breadsticks Foundation
Bristol Charities
John Bristow and Thomas Mason Trust
The British and Foreign School Society
*The British and Foreign Bible Society**
British Record Industry Trust
The Jack Brunton Charitable Trust
Buckingham Trust
Buckinghamshire Community Foundation
The Buffini Chao Foundation
The E. F. Bulmer Benevolent Fund
*The Burberry Foundation**
The Burden Trust
The Clara E. Burgess Charity
Consolidated Charity of Burton upon Trent
The Edward and Dorothy Cadbury Trust
CAFOD (Catholic Agency for Overseas Development)
The Cambridgeshire Community Foundation
*Canary Wharf Contractors Fund**
*The W. A. Cargill Fund**
The Richard Carne Trust
The Carnegie Dunfermline Trust
The Carrington Charitable Trust
The Casey Trust
Sir John Cass's Foundation
*The Chadwick Educational Foundation**
Chalfords Ltd
Chartered Accountants' Livery Charity (CALC)
The Church Burgesses Educational Foundation
The City Bridge Trust (Bridge House Estates)
*The Clan Trust Ltd**
*The Clark Foundation**
The Clothworkers' Foundation
The Robert Clutterbuck Charitable Trust
The Colchester Catalyst Charity
The Sir Jeremiah Colman Gift Trust
Col-Reno Ltd
Colyer-Fergusson Charitable Trust
The Comino Foundation
*The Thomas Cook Chidlren's Charity**
The Ernest Cook Trust
The Catherine Cookson Charitable Trust
The J. Reginald Corah Foundation Fund
The Worshipful Company of Cordwainers Charitable Trusts (Minges Gift and the Pooled Trusts)
The Duke of Cornwall's Benevolent Fund
*The Coulthurst Trust**
The Sir Tom Cowie Charitable Trust
The Craps Charitable Trust
Criffel Charitable Trust
The Ronald Cruickshanks Foundation
The Cumber Family Charitable Trust
The Daiwa Anglo-Japanese Foundation
*The Biss Davies Charitable Trust**
Margaret Davies Charity
The Hamilton Davies Trust
The Crispin Davis Family Trust
The Davis Foundation
*The Roger De Haan Charitable Trust**
The De Laszlo Foundation
William Dean Countryside and Educational Trust
The Denman Charitable Trust
The Duke of Devonshire's Charitable Trust
The Sandy Dewhirst Charitable Trust
The Dischma Charitable Trust
Dorset Community Foundation
The Dumbreck Charity
County Durham Community Foundation
The James Dyson Foundation
Earls Colne and Halstead Educational Charity
East End Community Foundation
Eastern Counties Educational Trust Ltd
The Sir John Eastwood Foundation
Echoes Of Service
*Edge Foundation**
Edinburgh Children's Holiday Fund
Dr Edwards Bishop King's Fulham Endowment Fund
The Maud Elkington Charitable Trust
The Elmley Foundation
EMI Music Sound Foundation
The Englefield Charitable Trust
The Enkalon Foundation
Entindale Ltd
Esh Foundation
The Essex Youth Trust
The Exilarch's Foundation
The F. P. Ltd Charitable Trust
The Fairstead Trust
Famos Foundation Trust
Samuel William Farmer Trust
The George Fentham Birmingham Charity
*The Fidelio Charitable Trust**
The Doris Field Charitable Trust
The Fifty Fund
Dixie Rose Findlay Charitable Trust
The Sir John Fisher Foundation
Fishmongers' Company's Charitable Trust
The Earl Fitzwilliam Charitable Trust
The Joyce Fletcher Charitable Trust
The Football Foundation
Ford Britain Trust
The Forman Hardy Charitable Trust
The Lord Forte Foundation
The Foyle Foundation
The Elizabeth Frankland Moore and Star Foundation
The Hugh Fraser Foundation
The Joseph Strong Frazer Trust
*The Raphael Freshwater Memorial Association**
Friends Provident Charitable Foundation
Mejer and Gertrude Miriam Frydman Foundation
G. M. C. Trust
The Gale Family Charity Trust
The Ganzoni Charitable Trust
The Garrard Family Foundation
The Robert Gavron Charitable Trust

The Jacqueline and Michael Gee Charitable Trust
The Generations Foundation
Genetic Disorders UK*
The G. C. Gibson Charitable Trust
The Simon Gibson Charitable Trust
Gloucestershire Community Foundation
Worshipful Company of Glovers of London Charitable Trust
Worshipful Company of Gold and Silver Wyre Drawers Charitable Trust Fund
The Goldman Sachs Charitable Gift Fund (UK)
Goldman Sachs Gives (UK)
The Goldsmiths' Company Charity
The Golf Foundation Ltd
Grahame Charitable Foundation Ltd
The Grantham Yorke Trust
GrantScape
The Gray Trust
The Great Britain Sasakawa Foundation
Greenham Common Community Trust Ltd
The Greggs Foundation
Hadras Kodesh Trust
The Hadrian Trust
The Helen Hamlyn Trust
The W. A. Handley Charity Trust
The Kathleen Hannay Memorial Charity
Harbinson Charitable Trust
Harbo Charities Ltd
William Harding's Charity
The Harebell Centenary Fund
The Harpur Trust
The Peter Harrison Foundation
The Alfred And Peggy Harvey Charitable Trust
The Maurice Hatter Foundation
Heathrow Community Fund (LHR Airport Communities Trust)
The Heathside Charitable Trust
The Charlotte Heber-Percy Charitable Trust
Ernest Hecht Charitable Foundation
The Percy Hedley 1990 Charitable Trust
Hedley Foundation Ltd (The Hedley Foundation)
The Helping Foundation
The Hemby Charitable Trust
Henley Educational Trust
Heritage Lottery Fund*
The Hesslewood Children's Trust (Hull Seamen's and General Orphanage)
P. and C. Hickinbotham Charitable Trust
The Hilden Charitable Fund
M. V. Hillhouse Trust*
The Hillingdon Community Trust
The Hintze Family Charity Foundation
The Jane Hodge Foundation
The Holden Charitable Trust
The Dorothy Holmes Charitable Trust
P. H. Holt Foundation
The Holywood Trust
The Homestead Charitable Trust
The Mary Homfray Charitable Trust
Sir Harold Hood's Charitable Trust
Hopmarket Charity
The Horizon Foundation
The Worshipful Company of Horners' Charitable Trusts
Horwich Shotter Charitable Trust*
House of Industry Estate
The Hudson Foundation
The Hull and East Riding Charitable Trust
Hulme Trust Estates (Educational)
The Albert Hunt Trust
The Hunter Foundation
The Huntingdon Foundation Ltd
Huntingdon Freemen's Trust
IBM United Kingdom Trust
Imagine Foundation
The Worshipful Company of Information Technologists*
The Innocent Foundation
The Worshipful Company of Insurers – First Charitable Trust Fund*
Integrated Education Fund*
The International Bankers Charitable Trust (The Worshipful Company of Interntional Bankers)
Irish Youth Foundation (UK) Ltd (incorporating The Lawlor Foundation)
The Ironmongers' Company
The J. A. R. Charitable Trust
John James Bristol Foundation
Lady Eda Jardine Charitable Trust
The Jarman Charitable Trust
John Jarrold Trust Ltd
Rees Jeffreys Road Fund
Nick Jenkins Foundation
The Jenour Foundation
The Jerusalem Trust
The Johnson Foundation
Johnnie Johnson Trust
Johnson Wax Ltd Charitable Trust
The Jones 1986 Charitable Trust
The Dezna Robins Jones Charitable Foundation
Kahal Chassidim Bobov
The Bernard Kahn Charitable Trust
C. S. Kaufman Charitable Trust
Kelsick's Educational Foundation
William Kendall's Charity (Wax Chandlers' Company)
The Nancy Kenyon Charitable Trust
The Peter Kershaw Trust
The Ursula Keyes Trust
The King Henry VIII Endowed Trust – Warwick
Kirkley Poor's Land Estate
Robert Kitchin (Saddlers' Company)
The Sir James Knott Trust
The Kohn Foundation
Kollel and Co. Ltd
Kreditor Charitable Trust
Kusuma Trust UK
The Kyte Charitable Trust
John Laing Charitable Trust
Maurice and Hilda Laing Charitable Trust
The Beatrice Laing Trust
The Lancashire Foundation*
Lancaster Foundation
The Jack Lane Charitable Trust
Langdale Trust
The Edgar E. Lawley Foundation
Lawson Beckman Charitable Trust
The Raymond and Blanche Lawson Charitable Trust
The David Lean Foundation
The Leathersellers' Company Charitable Fund
The Leche Trust
The Legal Education Foundation*
Leicestershire, Leicester and Rutland Community Foundation
P. Leigh-Bramwell Trust 'E'
The Lennox Hannay Charitable Trust
The Mark Leonard Trust
The Leverhulme Trade Charities Trust
The Leverhulme Trust
Lord Leverhulme's Charitable Trust
The John Spedan Lewis Foundation
The Sir Edward Lewis Foundation
Life Changes Trust*
Lifeline 4 Kids (Handicapped Children's Aid Committee)
The Linbury Trust

The Linden Charitable Trust
The Enid Linder Foundation
The Lister Charitable Trust
The Frank Litchfield Charitable Trust
The Charles Littlewood Hill Trust
The Second Joseph Aaron Littman Foundation
Jack Livingstone Charitable Trust
The Elaine and Angus Lloyd Charitable Trust
The Andrew Lloyd Webber Foundation
The Locker Foundation
The Lolev Charitable Trust
The London Marathon Charitable Trust Ltd
The Lord's Taverners
The Lower Green Foundation
The Henry Lumley Charitable Trust
Lord and Lady Lurgan Trust
John Lyon's Charity
The Sir Jack Lyons Charitable Trust
M. and C. Trust
The Mackintosh Foundation
The Mactaggart Third Fund
The Ian Mactaggart Trust (The Mactaggart Second Fund)
The Magdalen and Lasher Charity (General Fund)
The Magen Charitable Trust
Man Group PLC Charitable Trust
Manchester Airport Community Trust Fund
The Manchester Guardian Society Charitable Trust
R. W. Mann Trust
Marbeh Torah Trust
The J. P. Marland Charitable Trust
Charlotte Marshall Charitable Trust
Sir George Martin Trust
John Martin's Charity
The Dan Maskell Tennis Trust
The Mason Porter Charitable Trust
The Nancie Massey Charitable Trust
*The Master Charitable Trust**
The Matliwala Family Charitable Trust
Mayfair Charities Ltd
The Mayfield Valley Arts Trust
The Medlock Charitable Trust
Melodor Ltd
The Brian Mercer Charitable Trust
The Mercers' Charitable Foundation
The Merchant Taylors' Company Charities Fund
The Merchant Venturers' Charity
The Mickel Fund
The Masonic Province of Middlesex Charitable Trust (Middlesex Masonic Charity)
The Millichope Foundation
The Mills Charity
The Peter Minet Trust
Mobbs Memorial Trust Ltd
Mole Charitable Trust
*Moondance Foundation**
The George A. Moore Foundation
The Steve Morgan Foundation
Morgan Stanley International Foundation
The Morris Charitable Trust
The Moshal Charitable Trust
Moto in the Community
The Mugdock Children's Trust
MW (CL) Foundation
MW (GK) Foundation
MW (HO) Foundation
MW (RH) Foundation
*The National Gardens Scheme**
The Newcomen Collett Foundation
Alderman Newton's Educational Foundation
Norfolk Community Foundation
Educational Foundation of Alderman John Norman
The Norman Family Charitable Trust
*Provincial Grand Charity of Northamptonshire and Huntingdonshire**
The Norton Foundation
Norwich Town Close Estate Charity
The Notgrove Trust
The Nuffield Foundation
The Oakdale Trust
The Ogle Christian Trust
Oglesby Charitable Trust
Oizer Charitable Trust
Old Possum's Practical Trust
OneFamily Foundation
The Ouseley Church Music Trust
The Owen Family Trust
B. E. Perl Charitable Trust
Personal Assurance Charitable Trust
The Jack Petchey Foundation
*The Prince Philip Trust Fund**
Mr and Mrs J. A. Pye's Charitable Settlement
*Quercus Foundation**
The Radcliffe Trust
The Ravensdale Trust
The John Rayner Charitable Trust
The Sir James Reckitt Charity
Richard Reeve's Foundation
Reuben Foundation
The Clive and Sylvia Richards Charity Ltd
The Helen Roll Charity
Mrs L. D. Rope's Third Charitable Settlement
The Rose Foundation
*The Cissie Rosefield Charitable Trust**
*The David Ross Foundation**
Rowanville Ltd
Rugby Football Foundation
The Rugby Group Benevolent Fund Ltd
The Saga Charitable Trust
*The Salisbury New Pool Settlement**
Coral Samuel Charitable Trust
The Sands Family Trust
The Sants Charitable Trust
*Sarum St Michael Educational Charity**
*The Savoy Educational Trust**
The Scarfe Charitable Trust
The Annie Schiff Charitable Trust
The Schreiber Charitable Trust
The Seedfield Trust
The Shanly Foundation
The Shears Foundation
The Sheepdrove Trust
The Sylvia and Colin Shepherd Charitable Trust
SHINE (Support and Help in Education)
The Shipwrights' Company Charitable Fund
The Shirley Foundation
*Shulem B. Association Ltd**
The Sino-British Fellowship Trust
SITA Cornwall Trust Ltd
The Charles Skey Charitable Trust
Skipton Building Society Charitable Foundation
The John Slater Foundation
The Slaughter and May Charitable Trust
Sloane Robinson Foundation
Ruth Smart Foundation
The Henry Smith Charity
The WH Smith Group Charitable Trust
The Stanley Smith UK Horticultural Trust
The R. C. Snelling Charitable Trust
Solev Co. Ltd
David Solomons Charitable Trust
*Somerset Community Foundation**
The Southover Manor General Education Trust
The Spear Charitable Trust
Spears-Stutz Charitable Trust
The Spielman Charitable Trust

The Spoore, Merry and Rixman Foundation
Rosalyn and Nicholas Springer Charitable Trust
The Geoff and Fiona Squire Foundation
St James's Place Foundation
Sir Walter St John's Educational Charity
St Luke's College Foundation
*St Marylebone Educational Foundation**
St Olave's and St Saviour's Schools Foundation – Foundation Fund
St Peter's Saltley Trust
The Steel Charitable Trust
The Stevenage Community Trust
Stewards' Company Ltd
Sir Halley Stewart Trust
The Samuel Storey Family Charitable Trust
Peter Stormonth Darling Charitable Trust
Stratford upon Avon Town Trust
The W. O. Street Charitable Foundation
The Sudborough Foundation
Suffolk Community Foundation
*Sunninghill Fuel Allotment Trust**
Community Foundation for Surrey
The Sutasoma Trust
Sutton Coldfield Charitable Trust
The John Swire (1989) Charitable Trust
The Adrian Swire Charitable Trust
The Talbot Village Trust
Tallow Chandlers Benevolent Fund No. 2
The David Tannen Charitable Trust
The Tanner Trust
C. B. and H. H. Taylor 1984 Trust
Humphrey Richardson Taylor Charitable Trust
The Connie and Albert Taylor Charitable Trust
Tearfund
The Tedworth Charitable Trust
Tees Valley Community Foundation
The Tennis Foundation
The Thompson Family Charitable Trust
The Sir Jules Thorn Charitable Trust
The Thornton Trust
Mrs R. P. Tindall's Charitable Trust
The Tompkins Foundation
Tottenham Grammar School Foundation
The Tower Hill Trust
The Toy Trust
Toyota Manufacturing UK Charitable Trust
The Constance Travis Charitable Trust
The Treeside Trust
The Trefoil Trust
The Tudor Trust
The Tufton Charitable Trust
The Tuixen Foundation
The Roger and Douglas Turner Charitable Trust
Ulting Overseas Trust
The Ulverscroft Foundation
The Vail Foundation
The Vandervell Foundation
Variety The Children's Charity (Variety Club)
The Vintners' Foundation
Vivdale Ltd
Wade's Charity
The Walcot Foundation
Wales Council for Voluntary Action
The Walker Trust
Walton on Thames Charity
The Barbara Ward Children's Foundation
*Mrs N. E. M. Warren's Charitable Trust**
G. R. Waters Charitable Trust 2000
Wates Family Enterprise Trust
John Watson's Trust
Waynflete Charitable Trust
The Weavers' Company Benevolent Fund
West Derby Waste Lands Charity
The Westminster Foundation
The Garfield Weston Foundation
Westway Trust
White Stuff Foundation
The Whitecourt Charitable Trust
Williams Serendipity Trust
Dame Violet Wills Charitable Trust
*Brian Wilson Charitable Trust**
The Wilson Foundation
The W. Wing Yip and Brothers Foundation
The Wixamtree Trust
The Maurice Wohl Charitable Foundation
The Charles Wolfson Charitable Trust
The Wolfson Foundation
The Wood Foundation
Wooden Spoon Society
The F. Glenister Woodger Trust
Woodroffe Benton Foundation
The A. and R. Woolf Charitable Trust
Worcester Municipal Charities (CIO)
Yankov Charitable Trust
*York Children's Trust**
Yorkshire Building Society Charitable Foundation
Youth Music

Teacher training and development

The City Educational Trust Fund
The February Foundation
Hockerill Educational Foundation
*Integrated Education Fund**

Environment and animals

The W. A. Handley Charity Trust
The Kathleen Hannay Memorial Charity
Harbinson Charitable Trust
The Harebell Centenary Fund
The Harrison-Frank Family Foundation (UK) Ltd
The Hawthorne Charitable Trust
Heathrow Community Fund (LHR Airport Communities Trust)
The Charlotte Heber-Percy Charitable Trust
The Percy Hedley 1990 Charitable Trust
The Hemby Charitable Trust
The G. D. Herbert Charitable Trust
Herefordshire Community Foundation
Heritage Lottery Fund*
M. V. Hillhouse Trust*
The Hillingdon Community Trust
R. G. Hills Charitable Trust
The Henry C. Hoare Charitable Trust
The Hobson Charity Ltd
The Homestead Charitable Trust
The Mary Homfray Charitable Trust
The Daniel Howard Trust
Howman Charitable Trust*
The Michael and Shirley Hunt Charitable Trust
The Hutchinson Charitable Trust
The Idlewild Trust
The Iliffe Family Charitable Trust
The Ingram Trust
The Innocent Foundation
International Fund for Animal Welfare (IFAW)*
The Isle of Anglesey Charitable Trust
The J. J. Charitable Trust
The Jabbs Foundation
John Jarrold Trust Ltd
Rees Jeffreys Road Fund
The Jenour Foundation
The Jephcott Charitable Trust
Johnson Wax Ltd Charitable Trust
The Marjorie and Geoffrey Jones Charitable Trust
The Jordan Charitable Foundation
The Kennel Club Charitable Trust
The Graham Kirkham Foundation*
The Ernest Kleinwort Charitable Trust
The Sir James Knott Trust
Christopher Laing Foundation
The Kirby Laing Foundation
The Martin Laing Foundation
The Leonard Laity Stoate Charitable Trust
Lancashire Environmental Fund Ltd
The Jack Lane Charitable Trust
The Lauffer Family Charitable Foundation
Mrs F. B. Laurence Charitable Trust
The Raymond and Blanche Lawson Charitable Trust
The Leche Trust
Leng Charitable Trust*
The Lennox Hannay Charitable Trust
The Mark Leonard Trust
Lord Leverhulme's Charitable Trust
The John Spedan Lewis Foundation
John Lewis Partnership General Community Fund
The Limbourne Trust
Limoges Charitable Trust
The Linbury Trust
The Lindley Foundation (TLF)
The Lister Charitable Trust
The Frank Litchfield Charitable Trust
The Charles Littlewood Hill Trust
Trust for London
The London Community Foundation (LCF)
The William and Katherine Longman Trust
The C. L. Loyd Charitable Trust
The Lynn Foundation
The R. S. Macdonald Charitable Trust
The Macdonald-Buchanan Charitable Trust
The Mackay and Brewer Charitable Trust
The Mackintosh Foundation
GPS Macpherson Charitable Settlement*
The MacRobert Trust
The Mactaggart Third Fund
The Ian Mactaggart Trust (The Mactaggart Second Fund)
Manchester Airport Community Trust Fund
The Manifold Charitable Trust
R. W. Mann Trust
The Marcela Trust
The Marchig Animal Welfare Trust
The Michael Marks Charitable Trust
Marmot Charitable Trust
The Marsh Christian Trust
Sir George Martin Trust
The Master Charitable Trust*
The Medlock Charitable Trust
T. and J. Meyer Family Foundation Ltd
The Gerald Micklem Charitable Trust
Millennium Stadium Charitable Trust (Ymddiriedolaeth Elusennol Stadiwm Y. Mileniwm)
The Ronald Miller Foundation
The Millichope Foundation
The Millward Charitable Trust
Mitsubishi Corporation Fund for Europe and Africa*
The Monument Trust
The George A. Moore Foundation
Moto in the Community
The Frederick Mulder Foundation
The Edith Murphy Foundation
The National Gardens Scheme*
Network for Social Change Charitable Trust
The NFU Mutual Charitable Trust
Alice Noakes Memorial Charitable Trust
Nominet Charitable Foundation
The Community Foundation for Northern Ireland
The Northwick Trust*
The Sir Peter O'Sullevan Charitable Trust
The Oakdale Trust
The Ofenheim Charitable Trust
Oglesby Charitable Trust
The John Oldacre Foundation
The Oldham Foundation
The Onaway Trust*
One Community Foundation Ltd*
Open Gate
The Owen Family Trust
Oxfam (GB)
Oxfordshire Community Foundation
The Paget Charitable Trust
The Jack Patston Charitable Trust
Peacock Charitable Trust
Susanna Peake Charitable Trust
People's Postcode Trust
The Persula Foundation
Petplan Charitable Trust
The Phillips Charitable Trust
The Pilgrim Trust
Polden-Puckham Charitable Foundation
The Portrack Charitable Trust
Postcode Community Trust*
Postcode Dream Trust – Dream Fund
The Primrose Trust
The Prince of Wales's Charitable Foundation
The Princess Anne's Charities

Mr and Mrs J. A. Pye's Charitable Settlement
Quartet Community Foundation
The Racing Foundation
Richard Radcliffe Trust
The Ranworth Trust
The Sigrid Rausing Trust
Reed Family Foundation
The Rhododendron Trust
Daisie Rich Trust
The River Farm Foundation
The Roddick Foundation
The Helen Roll Charity
The Rothley Trust
The Roughley Charitable Trust
The Rowlands Trust
Royal Docks Trust (London)
Royal Society Of Wildlife Trusts*
The Rufford Foundation
The Michael and Nicola Sacher Charitable Trust
The Jean Sainsbury Animal Welfare Trust
The Saintbury Trust
The Salamander Charitable Trust
The Salisbury New Pool Settlement*
The Basil Samuel Charitable Trust
The M. J. Samuel Charitable Trust
The Samworth Foundation
The Sandra Charitable Trust
The Scarfe Charitable Trust
Schroder Charity Trust
The Scotshill Trust
Scott (Eredine) Charitable Trust
The ScottishPower Energy People Trust
The ScottishPower Foundation
The Scouloudi Foundation
The SDL Foundation
Seafarers UK (King George's Fund for Sailors)
SEM Charitable Trust
The Linley Shaw Foundation
The Shears Foundation
The Sheepdrove Trust
The Shipwrights' Company Charitable Fund
David and Jennifer Sieff Charitable Trust
SITA Cornwall Trust Ltd
The John Slater Foundation
Ruth Smart Foundation
The SMB Trust
The DS Smith Charitable Foundation
The N. Smith Charitable Settlement
The Martin Smith Foundation*
The Stanley Smith UK Horticultural Trust
Philip Smith's Charitable Trust
The R. C. Snelling Charitable Trust
The Sobell Foundation
The W. F. Southall Trust
R. H. Southern Trust
The Spear Charitable Trust
The Stafford Trust
The Steel Charitable Trust
The Stevenage Community Trust
The Andy Stewart Charitable Foundation
M. J. C. Stone Charitable Trust
The Stone Family Foundation
Support Adoption For Pets*
The Adrienne and Leslie Sussman Charitable Trust
The John Swire (1989) Charitable Trust
Sylvia Waddilove Foundation UK
The Tanner Trust
C. B. and H. H. Taylor 1984 Trust
The Connie and Albert Taylor Charitable Trust
Tearfund
The Tedworth Charitable Trust
The C. Paul Thackray General Charitable Trust
The Three Guineas Trust
The Tisbury Telegraph Trust
The Tolkien Trust
The Tower Hill Trust
Toyota Manufacturing UK Charitable Trust
The Roger and Douglas Turner Charitable Trust
Community Foundation serving Tyne and Wear and Northumberland
Ulster Garden Villages Ltd
The Underwood Trust
The Michael Uren Foundation
The Valentine Charitable Trust
Mrs Maud Van Norden's Charitable Foundation
The Vandervell Foundation
The William and Patricia Venton Charitable Trust
The Veolia Environmental Trust*
Roger Vere Foundation
The Virgin Foundation (Virgin Unite)
Viridor Credits Environmental Company*
Wales Council for Voluntary Action
Mrs Waterhouse Charitable Trust
The Waterloo Foundation
Wates Family Enterprise Trust
The Geoffrey Watling Charity*
Waynflete Charitable Trust
The David Webster Charitable Trust
The Weir Charitable Trust*
The Garfield Weston Foundation
Westway Trust
The Barbara Whatmore Charitable Trust
The Whitaker Charitable Trust
Colonel W. H. Whitbread Charitable Trust
The Whitley Animal Protection Trust
The Kay Williams Charitable Foundation
The Alfred Williams Charitable Trust*
The Williams Family Foundation*
The HDH Wills 1965 Charitable Trust
J. and J. R. Wilson Trust
The Wixamtree Trust
Woodroffe Benton Foundation
The A. and R. Woolf Charitable Trust
The Diana Edgson Wright Charitable Trust
Yorkshire and Clydesdale Bank Foundation
Yorkshire Building Society Charitable Foundation
Elizabeth and Prince Zaiger Trust*
Zephyr Charitable Trust

Agriculture and fishing

The Associated Country Women of the World
The Clan Trust Ltd*
The Elizabeth Creak Charitable Trust*
The Cumber Family Charitable Trust
The Davis Foundation
The Englefield Charitable Trust
Fishmongers' Company's Charitable Trust
The Worshipful Company of Gardeners of London
The Hutchinson Charitable Trust
The Innocent Foundation
The J. J. Charitable Trust
The Mark Leonard Trust
The Frank Litchfield Charitable Trust
The MacRobert Trust
Manchester Airport Community Trust Fund
Mitsubishi Corporation Fund for Europe and Africa*
The NFU Mutual Charitable Trust
The John Oldacre Foundation
Quartet Community Foundation
Seafarers UK (King George's Fund for Sailors)

The Stanley Smith UK Horticultural Trust
The Tanner Trust
The Waterloo Foundation
The Garfield Weston Foundation

Farming and food production

The Elizabeth Creak Charitable Trust*
The Hutchinson Charitable Trust
The Innocent Foundation
Mitsubishi Corporation Fund for Europe and Africa*
The NFU Mutual Charitable Trust
CLA Charitable Trust
The Gatsby Charitable Foundation
The Innocent Foundation
LSA Charitable Trust
The NFU Mutual Charitable Trust

Fishing and fisheries

Mr and Mrs J. A. Fishmongers' Company's Charitable Trust
The Seafarers UK (King George's Fund for Sailors)

Forestry

Manchester Airport Community Trust Fund
Mitsubishi Corporation Fund for Europe and Africa*

Horticulture

The Clan Trust Ltd*
The Davis Foundation
The Worshipful Company of Gardeners of London
The MacRobert Trust
The Stanley Smith UK Horticultural Trust

Animal care

The Alborada Trust
The Derrill Allatt Foundation
The Ancaster Trust*
The Animal Defence Trust
The Annandale Charitable Trust
The Ashden Trust
The Astor Foundation
The Harry Bacon Foundation
The Bellahouston Bequest Fund
Isabel Blackman Foundation
The Childwick Trust
The Robert Clutterbuck Charitable Trust
The Catherine Cookson Charitable Trust
The Marjorie Coote Animal Charity Trust
The Joan Lynette Dalton Charitable Trust
The Dischma Charitable Trust
The Dumbreck Charity
The EBM Charitable Trust
The Beryl Evetts and Robert Luff Animal Welfare Trust Ltd
Matthew Eyton Animal Welfare Trust
The Anna Rosa Forster Charitable Trust
The Joseph Strong Frazer Trust
The Gerrick Rose Animal Trust*
The Harebell Centenary Fund
M. V. Hillhouse Trust*
The Michael and Shirley Hunt Charitable Trust
International Fund for Animal Welfare (IFAW)*
The Jenour Foundation
The Jordan Charitable Foundation
The Kennel Club Charitable Trust
The William and Katherine Longman Trust
The R. S. Macdonald Charitable Trust
The Mackay and Brewer Charitable Trust
The Marchig Animal Welfare Trust
The Millward Charitable Trust
The Edith Murphy Foundation
Alice Noakes Memorial Charitable Trust
The Sir Peter O'Sullevan Charitable Trust
Open Gate
The Persula Foundation
Petplan Charitable Trust
The Phillips Charitable Trust
The Racing Foundation
The Jean Sainsbury Animal Welfare Trust
The Scotshill Trust
David and Jennifer Sieff Charitable Trust
The John Slater Foundation
Ruth Smart Foundation
The Stafford Trust
The Andy Stewart Charitable Foundation
Support Adoption For Pets*
The Adrienne and Leslie Sussman Charitable Trust
Mrs Maud Van Norden's Charitable Foundation
The William and Patricia Venton Charitable Trust
The Weir Charitable Trust*
The Kay Williams Charitable Foundation
J. and J. R. Wilson Trust
The Diana Edgson Wright Charitable Trust
Yorkshire Building Society Charitable Foundation
Elizabeth and Prince Zaiger Trust*

Animal conservation

The AEB Charitable Trust*
The Derrill Allatt Foundation
The Ian Askew Charitable Trust
Birmingham International Airport Community Trust Fund
The Blair Foundation
The Robert Clutterbuck Charitable Trust
The John S. Cohen Foundation
The Marjorie Coote Animal Charity Trust
William Dean Countryside and Educational Trust
The Dumbreck Charity
The Alan Evans Memorial Trust
Samuel William Farmer Trust
The Doris Field Charitable Trust
The Earl Fitzwilliam Charitable Trust
The Joseph Strong Frazer Trust
The Godinton Charitable Trust
Hamamelis Trust
The Harrison-Frank Family Foundation (UK) Ltd
M. V. Hillhouse Trust*
The Iliffe Family Charitable Trust
The Ingram Trust
International Fund for Animal Welfare (IFAW)*
The Lister Charitable Trust
The Marchig Animal Welfare Trust
Mitsubishi Corporation Fund for Europe and Africa*
The Oakdale Trust
The Owen Family Trust
The Jack Patston Charitable Trust
Postcode Community Trust*
The Primrose Trust
The Ranworth Trust
Reed Family Foundation
The Rhododendron Trust
The Rufford Foundation
The Michael and Nicola Sacher Charitable Trust

The Jean Sainsbury Animal Welfare Trust
SITA Cornwall Trust Ltd
Ruth Smart Foundation
Mrs Maud Van Norden's Charitable Foundation
The David Webster Charitable Trust
The Garfield Weston Foundation
J. and J. R. Wilson Trust
The Diana Edgson Wright Charitable Trust

Climate change

A2BD Foundation UK Ltd*
Anglo American Group Foundation
The Ashden Trust
The Ecology Trust
The Freshfield Foundation
H. C. D. Memorial Fund
The Mark Leonard Trust
Mitsubishi Corporation Fund for Europe and Africa*
The Frederick Mulder Foundation
The Northwick Trust*
SEM Charitable Trust
The Three Guineas Trust
The Waterloo Foundation
The Garfield Weston Foundation

Countryside

The Aberbrothock Skea Trust
The AEB Charitable Trust*
The Astor Foundation
The Big Lottery Fund (see also Awards for All)
The Bothwell Charitable Trust
CHK Charities Ltd
The Ernest Cook Trust
The Craignish Trust
The D'Oyly Carte Charitable Trust
The Dr and Mrs A. Darlington Charitable Trust
The Dunn Family Charitable Trust
The Ecology Trust
The Alan Evans Memorial Trust
The Earl Fitzwilliam Charitable Trust
The Girdlers' Company Charitable Trust
GrantScape
Gordon Gray Trust
The Greggs Foundation
Hamamelis Trust
Heathrow Community Fund (LHR Airport Communities Trust)
The G. D. Herbert Charitable Trust
The Idlewild Trust
The Leche Trust
Manchester Airport Community Trust Fund
Sir George Martin Trust
The Gerald Micklem Charitable Trust
Millennium Stadium Charitable Trust (Ymddiriedolaeth Elusennol Stadiwm Y. Mileniwm)
The Northwick Trust*
The Jack Patston Charitable Trust
The Pilgrim Trust
Quartet Community Foundation
The Ranworth Trust
The Rufford Foundation
Schroder Charity Trust
The Linley Shaw Foundation
The Shears Foundation
SITA Cornwall Trust Ltd
The Tanner Trust
The Connie and Albert Taylor Charitable Trust
Ulster Garden Villages Ltd
The Valentine Charitable Trust
The Vandervell Foundation
The Waterloo Foundation
Waynflete Charitable Trust
The David Webster Charitable Trust
The Garfield Weston Foundation
Colonel W. H. Whitbread Charitable Trust
The Alfred Williams Charitable Trust*
Woodroffe Benton Foundation
Zephyr Charitable Trust

Environmental education and research

A2BD Foundation UK Ltd*
Anglo American Group Foundation
The Ardwick Trust
The Ashden Trust
The Ian Askew Charitable Trust
The Associated Country Women of the World
Bergqvist Charitable Trust
The Big Lottery Fund (see also Awards for All)
Birmingham International Airport Community Trust Fund
The Cadbury Foundation
The Castansa Trust*
Community First (Landfill Communities Fund)
The Ernest Cook Trust
The Craignish Trust
William Dean Countryside and Educational Trust
The Delves Charitable Trust
The Dulverton Trust
The Dunn Family Charitable Trust
Eaga Charitable Trust
The Ecology Trust
Esh Foundation
Esmée Fairbairn Foundation
The Great Britain Sasakawa Foundation
The Greggs Foundation
Hampshire and Isle of Wight Community Foundation
Heathrow Community Fund (LHR Airport Communities Trust)
The J. J. Charitable Trust
The Mark Leonard Trust
Manchester Airport Community Trust Fund
The Marchig Animal Welfare Trust
Marmot Charitable Trust
Mitsubishi Corporation Fund for Europe and Africa*
The National Gardens Scheme*
Network for Social Change Charitable Trust
Nominet Charitable Foundation
The Community Foundation for Northern Ireland
The Northwick Trust*
Oglesby Charitable Trust
Oxfordshire Community Foundation
Quartet Community Foundation
The Rufford Foundation
The Saintbury Trust
The Linley Shaw Foundation
The Shears Foundation
The Martin Smith Foundation*
The Stanley Smith UK Horticultural Trust
The Sobell Foundation
The Stevenage Community Trust
The Tedworth Charitable Trust
The Tower Hill Trust
Ulster Garden Villages Ltd
The Waterloo Foundation
The David Webster Charitable Trust
The Garfield Weston Foundation

Natural environment

The 29th May 1961 Charitable Trust
A2BD Foundation UK Ltd*
The Adnams Community Trust
The AEB Charitable Trust*
The Ancaster Trust*
Anglo American Group Foundation

Arcadia Charitable Trust*
Ove Arup Partnership Charitable Trust
The Ashden Trust
The Ian Askew Charitable Trust
BC Partners Foundation
The Becht Family Charitable Trust*
Bergqvist Charitable Trust
Birmingham International Airport Community Trust Fund
Isabel Blackman Foundation
The Blair Foundation
Bridgepoint Charitable Trust
The Christopher Cadbury Charitable Trust
The Cadbury Foundation
Calouste Gulbenkian Foundation – UK Branch
The Castansa Trust*
The City Bridge Trust (Bridge House Estates)
The Robert Clutterbuck Charitable Trust
The Cole Charitable Trust
Community First (Landfill Communities Fund)
The Ernest Cook Trust
Mabel Cooper Charity
The Craignish Trust
The D'Oyly Carte Charitable Trust
The Dr and Mrs A. Darlington Charitable Trust
William Dean Countryside and Educational Trust
The Delves Charitable Trust
The Demigryphon Trust
The Dischma Charitable Trust
The Dulverton Trust
The Dunn Family Charitable Trust
County Durham Community Foundation
The Ericson Trust
The Alan Evans Memorial Trust
Esmée Fairbairn Foundation
Samuel William Farmer Trust
The Fidelity UK Foundation
The Doris Field Charitable Trust
Fisherbeck Charitable Trust
Fishmongers' Company's Charitable Trust
The Earl Fitzwilliam Charitable Trust
The Fort Foundation
The Gordon Fraser Charitable Trust
The Hugh Fraser Foundation
The Joseph Strong Frazer Trust
The Freshgate Trust Foundation
The Adrian and Jane Frost Charitable Trust
The Girdlers' Company Charitable Trust
The Godinton Charitable Trust
GrantScape
Gordon Gray Trust
H. C. D. Memorial Fund
The Hadrian Trust
Hamamelis Trust
Hampshire and Isle of Wight Community Foundation
The Harrison-Frank Family Foundation (UK) Ltd
Heathrow Community Fund (LHR Airport Communities Trust)
The Hemby Charitable Trust
The G. D. Herbert Charitable Trust
Heritage Lottery Fund*
M. V. Hillhouse Trust*
The Daniel Howard Trust
The Iliffe Family Charitable Trust
International Fund for Animal Welfare (IFAW)*
The Isle of Anglesey Charitable Trust
The J. J. Charitable Trust
The Jabbs Foundation
Rees Jeffreys Road Fund
The Jephcott Charitable Trust
The Marjorie and Geoffrey Jones Charitable Trust
The Kirby Laing Foundation
The Lauffer Family Charitable Foundation
The Charles Littlewood Hill Trust
Manchester Airport Community Trust Fund
Sir George Martin Trust
The Medlock Charitable Trust
T. and J. Meyer Family Foundation Ltd
The Gerald Micklem Charitable Trust
Mitsubishi Corporation Fund for Europe and Africa*
The Northwick Trust*
The Oakdale Trust
The Onaway Trust*
One Community Foundation Ltd*
The Owen Family Trust
The Jack Patston Charitable Trust
People's Postcode Trust
Polden-Puckham Charitable Foundation
Postcode Community Trust*
Quartet Community Foundation
The Ranworth Trust
The Sigrid Rausing Trust
The Rhododendron Trust
The Roughley Charitable Trust
The Rufford Foundation
The Saintbury Trust
Schroder Charity Trust
The Linley Shaw Foundation
SITA Cornwall Trust Ltd
Ruth Smart Foundation
The Martin Smith Foundation*
The Stanley Smith UK Horticultural Trust
The Stevenage Community Trust
The Tower Hill Trust
The Roger and Douglas Turner Charitable Trust
Ulster Garden Villages Ltd
The Valentine Charitable Trust
The Vandervell Foundation
The Waterloo Foundation
The David Webster Charitable Trust
The Garfield Weston Foundation
Westway Trust
Woodroffe Benton Foundation
Zephyr Charitable Trust

Pollution abatement and control

Anglo American Group Foundation
BC Partners Foundation
Birmingham International Airport Community Trust Fund
Esmée Fairbairn Foundation
GrantScape
H. C. D. Memorial Fund
Marmot Charitable Trust
Quartet Community Foundation
SITA Cornwall Trust Ltd
The Ashden Trust
The Big Lottery Fund (see also Awards for All)
The Delves Charitable Trust
The Garfield Weston Foundation
The Mark Leonard Trust
The Saintbury Trust
The Sigrid Rausing Trust
The Waterloo Foundation
Trust for London
Westway Trust
Woodroffe Benton Foundation
Zephyr Charitable Trust

Sustainable environment

The 1970 Trust
A2BD Foundation UK Ltd*
The Adnams Community Trust
Anglo American Group Foundation
Arcadia Charitable Trust*
Ove Arup Partnership Charitable Trust
The Ashden Trust

The Associated Country Women of the World
BC Partners Foundation
*The Becht Family Charitable Trust**
Bergqvist Charitable Trust
The Big Lottery Fund (see also Awards for All)
Birmingham International Airport Community Trust Fund
The Cadbury Foundation
Calouste Gulbenkian Foundation – UK Branch
*The Castansa Trust**
The City Bridge Trust (Bridge House Estates)
The Cole Charitable Trust
Community First (Landfill Communities Fund)
The Craignish Trust
The Delves Charitable Trust
The Dunn Family Charitable Trust
County Durham Community Foundation
Eaga Charitable Trust
The Ecology Trust
Esh Foundation
Esmée Fairbairn Foundation
The Fidelity UK Foundation
The Fort Foundation
The Gordon Fraser Charitable Trust
The Freshfield Foundation
The Generations Foundation
GrantScape
The Greggs Foundation
H. C. D. Memorial Fund
The Hadrian Trust
Hamamelis Trust
Hampshire and Isle of Wight Community Foundation
Heathrow Community Fund (LHR Airport Communities Trust)
The Hemby Charitable Trust
The Daniel Howard Trust
The J. J. Charitable Trust
The Mark Leonard Trust
The Limbourne Trust
Manchester Airport Community Trust Fund
Marmot Charitable Trust
Sir George Martin Trust
Millennium Stadium Charitable Trust (Ymddiriedolaeth Elusennol Stadiwm Y. Mileniwm)
*Mitsubishi Corporation Fund for Europe and Africa**
Nominet Charitable Foundation
The Community Foundation for Northern Ireland
*The Northwick Trust**
*The Onaway Trust**
*One Community Foundation Ltd**
Open Gate
Polden-Puckham Charitable Foundation
*Postcode Community Trust**
Quartet Community Foundation
The Sigrid Rausing Trust
The Rothley Trust
The Roughley Charitable Trust
The Rufford Foundation
The Saintbury Trust
The ScottishPower Energy People Trust
The SDL Foundation
SITA Cornwall Trust Ltd
*The Martin Smith Foundation**
The Stone Family Foundation
The Tedworth Charitable Trust
The Tisbury Telegraph Trust
The Tower Hill Trust
Ulster Garden Villages Ltd
The Vandervell Foundation
The Waterloo Foundation
Wates Family Enterprise Trust
The David Webster Charitable Trust
The Garfield Weston Foundation
Westway Trust
Woodroffe Benton Foundation
Zephyr Charitable Trust

Energy issues

The 1970 Trust
Eaga Charitable Trust
The Mark Leonard Trust
The Rothley Trust
The ScottishPower Energy People Trust

Loss of biodiversity

*The Onaway Trust**
The Rufford Foundation
The Tower Hill Trust

Transport

The 1970 Trust
The Big Lottery Fund (see also Awards for All)
County Durham Community Foundation
The Gosling Foundation Ltd
The Hillingdon Community Trust
The J. J. Charitable Trust
Rees Jeffreys Road Fund
Quartet Community Foundation
Seafarers UK (King George's Fund for Sailors)
The Shipwrights' Company Charitable Fund
The Garfield Weston Foundation
Westway Trust

General charitable purposes

The 1989 Willan Charitable Trust
The 29th May 1961 Charitable Trust
The 3Ts Charitable Trust*
A2BD Foundation UK Ltd*
The Aberdeen Foundation
ABF The Soldiers' Charity
The Acacia Charitable Trust
The Addleshaw Goddard Charitable Trust
D. G. Albright Charitable Trust
Allchurches Trust Ltd
D. C. R. Allen Charitable Trust
The Alliance Family Foundation
AM Charitable Trust
The Amalur Foundation Ltd
Sir John and Lady Amory's Charitable Trust
The Ampelos Trust
The AMW Charitable Trust
The Ancaster Trust*
The Mary Andrew Charitable Trust
The Annandale Charitable Trust
The Anne Duchess of Westminster's Charity*
The Anson Charitable Trust
AO Smile Foundation*
The Arah Foundation
The Arbib Foundation
The Ardeola Charitable Trust
The Ardwick Trust
The Argus Appeal
The John Armitage Charitable Trust
The Armourers' and Brasiers' Gauntlet Trust
The Arsenal Foundation Ltd
Ove Arup Partnership Charitable Trust
The Asda Foundation
The Ashburnham Thanksgiving Trust
The Ian Askew Charitable Trust
The Astor Foundation
The Atlas Fund
The Lord Austin Trust
Autonomous Research Charitable Trust (ARCT)
Awards for All (see also the Big Lottery Fund)
The Aylesford Family Charitable Trust
The Bacit Foundation
The Bagri Foundation
The Andrew Balint Charitable Trust
The Bamford Charitable Foundation
The Banbury Charities
The Band Trust
The Barbers' Company General Charities
The Barbour Foundation
The Barham Charitable Trust
The Barker-Mill Foundation
Lord Barnby's Foundation
The Barnsbury Charitable Trust
Misses Barrie Charitable Trust
Robert Barr's Charitable Trust*
The Paul Bassham Charitable Trust
The Batchworth Trust
The Battens Charitable Trust
The Battersea Power Station Foundation*
Bauer Radio's Cash for Kids Charities
The Bay Tree Charitable Trust
The Louis Baylis (Maidenhead Advertiser) Charitable Trust
BBC Children in Need
BCH Trust
The Bearder Charity
The James Beattie Charitable Trust
The Becker Family Charitable Trust
The Bedfordshire and Luton Community Foundation
The David and Ruth Behrend Fund
The Behrens Foundation*
The Benham Charitable Settlement
Bennett Lowell Ltd
The Rowan Bentall Charitable Trust*
The Berkshire Community Foundation
The Big Lottery Fund (see also Awards for All)
The Billmeir Charitable Trust
The Bingham Trust
Birthday House Trust
Miss Jeanne Bisgood's Charitable Trust
The Michael Bishop Foundation
The Bertie Black Foundation
The Morgan Blake Charitable Trust
Blakemore Foundation
The Sir Victor Blank Charitable Settlement
Bloom Foundation
The Bloomfield Charitable Trust*
The Bluston Charitable Settlement
The Marjory Boddy Charitable Trust
The Bonamy Charitable Trust
The Charlotte Bonham-Carter Charitable Trust
The Linda and Gordon Bonnyman Charitable Trust
The Boodle & Dunthorne Charitable Trust
The Booth Charities
Boots Charitable Trust
The Bordon Liphook Haslemere Charity
The Borrows Charitable Trust*
The Bothwell Charitable Trust
The Bowland Charitable Trust
The Frank Brake Charitable Trust
The William Brake Charitable Trust
The Liz and Terry Bramall Foundation
Bridge Trust
Bridgepoint Charitable Trust
The Harold and Alice Bridges Charity
Bristol Charities
British Humane Association
The J. and M. Britton Charitable Trust
The T. B. H. Brunner's Charitable Settlement
The Jack Brunton Charitable Trust
The Bruntwood Charity
Buckingham Trust
Buckinghamshire Community Foundation
The Buffini Chao Foundation
The Burden Trust
Consolidated Charity of Burton upon Trent
The Derek Butler Trust
The Butters Foundation (UK) Ltd*
The Christopher Cadbury Charitable Trust
The G. W. Cadbury Charitable Trust
The Cadbury Foundation
The Edward and Dorothy Cadbury Trust
The George Cadbury Trust
Community Foundation for Calderdale
Callander Charitable Trust
Calleva Foundation
The Cambridgeshire Community Foundation
The Frederick and Phyllis Cann Trust
Cardy Beaver Foundation
The Carpenters' Company Charitable Trust
The Carrington Charitable Trust
The Casey Trust
The Joseph and Annie Cattle Trust
The Thomas Sivewright Catto Charitable Settlement
The Wilfrid and Constance Cave Foundation
The Cayo Foundation
The B. G. S. Cayzer Charitable Trust
The Cazenove Charitable Trust
The CBD Charitable Trust

CBRE UK UK Charitable Trust
The Amelia Chadwick Trust
Charitworth Ltd
The Charter 600 Charity
Chartered Accountants' Livery Charity (CALC)
The Cheruby Trust
*Cheshire Community Foundation Ltd**
Cheshire Freemason's Charity
CHK Charities Ltd
The Chownes Foundation
Christian Aid
Chrysalis Trust
Stephen Clark 1957 Charitable Trust
The Hilda and Alice Clark Charitable Trust
The Roger and Sarah Bancroft Clark Charitable Trust
*The Clark Foundation**
The Cleopatra Trust
The Clover Trust
The Robert Clutterbuck Charitable Trust
Clydpride Ltd
The Coalfields Regeneration Trust
The John Coates Charitable Trust
The Cobalt Trust
The Cobtree Charity Trust Ltd
The John S. Cohen Foundation
John Coldman Charitable Trust
The Colefax Charitable Trust
The Douglas Compton James Charitable Trust
Martin Connell Charitable Trust
The Cooks Charity
The Catherine Cookson Charitable Trust
The Keith Coombs Trust
Mabel Cooper Charity
The Alice Ellen Cooper Dean Charitable Foundation
The Helen Jean Cope Trust
The Worshipful Company of Cordwainers Charitable Trusts (Minges Gift and the Pooled Trusts)
The Gershon Coren Charitable Foundation (also known as The Muriel and Gus Coren Charitable Foundation)
Michael Cornish Charitable Trust
Cornwall Community Foundation
The Cornwell Charitable Trust
The Cotton Industry War Memorial Trust
*The Coulthurst Trust**
The County Council of Dyfed Welsh Curch Fund
The Augustine Courtauld Trust
General Charity of Coventry
Coventry Building Society Charitable Foundation
The John Cowan Foundation
The Sir Tom Cowie Charitable Trust
The Lord Cozens-Hardy Trust
The Craignish Trust
The Craps Charitable Trust
The Cray Trust
The Crescent Trust
Cripplegate Foundation
The Ronald Cruickshanks Foundation
The Cuby Charitable Trust
Cullum Family Trust
Cumbria Community Foundation
The D. G. Charitable Settlement
Oizer Dalim Trust
The Joan Lynette Dalton Charitable Trust
The Davidson (Nairn) Charitable Trust
Michael Davies Charitable Settlement
*The Biss Davies Charitable Trust**
Margaret Davies Charity
*The John Grant Davies Trust**
The Crispin Davis Family Trust
The Henry and Suzanne Davis Foundation
The De Brye Charitable Trust
The Dellal Foundation
The Demigryphon Trust
The Denman Charitable Trust
Dentons UKMEA LLP Charitable Trust
Foundation Derbyshire
Provincial Grand Charity of the Province of Derbyshire
The Desmond Foundation
Devon Community Foundation
The Duke of Devonshire's Charitable Trust
The Sandy Dewhirst Charitable Trust
The Laduma Dhamecha Charitable Trust
Alan and Sheila Diamond Charitable Trust
The Dischma Charitable Trust
*C. H. Dixon Charitable Trust**
The DLM Charitable Trust
*The Dorfman Foundation**
Dorset Community Foundation
The Dorus Trust
The Double 'O' Charity Ltd
The Drapers' Charitable Fund
Dromintee Trust
The Dulverton Trust
The Dumbreck Charity
The Dunn Family Charitable Trust
The Charles Dunstone Charitable Trust
County Durham Community Foundation
The Mildred Duveen Charitable Trust
The Dyers' Company Charitable Trust
The James Dyson Foundation
Audrey Earle Charitable Trust
The Earley Charity
The Sir John Eastwood Foundation
The Economist Charitable Trust
Edinburgh Trust No 2 Account
Edupoor Ltd
The George Elias Charitable Trust
The Wilfred and Elsie Elkes Charity Fund
The Maud Elkington Charitable Trust
The Edith Maud Ellis 1985 Charitable Trust
The Vernon N. Ely Charitable Trust
The Englefield Charitable Trust
The Epigoni Trust
The Erskine Cunningham Hill Trust
Essex Community Foundation
Joseph Ettedgui Charitable Foundation
The Eventhall Family Charitable Trust
The Everard Foundation
The Exilarch's Foundation
The William and Christine Eynon Charity
G. F. Eyre Charitable Trust
The F. P. Ltd Charitable Trust
The Fairstead Trust
The Lord Faringdon Charitable Trust
The Thomas Farr Charity
The Farthing Trust
The February Foundation
The A. M. Fenton Trust
The Doris Field Charitable Trust
Dixie Rose Findlay Charitable Trust
The Sir John Fisher Foundation
Fisherbeck Charitable Trust
The Fitton Trust
The Earl Fitzwilliam Charitable Trust
The Joyce Fletcher Charitable Trust
The Follett Trust
Fordeve Ltd
*The Fore Trust**
Forest Hill Charitable Trust
Forever Manchester
The Forman Hardy Charitable Trust
Donald Forrester Trust
Gwyneth Forrester Trust
The Fort Foundation

The Forte Charitable Trust
The Elizabeth Frankland Moore and Star Foundation
The Gordon Fraser Charitable Trust
The Hugh Fraser Foundation
The Joseph Strong Frazer Trust
The Louis and Valerie Freedman Charitable Settlement
The Michael and Clara Freeman Charitable Trust
The Charles S. French Charitable Trust
The Anne French Memorial Trust
The Frognal Trust
The Adrian and Jane Frost Charitable Trust
The Patrick and Helena Frost Foundation
Mejer and Gertrude Miriam Frydman Foundation
The Fulmer Charitable Trust
G. M. C. Trust
The G. R. P. Charitable Trust
The Galanthus Trust
The Gale Family Charity Trust
The Ganzoni Charitable Trust
The Worshipful Company of Gardeners of London
The Garrard Family Foundation
Gatwick Airport Community Trust
The Robert Gavron Charitable Trust
The Gertner Charitable Trust
The G. C. Gibson Charitable Trust
The Simon Gibson Charitable Trust
The L. and R. Gilley Charitable Trust*
The B. and P. Glasser Charitable Trust
Global Charities
Gloucestershire Community Foundation
Worshipful Company of Glovers of London Charitable Trust
The Godinton Charitable Trust
Worshipful Company of Gold and Silver Wyre Drawers Charitable Trust Fund
The Golden Bottle Trust
The Goldman Sachs Charitable Gift Fund (UK)
Goldman Sachs Gives (UK)
The Goldsmiths' Company Charity
The Goodman Foundation
The Mike Gooley Trailfinders Charity
The Gordon Trust*
The Gosling Foundation Ltd
The Gould Charitable Trust
Gowling WLG (UK) Charitable Trust
The Hemraj Goyal Foundation
Grace Charitable Trust
Graff Foundation
E. C. Graham Belford Charitable Settlement
A. and S. Graham Charitable Trust
Grand Charitable Trust of the Order of Women Freemasons
GrantScape
The J. G. Graves Charitable Trust
The Gray Trust
The Kenneth and Susan Green Charitable Foundation
The Green Hall Foundation
Mrs H. R. Greene Charitable Settlement
Greenham Common Community Trust Ltd
The Gretna Charitable Trust
M. and R. Gross Charities Ltd
Guildry Incorporation of Perth
The Walter Guinness Charitable Trust
The Gunter Charitable Trust
H. and T. Clients Charitable Trust
H. C. D. Memorial Fund
H. P. Charitable Trust
The Haley Family Charitable Trust
Hampshire and Isle of Wight Community Foundation
Hampton Fuel Allotment Charity
The W. A. Handley Charity Trust
The Kathleen Hannay Memorial Charity
The Happold Foundation*
The Haramead Trust
Harbinson Charitable Trust
The Harbour Charitable Trust
The Harbour Foundation
William Harding's Charity
The Harebell Centenary Fund
The Peter and Teresa Harris Charitable Trust
The Edith Lilian Harrison 2000 Foundation
The Harrison-Frank Family Foundation (UK) Ltd
The Hartley Charitable Trust
The Hasluck Charitable Trust
The Hathaway Trust
The Maurice Hatter Foundation
The Hawthorne Charitable Trust
The Charles Hayward Foundation
May Hearnshaw Charitable Trust (May Hearnshaw's Charity)
Heart of England Community Foundation
The Heathcoat Trust
The Heathside Charitable Trust
The Charlotte Heber-Percy Charitable Trust
The Percy Hedley 1990 Charitable Trust
The Michael Heller Charitable Foundation
The Helping Foundation
The Hemby Charitable Trust
Henderson Firstfruits*
The Christina Mary Hendrie Trust for Scottish and Canadian Charities
Philip Henman Trust
The G. D. Herbert Charitable Trust
Herefordshire Community Foundation
Hertfordshire Community Foundation
P. and C. Hickinbotham Charitable Trust
The Alan Edward Higgs Charity
The Hilden Charitable Fund
M. V. Hillhouse Trust*
R. G. Hills Charitable Trust
Hinchley Charitable Trust
The Hintze Family Charity Foundation
The Hiscox Foundation
The Henry C. Hoare Charitable Trust
The Hobson Charity Ltd
The Jane Hodge Foundation
The Hollick Family Charitable Trust
The Holliday Foundation
The Dorothy Holmes Charitable Trust
P. H. Holt Foundation
The Homestead Charitable Trust
The Mary Homfray Charitable Trust
The Horizon Foundation
The Antony Hornby Charitable Trust
The Thomas J. Horne Memorial Trust
The Worshipful Company of Horners' Charitable Trusts
The Hospital of God at Greatham
The Sir Joseph Hotung Charitable Settlement
House of Industry Estate
The Daniel Howard Trust
Howman Charitable Trust*
The Hudson Foundation
The Hull and East Riding Charitable Trust
The Michael and Shirley Hunt Charitable Trust
The Albert Hunt Trust

The Hunting Horn General Charitable Trust
Huntingdon Freemen's Trust
The Hutchinson Charitable Trust
The Hutton Foundation
The Nani Huyu Charitable Trust
The P. Y. N. and B. Hyams Trust
*Ibbett Trust**
Ibrahim Foundation Ltd
*ICE Futures Charitable Trust**
IGO Foundation Ltd
The Iliffe Family Charitable Trust
Imagine Foundation
Incommunities Foundation
The Indigo Trust
*The Worshipful Company of Information Technologists**
The Ingram Trust
The Inman Charity
Interserve Employee Foundation Ltd
The Inverforth Charitable Trust
Investream Charitable Trust
The Ireland Fund of Great Britain
The Charles Irving Charitable Trust
The J. Isaacs Charitable Trust
The Isle of Anglesey Charitable Trust
The J. and J. Benevolent Foundation
The Jabbs Foundation
C. Richard Jackson Charitable Trust
John James Bristol Foundation
The Susan and Stephen James Charitable Settlement
Lady Eda Jardine Charitable Trust
The Jarman Charitable Trust
John Jarrold Trust Ltd
Nick Jenkins Foundation
The Jenour Foundation
The Jephcott Charitable Trust
Lillie Johnson Charitable Trust
The Johnson Foundation
Johnson Wax Ltd Charitable Trust
The Christopher and Kirsty Johnston Charitable Trust
The Joicey Trust
The Jones 1986 Charitable Trust
The Dezna Robins Jones Charitable Foundation
The Marjorie and Geoffrey Jones Charitable Trust
The Muriel Jones Foundation
The Jordan Charitable Foundation
The Joron Charitable Trust
J. E. Joseph Charitable Fund
The Cyril and Eve Jumbo Charitable Trust
Anton Jurgens Charitable Trust
The Jusaca Charitable Trust
Kahal Chassidim Bobov
The Stanley Kalms Foundation
Karaviotis Foundation
The Kasner Charitable Trust
The Michael and Ilse Katz Foundation
William Kendall's Charity (Wax Chandlers' Company)
Kent Community Foundation
The Nancy Kenyon Charitable Trust
Keren Association Ltd
E. and E. Kernkraut Charities Ltd
The Ursula Keyes Trust
*The Kildare Trust**
The King Henry VIII Endowed Trust – Warwick
The King/Cullimore Charitable Trust
Laura Kinsella Foundation
*The Graham Kirkham Foundation**
The Richard Kirkman Trust
Robert Kitchin (Saddlers' Company)
The Ernest Kleinwort Charitable Trust
The Sir James Knott Trust
The Kobler Trust
Kollel and Co. Ltd
The Kreitman Foundation
The Neil Kreitman Foundation
The Kyte Charitable Trust
Ladbrokes in the Community Charitable Trust
The K. P. Ladd Charitable Trust
John Laing Charitable Trust
Christopher Laing Foundation
The David Laing Foundation
The Martin Laing Foundation
The Leonard Laity Stoate Charitable Trust
Community Foundations for Lancashire and Merseyside
*The Lancashire Foundation**
Duchy of Lancaster Benevolent Fund
The Jack Lane Charitable Trust
Langdale Trust
The Langtree Trust
The LankellyChase Foundation
The Lauffer Family Charitable Foundation
Mrs F. B. Laurence Charitable Trust
The Kathleen Laurence Trust
The Edgar E. Lawley Foundation
The Herd Lawson and Muriel Lawson Charitable Trust
Lawson Beckman Charitable Trust
The Raymond and Blanche Lawson Charitable Trust
The Leathersellers' Company Charitable Fund
The Arnold Lee Charitable Trust
The William Leech Charity
Leeds Building Society Charitable Foundation
Leeds Community Foundation (LCF)
*Leicestershire and Rutland Masonic Charity Association**
Leicestershire, Leicester and Rutland Community Foundation
The Kennedy Leigh Charitable Trust
The Leigh Trust
P. Leigh-Bramwell Trust 'E'
*Leng Charitable Trust**
The Lennox Hannay Charitable Trust
The Mark Leonard Trust
*The Lethendy Charitable Trust**
The Leverhulme Trade Charities Trust
Lord Leverhulme's Charitable Trust
*Bernard Lewis Family Charitable Trust**
David and Ruth Lewis Family Charitable Trust
The Sir Edward Lewis Foundation
John Lewis Partnership General Community Fund
Liberum Foundation
*The Lidbury Family Trust**
*The Light Fund Company**
Limoges Charitable Trust
The Linbury Trust
Lincolnshire Community Foundation
The Lind Trust
The Linden Charitable Trust
The Enid Linder Foundation
The Lindley Foundation (TLF)
The Ruth and Stuart Lipton Charitable Trust
The Lister Charitable Trust
The Frank Litchfield Charitable Trust
Littlefield Foundation (UK) Ltd
The Second Joseph Aaron Littman Foundation
The George John and Sheilah Livanos Charitable Trust
Liverpool Charity and Voluntary Services (LCVS)
Jack Livingstone Charitable Trust
The Ian and Natalie Livingstone Charitable Trust
The Elaine and Angus Lloyd Charitable Trust

*The W. M. and B. W. Lloyd Trust**
Lloyd's Charities Trust
Localtrent Ltd
The Locker Foundation
*The Lockwood Charitable Foundation**
The Joyce Lomax Bullock Charitable Trust
The London Community Foundation (LCF)
The William and Katherine Longman Trust
The Loseley and Guildway Charitable Trust
*P. and M. Lovell Charitable Settlement**
*Michael Lowe's and Associated Charities**
The Lower Green Foundation
The C. L. Loyd Charitable Trust
LPW Ltd
The Henry Lumley Charitable Trust
Lord and Lady Lurgan Trust
The Lynn Foundation
The E. M. MacAndrew Trust
The Mackay and Brewer Charitable Trust
The Mackintosh Foundation
*GPS Macpherson Charitable Settlement**
The MacRobert Trust
The Mactaggart Third Fund
The Ian Mactaggart Trust (The Mactaggart Second Fund)
The Magen Charitable Trust
The Makers of Playing Cards Charity
The Mallinckrodt Foundation
The Manackerman Charitable Trust
The Manchester Guardian Society Charitable Trust
Lord Mayor of Manchester's Charity Appeal Trust
The Manifold Charitable Trust
The W. M. Mann Foundation
R. W. Mann Trust
Marbeh Torah Trust
The Marcela Trust
The Stella and Alexander Margulies Charitable Trust
The Marks Family Foundation
The Ann and David Marks Foundation
The Hilda and Samuel Marks Foundation
The J. P. Marland Charitable Trust
The Michael Marsh Charitable Trust
Charlotte Marshall Charitable Trust
D. G. Marshall of Cambridge Trust
*The Martin Charitable Trust**
John Martin's Charity
The Mason Porter Charitable Trust
The Violet Mauray Charitable Trust
Mazars Charitable Trust
The Robert McAlpine Foundation
McGreevy No. 5 Settlement
The Medlock Charitable Trust
Melodor Ltd
The Brian Mercer Charitable Trust
The Mercers' Charitable Foundation
Merchant Navy Welfare Board
The Merchant Venturers' Charity
The Metropolitan Masonic Charity
The Mickel Fund
The Masonic Province of Middlesex Charitable Trust (Middlesex Masonic Charity)
Hugh and Mary Miller Bequest Trust
The Ronald Miller Foundation
The Millichope Foundation
*Mills and Reeve Charitable Trust**
The Mills Charity
The Millward Charitable Trust
The Clare Milne Trust
Milton Keynes Community Foundation Ltd
The Edgar Milward Charity
The Mirianog Trust
The Laurence Misener Charitable Trust
The Brian Mitchell Charitable Settlement
The MITIE Foundation
The Mittal Foundation
Keren Mitzvah Trust
The Mizpah Trust
Mobbs Memorial Trust Ltd
Mole Charitable Trust
The Monatrea Charitable Trust
The Monument Trust
The George A. Moore Foundation
The Morgan Charitable Foundation
The Steve Morgan Foundation
The Diana and Allan Morgenthau Charitable Trust
The Morris Charitable Trust
The Willie and Mabel Morris Charitable Trust
G. M. Morrison Charitable Trust
*The Morrisons Foundation**
*The Morton Charitable Trust**
The Moshal Charitable Trust
Vyoel Moshe Charitable Trust
The Moss Family Charitable Trust
Moto in the Community
The Mulberry Trust
The Music Sales Charitable Trust
Muslim Hands
The Janet Nash Charitable Settlement
The NDL Foundation
The Worshipful Company of Needlemakers' Charitable Fund
The James Neill Trust Fund
Ner Foundation
Network for Social Change Charitable Trust
Norfolk Community Foundation
The Norman Family Charitable Trust
Normanby Charitable Trust
*North London Charities Ltd**
*Provincial Grand Charity of Northamptonshire and Huntingdonshire**
Northamptonshire Community Foundation
Northwood Charitable Trust
The Notgrove Trust
Nottinghamshire Community Foundation
The Oakley Charitable Trust
Odin Charitable Trust
The Ofenheim Charitable Trust
Oglesby Charitable Trust
Oizer Charitable Trust
The Olga Charitable Trust
*One Community Foundation Ltd**
OneFamily Foundation
The Ormsby Charitable Trust
The O'Sullivan Family Charitable Trust
Oxfordshire Community Foundation
P. F. Charitable Trust
The Doris Pacey Charitable Foundation
The Paget Charitable Trust
*Palmtree Memorial Trust**
The James Pantyfedwen Foundation
The Paphitis Charitable Trust
*Parabola Foundation**
Paradigm Foundation
The Paragon Trust
*Parish Estate of the Church of St Michael Spurriergate York**
The Patrick Trust
Peacock Charitable Trust
Susanna Peake Charitable Trust
The Dowager Countess Eleanor Peel Trust
The Pell Charitable Trust
The Pennycress Trust
People's Health Trust
Personal Assurance Charitable Trust

The Persula Foundation
The Pharsalia Charitable Trust
The Phillips and Rubens Charitable Trust
The Phillips Family Charitable Trust
The Bernard Piggott Charitable Trust
Pilkington Charities Fund
Miss A. M. Pilkington's Charitable Trust
The DLA Piper Charitable Trust
*The Polehampton Charity**
The George and Esme Pollitzer Charitable Settlement
Pollywally Charitable Trust
Edith and Ferdinand Porjes Charitable Trust
The Porta Pia 2012 Foundation
The Portrack Charitable Trust
The J. E. Posnansky Charitable Trust
*Powys Welsh Church Fund**
The W. L. Pratt Charitable Trust
Sir John Priestman Charity Trust
The Primrose Trust
*Princes Gate Trust**
The Princess Anne's Charities
The Privy Purse Charitable Trust
*The Professional Footballers' Association Charity**
*The Pye Foundation**
Mr and Mrs J. A. Pye's Charitable Settlement
Quartet Community Foundation
The Queen's Trust
Rachel Charitable Trust
The Rainford Trust
*The Edward Ramsden Charitable Trust**
The Joseph and Lena Randall Charitable Trust
The Rank Foundation Ltd
The Joseph Rank Trust
Rashbass Family Trust
The Ratcliff Foundation
The Ravensdale Trust
The Roger Raymond Charitable Trust
The John Rayner Charitable Trust
The Sir James Reckitt Charity
C. A. Redfern Charitable Foundation
Reed Family Foundation
The Rest Harrow Trust
Reuben Foundation
The Rhododendron Trust
Rhondda Cynon Taff Welsh Church Acts Fund
*Riada Trust**
Daisie Rich Trust
Richmond Parish Lands Charity
The Sir John Ritblat Family Foundation
The River Farm Foundation
Rivers Foundation
*Riverside Charitable Trust Ltd**
RJM Charity Trust
Robyn Charitable Trust
The Rofeh Trust
The Richard Rogers Charitable Settlement
Rokach Family Charitable Trust
The Sir James Roll Charitable Trust
The Helen Roll Charity
The Gerald Ronson Family Foundation
*Mrs L. D. Rope's Second Charitable Settlement**
Mrs L. D. Rope's Third Charitable Settlement
Rosca Trust
The Rose Foundation
*The Cissie Rosefield Charitable Trust**
The Rothermere Foundation
The Rothley Trust
The Rowlands Trust
Royal Artillery Charitable Fund
The Rubin Foundation Charitable Trust
The Rugby Group Benevolent Fund Ltd
The J. S. and E. C. Rymer Charitable Trust
*S. and R. Charitable Trust**
The Michael Sacher Charitable Trust
The Saddlers' Company Charitable Fund
The Saintbury Trust
The Saints and Sinners Trust Ltd
The Salamander Charitable Trust
*The Salisbury New Pool Settlement**
Salters' Charitable Foundation
The Andrew Salvesen Charitable Trust
Coral Samuel Charitable Trust
The Samworth Foundation
The Sandhu Charitable Foundation
The Sands Family Trust
The Sants Charitable Trust
The Scarfe Charitable Trust
The Schmidt-Bodner Charitable Trust
The Schreib Trust
O. and G. Schreiber Charitable Trust
Schroder Charity Trust
The Schroder Foundation
Foundation Scotland
The Scotshill Trust
Scott (Eredine) Charitable Trust
The Frieda Scott Charitable Trust
*The John Scott Trust Fund**
The ScottishPower Foundation
The Scouloudi Foundation
The SDL Foundation
The Searchlight Electric Charitable Trust
Sam and Bella Sebba Charitable Trust
*The Sellafield Charity Trust Fund**
The Cyril Shack Trust
The Shanly Foundation
The Shanti Charitable Trust
ShareGift (The Orr Mackintosh Foundation)
The Sheepdrove Trust
The Sheffield Town Trust
The Sheldon Trust
The Patricia and Donald Shepherd Charitable Trust
The Sylvia and Colin Shepherd Charitable Trust
*Sherling Charitable Trust**
The Archie Sherman Charitable Trust
Shlomo Memorial Fund Ltd
The Shoe Zone Trust
*Shulem B. Association Ltd**
*The Florence Shute Millennium Trust**
David and Jennifer Sieff Charitable Trust
Silver Family Charitable Trust
The Huntly and Margery Sinclair Charitable Trust
The Charles Skey Charitable Trust
Skipton Building Society Charitable Foundation
The John Slater Foundation
The Slaughter and May Charitable Trust
Rita and David Slowe Charitable Trust
The SMB Trust
The N. Smith Charitable Settlement
The Smith Charitable Trust
The Leslie Smith Foundation
The WH Smith Group Charitable Trust
Philip Smith's Charitable Trust
The R. C. Snelling Charitable Trust
Social Business Trust
*Social Investment Business Foundation**
Solev Co. Ltd
The Solo Charitable Settlement
*Somerset Community Foundation**
The South Square Trust
The W. F. Southall Trust
Spar Charitable Fund
Sparquote Ltd

The Spear Charitable Trust
Spears-Stutz Charitable Trust
The Jessie Spencer Trust
The Spielman Charitable Trust
Rosalyn and Nicholas Springer Charitable Trust
The Spurrell Charitable Trust
The Geoff and Fiona Squire Foundation
The Squires Foundation
The St James's Trust Settlement
*Staffordshire Community Foundation**
The Staples Trust
The Peter Stebbings Memorial Charity
The Hugh Stenhouse Foundation
The Sigmund Sternberg Charitable Foundation
The Stevenage Community Trust
Stevenson Family's Charitable Trust
The Andy Stewart Charitable Foundation
The Stoller Charitable Trust
M. J. C. Stone Charitable Trust
The Samuel Storey Family Charitable Trust
Peter Storrs Trust
Stratford upon Avon Town Trust
The Strawberry Charitable Trust
Sueberry Ltd
Suffolk Community Foundation
The Alan Sugar Foundation
*Sunninghill Fuel Allotment Trust**
Community Foundation for Surrey
The Sussex Community Foundation
The Adrienne and Leslie Sussman Charitable Trust
The Sutasoma Trust
Sutton Coldfield Charitable Trust
The Swann-Morton Foundation
The John Swire (1989) Charitable Trust
The Adrian Swire Charitable Trust
The Hugh and Ruby Sykes Charitable Trust
The Charles and Elsie Sykes Trust
Sylvia Waddilove Foundation UK
The Talbot Village Trust
Tallow Chandlers Benevolent Fund No. 2
The Lady Tangye Charitable Trust Ltd
The Tanner Trust
The Lili Tapper Charitable Foundation
The Taurus Foundation
The Tay Charitable Trust
C. B. and H. H. Taylor 1984 Trust
The Tedworth Charitable Trust
Tees Valley Community Foundation
The Templeton Goodwill Trust
The Thales Charitable Trust
The David Thomas Charitable Trust
The Arthur and Margaret Thompson Charitable Trust
The Thompson Family Charitable Trust
The Thornton Foundation
The Thousandth Man- Richard Burns Charitable Trust
The John Raymond Tijou Charitable Trust
Mrs R. P. Tindall's Charitable Trust
The Tobacco Pipe Makers and Tobacco Trade Benevolent Fund
The Toye Foundation
*The Trades House of Glasgow**
Annie Tranmer Charitable Trust
The Constance Travis Charitable Trust
The Treeside Trust
The Truemark Trust
Truemart Ltd
The Trusthouse Charitable Foundation
*The Trysil Charitable Trust**
The Tudor Trust
The Tuixen Foundation
The Florence Turner Trust
The G. J. W. Turner Trust
TVML Foundation
Two Ridings Community Foundation
Community Foundation serving Tyne and Wear and Northumberland
The Udlington Trust
UnLtd (Foundation for Social Entrepreneurs)
The Michael Uren Foundation
The David Uri Memorial Trust
*The Utley Family Charitable Trust**
The Vail Foundation
Vale of Glamorgan Welsh Church Fund
The Valentine Charitable Trust
The Valiant Charitable Trust
The Albert Van Den Bergh Charitable Trust
Mrs Maud Van Norden's Charitable Foundation
The Vandervell Foundation
The Vardy Foundation
Roger Vere Foundation
The Nigel Vinson Charitable Trust
The Vintners' Foundation
The Virgin Foundation (Virgin Unite)
The Virgin Money Foundation
The Vodafone Foundation
Voluntary Action Fund (VAF)
*The Wakefield Trust**
The Community Foundation in Wales
Wales Council for Voluntary Action
Robert and Felicity Waley-Cohen Charitable Trust
*Walton Foundation**
The Ward Blenkinsop Trust
*Mrs N. E. M. Warren's Charitable Trust**
*The Warwickshire Masonic Charitable Association Ltd**
G. R. Waters Charitable Trust 2000
*The Geoffrey Watling Charity**
Blyth Watson Charitable Trust
Waynflete Charitable Trust
The Weavers' Company Benevolent Fund
The William Webster Charitable Trust
The Weinstein Foundation
The Weinstock Fund
The James Weir Foundation
The Welton Foundation
The Wessex Youth Trust
West Derby Waste Lands Charity
The Garfield Weston Foundation
The Whitaker Charitable Trust
The Melanie White Foundation Ltd
White Stuff Foundation
The Whitecourt Charitable Trust
The Whitewater Charitable Trust
*The Wigoder Family Foundation**
The Lionel Wigram Memorial Trust
The Kay Williams Charitable Foundation
The Williams Charitable Trust
The Williams Family Charitable Trust
Williams Serendipity Trust
The HDH Wills 1965 Charitable Trust
The Dame Violet Wills Will Trust
The Wilmcote Charitrust
*Brian Wilson Charitable Trust**
Sumner Wilson Charitable Trust
Wiltshire Community Foundation
*The Wimbledon Foundation**

The W. Wing Yip and Brothers Foundation
The Harold Hyam Wingate Foundation
Winton Philanthropies
The Witzenfeld Foundation
The Michael and Anna Wix Charitable Trust
The Wixamtree Trust
The Maurice Wohl Charitable Foundation
The Charles Wolfson Charitable Trust
The James Wood Bequest Fund
The F. Glenister Woodger Trust
Woodroffe Benton Foundation
*The Woodstock Family Charitable Foundation**
The A. and R. Woolf Charitable Trust
*The Worwin UK Foundation**
The Diana Edgson Wright Charitable Trust
Wychdale Ltd
Wychville Ltd
*The Wyfold Charitable Trust**
The Wyndham Charitable Trust
Yorkshire Building Society Charitable Foundation
The South Yorkshire Community Foundation
The William Allen Young Charitable Trust
The Z. Foundation
*Elizabeth and Prince Zaiger Trust**
The Marjorie and Arnold Ziff Charitable Foundation
Stephen Zimmerman Charitable Trust
The Zochonis Charitable Trust
Zurich Community Trust (UK) Ltd
The Thales Charitable Trust
The Loke Wan Tho Memorial Foundation
The Thompson Family Charitable Trust
Thomson Reuters Foundation
The Thornton Foundation
The Thousandth Man- Richard Burns Charitable Trust
The Daniel Thwaites Charitable Trust
The Tisbury Telegraph Trust
The Tobacco Pipe Makers and Tobacco Trade Benevolent Fund
The Tolkien Trust
Tomchei Torah Charitable Trust
The Tower Hill Trust
The Toy Trust
Annie Tranmer Charitable Trust
The Constance Travis Charitable Trust
The Tresillian Trust
The Truemark Trust
Truemart Ltd
The Trusthouse Charitable Foundation
The Tudor Trust
Tuixen Foundation
The Douglas Turner Trust
The Florence Turner Trust
The G. J. W. Turner Trust
TVML Foundation
Two Ridings Community Foundation
Community Foundation Serving Tyne and Wear and Northumberland
The Udlington Trust
UKI Charitable Foundation
The Michael Uren Foundation
The Vail Foundation
The Valentine Charitable Trust
The Valiant Charitable Trust
The Albert Van Den Bergh Charitable Trust
Mrs Maud Van Norden's Charitable Foundation
The Vandervell Foundation
The Vardy Foundation
The Variety Club Children's Charity
Roger Vere Foundation
Victoria Homes Trust
The Nigel Vinson Charitable Trust
Virgin Atlantic Foundation
The Vodafone Foundation
Volant Charitable Trust
Voluntary Action Fund (VAF)
Wade's Charity
The Wakefield and Tetley Trust
The Community Foundation in Wales
Robert and Felicity Waley-Cohen Charitable Trust
The Ward Blenkinsop Trust
G. R. Waters Charitable Trust 2000
Blyth Watson Charitable Trust
Waynflete Charitable Trust
Weatherley Charitable Trust
The Weavers' Company Benevolent Fund
The William Webster Charitable Trust
The Weinstein Foundation
The James Weir Foundation
The Joir and Kato Weisz Foundation
Welsh Church Fund – Dyfed area (Carmarthenshire, Ceredigion and Pembrokeshire)
The Welton Foundation
The Wessex Youth Trust
The West Derby Wastelands Charity
The Garfield Weston Foundation
The Melanie White Foundation Ltd
White Stuff Foundation
The Whitecourt Charitable Trust
A. H. and B. C. Whiteley Charitable Trust
The Lionel Wigram Memorial Trust
The Kay Williams Charitable Foundation
The Williams Charitable Trust
Williams Serendipity Trust
The HDH Wills 1965 Charitable Trust
The Dame Violet Wills Will Trust
The Wilmcote Charitrust
Sumner Wilson Charitable Trust
David Wilson Foundation
The Community Foundation for Wiltshire and Swindon
The Harold Hyam Wingate Foundation
The Winton Charitable Foundation
The James Wise Charitable Trust
The Michael and Anna Wix Charitable Trust
The Wixamtree Trust
The Maurice Wohl Charitable Foundation
The Charles Wolfson Charitable Trust
The James Wood Bequest Fund
The F. Glenister Woodger Trust
Woodroffe Benton Foundation
The Woodward Charitable Trust
The Wragge and Co Charitable Trust
The Diana Edgson Wright Charitable Trust
The Matthews Wrightson Charity Trust
Wychdale Ltd
Wychville Ltd
The Wyndham Charitable Trust
The Yardley Great Trust
The W. Wing Yip and Brothers Foundation
Yorkshire Building Society Charitable Foundation
The South Yorkshire Community Foundation
The William Allen Young Charitable Trust
The Marjorie and Arnold Ziff Charitable Foundation
Stephen Zimmerman Charitable Trust
The Zochonis Charitable Trust
The Zolfo Cooper Foundation
Zurich Community Trust (UK) Ltd

Health

The 1989 Willan Charitable Trust
The 29th May 1961 Charitable Trust
The Aberdeen Foundation
ABF The Soldiers' Charity
The ACT Foundation
The Adint Charitable Trust
The Adnams Community Trust
*The AEB Charitable Trust**
The AIM Foundation
The Sylvia Aitken Charitable Trust
Ajahma Charitable Trust
Al-Fayed Charitable Foundation
The Derrill Allatt Foundation
The Ammco Trust
The Andrew Anderson Trust
Andor Charitable Trust
The Mary Andrew Charitable Trust
Anglo American Group Foundation
*The Anne Duchess of Westminster's Charity**
The Ardwick Trust
Ove Arup Partnership Charitable Trust
The Ashmore Foundation
The Lord Austin Trust
Autonomous Research Charitable Trust (ARCT)
The Harry Bacon Foundation
The Roy and Pixie Baker Charitable Trust
The Balcombe Charitable Trust
The Balfour Beatty Charitable Trust
The Ballinger Charitable Trust
The Barbour Foundation
The Barcapel Foundation
Barchester Healthcare Foundation
Misses Barrie Charitable Trust
The Bartlett Taylor Charitable Trust
The Batchworth Trust
The Bay Tree Charitable Trust
BBC Children in Need
Beefy's Charity Foundation
The Bellahouston Bequest Fund
*Benesco Charity Ltd**
The Benham Charitable Settlement
Bergqvist Charitable Trust
The Berkshire Community Foundation
The Billmeir Charitable Trust
The Lord Mayor of Birmingham's Charity
Isabel Blackman Foundation
The Blair Foundation
Bloom Foundation
The Booth Charities
Boots Charitable Trust
Sir Clive Bourne Family Trust
The Bowerman Charitable Trust
The Liz and Terry Bramall Foundation
The Bransford Trust
The Breadsticks Foundation
*The Brelms Trust CIO**
Bridgepoint Charitable Trust
British Humane Association
The Consuelo and Anthony Brooke Charitable Trust
The Rory and Elizabeth Brooks Foundation
R. S. Brownless Charitable Trust
BUPA UK Foundation
The Clara E. Burgess Charity
The William A. Cadbury Charitable Trust
The Edward and Dorothy Cadbury Trust
The George Cadbury Trust
CAFOD (Catholic Agency for Overseas Development)
Community Foundation for Calderdale
Callander Charitable Trust
*Canary Wharf Contractors Fund**
*The W. A. Cargill Charitable Trust**
The Carr-Gregory Trust
The Leslie Mary Carter Charitable Trust
Celtic Charity Fund
Champneys Charitable Foundation
The Charter 600 Charity
*Cheshire Community Foundation Ltd**
Chesterhill Charitable Trust
The Childwick Trust
Chrysalis Trust
Church Burgesses Trust
The City Bridge Trust (Bridge House Estates)
Stephen Clark 1957 Charitable Trust
The Cleopatra Trust
The Clothworkers' Foundation
Richard Cloudesley's Charity
The Clover Trust
The Robert Clutterbuck Charitable Trust
The Coalfields Regeneration Trust
The John Coates Charitable Trust
Denise Coates Foundation
The Denise Cohen Charitable Trust
The Vivienne and Samuel Cohen Charitable Trust
The Colchester Catalyst Charity
John Coldman Charitable Trust
Comic Relief
*The Thomas Cook Chidlren's Charity**
The Catherine Cookson Charitable Trust
The Keith Coombs Trust
The J. Reginald Corah Foundation Fund
The Worshipful Company of Cordwainers Charitable Trusts (Minges Gift and the Pooled Trusts)
The Gershon Coren Charitable Foundation (also known as The Muriel and Gus Coren Charitable Foundation)
Michael Cornish Charitable Trust
The Evan Cornish Foundation
Coutts Charitable Foundation
General Charity of Coventry
The John Cowan Foundation
The Lord Cozens-Hardy Trust
The Craps Charitable Trust
The Crerar Hotels Trust
The Violet and Milo Cripps Charitable Trust
The Croydon Relief in Need Charities
*CSIS Charity Fund**
The Cumber Family Charitable Trust
Cumbria Community Foundation
The Harry Cureton Charitable Trust
Itzchok Meyer Cymerman Trust Ltd
Roald Dahl's Marvellous Children's Charity
The Dr and Mrs A. Darlington Charitable Trust
The Davidson Family Charitable Trust
*The Biss Davies Charitable Trust**
Margaret Davies Charity
*The John Grant Davies Trust**
The Crispin Davis Family Trust
*The Roger De Haan Charitable Trust**
The De Laszlo Foundation
Debenhams Foundation
The Demigryphon Trust
The J. N. Derbyshire Trust
The Desmond Foundation
Devon Community Foundation
The Laduma Dhamecha Charitable Trust
The Dischma Charitable Trust
The Djanogly Foundation
The Derek and Eileen Dodgson Foundation
Dorset Community Foundation
The Dorus Trust
The Double 'O' Charity Ltd
Douglas Arter Foundation
Duchy Health Charity Ltd

The Royal Foundation of the Duke and Duchess of Cambridge and Prince Harry
The Dumbreck Charity
County Durham Community Foundation
The Dyers' Company Charitable Trust
*The ECHO Trust**
Echoes Of Service
Edupoor Ltd
The George Elias Charitable Trust
The Gerald Palmer Eling Trust Company
The Emerton-Christie Charity
The Epigoni Trust
Esh Foundation
Esher House Charitable Trust
Joseph Ettedgui Charitable Foundation
The Exilarch's Foundation
The F. P. Ltd Charitable Trust
Famos Foundation Trust
Samuel William Farmer Trust
The Farthing Trust
The A. M. Fenton Trust
The Fidelity UK Foundation
The Doris Field Charitable Trust
Dixie Rose Findlay Charitable Trust
The Earl Fitzwilliam Charitable Trust
The Follett Trust
The Forman Hardy Charitable Trust
The Fort Foundation
The Forte Charitable Trust
The Gordon Fraser Charitable Trust
The Louis and Valerie Freedman Charitable Settlement
The Freshfield Foundation
Friarsgate Trust
Friends of Wiznitz Ltd
The Adrian and Jane Frost Charitable Trust
The Patrick and Helena Frost Foundation
G. M. C. Trust
The Ganzoni Charitable Trust
The Jacqueline and Michael Gee Charitable Trust
The David Gibbons Foundation
The G. C. Gibson Charitable Trust
The Simon Gibson Charitable Trust
The B. and P. Glasser Charitable Trust
The Gloag Foundation
The Godinton Charitable Trust
Worshipful Company of Gold and Silver Wyre Drawers Charitable Trust Fund
The Goldman Sachs Charitable Gift Fund (UK)
Goldman Sachs Gives (UK)
The Goodman Foundation
Gowling WLG (UK) Charitable Trust
A. and S. Graham Charitable Trust
*The Graham Trust**
Grand Charitable Trust of the Order of Women Freemasons
Gordon Gray Trust
The Kenneth and Susan Green Charitable Foundation
Greenham Common Community Trust Ltd
The Greggs Foundation
The Grimmitt Trust
H. C. D. Memorial Fund
The Hadley Trust
Paul Hamlyn Foundation
The Helen Hamlyn Trust
Hampshire and Isle of Wight Community Foundation
The Hampstead Wells and Campden Trust
Hampton Fuel Allotment Charity
The Kathleen Hannay Memorial Charity
The Haramead Trust
Harbinson Charitable Trust
The Harbour Charitable Trust
The Harbour Foundation
The Harding Trust
The Harpur Trust
The Edith Lilian Harrison 2000 Foundation
The Harrison-Frank Family Foundation (UK) Ltd
The Hartley Charitable Trust
The Hasluck Charitable Trust
The Hathaway Trust
The Maurice Hatter Foundation
The Hawthorne Charitable Trust
The Headley Trust
May Hearnshaw Charitable Trust (May Hearnshaw's Charity)
Heart of England Community Foundation
The Heathcoat Trust
The Heathside Charitable Trust
*Heb Ffin (Without Frontier)**
The Charlotte Heber-Percy Charitable Trust
The Percy Hedley 1990 Charitable Trust
Hedley Foundation Ltd (The Hedley Foundation)
Help for Health
The Christina Mary Hendrie Trust for Scottish and Canadian Charities
The G. D. Herbert Charitable Trust
Herefordshire Community Foundation
Hertfordshire Community Foundation
P. and C. Hickinbotham Charitable Trust
The Alan Edward Higgs Charity
The Hilden Charitable Fund
R. G. Hills Charitable Trust
The Hinduja Foundation
The Hiscox Foundation
The Henry C. Hoare Charitable Trust
The Hobson Charity Ltd
The Hollick Family Charitable Trust
The Edward Holt Trust
The Homestead Charitable Trust
The Mary Homfray Charitable Trust
The Hoover Foundation
Hopmarket Charity
The Worshipful Company of Horners' Charitable Trusts
*Horwich Shotter Charitable Trust**
The Hospital of God at Greatham
House of Industry Estate
The Hudson Foundation
The Hull and East Riding Charitable Trust
The Humanitarian Trust
The Albert Hunt Trust
Hurdale Charity Ltd
The Hutton Foundation
The Nani Huyu Charitable Trust
*Ibbett Trust**
The Iliffe Family Charitable Trust
Incommunities Foundation
The Ingram Trust
The Inman Charity
Investream Charitable Trust
The Ireland Fund of Great Britain
The Charles Irving Charitable Trust
C. Richard Jackson Charitable Trust
The Ruth and Lionel Jacobson Trust (Second Fund) No. 2
John James Bristol Foundation
The Susan and Stephen James Charitable Settlement
John Jarrold Trust Ltd
The Jenour Foundation
The Jephcott Charitable Trust
Jewish Child's Day (JCD)
Lillie Johnson Charitable Trust
The Johnson Foundation
Johnson Wax Ltd Charitable Trust
The Dezna Robins Jones Charitable Foundation

The Marjorie and Geoffrey Jones Charitable Trust
J. E. Joseph Charitable Fund
The Cyril and Eve Jumbo Charitable Trust
Anton Jurgens Charitable Trust
The Jusaca Charitable Trust
Karaviotis Foundation
The Michael and Ilse Katz Foundation
The Ursula Keyes Trust
*The Graham Kirkham Foundation**
Kirkley Poor's Land Estate
The Richard Kirkman Trust
The Sir James Knott Trust
The Kobler Trust
Kreditor Charitable Trust
The Kreitman Foundation
The Neil Kreitman Foundation
The Kyte Charitable Trust
Ladbrokes in the Community Charitable Trust
Christopher Laing Foundation
The David Laing Foundation
The Beatrice Laing Trust
The Leonard Laity Stoate Charitable Trust
The Lambert Charitable Trust
Community Foundations for Lancashire and Merseyside
*The Lancashire Foundation**
The Jack Lane Charitable Trust
The R. J. Larg Family Charitable Trust
Laslett's (Hinton) Charity
The Lauffer Family Charitable Foundation
Mrs F. B. Laurence Charitable Trust
The Kathleen Laurence Trust
The Edgar E. Lawley Foundation
Lawson Beckman Charitable Trust
The Raymond and Blanche Lawson Charitable Trust
The Leathersellers' Company Charitable Fund
The Arnold Lee Charitable Trust
Leeds Building Society Charitable Foundation
Leicestershire, Leicester and Rutland Community Foundation
The Kennedy Leigh Charitable Trust
P. Leigh-Bramwell Trust 'E'
*Leng Charitable Trust**
The Lennox Hannay Charitable Trust
Lord Leverhulme's Charitable Trust
*The Maisie and Raphael Lewis Charitable Trust**
*Bernard Lewis Family Charitable Trust**
David and Ruth Lewis Family Charitable Trust
John Lewis Partnership General Community Fund
The Limbourne Trust
Limoges Charitable Trust
The Linbury Trust
Lincolnshire Community Foundation
The Linden Charitable Trust
The Lindley Foundation (TLF)
The Ruth and Stuart Lipton Charitable Trust
The Lister Charitable Trust
The Frank Litchfield Charitable Trust
The George John and Sheilah Livanos Charitable Trust
Jack Livingstone Charitable Trust
The Elaine and Angus Lloyd Charitable Trust
*The W. M. and B. W. Lloyd Trust**
Lloyds TSB Foundation for Scotland
The Locker Foundation
The Lolev Charitable Trust
London Catalyst
The London Community Foundation (LCF)
London Housing Foundation Ltd (LHF)
The William and Katherine Longman Trust
The Loseley and Guildway Charitable Trust
*P. and M. Lovell Charitable Settlement**
The C. L. Loyd Charitable Trust
The Henry Lumley Charitable Trust
The Lynn Foundation
M. and C. Trust
The M. K. Charitable Trust
The E. M. MacAndrew Trust
The Macdonald-Buchanan Charitable Trust
*Mace Foundation**
The Mackay and Brewer Charitable Trust
*GPS Macpherson Charitable Settlement**
The Mactaggart Third Fund
The Ian Mactaggart Trust (The Mactaggart Second Fund)
The Manackerman Charitable Trust
The Manchester Guardian Society Charitable Trust
R. W. Mann Trust
The Stella and Alexander Margulies Charitable Trust
The Marks Family Foundation
The Ann and David Marks Foundation
The Hilda and Samuel Marks Foundation
The J. P. Marland Charitable Trust
The Michael Marsh Charitable Trust
The Marsh Christian Trust
Charlotte Marshall Charitable Trust
D. G. Marshall of Cambridge Trust
*The Martin Charitable Trust**
*Masonic Charitable Foundation**
*The Master Charitable Trust**
The Matliwala Family Charitable Trust
The Violet Mauray Charitable Trust
The Medlock Charitable Trust
Merchant Navy Welfare Board
The Merchant Taylors' Company Charities Fund
The Merchant Venturers' Charity
The Metropolitan Masonic Charity
T. and J. Meyer Family Foundation Ltd
The Mickleham Trust
The Gerald Micklem Charitable Trust
Hugh and Mary Miller Bequest Trust
The Ronald Miller Foundation
The Millichope Foundation
The Mills Charity
*The James Milner Foundation**
The Laurence Misener Charitable Trust
The Mishcon Family Charitable Trust
Keren Mitzvah Trust
The Monmouthshire County Council Welsh Church Act Fund
The Monument Trust
*Moondance Foundation**
The George A. Moore Foundation
The Morel Charitable Trust
The Morgan Charitable Foundation
The Steve Morgan Foundation
Morgan Stanley International Foundation
The Diana and Allan Morgenthau Charitable Trust
The Morris Charitable Trust
The Willie and Mabel Morris Charitable Trust
G. M. Morrison Charitable Trust
*The Morton Charitable Trust**
Vyoel Moshe Charitable Trust
The Moss Family Charitable Trust
The Edith Murphy Foundation

Murphy-Neumann Charity Company Ltd
The Music Sales Charitable Trust
Muslim Hands
The Janet Nash Charitable Settlement
The National Gardens Scheme*
The NDL Foundation
Ner Foundation
Nesta*
Network for Social Change Charitable Trust
Newby Trust Ltd
Nominet Charitable Foundation
Norfolk Community Foundation
Normanby Charitable Trust
Northamptonshire Community Foundation
Northwood Charitable Trust
The Norton Foundation
The Norton Rose Fulbright Charitable Foundation
The Notgrove Trust
The Father O'Mahoney Memorial Trust
The Oakley Charitable Trust
The Ofenheim Charitable Trust
Oizer Charitable Trust
The Olga Charitable Trust
OneFamily Foundation
The O'Sullivan Family Charitable Trust
The Doris Pacey Charitable Foundation
The Paget Charitable Trust
Palmtree Memorial Trust*
The Paphitis Charitable Trust
The Patrick Trust
Peacock Charitable Trust
Susanna Peake Charitable Trust
People's Postcode Trust
Personal Assurance Charitable Trust
The Pharsalia Charitable Trust
The Phillips and Rubens Charitable Trust
The Phillips Charitable Trust
Pilkington Charities Fund
The Austin and Hope Pilkington Trust
The George and Esme Pollitzer Charitable Settlement
The Portrack Charitable Trust
The J. E. Posnansky Charitable Trust
Postcode Community Trust*
Princes Gate Trust*
The Princess Anne's Charities
Prison Service Charity Fund
The PwC Foundation
QBE European Operations Foundation*
The Queen Anne's Gate Foundation
Quercus Foundation*
The Monica Rabagliati Charitable Trust
Richard Radcliffe Trust
The Rambourg Foundation
Rashbass Family Trust
Elizabeth Rathbone Charity
The Ravensdale Trust
The Rayne Foundation
The John Rayner Charitable Trust
C. A. Redfern Charitable Foundation
The Rest Harrow Trust
Daisie Rich Trust
Rigby Foundation*
The River Farm Foundation
The Robertson Trust
Robyn Charitable Trust
The Roddick Foundation
The Richard Rogers Charitable Settlement
The Helen Roll Charity
The Cecil Rosen Foundation
The Rothley Trust
The J. S. and E. C. Rymer Charitable Trust
S. and R. Charitable Trust*
The Michael and Nicola Sacher Charitable Trust
The Michael Sacher Charitable Trust
The Saintbury Trust
The Saints and Sinners Trust Ltd
The Salamander Charitable Trust
Salters' Charitable Foundation
Coral Samuel Charitable Trust
The Basil Samuel Charitable Trust
The M. J. Samuel Charitable Trust
The Sandhu Charitable Foundation
The Sandra Charitable Trust
The Sants Charitable Trust
The Save the Children Fund*
The Schapira Charitable Trust
Schroder Charity Trust
The Scotshill Trust
Scott (Eredine) Charitable Trust
The Scouloudi Foundation
Sam and Bella Sebba Charitable Trust
The Sellafield Charity Trust Fund*
The Shanti Charitable Trust
The Shears Foundation
The Sylvia and Colin Shepherd Charitable Trust
Sherburn House Charity*
The Archie Sherman Cardiff Foundation
The Shoe Zone Trust
The Florence Shute Millennium Trust*
David and Jennifer Sieff Charitable Trust
The Huntly and Margery Sinclair Charitable Trust
The John Slater Foundation
The Mrs Smith and Mount Trust
The WH Smith Group Charitable Trust
The R. C. Snelling Charitable Trust
The Sobell Foundation
The Solo Charitable Settlement
Somerset Community Foundation*
Songdale Ltd
R. H. Southern Trust
Sparquote Ltd
Rosalyn and Nicholas Springer Charitable Trust
The Squires Foundation
The St James's Trust Settlement
St Monica Trust
Staffordshire Community Foundation*
The Stanley Foundation Ltd
The Peter Stebbings Memorial Charity
The Steel Charitable Trust
The Stevenage Community Trust
Stevenson Family's Charitable Trust
M. J. C. Stone Charitable Trust
The Stoneygate Trust*
Peter Stormonth Darling Charitable Trust
The Strangward Trust
The W. O. Street Charitable Foundation
Suffolk Community Foundation
The Bernard Sunley Charitable Foundation
The Sussex Community Foundation
The Adrienne and Leslie Sussman Charitable Trust
Sutton Coldfield Charitable Trust
The Swire Charitable Trust
The Talbot Trusts
C. B. and H. H. Taylor 1984 Trust
Khoo Teck Puat UK Foundation*
The C. Paul Thackray General Charitable Trust
The Thales Charitable Trust
DM Thomas Foundation for Young People*
The Thornton Trust
The Thousandth Man- Richard Burns Charitable Trust
The Three Guineas Trust
The Tompkins Foundation
The Tory Family Foundation

Toyota Manufacturing UK Charitable Trust
Annie Tranmer Charitable Trust
Trumros Ltd
The Trusthouse Charitable Foundation
The Trysil Charitable Trust*
The James Tudor Foundation
The Tuixen Foundation
Community Foundation serving Tyne and Wear and Northumberland
UKH Foundation*
Ulster Garden Villages Ltd
The Underwood Trust
The Utley Family Charitable Trust*
The Valentine Charitable Trust
The Albert Van Den Bergh Charitable Trust
Virgin Atlantic Foundation
Voluntary Action Fund (VAF)
The Community Foundation in Wales
Wales Council for Voluntary Action
Robert and Felicity Waley-Cohen Charitable Trust
The Walker Trust
Walton Foundation*
The Barbara Ward Children's Foundation
The Warwickshire Masonic Charitable Association Ltd*
Mrs Waterhouse Charitable Trust
Wates Family Enterprise Trust
The Wates Foundation
The Geoffrey Watling Charity*
The Watson Family Charitable Trust*
The Weir Charitable Trust*
The James Weir Foundation
The Welton Foundation
The Wessex Youth Trust
The West Looe Town Trust*
The Westfield Health Charitable Trust
The Garfield Weston Foundation
The Melanie White Foundation Ltd
The Williams Family Foundation*
Williams Serendipity Trust
The Dame Violet Wills Will Trust
The Michael and Anna Wix Charitable Trust
The Wixamtree Trust
The Maurice Wohl Charitable Foundation
The Wolfson Family Charitable Trust
The Wolfson Foundation
The Wood Foundation
The A. and R. Woolf Charitable Trust
The Worwin UK Foundation*
The Wyseliot Rose Charitable Trust
Yorkshire and Clydesdale Bank Foundation
Yorkshire Building Society Charitable Foundation
The William Allen Young Charitable Trust
Zephyr Charitable Trust
The Marjorie and Arnold Ziff Charitable Foundation
The Zochonis Charitable Trust
Zurich Community Trust (UK) Ltd

Alternative and complementary medicine

Disability Aid Fund (The Roger and Jean Jefcoate Trust)
The Onaway Trust*
The Pen Shell Project
The Joseph Rank Trust
The Roughley Charitable Trust

Health care

The 1970 Trust
The Alchemy Foundation
The John Armitage Charitable Trust
The Artemis Charitable Trust
The Barbers' Company General Charities
The Barclay Foundation
The Philip Barker Charity*
Barnwood Trust
The Berkeley Charitable Foundation
The Big Lottery Fund (see also Awards for All)
The Birmingham District Nursing Charitable Trust
The Boshier-Hinton Foundation
The Harry Bottom Charitable Trust
The Tony Bramall Charitable Trust
The Burdett Trust for Nursing
David William Traill Cargill Fund
The W. A. Cargill Fund*
The Elizabeth Casson Trust
The Amelia Chadwick Trust
The Chapman Charitable Trust
The Chownes Foundation
Christian Aid
The Clark Foundation*
Mabel Cooper Charity
The Marjorie Coote Old People's Charity
Dudley and Geoffrey Cox Charitable Trust
Cruden Foundation Ltd
The D'Oyly Carte Charitable Trust
Baron Davenport's Charity
Michael Davies Charitable Settlement
The Delves Charitable Trust
Dinwoodie Charitable Company
Disability Aid Fund (The Roger and Jean Jefcoate Trust)
The Dunhill Medical Trust
The Charles Dunstone Charitable Trust
The W. G. Edwards Charitable Foundation
The Eranda Rothschild Foundation
Euro Charity Trust
The Eveson Charitable Trust
G. F. Eyre Charitable Trust
The Lord Faringdon Charitable Trust
The February Foundation
Elizabeth Ferguson Charitable Trust Fund
The Sir John Fisher Foundation
The Joyce Fletcher Charitable Trust
Forest Hill Charitable Trust
The Lady Forester Trust
Donald Forrester Trust
The Elizabeth Frankland Moore and Star Foundation
Jill Franklin Trust
The Hugh Fraser Foundation
The Joseph Strong Frazer Trust
The Freshgate Trust Foundation
The Robert Gavron Charitable Trust
The General Nursing Council for England and Wales Trust
The Generations Foundation
Genetic Disorders UK*
The L. and R. Gilley Charitable Trust*
The Girdlers' Company Charitable Trust
The Goldsmiths' Company Charity
The Gordon Trust*
Grace Charitable Trust
The Green Hall Foundation
Guildry Incorporation of Perth
The W. A. Handley Charity Trust
Harbo Charities Ltd
The Harris Family Charitable Trust
The Charles Hayward Foundation
The Health Foundation
Ernest Hecht Charitable Foundation
The Hemby Charitable Trust
M. V. Hillhouse Trust*
The Hintze Family Charity Foundation

The Hollands-Warren Fund
The Homelands Charitable Trust
The Thomas J. Horne Memorial Trust
Hospice UK
The Hospital Saturday Fund
Human Relief Foundation
Miss Agnes H. Hunter's Trust
Huntingdon Freemen's Trust
The J. Isaacs Charitable Trust
The Joicey Trust
The Jones 1986 Charitable Trust
The Jordan Charitable Foundation
The Kelly Family Charitable Trust
The Peter Kershaw Trust
Kidney Research UK
The Kirschel Foundation
The Ernest Kleinwort Charitable Trust
Lancaster Foundation
Langdale Trust
Lifeline 4 Kids (Handicapped Children's Aid Committee)
The Charles Littlewood Hill Trust
Trust for London
The Lord's Taverners
Lord and Lady Lurgan Trust
The MacRobert Trust
John Martin's Charity
The Robert McAlpine Foundation
Merchant Taylors' Consolidated Charities for the Infirm
The Edwina Mountbatten and Leonora Children's Foundation
The Frances and Augustus Newman Foundation
The Nuffield Foundation
Odin Charitable Trust
The JGW Patterson Foundation*
The Mary Potter Convent Hospital Trust
Powys Welsh Church Fund*
The Prince of Wales's Charitable Foundation
Prostate Cancer UK*
Mr and Mrs J. A. Pye's Charitable Settlement
The Joseph Rank Trust
The Ranworth Trust
Reuben Foundation
The Clive and Sylvia Richards Charity Ltd
Riverside Charitable Trust Ltd*
The Rix-Thompson-Rothenberg Foundation
Thomas Roberts Trust
The Saga Charitable Trust
The Sheepdrove Trust
The Shetland Charitable Trust
The Henry Smith Charity
David Solomons Charitable Trust
The E. C. Sosnow Charitable Trust
St James's Place Foundation
The Andy Stewart Charitable Foundation
Sunninghill Fuel Allotment Trust*
Surgo Foundation UK Ltd*
The Connie and Albert Taylor Charitable Trust
The Tolkien Trust
The Trefoil Trust
Tropical Health and Education Trust*
The True Colours Trust
The Vandervell Foundation
Variety The Children's Charity (Variety Club)
Blyth Watson Charitable Trust
The Westcroft Trust
The Westminster Amalgamated Charity*
The Will Charitable Trust
J. and J. R. Wilson Trust
The Charles Wolfson Charitable Trust
The Yapp Charitable Trust
Yorkshire Cancer Research*

Health training

The Barbers' Company General Charities
Dinwoodie Charitable Company
The Nuffield Foundation

Therapy

The Artemis Charitable Trust
The Elizabeth Casson Trust
The Joyce Fletcher Charitable Trust
Jill Franklin Trust
The Kelly Family Charitable Trust
Trust for London

Medical equipment

Barnwood Trust
The Green Hall Foundation
The Jordan Charitable Foundation
Lifeline 4 Kids (Handicapped Children's Aid Committee)
The Lord's Taverners
The Frances and Augustus Newman Foundation
The Rix-Thompson-Rothenberg Foundation
The Saga Charitable Trust

Medical institutions (hospitals)

The Aberbrothock Skea Trust
The Aberbrothock Skea Trust
ABF The Soldiers' Charity
The ACT Foundation
Action Medical Research
The Adint Charitable Trust
Aid to the Church in Need (UK)
Al-Fayed Charitable Foundation
Alzheimer's Research UK*
Alzheimer's Society*
The AM Charitable Trust
Andor Charitable Trust
The Arbib Foundation
The Ardwick Trust
The John Armitage Charitable Trust
The Armourers' and Brasiers' Gauntlet Trust
Arthritis Research UK
The Ashburnham Thanksgiving Trust
The Ian Askew Charitable Trust
Asthma UK
The Astor Foundation
The Lord Austin Trust
Awards for All
Awards for All (see also the Big Lottery Fund)
The Bamford Charitable Foundation
The Band Trust
The Bank of Scotland Foundation
The Barbers' Company General Charities
The Barclay Foundation
Lord Barnby's Foundation
Misses Barrie Charitable Trust
The Paul Bassham Charitable Trust
The James Beattie Charitable Trust
The John Beckwith Charitable Trust
Beefy's Charity Foundation
Benesco Charity Ltd*
The Rowan Bentall Charitable Trust*
Bergqvist Charitable Trust
The Bestway Foundation
The Big Lottery Fund (see also Awards for All)
The Billmeir Charitable Trust
The Bingham Trust
The Birmingham District Nursing Charitable Trust
Birmingham International Airport Community Trust Fund
The Lord Mayor of Birmingham's Charity
The Sydney Black Charitable Trust
The Bertie Black Foundation

Isabel Blackman Foundation
Bloodwise
The Booth Charities
The Boshier-Hinton Foundation
The Harry Bottom Charitable Trust
The Tony Bramall Charitable Trust
The Breadsticks Foundation
*Breast Cancer Now**
The Breast Cancer Research Trust (BCRT)
*The British and Foreign Bible Society**
British Council for Prevention of Blindness (Save Eyes Everywhere)
*British Eye Research Foundation (Fight for Sight)**
British Heart Foundation (BHF)
British Humane Association
British Record Industry Trust
The J. and M. Britton Charitable Trust
The T. B. H. Brunner's Charitable Settlement
The Burden Trust
The Burdett Trust for Nursing
The Burry Charitable Trust
Consolidated Charity of Burton upon Trent
The G. W. Cadbury Charitable Trust
CAFOD (Catholic Agency for Overseas Development)
The Carrington Charitable Trust
The Wilfrid and Constance Cave Foundation
CBRE UK Charitable Trust
Chest Heart and Stroke Scotland
Children with Cancer UK
Children's Liver Disease Foundation
CHK Charities Ltd
Stephen Clark 1957 Charitable Trust
*The Clark Foundation**
The Cleopatra Trust
Clydpride Ltd
The Vivienne and Samuel Cohen Charitable Trust
The Colchester Catalyst Charity
The Coldman Charitable Trust
The Sir Jeremiah Colman Gift Trust
Colyer-Fergusson Charitable Trust
*The Thomas Cook Chidlren's Charity**
The Thomas Cook Children's Charity
The Cooks Charity
The Alice Ellen Cooper Dean Charitable Foundation
The Marjorie Coote Old People's Charity
The Worshipful Company of Cordwainers Charitable Trusts (Minges Gift and the Pooled Trusts)
The Duke of Cornwall's Benevolent Fund
*The Corporation of Trinity House of Deptford Strond**
The Cotton Trust
The Sir Tom Cowie Charitable Trust
Dudley and Geoffrey Cox Charitable Trust
The Craps Charitable Trust
The Crerar Hotels Trust
Criffel Charitable Trust
The Croydon Relief in Need Charities
The Peter Cruddas Foundation
*CSIS Charity Fund**
The Cumber Family Charitable Trust
The Cunningham Trust
The D. G. Charitable Settlement
The Joan Lynette Dalton Charitable Trust
Baron Davenport's Charity
Michael Davies Charitable Settlement
*The Biss Davies Charitable Trust**
Margaret Davies Charity
*The Roger De Haan Charitable Trust**
William Dean Countryside and Educational Trust
Dinwoodie Charitable Company
The Dinwoodie Settlement
The Djanogly Foundation
The Derek and Eileen Dodgson Foundation
The Double 'O' Charity Ltd
Dromintee Trust
Duchy Health Charity Ltd
The Dumbreck Charity
The Dunhill Medical Trust
The Charles Dunstone Charitable Trust
The Sir John Eastwood Foundation
*The ECHO Trust**
Echoes Of Service
The Gilbert and Eileen Edgar Foundation
The W. G. Edwards Charitable Foundation
The Maud Elkington Charitable Trust
The Epigoni Trust
Epilepsy Research UK
Esher House Charitable Trust
Joseph Ettedgui Charitable Foundation
Euro Charity Trust
The Everard Foundation
The Eveson Charitable Trust
The Beryl Evetts and Robert Luff Animal Welfare Trust Ltd
The Exilarch's Foundation
The Fairstead Trust
The Lord Faringdon Charitable Trust
Samuel William Farmer Trust
The George Fentham Birmingham Charity
The A. M. Fenton Trust
Elizabeth Ferguson Charitable Trust Fund
The Fidelity UK Foundation
The Doris Field Charitable Trust
The Fifty Fund
The Sir John Fisher Foundation
The Lady Forester Trust
Donald Forrester Trust
The Forte Charitable Trust
The Lord Forte Foundation
The Elizabeth Frankland Moore and Star Foundation
Jill Franklin Trust
The Hugh Fraser Foundation
The Joseph Strong Frazer Trust
The Freshgate Trust Foundation
The Frognal Trust
The Fulmer Charitable Trust
The G. D. Charitable Trust
The Gale Family Charity Trust
The Ganzoni Charitable Trust
The Robert Gavron Charitable Trust
The General Nursing Council for England and Wales Trust
The Generations Foundation
The Steven Gerrard Foundation
The G. C. Gibson Charitable Trust
The Simon Gibson Charitable Trust
*The L. and R. Gilley Charitable Trust**
The B. and P. Glasser Charitable Trust
Worshipful Company of Glovers of London Charitable Trust
The Gosling Foundation Ltd
The Gould Charitable Trust
Gowling WLG (UK) Charitable Trust
Grand Charitable Trust of the Order of Women Freemasons
The J. G. Graves Charitable Trust
Gordon Gray Trust
The Gray Trust
The Green Hall Foundation
The Greggs Foundation
The Walter Guinness Charitable Trust

The Gunter Charitable Trust
The Hadfield Charitable Trust
The Hadrian Trust
The Hampshire and Islands Historic Churches Trust
Hampton Fuel Allotment Charity
The W. A. Handley Charity Trust
The Harbour Foundation
William Harding's Charity
The Harebell Centenary Fund
The Harris Family Charitable Trust
The Harrison-Frank Family Foundation (UK) Ltd
The Maurice Hatter Foundation
The Health Foundation
May Hearnshaw Charitable Trust (May Hearnshaw's Charity)
Heart Research UK
The Charlotte Heber-Percy Charitable Trust
The Michael Heller Charitable Foundation
Help for Health
The Hemby Charitable Trust
Heritage Lottery Fund*
The Hesslewood Children's Trust (Hull Seamen's and General Orphanage)
P. and C. Hickinbotham Charitable Trust
The Hilden Charitable Fund
M. V. Hillhouse Trust*
The Hillingdon Community Trust
The Hintze Family Charity Foundation
The Hiscox Foundation
The Hobson Charity Ltd
The Jane Hodge Foundation
The Dorothy Holmes Charitable Trust
The Edward Holt Trust
The Holywood Trust
The Homelands Charitable Trust
The Homestead Charitable Trust
The Mary Homfray Charitable Trust
Sir Harold Hood's Charitable Trust
The Horizon Foundation
The Hospital of God at Greatham
The Hospital Saturday Fund
The Hull and East Riding Charitable Trust
Human Relief Foundation
The Albert Hunt Trust
The Hunter Foundation
Huntingdon Freemen's Trust
The Iliffe Family Charitable Trust
The Inverforth Charitable Trust
The Jabbs Foundation
John James Bristol Foundation
The Susan and Stephen James Charitable Settlement
Lady Eda Jardine Charitable Trust
The Jarman Charitable Trust
John Jarrold Trust Ltd
Lillie Johnson Charitable Trust
The Johnson Foundation
Johnnie Johnson Trust
The Dezna Robins Jones Charitable Foundation
The Marjorie and Geoffrey Jones Charitable Trust
The Muriel Jones Foundation
The Joron Charitable Trust
J. E. Joseph Charitable Fund
Anton Jurgens Charitable Trust
Kahal Chassidim Bobov
The Stanley Kalms Foundation
The Kasner Charitable Trust
The Kay Kendall Leukaemia Fund
The Peter Kershaw Trust
The Ursula Keyes Trust
Kidney Research UK
The King Henry VIII Endowed Trust – Warwick
The Mary Kinross Charitable Trust
The Sir James Knott Trust
The Kreitman Foundation
Maurice and Hilda Laing Charitable Trust
The Lancashire Foundation*
Langdale Trust
Laslett's (Hinton) Charity
The Kathleen Laurence Trust
The Edgar E. Lawley Foundation
The Raymond and Blanche Lawson Charitable Trust
The William Leech Charity
Leicestershire, Leicester and Rutland Community Foundation
The Lennox Hannay Charitable Trust
The Leverhulme Trust
The Maisie and Raphael Lewis Charitable Trust*
David and Ruth Lewis Family Charitable Trust
The Sir Edward Lewis Foundation
Lifeline 4 Kids
Lifeline 4 Kids (Handicapped Children's Aid Committee)
Lincolnshire Community Foundation
The Enid Linder Foundation
The Charles Littlewood Hill Trust
The Second Joseph Aaron Littman Foundation
The George John and Sheilah Livanos Charitable Trust
The Ian and Natalie Livingstone Charitable Trust
The Elaine and Angus Lloyd Charitable Trust
Loftus Charitable Trust
London Catalyst
The William and Katherine Longman Trust
The Loseley and Guildway Charitable Trust
The Lower Green Foundation
Robert Luff Foundation Ltd
The Henry Lumley Charitable Trust
Lord and Lady Lurgan Trust
The Lynn Foundation
M. and C. Trust
The R. S. Macdonald Charitable Trust
The Manackerman Charitable Trust
R. W. Mann Trust
The Marchig Animal Welfare Trust
D. G. Marshall of Cambridge Trust
The Martin Charitable Trust*
Maudsley Charity*
The Robert McAlpine Foundation
The Metropolitan Masonic Charity
T. and J. Meyer Family Foundation Ltd
T. and J. Meyer Family Foundation Ltd
The Masonic Province of Middlesex Charitable Trust (Middlesex Masonic Charity)
Hugh and Mary Miller Bequest Trust
The Millichope Foundation
The Laurence Misener Charitable Trust
The Monatrea Charitable Trust
The George A. Moore Foundation
Morgan Stanley International Foundation
G. M. Morrison Charitable Trust
Motor Neurone Disease Association
J. P. Moulton Charitable Foundation
The Edwina Mountbatten and Leonora Children's Foundation
The Mugdock Children's Trust
The Edith Murphy Foundation
The Janet Nash Charitable Settlement
The National Gardens Scheme*
Nesta*

The Frances and Augustus Newman Foundation
The NFU Mutual Charitable Trust
Norfolk Community Foundation
The Norman Family Charitable Trust
The Father O'Mahoney Memorial Trust
Oglesby Charitable Trust
The Oldham Foundation
The Doris Pacey Charitable Foundation
The Pen Shell Project
Petplan Charitable Trust
The Phillips Family Charitable Trust
The DLA Piper Charitable Trust
The George and Esme Pollitzer Charitable Settlement
*Postcode Community Trust**
The Mary Potter Convent Hospital Trust
Sir John Priestman Charity Trust
The Prince of Wales's Charitable Foundation
*Princes Gate Trust**
The Princess Anne's Charities
*Prostate Cancer UK**
The PwC Foundation
Mr and Mrs J. A. Pye's Charitable Settlement
Mr and Mrs J. A. Pyes Charitable Settlement
*Quercus Foundation**
Rachel Charitable Trust
The Radcliffe Trust
The Rambourg Foundation
The Joseph and Lena Randall Charitable Trust
The Sir James Reckitt Charity
Richard Reeve's Foundation
The Rest Harrow Trust
Reuben Foundation
The Clive and Sylvia Richards Charity Ltd
*Mrs L. D. Rope's Second Charitable Settlement**
*The Cissie Rosefield Charitable Trust**
Rosetrees Trust
The Royal Artillery Charitable Fund
The Royal British Legion
The Rugby Group Benevolent Fund Ltd
The Dr Mortimer and Theresa Sackler Foundation
Saint Sarkis Charity Trust
The Saintbury Trust
*The Salisbury New Pool Settlement**
The M. J. Samuel Charitable Trust
*The Savoy Educational Trust**
Scott (Eredine) Charitable Trust
Sir Samuel Scott of Yews Trust
The ScottishPower Foundation
The Jean Shanks Foundation
The Shirley Foundation
The Charles Skey Charitable Trust
The Mrs Smith and Mount Trust
The WH Smith Group Charitable Trust
Philip Smith's Charitable Trust
Sparks Charity (Sport Aiding Medical Research for Kids)
The Jessie Spencer Trust
Rosalyn and Nicholas Springer Charitable Trust
The Squires Foundation
St Monica Trust
The Andy Stewart Charitable Foundation
Sir Halley Stewart Trust
The Stoller Charitable Trust
*The Stoneygate Trust**
Peter Stormonth Darling Charitable Trust
The Sudborough Foundation
The Alan Sugar Foundation
Sutton Coldfield Charitable Trust
The Swann-Morton Foundation
The Charles and Elsie Sykes Trust
The Talbot Trusts
Talteg Ltd
The Connie and Albert Taylor Charitable Trust
*Khoo Teck Puat UK Foundation**
The Templeton Goodwill Trust
*Tenovus Scotland**
*DM Thomas Foundation for Young People**
The Thompson Family Charitable Trust
The Sir Jules Thorn Charitable Trust
The Thornton Foundation
The Thornton Trust
The Thriplow Charitable Trust
The Tompkins Foundation
Annie Tranmer Charitable Trust
The Constance Travis Charitable Trust
*Tropical Health and Education Trust**
*The Trysil Charitable Trust**
The Tuixen Foundation
Ulster Garden Villages Ltd
The Ulverscroft Foundation
The Underwood Trust
The Michael Uren Foundation
*The Utley Family Charitable Trust**
Mrs Maud Van Norden's Charitable Foundation
The Variety Club Children's Charity
Variety The Children's Charity (Variety Club)
The Walker Trust
Walton on Thames Charity
*The Warwickshire Masonic Charitable Association Ltd**
Mrs Waterhouse Charitable Trust
Wates Family Enterprise Trust
Blyth Watson Charitable Trust
The William Webster Charitable Trust
The Westfield Health Charitable Trust
The Garfield Weston Foundation
The Colonel W. H. Whitbread Charitable Trust
The Whitecourt Charitable Trust
The Whitley Animal Protection Trust
The Kay Williams Charitable Foundation
Sumner Wilson Charitable Trust
Wiltshire Community Foundation
The Francis Winham Foundation
The Charles Wolfson Charitable Trust
The Wolfson Family Charitable Trust
The Wolfson Foundation
The F. Glenister Woodger Trust
The Wyndham Charitable Trust
*York Children's Trust**
Yorkshire and Clydesdale Bank Foundation
*Yorkshire Cancer Research**
The William Allen Young Charitable Trust
The John Kirkhope Young Endowment Fund
The Z. Foundation
*Elizabeth and Prince Zaiger Trust**
The Marjorie and Arnold Ziff Charitable Foundation

Medical institutions (hospices)

The Aberbrothock Skea Trust
The Aberbrothock Skea Trust
ABF The Soldiers' Charity
The Acacia Charitable Trust
The ACT Foundation
The Addleshaw Goddard Charitable Trust
The Adint Charitable Trust
Age Scotland
Aid to the Church in Need (UK)
Al-Fayed Charitable Foundation
Allchurches Trust Ltd

The W. G. Edwards Charitable Foundation
*The Eighty Eight Foundation**
The Wilfred and Elsie Elkes Charity Fund
The Vernon N. Ely Charitable Trust
*The Emerald Foundation**
The Epigoni Trust
Ernest Hecht Charitable Foundation
Esh Foundation
Esher House Charitable Trust
The Everard Foundation
The Eveson Charitable Trust
The Exilarch's Foundation
G. F. Eyre Charitable Trust
The Fairstead Trust
The Lord Faringdon Charitable Trust
Samuel William Farmer Trust
The A. M. Fenton Trust
Elizabeth Ferguson Charitable Trust Fund
The Doris Field Charitable Trust
The Fifty Fund
Dixie Rose Findlay Charitable Trust
The Sir John Fisher Foundation
The Earl Fitzwilliam Charitable Trust
The Follett Trust
Ford Britain Trust
Forest Hill Charitable Trust
The Lady Forester Trust
Donald Forrester Trust
Gwyneth Forrester Trust
The John Spedan Foundation
The Elizabeth Frankland Moore and Star Foundation
Jill Franklin Trust
The Hugh Fraser Foundation
The Joseph Strong Frazer Trust
The Louis and Valerie Freedman Charitable Settlement
The Charles S. French Charitable Trust
The Freshgate Trust Foundation
Friarsgate Trust
The Patrick and Helena Frost Foundation
The Fulmer Charitable Trust
The G. D. Charitable Trust
The Gale Family Charity Trust
The Ganzoni Charitable Trust
Gardeners of London
The Generations Foundation
The G. C. Gibson Charitable Trust
The Simon Gibson Charitable Trust
*The L. and R. Gilley Charitable Trust**
The B. and P. Glasser Charitable Trust
The Gloag Foundation
Global Charities
The Godinton Charitable Trust
Worshipful Company of Gold and Silver Wyre Drawers Charitable Trust Fund
The Goshen Trust
The Gosling Foundation Ltd
Gowling WLG (UK) Charitable Trust
Grand Charitable Trust of the Order of Women Freemasons
The J. G. Graves Charitable Trust
Gordon Gray Trust
The Gray Trust
The Green Hall Foundation
Greenham Common Community Trust Ltd
The Greggs Foundation
The Grimmitt Trust
The Walter Guinness Charitable Trust
The Hadfield Charitable Trust
The Hadley Trust
The Hadrian Trust
Hampton Fuel Allotment Charity
The W. A. Handley Charity Trust
The Kathleen Hannay Memorial Charity
The Harding Trust
William Harding's Charity
The Harebell Centenary Fund
The Harris Family Charitable Trust
The Edith Lilian Harrison 2000 Foundation
The Harrison-Frank Family Foundation (UK) Ltd
The Hawthorne Charitable Trust
The Health Foundation
The Charlotte Heber-Percy Charitable Trust
Ernest Hecht Charitable Foundation
The Percy Hedley 1990 Charitable Trust
Hedley Foundation Ltd (The Hedley Foundation)
Help for Health
The Hemby Charitable Trust
The Christina Mary Hendrie Trust for Scottish and Canadian Charities
The G. D. Herbert Charitable Trust
*Heritage Lottery Fund**
The Hesslewood Children's Trust (Hull Seamen's and General Orphanage)
P. and C. Hickinbotham Charitable Trust
*M. V. Hillhouse Trust**
The Hillingdon Community Trust
R. G. Hills Charitable Trust
The Hiscox Foundation
The Hobson Charity Ltd
The Jane Hodge Foundation
The Hollands-Warren Fund
The Holliday Foundation
The Dorothy Holmes Charitable Trust
The Holywood Trust
The Homelands Charitable Trust
The Homestead Charitable Trust
Sir Harold Hood's Charitable Trust
The Hoover Foundation
The Horizon Foundation
The Antony Hornby Charitable Trust
The Thomas J. Horne Memorial Trust
*Horwich Shotter Charitable Trust**
Hospice UK
Hospice UK
The Hospital of God at Greatham
The Hospital Saturday Fund
House of Industry Estate
The Hudson Foundation
The Michael and Shirley Hunt Charitable Trust
The Albert Hunt Trust
Huntingdon Freemen's Trust
*Ibbett Trust**
*ICE Futures Charitable Trust**
The Ingram Trust
The Inman Charity
The Inverforth Charitable Trust
The Charles Irving Charitable Trust
The J. A. R. Charitable Trust
C. Richard Jackson Charitable Trust
The Susan and Stephen James Charitable Settlement
Lady Eda Jardine Charitable Trust
The Jarman Charitable Trust
John Jarrold Trust Ltd
Nick Jenkins Foundation
The Jenour Foundation
Lillie Johnson Charitable Trust
The Johnson Foundation
Johnnie Johnson Trust
The Christopher and Kirsty Johnston Charitable Trust
The Jones 1986 Charitable Trust
The Dezna Robins Jones Charitable Foundation
The Marjorie and Geoffrey Jones Charitable Trust
Anton Jurgens Charitable Trust
Kahal Chassidim Bobov

The Bernard Kahn Charitable Trust
The Michael and Ilse Katz Foundation
The Caron Keating Foundation
Kent Community Foundation
The Peter Kershaw Trust
The Ursula Keyes Trust
*The Kildare Trust**
The King Henry VIII Endowed Trust – Warwick
Kirkley Poor's Land Estate
The Richard Kirkman Trust
The Ernest Kleinwort Charitable Trust
The Kobler Trust
Kreditor Charitable Trust
The Kyte Charitable Trust
Ladbrokes in the Community Charitable Trust
Maurice and Hilda Laing Charitable Trust
The Beatrice Laing Trust
The Leonard Laity Stoate Charitable Trust
The Lambert Charitable Trust
*The Lancashire Foundation**
LandAid Charitable Trust (Land Aid)
Langdale Trust
The R. J. Larg Family Charitable Trust
Laslett's (Hinton) Charity
The Lauffer Family Charitable Foundation
The Edgar E. Lawley Foundation
The Herd Lawson and Muriel Lawson Charitable Trust
The Raymond and Blanche Lawson Charitable Trust
Leicestershire, Leicester and Rutland Community Foundation
P. Leigh-Bramwell Trust 'E'
P. Leigh-Bramwell Trust E
The Sir Edward Lewis Foundation
Lifeline 4 Kids
Lifeline 4 Kids (Handicapped Children's Aid Committee)
Limoges Charitable Trust
The Linden Charitable Trust
The Lindley Foundation
The Ruth and Stuart Lipton Charitable Trust
The Frank Litchfield Charitable Trust
The Charles Littlewood Hill Trust
The Second Joseph Aaron Littman Foundation
The George John and Sheilah Livanos Charitable Trust
The Elaine and Angus Lloyd Charitable Trust
The Andrew Lloyd Webber Foundation
*The Lockwood Charitable Foundation**
London Catalyst
The Loseley and Guildway Charitable Trust
The Lower Green Foundation
The C. L. Loyd Charitable Trust
Robert Luff Foundation Ltd
The Henry Lumley Charitable Trust
Lord and Lady Lurgan Trust
The Lynn Foundation
M. and C. Trust
The E. M. MacAndrew Trust
The Macdonald-Buchanan Charitable Trust
The Manchester Guardian Society Charitable Trust
R. W. Mann Trust
The Michael Marsh Charitable Trust
Charlotte Marshall Charitable Trust
D. G. Marshall of Cambridge Trust
*The Martin Charitable Trust**
Sir George Martin Trust
John Martin's Charity
John Martin's Charity
The Mason Porter Charitable Trust
*Masonic Charitable Foundation**
The Nancie Massey Charitable Trust
*The Master Charitable Trust**
The Violet Mauray Charitable Trust
Mazars Charitable Trust
The Robert McAlpine Foundation
D. D. McPhail Charitable Settlement
The Medlock Charitable Trust
Merchant Taylors' Consolidated Charities for the Infirm
The Metropolitan Masonic Charity
The Mickel Fund
The Mickleham Trust
The Gerald Micklem Charitable Trust
The Masonic Province of Middlesex Charitable Trust (Middlesex Masonic Charity)
The Millward Charitable Trust
The Mirianog Trust
The Laurence Misener Charitable Trust
The Brian Mitchell Charitable Settlement
Mobbs Memorial Trust Ltd
The Monmouthshire County Council Welsh Church Act Fund
The Monument Trust
The George A. Moore Foundation
The Willie and Mabel Morris Charitable Trust
G. M. Morrison Charitable Trust
*The Morrisons Foundation**
The Moss Family Charitable Trust
J. P. Moulton Charitable Foundation
The Edwina Mountbatten and Leonora Children's Foundation
The Mugdock Children's Trust
The Mulberry Trust
Murphy-Neumann Charity Company Ltd
The Music Sales Charitable Trust
*The National Gardens Scheme**
The NFU Mutual Charitable Trust
Provincial Grand Charity of Northamptonshire and Huntingdonshire
The Oakley Charitable Trust
Odin Charitable Trust
The Ofenheim Charitable Trust
The Oldham Foundation
The Olga Charitable Trust
*One Community Foundation Ltd**
OneFamily Foundation
The Paget Charitable Trust
The Paphitis Charitable Trust
The Paragon Trust
*The Pargiter Trust**
The Patrick Trust
The Jack Patston Charitable Trust
*The JGW Patterson Foundation**
Susanna Peake Charitable Trust
The Pears Family Charitable Foundation
The Dowager Countess Eleanor Peel Trust
Personal Assurance Charitable Trust
The Jack Petchey Foundation
The Phillips Charitable Trust
The Bernard Piggott Charitable Trust
*Pink Ribbon Foundation**
The George and Esme Pollitzer Charitable Settlement
The Mary Potter Convent Hospital Trust
The W. L. Pratt Charitable Trust
The Prince of Wales's Charitable Foundation
*The Prince Philip Trust Fund**
Prison Service Charity Fund

The Privy Purse Charitable Trust
Mr and Mrs J. A. Pye's Charitable Settlement
Mr and Mrs J. A. Pyes Charitable Settlement
Quartet Community Foundation
Richard Radcliffe Trust
The Rainford Trust
The Rambourg Foundation
The Rank Foundation Ltd
The Ratcliff Foundation
The Ravensdale Trust
The Rayne Foundation
The John Rayner Charitable Trust
C. A. Redfern Charitable Foundation
*Riada Trust**
Daisie Rich Trust
The Clive and Sylvia Richards Charity
*Rigby Foundation**
The River Trust
Thomas Roberts Trust
The Helen Roll Charity
*The David Ross Foundation**
The Rothley Trust
The Rowlands Trust
The Rugby Group Benevolent Fund Ltd
Michael Sacher Charitable Trust
The Saintbury Trust
The M. J. Samuel Charitable Trust
Schroder Charity Trust
John Scott Trust Fund
The ScottishPower Foundation
The Scouloudi Foundation
Seafarers UK (King George's Fund for Sailors)
The Shears Foundation
The Sheffield Town Trust
The Sylvia and Colin Shepherd Charitable Trust
The Sherling Charitable Trust
The Shoe Zone Trust
*The Florence Shute Millennium Trust**
*The Florence Shute Millennium Trust**
The David and Jennifer Sieff Charitable Trust
Skipton Building Society Charitable Foundation
The John Slater Foundation
The N. Smith Charitable Settlement
The Smith Charitable Trust
The Leslie Smith Foundation
The WH Smith Group Charitable Trust
The Sobell Foundation
David Solomons Charitable Trust
The Spear Charitable Trust
The Spielman Charitable Trust
The Spoore, Merry and Rixman Foundation
Rosalyn and Nicholas Springer Charitable Trust
The Spurrell Charitable Trust
The Squires Foundation
St James's Place Foundation
St Monica Trust
The Stafford Trust
The Stanley Foundation Ltd
The Peter Stebbings Memorial Charity
The Steel Charitable Trust
The Samuel Storey Family Charitable Trust
Peter Stormonth Darling Charitable Trust
The Strangward Trust
Stratford upon Avon Town Trust
The W. O. Street Charitable Foundation
*The Street Foundation**
The Bernard Sunley Charitable Foundation
Sutton Coldfield Charitable Trust
The Swann-Morton Foundation
The Charles and Elsie Sykes Trust
The Talbot Trusts
Tallow Chandlers Benevolent Fund No. 2
Talteg Ltd
The Tanner Trust
The Connie and Albert Taylor Charitable Trust
The Taylor Family Foundation
The C. Paul Thackray General Charitable Trust
*DM Thomas Foundation for Young People**
The Thompson Family Charitable Trust
The Sir Jules Thorn Charitable Trust
The Thornton Foundation
Tilney Charitable Trust
Tilney Charitable Trust
The Tompkins Foundation
The Toy Trust
Annie Tranmer Charitable Trust
The Trefoil Trust
*Tropical Health and Education Trust**
The True Colours Trust
The Trusthouse Charitable Foundation
The James Tudor Foundation
The Tudor Trust
The Tufton Charitable Trust
The Tuixen Foundation
The Roger and Douglas Turner Charitable Trust
The G. J. W. Turner Trust
*UKH Foundation**
Ulster Garden Villages Ltd
The Underwood Trust
The Albert Van Den Bergh Charitable Trust
Mrs Maud Van Norden's Charitable Foundation
The Variety Club Children's Charity
Variety The Children's Charity (Variety Club)
Roger Vere Foundation
Virgin Atlantic Foundation
*The Bruce Wake Charity**
The Walker Trust
The Ward Blenkinsop Trust
The Barbara Ward Children's Foundation
*Mrs N. E. M. Warren's Charitable Trust**
*The Warwickshire Masonic Charitable Association Ltd**
Mrs Waterhouse Charitable Trust
Wates Family Enterprise Trust
*The Geoffrey Watling Charity**
Blyth Watson Charitable Trust
The David Webster Charitable Trust
The William Webster Charitable Trust
The Weinstock Fund
The James Weir Foundation
The Welton Foundation
The Westfield Health Charitable Trust
*The Westminster Amalgamated Charity**
The Garfield Weston Foundation
Westway Trust
The Whitaker Charitable Trust
The Colonel W. H. Whitbread Charitable Trust
White Stuff Foundation
The Felicity Wilde Charitable Trust
The Will Charitable Trust
*The Alfred Williams Charitable Trust**
*The Willmott Dixon Foundation**
The Dame Violet Wills Will Trust
*Brian Wilson Charitable Trust**
J. and J. R. Wilson Trust
The Francis Winham Foundation
The Wixamtree Trust
The Charles Wolfson Charitable Trust
The Wolfson Family Charitable Trust
The Wolfson Foundation
The F. Glenister Woodger Trust
*The Woodstock Family Charitable Foundation**
The A. and R. Woolf Charitable Trust
*York Children's Trust**

Yorkshire and Clydesdale Bank Foundation
Yorkshire Building Society Charitable Foundation
The William Allen Young Charitable Trust
The Z. Foundation
The Marjorie and Arnold Ziff Charitable Foundation

Nursing

The Barbers' Company General Charities
The Birmingham District Nursing Charitable Trust
The General Nursing Council for England and Wales Trust
The Edwina Mountbatten and Leonora Children's Foundation

Medical research and clinical treatment

The Aberbrothock Skea Trust
The Alborada Trust
The Alchemy Foundation
The H. B. Allen Charitable Trust
The Alliance Family Foundation
The Arbib Foundation
The John Armitage Charitable Trust
The Armourers' and Brasiers' Gauntlet Trust
Arthritis Research UK
The Astor Foundation
The Baker Charitable Trust
The Barbers' Company General Charities
The Barclay Foundation
The John Beckwith Charitable Trust
The Ruth Berkowitz Charitable Trust
The Bestway Foundation
The Boltini Trust
The Bothwell Charitable Trust
P. G. and N. J. Boulton Trust
The British Dietetic Association General and Education Trust Fund
Bill Brown 1989 Charitable Trust
The Burden Trust
The Burry Charitable Trust
The Arnold Burton 1998 Charitable Trust
The Cadogan Charity
Calleva Foundation
David William Traill Cargill Fund
The W. A. Cargill Fund*
The Cayo Foundation
The B. G. S. Cayzer Charitable Trust
Children's Liver Disease Foundation
CHK Charities Ltd
The Clark Foundation*
The Colt Foundation
The Cotton Trust
Dudley and Geoffrey Cox Charitable Trust
Cruden Foundation Ltd
The Cunningham Trust
The Joan Lynette Dalton Charitable Trust
Michael Davies Charitable Settlement
The Delves Charitable Trust
Dinwoodie Charitable Company
Dromintee Trust
The Dunhill Medical Trust
The James Dyson Foundation
The EBM Charitable Trust
The Gilbert and Eileen Edgar Foundation
The Englefield Charitable Trust
The Eranda Rothschild Foundation
G. F. Eyre Charitable Trust
Elizabeth Ferguson Charitable Trust Fund
The Sir John Fisher Foundation
Fishmongers' Company's Charitable Trust
Donald Forrester Trust
The Anna Rosa Forster Charitable Trust
The Elizabeth Frankland Moore and Star Foundation
The Hugh Fraser Foundation
The Joseph Strong Frazer Trust
The Frognal Trust
Genetic Disorders UK*
The L. and R. Gilley Charitable Trust*
Sydney and Phyllis Goldberg Memorial Charitable Trust
The Mike Gooley Trailfinders Charity
The Great Britain Sasakawa Foundation
The Grocers' Charity
The Walter Guinness Charitable Trust
Hamamelis Trust
The Alfred And Peggy Harvey Charitable Trust
The Michael Heller Charitable Foundation
The Simon Heller Charitable Settlement
M. V. Hillhouse Trust*
The Homelands Charitable Trust
The Antony Hornby Charitable Trust
The Hospital Saturday Fund
The Sir Joseph Hotung Charitable Settlement
The Jabbs Foundation
The Jones 1986 Charitable Trust
The Jordan Charitable Foundation
The Joron Charitable Trust
The Stanley Kalms Foundation
The Peter Kershaw Trust
Kidney Research UK
The Mary Kinross Charitable Trust
The Kirschel Foundation
The Ernest Kleinwort Charitable Trust
The Kohn Foundation
Kollel and Co. Ltd
The Kirby Laing Foundation
The William Leech Charity
The Enid Linder Foundation
The Charles Littlewood Hill Trust
The Second Joseph Aaron Littman Foundation
The Lower Green Foundation
Robert Luff Foundation Ltd
Lord and Lady Lurgan Trust
The Madeline Mabey Trust
The W. M. Mann Foundation
The Manoukian Charitable Foundation
The Marcela Trust
The Nancie Massey Charitable Trust
The Robert McAlpine Foundation
D. D. McPhail Charitable Settlement
Medical Research Foundation*
Medical Research Scotland*
The Brian Mercer Charitable Trust
The Mickel Fund
Mills and Reeve Charitable Trust*
The Millward Charitable Trust
The Mosselson Charitable Trust
J. P. Moulton Charitable Foundation
The Frances and Augustus Newman Foundation
The Oakdale Trust
Oglesby Charitable Trust
The Dowager Countess Eleanor Peel Trust
The DLA Piper Charitable Trust
Mr and Mrs J. A. Pye's Charitable Settlement
Queen Mary's Roehampton Trust
The Ranworth Trust
Reuben Foundation
Rhondda Cynon Taff Welsh Church Acts Fund
Rosetrees Trust
The Rothermere Foundation

Mrs Gladys Row Fogo Charitable Trust
The Rowlands Trust
The Dr Mortimer and Theresa Sackler Foundation
The Sackler Trust
The Alan and Babette Sainsbury Charitable Fund
The Andrew Salvesen Charitable Trust
Sir Samuel Scott of Yews Trust
The Jean Shanks Foundation
The Sheepdrove Trust
The Bassil Shippam and Alsford Trust
The SMB Trust
The N. Smith Charitable Settlement
Sparks Charity (Sport Aiding Medical Research for Kids)
The Spear Charitable Trust
The Spielman Charitable Trust
The Spurrell Charitable Trust
The Geoff and Fiona Squire Foundation
The Stafford Trust
Sir Halley Stewart Trust
The Stewarts Law Foundation
The Stoller Charitable Trust
The Swann-Morton Foundation
The John Swire (1989) Charitable Trust
The Charles and Elsie Sykes Trust
Sylvia Waddilove Foundation UK
The Gay and Keith Talbot Trust
Tallow Chandlers Benevolent Fund No. 2
The Tanner Trust
The Templeton Goodwill Trust
*Tenovus Scotland**
The Sir Jules Thorn Charitable Trust
The John Raymond Tijou Charitable Trust
Tilney Charitable Trust
Mrs R. P. Tindall's Charitable Trust
The Tolkien Trust
The Trefoil Trust
The Roger and Douglas Turner Charitable Trust
The Michael Uren Foundation
Mrs Maud Van Norden's Charitable Foundation
The Vandervell Foundation
Roger Vere Foundation
The Wellcome Trust
The Felicity Wilde Charitable Trust
The Kay Williams Charitable Foundation
The Williams Family Charitable Trust
The W. Wing Yip and Brothers Foundation
The Harold Hyam Wingate Foundation
Winton Philanthropies
The Charles Wolfson Charitable Trust
The John Kirkhope Young Endowment Fund

History of medicine

The Joseph Rank Trust
The Wellcome Trust

Paediatrics and child health

Action Medical Research
The Eveson Charitable Trust
The Girdlers' Company Charitable Trust
The Jane Hodge Foundation
The Waterloo Foundation

Health education/ prevention/ development

The Sylvia Adams Charitable Trust
The Alchemy Foundation
The Associated Country Women of the World
The Big Lottery Fund (see also Awards for All)
Birmingham International Airport Community Trust Fund
The Tony Bramall Charitable Trust
The British Dietetic Association General and Education Trust Fund
The Derek Butler Trust
Chest Heart and Stroke Scotland
The Colt Foundation
The Marjorie Coote Old People's Charity
The Cotton Trust
Disability Aid Fund (The Roger and Jean Jefcoate Trust)
*Genetic Disorders UK**
The Health Foundation
Heart Research UK
The Hope Trust
The Hospital Saturday Fund
Human Relief Foundation
The Innocent Foundation
The Allen Lane Foundation
The Enid Linder Foundation
Trust for London
*Maudsley Charity**
Merchant Taylors' Consolidated Charities for the Infirm
Mercury Phoenix Trust
John Moores Foundation
The Community Foundation for Northern Ireland
People's Health Trust
*Prostate Cancer UK**
The Joseph Rank Trust
Responsible Gambling Trust (GambleAware)
Rosca Trust
The Roughley Charitable Trust
The Saga Charitable Trust
Sodexo Stop Hunger Foundation
*Tropical Health and Education Trust**
The Wellcome Trust
Westway Trust
*York Children's Trust**

Medical ethics

The Joseph Rank Trust
The Wellcome Trust

Overseas aid/projects

The A. S. Charitable Trust
The Acacia Charitable Trust
The Accenture Foundation
Age UK
Aid to the Church in Need (UK)
Ajahma Charitable Trust
The Alborada Trust
The Alchemy Foundation
The Allen & Overy Foundation*
The Allen Trust
The Ancaster Trust*
The Anchor Foundation
The Andrew Anderson Trust
Anglo American Group Foundation
The Apax Foundation
The Ardwick Trust
Ove Arup Partnership Charitable Trust
The Asfari Foundation*
The Ashworth Charitable Trust
The Ian Askew Charitable Trust
The Associated Country Women of the World
The Bagri Foundation
The Austin Bailey Foundation
The Baring Foundation
The Bartlett Taylor Charitable Trust
The Bay Tree Charitable Trust
The Becht Family Charitable Trust*
The John Beckwith Charitable Trust
The Benham Charitable Settlement
The Bestway Foundation
BHP Billiton Sustainable Communities*
The Big Lottery Fund (see also Awards for All)
The Blandford Lake Trust
Bloom Foundation
The Boltini Trust
The Borrows Charitable Trust*
The Breadsticks Foundation
The British and Foreign School Society
British Council for Prevention of Blindness (Save Eyes Everywhere)
The Consuelo and Anthony Brooke Charitable Trust
The Noel Buxton Trust
The William A. Cadbury Charitable Trust
CAFOD (Catholic Agency for Overseas Development)
Calleva Foundation
The Cheruby Trust
The Childwick Trust
Christadelphian Samaritan Fund
Christian Aid
Stephen Clark 1957 Charitable Trust
J. A. Clark Charitable Trust
The Clark Foundation*
The Clover Trust
Denise Coates Foundation
The Vivienne and Samuel Cohen Charitable Trust
The Coltstaple Trust
Comic Relief
The Thomas Cook Chidlren's Charity*
The Gershon Coren Charitable Foundation (also known as The Muriel and Gus Coren Charitable Foundation)
Michael Cornish Charitable Trust
The Cotton Trust
The Craps Charitable Trust
Credit Suisse EMEA Foundation*
The Cumber Family Charitable Trust
The Biss Davies Charitable Trust*
Dawat-E-Hadiyah Trust (United Kingdom)*
The Roger De Haan Charitable Trust*
The De La Rue Charitable Trust*
Debenhams Foundation
The Diageo Foundation
The Dischma Charitable Trust
The Dorus Trust
The Dulverton Trust
Echoes Of Service
The Ecology Trust
The Gilbert and Eileen Edgar Foundation
The Englefield Charitable Trust
The Epigoni Trust
The Ericson Trust
The Estelle Trust
Euro Charity Trust
The Expat Foundation
The Farthing Trust
Allan and Nesta Ferguson Charitable Settlement
The Earl Fitzwilliam Charitable Trust
The Follett Trust
Forest Hill Charitable Trust
Donald Forrester Trust
The Anna Rosa Forster Charitable Trust
The Forte Charitable Trust
The Freshfield Foundation
G. M. C. Trust
The Galanthus Trust
The Gatsby Charitable Foundation
The Jacqueline and Michael Gee Charitable Trust
The Generations Foundation
The Genesis Charitable Trust*
The Gibbs Charitable Trust
Global Care
The Goldman Sachs Charitable Gift Fund (UK)
Goldman Sachs Gives (UK)
The Goodman Foundation
The Green Hall Foundation
The Grimmitt Trust
The Walter Guinness Charitable Trust
H. C. D. Memorial Fund
The Hadley Trust
The Alfred Haines Charitable Trust
The Haramead Trust
Harbinson Charitable Trust
The Harbour Foundation
The Hartley Charitable Trust
The Hasluck Charitable Trust
The Hathaway Trust
The Hawthorne Charitable Trust
The Charles Hayward Foundation
The Headley Trust
Heb Ffin (Without Frontier)*
The Charlotte Heber-Percy Charitable Trust
The Michael Heller Charitable Foundation
The Simon Heller Charitable Settlement
Henderson Firstfruits*
Philip Henman Trust
The Hilden Charitable Fund
The Hillier Trust
R. G. Hills Charitable Trust
The Hinduja Foundation
Hockerill Educational Foundation
The Hollick Family Charitable Trust
The Thomas J. Horne Memorial Trust
Human Relief Foundation
The Hunter Foundation
The Hunting Horn General Charitable Trust
Ibrahim Foundation Ltd
The Indigo Trust
The Innocent Foundation
Interserve Employee Foundation Ltd
Investream Charitable Trust
The J. J. Charitable Trust
John Jarrold Trust Ltd
The Jephcott Charitable Trust
The Jerusalem Trust
Joffe Charitable Trust
The Elton John AIDS Foundation (EJAF)
The Joron Charitable Trust
The Cyril and Eve Jumbo Charitable Trust
The Jusaca Charitable Trust
The K. P. Ladd Charitable Trust
Maurice and Hilda Laing Charitable Trust

The David Laing Foundation
The Kirby Laing Foundation
The Martin Laing Foundation
The Beatrice Laing Trust
The Leonard Laity Stoate Charitable Trust
*The Lancashire Foundation**
Lancaster Foundation
Mrs F. B. Laurence Charitable Trust
Lawson Beckman Charitable Trust
The William Leech Charity
David and Ruth Lewis Family Charitable Trust
The Linbury Trust
The Lindley Foundation (TLF)
The Lister Charitable Trust
Lloyd's Charities Trust
Lloyds TSB Foundation for Scotland
Localtrent Ltd
*P. and M. Lovell Charitable Settlement**
Paul Lunn-Rockliffe Charitable Trust
Lord and Lady Lurgan Trust
The Lyndhurst Trust
The Madeline Mabey Trust
The Mackintosh Foundation
The Mactaggart Third Fund
The Manoukian Charitable Foundation
The Ann and David Marks Foundation
The Marr-Munning Trust
*Masonic Charitable Foundation**
The Matliwala Family Charitable Trust
The Violet Mauray Charitable Trust
The Millfield Trust
The Mirianog Trust
The Brian Mitchell Charitable Settlement
The Mittal Foundation
The Mizpah Trust
*Moondance Foundation**
The Morel Charitable Trust
The Morgan Charitable Foundation
The Diana and Allan Morgenthau Charitable Trust
The Morris Charitable Trust
Vyoel Moshe Charitable Trust
The Edwina Mountbatten and Leonora Children's Foundation
The Frederick Mulder Foundation
The Music Sales Charitable Trust
Muslim Hands
National Committee of the Women's World Day of Prayer for England and Wales and Northern Ireland
Network for Social Change Charitable Trust
The Norton Rose Fulbright Charitable Foundation
The Father O'Mahoney Memorial Trust
The Oakdale Trust
Odin Charitable Trust
Oizer Charitable Trust
*The Onaway Trust**
Open Gate
Oxfam (GB)
The Paget Charitable Trust
The Park House Charitable Trust
Susanna Peake Charitable Trust
The Persson Charitable Trust
The George and Esme Pollitzer Charitable Settlement
The Portrack Charitable Trust
The J. E. Posnansky Charitable Trust
David and Elaine Potter Foundation
The W. L. Pratt Charitable Trust
The Prince of Wales's Charitable Foundation
The Puebla Charitable Trust
The Puri Foundation
*Quercus Foundation**
The Bishop Radford Trust
The Ranworth Trust
The Eleanor Rathbone Charitable Trust
The Rhododendron Trust
The Clive and Sylvia Richards Charity Ltd
The River Farm Foundation
Rivers Foundation
Robyn Charitable Trust
The Roddick Foundation
The Richard Rogers Charitable Settlement
The Sir James Roll Charitable Trust
*Rozelle Trust**
The Michael and Nicola Sacher Charitable Trust
The Saga Charitable Trust
The Alan and Babette Sainsbury Charitable Fund
The Salamander Charitable Trust
The Basil Samuel Charitable Trust
The M. J. Samuel Charitable Trust
The Samworth Foundation
The Sandhu Charitable Foundation
*The Save the Children Fund**
Schroder Charity Trust
Scott (Eredine) Charitable Trust
The Scouloudi Foundation
The SDL Foundation
The Seedfield Trust
The Shanley Charitable Trust
The Shanti Charitable Trust
The Archie Sherman Cardiff Foundation
The Archie Sherman Charitable Trust
The Shoe Zone Trust
Rita and David Slowe Charitable Trust
The SMB Trust
The N. Smith Charitable Settlement
The Souter Charitable Trust
The W. F. Southall Trust
Spar Charitable Fund
The Stafford Trust
The Staples Trust
The Peter Stebbings Memorial Charity
Stevenson Family's Charitable Trust
Sir Halley Stewart Trust
The Stewarts Law Foundation
The Stobart Newlands Charitable Trust
The Stone Family Foundation
*Surgo Foundation UK Ltd**
The Sutasoma Trust
The Gay and Keith Talbot Trust
The Tanner Trust
C. B. and H. H. Taylor 1984 Trust
Tearfund
The C. Paul Thackray General Charitable Trust
The Thornton Trust
The Three Oaks Trust
Mrs R. P. Tindall's Charitable Trust
The Tinsley Foundation
The Tisbury Telegraph Trust
The Tolkien Trust
The Toy Trust
The Constance Travis Charitable Trust
*Tropical Health and Education Trust**
The True Colours Trust
*The Trysil Charitable Trust**
The Roger and Douglas Turner Charitable Trust
Ulting Overseas Trust
*The Utley Family Charitable Trust**
The Valentine Charitable Trust
The Albert Van Den Bergh Charitable Trust
The Van Neste Foundation
The Vandervell Foundation
The Vardy Foundation
Virgin Atlantic Foundation
The Virgin Foundation (Virgin Unite)

The Vodafone Foundation
The Waterloo Foundation
The Watson Family Charitable Trust*
The Westcroft Trust
The Westminster Foundation
The Harold Hyam Wingate Foundation
The Wixamtree Trust
The Wood Foundation
The Wyndham Charitable Trust
Zephyr Charitable Trust
The Zochonis Charitable Trust
Zurich Community Trust (UK) Ltd

Philanthropy and the voluntary sector

The Edward and Dorothy Cadbury Trust
Calouste Gulbenkian Foundation – UK Branch
The Comino Foundation
The Joseph Strong Frazer Trust
The W. A. Handley Charity Trust
The Hull and East Riding Charitable Trust
Community Foundations for Lancashire and Merseyside
Lloyds Bank Foundation for the Channel Islands
The Millfield House Foundation (1)
The Frederick Mulder Foundation
Nesta*
The Pears Family Charitable Foundation
The Joseph Rowntree Charitable Trust
The Tudor Trust
Two Ridings Community Foundation
The Westminster Foundation
Wiltshire Community Foundation
The Wood Foundation
The South Yorkshire Community Foundation

Voluntarism

The Big Lottery Fund (see also Awards for All)
Esmée Fairbairn Foundation
Gatwick Airport Community Trust
Heart of England Community Foundation
The Hemby Charitable Trust
The Henry C. Hoare Charitable Trust
The Allen Lane Foundation
The William Leech Charity
The Mark Leonard Trust
The London Community Foundation (LCF)
London Housing Foundation Ltd (LHF)
Lord Mayor of Manchester's Charity Appeal Trust
Milton Keynes Community Foundation Ltd
John Moores Foundation
The Jack Petchey Foundation
The Prince Philip Trust Fund*
Mrs L. D. Rope's Third Charitable Settlement
The Slaughter and May Charitable Trust
UnLtd (Foundation for Social Entrepreneurs)
Voluntary Action Fund (VAF)
The Wakeham Trust
Wales Council for Voluntary Action
Waynflete Charitable Trust

Community participation

The Big Lottery Fund (see also Awards for All)
The Hemby Charitable Trust
The Mark Leonard Trust
The Jack Petchey Foundation
The Prince Philip Trust Fund*
The Slaughter and May Charitable Trust
UnLtd (Foundation for Social Entrepreneurs)
The Wakeham Trust

Development of volunteers

Gatwick Airport Community Trust
The William Leech Charity
Mrs L. D. Rope's Third Charitable Settlement

Voluntary sector capacity building

The Asfari Foundation*
The Baring Foundation
The Barrow Cadbury Trust
The City Bridge Trust (Bridge House Estates)
The Legal Education Foundation*
Liverpool Charity and Voluntary Services (LCVS)
Trust for London
The London Community Foundation (LCF)
R. W. Mann Trust
John Moores Foundation
The Transform Foundation*
The Triangle Trust (1949) Fund
Tropical Health and Education Trust*
Voluntary Action Fund (VAF)
Wales Council for Voluntary Action
Walton on Thames Charity
The Wates Foundation
Waynflete Charitable Trust
The Westcroft Trust

Religious activities

The John Armitage Charitable Trust
The Austin Bailey Foundation
The Bellahouston Bequest Fund
Callander Charitable Trust
The Carpenters' Company Charitable Trust
The B. G. S. Cayzer Charitable Trust
Chartered Accountants' Livery Charity (CALC)
The Chownes Foundation
Church of Ireland Priorities Fund
The Catherine Cookson Charitable Trust
The Keith Coombs Trust
The Duke of Cornwall's Benevolent Fund
The Crerar Hotels Trust
The Cross Trust
Dorset Community Foundation
County Durham Community Foundation
Echoes Of Service
The Gerald Palmer Eling Trust Company
The F. P. Ltd Charitable Trust
The Thomas Farr Charity
The Fort Foundation
The Hugh Fraser Foundation
The Joseph Strong Frazer Trust
The Fulmer Charitable Trust
The G. C. Gibson Charitable Trust
A. and S. Graham Charitable Trust
The Kathleen Hannay Memorial Charity
The Haramead Trust
Harbinson Charitable Trust
The Harbour Foundation
The Hinduja Foundation
The Henry C. Hoare Charitable Trust
The Hobson Charity Ltd
The Jane Hodge Foundation
The Mary Homfray Charitable Trust
The Inlight Trust
John Jarrold Trust Ltd
The Joicey Trust
The Nancy Kenyon Charitable Trust
Duchy of Lancaster Benevolent Fund
The R. J. Larg Family Charitable Trust
Mrs F. B. Laurence Charitable Trust
The Lennox Hannay Charitable Trust
Lord Leverhulme's Charitable Trust
Paul Lunn-Rockliffe Charitable Trust
The Mactaggart Third Fund
*The Master Charitable Trust**
The Millward Charitable Trust
The Moss Family Charitable Trust
The Music Sales Charitable Trust
The Worshipful Company of Needlemakers' Charitable Fund
Pollywally Charitable Trust
The Joseph Rank Trust
Rashbass Family Trust
The Rofeh Trust
The Sandhu Charitable Foundation
*The Martin Smith Foundation**
The R. C. Snelling Charitable Trust
*The Street Foundation**
Sutton Coldfield Charitable Trust
The Tompkins Foundation
Community Foundation serving Tyne and Wear and Northumberland
The Garfield Weston Foundation

Christianity

Aid to the Church in Need (UK)
Allchurches Trust Ltd
Andrews Charitable Trust
Buckingham Trust
Criffel Charitable Trust
Dromintee Trust
Fisherbeck Charitable Trust
G. F. Eyre Charitable Trust
Grace Charitable Trust
*Heb Ffin (Without Frontier)**
*Henderson Firstfruits**
Hinchley Charitable Trust
*Ibbett Trust**
*International Bible Students Association**
John Martin's Charity
*M. V. Hillhouse Trust**
Maurice and Hilda Laing Charitable Trust
Mrs L. D. Rope's Third Charitable Settlement
*Mrs L. D. Rope's Second Charitable Settlement**
P. Leigh-Bramwell Trust 'E'
Rhondda Cynon Taff Welsh Church Acts Fund
Sir Halley Stewart Trust
St Peter's Saltley Trust
Tearfund
The A. S. Charitable Trust
The Anchor Foundation
*The Barrack Charitable Trust**
The Bassil Shippam and Alsford Trust
The Beatrice Laing Trust
The Benham Charitable Settlement
The Bishop of Guildford's Foundation
The Bowerman Charitable Trust
The Bowland Charitable Trust
The C. Paul Thackray General Charitable Trust
The Charles Littlewood Hill Trust
The Clover Trust
The Costa Family Charitable Trust
The Dorcas Trust
The Dulverton Trust
The Dyers' Company Charitable Trust
The Edgar Milward Charity
The Elaine and Angus Lloyd Charitable Trust
The Farthing Trust
The Ganzoni Charitable Trust
The Gloag Foundation
The Goshen Trust
The Harry Bottom Charitable Trust
The Hillier Trust
The Hintze Family Charity Foundation
The Homestead Charitable Trust
The Hope Trust
The Hunting Horn General Charitable Trust
The Hutton Foundation
*The Hyde Park Place Estate Charity – civil trustees**
The Iliffe Family Charitable Trust
The Jack Patston Charitable Trust
The James Pantyfedwen Foundation
The John Apthorp Charity
The K. P. Ladd Charitable Trust
The Kirby Laing Foundation
The Lady Tangye Charitable Trust Ltd
The Leonard Laity Stoate Charitable Trust
*The Lethendy Charitable Trust**
The Lind Trust
The Liz and Terry Bramall Foundation
The Lyndhurst Trust
The Mallinckrodt Foundation
The Marsh Christian Trust
The Mason Porter Charitable Trust
The Mercers' Charitable Foundation
The Merchant Taylors' Company Charities Fund
The Millfield Trust
The Mizpah Trust

P. G. and N. J. Boulton Trust
The Sants Charitable Trust
The Scarfe Charitable Trust
The Seedfield Trust
The Seven Fifty Trust
The Simon Gibson Charitable Trust
The SMB Trust
The Souter Charitable Trust
The Squires Foundation
The Tisbury Telegraph Trust
The Tory Family Foundation
The Toye Foundation
The Tufton Charitable Trust
The Van Neste Foundation
Ulting Overseas Trust

Christian causes

The Andrew Anderson Trust
The André Christian Trust
The Archer Trust
The Ashburnham Thanksgiving Trust
The Baird Trust
The Blandford Lake Trust
Bristol Archdeaconry Charity
Church Urban Fund
The John Grant Davies Trust*
The Englefield Charitable Trust
Fishmongers' Company's Charitable Trust
Forest Hill Charitable Trust
The Forte Charitable Trust
The Anne French Memorial Trust
The Gibbs Charitable Trust
The Girdlers' Company Charitable Trust
Global Care
Philip and Judith Green Trust
The Alfred Haines Charitable Trust
Sir Harold Hood's Charitable Trust
The Jerusalem Trust
Langdale Trust
The Herd Lawson and Muriel Lawson Charitable Trust
The William Leech Charity
The Martin Charitable Trust*
National Committee of the Women's World Day of Prayer for England and Wales and Northern Ireland
The Norwood and Newton Settlement
The Owen Family Trust
The Panacea Charitable Trust
The Park House Charitable Trust
Quothquan Trust
The River Trust
The Salamander Charitable Trust
Sarum St Michael Educational Charity*
The Shanti Charitable Trust
Stewards' Company Ltd
The Stobart Newlands Charitable Trust
Mrs R. P. Tindall's Charitable Trust
The Vardy Foundation
The Whitecourt Charitable Trust

Christian churches

The A. S. Charitable Trust
Age Scotland
Aid to the Church in Need (UK)
Allchurches Trust Ltd
The H. B. Allen Charitable Trust
Sir John and Lady Amory's Charitable Trust
Viscount Amory's Charitable Trust
The AMW Charitable Trust
The Ancaster Trust*
The Anchor Foundation
The Andrew Anderson Trust
The Mary Andrew Charitable Trust
The Anne Duchess of Westminster's Charity*
The John Armitage Charitable Trust
The Armourers' and Brasiers' Gauntlet Trust
The Ashley Family Foundation
The Astor Foundation
The Atlas Fund
The Aurelius Charitable Trust
Awards for All (see also the Big Lottery Fund)
The Austin Bailey Foundation
The Baird Trust
The Banbury Charities
The Barbour Foundation
The Barham Charitable Trust
Lord Barnby's Foundation
The Barnsbury Charitable Trust
The Paul Bassham Charitable Trust
BBC Children in Need
The Bearder Charity
The James Beattie Charitable Trust
The Bedfordshire and Hertfordshire Historic Churches Trust
The Bellahouston Bequest Fund
The Benham Charitable Settlement
The Rowan Bentall Charitable Trust*
The Big Lottery Fund (see also Awards for All)
Percy Bilton Charity
The Bingham Trust
Birmingham International Airport Community Trust Fund
The Sydney Black Charitable Trust
Isabel Blackman Foundation
The Blagrave Trust
The Booth Charities
The Oliver Borthwick Memorial Trust
The Harry Bottom Charitable Trust
P. G. and N. J. Boulton Trust
The Bowland Charitable Trust
The Liz and Terry Bramall Foundation
Bristol Archdeaconry Charity
Bristol Charities
The British and Foreign Bible Society*
The J. and M. Britton Charitable Trust
The T. B. H. Brunner's Charitable Settlement
The Jack Brunton Charitable Trust
Buckingham Trust
The Buckinghamshire Historic Churches Trust
Consolidated Charity of Burton upon Trent
The Edward and Dorothy Cadbury Trust
CAFOD (Catholic Agency for Overseas Development)
The Carrington Charitable Trust
The Leslie Mary Carter Charitable Trust
The Catholic Charitable Trust
The Catholic Trust for England and Wales
The CBD Charitable Trust
CEO Sleepout
The Chadwick Educational Foundation*
John Christie Trust*
Church Burgesses Trust
Church of Ireland Priorities Fund
Church Urban Fund
The City Bridge Trust (Bridge House Estates)
Stephen Clark 1957 Charitable Trust
The Clark Foundation*
The Clothworkers' Foundation
Richard Cloudesley's Charity
The Robert Clutterbuck Charitable Trust
The Francis Coales Charitable Foundation
The Coalfields Regeneration Trust
The Cobtree Charity Trust Ltd
The Sir Jeremiah Colman Gift Trust
Colyer-Fergusson Charitable Trust
Community First (Landfill Communities Fund)

The Congregational and General Charitable Trust
The Catherine Cookson Charitable Trust
The Keith Coombs Trust
The Helen Jean Cope Trust
The Worshipful Company of Cordwainers Charitable Trusts (Minges Gift and the Pooled Trusts)
Michael Cornish Charitable Trust
The Duke of Cornwall's Benevolent Fund
The Cornwell Charitable Trust
The Costa Family Charitable Trust
The County Council of Dyfed Welsh Curch Fund
The Sir Tom Cowie Charitable Trust
Criffel Charitable Trust
Cripplegate Foundation
The Croydon Relief in Need Charities
The Ronald Cruickshanks Foundation
The Cumber Family Charitable Trust
The Davidson (Nairn) Charitable Trust
Margaret Davies Charity
The Hamilton Davies Trust
The Davis Foundation
The De Brye Charitable Trust
The Roger De Haan Charitable Trust*
The Devon Historic Churches Trust
The Duke of Devonshire's Charitable Trust
The Sandy Dewhirst Charitable Trust
The Derek and Eileen Dodgson Foundation
Dorset Community Foundation
The Dorset Historic Churches Trust
The Dorus Trust
The Dumbreck Charity
County Durham Community Foundation
Echoes Of Service
The Gilbert and Eileen Edgar Foundation
Edinburgh Trust No 2 Account
The Maud Elkington Charitable Trust
The Emerald Foundation*
The Englefield Charitable Trust
The Enkalon Foundation
Esher House Charitable Trust
The Essex Heritage Trust
The Alan Evans Memorial Trust
The Everard Foundation
G. F. Eyre Charitable Trust
The Fairstead Trust
Famos Foundation Trust
The Farthing Trust
The Doris Field Charitable Trust
The Fifty Fund
Dixie Rose Findlay Charitable Trust
Fisherbeck Charitable Trust
The Earl Fitzwilliam Charitable Trust
The Forte Charitable Trust
Jill Franklin Trust
Friends of Essex Churches Trust
The Friends of Kent Churches
Friends Provident Charitable Foundation
The Gale Family Charity Trust
The Ganzoni Charitable Trust
The Simon Gibson Charitable Trust
The Girdlers' Company Charitable Trust
The Gloag Foundation
The Gloucestershire Historic Churches Trust
Worshipful Company of Glovers of London Charitable Trust
The Godinton Charitable Trust
The Golsoncott Foundation
The Goshen Trust
The Gould Charitable Trust
The J. G. Graves Charitable Trust
The Gray Trust
The Green Hall Foundation
Philip and Judith Green Trust
The Grimmitt Trust
The Grocers' Charity
The Bishop of Guildford's Foundation
The Hadrian Trust
The Hampshire and Islands Historic Churches Trust
The Hampstead Wells and Campden Trust
Hampton Fuel Allotment Charity
The W. A. Handley Charity Trust
The Kathleen Hannay Memorial Charity
Harbo Charities Ltd
William Harding's Charity
The Headley Trust
The Charlotte Heber-Percy Charitable Trust
The Percy Hedley 1990 Charitable Trust
Help the Homeless Ltd
The Helping Foundation
The Herefordshire Historic Churches Trust
The Hesslewood Children's Trust (Hull Seamen's and General Orphanage)
P. and C. Hickinbotham Charitable Trust
The Hilden Charitable Fund
M. V. Hillhouse Trust*
The Hillier Trust
The Hillingdon Community Trust
R. G. Hills Charitable Trust
The Hintze Family Charity Foundation
Hockerill Educational Foundation
The Jane Hodge Foundation
The Holden Charitable Trust
The Dorothy Holmes Charitable Trust
The Holywood Trust
The Homelands Charitable Trust
The Mary Homfray Charitable Trust
Sir Harold Hood's Charitable Trust
The Hope Trust
The Horizon Foundation
The Hospital of God at Greatham
The Hull and East Riding Charitable Trust
The Humanitarian Trust
The Albert Hunt Trust
The Hunting Horn General Charitable Trust
Huntingdon Freemen's Trust
The Hyde Park Place Estate Charity – civil trustees*
The Idlewild Trust
The Iliffe Family Charitable Trust
The Ironmongers' Company
The J. and J. Benevolent Foundation
The J. A. R. Charitable Trust
The Jarman Charitable Trust
John Jarrold Trust Ltd
The Jenour Foundation
The Jerusalem Trust
The Joicey Trust
The Nancy Kenyon Charitable Trust
The Kildare Trust*
The King Henry VIII Endowed Trust – Warwick
The Mary Kinross Charitable Trust
The Kohn Foundation
Kollel and Co. Ltd
The K. P. Ladd Charitable Trust
Maurice and Hilda Laing Charitable Trust
The Kirby Laing Foundation
The Beatrice Laing Trust
Duchy of Lancaster Benevolent Fund
The Jack Lane Charitable Trust
The Allen Lane Foundation
Laslett's (Hinton) Charity
The Lauffer Family Charitable Foundation

The Edgar E. Lawley Foundation
The Herd Lawson and Muriel Lawson Charitable Trust
The Leche Trust
The William Leech Charity
Leicester and Leicestershire Historic Churches Preservation Trust (Leicestershire Historic Churches Trust)
*Leicestershire and Rutland Masonic Charity Association**
Leicestershire, Leicester and Rutland Community Foundation
P. Leigh-Bramwell Trust 'E'
The Lennox Hannay Charitable Trust
The Sir Edward Lewis Foundation
Limoges Charitable Trust
The Linbury Trust
The Lind Trust
Lindale Educational Foundation
The Enid Linder Foundation
The Ruth and Stuart Lipton Charitable Trust
The Charles Littlewood Hill Trust
The Second Joseph Aaron Littman Foundation
Jack Livingstone Charitable Trust
The Elaine and Angus Lloyd Charitable Trust
*The Lockwood Charitable Foundation**
Trust for London
The Lower Green Foundation
The C. L. Loyd Charitable Trust
The Lyndhurst Trust
The Lynn Foundation
John Lyon's Charity
Sylvanus Lysons Charity
The Ian Mactaggart Trust (The Mactaggart Second Fund)
The Magdalen and Lasher Charity (General Fund)
The Manifold Charitable Trust
R. W. Mann Trust
Charity of John Marshall
Charlotte Marshall Charitable Trust
D. G. Marshall of Cambridge Trust
Sir George Martin Trust
John Martin's Charity
The Mason Porter Charitable Trust
The Medlock Charitable Trust
The Mercers' Charitable Foundation
The Merchant Taylors' Company Charities Fund
The Merchant Venturers' Charity
The Millfield Trust
The Millichope Foundation
The Millward Charitable Trust
The Edgar Milward Charity
The Peter Minet Trust
Mobbs Memorial Trust Ltd
The Monmouthshire County Council Welsh Church Act Fund
The George A. Moore Foundation
Vyoel Moshe Charitable Trust
The Music Sales Charitable Trust
The National Churches Trust
The National Express Foundation
*The Norfolk Churches Trust Ltd**
Norfolk Community Foundation
*Provincial Grand Charity of Northamptonshire and Huntingdonshire**
Northamptonshire Community Foundation
The Northumbria Historic Churches Trust
Norwich Town Close Estate Charity
The Norwood and Newton Settlement
The Notgrove Trust
The Nottinghamshire Historic Churches Trust
The Father O'Mahoney Memorial Trust
The Oakdale Trust
The Ogle Christian Trust
The Oldham Foundation
The Olga Charitable Trust
The Ouseley Church Music Trust
The Owen Family Trust
*Oxfordshire Historic Churches Trust**
The James Pantyfedwen Foundation
*Parish Estate of the Church of St Michael Spurriergate York**
The Jack Patston Charitable Trust
The Pennycress Trust
The Pilgrim Trust
*Powys Welsh Church Fund**
Sir John Priestman Charity Trust
*The Prince Philip Trust Fund**
Mr and Mrs J. A. Pye's Charitable Settlement
Quothquan Trust
The Bishop Radford Trust
The Rank Foundation Ltd
The Joseph Rank Trust
The Ratcliff Foundation
The Sir James Reckitt Charity
Rhondda Cynon Taff Welsh Church Acts Fund
Daisie Rich Trust
The Clive and Sylvia Richards Charity Ltd
The River Trust
*Robertson Hall Trust**
Mrs L. D. Rope's Third Charitable Settlement
Rosca Trust
The Rose Foundation
*The Cissie Rosefield Charitable Trust**
The Rothermere Foundation
The Rowlands Trust
The Rugby Group Benevolent Fund Ltd
The Saddlers' Company Charitable Fund
Saint Sarkis Charity Trust
The Salamander Charitable Trust
*The Salisbury New Pool Settlement**
Salters' Charitable Foundation
The Sants Charitable Trust
*Sarum St Michael Educational Charity**
The Scarfe Charitable Trust
The Seedfield Trust
The Seven Fifty Trust
The Shanti Charitable Trust
The Sylvia and Colin Shepherd Charitable Trust
The Shipwrights' Company Charitable Fund
SITA Cornwall Trust Ltd
The Charles Skey Charitable Trust
The R. C. Snelling Charitable Trust
*Somerset Community Foundation**
The Worshipful Company of Spectacle Makers' Charity
The Jessie Spencer Trust
The Spoore, Merry and Rixman Foundation
The Spurrell Charitable Trust
The St Hilda's Trust
St Luke's College Foundation
St Peter's Saltley Trust
The Stanley Foundation Ltd
The Steel Charitable Trust
The Hugh Stenhouse Foundation
Stevenson Family's Charitable Trust
Sir Halley Stewart Trust
The Stobart Newlands Charitable Trust
M. J. C. Stone Charitable Trust
*The Stoneygate Trust**
The Samuel Storey Family Charitable Trust
Stratford upon Avon Town Trust
*The Street Foundation**

The Suffolk Historic Churches Trust
Sunninghill Fuel Allotment Trust*
Sutton Coldfield Charitable Trust
The Adrian Swire Charitable Trust
Tabeel Trust
The Talbot Village Trust
Tallow Chandlers Benevolent Fund No. 2
The Lady Tangye Charitable Trust Ltd
The Tanner Trust
C. B. and H. H. Taylor 1984 Trust
Tearfund
The Thornton Trust
Mrs R. P. Tindall's Charitable Trust
The Tisbury Telegraph Trust
The Tompkins Foundation
The Toye Foundation
The Constance Travis Charitable Trust
The Tufton Charitable Trust
The Roger and Douglas Turner Charitable Trust
Community Foundation serving Tyne and Wear and Northumberland
Ulting Overseas Trust
Vale of Glamorgan Welsh Church Fund
The Albert Van Den Bergh Charitable Trust
The Vardy Foundation
Viridor Credits Environmental Company*
Wade's Charity
The Scurrah Wainwright Charity
The Wakefield and Tetley Trust
The Walker Trust
Mrs N. E. M. Warren's Charitable Trust*
Warwick Relief in Need Charity*
Mrs Waterhouse Charitable Trust
The Wates Foundation
The Geoffrey Watling Charity*
The William Webster Charitable Trust
The Welton Foundation
West Derby Waste Lands Charity
The Westcroft Trust
The Westminster Foundation
The Garfield Weston Foundation
The Barbara Whatmore Charitable Trust
The Whitaker Charitable Trust
The Whitecourt Charitable Trust
The Norman Whiteley Trust
The HDH Wills 1965 Charitable Trust
Dame Violet Wills Charitable Trust
The Wilmcote Charitrust
Wiltshire Community Foundation
The Wixamtree Trust
The Wolfson Foundation
The James Wood Bequest Fund
The Wyndham Charitable Trust
The Yorkshire Historic Churches Trust
The William Allen Young Charitable Trust
The Marjorie and Arnold Ziff Charitable Foundation

Ecumenicalism

The Gibbs Charitable Trust
Mariapolis Ltd

Missionary work, evangelism

The André Christian Trust
The Armourers' and Brasiers' Gauntlet Trust
The British and Foreign Bible Society*
John Christie Trust*
Philip and Judith Green Trust
Hockerill Educational Foundation
The Jerusalem Trust
Lancaster Foundation
National Committee of the Women's World Day of Prayer for England and Wales and Northern Ireland
The Father O'Mahoney Memorial Trust
The Ogle Christian Trust
The Owen Family Trust
The Persson Charitable Trust
Quothquan Trust
The River Trust
Stewards' Company Ltd
Tabeel Trust
The Thornton Trust
The Norman Whiteley Trust
Dame Violet Wills Charitable Trust

Inter-faith activities

All Saints Educational Trust
The Edward Cadbury Charitable Trust
The Edith Maud Ellis 1985 Charitable Trust
The Exilarch's Foundation
The Anne French Memorial Trust
The Harbour Charitable Trust
The Humanitarian Trust
The C. L. Loyd Charitable Trust
Mariapolis Ltd
The Community Foundation for Northern Ireland
The Rayne Trust
The Sir James Roll Charitable Trust
The Michael Sacher Charitable Trust
The Spalding Trust*
The Sigmund Sternberg Charitable Foundation
Sir Halley Stewart Trust
Roger Vere Foundation

Islam

Dawat-E-Hadiyah Trust (United Kingdom)*
Euro Charity Trust
The Matliwala Family Charitable Trust
Muslim Hands

Judaism

4 Charity Foundation
A. W. Charitable Trust
The Aberdeen Foundation
The Acacia Charitable Trust
Achisomoch Aid Company Ltd
Adenfirst Ltd
The Alliance Family Foundation
AM Charitable Trust
Amabrill Ltd
Anpride Ltd
The Ardwick Trust
The Baker Charitable Trust
The Andrew Balint Charitable Trust
Bay Charitable Trust
BCH Trust
Bear Mordechai Ltd
Beauland Ltd
The Becker Family Charitable Trust
Belljoe Tzedoko Ltd
The Ruth Berkowitz Charitable Trust
Asser Bishvil Foundation*
The Bertie Black Foundation
The Sir Victor Blank Charitable Settlement
The Bluston Charitable Settlement
The Bonamy Charitable Trust
Salo Bordon Charitable Trust
Sir Clive Bourne Family Trust
Bourneheights Ltd
Friends of Boyan Trust
Brushmill Ltd
The Arnold Burton 1998 Charitable Trust

The CH (1980) Charitable Trust
Chalfords Ltd
Charitworth Ltd
The Childwick Trust
The Clore Duffield Foundation
Closehelm Ltd
Clydpride Ltd
The Denise Cohen Charitable Trust
The Vivienne and Samuel Cohen Charitable Trust
Col-Reno Ltd
The Gershon Coren Charitable Foundation (also known as The Muriel and Gus Coren Charitable Foundation)
The Craps Charitable Trust
The Cuby Charitable Trust
Itzchok Meyer Cymerman Trust Ltd
Oizer Dalim Trust
The Davidson Family Charitable Trust
The Davis Foundation
Debmar Benevolent Trust Ltd
The Dellal Foundation
The Desmond Foundation
Alan and Sheila Diamond Charitable Trust
The Djanogly Foundation
The DM Charitable Trust
The Dollond Charitable Trust
The Dorfman Foundation*
The Doughty Charity Trust
Dushinsky Trust Ltd
Elanore Ltd*
The George Elias Charitable Trust
Ellador Ltd
The Ellinson Foundation Ltd
Entindale Ltd
The Esfandi Charitable Foundation
Esher House Charitable Trust
The Eventhall Family Charitable Trust
The Exilarch's Foundation
Extonglen Ltd
Famos Foundation Trust
Fordeve Ltd
The Isaac and Freda Frankel Memorial Charitable Trust
The Raphael Freshwater Memorial Association*
Friends of Biala Ltd
Friends of Wiznitz Ltd
Mejer and Gertrude Miriam Frydman Foundation
The G. R. P. Charitable Trust
The Gertner Charitable Trust
Grahame Charitable Foundation Ltd
M. and R. Gross Charities Ltd
N. and R. Grunbaum Charitable Trust
The Gur Trust
H. P. Charitable Trust
Hadras Kodesh Trust
Harbo Charities Ltd
The Harbour Charitable Trust
The Hathaway Trust
The Maurice Hatter Foundation
The Heathside Charitable Trust
Ernest Hecht Charitable Foundation
The Helping Foundation
Highcroft Charitable Trust
The Holden Charitable Trust
Horwich Shotter Charitable Trust*
The Huntingdon Foundation Ltd
Hurdale Charity Ltd
IGO Foundation Ltd
Investream Charitable Trust
The J. and J. Benevolent Foundation
The Ruth and Lionel Jacobson Trust (Second Fund) No. 2
The Susan and Stephen James Charitable Settlement
Jewish Child's Day (JCD)
The Jewish Youth Fund (JYF)
J. E. Joseph Charitable Fund
The Jusaca Charitable Trust
Kahal Chassidim Bobov
The Bernard Kahn Charitable Trust
The Stanley Kalms Foundation
Karaviotis Foundation
The Kasner Charitable Trust
The Michael and Ilse Katz Foundation
C. S. Kaufman Charitable Trust
Keren Association Ltd
E. and E. Kernkraut Charities Ltd
The Kirschel Foundation
The Kobler Trust
The Kohn Foundation
Kollel and Co. Ltd
Kreditor Charitable Trust
Kupath Gemach Chaim Bechesed Viznitz Trust
The Kyte Charitable Trust
The Lambert Charitable Trust
Largsmount Ltd
The Lauffer Family Charitable Foundation
Lawson Beckman Charitable Trust
The Arnold Lee Charitable Trust
The Kennedy Leigh Charitable Trust
Bernard Lewis Family Charitable Trust*
David and Ruth Lewis Family Charitable Trust
The Ruth and Stuart Lipton Charitable Trust
The Second Joseph Aaron Littman Foundation
Jack Livingstone Charitable Trust
Localtrent Ltd
The Locker Foundation
Loftus Charitable Trust
The Lolev Charitable Trust
LPW Ltd
The Sir Jack Lyons Charitable Trust
M. and C. Trust
M. B. Foundation*
The M. K. Charitable Trust
The M. Y. A. Charitable Trust
The Magen Charitable Trust
The Manackerman Charitable Trust
Marbeh Torah Trust
The Stella and Alexander Margulies Charitable Trust
The Marks Family Foundation
The Ann and David Marks Foundation
The Hilda and Samuel Marks Foundation
The Violet Mauray Charitable Trust
Mayfair Charities Ltd
Maypride Ltd*
Melodor Ltd
Menuchar Ltd
Mercaz Torah Vechesed Ltd
The Laurence Misener Charitable Trust
The Mishcon Family Charitable Trust
Keren Mitzvah Trust
Mole Charitable Trust
The Morgan Charitable Foundation
The Diana and Allan Morgenthau Charitable Trust
The Moshal Charitable Trust
Vyoel Moshe Charitable Trust
The Mosselson Charitable Trust
The Mutual Trust Group
MW (CL) Foundation
MW (GK) Foundation
MW (HO) Foundation
MW (RH) Foundation
Nemoral Ltd
Ner Foundation
Nesswall Ltd
Newpier Charity Ltd
NJD Charitable Trust
North London Charities Ltd*
Oizer Charitable Trust
The Doris Pacey Charitable Foundation
Palmtree Memorial Trust*
The Pears Family Charitable Foundation
B. E. Perl Charitable Trust
The Phillips and Rubens Charitable Trust
The Phillips Family Charitable Trust

The George and Esme Pollitzer Charitable Settlement
Edith and Ferdinand Porjes Charitable Trust
The J. E. Posnansky Charitable Trust
Premishlaner Charitable Trust
R. S. Charitable Trust
Rachel Charitable Trust
The Rayne Trust
The Rest Harrow Trust
Reuben Foundation
Ridgesave Ltd
RJM Charity Trust
Rokach Family Charitable Trust
The Gerald Ronson Family Foundation
*The Cissie Rosefield Charitable Trust**
*Rothschild Foundation (Hanadiv) Europe**
Rowanville Ltd
The Rubin Foundation Charitable Trust
S. F. Foundation
The Michael and Nicola Sacher Charitable Trust
The Michael Sacher Charitable Trust
The Ruzin Sadagora Trust
*Samjo Ltd**
The Schapira Charitable Trust
The Annie Schiff Charitable Trust
The Schmidt-Bodner Charitable Trust
The Schreib Trust
O. and G. Schreiber Charitable Trust
The Schreiber Charitable Trust
The Searchlight Electric Charitable Trust
Sam and Bella Sebba Charitable Trust
Sellata Ltd
The Archie Sherman Cardiff Foundation
The Archie Sherman Charitable Trust
Shlomo Memorial Fund Ltd
*Shulem B. Association Ltd**
David and Jennifer Sieff Charitable Trust
The Sobell Foundation
Solev Co. Ltd
The Solo Charitable Settlement
Songdale Ltd
The E. C. Sosnow Charitable Trust
Sparquote Ltd
Rosalyn and Nicholas Springer Charitable Trust
Springrule Ltd
*The Stanley Charitable Trust**
The Steinberg Family Charitable Trust
C. E. K. Stern Charitable Trust
The Sigmund Sternberg Charitable Foundation
Stervon Ltd
The Strawberry Charitable Trust
Sueberry Ltd
The Alan Sugar Foundation
The Adrienne and Leslie Sussman Charitable Trust
T. and S. Trust Fund
The Tajtelbaum Charitable Trust
*The Talmud Torah Machzikei Hadass Trust**
Talteg Ltd
The David Tannen Charitable Trust
The Lili Tapper Charitable Foundation
Tegham Ltd
Toras Chesed (London) Trust
Truedene Co. Ltd
Truemart Ltd
Trumros Ltd
TVML Foundation
Tzedakah
The Union of Orthodox Hebrew Congregations
The David Uri Memorial Trust
The Vail Foundation
Vivdale Ltd
The Weinstein Foundation
*The Wigoder Family Foundation**
The Williams Family Charitable Trust
The Harold Hyam Wingate Foundation
The Michael and Anna Wix Charitable Trust
The Maurice Wohl Charitable Foundation
The Charles Wolfson Charitable Trust
The Wolfson Family Charitable Trust
Woodlands Green Ltd
The A. and R. Woolf Charitable Trust
Wychdale Ltd
Wychville Ltd
Yankov Charitable Trust
The Marjorie and Arnold Ziff Charitable Foundation
Stephen Zimmerman Charitable Trust

Orthodox Judaism

A. W. Charitable Trust
Achisomoch Aid Company Ltd
Amabrill Ltd
Bay Charitable Trust
Beauland Ltd
The Becker Family Charitable Trust
Belljoe Tzedoko Ltd
Bourneheights Ltd
Friends of Boyan Trust
Chalfords Ltd
Clydpride Ltd
Itzchok Meyer Cymerman Trust Ltd
Oizer Dalim Trust
The Doughty Charity Trust
Dushinsky Trust Ltd
Entindale Ltd
Extonglen Ltd
The Famos Foundation Trust
Fordeve Ltd
The Isaac and Freda Frankel Memorial Charitable Trust
Friends of Biala Ltd
Friends of Wiznitz Ltd
M. and R. Gross Charities Ltd
The Gur Trust
H. P. Charitable Trust
Hadras Kodesh Trust
Harbo Charities Ltd
The Helping Foundation
The Holden Charitable Trust
Hurdale Charity Ltd
The J. and J. Benevolent Foundation
The Stanley Kalms Foundation
E. and E. Kernkraut Charities Ltd
The Kreditor Charitable Trust
Kupath Gemach Chaim Bechesed Viznitz Trust
Largsmount Ltd
Localtrent Ltd
The Lolev Charitable Trust
The M. K. Charitable Trust
The M. Y. A. Charitable Trust
Marbeh Torah Trust
Mayfair Charities Ltd
*Maypride Ltd**
Melodor Ltd
Menuchar Ltd
Mercaz Torah Vechesed Ltd
The Mutual Trust Group
MW (CL) Foundation
MW (GK) Foundation
MW (HO) Foundation
MW (RH) Foundation
Ner Foundation
Nesswall Ltd
Newpier Charity Ltd
*North London Charities Ltd**
Oizer Charitable Trust
B. E. Perl Charitable Trust
Premishlaner Charitable Trust
Rowanville Ltd
*Samjo Ltd**
O. and G. Schreiber Charitable Trust
Sellata Ltd
Sparquote Ltd
Springrule Ltd
C. E. K. Stern Charitable Trust
Stervon Ltd
T. and S. Trust Fund
The Tajtelbaum Charitable Trust

The Talmud Torah Machzikei Hadass Trust*
Talteg Ltd
Tegham Ltd
Toras Chesed (London) Trust
Truemart Ltd
The Union of Orthodox Hebrew Congregations
Vivdale Ltd
Woodlands Green Ltd
Wychdale Ltd
Wychville Ltd

Religious understanding

The Arah Foundation
The Edward Cadbury Charitable Trust
Itzchok Meyer Cymerman Trust Ltd
The Davis Foundation
Didymus
The Doughty Charity Trust
The Anne French Memorial Trust
Ibrahim Foundation Ltd
The Kennedy Leigh Charitable Trust
Mariapolis Ltd
Quothquan Trust
The Rayne Trust
Sir Halley Stewart Trust
The Tolkien Trust

Rights, law and conflict

The 1970 Trust
The A. B. Charitable Trust
The A. S. Charitable Trust
A2BD Foundation UK Ltd*
ABF The Soldiers' Charity
The Addleshaw Goddard Charitable Trust
Ajahma Charitable Trust
The Alchemy Foundation
The Allen & Overy Foundation*
The Arah Foundation
The Ashworth Charitable Trust
The Associated Country Women of the World
The Bank of Scotland Foundation
Barnwood Trust
The Big Lottery Fund (see also Awards for All)
British Gas (Scottish Gas) Energy Trust
The Bromley Trust
The William A. Cadbury Charitable Trust
The Barrow Cadbury Trust
CAFOD (Catholic Agency for Overseas Development)
Calouste Gulbenkian Foundation – UK Branch
Celtic Charity Fund
Christian Aid
J. A. Clark Charitable Trust
The Evan Cornish Foundation
Coutts Charitable Foundation
The Craignish Trust
The Daiwa Anglo-Japanese Foundation
The John Grant Davies Trust*
The Davis Foundation
The Henry and Suzanne Davis Foundation
The Delves Charitable Trust
The Diageo Foundation
The Dulverton Trust
Dunard Fund 2016
County Durham Community Foundation
EDF Energy Trust (EDFET)
The Edith Maud Ellis 1985 Charitable Trust
The Enkalon Foundation
The Ericson Trust
Esmée Fairbairn Foundation
The Farthing Trust
Allan and Nesta Ferguson Charitable Settlement
The Fort Foundation
The Elizabeth Frankland Moore and Star Foundation
Jill Franklin Trust
Friends Provident Charitable Foundation
The Adrian and Jane Frost Charitable Trust
The G. D. Charitable Trust
The Robert Gavron Charitable Trust
The Hemraj Goyal Foundation
Greenham Common Community Trust Ltd
H. C. D. Memorial Fund
The Hadrian Trust
The Alfred Haines Charitable Trust
Paul Hamlyn Foundation
The Helen Hamlyn Trust
Harbinson Charitable Trust
The Maurice Hatter Foundation
The Charles Hayward Foundation
Heart of England Community Foundation
The Hilden Charitable Fund
The Henry C. Hoare Charitable Trust
Human Relief Foundation
The Michael and Shirley Hunt Charitable Trust
The Hunter Foundation
The Indigo Trust
Integrated Education Fund*
The Ireland Fund of Great Britain
Irish Youth Foundation (UK) Ltd (incorporating The Lawlor Foundation)
The J. Isaacs Charitable Trust
The JRSST Charitable Trust
Joffe Charitable Trust
Laura Kinsella Foundation
Robert Kitchin (Saddlers' Company)
Community Foundations for Lancashire and Merseyside
The Lancashire Foundation*
The Allen Lane Foundation
The LankellyChase Foundation
The Law Society Charity
The Legal Education Foundation*
The Kennedy Leigh Charitable Trust
The Leigh Trust
The Lennox Hannay Charitable Trust
The Mark Leonard Trust
Lloyds Bank Foundation for England and Wales
Lloyds TSB Foundation for Scotland
Trust for London
The London Community Foundation (LCF)
London Legal Support Trust (LLST)
John Lyon's Charity
The Sir Jack Lyons Charitable Trust
M. and C. Trust
The Mactaggart Third Fund
The Ian Mactaggart Trust (The Mactaggart Second Fund)
Mariapolis Ltd

Marmot Charitable Trust
The Marr-Munning Trust
Masonic Charitable Foundation*
The Master Charitable Trust*
The Violet Mauray Charitable Trust
John Moores Foundation
The Morel Charitable Trust
The Miles Morland Foundation
The MSE Charity
Muslim Hands
The Nationwide Foundation
Nesta*
Network for Social Change Charitable Trust
The Community Foundation for Northern Ireland
The Nuffield Foundation
The Onaway Trust*
Oxfam (GB)
The Pears Family Charitable Foundation
People's Postcode Trust
The Persula Foundation
Polden-Puckham Charitable Foundation
The Polonsky Foundation
Postcode Community Trust*
David and Elaine Potter Foundation
Powys Welsh Church Fund*
The Professional Footballers' Association Charity*
Quartet Community Foundation
The Rambourg Foundation
The Eleanor Rathbone Charitable Trust
The Sigrid Rausing Trust
The Rayne Trust
Reed Family Foundation
The Roddick Foundation
The Richard Rogers Charitable Settlement
The Joseph Rowntree Charitable Trust
The Alan and Babette Sainsbury Charitable Fund
Santander UK Foundation Ltd
The Save the Children Fund*
The ScottishPower Energy People Trust
The ScottishPower Foundation
Sam and Bella Sebba Charitable Trust
The Severn Trent Water Charitable Trust Fund
Sherburn House Charity*
The Simmons & Simmons Charitable Foundation
The Slaughter and May Charitable Trust
The Henry Smith Charity
The W. F. Southall Trust
Standard Life Foundation*
The Staples Trust
The Stewarts Law Foundation
The Street Foundation*
The Sutasoma Trust
Tearfund
The Three Guineas Trust
The Tinsley Foundation
The Tolkien Trust
The Tudor Trust
United Utilities Trust Fund
Variety The Children's Charity (Variety Club)
The Nigel Vinson Charitable Trust
Voluntary Action Fund (VAF)
The Scurrah Wainwright Charity
The Wakefield and Tetley Trust
Warwick Relief in Need Charity*
The Watson Family Charitable Trust*
Webb Memorial Trust
The Westcroft Trust
The Wood Foundation
Worcester Municipal Charities (CIO)
The Wyndham Charitable Trust
York Children's Trust*
Yorkshire and Clydesdale Bank Foundation

Citizen participation

The Bromley Trust
The Davis Foundation
The Delves Charitable Trust
The Ericson Trust
Esmée Fairbairn Foundation
The Fort Foundation
The Adrian and Jane Frost Charitable Trust
Paul Hamlyn Foundation
The Henry C. Hoare Charitable Trust
The Michael and Shirley Hunt Charitable Trust
The Hunter Foundation
The Indigo Trust
The Legal Education Foundation*
The Leigh Trust
The Lennox Hannay Charitable Trust
Lloyds TSB Foundation for Scotland
The London Community Foundation (LCF)
Nesta*
The Nuffield Foundation
Polden-Puckham Charitable Foundation
Postcode Community Trust*
The Joseph Rowntree Charitable Trust
The ScottishPower Foundation
The W. F. Southall Trust
The Staples Trust
The Tinsley Foundation
The Nigel Vinson Charitable Trust
Webb Memorial Trust
The Wood Foundation

Conflict resolution

The A. S. Charitable Trust
A2BD Foundation UK Ltd*
The Arah Foundation
The William A. Cadbury Charitable Trust
Christian Aid
The Daiwa Anglo-Japanese Foundation
The Davis Foundation
The Dulverton Trust
County Durham Community Foundation
The Edith Maud Ellis 1985 Charitable Trust
The Enkalon Foundation
The Ericson Trust
Allan and Nesta Ferguson Charitable Settlement
H. C. D. Memorial Fund
The Hadrian Trust
Paul Hamlyn Foundation
Human Relief Foundation
Integrated Education Fund*
The Ireland Fund of Great Britain
Irish Youth Foundation (UK) Ltd (incorporating The Lawlor Foundation)
The J. Isaacs Charitable Trust
The Kennedy Leigh Charitable Trust
Mariapolis Ltd
Marmot Charitable Trust
John Moores Foundation
The Morel Charitable Trust
The Community Foundation for Northern Ireland
The Onaway Trust*
The Pears Family Charitable Foundation
People's Postcode Trust
Polden-Puckham Charitable Foundation
The Polonsky Foundation
Postcode Community Trust*
The Eleanor Rathbone Charitable Trust
The Rayne Trust
The Joseph Rowntree Charitable Trust
The W. F. Southall Trust
The Sutasoma Trust
Tearfund
The Tolkien Trust
The Westcroft Trust

Cross-border initiatives

Irish Youth Foundation (UK) Ltd (incorporating The Lawlor Foundation)

Cross-community work

The Arah Foundation
The William A. Cadbury Charitable Trust
The Daiwa Anglo-Japanese Foundation
The Davis Foundation
County Durham Community Foundation
The Enkalon Foundation
The Hadrian Trust
Paul Hamlyn Foundation
*Integrated Education Fund**
Irish Youth Foundation (UK) Ltd (incorporating The Lawlor Foundation)
The J. Isaacs Charitable Trust
Mariapolis Ltd
John Moores Foundation
The Morel Charitable Trust
*The Onaway Trust**
The Pears Family Charitable Foundation
People's Postcode Trust

Peace and disarmament

The A. S. Charitable Trust
The Edith Maud Ellis 1985 Charitable Trust
The Tolkien Trust

Legal advice and services

The Addleshaw Goddard Charitable Trust
The Bank of Scotland Foundation
The Big Lottery Fund (see also Awards for All)
British Gas (Scottish Gas) Energy Trust
The William A. Cadbury Charitable Trust
EDF Energy Trust (EDFET)
Friends Provident Charitable Foundation
The Hadrian Trust
The Alfred Haines Charitable Trust
The Law Society Charity
*The Legal Education Foundation**
Lloyds Bank Foundation for England and Wales
The London Community Foundation (LCF)
London Legal Support Trust (LLST)
*Masonic Charitable Foundation**
The MSE Charity
The Nationwide Foundation
The Community Foundation for Northern Ireland
The Nuffield Foundation
David and Elaine Potter Foundation
*Powys Welsh Church Fund**
Quartet Community Foundation
Santander UK Foundation Ltd
The ScottishPower Energy People Trust
The Severn Trent Water Charitable Trust Fund
*Sherburn House Charity**
The Simmons & Simmons Charitable Foundation
The Slaughter and May Charitable Trust
*Standard Life Foundation**
The Stewarts Law Foundation
The Three Guineas Trust
United Utilities Trust Fund
The Wakefield and Tetley Trust
*Warwick Relief in Need Charity**
Worcester Municipal Charities (CIO)
Yorkshire and Clydesdale Bank Foundation

Advice services

The Bank of Scotland Foundation
The Big Lottery Fund (see also Awards for All)
British Gas (Scottish Gas) Energy Trust
EDF Energy Trust (EDFET)
Friends Provident Charitable Foundation
The Hadrian Trust
The Alfred Haines Charitable Trust
Lloyds Bank Foundation for England and Wales
The London Community Foundation (LCF)
*Masonic Charitable Foundation**
The MSE Charity
The Community Foundation for Northern Ireland
Quartet Community Foundation
Santander UK Foundation Ltd
The ScottishPower Energy People Trust
The Severn Trent Water Charitable Trust Fund
*Sherburn House Charity**
*Standard Life Foundation**
United Utilities Trust Fund
The Wakefield and Tetley Trust
*Warwick Relief in Need Charity**
Worcester Municipal Charities (CIO)
Yorkshire and Clydesdale Bank Foundation

Legal issues

The Law Society Charity
The Nationwide Foundation
The Nuffield Foundation

Rights, equality and justice

The 1970 Trust
The A. B. Charitable Trust
*A2BD Foundation UK Ltd**
Ajahma Charitable Trust
*The Allen & Overy Foundation**
The Arah Foundation
The Associated Country Women of the World
Barnwood Trust
The Bromley Trust
The Barrow Cadbury Trust
Calouste Gulbenkian Foundation – UK Branch
Celtic Charity Fund
Christian Aid
J. A. Clark Charitable Trust
The Evan Cornish Foundation
Coutts Charitable Foundation
The Craignish Trust
*The John Grant Davies Trust**
The Davis Foundation
The Henry and Suzanne Davis Foundation
The Diageo Foundation
Dunard Fund 2016
County Durham Community Foundation
The Ericson Trust
Esmée Fairbairn Foundation
The Farthing Trust
The Elizabeth Frankland Moore and Star Foundation
Jill Franklin Trust
The G. D. Charitable Trust
The Robert Gavron Charitable Trust
The Hemraj Goyal Foundation
Greenham Common Community Trust Ltd
The Hadrian Trust
Paul Hamlyn Foundation
The Helen Hamlyn Trust
Harbinson Charitable Trust
The Maurice Hatter Foundation
The Charles Hayward Foundation

Human rights

Civil liberties

Cultural equity

Disability rights

Economic justice

Racial justice

Social justice

Women's rights

Paul Hamlyn Foundation
The Marr-Munning Trust
Polden-Puckham Charitable Foundation
The Staples Trust

Young people's rights

Paul Hamlyn Foundation
The Mark Leonard Trust
The Save the Children Fund*
Variety The Children's Charity (Variety Club)
The Yapp Charitable Trust
York Children's Trust*

Science and technology

The 1970 Trust
The Armourers' and Brasiers' Gauntlet Trust
Ove Arup Partnership Charitable Trust
The Barrack Charitable Trust*
The Big Lottery Fund (see also Awards for All)
The John Coates Charitable Trust
The Sir Jeremiah Colman Gift Trust
The De Laszlo Foundation
William Dean Countryside and Educational Trust
The Dunn Family Charitable Trust
County Durham Community Foundation
The James Dyson Foundation
The Beryl Evetts and Robert Luff Animal Welfare Trust Ltd
The Lord Faringdon Charitable Trust
The Adrian and Jane Frost Charitable Trust
The Gatsby Charitable Foundation
The Graham Trust*
The Granada Foundation
The Great Britain Sasakawa Foundation
The Happold Foundation*
The Harbour Foundation
The Michael Heller Charitable Foundation
The Simon Heller Charitable Settlement
IBM United Kingdom Trust
The Indigo Trust
The Worshipful Company of Information Technologists*
John Jarrold Trust Ltd
The Graham Kirkham Foundation*
The Kohn Foundation
The Kennedy Leigh Charitable Trust
The Lennox Hannay Charitable Trust
The Leverhulme Trust
The John Spedan Lewis Foundation
The Limbourne Trust
Lloyd's Register Foundation*
The MacRobert Trust
Man Group PLC Charitable Trust
The W. M. Mann Foundation
The Michael Marks Charitable Trust
The Nancie Massey Charitable Trust
Nesta*
The NFU Mutual Charitable Trust
Nominet Charitable Foundation
The Nuffield Foundation
Open Gate
Petplan Charitable Trust
The Prince Philip Trust Fund*
The Michael Sacher Charitable Trust
The Dr Mortimer and Theresa Sackler Foundation
The Sackler Trust
Salters' Charitable Foundation
David and Jennifer Sieff Charitable Trust
The Stanley Smith UK Horticultural Trust
Khoo Teck Puat UK Foundation*
Tenovus Scotland*
The Thales Charitable Trust
The Vodafone Foundation
The Waterloo Foundation
The Wellcome Trust
The Williams Family Foundation*
Winton Philanthropies
The Wolfson Family Charitable Trust
The Wolfson Foundation
Yorkshire and Clydesdale Bank Foundation
The John Kirkhope Young Endowment Fund

Engineering/ technology

The 1970 Trust
The Armourers' and Brasiers' Gauntlet Trust
County Durham Community Foundation
The James Dyson Foundation
The Gatsby Charitable Foundation
The Happold Foundation*
IBM United Kingdom Trust
The Indigo Trust
The Worshipful Company of Information Technologists*
Lloyd's Register Foundation*
Open Gate
The Thales Charitable Trust
The Vodafone Foundation

Life sciences

William Dean Countryside and Educational Trust
The Dunn Family Charitable Trust
The Beryl Evetts and Robert Luff Animal Welfare Trust Ltd

The Gatsby Charitable Foundation
John Jarrold Trust Ltd
The John Spedan Lewis Foundation
The Limbourne Trust
The Michael Marks Charitable Trust
Petplan Charitable Trust
The Stanley Smith UK Horticultural Trust
*Tenovus Scotland**
The Waterloo Foundation
The Wellcome Trust

Physical and earth sciences

The Armourers' and Brasiers' Gauntlet Trust
Man Group PLC Charitable Trust
The NFU Mutual Charitable Trust
The John Kirkhope Young Endowment Fund

Social sciences, policy and research

Age UK
All Saints Educational Trust
*The British Academy for the Promotion of Historical Philosophical and Philological Studies (The British Academy)**
The Edward Cadbury Charitable Trust
The Daiwa Anglo-Japanese Foundation
The Dawe Charitable Trust
Eaga Charitable Trust
The Lord Faringdon Charitable Trust
The Joseph Strong Frazer Trust
Friends Provident Charitable Foundation
The Gatsby Charitable Foundation
The Robert Gavron Charitable Trust
The Glass-House Trust
The Great Britain Sasakawa Foundation
The Hadley Trust
The Harbour Foundation
The Maurice Hatter Foundation
The Health Foundation
The Hinduja Foundation
The Humanitarian Trust
The Allen Lane Foundation
The LankellyChase Foundation
*The Legal Education Foundation**
The Leverhulme Trust
The Limbourne Trust
Trust for London
London Housing Foundation Ltd (LHF)
The Millfield House Foundation (1)
The Monmouthshire County Council Welsh Church Act Fund
The MSE Charity
*Nesta**
The Nuffield Foundation
*The Institute for Policy Research**
The Polonsky Foundation
David and Elaine Potter Foundation
The Sigrid Rausing Trust
The Joseph Rowntree Charitable Trust
The Joseph Rowntree Foundation
The Michael Sacher Charitable Trust
Sir Halley Stewart Trust
The Sutasoma Trust
The Nigel Vinson Charitable Trust
The Scurrah Wainwright Charity
Wates Family Enterprise Trust
Webb Memorial Trust
The Wellcome Trust

Economics

Age UK
All Saints Educational Trust
Friends Provident Charitable Foundation
The MSE Charity
*Standard Life Foundation**

Political science

The Dawe Charitable Trust
The Gatsby Charitable Foundation
The Maurice Hatter Foundation
The Allen Lane Foundation
The Sigrid Rausing Trust
The Joseph Rowntree Charitable Trust
The Joseph Rowntree Foundation
The Michael Sacher Charitable Trust

Social policy

Age UK
The Edward Cadbury Charitable Trust
The Robert Gavron Charitable Trust
The Glass-House Trust
The Hadley Trust
The Maurice Hatter Foundation
The Health Foundation
The Hinduja Foundation
The Humanitarian Trust
Trust for London
London Housing Foundation Ltd (LHF)
The Millfield House Foundation (1)
The Monmouthshire County Council Welsh Church Act Fund
The Sigrid Rausing Trust
The Joseph Rowntree Foundation
The Scurrah Wainwright Charity
The Wellcome Trust

Social welfare

The Walter Guinness Charitable Trust
The Gur Trust
H. C. D. Memorial Fund
H. P. Charitable Trust
Hackney Parochial Charities
The Hadfield Charitable Trust
The Hadley Trust
The Hadrian Trust
Halifax Foundation for Northern Ireland (previously known as Lloyds Bank Foundation for Northern Ireland)
The Helen Hamlyn Trust
*Hammersmith United Charities**
Hampshire and Isle of Wight Community Foundation
The Hampstead Wells and Campden Trust
Hampton Fuel Allotment Charity
The Kathleen Hannay Memorial Charity
The Haramead Trust
Harbo Charities Ltd
The Harbour Foundation
William Harding's Charity
The Harpur Trust
The Edith Lilian Harrison 2000 Foundation
The Harrison-Frank Family Foundation (UK) Ltd
The Hasluck Charitable Trust
The Maurice Hatter Foundation
*HC Foundation**
The Headley Trust
May Hearnshaw Charitable Trust (May Hearnshaw's Charity)
Heart of England Community Foundation
The Heathcoat Trust
*Heb Ffin (Without Frontier)**
The Charlotte Heber-Percy Charitable Trust
The Helping Foundation
The Hemby Charitable Trust
*Henderson Firstfruits**
The G. D. Herbert Charitable Trust
Herefordshire Community Foundation
Hertfordshire Community Foundation
P. and C. Hickinbotham Charitable Trust
The Alan Edward Higgs Charity
Highcroft Charitable Trust
The Hilden Charitable Fund
*M. V. Hillhouse Trust**
The Hillier Trust
R. G. Hills Charitable Trust
The Hinduja Foundation
The Henry C. Hoare Charitable Trust
The Hobson Charity Ltd
The Holden Charitable Trust
The Homelands Charitable Trust
The Homestead Charitable Trust
The Hoover Foundation
The Antony Hornby Charitable Trust
*Horwich Shotter Charitable Trust**
The Hospital of God at Greatham
House of Industry Estate
The Daniel Howard Trust
Human Relief Foundation
The Humanitarian Trust
The Albert Hunt Trust
Huntingdon Freemen's Trust
The Nani Huyu Charitable Trust
*The Hyde Park Place Estate Charity – civil trustees**
*Ibbett Trust**
Ibrahim Foundation Ltd
*ICE Futures Charitable Trust**
IGO Foundation Ltd
The Iliffe Family Charitable Trust
Imagine Foundation
Incommunities Foundation
The Inman Charity
*The Worshipful Company of Insurers – First Charitable Trust Fund**
Interserve Employee Foundation Ltd
Investream Charitable Trust
The Ireland Fund of Great Britain
The ITF Seafarers' Trust
The J. and J. Benevolent Foundation
The J. A. R. Charitable Trust
The Jarman Charitable Trust
The Jenour Foundation
The Johnson Foundation
Johnson Wax Ltd Charitable Trust
The Marjorie and Geoffrey Jones Charitable Trust
The Cyril and Eve Jumbo Charitable Trust
Anton Jurgens Charitable Trust
The Jusaca Charitable Trust
The Bernard Kahn Charitable Trust
The Michael and Ilse Katz Foundation
The Kelly Family Charitable Trust
William Kendall's Charity (Wax Chandlers' Company)
Kent Community Foundation
The Nancy Kenyon Charitable Trust
The Peter Kershaw Trust
Kirkley Poor's Land Estate
The Ernest Kleinwort Charitable Trust
The Sir James Knott Trust
Kollel and Co. Ltd
Kreditor Charitable Trust
The Kreitman Foundation
The Neil Kreitman Foundation
The Kyte Charitable Trust
Ladbrokes in the Community Charitable Trust
John Laing Charitable Trust
Maurice and Hilda Laing Charitable Trust
Christopher Laing Foundation
The David Laing Foundation
The Kirby Laing Foundation
The Beatrice Laing Trust
The Leonard Laity Stoate Charitable Trust
The Lambert Charitable Trust
Community Foundations for Lancashire and Merseyside
Lancaster Foundation
Langdale Trust
The LankellyChase Foundation
The R. J. Larg Family Charitable Trust
Largsmount Ltd
Laslett's (Hinton) Charity
The Kathleen Laurence Trust
Lawson Beckman Charitable Trust
The Raymond and Blanche Lawson Charitable Trust
Leeds Building Society Charitable Foundation
Leeds Community Foundation (LCF)
Leicestershire, Leicester and Rutland Community Foundation
The Kennedy Leigh Charitable Trust
*Leng Charitable Trust**
The Leverhulme Trade Charities Trust
*Bernard Lewis Family Charitable Trust**
David and Ruth Lewis Family Charitable Trust
John Lewis Partnership General Community Fund
Liberum Foundation
The Limbourne Trust
The Linbury Trust
Lincolnshire Community Foundation
The Enid Linder Foundation
The Charles Littlewood Hill Trust
The Second Joseph Aaron Littman Foundation
Liverpool Charity and Voluntary Services (LCVS)
The Elaine and Angus Lloyd Charitable Trust
*The W. M. and B. W. Lloyd Trust**
Lloyd's Charities Trust

Lloyds Bank Foundation for England and Wales
Lloyds Bank Foundation for the Channel Islands
Lloyds TSB Foundation for Scotland
Loftus Charitable Trust
The Lolev Charitable Trust
Trust for London
The London Community Foundation (LCF)
London Housing Foundation Ltd (LHF)
Inner London Magistrates Court's Poor Box and Feeder Charity
*P. and M. Lovell Charitable Settlement**
*Michael Lowe's and Associated Charities**
The C. L. Loyd Charitable Trust
LPW Ltd
The Henry Lumley Charitable Trust
Paul Lunn-Rockliffe Charitable Trust
The Lynn Foundation
Sylvanus Lysons Charity
M. and C. Trust
*M. B. Foundation**
The M. Y. A. Charitable Trust
The E. M. MacAndrew Trust
*Mace Foundation**
The Mactaggart Third Fund
The Ian Mactaggart Trust (The Mactaggart Second Fund)
The Magen Charitable Trust
Manchester Airport Community Trust Fund
The Manchester Guardian Society Charitable Trust
Lord Mayor of Manchester's Charity Appeal Trust
The Manifold Charitable Trust
The Manoukian Charitable Foundation
Marbeh Torah Trust
The Stella and Alexander Margulies Charitable Trust
The Ann and David Marks Foundation
The Hilda and Samuel Marks Foundation
The Michael Marsh Charitable Trust
The Marsh Christian Trust
Charlotte Marshall Charitable Trust
D. G. Marshall of Cambridge Trust
*Masonic Charitable Foundation**
*The Master Charitable Trust**
The Matliwala Family Charitable Trust
The Robert McAlpine Foundation
The Medlock Charitable Trust
Melodor Ltd
The Mercers' Charitable Foundation
Merchant Navy Welfare Board
The Merchant Venturers' Charity
The Metropolitan Masonic Charity
The Mickel Fund
The Mickleham Trust
The Ronald Miller Foundation
The Mills Charity
The Millward Charitable Trust
Milton Keynes Community Foundation Ltd
The Mirianog Trust
The Mishcon Family Charitable Trust
Keren Mitzvah Trust
*Moondance Foundation**
The George A. Moore Foundation
The Morel Charitable Trust
The Morgan Charitable Foundation
The Steve Morgan Foundation
The Diana and Allan Morgenthau Charitable Trust
The Morris Charitable Trust
G. M. Morrison Charitable Trust
*The Morton Charitable Trust**
Vyoel Moshe Charitable Trust
The Moss Family Charitable Trust
J. P. Moulton Charitable Foundation
The Edith Murphy Foundation
Murphy-Neumann Charity Company Ltd
Muslim Hands
The Mutual Trust Group
MW (CL) Foundation
MW (GK) Foundation
MW (HO) Foundation
MW (RH) Foundation
The Janet Nash Charitable Settlement
The Nationwide Foundation
The Worshipful Company of Needlemakers' Charitable Fund
Nemoral Ltd
Ner Foundation
Newby Trust Ltd
The NFU Mutual Charitable Trust
NJD Charitable Trust
Nominet Charitable Foundation
Norfolk Community Foundation
Normanby Charitable Trust
Northamptonshire Community Foundation
The Community Foundation for Northern Ireland
The Northmoor Trust
The Northumberland Village Homes Trust
*The Northwick Trust**
The Norton Rose Fulbright Charitable Foundation
Norwich Town Close Estate Charity
Nottinghamshire Community Foundation
The Oakdale Trust
The Oakley Charitable Trust
The Ofenheim Charitable Trust
Oglesby Charitable Trust
The Oldham Foundation
The Olga Charitable Trust
*One Community Foundation Ltd**
OneFamily Foundation
The O'Sullivan Family Charitable Trust
Oxfam (GB)
Oxfordshire Community Foundation
The Doris Pacey Charitable Foundation
*The Paddington Charitable Estate Educational Fund**
The Paget Charitable Trust
*Palmtree Memorial Trust**
The Panacea Charitable Trust
*Parabola Foundation**
*The Pargiter Trust**
*Parish Estate of the Church of St Michael Spurriergate York**
The Park House Charitable Trust
Peacock Charitable Trust
People's Postcode Trust
Personal Assurance Charitable Trust
The Phillips Family Charitable Trust
Pilkington Charities Fund
The DLA Piper Charitable Trust
Pollywally Charitable Trust
The Porta Pia 2012 Foundation
The Portrack Charitable Trust
The J. E. Posnansky Charitable Trust
Postcode Dream Trust – Dream Fund
Sir John Priestman Charity Trust
The Princess Anne's Charities
The Puebla Charitable Trust
The Puri Foundation
*QBE European Operations Foundation**
Quartet Community Foundation
The Queen's Trust
*Quercus Foundation**
Quothquan Trust
R. S. Charitable Trust
The Monica Rabagliati Charitable Trust
The Racing Foundation

The Rainford Trust
The Joseph Rank Trust
The Ranworth Trust
Rashbass Family Trust
The Ravensdale Trust
The Rayne Foundation
The Rayne Trust
The John Rayner Charitable Trust
The Sir James Reckitt Charity
C. A. Redfern Charitable Foundation
The Rest Harrow Trust
*Rhodi Charitable Trust**
Daisie Rich Trust
Ridgesave Ltd
*Rigby Foundation**
The River Farm Foundation
Rivers Foundation
*Riverside Charitable Trust Ltd**
Thomas Roberts Trust
Robyn Charitable Trust
The Roddick Foundation
*Mrs L. D. Rope's Second Charitable Settlement**
Mrs L. D. Rope's Third Charitable Settlement
Rosca Trust
The Cecil Rosen Foundation
*The David Ross Foundation**
The Roughley Charitable Trust
The Joseph Rowntree Foundation
Royal Artillery Charitable Fund
Royal Docks Trust (London)
*The Royal Navy And Royal Marines Charity**
*Rozelle Trust**
*S. and R. Charitable Trust**
Erach and Roshan Sadri Foundation
The Saga Charitable Trust
The Saints and Sinners Trust Ltd
The Salamander Charitable Trust
Salters' Charitable Foundation
Coral Samuel Charitable Trust
The Basil Samuel Charitable Trust
The M. J. Samuel Charitable Trust
The Sandhu Charitable Foundation
The Sands Family Trust
Santander UK Foundation Ltd
The Sants Charitable Trust
The Schreiber Charitable Trust
Schroder Charity Trust
Foundation Scotland
The Scotshill Trust
Scott (Eredine) Charitable Trust
The ScottishPower Foundation
The Scouloudi Foundation
The SDL Foundation
The Searchlight Electric Charitable Trust
Sam and Bella Sebba Charitable Trust
*The Sellafield Charity Trust Fund**
Sellata Ltd
The Severn Trent Water Charitable Trust Fund
The Shanley Charitable Trust
The Shanly Foundation
The Shears Foundation
The Sylvia and Colin Shepherd Charitable Trust
*Sherburn House Charity**
The Archie Sherman Charitable Trust
The Bassil Shippam and Alsford Trust
Shlomo Memorial Fund Ltd
The Shoe Zone Trust
The Simmons & Simmons Charitable Foundation
The Skelton Bounty
The Slaughter and May Charitable Trust
The Mrs Smith and Mount Trust
The N. Smith Charitable Settlement
The Henry Smith Charity
*The Martin Smith Foundation**
Philip Smith's Charitable Trust
The R. C. Snelling Charitable Trust
The Sobell Foundation
Social Business Trust
Sodexo Stop Hunger Foundation
The Solo Charitable Settlement
*Somerset Community Foundation**
Songdale Ltd
The E. C. Sosnow Charitable Trust
The Souter Charitable Trust
The W. F. Southall Trust
R. H. Southern Trust
Sparquote Ltd
Spears-Stutz Charitable Trust
The Spielman Charitable Trust
Rosalyn and Nicholas Springer Charitable Trust
The Spurrell Charitable Trust
The Geoff and Fiona Squire Foundation
The Squires Foundation
The St James's Trust Settlement
St James's Place Foundation
The Stafford Trust
*Staffordshire Community Foundation**
*Standard Life Foundation**
The Stanley Foundation Ltd
The Peter Stebbings Memorial Charity
The Steel Charitable Trust
The Steinberg Family Charitable Trust
The Hugh Stenhouse Foundation
The Stevenage Community Trust
Sir Halley Stewart Trust
The Stewarts Law Foundation
M. J. C. Stone Charitable Trust
The Stone Family Foundation
*The Stoneygate Trust**
Stratford upon Avon Town Trust
The W. O. Street Charitable Foundation
*The Street Foundation**
Suffolk Community Foundation
The Alan Sugar Foundation
The Bernard Sunley Charitable Foundation
*Sunninghill Fuel Allotment Trust**
Community Foundation for Surrey
The Sussex Community Foundation
The Sutasoma Trust
Sutton Coldfield Charitable Trust
The Swann-Morton Foundation
The John Swire (1989) Charitable Trust
The Swire Charitable Trust
The Charles and Elsie Sykes Trust
Sylvia Waddilove Foundation UK
The Tajtelbaum Charitable Trust
Talteg Ltd
The David Tannen Charitable Trust
C. B. and H. H. Taylor 1984 Trust
Tearfund
*Khoo Teck Puat UK Foundation**
Tees Valley Community Foundation
The C. Paul Thackray General Charitable Trust
The Sir Jules Thorn Charitable Trust
The Three Oaks Trust
Tilney Charitable Trust
Mrs R. P. Tindall's Charitable Trust
The Tobacco Pipe Makers and Tobacco Trade Benevolent Fund
The Tompkins Foundation
Toras Chesed (London) Trust
The Tory Family Foundation
The Tower Hill Trust
*The Trades House of Glasgow**
Annie Tranmer Charitable Trust
The Trefoil Trust

The Truemark Trust
Trumros Ltd
The Trusthouse Charitable Foundation
The Tudor Trust
The Tuixen Foundation
The Roger and Douglas Turner Charitable Trust
The Turtleton Charitable Trust
TVML Foundation
Two Ridings Community Foundation
Community Foundation serving Tyne and Wear and Northumberland
Tzedakah
Ulster Garden Villages Ltd
The Underwood Trust
UnLtd (Foundation for Social Entrepreneurs)
The Valentine Charitable Trust
The Valiant Charitable Trust
The Albert Van Den Bergh Charitable Trust
The Van Neste Foundation
The Vandervell Foundation
The Vardy Foundation
The Virgin Foundation (Virgin Unite)
The Virgin Money Foundation
The Vodafone Foundation
Volant Charitable Trust
Voluntary Action Fund (VAF)
The Scurrah Wainwright Charity
The Wakefield and Tetley Trust
The Wakefield Trust*
The Walcot Foundation
The Community Foundation in Wales
Wales Council for Voluntary Action
The Walker Trust
Walton Foundation*
Walton on Thames Charity
Warwick Relief in Need Charity*
The Warwickshire Masonic Charitable Association Ltd*
Mrs Waterhouse Charitable Trust
The Waterloo Foundation
Wates Family Enterprise Trust
The Wates Foundation
Blyth Watson Charitable Trust
The Weinstock Fund
The James Weir Foundation
The Wessex Youth Trust
West Derby Waste Lands Charity
The West Looe Town Trust*
The Westcroft Trust
The Westfield Health Charitable Trust
The Westminster Amalgamated Charity*
The Westminster Foundation
The Garfield Weston Foundation
Westway Trust
The Melanie White Foundation Ltd
White Stuff Foundation
The Lionel Wigram Memorial Trust
The Williams Family Foundation*
Williams Serendipity Trust
The Willmott Dixon Foundation*
Wiltshire Community Foundation
The W. Wing Yip and Brothers Foundation
The Michael and Anna Wix Charitable Trust
The Wixamtree Trust
The Maurice Wohl Charitable Foundation
The Charles Wolfson Charitable Trust
The Wolfson Foundation
The Wood Foundation
Woodlands Green Ltd
Woodroffe Benton Foundation
Worcester Municipal Charities (CIO)
The Diana Edgson Wright Charitable Trust
The Wyseliot Rose Charitable Trust
The Yapp Charitable Trust
Yorkshire and Clydesdale Bank Foundation
Yorkshire Building Society Charitable Foundation
The South Yorkshire Community Foundation
The William Allen Young Charitable Trust
Elizabeth and Prince Zaiger Trust*
Zephyr Charitable Trust
The Zochonis Charitable Trust
Zurich Community Trust (UK) Ltd

Community care services

The Avon and Somerset Police Community Trust
BBC Children in Need
The Boltini Trust
The Bothwell Charitable Trust
The Rory and Elizabeth Brooks Foundation
The Charter 600 Charity
The Charles Dunstone Charitable Trust
The Eveson Charitable Trust
The February Foundation
The Gordon Trust*
The J. G. Graves Charitable Trust
The Green Hall Foundation
The W. A. Handley Charity Trust
The Hillingdon Community Trust
Hopmarket Charity
The Horizon Foundation
The Hull and East Riding Charitable Trust
Miss Agnes H. Hunter's Trust
The Charles Irving Charitable Trust
The J. Isaacs Charitable Trust
The Isle of Anglesey Charitable Trust
The Kirschel Foundation
Duchy of Lancaster Benevolent Fund
The Edgar E. Lawley Foundation
London Catalyst
The Mackintosh Foundation
The Magdalen and Lasher Charity (General Fund)
The Millichope Foundation
Mills and Reeve Charitable Trust*
The Monmouthshire County Council Welsh Church Act Fund
The National Gardens Scheme*
Paradigm Foundation
People's Health Trust
The Austin and Hope Pilkington Trust
Postcode Community Trust*
Queen Mary's Roehampton Trust
The Robertson Trust
The Rothley Trust
The Michael and Nicola Sacher Charitable Trust
The Salisbury New Pool Settlement*
The Sheldon Trust
David and Jennifer Sieff Charitable Trust
David Solomons Charitable Trust
St Monica Trust
The Summerfield Charitable Trust
The Templeton Goodwill Trust
The Wakeham Trust
The Marjorie and Arnold Ziff Charitable Foundation

Services for and about children and young people

The 1989 Willan Charitable Trust
The AIM Foundation
The John Armitage Charitable Trust
The Barcapel Foundation

*The Philip Barker Charity**
Bauer Radio's Cash for Kids Charities
*The Burberry Foundation**
The Burden Trust
The Noel Buxton Trust
The Ellis Campbell Charitable Foundation
The Casey Trust
The Cayo Foundation
*The Thomas Cook Chidlren's Charity**
Dudley and Geoffrey Cox Charitable Trust
*Credit Suisse EMEA Foundation**
Baron Davenport's Charity
The Dumbreck Charity
Edinburgh Children's Holiday Fund
The Erskine Cunningham Hill Trust
The Essex Youth Trust
The A. M. Fenton Trust
Elizabeth Ferguson Charitable Trust Fund
The Joyce Fletcher Charitable Trust
The Hugh Fraser Foundation
The Generations Foundation
The Girdlers' Company Charitable Trust
The Glass-House Trust
Global Care
Worshipful Company of Gold and Silver Wyre Drawers Charitable Trust Fund
The Grantham Yorke Trust
The Grocers' Charity
Dr Guthrie's Association
The Alfred Haines Charitable Trust
The Harbour Charitable Trust
The Harris Charity
The Peter Harrison Foundation
The Alfred And Peggy Harvey Charitable Trust
Heathrow Community Fund (LHR Airport Communities Trust)
Hedley Foundation Ltd (The Hedley Foundation)
The Christina Mary Hendrie Trust for Scottish and Canadian Charities
Henley Educational Trust
Philip Henman Trust
The Hesslewood Children's Trust (Hull Seamen's and General Orphanage)
The Holywood Trust
The Reta Lila Howard Foundation
Irish Youth Foundation (UK) Ltd (incorporating The Lawlor Foundation)
The Ironmongers' Company
C. Richard Jackson Charitable Trust
The Ruth and Lionel Jacobson Trust (Second Fund) No. 2
Jewish Child's Day (JCD)
Lillie Johnson Charitable Trust
Johnnie Johnson Trust
The Jones 1986 Charitable Trust
Kelsick's Educational Foundation
The Mary Kinross Charitable Trust
The KPMG Foundation
LandAid Charitable Trust (Land Aid)
The Langtree Trust
The Lauffer Family Charitable Foundation
The Mark Leonard Trust
*The Lethendy Charitable Trust**
Lord Leverhulme's Charitable Trust
*Life Changes Trust**
The Lind Trust
The Lister Charitable Trust
The Lord's Taverners
John Lyon's Charity
The R. S. Macdonald Charitable Trust
The MacRobert Trust
R. W. Mann Trust
Mariapolis Ltd
Sir George Martin Trust
The Nancie Massey Charitable Trust
The Violet Mauray Charitable Trust
The Gerald Micklem Charitable Trust
Middlesex Sports Foundation
The Peter Minet Trust
The Monument Trust
John Moores Foundation
Morgan Stanley International Foundation
The Mosselson Charitable Trust
The Mugdock Children's Trust
The Mulberry Trust
The Music Sales Charitable Trust
The National Express Foundation
Alderman Newton's Educational Foundation
The Norton Foundation
The Nuffield Foundation
The Paphitis Charitable Trust
The Pears Family Charitable Foundation
The Jack Petchey Foundation
The George and Esme Pollitzer Charitable Settlement
The Ponton House Trust
The Portishead Nautical Trust
*Powys Welsh Church Fund**
Mr and Mrs J. A. Pye's Charitable Settlement
The Rank Foundation Ltd
The Eleanor Rathbone Charitable Trust
Elizabeth Rathbone Charity
Rhondda Cynon Taff Welsh Church Acts Fund
The Royal British Legion
The Andrew Salvesen Charitable Trust
The Sandra Charitable Trust
*The Save the Children Fund**
The Francis C. Scott Charitable Trust
The Frieda Scott Charitable Trust
Seafarers UK (King George's Fund for Sailors)
Leslie Sell Charitable Trust
The Shipwrights' Company Charitable Fund
Skipton Building Society Charitable Foundation
The Leslie Smith Foundation
The Spoore, Merry and Rixman Foundation
The St Hilda's Trust
The Andy Stewart Charitable Foundation
The Stoller Charitable Trust
Swan Mountain Trust
The Talbot Trusts
Tallow Chandlers Benevolent Fund No. 2
The Tanner Trust
The Connie and Albert Taylor Charitable Trust
The Taylor Family Foundation
The Tedworth Charitable Trust
*DM Thomas Foundation for Young People**
Tottenham Grammar School Foundation
The Toy Trust
Toyota Manufacturing UK Charitable Trust
The True Colours Trust
*The Trysil Charitable Trust**
*The Utley Family Charitable Trust**
Mrs Maud Van Norden's Charitable Foundation
Variety The Children's Charity (Variety Club)
Virgin Atlantic Foundation
Wade's Charity
Robert and Felicity Waley-Cohen Charitable Trust
The Barbara Ward Children's Foundation
John Watson's Trust
The Weavers' Company Benevolent Fund
The Felicity Wilde Charitable Trust
The Dame Violet Wills Will Trust

The Wilson Foundation
Wooden Spoon Society
The Woodstock Family Charitable Foundation*
York Children's Trust*
Youth Music

Services for and about older people

Age Scotland
Age UK
Barchester Healthcare Foundation
The Birmingham District Nursing Charitable Trust
The Burden Trust
The Childwick Trust
The Clan Trust Ltd*
Baron Davenport's Charity
The Dumbreck Charity
The Earley Charity
The Erskine Cunningham Hill Trust
The Hugh Fraser Foundation
The L. and R. Gilley Charitable Trust*
The Girdlers' Company Charitable Trust
The Grocers' Charity
The Alfred And Peggy Harvey Charitable Trust
The Charles Hayward Foundation
The Christina Mary Hendrie Trust for Scottish and Canadian Charities
The Hiscox Foundation
The Hudson Foundation
Hyde Charitable Trust (Youth Plus)
The Ruth and Lionel Jacobson Trust (Second Fund) No. 2
John James Bristol Foundation
The Jones 1986 Charitable Trust
The Jordan Charitable Foundation
The Allen Lane Foundation
The Herd Lawson and Muriel Lawson Charitable Trust
The Maisie and Raphael Lewis Charitable Trust*
Mariapolis Ltd
Sir George Martin Trust
The Nancie Massey Charitable Trust
Merchant Taylors' Consolidated Charities for the Infirm
The Gerald Micklem Charitable Trust
The Peter Minet Trust
The Music Sales Charitable Trust
Mrs Gladys Row Fogo Charitable Trust
The Rowlands Trust
The Andrew Salvesen Charitable Trust
Seafarers UK (King George's Fund for Sailors)
The Skerritt Trust*
Skipton Building Society Charitable Foundation
The Talbot Trusts
The Tanner Trust
The Connie and Albert Taylor Charitable Trust
The Utley Family Charitable Trust*
The William and Patricia Venton Charitable Trust
Wade's Charity
J. and J. R. Wilson Trust
The Francis Winham Foundation

Services for and about vulnerable people/people who are ill

The 1989 Willan Charitable Trust
The Archer Trust
The Artemis Charitable Trust
Barchester Healthcare Foundation
Barnwood Trust
The Birmingham District Nursing Charitable Trust
The Dumbreck Charity
The Forbes Charitable Foundation
The Oliver Ford Charitable Trust
Jill Franklin Trust
The Hugh Fraser Foundation
The Generations Foundation
Genetic Disorders UK*
The L. and R. Gilley Charitable Trust*
The Girdlers' Company Charitable Trust
The Alfred And Peggy Harvey Charitable Trust
The Hawthorne Charitable Trust
Help for Health
The Thomas J. Horne Memorial Trust
The Hudson Foundation
The Michael and Shirley Hunt Charitable Trust
Irish Youth Foundation (UK) Ltd (incorporating The Lawlor Foundation)
The Jabbs Foundation
C. Richard Jackson Charitable Trust
The Ruth and Lionel Jacobson Trust (Second Fund) No. 2
The Jones 1986 Charitable Trust
The Jordan Charitable Foundation
The Allen Lane Foundation
John Lyon's Charity
Merchant Taylors' Consolidated Charities for the Infirm
The Gerald Micklem Charitable Trust
The Peter Minet Trust
John Moores Foundation
The Mugdock Children's Trust
The Music Sales Charitable Trust
Odin Charitable Trust
The Pilgrim Trust
The Portishead Nautical Trust
The Mary Potter Convent Hospital Trust
Mr and Mrs J. A. Pye's Charitable Settlement
Richard Radcliffe Trust
Elizabeth Rathbone Charity
The Rix-Thompson-Rothenberg Foundation
The Rowlands Trust
The Andrew Salvesen Charitable Trust
The Frieda Scott Charitable Trust
Seafarers UK (King George's Fund for Sailors)
The Leslie Smith Foundation
Swan Mountain Trust
The Talbot Trusts
The Connie and Albert Taylor Charitable Trust
The True Colours Trust
The James Tudor Foundation
The Utley Family Charitable Trust*
The Vintners' Foundation
The Will Charitable Trust

Services for carers

The Astor Foundation
Disability Aid Fund (The Roger and Jean Jefcoate Trust)
Jill Franklin Trust
Genetic Disorders UK*
The Girdlers' Company Charitable Trust
Hedley Foundation Ltd (The Hedley Foundation)
The Ruth and Lionel Jacobson Trust (Second Fund) No. 2
The Gerald Micklem Charitable Trust
John Moores Foundation
Richard Radcliffe Trust
The Rix-Thompson-Rothenberg Foundation
The Frieda Scott Charitable Trust
The Triangle Trust (1949) Fund

The Will Charitable Trust

Services for victims of crime

The Allen Lane Foundation

Services for women

Coutts Charitable Foundation
The Jabbs Foundation
The Allen Lane Foundation
John Moores Foundation
The Mosselson Charitable Trust
The Pilgrim Trust
The Eleanor Rathbone Charitable Trust
Elizabeth Rathbone Charity

Activities and relationships between generations

The Earley Charity
Mariapolis Ltd

Community centres and activities

Allchurches Trust Ltd
The Anne Duchess of Westminster's Charity*
The Bank of Scotland Foundation
Barchester Healthcare Foundation
BBC Children in Need
The Carnegie Dunfermline Trust
The Charter 600 Charity
Community First (Landfill Communities Fund)
The Hamilton Davies Trust
Eastern Counties Educational Trust Ltd
The Football Association National Sports Centre Trust
The Mike Gooley Trailfinders Charity
The J. G. Graves Charitable Trust
The Grimmitt Trust
Paul Hamlyn Foundation
The W. A. Handley Charity Trust
Heathrow Community Fund (LHR Airport Communities Trust)
The Hillingdon Community Trust
P. H. Holt Foundation
The Charles Irving Charitable Trust
The Isle of Anglesey Charitable Trust
Jewish Child's Day (JCD)
The Allen Lane Foundation
The Edgar E. Lawley Foundation
Lord Leverhulme's Charitable Trust
London Catalyst
The Mackintosh Foundation
The Magdalen and Lasher Charity (General Fund)
John Martin's Charity
The Peter Minet Trust
North East Area Miners Welfare Trust Fund*
Paradigm Foundation
People's Health Trust
The George and Esme Pollitzer Charitable Settlement
Reed Family Foundation
The Sir James Roll Charitable Trust
The Salisbury New Pool Settlement*
The Frieda Scott Charitable Trust
The Sheldon Trust
The Archie Sherman Cardiff Foundation
SITA Cornwall Trust Ltd
Swan Mountain Trust
The Talbot Village Trust
Vale of Glamorgan Welsh Church Fund
Viridor Credits Environmental Company*
Wade's Charity
The Bruce Wake Charity*
The Wakeham Trust
The Wilson Foundation

Community and social centres

The Gannochy Trust
The J. Isaacs Charitable Trust
Lancashire Environmental Fund Ltd
Duchy of Lancaster Benevolent Fund
John Lyon's Charity
The Monmouthshire County Council Welsh Church Act Fund
The Owen Family Trust
Powys Welsh Church Fund*
Elizabeth Rathbone Charity
The Rhododendron Trust
The Shetland Charitable Trust

Community organisations

The John Grant Davies Trust*
The Gannochy Trust
The Holywood Trust
Impetus – The Private Equity Foundation (Impetus – PEF)
The Innocent Foundation
Lancashire Environmental Fund Ltd
Duchy of Lancaster Benevolent Fund
Jack Livingstone Charitable Trust
The London Marathon Charitable Trust Ltd
Mobbs Memorial Trust Ltd
Powys Welsh Church Fund*
The Rothley Trust

Community outings and holidays

Barnwood Trust
Edinburgh Children's Holiday Fund
The Alfred Haines Charitable Trust
Hedley Foundation Ltd (The Hedley Foundation)
The Hesslewood Children's Trust (Hull Seamen's and General Orphanage)
The Holywood Trust
Middlesex Sports Foundation
The Eleanor Rathbone Charitable Trust

Community transport

Rees Jeffreys Road Fund
The Lord's Taverners
Millennium Stadium Charitable Trust (Ymddiriedolaeth Elusennol Stadiwm Y. Mileniwm)
The Shetland Charitable Trust

Emergency response

BBC Children in Need
The Lennox Hannay Charitable Trust
The Loseley and Guildway Charitable Trust
The MacRobert Trust

The Laurence Misener Charitable Trust
The Monmouthshire County Council Welsh Church Act Fund
The Sir James Roll Charitable Trust
The Saintbury Trust
Spar Charitable Fund

Armed forces

The Robert Clutterbuck Charitable Trust
Edinburgh Trust No 2 Account
The Erskine Cunningham Hill Trust
Worshipful Company of Gold and Silver Wyre Drawers Charitable Trust Fund
The Grocers' Charity
The Hiscox Foundation
The Inverforth Charitable Trust
Mrs F. B. Laurence Charitable Trust
The William Leech Charity
Northwood Charitable Trust
Queen Mary's Roehampton Trust
The Royal British Legion
Mrs Maud Van Norden's Charitable Foundation
Colonel W. H. Whitbread Charitable Trust

Lifeboat service

Mrs F. B. Laurence Charitable Trust
The R. S. Macdonald Charitable Trust
Northwood Charitable Trust
The Phillips Charitable Trust

Relief assistance

Age UK
P. G. and N. J. Boulton Trust
Christadelphian Samaritan Fund
Harbinson Charitable Trust
The Innocent Foundation
The Madeline Mabey Trust
The Marr-Munning Trust
The Father O'Mahoney Memorial Trust
The Eleanor Rathbone Charitable Trust
The Sigrid Rausing Trust
The Rhododendron Trust
The SMB Trust
The Gay and Keith Talbot Trust
The Tisbury Telegraph Trust
Roger Vere Foundation

Socially preventative schemes

The Avon and Somerset Police Community Trust
Hyde Charitable Trust (Youth Plus)
Impetus – The Private Equity Foundation (Impetus – PEF)
Irish Youth Foundation (UK) Ltd (incorporating The Lawlor Foundation)
The Jabbs Foundation
Jewish Child's Day (JCD)
John Moores Foundation
The National Express Foundation
The Eleanor Rathbone Charitable Trust
Elizabeth Rathbone Charity
The Robertson Trust
*The Salisbury New Pool Settlement**
The Weavers' Company Benevolent Fund
*The Woodstock Family Charitable Foundation**

Crime prevention

The 1970 Trust
BBC Children in Need
The Cayo Foundation
Jill Franklin Trust
*The Gordon Trust**
The Charles Hayward Foundation
Hedley Foundation Ltd (The Hedley Foundation)
The Michael and Shirley Hunt Charitable Trust
The Charles Irving Charitable Trust
The Mary Kinross Charitable Trust
The KPMG Foundation
The Leigh Trust
The Mark Leonard Trust
John Lyon's Charity
The Pilgrim Trust
The Triangle Trust (1949) Fund

Family justice

BBC Children in Need
The Charles Hayward Foundation
John Lyon's Charity
The Nuffield Foundation

Family planning

The G. W. Cadbury Charitable Trust
John Lyon's Charity
The Monument Trust
The Pilgrim Trust

Prisons and penal reform

The 1970 Trust
The A. B. Charitable Trust
BBC Children in Need
The Bromley Trust
The Noel Buxton Trust
Sir John Cass's Foundation
The Evan Cornish Foundation
The Violet and Milo Cripps Charitable Trust
The Ericson Trust
Jill Franklin Trust
The Robert Gavron Charitable Trust
*The Gordon Trust**
The Charles Hayward Foundation
The Michael and Shirley Hunt Charitable Trust
The Charles Irving Charitable Trust
The Mary Kinross Charitable Trust
The Allen Lane Foundation
The Leigh Trust
The Monument Trust
Odin Charitable Trust
The Pilgrim Trust
The Austin and Hope Pilkington Trust
Saint Sarkis Charity Trust
The Triangle Trust (1949) Fund

Substance abuse and education

BBC Children in Need
*The Gordon Trust**
The Hope Trust
The Michael and Shirley Hunt Charitable Trust
The Leigh Trust
The Norton Foundation
The Portishead Nautical Trust
The Frieda Scott Charitable Trust
The Vintners' Foundation

Beneficial groups

Age

Babies

The Castang Foundation
G. F. Eyre Charitable Trust
Lifeline 4 Kids (Handicapped Children's Aid Committee)
The Edwina Mountbatten and Leonora Children's Foundation
Postcode Dream Trust – Dream Fund
*Quercus Foundation**
*The Save the Children Fund**
The Francis C. Scott Charitable Trust
Sparks Charity (Sport Aiding Medical Research for Kids)
The Toy Trust
*The Utley Family Charitable Trust**

Children and young people

The 1989 Willan Charitable Trust
The 29th May 1961 Charitable Trust
The Aberbrothock Skea Trust
Aberdeen Asset Management Charitable Foundation
The Accenture Foundation
Access Sport CIO
The ACT Foundation
Action Medical Research
The Sylvia Adams Charitable Trust
The Adint Charitable Trust
The Adnams Community Trust
The AIM Foundation
The Sylvia Aitken Charitable Trust
Ajahma Charitable Trust
D. G. Albright Charitable Trust
Aldgate and All Hallows' Foundation
Al-Fayed Charitable Foundation
The Derrill Allatt Foundation
D. C. R. Allen Charitable Trust
The Allen Trust
Viscount Amory's Charitable Trust
The AMW Charitable Trust
The Mary Andrew Charitable Trust
Anglo American Group Foundation
Anguish's Educational Foundation
*AO Smile Foundation**
The Arbib Foundation
The Ardwick Trust
The Armourers' and Brasiers' Gauntlet Trust
The Arsenal Foundation Ltd
*The Asfari Foundation**
The Associated Country Women of the World
The Astor Foundation
The Lord Austin Trust
Autonomous Research Charitable Trust (ARCT)
The Avon and Somerset Police Community Trust
*Bairdwatson Charitable Trust**
The Roy and Pixie Baker Charitable Trust
The Balfour Beatty Charitable Trust
The Ballinger Charitable Trust
The Band Trust
The Barbour Foundation
The Barcapel Foundation
The Barclay Foundation
*The Philip Barker Charity**
Misses Barrie Charitable Trust
Bauer Radio's Cash for Kids Charities
The Louis Baylis (Maidenhead Advertiser) Charitable Trust
BBC Children in Need
The John Beckwith Charitable Trust
The Bedfordshire and Luton Community Foundation
Beefy's Charity Foundation
*The Behrens Foundation**
The Benham Charitable Settlement
*The Rowan Bentall Charitable Trust**
Bergqvist Charitable Trust
The Berkeley Charitable Foundation
The Ruth Berkowitz Charitable Trust
The Berkshire Community Foundation
Percy Bilton Charity
The Lord Mayor of Birmingham's Charity
Isabel Blackman Foundation
The Blagrave Trust
The Blair Foundation
Blakemore Foundation
Bloom Foundation
The Bluston Charitable Settlement
The Boltini Trust
The Boodle & Dunthorne Charitable Trust
The Booth Charities
*Sir William Boreman's Foundation**
The Bothwell Charitable Trust
The Bowerman Charitable Trust
The Bowland Charitable Trust
The Bransford Trust
The Breadsticks Foundation
Bridge Trust
Bridgepoint Charitable Trust
British Record Industry Trust
The Britten-Pears Foundation (The Britten Pears Library)
The Bromley Trust
The Charles Brotherton Trust
The Bruntwood Charity
Buckingham Trust
The Buffini Chao Foundation
*The Burberry Foundation**
The Burden Trust
The Clara E. Burgess Charity
*The Butters Foundation (UK) Ltd**
The William A. Cadbury Charitable Trust
The Edward and Dorothy Cadbury Trust
Calleva Foundation
Calouste Gulbenkian Foundation – UK Branch
The Cambridgeshire Community Foundation
The Ellis Campbell Charitable Foundation
*Canary Wharf Contractors Fund**
*The W. A. Cargill Charitable Trust**
David William Traill Cargill Fund
*The W. A. Cargill Fund**
The Richard Carne Trust
The Carpenters' Company Charitable Trust
The Casey Trust
Sir John Cass's Foundation
The Castang Foundation
*The Castansa Trust**
The Cattanach Charitable Trust
The Joseph and Annie Cattle Trust
The Wilfrid and Constance Cave Foundation
The Cayo Foundation
The CBD Charitable Trust
*The Chadwick Educational Foundation**
The Amelia Chadwick Trust
The Charter 600 Charity
Chesterhill Charitable Trust
The Childhood Trust
Children with Cancer UK
Children's Liver Disease Foundation
CHK Charities Ltd
The Church Burgesses Educational Foundation
Church Urban Fund
The CIBC World Markets Children's Miracle Foundation
The Hilda and Alice Clark Charitable Trust
J. A. Clark Charitable Trust
*The Clark Foundation**
The Cleopatra Trust

The Patrick and Helena Frost Foundation
The Fulmer Charitable Trust
The Gale Family Charity Trust
The Gannochy Trust
The Garrard Family Foundation
Gatwick Airport Community Trust
The Robert Gavron Charitable Trust
The Generations Foundation
*Genetic Disorders UK**
The Steven Gerrard Foundation
Get Kids Going
The Gibbons Family Trust
The Simon Gibson Charitable Trust
*Gilchrist Educational Trust**
The Girdlers' Company Charitable Trust
The Glass-House Trust
The Gloag Foundation
Global Care
Global Charities
Gloucestershire Community Foundation
The Godinton Charitable Trust
Worshipful Company of Gold and Silver Wyre Drawers Charitable Trust Fund
The Goldsmiths' Company Charity
The Golf Foundation Ltd
The Goodman Foundation
The Mike Gooley Trailfinders Charity
The Gosling Foundation Ltd
Gowling WLG (UK) Charitable Trust
The Hemraj Goyal Foundation
A. and S. Graham Charitable Trust
Grand Charitable Trust of the Order of Women Freemasons
The Grantham Yorke Trust
Gordon Gray Trust
The Green Hall Foundation
Greenham Common Community Trust Ltd
The Greggs Foundation
The Grimmitt Trust
The Grocers' Charity
The Bishop of Guildford's Foundation
Guildry Incorporation of Perth
The Walter Guinness Charitable Trust
The Gur Trust
Dr Guthrie's Association
Hackney Parochial Charities
The Hadfield Charitable Trust
The Hadley Trust
The Hadrian Trust
The Alfred Haines Charitable Trust
Paul Hamlyn Foundation
*Hammersmith United Charities**
Hampton Fuel Allotment Charity
The W. A. Handley Charity Trust
The Kathleen Hannay Memorial Charity
The Haramead Trust
The Harbour Charitable Trust
The Harbour Foundation
William Harding's Charity
The Harebell Centenary Fund
The Harris Charity
The Harris Family Charitable Trust
The Edith Lilian Harrison 2000 Foundation
The Peter Harrison Foundation
The Harrison-Frank Family Foundation (UK) Ltd
The Hartley Charitable Trust
The Alfred And Peggy Harvey Charitable Trust
The Hasluck Charitable Trust
The Hathaway Trust
The Hawthorne Charitable Trust
May Hearnshaw Charitable Trust (May Hearnshaw's Charity)
Heart of England Community Foundation
The Heathcoat Trust
Heathrow Community Fund (LHR Airport Communities Trust)
*Heb Ffin (Without Frontier)**
The Charlotte Heber-Percy Charitable Trust
Ernest Hecht Charitable Foundation
Hedley Foundation Ltd (The Hedley Foundation)
The Hemby Charitable Trust
*Henderson Firstfruits**
The Christina Mary Hendrie Trust for Scottish and Canadian Charities
Henley Educational Trust
Philip Henman Trust
The G. D. Herbert Charitable Trust
Herefordshire Community Foundation
Hertfordshire Community Foundation
The Hesslewood Children's Trust (Hull Seamen's and General Orphanage)
P. and C. Hickinbotham Charitable Trust
The Alan Edward Higgs Charity
The Hilden Charitable Fund
The Derek Hill Foundation
*M. V. Hillhouse Trust**
The Hillier Trust
The Hillingdon Community Trust
R. G. Hills Charitable Trust
Hinchley Charitable Trust
The Hiscox Foundation
The Henry C. Hoare Charitable Trust
The Hobson Charity Ltd
The Jane Hodge Foundation
The Hollick Family Charitable Trust
The Holliday Foundation
The Dorothy Holmes Charitable Trust
The Holywood Trust
The Homelands Charitable Trust
The Homestead Charitable Trust
The Mary Homfray Charitable Trust
Sir Harold Hood's Charitable Trust
The Hoover Foundation
Hopmarket Charity
The Horizon Foundation
The Thomas J. Horne Memorial Trust
Hospice UK
The Hospital of God at Greatham
House of Industry Estate
The Reta Lila Howard Foundation
The Hull and East Riding Charitable Trust
Hulme Trust Estates (Educational)
The Humanitarian Trust
The Albert Hunt Trust
The Hunter Foundation
The Huntingdon Foundation Ltd
Huntingdon Freemen's Trust
The Nani Huyu Charitable Trust
*Ibbett Trust**
Ibrahim Foundation Ltd
*ICE Futures Charitable Trust**
IGO Foundation Ltd
The Iliffe Family Charitable Trust
Impetus – The Private Equity Foundation (Impetus – PEF)
Incommunities Foundation
The Ingram Trust
The International Bankers Charitable Trust (The Worshipful Company of Interntional Bankers)
The Inverforth Charitable Trust
Investream Charitable Trust
The Ireland Fund of Great Britain
Irish Youth Foundation (UK) Ltd (incorporating The Lawlor Foundation)
The Ironmongers' Company

The Charles Irving Charitable Trust
The J. Isaacs Charitable Trust
The J. J. Charitable Trust
The Jabbs Foundation
C. Richard Jackson Charitable Trust
The Ruth and Lionel Jacobson Trust (Second Fund) No. 2
John James Bristol Foundation
The Jarman Charitable Trust
John Jarrold Trust Ltd
The Jenour Foundation
Jewish Child's Day (JCD)
The Jewish Youth Fund (JYF)
Lillie Johnson Charitable Trust
The Johnson Foundation
Johnnie Johnson Trust
Johnson Wax Ltd Charitable Trust
The Joicey Trust
The Jones 1986 Charitable Trust
The Dezna Robins Jones Charitable Foundation
The Marjorie and Geoffrey Jones Charitable Trust
The Jordan Charitable Foundation
The Joron Charitable Trust
J. E. Joseph Charitable Fund
The Cyril and Eve Jumbo Charitable Trust
Anton Jurgens Charitable Trust
The Boris Karloff Charitable Foundation
The Michael and Ilse Katz Foundation
The Kelly Family Charitable Trust
Kelsick's Educational Foundation
The Nancy Kenyon Charitable Trust
The Ursula Keyes Trust
The Robert Kiln Charitable Trust
The Mary Kinross Charitable Trust
The Graham Kirkham Foundation*
Kirkley Poor's Land Estate
The Richard Kirkman Trust
Robert Kitchin (Saddlers' Company)
The Ernest Kleinwort Charitable Trust
The Sir James Knott Trust
The Kobler Trust
The KPMG Foundation
Kreditor Charitable Trust
Kusuma Trust UK
Ladbrokes in the Community Charitable Trust
The K. P. Ladd Charitable Trust
John Laing Charitable Trust
Maurice and Hilda Laing Charitable Trust
Christopher Laing Foundation
The David Laing Foundation
The Kirby Laing Foundation
The Martin Laing Foundation
The Beatrice Laing Trust
The Leonard Laity Stoate Charitable Trust
The Lambert Charitable Trust
Community Foundations for Lancashire and Merseyside
The Lancashire Foundation*
Duchy of Lancaster Benevolent Fund
Lancaster Foundation
LandAid Charitable Trust (Land Aid)
The Jack Lane Charitable Trust
Langdale Trust
The Langtree Trust
The R. J. Larg Family Charitable Trust
Laslett's (Hinton) Charity
The Lauffer Family Charitable Foundation
Mrs F. B. Laurence Charitable Trust
The Kathleen Laurence Trust
The Edgar E. Lawley Foundation
The Raymond and Blanche Lawson Charitable Trust
The David Lean Foundation
The Leathersellers' Company Charitable Fund
The William Leech Charity
Leeds Building Society Charitable Foundation
Leicestershire, Leicester and Rutland Community Foundation
The Leigh Trust
P. Leigh-Bramwell Trust 'E'
The Mark Leonard Trust
The Lethendy Charitable Trust*
The Leverhulme Trade Charities Trust
Lord Leverhulme's Charitable Trust
Bernard Lewis Family Charitable Trust*
David and Ruth Lewis Family Charitable Trust
John Lewis Partnership General Community Fund
Liberum Foundation
Life Changes Trust*
Lifeline 4 Kids (Handicapped Children's Aid Committee)
The Limbourne Trust
Limoges Charitable Trust
Lincolnshire Community Foundation
The Lind Trust
Lindale Educational Foundation
The Linden Charitable Trust
The Enid Linder Foundation
The Lindley Foundation (TLF)
The Lister Charitable Trust
The Frank Litchfield Charitable Trust
The Charles Littlewood Hill Trust
The George John and Sheilah Livanos Charitable Trust
Jack Livingstone Charitable Trust
The Ian and Natalie Livingstone Charitable Trust
The Elaine and Angus Lloyd Charitable Trust
The W. M. and B. W. Lloyd Trust*
Lloyd's Charities Trust
Lloyds Bank Foundation for England and Wales
Lloyds Bank Foundation for the Channel Islands
Lloyds TSB Foundation for Scotland
Localtrent Ltd
Loftus Charitable Trust
London Catalyst
The London Community Foundation (LCF)
Inner London Magistrates Court's Poor Box and Feeder Charity
The William and Katherine Longman Trust
The Lord's Taverners
The Loseley and Guildway Charitable Trust
The Lower Green Foundation
The C. L. Loyd Charitable Trust
The Henry Lumley Charitable Trust
Paul Lunn-Rockliffe Charitable Trust
C. F. Lunoe Trust Fund
Lord and Lady Lurgan Trust
The Lynn Foundation
John Lyon's Charity
The Sir Jack Lyons Charitable Trust
Sylvanus Lysons Charity
M. and C. Trust
The M. K. Charitable Trust
The Madeline Mabey Trust
The R. S. Macdonald Charitable Trust
The Macdonald-Buchanan Charitable Trust
Mace Foundation*
The Mackintosh Foundation
GPS Macpherson Charitable Settlement*
The MacRobert Trust
The Magdalen and Lasher Charity (General Fund)
The Magen Charitable Trust
The Mallinckrodt Foundation

Man Group PLC Charitable Trust
The Manackerman Charitable Trust
The Manchester Guardian Society Charitable Trust
The Manifold Charitable Trust
R. W. Mann Trust
The Manoukian Charitable Foundation
The Stella and Alexander Margulies Charitable Trust
Mariapolis Ltd
The Marks Family Foundation
The Ann and David Marks Foundation
The Marr-Munning Trust
The Michael Marsh Charitable Trust
The Marsh Christian Trust
Charlotte Marshall Charitable Trust
D. G. Marshall of Cambridge Trust
*The Martin Charitable Trust**
Sir George Martin Trust
John Martin's Charity
*Masonic Charitable Foundation**
The Nancie Massey Charitable Trust
The Matliwala Family Charitable Trust
The Violet Mauray Charitable Trust
The Robert McAlpine Foundation
McGreevy No. 5 Settlement
D. D. McPhail Charitable Settlement
The Medlock Charitable Trust
Melodor Ltd
Mercaz Torah Vechesed Ltd
The Mercers' Charitable Foundation
The Merchant Venturers' Charity
The Metropolitan Masonic Charity
T. and J. Meyer Family Foundation Ltd
The Mickel Fund
The Mickleham Trust
The Gerald Micklem Charitable Trust
Middlesex Sports Foundation
Millennium Stadium Charitable Trust (Ymddiriedolaeth Elusennol Stadiwm Y. Mileniwm)
The Ronald Miller Foundation
The Millfield House Foundation (1)
The Millfield Trust
The Millichope Foundation
*Mills and Reeve Charitable Trust**
The Mills Charity
The Millward Charitable Trust
*The James Milner Foundation**
The Edgar Milward Charity
The Mishcon Family Charitable Trust
The MITIE Foundation
The Mittal Foundation
Keren Mitzvah Trust
Mobbs Memorial Trust Ltd
Mole Charitable Trust
The Monmouthshire County Council Welsh Church Act Fund
The Monument Trust
*Moondance Foundation**
The George A. Moore Foundation
John Moores Foundation
The Morgan Charitable Foundation
The Steve Morgan Foundation
Morgan Stanley International Foundation
The Morris Charitable Trust
G. M. Morrison Charitable Trust
*The Morrisons Foundation**
Vyoel Moshe Charitable Trust
The Moss Family Charitable Trust
The Mosselson Charitable Trust
The Edwina Mountbatten and Leonora Children's Foundation
The Mugdock Children's Trust
The Mulberry Trust
The Edith Murphy Foundation
Murphy-Neumann Charity Company Ltd
The Music Sales Charitable Trust
Muslim Hands
The National Express Foundation
The NDL Foundation
The Newcomen Collett Foundation
Alderman Newton's Educational Foundation
The NFU Mutual Charitable Trust
Nominet Charitable Foundation
Norfolk Community Foundation
Educational Foundation of Alderman John Norman
The Norman Family Charitable Trust
Normanby Charitable Trust
Northamptonshire Community Foundation
The Northumberland Village Homes Trust
*The Northwick Trust**
The Norton Foundation
The Norton Rose Fulbright Charitable Foundation
The Notgrove Trust
Nottinghamshire Community Foundation
The Oakley Charitable Trust
Oizer Charitable Trust
Old Possum's Practical Trust
The Oldham Foundation
The Olga Charitable Trust
*One Community Foundation Ltd**
Open Gate
The Ormsby Charitable Trust
The O'Sullivan Family Charitable Trust
Oxfordshire Community Foundation
The Doris Pacey Charitable Foundation
*The Paddington Charitable Estate Educational Fund**
The Paget Charitable Trust
The Paphitis Charitable Trust
Peacock Charitable Trust
Susanna Peake Charitable Trust
The Pears Family Charitable Foundation
People's Postcode Trust
The Persula Foundation
The Jack Petchey Foundation
The Pharsalia Charitable Trust
The Phillips Charitable Trust
The Bernard Piggott Charitable Trust
Pilkington Charities Fund
The George and Esme Pollitzer Charitable Settlement
The Ponton House Trust
The Porta Pia 2012 Foundation
The Portishead Nautical Trust
The Portrack Charitable Trust
The J. E. Posnansky Charitable Trust
Postcode Dream Trust – Dream Fund
*Powys Welsh Church Fund**
The Prince of Wales's Charitable Foundation
*The Prince Philip Trust Fund**
*Princes Gate Trust**
The Princess Anne's Charities
*The Professional Footballers' Association Charity**
The Puri Foundation
*The Pye Foundation**
Mr and Mrs J. A. Pye's Charitable Settlement
Quartet Community Foundation
The Queen's Trust
*Quercus Foundation**
Quothquan Trust
The Monica Rabagliati Charitable Trust
The Radcliffe Trust
Richard Radcliffe Trust
The Rainford Trust
The Rambourg Foundation
The Rank Foundation Ltd

The Joseph Rank Trust
Rashbass Family Trust
Elizabeth Rathbone Charity
The Ravensdale Trust
The Rayne Foundation
The Rayne Trust
The John Rayner Charitable Trust
The Sir James Reckitt Charity
Red Hill Charitable Trust
Reed Family Foundation
Richard Reeve's Foundation
Reuben Foundation
Rhondda Cynon Taff Welsh Church Acts Fund
Richmond Parish Lands Charity
The River Farm Foundation
The Robertson Trust
Robyn Charitable Trust
The Sir James Roll Charitable Trust
*Mrs L. D. Rope's Second Charitable Settlement**
Mrs L. D. Rope's Third Charitable Settlement
Rosca Trust
*The David Ross Foundation**
The Rothermere Foundation
The Rothley Trust
The Roughley Charitable Trust
*Rozelle Trust**
*S. and R. Charitable Trust**
The Michael and Nicola Sacher Charitable Trust
The Michael Sacher Charitable Trust
The Saddlers' Company Charitable Fund
The Saga Charitable Trust
The Saintbury Trust
The Saints and Sinners Trust Ltd
The Salamander Charitable Trust
Salters' Charitable Foundation
The Andrew Salvesen Charitable Trust
Coral Samuel Charitable Trust
The Basil Samuel Charitable Trust
The Samworth Foundation
The Sandhu Charitable Foundation
Santander UK Foundation Ltd
The Sants Charitable Trust
*The Save the Children Fund**
The Scarfe Charitable Trust
Schroder Charity Trust
The Francis C. Scott Charitable Trust
The Frieda Scott Charitable Trust
*The John Scott Trust Fund**
The Scouloudi Foundation
Sam and Bella Sebba Charitable Trust
Leslie Sell Charitable Trust
The Shanly Foundation
The Shears Foundation
The Sheldon Trust
The Patricia and Donald Shepherd Charitable Trust
The Shetland Charitable Trust
SHINE (Support and Help in Education)
The Bassil Shippam and Alsford Trust
The Shipwrights' Company Charitable Fund
The Shoe Zone Trust
David and Jennifer Sieff Charitable Trust
The Skelton Bounty
Skipton Building Society Charitable Foundation
The Slaughter and May Charitable Trust
Sloane Robinson Foundation
The Smith Charitable Trust
The Henry Smith Charity
The Leslie Smith Foundation
The WH Smith Group Charitable Trust
The R. C. Snelling Charitable Trust
The Sobell Foundation
*Sofronie Foundation**
The Solo Charitable Settlement
*Somerset Community Foundation**
The E. C. Sosnow Charitable Trust
The South Square Trust
The Southover Manor General Education Trust
Spar Charitable Fund
Sparks Charity (Sport Aiding Medical Research for Kids)
The Spear Charitable Trust
The Spielman Charitable Trust
The Spoore, Merry and Rixman Foundation
The Spurrell Charitable Trust
The Geoff and Fiona Squire Foundation
The Squires Foundation
The St Hilda's Trust
The St James's Trust Settlement
St James's Place Foundation
Sir Walter St John's Educational Charity
*St Marylebone Educational Foundation**
St Olave's and St Saviour's Schools Foundation – Foundation Fund
The Stafford Trust
*Staffordshire Community Foundation**
The Hugh Stenhouse Foundation
C. E. K. Stern Charitable Trust
The Sigmund Sternberg Charitable Foundation
The Stewards' Charitable Trust
The Andy Stewart Charitable Foundation
The Stoller Charitable Trust
The Samuel Storey Family Charitable Trust
Stratford upon Avon Town Trust
The W. O. Street Charitable Foundation
The Sudborough Foundation
The Alan Sugar Foundation
The Summerfield Charitable Trust
The Bernard Sunley Charitable Foundation
Swan Mountain Trust
The Swann-Morton Foundation
The John Swire (1989) Charitable Trust
The Swire Charitable Trust
Sylvia Waddilove Foundation UK
The Talbot Trusts
The Talbot Village Trust
Tallow Chandlers Benevolent Fund No. 2
The Tanner Trust
The Lili Tapper Charitable Foundation
The Taurus Foundation
The Connie and Albert Taylor Charitable Trust
The Taylor Family Foundation
The Tedworth Charitable Trust
Tees Valley Community Foundation
The Templeton Goodwill Trust
The Tennis Foundation
The Thales Charitable Trust
*DM Thomas Foundation for Young People**
The Thornton Trust
The Thousandth Man- Richard Burns Charitable Trust
Tilney Charitable Trust
The Tobacco Pipe Makers and Tobacco Trade Benevolent Fund
The Tolkien Trust
Toras Chesed (London) Trust
Tottenham Grammar School Foundation
The Toy Trust
Toyota Manufacturing UK Charitable Trust
Annie Tranmer Charitable Trust
The Treeside Trust
The Trefoil Trust
The True Colours Trust
Trumros Ltd
The Trusthouse Charitable Foundation
*The Trysil Charitable Trust**
The Tudor Trust
The Tuixen Foundation
The Roger and Douglas Turner Charitable Trust

Older people

The Crerar Hotels Trust
Criffel Charitable Trust
The Ronald Cruickshanks Foundation
The Cumber Family Charitable Trust
Cumbria Community Foundation
The D'Oyly Carte Charitable Trust
The Joan Lynette Dalton Charitable Trust
The Dr and Mrs A. Darlington Charitable Trust
Baron Davenport's Charity
The Davis Foundation
The De Brye Charitable Trust
William Dean Countryside and Educational Trust
Debenhams Foundation
Foundation Derbyshire
Provincial Grand Charity of the Province of Derbyshire
The Dischma Charitable Trust
The Djanogly Foundation
The Derek and Eileen Dodgson Foundation
Dorset Community Foundation
The Dorus Trust
Douglas Arter Foundation
The Drapers' Charitable Fund
The Dumbreck Charity
The Dunhill Medical Trust
County Durham Community Foundation
The Earley Charity
The Sir John Eastwood Foundation
Echoes Of Service
The Economist Charitable Trust
Edupoor Ltd
Dr Edwards Bishop King's Fulham Endowment Fund
The W. G. Edwards Charitable Foundation
The Eighty Eight Foundation*
The Wilfred and Elsie Elkes Charity Fund
The Maud Elkington Charitable Trust
The Vernon N. Ely Charitable Trust
The Emerton-Christie Charity
The Englefield Charitable Trust
The Enkalon Foundation
The Epigoni Trust
The Ericson Trust
The Erskine Cunningham Hill Trust
Esh Foundation
The Essex and Southend Sports Trust
Joseph Ettedgui Charitable Foundation
Euro Charity Trust
The Everard Foundation
The Eveson Charitable Trust
The Expat Foundation
Esmée Fairbairn Foundation
The Fairstead Trust
The Lord Faringdon Charitable Trust
Samuel William Farmer Trust
The Doris Field Charitable Trust
The Football Association National Sports Centre Trust
The Lady Forester Trust
Forever Manchester
The Forman Hardy Charitable Trust
Donald Forrester Trust
The Hugh Fraser Foundation
The Joseph Strong Frazer Trust
The Charles S. French Charitable Trust
Friarsgate Trust
The Frognal Trust
The Adrian and Jane Frost Charitable Trust
The Patrick and Helena Frost Foundation
The Gale Family Charity Trust
Gatwick Airport Community Trust
The David Gibbons Foundation
The G. C. Gibson Charitable Trust
The Simon Gibson Charitable Trust
Gilchrist Educational Trust*
The L. and R. Gilley Charitable Trust*
The Gloag Foundation
Gloucestershire Community Foundation
Worshipful Company of Gold and Silver Wyre Drawers Charitable Trust Fund
The Goldsmiths' Company Charity
The Goodman Foundation
Gowling WLG (UK) Charitable Trust
Grand Charitable Trust of the Order of Women Freemasons
The Gray Trust
Gordon Gray Trust
The Green Hall Foundation
Greenham Common Community Trust Ltd
The Greggs Foundation
The Grimmitt Trust
The Grocers' Charity
The Bishop of Guildford's Foundation
The Walter Guinness Charitable Trust
The Hadfield Charitable Trust
The Hadrian Trust
The Alfred Haines Charitable Trust
The Helen Hamlyn Trust
Hampton Fuel Allotment Charity
The W. A. Handley Charity Trust
The Kathleen Hannay Memorial Charity
The Haramead Trust
The Harbour Charitable Trust
The Harbour Foundation
William Harding's Charity
The Harris Family Charitable Trust
The Edith Lilian Harrison 2000 Foundation
The Harrison-Frank Family Foundation (UK) Ltd
The Alfred And Peggy Harvey Charitable Trust
The Hasluck Charitable Trust
The Hathaway Trust
The Charles Hayward Foundation
May Hearnshaw Charitable Trust (May Hearnshaw's Charity)
Heart of England Community Foundation
The Heathcoat Trust
The Charlotte Heber-Percy Charitable Trust
Ernest Hecht Charitable Foundation
The Helping Foundation
The Hemby Charitable Trust
Henderson Firstfruits*
The Christina Mary Hendrie Trust for Scottish and Canadian Charities
The G. D. Herbert Charitable Trust
Herefordshire Community Foundation
M. V. Hillhouse Trust*
The Hillier Trust
The Hillingdon Community Trust
R. G. Hills Charitable Trust
The Hiscox Foundation
The Henry C. Hoare Charitable Trust
The Hobson Charity Ltd
The Jane Hodge Foundation
The Hollick Family Charitable Trust
The Dorothy Holmes Charitable Trust
The Edward Holt Trust
The Homestead Charitable Trust
The Mary Homfray Charitable Trust
Hopmarket Charity
The Thomas J. Horne Memorial Trust
Hospice UK
The Hospital of God at Greatham
House of Industry Estate

The Hudson Foundation
The Hull and East Riding Charitable Trust
The Albert Hunt Trust
Miss Agnes H. Hunter's Trust
Huntingdon Freemen's Trust
The Nani Huyu Charitable Trust
Hyde Charitable Trust (Youth Plus)
*Ibbett Trust**
IGO Foundation Ltd
The Iliffe Family Charitable Trust
The Inman Charity
Investream Charitable Trust
The Ireland Fund of Great Britain
The Charles Irving Charitable Trust
The J. Isaacs Charitable Trust
The Ruth and Lionel Jacobson Trust (Second Fund) No. 2
John James Bristol Foundation
The Jarman Charitable Trust
John Jarrold Trust Ltd
The Jenour Foundation
Lillie Johnson Charitable Trust
The Johnson Foundation
Johnson Wax Ltd Charitable Trust
The Joicey Trust
The Jones 1986 Charitable Trust
The Dezna Robins Jones Charitable Foundation
The Marjorie and Geoffrey Jones Charitable Trust
The Jordan Charitable Foundation
J. E. Joseph Charitable Fund
The Cyril and Eve Jumbo Charitable Trust
The Michael and Ilse Katz Foundation
Kent Community Foundation
The Ursula Keyes Trust
Kirkley Poor's Land Estate
The Richard Kirkman Trust
Robert Kitchin (Saddlers' Company)
The Ernest Kleinwort Charitable Trust
The Sir James Knott Trust
Kreditor Charitable Trust
Ladbrokes in the Community Charitable Trust
The K. P. Ladd Charitable Trust
John Laing Charitable Trust
Maurice and Hilda Laing Charitable Trust
Christopher Laing Foundation
The David Laing Foundation
The Kirby Laing Foundation
The Martin Laing Foundation
The Beatrice Laing Trust
The Lambert Charitable Trust
Duchy of Lancaster Benevolent Fund
The Jack Lane Charitable Trust
The Allen Lane Foundation
Langdale Trust
The R. J. Larg Family Charitable Trust
Laslett's (Hinton) Charity
Mrs F. B. Laurence Charitable Trust
The Kathleen Laurence Trust
The Edgar E. Lawley Foundation
The Herd Lawson and Muriel Lawson Charitable Trust
The Raymond and Blanche Lawson Charitable Trust
The Leathersellers' Company Charitable Fund
The William Leech Charity
Leeds Building Society Charitable Foundation
Leicestershire, Leicester and Rutland Community Foundation
P. Leigh-Bramwell Trust 'E'
The Leverhulme Trade Charities Trust
*The Maisie and Raphael Lewis Charitable Trust**
*Bernard Lewis Family Charitable Trust**
David and Ruth Lewis Family Charitable Trust
John Lewis Partnership General Community Fund
Lincolnshire Community Foundation
The Linden Charitable Trust
The Lindley Foundation (TLF)
The Frank Litchfield Charitable Trust
The George John and Sheilah Livanos Charitable Trust
Jack Livingstone Charitable Trust
*The W. M. and B. W. Lloyd Trust**
Lloyds Bank Foundation for England and Wales
Lloyds Bank Foundation for the Channel Islands
Lloyds TSB Foundation for Scotland
Loftus Charitable Trust
London Catalyst
The London Community Foundation (LCF)
The William and Katherine Longman Trust
*Michael Lowe's and Associated Charities**
Paul Lunn-Rockliffe Charitable Trust
C. F. Lunoe Trust Fund
Lord and Lady Lurgan Trust
The Lynn Foundation
M. and C. Trust
The Macdonald-Buchanan Charitable Trust
The Mackintosh Foundation
The Magdalen and Lasher Charity (General Fund)
The Manchester Guardian Society Charitable Trust
R. W. Mann Trust
The Stella and Alexander Margulies Charitable Trust
Mariapolis Ltd
The Marks Family Foundation
The Ann and David Marks Foundation
The Michael Marsh Charitable Trust
The Marsh Christian Trust
Charlotte Marshall Charitable Trust
*The Martin Charitable Trust**
Sir George Martin Trust
John Martin's Charity
*Masonic Charitable Foundation**
The Nancie Massey Charitable Trust
The Matliwala Family Charitable Trust
The Violet Mauray Charitable Trust
The Robert McAlpine Foundation
D. D. McPhail Charitable Settlement
The Medlock Charitable Trust
Mercaz Torah Vechesed Ltd
The Mercers' Charitable Foundation
Merchant Navy Welfare Board
Merchant Taylors' Consolidated Charities for the Infirm
The Merchant Venturers' Charity
The Metropolitan Masonic Charity
T. and J. Meyer Family Foundation Ltd
The Mickel Fund
The Mickleham Trust
The Gerald Micklem Charitable Trust
The Millfield House Foundation (1)
The Millfield Trust
The Mills Charity
The Millward Charitable Trust
The Mirianog Trust
The Mishcon Family Charitable Trust
The MITIE Foundation
Keren Mitzvah Trust
Mobbs Memorial Trust Ltd
The Monmouthshire County Council Welsh Church Act Fund
The George A. Moore Foundation

The Morgan Charitable Foundation
The Steve Morgan Foundation
The Morris Charitable Trust
G. M. Morrison Charitable Trust
*The Morrisons Foundation**
Vyoel Moshe Charitable Trust
The Moss Family Charitable Trust
The Mosselson Charitable Trust
The Mulberry Trust
The Edith Murphy Foundation
Murphy-Neumann Charity Company Ltd
The Music Sales Charitable Trust
Muslim Hands
Nominet Charitable Foundation
Norfolk Community Foundation
The Norman Family Charitable Trust
Normanby Charitable Trust
Northamptonshire Community Foundation
Northwood Charitable Trust
The Notgrove Trust
Nottinghamshire Community Foundation
The Oakley Charitable Trust
Oizer Charitable Trust
The Oldham Foundation
*One Community Foundation Ltd**
The Ormsby Charitable Trust
Oxfordshire Community Foundation
*The Paddington Charitable Estate Educational Fund**
The Paget Charitable Trust
*The Pargiter Trust**
Susanna Peake Charitable Trust
The Dowager Countess Eleanor Peel Trust
People's Postcode Trust
The Persula Foundation
The Pharsalia Charitable Trust
The Phillips and Rubens Charitable Trust
Pilkington Charities Fund
The George and Esme Pollitzer Charitable Settlement
The Porta Pia 2012 Foundation
The Portrack Charitable Trust
The J. E. Posnansky Charitable Trust
*Postcode Community Trust**
Sir John Priestman Charity Trust
*The Pye Foundation**
Quartet Community Foundation
Quothquan Trust
The Radcliffe Trust
The Rainford Trust
The Rank Foundation Ltd
The Joseph Rank Trust
Rashbass Family Trust
The Ravensdale Trust
The Rayne Foundation
The Rayne Trust
The John Rayner Charitable Trust
The Sir James Reckitt Charity
Reed Family Foundation
Reuben Foundation
Rhondda Cynon Taff Welsh Church Acts Fund
Richmond Parish Lands Charity
The River Farm Foundation
*Riverside Charitable Trust Ltd**
*Mrs L. D. Rope's Second Charitable Settlement**
Rosca Trust
The Cecil Rosen Foundation
The Roughley Charitable Trust
Mrs Gladys Row Fogo Charitable Trust
The Rowlands Trust
*S. and R. Charitable Trust**
The Saintbury Trust
The Saints and Sinners Trust Ltd
The Salamander Charitable Trust
The Andrew Salvesen Charitable Trust
Coral Samuel Charitable Trust
The Sandhu Charitable Foundation
Santander UK Foundation Ltd
The Scarfe Charitable Trust
Schroder Charity Trust
The Frieda Scott Charitable Trust
The Scouloudi Foundation
The Searchlight Electric Charitable Trust
The Shanly Foundation
The Shears Foundation
The Sheldon Trust
The Shetland Charitable Trust
The Bassil Shippam and Alsford Trust
The Skelton Bounty
*The Skerritt Trust**
Skipton Building Society Charitable Foundation
The Slaughter and May Charitable Trust
The Smith Charitable Trust
The Henry Smith Charity
The WH Smith Group Charitable Trust
The R. C. Snelling Charitable Trust
The Sobell Foundation
The Solo Charitable Settlement
*Somerset Community Foundation**
The Spear Charitable Trust
The Spielman Charitable Trust
The Spurrell Charitable Trust
The Squires Foundation
St Monica Trust
The Stafford Trust
*Staffordshire Community Foundation**
The Sigmund Sternberg Charitable Foundation
Stratford upon Avon Town Trust
The W. O. Street Charitable Foundation
The Alan Sugar Foundation
The Summerfield Charitable Trust
The Bernard Sunley Charitable Foundation
*Sunninghill Fuel Allotment Trust**
Sutton Coldfield Charitable Trust
The John Swire (1989) Charitable Trust
Sylvia Waddilove Foundation UK
The Talbot Trusts
The Talbot Village Trust
The Tanner Trust
The Lili Tapper Charitable Foundation
The Connie and Albert Taylor Charitable Trust
Tees Valley Community Foundation
The Templeton Goodwill Trust
The Thales Charitable Trust
The Thousandth Man- Richard Burns Charitable Trust
Tilney Charitable Trust
The Tobacco Pipe Makers and Tobacco Trade Benevolent Fund
The Tolkien Trust
The Tory Family Foundation
Annie Tranmer Charitable Trust
The Treeside Trust
Trumros Ltd
The Trusthouse Charitable Foundation
The Tudor Trust
The Roger and Douglas Turner Charitable Trust
Community Foundation serving Tyne and Wear and Northumberland
The Udlington Trust
Vale of Glamorgan Welsh Church Fund
The Valiant Charitable Trust
The Albert Van Den Bergh Charitable Trust
The Van Neste Foundation
The William and Patricia Venton Charitable Trust
Voluntary Action Fund (VAF)
Wade's Charity
Walton on Thames Charity
Wates Family Enterprise Trust
The Wates Foundation

Waynflete Charitable Trust
West Derby Waste Lands Charity
*The West Looe Town Trust**
*The Westminster Amalgamated Charity**
The Garfield Weston Foundation
*The Williams Family Foundation**
Williams Serendipity Trust
The Wilmcote Charitrust
J. and J. R. Wilson Trust
Wiltshire Community Foundation
The Francis Winham Foundation
The Michael and Anna Wix Charitable Trust
The Maurice Wohl Charitable Foundation
Woodroffe Benton Foundation
The Yapp Charitable Trust
Yorkshire and Clydesdale Bank Foundation
Yorkshire Building Society Charitable Foundation
*Elizabeth and Prince Zaiger Trust**
The Marjorie and Arnold Ziff Charitable Foundation
Zurich Community Trust (UK) Ltd

Class, group, occupation or former occupation

■ Armed forces

ABF The Soldiers' Charity
*The AEB Charitable Trust**
The Ammco Trust
*The Anne Duchess of Westminster's Charity**
The Armourers' and Brasiers' Gauntlet Trust
ASCB Charitable Fund
The Baltic Charitable Fund
The Band Trust
The Cadogan Charity
The Childwick Trust
The Robert Clutterbuck Charitable Trust
The Worshipful Company of Cordwainers Charitable Trusts (Minges Gift and the Pooled Trusts)
The Sandy Dewhirst Charitable Trust
The Royal Foundation of the Duke and Duchess of Cambridge and Prince Harry
The Gilbert and Eileen Edgar Foundation
Edinburgh Trust No 2 Account
The Englefield Charitable Trust
The Erskine Cunningham Hill Trust
The Everard Foundation
The Doris Field Charitable Trust
Donald Forrester Trust
The Elizabeth Frankland Moore and Star Foundation
The Joseph Strong Frazer Trust
The Godinton Charitable Trust
Worshipful Company of Gold and Silver Wyre Drawers Charitable Trust Fund
The Mike Gooley Trailfinders Charity
The Gosling Foundation Ltd
The Green Hall Foundation
The Grocers' Charity
The Walter Guinness Charitable Trust
The W. A. Handley Charity Trust
The Hawthorne Charitable Trust
The Christina Mary Hendrie Trust for Scottish and Canadian Charities
*M. V. Hillhouse Trust**
The Hiscox Foundation
The Hobson Charity Ltd
The Albert Hunt Trust
The Inman Charity
The Inverforth Charitable Trust
Lillie Johnson Charitable Trust
The Michael and Ilse Katz Foundation
*The Graham Kirkham Foundation**
The Richard Kirkman Trust
The Ernest Kleinwort Charitable Trust
The Sir James Knott Trust
The Beatrice Laing Trust
Duchy of Lancaster Benevolent Fund
Mrs F. B. Laurence Charitable Trust
The Raymond and Blanche Lawson Charitable Trust
John Lewis Partnership General Community Fund
The Charles Littlewood Hill Trust
The Henry Lumley Charitable Trust
Paul Lunn-Rockliffe Charitable Trust
The MacRobert Trust
*Masonic Charitable Foundation**
*The Master Charitable Trust**
The Medlock Charitable Trust
The Mickel Fund
The Laurence Misener Charitable Trust
The George A. Moore Foundation
G. M. Morrison Charitable Trust
The Norman Family Charitable Trust
The George and Esme Pollitzer Charitable Settlement
The Prince of Wales's Charitable Foundation
The Princess Anne's Charities
Queen Mary's Roehampton Trust
The Rothley Trust
Royal Artillery Charitable Fund
The Royal British Legion
*The Royal Navy And Royal Marines Charity**
The Saddlers' Company Charitable Fund
Salters' Charitable Foundation
Scott (Eredine) Charitable Trust
The Scouloudi Foundation
Seafarers UK (King George's Fund for Sailors)
The Leslie Smith Foundation
The Stafford Trust
The John Swire (1989) Charitable Trust
The Swire Charitable Trust
The Trefoil Trust
The Michael Uren Foundation
The Albert Van Den Bergh Charitable Trust
Mrs Maud Van Norden's Charitable Foundation
G. R. Waters Charitable Trust 2000
The James Weir Foundation
Colonel W. H. Whitbread Charitable Trust

■ Arts, culture,sports and recreation

Arts Council England
Arts Council of Northern Ireland
Arts Council of Wales (also known as Cyngor Celfyddydau Cymru)
*The Associated Board of the Royal Schools of Music**
British Record Industry Trust
The Britten-Pears Foundation (The Britten Pears Library)
The Richard Carne Trust
Colwinston Charitable Trust
The Worshipful Company of Cordwainers Charitable Trusts (Minges Gift and the Pooled Trusts)
The Cotton Industry War Memorial Trust
Creative Scotland
The D'Oyly Carte Charitable Trust
The Delius Trust
*The Eighty Eight Foundation**

The Elephant Trust
The Elmley Foundation
The Vernon N. Ely Charitable Trust
EMI Music Sound Foundation
Esmée Fairbairn Foundation
The Fidelio Charitable Trust*
The Foyle Foundation
The Garrick Charitable Trust
Worshipful Company of Glovers of London Charitable Trust
Worshipful Company of Gold and Silver Wyre Drawers Charitable Trust Fund
The Goldsmiths' Company Charity
Nicholas and Judith Goodison's Charitable Settlement
The Derek Hill Foundation
The Hinrichsen Foundation
The Sir Barry Jackson County Fund (incorporating the Hornton Fund)
The Jerwood Charitable Foundation
The Boris Karloff Charitable Foundation
The David Laing Foundation
The David Lean Foundation
The Leathersellers' Company Charitable Fund
The Leche Trust
Limoges Charitable Trust
The Linbury Trust
The Linden Charitable Trust
The Enid Linder Foundation
Lord and Lady Lurgan Trust
The Lynn Foundation
The Sir Jack Lyons Charitable Trust
The Mayfield Valley Arts Trust
The Brian Mercer Charitable Trust
The Millward Charitable Trust
The Henry Moore Foundation
British Motor Sports Training Trust
The Worshipful Company of Needlemakers' Charitable Fund
The Performing Right Society Foundation
The Racing Foundation
Racing Welfare
Royal Victoria Hall Foundation
The RVW Trust
The Shanly Foundation
The Spear Charitable Trust
The Stewards' Charitable Trust
The Taurus Foundation
Humphrey Richardson Taylor Charitable Trust
The Thistle Trust
The Valiant Charitable Trust
The Vandervell Foundation
The Wolfson Foundation

■ Environment and agriculture

The Elizabeth Creak Charitable Trust*
Fishmongers' Company's Charitable Trust
The Worshipful Company of Gardeners of London
The Hutchinson Charitable Trust
Rees Jeffreys Road Fund
The Joicey Trust
The Kennel Club Charitable Trust
The Mark Leonard Trust
The Frank Litchfield Charitable Trust
The NFU Mutual Charitable Trust
The John Oldacre Foundation
The Racing Foundation
Racing Welfare

■ Financial services

Chartered Accountants' Livery Charity (CALC)
The Worshipful Company of Insurers – First Charitable Trust Fund*
The International Bankers Charitable Trust (The Worshipful Company of Interntional Bankers)
Mrs F. B. Laurence Charitable Trust

■ Freemasons

Cheshire Freemason's Charity
Provincial Grand Charity of the Province of Derbyshire
Grand Charitable Trust of the Order of Women Freemasons
Leicestershire and Rutland Masonic Charity Association*
Masonic Charitable Foundation*
The Metropolitan Masonic Charity
The Masonic Province of Middlesex Charitable Trust (Middlesex Masonic Charity)
Provincial Grand Charity of Northamptonshire and Huntingdonshire*
The Warwickshire Masonic Charitable Association Ltd*

■ Law

The Addleshaw Goddard Charitable Trust
The Law Society Charity
The Legal Education Foundation*

■ Manufacturing and service industries

Canary Wharf Contractors Fund*
The Cooks Charity
The Worshipful Company of Cordwainers Charitable Trusts (Minges Gift and the Pooled Trusts)
The Cotton Industry War Memorial Trust
The Crerar Hotels Trust
Debenhams Foundation
Worshipful Company of Glovers of London Charitable Trust
Worshipful Company of Gold and Silver Wyre Drawers Charitable Trust Fund
The Goldsmiths' Company Charity
The Worshipful Company of Horners' Charitable Trusts
The Leathersellers' Company Charitable Fund
The Leverhulme Trade Charities Trust
C. F. Lunoe Trust Fund
The Makers of Playing Cards Charity
The Worshipful Company of Needlemakers' Charitable Fund
Daisie Rich Trust
Riverside Charitable Trust Ltd*
The Rugby Group Benevolent Fund Ltd
The Savoy Educational Trust*
Spar Charitable Fund

■ Medicine and health

Bloodwise
The British Dietetic Association General and Education Trust Fund
British Heart Foundation (BHF)
The Burdett Trust for Nursing
The Colt Foundation
The Harry Cureton Charitable Trust
Dinwoodie Charitable Company
The General Nursing Council for England and Wales Trust
The Health Foundation
The Ursula Keyes Trust
The Leverhulme Trade Charities Trust
John Lewis Partnership General Community Fund

The Enid Linder Foundation
The Edwina Mountbatten and Leonora Children's Foundation
The Pen Shell Project
Sir John Priestman Charity Trust
The Sandra Charitable Trust
The Jean Shanks Foundation
The Swann-Morton Foundation
*Tropical Health and Education Trust**
The James Weir Foundation
The Wellcome Trust

■ Religion

All Saints Educational Trust
The Ashburnham Thanksgiving Trust
The Bellahouston Bequest Fund
The Anne French Memorial Trust
The Goshen Trust
Philip and Judith Green Trust
*Heb Ffin (Without Frontier)**
Hockerill Educational Foundation
Sir Harold Hood's Charitable Trust
The Hope Trust
The Lyndhurst Trust
Sylvanus Lysons Charity
Charity of John Marshall
The Father O'Mahoney Memorial Trust
Sir John Priestman Charity Trust
The Bishop Radford Trust
The River Trust
The Seedfield Trust
The Seven Fifty Trust
The Souter Charitable Trust
The Sigmund Sternberg Charitable Foundation
Mrs R. P. Tindall's Charitable Trust
Ulting Overseas Trust
The Norman Whiteley Trust
The James Wood Bequest Fund

■ Science, technology and engineering

The Colt Foundation
*The Happold Foundation**
The Worshipful Company of Horners' Charitable Trusts
*The Worshipful Company of Information Technologists**
The Leverhulme Trade Charities Trust
*North East Area Miners Welfare Trust Fund**
Winton Philanthropies

■ Seafarers and ex-seafarers

The Baltic Charitable Fund
The Frederick and Phyllis Cann Trust
*The Corporation of Trinity House of Deptford Strond**
Edinburgh Trust No 2 Account
The Erskine Cunningham Hill Trust
Dixie Rose Findlay Charitable Trust
The Sir John Fisher Foundation
Fishmongers' Company's Charitable Trust
The Joseph Strong Frazer Trust
The Gosling Foundation Ltd
The W. A. Handley Charity Trust
The ITF Seafarers' Trust
The Joicey Trust
The Sir James Knott Trust
Mrs F. B. Laurence Charitable Trust
Limoges Charitable Trust
The George John and Sheilah Livanos Charitable Trust
The MacRobert Trust
Merchant Navy Welfare Board
The Norman Family Charitable Trust
The Phillips Charitable Trust
The George and Esme Pollitzer Charitable Settlement
*The Royal Navy And Royal Marines Charity**
The Scouloudi Foundation
Seafarers Hospital Society
Seafarers UK (King George's Fund for Sailors)
The Shipwrights' Company Charitable Fund
The James Weir Foundation

■ Social welfare

*CSIS Charity Fund**
The Norman Family Charitable Trust
*Tropical Health and Education Trust**
The Wellcome Trust

■ Transport

Rees Jeffreys Road Fund
D. G. Marshall of Cambridge Trust

Disability

The ACT Foundation
The Adint Charitable Trust
The Sylvia Aitken Charitable Trust
Ajahma Charitable Trust
The Alchemy Foundation
The Ammco Trust
*The Ancaster Trust**
Andor Charitable Trust
The Mary Andrew Charitable Trust
*The Anne Duchess of Westminster's Charity**
The Archer Trust
The Argus Appeal
The Astor Foundation
The Lord Austin Trust
Autonomous Research Charitable Trust (ARCT)
The Roy and Pixie Baker Charitable Trust
The Baker Charitable Trust
The Band Trust
Barchester Healthcare Foundation
The Barclay Foundation
Barnwood Trust
Bauer Radio's Cash for Kids Charities
The Benham Charitable Settlement
*The Rowan Bentall Charitable Trust**
Bergqvist Charitable Trust
The Berkeley Charitable Foundation
Percy Bilton Charity
Birmingham International Airport Community Trust Fund
Blakemore Foundation
BOOST Charitable Trust
The Boshier-Hinton Foundation
The Bothwell Charitable Trust
The Harry Bottom Charitable Trust
P. G. and N. J. Boulton Trust
The Liz and Terry Bramall Foundation
*The Brelms Trust CIO**
Bridge Trust
Bristol Charities
John Bristow and Thomas Mason Trust
Bill Brown 1989 Charitable Trust
R. S. Brownless Charitable Trust
The Bruntwood Charity
The Burry Charitable Trust
The William A. Cadbury Charitable Trust
The Cadbury Foundation
The Casey Trust
Champneys Charitable Foundation
Chesterhill Charitable Trust

The Childwick Trust
CHK Charities Ltd
Chrysalis Trust
Church Burgesses Trust
The Cleopatra Trust
The Clothworkers' Foundation
The Clover Trust
The Robert Clutterbuck Charitable Trust
The John Coates Charitable Trust
The Vivienne and Samuel Cohen Charitable Trust
The Catherine Cookson Charitable Trust
The Keith Coombs Trust
The J. Reginald Corah Foundation Fund
Michael Cornish Charitable Trust
The Cotton Industry War Memorial Trust
The Sir Tom Cowie Charitable Trust
The Lord Cozens-Hardy Trust
Criffel Charitable Trust
Cruden Foundation Ltd
The Ronald Cruickshanks Foundation
The Cumber Family Charitable Trust
Cumbria Community Foundation
The Dr and Mrs A. Darlington Charitable Trust
The Davis Foundation
*The Roger De Haan Charitable Trust**
William Dean Countryside and Educational Trust
The J. N. Derbyshire Trust
Devon Community Foundation
The Sandy Dewhirst Charitable Trust
Disability Aid Fund (The Roger and Jean Jefcoate Trust)
The Dischma Charitable Trust
Dorset Community Foundation
The Dorus Trust
The Charles Dunstone Charitable Trust
County Durham Community Foundation
The Sir John Eastwood Foundation
Echoes Of Service
The Economist Charitable Trust
Edupoor Ltd
The George Elias Charitable Trust
The Vernon N. Ely Charitable Trust
The Emerton-Christie Charity
The Englefield Charitable Trust
The Epigoni Trust
The Eranda Rothschild Foundation
Esh Foundation
Euro Charity Trust
G. F. Eyre Charitable Trust
Esmée Fairbairn Foundation
The Fairstead Trust
The Lord Faringdon Charitable Trust
Samuel William Farmer Trust
The Thomas Farr Charity
The February Foundation
The George Fentham Birmingham Charity
The A. M. Fenton Trust
The Doris Field Charitable Trust
Dixie Rose Findlay Charitable Trust
The Sir John Fisher Foundation
Fishmongers' Company's Charitable Trust
The Earl Fitzwilliam Charitable Trust
The Joyce Fletcher Charitable Trust
Ford Britain Trust
Forest Hill Charitable Trust
The Lady Forester Trust
Forever Manchester
The Forman Hardy Charitable Trust
Donald Forrester Trust
The Elizabeth Frankland Moore and Star Foundation
The Gordon Fraser Charitable Trust
The Hugh Fraser Foundation
The Joseph Strong Frazer Trust
The Charles S. French Charitable Trust
Friarsgate Trust
The Frognal Trust
The Adrian and Jane Frost Charitable Trust
The Patrick and Helena Frost Foundation
The Fulmer Charitable Trust
The G. D. Charitable Trust
The Gale Family Charity Trust
Gatwick Airport Community Trust
The Robert Gavron Charitable Trust
The Generations Foundation
*Genetic Disorders UK**
Get Kids Going
The David Gibbons Foundation
The G. C. Gibson Charitable Trust
The Simon Gibson Charitable Trust
*Gilchrist Educational Trust**
*The L. and R. Gilley Charitable Trust**
The Girdlers' Company Charitable Trust
The B. and P. Glasser Charitable Trust
Gloucestershire Community Foundation
Worshipful Company of Gold and Silver Wyre Drawers Charitable Trust Fund
Sydney and Phyllis Goldberg Memorial Charitable Trust
The Goldsmiths' Company Charity
The Goodman Foundation
*The Gordon Trust**
The Gosling Foundation Ltd
Gowling WLG (UK) Charitable Trust
The Hemraj Goyal Foundation
Grand Charitable Trust of the Order of Women Freemasons
The J. G. Graves Charitable Trust
Gordon Gray Trust
The Green Hall Foundation
Greenham Common Community Trust Ltd
The Greggs Foundation
The Bishop of Guildford's Foundation
Guildry Incorporation of Perth
The Walter Guinness Charitable Trust
The Gur Trust
The Hadley Trust
The Hadrian Trust
The Alfred Haines Charitable Trust
Hampshire and Isle of Wight Community Foundation
The Hampstead Wells and Campden Trust
Hampton Fuel Allotment Charity
The W. A. Handley Charity Trust
The Haramead Trust
Harbinson Charitable Trust
Harbo Charities Ltd
The Harbour Foundation
William Harding's Charity
The Harebell Centenary Fund
The Harris Charity
The Harris Family Charitable Trust
The Edith Lilian Harrison 2000 Foundation
The Peter Harrison Foundation
The Harrison-Frank Family Foundation (UK) Ltd
The Hartley Charitable Trust
The Alfred And Peggy Harvey Charitable Trust
The Hasluck Charitable Trust
The Hathaway Trust
The Hawthorne Charitable Trust
May Hearnshaw Charitable Trust (May Hearnshaw's Charity)

Heart of England Community Foundation
The Heathcoat Trust
Ernest Hecht Charitable Foundation
Hedley Foundation Ltd (The Hedley Foundation)
Help for Health
The Hemby Charitable Trust
*Henderson Firstfruits**
The G. D. Herbert Charitable Trust
Herefordshire Community Foundation
*M. V. Hillhouse Trust**
The Hillier Trust
R. G. Hills Charitable Trust
The Hiscox Foundation
The Henry C. Hoare Charitable Trust
The Hobson Charity Ltd
The Jane Hodge Foundation
The Hollick Family Charitable Trust
The Dorothy Holmes Charitable Trust
The Edward Holt Trust
The Homestead Charitable Trust
The Mary Homfray Charitable Trust
The Hoover Foundation
Hopmarket Charity
The Antony Hornby Charitable Trust
The Thomas J. Horne Memorial Trust
The Worshipful Company of Horners' Charitable Trusts
Hospice UK
The Hospital of God at Greatham
The Hospital Saturday Fund
House of Industry Estate
The Hudson Foundation
The Hull and East Riding Charitable Trust
The Humanitarian Trust
The Albert Hunt Trust
Miss Agnes H. Hunter's Trust
Huntingdon Freemen's Trust
*ICE Futures Charitable Trust**
The Iliffe Family Charitable Trust
Incommunities Foundation
The Ingram Trust
The Inman Charity
Investream Charitable Trust
Irish Youth Foundation (UK) Ltd (incorporating The Lawlor Foundation)
The Ruth and Lionel Jacobson Trust (Second Fund) No. 2
John James Bristol Foundation
John Jarrold Trust Ltd
Jewish Child's Day (JCD)
Lillie Johnson Charitable Trust
The Johnson Foundation
Johnnie Johnson Trust
Johnson Wax Ltd Charitable Trust
The Joicey Trust
The Jones 1986 Charitable Trust
The Dezna Robins Jones Charitable Foundation
The Marjorie and Geoffrey Jones Charitable Trust
The Jordan Charitable Foundation
J. E. Joseph Charitable Fund
The Cyril and Eve Jumbo Charitable Trust
Anton Jurgens Charitable Trust
The Boris Karloff Charitable Foundation
The Michael and Ilse Katz Foundation
Kent Community Foundation
The Ursula Keyes Trust
Kirkley Poor's Land Estate
The Richard Kirkman Trust
The Kirschel Foundation
The Ernest Kleinwort Charitable Trust
The Sir James Knott Trust
The Kobler Trust
The Kohn Foundation
Ladbrokes in the Community Charitable Trust
The K. P. Ladd Charitable Trust
Maurice and Hilda Laing Charitable Trust
Christopher Laing Foundation
The David Laing Foundation
The Kirby Laing Foundation
The Beatrice Laing Trust
The Leonard Laity Stoate Charitable Trust
The Lambert Charitable Trust
*The Lancashire Foundation**
Duchy of Lancaster Benevolent Fund
The Jack Lane Charitable Trust
Langdale Trust
The R. J. Larg Family Charitable Trust
Laslett's (Hinton) Charity
The Lauffer Family Charitable Foundation
Mrs F. B. Laurence Charitable Trust
The Kathleen Laurence Trust
The Edgar E. Lawley Foundation
Lawson Beckman Charitable Trust
The Raymond and Blanche Lawson Charitable Trust
The Leathersellers' Company Charitable Fund
The William Leech Charity
Leeds Building Society Charitable Foundation
*Leicestershire and Rutland Masonic Charity Association**
Leicestershire, Leicester and Rutland Community Foundation
The Kennedy Leigh Charitable Trust
P. Leigh-Bramwell Trust 'E'
Lord Leverhulme's Charitable Trust
David and Ruth Lewis Family Charitable Trust
John Lewis Partnership General Community Fund
Lifeline 4 Kids (Handicapped Children's Aid Committee)
The Linbury Trust
The Linden Charitable Trust
The Enid Linder Foundation
The Lindley Foundation (TLF)
The Frank Litchfield Charitable Trust
The Charles Littlewood Hill Trust
The George John and Sheilah Livanos Charitable Trust
Jack Livingstone Charitable Trust
The Elaine and Angus Lloyd Charitable Trust
*The W. M. and B. W. Lloyd Trust**
Lloyds Bank Foundation for the Channel Islands
Lloyds TSB Foundation for Scotland
London Catalyst
The William and Katherine Longman Trust
The Lord's Taverners
The Loseley and Guildway Charitable Trust
*Michael Lowe's and Associated Charities**
The C. L. Loyd Charitable Trust
The Henry Lumley Charitable Trust
Paul Lunn-Rockliffe Charitable Trust
Lord and Lady Lurgan Trust
The Lynn Foundation
M. and C. Trust
The M. K. Charitable Trust
The E. M. MacAndrew Trust
The Macdonald-Buchanan Charitable Trust
The Mackintosh Foundation
*GPS Macpherson Charitable Settlement**
The MacRobert Trust
The Manackerman Charitable Trust
The Manchester Guardian Society Charitable Trust
The Ann and David Marks Foundation

The Michael Marsh Charitable Trust
The Marsh Christian Trust
Charlotte Marshall Charitable Trust
D. G. Marshall of Cambridge Trust
Sir George Martin Trust
John Martin's Charity
Masonic Charitable Foundation*
The Robert McAlpine Foundation
D. D. McPhail Charitable Settlement
Merchant Taylors' Consolidated Charities for the Infirm
The Metropolitan Masonic Charity
T. and J. Meyer Family Foundation Ltd
The Mickleham Trust
The Gerald Micklem Charitable Trust
Middlesex Sports Foundation
Millennium Stadium Charitable Trust (Ymddiriedolaeth Elusennol Stadiwm Y. Mileniwm)
Hugh and Mary Miller Bequest Trust
The Ronald Miller Foundation
The Millfield House Foundation (1)
The Millichope Foundation
Mills and Reeve Charitable Trust*
The Mills Charity
The Millward Charitable Trust
The Clare Milne Trust
The Peter Minet Trust
The Laurence Misener Charitable Trust
The Mishcon Family Charitable Trust
The MITIE Foundation
Keren Mitzvah Trust
Mobbs Memorial Trust Ltd
Mole Charitable Trust
The Monmouthshire County Council Welsh Church Act Fund
The George A. Moore Foundation
The Morgan Charitable Foundation
The Steve Morgan Foundation
The Morris Charitable Trust
G. M. Morrison Charitable Trust
The Morrisons Foundation*
Vyoel Moshe Charitable Trust
The Moss Family Charitable Trust
The Mosselson Charitable Trust
The MSE Charity
The Mugdock Children's Trust
The Edith Murphy Foundation
Murphy-Neumann Charity Company Ltd
The Music Sales Charitable Trust
Muslim Hands
The Janet Nash Charitable Settlement
Norfolk Community Foundation
The Norman Family Charitable Trust
Normanby Charitable Trust
Northamptonshire Community Foundation
The Northwick Trust*
The Norton Foundation
The Notgrove Trust
Oizer Charitable Trust
Old Possum's Practical Trust
The Oldham Foundation
OneFamily Foundation
Open Gate
The Ormsby Charitable Trust
The O'Sullivan Family Charitable Trust
The Doris Pacey Charitable Foundation
Peacock Charitable Trust
Susanna Peake Charitable Trust
The Pears Family Charitable Foundation
People's Postcode Trust
The Persula Foundation
The Pharsalia Charitable Trust
The Phillips and Rubens Charitable Trust
Pilkington Charities Fund
The George and Esme Pollitzer Charitable Settlement
The Portrack Charitable Trust
The Prince Philip Trust Fund*
Princes Gate Trust*
Prison Service Charity Fund
The Pye Foundation*
QBE European Operations Foundation*
The Radcliffe Trust
The Rainford Trust
The Joseph Rank Trust
The Ranworth Trust
Rashbass Family Trust
Elizabeth Rathbone Charity
The Rayne Foundation
The John Rayner Charitable Trust
The Clive and Sylvia Richards Charity Ltd
The River Farm Foundation
Thomas Roberts Trust
The Helen Roll Charity
Mrs L. D. Rope's Second Charitable Settlement*
Rosca Trust
The Cecil Rosen Foundation
The David Ross Foundation*
The Rothley Trust
The Roughley Charitable Trust
The Rowlands Trust
Rozelle Trust*
S. and R. Charitable Trust*
The Michael Sacher Charitable Trust
The Saga Charitable Trust
The Saints and Sinners Trust Ltd
The Salamander Charitable Trust
The Basil Samuel Charitable Trust
The M. J. Samuel Charitable Trust
The Sandhu Charitable Foundation
The Scarfe Charitable Trust
Scott (Eredine) Charitable Trust
The Francis C. Scott Charitable Trust
The Frieda Scott Charitable Trust
The John Scott Trust Fund*
The Scouloudi Foundation
Sam and Bella Sebba Charitable Trust
The Shanly Foundation
The Shears Foundation
The Sheldon Trust
The Shipwrights' Company Charitable Fund
The Florence Shute Millennium Trust*
The Skelton Bounty
The Smith Charitable Trust
The Henry Smith Charity
The R. C. Snelling Charitable Trust
The Sobell Foundation
The Solo Charitable Settlement
Songdale Ltd
R. H. Southern Trust
The Spielman Charitable Trust
The Spurrell Charitable Trust
The Geoff and Fiona Squire Foundation
The St James's Trust Settlement
St James's Place Foundation
St Monica Trust
Staffordshire Community Foundation*
The Peter Stebbings Memorial Charity
The Sigmund Sternberg Charitable Foundation
The Andy Stewart Charitable Foundation
The W. O. Street Charitable Foundation
The Street Foundation*
The Summerfield Charitable Trust
The Bernard Sunley Charitable Foundation

The Swann-Morton Foundation
The John Swire (1989) Charitable Trust
The Swire Charitable Trust
Sylvia Waddilove Foundation UK
The Talbot Trusts
The Talbot Village Trust
Tallow Chandlers Benevolent Fund No. 2
The Tanner Trust
The Lili Tapper Charitable Foundation
C. B. and H. H. Taylor 1984 Trust
The Templeton Goodwill Trust
The Tennis Foundation
The Thales Charitable Trust
*DM Thomas Foundation for Young People**
The Sir Jules Thorn Charitable Trust
The Thousandth Man- Richard Burns Charitable Trust
The Three Oaks Trust
Tilney Charitable Trust
The Tobacco Pipe Makers and Tobacco Trade Benevolent Fund
The Tory Family Foundation
The Toy Trust
Annie Tranmer Charitable Trust
The Treeside Trust
The Trefoil Trust
The True Colours Trust
The Trusthouse Charitable Foundation
The James Tudor Foundation
The Tudor Trust
The Tuixen Foundation
The Roger and Douglas Turner Charitable Trust
Community Foundation serving Tyne and Wear and Northumberland
The Udlington Trust
The Valiant Charitable Trust
The Albert Van Den Bergh Charitable Trust
The Van Neste Foundation
Mrs Maud Van Norden's Charitable Foundation
Variety The Children's Charity (Variety Club)
Volant Charitable Trust
*The Bruce Wake Charity**
The Walker Trust
*The Warwickshire Masonic Charitable Association Ltd**
Wates Family Enterprise Trust
The Wates Foundation
*The Geoffrey Watling Charity**
John Watson's Trust
Waynflete Charitable Trust
The James Weir Foundation
The Welton Foundation
The Wessex Youth Trust
The Westcroft Trust
The Westfield Health Charitable Trust
*The Westminster Amalgamated Charity**
The Garfield Weston Foundation
White Stuff Foundation
The Lionel Wigram Memorial Trust
The Kay Williams Charitable Foundation
*The Williams Family Foundation**
Williams Serendipity Trust
The Wilmcote Charitrust
The Michael and Anna Wix Charitable Trust
The Maurice Wohl Charitable Foundation
The Wolfson Family Charitable Trust
The Wolfson Foundation
The Wolfson Foundation
Wooden Spoon Society
The Wyseliot Rose Charitable Trust
The Yapp Charitable Trust
*York Children's Trust**
Yorkshire and Clydesdale Bank Foundation
Yorkshire Building Society Charitable Foundation
Youth Music
*Elizabeth and Prince Zaiger Trust**
Zurich Community Trust (UK) Ltd

■ People with a mental/mental health disability

The Artemis Charitable Trust
The Berkshire Community Foundation
The Cambridgeshire Community Foundation
The Eveson Charitable Trust
Jill Franklin Trust
G. M. C. Trust
The Charles Irving Charitable Trust
*Life Changes Trust**
The Norman Family Charitable Trust
*Postcode Community Trust**
Mr and Mrs J. A. Pye's Charitable Settlement
David Solomons Charitable Trust
The Peter Stebbings Memorial Charity
The Strangward Trust
The Barbara Ward Children's Foundation

■ People with autism

The Shirley Foundation
The Three Guineas Trust

■ People with dyslexia

The Joseph and Annie Cattle Trust
The Follett Trust
Odin Charitable Trust

■ People with learning difficulties

The Aberbrothock Skea Trust
The Baily Thomas Charitable Fund
Douglas Arter Foundation
The Drapers' Charitable Fund
The Dumbreck Charity
Eastern Counties Educational Trust Ltd
The EBM Charitable Trust
The Forbes Charitable Foundation
The Oliver Ford Charitable Trust
The Foyle Foundation
Kelsick's Educational Foundation
Lloyds Bank Foundation for England and Wales
The Dan Maskell Tennis Trust
The Ponton House Trust
The Rix-Thompson-Rothenberg Foundation
The Sir James Roll Charitable Trust
The Saddlers' Company Charitable Fund
The Mrs Smith and Mount Trust
The Will Charitable Trust

■ People with a physical impairment

The Aberbrothock Skea Trust
The De Brye Charitable Trust
Douglas Arter Foundation
The Drapers' Charitable Fund
The Dumbreck Charity
The EBM Charitable Trust
The Eveson Charitable Trust
The Charles Irving Charitable Trust
Lloyds Bank Foundation for England and Wales
The Dan Maskell Tennis Trust
The Dowager Countess Eleanor Peel Trust
The Ponton House Trust
Mr and Mrs J. A. Pye's Charitable Settlement

Richard Radcliffe Trust
Mrs L. D. Rope's Third Charitable Settlement
The Saddlers' Company Charitable Fund
The Strangward Trust

People with a sensory impairment

The Dan Maskell Tennis Trust
Richard Radcliffe Trust

Hearing loss

The H. B. Allen Charitable Trust
The Wilfred and Elsie Elkes Charity Fund
Northwood Charitable Trust

Sight loss

The H. B. Allen Charitable Trust
British Council for Prevention of Blindness (Save Eyes Everywhere)
*British Eye Research Foundation (Fight for Sight)**
The Worshipful Company of Cordwainers Charitable Trusts (Minges Gift and the Pooled Trusts)
The De Brye Charitable Trust
The Wilfred and Elsie Elkes Charity Fund
The R. S. Macdonald Charitable Trust
The Brian Mercer Charitable Trust
Rhondda Cynon Taff Welsh Church Acts Fund
The Worshipful Company of Spectacle Makers' Charity
The Ulverscroft Foundation
The Michael Uren Foundation
The Will Charitable Trust

Ethnicity

The Bagri Foundation
The Berkshire Community Foundation
The Clothworkers' Foundation
Foundation Derbyshire
County Durham Community Foundation
The Englefield Charitable Trust
The Football Association National Sports Centre Trust
Gloucestershire Community Foundation
Greenham Common Community Trust Ltd
The Hadrian Trust
Hampton Fuel Allotment Charity
The Hinduja Foundation
The Homestead Charitable Trust
The Mary Homfray Charitable Trust
The Albert Hunt Trust
The Joicey Trust
The LankellyChase Foundation
Leicestershire, Leicester and Rutland Community Foundation
Lloyds Bank Foundation for England and Wales
Lloyds TSB Foundation for Scotland
London Catalyst
The London Community Foundation (LCF)
The Ann and David Marks Foundation
The Marsh Christian Trust
The Millfield House Foundation (1)
John Moores Foundation
The Morris Charitable Trust
Norfolk Community Foundation
Normanby Charitable Trust
Northamptonshire Community Foundation
Oxfordshire Community Foundation
The Jack Petchey Foundation
Quartet Community Foundation
Rashbass Family Trust
The Eleanor Rathbone Charitable Trust
The Sigrid Rausing Trust
Reed Family Foundation
The Henry Smith Charity
*Staffordshire Community Foundation**
Tees Valley Community Foundation
The Trusthouse Charitable Foundation
Community Foundation serving Tyne and Wear and Northumberland
The Wates Foundation
*The Westminster Amalgamated Charity**

Faith

The AMW Charitable Trust
*The British and Foreign Bible Society**
Echoes Of Service
The Kathleen Hannay Memorial Charity
The Hinduja Foundation
The Inlight Trust
*Leicestershire and Rutland Masonic Charity Association**
The Lennox Hannay Charitable Trust
Lord Leverhulme's Charitable Trust
The C. L. Loyd Charitable Trust
The Metropolitan Masonic Charity
The Millward Charitable Trust
The Sir James Roll Charitable Trust
The Rothermere Foundation
*The Spalding Trust**
Community Foundation serving Tyne and Wear and Northumberland
Vale of Glamorgan Welsh Church Fund

People of the Christian faith

Aid to the Church in Need (UK)
All Saints Educational Trust
Allchurches Trust Ltd
The Anchor Foundation
Andrews Charitable Trust
*The Anne Duchess of Westminster's Charity**
The Ashburnham Thanksgiving Trust
The Baird Trust
The Bedfordshire and Hertfordshire Historic Churches Trust
The Harry Bottom Charitable Trust
P. G. and N. J. Boulton Trust
The Liz and Terry Bramall Foundation
Bristol Archdeaconry Charity
Buckingham Trust
The Buckinghamshire Historic Churches Trust
The William A. Cadbury Charitable Trust
The Catholic Charitable Trust
The Catholic Trust for England and Wales
Church of Ireland Priorities Fund
The Roger and Sarah Bancroft Clark Charitable Trust
The Hilda and Alice Clark Charitable Trust
Richard Cloudesley's Charity
The Clover Trust
The Congregational and General Charitable Trust
The Costa Family Charitable Trust
The County Council of Dyfed Welsh Curch Fund
The Devon Historic Churches Trust

The Gerald Palmer Eling Trust Company
The Edith Maud Ellis 1985 Charitable Trust
Fisherbeck Charitable Trust
Forest Hill Charitable Trust
The Forte Charitable Trust
Friends of Essex Churches Trust
The Friends of Kent Churches
The Ganzoni Charitable Trust
The Gibbs Charitable Trust
The Gloag Foundation
Global Care
The Gloucestershire Historic Churches Trust
The Goshen Trust
Grace Charitable Trust
The Hampshire and Islands Historic Churches Trust
*Henderson Firstfruits**
The Herefordshire Historic Churches Trust
Hinchley Charitable Trust
The Hintze Family Charity Foundation
Hockerill Educational Foundation
Sir Harold Hood's Charitable Trust
The Hope Trust
The Hutton Foundation
*Integrated Education Fund**
*International Bible Students Association**
The J. A. R. Charitable Trust
The Jerusalem Trust
Maurice and Hilda Laing Charitable Trust
The Leonard Laity Stoate Charitable Trust
Lancaster Foundation
The Herd Lawson and Muriel Lawson Charitable Trust
The William Leech Charity
Leicester and Leicestershire Historic Churches Preservation Trust (Leicestershire Historic Churches Trust)
The Lind Trust
Lindale Educational Foundation
The Charles Littlewood Hill Trust
*P. and M. Lovell Charitable Settlement**
The Lyndhurst Trust
Sylvanus Lysons Charity
The Mallinckrodt Foundation
Mariapolis Ltd
Charity of John Marshall
Charlotte Marshall Charitable Trust
John Martin's Charity
The Mason Porter Charitable Trust
The Mercers' Charitable Foundation
The Millfield Trust
The Edgar Milward Charity
The Mizpah Trust
The Mulberry Trust
The National Churches Trust
National Committee of the Women's World Day of Prayer for England and Wales and Northern Ireland
*The Norfolk Churches Trust Ltd**
The Northumbria Historic Churches Trust
The Norwood and Newton Settlement
The Nottinghamshire Historic Churches Trust
The Ogle Christian Trust
The Ouseley Church Music Trust
The Owen Family Trust
*Oxfordshire Historic Churches Trust**
The Panacea Charitable Trust
*Parish Estate of the Church of St Michael Spurriergate York**
The Park House Charitable Trust
The Park House Charitable Trust
The Persson Charitable Trust
Sir John Priestman Charity Trust
Quothquan Trust
The Bishop Radford Trust
The Joseph Rank Trust
The Sir James Reckitt Charity
Rhondda Cynon Taff Welsh Church Acts Fund
The River Trust
*Robertson Hall Trust**
The Sants Charitable Trust
*Sarum St Michael Educational Charity**
The Scarfe Charitable Trust
The Seedfield Trust
The Seven Fifty Trust
The Shanti Charitable Trust
*The Shropshire Historic Churches Trust**
The SMB Trust
The Souter Charitable Trust
The W. F. Southall Trust
The Squires Foundation
St Luke's College Foundation
St Peter's Saltley Trust
Stewards' Company Ltd
The Stobart Newlands Charitable Trust
The Samuel Storey Family Charitable Trust
The Suffolk Historic Churches Trust
The Talbot Village Trust
C. B. and H. H. Taylor 1984 Trust
The Thornton Trust
The Tisbury Telegraph Trust
The Tory Family Foundation
The Toye Foundation
The Tufton Charitable Trust
The Van Neste Foundation
*The Warrington Church of England Educational Trust**
The Whitecourt Charitable Trust
Dame Violet Wills Charitable Trust
The James Wood Bequest Fund
The Yorkshire Historic Churches Trust

■ People of the Jewish faith

4 Charity Foundation
A. W. Charitable Trust
The Acacia Charitable Trust
Achisomoch Aid Company Ltd
Adenfirst Ltd
The Alliance Family Foundation
Amabrill Ltd
Anpride Ltd
The Baker Charitable Trust
Bay Charitable Trust
BCH Trust
Bear Mordechai Ltd
Beauland Ltd
The Becker Family Charitable Trust
Belljoe Tzedoko Ltd
*Benesco Charity Ltd**
The Ruth Berkowitz Charitable Trust
*Asser Bishvil Foundation**
The Sir Victor Blank Charitable Settlement
The Bonamy Charitable Trust
Salo Bordon Charitable Trust
Sir Clive Bourne Family Trust
Bourneheights Ltd
Friends of Boyan Trust
Brushmill Ltd
The Arnold Burton 1998 Charitable Trust
The CH (1980) Charitable Trust
Chalfords Ltd
Charitworth Ltd
The Childwick Trust
The Clore Duffield Foundation
Closehelm Ltd
Clydpride Ltd
The Vivienne and Samuel Cohen Charitable Trust
Col-Reno Ltd
The Gershon Coren Charitable Foundation (also known as The Muriel and Gus Coren Charitable Foundation)
The Cuby Charitable Trust

Itzchok Meyer Cymerman Trust Ltd
Oizer Dalim Trust
The Davidson Family Charitable Trust
The Davis Foundation
Debmar Benevolent Trust Ltd
The Dellal Foundation
The Desmond Foundation
Alan and Sheila Diamond Charitable Trust
The Djanogly Foundation
The DM Charitable Trust
The Dollond Charitable Trust
*The Dorfman Foundation**
The Doughty Charity Trust
Dushinsky Trust Ltd
*Elanore Ltd**
The George Elias Charitable Trust
Ellador Ltd
The Ellinson Foundation Ltd
Entindale Ltd
The Eranda Rothschild Foundation
The Esfandi Charitable Foundation
Esher House Charitable Trust
The Eventhall Family Charitable Trust
The Exilarch's Foundation
Extonglen Ltd
Famos Foundation Trust
Fordeve Ltd
The Isaac and Freda Frankel Memorial Charitable Trust
*The Raphael Freshwater Memorial Association**
Friends of Biala Ltd
Friends of Wiznitz Ltd
The G. R. P. Charitable Trust
The Jacqueline and Michael Gee Charitable Trust
The Gertner Charitable Trust
The B. and P. Glasser Charitable Trust
The Gould Charitable Trust
Grahame Charitable Foundation Ltd
M. and R. Gross Charities Ltd
N. and R. Grunbaum Charitable Trust
The Gur Trust
H. P. Charitable Trust
Hadras Kodesh Trust
Harbo Charities Ltd
The Harbour Charitable Trust
The Hathaway Trust
The Maurice Hatter Foundation
The Heathside Charitable Trust
The Simon Heller Charitable Settlement
The Helping Foundation
Highcroft Charitable Trust
The Holden Charitable Trust
*Horwich Shotter Charitable Trust**
The Daniel Howard Trust
The Humanitarian Trust
The Huntingdon Foundation Ltd
Hurdale Charity Ltd
IGO Foundation Ltd
Investream Charitable Trust
The J. Isaacs Charitable Trust
The J. and J. Benevolent Foundation
The Ruth and Lionel Jacobson Trust (Second Fund) No. 2
The Susan and Stephen James Charitable Settlement
Jewish Child's Day (JCD)
The Jewish Youth Fund (JYF)
J. E. Joseph Charitable Fund
The Jusaca Charitable Trust
Kahal Chassidim Bobov
The Bernard Kahn Charitable Trust
The Stanley Kalms Foundation
Karaviotis Foundation
The Kasner Charitable Trust
The Michael and Ilse Katz Foundation
C. S. Kaufman Charitable Trust
Keren Association Ltd
E. and E. Kernkraut Charities Ltd
The Kirschel Foundation
The Kobler Trust
The Kohn Foundation
Kollel and Co. Ltd
Kreditor Charitable Trust
Kupath Gemach Chaim Bechesed Viznitz Trust
The Kyte Charitable Trust
The Lambert Charitable Trust
Largsmount Ltd
The Lauffer Family Charitable Foundation
Lawson Beckman Charitable Trust
The Arnold Lee Charitable Trust
The Kennedy Leigh Charitable Trust
*The Maisie and Raphael Lewis Charitable Trust**
*Bernard Lewis Family Charitable Trust**
David and Ruth Lewis Family Charitable Trust
The Ruth and Stuart Lipton Charitable Trust
The Second Joseph Aaron Littman Foundation
Jack Livingstone Charitable Trust
Localtrent Ltd
The Locker Foundation
Loftus Charitable Trust
The Lolev Charitable Trust
LPW Ltd
The Sir Jack Lyons Charitable Trust
M. and C. Trust
*M. B. Foundation**
The M. K. Charitable Trust
The M. Y. A. Charitable Trust
The Magen Charitable Trust
The Manackerman Charitable Trust
Marbeh Torah Trust
The Stella and Alexander Margulies Charitable Trust
The Marks Family Foundation
The Ann and David Marks Foundation
The Hilda and Samuel Marks Foundation
The Violet Mauray Charitable Trust
Mayfair Charities Ltd
*Maypride Ltd**
Melodor Ltd
Menuchar Ltd
Mercaz Torah Vechesed Ltd
The Laurence Misener Charitable Trust
The Mishcon Family Charitable Trust
Keren Mitzvah Trust
Mole Charitable Trust
The Morgan Charitable Foundation
The Diana and Allan Morgenthau Charitable Trust
The Moshal Charitable Trust
Vyoel Moshe Charitable Trust
The Moss Family Charitable Trust
The Mutual Trust Group
MW (CL) Foundation
MW (GK) Foundation
MW (HO) Foundation
MW (RH) Foundation
Nemoral Ltd
Ner Foundation
Nesswall Ltd
Newpier Charity Ltd
NJD Charitable Trust
*North London Charities Ltd**
Oizer Charitable Trust
*Palmtree Memorial Trust**
The Pears Family Charitable Foundation
B. E. Perl Charitable Trust
The Phillips and Rubens Charitable Trust
The Phillips Family Charitable Trust
The George and Esme Pollitzer Charitable Settlement
Edith and Ferdinand Porjes Charitable Trust
Premishlaner Charitable Trust
R. S. Charitable Trust
Rachel Charitable Trust
The Rayne Trust
The Rest Harrow Trust
Ridgesave Ltd
RJM Charity Trust

The Rofeh Trust
Rokach Family Charitable Trust
The Gerald Ronson Family Foundation
*The Cissie Rosefield Charitable Trust**
*Rothschild Foundation (Hanadiv) Europe**
Rowanville Ltd
The Rubin Foundation Charitable Trust
S. F. Foundation
The Michael and Nicola Sacher Charitable Trust
The Ruzin Sadagora Trust
*Samjo Ltd**
The Schapira Charitable Trust
The Annie Schiff Charitable Trust
The Schmidt-Bodner Charitable Trust
The Schreib Trust
O. and G. Schreiber Charitable Trust
The Schreiber Charitable Trust
The Searchlight Electric Charitable Trust
Sam and Bella Sebba Charitable Trust
Sellata Ltd
The Cyril Shack Trust
The Archie Sherman Charitable Trust
Shlomo Memorial Fund Ltd
*Shulem B. Association Ltd**
Solev Co. Ltd
The Solo Charitable Settlement
Songdale Ltd
The E. C. Sosnow Charitable Trust
Sparquote Ltd
Rosalyn and Nicholas Springer Charitable Trust
Springrule Ltd
*The Stanley Charitable Trust**
The Steinberg Family Charitable Trust
C. E. K. Stern Charitable Trust
Stervon Ltd
The Strawberry Charitable Trust
T. and S. Trust Fund
The Tajtelbaum Charitable Trust
*The Talmud Torah Machzikei Hadass Trust**
Talteg Ltd
The David Tannen Charitable Trust
The Lili Tapper Charitable Foundation
Toras Chesed (London) Trust
Truedene Co. Ltd
Truemart Ltd
Trumros Ltd
TVML Foundation
Tzedakah
The Union of Orthodox Hebrew Congregations
The David Uri Memorial Trust
The Vail Foundation
Vivdale Ltd
*Walton Foundation**
The Weinstein Foundation
*The Wigoder Family Foundation**
The Williams Family Charitable Trust
The Harold Hyam Wingate Foundation
The Maurice Wohl Charitable Foundation
The Charles Wolfson Charitable Trust
The Wolfson Family Charitable Trust
Woodlands Green Ltd
Wychdale Ltd
Wychville Ltd
Yankov Charitable Trust
The Marjorie and Arnold Ziff Charitable Foundation

People of the Muslim faith

*Dawat-E-Hadiyah Trust (United Kingdom)**
Ibrahim Foundation Ltd
The Matliwala Family Charitable Trust
Muslim Hands

People of the Zoroastrian faith

Erach and Roshan Sadri Foundation

Gender and relationships

Adopted or fostered children

Hampton Fuel Allotment Charity
The Hemby Charitable Trust
The Albert Hunt Trust
Lloyds TSB Foundation for Scotland
John Lyon's Charity
The Walker Trust

Bereaved

Baron Davenport's Charity
Jill Franklin Trust
*M. V. Hillhouse Trust**
The Albert Hunt Trust
Sylvanus Lysons Charity
The MSE Charity
Northwood Charitable Trust

Carers

The Alchemy Foundation
The Berkshire Community Foundation
The Birmingham District Nursing Charitable Trust
BUPA UK Foundation
The Cambridgeshire Community Foundation
Chesterhill Charitable Trust
The D'Oyly Carte Charitable Trust
Disability Aid Fund (The Roger and Jean Jefcoate Trust)
Esmée Fairbairn Foundation
Jill Franklin Trust
The Goldsmiths' Company Charity
The Hadrian Trust
Hampton Fuel Allotment Charity
Hedley Foundation Ltd (The Hedley Foundation)
Help for Health
The Richard Kirkman Trust
The Martin Laing Foundation
Leicestershire, Leicester and Rutland Community Foundation
John Lewis Partnership General Community Fund
Lloyds Bank Foundation for England and Wales
Lloyds TSB Foundation for Scotland
London Catalyst
The Lord's Taverners
John Lyon's Charity
M. and C. Trust
The E. M. MacAndrew Trust
The Gerald Micklem Charitable Trust
John Moores Foundation
The Steve Morgan Foundation
The MSE Charity
Norfolk Community Foundation
The Rix-Thompson-Rothenberg Foundation
The Frieda Scott Charitable Trust
The Skelton Bounty
St James's Place Foundation
The Triangle Trust (1949) Fund
The True Colours Trust
The Will Charitable Trust

Families

The Noel Buxton Trust
The Cambridgeshire Community Foundation
Colwinston Charitable Trust

Cumbria Community Foundation
The John Grant Davies Trust*
Devon Community Foundation
County Durham Community Foundation
The Gloag Foundation
Gloucestershire Community Foundation
The Godinton Charitable Trust
The Walter Guinness Charitable Trust
Hackney Parochial Charities
The Alfred Haines Charitable Trust
Hammersmith United Charities*
Hampshire and Isle of Wight Community Foundation
Hampton Fuel Allotment Charity
The Hemby Charitable Trust
Philip Henman Trust
The Albert Hunt Trust
The Nani Huyu Charitable Trust
The Jabbs Foundation
The Kelly Family Charitable Trust
The Beatrice Laing Trust
Community Foundations for Lancashire and Merseyside
The Lauffer Family Charitable Foundation
The Leverhulme Trade Charities Trust
The Limbourne Trust
The Lister Charitable Trust
Lloyds Bank Foundation for England and Wales
Lloyds TSB Foundation for Scotland
London Catalyst
Inner London Magistrates Court's Poor Box and Feeder Charity
Paul Lunn-Rockliffe Charitable Trust
John Lyon's Charity
Sylvanus Lysons Charity
Mariapolis Ltd
Charlotte Marshall Charitable Trust
The Monument Trust
John Moores Foundation
The Steve Morgan Foundation
Vyoel Moshe Charitable Trust
The Mulberry Trust
Northwood Charitable Trust
OneFamily Foundation
People's Postcode Trust
The George and Esme Pollitzer Charitable Settlement
Quartet Community Foundation
Quothquan Trust
The Save the Children Fund*
The ScottishPower Energy People Trust
The Henry Smith Charity
Somerset Community Foundation*
The Peter Stebbings Memorial Charity
The Tedworth Charitable Trust
The C. Paul Thackray General Charitable Trust
The Walker Trust

■ LGBT

The Elton John AIDS Foundation (EJAF)
The Allen Lane Foundation
People's Postcode Trust
The Sigrid Rausing Trust
The Henry Smith Charity

■ Orphans

The Clara E. Burgess Charity
John Christie Trust*
The De Brye Charitable Trust
The Gloag Foundation
Philip Henman Trust
Human Relief Foundation
Kollel and Co. Ltd
Muslim Hands
The Walker Trust

■ Parents

The John Armitage Charitable Trust
The Artemis Charitable Trust
Philip Henman Trust
The Albert Hunt Trust
The Kelly Family Charitable Trust
Lloyds Bank Foundation for England and Wales
Lloyds TSB Foundation for Scotland
Inner London Magistrates Court's Poor Box and Feeder Charity
The Tedworth Charitable Trust

■ Lone parents

The Jarman Charitable Trust
The MSE Charity
Quothquan Trust
The Walker Trust

■ Women

The A. B. Charitable Trust
Ove Arup Partnership Charitable Trust
The Associated Country Women of the World
The Bromley Trust
J. A. Clark Charitable Trust
Comic Relief
Coutts Charitable Foundation
Baron Davenport's Charity
The Diageo Foundation
Didymus
The Dischma Charitable Trust
Esmée Fairbairn Foundation
Forever Manchester
The Gloag Foundation
The Goldsmiths' Company Charity
The Hemraj Goyal Foundation
The Hadrian Trust
Paul Hamlyn Foundation
Harbinson Charitable Trust
The Hemby Charitable Trust
Philip Henman Trust
P. and C. Hickinbotham Charitable Trust
The Hilden Charitable Fund
M. V. Hillhouse Trust*
The Horizon Foundation
The Hull and East Riding Charitable Trust
The Albert Hunt Trust
The Nani Huyu Charitable Trust
The Jabbs Foundation
The Elton John AIDS Foundation (EJAF)
The Mary Kinross Charitable Trust
The Beatrice Laing Trust
The Allen Lane Foundation
The LankellyChase Foundation
London Catalyst
The London Community Foundation (LCF)
The Henry Lumley Charitable Trust
John Lyon's Charity
The Marr-Munning Trust
The Monument Trust
John Moores Foundation
The Mosselson Charitable Trust
National Committee of the Women's World Day of Prayer for England and Wales and Northern Ireland
The NDL Foundation
Northwood Charitable Trust
Oxfam (GB)
The Pilgrim Trust
The Eleanor Rathbone Charitable Trust
Elizabeth Rathbone Charity
The Sigrid Rausing Trust
The Saga Charitable Trust
The Henry Smith Charity
The Staples Trust
The Peter Stebbings Memorial Charity
The Vodafone Foundation
Volant Charitable Trust
Voluntary Action Fund (VAF)

Ill health

The 29th May 1961 Charitable Trust
The Aberbrothock Skea Trust
The Aberdeen Foundation
The Adint Charitable Trust
The Adnams Community Trust
The Derrill Allatt Foundation
The H. B. Allen Charitable Trust
AM Charitable Trust
The AMW Charitable Trust
Andor Charitable Trust
The Mary Andrew Charitable Trust
*The Anne Duchess of Westminster's Charity**
The Arbib Foundation
The Ardwick Trust
The Arsenal Foundation Ltd
Ove Arup Partnership Charitable Trust
The Lord Austin Trust
The Harry Bacon Foundation
The Baker Charitable Trust
The Balcombe Charitable Trust
The Barbers' Company General Charities
The Barbour Foundation
The Barcapel Foundation
Barnwood Trust
Misses Barrie Charitable Trust
The Bay Tree Charitable Trust
*Benesco Charity Ltd**
The Benham Charitable Settlement
The Ruth Berkowitz Charitable Trust
The Bestway Foundation
The Birmingham District Nursing Charitable Trust
Isabel Blackman Foundation
The Bluston Charitable Settlement
The Booth Charities
The Tony Bramall Charitable Trust
The Liz and Terry Bramall Foundation
Bridge Trust
Bridgepoint Charitable Trust
Bristol Charities
John Bristow and Thomas Mason Trust
The British Dietetic Association General and Education Trust Fund
R. S. Brownless Charitable Trust
The Bruntwood Charity
Buckingham Trust
The E. F. Bulmer Benevolent Fund
BUPA UK Foundation
The Burden Trust
The Burry Charitable Trust
The Edward and Dorothy Cadbury Trust
Calleva Foundation
David William Traill Cargill Fund
The Carr-Gregory Trust
The Elizabeth Casson Trust
The Wilfrid and Constance Cave Foundation
The Amelia Chadwick Trust
Champneys Charitable Foundation
Children's Liver Disease Foundation
The Childwick Trust
Church Burgesses Trust
The Clover Trust
The Robert Clutterbuck Charitable Trust
Denise Coates Foundation
The Denise Cohen Charitable Trust
The Colchester Catalyst Charity
John Coldman Charitable Trust
The J. Reginald Corah Foundation Fund
The Worshipful Company of Cordwainers Charitable Trusts (Minges Gift and the Pooled Trusts)
The Gershon Coren Charitable Foundation (also known as The Muriel and Gus Coren Charitable Foundation)
The Cotton Trust
The John Cowan Foundation
The Lord Cozens-Hardy Trust
The Craps Charitable Trust
The Crerar Hotels Trust
Criffel Charitable Trust
The Violet and Milo Cripps Charitable Trust
The Croydon Relief in Need Charities
Cruden Foundation Ltd
The Cumber Family Charitable Trust
The Cunningham Trust
The Harry Cureton Charitable Trust
The D'Oyly Carte Charitable Trust
Roald Dahl's Marvellous Children's Charity
*The Roger De Haan Charitable Trust**
The Demigryphon Trust
Provincial Grand Charity of the Province of Derbyshire
The J. N. Derbyshire Trust
The Sandy Dewhirst Charitable Trust
The Laduma Dhamecha Charitable Trust
The Dorcas Trust
The Dorus Trust
Dromintee Trust
Duchy Health Charity Ltd
County Durham Community Foundation
The Earley Charity
Edupoor Ltd
The Gerald Palmer Eling Trust Company
The Vernon N. Ely Charitable Trust
The Emerton-Christie Charity
The Englefield Charitable Trust
The Eranda Rothschild Foundation
Esh Foundation
Esher House Charitable Trust
Joseph Ettedgui Charitable Foundation
Euro Charity Trust
The Everard Foundation
The Exilarch's Foundation
G. F. Eyre Charitable Trust
The Lord Faringdon Charitable Trust
Samuel William Farmer Trust
The Thomas Farr Charity
The February Foundation
The George Fentham Birmingham Charity
The A. M. Fenton Trust
The Doris Field Charitable Trust
Dixie Rose Findlay Charitable Trust
The Sir John Fisher Foundation
The Earl Fitzwilliam Charitable Trust
The Follett Trust
Forest Hill Charitable Trust
Forever Manchester
The Forman Hardy Charitable Trust
Donald Forrester Trust
Gwyneth Forrester Trust
The Elizabeth Frankland Moore and Star Foundation
The Gordon Fraser Charitable Trust
The Hugh Fraser Foundation
The Joseph Strong Frazer Trust
The Charles S. French Charitable Trust
The Freshfield Foundation
The Freshgate Trust Foundation
Friarsgate Trust
The Adrian and Jane Frost Charitable Trust
The Patrick and Helena Frost Foundation
The Fulmer Charitable Trust
The Ganzoni Charitable Trust
The Jacqueline and Michael Gee Charitable Trust
The Generations Foundation
*Genetic Disorders UK**
The David Gibbons Foundation
The Simon Gibson Charitable Trust

The Girdlers' Company Charitable Trust
The B. and P. Glasser Charitable Trust
The Gloag Foundation
Global Charities
Gloucestershire Community Foundation
The Godinton Charitable Trust
Worshipful Company of Gold and Silver Wyre Drawers Charitable Trust Fund
The Goldsmiths' Company Charity
The Goodman Foundation
The Gosling Foundation Ltd
Gowling WLG (UK) Charitable Trust
Grace Charitable Trust
The Graham Trust*
The J. G. Graves Charitable Trust
Gordon Gray Trust
The Kenneth and Susan Green Charitable Foundation
The Green Hall Foundation
Greenham Common Community Trust Ltd
The Greggs Foundation
The Grimmitt Trust
The Bishop of Guildford's Foundation
Guildry Incorporation of Perth
The Gunter Charitable Trust
The Hadley Trust
The Hadrian Trust
The Helen Hamlyn Trust
Hampshire and Isle of Wight Community Foundation
The Hampstead Wells and Campden Trust
Hampton Fuel Allotment Charity
The W. A. Handley Charity Trust
The Kathleen Hannay Memorial Charity
The Haramead Trust
Harbinson Charitable Trust
Harbo Charities Ltd
The Harding Trust
The Harebell Centenary Fund
The Harris Family Charitable Trust
The Edith Lilian Harrison 2000 Foundation
The Harrison-Frank Family Foundation (UK) Ltd
The Hasluck Charitable Trust
The Hathaway Trust
The Hawthorne Charitable Trust
The Charles Hayward Foundation
The Health Foundation
May Hearnshaw Charitable Trust (May Hearnshaw's Charity)
Heart of England Community Foundation
Heb Ffin (Without Frontier)*
The Charlotte Heber-Percy Charitable Trust
Ernest Hecht Charitable Foundation
Help for Health
The Hemby Charitable Trust
The G. D. Herbert Charitable Trust
Herefordshire Community Foundation
P. and C. Hickinbotham Charitable Trust
M. V. Hillhouse Trust*
The Hillingdon Community Trust
R. G. Hills Charitable Trust
The Hintze Family Charity Foundation
The Henry C. Hoare Charitable Trust
The Hobson Charity Ltd
The Jane Hodge Foundation
The Hollands-Warren Fund
The Hollick Family Charitable Trust
The Dorothy Holmes Charitable Trust
The Edward Holt Trust
The Homestead Charitable Trust
Sir Harold Hood's Charitable Trust
The Hoover Foundation
Hopmarket Charity
The Antony Hornby Charitable Trust
The Thomas J. Horne Memorial Trust
The Worshipful Company of Horners' Charitable Trusts
Hospice UK
The Hospital of God at Greatham
The Hospital Saturday Fund
House of Industry Estate
The Hudson Foundation
The Hull and East Riding Charitable Trust
Human Relief Foundation
The Humanitarian Trust
The Albert Hunt Trust
Huntingdon Freemen's Trust
Hurdale Charity Ltd
The Hutton Foundation
The Nani Huyu Charitable Trust
The Iliffe Family Charitable Trust
The Ingram Trust
The Inman Charity
The Inverforth Charitable Trust
Investream Charitable Trust
The J. Isaacs Charitable Trust
The J. and J. Benevolent Foundation
C. Richard Jackson Charitable Trust
The Ruth and Lionel Jacobson Trust (Second Fund) No. 2
John James Bristol Foundation
The Susan and Stephen James Charitable Settlement
John Jarrold Trust Ltd
The Jenour Foundation
Jewish Child's Day (JCD)
Lillie Johnson Charitable Trust
The Johnson Foundation
Johnson Wax Ltd Charitable Trust
The Jones 1986 Charitable Trust
The Dezna Robins Jones Charitable Foundation
The Jordan Charitable Foundation
The Joron Charitable Trust
Anton Jurgens Charitable Trust
The Jusaca Charitable Trust
Karaviotis Foundation
The Michael and Ilse Katz Foundation
Kent Community Foundation
The Ursula Keyes Trust
Kidney Research UK
The Mary Kinross Charitable Trust
The Graham Kirkham Foundation*
The Ernest Kleinwort Charitable Trust
The Kobler Trust
The Kohn Foundation
Kollel and Co. Ltd
The Kreitman Foundation
Ladbrokes in the Community Charitable Trust
Christopher Laing Foundation
The Kirby Laing Foundation
The Leonard Laity Stoate Charitable Trust
Community Foundations for Lancashire and Merseyside
Duchy of Lancaster Benevolent Fund
Langdale Trust
The R. J. Larg Family Charitable Trust
The Lauffer Family Charitable Foundation
The Kathleen Laurence Trust
The Edgar E. Lawley Foundation
Lawson Beckman Charitable Trust
The Raymond and Blanche Lawson Charitable Trust
The William Leech Charity
Leeds Building Society Charitable Foundation
Leicestershire and Rutland Masonic Charity Association*

Leicestershire, Leicester and Rutland Community Foundation
The Kennedy Leigh Charitable Trust
P. Leigh-Bramwell Trust 'E'
The Lennox Hannay Charitable Trust
Lord Leverhulme's Charitable Trust
The Limbourne Trust
Limoges Charitable Trust
The Linbury Trust
Lincolnshire Community Foundation
The Linden Charitable Trust
The Enid Linder Foundation
The Ruth and Stuart Lipton Charitable Trust
The Lister Charitable Trust
The Frank Litchfield Charitable Trust
The Charles Littlewood Hill Trust
The George John and Sheilah Livanos Charitable Trust
Jack Livingstone Charitable Trust
The Elaine and Angus Lloyd Charitable Trust
Lloyds Bank Foundation for the Channel Islands
Lloyds TSB Foundation for Scotland
The William and Katherine Longman Trust
The Loseley and Guildway Charitable Trust
P. and M. Lovell Charitable Settlement*
The Lower Green Foundation
The C. L. Loyd Charitable Trust
Robert Luff Foundation Ltd
The Henry Lumley Charitable Trust
Lord and Lady Lurgan Trust
The Lynn Foundation
M. and C. Trust
The M. K. Charitable Trust
The E. M. MacAndrew Trust
The Manackerman Charitable Trust
The Manchester Guardian Society Charitable Trust
R. W. Mann Trust
The Manoukian Charitable Foundation
The Stella and Alexander Margulies Charitable Trust
The Marsh Christian Trust
Charlotte Marshall Charitable Trust
D. G. Marshall of Cambridge Trust
Sir George Martin Trust
John Martin's Charity
The Nancie Massey Charitable Trust
The Matliwala Family Charitable Trust
D. D. McPhail Charitable Settlement
Medical Research Foundation*
Medical Research Scotland*
The Merchant Taylors' Company Charities Fund
Merchant Taylors' Consolidated Charities for the Infirm
The Merchant Venturers' Charity
The Metropolitan Masonic Charity
T. and J. Meyer Family Foundation Ltd
The Mickleham Trust
The Ronald Miller Foundation
The Millichope Foundation
The Mills Charity
The Millward Charitable Trust
Milton Keynes Community Foundation Ltd
The Laurence Misener Charitable Trust
The Brian Mitchell Charitable Settlement
Keren Mitzvah Trust
The Monmouthshire County Council Welsh Church Act Fund
The Monument Trust
Moondance Foundation*
The George A. Moore Foundation
The Morris Charitable Trust
The Willie and Mabel Morris Charitable Trust
G. M. Morrison Charitable Trust
J. P. Moulton Charitable Foundation
The Edith Murphy Foundation
The Music Sales Charitable Trust
The Janet Nash Charitable Settlement
Newby Trust Ltd
The Frances and Augustus Newman Foundation
Northwood Charitable Trust
The Norton Rose Fulbright Charitable Foundation
The Oakdale Trust
The Olga Charitable Trust
OneFamily Foundation
The Ormsby Charitable Trust
The Doris Pacey Charitable Foundation
The Paget Charitable Trust
The Panacea Charitable Trust
Susanna Peake Charitable Trust
The Pen Shell Project
Personal Assurance Charitable Trust
The Pharsalia Charitable Trust
The Bernard Piggott Charitable Trust
The DLA Piper Charitable Trust
Pollywally Charitable Trust
The J. E. Posnansky Charitable Trust
The Mary Potter Convent Hospital Trust
Sir John Priestman Charity Trust
Prison Service Charity Fund
QBE European Operations Foundation*
Quothquan Trust
The Rainford Trust
The Ranworth Trust
Elizabeth Rathbone Charity
The Ravensdale Trust
The Rayne Foundation
The John Rayner Charitable Trust
Reuben Foundation
Daisie Rich Trust
The Clive and Sylvia Richards Charity Ltd
Rigby Foundation*
Riverside Charitable Trust Ltd*
Thomas Roberts Trust
The Helen Roll Charity
Rosetrees Trust
The Rothermere Foundation
The Rowlands Trust
The Michael and Nicola Sacher Charitable Trust
The Saga Charitable Trust
The Saintbury Trust
The Saints and Sinners Trust Ltd
The Andrew Salvesen Charitable Trust
The Basil Samuel Charitable Trust
Coral Samuel Charitable Trust
The Sandhu Charitable Foundation
Schroder Charity Trust
Sir Samuel Scott of Yews Trust
The John Scott Trust Fund*
The Scouloudi Foundation
The Searchlight Electric Charitable Trust
The Sellafield Charity Trust Fund*
The Jean Shanks Foundation
The Shanly Foundation
The Shanti Charitable Trust
The Shears Foundation
The Florence Shute Millennium Trust*
David and Jennifer Sieff Charitable Trust
The Henry Smith Charity
The Solo Charitable Settlement
Somerset Community Foundation*
Songdale Ltd

Sparks Charity (Sport Aiding Medical Research for Kids)
Sparquote Ltd
The Spielman Charitable Trust
Rosalyn and Nicholas Springer Charitable Trust
The Squires Foundation
The Stafford Trust
The Hugh Stenhouse Foundation
The Sigmund Sternberg Charitable Foundation
The Andy Stewart Charitable Foundation
The Stoller Charitable Trust
Sunninghill Fuel Allotment Trust*
The Adrienne and Leslie Sussman Charitable Trust
The Charles and Elsie Sykes Trust
The Talbot Trusts
Tallow Chandlers Benevolent Fund No. 2
C. B. and H. H. Taylor 1984 Trust
Khoo Teck Puat UK Foundation*
Tees Valley Community Foundation
The Templeton Goodwill Trust
Tenovus Scotland*
The C. Paul Thackray General Charitable Trust
The Thales Charitable Trust
DM Thomas Foundation for Young People*
The Sir Jules Thorn Charitable Trust
The Thornton Trust
The Tolkien Trust
The Tory Family Foundation
The Toy Trust
The Constance Travis Charitable Trust
The Trefoil Trust
The True Colours Trust
The James Tudor Foundation
The Roger and Douglas Turner Charitable Trust
UKH Foundation*
The Albert Van Den Bergh Charitable Trust
The Vandervell Foundation
Variety The Children's Charity (Variety Club)
Volant Charitable Trust
Robert and Felicity Waley-Cohen Charitable Trust
The Warwickshire Masonic Charitable Association Ltd*
Mrs Waterhouse Charitable Trust
The Geoffrey Watling Charity*
Blyth Watson Charitable Trust
The James Weir Foundation
The Welton Foundation
The Westfield Health Charitable Trust
The Garfield Weston Foundation
The Melanie White Foundation Ltd
White Stuff Foundation
The Lionel Wigram Memorial Trust
The Felicity Wilde Charitable Trust
The Kay Williams Charitable Foundation
The Michael and Anna Wix Charitable Trust
The Maurice Wohl Charitable Foundation
The Wolfson Family Charitable Trust
The A. and R. Woolf Charitable Trust
The Wyseliot Rose Charitable Trust
Yorkshire and Clydesdale Bank Foundation
Yorkshire Building Society Charitable Foundation
The John Kirkhope Young Endowment Fund
Zephyr Charitable Trust
The Zochonis Charitable Trust
Zurich Community Trust (UK) Ltd

People with cardiovascular disorders

British Heart Foundation (BHF)
Chest Heart and Stroke Scotland
General Charity of Coventry
Heart Research UK
The Connie and Albert Taylor Charitable Trust

People with glandular and endocrine disorders

Diabetes UK

People with HIV/AIDS

Anglo American Group Foundation
The Derek Butler Trust
The Elton John AIDS Foundation (EJAF)
The Mackintosh Foundation
Mercury Phoenix Trust
John Moores Foundation

People with a mental illness

The Artemis Charitable Trust
The Baily Thomas Charitable Fund
The Berkshire Community Foundation
The Cambridgeshire Community Foundation
Eastern Counties Educational Trust Ltd
The Eveson Charitable Trust
Esmée Fairbairn Foundation
G. M. C. Trust
The Peter Harrison Foundation
Miss Agnes H. Hunter's Trust
The Charles Irving Charitable Trust
The Beatrice Laing Trust
The Allen Lane Foundation
The LankellyChase Foundation
Maudsley Charity*
John Moores Foundation
The MSE Charity
Norfolk Community Foundation
The Norman Family Charitable Trust
Nottinghamshire Community Foundation
Postcode Community Trust*
Mr and Mrs J. A. Pye's Charitable Settlement
The Mrs Smith and Mount Trust
The Peter Stebbings Memorial Charity
The Stone Family Foundation
Swan Mountain Trust
The Tuixen Foundation

People with musculoskeletal disorders

Arthritis Research UK
The Bingham Trust
Miss Agnes H. Hunter's Trust
The JGW Patterson Foundation*
The Andy Stewart Charitable Foundation

People with neurological disorders

Alzheimer's Research UK*
Alzheimer's Society*
The Baily Thomas Charitable Fund
The Castang Foundation
Chest Heart and Stroke Scotland
The Dunn Family Charitable Trust
The Eighty Eight Foundation*

Epilepsy Research UK
The Girdlers' Company Charitable Trust
The Harebell Centenary Fund
*Life Changes Trust**
The R. S. Macdonald Charitable Trust
*Maudsley Charity**
Motor Neurone Disease Association
*Multiple Sclerosis Society**
Odin Charitable Trust
*Parkinson's Disease Society of the United Kingdom**
The Shirley Foundation
Volant Charitable Trust

People with oncological disorders

The Bacit Foundation
Bloodwise
*Breast Cancer Now**
The Breast Cancer Research Trust (BCRT)
The Derek Butler Trust
*The Castansa Trust**
Children with Cancer UK
General Charity of Coventry
The Joan Lynette Dalton Charitable Trust
*The Eighty Eight Foundation**
The Girdlers' Company Charitable Trust
The Jane Hodge Foundation
Miss Agnes H. Hunter's Trust
The Caron Keating Foundation
The Kay Kendall Leukaemia Fund
The Mackintosh Foundation
The Mickel Fund
The Edwina Mountbatten and Leonora Children's Foundation
North West Cancer Research (incorporating Clatterbridge Cancer Research)
*The JGW Patterson Foundation**
*Pink Ribbon Foundation**
*Prostate Cancer UK**
St James's Place Foundation
The Connie and Albert Taylor Charitable Trust
The Will Charitable Trust

People with respiratory disorders

Asthma UK
Chest Heart and Stroke Scotland

People who are substance misusers

The Berkshire Community Foundation
Esmée Fairbairn Foundation
*The Gordon Trust**
The Hope Trust
The LankellyChase Foundation
The Leigh Trust
*Maudsley Charity**
John Moores Foundation
Norfolk Community Foundation
The Norman Family Charitable Trust
Responsible Gambling Trust (GambleAware)
The Frieda Scott Charitable Trust
The Peter Stebbings Memorial Charity
The C. Paul Thackray General Charitable Trust
The Vintners' Foundation

Nationality

Armenian

The Manoukian Charitable Foundation
Saint Sarkis Charity Trust

Asian

The Matliwala Family Charitable Trust
The Sino-British Fellowship Trust
The W. Wing Yip and Brothers Foundation

Irish

Arts Council of Northern Ireland
*Integrated Education Fund**
The Ireland Fund of Great Britain
Irish Youth Foundation (UK) Ltd (incorporating The Lawlor Foundation)

Social or economic circumstances

The Aberdeen Foundation
ABF The Soldiers' Charity
The ACT Foundation
The Adnams Community Trust
Ajahma Charitable Trust
Al-Fayed Charitable Foundation
The Derrill Allatt Foundation
Allchurches Trust Ltd
AM Charitable Trust
The AMW Charitable Trust
*The Ancaster Trust**
The Mary Andrew Charitable Trust
Andrews Charitable Trust
The Arbib Foundation
The Ardwick Trust
The Arsenal Foundation Ltd
Ove Arup Partnership Charitable Trust
Autonomous Research Charitable Trust (ARCT)
The Austin Bailey Foundation
The Balcombe Charitable Trust
The Barbour Foundation
The Bay Tree Charitable Trust
The Bearder Charity
The Bedfordshire and Luton Community Foundation
The Benham Charitable Settlement
The Bingham Trust
Isabel Blackman Foundation
The Bluston Charitable Settlement
The Booth Charities
The Liz and Terry Bramall Foundation
The Breadsticks Foundation
Bridge Trust
Buckinghamshire Community Foundation
The Edward and Dorothy Cadbury Trust
The Carr-Gregory Trust
The Wilfrid and Constance Cave Foundation
Celtic Charity Fund
The Amelia Chadwick Trust
The Cleopatra Trust
The Clover Trust
Denise Coates Foundation
The Vivienne and Samuel Cohen Charitable Trust
The Denise Cohen Charitable Trust
John Coldman Charitable Trust
Comic Relief
The Cooks Charity
Cornwall Community Foundation
The Cotton Trust
General Charity of Coventry
Coventry Building Society Charitable Foundation
The John Cowan Foundation
The Lord Cozens-Hardy Trust
The Crerar Hotels Trust
Criffel Charitable Trust
Cripplegate Foundation
The Cross Trust
The Croydon Relief in Need Charities
Cruden Foundation Ltd
The Ronald Cruickshanks Foundation
The Cumber Family Charitable Trust

Cumbria Community Foundation
The Roger De Haan Charitable Trust*
The De La Rue Charitable Trust*
Debenhams Foundation
Foundation Derbyshire
The J. N. Derbyshire Trust
The Diageo Foundation
The Dorcas Trust
Dorset Community Foundation
The Dorus Trust
Dromintee Trust
The Dulverton Trust
County Durham Community Foundation
Eaga Charitable Trust
The Earley Charity
Dr Edwards Bishop King's Fulham Endowment Fund
The Eighty Eight Foundation*
The George Elias Charitable Trust
The Gerald Palmer Eling Trust Company
The Vernon N. Ely Charitable Trust
The Englefield Charitable Trust
The Epigoni Trust
The Eranda Rothschild Foundation
Essex Community Foundation
The Eventhall Family Charitable Trust
The Everard Foundation
The Exilarch's Foundation
The Expat Foundation
G. F. Eyre Charitable Trust
Esmée Fairbairn Foundation
The Lord Faringdon Charitable Trust
Samuel William Farmer Trust
The Thomas Farr Charity
The Farthing Trust
The February Foundation
The George Fentham Birmingham Charity
The Doris Field Charitable Trust
Fishmongers' Company's Charitable Trust
The Earl Fitzwilliam Charitable Trust
The Follett Trust
Forest Hill Charitable Trust
Forever Manchester
The Forman Hardy Charitable Trust
Donald Forrester Trust
The Elizabeth Frankland Moore and Star Foundation
The Gordon Fraser Charitable Trust
The Joseph Strong Frazer Trust
The Charles S. French Charitable Trust
The Freshfield Foundation
The Freshgate Trust Foundation
The Adrian and Jane Frost Charitable Trust
The Patrick and Helena Frost Foundation
The Fulmer Charitable Trust
The Generations Foundation
The Genesis Charitable Trust*
The Gibbs Charitable Trust
The Simon Gibson Charitable Trust
The Gloag Foundation
Global Charities
Gloucestershire Community Foundation
The Godinton Charitable Trust
Gowling WLG (UK) Charitable Trust
Grace Charitable Trust
The Graham Trust*
The Greggs Foundation
The Bishop of Guildford's Foundation
The Hampstead Wells and Campden Trust
The Kathleen Hannay Memorial Charity
The Haramead Trust
The Hasluck Charitable Trust
The Hawthorne Charitable Trust
HC Foundation*
Heart of England Community Foundation
The Charlotte Heber-Percy Charitable Trust
Ernest Hecht Charitable Foundation
The Hemby Charitable Trust
Henderson Firstfruits*
R. G. Hills Charitable Trust
The Hinduja Foundation
The Hobson Charity Ltd
The Hollick Family Charitable Trust
The Dorothy Holmes Charitable Trust
P. H. Holt Foundation
Sir Harold Hood's Charitable Trust
The Hospital of God at Greatham
Human Relief Foundation
The Humanitarian Trust
The Albert Hunt Trust
Ibrahim Foundation Ltd
Imagine Foundation
Impetus – The Private Equity Foundation (Impetus – PEF)
Interserve Employee Foundation Ltd
Investream Charitable Trust
The Ironmongers' Company
The Jarman Charitable Trust
John Jarrold Trust Ltd
The Jenour Foundation
Joffe Charitable Trust
Lillie Johnson Charitable Trust
Johnson Wax Ltd Charitable Trust
Anton Jurgens Charitable Trust
The Michael and Ilse Katz Foundation
Kent Community Foundation
The Mary Kinross Charitable Trust
Kollel and Co. Ltd
The Kreitman Foundation
The Leonard Laity Stoate Charitable Trust
Duchy of Lancaster Benevolent Fund
Lancaster Foundation
The R. J. Larg Family Charitable Trust
The Raymond and Blanche Lawson Charitable Trust
Leeds Building Society Charitable Foundation
Leicestershire and Rutland Masonic Charity Association*
The Lennox Hannay Charitable Trust
David and Ruth Lewis Family Charitable Trust
Lincolnshire Community Foundation
The Lister Charitable Trust
The Charles Littlewood Hill Trust
Liverpool Charity and Voluntary Services (LCVS)
The W. M. and B. W. Lloyd Trust*
Lloyd's Charities Trust
Lloyds Bank Foundation for the Channel Islands
Trust for London
London Legal Support Trust (LLST)
P. and M. Lovell Charitable Settlement*
The C. L. Loyd Charitable Trust
C. F. Lunoe Trust Fund
Sylvanus Lysons Charity
The Makers of Playing Cards Charity
The Manchester Guardian Society Charitable Trust
Lord Mayor of Manchester's Charity Appeal Trust
R. W. Mann Trust
The Marsh Christian Trust
Charlotte Marshall Charitable Trust
D. G. Marshall of Cambridge Trust
John Martin's Charity
The Matliwala Family Charitable Trust
The Mickleham Trust
The Millichope Foundation
Milton Keynes Community Foundation Ltd

The Brian Mitchell Charitable Settlement
*Moondance Foundation**
The Morgan Charitable Foundation
G. M. Morrison Charitable Trust
*The Morrisons Foundation**
The Moss Family Charitable Trust
J. P. Moulton Charitable Foundation
The Janet Nash Charitable Settlement
The Nationwide Foundation
Newby Trust Ltd
The NFU Mutual Charitable Trust
Nominet Charitable Foundation
Northamptonshire Community Foundation
Norwich Town Close Estate Charity
OneFamily Foundation
Oxfordshire Community Foundation
*The Paddington Charitable Estate Educational Fund**
The Paget Charitable Trust
*Parabola Foundation**
The Park House Charitable Trust
Peacock Charitable Trust
Personal Assurance Charitable Trust
Pilkington Charities Fund
The DLA Piper Charitable Trust
The J. E. Posnansky Charitable Trust
*Postcode Community Trust**
Mr and Mrs J. A. Pye's Charitable Settlement
*QBE European Operations Foundation**
The Rainford Trust
The Rambourg Foundation
The Ranworth Trust
The Ravensdale Trust
The Rayne Foundation
Responsible Gambling Trust (GambleAware)
Reuben Foundation
*Rhodi Charitable Trust**
Daisie Rich Trust
Richmond Parish Lands Charity
*Rigby Foundation**
The River Farm Foundation
The Sir James Roll Charitable Trust
*Mrs L. D. Rope's Second Charitable Settlement**
The Michael and Nicola Sacher Charitable Trust
Erach and Roshan Sadri Foundation
The Saga Charitable Trust
The Saintbury Trust
The Salamander Charitable Trust
Salters' Charitable Foundation
The Basil Samuel Charitable Trust
Coral Samuel Charitable Trust
The Samworth Foundation
The Sandhu Charitable Foundation
The Sants Charitable Trust
*The Save the Children Fund**
Schroder Charity Trust
*The John Scott Trust Fund**
The Scouloudi Foundation
The SDL Foundation
Sam and Bella Sebba Charitable Trust
The Seedfield Trust
*The Sellafield Charity Trust Fund**
The Shanly Foundation
The Shanti Charitable Trust
The Shears Foundation
The Sheldon Trust
*Sherburn House Charity**
The Archie Sherman Cardiff Foundation
The Shoe Zone Trust
The Skelton Bounty
Rita and David Slowe Charitable Trust
The Henry Smith Charity
Philip Smith's Charitable Trust
Sodexo Stop Hunger Foundation
The Solo Charitable Settlement
*Somerset Community Foundation**
The E. C. Sosnow Charitable Trust
The Souter Charitable Trust
The W. F. Southall Trust
The Spear Charitable Trust
The Spielman Charitable Trust
The St Hilda's Trust
The Hugh Stenhouse Foundation
The Stone Family Foundation
Stratford upon Avon Town Trust
*The Street Foundation**
The Alan Sugar Foundation
The Sussex Community Foundation
The Adrienne and Leslie Sussman Charitable Trust
The Sutasoma Trust
Sutton Coldfield Charitable Trust
The Swann-Morton Foundation
The Charles and Elsie Sykes Trust
The Talbot Village Trust
The Taurus Foundation
C. B. and H. H. Taylor 1984 Trust
Tearfund
*Khoo Teck Puat UK Foundation**
Tees Valley Community Foundation
The Sir Jules Thorn Charitable Trust
The Three Oaks Trust
Tilney Charitable Trust
The Tisbury Telegraph Trust
The Tobacco Pipe Makers and Tobacco Trade Benevolent Fund
The Toy Trust
Annie Tranmer Charitable Trust
The Constance Travis Charitable Trust
The Truemark Trust
The Trusthouse Charitable Foundation
The Tudor Trust
TVML Foundation
Community Foundation serving Tyne and Wear and Northumberland
Ulster Garden Villages Ltd
Vale of Glamorgan Welsh Church Fund
The Vandervell Foundation
The Vardy Foundation
The Vodafone Foundation
Volant Charitable Trust
Voluntary Action Fund (VAF)
The Wakefield and Tetley Trust
Walton on Thames Charity
Mrs Waterhouse Charitable Trust
The Waterloo Foundation
Wates Family Enterprise Trust
The Wates Foundation
*The Geoffrey Watling Charity**
Blyth Watson Charitable Trust
The James Weir Foundation
The Westminster Foundation
The Garfield Weston Foundation
Westway Trust
*The Williams Family Foundation**
Williams Serendipity Trust
The Michael and Anna Wix Charitable Trust
The Wolfson Foundation
The Wood Foundation
The Wyseliot Rose Charitable Trust
*York Children's Trust**
Yorkshire and Clydesdale Bank Foundation
Yorkshire Building Society Charitable Foundation
The Zochonis Charitable Trust

People with an alternative lifestyle (including travellers)

The Allen Lane Foundation
Odin Charitable Trust
*The Onaway Trust**

People who are educationally disadvantaged

*The Allen & Overy Foundation**
The Ellis Campbell Charitable Foundation
*Sir Ernest Cassel Educational Trust**
Colyer-Fergusson Charitable Trust
Eastern Counties Educational Trust Ltd
The Foyle Foundation
The Hugh Fraser Foundation
Global Care
*The Gordon Trust**
Philip and Judith Green Trust
H. C. D. Memorial Fund
The Hadley Trust
Paul Hamlyn Foundation
Harbinson Charitable Trust
The Hathaway Trust
The Hillingdon Community Trust
Miss Agnes H. Hunter's Trust
The KPMG Foundation
Kreditor Charitable Trust
Kusuma Trust UK
The Beatrice Laing Trust
Community Foundations for Lancashire and Merseyside
The Manifold Charitable Trust
The Marr-Munning Trust
The Michael Marsh Charitable Trust
The Merchant Venturers' Charity
John Moores Foundation
Paradigm Foundation
SHINE (Support and Help in Education)
The Simmons & Simmons Charitable Foundation
The Harold Hyam Wingate Foundation

People who are homeless

The 29th May 1961 Charitable Trust
The A. B. Charitable Trust
The Argus Appeal
The Ashden Trust
The Berkeley Charitable Foundation
The Berkshire Community Foundation
The Oliver Borthwick Memorial Trust
Community Foundation for Calderdale
The Cambridgeshire Community Foundation
CEO Sleepout
CHK Charities Ltd
The Clothworkers' Foundation
The Cole Charitable Trust
The Coltstaple Trust
The Evan Cornish Foundation
*Crisis UK**
*The John Grant Davies Trust**
The Dawe Charitable Trust
The Drapers' Charitable Fund
The Wilfred and Elsie Elkes Charity Fund
The Ericson Trust
The Eveson Charitable Trust
Fisherbeck Charitable Trust
The Hugh Fraser Foundation
The G. D. Charitable Trust
The Goldsmiths' Company Charity
*The Gordon Trust**
The Hadrian Trust
The Alfred Haines Charitable Trust
Hampshire and Isle of Wight Community Foundation
Hampton Fuel Allotment Charity
The Harbour Foundation
*Heb Ffin (Without Frontier)**
Help the Homeless Ltd
The Hilden Charitable Fund
*M. V. Hillhouse Trust**
The Thomas J. Horne Memorial Trust
The Ingram Trust
The Charles Irving Charitable Trust
The Jusaca Charitable Trust
Ladbrokes in the Community Charitable Trust
John Laing Charitable Trust
Maurice and Hilda Laing Charitable Trust
The Beatrice Laing Trust
The Leathersellers' Company Charitable Fund
The London Community Foundation (LCF)
Paul Lunn-Rockliffe Charitable Trust
The Mackintosh Foundation
*Masonic Charitable Foundation**
The Merchant Venturers' Charity
The Mickel Fund
The Monument Trust
John Moores Foundation
The MSE Charity
Network for Social Change Charitable Trust
Norfolk Community Foundation
The Norman Family Charitable Trust
Odin Charitable Trust
People's Postcode Trust
The Persula Foundation
The Austin and Hope Pilkington Trust
The Portishead Nautical Trust
Quartet Community Foundation
Mrs L. D. Rope's Third Charitable Settlement
The Francis C. Scott Charitable Trust
The Mrs Smith and Mount Trust
The Sobell Foundation
The Peter Stebbings Memorial Charity
The Summerfield Charitable Trust
The Swire Charitable Trust
The Tolkien Trust
The Tuixen Foundation
Mrs Maud Van Norden's Charitable Foundation

People who are housebound

The Goldsmiths' Company Charity
Community Foundations for Lancashire and Merseyside
The London Community Foundation (LCF)

People who are unemployed

The Accenture Foundation
*Bairdwatson Charitable Trust**
The Cadbury Foundation
CHK Charities Ltd
Colyer-Fergusson Charitable Trust
The Enkalon Foundation
H. C. D. Memorial Fund
The Alfred Haines Charitable Trust
Hampshire and Isle of Wight Community Foundation
The Hillingdon Community Trust
Miss Agnes H. Hunter's Trust
Incommunities Foundation
The KPMG Foundation
Kusuma Trust UK
Maurice and Hilda Laing Charitable Trust
Paul Lunn-Rockliffe Charitable Trust
The Marr-Munning Trust
The Mathew Trust
Vyoel Moshe Charitable Trust

The MSE Charity
Paradigm Foundation
The Simmons & Simmons Charitable Foundation
The Willmott Dixon Foundation*

Migrants

The Barrow Cadbury Trust
Paul Hamlyn Foundation
The Manoukian Charitable Foundation
The Marr-Munning Trust
The MSE Charity
People's Postcode Trust

People who have offended

The 29th May 1961 Charitable Trust
The Alchemy Foundation
The John Armitage Charitable Trust
The Sydney Black Charitable Trust
The Bromley Trust
The Noel Buxton Trust
The William A. Cadbury Charitable Trust
Sir John Cass's Foundation
Chesterhill Charitable Trust
The City Bridge Trust (Bridge House Estates)
The Clothworkers' Foundation
The Violet and Milo Cripps Charitable Trust
The Drapers' Charitable Fund
Jill Franklin Trust
The Robert Gavron Charitable Trust
The Goldsmiths' Company Charity
The Gordon Trust*
The Walter Guinness Charitable Trust
H. C. D. Memorial Fund
The Hadley Trust
The Hadrian Trust
Paul Hamlyn Foundation
The Charles Hayward Foundation
The Hilden Charitable Fund
The Michael and Shirley Hunt Charitable Trust
The Ingram Trust
The Charles Irving Charitable Trust
The J. J. Charitable Trust
The Jabbs Foundation
The KPMG Foundation
Maurice and Hilda Laing Charitable Trust
The Beatrice Laing Trust
The Allen Lane Foundation
The Law Society Charity
The Leathersellers' Company Charitable Fund
Inner London Magistrates Court's Poor Box and Feeder Charity
The William and Katherine Longman Trust
Paul Lunn-Rockliffe Charitable Trust
The Monument Trust
The MSE Charity
The Oakdale Trust
The Pilgrim Trust
The Austin and Hope Pilkington Trust
Saint Sarkis Charity Trust
The Francis C. Scott Charitable Trust
The Frieda Scott Charitable Trust
The Peter Stebbings Memorial Charity
The Triangle Trust (1949) Fund
The Woodstock Family Charitable Foundation*
H. and T. Clients Charitable Trust
Heb Ffin (Without Frontier)*
The Mercers' Charitable Foundation
The C. Paul Thackray General Charitable Trust
The Weavers' Company Benevolent Fund

Prisoners and their families

The A. B. Charitable Trust
Odin Charitable Trust
The Weavers' Company Benevolent Fund

Young people at risk of offending

The Avon and Somerset Police Community Trust
Mrs H. R. Greene Charitable Settlement
H. and T. Clients Charitable Trust
The Mark Leonard Trust
The London Community Foundation (LCF)
The Merchant Venturers' Charity
The Norman Family Charitable Trust
People's Postcode Trust
The Portishead Nautical Trust
Rhondda Cynon Taff Welsh Church Acts Fund
The Weavers' Company Benevolent Fund

People who are poor, on low incomes

The 29th May 1961 Charitable Trust
The Accenture Foundation
Achisomoch Aid Company Ltd
The Alliance Family Foundation
Sir John and Lady Amory's Charitable Trust
The Archer Trust
The Bellahouston Bequest Fund
The Bestway Foundation
P. G. and N. J. Boulton Trust
The Bridging Fund Charitable Trust
John Bristow and Thomas Mason Trust
British Gas (Scottish Gas) Energy Trust
Brushmill Ltd
Buckingham Trust
The E. F. Bulmer Benevolent Fund
CAFOD (Catholic Agency for Overseas Development)
Community Foundation for Calderdale
Charitworth Ltd
Christian Aid
Church Urban Fund
Clydpride Ltd
The R. and S. Cohen Foundation
Colyer-Fergusson Charitable Trust
The John Grant Davies Trust*
The Double 'O' Charity Ltd
The Doughty Charity Trust
The Drapers' Charitable Fund
Eastern Counties Educational Trust Ltd
The EBM Charitable Trust
EDF Energy Trust (EDFET)
Elanore Ltd*
The Enkalon Foundation
Entindale Ltd
The Fifty Fund
Fisherbeck Charitable Trust
The Lord Forte Foundation
The Hugh Fraser Foundation
The Raphael Freshwater Memorial Association*
Friends of Wiznitz Ltd
The David Gibbons Foundation
Global Care
The Goodman Foundation
The Gordon Trust*
The Gosling Foundation Ltd
Grahame Charitable Foundation Ltd
The Kenneth and Susan Green Charitable Foundation
Mrs H. R. Greene Charitable Settlement
H. C. D. Memorial Fund

The Hadley Trust
The Hadrian Trust
The Alfred Haines Charitable Trust
Paul Hamlyn Foundation
Hampshire and Isle of Wight Community Foundation
Hampton Fuel Allotment Charity
The W. A. Handley Charity Trust
Harbinson Charitable Trust
Harbo Charities Ltd
The Harbour Foundation
The Harpur Trust
The Edith Lilian Harrison 2000 Foundation
The Hathaway Trust
May Hearnshaw Charitable Trust (May Hearnshaw's Charity)
The Helping Foundation
Henley Educational Trust
Herefordshire Community Foundation
The Hesslewood Children's Trust (Hull Seamen's and General Orphanage)
*M. V. Hillhouse Trust**
The Hillingdon Community Trust
The Holden Charitable Trust
The Mary Homfray Charitable Trust
Hopmarket Charity
The Daniel Howard Trust
The Hunter Foundation
Huntingdon Freemen's Trust
IGO Foundation Ltd
Incommunities Foundation
The Innocent Foundation
The Charles Irving Charitable Trust
The J. and J. Benevolent Foundation
The J. A. R. Charitable Trust
The Johnson Foundation
The Joicey Trust
J. E. Joseph Charitable Fund
The Cyril and Eve Jumbo Charitable Trust
The Jusaca Charitable Trust
The Bernard Kahn Charitable Trust
William Kendall's Charity (Wax Chandlers' Company)
The Nancy Kenyon Charitable Trust
The Kohn Foundation
Kreditor Charitable Trust
Kupath Gemach Chaim Bechesed Viznitz Trust
Kusuma Trust UK
The Kirby Laing Foundation
The Beatrice Laing Trust
Community Foundations for Lancashire and Merseyside
The Jack Lane Charitable Trust
Largsmount Ltd
Laslett's (Hinton) Charity
The Edgar E. Lawley Foundation
Lawson Beckman Charitable Trust
The Leathersellers' Company Charitable Fund
The Kennedy Leigh Charitable Trust
The Enid Linder Foundation
The Frank Litchfield Charitable Trust
Localtrent Ltd
Loftus Charitable Trust
London Catalyst
The London Community Foundation (LCF)
Inner London Magistrates Court's Poor Box and Feeder Charity
*Michael Lowe's and Associated Charities**
The Henry Lumley Charitable Trust
Paul Lunn-Rockliffe Charitable Trust
The Lynn Foundation
The M. K. Charitable Trust
The E. M. MacAndrew Trust
The Mackintosh Foundation
The Magdalen and Lasher Charity (General Fund)
The Magen Charitable Trust
The Manackerman Charitable Trust
The Manoukian Charitable Foundation
Marbeh Torah Trust
Mariapolis Ltd
The Marr-Munning Trust
The Michael Marsh Charitable Trust
*Masonic Charitable Foundation**
Mayfair Charities Ltd
Melodor Ltd
Mercaz Torah Vechesed Ltd
The Merchant Taylors' Company Charities Fund
Merchant Taylors' Consolidated Charities for the Infirm
The Merchant Venturers' Charity
The Metropolitan Masonic Charity
T. and J. Meyer Family Foundation Ltd
The Mills Charity
Keren Mitzvah Trust
The Mizpah Trust
The Monmouthshire County Council Welsh Church Act Fund
The Morel Charitable Trust
The Morris Charitable Trust
Vyoel Moshe Charitable Trust
The MSE Charity
The Edith Murphy Foundation
Muslim Hands
Newpier Charity Ltd
Norfolk Community Foundation
The Northmoor Trust
The Olga Charitable Trust
Oxfam (GB)
Paradigm Foundation
Pollywally Charitable Trust
The Portishead Nautical Trust
Sir John Priestman Charity Trust
The Puebla Charitable Trust
The Puri Foundation
Quartet Community Foundation
Quothquan Trust
Rachel Charitable Trust
Rhondda Cynon Taff Welsh Church Acts Fund
*Riverside Charitable Trust Ltd**
Mrs L. D. Rope's Third Charitable Settlement
The Rowlands Trust
The Joseph Rowntree Charitable Trust
*Rozelle Trust**
S. F. Foundation
The ScottishPower Energy People Trust
The Severn Trent Water Charitable Trust Fund
The Shanley Charitable Trust
The Simmons & Simmons Charitable Foundation
Songdale Ltd
R. H. Southern Trust
Sparquote Ltd
Spears-Stutz Charitable Trust
Springrule Ltd
The Squires Foundation
The Peter Stebbings Memorial Charity
The Sigmund Sternberg Charitable Foundation
Stervon Ltd
The Summerfield Charitable Trust
Tegham Ltd
The Thornton Trust
The Tuixen Foundation
United Utilities Trust Fund
The Walcot Foundation
The Walker Trust
West Derby Waste Lands Charity
The Norman Whiteley Trust
*The Willmott Dixon Foundation**
The Maurice Wohl Charitable Foundation
Woodlands Green Ltd
*The Worwin UK Foundation**

Refugees and asylum seekers

The A. B. Charitable Trust
The Bromley Trust
Christian Aid
The Evan Cornish Foundation
The Edith Maud Ellis 1985 Charitable Trust
The Ericson Trust
Jill Franklin Trust
H. C. D. Memorial Fund
Paul Hamlyn Foundation
The Harbour Foundation
The Hilden Charitable Fund
M. V. Hillhouse Trust*
The KPMG Foundation
The Allen Lane Foundation
The Leigh Trust
M. and C. Trust
The Mackintosh Foundation
John Moores Foundation
Network for Social Change Charitable Trust
Odin Charitable Trust
People's Postcode Trust
The Austin and Hope Pilkington Trust
The Portrack Charitable Trust
Postcode Dream Trust – Dream Fund
Elizabeth Rathbone Charity
The Sigrid Rausing Trust
Swan Mountain Trust
The Tolkien Trust

Sex workers

The Elton John AIDS Foundation (EJAF)
The Pilgrim Trust

Victims, oppressed people

A2BD Foundation UK Ltd*
The Bay Tree Charitable Trust
BHP Bhilliton Sustainable Communities
The Bromley Trust
Christian Aid
Denise Coates Foundation
The Dorcas Trust
The Emerton-Christie Charity
Jill Franklin Trust
The Gunter Charitable Trust
The Horizon Foundation
The Ireland Fund of Great Britain
Irish Youth Foundation (UK) Ltd (incorporating The Lawlor Foundation)
The Elton John AIDS Foundation (EJAF)
The LankellyChase Foundation
The William Leech Charity
The Loseley and Guildway Charitable Trust
The Marr-Munning Trust
The Mirianog Trust
The Morel Charitable Trust
The Steve Morgan Foundation
The Eleanor Rathbone Charitable Trust
The Roughley Charitable Trust
The Samworth Foundation
The Save the Children Fund*
The Shanti Charitable Trust
The Souter Charitable Trust
The W. F. Southall Trust
The Spear Charitable Trust
The Swire Charitable Trust
The Gay and Keith Talbot Trust
The Three Oaks Trust
The Tinsley Foundation
The Tisbury Telegraph Trust
Voluntary Action Fund (VAF)
Blyth Watson Charitable Trust
The Westcroft Trust

People who have suffered abuse, violence or torture

The Brelms Trust CIO*
The Cambridgeshire Community Foundation
The Hadrian Trust
Harbinson Charitable Trust
Heb Ffin (Without Frontier)*
P. and C. Hickinbotham Charitable Trust
The Charles Irving Charitable Trust
The Kelly Family Charitable Trust
The Allen Lane Foundation
The London Community Foundation (LCF)
Inner London Magistrates Court's Poor Box and Feeder Charity
The R. S. Macdonald Charitable Trust
The MSE Charity
People's Postcode Trust
The Austin and Hope Pilkington Trust
The Portishead Nautical Trust
The Sigrid Rausing Trust
The Francis C. Scott Charitable Trust
The Frieda Scott Charitable Trust
The Peter Stebbings Memorial Charity
The C. Paul Thackray General Charitable Trust
The Three Guineas Trust

Victims of disasters

The A. S. Charitable Trust
The Allen & Overy Foundation*
The Austin Bailey Foundation
Bergqvist Charitable Trust
The Bestway Foundation
The Blandford Lake Trust
Christadelphian Samaritan Fund
The De La Rue Charitable Trust*
The Diageo Foundation
The Freshfield Foundation
Interserve Employee Foundation Ltd
The Leathersellers' Company Charitable Fund
The Monmouthshire County Council Welsh Church Act Fund
Muslim Hands
The Norton Rose Fulbright Charitable Foundation
Oxfam (GB)
The W. L. Pratt Charitable Trust
The Sir James Reckitt Charity
Rhodi Charitable Trust*

People suffering from famine

The A. S. Charitable Trust
The Alchemy Foundation
The Andrew Anderson Trust
The Austin Bailey Foundation
Bergqvist Charitable Trust
The Blandford Lake Trust
CAFOD (Catholic Agency for Overseas Development)
Christadelphian Samaritan Fund
The Coltstaple Trust
The Anna Rosa Forster Charitable Trust
Oxfam (GB)
The Constance Travis Charitable Trust

People suffering injustice

Network for Social Change Charitable Trust
The Allen Lane Foundation
The Joseph Rowntree Charitable Trust
The Law Society Charity
The Leigh Trust
The Michael and Shirley Hunt Charitable Trust
The Sigrid Rausing Trust

■ Victims of war or conflict

The A. S. Charitable Trust
The Austin Bailey Foundation
The Blandford Lake Trust
CAFOD (Catholic Agency for Overseas Development)
H. C. D. Memorial Fund
The Kennedy Leigh Charitable Trust
*P. and M. Lovell Charitable Settlement**
Marmot Charitable Trust
Vyoel Moshe Charitable Trust
Muslim Hands
Oxfam (GB)

Grant-makers by type of grant

This index contains two separate listings:

List of types of grant: This lists all the headings used in DGMT to categorise types of grant.

Grant-makers by type of grant: This lists funders under the types of grant for which they have expressed a funding preference. Asterisks mark funders which have not been featured in DGMT before.

Grant-makers by type of grant

These pages contain two separate listings

List of type of grants
This lists all of the headings used in DGMT to categorise types of grants

Grant-makers by type of grant
This lists funders under the types of grants for which they have expressed a funding preference

Type of support

Capital support

The 1970 Trust
The 29th May 1961 Charitable Trust
*The 3Ts Charitable Trust**
4 Charity Foundation
*A2BD Foundation UK Ltd**
Aberdeen Asset Management Charitable Foundation
The Aberdeen Foundation
The Acacia Charitable Trust
The ACT Foundation
The Sylvia Adams Charitable Trust
The Addleshaw Goddard Charitable Trust
Adenfirst Ltd
The Adint Charitable Trust
AF Trust Company
*AKO Foundation**
The Alborada Trust
D. G. Albright Charitable Trust
Allchurches Trust Ltd
*The Allen & Overy Foundation**
D. C. R. Allen Charitable Trust
The H. B. Allen Charitable Trust
The Allen Trust
*Alzheimer's Society**
AM Charitable Trust
The Ampelos Trust
The Andrew Anderson Trust
Andor Charitable Trust
Anglo American Group Foundation
The Animal Defence Trust
The Annandale Charitable Trust
*The Anne Duchess of Westminster's Charity**
The Anson Charitable Trust
*AO Smile Foundation**
The Apax Foundation
The John Apthorp Charity
The Arah Foundation
The Arbib Foundation
The Archer Trust
The Architectural Heritage Fund
The Ardeola Charitable Trust
The John Armitage Charitable Trust
Ove Arup Partnership Charitable Trust
*The Asfari Foundation**
The Ashley Family Foundation
*The Associated Board of the Royal Schools of Music**
The Atlas Fund
The Aurelius Charitable Trust
The Lord Austin Trust
Autonomous Research Charitable Trust (ARCT)
Awards for All (see also the Big Lottery Fund)
The Aylesford Family Charitable Trust
Backstage Trust
The Harry Bacon Foundation
The Baker Charitable Trust
The Roy and Pixie Baker Charitable Trust
The Balfour Beatty Charitable Trust
The Andrew Balint Charitable Trust
The Band Trust
The Barclay Foundation
The Barham Charitable Trust
The Baring Foundation
The Barker-Mill Foundation
Lord Barnby's Foundation
Barnwood Trust
Bay Charitable Trust
The Bay Tree Charitable Trust
The Louis Baylis (Maidenhead Advertiser) Charitable Trust
BBC Children in Need
BC Partners Foundation
BCH Trust
Bear Mordechai Ltd
Beauland Ltd
The Becker Family Charitable Trust
The Bedfordshire and Luton Community Foundation
Beefy's Charity Foundation
*Benesco Charity Ltd**
The Berkeley Charitable Foundation
The Ruth Berkowitz Charitable Trust
The Berkshire Community Foundation
The Bestway Foundation
The Big Lottery Fund (see also Awards for All)
Birthday House Trust
Miss Jeanne Bisgood's Charitable Trust
*Asser Bishvil Foundation**
The Bertie Black Foundation
Isabel Blackman Foundation
Blakemore Foundation
The Blandford Lake Trust
The Bluston Charitable Settlement
The Bonamy Charitable Trust
The Boodle & Dunthorne Charitable Trust
The Booth Charities
Salo Bordon Charitable Trust
The Boshier-Hinton Foundation
P. G. and N. J. Boulton Trust
Sir Clive Bourne Family Trust
Bourneheights Ltd
Friends of Boyan Trust
The Tony Bramall Charitable Trust
The Liz and Terry Bramall Foundation
The Bransford Trust
The Breadsticks Foundation
Bridgepoint Charitable Trust
The Harold and Alice Bridges Charity
Bristol Archdeaconry Charity
Bristol Charities
John Bristow and Thomas Mason Trust
The British and Foreign School Society
British Council for Prevention of Blindness (Save Eyes Everywhere)
The British Dietetic Association General and Education Trust Fund
The J. and M. Britton Charitable Trust
The Consuelo and Anthony Brooke Charitable Trust
The Rory and Elizabeth Brooks Foundation
R. S. Brownless Charitable Trust
The T. B. H. Brunner's Charitable Settlement
The Bruntwood Charity
Brushmill Ltd
Buckingham Trust
The Buffini Chao Foundation
The E. F. Bulmer Benevolent Fund
BUPA UK Foundation
*The Burberry Foundation**
The Burdett Trust for Nursing
The Derek Butler Trust
*The Butters Foundation (UK) Ltd**
The Edward Cadbury Charitable Trust
The William A. Cadbury Charitable Trust
The Cadbury Foundation
The Edward and Dorothy Cadbury Trust
The Cadogan Charity
Calleva Foundation
The Cambridgeshire Community Foundation
The Ellis Campbell Charitable Foundation
The Campden Charities Trustee
*Canary Wharf Contractors Fund**
The Frederick and Phyllis Cann Trust
Cardy Beaver Foundation
David William Traill Cargill Fund
The Richard Carne Trust
The Carnegie Dunfermline Trust

The Casey Trust
The Catholic Charitable Trust
The Catholic Trust for England and Wales
The Cayo Foundation
The Cazenove Charitable Trust
The CBD Charitable Trust
CBRE UK Charitable Trust
The CH (1980) Charitable Trust
*The Chadwick Educational Foundation**
The Amelia Chadwick Trust
The Chapman Charitable Trust
The Charter 600 Charity
Chartered Accountants' Livery Charity (CALC)
*Cheshire Community Foundation Ltd**
Chesterhill Charitable Trust
The Childhood Trust
Children with Cancer UK
The Childwick Trust
CHK Charities Ltd
The CIBC World Markets Children's Miracle Foundation
Stephen Clark 1957 Charitable Trust
The Cleopatra Trust
The Clover Trust
The Coalfields Regeneration Trust
The Cobalt Trust
John Coldman Charitable Trust
The Sir Jeremiah Colman Gift Trust
Col-Reno Ltd
Colyer-Fergusson Charitable Trust
Community First (Landfill Communities Fund)
The Douglas Compton James Charitable Trust
The Congregational and General Charitable Trust
Martin Connell Charitable Trust
*The Thomas Cook Chidlren's Charity**
The Cooks Charity
The Catherine Cookson Charitable Trust
The Keith Coombs Trust
The Alice Ellen Cooper Dean Charitable Foundation
The J. Reginald Corah Foundation Fund
The Worshipful Company of Cordwainers Charitable Trusts (Minges Gift and the Pooled Trusts)
*The Corporation of Trinity House of Deptford Strond**
The County Council of Dyfed Welsh Curch Fund
Coutts Charitable Foundation
Coventry Building Society Charitable Foundation
The John Cowan Foundation
The Craignish Trust
*Credit Suisse EMEA Foundation**
The Crescent Trust
*England and Wales Cricket Trust**
Criffel Charitable Trust
*Crisis UK**
The Peter Cruddas Foundation
*CSIS Charity Fund**
The Cuby Charitable Trust
Cullum Family Trust
The D'Oyly Carte Charitable Trust
Roald Dahl's Marvellous Children's Charity
Oizer Dalim Trust
*The Biss Davies Charitable Trust**
*Dawat-E-Hadiyah Trust (United Kingdom)**
*The Roger De Haan Charitable Trust**
*The De La Rue Charitable Trust**
Debmar Benevolent Trust Ltd
Provincial Grand Charity of the Province of Derbyshire
The J. N. Derbyshire Trust
The Sandy Dewhirst Charitable Trust
The Laduma Dhamecha Charitable Trust
The Diageo Foundation
Alan and Sheila Diamond Charitable Trust
Dinwoodie Charitable Company
The Dischma Charitable Trust
*C. H. Dixon Charitable Trust**
The Djanogly Foundation
The DM Charitable Trust
The Dorcas Trust
*The Dorfman Foundation**
Dorset Community Foundation
The Dorus Trust
The Double 'O' Charity Ltd
The Drapers' Charitable Fund
Dromintee Trust
Duchy Health Charity Ltd
The Royal Foundation of the Duke and Duchess of Cambridge and Prince Harry
The Dulverton Trust
Dunard Fund 2016
The Dunhill Medical Trust
The Charles Dunstone Charitable Trust
Dushinsky Trust Ltd
The Mildred Duveen Charitable Trust
The James Dyson Foundation
Audrey Earle Charitable Trust
The Earley Charity
Eastern Counties Educational Trust Ltd
*The ECHO Trust**
Echoes Of Service
The Ecology Trust
The Economist Charitable Trust
EDF Energy Trust (EDFET)
The Gilbert and Eileen Edgar Foundation
Edinburgh Children's Holiday Fund
Edupoor Ltd
Ellador Ltd
The Ellinson Foundation Ltd
The Elmley Foundation
*The Emerald Foundation**
The Enkalon Foundation
Entindale Ltd
The Ericson Trust
The Erskine Cunningham Hill Trust
The Esfandi Charitable Foundation
Esh Foundation
Esher House Charitable Trust
Essex Community Foundation
The Essex Youth Trust
The Estelle Trust
Joseph Ettedgui Charitable Foundation
Euro Charity Trust
The Alan Evans Memorial Trust
The Eveson Charitable Trust
The Beryl Evetts and Robert Luff Animal Welfare Trust Ltd
The Exilarch's Foundation
The Expat Foundation
Extonglen Ltd
The William and Christine Eynon Charity
G. F. Eyre Charitable Trust
Matthew Eyton Animal Welfare Trust
The F. P. Ltd Charitable Trust
The Fairstead Trust
Famos Foundation Trust
The Lord Faringdon Charitable Trust
Samuel William Farmer Trust
The Thomas Farr Charity
The Farthing Trust
The February Foundation
The John Feeney Charitable Bequest
The George Fentham Birmingham Charity
The A. M. Fenton Trust
Allan and Nesta Ferguson Charitable Settlement
Elizabeth Ferguson Charitable Trust Fund
The Fidelity UK Foundation

The Alfred And Peggy Harvey Charitable Trust
The Hasluck Charitable Trust
The Hathaway Trust
The Maurice Hatter Foundation
The Hawthorne Charitable Trust
The Charles Hayward Foundation
The Headley Trust
May Hearnshaw Charitable Trust (May Hearnshaw's Charity)
Heart of England Community Foundation
Heart Research UK
The Heathcoat Trust
Heathrow Community Fund (LHR Airport Communities Trust)
The Heathside Charitable Trust
*Heb Ffin (Without Frontier)**
The Charlotte Heber-Percy Charitable Trust
Ernest Hecht Charitable Foundation
The Percy Hedley 1990 Charitable Trust
Hedley Foundation Ltd (The Hedley Foundation)
The Michael Heller Charitable Foundation
The Simon Heller Charitable Settlement
Help for Health
The Helping Foundation
The Hemby Charitable Trust
*Henderson Firstfruits**
The Christina Mary Hendrie Trust for Scottish and Canadian Charities
Henley Educational Trust
The G. D. Herbert Charitable Trust
Herefordshire Community Foundation
Hertfordshire Community Foundation
P. and C. Hickinbotham Charitable Trust
The Alan Edward Higgs Charity
Highcroft Charitable Trust
The Hilden Charitable Fund
The Derek Hill Foundation
*M. V. Hillhouse Trust**
The Hillier Trust
The Hillingdon Community Trust
R. G. Hills Charitable Trust
Hinchley Charitable Trust
The Hinduja Foundation
The Hintze Family Charity Foundation
The Hiscox Foundation
The Henry C. Hoare Charitable Trust
The Hobson Charity Ltd
Hockerill Educational Foundation
The Jane Hodge Foundation
The Holden Charitable Trust
The Hollands-Warren Fund
The Hollick Family Charitable Trust
The Holliday Foundation
The Dorothy Holmes Charitable Trust
P. H. Holt Foundation
The Holywood Trust
The Homelands Charitable Trust
The Homestead Charitable Trust
The Mary Homfray Charitable Trust
Sir Harold Hood's Charitable Trust
The Hope Trust
Hopmarket Charity
The Horizon Foundation
The Antony Hornby Charitable Trust
The Thomas J. Horne Memorial Trust
The Worshipful Company of Horners' Charitable Trusts
Hospice UK
The Hospital Saturday Fund
The Sir Joseph Hotung Charitable Settlement
House of Industry Estate
The Reta Lila Howard Foundation
The Daniel Howard Trust
*Howman Charitable Trust**
The Hudson Foundation
The Hull and East Riding Charitable Trust
Hulme Trust Estates (Educational)
Human Relief Foundation
The Humanitarian Trust
The Michael and Shirley Hunt Charitable Trust
The Albert Hunt Trust
The Hunter Foundation
Miss Agnes H. Hunter's Trust
The Hunting Horn General Charitable Trust
The Huntingdon Foundation Ltd
Huntingdon Freemen's Trust
Hurdale Charity Ltd
The Hutchinson Charitable Trust
The Hutton Foundation
The Nani Huyu Charitable Trust
The P. Y. N. and B. Hyams Trust
Hyde Charitable Trust (Youth Plus)
*Ibbett Trust**
Ibrahim Foundation Ltd
*ICE Futures Charitable Trust**
The Idlewild Trust
IGO Foundation Ltd
The Iliffe Family Charitable Trust
Imagine Foundation
Impetus – The Private Equity Foundation (Impetus – PEF)
Incommunities Foundation
The Indigo Trust
*The Worshipful Company of Information Technologists**
The Ingram Trust
The Inlight Trust
The Inman Charity
The Innocent Foundation
*The Worshipful Company of Insurers – First Charitable Trust Fund**
*Integrated Education Fund**
The International Bankers Charitable Trust (The Worshipful Company of Interntional Bankers)
*International Bible Students Association**
*International Fund for Animal Welfare (IFAW)**
Interserve Employee Foundation Ltd
The Inverforth Charitable Trust
Investream Charitable Trust
The Ireland Fund of Great Britain
Irish Youth Foundation (UK) Ltd (incorporating The Lawlor Foundation)
The Ironmongers' Company
The Charles Irving Charitable Trust
The J. Isaacs Charitable Trust
The Isle of Anglesey Charitable Trust
The ITF Seafarers' Trust
The J. and J. Benevolent Foundation
The J. A. R. Charitable Trust
The J. J. Charitable Trust
The Jabbs Foundation
C. Richard Jackson Charitable Trust
The Sir Barry Jackson County Fund (incorporating the Hornton Fund)
The Ruth and Lionel Jacobson Trust (Second Fund) No. 2
John James Bristol Foundation
The Susan and Stephen James Charitable Settlement
The Jarman Charitable Trust
John Jarrold Trust Ltd
Rees Jeffreys Road Fund
Nick Jenkins Foundation
The Jenour Foundation

The Jephcott Charitable Trust
The Jerusalem Trust
The Jewish Youth Fund (JYF)
Joffe Charitable Trust
Lillie Johnson Charitable Trust
The Johnson Foundation
Johnnie Johnson Trust
Johnson Wax Ltd Charitable Trust
The Christopher and Kirsty Johnston Charitable Trust
The Joicey Trust
The Jones 1986 Charitable Trust
The Dezna Robins Jones Charitable Foundation
The Marjorie and Geoffrey Jones Charitable Trust
The Muriel Jones Foundation
The Jordan Charitable Foundation
The Joron Charitable Trust
J. E. Joseph Charitable Fund
The Cyril and Eve Jumbo Charitable Trust
Anton Jurgens Charitable Trust
The Jusaca Charitable Trust
Kahal Chassidim Bobov
The Bernard Kahn Charitable Trust
The Stanley Kalms Foundation
Karaviotis Foundation
The Boris Karloff Charitable Foundation
The Kasner Charitable Trust
The Michael and Ilse Katz Foundation
C. S. Kaufman Charitable Trust
The Caron Keating Foundation
The Kelly Family Charitable Trust
Kelsick's Educational Foundation
The Kay Kendall Leukaemia Fund
William Kendall's Charity (Wax Chandlers' Company)
The Kennel Club Charitable Trust
Kent Community Foundation
The Nancy Kenyon Charitable Trust
Keren Association Ltd
E. and E. Kernkraut Charities Ltd
The Peter Kershaw Trust
The Ursula Keyes Trust
The Robert Kiln Charitable Trust
The King Henry VIII Endowed Trust – Warwick
The King/Cullimore Charitable Trust
Laura Kinsella Foundation
The Graham Kirkham Foundation*
Kirkley Poor's Land Estate
The Richard Kirkman Trust
The Kirschel Foundation
Robert Kitchin (Saddlers' Company)
The Ernest Kleinwort Charitable Trust
The Kobler Trust
The Kohn Foundation
Kollel and Co. Ltd
Kreditor Charitable Trust
The Kreitman Foundation
The Neil Kreitman Foundation
Kupath Gemach Chaim Bechesed Viznitz Trust
Kusuma Trust UK
The Kyte Charitable Trust
Ladbrokes in the Community Charitable Trust
The K. P. Ladd Charitable Trust
John Laing Charitable Trust
Maurice and Hilda Laing Charitable Trust
Christopher Laing Foundation
The David Laing Foundation
The Kirby Laing Foundation
The Martin Laing Foundation
The Beatrice Laing Trust
The Leonard Laity Stoate Charitable Trust
The Lambert Charitable Trust
Community Foundations for Lancashire and Merseyside
Lancashire Environmental Fund Ltd
The Lancashire Foundation*
Duchy of Lancaster Benevolent Fund
Lancaster Foundation
LandAid Charitable Trust (Land Aid)
The Jack Lane Charitable Trust
Langdale Trust
The Langtree Trust
The R. J. Larg Family Charitable Trust
Largsmount Ltd
Laslett's (Hinton) Charity
The Lauffer Family Charitable Foundation
Mrs F. B. Laurence Charitable Trust
The Kathleen Laurence Trust
The Edgar E. Lawley Foundation
The Herd Lawson and Muriel Lawson Charitable Trust
Lawson Beckman Charitable Trust
The Raymond and Blanche Lawson Charitable Trust
The David Lean Foundation
The Leathersellers' Company Charitable Fund
The Leche Trust
The Arnold Lee Charitable Trust
Leeds Building Society Charitable Foundation
Leeds Community Foundation (LCF)
The Legal Education Foundation*
Leicestershire, Leicester and Rutland Community Foundation
The Kennedy Leigh Charitable Trust
The Leigh Trust
P. Leigh-Bramwell Trust 'E'
The Lennox Hannay Charitable Trust
The Mark Leonard Trust
The Leverhulme Trade Charities Trust
Lord Leverhulme's Charitable Trust
David and Ruth Lewis Family Charitable Trust
The John Spedan Lewis Foundation
The Sir Edward Lewis Foundation
John Lewis Partnership General Community Fund
The Light Fund Company*
The Limbourne Trust
Limoges Charitable Trust
The Linbury Trust
Lincolnshire Community Foundation
The Lind Trust
Lindale Educational Foundation
The Linden Charitable Trust
The Enid Linder Foundation
The Ruth and Stuart Lipton Charitable Trust
The Lister Charitable Trust
The Frank Litchfield Charitable Trust
Littlefield Foundation (UK) Ltd
The Charles Littlewood Hill Trust
The George John and Sheilah Livanos Charitable Trust
Liverpool Charity and Voluntary Services (LCVS)
Jack Livingstone Charitable Trust
The Elaine and Angus Lloyd Charitable Trust
Lloyd's Charities Trust
Lloyds Bank Foundation for the Channel Islands
Localtrent Ltd
The Locker Foundation
Loftus Charitable Trust

The Lolev Charitable Trust
The Joyce Lomax Bullock Charitable Trust
Trust for London
London Catalyst
The London Community Foundation (LCF)
London Housing Foundation Ltd (LHF)
London Legal Support Trust (LLST)
Inner London Magistrates Court's Poor Box and Feeder Charity
The London Marathon Charitable Trust Ltd
The William and Katherine Longman Trust
The Loseley and Guildway Charitable Trust
P. and M. Lovell Charitable Settlement*
The Lower Green Foundation
The C. L. Loyd Charitable Trust
The Henry Lumley Charitable Trust
Paul Lunn-Rockliffe Charitable Trust
Lord and Lady Lurgan Trust
The Lynn Foundation
John Lyon's Charity
The Sir Jack Lyons Charitable Trust
M. and C. Trust
M. B. Foundation*
The M. K. Charitable Trust
The M. Y. A. Charitable Trust
The E. M. MacAndrew Trust
The R. S. Macdonald Charitable Trust
The Mackay and Brewer Charitable Trust
The Mackintosh Foundation
GPS Macpherson Charitable Settlement*
The MacRobert Trust
The Mactaggart Third Fund
The Ian Mactaggart Trust (The Mactaggart Second Fund)
The Magen Charitable Trust
The Makers of Playing Cards Charity
The Mallinckrodt Foundation
The Manackerman Charitable Trust
The Manchester Guardian Society Charitable Trust
Lord Mayor of Manchester's Charity Appeal Trust
The Manifold Charitable Trust
The W. M. Mann Foundation
The Manoukian Charitable Foundation
Marbeh Torah Trust
The Marcela Trust
The Marchig Animal Welfare Trust
The Stella and Alexander Margulies Charitable Trust
Mariapolis Ltd
The Michael Marks Charitable Trust
The Marks Family Foundation
The Ann and David Marks Foundation
The Hilda and Samuel Marks Foundation
The J. P. Marland Charitable Trust
Marmot Charitable Trust
The Marr-Munning Trust
The Michael Marsh Charitable Trust
The Marsh Christian Trust
Charlotte Marshall Charitable Trust
D. G. Marshall of Cambridge Trust
The Martin Charitable Trust*
Sir George Martin Trust
John Martin's Charity
The Mason Porter Charitable Trust
Masonic Charitable Foundation*
The Nancie Massey Charitable Trust
The Mathew Trust
The Matliwala Family Charitable Trust
The Violet Mauray Charitable Trust
Mayfair Charities Ltd
The Mayfield Valley Arts Trust
Mazars Charitable Trust
The Robert McAlpine Foundation
McGreevy No. 5 Settlement
D. D. McPhail Charitable Settlement
Medical Research Foundation*
The Medlock Charitable Trust
Melodor Ltd
Menuchar Ltd
Mercaz Torah Vechesed Ltd
The Brian Mercer Charitable Trust
The Mercers' Charitable Foundation
Merchant Navy Welfare Board
Merchant Taylors' Consolidated Charities for the Infirm
The Merchant Venturers' Charity
Mercury Phoenix Trust
The Metropolitan Masonic Charity
T. and J. Meyer Family Foundation Ltd
The Mickel Fund
The Mickleham Trust
The Gerald Micklem Charitable Trust
The Masonic Province of Middlesex Charitable Trust (Middlesex Masonic Charity)
Middlesex Sports Foundation
Millennium Stadium Charitable Trust (Ymddiriedolaeth Elusennol Stadiwm Y. Mileniwm)
Hugh and Mary Miller Bequest Trust
The Ronald Miller Foundation
The Millfield House Foundation (1)
The Millfield Trust
The Millichope Foundation
Mills and Reeve Charitable Trust*
The Mills Charity
The Millward Charitable Trust
The Clare Milne Trust
The James Milner Foundation*
Milton Keynes Community Foundation Ltd
The Edgar Milward Charity
The Peter Minet Trust
The Mirianog Trust
The Laurence Misener Charitable Trust
The Mishcon Family Charitable Trust
The Brian Mitchell Charitable Settlement
Mitsubishi Corporation Fund for Europe and Africa*
The Mittal Foundation
Keren Mitzvah Trust
The Mizpah Trust
Mobbs Memorial Trust Ltd
Mole Charitable Trust
The Monatrea Charitable Trust
The Monmouthshire County Council Welsh Church Act Fund
The Monument Trust
Moondance Foundation*
The George A. Moore Foundation
John Moores Foundation
The Morel Charitable Trust
The Morgan Charitable Foundation
The Steve Morgan Foundation
Morgan Stanley International Foundation
The Diana and Allan Morgenthau Charitable Trust
The Miles Morland Foundation
The Morris Charitable Trust
The Willie and Mabel Morris Charitable Trust

G. M. Morrison Charitable Trust
The Morrisons Foundation*
The Morton Charitable Trust*
The Moshal Charitable Trust
Vyoel Moshe Charitable Trust
The Moss Family Charitable Trust
The Mosselson Charitable Trust
Moto in the Community
The Edwina Mountbatten and Leonora Children's Foundation
The Mugdock Children's Trust
The Mulberry Trust
The Frederick Mulder Foundation
The Edith Murphy Foundation
Murphy-Neumann Charity Company Ltd
The John R. Murray Charitable Trust
The Music Sales Charitable Trust
Muslim Hands
The Mutual Trust Group
MW (CL) Foundation
MW (GK) Foundation
MW (HO) Foundation
MW (RH) Foundation
The Janet Nash Charitable Settlement
The National Express Foundation
The National Gardens Scheme*
The Worshipful Company of Needlemakers' Charitable Fund
Nemoral Ltd
Ner Foundation
Nesswall Ltd
Newby Trust Ltd
Newpier Charity Ltd
Alderman Newton's Educational Foundation
The NFU Mutual Charitable Trust
NJD Charitable Trust
Alice Noakes Memorial Charitable Trust
Norfolk Community Foundation
Educational Foundation of Alderman John Norman
The Norman Family Charitable Trust
Normanby Charitable Trust
North East Area Miners Welfare Trust Fund*
North London Charities Ltd*
Provincial Grand Charity of Northamptonshire and Huntingdonshire*
Northamptonshire Community Foundation
The Community Foundation for Northern Ireland
The Northumberland Village Homes Trust
Northwood Charitable Trust
The Norton Foundation
The Norton Rose Fulbright Charitable Foundation
Norwich Town Close Estate Charity
Nottinghamshire Community Foundation
The Father O'Mahoney Memorial Trust
The Sir Peter O'Sullevan Charitable Trust
The Oakdale Trust
The Oakley Charitable Trust
Odin Charitable Trust
The Ofenheim Charitable Trust
The Ogle Christian Trust
Oizer Charitable Trust
Old Possum's Practical Trust
The Oldham Foundation
The Olga Charitable Trust
The Onaway Trust*
OneFamily Foundation
Open Gate
The O'Sullivan Family Charitable Trust
The Ouseley Church Music Trust
The Owen Family Trust
Oxfam (GB)
Oxfordshire Community Foundation
P. F. Charitable Trust
The Doris Pacey Charitable Foundation
The Paget Charitable Trust
Palmtree Memorial Trust*
The Paphitis Charitable Trust
Parabola Foundation*
Paradigm Foundation
The Paragon Trust
Parish Estate of the Church of St Michael Spurriergate York*
The Park House Charitable Trust
The Patrick Trust
The Jack Patston Charitable Trust
Peacock Charitable Trust
Susanna Peake Charitable Trust
The Pears Family Charitable Foundation
The Dowager Countess Eleanor Peel Trust
The Pell Charitable Trust
The Pennycress Trust
People's Postcode Trust
The Performing Right Society Foundation
B. E. Perl Charitable Trust
Personal Assurance Charitable Trust
The Persson Charitable Trust
The Persula Foundation
The Jack Petchey Foundation
Petplan Charitable Trust
The Pharsalia Charitable Trust
The Phillips and Rubens Charitable Trust
The Phillips Charitable Trust
The Phillips Family Charitable Trust
Pilkington Charities Fund
Miss A. M. Pilkington's Charitable Trust
The DLA Piper Charitable Trust
The George and Esme Pollitzer Charitable Settlement
Pollywally Charitable Trust
The Polonsky Foundation
The Ponton House Trust
Edith and Ferdinand Porjes Charitable Trust
The Porta Pia 2012 Foundation
The Portrack Charitable Trust
The J. E. Posnansky Charitable Trust
Postcode Community Trust*
Postcode Dream Trust – Dream Fund
The Mary Potter Convent Hospital Trust
Power to Change Trust*
Powys Welsh Church Fund*
Premishlaner Charitable Trust
Sir John Priestman Charity Trust
The Primrose Trust
The Prince Philip Trust Fund*
Princes Gate Trust*
The Princess Anne's Charities
The Privy Purse Charitable Trust
The Professional Footballers' Association Charity*
Prostate Cancer UK*
The Puebla Charitable Trust
The Puri Foundation
The PwC Foundation
The Pye Foundation*
Mr and Mrs J. A. Pye's Charitable Settlement
Quartet Community Foundation
The Queen Anne's Gate Foundation
Queen Mary's Roehampton Trust
The Queen's Trust
Quothquan Trust
R. S. Charitable Trust
Rachel Charitable Trust
The Racing Foundation
Racing Welfare
Richard Radcliffe Trust
The Radcliffe Trust

The Bishop Radford Trust
The Rainford Trust
*The Edward Ramsden Charitable Trust**
The Joseph and Lena Randall Charitable Trust
The Joseph Rank Trust
The Ranworth Trust
Rashbass Family Trust
The Ratcliff Foundation
The Eleanor Rathbone Charitable Trust
Elizabeth Rathbone Charity
The Sigrid Rausing Trust
The Ravensdale Trust
The Roger Raymond Charitable Trust
The Rayne Trust
The John Rayner Charitable Trust
The Sir James Reckitt Charity
C. A. Redfern Charitable Foundation
Reed Family Foundation
Richard Reeve's Foundation
Reuben Foundation
*Rhodi Charitable Trust**
The Rhododendron Trust
Daisie Rich Trust
The Clive and Sylvia Richards Charity Ltd
Ridgesave Ltd
The Sir John Ritblat Family Foundation
The River Farm Foundation
Rivers Foundation
*Riverside Charitable Trust Ltd**
The Rix-Thompson-Rothenberg Foundation
RJM Charity Trust
Thomas Roberts Trust
Robyn Charitable Trust
The Rofeh Trust
The Richard Rogers Charitable Settlement
Rokach Family Charitable Trust
The Sir James Roll Charitable Trust
The Helen Roll Charity
The Gerald Ronson Family Foundation
*Mrs L. D. Rope's Second Charitable Settlement**
The Rothermere Foundation
*Rothschild Foundation (Hanadiv) Europe**
The Roughley Charitable Trust
Rowanville Ltd
The Rowlands Trust
The Joseph Rowntree Charitable Trust
Royal Artillery Charitable Fund
The Royal British Legion
*Royal Society Of Wildlife Trusts**
*Rozelle Trust**
Rugby Football Foundation
The Rugby Group Benevolent Fund Ltd
The RVW Trust
The J. S. and E. C. Rymer Charitable Trust
S. F. Foundation
The Michael and Nicola Sacher Charitable Trust
The Michael Sacher Charitable Trust
The Dr Mortimer and Theresa Sackler Foundation
The Sackler Trust
The Ruzin Sadagora Trust
The Saddlers' Company Charitable Fund
Erach and Roshan Sadri Foundation
The Saga Charitable Trust
The Jean Sainsbury Animal Welfare Trust
The Alan and Babette Sainsbury Charitable Fund
Saint Sarkis Charity Trust
The Saintbury Trust
The Saints and Sinners Trust Ltd
The Salamander Charitable Trust
*The Salisbury New Pool Settlement**
Salters' Charitable Foundation
The Andrew Salvesen Charitable Trust
*Samjo Ltd**
Coral Samuel Charitable Trust
The Basil Samuel Charitable Trust
The M. J. Samuel Charitable Trust
The Samworth Foundation
The Sandhu Charitable Foundation
The Sandra Charitable Trust
The Sands Family Trust
The Sants Charitable Trust
*The Save the Children Fund**
The Annie Schiff Charitable Trust
The Schreib Trust
O. and G. Schreiber Charitable Trust
Schroder Charity Trust
The Schroder Foundation
The Scotshill Trust
Scott (Eredine) Charitable Trust
The ScottishPower Foundation
The SDL Foundation
The Searchlight Electric Charitable Trust
Sam and Bella Sebba Charitable Trust
The Seedfield Trust
Leslie Sell Charitable Trust
*The Sellafield Charity Trust Fund**
Sellata Ltd
SEM Charitable Trust
The Severn Trent Water Charitable Trust Fund
The Cyril Shack Trust
The Shanley Charitable Trust
The Shanti Charitable Trust
ShareGift (The Orr Mackintosh Foundation)
The Shears Foundation
The Sheepdrove Trust
The Sheffield Town Trust
The Patricia and Donald Shepherd Charitable Trust
The Sylvia and Colin Shepherd Charitable Trust
The Archie Sherman Charitable Trust
SHINE (Support and Help in Education)
The Shirley Foundation
Shlomo Memorial Fund Ltd
The Shoe Zone Trust
*Shulem B. Association Ltd**
*The Florence Shute Millennium Trust**
Silver Family Charitable Trust
SITA Cornwall Trust Ltd
The John Slater Foundation
The Slaughter and May Charitable Trust
Sloane Robinson Foundation
Rita and David Slowe Charitable Trust
Ruth Smart Foundation
The SMB Trust
The Mrs Smith and Mount Trust
The DS Smith Charitable Foundation
The N. Smith Charitable Settlement
The Smith Charitable Trust
The WH Smith Group Charitable Trust
Philip Smith's Charitable Trust
The R. C. Snelling Charitable Trust
The Sobell Foundation
Social Business Trust
*Social Investment Business Foundation**
Sodexo Stop Hunger Foundation
Solev Co. Ltd
David Solomons Charitable Trust
*Somerset Community Foundation**
Songdale Ltd
R. H. Southern Trust
*The Spalding Trust**
Spar Charitable Fund
Sparquote Ltd

The Spear Charitable Trust
Spears-Stutz Charitable Trust
The Spoore, Merry and Rixman Foundation
Rosalyn and Nicholas Springer Charitable Trust
Springrule Ltd
The Spurrell Charitable Trust
The St James's Trust Settlement
Sir Walter St John's Educational Charity
*St Marylebone Educational Foundation**
St Monica Trust
St Olave's and St Saviour's Schools Foundation – Foundation Fund
The Stafford Trust
*Staffordshire Community Foundation**
*Standard Life Foundation**
*The Stanley Charitable Trust**
The Peter Stebbings Memorial Charity
The Steel Charitable Trust
The Steinberg Family Charitable Trust
The Hugh Stenhouse Foundation
C. E. K. Stern Charitable Trust
The Sigmund Sternberg Charitable Foundation
Stervon Ltd
The Stevenage Community Trust
Stevenson Family's Charitable Trust
Stewards' Company Ltd
The Andy Stewart Charitable Foundation
The Stewarts Law Foundation
The Stobart Newlands Charitable Trust
The Stoller Charitable Trust
M. J. C. Stone Charitable Trust
The Stone Family Foundation
The Samuel Storey Family Charitable Trust
Peter Storrs Trust
The Strangward Trust
Stratford upon Avon Town Trust
The Strawberry Charitable Trust
The W. O. Street Charitable Foundation
*The Street Foundation**
The Sudborough Foundation
Sueberry Ltd
Suffolk Community Foundation
The Suffolk Historic Churches Trust
The Alan Sugar Foundation
The Summerfield Charitable Trust
*Sunninghill Fuel Allotment Trust**
*Support Adoption For Pets**
Community Foundation for Surrey
The Sussex Community Foundation
The Adrienne and Leslie Sussman Charitable Trust
The Sutasoma Trust
Sutton Coldfield Charitable Trust
Swan Mountain Trust
The Swann-Morton Foundation
The Adrian Swire Charitable Trust
The Swire Charitable Trust
The Hugh and Ruby Sykes Charitable Trust
The Charles and Elsie Sykes Trust
Sylvia Waddilove Foundation UK
T. and S. Trust Fund
Tabeel Trust
The Tajtelbaum Charitable Trust
The Gay and Keith Talbot Trust
The Talbot Trusts
The Talbot Village Trust
Tallow Chandlers Benevolent Fund No. 2
*The Talmud Torah Machzikei Hadass Trust**
Talteg Ltd
The Lady Tangye Charitable Trust Ltd
The David Tannen Charitable Trust
The Tanner Trust
The Lili Tapper Charitable Foundation
The Taurus Foundation
The Tay Charitable Trust
C. B. and H. H. Taylor 1984 Trust
Humphrey Richardson Taylor Charitable Trust
The Connie and Albert Taylor Charitable Trust
The Taylor Family Foundation
Tearfund
*Khoo Teck Puat UK Foundation**
The Tedworth Charitable Trust
Tees Valley Community Foundation
Tegham Ltd
The Templeton Goodwill Trust
The Tennis Foundation
*Tenovus Scotland**
The C. Paul Thackray General Charitable Trust
The Thales Charitable Trust
The Thistle Trust
The David Thomas Charitable Trust
*DM Thomas Foundation for Young People**
The Arthur and Margaret Thompson Charitable Trust
The Thompson Family Charitable Trust
The Sir Jules Thorn Charitable Trust
The Thornton Foundation
The Thousandth Man- Richard Burns Charitable Trust
The Three Oaks Trust
The Thriplow Charitable Trust
The John Raymond Tijou Charitable Trust
Tilney Charitable Trust
Mrs R. P. Tindall's Charitable Trust
The Tinsley Foundation
The Tisbury Telegraph Trust
The Tobacco Pipe Makers and Tobacco Trade Benevolent Fund
The Tolkien Trust
The Tompkins Foundation
Toras Chesed (London) Trust
The Tory Family Foundation
Tottenham Grammar School Foundation
The Tower Hill Trust
The Toy Trust
The Toye Foundation
Toyota Manufacturing UK Charitable Trust
*The Trades House of Glasgow**
Annie Tranmer Charitable Trust
The Constance Travis Charitable Trust
The Treeside Trust
The Trefoil Trust
The Triangle Trust (1949) Fund
*Tropical Health and Education Trust**
The True Colours Trust
Truedene Co. Ltd
The Truemark Trust
Truemart Ltd
Trumros Ltd
The Trusthouse Charitable Foundation
*The Trysil Charitable Trust**
The Tudor Trust
The Tufton Charitable Trust
The Tuixen Foundation
The Florence Turner Trust
The G. J. W. Turner Trust
The Turtleton Charitable Trust
TVML Foundation
Two Ridings Community Foundation
Community Foundation serving Tyne and Wear and Northumberland

Tzedakah
The Udlington Trust
UKH Foundation*
Ulster Garden Villages Ltd
The Union of Orthodox Hebrew Congregations
United Utilities Trust Fund
The Michael Uren Foundation
The David Uri Memorial Trust
The Utley Family Charitable Trust*
The Vail Foundation
The Valentine Charitable Trust
The Valiant Charitable Trust
The Albert Van Den Bergh Charitable Trust
The Van Neste Foundation
Mrs Maud Van Norden's Charitable Foundation
The Vandervell Foundation
The Vardy Foundation
Variety The Children's Charity (Variety Club)
The William and Patricia Venton Charitable Trust
The Veolia Environmental Trust*
Roger Vere Foundation
Virgin Atlantic Foundation
The Virgin Foundation (Virgin Unite)
The Virgin Money Foundation
Vivdale Ltd
The Vodafone Foundation
Voluntary Action Fund (VAF)
Wade's Charity
The Scurrah Wainwright Charity
The Bruce Wake Charity*
The Wakefield Trust*
The Walcot Foundation
The Community Foundation in Wales
Wales Council for Voluntary Action
Robert and Felicity Waley-Cohen Charitable Trust
The Walker Trust
Walton Foundation*
Walton on Thames Charity
Sir Siegmund Warburg's Voluntary Settlement
The Ward Blenkinsop Trust
The Barbara Ward Children's Foundation
Mrs N. E. M. Warren's Charitable Trust*
Warwick Relief in Need Charity*
The Warwickshire Masonic Charitable Association Ltd*
Mrs Waterhouse Charitable Trust
The Waterloo Foundation
G. R. Waters Charitable Trust 2000
Wates Family Enterprise Trust
The Wates Foundation
The Geoffrey Watling Charity*
Blyth Watson Charitable Trust
John Watson's Trust
Waynflete Charitable Trust
The Weavers' Company Benevolent Fund
Webb Memorial Trust
The David Webster Charitable Trust
The William Webster Charitable Trust
The Weinstein Foundation
The Weinstock Fund
The James Weir Foundation
The Wellcome Trust
The Welton Foundation
The Wessex Youth Trust
West Derby Waste Lands Charity
The Westcroft Trust
The Westfield Health Charitable Trust
The Westminster Foundation
The Garfield Weston Foundation
Westway Trust
The Barbara Whatmore Charitable Trust
The Whitaker Charitable Trust
Colonel W. H. Whitbread Charitable Trust
The Melanie White Foundation Ltd
White Stuff Foundation
The Whitecourt Charitable Trust
The Norman Whiteley Trust
The Whitewater Charitable Trust
The Whitley Animal Protection Trust
The Wigoder Family Foundation*
The Lionel Wigram Memorial Trust
The Felicity Wilde Charitable Trust
The Will Charitable Trust
The Kay Williams Charitable Foundation
The Alfred Williams Charitable Trust*
The Williams Charitable Trust
The Williams Family Charitable Trust
Williams Serendipity Trust
The Willmott Dixon Foundation*
The HDH Wills 1965 Charitable Trust
Dame Violet Wills Charitable Trust
The Dame Violet Wills Will Trust
The Wilmcote Charitrust
Brian Wilson Charitable Trust*
Sumner Wilson Charitable Trust
The Wilson Foundation
J. and J. R. Wilson Trust
Wiltshire Community Foundation
The W. Wing Yip and Brothers Foundation
The Francis Winham Foundation
Winton Philanthropies
The Witzenfeld Foundation
The Michael and Anna Wix Charitable Trust
The Wixamtree Trust
The Maurice Wohl Charitable Foundation
The Charles Wolfson Charitable Trust
The Wolfson Family Charitable Trust
The Wolfson Foundation
The James Wood Bequest Fund
The Wood Foundation
Wooden Spoon Society
The F. Glenister Woodger Trust
Woodlands Green Ltd
The Woodstock Family Charitable Foundation*
The A. and R. Woolf Charitable Trust
Worcester Municipal Charities (CIO)
The Worwin UK Foundation*
The Diana Edgson Wright Charitable Trust
Wychdale Ltd
Wychville Ltd
The Wyfold Charitable Trust*
The Wyndham Charitable Trust
The Wyseliot Rose Charitable Trust
Yankov Charitable Trust
York Children's Trust*
Yorkshire Building Society Charitable Foundation
Yorkshire Cancer Research*
The South Yorkshire Community Foundation
The William Allen Young Charitable Trust
The John Kirkhope Young Endowment Fund
The Z. Foundation
Zephyr Charitable Trust
The Marjorie and Arnold Ziff Charitable Foundation
Stephen Zimmerman Charitable Trust
The Zochonis Charitable Trust

Building/renovation

The 1989 Willan Charitable Trust
The A. S. Charitable Trust
A. W. Charitable Trust
The Aberbrothock Skea Trust
*The Neville Abraham Foundation**
Access Sport CIO
Achisomoch Aid Company Ltd
Action Medical Research
The Adnams Community Trust
*The AEB Charitable Trust**
Age UK
Aid to the Church in Need (UK)
The Sylvia Aitken Charitable Trust
Al-Fayed Charitable Foundation
The Alliance Family Foundation
Amabrill Ltd
The Amalur Foundation Ltd
The Ammco Trust
Sir John and Lady Amory's Charitable Trust
Viscount Amory's Charitable Trust
The AMW Charitable Trust
The Anchor Foundation
The André Christian Trust
Anpride Ltd
The Ardwick Trust
The Argus Appeal
The Armourers' and Brasiers' Gauntlet Trust
The Arsenal Foundation Ltd
The Artemis Charitable Trust
Arts Council England
Arts Council of Northern Ireland
Arts Council of Wales (also known as Cyngor Celfyddydau Cymru)
ASCB Charitable Fund
The Asda Foundation
The Ian Askew Charitable Trust
The Astor Foundation
The Bagri Foundation
The Baily Thomas Charitable Fund
The Baird Trust
*Bairdwatson Charitable Trust**
The Balcombe Charitable Trust
The Baltic Charitable Fund
The Banbury Charities
The Bank of Scotland Foundation
The Barbers' Company General Charities
The Barcapel Foundation
*The Philip Barker Charity**
The Barnsbury Charitable Trust
*The Barrack Charitable Trust**
Misses Barrie Charitable Trust
*Robert Barr's Charitable Trust**
The Bartlett Taylor Charitable Trust
The Paul Bassham Charitable Trust
The Batchworth Trust
The Battens Charitable Trust
The Bearder Charity
The James Beattie Charitable Trust
*The Becht Family Charitable Trust**
The John Beckwith Charitable Trust
The Bedfordshire and Hertfordshire Historic Churches Trust
The David and Ruth Behrend Fund
*The Behrens Foundation**
The Bellahouston Bequest Fund
Belljoe Tzedoko Ltd
The Benham Charitable Settlement
*The Rowan Bentall Charitable Trust**
Bergqvist Charitable Trust
The Billmeir Charitable Trust
Percy Bilton Charity
The Bingham Trust
The Birmingham District Nursing Charitable Trust
The Lord Mayor of Birmingham's Charity
The Michael Bishop Foundation
The Blair Foundation
The Morgan Blake Charitable Trust
The Sir Victor Blank Charitable Settlement
Bloom Foundation
The Marjory Boddy Charitable Trust
The Boltini Trust
The Charlotte Bonham-Carter Charitable Trust
The Linda and Gordon Bonnyman Charitable Trust
BOOST Charitable Trust
Boots Charitable Trust
The Bordon Liphook Haslemere Charity
*Sir William Boreman's Foundation**
*The Borrows Charitable Trust**
The Oliver Borthwick Memorial Trust
The Harry Bottom Charitable Trust
The Bowerman Charitable Trust
The Bowland Charitable Trust
The Frank Brake Charitable Trust
The William Brake Charitable Trust
*The Brelms Trust CIO**
Bridge Trust
British Humane Association
The Charles Brotherton Trust
The Jack Brunton Charitable Trust
Buckinghamshire Community Foundation
The Buckinghamshire Historic Churches Trust
The Burry Charitable Trust
The Arnold Burton 1998 Charitable Trust
Consolidated Charity of Burton upon Trent
The Christopher Cadbury Charitable Trust
The George Cadbury Trust
CAFOD (Catholic Agency for Overseas Development)
Community Foundation for Calderdale
Callander Charitable Trust
*The W. A. Cargill Charitable Trust**
*The W. A. Cargill Fund**
The Carpenters' Company Charitable Trust
The Carr-Gregory Trust
The Carrington Charitable Trust
The Leslie Mary Carter Charitable Trust
*The Castansa Trust**
The Joseph and Annie Cattle Trust
The Thomas Sivewright Catto Charitable Settlement
The Wilfrid and Constance Cave Foundation
Elizabeth Cayzer Charitable Trust
The B. G. S. Cayzer Charitable Trust
Celtic Charity Fund
CEO Sleepout
Charitworth Ltd
The Cheruby Trust
Cheshire Freemason's Charity
The Chownes Foundation
Christadelphian Samaritan Fund
Christian Aid
Chrysalis Trust
The Church Burgesses Educational Foundation
Church Burgesses Trust
The City Bridge Trust (Bridge House Estates)
*The Clan Trust Ltd**
The Hilda and Alice Clark Charitable Trust
The Roger and Sarah Bancroft Clark Charitable Trust

The Clark Foundation*
The Clore Duffield Foundation
Closehelm Ltd
The Clothworkers' Foundation
Richard Cloudesley's Charity
The Robert Clutterbuck Charitable Trust
Clydpride Ltd
The Francis Coales Charitable Foundation
The John Coates Charitable Trust
The Cobtree Charity Trust Ltd
The Denise Cohen Charitable Trust
The Vivienne and Samuel Cohen Charitable Trust
The John S. Cohen Foundation
The R. and S. Cohen Foundation
The Colchester Catalyst Charity
The Cole Charitable Trust
The Colefax Charitable Trust
John and Freda Coleman Charitable Trust
The Coltstaple Trust
Colwinston Charitable Trust
Mabel Cooper Charity
The Marjorie Coote Animal Charity Trust
The Marjorie Coote Old People's Charity
The Helen Jean Cope Trust
The Gershon Coren Charitable Foundation
Cornwall Community Foundation
The Duke of Cornwall's Benevolent Fund
The Cornwell Charitable Trust
The Costa Family Charitable Trust
The Cotton Industry War Memorial Trust
The Cotton Trust
The Coulthurst Trust*
Country Houses Foundation
The Augustine Courtauld Trust
General Charity of Coventry
The Sir Tom Cowie Charitable Trust
Dudley and Geoffrey Cox Charitable Trust
The Lord Cozens-Hardy Trust
The Craps Charitable Trust
The Cray Trust
The Elizabeth Creak Charitable Trust*
The Crerar Hotels Trust
Cripplegate Foundation
The Violet and Milo Cripps Charitable Trust
The Cross Trust
The Cross Trust
Cruden Foundation Ltd
The Ronald Cruickshanks Foundation
The Cumber Family Charitable Trust
Cumbria Community Foundation
Itzchok Meyer Cymerman Trust Ltd
The D. G. Charitable Settlement
The Joan Lynette Dalton Charitable Trust
The Dr and Mrs A. Darlington Charitable Trust
Baron Davenport's Charity
The Davidson Family Charitable Trust
Michael Davies Charitable Settlement
Margaret Davies Charity
The Hamilton Davies Trust
The Crispin Davis Family Trust
The Dawe Charitable Trust
The De Brye Charitable Trust
William Dean Countryside and Educational Trust
The Dellal Foundation
The Delves Charitable Trust
The Demigryphon Trust
Dentons UKMEA LLP Charitable Trust
Foundation Derbyshire
The Desmond Foundation
The Devon Historic Churches Trust
The Duke of Devonshire's Charitable Trust
The Gillian Dickinson Trust
Didymus
The DLM Charitable Trust
The Derek and Eileen Dodgson Foundation
The Dollond Charitable Trust
The Dorset Historic Churches Trust
The Doughty Charity Trust
The Dumbreck Charity
The Dunn Family Charitable Trust
County Durham Community Foundation
The Dyers' Company Charitable Trust
Earls Colne and Halstead Educational Charity
The Sir John Eastwood Foundation
The EBM Charitable Trust
The W. G. Edwards Charitable Foundation
The Eighty Eight Foundation*
Elanore Ltd*
The Elephant Trust
The George Elias Charitable Trust
The Gerald Palmer Eling Trust Company
The Wilfred and Elsie Elkes Charity Fund
The Maud Elkington Charitable Trust
The Edith Maud Ellis 1985 Charitable Trust
The Vernon N. Ely Charitable Trust
The Emerton-Christie Charity
The Englefield Charitable Trust
The Epigoni Trust
The Essex Heritage Trust
The Eventhall Family Charitable Trust
The Everard Foundation
The Football Association National Sports Centre Trust
The Foyle Foundation
Friends of Essex Churches Trust
The Friends of Kent Churches
Gatwick Airport Community Trust
The Gerrick Rose Animal Trust*
The Girdlers' Company Charitable Trust
The Glass-House Trust
Global Charities
The Gloucestershire Historic Churches Trust
The Mike Gooley Trailfinders Charity
The Graham Trust*
The Gray Trust
Greenham Common Community Trust Ltd
The Greggs Foundation
The Grocers' Charity
Dr Guthrie's Association
Hackney Parochial Charities
The Hadfield Charitable Trust
Halifax Foundation for Northern Ireland
Hammersmith United Charities*
The Hampshire and Islands Historic Churches Trust
The Harpur Trust
The Harris Charity
The Peter Harrison Foundation
HC Foundation*
The Herefordshire Historic Churches Trust
The Hesslewood Children's Trust (Hull Seamen's and General Orphanage)
Horwich Shotter Charitable Trust*
The Hyde Park Place Estate Charity – civil trustees*
Lady Eda Jardine Charitable Trust

The Kildare Trust*
The Mary Kinross Charitable Trust
The Sir James Knott Trust
The William Leech Charity
Leicester and Leicestershire Historic Churches Preservation Trust (Leicestershire Historic Churches Trust)
Leicestershire and Rutland Masonic Charity Association*
Leng Charitable Trust*
The Lethendy Charitable Trust*
The Maisie and Raphael Lewis Charitable Trust*
Bernard Lewis Family Charitable Trust*
Life Changes Trust*
Lifeline 4 Kids (Handicapped Children's Aid Committee)
The W. M. and B. W. Lloyd Trust*
The Lockwood Charitable Foundation*
Michael Lowe's and Associated Charities*
The Madeline Mabey Trust
The Macdonald-Buchanan Charitable Trust
Mace Foundation*
Charity of John Marshall
The Master Charitable Trust*
The National Churches Trust
The Nationwide Foundation
The James Neill Trust Fund
The Norfolk Churches Trust Ltd*
The Northumbria Historic Churches Trust
The Northwick Trust*
The Norwood and Newton Settlement
The Notgrove Trust
The Nottinghamshire Historic Churches Trust
Oglesby Charitable Trust
One Community Foundation Ltd*
The Ormsby Charitable Trust
Oxfordshire Historic Churches Trust*
The Paddington Charitable Estate Educational Fund*
The James Pantyfedwen Foundation
The Pargiter Trust*
The JGW Patterson Foundation*
The Bernard Piggott Charitable Trust
The Pilgrim Trust
Pink Ribbon Foundation*
The Polehampton Charity*
The Portishead Nautical Trust
The Prince of Wales's Charitable Foundation
QBE European Operations Foundation*
Quercus Foundation*
The Monica Rabagliati Charitable Trust
The Rayne Foundation
Red Hill Charitable Trust
The Rest Harrow Trust
Rhondda Cynon Taff Welsh Church Acts Fund
Riada Trust*
Richmond Parish Lands Charity
Mrs L. D. Rope's Third Charitable Settlement
Rosca Trust
The Rose Foundation
The Cissie Rosefield Charitable Trust*
The Cecil Rosen Foundation
The David Ross Foundation*
The Rothley Trust
Royal Docks Trust (London)
The Royal Navy And Royal Marines Charity*
Royal Victoria Hall Foundation
The Rubin Foundation Charitable Trust
The Sainsbury Family Charitable Trusts
Santander UK Foundation Ltd
The Scarfe Charitable Trust
The Schapira Charitable Trust
The Schmidt-Bodner Charitable Trust
The Schreiber Charitable Trust
Foundation Scotland
The Francis C. Scott Charitable Trust
The Frieda Scott Charitable Trust
The John Scott Trust Fund*
The Scouloudi Foundation
Seafarers Hospital Society
Seafarers UK (King George's Fund for Sailors)
The Seven Fifty Trust
The Shanly Foundation
The Linley Shaw Foundation
Sherling Charitable Trust*
The Archie Sherman Cardiff Foundation
The Shetland Charitable Trust
The Bassil Shippam and Alsford Trust
The Shipwrights' Company Charitable Fund
The Shropshire Historic Churches Trust*
David and Jennifer Sieff Charitable Trust
The Huntly and Margery Sinclair Charitable Trust
The Skelton Bounty
The Skerritt Trust*
The Charles Skey Charitable Trust
The Henry Smith Charity
The Leslie Smith Foundation
The Martin Smith Foundation*
The Stanley Smith UK Horticultural Trust
Sofronie Foundation*
The Solo Charitable Settlement
The E. C. Sosnow Charitable Trust
The South Square Trust
The W. F. Southall Trust
The Southover Manor General Education Trust
The Worshipful Company of Spectacle Makers' Charity
The Jessie Spencer Trust
The Spielman Charitable Trust
The Geoff and Fiona Squire Foundation
The Squires Foundation
St James's Place Foundation
The Stanley Foundation Ltd
The Staples Trust
The Stoneygate Trust*
Peter Stormonth Darling Charitable Trust
The Bernard Sunley Charitable Foundation
Surgo Foundation UK Ltd*
The John Swire (1989) Charitable Trust
The Thornton Trust
The Roger and Douglas Turner Charitable Trust
The Turtleton Charitable Trust
The Underwood Trust
Vale of Glamorgan Welsh Church Fund
The Nigel Vinson Charitable Trust
Viridor Credits Environmental Company*
The Warrington Church of England Educational Trust*
The Watson Family Charitable Trust*
The Weir Charitable Trust*
The West Looe Town Trust*
The Wheeler Family Charitable Trust*
The Williams Family Foundation*
The Wimbledon Foundation*
Yorkshire and Clydesdale Bank Foundation
The Yorkshire Historic Churches Trust
Zurich Community Trust (UK) Ltd

Collections or acquisitions

The Arts Council
Elizabeth Cayzer Charitable Trust
The Francis Coales Charitable Foundation
The Delius Trust
The Essex Heritage Trust
The Henry Moore Foundation
The National Art Collections Fund
Oglesby Charitable Trust
The Pilgrim Trust
The Rothschild Foundation (Hanadiv) Europe

Equipment (including computers)

The 1989 Willan Charitable Trust
The A. S. Charitable Trust
A. W. Charitable Trust
The Aberbrothock Skea Trust
*The Neville Abraham Foundation**
Access Sport CIO
Achisomoch Aid Company Ltd
Action Medical Research
The Adnams Community Trust
*The AEB Charitable Trust**
Age Scotland
Age UK
Aid to the Church in Need (UK)
The Sylvia Aitken Charitable Trust
Aldgate and All Hallows' Foundation
Al-Fayed Charitable Foundation
The Alliance Family Foundation
*Alzheimer's Research UK**
Amabrill Ltd
The Amalur Foundation Ltd
The Ammco Trust
Sir John and Lady Amory's Charitable Trust
Viscount Amory's Charitable Trust
The AMW Charitable Trust
The Anchor Foundation
The André Christian Trust
Anguish's Educational Foundation
Anpride Ltd
The Ardwick Trust
The Argus Appeal
The Armourers' and Brasiers' Gauntlet Trust
The Arsenal Foundation Ltd
The Artemis Charitable Trust
Arts Council England
Arts Council of Northern Ireland
Arts Council of Wales (also known as Cyngor Celfyddydau Cymru)
The Ove Arup Foundation
ASCB Charitable Fund
The Asda Foundation
The Ashworth Charitable Trust
The Ian Askew Charitable Trust
The Associated Country Women of the World
Asthma UK
The Astor Foundation
The Avon and Somerset Police Community Trust
The Bagri Foundation
The Baily Thomas Charitable Fund
The Baird Trust
*Bairdwatson Charitable Trust**
The Balcombe Charitable Trust
The Ballinger Charitable Trust
The Baltic Charitable Fund
The Bamford Charitable Foundation
The Banbury Charities
The Bank of Scotland Foundation
The Barbers' Company General Charities
The Barcapel Foundation
Barchester Healthcare Foundation
*The Philip Barker Charity**
The Barnsbury Charitable Trust
*The Barrack Charitable Trust**
Misses Barrie Charitable Trust
*Robert Barr's Charitable Trust**
The Bartlett Taylor Charitable Trust
The Paul Bassham Charitable Trust
The Batchworth Trust
The Battens Charitable Trust
Bauer Radio's Cash for Kids Charities
The Bearder Charity
The James Beattie Charitable Trust
*The Becht Family Charitable Trust**
The John Beckwith Charitable Trust
The David and Ruth Behrend Fund
*The Behrens Foundation**
The Bellahouston Bequest Fund
Belljoe Tzedoko Ltd
The Benham Charitable Settlement
*The Rowan Bentall Charitable Trust**
Bergqvist Charitable Trust
The Billmeir Charitable Trust
Percy Bilton Charity
The Bingham Trust
The Birmingham District Nursing Charitable Trust
Birmingham International Airport Community Trust Fund
The Lord Mayor of Birmingham's Charity
The Michael Bishop Foundation
The Blair Foundation
The Morgan Blake Charitable Trust
The Sir Victor Blank Charitable Settlement
Bloodwise
Bloom Foundation
The Boltini Trust
The Charlotte Bonham-Carter Charitable Trust
The Linda and Gordon Bonnyman Charitable Trust
BOOST Charitable Trust
Boots Charitable Trust
The Bordon Liphook Haslemere Charity
*Sir William Boreman's Foundation**
*The Borrows Charitable Trust**
The Oliver Borthwick Memorial Trust
The Harry Bottom Charitable Trust
The Bowerman Charitable Trust
The Bowland Charitable Trust
The Frank Brake Charitable Trust
The William Brake Charitable Trust
*The Brelms Trust CIO**
Bridge Trust
*The British and Foreign Bible Society**
*British Eye Research Foundation (Fight for Sight)**
British Gas (Scottish Gas) Energy Trust
British Heart Foundation (BHF)
British Humane Association
The Charles Brotherton Trust
Bill Brown 1989 Charitable Trust
The Jack Brunton Charitable Trust
Buckinghamshire Community Foundation
The Burry Charitable Trust
The Arnold Burton 1998 Charitable Trust
Consolidated Charity of Burton upon Trent
The Noel Buxton Trust
The Christopher Cadbury Charitable Trust

The G. W. Cadbury Charitable Trust
The Barrow Cadbury Trust
The George Cadbury Trust
CAFOD (Catholic Agency for Overseas Development)
Community Foundation for Calderdale
Callander Charitable Trust
The W. A. Cargill Charitable Trust*
The W. A. Cargill Fund*
The Carnegie Trust for the Universities of Scotland
The Carpenters' Company Charitable Trust
The Carr-Gregory Trust
The Carrington Charitable Trust
The Leslie Mary Carter Charitable Trust
Sir John Cass's Foundation
Sir Ernest Cassel Educational Trust*
The Elizabeth Casson Trust
The Castang Foundation
The Castansa Trust*
The Joseph and Annie Cattle Trust
The Thomas Sivewright Catto Charitable Settlement
The Wilfrid and Constance Cave Foundation
Elizabeth Cayzer Charitable Trust
The B. G. S. Cayzer Charitable Trust
Celtic Charity Fund
CEO Sleepout
Champneys Charitable Foundation
Charitworth Ltd
The Cheruby Trust
Cheshire Freemason's Charity
Children's Liver Disease Foundation
The Chownes Foundation
Christadelphian Samaritan Fund
Christian Aid
Chrysalis Trust
The Church Burgesses Educational Foundation
Church Burgesses Trust
Church Urban Fund
The City Bridge Trust (Bridge House Estates)
The City Educational Trust Fund
The Clan Trust Ltd*
J. A. Clark Charitable Trust
The Hilda and Alice Clark Charitable Trust
The Roger and Sarah Bancroft Clark Charitable Trust
The Clark Foundation*
The Clore Duffield Foundation
Closehelm Ltd
The Clothworkers' Foundation
Richard Cloudesley's Charity
The Robert Clutterbuck Charitable Trust
Clydpride Ltd
The John Coates Charitable Trust
The Cobtree Charity Trust Ltd
The Denise Cohen Charitable Trust
The Vivienne and Samuel Cohen Charitable Trust
The John S. Cohen Foundation
The R. and S. Cohen Foundation
The Colchester Catalyst Charity
The Cole Charitable Trust
The Colefax Charitable Trust
John and Freda Coleman Charitable Trust
The Coltstaple Trust
Colwinston Charitable Trust
Comic Relief
The Comino Foundation
The Ernest Cook Trust
Mabel Cooper Charity
The Marjorie Coote Animal Charity Trust
The Marjorie Coote Old People's Charity
The Helen Jean Cope Trust
The Gershon Coren Charitable Foundation (also known as The Muriel and Gus Coren Charitable Foundation)
Cornwall Community Foundation
The Duke of Cornwall's Benevolent Fund
The Cornwell Charitable Trust
The Costa Family Charitable Trust
The Cotton Industry War Memorial Trust
The Cotton Trust
The Coulthurst Trust*
The Augustine Courtauld Trust
General Charity of Coventry
The Sir Tom Cowie Charitable Trust
Dudley and Geoffrey Cox Charitable Trust
The Lord Cozens-Hardy Trust
The Craps Charitable Trust
The Cray Trust
The Elizabeth Creak Charitable Trust*
Creative Scotland
The Crerar Hotels Trust
Cripplegate Foundation
The Violet and Milo Cripps Charitable Trust
The Cross Trust
The Cross Trust
Cruden Foundation Ltd
The Ronald Cruickshanks Foundation
The Cumber Family Charitable Trust
Cumbria Community Foundation
The Cunningham Trust
The Harry Cureton Charitable Trust
Itzchok Meyer Cymerman Trust Ltd
The D. G. Charitable Settlement
The Daiwa Anglo-Japanese Foundation
The Joan Lynette Dalton Charitable Trust
The Dr and Mrs A. Darlington Charitable Trust
Baron Davenport's Charity
The Davidson (Nairn) Charitable Trust
The Davidson Family Charitable Trust
Michael Davies Charitable Settlement
Margaret Davies Charity
The Hamilton Davies Trust
The John Grant Davies Trust*
The Crispin Davis Family Trust
The Dawe Charitable Trust
The De Brye Charitable Trust
William Dean Countryside and Educational Trust
The Dellal Foundation
The Delves Charitable Trust
The Demigryphon Trust
Dentons UKMEA LLP Charitable Trust
Foundation Derbyshire
The Desmond Foundation
Devon Community Foundation
The Devon Historic Churches Trust
The Duke of Devonshire's Charitable Trust
Diabetes UK
The Gillian Dickinson Trust
Didymus
Disability Aid Fund (The Roger and Jean Jefcoate Trust)
The DLM Charitable Trust
The Derek and Eileen Dodgson Foundation
The Dollond Charitable Trust
The Dorset Historic Churches Trust
The Doughty Charity Trust
Douglas Arter Foundation
The Dumbreck Charity
The Dunn Family Charitable Trust
County Durham Community Foundation

The Dyers' Company Charitable Trust
Earls Colne and Halstead Educational Charity
East End Community Foundation
The Sir John Eastwood Foundation
The EBM Charitable Trust
The W. G. Edwards Charitable Foundation
*The Eighty Eight Foundation**
*Elanore Ltd**
The Elephant Trust
The George Elias Charitable Trust
The Gerald Palmer Eling Trust Company
The Wilfred and Elsie Elkes Charity Fund
The Maud Elkington Charitable Trust
The Edith Maud Ellis 1985 Charitable Trust
The Vernon N. Ely Charitable Trust
The Emerton-Christie Charity
EMI Music Sound Foundation
The Englefield Charitable Trust
The Epigoni Trust
Epilepsy Research UK
The Essex and Southend Sports Trust
The Eventhall Family Charitable Trust
The Everard Foundation
The Football Association National Sports Centre Trust
Ford Britain Trust
The Foyle Foundation
Gatwick Airport Community Trust
*The Genesis Charitable Trust**
*The Gerrick Rose Animal Trust**
Get Kids Going
*Gilchrist Educational Trust**
The Girdlers' Company Charitable Trust
The Glass-House Trust
Global Charities
The Golf Foundation Ltd
The Mike Gooley Trailfinders Charity
*The Graham Trust**
The Gray Trust
Greenham Common Community Trust Ltd
The Greggs Foundation
The Grocers' Charity
Dr Guthrie's Association
Hackney Parochial Charities
The Hadfield Charitable Trust
The Hadrian Trust
Halifax Foundation for Northern Ireland (previously known as Lloyds Bank Foundation for Northern Ireland)
*Hammersmith United Charities**
The Hampshire and Islands Historic Churches Trust
The Hampstead Wells and Campden Trust
The Harpur Trust
The Harris Charity
The Peter Harrison Foundation
*HC Foundation**
Philip Henman Trust
The Herefordshire Historic Churches Trust
The Hesslewood Children's Trust (Hull Seamen's and General Orphanage)
The Hoover Foundation
*Horwich Shotter Charitable Trust**
*The Hyde Park Place Estate Charity – civil trustees**
IBM United Kingdom Trust
Lady Eda Jardine Charitable Trust
Jewish Child's Day (JCD)
Kidney Research UK
*The Kildare Trust**
The Mary Kinross Charitable Trust
The Sir James Knott Trust
The William Leech Charity
Leicester and Leicestershire Historic Churches Preservation Trust (Leicestershire Historic Churches Trust)
*Leicestershire and Rutland Masonic Charity Association**
*Leng Charitable Trust**
*The Lethendy Charitable Trust**
*The Maisie and Raphael Lewis Charitable Trust**
*Bernard Lewis Family Charitable Trust**
*Life Changes Trust**
Lifeline 4 Kids (Handicapped Children's Aid Committee)
*The W. M. and B. W. Lloyd Trust**
Lloyds Bank Foundation for England and Wales
*The Lockwood Charitable Foundation**
The Lord's Taverners
*Michael Lowe's and Associated Charities**
Robert Luff Foundation Ltd
The Lyndhurst Trust
Sylvanus Lysons Charity
The Madeline Mabey Trust
The Macdonald-Buchanan Charitable Trust
*Mace Foundation**
Manchester Airport Community Trust Fund
Charity of John Marshall
The Dan Maskell Tennis Trust
*The Master Charitable Trust**
*Maypride Ltd**
British Motor Sports Training Trust
The James Neill Trust Fund
The Newcomen Collett Foundation
The Frances and Augustus Newman Foundation
The Northmoor Trust
The Northumbria Historic Churches Trust
*The Northwick Trust**
The Notgrove Trust
The Nottinghamshire Historic Churches Trust
*One Community Foundation Ltd**
The Ormsby Charitable Trust
*Oxfordshire Historic Churches Trust**
*The Paddington Charitable Estate Educational Fund**
The James Pantyfedwen Foundation
*The Pargiter Trust**
*The JGW Patterson Foundation**
The Bernard Piggott Charitable Trust
*Pink Ribbon Foundation**
*The Polehampton Charity**
The Portishead Nautical Trust
The Prince of Wales's Charitable Foundation
*QBE European Operations Foundation**
*Quercus Foundation**
The Monica Rabagliati Charitable Trust
The Rank Foundation Ltd
The Rayne Foundation
Red Hill Charitable Trust
The Rest Harrow Trust
Rhondda Cynon Taff Welsh Church Acts Fund
*Riada Trust**
Richmond Parish Lands Charity
*Rigby Foundation**
The River Trust
The Robertson Trust
Mrs L. D. Rope's Third Charitable Settlement
Rosca Trust
*The Cissie Rosefield Charitable Trust**
The Cecil Rosen Foundation
*The David Ross Foundation**

The Rothley Trust
Royal Docks Trust (London)
The Royal Navy And Royal Marines Charity*
Royal Victoria Hall Foundation
The Rubin Foundation Charitable Trust
The Sainsbury Family Charitable Trusts
Santander UK Foundation Ltd
The Savoy Educational Trust*
The Scarfe Charitable Trust
The Schapira Charitable Trust
The Schmidt-Bodner Charitable Trust
The Schreiber Charitable Trust
Foundation Scotland
The Francis C. Scott Charitable Trust
The Frieda Scott Charitable Trust
Sir Samuel Scott of Yews Trust
The John Scott Trust Fund*
The Scouloudi Foundation
Seafarers Hospital Society
Seafarers UK (King George's Fund for Sailors)
The Seven Fifty Trust
The Shanly Foundation
The Linley Shaw Foundation
The Sheldon Trust
Sherburn House Charity*
Sherling Charitable Trust*
The Archie Sherman Cardiff Foundation
The Shetland Charitable Trust
The Bassil Shippam and Alsford Trust
The Shipwrights' Company Charitable Fund
The Shropshire Historic Churches Trust*
David and Jennifer Sieff Charitable Trust
The Huntly and Margery Sinclair Charitable Trust
The Skelton Bounty
The Skerritt Trust*
The Charles Skey Charitable Trust
Skipton Building Society Charitable Foundation
The Henry Smith Charity
The Leslie Smith Foundation
The Martin Smith Foundation*
The Stanley Smith UK Horticultural Trust
Sofronie Foundation*
The Solo Charitable Settlement
The E. C. Sosnow Charitable Trust
The South Square Trust
The W. F. Southall Trust
The Southover Manor General Education Trust
Sparks Charity (Sport Aiding Medical Research for Kids)
The Worshipful Company of Spectacle Makers' Charity
The Jessie Spencer Trust
The Spielman Charitable Trust
The Geoff and Fiona Squire Foundation
The Squires Foundation
St James's Place Foundation
The Stanley Foundation Ltd
The Staples Trust
The Stoneygate Trust*
Peter Stormonth Darling Charitable Trust
The Bernard Sunley Charitable Foundation
Surgo Foundation UK Ltd*
The Thornton Trust
The Transform Foundation*
The James Tudor Foundation
The Roger and Douglas Turner Charitable Trust
The Ulverscroft Foundation
The Underwood Trust
Vale of Glamorgan Welsh Church Fund
The Nigel Vinson Charitable Trust
The Vintners' Foundation
Viridor Credits Environmental Company*
The Warrington Church of England Educational Trust*
The Watson Family Charitable Trust*
The Weir Charitable Trust*
The West Looe Town Trust*
The Wheeler Family Charitable Trust*
The Williams Family Foundation*
The Wimbledon Foundation*
Yorkshire and Clydesdale Bank Foundation
Zurich Community Trust (UK) Ltd

■ Vehicles

The 1989 Willan Charitable Trust
The A. S. Charitable Trust
A. W. Charitable Trust
The Aberbrothock Skea Trust
The Neville Abraham Foundation*
Achisomoch Aid Company Ltd
Action Medical Research
The Adnams Community Trust
The AEB Charitable Trust*
Age UK
Aid to the Church in Need (UK)
The Sylvia Aitken Charitable Trust
The Alliance Family Foundation
The Amalur Foundation Ltd
The Ammco Trust
Sir John and Lady Amory's Charitable Trust
Viscount Amory's Charitable Trust
The AMW Charitable Trust
The Anchor Foundation
The André Christian Trust
Anpride Ltd
The Ardwick Trust
The Argus Appeal
The Armourers' and Brasiers' Gauntlet Trust
The Arsenal Foundation Ltd
The Artemis Charitable Trust
Arts Council of Northern Ireland
Arts Council of Wales (also known as Cyngor Celfyddydau Cymru)
The Astor Foundation
The Avon and Somerset Police Community Trust
The Bagri Foundation
Bairdwatson Charitable Trust*
The Balcombe Charitable Trust
The Baltic Charitable Fund
The Banbury Charities
The Bank of Scotland Foundation
The Barbers' Company General Charities
The Barcapel Foundation
Barchester Healthcare Foundation
The Philip Barker Charity*
The Barnsbury Charitable Trust
The Barrack Charitable Trust*
Misses Barrie Charitable Trust
Robert Barr's Charitable Trust*
The Bartlett Taylor Charitable Trust
The Paul Bassham Charitable Trust
The Batchworth Trust
The Battens Charitable Trust
Bauer Radio's Cash for Kids Charities
The Bearder Charity
The James Beattie Charitable Trust
The Becht Family Charitable Trust*
The John Beckwith Charitable Trust
The David and Ruth Behrend Fund
The Behrens Foundation*
The Bellahouston Bequest Fund
Belljoe Tzedoko Ltd

The Benham Charitable Settlement
The Rowan Bentall Charitable Trust*
Bergqvist Charitable Trust
The Billmeir Charitable Trust
Percy Bilton Charity
The Bingham Trust
Birmingham International Airport Community Trust Fund
The Lord Mayor of Birmingham's Charity
The Michael Bishop Foundation
The Blair Foundation
The Morgan Blake Charitable Trust
The Sir Victor Blank Charitable Settlement
The Boltini Trust
The Charlotte Bonham-Carter Charitable Trust
The Linda and Gordon Bonnyman Charitable Trust
BOOST Charitable Trust
Boots Charitable Trust
The Bordon Liphook Haslemere Charity
Sir William Boreman's Foundation*
The Borrows Charitable Trust*
The Oliver Borthwick Memorial Trust
The Harry Bottom Charitable Trust
The Bowerman Charitable Trust
The Bowland Charitable Trust
The Frank Brake Charitable Trust
The William Brake Charitable Trust
The Brelms Trust CIO*
Bridge Trust
British Humane Association
The Charles Brotherton Trust
Bill Brown 1989 Charitable Trust
The Jack Brunton Charitable Trust
Buckinghamshire Community Foundation
The Burry Charitable Trust
The Arnold Burton 1998 Charitable Trust
Consolidated Charity of Burton upon Trent
The Noel Buxton Trust
The Christopher Cadbury Charitable Trust
The G. W. Cadbury Charitable Trust
The George Cadbury Trust
CAFOD (Catholic Agency for Overseas Development)
Community Foundation for Calderdale
Callander Charitable Trust
The W. A. Cargill Charitable Trust*
The W. A. Cargill Fund*
The Carpenters' Company Charitable Trust
The Carr-Gregory Trust
The Carrington Charitable Trust
The Leslie Mary Carter Charitable Trust
The Castansa Trust*
The Joseph and Annie Cattle Trust
The Thomas Sivewright Catto Charitable Settlement
The Wilfrid and Constance Cave Foundation
The B. G. S. Cayzer Charitable Trust
Celtic Charity Fund
Charitworth Ltd
The Cheruby Trust
Cheshire Freemason's Charity
The Chownes Foundation
Christadelphian Samaritan Fund
Christian Aid
The Church Burgesses Educational Foundation
Church Burgesses Trust
Church Urban Fund
The Clan Trust Ltd*
J. A. Clark Charitable Trust
The Hilda and Alice Clark Charitable Trust
The Roger and Sarah Bancroft Clark Charitable Trust
The Clark Foundation*
The Clore Duffield Foundation
Closehelm Ltd
The Clothworkers' Foundation
Richard Cloudesley's Charity
The Robert Clutterbuck Charitable Trust
Clydpride Ltd
The John Coates Charitable Trust
The Cobtree Charity Trust Ltd
The Denise Cohen Charitable Trust
The Vivienne and Samuel Cohen Charitable Trust
The John S. Cohen Foundation
The R. and S. Cohen Foundation
The Colchester Catalyst Charity
The Cole Charitable Trust
The Colefax Charitable Trust
John and Freda Coleman Charitable Trust
The Coltstaple Trust
Colwinston Charitable Trust
The Ernest Cook Trust
Mabel Cooper Charity
The Marjorie Coote Animal Charity Trust
The Helen Jean Cope Trust
The Gershon Coren Charitable Foundation (also known as The Muriel and Gus Coren Charitable Foundation)
Cornwall Community Foundation
The Duke of Cornwall's Benevolent Fund
The Cornwell Charitable Trust
The Costa Family Charitable Trust
The Cotton Industry War Memorial Trust
The Cotton Trust
The Augustine Courtauld Trust
General Charity of Coventry
The Sir Tom Cowie Charitable Trust
Dudley and Geoffrey Cox Charitable Trust
The Lord Cozens-Hardy Trust
The Craps Charitable Trust
The Cray Trust
The Elizabeth Creak Charitable Trust*
Creative Scotland
The Crerar Hotels Trust
Cripplegate Foundation
The Violet and Milo Cripps Charitable Trust
The Cross Trust
The Cross Trust
Cruden Foundation Ltd
The Ronald Cruickshanks Foundation
The Cumber Family Charitable Trust
Cumbria Community Foundation
Itzchok Meyer Cymerman Trust Ltd
The D. G. Charitable Settlement
The Joan Lynette Dalton Charitable Trust
The Dr and Mrs A. Darlington Charitable Trust
Baron Davenport's Charity
The Davidson (Nairn) Charitable Trust
The Davidson Family Charitable Trust
Michael Davies Charitable Settlement
Margaret Davies Charity
The John Grant Davies Trust*
The Crispin Davis Family Trust
The Dawe Charitable Trust
The De Brye Charitable Trust
William Dean Countryside and Educational Trust

The Dellal Foundation
The Delves Charitable Trust
The Demigryphon Trust
Dentons UKMEA LLP Charitable Trust
Foundation Derbyshire
The Desmond Foundation
The Duke of Devonshire's Charitable Trust
The Gillian Dickinson Trust
Didymus
The DLM Charitable Trust
The Derek and Eileen Dodgson Foundation
The Dollond Charitable Trust
The Doughty Charity Trust
Douglas Arter Foundation
The Dumbreck Charity
The Dunn Family Charitable Trust
The Dyers' Company Charitable Trust
Earls Colne and Halstead Educational Charity
The Sir John Eastwood Foundation
The EBM Charitable Trust
The W. G. Edwards Charitable Foundation
*The Eighty Eight Foundation**
*Elanore Ltd**
The Elephant Trust
The George Elias Charitable Trust
The Gerald Palmer Eling Trust Company
The Wilfred and Elsie Elkes Charity Fund
The Maud Elkington Charitable Trust
The Edith Maud Ellis 1985 Charitable Trust
The Vernon N. Ely Charitable Trust
The Emerton-Christie Charity
The Englefield Charitable Trust
The Epigoni Trust
The Eventhall Family Charitable Trust
The Everard Foundation
The Football Association National Sports Centre Trust
Ford Britain Trust
Gatwick Airport Community Trust
*The Genesis Charitable Trust**
*The Gerrick Rose Animal Trust**
Get Kids Going
*Gilchrist Educational Trust**
The Girdlers' Company Charitable Trust
The Glass-House Trust
The Mike Gooley Trailfinders Charity
*The Graham Trust**
The Gray Trust
Greenham Common Community Trust Ltd
The Greggs Foundation
The Grocers' Charity
Dr Guthrie's Association
Hackney Parochial Charities
The Hadfield Charitable Trust
*Hammersmith United Charities**
The Hampstead Wells and Campden Trust
The Harpur Trust
The Harris Charity
*HC Foundation**
*Horwich Shotter Charitable Trust**
*The Hyde Park Place Estate Charity – civil trustees**
Lady Eda Jardine Charitable Trust
Jewish Child's Day (JCD)
*The Kildare Trust**
The Mary Kinross Charitable Trust
The Sir James Knott Trust
The William Leech Charity
*Leicestershire and Rutland Masonic Charity Association**
*Leng Charitable Trust**
*The Lethendy Charitable Trust**
*The Maisie and Raphael Lewis Charitable Trust**
*Bernard Lewis Family Charitable Trust**
*Life Changes Trust**
Lifeline 4 Kids (Handicapped Children's Aid Committee)
*The W. M. and B. W. Lloyd Trust**
Lloyds Bank Foundation for England and Wales
*The Lockwood Charitable Foundation**
The Lord's Taverners
*Michael Lowe's and Associated Charities**
The Lyndhurst Trust
Sylvanus Lysons Charity
The Madeline Mabey Trust
The Macdonald-Buchanan Charitable Trust
*Mace Foundation**
*The Master Charitable Trust**
*Maypride Ltd**
The James Neill Trust Fund
The Newcomen Collett Foundation
The Northmoor Trust
*The Northwick Trust**
The Notgrove Trust
*One Community Foundation Ltd**
The Ormsby Charitable Trust
*The Paddington Charitable Estate Educational Fund**
The James Pantyfedwen Foundation
*The Pargiter Trust**
*The JGW Patterson Foundation**
The Bernard Piggott Charitable Trust
*Pink Ribbon Foundation**
*The Polehampton Charity**
The Portishead Nautical Trust
The Prince of Wales's Charitable Foundation
*QBE European Operations Foundation**
*Quercus Foundation**
The Monica Rabagliati Charitable Trust
The Rank Foundation Ltd
The Rayne Foundation
The Rest Harrow Trust
Rhondda Cynon Taff Welsh Church Acts Fund
*Riada Trust**
Richmond Parish Lands Charity
*Rigby Foundation**
The River Trust
The Robertson Trust
Rosca Trust
*The Cissie Rosefield Charitable Trust**
The Cecil Rosen Foundation
*The David Ross Foundation**
The Rothley Trust
Royal Docks Trust (London)
*The Royal Navy And Royal Marines Charity**
Royal Victoria Hall Foundation
The Rubin Foundation Charitable Trust
The Sainsbury Family Charitable Trusts
Santander UK Foundation Ltd
*The Savoy Educational Trust**
The Scarfe Charitable Trust
The Schapira Charitable Trust
The Schmidt-Bodner Charitable Trust
The Schreiber Charitable Trust
Foundation Scotland
The Francis C. Scott Charitable Trust
The Frieda Scott Charitable Trust
*The John Scott Trust Fund**
The Scouloudi Foundation
Seafarers Hospital Society
Seafarers UK (King George's Fund for Sailors)
The Seven Fifty Trust
The Shanly Foundation
The Linley Shaw Foundation
*Sherburn House Charity**
*Sherling Charitable Trust**

The Archie Sherman Cardiff Foundation
The Shetland Charitable Trust
The Bassil Shippam and Alsford Trust
The Shipwrights' Company Charitable Fund
David and Jennifer Sieff Charitable Trust
The Huntly and Margery Sinclair Charitable Trust
The Skelton Bounty
*The Skerritt Trust**
The Charles Skey Charitable Trust
The Henry Smith Charity
The Leslie Smith Foundation
*The Martin Smith Foundation**
The Stanley Smith UK Horticultural Trust
*Sofronie Foundation**
The Solo Charitable Settlement
The E. C. Sosnow Charitable Trust
The South Square Trust
The W. F. Southall Trust
The Southover Manor General Education Trust
The Worshipful Company of Spectacle Makers' Charity
The Jessie Spencer Trust
The Spielman Charitable Trust
The Geoff and Fiona Squire Foundation
The Squires Foundation
St James's Place Foundation
The Stanley Foundation Ltd
The Staples Trust
*The Stoneygate Trust**
Peter Stormonth Darling Charitable Trust
The Bernard Sunley Charitable Foundation
*Surgo Foundation UK Ltd**
The Thornton Trust
The Roger and Douglas Turner Charitable Trust
The Ulverscroft Foundation
The Nigel Vinson Charitable Trust
The Vintners' Foundation
*The Watson Family Charitable Trust**
*The Weir Charitable Trust**
*The West Looe Town Trust**
*The Wheeler Family Charitable Trust**
*The Williams Family Foundation**
*The Wimbledon Foundation**
Yorkshire and Clydesdale Bank Foundation
Zurich Community Trust (UK) Ltd

Core support

■ Core costs

The 29th May 1961 Charitable Trust
The A. B. Charitable Trust
Aberdeen Asset Management Charitable Foundation
ABF The Soldiers' Charity
The Adint Charitable Trust
The Adnams Community Trust
The AIM Foundation
Ajahma Charitable Trust
The Alchemy Foundation
D. C. R. Allen Charitable Trust
The H. B. Allen Charitable Trust
*Alzheimer's Research UK**
The Ammco Trust
The Anchor Foundation
The Andrew Anderson Trust
Anglo American Group Foundation
*The Anne Duchess of Westminster's Charity**
*Arcadia Charitable Trust**
The Ardwick Trust
The Armourers' and Brasiers' Gauntlet Trust
The Asda Foundation
The Ashden Trust
The Ashley Family Foundation
The Astor Foundation
The Lord Austin Trust
The Aylesford Family Charitable Trust
The Austin Bailey Foundation
The Baily Thomas Charitable Fund
*Bairdwatson Charitable Trust**
Lord Barnby's Foundation
*The Battersea Power Station Foundation**
BBC Children in Need
*The Becht Family Charitable Trust**
The John Beckwith Charitable Trust
The Bedfordshire and Luton Community Foundation
The Bellahouston Bequest Fund
The Berkeley Charitable Foundation
The Berkshire Community Foundation
The Blagrave Trust
The Blandford Lake Trust
The Marjory Boddy Charitable Trust
The Boltini Trust
The Harry Bottom Charitable Trust
The Breadsticks Foundation
The Breast Cancer Research Trust (BCRT)
The British Dietetic Association General and Education Trust Fund
British Gas (Scottish Gas) Energy Trust
British Record Industry Trust
The Bromley Trust
The Charles Brotherton Trust
Buckinghamshire Community Foundation
The E. F. Bulmer Benevolent Fund
The Clara E. Burgess Charity
Consolidated Charity of Burton upon Trent
The William A. Cadbury Charitable Trust
The Cadbury Foundation
The Barrow Cadbury Trust
The Cambridgeshire Community Foundation
The Campden Charities Trustee
The Richard Carne Trust
The Casey Trust
The Cattanach Charitable Trust
The Childwick Trust
*John Christie Trust**
Chrysalis Trust
The City Bridge Trust (Bridge House Estates)
Stephen Clark 1957 Charitable Trust
J. A. Clark Charitable Trust
The Cole Charitable Trust
John and Freda Coleman Charitable Trust
The Colt Foundation
Colyer-Fergusson Charitable Trust
Comic Relief
The Ernest Cook Trust
The Helen Jean Cope Trust
The J. Reginald Corah Foundation Fund
Cornwall Community Foundation
*The Coulthurst Trust**
The County Council of Dyfed Welsh Curch Fund
The Augustine Courtauld Trust
*Credit Suisse EMEA Foundation**
*England and Wales Cricket Trust**
Cripplegate Foundation
The Croydon Relief in Need Charities
The Peter Cruddas Foundation
Cruden Foundation Ltd
Cullum Family Trust
The Cumber Family Charitable Trust

Cumbria Community Foundation
Roald Dahl's Marvellous Children's Charity
Baron Davenport's Charity
The Hamilton Davies Trust
William Dean Countryside and Educational Trust
Disability Aid Fund (The Roger and Jean Jefcoate Trust)
The Dischma Charitable Trust
The Djanogly Foundation
The DLM Charitable Trust
The Derek and Eileen Dodgson Foundation
Dorset Community Foundation
The Double 'O' Charity Ltd
The Drapers' Charitable Fund
The Dulverton Trust
The Dunhill Medical Trust
The Charles Dunstone Charitable Trust
County Durham Community Foundation
The Ecology Trust
EDF Energy Trust (EDFET)
Dr Edwards Bishop King's Fulham Endowment Fund
The John Ellerman Foundation
The Elmley Foundation
The Englefield Charitable Trust
Epilepsy Research UK
Esh Foundation
The Essex and Southend Sports Trust
Essex Community Foundation
The Essex Youth Trust
Euro Charity Trust
The Eveson Charitable Trust
The Expat Foundation
Esmée Fairbairn Foundation
The Doris Field Charitable Trust
Ford Britain Trust
Donald Forrester Trust
The Foyle Foundation
The Elizabeth Frankland Moore and Star Foundation
Jill Franklin Trust
Friends Provident Charitable Foundation
The Galanthus Trust
The Gale Family Charity Trust
The Gannochy Trust
The Garrick Charitable Trust
The Gatsby Charitable Foundation
*Genetic Disorders UK**
The Gibbs Charitable Trust
The G. C. Gibson Charitable Trust
The Simon Gibson Charitable Trust
*The L. and R. Gilley Charitable Trust**
The Girdlers' Company Charitable Trust
The Glass-House Trust
The Gloag Foundation
Gloucestershire Community Foundation
The Goldsmiths' Company Charity
The Golsoncott Foundation
Nicholas and Judith Goodison's Charitable Settlement
The Gosling Foundation Ltd
The Gould Charitable Trust
Grahame Charitable Foundation Ltd
The Greggs Foundation
H. C. D. Memorial Fund
The Hadfield Charitable Trust
The Hadley Trust
The Hadrian Trust
Halifax Foundation for Northern Ireland (previously known as Lloyds Bank Foundation for Northern Ireland)
Paul Hamlyn Foundation
Hampshire and Isle of Wight Community Foundation
The Hampstead Wells and Campden Trust
The W. A. Handley Charity Trust
The Kathleen Hannay Memorial Charity
The Haramead Trust
William Harding's Charity
The Harebell Centenary Fund
The Harpur Trust
The Peter Harrison Foundation
The Hartley Charitable Trust
The Hasluck Charitable Trust
The Headley Trust
May Hearnshaw Charitable Trust (May Hearnshaw's Charity)
Heart of England Community Foundation
The Charlotte Heber-Percy Charitable Trust
The Percy Hedley 1990 Charitable Trust
The Helping Foundation
The Hemby Charitable Trust
Henley Educational Trust
The G. D. Herbert Charitable Trust
Herefordshire Community Foundation
The Herefordshire Historic Churches Trust
Hertfordshire Community Foundation
The Alan Edward Higgs Charity
The Hilden Charitable Fund
*M. V. Hillhouse Trust**
The Hillingdon Community Trust
Hinchley Charitable Trust
The Hintze Family Charity Foundation
The Henry C. Hoare Charitable Trust
The Dorothy Holmes Charitable Trust
The Edward Holt Trust
The Holywood Trust
The Homelands Charitable Trust
The Homestead Charitable Trust
The Mary Homfray Charitable Trust
Sir Harold Hood's Charitable Trust
Hopmarket Charity
The Worshipful Company of Horners' Charitable Trusts
The Hospital of God at Greatham
The Hospital Saturday Fund
House of Industry Estate
The Daniel Howard Trust
The Hull and East Riding Charitable Trust
The Albert Hunt Trust
The Hunter Foundation
Miss Agnes H. Hunter's Trust
Ibrahim Foundation Ltd
The Indigo Trust
The Inverforth Charitable Trust
Irish Youth Foundation (UK) Ltd (incorporating The Lawlor Foundation)
The ITF Seafarers' Trust
John James Bristol Foundation
The Susan and Stephen James Charitable Settlement
Nick Jenkins Foundation
The Jerusalem Trust
Joffe Charitable Trust
The Elton John AIDS Foundation (EJAF)
The Jordan Charitable Foundation
The Joron Charitable Trust
The Jusaca Charitable Trust
The Boris Karloff Charitable Foundation
The Caron Keating Foundation
The Kelly Family Charitable Trust
Kent Community Foundation
The Robert Kiln Charitable Trust
The King/Cullimore Charitable Trust
The Mary Kinross Charitable Trust
The Sir James Knott Trust
The Neil Kreitman Foundation

The K. P. Ladd Charitable Trust
Community Foundations for Lancashire and Merseyside
The Allen Lane Foundation
The LankellyChase Foundation
The R. J. Larg Family Charitable Trust
Mrs F. B. Laurence Charitable Trust
The Edgar E. Lawley Foundation
The Leathersellers' Company Charitable Fund
The William Leech Charity
Leicestershire, Leicester and Rutland Community Foundation
The Kennedy Leigh Charitable Trust
The Leigh Trust
The Lennox Hannay Charitable Trust
The Leverhulme Trust
The Sir Edward Lewis Foundation
Life Changes Trust*
Lincolnshire Community Foundation
Lindale Educational Foundation
The Frank Litchfield Charitable Trust
The Charles Littlewood Hill Trust
The Second Joseph Aaron Littman Foundation
Lloyds Bank Foundation for England and Wales
Lloyds Bank Foundation for the Channel Islands
Lloyds TSB Foundation for Scotland
The Lolev Charitable Trust
Trust for London
London Catalyst
The London Community Foundation (LCF)
London Housing Foundation Ltd (LHF)
London Legal Support Trust (LLST)
The Henry Lumley Charitable Trust
John Lyon's Charity
The R. S. Macdonald Charitable Trust
The MacRobert Trust
Man Group PLC Charitable Trust
The Manchester Guardian Society Charitable Trust
The W. M. Mann Foundation
R. W. Mann Trust
The Ann and David Marks Foundation
Marmot Charitable Trust
The Marr-Munning Trust
The Marsh Christian Trust
John Martin's Charity
Masonic Charitable Foundation*
The Nancie Massey Charitable Trust
The Mathew Trust
The Matliwala Family Charitable Trust
Mayfair Charities Ltd
D. D. McPhail Charitable Settlement
Medical Research Foundation*
The Medlock Charitable Trust
The Mercers' Charitable Foundation
The Merchant Taylors' Company Charities Fund
Merchant Taylors' Consolidated Charities for the Infirm
The Merchant Venturers' Charity
Mercury Phoenix Trust
The Mickel Fund
The Gerald Micklem Charitable Trust
Middlesex Sports Foundation
The Millfield House Foundation (1)
The Clare Milne Trust
The Monmouthshire County Council Welsh Church Act Fund
John Moores Foundation
The Morgan Charitable Foundation
The Steve Morgan Foundation
The Mugdock Children's Trust
The Frederick Mulder Foundation
Murphy-Neumann Charity Company Ltd
National Committee of the Women's World Day of Prayer for England and Wales and Northern Ireland
The National Express Foundation
The National Gardens Scheme*
The Nationwide Foundation
Network for Social Change Charitable Trust
The Frances and Augustus Newman Foundation
Alice Noakes Memorial Charitable Trust
Norfolk Community Foundation
The Northmoor Trust
The Notgrove Trust
The Oakdale Trust
The Oakley Charitable Trust
Open Gate
The Ouseley Church Music Trust
The Owen Family Trust
P. F. Charitable Trust
Peacock Charitable Trust
The Pears Family Charitable Foundation
The Pennycress Trust
The Jack Petchey Foundation
The Pilgrim Trust
Pilkington Charities Fund
Polden-Puckham Charitable Foundation
Pollywally Charitable Trust
The Mary Potter Convent Hospital Trust
David and Elaine Potter Foundation
The Primrose Trust
The Princess Anne's Charities
Mr and Mrs J. A. Pye's Charitable Settlement
Queen Mary's Roehampton Trust
The Racing Foundation
The Joseph Rank Trust
Elizabeth Rathbone Charity
The Sigrid Rausing Trust
The Ravensdale Trust
The Rayne Foundation
The Rayne Trust
The John Rayner Charitable Trust
The Sir James Reckitt Charity
C. A. Redfern Charitable Foundation
The Rhododendron Trust
Daisie Rich Trust
Richmond Parish Lands Charity
Rivers Foundation
The Rix-Thompson-Rothenberg Foundation
The Robertson Trust
The Helen Roll Charity
Rosca Trust
Mrs Gladys Row Fogo Charitable Trust
The Joseph Rowntree Charitable Trust
The Royal British Legion
The Saddlers' Company Charitable Fund
The Jean Sainsbury Animal Welfare Trust
The Alan and Babette Sainsbury Charitable Fund
The Saintbury Trust
Santander UK Foundation Ltd
The Scarfe Charitable Trust
The Francis C. Scott Charitable Trust
The Frieda Scott Charitable Trust
Seafarers UK (King George's Fund for Sailors)
The Shanly Foundation

ShareGift (The Orr Mackintosh Foundation)
The Sheldon Trust
SHINE (Support and Help in Education)
The Shirley Foundation
SITA Cornwall Trust Ltd
The Charles Skey Charitable Trust
The Mrs Smith and Mount Trust
The Henry Smith Charity
The R. C. Snelling Charitable Trust
The Sobell Foundation
Social Business Trust
*Somerset Community Foundation**
The Souter Charitable Trust
R. H. Southern Trust
The Spurrell Charitable Trust
Sir Walter St John's Educational Charity
The Stafford Trust
The Staples Trust
The Peter Stebbings Memorial Charity
The Steel Charitable Trust
The Stone Family Foundation
The Samuel Storey Family Charitable Trust
Peter Storrs Trust
Stratford upon Avon Town Trust
Suffolk Community Foundation
*Sunninghill Fuel Allotment Trust**
Community Foundation for Surrey
The Sussex Community Foundation
Sutton Coldfield Charitable Trust
The Swire Charitable Trust
Sylvia Waddilove Foundation UK
Tallow Chandlers Benevolent Fund No. 2
The Tedworth Charitable Trust
The Sir Jules Thorn Charitable Trust
Mrs R. P. Tindall's Charitable Trust
The Tisbury Telegraph Trust
The Constance Travis Charitable Trust
The Treeside Trust
The Triangle Trust (1949) Fund
The True Colours Trust
The Trusthouse Charitable Foundation
The James Tudor Foundation
The Tudor Trust
The Tuixen Foundation
The Roger and Douglas Turner Charitable Trust
Two Ridings Community Foundation
United Utilities Trust Fund
The Valentine Charitable Trust
The Vandervell Foundation
The Virgin Money Foundation
Volant Charitable Trust
Voluntary Action Fund (VAF)
The Scurrah Wainwright Charity
The Wakefield and Tetley Trust
Walton on Thames Charity
Sir Siegmund Warburg's Voluntary Settlement
The Barbara Ward Children's Foundation
The Waterloo Foundation
The Wates Foundation
Waynflete Charitable Trust
The Weavers' Company Benevolent Fund
Webb Memorial Trust
The Weinstock Fund
*The Weir Charitable Trust**
The James Weir Foundation
*The Westminster Amalgamated Charity**
The Westminster Foundation
The Garfield Weston Foundation
Westway Trust
The Whitaker Charitable Trust
White Stuff Foundation
The Norman Whiteley Trust
The Whitley Animal Protection Trust
The Lionel Wigram Memorial Trust
The Will Charitable Trust
Dame Violet Wills Charitable Trust
The Dame Violet Wills Will Trust
The Wilson Foundation
Wiltshire Community Foundation
The Harold Hyam Wingate Foundation
The Wixamtree Trust
The Wood Foundation
Wooden Spoon Society
Woodroffe Benton Foundation
Worcester Municipal Charities (CIO)
The Wyndham Charitable Trust
The Yapp Charitable Trust
The South Yorkshire Community Foundation
The John Kirkhope Young Endowment Fund
Youth Music
Zurich Community Trust (UK) Ltd

■ Development funding

The 1970 Trust
The 1989 Willan Charitable Trust
*The 3Ts Charitable Trust**
4 Charity Foundation
The A. S. Charitable Trust
A. W. Charitable Trust
*A2BD Foundation UK Ltd**
The Aberbrothock Skea Trust
The Aberdeen Foundation
ABF The Soldiers' Charity
*The Neville Abraham Foundation**
The Acacia Charitable Trust
The Accenture Foundation
Access Sport CIO
Achisomoch Aid Company Ltd
The ACT Foundation
Action Medical Research
The Sylvia Adams Charitable Trust
The Addleshaw Goddard Charitable Trust
Adenfirst Ltd
The Adint Charitable Trust
*The AEB Charitable Trust**
AF Trust Company
Age Scotland
Age UK
Aid to the Church in Need (UK)
The Sylvia Aitken Charitable Trust
Ajahma Charitable Trust
*AKO Foundation**
The Alborada Trust
D. G. Albright Charitable Trust
The Alchemy Foundation
Aldgate and All Hallows' Foundation
Al-Fayed Charitable Foundation
All Saints Educational Trust
The Derrill Allatt Foundation
Allchurches Trust Ltd
*The Allen & Overy Foundation**
The H. B. Allen Charitable Trust
The Allen Trust
The Alliance Family Foundation
AM Charitable Trust
Amabrill Ltd
The Amalur Foundation Ltd
The Ammco Trust
Sir John and Lady Amory's Charitable Trust
Viscount Amory's Charitable Trust
The Ampelos Trust
The AMW Charitable Trust
*The Ancaster Trust**
The Andrew Anderson Trust
Andor Charitable Trust
The Mary Andrew Charitable Trust
Andrews Charitable Trust

Anglo American Group Foundation
Anguish's Educational Foundation
The Annandale Charitable Trust
*The Anne Duchess of Westminster's Charity**
Anpride Ltd
The Anson Charitable Trust
*AO Smile Foundation**
The Apax Foundation
The John Apthorp Charity
The Arah Foundation
The Arbib Foundation
The Archer Trust
The Architectural Heritage Fund
The Ardeola Charitable Trust
The Argus Appeal
The Armourers' and Brasiers' Gauntlet Trust
The Arsenal Foundation Ltd
The Artemis Charitable Trust
Arts Council England
Arts Council of Northern Ireland
Arts Council of Wales (also known as Cyngor Celfyddydau Cymru)
The Ove Arup Foundation
Ove Arup Partnership Charitable Trust
*The Asfari Foundation**
The Ashburnham Thanksgiving Trust
The Ashden Trust
The Ashley Family Foundation
The Ian Askew Charitable Trust
*The Associated Board of the Royal Schools of Music**
The Associated Country Women of the World
The Astor Foundation
The Aurelius Charitable Trust
Autonomous Research Charitable Trust (ARCT)
The Avon and Somerset Police Community Trust
Awards for All (see also the Big Lottery Fund)
The Aylesford Family Charitable Trust
The Harry Bacon Foundation
The Bagri Foundation
The Baird Trust
The Baker Charitable Trust
The Roy and Pixie Baker Charitable Trust
The Balcombe Charitable Trust
The Balfour Beatty Charitable Trust
The Ballinger Charitable Trust
The Baltic Charitable Fund
The Bamford Charitable Foundation
The Banbury Charities
The Band Trust
The Bank of Scotland Foundation
The Barbers' Company General Charities
The Barbour Foundation
Barchester Healthcare Foundation
The Barclay Foundation
The Barham Charitable Trust
The Baring Foundation
*The Philip Barker Charity**
The Barker-Mill Foundation
Lord Barnby's Foundation
The Barnsbury Charitable Trust
*The Barrack Charitable Trust**
Misses Barrie Charitable Trust
The Bartlett Taylor Charitable Trust
The Paul Bassham Charitable Trust
The Batchworth Trust
The Battens Charitable Trust
Bauer Radio's Cash for Kids Charities
Bay Charitable Trust
The Bay Tree Charitable Trust
The Louis Baylis (Maidenhead Advertiser) Charitable Trust
BBC Children in Need
BC Partners Foundation
BCH Trust
Bear Mordechai Ltd
The Bearder Charity
The James Beattie Charitable Trust
Beauland Ltd
The Becker Family Charitable Trust
The John Beckwith Charitable Trust
The Bedfordshire and Luton Community Foundation
Beefy's Charity Foundation
The David and Ruth Behrend Fund
*The Behrens Foundation**
The Bellahouston Bequest Fund
Belljoe Tzedoko Ltd
*Benesco Charity Ltd**
The Benham Charitable Settlement
Bennett Lowell Ltd
*The Rowan Bentall Charitable Trust**
The Berkeley Charitable Foundation
The Ruth Berkowitz Charitable Trust
The Berkshire Community Foundation
The Bestway Foundation
The Big Lottery Fund (see also Awards for All)
The Billmeir Charitable Trust
The Bingham Trust
The Birmingham District Nursing Charitable Trust
Birmingham International Airport Community Trust Fund
The Lord Mayor of Birmingham's Charity
Birthday House Trust
Miss Jeanne Bisgood's Charitable Trust
The Michael Bishop Foundation
*Asser Bishvil Foundation**
The Sydney Black Charitable Trust
The Bertie Black Foundation
Isabel Blackman Foundation
The Blagrave Trust
The Blair Foundation
The Morgan Blake Charitable Trust
Blakemore Foundation
The Blandford Lake Trust
The Sir Victor Blank Charitable Settlement
Bloom Foundation
The Bluston Charitable Settlement
The Marjory Boddy Charitable Trust
The Boltini Trust
The Bonamy Charitable Trust
The Charlotte Bonham-Carter Charitable Trust
The Linda and Gordon Bonnyman Charitable Trust
The Boodle & Dunthorne Charitable Trust
BOOST Charitable Trust
The Booth Charities
Boots Charitable Trust
Salo Bordon Charitable Trust
The Bordon Liphook Haslemere Charity
*Sir William Boreman's Foundation**
*The Borrows Charitable Trust**
The Oliver Borthwick Memorial Trust
The Boshier-Hinton Foundation
The Bothwell Charitable Trust
The Harry Bottom Charitable Trust
P. G. and N. J. Boulton Trust
Sir Clive Bourne Family Trust
Bourneheights Ltd
The Bowerman Charitable Trust
The Bowland Charitable Trust
Friends of Boyan Trust
The Frank Brake Charitable Trust
The William Brake Charitable Trust

The Tony Bramall Charitable Trust
The Liz and Terry Bramall Foundation
The Bransford Trust
The Breadsticks Foundation
*The Brelms Trust CIO**
Bridgepoint Charitable Trust
Bristol Archdeaconry Charity
Bristol Charities
John Bristow and Thomas Mason Trust
The British and Foreign School Society
British Council for Prevention of Blindness (Save Eyes Everywhere)
The British Dietetic Association General and Education Trust Fund
British Gas (Scottish Gas) Energy Trust
British Heart Foundation (BHF)
British Humane Association
British Record Industry Trust
The J. and M. Britton Charitable Trust
The Bromley Trust
The Consuelo and Anthony Brooke Charitable Trust
The Rory and Elizabeth Brooks Foundation
The Charles Brotherton Trust
Bill Brown 1989 Charitable Trust
R. S. Brownless Charitable Trust
The T. B. H. Brunner's Charitable Settlement
The Bruntwood Charity
Brushmill Ltd
Buckingham Trust
The E. F. Bulmer Benevolent Fund
BUPA UK Foundation
*The Burberry Foundation**
The Burden Trust
The Burdett Trust for Nursing
The Clara E. Burgess Charity
The Burry Charitable Trust
The Arnold Burton 1998 Charitable Trust
Consolidated Charity of Burton upon Trent
The Derek Butler Trust
*The Butters Foundation (UK) Ltd**
The Noel Buxton Trust
The Christopher Cadbury Charitable Trust
The Edward Cadbury Charitable Trust
The G. W. Cadbury Charitable Trust
The William A. Cadbury Charitable Trust
The Cadbury Foundation
The Barrow Cadbury Trust
The Edward and Dorothy Cadbury Trust
The George Cadbury Trust
The Cadogan Charity
CAFOD (Catholic Agency for Overseas Development)
Community Foundation for Calderdale
Callander Charitable Trust
Calleva Foundation
Calouste Gulbenkian Foundation – UK Branch
The Cambridgeshire Community Foundation
The Ellis Campbell Charitable Foundation
The Campden Charities Trustee
*Canary Wharf Contractors Fund**
Cardy Beaver Foundation
*The W. A. Cargill Charitable Trust**
David William Traill Cargill Fund
*The W. A. Cargill Fund**
The Richard Carne Trust
The Carnegie Dunfermline Trust
The Carnegie Trust for the Universities of Scotland
The Carpenters' Company Charitable Trust
The Carr-Gregory Trust
The Carrington Charitable Trust
The Leslie Mary Carter Charitable Trust
The Casey Trust
Sir John Cass's Foundation
*Sir Ernest Cassel Educational Trust**
The Elizabeth Casson Trust
*The Castansa Trust**
The Catholic Charitable Trust
The Catholic Trust for England and Wales
The Joseph and Annie Cattle Trust
The Thomas Sivewright Catto Charitable Settlement
The Wilfrid and Constance Cave Foundation
The Cayo Foundation
Elizabeth Cayzer Charitable Trust
The B. G. S. Cayzer Charitable Trust
The Cazenove Charitable Trust
The CBD Charitable Trust
CBRE UK Charitable Trust
Celtic Charity Fund
The CH (1980) Charitable Trust
The Amelia Chadwick Trust
Chalfords Ltd
The Chapman Charitable Trust
Charitworth Ltd
The Charter 600 Charity
Chartered Accountants' Livery Charity (CALC)
The Cheruby Trust
Cheshire Freemason's Charity
Chesterhill Charitable Trust
The Childwick Trust
CHK Charities Ltd
The Chownes Foundation
Christadelphian Samaritan Fund
Christian Aid
Chrysalis Trust
The Church Burgesses Educational Foundation
Church Burgesses Trust
Church Urban Fund
The CIBC World Markets Children's Miracle Foundation
The City Bridge Trust (Bridge House Estates)
The City Educational Trust Fund
*The Clan Trust Ltd**
Stephen Clark 1957 Charitable Trust
J. A. Clark Charitable Trust
The Hilda and Alice Clark Charitable Trust
The Roger and Sarah Bancroft Clark Charitable Trust
*The Clark Foundation**
The Cleopatra Trust
The Clore Duffield Foundation
Richard Cloudesley's Charity
The Clover Trust
The Robert Clutterbuck Charitable Trust
Clydpride Ltd
The Coalfields Regeneration Trust
The John Coates Charitable Trust
Denise Coates Foundation
The Cobalt Trust
The Cobtree Charity Trust Ltd
The Denise Cohen Charitable Trust
The Vivienne and Samuel Cohen Charitable Trust
The John S. Cohen Foundation
The R. and S. Cohen Foundation
John Coldman Charitable Trust
The Colefax Charitable Trust
John and Freda Coleman Charitable Trust
The Sir Jeremiah Colman Gift Trust
Col-Reno Ltd
The Colt Foundation

The Coltstaple Trust
Colwinston Charitable Trust
Colyer-Fergusson Charitable Trust
Comic Relief
The Comino Foundation
The Douglas Compton James Charitable Trust
Martin Connell Charitable Trust
*The Thomas Cook Chidlren's Charity**
The Ernest Cook Trust
The Cooks Charity
The Catherine Cookson Charitable Trust
The Keith Coombs Trust
Mabel Cooper Charity
The Alice Ellen Cooper Dean Charitable Foundation
The Marjorie Coote Animal Charity Trust
The Marjorie Coote Old People's Charity
The J. Reginald Corah Foundation Fund
The Worshipful Company of Cordwainers Charitable Trusts (Minges Gift and the Pooled Trusts)
The Gershon Coren Charitable Foundation (also known as The Muriel and Gus Coren Charitable Foundation)
Cornwall Community Foundation
The Duke of Cornwall's Benevolent Fund
The Cornwell Charitable Trust
The Costa Family Charitable Trust
The Cotton Industry War Memorial Trust
The County Council of Dyfed Welsh Curch Fund
The Augustine Courtauld Trust
Coutts Charitable Foundation
General Charity of Coventry
Coventry Building Society Charitable Foundation
The John Cowan Foundation
The Sir Tom Cowie Charitable Trust
Dudley and Geoffrey Cox Charitable Trust
The Craignish Trust
The Craps Charitable Trust
The Cray Trust
*The Elizabeth Creak Charitable Trust**
Creative Scotland
*Credit Suisse EMEA Foundation**
The Crescent Trust
*England and Wales Cricket Trust**
Criffel Charitable Trust
Cripplegate Foundation
The Violet and Milo Cripps Charitable Trust
*Crisis UK**
The Peter Cruddas Foundation
Cruden Foundation Ltd
The Ronald Cruickshanks Foundation
*CSIS Charity Fund**
The Cuby Charitable Trust
The Cumber Family Charitable Trust
The Harry Cureton Charitable Trust
Itzchok Meyer Cymerman Trust Ltd
The D'Oyly Carte Charitable Trust
Roald Dahl's Marvellous Children's Charity
Oizer Dalim Trust
The Joan Lynette Dalton Charitable Trust
The Dr and Mrs A. Darlington Charitable Trust
The Davidson (Nairn) Charitable Trust
The Davidson Family Charitable Trust
Michael Davies Charitable Settlement
*The Biss Davies Charitable Trust**
Margaret Davies Charity
*The John Grant Davies Trust**
The Crispin Davis Family Trust
The Davis Foundation
The Henry and Suzanne Davis Foundation
*Dawat-E-Hadiyah Trust (United Kingdom)**
The Dawe Charitable Trust
The De Brye Charitable Trust
Peter De Haan Charitable Trust
*The Roger De Haan Charitable Trust**
*The De La Rue Charitable Trust**
The De Laszlo Foundation
William Dean Countryside and Educational Trust
Debmar Benevolent Trust Ltd
The Delius Trust
The Dellal Foundation
The Delves Charitable Trust
The Demigryphon Trust
The Denman Charitable Trust
Dentons UKMEA LLP Charitable Trust
Foundation Derbyshire
Provincial Grand Charity of the Province of Derbyshire
The Desmond Foundation
Devon Community Foundation
The Sandy Dewhirst Charitable Trust
The Laduma Dhamecha Charitable Trust
Diabetes UK
The Diageo Foundation
Alan and Sheila Diamond Charitable Trust
The Gillian Dickinson Trust
Didymus
Dinwoodie Charitable Company
The Dischma Charitable Trust
*C. H. Dixon Charitable Trust**
The Djanogly Foundation
The DLM Charitable Trust
The DM Charitable Trust
The Derek and Eileen Dodgson Foundation
The Dollond Charitable Trust
The Dorcas Trust
Dorset Community Foundation
The Dorus Trust
The Double 'O' Charity Ltd
The Doughty Charity Trust
Douglas Arter Foundation
The Drapers' Charitable Fund
Dromintee Trust
Duchy Health Charity Ltd
The Royal Foundation of the Duke and Duchess of Cambridge and Prince Harry
The Dulverton Trust
The Dumbreck Charity
Dunard Fund 2016
The Dunhill Medical Trust
The Dunn Family Charitable Trust
The Charles Dunstone Charitable Trust
County Durham Community Foundation
Dushinsky Trust Ltd
The Mildred Duveen Charitable Trust
The Dyers' Company Charitable Trust
The James Dyson Foundation
Audrey Earle Charitable Trust
The Earley Charity
Earls Colne and Halstead Educational Charity
East End Community Foundation
Eastern Counties Educational Trust Ltd
The Sir John Eastwood Foundation
The EBM Charitable Trust
*The ECHO Trust**
Echoes Of Service
The Ecology Trust
The Economist Charitable Trust
EDF Energy Trust (EDFET)
The Gilbert and Eileen Edgar Foundation

Global Care
Global Charities
Gloucestershire Community Foundation
Worshipful Company of Glovers of London Charitable Trust
The Godinton Charitable Trust
Worshipful Company of Gold and Silver Wyre Drawers Charitable Trust Fund
Sydney and Phyllis Goldberg Memorial Charitable Trust
The Golden Bottle Trust
The Goldman Sachs Charitable Gift Fund (UK)
Goldman Sachs Gives (UK)
The Goldsmiths' Company Charity
The Golf Foundation Ltd
The Golsoncott Foundation
Nicholas and Judith Goodison's Charitable Settlement
The Goodman Foundation
The Mike Gooley Trailfinders Charity
The Goshen Trust
The Gosling Foundation Ltd
The Gould Charitable Trust
Gowling WLG (UK) Charitable Trust
The Hemraj Goyal Foundation
Grace Charitable Trust
Graff Foundation
E. C. Graham Belford Charitable Settlement
A. and S. Graham Charitable Trust
The Graham Trust*
Grahame Charitable Foundation Ltd
The Granada Foundation
Grand Charitable Trust of the Order of Women Freemasons
The Grantham Yorke Trust
GrantScape
Gordon Gray Trust
The Gray Trust
The Great Britain Sasakawa Foundation
The Kenneth and Susan Green Charitable Foundation
The Green Hall Foundation
Philip and Judith Green Trust
Mrs H. R. Greene Charitable Settlement
Greenham Common Community Trust Ltd
The Greggs Foundation
The Gretna Charitable Trust
Greys Charitable Trust
The Grimmitt Trust
The Grocers' Charity
M. and R. Gross Charities Ltd
N. and R. Grunbaum Charitable Trust
The Bishop of Guildford's Foundation
Guildry Incorporation of Perth
The Walter Guinness Charitable Trust
The Gunter Charitable Trust
The Gur Trust
Dr Guthrie's Association
H. C. D. Memorial Fund
H. P. Charitable Trust
Hackney Parochial Charities
The Hadfield Charitable Trust
The Hadley Trust
Hadras Kodesh Trust
The Hadrian Trust
The Alfred Haines Charitable Trust
The Haley Family Charitable Trust
Hamamelis Trust
Paul Hamlyn Foundation
The Helen Hamlyn Trust
Hammersmith United Charities*
Hampshire and Isle of Wight Community Foundation
Hampton Fuel Allotment Charity
The W. A. Handley Charity Trust
The Kathleen Hannay Memorial Charity
The Happold Foundation*
The Haramead Trust
Harbinson Charitable Trust
Harbo Charities Ltd
The Harbour Charitable Trust
The Harbour Foundation
The Harding Trust
William Harding's Charity
The Harebell Centenary Fund
The Peter and Teresa Harris Charitable Trust
The Harris Family Charitable Trust
The Edith Lilian Harrison 2000 Foundation
The Harrison-Frank Family Foundation (UK) Ltd
The Hartley Charitable Trust
The Alfred And Peggy Harvey Charitable Trust
The Hasluck Charitable Trust
The Hathaway Trust
The Maurice Hatter Foundation
The Hawthorne Charitable Trust
The Charles Hayward Foundation
HC Foundation*
The Headley Trust
May Hearnshaw Charitable Trust (May Hearnshaw's Charity)
Heart of England Community Foundation
Heart Research UK
The Heathcoat Trust
Heathrow Community Fund (LHR Airport Communities Trust)
The Heathside Charitable Trust
Heb Ffin (Without Frontier)*
The Charlotte Heber-Percy Charitable Trust
Ernest Hecht Charitable Foundation
The Percy Hedley 1990 Charitable Trust
Hedley Foundation Ltd (The Hedley Foundation)
The Michael Heller Charitable Foundation
The Simon Heller Charitable Settlement
Help for Health
Help the Homeless Ltd
The Helping Foundation
The Hemby Charitable Trust
Henderson Firstfruits*
The Christina Mary Hendrie Trust for Scottish and Canadian Charities
Henley Educational Trust
Philip Henman Trust
The G. D. Herbert Charitable Trust
Herefordshire Community Foundation
The Herefordshire Historic Churches Trust
Hertfordshire Community Foundation
The Hesslewood Children's Trust (Hull Seamen's and General Orphanage)
P. and C. Hickinbotham Charitable Trust
The Alan Edward Higgs Charity
Highcroft Charitable Trust
The Hilden Charitable Fund
The Derek Hill Foundation
M. V. Hillhouse Trust*
The Hillier Trust
The Hillingdon Community Trust
R. G. Hills Charitable Trust
Hinchley Charitable Trust
The Hinduja Foundation
The Hinrichsen Foundation
The Hintze Family Charity Foundation
The Hiscox Foundation
The Henry C. Hoare Charitable Trust
The Hobson Charity Ltd
Hockerill Educational Foundation
The Jane Hodge Foundation
The Holden Charitable Trust

The King/Cullimore Charitable Trust
The Mary Kinross Charitable Trust
Laura Kinsella Foundation
The Graham Kirkham Foundation*
Kirkley Poor's Land Estate
The Richard Kirkman Trust
The Kirschel Foundation
Robert Kitchin (Saddlers' Company)
The Ernest Kleinwort Charitable Trust
The Kobler Trust
The Kohn Foundation
Kollel and Co. Ltd
The KPMG Foundation
Kreditor Charitable Trust
The Kreitman Foundation
The Neil Kreitman Foundation
Kupath Gemach Chaim Bechesed Viznitz Trust
Kusuma Trust UK
The Kyte Charitable Trust
Ladbrokes in the Community Charitable Trust
The K. P. Ladd Charitable Trust
John Laing Charitable Trust
Christopher Laing Foundation
The David Laing Foundation
The Leonard Laity Stoate Charitable Trust
The Lambert Charitable Trust
Community Foundations for Lancashire and Merseyside
The Lancashire Foundation*
Duchy of Lancaster Benevolent Fund
Lancaster Foundation
The Jack Lane Charitable Trust
The Allen Lane Foundation
Langdale Trust
The LankellyChase Foundation
The R. J. Larg Family Charitable Trust
Largsmount Ltd
Laslett's (Hinton) Charity
The Lauffer Family Charitable Foundation
Mrs F. B. Laurence Charitable Trust
The Kathleen Laurence Trust
The Law Society Charity
The Edgar E. Lawley Foundation
The Herd Lawson and Muriel Lawson Charitable Trust
Lawson Beckman Charitable Trust
The Raymond and Blanche Lawson Charitable Trust
The David Lean Foundation
The Leathersellers' Company Charitable Fund
The Arnold Lee Charitable Trust
The William Leech Charity
Leeds Community Foundation (LCF)
The Legal Education Foundation*
Leicestershire and Rutland Masonic Charity Association*
Leicestershire, Leicester and Rutland Community Foundation
The Kennedy Leigh Charitable Trust
The Leigh Trust
P. Leigh-Bramwell Trust 'E'
Leng Charitable Trust*
The Lennox Hannay Charitable Trust
The Mark Leonard Trust
The Lethendy Charitable Trust*
The Leverhulme Trade Charities Trust
The Leverhulme Trust
Bernard Lewis Family Charitable Trust*
David and Ruth Lewis Family Charitable Trust
The John Spedan Lewis Foundation
The Sir Edward Lewis Foundation
John Lewis Partnership General Community Fund
Liberum Foundation
The Lidbury Family Trust*
Life Changes Trust*
The Light Fund Company*
The Limbourne Trust
Limoges Charitable Trust
The Linbury Trust
Lincolnshire Community Foundation
The Lind Trust
Lindale Educational Foundation
The Linden Charitable Trust
The Enid Linder Foundation
The Lindley Foundation (TLF)
The Ruth and Stuart Lipton Charitable Trust
The Lister Charitable Trust
The Frank Litchfield Charitable Trust
Littlefield Foundation (UK) Ltd
The Charles Littlewood Hill Trust
The Second Joseph Aaron Littman Foundation
The George John and Sheilah Livanos Charitable Trust
Liverpool Charity and Voluntary Services (LCVS)
Jack Livingstone Charitable Trust
The Ian and Natalie Livingstone Charitable Trust
The Elaine and Angus Lloyd Charitable Trust
The W. M. and B. W. Lloyd Trust*
The Andrew Lloyd Webber Foundation
Lloyd's Charities Trust
Lloyds Bank Foundation for England and Wales
Lloyds Bank Foundation for the Channel Islands
Lloyds TSB Foundation for Scotland
Localtrent Ltd
The Locker Foundation
The Lockwood Charitable Foundation*
Loftus Charitable Trust
The Lolev Charitable Trust
The Joyce Lomax Bullock Charitable Trust
Trust for London
London Catalyst
The London Community Foundation (LCF)
London Housing Foundation Ltd (LHF)
London Legal Support Trust (LLST)
Inner London Magistrates Court's Poor Box and Feeder Charity
The William and Katherine Longman Trust
The Loseley and Guildway Charitable Trust
Michael Lowe's and Associated Charities*
The Lower Green Foundation
The C. L. Loyd Charitable Trust
LPW Ltd
Robert Luff Foundation Ltd
The Henry Lumley Charitable Trust
Paul Lunn-Rockliffe Charitable Trust
C. F. Lunoe Trust Fund
Lord and Lady Lurgan Trust
The Lyndhurst Trust
The Lynn Foundation
John Lyon's Charity
The Sir Jack Lyons Charitable Trust
Sylvanus Lysons Charity
M. and C. Trust
M. B. Foundation*
The M. K. Charitable Trust
The M. Y. A. Charitable Trust
The Madeline Mabey Trust
The E. M. MacAndrew Trust
The R. S. Macdonald Charitable Trust

The James Neill Trust Fund
Nemoral Ltd
Nesswall Ltd
*Nesta**
Network for Social Change Charitable Trust
Newby Trust Ltd
The Newcomen Collett Foundation
Newpier Charity Ltd
Alderman Newton's Educational Foundation
NJD Charitable Trust
Alice Noakes Memorial Charitable Trust
Norfolk Community Foundation
Educational Foundation of Alderman John Norman
The Norman Family Charitable Trust
Normanby Charitable Trust
*North London Charities Ltd**
*Provincial Grand Charity of Northamptonshire and Huntingdonshire**
Northamptonshire Community Foundation
The Community Foundation for Northern Ireland
The Northmoor Trust
The Northumberland Village Homes Trust
*The Northwick Trust**
Northwood Charitable Trust
The Norton Foundation
Norwich Town Close Estate Charity
Nottinghamshire Community Foundation
The Nottinghamshire Historic Churches Trust
The Nuffield Foundation
The Father O'Mahoney Memorial Trust
The Sir Peter O'Sullevan Charitable Trust
The Oakdale Trust
The Oakley Charitable Trust
Odin Charitable Trust
The Ofenheim Charitable Trust
The Ogle Christian Trust
Oizer Charitable Trust
Old Possum's Practical Trust
The Olga Charitable Trust
*The Onaway Trust**
*One Community Foundation Ltd**
OneFamily Foundation
Open Gate
The Ormsby Charitable Trust
The O'Sullivan Family Charitable Trust
The Ouseley Church Music Trust
The Owen Family Trust
Oxfam (GB)
Oxfordshire Community Foundation
P. F. Charitable Trust
The Doris Pacey Charitable Foundation
*The Paddington Charitable Estate Educational Fund**
The Paget Charitable Trust
*Palmtree Memorial Trust**
The Panacea Charitable Trust
The Paphitis Charitable Trust
*Parabola Foundation**
The Paragon Trust
*The Pargiter Trust**
*Parish Estate of the Church of St Michael Spurriergate York**
The Park House Charitable Trust
The Patrick Trust
The Jack Patston Charitable Trust
Peacock Charitable Trust
Susanna Peake Charitable Trust
The Pears Family Charitable Foundation
The Dowager Countess Eleanor Peel Trust
The Pell Charitable Trust
The Pen Shell Project
The Pennycress Trust
People's Health Trust
People's Postcode Trust
The Performing Right Society Foundation
B. E. Perl Charitable Trust
Personal Assurance Charitable Trust
The Persson Charitable Trust
The Persula Foundation
The Jack Petchey Foundation
Petplan Charitable Trust
The Pharsalia Charitable Trust
The Phillips and Rubens Charitable Trust
The Phillips Charitable Trust
The Phillips Family Charitable Trust
The Pilgrim Trust
Pilkington Charities Fund
The Austin and Hope Pilkington Trust
Miss A. M. Pilkington's Charitable Trust
*Pink Ribbon Foundation**
The DLA Piper Charitable Trust
Polden-Puckham Charitable Foundation
*The Polehampton Charity**
The George and Esme Pollitzer Charitable Settlement
The Polonsky Foundation
Edith and Ferdinand Porjes Charitable Trust
The Porta Pia 2012 Foundation
The Portrack Charitable Trust
The J. E. Posnansky Charitable Trust
*Postcode Community Trust**
The Mary Potter Convent Hospital Trust
David and Elaine Potter Foundation
*Powys Welsh Church Fund**
Premishlaner Charitable Trust
Sir John Priestman Charity Trust
The Primrose Trust
The Prince of Wales's Charitable Foundation
*The Prince Philip Trust Fund**
The Princess Anne's Charities
The Privy Purse Charitable Trust
*The Professional Footballers' Association Charity**
The Puebla Charitable Trust
The Puri Foundation
*The Pye Foundation**
Mr and Mrs J. A. Pye's Charitable Settlement
*QBE European Operations Foundation**
Quartet Community Foundation
The Queen Anne's Gate Foundation
The Queen's Trust
*Quercus Foundation**
Quothquan Trust
R. S. Charitable Trust
The Monica Rabagliati Charitable Trust
Rachel Charitable Trust
The Racing Foundation
Richard Radcliffe Trust
The Radcliffe Trust
The Bishop Radford Trust
The Rainford Trust
The Rambourg Foundation
*The Edward Ramsden Charitable Trust**
The Joseph and Lena Randall Charitable Trust
The Joseph Rank Trust
The Ranworth Trust
Rashbass Family Trust
The Ratcliff Foundation
The Eleanor Rathbone Charitable Trust
Elizabeth Rathbone Charity
The Sigrid Rausing Trust
The Ravensdale Trust
The Roger Raymond Charitable Trust
The Rayne Trust
The John Rayner Charitable Trust
The Sir James Reckitt Charity

C. A. Redfern Charitable Foundation
Reed Family Foundation
Richard Reeve's Foundation
The Rest Harrow Trust
Reuben Foundation
The Rhododendron Trust
Riada Trust*
Daisie Rich Trust
The Clive and Sylvia Richards Charity Ltd
Richmond Parish Lands Charity
Ridgesave Ltd
Rigby Foundation*
The Sir John Ritblat Family Foundation
The River Farm Foundation
The River Trust
Rivers Foundation
Riverside Charitable Trust Ltd*
The Rix-Thompson-Rothenberg Foundation
RJM Charity Trust
Thomas Roberts Trust
Robyn Charitable Trust
The Roddick Foundation
The Rofeh Trust
The Richard Rogers Charitable Settlement
Rokach Family Charitable Trust
The Sir James Roll Charitable Trust
The Helen Roll Charity
Mrs L. D. Rope's Second Charitable Settlement*
Mrs L. D. Rope's Third Charitable Settlement
Rosca Trust
The Cissie Rosefield Charitable Trust*
The Cecil Rosen Foundation
Rosetrees Trust
The David Ross Foundation*
The Rothermere Foundation
Rothschild Foundation (Hanadiv) Europe*
The Roughley Charitable Trust
Mrs Gladys Row Fogo Charitable Trust
Rowanville Ltd
The Rowlands Trust
The Joseph Rowntree Charitable Trust
The Joseph Rowntree Foundation
Royal Artillery Charitable Fund
The Royal British Legion
Royal Docks Trust (London)
The Royal Navy And Royal Marines Charity*
Royal Victoria Hall Foundation
Rozelle Trust*
The Rubin Foundation Charitable Trust
Rugby Football Foundation
The RVW Trust
The J. S. and E. C. Rymer Charitable Trust
S. F. Foundation
The Michael and Nicola Sacher Charitable Trust
The Michael Sacher Charitable Trust
The Dr Mortimer and Theresa Sackler Foundation
The Sackler Trust
The Ruzin Sadagora Trust
The Saddlers' Company Charitable Fund
The Saga Charitable Trust
The Jean Sainsbury Animal Welfare Trust
The Alan and Babette Sainsbury Charitable Fund
The Sainsbury Family Charitable Trusts
Saint Sarkis Charity Trust
The Saintbury Trust
The Saints and Sinners Trust Ltd
The Salamander Charitable Trust
The Salisbury New Pool Settlement*
Salters' Charitable Foundation
The Andrew Salvesen Charitable Trust
Samjo Ltd*
Coral Samuel Charitable Trust
The Basil Samuel Charitable Trust
The M. J. Samuel Charitable Trust
The Samworth Foundation
The Sandhu Charitable Foundation
The Sandra Charitable Trust
The Sands Family Trust
Santander UK Foundation Ltd
The Sants Charitable Trust
Sarum St Michael Educational Charity*
The Save the Children Fund*
The Scarfe Charitable Trust
The Schapira Charitable Trust
The Annie Schiff Charitable Trust
The Schmidt-Bodner Charitable Trust
The Schreib Trust
O. and G. Schreiber Charitable Trust
The Schreiber Charitable Trust
Schroder Charity Trust
The Schroder Foundation
Foundation Scotland
The Scotshill Trust
Scott (Eredine) Charitable Trust
The Francis C. Scott Charitable Trust
The Frieda Scott Charitable Trust
Sir Samuel Scott of Yews Trust
The John Scott Trust Fund*
The ScottishPower Foundation
The Scouloudi Foundation
The SDL Foundation
Seafarers Hospital Society
Seafarers UK (King George's Fund for Sailors)
The Searchlight Electric Charitable Trust
Sam and Bella Sebba Charitable Trust
The Seedfield Trust
Leslie Sell Charitable Trust
The Sellafield Charity Trust Fund*
Sellata Ltd
SEM Charitable Trust
The Seven Fifty Trust
The Severn Trent Water Charitable Trust Fund
The Cyril Shack Trust
The Jean Shanks Foundation
The Shanly Foundation
The Shanti Charitable Trust
ShareGift (The Orr Mackintosh Foundation)
The Linley Shaw Foundation
The Shears Foundation
The Sheepdrove Trust
The Sheffield Town Trust
The Sheldon Trust
The Patricia and Donald Shepherd Charitable Trust
The Sylvia and Colin Shepherd Charitable Trust
Sherburn House Charity*
Sherling Charitable Trust*
The Archie Sherman Cardiff Foundation
The Archie Sherman Charitable Trust
The Shetland Charitable Trust
SHINE (Support and Help in Education)
The Bassil Shippam and Alsford Trust
The Shipwrights' Company Charitable Fund
The Shirley Foundation
Shlomo Memorial Fund Ltd
The Shoe Zone Trust
The Shropshire Historic Churches Trust*
Shulem B. Association Ltd*
The Florence Shute Millennium Trust*
David and Jennifer Sieff Charitable Trust
Silver Family Charitable Trust
The Simmons & Simmons Charitable Foundation

The Huntly and Margery Sinclair Charitable Trust
SITA Cornwall Trust Ltd
The Skelton Bounty
*The Skerritt Trust**
The Charles Skey Charitable Trust
Skipton Building Society Charitable Foundation
The John Slater Foundation
The Slaughter and May Charitable Trust
Rita and David Slowe Charitable Trust
Ruth Smart Foundation
The SMB Trust
The Mrs Smith and Mount Trust
The DS Smith Charitable Foundation
The N. Smith Charitable Settlement
The Smith Charitable Trust
The Henry Smith Charity
The Leslie Smith Foundation
*The Martin Smith Foundation**
The WH Smith Group Charitable Trust
The Stanley Smith UK Horticultural Trust
Philip Smith's Charitable Trust
The R. C. Snelling Charitable Trust
The Sobell Foundation
Social Business Trust
*Social Investment Business Foundation**
Sodexo Stop Hunger Foundation
*Sofronie Foundation**
Solev Co. Ltd
The Solo Charitable Settlement
David Solomons Charitable Trust
*Somerset Community Foundation**
Songdale Ltd
The E. C. Sosnow Charitable Trust
The Souter Charitable Trust
The South Square Trust
The W. F. Southall Trust
R. H. Southern Trust
The Southover Manor General Education Trust
*The Spalding Trust**
Spar Charitable Fund
Sparks Charity (Sport Aiding Medical Research for Kids)
Sparquote Ltd
Spears-Stutz Charitable Trust
The Worshipful Company of Spectacle Makers' Charity
The Jessie Spencer Trust
The Spielman Charitable Trust
The Spoore, Merry and Rixman Foundation
Rosalyn and Nicholas Springer Charitable Trust
Springrule Ltd
The Spurrell Charitable Trust
The Geoff and Fiona Squire Foundation
The Squires Foundation
The St Hilda's Trust
The St James's Trust Settlement
Sir Walter St John's Educational Charity
St Luke's College Foundation
St Monica Trust
St Olave's and St Saviour's Schools Foundation – Foundation Fund
St Peter's Saltley Trust
The Stafford Trust
*Staffordshire Community Foundation**
*Standard Life Foundation**
*The Stanley Charitable Trust**
The Stanley Foundation Ltd
The Staples Trust
The Peter Stebbings Memorial Charity
The Steel Charitable Trust
The Steinberg Family Charitable Trust
The Hugh Stenhouse Foundation
C. E. K. Stern Charitable Trust
The Sigmund Sternberg Charitable Foundation
Stervon Ltd
The Stevenage Community Trust
Stevenson Family's Charitable Trust
The Stewards' Charitable Trust
The Andy Stewart Charitable Foundation
Sir Halley Stewart Trust
The Stewarts Law Foundation
The Stobart Newlands Charitable Trust
The Stoller Charitable Trust
M. J. C. Stone Charitable Trust
The Stone Family Foundation
*The Stoneygate Trust**
The Samuel Storey Family Charitable Trust
Peter Stormonth Darling Charitable Trust
Peter Storrs Trust
The Strangward Trust
Stratford upon Avon Town Trust
The Strawberry Charitable Trust
The W. O. Street Charitable Foundation
*The Street Foundation**
The Sudborough Foundation
Sueberry Ltd
Suffolk Community Foundation
The Suffolk Historic Churches Trust
The Alan Sugar Foundation
The Summerfield Charitable Trust
The Bernard Sunley Charitable Foundation
*Sunninghill Fuel Allotment Trust**
*Support Adoption For Pets**
*Surgo Foundation UK Ltd**
Community Foundation for Surrey
The Sussex Community Foundation
The Adrienne and Leslie Sussman Charitable Trust
The Sutasoma Trust
Sutton Coldfield Charitable Trust
Swan Mountain Trust
The Swann-Morton Foundation
The John Swire (1989) Charitable Trust
The Adrian Swire Charitable Trust
The Swire Charitable Trust
The Hugh and Ruby Sykes Charitable Trust
The Charles and Elsie Sykes Trust
Sylvia Waddilove Foundation UK
T. and S. Trust Fund
Tabeel Trust
The Tajtelbaum Charitable Trust
The Talbot Trusts
The Talbot Village Trust
Tallow Chandlers Benevolent Fund No. 2
*The Talmud Torah Machzikei Hadass Trust**
Talteg Ltd
The Lady Tangye Charitable Trust Ltd
The David Tannen Charitable Trust
The Tanner Trust
The Lili Tapper Charitable Foundation
The Taurus Foundation
The Tay Charitable Trust
C. B. and H. H. Taylor 1984 Trust
Humphrey Richardson Taylor Charitable Trust
The Connie and Albert Taylor Charitable Trust
The Taylor Family Foundation
Tearfund
*Khoo Teck Puat UK Foundation**

The Tedworth Charitable Trust
Tees Valley Community Foundation
Tegham Ltd
The Templeton Goodwill Trust
The Tennis Foundation
*Tenovus Scotland**
The C. Paul Thackray General Charitable Trust
The Thales Charitable Trust
The Thistle Trust
The David Thomas Charitable Trust
*DM Thomas Foundation for Young People**
The Arthur and Margaret Thompson Charitable Trust
The Thompson Family Charitable Trust
The Sir Jules Thorn Charitable Trust
The Thornton Foundation
The Thornton Trust
The Thousandth Man- Richard Burns Charitable Trust
The Three Guineas Trust
The Three Oaks Trust
The Thriplow Charitable Trust
The John Raymond Tijou Charitable Trust
Tilney Charitable Trust
Mrs R. P. Tindall's Charitable Trust
The Tinsley Foundation
The Tisbury Telegraph Trust
The Tobacco Pipe Makers and Tobacco Trade Benevolent Fund
The Tolkien Trust
The Tompkins Foundation
Toras Chesed (London) Trust
The Tory Family Foundation
Tottenham Grammar School Foundation
The Tower Hill Trust
The Toy Trust
The Toye Foundation
Toyota Manufacturing UK Charitable Trust
*The Trades House of Glasgow**
Annie Tranmer Charitable Trust
The Constance Travis Charitable Trust
The Treeside Trust
The Trefoil Trust
The Triangle Trust (1949) Fund
*Tropical Health and Education Trust**
The True Colours Trust
Truedene Co. Ltd
The Truemark Trust
Truemart Ltd
Trumros Ltd
The Trusthouse Charitable Foundation
*The Trysil Charitable Trust**
The James Tudor Foundation
The Tudor Trust
The Tufton Charitable Trust
The Tuixen Foundation
The Roger and Douglas Turner Charitable Trust
The Florence Turner Trust
The G. J. W. Turner Trust
The Turtleton Charitable Trust
TVML Foundation
Two Ridings Community Foundation
Community Foundation serving Tyne and Wear and Northumberland
Tzedakah
The Udlington Trust
*UKH Foundation**
Ulster Garden Villages Ltd
Ulting Overseas Trust
The Ulverscroft Foundation
The Underwood Trust
The Union of Orthodox Hebrew Congregations
United Utilities Trust Fund
UnLtd (Foundation for Social Entrepreneurs)
The Michael Uren Foundation
The David Uri Memorial Trust
*The Utley Family Charitable Trust**
The Vail Foundation
The Valentine Charitable Trust
The Valiant Charitable Trust
The Albert Van Den Bergh Charitable Trust
The Van Neste Foundation
Mrs Maud Van Norden's Charitable Foundation
The Vandervell Foundation
The Vardy Foundation
Variety The Children's Charity (Variety Club)
The William and Patricia Venton Charitable Trust
*The Veolia Environmental Trust**
Roger Vere Foundation
The Nigel Vinson Charitable Trust
The Vintners' Foundation
Virgin Atlantic Foundation
The Virgin Foundation (Virgin Unite)
The Virgin Money Foundation
*Viridor Credits Environmental Company**
Vivdale Ltd
The Vodafone Foundation
Volant Charitable Trust
Voluntary Action Fund (VAF)
Wade's Charity
The Scurrah Wainwright Charity
*The Bruce Wake Charity**
The Wakefield and Tetley Trust
*The Wakefield Trust**
The Wakeham Trust
The Walcot Foundation
The Community Foundation in Wales
Wales Council for Voluntary Action
Robert and Felicity Waley-Cohen Charitable Trust
The Walker Trust
*Walton Foundation**
Walton on Thames Charity
Sir Siegmund Warburg's Voluntary Settlement
The Ward Blenkinsop Trust
The Barbara Ward Children's Foundation
*Mrs N. E. M. Warren's Charitable Trust**
*The Warrington Church of England Educational Trust**
*Warwick Relief in Need Charity**
*The Warwickshire Masonic Charitable Association Ltd**
Mrs Waterhouse Charitable Trust
The Waterloo Foundation
G. R. Waters Charitable Trust 2000
Wates Family Enterprise Trust
The Wates Foundation
*The Geoffrey Watling Charity**
Blyth Watson Charitable Trust
*The Watson Family Charitable Trust**
John Watson's Trust
Waynflete Charitable Trust
The Weavers' Company Benevolent Fund
The David Webster Charitable Trust
The Weinstein Foundation
The Weinstock Fund
The James Weir Foundation
The Wellcome Trust
The Welton Foundation
The Wessex Youth Trust
West Derby Waste Lands Charity
*The West Looe Town Trust**
The Westcroft Trust
The Westfield Health Charitable Trust
*The Westminster Amalgamated Charity**
The Westminster Foundation
The Garfield Weston Foundation
Westway Trust
The Barbara Whatmore Charitable Trust
*The Wheeler Family Charitable Trust**
The Whitaker Charitable Trust

Colonel W. H. Whitbread Charitable Trust
The Melanie White Foundation Ltd
White Stuff Foundation
The Whitecourt Charitable Trust
The Norman Whiteley Trust
The Whitewater Charitable Trust
The Whitley Animal Protection Trust
*The Wigoder Family Foundation**
The Lionel Wigram Memorial Trust
The Felicity Wilde Charitable Trust
The Will Charitable Trust
The Kay Williams Charitable Foundation
*The Alfred Williams Charitable Trust**
The Williams Charitable Trust
The Williams Family Charitable Trust
Williams Serendipity Trust
*The Willmott Dixon Foundation**
The HDH Wills 1965 Charitable Trust
Dame Violet Wills Charitable Trust
The Dame Violet Wills Will Trust
The Wilmcote Charitrust
*Brian Wilson Charitable Trust**
Sumner Wilson Charitable Trust
The Wilson Foundation
J. and J. R. Wilson Trust
Wiltshire Community Foundation
*The Wimbledon Foundation**
The W. Wing Yip and Brothers Foundation
The Harold Hyam Wingate Foundation
The Francis Winham Foundation
Winton Philanthropies
The Witzenfeld Foundation
The Michael and Anna Wix Charitable Trust
The Wixamtree Trust
The Maurice Wohl Charitable Foundation
The Charles Wolfson Charitable Trust
The James Wood Bequest Fund
The Wood Foundation
Wooden Spoon Society
The F. Glenister Woodger Trust
Woodlands Green Ltd
Woodroffe Benton Foundation
*The Woodstock Family Charitable Foundation**
The A. and R. Woolf Charitable Trust
Worcester Municipal Charities (CIO)
*The Worwin UK Foundation**
The Diana Edgson Wright Charitable Trust
Wychdale Ltd
Wychville Ltd
*The Wyfold Charitable Trust**
The Wyndham Charitable Trust
The Wyseliot Rose Charitable Trust
Yankov Charitable Trust
*York Children's Trust**
Yorkshire and Clydesdale Bank Foundation
Yorkshire Building Society Charitable Foundation
*Yorkshire Cancer Research**
The South Yorkshire Community Foundation
The William Allen Young Charitable Trust
The John Kirkhope Young Endowment Fund
Youth Music
The Z. Foundation
*Elizabeth and Prince Zaiger Trust**
Zephyr Charitable Trust
The Marjorie and Arnold Ziff Charitable Foundation
Stephen Zimmerman Charitable Trust
The Zochonis Charitable Trust

■ Salaries

ABF The Soldiers' Charity
The AIM Foundation
The Alchemy Foundation
The Anchor Foundation
Anglo American Group Foundation
The Ardwick Trust
The Ashley Family Foundation
The Aylesford Family Charitable Trust
*Bairdwatson Charitable Trust**
Lord Barnby's Foundation
BBC Children in Need
*The Becht Family Charitable Trust**
The Bedfordshire and Luton Community Foundation
The Berkshire Community Foundation
The Blagrave Trust
The Blandford Lake Trust
The Boshier-Hinton Foundation
The Breadsticks Foundation
The Breast Cancer Research Trust (BCRT)
The British Dietetic Association General and Education Trust Fund
British Heart Foundation (BHF)
British Record Industry Trust
The Charles Brotherton Trust
The E. F. Bulmer Benevolent Fund
The Clara E. Burgess Charity
The Cadbury Foundation
The Cambridgeshire Community Foundation
The Campden Charities Trustee
The Richard Carne Trust
The Castang Foundation
The Cattanach Charitable Trust
Church Urban Fund
The City Bridge Trust (Bridge House Estates)
J. A. Clark Charitable Trust
The Sir Jeremiah Colman Gift Trust
The Colt Foundation
The Ernest Cook Trust
*Credit Suisse EMEA Foundation**
Cripplegate Foundation
Cumbria Community Foundation
The Cunningham Trust
Roald Dahl's Marvellous Children's Charity
Baron Davenport's Charity
The Hamilton Davies Trust
Disability Aid Fund (The Roger and Jean Jefcoate Trust)
The Dischma Charitable Trust
Dorset Community Foundation
The Drapers' Charitable Fund
The Dunhill Medical Trust
County Durham Community Foundation
The John Ellerman Foundation
Epilepsy Research UK
Essex Community Foundation
The Essex Youth Trust
The Eveson Charitable Trust
The Expat Foundation
Esmée Fairbairn Foundation
Ford Britain Trust
Donald Forrester Trust
The Foyle Foundation
The Gannochy Trust
The Garrick Charitable Trust
*Genetic Disorders UK**
The Girdlers' Company Charitable Trust
The Glass-House Trust
The Goldsmiths' Company Charity
The Golsoncott Foundation
The Greggs Foundation
The Hadfield Charitable Trust
The Hadley Trust
The Hadrian Trust

Halifax Foundation for Northern Ireland (previously known as Lloyds Bank Foundation for Northern Ireland)
Paul Hamlyn Foundation
Hampshire and Isle of Wight Community Foundation
William Harding's Charity
The Harebell Centenary Fund
The Harpur Trust
The Peter Harrison Foundation
The Hasluck Charitable Trust
May Hearnshaw Charitable Trust (May Hearnshaw's Charity)
Heart of England Community Foundation
Heart Research UK
The Percy Hedley 1990 Charitable Trust
The Helping Foundation
Herefordshire Community Foundation
P. and C. Hickinbotham Charitable Trust
The Alan Edward Higgs Charity
The Hilden Charitable Fund
The Hintze Family Charity Foundation
The Edward Holt Trust
The Holywood Trust
Sir Harold Hood's Charitable Trust
Hopmarket Charity
The Worshipful Company of Horners' Charitable Trusts
The Hospital of God at Greatham
Miss Agnes H. Hunter's Trust
The Innocent Foundation
*Integrated Education Fund**
Irish Youth Foundation (UK) Ltd (incorporating The Lawlor Foundation)
The JRSST Charitable Trust
Nick Jenkins Foundation
The Elton John AIDS Foundation (EJAF)
The Jusaca Charitable Trust
The Boris Karloff Charitable Foundation
The Caron Keating Foundation
The Kelly Family Charitable Trust
William Kendall's Charity (Wax Chandlers' Company)
The Kennel Club Charitable Trust
The Mary Kinross Charitable Trust
The Sir James Knott Trust
The K. P. Ladd Charitable Trust
Community Foundations for Lancashire and Merseyside
LandAid Charitable Trust (Land Aid)
The Allen Lane Foundation
The R. J. Larg Family Charitable Trust
The Edgar E. Lawley Foundation
The Leathersellers' Company Charitable Fund
Leicestershire, Leicester and Rutland Community Foundation
The Leigh Trust
The Leverhulme Trust
The Sir Edward Lewis Foundation
Lincolnshire Community Foundation
Lloyds Bank Foundation for England and Wales
Lloyds Bank Foundation for the Channel Islands
*Lloyd's Register Foundation**
Lloyds TSB Foundation for Scotland
Trust for London
London Catalyst
The London Community Foundation (LCF)
London Legal Support Trust (LLST)
John Lyon's Charity
The R. S. Macdonald Charitable Trust
The MacRobert Trust
Man Group PLC Charitable Trust
The W. M. Mann Foundation
R. W. Mann Trust
The Marsh Christian Trust
John Martin's Charity
*Masonic Charitable Foundation**
The Nancie Massey Charitable Trust
The Mathew Trust
The Robert McAlpine Foundation
D. D. McPhail Charitable Settlement
*Medical Research Foundation**
The Mercers' Charitable Foundation
The Mickel Fund
The Gerald Micklem Charitable Trust
The Millfield House Foundation (1)
The Clare Milne Trust
The Edgar Milward Charity
John Moores Foundation
The Mugdock Children's Trust
*The National Gardens Scheme**
Network for Social Change Charitable Trust
The Frances and Augustus Newman Foundation
Norfolk Community Foundation
The Northmoor Trust
The Nuffield Foundation
People's Health Trust
People's Postcode Trust
The Pilgrim Trust
Pilkington Charities Fund
Polden-Puckham Charitable Foundation
The Princess Anne's Charities
*Prostate Cancer UK**
The Racing Foundation
The Rainford Trust
The Joseph Rank Trust
The Rayne Foundation
The Rayne Trust
The Rhododendron Trust
The Rix-Thompson-Rothenberg Foundation
The Robertson Trust
The Roddick Foundation
Mrs L. D. Rope's Third Charitable Settlement
*Rothschild Foundation (Hanadiv) Europe**
The Joseph Rowntree Charitable Trust
The Royal British Legion
The Saddlers' Company Charitable Fund
The Saintbury Trust
Santander UK Foundation Ltd
The Francis C. Scott Charitable Trust
The Frieda Scott Charitable Trust
The ScottishPower Energy People Trust
Seafarers UK (King George's Fund for Sailors)
The Shanly Foundation
The Sheldon Trust
SHINE (Support and Help in Education)
The Shirley Foundation
The Mrs Smith and Mount Trust
The Henry Smith Charity
The R. C. Snelling Charitable Trust
Social Business Trust
R. H. Southern Trust
Sparks Charity (Sport Aiding Medical Research for Kids)
St James's Place Foundation
Sir Walter St John's Educational Charity
The Steel Charitable Trust
Sir Halley Stewart Trust
Stratford upon Avon Town Trust
Suffolk Community Foundation
The Sussex Community Foundation

The Swire Charitable Trust
The Connie and Albert Taylor Charitable Trust
The Thriplow Charitable Trust
Mrs R. P. Tindall's Charitable Trust
The Constance Travis Charitable Trust
The Triangle Trust (1949) Fund
The True Colours Trust
The Trusthouse Charitable Foundation
The James Tudor Foundation
The Tudor Trust
Two Ridings Community Foundation
United Utilities Trust Fund
Volant Charitable Trust
Voluntary Action Fund (VAF)
The Scurrah Wainwright Charity
The Wakefield and Tetley Trust
Sir Siegmund Warburg's Voluntary Settlement
The Barbara Ward Children's Foundation
The Waterloo Foundation
The Wates Foundation
Waynflete Charitable Trust
The Weinstock Fund
The Weir Charitable Trust*
The Westminster Foundation
The Garfield Weston Foundation
White Stuff Foundation
The Norman Whiteley Trust
The Whitley Animal Protection Trust
Dame Violet Wills Charitable Trust
Wiltshire Community Foundation
The Wixamtree Trust
The Wood Foundation
The Yapp Charitable Trust
The South Yorkshire Community Foundation
The John Kirkhope Young Endowment Fund
Youth Music

■ Strategic funding

The 1970 Trust
The 1989 Willan Charitable Trust
The 3Ts Charitable Trust*
4 Charity Foundation
The A. S. Charitable Trust
A. W. Charitable Trust
A2BD Foundation UK Ltd*
The Aberbrothock Skea Trust
Aberdeen Asset Management Charitable Foundation
The Aberdeen Foundation
ABF The Soldiers' Charity
The Neville Abraham Foundation*
The Acacia Charitable Trust
The Accenture Foundation
Achisomoch Aid Company Ltd
The ACT Foundation
Action Medical Research
The Sylvia Adams Charitable Trust
The Addleshaw Goddard Charitable Trust
Adenfirst Ltd
The Adint Charitable Trust
The AEB Charitable Trust*
AF Trust Company
Age Scotland
Age UK
Aid to the Church in Need (UK)
The Sylvia Aitken Charitable Trust
AKO Foundation*
The Alborada Trust
D. G. Albright Charitable Trust
The Alchemy Foundation
All Saints Educational Trust
Allchurches Trust Ltd
The Allen & Overy Foundation*
The H. B. Allen Charitable Trust
The Alliance Family Foundation
AM Charitable Trust
Amabrill Ltd
The Amalur Foundation Ltd
The Ammco Trust
Sir John and Lady Amory's Charitable Trust
Viscount Amory's Charitable Trust
The Ampelos Trust
The AMW Charitable Trust
The Andrew Anderson Trust
Andor Charitable Trust
The Mary Andrew Charitable Trust
Andrews Charitable Trust
Anglo American Group Foundation
Anguish's Educational Foundation
The Annandale Charitable Trust
The Anne Duchess of Westminster's Charity*
Anpride Ltd
The Anson Charitable Trust
AO Smile Foundation*
The Apax Foundation
The John Apthorp Charity
The Arah Foundation
The Arbib Foundation
The Archer Trust
The Architectural Heritage Fund
The Ardeola Charitable Trust
The Ardwick Trust
The Argus Appeal
The Armourers' and Brasiers' Gauntlet Trust
The Arsenal Foundation Ltd
The Artemis Charitable Trust
Arts Council England
Arts Council of Northern Ireland
Arts Council of Wales (also known as Cyngor Celfyddydau Cymru)
The Ove Arup Foundation
Ove Arup Partnership Charitable Trust
The Asda Foundation
The Asfari Foundation*
The Ashburnham Thanksgiving Trust
The Ashden Trust
The Ashley Family Foundation
The Ian Askew Charitable Trust
The Associated Board of the Royal Schools of Music*
Asthma UK
The Astor Foundation
The Aurelius Charitable Trust
Autonomous Research Charitable Trust (ARCT)
The Avon and Somerset Police Community Trust
Awards for All (see also the Big Lottery Fund)
The Aylesford Family Charitable Trust
The Harry Bacon Foundation
The Bagri Foundation
The Baird Trust
The Baker Charitable Trust
The Roy and Pixie Baker Charitable Trust
The Balcombe Charitable Trust
The Balfour Beatty Charitable Trust
The Ballinger Charitable Trust
The Baltic Charitable Fund
The Bamford Charitable Foundation
The Banbury Charities
The Band Trust
The Bank of Scotland Foundation
The Barbers' Company General Charities
The Barbour Foundation
Barchester Healthcare Foundation
The Barclay Foundation
The Barham Charitable Trust
The Baring Foundation
The Philip Barker Charity*
The Barker-Mill Foundation
Lord Barnby's Foundation
The Barnsbury Charitable Trust
The Barrack Charitable Trust*
Misses Barrie Charitable Trust
The Bartlett Taylor Charitable Trust

The Paul Bassham Charitable Trust
The Battens Charitable Trust
Bauer Radio's Cash for Kids Charities
Bay Charitable Trust
The Bay Tree Charitable Trust
The Louis Baylis (Maidenhead Advertiser) Charitable Trust
BBC Children in Need
BC Partners Foundation
Bear Mordechai Ltd
The Bearder Charity
The James Beattie Charitable Trust
Beauland Ltd
*The Becht Family Charitable Trust**
The Becker Family Charitable Trust
The John Beckwith Charitable Trust
The Bedfordshire and Luton Community Foundation
The David and Ruth Behrend Fund
*The Behrens Foundation**
The Bellahouston Bequest Fund
Belljoe Tzedoko Ltd
The Benham Charitable Settlement
*The Rowan Bentall Charitable Trust**
Bergqvist Charitable Trust
The Berkeley Charitable Foundation
The Ruth Berkowitz Charitable Trust
The Berkshire Community Foundation
The Bestway Foundation
The Big Lottery Fund (see also Awards for All)
The Billmeir Charitable Trust
The Bingham Trust
The Birmingham District Nursing Charitable Trust
Birmingham International Airport Community Trust Fund
The Lord Mayor of Birmingham's Charity
Birthday House Trust
Miss Jeanne Bisgood's Charitable Trust
The Michael Bishop Foundation
*Asser Bishvil Foundation**
The Sydney Black Charitable Trust
The Bertie Black Foundation
Isabel Blackman Foundation
The Blagrave Trust
The Blair Foundation
The Morgan Blake Charitable Trust
Blakemore Foundation
The Blandford Lake Trust
The Sir Victor Blank Charitable Settlement
Bloodwise
Bloom Foundation
The Bluston Charitable Settlement
The Boltini Trust
The Bonamy Charitable Trust
The Charlotte Bonham-Carter Charitable Trust
The Boodle & Dunthorne Charitable Trust
BOOST Charitable Trust
The Booth Charities
Salo Bordon Charitable Trust
The Bordon Liphook Haslemere Charity
*Sir William Boreman's Foundation**
*The Borrows Charitable Trust**
The Oliver Borthwick Memorial Trust
The Boshier-Hinton Foundation
The Bothwell Charitable Trust
The Harry Bottom Charitable Trust
P. G. and N. J. Boulton Trust
Sir Clive Bourne Family Trust
Bourneheights Ltd
The Bowerman Charitable Trust
The Bowland Charitable Trust
Friends of Boyan Trust
The Frank Brake Charitable Trust
The William Brake Charitable Trust
The Tony Bramall Charitable Trust
The Liz and Terry Bramall Foundation
The Bransford Trust
The Breadsticks Foundation
*The Brelms Trust CIO**
Bridgepoint Charitable Trust
Bristol Archdeaconry Charity
John Bristow and Thomas Mason Trust
The British and Foreign School Society
British Council for Prevention of Blindness (Save Eyes Everywhere)
The British Dietetic Association General and Education Trust Fund
British Gas (Scottish Gas) Energy Trust
British Heart Foundation (BHF)
British Humane Association
British Record Industry Trust
The J. and M. Britton Charitable Trust
The Bromley Trust
The Consuelo and Anthony Brooke Charitable Trust
The Rory and Elizabeth Brooks Foundation
Bill Brown 1989 Charitable Trust
R. S. Brownless Charitable Trust
The T. B. H. Brunner's Charitable Settlement
The Bruntwood Charity
Brushmill Ltd
Buckingham Trust
The E. F. Bulmer Benevolent Fund
BUPA UK Foundation
*The Burberry Foundation**
The Burden Trust
The Burdett Trust for Nursing
The Clara E. Burgess Charity
The Burry Charitable Trust
The Arnold Burton 1998 Charitable Trust
Consolidated Charity of Burton upon Trent
The Derek Butler Trust
*The Butters Foundation (UK) Ltd**
The Noel Buxton Trust
The Christopher Cadbury Charitable Trust
The G. W. Cadbury Charitable Trust
The William A. Cadbury Charitable Trust
The Cadbury Foundation
The Barrow Cadbury Trust
The Edward and Dorothy Cadbury Trust
The George Cadbury Trust
The Cadogan Charity
CAFOD (Catholic Agency for Overseas Development)
Community Foundation for Calderdale
Callander Charitable Trust
Calleva Foundation
Calouste Gulbenkian Foundation – UK Branch
The Cambridgeshire Community Foundation
The Ellis Campbell Charitable Foundation
The Campden Charities Trustee
*Canary Wharf Contractors Fund**
Cardy Beaver Foundation
*The W. A. Cargill Charitable Trust**
David William Traill Cargill Fund
The Richard Carne Trust

The Carnegie Dunfermline Trust
The Carnegie Trust for the Universities of Scotland
The Carpenters' Company Charitable Trust
The Carr-Gregory Trust
The Carrington Charitable Trust
The Leslie Mary Carter Charitable Trust
The Casey Trust
Sir John Cass's Foundation
*Sir Ernest Cassel Educational Trust**
The Elizabeth Casson Trust
*The Castansa Trust**
The Catholic Charitable Trust
The Catholic Trust for England and Wales
The Joseph and Annie Cattle Trust
The Thomas Sivewright Catto Charitable Settlement
The Wilfrid and Constance Cave Foundation
The Cayo Foundation
Elizabeth Cayzer Charitable Trust
The B. G. S. Cayzer Charitable Trust
The Cazenove Charitable Trust
The CBD Charitable Trust
CBRE UK Charitable Trust
Celtic Charity Fund
The CH (1980) Charitable Trust
The Amelia Chadwick Trust
Chalfords Ltd
The Chapman Charitable Trust
The Charter 600 Charity
Chartered Accountants' Livery Charity (CALC)
The Cheruby Trust
*Cheshire Community Foundation Ltd**
Cheshire Freemason's Charity
Chesterhill Charitable Trust
The Childwick Trust
CHK Charities Ltd
The Chownes Foundation
Christadelphian Samaritan Fund
Christian Aid
Chrysalis Trust
Church Burgesses Trust
Church Urban Fund
The CIBC World Markets Children's Miracle Foundation
The City Bridge Trust (Bridge House Estates)
The City Educational Trust Fund
*The Clan Trust Ltd**
Stephen Clark 1957 Charitable Trust
J. A. Clark Charitable Trust
The Hilda and Alice Clark Charitable Trust
The Roger and Sarah Bancroft Clark Charitable Trust
*The Clark Foundation**
The Cleopatra Trust
The Clore Duffield Foundation
Richard Cloudesley's Charity
The Clover Trust
The Robert Clutterbuck Charitable Trust
The Coalfields Regeneration Trust
The John Coates Charitable Trust
The Cobalt Trust
The Cobtree Charity Trust Ltd
The Denise Cohen Charitable Trust
The Vivienne and Samuel Cohen Charitable Trust
The John S. Cohen Foundation
The R. and S. Cohen Foundation
John Coldman Charitable Trust
The Colefax Charitable Trust
John and Freda Coleman Charitable Trust
The Sir Jeremiah Colman Gift Trust
Col-Reno Ltd
The Colt Foundation
The Coltstaple Trust
Colwinston Charitable Trust
Colyer-Fergusson Charitable Trust
Community First (Landfill Communities Fund)
The Douglas Compton James Charitable Trust
Martin Connell Charitable Trust
*The Thomas Cook Chidlren's Charity**
The Ernest Cook Trust
The Cooks Charity
The Catherine Cookson Charitable Trust
The Keith Coombs Trust
Mabel Cooper Charity
The Alice Ellen Cooper Dean Charitable Foundation
The Marjorie Coote Animal Charity Trust
The Marjorie Coote Old People's Charity
The J. Reginald Corah Foundation Fund
The Worshipful Company of Cordwainers Charitable Trusts (Minges Gift and the Pooled Trusts)
The Gershon Coren Charitable Foundation (also known as The Muriel and Gus Coren Charitable Foundation)
Cornwall Community Foundation
The Duke of Cornwall's Benevolent Fund
The Cornwell Charitable Trust
*The Corporation of Trinity House of Deptford Strond**
The Costa Family Charitable Trust
The Cotton Industry War Memorial Trust
*The Coulthurst Trust**
The County Council of Dyfed Welsh Curch Fund
The Augustine Courtauld Trust
Coutts Charitable Foundation
General Charity of Coventry
Coventry Building Society Charitable Foundation
The John Cowan Foundation
The Sir Tom Cowie Charitable Trust
Dudley and Geoffrey Cox Charitable Trust
The Craignish Trust
The Craps Charitable Trust
The Cray Trust
*The Elizabeth Creak Charitable Trust**
Creative Scotland
*Credit Suisse EMEA Foundation**
The Crescent Trust
*England and Wales Cricket Trust**
Criffel Charitable Trust
Cripplegate Foundation
The Violet and Milo Cripps Charitable Trust
*Crisis UK**
The Cross Trust
Cruden Foundation Ltd
The Ronald Cruickshanks Foundation
The Cuby Charitable Trust
The Cumber Family Charitable Trust
Itzchok Meyer Cymerman Trust Ltd
The D. G. Charitable Settlement
The D'Oyly Carte Charitable Trust
Roald Dahl's Marvellous Children's Charity
Oizer Dalim Trust
The Joan Lynette Dalton Charitable Trust
The Dr and Mrs A. Darlington Charitable Trust
The Davidson (Nairn) Charitable Trust

The Davidson Family Charitable Trust
Michael Davies Charitable Settlement
*The Biss Davies Charitable Trust**
Margaret Davies Charity
*The John Grant Davies Trust**
The Crispin Davis Family Trust
The Henry and Suzanne Davis Foundation
*Dawat-E-Hadiyah Trust (United Kingdom)**
The Dawe Charitable Trust
The De Brye Charitable Trust
Peter De Haan Charitable Trust
*The De La Rue Charitable Trust**
The De Laszlo Foundation
William Dean Countryside and Educational Trust
Debmar Benevolent Trust Ltd
The Dellal Foundation
The Delves Charitable Trust
The Demigryphon Trust
The Denman Charitable Trust
Dentons UKMEA LLP Charitable Trust
Foundation Derbyshire
Provincial Grand Charity of the Province of Derbyshire
The J. N. Derbyshire Trust
The Desmond Foundation
Devon Community Foundation
The Sandy Dewhirst Charitable Trust
The Laduma Dhamecha Charitable Trust
The Diageo Foundation
Alan and Sheila Diamond Charitable Trust
The Gillian Dickinson Trust
Didymus
Dinwoodie Charitable Company
The Dischma Charitable Trust
*C. H. Dixon Charitable Trust**
The DM Charitable Trust
The Derek and Eileen Dodgson Foundation
The Dollond Charitable Trust
The Dorcas Trust
*The Dorfman Foundation**
Dorset Community Foundation
The Dorus Trust
The Double 'O' Charity Ltd
The Doughty Charity Trust
Douglas Arter Foundation
The Drapers' Charitable Fund
Dromintee Trust
Duchy Health Charity Ltd
The Royal Foundation of the Duke and Duchess of Cambridge and Prince Harry
The Dulverton Trust
The Dumbreck Charity
Dunard Fund 2016
The Dunhill Medical Trust
The Dunn Family Charitable Trust
The Charles Dunstone Charitable Trust
County Durham Community Foundation
Dushinsky Trust Ltd
The Mildred Duveen Charitable Trust
The Dyers' Company Charitable Trust
The James Dyson Foundation
Audrey Earle Charitable Trust
The Earley Charity
Earls Colne and Halstead Educational Charity
East End Community Foundation
Eastern Counties Educational Trust Ltd
The Sir John Eastwood Foundation
The EBM Charitable Trust
*The ECHO Trust**
Echoes Of Service
The Economist Charitable Trust
The Gilbert and Eileen Edgar Foundation
*Edge Foundation**
Edinburgh Children's Holiday Fund
Edinburgh Trust No 2 Account
Edupoor Ltd
*The Eighty Eight Foundation**
*Elanore Ltd**
The Elephant Trust
The George Elias Charitable Trust
The Gerald Palmer Eling Trust Company
The Wilfred and Elsie Elkes Charity Fund
Ellador Ltd
The John Ellerman Foundation
The Ellinson Foundation Ltd
The Edith Maud Ellis 1985 Charitable Trust
The Elmley Foundation
The Vernon N. Ely Charitable Trust
The Emerton-Christie Charity
The Englefield Charitable Trust
The Enkalon Foundation
Entindale Ltd
The Epigoni Trust
The Eranda Rothschild Foundation
The Ericson Trust
The Erskine Cunningham Hill Trust
Esh Foundation
Esher House Charitable Trust
Essex Community Foundation
The Essex Heritage Trust
The Essex Youth Trust
The Estelle Trust
Joseph Ettedgui Charitable Foundation
Euro Charity Trust
The Alan Evans Memorial Trust
The Eventhall Family Charitable Trust
The Eveson Charitable Trust
The Beryl Evetts and Robert Luff Animal Welfare Trust Ltd
The Exilarch's Foundation
The Expat Foundation
Extonglen Ltd
The William and Christine Eynon Charity
G. F. Eyre Charitable Trust
Matthew Eyton Animal Welfare Trust
The F. P. Ltd Charitable Trust
Esmée Fairbairn Foundation
The Fairstead Trust
Famos Foundation Trust
The Lord Faringdon Charitable Trust
Samuel William Farmer Trust
The Thomas Farr Charity
The Farthing Trust
The February Foundation
The John Feeney Charitable Bequest
The George Fentham Birmingham Charity
The A. M. Fenton Trust
Allan and Nesta Ferguson Charitable Settlement
Elizabeth Ferguson Charitable Trust Fund
The Fidelity UK Foundation
The Doris Field Charitable Trust
The Fifty Fund
Dixie Rose Findlay Charitable Trust
Fisherbeck Charitable Trust
Fishmongers' Company's Charitable Trust
The Fitton Trust
The Earl Fitzwilliam Charitable Trust
The Joyce Fletcher Charitable Trust
The Follett Trust
The Football Association National Sports Centre Trust
The Football Foundation
The Forbes Charitable Foundation
Ford Britain Trust
The Oliver Ford Charitable Trust
Fordeve Ltd
Forest Hill Charitable Trust

The Lady Forester Trust
Forever Manchester
The Forman Hardy Charitable Trust
Donald Forrester Trust
Gwyneth Forrester Trust
The Anna Rosa Forster Charitable Trust
The Fort Foundation
The Forte Charitable Trust
The Lord Forte Foundation
The Foyle Foundation
The Isaac and Freda Frankel Memorial Charitable Trust
The Elizabeth Frankland Moore and Star Foundation
Jill Franklin Trust
The Gordon Fraser Charitable Trust
The Hugh Fraser Foundation
The Joseph Strong Frazer Trust
The Louis and Valerie Freedman Charitable Settlement
The Michael and Clara Freeman Charitable Trust
The Charles S. French Charitable Trust
The Anne French Memorial Trust
The Freshfield Foundation
The Freshgate Trust Foundation
*The Raphael Freshwater Memorial Association**
Friarsgate Trust
Friends of Biala Ltd
Friends of Wiznitz Ltd
Friends Provident Charitable Foundation
The Frognal Trust
The Adrian and Jane Frost Charitable Trust
The Patrick and Helena Frost Foundation
Mejer and Gertrude Miriam Frydman Foundation
The Fulmer Charitable Trust
The G. D. Charitable Trust
G. M. C. Trust
The G. R. P. Charitable Trust
The Gale Family Charity Trust
The Gannochy Trust
The Ganzoni Charitable Trust
The Worshipful Company of Gardeners of London
The Garrard Family Foundation
The Garrick Charitable Trust
The Gatsby Charitable Foundation
Gatwick Airport Community Trust
The Robert Gavron Charitable Trust
The Jacqueline and Michael Gee Charitable Trust
The General Nursing Council for England and Wales Trust
The Generations Foundation
*The Genesis Charitable Trust**
The Steven Gerrard Foundation
*The Gerrick Rose Animal Trust**
The Gertner Charitable Trust
The Gibbons Family Trust
The David Gibbons Foundation
The Gibbs Charitable Trust
The G. C. Gibson Charitable Trust
The Simon Gibson Charitable Trust
*Gilchrist Educational Trust**
*The L. and R. Gilley Charitable Trust**
The Girdlers' Company Charitable Trust
The B. and P. Glasser Charitable Trust
The Glass-House Trust
The Gloag Foundation
Global Care
Global Charities
Gloucestershire Community Foundation
Worshipful Company of Glovers of London Charitable Trust
The Godinton Charitable Trust
Worshipful Company of Gold and Silver Wyre Drawers Charitable Trust Fund
Sydney and Phyllis Goldberg Memorial Charitable Trust
The Golden Bottle Trust
The Goldman Sachs Charitable Gift Fund (UK)
Goldman Sachs Gives (UK)
The Goldsmiths' Company Charity
The Golf Foundation Ltd
The Golsoncott Foundation
Nicholas and Judith Goodison's Charitable Settlement
The Goodman Foundation
The Mike Gooley Trailfinders Charity
The Goshen Trust
The Gosling Foundation Ltd
The Gould Charitable Trust
Gowling WLG (UK) Charitable Trust
The Hemraj Goyal Foundation
Grace Charitable Trust
Graff Foundation
E. C. Graham Belford Charitable Settlement
A. and S. Graham Charitable Trust
*The Graham Trust**
Grahame Charitable Foundation Ltd
The Granada Foundation
Grand Charitable Trust of the Order of Women Freemasons
The Grantham Yorke Trust
GrantScape
Gordon Gray Trust
The Gray Trust
The Great Britain Sasakawa Foundation
The Kenneth and Susan Green Charitable Foundation
The Green Hall Foundation
Philip and Judith Green Trust
Mrs H. R. Greene Charitable Settlement
Greenham Common Community Trust Ltd
The Greggs Foundation
The Gretna Charitable Trust
Greys Charitable Trust
The Grimmitt Trust
The Grocers' Charity
M. and R. Gross Charities Ltd
The Bishop of Guildford's Foundation
Guildry Incorporation of Perth
The Walter Guinness Charitable Trust
The Gunter Charitable Trust
The Gur Trust
Dr Guthrie's Association
H. C. D. Memorial Fund
H. P. Charitable Trust
Hackney Parochial Charities
The Hadfield Charitable Trust
The Hadley Trust
Hadras Kodesh Trust
The Hadrian Trust
The Alfred Haines Charitable Trust
The Haley Family Charitable Trust
Hamamelis Trust
Paul Hamlyn Foundation
The Helen Hamlyn Trust
*Hammersmith United Charities**
Hampshire and Isle of Wight Community Foundation
Hampton Fuel Allotment Charity
The W. A. Handley Charity Trust
The Kathleen Hannay Memorial Charity
*The Happold Foundation**
The Haramead Trust
Harbinson Charitable Trust
Harbo Charities Ltd
The Harbour Charitable Trust
The Harbour Foundation
The Harding Trust
William Harding's Charity

The Harebell Centenary Fund
The Peter and Teresa Harris Charitable Trust
The Harris Family Charitable Trust
The Edith Lilian Harrison 2000 Foundation
The Harrison-Frank Family Foundation (UK) Ltd
The Hartley Charitable Trust
The Alfred And Peggy Harvey Charitable Trust
The Hasluck Charitable Trust
The Hathaway Trust
The Maurice Hatter Foundation
The Hawthorne Charitable Trust
The Charles Hayward Foundation
*HC Foundation**
The Headley Trust
The Health Foundation
May Hearnshaw Charitable Trust (May Hearnshaw's Charity)
Heart of England Community Foundation
Heart Research UK
The Heathcoat Trust
Heathrow Community Fund (LHR Airport Communities Trust)
The Heathside Charitable Trust
*Heb Ffin (Without Frontier)**
The Charlotte Heber-Percy Charitable Trust
Ernest Hecht Charitable Foundation
The Percy Hedley 1990 Charitable Trust
Hedley Foundation Ltd (The Hedley Foundation)
The Michael Heller Charitable Foundation
The Simon Heller Charitable Settlement
Help for Health
The Helping Foundation
The Hemby Charitable Trust
*Henderson Firstfruits**
The Christina Mary Hendrie Trust for Scottish and Canadian Charities
Henley Educational Trust
Philip Henman Trust
The G. D. Herbert Charitable Trust
Herefordshire Community Foundation
Hertfordshire Community Foundation
The Hesslewood Children's Trust (Hull Seamen's and General Orphanage)
P. and C. Hickinbotham Charitable Trust
The Alan Edward Higgs Charity
Highcroft Charitable Trust
The Hilden Charitable Fund
The Derek Hill Foundation
*M. V. Hillhouse Trust**
The Hillier Trust
The Hillingdon Community Trust
R. G. Hills Charitable Trust
Hinchley Charitable Trust
The Hinduja Foundation
The Hintze Family Charity Foundation
The Hiscox Foundation
The Henry C. Hoare Charitable Trust
The Hobson Charity Ltd
Hockerill Educational Foundation
The Jane Hodge Foundation
The Holden Charitable Trust
The Hollands-Warren Fund
The Hollick Family Charitable Trust
The Holliday Foundation
The Dorothy Holmes Charitable Trust
P. H. Holt Foundation
The Holywood Trust
The Homelands Charitable Trust
The Homestead Charitable Trust
The Mary Homfray Charitable Trust
Sir Harold Hood's Charitable Trust
The Hoover Foundation
The Hope Trust
Hopmarket Charity
The Horizon Foundation
The Antony Hornby Charitable Trust
The Thomas J. Horne Memorial Trust
The Worshipful Company of Horners' Charitable Trusts
*Horwich Shotter Charitable Trust**
The Hospital of God at Greatham
The Hospital Saturday Fund
The Sir Joseph Hotung Charitable Settlement
The Reta Lila Howard Foundation
The Daniel Howard Trust
*Howman Charitable Trust**
The Hudson Foundation
The Hull and East Riding Charitable Trust
Hulme Trust Estates (Educational)
Human Relief Foundation
The Humanitarian Trust
The Albert Hunt Trust
The Hunter Foundation
Miss Agnes H. Hunter's Trust
The Hunting Horn General Charitable Trust
The Huntingdon Foundation Ltd
Huntingdon Freemen's Trust
Hurdale Charity Ltd
The Hutchinson Charitable Trust
The Hutton Foundation
The Nani Huyu Charitable Trust
The P. Y. N. and B. Hyams Trust
Hyde Charitable Trust (Youth Plus)
*The Hyde Park Place Estate Charity – civil trustees**
*Ibbett Trust**
Ibrahim Foundation Ltd
*ICE Futures Charitable Trust**
The Idlewild Trust
IGO Foundation Ltd
The Iliffe Family Charitable Trust
Imagine Foundation
Impetus – The Private Equity Foundation (Impetus – PEF)
Incommunities Foundation
The Indigo Trust
*The Worshipful Company of Information Technologists**
The Ingram Trust
The Inlight Trust
The Inman Charity
The Innocent Foundation
*The Worshipful Company of Insurers – First Charitable Trust Fund**
*Integrated Education Fund**
The International Bankers Charitable Trust (The Worshipful Company of Interntional Bankers)
*International Bible Students Association**
*International Fund for Animal Welfare (IFAW)**
Interserve Employee Foundation Ltd
The Inverforth Charitable Trust
Investream Charitable Trust
The Ireland Fund of Great Britain
Irish Youth Foundation (UK) Ltd (incorporating The Lawlor Foundation)
The Ironmongers' Company
The Charles Irving Charitable Trust
The J. Isaacs Charitable Trust
The Isle of Anglesey Charitable Trust
The ITF Seafarers' Trust
The J. and J. Benevolent Foundation

The J. A. R. Charitable Trust
The J. J. Charitable Trust
The Jabbs Foundation
C. Richard Jackson Charitable Trust
The Sir Barry Jackson County Fund (incorporating the Hornton Fund)
The Ruth and Lionel Jacobson Trust (Second Fund) No. 2
John James Bristol Foundation
The Susan and Stephen James Charitable Settlement
Lady Eda Jardine Charitable Trust
The Jarman Charitable Trust
John Jarrold Trust Ltd
Rees Jeffreys Road Fund
Nick Jenkins Foundation
The Jenour Foundation
The Jephcott Charitable Trust
The Jerusalem Trust
The Jerwood Charitable Foundation
Jewish Child's Day (JCD)
The Jewish Youth Fund (JYF)
Joffe Charitable Trust
The Elton John AIDS Foundation (EJAF)
Lillie Johnson Charitable Trust
The Johnson Foundation
Johnnie Johnson Trust
Johnson Wax Ltd Charitable Trust
The Christopher and Kirsty Johnston Charitable Trust
The Joicey Trust
The Jones 1986 Charitable Trust
The Dezna Robins Jones Charitable Foundation
The Marjorie and Geoffrey Jones Charitable Trust
The Muriel Jones Foundation
The Jordan Charitable Foundation
The Joron Charitable Trust
J. E. Joseph Charitable Fund
The Cyril and Eve Jumbo Charitable Trust
Anton Jurgens Charitable Trust
The Jusaca Charitable Trust
Kahal Chassidim Bobov
The Bernard Kahn Charitable Trust
The Stanley Kalms Foundation
Karaviotis Foundation
The Boris Karloff Charitable Foundation
The Kasner Charitable Trust
The Michael and Ilse Katz Foundation
C. S. Kaufman Charitable Trust
The Caron Keating Foundation
The Kelly Family Charitable Trust
Kelsick's Educational Foundation
The Kay Kendall Leukaemia Fund
William Kendall's Charity (Wax Chandlers' Company)
The Kennel Club Charitable Trust
Kent Community Foundation
The Nancy Kenyon Charitable Trust
Keren Association Ltd
E. and E. Kernkraut Charities Ltd
The Peter Kershaw Trust
The Ursula Keyes Trust
*The Kildare Trust**
The King/Cullimore Charitable Trust
The Mary Kinross Charitable Trust
Laura Kinsella Foundation
*The Graham Kirkham Foundation**
Kirkley Poor's Land Estate
The Richard Kirkman Trust
The Kirschel Foundation
Robert Kitchin (Saddlers' Company)
The Ernest Kleinwort Charitable Trust
The Sir James Knott Trust
The Kobler Trust
The Kohn Foundation
Kollel and Co. Ltd
The KPMG Foundation
Kreditor Charitable Trust
The Kreitman Foundation
The Neil Kreitman Foundation
Kupath Gemach Chaim Bechesed Viznitz Trust
Kusuma Trust UK
The Kyte Charitable Trust
Ladbrokes in the Community Charitable Trust
The K. P. Ladd Charitable Trust
John Laing Charitable Trust
Christopher Laing Foundation
The David Laing Foundation
The Leonard Laity Stoate Charitable Trust
The Lambert Charitable Trust
Community Foundations for Lancashire and Merseyside
*The Lancashire Foundation**
Duchy of Lancaster Benevolent Fund
Lancaster Foundation
The Jack Lane Charitable Trust
The Allen Lane Foundation
Langdale Trust
The LankellyChase Foundation
The R. J. Larg Family Charitable Trust
Largsmount Ltd
Laslett's (Hinton) Charity
The Lauffer Family Charitable Foundation
Mrs F. B. Laurence Charitable Trust
The Kathleen Laurence Trust
The Law Society Charity
The Edgar E. Lawley Foundation
The Herd Lawson and Muriel Lawson Charitable Trust
Lawson Beckman Charitable Trust
The Raymond and Blanche Lawson Charitable Trust
The David Lean Foundation
The Leathersellers' Company Charitable Fund
The Arnold Lee Charitable Trust
The William Leech Charity
Leeds Community Foundation (LCF)
*The Legal Education Foundation**
*Leicestershire and Rutland Masonic Charity Association**
Leicestershire, Leicester and Rutland Community Foundation
The Kennedy Leigh Charitable Trust
The Leigh Trust
P. Leigh-Bramwell Trust 'E'
*Leng Charitable Trust**
The Lennox Hannay Charitable Trust
The Mark Leonard Trust
*The Lethendy Charitable Trust**
The Leverhulme Trade Charities Trust
The Leverhulme Trust
*Bernard Lewis Family Charitable Trust**
David and Ruth Lewis Family Charitable Trust
The John Spedan Lewis Foundation
The Sir Edward Lewis Foundation
John Lewis Partnership General Community Fund
Liberum Foundation
*The Light Fund Company**
The Limbourne Trust
Limoges Charitable Trust
The Linbury Trust
Lincolnshire Community Foundation
The Lind Trust

Lindale Educational Foundation
The Linden Charitable Trust
The Enid Linder Foundation
The Lindley Foundation (TLF)
The Ruth and Stuart Lipton Charitable Trust
The Lister Charitable Trust
The Frank Litchfield Charitable Trust
The Charles Littlewood Hill Trust
The Second Joseph Aaron Littman Foundation
The George John and Sheilah Livanos Charitable Trust
Liverpool Charity and Voluntary Services (LCVS)
Jack Livingstone Charitable Trust
The Elaine and Angus Lloyd Charitable Trust
*The W. M. and B. W. Lloyd Trust**
The Andrew Lloyd Webber Foundation
Lloyd's Charities Trust
Lloyds Bank Foundation for England and Wales
Lloyds Bank Foundation for the Channel Islands
*Lloyd's Register Foundation**
Lloyds TSB Foundation for Scotland
Localtrent Ltd
The Locker Foundation
*The Lockwood Charitable Foundation**
Loftus Charitable Trust
The Lolev Charitable Trust
The Joyce Lomax Bullock Charitable Trust
Trust for London
London Catalyst
The London Community Foundation (LCF)
London Housing Foundation Ltd (LHF)
London Legal Support Trust (LLST)
Inner London Magistrates Court's Poor Box and Feeder Charity
The William and Katherine Longman Trust
The Loseley and Guildway Charitable Trust
*Michael Lowe's and Associated Charities**
The Lower Green Foundation
The C. L. Loyd Charitable Trust
Robert Luff Foundation Ltd
The Henry Lumley Charitable Trust
Paul Lunn-Rockliffe Charitable Trust
C. F. Lunoe Trust Fund
Lord and Lady Lurgan Trust
The Lyndhurst Trust
The Lynn Foundation
John Lyon's Charity
The Sir Jack Lyons Charitable Trust
Sylvanus Lysons Charity
M. and C. Trust
*M. B. Foundation**
The M. K. Charitable Trust
The M. Y. A. Charitable Trust
The Madeline Mabey Trust
The E. M. MacAndrew Trust
The R. S. Macdonald Charitable Trust
The Macdonald-Buchanan Charitable Trust
*Mace Foundation**
The Mackay and Brewer Charitable Trust
The Mackintosh Foundation
*GPS Macpherson Charitable Settlement**
The MacRobert Trust
The Mactaggart Third Fund
The Ian Mactaggart Trust (The Mactaggart Second Fund)
The Magdalen and Lasher Charity (General Fund)
The Magen Charitable Trust
The Makers of Playing Cards Charity
The Mallinckrodt Foundation
The Manackerman Charitable Trust
Manchester Airport Community Trust Fund
The Manchester Guardian Society Charitable Trust
Lord Mayor of Manchester's Charity Appeal Trust
The Manifold Charitable Trust
The W. M. Mann Foundation
R. W. Mann Trust
The Manoukian Charitable Foundation
Marbeh Torah Trust
The Marchig Animal Welfare Trust
The Stella and Alexander Margulies Charitable Trust
Mariapolis Ltd
The Michael Marks Charitable Trust
The Marks Family Foundation
The Ann and David Marks Foundation
The Hilda and Samuel Marks Foundation
The J. P. Marland Charitable Trust
Marmot Charitable Trust
The Marr-Munning Trust
The Michael Marsh Charitable Trust
The Marsh Christian Trust
Charlotte Marshall Charitable Trust
D. G. Marshall of Cambridge Trust
*The Martin Charitable Trust**
Sir George Martin Trust
John Martin's Charity
The Mason Porter Charitable Trust
*Masonic Charitable Foundation**
The Nancie Massey Charitable Trust
*The Master Charitable Trust**
The Mathew Trust
The Matliwala Family Charitable Trust
*Maudsley Charity**
The Violet Mauray Charitable Trust
The Mayfield Valley Arts Trust
*Maypride Ltd**
Mazars Charitable Trust
The Robert McAlpine Foundation
McGreevy No. 5 Settlement
D. D. McPhail Charitable Settlement
The Medlock Charitable Trust
Melodor Ltd
Menuchar Ltd
Mercaz Torah Vechesed Ltd
The Brian Mercer Charitable Trust
The Mercers' Charitable Foundation
The Merchant Taylors' Company Charities Fund
Merchant Taylors' Consolidated Charities for the Infirm
The Merchant Venturers' Charity
Mercury Phoenix Trust
The Metropolitan Masonic Charity
T. and J. Meyer Family Foundation Ltd
The Mickel Fund
The Mickleham Trust
The Gerald Micklem Charitable Trust
The Masonic Province of Middlesex Charitable Trust (Middlesex Masonic Charity)
Middlesex Sports Foundation
Millennium Stadium Charitable Trust (Ymddiriedolaeth Elusennol Stadiwm Y. Mileniwm)
Hugh and Mary Miller Bequest Trust
The Ronald Miller Foundation

The Millfield House Foundation (1)
The Millfield Trust
The Millichope Foundation
*Mills and Reeve Charitable Trust**
The Mills Charity
The Millward Charitable Trust
The Clare Milne Trust
*The James Milner Foundation**
Milton Keynes Community Foundation Ltd
The Edgar Milward Charity
The Peter Minet Trust
The Mirianog Trust
The Laurence Misener Charitable Trust
The Mishcon Family Charitable Trust
The Brian Mitchell Charitable Settlement
*Mitsubishi Corporation Fund for Europe and Africa**
Keren Mitzvah Trust
The Mizpah Trust
Mobbs Memorial Trust Ltd
Mole Charitable Trust
The Monatrea Charitable Trust
The Monmouthshire County Council Welsh Church Act Fund
The Monument Trust
*Moondance Foundation**
The George A. Moore Foundation
The Henry Moore Foundation
The Morel Charitable Trust
The Morgan Charitable Foundation
The Steve Morgan Foundation
Morgan Stanley International Foundation
The Diana and Allan Morgenthau Charitable Trust
The Miles Morland Foundation
The Morris Charitable Trust
The Willie and Mabel Morris Charitable Trust
G. M. Morrison Charitable Trust
*The Morton Charitable Trust**
The Moshal Charitable Trust
Vyoel Moshe Charitable Trust
The Moss Family Charitable Trust
The Mosselson Charitable Trust
Moto in the Community
The Edwina Mountbatten and Leonora Children's Foundation
The Mugdock Children's Trust
The Mulberry Trust
The Frederick Mulder Foundation
The Edith Murphy Foundation
Murphy-Neumann Charity Company Ltd
The John R. Murray Charitable Trust
The Music Sales Charitable Trust
Muslim Hands
The Mutual Trust Group
MW (CL) Foundation
MW (GK) Foundation
MW (HO) Foundation
MW (RH) Foundation
The Janet Nash Charitable Settlement
The National Churches Trust
The National Express Foundation
*The National Gardens Scheme**
The Nationwide Foundation
The James Neill Trust Fund
Nemoral Ltd
Nesswall Ltd
*Nesta**
Network for Social Change Charitable Trust
Newby Trust Ltd
The Newcomen Collett Foundation
Newpier Charity Ltd
Alderman Newton's Educational Foundation
NJD Charitable Trust
Alice Noakes Memorial Charitable Trust
*The Norfolk Churches Trust Ltd**
Norfolk Community Foundation
Educational Foundation of Alderman John Norman
The Norman Family Charitable Trust
Normanby Charitable Trust
*North East Area Miners Welfare Trust Fund**
*North London Charities Ltd**
*Provincial Grand Charity of Northamptonshire and Huntingdonshire**
Northamptonshire Community Foundation
The Community Foundation for Northern Ireland
The Northmoor Trust
The Northumberland Village Homes Trust
*The Northwick Trust**
Northwood Charitable Trust
The Norton Foundation
Norwich Town Close Estate Charity
The Norwood and Newton Settlement
Nottinghamshire Community Foundation
The Nottinghamshire Historic Churches Trust
The Father O'Mahoney Memorial Trust
The Sir Peter O'Sullevan Charitable Trust
The Oakdale Trust
The Oakley Charitable Trust
Odin Charitable Trust
The Ofenheim Charitable Trust
The Ogle Christian Trust
Oizer Charitable Trust
Old Possum's Practical Trust
The Oldham Foundation
The Olga Charitable Trust
*One Community Foundation Ltd**
OneFamily Foundation
Open Gate
The Ormsby Charitable Trust
The O'Sullivan Family Charitable Trust
The Ouseley Church Music Trust
The Owen Family Trust
Oxfam (GB)
Oxfordshire Community Foundation
*Oxfordshire Historic Churches Trust**
P. F. Charitable Trust
The Doris Pacey Charitable Foundation
*The Paddington Charitable Estate Educational Fund**
The Paget Charitable Trust
*Palmtree Memorial Trust**
The Panacea Charitable Trust
The Paphitis Charitable Trust
*Parabola Foundation**
The Paragon Trust
*The Pargiter Trust**
*Parish Estate of the Church of St Michael Spurriergate York**
The Park House Charitable Trust
The Patrick Trust
The Jack Patston Charitable Trust
Susanna Peake Charitable Trust
The Pears Family Charitable Foundation
The Dowager Countess Eleanor Peel Trust
The Pell Charitable Trust
The Pennycress Trust
People's Health Trust
People's Postcode Trust
The Performing Right Society Foundation
B. E. Perl Charitable Trust
Personal Assurance Charitable Trust
The Persson Charitable Trust

The Persula Foundation
The Jack Petchey Foundation
Petplan Charitable Trust
The Pharsalia Charitable Trust
The Phillips and Rubens Charitable Trust
The Phillips Charitable Trust
The Phillips Family Charitable Trust
The Pilgrim Trust
Pilkington Charities Fund
The Austin and Hope Pilkington Trust
Miss A. M. Pilkington's Charitable Trust
Pink Ribbon Foundation*
The DLA Piper Charitable Trust
Polden-Puckham Charitable Foundation
The Polehampton Charity*
The George and Esme Pollitzer Charitable Settlement
Pollywally Charitable Trust
The Polonsky Foundation
The Ponton House Trust
Edith and Ferdinand Porjes Charitable Trust
The Porta Pia 2012 Foundation
The Portrack Charitable Trust
The J. E. Posnansky Charitable Trust
Postcode Community Trust*
Postcode Dream Trust – Dream Fund
The Mary Potter Convent Hospital Trust
David and Elaine Potter Foundation
Powys Welsh Church Fund*
Premishlaner Charitable Trust
Sir John Priestman Charity Trust
The Primrose Trust
The Prince of Wales's Charitable Foundation
The Prince Philip Trust Fund*
Princes Gate Trust*
The Princess Anne's Charities
The Privy Purse Charitable Trust
The Professional Footballers' Association Charity*
The Puebla Charitable Trust
The Puri Foundation
The Pye Foundation*
Mr and Mrs J. A. Pye's Charitable Settlement
QBE European Operations Foundation*
Quartet Community Foundation
The Queen Anne's Gate Foundation
Queen Mary's Roehampton Trust
The Queen's Trust
Quercus Foundation*
Quothquan Trust
R. S. Charitable Trust
The Monica Rabagliati Charitable Trust
Rachel Charitable Trust
The Racing Foundation
Richard Radcliffe Trust
The Radcliffe Trust
The Bishop Radford Trust
The Rainford Trust
The Rambourg Foundation
The Edward Ramsden Charitable Trust*
The Joseph and Lena Randall Charitable Trust
The Joseph Rank Trust
The Ranworth Trust
Rashbass Family Trust
The Ratcliff Foundation
The Eleanor Rathbone Charitable Trust
Elizabeth Rathbone Charity
The Sigrid Rausing Trust
The Ravensdale Trust
The Roger Raymond Charitable Trust
The Rayne Trust
The John Rayner Charitable Trust
C. A. Redfern Charitable Foundation
Reed Family Foundation
Richard Reeve's Foundation
Reuben Foundation
The Rhododendron Trust
Riada Trust*
Daisie Rich Trust
The Clive and Sylvia Richards Charity Ltd
Richmond Parish Lands Charity
Ridgesave Ltd
Rigby Foundation*
The Sir John Ritblat Family Foundation
The River Farm Foundation
The River Trust
Rivers Foundation
Riverside Charitable Trust Ltd*
The Rix-Thompson-Rothenberg Foundation
RJM Charity Trust
Thomas Roberts Trust
The Robertson Trust
Robyn Charitable Trust
The Roddick Foundation
The Rofeh Trust
The Richard Rogers Charitable Settlement
Rokach Family Charitable Trust
The Sir James Roll Charitable Trust
The Helen Roll Charity
Mrs L. D. Rope's Second Charitable Settlement*
Mrs L. D. Rope's Third Charitable Settlement
Rosca Trust
The Cissie Rosefield Charitable Trust*
The Cecil Rosen Foundation
Rosetrees Trust
The David Ross Foundation*
The Rothermere Foundation
Rothschild Foundation (Hanadiv) Europe*
The Roughley Charitable Trust
Mrs Gladys Row Fogo Charitable Trust
Rowanville Ltd
The Rowlands Trust
The Joseph Rowntree Charitable Trust
Royal Artillery Charitable Fund
The Royal British Legion
Royal Docks Trust (London)
The Royal Navy And Royal Marines Charity*
Rozelle Trust*
The Rubin Foundation Charitable Trust
Rugby Football Foundation
The RVW Trust
The J. S. and E. C. Rymer Charitable Trust
S. F. Foundation
The Michael and Nicola Sacher Charitable Trust
The Michael Sacher Charitable Trust
The Dr Mortimer and Theresa Sackler Foundation
The Sackler Trust
The Ruzin Sadagora Trust
The Saddlers' Company Charitable Fund
The Saga Charitable Trust
The Jean Sainsbury Animal Welfare Trust
The Alan and Babette Sainsbury Charitable Fund
The Sainsbury Family Charitable Trusts
Saint Sarkis Charity Trust
The Saintbury Trust
The Saints and Sinners Trust Ltd
The Salamander Charitable Trust
The Salisbury New Pool Settlement*
Salters' Charitable Foundation
The Andrew Salvesen Charitable Trust
Samjo Ltd*
Coral Samuel Charitable Trust
The Basil Samuel Charitable Trust
The M. J. Samuel Charitable Trust
The Samworth Foundation

The Sandhu Charitable Foundation
The Sandra Charitable Trust
The Sands Family Trust
Santander UK Foundation Ltd
The Sants Charitable Trust
*Sarum St Michael Educational Charity**
*The Save the Children Fund**
The Scarfe Charitable Trust
The Schapira Charitable Trust
The Annie Schiff Charitable Trust
The Schmidt-Bodner Charitable Trust
The Schreib Trust
O. and G. Schreiber Charitable Trust
The Schreiber Charitable Trust
Schroder Charity Trust
The Schroder Foundation
Foundation Scotland
The Scotshill Trust
Scott (Eredine) Charitable Trust
The Francis C. Scott Charitable Trust
*The John Scott Trust Fund**
The ScottishPower Foundation
The Scouloudi Foundation
The SDL Foundation
Seafarers Hospital Society
Seafarers UK (King George's Fund for Sailors)
The Searchlight Electric Charitable Trust
Sam and Bella Sebba Charitable Trust
The Seedfield Trust
Leslie Sell Charitable Trust
*The Sellafield Charity Trust Fund**
Sellata Ltd
SEM Charitable Trust
The Seven Fifty Trust
The Severn Trent Water Charitable Trust Fund
The Cyril Shack Trust
The Jean Shanks Foundation
The Shanly Foundation
The Shanti Charitable Trust
ShareGift (The Orr Mackintosh Foundation)
The Linley Shaw Foundation
The Shears Foundation
The Sheepdrove Trust
The Sheffield Town Trust
The Sheldon Trust
The Patricia and Donald Shepherd Charitable Trust
The Sylvia and Colin Shepherd Charitable Trust
*Sherburn House Charity**
*Sherling Charitable Trust**
The Archie Sherman Cardiff Foundation
The Archie Sherman Charitable Trust
The Shetland Charitable Trust
SHINE (Support and Help in Education)
The Bassil Shippam and Alsford Trust
The Shipwrights' Company Charitable Fund
The Shirley Foundation
Shlomo Memorial Fund Ltd
The Shoe Zone Trust
*The Shropshire Historic Churches Trust**
*Shulem B. Association Ltd**
*The Florence Shute Millennium Trust**
David and Jennifer Sieff Charitable Trust
Silver Family Charitable Trust
The Simmons & Simmons Charitable Foundation
The Huntly and Margery Sinclair Charitable Trust
SITA Cornwall Trust Ltd
The Skelton Bounty
*The Skerritt Trust**
Skipton Building Society Charitable Foundation
The John Slater Foundation
The Slaughter and May Charitable Trust
Rita and David Slowe Charitable Trust
Ruth Smart Foundation
The SMB Trust
The Mrs Smith and Mount Trust
The DS Smith Charitable Foundation
The N. Smith Charitable Settlement
The Smith Charitable Trust
The Henry Smith Charity
The Leslie Smith Foundation
*The Martin Smith Foundation**
The WH Smith Group Charitable Trust
The Stanley Smith UK Horticultural Trust
Philip Smith's Charitable Trust
The R. C. Snelling Charitable Trust
The Sobell Foundation
Social Business Trust
*Social Investment Business Foundation**
Sodexo Stop Hunger Foundation
*Sofronie Foundation**
Solev Co. Ltd
The Solo Charitable Settlement
David Solomons Charitable Trust
*Somerset Community Foundation**
Songdale Ltd
The E. C. Sosnow Charitable Trust
The Souter Charitable Trust
The South Square Trust
The W. F. Southall Trust
R. H. Southern Trust
The Southover Manor General Education Trust
*The Spalding Trust**
Spar Charitable Fund
Sparks Charity (Sport Aiding Medical Research for Kids)
Sparquote Ltd
The Spear Charitable Trust
Spears-Stutz Charitable Trust
The Worshipful Company of Spectacle Makers' Charity
The Jessie Spencer Trust
The Spielman Charitable Trust
The Spoore, Merry and Rixman Foundation
Rosalyn and Nicholas Springer Charitable Trust
Springrule Ltd
The Spurrell Charitable Trust
The Squires Foundation
The St Hilda's Trust
The St James's Trust Settlement
Sir Walter St John's Educational Charity
St Luke's College Foundation
*St Marylebone Educational Foundation**
St Monica Trust
St Olave's and St Saviour's Schools Foundation – Foundation Fund
St Peter's Saltley Trust
The Stafford Trust
*Staffordshire Community Foundation**
*Standard Life Foundation**
*The Stanley Charitable Trust**
The Stanley Foundation Ltd
The Staples Trust
The Peter Stebbings Memorial Charity
The Steel Charitable Trust
The Steinberg Family Charitable Trust
The Hugh Stenhouse Foundation
C. E. K. Stern Charitable Trust
The Sigmund Sternberg Charitable Foundation
Stervon Ltd
The Stevenage Community Trust
Stevenson Family's Charitable Trust
The Stewards' Charitable Trust

The Andy Stewart Charitable Foundation
Sir Halley Stewart Trust
The Stewarts Law Foundation
The Stobart Newlands Charitable Trust
The Stoller Charitable Trust
M. J. C. Stone Charitable Trust
The Stone Family Foundation
*The Stoneygate Trust**
The Samuel Storey Family Charitable Trust
Peter Stormonth Darling Charitable Trust
Peter Storrs Trust
The Strangward Trust
Stratford upon Avon Town Trust
The Strawberry Charitable Trust
The W. O. Street Charitable Foundation
The Sudborough Foundation
Sueberry Ltd
Suffolk Community Foundation
The Suffolk Historic Churches Trust
The Alan Sugar Foundation
The Summerfield Charitable Trust
The Bernard Sunley Charitable Foundation
*Sunninghill Fuel Allotment Trust**
*Support Adoption For Pets**
*Surgo Foundation UK Ltd**
Community Foundation for Surrey
The Sussex Community Foundation
The Adrienne and Leslie Sussman Charitable Trust
The Sutasoma Trust
Sutton Coldfield Charitable Trust
Swan Mountain Trust
The Swann-Morton Foundation
The John Swire (1989) Charitable Trust
The Adrian Swire Charitable Trust
The Swire Charitable Trust
The Hugh and Ruby Sykes Charitable Trust
The Charles and Elsie Sykes Trust
Sylvia Waddilove Foundation UK
T. and S. Trust Fund
Tabeel Trust
The Tajtelbaum Charitable Trust
The Talbot Trusts
The Talbot Village Trust
Tallow Chandlers Benevolent Fund No. 2
*The Talmud Torah Machzikei Hadass Trust**
Talteg Ltd
The Lady Tangye Charitable Trust Ltd
The David Tannen Charitable Trust
The Tanner Trust
The Lili Tapper Charitable Foundation
The Taurus Foundation
The Tay Charitable Trust
C. B. and H. H. Taylor 1984 Trust
Humphrey Richardson Taylor Charitable Trust
The Connie and Albert Taylor Charitable Trust
The Taylor Family Foundation
Tearfund
*Khoo Teck Puat UK Foundation**
The Tedworth Charitable Trust
Tees Valley Community Foundation
Tegham Ltd
The Templeton Goodwill Trust
The Tennis Foundation
*Tenovus Scotland**
The C. Paul Thackray General Charitable Trust
The Thales Charitable Trust
The Thistle Trust
The David Thomas Charitable Trust
*DM Thomas Foundation for Young People**
The Arthur and Margaret Thompson Charitable Trust
The Thompson Family Charitable Trust
The Sir Jules Thorn Charitable Trust
The Thornton Foundation
The Thornton Trust
The Thousandth Man- Richard Burns Charitable Trust
The Three Oaks Trust
The Thriplow Charitable Trust
Tilney Charitable Trust
Mrs R. P. Tindall's Charitable Trust
The Tinsley Foundation
The Tisbury Telegraph Trust
The Tobacco Pipe Makers and Tobacco Trade Benevolent Fund
The Tolkien Trust
The Tompkins Foundation
Toras Chesed (London) Trust
The Tory Family Foundation
Tottenham Grammar School Foundation
The Tower Hill Trust
The Toy Trust
The Toye Foundation
Toyota Manufacturing UK Charitable Trust
*The Trades House of Glasgow**
Annie Tranmer Charitable Trust
The Constance Travis Charitable Trust
The Treeside Trust
The Trefoil Trust
The Triangle Trust (1949) Fund
*Tropical Health and Education Trust**
The True Colours Trust
Truedene Co. Ltd
The Truemark Trust
Truemart Ltd
Trumros Ltd
The Trusthouse Charitable Foundation
*The Trysil Charitable Trust**
The Tudor Trust
The Tufton Charitable Trust
The Roger and Douglas Turner Charitable Trust
The Florence Turner Trust
The G. J. W. Turner Trust
The Turtleton Charitable Trust
TVML Foundation
Two Ridings Community Foundation
Community Foundation serving Tyne and Wear and Northumberland
Tzedakah
The Udlington Trust
*UKH Foundation**
Ulster Garden Villages Ltd
Ulting Overseas Trust
The Ulverscroft Foundation
The Underwood Trust
The Union of Orthodox Hebrew Congregations
United Utilities Trust Fund
UnLtd (Foundation for Social Entrepreneurs)
The Michael Uren Foundation
The David Uri Memorial Trust
*The Utley Family Charitable Trust**
The Vail Foundation
Vale of Glamorgan Welsh Church Fund
The Valentine Charitable Trust
The Valiant Charitable Trust
The Albert Van Den Bergh Charitable Trust
The Van Neste Foundation
Mrs Maud Van Norden's Charitable Foundation
The Vandervell Foundation
The Vardy Foundation
Variety The Children's Charity (Variety Club)
The William and Patricia Venton Charitable Trust

*The Veolia Environmental Trust**
Roger Vere Foundation
The Nigel Vinson Charitable Trust
The Vintners' Foundation
The Virgin Foundation (Virgin Unite)
The Virgin Money Foundation
*Viridor Credits Environmental Company**
Vivdale Ltd
The Vodafone Foundation
Volant Charitable Trust
Voluntary Action Fund (VAF)
Wade's Charity
The Scurrah Wainwright Charity
*The Bruce Wake Charity**
The Wakefield and Tetley Trust
*The Wakefield Trust**
The Wakeham Trust
The Community Foundation in Wales
Wales Council for Voluntary Action
Robert and Felicity Waley-Cohen Charitable Trust
The Walker Trust
*Walton Foundation**
Walton on Thames Charity
Sir Siegmund Warburg's Voluntary Settlement
The Ward Blenkinsop Trust
The Barbara Ward Children's Foundation
*Mrs N. E. M. Warren's Charitable Trust**
*The Warrington Church of England Educational Trust**
*Warwick Relief in Need Charity**
*The Warwickshire Masonic Charitable Association Ltd**
Mrs Waterhouse Charitable Trust
The Waterloo Foundation
G. R. Waters Charitable Trust 2000
Wates Family Enterprise Trust
The Wates Foundation
Blyth Watson Charitable Trust
*The Watson Family Charitable Trust**
John Watson's Trust
Waynflete Charitable Trust
The Weavers' Company Benevolent Fund
The David Webster Charitable Trust
The Weinstein Foundation
The James Weir Foundation
The Wellcome Trust
The Welton Foundation
The Wessex Youth Trust
West Derby Waste Lands Charity
*The West Looe Town Trust**
The Westcroft Trust
The Westfield Health Charitable Trust
*The Westminster Amalgamated Charity**
The Westminster Foundation
The Garfield Weston Foundation
Westway Trust
The Barbara Whatmore Charitable Trust
*The Wheeler Family Charitable Trust**
The Whitaker Charitable Trust
Colonel W. H. Whitbread Charitable Trust
The Melanie White Foundation Ltd
White Stuff Foundation
The Whitecourt Charitable Trust
The Norman Whiteley Trust
The Whitewater Charitable Trust
The Whitley Animal Protection Trust
*The Wigoder Family Foundation**
The Lionel Wigram Memorial Trust
The Felicity Wilde Charitable Trust
The Will Charitable Trust
The Kay Williams Charitable Foundation
*The Alfred Williams Charitable Trust**
The Williams Charitable Trust
The Williams Family Charitable Trust
Williams Serendipity Trust
*The Willmott Dixon Foundation**
The HDH Wills 1965 Charitable Trust
Dame Violet Wills Charitable Trust
The Dame Violet Wills Will Trust
The Wilmcote Charitrust
*Brian Wilson Charitable Trust**
Sumner Wilson Charitable Trust
The Wilson Foundation
J. and J. R. Wilson Trust
Wiltshire Community Foundation
*The Wimbledon Foundation**
The W. Wing Yip and Brothers Foundation
The Harold Hyam Wingate Foundation
The Francis Winham Foundation
Winton Philanthropies
The Witzenfeld Foundation
The Michael and Anna Wix Charitable Trust
The Wixamtree Trust
The Maurice Wohl Charitable Foundation
The Charles Wolfson Charitable Trust
The James Wood Bequest Fund
The Wood Foundation
Wooden Spoon Society
The F. Glenister Woodger Trust
Woodlands Green Ltd
Woodroffe Benton Foundation
*The Woodstock Family Charitable Foundation**
The A. and R. Woolf Charitable Trust
Worcester Municipal Charities (CIO)
*The Worwin UK Foundation**
The Diana Edgson Wright Charitable Trust
Wychdale Ltd
Wychville Ltd
*The Wyfold Charitable Trust**
The Wyndham Charitable Trust
The Wyseliot Rose Charitable Trust
Yankov Charitable Trust
*York Children's Trust**
Yorkshire and Clydesdale Bank Foundation
Yorkshire Building Society Charitable Foundation
*Yorkshire Cancer Research**
The South Yorkshire Community Foundation
The William Allen Young Charitable Trust
The John Kirkhope Young Endowment Fund
Youth Music
The Z. Foundation
Zephyr Charitable Trust
The Marjorie and Arnold Ziff Charitable Foundation
Stephen Zimmerman Charitable Trust
The Zochonis Charitable Trust

Project funding

The 1970 Trust
The 1989 Willan Charitable Trust
The 29th May 1961 Charitable Trust
The A. B. Charitable Trust
The A. S. Charitable Trust
A. W. Charitable Trust
The Aberbrothock Skea Trust
The Aberdeen Foundation
ABF The Soldiers' Charity
The Acacia Charitable Trust

The Accenture Foundation
Access Sport CIO
Achisomoch Aid Company Ltd
The ACT Foundation
Action Medical Research
Adenfirst Ltd
The Adint Charitable Trust
*The AEB Charitable Trust**
AF Trust Company
Age Scotland
Age UK
Aid to the Church in Need (UK)
Ajahma Charitable Trust
*AKO Foundation**
The Alborada Trust
D. G. Albright Charitable Trust
The Alchemy Foundation
All Saints Educational Trust
Allchurches Trust Ltd
The H. B. Allen Charitable Trust
The Alliance Family Foundation
*Alzheimer's Society**
AM Charitable Trust
Viscount Amory's Charitable Trust
The Ampelos Trust
The AMW Charitable Trust
The Andrew Anderson Trust
Andor Charitable Trust
Anglo American Group Foundation
The Annandale Charitable Trust
Anpride Ltd
The Anson Charitable Trust
The Apax Foundation
The Arbib Foundation
The Archer Trust
The Architectural Heritage Fund
The Ardeola Charitable Trust
The Argus Appeal
The John Armitage Charitable Trust
The Arsenal Foundation Ltd
The Artemis Charitable Trust
Arts Council England
Arts Council of Northern Ireland
Arts Council of Wales (also known as Cyngor Celfyddydau Cymru)
The Ove Arup Foundation
ASCB Charitable Fund
The Ashburnham Thanksgiving Trust
The Ashley Family Foundation
*The Associated Board of the Royal Schools of Music**
The Astor Foundation
The Atlas Fund
Autonomous Research Charitable Trust (ARCT)
The Avon and Somerset Police Community Trust
Awards for All (see also the Big Lottery Fund)
The Aylesford Family Charitable Trust
The Bacit Foundation
Backstage Trust
The Harry Bacon Foundation
The Bagri Foundation
The Baird Trust
*Bairdwatson Charitable Trust**
The Roy and Pixie Baker Charitable Trust
The Balfour Beatty Charitable Trust
The Baltic Charitable Fund
The Banbury Charities
The Band Trust
The Barbers' Company General Charities
The Barbour Foundation
Barchester Healthcare Foundation
The Barclay Foundation
The Baring Foundation
*The Philip Barker Charity**
The Barker-Mill Foundation
Lord Barnby's Foundation
The Barnsbury Charitable Trust
Barnwood Trust
*The Barrack Charitable Trust**
Misses Barrie Charitable Trust
The Bartlett Taylor Charitable Trust
The Batchworth Trust
Bay Charitable Trust
The Bay Tree Charitable Trust
The Louis Baylis (Maidenhead Advertiser) Charitable Trust
BBC Children in Need
BC Partners Foundation
BCH Trust
Bear Mordechai Ltd
The Bearder Charity
The James Beattie Charitable Trust
Beauland Ltd
*The Becht Family Charitable Trust**
The John Beckwith Charitable Trust
The David and Ruth Behrend Fund
*The Behrens Foundation**
The Bellahouston Bequest Fund
Belljoe Tzedoko Ltd
*Benesco Charity Ltd**
The Benham Charitable Settlement
*The Rowan Bentall Charitable Trust**
The Ruth Berkowitz Charitable Trust
The Berkshire Community Foundation
The Bestway Foundation
The Big Lottery Fund (see also Awards for All)
The Billmeir Charitable Trust
The Bingham Trust
The Birmingham District Nursing Charitable Trust
Birmingham International Airport Community Trust Fund
The Lord Mayor of Birmingham's Charity
Birthday House Trust
Miss Jeanne Bisgood's Charitable Trust
The Michael Bishop Foundation
The Bertie Black Foundation
Isabel Blackman Foundation
The Blagrave Trust
The Blair Foundation
The Morgan Blake Charitable Trust
Blakemore Foundation
The Sir Victor Blank Charitable Settlement
*The Bloomfield Charitable Trust**
The Marjory Boddy Charitable Trust
The Bonamy Charitable Trust
The Charlotte Bonham-Carter Charitable Trust
The Linda and Gordon Bonnyman Charitable Trust
The Booth Charities
Boots Charitable Trust
Salo Bordon Charitable Trust
The Bordon Liphook Haslemere Charity
*Sir William Boreman's Foundation**
*The Borrows Charitable Trust**
The Oliver Borthwick Memorial Trust
The Bothwell Charitable Trust
The Harry Bottom Charitable Trust
P. G. and N. J. Boulton Trust
Sir Clive Bourne Family Trust
Bourneheights Ltd
The Bowerman Charitable Trust
The Bowland Charitable Trust
The Frank Brake Charitable Trust
The William Brake Charitable Trust
The Tony Bramall Charitable Trust
The Liz and Terry Bramall Foundation
The Bransford Trust
The Breadsticks Foundation
*The Brelms Trust CIO**
Bridge Trust
Bridgepoint Charitable Trust

Bristol Archdeaconry Charity
Bristol Charities
The British and Foreign School Society
British Council for Prevention of Blindness (Save Eyes Everywhere)
The British Dietetic Association General and Education Trust Fund
*British Eye Research Foundation (Fight for Sight)**
British Gas (Scottish Gas) Energy Trust
British Heart Foundation (BHF)
British Humane Association
British Record Industry Trust
The Britten-Pears Foundation (The Britten Pears Library)
The Bromley Trust
The Rory and Elizabeth Brooks Foundation
The Charles Brotherton Trust
Bill Brown 1989 Charitable Trust
R. S. Brownless Charitable Trust
The T. B. H. Brunner's Charitable Settlement
The Bruntwood Charity
Brushmill Ltd
Buckingham Trust
Buckinghamshire Community Foundation
The Buffini Chao Foundation
The E. F. Bulmer Benevolent Fund
BUPA UK Foundation
*The Burberry Foundation**
The Burdett Trust for Nursing
The Burry Charitable Trust
The Arnold Burton 1998 Charitable Trust
Consolidated Charity of Burton upon Trent
The Derek Butler Trust
The Noel Buxton Trust
The Edward Cadbury Charitable Trust
The William A. Cadbury Charitable Trust
The Christopher Cadbury Charitable Trust
The G. W. Cadbury Charitable Trust
The Cadbury Foundation
The Barrow Cadbury Trust
The George Cadbury Trust
The Cadogan Charity
CAFOD (Catholic Agency for Overseas Development)
Community Foundation for Calderdale
Callander Charitable Trust
Calleva Foundation
Calouste Gulbenkian Foundation – UK Branch
The Frederick and Phyllis Cann Trust
Cardy Beaver Foundation
*The W. A. Cargill Charitable Trust**
David William Traill Cargill Fund
*The W. A. Cargill Fund**
The Richard Carne Trust
The Carnegie Dunfermline Trust
The Carpenters' Company Charitable Trust
The Carrington Charitable Trust
The Leslie Mary Carter Charitable Trust
The Casey Trust
Sir John Cass's Foundation
*Sir Ernest Cassel Educational Trust**
The Elizabeth Casson Trust
The Castang Foundation
The Catholic Charitable Trust
The Catholic Trust for England and Wales
The Joseph and Annie Cattle Trust
The Thomas Sivewright Catto Charitable Settlement
The Wilfrid and Constance Cave Foundation
The Cayo Foundation
Elizabeth Cayzer Charitable Trust
The B. G. S. Cayzer Charitable Trust
The CBD Charitable Trust
CBRE UK Charitable Trust
The CH (1980) Charitable Trust
The Amelia Chadwick Trust
Charitworth Ltd
Chartered Accountants' Livery Charity (CALC)
*Cheshire Community Foundation Ltd**
Chesterhill Charitable Trust
Children with Cancer UK
Children's Liver Disease Foundation
The Childwick Trust
CHK Charities Ltd
Christadelphian Samaritan Fund
Christian Aid
The Church Burgesses Educational Foundation
Church Burgesses Trust
Church of Ireland Priorities Fund
Church Urban Fund
The City Bridge Trust (Bridge House Estates)
The City Educational Trust Fund
*The Clan Trust Ltd**
Stephen Clark 1957 Charitable Trust
J. A. Clark Charitable Trust
The Roger and Sarah Bancroft Clark Charitable Trust
*The Clark Foundation**
The Cleopatra Trust
The Clore Duffield Foundation
Richard Cloudesley's Charity
The Clover Trust
The Robert Clutterbuck Charitable Trust
Clydpride Ltd
The Coalfields Regeneration Trust
The John Coates Charitable Trust
The Cobalt Trust
The Cobtree Charity Trust Ltd
The Denise Cohen Charitable Trust
The Vivienne and Samuel Cohen Charitable Trust
The John S. Cohen Foundation
The Colchester Catalyst Charity
John Coldman Charitable Trust
The Colefax Charitable Trust
The Sir Jeremiah Colman Gift Trust
Col-Reno Ltd
The Colt Foundation
The Coltstaple Trust
Comic Relief
The Comino Foundation
Community First (Landfill Communities Fund)
Martin Connell Charitable Trust
*The Thomas Cook Chidlren's Charity**
The Ernest Cook Trust
The Cooks Charity
The Catherine Cookson Charitable Trust
Mabel Cooper Charity
The Alice Ellen Cooper Dean Charitable Foundation
The J. Reginald Corah Foundation Fund
The Worshipful Company of Cordwainers Charitable Trusts (Minges Gift and the Pooled Trusts)
The Gershon Coren Charitable Foundation (also known as The Muriel and Gus Coren Charitable Foundation)
The Costa Family Charitable Trust
The Cotton Industry War Memorial Trust

The County Council of Dyfed Welsh Curch Fund
Coutts Charitable Foundation
General Charity of Coventry
The Craignish Trust
The Cray Trust
*Credit Suisse EMEA Foundation**
The Crescent Trust
*England and Wales Cricket Trust**
Cripplegate Foundation
The Violet and Milo Cripps Charitable Trust
*Crisis UK**
The Cross Trust
The Peter Cruddas Foundation
Cruden Foundation Ltd
*CSIS Charity Fund**
The Cuby Charitable Trust
The Cunningham Trust
The Harry Cureton Charitable Trust
Roald Dahl's Marvellous Children's Charity
The Daiwa Anglo-Japanese Foundation
Oizer Dalim Trust
The Dr and Mrs A. Darlington Charitable Trust
Baron Davenport's Charity
The Davidson (Nairn) Charitable Trust
The Davidson Family Charitable Trust
*The John Grant Davies Trust**
The Davis Foundation
The Henry and Suzanne Davis Foundation
*Dawat-E-Hadiyah Trust (United Kingdom)**
The Dawe Charitable Trust
*The Roger De Haan Charitable Trust**
Peter De Haan Charitable Trust
*The De La Rue Charitable Trust**
William Dean Countryside and Educational Trust
The Delius Trust
The Dellal Foundation
The Delves Charitable Trust
The Demigryphon Trust
Foundation Derbyshire
Devon Community Foundation
Diabetes UK
The Diageo Foundation
Alan and Sheila Diamond Charitable Trust
The Gillian Dickinson Trust
Dinwoodie Charitable Company
The Dischma Charitable Trust
The DLM Charitable Trust
The DM Charitable Trust
The Dollond Charitable Trust
Dorset Community Foundation
The Dorus Trust
The Double 'O' Charity Ltd
The Doughty Charity Trust
Douglas Arter Foundation
The Drapers' Charitable Fund
Dromintee Trust
Duchy Health Charity Ltd
The Dulverton Trust
The Dumbreck Charity
The Dunn Family Charitable Trust
The Charles Dunstone Charitable Trust
County Durham Community Foundation
Dushinsky Trust Ltd
The Mildred Duveen Charitable Trust
The Dyers' Company Charitable Trust
Audrey Earle Charitable Trust
The Earley Charity
Earls Colne and Halstead Educational Charity
East End Community Foundation
The Sir John Eastwood Foundation
The EBM Charitable Trust
*Edge Foundation**
Edinburgh Trust No 2 Account
*The Eighty Eight Foundation**
*Elanore Ltd**
The Elephant Trust
The George Elias Charitable Trust
The Gerald Palmer Eling Trust Company
The Wilfred and Elsie Elkes Charity Fund
The Maud Elkington Charitable Trust
Ellador Ltd
The John Ellerman Foundation
The Elmley Foundation
The Vernon N. Ely Charitable Trust
The Emerton-Christie Charity
The Englefield Charitable Trust
The Epigoni Trust
Epilepsy Research UK
The Erskine Cunningham Hill Trust
The Esfandi Charitable Foundation
Esh Foundation
The Essex and Southend Sports Trust
The Essex Heritage Trust
The Alan Evans Memorial Trust
The Eventhall Family Charitable Trust
Matthew Eyton Animal Welfare Trust
The Farthing Trust
The John Feeney Charitable Bequest
Elizabeth Ferguson Charitable Trust Fund
*The Fidelio Charitable Trust**
Fishmongers' Company's Charitable Trust
Marc Fitch Fund
The Follett Trust
The Football Association National Sports Centre Trust
Fordeve Ltd
Forest Hill Charitable Trust
Forever Manchester
Donald Forrester Trust
The Anna Rosa Forster Charitable Trust
The Lord Forte Foundation
The Foyle Foundation
*The Raphael Freshwater Memorial Association**
Friends Provident Charitable Foundation
Mejer and Gertrude Miriam Frydman Foundation
Gatwick Airport Community Trust
The General Nursing Council for England and Wales Trust
*The Genesis Charitable Trust**
*Genetic Disorders UK**
The Steven Gerrard Foundation
*The Gerrick Rose Animal Trust**
*Gilchrist Educational Trust**
The Girdlers' Company Charitable Trust
Global Charities
The Golsoncott Foundation
The Mike Gooley Trailfinders Charity
The Goshen Trust
A. and S. Graham Charitable Trust
*The Graham Trust**
The Gray Trust
The Great Britain Sasakawa Foundation
Mrs H. R. Greene Charitable Settlement
Greenham Common Community Trust Ltd
The Greggs Foundation
The Grocers' Charity
N. and R. Grunbaum Charitable Trust
The Bishop of Guildford's Foundation
Dr Guthrie's Association
H. and T. Clients Charitable Trust
Hackney Parochial Charities
The Hadfield Charitable Trust

Halifax Foundation for Northern Ireland (previously known as Lloyds Bank Foundation for Northern Ireland)
*Hammersmith United Charities**
The Hampshire and Islands Historic Churches Trust
Hampshire and Isle of Wight Community Foundation
The Harbour Charitable Trust
The Peter Harrison Foundation
The Hartley Charitable Trust
The Maurice Hatter Foundation
*HC Foundation**
The Headley Trust
The Health Foundation
Heart of England Community Foundation
Heart Research UK
The Heathcoat Trust
Help for Health
Help the Homeless Ltd
The Christina Mary Hendrie Trust for Scottish and Canadian Charities
Henley Educational Trust
Philip Henman Trust
Herefordshire Community Foundation
The Herefordshire Historic Churches Trust
The Hilden Charitable Fund
The Hillingdon Community Trust
Hinchley Charitable Trust
The Hinduja Foundation
The Hinrichsen Foundation
The Hiscox Foundation
Hockerill Educational Foundation
The Hollands-Warren Fund
P. H. Holt Foundation
The Holywood Trust
The Homelands Charitable Trust
The Homestead Charitable Trust
The Hoover Foundation
The Hope Trust
The Horizon Foundation
The Worshipful Company of Horners' Charitable Trusts
*Horwich Shotter Charitable Trust**
The Hospital of God at Greatham
The Hospital Saturday Fund
House of Industry Estate
Human Relief Foundation
The Michael and Shirley Hunt Charitable Trust
The Hunter Foundation
Miss Agnes H. Hunter's Trust
The Huntingdon Foundation Ltd
The Hutton Foundation
The P. Y. N. and B. Hyams Trust
Hyde Charitable Trust (Youth Plus)
*The Hyde Park Place Estate Charity – civil trustees**
IBM United Kingdom Trust
The Idlewild Trust
Imagine Foundation
Incommunities Foundation
The Indigo Trust
*The Worshipful Company of Information Technologists**
The Inman Charity
*The Worshipful Company of Insurers – First Charitable Trust Fund**
The International Bankers Charitable Trust (The Worshipful Company of Interntional Bankers)
The Inverforth Charitable Trust
The Ireland Fund of Great Britain
Irish Youth Foundation (UK) Ltd (incorporating The Lawlor Foundation)
The Isle of Anglesey Charitable Trust
The ITF Seafarers' Trust
The J. J. Charitable Trust
The JRSST Charitable Trust
The Ruth and Lionel Jacobson Trust (Second Fund) No. 2
John James Bristol Foundation
Lady Eda Jardine Charitable Trust
The Jarman Charitable Trust
Rees Jeffreys Road Fund
The Jephcott Charitable Trust
The Jerusalem Trust
The Jerwood Charitable Foundation
Jewish Child's Day (JCD)
The Jewish Youth Fund (JYF)
Joffe Charitable Trust
The Elton John AIDS Foundation (EJAF)
Johnson Wax Ltd Charitable Trust
The Joicey Trust
The Dezna Robins Jones Charitable Foundation
J. E. Joseph Charitable Fund
The Cyril and Eve Jumbo Charitable Trust
The Kasner Charitable Trust
The Kelly Family Charitable Trust
Kelsick's Educational Foundation
The Kay Kendall Leukaemia Fund
The Kennel Club Charitable Trust
Kent Community Foundation
The Nancy Kenyon Charitable Trust
Keren Association Ltd
The Peter Kershaw Trust
Kidney Research UK
*The Kildare Trust**
The Robert Kiln Charitable Trust
The King Henry VIII Endowed Trust – Warwick
The King/Cullimore Charitable Trust
The Mary Kinross Charitable Trust
*The Graham Kirkham Foundation**
Kirkley Poor's Land Estate
The Richard Kirkman Trust
The Kirschel Foundation
Robert Kitchin (Saddlers' Company)
The Ernest Kleinwort Charitable Trust
The Kobler Trust
The Kohn Foundation
The KPMG Foundation
Kreditor Charitable Trust
The Neil Kreitman Foundation
Kupath Gemach Chaim Bechesed Viznitz Trust
Kusuma Trust UK
The Kyte Charitable Trust
Ladbrokes in the Community Charitable Trust
The K. P. Ladd Charitable Trust
John Laing Charitable Trust
Christopher Laing Foundation
Community Foundations for Lancashire and Merseyside
Duchy of Lancaster Benevolent Fund
Lancaster Foundation
LandAid Charitable Trust (Land Aid)
The Jack Lane Charitable Trust
The Allen Lane Foundation
Langdale Trust
The Langtree Trust
The LankellyChase Foundation
The R. J. Larg Family Charitable Trust
Largsmount Ltd
The Lauffer Family Charitable Foundation
Mrs F. B. Laurence Charitable Trust
The Kathleen Laurence Trust
The Law Society Charity
The Edgar E. Lawley Foundation
The Herd Lawson and Muriel Lawson Charitable Trust

Lawson Beckman Charitable Trust
The Raymond and Blanche Lawson Charitable Trust
The David Lean Foundation
The Leathersellers' Company Charitable Fund
The Leche Trust
The Arnold Lee Charitable Trust
Leeds Community Foundation (LCF)
*The Legal Education Foundation**
*Leicestershire and Rutland Masonic Charity Association**
Leicestershire, Leicester and Rutland Community Foundation
The Kennedy Leigh Charitable Trust
The Leigh Trust
P. Leigh-Bramwell Trust 'E'
*Leng Charitable Trust**
The Lennox Hannay Charitable Trust
The Mark Leonard Trust
*The Lethendy Charitable Trust**
The Leverhulme Trust
Lord Leverhulme's Charitable Trust
David and Ruth Lewis Family Charitable Trust
*Bernard Lewis Family Charitable Trust**
The John Spedan Lewis Foundation
The Sir Edward Lewis Foundation
John Lewis Partnership General Community Fund
Liberum Foundation
*The Lidbury Family Trust**
The Limbourne Trust
Limoges Charitable Trust
The Linbury Trust
Lincolnshire Community Foundation
Lindale Educational Foundation
The Linden Charitable Trust
The Enid Linder Foundation
The Lindley Foundation (TLF)
The Ruth and Stuart Lipton Charitable Trust
The Lister Charitable Trust
The Frank Litchfield Charitable Trust
The Charles Littlewood Hill Trust
The Second Joseph Aaron Littman Foundation
The George John and Sheilah Livanos Charitable Trust
Liverpool Charity and Voluntary Services (LCVS)
Jack Livingstone Charitable Trust
The Elaine and Angus Lloyd Charitable Trust
*The W. M. and B. W. Lloyd Trust**
Lloyd's Charities Trust
Lloyds Bank Foundation for England and Wales
Lloyds Bank Foundation for the Channel Islands
Lloyds TSB Foundation for Scotland
Localtrent Ltd
The Locker Foundation
*The Lockwood Charitable Foundation**
Loftus Charitable Trust
The Lolev Charitable Trust
The Joyce Lomax Bullock Charitable Trust
Trust for London
London Catalyst
The London Community Foundation (LCF)
London Housing Foundation Ltd (LHF)
London Legal Support Trust (LLST)
Inner London Magistrates Court's Poor Box and Feeder Charity
The William and Katherine Longman Trust
The Loseley and Guildway Charitable Trust
*P. and M. Lovell Charitable Settlement**
*Michael Lowe's and Associated Charities**
The Lower Green Foundation
The C. L. Loyd Charitable Trust
Robert Luff Foundation Ltd
The Henry Lumley Charitable Trust
Paul Lunn-Rockliffe Charitable Trust
C. F. Lunoe Trust Fund
Lord and Lady Lurgan Trust
The Lyndhurst Trust
The Lynn Foundation
John Lyon's Charity
The Sir Jack Lyons Charitable Trust
Sylvanus Lysons Charity
M. and C. Trust
The M. K. Charitable Trust
The M. Y. A. Charitable Trust
The Madeline Mabey Trust
The E. M. MacAndrew Trust
The Macdonald-Buchanan Charitable Trust
*Mace Foundation**
The Mackay and Brewer Charitable Trust
The MacRobert Trust
The Mactaggart Third Fund
The Magdalen and Lasher Charity (General Fund)
The Makers of Playing Cards Charity
The Manackerman Charitable Trust
The Manchester Guardian Society Charitable Trust
The Manoukian Charitable Foundation
The Marcela Trust
The Michael Marks Charitable Trust
The Ann and David Marks Foundation
The Marr-Munning Trust
Charity of John Marshall
D. G. Marshall of Cambridge Trust
John Martin's Charity
The Matliwala Family Charitable Trust
*Maudsley Charity**
*Maypride Ltd**
Mazars Charitable Trust
McGreevy No. 5 Settlement
Mercury Phoenix Trust
The Masonic Province of Middlesex Charitable Trust (Middlesex Masonic Charity)
Milton Keynes Community Foundation Ltd
The Edgar Milward Charity
The Peter Minet Trust
The Laurence Misener Charitable Trust
*Mitsubishi Corporation Fund for Europe and Africa**
The Mittal Foundation
Keren Mitzvah Trust
The Monatrea Charitable Trust
The Monmouthshire County Council Welsh Church Act Fund
John Moores Foundation
*The Morrisons Foundation**
The Mosselson Charitable Trust
Motor Neurone Disease Association
J. P. Moulton Charitable Foundation
The Frederick Mulder Foundation
Murphy-Neumann Charity Company Ltd
The John R. Murray Charitable Trust
Muslim Hands
MW (GK) Foundation
MW (HO) Foundation

MW (RH) Foundation
*The National Gardens Scheme**
The National Manuscripts Conservation Trust
The James Neill Trust Fund
Ner Foundation
Nesswall Ltd
*Nesta**
Network for Social Change Charitable Trust
Newby Trust Ltd
The Newcomen Collett Foundation
Newpier Charity Ltd
The NFU Mutual Charitable Trust
NJD Charitable Trust
Alice Noakes Memorial Charitable Trust
*The Norfolk Churches Trust Ltd**
Educational Foundation of Alderman John Norman
North West Cancer Research (incorporating Clatterbridge Cancer Research)
Northamptonshire Community Foundation
The Community Foundation for Northern Ireland
The Northmoor Trust
*The Northwick Trust**
The Norton Foundation
The Norton Rose Fulbright Charitable Foundation
The Norwood and Newton Settlement
Nottinghamshire Community Foundation
The Nottinghamshire Historic Churches Trust
The Oakdale Trust
Oglesby Charitable Trust
Oizer Charitable Trust
Old Possum's Practical Trust
The Oldham Foundation
*One Community Foundation Ltd**
OneFamily Foundation
Open Gate
The Ormsby Charitable Trust
The O'Sullivan Family Charitable Trust
The Ouseley Church Music Trust
Oxfam (GB)
Oxfordshire Community Foundation
*Oxfordshire Historic Churches Trust**
*The Paddington Charitable Estate Educational Fund**
The Panacea Charitable Trust
The Paphitis Charitable Trust
Paradigm Foundation
*The Pargiter Trust**
The Park House Charitable Trust
*The JGW Patterson Foundation**
Peacock Charitable Trust
The Pears Family Charitable Foundation
The Pell Charitable Trust
People's Health Trust
People's Postcode Trust
B. E. Perl Charitable Trust
Personal Assurance Charitable Trust
Petplan Charitable Trust
Miss A. M. Pilkington's Charitable Trust
Polden-Puckham Charitable Foundation
*The Polehampton Charity**
Pollywally Charitable Trust
The Polonsky Foundation
The Portishead Nautical Trust
Postcode Dream Trust – Dream Fund
*Power to Change Trust**
Premishlaner Charitable Trust
Sir John Priestman Charity Trust
The Prince of Wales's Charitable Foundation
The Princess Anne's Charities
*Prostate Cancer UK**
The PwC Foundation
*QBE European Operations Foundation**
Quartet Community Foundation
The Queen Anne's Gate Foundation
Queen Mary's Roehampton Trust
*Quercus Foundation**
Quothquan Trust
The Monica Rabagliati Charitable Trust
Rachel Charitable Trust
Racing Welfare
The Bishop Radford Trust
The Rambourg Foundation
The Joseph Rank Trust
The Ranworth Trust
The Ravensdale Trust
The Rayne Trust
The Sir James Reckitt Charity
The Rest Harrow Trust
Reuben Foundation
*Rhodi Charitable Trust**
Rhondda Cynon Taff Welsh Church Acts Fund
*Riada Trust**
Daisie Rich Trust
The Clive and Sylvia Richards Charity Ltd
Richmond Parish Lands Charity
Ridgesave Ltd
*Rigby Foundation**
The Sir John Ritblat Family Foundation
The River Trust
Rivers Foundation
*Riverside Charitable Trust Ltd**
The Rix-Thompson-Rothenberg Foundation
RJM Charity Trust
Robyn Charitable Trust
The Roddick Foundation
The Gerald Ronson Family Foundation
Rosca Trust
The Rose Foundation
*The Cissie Rosefield Charitable Trust**
The Cecil Rosen Foundation
Rosetrees Trust
*The David Ross Foundation**
The Rothley Trust
*Rothschild Foundation (Hanadiv) Europe**
The Roughley Charitable Trust
Mrs Gladys Row Fogo Charitable Trust
Rowanville Ltd
The Rowlands Trust
The Joseph Rowntree Foundation
Royal Artillery Charitable Fund
Royal Docks Trust (London)
*The Royal Navy And Royal Marines Charity**
Royal Victoria Hall Foundation
The Rufford Foundation
Rugby Football Foundation
The Rugby Group Benevolent Fund Ltd
The Sainsbury Family Charitable Trusts
Saint Sarkis Charity Trust
The Saintbury Trust
Salters' Charitable Foundation
The Andrew Salvesen Charitable Trust
The M. J. Samuel Charitable Trust
The Sandhu Charitable Foundation
The Sands Family Trust
Santander UK Foundation Ltd
The Sants Charitable Trust
*Sarum St Michael Educational Charity**
*The Save the Children Fund**
The Scarfe Charitable Trust
The Annie Schiff Charitable Trust
The Schreiber Charitable Trust
Schroder Charity Trust
Foundation Scotland
The Scotshill Trust
Scott (Eredine) Charitable Trust
The Francis C. Scott Charitable Trust

Sir Samuel Scott of Yews Trust
*The John Scott Trust Fund**
The Scouloudi Foundation
The SDL Foundation
Seafarers Hospital Society
Seafarers UK (King George's Fund for Sailors)
The Searchlight Electric Charitable Trust
The Seedfield Trust
*The Sellafield Charity Trust Fund**
Sellata Ltd
The Seven Fifty Trust
The Severn Trent Water Charitable Trust Fund
The Jean Shanks Foundation
The Shanley Charitable Trust
The Shanly Foundation
ShareGift (The Orr Mackintosh Foundation)
The Sheepdrove Trust
The Sheldon Trust
The Patricia and Donald Shepherd Charitable Trust
The Sylvia and Colin Shepherd Charitable Trust
*Sherburn House Charity**
*Sherling Charitable Trust**
The Archie Sherman Charitable Trust
The Shetland Charitable Trust
SHINE (Support and Help in Education)
The Shirley Foundation
Shlomo Memorial Fund Ltd
The Shoe Zone Trust
*The Shropshire Historic Churches Trust**
Silver Family Charitable Trust
The Simmons & Simmons Charitable Foundation
The Huntly and Margery Sinclair Charitable Trust
The Sino-British Fellowship Trust
The Skelton Bounty
*The Skerritt Trust**
The John Slater Foundation
Sloane Robinson Foundation
Rita and David Slowe Charitable Trust
Ruth Smart Foundation
The Mrs Smith and Mount Trust
The N. Smith Charitable Settlement
The Henry Smith Charity
The Leslie Smith Foundation
The WH Smith Group Charitable Trust
The Stanley Smith UK Horticultural Trust
Social Business Trust
Sodexo Stop Hunger Foundation
*Sofronie Foundation**
The Solo Charitable Settlement
David Solomons Charitable Trust
*Somerset Community Foundation**
Songdale Ltd
The Souter Charitable Trust
The South Square Trust
The W. F. Southall Trust
R. H. Southern Trust
The Southover Manor General Education Trust
*The Spalding Trust**
Spar Charitable Fund
Sparks Charity (Sport Aiding Medical Research for Kids)
The Spear Charitable Trust
Spears-Stutz Charitable Trust
Rosalyn and Nicholas Springer Charitable Trust
Springrule Ltd
The Spurrell Charitable Trust
The Geoff and Fiona Squire Foundation
The Squires Foundation
The St Hilda's Trust
St James's Place Foundation
Sir Walter St John's Educational Charity
St Monica Trust
St Olave's and St Saviour's Schools Foundation – Foundation Fund
St Peter's Saltley Trust
The Stafford Trust
*Standard Life Foundation**
The Stanley Foundation Ltd
The Staples Trust
C. E. K. Stern Charitable Trust
The Stevenage Community Trust
The Stewards' Charitable Trust
Sir Halley Stewart Trust
The Stone Family Foundation
*The Stoneygate Trust**
The Samuel Storey Family Charitable Trust
Peter Storrs Trust
The Strangward Trust
Stratford upon Avon Town Trust
The Strawberry Charitable Trust
The W. O. Street Charitable Foundation
*The Street Foundation**
The Sudborough Foundation
Sueberry Ltd
Suffolk Community Foundation
The Suffolk Historic Churches Trust
The Alan Sugar Foundation
The Bernard Sunley Charitable Foundation
*Sunninghill Fuel Allotment Trust**
*Surgo Foundation UK Ltd**
Community Foundation for Surrey
The Sussex Community Foundation
The Sutasoma Trust
Sutton Coldfield Charitable Trust
Swan Mountain Trust
The Swire Charitable Trust
The Charles and Elsie Sykes Trust
Sylvia Waddilove Foundation UK
The Tajtelbaum Charitable Trust
The Gay and Keith Talbot Trust
The Talbot Trusts
The Talbot Village Trust
Tallow Chandlers Benevolent Fund No. 2
Talteg Ltd
The Taurus Foundation
C. B. and H. H. Taylor 1984 Trust
The Connie and Albert Taylor Charitable Trust
Tearfund
Tees Valley Community Foundation
Tegham Ltd
The Templeton Goodwill Trust
The Tennis Foundation
*Tenovus Scotland**
The David Thomas Charitable Trust
*DM Thomas Foundation for Young People**
The Thompson Family Charitable Trust
The Sir Jules Thorn Charitable Trust
The Thornton Trust
The Thousandth Man- Richard Burns Charitable Trust
The Thriplow Charitable Trust
Tilney Charitable Trust
Mrs R. P. Tindall's Charitable Trust
The Tinsley Foundation
The Tobacco Pipe Makers and Tobacco Trade Benevolent Fund
The Tolkien Trust
Toras Chesed (London) Trust
Tottenham Grammar School Foundation
The Tower Hill Trust
The Toy Trust
Annie Tranmer Charitable Trust
The Constance Travis Charitable Trust

The Treeside Trust
The Trefoil Trust
Tropical Health and Education Trust*
The True Colours Trust
The Truemark Trust
Truemart Ltd
Trumros Ltd
The Trusthouse Charitable Foundation
The Trysil Charitable Trust*
The James Tudor Foundation
The Tudor Trust
The Tufton Charitable Trust
The Tuixen Foundation
The Roger and Douglas Turner Charitable Trust
The Turtleton Charitable Trust
Two Ridings Community Foundation
Community Foundation serving Tyne and Wear and Northumberland
The Udlington Trust
Ulting Overseas Trust
The Ulverscroft Foundation
United Utilities Trust Fund
The Michael Uren Foundation
Vale of Glamorgan Welsh Church Fund
The Valentine Charitable Trust
The Valiant Charitable Trust
The Albert Van Den Bergh Charitable Trust
Mrs Maud Van Norden's Charitable Foundation
The Vardy Foundation
Variety The Children's Charity (Variety Club)
The William and Patricia Venton Charitable Trust
Roger Vere Foundation
The Nigel Vinson Charitable Trust
The Vintners' Foundation
The Virgin Foundation (Virgin Unite)
The Virgin Money Foundation
Viridor Credits Environmental Company*
Volant Charitable Trust
Voluntary Action Fund (VAF)
Wade's Charity
The Scurrah Wainwright Charity
The Wakefield and Tetley Trust
The Wakeham Trust
The Community Foundation in Wales
Wales Council for Voluntary Action
Robert and Felicity Waley-Cohen Charitable Trust
Walton on Thames Charity
Sir Siegmund Warburg's Voluntary Settlement
The Barbara Ward Children's Foundation
The Warrington Church of England Educational Trust*
Warwick Relief in Need Charity*
The Warwickshire Masonic Charitable Association Ltd*
The Waterloo Foundation
G. R. Waters Charitable Trust 2000
Wates Family Enterprise Trust
The Wates Foundation
The Geoffrey Watling Charity*
Blyth Watson Charitable Trust
John Watson's Trust
Waynflete Charitable Trust
The Weavers' Company Benevolent Fund
Webb Memorial Trust
The David Webster Charitable Trust
The William Webster Charitable Trust
The James Weir Foundation
The Welton Foundation
The Wessex Youth Trust
West Derby Waste Lands Charity
The West Looe Town Trust*
The Westcroft Trust
The Westminster Amalgamated Charity*
The Garfield Weston Foundation
The Barbara Whatmore Charitable Trust
The Whitaker Charitable Trust
Colonel W. H. Whitbread Charitable Trust
The Melanie White Foundation Ltd
White Stuff Foundation
The Whitecourt Charitable Trust
The Norman Whiteley Trust
The Whitley Animal Protection Trust
The Wigoder Family Foundation*
The Lionel Wigram Memorial Trust
The Felicity Wilde Charitable Trust
The Will Charitable Trust
The Williams Charitable Trust
Williams Serendipity Trust
The HDH Wills 1965 Charitable Trust
Dame Violet Wills Charitable Trust
The Dame Violet Wills Will Trust
The Wilson Foundation
J. and J. R. Wilson Trust
Wiltshire Community Foundation
The W. Wing Yip and Brothers Foundation
The Harold Hyam Wingate Foundation
The Francis Winham Foundation
Winton Philanthropies
The Michael and Anna Wix Charitable Trust
The Wixamtree Trust
The Charles Wolfson Charitable Trust
The Wolfson Family Charitable Trust
The James Wood Bequest Fund
The Wood Foundation
Wooden Spoon Society
Woodlands Green Ltd
Woodroffe Benton Foundation
The A. and R. Woolf Charitable Trust
Worcester Municipal Charities (CIO)
The Diana Edgson Wright Charitable Trust
Wychdale Ltd
Wychville Ltd
The Wyndham Charitable Trust
The Wyseliot Rose Charitable Trust
Yankov Charitable Trust
York Children's Trust*
Yorkshire and Clydesdale Bank Foundation
Yorkshire Cancer Research*
The South Yorkshire Community Foundation
The William Allen Young Charitable Trust
The John Kirkhope Young Endowment Fund
Youth Music
The Z. Foundation
Zephyr Charitable Trust
The Marjorie and Arnold Ziff Charitable Foundation
Zurich Community Trust (UK) Ltd

■ Full project funding

The 1989 Willan Charitable Trust
The 3Ts Charitable Trust*
4 Charity Foundation
The A. S. Charitable Trust
A. W. Charitable Trust
A2BD Foundation UK Ltd*
The Aberbrothock Skea Trust
Aberdeen Asset Management Charitable Foundation
ABF The Soldiers' Charity

The Neville Abraham Foundation*
Achisomoch Aid Company Ltd
Action Medical Research
The Sylvia Adams Charitable Trust
The Addleshaw Goddard Charitable Trust
The AEB Charitable Trust*
Age UK
Aid to the Church in Need (UK)
The Sylvia Aitken Charitable Trust
Ajahma Charitable Trust
Aldgate and All Hallows' Foundation
The Derrill Allatt Foundation
The Allen & Overy Foundation*
The H. B. Allen Charitable Trust
The Alliance Family Foundation
Alzheimer's Research UK*
Amabrill Ltd
The Amalur Foundation Ltd
The Ammco Trust
Sir John and Lady Amory's Charitable Trust
The AMW Charitable Trust
The Ancaster Trust*
The Mary Andrew Charitable Trust
Andrews Charitable Trust
Anguish's Educational Foundation
The Animal Defence Trust
The Anne Duchess of Westminster's Charity*
Anpride Ltd
AO Smile Foundation*
The John Apthorp Charity
The Arah Foundation
Arcadia Charitable Trust*
The Argus Appeal
The Armourers' and Brasiers' Gauntlet Trust
The Arsenal Foundation Ltd
Arthritis Research UK
Arts Council England
Arts Council of Northern Ireland
Arts Council of Wales (also known as Cyngor Celfyddydau Cymru)
The Ove Arup Foundation
Ove Arup Partnership Charitable Trust
The Asfari Foundation*
The Ashden Trust
The Ashmore Foundation
The Ashworth Charitable Trust
The Ian Askew Charitable Trust
The Associated Country Women of the World
The Association of Colleges Charitable Trust
Asthma UK
The Astor Foundation
The Aurelius Charitable Trust
The Bacit Foundation
The Bagri Foundation
The Austin Bailey Foundation
The Baily Thomas Charitable Fund
The Baird Trust
Bairdwatson Charitable Trust*
The Baker Charitable Trust
The Balcombe Charitable Trust
The Andrew Balint Charitable Trust
The Ballinger Charitable Trust
The Baltic Charitable Fund
The Bamford Charitable Foundation
The Banbury Charities
The Bank of Scotland Foundation
The Barbers' Company General Charities
The Barcapel Foundation
The Barham Charitable Trust
The Philip Barker Charity*
The Barnsbury Charitable Trust
Barnwood Trust
The Barrack Charitable Trust*
Misses Barrie Charitable Trust
The Bartlett Taylor Charitable Trust
The Paul Bassham Charitable Trust
The Batchworth Trust
The Battens Charitable Trust
Bauer Radio's Cash for Kids Charities
The Bearder Charity
The James Beattie Charitable Trust
The Becht Family Charitable Trust*
The Becker Family Charitable Trust
The John Beckwith Charitable Trust
The Bedfordshire and Luton Community Foundation
Beefy's Charity Foundation
The David and Ruth Behrend Fund
The Behrens Foundation*
The Bellahouston Bequest Fund
Belljoe Tzedoko Ltd
The Benham Charitable Settlement
Bennett Lowell Ltd
The Rowan Bentall Charitable Trust*
The Berkeley Charitable Foundation
BHP Billiton Sustainable Communities*
The Billmeir Charitable Trust
The Bingham Trust
The Birmingham District Nursing Charitable Trust
The Lord Mayor of Birmingham's Charity
The Michael Bishop Foundation
Asser Bishvil Foundation*
The Sydney Black Charitable Trust
The Blagrave Trust
The Blair Foundation
The Morgan Blake Charitable Trust
The Blandford Lake Trust
The Sir Victor Blank Charitable Settlement
Bloodwise
Bloom Foundation
The Bluston Charitable Settlement
The Boltini Trust
The Charlotte Bonham-Carter Charitable Trust
The Boodle & Dunthorne Charitable Trust
BOOST Charitable Trust
Boots Charitable Trust
The Bordon Liphook Haslemere Charity
Sir William Boreman's Foundation*
The Borrows Charitable Trust*
The Oliver Borthwick Memorial Trust
The Boshier-Hinton Foundation
The Harry Bottom Charitable Trust
The Bowerman Charitable Trust
The Bowland Charitable Trust
Friends of Boyan Trust
The Frank Brake Charitable Trust
The William Brake Charitable Trust
The Breast Cancer Research Trust (BCRT)
The Brelms Trust CIO*
The Harold and Alice Bridges Charity
John Bristow and Thomas Mason Trust
The British and Foreign Bible Society*
British Humane Association
The J. and M. Britton Charitable Trust
The Consuelo and Anthony Brooke Charitable Trust
The Charles Brotherton Trust
Buckinghamshire Community Foundation
The Burry Charitable Trust
The Arnold Burton 1998 Charitable Trust

Consolidated Charity of Burton upon Trent
*The Butters Foundation (UK) Ltd**
The Christopher Cadbury Charitable Trust
The G. W. Cadbury Charitable Trust
The Edward and Dorothy Cadbury Trust
CAFOD (Catholic Agency for Overseas Development)
Community Foundation for Calderdale
Callander Charitable Trust
The Cambridgeshire Community Foundation
*The W. A. Cargill Fund**
The Carnegie Trust for the Universities of Scotland
The Carpenters' Company Charitable Trust
The Carr-Gregory Trust
The Carrington Charitable Trust
The Leslie Mary Carter Charitable Trust
*Sir Ernest Cassel Educational Trust**
The Elizabeth Casson Trust
The Castang Foundation
*The Castansa Trust**
The Cattanach Charitable Trust
The Joseph and Annie Cattle Trust
The Thomas Sivewright Catto Charitable Settlement
The Wilfrid and Constance Cave Foundation
The B. G. S. Cayzer Charitable Trust
The Cazenove Charitable Trust
Celtic Charity Fund
CEO Sleepout
*The Chadwick Educational Foundation**
Chalfords Ltd
The Chapman Charitable Trust
Charitworth Ltd
The Charter 600 Charity
The Cheruby Trust
Cheshire Freemason's Charity
CHK Charities Ltd
The Chownes Foundation
Christadelphian Samaritan Fund
Christian Aid
Chrysalis Trust
The Church Burgesses Educational Foundation
Church Burgesses Trust
Church of Ireland Priorities Fund
The CIBC World Markets Children's Miracle Foundation
The City Educational Trust Fund
*The Clan Trust Ltd**
The Hilda and Alice Clark Charitable Trust
The Roger and Sarah Bancroft Clark Charitable Trust
The Clore Duffield Foundation
Closehelm Ltd
Richard Cloudesley's Charity
The Robert Clutterbuck Charitable Trust
Clydpride Ltd
The John Coates Charitable Trust
Denise Coates Foundation
The Cobtree Charity Trust Ltd
The Denise Cohen Charitable Trust
The Vivienne and Samuel Cohen Charitable Trust
The John S. Cohen Foundation
The R. and S. Cohen Foundation
The Colchester Catalyst Charity
The Cole Charitable Trust
The Colefax Charitable Trust
John and Freda Coleman Charitable Trust
The Colt Foundation
The Coltstaple Trust
Colwinston Charitable Trust
Colyer-Fergusson Charitable Trust
Comic Relief
The Comino Foundation
The Douglas Compton James Charitable Trust
The Congregational and General Charitable Trust
The Ernest Cook Trust
The Cooks Charity
The Keith Coombs Trust
Mabel Cooper Charity
The Marjorie Coote Old People's Charity
The Helen Jean Cope Trust
The Gershon Coren Charitable Foundation (also known as The Muriel and Gus Coren Charitable Foundation)
Michael Cornish Charitable Trust
The Evan Cornish Foundation
Cornwall Community Foundation
The Duke of Cornwall's Benevolent Fund
The Cornwell Charitable Trust
*The Corporation of Trinity House of Deptford Strond**
The Costa Family Charitable Trust
The Cotton Industry War Memorial Trust
The Cotton Trust
*The Coulthurst Trust**
The Augustine Courtauld Trust
General Charity of Coventry
Coventry Building Society Charitable Foundation
The John Cowan Foundation
The Sir Tom Cowie Charitable Trust
Dudley and Geoffrey Cox Charitable Trust
The Lord Cozens-Hardy Trust
The Craps Charitable Trust
The Cray Trust
*The Elizabeth Creak Charitable Trust**
Creative Scotland
The Crerar Hotels Trust
Criffel Charitable Trust
The Violet and Milo Cripps Charitable Trust
The Cross Trust
The Cross Trust
The Croydon Relief in Need Charities
Cruden Foundation Ltd
The Ronald Cruickshanks Foundation
Cullum Family Trust
Cumbria Community Foundation
Itzchok Meyer Cymerman Trust Ltd
The D. G. Charitable Settlement
The D'Oyly Carte Charitable Trust
Roald Dahl's Marvellous Children's Charity
The Daiwa Anglo-Japanese Foundation
The Joan Lynette Dalton Charitable Trust
The Dr and Mrs A. Darlington Charitable Trust
Baron Davenport's Charity
The Davidson (Nairn) Charitable Trust
The Davidson Family Charitable Trust
Michael Davies Charitable Settlement
*The Biss Davies Charitable Trust**
Margaret Davies Charity
*The John Grant Davies Trust**
The Crispin Davis Family Trust
The Dawe Charitable Trust
The De Brye Charitable Trust
Peter De Haan Charitable Trust
The De Laszlo Foundation
Debenhams Foundation
Debmar Benevolent Trust Ltd
The Dellal Foundation
The Delves Charitable Trust

The Demigryphon Trust
The Denman Charitable Trust
Dentons UKMEA LLP Charitable Trust
Foundation Derbyshire
Provincial Grand Charity of the Province of Derbyshire
The J. N. Derbyshire Trust
The Desmond Foundation
The Sandy Dewhirst Charitable Trust
The Laduma Dhamecha Charitable Trust
Diabetes UK
The Gillian Dickinson Trust
Didymus
C. H. Dixon Charitable Trust*
The Djanogly Foundation
The DLM Charitable Trust
The Derek and Eileen Dodgson Foundation
The Dollond Charitable Trust
The Dorcas Trust
The Dorfman Foundation*
The Doughty Charity Trust
The Royal Foundation of the Duke and Duchess of Cambridge and Prince Harry
The Dumbreck Charity
Dunard Fund 2016
The Dunhill Medical Trust
The Dunn Family Charitable Trust
County Durham Community Foundation
The Dyers' Company Charitable Trust
The James Dyson Foundation
Eaga Charitable Trust
Earls Colne and Halstead Educational Charity
East End Community Foundation
Eastern Counties Educational Trust Ltd
The EBM Charitable Trust
The ECHO Trust*
Echoes Of Service
The Ecology Trust
The Economist Charitable Trust
EDF Energy Trust (EDFET)
The Gilbert and Eileen Edgar Foundation
Edge Foundation*
Edinburgh Children's Holiday Fund
Edinburgh Trust No 2 Account
Edupoor Ltd
Dr Edwards Bishop King's Fulham Endowment Fund
The W. G. Edwards Charitable Foundation
The Eighty Eight Foundation*
Elanore Ltd*
The Elephant Trust
The George Elias Charitable Trust
The Gerald Palmer Eling Trust Company
The Wilfred and Elsie Elkes Charity Fund
The Maud Elkington Charitable Trust
The John Ellerman Foundation
The Ellinson Foundation Ltd
The Vernon N. Ely Charitable Trust
The Emerald Foundation*
The Emerton-Christie Charity
The Englefield Charitable Trust
The Enkalon Foundation
Entindale Ltd
The Epigoni Trust
Epilepsy Research UK
The Eranda Rothschild Foundation
The Ericson Trust
Esher House Charitable Trust
Essex Community Foundation
The Essex Youth Trust
The Estelle Trust
Joseph Ettedgui Charitable Foundation
Euro Charity Trust
The Eventhall Family Charitable Trust
The Eveson Charitable Trust
The Beryl Evetts and Robert Luff Animal Welfare Trust Ltd
The Exilarch's Foundation
Extonglen Ltd
The William and Christine Eynon Charity
G. F. Eyre Charitable Trust
The F. P. Ltd Charitable Trust
Esmée Fairbairn Foundation
The Fairstead Trust
Famos Foundation Trust
The Lord Faringdon Charitable Trust
Samuel William Farmer Trust
The Thomas Farr Charity
The February Foundation
The George Fentham Birmingham Charity
The A. M. Fenton Trust
Allan and Nesta Ferguson Charitable Settlement
The Fidelity UK Foundation
The Doris Field Charitable Trust
The Fifty Fund
Dixie Rose Findlay Charitable Trust
The Sir John Fisher Foundation
Fisherbeck Charitable Trust
The Fitton Trust
The Earl Fitzwilliam Charitable Trust
The Joyce Fletcher Charitable Trust
The Football Association National Sports Centre Trust
The Football Foundation
The Forbes Charitable Foundation
Ford Britain Trust
The Oliver Ford Charitable Trust
The Lady Forester Trust
The Forman Hardy Charitable Trust
Gwyneth Forrester Trust
The Fort Foundation
The Forte Charitable Trust
The Foyle Foundation
The Isaac and Freda Frankel Memorial Charitable Trust
The Elizabeth Frankland Moore and Star Foundation
Jill Franklin Trust
The Gordon Fraser Charitable Trust
The Hugh Fraser Foundation
The Joseph Strong Frazer Trust
The Louis and Valerie Freedman Charitable Settlement
The Michael and Clara Freeman Charitable Trust
The Charles S. French Charitable Trust
The Anne French Memorial Trust
The Freshfield Foundation
The Freshgate Trust Foundation
Friarsgate Trust
Friends of Biala Ltd
Friends of Wiznitz Ltd
Friends Provident Charitable Foundation
The Frognal Trust
The Adrian and Jane Frost Charitable Trust
The Patrick and Helena Frost Foundation
The Fulmer Charitable Trust
The G. D. Charitable Trust
G. M. C. Trust
The G. R. P. Charitable Trust
The Galanthus Trust
The Gale Family Charity Trust
The Gannochy Trust
The Ganzoni Charitable Trust
The Worshipful Company of Gardeners of London
The Garrard Family Foundation
The Gatsby Charitable Foundation
The Robert Gavron Charitable Trust
The Jacqueline and Michael Gee Charitable Trust

The General Nursing Council for England and Wales Trust
The Generations Foundation
*The Genesis Charitable Trust**
*The Gerrick Rose Animal Trust**
The Gertner Charitable Trust
The Gibbons Family Trust
The David Gibbons Foundation
The Gibbs Charitable Trust
The G. C. Gibson Charitable Trust
The Simon Gibson Charitable Trust
*Gilchrist Educational Trust**
*The L. and R. Gilley Charitable Trust**
The Girdlers' Company Charitable Trust
The B. and P. Glasser Charitable Trust
The Glass-House Trust
The Gloag Foundation
Global Care
Global Charities
Gloucestershire Community Foundation
The Gloucestershire Historic Churches Trust
Worshipful Company of Glovers of London Charitable Trust
The Godinton Charitable Trust
Worshipful Company of Gold and Silver Wyre Drawers Charitable Trust Fund
Sydney and Phyllis Goldberg Memorial Charitable Trust
The Golden Bottle Trust
The Goldman Sachs Charitable Gift Fund (UK)
Goldman Sachs Gives (UK)
The Goldsmiths' Company Charity
The Golf Foundation Ltd
Nicholas and Judith Goodison's Charitable Settlement
The Goodman Foundation
The Mike Gooley Trailfinders Charity
*The Gordon Trust**
The Gosling Foundation Ltd
The Gould Charitable Trust
Gowling WLG (UK) Charitable Trust
The Hemraj Goyal Foundation
Grace Charitable Trust
Graff Foundation
E. C. Graham Belford Charitable Settlement
*The Graham Trust**
Grahame Charitable Foundation Ltd
The Granada Foundation
Grand Charitable Trust of the Order of Women Freemasons
The Grantham Yorke Trust
GrantScape
The J. G. Graves Charitable Trust
Gordon Gray Trust
The Gray Trust
The Kenneth and Susan Green Charitable Foundation
The Green Hall Foundation
Philip and Judith Green Trust
Greenham Common Community Trust Ltd
The Greggs Foundation
The Gretna Charitable Trust
Greys Charitable Trust
The Grimmitt Trust
The Grocers' Charity
M. and R. Gross Charities Ltd
N. and R. Grunbaum Charitable Trust
Guildry Incorporation of Perth
The Walter Guinness Charitable Trust
The Gunter Charitable Trust
The Gur Trust
H. C. D. Memorial Fund
H. P. Charitable Trust
Hackney Parochial Charities
The Hadfield Charitable Trust
The Hadley Trust
Hadras Kodesh Trust
The Hadrian Trust
The Alfred Haines Charitable Trust
The Haley Family Charitable Trust
Halifax Foundation for Northern Ireland (previously known as Lloyds Bank Foundation for Northern Ireland)
Hamamelis Trust
Paul Hamlyn Foundation
The Helen Hamlyn Trust
*Hammersmith United Charities**
The Hampshire and Islands Historic Churches Trust
Hampton Fuel Allotment Charity
The W. A. Handley Charity Trust
The Kathleen Hannay Memorial Charity
*The Happold Foundation**
The Haramead Trust
Harbinson Charitable Trust
Harbo Charities Ltd
The Harbour Foundation
The Harding Trust
William Harding's Charity
The Harebell Centenary Fund
The Peter and Teresa Harris Charitable Trust
The Harris Charity
The Harris Family Charitable Trust
The Edith Lilian Harrison 2000 Foundation
The Peter Harrison Foundation
The Harrison-Frank Family Foundation (UK) Ltd
The Alfred And Peggy Harvey Charitable Trust
The Hasluck Charitable Trust
The Hathaway Trust
The Hawthorne Charitable Trust
The Charles Hayward Foundation
*HC Foundation**
May Hearnshaw Charitable Trust (May Hearnshaw's Charity)
Heathrow Community Fund (LHR Airport Communities Trust)
The Heathside Charitable Trust
*Heb Ffin (Without Frontier)**
The Charlotte Heber-Percy Charitable Trust
Ernest Hecht Charitable Foundation
The Percy Hedley 1990 Charitable Trust
Hedley Foundation Ltd (The Hedley Foundation)
The Michael Heller Charitable Foundation
The Simon Heller Charitable Settlement
The Helping Foundation
The Hemby Charitable Trust
*Henderson Firstfruits**
The G. D. Herbert Charitable Trust
Hertfordshire Community Foundation
The Hesslewood Children's Trust (Hull Seamen's and General Orphanage)
The Alan Edward Higgs Charity
Highcroft Charitable Trust
The Derek Hill Foundation
*M. V. Hillhouse Trust**
The Hillier Trust
R. G. Hills Charitable Trust
The Hintze Family Charity Foundation
The Henry C. Hoare Charitable Trust
The Hobson Charity Ltd
The Jane Hodge Foundation
The Holden Charitable Trust
The Hollick Family Charitable Trust
The Holliday Foundation

The Dorothy Holmes Charitable Trust
The Mary Homfray Charitable Trust
Sir Harold Hood's Charitable Trust
The Hoover Foundation
Hopmarket Charity
The Antony Hornby Charitable Trust
The Thomas J. Horne Memorial Trust
*Horwich Shotter Charitable Trust**
The Sir Joseph Hotung Charitable Settlement
The Reta Lila Howard Foundation
The Daniel Howard Trust
*Howman Charitable Trust**
The Hudson Foundation
The Hull and East Riding Charitable Trust
Hulme Trust Estates (Educational)
The Humanitarian Trust
The Albert Hunt Trust
The Hunting Horn General Charitable Trust
Huntingdon Freemen's Trust
Hurdale Charity Ltd
The Hutchinson Charitable Trust
*The Hyde Park Place Estate Charity – civil trustees**
IBM United Kingdom Trust
*ICE Futures Charitable Trust**
IGO Foundation Ltd
The Iliffe Family Charitable Trust
Impetus – The Private Equity Foundation (Impetus – PEF)
The Ingram Trust
The Inlight Trust
The Innocent Foundation
*Integrated Education Fund**
*International Bible Students Association**
*International Fund for Animal Welfare (IFAW)**
Interserve Employee Foundation Ltd
Investream Charitable Trust
The Ironmongers' Company
The Charles Irving Charitable Trust
The J. Isaacs Charitable Trust
The J. and J. Benevolent Foundation
The J. A. R. Charitable Trust
The Jabbs Foundation
C. Richard Jackson Charitable Trust
The Sir Barry Jackson County Fund (incorporating the Hornton Fund)
The Susan and Stephen James Charitable Settlement
Lady Eda Jardine Charitable Trust
John Jarrold Trust Ltd
Nick Jenkins Foundation
The Jenour Foundation
The Jerwood Charitable Foundation
Lillie Johnson Charitable Trust
The Johnson Foundation
Johnnie Johnson Trust
The Christopher and Kirsty Johnston Charitable Trust
The Jones 1986 Charitable Trust
The Marjorie and Geoffrey Jones Charitable Trust
The Muriel Jones Foundation
The Jordan Charitable Foundation
The Joron Charitable Trust
Anton Jurgens Charitable Trust
The Jusaca Charitable Trust
Kahal Chassidim Bobov
The Bernard Kahn Charitable Trust
The Stanley Kalms Foundation
Karaviotis Foundation
The Boris Karloff Charitable Foundation
The Michael and Ilse Katz Foundation
C. S. Kaufman Charitable Trust
The Caron Keating Foundation
William Kendall's Charity (Wax Chandlers' Company)
E. and E. Kernkraut Charities Ltd
The Ursula Keyes Trust
Kidney Research UK
*The Kildare Trust**
Laura Kinsella Foundation
Kollel and Co. Ltd
The Kreitman Foundation
Maurice and Hilda Laing Charitable Trust
The David Laing Foundation
The Kirby Laing Foundation
The Martin Laing Foundation
The Beatrice Laing Trust
The Leonard Laity Stoate Charitable Trust
*The Lancashire Foundation**
Laslett's (Hinton) Charity
The Leche Trust
*Leicestershire and Rutland Masonic Charity Association**
*Leng Charitable Trust**
*The Lethendy Charitable Trust**
The Leverhulme Trade Charities Trust
*The Maisie and Raphael Lewis Charitable Trust**
*Bernard Lewis Family Charitable Trust**
*The Lidbury Family Trust**
*Life Changes Trust**
*The Light Fund Company**
Littlefield Foundation (UK) Ltd
The Ian and Natalie Livingstone Charitable Trust
*The W. M. and B. W. Lloyd Trust**
The Andrew Lloyd Webber Foundation
*Lloyd's Register Foundation**
*The Lockwood Charitable Foundation**
*Michael Lowe's and Associated Charities**
LPW Ltd
*M. B. Foundation**
The R. S. Macdonald Charitable Trust
The Mackintosh Foundation
*GPS Macpherson Charitable Settlement**
The Ian Mactaggart Trust (The Mactaggart Second Fund)
The Magen Charitable Trust
The Mallinckrodt Foundation
Man Group PLC Charitable Trust
Manchester Airport Community Trust Fund
Lord Mayor of Manchester's Charity Appeal Trust
The Manifold Charitable Trust
The W. M. Mann Foundation
Marbeh Torah Trust
The Marchig Animal Welfare Trust
The Stella and Alexander Margulies Charitable Trust
Mariapolis Ltd
The Marks Family Foundation
The Hilda and Samuel Marks Foundation
The J. P. Marland Charitable Trust
Marmot Charitable Trust
The Michael Marsh Charitable Trust
Charlotte Marshall Charitable Trust
*The Martin Charitable Trust**
Sir George Martin Trust
The Mason Porter Charitable Trust
*Masonic Charitable Foundation**
The Nancie Massey Charitable Trust
*The Master Charitable Trust**
The Mathew Trust
The Violet Mauray Charitable Trust

The Mayfield Valley Arts Trust
Maypride Ltd*
D. D. McPhail Charitable Settlement
The Medlock Charitable Trust
Melodor Ltd
Menuchar Ltd
Mercaz Torah Vechesed Ltd
The Brian Mercer Charitable Trust
The Mercers' Charitable Foundation
The Merchant Venturers' Charity
The Metropolitan Masonic Charity
T. and J. Meyer Family Foundation Ltd
The Mickel Fund
The Mickleham Trust
The Gerald Micklem Charitable Trust
Millennium Stadium Charitable Trust (Ymddiriedolaeth Elusennol Stadiwm Y. Mileniwm)
Hugh and Mary Miller Bequest Trust
The Ronald Miller Foundation
The Millfield House Foundation (1)
The Millfield Trust
The Millichope Foundation
Mills and Reeve Charitable Trust*
The Mills Charity
The Millward Charitable Trust
The James Milner Foundation*
The Mirianog Trust
The Mishcon Family Charitable Trust
The Brian Mitchell Charitable Settlement
The MITIE Foundation
The Mizpah Trust
Mobbs Memorial Trust Ltd
Mole Charitable Trust
The Monument Trust
Moondance Foundation*
The George A. Moore Foundation
The Morel Charitable Trust
The Morgan Charitable Foundation
The Steve Morgan Foundation
Morgan Stanley International Foundation
The Diana and Allan Morgenthau Charitable Trust
The Miles Morland Foundation
The Morris Charitable Trust
The Willie and Mabel Morris Charitable Trust
G. M. Morrison Charitable Trust
The Morrisons Foundation*
The Morton Charitable Trust*
The Moshal Charitable Trust
Vyoel Moshe Charitable Trust
The Moss Family Charitable Trust
Moto in the Community
The Edwina Mountbatten and Leonora Children's Foundation
The MSE Charity
The Mugdock Children's Trust
The Mulberry Trust
The Edith Murphy Foundation
The Music Sales Charitable Trust
The Mutual Trust Group
MW (CL) Foundation
The Janet Nash Charitable Settlement
The National Churches Trust
National Committee of the Women's World Day of Prayer for England and Wales and Northern Ireland
The National Express Foundation
The Worshipful Company of Needlemakers' Charitable Fund
The James Neill Trust Fund
Nemoral Ltd
The Frances and Augustus Newman Foundation
Alderman Newton's Educational Foundation
Nominet Charitable Foundation
Norfolk Community Foundation
The Norman Family Charitable Trust
Normanby Charitable Trust
North London Charities Ltd*
Provincial Grand Charity of Northamptonshire and Huntingdonshire*
The Northmoor Trust
The Northumberland Village Homes Trust
The Northwick Trust*
Northwood Charitable Trust
Norwich Town Close Estate Charity
The Nottinghamshire Historic Churches Trust
The Nuffield Foundation
The Father O'Mahoney Memorial Trust
The Sir Peter O'Sullevan Charitable Trust
The Oakley Charitable Trust
Odin Charitable Trust
The Ofenheim Charitable Trust
The Ogle Christian Trust
Oglesby Charitable Trust
The Olga Charitable Trust
One Community Foundation Ltd*
The Ormsby Charitable Trust
The Owen Family Trust
P. F. Charitable Trust
The Doris Pacey Charitable Foundation
The Paddington Charitable Estate Educational Fund*
The Paget Charitable Trust
Palmtree Memorial Trust*
Parabola Foundation*
The Paragon Trust
The Pargiter Trust*
Parish Estate of the Church of St Michael Spurriergate York*
The Patrick Trust
The Jack Patston Charitable Trust
The JGW Patterson Foundation*
Susanna Peake Charitable Trust
The Dowager Countess Eleanor Peel Trust
The Pen Shell Project
The Pennycress Trust
The Performing Right Society Foundation
The Persson Charitable Trust
The Persula Foundation
The Jack Petchey Foundation
The Pharsalia Charitable Trust
The Phillips and Rubens Charitable Trust
The Phillips Charitable Trust
The Phillips Family Charitable Trust
The Pilgrim Trust
Pilkington Charities Fund
The Austin and Hope Pilkington Trust
Pink Ribbon Foundation*
The DLA Piper Charitable Trust
The Polehampton Charity*
The Institute for Policy Research*
The George and Esme Pollitzer Charitable Settlement
The Ponton House Trust
Edith and Ferdinand Porjes Charitable Trust
The Porta Pia 2012 Foundation
The Portrack Charitable Trust
The J. E. Posnansky Charitable Trust
Postcode Community Trust*
The Mary Potter Convent Hospital Trust
David and Elaine Potter Foundation
Powys Welsh Church Fund*
The Primrose Trust

The Prince of Wales's Charitable Foundation
*The Prince Philip Trust Fund**
The Privy Purse Charitable Trust
*The Professional Footballers' Association Charity**
The Puebla Charitable Trust
The Puri Foundation
*The Pye Foundation**
Mr and Mrs J. A. Pye's Charitable Settlement
*QBE European Operations Foundation**
The Queen's Trust
*Quercus Foundation**
R. S. Charitable Trust
The Monica Rabagliati Charitable Trust
The Racing Foundation
Richard Radcliffe Trust
The Radcliffe Trust
The Rainford Trust
*The Edward Ramsden Charitable Trust**
The Joseph and Lena Randall Charitable Trust
The Rank Foundation Ltd
Rashbass Family Trust
The Ratcliff Foundation
The Eleanor Rathbone Charitable Trust
Elizabeth Rathbone Charity
The Sigrid Rausing Trust
The Roger Raymond Charitable Trust
The Rayne Foundation
The John Rayner Charitable Trust
The Sir James Reckitt Charity
Red Hill Charitable Trust
C. A. Redfern Charitable Foundation
Reed Family Foundation
Richard Reeve's Foundation
The Rhododendron Trust
*Riada Trust**
The Clive and Sylvia Richards Charity Ltd
Richmond Parish Lands Charity
*Rigby Foundation**
The River Farm Foundation
Thomas Roberts Trust
The Rofeh Trust
The Richard Rogers Charitable Settlement
Rokach Family Charitable Trust
The Sir James Roll Charitable Trust
The Helen Roll Charity
*Mrs L. D. Rope's Second Charitable Settlement**
Mrs L. D. Rope's Third Charitable Settlement
Rosca Trust
*The Cissie Rosefield Charitable Trust**
The Cecil Rosen Foundation
*The David Ross Foundation**
The Rothermere Foundation
The Joseph Rowntree Charitable Trust
The Joseph Rowntree Foundation
*Royal Society Of Wildlife Trusts**
Royal Victoria Hall Foundation
*Rozelle Trust**
The Rubin Foundation Charitable Trust
The RVW Trust
The J. S. and E. C. Rymer Charitable Trust
S. F. Foundation
The Michael and Nicola Sacher Charitable Trust
The Michael Sacher Charitable Trust
The Dr Mortimer and Theresa Sackler Foundation
The Sackler Trust
The Ruzin Sadagora Trust
The Saddlers' Company Charitable Fund
Erach and Roshan Sadri Foundation
The Saga Charitable Trust
The Jean Sainsbury Animal Welfare Trust
The Alan and Babette Sainsbury Charitable Fund
The Sainsbury Family Charitable Trusts
The Saints and Sinners Trust Ltd
The Salamander Charitable Trust
*The Salisbury New Pool Settlement**
*Samjo Ltd**
Coral Samuel Charitable Trust
The Basil Samuel Charitable Trust
The Samworth Foundation
The Sandra Charitable Trust
*Sarum St Michael Educational Charity**
*The Savoy Educational Trust**
The Scarfe Charitable Trust
The Schapira Charitable Trust
The Schmidt-Bodner Charitable Trust
O. and G. Schreiber Charitable Trust
The Schreiber Charitable Trust
The Schroder Foundation
Foundation Scotland
The Francis C. Scott Charitable Trust
The Frieda Scott Charitable Trust
*The John Scott Trust Fund**
The ScottishPower Energy People Trust
The ScottishPower Foundation
The Scouloudi Foundation
Seafarers Hospital Society
Seafarers UK (King George's Fund for Sailors)
Sam and Bella Sebba Charitable Trust
Leslie Sell Charitable Trust
*The Sellafield Charity Trust Fund**
SEM Charitable Trust
The Seven Fifty Trust
The Cyril Shack Trust
The Jean Shanks Foundation
The Shanti Charitable Trust
The Linley Shaw Foundation
The Shears Foundation
The Sheffield Town Trust
The Sheldon Trust
*Sherling Charitable Trust**
The Archie Sherman Cardiff Foundation
The Bassil Shippam and Alsford Trust
The Shipwrights' Company Charitable Fund
*The Shropshire Historic Churches Trust**
*Shulem B. Association Ltd**
*The Florence Shute Millennium Trust**
David and Jennifer Sieff Charitable Trust
The Huntly and Margery Sinclair Charitable Trust
The Skelton Bounty
The Charles Skey Charitable Trust
Skipton Building Society Charitable Foundation
The Slaughter and May Charitable Trust
The SMB Trust
The DS Smith Charitable Foundation
The Smith Charitable Trust
The Leslie Smith Foundation
*The Martin Smith Foundation**
The Stanley Smith UK Horticultural Trust
Philip Smith's Charitable Trust
The R. C. Snelling Charitable Trust
The Sobell Foundation
*Social Investment Business Foundation**
*Sofronie Foundation**
The Solo Charitable Settlement
The E. C. Sosnow Charitable Trust
The Souter Charitable Trust
The South Square Trust

The W. F. Southall Trust
Sparquote Ltd
The Worshipful Company of Spectacle Makers' Charity
The Jessie Spencer Trust
The Spielman Charitable Trust
The Spoore, Merry and Rixman Foundation
The Geoff and Fiona Squire Foundation
The Squires Foundation
The St James's Trust Settlement
St Luke's College Foundation
Staffordshire Community Foundation*
The Stanley Charitable Trust*
The Stanley Foundation Ltd
The Staples Trust
The Peter Stebbings Memorial Charity
The Steel Charitable Trust
The Steinberg Family Charitable Trust
The Hugh Stenhouse Foundation
The Sigmund Sternberg Charitable Foundation
Stervon Ltd
Stevenson Family's Charitable Trust
The Stewards' Charitable Trust
Stewards' Company Ltd
The Andy Stewart Charitable Foundation
The Stobart Newlands Charitable Trust
The Stoller Charitable Trust
M. J. C. Stone Charitable Trust
The Stoneygate Trust*
Peter Stormonth Darling Charitable Trust
The Summerfield Charitable Trust
Support Adoption For Pets*
Surgo Foundation UK Ltd*
The Adrienne and Leslie Sussman Charitable Trust
The Swann-Morton Foundation
The John Swire (1989) Charitable Trust
The Adrian Swire Charitable Trust
The Hugh and Ruby Sykes Charitable Trust
T. and S. Trust Fund
Tabeel Trust
The Talmud Torah Machzikei Hadass Trust*
The Lady Tangye Charitable Trust Ltd
The David Tannen Charitable Trust
The Tanner Trust
The Lili Tapper Charitable Foundation
The Tay Charitable Trust
Humphrey Richardson Taylor Charitable Trust
The Taylor Family Foundation
Khoo Teck Puat UK Foundation*
The Tedworth Charitable Trust
The C. Paul Thackray General Charitable Trust
The Thales Charitable Trust
The Thistle Trust
The Arthur and Margaret Thompson Charitable Trust
The Thornton Foundation
The Thornton Trust
The Three Guineas Trust
The Three Oaks Trust
The John Raymond Tijou Charitable Trust
The Tisbury Telegraph Trust
The Tompkins Foundation
The Tory Family Foundation
The Toy Trust
The Toye Foundation
Toyota Manufacturing UK Charitable Trust
The Trades House of Glasgow*
The Transform Foundation*
Truedene Co. Ltd
The Trusthouse Charitable Foundation
The Roger and Douglas Turner Charitable Trust
The Florence Turner Trust
The G. J. W. Turner Trust
TVML Foundation
Tzedakah
UKH Foundation*
Ulster Garden Villages Ltd
Ulting Overseas Trust
The Ulverscroft Foundation
The Underwood Trust
The Union of Orthodox Hebrew Congregations
The David Uri Memorial Trust
The Utley Family Charitable Trust*
The Vail Foundation
The Van Neste Foundation
The Vandervell Foundation
The Veolia Environmental Trust*
The Nigel Vinson Charitable Trust
Virgin Atlantic Foundation
Vivdale Ltd
The Vodafone Foundation
Wade's Charity
The Bruce Wake Charity*
The Wakefield Trust*
The Walcot Foundation
The Walker Trust
Walton Foundation*
The Ward Blenkinsop Trust
Mrs N. E. M. Warren's Charitable Trust*
The Warrington Church of England Educational Trust*
Mrs Waterhouse Charitable Trust
The Watson Family Charitable Trust*
The Weinstein Foundation
The Weinstock Fund
The Weir Charitable Trust*
The Wellcome Trust
The West Looe Town Trust*
The Westfield Health Charitable Trust
The Westminster Foundation
Westway Trust
The Wheeler Family Charitable Trust*
The Whitewater Charitable Trust
The Kay Williams Charitable Foundation
The Alfred Williams Charitable Trust*
The Williams Family Charitable Trust
The Williams Family Foundation*
The Willmott Dixon Foundation*
The Wilmcote Charitrust
Brian Wilson Charitable Trust*
Sumner Wilson Charitable Trust
The Wimbledon Foundation*
The Witzenfeld Foundation
The Maurice Wohl Charitable Foundation
The F. Glenister Woodger Trust
The Woodstock Family Charitable Foundation*
The Worwin UK Foundation*
The Wyfold Charitable Trust*
The Yapp Charitable Trust
Yorkshire and Clydesdale Bank Foundation
Yorkshire Building Society Charitable Foundation
Stephen Zimmerman Charitable Trust
The Zochonis Charitable Trust
Zurich Community Trust (UK) Ltd

■ Seed funding

The 1989 Willan Charitable Trust
The 3Ts Charitable Trust*
The A. S. Charitable Trust
A. W. Charitable Trust
The Aberbrothock Skea Trust
ABF The Soldiers' Charity
Achisomoch Aid Company Ltd
Action Medical Research

Age UK
Aid to the Church in Need (UK)
All Saints Educational Trust
The Alliance Family Foundation
The Ammco Trust
Viscount Amory's Charitable Trust
The AMW Charitable Trust
*The Anne Duchess of Westminster's Charity**
Anpride Ltd
The Ardwick Trust
The Argus Appeal
The Arsenal Foundation Ltd
Arts Council England
Arts Council of Northern Ireland
Arts Council of Wales (also known as Cyngor Celfyddydau Cymru)
The Ove Arup Foundation
The Astor Foundation
The Aurelius Charitable Trust
The Bagri Foundation
The Baird Trust
The Baltic Charitable Fund
The Banbury Charities
The Barbers' Company General Charities
*The Philip Barker Charity**
The Barnsbury Charitable Trust
Barnwood Trust
Misses Barrie Charitable Trust
The Bartlett Taylor Charitable Trust
The Batchworth Trust
The Battens Charitable Trust
The Bearder Charity
The James Beattie Charitable Trust
The John Beckwith Charitable Trust
The David and Ruth Behrend Fund
*The Behrens Foundation**
The Bellahouston Bequest Fund
Belljoe Tzedoko Ltd
The Benham Charitable Settlement
*The Rowan Bentall Charitable Trust**
The Billmeir Charitable Trust
The Bingham Trust
The Birmingham District Nursing Charitable Trust
The Lord Mayor of Birmingham's Charity
The Michael Bishop Foundation
The Sir Victor Blank Charitable Settlement
The Charlotte Bonham-Carter Charitable Trust
Boots Charitable Trust
The Bordon Liphook Haslemere Charity
*Sir William Boreman's Foundation**
The Oliver Borthwick Memorial Trust
The Boshier-Hinton Foundation
The Harry Bottom Charitable Trust
The Bowerman Charitable Trust
The Bowland Charitable Trust
The Frank Brake Charitable Trust
The William Brake Charitable Trust
British Humane Association
The Charles Brotherton Trust
The Burry Charitable Trust
The Arnold Burton 1998 Charitable Trust
Consolidated Charity of Burton upon Trent
The Christopher Cadbury Charitable Trust
The G. W. Cadbury Charitable Trust
The George Cadbury Trust
CAFOD (Catholic Agency for Overseas Development)
Community Foundation for Calderdale
Callander Charitable Trust
Calouste Gulbenkian Foundation – UK Branch
*The W. A. Cargill Fund**
The Carpenters' Company Charitable Trust
The Carrington Charitable Trust
The Leslie Mary Carter Charitable Trust
*Sir Ernest Cassel Educational Trust**
The Elizabeth Casson Trust
The Joseph and Annie Cattle Trust
The Wilfrid and Constance Cave Foundation
The B. G. S. Cayzer Charitable Trust
Charitworth Ltd
CHK Charities Ltd
Christian Aid
Chrysalis Trust
The Church Burgesses Educational Foundation
Church Burgesses Trust
Church of Ireland Priorities Fund
The City Educational Trust Fund
*The Clan Trust Ltd**
The Hilda and Alice Clark Charitable Trust
The Roger and Sarah Bancroft Clark Charitable Trust
The Clore Duffield Foundation
Closehelm Ltd
Richard Cloudesley's Charity
The Robert Clutterbuck Charitable Trust
Clydpride Ltd
The John Coates Charitable Trust
The Cobtree Charity Trust Ltd
The Denise Cohen Charitable Trust
The Vivienne and Samuel Cohen Charitable Trust
The John S. Cohen Foundation
The R. and S. Cohen Foundation
The Colefax Charitable Trust
John and Freda Coleman Charitable Trust
The Coltstaple Trust
Comic Relief
The Comino Foundation
The Ernest Cook Trust
The Cooks Charity
Mabel Cooper Charity
The Gershon Coren Charitable Foundation (also known as The Muriel and Gus Coren Charitable Foundation)
The Costa Family Charitable Trust
General Charity of Coventry
Dudley and Geoffrey Cox Charitable Trust
The Cray Trust
Creative Scotland
The Violet and Milo Cripps Charitable Trust
Cruden Foundation Ltd
Roald Dahl's Marvellous Children's Charity
The Daiwa Anglo-Japanese Foundation
The Dr and Mrs A. Darlington Charitable Trust
The Davidson (Nairn) Charitable Trust
The Davidson Family Charitable Trust
Michael Davies Charitable Settlement
Margaret Davies Charity
The Hamilton Davies Trust
*The John Grant Davies Trust**
The Dawe Charitable Trust
The De Brye Charitable Trust
The Dellal Foundation
The Delves Charitable Trust
The Demigryphon Trust
The Denman Charitable Trust
Foundation Derbyshire
Devon Community Foundation
Diabetes UK
Dinwoodie Charitable Company

Disability Aid Fund (The Roger and Jean Jefcoate Trust)
The Djanogly Foundation
The DLM Charitable Trust
The Derek and Eileen Dodgson Foundation
The Doughty Charity Trust
Douglas Arter Foundation
The Dumbreck Charity
The Dunn Family Charitable Trust
County Durham Community Foundation
The Dyers' Company Charitable Trust
Earls Colne and Halstead Educational Charity
East End Community Foundation
The EBM Charitable Trust
*Elanore Ltd**
The Elephant Trust
The George Elias Charitable Trust
The Gerald Palmer Eling Trust Company
The Wilfred and Elsie Elkes Charity Fund
The Maud Elkington Charitable Trust
The John Ellerman Foundation
The Edith Maud Ellis 1985 Charitable Trust
The Vernon N. Ely Charitable Trust
*The Emerald Foundation**
The Emerton-Christie Charity
The Englefield Charitable Trust
The Epigoni Trust
The Essex Heritage Trust
The Eventhall Family Charitable Trust
The Expat Foundation
The Football Association National Sports Centre Trust
*The Fore Trust**
The Foyle Foundation
Friends Provident Charitable Foundation
Gatwick Airport Community Trust
The Gibbs Charitable Trust
*Gilchrist Educational Trust**
The Girdlers' Company Charitable Trust
Global Charities
The Mike Gooley Trailfinders Charity
The Granada Foundation
The J. G. Graves Charitable Trust
The Gray Trust
Greenham Common Community Trust Ltd
The Greggs Foundation
The Gretna Charitable Trust
The Grocers' Charity
H. C. D. Memorial Fund
Hackney Parochial Charities
The Hadfield Charitable Trust
The Health Foundation
P. and C. Hickinbotham Charitable Trust
The Hoover Foundation
*Horwich Shotter Charitable Trust**
*The Hyde Park Place Estate Charity – civil trustees**
The Innocent Foundation
*Integrated Education Fund**
Lady Eda Jardine Charitable Trust
The Sir James Knott Trust
The Langtree Trust
The William Leech Charity
*Leicestershire and Rutland Masonic Charity Association**
*Leng Charitable Trust**
*The Lethendy Charitable Trust**
*The Maisie and Raphael Lewis Charitable Trust**
*The W. M. and B. W. Lloyd Trust**
*Michael Lowe's and Associated Charities**
The R. S. Macdonald Charitable Trust
*Maypride Ltd**
D. D. McPhail Charitable Settlement
The Merchant Taylors' Company Charities Fund
Merchant Taylors' Consolidated Charities for the Infirm
The Mickleham Trust
*The Morrisons Foundation**
National Committee of the Women's World Day of Prayer for England and Wales and Northern Ireland
The Nationwide Foundation
The Worshipful Company of Needlemakers' Charitable Fund
The James Neill Trust Fund
The Newcomen Collett Foundation
The Northmoor Trust
The Nottinghamshire Historic Churches Trust
Oglesby Charitable Trust
*The Onaway Trust**
*The Paddington Charitable Estate Educational Fund**
*The JGW Patterson Foundation**
The Pilgrim Trust
*The Polehampton Charity**
David and Elaine Potter Foundation
The Prince of Wales's Charitable Foundation
The Monica Rabagliati Charitable Trust
The Rank Foundation Ltd
Richmond Parish Lands Charity
Rosca Trust
*The Cissie Rosefield Charitable Trust**
The Cecil Rosen Foundation
The Joseph Rowntree Foundation
Royal Victoria Hall Foundation
The Saddlers' Company Charitable Fund
Erach and Roshan Sadri Foundation
The Saga Charitable Trust
The Sainsbury Family Charitable Trusts
*Sarum St Michael Educational Charity**
The Scarfe Charitable Trust
The Schreiber Charitable Trust
Foundation Scotland
The Francis C. Scott Charitable Trust
The Frieda Scott Charitable Trust
*The John Scott Trust Fund**
The Scouloudi Foundation
Seafarers Hospital Society
Seafarers UK (King George's Fund for Sailors)
*The Sellafield Charity Trust Fund**
The Seven Fifty Trust
The Jean Shanks Foundation
The Sheldon Trust
*Sherling Charitable Trust**
*The Shropshire Historic Churches Trust**
The Huntly and Margery Sinclair Charitable Trust
The Skelton Bounty
The Leslie Smith Foundation
The Stanley Smith UK Horticultural Trust
The R. C. Snelling Charitable Trust
The Solo Charitable Settlement
The Souter Charitable Trust
The South Square Trust
The W. F. Southall Trust
The Geoff and Fiona Squire Foundation
The Squires Foundation
The Stanley Foundation Ltd
The Staples Trust
The Stewards' Charitable Trust
Stewards' Company Ltd
The Thornton Trust
The Ulverscroft Foundation

UnLtd (Foundation for Social Entrepreneurs)
The Nigel Vinson Charitable Trust
Wade's Charity
*The Warrington Church of England Educational Trust**
*The Watson Family Charitable Trust**
*The West Looe Town Trust**
Zurich Community Trust (UK) Ltd

Campaigning

ABF The Soldiers' Charity
Access Sport CIO
Action Medical Research
Age UK
Arts Council of Wales (also known as Cyngor Celfyddydau Cymru)
The Avon and Somerset Police Community Trust
*The Philip Barker Charity**
The Barnsbury Charitable Trust
*The Rowan Bentall Charitable Trust**
CAFOD (Catholic Agency for Overseas Development)
Calouste Gulbenkian Foundation – UK Branch
Christian Aid
*The Clan Trust Ltd**
J. A. Clark Charitable Trust
The Cobalt Trust
The Coltstaple Trust
The Violet and Milo Cripps Charitable Trust
The Dellal Foundation
Dorset Community Foundation
*Elanore Ltd**
The Elephant Trust
The John Ellerman Foundation
Matthew Eyton Animal Welfare Trust
Elizabeth Ferguson Charitable Trust Fund
The Elizabeth Frankland Moore and Star Foundation
Harbinson Charitable Trust
The Health Foundation
*Horwich Shotter Charitable Trust**
Hospice UK
The JRSST Charitable Trust
Lady Eda Jardine Charitable Trust
The Muriel Jones Foundation
The Kirschel Foundation
*Leng Charitable Trust**
*The Lethendy Charitable Trust**
*The W. M. and B. W. Lloyd Trust**
*Medical Research Foundation**
The Millfield House Foundation (1)
The Frederick Mulder Foundation
*The Onaway Trust**
Petplan Charitable Trust
Polden-Puckham Charitable Foundation
*The Polehampton Charity**
The Prince of Wales's Charitable Foundation
Quartet Community Foundation
The Sigrid Rausing Trust
The Roddick Foundation
The Joseph Rowntree Foundation
*The Shropshire Historic Churches Trust**
The Slaughter and May Charitable Trust
The DS Smith Charitable Foundation
The Souter Charitable Trust
The Ulverscroft Foundation
The Yapp Charitable Trust

Loan finance

The ACT Foundation
The Architectural Heritage Fund
The British Dietetic Association General and Education Trust Fund
Buckinghamshire Community Foundation
The Coalfields Regeneration Trust
*England and Wales Cricket Trust**
The Dawe Charitable Trust
The Edith Maud Ellis 1985 Charitable Trust
Friends Provident Charitable Foundation
The Hathaway Trust
The Maurice Hatter Foundation
Joffe Charitable Trust
Christopher Laing Foundation
The William Leech Charity
The M. Y. A. Charitable Trust
Marbeh Torah Trust
Charity of John Marshall
Rugby Football Foundation
Ulster Garden Villages Ltd

The alphabetical register of grant-making charities

This section lists the individual entries for the grant-making charities.

■ The 1970 Trust

SC NO SC008788 **ESTABLISHED** 1970
WHERE FUNDING CAN BE GIVEN UK.
WHO CAN BENEFIT Charities which support disadvantaged minorities.
WHAT IS FUNDED The trust states it supports small UK charities 'doing innovative, educational, or experimental work' in the following fields: civil liberties (e.g. freedom of information; constitutional reform; humanising work; children's welfare); the public interest in the face of vested interest groups (such as the advertising, alcohol, road, war, pharmaceuticals, and tobacco industries); disadvantaged minorities, multiracial work, prison reform; new economics and intermediate technology; public transport, pedestrians, bicycling, road crash prevention, traffic-calming, low-energy lifestyles; and preventative health.
WHAT IS NOT FUNDED Larger charities or those with religious connections; individuals (except in rare cases – and then only through registered charities or educational bodies); central or local government agencies.
TYPE OF GRANT Usually one to three years.
SAMPLE GRANTS BackCare; Earth Resources; Public Interest Research Centre; Parent to Parent; Prisoners' Wives; Roadpeace; Shelter Winter Night; Slower Speeds Trust.
FINANCES *Year* 2015/16 *Income* £9,516 *Grants* £200,000 *Grants to organisations* £200,000
OTHER INFORMATION This charity's latest accounts were not available to view on the OSCR website. We have therefore estimated the grant total based on the charity's expenditure.
HOW TO APPLY Apply in writing to the correspondent. Proposals should be summarised on one page with one or two more pages of supporting information. The trust has previously stated that regrettably it only has time to reply to the very few applications it is able to fund.
WHO TO APPLY TO The Trustees, 12 St Catherine Street, Cupar, Fife KY15 4HN *Tel.* 01334 653777

■ The 1989 Willan Charitable Trust

CC NO 802749 **ESTABLISHED** 1989
WHERE FUNDING CAN BE GIVEN Tyne and Wear; Northumberland; County Durham; Teesside.
WHO CAN BENEFIT Registered charities.
WHAT IS FUNDED General charitable purposes including: growth and employment; children and young people; health; community cohesion; older people.
WHAT IS NOT FUNDED Statutory organisations, including schools or activities eligible for public funding; trips abroad; projects focused on: heritage and the environment, religion and the promotion of faith, scientific and/or medical research.
RANGE OF GRANTS Up to £10,000.
SAMPLE GRANTS SAFC Foundation and Cancer Connexions (£10,000 each); Amble Multi Agency Crime Prevention Initiative (£6,000); Durham City Centre Youth Project, The Children's Society and the Calvert Trust (£5,000 each); Chester le Street Youth Centre (£4,000); Different Strokes North East, Northern Roots and People and Drugs (£3,000 each); Leukaemia Research and Coast Video Club (£2,000 each); Northumberland Mountain Rescue and the Association of British Poles (£1,000 each); Healthwise and Newcastle Gang Show (£500).
FINANCES *Year* 2014/15 *Income* £546,970 *Grants* £498,284 *Grants to organisations* £491,284 *Assets* £16,681,776
TRUSTEES Francis Chapman; Alex Ohlsson; Willan Trustee Ltd.
OTHER INFORMATION The 2014/15 accounts were the latest available at the time of writing (June 2017). Grants were distributed in the following categories: building our children's future (£193,500); taking part in community life (£173,500); improving health (£101,500); enjoying later life (£24,500); stimulating growth and employment (£3,500); environment (£1,600).
HOW TO APPLY Apply in writing to the correspondent at the Community Foundation Serving Tyne and Wear. Refer to the very helpful website for full details before making application. The trustees meet in March, June, September and December. Applications will generally be considered at the next scheduled trustee meeting, provided they are received by the 15th of the preceding month. However, applicants are encouraged to submit their applications as early as possible to ensure they are considered at the next available trustees' meeting.
WHO TO APPLY TO Community Foundation Tyne and Wear and Northumberland, The 1989 Willan Charitable Trust, c/o Community Foundation, Philanthropy House, Woodbine Road, Gosforth, Newcastle upon Tyne NE3 1DD *Tel.* 0191 222 0945 *Email* general@communityfoundation.org.uk *Website* www.communityfoundation.org.uk/funds/the-1989-willan-charitable-trust

■ The 29th May 1961 Charitable Trust

CC NO 200198 **ESTABLISHED** 1961
WHERE FUNDING CAN BE GIVEN UK with a preference for the West Midlands and in particular the Coventry and Warwickshire area. The trustees do not typically fund projects outside the UK.
WHO CAN BENEFIT Charitable organisations in the UK.
WHAT IS FUNDED General charitable purposes including: arts and museums; conservation and protection; employment, education and training; homelessness and housing; leisure, recreation and youth; medical causes; people who have offended; social welfare.
WHAT IS NOT FUNDED Individuals. Grants are only made to registered charities.
TYPE OF GRANT One-off, recurring and some spread over two to three years. Grants are given for capital and revenue purposes.
RANGE OF GRANTS Up to £100,000 but typically £6,000 to £40,000.
SAMPLE GRANTS Coventry City of Culture Trust (£100,000); Crisis (£50,000); Law Works (£45,000); Chance to Shine and South Bank Centre (£30,000 each); Coventry University (£15,000); Prison Reform Trust (£10,000); Firm Foundation and Surfers Against Sewage (£9,000 each); Devon In Sight, The Lighthouse and Merlin MS Centre (£6,000 each).
FINANCES *Year* 2015/16 *Income* £3,381,798 *Grants* £3,724,725 *Grants to organisations* £3,724,725 *Assets* £103,076,759
TRUSTEES Vanni Emanuele Treves; Andrew Jones; Elizabeth Rantzen; Paul Varney.
OTHER INFORMATION Grants were awarded to 360 organisations during the year.
HOW TO APPLY Apply to the secretary in writing, enclosing in triplicate the most recent annual report and accounts. The trustees normally meet in February, May, August and November.

Due to the large number of applications received, they cannot be acknowledged.

WHO TO APPLY TO Vanni Emanuele Treves, Trustee, Ryder Court, 14 Ryder Street, London SW1 Y. 6QB *Tel.* 020 7024 9034 *Email* enquiries@29may1961charity.org.uk

■ The 3Ts Charitable Trust

CC NO 1109733 **ESTABLISHED** 2005

WHERE FUNDING CAN BE GIVEN UK and India.

WHO CAN BENEFIT Registered charities.

WHAT IS FUNDED General charitable purposes.

RANGE OF GRANTS Up to £100,000 but typically £500 to £10,000.

SAMPLE GRANTS Haileybury Independent School – Youth Trust (£50,000); Supporting Dalit Children (£30,000); Harvard College (£16,500); Royal Botanical Gardens – Kew (£10,000); Alpenglow Foundation (£6,500); Breast Cancer Now (£4,000).

FINANCES *Year* 2015/16 *Income* £219,221 *Grants* £182,344 *Grants to organisations* £182,344 *Assets* £9,854,082

TRUSTEES Charles Sherwood; Rosemary Sherwood; Tim Sherwood; William Medlicott; Tabitha Sherwood; Tatiana Sherwood.

OTHER INFORMATION The trust made 25 grants during the year.

HOW TO APPLY The trustees adopt a proactive approach in seeking worthy causes requiring support.

WHO TO APPLY TO The Trustees, PO Box 68, Knebworth, Hertfordshire SG3 6UZ *Email* info@3tscharitabletrust.com

■ 4 Charity Foundation

CC NO 1077143 **ESTABLISHED** 1999

WHERE FUNDING CAN BE GIVEN UK and Israel.

WHO CAN BENEFIT Jewish charities and causes.

WHAT IS FUNDED Religious activities and education.

RANGE OF GRANTS Up to £570,000.

SAMPLE GRANTS Tikvah UK (£571,000); Shaare Zedek Medical Centre (£143,000); Shuvo Yisroel (£50,000); The Alder Trust (£33,000); Asser Bishvil Foundation (£26,000); Friends of Mur (£25,000).

FINANCES *Year* 2015/16 *Income* £4,491,377 *Grants* £2,612,234 *Grants to organisations* £2,612,234 *Assets* £21,349,590

TRUSTEES Jacob Schimmel; Verette Schimmel; Jonathan Schimmel.

HOW TO APPLY This trust does not respond to unsolicited applications.

WHO TO APPLY TO Jacob Schimmel, Trustee, 121 Princes Park Avenue, London NW11 0JS *Tel.* 020 8455 0100 *Email* four4charities@gmail.com

■ The A. B. Charitable Trust

CC NO 1000147 **ESTABLISHED** 1990

WHERE FUNDING CAN BE GIVEN Mainly UK.

WHO CAN BENEFIT Charities registered and working in the UK. The trust favours those charities with an annual income between £150,000 and £1.5 million, which do not have substantial investments or surpluses.

WHAT IS FUNDED The trust supports charities that defend human rights and promote respect for vulnerable individuals whatever their circumstances. The trust is particularly interested in charities that work with marginalised and excluded people in society, with a focus on: migrants, refugees and asylum seekers; prisoners and penal reform; human rights, particularly access to justice.

TYPE OF GRANT Project funding and core costs.

RANGE OF GRANTS Typically £10,000 to £20,000.

SAMPLE GRANTS British Red Cross Society – Families Together Initiative (£50,000); Shannon Trust and The Civil Liberties Trust (£30,000 each); Greater Manchester Law Centre (£25,000); Barnet Refugee Service, Changing Tunes and JUSTICE (£15,000 each); Asylum Welcome (£10,000); North East Prison After Care Society (£7,500); Piers Road New Communities Centre Association (£5,000).

FINANCES *Year* 2016/17 *Income* £497,231 *Grants* £1,117,500 *Grants to organisations* £1,117,500 *Assets* £304,140

TRUSTEES Claire Bonavero; Olivier Bonavero; Philippe Bonavero; Anne Bonavero; Yves Bonavero; Athol Harley; Alison Swan Parente; Peter Day.

HOW TO APPLY Applications can be completed online at the trust's website.

WHO TO APPLY TO Sara Harrity, Director, Monmouth House, 87–93 Westbourne Grove, London W2 4UL *Tel.* 020 7313 8070 *Fax* 020 7313 9607 *Email* mail@abcharitabletrust.org.uk *Website* www.abcharitabletrust.org.uk

■ The A. S. Charitable Trust

CC NO 242190 **ESTABLISHED** 1965

WHERE FUNDING CAN BE GIVEN UK and overseas.

WHO CAN BENEFIT Preference for charities in which the trust has special interest, knowledge of or association with. Christian organisations will benefit. Support may go to victims of famine, man-made or natural disasters, and war.

WHAT IS FUNDED The trust is sympathetic to projects which combine the advancement of the Christian religion with Christian lay leadership, international development, peacemaking and reconciliation, or other areas of social concern.

WHAT IS NOT FUNDED Grants to individuals or large charities are very rare. Such applications are discouraged.

SAMPLE GRANTS GRACE (£28,500 in 12 grants); St Michael's Centre (£9,500); CHIPS (£6,100); Uganda Development Service (£4,500); Uganda Church Association (£3,000); Discover and The Message Trust (£1,500 each); Frontiers and International Service Fellowship Trust (£1,000 each).

FINANCES *Year* 2015/16 *Income* £369,876 *Grants* £101,680 *Grants to organisations* £101,680 *Assets* £13,013,476

TRUSTEES Caroline Eady; George Calvocoressi; Simon Sampson.

HOW TO APPLY Apply in writing to the correspondent.

WHO TO APPLY TO George Calvocoressi, Trustee, Bix Bottom Farm, Henley-on-Thames, Oxfordshire RG9 6BH

■ A. W. Charitable Trust

CC NO 283322 **ESTABLISHED** 1961

WHERE FUNDING CAN BE GIVEN London, Gateshead, Manchester and Salford; Israel.

WHO CAN BENEFIT Jewish educational and religious organisations; registered charities.

WHAT IS FUNDED Orthodox Jewish causes.

SAMPLE GRANTS Asser Bishvil Foundation; Beenstock Home; British Friends of Kupat Hair; Chevras Oneg Shabbos-Yomtov; Friends of Mir; Purim Fund; Toimchei Shabbos Manchester; Zoreya Tzedokos.

FINANCES *Year* 2015/16 *Income* £14,893,253 *Grants* £1,570,777 *Grants to organisations* £1,570,777 *Assets* £157,232,069

TRUSTEES Rabbi Aubrey Weis; Rachel Weis; Sir Weis.

HOW TO APPLY Apply in writing to the correspondent.

WHO TO APPLY TO Rabbi Aubrey Weis, Trustee, 66 Waterpark Road, Manchester M7 4JL *Tel.* 0161 740 0116

■ A2BD Foundation UK Ltd

CC NO 1157596 **ESTABLISHED** 2014

WHERE FUNDING CAN BE GIVEN England and Wales.

WHO CAN BENEFIT Registered charities.

WHAT IS FUNDED General charitable purposes with an initial focus on: focus on the advancement of education; conflict resolution and human rights; sustainable development and the protection; enhancement and rehabilitation of the environment.

SAMPLE GRANTS Social Finance (£75,000).

FINANCES *Year* 2015 *Income* £90,000 *Grants* £75,000 *Grants to organisations* £75,000 *Assets* £11,088

TRUSTEES David Blood; Peter Harris; Beth Blood.

HOW TO APPLY Apply in writing to the correspondent. The trustees meet on an annual basis to decide how grants will be distributed.

WHO TO APPLY TO Withers LLP, 16 Old Bailey, London EC4M 7EG *Tel.* 020 7597 6257

■ The Aberbrothock Skea Trust

SC NO SC039202 **ESTABLISHED** 1971/2008

WHERE FUNDING CAN BE GIVEN East of Scotland, north of the Firth of Tay.

WHO CAN BENEFIT Organisations benefitting the community with charitable status.

WHAT IS FUNDED Children/young people; disability; environment/conservation; hospitals/hospices; medical research.

WHAT IS NOT FUNDED The geographical restriction is strictly adhered to. Applications from outside the area, and/or from individuals, will not be considered.

TYPE OF GRANT One-off, including project, research, capital and core costs.

RANGE OF GRANTS Up to £2,500.

SAMPLE GRANTS Colon Cancer Care; Dundee Heritage Trust; International League of Horses; Kids Out; Princess Royal Trust; Red Cross.
FINANCES *Year* 2015/16 *Income* £138,395 *Grants* £142,960 *Grants to organisations* £142,960 *Assets* £3,828,040
HOW TO APPLY Apply in writing to the correspondent. The trustees meet to consider grants in March, July and December.
WHO TO APPLY TO The Trustees, Thorntons Law LLP, Brothockbank House, Arbroath, Angus DD11 1NE

■ Aberdeen Asset Management Charitable Foundation

SC NO SC042597 **ESTABLISHED** 2011
WHERE FUNDING CAN BE GIVEN UK and overseas where the company has a presence.
WHO CAN BENEFIT Registered charities and non-profit organisations.
WHAT IS FUNDED Providing education and opportunities for underprivileged young people. Each year the foundation will select an emerging market and focus its investment in that area. The emerging markets allocation will be focused on a small number of long-term partnerships (average duration of three years). Grants are also made to charities local to its offices.
WHAT IS NOT FUNDED The foundation does not support political causes, parties or organisations or charities with a religious focus.
SAMPLE GRANTS A list of beneficiaries was not available.
FINANCES *Year* 2014/15 *Income* £2,030,018 *Grants* £856,076 *Grants to organisations* £856,076
OTHER INFORMATION The 2014/15 accounts were the latest available at the time of writing.
HOW TO APPLY Application forms are available to download from the foundation's page on the company's website. Completed application forms should be emailed to the foundation for consideration. Successful applicants will be notified within a three month period following application. The foundation is not able to respond to all unsuccessful applications.
WHO TO APPLY TO The Trustees, 10 Queen's Terrace, Aberdeen AB10 1YG *Email* foundation.uk@aberdeen-asset.com *Website* aboutus.aberdeen-asset.com/en/aboutus/responsible-business/aberdeen-charitable

■ The Aberdeen Foundation

CC NO 1151506 **ESTABLISHED** 2013
WHERE FUNDING CAN BE GIVEN UK and Israel; overseas including Chile and USA.
WHO CAN BENEFIT Charitable organisations.
WHAT IS FUNDED Jewish causes; health; social welfare; education.
RANGE OF GRANTS Up to £1 million.
SAMPLE GRANTS Colegio Maimonides (£1.1 million); Ptach (£1 million) Encyclopedia Talmudit (£770,000); Harchavat Hamaagalim (£683,000); Instituto Hebreo (£234,000); Friedberg Economic Institute (£181,000); Hapotential Haleumi (£120,000).
FINANCES *Year* 2015/16 *Income* £37,749 *Grants* £4,302,484 *Grants to organisations* £4,302,484 *Assets* £55,631,496
TRUSTEES Irwin Weiler; Albert Friedberg; Irwin Weiler; Nancy Friedberg.
HOW TO APPLY Unsolicited applications are not accepted.
WHO TO APPLY TO Yedidut Toronto, 7 Hartom Street, 2nd Floor, Har Hotzvim, Jerusalem, Israel *Tel.* 0526 130910 *Email* aberdeenfoundation@gmail.com

■ ABF The Soldiers' Charity

CC NO 1146420 **ESTABLISHED** 1944
WHERE FUNDING CAN BE GIVEN Worldwide.
WHO CAN BENEFIT Charities supporting people serving, or who have served, in the British Army, or their families/dependants. Individuals.
WHAT IS FUNDED Supporting individuals through the Regimental and Corps Benevolence Funds, and other military and national charities which look after the needs of the serving and retired army community.
TYPE OF GRANT One-off grants.
SAMPLE GRANTS SSAFA (£297,000); Royal Commonwealth Ex-Services (£240,000); Gurkha Welfare Trust (£50,000); Home-Start UK (£35,000); Music in Hospitals (£21,000); The Ripple Pond (£15,000); Hostage UK (£10,000); Hospice UK (£5,000); QEHB Fisher House (£2,000); Stand Easy (£1,100).
FINANCES *Year* 2015/16 *Income* £22,842,918 *Grants* £6,573,000 *Grants to organisations* £3,204,000
TRUSTEES Andrew Gregory; Brig. Andrew Freemantle; Maj. Gen. George Kennedy; Simon Martin; Maj. Gen. David Wood; Maj. Gen. Robert Nitsch; Damien Francis; Peter Baynam; Paul Hearn; Glenn Haughton; Mary Fagan.
HOW TO APPLY Application forms are available from the charity's website and should be emailed to externalgrants@soldierscharity.org. The website states: 'The main Grants Committee sits three times a year in February, June and October, with the Scottish Committee being held in April. Applications received for the main Grants Committee from organisations that have not applied to the Charity within the last two years, and who are requesting grants of over £35,000, will only be considered at the February Grants Committee.' Individual cases should be referred initially to the appropriate Corps or Regimental Association.
WHO TO APPLY TO Temidayo Ajakaiye, Director of Finance, Mountbarrow House, 6–20 Elizabeth Street, London SW1W 9RB *Tel.* 020 7901 8900 *Fax* 020 7901 8901 *Email* info@soldierscharity.org *Website* www.soldierscharity.org

■ The Neville Abraham Foundation

CC NO 328636 **ESTABLISHED** 1990
WHERE FUNDING CAN BE GIVEN England and Wales.
WHO CAN BENEFIT Registered charities.
WHAT IS FUNDED Promotion of education through the performing arts.
SAMPLE GRANTS A list of beneficiaries was not available.
FINANCES *Year* 2015/16 *Income* £15,886 *Grants* £200,000 *Grants to organisations* £200,000
TRUSTEES Neville Abraham; Nicola Leach.
HOW TO APPLY Apply in writing to the correspondent.
WHO TO APPLY TO Neville Abraham, 85 Cadogan Gardens, London SW3 2RD

■ The Acacia Charitable Trust

CC NO 274275 **ESTABLISHED** 1977

WHERE FUNDING CAN BE GIVEN UK and Israel.

WHO CAN BENEFIT Registered charities.

WHAT IS FUNDED Arts and culture; community and welfare; overseas aid; medical causes and disability; education; environment; Jewish causes.

WHAT IS NOT FUNDED Individuals.

TYPE OF GRANT Core and project costs will be considered.

RANGE OF GRANTS Up to £36,000, although most for under £5,000.

SAMPLE GRANTS The Jewish Museum (£36,500); World Jewish Relief (£6,000); Spanish and Portuguese Jews' Congregation (£3,700), Jewish Care, (£2,800); Community Security Trust, Parayhouse School (£2,000 each); Norwood Children's Home (£1,000); NSPCC (£500); Royal Academy of Arts (£150); Wormwood Scrubbs Pony Centre, Shelter (£100 each).

FINANCES *Year* 2014/15 *Income* £60,814 *Grants* £63,317 *Grants to organisations* £63,317 *Assets* £144,943

TRUSTEES Kenneth Rubens; Angela Gillian Rubens; Simon Rubens; Paul Rubens.

OTHER INFORMATION A total of 49 grants were made in the following areas: arts and culture (£38,500); community and welfare (£12,300); overseas aid (£5,700); medical and disability (£3,800); education (£3,100); environment (£100). The 2014/15 accounts were the latest available at the time of writing (May 2017).

HOW TO APPLY Apply in writing to the correspondent.

WHO TO APPLY TO The Secretary, c/o H. W. Fisher and Co., Acre House, 11–15 William Road, London NW1 3ER *Tel.* 020 7486 1884 *Email* acacia@dircon.co.uk

■ The Accenture Foundation

CC NO 1057696 **ESTABLISHED** 1996

WHERE FUNDING CAN BE GIVEN UK and overseas.

WHO CAN BENEFIT Registered charities.

WHAT IS FUNDED General charitable purposes; education; medical causes; community; culture.

SAMPLE GRANTS Cherie Blair Foundation for Women (£576,000); Voluntary Service Overseas (£560,500); The Prince of Wales Youth Business International (£528,500); Onside Northwest Ltd (£127,500).

FINANCES *Year* 2014/15 *Income* £85,178 *Grants* £1,845,734 *Grants to organisations* £1,845,734 *Assets* £2,752,030

TRUSTEES Peter Webb; Camilla Drejer; Fiona Gibson; Gareth Newton.

OTHER INFORMATION The 2014/15 accounts were the latest available at the time of writing (May 2017).

HOW TO APPLY The foundation's Charity Commission record states: 'Proposals are generally invited by the trustees or initiated at their request. Unsolicited applications are discouraged and are unlikely to be successful, even if they fall within the an area in which the trustees are interested.'

WHO TO APPLY TO Anthony Richardson, Administrator, 1 Plantation Place, 30 Fenchurch Street, London EC3M 3BD *Tel.* 020 7844 4000 *Email* corporatecitizenship@accenture.com *Website* www.accenture.com

■ Access Sport CIO

CC NO 1156819 **ESTABLISHED** 2004

WHERE FUNDING CAN BE GIVEN UK.

WHO CAN BENEFIT Sports clubs; registered charities.

WHAT IS FUNDED Improving access to sport for young people in disadvantaged communities.

TYPE OF GRANT One-off and ongoing grants to organisations.

SAMPLE GRANTS A list of beneficiaries was not available.

FINANCES *Year* 2015/16 *Income* £1,061,277 *Grants* £271,206 *Grants to organisations* £271,206 *Assets* £346,580

TRUSTEES Paul Lee; Fraser Hardie; Tim Jones; Grace Clancey; Phil Veasey; Marc Donnelly; John Sarsby; Tina Kokkinos; Keith Wishart; Greg Searle; Mark Burgess; John Baker; Preston Rabl; Martin McPhee.

HOW TO APPLY Contact details for each of the projects can be found on the trust's website. General enquiries should be directed to the correspondent.

WHO TO APPLY TO Sue Wheeler, Correspondent, 3 Durham Yard, Teesdale Street, London E2 6QF *Tel.* 020 7993 9883 *Email* info@accesssport.co.uk *Website* www.accesssport.org.uk

■ Achisomoch Aid Company Ltd

CC NO 278387 **ESTABLISHED** 1979

WHERE FUNDING CAN BE GIVEN UK and overseas.

WHO CAN BENEFIT Jewish schools and charities.

WHAT IS FUNDED The advancement of religion in accordance with the Jewish faith.

RANGE OF GRANTS Up to £670,000.

SAMPLE GRANTS Hasmonean High School Charitable Trust (£668,000); Yesamach Levav Trust (£383,500); The Friends of Ohr Someach (£251,500); Dover Sholem Community Trust (£210,000); Kollel Skver Trust (£139,500); Kisharon (£102,500); École Juive De Lyon (£100,000); Hadras Kodesh Trust (£85,500); Torah Temimah Primary School (£80,500).

FINANCES *Year* 2015/16 *Income* £17,088,490 *Grants* £16,540,372 *Grants to organisations* £16,540,372 *Assets* £4,837,393

TRUSTEES Jack Emanuel; Isaac Katz; Michael Hockenbroch.

OTHER INFORMATION The following information about how the trust operates is given on the its website: 'Achisomoch is a charity voucher agency – it is like a bank. You open an account with us and then pay money into the account. You are given a cheque (voucher) book and can then make (charitable) payments by using these vouchers. As a charity in its own right, we can reclaim the tax rebate under Gift Aid to increase the money in your account and available for distribution to charities. Donations, via vouchers can be made only to registered charities. You get regular statements and can arrange to speak to client services for any help or special instructions.'

HOW TO APPLY Apply in writing to the correspondent.

WHO TO APPLY TO Isaac Katz, Trustee, 26 Hoop Lane, London NW11 8BU *Tel.* 020 8731 8988 *Email* admin@achisomoch.org *Website* www.achisomoch.org

■ The ACT Foundation

CC NO 1068617 **ESTABLISHED** 1998
WHERE FUNDING CAN BE GIVEN UK and overseas.
WHO CAN BENEFIT Registered charities; hospices; individuals.
WHAT IS FUNDED Grants are made with the aim of enhancing the quality of life for people in need with a focus on: people with disabilities; older people; hospices and end of life care; young carers. Grants generally fall into the following areas: building – funding modifications to homes, schools, hospices, etc.; equipment – provision of specialised wheelchairs, other mobility aids and equipment including medical equipment to assist independent living; financial assistance – towards the cost of short-term respite breaks at a registered respite centre.
WHAT IS NOT FUNDED The foundation will not make grants: to charities that have not been registered for at least three years; which would replace statutory funding; which would pay for work that has already commenced or equipment already purchased or on order; towards the operating costs of other charities except in connection with setting up new services; for projects which promote a particular religion or faith; to community centres and youth clubs except where those served are in special need of help (e.g. older people or persons with special needs); to local authorities; to umbrella or grant-making organisations except where they undertake special assessments not readily available from the foundation's own resources; to universities and colleges and grant maintained, private or local education authority schools or their PTAs, except if those schools are for students with special needs; for costs associated with political or publicity campaigns.
RANGE OF GRANTS Up to £100,000.
SAMPLE GRANTS Shelterbox (£250,000); Alexander Devine Children's Hospice (£75,000); Action for Kids (£30,000); The Exaireo Trust (£27,500); Ambitious Abourautism (£25,000); East Park (£20,000); Friends of Thomas Wolsey School (£15,300); Cardiac Risk in the Young and Thames Valley Adventure Playground (£10,000 each); Winchester Young Carers (£8,900); Hampshire Riding Therapy Centre (£4,900).
FINANCES *Year* 2015/16 *Income* £21,023,533 *Grants* £1,750,645 *Grants to organisations* £1,522,547 *Assets* £65,389,574
TRUSTEES Michael Street; John O'Sullivan; Andrew Ross; Robert White; Denis Taylor; Christine Erwood; Russell Meadows; Colin Clarkson.
OTHER INFORMATION Grants were made to 274 organisations and 345 individuals during the year.
HOW TO APPLY Apply in writing to the correspondent. The website provides detailed information on the application process and what to include in an application.
WHO TO APPLY TO Grants Manager, 61 Thames Street, Windsor, Berkshire SL4 1QW *Tel.* 01753 753900 *Fax* 01753 753901 *Email* info@theactfoundation.co.uk *Website* www.theactfoundation.co.uk

■ Action Medical Research

CC NO 208701 **ESTABLISHED** 1952
WHERE FUNDING CAN BE GIVEN UK.
WHO CAN BENEFIT University departments, hospitals and research institutes for specific research projects.
WHAT IS FUNDED Research focusing on children's health including problems affecting pregnancy, childbirth, babies, children and young people. Within this a broad spectrum of research is supported with the objective of preventing disease and disability and of alleviating physical disability.
WHAT IS NOT FUNDED The charity does not provide: grants towards service provision or audit studies; grants purely for higher education, e.g. BSc/MSc/PhD course fees and subsistence costs; grants for medical or dental electives; grants for work undertaken outside the UK; any indirect costs such as administrative or other overheads imposed by the university or other institution; costs associated with advertising and recruitment; top-up funding for work supported by other funding bodies; costs to attend conferences and meetings (current Action Medical Research grantholders may apply separately); grants to other charities – applications would normally come directly from research teams and projects need to be passed through the charity's scientific peer review system; grants for research into complementary/alternative medicine; grants on how best to train clinical staff; grants for psychosocial aspects of treatment; grants on social research, family relationships or socio-economic research; grants for very basic research with little likelihood of clinical impact within the short to medium term. Applicants based in core funded units can apply but need to demonstrate added value.
TYPE OF GRANT Research comprising: project grants and Research Training Fellowship scheme.
RANGE OF GRANTS The average award is about £80,000. It is unusual to fund projects over £150,000 in their entirety.
SAMPLE GRANTS Department of Pharmacology and Sir William Dunn School of Pathology both at the University of Oxford (£200,000 each); University of Manchester and St Mary's Hospital Manchester (£134,000); Molecular Immunology Unit, Institute of Child Health – London (£106,000); Royal College of Obstetricians and Gynaecologists, London (£5,000).
FINANCES *Year* 2015 *Income* £7,467,871 *Grants* £3,538,935 *Grants to organisations* £3,538,935 *Assets* £6,978,793
TRUSTEES Charles Jackson; Valerie Remington-Hobbs; Prof. Sarah Bray; Esther Alderson; Nick Peters; Luke Bordewich; Prof. David Edwards; Prof. Nigel Klein.
HOW TO APPLY Full details of applying for both project and research grants are given on the charity's website together with current closing dates. Read the guidelines (given in the general section of this entry) before making application online.
WHO TO APPLY TO Martin Richardson, Director of Finance, IT and Operations, Vincent House, 31 North Parade, Horsham, West Sussex RH12 2DP *Tel.* 01403 210406 *Email* info@action.org.uk *Website* www.action.org.uk

■ The Sylvia Adams Charitable Trust

CC NO 1050678 **ESTABLISHED** 1995
WHERE FUNDING CAN BE GIVEN England and Wales.
WHO CAN BENEFIT UK-registered charities.
WHAT IS FUNDED Projects improving the life chances of disadvantaged 0- to 3-year-olds in England and Wales; work supporting and informing families and communities affected by genetic conditions; development work in Kenya, Tanzania and Uganda.

RANGE OF GRANTS Generally £5,000 to £20,000.
SAMPLE GRANTS Alstrom Syndrome UK (£20,000); African Initiatives and Chance for Childhood (£15,000 each); Advantage Africa (£10,000); Chellington Centre and The Daisy Garland (£5,000 each).
FINANCES *Year* 2015/16 *Income* £194,954 *Grants* £95,000 *Grants to organisations* £95,000
TRUSTEES Richard Golland; Matthew McBryde; Alex Butler; Jane Young.
HOW TO APPLY Applications can be made through the trust's website. At the time of writing (March 2017) the trust was only accepting applications for preventative work for 0- to 3-year-olds.
WHO TO APPLY TO Jane Young, Director, Sylvia Adams House, 24 The Common, Hatfield, Hertfordshire AL10 0NB *Tel.* 01707 259259 *Email* Jane.Young@sylvia-adams.org.uk *Website* www.sylvia-adams.org.uk

■ The Addleshaw Goddard Charitable Trust

CC NO 286887 **ESTABLISHED** 1983
WHERE FUNDING CAN BE GIVEN Greater London, Manchester and Leeds.
WHO CAN BENEFIT Registered charities.
WHAT IS FUNDED Education; health; social welfare; people in the legal profession; legal education; general charitable purposes.
SAMPLE GRANTS Martin House Children's Hospice (£7,400).
FINANCES *Year* 2015/16 *Income* £63,327 *Grants* £43,041 *Grants to organisations* £43,041 *Assets* £171,966
TRUSTEES Bruce Lightbody; Jonathan Cheney; Lisa Rodgers; Pervinder Kaur; Christopher Noel; Therese Ryan.
OTHER INFORMATION A list of beneficiaries was not included in the 2015/16 accounts, but the following breakdown was given: matching Addleshaw Goddard staff fundraising (£32,000); Leeds charities (£7,400); national and other charities (£3,500).
HOW TO APPLY Apply in writing to the correspondent.
WHO TO APPLY TO Christopher Noel, Trustee, Addleshaw Goddard LLP, One St Peter's Square, Manchester M2 3DE *Tel.* 0161 934 6000 *Email* christopher.noel@addleshawgoddard.com

■ Adenfirst Ltd

CC NO 291647 **ESTABLISHED** 1984
WHERE FUNDING CAN BE GIVEN Worldwide.
WHO CAN BENEFIT Jewish organisations only.
WHAT IS FUNDED Jewish causes related to education, medical care, relief of poverty and the advancement of religion.
SAMPLE GRANTS Beis Aaron Trust (£30,000); Ezer Vehatzolo and Kahal Chassidim Wiznitz (£20,000 each); Beis Rochel D'Satmar, Lolev Charitable Trust and Mercaz Hatorah Belz Machnovke (£10,000 each).
FINANCES *Year* 2015 *Income* £232,698 *Grants* £118,500 *Grants to organisations* £118,500 *Assets* £4,543,447
TRUSTEES Leonard Bondi; Mrs H. F. Bondi; Ian Heitner; Sarah Heitner.
HOW TO APPLY Apply in writing to the correspondent.
WHO TO APPLY TO Leonard Bondi, Trustee, c/o 479 Holloway Road, London N7 6LE *Tel.* 020 7272 2255 *Email* mail@cohenarnold.com

■ The Adint Charitable Trust

CC NO 265290 **ESTABLISHED** 1973
WHERE FUNDING CAN BE GIVEN UK.
WHO CAN BENEFIT Registered charities.
WHAT IS FUNDED Health and social welfare.
WHAT IS NOT FUNDED Individuals.
TYPE OF GRANT One-off grants and recurrent grants for more than three years are considered, for capital costs (including buildings) and core costs.
RANGE OF GRANTS Mostly £5,000 or £10,000.
SAMPLE GRANTS Aldis Trust, Independent Age, Macmillan Cancer Support and The Spring Board Charity (£10,000 each); Noah's Ark Children's Hospice (£6,000); Great Ormond Street Hospital, Listening Books and Shelter (£5,000 each); The WCII Charity (£1,000).
FINANCES *Year* 2015/16 *Income* £220,362 *Grants* £302,000 *Grants to organisations* £302,000 *Assets* £7,601,612
TRUSTEES Anthony Edwards; Douglas Oram; Margaret Edwards; Brian Pate.
HOW TO APPLY Apply in writing to the correspondent. Each applicant should make its own case in the way it considers best, but the application should include full details of the applicant charity. The trust states that it cannot enter into correspondence and unsuccessful applicants will not be notified.
WHO TO APPLY TO Douglas Oram, Trustee, Suite 512, 571 Finchley Road, London NW3 7BN *Email* adintct@gmail.com

■ The Adnams Community Trust

CC NO 1000203 **ESTABLISHED** 1990
WHERE FUNDING CAN BE GIVEN Within a 25-mile radius of St Edmund's Church, Southwold.
WHO CAN BENEFIT Local charities, schools, CICs and community organisations.
WHAT IS FUNDED Education; health and social welfare; the arts; recreation; buildings/community facilities; the environment/conservation; history.
WHAT IS NOT FUNDED Grants are never made to individuals, but may be channelled through recognised organisations that are prepared to sponsor needy individuals and to ensure that the money is well spent. Grants are made for specific purposes only, and are rarely made to the same organisation two years in succession.
TYPE OF GRANT The trustees prefer applications for specific items. Grants are generally of a one-off nature.
RANGE OF GRANTS £500 to £2,000.
SAMPLE GRANTS Prisoners' Education Trust (£2,100); Great Yarmouth Haven Rotary Club and Seagull Lowestoft CIC (£1,300); Teacher Scientist Network (£1,200); Suffolk Coastal Young People's Project (£700); Blythburgh Carpet Bowls Club (£540); St Edmund's Catholic Primary School (£500); Brockdish Village Hall (£350).
FINANCES *Year* 2015/16 *Income* £44,366 *Grants* £72,867 *Grants to organisations* £72,867 *Assets* £10,560
TRUSTEES Melvyn Horn; Simon Loftus; Andy Wood; Jonathan Admans; Emma Hibbert; Guy Heald; Ann-Marie Cross; Tracey Clark; Sarah Churchyard.
OTHER INFORMATION Grants were made to 67 organisations during the year.
HOW TO APPLY For further information, an application form, the full Adnams Charity application guidelines and application deadline dates,

contact Rebecca Abrahall, Adnams Charity Administrator.

WHO TO APPLY TO Rebecca Abrahall, Adnams Community Trust Administrator, Adnams PLC, Sole Bay Brewery, East Green, Southwold, Suffolk IP18 6JW *Tel.* 01502 727200 *Email* communitytrust@adnams.co.uk *Website* adnams.co.uk/about/the-adnams-community-trust

■ The AEB Charitable Trust

SC NO SC028858 **ESTABLISHED** 1998

WHERE FUNDING CAN BE GIVEN Scotland with a preference for the Lothian and Borders regions.

WHO CAN BENEFIT Registered charities.

WHAT IS FUNDED Arts and museums; older people; health; wildlife and nature.

WHAT IS NOT FUNDED Individuals.

SAMPLE GRANTS Hearts and Minds and The Gurkha Welfare Trust (£10,000 each); Edinburgh International Book Festival (£8,000); Royal Botanic Garden – Edinburgh (£7,500); Contact the Elderly, Horatio's Garden and Trellis (£5,000 each); John Muir Trust (£3,000); The Eric Liddell Centre (£2,000).

FINANCES *Year* 2015/16 *Income* £94,951 *Grants* £80,500 *Grants to organisations* £80,500 *Assets* £2,375,603

HOW TO APPLY Applications should be made in writing on no more than three sides of A4 via the online application form on website. Hard copies can also be requested from the correspondent. The trustees meet once a year in spring to decide on grants for the following 12 months. The application deadline is 31 January each year. The trustees normally pay grants prior to 31 March in each year. Applications are not normally acknowledged on receipt; however, successful applicants will be contacted after the trustees have held their annual meeting.

WHO TO APPLY TO Kenneth Pinkerton, Princes Exchange, 1 Earl Grey Street, Edinburgh *Website* www.turcanconnell.com/the-aeb-charitable-trust

■ AF Trust Company

CC NO 1060319 **ESTABLISHED** 1996

WHERE FUNDING CAN BE GIVEN England.

WHO CAN BENEFIT Higher education institutions.

WHAT IS FUNDED Charitable purposes connected with the provision of higher education.

WHAT IS NOT FUNDED Individuals.

SAMPLE GRANTS University of Nottingham (£24,000); University of Reading (£21,000); University of Exeter (£3,000).

FINANCES *Year* 2015/16 *Income* £718,328 *Grants* £50,000 *Grants to organisations* £50,000 *Assets* £355,107

TRUSTEES Martin Wynne-Jones; Andrew Connolly; David Leah; Carol Wright.

OTHER INFORMATION The income figure also relates to funds used to lease buildings from educational establishments and then enter into lease-back arrangements rather than indicating the size of funds available.

HOW TO APPLY Apply in writing to the correspondent. However, unsolicited applications are only accepted from higher education institutions within England.

WHO TO APPLY TO Paul Welch, Secretary, 34 Chapel Street, Thatcham RG18 4QL *Tel.* 01635 867222

■ Age Scotland

SC NO SC010100 **ESTABLISHED** 2009

WHERE FUNDING CAN BE GIVEN Scotland.

WHO CAN BENEFIT Registered charities and community groups.

WHAT IS FUNDED Projects benefitting older people. Recent funding themes have included: tacking loneliness and isolation; grant funding for men's sheds.

WHAT IS NOT FUNDED Statutory authorities; commercial organisations; individuals.

TYPE OF GRANT Capital; one-off; seed funding start-up costs.

SAMPLE GRANTS Glasgow Old People's Welfare Association (£22,500); Luminate (£5,300); Kinloch Historical Society (£3,300); Age Concern – Vale of Leven (£3,000); Abbeyview Day Centre (£1,700); CLASP and Merkinch Community Centre (£1,200 each); Dalbeattie Men's Shed (£1,100).

FINANCES *Year* 2015/16 *Income* £3,079,777 *Grants* £81,426 *Grants to organisations* £81,426 *Assets* £500,083

HOW TO APPLY Details of current grant programmes and how to apply can be found on the charity's website.

WHO TO APPLY TO Community Development Team, Causewayside House, 160 Causewayside, Edinburgh EH9 1PR *Tel.* 0333 323 2400 *Email* members@agescotland.org.uk *Website* www.ageuk.org.uk/scotland

■ Age UK

CC NO 1128267 **ESTABLISHED** 1977

WHERE FUNDING CAN BE GIVEN UK and overseas.

WHO CAN BENEFIT Independently constituted, not-for-profit organisations that are accessible to all people in later life. Research organisations.

WHAT IS FUNDED The charity administers a variety of grant programmes aimed at organisations working to make life better for older people by addressing people's immediate needs or tackling the root causes of problems they are experiencing. Research grants, designed to increase understanding of the ageing process, of what it means to grow old and the implications for society and the economy, are also made.

WHAT IS NOT FUNDED Individuals.

TYPE OF GRANT Capital; one-off; running costs; salaries; and start-up costs. Funding is available for up to three years.

SAMPLE GRANTS A list of beneficiaries was not available.

FINANCES *Year* 2015/16 *Income* £168,071,000 *Grants* £24,686,000 *Grants to organisations* £24,686,000 *Assets* £41,137,000

TRUSTEES Sir Brian Pomeroy; Dianne Jeffrey; Suzanna Townsend; Mark Lunney; Dr Bernadette Fuge; David Hunter; Nick Wilkinson; Lawrence Churchill.

HOW TO APPLY For further information on general grant programmes currently open to applications, contact the Grants Team. Applicants interested in research funding should contact the Research Department at Tavis House, 1–6 Tavistock Square, London WC1H 9NA or email research@ageuk.org.uk.

WHO TO APPLY TO Jayne Moore, Marketing, Communications and Fundraising Officer, Tavis House, 1–6 Tavistock Square, London WC1H 9NA *Tel.* 0800 169 8080 *Email* contact@ageuk.org.uk *Website* www.ageuk.org.uk

■ Aid to the Church in Need (UK)

CC NO 1097984 **ESTABLISHED** 1947
WHERE FUNDING CAN BE GIVEN Worldwide.
WHO CAN BENEFIT Churches; religious projects.
WHAT IS FUNDED Christians who are persecuted, oppressed or in pastoral need.
TYPE OF GRANT Buildings, capital, core costs, endowment, one-off, project, running costs, salaries and start-up costs.
SAMPLE GRANTS A list of beneficiaries was not available.
FINANCES *Year* 2015 *Income* £10,055,178 *Grants* £7,510,437 *Grants to organisations* £7,510,437 *Assets* £1,995,010
TRUSTEES Philipp Habsburg-Lothringen; Graham Hutton; Lisa Simpson; Simon Sheldon; John Marsden; Lord David Alton; Canon Christopher Tuckwell.
OTHER INFORMATION **Note:** The focus of this charity is the church overseas and individuals without the backing as required may not apply for funding.
HOW TO APPLY Applicants are directed, where possible, to the charity's website where the criteria, guidelines and application process are posted. All applications by individuals must have the backing of a Catholic bishop or religious superior.
WHO TO APPLY TO The Trustees, 12–14 Benhill Avenue, Sutton, Surrey SM1 4DA *Tel.* 020 8642 8668 *Email* acn@acnuk.org *Website* www.acnuk.org

■ The AIM Foundation

CC NO 263294 **ESTABLISHED** 1971
WHERE FUNDING CAN BE GIVEN UK.
WHO CAN BENEFIT Charitable organisations.
WHAT IS FUNDED Health and well-being; social change; youth care and development; community development.
WHAT IS NOT FUNDED Individuals.
TYPE OF GRANT Revenue grants: core costs and salaries.
RANGE OF GRANTS Up to £75,000.
SAMPLE GRANTS Impetus Trust – PEF (£75,000); New Economics Foundation (£55,000); The Children's Society (£45,000); Essex Community Foundation (£27,000); Wave Trust (£25,000); The Lighthouse Group (£20,000); The Who Cares Trust (£10,000); Families In Focus (£5,000).
FINANCES *Year* 2014/15 *Income* £3,775,476 *Grants* £327,000 *Grants to organisations* £327,000 *Assets* £10,025,036
TRUSTEES Nicholas Marks; Ian Marks; Caroline Marks; Angela Marks; Joanna Precious; Philippa Bailey.
OTHER INFORMATION The 2014/15 accounts were the latest available at the time of writing (May 2017).
HOW TO APPLY The foundation 'is proactive in its approach' and does not wish to receive applications. Unsolicited requests for assistance will not be responded to under any circumstance.
WHO TO APPLY TO Sean Grinsted, Francis Clark LLP, Vantage Point, Woodwater Park, Pynes Hill, Exeter EX2 5FD *Tel.* 01392 667000 *Email* info@francisclark.co.uk

■ The Sylvia Aitken Charitable Trust

SC NO SC010556 **ESTABLISHED** 1985
WHERE FUNDING CAN BE GIVEN UK, with a preference for Scotland.
WHO CAN BENEFIT Registered charities; charitable organisations.
WHAT IS FUNDED Medical causes; children and young people; countryside, wildlife and animals; educational, cultural and religious; older people, disadvantaged people; disability.
WHAT IS NOT FUNDED Individuals. The trust can only support UK-registered charities.
SAMPLE GRANTS Association for International Cancer Research; Barn Owl Trust; British Lung Foundation; British Stammering Association; Disabled Living Foundation; Epilepsy Research Trust; Royal Scots Dragoon Guards Museum Trust; Sense Scotland; Scottish Child Psychotherapy Trust; Tall Ships Youth Trust; Tenovus Scotland.
FINANCES *Year* 2015/16 *Income* £76,311 *Grants* £161,550 *Grants to organisations* £161,550 *Assets* £1,852,641
HOW TO APPLY Apply in writing to the correspondent. Applicants should outline the charity's objectives and current projects for which funding may be required. The trustees meet at least twice a year, usually in March/April and September/October.
WHO TO APPLY TO The Trustees, Fergusons Chartered Accountants, 24 Woodside, Houston, Renfrewshire PA6 7DD

■ The Ajahma Charitable Trust

CC NO 273823 **ESTABLISHED** 1977
WHERE FUNDING CAN BE GIVEN UK and overseas.
WHO CAN BENEFIT Registered charities.
WHAT IS FUNDED General charitable purposes including: development; health; disability; social welfare; human rights.
TYPE OF GRANT Core and running costs, projects and salaries.
SAMPLE GRANTS Prisoners Abroad and Pump Aid (£50,000 each); Disability Rights UK (£35,000); Southall Black Sisters and Tender (£12,000 each); Age UK Kensington and Chelsea, Change Foundation and Gospel Oak Action Link (£4,500 each).
FINANCES *Year* 2015/16 *Income* £75,535 *Grants* £322,500 *Grants to organisations* £322,500 *Assets* £2,507,553
TRUSTEES Roger Paffard; Elizabeth Simpson; Jenny Sheridan; James Taylor; Carole Pound.
HOW TO APPLY The trust no longer accepts unsolicited applications. The 2015/16 annual report states: 'The Trustees have adopted a policy of seeking and considering applications for charitable funding generally from established charities. They seek to maintain a reasonable balance between charitable activities overseas and in the United Kingdom.'
WHO TO APPLY TO Suzanne Hunt, 275 Dover House Road, London SW15 5BP *Tel.* 020 8788 5388

■ AKO Foundation

CC NO 1151815 **ESTABLISHED** 2013
WHERE FUNDING CAN BE GIVEN England; USA; Africa; Norway.
WHO CAN BENEFIT Registered charities.
WHAT IS FUNDED Education; the arts.
RANGE OF GRANTS Up to £4.5 million.

SAMPLE GRANTS AKO Kunststiftelse (£4.6 million); University of Pennsylvania (£1.1 million); Center for Human Rights and Diplomacy (£613,000); London School of Economics (£337,000); The Jamie Oliver Food Foundation (£150,000); Maytree (£100,000); National Society for Prevention of Cruelty to Children (£50,000); Zeitz MOCAA Curatorial Training Programme (£44,000); Bowel Disease UK (£40,000); The Special Yoga Foundation (£19,000).
FINANCES *Year* 2015 *Income* £11,951,992 *Grants* £8,061,588 *Grants to organisations* £8,061,558 *Assets* £44,477,106
TRUSTEES Nicolai Tangen; David Woodburn; Henrik Syse; Martin Byman.
OTHER INFORMATION There were 17 grants made during the year and distributed as follows: art (£4.7 million); education (£3.3 million); AKO Give Back Initiative (£100,000).
HOW TO APPLY The foundation does not accept unsolicited applications.
WHO TO APPLY TO David Woodburn, Trustee, c/o Ako Capital LLP, 61 Conduit Street, London W1S 2GB *Tel.* 020 7070 2420 *Email* akofoundation@akocapital.com *Website* www.akocapital.com/40/ako-foundation

■ The Al-Fayed Charitable Foundation

CC NO 297114 **ESTABLISHED** 1987
WHERE FUNDING CAN BE GIVEN Worldwide with a preference for the UK.
WHO CAN BENEFIT Registered charities; schools; hospices; hospitals; individuals.
WHAT IS FUNDED Health, well-being and education of disadvantaged children and young people.
TYPE OF GRANT One-off and recurring.
RANGE OF GRANTS £1,000 to £180,000.
SAMPLE GRANTS Francis House (£157,500); Face for Children in Need (£120,000); Facing the World (£90,000); Zoë's Place (£91,000); Lotus Children Centre (£80,000); Great Ormond Street (£60,000); Naked Heart Foundation (£7,000); Unicef UK (£4,000); Nowzad Dogs (£3,000); Helping Rhinos (£1,000).
FINANCES *Year* 2015 *Income* £844,104 *Grants* £802,485 *Grants to organisations* £802,485 *Assets* £108,523
TRUSTEES Mohamed Al-Fayed; Camilla Fayed; Heini Fayed; Omar Fayed.
HOW TO APPLY Apply in writing to the correspondent.
WHO TO APPLY TO Charity Manager, Hyde Park Residence Ltd, 55 Park Lane, London W1K 1NA *Email* acf@alfayed.com *Website* www.the-acf.com

■ The Alborada Trust

CC NO 1091660 **ESTABLISHED** 2001
WHERE FUNDING CAN BE GIVEN Worldwide.
WHO CAN BENEFIT Charitable organisations.
WHAT IS FUNDED Medical and veterinary causes; research and education; welfare of animals; disaster relief.
RANGE OF GRANTS Over £25,000.
SAMPLE GRANTS Alzheimer's Research UK (£364,000); Médecins Sans Frontières (£220,000); The Langford Trust for Animal Health and Welfare (£200,00); Wildlife SOS India (£87,000); Action Aid UK (£100,000); Animal Health Trust (£50,000); Wolfson College, Cambridge (£10,000).
FINANCES *Year* 2015 *Income* £70,756 *Grants* £1,770,637 *Grants to organisations* £1,770,637 *Assets* £9,322,688
TRUSTEES Eva Rausing; David Way; Roland Lerner; Capt. James Nicholson; Robert Goff.
OTHER INFORMATION Grants were made to 14 organisations during the year.
HOW TO APPLY Application forms are available from the trust's website.
WHO TO APPLY TO Jeremy Richardson, Secretary, Fladgate LLP, 16 Great Queen Street, London WC2B 5DG *Tel.* 01638 750222 *Website* www.alboradatrust.com

■ D. G. Albright Charitable Trust

CC NO 277367 **ESTABLISHED** 1978
WHERE FUNDING CAN BE GIVEN UK, with a preference for Gloucestershire.
WHO CAN BENEFIT Registered charities.
WHAT IS FUNDED General charitable purposes.
WHAT IS NOT FUNDED Grants are not usually made to individuals.
TYPE OF GRANT One-off and recurrent.
RANGE OF GRANTS £500 to £5,000.
SAMPLE GRANTS Great Somerford Church Appeal (£5,000); The Family Haven – Gloucester (£3,000); The Shop at Bromesberrow (£2,000); Fields in Trust and Hope and Homes for Children (£1,000 each); Dymock Rectory (£750); Almshouse Association, OSCAR and War Memorials Trust (£500 each).
FINANCES *Year* 2015/16 *Income* £58,650 *Grants* £47,745 *Grants to organisations* £47,745 *Assets* £1,377,893
TRUSTEES Hon. Dr Gilbert Greenall; Richard Wood.
HOW TO APPLY Apply in writing to the correspondent.
WHO TO APPLY TO Richard Wood, Trustee, Old Church School, Hollow Street, Great Somerford, Chippenham, Wiltshire SN15 5JD *Tel.* 01249 720760

■ The Alchemy Foundation

CC NO 292500 **ESTABLISHED** 1985
WHERE FUNDING CAN BE GIVEN UK and overseas.
WHO CAN BENEFIT Community projects; voluntary organisations; registered charities.
WHAT IS FUNDED The focus is on: The Alchemist Scheme (funding the costs of fundraisers assigned to other charities to assist with their fundraising efforts), water projects in financially developing countries, disability (particularly mobility, access, helplines and communications), social welfare (inner city community projects, disaffected young people, family mediation, homelessness), personal reform, penal reform (work with prisoners, especially young prisoners, and their families), medical research and aid (especially in areas of blindness and disfigurement), individual enterprise (by helping Raleigh International and similar organisations to give opportunities to young people according to need) and respite for carers.
WHAT IS NOT FUNDED Organisations exclusive to one faith or political belief.
TYPE OF GRANT Capital; revenue; one-off; salaries.
SAMPLE GRANTS A list of beneficiaries was not available.
FINANCES *Year* 2015/16 *Income* £501,968 *Grants* £397,387 *Grants to organisations* £397,387 *Assets* £3,020,263
TRUSTEES Dr Jemima Stilgoe; Holly Stilgoe; Jack Stilgoe; Rufus Stilgoe; Richard Stilgoe;

Alexander Armitage; Andrew Murison; Annabel Stilgoe; Joseph Stilgoe; Antoun Elias.

HOW TO APPLY Apply in writing to the correspondent.

WHO TO APPLY TO Richard Stilgoe, Trustee, Trevereux Manor, Limpsfield Chart, Oxted, Surrey RH8 0TL

■ Aldgate and All Hallows' Foundation

CC NO 312500 **ESTABLISHED** 1893

WHERE FUNDING CAN BE GIVEN City of London and the London borough of Tower Hamlets.

WHO CAN BENEFIT Registered charities; schools; individuals.

WHAT IS FUNDED The foundation can only consider applications for education projects from schools and organisations that will benefit: children or young people who are: under the age of 30; residents of Tower Hamlets or the City of London; in full-time education or studying for a recognised qualification; and from disadvantaged backgrounds or areas of high deprivation.

WHAT IS NOT FUNDED Equipment or teachers' salaries that are the responsibility of education authorities; youth groups; supplementary schools or mother tongue teaching; the purchase, repair or furnishing of buildings; conferences or seminars; stage, film, publication or video production costs; performances or exhibitions; retrospective requests (i.e. any activity that has already taken place); requests to substitute for the withdrawal or reduction of statutory funding; general fundraising campaigns or appeals.

RANGE OF GRANTS Up to £45,000.

SAMPLE GRANTS Rich Mix (£35,000); Charles Dickens Museum (£19,000); Chain Reaction Theatre Company (£18,100); National Maritime Museum (£17,200); Bow Arts (£15,000); First Story (£14,600); The Country Trust (£10,300); Magic Me (£10,000).

FINANCES *Year* 2015 *Income* £70,517 *Grants* £296,879 *Grants to organisations* £255,379 *Assets* £7,013,961

TRUSTEES Cllr Denise Jones; David Mash; Robin Hazlewood; Revd Bertrand Olivier; Graham Forbes; John Hall; William Hamilton-Hinds; Billy Whitbread; Susan Knowles; Cllr Sirajul Islam; Revd Laura Jorgenson; Kevon Everett; Michael O'Dwyer.

OTHER INFORMATION During the year there were 23 grants made to institutions totalling £235,500 and 37 grants made to individuals totalling £41,500.

HOW TO APPLY Apply in writing to the correspondent. Full details of what should be included in an application can be found on the foundation's website. Applications can be submitted throughout the year. There is no closing date, but applications must be received in good time before meeting dates to enable the foundation to complete its assessment process. Decisions are made by the foundation's governors who meet twice a year, in April and September.

WHO TO APPLY TO Richard Foley, Clerk and Chief Executive, 31 Jewry Street, London EC3N 2EY *Tel.* 020 7488 2518 *Email* aldgateandallhallows@sirjohncass.org *Website* www.aldgateallhallows.org.uk

■ All Saints Educational Trust

CC NO 312934 **ESTABLISHED** 1978

WHERE FUNDING CAN BE GIVEN UK and overseas.

WHO CAN BENEFIT Charities; individuals.

WHAT IS FUNDED Projects that promote the development of education, particularly in the areas of religious education, home economics and related areas or subjects, and multi-cultural/inter-faith education.

WHAT IS NOT FUNDED General or core funds of any organisation; public appeals; school buildings, equipment or supplies (except library resources); the establishment of new departments in universities and colleges; general bursary funds of other organisations.

TYPE OF GRANT One-off, project or annual grants for a limited period. Funding may be given for more than three years. Preference will be given to pump-priming projects.

RANGE OF GRANTS Up to £40,000.

SAMPLE GRANTS British Nutrition Foundation (£40,000); Southall Christian Schools' Worker Project (£15,000); Bible Reading Fellowship and University of Manchester (£10,000 each); RE Today (£8,000); Friends of Bruce Castle (£5,000); Wilde Food (£2,600); Priory School (£750).

FINANCES *Year* 2015/16 *Income* £716,932 *Grants* £425,288 *Grants to organisations* £251,058 *Assets* £11,744,927

TRUSTEES Diane McCrea; The Revd John Trillo; Stephen Brooker; Barbara Harvey; Dr Augur Pearce; The Ven. Stephen Welch; Prof. Anthony Leeds; Stephanie Valentine; Frances Smith; Anna Cumbers; Michael Jacob; Dorothy Garland; Revd Tim Elbourne; Derek Charles Holloway; Michael Blackpool.

OTHER INFORMATION Grants are made to individuals who are or intend to become engaged as teachers or in other capacities connected with education, in particular home economics and religious subjects, and those who teach or intend to teach in multicultural areas.

HOW TO APPLY For applications from organisations (not individuals): applicants are invited to discuss their ideas informally with the clerk before making an application. In some cases, a 'link trustee' is appointed to assist the organisation in preparing the application and who will act in a liaison role with the trust. Completed applications are put before the awards committee in April/May, with final decisions made in June. Application forms are available on the trust's website, either in interactive or printable form.

WHO TO APPLY TO The Trustees, Knightrider House, 2 Knightrider Court, London EC4V 5AR *Tel.* 020 7248 8380 *Email* aset@aset.org.uk *Website* www.aset.org.uk

■ The Derrill Allatt Foundation

CC NO 1148440 **ESTABLISHED** 2012

WHERE FUNDING CAN BE GIVEN Worldwide with a preference for South America; Central America; The Caribbean; Africa; Russia; Iraq; Pakistan; Portugal; UK.

WHO CAN BENEFIT Registered charities.

WHAT IS FUNDED Social welfare; social inclusion; health; training; arts; animals.

RANGE OF GRANTS Up to £40,000.

SAMPLE GRANTS Hazara Charitable Trust (£40,000); Build Africa (£30,000); Oxford Lieder (£20,000); Southbank Sinfonia (£13,500); Parliament Choir and St Clement Danes (£10,000 each); HM Tower of London Chapels Royal Foundation

(£8,000); Get Connected Helpline (£5,000); Winchester District Council Scouts Pinsent Building Appeal (£2,000).

FINANCES *Year* 2015/16 *Income* £255,681 *Grants* £212,670 *Grants to organisations* £212,670 *Assets* £1,187,842

TRUSTEES Diana Hargreaves; Clare Matthews; Payne Hicks Beach Trust Corporation Ltd.

HOW TO APPLY No grants are given to unsolicited applications.

WHO TO APPLY TO The Trustees, Payne Hicks Beach, 10 New Square, Lincoln's Inn, London WC2A 3QG *Tel.* 020 7465 4300

■ Allchurches Trust Ltd

CC NO 263960 **ESTABLISHED** 1972

WHERE FUNDING CAN BE GIVEN UK and overseas.

WHO CAN BENEFIT Church of England dioceses; Church of England cathedrals; religious charities; charities preserving UK heritage; hospices; schools.

WHAT IS FUNDED Promotion of the Christian religion; heritage, care and the community; church restoration; training and development. Charitable projects should have a Christian foundation.

WHAT IS NOT FUNDED The trust's grant-giving policy states: 'The following will only be supported in exceptional circumstances: charities with a political association; national charities; individuals or causes that will benefit only one person such as student grants and bursaries; appeals for running costs or salaries; healthcare though hospices can apply for funding towards the provision of chapel and chaplaincy space; work that is primarily the responsibility of statutory authorities including residential, respite, day care and housing provision; animal welfare, zoos, captive breeding or animal rescue centres; retrospective grants although we may be prepared to consider applications for work already done which was urgent (such as essential emergency roof repairs) or for major capital projects (where work has started before all funding has been raised); more than one appeal from the same applicant within a 24 month period.'

TYPE OF GRANT Primarily one-off.

RANGE OF GRANTS Most grants are £1,000 to £5,000 but larger grants are considered.

SAMPLE GRANTS The Representative Body of the Church in Wales (£183,000); Dumfries Baptist Church (£40,000); Centre for Theology and Community (£25,000); Birmingham Cathedral (£22,000); Civic Voice – Liverpool (£3,000); The Church of the Ascension, Bath (£2,000); Aberdeen Passion Plays and Love Bristol (£1,000 each).

FINANCES *Year* 2015 *Income* £21,681,000 *Grants* £11,691,684 *Grants to organisations* £11,691,684 *Assets* £432,999

TRUSTEES Archdeacon Annette Cooper; Sir Philip Mawer; Christopher Smith; Denise Wilson; Sir Laurence Magnus; Michael Arlington; Timothy Carroll; Steven Hudson.

OTHER INFORMATION Income is derived from its wholly owned subsidiary company Ecclesiastical Insurance Office PLC. A total of 1,221 grants were made during the year.

HOW TO APPLY Applications should be submitted online via the trust's website.

WHO TO APPLY TO Iain Hearn, Grants Administrator, Beaufort House, Brunswick Road, Gloucester GL1 1JZ *Tel.* 01452 873184 *Email* atl@allchurches.co.uk *Website* www.allchurches.co.uk

■ The Allen & Overy Foundation

CC NO 1153738 **ESTABLISHED** 2013

WHERE FUNDING CAN BE GIVEN London; Northern Ireland; India; Nepal; Syria; Tanzania; Uganda.

WHO CAN BENEFIT Registered charities.

WHAT IS FUNDED Disaster relief; access to justice; access to education, employment and training.

SAMPLE GRANTS Amref Health Africa (£300,500); UN High Commissioner for Refugees (£25,000); Save the Children (£13,000); Child Poverty Action Group (£8,000); Beyond Food Foundation (£5,100); Alice's Arc, Switchback and YoungMinds (£5,000 each); International Law Book Facility (£2,000); Horn of Africa People's Aid (£1,500).

FINANCES *Year* 2015/16 *Income* £731,998 *Grants* £730,458 *Grants to organisations* £730,458 *Assets* £544,526

TRUSTEES Mark Mansell; Andrew Wedderburn-Day; Jane Finlayson-Brown; Jane Townsend; Philip Mansfield; Annelies van der Pauw.

HOW TO APPLY The Allen & Overy Foundation (London) – email the foundation to request an application form. Global grants programme (worldwide funding and disaster relief) – apply in writing to the Global Foundation (GlobalFoundation@AllenOvery.com).

WHO TO APPLY TO The Trustees, One Bishops Square, London E1 6AD *Tel.* 020 3088 0000 *Email* allenoveryfoundation@allenovery.com *Website* www.allenovery.com/corporate-responsibility/charitable-giving/Pages/Local-charitable-giving.aspx

■ D. C. R. Allen Charitable Trust

CC NO 277293 **ESTABLISHED** 1979

WHERE FUNDING CAN BE GIVEN UK.

WHO CAN BENEFIT Registered charities.

WHAT IS FUNDED General charitable purposes, especially disadvantaged young people. There is a preference for small to medium-sized charities.

WHAT IS NOT FUNDED Individuals; funding of services usually provided by statutory sources; causes outside the UK; evangelical or worship activities; animal welfare; medical research; heritage conservation/preservation; arts or collections.

TYPE OF GRANT One-off. Funding for capital projects may be given.

RANGE OF GRANTS From £2,000 to £20,000. Larger amounts may be considered, especially for innovative or capital projects.

SAMPLE GRANTS Centrepoint and The Northamptonshire Parent Infant Partnership (£25,000 each); Katherine House Hospice (£11,200); Greenham Community Trust and Suffolk Young Carers (£10,000 each); Home-Start UK (£5,000); Brainwave (£3,500); Pelton Youth Project (£3,000); Choysez (£2,500); Great Ormond Street (£1,000); Suffolk Art Link (£900).

FINANCES *Year* 2015/16 *Income* £434,000 *Grants* £228,200 *Grants to organisations* £228,200 *Assets* £4,880,708

TRUSTEES Julie Frusher; Martin Allen; Colin Allen.

HOW TO APPLY Applications should be made in writing to the correspondent. The trustees normally meet monthly, so decisions can be made fairly promptly. It is not possible for the trustees to respond to unsuccessful applicants, so if no positive response has been received within eight weeks of the application date, then applicants may assume that they have not been successful.

WHO TO APPLY TO Julie Frusher, Estate Office, Edgcote House, Edgcote, Banbury, Oxfordshire OX17 1AG *Email* edgcotehouse@outlook.com

■ The H. B. Allen Charitable Trust

CC NO 802306 **ESTABLISHED** 1985

WHERE FUNDING CAN BE GIVEN Worldwide.

WHO CAN BENEFIT Registered charities; museums; hospices; churches.

WHAT IS FUNDED Current priorities: blindness/deafness research; medical research; museums, galleries and heritage; churches (built heritage only); environment, wildlife and animals.

WHAT IS NOT FUNDED Individuals.

TYPE OF GRANT One-off and recurrent up to three years, revenue and capital including core costs.

RANGE OF GRANTS Mainly £5,000 to £25,000.

SAMPLE GRANTS Canterbury Cathedral (£220,000); Hereford Cathedral Perpetual Trust (£125,000); The Rowans Hospice (£100,000); Skeletal Cancer Action Trust (£84,000); Spetchley Gardens Charitable Trust (£50,000); Bowel Disease Research Foundation (£20,000); The Hawk and Owl Trust and Trees for Life (£10,000 each); War Memorials Trust (£5,000).

FINANCES *Year* 2015 *Income* £1,645,860 *Grants* £1,919,000 *Grants to organisations* £1,919,000 *Assets* £38,757,605

TRUSTEES Helen Ratcliffe; Peter Shone.

HOW TO APPLY Apply by letter to the correspondent enclosing the latest annual report and accounts. Email applications are not accepted but enquiries can be made by email. Applications are considered at the main annual meeting which takes place in the first few months of the year. Although applications can be made at any time, it states on the trust's website that it would be preferable if applications were only made in the last quarter of the calendar year. Only successful applicants are acknowledged.

WHO TO APPLY TO Peter Shone, Trustee, Homefield, Chidden Holt, Hambledon, Waterlooville, Hampshire PO7 4TG *Tel.* 023 9263 2406 *Email* mail@hballenct.org.uk *Website* www.hballenct.org.uk

■ The Allen Trust

CC NO 1146388 **ESTABLISHED** 2012

WHERE FUNDING CAN BE GIVEN Worldwide.

WHO CAN BENEFIT Registered charities.

WHAT IS FUNDED Social welfare.

SAMPLE GRANTS African Revival (£29,000); Jubilee Life Ministries (£10,000); Tamama Construction (£5,000); Chairna Christian institute (£3,500); Diocese of Maridi (£3,500); Church Mission Society Ireland (£2,500); Len Treneary (£2,000).

FINANCES *Year* 2015/16 *Income* £13,427 *Grants* £1,000,000 *Grants to organisations* £1,000,000

TRUSTEES Tony Allen; Andreas Triteos.

OTHER INFORMATION This charity's latest accounts were not available to view on the Charity Commission's website due to its low income. We have therefore estimated the grant total based on previous years' information.

HOW TO APPLY Apply in writing to the correspondent.

WHO TO APPLY TO Tony Allen, Trustee, Oakmead Farm, Ockham Lane, Cobham, SURREY, KTLL 1LY *Tel.* 020 8939 3905

■ The Alliance Family Foundation

CC NO 258721 **ESTABLISHED** 1968

WHERE FUNDING CAN BE GIVEN UK and Israel.

WHO CAN BENEFIT Organisations, particularly Jewish causes, benefitting young people and people disadvantaged by poverty.

WHAT IS FUNDED The relief of poverty; advancement of religion; education and medical knowledge.

SAMPLE GRANTS University of Manchester (£86,000); Weizmann Institute (£70,000); Shaare Hayim (£45,500); Fariboz Fred Matloob Foundation (£36,000); Tel Aviv University (£58,500 in two grants).

FINANCES *Year* 2015/16 *Income* £700,231 *Grants* £663,884 *Grants to organisations* £409,341 *Assets* £3,444,338

TRUSTEES Lord David Alliance; Graham Alliance; Sara Esterkin; Joshua Alliance.

OTHER INFORMATION Donations to individuals totalled £121,000.

HOW TO APPLY Apply in writing to the trustees. The 2015/16 annual report states: 'The trustees' policy is to review requests for financial support and make donations at their discretion.'

WHO TO APPLY TO The Trustees, Spencer House, 27 St James's Place, London SW1A 1NR *Email* aff@alliance.me

■ Alzheimer's Research UK

CC NO 1077089 **ESTABLISHED** 1998

WHERE FUNDING CAN BE GIVEN UK.

WHO CAN BENEFIT Universities; charities; hospitals; research institutions.

WHAT IS FUNDED Alzheimer's research.

SAMPLE GRANTS A list of beneficiaries was not available.

FINANCES *Year* 2015/16 *Income* £22,014,026 *Grants* £14,819,168 *Grants to organisations* £14,819,168 *Assets* £3,740,220

TRUSTEES Barry Townsley; Shirley Cramer; Dr Rupert Everett; Prof. James Fawcett; David Mayhew; Dr Fiona Marshall; Michael Cooper; Nicholas Antil; Christopher Carter; Caroline van den Brul; Giles Dennison.

HOW TO APPLY There are a number of grant schemes available, details of which can be found on the charity's website. Applications also can be made on the website.

WHO TO APPLY TO Lizzie Ashley-Webb, 3 Riverside, Granta Park, Cambridge CB21 6AD *Tel.* 01223 824581 *Email* enquiries@alzheimersresearchuk.org *Website* www.alzheimersresearchuk.org

■ Alzheimer's Society

CC NO 296645 **ESTABLISHED** 1987

WHERE FUNDING CAN BE GIVEN UK.

WHO CAN BENEFIT Universities; hospitals; research institutions.

WHAT IS FUNDED Research into dementia.

SAMPLE GRANTS University of Edinburgh (£850,000); King's College London (£397,000) University of Liverpool (£361,000); London School of Hygiene and Tropical Medicine (£55,000); University of Northumbria (£2,000).

FINANCES *Year* 2015/16 *Income* £97,949,000 *Grants* £6,499,000 *Grants to organisations* £6,499,000 *Assets* £44,253,000

TRUSTEES Prof. Gordon Wilcock; Dr Bernard Herdan; Sir John Powell; Richard Ford; Sarah Weir; Dr Emyr Roberts; Manish Shah; Margaret Joy; Jennifer Owen; Hazel Blears; David Kelham; Stephen Hill; Alison Harrison; Duncan Jones.

HOW TO APPLY For information on how to apply to one of Alzheimer's Society's current grant schemes, refer to the website. Funding calls are advertised on the website and applications should be submitted online. Guidelines for applicants are available to download from the website.

WHO TO APPLY TO Research Team, 43–44 Crutched Friars, London EC3N 2AE *Tel.* 020 7423 5136 *Email* governance@alzheimer's.org.uk *Website* www.alzheimer's.org.uk

■ The AM Charitable Trust

CC NO 256283 **ESTABLISHED** 1968

WHERE FUNDING CAN BE GIVEN UK and overseas.

WHO CAN BENEFIT Registered charities; Jewish organisations.

WHAT IS FUNDED General charitable purposes including: medical causes; welfare; arts; and conservation causes.

WHAT IS NOT FUNDED Individuals.

TYPE OF GRANT Certain charities are supported for more than one year, although no commitment is usually given to the recipients.

SAMPLE GRANTS British Heart Foundation and Cancer Research Campaign (£20,000 each); Israel Free Loan Association (£5,000); Alzheimer's Research Trust and Help the Aged (£1,000 each); Bletchley park Trust (£500); Brain Research Trust (£400); Alder Hey Children's Hospital (£200); Children's Country Holiday Fund (£150).

FINANCES *Year* 2015/16 *Income* £100,451 *Grants* £92,100 *Grants to organisations* £92,100 *Assets* £1,768,855

TRUSTEE Kleinwort Benson Trustees Ltd.

HOW TO APPLY The 2015/16 accounts state: 'Donations are decided periodically by the trustee having regard to the wishes of the Settlor, and unsolicited appeals are considered as well as causes which have already been supported. Only successful applicants are notified of the trustee's decision. Certain charities are supported for more than one year, although no commitment is usually given to the recipients. A range of general charitable causes is considered, as well as Jewish charities. There is no facility for processing applications from individuals for financial support, and these cannot be considered.'

WHO TO APPLY TO The Trustees, SG Kleinwort Hambros Trust Company (UK) Ltd, 8 St James's Square, London SW19 4JU *Tel.* 020 3207 7091

■ Amabrill Ltd

CC NO 1078968 **ESTABLISHED** 2000

WHERE FUNDING CAN BE GIVEN UK with a preference for North West London.

WHO CAN BENEFIT Jewish charities.

WHAT IS FUNDED The advancement of education and religious practice in accordance with the teachings of the Orthodox Jewish faith; and social welfare.

SAMPLE GRANTS SOFT (Support Organisation for Trisomy) (£247,000); Kahal Chasidim Bobov (£170,000); United Talmudical Associates Ltd (£103,000); BFON Trust (£72,000); Torah Vodaas (£64,500); FOSI (£59,500); The Talmud Torah Machzikei Hadass Trust (£51,500); Yesamach Levav Trust (£38,000); FOBM (£18,000).

FINANCES *Year* 2015/16 *Income* £2,733,150 *Grants* £2,112,804 *Grants to organisations* £2,112,804 *Assets* £8,023,487

TRUSTEES Charles Lerner; Frances Lerner; Israel Grossnass; Irving Lerner.

OTHER INFORMATION Grants were distributed as follows: relief of poverty (£915,500); advancement of the Jewish faith (£897,000); educational grants (£300,500).

HOW TO APPLY Apply in writing to the correspondent. Appeal letters are received from, and personal visits made by representatives of Jewish charitable, religious and educational institutions. These requests are then considered by the trustees and grants are made in accordance with the trustees' decisions.

WHO TO APPLY TO Charles Lerner, Trustee, 1 Golders Manor Drive, London NW11 9HU *Tel.* 020 8455 6785 *Email* mail@venittandgreaves.com

■ The Amalur Foundation Ltd

CC NO 1090476 **ESTABLISHED** 2002

WHERE FUNDING CAN BE GIVEN Worldwide.

WHO CAN BENEFIT Charitable organisations.

WHAT IS FUNDED General charitable purposes.

SAMPLE GRANTS Absolute Return for Kids (£110,000); St Patrick's Catholic Church (£50,000); Prostate Research Campaign UK (£10,000); Brain Tumour Research Campaign (£5,500); Breakthrough Breast Cancer (£3,000); the Extra Care Charitable Trust (£2,000).

FINANCES *Year* 2014/15 *Income* £517,160 *Grants* £529,094 *Grants to organisations* £529,094 *Assets* £622,022

TRUSTEES Claudia Garuti; David Way; Helen Mellor.

OTHER INFORMATION The 2014/15 accounts were the latest available at the time of writing (May 2017).

HOW TO APPLY Apply in writing to the correspondent.

WHO TO APPLY TO David Way, Trustee, Fladgate LLP, 16 Great Queen Street, London WC2B 5DG *Tel.* 020 3036 7000

■ The Ammco Trust

CC NO 327962 **ESTABLISHED** 1988

WHERE FUNDING CAN BE GIVEN Oxfordshire and adjoining counties.

WHO CAN BENEFIT Registered local charities.

WHAT IS FUNDED General charitable purposes; disability; health; medical causes; special needs education; ex-services; sport and arts/heritage.

WHAT IS NOT FUNDED Individuals.

TYPE OF GRANT One-off.

RANGE OF GRANTS Usually up to £2,000, except in exceptional circumstances.

SAMPLE GRANTS A list of beneficiaries was not available.

FINANCES *Year* 2015/16 *Income* £57,553 *Grants* £53,837 *Grants to organisations* £53,837 *Assets* £1,565,736

TRUSTEES Esther Lewis; Rowena Vickers; Nicholas Cobbold.

OTHER INFORMATION A list of beneficiaries for the year could not be obtained. During the year the charity spent £14,500 in welfare grants; £9,000 in medical grants; £8,500 in disability grants and £6,600 on other causes. No grants were awarded to individuals.

HOW TO APPLY Apply in writing to the correspondent.

WHO TO APPLY TO Esther Lewis, Glebe Farm, Hinton Waldrist, Faringdon, Oxfordshire SN7 8RX *Tel.* 01865 820269

■ Viscount Amory's Charitable Trust

CC NO 204958 **ESTABLISHED** 1962

WHERE FUNDING CAN BE GIVEN Devon.

WHO CAN BENEFIT Registered charities; schools; churches; individuals.

WHAT IS FUNDED General charitable purposes including: education; religion.

WHAT IS NOT FUNDED Applications from individuals for the relief of poverty; applications for grants or short-term loans for individuals' immediate needs or wants.

TYPE OF GRANT Usually one-off including capital.

RANGE OF GRANTS £5,00 to £95,000.

SAMPLE GRANTS Rona Sailing Project (£95,000); Devon Young Farmers Club (£50,000); Exeter Cathedral School (£31,500); Blundell's School (£30,500); Exeter Cathedral (£15,000); Tiverton Market Centre (£12,000); St Peter's Church – Tiverton (£10,000); Tiverton Museum of Mid Devon Life (£6,900); Exmoor Society (£5,000).

FINANCES *Year* 2015/16 *Income* £469,681 *Grants* £404,004 *Grants to organisations* £400,367 *Assets* £12,954,897

TRUSTEES Sir Ian Heathcoat Amory; Catherine Cavender.

OTHER INFORMATION The trustees do not consider applications from individuals unless as part of an activity sponsored or promoted by an organisation.

HOW TO APPLY Apply in writing to the correspondent by letter, not by email. Applications should include the following: your address; your email address, if available; general background information about your appeal; the nature of the sponsoring or associated organisation; the total amount you are looking to raise; how much has been raised to date; how you propose raising any shortfall; any further information you feel would be relevant for the attention of the trustees. The trustees aim to meet on a monthly basis and expect to inform applicants of the trustees' decision either way.

WHO TO APPLY TO The Trustees, The Island, Lowman Green, Tiverton, Devon EX16 4LA *Tel.* 01884 254899 *Email* office@vact.org.uk *Website* www.vact.org.uk

■ Sir John and Lady Amory's Charitable Trust

CC NO 203970 **ESTABLISHED** 1961

WHERE FUNDING CAN BE GIVEN UK, with a preference the South West.

WHO CAN BENEFIT Local organisations, plus a few UK-wide charities.

WHAT IS FUNDED General charitable purposes.

TYPE OF GRANT One-off grants for capital expenditure.

SAMPLE GRANTS National Trust (£8,000); Project Trust (£5,000).

FINANCES *Year* 2015/16 *Income* £380,833 *Grants* £53,947 *Grants to organisations* £53,947 *Assets* £2,315,144

TRUSTEES Lady Amory; Sir Ian Heathcoat Amory; Mr W. F. Heathcoat Amory.

HOW TO APPLY Apply in writing to the correspondent.

WHO TO APPLY TO Mrs S. Curtis, The Island, Lowman Green, Tiverton, Devon EX16 4LA *Tel.* 01884 254899 *Email* charities@lowman.co.uk

■ The Ampelos Trust

CC NO 1048778 **ESTABLISHED** 1995

WHERE FUNDING CAN BE GIVEN UK.

WHO CAN BENEFIT Registered charities.

WHAT IS FUNDED General charitable purposes.

TYPE OF GRANT Usually one-off.

SAMPLE GRANTS Shelter (£25,000); Handel House Trust, Little Hearts Matter and RNIB (£10,000 each); National Clinical Group (£6,000); AIDS Life Cycle and Kingston Citizens Advice (£1,000 each).

FINANCES *Year* 2015/16 *Income* £6,640 *Grants* £175,000 *Grants to organisations* £175,000

TRUSTEES Ann Marie; Simon Rendell; MMH. Trustees Ltd.

OTHER INFORMATION This charity's latest accounts were not available to view on the Charity Commission's website due to its low income. We have therefore estimated the grant total based on previous years' information.

HOW TO APPLY The trust has previously stated that it does not accept unsolicited applications.

WHO TO APPLY TO Philip Hitchinson, Secretary, c/o Menzies LLP, Ashcombe House, 5 The Crescent, Leatherhead, Surrey KT22 8DY *Email* phitchinson@menzies.co.uk

■ The AMW Charitable Trust

SC NO SC006959 **ESTABLISHED** 1974

WHERE FUNDING CAN BE GIVEN Scotland only, with a priority for the west of Scotland.

WHO CAN BENEFIT Charitable organisations.

WHAT IS FUNDED General charitable purposes.

WHAT IS NOT FUNDED Individuals; organisations outside Scotland.

RANGE OF GRANTS £1,000 to £10,000.

SAMPLE GRANTS National Library for Scotland (£10,000); Accord Hospice, Beatson Cancer Charity and Epilepsy Society (£5,000 each); Frontier Youth Trust (£4,000); Fostering Network and John Muir Trust (£3,000 each); Brain Tumour Charity (£2,000); Headway and Scottish Ballet (£1,000 each).

FINANCES *Year* 2015/16 *Income* £178,103 *Grants* £164,500 *Grants to organisations* £164,500 *Assets* £4,470,671

OTHER INFORMATION The trust made 58 donations during the year.

HOW TO APPLY Apply in writing to the correspondent. Appeals are not acknowledged and the trust only advises successful applicants.

WHO TO APPLY TO The Trustees, c/o KPMG LLP, 319 St Vincent Street, Glasgow G2 5AS

■ The Ancaster Trust

CC NO 270822 **ESTABLISHED** 1965

WHERE FUNDING CAN BE GIVEN There is some preference for work in Lincolnshire.

WHO CAN BENEFIT Registered charities; schools.

WHAT IS FUNDED Welfare; environment and disability.

TYPE OF GRANT Normally small, recurring types of grant.

SAMPLE GRANTS Glenalmond College (£12,000); Cheltenham College (£10,500); Beestone School (£7,500); Cheltenham Ladies College (£4,500); Small Library Appeal (£1,000); WaterAid, Wells for India and Womankind (£500); New Bridge (£300); St Mungo Housing (£200); Royal Literary Fund and Scottish Wildlife Fund (£100).

FINANCES *Year* 2015/16 *Income* £77,286 *Grants* £76,014 *Grants to organisations* £76,014 *Assets* £2,416,854

TRUSTEES Baroness Jane Willoughby de Eresby; Susan Simmons; David Genders.

HOW TO APPLY Apply in writing to the correspondent, although note that the trustees have stated that available income is fully committed to existing beneficiaries.

WHO TO APPLY TO Sue Simmons, Trustee, c/o Sayers Butterworth LLP, 3rd Floor, 12 Gough Square, London EC4A 3DW *Tel.* 020 7936 1910

■ The Anchor Foundation

CC NO 1082485 **ESTABLISHED** 2000

WHERE FUNDING CAN BE GIVEN UK and overseas.

WHO CAN BENEFIT Christian charities.

WHAT IS FUNDED Social inclusion, particularly through ministries of healing and the arts.

WHAT IS NOT FUNDED Individuals. Support is rarely given for building work.

TYPE OF GRANT Applications for capital and revenue funding are considered. Only in very exceptional circumstances will grants be given for building work. It is not the normal practice of the charity to support the same project for more than three years (projects which have had three years funding may apply again two years from the payment of the last grant).

RANGE OF GRANTS £500 to £10,000.

SAMPLE GRANTS All Saints Community Arts (£7,000); Haven Project – Liverpool, Justice Mission and Operation Mobilisation UK (£5,000 each); Aberdeen Passion Plays and Mabona Community Health Initiative (£4,000 each); Christian Solidarity Worldwide (£3,000); Crisis Islington (£2,000); Still Waters Perth (£1,000); New Hope Trust (£750).

FINANCES *Year* 2015/16 *Income* £228,741 *Grants* £214,715 *Grants to organisations* £214,715 *Assets* £6,806,841

TRUSTEES Revd Michael Mitton; Revd Robin Anker-Petersen; Nina Catherine Stewart; Sue Mayfield.

HOW TO APPLY An initial application form can be completed online at the Anchor Foundation website. Full guidelines for applicants are also available online. If the trustees decide they are interested in your application you will be contacted and asked to send further relevant information such as a project budget and your annual accounts. **Do not send these with your application form.** Also note that applications should not be sent to the registered office in Nottingham. Applications are considered at twice yearly trustee meetings in April and November and need to be received by 31 January and 31 July each year. The foundation regrets that applications cannot be acknowledged. Successful applicants will be notified as soon as possible after trustees' meetings – usually before the end of May or the end of November. Unsuccessful applicants may re-apply after twelve months.

WHO TO APPLY TO Catherine Middleton, Company Secretary, PO Box 21107, Alloa FK12 5WA *Tel.* 0115 950 0055 *Email* secretary@theanchorfoundation.org.uk *Website* www.theanchorfoundation.org.uk

■ The Andrew Anderson Trust

CC NO 212170 **ESTABLISHED** 1954

WHERE FUNDING CAN BE GIVEN UK and overseas.

WHO CAN BENEFIT Organisations benefitting: Christians and evangelists; at risk groups; carers; people with disabilities; people disadvantaged by poverty; socially isolated people; and victims of abuse, crime and domestic violence.

WHAT IS FUNDED General charitable purposes with a focus on religious activities; education and training; medical causes, health and sickness; overseas aid.

WHAT IS NOT FUNDED Individuals should not apply for travel or education.

SAMPLE GRANTS A list of beneficiaries was not available.

FINANCES *Year* 2015/16 *Income* £495,652 *Grants* £481,750 *Grants to organisations* £410,750 *Assets* £11,999,596

TRUSTEES Anne Anderson; Margaret Anderson; Andrew Anderson; Fiona West; Colleen Rosser.

OTHER INFORMATION The amount of grants given to individuals totalled £71,000.

HOW TO APPLY Unsolicited applications are not accepted.

WHO TO APPLY TO Andrew Robertson, 1 Cote House Lane, Bristol BS9 3UW *Tel.* 0117 962 1588

■ Andor Charitable Trust

CC NO 1083572 **ESTABLISHED** 2000

WHERE FUNDING CAN BE GIVEN UK and overseas.

WHO CAN BENEFIT Charitable organisations.

WHAT IS FUNDED Health; education; social welfare; disability; the arts.

RANGE OF GRANTS Mostly £1,000 to £5,000.

SAMPLE GRANTS British Library (£5,000); Cove Park (£3,000); Practical Action (£2,900); Glyndebourne Arts Trust and National Brain Appeal (£2,500 each); Music in Hospitals and Sistema England (£2,000 each); Anne Frank Trust UK (£1,500); Macular Disease Society and The Virtual Doctors (£1,000 each).

FINANCES *Year* 2015/16 *Income* £100,811 *Grants* £160,225 *Grants to organisations* £160,255 *Assets* £3,000,834

TRUSTEES David Rothenberg; Nicholas Lederer; Claire Walford; Karen Andor.

OTHER INFORMATION There were 84 grants made during the year.

HOW TO APPLY The trust is no longer accepting applications.

WHO TO APPLY TO David Rothenberg, Trustee, c/o Blick Rothenberg Chartered Accountants, 16 Great Queen Street, Covent Garden, London WC2B 5AH *Tel.* 020 7544 8865 *Email* robin@blickrothenberg.com

■ The André Christian Trust

CC NO 248466 **ESTABLISHED** 1950

WHERE FUNDING CAN BE GIVEN UK.

WHO CAN BENEFIT Christian organisations.

WHAT IS FUNDED Christian missionary work; promotion of Christianity.

TYPE OF GRANT Typically recurrent, to charities named in the trust deed.

RANGE OF GRANTS £1,000 to £22,000.

SAMPLE GRANTS Palm Tree Associates (£22,000); Exeter Peartree (£9,000); Care for the Family (£5,000); Choices Pregnancy Centre (£4,400); Tiverton Street Pastors and Tiverton Vineyard Church (£1,500 each); Bible Society and Overseas Missionary Fellowship (£1,000 each).

FINANCES *Year* 2015 *Income* £52,490 *Grants* £53,850 *Grants to organisations* £50,850 *Assets* £1,385,279

TRUSTEES Andrew Kilvinton Mowll; Stephen Daykin.

OTHER INFORMATION Grants were made to two individuals, including one of the trustees, and totalled £3,000.
HOW TO APPLY Apply in writing to the correspondent.
WHO TO APPLY TO Andrew Kilvinton Mowll, Trustee, 24 Hellings Gardens, Broadclyst, Exeter EX5 3DX *Tel.* 01392 759836

■ The Mary Andrew Charitable Trust

SC NO SC021977 **ESTABLISHED** 1993
WHERE FUNDING CAN BE GIVEN UK, with a preference for Scotland.
WHO CAN BENEFIT Registered charities only.
WHAT IS FUNDED A wide range of charitable causes are supported, including: health; social welfare; education and training; children and young people; arts; environment; churches.
WHAT IS NOT FUNDED Individuals.
RANGE OF GRANTS Mostly £500 or £1,000.
SAMPLE GRANTS Children's Classic Concerts (£2,500); Oxfam – Nepal Earthquake Appeal (£2,000); Bumblebee Conservation Trust, Gullane Parish Church and Scottish Opera (£1,000 each); Citizens Theatre (£850); Children with Cancer and Leukaemia (£750); Carers Trust Scotland, Headway Glasgow and St Andrew's First Aid (£500 each).
FINANCES *Year* 2014/15 *Income* £45,745 *Grants* £49,595 *Grants to organisations* £49,595 *Assets* £987,382
OTHER INFORMATION At the time of writing (June 2017) the 2014/15 accounts were the most recent available to view on the OSCR website.
HOW TO APPLY Apply in writing to the correspondent.
WHO TO APPLY TO The Trustees, Mitchells Roberton Solicitors, George House, 36 North Hanover Street, Glasgow G1 2AD

■ Andrews Charitable Trust

CC NO 243509 **ESTABLISHED** 1965
WHERE FUNDING CAN BE GIVEN UK.
WHO CAN BENEFIT Christian charities and community groups.
WHAT IS FUNDED Social welfare and Christian causes.
RANGE OF GRANTS Up to £2,000.
SAMPLE GRANTS 2nd Chance and Inspira Farms (£100,000); Dementia Adventure (£81,000); The Together Group (£70,000); Restored (£54,000); Ekklesia (£46,500).
FINANCES *Year* 2015 *Income* £38,501,965 *Grants* £457,500 *Grants to organisations* £457,500 *Assets* £15,447,338
TRUSTEES David Westgate; Nicholas Wright; Helen Battrick; Paul Heal; Alastair Page; Elizabeth Hughes; Chris Chapman; Marcus Olliffe; Ami Davis; Alison Kelly; Ruth Knagg.
HOW TO APPLY The trust only accepts applications for its Christian Innovation Grants programme which provides small grants to Christian organisations that promote the Christian faith and provide practical help for disadvantaged and marginalised people within communities. Applications to this programme can be made online.
WHO TO APPLY TO Ms Sian Edwards, Director, The Clockhouse, Bath Hill, Keynsham, Bristol BS31 1HL *Tel.* 0117 946 1834 *Email* info@andrewscharitabletrust.org.uk *Website* www.andrewscharitabletrust.org.uk

■ Anglo American Group Foundation

CC NO 1111719 **ESTABLISHED** 2005
WHERE FUNDING CAN BE GIVEN UK with a preference for Westminster, Southwark and Lambeth; Brazil; Chile; Peru; Colombia; China; India; Zimbabwe.
WHO CAN BENEFIT Registered charities.
WHAT IS FUNDED Education, international development, health/HIV, environment and London-based community development.
WHAT IS NOT FUNDED Organisations which are not registered charities.
TYPE OF GRANT Support to ongoing projects by organisations.
SAMPLE GRANTS Technoserve (£676,000); Royal Academy of Engineering (£500,000); Diamond Development Initiative (£195,000); International Women's Health Coalition (£157,000); Sentebale (£148,000).
FINANCES *Year* 2015 *Income* £1,203,120 *Grants* £1,673,299 *Grants to organisations* £1,673,299 *Assets* £1,636,436
TRUSTEES Angela Bromfield; Duncan Wanblad; Jonathan Samuel.
OTHER INFORMATION The foundation was established in 2005 by Anglo American PLC, a large multinational mining company.
HOW TO APPLY Apply in writing to the correspondent.
WHO TO APPLY TO Laura Dunne, Anglo American PLC, 20 Carlton House Terrace, London SW1Y 5AN *Tel.* 020 7968 8888 *Email* aagf@angloamerican.com *Website* www.angloamericangroupfoundation.org

■ Anguish's Educational Foundation

CC NO 311288 **ESTABLISHED** 1605
WHERE FUNDING CAN BE GIVEN Norwich and the parishes of Costessey, Hellesdon, Catton, Sprowston, Thorpe St Andrew and Corpusty.
WHO CAN BENEFIT Registered charities; schools; community groups that support residents of the area of benefit under the age of 25.
WHAT IS FUNDED Promoting speech and language development and socialisation in disadvantaged children; raising the aspirations and personal skills of disadvantaged young people; broadening young people's experience of life.
RANGE OF GRANTS £2,000 to £30,000.
SAMPLE GRANTS Bowthorpe Children's Centre and Clover Hill Nursery School (£30,000 each); Stepping Stones (£9,700); East Norwich Youth Projects (£8,100); Lakenham Pre-school Play Group (£7,000); Earlham Scout Group (£5,000); Chermond Trust (£3,000); Earlham Early Years Centre (£2,500); Catton Grove Primary School (£2,000).
FINANCES *Year* 2015/16 *Income* £886,431 *Grants* £539,218 *Grants to organisations* £75,690 *Assets* £21,933,726
TRUSTEES David Fullman; Brenda Ferris; Geoffrey Loades; Pamela Scutter; Philip Blanchflower; Dr Iain Brooksby; Jeremy Hooke; Roy Blower; Jeanne Southgate; Brenda Arthur; Heather Tyrrell; Peter Shields; Michael Flynn; Lesley Grahame.
OTHER INFORMATION Grants are also made to/for: individuals for school clothing; university maintenance; further education; education travel; and college fees.
HOW TO APPLY Apply in writing to the correspondent. Individuals are usually invited to the office for an informal interview.

WHO TO APPLY TO David Walker, Clerk to the Trustees, 1 Woolgate Court, St Benedicts Street, Norwich NR2 4AP *Tel.* 01603 621023 *Email* info@norwichcharitabletrusts.org.uk *Website* www.norwichcharitabletrusts.org.uk

■ The Animal Defence Trust

CC NO 263095 **ESTABLISHED** 1971

WHERE FUNDING CAN BE GIVEN UK or Ireland.

WHO CAN BENEFIT UK organisations benefitting animals.

WHAT IS FUNDED Animal welfare/protection.

TYPE OF GRANT Usually one-off payments for capital projects.

RANGE OF GRANTS Usually £1,500 or £2,500.

SAMPLE GRANTS Animals Asia, Help in Suffering and Worldwide Veterinary Society (£2,500 each); British Hen Welfare, Dartmoor Livestock Protection Society and Dogstar Foundation (£1,500 each); Otter Sanctuary (£100).

FINANCES *Year* 2014/15 *Income* £67,162 *Grants* £77,850 *Grants to organisations* £77,850 *Assets* £1,297,736

TRUSTEES Marion Saunders; Carole Bowles; Richard Vines; Jenny Wheadon.

OTHER INFORMATION The 2014/15 accounts were the latest available at the time of writing (June 2017).

HOW TO APPLY Apply on a form which together with guidelines can be downloaded from the trust's website. The closing date for applications is 31 March each year.

WHO TO APPLY TO Roy Stokes, Grants Application Secretary, PO Box 44, Plymouth PL7 5YW *Tel.* 020 7222 8844 *Email* ameyer@horseylightly.com *Website* www.animaldefencetrust.org

■ The Annandale Charitable Trust

CC NO 1049193 **ESTABLISHED** 1995

WHERE FUNDING CAN BE GIVEN UK.

WHO CAN BENEFIT Registered charities.

WHAT IS FUNDED General charitable purposes including animal protection.

SAMPLE GRANTS Action for Sick Children and North London Hospice (£5,300 each); The Donkey Sanctuary and Victim Support (£4,200 each); People's Dispensary for Sick Animals (PDSA) (£3,300); Royal Marsden Cancer Trust (£2,700); A Change of Scene for Children and Battersea Cats and Dogs Home (£2,300 each).

FINANCES *Year* 2015/16 *Income* £321,554 *Grants* £227,850 *Grants to organisations* £227,850 *Assets* £12,185,691

TRUSTEES Carole Duggan; HSBC. Trust Company (UK) Ltd.

HOW TO APPLY Unsolicited applications are not accepted.

WHO TO APPLY TO The Trustees, HSBC Trust Company UK Ltd, Second Floor, 1 The Forum, Parkway, Whiteley, Fareham PO15 7PA *Tel.* 023 8072 3344

■ The Anne Duchess of Westminster's Charity

CC NO 245177 **ESTABLISHED** 1965

WHERE FUNDING CAN BE GIVEN Cheshire and surrounding areas (Wirral, Merseyside and North Wales); Highlands of Scotland. Military welfare grants are made throughout the UK.

WHO CAN BENEFIT Registered charities.

WHAT IS FUNDED Equestrian welfare, horse and racing-related charities (especially charities concerned with those who may have suffered injury from racing or using horses to help those with a disability or other difficulties); accommodation and housing; religious activities; education and training; medical research; health and sickness; disability; economic and community, development and employment; environment, conservation and heritage; military welfare.

WHAT IS NOT FUNDED General appeals or letters requesting donations; organisations that do not have charitable aims (e.g. commercial companies and companies limited by shares); overtly political projects (including party political and campaigning projects); individuals (or organisations applying on behalf of an individual); student fees/bursaries; projects taking place or benefitting people outside the UK; projects/work benefitting people outside the charity's specific geographical criteria unless they relate to military welfare; organisations that have applied unsuccessfully within the previous 12 months (unless invited to apply again); organisations who have been awarded a grant within the previous two years; grant applications seeking the entire costs of a project.

TYPE OF GRANT One-off grants of up to £10,000 (including start up and running costs) and recurring grants made over one to three years (up to a total maximum of £15,000).

SAMPLE GRANTS The Injured Jockeys Fund (£50,000); Clatterbridge Cancer Research Trust (£37,000); St John's Hospice (£20,000); Hospice of the Good Shepherd (£15,000); Beechwood House, Combat Stress, Holy Trinity Parochial Church Council, St Chad's Parochial Church Council (£10,000 each); Chester Citizens Advice (£7,000); Community Foundation in Wales (£6,000).

FINANCES *Year* 2015/16 *Income* £136,516 *Grants* £218,586 *Grants to organisations* £218,586 *Assets* £7,019,290

TRUSTEES Timothy Marshall; Sir Michael Ridley; Andrew Clowes; Mark Ridley; John Ridley; Richard Henniker-Wilson.

OTHER INFORMATION There were 54 grants made during the year.

HOW TO APPLY Applications can be made through the charity's website.

WHO TO APPLY TO Kate Williams, Eaton Estate Office, Eaton Hall, Eaton Park, Eaton, Chester CH4 9ET *Tel.* 01244 684433 *Email* enquiries@adwc.org.uk *Website* www.adwc.org.uk

■ Anpride Ltd

CC NO 288978 **ESTABLISHED** 1984

WHERE FUNDING CAN BE GIVEN London and Israel.

WHO CAN BENEFIT Registered charities.

WHAT IS FUNDED Advancement of the Jewish faith and the relief of poverty.

WHAT IS NOT FUNDED Individuals. Grants to state-aided institutions will generally not be considered.

SAMPLE GRANTS A list of beneficiaries was not available.

FINANCES *Year* 2015/16 *Income* £418,700 *Grants* £188,096 *Grants to organisations* £188,096 *Assets* £362,201

TRUSTEES Chaim Benedikt; Golda Benedikt.

HOW TO APPLY Apply in writing to the correspondent.

WHO TO APPLY TO Golda Benedikt, Trustee, 99 Geldeston Road, London E5 8RS *Tel.* 020 8806 1011

■ The Anson Charitable Trust

CC NO 1111010 **ESTABLISHED** 2005

WHERE FUNDING CAN BE GIVEN UK.

WHO CAN BENEFIT Charitable organisations and individuals.

WHAT IS FUNDED General charitable purposes, there is a preference for work with children and older people. Health and medical research causes are also supported.

RANGE OF GRANTS £100 to £30,000.

SAMPLE GRANTS ABF The Soldiers' Charity (£5,000); Changing Faces and Youth Concern (£3,000 each); British Stammering and Rennie Grove Hospice (£2,000 each); Bipolar UK, British Blind Spot and Child Autism UK (£1,000 each); Woodland Trust (£1,000) Rescue Dog Association (£900); WWF (£420).

FINANCES *Year* 2015/16 *Income* £187,500 *Grants* £241,774 *Grants to organisations* £241,774 *Assets* £558,461

TRUSTEES George Anson; Kirsty Anson; Lady Pauncefort-Duncombe.

HOW TO APPLY Apply in writing to the correspondent.

WHO TO APPLY TO George Anson, Trustee, The Lilies, High Street, Weedon, Aylesbury, Buckinghamshire HP22 4NS *Tel.* 01296 640331 *Email* ansonctrust@btinternet.com

■ AO Smile Foundation

CC NO 1157111 **ESTABLISHED** 2014

WHERE FUNDING CAN BE GIVEN England and Wales.

WHO CAN BENEFIT Registered charities.

WHAT IS FUNDED General charitable purposes.

SAMPLE GRANTS Onside Youth Zones (£139,200); Derian House (£56,000); Duke of Edinburgh Award Scheme (£50,000).

FINANCES *Year* 2015/16 *Income* £738,409 *Grants* £283,286 *Grants to organisations* £283,286 *Assets* £309,111

TRUSTEES John Roberts; Stephen Caunce; Karen Hunter.

HOW TO APPLY Apply in writing to the correspondent.

WHO TO APPLY TO Karen Hunter, Trustee, AO Park, 5A The Parklands, Lostock, Bolton BL6 4SD *Tel.* 07713 312014 *Email* Karen@AOSmileFoundation.org

■ The Apax Foundation

CC NO 1112845 **ESTABLISHED** 2006

WHERE FUNDING CAN BE GIVEN UK and overseas.

WHO CAN BENEFIT Registered charities and community groups.

WHAT IS FUNDED Social entrepreneurship; relief of poverty; education.

RANGE OF GRANTS Up to £215,000.

SAMPLE GRANTS Grameen America (£310,000); Joblinge (£225,000); Mosaic – Business in the Community (£86,000); Institute for the Development of Social Investment (£50,000); Impetus – The Private Equity Foundation (£41,500); B Lab UK (£20,000); Special Olympics (£17,100); Inner City (£16,000); Pilot Light (£14,400); Crisis UK (£13,500).

FINANCES *Year* 2015/16 *Income* £3,530,806 *Grants* £991,394 *Grants to organisations* £991,394 *Assets* £21,579,364

TRUSTEES Sir Ronald Cohen; David Marks; Dr Peter Englander; John Megrue; Simon Cresswell; Mitch Truwit; Shashank Singh; Rohan Haldea; Jason Wright.

OTHER INFORMATION 'The Apax Foundation is the formal channel for Apax Partners' charitable giving and receives a percentage of the firm's profits and carried interest.'

HOW TO APPLY Apply in writing to the correspondent.

WHO TO APPLY TO Kate Albert, Apax Partners, 33 Jermyn Street, London SW1Y 6DN *Tel.* 020 7872 6300 *Email* foundation@apax.com *Website* www.apax.com/responsibility/apax-foundation

■ The John Apthorp Charity

CC NO 1102472 **ESTABLISHED** 2004

WHERE FUNDING CAN BE GIVEN UK, with a preference for Hertfordshire.

WHO CAN BENEFIT Charitable organisations and individuals.

WHAT IS FUNDED Education; religion; social welfare.

RANGE OF GRANTS Up to £40,000.

SAMPLE GRANTS Community Home Enrichment Xtra-mile Support (£40,000); Christ Church Radlett (£30,000); Families United Network (£25,000); Marie Curie (£15,000); Demand (£10,000); Belstone Football Club (£6,000); Blesma (£5,000); Bowel Cancer UK (£2,500); Dance Pad (£1,000).

FINANCES *Year* 2015 *Income* £476,732 *Grants* £460,679 *Grants to organisations* £460,679 *Assets* £97,688

TRUSTEES John Apthorp; Duncan Apthorp; Justin Apthorp; Kate Arnold.

OTHER INFORMATION Grants totalling £4,700 were made to individuals.

HOW TO APPLY Apply in writing to the correspondent.

WHO TO APPLY TO Jenny Dunford, The Field House Farm, 29 Newlands Avenue, Radlett, Hertfordshire WD7 8EJ *Email* johnapthorpcharity@hotmail.com

■ The Arah Foundation

CC NO 1154244 **ESTABLISHED** 2013

WHERE FUNDING CAN BE GIVEN England and Wales, particularly London; St Vincent and the Grenadines; Turkey.

WHO CAN BENEFIT Charitable organisations.

WHAT IS FUNDED General charitable purposes; education and training; arts and culture; human rights; religious and racial harmony.

SAMPLE GRANTS A list of beneficiaries was not available.

FINANCES *Year* 2015/16 *Income* £125,000 *Grants* £41,456 *Grants to organisations* £41,456 *Assets* £82,574

TRUSTEES Asli Arah; William Arah.

OTHER INFORMATION A list of recent beneficiaries was not provided in the accounts.

HOW TO APPLY Apply in writing to the correspondent.

WHO TO APPLY TO Asli Arah, Trustee, c/o Macfarlanes LLP, 10 Norwich Street, London EC4A 1 BD *Tel.* 07435 883224 *Email* info@arahfoundation.org

■ The Annabel Arbib Foundation

CC NO 296358 **ESTABLISHED** 1987

WHERE FUNDING CAN BE GIVEN UK.

WHO CAN BENEFIT Registered charities and local organisations with charitable purposes.

WHAT IS FUNDED Social welfare; children's welfare; medical causes; education.

WHAT IS NOT FUNDED Individuals.

TYPE OF GRANT Recurrent and single donations.

RANGE OF GRANTS £100 to £125,000.

SAMPLE GRANTS Langley Academy Trust (£1 million); Eton College (£230,00); Barbados Community

Foundation (£25,000); Henley Festival Trust (£2,500); The Teenage Wilderness Trust (£1,000); Marie Curie (£250); Meningitis Research (£200).

FINANCES *Year* 2015/16 *Income* £12,728,793 *Grants* £1,671,455 *Grants to organisations* £1,671,455 *Assets* £11,544,117

TRUSTEES Sir Martyn Arbib; Paddy Nicoll; Annabel Nicoll.

OTHER INFORMATION Grants were distributed as follows: education (£1.27 million); social welfare (£28,500); medical causes (£17,500); children's welfare (£6,700).

HOW TO APPLY Apply in writing to the correspondent, although note the trustees have stressed that grants are largely made to organisations with which the trustees have a connection, and therefore unsolicited applications are unlikely to be successful.

WHO TO APPLY TO Paula Doraisamy, 61 Grosvenor Street, London W1K 3JE *Tel.* 020 3011 1100 *Email* admin@61grosvenorstreet.com

Arcadia Charitable Trust

CC NO 1170621 **ESTABLISHED** 2001

WHERE FUNDING CAN BE GIVEN Worldwide.

WHO CAN BENEFIT Registered charities; educational institutions.

WHAT IS FUNDED Preserving endangered culture; protecting endangered nature; promoting open access to information.

TYPE OF GRANT Capital and project costs.

RANGE OF GRANTS From tens of thousands to multi-millions.

SAMPLE GRANTS Fauna and Flora International ($3.75 million over three years); Internews ($450,000 over three years); Harvard University Library ($100,000); University College London ($83,000); Cambridge University Library ($80,000).

FINANCES *Year* 2015 *Grants* £19,481,500 *Grants to organisations* £19,481,500

TRUSTEES Iona Hemphill; Geoffrey Hemphill; Erica Cobb; Scott Cobb.

OTHER INFORMATION The grant total was taken from trust's Triennial Review 2013–15 and was converted to GBP using the exchange rate at the time of writing (May 2017).

HOW TO APPLY Unsolicited applications are not accepted.

WHO TO APPLY TO Grants Team, Sixth Floor, 5 Young Street, London W8 5EH *Email* info@arcadiafund.org.uk *Website* www.arcadiafund.org.uk

The Archer Trust

CC NO 1033534 **ESTABLISHED** 1994

WHERE FUNDING CAN BE GIVEN UK.

WHO CAN BENEFIT Voluntary organisations, especially those which make good use of volunteers or are located in areas of high unemployment or disadvantage. Preference is given to smaller organisations.

WHAT IS FUNDED Provision of aid and support to a defined group of needy or deserving people, such as people with mental or physical disabilities or people who are otherwise disadvantaged; Christian causes.

WHAT IS NOT FUNDED Individuals; conservation, heritage and environmental projects; conversions for disability access; charities supporting animals; research.

RANGE OF GRANTS Usually £250 to £3,000.

SAMPLE GRANTS Lilias Graham Trust (£4,000); Ashford Place, Maytree Respite Centre and Waste Not Want Not (£3,000 each); The Datic Trust, Leonard Cheshire Disability and Low Mill Outdoor Centre (£2,000 each); Sorted and Tracks Autism (£1,500 each); Prison! Me! No Way! and Wells for India (£1,000 each); Heartbeat and Spacious Places (£500 each).

FINANCES *Year* 2015/16 *Income* £119,950 *Grants* £119,950 *Grants to organisations* £119,950 *Assets* £1,915,187

TRUSTEES Catherine Archer; Lyn Packman; James Archer; Michael Baker.

OTHER INFORMATION The trust made 90 grants during the year.

HOW TO APPLY Apply in writing to the correspondent. Unsuccessful applicants will not receive a response, even if an sae is enclosed. Applications are considered twice a year, usually in March and September.

WHO TO APPLY TO The Secretary, Bourne House, Wadesmill, Ware, Hertfordshire SG12 0TT *Tel.* 01920 462312 *Website* www.archertrust.org.uk

The Architectural Heritage Fund

CC NO 266780 **ESTABLISHED** 1973

WHERE FUNDING CAN BE GIVEN UK (excluding the Channel Islands and the Isle of Man).

WHO CAN BENEFIT Formally constituted and incorporated charities or social enterprises whose members have limited liability. These include: CIOs; charitable companies limited by guarantee; not-for-private-profit Companies limited by guarantee; CICs limited by guarantee; community benefit societies; parish and town councils; community councils (in Scotland and Wales).

WHAT IS FUNDED Support is given in the form of grants, loans, advice and information for the preservation and sustainable re-use of historic buildings. Grants may be given for purposes including project viability studies and project development. Up-to-date information on the grants and support available can be found on the fund's website.

WHAT IS NOT FUNDED Private individuals; unincorporated trusts or associations; local authorities and other public sector bodies; for-private-profit companies, unless in a partnership led by a charity or social enterprise; churches or other places of worship, where the building will remain in use primarily as a place of religious worship; projects that simply involve upgrading existing uses within a building and do not involve a change of ownership; capital works (such as building repairs, installation of services, landscaping, access improvements or heritage interpretation displays).

TYPE OF GRANT Loans; feasibility study grants; project development grants; refundable and non-refundable grants.

RANGE OF GRANTS Grants of up to £25,000; loans up to £500,000 (more in exceptional circumstances).

SAMPLE GRANTS Dundee Museum of Transport Trust (£23,000); Urras Dualchas Shiaboist (£15,000); Lochgilphead Phoenix (£11,900); Willow Tea Rooms Trust (£10,000); Edinburgh Fruitmarket Gallery (£6,500); Citizens Theatre and Saltdean Lido CIC (£5,000 each); Providence Chapel Charlwood Trust (£2,500); The Historical Diving Society (£2,400); The Cross Keys Community Society (Pub) Ltd (£2,000).

FINANCES *Year* 2015/16 *Income* £2,136,909 *Grants* £375,033 *Grants to organisations* £375,033 *Assets* £14,022,970

TRUSTEES John Duggan; Philip Kirby; Liz Davidson; Rita Harkin; Kate Dickson; Myra Barnes; Richard Keen; Liz Peace.

HOW TO APPLY Detailed notes for applicants for loans and feasibility studies are supplied with the application forms, all of which are available from the fund's website. Applications for grants of less than £5,000 can be made at any time. Decisions on grants requesting £5,000 and over are made by trustees at their quarterly meetings. The deadlines for these meetings can be found on the fund's website.

WHO TO APPLY TO Regional Project Support Officers, 3 Spital Yard, Spitalfields, London E1 6AQ *Tel.* 020 7925 0199 *Email* ahf@ahfund.org.uk *Website* www.ahfund.org.uk

■ The Ardeola Charitable Trust

CC NO 1124380 **ESTABLISHED** 2008

WHERE FUNDING CAN BE GIVEN UK.

WHO CAN BENEFIT Registered charities.

WHAT IS FUNDED General charitable purposes, although the main beneficiary each year is Target Ovarian Cancer.

RANGE OF GRANTS £3,000 to £100,000.

SAMPLE GRANTS Target Ovarian Cancer (£221,500); Durham Cathedral and St Francis Hospice (£100,000 each); Royal National Theatre (£75,000); Royal National Theatre (£60,000); University of Oxford (£18,000); London Symphony Orchestra (£5,000); St Mary's Church, Maidenhead (£3,000).

FINANCES *Year* 2015/16 *Income* £1,965,715 *Grants* £583,000 *Grants to organisations* £583,000 *Assets* £6,449,354

TRUSTEES Graham Barker; Joanna Barker; Coutts & Co.; Prof. John Mark Cornwall; William Hiscocks.

HOW TO APPLY Apply in writing to the correspondent, although potential applicants should note that the trust's main beneficiary is connected with the trustees.

WHO TO APPLY TO The Trustees, Coutts & Co., Trustee Department, 6th Floor, Trinity Quay 2, Avon Street, Bristol BS2 0PT *Tel.* 020 7663 6825 *Email* couttscharities@coutts.com

■ The Ardwick Trust

CC NO 266981 **ESTABLISHED** 1975

WHERE FUNDING CAN BE GIVEN UK and Israel.

WHO CAN BENEFIT Institutions and registered charities (mainly UK charities) benefitting people of all ages.

WHAT IS FUNDED Jewish welfare, along with a wide range of non-Jewish causes to include social welfare, health, education, older people, conservation and the environment, children's welfare, disability and medical research. In general most of the largest grants go to Jewish organisations, with most of the smaller grants to non-Jewish organisations.

WHAT IS NOT FUNDED Individuals.

RANGE OF GRANTS Up to £3,000 but usually £100 to £500.

SAMPLE GRANTS Weizmann UK (£3,000); Techion UK (£2,000); World Jewish Relief (£1,000); Alzheimer's Research, Beating Bowel Cancer and Rivertime Boat Trust (£500 each); Breast Cancer, Crisis and Hearing Link (£200 each); Coeliac UK, Coram and React (£100 each).

FINANCES *Year* 2015/16 *Income* £80,378 *Grants* £71,400 *Grants to organisations* £71,400 *Assets* £1,240,764

TRUSTEES Janet Bloch; Dominic Flynn; Judith Portrait.

HOW TO APPLY Apply in writing to the correspondent.

WHO TO APPLY TO Janet Bloch, Trustee, 24 Petworth Road, Haslemere, Surrey GU27 2HR *Tel.* 01428 652788 *Email* haslemere@knoxcropper.com

■ The Argus Appeal

CC NO 1013647 **ESTABLISHED** 1992

WHERE FUNDING CAN BE GIVEN Sussex.

WHO CAN BENEFIT Registered charities; hospices.

WHAT IS FUNDED Community development; disability; older people; animals; homelessness.

RANGE OF GRANTS Up to £16,500.

SAMPLE GRANTS A list of beneficiaries was not available.

FINANCES *Year* 2015 *Income* £77,065 *Grants* £88,436 *Grants to organisations* £68,902 *Assets* £285,525

TRUSTEES Elsa Gillio; David Goldin; Roger French; Sue Addis; Lucy Pearce; Dawn Sweeney; Michael Gilson.

OTHER INFORMATION The amount of grants given to individuals totalled £19,534. Grants to organisations were broken down as follows: disability (£19,400); homelessness (£16,600); community charities (£10,400); hospices (£1,900); older people (£1,100); animals (£1,600).

HOW TO APPLY Apply in writing to the correspondent.

WHO TO APPLY TO Elsa Gillio, Trustee, Argus House, Crowhurst Road, Hollingbury, Brighton BN1 8AR *Tel.* 01273 544465 *Email* elsa.gillio@theargus.co.uk *Website* www.theargus.co.uk/argusappeal

■ The John Armitage Charitable Trust

CC NO 1079688 **ESTABLISHED** 2000

WHERE FUNDING CAN BE GIVEN England and Wales.

WHO CAN BENEFIT Institutions and registered charities.

WHAT IS FUNDED Parenting support; education; support for people who have offended; medical research/medical care; youth support; religion; museums and arts.

RANGE OF GRANTS Up to £100,000.

SAMPLE GRANTS Greenhouse Schools, Policy Exchange and Westminster Abbey Foundation (£100,000 each).

FINANCES *Year* 2015/16 *Income* £9,949,969 *Grants* £2,204,166 *Grants to organisations* £2,204,166 *Assets* £59,942,910

TRUSTEES John Armitage; Catherine Armitage; William Francklin; Celina Francklin.

OTHER INFORMATION Grants were distributed in the following categories: other (£514,500); youth support (£464,000); education (£260,000); medical research/care (£213,000); museum and arts (£186,000); support for people who have offended (£181,000); religion (£180,000).

HOW TO APPLY Apply in writing to the correspondent.

WHO TO APPLY TO John Armitage, Trustee, c/o Sampson West, 12–14 Mitre House, London EC3A 5BU

The Armourers' and Brasiers' Gauntlet Trust

CC NO 279204 **ESTABLISHED** 1979

WHERE FUNDING CAN BE GIVEN UK, with some preference for London.

WHO CAN BENEFIT Registered charities.

WHAT IS FUNDED Education and research in materials science and technology; basic science in schools; understanding and preservation of historic armour; encouragement of the armourer's trade in the armed services; community and armed forces; children, youth and general education; medical and health causes; the arts, arms and armour; Christian mission.

WHAT IS NOT FUNDED The guidelines state that in general grants are not made: 'to organisations or groups that are not registered charities; in response to applications for the benefit of individuals; to organisations or groups whose main object is to fund or support other charitable bodies; which are in direct relief of, or will lead to, a reduction of financial support from public funds; to charities with gross income in excess of £500,000; to charities which spend over 10% of their income on fund-raising activities; towards general maintenance, repair or restoration of buildings, including ecclesiastical buildings, unless there is a connection with the Armourers and Brasiers' Company, or unless of outstanding importance to the national heritage; to appeals for charitable sponsorship from individuals; to locally focused charities outside London, or to support projects being delivered outside the UK'.

TYPE OF GRANT One-off.

SAMPLE GRANTS Youth Action for Change International (£1,800); Coeliac UK (£1,500); Association of Visitors to Immigration Detainees, City of London Police, Widows' and Orphans' Fund, Disasters Emergency Committee – Philippines Appeal, First Aid Nursing Yeomanry, Inns of Court and City Yeomanry, Keep Out – The Crime Diversion Scheme, Kingston Bereavement Service, The Royal British Legion and Sheriffs' and Recorder's Fund (£500 each).

FINANCES *Year* 2015/16 *Income* £470,465 *Grants* £312,814 *Grants to organisations* £312,814 *Assets* £6,790,182

TRUSTEES Prof. William Bonfield; Sir Timothy Ruggles-Brise; Christopher Simons; Edward Pitt; Anthony Pontifex; Anthony Beare.

OTHER INFORMATION The trust's website states that around three quarters of its giving is directed towards education and research in material science. The trustees prefer to make grants to smaller and less well known charitable organisations rather than to those with a high public profile. Over 100 such charities receive grants each year.

HOW TO APPLY Apply in writing to the correspondent, with a copy of the latest annual report and audited accounts. The trustees meet three times a year in February, May and September.

WHO TO APPLY TO Charity and Partnership Manager, Armourers' Hall, 81 Coleman Street, London EC2R 5BJ *Tel.* 020 7374 4000 *Email* charities@armourershall.co.uk *Website* www.armourershall.co.uk/gauntlet-trust

The Arsenal Foundation

CC NO 1145668 **ESTABLISHED** 2012

WHERE FUNDING CAN BE GIVEN UK with a preference for London.

WHO CAN BENEFIT Organisations and individuals.

WHAT IS FUNDED Social welfare; the provision of sports facilities; education of younger people.

SAMPLE GRANTS Save the Children (£62,000); Islington Giving (£50,000); Premier League Charitable Fund (£25,000).

FINANCES *Year* 2015/16 *Income* £872,214 *Grants* £409,959 *Grants to organisations* £409,959 *Assets* £1,340,735

TRUSTEES Kenneth Friar; David Miles; Alan Sefton; Ivan Gazidis; Svenja Geissmar; Andrew Jolly.

OTHER INFORMATION The Gunners Fund provides grants of up to £2,500 to local projects in Islington, Camden and Hackney.

HOW TO APPLY **The Arsenal Foundation** – application forms are available on the foundation's website and can be returned by email or post once completed. At the time of writing (May 2017) the foundation's website states: 'Note that due to the high volume of applications currently being received from international organisations, grants are currently only being considered for UK-based charities in order to ensure that The Arsenal Foundation is able to carry out effective assessment of applications and monitoring of grants made.' **The Gunners Fund –** application forms are available on the foundation's website and can be returned by email to ssingh@arsenal.co.uk or post once completed.

WHO TO APPLY TO Svenja Geissmar, Trustee, Highbury House, 75 Drayton Park, London N5 1BU *Email* thearsenalfoundation@arsenal.co.uk *Website* www.arsenal.com/thearsenalfoundation

The Artemis Charitable Trust

CC NO 291328 **ESTABLISHED** 1985

WHERE FUNDING CAN BE GIVEN UK.

WHO CAN BENEFIT Registered charities benefitting parents, counsellors and psychotherapists.

WHAT IS FUNDED Counselling, psychotherapy, parenting, and human relationship training.

TYPE OF GRANT Recurring.

SAMPLE GRANTS Chester University (£110,000 in four grants); Get Stable (£25,500); Friends of Chichester Harbour (£10,000); Coaching Inside and Out (£8,000); The Chichester Art Trust (£1,000); 21st Century (£500).

FINANCES *Year* 2015 *Income* £41,959 *Grants* £155,000 *Grants to organisations* £155,000 *Assets* £1,277,204

TRUSTEES Richard Evans; Dawn Bergin; David Evans; Mark Evans; Wendy Menke.

HOW TO APPLY Applicants should be aware that most of the trust's funds are committed to a number of major ongoing projects and that spare funds available to meet new applications are very limited.'

WHO TO APPLY TO Richard Evans, Trustee, Brook House, Quay Meadow, Bosham, Chichester PO18 8LY *Tel.* 01243 573475 *Email* ritchie80@outlook.com

Arthritis Research UK

CC NO 207711 **ESTABLISHED** 1936
WHERE FUNDING CAN BE GIVEN Mainly UK.
WHO CAN BENEFIT Universities; research institutions.
WHAT IS FUNDED Research into the cause and cure of arthritis and related musculoskeletal diseases.
WHAT IS NOT FUNDED Applications for welfare and social matters will not be considered.
TYPE OF GRANT One-off, project, recurring, running costs, and salaries. Programme support is for five years; project grants are usually for three years.
RANGE OF GRANTS Up to £126,000.
SAMPLE GRANTS University of Manchester (£403,000 in eleven grants); University of Oxford (£291,000 in seven grants); Design Council (£126,000); Royal College of Art (£48,000); Cambridge University Hospital (£41,000); The Royal Veterinary College (£33,000 in two grants); Norfolk and Norwich University Hospital (£32,000); University of Sussex (£21,000); University of East Anglia (£12,000).
FINANCES *Year* 2015/16 *Income* £36,677,000 *Grants* £21,400,000 *Grants to organisations* £21,400,000 *Assets* £170,389,000
TRUSTEES Prof. David Isenberg; Phillip Gray; Prof. David Marsh; Sylvie Jackson; Tom Hayhoe; Prof. Jonathan Cohen; Dr Rodger Macmillan; Karin Hogsander; Juliette Scott; Alex Hesz; Prof. Sarah Lamb.
OTHER INFORMATION The charity made 68 awards over £10,000 during the year.
HOW TO APPLY Application forms and guidelines are available from the Arthritis Research UK website. Although the application process has strict criteria, the procedure is clearly explained on the charity's website.
WHO TO APPLY TO Research Department, Copeman House, St Mary's Court, St Mary's Gate, Chesterfield S41 7TD *Tel.* 0300 790 0400 *Email* research@arthritisresearchuk.org *Website* www.arthritisresearchuk.org

Arts Council England

CC NO 1036733 **ESTABLISHED** 1994
WHERE FUNDING CAN BE GIVEN England.
WHO CAN BENEFIT Arts organisations; galleries; museums; libraries; artists and creative professionals.
WHAT IS FUNDED Developing, sustaining and promoting the arts.
SAMPLE GRANTS Artlink West Yorkshire; Bedford Creative Arts; Book Works; Canterbury Festival; East Street Arts; Harrogate Theatre; Hull City Council; More Music; Northern Ballet; The Bluecoat; Young Vic Company.
FINANCES *Year* 2015/16 *Income* £733,516,000 *Grants* £570,195,000 *Grants to organisations* £570,195,000 *Assets* £164,378,000
TRUSTEES David Bryan; Nicholas Kenyon; Nicholas Serota; Matthew Bowcock; Jon Cook; Alastair Spalding; Veronica Wadley; Sheila Healy; Peter Phillips; Joe Docherty; Dr Maria Balshaw; David Joseph; Nazo Moosa.
HOW TO APPLY Grants can be made through the council's website. The website stresses that it is important to read the guidelines for each grant programme carefully before making an application or expression of interest. We would advise that potential applicants phone and speak to a member of the enquiries team if any clarification of the process, or your organisation's eligibility is required.
WHO TO APPLY TO Enquiries Team, 21 Bloomsbury Street, London WC1B 3HF *Tel.* 0845 300 6200 *Email* enquiries@artscouncil.org.uk *Website* www.artscouncil.org.uk

Arts Council of Northern Ireland

ESTABLISHED 1995
WHERE FUNDING CAN BE GIVEN Northern Ireland.
WHO CAN BENEFIT Artists and arts organisations and individuals.
WHAT IS FUNDED The Arts Council of Northern Ireland (ACNI) is the development and funding agency for the Arts in Northern Ireland. it distributes public money and National Lottery funds to develop and deliver a wide variety of arts projects, events and initiatives across Northern Ireland.
SAMPLE GRANTS BEAM Creative Network (£31,000); Ulster Orchestra Society (£15,000); Waterside Theatre Company Ltd (£12,000); Arts Care (£10,000); Play Resource Warehouse (£8,000) and In Your Space (NI) Ltd (£4,000).
FINANCES *Year* 2015/16 *Income* £1,713,792 *Grants* £9,930,626 *Grants to organisations* £9,930,626 *Assets* -£2,213,810
TRUSTEES Bob Collins; Damien Coyle; Dr Katy Radford; David Alderdice; Anna Carragher; Noelle McAlinden; Katherine McCloskey; Paul Mullan; Nisha Tandon; Conor Shields; Eibhlín Ní Dhochartaigh; Dr Leon Litvack; Siún Hanrahan; Roisin Mohan; Jarlath Kearney; Cian Smyth.
HOW TO APPLY Guidelines and full details of how to apply can be found at the Arts Council of Northern Ireland website.
WHO TO APPLY TO The Arts Development Department, 1 The Sidings, Antrim Road, Lisburn BT28 3AJ *Tel.* 028 9262 3555 *Email* info@artscouncil-ni.org *Website* www.artscouncil-ni.org

Arts Council of Wales (also known as Cyngor Celfyddydau Cymru)

CC NO 1034245 **ESTABLISHED** 1994
WHERE FUNDING CAN BE GIVEN Wales.
WHO CAN BENEFIT Arts organisations and individuals based in Wales.
WHAT IS FUNDED Arts activities and projects based in or mainly in Wales.
WHAT IS NOT FUNDED Individuals and organisations not meeting the eligibility criteria.
TYPE OF GRANT Both recurrent and one-off grants.
SAMPLE GRANTS Wrexham County Borough Council (£2.3 million); Wales Millennium Centre (£250,000); Beyond the Border (£100,000); Bombastic (£40,500); Conwy Arts Trust (£30,000); Ruthin Craft Centre (£16,800); Fieldwork (£9,300); Standpoint (£5,200); Warriors International (£5,000); engage (£1,100); Ysgol Hafod Lon (£360).
FINANCES *Year* 2015/16 *Income* £36,214,000 *Grants* £29,835,500 *Grants to organisations* £29,835,500 *Assets* £1,993,000
TRUSTEES Marian Jones; Alan Watkin; Dr Philip George; Richard Turner; John Williams; Dr Lesely Hodgson; Michael Griffiths; Melanie Hawthorne; Andrew Miller; Dafydd Rhys; Andrew Eagle; Iwan Bala; Kate Eden; Dr Rachel O'Riordan.
HOW TO APPLY Details of the application process and application deadlines for each programme can be found on the council's website.
WHO TO APPLY TO Information Team, Bute Place, Cardiff CF10 5AL *Tel.* 0845 873 4900 *Email* information@arts.wales *Website* www.arts.wales

The Ove Arup Foundation

CC NO 328138 **ESTABLISHED** 1989

WHERE FUNDING CAN BE GIVEN UK and overseas.

WHO CAN BENEFIT Universities; organisations benefitting research workers and designers.

WHAT IS FUNDED Education and research in matters related to the built environment, particularly if related to multi-disciplinary design, through educational institutions and charities.

WHAT IS NOT FUNDED Individuals.

TYPE OF GRANT Research and project, including start-up and feasibility costs. They can be one-off or recurrent.

RANGE OF GRANTS Up to £40,000.

SAMPLE GRANTS University of Edinburgh (£40,500); Chongqing University (£28,500); Useful Simple Projects Ltd (£20,000); The Edge, The University of Queensland and The University of Sheffield (£10,000 each); Expedition and RNIB (£5,000 each); The Anglo Danish Society (£2,000).

FINANCES *Year* 2016/17 *Income* £301,765 *Grants* £146,684 *Grants to organisations* £146,684

TRUSTEES Joanna Kennedy; Caroline Cole; Terry Hill; Richard Haryott; Gregory Hodkinson; Dr Andrew Chan; Mahadev Raman; Tim Chapman.

HOW TO APPLY Apply using a form available to download from the foundation's website.

WHO TO APPLY TO John Ward, Secretary, Ove Arup and Partners, 13 Fitzroy Street, London W1T 4BQ *Email* ovarfound@arup.com *Website* www.ovearupfoundation.org

Ove Arup Partnership Charitable Trust

CC NO 1038737 **ESTABLISHED** 1978

WHERE FUNDING CAN BE GIVEN UK.

WHO CAN BENEFIT Registered charities.

WHAT IS FUNDED Education; social care; health; welfare; disaster relief; the alleviation of poverty; local community development; sustainability; the environment; technology.

RANGE OF GRANTS Up to £50,000.

SAMPLE GRANTS The Ove Arup Foundation (£165,000); RedR UK (£53,000); Young Woman's Trust (£50,000); Engineers Without Borders (£29,000); Bridges to Prosperity (£20,000); Ellen MacArthur Cancer Trust (£5,000); Opera North and The Francis Crick Institute (£1,000 each); Brain Tumour Research (£600).

FINANCES *Year* 2015/16 *Income* £457,827 *Grants* £465,830 *Grants to organisations* £465,830 *Assets* £16,326

TRUSTEE Ove Arup Partnership Trust Corporation Ltd.

HOW TO APPLY Apply in writing to the correspondent.

WHO TO APPLY TO Stephanie Wilde, Ove Arup and Partners, 13 Fitzroy Street, London W1T 4BQ *Email* stephanie.wilde@arup.com

ASCB Charitable Fund

CC NO 1123854 **ESTABLISHED** 2008

WHERE FUNDING CAN BE GIVEN UK.

WHO CAN BENEFIT Individual sports people, sports unions and associations that benefit members/ ex-members of the armed forces; garrisons/ units of the army.

WHAT IS FUNDED Annual grants to sports unions and associations; capital project grants for sports equipment/infrastructure; Army Sports Lottery Grants.

TYPE OF GRANT Annual grants and capital grants.

RANGE OF GRANTS Mostly £20,000 or less.

SAMPLE GRANTS Sailing Association (£27,500); Rifle Association (£24,500); Angling Association (£19,000); Swimming Union (£13,500); Volleyball Association (£6,500); Fencing Union (£3,500); Badminton Association (£2,400).

FINANCES *Year* 2015/16 *Income* £3,727,114 *Grants* £581,870 *Grants to organisations* £581,870 *Assets* £6,770,226

TRUSTEES Brig. John Donnelly; David Rowe; Lt General James Bashall; Maj. General Richard Stanford; Brig. Stephen Potter; WO1 Carl Burnett; Suzanne Anderson; Brig. Robert Knight; Brig. Paul Harkness; Brig. James Woodham.

HOW TO APPLY Applicants should first consider the information available on grants – from both the charitable fund and from the ASL lottery – which is contained on the 'Funding' page of the ASCB website and on the ASL website

WHO TO APPLY TO Major General Shaun Burley, Mackenzie Building, Fox Lines, Queen's Avenue, Aldershot GU11 2LB *Tel.* 01252 787057 *Email* RWard@ascb.uk.com *Website* www.armysportcontrolboard.org

The Asda Foundation

CC NO 1124268 **ESTABLISHED** 2008

WHERE FUNDING CAN BE GIVEN England and Wales.

WHO CAN BENEFIT Registered charities and voluntary sector organisations.

WHAT IS FUNDED Sport and recreation; community development; general charitable purposes.

WHAT IS NOT FUNDED Asda Foundation does not fund expeditions or sponsor charitable activities by people other than Asda colleagues.

RANGE OF GRANTS Up to £250,000.

SAMPLE GRANTS Silver Line, and Social Investment Business Foundation (£250,000 each); FareShare (£142,500); Run For All (£137,000); the Trussell Trust (£80,000); Motability (£74,000); YMCA Northumberland (£20,000); Help For Heroes (£1,600); Martin House (£1,400); Alva Primary School, Cransley Hospice, Bethel Community Church, and Rotary Club of Sowerby Bridge (£1,000 each).

FINANCES *Year* 2015 *Income* £8,231,526 *Grants* £6,722,805 *Grants to organisations* £6,722,805 *Assets* £8,123,963

TRUSTEES Paul Rowland; John Cookman; Lorraine Jackson; Annmarie Rocks; Jane Earnshaw; Francesca Haynes; James Jefcoate; Alex Simpson; Alison Seabrook; Gerald Oppenheim; Paul Rowland; Lynne Tooms.

OTHER INFORMATION The Asda Foundation is Asda's charitable trust. It supplements the good causes that colleagues support locally, as well as a number of bigger ad hoc projects in local communities. It also manages all funds raised for national charities and monies raised in Asda House.

HOW TO APPLY In the first instance, contact your local store or depot with your proposal/ application. This will then be passed on to the trustees who will make a final decision. There is an eligibility tool and 'store locator' on the website.

WHO TO APPLY TO Julie Ward, Asda Foundation, Asda House, Great Wilson Street, Leeds LS11 5AD *Tel.* 0113 243 5435 *Website* www.asdafoundation.org

■ The Asfari Foundation

CC NO 1116751 **ESTABLISHED** 2006

WHERE FUNDING CAN BE GIVEN UK; Syria; Israel; Palestine.

WHO CAN BENEFIT Registered charities; universities.

WHAT IS FUNDED Youth empowerment; civil society development; social welfare; humanitarian relief.

SAMPLE GRANTS Chatham House (£570,000); The American University of Beirut (£333,000); University of East Anglia (£72,000); The Asfari Institute for Civil Society and Citizenship at AUB (£149,000); St Andrews University (Centre Eor Syria Studies) (£66,500); Refugee Studies Centre, Oxford University (£10,000).

FINANCES *Year* 2015 *Income* £3,426,403 *Grants* £3,063,578 *Grants to organisations* £3,063,578 *Assets* £11,668,649

TRUSTEES Sawsan Asfari; Adeeb Asfari; Ayman Asfari; John Ferguson; Dr Marwan Muasher.

HOW TO APPLY The charity's 2015 accounts state: 'The Asfari Foundation is a grant-making organisation. All its objectives are achieved through partnerships with specialised, capable and reputable grantee organisations which are non-political and non-sectarian and share the Foundation's goals and values. The Asfari Foundation accepts applications from partner organisations and also identifies potential partners itself.'

WHO TO APPLY TO Mr C. Ridley, Unit A, 1–3 Canfield Place, London NW6 3BT *Tel.* 020 7372 3889 *Email* info@asfarifoundation.org.uk *Website* www.asfarifoundation.org.uk

■ The Ashburnham Thanksgiving Trust

CC NO 249109 **ESTABLISHED** 1965

WHERE FUNDING CAN BE GIVEN UK and worldwide.

WHO CAN BENEFIT Individuals and organisations benefitting Christians and evangelists.

WHAT IS FUNDED Only Christian work already known to the trustees is supported, particularly evangelical overseas missionary work.

WHAT IS NOT FUNDED Grants for buildings.

RANGE OF GRANTS Up to £5,000.

SAMPLE GRANTS Lawrence Barham Memorial Trust (£5,000); New Destiny Ashburnham Chapel (£3,000); Genesis Arts Trust (£2,000); Latin Link (£1,300); Chasah Trust (£1,100); Prison Fellowship (£1,000); Tear Fund (£750); Media Watch UK (£200); Lee Abbey Fellowship (£150); Royal Marsden Hospital (£100).

FINANCES *Year* 2015/16 *Income* £235,487 *Grants* £81,219 *Grants to organisations* £72,269 *Assets* £7,014,762

TRUSTEES Edward Bickersteth; Robert Bickersteth; Dr Charles Warren.

HOW TO APPLY The trustees state they are fully committed to supporting existing beneficiaries and otherwise proactive in their grant-making and so do not accept unsolicited applications, nor do they respond to such applications.

WHO TO APPLY TO The Charity Secretary, Agmerhurst House, Kitchenham Road, Ashburnham, Battle, East Sussex TN33 9NB *Email* att@lookingforward.biz

■ The Ashden Trust

CC NO 802623 **ESTABLISHED** 1989

WHERE FUNDING CAN BE GIVEN UK and overseas.

WHO CAN BENEFIT Registered charities.

WHAT IS FUNDED Sustainable development – UK and international; people at risk; sustainable regeneration; arts and sustainability.

TYPE OF GRANT Project funding; core costs.

SAMPLE GRANTS Carbon Tracker (£79,000); Client Earth (£75,00); Christian Aid (£40,000); Greenpeace (£37,500); Soil Association (£25,000); Garage Sale Trail (£20,000); Shift (£15,000); 350.org, Green Alliance, People and Planet (£10,000 each); Syria Relief (£5,000); Share Action (£4,000); Beat the Cold (£2,500).

FINANCES *Year* 2015/16 *Income* £1,135,154 *Grants* £1,037,320 *Grants to organisations* £1,037,320 *Assets* £33,602,289

TRUSTEES Judith Portrait; Robert Butler-Sloss; Sarah Butler-Sloss.

OTHER INFORMATION The trust is one of the Sainsbury Family Charitable Trusts which share a common administration. An application to one is taken as an application to all. The trust also supports charitable activities through loans, interest-free loans and in some cases an equity stake in organisations which meet the charitable objectives of the trust. Currently, priority is given to Ashden Award winners.

HOW TO APPLY The 2015/16 accounts state: 'Proposals to The Ashden Trust are generally invited by the Trustees or initiated at their request. Unsolicited applications are only considered if they are aligned with the Trust's interests. The Trustees prefer to support innovative schemes that can be successfully replicated or become self-sustaining. Grants are not normally made to individuals.'

WHO TO APPLY TO Alan Bookbinder, Director, The Peak, 5 Wilton Road, London SW1V 1AP *Tel.* 020 7410 0330 *Email* ashdentrust@sfct.org.uk *Website* www.ashdentrust.org.uk

■ The Ashley Family Foundation

CC NO 288099 **ESTABLISHED** 1985

WHERE FUNDING CAN BE GIVEN England and Wales.

WHO CAN BENEFIT Charitable organisations, including registered charities; unincorporated organisations; or community groups with a constitution or terms of reference and a charitable purpose.

WHAT IS FUNDED Development of rural communities; participation in the arts. The website states: 'We are keen to fund good small scale arts projects in England and Wales and welcome proposals from small scale community textile museums/organisations.'

WHAT IS NOT FUNDED Individuals; business ventures; overseas projects; projects in the field of religion; dance-related projects; direct funding toward schools; retrospective funding for activities that have already taken place.

TYPE OF GRANT Revenue proposals are favoured over capital requests. Funding is generally awarded to one-off projects but the trustees will consider funding over a number of years (up to three) if the project requires it.

RANGE OF GRANTS Up to £50,000 but mainly £1,000 to £10,000.

SAMPLE GRANTS Cambrian Heritage Regeneration Trust (£50,000); Joe Strummer Foundation (£20,000); Velvet Coalmine (£7,500); Dorothy Parkes Centre (£5,500); Steam Collective (£5,000); It's Your Life (£4,100); St Martin-in-the-Fields Trust (£3,000); Tall Ships Youth Trust (£900); Eisteddfod Org UK (£54).

FINANCES *Year* 2014/15 *Income* £300,159 *Grants* £530,726 *Grants to organisations* £530,726

TRUSTEES Oriana Baddeley; Emma Suckburgh; Martyn Gowar; Laura Ashley; Mike Hodgson; Sue Timney; Jeremy McIlroy.

OTHER INFORMATION The 2014/15 accounts were the latest available at the time of writing (May 2015). For the past few years the foundation has had policy of giving half its funds to Welsh projects.

HOW TO APPLY Applications can be made online through the foundation's website. Applicants are encouraged to read the grants criteria on the website and speak to the foundation before applying. If you have submitted an application and have not heard within twelve weeks assume you have been unsuccessful. Unsolicited requests, which sit outside the foundation's criteria will not be answered.

WHO TO APPLY TO Mia Duddridge, Administrator, 6 Trull Farm Buildings, Trull, Tetbury, Gloucestershire GL8 8SQ *Tel.* 0303 040 1005 *Email* info@ashleyfamilyfoundation.org.uk *Website* www.ashleyfamilyfoundation.org.uk

■ The Ashmore Foundation

CC NO 1122351 **ESTABLISHED** 2007

WHERE FUNDING CAN BE GIVEN Overseas. Priority countries are: Brazil, Colombia, Mexico, India, Philippines, Indonesia and Turkey.

WHO CAN BENEFIT Registered charities and voluntary organisations.

WHAT IS FUNDED Community and economic development; education and training; health.

TYPE OF GRANT One-off and multi-year grants for projects of up to three years.

SAMPLE GRANTS Lend a Hand (£101,000); IDEP Foundation (£66,000); Yunus Social Business (£44,000); Unltd Indonesia (£32,000); Children Change Colombia (£21,000); Yuva (£17,000); Adana (£11,000); Child Workers in Nepal (£5,000).

FINANCES *Year* 2015 *Income* £573,000 *Grants* £505,000 *Grants to organisations* £505,000 *Assets* £6,476,000

TRUSTEES James Carleton; Christoph Hofmann; Romain Bocket; John Gregory; Victoria Rogova; Elaine Cheung; Ibrahim Assem; Adrian Petreanu.

HOW TO APPLY The foundation's website states: 'The Ashmore Foundation does not accept unsolicited applications. We source new partners through recommendations from experts, existing partners, suggestions from Ashmore staff and detailed research by the Foundation team.'

WHO TO APPLY TO The Trustees, Ashmore Group, 5th Floor, 61 Aldwych, London WC2B 4AE *Tel.* 020 3077 6153 *Email* info@ashmorefoundation.org *Website* www.ashmorefoundation.org

■ The Ashworth Charitable Trust

CC NO 1045492 **ESTABLISHED** 1995

WHERE FUNDING CAN BE GIVEN UK and worldwide, with some preference for certain specific needs in Honiton, Ottery St Mary, Sidmouth and Wonford Green surgery, Exeter.

WHO CAN BENEFIT Registered UK charities.

WHAT IS FUNDED Humanitarian causes operating locally, nationally or internationally.

WHAT IS NOT FUNDED The website states that the trust never funds: 'charities which do not have a United Kingdom Registered Charity Number; non-humanitarian charities (with the single exception of The Ironbridge Gorge Museum); individuals – including gap year funding, travel overseas for charity work and medical treatment; professionals representing individuals, unless they are applying from a registered charity; charities with a turnover of more than one million pounds; charities with disproportionately large reserves, unless there is an exceptional reason (in such a case, we will require an explanation); animal welfare; projects promoting religious proselytisation or partisan political activities; charities mainly involved in research, whether medical or otherwise; heritage; museums (with the sole exception of the Ironbridge Gorge Museum); United Kingdom hospices (as the Trustees already sponsor a hospice of their choice within the Southwest)'.

TYPE OF GRANT For the most part, the trust looks to fund projects and not core funding.

RANGE OF GRANTS Levels of grant do not usually exceed £3,000. Very occasionally, a grant of up to £5,000 may be made.

SAMPLE GRANTS Manisha UK (£15,000); Action Coalition and Amigos Worldwide (£4,000 each); Devon and Cornwall Food Association and Green Shoots Foundation (£3,000 each); Bees for Development Trust (£2,500); React and The Quicken Trust (£2,000 each); Serian and South Hampshire Lifestyles (£1,000 each); Naserian (£250).

FINANCES *Year* 2015/16 *Income* £161,284 *Grants* £161,750 *Grants to organisations* £161,750 *Assets* £4,838,988

TRUSTEES Hoshmand Rouhipour; Sharareh Rouhipour; Dr Wendi Momen; Ian Miles; Kian Golestani; Katherine Gray.

OTHER INFORMATION Grants were broken down as follows: international (£108,000); national (£29,000); other (£15,000); local (£10,000).

HOW TO APPLY Applications can be made through the trust's website. Trustee meetings are held in May and November. Successful applicants will be informed within six weeks of the relevant meeting.

WHO TO APPLY TO Mandy Walsom, Foot Anstey, Senate Court, Southernhay Gardens, Exeter EX1 1NT *Tel.* 01392 411221 *Email* ashworthtrust@btinternet.com *Website* www.ashworthtrust.org

■ The Ian Askew Charitable Trust

CC NO 264515 **ESTABLISHED** 1972

WHERE FUNDING CAN BE GIVEN UK, with a preference for Sussex; overseas.

WHO CAN BENEFIT Charitable organisations.

WHAT IS FUNDED General charitable purposes including: conservation of historic buildings; environment; education.

RANGE OF GRANTS Up to £10,000 but the majority of grants are for £500 or less.

SAMPLE GRANTS The Royal Ballet School (£10,000); The Barn Owl Trust and The Charleston Trust (£2,000 each); Churches Conservation Trust (£1,500); Sir John Soanne's Museum, React and The Children's Trust (£1,000 each); Bumblebee Conservation Trust (£500).

FINANCES *Year* 2015/16 *Income* £563,325 *Grants* £145,346 *Grants to organisations* £145,346 *Assets* £17,664,920

TRUSTEES Cleone St Quentin; Rory Askew; James Rank; John Hecks; Richard Lewis; Henrietta Marshall; Venetia.

OTHER INFORMATION Grants were made to 191 organisations during the year.

HOW TO APPLY Apply in writing to the correspondent. Applications are considered every other month.

WHO TO APPLY TO Paul Hodge, RSM Tax and Accounting Ltd, 18 Mount Ephraim Road, Tunbridge Wells, Kent TN1 1ED *Tel.* 01892 511944 *Email* paul.hodge@rsmuk.com

■ The Associated Board of the Royal Schools of Music

CC NO 292182 **ESTABLISHED** 1985

WHERE FUNDING CAN BE GIVEN Worldwide.

WHO CAN BENEFIT Registered charities.

WHAT IS FUNDED Music education.

RANGE OF GRANTS Up to £38,000.

SAMPLE GRANTS Music For Youth (£38,000); National Youth Orchestra (£21,000); The Mayor of London's Fund for Young Musicians (£20,000); Royal Philharmonic Society (£12,000); National Youth Choir, Music Centre of Christ Church and The Johor Society for the Performing Arts (£10,000 each); Chamber Music New Zealand (£7,000).

FINANCES *Year* 2015/16 *Income* £39,052,000 *Grants* £5,914,000 *Grants to organisations* £4,956,000 *Assets* £14,019,000

TRUSTEES Anthony Travis; Colette Bowe; Prof. Colin Lawson; Alan Smith; Prof. Jonathan Freeman-Attwood; Kevin Porter; Judith Barber; Linda Merrick; John Gallacher; David Roper; Robin Downie; Douglas Gardner; Jeffrey Sharkey; Jeremy Heap.

OTHER INFORMATION There were 86 individual scholars (£958,000) supported during the year. The charity makes four annual donations to the trustees of the Royal Academy of Music, Royal College of Music, Royal Northern College of Music Endowment Fund, Royal Conservatoire of Scotland Trust, all of which receive £1.2 million each and represent the majority of the grant total.

HOW TO APPLY Check the website for the latest information before applying in writing to the correspondent.

WHO TO APPLY TO Susan Cambridge, Executive Director of Finance and Administration, Associated Board of the Royal Schools of Music, 4 London Wall Place, London EC2Y 5AU *Tel.* 020 7467 8223 *Email* abrsm@abrsm.ac.uk *Website* www.abrsm.org

■ The Associated Country Women of the World (ACWW)

CC NO 290367 **ESTABLISHED** 1933

WHERE FUNDING CAN BE GIVEN Overseas, mainly Africa and Asia.

WHO CAN BENEFIT NGOs, umbrella organisations, women's organisations, educational institutions; any organisation applying must have been registered in its home country for at least two years (with suitable registration for receiving foreign donations) and be able to provide all of the supporting documents required.

WHAT IS FUNDED Sustainable projects worldwide to improve the standard of living of women and their families. Projects should meet at least one of the following criteria: education and capacity building; health education; nutrition and home economics; civic consciousness and community involvement; income generation; water and sanitation; agricultural training and development.

WHAT IS NOT FUNDED The following are not funded: land; motor vehicles; items of large mechanical equipment; emergency relief work; capital infrastructure projects; office administration; ongoing salary expenses.

TYPE OF GRANT One-off grants for projects for organisations.

RANGE OF GRANTS The maximum grants for non-members is £5,000. For members it is £10,000.

SAMPLE GRANTS Annai Theresa Social Welfare Action Trust – India and NEST – Sri Lanka (£6,100 each); Cameroon Gender and Environment Watch (£4,700); Our Lady of Mercy Community Services – Ghana (£2,800); Safeplan Uganda (£2,500).

FINANCES *Year* 2015 *Income* £520,626 *Grants* £139,767 *Grants to organisations* £139,767 *Assets* £2,496,414

TRUSTEES Jo Almond; Ruth Shanks; Margaret Yetman; Henrietta Schoeman; Mabel Moyo; Sheila Needham; Dotsie Gordon; Heather Brenan; Margaret Macmillan; Gail Commens; Magdalena de Kock; Anne Hovstad; Thilaka Perera; Irene Chinje; Enny Karim; Kerry Maw-Smith.

OTHER INFORMATION Grants were awarded to 28 projects in 12 countries.

HOW TO APPLY Application forms can be downloaded from the organisation's website.

WHO TO APPLY TO The Trustees, 24 Tufton Street, London SW1P 3RB *Tel.* 020 7799 3875 *Email* info@acww.org.uk *Website* www.acww.org.uk

■ The Association of Colleges Charitable Trust

CC NO 1040631 **ESTABLISHED** 1994

WHERE FUNDING CAN BE GIVEN UK.

WHO CAN BENEFIT Further education establishments.

WHAT IS FUNDED Further education. The charitable trust is responsible for administering two programmes. The largest of these is the Beacon Awards, which provide monetary grants to award-winning initiatives within further education colleges. The other scheme is the AoC Gold Awards for Further Education Alumni, which reward former members of further education colleges who have since excelled in their chosen field or profession.

WHAT IS NOT FUNDED Individuals.

RANGE OF GRANTS £3,000 to £5,000.

SAMPLE GRANTS Abingdon and Witney, City of Wolverhampton College, Reading College and South Eastern Regional College (£5,000 each); Weston College (£2,000).

FINANCES *Year* 2015/16 *Income* £225,403 *Grants* £56,000 *Grants to organisations* £56,000 *Assets* £206,328

TRUSTEES Alice Thiagaraj; Peter Brophy; David Forrester; John Bingham; Martin Doel; Carole Stott; Dame Pat Bacon, Jane Samuels; Simon Francis; Shahida Aslam.

HOW TO APPLY Full details including application packs can be found on the trust's website.

WHO TO APPLY TO Alice Thiagaraj, Managing Trustee, 2–5 Stedham Place, London WC1A 1HU *Tel.* 020 7034 9977 *Email* alice_thiagaraj@aoc.co.uk *Website* www.aoc.co.uk/beaconawards

■ Asthma UK

CC NO 802364 **ESTABLISHED** 1990

WHERE FUNDING CAN BE GIVEN UK.

WHO CAN BENEFIT Research organisations; universities; medical and academic professionals.

WHAT IS FUNDED Research into asthma. Priority areas can be broadly split into six themes: asthma biology; asthma types; asthma management; asthma diagnosis; asthma prevention; asthma treatments.

TYPE OF GRANT Project grants; research; fellowships and studentships; up to five years.

SAMPLE GRANTS Imperial College of Science, Technology and Medicine (£2 million).

FINANCES *Year* 2016 *Income* £8,762,000 *Grants* £2,649,000 *Grants to organisations* £2,649,000 *Assets* £6,807,000

TRUSTEES John Garbutt; Jane Tozer; John Tucker; Barbara Herts; John Lelliott; Dr Robert Wilson; Mary Leadbeater; Matthew Smith; Martin Sinclair; Kate Clarke; George Anson; Dr Paul Hodgkin; Prof. Sir Lewis Ritchie; Jean-Francois Bessiron; James Bowes.

HOW TO APPLY Details of how and when to apply for grants can be found on the charity's website.

WHO TO APPLY TO Harriet Jones, Director of Finance and Resources, 18 Mansell Street, London E1 8AA *Tel.* 0300 222 5800 *Email* info@asthma.org.uk *Website* www.asthma.org.uk/research/for-researchers

■ The Astor Foundation

CC NO 225708 **ESTABLISHED** 1963

WHERE FUNDING CAN BE GIVEN UK.

WHO CAN BENEFIT Medical research organisations and registered charities.

WHAT IS FUNDED General charitable purposes including medical research; disability; social welfare; children.

WHAT IS NOT FUNDED Individuals; salaries.

RANGE OF GRANTS £500 to £45,000; generally £500 to £2,500.

SAMPLE GRANTS Friends of University College London Hospitals (£5,000); Heartsurge Fund (£3,500); Alzheimer's Society and Samaritans (£3,000 each); Multiple Sclerosis Trust (£2,000); Snowdon Trust (£1,500); Aidis Trust and Coeliac UK (£1,000 each); Atlantic Lions and National Tremor Foundation (£500 each).

FINANCES *Year* 2015/16 *Income* £127,243 *Grants* £117,000 *Grants to organisations* £117,000 *Assets* £3,808,825

TRUSTEES Robert Astor; Lord Latymer; Dr Howard Swanton; Prof. Sir John Cunningham; Charles Astor; Tania Astor.

HOW TO APPLY There are no deadline dates or application forms. Applications should be in writing to the correspondent and must include accounts and an annual report if available. The trustees meet twice yearly, usually in October and April. If the appeal arrives too late for one meeting it will automatically be carried over for consideration at the next. An acknowledgement will be sent on receipt of an appeal. No further communication will be entered into unless the trustees raise any queries regarding the appeal, or unless the appeal is subsequently successful.

WHO TO APPLY TO Lisa Rothwell-Orr, Secretary, PO Box 168, Bideford EX39 6WB *Tel.* 07901 737488 *Email* astor.foundation@gmail.com

■ The Atlas Fund

CC NO 278030 **ESTABLISHED** 1979

WHERE FUNDING CAN BE GIVEN UK.

WHO CAN BENEFIT Registered charities; churches; schools.

WHAT IS FUNDED General charitable purposes.

RANGE OF GRANTS Up to £30,000 but generally £1,000 to £5,000.

SAMPLE GRANTS Friends of St Margaret's Church (£30,000); Canterbury Cathedral Trust (£10,000); Westcott Church Fund (£4,000); British Museum Friends and Royal Academy of Arts (£3,000 each); British Red Cross and Radley Foundation (£2,000 each); Age UK and Ashmolean Museum (£1,000 each).

FINANCES *Year* 2015/16 *Income* £79,173 *Grants* £114,000 *Grants to organisations* £114,000 *Assets* £2,046,447

TRUSTEES Lady Hester Touche; William Touche; Sir Anthony Touche; Helen Hofmann.

HOW TO APPLY Apply in writing to the correspondent.

WHO TO APPLY TO Lady Hester Touche, Trustee, Stane House, Ockley, Dorking, Surrey RH5 5TQ *Tel.* 01306 627397 *Email* toucheockley@btinternet.com

■ The Aurelius Charitable Trust

CC NO 271333 **ESTABLISHED** 1975

WHERE FUNDING CAN BE GIVEN UK.

WHO CAN BENEFIT Registered charities; historic societies; museums/galleries; academic institutions.

WHAT IS FUNDED Conservation/preservation of culture inherited from the past; the dissemination of knowledge, particularly in the humanities field; research or publications.

WHAT IS NOT FUNDED Individuals.

TYPE OF GRANT Seed funding or completion funding not otherwise available; usually one-off.

RANGE OF GRANTS Generally £500 to £3,000.

SAMPLE GRANTS British Institute at Ankara and British Academy (£5,000 each); Ironbridge Gorge Museum Trust (£3,000); Fife Cultural Trust (£2,500); Suffolk Building Preservation Trust (£1,700); Worcestershire Historical Society (£1,300); RAF Benevolent Fund (£1,100); Charing and District Local History Society (£500); Hosking Houses Trust (£430).

FINANCES *Year* 2015/16 *Income* £86,400 *Grants* £89,722 *Grants to organisations* £89,722 *Assets* £2,190,677

TRUSTEES William Wallis; Philip Haynes.

HOW TO APPLY Apply in writing to the correspondent. Donations are generally made on the recommendation of the trust's board of advisors. Unsolicited applications will only be responded to if an sae is included. The trustees meet twice a year.

WHO TO APPLY TO Philip Haynes, Trustee, Briarsmead, Old Road, Buckland, Betchworth, Surrey RH3 7DU *Tel.* 01737 842186 *Email* philip.haynes@tiscali.co.uk

■ The Lord Austin Trust

CC NO 208394 **ESTABLISHED** 1937

WHERE FUNDING CAN BE GIVEN Birmingham and its immediate area.

WHO CAN BENEFIT Hospitals, medical institutions and charities in England, restricted to: local charities based in Birmingham and West Midlands; and national organisations (but not their provincial branches).

WHAT IS FUNDED Children; older people; medical institutions and research.
WHAT IS NOT FUNDED Appeals from, or on behalf of, individual applicants.
TYPE OF GRANT One-off.
SAMPLE GRANTS Birmingham St Mary's Hospice (£5,000); City of Birmingham Symphony Orchestra (£4,500); Acorns Children's Hospice Trust (£3,000); Tamworth Nursery (Special Needs) (£2,500); Saltley Neighbourhood Pensioner's Centre and Queen Elizabeth Hospital Birmingham (£2,000 each); Children's Heart Foundation (£1,500) and All Saints Youth Project, Army Benevolent Fund, Avoncroft Museum, Broadening Choices for Older People and St Martin's Centre for Health and Healing (£1,000 each).
FINANCES *Year* 2015/16 *Income* £103,211 *Grants* £100,850 *Grants to organisations* £100,850 *Assets* £3,385,061
TRUSTEES Rodney Kettel; Keith Dudley; Neil Andrews.
OTHER INFORMATION Grants were made to 64 organisations and broken down as follows: miscellaneous (£25,000); medical (£24,500); children and young people (£22,500); older people (£7,000).
HOW TO APPLY Apply in writing to the correspondent, including a set of recent accounts. The trustees meet twice a year in or around May and November to consider grants.
WHO TO APPLY TO Chrissy Norgrove, c/o Shakespeare Martineau, 1 Colmore Square, Birmingham B4 6AA *Tel.* 0121 214 0487

■ Autonomous Research Charitable Trust (ARCT)

CC NO 1137503 **ESTABLISHED** 2010
WHERE FUNDING CAN BE GIVEN UK with a preference for London; overseas.
WHO CAN BENEFIT Registered charities.
WHAT IS FUNDED Helping disadvantaged people get a step up in life and empowering individuals to improve the quality of their lives. The trust focuses its resources upon a small number of key partner charities – both in London and abroad – where it feels it can make a difference and establish long-term relationships.
SAMPLE GRANTS Find Your Feet (£101,000); Food Cycle (£100,000); Honeypot Children's Charity (£15,000); Contact the Elderly (£10,000); Marie Curie (£5,500); Nordoff Robbins (£2,000); Plan International UK and The Leukemia and Lymphoma Society (£1,500 each); Alec's Angels and The Prince's Trust (£1,000 each).
FINANCES *Year* 2015/16 *Income* £217,621 *Grants* £266,347 *Grants to organisations* £266,347 *Assets* £171,616
TRUSTEES Jonathan Firkins; Andrew Crean; Donald Betson.
HOW TO APPLY Apply in writing to the correspondent.
WHO TO APPLY TO Martin Pollock, Trust Administrator, 150 Aldersgate Street, London EC1A 4AB *Tel.* 020 7334 9191 *Email* martin.pollock@moorestephens.com

■ The Avon and Somerset Police Community Trust

CC NO 1076770 **ESTABLISHED** 1999
WHERE FUNDING CAN BE GIVEN The Avon and Somerset Constabulary area.
WHO CAN BENEFIT Charitable organisations.
WHAT IS FUNDED The trustees favour projects that: promote safety and quality of life in the Avon and Somerset Constabulary area; through the prevention of crime and disorder, protect young people, people who are vulnerable and older people from criminal acts; advance education, including that related to alcohol, drugs, solvent abuse, community relations and responsible citizenship.
WHAT IS NOT FUNDED Individuals, including students; expeditions and trips; bursaries or scholarships; replacements of statutory funding and salaries; projects that fall outside the Avon and Somerset Constabulary area; building costs are given a very low priority by the trustees; further applications within a period of three years.
RANGE OF GRANTS Usually up to £50,000.
SAMPLE GRANTS Bobby Van Scheme (£54,500); Hartcliffe and Withywood Angling Club, Stand Against Violence, The National Smelting Co. Amateur Boxing Club, Henbury Football Club and Priory Community Association (£1,000 each); Sandford Scouts (£880); Wolverhampton Playing Fields and Thornbury Sea Cadets (£600 each); Oasis Community Club (£500) and Clevedon YMCA and Bath and North East Somerset Youth Offending Team (£250 each).
FINANCES *Year* 2015/16 *Income* £473,599 *Grants* £343,099 *Grants to organisations* £413,747 *Assets* £615,339
TRUSTEES Patricia Hunt; Paul Hooper; Beatrice Salter; Mary Prior; Dame Janet Trotter; Alan Bell; Sean Connolly; Sue Mountstevens.
OTHER INFORMATION The grant total includes funds used to run the trust's own projects and initiatives.
HOW TO APPLY Application forms are available to download, together with criteria and guidelines, on the website. For further information about the trust or advice on obtaining or completing the trust's application form contact the Trust Manager. The trustees usually meet in January, April, July and October. Applications need to be received at least six weeks before each meeting.
WHO TO APPLY TO Tracey Clegg, Trust Manager, PO Box 37, Valley Road, Portishead, Bristol BS20 8QJ *Tel.* 01275 816240 *Email* tracey.clegg@avonandsomerset.police.uik *Website* www.avonandsomerset.police.uk/services/police-community-trust

■ Awards for All

WHERE FUNDING CAN BE GIVEN UK.
WHO CAN BENEFIT Voluntary and community organisations; schools; parish or town councils; health bodies; registered and unregistered charities; co-operatives; friendly societies; industrial and provident societies; not-for-profit companies; not-for-profit unincorporated associations; clinical commissioning groups; NHS hospital trusts; foundation hospitals.
WHAT IS FUNDED Grassroots and community activity that aims to improve life for local people and neighbourhoods.
WHAT IS NOT FUNDED Full exclusions are included in the guidance notes available from the programme's website.
TYPE OF GRANT Activities that can be funded include: hosting an event, activity or performance; purchasing new equipment or materials; running training courses; setting up a pilot project or starting up a new group; carrying out special repairs or conservation work; expenses for

volunteers, pay for workers and professional fees; transport costs.

RANGE OF GRANTS England: £300 to £10,000; Northern Ireland: £500 to £10,000; Scotland: £500 to £10,000; Wales: £500 to £5,000.

SAMPLE GRANTS Family Action, Park View School and The Rock Youth Club (£10,000 each); Binton Parish Council (£2,700); Support Trough Sport UK (£2,400); Elloughton Village Hall (£1,900); Runnymede Swimming Club (£1,500); The Young Pensioners Club (£650).

OTHER INFORMATION For details on the Big Lottery Fund also see a separate entry. The amount given through the scheme appears to be included in the overall total distributed by the Big Lottery Fund. The grant search facility available on the website shows that in the 2015/16 period there were 10,231 awards made totalling around £83.8 million, allocated as follows: England (£64.1 million in 7,250 awards); Scotland (£12.1 million in 1,644 awards); Wales (£3.2 million in 809 awards); Northern Ireland (£4.4 million in 528 awards).

HOW TO APPLY All information, application forms and guidelines are available online. If you need further support or have any questions get in touch with the organisation. Note that there are separate programmes for each country of the UK.

WHO TO APPLY TO c/o Big Lottery Fund, 1 Plough Place, London EC4A 1DE *Tel.* 0345 410 2030 *Email* general.enquiries@awardsforall.org.uk *Website* www.awardsforall.org.uk

■ The Aylesford Family Charitable Trust

CC NO 328299 **ESTABLISHED** 1989

WHERE FUNDING CAN BE GIVEN West Midlands and Warwickshire.

WHO CAN BENEFIT Registered charities.

WHAT IS FUNDED General charitable purposes.

WHAT IS NOT FUNDED Grants are not normally given to individuals.

TYPE OF GRANT Recurrent; one-off.

RANGE OF GRANTS Usually £100 to £5,000.

SAMPLE GRANTS Game and Wildlife Conservation Trust (£4,400); Lewa UK (£1,500); Henry Plumb Foundation and North Warwickshire First Responders (£1,000 each); Cerebra, Guy's Gift, Meningitis Now and Support Dogs (£500 each); Highland Hospice and NARA (£300 each).

FINANCES *Year* 2015/16 *Income* £55,531 *Grants* £79,500 *Grants to organisations* £79,500 *Assets* £1,779,084

TRUSTEES Lord Charles Aylesford; Lady Aylesford.

HOW TO APPLY Apply in writing to the correspondent at any time.

WHO TO APPLY TO The Trustees, Packington Hall, Meriden, Warwickshire CV7 7HF *Tel.* 01676 522020 *Email* sam@packingtonestate.co.uk

The Bacit Foundation

CC NO 1149202 **ESTABLISHED** 2012

WHERE FUNDING CAN BE GIVEN UK.

WHO CAN BENEFIT Charities and research institutes.

WHAT IS FUNDED General charitable purposes including research into cancer and related diseases.

SAMPLE GRANTS The Institute of Cancer Research (£148,000); Alzheimer's Research UK (£128,500); Women for Women International (£116,500); The Louis Dundas Centre for Children's Palliative Care (£125,500); Beating Bowel Cancer, Cure Leukaemia and SSAFA (£112,000 each).

FINANCES *Year* 2015/16 *Income* £2,646,975 *Grants* £2,371,000 *Grants to organisations* £2,371,000 *Assets* £305,094

TRUSTEES Martin Thomas; Catherine Scivier; Thomas Henderson; Rupert Adams.

HOW TO APPLY Unsolicited applications are not accepted. The foundation's Charity Commission record states that: 'The foundation grants those funds to charities selected by its trustees in furtherance of the foundation's objects, in proportions determined each year by shareholders of Bacit Ltd.'

WHO TO APPLY TO Martin Thomas, Trustee, 91 Gower Street, London WC1E 6AB *Tel.* 020 7968 6460 *Email* MThomas@altimapartners.com

Backstage Trust

CC NO 1145887 **ESTABLISHED** 2012

WHERE FUNDING CAN BE GIVEN UK.

WHO CAN BENEFIT Small scale arts organisations, particularly those benefitting the young and disadvantaged.

WHAT IS FUNDED Theatre and the performing arts.

SAMPLE GRANTS Royal Academy of Music (£4.3 million); Shoreditch Town Hall (£1 million); Hightide Theatre Festival (£130,000); Chrisalys Circus (£15,500); North Wall Arts Centre (£10,000).

FINANCES *Year* 2015/16 *Income* £1,697,169 *Grants* £7,128,932 *Grants to organisations* £7,128,932 *Assets* £1,003,676

TRUSTEES Lady Susan Sainsbury; Dominic Flynn; David Wood.

OTHER INFORMATION The trust was established in February 2012 by Lady Susan Sainsbury for general charitable purposes. In practice, the trust's priorities are likely to be focused on the arts, particularly theatre and the performing arts. Lady Sainsbury is the deputy chair of both the Royal Shakespeare Company and the Royal Academy of Music, and she and her husband, Lord David Sainsbury of Turville, are high profile patrons of the arts.

HOW TO APPLY Apply in writing to the correspondent. Proposals for support should be relevant, realistic and demonstrate a clearly expressed set of aims. It should contain a realistic expression of potential viability and ideas for how the organisation would augment charitable funding. The 2015/16 annual report states: 'Trustees will want to see evidence of fundraising plans, and to know that Backstage could act as a catalyst to encourage other grant-giving bodies, but not be expected to be sole benefactor.'

WHO TO APPLY TO Kathryn Thompson, Trustee, North House, 27 Great Peter Street, London SW1P 3LN *Tel.* 020 7072 4498 *Email* info@backstagetrust.org.uk

Harry Bacon Foundation

CC NO 1056500 **ESTABLISHED** 1996

WHERE FUNDING CAN BE GIVEN UK.

WHO CAN BENEFIT Registered charities.

WHAT IS FUNDED Health/medical charities; animal welfare.

RANGE OF GRANTS Around £6,000.

SAMPLE GRANTS Arthritis Research Campaign; British Heart Foundation; Cancer Research UK; Donkey Sanctuary; Parkinson's Disease Society; RNLI; World Horse Welfare.

FINANCES *Year* 2015/16 *Income* £67,863 *Grants* £55,360 *Grants to organisations* £55,360 *Assets* £54,441

TRUSTEE NatWest Bank PLC.

HOW TO APPLY Apply in writing to the correspondent. The same charities are generally supported every year at the request of the founder.

WHO TO APPLY TO The Trustees, Ground Floor, Eastwood House, Glebe House, Chelmsford CM1 1RS *Tel.* 01245 292492 *Email* nwb.charities@natwest.com

The Bagri Foundation

CC NO 1000219 **ESTABLISHED** 1990

WHERE FUNDING CAN BE GIVEN Mainly UK and India.

WHO CAN BENEFIT Organisations and individuals.

WHAT IS FUNDED Education; overseas aid; health; the preservation of India's cultural heritage.

SAMPLE GRANTS A list of beneficiaries was not available.

FINANCES *Year* 2015/16 *Income* £618,540 *Grants* £875,437 *Grants to organisations* £875,437 *Assets* £13,250,830

TRUSTEES Lady Bagri; The Hon. Apurv Bagri; The Hon. Alka Bagri.

HOW TO APPLY The foundation has in the past stated that it does not accept unsolicited applications.

WHO TO APPLY TO D. M. Beaumont, Correspondent, 80 Cannon Street, London EC4N 6EJ *Tel.* 020 7280 0000 *Email* enquiries@bagrifoundation.org *Website* bagrifoundation.org

The Austin Bailey Trust

CC NO 514912 **ESTABLISHED** 1984

WHERE FUNDING CAN BE GIVEN Swansea and overseas.

WHO CAN BENEFIT Churches; overseas aid organisations; local organisations.

WHAT IS FUNDED Health; social welfare; churches; overseas aid.

WHAT IS NOT FUNDED Individuals.

TYPE OF GRANT Core costs; start-up costs. One-off, up to three years.

RANGE OF GRANTS Up to £8,000.

SAMPLE GRANTS Y-Care International (£3,300); Chernobyl Children's Lifeline (£1,200); Microloan Foundation (£1,000); African Revival, International Refugee Trust, Sailors Trust and Global Care (£500 each); St James' Church – Swansea (£450); Arts Migration CIC (£400); Child's Foundation (£200).

FINANCES *Year* 2015/16 *Income* £83,911 *Grants* £81,846 *Grants to organisations* £81,846 *Assets* £671,748

TRUSTEES Penny Ryan; Clive Bailey; The Ven. Robert Williams; Sandra Morton; Jonathan Davies; Sian Popper.

HOW TO APPLY Application forms are available to download from the trust's website and should be submitted by email. The trustees of the Austin Bailey Foundation normally meet in May and December. Therefore, you should submit your grant application by mid-April and mid-November to be reviewed in time for the next meeting.

WHO TO APPLY TO Clive Bailey, Trustee, 64 Bosworth Road, Barnet EN5 5LP *Tel.* 020 8449 4327 *Email* localcharities@austinbaileyfoundation.org *Website* www.austinbaileyfoundation.org

■ The Baily Thomas Charitable Trust

CC NO 262334 **ESTABLISHED** 1970

WHERE FUNDING CAN BE GIVEN UK.

WHO CAN BENEFIT Registered charities. Schools and PTAs, industrial and provident societies and other such exempt charities can also apply.

WHAT IS FUNDED Research into learning disability; the care and relief of those affected by learning disability. The following areas of work normally fall within the fund's current policy providing they benefit people with learning disabilities: capital building/renovation/refurbishment works for residential, nursing and respite care, and schools; employment schemes including woodwork, crafts, printing and horticulture; play schemes and play therapy schemes; day and social activities centres including building costs and running costs; support for families, including respite schemes; independent living schemes; support in the community schemes; snoezelen rooms.

WHAT IS NOT FUNDED Individuals; CICs; hospices; minibuses except those for residential and/or day care services for people with learning disabilities; advocacy projects; conductive education projects; arts and theatre projects; swimming and hydro-therapy pools; physical disabilities unless accompanied by significant learning disabilities; grants for acquired brain injury unless the resulting learning disabilities occur early in the developmental period (i.e. birth, infancy or childhood), impacting on brain maturation and development and learning in childhood; appeals which are ethnically or religiously selective which the fund defines as therefore not benefitting the wider community.

TYPE OF GRANT Funding is normally considered for capital and revenue costs and for both specific projects and for general running/core costs.

RANGE OF GRANTS £250 to £130,000.

SAMPLE GRANTS Queen's University Belfast (£123,500); Development Trust and The JPK Sussex Project (£100,000 each); Rix-Thompson-Rothenberg Foundation (£70,000); Avon Riding Centre for the Disabled, Ferring Country Centre and The Hextol Foundation (£30,000 each).

FINANCES *Year* 2015/16 *Income* £1,833,528 *Grants* £2,807,181 *Grants to organisations* £2,807,181 *Assets* £89,397,049

TRUSTEES Kenneth Young; Suzanne Marriott; Prof. Sally-Ann Cooper; Jonathan Snow.

HOW TO APPLY Applications can be made through the fund's website. Details of application deadlines can also be found on the site.

WHO TO APPLY TO Ann Cooper, Secretary to the Trustees, c/o TMF Management (UK) Ltd, 400 Capability Green, Luton LU1 3AE *Tel.* 01582 439205 *Email* info@bailythomas.org.uk *Website* www.bailythomas.org.uk

■ The Baird Trust

SC NO SC016549 **ESTABLISHED** 1873

WHERE FUNDING CAN BE GIVEN Scotland.

WHO CAN BENEFIT Generally, the Church of Scotland.

WHAT IS FUNDED The trust is chiefly concerned with supporting the repair and refurbishment of the churches and halls belonging to the Church of Scotland. It also endows parishes and gives help to the Church of Scotland in its work.

TYPE OF GRANT One-off for capital and revenue.

SAMPLE GRANTS Grassmarket Community Project and Lodging House Mission (£10,000 each); Greenock East End Parish Church (£5,000); Rainbow Care Centre The GK Experience (£3,000 each); Scotland's Churches Trust (£2,000); Murrayfield United Free Church and Priesthill United Reformed Church (£1,000 each).

FINANCES *Year* 2016 *Income* £404,982 *Grants* £404,982 *Grants to organisations* £404,982 *Assets* £10,840,284

TRUSTEES The Hon. Mrs M. Coleman; Maj. J. M. K. Erskine; Revd Dr J. R. McKay; Mr A. Borthwick; Dr A. Elliot; Mr W. H. Barbour; Mr L. M. Borthwick; Lt Col. R. Callander; Lt Col. C. B. C. Ball.

HOW TO APPLY Application forms are available to download from the trust's website.

WHO TO APPLY TO Iain Mowat, Secretary, 182 Bath Street, Glasgow G2 4HG *Tel.* 0141 332 0476 *Email* info@bairdtrust.org.uk *Website* www.bairdtrust.org.uk

■ Bairdwatson Charitable Trust

SC NO SC038468 **ESTABLISHED** 2007

WHERE FUNDING CAN BE GIVEN Aye; Airdrie; West Bengal.

WHO CAN BENEFIT Registered charities. The trust may also consider applications from social enterprises and similar organisations for work which is charitable in nature. The trust will, in some instances, fund individuals.

WHAT IS FUNDED Education or training for employment; re-training; supporting people into work; vocational training, especially for young people.

WHAT IS NOT FUNDED Hospices and palliative care; appliances for illness or disability; organisations concerned with specific diseases or medical research; animal charities. The trust will not normally support projects in England, Wales or Northern Ireland, nor will it normally contribute to especially large projects where its contribution would not make a material difference.

TYPE OF GRANT Revenue; capital funding, project funding; core costs.

RANGE OF GRANTS £4,000 to £14,000.

SAMPLE GRANTS The Health and Wellness Hub (£13,500); Young Enterprises Scotland (£11,000); Active 4 All, The Prince's Trust, South Asia Voluntary Enterprise UK and Utheo Ltd (£10,000 each); Right Track Scotland (£9,500); National Trust for Scotland (£8,000); Clydesdale Community Initiatives (£4,000).

FINANCES *Year* 2015/16 *Income* £90,326 *Grants* £85,478 *Grants to organisations* £85,478 *Assets* £2,238,099

TRUSTEES Robert Kerr; John Ramsay; Jacqueline Leslie.
HOW TO APPLY Application forms are available from the trust's website and can be returned by email or post. The trustees meet three times a year for grant-making, in January, May and September. Application deadlines are posted on the trust's website.
WHO TO APPLY TO Linda Anderson, 27 Balfour Terrace, Murray, East Kilbride G75 0JQ *Tel.* 07982 915666 *Email* linda@bairdwatson.org.uk *Website* www.bairdwatson.org.uk

■ The Baker Charitable Trust

CC NO 273629 **ESTABLISHED** 1977
WHERE FUNDING CAN BE GIVEN UK and overseas.
WHO CAN BENEFIT Registered charities.
WHAT IS FUNDED Our previous research has indicated that there is particular interest in: social welfare in the Jewish community; older people; people with disabilities; neurological research; and people with diabetes and epilepsy. Preference is given to charities in which the trust has special interest, knowledge or association.
WHAT IS NOT FUNDED Individuals.
RANGE OF GRANTS Mostly under £1,000.
SAMPLE GRANTS British Council Shaare Zedek Medical Centre, Chai Cancer Care, Community Security Trust, Disabled Living Foundation, Friends of Magen David Adom in Great Britain, Hillel Foundation, Institute of Jewish Policy Research, Jewish Care; Jewish Women's Aid, Marie Curie Cancer Care, National Society for Epilepsy, Norwood; United Jewish Israel Appeal (UJIA), St John's Hospice, United Synagogue, Winged Fellowship and World Jewish Relief.
FINANCES *Year* 2015/16 *Income* £65,578 *Grants* £54,030 *Grants to organisations* £54,030 *Assets* £1,412,934
TRUSTEES Dr Harvey Baker; Dr Adrienne Baker.
OTHER INFORMATION Grants were made to 54 organisations in 2015/16. A list of recent beneficiaries was not provided in the accounts.
HOW TO APPLY Apply in writing to the correspondent.
WHO TO APPLY TO Dr Harvey Baker, Trustee, 16 Sheldon Avenue, Highgate, London N6 4JT *Tel.* 020 8340 5970 *Email* harbaker@doctors.org.uk

■ The Roy and Pixie Baker Charitable Trust

CC NO 1101988 **ESTABLISHED** 1995
WHERE FUNDING CAN BE GIVEN North East England.
WHO CAN BENEFIT Registered charities.
WHAT IS FUNDED Medical research, education, rural and urban heritage.
WHAT IS NOT FUNDED Individuals.
TYPE OF GRANT One-off and recurrent.
RANGE OF GRANTS Up to £10,000.
SAMPLE GRANTS Diocese of Hexham and Newcastle (£5,000); Nunnykirk Centre for Dyslexia, Northumberland Clubs for Young People and Percy Park Youth Trust (£3,000 each); Hospice Care North Northumberland and Tyneside Centre Against Unemployment (£2,500 each); The Sick Children's Trust (£2,000); Marine Society and Sea Cadets (£1,000); Amble Community Sports Development Centre (£500).
FINANCES *Year* 2015/16 *Income* £75,580 *Grants* £54,500 *Grants to organisations* £54,500 *Assets* £3,149,413
TRUSTEES Tony Glenton; George Straker; Lesley Caisley; David Irvin; Bill Dryden.
OTHER INFORMATION Grants were made to 23 organisations during the year.
HOW TO APPLY Apply in writing to the correspondent, providing full back up information. Trustees' meetings are held half yearly. The trustees require a receipt from the donee in respect of each grant.
WHO TO APPLY TO The Trustees, c/o Ryecroft Glenton, 32 Portland Terrace, Newcastle upon Tyne NE2 1QP *Tel.* 0191 281 1292 *Email* bakercharitabletrust@ryecroft-glenton.co.uk

■ The Balcombe Charitable Trust

CC NO 267172 **ESTABLISHED** 1975
WHERE FUNDING CAN BE GIVEN UK and overseas.
WHO CAN BENEFIT Registered charities.
WHAT IS FUNDED Education; the environment; health and welfare.
TYPE OF GRANT One-off and recurrent grants.
RANGE OF GRANTS £15,000 to £50,000.
SAMPLE GRANTS Durrell Wildlife Conservation Trust (£76,000); Blue Ventures Conservation Trust (£43,000); Connect and Global Feedback Ltd (£20,000); Womankind Worldwide (£17,300); Centrepoint (£15,000); The Martlets Hospice Ltd (£10,000); Body and Soul (£8,000); Age UK (£5,000); Bath Festivals (£2,500); Greenwich Theatre (£1,000).
FINANCES *Year* 2015/16 *Income* £250,484 *Grants* £301,250 *Grants to organisations* £301,250 *Assets* £26,767,519
TRUSTEES Nicholas Brown; R. A. Kreitman; Patricia Kreitman.
OTHER INFORMATION At the time of writing (May 2017) the trust's website stated: 'For the current funding period we are restricting applications to those working in the UK with young people who are homeless or not in education, employment or training (NEETs). We are particularly interested in projects working with young women.' Applicant charities should have an annual income of between £500,000 and £5 million.
HOW TO APPLY Applications should be made by email only to: lee@balcombetrust.org.uk. Applicants should apply with short (maximum 1,000 words) proposal plus budget and latest annual report and financial statements.
WHO TO APPLY TO Jonathan W. Prevezer, c/o Citroen Wells, Devonshire House, 1 Devonshire Street, London W1W 5DR *Tel.* 020 7304 2000 *Email* jonathan@balcombetrust.org.uk *Website* www.balcombetrust.org.uk

■ The Balfour Beatty Charitable Trust

CC NO 1127453 **ESTABLISHED** 2009
WHERE FUNDING CAN BE GIVEN UK.
WHO CAN BENEFIT Registered charities.
WHAT IS FUNDED The education and training of young people; health, sport and well-being.
RANGE OF GRANTS Up to £50,000.
SAMPLE GRANTS The Prince's Trust (£50,000); Barnardo's (£6,700); The Thomas Coram Foundation (£6,300).
FINANCES *Year* 2016 *Income* £166,356 *Grants* £68,849 *Grants to organisations* £68,849 *Assets* £162,322
TRUSTEES Paul Raby; Adrian McManus; Andrea Holt.
HOW TO APPLY The trustees work together with the Balfour Beatty Community Engagement Working

Group (CEWG) to identify suitable charities to support.

WHO TO APPLY TO Paul Raby, Trustee, The Curve, Axis Business Park, Hurricane Way, Langley, Slough SL3 8AG *Tel.* 01753 211121 *Email* bbfutures@balfourbeatty.com *Website* www.balfourbeatty.com/sustainability/involved/building-better-futures

■ The Andrew Balint Charitable Trust

CC NO 273691 **ESTABLISHED** 1961

WHERE FUNDING CAN BE GIVEN UK; Israel; Hungary and Romania.

WHO CAN BENEFIT Charitable organisations; Jewish organisations.

WHAT IS FUNDED General charitable causes; health; older people; ex-service people; Jewish faith; disability.

TYPE OF GRANT One-off and recurring.

RANGE OF GRANTS £100 to £20,000.

SAMPLE GRANTS Nightingale House (£20,000); Former Employee Trust and Hungarian Senior Citizens (£6,000 each); Jewish Care (£5,000); United Jewish Israel Appeal (UJIA) and Toth Gabor £5,000 each); The Board of Deputies of British Jews and World Jewish Relief (£500 each); British Friends of Children's Town (£250).

FINANCES *Year* 2015/16 *Income* £43,398 *Grants* £61,500 *Grants to organisations* £61,500 *Assets* £1,582,157

TRUSTEES Dr Gabriel Balint-Kurti; Angela Balint; Roy Balint-Kurti; Daniel Balint-Kurti.

OTHER INFORMATION The Andrew Balint Charitable Trust, The George Balint Charitable Trust, The Paul Charitable Trust and the Trust for Former Employees of Balint Companies are jointly administered. They have some trustees in common and are independent in other matters. Accounts had been received at the Charity Commission but because of the low income were not published.

HOW TO APPLY Apply in writing to the correspondent.

WHO TO APPLY TO David Kramer, Administrator, c/o Carter Backer Winter, Enterprise House, 21 Buckle Street, London E1 8NN *Tel.* 020 7309 3800 *Email* david.kramer@cbw.co.uk

■ The Ballinger Charitable Trust

CC NO 1121739 **ESTABLISHED** 1994

WHERE FUNDING CAN BE GIVEN North East England, Tyne and Wear.

WHO CAN BENEFIT Registered charities only.

WHAT IS FUNDED The health, development and well-being of young people; older people; promote cultural/arts projects based in the north east of England.

WHAT IS NOT FUNDED Individuals; sponsorships.

SAMPLE GRANTS Percy Hedley Foundation (£500,000); Age UK (£294,500); Alzheimer's Society (£249,000); Streetwise Young People's Project (£55,500); Pennywell Youth Project (£35,000); St Cuthbert's Care (£30,000); Patch Family Support (£25,000); Search Rights for the Elderly (£17,500); Children North East (£10,000).

FINANCES *Year* 2015 *Income* £3,108,915 *Grants* £2,732,569 *Grants to organisations* £2,732,569 *Assets* £36,180,859

TRUSTEES Diana Ballinger; John Flynn; Andrew Ballinger; Nicola Crowther.

HOW TO APPLY The following information is taken from the trust's website: '**Amounts up to £5,000** – A letter will suffice and should be forwarded to our P O Box address. **Amounts over £5,000** – Complete the initial application form and submit via the website. In both cases you will be acknowledged as soon as possible.'

WHO TO APPLY TO Nicola Crowther, Trustee, PO Box 166, Ponteland, Newcastle upon Tyne NE20 2BL *Tel.* 0191 488 0520 *Email* info@ballingercharitabletrust.org.uk *Website* www.ballingercharitabletrust.org.uk

■ The Baltic Charitable Fund

CC NO 279194 **ESTABLISHED** 1979

WHERE FUNDING CAN BE GIVEN UK, with a preference for the City of London.

WHO CAN BENEFIT Registered charities; organisations which carry out maritime activities.

WHAT IS FUNDED Education; training; shipping; maritime activities; armed forces.

TYPE OF GRANT One-off and recurrent.

RANGE OF GRANTS £300 to £36,000.

SAMPLE GRANTS Lord Mayor's Appeal, National Maritime Museum (£10,000 each); Sailor's Society (£8,360) Mission to Seafarers and SSAFA (£5,000 each); The Institute of Chartered Shipbrokers (£4,200); Moonwalk, The Royal British Legion Poppy Appeal (£1,000); Challenge Adventure Charities, Ocean Reunion Atlantic Row (£300 each).

FINANCES *Year* 2015/16 *Income* £93,352 *Grants* £57,275 *Grants to organisations* £57,275 *Assets* £2,418,735

TRUSTEE The directors of the Baltic Exchange Ltd.

OTHER INFORMATION The charity also awards grants through the Bonno Krull Fund. This is a separate fund which awarded five grants totalling £7,800.

HOW TO APPLY Unsolicited applications are usually not considered.

WHO TO APPLY TO Clive Weston, Secretary to the Trustee, The Baltic Exchange, 38 St Mary Axe, London EC3A 8BH *Tel.* 020 7623 5501

■ The Bamford Charitable Foundation

CC NO 279848 **ESTABLISHED** 1979

WHERE FUNDING CAN BE GIVEN UK and overseas but mainly within a 40-mile radius of Rocester.

WHO CAN BENEFIT Mainly local organisations.

WHAT IS FUNDED General charitable purposes.

TYPE OF GRANT One-off.

SAMPLE GRANTS Barbados Children's Trust (£250,000); Royal Yacht Squadron (£150,000); Denstone Foundation (£100,000); National Autistic Society (£20,000); Farm Stret Church (£10,000); Reed's School Charity (£7,500); Encompass (£5,000); Macmillan Cancer Support (£3,000); The Milgis Trust (£1,000).

FINANCES *Year* 2015/16 *Income* £58,540 *Grants* £704,341 *Grants to organisations* £704,341 *Assets* £1,164,104

TRUSTEES The Lord Bamford; Lady Bamford.

HOW TO APPLY Apply in writing to the correspondent. The 2015/16 accounts state: 'Successful applicants are required to demonstrate to the trustees that the receipt of the grant is wholly necessary to enable them to fulfil their own objectives.'

WHO TO APPLY TO Steven Ovens, Administrator, c/o J. C. Bamford Excavators Ltd, Lakeside Works, Denstone Road, Rocester, Uttoxeter ST14 5JP *Tel.* 01889 593140

■ The Banbury Charities

CC NO 201418 **ESTABLISHED** 1961
WHERE FUNDING CAN BE GIVEN Banbury and surrounding areas.
WHO CAN BENEFIT Charitable organisations; individuals.
WHAT IS FUNDED General charitable purposes.
TYPE OF GRANT One-off grants.
RANGE OF GRANTS Up to £35,000.
SAMPLE GRANTS Banbury Welfare Trust (£33,000); Banbury Cricket Club (£15,000); Banbury Squadron Air Cadets (£10,000); Dogs for Good (£8,700); The Mill Arts Centre £5,000); Footsteps Foundation (£2,100); See Saw (£2,000); Frank Wise School (£1,500); Banbury Citizens Advice (£1,500); Nicodemus Trust (£1,000).
FINANCES *Year* 2015 *Income* £421,450 *Grants* £333,190 *Grants to organisations* £333,190 *Assets* £5,645,295
TRUSTEES Fred Blackwell; Judy May; Julia Colegrave; Angela Heritage; Nigel Morris; Helen Madeiros; Colin Clarke; Martin Humphris; Jamie Briggs; Kieron Mallon; Valerie Fisher; Tom Blinkhorn.
OTHER INFORMATION There were 273 grants made to individuals totalling £79,000.
HOW TO APPLY Apply in writing to the correspondent.
WHO TO APPLY TO Nigel Yeadon, Clerk to the Trustees, 36 West Bar, Banbury, Oxfordshire OX16 9RU *Tel.* 01295 251234

■ The Band Trust

CC NO 279802 **ESTABLISHED** 1976
WHERE FUNDING CAN BE GIVEN UK.
WHO CAN BENEFIT Registered UK charities.
WHAT IS FUNDED General charitable purposes including: armed forces; children and young people; disability; education; the arts; older people; nursing care.
WHAT IS NOT FUNDED Individuals; political activities commercial ventures or publications; retrospective grants or loans; direct replacement of statutory funding; activities that are primarily the responsibility of central or local government.
TYPE OF GRANT One-off and recurring.
RANGE OF GRANTS £1,000 to £30,000.
SAMPLE GRANTS CLIC Sargent (£30,000); Ambitious About Autism and Breakthrough Breast Cancer (£15,000 each); Resurgo Trust (£12,500); Willow Foundation (£10,000); Cirdan Trust (£7,500); Cleanup UK (£5,000); The Sixteen (£3,000); Barristers' Benevolent Fund (£2,000).
FINANCES *Year* 2015/16 *Income* £956,174 *Grants* £875,777 *Grants to organisations* £875,777 *Assets* £27,351,613
TRUSTEES The Hon. Nicholas Wallop; The Hon. Nicholas Wallop; Richard Mason; Bruce Streather; Victoria Wallop.
HOW TO APPLY **Unsolicited applications are not accepted.** Only make an application if you have been invited to do so. Applicants who have been specifically invited to apply must submit an application and send it to the trustee with whom they have been in contact, together with a copy of their latest report and accounts.
WHO TO APPLY TO Richard Mason, Trustee, The Band Trust, BM BOX 2144, London WC1N 3XX *Tel.* 020 7702 4243 *Email* rjsmason32@gmail.com *Website* www.bandtrust.co.uk

■ The Bank of Scotland Foundation

SC NO SC032942 **ESTABLISHED** 2002
WHERE FUNDING CAN BE GIVEN Scotland.
WHO CAN BENEFIT OSCR registered charities.
WHAT IS FUNDED Developing and improving local communities; financial literacy and financial inclusion.
WHAT IS NOT FUNDED Discriminatory or political organisations; religion; animal charities; medical research; organisations that redistribute funding for subsequent grant-making to other organisations and/or individuals; individuals; advertising; sponsorship.
RANGE OF GRANTS The foundation operates the following programmes: small grants (£1,000 to £10,000); medium grants (£10,000 to £25,000); large grants (£50,000 to £100,000).
SAMPLE GRANTS Quarriers (£98,000); Financial Fitness Resource Team (£63,000); Signpost (£22,000); YMCA Edinburgh (£20,000); Lothian Community Transport Services (£11,300); Music in Hospitals (£8,300); The DASH Club (Gardening Leave (£5,000); Scottish Chamber Orchestra (£3,000); Craigentinny Lochend Social Centre (£1,000).
FINANCES *Year* 2015 *Income* £2,347,299 *Grants* £1,998,100 *Grants to organisations* £1,998,100 *Assets* £659,553
TRUSTEES Philip Grant; Robin Bulloch; Sarah Deas; Martin Flemming; Donald Gately; Paul Grice.
OTHER INFORMATION The foundation also has a Matched Giving Programme whereby Lloyds Banking Group colleagues can receive matched funding for their charitable activities. Matched funding totalled £808,000 during the year. The 2015 annual accounts state: 'During 2015 the Foundation made 79 grants to developing and improving local communities ranging from £1,000 to £98,218 and nine grants to money advice and financial literacy causes ranging from £3,000 to £62,830.'
HOW TO APPLY Application forms are available from the foundation's website, where detailed criteria and guidelines are also posted. Appeals for small and medium grants can be made once every 12 months and for large grants can be submitted only after two years have passed from the receipt of an award. Unsuccessful organisations should wait one year before trying again. The submission deadlines for each programme may vary – see the website for most up-to-date information.
WHO TO APPLY TO Lorraine O'Neill, Finance and Grants Manager, The Mound, Edinburgh EH1 1YZ *Tel.* 0131 655 2599 *Email* enquiries@bankofscotlandfoundation.co.uk *Website* www.bankofscotlandfoundation.org

■ The Barbers' Company General Charities

CC NO 265579 **ESTABLISHED** 1973
WHERE FUNDING CAN BE GIVEN UK with a preference for London.
WHO CAN BENEFIT Charitable organisations and individuals.
WHAT IS FUNDED General charitable purposes, including medical education and nursing.
RANGE OF GRANTS £1,000 to £60,000.
SAMPLE GRANTS King's College London (£62,000); Royal College of Surgeons (£50,000); Phyllis Tuckwell Hospice (£30,000); Michaela Community School and Treloar Trust (£5,000 each); Spitalfields Music (£2,500); Headway

East London (£2,400); Selfless and Tower Hamlets Parents' Centre (£1,000 each).

FINANCES *Year* 2015/16 *Income* £156,629 *Grants* £223,980 *Grants to organisations* £223,980 *Assets* £1,534,396

TRUSTEE The Barbers Company.

HOW TO APPLY Visit the 'How to Apply' section on the Barbers' Company's website.

WHO TO APPLY TO Col. Peter Durrant, Barber-Surgeons' Hall, 1A Monkwell Square, Wood Street, London EC2Y 5BL *Tel.* 020 7606 0741 *Email* clerk@barberscompany.org *Website* barberscompany.org.uk

■ The Barbour Foundation

CC NO 328081 **ESTABLISHED** 1988

WHERE FUNDING CAN BE GIVEN Mainly Tyne and Wear, Northumberland and South Tyneside.

WHO CAN BENEFIT Local charities and organisations dealing with community welfare, housing and social deprivation. Also supports local branches of national charities.

WHAT IS FUNDED Relief of patients suffering from any form of illness or disease, promotion of research into causes of such illnesses; furtherance of education; preservation of buildings and countryside of environmental, historical or architectural interest; relief of people in need; disaster relief (in England).

WHAT IS NOT FUNDED Requests from outside the geographical area; individual applications, unless backed by a particular charitable organisation; capital grants for building projects.

TYPE OF GRANT Core costs; start-up costs; full project costs. Funding for up to one year will be considered.

RANGE OF GRANTS Up to £200,000 but normally £1,000 to £5,000.

SAMPLE GRANTS North Music Trust (£200,000); Customs House (£50,000); Daft as a Bush (£10,000); Scope (£5,000); Place2Be and YMCA Sunderland (£2,000 each); Salvation Army (£1,500); Whizz-Kidz (£1,200); Pelton Youth Project and Quarriers (£1,000 each).

FINANCES *Year* 2015/16 *Income* £606,652 *Grants* £948,332 *Grants to organisations* £948,332 *Assets* £12,219,879

TRUSTEES Helen Humphrey; Dame Margaret Barbour; Nichola Bellaby.

OTHER INFORMATION In 2015/16 grants were made in the following areas: community welfare; youth/children; medical causes; disability; older people; conservation; heritage/museums; service charities; the arts; housing/ homelessness; maritime; animal welfare; special appeals; education; deprivation.

HOW TO APPLY Applications should be made in writing to Mrs A. Harvey, PO Box 21, Guisborough, Cleveland, TS14 8YH. The application should include full back-up information, a statement of accounts and the official charity number of the applicant.

WHO TO APPLY TO Mrs A. Harvey, PO Box 21, Guisborough, Cleveland TS14 8YH *Tel.* 0191 427 4221 *Email* barbour.foundation@barbour.com

■ The Barcapel Foundation

SC NO SC009211 **ESTABLISHED** 1964

WHERE FUNDING CAN BE GIVEN Mainly Scotland, also other parts of the UK.

WHO CAN BENEFIT Charitable organisations.

WHAT IS FUNDED **Health** – all areas of medicine and healing are supported by the foundation, with a particular interest in complementary and alternative therapies. **Heritage** – the foundation supports our artistic and cultural heritage, especially with reference to the built environment. **Youth** – the foundation supports all areas of development for young people especially those from socially disadvantaged backgrounds.

WHAT IS NOT FUNDED Individual applications for travel or similar; organisations or individuals engaged in promoting religious or political beliefs; applications for funding costs of feasibility studies or similar.

RANGE OF GRANTS Up to £100,000.

SAMPLE GRANTS The Citizens Theatre (£50,000); The Brain Tumor Charity (£30,000); Fetlor Youth Club (£25,000); The Daisy Garland (£22,500); Wee Gardens Project (£17,500); Strongbones Children's Charity (£13,800); Bobath Scotland, Horatio's Garden and Phoenix Safe Harbour (£10,000 each).

FINANCES *Year* 2015 *Income* £139,672 *Grants* £671,870 *Grants to organisations* £671,870 *Assets* £3,864,079

TRUSTEES Robert Wilson; Jed Wilson; Clement Wilson; Niall Scott; Amanda Richards.

HOW TO APPLY Application forms are available from the foundation's website. These should be returned by post with a covering letter and a copy of your annual accounts. In the first instance do not send any additional information. If you have particularly important further documents and information refer to them in the covering letter so the trustees can request them if required. The foundation does not accept applications by email. Application deadlines are posted on the foundation's website.

WHO TO APPLY TO The Trustees, The Mews, Skelmorlie Castle, Skelmorlie, Ayrshire PA17 5EY *Tel.* 01475 521616 *Email* admin@barcapelfoundation.org *Website* www.barcapelfoundation.org

■ Barchester Healthcare Foundation

CC NO 1083272 **ESTABLISHED** 2000

WHERE FUNDING CAN BE GIVEN England, Scotland and Wales.

WHO CAN BENEFIT Individuals and small community groups and charities that support older people (65+) and adults (18+) with disabilities.

WHAT IS FUNDED The foundation favours applications that help improve people's mobility, independence and quality of life.

WHAT IS NOT FUNDED Core/running costs or salaries, or financial support to general projects; indirect services such as help lines, newsletters, leaflets or research; major building projects or large capital projects; training of staff and volunteers.

TYPE OF GRANT One-off costs towards activities, outings, equipment, etc.

RANGE OF GRANTS Up to £5,000.

SAMPLE GRANTS Warwickshire Bears Wheelchair Academy (£2,500); Canterbury Shopmobility (£2,000); Winchester Live at Home (£1,700); Find a Voice and Marches Family Network (£1,500 each) Willow Tree Group (£1,300); Age UK Mid Devon and Dumfries and Galloway Carers Centre (£1,300 each); Oyster Project Charity and Tendering Eldercare (£1,000 each).

FINANCES *Year* 2015 *Income* £200,000 *Grants* £143,280 *Grants to organisations* £58,280 *Assets* £67,000

TRUSTEES David Walden; Dr Jackie Morris; Andrew Cozens; Ann Mackay; Caroline Baker; Kate Mansfield-Loynes; Michael Butler; Dr Pete Calveley.
OTHER INFORMATION Grants were awarded to 100 individuals totalling £85,000.
HOW TO APPLY Application can be made via the foundation's website. A decision usually takes approximately ten weeks from the date of application. All applications supported by Barchester Healthcare staff will be given priority.
WHO TO APPLY TO Grants Management Team, Suite 304, Third Floor, Design Centre East, Chelsea Harbour, London SW10 0XF *Tel.* 0800 328 3328 *Fax* 020 7352 2229 *Email* info@bhcfoundation.org.uk *Website* www.bhcfoundation.org.uk

■ The Barclay Foundation

CC NO 803696 **ESTABLISHED** 1990
WHERE FUNDING CAN BE GIVEN UK.
WHO CAN BENEFIT Registered charities, hospitals, universities and individuals.
WHAT IS FUNDED The charitable objectives of the foundation are to fund: medical research; young people; people with disabilities; individuals who are sick; and disadvantaged people.
TYPE OF GRANT Projects and one-off grants. Some recurrent.
SAMPLE GRANTS Frederick Hugh Trust (£300,000); Nora Doherty Charitable Foundation (£127,500); Thrombosis Research Institute and Weidenfeld Fund (£100,000 each); Duke of Edinburgh's Foundation (£15,000); Cometa Foundation (£10,000); Reina Sophia School of Music (£2,000).
FINANCES *Year* 2016 *Income* £790,496 *Grants* £684,786 *Grants to organisations* £654,786 *Assets* £61,928
TRUSTEES Sir David Barclay; Sir Frederick Barclay; Aidan Barclay; Howard Barclay.
OTHER INFORMATION The amount of grants given to individuals totalled £30,000.
HOW TO APPLY Applications should be in writing, clearly outlining the details of the proposed project, (for medical research, as far as possible in lay terms). The total cost and duration should be stated; also the amount, if any, which has already been raised. Following an initial screening, applications are selected according to their merits, suitability and funds available. Visits are usually made to projects where substantial funds are involved. The foundation welcomes reports as to progress and requires these on the completion of a project.
WHO TO APPLY TO Michael Seal, Administrator, 2nd Floor, 14 St George Street, London W1S 1FE *Tel.* 020 7915 0915 *Email* mseal@ellerman.co.uk

■ The Barham Charitable Trust

CC NO 1129728 **ESTABLISHED** 2009
WHERE FUNDING CAN BE GIVEN UK and worldwide.
WHO CAN BENEFIT Charitable organisations.
WHAT IS FUNDED General charitable purposes.
SAMPLE GRANTS The Funding Network; Humanitarian Support Agency; Imperial College London; Medical Aid Palestinians; Merimma; Reprieve; War on Want.
FINANCES *Year* 2015/16 *Income* £121,630 *Grants* £64,390 *Grants to organisations* £64,390 *Assets* £39,980
TRUSTEES Dr John Barham; Dr Eugenia Metaxa-Barham; Coutts & Co.
HOW TO APPLY Apply in writing to the correspondent.
WHO TO APPLY TO The Trustees, Coutts & Co., 440 Strand, London WC2R 0QS *Tel.* 020 7663 6825 *Email* couttscharities@coutts.com

■ The Baring Foundation

CC NO 258583 **ESTABLISHED** 1969
WHERE FUNDING CAN BE GIVEN UK and overseas (UK charities working with NGO partners in financially developing countries), with a special interest in London, Merseyside, Cornwall and Devon.
WHO CAN BENEFIT Charitable organisations; UK charities working with NGO partners in financially developing countries.
WHAT IS FUNDED **Arts** – engaging the talent, experience and enthusiasm of older people in the creative arts; **International development** – leaving no one behind, challenging discrimination and disadvantage; **Strengthening the voluntary sector** – supporting the use of the law and human rights based approaches.
RANGE OF GRANTS Up to £494,500.
SAMPLE GRANTS STVS Advice Provider programme (£494,500); STVS Advice Strategic grants (£290,000); Africa Educational Trust and Arts Council England (£250,000 each); Arts Council Northern Ireland (£150,000); StreetInvest (£131,000); Youth Access (£100,000); Public Law Project (£80,000); Advice UK (£56,000); Comic Relief (£50,000); Anti Trafficking and Labour Exploitation Unit (£30,00); Cambridge House (£24,000); Centre for Mental Health (£20,000); Fair Money Advice (£17,000); Voluntary Arts Network (£10,000); ABF The Soldiers' Charity and Protimos Educational Trust (£5,000 each); Spinal Research (£2,500); Women and Children First (£2,000); Winston Churchill Memorial Trust (£750).
FINANCES *Year* 2015 *Income* £869,786 *Grants* £1,105,624 *Grants to organisations* £1,105,624 *Assets* £69,055,042
TRUSTEES David Elliott; Dr Robert Berkeley; Amanda Jordan; Mark Baring; Myles Wickstead; Katherine Garrett-Cox; Shauneen Lambe; Janet Morrison; Andrew Hind; Lucy de Groot; Dr Dhananjayan Sriskandarajah; Edward Brown; Marie Staunton; Francois Matarasso.
HOW TO APPLY Check the foundation's website for the latest information on open programmes.
WHO TO APPLY TO David Cutler, Director, 8–10 Moorgate, London EC2R 6DA *Tel.* 020 7767 1348 *Email* baring.foundation@uk.ing.com *Website* www.baringfoundation.org.uk

■ The Philip Barker Charity

CC NO 1000227 **ESTABLISHED** 1990
WHERE FUNDING CAN BE GIVEN Cheshire.
WHO CAN BENEFIT Registered charities and community organisations.
WHAT IS FUNDED Young people; community development; medical causes.
TYPE OF GRANT Principally one-off grants. Will consider contribution towards recurring costs, core costs, and projects. Funding is available for up to two years.
SAMPLE GRANTS Manchester Camerata (£18,000); Chester Zoological Society (£15,000); Chester Performs (£15,000); Youth Federation (£12,000).
FINANCES *Year* 2014/15 *Income* £51,317 *Grants* £74,000 *Grants to organisations* £74,000 *Assets* £1,484,985
TRUSTEES Lady Burton; Sir Edmund Burton; Janet Groves; Terry Groves.

OTHER INFORMATION The 2014/15 accounts were the latest available at the time of writing (May 2017).
HOW TO APPLY Apply in writing to the correspondent.
WHO TO APPLY TO Lady Burton, Trustee, Bay Tree Cottage, Barbary Close, South Cheriton, Templecombe BA8 0BG *Tel.* 07967 204685

■ The Barker-Mill Memorial Foundation

CC NO 1045479 **ESTABLISHED** 1995
WHERE FUNDING CAN BE GIVEN The south west of Hampshire, including Southampton.
WHO CAN BENEFIT Charitable organisations; local groups; schools; individuals.
WHAT IS FUNDED General charitable purposes, including: education; health; performing arts and culture; sport and leisure; and animal welfare.
WHAT IS NOT FUNDED Only in exceptional circumstances does the foundation make donations to national charities.
TYPE OF GRANT One-off donations of up to £5,000.
RANGE OF GRANTS Generally up to £5,000.
SAMPLE GRANTS A Space' Arts (£100,000); Sussex House School (£41,000); Tate (£12,000); Lymington Museum Trust (£7,500); Winchester Cathedral Trust (£5,000); English National Ballet School (£4,000); Wessex Chalk Stream and Rivers Trust (£2,500); Community First New Forest (£1,000); Team Fusion Netball (£500); New Milton Hedgehog Rescue (£400).
FINANCES *Year* 2015/16 *Income* £76,517 *Grants* £307,133 *Grants to organisations* £307,133 *Assets* £3,096,052
TRUSTEES Christopher Gwyn-Evans; Tim Jobling; Richard Moyse.
OTHER INFORMATION Around 60 grants were awarded during the year.
HOW TO APPLY Applications should be made through the foundation's website. Guidelines are also available on the site. The trustees meet quarterly to consider applications.
WHO TO APPLY TO Christopher Gwyn-Evans, Trustee, The Estate Office, Longdown, Marchwood, Southampton SO40 4UH *Tel.* 023 8029 2107 *Email* info@barkermillfoundation.com *Website* www.barkermillfoundation.com

■ Lord Barnby's Foundation

CC NO 251016 **ESTABLISHED** 1966
WHERE FUNDING CAN BE GIVEN UK.
WHO CAN BENEFIT Registered charities.
WHAT IS FUNDED General charitable purposes.
WHAT IS NOT FUNDED Individuals.
TYPE OF GRANT One-off and recurrent.
RANGE OF GRANTS Grants range from £500 to £10,000; however, the awards are generally for £1,000 to £2,000.
SAMPLE GRANTS Canine Partners (£10,000); RAF Benevolent Fund (£5,000); Bradford Sea Scouts (£3,000); Antibiotic Research (£2,500); Durham Cathedral (£2,000); Motability and One in a Million (£1,000 each); The Elephant Family (£750); The Keppleway Project (£500); Send a Cow (£250).
FINANCES *Year* 2015/16 *Income* £234,303 *Grants* £227,799 *Grants to organisations* £227,799 *Assets* £6,023,801
TRUSTEES Hon. George Lopes; Countess Peel; Sir Michael Farquhar; Algy Smith-Maxwell; Laura Greenall.
HOW TO APPLY Applications will only be considered if received in writing accompanied by a set of the latest accounts.
WHO TO APPLY TO Jane Lethbridge, Secretary, PO Box 71, Yealmpton, Plymouth PL8 2YP *Email* nlethbridge@btinternet.com

■ The Barnsbury Charitable Trust

CC NO 241383 **ESTABLISHED** 1964
WHERE FUNDING CAN BE GIVEN UK with a strong preference for Oxfordshire.
WHO CAN BENEFIT Charitable organisations.
WHAT IS FUNDED General charitable purposes.
WHAT IS NOT FUNDED Individuals.
RANGE OF GRANTS Up to 10,000.
SAMPLE GRANTS Oxfordshire Historic Churches Trust (£10,000); Home-Start Oxford (£2,500); Landmark Trust (£1,500); Bookfeast and Ucare (£1,000 each); Dalai Lama Centre For Compassion Oxfordshire and Music at Oxford (£500 each); Blackfriars Overseas Aid and Cutteslowe Community Association (£250 each); Oxfordshire Museum (£100); South West Coast Path Association (£25).
FINANCES *Year* 2015/16 *Income* £103,206 *Grants* £97,225 *Grants to organisations* £97,225 *Assets* £3,533,126
TRUSTEES Hugo Brunner; Mary Brunner; Timothy Yates.
OTHER INFORMATION Grants were made to 49 organisations during the year.
HOW TO APPLY Apply in writing to the correspondent.
WHO TO APPLY TO Hugo Brunner, Trustee, 26 Norham Road, Oxford OX2 6SF *Tel.* 01865 316431 *Email* hmrbrunner@gmail.com

■ The Barnwood Trust

CC NO 1162855 **ESTABLISHED** 1972
WHERE FUNDING CAN BE GIVEN Gloucestershire.
WHO CAN BENEFIT Gloucestershire-based charitable organisations and community groups; individuals.
WHAT IS FUNDED Improving the quality of life of people in Gloucestershire with disabilities and mental health challenges. The trust also provides relief of persons in need by providing housing or other accommodation, care nursing and attention. Grants for individuals fall into the categories of either well-being or opportunities. Grants are awarded to organisations providing activities, services, holidays or play schemes to improve the lives of people with disabilities or mental health challenges. Small Sparks grants are given to small groups of people for shared activities which are inclusive of people with disabilities or mental health challenges.
WHAT IS NOT FUNDED People or organisations outside Gloucestershire. Specific exclusions and criteria apply to each of the grants programmes for individuals, as well as the Small Sparks grants, which are published on the trust's website.
TYPE OF GRANT Small grants to organisations and grants to individuals. Project costs, start-up costs, capital costs.
RANGE OF GRANTS Small grants of up to £1,000 for organisations; no limit specified for holidays and play schemes. Individual well-being grants range between £50 and £750, while the average opportunity grant is £850.
SAMPLE GRANTS Consortium of Mental Health Day Support Providers (£305,000); Crossroads Care – Cheltenham and Tewkesbury, Independence Trust and People and Places in Gloucestershire (£30,000 each); Whitefriars Sailing Club

(£27,500); Stroke Association (£25,000); Forest of Dean Citizens Advice and Hop, Skip and Jump (Cotswold) (£18,000 each); Art Shape Ltd, Barnwood Residents Association and Watershed Riding for the Disabled (£10,000 each).

FINANCES *Year* 2015 *Income* £2,717,284 *Grants* £515,813 *Grants to organisations* £184,075

TRUSTEES James Davidson; Sally Pullen; Annabella Scott; Lucy Floyer-Acland; Michael North; Prof. Clair Chilvers; Dr Jean Waters; Suzanne Beech; Shaun Parson; Rachel Robinson.

OTHER INFORMATION Note that the financial information in this entry relates to the Barnwood House Trust (Charity Commission no. 218401) whose assets were transferred to the Barnwood Trust on 1 October 2015.

HOW TO APPLY Application forms are available to download from the trust's website. For any queries or to talk through your idea before applying, contact Gail Rodway, Grants Manager, on 01452 611292 or email gail.rodway@barnwoodtrust.org. More specific information about applying for village hall adaptations or individual grants are given on the trust's website.

WHO TO APPLY TO Gail Rodway, Head of Grants, Ullenwood Manor Farm, Ullenwood, Cheltenham GL53 9QT *Tel.* 01452 611292 *Email* gail.rodway@barnwoodtrust.org *Website* www.barnwoodtrust.org

■ The Barrack Charitable Trust

SC NO SC040677 **ESTABLISHED** 2009

WHERE FUNDING CAN BE GIVEN UK.

WHO CAN BENEFIT Registered charities.

WHAT IS FUNDED Education; Christian causes; community development; art and science; recreational facilities.

RANGE OF GRANTS Up to £10,000.

SAMPLE GRANTS Robert Gordon University Foundation (£10,000); Business in the Community (£9,200); Archie Foundation, Camphill Wellbeing Trust, Edinburgh Printmakers, Hopscotch Children's Charity, Prince and Princess of Wales Hospice; St John's Church Development (£5,000 each).

FINANCES *Year* 2015/16 *Income* £96,625 *Grants* £96,625 *Grants to organisations* £96,625 *Assets* £596,005

TRUSTEES James Barrack; Louise Barrack; Robert Anderson.

OTHER INFORMATION There were 35 grants made during the year.

HOW TO APPLY Application forms can be downloaded from the trust's website and should be returned by post.

WHO TO APPLY TO Pamela Bryce, Burnbrae, 25A Rubislaw Den North, Aberdeen AB15 4AL *Email* trust@barrack.org *Website* thebarrackcharitabletrust.co.uk

■ Misses Barrie Charitable Trust

CC NO 279459 **ESTABLISHED** 1979

WHERE FUNDING CAN BE GIVEN UK.

WHO CAN BENEFIT Registered charities.

WHAT IS FUNDED General charitable purposes in particular medical/health causes.

WHAT IS NOT FUNDED Individuals.

TYPE OF GRANT Mainly one-off.

RANGE OF GRANTS Average £1,000 to £5,000.

SAMPLE GRANTS East Neuk Festival (£25,000); V&A Museum of Design – Dundee (£15,000); Scottish Opera (£3,500); Abbotsford Trust and Sistema Scotland (£3,000 each); The National Piping Centre (£2,500); Alzheimer Scotland and Brain Research Trust (£2,000 each); Music in Hospitals (£1,500); Action for Kids and Move On (£1,000 each).

FINANCES *Year* 2015/16 *Income* £246,181 *Grants* £211,250 *Grants to organisations* £211,250 *Assets* £6,132,539

TRUSTEES John Carter; Robin Ogg; Rachel Fraser; Sally Abell.

HOW TO APPLY Apply in writing to the correspondent accompanied by up-to-date accounts or financial information. The trustees are not able to notify unsuccessful applicants.

WHO TO APPLY TO The Trustees, Raymond Carter and Co., 14A High Street, Reigate, Surrey RH2 9AY *Tel.* 01737 248065 *Email* charlotte@raymondcarter.co.uk

■ Robert Barr's Charitable Trust

SC NO SC007613 **ESTABLISHED** 1970

WHERE FUNDING CAN BE GIVEN Scotland and overseas.

WHO CAN BENEFIT Charities; CICs; schools.

WHAT IS FUNDED General charitable purposes.

TYPE OF GRANT The trustees tend to favour capital projects rather than running costs.

RANGE OF GRANTS £1,000 to £50,000.

SAMPLE GRANTS Citizens Theatre (£50,000); Cancer Research UK (£30,000); Revive MS Support (£20,000); Dundonnell Mountain Rescue Team (£15,000); Canine Partners (£10,000); Paws for Progress CIC (£7,500); Clyde River Foundation and Stonehaven Sea Cadets (£5,000 each); Borders Children's Charity (£3,000); Inverclyde Amateur Swimming Club (£1,000).

FINANCES *Year* 2015/16 *Income* £671,952 *Grants* £556,500 *Grants to organisations* £556,500 *Assets* £1,161,309

HOW TO APPLY Apply in writing to the correspondent using the reference Ref: SMG/AIG/BAR/352/1. The trustees meet in March to consider applications. If you have not received a donation by the end of May then your application has not been successful.

WHO TO APPLY TO Sandra Graham, Maclay Murray and Spens, 1 George Square, Glasgow G2 1AL *Website* www.mms.co.uk/What-We-Do/Practice-Groups/Private-Client-and-Charities/Private-Client-Charities-List

■ The Bartlett Taylor Charitable Trust

CC NO 285249 **ESTABLISHED** 1982

WHERE FUNDING CAN BE GIVEN West Oxfordshire.

WHO CAN BENEFIT Registered charities; individuals (social welfare and education).

WHAT IS FUNDED Medical causes; social welfare; international appeals.

RANGE OF GRANTS £100 to £1,000.

SAMPLE GRANTS There was no list of beneficiaries available.

FINANCES *Year* 2015/16 *Income* £88,238 *Grants* £51,475 *Grants to organisations* £46,080 *Assets* £2,273,588

TRUSTEES Richard Bartlett; Gareth Alty; Katherine Bradley; Brenda Cook; James W. Dingle; Rosemary Warner; Ms S. Boyd; Jonathan Smith.

HOW TO APPLY Applications can be made via the trust's website. The trustees meet six times per year.

WHO TO APPLY TO Gareth Alty, Trustee, John Welch and Stammers Solicitors, 24 Church Green,

Witney, Oxfordshire OX28 4AT *Tel.* 01993 703941 *Email* info@btctrust.org.uk *Website* www.btctrust.org.uk

■ The Paul Bassham Charitable Trust

CC NO 266842 **ESTABLISHED** 1973
WHERE FUNDING CAN BE GIVEN UK with strong preference for Norfolk.
WHO CAN BENEFIT UK-registered charities.
WHAT IS FUNDED General charitable purposes. Preference given to Norfolk charitable causes.
WHAT IS NOT FUNDED Individuals; unregistered organisations.
SAMPLE GRANTS Norfolk Theatre Royal Trust (£30,000); Norfolk Community Foundation (£25,000); Norwich Hebrew Congregation (£10,000); Norfolk and Norwich Scope Association, Centre 81, Eagle Canoe Club and Sea Scouts (£10,000 each).
FINANCES *Year* 2015/16 *Income* £382,961 *Grants* £530,190 *Grants to organisations* £530,190 *Assets* £11,534,592
TRUSTEES Alexander Munro; Richard Lovett; Graham Tuttle; Patrick Harris.
HOW TO APPLY Only in writing to the correspondent. The trustees meet quarterly to consider general applications.
WHO TO APPLY TO Richard Lovett, Trustee, c/o Howes Percival, The Guildyard, 51 Colegate, Norwich NR3 1DD *Tel.* 01603 762103

■ The Batchworth Trust

CC NO 245061 **ESTABLISHED** 1965
WHERE FUNDING CAN BE GIVEN UK and overseas.
WHO CAN BENEFIT Major UK and international charities.
WHAT IS FUNDED General charitable purposes including: health; and social welfare.
WHAT IS NOT FUNDED Individuals.
RANGE OF GRANTS Up to £110,000 but generally £1,000 to £25,000.
SAMPLE GRANTS Cancer Research UK (£110,000); Murray Edwards College and Nepal Earthquake Appeal (£50,000 each); Street Child (£25,000); Sunama (£18,500); Cambridge House (£15,000); Age UK (£10,000); Friends of Plockton Music School (£7,500); Oxford Hub (£5,000).
FINANCES *Year* 2015/16 *Income* £948,961 *Grants* £762,000 *Grants to organisations* £762,000 *Assets* £12,475,032
TRUSTEE Lockwell Trustees Ltd.
OTHER INFORMATION Grants were made to 55 charities during the year.
HOW TO APPLY Apply in writing to the correspondent. An sae should be included if a reply is required.
WHO TO APPLY TO James Peach, Administrative Executive, Kreston Reeves LLP, Griffin House, 135 High Street, Crawley RH10 1DQ *Tel.* 01209 377 615 *Email* james.peach@krestonreeves.com

■ The Battens Charitable Trust

CC NO 293500 **ESTABLISHED** 1985
WHERE FUNDING CAN BE GIVEN Dorset; Somerset; Wiltshire.
WHO CAN BENEFIT Registered charities and local organisations.
WHAT IS FUNDED General charitable purposes.
RANGE OF GRANTS Mostly up to £5,000.
SAMPLE GRANTS Dorset Wildlife Trust (£13,500); LV Streetwise Safety Centre (£10,000); Citizens Advice, Dorset and Somerset Air Ambulance and RSPB (£5,000 each).
FINANCES *Year* 2015/16 *Income* £19,658 *Grants* £60,000 *Grants to organisations* £60,000
TRUSTEES Rupert Vaughan; Stuart Allen; Raymond Edwards; Robert Randall.
OTHER INFORMATION This charity's latest accounts were not available to view on the Charity Commission's website due to its low income. We have therefore estimated the grant total based on previous years' information.
HOW TO APPLY Apply in writing to the correspondent.
WHO TO APPLY TO Kelly Payne, c/o Battens Solicitors, Mansion House, 54–58 Princes Street, Yeovil, Somerset BA20 1EP *Tel.* 01935 846237 *Email* kelly.payne@battens.co.uk

■ The Battersea Power Station Foundation

CC NO 1161232 **ESTABLISHED** 2014
WHERE FUNDING CAN BE GIVEN Lambeth and Wandsworth.
WHO CAN BENEFIT Constituted groups that have a charitable purpose, such as registered charities, CICs, CIOs, non-profits, voluntary or community groups, social enterprises and resident associations. Non-registered charities will need to provide a written constitution.
WHAT IS FUNDED General charitable purposes; community development.
WHAT IS NOT FUNDED The website notes that the foundation does not fund: 'individuals or causes that will benefit only one person, including student grants or bursaries; general and round-robin appeals; promotion of religion and places of worship; replacement or subsidy of statutory funding, or for work we consider should be funded by government, such as residential and day care, housing provision, individual schools, nurseries and colleges, or a combination of any of these; individual campaigns; organisations seeking to distribute grants or funds to others; capital developments and individual items of equipment; one-off events, such as conferences, seminars, galas, or summer schools; educational initiatives linked to the national curriculum; medical research or treatment, including drug and alcohol rehabilitation services; counselling and psychotherapy services; animal welfare, zoos, captive breeding and animal rescue centres; retrospective funding, meaning support for work that has already taken place; work that is not legally charitable; organisations who have applied unsuccessfully within the previous 12-months'.
TYPE OF GRANT One-off. Revenue costs.
RANGE OF GRANTS Up to £5,000.
SAMPLE GRANTS Battersea Arts Centre (£100,000).
FINANCES *Year* 2015 *Income* £224,500 *Grants* £100,000 *Grants to organisations* £100,000 *Assets* £41,690
TRUSTEES Marquess of Salisbury Robert Michael James Gascoyne Cecil; Right Hon. Lord Strathclyde; Dato' Ir Jauhari Hamidi.
HOW TO APPLY Applications can be made through the foundation's website. Applicants should first complete the eligibility test and they will then be sent a link to the application page.

WHO TO APPLY TO Barbra Mazur, 188 Kirting Street, London SW8 5BN *Tel.* 020 7501 0715 *Email* info@bpsfoundation.org.uk *Website* bpsfoundation.org.uk

■ Bauer Radio's Cash for Kids Charities

CC NO 1122062 **ESTABLISHED** 2007

WHERE FUNDING CAN BE GIVEN 22 areas around the UK where Bauer Radio have a local radio station.

WHO CAN BENEFIT Registered charities.

WHAT IS FUNDED Children and young people under the age of 18.

WHAT IS NOT FUNDED Generally the charity will not fund the following: salaries/volunteer expenses; home improvements (windows and doors/ extensions); holidays abroad for families; furniture that will not be used specifically by children; school trips abroad; general operational costs; televisions; rent/rates for premises; driving lessons for parents/carers; medical treatment abroad; PTAs; sporting events for individuals to participate in; CICs. See your local radio's website for specific exclusions in your area.

TYPE OF GRANT Equipment and project costs.

SAMPLE GRANTS A list of beneficiaries was not available.

FINANCES *Year* 2015 *Income* £13,636,627 *Grants* £11,775,262 *Grants to organisations* £11,775,262 *Assets* £2,057,965

TRUSTEES Sally Aitchison; Martin Ball; Mark Mahaffy; Sean Marley; Owen Ryan; Danny Simpson.

OTHER INFORMATION This is the corporate umbrella charity for Bauer Radio who own radio stations in 22 areas of the UK. Each station has its own charity and operates a grant-making strategy to benefit children in the local area. A full list of the types of causes that the local charities have made grants to is listed in the accounts. The charity prefers to make a large amount of one-off small donation; however, the amount varies from station to station.

HOW TO APPLY To apply for a grant, first visit the locations page of the charity's website to find your local radio station and grant team. Application forms, eligibility criteria and deadlines are available on the local websites. The charity encourages you to discuss your application with your local grant team.

WHO TO APPLY TO Tracey Butler, Company Secretary, Hampdon House, Unit 3 Falcon Court, Preston Farm, Stockton-on-Tees TS18 3TS *Tel.* 01642 675788 *Email* tracey.butler@bauermedia.co.uk *Website* www.cashforkids.uk.com

■ Bay Charitable Trust

CC NO 1060537 **ESTABLISHED** 1997

WHERE FUNDING CAN BE GIVEN UK and overseas.

WHO CAN BENEFIT Jewish organisations.

WHAT IS FUNDED The latest annual report states: 'The objectives of the charity are to give charity for the relief of poverty and the advancement of traditions of the Orthodox Jewish Religion and the study of Torah.'

SAMPLE GRANTS A list of beneficiaries was not available.

FINANCES *Year* 2015 *Income* £558,000 *Grants* £629,271 *Grants to organisations* £629,271 *Assets* £303,871

TRUSTEES Ian Kreditor; Michael Lisser.

OTHER INFORMATION The grant total includes awards made to individuals.

HOW TO APPLY Apply in writing to the correspondent.

WHO TO APPLY TO Ian Kreditor, Trustee, 21 Woodlands Close, London NW11 9QR *Tel.* 020 8810 4321

■ The Bay Tree Charitable Trust

CC NO 1044091 **ESTABLISHED** 1994

WHERE FUNDING CAN BE GIVEN UK and overseas.

WHO CAN BENEFIT Charitable organisations.

WHAT IS FUNDED General charitable purposes including: development work; health social welfare.

WHAT IS NOT FUNDED Individuals.

RANGE OF GRANTS £5,000 to £40,000.

SAMPLE GRANTS British Red Cross (£40,000); Médecins Sans Frontières UK (£15,000); Alzheimer's Researck UK and Combat Stress (£10,000 each); Carers Trust, Friends of the Earth, Salvation Army and The Rainforest Foundation UK (£5,000 each).

FINANCES *Year* 2015 *Income* £156,117 *Grants* £130,000 *Grants to organisations* £130,000 *Assets* £4,141,375

TRUSTEES Ian Benton; Emma Benton; Paul Benton.

OTHER INFORMATION Grants were made to 15 organisations during the year.

HOW TO APPLY All appeals should be by letter containing the following: aims and objectives of the charity; nature of appeal; total target if for a specific project; contributions received against target; registered charity number; any other relevant factors. Letters should be accompanied by a set of the charitable organisation's latest report and full accounts.

WHO TO APPLY TO The Trustees, PO Box 53983, London SW15 1VT

■ The Louis Baylis (Maidenhead Advertiser) Charitable Trust

CC NO 210533 **ESTABLISHED** 1962

WHERE FUNDING CAN BE GIVEN UK but mainly Berkshire, Buckinghamshire and Oxfordshire, with a preference for Maidenhead.

WHO CAN BENEFIT Local, regional and national charities.

WHAT IS FUNDED General charitable purposes with a preference for older people and young people.

WHAT IS NOT FUNDED Individuals.

SAMPLE GRANTS Alexander Divine Children's Charity Trust (£100,000); Cash for Schools (£20,000); Maidenhead Heritage Trust (£6,000); Maidenhead Mencap and Relate (£4,000 each); Beating Bowel Cancer and Target Ovarian Cancer (£2,000); Vitalise (£1,000); Dementia Care Nurses (£750); Berkshire Women's Cricket (£500); Reading Myeloma Support Group (£300).

FINANCES *Year* 2015/16 *Income* £3,876,049 *Grants* £360,868 *Grants to organisations* £360,868 *Assets* £14,282,064

TRUSTEES Peter Murcott; Peter Sands; John Robertson; Patricia Lattimer.

HOW TO APPLY Application forms are available to download on the website and should be returned to the trust by email or post.

WHO TO APPLY TO Peter Murcott, Hale and Co. LLP, Belmont Place, Belmont Road, Maidenhead Sl6 6TB *Tel.* 01628 626333 *Email* lbctrust@baylismedia.co.uk *Website* www.baylis-trust.org.uk

■ BBC Children in Need

CC NO 802052 **ESTABLISHED** 1989

WHERE FUNDING CAN BE GIVEN UK (including the Channel Islands and the Isle of Man).

WHO CAN BENEFIT Voluntary projects; community groups; registered charities; not-for-profit organisations; churches; schools.

WHAT IS FUNDED Children and young people under the age of 18 experiencing disadvantage through illness, distress, abuse or neglect, any kind of disability, behavioural or psychological difficulties, are living in poverty or experiencing situations of deprivation. The charity's vision is 'that every child in the UK has a safe, happy and secure childhood and the chance to reach their potential'. The charity offers support through: Main Grants Programme (over £10,000 a year for up to three years); Small Grants Programme (up to £10,000 a year for one year); Emergency Essentials (administered on behalf of Buttle UK 'to meet the most basic needs of children and young people living with acute poverty and deprivation', grants are available to individuals and families).

WHAT IS NOT FUNDED Funding is not given: for work which statutory bodies (such as schools or local authorities) have a duty to fund; to local government or NHS bodies; for building projects requiring more than £20,000 from the charity; for projects which promote religion; to fund trips or projects abroad; for medical treatment or research; for pregnancy testing or advice, information or counselling on pregnancy choices; for awareness-raising work, except where it is targeted at those children or young people most at risk; for bursaries, sponsored places, fees or equivalent; to individuals (unless an eligible organisation is applying on their behalf or through the Emergency Essentials Programme); to be passed on to other organisations, for example, PTAs applying on behalf of schools; for general appeals or endowment funds; to help with budget shortfalls or debt repayments; to projects where the grant expenditure is due to start before the grant award date (retrospective funding); to organisations which have applied in the last 12 months; to projects unable to start within 12 months of the grant award date; for unspecified expenditure; for organisational overheads or running costs which the organisation would incur whether the project was running or not (although funding support costs incurred as a direct result of running the project will be considered).

TYPE OF GRANT Capital expenditure; projects; salaries; recurrent grants; project-related core expenditure but not the organisation running costs.

RANGE OF GRANTS Generally up to £100,000 for main grants and up to £10,000 for small grants.

SAMPLE GRANTS Children 1st (£132,500); Stable Life (£121,000); Active Luton (£29,000); Chillax (£10,000); Beaver Arts Ltd (£9,100); Pembrokeshire People First (£3,900); Buxton and District Summer Club (£2,500). A full list of beneficiaries for each region can be found on the charity's website.

FINANCES *Year* 2015/16 *Income* £64,829,000 *Grants* £51,447,000 *Grants to organisations* £51,447,000 *Assets* £80,778,000

TRUSTEES Phil Hodkinson; Charlotte Moore; Peter McBride; Steve Spring; Anne Bulford; Bob Shennan; Luke Mayhew; Donalda Mackinnon; Gillian Sheldon; Matthew Baker; Joanna Berry.

OTHER INFORMATION During the year £51.4 million was awarded in grants of which £48.9 million related to responsive funding of 1,342 projects. A further £2.3 million was awarded to 8,943 individuals through the Emergency Essentials programme. Grant funding was geographically distributed as follows: England (73%); Scotland (10%); Northern Ireland (7%); Wales (6%); UK-wide grants (4%).

HOW TO APPLY Applications can be made via the charity's website which also has details of guidelines and application deadlines. If you have a general enquiry, are unsure about anything you have read or are looking for support regarding your application contact the charity via phone or email. You can also contact your local regional or national office. All applicants to the main grants programme need to complete an 'Initial Application' form. After this assessment successful applicants are invited to make a full application. Decisions are usually made within five months, some applicants will hear much sooner if they are not going to get a grant. For applications to the Small Grants Programme there are four application dates throughout the year with a shortened period of consideration.

WHO TO APPLY TO Simon Antrobus, Chief Executive, Grants, BBC Children in Need, PO Box 649, Salford M5 0LD *Tel.* 0345 609 0015 *Email* pudseygrants@bbc.co.uk *Website* www.bbc.co.uk/pudsey

■ BC Partners Foundation

CC NO 1136956 **ESTABLISHED** 2010

WHERE FUNDING CAN BE GIVEN UK.

WHO CAN BENEFIT Registered charities in the UK and worldwide.

WHAT IS FUNDED Community development; conservation of the environment; arts and education.

RANGE OF GRANTS Up to £100,000.

SAMPLE GRANTS Private Equity Foundation (£103,000); American School in London Foundation (£50,000); Over the Wall (£23,000) I Right to Play (£14,000); Wildlife Heritage Trust (£10,000); Serious Fun Children's Network (£8,500); Pro Bono Economics (£5,000); Opera North (£2,500); Jo's Trust (£1,000).

FINANCES *Year* 2015 *Income* £634,112 *Grants* £542,912 *Grants to organisations* £542,912 *Assets* £614,687

TRUSTEES Nikos Stathopolous; Joseph Cronley; Lorna Parker; Michael Pritchard; Richard Kunzer; Cedric Dubourdieu; Francesco Loredan.

OTHER INFORMATION This is the foundation of private equity firm BC Partners.

HOW TO APPLY The foundation does not accept unsolicited applications – charities must be nominated by BC Partners employees or trustees of the foundation.

WHO TO APPLY TO The Trustees, BC Partners Ltd, 40 Portman Square, London W1H 6DA *Tel.* 020 7009 4800 *Email* bcpfoundation@bcpartners.com *Website* www.bcpartners.com/about-us/bcp-foundation.aspx

■ BCH Trust

CC NO 1138652 **ESTABLISHED** 2010

WHERE FUNDING CAN BE GIVEN Manchester and surrounding areas.

WHO CAN BENEFIT Schools and higher education institutions.

WHAT IS FUNDED General charitable purposes with a stated interest in education, social welfare, the Jewish faith and disability.

SAMPLE GRANTS Manchester Senior Girls School (£47,500); Chesed L 'Yisroel (£15,500); Prestwich Cost Shop (£1,000).
FINANCES *Year* 2014/15 *Income* £88,312 *Grants* £66,813 *Grants to organisations* £66,813 *Assets* £220,024
TRUSTEES Benny Stone; Charles Bernstein; Yossef Bowden.
HOW TO APPLY Apply in writing to the correspondent.
WHO TO APPLY TO Benny Stone, Trustee, 59 Kings Road, Prestwich, Manchester M25 0LQ *Tel.* 0161 773 0512 *Email* mail@bchtrust.org

■ Bear Mordechai Ltd

CC NO 286806 **ESTABLISHED** 1982
WHERE FUNDING CAN BE GIVEN Worldwide.
WHO CAN BENEFIT Jewish charities.
WHAT IS FUNDED Individuals, small local projects and national organisations benefitting Jewish people.
TYPE OF GRANT One-off and recurrent costs.
SAMPLE GRANTS Chochmas Lev (£40,000); Hod Yerushlaim (£31,000); Pinebent (£21,000); Tzedaka Vchesed (£15,000); Inspiration (£5,000); Tevini (£3,200); SOFT (Support Organisation for Trisomy) (£4,000); Kollel Penina Lev (£2,000); KEF Manchester (£1,000); Talmud Torah Gur (£500).
FINANCES *Year* 2015/16 *Income* £385,077 *Grants* £166,943 *Grants to organisations* £166,943 *Assets* £475,085
TRUSTEES Chaim Benedikt; Eliezer Benedikt; Yechiel Benedikt.
OTHER INFORMATION Grants were made to 21 organisations during the year.
HOW TO APPLY Apply in writing to the correspondent.
WHO TO APPLY TO Yechiel Benedikt, Trustee, 40 Fountayne Road, London N16 7DT *Email* DP.WHITESIDE@GMAIL.COM

■ The Bearder Charity

CC NO 1010529 **ESTABLISHED** 1992
WHERE FUNDING CAN BE GIVEN Calderdale.
WHO CAN BENEFIT Registered charities and individuals.
WHAT IS FUNDED Social welfare.
RANGE OF GRANTS Up to £5,000.
SAMPLE GRANTS Calderdale Smart Move (£3,000); Macmillan Cancer Support (£2,000); Alpha House (£1,500); Alzheimer's Society, Eureka Children's Museum, Illingworth Cricket Club (£1,000 each); Waring Green Community Association (£500); Sowerby Bridge Fire and Water (£250).
FINANCES *Year* 2015/16 *Income* £129,850 *Grants* £193,414 *Grants to organisations* £55,752 *Assets* £3,552,156
TRUSTEES Leyland Smith; Trevor Simpson; Richard Smithies; Brendan Mowforth; David Normanton.
OTHER INFORMATION Grants were made to 49 organisations during the year. The amount of grants given to individuals totalled £137,500.
HOW TO APPLY Apply in writing to the correspondent, detailing requirements and costings. Trustee board meetings are held six times a year.
WHO TO APPLY TO Richard Smithies, Trustee, 5 King Street, Brighouse, West Yorkshire HD6 1NX *Tel.* 01484 710571 *Email* bearders@btinternet.com

■ The James Beattie Charitable Trust

CC NO 265654 **ESTABLISHED** 1961
WHERE FUNDING CAN BE GIVEN Wolverhampton area.
WHO CAN BENEFIT Local projects and organisations, hospitals, churches and schools benefitting the people of Wolverhampton.
WHAT IS FUNDED General charitable purposes.
WHAT IS NOT FUNDED Individuals; organisations outside the West Midlands; exclusive organisations (e.g. all-white or all-Asian groups).
TYPE OF GRANT Grants awarded for capital, project funding and revenue costs. Grants may be one-off or recurring and funding for a single project may be available for less than one year to more than three.
SAMPLE GRANTS Barnardo's, James Beattie House; Cottage Homes; Marie Curie Cancer Care; St Chad's – Pattingham; St Martin's School; Whizz-Kidz; Wolverhampton Grammar School; YMCA.
FINANCES *Year* 2015/16 *Income* £75,639 *Grants* £135,475 *Grants to organisations* £135,475 *Assets* £3,273,285
TRUSTEES Jane Redshaw; Michael Redshaw; Kenneth Dolman; Susannah Norbury.
HOW TO APPLY Apply in writing to the correspondent, including accounts.
WHO TO APPLY TO The Trustees, PO Box 12, Bridgnorth, Shropshire WV15 5LQ

■ Beauland Ltd

CC NO 511374 **ESTABLISHED** 1981
WHERE FUNDING CAN BE GIVEN Worldwide, with some preference for the Manchester area.
WHO CAN BENEFIT Registered charities; Jewish educational institutions; religious institutions.
WHAT IS FUNDED Advancement of the Orthodox Jewish faith; social welfare.
SAMPLE GRANTS Yeshiva Tifres Yaacov (£50,000); Machnof Belz (£30,000); Chareidim (£20,000); Rabbinical Research College (£12,500).
FINANCES *Year* 2015/16 *Income* £656,262 *Grants* £173,815 *Grants to organisations* £173,815 *Assets* £7,306,548
TRUSTEES Henry Neumann; Pinchas Neumann; Maurice Neumann; Mr Neumann; Esther Henry; Janet Bleier; Miriam Friedlander; Rebecca Delange; Hannah Roseman.
OTHER INFORMATION Grants were distributed as follows: social and relief of poverty (£70,500); education (£62,500); religious institutions (£36,500); general charitable purposes (£4,100).
HOW TO APPLY Apply in writing to the correspondent.
WHO TO APPLY TO Maurice Neumann, Trustee, 32 Stanley Road, Salford M7 4ES

■ The Becht Family Charitable Trust

CC NO 1116657 **ESTABLISHED** 2006
WHERE FUNDING CAN BE GIVEN Worldwide.
WHO CAN BENEFIT Registered charities.
WHAT IS FUNDED Conservation of the natural environment; education; humanitarian aid.
SAMPLE GRANTS Save the Children (£2.6 million); Human Rights Watch (£262,000); Excellent Development and WaterAid (£50,000 each); DKMS Delete Blood Cancer (£32,500); University of Chicago – Booth School (£32,000); Sightsavers (£30,000); Room to Read (£15,000); Covenant Habor Bible Camp (£3,300).

FINANCES *Year* 2014/15 *Income* £4,463,686 *Grants* £3,067,193 *Grants to organisations* £3,067,193 *Assets* £225,407,903
TRUSTEES Lambertus Johannes Hermanus Becht; Ann Marie Becht; Rathbone Trust Company Ltd.
OTHER INFORMATION The 2014/15 accounts were the latest available at the time of writing (June 2017).
HOW TO APPLY Apply in writing to the correspondent.
WHO TO APPLY TO Alex Richmond, Rathbone Trust Company Ltd, 4th Floor, Port of Liverpool Building, Pier Head, Liverpool L3 1NW *Tel.* 0151 236 6666

■ The Becker Family Charitable Trust

CC NO 1047968 **ESTABLISHED** 1995
WHERE FUNDING CAN BE GIVEN Worldwide.
WHO CAN BENEFIT Registered charities.
WHAT IS FUNDED General charitable purposes, particularly Orthodox Jewish causes.
WHAT IS NOT FUNDED Individuals.
SAMPLE GRANTS A list of beneficiaries was not included in the accounts.
FINANCES *Year* 2015/16 *Income* £142,613 *Grants* £102,041 *Grants to organisations* £102,041 *Assets* £664,086
TRUSTEES Allan Becker; Ruth Becker; Deanna Fried; Andrew Guttentag.
HOW TO APPLY Apply in writing to the correspondent. However, note that the trust has previously stated that its funds were fully committed.
WHO TO APPLY TO Allan Becker, Trustee, 33 Sinclair Grove, London NW11 9JH

■ The John Beckwith Charitable Trust

CC NO 800276 **ESTABLISHED** 1987
WHERE FUNDING CAN BE GIVEN UK and overseas.
WHO CAN BENEFIT Registered charities.
WHAT IS FUNDED Art; education; medical research; sport; social welfare.
TYPE OF GRANT Capital, one-off and recurring.
SAMPLE GRANTS Institute of Cancer Research (£250,000); Serpentine Galleries (£70,000); David Ross Foundation (£40,000); Dalliaglo Foundation (£11,000); Médecins Sans Frontières UK (£2,000); Crimestoppers, Facing the World, Shelter and Youth Sport Trust (£1,000 each); IT Schools Africa (£500); Great Ormond Street Hospital (GOSH) (£250).
FINANCES *Year* 2015/16 *Income* £253,451 *Grants* £603,078 *Grants to organisations* £603,078 *Assets* £1,254,824
TRUSTEES Sir John Beckwith; Heather Beckwith; Christopher Meech.
HOW TO APPLY Apply in writing to the correspondent.
WHO TO APPLY TO Sally Holder, 124 Sloane Street, London SW1X 9BW *Tel.* 020 7225 2250 *Email* info@beckwithlondon.com

■ The Bedfordshire and Hertfordshire Historic Churches Trust

CC NO 1005697 **ESTABLISHED** 1991
WHERE FUNDING CAN BE GIVEN Bedfordshire, Hertfordshire and that part of Barnet within the Diocese of St Albans.
WHO CAN BENEFIT Places of active Christian worship.
WHAT IS FUNDED Restoration, repair and development of Christian places of worship.
WHAT IS NOT FUNDED Individuals.
TYPE OF GRANT One-off and buildings. Funding may be given for one year or less.
RANGE OF GRANTS £1,000 to £15,000.
SAMPLE GRANTS St Mary the Virgin – Eaton Bray (£16,000); St Alban – Hemel Hempstead and All Saints – Luton (£10,000 each); St Mary the Virgin – Braughing (£2,500); All Saints – Renhold (£1,500).
FINANCES *Year* 2015/16 *Income* £332,220 *Grants* £152,000 *Grants to organisations* £152,000 *Assets* £328,804
TRUSTEES Stuart Russell; Dr Christopher Green; Richard Genochio; Judith Howard; William Marsterson; Jim May; Kevin Macan-Lind; Nico Rodenburg; Madeline Russell.
OTHER INFORMATION Annual income comes from member subscription and from the annual Bike 'n Hike event. The trust also acts as a distributive agent for church grants made by the Wixamtree Trust.
HOW TO APPLY Initial enquiries should be made to the Grants Secretary. Applications can only be made by members of the trust.
WHO TO APPLY TO Archie Russell, Grants Secretary and Trustee, Wychbrook, 31 Ivel Gardens, Biggleswade, Bedfordshire SG18 0AN *Tel.* 01767 312966 *Email* grants@bedshertshct.org.uk *Website* www.bedshertshct.org.uk

■ The Bedfordshire and Luton Community Foundation

CC NO 1086516 **ESTABLISHED** 2001
WHERE FUNDING CAN BE GIVEN The county of Bedfordshire and the borough of Luton.
WHO CAN BENEFIT The grant schemes aim to assist community voluntary organisations and groups in Bedfordshire and Luton in new or exciting projects that can help make a positive difference in the local community.
WHAT IS FUNDED The foundation is dedicated to improving the quality of community life of those in Bedfordshire and Luton and in particular those in special need by reason of disability, age, financial or other disadvantage. The foundation manages a number of grants programmes awarding a range of grants for such causes.
WHAT IS NOT FUNDED Criteria for each of the foundation's grants programmes are available on the website.
SAMPLE GRANTS Centre for Youth and Community Development (£140,000); Walk to Freedom (£43,500); Noah Enterprises (£15,000); Ameina Centre CIC (£10,000); Pink Rooster (£5,000); Young Enterprise (£2,500); Gravenhurst Village Hall (£1,800); OM Group (£1,500); Sundon Park Junior School (£400); Whitefield Primary School (£45).
FINANCES *Year* 2015/16 *Income* £1,572,457 *Grants* £1,106,594 *Grants to organisations* £1,106,594 *Assets* £2,164,136
TRUSTEES Janet Ridge; Andrew Rayment; Dr Wendi Momen; Geoff Lambert; Keith Rawlings; Pauline Stewart; Julia Siegler; Steve Leverton.
HOW TO APPLY The foundation manages a number of schemes which have their own deadlines and application methods. Check the foundation's website for details.

WHO TO APPLY TO Fozia Irfan, Head of Grant-making, The Old School, Southill Road, Cardington MK44 3SX *Tel.* 01234 834930 *Email* administrator@blcf.org.uk *Website* www.blcf.org.uk

■ Beefy's Charity Foundation

CC NO 1151516 **ESTABLISHED** 2013
WHERE FUNDING CAN BE GIVEN UK.
WHO CAN BENEFIT Registered charities.
WHAT IS FUNDED Chronic illness in children.
WHAT IS NOT FUNDED Individuals.
TYPE OF GRANT One-off or up to three years.
SAMPLE GRANTS Batten Disease Family Association; Bloodwise; Brain Tumour Research Yorkshire; Cardiac Risk in the Young; Juvenile Diabetes Research Foundation; Royal Victoria Hospital Belfast; Ravensworth Defibrillator Appeal.
FINANCES *Year* 2015/16 *Income* £241,655 *Grants* £191,000 *Grants to organisations* £191,000 *Assets* £91,913
TRUSTEES Douglas Osborne; Naynesh Desai; Paul Monk.
HOW TO APPLY The foundation tends to support the same charities each year.
WHO TO APPLY TO The Trustees, DDO Solicitors, 36 Upper Brook Street, Mayfair, London W1K 7QJ *Tel.* 020 7499 5353 *Email* info@beefysfoundation.org *Website* www.beefysfoundation.org

■ The David and Ruth Behrend Fund

CC NO 261567 **ESTABLISHED** 1969
WHERE FUNDING CAN BE GIVEN UK, with a preference for Merseyside.
WHO CAN BENEFIT Registered charities.
WHAT IS FUNDED General charitable purposes. The fund only gives funding to charities known to the settlors.
RANGE OF GRANTS Up to £16,000.
SAMPLE GRANTS Amelian Chadwick Trust and Save the Children (£6,000 each); Adelaide House and Big Help Project (£2,000 each); Fazakerley Community Federation (£1,800); Marybone Youth and Community Association (£1,600); Steps to Freedom (£1,300); Clapperboard UK and Sheila Kay Fund (£1,000 each).
FINANCES *Year* 2015/16 *Income* £94,766 *Grants* £101,918 *Grants to organisations* £101,918 *Assets* £1,368,124
TRUSTEE Liverpool Charity and Voluntary Services.
HOW TO APPLY The trustees state that they do not respond to unsolicited applications. The latest annual report states: 'Grants are only made to charities known to the settlor and unsolicited applications are therefore not considered.'
WHO TO APPLY TO The Trustees, 151 Dale Street, Liverpool L2 2AH *Tel.* 0151 227 5177 *Website* www.merseytrusts.org.uk

■ The Behrens Foundation

CC NO 266324 **ESTABLISHED** 1973
WHERE FUNDING CAN BE GIVEN UK.
WHO CAN BENEFIT UK-registered charities.
WHAT IS FUNDED General charitable purposes with a preference for music and the arts.
WHAT IS NOT FUNDED Non-registered charities.
SAMPLE GRANTS Lettering and Commemorative Arts Trust (£35,000); English National Opera (£20,000); Garsington Opera and Royal National Theatre Education Programme (£10,000 each); Bletchley Park (£8,400); Dynamic Earth (£6,500); Brighton Early Music Festival, Sir John Soanne's Museum and Trinity Sailing Foundation (£5,000 each).
FINANCES *Year* 2015/16 *Income* £128,363 *Grants* £186,850 *Grants to organisations* £186,850 *Assets* £3,644,726
TRUSTEES Mr Parish; Stephen Cockburn; Jonna Behrens.
HOW TO APPLY The foundation has previously stated that it does not respond to unsolicited applications.
WHO TO APPLY TO Mrs A. Slaughter, Suite 359, Salisbury House, London Wall, London EC2M 5QS *Tel.* 020 7448 4700 *Email* info@fiskeplc.com

■ The Bellahouston Bequest Fund

SC NO SC011781 **ESTABLISHED** 1888
WHERE FUNDING CAN BE GIVEN Glasgow and district, but not more than five miles beyond the Glasgow city boundary (churches only).
WHO CAN BENEFIT Churches and registered charities in Glasgow or within five miles especially those benefitting Protestant evangelical denominations and clergy of such churches, as well as people disadvantaged by poverty.
WHAT IS FUNDED The trust supports a wide variety of causes. Its main priority is to help build, expand and repair Protestant evangelical churches or places of religious worship, as well as supporting the clergy of these churches. It further states that it is set up to give grants to charities for the relief of poverty or disease and to organisations concerned with promotion of the Protestant religion, education, and conservation of places of historical and artistic significance.
RANGE OF GRANTS Usually between £1,000 and £5,000.
SAMPLE GRANTS Horatio's Garden (£5,000); Chryston Parish Church (£4,000); Castlemilk Parish Church (£3,000); Glasgow Women's Aid and Rape Crisis Centre (£2,000 each); Hearing Dogs for Deaf People and SAM's Charity (£1,500 each); Brittle Bone Society and Home-Start Glasgow North (£1,000 each).
FINANCES *Year* 2015/16 *Income* £212,172 *Grants* £146,150 *Grants to organisations* £146,150 *Assets* £5,127,995
HOW TO APPLY Application forms are available from the trust for church applications only. Other charitable organisations can apply in writing to the correspondent. The trustees meet to consider grants in March, July, October and December.
WHO TO APPLY TO Edward Barry, Mitchells Roberton Solicitors, George House, 36 North Hanover Street, Glasgow G1 2AD *Tel.* 0141 552 3422 *Email* emb@mitchells-roberton.co.uk

■ Belljoe Tzedoko Ltd

CC NO 282726 **ESTABLISHED** 1981
WHERE FUNDING CAN BE GIVEN UK.
WHO CAN BENEFIT Registered charities and institutions.
WHAT IS FUNDED Advancement of religion in accordance with the Orthodox Jewish faith and the relief of poverty.
SAMPLE GRANTS Adath Yisroel Synagogue, Beer Miriam, Children with Cancer, Kupat Hair, Marbe Torah, Shomre Hachomos, Yeshivo Horomo and Yesodey Hatora.

FINANCES *Year* 2015 *Income* £488,501 *Grants* £172,710 *Grants to organisations* £172,710 *Assets* £4,269,518

TRUSTEES Morris Lobenstein; Karen Lobenstein.

HOW TO APPLY Apply in writing to the correspondent.

WHO TO APPLY TO H. J. Lobenstein, 27 Fairholt Road, London N16 5EW

■ Benesco Charity Ltd

CC NO 269181 **ESTABLISHED** 1970

WHERE FUNDING CAN BE GIVEN UK.

WHO CAN BENEFIT Registered charities.

WHAT IS FUNDED Medicine; education.

WHAT IS NOT FUNDED Individuals.

SAMPLE GRANTS A list of beneficiaries was not available.

FINANCES *Year* 2015/16 *Income* £7,517,310 *Grants* £6,925,416 *Grants to organisations* £6,925,416 *Assets* £226,393,911

TRUSTEES Jonathan Ragol-Levy; Hon. Andrew Wolfson; Lord David Wolfson.

OTHER INFORMATION A large proportion (£6.3 million) of the grant total was given to The Charles Wolfson Charitable Trust. The remaining £625,500 was donated to medical causes.

HOW TO APPLY Apply in writing to the correspondent.

WHO TO APPLY TO Joanne Cowan, Benesco Charity Ltd, 8/10 Hallam Street, London W1W 6NS

■ The Benham Charitable Settlement

CC NO 239371 **ESTABLISHED** 1964

WHERE FUNDING CAN BE GIVEN UK, with strong preference for Northamptonshire.

WHO CAN BENEFIT Registered charities.

WHAT IS FUNDED General charitable purposes; medical charities; Christian Mission; disability; overseas aid and mission; older people; children, schools and young people; conservation; art and sport; churches; animal welfare.

WHAT IS NOT FUNDED Individuals.

TYPE OF GRANT One-off and recurring grants will be considered.

RANGE OF GRANTS Mostly between £500 and £800 with some larger grants of up to £25,000.

SAMPLE GRANTS Northamptonshire Association of Youth Clubs (£25,000); The Filling Station Trust (£12,000); The Royal British Legion (£1,300); Motability, MS Therapy Centre and Prostate Cancer UK (£800 each); Bibles for Children, Independence at Home and Northampton Volunteering Centre (£700 each); Northampton Festival of Dance (£500).

FINANCES *Year* 2015/16 *Income* £236,658 *Grants* £186,700 *Grants to organisations* £186,700 *Assets* £5,631,882

TRUSTEES Mrs M. M. Tittle; Lady Hutton; David Tittle; Revd J. A. Nickols.

OTHER INFORMATION The trust's policy is to make a large number of relatively small grants to groups working in many charitable fields. There were 166 grants made during the year.

HOW TO APPLY Apply in writing to the correspondent.

WHO TO APPLY TO The Secretary, 1 Virginia Drive, Virginia Water, Surrey GU25 4RX

■ Bennett Lowell Ltd

CC NO 1149726 **ESTABLISHED** 2012

WHERE FUNDING CAN BE GIVEN UK and USA.

WHO CAN BENEFIT Registered charities.

WHAT IS FUNDED General charitable purposes including: art and culture; heritage.

SAMPLE GRANTS Sir John Soane's Museum Foundation (£67,000); Campaign for the Mary Rose (£48,000); American Friends of Covent Garden (£8,000); American Association of the Old Vic (£5,000); Human Rights Watch (£3,500); American Friends of Leket Israel (£1,600).

FINANCES *Year* 2015 *Income* £143 *Grants* £160,000 *Grants to organisations* £160,000

TRUSTEES David Borthwick; John Attree; Molly Borthwick; William Borthwick.

OTHER INFORMATION This charity's latest accounts were not available to view on the Charity Commission's website due to its low income. We have therefore estimated the grant total based on previous years' information.

HOW TO APPLY Apply in writing to the correspondent.

WHO TO APPLY TO The Administrator of Bennett Lowell Ltd, 176161–00001, Charles Russell Speechlys LLP, 5 Fleet Place, London EC4M 7RD *Tel.* 020 7203 5000 *Email* information@crsblaw.com

■ The Rowan Bentall Charitable Trust

CC NO 273818 **ESTABLISHED** 1960

WHERE FUNDING CAN BE GIVEN Southern England.

WHO CAN BENEFIT Registered charities; churches; organisations.

WHAT IS FUNDED Medical causes; churches; children; older people; special needs; education; environment; animal welfare; national disasters. The trustees are requested to have regard to the following purposes of an exclusively charitable nature – relief, maintenance, support and provision of amenities for such former employees of Bentalls PLC and associated companies and their widows, widowers, children and dependants as the trustees consider to be in need.

WHAT IS NOT FUNDED Individuals.

TYPE OF GRANT Capital; core costs; full projects; one-off; recurrent.

RANGE OF GRANTS £100 to £3,000.

SAMPLE GRANTS A list of beneficiaries was not available.

FINANCES *Year* 2015/16 *Income* £54,433 *Grants* £45,210 *Grants to organisations* £45,210 *Assets* £1,875,853

TRUSTEES L. Edward Bentall; Alastair R. Bentall; Kate C. Bentall.

HOW TO APPLY Apply in writing to the correspondent. The trustees meet twice a year in January and September to consider applications.

WHO TO APPLY TO L. Edward Bentall, Trustee, PO Box 1268, Chobham GU24 8WE *Email* rowanbentallcharitabletrust@hotmail.co.uk

■ Bergqvist Charitable Trust

CC NO 1015707 **ESTABLISHED** 1992

WHERE FUNDING CAN BE GIVEN Buckinghamshire and neighbouring counties.

WHO CAN BENEFIT Registered charities and community organisations.

WHAT IS FUNDED Education; medical causes; health; environment; disaster and famine relief.

TYPE OF GRANT One-off and recurrent grants.
SAMPLE GRANTS Abracadabra; British Epilepsy Association; British Heart Foundation; Church Urban Fund; Generation Trust; PACE; Sight Savers International; Stoke Mandeville Hospital.
FINANCES *Year* 2015 *Income* £47,912 *Grants* £44,480 *Grants to organisations* £44,480 *Assets* £1,869,983
TRUSTEES Patricia Bergqvist; Philip Bergqvist; Sophia Bergqvist.
HOW TO APPLY Apply in writing to the correspondent.
WHO TO APPLY TO Patricia Bergqvist, Trustee, Moat Farm, Water Lane, Ford, Aylesbury, Buckinghamshire HP17 8XD *Tel.* 01296 748560 *Email* tsaukltd@gmail.com

■ The Berkeley Charitable Foundation

CC NO 1152596 **ESTABLISHED** 2011
WHERE FUNDING CAN BE GIVEN England and Wales with a focus on communities in which the Berkeley Group works.
WHO CAN BENEFIT Registered charities and community groups.
WHAT IS FUNDED Homelessness; illness and disability; training and employment schemes for young people.
SAMPLE GRANTS The Lord's Taverners (£330,000); Headstart – London (£100,000).
FINANCES *Year* 2015/16 *Income* £1,760,059 *Grants* £923,081 *Grants to organisations* £923,081 *Assets* £817,112
TRUSTEES Anthony Pidgley; Robert Perrins; Wendy Pritchard; Elaine Driver.
OTHER INFORMATION The foundation was established by Anthony Pidgley founder and chair of the Berkeley Group, a British housebuilding company based in Surrey.
HOW TO APPLY The foundation has stated that it very rarely makes unsolicited donations; however, organisations can write to the correspondent if they believe there is a partnership that could be explored.
WHO TO APPLY TO Stuart Cowen, The Berkeley Foundation, Berkeley House, 19 Portsmouth Road, Cobham, Surrey KT11 1JG *Tel.* 01932 868555 *Email* info@berkeleyfoundation.org.uk *Website* www.berkeleyfoundation.org.uk

■ The Ruth Berkowitz Charitable Trust

CC NO 1111673 **ESTABLISHED** 2005
WHERE FUNDING CAN BE GIVEN UK and overseas.
WHO CAN BENEFIT Mainly Jewish charitable organisations.
WHAT IS FUNDED Medical causes; children, young people and education; community.
RANGE OF GRANTS £2,000 to £50,000.
SAMPLE GRANTS University Jewish Chaplaincy (£50,000); Community Security Trust (£40,000); Jewish Leadership Council (£24,000); Norwood Ravenswood (£20,000); Marie Curie Cancer Care (£15,000); Nightingale House (£12,500); Cancer Research UK (£7,500); Jewish Deaf Association (£5,000); Chana (£3,500).
FINANCES *Year* 2015/16 *Income* £51,201 *Grants* £536,900 *Grants to organisations* £536,900 *Assets* £2,637,752
TRUSTEES Philip Beckman; Brian Beckman; Philip Goodman.
OTHER INFORMATION Grants were broken down as follows: children/youth/education (£261,500); community (£147,500); medical (£128,000).
HOW TO APPLY The 2015/16 annual report states: 'As the Trust is not a reactive trust the Trustees will generally only make grants to charities which are known to them and will not normally respond to unsolicited requests for assistance.'
WHO TO APPLY TO The Trustees of The Ruth Berkowitz Charitable Trust, 63/66 Hatton Garden, London EC1N 9LE *Tel.* 020 7408 8888

■ The Berkshire Community Foundation

CC NO 1155173 **ESTABLISHED** 1985
WHERE FUNDING CAN BE GIVEN Berkshire (the unitary authorities of Bracknell, Reading, Slough, Windsor and Maidenhead, West Berkshire and Wokingham).
WHO CAN BENEFIT Not-for profit organisations; voluntary or community groups; social enterprise/CICs; registered charities.
WHAT IS FUNDED The foundation manages a number of different funds. Grants are made for a range of purposes including: health and well-being; community development; housing and homelessness; children and young people; carers; environment; education and skills.
WHAT IS NOT FUNDED Organisations that are regional or national charities (unless locally led and run); organisations that have substantial unrestricted funds; statutory work (in educational institutions or replacing statutory funding); building improvements/projects or capital appeals (unless flood damaged); promotion of religious or political causes; projects benefitting those outside the county; retrospective funding; medical research or equipment; sponsorship or one-off events; individuals over the age of 18 (except those up to 25 for those with learning/ physical disabilities); organisations primarily concerned with conservation of plants or animal welfare; overseas travel/expeditions.
TYPE OF GRANT Capital and core costs; salaries; projects; one-off and up to three years; unrestricted funding.
SAMPLE GRANTS A list of beneficiaries was not available.
FINANCES *Year* 2015/16 *Income* £1,034,116 *Grants* £918,174 *Grants to organisations* £918,174 *Assets* £8,161,081
TRUSTEES Susie Tremlett; David Seward; Torquil Montague-Johnstone; Lady Catherine Stevenson; Chris Barrett; Sean Taylor; Nick Burrorws; David Oram; Anthony Wood; Gordon Anderson; Chris Dodson; Jesal Dhokia.
HOW TO APPLY Full details of how to apply to the specific funding streams can be found on the foundation's website. Note that organisations are required to submit audited accounts for the past three financial years and their governing document.
WHO TO APPLY TO Grants Team, 100 Longwater Avenue, Green Park, Reading RG2 6GP *Tel.* 0118 945 0252 *Email* grants@berkshirecf.org *Website* www.berkshirecf.org

■ The Bestway Foundation

CC NO 297178 **ESTABLISHED** 1987

WHERE FUNDING CAN BE GIVEN UK; overseas with a preference for Pakistan.

WHO CAN BENEFIT Registered charities; unregistered organisations; overseas charitable bodies; individuals; educational establishments.

WHAT IS FUNDED Education and training; health; social welfare; disaster aid.

WHAT IS NOT FUNDED Trips/travel abroad.

TYPE OF GRANT The majority of the grants are made on an annual basis.

RANGE OF GRANTS £500 to £100,000.

SAMPLE GRANTS Grocery Aid (£110,000); Crimestoppers (£74,000); British Asian Trust (£30,000); Duke of Edinburgh's Award (£15,000); Developments in Literacy Trust UK (£10,000); Springboard Charity (£8,000); Shelter (£1,000); Macmillan Cancer Support (£200).

FINANCES *Year* 2015/16 *Income* £251,009 *Grants* £254,200 *Grants to organisations* £254,200 *Assets* £6,261,915

TRUSTEES Mohammed Sheikh; Sir Anwar Pervez; Zameer Choudrey; Dawood Pervez; Rizwan Pervez.

OTHER INFORMATION Grants were made to ten organisations during the year.

HOW TO APPLY Applications may be made in writing to the correspondent, enclosing an sae. Appeals are normally considered in March/April. The foundation has previously noted that telephone calls are not invited.

WHO TO APPLY TO Mohammed Younus Sheikh, Trustee, Abbey Road, London NW10 7BW *Tel.* 020 8453 1234 *Email* zulfikaur.wajid-hasan@bestway.co.uk *Website* www.bestwaygroup.co.uk/responsibility/bestway-foundation

■ BHP Billiton Sustainable Communities

CC NO 1131066 **ESTABLISHED** 2009

WHERE FUNDING CAN BE GIVEN Financially developing countries; countries in BHP Billiton operates or has a business interest.

WHO CAN BENEFIT Registered charities; NGOs.

WHAT IS FUNDED The charity actively identifies and provides funds to key NGOs for significant longer-term national or international social or environmental programs that directly address the Sustainable Development Goals in financially developing countries. Natural disaster relief.

SAMPLE GRANTS A list of beneficiaries was not available.

FINANCES *Year* 2015/16 *Income* £359,579 *Grants* £11,733,400 *Grants to organisations* £11,733,400 *Assets* £82,076,000

TRUSTEES Ian Wood; Melinda Buckland; Robert McDonald; Fiona Wild; Christine Barnesby.

OTHER INFORMATION The financial information has been converted from US dollars using the exchange rate at the time of writing (27 June 2017).

HOW TO APPLY The 2015/16 annual report states: 'The Charity does not encourage unsolicited requests from charitable organisations but it may consider requests from the BHP Billiton businesses to support charitable projects in their region of operation.'

WHO TO APPLY TO The Trustees, Nova South, 160 Victoria Street, London SW1E 5LB *Email* hsec@bhpbilliton.com

■ The Big Lottery Fund (see also Awards for All)

ESTABLISHED 2004

WHERE FUNDING CAN BE GIVEN UK, also overseas.

WHO CAN BENEFIT Charitable organisations; statutory bodies; local groups; large national institutions; social enterprises.

WHAT IS FUNDED BIG runs a range of different programmes aimed at improving communities and people's lives. Some are UK-wide and others specific to each region. New programmes are introduced from time to time, and others close. Potential applicants are advised to check the fund's website for up-to-date information on current and upcoming programmes. There are also international funding programmes.

WHAT IS NOT FUNDED There will be specific and detailed conditions for each separate programme – see specific details.

RANGE OF GRANTS Mostly up to £10,000.

SAMPLE GRANTS Homeless Link (£2.8 million); Crisis (£739,000); Community Shop CIC (£611,000); Green Thyme (£10,000); Off the Scale CIC (£6,300); SHEDNET (£5,000); Tavistock Community Sensory Garden (£4,800); Arts Factory Ltd (£4,000); Stroud High School (£3,300). Details of projects supported can be find online.

FINANCES *Year* 2015/16 *Income* £820,210,000 *Grants* £585,260,000 *Grants to organisations* £585,260,000 *Assets* £480,499,000

TRUSTEES Board members: Peter Ainsworth; Tony Burton; Nat Sloane; Sir Adrian Webb; Maureen McGinn; Julie Harrison; Dr Astrid Bonfield; David Isaac; Elizabeth Passey; Perdita Fraser; Natalie Campbell; Rachael Robaton.

OTHER INFORMATION BIG distributes money from the National Lottery to good causes as well as non-Lottery funding on behalf of public bodies, for example the Department for Education and the Office for Civil Society. The fund's 2015/16 annual report states: 'As the UK's largest community funder, we gave out over 11,700 grants to the tune of £583 million this year, the vast majority of which were for less than £10,000.' The organisation's website gives extensive information on the background of the funds, support available, application procedures and so on, which is also subject to change. It would not be practicable to replicate all the details here and potential applicants are advised to study the helpful website to learn more about the funder. For Awards for All programme also see a separate entry.

HOW TO APPLY Note there are different regional offices and contact details for England, Northern Ireland, Scotland and Wales (see the website for full details). All application forms and guidelines are given on the charity's website. If you need further guidance you can also call the BIG advice line at 0345 4 10 20 30.

WHO TO APPLY TO See 'How to apply', 1 Plough Place, London EC4A 1DE *Tel.* 0345 410 2030 *Email* general.enquiries@biglotteryfund.org.uk *Website* www.biglotteryfund.org.uk

■ The Billmeir Charitable Trust

CC NO 208561 **ESTABLISHED** 1956

WHERE FUNDING CAN BE GIVEN UK, with a preference for the Surrey area, specifically Elstead, Tilford, Farnham and Frensham.

WHO CAN BENEFIT Charitable organisations.

WHAT IS FUNDED General charitable purposes. About a quarter of the grants are for health and medical causes and many are given to charities in Surrey.

RANGE OF GRANTS £500 to £12,000.

SAMPLE GRANTS Reed's School – Cobham (£15,000); ABF The Soldiers' Charity (£10,000); Surrey AirMotor Neurone Association (£5,000); Disability Challengers – Farnham (£2,500); Music in Hospitals and Sparks (£2,000 each); Farham Explorers (£1,000).

FINANCES *Year* 2015/16 *Income* £224,724 *Grants* £154,500 *Grants to organisations* £154,500 *Assets* £4,991,577

TRUSTEES Max Whitaker; Suzanne Marriott; Jason Whitaker.

HOW TO APPLY The trust states that 'unsolicited applications are not welcome and are rarely successful'.

WHO TO APPLY TO Martin Pollock, Moore Stephens, 150 Aldersgate Street, London EC1A 4AB *Email* martin.pollock@moorestephens.com

■ Percy Bilton Charity

CC NO 1094720 **ESTABLISHED** 1962

WHERE FUNDING CAN BE GIVEN UK.

WHO CAN BENEFIT Large grants are only available to registered charities. Unregistered organisations can apply for a small grant but a reference from another charity, Council for Voluntary Service or the local authority youth service will be required.

WHAT IS FUNDED Projects working with disadvantaged and underprivileged young people (under 25), people with disabilities (physical or learning disabilities or mental health problems) and/or older people (aged over 60).

WHAT IS NOT FUNDED According to its website, the charity will not consider the following (the list is not exhaustive): 'running expenses for the organisation or individual projects; salaries, training costs or office equipment/furniture; projects for general community use e.g. community centre and church halls; disability access to community buildings; publication costs e.g. printing/distributing promotional and information leaflets; projects that have been completed; items that have already been purchased; provision of disabled facilities in schemes mainly for the able-bodied; general funding/circularised appeals; pre-schools or playgroups (other than predominantly for disabled children); play schemes/summer schemes; holidays or expeditions for individuals or groups; trips, activities or events; community sports/play area facilities; exterior works such as paving, roofing and garden landscaping; consumables (e.g. stationery, arts and crafts materials); refurbishment or repair of places of worship/church halls; research projects; mainstream pre-schools, schools, colleges and universities (other than special schools); welfare funds for individuals; hospital/medical equipment; works to premises not used primarily by the eligible groups'.

TYPE OF GRANT Capital expenditure.

RANGE OF GRANTS Small grants to organisations: up to £500 towards furnishing and equipment for small projects. Large grants for capital expenditure: usually £2,000 to £5,000.

SAMPLE GRANTS Ellie's Haven (£31,500); Hertline Families (£11,000); Wingate Special Children's Trust (£7,500); St Andrew's Children's Hospice – Grimsby (£6,300); Living Paintings Trust (£5,500); KIDS – Bristol (£4,900); Victoria School – Birmingham (£4,700); Doncaster Deaf Trust (£4,500); National Star (£3,000); Childhood First (£500); Friendship Works (£150).

FINANCES *Year* 2015/16 *Income* £839,135 *Grants* £664,040 *Grants to organisations* £664,040 *Assets* £22,525,298

TRUSTEES James Lee; Stefan Paciorek; Kim Lansdown; Hayley Bilton.

OTHER INFORMATION Urgent one-off assistance is given to older people (over 65) and people with disabilities to purchase essential items.

HOW TO APPLY The following information has been taken form the charity's website: **'Large grants (£2,000 and over)** – apply on your organisation's headed notepaper giving or attaching the following information: summary outlining the amount you are requesting and what the funding is for; a brief history of your Charity including year established, its objectives and work; description of the project and what you intend to achieve; an itemised list of the equipment/furniture with estimate of costs. Obtain at least two competitive estimates except where this is not practicable e.g. specialised equipment; when you expect to purchase the equipment/furniture; details of funds already raised and other sources that you have approached; proposals to monitor and evaluate the project; a copy of your most recent Annual Report and audited Accounts; any other relevant information that will help to explain your application. **Small grants (up to £500)** – apply on your organisation's headed notepaper with the following information: brief details about your organisation and its work; a copy of your most recent annual accounts; outline of the project and its principal aims; breakdown of the cost of item/s required; the organisation's bank account name to which the cheque should be made payable if a grant is approved. (We cannot make cheques payable to individuals); if your organisation is not a registered charity, supply a reference from a registered charity with whom you work or from the local Voluntary Service Council.'

WHO TO APPLY TO Tara Smith, Charity Administrator, Bilton House, 7 Culmington Road, Ealing, London W13 9NB *Tel.* 020 8579 2829 *Email* percybilton@aol.com *Website* www.percy-bilton-charity.org

■ The Bingham Trust

CC NO 287636 **ESTABLISHED** 1977

WHERE FUNDING CAN BE GIVEN Buxton and district.

WHO CAN BENEFIT Registered charities; individuals.

WHAT IS FUNDED Community needs; social welfare; churches; the arts; arthritis research throughout the UK.

WHAT IS NOT FUNDED Repayment of existing debts; grants for businesses; profit-making organisations; for higher educational purposes (university and college level).

TYPE OF GRANT The trust prefers to fund capital projects rather than revenue expenses.

RANGE OF GRANTS Up to £5,000.

SAMPLE GRANTS Good News Family Care (£37,500); Warslow Village Hall (£5,000); High Peak Foodbank (£4,900); Step By Step (£4,000); Buxton Community School and High Peak CVS (£3,100 each); Samaritans and Volunteer Centre Buxton (£2,000 each); Churches Together and Buxton Well Dressing (£1,000 each); People's Dispensary for Sick Animals (PDSA) (£50).

FINANCES *Year* 2015/16 *Income* £193,539 *Grants* £160,578 *Grants to organisations* £160,578 *Assets* £4,284,277

TRUSTEES Roger Horne; Alexandra Hurst; Eric Butterly; Helen Mirtle; Christine McMullen.

OTHER INFORMATION Grants were made to 64 organisations during the year. Grants totalling £20,500 were also made to individuals.
HOW TO APPLY Application forms and application guidelines are available from the trust's very helpful website. Applications can also be made by post but these may take longer to deal with.
WHO TO APPLY TO Roger Horne, Trustee, Unit 1, Tongue Lane Industrial Estate, Dew Pond Lane, Buxton, Derbyshire SK17 7LN *Tel.* 01298 600591 *Email* binghamtrust@aol.com *Website* www.binghamtrust.org.uk

■ The Birmingham District Nursing Charitable Trust

CC NO 215652 **ESTABLISHED** 1960
WHERE FUNDING CAN BE GIVEN Within a 20-mile radius of the Council House in Birmingham.
WHO CAN BENEFIT Local organisations benefitting medical professionals. Grants may be made to local branches of national organisations.
WHAT IS FUNDED Medical or nursing organisations; convalescent homes; convalescent homes or rest homes for nurses or other medical or nursing institution; amenities for patients or nursing staff of Birmingham Domiciliary Nursing Service; amenities for patients or nursing staff of any state hospital.
WHAT IS NOT FUNDED Individuals.
TYPE OF GRANT One-off and recurrent.
RANGE OF GRANTS £1,000 to £5,000.
SAMPLE GRANTS Birmingham PHAB Camps (£5,000); Freedom from Torture (£4,000); Interact Stroke Support (£2,500); Birmingham Samaritans, Shakespeare Hospice and The Mobility Trust (£2,000 each); Huntington's Disease Association and Well Child (£1,500 each).
FINANCES *Year* 2015/16 *Income* £71,660 *Grants* £51,500 *Grants to organisations* £51,500 *Assets* £1,994,805
TRUSTEES Anthony Jones; Dr Mayer; Stuart Reynolds; Dr Mary Honeyman; Prof. Fiona Irvine; Jonathan Tuckey.
HOW TO APPLY Apply in writing to the correspondent with a copy of the latest accounts. Applications should be sent in August/September. The trustees meet to consider grants in the first week of November.
WHO TO APPLY TO Mr M. Parr, Shakespeare Martineau, Homer House, 8 Homer Road, Solihull B91 3QQ *Tel.* 0121 631 5369 *Email* matthew.parr@shma.co.uk

■ Birmingham International Airport Community Trust

CC NO 1071176 **ESTABLISHED** 1998
WHERE FUNDING CAN BE GIVEN The areas affected by the airport's operation, particularly the east of Birmingham and the north of Solihull – a full list of postcodes is provided on the website.
WHO CAN BENEFIT Established local charities. Priority is given to groups based locally and under local control and management.
WHAT IS FUNDED Heritage conservation; environmental improvement; community development; community recreation facilities; health and well-being.
WHAT IS NOT FUNDED Organisations with statutory responsibilities; medical treatment; purchase of land or buildings; repair and maintenance; uniforms; sports kit; trips or projects resulting in short-term benefits, e.g. events, performances or visits.
TYPE OF GRANT Grants may be for capital or revenue projects, although the trust will not commit to recurrent or running costs, such as salaries.
RANGE OF GRANTS The maximum grant is £3,000.
SAMPLE GRANTS John Taylor Hospice – Men's Shed and Training Ship Stirling (£3,000 each); Spotlight Stage School (£2,000); Coleshill Parish Church (£1,000).
FINANCES *Year* 2015/16 *Income* £80,205 *Grants* £74,522 *Grants to organisations* £74,522 *Assets* £17,562
TRUSTEES Cllr Michael Ward; Paul Orton; Andrew Holding; Edward Richards; Margaret Kennett; Cllr Majid Mahmood; David Cuthbert; Cllr Jeff Potts; Cllr Robert Grinsell.
HOW TO APPLY Application packs can be requested by completing a form on the trust's website.
WHO TO APPLY TO Andrew Holding, Trustee, Birmingham International Airport Ltd, Diamond House, Birmingham B26 3QJ *Tel.* 0121 767 7448 *Email* andy.holding@birminghamairport.co.uk *Website* www.birminghamairport.co.uk

■ The Lord Mayor of Birmingham's Charity

CC NO 1036968 **ESTABLISHED** 1994
WHERE FUNDING CAN BE GIVEN Birmingham.
WHO CAN BENEFIT Charities determined by the Lord Mayor at the commencement of term of office.
WHAT IS FUNDED Disability and ill health; community; young people.
TYPE OF GRANT One-off.
SAMPLE GRANTS Focus Birmingham and Queen Elizabeth Hospital Birmingham (£10,000 each); The Guide Association and The Scout Association (£12,900 each); Brandwood Centre Community Association (£8,000); St Margaret's Community Trust (£2,500); The Royal British Legion (£500); Workplace Matters (£100).
FINANCES *Year* 2015/16 *Income* £41,186 *Grants* £99,392 *Grants to organisations* £99,392 *Assets* £95,095
TRUSTEES Lord Mayor of Birmingham; Deputy Lord Mayor of Birmingham; Clive Stone; Anita Ward; Mike Leddy; Randal Brew; Phil Davis; Saqib Bhatti; Marc Reeves; Paul Kehoe.
HOW TO APPLY Apply in writing to the correspondent. Although the beneficiaries are often predetermined, applications can be sent in January/February for the new Lord Mayor to consider.
WHO TO APPLY TO Leigh Nash, Secretary to the Trustees, Development Section, Room 403, 4th Floor, Council House, Birmingham B1 1BB *Tel.* 0121 303 2691 *Email* leigh_nash@birmingham.gov.uk *Website* www.birmingham.gov.uk

■ Birthday House Trust

CC NO 248028 **ESTABLISHED** 1966
WHERE FUNDING CAN BE GIVEN England and Wales.
WHO CAN BENEFIT Charitable organisations; individuals.
WHAT IS FUNDED General charitable purposes.
WHAT IS NOT FUNDED Individuals; non-charitable organisations.
TYPE OF GRANT One-off and recurrent.
SAMPLE GRANTS Easebourne Church of England Primary School (£13,100); Greenpeace Environment Trust, Live to Love Charity and Merton Park Explorer Scouts (£10,000 each); The Ecology Trust (£7,500).

FINANCES *Year* 2015/16 *Income* £208,485 *Grants* £107,823 *Grants to organisations* £67,471 *Assets* £7,165,624

TRUSTEE The Dickinson Trust Ltd and Rathbone Trust Company Ltd.

OTHER INFORMATION The main work of the trust is the running of a residential home for Midhurst, West Sussex. The amount of grants given to individuals totalled £40,500.

HOW TO APPLY Apply in writing to the correspondent, including an sae. No application forms are issued and there is no deadline. Only successful applicants are acknowledged.

WHO TO APPLY TO Anina Cheng, Millbank Financial Services Ltd, 4th Floor, Swan House, 17–19 Stratford Place, London W1C 1BQ *Tel.* 020 7907 2100 *Email* charity@mfs.co.uk

■ The Bisgood Charitable Trust

CC NO 208714 **ESTABLISHED** 1963

WHERE FUNDING CAN BE GIVEN UK with a preference for Bournemouth and Dorset, especially Poole.

WHO CAN BENEFIT Registered charities.

WHAT IS FUNDED General charitable purposes. Preference is given to charities: operating under Roman Catholic auspices; operating in Poole, Bournemouth and the county of Dorset; national charities concerned with older people.

WHAT IS NOT FUNDED Individuals; non-registered charities.

TYPE OF GRANT One-off, capital and recurring.

RANGE OF GRANTS £25 to £2,500.

SAMPLE GRANTS Apex Trust; ITDG; Horder Centre for Arthritis; Impact; The St Barnabas Society; St Francis Leprosy Guild; Sight Savers International; YMCA.

FINANCES *Year* 2015/16 *Income* £201,296 *Grants* £199,150 *Grants to organisations* £199,150 *Assets* £6,359,120

TRUSTEES Jeanne Bisgood; Patrick Bisgood; Paula Schulte.

OTHER INFORMATION The trust operates a sub-fund – the Bertram Fund from which grants made for Roman Catholic purposes. Preference is given to charities whose fundraising and administrative expenses are proportionally low.

HOW TO APPLY Apply in writing to the correspondent, quoting the UK registration number and registered name of the charity and including recent income and expenditure accounts. The trustees normally meet in late February/early March and September.

WHO TO APPLY TO Jeanne Bisgood, Trustee, Flat 12, Waters Edge, Brudenell Road, Poole BH13 7NN *Tel.* 01202 708460 *Email* bisgoodchtr123@btinternet.com

■ The Michael Bishop Foundation

CC NO 297627 **ESTABLISHED** 1987

WHERE FUNDING CAN BE GIVEN Worldwide with a preference for the Midlands.

WHO CAN BENEFIT Registered charities.

WHAT IS FUNDED General charitable purposes.

SAMPLE GRANTS Baker Dearing Educational Trust (£500,000); Brooklands Museum (£250,000); Glendonbrook Foundation (£163,000); Exeter Northcote Museum (£50,000); Foundling Museum (£25,000); Royal Naval Benevolent Trust and Terrance Higgins Trust (£10,000 each); National Aids Trust (£1,000); ABF The Soldiers' Charity (£500).

FINANCES *Year* 2015/16 *Income* £2,626,393 *Grants* £1,187,696 *Grants to organisations* £1,187,696 *Assets* £26,952,754

TRUSTEES Grahame Elliott; Baron Glendonbrook of Bowdon; Martin Ritchie; Timothy Bye.

HOW TO APPLY Apply in writing to the correspondent.

WHO TO APPLY TO Pat Robinson, Staunton House, Ashby-de-la-Zouch, Leicestershire LE65 1RW *Tel.* 01530 564388 *Email* patannrob@btconnect.com

■ Asser Bishvil Foundation

CC NO 1112477 **ESTABLISHED** 2005

WHERE FUNDING CAN BE GIVEN Manchester and London.

WHO CAN BENEFIT Registered charities.

WHAT IS FUNDED The relief of poverty among the Jewish community; the advancement of Jewish education and the Jewish faith.

SAMPLE GRANTS A list of beneficiaries was not available.

FINANCES *Year* 2015/16 *Income* £7,394,492 *Grants* £7,400,857 *Grants to organisations* £7,400,857 *Assets* £1,072,618

TRUSTEES Rabbi D. Orzel; Mrs S. Orzel; C. S. Ehrenteu.

OTHER INFORMATION Grants were distributed in the following categories: relief of poverty (£4.7 million); educational grants (£1.9 million); religious grants (£814,000).

HOW TO APPLY According to the 2015/16 annual report: 'The charity invites applications for funding through contacting local philanthropists to contribute towards projects that both the trustees and the philanthropists feel are appropriate for the charities objects.'

WHO TO APPLY TO Mr D. Orzel, 2 New Hall Road, Salford M7 4EL

■ The Sydney Black Charitable Trust

CC NO 219855 **ESTABLISHED** 1949

WHERE FUNDING CAN BE GIVEN UK.

WHO CAN BENEFIT Charitable organisations.

WHAT IS FUNDED Older people; education; advancement of religion; prisoner welfare.

TYPE OF GRANT One-off grants for core support, equipment and vehicles.

SAMPLE GRANTS Endeavour Youth Club – Merton (£10,000).

FINANCES *Year* 2015/16 *Income* £80,305 *Grants* £55,909 *Grants to organisations* £55,909 *Assets* £3,220,077

TRUSTEES Jennifer Crabtree; Hilary Dickenson; Stephen Crabtree; Philip Crabtree.

OTHER INFORMATION Grants were broken down as follows: education and children (£33,000); social welfare (£13,200); religion (£4,500); prisoners (£1,500). Grants are generally in the region of £125 and £250 each.

HOW TO APPLY Applications should be made in writing to the correspondent.

WHO TO APPLY TO Jennifer Crabtree, Trustee, 30 Welford Place, London SW19 5AJ

■ The Bertie Black Foundation

CC NO 245207 **ESTABLISHED** 1965

WHERE FUNDING CAN BE GIVEN UK; Israel.

WHO CAN BENEFIT Registered charities.

WHAT IS FUNDED General charitable purposes including: social welfare; the advancement of education and religion. Particular support is given to Jewish causes.

SAMPLE GRANTS I Rescue (£50,000); Magen David Adom (£47,000 in three grants); Alyn Hospital (£49,000 in two grants); Emunah (£38,000); Laniardo Hospital and Shaare Zedek (£25,000 each); Friends of Israel Sports Centre for Disabled (£20,000); Child Resettlement Trust (£10,000 in four grants); Norwood (£7,600 in four grants); Hope (£5,200 in four grants).
FINANCES *Year* 2015/16 *Income* £114,969 *Grants* £70,591 *Grants to organisations* £70,591 *Assets* £3,222,484
TRUSTEES Doris Black; Harry Black; Isabelle Seddon; Ivor Seddon; Carolyn Black.
OTHER INFORMATION Grants were made to 35 organisations in 2015/16, of which five received £5,000. The largest grant was £15,000.
HOW TO APPLY The trust has previously stated that it 'supports causes known to the trustees' and that the trustees 'do not respond to unsolicited requests'.
WHO TO APPLY TO Harry Black, Trustee, Abbots House, 13 Beaumont Gate, Shenley Hill, Radlett, Hertfordshire WD7 7AR *Tel.* 01923 850096 *Email* sonneborn@btconnect.com

■ Isabel Blackman Foundation

CC NO 313577 **ESTABLISHED** 1966
WHERE FUNDING CAN BE GIVEN Hastings and St Leonards-on-sea.
WHO CAN BENEFIT Charitable organisations; hospices; schools; individuals.
WHAT IS FUNDED General charitable purposes including: health; social services; education; culture and recreation; youth clubs and organisations; religion; environment.
WHAT IS NOT FUNDED Note only applications from Hastings and St Leonards-on-Sea are considered.
TYPE OF GRANT One-off; capital costs.
RANGE OF GRANTS Up to £60,000 but generally £500 to £5,000.
SAMPLE GRANTS St Michael's Hospice (£30,000); Surviving Christmas (£4,000); Little Gate Farm (£3,000); Blind Veterans UK and Hastings Christian Trust (£2,500 each); Fire Fighters Charity (£2,000); People's Dispensary for Sick Animals (PDSA) (£1,500); Bag Books (£1,000); Caudwell Children and Hastings Pensioners Association (£500 each).
FINANCES *Year* 2015/16 *Income* £300,318 *Grants* £200,687 *Grants to organisations* £171,325 *Assets* £5,694,683
TRUSTEES Denis Jukes; Patricia Connolly; Margaret Haley; John Lamplugh; Evelyn Williams; Christine Deacon.
OTHER INFORMATION Grants were made to 85 organisations and broken down as follows: health (£102,000); social services (£48,500); education (£38,500); culture and recreation (£4,700); youth clubs and organisations (£3,100); religion (£2,500); environment (£1,500). The amount of grants given to individuals totalled £29,500.
HOW TO APPLY Apply in writing to the correspondent. The trustees meet bi-monthly to consider applications.
WHO TO APPLY TO The Trustees, Stonehenge, 13 Laton Road, Hastings, East Sussex TN34 2ES *Tel.* 01424 431756 *Email* ibfoundation@uwclub.net

■ The Blagrave Trust

CC NO 1164021 **ESTABLISHED** 1978
WHERE FUNDING CAN BE GIVEN Berkshire; Hampshire; Sussex; Wiltshire.
WHO CAN BENEFIT Registered charities; CICs where they satisfy due diligence and demonstrate impact.
WHAT IS FUNDED Youth organisations whose mission is to help young people aged 12–25 in Berkshire, Hampshire, Sussex and Wiltshire make a successful transition to adulthood. Services that help these young people develop the skills, experience and capabilities to succeed at school, work and in life.
WHAT IS NOT FUNDED Grants are not given for: capital grants or building projects; grants for more than 20% of a charity's total turnover; general recreational or social activities; promotion of religion; young people living with mental health issues.
TYPE OF GRANT Funding is given for three year periods and no less. Core costs; unrestricted.
RANGE OF GRANTS Between £10,000 and £100,000.
SAMPLE GRANTS Sussex Community Foundation (£107,000); Achievement For All (£100,000); Resurgo Trust (£50,000); Splitz Support Service (£45,000); Youth Adventure Trust (£30,000); Ellen MacArthur Cancer Trust (£15,000); Greatwood Charity (£13,000); Hampshire County Learning (£9,000).
FINANCES *Year* 2015/16 *Income* £1,625,682 *Grants* £1,557,855 *Grants to organisations* £1,557,855 *Assets* £37,368,705
TRUSTEES Julian Whately; Timothy Jackson-Stops; Diana Leat; Sir Paul Neave; Clare Cannock.
HOW TO APPLY Applications can be made through the trust's website.
WHO TO APPLY TO Jo Wells, Trust Director, c/o Rathbone Trust Company Ltd, 1 Curzon Street, London W1J 5FB *Tel.* 020 7399 0370 *Email* jo.wells@blagravetrust.org *Website* www.blagravetrust.org

■ The Blair Foundation

CC NO 801755 **ESTABLISHED** 1989
WHERE FUNDING CAN BE GIVEN Scotland.
WHO CAN BENEFIT Organisations, particularly disability and wildlife groups.
WHAT IS FUNDED Wildlife; young people; medical issues.
WHAT IS NOT FUNDED Charities that have objectives which the trustees consider harmful to the environment are not supported.
RANGE OF GRANTS Up to £12,000.
SAMPLE GRANTS Ayrshire Wildlife Services (£12,000); King's School – Canterbury and Ayrshire Fiddler Orchestra (£10,000 each); Scottish National Trust (£7,000); Home Farm Trust (£5,000); CHAS (£2,000); Penny Brohn Cancer Care (£1,500); Ro-Ro Sailing Project and Sustrans (£1,000 each).
FINANCES *Year* 2015/16 *Income* £16,257 *Grants* £60,000 *Grants to organisations* £60,000
TRUSTEES Graham Healy; Jennifer Thornton; Alan Thornton.
OTHER INFORMATION The foundation's latest accounts were not available to view on the Charity Commission's website due to its low income. We have therefore estimated the grant total.
HOW TO APPLY Apply in writing to the correspondent, for consideration at trustees' meetings held at least once a year.

WHO TO APPLY TO The Trustees, Smith and Williamson, 1 Bishops Wharf, Walnut Tree Close, Guildford, Surrey GU1 4RA *Tel.* 01483 407100 *Email* luke.west@smith.williamson.co.uk

■ The Morgan Blake Charitable Trust

CC NO 293706 **ESTABLISHED** 1985
WHERE FUNDING CAN BE GIVEN UK with a preference for East Anglia.
WHO CAN BENEFIT Registered charities.
WHAT IS FUNDED General charitable purposes.
WHAT IS NOT FUNDED Individuals.
RANGE OF GRANTS Up to £5,000.
SAMPLE GRANTS Alzheimer's Research UK, Child Autism UK, Churches Conservation Trust, Sunny Days Children's Fund, The Brain Research Trust, The Ellen McArthur Cancer Trust, Sunny Days Children's Fund (£5,000 each); Pre-School Music Association (£1,000).
FINANCES *Year* 2015/16 *Income* £29,630 *Grants* £56,000 *Grants to organisations* £56,000 *Assets* £755,451
TRUSTEES Jeremy Whigham; John Hall.
HOW TO APPLY Apply in writing to the correspondent.
WHO TO APPLY TO Sophie Thurston, Spire Solicitors LLP, 3 Burgh Road, Aylsham, Norwich NR11 6AH *Tel.* 01263 732123 *Email* sophie.thurston@spiresolicitors.co.uk

■ Blakemore Foundation

CC NO 1015938 **ESTABLISHED** 1992
WHERE FUNDING CAN BE GIVEN England and Wales excluding parts of the Southwest.
WHO CAN BENEFIT The trust supports local and national charitable organisations.
WHAT IS FUNDED General charitable purposes.
TYPE OF GRANT One-off.
SAMPLE GRANTS Foundation for Conductive Education; St Andrew's Church – Biggleswade and Wenlock Poetry Festival.
FINANCES *Year* 2015/16 *Income* £195,053 *Grants* £78,882 *Grants to organisations* £78,882 *Assets* £110,052
TRUSTEES Peter Blakemore; Ita McAuley.
OTHER INFORMATION Charities can also apply for in-kind support in the forms of goods for local charity and community events.
HOW TO APPLY Applications can be made through the foundation's website. Applications are decided upon on the last Friday of every month.
WHO TO APPLY TO Peter Blakemore, Trustee, A. F. Blakemore and Sons Ltd, Longacre, Willenhall WV13 2JP *Tel.* 01902 366066 *Website* www.afblakemore.com/blakemore-foundation/blakemore-foundation

■ The Blandford Lake Trust

CC NO 1069630 **ESTABLISHED** 1998
WHERE FUNDING CAN BE GIVEN North Wales and overseas.
WHO CAN BENEFIT Registered charities.
WHAT IS FUNDED Overseas aid and development; Christian extension work in North Wales.
SAMPLE GRANTS Christian Aid (£30,000); Bible Society (£15,000); Open Door and Peace Direct (£10,000 each); Feed the Minds (£6,700); Concordis, Urban Saints and Viva (£5,000 each); Scholarships for Street Kids (£1,000); Mission Aviation Fellowship (£500).
FINANCES *Year* 2016 *Income* £126,440 *Grants* £127,000 *Grants to organisations* £127,000 *Assets* £29,909
TRUSTEES Lucy Lake; Richard Lake; Jonathan Lake; Mathew Lake.
HOW TO APPLY Apply in writing to the correspondent including budgets and accounts.
WHO TO APPLY TO Lucy Lake, The Courts, Park Street, Denbigh, Denbighshire LL16 3DE *Tel.* 01745 813174

■ The Sir Victor Blank Charitable Settlement

CC NO 1084187 **ESTABLISHED** 2000
WHERE FUNDING CAN BE GIVEN Worldwide.
WHO CAN BENEFIT Jewish organisations and other registered charities.
WHAT IS FUNDED Jewish causes and general charitable purposes.
SAMPLE GRANTS Jewish Care (£27,500); Norwood Ravenswood (£23,500); One Voice Europe (£18,000); Work Adventure Foundation (£15,000); Best Beginning (£7,500); Friends of the Earth (£3,400); The Langdon Foundation (£3,000); Maccabi UK (£2,000); St John's Hospice (£1,000); The Marwyn Trust (£500).
FINANCES *Year* 2015/16 *Income* £468,951 *Grants* £235,451 *Grants to organisations* £235,451 *Assets* £2,264,624
TRUSTEES Sir Maurice Blank; Lady Sylvia Blank; Simon Blank.
OTHER INFORMATION Grants of less than £1,000 totalled £11,200.
HOW TO APPLY Apply in writing to the correspondent.
WHO TO APPLY TO The Trustees, c/o Wilkins Kennedy, Bridge House, London Bridge, London SE1 9QR *Tel.* 020 7403 1877 *Email* enquiries@sirvictorblankcharitablesettlement.com

■ Bloodwise

CC NO 216032/SC037529 **ESTABLISHED** 1960
WHERE FUNDING CAN BE GIVEN UK.
WHO CAN BENEFIT Hospitals; university medical centres; medical professionals; academics; medical research projects.
WHAT IS FUNDED Research into blood cancers. The charity supports specialist programmes, clinical trials, research projects and academic training and career development.
TYPE OF GRANT Equipment; feasibility studies; recurring costs; research; salaries.
RANGE OF GRANTS Up to £3.5 million.
SAMPLE GRANTS University of York (£3.5 million); University of Newcastle (£3 million); Cardiff University (£997,000); University of Glasgow (£510,000); King's College London (£275,000); Newcastle upon Tyne Hospital NHS Foundation (£168,000); St James's University Hospital (£65,000).
FINANCES *Year* 2015/16 *Income* £16,850,000 *Grants* £18,190,000 *Grants to organisations* £18,190,000 *Assets* £7,379,000
TRUSTEES Maria Clarke; John Reeve; Charles Metcalfe; Jeremy Bird; Pelham Allen; Suzanna Floyd; Simon Guild; Michael Prescott; Glen Lucken.
HOW TO APPLY All applications for all forms of funding must be submitted via the fund's online application system. See the website for details on the application and decision process as well as submission deadlines.

WHO TO APPLY TO Research Team, 39–40 Eagle Street, London WC1R 4TH *Tel.* 020 7504 2200 *Email* research@bloodwise.org.uk *Website* www.bloodwise.org.uk

■ Bloom Foundation

CC NO 1140213 **ESTABLISHED** 2011

WHERE FUNDING CAN BE GIVEN Worldwide.

WHO CAN BENEFIT Registered charities.

WHAT IS FUNDED Education, training and health care in financially developing countries; community development; advocacy; overseas aid.

SAMPLE GRANTS Save the Children (£125,000); Jewish Care (£100,000); Action Aid (£80,000); Kick 4 Life (£50,000); GIFT and Myleloma UK (£45,000 each); Yedid (£25,000); Israel Sport and Education (£23,000); Ahava and Mango Tree (£20,000 each).

FINANCES *Year* 2015/16 *Income* £4,258,679 *Grants* £2,280,551 *Grants to organisations* £2,280,551 *Assets* £0

TRUSTEES Adam Franks; Tony Bloom; Linda Bloom; Marc Sugarman; Marcelle Lester.

OTHER INFORMATION All assets (around £3 million) were transferred to the successor charity The Bloom Foundation (Charity Commission no. 1166112). Grants were distributed for the following purposes: welfare (£648,500); education (£644,000); community development (£389,500); advocacy (£212,500); health care (£211,00); overseas aid (£175,000).

HOW TO APPLY Apply in writing to the correspondent.

WHO TO APPLY TO The Trustees, 34 Jamestown Road, London NW1 7BY *Email* info@thebloomfoundation.com

■ The Bloomfield Charitable Trust

CC NO 1145866 **ESTABLISHED** 2012

WHERE FUNDING CAN BE GIVEN UK.

WHO CAN BENEFIT Registered charities.

WHAT IS FUNDED General charitable purposes.

TYPE OF GRANT Project funding.

SAMPLE GRANTS Dreams Come True; Resources for Autism; Riverside School – Out and About; The Friends of The Harington Scheme; The Markfield Project; Tree of Hope.

FINANCES *Year* 2015/16 *Income* £136,231 *Grants* £66,495 *Grants to organisations* £66,495 *Assets* £227,829

TRUSTEES Martin Hellawell; Mary Hellawell; Coutts & Co.

HOW TO APPLY Apply in writing to the correspondent.

WHO TO APPLY TO The Trustees, Coutts & Co., Trustee Department, 440 Strand, London WC2R 0QS *Tel.* 020 7663 6825 *Email* couttscharities@coutts.com

■ The Bluston Charitable Settlement

CC NO 256691 **ESTABLISHED** 1968

WHERE FUNDING CAN BE GIVEN UK and Israel.

WHO CAN BENEFIT Registered charities, particularly Jewish organisations.

WHAT IS FUNDED General charitable purposes including: education; welfare; and medical causes.

WHAT IS NOT FUNDED Individuals.

RANGE OF GRANTS £5,000 to £100,000.

SAMPLE GRANTS The Langdon Foundation (£100,000); The Weizmann Institute Foundation (£100,000); Ohel Sarah (£50,000); Prisoners Abroad and The Shaarei Torah Trust (£25,000 each); Keren Hatorah (£15,000); The Welfare Fund (£10,000); Farms for City Children (£5,000).

FINANCES *Year* 2015/16 *Income* £587,959 *Grants* £677,500 *Grants to organisations* £677,500 *Assets* £8,309,505

TRUSTEES Daniel Dover; Martin Paisner.

OTHER INFORMATION The were 21 grants made during the year.

HOW TO APPLY Apply in writing to the correspondent. The trustees meet annually in the spring.

WHO TO APPLY TO Martin Paisner, Trustee, 20 Gloucester Place, London W1U 8HA *Tel.* 020 7486 7760

■ The Marjory Boddy Charitable Trust

CC NO 1091356 **ESTABLISHED** 2002

WHERE FUNDING CAN BE GIVEN Cheshire, Wirral, North Wales and elsewhere in the North West.

WHO CAN BENEFIT Organisations and individuals.

WHAT IS FUNDED General charitable purposes.

RANGE OF GRANTS Normally £500 to £4,000.

SAMPLE GRANTS Hospice of the Good Shepherd (£40,000); Chester Mystery Plays (£4,000).

FINANCES *Year* 2015/16 *Income* £98,948 *Grants* £97,000 *Grants to organisations* £97,000 *Assets* £3,117,850

TRUSTEES Edward Walton; Elizabeth Roberts; William Benoy; Hems de Winter.

OTHER INFORMATION Grants were awarded to 28 organisations during the year.

HOW TO APPLY Apply in writing to the correspondent.

WHO TO APPLY TO Karen Welch, c/o Cullimore Dutton Solicitors, 20 White Friars, Chester CH1 1XS *Tel.* 01244 356789

■ The Boltini Trust

CC NO 1123129 **ESTABLISHED** 2008

WHERE FUNDING CAN BE GIVEN UK, with a focus the home counties, particularly Surrey and West Sussex. International support to financially developing countries including Africa, Asia and West Indies.

WHO CAN BENEFIT Charitable organisations.

WHAT IS FUNDED Overseas aid; children who have disabilities or are disadvantaged; homelessness; medical research; music art and culture.

WHAT IS NOT FUNDED Individuals.

SAMPLE GRANTS Midhurst Youth Club (£25,000); Pallant House Gallery (£20,000); Plan International (£10,000); Breast Cancer Haven (£9,500); Life Centre and Snowdon Trust (£5,000 each); The Honeypot Children's Charity (£2,500); Penny Brohn Cancer Care (£2,000); Friends of St Mary's (£1,000).

FINANCES *Year* 2015/16 *Income* £740,138 *Grants* £906,719 *Grants to organisations* £906,719 *Assets* £11,936,408

TRUSTEES Anthony Bolton; Sarah Bolton; James Nelson; Emma Nelson; Oliver Bolton; Benjamin Bolton; Fiona Bolton; Phoebe Moore.

HOW TO APPLY Initial enquiries should be made in writing to the correspondent. The trustees meet twice a year to consider applications.

WHO TO APPLY TO Anthony Bolton, Trustee, Woolbeding Glebe, Woolbeding, Midhurst, West Sussex GU29 9RR *Email* boltinitrust@gmail.com

■ The Bonamy Charitable Trust

CC NO 326424 **ESTABLISHED** 1983

WHERE FUNDING CAN BE GIVEN UK and overseas, with a preference for North West England.

WHO CAN BENEFIT Charitable organisations.

WHAT IS FUNDED Jewish causes; general charitable purposes.

RANGE OF GRANTS Up to £17,000.

SAMPLE GRANTS Shaare Hayim Synagogue (£100,000); Bet Haknesset Hara Synagogue (£17,000); South Manchester Synagogue (£7,800); North Cheshire Jewish Primary School (£4,500).

FINANCES *Year* 2015 *Income* £208,905 *Grants* £208,261 *Grants to organisations* £208,261 *Assets* £338,061

TRUSTEES Max Moryoussef; James Moryoussef; Robert Moryoussef.

HOW TO APPLY Apply in writing to the correspondent.

WHO TO APPLY TO Max Moryoussef, Trustee, Flat 2, Forrest Hills, South Downs Road, Altrincham, Cheshire WA14 3HD *Tel.* 01706 345868

■ The Charlotte Bonham-Carter Charitable Trust

CC NO 292839 **ESTABLISHED** 1985

WHERE FUNDING CAN BE GIVEN UK, with a preference for Hampshire.

WHO CAN BENEFIT Registered charities.

WHAT IS FUNDED General charitable purposes which were of particular concern to Lady Charlotte Bonham-Carter during her lifetime or are within the county of Hampshire.

WHAT IS NOT FUNDED Individuals; non-registered charities.

TYPE OF GRANT One-off grants.

RANGE OF GRANTS £500 to £10,000.

SAMPLE GRANTS National Trust (£10,000); British Museum and The Wakes (£3,000 each); Wessex Heritage Trust (£2,500); Birmingham Royal Ballet (£2,000); Launderdale House (£1,500); Mobility Trust and Revitalise (£1,000 each); Rowans Hospice and Southampton Sight (£500 each).

FINANCES *Year* 2015/16 *Income* £154,621 *Grants* £115,900 *Grants to organisations* £115,900 *Assets* £4,902,270

TRUSTEES Sir Matthew Farrer; David Bonham-Carter; Eliza Bonham-Carter; Georgina Nayler.

HOW TO APPLY Apply in writing to the correspondent. The 2015/16 accounts state: 'The trustees continue to support a core number of charities to whom they have made grants in the past as well as reviewing all applications received and making grants to new charities within their grant-giving criteria.'

WHO TO APPLY TO Jenny Cannon, Chelwood, Rectory Road, East Carleton, Norwich NR14 8HT *Tel.* 01508 571230 *Email* jmc.charities@btinternet.com

■ The Linda and Gordon Bonnyman Charitable Trust

CC NO 1123441 **ESTABLISHED** 2008

WHERE FUNDING CAN BE GIVEN UK; USA.

WHO CAN BENEFIT Registered charities.

WHAT IS FUNDED General charitable purposes.

SAMPLE GRANTS Hospice in the Weald (£15,000); Aspire Fundraising, Blond McIndoe Research Foundation and Reach Volunteering (£5,000 each).

FINANCES *Year* 2015/16 *Income* £2,318 *Grants* £150,000 *Grants to organisations* £150,000

TRUSTEES James Gordon Bonnyman; Linda Bonnyman; James Wallace Taylor Bonnyman.

OTHER INFORMATION This charity's latest accounts were not available to view on the Charity Commission's website due to its low income. We have therefore estimated the grant total based on previous years' information.

HOW TO APPLY Apply in writing to the correspondent.

WHO TO APPLY TO Linda Bonnyman, Trustee, Ely Grange, Bells Yew Green Road, Frant, Tunbridge Wells, East Sussex TN3 9DY *Tel.* 01732 450744 *Email* da@csw-uk.com

■ The Boodle & Dunthorne Charitable Trust

CC NO 1077748 **ESTABLISHED** 1999

WHERE FUNDING CAN BE GIVEN UK.

WHO CAN BENEFIT Registered charities and voluntary organisations.

WHAT IS FUNDED General charitable purposes.

TYPE OF GRANT One-off.

RANGE OF GRANTS Up to £20,000.

SAMPLE GRANTS The Gordon Ramsay Foundation and Rainbow Trust (£20,000); The Message Trust (£15,000); Alder Hey Children's Charity and Shining Faces in India (£10,000 each).

FINANCES *Year* 2015/16 *Income* £209,408 *Grants* £141,336 *Grants to organisations* £141,336 *Assets* £611,884

TRUSTEES Nicholas Wainwright; Michael Wainwright.

OTHER INFORMATION Established in 1999 this is the charitable trust of Boodles, a family jewellers based in North West England.

HOW TO APPLY Apply in writing to the correspondent.

WHO TO APPLY TO Nicholas Wainwright, Boodle & Dunthorne, 35 Lord Street, Liverpool L2 9SQ *Tel.* 0151 224 0580

■ BOOST Charitable Trust

CC NO 1111961 **ESTABLISHED** 2005

WHERE FUNDING CAN BE GIVEN UK.

WHO CAN BENEFIT Registered charities; not-for-profit organisations involved in sports and aiding individuals with disabilities or socially and economically disadvantaged people.

WHAT IS FUNDED Access to sport for socially or economically disadvantaged individuals, people with disabilities.

WHAT IS NOT FUNDED Only charities or non-profit-making organisations with a focus on sport can be supported.

RANGE OF GRANTS Up to £500 for small awards.

SAMPLE GRANTS Boccia England (£17,200); Southwark City Tennis Club (£10,400); Westminster Befriend A Family (£9,000); Be Strong project (£8,000); Sport In Mind (£6,000); Amputee Games (£2,500).

FINANCES *Year* 2014/15 *Income* £100,443 *Grants* £86,249 *Grants to organisations* £86,249 *Assets* £11,704,602

TRUSTEES Robert Houston; Rachel Booth; Alurie Dutton; Oliver Bartrum.

OTHER INFORMATION The 2014/15 accounts were the latest available at the time of writing (April 2017).

HOW TO APPLY Apply in writing to the correspondent by email or post. The application should be no longer than two sides of A4 and include: the name of your organisation – what you do and who your beneficiaries are; funding – why you

need funding, details of the project and approximate funding requirements.
WHO TO APPLY TO Liz Turtle, Administrator, 5 St Bride Street, London EC4A 4AS *Tel.* 020 7078 1966 *Email* liz.turtle@boostct.org *Website* www.boostct.org

The Booth Charities

CC NO 221800 **ESTABLISHED** 1963
WHERE FUNDING CAN BE GIVEN Salford.
WHO CAN BENEFIT Organisations supporting the inhabitants of the City of Salford, especially older people; individuals.
WHAT IS FUNDED General charitable purposes; social welfare; sport and recreation; education.
TYPE OF GRANT Capital and revenue funding; salaries; one-off and up to three years.
RANGE OF GRANTS £100 to £25,000.
SAMPLE GRANTS START in Salford (£15,000); The Christie Charity (£10,700); Salford Mayoral Charity Appeal (£7,500); Barton Athletic Club (£5,000); Mustard Tree (£1,500); Age UK Salford (£1,000); Salford Stroke Club (£750); Tall Ships Youth Trust (£600); Salford Mental Health Forum (£500).
FINANCES *Year* 2015/16 *Income* £1,014,000 *Grants* £363,000 *Grants to organisations* £363,000 *Assets* £36,783,000
TRUSTEES John Willis; David Tully; Philip Okell; Richard Kershaw; Edward Hunt; Roger Weston; William Whittle; Richard Fildes; Alan Dewhurst; Jonathan Shelmerdine.
OTHER INFORMATION Grants totalling £1,000 were made to individuals.
HOW TO APPLY Applications may be made in writing to the correspondent.
WHO TO APPLY TO Jonathan Aldersley, Clerk to the Trustees, c/o Butcher and Barlow LLP, 3 Royal Mews, Gadbrook Road, Northwich, Cheshire CW9 7UD *Tel.* 01606 334309 *Email* jaldersley@butcher-barlow.co.uk

Boots Charitable Trust

CC NO 1045927 **ESTABLISHED** 1971
WHERE FUNDING CAN BE GIVEN Nottinghamshire and Nottingham.
WHO CAN BENEFIT Charitable organisations benefitting people who live in Nottinghamshire.
WHAT IS FUNDED Health; lifelong learning; community development; social care.
WHAT IS NOT FUNDED Projects benefitting people outside Nottinghamshire; individuals; organisations which are not registered charities and which have income or expenditure of more than £5,000 per year; charities seeking funds to redistribute to other charities; projects for which there is a legal statutory obligation or which replace statutory funding.
RANGE OF GRANTS Up to £10,000.
SAMPLE GRANTS Citizens Advice Newark, Ecoworks, Groundwork Greater Nottingham, Hope Nottingham, Nottinghamshire Hospice, Signpost to Polish Success and Stonebridge City Farm (£10,000 each).
FINANCES *Year* 2015/16 *Income* £281,799 *Grants* £282,688 *Grants to organisations* £282,688 *Assets* £10,528
TRUSTEES Judith Lyons; Helen Jeremiah; Lavina Moxley; Adrian Bremner; Una Kent.
OTHER INFORMATION The trust made a total of 59 grants which were broken down as follows: health (£114,000); social care (£96,500); lifelong learning (£41,000); community development (£31,000).
HOW TO APPLY Application forms and guidelines are available from the trust's website or can be requested by post. Completed forms should be sent to the correspondent with the latest annual report and accounts. For applications over £2,000 the deadlines are on the 7th of February, April, June, August, October and December. These applications take between two and four months to process. There is no deadline for applications under £2,000, and these take between one and two months to be processed.
WHO TO APPLY TO James Kirkpatrick, Funding Support, Boots UK Ltd, 1698 Melton Road, Rearsby, Leicester LE7 4YR *Tel.* 07739 835909 *Email* james@fundingsupport.co.uk *Website* www.boots-uk.com/corporate_social_responsibility/community/boots-charitable-trust.aspx

Salo Bordon Charitable Trust

CC NO 266439 **ESTABLISHED** 1973
WHERE FUNDING CAN BE GIVEN UK and worldwide.
WHO CAN BENEFIT Organisations, primarily Jewish.
WHAT IS FUNDED Religious education; social welfare.
SAMPLE GRANTS Agudas Israel Housing Association Ltd; Baer Hatorah; Beth Jacob Grammar School; Brisk Yeshivas; Golders Green Beth Hamedrash Congregation; Jaffa Institute; Jewish Learning Exchange; London Academy of Jewish Studies; Society of Friends of Torah; WST Charity.
FINANCES *Year* 2015/16 *Income* £162,476 *Grants* £166,461 *Grants to organisations* £166,461 *Assets* £7,266,791
TRUSTEES Marcel Bordon; Salo Bordon; Lilly Bordon.
HOW TO APPLY Apply in writing to the correspondent.
WHO TO APPLY TO Marcel Bordon, Trustee, 39 Gresham Gardens, London NW11 8PA *Tel.* 020 8458 6622

The Bordon Liphook Haslemere Charity

CC NO 1032428 **ESTABLISHED** 1994
WHERE FUNDING CAN BE GIVEN Bordon, Liphook, Haslemere and surrounding areas, Hampshire.
WHO CAN BENEFIT Organisations and individuals.
WHAT IS FUNDED General charitable purposes.
WHAT IS NOT FUNDED Non-priority loans.
SAMPLE GRANTS British Kidney Patient Association; Breast Cancer Campaign; British Red Cross; Bordon Day Care Unit; Bordon Infants School; Cranstoun Drug Services Crossways Counselling; East Hants Advocacy Scheme (EHAS); Senior Luncheon Club Liphook (SCLC); St Francis Church; St John Ambulance; Stroke Association and Weyford County Junior School.
FINANCES *Year* 2013 *Income* £36,718 *Grants* £67,870 *Grants to organisations* £67,870 *Assets* £126,593
TRUSTEES Toni Shaw; Jennifer Vernon-Smith; Michael Gallagher; Vanessa Moss; Seona Rivett; Alison Bedford; Alan Finn.
OTHER INFORMATION The 2013 accounts were the latest available at the time of writing (May 2017). The grant total includes grants to organisations and individuals.
HOW TO APPLY Apply on a form available to download, together with criteria and guidelines, from the website. Alternatively, applicants can request forms to be sent out by post.

WHO TO APPLY TO Robert Monteath, Room 29, The Forest Centre, Bordon, Hampshire GU35 0TN *Tel.* 01420 477787 *Email* info@blhcharity.co.uk *Website* www.blhcharity.co.uk

■ Sir William Boreman's Foundation

CC NO 312796 **ESTABLISHED** 1962

WHERE FUNDING CAN BE GIVEN London boroughs of Greenwich and Lewisham.

WHO CAN BENEFIT Charities; individuals; educational establishments.

WHAT IS FUNDED Providing educational awards to people under 25, and to organisations benefitting eligible individuals, including youth clubs, colleges and educational projects in the beneficial area.

WHAT IS NOT FUNDED Grants to replace or subsidise statutory funding. Grants to organisations must mainly benefit qualified beneficiaries (under 25, resident in Lewisham or Greenwich, in financial need).

TYPE OF GRANT One-off.

SAMPLE GRANTS Carers Lewisham (£12,000); Lewisham Education Service (£8,000 in two awards); Somerville Youth and Play Provision (£7,500); Ahoy Centre (£5,000); For Jimmy (£4,200); New Cross and Depford Families First (£4,000); Tall Ships Youth Trust (£2,500).

FINANCES *Year* 2015/16 *Income* £128,496 *Grants* £116,943 *Grants to organisations* £97,493 *Assets* £3,776,562

TRUSTEE The Drapers' Company.

OTHER INFORMATION Grants to 16 individuals totalled £19,450.

HOW TO APPLY According to the foundation's website: registered charities and educational organisations can apply by setting out in writing: which projects or activities you need funds for; how this will benefit the education of young people living in Greenwich or Lewisham; your operational/project budget; any other funding you have received or applied for. Also include your most recent annual report and accounts. Applications can be made at any time and are considered at meetings in November, February and June. In order to be considered, completed applications should be submitted at least three weeks before these meeting dates.

WHO TO APPLY TO The Clerk to the Governors, The Drapers' Company, Drapers' Hall, Throgmorton Avenue, London EC2N 2DQ *Tel.* 020 7588 5001 *Email* charities@thedrapers.co.uk *Website* www.thedrapers.co.uk/Charities/Grant-making-trusts/Sir-William-Boremans-Foundation.aspx

■ The Borrows Charitable Trust

CC NO 1140591 **ESTABLISHED** 2011

WHERE FUNDING CAN BE GIVEN UK and overseas.

WHO CAN BENEFIT Registered charities.

WHAT IS FUNDED General charitable purposes.

SAMPLE GRANTS Footsteps International (£20,000); Medical Detection Dogs (£11,000); London Business School, Prostate Cancer UK, Supporting West Africa Through Schooling and Noah's Ark Children's Charity (£10,000 each); King's College London and The Martin Lawrence Fund (£5,000 each).

FINANCES *Year* 2015/16 *Income* £90,708 *Grants* £255,350 *Grants to organisations* £255,350 *Assets* £6,375,239

TRUSTEES Sally Borrows; Simon Borrows.

HOW TO APPLY Apply in writing to the correspondent.

WHO TO APPLY TO Simon Borrows, Kingston Smith and Partners LLP, Devonshire House, 60 Goswell Road, London EC1M 7AD *Tel.* 020 7566 4000

■ The Oliver Borthwick Memorial Trust

CC NO 256206 **ESTABLISHED** 1968

WHERE FUNDING CAN BE GIVEN UK.

WHO CAN BENEFIT Registered charities benefitting homeless people and people disadvantaged by poverty.

WHAT IS FUNDED Currently the main areas of interest are to provide shelter and help for homeless people.

WHAT IS NOT FUNDED Grants are not made to individuals, including people working temporarily overseas for a charity where the request is for living expenses, together with applications relating to health, disability and those from non-registered charitable organisations.

TYPE OF GRANT Mainly one-off.

SAMPLE GRANTS CHAS Bristol, Christian Action, Response Society, Cirencester Housing (£5,000 each); Deptford Reach (£3,000); Network Community (£2,000).

FINANCES *Year* 2015/16 *Income* £52,804 *Grants* £49,000 *Grants to organisations* £49,000 *Assets* £1,325,744

TRUSTEES David Scott; The Earl Bathurst; John Toth; Andrew Impey; Sebastian Cresswell-Turner; Virginia Buckley; Sarah Mudd; George Impey.

OTHER INFORMATION Grants were awarded to 11 organisations during the year.

HOW TO APPLY Apply in writing to the correspondent. Letters should be set out on a maximum of two sides of A4, giving full details of the project with costs, who the project will serve and the anticipated outcome of the project. The 2015/16 accounts state: 'The Trustees welcome applications from small but viable charities where they are able to make a significant contribution to the practical work of the charity.'

WHO TO APPLY TO Tony Blake, 2B Vicarage Drive, London SW14 8RX *Tel.* 020 8876 0582 *Email* tblake@charaplus.co.uk

■ The Boshier-Hinton Foundation

CC NO 1108886 **ESTABLISHED** 2005

WHERE FUNDING CAN BE GIVEN England and Wales.

WHO CAN BENEFIT Charitable organisations; hospices; schools.

WHAT IS FUNDED Work with children and adults with special educational or other needs.

WHAT IS NOT FUNDED No repeat grants are made within two years.

TYPE OF GRANT One-off grants.

RANGE OF GRANTS £250 to £20,000. Generally around £1,000 to £2,000.

SAMPLE GRANTS Designability (£50,000); Action for Kids (£10,000); Hospice Service (£5,000); Cauldwell Children (£4,200); Hospice of St Francis (£3,000); Compaid (£2,500); Breakthrough UK (£2,000); Child Autism (£1,000).

FINANCES *Year* 2015/16 *Income* £449,738 *Grants* £649,935 *Grants to organisations* £649,935 *Assets* £1,463,698

TRUSTEES Thea Boshier, Chair; Dr Peter Boshier; Colin Flint; Janet Beale.

HOW TO APPLY The foundation accepts applications for grants in writing and via electronic communication, using a grant application form, which includes some notes for guidance, and is regularly monitored and updated. The application form can be downloaded from the website. The foundation welcomes informal email enquiries prior to the submission of a formal application.

WHO TO APPLY TO Dr Peter Boshier, Trustee, Yeomans, Aythorpe Roding, Great Dunmow, Essex CM6 1PD *Tel.* 01245 231032 *Email* boshierhinton@yahoo.co.uk *Website* www.boshierhintonfoundation.org.uk

■ The Bothwell Charitable Trust

CC NO 299056 **ESTABLISHED** 1987

WHERE FUNDING CAN BE GIVEN UK.

WHO CAN BENEFIT Registered charities; hospices.

WHAT IS FUNDED Children's causes; countryside projects; medical research; disability/social work.

WHAT IS NOT FUNDED Animal charities; overseas causes; individuals; charities not registered with the Charity Commission.

RANGE OF GRANTS Usually £1,000 or £2,000.

SAMPLE GRANTS Arthritis Research UK, Blackthorn Trust, British Heart Foundation, ECHO International Health Services Ltd, Friends of the Elderly, Invalid Children's Aid Nationwide, Leukaemia Research Fund (£2,000 each); Brain Research Trust, British Trust for Conservation Volunteers, Childlink Adoption Society, Multiple Sclerosis Society and Riding for the Disabled Association (£1,000 each).

FINANCES *Year* 2015/16 *Income* £191,791 *Grants* £276,000 *Grants to organisations* £276,000 *Assets* £3,926,987

TRUSTEES Paul James; Crispian Howard; Theresa McGregor.

OTHER INFORMATION Grants were distributed as follows: disability/social work (£107,500); children's causes (£68,000); medical research (£67,500); hospices (£22,500); countryside projects (£10,500).

HOW TO APPLY Apply in writing to the correspondent. Distributions are usually made in February or March each year.

WHO TO APPLY TO Paul James, Trustee, 25 Ellenbridge Way, South Croydon CR2 0EW *Tel.* 020 8657 6884

■ The Harry Bottom Charitable Trust

CC NO 204675 **ESTABLISHED** 1960

WHERE FUNDING CAN BE GIVEN Sheffield; Rotherham; Barnsley; North East Derbyshire.

WHO CAN BENEFIT Registered charities.

WHAT IS FUNDED Medical causes; religious activities; education.

WHAT IS NOT FUNDED Individuals.

SAMPLE GRANTS Yorkshire Baptist Association (£30,000); Sheffield Mencap (£3,000); Contact the Elderly (£2,500); Asperger's Children and Carers Together, Lost Chord, Sheffield Dial A Ride and The Action Trust (£2,000 each).

FINANCES *Year* 2015/16 *Income* £231,860 *Grants* £69,410 *Grants to organisations* £69,410 *Assets* £6,281,495

TRUSTEES Revd William Shaw; Prof. Andrew Rawlinson; Helen Woolley; Derek Handforth.

OTHER INFORMATION Grants were broken down as follows: religious activities (£32,000); educational and other activities (£27,000); medical activities (£10,700).

HOW TO APPLY Apply in writing to the correspondent at any time enclosing your most recent set of annual accounts.

WHO TO APPLY TO John Hinsley, c/o Westons, Chartered Accountants, 1 Vincent House, 149 Solly Street, Sheffield S1 4BB *Tel.* 0114 273 8341

■ P. G. and N. J. Boulton Trust

CC NO 1158431 **ESTABLISHED** 1976

WHERE FUNDING CAN BE GIVEN Worldwide.

WHO CAN BENEFIT Registered charities, particularly smaller charities.

WHAT IS FUNDED Christian missionary work; social welfare and disaster relief; medical research and health care.

WHAT IS NOT FUNDED Individuals.

SAMPLE GRANTS Vision for China (£21,500); Longford Christian Trust (£15,500); Shalom Christian Trust (£6,000); Avail Mission (£5,500); Christian Institute (£4,000); Aurora Christian Association (£3,000); Charles Thompson Mission (£1,500); Anglo-Peruvian Child Care, Just Care and Asia Link (£1,000 each).

FINANCES *Year* 2015/16 *Income* £156,622 *Grants* £82,000 *Grants to organisations* £82,000 *Assets* £4,372,341

TRUSTEES Andrew L. Perry; Shirley Perry; Peter Stafford; Margaret Jardine-Smith.

HOW TO APPLY The trust's website states: 'The grant making policy has however undergone considerable change and shift of emphasis over the years. The original stated purpose of the Trust was to provide relief for the victims of disaster and to give to support to any other charitable cause as the Trustees saw fit. In earlier years we were open to applications for grants from a wide variety of causes, but due to ongoing financial and manpower constraints over more recent years, we are now no longer able to process numerous requests for grants in the same way. Instead our support is now largely limited to a list of charitable projects that are of special interest to the Trustees. Our interests are mainly centred around Christian missionary work, although many of the projects supported are concerned with the humanitarian relief of poverty and sickness in addition to the proclamation of the Gospel of Jesus Christ. Due to ongoing changes in policy [...] we are now largely unable to honour unsolicited requests for grants. If you would however like to share something of your work with us, then we are happy for you to do so, but would be grateful if you would do so by conventional post, rather than by e-mail. We are unable to respond to all correspondence, but as a general guideline, the Trustees meet every three months and if you do not receive any response within that timeframe, then you may reasonably assume that we are unable to provide any help at the present time.'

WHO TO APPLY TO Andrew Perry, Trustee, PO Box 72, Wirral CH28 9AE *Website* www.boultontrust.org.uk

■ Sir Clive Bourne Family Trust

CC NO 290620 **ESTABLISHED** 1984

WHERE FUNDING CAN BE GIVEN UK.

WHO CAN BENEFIT Individuals and institutions benefitting Jewish people.

WHAT IS FUNDED The trustees favour Jewish causes. A number of health and medical charities (particularly relating to cancer) have also benefitted.

SAMPLE GRANTS Prostate Cancer (£16,700); Jewish Care (£15,500); Magen David Adom UK (£10,000); Norwood (£9,300); Chai Community Care (£5,000); Chana (£1,800); Viscardi Center (£1,000); WIZO UK (£900); Simon Marks Primary School (£500).

FINANCES *Year* 2015/16 *Income* £188,399 *Grants* £97,300 *Grants to organisations* £97,300 *Assets* £5,135,997

TRUSTEES Lady Joy Bourne; Lucy Furman; Katie Cohen; Claire Lefton; Merryl Flitterman.

HOW TO APPLY Apply in writing to the correspondent.

WHO TO APPLY TO Janet Bater, Gardiner House, 6B Hemnall Street, Epping, Essex CM16 4LW *Tel.* 01992 560500 *Email* jbater@seabourne-group.com

■ Bourneheights Ltd

CC NO 298359 **ESTABLISHED** 1984

WHERE FUNDING CAN BE GIVEN UK.

WHO CAN BENEFIT Orthodox Jewish organisations and registered charities.

WHAT IS FUNDED Social welfare; education.

SAMPLE GRANTS Moreshet Hatorah; Mercaz Torah Vahesed Ltd; Belz Synagogue; Telz Academy Trust; Gevurath Ari Academy; UTA; Toreth Emeth; Olam Chesed Yiboneh; Before Trust; Heaven Point; Yeshivas Avas Torah; Lubavitch Mechina.

FINANCES *Year* 2014/15 *Income* £1,378,141 *Grants* £613,930 *Grants to organisations* £613,930 *Assets* £6,872,994

TRUSTEES Chaskel Rand; Esther Rand; Erno Berger; Yechiel Chersky; Schloime Rand.

OTHER INFORMATION The 2014/15 accounts were the latest available at the time of writing.

HOW TO APPLY Apply in writing to the correspondent.

WHO TO APPLY TO Schloime Rand, Trustee, Flat 10, Palm Court, Queen Elizabeth's Walk, London N16 5XA *Tel.* 020 8809 7398

■ The Bowerman Charitable Trust

CC NO 289446 **ESTABLISHED** 1984

WHERE FUNDING CAN BE GIVEN UK, with a preference for West Sussex.

WHO CAN BENEFIT Registered charities; churches.

WHAT IS FUNDED Church activities; the arts and music; medical causes; youth work; education.

TYPE OF GRANT One-off.

SAMPLE GRANTS St Margaret's Church (£84,500); St Mary's Maidenhead (£20,000); Petworth Festival (£11,000); Christianity Explored (£10,000); Imogen Cooper Music Trust, Lyminster Church and London Conducting Workshop (£5,000 each).

FINANCES *Year* 2015/16 *Income* £544,981 *Grants* £228,356 *Grants to organisations* £228,356 *Assets* £18,926,126

TRUSTEES David Bowerman; Anna Downham; Clarice Bowerman; Janet Taylor; Julyan Capper; Katharine Bowerman; Michael Follis.

HOW TO APPLY Unsolicited applications are not accepted.

WHO TO APPLY TO David Bowerman, Trustee, Champs Hill, Coldwaltham, Pulborough, West Sussex RH20 1LY *Tel.* 01798 831205

■ The Bowland Charitable Trust

CC NO 292027 **ESTABLISHED** 1985

WHERE FUNDING CAN BE GIVEN North West England.

WHO CAN BENEFIT Registered charities; institutions.

WHAT IS FUNDED Young people; education; general charitable purposes.

SAMPLE GRANTS Ron Clark Academy (£660,000); LEB Partnership (£306,000); The Brantwood Trust (£75,000); North Music Trust (£50,000); The Rosemere Cancer Foundation (£30,000); Blackburn Cathedral Trust (£25,000); Bowland High School (£20,000); Nazareth Unitarian Chapel (£15,000); The Lowry Centre Trust (£2,000); Ribble FM (£1,000).

FINANCES *Year* 2015 *Income* £52,385 *Grants* £1,610,197 *Grants to organisations* £1,610,197 *Assets* £7,737,203

TRUSTEES Tony Cann; Ruth Cann; Carole Fahy; Hugh Turner.

HOW TO APPLY The charity invites applications for funding of projects from individuals, institutions and charitable organisations. The applications are made directly to the trustees, who meet regularly to assess them.

WHO TO APPLY TO Carole Fahy, Trustee, Activhouse, Philips Road, Blackburn, Lancashire BB1 5RD *Tel.* 01254 688051 *Email* carole.fahy@cannco.co.uk

■ Friends of Boyan Trust

CC NO 1114498 **ESTABLISHED** 2006

WHERE FUNDING CAN BE GIVEN Worldwide.

WHO CAN BENEFIT Orthodox Jews.

WHAT IS FUNDED Jewish causes.

SAMPLE GRANTS A list of beneficiaries was not available.

FINANCES *Year* 2015 *Income* £703,908 *Grants* £705,611 *Grants to organisations* £705,611 *Assets* £65,977

TRUSTEES Jacob Getter; Mordechai Freund; Nathan Kuflik.

HOW TO APPLY Apply in writing to the correspondent.

WHO TO APPLY TO Jacob Getter, Trustee, 23 Durley Road, London N16 5JW *Tel.* 020 8809 6051

■ The Frank Brake Charitable Trust

CC NO 1023245 **ESTABLISHED** 1993

WHERE FUNDING CAN BE GIVEN Kent.

WHO CAN BENEFIT Registered charities.

WHAT IS FUNDED General charitable purposes.

RANGE OF GRANTS £1,000 to £30,000.

SAMPLE GRANTS Parkinson's UK (£30,000); Canterbury Cathedral Trust Fund and NSPCC (£10,000 each); Home-Start Ashford (£6,800); Children With Special Needs (£3,000); The Prostate Cancer Charity (£2,000); Ashford Borough Museum Society and BLISS (£1,000 each).

FINANCES *Year* 2015/16 *Income* £526,247 *Grants* £120,825 *Grants to organisations* £120,825 *Assets* £8,438,344

TRUSTEES Philip Wilson; Michael Trigg; Michelle Leveridge; Richard Brake.

HOW TO APPLY The 2015/16 accounts note: 'The charity invites applications from the Frank Blake family for funding of worthy registered charities each year, with a particular emphasis on local charities where the family know the charity's representative.'

WHO TO APPLY TO Michael Trigg, Trustee, Colman House, King Street, Maidstone, Kent ME14 1JE *Tel.* 01622 759051 *Email* michael.trigg@gillturnertucker.com

■ The William Brake Charitable Trust

CC NO 1023244 **ESTABLISHED** 1984

WHERE FUNDING CAN BE GIVEN UK, with a preference for Kent.

WHO CAN BENEFIT Registered charities; universities; hospices.

WHAT IS FUNDED General charitable purposes.

RANGE OF GRANTS £1,000 to £50,000.

SAMPLE GRANTS NSPCC (£52,000); The Whitley Fund for Nature (£50,000); Royal Academy of Arts (£15,000); The Kent MS Therapy Unit (£10,000); Jessie's Fund (£5,000); Magic Breakfast (£2,500); The Salvation Army (£2,000); Mane Chance, Purely Overseas Trust and Rutland Citizens Advice (£1,000 each).

FINANCES *Year* 2015/16 *Income* £112,863 *Grants* £457,556 *Grants to organisations* £457,556 *Assets* £10,316,774

TRUSTEES Philip Wilson; Deborah Isaac; Penelope Lang; Michael Trigg.

HOW TO APPLY The 2015/16 accounts note that: 'The charity invites applications from the William Brake family for funding of worthy registered charities each year, with a particular emphasis on local charities where the family know the charity's representative.'

WHO TO APPLY TO Michael Trigg, Trustee, Colman House, King Street, Maidstone, Kent ME14 1JE *Tel.* 01622 759051 *Email* michael.trigg@gillturnertucker.com

■ The Tony Bramall Charitable Trust

CC NO 1001522 **ESTABLISHED** 1990

WHERE FUNDING CAN BE GIVEN UK, with some preference for Yorkshire.

WHO CAN BENEFIT Local charities within Yorkshire and national medical institutions.

WHAT IS FUNDED Medical research, ill health and social welfare.

RANGE OF GRANTS Usually £1,000 to £5,000.

SAMPLE GRANTS University of Leeds – Cancer Research (£193,000); Shift.ms (£17,500); Saint Michael's Hospice (£5,600); Children with Cancer (£3,000); Wellbeing of Women (£2,500); Cystic Fibrosis Care (£2,000); Claire House Children's Hospice (£1,500); Barnardo's (£1,000); Tall Ships Youth Trust (£750); World Cancer Research (£500).

FINANCES *Year* 2015/16 *Income* £157,758 *Grants* £247,670 *Grants to organisations* £247,670 *Assets* £4,020,696

TRUSTEES Tony Bramall; Karen Bramall Odgen; Melanie Foody; Geoffrey Tate; Anna Bramall.

HOW TO APPLY Apply in writing to the correspondent.

WHO TO APPLY TO The Trustees, 12 Cardale Court, Beckwith Head Road, Harrogate, North Yorkshire HG3 1RY *Tel.* 01423 535300 *Email* alison.lockwood@bramallproperties.co.uk

■ The Liz and Terry Bramall Foundation

CC NO 1121670 **ESTABLISHED** 2007

WHERE FUNDING CAN BE GIVEN UK, in practice mainly Yorkshire.

WHO CAN BENEFIT Charitable organisations; churches.

WHAT IS FUNDED Support of the Christian faith; promotion of urban or rural regeneration in areas of social and economic deprivation; relief of sickness and the advancement of health; education; arts and culture.

RANGE OF GRANTS £1,000 to £1 million.

SAMPLE GRANTS The Prince's Trust (£1.05 million); NSPCC (£400,000); Yorkshire Air Ambulance (£200,000); Birmingham University (£97,500); Bradford Cathedral (£40,000); Action on Hearing Loss (£35,000); Mark Scott Foundation (£25,000); Ashwell Academy (£10,000); Unity in Poverty Action (£3,500); The National Motor Museum (£2,500); The Rotary Club of Humberside (£1,400); Jericho House Production (£500).

FINANCES *Year* 2015/16 *Income* £2,073,280 *Grants* £6,176,475 *Grants to organisations* £5,212,972 *Assets* £107,616,639

TRUSTEES Dr Terence Bramall; Elizabeth Bramall; Suzannah Allard; Rebecca Bletcher; Rachel Tunnicliffe; Anthony Sharp.

HOW TO APPLY Applications can be made in writing to the correspondent. The foundation has previously stated that 'unsolicited requests from national charities will generally only be considered if there is some public benefit to the Yorkshire region'.

WHO TO APPLY TO Dr Terence Bramall, Trustee, c/o Raworths LLP, Eton House, 89 Station Parade, Harrogate, North Yorkshire HG1 1HF *Tel.* 01423 566666

■ The Bransford Trust

CC NO 1106554 **ESTABLISHED** 2004

WHERE FUNDING CAN BE GIVEN Worcester and surrounding areas.

WHO CAN BENEFIT Registered charities; hospices; educational establishments.

WHAT IS FUNDED Culture; education; sport; community health care.

RANGE OF GRANTS Up to £120,000.

SAMPLE GRANTS St Richard's Hospice (£120,000); Acorn Children's Hospice (£40,000); The Prince's Trust (£20,000); Worcester Festival (£18,000); Young Enterprise (£15,000); Earth Heritage Trust (£11,000); Elgar School of Music (£8,000); Severn Valley Railway Charitable Trust, Vamos Young Children's' Theatre and Worcester Haven Unit (£5,000 each).

FINANCES *Year* 2015/16 *Income* £497,016 *Grants* £438,050 *Grants to organisations* £438,050 *Assets* £16,018,182

TRUSTEES Arthur Neil; Colin Kinnear; Brenda Kinnear; John Carver.

HOW TO APPLY Applications can be made through the trust's website. The trustees meet in July/August and December/January to discuss applications. The closing dates for applications are 15 June and 15 December each year.

WHO TO APPLY TO Julia Kirkham, Administrator, 6 Edgar Street, Worcester WR1 2LR *Website* www.bransfordtrust.org

■ The Breadsticks Foundation

CC NO 1125396 **ESTABLISHED** 2008

WHERE FUNDING CAN BE GIVEN UK; Sudan; South Sudan; Kenya; Rwanda; Zambia; Zimbabwe; South Africa; India; Indonesia; Laos.

WHO CAN BENEFIT Charities and community groups.

WHAT IS FUNDED Health; education; youth development.

TYPE OF GRANT Core funding; project funding.

SAMPLE GRANTS Hope and Homes for Children (£250,000); Freedom from Torture (£150,000); Kids in Need of Education (£146,000); Mumbai Mobile Crèches (£103,500).

FINANCES *Year* 2014/15 *Income* £1,013,533 *Grants* £1,151,416 *Grants to organisations* £1,151,416 *Assets* £247,462

TRUSTEES Beatrix Payne; Dr Kirsty Le Doare; Dr Paul Ballantyne; Beatrice Roberts; Trevor Macy; Alison Bukhari.

OTHER INFORMATION The 2014/15 accounts were the latest available at the time of writing (May 2017).

HOW TO APPLY Applications are by invitation only, and unsolicited applications will not be considered.

WHO TO APPLY TO Beatrix Payne, Trustee, 35 Canonbury Square, London N1 2AN *Tel.* 020 7288 0667 *Email* info@breadsticksfoundation.org *Website* www.breadsticksfoundation.org

■ Breast Cancer Now

CC NO 1160558 **ESTABLISHED** 2014

WHERE FUNDING CAN BE GIVEN UK and Ireland.

WHO CAN BENEFIT Research institutions.

WHAT IS FUNDED Breast cancer research.

TYPE OF GRANT Research.

SAMPLE GRANTS A list of beneficiaries was not available.

FINANCES *Year* 2015/16 *Income* £27,616,000 *Grants* £13,147,000 *Grants to organisations* £13,147,000 *Assets* £11,211,000

TRUSTEES Susan Johnson; Prof. Powles; Lynne Berry; Prof. Robert Coleman; Prof. Harris; Prof. Evans; Pascale Guely; Dr Veronique Bouchet; Laura Simons; Susan Gallone.

HOW TO APPLY Applications can be made via the charity's website.

WHO TO APPLY TO Hannah Hinton, 5th Floor, Ibex House, 42–47 Minories, London EC3N 1DY *Tel.* 0333 207 0300 *Website* www.breastcancernow.org

■ The Breast Cancer Research Trust (BCRT)

CC NO 272214 **ESTABLISHED** 1961

WHERE FUNDING CAN BE GIVEN UK.

WHO CAN BENEFIT Specific units in teaching hospitals; universities.

WHAT IS FUNDED Clinical and translational research into the prevention, early diagnosis and treatment of breast cancer.

TYPE OF GRANT Project; research; core costs; salaries; up to a term of three years (reviewed annually).

SAMPLE GRANTS Breakthrough Breast Cancer, The Institute of Cancer Research (£50,000); King's College London (£24,500); University of South Manchester (£20,000).

FINANCES *Year* 2015/16 *Income* £68,140 *Grants* £94,500 *Grants to organisations* £94,500 *Assets* £140,835

TRUSTEES Dame Vera Lynn; Bob Potter; Prof. Trevor Powles; Dr Margaret Spittle; Mr R. Rainsbury; Prof. Charles Coombes; Ms Lewis-Jones.

HOW TO APPLY Application forms are available only from the trust's website. Awards are made once or twice a year. Note that seven copies of the form are required. All appeals are assessed by a peer group.

WHO TO APPLY TO Rosemary Sutcliffe, Executive Administrator, PO Box 861, Bognor Regis, West Sussex PO21 9HW *Tel.* 01243 583143 *Email* bcrtrust@btinternet.com *Website* www.breastcancerresearchtrust.org.uk

■ The Brelms Trust CIO

CC NO 1153372 **ESTABLISHED** 2013

WHERE FUNDING CAN BE GIVEN Yorkshire.

WHO CAN BENEFIT Registered charities.

WHAT IS FUNDED Health; social welfare; the arts; sport; disability; community.

WHAT IS NOT FUNDED The charity's website lists the following restrictions: 'Organisations without charitable status; organisations not registered at the Charity Commission; large charitable organisations with an annual income of more than £500,000; national charities, unless the project is based in Yorkshire and for the specific benefit of the Yorkshire community, with clear evidence of embedded local management and financial control of budgetary spending and grant funding, usually evidenced by a set of Accounts; applications from individuals or student gap year costs; charities which send out general appeal letters for donations; organisations which advance religion or promote faith-based activities as stated within the charitable objects registered at the Charity Commission (if this does not in any way apply to the Project for which you are applying for funding, then it is your responsibility to demonstrate to us within your application that such is the case); party political organisations; animal welfare; medical research; work requiring retrospective funding.'

RANGE OF GRANTS Up to £15,000 but mostly £1,000 to £5,000.

SAMPLE GRANTS Behind Closed Doors and Calderdale Wellbeing (£15,000 each); Castle Community Network (£9,000); Hale Project and Sobriety Project (£7,500 each); Faceless Company (£6,000); Imagine Theatre (£5,000); Orb Comm Enterprise (£2,100); Football Unites Racism Divides (£1,900).

FINANCES *Year* 2015/16 *Income* £705,840 *Grants* £436,527 *Grants to organisations* £436,527 *Assets* £2,133,427

TRUSTEES Mary Cornish; Lesley Faithful; Juliet Kemp; Christine Gamble; Glynis Jones; Stephen Stroud.

OTHER INFORMATION There were 51 grants made during the year.

HOW TO APPLY Applications can be made via the trust's website.

WHO TO APPLY TO Chris Goldson, Metro House, 57 Pepper Road, Leeds, West Yorkshire LS10 2RU *Email* admin@brelmstrust.org.uk *Website* www.brelmstrust.org.uk

■ Bridge Trust

CC NO 201288 **ESTABLISHED** 1961

WHERE FUNDING CAN BE GIVEN Barnstaple (within a five-mile radius of Barnstaple Guildhall).

WHO CAN BENEFIT Local charitable and amenity groups within the area of benefit; national organisations providing support to individuals or groups within the area of benefit; and individuals within the area of benefit, deserving and in need.

WHAT IS FUNDED General charitable purpose including: welfare; older people; young people, health and medical causes; schools; and sport.

TYPE OF GRANT Capital including buildings, core costs, one-off, project, research, running costs, recurring costs and start-up costs will be considered. Funding may be given for up to one year.

SAMPLE GRANTS Barnstaple Football Club; Barnstaple Town Youth Marching Band; Brauton Youth Club; North Devon Family Mediation

Service; North Devon Hospice; Orchard Vale School; Tarka Velo; Westward Housing.

FINANCES *Year* 2015 *Income* £309,752 *Grants* £87,789 *Grants to organisations* £87,789 *Assets* £4,924,887

TRUSTEES David Trueman; Cllr Jeremy Phillips; Valerie Elkins; Graham Lofthouse; Stephen Upcott; Suzanne Haywood; Keith Luckhurst; Christopher Haywood; Amanda Isaac; Julie Hunt; Graham Townsend; David Wright.

HOW TO APPLY Application forms are available to download from the trust's website. The grants subcommittee meets three times per year in February, May and November. Applications must be received by the 25th of the previous month.

WHO TO APPLY TO Peter Laurie, Chamberlain, 7 Bridge Chambers, The Strand, Barnstaple, Devon EX31 1HB *Tel.* 01271 343995 *Email* chamberlain@barumbridgetrust.org *Website* www.barumbridgetrust.org

■ Bridgepoint Charitable Trust

CC NO 1134525 **ESTABLISHED** 2010

WHERE FUNDING CAN BE GIVEN UK; France; Germany; Italy; Luxembourg; Poland; Spain.

WHO CAN BENEFIT Registered charities.

WHAT IS FUNDED General charitable purposes, especially education, health, environment and children. The trust aims to help 'where its donation can make a meaningful difference'.

RANGE OF GRANTS Up to £64,000.

SAMPLE GRANTS Teens and Toddlers (£103,500); Fundacja Dzieci Niczyje (£53,000); Fryshuset (£50,000); Aenilce (£45,500); Orchestre a l'Ecole (£44,500).

FINANCES *Year* 2015 *Income* £104,400 *Grants* £203,303 *Grants to organisations* £203,303 *Assets* £254,051

TRUSTEES Michael Walton; James Murray; Ruth McIntosh; P. R. Gunner; Jamie Wyatt; David Hankin; Emma Watford; Stefanie Arensmann; Mathew Legg; Vincent-Gael Baudet.

OTHER INFORMATION The trust is linked to the international private equity firm, Bridgepoint. It also operates an employee matched funding scheme (matched donations of below £10,000 totalled £11,600).

HOW TO APPLY The trust does not appear to be accepting unsolicited applications.

WHO TO APPLY TO Benjamin Marten, Secretary, 95 Wigmore Street, London W1U 1FB *Tel.* 020 7432 3500 *Website* www.bridgepoint.eu

■ The Harold and Alice Bridges Charity

CC NO 236654 **ESTABLISHED** 1963

WHERE FUNDING CAN BE GIVEN Lancashire and South Cumbria, particularly the area north of the River Ribble, eastwards towards the Blackburn area and into South Lakes.

WHO CAN BENEFIT Registered charities; village halls; churches.

WHAT IS FUNDED General charitable purposes, particularly young people, older people and capital projects supporting rural and village life.

WHAT IS NOT FUNDED Individuals.

TYPE OF GRANT The trustees prefer mainly capital projects which have an element of self-help.

RANGE OF GRANTS Usually £500 to £5,000.

SAMPLE GRANTS St John the Baptist, Tunstall (£5,000); Newton in Bowland Village Hall (£4,000); Stalmine Village Hall (£3,000); Pendleton Village Hall and Swarthmoor Sports and Community Club (£2,000 each); British Wireless for the Blind (£1,000); Arnside Bowling Club (£600); Luneside and Rosebank Bowling Club (£500).

FINANCES *Year* 2015/16 *Income* £131,104 *Grants* £122,700 *Grants to organisations* £122,700 *Assets* £3,481,530

TRUSTEES Richard N. Hardy; Irene Greenwood; John Hinchliffe; Christopher Calvert.

HOW TO APPLY Refer to the charity's website for full application details including a downloadable form. The application deadlines are 15 January, 15 May and 15 September each year.

WHO TO APPLY TO Richard N. Hardy, Trustee, Linder Myers Solicitors, 21–23 Park Street, Lytham FY8 5LU *Tel.* 0844 984 6001 *Email* david.hinchliffe@lindermyers.co.uk *Website* www.haroldandalicebridgescharity.co.uk

■ The Bridging Fund Charitable Trust

CC NO 1119171 **ESTABLISHED** 2007

WHERE FUNDING CAN BE GIVEN UK.

WHO CAN BENEFIT Charitable organisations that help individuals in need.

WHAT IS FUNDED Social welfare and the relief of poverty.

WHAT IS NOT FUNDED Running costs; grants directly to individuals.

SAMPLE GRANTS A list of beneficiaries was not available.

FINANCES *Year* 2015 *Income* £6,035 *Grants* £100,000 *Grants to organisations* £100,000

TRUSTEES David Reeds; Mike Richardson; Rosemary Mackay; Debbie Cockrill; Gordon Hayes; Rosemary Williamson.

OTHER INFORMATION This charity's latest accounts were not available to view on the Charity Commission's website due to its low income. We have therefore estimated the grant total based on its annual expenditure.

HOW TO APPLY Apply in writing to the correspondent.

WHO TO APPLY TO Debbie Cockrill, Trustee, PO Box 3106, Lancing, West Sussex BN15 5BL *Tel.* 01903 750008 *Email* info@bridgingfund.org

■ Bristol Archdeaconry Charity

CC NO 1058853 **ESTABLISHED** 1996

WHERE FUNDING CAN BE GIVEN Archdeaconry of Bristol and the surrounding area including the Deanery of Kingswood in South Gloucestershire, and the Benefice of Marshfield with Cold Ashton and Tormarton with West Littleton.

WHO CAN BENEFIT Registered charities; religious bodies; individuals.

WHAT IS FUNDED Religious and other charitable purposes of the Church of England in the area of benefit. The 2015 accounts state: 'Grants should generally be associated with church-based ministry and community projects in Urban Priority Area parishes, and made wherever possible by way of start-up funding.'

TYPE OF GRANT One-off and recurrent; capital costs; projects; start-up costs.

RANGE OF GRANTS £60 to£70,000.

SAMPLE GRANTS Diocese of Bristol (£75,000); Redland Education Centre (£15,000); East Bristol Partnership and St Luke's Church, Barton Hill (£5,000 each); St Martin's Church, Knowle (£2,000); Christ Church, Downend (£500).

FINANCES *Year* 2015 *Income* £138,697 *Grants* £150,500 *Grants to organisations* £150,500 *Assets* £3,506,097

TRUSTEES David Worthington; Timothy Thom; Roger Metcalfe; Anthony Brown; Peter Wolf; The Ven. Christine Froude, Archdeacon of Malmesbury; Revd Lee Barnes; Stephen Gisby; Oliver Home.

OTHER INFORMATION In 2015 grants were made to 15 organisations.

HOW TO APPLY Applications may be made in writing to the correspondent. The trustees meet twice during the year.

WHO TO APPLY TO Philippa Drewett, Clerk to the Trustees, All Saints Centre, 1 All Saints Court, Bristol BS1 1JN *Tel.* 0117 929 2709

■ Bristol Charities

CC NO 1109141 **ESTABLISHED** 1960

WHERE FUNDING CAN BE GIVEN In practice the City of Bristol, North Somerset and South Gloucestershire; mainly within a ten-mile radius of Bristol city centre.

WHO CAN BENEFIT Educational and religious establishments; individuals.

WHAT IS FUNDED Educational assistance to schools and educational charities (via Barry Theo Jones Fund). A great part of support is given to individual beneficiaries for the relief of sickness and need and supporting carers, especially women.

RANGE OF GRANTS Up to £57,500.

SAMPLE GRANTS Bristol Grammar School (£64,000 in two grants); Red Maids School (£4,800); Clifton High School (£2,200); Wesleyan Memorial Methodist Church (£1,800).

FINANCES *Year* 2015/16 *Income* £1,673,707 *Grants* £159,181 *Grants to organisations* £90,189 *Assets* £12,257,687

TRUSTEES David Watts; Susan Hampton; Dudley Lewis; Sonia Mills; Kamala Das; Andew Hillman; Laura Claydon; John Webster; Anthony Harris; Paul Staples; Richard Gore; Dr Ros Kennedy; Michelle Meredith; Dr Shaheen Chaudhry; Melanie Tiley; Nolan Webber.

OTHER INFORMATION The charity also provides housing and day care services for older people.

HOW TO APPLY Application forms are available to download from the charity's website, together with full criteria and guidelines.

WHO TO APPLY TO Andy Dixon, 17 St Augustine's Parade, Bristol BS1 4UL *Tel.* 0117 930 0301 *Email* info@bristolcharities.org.uk *Website* www.bristolcharities.org.uk

■ John Bristow and Thomas Mason Trust

CC NO 1075971 **ESTABLISHED** 1999

WHERE FUNDING CAN BE GIVEN Parish of Charlwood (as the boundaries stood in 1926).

WHO CAN BENEFIT Charitable organisations; individuals.

WHAT IS FUNDED Community purposes; social welfare; education. Grants are also made to individuals for welfare and educational purposes.

WHAT IS NOT FUNDED Any application that will not benefit the residents of the Parish of Charlwood (as the boundaries stood in 1926) will not be considered.

RANGE OF GRANTS Generally under £5,000.

SAMPLE GRANTS St Nicholas Parochial Church Council (£11,200 in two grants); Charlwood Parish Council and Charlwood Pre-School (£5,000 each); St Catherine's Hospice (£3,600); Charlwood Residents FC (£880); Lowfield Heath Windmill Trust (£520); Charlwood Mothers Union (£300); The Royal British Legion Charlwood – Women's Section (£130).

FINANCES *Year* 2015/16 *Income* £94,874 *Grants* £55,788 *Grants to organisations* £41,315 *Assets* £2,693,713

TRUSTEES Richard Parker; Graham Shoubridge; Alison Martin; Julie King; Carole Jordan; Christopher Peters; Margaret Hensman; Revd Sue Weakley.

OTHER INFORMATION In 2015/16 there were three grants to individuals for welfare purposes, amounting to £11,500, as well as three grants for educational purposes, which totalled £3,000.

HOW TO APPLY Applications should be made on a form available to download from the trust's website. Applications are usually considered within a fortnight. The trust welcomes contact from potential applicants to discuss eligibility and the application process.

WHO TO APPLY TO Sam Songhurst, Secretary, Beech Hay, Ifield Road, Charlwood, Surrey RH6 0DR *Tel.* 01293 862734 *Email* trust.secretary@jbtmt.org.uk *Website* www.jbtmt.org.uk

■ The British Academy for the Promotion of Historical Philosophical and Philological Studies (The British Academy)

CC NO 233176 **ESTABLISHED** 1902

WHERE FUNDING CAN BE GIVEN UK and overseas.

WHO CAN BENEFIT Postdoctoral scholars in the humanities and social sciences, ordinarily resident in the UK.

WHAT IS FUNDED Research grants, international joint activities, appointments, research projects and conferences.

WHAT IS NOT FUNDED Loans for graduate studies.

TYPE OF GRANT All awards are at postdoctoral level only.

SAMPLE GRANTS University of Oxford (£3.7 million); British School at Rome (£1 million); London School of Economics (£771,500); Council for British Research in the Levant (£686,000); School of Oriental and African Studies (£285,500); Medical Research Council (£249,000); Overseas Development Institute (£147,500); Institute for Fiscal Studies (£136,500); British Institute of Persian Studies (£114,500); Northumbria University (£86,000).

FINANCES *Year* 2015/16 *Income* £36,223,527 *Grants* £27,702,620 *Grants to organisations* £27,702,620 *Assets* £16,950,244

TRUSTEES Prof. Genevra Richardson; Prof. Richard McCabe; Prof. David Abulafia; Prof. Alan Bowman; Prof. Sarah Worthington; Prof. Bencie Woll; Prof. Ash Amin; Lord Stern of Brentford; Prof. Mary Morgan; Prof. Dominic Abrams; Prof. Sally Shuttleworth; Prof. Janet Watson; Prof. Nicholas Vincent; Prof. Gillian Clark; Prof. Archibald Brown; Prof. John Baines; Prof. Roger Kain; Prof. Glynis Jones; Prof. Maxine Berg; Prof. Marianne Elliott; Prof. Michael Keating; Revd Prof. Diarmaid MacCulloch; Prof. Terence Irwin; Prof. Anne Phillips; Prof. John Scott.

HOW TO APPLY Comprehensive details of grants and awards are available from the academy's website.

WHO TO APPLY TO Grants Team, British Academy, 10 Carlton House Terrace, London SW1Y 5AH *Tel.* 020 7969 5217 *Email* grants@britac.ac.uk *Website* www.britac.ac.uk

■ The British and Foreign Bible Society

CC NO 232759 **ESTABLISHED** 1948

WHERE FUNDING CAN BE GIVEN Worldwide.

WHO CAN BENEFIT Charities; prisons; immigration centres; educational institutions.

WHAT IS FUNDED Projects that make the Bible available and accessible to people around the world.

SAMPLE GRANTS A list of beneficiaries was not available.

FINANCES *Year* 2015/16 *Income* £18,146,000 *Grants* £3,649,000 *Grants to organisations* £3,649,000 *Assets* £2,219,000

TRUSTEES Arfon Jones; John Grifiths; Col. Richard Sandy; Christina Rees; Peter Muir; Catherine Pepinster; Dr Bunmi Olayisade; Sue Heatherington; Paul Chandler; Alan Eccles; James Featherby; Ian Dighe; Paul Bosson; Prof. Paul Williams.

OTHER INFORMATION A total of 522 grants were made during the year. Grants to UK organisations totalled £259,000.

HOW TO APPLY According the annual report for 2015/16: 'Project proposals are discussed with those Bible Societies and project briefs are agreed and documented, to a formal approval process. An agreed monitoring process is undertaken during the life cycle of the project. In addition, interim and final evaluations are carried out on a sample of the larger projects, to ensure that lessons are learned. A summary of the largest grants made by Bible Society is shown in note nine to the accounts.'

WHO TO APPLY TO The Trustees, Stonehill Green, Westlea, Swindon SN5 7DG *Tel.* 01793 418100 *Email* info@biblesociety.org.uk *Website* www.biblesociety.org.uk

■ The British and Foreign School Society

CC NO 314286 **ESTABLISHED** 1964

WHERE FUNDING CAN BE GIVEN UK and overseas.

WHO CAN BENEFIT Educational or training institutions which have UK charitable status or, in the case of schools, colleges, universities and churches, 'exempt charity' status.

WHAT IS FUNDED Education and training for children and young people (up to 25).

WHAT IS NOT FUNDED Health projects without a clear education link (except where used as a means of achieving educational outcomes); water and sanitation projects without a clear education link (except where there is a very clear link to education access/attainment); transport or other travel costs; the arts (unless where used as a means of achieving educational outcomes); sport and sports facilities (unless where used as a means of achieving educational outcomes); special or one-off events, e.g. conferences, seminars, expeditions, summer camps; bursaries, scholarships and endowments; expeditions and overseas travel; individual volunteering overseas; ongoing programmes; salaries and running costs; research other than on educational service development.

TYPE OF GRANT One-off and recurring.

RANGE OF GRANTS Up to £35,000.

SAMPLE GRANTS Children on the Edge (£41,000); Afghan Association Paiwand (£33,000); War Child (£27,500); Care Pakistan (£24,000); International Children's Trust (£16,000); Children in Crisis (£14,500); Egerton Schools Foundation (£6,300); Phase Worldwide (£4,400); Chhahari Schools UK (£4,000); Sensory Trust (£3,000).

FINANCES *Year* 2015 *Income* £669,956 *Grants* £731,554 *Grants to organisations* £731,554 *Assets* £21,685,169

TRUSTEES Graham Kingsley; Leslie Stephen; David Swain; Prof. Steve Hodkinson; Revd David Tennant; Stephen King; Stephen Ross; Dr Emily Ross; Dr Jaz Saggu; Stephen Wordsworth; Ms E. J. Weale; Diana Hoy; Peter Miller; Karen Hughes; Prof. Joy Palmer.

HOW TO APPLY There is an online application form. Applications from charitable organisations which meet the grant criteria are considered by the grants committee, which normally meets quarterly. Refer to the society's website for more details, including deadline dates.

WHO TO APPLY TO Belinda Lawrence, Maybrook House, 97 Godstone Road, Caterham, Surrey CR3 6RE *Tel.* 01883 331177 *Email* enquiries@bfss.org.uk *Website* www.bfss.org.uk

■ British Council for Prevention of Blindness (Save Eyes Everywhere)

CC NO 270941 **ESTABLISHED** 1976

WHERE FUNDING CAN BE GIVEN Worldwide.

WHO CAN BENEFIT Organisations benefitting people with sight loss; research bodies; medical professionals, research workers and scientists in the field.

WHAT IS FUNDED According to its website the charity focuses on 'funding research, including fellowships, which has the potential to make breakthroughs in understanding and treating currently incurable eye diseases, and on operational research to improve best practice and delivery of eye care services'.

WHAT IS NOT FUNDED Completion of an existing project, including a PhD or MD, when previous funding has ended; laboratory-based research of a basic molecular or cell biological nature, unless strong relevance to VISION 2020 aims can be demonstrated to the satisfaction of the advisory panel.

TYPE OF GRANT Fellowships; funding for studentships; research grants over one, two or three years.

SAMPLE GRANTS International Centre for Eye Health (£242,000 in four grants); Boulter Fellowship Awards (£62,500).

FINANCES *Year* 2015/16 *Income* £196,877 *Grants* £290,482 *Grants to organisations* £290,482 *Assets* £690,982

TRUSTEE BCPB. Management Ltd.

HOW TO APPLY Application forms are accessible on the charity's website. See online for full guidelines and submission deadlines.

WHO TO APPLY TO Diana Bramson, Charity Manager, 4 Bloomsbury Square, London WC1A 2RP *Tel.* 020 7404 7114 *Email* info@bcpb.org *Website* www.bcpb.org

■ The British Dietetic Association General and Education Trust Fund

CC NO 282553 **ESTABLISHED** 1981

WHERE FUNDING CAN BE GIVEN UK.

WHO CAN BENEFIT Organisations; individuals; recognised associations; groups of people engaged in dietetic research and associated activities.

WHAT IS FUNDED Education; research; anything related to the science of dietetics.

WHAT IS NOT FUNDED Buying buildings; expenses for postgraduate qualifications; support dietetic students in training; conference attendance, unless the attendee is presenting a poster, a lecture, leading a workshop, etc. and the conference will promote the science of dietetics or dietetic practice.

TYPE OF GRANT Running costs; project costs; salary costs.

SAMPLE GRANTS A list of beneficiaries was not available.

FINANCES *Year* 2015/16 *Income* £65,235 *Grants* £40,826 *Grants to organisations* £41,760 *Assets* £1,660,218

TRUSTEES Peter Brindley; William Seddon; Michele Mackintosh; Prof. Martin Wiseman; Sian O'Shea.

OTHER INFORMATION A list of beneficiaries could not be obtained. The trust has various different award schemes; full details can be found on the website. The trustees awarded £1,500 for the Dame Barbara Clayton Award, along with a Rose Simmonds Memorial Fund award of £2,000 for work published or delivered by dietitians in the previous year.

HOW TO APPLY Application forms can be downloaded from the trust's website. They should be submitted at least six weeks before the trustees' meeting – mid-March for the May meeting and mid-September for the November meeting. Supporting documentation is welcome. Full and detailed guidelines are available online.

WHO TO APPLY TO The Secretary to the Trustees, 5th Floor, Charles House, 148–149 Great Charles Street, Queensway, Birmingham B3 3HT *Tel.* 0121 200 8080 *Fax* 0121 200 8081 *Email* info@bda.uk.com *Website* www.bda.uk.com/about/trustfund/home

■ British Eye Research Foundation (Fight for Sight)

CC NO 1111438 **ESTABLISHED** 2005

WHERE FUNDING CAN BE GIVEN UK.

WHO CAN BENEFIT Research institutions; hospitals; universities.

WHAT IS FUNDED Ophthalmology and eye research. The charity's six priority research areas are: developing and testing new and more effective treatments; improving the understanding of the causes of eye diseases and conditions; developing ways of preventing age-related macular degeneration, glaucoma, cataract and diabetic eye disease; improving the early detection of eye diseases and conditions; improving through eye research the quality of life for adults and children living with sight loss; identifying and assessing emerging threats to sight.

SAMPLE GRANTS University College London Institute of Ophthalmology (£827,000); University of Liverpool (£219,000); University College London (£145,000); King's College London (£100,000); Moorfields Eye Hospital NHS Foundation Trust (£60,000); Imperial College London (£25,000); University of Nottingham (£15,000); Guy's and St Thomas' NHS Foundation Trust (£2,000).

FINANCES *Year* 2015/16 *Income* £4,011,000 *Grants* £3,163,000 *Grants to organisations* £3,163,000 *Assets* £10,208,000

TRUSTEES Alistair Rae; Nigel Panting; Jennifer Williams; Louisa Vincent; Ginny Greenwood; Fiona Hathorn; Prof. David Spalton; Joanna Baldwin; Barbara Merry; Roy Quinlan; Thomas Bjorn; Prof. Maria Cordeiro; Simon Craddock; Prof. Johnathan Grant.

HOW TO APPLY Apply online via the charity's website. Details of open programmes and application deadlines can also be found on the site.

WHO TO APPLY TO Zoe Marshall, Fight For Sight, 18 Mansell Street, London E1 8AA *Tel.* 020 7264 3904 *Email* info@fightforsight.org.uk *Website* www.fightforsight.org.uk

■ British Gas Energy Trust

CC NO 1106218 **ESTABLISHED** 2004

WHERE FUNDING CAN BE GIVEN England, Scotland and Wales.

WHO CAN BENEFIT Charities and other voluntary sector organisations; charitable advice agencies; current domestic customers of British Gas or Scottish Gas. Organisations must operate or serve people in the main regions of the trust's operation.

WHAT IS FUNDED Relief in need for individuals and families; agencies providing money and debt prevention advice and education, often with a particular fuel poverty emphasis. The main aim of the fund is to address health problems that are exacerbated by fuel poverty.

TYPE OF GRANT One-off grants for individuals; one-off and recurrent, capital and revenue grants for organisations.

SAMPLE GRANTS Shelter (£1.7 million); Energy Project (£125,000); Zinthyia (£106,000); Preston Citizens Advice (£96,000); Speakeasy (£83,000); St Helen's Citizens Advice (Bromley by Bow (£70,000); Local Solutions (£69,000); St Ann's Advice (£68,500); Dawn (£22,000).

FINANCES *Year* 2015/16 *Income* £28,641,803 *Grants* £28,641,803 *Grants to organisations* £14,924,468 *Assets* £2,488,824

TRUSTEES Imelda Redmond; Andrew Brown; John Kolm-Murray; Daksha Piparia; Colin Trend; Peter Smith.

OTHER INFORMATION Grants to individuals for energy debt totalled £5.8 million. Around £10.9 million of the grants to organisations were made under the Health Homes Funding agreement.

HOW TO APPLY Funding rounds for organisations are normally publicised on the trust's website and in its newsletter. Applications from individuals should be made through the online application form or by post using a form available from the trust's website. Successful applicant cannot re-apply for a period of two years; unsuccessful applicants can re-apply if their circumstances change.

WHO TO APPLY TO The Trustees, 3rd Floor, Trinity Court, Trinity Street, Peterborough PE1 1DA *Tel.* 01733 421060 *Email* bget@charisgrants.com *Website* www.britishgasenergytrust.org.uk

British Heart Foundation (BHF)

CC NO 225971 **ESTABLISHED** 1961

WHERE FUNDING CAN BE GIVEN Unrestricted, in practice UK.

WHO CAN BENEFIT Organisations; research bodies; educational and medical institutions; academics; medical professionals; students.

WHAT IS FUNDED Medical research into all aspects of heart disease. There are a range of awards available, all schemes being detailed on the foundation's website.

WHAT IS NOT FUNDED Applications are accepted only from appropriately qualified individuals.

TYPE OF GRANT Projects; research; programmes; fellowship grants; salaries.

RANGE OF GRANTS Unrestricted.

SAMPLE GRANTS University of Oxford (£17.4 million in 11 grants); King's College London (£2.3 million in three grants); University of Glasgow (£2 million in three grants); University of Bristol (£1.5 million); University of Leeds (£1.4 million); University of Loughborough (£500,000).

FINANCES *Year* 2015/16 *Income* £124,700,000 *Grants* £104,300,000 *Grants to organisations* £116,700,000 *Assets* £46,200,000

TRUSTEES Richard Hytner; Dr Simon Ray; Prof. Liam Smeeth; Dr Evan Harris; Andrew Balfour; Prof. John Iredale; Dr Robert Easton; Prof. Anna Domini.

HOW TO APPLY Detailed and helpful criteria, guidelines, forms and application procedure are all fully explained on the foundation's website.

WHO TO APPLY TO Research Funds Department, Greater London House, 180 Hampstead Road, London NW1 7AW *Tel.* 020 7554 0434 *Email* research@bhf.org.uk *Website* www.bhf.org.uk

British Humane Association

CC NO 207120 **ESTABLISHED** 1922

WHERE FUNDING CAN BE GIVEN UK.

WHO CAN BENEFIT Charities directly involved in humanitarian activities; charities distributing grants to individuals; charities providing relief of poverty or sickness, or benefit to the community.

WHAT IS FUNDED Welfare.

TYPE OF GRANT One-off, capital and recurring grants will be considered.

RANGE OF GRANTS £1,000 to £15,000.

SAMPLE GRANTS White Chapel Mission (£20,000); St John of Jerusalem Eye Hospital (£15,000); Send a Cow (£10,000); The Amber Trust (£7,000); New Generation – Burundi (£6,000); Tilden Project – Nepal (£5,000); Genesis Trust (£3,000); Off the Fence (£2,000); Cancer Research UK (£1,000).

FINANCES *Year* 2015 *Income* £135,102 *Grants* £104,000 *Grants to organisations* £104,000 *Assets* £4,394,867

TRUSTEES Philip Gee; Duncan Cantlay; Anthony Chignell; John Breen; Michael Nemko; Rachel Campbell-Johnston; Edward Campbell-Johnston; Dr John Smail; Sarah Fox.

HOW TO APPLY Applications are not considered by the charity. The charity's 2015 annual report states: 'The directors of the Association have decided, that in order to increase the amount available for grant distribution to beneficiaries, they will transfer funds to other charitable organisations, which have in place systems for identifying and assisting deserving cases in need. By so doing, they will not duplicate selection processes and the resultant costs. It is the intention that any one or more of the directors will examine requests for assistance received and submit a proposal to the board to award a one-off, set period or continuing grant to any body, which has applied for assistance.'

WHO TO APPLY TO Sarah Fox, Secretary, Suite 1, Bessemer Road, Cardiff CF11 8BA

British Record Industry Trust (BRIT Trust)

CC NO 1000413 **ESTABLISHED** 1989

WHERE FUNDING CAN BE GIVEN Worldwide, in practice UK.

WHO CAN BENEFIT Registered charities benefitting young people involved in the arts, particularly music; schools.

WHAT IS FUNDED The BRIT Trust considers all applications which meet the criteria within its mission statement: 'To encourage young people in the exploration and pursuit of educational, cultural or therapeutic benefits emanating from music.'

WHAT IS NOT FUNDED Scholarships or grants to individuals; capital funding projects; unregistered charities; grants outside the UK.

TYPE OF GRANT One-off and recurring grants; capital and core costs; salaries; projects; unrestricted funding.

SAMPLE GRANTS Nordoff Robbins Music Therapy (£410,000); BRIT School for Performing Arts and Technology (£400,000); Warchild (£172,000); Creative Access (£40,000); Key4Life (£30,000); Chelsea and Westminster Hospital (£10,000); Buckinghamshire University (£5,000).

FINANCES *Year* 2015 *Income* £1,826,717 *Grants* £1,041,613 *Grants to organisations* £1,032,113 *Assets* £9,502,861

TRUSTEES John Deacon; John Craig; Andy Cleary; Jonathan Morrish; Rob Dickins; Tony Wandsworth; David Kassner; Geoff Taylor; Korda Marshall; David Sharpe; William Rowe; David Munns; Margaret Crowe; Angela Watts; Simon Presswell; Melanie Fox; Gerald Doherty.

OTHER INFORMATION The accounts note: 'After meeting the larger commitments of the BRIT School and Nordoff Robbins, if possible, it is the Trustees' policy to make a number of smaller donations to various charities.'

HOW TO APPLY Application forms are available from the trust's website.

WHO TO APPLY TO Maggie Crowe, Trustee, c/o BPI, Riverside Building, County Hall, Westminster Bridge Road, London SE1 7JA *Tel.* 020 7803 1351 *Email* maggie.crowe@bpi.co.uk *Website* www.brittrust.co.uk

The Britten-Pears Foundation

CC NO 295595 **ESTABLISHED** 1986

WHERE FUNDING CAN BE GIVEN UK, with a preference for East Anglia and Suffolk in particular.

WHO CAN BENEFIT Registered charities; arts organisations, including opera companies, orchestras and music ensembles; individual performers, authors and scholars; institutions with charitable objectives; UK-based commissioning bodies; local organisations.

WHAT IS FUNDED The foundation is not currently accepting applications as it is conducting a review of its grant-making. The foundation has in the past supported: projects that promote the music of Benjamin Britten in areas of the world where it is less well known; support to new, substantial music commissions; local grants within the vicinity of Aldeburgh (within 20 miles, especially Orford, Snape and Blythburgh) for grassroots projects in a range of fields and activities 'that promote the vitality of community life', with preference for causes involving young people, good environmental practice or environment and local amenities.

WHAT IS NOT FUNDED The following have previously been excluded: grants of a capital nature (including those for instrumental purchase or restoration); ongoing running costs; retrospective awards; tuition fees; copying or rehearsal fees; performance costs; recordings; educational or non-musical projects; applications for support for performances or recordings of the works of Benjamin Britten, of whose estate it is the beneficiary; subsidy for works by Britten which, in the estate's view, need further promotion can be sought from the Britten Estate Ltd.

TYPE OF GRANT One-off and recurring; projects. Partnership funding will be considered, although the foundation will wish to be a major contributor in all cases. Matching funding will not be a condition of grant.

SAMPLE GRANTS Royal Liverpool Philharmonic (£4,000); London Music Masters (£2,500); Eyke Parish Council Play Area (£2,000); Dig It and London Chamber Orchestra (£1,500 each); Judith Green Memorial Playground and Kyson Primary School (£1,000 each); Three Choirs Festival (£750).

FINANCES *Year* 2015 *Income* £1,440,072 *Grants* £396,925 *Grants to organisations* £396,925 *Assets* £26,207,560

TRUSTEES Andrew Fane; Dr Sally Irvine; Dr Colin Matthews; Sir Christopher Howes; Nicholas Prettejohn; Edward Blakeman; Janis Susskind; Caroline Brazier; Penelope Heath; Jane Hay; Oliver Rivers.

HOW TO APPLY At the time of writing (June 2017) the foundation's website states: 'Currently, no applications are being accepted for Britten Awards, New Music Commissions and Local Grants. A full review of the Foundation's grant-giving will take place in 2017 and further information will be put on the website thereafter. Send any related enquiries to grants@brittenpears.org.'

WHO TO APPLY TO Amanda Arnold, Company Secretary, The Red House, Golf Lane, Aldeburgh, Suffolk IP15 5PZ *Tel.* 01728 451700 *Email* grants@brittenpears.org *Website* www.brittenpears.org

■ The J. and M. Britton Charitable Trust

CC NO 1081979 **ESTABLISHED** 1996

WHERE FUNDING CAN BE GIVEN Mainly Bristol and the former county of Avon.

WHO CAN BENEFIT Local charities such as hospital appeals and other charities that the trustees are involved in.

WHAT IS FUNDED General charitable purposes; education.

WHAT IS NOT FUNDED Individuals; non-registered charities.

RANGE OF GRANTS Up to £10,000.

SAMPLE GRANTS Cancer Research UK and Nepali Children's Trust (£10,000 each); Home Farm Trust (£5,300); St George's, Bristol and Teenage Cancer Trust (£5,000 each); Fair Shares (£3,000); Door Youth Project (£1,500); Colstons Girls School (£1,400).

FINANCES *Year* 2015/16 *Income* £97,124 *Grants* £76,050 *Grants to organisations* £76,050 *Assets* £3,013,519

TRUSTEES Robert Bernays; Mr R. Bernays; Lady Merrison; Alison Bernays.

OTHER INFORMATION Grants of less than £1,000 totalled £31,500.

HOW TO APPLY Apply in writing to the correspondent enclosing an sae. Charities can apply at any time, but the trust makes distributions twice a year, usually in May and November.

WHO TO APPLY TO Mr R. E. J. Bernays, Trustee, Kilcot House, Lower Kilcot, Hillesley, Wotton-Under-Edge, Gloucestershire GL12 7RL *Tel.* 01454 238571

■ The Bromley Trust

CC NO 801875 **ESTABLISHED** 1989

WHERE FUNDING CAN BE GIVEN Worldwide.

WHO CAN BENEFIT UK-registered charities only. The trust is happy to work with other charities and particularly encourages crossover between the different funding streams and focus areas.

WHAT IS FUNDED Prevention of violations of human rights, helping help victims of torture, refugees, people suffering from oppression and those who have been falsely imprisoned, assisting those who have suffered severe bodily or mental harm through no fault of their own (and, if need be, their dependants); prison reform within the UK with particular emphasis on the reduction of re-offending; oppose the extinction of the world's fauna and flora and the destruction of the environment for wildlife and for mankind worldwide.

TYPE OF GRANT Unrestricted.

RANGE OF GRANTS £5,000 to £20,000.

SAMPLE GRANTS Landlife and Redress Trust (£20,000 each); Changing Paths and One in Four (£15,000 each); Butler Trust (£13,000); British Institute of Human Rights, Froglife and Platform (£10,000 each); Koestler Award Trust (£8,000); Detention Action and Hardman Trust (£5,000 each).

FINANCES *Year* 2015/16 *Income* £734,789 *Grants* £641,000 *Grants to organisations* £641,000 *Assets* £15,558,333

TRUSTEES Anthony Roberts; Peter Edwards; Jean Ritchie; Anne-Marie Edgell; Dr Judith Brett; Fiona Cramb; Terrence Davies.

OTHER INFORMATION Grants were made to 55 organisations and were broken down as follows: human rights (£300,000); prison reform (£226,000); sustainability and conservation (£115,000).

HOW TO APPLY Application forms and guidelines are available from the trust's website. Note that at the time of writing (April 2017), the environmental funding stream was closed while the trustees review the funding strategy.

WHO TO APPLY TO The Trustees, Studio 7, 2 Pinchin Street, Whitechapel, London E1 1SA *Tel.* 020 7481 4899 *Email* info@thebromleytrust.org.uk *Website* www.thebromleytrust.org.uk

■ The Consuelo and Anthony Brooke Charitable Trust

CC NO 1150569 **ESTABLISHED** 2013

WHERE FUNDING CAN BE GIVEN UK and overseas, particularly Barnet, Camden, City of Westminster, East Sussex, Kensington and Chelsea, West Sussex and Uganda.

WHO CAN BENEFIT Charitable organisations.

WHAT IS FUNDED Education; the arts and heritage; health; economic and community development.
SAMPLE GRANTS A list of beneficiaries was not available.
FINANCES *Year* 2015/16 *Income* £143,230 *Grants* £61,750 *Grants to organisations* £61,750 *Assets* £20,116
TRUSTEES Carol Consuelo Brooke; Anthony Brooke; Charlotte Eade; Alexander Brooke.
HOW TO APPLY Apply in writing to the correspondent.
WHO TO APPLY TO Anthony Brooke, Trustee, 20 Caroline Place, London W2 4AN *Tel.* 07802 796416 *Email* anthonylbrooke@btinternet.com

■ The Rory and Elizabeth Brooks Foundation

CC NO 1111587 **ESTABLISHED** 2005
WHERE FUNDING CAN BE GIVEN Worldwide.
WHO CAN BENEFIT Charitable organisations.
WHAT IS FUNDED Education; medical research; health care; community care; arts and culture.
SAMPLE GRANTS A list of beneficiaries was not available.
FINANCES *Year* 2015/16 *Income* £544,774 *Grants* £460,845 *Grants to organisations* £460,845 *Assets* £1,292,445
TRUSTEES Elizabeth Brooks; Roderick Brooks; Bridget Fury.
HOW TO APPLY Apply in writing to the correspondent.
WHO TO APPLY TO Robyn Bryson, Robyn Bryson, Orion House 5 Upper *Tel.* 020 7024 2217 *Email* RBryson@mmlcapital.com

■ The Charles Brotherton Trust

CC NO 227067 **ESTABLISHED** 1940
WHERE FUNDING CAN BE GIVEN Birmingham; Bebington and Wirral; Leeds; Liverpool; Wakefield; York.
WHO CAN BENEFIT Charitable organisations.
WHAT IS FUNDED 'The charity is principally directed to encourage young people to improve their own lives by taking advantage of educational opportunities and organised recreational activities. The charity is also empowered to help improve the standard of living of older people and people with disabilities and relieve the suffering caused by illness.'
WHAT IS NOT FUNDED Individuals. Grants are only made to registered charities and recognised bodies.
TYPE OF GRANT One-off.
RANGE OF GRANTS Up to £6,000 but generally £150 to £375.
SAMPLE GRANTS University of Leeds – Brotherton Library (£6,000); Brotherton Charity Trust (£1,200); Meanwood Valley Urban Farm and Opera North Education (£300 each); York Mind (£250); Barnstondale Centre, Focus Birmingham and Wildlife Trust for Birmingham (£200 each); Tall Ships Youth Trust and Tranmere Youth Project (£150 each).
FINANCES *Year* 2015/16 *Income* £72,320 *Grants* £68,000 *Grants to organisations* £68,000 *Assets* £188,712
TRUSTEES David Brotherton; Christopher Brotherton-Ratcliffe; Helen Brotherton-Ratcliffe; Dominic Jones.
OTHER INFORMATION Grants were distributed as follows: Leeds (£26,000); Birmingham (£13,100); Liverpool, Wakefield and York (£6,700 each); Bebington and Wirral (£6,600).
HOW TO APPLY Apply in writing to the correspondent. The application should clearly show the organisation's activities, geographical area of operations, and for what the funds are required. Applications should be accompanied by the organisation's most recent set of accounts. There is no formal application form and applications are not acknowledged. Grants are considered by the trustees at the start of the trust's accounting year in April, and a single payment made to successful applicants in October.
WHO TO APPLY TO The Secretary, PO Box 374, Harrogate, North Yorkshire HG1 4YW *Email* admin@charlesbrothertontrust.com *Website* www.charlesbrothertontrust.com

■ Bill Brown 1989 Charitable Trust

CC NO 801756 **ESTABLISHED** 1989
WHERE FUNDING CAN BE GIVEN UK, mainly South England.
WHO CAN BENEFIT Charities registered in the UK.
WHAT IS FUNDED Research into blindness; medical research; deaf and blind people; older people; people with disabilities; general welfare; hospices.
WHAT IS NOT FUNDED Individuals; animal welfare; small (local) charitable causes; appeals from regional branches of national charitable organisations; wildlife and environmental conservation; maintenance of buildings; religious charities.
TYPE OF GRANT Mainly recurrent.
SAMPLE GRANTS Moorfields Eye Charity (£72,000); Charities Aid Foundation Trust (£75,000); Arthritis Research (£22,000); Macmillan Cancer Support and Salvation Army (£15,000 each); Crohn's and Colitis UK (£7,500); Blind Veterans UK (£5,000); Barnardo's (£3,800).
FINANCES *Year* 2015/16 *Income* £571,067 *Grants* £487,500 *Grants to organisations* £487,500 *Assets* £14,924,355
TRUSTEES Graham Brown; Anthony Barnett.
HOW TO APPLY Apply by letter confirming your registered charity number, the aims and objectives of your charity, and any other relevant facts. Applicants must also include a copy of their latest annual report and most recent audited accounts. The trustees will consider supporting specific projects, in this case provide details of the total amount required, contributions received to date and proposed timing to completion. Depending on the nature of the project, the trustees will sometimes make a grant commitment, but defer payment until assurances are received that sufficient funds have been raised or pledged. Applications will only be considered from English registered charities and the trustees concentrate on supporting charities mainly in the south of England. Applications must be received by the end of May or the end of October to be sure of consideration at the summer and winter meetings.
WHO TO APPLY TO The Trustees, BM Box 4567, London WC1N 3XX *Website* www.billbrowncharity.org

■ R. S. Brownless Charitable Trust

CC NO 1000320 **ESTABLISHED** 1990
WHERE FUNDING CAN BE GIVEN UK.
WHO CAN BENEFIT Registered charities.
WHAT IS FUNDED General charitable purposes including: disability; illness; social welfare.
WHAT IS NOT FUNDED Grants are rarely given to individuals for educational projects, educational or conservational causes or overseas aid.

TYPE OF GRANT Usually one-off; sometimes annual.
RANGE OF GRANTS Up to £2,000 (occasionally more); usually £100 to £500.
SAMPLE GRANTS Alzheimer's Society; Camp Mohawk; Casa Allianza UK; Crisis; Foundation for Study of Infant Deaths; Prader-Willi Foundation; St Andrew's Hall; Unicef; Wargrave Parochial Church Council.
FINANCES *Year* 2015/16 *Income* £56,796 *Grants* £54,644 *Grants to organisations* £56,644 *Assets* £1,313,430
TRUSTEES Frances Plummer; Philippa Nicolai.
HOW TO APPLY Apply in writing to the correspondent. The trustees meet twice a year, but in special circumstances will meet at other times. The trust is unable to acknowledge all requests.
WHO TO APPLY TO Philippa Nicolai, Trustee, Hennerton Holt, Hennerton, Wargrave, Reading RG10 8PD *Tel.* 0118 940 4029

■ The T. B. H. Brunner's Charitable Settlement

CC NO 260604 **ESTABLISHED** 1969
WHERE FUNDING CAN BE GIVEN UK with some preference for Oxfordshire.
WHO CAN BENEFIT Registered charities and individuals.
WHAT IS FUNDED Church of England preservation projects and other charities dealing with historical preservation, both local to Oxfordshire and nationally; the arts; music; general charitable purposes.
RANGE OF GRANTS £100 to £3,000.
SAMPLE GRANTS Trinity College, Oxford (£10,000); Oxfordshire Historic Churches Trust and Institute of Economic Affairs (£2,500 each); British Red Cross, The Art Fund and The Landmark Trust (£1,000 each); The Children's Society (£500); Breast Cancer Care (£250); Moorfields Eye Hospital (£100).
FINANCES *Year* 2015/16 *Income* £61,255 *Grants* £64,950 *Grants to organisations* £64,950 *Assets* £201,516
TRUSTEES Helen Brunner; Dr Imogen Brunner; Timothy Brunner.
OTHER INFORMATION Grants were made to 50 organisations during the year.
HOW TO APPLY Apply in writing to the correspondent.
WHO TO APPLY TO Timothy Brunner, Trustee, Flat 4, 2 Inverness Gardens, London W8 4RN *Tel.* 020 7727 6277 *Email* p.roberts@robco.uk.com

■ The Jack Brunton Charitable Trust

CC NO 518407 **ESTABLISHED** 1986
WHERE FUNDING CAN BE GIVEN North Riding area of Yorkshire prior to the 1974 boundary changes.
WHO CAN BENEFIT Registered charities for the benefit of the population of the rural villages and towns within the beneficial area.
WHAT IS FUNDED General charitable purposes.
TYPE OF GRANT One-off for capital costs.
RANGE OF GRANTS Between £100 and £40,000.
SAMPLE GRANTS York Minster (£39,500); Cleveland Mountain Rescue Team (£5,000); Goathland Village Hall Trust and Holy Cross Church – Bilsdale (£3,000 each); Home-Start – Ryedale; (£2,500); Motability – North Yorkshire and Samaritans – York (£2,000 each); Great Ayton Dramatic Society and Reeth and District Community Transport (£1,500).
FINANCES *Year* 2015/16 *Income* £157,677 *Grants* £128,600 *Grants to organisations* £128,600 *Assets* £5,078,315
TRUSTEES Dr Clair Hurst; Derek Noble; James Lamb; Joan Brunton.
OTHER INFORMATION Grants were made to 55 organisations during the year.
HOW TO APPLY Apply in writing to the correspondent including full details of costings if relevant.
WHO TO APPLY TO David Swallow, 10 Bridge Road, Stokesley, North Yorkshire TS9 5AA *Tel.* 01642 711407 *Email* margaretc@swallco.co.uk

■ The Bruntwood Charity

CC NO 1135777 **ESTABLISHED** 2010
WHERE FUNDING CAN BE GIVEN Birmingham; Leeds; Liverpool; Manchester.
WHO CAN BENEFIT Registered charities.
WHAT IS FUNDED General charitable purposes and social welfare, especially with regards to children and disability causes.
SAMPLE GRANTS Factory Youth Zone – Manchester (£28,500); Onside – Manchester (£20,000); Whizz-Kidz (£10,000); Gemma's Hospice (£4,500).
FINANCES *Year* 2014/15 *Income* £100,614 *Grants* £65,047 *Grants to organisations* £65,047 *Assets* £46,855
TRUSTEES Kate Vokes; Sally Hill; Kathryn Graham; Jane Williams; Peter Crowther.
OTHER INFORMATION This is the charity of Bruntwood Ltd, a company which owns and manages commercial property and offices space in Birmingham, Leeds, Manchester and Liverpool. The 2014/15 accounts were the latest available at the time of writing (May 2017).
HOW TO APPLY Charities are chosen following discussions with the company and its employees. Funds are fully committed and the charity therefore does not accept unsolicited applications.
WHO TO APPLY TO Kathryn Graham, Trustee, Bruntwood Ltd, York House, York Street, Manchester M2 3BB

■ Brushmill Ltd

CC NO 285420 **ESTABLISHED** 1982
WHERE FUNDING CAN BE GIVEN Worldwide.
WHO CAN BENEFIT Organisations benefitting Jewish people.
WHAT IS FUNDED Jewish charitable purposes; education; social welfare.
SAMPLE GRANTS Ezer V'Hatzalah Ltd (£117,500); Friends of Boyan Trust (£31,000); Toras Chessed (£12,500); Beis Rizhin Trust (£23,500); Bais Rochel (£7,500); Yetev Lev (£7,000).
FINANCES *Year* 2015/16 *Income* £532,560 *Grants* £285,101 *Grants to organisations* £285,101 *Assets* £212,928
TRUSTEES Mr C. Getter; Mr J. Weinberger; Mrs E. Weinberger.
HOW TO APPLY Apply in writing to the correspondent.
WHO TO APPLY TO Mrs M. Getter, Secretary, 76 Fairholt Road, London N16 5HN *Email* mail@cohenarnold.com

■ Buckingham Trust

CC NO 237350 **ESTABLISHED** 1962
WHERE FUNDING CAN BE GIVEN UK and overseas.
WHO CAN BENEFIT Charitable organisations and churches.

WHAT IS FUNDED Advancement of religion (including missionary activities); relief of people disadvantaged by poverty and older people or those who are ill.
TYPE OF GRANT One-off and recurrent grants.
SAMPLE GRANTS Overseas Missionary Fellowship (£39,000); Battle Methodist Church (£14,700); St Andrews Parochial Church Council (£9,500); Tearafund (£5,800); St Helen's Church (£3,000); Godalming Baptist Church (£2,800); Echoes of Service (£1,900); Disasters Emergency Committee – Ebola Appeal (£500).
FINANCES *Year* 2014/15 *Income* £306,164 *Grants* £192,143 *Grants to organisations* £182,068 *Assets* £229,662
TRUSTEES Richard Foot; Tina Clay.
OTHER INFORMATION The 2014/15 accounts were the latest available at the time of writing (June 2017). The trust acts mainly as an agency charity acting on behalf of other donors. The grant total also includes £10,100 in grants to individuals.
HOW TO APPLY Apply in writing to the correspondent. Preference is given to charities of which the trustees have personal interest, knowledge, or association.
WHO TO APPLY TO Tina Clay, Trustee, Foot Davson Ltd, 17 Church Road, Tunbridge Wells, Kent TN1 1LG *Tel.* 01892 774774

■ Buckinghamshire Community Foundation

CC NO 1073861 **ESTABLISHED** 1998
WHERE FUNDING CAN BE GIVEN Buckinghamshire.
WHO CAN BENEFIT Charities and community groups whose work benefits local people.
WHAT IS FUNDED Community development.
WHAT IS NOT FUNDED Organisations and projects operating solely outside the county of Buckinghamshire; activities promoting a particular religious or political belief; overseas travel; individuals; statutory organisations (with the exception of parish councils); organisations whose principal concern is animal welfare; relief of statutory responsibilities; schools; projects which are already completed. Funding cannot be granted retrospectively.
TYPE OF GRANT Project funding; core running costs; capital expenditure.
SAMPLE GRANTS Haddenham Community Vehicle (£37,000); Community Impact (£20,000); Open House – Mickelfield (£15,000); Chiltern and South Buckinghamshire Dial-A-Ride (£14,700); The Princes Risborough Centre Ltd (£10,000); Wrights Meadow Centre (£9,900); Buckinghamshire Mind (£6,500); Inspire All CIC (£5,000).
FINANCES *Year* 2015/16 *Income* £1,050,351 *Grants* £692,005 *Grants to organisations* £692,005 *Assets* £527,719
TRUSTEES Roy Collis; Joe Barclay; Colin Hayfield; Simon Deans; The Countess Howe; Graham Corney; Linda Clegg; Lynda Marston-Weston; Masaud Subedar.
OTHER INFORMATION A total of 257 grants were made during the year. The foundation also provides loans.
HOW TO APPLY Visit the foundation's website for details of up-to-date schemes.
WHO TO APPLY TO Peter Costello, Sunley House, 4th Floor, Oxford Road, Aylesbury HP19 8EZ *Tel.* 01296 330134 *Email* info@buckscf.org.uk *Website* heartofbucks.org

■ The Buckinghamshire Historic Churches Trust

CC NO 206471 **ESTABLISHED** 1957
WHERE FUNDING CAN BE GIVEN The county or archdeaconry of Buckingham.
WHO CAN BENEFIT Parochial church councils or trustees of Christian churches and chapels, including Baptist, Anglican, Methodist and Catholic.
WHAT IS FUNDED The preservation, repair, maintenance and upkeep of the fabric of churches or chapels in Buckinghamshire. Grants are made to churches and chapels embarking upon restoration.
WHAT IS NOT FUNDED Grants are not usually given for repairs to bells, bell frames, organs, furnishings, work on heating, lighting, decoration or churchyard structures, installation of kitchen facilities and lavatories.
TYPE OF GRANT One-off.
RANGE OF GRANTS £500 to £20,000.
SAMPLE GRANTS St Mary Ludgershall (£20,000); St Mary the Virgin Long Crendon (£15,000); Baptist Church Princes Risborough (£14,000); St James the Less Dorney, (£10,000 each); All Saints Bisham, Former Methodist Church Wolverton, St Mary Cold Brayfield, St Mary Farnham Royal (£5,000 each); St Dunstan Monks Risborough (£4,000); St Nicholas Ickford (£2,000); St John, Ashley Green (£500).
FINANCES *Year* 2015/16 *Income* £72,261 *Grants* £113,000 *Grants to organisations* £113,000 *Assets* £786,322
TRUSTEES Sir Henry Aubrey-Fletcher; Cherry Aston; The Hon. Jenefer Farncombe; Mary Villiers; Roger Evans; The Rt Revd Alan Wilson; The Revd Canon Herbert Cavell-Northam; Jennifer Moss; Rupert Carington; Timothy Oliver; Caroline Abel-Smith.
HOW TO APPLY An application form is available from the correspondent: Mrs Penny Keens, 377 Japonica Lane, Willen Park, Milton Keynes, MK15 9EG.
WHO TO APPLY TO Mrs Penny Keens, Hon. Secretary, c/o Community Impact Buckinghamshire, 6 Centre Parade Parade, Place Farm Way, Monks Risborough, Princes Risborough HP27 9JS *Tel.* 01844 274162 *Email* penny@pkeens.plus.com *Website* www.bucks-historic-churches.org

■ The Buffini Chao Foundation

CC NO 1111022 **ESTABLISHED** 2005
WHERE FUNDING CAN BE GIVEN England and Wales.
WHO CAN BENEFIT Charitable organisations.
WHAT IS FUNDED General charitable purposes, especially organisations working in the field of education and with children.
RANGE OF GRANTS Up to £50,000.
SAMPLE GRANTS Royal Shakespeare Company (£50,000); The Community Foundation Surrey (£30,000); Beneden School Trust (£25,000); National Deaf Children Society (£18,000); Suburban Hockey (£15,000); Auditory Verbal UK (£4,500); Build Africa (£1,300); West Kent YMCA (£1,000).
FINANCES *Year* 2015/16 *Income* £10,066,471 *Grants* £214,000 *Grants to organisations* £214,000 *Assets* £5,982,515
TRUSTEES Lady Buffini; Sir Damon Buffini; Maria Hindmarsh; Sue Gutierrez.
HOW TO APPLY Apply in writing to the correspondent.
WHO TO APPLY TO Lady Buffini, Trustee, PO Box 1427, Northampton NN1 9FP *Tel.* 01892 701801 *Email* trustees@buffinichao.com

■ The E. F. Bulmer Benevolent Fund

CC NO 214831 **ESTABLISHED** 1938
WHERE FUNDING CAN BE GIVEN Herefordshire.
WHO CAN BENEFIT Organisations; former employees of H. P. Bulmer Holdings PLC or its subsidiaries and individuals.
WHAT IS FUNDED Organisations benefitting people who are sick or disadvantaged by poverty. Former employees of H. P. Bulmer Holdings PLC and individuals who are in need.
WHAT IS NOT FUNDED Large UK charities and those from outside Herefordshire are unlikely to be supported.
TYPE OF GRANT One-off for capital (including buildings), core costs, feasibility studies, project, research, running costs, salaries and start-up costs. Funding may be given for up to three years.
RANGE OF GRANTS Up to £12,000.
SAMPLE GRANTS Herefordshire Citizens Advice (£12,000); Herefordshire Headway (£7,500); Basement Youth Trust (£6,000); Bulmer Foundation (£5,000); Jumpstart Kidz (£4,000); Herefordshire Wildlife Trust (£3,500); Acorn Children's Hospice and Deaf Direct (£3,000 each); Happy Days (£2,300).
FINANCES *Year* 2015/16 *Income* £455,949 *Grants* £255,079 *Grants to organisations* £195,654 *Assets* £13,260,464
TRUSTEES Nigel Bulmer; Edward Bulmer; Richard Bulmer; Caroline Bulmer; Timothy Bulmer.
OTHER INFORMATION Grants to 129 H. P. Bulmer pensioners totalled £37,000 and grants to 45 other individuals totalled £22,500.
HOW TO APPLY Apply in writing to the correspondent, although a voluntary application form is available and will be sent if requested. Applications should be accompanied by a copy of the latest report and accounts. The administrator is very happy to discuss applications by email or telephone prior to the application being submitted. The trustees usually meet four times a year. Smaller groups who may have difficulty in receiving support from large national trusts are normally given priority. More detailed information on applying for grants is available on the fund's website.
WHO TO APPLY TO James Greenfield, Fred Bulmer Centre, Wall Street, Hereford, Herefordshire HR4 9HP *Tel.* 01432 271293 *Email* efbulmer@gmail.com *Website* www.efbulmer.co.uk

■ Bupa UK Foundation

CC NO 1162759 **ESTABLISHED** 2015
WHERE FUNDING CAN BE GIVEN UK.
WHO CAN BENEFIT Registered charities.
WHAT IS FUNDED Health and well-being; mental health; carers.
WHAT IS NOT FUNDED Work that does not fall within the scope of the Bupa UK Foundation's charitable purposes; work that is not clearly aligned with the stated funding priorities of a specific funding programme; projects delivered outside the UK; long-term projects and initiatives (the vast majority of projects funded are expected to be delivered within 12 to 18 months); work which is delivered by local authorities and housing associations; work which might reasonably be eligible for funding from statutory bodies; general awareness and information campaigns; sponsorship of or attendance at meetings, events and conferences; fundraising appeals, including requests for contributions to capital or equipment costs; unrestricted funding for charities or other organisations; educational bursaries or grants for university or postgraduate education, school trips or projects, gap year or elective year projects; academic research, including funding for educational or research posts.
SAMPLE GRANTS Age UK Enfield; Asian Lone Women Parents Association; Bipolar UK; Carers UK; Cascade Theatre Company; Down to Earth; Men's Health Forum; Sinfonia Viva; The Dove Service; Tomorrow's People Trust.
FINANCES *Year* 2015 *Income* £460,462 *Grants* £106,260 *Grants to organisations* £106,260 *Assets* £235,202
TRUSTEES Andrea Spyropoulos; Catherine Barton; David Hynam; Helen Cliffe; Helen Vauhan-Jones; Paula Franklin; Ruth Owen.
HOW TO APPLY Applicants should first refer to the website to see which grants programmes are currently open for application, along with eligibility criteria and deadlines. Applicants can submit an initial expression of interest online. Applicants will be notified within six weeks of the closing date for Stage 1 applications whether they are invited to submit a more detailed application. Final decisions are made by the trustees.
WHO TO APPLY TO Tina Gwynne-Evans, Head of Bupa UK Foundation, Bupa House, 15–19 Bloomsbury Way, London WC1A 2BA *Tel.* 020 7656 2738 *Email* bupaukfoundation@bupa.com *Website* www.bupaukfoundation.org

■ The Burberry Foundation

CC NO 1154468 **ESTABLISHED** 2013
WHERE FUNDING CAN BE GIVEN UK; Brazil; Hong Kong; Japan; Korea; USA.
WHO CAN BENEFIT Registered charities.
WHAT IS FUNDED The foundation supports organisations which help young people to: gain confidence in their daily lives and develop self-esteem; build connections to their families, friends, partners and society at large; develop the ability to reach for opportunities in school, work and life.
RANGE OF GRANTS Up to £250,000.
SAMPLE GRANTS County Durham Groundwork and Place2Be (£250,000 each); City Year UK (£200,000); IntoUniversity, National Theatre, Spear – Resurgo Trust and The Prince's Trust (£50,000 each).
FINANCES *Year* 2015/16 *Income* £2,768,996 *Grants* £1,495,938 *Grants to organisations* £145,938 *Assets* £6,502,690
TRUSTEES Christopher Baily; Sir John Peace; Leanne Wood.
HOW TO APPLY Apply in writing to the correspondent.
WHO TO APPLY TO Foundation Director, Burberry Ltd, Horseferry House, Horseferry Road, London SW1P 2AW *Email* enquiries@burberryfoundation.com *Website* www.burberryfoundation.org

■ The Burden Trust

CC NO 235859 **ESTABLISHED** 1913
WHERE FUNDING CAN BE GIVEN UK with a preference for Bristol.
WHO CAN BENEFIT Charitable organisations; hospitals; retirement homes; schools and training institutions.
WHAT IS FUNDED Medical research; hospitals; retirement homes; educational institutions; homes and care for the young; other charitable work which helps people in need.

WHAT IS NOT FUNDED Individuals.
TYPE OF GRANT Recurring and one-off.
SAMPLE GRANTS Crisis Centre Ministries (£14,000); Bristol Hospitality Network (£7,000); Changing Tunes (£6,000); Barton Camp and FareShare SW (£5,000 each); Personal Support Unit (£3,000); Mission Direct (£2,500); Seed International (£1,500).
FINANCES *Year* 2015/16 *Grants* £138,500 *Grants to organisations* £138,500 *Assets* £4,431,524
TRUSTEES Anthony Miles; Prof. Andrew Halestrap; Dr Joanna Bacon; Annie Crawley.
HOW TO APPLY Apply via the online form available on the trust's website by 31 March each year in preparation for the trustee meeting in June. Once an online application is submitted the trustees will make further contact before the June meeting if they want a full application.
WHO TO APPLY TO Patrick O'Conor, Secretary, 51 Downs Park West, Westbury Park, Bristol BS6 7QL *Tel.* 0117 962 8611 *Email* p.oconor@netgates.co.uk *Website* www.burdentrustbristol.co.uk

■ The Burdett Trust for Nursing

CC NO 1089849 **ESTABLISHED** 2001
WHERE FUNDING CAN BE GIVEN Mostly UK.
WHO CAN BENEFIT Charities supporting nurses and research into nursing.
WHAT IS FUNDED The trust makes grants to support the nursing contribution to health care. The trust's website states three key priority areas: **Building nursing research capacity** – 'supporting clinical nursing research and research addressing policy, leadership development and delivery of nursing care'. **Building nurse leadership capacity** – 'supporting nurses in their professional development to create a cadre of excellent nursing and allied health professionals who will become leaders of the future and foster excellence and capacity-building in advancing the nursing profession'. **Supporting local nurse-led initiatives** – 'supporting nurse-led initiatives that make a difference at local level and are focused explicitly on improving care for patients and users of services'. Details on the current grant programmes can be found on the trust's website.
WHAT IS NOT FUNDED Consult the relevant programme guidance for information on the funding criteria.
TYPE OF GRANT Usually one-off, although up to three years will be considered.
RANGE OF GRANTS Up to £400,000.
SAMPLE GRANTS University of Oxford (£300,000); St Marks Hospital Foundation (£250,000); Tenovus Cancer Centre (£100,000); St Christopher's Hospice (£39,500); Children's Hospital Trust (£7,000); World Orthopaedic (£2,700).
FINANCES *Year* 2015 *Income* £1,533,973 *Grants* £3,045,843 *Grants to organisations* £3,045,843 *Assets* £72,790,470
TRUSTEES Alan Gibbs; Dame Christine Beasley; Andrew Smith; David Sines; Dame Eileen Sills; Lady Henrietta St George; Joanna Webber; Jack Gibbs; William Gordon; Evy Hambro; Dr Michael Gormley; Andrew Gibbs.
HOW TO APPLY See the trust's website for information on the current grant programmes and details on how to apply.
WHO TO APPLY TO Shirley Baines, Charity Grants Director, Rathbone Trust Company Ltd, 8 Finsbury Circus, London EC2M 7AZ *Tel.* 020 7399 0102 *Email* administrator@btfn.org.uk *Website* www.btfn.org.uk

■ The Clara E. Burgess Charity

CC NO 1072546 **ESTABLISHED** 1998
WHERE FUNDING CAN BE GIVEN UK and overseas.
WHO CAN BENEFIT Registered charities benefitting children.
WHAT IS FUNDED Children and young people; facilities of and assistance for education, health and physical well-being. Preference may be given to younger children under the age of ten who have lost one or both parents.
WHAT IS NOT FUNDED Non-registered charities.
TYPE OF GRANT One-off and recurrent (up to three years).
RANGE OF GRANTS £500 to £10,000.
SAMPLE GRANTS Build Aid and Childhood First (£10,000 each); Bereavement Matters and See Ability (£7,500 each); Hearing Dogs for Deaf People and YMCA East Surrey (£5,000 each); Goodwill Children's Home (£3,500); Hollybank Trust (£2,500); ACE Cardiff, Books Abroad and Tree Hope (£2,000 each).
FINANCES *Year* 2015/16 *Income* £355,402 *Grants* £349,000 *Grants to organisations* £349,000 *Assets* £11,441,106
TRUSTEE The Royal Bank of Scotland PLC.
HOW TO APPLY Applications can be made in writing to the correspondent and are considered in January and July.
WHO TO APPLY TO The Trust Section Manager, c/o RBS Trust Administration, Eastwood House, Glebe Road, Chelmsford, Essex CM1 1RS *Tel.* 01245 292492 *Email* rbscharities@rbs.com

■ The Burry Charitable Trust

CC NO 281045 **ESTABLISHED** 1961
WHERE FUNDING CAN BE GIVEN UK, with a preference for Dorset and Hampshire.
WHO CAN BENEFIT Charities, voluntary groups and other not-for-profit organisations.
WHAT IS FUNDED Medicine; health; disability; welfare.
WHAT IS NOT FUNDED Individuals or students.
RANGE OF GRANTS Up to £20,000 but generally £1,000 to £2,500.
SAMPLE GRANTS Oakhaven Hospital Trust (£20,000); Not Forgotten Association (£5,000); Canine Partners and Salvation Army (£2,500 each); Alzheimer's Research (£2,000); Autism Wessex (£1,500); British Red Cross and Parkinson's UK (£1,000); Lymington Hospital (£100).
FINANCES *Year* 2015/16 *Income* £53,319 *Grants* £53,100 *Grants to organisations* £53,100 *Assets* £802,715
TRUSTEES Robert Burry; Adrian Osman; John Kennar; Sarah Teague.
HOW TO APPLY This trust states that it does not respond to unsolicited applications.
WHO TO APPLY TO Sarah Teague, Trustee, 261 Lymington Road, Highcliffe, Christchurch, Dorset BH23 5EE *Tel.* 01425 277661 *Email* sarahteague@hoburne.com

■ The Arnold Burton 1998 Charitable Trust

CC NO 1074633 **ESTABLISHED** 1998
WHERE FUNDING CAN BE GIVEN Worldwide with a preference for Yorkshire.
WHO CAN BENEFIT Registered charities.
WHAT IS FUNDED Arts and amenities; education; health; Jewish/Israel; social welfare.
WHAT IS NOT FUNDED Individuals.
RANGE OF GRANTS £100 to £40,000.

SAMPLE GRANTS Gladrags Community Costume Resource and Yorkshire Sculpture Park (£10,000 each); Pulmonary Hypertension and Special Boat Service Association (£5,000); Alliance Francais De Leeds and Yorkshire Air Museum (£2,500 each).
FINANCES *Year* 2015/16 *Income* £160,257 *Grants* £60,150 *Grants to organisations* £60,150 *Assets* £4,458,637
TRUSTEES Mark Burton; Jeremy Burton; Nicholas Burton.
OTHER INFORMATION There were ten grants made during the year. Grants were broken down as follows: arts and amenities (£22,500); social welfare (£17,500); other (£9,000); health (£6,000); education (£5,000).
HOW TO APPLY Apply in writing to the trust managers. Unsuccessful appeals will not necessarily be acknowledged.
WHO TO APPLY TO The Trust Managers, c/o Trustee Management Ltd, 19 Cookridge Street, Leeds LS2 3AG

■ Consolidated Charity of Burton upon Trent

CC NO 239072 **ESTABLISHED** 1981
WHERE FUNDING CAN BE GIVEN The former county borough of Burton upon Trent and the parishes of Branston, Stretton and Outwoods.
WHO CAN BENEFIT Registered charities; voluntary groups; churches; individuals.
WHAT IS FUNDED General charitable purposes.
WHAT IS NOT FUNDED Grants for salaries.
TYPE OF GRANT Capital and revenue grants.
RANGE OF GRANTS Up to £20,000.
SAMPLE GRANTS Burton Hockey Club (£21,000); Burton Hospital League of Friends (£10,000); Star Foundation (£7,500); St George Knights Power Wheelchair Football Club (£5,000); Burton Musical Theatre Company (£3,500); One Recovery Burton (£1,400); Riverside Lunch Club (£900).
FINANCES *Year* 2015 *Income* £576,371 *Grants* £200,186 *Grants to organisations* £122,904 *Assets* £12,556,201
TRUSTEES Cllr Dennis Fletcher; Cllr Beryl Toon; John Peach; Margaret Heather; Cllr Patricia Ackroyd; Gerald Hamilton; Alderman Peter Davies; Ben Robinson; Cllr David Leese; Revd Robert Styles; Cllr Leonard Milner; George Fargher; Cllr Ronald Clarke; Geoffrey Brown; Sandra Phillips; Nigel Powlson; Cllr Simon Gaskin.
OTHER INFORMATION The amount of grants given to individuals totalled £77,000 and are available for both welfare and education.
HOW TO APPLY Applications can be made through the charity's website or by using an application form which is available to download from the website.
WHO TO APPLY TO J. P. Southwell, Clerk to the Trustees, Dains LLP, 1st Floor, Gibraltar House, Crown Square, First Avenue, Burton-on-Trent *Tel.* 01283 527067 *Email* clerk@consolidatedcharityburton.org.uk *Website* www.consolidatedcharityburton.org.uk

■ The Derek Butler Trust

CC NO 1081995 **ESTABLISHED** 2000
WHERE FUNDING CAN BE GIVEN Worldwide, in practice UK.
WHO CAN BENEFIT Institutions and charitable organisations.
WHAT IS FUNDED Music; music education; cancer; HIV.
SAMPLE GRANTS The Digestive Disorders Foundation (£2.5 million); Countess of Munster Musical Trust (£1 million); Trinity Laban Conservatoire of Music and Drama and The Guildhall School Trust (£500,000 each); British Library; Holidays for Carers (£20,000); St Luke's Hospice Harrow (£15,000); Great Western Air Ambulance Charity, Cancer Research (£10,000 each); Royal Academy of Music Scholarship Award (£9,000); Guildhall School of Music and Drama and Guildford Cathedral Choir School (£5,000 each); The Wigmore Hall Trust (£1,700).
FINANCES *Year* 2015/16 *Income* £1,545 *Grants* £370,000 *Grants to organisations* £370,000
TRUSTEES Hilary Guest; Donald Freeman; The Revd Michael Fuller; James McLean.
OTHER INFORMATION This charity's latest accounts were not available to view on the Charity Commission's website due to its low income. We have therefore estimated the grant total based on previous years' information. Scholarship awards for students at Trinity College, Royal College of Music, Royal Academy of Music, and Guildhall School of Music and Drama are paid under the Derek Butler Trust London Scholarship and Prize.
HOW TO APPLY Apply in writing to the correspondent.
WHO TO APPLY TO James McLean, Trustee, c/o Underwood Solicitors LLP, 40 Welbeck Street, London W1G 8LN *Tel.* 020 7526 6000 *Email* info@thederekbutlertrust.org.uk *Website* www.thederekbutlertrust.org.uk

■ The Butters Foundation (UK) Ltd

CC NO 1157301 **ESTABLISHED** 2014
WHERE FUNDING CAN BE GIVEN England and Wales.
WHO CAN BENEFIT Registered charities.
WHAT IS FUNDED General charitable purposes including: relieving poverty, especially in urban areas; advancing and improving education, particularly for disadvantaged children.
RANGE OF GRANTS Up to £60,000.
SAMPLE GRANTS St Giles Trust (£60,000); Ummah Help (£50,000); Elton John AIDS Foundation (£10,000).
FINANCES *Year* 2015 *Income* £5,303,852 *Grants* £120,000 *Grants to organisations* £120,000 *Assets* £5,166,929
TRUSTEES Alfred Cavallaro; Belma Gaudio; Julius Gaudio.
HOW TO APPLY Applications can be made in writing to the foundation. Grant recipients will be required to produce project reports.
WHO TO APPLY TO The Trustees, Withers LLP, Withers Ltd, 16 Old Bailey, London EC4M 7EG *Tel.* 020 7597 6427

■ The Noel Buxton Trust

CC NO 220881 **ESTABLISHED** 1919
WHERE FUNDING CAN BE GIVEN UK and Africa, particularly Ethiopia, Kenya, Uganda, Sudan and South Sudan.
WHO CAN BENEFIT Registered charities.
WHAT IS FUNDED **Africa grants** – community-led organisations working to build local sustainable livelihoods; **family grants** – focusing on the issue of domestic abuse; penal grants – organisations working with people who have offended.
WHAT IS NOT FUNDED In addition to each programme's specific exclusions, grants are not made for: academic research; advice centres; animal charities; the arts for their own sake;

buildings; conferences; counselling for individuals; expeditions, exchanges, holidays, study tours, visits; housing and homelessness; human rights; HIV/AIDS programmes; individuals; Northern Ireland; organisations set up primarily to treat medical conditions, physical disabilities or mental health issues; playgrounds; prizes; race relations; contribution to a specific salaried post; schools, including school infrastructure and teaching equipment; vehicles; victims of crime (except those affected by domestic violence and victims involved with restorative justice projects); videos and IT.

TYPE OF GRANT One-off or recurrent. Not for buildings or salaries.

RANGE OF GRANTS £1,000 to £5,000.

SAMPLE GRANTS AFFORD – The African Foundation for Development (£10,000); Mango Tree – Kenya and Southern Domestic Abuse Service (£5,000 each); Hampton Trust (£3,000); Age UK – Cheshire (£1,500); Darlington Landworks (£1,000); Irene Taylor Trust (£1,000).

FINANCES *Year* 2015 *Income* £122,431 *Grants* £113,612 *Grants to organisations* £113,612 *Assets* £2,686,371

TRUSTEES Simon Buxton; Jo Tunnard; John Littlewood; Brendan Gormley; Emma Compton-Burnett; Katie Aston; Katie Buxton.

HOW TO APPLY Visit the trust's website for guidance on how to apply to each programme.

WHO TO APPLY TO The Trustees, PO Box 520, Fleet, Hampshire GU51 9GX *Website* www.noelbuxtontrust.org.uk

■ The Christopher Cadbury Charitable Trust

CC NO 231859 **ESTABLISHED** 1922

WHERE FUNDING CAN BE GIVEN UK, with a strong preference for the Midlands.

WHO CAN BENEFIT Registered charities.

WHAT IS FUNDED To support approved charities by annual contribution. The trustees have drawn up a schedule of commitments covering charities which they have chosen to support.

WHAT IS NOT FUNDED Individuals.

RANGE OF GRANTS £500 to £10,000.

SAMPLE GRANTS Fircroft College and Island Conservation (£10,500 each); Playthings Past (£7,500); Devon Wildlife (£6,000); The Wildlife Trust (£4,000); Sarnia Charitable Trust (£3,000); Survival International (£1,000); Selly Oak Nursery School (£500).

FINANCES *Year* 2015/16 *Income* £84,918 *Grants* £69,450 *Grants to organisations* £69,450 *Assets* £2,204,264

TRUSTEES Roger Cadbury; Tim Peet; Dr James Cadbury; Tina Benfield; Virginia Reekie; Peter Cadbury.

HOW TO APPLY Unsolicited applications are unlikely to be successful.

WHO TO APPLY TO Sarah Moss, BDO, 2 Snow Hill, Birmingham B4 6GA *Tel.* 0121 265 7288

■ The Edward Cadbury Charitable Trust

CC NO 1160334 **ESTABLISHED** 2015

WHERE FUNDING CAN BE GIVEN Midlands region, including: Herefordshire; Shropshire; Staffordshire; Warwickshire; and Worcestershire.

WHO CAN BENEFIT Registered charities.

WHAT IS FUNDED Arts and culture; community projects; social welfare; environment and conservation; religious activities such as interfaith and multi-faith relations; education and training; research.

RANGE OF GRANTS Mostly £2,000 to £5,000.

SAMPLE GRANTS Ashton University Medical School (£250,000); Sense (£100,000); Heart of England Community Foundation (£50,000); Dodford Children's Holiday Farm (£10,000); Birmingham Samaritans (£5,000); Trailblazers Mentoring (£4,000); Myton Hospice (£3,000); Horsham Quaker Meeting (£2,500); Relate Worcester (£2,000).

FINANCES *Year* 2015/16 *Income* £39,680,627 *Grants* £692,600 *Grants to organisations* £692,600 *Assets* £36,019,860

TRUSTEES James Midgley; Ralph Fiennes; Julian Wadam.

OTHER INFORMATION Grants were made to 129 organisations during the year.

HOW TO APPLY Applications can be made by writing to the correspondent by post or email or online on the trust's website (www.edwardcadburytrust.org.uk/applyForGrant.asp). Applications are accepted all year round and are normally considered within a three-month timescale. Letters of application should provide a clear and concise description of the project requiring funding as well as the outcomes and benefits that are likely to be achieved. The trustees also require an outline budget and explanation of how the project is to be funded initially and in the future together with the latest annual report and accounts for the charity.

WHO TO APPLY TO Susan Anderson, Trust Manager, Rokesley, University of Birmingham, Bristol Road, Selly Oak, Birmingham B29 6QF *Tel.* 0121 472 1838 *Email* ecadburytrust@btconnect.com *Website* www.edwardcadburytrust.org.uk

■ The G. W. Cadbury Charitable Trust

CC NO 231861 **ESTABLISHED** 1922

WHERE FUNDING CAN BE GIVEN UK and USA.

WHO CAN BENEFIT Registered charities.

WHAT IS FUNDED General charitable purposes.

WHAT IS NOT FUNDED Individuals; non-registered charities; scholarships.

RANGE OF GRANTS Up to £20,000.

SAMPLE GRANTS Gender and Development Network (£20,000); Seattle Academy of American Ballet (£12,700); Bobath Centre (£6,000); Brook (£5,000); Joseph Rowntree Charitable Trust (£3,000); Henry Art Gallery (£2,100); Fessenden School (£2,000); Swaledale Festival (£1,000).

FINANCES *Year* 2015/16 *Income* £242,343 *Grants* £223,575 *Grants to organisations* £223,575 *Assets* £6,842,278

TRUSTEES Jennifer Boal; Lyndall Boal; Nick Woodroffe; Peter Boal; Caroline Woodroffe.

HOW TO APPLY Apply in writing to the correspondent.

WHO TO APPLY TO Sarah Moss, BDO LLP, 2 Snowhill Queensway, Birmingham B4 6GA *Tel.* 0121 265 7288

■ The William A. Cadbury Charitable Trust

CC NO 213629 **ESTABLISHED** 1923

WHERE FUNDING CAN BE GIVEN West Midlands, especially Birmingham and to a lesser extent, UK, Ireland and overseas.

WHO CAN BENEFIT Organisations serving Birmingham and the West Midlands; organisations whose work has a national significance; organisations outside the West Midlands where the trust has well-established links; organisations in Northern Ireland, and UK-based charities working overseas. UK bodies legally exempt from registration with the Charity Commission can apply and small grants are occasionally made to unregistered groups in the West Midlands.

WHAT IS FUNDED **Birmingham and the West Midlands:** community action; venerable groups; advice, mediation and counselling; education and training; environment conservation; medical and health care; the arts; penal affairs. **United Kingdom:** the Religious Society of Friends – support for groups with a clear Quaker connection and support for the work of the Religious Society of Friends in the UK; penal affairs – restorative justice, prison-based projects and work with people who have offended aimed at reducing re-offending. **Ireland:** peace and reconciliation. **International development:** Africa – the international development programme is concentrated on West Africa and work to reduce poverty on a sustainable basis in both rural and urban communities – schemes that help children access education are also supported; Asia and

Eastern Europe; South America. **Note:** The international development programme is heavily oversubscribed and unsolicited applications are unlikely to be successful.

WHAT IS NOT FUNDED Individuals (whether for research, expeditions, educational purposes or medical treatment); projects concerned with travel, adventure, sports or recreation; organisations which do not have UK charity registration (except those legally exempt from registration and, in exceptional circumstances, West Midlands-based small grant applications).

TYPE OF GRANT Core costs; development funding; project funding. Grants are normally one-off.

RANGE OF GRANTS Small grants of up to £2,000; large grants usually range from £10,000 to £20,000 with an occasional maximum of £50,000.

SAMPLE GRANTS Concern Universal (£90,000); Jericho Foundation (£30,000); Freedom from Torture and The Ironbridge Gorge Museum (£20,000 each); Birmingham Tribunal Unit (£11,000); Craftspace (£10,000); Colwall Orchard Trust (£8,000); St Anne's Hostel (£7,000); Birmingham Settlement (£3,000).

FINANCES *Year* 2015/16 *Income* £1,034,039 *Grants* £741,250 *Grants to organisations* £741,250 *Assets* £31,927,869

TRUSTEES Margaret Salmon; Rupert Cadbury; Sarah Stafford; Katherine Cadbury; Adrian Thomas; John Penny; Sophy Blandy; Janine Cobaine; Victoria Mohan.

HOW TO APPLY Grant applications can be submitted on-line (preferred) or by post. Small grants (up to a maximum of £2,000) are awarded monthly). The trustees meet in May and November to award large grants ranging in value from £10,000 to £20,000 with an occasional maximum of £50,000. The cut-off for applications to the May meeting is early March while for November the cut-off is early to mid-September.

WHO TO APPLY TO Carolyn Bettis, Rokesley, University of Birmingham, Bristol Road, Selly Oak, Birmingham B29 6QF *Tel.* 0121 472 1464 *Email* info@wa-cadbury.org.uk *Website* www.wa-cadbury.org.uk

■ The Cadbury Foundation

CC NO 1050482 **ESTABLISHED** 1994

WHERE FUNDING CAN BE GIVEN UK and Africa, particularly in areas where the company has operations.

WHO CAN BENEFIT Registered charities and voluntary organisations.

WHAT IS FUNDED Education and enterprise; poverty and homelessness; the environment and international development.

RANGE OF GRANTS Between £5,000 and £100,000.

SAMPLE GRANTS Taste of Work (£100,000); Grocery Aid (£75,000); Northside Partnership (£50,000); Ready for Work (£25,000); Help for Heroes; Launchpad and Acorn Children's Hospice (£5,000 each); Cocoa Life Source Project (£3,100); Moreton Hamsptead Swimming Pool (£2,500); St Hilda's Church Scout Group (£2,000).

FINANCES *Year* 2015 *Income* £649,828 *Grants* £662,603 *Grants to organisations* £662,603 *Assets* £120,819

TRUSTEES Jonathan Horrell; Neil Chapman; Mary Barnard; Eoin Kellett; Glenn Caton; Alex Blanchard; Suzanne Perry; Josephine Bradley.

OTHER INFORMATION The Cadbury Foundation was set up in 1935 in recognition of the company founders George and Richard Cadbury and their investment in the welfare of their employees and wider communities. In 2010 Kraft Foods Inc. gained control of Cadbury PLC. In 2012 Kraft Foods Inc. was split into Kraft Food Group PLC and Mondelez which now funds the Cadbury Foundation.

HOW TO APPLY The foundations actively seeks out projects to support and therefore cannot accept any unsolicited requests for funding.

WHO TO APPLY TO Kelly Farrell, Community Affairs Manager, Cadbury Ltd, PO BOX 12, Bourneville, Birmingham B30 2LU *Tel.* 0121 787 2421 *Email* kelly.farrell@mdlz.com

■ The Barrow Cadbury Trust

CC NO 1115476 **ESTABLISHED** 1920

WHERE FUNDING CAN BE GIVEN UK and overseas, with a preference for Birmingham and the surrounding area.

WHO CAN BENEFIT Charities; voluntary organisations; preferably grassroots community groups and user-led projects.

WHAT IS FUNDED Criminal justice; migration; economic justice.

TYPE OF GRANT Projects; recurring costs; running expenditure.

SAMPLE GRANTS ShareAction (£70,000); Citizens UK (£60,000); Fawcett Society (£57,500); Young Women's Trust (£45,000); Localise West Midlands (£44,500); Community Development Finance Association (£41,000); Uturn UK CIC (£40,000); The School for Social Entrepreneurs (£10,000).

FINANCES *Year* 2015/16 *Income* £3,048,000 *Grants* £4,193,000 *Grants to organisations* £4,193,000 *Assets* £69,511,000

TRUSTEES Erica Cadbury; Anna Southall; Nicola Cadbury; Helen Cadbury; Catherina Pharoah; Tamsin Rupprechter; Harry Serle; John Serle; Steven Skakel; Binita Mehta; Esther McConnell.

OTHER INFORMATION The trust made 117 grants during the year. The trust also provides social investment. It will consider investments which further the aims of the charity to promote social justice, in particular, but not exclusively, in line with the following interests of the trust: criminal justice; gender justice; racial justice; economic justice.

HOW TO APPLY Applicants should initially complete an enquiry form which is available on the trust's website. Applicants can then complete the application form once they have discussed the project with the trust and have been asked to make an application. Applications can be made at any time.

WHO TO APPLY TO Mark O'Kelly, Head of Finance and Administration, Kean House, 6 Kean Street, London WC2B 4AS *Tel.* 020 7632 9075 *Email* info@barrowcadbury.org.uk *Website* www.barrowcadbury.org.uk

■ The Edward and Dorothy Cadbury Trust

CC NO 1107327 **ESTABLISHED** 1928

WHERE FUNDING CAN BE GIVEN Preference for the West Midlands area.

WHO CAN BENEFIT Registered charities.

WHAT IS FUNDED The trust continues to support, where appropriate, the interests of the founders and the particular charitable interests of the trustees. Grants are grouped under six main headings: arts and culture; community projects and integration; compassionate support;

education and training; conservation and environment; and research.
WHAT IS NOT FUNDED Individuals.
TYPE OF GRANT Grants are made on a one-off basis for a specific purpose or part of a project.
RANGE OF GRANTS £500 to £5,000.
SAMPLE GRANTS Birmingham St Mary's Hospice (£10,000); Haven Breast Cancer Centre (£5,000); Age UK Bromsgrove and District (£3,900); Willow Trust (£1,500); Caudwell Children (£1,000); Worcester Live (£600); Birmingham Contemporary Music (£500).
FINANCES *Year* 2015/16 *Income* £185,197 *Grants* £108,239 *Grants to organisations* £108,239 *Assets* £6,646,204
TRUSTEES Philippa Ward; Susan Anfilogoff; Julia Gillet; Julie Cadbury; Dr Johanna Russell; Jayne Higgins.
HOW TO APPLY The trust's website states: 'An application for funding may be made at any time and should be submitted in writing to the Trust Manager either by post or email. Trustees request that the letter of application should provide a clear and concise description of the project for which the funding is required as well as the outcomes and benefits that it is intended to achieve. They also require an outline budget and explanation of how the project is to be funded initially and in the future together with the latest annual report and accounts for the charity. Applications for funding are generally considered within a three month timescale. Note that applications which fall outside the Trust's stated areas of interest may not be considered or acknowledged.'
WHO TO APPLY TO Sue Anderson, Trust Manager, Rokesley, University of Birmingham – Selly Oak, Bristol Road, Selly Oak, Birmingham B29 6QF *Tel.* 0121 472 1838 *Fax* 0121 472 1838 *Email* e-dcadburytrust@btconnect.com *Website* www.e-dcadburytrust.org.uk

■ The George Cadbury Trust

CC NO 1040999 **ESTABLISHED** 1924
WHERE FUNDING CAN BE GIVEN Preference for the West Midlands, Hampshire and Gloucestershire.
WHO CAN BENEFIT Registered charities.
WHAT IS FUNDED General charitable purposes.
WHAT IS NOT FUNDED Grants to individuals for projects, courses of study, expeditions or sporting tour; overseas appeals.
RANGE OF GRANTS £1,000 to £30,000.
SAMPLE GRANTS Birmingham Royal Ballet and King's School – Burton (£30,000 each); Dean and Chapter Gloucester Cathedral (£20,000); Grange Park Opera (£11,000); Age UK Warwickshire and Birmingham Children's Hospital, The Old Vic and West Green Opera (£5,000 each); Nordoff Robbins (£1,000).
FINANCES *Year* 2015/16 *Income* £410,889 *Grants* £283,023 *Grants to organisations* £283,023 *Assets* £12,398,199
TRUSTEES Roger Cadbury; Benedict Cadbury; Annette Cadbury; Angela Cadbury; Mark Cadbury.
OTHER INFORMATION Grants were made to 140 charities during the year.
HOW TO APPLY Apply in writing to the correspondent to be considered quarterly. Note that very few new applications are supported due to ongoing and alternative commitments.
WHO TO APPLY TO Sarah Moss, BDO, 2 Snow Hill, Birmingham B4 6GA *Tel.* 0121 265 7288

■ The Cadogan Charity

CC NO 247773 **ESTABLISHED** 1966
WHERE FUNDING CAN BE GIVEN UK with a preference for London and Scotland.
WHO CAN BENEFIT Registered charities.
WHAT IS FUNDED General charitable purposes including: social welfare; medical research; military charities; conservation and the environment; education; animal welfare.
WHAT IS NOT FUNDED Individuals.
TYPE OF GRANT Support is usually given over one to two years, although some one-off grants may be made.
RANGE OF GRANTS Up to £600,000.
SAMPLE GRANTS Natural History Museum (£600,000); Historic Royal Palaces (£250,000); London Playing Fields Foundation (£50,000); Downside Fisher Youth Club (£7,500); SeeSaw (£6,000); Gurkha Welfare Trust (£5,000); Multiple Sclerosis Society (£3,500); Mary Hare Foundation and World Sight Foundation (£2,000 each); Epilepsy Research UK (£1,000).
FINANCES *Year* 2015/16 *Income* £2,967,898 *Grants* £1,983,500 *Grants to organisations* £1,983,500 *Assets* £66,583,584
TRUSTEES Earl Cadogan; Countess Cadogan; Viscount Chelsea; Lady Anna Thomson; The Hon. William Cadogan.
OTHER INFORMATION The charity was created with a gift from Cadogan Holdings Company in 1985. Grants were broken down as follows: social welfare (£1.4 million); medical research (£287,500); military charities (£209,500); education (£47,000); animal welfare (£42,000); conservation and the environment (£25,000).
HOW TO APPLY Apply in writing to the correspondent.
WHO TO APPLY TO Paul Loutit, Secretary, The Cadogan Group, 10 Duke of York Square, London SW3 4LY *Tel.* 020 7730 4567 *Email* paul.loutit@cadogan.co.uk

■ CAFOD (Catholic Agency for Overseas Development)

CC NO 1160384 **ESTABLISHED** 1962
WHERE FUNDING CAN BE GIVEN Predominantly overseas, with some funding to partners in England and Wales.
WHO CAN BENEFIT Poorer communities overseas and victims of famine, disasters or war.
WHAT IS FUNDED Long-term development work with some of the world's poorest communities. In almost all cases work overseas is planned and run by local people. Programmes include conflict resolution; disaster relief; economic advocacy; education; health; HIV/AIDS; human right; sustainable livelihoods.
WHAT IS NOT FUNDED CAFOD does not make grants to individuals or to organisations whose aims are primarily political.
TYPE OF GRANT Partnership, programme and project.
SAMPLE GRANTS A list of beneficiaries was not available.
FINANCES *Year* 2015/16 *Income* £53,097,000 *Grants* £31,422,000 *Grants to organisations* £31,422,000 *Assets* £28,655,000
TRUSTEES Joanne Rule; Mary Ney; John Darley; Jim O'Keefe; Dominic Jeremy; Margaret Mwaniki; Bishop John Arnold; Catherine Newman; Bishop John Sherrington; Megan Russell; Mary Ward; Dr John Guy; Prof. Karen Kilby; Christopher Perry.
OTHER INFORMATION During the year, 577 grants were distributed for the following purposes: disaster relief (£16 million); sustainable livelihoods (£6.2 million); human rights (£3.4 million); economic advocacy

(£1.6 million); health (£1.4 million); HIV/AIDS (£1.4 million); conflict resolution (£1.1 million); education (£340,000).

HOW TO APPLY Grants are mainly made to partner organisations. Contact the charity for further information.

WHO TO APPLY TO Education Fund Co-ordinator, Romero House, 55 Westminster Bridge Road, London SE1 7JB *Tel.* 0303 303 3030 *Email* cafod@cafod.org.uk *Website* www.cafod.org.uk

■ Community Foundation for Calderdale

CC NO 1002722 **ESTABLISHED** 1991

WHERE FUNDING CAN BE GIVEN Calderdale, with ability to manage funds outside this area.

WHO CAN BENEFIT Constituted voluntary, community and faith groups, run for and by local people and registered charities working in Calderdale; individuals.

WHAT IS FUNDED General charitable purposes including: health; social welfare; health; community development; older people.

TYPE OF GRANT Revenue; capital; one-off.

RANGE OF GRANTS £100 to £40,000, depending upon scheme.

SAMPLE GRANTS Age UK Calderdale and Kirklees (£19,300); Artworks Yorkshire CIC (£14,000); St Augustine Centre (£10,000); Todmorden Food Drop In (£6,000); Rastrick Big Local (£5,000); Music and the Deaf (£3,500); Calder Valley Youth Theatre (£2,000); Allan Park Bowling Club (£1,200).

FINANCES *Year* 2015/16 *Income* £3,772,223 *Grants* £1,724,085 *Grants to organisations* £488,729 *Assets* £3,748,448

TRUSTEES Brenda Hodgson; Juliet Chambers; Wim Batist; Lee Kenny; Stuart Rumney; Andrew Banks; Liz Bavidge; Christopher Harris; Dr Roger Moore; Russell Galley.

OTHER INFORMATION Grants were split between 1,823 individuals (£598,500) and 233 organisations (£1.1 million).

HOW TO APPLY The foundation's website has details of the grant schemes currently being administered. Application packs for all of the programmes are available to download from the website. Alternatively, contact the foundation directly and it will send a pack in the post. If you wish to discuss your project before applying, the grants team are always happy to answer any queries. The foundation also runs a monthly drop-in, where groups can go for advice and support on their applications.

WHO TO APPLY TO Danni Bailey, Grants Officer, The 1855 Building (first floor), Discovery Road, Halifax HX1 2NG *Tel.* 01422 438738 *Email* grants@cffc.co.uk *Website* www.cffc.co.uk

■ Callander Charitable Trust

SC NO SC016609 **ESTABLISHED** 1972

WHERE FUNDING CAN BE GIVEN Primarily Scotland, but also other parts of the UK.

WHO CAN BENEFIT Charitable organisations.

WHAT IS FUNDED General charitable purposes including: the advancement of religion; education; well-being; social welfare.

WHAT IS NOT FUNDED Individuals; non-registered charities.

SAMPLE GRANTS Médecins Sans Frontières (£9,000); Coldsteam Guards Charitable Trust and Holidays for Heroes (£3,000); Age Concern Falkirk (£1,800); British Red Cross (£1,300); Alzheimer's Scotland and University of St Andrews (£1,000 each); ABF The Soldiers' Charity (£500); Birse Community Trust (£250).

FINANCES *Year* 2015/16 *Income* £72,875 *Grants* £77,250 *Grants to organisations* £77,250 *Assets* £1,748,726

HOW TO APPLY Apply in writing to the correspondent.

WHO TO APPLY TO The Secretary, Anderson Strathern LLP, 1 Rutland Court, Edinburgh EH3 8EY

■ Calleva Foundation

CC NO 1078808 **ESTABLISHED** 1999

WHERE FUNDING CAN BE GIVEN UK.

WHO CAN BENEFIT Charitable organisations.

WHAT IS FUNDED Education and academic research; children's holidays; social services; medical research; overseas/international relief; environment; community; animal welfare.

SAMPLE GRANTS Kew CF Phylogenics Research Project (£2 million); Natural History Museum (£1.7 million); Reading University (£600,000); Royal Ballet School (£58,000); Kensington and Chelsea Foundation (£50,000); University of Cape Town Trust (£7,500); Salvation Army William Booth Centre (£2,000); Silchester Playground Association (£1,000).

FINANCES *Year* 2015 *Income* £2,875,000 *Grants* £1,799,841 *Grants to organisations* £1,799,841 *Assets* £1,086,084

TRUSTEES Stephen Butt; Caroline Butt.

OTHER INFORMATION Grants were made to 11 organisations during the year.

HOW TO APPLY The foundation does not accept unsolicited applications.

WHO TO APPLY TO The Trustees, PO Box 22554, London W8 5GN *Email* contactcalleva@btopenworld.com

■ Calouste Gulbenkian Foundation – UK Branch

ESTABLISHED 1956

WHERE FUNDING CAN BE GIVEN UK and the Republic of Ireland.

WHO CAN BENEFIT Registered charities or tax exempt organisations.

WHAT IS FUNDED The foundation's UK Branch Strategy 2014/2019 focuses on four areas of work: '**Creating the Conditions for Change** – promoting social innovation, strengthening civil society and working to advance our own and others' philanthropic practice; **Participatory Performing Arts** – widening participation in the performing arts to people from all walks of life, especially from the most vulnerable; **Valuing the Ocean** – connecting and building relationships designed to help protect our oceans; **Transitions in Later Life** – helping people in mid to later life feel better supported to manage changes as they age.'

WHAT IS NOT FUNDED Work that does not have a direct benefit in the UK or the Republic of Ireland; individuals; curriculum-based activities in statutory education; student grants or scholarships for tuition and maintenance; vocational training; teaching or research posts or visiting fellowships; educational resources and equipment; gap year activities; group or individual visits abroad, including to Portugal; core services and standard provisions; routine information and advice services; capital costs for housing or the purchase, construction, repair or furnishing of buildings; equipment, including vehicles, IT, or musical instruments; scientific or medical research; medicine or related therapies such as complementary medicine, hospices, counselling and therapy; promoting religion or a belief system; website development; sports; holidays of any sort; animal welfare; loans; retrospective grants; the payment of deficits or loans; the replacement of statutory funding; capital, endowment or widely distributed appeals. Historically the foundation has supported arts-related applications (arts, arts and science and arts education); however, these will no longer be accepted unless they meet the foundation's current aims.

TYPE OF GRANT Generally one-off grants, occasionally recurring for a maximum of three years.

SAMPLE GRANTS Recent beneficiaries listed on the foundation's website have included: Social Finance (£200,000); SP Transitions Ltd (£100,000); Volunteering Matters (£60,000); Forum for the Future (£50,000); Marine Conservation Society (£47,000); Battersea Arts Centre and Common Seas (£20,000 each); Fevered Sleep and Green Alliance Trust (£15,000 each).

FINANCES *Year* 2015/16 *Grants* £1,672,394 *Grants to organisations* £1,672,394

TRUSTEE The foundation's board of administration is based in Lisbon. The UK-resident trustee is Martin Essayan.

OTHER INFORMATION The foundation, which was established in Portugal, is headquartered in Lisbon and has offices in Paris and London.

HOW TO APPLY The charity's website states: 'The majority of support is determined proactively on the basis of the research we undertake. We consider some unsolicited proposals to our open fund through which we hope to attract exceptional organisations and ideas that our research has not identified.'

WHO TO APPLY TO Andrew Barnett, Director, 50 Hoxton Square, London N1 6PB *Tel.* 020 7012 1400 *Fax* 020 7739 1961 *Email* info@gulbenkian.org.uk *Website* www.gulbenkian.org.uk

■ The Cambridgeshire Community Foundation

CC NO 1103314 **ESTABLISHED** 2003

WHERE FUNDING CAN BE GIVEN Cambridgeshire and Peterborough.

WHO CAN BENEFIT Registered charities; formally constituted community and voluntary sector groups; individuals.

WHAT IS FUNDED Community projects seeking to tackle a need or disadvantage. The foundation administers a number of funds. For up-to-date details, see its website.

WHAT IS NOT FUNDED Activities not considered to be charitable; groups that do not operate in accordance with best practice (for example, groups must have a governing document equal opportunity policy, three or more independent members of management committee, etc.); registered charities whose submissions to the Charity Commission are not up to date; unincorporated bodies – voluntary groups that have income above the threshold for registration (of £5,000 per annum) with the Charity Commission but who have not registered with the Charity Commission; groups that have been turned down by the Charity Commission; statutory responsibilities (i.e. projects which should be funded by a statutory body); sponsored events or fundraising for other beneficiaries; improvements to land/buildings that are not open to the general public at convenient hours; projects promoting political activities; animal welfare; projects lobbying for a particular cause or action; deficit or retrospective funding (i.e. grants for activities which have already taken place); overseas travel; organisations that state their purpose to be the promotion of a religion; other grant-making charities.

TYPE OF GRANT Running costs; one-off revenue and capital costs.

RANGE OF GRANTS The majority of the grants awarded are for small amounts of between £500 and £5,000.

SAMPLE GRANTS A list of beneficiaries was not available.

FINANCES *Year* 2015/16 *Income* £2,023,611 *Grants* £1,541,960 *Grants to organisations* £1,497,731 *Assets* £6,086,456

TRUSTEES Robert Satchwell; Iain Crighton; William Dastur; Richard Barnwell; Sam Weller; Chris Belcher; Catherine Stewart; Philip Woolner; Simon Humphrey; Alison Griffiths.

OTHER INFORMATION The amount of grants given to individuals totalled £44,000.

HOW TO APPLY Applications can be made through the foundation's website. Consult the 'Is Your Group ready to Apply for a Grant?' page of the website before applying.

WHO TO APPLY TO Jane Darlington, Chief Executive, Hangar One, The Airport, Newmarket Road, Cambridge CB5 8TG *Tel.* 01223 410535 *Email* info@cambscf.org.uk *Website* www.cambscf.org.uk

■ The Ellis Campbell Foundation

CC NO 802717 **ESTABLISHED** 1989

WHERE FUNDING CAN BE GIVEN London, Hampshire and Perthshire.

WHO CAN BENEFIT Organisations benefitting young disadvantaged people. Maintenance and preservation of buildings is also considered.

WHAT IS FUNDED Youth; education; heritage.

WHAT IS NOT FUNDED Individuals; annual running costs. Other than the grants made annually over a period, no grants will be made more regularly than every other year.

TYPE OF GRANT Usually one-off funding, although grants may be given for over three to five years.

RANGE OF GRANTS Average grants of £2,000.

SAMPLE GRANTS Anvil Trust; Scottish Community Foundation; The Prince's Trust; Bhutan Society; Meridian Trust Association; Hampshire Scouting; Hampshire Country Learning; Martin Sailing Project; Ro-Ro Sailing Project; Wheatsheaf Trust.

FINANCES *Year* 2015 *Income* £136,488 *Grants* £165,440 *Grants to organisations* £165,440 *Assets* £2,017,058

TRUSTEES Michael Campbell, Chair; Linda Campbell; Jamie Campbell; Alexandra Andrews; Laura Montgomery.

HOW TO APPLY Apply in writing to the correspondent. The trustees meet in April and November.

WHO TO APPLY TO Laura Montgomery, Grants Co-ordinator, c/o The Ellis Campbell Group, 10–12 Blandford Street, London W1U 4AZ *Email* sarah@elliscampbell.co.uk *Website* www.elliscampbellfoundation.org

The Campden Charities Trustee

CC NO 1104616 **ESTABLISHED** 1629

WHERE FUNDING CAN BE GIVEN The former parish of Kensington, London; a north-south corridor, roughly from the north of the Fulham Road to the north of Ladbroke Grove (a map can be viewed on the website).

WHO CAN BENEFIT Individuals and non-statutory not-for-profit organisations which refer and support individuals.

WHAT IS FUNDED Social welfare and education.

TYPE OF GRANT One-off and recurrent. Pensions to older people, grants in cash or in kind to relieve need, bursaries and grants to Kensington-based organisations.

SAMPLE GRANTS Nova (£110,000); Westway Community Transport (£88,000); Nucleus Legal Advice Centre (£74,500); Volunteer Centre (£74,000); Blenheim CDP (£36,000); Open Age Project (£18,000); Clement James Centre (£14,000).

FINANCES *Year* 2015/16 *Income* £3,374,616 *Grants* £1,897,037 *Grants to organisations* £1,483,037 *Assets* £144,410,758

TRUSTEES Revd Gillean Craig; David Banks; Susan Lockhart; Dr Kit Davis; Richard Arnott; Terry Myers; Sam Berwick; Dr Christopher Calman; Marta Rodkina; Michael Finney; Robert Atkinson; Julie Mills; Timothy Harvey-Samuel; Robert Orr-Ewing; Daniel Hawkins; Angela McLennon.

OTHER INFORMATION During the year, the charity gave seven 'partnership' grants totalling £414,000. Fourteen 'referral' grants amounted to £14,000. An additional £1.4 million was given in grants to individuals.

HOW TO APPLY The following information is taken from the website: 'We are trying to target our resources where they can be of the most direct benefit to financially disadvantaged individuals. **We therefore do not receive unsolicited applications from organisations.** However, the Charities officers are eager to meet with colleagues from other not-for-profit organisations to explore ways in which we can work together to help individuals to end dependency on benefits or improve a low wage. We make incentive payments to any not-for-profit non-statutory organisations that successfully refer individuals and families to us. The best way to show us that you are working with the people that we want to help is to refer individuals to us and at the same time you will benefit your organisation. **Referrals:** Non-statutory not-for-profit organisations that are working directly with low-income residents of Kensington are eligible to receive £1,000 for each individual or family that they refer successfully (i.e. each individual or family that is awarded a grant or pension).'

WHO TO APPLY TO Chris Stannard, Chief Executive Officer, Studios 3, 27A Pembridge Villas, London W11 3EP *Tel.* 020 7243 0551 *Email* chris-stannard@campdencharities.org.uk *Website* www.campdencharities.org.uk

Canary Wharf Contractors Fund

CC NO 1097007 **ESTABLISHED** 2002

WHERE FUNDING CAN BE GIVEN UK, with a preference for East London.

WHO CAN BENEFIT Individuals; charities and community groups.

WHAT IS FUNDED Communities; social welfare and education, with a focus on people engaged in the construction industry.

SAMPLE GRANTS Lighthouse Club (£51,000); WheelPower (£20,500); Chickenshed (£15,000); Mayors Music Fund Donation (£10,000); Discovery Sailing Project (£9,500); Friends of Ifield School (£5,000); Tower Hamlets Judo (£1,400); Bangladesh Football Association, Caizen Academy and Bethnal Green Swimming Club (£1,000 each).

FINANCES *Year* 2015/16 *Income* £379,426 *Grants* £237,432 *Grants to organisations* £237,432 *Assets* £116,578

TRUSTEES Cormac MacCrain; James Ward.

HOW TO APPLY Apply in writing to the correspondent. The 2015/16 annual report states: 'applicants are invited to submit a summary of their proposals in a specific format'. The trustees meet at least quarterly to assess applications.

WHO TO APPLY TO Alan Ruddy, Ruddy Joinery Ltd, Enterprise Way, Flitwick, Bedford MK45 5BS *Tel.* 01525 716603

The Frederick and Phyllis Cann Trust

CC NO 1087863 **ESTABLISHED** 1998

WHERE FUNDING CAN BE GIVEN Northamptonshire.

WHO CAN BENEFIT The trust deed names seven charities, but trustees are prepared to consider other charities that fall within the charitable objects of the trust.

WHAT IS FUNDED Animal welfare; welfare of children; safety at sea.

RANGE OF GRANTS Up to £20,000.

SAMPLE GRANTS People's Dispensary for Sick Animals (PDSA) (£5,000); Listening Books (£4,500); Brainwave (£3,500); British Horse Society (£3,000); Lakeland Day Care Hospice and Whizz-Kidz (£2,000 each); Childhood Fist (£1,500); Cransley Hospice (£1,400); Aspire and Free to Talk (£1,000 each); Tall Ships (£900); St Giles' Church (£500).

FINANCES *Year* 2015/16 *Income* £0 *Grants* £70,000 *Grants to organisations* £70,000

TRUSTEES Keith Panter; Michael Percival; Philip Saunderson; David Sharp; Christopher Toller; Laura Steedman.

OTHER INFORMATION This charity's latest accounts were not available to view on the Charity Commission's website due to its low income. We have therefore estimated the grant total based on previous years' information.

HOW TO APPLY Apply in writing to the correspondent.

WHO TO APPLY TO Mrs Angela Moon, c/o Hewitsons, Elgin House, Billing Road, Northampton NN1 5 AU *Tel.* 01604 233233 *Email* angelamoon@hewitsons.com

Cardy Beaver Foundation

CC NO 265763 **ESTABLISHED** 1973

WHERE FUNDING CAN BE GIVEN UK with preference for Berkshire.

WHO CAN BENEFIT National and local registered charities.

WHAT IS FUNDED General charitable purposes.

RANGE OF GRANTS Usually under £5,000.

SAMPLE GRANTS Adventure Dolphin; Asthma Relief; Berkshire Blind Society; Cancer Research UK; Church House Trust; Elizabeth Foundation; RNLI; St Peter's Parochial Church Council; Wallingford Museum; Watermill Theatre Appeal.

FINANCES *Year* 2015/16 *Income* £151,352 *Grants* £98,000 *Grants to organisations* £98,000 *Assets* £3,061,117

TRUSTEES John James; Mary Cardy; Sandra Rice.

HOW TO APPLY Apply in writing to the correspondent.

WHO TO APPLY TO John James, Trustee, Clifton House, 17 Reading Road, Pangbourne, Berkshire RG8 7LU *Tel.* 0118 961 4260 *Email* jjames@valewest.com

■ The W. A. Cargill Charitable Trust

SC NO SC012076 **ESTABLISHED** 1954
WHERE FUNDING CAN BE GIVEN Scotland.
WHO CAN BENEFIT Registered charities.
WHAT IS FUNDED Care of older people; care and support of children; medical causes.
WHAT IS NOT FUNDED Individuals; organisations which have been nationalised or taken over by state/local authorities.
SAMPLE GRANTS Tak Tent (£10,000); Glasgow Children Holiday Scheme (£6,000); Brainwave (£4,000); Crossroads and Raleigh International (£3,000 each); Action Medical Research (£2,000); Borderline and Deafblind Scotland (£1,000 each).
FINANCES *Year* 2014/15 *Income* £172,496 *Grants* £77,000 *Grants to organisations* £77,000 *Assets* £5,171,768
OTHER INFORMATION The 2014/15 accounts were the latest available at the time of writing (June 2017).
HOW TO APPLY Apply in writing to the correspondent.
WHO TO APPLY TO The Trustees, Miller Beckett and Jackson Solicitors, 190 St Vincent Street, Glasgow G2 5SP

■ David William Traill Cargill Fund

SC NO SC012703 **ESTABLISHED** 1939
WHERE FUNDING CAN BE GIVEN Scotland.
WHO CAN BENEFIT Registered charities; universities; hospices.
WHAT IS FUNDED Medical research; medical care; care of children; care in the community; care for older people; heritage and arts.
WHAT IS NOT FUNDED Individuals.
TYPE OF GRANT One-off and recurrent.
SAMPLE GRANTS Ardgowan Hospice (£40,000); Beatson Cancer Charity (£15,000); Glasgow Care Foundation and Mary's Meals (£5,000 each); Aberlour and Shelter Scotland (£2,000 each); Enable and Heart and Minds – Glasgow (£1,000 each).
FINANCES *Year* 2014/15 *Income* £344,341 *Grants* £219,613 *Grants to organisations* £218,613 *Assets* £8,467,340
OTHER INFORMATION The 2014/15 accounts were the latest available at the time of writing (June 2017).
HOW TO APPLY Applications may be made in writing to the correspondent, supported by up-to-date accounts. The trustees meet quarterly.
WHO TO APPLY TO The Trustees, Miller Beckett and Jackson Ltd, 190 St Vincent Street, Glasgow G2 5SP

■ The W. A. Cargill Fund

SC NO SC008456 **ESTABLISHED** 1962
WHERE FUNDING CAN BE GIVEN Scotland.
WHO CAN BENEFIT Registered charities; hospices; schools.
WHAT IS FUNDED Medical research; medical care; care of children; care of older people; youth organisations; heritage and arts; educational; religious organisations; general charitable purposes.
WHAT IS NOT FUNDED Individuals.
TYPE OF GRANT One-off or recurrent.
RANGE OF GRANTS Up to £50,000 but generally £500 to £5,000.
SAMPLE GRANTS Erskine (£50,000); People's Welfare Association (£25,000); High School of Glasgow (£20,000); Tenovus (£8,000); Accord Hospice (£7,000); Cancer Research UK (£5,000); The Girls' Brigade (£3,000); Glasgow Cathedral (£2,200); Volunteer Tutors Organisation (£1,000).
FINANCES *Year* 2014/15 *Income* £520,566 *Grants* £410,050 *Grants to organisations* £410,050 *Assets* £16,118,980
OTHER INFORMATION The 2014/15 accounts were the latest available at the time of writing (June 2017).
HOW TO APPLY Apply in writing to the correspondent, including a copy of the charity's latest accounts or details of its financial position.
WHO TO APPLY TO The Trustees, Miller Beckett and Jackson Ltd, 190 St Vincent Street, Glasgow G2 5SP

■ The Richard Carne Trust

CC NO 1115903 **ESTABLISHED** 2006
WHERE FUNDING CAN BE GIVEN UK.
WHO CAN BENEFIT Registered charities; arts institutions; educational establishments; individuals; theatrical groups or musical groups in the early stages of their careers.
WHAT IS FUNDED Children and young people in the performing arts, especially music and theatre. A number of selected charities are supported on an ongoing basis.
TYPE OF GRANT One-off and recurrent.
SAMPLE GRANTS LAMDA (£310,000); Trinity Laban Conservatoire of Music and Dance (£26,000); Welsh College of Music and Drama (£20,000); ChamberStudio (£10,000); JMK Trust (£5,300); Classical Opera Company and RADA (Royal Academy of Dramatic Art) (£5,000 each); Carducci Trust (£1,000).
FINANCES *Year* 2015 *Income* £372,308 *Grants* £491,410 *Grants to organisations* £407,950 *Assets* £919,849
TRUSTEES Philip Carne; Marjorie Carne; SC. Kleinwort Hambros Trust Company UK. Ltd.
HOW TO APPLY Apply in writing to the correspondent. The 2015 accounts state: 'The trustees' current policy is to consider all written appeals received, but only successful applicants are notified of the trustees' decision.'
WHO TO APPLY TO Karen Wall, Administrator, Kleinwort Hambros Trust Company UK, 14 St George Street, London W1S 1FE *Tel.* 020 3207 7014 *Email* Karen.Wall@kleinwortbenson.com

■ The Carnegie Dunfermline Trust

SC NO SC015710 **ESTABLISHED** 1903
WHERE FUNDING CAN BE GIVEN Dunfermline and Rosyth.
WHO CAN BENEFIT Registered charities; voluntary sector organisations; schools; sports clubs; societies.
WHAT IS FUNDED Projects, activities and schemes with social, community, educational, cultural, sport and recreational purposes for the benefit of those within the defined geographic area of the operation of the trust. The trust looks for proposals that are innovative and far reaching together with those that particularly impact on young people. It is also interested in active partnerships where organisations decide to work

together and adopt a joint approach. Start-up funding is offered on a one-off basis. Additional guidelines are available for schools.

WHAT IS NOT FUNDED Individuals; closed groups (with the exception of those catering for specialist needs); political, military or sectarian bodies; activities outside the geographic scope of the trust; medical organisations; routine running or salary costs; costs which are the responsibility of a government body.

TYPE OF GRANT Principally single grants and capital funding. The trust does not usually provide annual recurrent funding for events, schools, clubs and societies.

RANGE OF GRANTS A typical grant lies between £300 and £10,000.

SAMPLE GRANTS Primary Schools Sports Festivals (£5,500); Carnegie Swimming Club (£2,500); West Fife Woodlands Group, 4th Dunfermline Boys' Brigade (£2,000); Fife Festival of Music, Fresh Air Festival (£1,000 each).

FINANCES *Year* 2015 *Income* £539,311 *Grants* £121,489 *Grants to organisations* £121,489 *Assets* £15,691,963

TRUSTEES Andrew Croxford; Dr Colin Firth; David Fleetwood; Keith Harrison; Jane Livingstone; Danny McArthur; Janet McCauslin; Gillian Mann; George Murray; Dr Ruth Ray; Revd Mary Rennie; Fiona Robertson; Douglas Scott; David Walker; Ian Wilson.

HOW TO APPLY The trust's website provides the following information on applications: 'Trustees meet every two months and applications can be submitted at any time. Application forms are available from the website or from the office and initial discussion with the Grants Officer is encouraged. Where possible applications will be acknowledged and further information may be sought. Once all the necessary background is available the application will be considered by the appropriate assessing Trustee in the first instance who will decide if a grant under delegated powers is applicable, if it should go to the Board, or if it is not suitable to progress. When a grant is awarded the recipient will be notified in writing with any related terms and conditions which will include the take up of the grant within a twenty four month period. If an application is unsuccessful, the Trust is unlikely to consider a further application within twelve months.'

WHO TO APPLY TO Elaine Stewart, Grants Officer, Andrew Carnegie House, Pittencrief Street, Dunfermline KY12 8AW *Tel.* 01383 749789 *Fax* 01383 749799 *Email* grants@carnegietrust.com *Website* www.andrewcarnegie.co.uk

■ The Carnegie Trust for the Universities of Scotland

SC NO SC015600 **ESTABLISHED** 1901

WHERE FUNDING CAN BE GIVEN Scotland.

WHO CAN BENEFIT The 15 universities of Scotland, their staff and students.

WHAT IS FUNDED The enrichment of the scholarly capability of Scotland's Universities and assistance for people of limited means to benefit from higher education. The trust operates a number of funding streams to achieve this, which are: fee support for Scottish students unable to fund their course at a Scottish University; Vacation Scholarships for undergraduates who have a talent and an interest for research; bursaries to cover the cost of tuition fees of one year of postgraduate study at a Scottish university; Scholarships for PhD study; Research Incentive Grants to fund high-quality research in any academic field; Collaborative Research Grants to encourage academic researchers to initiate joint research projects to the benefit of Scottish universities as a whole; the Centenary Professorship scheme to support visits to Scotland from leading international researchers.

WHAT IS NOT FUNDED See the website for exclusions of individual schemes.

TYPE OF GRANT Funding for projects of value to the Scottish universities; scholarships; professorships; bursaries.

SAMPLE GRANTS University of Aberdeen; University of Dundee; University of Glasgow; University of Strathclyde.

FINANCES *Year* 2015/16 *Income* £2,983,845 *Grants* £2,376,392 *Grants to organisations* £2,376,392 *Assets* £74,008,235

TRUSTEES Prof. Ian Diamond; Prof. Nigel Seaton; Prof. Sir Peter Downes; Prof. Sir Timothy O'Shea; Prof. Andrea Nolan; Prof. Antonio Muscatelli; Prof. Pamela Gillies; Prof. Richard A. Williams; Prof. Clive Mulholland; Prof. Petra Wend; Prof. Ferdinand von Prondzynski; Prof. Louise Richardson; Prof. Sally Mapstone; Prof. Gerry McCormac; Prof. Jim MacDonald; Prof. Craig Mahoney.

OTHER INFORMATION The grant total above includes funding given both to Universities and to individuals.

HOW TO APPLY Details of the various schemes operated by the trust are available from its website.

WHO TO APPLY TO The Trustees, Andrew Carnegie House, Pittencrieff Street, Dunfermline, Fife KY12 8AW *Tel.* 01383 724990 *Website* www.carnegie-trust.org

■ The Carpenters' Company Charitable Trust

CC NO 276996 **ESTABLISHED** 1978

WHERE FUNDING CAN BE GIVEN UK. Mainly Greater London.

WHO CAN BENEFIT Individuals and schools, colleges, universities and other charitable organisations promoting the craft of carpentry and individuals within the building craft.

WHAT IS FUNDED General charitable purposes including; craft activities; children and young people; religion; education.

WHAT IS NOT FUNDED Grants are not normally made to individual churches or cathedrals, or to educational establishments having no association to the Carpenters' Company. No grants (except educational grants) are made to individual applicants. Funds are usually only available to charities registered with the Charity Commission or exempt from registration.

SAMPLE GRANTS Building Crafts College (£764,000); Carpenters and Dockland Centre and Carpenters Primary School (£15,000 each); Institute of Carpenters (£6,000).

FINANCES *Year* 2015/16 *Income* £1,484,451 *Grants* £904,526 *Grants to organisations* £904,526

TRUSTEES Guy Morton-Smith; Peter Luton; Michael Mathews; Martin Samuel.

HOW TO APPLY Contact the correspondent for details of charitable grants and how to apply.

WHO TO APPLY TO Clerk to the Carpenters' Company, Carpenters' Hall, 1 Throgmorton Avenue, London EC2N 2JJ *Tel.* 020 7588 7001 *Email* info@carpentersco.com *Website* www.carpentersco.com

■ The Carr-Gregory Trust

CC NO 1085580 **ESTABLISHED** 2001
WHERE FUNDING CAN BE GIVEN London; Bristol.
WHO CAN BENEFIT Charitable organisations.
WHAT IS FUNDED Performing arts; health; social welfare.
WHAT IS NOT FUNDED Individuals.
SAMPLE GRANTS National Theatre (£20,000); St George's – Bristol (£16,000); Royal Academy of Music (£15,000); Alzheimer's Research UK (£6,000); Prisoner's Education Trust and University of Bristol (£5,000 each); Hospice UK, St Mungo's and The Salvation Army (£1,000).
FINANCES *Year* 2016 *Income* £110,219 *Grants* £111,991 *Grants to organisations* £111,991 *Assets* £586,344
TRUSTEES Russ Carr; Heather Wheelhouse; Linda Carr.
OTHER INFORMATION Grants over £1,000 were made to 29 organisations during the year.
HOW TO APPLY Apply in writing to the correspondent and should not exceed two A4 pages. An email address should also be provided.
WHO TO APPLY TO Russ Carr, Trustee, 56 Pembroke Road, Clifton, Bristol BS8 3DT

■ The Carrington Charitable Trust

CC NO 265824 **ESTABLISHED** 1973
WHERE FUNDING CAN BE GIVEN UK with a preference for Buckinghamshire.
WHO CAN BENEFIT Registered charities.
WHAT IS FUNDED General charitable purposes; armed forces.
WHAT IS NOT FUNDED Individuals.
RANGE OF GRANTS Up to £25,000 but mostly £50 to £1,000.
SAMPLE GRANTS A list of beneficiaries was not available.
FINANCES *Year* 2015/16 *Income* £85,629 *Grants* £85,629 *Grants to organisations* £85,629 *Assets* £6,043,849
TRUSTEES Jeffrey Cloke; The Rt Hon. Lord Peter Rupert; The Hon. Virginia Carington.
HOW TO APPLY Applications should be made in writing to the correspondent.
WHO TO APPLY TO Jeffrey Cloke, Trustee, The Courtyard, Manor Farm, Church End, Bledlow, Buckinghamshire HP27 9PD *Tel.* 01844 273508 *Email* jeff@cloke.co.uk

■ The Leslie Mary Carter Charitable Trust

CC NO 284782 **ESTABLISHED** 1982
WHERE FUNDING CAN BE GIVEN Norfolk; Suffolk; Essex.
WHO CAN BENEFIT Registered charities; hospices.
WHAT IS FUNDED General charitable purposes including: health; conservation; social welfare.
WHAT IS NOT FUNDED Individuals.
TYPE OF GRANT Capital including buildings; core costs; one-off; project; research; running costs and recurring costs will be considered.
RANGE OF GRANTS £1,000 to £7,000.
SAMPLE GRANTS Norfolk Wildlife Trust (£7,000); Animal Health Trust (£6,000); Acorn Villages and Save the Children (£5,000 each); War Memorials Trust (£3,000); Barn Owl Trust (£2,000); Tall Ships Trust (£1,500); Waveney Stardust (£1,000).
FINANCES *Year* 2015 *Income* £106,500 *Grants* £106,500 *Grants to organisations* £118,500 *Assets* £3,819,855
TRUSTEES Sam Wilson; Leslie Carter; Martyn Carr.
HOW TO APPLY Apply in writing to the correspondent. Telephone calls are not welcome. There is no need to enclose an sae unless applicants wish to have materials returned. Applications made outside the preferred areas for grant-giving will be considered, but acknowledgements may not always be sent.
WHO TO APPLY TO Stephen Richard, c/o Birketts, 24–26 Museum Street, Ipswich IP1 1HZ *Tel.* 01473 232300

■ The Casey Trust

CC NO 1055726 **ESTABLISHED** 1996
WHERE FUNDING CAN BE GIVEN UK and financially developing countries.
WHO CAN BENEFIT Registered (or UK affiliate) charities benefitting children. The trust works with established UK charities.
WHAT IS FUNDED Children (up to the age of 18). The trust is currently looking to support children's projects connected with the arts, metal health, child refugees in the UK and inner-London-based projects. The trustees are looking for start-up projects or identifiable new initiatives within existing projects rather than contributing to recurring events or continuing events.
WHAT IS NOT FUNDED Individual applicants requesting funds to continue studies or travel; unregistered organisations; projects that are not exclusively for children.
TYPE OF GRANT Project funding; start-up costs; up to three years.
RANGE OF GRANTS £1,000 to £12,500; average grant was £2,150.
SAMPLE GRANTS Raw Material (£12,500); World Monuments Fund (£11,000); Buttle UK (£2,500); Acorns (£2,400); The Children's Adventure Farm Trust (£2,300); Lifelites (£2,100); Malaika Kids UK, Motability and Sightsavers (£2,000 each); Street Child – Liberia (£1,800); Perthes Association (£1,600); Sunny Days Children's Fund (£1,500); Edinburgh Young Carers Project and St Luke's Cares (£1,000 each).
FINANCES *Year* 2015/16 *Income* £107,551 *Grants* £87,942 *Grants to organisations* £87,942 *Assets* £3,385,815
TRUSTEES Kenneth Howard; Benjamin Shorten; Sam Howard; Alex Krikler.
HOW TO APPLY Appeals may be made in writing to the correspondent, providing a brief outline of your work and project for which the money is required as well as a clear budget and a recent set of accounts, if possible. If you require a response enclose an sae.
WHO TO APPLY TO Kenneth Howard, Trustee, 27 Arkwright Road, London NW3 6BJ *Tel.* 020 7435 9601 *Email* caseytrust@icloud.com *Website* www.caseytrust.org

■ Sir John Cass's Foundation

CC NO 312425 **ESTABLISHED** 1748
WHERE FUNDING CAN BE GIVEN The inner London boroughs – Camden, Greenwich, Hackney, Hammersmith and Fulham, Islington, Kensington and Chelsea, Lambeth, Lewisham, Newham,

Southwark, Tower Hamlets, Wandsworth, Westminster and the City of London.

WHO CAN BENEFIT Charitable organisations; schools; individuals.

WHAT IS FUNDED Education. The foundation's focus areas are: widening participation in further and higher education; truancy, exclusion and behaviour management; prisoner education; new initiatives. Funding applications should benefit children and young people under the age of 25 who are: residents of the named inner London Boroughs; from a low income background; from disadvantaged backgrounds or areas of high deprivation.

WHAT IS NOT FUNDED Projects that do not meet a foundation priority; holiday projects, school journeys, trips abroad or exchange visits; supplementary schools or mother tongue teaching; independent schools; youth and community groups, or projects taking place in these settings; pre-school and nursery education; general fundraising campaigns or appeals; costs for equipment or salaries that are the statutory responsibility of education authorities; costs to substitute for the withdrawal or reduction of statutory funding; costs for work or activities that have already taken place prior to the grant application; costs already covered by core funding or other grants; capital costs, that are exclusively for the purchase, repair or furnishing of buildings, purchase of vehicles, computers, sports equipment or improvements to school grounds.

TYPE OF GRANT Recurrent for individuals; project, recurrent or one-off support for groups, organisations and schools. Funding may be given for up to three years.

SAMPLE GRANTS London Metropolitan University (£2.6 million); City Business School (£100,000); The Charterhouse (£50,000); British Academy (£40,000); Pembroke College (£30,000); Country Trust (£21,500); Mayor of London's Fund for Young Musicians (£6,000); Roundabout (£5,000).

FINANCES *Year* 2015/16 *Income* £5,510,307 *Grants* £3,433,778 *Grants to organisations* £3,286,278 *Assets* £147,617,532

TRUSTEES Kevin Everett; HH. Brian Barker; Graham Forbes; John Hall; Helen Meixner; David Hogben; Prof. Michael Thorne; Revd Laura Jorgensen; Revd Trevor Critchlow; Pail Bloomfield; Jennifer Moseley; Sophie Fernandes.

OTHER INFORMATION Educational grants are also made to individuals and totalled £147,500.

HOW TO APPLY Applicants should submit an initial enquiry form. The form asks for: outline information about your proposed project; information about how the project meets the foundation's priorities; a summary of the project that includes the following information; the aims of the project including outputs and outcomes; how the project will be delivered; the duration of the project, including when and where it will take place; a budget covering project costs. If successful, applicants will be sent a copy of the stage two application form and guidelines.

WHO TO APPLY TO Richard Foley, Clerk/Chief Executive, 31 Jewry Street, London EC3N 2EY *Tel.* 020 7480 5884 *Email* contactus@sirjohncass.org *Website* sirjohncassfoundation.com

■ Sir Ernest Cassel Educational Trust

CC NO 313820 **ESTABLISHED** 1919

WHERE FUNDING CAN BE GIVEN UK and overseas.

WHO CAN BENEFIT Educational institutions in the UK and in financially developing countries; UK-registered charities; organisations.

WHAT IS FUNDED Educational projects; research; students from overseas studying in the UK; UK charities working overseas in educational development.

WHAT IS NOT FUNDED Individuals directly.

RANGE OF GRANTS £500 to £5,000.

SAMPLE GRANTS CISN Hardship Fund (£9,900); Overseas Research Grants – British Academy (£8,000); Afrikids and Mountbatten Memorial Award at Christ's College – Cambridge (£5,000 each); Budiriro Trust, The Zambia Society Trust (£2,000 each); The Burnbake Trusts Art Project (£1,500); Project Trusts (£1,000).

FINANCES *Year* 2015/16 *Income* £63,481 *Grants* £52,900 *Grants to organisations* £38,000 *Assets* £1,541,831

TRUSTEES Kit Gordon; Ann Kennedy; Anne Sofer; Lady Amanda Ellingworth; Dr Gordon Johnson; Nicholas Allan; Prof. Francis Robinson.

OTHER INFORMATION The Mountbatten Memorial Grant (awards to students from developing countries) awarded a total of £14,900. Grants to organisations working in education in financially developing countries totalled £23,300. The trust awarded £14,700 in grants to UK organisations.

HOW TO APPLY As the trust funds a number of different schemes in partnership with third party organisations applicants are advised to check the website for details on how to apply.

WHO TO APPLY TO Mrs Kathryn Hodges, Trust Secretary, 5 Grimston Park Mews, Grimston Park, Tadcaster, North Yorkshire LS24 9DB *Tel.* 01937 834730 *Email* casseltrust@btinternet.com *Website* www.casseltrust.co.uk

■ The Elizabeth Casson Trust

CC NO 227166 **ESTABLISHED** 1930

WHERE FUNDING CAN BE GIVEN Worldwide.

WHO CAN BENEFIT Occupational therapy schools/departments; individual occupational therapists.

WHAT IS FUNDED The training and development of occupational therapists. Ongoing support is given to Oxford Brookes University.

WHAT IS NOT FUNDED Anything other than occupational therapy education and training.

TYPE OF GRANT Research projects and courses/travel bursaries that will benefit the profession as well as the individual.

RANGE OF GRANTS £400 to £30,000.

SAMPLE GRANTS Fit to Work Project (£30,000); Scholarship at Tufts University (£18,700); Combat Stress, Multiple Sclerosis Trust, Resurge Africa and UK Occupational Therapy Research Foundation (a total of £11,500); College of Occupational Therapy and Ugandan Association of Occupational Therapists (£1,000 each); Oxford Research Group (£400).

FINANCES *Year* 2015/16 *Income* £243,214 *Grants* £339,713 *Grants to organisations* £250,000 *Assets* £7,762,128

TRUSTEES Peter Agulnik; Dr David Parker; Rosemary Hallam; sally Townsend; Marin McNamara; Prof. Elizabeth Turner; Tai Frater; Shelley Grey; Anne Lawson-Porter.

OTHER INFORMATION Grants, scholarships and prizes to individuals totalled £89,500.

HOW TO APPLY Apply in writing to the correspondent.

WHO TO APPLY TO Pamela Anderson, Secretary, 6 Langdale Court, Witney OX28 6FG *Tel.* 01993 850716 *Email* ec.trust@btinternet.com *Website* www.elizabethcassontrust.org.uk

■ The Castang Foundation

CC NO 1003867 **ESTABLISHED** 1991

WHERE FUNDING CAN BE GIVEN UK.

WHO CAN BENEFIT Registered charities; universities; research institutions.

WHAT IS FUNDED Research into neurodevelopmental disorders in children.

SAMPLE GRANTS Sparks (£57,500); Oxford University (£73,500); Royal United NHS Trust – Bath (£35,500); Newcastle University (£20,000); Manchester University (£11,500).

FINANCES *Year* 2015/16 *Income* £261,567 *Grants* £216,829 *Grants to organisations* £216,829 *Assets* £1,884,289

TRUSTEES Michael Glynn; Ian Burman; Dr Paul Euson; Dr Jeremy Parr; Dr Ian Crocker; Carol Barfoot.

HOW TO APPLY Apply in writing to the correspondent.

WHO TO APPLY TO Ian Burman, Trustee, Laytons, 50 Victoria Embankment, London EC4Y 0LS *Tel.* 020 7842 8000 *Email* ian.burnham@laytons.com *Website* www.castangfoundation.net

■ The Castansa Trust

SC NO SC037414 **ESTABLISHED** 2008

WHERE FUNDING CAN BE GIVEN The Central Belt of Scotland and Dumfries and Galloway.

WHO CAN BENEFIT Registered charities.

WHAT IS FUNDED Education; children and young people; support for those diagnosed with dementia or cancer; social inclusion; arts and culture; health; environment.

WHAT IS NOT FUNDED Individuals.

SAMPLE GRANTS Women's Fund for Scotland (£66,500); VOCAL (£10,000); Community Transport Glasgow and Peeblesshire Youth Trust (£5,000 each).

FINANCES *Year* 2015/16 *Income* £556,513 *Grants* £556,513 *Grants to organisations* £556,513 *Assets* £2,641,677

OTHER INFORMATION The average success rate for applicants is currently around 1 in 7.

HOW TO APPLY Application forms are available from the trust's website. Applications are considered quarterly with deadlines of 28 February, 31 May, 31 August and 30 November.

WHO TO APPLY TO The Trustees, c/o Turcan Connell, Princes Exchange, 1 Earl Grey Street, Edinburgh *Website* www.turcanconnell.com/the-castansa-trust

■ The Catholic Charitable Trust

CC NO 215553 **ESTABLISHED** 1935

WHERE FUNDING CAN BE GIVEN America and Europe.

WHO CAN BENEFIT Traditional Catholic organisations.

WHAT IS FUNDED The traditional teachings of the Roman Catholic faith. The trust's income is usually fully committed.

WHAT IS NOT FUNDED The trust does not normally support a charity unless it is known to the trustees. Grants are not made to individuals.

RANGE OF GRANTS £1,500 to £16,000.

SAMPLE GRANTS Society of Saint Pius X – England (£16,000); White Fathers (£5,000); Little Sisters of the Poor and Mission (£4,000 each); White Sisters (£3,000); Friends of Ordinarite and Sisters of the Blessed Virgin Mary Trust (£2,000 each); Holy Cross Catholic Church Fulham (£1,500).

FINANCES *Year* 2015 *Income* £76,204 *Grants* £63,480 *Grants to organisations* £63,480 *Assets* £2,096,287

TRUSTEES John Miles; Wilfrid Miles; David Orr; Jennifer Vernor-Miles.

HOW TO APPLY Applications can only be accepted from registered charities and should be in writing to the correspondent. The trust does not normally support a charity unless it is known to the trustees. In order to save administration costs replies are not sent to unsuccessful applicants. For the most part funds are fully committed.

WHO TO APPLY TO Wilfrid Vernor Miles, Trustee, c/o Hunters Solicitors, 9 New Square, London WC2A 3QN *Tel.* 020 7412 0050 *Email* gt@hunters-solicitors.co.uk

■ The Catholic Trust for England and Wales

CC NO 1097482 **ESTABLISHED** 1968

WHERE FUNDING CAN BE GIVEN England and Wales.

WHO CAN BENEFIT Roman Catholic organisations.

WHAT IS FUNDED The advancement of the Roman Catholic religion in England and Wales.

WHAT IS NOT FUNDED Individuals; local projects; projects not immediately advancing the Roman Catholic religion in England and Wales.

SAMPLE GRANTS Anscombe Bioethics Centre (£100,000); CARITAS Social Action Network (£90,000); Diocese of Cardiff (£12,500); National Board of Catholic Women (£10,000); National Council Lay Association (£9,000); Walsingham Trust (£6,800); Lisbonian Society (£4,100).

FINANCES *Year* 2015 *Income* £12,264,111 *Grants* £733,900 *Grants to organisations* £733,900 *Assets* £37,137,188

TRUSTEES John Gibbs; Rt, Revd Malcolm McMahon; Dr James Whiston; Kathleen Smith; Edward Nally; Pauline Stuart; Michael Prior; Edward Poyser; Nigel Newton; Dr Elizabeth Walmsley; Austin King; Revd David Roberts; Kees Kempenaar.

HOW TO APPLY The trust has stated previously that it does not respond to unsolicited applications.

WHO TO APPLY TO Revd Christopher Thomas, Secretary, 39 Eccleston Square, London SW1V 1BX *Tel.* 020 7901 4808 *Email* secretariat@cbcew.org.uk *Website* www.catholic-ew.org.uk

■ The Cattanach Charitable Trust

SC NO SC020902 **ESTABLISHED** 1992

WHERE FUNDING CAN BE GIVEN Scotland.

WHO CAN BENEFIT The trust will fund charities registered either in Scotland or in England for work done exclusively in Scotland. Organisations should be registered, or in the process of registering, with the Office of the Scottish Charity Regulator.

WHAT IS FUNDED Projects which support children from pre-birth to three years old, who are affected by deprivation.

WHAT IS NOT FUNDED Individuals; personal study or travel; hospices and palliative care; animal charities; appliances for illness or disability; organisations concerned with specific diseases; large capital projects (more than £100,000); projects costing less than £3,000; crèches where parents are not involved; organisations or activities where religious content is compulsory for users; general appeals.

TYPE OF GRANT The trust's website states: 'Grants may be for project funding, or for core funding including salaries and general running costs in smaller organisations. We prefer to fund revenue costs and a grant towards a capital project will usually only be associated with staff costs or some other aspect of revenue funding. The Trust prefers to make a grant which is a sizeable contribution to a project and so is unlikely to make a small grant towards a very large project.' Applicants can initially apply for a one, two or three year grant.

SAMPLE GRANTS Working on Wheels (£33,000); Barnardo's – Paisley (£29,500); Children First (£20,000); Hawick Congregational Community Church and Home Start Majik (£12,000 each); Hidden Garden Trust (£11,000); Step by Step – Moray (£10,000); Barra Children's Centre (£9,300).

FINANCES *Year* 2015 *Income* £523,708 *Grants* £269,141 *Grants to organisations* £269,141 *Assets* £16,696,595

TRUSTEES Alastair Wilson; Andrew Millington; Anne Houston; Duncan McEachran; Helen Healy; Ian McLaughlan; Mafe Marwick; Neil Wood; Rhoda Reid; Steven Murray; Rachel Campbell.

HOW TO APPLY Applications should be made via a form which can be completed online or downloaded from the trust's website. The trust does not normally accept postal applications. The trust no longer has application deadlines, but works on a rolling programme. Trust meetings are listed on its website. There is no deadline for applications, following submission your application the trust will provide guidance on when your application will be considered.

WHO TO APPLY TO Rachel Campbell, c/o Lloyds TSB, Foundation for Scotland, Riverside House, 502 Gorgie Road, Edinburgh EH11 3AF *Tel.* 0131 281 0369 *Email* info@cattanach.org.uk *Website* www.cattanach.org.uk

■ The Joseph and Annie Cattle Trust

CC NO 262011 **ESTABLISHED** 1970

WHERE FUNDING CAN BE GIVEN Hull and East Riding of Yorkshire.

WHO CAN BENEFIT Charitable organisations and statutory authorities.

WHAT IS FUNDED Older people; people with disabilities; disadvantaged people; children; children with dyslexia.

WHAT IS NOT FUNDED Grants are not made directly to individuals. However, applications can be made by charitable or statutory bodies on behalf of individuals or families.

TYPE OF GRANT One-off, capital, recurring and interest-free loans are considered.

RANGE OF GRANTS Up to £15,000.

SAMPLE GRANTS Sobriety Project (£15,000); Dyslexia Action (£14,000); Anlaby Park Methodist Church and The Prince's Trust (£5,000 each); Hull and East Riding Institution for the Blind (£3,000); Bath Institute of Medical Engineering and Ocean Youth Trust (£2,000 each); Age UK East Riding, Longhill Primary School and Prison Fellowship (£1,000 each).

FINANCES *Year* 2015/16 *Income* £380,801 *Grants* £318,655 *Grants to organisations* £318,655 *Assets* £8,770,663

TRUSTEES Michael Gyte; Paul Anthony Edwards; Mr S. C. Jowers; Christopher Munday.

HOW TO APPLY Apply in writing to the correspondent. The trust's website provides the following information on applications: 'There are two main types of application that we are looking to support. Firstly, there are applications by charitable or statutory bodies on behalf of individuals or families. The application form available through this web page must be completed by the charitable organisation/ statutory body concerned and not the individual/ family. Supporting papers should be attached where necessary. Secondly, there are applications for projects and work with the groups of people who are outlined in our key objective above. Please submit full details to the address shown below including the following: the charitable organisation including contact details and the latest financial statements; projects/work successfully completed to date that support the current application. Please outline work already carried out in the Hull & East Riding area. Because we will request that our grants are used exclusively in the Hull & East Riding area please identify how your organisation will guarantee this is achieved; the project/work together with detailed costings and supporting information. (e.g. estimates/planning permission and so on); identify other grants received or currently being considered by other bodies; how the grant is to be spent.'

WHO TO APPLY TO The Administrator, PO Box 23, Patrington, Hull HU12 0WF *Tel.* 01964 671742 *Email* rogerwaudby@hotmail.co.uk *Website* www.jacattletrust.co.uk

■ The Thomas Sivewright Catto Charitable Settlement

CC NO 279549 **ESTABLISHED** 1979

WHERE FUNDING CAN BE GIVEN Unrestricted (for UK-based registered charities).

WHO CAN BENEFIT Registered charities only.

WHAT IS FUNDED General charitable purposes.

WHAT IS NOT FUNDED Non-registered charities; expeditions; travel bursaries; unsolicited applications from churches of any denomination. Grants are unlikely to be considered in the areas of community care, play schemes and drug abuse, or for local branches of national organisations.

RANGE OF GRANTS Up to £14,000.

SAMPLE GRANTS Médecins Sans Frontières (£20,000); Society (£8,000); Good for Life Charity (£5,000); Arthritis Care and DEMAND (£1,000 each); Ruddi's Retreat (£800); Cystic Fibrosis Trust and Macular Society (£750 each); Climbing Out, Fight for Sight and Lepra (£500 each).

FINANCES *Year* 2015/16 *Income* £480,908 *Grants* £216,780 *Grants to organisations* £216,780 *Assets* £11,261,479

TRUSTEES Lord Catto; Olivia Marchant; Zoe Richmond-Watson.

HOW TO APPLY Apply in writing to the correspondent, including an sae.

WHO TO APPLY TO The Secretary to the Trustees, PO Box 47408, London N21 1YW *Email* office@tscatto.org.uk

■ The Wilfrid and Constance Cave Foundation

CC NO 241900 **ESTABLISHED** 1965

WHERE FUNDING CAN BE GIVEN UK, with preference for Berkshire, Cornwall, Devon, Dorset, Hampshire, Oxfordshire, Somerset, Warwickshire and Wiltshire.

WHO CAN BENEFIT Registered charities. Mainly local charities or charities which the trustees have personal knowledge of, interest in, or association with are considered.

WHAT IS FUNDED General charitable purposes including conservation, animal welfare, health and social welfare.

WHAT IS NOT FUNDED Individuals.

TYPE OF GRANT Buildings; core costs; one-off; project. Grants may be given for up to three years.

RANGE OF GRANTS £1,000 to £71,000.

SAMPLE GRANTS Oxford Museum of Children's Literature (£71,000); The Atlantic Salmon Trust (£20,000); The Farmer's Club Pinnacle Award (£7,000); Braunton Academy and Shelter Box (£5,000 each); Swan Support and Thames Rivers Restoration Trust (£3,000 each); Wiltshire Air Ambulance (£2,000); Watton Diabetes UK (£1,000).

FINANCES *Year* 2015/16 *Income* £147,970 *Grants* £176,000 *Grants to organisations* £176,000 *Assets* £4,340,276

TRUSTEES Toni Jones; Francois Jones; Jacqueline Archer; Janet Pickin; Mark Pickin; Melanie Waterworth; Roy Walker; Glyn Howells; William Howells; Matthew Pickin; Emily Pickin; Lucy Howells; Joshua Thorne.

HOW TO APPLY Apply in writing to the correspondent, ensuring that applications are received a month before the trustees' meetings which are held twice each year, in May and October.

WHO TO APPLY TO The Trustees, New Lodge Farm, Drift Road, Winkfield, Windsor SL4 4QQ *Email* tcf@eamo.co.uk

■ The Cayo Foundation

CC NO 1080607 **ESTABLISHED** 1999

WHERE FUNDING CAN BE GIVEN UK.

WHO CAN BENEFIT Registered charities.

WHAT IS FUNDED General charitable purposes; medical research; crime prevention; children and young people; performing arts.

TYPE OF GRANT Grants and loans.

RANGE OF GRANTS £1,000 to £125,000.

SAMPLE GRANTS NSPCC (£125,000); Disability Foundation, PACT and The Royal Opera House (£25,000 each); Princes Foundation (£20,000); Wessex Youth Trust (£10,000); Christian Blind Mission (£6,000); Wellbeing of Women (£3,000); Institute for Policy Research and Royal Humane Society (£2,500 each); Sue Ryder Care – St John's Hospice (£1,000).

FINANCES *Year* 2014/15 *Income* £1,323,093 *Grants* £1,248,893 *Grants to organisations* £1,248,893 *Assets* £2,373,261

TRUSTEES Angela McCarville; Stewart Harris.

HOW TO APPLY Applications can be made in writing to the correspondent.

WHO TO APPLY TO Angela McCarville, Trustee, 7 Cowley Street, London SW1P 3NB *Tel.* 020 7248 6700

■ Elizabeth Cayzer Charitable Trust

CC NO 1059265 **ESTABLISHED** 1996

WHERE FUNDING CAN BE GIVEN UK.

WHO CAN BENEFIT Museums, galleries and other arts organisations and projects.

WHAT IS FUNDED Funds are used in promoting activities related to art, including education, restoration, research, conservation and conferences and exhibitions.

SAMPLE GRANTS The Landmark Trust and the Wallace Collection (£20,000 each); The Dulwich Picture Gallery (£14,500); The House of Illustration (£7,000); The National Gallery (£6,000).

FINANCES *Year* 2015/16 *Income* £773,821 *Grants* £67,500 *Grants to organisations* £67,500 *Assets* £6,310,938

TRUSTEES The Hon. Elizabeth Gilmour; Dominic Gibbs; Diana Lloyd.

OTHER INFORMATION This charity was established by The Hon. Elizabeth Gilmour, who has made significant donations to the charity since 1996. In formulating policy the trustees have taken into account the wishes of the Settlor, which are that the assets of the charity should be used in supporting and promoting activities relating to art.

HOW TO APPLY The 2015/16 accounts state: 'The trustees identify the projects and organisations they wish to support and that benefit the public. These include supporting exhibitions, the restoration of paintings and sculpture, academic research, art historical publications and architectural conservation. They do not consider grants to people or organisations who apply speculatively. The trust also has a policy of not responding to any correspondence unless it relates to grants it has agreed to make or to the general management of the trust.'

WHO TO APPLY TO The Hon. Elizabeth Gilmour, Trustee, The Cayzer Trust Company Ltd, 2nd Floor, Stratton House, Stratton Street, London W1J 8LA *Tel.* 020 7802 8080 *Email* admin@cayzertrust.com

■ The B. G. S. Cayzer Charitable Trust

CC NO 286063 **ESTABLISHED** 1982

WHERE FUNDING CAN BE GIVEN UK.

WHO CAN BENEFIT Registered charities.

WHAT IS FUNDED General charitable purposes.

WHAT IS NOT FUNDED Organisations outside the UK.

SAMPLE GRANTS A list of beneficiaries was not available.

FINANCES *Year* 2015/16 *Income* £241,717 *Grants* £75,200 *Grants to organisations* £75,200 *Assets* £4,501,602

TRUSTEES Mr P. R. Davies; Mary Buckley; Arabella Hunter; Roseanna Leslie.

HOW TO APPLY The 2015/16 accounts state: 'The trustees identify the projects and organisations they wish to support and so do not consider unsolicited applications from people or organisations. To preserve the trust's funds the trust also has a policy of not responding to any such applications.'

WHO TO APPLY TO Sonia Barry, The Cayzer Trust Company Ltd, Cayzer House, 30 Buckingham Gate, London SW1E 6NN *Tel.* 020 7802 8439 *Email* admin@cayzertrust.com

■ The Cazenove Charitable Trust

CC NO 1086899 **ESTABLISHED** 1969
WHERE FUNDING CAN BE GIVEN UK.
WHO CAN BENEFIT Charitable organisations.
WHAT IS FUNDED General charitable purposes.
RANGE OF GRANTS Up to £12,000.
SAMPLE GRANTS Alzheimer's Research UK (£12,000); Tall Ships Youth Trust, The Ditchley Foundation and The Macular Society (£7,000 each); PACE, Skinners' Almshouse Charity, Royal Society of Wildlife Trusts and The Royal Foundation (£4,000 each); Winston Churchill Memorial Trust (£2,500); Darwin College and St Margaret Lothbury Church (£1,000 each).
FINANCES *Year* 2015 *Income* £82,204 *Grants* £75,570 *Grants to organisations* £75,570 *Assets* £2,709,804
TRUSTEES David Mayhew; Edward Harley; Michael Wentworth-Stanley; Michael Power; Lucinda Napier.
OTHER INFORMATION In 2015 58 grants were made. Grants of less than £1,000 each totalled £22,000. The trust primarily supports fundraising activities by employees and ex-employees of JP Morgan Cazenove and Cazenove Capital Management via a matched giving scheme.
HOW TO APPLY Apply in writing to the correspondent.
WHO TO APPLY TO Lucinda Napier, Trustee, Cazenove Capital Management Ltd, 12 Moorgate, London EC2R 6DA *Tel.* 020 7658 1106

■ The CBD Charitable Trust

CC NO 1136702 **ESTABLISHED** 2010
WHERE FUNDING CAN BE GIVEN Worldwide.
WHO CAN BENEFIT Registered charities, particularly organisations benefitting children and young people.
WHAT IS FUNDED General charitable purposes; children and young people.
RANGE OF GRANTS £100 to £152,000.
SAMPLE GRANTS Action Aid; Athena; Avaaz; Charities Advisory Trust; Global White Lion; Medical Aid for Palestinians; Morning Star Children; Oxfam; Salvation Army; The Funding Network; Whizz-Kidz; Womankind Worldwide.
FINANCES *Year* 2015/16 *Income* £81,466 *Grants* £103,547 *Grants to organisations* £103,547 *Assets* £36,091
TRUSTEES Coutts & Co.; Ingrid Scott.
OTHER INFORMATION Grants were made to 20 organisations during the year.
HOW TO APPLY Applications may be made in writing to the correspondent.
WHO TO APPLY TO The Trustees, c/o Coutts & Co., Trustee Department, 440 Strand, London WC2R 0QS *Tel.* 020 7663 6825 *Email* couttscharities@coutts.com

■ CBRE UK Charitable Trust

CC NO 299026 **ESTABLISHED** 1987
WHERE FUNDING CAN BE GIVEN UK.
WHO CAN BENEFIT Registered charities.
WHAT IS FUNDED General charitable purposes.
WHAT IS NOT FUNDED Third parties, such as fundraising organisations or publication companies producing charity awareness materials.
RANGE OF GRANTS £100 to £9,500.
SAMPLE GRANTS Shelter (£9,500); Plan International (£6,600); Marion's Still Smiling (£2,200); Haven House (£1,700); Muscular Dystrophy UK (£1,500); Great Ormond Street Hospital Children's Charity (£1,300); Club Peloton (£1,000); Cancer Research UK (£750); Breast Cancer Campaign (£500); Action For Children (£250); Wessex Children's Hospice Trust (£50).
FINANCES *Year* 2015/16 *Income* £43,533 *Grants* £53,766 *Grants to organisations* £53,766 *Assets* £66,734
TRUSTEES Alex Naftis; Guy Gregory; Emma Warren; Lucy Aldrich-Smith; Rachel Lee.
OTHER INFORMATION The trust made 129 donations to 87 charities during the year. Formerly known as the CB Richard Ellis Charitable Trust, this is the corporate charity of CBRE, a commercial property and real estate provider. Support is generally given to organisations that are recommended by CBRE's employees or whose work is closely aligned to that of CBRE.
HOW TO APPLY Apply in writing to the correspondent.
WHO TO APPLY TO Tilly Harvey, CBRE UK, St Martin's Court, 10 Paternoster Row, London EC4M 7HP *Tel.* 020 7182 2000

■ Celtic Charity Fund

SC NO SC024648 **ESTABLISHED** 1995
WHERE FUNDING CAN BE GIVEN Worldwide but with a preference for Scotland and Ireland.
WHO CAN BENEFIT Charitable organisations.
WHAT IS FUNDED Health; equality; education; social welfare.
SAMPLE GRANTS No details regarding individual grant beneficiaries are provided.
FINANCES *Year* 2015/16 *Income* £1,550,117 *Grants* £253,982 *Grants to organisations* £196,812 *Assets* £909,356
TRUSTEES Chris Traynor; Peter Lawwell; Gavin Kelly; Eric Riley; Adrian Filby; Stephen Glancey.
HOW TO APPLY Apply in writing to the correspondent.
WHO TO APPLY TO Jane Maguire, Celtic Football Club, Celtic Park, Glasgow G40 3RE *Email* cfcfoundation@celticfc.co.uk *Website* www.celticfc.net

■ CEO Sleepout

CC NO 1154963 **ESTABLISHED** 2013
WHERE FUNDING CAN BE GIVEN UK.
WHO CAN BENEFIT Registered charities.
WHAT IS FUNDED Homelessness.
SAMPLE GRANTS A list of beneficiaries was not available.
FINANCES *Year* 2015/16 *Income* £321,385 *Grants* £158,789 *Grants to organisations* £158,789 *Assets* £196,976
TRUSTEES Andy Preston; Niklas Tunley; Abu Ali.
HOW TO APPLY Applications can be made in writing to the correspondent.
WHO TO APPLY TO Andy Preston, Trustee, Boho Number One, Bridge Street West, Middlesbrough, Cleveland TS2 1AE *Tel.* 07922 478994 *Email* info@ceosleepoutuk.com *Website* www.ceosleepoutuk.com

■ The CH (1980) Charitable Trust

CC NO 279481 **ESTABLISHED** 1980
WHERE FUNDING CAN BE GIVEN UK and Israel.
WHO CAN BENEFIT Jewish organisations.
WHAT IS FUNDED Jewish causes.
RANGE OF GRANTS £500 to £37,000.
SAMPLE GRANTS Jerusalem Foundation (£38,000); Jewish Care, William Sharon Memorial Fund and World Jewish Relief (£20,000 each); United Jewish Israel Appeal (UJIA) (£10,000); Israel

Diaspora Trust (£3,000); Institute of Jewish Policy (£1,000); Anne Frank Trust (£500).

FINANCES *Year* 2015/16 *Income* £32,021 *Grants* £171,080 *Grants to organisations* £171,080 *Assets* £926,080

TRUSTEE SG. Kleinwort Hambros Trust Company (UK) Ltd.

HOW TO APPLY Unsolicited applications are not accepted.

WHO TO APPLY TO The Trustees, Kleinwort Benson Trustees Ltd, 14 St George Street, London W1S 1FE *Tel.* 020 3207 7000

■ The Chadwick Educational Foundation

CC NO 526373 **ESTABLISHED** 1963

WHERE FUNDING CAN BE GIVEN The borough of Bolton and former urban district of Turton.

WHO CAN BENEFIT Schools; individuals; organisations.

WHAT IS FUNDED Education.

TYPE OF GRANT Mainly capital grants.

RANGE OF GRANTS £100 to £18,000.

SAMPLE GRANTS Johnson Fold County Primary School (£18,000); Red Lane Primary School (£16,000); Clarendon Primary School (£12,500); Moorgate Primary School (£8,000); Devonshire Road Primary School (£7,500); Pikes Lane Primary School (£4,900); Beanstalk (£2,500); Bolton Parish Church (£140).

FINANCES *Year* 2015 *Income* £167,062 *Grants* £156,185 *Grants to organisations* £156,185 *Assets* £98,481

TRUSTEES Peter Liptrott; Stan Wilson; Canon Smith; Canon Matt Thompson; Esther Gelling; Rachel Cole; Ian Tomkin.

HOW TO APPLY The 2015 accounts state: 'The Charity invites applications for grants through headteachers at Bolton schools and with the co-operation of Bolton's Local Education Authority. Preference is given to the underprivileged.'

WHO TO APPLY TO Simon Warswick, 71 Chorley Old Road, Bolton BL1 3AJ *Tel.* 01204 534421

■ The Amelia Chadwick Trust

CC NO 213795 **ESTABLISHED** 1960

WHERE FUNDING CAN BE GIVEN UK, especially Merseyside.

WHO CAN BENEFIT Local charities and community organisations; hospices; some UK organisations.

WHAT IS FUNDED General charitable purposes including: education; health; the arts; social welfare; the environment.

WHAT IS NOT FUNDED Individuals.

TYPE OF GRANT Mostly recurring.

RANGE OF GRANTS £1,000 to £39,000.

SAMPLE GRANTS Merseyside Development Foundation (£39,000); Save the Children (£10,000); L'Arche Ltd – Liverpool (£2,500); Beanstalk (£2,000); Sheila Kay Fund (£1,800); Age Concern Liverpool and Wirral Women and Children's Aid (£1,300 each); Oxfam (£1,000).

FINANCES *Year* 2015/16 *Income* £150,452 *Grants* £155,738 *Grants to organisations* £155,738 *Assets* £4,122,033

TRUSTEES Liverpool Charity and Voluntary Services; Ruth Behrend; Matthew Dawson.

HOW TO APPLY All donations are made through Liverpool Charity and Voluntary Services. Grants are only made to charities known to the trustees, and unsolicited applications are not considered.

WHO TO APPLY TO The Trustees, c/o Liverpool Charity and Voluntary Services, 151 Dale Street, Liverpool L2 2AH *Tel.* 0151 227 5177 *Email* info@lcvs.org.uk

■ Chalfords Ltd

CC NO 287322 **ESTABLISHED** 1983

WHERE FUNDING CAN BE GIVEN England and Wales.

WHO CAN BENEFIT Orthodox Jewish institutions.

WHAT IS FUNDED Religious education; social welfare.

SAMPLE GRANTS A list of beneficiaries was not available.

FINANCES *Year* 2015 *Income* £2,040,138 *Grants* £1,675,619 *Grants to organisations* £1,675,619 *Assets* £38,740,132

TRUSTEES Irwin Weiler; Nicky Rosenthal; Paula Weiler; Monica Rosenthal; Riki Weiler; Talia Rosenthal; Daniella Rosenthal; Mr A. Weiler; Mr M. Weiler.

HOW TO APPLY Apply in writing to the correspondent.

WHO TO APPLY TO The Trustees, New Burlington House, 1075 Finchley Road, London NW11 0PU *Tel.* 020 8455 6075

■ Champneys Charitable Foundation

CC NO 1114429 **ESTABLISHED** 2006

WHERE FUNDING CAN BE GIVEN UK.

WHO CAN BENEFIT Charitable organisations.

WHAT IS FUNDED Health; medical causes; disability.

TYPE OF GRANT Equipment.

RANGE OF GRANTS Up to £60,000.

SAMPLE GRANTS Pink Ribbon Foundation (£60,000); Cystic Fibrosis (£43,500); Disability Snowsport (£6,000); Wyvern School (£5,400); Rainbow Hospice (£5,000); Silver Star Appeal (£3,500); Hertfordshire MS Therapy (£3,000).

FINANCES *Year* 2015/16 *Income* £101,676 *Grants* £138,838 *Grants to organisations* £138,838 *Assets* £21,914

TRUSTEES Dorothy Purdew; Stephen Purdew; Michael Hawkins.

HOW TO APPLY Apply in writing to the correspondent.

WHO TO APPLY TO Dorothy Purdew, Chair, Henlow Grange, Henlow, Bedfordshire SG16 6DB *Tel.* 01462 811111 *Email* charity@champneys.co.uk *Website* www.champneys.com

■ The Chapman Charitable Trust

CC NO 232791 **ESTABLISHED** 1963

WHERE FUNDING CAN BE GIVEN The trust mainly supports national charities but also supports local charities in North Wales, London and South East England.

WHO CAN BENEFIT Any recognised charity can apply but special consideration is given to those of personal interest to the late settlor or to the current trustees.

WHAT IS FUNDED Activity, health and well-being, including research; culture, the natural environment and heritage; care; community; counselling.

WHAT IS NOT FUNDED Local branches of national charities; overseas charities; animal welfare organisations; sports tours; research expeditions; sponsored adventure holidays; applications for individuals.

RANGE OF GRANTS Mostly £1,000 to £2,000.

SAMPLE GRANTS Pesticide Action Network UK (£20,000); Action for Children, Aldeburgh Music, Fragile X Society, Methodist Homes for the Aged

(£12,000 each); Ambitious about Autism and Cherry Trees (£6,000 each); British Film Institute (£4,000); Woodland Trust (£3,000); Braille Chess Association, Pain Relief Foundation and University of Surrey (£2,000 each).

FINANCES *Year* 2015/16 *Income* £316,093 *Grants* £142,000 *Grants to organisations* £142,000 *Assets* £7,404,721

TRUSTEES Roger Chapman; Guy Chapman; Richard Chapman; Byrony Chapman; Thomas Williams.

OTHER INFORMATION There were 149 grants made during the year. A full list of grants made is available on the trust's website. Grants were broken down as follows: social care (£90,500); culture and heritage (£70,500); environment (£57,000); activity, health and well-being (£48,000); education and research (£37,000).

HOW TO APPLY Apply in writing to the correspondent. The trust's website states: 'It is helpful to us if your application begins with a short paragraph giving a succinct summary of your project. The trustees meet twice a year, in March and September. Applications received before the beginning of those months will be considered at the relevant meeting. We receive a great many applications and regret that we cannot acknowledge receipt. Regard the absence of any communication for six months as an indication that we have considered the application but it has been unsuccessful.'

WHO TO APPLY TO Roger S. Chapman, Trustee, Roger Chapman, 62 Wilson Street, London EC2A 2BU *Tel.* 020 7782 0007 *Email* cct@rpgcrouchchapman.co.uk *Website* www.chapmancharitabletrust.org.uk

■ Charitworth Ltd

CC NO 286908 **ESTABLISHED** 1983

WHERE FUNDING CAN BE GIVEN Worldwide, mainly UK and Israel.

WHO CAN BENEFIT Charitable organisations.

WHAT IS FUNDED Religion, education and the relief of poverty. In practice, mainly Jewish causes are supported.

TYPE OF GRANT One-off and recurring.

SAMPLE GRANTS Be'er Ya'akov; Beis Soroh Schneirer; British Friends of Tshernobil; Centre for Torah Education Trust; Chevras Maoz Ladal; Cosmon Belz; Dushinsky Trust; Finchley Road Synagogue; Friends of Viznitz; Zichron Nahum.

FINANCES *Year* 2015/16 *Income* £1,141,812 *Grants* £1,260,000 *Grants to organisations* £1,260,000 *Assets* £32,845,807

TRUSTEES Samuel Halpern; Sidney Halpern; David Halpern; Relly Halpern.

HOW TO APPLY Apply in writing to the correspondent.

WHO TO APPLY TO David Halpern, Trustee, New Burlington House, 1075 Finchley Road, London NW11 0PU

■ The Charter 600 Charity

CC NO 1051146 **ESTABLISHED** 1994

WHERE FUNDING CAN BE GIVEN UK and occasionally overseas.

WHO CAN BENEFIT Registered charities; community-based, grassroots organisations.

WHAT IS FUNDED General charitable purposes, with particular emphasis on education, older people; social and medical welfare; material conservation; the arts; wildlife; Christianity; youth and community welfare.

TYPE OF GRANT Typically one-off.

RANGE OF GRANTS £250 to £2,500.

SAMPLE GRANTS Royal Green Jackets Museum (£2,500); Arts Together, Bumblebee Conservation Trust, Chiltern Food Bank and Education Partnerships Africa (£1,500 each); Wymondham College (£1,000); Wolfson Social Activity and Transport Fund (£750); Football Beyond Borders and Juvenile Diabetes Research Foundation (£500 each); Salaam Peace (£250).

FINANCES *Year* 2015/16 *Income* £180,024 *Grants* £46,641 *Grants to organisations* £45,641 *Assets* £1,289,043

TRUSTEE The Mercers Company.

OTHER INFORMATION A grant of £1,000 was made to one individual during the year and 37 grants were made to organisations.

HOW TO APPLY Applications for charitable grants will only be accepted when put forward by a member of the Mercers' Company. The charity does not consider unsolicited applications.

WHO TO APPLY TO Mimi Phung, Grants Team, Mercers' Hall, Ironmongers Lane, London EC2V 8HE *Tel.* 020 7726 4991 *Email* grants@mercers.co.uk *Website* www.mercers.co.uk

■ Chartered Accountants' Livery Charity (CALC)

CC NO 327681 **ESTABLISHED** 1988

WHERE FUNDING CAN BE GIVEN UK.

WHO CAN BENEFIT Registered charities; voluntary organisations.

WHAT IS FUNDED General charitable purposes including: social welfare; education; religion.

RANGE OF GRANTS £1,500 to £75,000.

SAMPLE GRANTS MyBnk (£75,000); SBS Association and 47 Squadron (£6,800); Centrepoint (£5,000); PACE and The Lord Mayors Appeal (£2,500 each); Harrow and Wembley Sea Cadets (£1,500).

FINANCES *Year* 2014/15 *Income* £160,250 *Grants* £123,850 *Grants to organisations* £123,850 *Assets* £1,568,508

TRUSTEES William Fowle; Miles Hedges; Richard Dyson; Adam Vere Broke; Andrew Popham; Nigel Turnbull; Andrew Pianca.

OTHER INFORMATION The 2014/15 accounts were the latest available at the time of writing.

HOW TO APPLY Apply in writing to the correspondent. Applications must be sponsored by a liveryman of the company.

WHO TO APPLY TO Barbara Brooks, 18 Bosman Drive, Windlesham GU20 6JW *Tel.* 01276 850195 *Email* charity@accountantslivery.org

■ The Cheruby Trust

CC NO 327069 **ESTABLISHED** 1986

WHERE FUNDING CAN BE GIVEN UK and worldwide.

WHO CAN BENEFIT Registered charities.

WHAT IS FUNDED General charitable purposes including: the relief of poverty anywhere in the world; the advancement of public education anywhere in the world.

RANGE OF GRANTS £100 to £5,000.

SAMPLE GRANTS Age UK (£5,000); Crisis at Christmas (£4,000); Action on Poverty (£3,000); British Humanitarian Aid and Childhope (£2,000 each); Concern Worldwide (£1,500); Winston's Wish (£1,000); Rainforest Concern (£500); Listening Books (£200).

FINANCES *Year* 92516 *Income* £92,516 *Grants* £100,050 *Grants to organisations* £100,050

TRUSTEES Alison Corob; Laura Corob; Christopher Cook; Sheila Wechsler; Tricia Corob.

HOW TO APPLY Apply in writing to the correspondent.
WHO TO APPLY TO Sheila Wechsler, Trustee, 62 Grosvenor Street, London W1K 3JF *Tel.* 020 7499 4301

■ Cheshire Community Foundation Ltd

CC NO 1143711 **ESTABLISHED** 2011
WHERE FUNDING CAN BE GIVEN Cheshire.
WHO CAN BENEFIT Registered charities; community organisations; CICs.
WHAT IS FUNDED General charitable purposes.
WHAT IS NOT FUNDED According to its website, the foundation will not fund the following organisations: that are statutory bodies (such as schools, parish councils and hospitals) or private businesses, including sole traders; whose work does not support people living within one of the three local authorities of Cheshire East, Cheshire West and Chester or Warrington; which do not have a minimum of two unrelated cheque signatories; CICs which do not have a minimum of three unrelated directors to the company. In general the foundation will not fund: general appeals and political promotion, including political party activity; the support or promotion of a religious doctrine; mission; proselytism or promotion of the beliefs of a particular faith (beyond basic religious/cultural awareness raising); medical research, medical equipment or medical treatment; activities that are for the sole relief or benefit of animals or plants; retrospective or deficit funding; activities which a statutory body is responsible for.
SAMPLE GRANTS A full list of all charities supported is available from the foundation's website.
FINANCES *Year* 2015 *Income* £565,489 *Grants* £421,974 *Grants to organisations* £421,974 *Assets* £5,235,571
TRUSTEES David Briggs; Norman Banner; Joëlle Warren; Sue Craven; Nicholas Mason; Robert Barrow; Heather Cunningham; John Farrell.
HOW TO APPLY The foundation has a grants team that is available to talk to potential applicants about the eligibility and suitability of the project. It advises that applicants apply to the most appropriate grant programme, read the relevant guidelines and regularly check the deadline section of the website. Once a suitable programme has been identified, applications can be made online.
WHO TO APPLY TO Sarah Mitchell, Cheshire Community Foundation, Sension House, Denton Drive, Northwich, Cheshire CW9 7LU *Tel.* 01606 330607 *Email* office@cheshirecommunityfoundation.org.uk *Website* www.cheshirecommunityfoundation.org.uk

■ Cheshire Freemason's Charity

CC NO 219177 **ESTABLISHED** 1963
WHERE FUNDING CAN BE GIVEN Cheshire and parts of Greater Manchester and Merseyside.
WHO CAN BENEFIT Individuals and organisations benefitting Masons and their families.
WHAT IS FUNDED The relief of Masons and their dependants, Masonic charities and other charities, especially medical.
SAMPLE GRANTS Children's Cancer Support Group; Mencap, Wirral Autistic Society; Bollington and Macclesfield Sea Cadets; Cathedral Road Kids Project.
FINANCES *Year* 2015/16 *Income* £193,350 *Grants* £445,687 *Grants to organisations* £445,687 *Assets* £4,015,275
TRUSTEES Peter Carroll; Paul Richards; Stephen Kinsey; Alisdair Macdonald; Graham Scott; Leo Saunders.
OTHER INFORMATION Grants made during the year were divided between Masonic institutions (£303,500) and individuals and charities (£142,000).
HOW TO APPLY Apply in writing to the correspondent.
WHO TO APPLY TO Christopher Renshaw, 6 Auden Close, Ewloe, Deeside CH5 3TY *Tel.* 01244 534343 *Email* enquiries@cheshiremasons.co.uk *Website* www.cheshiremasons.co.uk

■ Chest Heart and Stroke Scotland

SC NO SC018761 **ESTABLISHED** 1991
WHERE FUNDING CAN BE GIVEN Scotland.
WHO CAN BENEFIT Research institutions; hospitals; individuals.
WHAT IS FUNDED Research into all aspects of the prevention and treatment of chest, heart and stroke illness, and in the rehabilitation and care of those affected. The charity is particularly focused on research which has the potential to impact directly on health improvement and patient care, and on pilot studies which have the potential to stimulate further research from funders with greater resources.
WHAT IS NOT FUNDED Research projects involving animals; research studies whose primary focus is lung or other cancers.
TYPE OF GRANT Research fellowships; project grants; travel and equipment grants; career development awards; research secondments; student electives. Funding may be given for up to three years.
SAMPLE GRANTS Western General Hospital (£85,000); University of Aberdeen (£60,000); Glasgow Royal Infirmary (£48,000); University of Edinburgh (£76,000); University of Glasgow (£37,000); University of Strathclyde (£25,300); Glasgow Royal Infirmary (£14,300).
FINANCES *Year* 2015/16 *Income* £8,572,893 *Grants* £695,498 *Grants to organisations* £523,572 *Assets* £5,404,379
OTHER INFORMATION Welfare grants are awarded to individuals affected by chest, heart and stroke illnesses totalled £172,000.
HOW TO APPLY At the time of writing (May 2017) the charity was reviewing its funding strategy. Check the charity's website for the latest details on funding programmes.
WHO TO APPLY TO Research Committee, Third Floor, Rosebery House, 9 Haymarket Terrace, Edinburgh EH12 5EZ *Tel.* 0131 225 6963 *Email* webmaster@chss.org.uk *Website* www.chss.org.uk

■ Chesterhill Charitable Trust

CC NO 1147108 **ESTABLISHED** 2012
WHERE FUNDING CAN BE GIVEN UK.
WHO CAN BENEFIT Charitable organisations.
WHAT IS FUNDED Disadvantaged children and young people, young people who have offended and carers.
SAMPLE GRANTS A list of beneficiaries was not included in the accounts.
FINANCES *Year* 2015/16 *Income* £100,000 *Grants* £46,850 *Grants to organisations* £46,850 *Assets* £236,592

TRUSTEES Brian Binstock; Alan Graham; Pauline Binstock; Roy Kemp.
HOW TO APPLY Apply in writing to the correspondent.
WHO TO APPLY TO Brian Binstock, Trustee, 10 Wood Street, Barnet EN5 4BW *Tel.* 020 8449 9192 *Email* info@chesterhill-ct.org.uk

■ The Childhood Trust

CC NO 1154032 **ESTABLISHED** 2013
WHERE FUNDING CAN BE GIVEN London.
WHO CAN BENEFIT Registered charities.
WHAT IS FUNDED Children (4 to 18 years of age) who are living in poverty in London. The trust channels its funding into three thematic areas: **practical** (ensuring that children have access to the basic necessities); **emotional** (offering emotional support and motivation to break the cycle of poverty); **inspirational** (providing opportunities to try new experiences and develop new skills).
WHAT IS NOT FUNDED Activities which are aimed at services provided by the state; religious groups; individuals; events.
SAMPLE GRANTS A list of beneficiaries was not available.
FINANCES *Year* 2015/16 *Income* £679,433 *Grants* £467,583 *Grants to organisations* £467,583 *Assets* £66,457
TRUSTEES Dame Sylvia Morris; Grant Gordon; David Lewis; Katie Partridge; David Ayre; Clive Sparrow; Sonal Shenai.
HOW TO APPLY The charity's websites states: 'Charities should contact us by email at info@childhoodtrust.org.uk if they feel that the work they do is relevant to our mission – which is to alleviate the impact of child poverty across London. Charities are advised not to send speculative letters or emails to us requesting a donation as these will not be replied to. We do not make grants directly. We mostly work with small grassroots charities to embrace digital fundraising by matchfunding individual donor's gifts. There are two funding rounds each year; in December, via The Christmas Give campaign and June, via our Summer Give campaign. We make grants through both of these campaigns that are facilitated by our platform partner The Big Give. Contact us at info@childhoodtrust.org.uk to arrange an initial chat and eligibility check. Once accepted onto a campaign with us, we will help you to aim for the right amount and support you to market your project effectively in the run up to the campaign. The campaign application windows are June for December and January for May each year.'
WHO TO APPLY TO Laurence Guinness, Chief Executive, The Workary, Chelsea Old Town Hall, King's Road, London SW3 5EZ *Tel.* 020 8788 9637 *Email* info@childhoodtrust.org *Website* www.childhoodtrust.org.uk

■ Children with Cancer UK

CC NO 298405 **ESTABLISHED** 2003
WHERE FUNDING CAN BE GIVEN UK.
WHO CAN BENEFIT Registered charities; research institutions.
WHAT IS FUNDED Research into childhood cancer; welfare projects for young cancer patients and their families.
SAMPLE GRANTS CLIC Sargent (£629,500); University of Edinburgh (£249,500); Institute of Cancer Research (£236,000); Together for Short Lives (£180,000); Lifelites and Shooting Star Chase (£60,000 each).
FINANCES *Year* 2015 *Income* £17,544,264 *Grants* £13,753,822 *Grants to organisations* £13,753,822 *Assets* £14,209,860
TRUSTEES The Earl Cadogan; Edward O'Gorman; Linda Robson; Sandra Mileham; Alasdair Philips.
HOW TO APPLY For information on current funding opportunities and how to apply, refer to the charity's website.
WHO TO APPLY TO Neil Meemaduma, Research Grants Manager, Children with Cancer UK, 51 Great Ormond Street, London WC1N 3JQ *Tel.* 020 7404 0808 *Email* info@childrenwithcancer.org.uk *Website* www.childrenwithcancer.org.uk

■ Children's Liver Disease Foundation

CC NO 1067331 **ESTABLISHED** 1998
WHERE FUNDING CAN BE GIVEN UK.
WHO CAN BENEFIT Hospitals; universities; research organisations.
WHAT IS FUNDED Clinical and laboratory-based research and social research which looks at topics such as how to improve quality of life.
WHAT IS NOT FUNDED Individuals, whether medical professionals or patients; travel or personal education; general appeals. The charity does not accept applications from organisations whose work is not associated with paediatric liver disease.
TYPE OF GRANT Research and project. Occasionally medical equipment.
RANGE OF GRANTS Small grant programme: up to £5,000; main grants programme: up to £10,000.
SAMPLE GRANTS University of London (£139,500); University of Manchester (£81,000); King's College Hospital (£79,500); Coventry University (£50,500); University of Surrey (£2,800); Aston University (£2,600).
FINANCES *Year* 2015/16 *Income* £721,695 *Grants* £141,390 *Grants to organisations* £141,390 *Assets* £520,419
TRUSTEES Thomas Ross; Kellie Charge; David Tildsley; Nicholas Budd; Mairi Everard; Georgina Sugden; Theresa Martin; Karen Redgate.
HOW TO APPLY Details of programmes and application forms are available on the foundation's website.
WHO TO APPLY TO Alison Taylor, Chief Executive, 36 Great Charles Street, Queensway, Birmingham B3 3JY *Tel.* 0121 212 3839 *Email* info@childliverdisease.org *Website* www.childliverdisease.org

■ The Childwick Trust

CC NO 1150413 **ESTABLISHED** 1985
WHERE FUNDING CAN BE GIVEN South and South East England; South Africa.
WHO CAN BENEFIT Registered charities only.
WHAT IS FUNDED In the UK: health, people with disabilities and older people; welfare and research in connection with the (horses) bloodstock industry; Jewish charities; in South Africa: education.
WHAT IS NOT FUNDED Complementary health and therapy projects; charities offering legal advice; charities offering counselling; hospices outside the south east of England; NHS hospitals and other statutory bodies; universities academic research, scholarships and bursaries; homelessness charities; projects related to drugs or alcohol addiction; HIV/AIDS-related

projects; charities which are part of a wider network, i.e. Age UK, Mind, Mencap, etc. (only those that are based within the South East can apply); individuals or organisations applying on behalf of an individual (other than in relation to South African educational grants); students seeking sponsorship for educational or gap year projects; animal charities, unless they are connected to thoroughbred racehorses; national appeals; conferences, seminars and workshops; organisations that have received a grant within the previous two years; funding outside the UK (apart from South Africa). Larger charities with widespread support are less likely to be considered unless they support local causes in Hertfordshire/Bedfordshire.

TYPE OF GRANT Mainly one-off, project and capital for research and medical equipment.

SAMPLE GRANTS UK: Racing Welfare – Newmarket (£200,000); British Racing School – Newmarket (£100,000); Early Learning Resource Unit (£40,000); Iain Rennie Grove House Hospice – St Albans (£30,000); Deafblind UK – Peterborough and St Elizabeth's Centre – Hertfordshire (£20,000 each); J's Hospice – Chelmsford (£18,000); Hop, Skip and Jump – Gloucestershire and Not Forgotten Association – London (£15,000 each). South Africa: Ntataise Trust (£65,500); Tree – South Africa (£41,000); Little Elephant Training Centre (£29,000); Sekhukhune Educare Project (£21,000); Thusanang Association (£20,000); Sego Monene and Sunshine Centre Association (£16,000).

FINANCES *Year* 2015/16 *Income* £2,257,168 *Grants* £2,818,063 *Grants to organisations* £2,818,063 *Assets* £76,434,945

TRUSTEES Clare Maurice; Mark Farmar; Peter Harris; Anthony Cane; John Wood; Dr Alan Stranders.

HOW TO APPLY Applications can be made through the trust's website. Applications are normally open in October and April each year.

WHO TO APPLY TO Karen Groom, Trust Administrator, 9 Childwick Green, Childwicksbury, St Albans AL3 6JJ *Tel.* 01727 844666 *Email* karen@childwicktrust.org *Website* www.childwicktrust.org

■ CHK Charities Ltd

CC NO 1050900 **ESTABLISHED** 1995

WHERE FUNDING CAN BE GIVEN Worldwide, in practice mainly UK with a preference for national and West Midlands charities.

WHO CAN BENEFIT Registered charities.

WHAT IS FUNDED Artistic causes; conservation/preservation; countryside matters and animal welfare and disease; care of older people; crime prevention; disability care and treatment; drug prevention and treatment; education; employment and job creation; general medical research (note, the trustees do not normally support general medical research projects, but do occasionally consider appeals for areas where they have specific knowledge); general welfare and social problems; homeless/housing; hospices; hospital/nursing home building and equipment; miscellaneous; population control; research into blindness; research into deafness; youth care.

WHAT IS NOT FUNDED Organisations not registered as charities or those that have been registered for less than a year; pre-school groups; out of school play schemes including pre-school and holiday schemes; 'bottomless pits' and unfocused causes; very small and narrowly specialised activities; community centres; local authorities; umbrella or grant-making organisations; universities and colleges and grant-maintained private or local education authority schools or their PTAs, except if these schools are for students with special needs; individuals or charities applying on behalf of individuals; general requests for donations; professional associations and training of professionals; projects which are abroad even though the charity is based in the UK; expeditions or overseas travel; campaigning organisations or Citizens Advice projects providing legal advice; community transport projects; general counselling projects, except those in areas of considerable deprivation and with a clearly defined client group.

TYPE OF GRANT One-off; conditionally renewable; large grants (over £25,000).

RANGE OF GRANTS Up to £100,000 but generally £3,000 to £20,000.

SAMPLE GRANTS Emmaus Oxford (£100,000); St Christopher's Hospice (£75,000); Hand in Hand for Syria (£50,000); Home-Start UK (£40,000); Police Rehabilitation Trust (£20,000); RNIB (£10,000); FareShare (£8,000); St Anne's Hostel (£5,000); British Museum Development Trust (£1,500); Delete Blood Cancer UK (£1,000).

FINANCES *Year* 2015/16 *Income* £3,134,752 *Grants* £2,240,410 *Grants to organisations* £2,240,410 *Assets* £93,899,715

TRUSTEES Charlotte Percy; Joanna Prest; Katherine Lloyd; Lucy Morris; Rupert Prest; Serena Acland; Susanna Peake; Edward Peake; Diana Acland.

OTHER INFORMATION This trust has a very useful website that should be referred to when considering making an application.

HOW TO APPLY The following information is taken from the trust's website: 'Preference is given to National or West Midlands charities, and the organization will normally be based within the United Kingdom. The trustees do not require applicants to use a special application form, but suggest that the following guidelines be used: Applications should be no longer than four A4 sides, and should incorporate a short (half page) summary. Applications should also include a detailed budget for the project and the applicant's most recent audited accounts. If those accounts show a significant surplus or deficit of income, explain how this has arisen.'

WHO TO APPLY TO Katie Styles, Trust Officer, SG Kleinwort Hambros Trust Company, 5th Floor, 8 St James's Square, London SW1Y 4JU *Tel.* 020 3207 7041 *Email* scott.rice@kleinwortbenson.com *Website* www.chkcharities.co.uk

■ The Chownes Foundation

CC NO 327451 **ESTABLISHED** 1987

WHERE FUNDING CAN BE GIVEN UK, priority is given to charities based in Sussex, particularly in mid-Sussex.

WHO CAN BENEFIT Organisations and individuals.

WHAT IS FUNDED The advancement of religion, the advancement of education among the young, the amelioration of social problems, and the relief of poverty among older people and the former members of Sound Diffusion PLC who lost their pensions when the company went into receivership. Preference will be given to projects where a donation may have some meaningful impact on an identified need rather than simply being absorbed into a larger funding requirement. Applications from smaller charities

whose aims mirror those of the founder, Paul Stonor, will be favoured.
TYPE OF GRANT One-off, recurrent, buildings, capital, core costs, research and running costs. Funding is available for up to and over three years.
RANGE OF GRANTS Up to £7,500.
SAMPLE GRANTS Relief of hardship of former employees of Sound Diffusion (five grants totalling £17,000); Age Unlimited (£7,500); St Catherine's Hospice, St Peter and St James Hospice (£3,000 each) Amnesty International (£2,500); Mencap, NSPCC (£1,000 each).
FINANCES *Year* 2015/16 *Income* £8,238 *Grants* £1,000,000 *Grants to organisations* £9,980,000
TRUSTEES Mrs U. Hazeel; The Rt Revd S. Ortiger; M. Woolley.
OTHER INFORMATION The full accounts were not available on the Charity Commission's website due to the foundation's low income. The grant total has therefore been estimated based on grant-making in previous years. Spending was usually high in 2015/16 and is usually around £100,000 per year.
HOW TO APPLY Apply in writing to the correspondent.
WHO TO APPLY TO Sylvia Spencer, Trust Secretary, The Courtyard, Beeding Court, Shoreham Road, Steyning, West Sussex BN44 3TN *Tel.* 01903 816699 *Email* sylvia@russellnew.com

■ Christadelphian Samaritan Fund

CC NO 1004457 **ESTABLISHED** 1991
WHERE FUNDING CAN BE GIVEN Worldwide.
WHO CAN BENEFIT Registered charities.
WHAT IS FUNDED Human causes and overseas aid.
WHAT IS NOT FUNDED Individuals; non-registered charities.
TYPE OF GRANT Single donations.
SAMPLE GRANTS Disasters Emergency Committee – Nepal Earthquake Appeal (£17,100); Save the Children – Refugee Crisis (£8,000); Oxfam – Strength to Survive (£5,000); Heritage Children (£3,700); Action Aid and British Red Cross (£2,000 each); Jewish Clothing Relief (£1,000).
FINANCES *Year* 2015 *Income* £98,973 *Grants* £120,403 *Grants to organisations* £120,403 *Assets* £58,766
TRUSTEES K. H. A. Smith; David Ensell; William Moss; John Buckler; Roger Miles; Pauline Bromage; Elizabeth Briley; Ruth Meryl Deedman; Mark Halstead.
HOW TO APPLY Apply in writing to the correspondent.
WHO TO APPLY TO Kenneth Smith, Treasurer, Westhaven House, Arleston Way, Shirley, Solihull, West Midlands B90 4LH *Tel.* 0121 713 7100

■ Christian Aid

CC NO 1105851 **ESTABLISHED** 1945
WHERE FUNDING CAN BE GIVEN Mainly low- and middle-income countries. Limited assistance for development education projects in the UK.
WHO CAN BENEFIT Councils of churches; other ecumenical bodies, development and relief groups; UN agencies which benefit at risk groups; people disadvantaged by poverty; homeless people; refugees; immigrants; socially isolated people; victims of famine, man-made or natural disasters, and war.
WHAT IS FUNDED Organisations which work with the world's poorest people and communities. Funding is given to partner organisations only.
WHAT IS NOT FUNDED Individuals; political causes; organisations whose aims are primarily political.
SAMPLE GRANTS A list of beneficiaries was not available.
FINANCES *Year* 2015/16 *Income* £106,976,000 *Grants* £42,969,000 *Grants to organisations* £42,969,000 *Assets* £40,066,000
TRUSTEES Dr Rowan Williams; Jennifer Cormack; Wilton Powell; Rt Revd John Davies; Bala Gnanapragasam; Alexis Chapman; Revd Bob Fyffe; Thomas Hinton; Paul Spray; Trevor Williams; Alan McDonald; Victoria Hardman; Mervyn McCullagh; Valerie Traore; Amanda Mukwashi; Pippa Greenslade; Hazel Baird; Helene Bradley-Ritt; Mukami McCrum.
OTHER INFORMATION Grants were distributed as follows: Africa (£19.9 million); Asia and the Middle East (£16.5 million); Latin America and the Caribbean (£5.1 million); Europe (£1 million); global (£495,000).
HOW TO APPLY Initial approaches by potential partner organisations should be made in writing.
WHO TO APPLY TO Martin Birch, Director of Finance and Operations, 35 Lower Marsh, Waterloo, London SE1 7RL *Tel.* 020 7620 4444 *Email* info@christian-aid.org *Website* www.christianaid.org.uk

■ John Christie Trust

SC NO SC005291 **ESTABLISHED** 1904
WHERE FUNDING CAN BE GIVEN Scotland.
WHO CAN BENEFIT Charities; missions; churches.
WHAT IS FUNDED Religion, missions, welfare of orphans. The same organisations, as listed in the trust deed, are supported each year and receive an income in fixed, but not equal, proportions. Most are concerned with religion, missionary work or the welfare of orphans.
SAMPLE GRANTS Governors of the Lothian Homes Trust (£69,500); Home Missions of the Church of Scotland (£11,500); Quarriers, Scottish Bible Society, The London Association in Aid of Moravian Missions and United Reformed Church (£5,800 each).
FINANCES *Year* 2015/16 *Income* £92,313 *Grants* £88,113 *Grants to organisations* £88,113 *Assets* £2,321,621
HOW TO APPLY Due to the nature of this trust unsolicited applications cannot be considered.
WHO TO APPLY TO The Trustees, Shepherd and Wedderburn LLP, 1 Exchange Crescent, Conference Square, Edinburgh EH3 8UL

■ Chrysalis Trust

CC NO 1133525 **ESTABLISHED** 2010
WHERE FUNDING CAN BE GIVEN The north east of England; UK national organisations providing benefit across the UK; overseas.
WHO CAN BENEFIT Charities, community groups and educational projects.
WHAT IS FUNDED Social welfare. The trust's current priorities are: the relief of poverty and disability; provision of access to shelter, education, health care and water.
WHAT IS NOT FUNDED Research – academic or medical; holidays or outings; arts or entertainment activities; animal welfare; local appeals outside the north east of England; general appeals. There will be no response to general appeal communications.
TYPE OF GRANT One-off grants to support capital costs and core funding.
RANGE OF GRANTS £1,000 to £10,000.
SAMPLE GRANTS Build It International, Excellent Development and Greggs Foundation (£10,000 each); Deafway (£6,300); Village Water

(£4,000); CURE International UK (£3,500); British Wireless for the Blind (£1,100); Key Project (£1,000).

FINANCES *Year* 2015/16 *Income* £47,985 *Grants* £82,004 *Grants to organisations* £82,004 *Assets* £1,810,958

TRUSTEES Mark Evans; Sarah Evans; Andrew Playle; Thomas Evans.

HOW TO APPLY Apply in writing to the correspondent. A full application checklist is available on the trust's website.

WHO TO APPLY TO Sarah Evans, Trustee, Piper Close House, Aydon Road, Corbridge, Northumberland NE45 5PW *Email* info@chrysalis-trust.co.uk *Website* www.chrysalis-trust.co.uk

■ The Church Burgesses Educational Foundation

CC NO 529357 **ESTABLISHED** 1963

WHERE FUNDING CAN BE GIVEN Sheffield.

WHO CAN BENEFIT Charities and voluntary groups; schools; individuals (under 25).

WHAT IS FUNDED Education. Funding is given to a wide range of projects including musical activities in schools.

TYPE OF GRANT Core costs, one-off and running costs. Funding may be given for up to three years.

SAMPLE GRANTS Dyslexia Institute; Flower Estate Community Association; Pitstop, Sheffield County Guide Association; Sheffield YMCA; South Yorkshire and Hallam Clubs for Young People; Whirlow Hall Farm Trust; Wybourn Youth Trust.

FINANCES *Year* 2015 *Income* £235,707 *Grants* £188,536 *Grants to organisations* £106,853 *Assets* £145,617

TRUSTEES David Booker; Mr D. Stanley; Revd Stephen Hunter; Mr W. H. Thomas; Mrs B. R. Hickman; Prof. D. E. Luscombe; Susan Bain.

OTHER INFORMATION In 2015 grants were made in the following categories: individual grants for education (£81,500); church school grants (£35,500); church-based youth work (£27,500); Music in the City (£16,500); special individual grants (£10,500).

HOW TO APPLY On forms available to download, together with criteria and guidelines, from the foundation's website. The trustees meet four times a year. Initial telephone calls are welcome.

WHO TO APPLY TO Mr G. J. Smallman, Law Clerk, 3rd Floor, Fountain Precinct, Balm Green, Sheffield S1 2JA *Tel.* 0114 267 5594 *Fax* 0114 276 3176 *Email* sheffieldchurchburgesses@wrigleys.co.uk *Website* www.sheffieldchurchburgesses.org.uk

■ Church Burgesses Trust

CC NO 221284 **ESTABLISHED** 1554

WHERE FUNDING CAN BE GIVEN Sheffield.

WHO CAN BENEFIT Voluntary organisations,; registered charities; churches.

WHAT IS FUNDED Social welfare; health; recreation facilities; educational facilities; Anglican churches.

WHAT IS NOT FUNDED Individuals. (Individuals under 25 can apply to the Church Burgesses Educational Foundation for specific educational help.)

TYPE OF GRANT One-off and recurring.

RANGE OF GRANTS £5,000 to £10,000.

SAMPLE GRANTS St Chad's Woodseats (£40,000); SDBF Mission (£18,500); St Luke's Hospice (£15,000); Christchurch – Pitsmoor (£10,000); Cavendish Centre for Cancer Care (£6,000); Newlife Foundation (£2,500); Sheffield Street Pastors (£2,000); Carmel Care (£1,000); Broomhall Girls' Youth Club (£500); Grenoside Community Association (£400).

FINANCES *Year* 2015 *Income* £2,139,046 *Grants* £588,289 *Grants to organisations* £588,289 *Assets* £36,758,544

TRUSTEES Peter Lee; Nicholas Hutton; Michael Woffenden; Mr D. F. Booker; Mr D. Stanley; Revd S. A. P. Hunter; Ian Walker; Prof. Peter Ainsworth; Mrs B. R. Hickman; Dr Julie Banham; Mrs S. Bain.

OTHER INFORMATION The trust's website is very useful and should be referred to.

HOW TO APPLY Application packs can be downloaded form the trust's website.

WHO TO APPLY TO Godfrey Smallman, Law Clerk, Sheffield Church Burgesses Trust, 3rd Floor, Fountain Precinct, Balm Green, Sheffield S1 2JA *Tel.* 0114 267 5594 *Fax* 0114 276 3176 *Email* sheffieldchurchburgesses@wrigleys.co.uk *Website* www.sheffieldchurchburgesses.org.uk

■ Church of Ireland Priorities Fund

ESTABLISHED 1980

WHERE FUNDING CAN BE GIVEN Ireland.

WHO CAN BENEFIT Projects within the Church of Ireland.

WHAT IS FUNDED **Training (lay and ordained)** – training in the following areas: post-ordination, clergy in-service, lay ministry, youth ministry, children's ministry, student chaplaincy. **Christian education** – development of religious education in schools, children's ministry, youth work, adult education. **Outreach initiatives** – to encourage creative and innovative projects, which reach out to the communities that parishes serve, including church plants and missional areas. **Innovative ministry in a rural context** – to encourage creative and innovative ministry projects in the sparsely populated areas of the country, in rural or village settings.

RANGE OF GRANTS Up to €40,000.

SAMPLE GRANTS The House of Bishops (€40,000); Diocese of Connor (€11,700); SEEDS Children's Ministry (€9,400); Dundalk Grammar School (€5,000); Cork Diocesan Children's Council and Love for Life (€3,500 each); Crosslinks (€1,300).

FINANCES *Year* 2016 *Income* €531,117 *Grants* €512,780 *Grants to organisations* €512,780

OTHER INFORMATION Grants were made to 56 organisations.

HOW TO APPLY Application forms are available, together with criteria and guidelines, from the fund's website. Applications must be made by 31 October each year.

WHO TO APPLY TO Sylvia Simpson, Organiser, Church of Ireland House, Church Avenue, Rathmines, Dublin 6 *Tel.* +353-(0) 1-4125607 *Email* priorities@ireland.anglican.org *Website* www.priorities.ireland.anglican.org

■ Church Urban Fund

CC NO 297483 **ESTABLISHED** 1988

WHERE FUNDING CAN BE GIVEN England.

WHO CAN BENEFIT Local faith-based organisations; voluntary groups; charities.

WHAT IS FUNDED **Near Neighbours** – funding for local groups who are working to bring together neighbours to develop relationships and to improve their communities. **Together Grants** – grants for faith-based organisations to engage in social activity, ether for initiating or developing community work.

WHAT IS NOT FUNDED The fund's grant guidance lists the following restrictions: 'projects that will not run in one of our eligible areas; repeated activities (such as an annual summer camp or regular training sessions that have happened previously); activities open only to one faith/ ethnic group; activity promoting a specific faith; projects that are the normal curriculum work of schools and colleges or would fall under statutory health care provision; faith leaders' salaries; individuals; organisations with a high annual turnover (more than £150,000), with significant free reserves, or with a weak financial position; national organisations that are working locally; existing salary costs, except where there is a significant increase in hours in order to begin new work or expand an existing project to new people; organisational costs not associated with the funded project; major capital costs (though small items of equipment will be considered i.e. the cost of a kettle but not the cost of a kitchen); unspecified or excessive volunteer expenses or high staff costs/expenses; work that has already been completed or started (retrospective funding) – we will not accept applications for projects that will begin within 14 calendar days of us receiving your application; deficits or loans; campaigning and fundraising activity; revenue and capital funding for national voluntary/ community organisations and public and private sector organisations; general repairs and refurbishment of buildings, or internal re-ordering of places of worship, maintenance or DDA (Disability Discrimination Act) compliance; general appeals'.

TYPE OF GRANT Capital, project and revenue funding for up to three years.

RANGE OF GRANTS Up to £5,000.

SAMPLE GRANTS All Saints Hanley, The Bridge Pregnancy Crisis, Community Money Advice, Faith Drama Productions Project, Freedom Trust, Housing Justice, Reading Refugee Support Group and Sussex Pathways (£5,000 each); Bristol Inter Faith Group, Church Action on Poverty and Keeping Health in Mind (£4,500 each) Youth Project @ Apostles and Cuthbert's (£4,200); St Andrews Community Network (£4,000).

FINANCES *Year* 2015 *Income* £4,432,000 *Grants* £4,206,000 *Grants to organisations* £4,206,000 *Assets* £3,639,000

TRUSTEES Andrew Dorton; Revd Canon Denise Poole; Patrick Coldstream; Rt Revd Christopher Chessun; Alison Grieve; Derek Twine; Canon Paul Hackwood; Philip Fletcher; Brian Carroll; John Graham.

HOW TO APPLY Details of the application procedure for each programme can be found on the fund's website.

WHO TO APPLY TO Ali Khimji, Grants Co-ordinator, Church House, 27 Great Smith Street, Westminster, London SW1P 3AZ *Tel.* 020 7898 1647 *Email* enquiries@cuf.org.uk *Website* www.cuf.org.uk

■ The CIBC World Markets Children's Miracle Foundation

CC NO 1105094 **ESTABLISHED** 2004

WHERE FUNDING CAN BE GIVEN UK and the Netherlands.

WHO CAN BENEFIT UK/European registered charities that are well administered, with a record of achievement or potential for success in line with the foundation's overall goals.

WHAT IS FUNDED Projects or programs that provide a tangible benefit to European children and the communities where they live; which may also have potential for CIBC to donate time and resources in a non-financial capacity.

WHAT IS NOT FUNDED Donations to individuals; political or advocacy groups; private schools and groups that limit their activities to benefitting persons of a designated ethnic or religious affiliation; endowments, funds given permanently to a foundation so it may produce its own income for grant-making purposes; multi-year projects or commitments; no one charity will be chosen as an annual charity more than twice in any one five-year period; charities with an income of over £5 million.

RANGE OF GRANTS Up to £62,500.

SAMPLE GRANTS Noah's Ark Children's Hospice, React and The Sick Children's Trust (£62,500 each).

FINANCES *Year* 2015/16 *Income* £162,037 *Grants* £187,500 *Grants to organisations* £187,500 *Assets* £41,585

TRUSTEES Mark Beels; Howard Redgwell; Martin Autotte; Andrew Ryde; Paul Weideman; Samantha Orozco.

HOW TO APPLY Application forms, eligibility guidelines and details of application deadlines are available on the foundation's website. Grant rounds normally open in January each year.

WHO TO APPLY TO Howard Redgwell, Trustee, Canadian Imperial Bank of Commerce, 150 Cheapside, London EC2V 6ET *Tel.* 020 7234 6387 *Email* ukchildrensmiracle@cibc.co.uk *Website* www.cibc.com/ca/miracleday/international/childrens-foundation.html

■ The City Bridge Trust (Bridge House Estates)

CC NO 1035628 **ESTABLISHED** 1995

WHERE FUNDING CAN BE GIVEN Greater London.

WHO CAN BENEFIT Registered charities; registered CICs; registered CIOs; charitable companies; exempt or excepted charities; registered charitable industrial and provident society or charitable co-operatives.

WHAT IS FUNDED English language courses; mental health; environment; inclusion; safety; older people; social welfare; people who have offended; strengthening the voluntary sector.

WHAT IS NOT FUNDED Political parties; political lobbying; non-charitable activities; work which does not benefit the inhabitants of Greater London; individuals (except through nominated agencies); grant-making bodies to make grants on the trust's behalf (except through a nominated agency); schools, PTAs, universities or other educational establishments; medical or academic research; churches or other religious bodies where the monies will be used for religious purposes; hospitals or NHS trusts; projects which have already taken place or building work which has already been completed; statutory bodies, such as local authorities; charities established/registered outside the UK; festivals or events which last no longer than a few days; residential care services; residential facilities (except where they provide short-term emergency accommodation).

TYPE OF GRANT Capital and revenue.

SAMPLE GRANTS The Prince's Trust (£1 million); London's Air Ambulance (£214,000); Survivors UK (£180,000); Lambeth and Southwark Mind (£147,500); Shpresa Programme (£71,000); Blackfriars Settlement (£39,000); Orchestras for All (£4,000); Bethel – London's Riverside Church (£3,600); The Albany (£2,000).

FINANCES *Year* 2015/16 *Income* £31,400,000 *Grants* £18,342,301 *Grants to organisations* £18,342,301 *Assets* £1,196,700,000

TRUSTEE The Mayor and Commonalty and Citizens of the City of London.

OTHER INFORMATION The City Bridge Trust is the grant-making arm of the Bridge House Estates charity whose prime objective is the provision and maintenance of the four bridges across the Thames into the City of London.

HOW TO APPLY Applications are made through the trust's website. Applications will have to set up an online account using an email address.

WHO TO APPLY TO Steven Reynolds, City of London Corporation, PO Box 270, Guildhall, London EC2P 2EJ *Tel.* 020 7332 3710 *Email* citybridgetrust@cityoflondon.gov.uk *Website* www.citybridgetrust.org.uk

■ The City Educational Trust Fund

CC NO 290840 **ESTABLISHED** 1967

WHERE FUNDING CAN BE GIVEN Generally Greater London.

WHO CAN BENEFIT Organisations in London benefitting young adults, research workers, students and teachers.

WHAT IS FUNDED The promotion of teaching and training in areas such as science, technology, business management, commerce, biology, ecology and the cultural arts.

WHAT IS NOT FUNDED Individuals.

TYPE OF GRANT One-off, ongoing and fixed period grants.

RANGE OF GRANTS Up to £60,000.

SAMPLE GRANTS City University (£60,000); Spitalfields Festival (£45,000); Wilton's Music Hall (£25,000); St Paul's Cathedral School (£15,000); Dr Johnson's House (£8,800); City of London Symphonia (£5,000).

FINANCES *Year* 2015/16 *Income* £126,105 *Grants* £87,500 *Grants to organisations* £87,500 *Assets* £3,432,337

TRUSTEE The Corporation of London.

HOW TO APPLY Apply in writing to the correspondent.

WHO TO APPLY TO Mr Steven Reynolds, c/o Corporation of London, PO Box 270, Guildhall, London EC2P 2EJ *Tel.* 020 7332 1382 *Email* steven.reynolds@cityoflondon.gov.uk *Website* www.cityoflondon.gov.uk

■ Clan Trust

CC NO 803661 **ESTABLISHED** 1990

WHERE FUNDING CAN BE GIVEN Norfolk; Suffolk; Cambridgeshire; Lincolnshire.

WHO CAN BENEFIT Individuals and organisations benefitting people studying agriculture and horticulture.

WHAT IS FUNDED To encourage young people from all walks of life the opportunity to gain a deeper understanding of agriculture; to provide them with support into either a career in farming or simply to be able appreciate the farming and food production around them; to support retirement homes and clubs looking to provide enjoyment and additional comfort to those who need it.

TYPE OF GRANT One-off and recurrent; capital, feasibility, project, research and start-up costs. Interest-free loans are considered. Grants may be for up to and more than three years.

SAMPLE GRANTS Norfolk YFC (£16,200); Country Trust (£2,500); Farming is Magic (£1,500); Deafblind UK (£520); Glaven Care (£500); Royal Voluntary Service (£500); Friends of Garrick Green and Liveability (£250 each).

FINANCES *Year* 2015/16 *Income* £84,850 *Grants* £52,991 *Grants to organisations* £52,991 *Assets* £5,719,814

TRUSTEES Ian Alston; Sir Nicholas Bacon; Richard Hirst; Stephen Oldfield; James Alston; Rob Alston; Timothy Papworth; Alison Ritchie; Henry Raker.

HOW TO APPLY Apply in writing to the correspondent.

WHO TO APPLY TO R. H. C. Hughes, Secretary, Brown and Co., Market Chambers, 25–26 Tuesday Market Place, King's Lynn, Norfolk PE30 1JJ *Tel.* 01553 770771 *Email* rob.hughes@brown-co.com *Website* www.theclantrust.co.uk

■ Stephen Clark 1957 Charitable Trust

CC NO 258690 **ESTABLISHED** 1969

WHERE FUNDING CAN BE GIVEN Some preference for Bath and Somerset.

WHO CAN BENEFIT Registered charities.

WHAT IS FUNDED The trust's priorities are 'to make donations to charities in respect of the preservation, embellishment, maintenance, improvement or development of any monuments, churches or other buildings', but also general charitable purposes. The trust prefers local charities to national ones.

WHAT IS NOT FUNDED Animal charities; individuals.

TYPE OF GRANT One-off.

RANGE OF GRANTS Up to £30,000 but usually £100 to £1,000.

SAMPLE GRANTS BIHT (£28,500); Friends of Museum of Bath at Work (£20,000); The Roman Bath Foundation (£5,000); St Peter's Church – Marksbury (£3,000); Refugee Council (£1,000); PLAN International (UK) (£500); Mission Direct (£300); Starlight Children's Foundation (£200); Suffolk Preservation Society (£100).

FINANCES *Year* 2015 *Income* £171,241 *Grants* £109,898 *Grants to organisations* £109,898 *Assets* £2,912,090

TRUSTEES Dr Marianna Clark; Mary Lovell; Harriet Hall.

HOW TO APPLY Apply in writing to the correspondent. Note, replies are not usually made to unsuccessful applications. Include an sae for reply.

WHO TO APPLY TO Dr Marianna Clark, Trustee, 16 Lansdown Place East, Bath BA1 5ET

■ J. A. Clark Charitable Trust

CC NO 1010520 **ESTABLISHED** 1992

WHERE FUNDING CAN BE GIVEN UK, with a preference for South West England; Asia; Africa.

WHO CAN BENEFIT Charitable organisations for the benefit of the general public.

WHAT IS FUNDED Women's empowerment in Africa and Asia; disadvantaged youths in deprived areas of the UK, specifically East London and the North East.

SAMPLE GRANTS Eucalyptus Foundation (£189,000); Khwendo Kor (£50,000); Afghanaid (£48,000); Christian Aid (£22,000); Conflicts Forum and Skyway (£20,000 each); Pauline Probey Foundation (£10,000).
FINANCES *Year* 2015 *Income* £1,168,301 *Grants* £722,208 *Grants to organisations* £722,208 *Assets* £24,025,863
TRUSTEE William Pym.
OTHER INFORMATION There were 29 grants made during the year and distributed in the following categories: family fund (£359,000); women's empowerment fund (£285,500); youth projects (£63,000); other grants (£14,000).
HOW TO APPLY Unsolicited applications are not accepted.
WHO TO APPLY TO Lynette Cooper, Trust Secretary, PO Box 1704, Glastonbury, Somerset BA16 0YB *Website* jaclarktrust.com

■ The Hilda and Alice Clark Charitable Trust

CC NO 290916 **ESTABLISHED** 1953
WHERE FUNDING CAN BE GIVEN Worldwide with a preference for UK.
WHO CAN BENEFIT Registered charities.
WHAT IS FUNDED General charitable purposes. There is a preference given to the Society of Friends (Quakers) and to children and young adults.
WHAT IS NOT FUNDED Only registered charities are considered.
RANGE OF GRANTS £1,000 to £22,000.
SAMPLE GRANTS Britain Yearly Meeting (£25,000); Greenbank Swimming Pool (£15,000); Medical Aid for Palestinians and UK Friends of Hope Flowers (£10,000 each); Crispin Hall (£5,000) Quaker Social Action and Sightsavers International (£1,000 each); Leaveners (£500).
FINANCES *Year* 2015 *Income* £131,536 *Grants* £101,548 *Grants to organisations* £101,548 *Assets* £2,642,228
TRUSTEES Richard Clark; Thomas Clark; Martin Lovell; Alice Clark; Susannah Clark.
OTHER INFORMATION Grants were made to 14 organisations.
HOW TO APPLY Apply in writing to the correspondent by 30 September. The trustees meet in December each year.
WHO TO APPLY TO Susan Brown, 40 High Street, Somerset BA16 0EQ *Tel.* 0117 905 4000 *Email* angela.southern@clarks.com

■ The Roger and Sarah Bancroft Clark Charitable Trust

CC NO 211513 **ESTABLISHED** 1960
WHERE FUNDING CAN BE GIVEN UK and overseas, with preference for Somerset.
WHO CAN BENEFIT Religious Society of Friends, registered charities and individuals. Preference is given to local appeals.
WHAT IS FUNDED General charitable purposes with particular reference to: Religious Society of Friends and associated bodies; charities connected with Somerset; education.
WHAT IS NOT FUNDED Students.
TYPE OF GRANT Recurrent grants.
RANGE OF GRANTS Up to £16,000 but mostly £500 to £5,000.
SAMPLE GRANTS Quaker Peace and Social Witness (£16,000); Street Friends Meeting House (£15,000); Hillsborough Meeting House (£5,000); Quaker Service (£4,000); Historic Chapels Trust and The Retreat (£3,000 each); Bridge Care (£2,000); Karuma Trust (£500).
FINANCES *Year* 2015 *Income* £563,277 *Grants* £297,994 *Grants to organisations* £297,994 *Assets* £878,824
TRUSTEES Alice Clark; Martin Lovell; Caroline Gould; Priscilla Gouldby; Robert Robertson.
OTHER INFORMATION Grants were made to 160 organisations during the year. No grants were made to individuals.
HOW TO APPLY Apply in writing to the correspondent.
WHO TO APPLY TO The Secretary, 100 Temple Street, Bristol BS1 1AG *Email* susan.bowman@clarks.com

■ The Clark Foundation

CC NO 313143 **ESTABLISHED** 1959
WHERE FUNDING CAN BE GIVEN Preference for areas where there are significant numbers of employees of C&J Clark and its subsidiaries.
WHO CAN BENEFIT Registered charities; schools; voluntary organisations; churches.
WHAT IS FUNDED General charitable purposes including: arts; countryside; overseas; older people; religion; family; education; young people; medicine; social welfare.
WHAT IS NOT FUNDED Individuals.
TYPE OF GRANT One-off capital projects and organisation start-up costs.
RANGE OF GRANTS £1,000 to £100,000.
SAMPLE GRANTS Strode College (£48,500); Brewery Arts Centre – Kendal (£40,000); Glastonbury Abbey (£25,000); St Margaret's Hospice (£10,000); Somerset Wildlife Trust (£5,000); Feed Avalon CIC (£1,000); Kendal Lads and Girls Club (£600); Norden Community Primary School (£500); Stanchester Academy (£350).
FINANCES *Year* 2014/15 *Income* £989,921 *Grants* £682,818 *Grants to organisations* £682,818 *Assets* £20,289,005
TRUSTEES Richard Clark; Judith Derbyshire; Martin Lovell; Gloria Clark.
OTHER INFORMATION The 2014/15 accounts were the latest available at the time of writing (June 2016).
HOW TO APPLY Apply in writing to the correspondent.
WHO TO APPLY TO Mrs Lesley Hide, Clarks International, 40 High Street, Somerset BA16 0EQ *Tel.* 01458 842553 *Email* trustgrants@clarks.com

■ The Cleopatra Trust

CC NO 1004551 **ESTABLISHED** 1990
WHERE FUNDING CAN BE GIVEN Mainly UK.
WHO CAN BENEFIT Registered charities with a national focus.
WHAT IS FUNDED General charitable purposes; health and disability.
WHAT IS NOT FUNDED Individuals.
RANGE OF GRANTS £1,000 to £10,000.
SAMPLE GRANTS Envision and Progressive Supranuclear Palsy Association (£10,000 each); Vision for a Nation (£7,500); AHOY Centre (£5,000); National Theatre (£3,000); Crisis, Dimberley Cancer Trust and Theatre in Prison and Probation (£1,000 each).
FINANCES *Year* 2015 *Income* £32,279 *Grants* £47,460 *Grants to organisations* £47,460 *Assets* £3,859,817
TRUSTEES Bettine Bond; Charles Peacock; Dr Clare Peacock.
HOW TO APPLY Apply in writing to the correspondent.
WHO TO APPLY TO Charles Peacock, Trustee, Charities Aid Foundation, 25 Kings Hill Avenue,

Kings Hill, West Malling ME19 4TA *Tel.* 01732 520028

■ The Clore Duffield Foundation

CC NO 1084412 **ESTABLISHED** 2000

WHERE FUNDING CAN BE GIVEN UK.

WHO CAN BENEFIT Registered charities. Local authority cultural organisations are also eligible to apply.

WHAT IS FUNDED The cultural sector, in particular to cultural learning and to museum, gallery, heritage and performing arts learning spaces.

WHAT IS NOT FUNDED The foundation does not fund projects retrospectively and will not accept (or respond to) applications from the following: individuals; general appeals and circulars; projects outside the UK. It should also be noted that the following are very rarely funded: staff posts; local branches of national charities; academic or project research; conference costs.

RANGE OF GRANTS £10,000 to £1 million.

SAMPLE GRANTS Tate Britain (£937,500); Lady Margaret Hall (£350,000); Royal Academy of Arts (£200,000); The Art Room (£133,500); Historic Royal Palaces (£100,000); Tate Liverpool (£60,000); Glyndebourne Arts Trust (£50,000); Future Box (£25,000); Fixperts (£10,000); British Library (£5,000); Cancer Research UK (£2,000).

FINANCES *Year* 2015 *Income* £260,484 *Grants* £7,481,899 *Grants to organisations* £7,481,899 *Assets* £44,948,769

TRUSTEES David Harrell; Dame Vivien Duffield; Richard Oldfield; James Harding; Melanie Core; Jeremy Sandelson.

OTHER INFORMATION Grants were distributed in the following categories: arts, heritage and education (£5.1 million); leadership training (£2 million); Jewish support (£214,000); health and social care (£157,000).

HOW TO APPLY The foundation's website states: 'If your project falls within the Foundation's areas of interest, please send a letter of application. This letter should be no longer than two sides of A4 paper and must be written on your organisation's headed paper with your contact details and charity number clearly displayed. The letter should include the following information: a title (of no more than fifteen words) for the project/programme for which you are requesting funding; a brief overview of the work of your organisation; a concise account of the project you are seeking funding for; clear statement of the sum you are seeking from the Foundation and the total cost of the wider project if applicable; no annual accounts or additional information should be included at this stage. Please note that the Foundation will only be able to respond to your application if you enclose a standard-sized (DL), stamped, self-addressed envelope. Email applications will not be accepted, and please do not send it by recorded delivery as the Foundation is not able to guarantee that a member of staff will be on site to receive it. Only if your request is progressed to the relevant stage of the assessment process will you be sent an application form. The form is not available on this website.'

WHO TO APPLY TO Sally Bacon, Executive Director, Unit 3, Chelsea Manor Studios, Flood Street, London SW3 5SR *Tel.* 020 7351 6061 *Fax* 020 7351 5308 *Email* info@cloreduffield.org.uk *Website* www.cloreduffield.org.uk

■ Closehelm Ltd

CC NO 291296 **ESTABLISHED** 1983

WHERE FUNDING CAN BE GIVEN UK and Israel.

WHO CAN BENEFIT Individuals and institutions benefitting Jewish people and people disadvantaged by poverty.

WHAT IS FUNDED The advancement of religion in accordance with the Jewish faith; the relief of poverty; general charitable purposes.

RANGE OF GRANTS Up to £72,500.

SAMPLE GRANTS Zaks (£72,500); Beanstalk Home (£1,800); D Sassoon (£1,500); Chanichel Yeshivas Jewish Teacher (£1,400); Hayomi Trust (£1,100); Friends of Mir (£500).

FINANCES *Year* 2015/16 *Income* £207,805 *Grants* £131,590 *Grants to organisations* £79,162 *Assets* £2,710,497

TRUSTEES A. Van Praagh; Hanna Grosberg; Henrietta Van Praagh.

OTHER INFORMATION The amount of grants given to individuals totalled £52,500.

HOW TO APPLY Apply in writing to the correspondent.

WHO TO APPLY TO A. Van Praagh, Trustee, 30 Armitage Road, London NW11 8RD *Tel.* 020 8201 8688

■ The Clothworkers' Foundation

CC NO 274100 **ESTABLISHED** 1977

WHERE FUNDING CAN BE GIVEN UK.

WHO CAN BENEFIT Charitable organisations.

WHAT IS FUNDED Alcohol and substance misuse; disadvantaged young people; people with disabilities; domestic and sexual violence; disadvantaged minority communities; older people; homelessness; prisoners and ex-offenders; visual impairment.

WHAT IS NOT FUNDED Salaries; overheads; training; volunteer expenses; rent; lease of property; websites; databases/software; professional fees; hospices; NHS charities; setting-up/refurbishment of charity shops; events; projects previously declined; grant-making organisations; general mailings; medical research or equipment; emergency appeals; marketing/literature/leaflets; political projects; heritage projects. **In the main grants programme:** IT equipment which will only be used by staff; arts or education projects unless they exclusively work with people from groups described in the foundation's programme areas; schools, colleges and universities unless they work with physical and/or learning difficulties; students or individuals; organisations with an annual income of more than £15 million; organisations which have received a grant in the last five years; overseas work; statutory/public bodies; organisations that promote religion or only provide services to people of a particular faith.

TYPE OF GRANT Capital grants.

RANGE OF GRANTS **Main grants:** grants of up to £100,000 (larger grants awarded on very rare occasions). Average grant size of £20,000, grants size is relative to project size – smaller projects usually receive smaller grants and vice versa. **Small grants:** grants of between £500 and £10,000 for capital costs.

SAMPLE GRANTS Kibbleworks (£200,000); Deafblind Scotland (£85,000); Action Mental Health (£25,000); Unseen (£24,000); Gibside School (£15,000); Islington Boat Club (£20,000); Rainbow Film Society (£10,000); Birmingham Asian Resource Centre (£8,000); Swale Action to End Domestic Abuse (£3,000); Health Action Charity Organisation (£1,300).

FINANCES *Year* 2015 *Income* £10,115,211 *Grants* £4,984,732 *Grants to organisations* £4,984,732

TRUSTEES Anne Luttman-Johnson; Dr Carolyn Boulter; Michael Jarvis; Melville Haggard; Joanna Dodd; Andrew Blessley; Alexander Nelson; John Wake; Dr Lucy Rawson; Nicholas Horne; John Coombe-Tennant.

HOW TO APPLY Refer to the foundation's very helpful and detailed guidelines on how to apply for either main or small grants, which can be downloaded from the foundation's website.

WHO TO APPLY TO Jocelyn Stuart-Grumbar, Chief Executive, Clothworkers' Hall, Dunster Court, Mincing Lane, London EC3R 7AH *Tel.* 020 7623 7041 *Email* foundation@clothworkers.co.uk *Website* foundation.clothworkers.co.uk

■ Richard Cloudesley's Charity

CC NO 205959 **ESTABLISHED** 1517

WHERE FUNDING CAN BE GIVEN Islington.

WHO CAN BENEFIT Voluntary and charitable organisations. Individuals are assisted through the trust's welfare fund.

WHAT IS FUNDED **Health grants:** organisations supporting Islington residents who are affected by illness or disability and who are facing financial hardship; **Islington churches:** the upkeep and repair of the 25 Church of England churches in the Islington Deanery.

TYPE OF GRANT One-off grants are preferred; the vast majority of grants are free of restrictions. Grants for capital, core, recurring, running and start-up costs will be considered, as will grants for buildings, feasibility studies, project, research and salaries.

RANGE OF GRANTS Up to £60,000.

SAMPLE GRANTS Centre 404 and Solace Women's Aid (£60,000 each); The Manna and Women's Therapy Centre (£59,500 each); Blenheim CDP CASA Family Service (£56,500); The Maya Centre (£53,300); St Stephen – Canonbury (£38,500); St Andrew's – Thornhill Square (£10,000).

FINANCES *Year* 2015/16 *Income* £1,430,473 *Grants* £935,085 *Grants to organisations* £789,587 *Assets* £47,160,107

TRUSTEE Richard Cloudesley Trustee Ltd.

OTHER INFORMATION Grants totalling £145,500 were made to individuals during the year.

HOW TO APPLY Health grants: there are three programmes for health grants: the main grants fund, the small grants fund and the strategic grants fund. Check the charity's website for details. Church Grants: the charity currently holds two funding rounds for the eligible churches each year, in spring and autumn. Applications can be made online or by using a downloadable application form. See the charity's website for full details.

WHO TO APPLY TO Melanie Griffiths, Director, Office 1.1, Resource for London, 356 Holloway Road, London N7 6PA *Tel.* 020 7697 4094 *Email* info@richardcloudesleyscharity.org.uk *Website* www.richardcloudesleyscharity.org.uk

■ The Clover Trust

CC NO 213578 **ESTABLISHED** 1961

WHERE FUNDING CAN BE GIVEN UK, and occasionally overseas, with a slight preference for West Dorset.

WHO CAN BENEFIT Registered charities.

WHAT IS FUNDED Older people; young people; Catholicism; health; disability.

TYPE OF GRANT Up to three years.

RANGE OF GRANTS £2,000 to £37,000.

SAMPLE GRANTS Friends of Children in Romania (£37,000); Farms for City Children (£10,000); Children with Cancer (£8,000); Action Medical Research (£7,000); Cotswold Care (£6,000); Childhood First (£5,000); CLAPA (£4,000); Essex Association of Boys Clubs (£3,000); Disability Snowsport UK (£2,000).

FINANCES *Year* 2015 *Income* £379,704 *Grants* £196,500 *Grants to organisations* £196,500 *Assets* £4,968,163

TRUSTEES Sara Woodhouse; Nicholas Haydon; Benedict Woodhouse; Charlotte Morrison.

HOW TO APPLY The trust's Charity Commission record states: 'The Trustees prefer to make regular donations to a designated selection of recipients and intend to continue with this policy for the foreseeable future. The trustees are currently not accepting any further applications for grant funding from other individuals or organisations.'

WHO TO APPLY TO Charlotte Robinson, Trustee, The Clover Trust, c/o Smith and Williamson, 21 Chipper Street, Salisbury, Wiltshire SP1 1BG *Tel.* 01724 31087 *Email* jeremycb.major@smith.williamson.co.uk

■ The Robert Clutterbuck Charitable Trust

CC NO 1010559 **ESTABLISHED** 1992

WHERE FUNDING CAN BE GIVEN UK, with preference for Cheshire and Hertfordshire.

WHO CAN BENEFIT Registered charities and other organisations with a charitable focus.

WHAT IS FUNDED Personnel within the armed forces and ex-servicemen and women; sport and recreational facilities for young people benefitting Cheshire and Hertfordshire; the welfare, protection and preservation of domestic animal life benefitting Cheshire and Hertfordshire; natural history and wildlife; other charities associated with the counties of Cheshire and Hertfordshire; charities which have particular appeal to the founder, Robert Clutterbuck.

WHAT IS NOT FUNDED Individuals.

TYPE OF GRANT Specific items and projects rather than running costs. One-off.

RANGE OF GRANTS Up to £5,000 but generally £1,000 to £3,000.

SAMPLE GRANTS Barbers Company (£5,000); Erskine (£3,000); John Warner School (£2,500); Four Estates (£2,000); Barnstondale Centre (£1,500); Gurkha Welfare Trust and The Welcome (£1,000 each); Prickles Hedgehog Rescue (£750); Medlock and Tame Conservation (£600); Knutsford Methodist Church (£500).

FINANCES *Year* 2015/16 *Income* £56,517 *Grants* £66,640 *Grants to organisations* £66,640 *Assets* £1,774,263

TRUSTEES Roger Pincham; Ian Pearson; Lucy Pitman.

HOW TO APPLY The trust's website states: 'There are no application forms and charities wishing to apply should write to the Secretary giving details of what they propose to do with any grant made and of their current financial position. The Trustees generally meet twice in each year to approve grants. The deadlines for the rounds of applications are 30 June and 31 December in each year. The Trustees generally meet in March and September. The Trustees will not normally consider appeals from charities within two years of a previous grant being approved.'

WHO TO APPLY TO George Wolfe, Secretary, 28 Brookfields, Calver, Hope Valley, Derbyshire S32 3XB *Tel.* 01433 631308 *Email* secretary@clutterbucktrust.org.uk *Website* www.clutterbucktrust.org.uk

■ Clydpride Ltd

CC NO 295393 **ESTABLISHED** 1982

WHERE FUNDING CAN BE GIVEN UK.

WHO CAN BENEFIT Individuals and institutions benefitting Jewish people and people disadvantaged by poverty.

WHAT IS FUNDED Advancement of the Orthodox Jewish faith; relief of poverty; general charitable purposes. The main focus is to support the 'renaissance of religious study and to alleviate the plight of poor scholars'.

SAMPLE GRANTS Achiezer; Achisomoch Aid Company; Beis Chinuch Lebonos; Beis Soroh Scheneirer Seminary; Bnei Braq Hospital; Comet Charities Ltd; EM Shasha Foundation; Friends of Mir; Gevurath Ari Torah Academy Trust; Mosdos Tshernobil; Notzar Chesed; Seed; Society of Friends of Torah; Telz Talmudical Academy Trust.

FINANCES *Year* 2015 *Income* £3,279,397 *Grants* £3,177,220 *Grants to organisations* £3,177,220 *Assets* £2,642,353

TRUSTEES L. Faust; M. H. Linton; A. Faust.

HOW TO APPLY The charity considers all grant requests from organisations that fall within the criteria of the charity's objects. The trustees' policy is to award grants on the basis of educational, religious or charitable need, subject to the general objects of the charity and cash resources available.

WHO TO APPLY TO Leon Faust, Trustee, c/o Rayner Essex Accountants, Entrance D, Tavistock House South, Tavistock Square, London WC1H 9LG

■ The Francis Coales Charitable Foundation

CC NO 270718 **ESTABLISHED** 1975

WHERE FUNDING CAN BE GIVEN UK, with a preference for Bedfordshire, Buckinghamshire, Hertfordshire and Northamptonshire.

WHO CAN BENEFIT Old buildings open to the public, usually churches. Monuments and monumental brasses.

WHAT IS FUNDED The structural repair of buildings (built before 1875) which are open to the public. Preference is given to churches in the counties of Buckinghamshire, Bedfordshire, Hertfordshire and Northamptonshire. There is no geographical restriction in respect of the conservation of monuments and monumental brasses. Grants are occasionally made towards publication for architectural and architectural books and papers; towards the purchase of documents and items for record offices and museums; for archaeological research and related causes.

WHAT IS NOT FUNDED In respect of buildings, assistance is only given towards fabric repairs, but not to 'domestic' items such as heating, lighting, wiring, installation of facilities and so on.

TYPE OF GRANT Largely one-off.

SAMPLE GRANTS Smisby – Derbyshire (£4,250); Hertfordshire Buildings Trust (£3,000); Great Brighton – Northamptonshire (£2,500); London Record Society and Selby Abbey (£750 each); Monumental Brass Society (£500).

FINANCES *Year* 2015 *Income* £123,166 *Grants* £92,826 *Grants to organisations* £92,826 *Assets* £4,078,357

TRUSTEES Martin Stuchfield; Pamela Ward; Revd Brian Wilcox; Ian Barnett; Matthew Saunders.

HOW TO APPLY Application forms can be downloaded from the foundation's website. The website states: 'In respect of a building or contents, include a copy of the relevant portion only of the architect's (or conservator's) specification showing the actual work proposed. Photographs illustrating this are a necessity, and only in exceptional circumstances will an application be considered without supporting photographs here. It is of help if six copies of any supporting documentation are submitted in order that each trustee may have a copy in advance of the meeting.'

WHO TO APPLY TO Trevor Parker, The Bays, Hillcote, Bleadon Hill, Weston-super-Mare, Somerset BS24 9JS *Tel.* 01934 814009 *Email* fccf45@hotmail.com *Website* franciscoales.co.uk

■ The Coalfields Regeneration Trust

CC NO 1074930 **ESTABLISHED** 1999

WHERE FUNDING CAN BE GIVEN Coalfield and former coalfield communities in England (North West and North East, Yorkshire, West Midlands and East Midlands, Kent), Scotland (west and east) and Wales.

WHO CAN BENEFIT Most voluntary and community organisations and groups working to regenerate coalfield communities are eligible to apply for funding as long as they are not for personal profit. These include registered charities, companies limited by guarantee, community benefit societies, CICs, CIOs and community amateur sports clubs (CASCs).

WHAT IS FUNDED Welfare of coalfield communities. The trust focuses on: improving health; providing opportunities for children and young people; employment, skills and training programmes; supporting community enterprise; practical help and community investment.

WHAT IS NOT FUNDED Individuals; private businesses; companies limited by shares; statutory bodies including local authorities, schools, colleges, hospitals, GPs; national organisations as defined in their governing document; parish, town and community councils; organisations with unrestricted income above £250,000; organisations that are in a poor financial position or whose financial management systems are not in good order i.e. overdrawn bank account and/or operational deficit/net current liabilities in the annual accounts; organisations whose purpose is to raise funds for a specific project; 'Friends of Groups' where the end beneficiary will clearly be a statutory body; organisations not established in the UK; pigeon clubs.

TYPE OF GRANT Usually one-off grants.

RANGE OF GRANTS Up to £200,000.

SAMPLE GRANTS Aylesham Neighbourhood Project (£210,000); Haswell and District Mencap Society – The Community Anchor (£98,000); Derbyshire Rural Community Council – Wheels to Work (£89,000); The Cornforth Partnership – The Reach project (£75,000); Nottinghamshire Independent Domestic Abuse Link Workers (£66,000); Stoke-on-Trent and District

Gingerbread Centre Ltd – Peer Mentoring (£37,000); St John's Church – A Building in Which to Serve Our Community (£10,000); Mansfield and Dukeries Irish Association – Luncheon Club (£5,000); City of Durham Air Cadets – Achieving Duke of Edinburgh's Awards (£3,800); Thornycroft Art Club – Christmas Tree Exhibition (£520).

FINANCES *Year* 2015/16 *Income* £4,390,000 *Grants* £834,000 *Grants to organisations* £834,000 *Assets* £34,130

TRUSTEES Wayne Thomas; Sylvia Wileman; Nicholas Wilson; Peter McNestry; Vernon Jones; Dawn Davies; Michael Clapham; Terrence O'Neill; Robert Young.

OTHER INFORMATION The trust provides advice, support and financial assistance to community and voluntary organisations who are working to tackle problems at grassroots level within coalfield communities. It is closely connected with the areas it serves, operating through a network of staff based at offices located within coalfield regions themselves.

HOW TO APPLY Application details are different for each programme. Details for each programme can be found on the trust's website.

WHO TO APPLY TO Louise Dyson, Head of Finance and Corporate Services, 1 Waterside Park, Valley Way, Wombwell, Barnsley S73 0BB *Tel.* 01226 272810 *Email* info@coalfields-regen.org.uk *Website* www.coalfields-regen.org.uk

■ The John Coates Charitable Trust

CC NO 262057 **ESTABLISHED** 1969

WHERE FUNDING CAN BE GIVEN UK, mainly southern England.

WHO CAN BENEFIT Institutions either national or of personal or local interest to one or more of the trustees.

WHAT IS FUNDED General charitable purposes including: education; arts and culture; children; environment and health.

WHAT IS NOT FUNDED Grants are given to individuals only in exceptional circumstances.

TYPE OF GRANT Capital and recurring.

RANGE OF GRANTS £1,000 to £10,000.

SAMPLE GRANTS Sebastian's Action Trust (£10,000); Parkinson's UK and St Catherine's Hospice Ltd (£5,000 each); Big Issue Foundation and Pathways through Dementia (£3,000 each); Dreams Come True and Rowdeford Charity Trust (£2,000 each); The Barn Owl Trust (£1,000).

FINANCES *Year* 2015/16 *Income* £421,255 *Grants* £398,000 *Grants to organisations* £398,000 *Assets* £12,736,405

TRUSTEES Gillian McGregor; Rebecca Lawes; Phyllida Youngman; Catharine Kesley; Claire Cartledge.

HOW TO APPLY Apply in writing to the correspondent. Note that the trust does not invite phone calls – any communication should be made in writing. Small local charities are visited by the trust. It is the trust's policy to request a post-grant report detailing how a donation has been spent for any single donation over £15,000.

WHO TO APPLY TO Rebecca Lawes, Trustee, 3 Grange Road, Cambridge CB3 9AS

■ Denise Coates Foundation

CC NO 1149110 **ESTABLISHED** 2012

WHERE FUNDING CAN BE GIVEN UK and overseas.

WHO CAN BENEFIT Charities and community groups.

WHAT IS FUNDED Health and welfare; education and training; medical research; disaster relief; arts and culture.

SAMPLE GRANTS Abbotsholme School (£444,000); Douglas Macmillan Hospice (£343,000); mothers2mothers (£252,000); The Donna Louise Children's Hospice (£250,000); Keele University (£190,500 in two donations); Staffordshire University (£150,000).

FINANCES *Year* 2015/16 *Income* £127,126 *Grants* £3,086,649 *Grants to organisations* £3,086,649 *Assets* £129,480,829

TRUSTEES Denise Coates; John Coates; Peter Coates; Simon Adlington; James White; Simon Galletley.

OTHER INFORMATION Grants were distributed as follows: education and training (£1.8 million); health and welfare (£1 million); medical research and development (£200,000); arts and culture (£54,000).

HOW TO APPLY Apply in writing to the correspondent.

WHO TO APPLY TO Simon Galletley, Trustee, c/o RSM Tenon, Festival Way, Festival Park, Stoke-on-Trent, Staffordshire ST1 5BB *Tel.* 0845 600 0365

■ The Cobalt Trust

CC NO 1096342 **ESTABLISHED** 2002

WHERE FUNDING CAN BE GIVEN UK and overseas.

WHO CAN BENEFIT Registered charities known to the trustees.

WHAT IS FUNDED General charitable purposes.

SAMPLE GRANTS Impetus Trust (£169,000); European Venture Philanthropy Association (£26,000); Streets Ltd (£14,000); Enable Ethiopia and Tree Aid (£12,000 each); Rosetrees Trust and Money for Madagascar (£10,000 each); Beat – Eating Disorders Association (£5,000); Wherever the Need (£1,000); Red Squirrel Survival Trust (£500); Wessex MS Therapy Centre (£100); Bath RSPB (£50).

FINANCES *Year* 2015/16 *Income* £23,928 *Grants* £200,000 *Grants to organisations* £200,000

TRUSTEES Stephen Dawson; Brigitte Dawson.

HOW TO APPLY The trustees do not respond to unsolicited applications

WHO TO APPLY TO Stephen Dawson, Trustee, 17 New Row, London WC2N 4LA *Tel.* 07720 345880

■ The Cobtree Charity Trust Ltd

CC NO 208455 **ESTABLISHED** 1951

WHERE FUNDING CAN BE GIVEN Maidstone and surrounding area.

WHO CAN BENEFIT Registered charities; churches; hospices.

WHAT IS FUNDED The maintenance and development of Cobtree Manor Estate, and other general charitable purposes by other charities in the Maidstone and district area.

WHAT IS NOT FUNDED Individuals; non-registered charities; charities outside Maidstone and district.

TYPE OF GRANT Largely recurrent.

RANGE OF GRANTS £700 to £5,300.

SAMPLE GRANTS Heart of Kent Hospice (£5,300); Young Kent (£4,100); All Saints Church – Maidstone (£3,800); Spadework (£2,500); Hi

Kent (£2,000); Action for Children (£1,800); Five Acre Wood Special School (£1,300); Relate in Kent (£1,200); The Singalong Group (£900); Maidstone Day Centre (£700).

FINANCES *Year* 2015/16 *Income* £183,808 *Grants* £99,815 *Grants to organisations* £99,815 *Assets* £5,811,517

TRUSTEES John Fletcher; David Wigg; Lawrence Martin; Roger Hext; Michael Startup; Michael Lawrence; Stephen Beck; Stefan Jordan; Mike Sharp.

HOW TO APPLY Apply in writing to the correspondent. The trustees meet quarterly.

WHO TO APPLY TO Bernard Mee, Northdown, Church Lane, Bearsted, Maidstone ME14 4EF *Tel.* 01622 737267 *Email* cobtreecharitytrust@outlook.com *Website* thecobtreecharitytrust.co.uk

■ The Denise Cohen Charitable Trust

CC NO 276439 **ESTABLISHED** 1977

WHERE FUNDING CAN BE GIVEN UK.

WHO CAN BENEFIT Registered charities.

WHAT IS FUNDED Jewish causes; education; health and welfare of older people, illness; children; humanities; arts and culture.

RANGE OF GRANTS Up to £7,000.

SAMPLE GRANTS Nightingale Hammerson (£7,000); Chai Cancer Care (£6,000); Devonshire Street Charitable Foundation (£2,000); Save a Child's Heart (£1,000); Fight for Sight (£500); Starlight Children's Foundation (£400); The Salvation Army (£300); Cystic Fibrosis Trust (£250).

FINANCES *Year* 2015/16 *Income* £39,607 *Grants* £72,519 *Grants to organisations* £72,519 *Assets* £1,316,347

TRUSTEES Denise Cohen; Martin Paisner; Sara Cohen.

HOW TO APPLY Apply in writing to the correspondent incorporating full details of the charity for which funding is requested. No acknowledgements will be sent out to unsuccessful applicants.

WHO TO APPLY TO Dr Vivienne Cohen, Trustee, Clayton Start and Co., 5th Floor, Charles House, 108–110 Finchley Road, London NW3 5JJ *Tel.* 020 3400 1000

■ The Vivienne and Samuel Cohen Charitable Trust

CC NO 255496 **ESTABLISHED** 1965

WHERE FUNDING CAN BE GIVEN UK and Israel.

WHO CAN BENEFIT Charitable organisations.

WHAT IS FUNDED Jewish causes; education; health; medical purposes; culture; general charitable purposes.

WHAT IS NOT FUNDED Individuals.

RANGE OF GRANTS Up to £8,000.

SAMPLE GRANTS Ariel (£8,000); The Spiro Ark (£7,000); Keren Nevo (£3,000); Israel Foulkes Fund and Friends of the Royal Hospital (£2,000 each); Boys Town Jerusalem and Elimination of Leukaemia Fund (£1,000 each).

FINANCES *Year* 2015/26 *Income* £156,464 *Grants* £179,070 *Grants to organisations* £179,070 *Assets* £3,780,436

TRUSTEES Jonathan Lauffer; Gershon Cohen; Michael Ben-Gershon; Dr Vivienne Cohen; Gideon Lauffer.

OTHER INFORMATION Grants were made to 250 organisations during the year and 190 were under £1,000.

HOW TO APPLY Apply in writing only, to the correspondent.

WHO TO APPLY TO Martin Paisner, Trustee, Berwin Leighton and Paisner, Adelaide House, London Bridge, London EC4R 9HA *Tel.* 020 7431 4200 *Email* csco@claytonstark.co.uk

■ The John S. Cohen Foundation

CC NO 241598 **ESTABLISHED** 1965

WHERE FUNDING CAN BE GIVEN Worldwide, in practice mainly UK.

WHO CAN BENEFIT Registered charities.

WHAT IS FUNDED Arts; conservation and environment; education and academic; social and media.

TYPE OF GRANT One-off and recurring.

RANGE OF GRANTS £500 to £50,000.

SAMPLE GRANTS Royal Opera House (£50,000); National Portrait Gallery and Zoological Society of London (£10,000 each); Natural History Museum (£6,000); SJP Charity Trust (£3,000); Lincoln Cathedral (£2,000); Hardman Trust (£1,300); Environmental Law Foundation and Woodland Trust (£1,000 each); Courtauld Institute of Art and Friary Guilford Brass Band (£500 each).

FINANCES *Year* 2015/16 *Income* £571,193 *Grants* £465,362 *Grants to organisations* £465,362 *Assets* £10,982,851

TRUSTEES Dr David Cohen; Imogen Cohen; Olivia Cohen; Veronica Cohen.

HOW TO APPLY Apply in writing to the correspondent.

WHO TO APPLY TO Martin Dodd, 3 Stanley Crescent, London W11 2NB

■ The R. and S. Cohen Foundation

CC NO 1078225 **ESTABLISHED** 1999

WHERE FUNDING CAN BE GIVEN Worldwide.

WHO CAN BENEFIT Educational, theatrical, operatic, medical and Jewish charitable organisations.

WHAT IS FUNDED Education, relief in need and arts.

TYPE OF GRANT One-off and recurrent.

RANGE OF GRANTS Up to £1 million.

SAMPLE GRANTS Exeter College – Oxford (£1 million); The Portland Trust (£492,500); Tate Foundation (£100,000); Fight for Peace International (£75,000); Community Security Trust (£40,000); Ashoka (£24,000); The Weidenfeld Fund (£20,000); Victoria and Albert Museum (£15,000); The Old Vic Theatre Trust (£10,000); Royal Academy of The Arts (£1,200).

FINANCES *Year* 2015 *Income* £1,192,719 *Grants* £1,868,983 *Grants to organisations* £1,868,983 *Assets* £4,790,252

TRUSTEES Sir Ronald Cohen; Lady Sharon Harel-Cohen; Tamara Harel-Cohen; David Marks; Jonathan Harel-Cohen.

OTHER INFORMATION Grants were made to 19 organisations during the year.

HOW TO APPLY Apply in writing to the correspondent.

WHO TO APPLY TO Diana Helme, Foundation Administrator, PO Box 21277, London W9 2YH

■ Col-Reno Ltd

CC NO 274896 **ESTABLISHED** 1977

WHERE FUNDING CAN BE GIVEN UK and Israel.

WHO CAN BENEFIT Religious and educational institutions benefitting children, young adults, students and Jewish people.

WHAT IS FUNDED Jewish religion and education.

RANGE OF GRANTS Mostly under £2,000.

SAMPLE GRANTS Lubavitch of Liverpool (£14,700); Friends of Religious Settlements (£9,900); UK

Toremet Ltd (£6,800); Friends of Shamir (£4,800); Chabad of Wimbledon (£3,100); Hendon Adath Congregation (£2,100); Jerusalem Parks Authority (£1,000); Alzheimer's Research UK (£100).

FINANCES *Year* 2015/16 *Income* £113,437 *Grants* £79,471 *Grants to organisations* £79,471 *Assets* £2,100,858

TRUSTEES Alan Stern; Rhona Davis; Keith Davis; Chaim Stern; Libbie Goldstein; Martin Stern.

HOW TO APPLY Apply in writing to the correspondent.

WHO TO APPLY TO Martin Stern, Trustee, 10 Hampshire Court, 9 Brent Street, London NW4 2EW *Tel.* 020 8202 7013

■ The Colchester Catalyst Charity

CC NO 228352 **ESTABLISHED** 1959

WHERE FUNDING CAN BE GIVEN North East Essex.

WHO CAN BENEFIT Health organisations; individuals.

WHAT IS FUNDED Provision of support by direct contributions to health organisations for specific and well-designed projects in order to improve health care. Grants are also made to individuals for specialised equipment that is not available through statutory organisations.

WHAT IS NOT FUNDED No support is given for general funding, staff or running costs (usually). Retrospective funding is not considered. The charity is unable to consider applications for any item where there is an obligation for provision by a statutory authority.

TYPE OF GRANT Project funding; equipment.

SAMPLE GRANTS Community Voluntary Services Tendring (£95,000); Basics Essex Accident Rescue Service (£28,000); Autism Anglia (£15,000); Beacon House (£9,300); Bright Lives (£5,100); Essex Fire and Rescue (£4,000); St Helena Hospice (£2,500); Colchester Hospital Charity (£1,000).

FINANCES *Year* 2016 *Income* £519,145 *Grants* £473,413 *Grants to organisations* £473,413 *Assets* £11,272,036

TRUSTEES Peter Fitt; Christine Hayward; Mark Pertwee; Dr Thilaka Rudra; Dr Max Hickman; Dr Naomi Busfield; Elizabeth Thrower; Keith Songhurst.

OTHER INFORMATION Grants were broken down as follows: charities (£235,500); respite care (£145,000; special needs individuals (£89,000); equipment pools (£3,500).

HOW TO APPLY Application forms for general and individual grants can be downloaded from the charity's website. Grants for respite care and counselling are administered through partner organisations. Contact the charity for more information on partnership grants.

WHO TO APPLY TO Peter Fitt, Company Secretary, 7 Coast Road, West Mersea, Colchester CO5 8QE *Tel.* 01206 752545 *Email* info@colchestercatalyst.co.uk *Website* www.colchestercatalyst.co.uk

■ The Coldman Charitable Trust

CC NO 1050110 **ESTABLISHED** 1995

WHERE FUNDING CAN BE GIVEN Kent.

WHO CAN BENEFIT Registered charities.

WHAT IS FUNDED General charitable purposes, particularly community and Christian groups and UK organisations whose work benefits the community, such as children's and medical charities and schools.

SAMPLE GRANTS Chiddingstone Church of England School (£50,000); The Prince's Trust, NSPCC (£20,000 each); Celtic FC Charity Fund (£15,000); National Gardens Scheme (£11,400); African Promise (£13,400); St Peter's Church – Hever (£10,000); The Sick Children's Trust (£5,000); Cancer Research UK, Darent Valley Hospital Charity Fund, The Gurkha Welfare Trust (£1,000 each); Movember (£250).

FINANCES *Year* 2015/16 *Income* £20,253 *Grants* £150,000 *Grants to organisations* £150,000

TRUSTEES John Coldman; Graham Coldman; Charles Warner.

OTHER INFORMATION This charity's latest accounts were not available to view on the Charity Commission's website due to its low income. We have therefore estimated the grant total based on previous years' information.

HOW TO APPLY Apply in writing to the correspondent.

WHO TO APPLY TO The Trustees, Lockskinners Farmhouse, Chiddingstone, Edenbridge, Kent TN8 7NA *Email* johncoldman@benfieldpartners.com

■ The Cole Charitable Trust

CC NO 264033 **ESTABLISHED** 1972

WHERE FUNDING CAN BE GIVEN Birmingham City; Coventry City; Dudley; Sandwell; Solihull; Walsall; Wolverhampton; Kent; Cambridge.

WHO CAN BENEFIT Registered charities.

WHAT IS FUNDED Social welfare; community development; environmental development; young people; community development.

WHAT IS NOT FUNDED Large building appeals; animal welfare charities; research or further education; individuals.

TYPE OF GRANT Small capital or project grants; normally one-off; core costs.

RANGE OF GRANTS Up to £50,000 but generally £500 to £1,000.

SAMPLE GRANTS Hope Projects Ltd (£50,000); Emmaus (£2,000); Black Country Foodbank and Kingswood Trust (£1,000 each); Books Abroad (£750); Birmingham Care Group and Young Lives Foundation (£700 each); Stretham Youth Club (£650); Rage Arts and Woodside Community Association (£500 each).

FINANCES *Year* 2015/16 *Income* £146,741 *Grants* £120,050 *Grants to organisations* £120,050

TRUSTEES Ranjit Sondhi; Tim Cole; George Cole; Tom Cole; James Cole; Jont Cole; Maya Sondhi.

HOW TO APPLY Application forms are available to download from the trust's websites. Completed forms should be returned by email (preferred) or post along with a one page letter and latest accounts if they are not showing on the Charity Commission's website.

WHO TO APPLY TO Lise Jackson, PO Box 955, Haslingfield, Cambridge CB23 1WX *Tel.* 01223 871676 *Email* thecoletrust@gmail.com *Website* www.colecharitabletrust.org.uk

■ The Colefax Charitable Trust

CC NO 1017285 **ESTABLISHED** 1993

WHERE FUNDING CAN BE GIVEN Hampshire and Berkshire.

WHO CAN BENEFIT Registered charities.

WHAT IS FUNDED General charitable purposes.

WHAT IS NOT FUNDED Individuals.

SAMPLE GRANTS Church on the Heath; Home-Start; Jumbulance; Living Paintings Trust; Newbury District OAP Association; Newbury Spring Festival; Prospect Educational Trust; Reading Voluntary Action; Reliance Cancer Foundation;

Southend Residents' Association; Watership Brass.

FINANCES *Year* 2014/15 *Income* £339,419 *Grants* £114,850 *Grants to organisations* £114,850 *Assets* £339,419

TRUSTEES John Heath; Hans Krohn; Daniela Fienes-Cox.

HOW TO APPLY Unsolicited applications are not accepted.

WHO TO APPLY TO Hans Krohn, Trustee, Westbrook House, St Helens Gardens, The Pitchens, Wroughton, Wiltshire SN4 0RU *Tel.* 01635 200415 *Email* newbury@griffins.co.uk

■ The John and Freda Coleman Charitable Trust

CC NO 278223 **ESTABLISHED** 1979

WHERE FUNDING CAN BE GIVEN Hampshire; Surrey.

WHO CAN BENEFIT Registered charities; education and training centres.

WHAT IS FUNDED Small grants to organisations helping young people to obtain the skills they need for both work and life. Principal donations are currently directed to organisations in Surrey and Hampshire focused on providing practical training, skills and support where the education system is not enabling young people to reach their full potential.'

WHAT IS NOT FUNDED No grants are made to students.

TYPE OF GRANT One-off and recurrent.

RANGE OF GRANTS Up to £20,000.

SAMPLE GRANTS Surrey SATRO (£25,000); Surrey Care Trust (£10,000); Therapy Garden – Green School (£5,100); Second Chance (£3,000); GASP Car Project (£2,800); Smallpiece and Waverley Federation (£2,000 each); Step By Step (£1,500); St Joseph's Specialist School (£1,000).

FINANCES *Year* 2015/16 *Income* £32,601 *Grants* £70,870 *Grants to organisations* £70,870 *Assets* £722,987

TRUSTEES Paul Coleman; Jeanette Bird; Brian Coleman; Nicole Coleman.

HOW TO APPLY Apply in writing to the correspondent via post or email. Telephone calls are welcome.

WHO TO APPLY TO Jeanette Bird, Trustee, 3 Gasden Drive, Witley, Godalming, Surrey GU8 5QQ *Tel.* 01428 681333 *Email* questrum.holdings@gmail.com

■ The Sir Jeremiah Colman Gift Trust

CC NO 229553 **ESTABLISHED** 1920

WHERE FUNDING CAN BE GIVEN Hampshire.

WHO CAN BENEFIT Registered charities; churches. Projects should have a well-established needs for support.

WHAT IS FUNDED Advancement of education and literary scientific knowledge; moral and social improvement of people; maintenance of churches of the Church of England and gifts and offerings to the churches.

WHAT IS NOT FUNDED Grants are not made to individuals requiring support for personal education, or to individual families for welfare purposes.

RANGE OF GRANTS Up to £20,000.

SAMPLE GRANTS St Leonard's – Oakley and Wootton (£20,000); Basingstoke Mencap (£3,000); See Ability (£2,500); Bible Society and The Art Fund (£2,000 each); National Trust and Royal Horticultural Society (£1,500 each); Hampton Trust, Mercy Ships and Winchester Cathedral Trust (£1,000 each).

FINANCES *Year* 2015/16 *Income* £175,475 *Grants* £105,800 *Grants to organisations* £105,800 *Assets* £6,925,258

TRUSTEES Hon. Cynthia Colman; Jeremiah Colman; Lady Judith Colman; Sir Michael Colman; Oliver Colman; Sue Colman; Camilla Adeney; Louisa Whitworth.

OTHER INFORMATION Grants were broken down as follows: new appeals (£33,300); long term (£72,500).

HOW TO APPLY Unsolicited applications are not accepted.

WHO TO APPLY TO Sir Michael Colman, Malshanger, Basingstoke, Hampshire RG23 7EY *Tel.* 01256 780252 *Email* rosepersson@btinternet.com

■ The Colt Foundation

CC NO 277189 **ESTABLISHED** 1978

WHERE FUNDING CAN BE GIVEN UK.

WHO CAN BENEFIT Universities and research establishments benefitting research workers and students taking higher degrees.

WHAT IS FUNDED Research projects in the field of occupational and environmental health, particularly those aimed at discovering the cause of illnesses arising from conditions at the place of work. The trustees are particularly keen to fund research that is likely to inform government policy or change working practices.

WHAT IS NOT FUNDED Grants are not made for the general funds of another charity, directly to individuals or projects overseas.

TYPE OF GRANT Research; project.

SAMPLE GRANTS University of Edinburgh (£119,000 in two grants); Imperial College (£31,000); London School of Hygiene and Tropical Medicine (£26,500); City University (£17,000); Royal Society of Medicine (£3,200); University of Manchester (£210).

FINANCES *Year* 2015 *Income* £677,601 *Grants* £426,989 *Grants to organisations* £286,862 *Assets* £19,558,756

TRUSTEES Jerome O'Hea; Claire Gilchrist; Patricia Lebus; Peter O'Hea; Alan O'Hea; Prof. David Coggon; Natasha Heydon; Prof. Sir Anthony Taylor.

OTHER INFORMATION Grants were made to 13 organisations. Student fellowships totalled £140,000.

HOW TO APPLY Apply in writing to the correspondent. Full details of what should be included in an application can be found on the 'grants' section of the foundation's website. The trustees meet twice a year to review applications, in the spring and in the autumn, and applications normally need to be received approximately eight weeks beforehand to be considered at the meetings. Exact deadlines can be found on the foundation's website. Applicants can submit a single sheet lay summary at any time during the year prior to working on a full application, so that advice can be given on whether the work is likely to fall within the remit of the foundation.

WHO TO APPLY TO Jackie Douglas, Director, New Lane, Havant, Hampshire PO9 2LY *Tel.* 023 9249 1400 *Email* jackie.douglas@uk.coltgroup.com *Website* www.coltfoundation.org.uk

■ The Coltstaple Trust

CC NO 1085500 **ESTABLISHED** 2001
WHERE FUNDING CAN BE GIVEN Worldwide.
WHO CAN BENEFIT Charitable organisations.
WHAT IS FUNDED The relief of persons in need, poverty or distress in financially developing countries and the relief of persons who are homeless or in housing need in the UK or any other part of the world.
TYPE OF GRANT Recurrent.
SAMPLE GRANTS Oxfam (£130,000); Opportunity International (£40,000); Emmaus UK (£30,000); Whitechapel Mission (£30,000); St Mungo's (£20,000).
FINANCES *Year* 2015/16 *Income* £199,177 *Grants* £250,000 *Grants to organisations* £250,000 *Assets* £5,856,050
TRUSTEES Matthew Oakeshott; Lord Stoneham of Droxford; Elaine Colville; Dr Philippa Oakeshott.
HOW TO APPLY Unsolicited applications are unlikely to be successful. The trust's 2015/16 accounts state: 'The trustees intend to continue providing grants in a similar way to the recent past while retaining flexibility as to the timing and scale of grants.'
WHO TO APPLY TO Matthew Oakeshott, Trustee, 2 Queen Anne's Gate Buildings, Dartmouth Street, London SW1H 9BP *Tel.* 020 7647 6701 *Email* debbie.neal@olimproperty.co.uk

■ Colwinston Charitable Trust

CC NO 1049189 **ESTABLISHED** 1995
WHERE FUNDING CAN BE GIVEN UK. Over 80% of grants are made in Wales.
WHO CAN BENEFIT UK-registered charities.
WHAT IS FUNDED The trust seeks to sustain and support high quality artistic activities that add to the cultural life and experiences available in the UK and especially in Wales. Funding is particularly but not exclusively directed to the support of opera, music and the visual arts, libraries and archives.
WHAT IS NOT FUNDED Retrospective funding; funding for projects that have already started; applications from individuals or for individual research or study; funding for publications, conferences and seminars; general appeals; activity that takes place outside the UK, even if the organisation is UK registered; commercial recordings other than those benefitting the careers of emerging or mid-career Welsh composers. Social and community welfare organisations, where the dominant purpose is not art, and community arts projects and performances by amateur groups will not generally be supported. Capital or refurbishment projects will only be considered in exceptional circumstances and only when the applicant is an arts organisation or gallery in Wales. An organisation may only apply for one grant, in any one financial year. The trust will only consider applications from fully UK-registered charities and it will not consider applications from 'Friends of' charities.
RANGE OF GRANTS Generally grants of up to £50,000. Majority in the range of £5,000 to £20,000.
SAMPLE GRANTS Artes Mundi and Welsh National Opera (£170,000 each); Wales Millennium Centre (£150,000); Music Theatre Wales (£125,000); National Museum of Wales (£25,000); The Aloud Charity (£15,000); Cowbridge Music Festival (£5,000); Morley College (£2,500).
FINANCES *Year* 2015/16 *Income* £628,160 *Grants* £931,075 *Grants to organisations* £931,075 *Assets* £1,176,466
TRUSTEES Matthew Pritchard; Martin Tinney; Sian Williams; Lucinda Pritchard; Rebecca Evans.
OTHER INFORMATION The trust derives its income from the royalties from the West End production of *The Mousetrap*, the Agatha Christie's play, which opened in 1952.
HOW TO APPLY Application forms and guidelines are available to download from the trust's website. Grant applications should be received no later than 30 September, for consideration at the November meeting, or 31 March for consideration at the May meeting of trustees.
WHO TO APPLY TO Chris Bliss, Partner, Rawlinson and Hunter, 8th Floor, 6 New Street Square, London EC4A 3AQ *Tel.* 020 7842 2000 *Email* colwinston.trust@ntlworld.com *Website* www.colwinston.org.uk

■ Colyer-Fergusson Charitable Trust

CC NO 258958 **ESTABLISHED** 1969
WHERE FUNDING CAN BE GIVEN Kent.
WHO CAN BENEFIT Registered charities; CICs.
WHAT IS FUNDED Social welfare and education of young people. The trust is currently focused on 'young people with poverty of opportunity'.
WHAT IS NOT FUNDED Individuals – unless appeals are made via a referral partner or Hardship Awards Programme; national charities receiving widespread support; statutory bodies; hospitals and health authorities; medical care, medical equipment or medical research; academic research, scholarships or bursaries; animal charities; the promotion of religion; the restoration or conservation of buildings; work outside Kent; endowment appeals; work that has already taken place i.e. retrospective funding; round-robin, widely circulated appeals.
TYPE OF GRANT One-off, recurring, capital, core, running and start-up costs will all be considered, as will salaries, buildings, project and research costs. Funding may be given for up to three years.
RANGE OF GRANTS Up to £72,000.
SAMPLE GRANTS The Music Hub Plus (£72,500); Dandelion Time (£60,000); Canterbury Cathedral (£54,000); West Kent YMCA (£50,000); Thanet Community Development Trust (£41,000); PACE Foundation CIC (£27,000); Addaction (£20,000); Kent Community Foundation (£5,000).
FINANCES *Year* 2015/16 *Income* £479,938 *Grants* £1,001,161 *Grants to organisations* £1,001,161 *Assets* £23,678,932
TRUSTEES Nicholas Fisher; Robert North; Ruth Murphy; Rosalind Riley; James Thorne; Barbara Long.
HOW TO APPLY Applications can be made through the trust's website.
WHO TO APPLY TO David Williams, Marcar House, Parkshot, Richmond, Surrey TW9 2RG *Tel.* 020 8948 3388 *Email* grantadmin@cfct.org.uk *Website* www.cfct.org.uk

■ Comic Relief

CC NO 326568 **ESTABLISHED** 1985
WHERE FUNDING CAN BE GIVEN UK and overseas (mainly sub-Saharan Africa).
WHO CAN BENEFIT UK-registered charities; voluntary organisations.

WHAT IS FUNDED The charity's four programme areas are: investing in children and young people to be ready for the future; empowering women and girls so they're safe and free to lead the lives they choose; improving health and well-being of vulnerable and disadvantaged people; building stronger communities in areas of disadvantage, deprivation and poverty.
WHAT IS NOT FUNDED General appeals; individual and group sponsorship; marketing appeals; proposals for bursaries from individuals or proposals from individuals for the funding of study or attainment of qualifications; activities which evangelise (the practice of preaching or spreading religious beliefs), or proselytise (the practice of trying to convert people to one's own belief or religious views); one-off conferences or workshops; organisations which adopt a partisan political stance or activities which are party political.
SAMPLE GRANTS A list of beneficiaries was not available.
FINANCES *Year* 2015/16 *Income* £92,221,000 *Grants* £99,487,000 *Grants to organisations* £99,487,000 *Assets* £93,394,000
TRUSTEES Michael Harris; Colin Howes; Dr Dhananjayan Sriskandarajah; Richard Curtis; Timothy Davie; Theo Sowa; Diana Barran; Tristia Clarke; Suzie Aplin; Robert Webb; Saul Klein; Charlotte Moore.
OTHER INFORMATION The grant total includes £30.1 million in UK grants and £68.5 million in international grants.
HOW TO APPLY Applications are made online via the charity's website, where full guidance is also provided. Potential applicants must register and complete Stage 1 of the process, an initial proposal. Applicants are shortlisted from those successfully completing Stage 1.
WHO TO APPLY TO Ruth Ruderham, Grants Director, 1st Floor, 89 Albert Embankment, London SE1 7TP *Tel.* 020 7820 2000 *Email* grantsinfo@comicrelief.com *Website* www.comicrelief.com

■ The Comino Foundation

CC NO 312875 **ESTABLISHED** 1971
WHERE FUNDING CAN BE GIVEN UK.
WHO CAN BENEFIT Charities; schools; universities; social enterprises.
WHAT IS FUNDED Support of educational activities for young people which: improve practical and personal capabilities; enrich learning in science, engineering and technology; transform services for young people with complex needs; and improve social opportunity.
TYPE OF GRANT One-off.
RANGE OF GRANTS Up to 56,000.
SAMPLE GRANTS Ideas Foundation (£56,000); The RSA (£50,000); University of Winchester (£45,000); Local Solutions – Liverpool (£34,000); Royal College of Engineering (£15,000); Creative Academies (£10,000); Institute of Marketing (£4,600); Foundation for Science and Technology (£3,000).
FINANCES *Year* 2015/16 *Income* £146,127 *Grants* £153,557 *Grants to organisations* £153,557 *Assets* £3,766,038
TRUSTEES Anna Comino-James; John Slater; David Perry; James Westhead; Paul Pritchard; John Cridland.
OTHER INFORMATION Grants were made to 15 organisations during the year.
HOW TO APPLY All funding proposals and applications should be sent to the administrator. The foundation's website states: 'The Foundation currently gives consideration ONLY to grant applications that provide evidence showing that the new proposal will have an extremely close fit to existing work. The Foundation has a wide range of established longer-term funding commitments and has limited capacity to make further grants. The Foundation does not fund any research or activities outside the UK.'
WHO TO APPLY TO Anthony Darbyshire, Administrator, Firs House, Bilby, Retford, Nottinghamshire DN22 8JB *Tel.* 01777 711141 *Email* anthony.darbyshire@cominofoundation.org.uk *Website* www.cominofoundation.org.uk

■ Community First (Landfill Communities Fund)

CC NO 288117 **ESTABLISHED** 1983
WHERE FUNDING CAN BE GIVEN Wiltshire and Swindon.
WHO CAN BENEFIT Charities, community organisations, parish or town councils for persons in Wiltshire and Swindon.
WHAT IS FUNDED Community, built heritage and environmental projects in the vicinity of landfill sites and/or landfill operator depots.
WHAT IS NOT FUNDED Running costs and staff costs are not normally eligible.
TYPE OF GRANT Project costs.
RANGE OF GRANTS Mostly £2,000 to £15,000.
SAMPLE GRANTS Wootton Bassett Cricket Club (£39,000); Salisbury Playhouse (£35,000); Chiseldon Tennis Club (£15,000); Atworth Children's Playground Regeneration (£13,500); Swindon Restore Carpark (£10,600); Devizes Canoe Club (£10,000).
FINANCES *Year* 2015/16 *Income* £1,984,219 *Grants* £1,480,128 *Grants to organisations* £1,480,128 *Assets* £1,599,918
TRUSTEES Jane James; Piers Dibbin; Dr Martin Hamer; Brian Clake; Edward Heard; Jane Rowell; Anthony Pooley; Peter Duke; Steven Boocock.
OTHER INFORMATION If you wish to apply for a Landfill Communities Fund grant, your project will need to find 10% of the total grant applied for from a contributing third party.
HOW TO APPLY In the first instance download and complete the expression of interest form from the website then email to grants@communityfirst.org.uk. If you have been advised that your project is eligible for LCF funding, then download and complete the application form on the website, and submit with supporting documents as specified in the form.
WHO TO APPLY TO Grants Team, Unit C2 Brecon Business Centre, Hopton Park, Devizes, Wiltshire SN10 2EY *Tel.* 01380 732802 *Email* grants@communityfirst.org.uk *Website* www.communityfirst.org.uk

■ The Douglas Compton James Charitable Trust

CC NO 1091125 **ESTABLISHED** 2002
WHERE FUNDING CAN BE GIVEN Northamptonshire.
WHO CAN BENEFIT Registered charities.
WHAT IS FUNDED General charitable purposes including: education and social welfare. Some preference is given for Masonic charities.
TYPE OF GRANT One-off and recurrent.
RANGE OF GRANTS Up to £27,000.
SAMPLE GRANTS Stephen Perse Foundation (£31,500); Wellingborough School (£16,300); Kettering Masonic Club and Nepal Earthquake (£10,000 each); KHG Charity Fund (£5,000)

Lakeland Day Care Hospice (£4,000); Samaritans – Northampton (£2,000); International Rescue Corps (£1,000).

FINANCES *Year* 2015/16 *Income* £116,692 *Grants* £138,616 *Grants to organisations* £138,616 *Assets* £5,420,817

TRUSTEES Ian Clarke; John Humphrey; Richard Ongley.

HOW TO APPLY Apply in writing to the correspondent.

WHO TO APPLY TO Louise Davies, Montague House, Chancery Lane, Thrapston, Northamptonshire NN14 4LN *Tel.* 01832 732161 *Email* louise.davies@vshlaw.co.uk

■ The Congregational & General Charitable Trust

CC NO 297013 **ESTABLISHED** 1987

WHERE FUNDING CAN BE GIVEN UK.

WHO CAN BENEFIT Protestant churches and community projects, in particular those associated with United Reformed and Congregational denominations.

WHAT IS FUNDED The overall care, upkeep and extension of churches; church community projects; promotion of the Christian religion and, in particular, the United Reformed and Congregational denominations, and other churches of the Protestant tradition.

TYPE OF GRANT One-off for property projects and capital costs.

RANGE OF GRANTS £1,000 to £10,000.

SAMPLE GRANTS A list of beneficiaries was not available.

FINANCES *Year* 2015 *Income* £212,000 *Grants* £118,000 *Grants to organisations* £142,000 *Assets* £27,205,000

TRUSTEES Revd Arnold Harrison; Margaret Atkinson; Revd William Adams; Pamela Ward; Jacqueline Haws; Gordon Pullan; John Holmes.

HOW TO APPLY Applications should be made using a form which can be downloaded from the trust's website. The website notes: 'You will need to attach your church accounts including balance sheet, and any documentation supporting the estimated cost of the project. Appeal leaflets and project literature will be helpful; but you must fill in all the details requested on the form. **It is not enough to write See attached document.** You may be refused a grant if the only accounts you submit are those for the project; or if you fail to show the church's capital assets, or any other grants you have received. The receipt of the Application Form will be acknowledged, preferably by email. Provide a contact email address, if possible. Otherwise we will use regular postal mail.'

WHO TO APPLY TO Trish Thorpe, Trust Administrator, PO Box 1111, Lincoln LN5 OWJ *Email* enquiries@candgtrust.org.uk *Website* www.candgtrust.org.uk

■ Martin Connell Charitable Trust

SC NO SC009842 **ESTABLISHED** 1972

WHERE FUNDING CAN BE GIVEN Scotland.

WHO CAN BENEFIT Local charities.

WHAT IS FUNDED General charitable purposes.

WHAT IS NOT FUNDED Individuals.

RANGE OF GRANTS £1,000 to £4,000.

SAMPLE GRANTS Roxburghe House – Aberdeen and YWCA (Young Women's Christian Association) (£4,000 each) Aberdeen Voluntary Service, Asthma UK Scotland, Citizens Theatre and Scottish Cot Death Trust (£2,000 each); The Eric Liddell Centre, Inspire, Motability, Scottish Ballet (£1,000 each).

FINANCES *Year* 2015/16 *Income* £271,000 *Grants* £271,000 *Grants to organisations* £307,000 *Assets* £7,612,930

OTHER INFORMATION The trust made 192 grants during the year.

HOW TO APPLY Apply in writing to the correspondent.

WHO TO APPLY TO The Trustees, c/o Maclay Murray and Spens LLP, 1 George Square, Glasgow G2 1AL *Tel.* 0330 222 0050

■ The Thomas Cook Children's Charity

CC NO 1091673 **ESTABLISHED** 2000

WHERE FUNDING CAN BE GIVEN UK and overseas.

WHO CAN BENEFIT Registered charities.

WHAT IS FUNDED Children's health and education.

RANGE OF GRANTS Up to £150,000.

SAMPLE GRANTS Alder Hey Children's Hospital (£150,000); CLIC Sargent (£100,000); Happy Days (£60,000); British Red Cross (£50,000); Designability (£42,500); Little Miracles (£22,000); SWAN UK (£18,000); Welfare Concern (£10,000); Park House School (£4,000); Carefree Kids (£1,500); ALD Life (£500).

FINANCES *Year* 2015 *Income* £864,644 *Grants* £1,158,544 *Grants to organisations* £1,158,544 *Assets* £1,008,861

TRUSTEES Chris Mottershead; Lee Bradley; Rachael Gillet; Jamie Queen; Simon Lindsay; Bill Scott; Matthew Harding.

OTHER INFORMATION Grants were broken down as follows: UK projects (£979,500); overseas projects (£179,000).

HOW TO APPLY The charity's website states: 'We welcome nominations for charities to support from both customers and staff.' To nominate a charity send an email to thomascook.childrenscharity@thomascook.com or complete the form on the charity's website.

WHO TO APPLY TO Aoife McDonogh, Charitable Relations Manager, Thomas Cook Ltd Unit 15–30, The Thomas Cook Business Park, Coningsby Road, Bretton, Peterborough PE3 8SB *Tel.* 01733 417436 *Email* thomascook.childrenscharity@thomascook.com *Website* thomascookchildrenscharity.com

■ The Ernest Cook Trust

CC NO 1146629 **ESTABLISHED** 1952

WHERE FUNDING CAN BE GIVEN UK.

WHO CAN BENEFIT State schools; registered charities; other recognised not-for-profit organisations.

WHAT IS FUNDED Grants are given for educational work only, focusing on children and young people in the fields of countryside and environment, the arts, science and literacy and numeracy.

WHAT IS NOT FUNDED Grants are not made: retrospectively; to pre-school groups, individuals, agricultural colleges, independent schools or local authorities; for building work, infrastructure or refurbishment work; for youth work, social support, therapy and medical treatment, including projects using the arts, environment or literacy and numeracy for these purposes; for projects related to sports, outward bound type activities or recreation; for overseas projects; for Wildlife Trusts and for Farming and Wildlife

Advisory Groups other than those which are based in counties in which the trust owns land (Buckinghamshire, Dorset, Gloucestershire, Leicestershire and Oxfordshire).

TYPE OF GRANT Conditional awards; annual and one-off awards; project grants; research; start-up costs. Funding may be given for up to three years.

RANGE OF GRANTS £500 to £10,000.

SAMPLE GRANTS National Portrait Gallery (£10,000); Eco Drama (£9,800); Cogges Heritage Trust (£9,000); Echo Echo Dance Theatre (£6,700); Architecture Centre (£6,000); Petroc (£4,900); Marine Conservation Research (£4,500); Clio's Company (£3,000); Great Chart Primary School (£2,200); Endelienta (£1,000).

FINANCES *Year* 2015/16 *Income* £4,363,145 *Grants* £1,849,253 *Grants to organisations* £1,849,253 *Assets* £132,958,118

TRUSTEE This charity has been given a dispensation by the Charity Commission from publishing the names of its trustees.

OTHER INFORMATION There were 540 grants awarded during the year. Grants were broken down as follows: environment (£663,500); arts, crafts and architecture (£609,000); literacy and STEM (£539,500); other (£36,500).

HOW TO APPLY The website states: 'There are no application forms. All applicants are asked to post a covering letter on the official headed paper of the applicant organisation (letters from schools must be signed by the headteacher) and also include: up to two additional sheets of A4 describing the organisation, outlining the project and specifying its educational elements and the way in which it fits in with the interests of the ECT [Ernest Cook Trust]; a simple budget for the project, outlining the way in which the grant would be spent; a list of any other funding applications; the latest annual report and accounts for the organisation (schools are not required to send one). Do not send further supporting material or email applications, which are not accepted. It is advisable to read the examples of projects supported before making an application. Questions (not applications) can be addressed to the Grants Administrator grants@ernestcooktrust.org.uk or on 01285 712492. Applications must be posted to: The Grants Administrator.'

WHO TO APPLY TO The Grants Administrator, The Estate Office, Fairford Park, Fairford, Gloucestershire GL7 4JH *Tel.* 01285 712492 *Email* grants@ernestcooktrust.org.uk *Website* www.ernestcooktrust.org.uk

■ The Cooks Charity

CC NO 297913 **ESTABLISHED** 1987

WHERE FUNDING CAN BE GIVEN UK, especially City of London.

WHO CAN BENEFIT Charities and individuals within the city of London.

WHAT IS FUNDED The advancement of the education and general welfare of persons who are associated with the catering trade; support of any charitable purpose associated with the City of London.

WHAT IS NOT FUNDED Individuals. Applicants outside the City of London (except in exceptional circumstances, when close proximity to London is required).

RANGE OF GRANTS £3,000 to £50,000.

SAMPLE GRANTS Academy of Culinary Arts (£49,000); Cooks Company Apprenticeship Programme (£24,000); Springboard (£19,000); Hackney Community College (£17,500); Treloar Trust (£14,500); Crisis Skylight Cafe (£3,300).

FINANCES *Year* 2015/16 *Income* £250,576 *Grants* £132,844 *Grants to organisations* £132,844 *Assets* £4,989,804

TRUSTEES Peter Wright, Bev Puxley; Oliver Goodinge; Graham Price.

HOW TO APPLY Apply in writing to the correspondent.

WHO TO APPLY TO Peter Wilkinson, 18 Solent Drive, Warsash, Southampton SO31 9HB *Tel.* 01489 579511 *Email* clerk@cookslivery.org.uk *Website* www.cookslivery.org.uk

■ The Catherine Cookson Charitable Trust

CC NO 272895 **ESTABLISHED** 1977

WHERE FUNDING CAN BE GIVEN UK, with a preference for the north east of England.

WHO CAN BENEFIT Charitable organisations, including those benefitting children and young people, individuals with disabilities and older people.

WHAT IS FUNDED General charitable purposes, including: education and training; medical causes, health and sickness; children and young people; religious activities; animal welfare; disability; art and culture.

SAMPLE GRANTS Cardioproof CIC (£150,000); Live Theatre (£100,000); The Early Birth Association (£60,000); Beamish Museum (£50,000); Northern Stage (£25,000); The Donkey Sanctuary (£5,000); Hearing Dogs for Deaf People (£1,000); British Forces Foundation (£250); South Tyneside Women's Aid (£100).

FINANCES *Year* 2015/16 *Income* £1,153,957 *Grants* £1,018,480 *Grants to organisations* £1,018,480 *Assets* £28,130,426

TRUSTEES Peter Magnay; David Hawkins; Hugo Marshall; Jack Ravenscroft; Daniel Sallows.

OTHER INFORMATION There were a total of 190 awards made during the year.

HOW TO APPLY Applications can be made in writing to the correspondent.

WHO TO APPLY TO Peter Magnay, Trustee, Thomas Magnay and Co., 8 St Mary's Green, Whickham, Newcastle upon Tyne NE16 4DN *Tel.* 0191 488 7459 *Email* enquiries@thomasmagnay.co.uk

■ The Keith Coombs Trust

CC NO 1149791 **ESTABLISHED** 2012

WHERE FUNDING CAN BE GIVEN UK, with a preference for the West Midlands.

WHO CAN BENEFIT Registered charities.

WHAT IS FUNDED General charitable purposes with a preference for children and young people and individuals with disabilities.

SAMPLE GRANTS A list of beneficiaries was not included in the accounts.

FINANCES *Year* 2015/16 *Income* £60,025 *Grants* £63,494 *Grants to organisations* £63,494 *Assets* £3,376

TRUSTEES Anthony Coombs; Graham Coombs; Demetrios Markou; Christine Ingram; John Hanson; Chris Redford.

HOW TO APPLY Apply in writing to the correspondent.

WHO TO APPLY TO Anthony Coombs, Trustee, c/o S. & U. PLC, 6 The Quadrangle, Cranmore Avenue, Solihull, West Midlands B90 4LE *Tel.* 0121 705 7777 *Email* christineingram@suplc.co.uk

■ Mabel Cooper Charity

CC NO 264621 **ESTABLISHED** 1972

WHERE FUNDING CAN BE GIVEN UK, with a possible interest in South Devon.

WHO CAN BENEFIT Registered charities.

WHAT IS FUNDED General charitable purposes. Preference is given to projects with low overheads.

WHAT IS NOT FUNDED Individuals.

SAMPLE GRANTS Devon Air Ambulance (£10,000); Alzheimer's Research UK, Crisis, Cancer Research, Macmillan Cancer Support, St Luke's Hospice and St Peter's Hospice (£5,000 each); Rowcroft House Foundation, Salvation Army, and Shelter (£2,500 each); CLIC Sargent and Future Trees Trust (£1,000 each).

FINANCES *Year* 2014/15 *Income* £89,877 *Grants* £60,000 *Grants to organisations* £60,000

TRUSTEES Ian Harbottle; David Harbottle; Alison Harbottle.

OTHER INFORMATION The 2014/15 accounts were the latest available at the time of writing (June 2017).

HOW TO APPLY The trustees have previously stated that they do not welcome, or reply to, unsolicited applications.

WHO TO APPLY TO Ian Harbottle, Trustee, Middle Manor, Lascot Hill, Wedmore BS28 4AF *Tel.* 01934 712102

■ The Alice Ellen Cooper Dean Charitable Foundation

CC NO 273298 **ESTABLISHED** 1977

WHERE FUNDING CAN BE GIVEN Worldwide, with a preference for UK charities in Dorset and West Hampshire.

WHO CAN BENEFIT Registered charities.

WHAT IS FUNDED General charitable purposes; overseas aid.

WHAT IS NOT FUNDED Individuals; charitable entities not registered in the UK.

TYPE OF GRANT One-off and recurring.

RANGE OF GRANTS Up to £100,000.

SAMPLE GRANTS Dorset County Hospital NHS Foundation Trust (£103,000); Townsend Youth Partnership (£30,000); Dorchester Agricultural Society (£20,000); Inspire Foundation (£15,000); Scope (£5,000); Happy Days Children's' Society (£3,000); Poole Arts Trust (£2,000); National Childbirth Trust (£1,000).

FINANCES *Year* 2015/16 *Income* £1,252,359 *Grants* £1,202,000 *Grants to organisations* £1,202,000 *Assets* £28,774,874

TRUSTEES Linda Bowditch; Douglas Neville-Jones; Rupert Edwards; John Bowditch; Alastair Cowen.

OTHER INFORMATION Grants were broken down as follows: charities based in Dorset and West Hampshire (£722,500); national charitable bodies benefitting the residents of Dorset and West Hampshire (£283,000); UK charitable bodies for overseas projects (£94,500).

HOW TO APPLY Apply in writing to the correspondent. The foundation considers applications for funding of projects and appeals from local and national charitable bodies registered with the Charity Commission. Applicants are asked to provide a summary of the project together with costings, financial accounts and details of fundraising activities.

WHO TO APPLY TO Rupert Edwards, Trustee, Unity Chambers, 34 High East Street, Dorchester, Dorset DT1 1HA *Tel.* 01305 251333 *Email* rupertedwards@edwardsandkeeping.co.uk

■ The Marjorie Coote Animal Charity Trust

CC NO 208493 **ESTABLISHED** 1954

WHERE FUNDING CAN BE GIVEN Worldwide.

WHO CAN BENEFIT Registered charities for the benefit of animals.

WHAT IS FUNDED The care and protection of horses, dogs and other animals and birds.

WHAT IS NOT FUNDED Individuals.

TYPE OF GRANT One-off and recurrent.

RANGE OF GRANTS Grants are usually in the range of £250 to £20,000.

SAMPLE GRANTS Animal Health Trust (£20,000); Support Dogs (£10,000); The Barn Owl Trust (£7,000); Elephant Family and Tusk Trust (£2,000 each); Animals in Asia (£1,000); Devon Wildlife Trust and International Otter Survival Fund (£500 each); Greatwood (£250).

FINANCES *Year* 2015/16 *Income* £149,477 *Grants* £128,500 *Grants to organisations* £128,500 *Assets* £3,604,188

TRUSTEES Jill Holah; Lady Neil; Nicola Baguley; Sarah Neill.

HOW TO APPLY Apply in writing to the correspondent. The 2015/16 accounts state: 'The Trustees usually meet in Autumn each year to consider appeals, which should be submitted during the month of September. Appeals received at other times of the year are deferred until the following Autumn unless they require consideration for an urgent "one-off" grant for a specific project.'

WHO TO APPLY TO Mrs Jill P. Holah, Trustee, End Cottage, Terrington, York YO60 6PU *Email* j.holah@mcacharity.org.uk

■ The Marjorie Coote Old People's Charity

CC NO 226747 **ESTABLISHED** 1958

WHERE FUNDING CAN BE GIVEN South Yorkshire.

WHO CAN BENEFIT Charitable organisations which work actively for the benefit of old people in the area of jurisdiction.

WHAT IS FUNDED Older people.

WHAT IS NOT FUNDED Individuals.

RANGE OF GRANTS Up to £15,000.

SAMPLE GRANTS St Luke's Hospice (£15,000); Sheffield Dial-A-Ride (£10,000); Age UK Barnsley (£5,000); British Red Cross (£2,000); Sheffield Hospitals Charity (£1,000); Deafblind UK (£500); The Almshouse Association (£200).

FINANCES *Year* 2015/16 *Income* £126,483 *Grants* £107,200 *Grants to organisations* £107,200 *Assets* £3,174,970

TRUSTEES Lady Neill; Mrs J. A. Lee; Mr N. J. A. Hutton; Dr Caroline Lawrenson; Sarah Neill.

HOW TO APPLY Apply in writing to the correspondent during May. Appeals received at other times of the year are deferred unless for an urgent grant for a specific one-off project.

WHO TO APPLY TO Lady Neill, Trustee, Barn Cottage, Lindrick Common, Worksop S81 8BA *Email* neillcharities@me.com

■ The Helen Jean Cope Trust

CC NO 1125937 **ESTABLISHED** 1998

WHERE FUNDING CAN BE GIVEN East Midlands.

WHO CAN BENEFIT Registered charities only.

WHAT IS FUNDED General charitable purposes, supporting single projects.

WHAT IS NOT FUNDED Individuals; unregistered charities.

TYPE OF GRANT Generally single projects; capital and core costs.
RANGE OF GRANTS £500 to £5,000.
SAMPLE GRANTS Anthony Nolan Trust, Bradgate Park Trust, Steps, Twenty Twenty (£5,000 each); Marie Curie Cancer Care (£4,000); Charnwood Toys, Derbyshire Leicestershire Rutland Air Ambulance, Peter Le Marchant Trust, 1st Rothley Scout Group (£2,500 each); Nottingham Music School, Shepshed Volunteer Centre, St Peter's Church – Redmile, Veronica House Project (£1,000 each); Selston Music Festival, St Botolph's Church Shepshed, (£500 each).
FINANCES *Year* 2015 *Income* £94,837 *Grants* £140,000 *Grants to organisations* £140,000
TRUSTEES Alan Roberts; Malcolm Carrington; Graham Freckelton; Lindsay Brydson.
OTHER INFORMATION The charity's accounts were not available to view on the Charity Commission's website. We have therefore had to estimate the grant total.
HOW TO APPLY Apply in writing to the correspondent including the following: the full name and address of the charity to which correspondence should be sent and cheques made payable in the event of a grant being made; your charity number; a brief description of your charity and its activities if this is a first application; what the grant is for; who will benefit; how much any specific items will cost; other fundraising activities being carried out and the amount raised so far; a set of audited accounts where available; a copy of your reserves policy. The trustees meet about five times a year.
WHO TO APPLY TO The Trustees, 1 Woodgate, Loughborough, Leicestershire LE11 2TY *Tel.* 01509 218298 *Email* info@thehelenjeancopecharity.co.uk *Website* www.thehelenjeancopecharity.co.uk

■ The J. Reginald Corah Foundation Fund

CC NO 220792 **ESTABLISHED** 1953
WHERE FUNDING CAN BE GIVEN Leicester, Leicestershire and Rutland.
WHO CAN BENEFIT Charitable organisations. However, particular favour is given to hosiery firms carrying out their business in the city or county of Leicester and Rutland.
WHAT IS FUNDED Children; disability; education; medical causes; social welfare; special needs.
WHAT IS NOT FUNDED Applications from individuals are not considered unless made by, or supported by, a recognised charitable organisation.
TYPE OF GRANT One-off and recurrent.
SAMPLE GRANTS LOROS (£2,000); Air Ambulance (£1,700); British Red Cross (£1,600); Jubilee Sailing Trust (£1,500); Mobility Trust (£1,300).
FINANCES *Year* 2015/16 *Income* £124,352 *Grants* £99,965 *Grants to organisations* £99,965 *Assets* £4,630,014
TRUSTEES Geoffrey Makings; David Corah; Roger Bowder.
OTHER INFORMATION There were 100 grants made during the year. Grants were broken down as follows: welfare in the community (£18,600); special needs (£16,100); medical/disability (£15,500); children's organisations (£11,600); education (£9,000).
HOW TO APPLY Apply in writing to the correspondent. The trustees meet about every two months.
WHO TO APPLY TO Hannah Makings-Hone, Clerk, The Park House, Glaston Park, Spring Lane, Glaston LE15 9BW *Tel.* 01572 824000 *Email* gsmfambus@btconnect.com

■ The Worshipful Company of Cordwainers Charitable Trusts (Minges Gift and the Pooled Trusts)

CC NO 266073 **ESTABLISHED** 1972
WHERE FUNDING CAN BE GIVEN UK, with some preference for the City of London.
WHO CAN BENEFIT Registered charities; educational establishments; hospitals; churches; organisations associated with the shoe and leather trade; individuals.
WHAT IS FUNDED General charitable purposes; medical causes; disability; education and training; disadvantaged individuals; fashion and shoemaking industries; blind and partially sighted people; servicemen and women.
TYPE OF GRANT Grants of up to, and in some cases over, three years; core costs; projects; research; recurring costs; start-up costs may be considered.
RANGE OF GRANTS £100 to £20,000.
SAMPLE GRANTS University of Northampton (£20,000); Guildhall School of Music and Drama (£10,000); Footwear Friends (£7,500); Royal Marsden Cancer Charity (£5,000); British Footwear Development Trust (£4,500); SSAFA (£3,500); Fusiliers Aid Society (£2,500); Blind Veterans UK (£2,000); St Mary Magdalene – Enfield (£600); City of London Guildhall Library (£250).
FINANCES *Year* 2015/16 *Income* £288,389 *Grants* £178,141 *Grants to organisations* £158,441 *Assets* £4,401,028
TRUSTEES Patrick Peal; Jeremy Blanford; Jonathan Hooper.
OTHER INFORMATION In 2015/16 a total of £19,700 was given to individuals (£9,000 from Minge's Gift and £10,700 from Pooled Trusts). Grants were made to 38 organisations during the year.
HOW TO APPLY Apply in writing to the correspondent.
WHO TO APPLY TO John Miller, Secretary, The Cordwainers' Company, Clothworkers' Hall, Dunster Court, Mincing Lane, London EC3R 7AH *Tel.* 020 7929 1121 *Email* office@cordwainers.org *Website* www.cordwainers.org

■ The Gershon Coren Charitable Foundation

CC NO 257615 **ESTABLISHED** 1968
WHERE FUNDING CAN BE GIVEN UK and the financially developing countries.
WHO CAN BENEFIT Charitable organisations, particularly Jewish organisations.
WHAT IS FUNDED General charitable purposes; social welfare; Jewish causes.
RANGE OF GRANTS Up to £120,000.
SAMPLE GRANTS Muriel and Gershon Coren Charitable Foundation (£2.1 million); Gategi Village Self Help Group (£120,000); South Aliyah Child Rescue (£40,000); JNF Charitable Trust and MANNA UK (£30,000 each); J Trails (£9,000); Aish UK and Centre for Jewish Life (£5,000 each); Kisharon (£2,000); St John Ambulance (£1,000).
FINANCES *Year* 2015/16 *Income* £279,975 *Grants* £2,443,520 *Grants to organisations* £2,443,520 *Assets* £279,957
TRUSTEES Walter Stanton; Anthony Coren; Muriel Coren.

OTHER INFORMATION A grant of £2.1 million was made to The Muriel and Gershon Coren Charitable Foundation (Charity Commission no. 1160879).

HOW TO APPLY Apply in writing to the correspondent.

WHO TO APPLY TO Muriel Cohen, Trustee, 5 Golders Park Close, London NW11 7QR *Email* graham.weinberg@mhllp.co.uk

■ Michael Cornish Charitable Trust

CC NO 1107890 **ESTABLISHED** 2005

WHERE FUNDING CAN BE GIVEN UK and overseas, with preference of Lincolnshire.

WHO CAN BENEFIT Registered charities, individual supported only in exceptional circumstances. Preference for charities in the Lincolnshire area and charities involving children.

WHAT IS FUNDED General charitable purposes including: children/young people; people with disabilities; economic/community development; amateur sport; advancement of health or saving lives.

TYPE OF GRANT Project funding.

RANGE OF GRANTS £250 to £2,500.

SAMPLE GRANTS Pelican Trust (£2,500); Family Action, My Aware, Whizz-Kidz and Young Minds (£1,000 each); Children's Link and Emily Harris Foundation (£500 each); Bransby Horses Rest Home and Cancer Research (£250 each).

FINANCES *Year* 2015 *Income* £79,540 *Grants* £88,627 *Grants to organisations* £88,627 *Assets* £16,381,510

TRUSTEES Michael Cornish; Harriet Cornish; Richard Vigar.

HOW TO APPLY Applications can be made through the trust's website. The website states: 'Applications are reviewed quarterly in March, June, September and December. Once you submit an application you will receive an email confirming the date your application will be reviewed. We will confirm the outcome of your application within 30 days of the given review date.'

WHO TO APPLY TO Mrs Philippa Cridland, Trust Administrator, Michael Cornish Charitable Trust, c/o Wright Vigar Ltd, 15 Newland, Lincoln, Lincolnshire LN1 1XG *Tel.* 01522 531341 *Email* phillipa.cridland@wrightvigar.co.uk

■ The Evan Cornish Foundation

CC NO 1112703 **ESTABLISHED** 2005

WHERE FUNDING CAN BE GIVEN Worldwide; UK with a preference for: Northumberland, Cumbria, Durham, Yorkshire, Lancashire, Cheshire, Derbyshire, Nottinghamshire, Lincolnshire, Rutland, Shropshire, Staffordshire, Leicestershire, West Midlands, Norfolk, northern parts of Cambridgeshire.

WHO CAN BENEFIT Charities; not-for-profits; CICs.

WHAT IS FUNDED Human rights; social and economic inequality; education; health; criminal justice system; older people; refugees and asylum seekers; homelessness. International applications will be prioritised which: promote tolerance and equality for women; combat human rights violations. International applicants must have a registered UK office.

WHAT IS NOT FUNDED Building work or repairs; political activities and purpose; animal welfare; medical research; individuals/gap year students; holiday club providers. Religious organisations/religious or evangelical causes – the trustees will not consider applications: for projects that promote or evangelise any particular faith; from organisations whose goals include the promotion of their faith; from organisations who discriminate internally or externally based on faith. The trustees will consider applications from organisations that grew from a religious basis but now have a multi-faith and secular approach. Organisations must not discriminate on the grounds of faith. Trustees, staff, volunteers and beneficiaries should not be required to be of any particular faith. Organisations should work with people of all faiths as well as those with no faith.

TYPE OF GRANT Project funding.

RANGE OF GRANTS Up to £35,000 but normally £1,000 to £10,000. First time applicants should not apply for more than £5,000.

SAMPLE GRANTS Doctors of the World (£35,500); Age UK (£15,000); Asylum Aid (£10,000); Freedom From Torture (£8,000); Excellent Development (£7,000); Motivation (£6,500); Practical Action (£5,000); Vista (£3,500); Jericho House Productions (£2,500); Dukes (£1,000).

FINANCES *Year* 2015/16 *Income* £266,097 *Grants* £1,209,693 *Grants to organisations* £1,209,693 *Assets* £10,767,885

TRUSTEES Rachel Cornish; Barbara Ward; Sally Cornish.

OTHER INFORMATION Organisations with projects in other areas of England or the UK may still apply if their project: is unique in the UK; involves advocacy/policy work; or affects people in the UK prison system.

HOW TO APPLY Applications can be made through the foundation's website. Applicants should submit: a copy of your most recent accounts; a copy of your project budge; details of an independent, UK-based referee, not affiliated to your organisation; supporting information about your project. The trustees meet three times per years. Check the website for application deadlines.

WHO TO APPLY TO Rachel Cornish, Trustee, The Innovation Centre, 217 Portobello, Sheffield S1 4DP *Tel.* 0114 224 2230 *Email* contactus@evancornishfoundation.org.uk *Website* www.evancornishfoundation.org.uk

■ Cornwall Community Foundation

CC NO 1099977 **ESTABLISHED** 2003

WHERE FUNDING CAN BE GIVEN Cornwall and the Isles of Scilly.

WHO CAN BENEFIT Registered charities; voluntary or community groups; social enterprises; individuals.

WHAT IS FUNDED Disadvantage; exclusion; poverty.

WHAT IS NOT FUNDED Profit-making organisations including CICs limited by shares; statutory/public sector organisations such as health authorities, schools, hospitals, parish or town councils; award-making organisations or bodies who fundraise or distribute grants on behalf of other organisations; regional offices of national bodies if they are not independent, i.e. you must have your own local accounts and management committee; groups whose beneficiaries are not people; projects that help only one individual; groups that have had a previous grant which has not been managed satisfactorily; works or equipment already committed, bought or completed (including trips); projects where beneficiaries live outside Cornwall or the Isles of Scilly; unspecified expenditure; projects primarily for the advancement of religion or politics.

SAMPLE GRANTS The Frederick Foundation (£91,000); Goonhilly Wind Farm Community Fund (£48,000); Wellbeing and Prevention (£27,700), Winter Fuel Payments Fund (£21,000); The Lord and Lady St Levan Fund (£19,000); Caradon Area Community Fund (£11,500); Lord Lieutenant's Fund for Youth (£8,500); Benefitting Older People (£3,000); The Cornwall Crimebeat Fund (£1,100); Albert Van Den Bergh/Jane Hartley Fund (£320).
FINANCES *Year* 2015 *Income* £769,246 *Grants* £504,872 *Grants to organisations* £504,872 *Assets* £4,021,708
TRUSTEES Deborah Hinton; Philip Reed; The Hon. Evelyn Boscawen; The Lady Mary Holborow; Jane Hartley; James Williams; Daphne Skinnard; John Ede; Lady George; Tim Smith; Elaine Hunt; Mark Mitchell; Nicola Marquis; Meg Weir; Toby Ashworth.
HOW TO APPLY Applications should be made via a form available from the foundation. For general information about grants contact the grants team (tel.: 01566 779333 or email: grants@cornwallfoundation.com). Criteria, guidelines and application process are also posted on the foundation's website.
WHO TO APPLY TO Donna Wheadon, Grants Officer, Suite 1, Sheers Barton Barns, Lawhitton, Launceston, Cornwall PL15 9NJ *Tel.* 01566 779333/779865 *Email* office@cornwallfoundation.com *Website* www.cornwallfoundation.com

■ The Duke of Cornwall's Benevolent Fund

CC NO 269183 **ESTABLISHED** 1975
WHERE FUNDING CAN BE GIVEN Cornwall.
WHO CAN BENEFIT Charitable organisations.
WHAT IS FUNDED The relief of people in need of assistance because of sickness, poverty or age; the provision of almshouses, homes of rest, hospitals and convalescent homes; the advancement of education; the advancement of the arts and religion; and the preservation for the benefit of the public of lands and buildings.
WHAT IS NOT FUNDED Individuals.
TYPE OF GRANT One-off.
RANGE OF GRANTS Up to £35,000 but generally £1,000 to £10,000.
SAMPLE GRANTS Cornwall Community Foundation (£35,000); Cornwall Historic Churches and Cornish Red Squirrel Project (£15,000 each); Farm Cornwall (£10,000); Soil Association (£2,500); Surf Life Saving GB (£2,000); Friends of Bude Sea Pool (£1,500); Hearing Loss Cornwall, Plantlife and Helford River Children's Sailing Trust (£1,000 each).
FINANCES *Year* 2015/16 *Income* £290,463 *Grants* £126,800 *Grants to organisations* £126,800 *Assets* £4,311,377
TRUSTEES Col. Edward Bolitho; The Hon. James Leigh-Pemberton; Alastair Martin; Catherine Mead.
OTHER INFORMATION Grants under £1,000 totalled £20,000.
HOW TO APPLY Apply in writing to the correspondent.
WHO TO APPLY TO Terry Cotter, Duchy of Cornwall, 10 Buckingham Gate, London SW1E 6LA *Tel.* 020 7834 7346

■ The Cornwell Charitable Trust

CC NO 1012467 **ESTABLISHED** 1992
WHERE FUNDING CAN BE GIVEN Cornwall.
WHO CAN BENEFIT Registered charities; individuals.
WHAT IS FUNDED General charitable purposes, funding projects and individuals specifically and primarily in the Cornwall area.
WHAT IS NOT FUNDED Travel; expeditions; university grants.
TYPE OF GRANT Project and capital.
RANGE OF GRANTS Up to £50,000 – the majority are for £1,000 or less.
SAMPLE GRANTS Save the Children (£52,000); Age UK Cornwall (£30,000); Lincoln College Oxford (£25,000); Hemoglobin (£5,000); Little Harbour Children's Hospice South West and Macmillan Cancer Support (£1,000 each).
FINANCES *Year* 2015/16 *Income* £50,852 *Grants* £121,540 *Grants to organisations* £120,890 *Assets* £1,342,237
TRUSTEES David Cornwell; Valerie Cornwell; Mark Bailey; Matthew Bennett.
OTHER INFORMATION The amount of grants given to individuals totalled £650.
HOW TO APPLY Apply in writing to the correspondent.
WHO TO APPLY TO Mark Bailey, Trustee, Devonshire House, 1 Devonshire Street, London W1W 5DR *Tel.* 020 7304 2000 *Email* cw@citroenwells.co.uk

■ The Corporation of Trinity House of Deptford Strond

CC NO 211869 **ESTABLISHED** 1685
WHERE FUNDING CAN BE GIVEN England and Wales.
WHO CAN BENEFIT Registered charities; hospitals.
WHAT IS FUNDED Social welfare and training for seafarers; maritime safety and education.
RANGE OF GRANTS £5,000 to £165,000.
SAMPLE GRANTS Jubilee Sailing Trust (£165,000); Marine Society and Sea Scouts (£100,000); The Scout Association (£48,000); Merchant Navy Welfare Board (£40,000); Royal Liverpool Seaman's Orphan Institution (£32,000); Royal Naval Benevolent Trust (£10,000); Hospital of Sir John Hawkins (£5,000).
FINANCES *Year* 2015/16 *Income* £8,841,000 *Grants* £1,054,000 *Grants to organisations* £1,054,000 *Assets* £263,136,000
TRUSTEES Capt. Nigel Palmer; Capt. Ian McNaught; Cdre William Walworth; Capt. Roget Barker; Rear Admiral David Snelson; Capt. Nigel Hope; Capt. Stephen Gobbi; Richard Sadler; Malcolm Glaister.
HOW TO APPLY Apply in writing to the correspondent.
WHO TO APPLY TO Graham Hockley, Trinity House, Tower Hill, London EC3N 4DH *Tel.* 020 7481 6900 *Email* graham.hockley@thls.org *Website* www.trinityhouse.co.uk

■ The Costa Family Charitable Trust

CC NO 221604 **ESTABLISHED** 1964
WHERE FUNDING CAN BE GIVEN UK.
WHO CAN BENEFIT Christian organisations.
WHAT IS FUNDED Religious charities; charities with which the trustees have some connection.
RANGE OF GRANTS Up to £200,000.
SAMPLE GRANTS Alpha International (£200,000); Holy Trinity – Brompton (£13,500); Light and The Philo Trust (£5,000 each); Royal Academy of Arts (£1,200); Emmaus Church and Queen College (£500 each): The Toy Trust (£250);

Africa Foundation and The Amber Trust (£100 each).

FINANCES *Year* 2015/16 *Income* £312,900 *Grants* £246,215 *Grants to organisations* £237,675 *Assets* £102,768

TRUSTEES Kenneth Costa; Ann Costa.

HOW TO APPLY The trust's Charity Commission record states that: 'No funding requests are solicited or acknowledged.'

WHO TO APPLY TO Kenneth Costa, Trustee, 43 Chelsea Square, London SW3 6LH *Tel.* 07785 467441

■ The Cotton Industry War Memorial Trust

CC NO 242721 **ESTABLISHED** 1947

WHERE FUNDING CAN BE GIVEN UK.

WHO CAN BENEFIT Individuals and organisations.

WHAT IS FUNDED This trust makes grants to all aspects of aid and assistance to employees, former employees and students of the textile industry.

RANGE OF GRANTS Up to £40,000.

SAMPLE GRANTS The Society of Dyers and Colourists (£45,000); Lancashire Textile Manufacturers' Association (£40,000); Children's Adventure Farm Trust (£30,000); Participation Works (£17,500); Orchid (£5,000); Save Our Soldier (£3,000); Caudwell Children (£1,500).

FINANCES *Year* 2016 *Income* £332,384 *Grants* £184,267 *Grants to organisations* £184,267 *Assets* £7,130,587

TRUSTEES Christopher Trotter; Prof. Lockett; Keith Garbett; Peter Reid; Philip Roberts; Dr Michael Bartle; George Pope; Alan Robinson.

HOW TO APPLY Apply in writing to the correspondent. The trust meets at least four times a year to consider requests for funds and grants.

WHO TO APPLY TO Peter Booth, Stables Barn, Coldstones Farm, Bewerley, Harrogate, North Yorkshire HG3 5BJ *Tel.* 01423 711205

■ The Cotton Trust

CC NO 1094776 **ESTABLISHED** 1956

WHERE FUNDING CAN BE GIVEN UK and overseas.

WHO CAN BENEFIT UK-registered charities.

WHAT IS FUNDED Community and welfare; education (non-UK); medical causes and disability; overseas aid; respite.

TYPE OF GRANT Project funding and capital costs.

RANGE OF GRANTS The majority of grants are between £250 and £2,000.

SAMPLE GRANTS Leicester Charity Link (£30,500); Merlin (£25,000); Camfed (£15,000); Earl Shilton Social Institute, British Red Cross, Save The Children and Concern Worldwide (£5,000 each); Cecily's Fund and Queen Alexandra Hospital Home (£2,000 each); Computer Aid International, Health Poverty Action and Resolve International (£1,000 each); Special Toys Educational Postal Service, Strongbones Children's Charitable Trust and Inter Care (£500 each); Orcadia Creative Learning Centre (£250); Leysian Mission (£10).

FINANCES *Year* 2015/16 *Income* £205,326 *Grants* £196,334 *Grants to organisations* £196,334 *Assets* £6,519,464

TRUSTEES Joanne Congdon; Erica Cotton; Tenney Cotton.

OTHER INFORMATION A total of 111 organisations were supported through 118 grants. Grants to projects overseas totalled £112,000 and grants to UK charities totalled £84,000.

HOW TO APPLY Apply in writing to the correspondent.

WHO TO APPLY TO Joanne Burgess, Trustee, PO Box 6895, Earl Shilton, Leicester LE9 8ZE *Tel.* 01455 440917

■ The Coulthurst Trust

CC NO 209690 **ESTABLISHED** 1947

WHERE FUNDING CAN BE GIVEN North Yorkshire.

WHO CAN BENEFIT Registered charities.

WHAT IS FUNDED Principally to make recurring donations to specific charities, with surplus funds being used towards the support of specific charitable objects in the North Yorkshire area and then, at discretion, occasionally funding will be provided towards UK appeals.

SAMPLE GRANTS Cleveland Bay Horse Society, Riding for the Disabled Association (£2,000 each); Craven Trust, Heather Trust, RNLI, Trustees of the Gregory Village Hall, and St Andrew's Church – Gargrave (£1,000 each); Dales Care (£500).

FINANCES *Year* 2014/15 *Income* £33,747 *Grants* £53,078 *Grants to organisations* £53,078

TRUSTEES Michael Fenwick; Robert Forster; Iain Henderson.

OTHER INFORMATION The 2014/15 accounts were the latest available at the time of writing (June 2017).

HOW TO APPLY Apply in writing to the correspondent. The 2014/15 annual report states: 'The trustees identify registered charitable organisations as appropriate recipients of funds, but may also choose to donate to local charitable projects. Charitable donations are grants without condition. The Trust does not advertise in the press for applications.'

WHO TO APPLY TO Robert Foster, Foster Law, The North Barn, Broughton Hall, Skipton BD23 3AE *Tel.* 01756 700110 *Email* mail@fosterlawsolicitors.com

■ Country Houses Foundation

CC NO 1111049 **ESTABLISHED** 2005

WHERE FUNDING CAN BE GIVEN England.

WHO CAN BENEFIT Registered charities; building preservation trusts; private owners.

WHAT IS FUNDED The repair and conservation of rural historic buildings and structures located in England and Wales, including where appropriate their gardens, grounds and outbuildings.

WHAT IS NOT FUNDED According to the foundation's website grants are not offered for the following: 'buildings and structures which have been the subject of recent purchase and where the cost of works for which grant is sought should have been recognised in the purchase price paid; projects which do not principally involve the repair or conservation of a historic building or structure; churches and chapels unless now or previously linked to a country house or estate; alterations and improvements, and repairs to non historic fabric or services; routine maintenance and minor repairs; general running costs; demolition unless agreed as part of a repair and conservation programme; rent, loan or mortgage payments; conservation of furniture, fittings and equipment except where they are themselves of historic or architectural significance, have a historic relationship with the site, are relevant to the project, and can be secured long term from sale or disposal; work carried out before a grant offer has been made in writing and accepted'.

RANGE OF GRANTS £2,500 to £76,500.

SAMPLE GRANTS Bramall Hall and Castle Drogo (£60,000 each); Millichope Park (£45,000); Prior Park College (£38,500); Felton Park (£28,000); Plumpton Rocks (£22,000); Watton Priory (£18,000); Heritage Alliance and Woodchester Mansion (£2,000 each); Lullingstone Castle (£1,000).

FINANCES *Year* 2015/16 *Income* £307,286 *Grants* £897,751 *Grants to organisations* £897,751 *Assets* £11,501,193

TRUSTEES Oliver Pearcey; Nicholas Barber; Michael Clifton; Norman Hudson; Christopher Taylor; Sir John Parsons; Mary King.

HOW TO APPLY Refer to the foundation's very helpful website for full information on how to make an application. The foundation requires applicants to complete a pre-application form to confirm that projects fit its criteria. Pre-application forms and application forms can be downloaded from the foundation's website.

WHO TO APPLY TO David Price, Secretary, Sheephouse Farm, Uley Road, Dursley, Gloucestershire GL11 5AD *Tel.* 0845 402 4102 *Email* info@countryhousesfoundation.org.uk *Website* www.countryhousesfoundation.org.uk

■ The County Council of Dyfed Welsh Church Fund

CC NO 506583 **ESTABLISHED** 1977

WHERE FUNDING CAN BE GIVEN Carmarthenshire, Ceredigion and Pembrokeshire.

WHO CAN BENEFIT Churches; chapels; registered charities; individuals.

WHAT IS FUNDED Grants are mainly awarded towards the costs of maintaining places of worship. Funding is also given to registered charities which benefit local residents.

TYPE OF GRANT One-off and recurrent; project costs; capital costs; core costs.

RANGE OF GRANTS £1,000 to £10,000.

SAMPLE GRANTS Antioch Christian Centre and St Twrog's Church (£10,000 each); HUTS (£8,000); St Dogmael's Church (£5,000); Tabor Baptist Church (£4,200); Splat Development Committee and St John's Church (£3,000 each); St David's Church Bettws (£1,700); Aberystwyth Swimming Club (£1,600).

FINANCES *Year* 2015/16 *Income* £92,048 *Grants* £195,075 *Grants to organisations* £195,075 *Assets* £4,661,197

TRUSTEE Selected members of Carmarthenshire, Ceredigion and Pembrokeshire County Councils.

OTHER INFORMATION Grants were split between three regional areas – Carmarthenshire; Ceredigion and Pembrokeshire.

HOW TO APPLY Apply in writing to the correspondent.

WHO TO APPLY TO Anthony Parnell, Resources Department, Carmarthenshire County Council, County Hall, Carmarthen, Dyfed SA31 1JP *Tel.* 01267 224180 *Email* AParnell@carmarthenshire.gov.uk *Website* www.carmarthenshire.gov.uk

■ The Augustine Courtauld Trust

CC NO 226217 **ESTABLISHED** 1956

WHERE FUNDING CAN BE GIVEN UK with a preference for Essex.

WHO CAN BENEFIT Registered charities benefitting people in Essex; organisations involved in polar exploration.

WHAT IS FUNDED Grants are made to charities within Essex, to help disadvantaged people (particularly the young), to help conservation in the county and to support Artic and Antarctic expeditions.

WHAT IS NOT FUNDED Individuals; individual churches for fabric repairs or maintenance.

TYPE OF GRANT One-off grants for projects and core costs, which may be made for multiple years if an application is submitted for each year.

RANGE OF GRANTS £500 to £9,000.

SAMPLE GRANTS Gino Watkins Memorial Fund (£9,000); Essex Boys and Girls Trust (£6,000); The Cirdan Sailing Trust (£5,000); The Daws Hall Trust and The Stubbers Adventure Centre (£2,000); Essex Planning Fields Association (£1,000); Braintree Youth Project, Families in Focus, SNAP and The Conservation Volunteers (£500 each).

FINANCES *Year* 2015/16 *Income* £51,758 *Grants* £47,000 *Grants to organisations* £47,000 *Assets* £1,267,764

TRUSTEES Julien Courtauld; Derek Fordham; Sir A. Dennison Smith; Lord John Petre; Thomas Courtauld; Bruce Ballard; The Rt Revd Stephen Cottrell.

OTHER INFORMATION This trust was founded in 1956 by Augustine Courtauld, an Arctic explorer who was proud of his Essex roots. His charitable purpose was simple: 'My idea is to make available something that will do some good.'

HOW TO APPLY Applications must be submitted via the online form on the trust's website. Written applications will not be accepted.

WHO TO APPLY TO Bruce Ballard, Birkett Long Solicitors, Essex House, 42 Crouch Street, Colchester CO3 3HH *Tel.* 01206 217300 *Email* bruce.ballard@birkettlong.co.uk *Website* www.augustinecourtauldtrust.org

■ Coutts Charitable Foundation

CC NO 1150784 **ESTABLISHED** 2013

WHERE FUNDING CAN BE GIVEN UK.

WHO CAN BENEFIT Charitable organisations.

WHAT IS FUNDED The foundation's focus is supporting UK organisations or programmes that support women and girls, with a particular focus on addressing the causes and consequences of poverty. It is especially interested in organisations that are developing innovative solutions and/or those whose successful work has the potential to be scaled up.

RANGE OF GRANTS £5,000 to £150,000.

SAMPLE GRANTS Citizens UK (£150,000); Southall Black Sisters Trust (£120,000); Working Chance (£105,000); Safe Lives Ltd and The Fairlight Trust Anawim (£90,000 each); End Violence Against Women Coalition and Women For Refugee Women (£75,000 each); Women Centre Calderdale and Kirklees (£30,000); Sentebale (£20,000); City Gateway (£10,000).

FINANCES *Year* 2015/16 *Income* £1,156,874 *Grants* £855,052 *Grants to organisations* £855,052 *Assets* £2,875,149

TRUSTEES Sir Christopher Geidt; Dr Linda Yueh; Lord Waldegrave of North Hill; Leslie Gent; Michael Morley; Ali Hammad; Alison Rose-Slade; Thomas Kenrick; Peter Flavel; Camilla Stowell.

OTHER INFORMATION Grants were made to 11 organisations.

HOW TO APPLY The foundation does not accept unsolicited applications. However, if you wish to bring your organisation to the foundation's attention there is a information submission form which can be downloaded from the website and emailed or posted to the correspondent. The foundation will then be in touch if they wish to learn more about your organisation.

WHO TO APPLY TO Stella Musham, Coutts & Co., Strand, 440 London WC2R 0QS *Tel.* 020 7957 2822 *Email* coutts.foundation@coutts.com *Website* www.coutts.com/coutts-foundation.html

■ General Charity of Coventry

CC NO 216235 **ESTABLISHED** 1983

WHERE FUNDING CAN BE GIVEN Within the boundary of the City of Coventry.

WHO CAN BENEFIT Charitable organisations benefitting residents of Coventry.

WHAT IS FUNDED Social welfare; health; medical causes; education.

SAMPLE GRANTS The David Scott's Coventry Jubilee Community Care Trust (£100,000); Warwickshire and Northampton Air Ambulance (£70,000); Coventry Sports Foundation (£20,000); Relate Coventry (£6,000); Coventry Music Museum (£5,600); Coventry Godiva Harriers (£5,000); The Light House Christian Care Ministry (£3,000); St Andrew's Church (£1,500); Hillfields Readers Group (£400).

FINANCES *Year* 2015 *Income* £1,504,114 *Grants* £1,250,994 *Grants to organisations* £1,250,994 *Assets* £9,775,712

TRUSTEES David Mason; Richard Smith; Michael Harris; Edna Eaves; Edward Curtis; Margaret Lancaster; Nigel Lee; Cllr Ram Lakha; Julia McNaney; David Evans; Terry Proctor; Cllr Marcus Lapsa; Vivian Kershaw; Cllr Catherine Miks; Patricia Hetherton; James Parry; Dr Roger Davies.

HOW TO APPLY Apply in writing to the correspondent. Applications are not accepted directly from the general public for relief in need (individuals).

WHO TO APPLY TO Susan Hanrahan, Old Bablake, Hill Street, Coventry CV1 4AN *Tel.* 024 7622 2769 *Email* cov.genchar@btconnect.com

■ Coventry Building Society Charitable Foundation

CC NO 1072244 **ESTABLISHED** 1998

WHERE FUNDING CAN BE GIVEN Coventry and Warwickshire; Birmingham and Black Country; Gloucestershire; Oxfordshire; Bristol; Wiltshire and Swindon; Leicestershire and Rutland; Northamptonshire; Somerset; Milton Keynes; Nottinghamshire; Staffordshire; South Yorkshire; Wales.

WHO CAN BENEFIT Registered charities.

WHAT IS FUNDED Priority is given to groups or activates aimed at improving the quality of life and opportunities in communities affected by disadvantage, deprivation and social exclusion.

WHAT IS NOT FUNDED Charities or community groups with an annual income in excess of £250,000.

TYPE OF GRANT One-off.

SAMPLE GRANTS Heart of England Community Foundation (£20,500); Birmingham and Black Country Community Foundation (£7,600); Oxfordshire Community Foundation (£6,000); Quartet Community Foundation (£4,200); Somerset Community Foundation, Staffordshire Community Foundation and Milton Keynes Community Foundation (£1,000 each).

FINANCES *Year* 2015 *Income* £60,002 *Grants* £60,000 *Grants to organisations* £60,000 *Assets* £5,247

TRUSTEES Darin Landon; Thomas Crane.

HOW TO APPLY Applications can be made online through the community foundation for your area. In order to do this choose the area closest to where your charity operates from the table at the bottom of the Coventry Building Society Charitable Foundation website and click on the relevant link. This will take you to go to the community foundation website for your area. From here, you will be able to find out more about your local community foundation and all of the information that you'll need to apply for a grant.

WHO TO APPLY TO Christian Fleischmann, Coventry Building Society, Oak Tree Court, Harry Weston Road, Coventry CV3 2UN *Tel.* 024 7643 5229 *Website* www.coventrybuildingsociety.co.uk/consumer/who-we-are/charities/charitable-foundation.html

■ The John Cowan Foundation

CC NO 327613 **ESTABLISHED** 1987

WHERE FUNDING CAN BE GIVEN UK, with a preference for projects in Surrey.

WHO CAN BENEFIT Registered charities.

WHAT IS FUNDED General charitable purposes and community development in Surrey; national health and welfare charities.

WHAT IS NOT FUNDED Individuals; community projects outside Surrey area; overseas projects.

RANGE OF GRANTS £250 to £5,000.

SAMPLE GRANTS The Prince's Trust (£5,000); Kent, Surrey and Sussex Air Ambulance, Rape and Sexual Abuse Support Centre and The Royal Marsden Cancer Charity (£2,000 each); Dame Vera Lynn Trust, Friends of Grange Park, Marine Conservation Society and WheelPower (£1,000 each); Battersea Dogs and Cats Home, Pain Relief Foundation and The Therapy Garden (£500 each).

FINANCES *Year* 2015/16 *Income* £29,912 *Grants* £48,250 *Grants to organisations* £48,250 *Assets* £590,099

TRUSTEES Susan Arkoulis; James Arkoulis; Christine Foster; Kate Phillips.

OTHER INFORMATION Grants were made to 46 organisations during the year.

HOW TO APPLY Apply in writing to the correspondent.

WHO TO APPLY TO Christine Foster, Flat 12, Kingswood Place, 119 Croydon Road, Caterham CR3 6DJ *Tel.* 01883 344930 *Email* johncowanfoundation@gmail.com

■ The Sir Tom Cowie Charitable Trust

CC NO 1096936 **ESTABLISHED** 2003

WHERE FUNDING CAN BE GIVEN City of Sunderland and County Durham.

WHO CAN BENEFIT Registered charities.

WHAT IS FUNDED General charitable purposes.

RANGE OF GRANTS Usually up to £20,000.

SAMPLE GRANTS Beamish Museum (£162,000); University of Sunderland (£20,000); Outward Bound Trust (£11,600); St Mark's Community Foundation (£5,000); Sunderland Sports Fund (£4,000); Blind Veterans UK (£3,300).

FINANCES *Year* 2015/16 *Income* £143,202 *Grants* £227,186 *Grants to organisations* £227,186 *Assets* £5,056,479

TRUSTEES Peter Blackett; David Gray; Lady Diana Cowie.

HOW TO APPLY Apply in writing to the correspondent.

WHO TO APPLY TO Loraine Maddison, Estate Office, Broadwood Hall, Lanchester, Durham DH7 0TN *Tel.* 01207 529663 *Email* lorraine@sirtomcowie.com *Website* www.stcct.co.uk

■ Dudley and Geoffrey Cox Charitable Trust

CC NO 277761 **ESTABLISHED** 1979

WHERE FUNDING CAN BE GIVEN UK with a preference for West London.

WHO CAN BENEFIT Organisations benefitting children and young adults; former employees of Haymills; at-risk groups; people who are disadvantaged by poverty and socially isolated people.

WHAT IS FUNDED Education; young people; medical causes.

WHAT IS NOT FUNDED Charities registered outside the United Kingdom; political parties; unsolicited applications from individuals.

RANGE OF GRANTS Usually £1,000 to £6,000.

SAMPLE GRANTS Merchant Taylors' School Geoffrey Cox Scholarships (£40,000); Alzheimer's Research (£10,000); Childhood First, Girlguiding, Cure Parkinson's Trust, Dream Arts, WheelPower and the MS Society (£5,000 each); Derma Trust (£4,000); Haymills Pensioners (£1,000).

FINANCES *Year* 2015/16 *Income* £246,519 *Grants* £227,300 *Grants to organisations* £227,300 *Assets* £7,355,509

TRUSTEES Ian Ferres; Bill Underwood; Peter Watkins; John Wosner; Peter Magill; Michael Boyle.

OTHER INFORMATION The trustees prefer to support smaller charities or projects where there is evidence of real need. Grants were broken down as follows: youth and welfare (£115,000); medical (£65,000); educational (£47,500).

HOW TO APPLY Apply in writing to the correspondent. Full guidelines are available on the trust's website. The trustees meet at least twice a year in March and September. The application deadlines are 31 January for the March meeting and 20 July for the September meeting.

WHO TO APPLY TO Giles Hutchinson, Charities Officer, c/o Giles Hutchinson, Charities Officer, Merchant Taylors' Company, 30 Threadneedle Street, London EC2R 8JB *Tel.* 020 7450 4440 *Email* charities@merchant-taylors.co.uk *Website* www.merchant-taylors.co.uk/charities/charities-the-dudley-and-geoffrey-cox-charitable-trust

■ The Lord Cozens-Hardy Trust

CC NO 264237 **ESTABLISHED** 1972

WHERE FUNDING CAN BE GIVEN Merseyside and Norfolk.

WHO CAN BENEFIT Registered charities.

WHAT IS FUNDED General charitable purposes including: medicine; health; and welfare.

WHAT IS NOT FUNDED Individuals.

TYPE OF GRANT One-off and recurrent.

RANGE OF GRANTS Up to £15,000, mostly for smaller amounts of £1,000 or less.

SAMPLE GRANTS Huntington's Disease Association (£20,000); Arthritis Care (£5,000); Cromer and District Food Bank (£4,500); Norfolk Carers Support (£3,500); Norfolk Wildlife Trust (£1,300); Crisis; Norfolk Carers Support and Shelter (£1,000 each).

FINANCES *Year* 2015/16 *Income* £117,250 *Grants* £97,770 *Grants to organisations* £97,770 *Assets* £3,010,472

TRUSTEES Justin Ripman; John Phelps; Linda Phelps.

HOW TO APPLY Apply in writing to the correspondent. Applications are reviewed quarterly.

WHO TO APPLY TO The Trustees, PO Box 28, Holt, Norfolk NR25 7WH

■ The Craignish Trust

SC NO SC016882 **ESTABLISHED** 1961

WHERE FUNDING CAN BE GIVEN UK, with a preference for Scotland.

WHO CAN BENEFIT Charitable organisations.

WHAT IS FUNDED General charitable purposes; environment; human rights.

TYPE OF GRANT Project grants.

RANGE OF GRANTS Up to £10,000.

SAMPLE GRANTS Soil Association Scotland (£10,000); Scottish Environmental LINK (£5,000); Waverley Care (£3,000); Glasgow Film Festival (£2,000); Amphibian and Reptile Conservation (£2,500); Glasgow Life (£1,500); Fields in Trust (£1,000); RSPB Scotland (£500).

FINANCES *Year* 2015/16 *Income* £143,942 *Grants* £107,500 *Grants to organisations* £107,500 *Assets* £5,403,191

HOW TO APPLY Apply in writing to the correspondent. Details of the project should be included together with a copy of the most recent audited accounts.

WHO TO APPLY TO The Trustees, c/o Geoghegans Chartered Accountants, 6 St Colme Street, Edinburgh EH3 6AD

■ The Craps Charitable Trust

CC NO 271492 **ESTABLISHED** 1976

WHERE FUNDING CAN BE GIVEN UK, Israel.

WHO CAN BENEFIT Charitable organisations.

WHAT IS FUNDED General charitable purposes, particularly Jewish organisations.

RANGE OF GRANTS Up to £25,000.

SAMPLE GRANTS British Technion Society (£25,000); Jewish Care (£20,000); The New Israel Fund (£13,000); British Friends of Haifa University (£4,000); The United Jewish Israel Appeal (UJIA) (£3,000); Motor Neurone Disease Association (£2,000); Anglo Israel Association and National Theatre (£1,000 each).

FINANCES *Year* 2015/16 *Income* £339,275 *Grants* £186,500 *Grants to organisations* £186,500 *Assets* £4,269,873

TRUSTEES Caroline Dent; Jonathan Dent; Louisa Dent.

HOW TO APPLY Apply in writing to the correspondent.

WHO TO APPLY TO The Trustees, Grant Thornton, 202 Silbury Boulevard, Milton Keynes MK9 1LW *Tel.* 01908 660666 *Email* nevena.y.manolova@uk.gt.com

■ The Cray Trust

SC NO SC005592 **ESTABLISHED** 1976

WHERE FUNDING CAN BE GIVEN Mainly the east of Scotland.

WHO CAN BENEFIT Charitable organisations and community groups in Scotland.

WHAT IS FUNDED General charitable purposes.

WHAT IS NOT FUNDED Political appeals; large UK or international charities; individuals.

TYPE OF GRANT One-off grants.

SAMPLE GRANTS Macmillan Cancer Support (£6,200); Maggie's Centre (£5,600); Carers Trust, The Blair Trust and Winning Scotland (£5,000 each); Carers of West Lothian (£4,100); CCLASP (£3,900); Morham Village Hall and St Mary's Cathedral Workshop (£2,000 each); Leuchie House (£1,600).

FINANCES *Year* 2015/16 *Income* £43,085 *Grants* £56,190 *Grants to organisations* £56,190 *Assets* £1,079,646

HOW TO APPLY This trust does not accept unsolicited applications.

WHO TO APPLY TO The Trustees, c/o Springfords Accountants, Dundas House, Westfield Park, Eskbank, Edinburgh EH22 3FB

The Elizabeth Creak Charitable Trust

CC NO 286838 **ESTABLISHED** 1983

WHERE FUNDING CAN BE GIVEN UK, with preference for Warwickshire.

WHO CAN BENEFIT Charities; training bodies; universities.

WHAT IS FUNDED Agricultural education and support; life sciences education.

SAMPLE GRANTS Royal Agricultural University (£325,000); Innovation for Agriculture (£150,000); Warwick University (£66,000); Henry Plumb Foundation (£50,000); Studley (£30,000); Harper Adams (£25,000).

FINANCES *Year* 2015/16 *Income* £1,258,538 *Grants* £985,988 *Grants to organisations* £985,988 *Assets* £25,587,615

TRUSTEES John Hulse; Johnathan May; Nicholas Abell.

OTHER INFORMATION Grants were broken down as follows: agricultural national support (£397,000); capital projects (£300,000); life sciences education (£227,000); other local projects (£62,000).

HOW TO APPLY The trustees usually meet every two months to consider grant applications. Apply in writing to the correspondent.

WHO TO APPLY TO John Hulse, Trustee, 27 Widney Road, Knowle, Solihull B93 9DX *Tel.* 01564 773951 *Email* creakcharity@hotmail.com

Creative Scotland

ESTABLISHED 2010

WHERE FUNDING CAN BE GIVEN Scotland.

WHO CAN BENEFIT Organisations and individuals.

WHAT IS FUNDED Creative Scotland is a public body that, through a range of programmes, distributes funding from the Scottish government and The National Lottery. It supports the arts, screen and creative industries across the whole of Scotland by 'helping others to develop great ideas and bring them to life'.

WHAT IS NOT FUNDED Most programmes have their own specific exclusions, more details of which are available on the Creative Scotland website.

SAMPLE GRANTS Screen Education Edinburgh (£110,000); Scottish Music Centre (£57,000); Centre for the Moving Image (£65,000); City of Edinburgh Council (£6,000). A full list of beneficiaries is available from Creative Scotland's website.

FINANCES *Year* 2015/16 *Income* £2,837,000 *Grants* £46,551,000 *Grants to organisations* £46,551,000 *Assets* -£5,252,000

TRUSTEES Richard Findlay, Iain Aitchinson; David Brew; Karen Forbes; Erin Forster; Prof. Maggie Kinloch; Sheila Murray; Cate Nelson-Shaw; Barclay Price; Karthik Subramanya; Ruth Wishart.

HOW TO APPLY For information on the various funding programmes available, visit the Creative Scotland website.

WHO TO APPLY TO Enquiries Service, Waverley Gate, 2–4 Waterloo Place, Edinburgh EH1 3EG *Tel.* 0845 603 6000 *Email* enquiries@creativescotland.com *Website* www.creativescotland.com

Credit Suisse EMEA Foundation

CC NO 1122472 **ESTABLISHED** 2007

WHERE FUNDING CAN BE GIVEN Countries where Credit Suisse has offices, in Europe, the Middle East and Africa.

WHO CAN BENEFIT Registered charities.

WHAT IS FUNDED Education and training; young people.

WHAT IS NOT FUNDED Grants to directly replace or subsidise statutory funding or for activities that are the responsibility of statutory bodies; administration and costs not directly associated with the application; individuals; promotion of religious or political causes; holidays; retrospective funding; general appeals; animal welfare; festivals, sports and leisure activities.

SAMPLE GRANTS Fight for Peace (£333,000); Scope (£299,000); LEAP South Africa (£220,000); ThinkForward UK (£200,000); Rock Your Company (£194,500); Polish Children and Youth Foundation (£164,000); Orphan Opportunity Fund – Step Up (£39,500); Disasters Emergency Committee – Nepal Earthquake Appeal (£10,000).

FINANCES *Year* 2015 *Income* £1,705,616 *Grants* £1,460,175 *Grants to organisations* £1,460,175 *Assets* £1,147,815

TRUSTEES Stefano Toffolo; Patrick Flaherty; Russell Chambers; Michelle Mendelsson; Nicholas Wilcock; Markus Lammer; Colin Hely-Hutchinson; Mr I. Dembinski; Marisa Drew; Marc Pereira-Mendoza.

HOW TO APPLY Apply in writing to the correspondent.

WHO TO APPLY TO Kate Butchart, Credit Suisse, 1 Cabot Square, London E14 4QJ *Email* emea.corporatecitizenship@credit-suisse.com

The Crerar Hotels Trust

CC NO 221335 **ESTABLISHED** 1903

WHERE FUNDING CAN BE GIVEN Scotland.

WHO CAN BENEFIT Mainly registered charities.

WHAT IS FUNDED General charitable purposes including: medical research; and social welfare.

WHAT IS NOT FUNDED Individuals.

TYPE OF GRANT Capital; project funding.

RANGE OF GRANTS Up to £25,000.

SAMPLE GRANTS The Hospitality Industry Trust (£25,000); Glasgow Caledonian University (£15,000); Befriend a Child (£10,000); Bethany Christian Trust (£5,000); Dyslexia Action (£3,500); The Discovery Camps (£3,000); Disability Snowsport UK (£1,100); Nil by Mouth Charitable Trust (£1,000); Balloch Over 60's Club (£450).

FINANCES *Year* 2015/16 *Income* £669,558 *Grants* £444,254 *Grants to organisations* £444,254 *Assets* £10,537,572

TRUSTEES Patrick Crerar; James Barrack; Jeanette Crerar.

HOW TO APPLY Apply in writing to the correspondent.

WHO TO APPLY TO Patrick Crerar, 1 Queen Charlotte Lane, Edinburgh EH6 6BL *Tel.* 0131 554 7173 *Email* crerarhotelstrust@samuelston.com

The Crescent Trust

CC NO 327644 **ESTABLISHED** 1987

WHERE FUNDING CAN BE GIVEN UK.

WHO CAN BENEFIT Charitable organisations; museums; galleries.

WHAT IS FUNDED The arts, heritage and ecology.

TYPE OF GRANT One-off and recurrent.

RANGE OF GRANTS £100 to £11,000.

SAMPLE GRANTS Victoria and Albert Museum (£40,000); Public Monuments and Sculpture Association (£17,500); Chalke Valley History Trust (£12,000); Team Domenica (£10,000); The Garden Museum (£3,200); Mayor's Music Fund and National Youth Theatre (£1,000 each); Donhead St Mary Village Hall (£500); Wiltshire Air Ambulance (£250); Cancer Research UK (£150).

FINANCES *Year* 2015/16 *Income* £204,191 *Grants* £86,351 *Grants to organisations* £86,351 *Assets* £642,685

TRUSTEES John Tham; Richard Lascelles.

OTHER INFORMATION The trust made grants to 12 organisations during the year.

HOW TO APPLY Apply in writing to the correspondent.

WHO TO APPLY TO Anne Sheaf, 9 Queripel House, 1 Duke of York Square, London SW3 4LY *Tel.* 020 7730 5420 *Email* mail@thecrescenttrust.co.uk

■ England and Wales Cricket Trust

CC NO 1112540 **ESTABLISHED** 2005

WHERE FUNDING CAN BE GIVEN England and Wales.

WHO CAN BENEFIT County cricket boards; cricket charities; cricket clubs.

WHAT IS FUNDED Promotion and development of cricket; recreation.

SAMPLE GRANTS A list of beneficiaries was not available.

FINANCES *Year* 2015/16 *Income* £5,107,264 *Grants* £9,888,679 *Grants to organisations* £9,888,679 *Assets* £50,182,717

TRUSTEES Mr C. D. Fearnley; Rear Admiral Roger Moylan-Jones; Ian Lovett; Ebony-Jewel Rainford-Brent; Tom Harrison; Colin Graves; Scott Smith.

HOW TO APPLY Details of available funding and how to apply can be found on the 'Programme Support' and 'Club Support' sections of the website.

WHO TO APPLY TO Claire Harris, Curtis and Co. Ltd, 22 West Street, Oundle, Peterborough PE8 4EG *Email* claire.harris@ecb.co.uk *Website* www.ecb.co.uk

■ Criffel Charitable Trust

CC NO 1040680 **ESTABLISHED** 1994

WHERE FUNDING CAN BE GIVEN UK and overseas.

WHO CAN BENEFIT Registered charities, churches and schools.

WHAT IS FUNDED The advancement of Christianity; social welfare; education.

TYPE OF GRANT Up to three years.

SAMPLE GRANTS A list of beneficiaries was not available.

FINANCES *Year* 2015/16 *Income* £283,896 *Grants* £193,440 *Grants to organisations* £193,440 *Assets* £2,221,727

TRUSTEES Jim Lees; Joy Harvey; Juliet Lees; Murray Lees.

HOW TO APPLY The trust has previously stated that unsolicited applications are not accepted.

WHO TO APPLY TO The Trustees, 68 Liverpool Road, Stoke-on-Trent ST4 1BG *Tel.* 01782 847952 *Email* info@geens.co.uk

■ Cripplegate Foundation

CC NO 207499 **ESTABLISHED** 1891

WHERE FUNDING CAN BE GIVEN London borough of Islington and part of the City of London.

WHO CAN BENEFIT Charitable organisations; schools; organisations working with schools; individuals.

WHAT IS FUNDED Grants which aim to improve the quality of life in the area of benefit and provide opportunities for local residents. All of the foundation's work is informed by the following programme objectives: financial inclusion and capability; advice and access to services; supporting families; investing in young people; mental health and well-being; and confronting isolation.

TYPE OF GRANT Grants for core costs, project funding, salary costs and capital costs, up to three years.

SAMPLE GRANTS Help on Your Doorstep (£100,000); Family Action Islington (£65,000); North London Cares (£19,500); Islington Age UK (£10,000); Another Way (£8,300); The Kaizen Partnership Ltd (£6,000); Freightliners Farm (£2,500); Ben Kinsella Trust (£1,500); House of Illustration (£500).

FINANCES *Year* 2015 *Income* £2,248,899 *Grants* £1,207,295 *Grants to organisations* £1,070,278 *Assets* £36,240,455

TRUSTEE Cripplegate Foundation Ltd.

OTHER INFORMATION The amount of grants given to individuals totalled £137,000.

HOW TO APPLY Due to finite resources in recent years grants have been limited to organisations that have been previously funded. However, the foundation's website states: 'Cripplegate Foundation takes an active approach and we are keen to talk to groups working in Islington to deepen our understanding of need and activities in the Borough and to share knowledge and networking possibilities. If you feel that your aims are a close match to ours and would like to get in touch email us at grants@cripplegate.org.uk.'

WHO TO APPLY TO Kristina Glenn, 13 Elliott's Place, Islington, London N1 8HX *Tel.* 020 7288 6940 *Email* grants@cripplegate.org.uk *Website* www.cripplegate.org

■ The Violet and Milo Cripps Charitable Trust

CC NO 289404 **ESTABLISHED** 1984

WHERE FUNDING CAN BE GIVEN UK.

WHO CAN BENEFIT Charitable organisations.

WHAT IS FUNDED Prison welfare; health; education.

SAMPLE GRANTS Dudley Metropolitan Borough Council (£425,500); Alzheimer's Research UK, Dorothy House Hospice Care, The Frank Longford Charitable Trust (£25,000 each); Prisoners' Education Trust (£5,000).

FINANCES *Year* 2015/16 *Income* £2,013 *Grants* £130,000 *Grants to organisations* £130,000

TRUSTEES Richard Linenthal; Anthony Newhouse; Jennifer Beattie.

OTHER INFORMATION This charity's latest accounts were not available to view on the Charity Commission's website. We have therefore estimated the grant total based on previous years' information.

HOW TO APPLY The trustees have previously stated that unsolicited applications will not receive a response.

WHO TO APPLY TO The Trustees, Wedlake Bell LLP, 71 Queen Victoria Street, London EC4V 4AY

Crisis UK

CC NO 1082947 **ESTABLISHED** 2000

WHERE FUNDING CAN BE GIVEN UK.

WHO CAN BENEFIT Registered charities; housing associations; individuals.

WHAT IS FUNDED Homelessness and housing.

SAMPLE GRANTS Citizens Advice WHABAC Worcestershire; CRI Leeds; Hope North East; Isle of Wight Law Centre; Justlife; No Limits – Southampton; Refugee Council; Shropshire Housing Alliance; Vision Housing; Whitechapel Centre.

FINANCES *Year* 2015/16 *Income* £29,500,000 *Grants* £209,000 *Grants to organisations* £116,000 *Assets* £15,676,000

TRUSTEES Martin Cheeseman; Andrew Newell; Jason Warriner; Steven Holliday; Richard Murley; Peter Redfern; Emma Foulds; Caroline Lee-Davey; Terrie Alafat; Ann McIvor.

OTHER INFORMATION The amount of grants given to individuals totalled £93,000.

HOW TO APPLY Refer to the website for application forms and deadlines for any current grant schemes.

WHO TO APPLY TO Housing Team, 66 Commercial Street, London E1 6LT *Tel.* 0300 636 1967 *Email* enquiries@crisis.org.uk *Website* www.crisis.org.uk

The Cross Trust

SC NO SC008620 **ESTABLISHED** 1943

WHERE FUNDING CAN BE GIVEN Scotland.

WHO CAN BENEFIT Individuals and organisations.

WHAT IS FUNDED The promotion among the young people of Scotland of a love of nature and Scottish scenery. (Awards are made to organisations which provide opportunities for the education or advancement of their members including assistance with expeditions in furtherance of their objects, and for building and other renovation works for their premises). The promotion of drama, opera and similar works (in particular, the works of Shakespeare, and of Gilbert and Sullivan).

TYPE OF GRANT Normally one-off. Building and renovation.

SAMPLE GRANTS Perth Festival of Fine Arts (£10,000); Perth Theatre and Concert Hall, Out of the Blue Arts and Education Trust (£5,000 each); Byre Theatre (£2,000).

FINANCES *Year* 2015/16 *Income* £227,148 *Grants* £181,625 *Grants to organisations* £57,465 *Assets* £5,215,022

TRUSTEES Dougal Philip; Beppo Buchanan-Smith; Prof. R. H. MacDougal; Mark Webster; Prof. Hannah Buchanan-Smith; Clare Meredith; Richard Ingham.

OTHER INFORMATION The amount of grants given to individuals totalled £124,000 and are made to young Scottish men and women to 'extend the boundaries of their knowledge of human life.'

HOW TO APPLY Application forms are available from the correspondent. The trustees meet twice a year. Consult the website for application deadlines.

WHO TO APPLY TO The Secretaries of The Cross Trust, McCash and Hunter Solicitors, 25 South Methven Street, Perth PH1 5ES *Tel.* 01738 620451 *Email* kathleencarnegie@mccash.co.uk *Website* www.thecrosstrust.org.uk

The Cross Trust

CC NO 1127046 **ESTABLISHED** 2008

WHERE FUNDING CAN BE GIVEN UK and overseas.

WHO CAN BENEFIT Registered charities; religious organisations.

WHAT IS FUNDED Social welfare; advancement of religious and secular education; the advancement of the Christian faith in the UK and overseas.

SAMPLE GRANTS George Whitefield College (£300,00); Anglican Futures Ltd (£125,000); Gospel Partners Trust (£100,000); Lambeth Partnership (£35,000); Church of England Evangelical Council (£28,000); Diocese of York and The Oxford Centre (£6,000 each).

FINANCES *Year* 2015/16 *Income* £390,498 *Grants* £575,048 *Grants to organisations* £440,232 *Assets* £440,070

TRUSTEES Douglas Olsen; Jenny Farmer; Michael Farmer; David Lilley.

OTHER INFORMATION The amount of grants given to individuals totalled £135,000.

HOW TO APPLY Apply in writing to the correspondent.

WHO TO APPLY TO James Foskett, The Cross Trust, Cansdales, Bourbon Court, Nightingales Corner, Amersham HP7 9QS *Tel.* 01494 765428 *Email* mailto@cansdales.co.uk

The Croydon Relief in Need Charities

CC NO 810114 **ESTABLISHED** 1962

WHERE FUNDING CAN BE GIVEN The borough of Croydon.

WHO CAN BENEFIT Local charities; individuals.

WHAT IS FUNDED Health and social welfare.

TYPE OF GRANT Preference for one-off project grants but core costs also considered.

RANGE OF GRANTS Up to £30,000.

SAMPLE GRANTS Macmillan Cancer (£30,000); Croydon Drop In (£22,500); Croydon Mencap (£16,000); Refugee Support Network (£10,300); South East Cancer Help Centre (£6,000); Summer Centre (£5,000); Mobility Trust (£2,500); Happy Days Children's Charity (£1,200); Carers Information Centre (£100).

FINANCES *Year* 2015 *Income* £243,639 *Grants* £191,064 *Grants to organisations* £191,064 *Assets* £45,063

TRUSTEES Christopher Clementi; The Revd Canon Colin Boswell; Mrs C. D. A. Trower; Lynda Talbot; Noel Hepworth; Diana Hemmings; Diana Harries; John Tough; Caroline Melrose; Karen Ip; Gail Winter; Cllr Andrew Pelling; Deborah Knight; Martin Evans; Cllr Patrick Ryan; Susan Woolley; Revd David Pennells; Paul Smith.

HOW TO APPLY Application forms are available from the charity's website. Completed forms can be returned by email or post. The grants committee meets quarterly.

WHO TO APPLY TO Tessa Damer, Elis David Almshouses, Duppas Hill Terrace, Croydon CR0 4BT *Tel.* 020 8688 2649 *Email* tessadamer@croydonalmshouses.org.uk *Website* www.croydonalmshousecharities.org.uk

The Peter Cruddas Foundation

CC NO 1117323 **ESTABLISHED** 2006

WHERE FUNDING CAN BE GIVEN England and Wales.

WHO CAN BENEFIT Registered charities.

WHAT IS FUNDED The foundation gives priority to programmes designed to help disadvantaged and disengaged young people in the age range of 14 to 30, to pursue pathways to education, training and employment with the ultimate aim of helping them to become financially independent.

WHAT IS NOT FUNDED CICs; social enterprises; capital appeals.

RANGE OF GRANTS Up to £200,000.

SAMPLE GRANTS Royal Opera House Foundation (£207,500 in five grants); Great Ormond Street Hospital Children's Charity (£34,500 in two grants); Harris Manchester College (£20,000); Bootstrap Company (£10,000); Ignite Trust, Renaissance Foundation, The Royal Aero Club Trust, Woolf Institute (£5,000 each); Bounce Back Foundation (£2,500); Nikki's Wishes (£2,000).

FINANCES *Year* 2015/16 *Income* £522,738 *Grants* £453,052 *Grants to organisations* £453,052 *Assets* £11,091

TRUSTEES Lord Young; Peter Cruddas; Martin Paisner.

OTHER INFORMATION No grants were given to individuals.

HOW TO APPLY Application forms are available to download from the foundation's website.

WHO TO APPLY TO Stephen Cox, 133 Houndsditch, London EC3A 7BX *Tel.* 020 3003 8360 *Email* s.cox@petercruddasfoundation.org.uk *Website* www.petercruddasfoundation.org.uk

■ Cruden Foundation Ltd

SC NO SC004987 **ESTABLISHED** 1956

WHERE FUNDING CAN BE GIVEN Mainly Scotland.

WHO CAN BENEFIT Registered charities.

WHAT IS FUNDED Social welfare; medical causes; arts; education; heritage and conservation.

WHAT IS NOT FUNDED Individuals.

TYPE OF GRANT Recurrent and one-off.

RANGE OF GRANTS Up to £20,000.

SAMPLE GRANTS Edinburgh International Festival and Royal College of Physicians and Surgeons of Glasgow (£20,000 each); Cure Parkinson's Trust (£15,000); Edinburgh Headway Group (£10,000); Scottish Ballet (£5,000); St Andrews Hospice (£3,000); Bobath Scotland and Macmillan Cancer Support (£2,500 each).

FINANCES *Year* 2015/16 *Income* £493,202 *Grants* £326,500 *Grants to organisations* £326,500 *Assets* £8,947,769

HOW TO APPLY Apply in writing to the correspondent, accompanied by most recent accounts.

WHO TO APPLY TO The Trustees, Baberton House, Juniper Green, Edinburgh EH14 3HN

■ The Ronald Cruickshanks Foundation

CC NO 296075 **ESTABLISHED** 1987

WHERE FUNDING CAN BE GIVEN UK, with some preference for Folkestone, Faversham and the surrounding area.

WHO CAN BENEFIT Individuals and organisations, including various local churches.

WHAT IS FUNDED General charitable purposes including: social welfare; and education.

TYPE OF GRANT Recurrent.

RANGE OF GRANTS Up to £10,000.

SAMPLE GRANTS Demelza House Children's Hospice (£10,000); Kent Air Ambulance (£7,500); Holy Trinity Church (£5,000); Operation Sunshine (£4,500); Folkestone Rainbow Centre (£2,000); Independent Age, Epilepsy Here and Sense (£1,000 each); Action for Kids, Beanstalk and Missing People (£500); Samaritans (£250).

FINANCES *Year* 2015/16 *Income* £469,995 *Grants* £190,750 *Grants to organisations* £190,750 *Assets* £1,292,210

TRUSTEES Susan Cloke; Ian Cloke; Jan Schilder.

HOW TO APPLY Apply in writing to the correspondent. Applications should be received by the end of September for consideration on a date coinciding closely with the anniversary of the death of the founder, which was 7 December.

WHO TO APPLY TO Ian Cloke, Trustee, Rivendell, Teddars Leas, Etchinghill, Folkestone CT18 8AE *Tel.* 01303 862812 *Email* ian@iancloke.co.uk

■ CSIS Charity Fund

CC NO 1121671 **ESTABLISHED** 2007

WHERE FUNDING CAN BE GIVEN UK.

WHO CAN BENEFIT Serving, former and retired civil and public servants and organisations supporting them.

WHAT IS FUNDED Organisations whose beneficiaries will include former, serving and retired civil and public servants and their dependants and which are very clearly and directly relieving need, hardship and distress among those they support.

TYPE OF GRANT Normally one-off.

RANGE OF GRANTS Up to £250,000 but normally £5,000 to £60,000.

SAMPLE GRANTS The Charity for Civil Servants (£250,000); Help the Hospices (£100,500); Rowland Hill Fund (£54,000); Railway Benefit Fund (£40,000); Officers Association (£18,000); Prison Officers Association Welfare Fund (£15,000); Public and Commercial Services Union (£10,000); Omagh Independent Advice Services (£5,000).

FINANCES *Year* 2015 *Income* £831,458 *Grants* £818,346 *Grants to organisations* £791,005 *Assets* £2,513,639

TRUSTEES Gillian Noble; Charles Cochrane; Ray Flanigan; Beryl Evans; Kevin Holliday; Christopher Furlong; Tunde Ojetola; Brian Sturtevant; Sally Bundock; Julia Wood; Craig Pemberton; Rebecca Gooch; Tom Hoyle; Daniel Hewitt.

OTHER INFORMATION The amount of grants given to individuals totalled £27,500.

HOW TO APPLY Contact the fund's secretary in the first instance.

WHO TO APPLY TO Helen Harris, Secretary, 7 Colman House, King Street, Maidstone, Kent ME14 1DD *Tel.* 01622 766963 *Email* info@csischarityfund.org *Website* www.csischarityfund.org

■ The Cuby Charitable Trust

CC NO 328585 **ESTABLISHED** 1990

WHERE FUNDING CAN BE GIVEN UK; overseas.

WHO CAN BENEFIT Registered charities.

WHAT IS FUNDED Jewish causes.

SAMPLE GRANTS A list of beneficiaries was not available.

FINANCES *Year* 2014/15 *Income* £362,492 *Grants* £63,348 *Grants to organisations* £63,348 *Assets* £1,071,251

TRUSTEES C. Cuby; Sidney Cuby; Jonathan Cuby; Raquel Talmor.

OTHER INFORMATION The 2014/15 accounts were the latest available at the time of writing (June 2017).

HOW TO APPLY Apply in writing to the correspondent.

WHO TO APPLY TO Sidney Cuby, Trustee, 16 Mowbray Road, Edgware HA8 8JQ *Tel.* 020 7563 6868

■ Cullum Family Trust

CC NO 1117056 **ESTABLISHED** 2006

WHERE FUNDING CAN BE GIVEN UK.

WHO CAN BENEFIT Registered charities and institutions.

WHAT IS FUNDED General charitable purposes including: social welfare and education.

SAMPLE GRANTS The National Autistic Society (£1.7 million); City University (£221,000); The Sussex Community Foundation (£100,000); Lancing Prep PTA (£4,500); The Chestnut Tree (£4,300).

FINANCES *Year* 2015/16 *Income* £1,168,371 *Grants* £2,031,405 *Grants to organisations* £2,031,405 *Assets* £27,103,200

TRUSTEES Ann Cullum; Claire Cullum; Peter Cullum; Simon Cullum.

HOW TO APPLY Apply in writing to the correspondent.

WHO TO APPLY TO Peter Cullum, Trustee, Wealden Hall, Parkfield, Sevenoaks TN15 0HX

■ The Cumber Family Charitable Trust

CC NO 291009 **ESTABLISHED** 1985

WHERE FUNDING CAN BE GIVEN UK with a preference for Berkshire and Oxfordshire; overseas.

WHO CAN BENEFIT Charitable organisations.

WHAT IS FUNDED Overseas (preferably with an emphasis on active involvement in agriculture or rural development), housing and welfare; children, youth and education; medical causes and disability; agriculture/conservation.

WHAT IS NOT FUNDED Individuals are not usually supported, although individuals with local connections and who are personally known to the trustees are occasionally assisted.

TYPE OF GRANT One-off grants.

RANGE OF GRANTS £500 to £1,000.

SAMPLE GRANTS Action on Addiction, Institute of Cancer Research and Whizz-Kidz (£1,000 each); Demand, Global Care, Reading Quest and The Quicken Trust (£500 each).

FINANCES *Grants* £43,250 *Grants to organisations* £43,250

TRUSTEES Mary Tearney; Margaret Freeman; Julia Mearns; William Cumber; Kellie Davey.

HOW TO APPLY Applications must be sent in paper format and not via email. There is no formal application; however, the trust has provided guidelines which can be found on the trust's website. Applications must be sent to the secretary. The trustees meet twice a year to consider applications, usually in March and October. Applications need to be made at least a month before the meeting date. First time applicants must provide a copy of the latest annual report and accounts.

WHO TO APPLY TO The Secretary, Manor Farm, Mill Road, Marcham, Abingdon OX13 6NZ *Tel.* 01865 391327 *Email* mary.tearney@hotmail.co.uk *Website* www.cumberfamilycharitabletrust.org.uk

■ Cumbria Community Foundation

CC NO 1075120 **ESTABLISHED** 1999

WHERE FUNDING CAN BE GIVEN Cumbria.

WHO CAN BENEFIT Registered and non-registered charities, CIOs, CICs limited by guarantee and social enterprises that are engaged in legally charitable work with at least three unrelated trustees or directors. Individuals.

WHAT IS FUNDED Improving the lives of disadvantaged children and families; improving the life skills, education, employability and enterprise of disadvantaged people; older people; health and well-being; community development.

WHAT IS NOT FUNDED Animal welfare; contact boxing (unless you are applying to Comic Relief); businesses; deficit funding; general large appeals; medical research; activities which are normally the statutory duties of public bodies; statutory bodies; applications to a fund where you have had a grant from that fund within the last 12 months; projects which duplicate an existing service in an area; one-off or sponsored events; general large fundraising appeals; the advancement of religion; medical research and equipment; party political activities.

TYPE OF GRANT Core costs; salaries; capital projects.

SAMPLE GRANTS Eden Flood Volunteers (£100,000); Phoenix Enterprise Centre (£40,000); Cumbria Drug and Alcohol Advisory Service (£35,000); Rockcliffe Church of England School (£20,000); Ambleside Football Club (£15,000); The Whitehaven Foyer (£10,000); Cumbria Wheelchair Sports Club (£9,000); Distington Club for Young People (£6,500); Carlisle City Football Club (£5,000).

FINANCES *Year* 2015/16 *Income* £12,377,798 *Grants* £4,694,815 *Grants to organisations* £1,980,328 *Assets* £17,381,121

TRUSTEES Mr R. A. Roberts; Mr J. F. Whittle; Mr I. W. Brown; Mr T. Cartmell; Dr A. Naylor; Mrs E. Porter; Mr M. Casson; Mr W. Slavin; Mrs J. E. Humphries; Ms C. Thomson; Mrs C. Tomlinson; Mrs V. Young; Mr T. J. Knowles; Mrs C. A. Giel; Mr A. Burbridge; Mrs S. Cockayne; Mike Starkie; Mr A. B. Keen; Mr D. Beeby.

OTHER INFORMATION There were 363 grants made to organisations during the year.

HOW TO APPLY Each fund is subject to its own criteria, which are detailed on the individual web pages of each. Most funds share the same online application form, with the foundation deciding the fund to which your application is most suited. Applications are subject to deadline dates which can be found, along with further guidelines, on the website.

WHO TO APPLY TO Andrew Beeforth, Chief Executive, Dovenby Hall, Dovenby, Cockermouth, Cumbria CA13 0PN *Tel.* 01900 825760 *Email* enquiries@cumbriafoundation.org *Website* www.cumbriafoundation.org

■ The Cunningham Trust

SC NO SC013499 **ESTABLISHED** 1984

WHERE FUNDING CAN BE GIVEN Scotland.

WHO CAN BENEFIT Universities and research institutions.

WHAT IS FUNDED Medical research.

WHAT IS NOT FUNDED Grants are unlikely to be made available to non-regular beneficiaries.

TYPE OF GRANT Revenue and project funding for up to two years.

SAMPLE GRANTS University of Aberdeen (£84,500); University of Glasgow (£83,000); University of Strathclyde (£81,500).

FINANCES *Year* 2015/16 *Income* £284,567 *Grants* £244,671 *Grants to organisations* £244,671 *Assets* £9,365,346

HOW TO APPLY Contact the trust for an application form.

WHO TO APPLY TO Kim Falconer, Administrator, Murray Donald Drummond Cook LLP, Kinburn Castle, St Andrews, Fife KY16 9DR

■ The Harry Cureton Charitable Trust

CC NO 1106206 **ESTABLISHED** 2005

WHERE FUNDING CAN BE GIVEN The area covered by Peterborough and Stamford hospitals.

WHO CAN BENEFIT Organisations; individuals.

WHAT IS FUNDED Health issues; physical illness; mental illness; health and well-being education; palliative care; medical equipment; medical research.

WHAT IS NOT FUNDED Grants for the activity that can be paid for by the NHS, the surgery or another source; expenditure already incurred; support in situations where the grant results in financial benefit to one person or certain group of people, for example improvements or alterations in property.

TYPE OF GRANT One-off and recurrent; capital and revenue costs.

RANGE OF GRANTS Up to £20,000.

SAMPLE GRANTS Peterborough Association for the Blind (£17,000); Boroughbury Medical Centre (£14,200); Peterborough City Council (£8,000); Kidney Research UK (£3,000); Shine (£1,000); Thomas Walker Surgery (£750); The Surgery Hodgson Centre (£380).

FINANCES *Year* 2015/16 *Income* £91,210 *Grants* £76,407 *Grants to organisations* £61,737 *Assets* £3,808,534

TRUSTEES Nick Monsell; Simon Richards; Nick Plumb; Christopher Banks.

OTHER INFORMATION During 2015/16, grants in total of £16,000 were awarded to local individuals towards the purchase of equipment for use by persons with chronic illness.

HOW TO APPLY Cambridgeshire Community Foundation manages the administration of The Harry Cureton Charitable Trust. All applications must be made online through the Cambridgeshire Community Foundation website. Individual applications and applications for equipment for individuals should be made by an occupational therapist (or other medical professional who has full knowledge of the individuals overall health and financial position) using the 'Support for Individuals' form online. A 'Grants for Organisations' application form is available online also. Organisations can apply either with a small grant or large grant application form. When submitting the form organisations must also attach: a signed copy of your organisation's set of rules/terms of reference/constitution; the names and addresses of management committee members, with cheque signatories identified; a copy of bank paying in slip or bank statement to allow the trust to verify your organisation's bank details; your equality policy; your safeguarding policy (children and/or adults); your organisation's accounts for the past two financial years; three different quotes for any capital items over £500. Full guidelines are available via the Community Foundation Cambridge website.

WHO TO APPLY TO Jane Darlington, c/o Cambridgeshire Community Foundation, The Quorum, Barnwell Road, Cambridge CB5 8RE *Tel.* 01223 410535 *Email* hcct@cambscf.org.uk *Website* www.cambscf.org.uk/the-harry-cureton-charitable-trust.html

■ Itzchok Meyer Cymerman Trust Ltd

CC NO 265090 **ESTABLISHED** 1972

WHERE FUNDING CAN BE GIVEN UK and Israel.

WHO CAN BENEFIT Registered charities.

WHAT IS FUNDED Advancement of the Orthodox Jewish faith; education; social welfare; medical aid.

TYPE OF GRANT Mostly recurrent.

RANGE OF GRANTS Up to £161,000.

SAMPLE GRANTS Russian Immigrant Aid Fund (£161,000); Ichud Mosdos Gur (£115,050); Yeshiva Kollel Breslov (£53,000); Beth Hamidrash Gur (£50,000); Kollel Polin Kupath Ramban (£39,800); Telz Academy Trust (£35,000); Society of Friends of the Torah Ltd (£25,000).

FINANCES *Year* 2015/16 *Income* £1,072,391 *Grants* £530,210 *Grants to organisations* £530,210 *Assets* £11,649,480

TRUSTEES Mrs H. F. Bondi; Mrs S. Cymerman; Sara Heitner; Ian Heitner; Michael Cymerman; Leonard Bondi.

OTHER INFORMATION Grants were distributed in the following categories: relief of poverty (£190,500); advancement of religion (£189,500); religious education (£129,000); medical aid (£21,000).

HOW TO APPLY Apply in writing to the correspondent.

WHO TO APPLY TO Ian Heitner, Trustee, 497 Holloway Road, London N7 6LE

■ The D. G. Charitable Settlement

CC NO 1040778 **ESTABLISHED** 1994
WHERE FUNDING CAN BE GIVEN UK.
WHO CAN BENEFIT Registered charities.
WHAT IS FUNDED General charitable purposes mainly supporting a fixed list of charities.
RANGE OF GRANTS Up to £200,000.
SAMPLE GRANTS Oxfam (£100,000); Crisis (£40,000); Great Ormond Street Hospital and Shelter (£25,000 each); Cancer Research UK, Environmental Investigation Agency Charitable Trust, Friends of the Earth and Reprieve UK (£10,000 each); Defend the Right to Protest, Media Standards Trust – Hacked Off and University of St Andrews (£5,000 each); Terrence Higgins Trust (£2,000).
FINANCES *Year* 2015/16 *Income* £991 *Grants* £275,000 *Grants to organisations* £275,000
TRUSTEES David Gilmour; Patrick Grafton-Green; Polly Samson.
OTHER INFORMATION This charity's latest accounts were not available to view on the Charity Commission's website due to its low income. We have therefore estimated the grant total based on previous years' information.
HOW TO APPLY This charity does not consider unsolicited applications.
WHO TO APPLY TO Polly Samson, Basement Flat, 7 Medina Terrace, Hove, East Sussex BN3 2WL *Tel.* 01273 780245 *Email* nicola@gilmour-dj.co.uk

■ The D'Oyly Carte Charitable Trust

CC NO 1112457 **ESTABLISHED** 1972
WHERE FUNDING CAN BE GIVEN UK.
WHO CAN BENEFIT Registered charities.
WHAT IS FUNDED The arts; health and medical welfare; environmental protection or improvement.
WHAT IS NOT FUNDED According to its website, the trust is not likely to fund: 'advocacy; animal welfare; campaigning or lobbying; capital projects (unless a specific element falls within the Trust's remit); community transport organisations or services; conferences and seminars; counselling and psychotherapy services; cultural festivals; drug abuse or alcoholism rehabilitation; educational projects linked to the National Curriculum; endowments; exhibitions; expeditions and overseas travel; Friend/Parent Teacher Associations; general and round-robin appeals; individuals; large national charities; medical research; NHS hospitals for operational and building costs; organisations that are not Registered Charities (or accepted as Exempt Charities); projects taking place or benefiting people outside the UK; recordings and commissioning of new works; religious causes and activities; routine maintenance of religious or historic buildings; replacement or subsidy of statutory funding or for work we consider should be funded by Government; sport; umbrella organisations; universities, colleges and schools (other than those dedicated to the arts); schools, Nurseries and Playgroups (other than those for special needs children); works to enable a building to comply with the Disability Discrimination Act 2010'.
TYPE OF GRANT Mainly one-off.
SAMPLE GRANTS Hospices UK (£15,000); City and Guilds of London Art School (£10,000); Age Exchange (£5,000); Alternative Theatre Company Ltd (£4,000); Deafblind UK (£3,500); Aidis Trust (£3,000); Compaid Trust (£2,300); Erskine (£2,000); Garden Science Trust (£700).
FINANCES *Year* 2015/16 *Income* £1,303,690 *Grants* £1,246,356 *Grants to organisations* £1,246,356 *Assets* £49,462,164
TRUSTEES Francesca Radcliffe; Henry Freeland; Jeremy Pemberton; Julia Sibley; Dr Michael O'Brien; Andrew Wimble; Andrew Jackson.
OTHER INFORMATION A total of 357 grants were made during the year and distributed as follows: the arts (£573,000); medical welfare (£508,000); the environment (£165,000).
HOW TO APPLY Applications can be made online. Guidelines and application deadlines are also available on the trust's website.
WHO TO APPLY TO Sarah Conley, Grants Administrator, 6 Trull Farm Buildings, Tetbury, Gloucestershire GL8 8SQ *Tel.* 020 3637 3003 *Email* info@doylycartecharitabletrust.org *Website* www.doylycartecharitabletrust.org

■ Roald Dahl's Marvellous Children's Charity

CC NO 1137409 **ESTABLISHED** 1991
WHERE FUNDING CAN BE GIVEN UK.
WHO CAN BENEFIT Registered charities and individuals. In general, the charity aims to provide help to organisations where funds are not readily available. Preference for small or new organisations rather than long-established, large or national organisations.
WHAT IS FUNDED Children and young people with serious illness or disability, and their families.
WHAT IS NOT FUNDED Refer to the website for specific exclusions for different funding programmes.
TYPE OF GRANT One-off, start-up costs, salaries, projects for up to two years.
SAMPLE GRANTS A list of beneficiaries was not available.
FINANCES *Year* 2015/16 *Income* £940,259 *Grants* £415,206 *Grants to organisations* £415,206 *Assets* £1,172,188
TRUSTEES Martin Goodwin; Virginia Myer; Graham Faulkner; Donald Sturrock; Dr Husain Khaki; Niels Kirk; Michelle Johnson; Alex Hyde-Parker.
OTHER INFORMATION The Marvellous Family grants programme, providing direct support to families with seriously ill children, awarded 101 grants in 2015/16 totalling £244,500.
HOW TO APPLY Visit the charity's website for full and current information on whether funding programmes are open to application, and how to apply.
WHO TO APPLY TO Hannah Winter, Head of Policy and Programmes, Montague House, 23 Woodside Road, Amersham, Buckinghamshire HP6 6AA *Tel.* 01494 890465 *Email* enquiries@roalddahlcharity.org *Website* www.roalddahlcharity.org

■ The Daiwa Anglo-Japanese Foundation

CC NO 299955 **ESTABLISHED** 1988
WHERE FUNDING CAN BE GIVEN UK, Japan.
WHO CAN BENEFIT Individuals and organisations (UK or Japanese) benefitting young adults, students and Japanese people – including schools, universities, grassroots and professional groups.
WHAT IS FUNDED The education of citizens of the UK and Japan in each other's culture, institutions, arts, and so on. Scholarships, bursaries and awards to enable students and academics in the UK and Japan to pursue their education abroad. Grants to charitable organisations and institutions promoting education in the UK or Japan, and research.
WHAT IS NOT FUNDED Daiwa Foundation Small Grants cannot be used for: general appeals; capital expenditure (e.g. building refurbishment, equipment acquisition, etc.); consumables (e.g. stationery, scientific supplies, etc.); school, college or university fees; research or study by an individual school/college/university student; salary costs or professional fees; commissions for works of art; retrospective grants; replacement of statutory funding; commercial activities. Daiwa Foundation Awards cannot be used for: any project that does not involve both a British and a Japanese partner; general appeals; capital expenditure (e.g. building refurbishment, equipment acquisition, etc.); salary costs or professional fees; commissions for works of art; retrospective grants; commercial activities.
TYPE OF GRANT Outright or partnership grants, paid in sterling or Japanese yen. One-year funding.
SAMPLE GRANTS Museum of London (£10,000); Norfolk Museum Service (£8,000); University of Liverpool (£7,800); FellSwoop Theatre (£4,000); Amino and Watershed Arts Trust (£3,000 each); John Port School (£2,000).
FINANCES *Year* 2015/16 *Income* £407,152 *Grants* £607,926 *Grants to organisations* £607,926 *Assets* £36,411,185
TRUSTEES Lady Judge; Paul Dimond; Sir Peter Williams; Prof. Richard Browning; Mami Mizutori; Yusuke Kawamura; Masaki Orita; Shigeharu Suzuki; Prof. Hirotaka Takeuchi; Elizabeth Davidson; Stephen Barber; Stuart Chambers.
OTHER INFORMATION The grant total includes grants for scholarships.
HOW TO APPLY Applications can be made through the foundation's website.
WHO TO APPLY TO Jason James, Director General and Secretary, 13/14 Cornwall Terrace, London NW1 4QP *Email* office@dajf.org.uk *Website* www.dajf.org.uk

■ Oizer Dalim Trust

CC NO 1045296 **ESTABLISHED** 1994
WHERE FUNDING CAN BE GIVEN UK and overseas.
WHO CAN BENEFIT Registered charities.
WHAT IS FUNDED To alleviate poverty and further education within the Orthodox Jewish community.
SAMPLE GRANTS A list of beneficiaries was not available.
FINANCES *Year* 2015/16 *Income* £292,302 *Grants* £225,780 *Grants to organisations* £225,780 *Assets* £89,972
TRUSTEES Mordechai Cik; Maurice Freund; Moshe Cohen.
HOW TO APPLY Apply in writing to the correspondent.
WHO TO APPLY TO Mordechai Cik, Trustee, 68 Osbaldeston Road, London N16 7DR

■ The Joan Lynette Dalton Charitable Trust

CC NO 1154521 **ESTABLISHED** 2012
WHERE FUNDING CAN BE GIVEN England and Wales.
WHO CAN BENEFIT Registered charities.
WHAT IS FUNDED General charitable purposes including: health; animal welfare.
RANGE OF GRANTS Up to £9,000.
SAMPLE GRANTS Arthritis Research UK, Cancer Research UK, National Animal Welfare Trust, NSPCC, People's Dispensary for Sick Animals (PDSA), Scope and The Stroke Unit (£9,200 each in three grants).
FINANCES *Year* 2015/16 *Income* £41,745 *Grants* £64,400 *Grants to organisations* £64,400 *Assets* £1,593,937
TRUSTEE HSBC. Trust Company UK. Ltd.
OTHER INFORMATION The trust awarded a total of 21 grants during the year.
HOW TO APPLY Apply in writing to the correspondent.
WHO TO APPLY TO HSBC Trust Company UK Ltd, HSBC Trust Company UK Ltd – Trust Services, Second Floor, 1 The Forum, Parkway, Whiteley, Fareham PO15 7PA *Tel.* 023 8072 2243

■ The Dr and Mrs A. Darlington Charitable Trust

CC NO 283308 **ESTABLISHED** 1981
WHERE FUNDING CAN BE GIVEN Devon, in particular Sidmouth and East Devon.
WHO CAN BENEFIT Registered charities.
WHAT IS FUNDED The trust mainly supports: medical causes; people with disabilities; older people; and socially isolated people. Grants also given in the fields of nature conservation and preservation.
WHAT IS NOT FUNDED Applications from individuals, including students, are unlikely to be successful. Applications for donations to be used outside Devon (particularly outside Sidmouth and East Devon) are also not likely to be fruitful.
TYPE OF GRANT One-off, some recurring.
SAMPLE GRANTS Brainwave; Children's Health and Exercise Research Centre; Countryside Foundation; Freedom Wheels; MS Therapy Centre; Peninsula Medical School Foundation; Salcombe Regis Church; West of England School and College.
FINANCES *Year* 2015/16 *Income* £53,084 *Grants* £57,103 *Grants to organisations* £57,103 *Assets* £83,026
TRUSTEE Lloyds TSB. Bank PLC.
HOW TO APPLY Apply in writing to the correspondent. The trustees regret that they cannot send replies to unsuccessful applicants. The trustees meet quarterly in March, June, September and December; applications should be received the previous month.
WHO TO APPLY TO The Trustees, Lloyds TSB Bank PLC, UK Trust Centre, The Clock House, 22–26 Ock Street, Abingdon, Oxfordshire OX14 5SW *Tel.* 01235 232700

■ Baron Davenport's Charity

CC NO 217307 **ESTABLISHED** 1930
WHERE FUNDING CAN BE GIVEN Birmingham and the West Midlands counties. Applicants must be within 60 miles of Birmingham Town Hall.
WHO CAN BENEFIT Registered charities; almshouses; hospices; residential homes; individuals.
WHAT IS FUNDED Almshouses and hospitals; children and young people (under 25); older people (60 and over).
WHAT IS NOT FUNDED Statutory services including state schools (unless these are specifically for pupils with disabilities), local authorities, prisons, NHS hospitals or services; universities and further education colleges; start-up organisations that have not yet produced their first year's audited accounts; retrospective expenditure; capital appeals for places of worship unless these are primarily for community use, such as an adjoining church hall or clearly defined community area within a place of worship; medical research.
TYPE OF GRANT Project funding; equipment; running costs.
RANGE OF GRANTS Up to £20,000.
SAMPLE GRANTS Acorns Children's Hospice Trust (£24,000); Compton Hospice, Zoë's Place Trust (£20,000 each); Douglas Macmillan Hospice (£15,000); Lench's Trust, Rainbow Children's Hospice, Shakespeare Hospice, Stonehouse Gang (£10,000 each).
FINANCES *Year* 2015 *Income* £1,213,162 *Grants* £1,446,429 *Grants to organisations* £925,990 *Assets* £32,025,000
TRUSTEES William Colacicchi; Sue Ayres; Martin Easton; Lisa Bryan; Peter Horton; Alec Jones; Ashvin Pimpalnerkar; Victoria Milligan.
OTHER INFORMATION There were 517 grants made to organisations during the year. There were also 1,865 grants made to individuals totalling £520,500.
HOW TO APPLY Applications can be made through the charity's website. Applications are considered twice yearly and distributions are made at the end of May (spring) and at the end of November (autumn). Applications for the spring distribution should be received no later than 15 March and for the autumn no later than 15 September. No more than one application be made in each twelve-month period.
WHO TO APPLY TO Kate Slater, Charity Administrator, Portman House, 5–7 Temple Row West, Birmingham B2 5NY *Tel.* 0121 236 8004 *Email* enquiries@barondavenportscharity.org *Website* www.barondavenportscharity.org

■ The Davidson (Nairn) Charitable Trust

SC NO SC024273 **ESTABLISHED** 1995
WHERE FUNDING CAN BE GIVEN Nairn area.
WHO CAN BENEFIT Social welfare organisations and all charities recognised in Scottish Law.
WHAT IS FUNDED General charitable purposes.
WHAT IS NOT FUNDED Only registered charities or charities recognised in Scottish law are supported.
SAMPLE GRANTS Nairnshire Farming Society (£45,000); The Pentecostal Church of God and Nairn Old Parish Church (£20,000 each); Highland Hospice (£10,000); Vision Mechanics (£5,000); Nairn Book and Arts Festival (£3,000); Nairn Museum Ltd (£1,000).
FINANCES *Year* 2014/15 *Income* £40,409 *Grants* £106,724 *Grants to organisations* £106,724 *Assets* £1,692,340
HOW TO APPLY Contact the trust for an application form.
WHO TO APPLY TO The Trustees, 20 High Street, Nairn IV12 4AX

■ The Davidson Family Charitable Trust

CC NO 262937 **ESTABLISHED** 1971
WHERE FUNDING CAN BE GIVEN UK.
WHO CAN BENEFIT Mainly Jewish organisations.
WHAT IS FUNDED Education; medical causes; religious organisations; the arts; welfare.
RANGE OF GRANTS Up to £425,000.
SAMPLE GRANTS The Jerusalem Foundation (£1 million); Bowel and Cancer Research (£100,000); Western Marble Arch Synagogue (£24,000); British Ort Foundation (£12,000); Nightingale Hammerson and The Mental Health Foundation (£5,000); Friends of Tad Sarah (£1,800); Heart Cells Foundation (£500).
FINANCES *Year* 2015/16 *Income* £937,850 *Grants* £1,184,682 *Grants to organisations* £1,184,682 *Assets* £216,542
TRUSTEES Gerald Davidson; Maxine Davidson.
HOW TO APPLY Apply in writing to the correspondent.
WHO TO APPLY TO Gerald Davidson, Trustee, c/o Queen Anne Street Capital, 58 Queen Anne Street, London W1G 8HW *Tel.* 020 7224 1030

■ Michael Davies Charitable Settlement

CC NO 1000574 **ESTABLISHED** 1990
WHERE FUNDING CAN BE GIVEN UK.
WHO CAN BENEFIT Charities.
WHAT IS FUNDED General charitable purposes.
RANGE OF GRANTS £1,000 to £20,000.
SAMPLE GRANTS University of Sunderland Development Trust (£20,000); Camp and Trek, Camden Arts Centre and Royal National Orthopaedic Hospital Trust (£10,000 each); Marie Curie Cancer Care, Design Museum and The Markfield Project (£5,000 each); Royal Parks Foundation (£2,500); Cycle to Cannes (£1,000).
FINANCES *Year* 2015/16 *Income* £215,085 *Grants* £110,500 *Grants to organisations* £110,500 *Assets* £1,046,434
TRUSTEES Michael Davies; Kenneth Hawkins.
HOW TO APPLY Apply in writing to the correspondent.
WHO TO APPLY TO Kenneth Hawkins, Trustee, HW Lee Associates, New Derwent House, 69/73 Theobalds Road, London WC1X 8TA *Tel.* 020 7025 4600

■ The Biss Davies Charitable Trust

CC NO 296824 **ESTABLISHED** 1987
WHERE FUNDING CAN BE GIVEN UK and overseas.
WHO CAN BENEFIT Charitable organisations.
WHAT IS FUNDED General charitable purposes including: education/training; the advancement of health and saving lives; overseas aid.
RANGE OF GRANTS Up to £15,000.
SAMPLE GRANTS Médecins Sans Frontières (£15,000); GiveDirectly.org (£10,000); Macmillan Cancer Support (£7,000); St John's Hospice and UCL Development Fund (£5,000 each); MND Association (£1,000); Contact the Elderly (£500).
FINANCES *Year* 2015/16 *Income* £215,085 *Grants* £58,847 *Grants to organisations* £46,300 *Assets* £2,640,101

TRUSTEES Roger Davies; Adele Biss; Robert Davies.

OTHER INFORMATION The amount of grants given to individuals totalled £12,500.

HOW TO APPLY This trust does its own research and does not seek or respond to unsolicited applications.

WHO TO APPLY TO Roger Davies, Trustee, 7 Elsworthy Road, London NW3 3DS *Tel.* 020 7586 3999 *Email* rogdaviesbiss@gmail.com

■ Margaret Davies Charity

CC NO 235589 **ESTABLISHED** 1934

WHERE FUNDING CAN BE GIVEN Wales.

WHO CAN BENEFIT Registered charities only.

WHAT IS FUNDED General charitable purposes including: arts; education; health; and social welfare.

TYPE OF GRANT Mainly one-off, occasionally recurrent for specific capital projects.

RANGE OF GRANTS £1,000 to £50,000.

SAMPLE GRANTS University of Wales (£50,000); Welsh National Opera (£25,000); Gregynog Festival (£10,000); Valley Kids and Zoom Cymru (£5,000 each); Rekindle (£4,000); React (£3,000); Happy Days (£2,000); Centre for Alternative Technology (£1,800); Mid Wales Opera (£1,000).

FINANCES *Year* 2015/16 *Income* £258,589 *Grants* £222,424 *Grants to organisations* £222,424 *Assets* £7,401,568

TRUSTEES Lord David Davies; Dr Denis Balsom; Dr Janet Lewis; Daniel Davies; Thomas Williams.

HOW TO APPLY Apply in writing to the correspondent. The charity has previously stated the following information should be included in applications: whether the organisation is a registered charity; details of the reason for the application – the type of work and so on; the cost; how much has been raised so far towards the cost; the source of the sums raised; a copy of the last audited accounts if available; and any other information that the applicant may consider would help the application. Unsuccessful appeals are not informed unless an sae is enclosed.

WHO TO APPLY TO Mrs Susan Hamer, Secretary, The Offices, Plas Dolerw, Milford Road, Newtown, Powys SY16 2EH *Tel.* 01686 625228 *Email* susan@daviescharities.freeserve.co.uk

■ The Hamilton Davies Trust

CC NO 1106123 **ESTABLISHED** 2004

WHERE FUNDING CAN BE GIVEN Irlam and Cadishead (in Salford) and Rixton with Glazebrook (in Warrington).

WHO CAN BENEFIT Not-for-profit organisations with a governing body or committee, its own bank account and constitution. Individuals.

WHAT IS FUNDED Community; education; recreation; regeneration.

SAMPLE GRANTS Manchester Tech Trust (£200,000 in three grants); Manchester United Foundation (£22,000); Cadishead Primary School (£6,000); Irlam Gems (£3,000); The Meadows (£1,500); Irlam Royalettes (£500); Irlam Vets Bowling Club (£200); Salford Veterans Breakfast Club (£100).

FINANCES *Year* 2015/16 *Income* £785,725 *Grants* £488,927 *Grants to organisations* £488,927 *Assets* £7,191,895

TRUSTEES Neil McArthur; Graham Chisnall; Frank Cocker.

OTHER INFORMATION The trust also supports young people looking to develop practical skills and employability through the Chris Stocks Fund.

HOW TO APPLY For applications under £150, you simply need to send in a letter detailing: brief outline of the project and its benefits; who will be involved; how many people will be involved; who will benefit; how many will benefit; what area will the project benefit; the amount of financial support required; details of any other funding received or applied for. Application forms for applications over £150 can be downloaded from the trust's website.

WHO TO APPLY TO Jonathan Dale, Trustee, 48 Coronation Street, Salford M5 3SA *Tel.* 0161 222 4003 *Email* hello@hamiltondavies.org.uk *Website* www.hamiltondavies.org.uk

■ The John Grant Davies Trust

CC NO 1041001 **ESTABLISHED** 1994

WHERE FUNDING CAN BE GIVEN Greater Manchester.

WHO CAN BENEFIT Charitable organisation; registered charities; social groups.

WHAT IS FUNDED Poverty; economic/community development; children and young people; old people; ethnic minorities; deprived areas; education.

WHAT IS NOT FUNDED Priority is given to groups in hard-pressed areas.

TYPE OF GRANT One-off, capital, core costs, feasibility studies, project, research, salaries and start-up costs.

RANGE OF GRANTS £100 to £3,000.

SAMPLE GRANTS A list of beneficiaries was not available.

FINANCES *Year* 2015 *Grants* £60,000 *Grants to organisations* £60,000

TRUSTEES Maxine Rawlings; Jonathan Dale; Kate Davie; John Hughes; Graham Cooper.

OTHER INFORMATION A list of beneficiaries could not be located. There were no accounts available for this charity, therefore the amount spent on grants was estimated based on the charity's expenditure.

HOW TO APPLY Apply in writing to the correspondent.

WHO TO APPLY TO Mandy Coleman, General Manager, Hamilton Davies House, 117C Liverpool Road, Cadishead, Manchester M44 5BG *Email* johngrantdaviestrust@tiscali.co.uk

■ The Crispin Davis Family Trust

CC NO 1150637 **ESTABLISHED** 2013

WHERE FUNDING CAN BE GIVEN Worldwide with a preference for Africa.

WHO CAN BENEFIT Registered charities; schools.

WHAT IS FUNDED Children and young people across the world who are in need of help as a result of poverty, lack of education or illness.

SAMPLE GRANTS Tushinde Children's Trust (£20,000); Optimus Foundation (£180,000); Cavoequiva and Glyndebourne (£5,000 each); Gorrann School (£3,100).

FINANCES *Year* 2015/16 *Income* £120,203 *Grants* £213,195 *Grants to organisations* £213,195 *Assets* £5,612,694

TRUSTEES Sir Crispin Davis; Lady Jean Davis; Cripps Trust Corporation Ltd; Dr Julia Davis; Caroline Davis King; Angela Spaid.

HOW TO APPLY Apply in writing to the correspondent.

WHO TO APPLY TO The Trustees, Heartwood, Heartwood Wealth Management, 77 Mount Ephraim, Tunbridge Wells, Kent TN4 8BS *Tel.* 01892 701801 *Email* info@heartwoodgroup.co.uk

■ The Davis Foundation

CC NO 1152998 **ESTABLISHED** 2013
WHERE FUNDING CAN BE GIVEN England and Israel.
WHO CAN BENEFIT Organisations.
WHAT IS FUNDED Jewish causes; young people; older people; disability; the arts; horticulture; religious harmony; religious education; citizenship.
SAMPLE GRANTS A list of beneficiaries was not available.
FINANCES *Year* 2014/15 *Income* £1,781,940 *Grants* £2,213,511 *Grants to organisations* £2,213,511 *Assets* £5,141,469
TRUSTEES Michael Davis; Barbara Davis; Sarah Davis.
OTHER INFORMATION The 2014/15 accounts were the latest available at the time of writing (June 2017).
HOW TO APPLY Apply in writing to the correspondent.
WHO TO APPLY TO Robert Craig, Trustee, Howard Kennedy LLP, No. 1 London Bridge, London SE1 9BG *Tel.* 020 7389 9504 *Email* mick@thedavisfoundation.com

■ The Henry and Suzanne Davis Foundation

CC NO 1153199 **ESTABLISHED** 2013
WHERE FUNDING CAN BE GIVEN England and Wales.
WHO CAN BENEFIT Charitable organisations and individuals.
WHAT IS FUNDED General charitable purposes; education and training; arts and culture; human rights.
SAMPLE GRANTS A list of beneficiaries was not available.
FINANCES *Year* 2015/16 *Income* £195,000 *Grants* £158,045 *Grants to organisations* £158,045 *Assets* £204,256
TRUSTEES Robert Craig; Henry Davis; Suzanne Davis.
HOW TO APPLY Apply in writing to the correspondent.
WHO TO APPLY TO Michael Davis, Trustee, 3 Beechworth Close, London NW3 7UT *Tel.* 020 3755 5421 *Email* robert.craig@howardkennedy.com

■ Dawat-E-Hadiyah Trust (United Kingdom)

CC NO 294807 **ESTABLISHED** 1986
WHERE FUNDING CAN BE GIVEN UK and overseas.
WHO CAN BENEFIT Registered charities; individuals.
WHAT IS FUNDED The advancement of the Islamic religion; education; social welfare and relief in need.
SAMPLE GRANTS Saifee Burhani Upliftment Trust (£5.1 million); Al Jameah Al-Sayfiyah Trust (£125,500); Husaini Masjid and Mohammedi Park Management Trust (£52,000); Anjum-e-Saifee, Leicester (£26,000); Anjuman-e-Burhani, London (£11,800).
FINANCES *Year* 2015 *Income* £6,560,883 *Grants* £5,506,792 *Grants to organisations* £5,409,775 *Assets* £9,889,225
TRUSTEE The 53rd Dai Al-Mutlaq, His Holiness Syedna Mufaddal Saifuddin.
OTHER INFORMATION The amount of grants given to individuals totalled £97,000.
HOW TO APPLY Apply in writing to the correspondent.
WHO TO APPLY TO Dawat-E-Hadiyah Trust (United Kingdom), 6 Mohammedi Park Complex, Rowdell Road, Northolt, Middlesex UB5 6AG *Tel.* 020 8839 0750 *Email* farazdaqz@yahoo.com

■ The Dawe Charitable Trust

CC NO 1060314 **ESTABLISHED** 1997
WHERE FUNDING CAN BE GIVEN UK and overseas with a preference for Cambridgeshire.
WHO CAN BENEFIT Charitable organisations.
WHAT IS FUNDED Disadvantaged people and homelessness; research into international socio-economic issues.
SAMPLE GRANTS The Prince's Trust (£50,000); St Theresa Charity and Manda Wilderness Agricultural Project (£5,000 each).
FINANCES *Year* 2015/16 *Income* £25,950 *Grants* £161,593 *Grants to organisations* £161,593 *Assets* £1,254,276
TRUSTEES Dr Peter Dawe; Mark Turner; David Kerr.
HOW TO APPLY Apply in writing to the correspondent. The trust's 2015/16 annual report states: 'The trustees do not actively solicit the making of grants or loans, but will consider applications on their merits.'
WHO TO APPLY TO Dr Peter Dawe, Trustee, 17A Broad Street, Ely, Cambridgeshire CB7 4AJ *Tel.* 01353 634662 *Email* office@dawe.co.uk

■ The De Brye Charitable Trust

CC NO 326226 **ESTABLISHED** 1982
WHERE FUNDING CAN BE GIVEN UK.
WHO CAN BENEFIT Charitable organisations.
WHAT IS FUNDED General charitable purposes, preference may be given to the activities affecting the orphans, neglected children and children with physical disabilities, older people and the blind.
TYPE OF GRANT One-off grants to organisations.
RANGE OF GRANTS £500 to £10,000.
SAMPLE GRANTS British Red Cross and The Stars Appeal (£10,000 each); Newlife Foundation for Disabled Children and Winston's Wish (£3,000 each); Bag Books, Medical Detection Dogs and Sense (£2,000 each); CHICKS and WheelPower (£1,000 each); NSPCC (£500).
FINANCES *Year* 2015/16 *Income* £60,643 *Grants* £61,000 *Grants to organisations* £61,000 *Assets* £2,673,438
TRUSTEES Alexander de Brye; Jennifer de Brye; Phillip Sykes.
HOW TO APPLY Apply in writing to the correspondent.
WHO TO APPLY TO George Georghiou, Mercer and Hole, 72 London Road, St Albans, Hertfordshire AL1 1NS *Tel.* 01727 869141

■ Peter De Haan Charitable Trust

CC NO 1077005 **ESTABLISHED** 1999
WHERE FUNDING CAN BE GIVEN UK.
WHO CAN BENEFIT Charitable organisations.
WHAT IS FUNDED The arts; the environment; social welfare.
TYPE OF GRANT Project grants or core costs.
SAMPLE GRANTS Leicestershire and Rutland Wildlife Trust; National Youth Theatre; Old Vic New Voices; Yorkshire Wildlife Trust.
FINANCES *Year* 2015/16 *Income* £383,000 *Grants* £1,396,000 *Grants to organisations* £1,396,000 *Assets* £4,266,000
TRUSTEES Peter Charles De Haan; Janette McKay; Dr Rob Stoneman; Opus Corporate Trustees Ltd.
HOW TO APPLY The website states: 'The Trust does not fund unsolicited applications.'
WHO TO APPLY TO Simon Johnson, Finance Director, Wool Yard, 54 Bermondsey Street, London SE1 3UD *Tel.* 020 7232 5465 *Email* sjohnson@pdhct.org.uk *Website* www.pdhct.org.uk

■ The Roger De Haan Charitable Trust

CC NO 276274 **ESTABLISHED** 1978

WHERE FUNDING CAN BE GIVEN East Kent, particularly Folkestone, Hythe and Romney Marsh.

WHO CAN BENEFIT Registered charities; schools; community organisations; churches.

WHAT IS FUNDED Arts and culture; education; health and welfare; sports; community and young people; heritage and regeneration; overseas.

WHAT IS NOT FUNDED Applications that are unlikely to receive the trustees' support include: those where a grant would directly replace or subsidise statutory funding; those intended to develop business ventures, publications, websites or arrange conferences; any grant that would primarily benefit an individual or individuals; requests from students for the purpose of personal study or travel; funding for expeditions or overseas travel. The trust will not consider applications for projects that promote political or religious beliefs or causes, from animal welfare charities, or from national charities, unless there is a significant benefit to a local office or project. Repeat applications from a single organisation within a twelve-month period will not normally be considered.

SAMPLE GRANTS The Creative Foundation (£1.3 million); Age UK (£105,500); Folkestone Baptist Church (£31,000); Folkestone Academy (£21,000); Hythe Venetian Fete (£17,500); Cancer Research (£10,000); Childhood First (£5,000); Planet Folkestone (£3,500); Dover Sea Cadets (£2,000); In Step Dance Studio and Kent Gardens Trust (£1,000 each); Tenterden Folk Festival (£500).

FINANCES *Year* 2015/16 *Income* £795,000 *Grants* £3,318,317 *Grants to organisations* £3,318,317 *Assets* £26,872,000

TRUSTEES Benjamin De Haan; Joshua De Haan; Sir Roger De Haan; Lady De Haan.

HOW TO APPLY Applications can be made through the trust's website. Alternatively applicants may download or print the form available on this website for completion return to the trust by post.

WHO TO APPLY TO Sir Roger De Haan, Trustee, Strand House, Pilgrims Way, Monks Horton, Ashford, Kent TN25 6DR *Website* www.rdhct.org.uk

■ The De La Rue Charitable Trust

CC NO 274052 **ESTABLISHED** 1977

WHERE FUNDING CAN BE GIVEN Worldwide.

WHO CAN BENEFIT Charitable organisations.

WHAT IS FUNDED Educational projects which promote relevant skills, international understanding and bring relief from suffering.

TYPE OF GRANT Usually one-off for a specific project or part thereof.

SAMPLE GRANTS Afrikids; Cameo Aid; Cecily's Fund; Concern Universal – Bangladesh; Disasters Emergency Committee – Nepal Earthquake Appeal; Disability Africa; Handicapped Children's Action Group; International Refugee Trust; Newcastle Society for the Blind; Second Chance; Their Future Today; Zambia Orphans Aid.

FINANCES *Year* 2015/16 *Income* £60,978 *Grants* £69,999 *Grants to organisations* £69,999 *Assets* £33,441

TRUSTEES Bill Taylor; Ed Peppiatt; Amanda Wiltshire; Sarah Gilbert; Francis Carne.

HOW TO APPLY Apply in writing to the correspondent.

WHO TO APPLY TO Gill Hugill, De La Rue House, Jays Close, Basingstoke, Hampshire RG22 4BS *Tel.* 01256 605000 *Email* appeals.secretary@uk.delarue.com *Website* www.delarue.com

■ The De Laszlo Foundation

CC NO 327383 **ESTABLISHED** 1978

WHERE FUNDING CAN BE GIVEN UK.

WHO CAN BENEFIT Arts organisations and registered charities.

WHAT IS FUNDED Promotion of the arts; general charitable purposes.

SAMPLE GRANTS The De Laszlo Archive Trust (£188,000); Gordonstoun School Arts Centre (£20,000); Durham University and Royal Marsden (£10,000 each); Foundation for Liver Research (£8,000); Southampton University (£5,000); Federation of British Artists (£3,000); AGORA (£2,500); National Youth Orchestra (£1,500); Tate Foundation (£1,000); Cardboard Citizens (£500); Chelsea Open Air Nursery School (£250).

FINANCES *Year* 2015/16 *Income* £657,804 *Grants* £471,021 *Grants to organisations* £471,021 *Assets* £2,312,207

TRUSTEES Damon De Laszlo; Lucy Birkbeck; Robert De Laszlo; William De Laszlo.

OTHER INFORMATION The foundation was set up to promote the advancement and promotion of education and interest in the visual arts with special reference to encouraging knowledge of the works of contemporary painters, in particular those of the late Philip de Laszlo.

HOW TO APPLY No grants are given to unsolicited applications.

WHO TO APPLY TO Christabel Wood, 5 Albany Courtyard, London W1J 0HF *Tel.* 020 7437 1982 *Email* catalogue@delaszlo.com

■ William Dean Countryside and Educational Trust

CC NO 1044567 **ESTABLISHED** 1995

WHERE FUNDING CAN BE GIVEN UK with a preference for Cheshire; also Derbyshire, Lancashire, Staffordshire and the Wirral.

WHO CAN BENEFIT Organisations; individuals.

WHAT IS FUNDED The trust gives grants to individuals and organisations in its immediate locality which promote education in natural history, ecology and the conservation of the natural environment. Support can be given to wildlife trusts, schools for ecological and conservation projects, and parks and pleasure grounds for similar purposes.

WHAT IS NOT FUNDED Education is not funded, unless directly associated with one of the stated eligible categories.

TYPE OF GRANT Capital, core costs. One-off grants.

RANGE OF GRANTS £500 to £30,000.

SAMPLE GRANTS Cheshire Wildlife Trust (£30,000); Donna Louise Trust (£3,100); Congleton Community Projects (£2,800); Eaton Bank Academy (£2,000); Astbury Mere Trust and Bromley Farm Development Trust (£1,000 each); Cheshire Beekeepers' Association and Scottish Seabirds Centre (£500 each).

FINANCES *Year* 2015 *Income* £61,527 *Grants* £61,855 *Grants to organisations* £61,855 *Assets* £1,448,462

TRUSTEES John Ward; David Daniel; Prof. David Parsons; David Crawford; Rebecca Franklin; Patricia Pinto.

HOW TO APPLY Apply in writing to the correspondent. The trustees meet four times each year in March, June, September and December when applications for grants are considered.
WHO TO APPLY TO Clare Amare, 51 Moss Road, Congleton CW12 3BN *Tel.* 01260 276970 *Email* clare.amare@ellanet.co.uk

■ Debenhams Foundation

CC NO 1147682 **ESTABLISHED** 2012
WHERE FUNDING CAN BE GIVEN UK.
WHO CAN BENEFIT Local charities working in areas in which Debenhams have stores.
WHAT IS FUNDED Community projects; health; social welfare; disaster relief; support to charity partners.
SAMPLE GRANTS Help for Heroes (£440,000); BBC Children in Need (£382,000); Breast Cancer Now (£300,500); Make a Wish Foundation (£75,000); Breast Cancer Ireland (£14,500); NSPCC (£5,500); Allegra UK (£2,100); CLIC Sargent (£660); St Giles Hospice (£57).
FINANCES *Year* 2015/16 *Income* £2,099,828 *Grants* £2,099,828 *Grants to organisations* £1,575,112 *Assets* £1
TRUSTEES Keith Markham; Nicola Zamblera; Patricia Skinner.
OTHER INFORMATION Grants were made to 26 organisations during the year. The foundation's website states: 'In addition to our key charity partners, the Debenhams Foundation also supports local charities which operate in the Debenhams store community, ad hoc international relief via the Disasters Emergency Committee and other charity activity as deemed suitable by the Foundation's Trustees.'
HOW TO APPLY Contact your local Debenhams store.
WHO TO APPLY TO Lisa Hunt, Debenhams PLC, 10 Brock Street, London NW1 3FG *Email* lisa.hunt@debenhams.com *Website* sustainability.debenhamsplc.com/debenhams-foundation

■ Debmar Benevolent Trust Ltd

CC NO 283065 **ESTABLISHED** 1979
WHERE FUNDING CAN BE GIVEN UK and Israel.
WHO CAN BENEFIT Jewish organisations.
WHAT IS FUNDED Jewish causes; the advancement of the Jewish religion.
RANGE OF GRANTS Up to £102,500 but typically under £25,000.
SAMPLE GRANTS MW (RH) (HO) (GK) and (CL) Foundations (£102,500 each); Matono (£25,000); Asser Bishvil Foundation and Talmud Torah Chinuch Norim (£20,000 each); Kol Yom Trust (£10,000).
FINANCES *Year* 2015/16 *Income* £830,963 *Grants* £488,900 *Grants to organisations* £488,900 *Assets* £5,343,838
TRUSTEES David Olsberg; Jacob Halpern.
OTHER INFORMATION Other grants for less than £2,500 totalled £3,700. The associated MW Foundations received almost half of the grant total (£410,000).
HOW TO APPLY Apply in writing to the correspondent.
WHO TO APPLY TO David Olsberg, Trustee, 16 Stanley Road, Salford M7 4RW

■ The Delius Trust

CC NO 207324 **ESTABLISHED** 1935
WHERE FUNDING CAN BE GIVEN UK and overseas.
WHO CAN BENEFIT Orchestras; musical societies; individual performers.
WHAT IS FUNDED The promotion of the works of the composer Frederick Delius and any other composer born or at any time permanently resident in Great Britain or Ireland from 1860 to the present day, with a preference for contemporaries of Delius.
WHAT IS NOT FUNDED Capital projects.
RANGE OF GRANTS £500 to £10,000.
SAMPLE GRANTS American Symphony Orchestra (£10,000); Victorian Opera, Melbourne (£8,000); Royal Philharmonic Society (£3,000); Delius Society UK (£2,000); Epsom Symphony Orchestra (£1,000); Haslemere Music Society (£500).
FINANCES *Year* 2015 *Income* £111,941 *Grants* £59,340 *Grants to organisations* £59,340 *Assets* £2,373,452
TRUSTEES Musicians' Benevolent Fund; David Lloyd-Jones; Martin Williams.
HOW TO APPLY Apply in writing for consideration by the trustees and the advisers. See the trust's website for further details. The trustees meet three times a year, in February, June and October. Applications should be received early in the month before each meeting. The trust will not usually make retrospective grants. There is no standard application form.
WHO TO APPLY TO Helen Faulkner, Secretary to the Trust, 13 Calico Row, London SW11 3YH *Tel.* 020 7924 4250 *Email* delius.trust@helpmusicians.org.uk *Website* www.delius.org.uk

■ The Dellal Foundation

CC NO 265506 **ESTABLISHED** 1973
WHERE FUNDING CAN BE GIVEN UK.
WHO CAN BENEFIT Registered charities only.
WHAT IS FUNDED Mostly 'the welfare and benefit of Jewish people'.
WHAT IS NOT FUNDED Individuals.
TYPE OF GRANT One-off.
SAMPLE GRANTS A list of beneficiaries was not available.
FINANCES *Year* 2015/16 *Income* £100,000 *Grants* £142,135 *Grants to organisations* £142,135 *Assets* £72,663
TRUSTEES Edward Azouz; Guy Dellal; Jeffrey Azouz; Alexander Dellal.
HOW TO APPLY Apply in writing to the correspondent.
WHO TO APPLY TO S. Hosier, 25 Harley Street, London W1G 9BR *Tel.* 020 7299 1400 *Email* DellalFoundation@gmail.com

■ The Delves Charitable Trust

CC NO 231860 **ESTABLISHED** 1922
WHERE FUNDING CAN BE GIVEN UK and overseas.
WHO CAN BENEFIT Registered charities.
WHAT IS FUNDED Medical research; medical care; self-sustaining communities and economic independence; environment; social responsibility.
WHAT IS NOT FUNDED The trust does not give sponsorships or personal educational grants.
SAMPLE GRANTS British Heart Foundation (£16,100); Macular Disease Society (£10,000); Médecins Sans Frontières (£8,000); Motivation and Samaritans (£5,000 each); Tree Aid (£2,500); Plantlife (£2,200); Combat Stress and David Sheldrick Wildlife Trust (£1,500 each); Leatherhead Coral Society (£1,000).
FINANCES *Year* 2015/16 *Income* £252,982 *Grants* £198,400 *Grants to organisations* £198,400 *Assets* £7,875,791

TRUSTEES Dr Elizabeth Breeze; Dr Charles Breeze; George Breeze; John Breeze; Mark Breeze; William Breeze.
HOW TO APPLY The trust does not accept unsolicited applications for funding.
WHO TO APPLY TO The Trust Administrator, Luminary Finance LLP, PO Box 135, Longfield, Kent DA3 8WF *Tel.* 01732 822114

■ The Demigryphon Trust

CC NO 275821 **ESTABLISHED** 1978
WHERE FUNDING CAN BE GIVEN UK, with a preference for Scotland.
WHO CAN BENEFIT Registered charities only.
WHAT IS FUNDED General charitable purposes. The trust supports a wide range of organisations and appears to have a preference for education, medical, children and Scottish organisations.
WHAT IS NOT FUNDED Individuals. Only registered charities are supported.
TYPE OF GRANT Mainly one-off grants.
RANGE OF GRANTS Mostly up to £10,000.
SAMPLE GRANTS Bomber Command Association (£10,000); Chichester Access Group, Game and Wildlife Conservation Trust (£5,000 each); Friends of Tillington Church (£2,000); The Amber Foundation (£1,000); Breast Cancer Care, Royal National Countryside Initiative (£500 each); Prostate Cancer UK, RNLI (£100 each).
FINANCES *Year* 2015/16 *Income* £43,984 *Grants* £84,838 *Grants to organisations* £41,703 *Assets* £2,714,481
TRUSTEE The Cowdray Trust Ltd.
HOW TO APPLY No grants are given to unsolicited applications.
WHO TO APPLY TO Anina Cheng, Swan House, 17–19 Stratford Place, London W1C 1BQ *Tel.* 020 7907 2100 *Email* charity@mfs.co.uk

■ The Denman Charitable Trust

CC NO 326532 **ESTABLISHED** 1983
WHERE FUNDING CAN BE GIVEN Bath, North East Somerset, Bristol and Gloucestershire.
WHO CAN BENEFIT Registered charities only.
WHAT IS FUNDED General charitable purposes.
WHAT IS NOT FUNDED Individuals; non-charitable organisations.
TYPE OF GRANT Pump-priming rather than running costs.
RANGE OF GRANTS £100 to £25,000. Mostly under £5,000.
SAMPLE GRANTS St George's Music Trust (£25,000); At Bristol (£12,500); South Bristol Youth (£10,000); The Rock Community Centre (£5,000); Genesis Trust Bath (£2,000); Brain Tumour Support and Criminon (£1,000 each); Anchor Society and Grateful Society (£600 each); Douglas and Helen House Hospice (£300); Macmillan Cancer Support (£110).
FINANCES *Year* 2015/16 *Income* £72,329 *Grants* £101,388 *Grants to organisations* £101,388 *Assets* £15,661
TRUSTEES David Marsh; Arnold Denman; Dorothy Denman; Sue Blatchford; Joanna Denman.
HOW TO APPLY Apply in writing to the correspondent. Applications must contain: full contact details including address, phone number and email address; registered charity number; aims and main activities of the charity; latest financial accounts; income sources split between donations, grants and activities; if you are asking for funding for a particular project; details of the project that you would like the trust to fund; the benefits and outcomes that you hope to achieve as a result of the funding; full breakdown of costs. The trustees meet to consider applications four times a year in March, June, September and December.
WHO TO APPLY TO Dorothy Denman, Trustee, c/o Steeple Group, PO Box 1881, Old Sodbury, Bristol BS37 6WS *Email* enquiries@denmancharitabletrust.org.uk *Website* www.denmancharitabletrust.org.uk/index.html

■ Dentons UKMEA LLP Charitable Trust

CC NO 1041204 **ESTABLISHED** 1994
WHERE FUNDING CAN BE GIVEN UK with a preference for Milton Keynes and London.
WHO CAN BENEFIT Registered charities; hospices; community organisations.
WHAT IS FUNDED General charitable purposes with a preference is also given to organisations which have a connection with SNR Denton UK LLP.
WHAT IS NOT FUNDED Individuals; education and scholarships.
TYPE OF GRANT One-off and recurrent.
RANGE OF GRANTS Up to £6,800 but mainly £500 to £1,500.
SAMPLE GRANTS Dogs for Good (£6,800 in three grants); Whitechapel Mission (£6,500 in three grants); Time and Talents (£3,800); Blind in Business, React and Youth Aid (£1,500 each); Action for Kids, Prisoners' Education Trust and Willen Hospice (£750 each); Cancer Research UK (£500 in two grants); Coppafeel (£250).
FINANCES *Year* 2015/16 *Income* £135,690 *Grants* £126,150 *Grants to organisations* £126,150 *Assets* £26,712
TRUSTEES Virginia Glastonbury; Matthew Harvey; Brandon Ransley.
HOW TO APPLY Apply in writing to the correspondent. The trustees meet quarterly.
WHO TO APPLY TO Bernadette O'Sullivan, One Fleet Place, London EC4M 7WS *Tel.* 020 7242 1212

■ Foundation Derbyshire

CC NO 1039485 **ESTABLISHED** 1996
WHERE FUNDING CAN BE GIVEN Derbyshire and the city of Derby.
WHO CAN BENEFIT Voluntary groups and volunteers.
WHAT IS FUNDED General charitable purposes; social welfare; community.
WHAT IS NOT FUNDED The foundation's general exclusions are: profit-making organisations/businesses; medical equipment; animal charities; any project which promotes faith or involves the refurbishment/building of a place of worship; statutory bodies – schools, hospitals, police, etc.; any project which directly replaces statutory obligations; projects which benefit people outside Derbyshire; any project which promotes a political party; retrospective funding (grants for activities which have already taken place); sponsored events. Specific programs may have additional exclusions.
RANGE OF GRANTS Mainly between £100 and £5,000; possibly more for managed programmes depending on their criteria.
SAMPLE GRANTS Jonathan Vickers Fine Art Award (£17,100); Derbyshire Domestic Violence and Sexual Abuse Service (£15,000); Repton Foundation, Sinfonia Viva and Bamblebrook Community Association (£10,000 each); Play and Recycling Centre (£9,500); Sporting Communities (£8,600).

FINANCES *Year* 2015/16 *Income* £453,965 *Grants* £241,829 *Grants to organisations* £241,829 *Assets* £6,772,236

TRUSTEES Arthur Blackwood; Robin Wood; Michael Hall; Lucy Palmer; David Coleman; Nicholas Mirfin; David Walker; Matthew Montague; Louise Pinder; Nicola Phillips; Peter Pimm; Philip Boxham.

OTHER INFORMATION Grants were made to 214 organisations during the year.

HOW TO APPLY Applications can be made through the foundation's website. The foundation recommends contacting them before making an application and are happy to speak to applicants. Before proceeding also ensure that you have read the Journey Sheet and Success Guide which are available on the foundation's website.

WHO TO APPLY TO Emma Hanson, Secretary, c/o RSM UK, 7th Floor, City Gate East, Tollhouse Hill, Nottingham NG1 5FS *Tel.* 01773 525860 *Email* hello@foundationderbyshire.org *Website* www.foundationderbyshire.org

■ Provincial Grand Charity of the Province of Derbyshire

CC NO 701963 **ESTABLISHED** 1989

WHERE FUNDING CAN BE GIVEN Derbyshire.

WHO CAN BENEFIT Masons and their dependants; other charitable organisations.

WHAT IS FUNDED Masonic charities and general charitable purposes.

SAMPLE GRANTS Blythe House Hospice; WORK; Derby Kids' Camp; Ryder-Cheshire Volunteers; Brin's Cottage; Lennox Children's Cancer Fund; Ian Appeal; Guide Association Chesterfield HQ; 3rd Wingerworth Scout Group; Muscular Dystrophy Campaign; Nicholson Court Social Club.

FINANCES *Year* 2015/16 *Income* £74,324 *Grants* £59,461 *Grants to organisations* £54,861 *Assets* £1,327,453

OTHER INFORMATION We have estimated that donations to individuals total £4,600.

HOW TO APPLY Apply in writing to the correspondent.

WHO TO APPLY TO Martyn Bailey, Trustee, Derby Masonic Hall, 457 Burton Road, Littleover, Derby DE23 6XX *Tel.* 01332 272202 *Email* secretary@derbyshiremason.org *Website* www.derbyshiremason.org

■ The J. N. Derbyshire Trust

CC NO 231907 **ESTABLISHED** 1944

WHERE FUNDING CAN BE GIVEN Mainly Nottingham and Nottinghamshire.

WHO CAN BENEFIT Charitable organisations.

WHAT IS FUNDED General charitable purposes, including: the promotion of health; the development of physical improvement; the advancement of education; and the relief of poverty, distress and sickness. Local charities receive preferential consideration.

WHAT IS NOT FUNDED Individuals; costs of study.

TYPE OF GRANT Buildings; capital; project funding. Funding may be given for up to three years.

RANGE OF GRANTS Up to £15,000.

SAMPLE GRANTS St Paul's – West Bridgford (£15,000); Dance4 Ltd, Emmanuel House and Jericho Road Project Nottingham Nightspot (£5,000 each); Elizabeth Finn Care (£4,600); The Rainbow Project and Citizens Advice – Broxtowe (£4,000 each); Nottinghamshire Clubs for Young People (£3,300).

FINANCES *Year* 2015/16 *Income* £215,189 *Grants* £188,700 *Grants to organisations* £188,700 *Assets* £4,887,575

TRUSTEES Peter Moore; Andora Carver; Lucy Whittle; Charles George; Belinda Lawrie; Andrew Little.

OTHER INFORMATION Grants were broken down as follows: relief of poverty (£32,500); miscellaneous (£30,300); women and children (£28,900); youth organisations (£27,500); health and disability (£22,000); older people (£13,100); education (£11,500).

HOW TO APPLY Application forms are available from the correspondent. Applications can be made at any time but trustees usually only meet to consider them twice a year in March and September. Details of the project are required. A reply is only given to unsuccessful applicants if they enclose an sae.

WHO TO APPLY TO The Grants Team, Unit 2, Heritage Business Centre, Belper, Derbyshire DE56 1SW *Tel.* 0115 964 4450 *Email* emma.hanson@rsmuk.com

■ The Desmond Foundation

CC NO 1014352 **ESTABLISHED** 1992

WHERE FUNDING CAN BE GIVEN Worldwide.

WHO CAN BENEFIT Charitable organisations.

WHAT IS FUNDED General charitable purposes; the relief of poverty and sickness, particularly among children.

TYPE OF GRANT One-off grants.

RANGE OF GRANTS Up to £250,000.

SAMPLE GRANTS Canal and River Trust (£237,000); Centre for Vision in the Developing World (£50,000); Sue Ryder (£40,000); Good Deed Foundation (£30,000); Diabetes UK and Friends of the HSC (£10,000); Chai Cancer Centre (£5,000); The Marwyn Trust (£2,500); Royal Marsden Cancer Charity (£1,000).

FINANCES *Year* 2015 *Income* £2,142,335 *Grants* £903,788 *Grants to organisations* £903,788 *Assets* £1,759,487

TRUSTEES Richard Desmond; Northern & Shell Services Ltd; Northern & Shell Media Group Ltd.

HOW TO APPLY Apply in writing to the correspondent.

WHO TO APPLY TO Allison Racher, Northern & Shell Media Group Ltd, The Northern & Shell Building, 10 Lower Thames Street, London EC3R 6EN *Tel.* 020 8612 7760 *Email* allison.racher@express.co.uk

■ Devon Community Foundation

CC NO 1057923 **ESTABLISHED** 1996

WHERE FUNDING CAN BE GIVEN Devon.

WHO CAN BENEFIT Voluntary and community groups.

WHAT IS FUNDED Families in need; community cohesion; developing life skills; people with disabilities; safety and resilience; safety; helping people find a home; training and work opportunities; access to arts, culture and nature.

WHAT IS NOT FUNDED Previously funded groups/organisations that have overdue evaluations; large projects where a small grant would not make a significant difference; organisations that have unrestricted funds of more than one years' running costs; grant-making organisations; schools; building works; capital purchases over £1,000 (except for funding through the Wind and Solar Community Benefit Funds which cover specific areas); overseas travel; consultancy fees or feasibility studies; promoting political or religious beliefs; organisations or activities that primarily support animals or plants; sponsorship and/or fundraising events; funding for works that have already happened or been committed.

TYPE OF GRANT Predominantly one-off small grants for projects. Running costs and start-up costs will be considered. Funding may be given for up to one year, and very occasionally for two years.

SAMPLE GRANTS Balloons (£15,000); Moorvision (£5,000); Exwick Youth Council (£4,000); Devon and Cornwall Refugee Support and Pete's Dragons (£3,000 each); Ladies Lounge, Oasis Project and Tavistock Edge (£1,000); Exeter Network Church (£950); Plymouth Heartbeat (£500); Black Torrington Youth Club (£380).

FINANCES *Year* 2015/16 *Income* £878,427 *Grants* £401,615 *Grants to organisations* £398,618 *Assets* £5,962,426

TRUSTEES Steve Hindley; Caroline Marks; Nigel Arnold; James Cross; Christine Allison; Caroline Harlow; Rt Revd Robert Atwell Bishop of Exeter; Peter Holden; Sally Wace; Stewart Wallace; Jeremy Colson.

HOW TO APPLY The foundation's website has details of the grant schemes currently being administered and how to apply.

WHO TO APPLY TO Grants team, The Factory, Leat Street, Tiverton, Devon EX16 5LL *Tel.* 01884 235887 *Email* grants@devoncf.com *Website* www.devoncf.com

■ The Devon Historic Churches Trust

CC NO 265594 **ESTABLISHED** 1973

WHERE FUNDING CAN BE GIVEN Devon and diocese of Exeter.

WHO CAN BENEFIT Churches and chapels.

WHAT IS FUNDED The trust gives grants/loans for 'the preservation, repair, maintenance, improvement and upkeep of churches in the County of Devon.'

WHAT IS NOT FUNDED Redundant churches/chapels; bells; plumbing; disability facilities; routine maintenance.

TYPE OF GRANT Capital costs.

RANGE OF GRANTS £300 to £5,000.

SAMPLE GRANTS Jacobstowe Parochial Church Council (£5,000); Ashburton Parochial Church Council (£4,000); Thurlestone Parochial Church Council (£3,000); Walkhampton Parochial Church Council (£2,000); Cornworthy Parochial Church Council (£1,500); Atherington Parochial Church Council (£1,000); Plymtree Parochial Church Council (£300).

FINANCES *Year* 2015/16 *Income* £137,719 *Grants* £66,164 *Grants to organisations* £66,164 *Assets* £1,337,167

TRUSTEES Hugh Harrison; Lady Boles; Carol Plumstead; Lt Cdr Christopher Tuke; Lt Col. James Michie; Judith Kauntze; Rosemary Howell; Lee Martin; Lady Burnell-Nugent; The Revd Dr David Keep; Philip Tuckett; John Mills; Hendrik Vollers; Charlie Hutchings; John Rawlings.

HOW TO APPLY Apply in writing to the correspondent. The trustees meet quarterly to receive reports from officers and committees and to consider grant applications.

WHO TO APPLY TO John Mills, Dolphins, Popes Lane, Colyford, Colyton EX24 6QR *Tel.* 01297 553666 *Email* contact@devonhistoricchurches.co.uk *Website* www.devonhistoricchurches.co.uk

■ The Duke of Devonshire's Charitable Trust

CC NO 213519 **ESTABLISHED** 1949

WHERE FUNDING CAN BE GIVEN UK with a preference for North East Derbyshire, North Yorkshire and the Eastbourne area.

WHO CAN BENEFIT UK-registered charities only.

WHAT IS FUNDED General charitable purposes.

WHAT IS NOT FUNDED According to the website, the trust: 'will not normally consider any funding request made within 12 months of the outcome of a previously unsuccessful application or 5 years of a successful one. This is to ensure that the Trust can assist as wide a spread of worthwhile organisations as possible'; 'only considers applications from UK registered charities and your registration number is required (unless you have exempt status as a church, educational establishment, hospital etc)'; 'does not typically fund projects outside the UK, even if the organisation is a registered charity within Britain'; 'is not able to accept applications from individuals or for individual research or study. This includes gap year activities, study trips, fundraising expeditions and sponsorship'; 'does not normally make funding commitments over several years – grants made are typically for a single year with few exceptions'; 'does not normally fund specific salaries and positions. This is primarily because grants are single-year commitments and the Trustees would not wish a specific job to become unsustainable'; '[will not usually] consider making a grant to organisations who cannot demonstrate significant progress with fundraising, so please bear this in mind when considering the timing of your application'; '[will not consider applications] until all the information [it has] requested has been provided. Please keep your answers concise and avoid including protracted "Mission Statements", jargon and acronyms. Failure to do so may result in your application being overlooked.'

TYPE OF GRANT Capital projects.

RANGE OF GRANTS Typically £250 to £10,000.

SAMPLE GRANTS Boyle and Petyt Foundation (£25,000); Devonshire Educational Trust (£23,000); Ashford War Memorial Trust (£5,000); Child Bereavement UK (£2,500); Pod Charitable Trust (£2,400); Grindleford Playing Field Trust (£1,000); Living Paintings and Panathlon Foundation (£500 each).

FINANCES *Year* 2015/16 *Income* £199,264 *Grants* £105,985 *Grants to organisations* £105,985 *Assets* £12,419,412

TRUSTEES Earl William Cavendish Earl of Burlington; Sir Richard Gervase Beckett; Duke Peregrine Andrew Morny Cavendish Duke of Devonshire.

HOW TO APPLY Application forms are available on the trust's website, along with guidelines and details of current application deadlines. The website states: 'Do not attach additional support materials or case studies as these will not be considered. Do not exceed the space provided on the form.' The trustees meet three or four times per year.

WHO TO APPLY TO Mollie Moseley, Chatsworth, Bakewell, Derbyshire DE45 1PP *Tel.* 01246 565437 *Website* www.ddct.org.uk

The Sandy Dewhirst Charitable Trust

CC NO 279161 **ESTABLISHED** 1979

WHERE FUNDING CAN BE GIVEN UK, with a strong preference for East and North Yorkshire.

WHO CAN BENEFIT Charitable organisations; individuals connected with I. J. Dewhirst Holdings Ltd.

WHAT IS FUNDED General charitable purposes.

SAMPLE GRANTS Sargent Cancer Care for Children (£10,000); Help for Heroes (£5,000); Salvation Army, the Army Benevolent Fund and Yorkshire Air Ambulance (£3,000 each); Action Medical Research (£2,000); Driffield Town Cricket and Recreation Club (£1,500); St Catherine's Hospice, Hull Sea Cadets and All Saints Church – Nafferton (£500 each).

FINANCES *Year* 2015 *Income* £28,900 *Grants* £80,000 *Grants to organisations* £80,000

TRUSTEES Paul Howell; Timothy Dewhirst.

OTHER INFORMATION The trust's latest accounts were not available to view on the Charity Commission's website due to its low income. We have therefore estimated the grant total based on previous years' information.

HOW TO APPLY The trust does not accept unsolicited applications.

WHO TO APPLY TO Louise Cliffe, Addleshaw Goddard, 100 Barbirolli Square, Manchester M2 3AB *Tel.* 0161 934 6373

The Laduma Dhamecha Charitable Trust

CC NO 328678 **ESTABLISHED** 1990

WHERE FUNDING CAN BE GIVEN UK and overseas.

WHO CAN BENEFIT Charitable organisations.

WHAT IS FUNDED Health; education; general charitable purposes.

SAMPLE GRANTS A list of beneficiaries was not available.

FINANCES *Year* 2015/16 *Income* £594,037 *Grants* £1,525,648 *Grants to organisations* £1,525,648 *Assets* £2,229,330

TRUSTEES Mr K. R. Dhamecha; Pradip Dhamecha; Shantilal Dhamecha.

OTHER INFORMATION The trust received £451,000 from Dhamecha Foods Ltd. Grants to UK organisations totalled £438,000.

HOW TO APPLY Apply in writing to the correspondent.

WHO TO APPLY TO Pradip Dhamecha, Trustee, The Dhamecha Group, 2 Hathaway Close, Stanmore, Middlesex HA7 3NR *Tel.* 020 8903 8181 *Email* info@dhamecha.com

Diabetes UK

CC NO 215199 **ESTABLISHED** 1934

WHERE FUNDING CAN BE GIVEN UK.

WHO CAN BENEFIT Research institutions; universities.

WHAT IS FUNDED To promote and fund research into the causes and effects of diabetes, and the treatment and alleviation of the effects of diabetes to minimise the potential serious complications that can arise.

TYPE OF GRANT Equipment, fellowships, research grants, small grants, and studentships will be considered.

RANGE OF GRANTS Up to £885,000.

SAMPLE GRANTS King's College London (£885,000); Imperial College London (£638,000); University of Glasgow (£589,000); University of Exeter (£375,000); University of Manchester (£216,000); Queen's University Belfast (£158,000); University of York (£112,000); University of Ulster (£106,000).

FINANCES *Year* 2015 *Income* £37,028,000 *Grants* £5,549,000 *Grants to organisations* £5,549,000 *Assets* £22,396,000

TRUSTEES Sir Peter Dixon; Julian Baust; Noah Franklin; Dr Robert Young; Prof. David Williams; Helen McCallum; James McCall; Gareth Hoskin; Janice Watson; Prof. Mohamed Hanif; Sir Henry Burns.

OTHER INFORMATION Research grants to institutions were made for the following purposes: care (£4.1 million); prevention (£1.2 million); cure (£556,000).

HOW TO APPLY Potential applicants are first advised to read the 'General guidelines for research grant applicants' on the charity's website. Information on the application process and deadlines for each specific scheme is also available on the website or by contacting the charity directly.

WHO TO APPLY TO Research Department, Wells Lawrence House, 126 Back Church Lane, London E1 1FH *Tel.* 020 7424 1076 *Email* research@diabetes.org.uk *Website* www.diabetes.org.uk

Diageo Foundation

CC NO 1014681 **ESTABLISHED** 1992

WHERE FUNDING CAN BE GIVEN Worldwide with a focus on Africa, Latin America and Asia.

WHO CAN BENEFIT Charities and NGOs.

WHAT IS FUNDED Access to water and sanitation; skills and employability; women and girls.

SAMPLE GRANTS A list of beneficiaries was not available.

FINANCES *Year* 2015/16 *Income* £676,622 *Grants* £273,495 *Grants to organisations* £273,495 *Assets* £700,175

TRUSTEES Geoffrey Bush; William Bullard; Georgie Passalaris.

HOW TO APPLY The foundation has previously stated that it does not accept unsolicited applications.

WHO TO APPLY TO Lynne Smethurst, Head of Community Investment, Diageo PLC, Lakeside Drive, Park Royal, London NW10 7HQ *Tel.* 020 8978 6000 *Email* diageofoundation@diageo.com *Website* www.diageo.com

Alan and Sheila Diamond Charitable Trust

CC NO 274312 **ESTABLISHED** 1977

WHERE FUNDING CAN BE GIVEN UK.

WHO CAN BENEFIT Registered charities only, particularly Jewish charities.

WHAT IS FUNDED Jewish causes and general charitable purposes.

WHAT IS NOT FUNDED Individuals.

RANGE OF GRANTS Up to £12,500.

SAMPLE GRANTS Norwood (£12,500); Community Security Trust (£6,000); Youth Aliyah Child Rescue (£5,500); British ORT and Fight for Sight (£4,000 each); British WIZO (£3,000); Alzheimer's Research UK (£2,000).

FINANCES *Year* 2015/16 *Income* £246,658 *Grants* £761,654 *Grants to organisations* £76,154 *Assets* £1,925,924

TRUSTEES Dr Alan Diamond; Jonathan Kropman; Kate Goldberg; Sheila Diamond; Jerrold Bennett.

HOW TO APPLY The trust states that it will not consider unsolicited applications. No preliminary telephone calls. There are no regular trustees'

meetings. The trustees frequently decide how the funds should be allocated. The trustees have their own guidelines, which are not published.

WHO TO APPLY TO Carla Hobby, Mazars LLP, 5th Floor, Merck House, Seldown Lane, Poole, Dorset BH15 1TW *Tel.* 01202 680777 *Email* carla.hobby@mazars.co.uk

■ The Gillian Dickinson Trust

CC NO 1094362 **ESTABLISHED** 2002

WHERE FUNDING CAN BE GIVEN County Durham, Northumberland and Tyne and Wear.

WHO CAN BENEFIT Registered charities, museums, arts and theatre groups.

WHAT IS FUNDED The promotion of creativity in young people from disadvantaged backgrounds.

WHAT IS NOT FUNDED Individuals.

TYPE OF GRANT One-off or capital grants.

RANGE OF GRANTS Up to £50,000.

SAMPLE GRANTS Darlington Civic Theatre (£50,000); Sill (£25,000); Cheeseburn Sculpture (£20,000); Enter CIC (£16,000); Fertile Ground (£14,000); Northern Chords and Sage (£10,000 each).

FINANCES *Year* 2015/16 *Income* £68,817 *Grants* £170,000 *Grants to organisations* £199,551 *Assets* £1,685,921

TRUSTEES Alexander Dickinson; Piers Dickinson; Adrian Gifford; James Ramsbotham.

OTHER INFORMATION Grants were made to ten organisations.

HOW TO APPLY Applications can be made through the trust's website.

WHO TO APPLY TO Mary Waugh, Administrator, c/o Dickinson Dees LLP, One Trinity Gardens, Broad Chare, Newcastle upon Tyne NE1 2HF *Email* grants@gilliantrust.org.uk *Website* www.gilliandickinsontrust.org.uk

■ Didymus

CC NO 1152432 **ESTABLISHED** 2013

WHERE FUNDING CAN BE GIVEN England; Wales; Africa; South America.

WHO CAN BENEFIT Registered charities.

WHAT IS FUNDED Social inclusion; education; the arts; religious understanding; to advance equality and diversity by creating opportunities for women.

WHAT IS NOT FUNDED The charity will not normally consider applications: that fall outside the charity's geographical coverage; from large national charities i.e. those with an annual income in excess of £10 million or with £100 million and more in assets; from charities dedicated to issues deemed by the trustees to be already well funded within the UK; from organisations that carry out work that is the statutory responsibility of the UK government; for ongoing recurring expenses, such as mortgages.

RANGE OF GRANTS The charity will not normally consider applications in excess on £5,000.

SAMPLE GRANTS Bees for Development (£4,700); Theatre in the Quarter (£3,000); Centre for Movement Disorder (£2,900); Kreative Culture Club (£2,500); Genie Network and Trustlinks (£2,000 each); Warrington Youth Club (£1,500); Action for ME and Womankind (£1,000 each).

FINANCES *Year* 2014/15 *Income* £359,278 *Grants* £209,995 *Grants to organisations* £209,995 *Assets* £2,419,043

TRUSTEES Alan Wall; Caroline Cummins; Revd Dr Daphne Green; Helen Wall; Olivia Houlihan; William Corbett.

HOW TO APPLY Application forms are available to download from the charity's website.

WHO TO APPLY TO The Trustees, Cresswell Crabtree and Sons, 12 Market Street, Hebden Bridge HX7 6AD *Tel.* 01422 842431 *Email* apply@didymus-charity.org.uk *Website* www.didymus-charity.org.uk

■ The Dinwoodie Settlement

CC NO 1151139 **ESTABLISHED** 1968

WHERE FUNDING CAN BE GIVEN UK.

WHO CAN BENEFIT Organisations benefitting academics and postgraduate research workers.

WHAT IS FUNDED Postgraduate medical education centres (PMCs) and research fellowships for suitably qualified medical practitioners of registrar status in general medicine or general surgery.

WHAT IS NOT FUNDED Anything falling outside the main areas of work referred to above. The trustees do not expect to fund consumable or equipment costs or relieve the NHS of its financial responsibilities.

SAMPLE GRANTS Northumbria Healthcare NHS Trust (£200,000); Countess of Chester Hospital and Royal College of Psychiatrists (£53,500 each); Royal College of Surgeons (£46,000); Medical Research Council (£14,500).

FINANCES *Year* 2015/16 *Income* £316,977 *Grants* £395,263 *Grants to organisations* £395,263 *Assets* £3,834,231

TRUSTEES John Black; Dr Patrick Cadigan; Richard Arkle; Ian Goalen; John Pears.

HOW TO APPLY The trustees state they are proactive rather than reactive in their grant-giving. Negotiating for new PMCs and monitoring their construction invariably takes a number of years.

WHO TO APPLY TO Ian Goalen, Trustee, 4 Tytherington Green, Macclesfield SK10 2FA *Tel.* 01625 610549 *Email* dinwoodie@irwinmitchell.com

■ Disability Aid Fund

CC NO 1096211 **ESTABLISHED** 2002

WHERE FUNDING CAN BE GIVEN Buckinghamshire, Milton Keynes and adjacent counties.

WHO CAN BENEFIT Local, regional and small national health care charities for older people.

WHAT IS FUNDED Health care; disability. The fund is especially interested in charities which promote health and well-being through information, advice and practical help such as developing or providing special needs technology.

TYPE OF GRANT Building and refurbishment, equipment, training and general costs.

RANGE OF GRANTS £2,000 to £12,000.

SAMPLE GRANTS Dog Aid (£12,000); CEDA (Community, Equality, Disability Action) (£10,000); British Wireless for the Blind (£7,000); Designability – Bath (£6,000); Livability (£5,000); Action4Youth (£4,000); Action Against Elder Abuse (£3,000); Colostomy Association and Pituitary Foundation (£2,000 each).

FINANCES *Year* 2015/16 *Income* £201,297 *Grants* £147,000 *Grants to organisations* £147,000 *Assets* £4,490,764

TRUSTEES Roger Jefcoate; Rosemary McCloskey; Valerie Henchoz; Vivien Dinning; Carol Wemyss; Jean Jefcoate.

HOW TO APPLY The trust has previously provided the following information: 'If you think that your charity might fit our remit telephone Roger Jefcoate on 01296 715466 weekdays before 7pm to discuss your proposal. You may then be invited to submit a written application summarising your request on just one side of paper, with minimal supporting information like a single sheet general leaflet or a magazine article; do not send your annual review, we would ask for that if we need it. We would normally only consider a further request after two years, and then only by invitation.'

WHO TO APPLY TO Roger Jefcoate, Trustee, 2 Copse Gate, Winslow, Buckingham MK18 3HX *Tel.* 01296 715466

■ Dischma Charitable Trust

CC NO 1077501 **ESTABLISHED** 1999

WHERE FUNDING CAN BE GIVEN Worldwide, with a strong preference for London and the south east of England.

WHO CAN BENEFIT Charitable organisations.

WHAT IS FUNDED General charitable purposes, including: wildlife and conservation; health and disability; children and youth welfare; education; older people; the relief of poverty; arts and culture.

WHAT IS NOT FUNDED Medical research charities.

RANGE OF GRANTS Up to £29,000.

SAMPLE GRANTS Chickenshed Theatre (£29,000); University of East Anglia (£15,000); British Red Cross (£11,000); Womankind Worldwide (£4,000); West London Day Centre (£2,000); Wild Things (£1,500); Happy Days (£1,000); Down Syndrome International (£650); Yes Outdoors (£500).

FINANCES *Year* 2015 *Income* £146,580 *Grants* £188,150 *Grants to organisations* £188,150 *Assets* £5,086,071

TRUSTEES Simon Robertson; Edward Robertson; Lorna Robertson Timmis; Virginia Robertson; Selina Robertson; Arabella Brooke.

HOW TO APPLY The trustees meet half-yearly to review applications for funding. Only successful applicants are notified of the trustees' decision. Certain charities are supported annually, although no commitment is given.

WHO TO APPLY TO Linda Cousins, Secretary, Rathbones, 8 Finsbury Circus, London EC2M 7AZ *Tel.* 020 7399 0820 *Email* linda.cousins@rathbones.com

■ C. H. Dixon Charitable Trust

CC NO 282936 **ESTABLISHED** 1981

WHERE FUNDING CAN BE GIVEN England; Ghana.

WHO CAN BENEFIT Charitable organisations.

WHAT IS FUNDED General charitable purposes.

SAMPLE GRANTS Perspectives and River Thames Boat Project (£17,000 each); Sherborne Girls (£5,000); Treloar Trust (£2,300); Glyndebourne Arts Trust (£1,500); The Royal National Children's Foundation and Wulugu Project (£1,000 each).

FINANCES *Year* 2015/16 *Income* £51,181 *Grants* £44,750 *Grants to organisations* £44,750 *Assets* £1,380,621

TRUSTEES June Taylor; Richard Robinson.

HOW TO APPLY Apply in writing to the correspondent.

WHO TO APPLY TO Richard Robinson, Trustee, 22 Vicarage Drive, London SW14 8RX *Tel.* 020 8274 0744 *Email* rrobin4022@gmail.com

■ The Djanogly Foundation

CC NO 280500 **ESTABLISHED** 1980

WHERE FUNDING CAN BE GIVEN UK and overseas, mainly Israel.

WHO CAN BENEFIT Registered charities; schools and universities.

WHAT IS FUNDED Developments in medicine, education, social welfare and the arts. Welfare of older and younger people. Jewish charities.

SAMPLE GRANTS Tate Gallery (£207,000); Nottingham Girls' School (£125,000); Great Ormond Street Children's Hospital (£100,000); Animal Health Trust (£10,000); Art Fund (£3,000); Institute of Jewish Policy Research (£2,000); Jerusalem Music Centre (£1,000); River and Rowing Museum (£300); British Museum (£200).

FINANCES *Year* 2015/16 *Income* £205,730 *Grants* £667,724 *Grants to organisations* £667,724 *Assets* £4,942,776

TRUSTEES Sir Harry Djanogly; Michael Djanogly; Lady Carol Djanogly.

HOW TO APPLY Apply in writing to the correspondent. The 2015/16 accounts state 'The charity achieves its objectives receiving and evaluating grant applications.'

WHO TO APPLY TO Christopher Sills, 3 Angel Court, London SW1Y 6QF *Tel.* 020 7930 9845

■ The DLM Charitable Trust

CC NO 328520 **ESTABLISHED** 1990

WHERE FUNDING CAN BE GIVEN UK, especially the Oxford area.

WHO CAN BENEFIT Organisations benefitting: children; young adults; older people; medical professionals, nurses and doctors; and people with head and other injuries, heart disease or blindness.

WHAT IS FUNDED Charities operating in Oxford and the surrounding areas, particularly charities working in the fields of: arts, culture and recreation; religious buildings; self-help groups; the conservation of historic buildings; memorials; monuments and waterways; schools; community centres and village halls; parks; various community services and other charitable purposes.

WHAT IS NOT FUNDED Individuals.

TYPE OF GRANT Feasibility studies, one-off, research, recurring costs, running costs and start-up costs. Funding of up to three years will be considered.

SAMPLE GRANTS SeeSaw (£15,000); Home-Start – Oxford and Whizz-Kidz (£5,000 each); Brainwave (£4,000); Prison Phoenix Trust and Winston's Wish (£2,500 each); Footsteps Foundation and Keen Oxford (£2,000 each); Adventure Plus and Scope (£1,000 each).

FINANCES *Year* 2015/16 *Income* £201,310 *Grants* £109,000 *Grants to organisations* £109,000 *Assets* £5,959,256

TRUSTEES Dr Eric De La Mare; Jeffrey Cloke; Jennifer Pyper; Philippa Sawyer.

OTHER INFORMATION Grants were made to 29 organisations during the year.

HOW TO APPLY Apply in writing to the correspondent. The trustees meet in February, July and November to consider applications.

WHO TO APPLY TO Jeffrey Alan Cloke, Trustee, Water Eaton Manor, Water Eaton, Oxford OX2 8HE *Tel.* 01865 515753 *Email* clokejeff@gmail.com

■ The DM Charitable Trust

CC NO 1110419 **ESTABLISHED** 2005
WHERE FUNDING CAN BE GIVEN UK and Israel.
WHO CAN BENEFIT Jewish registered charities.
WHAT IS FUNDED Social welfare; education; promoting of the Jewish religion.
SAMPLE GRANTS Employment Resource Centre (£100,000); WST Charity Ltd (£72,000); Kisharon (£40,000); Community Concern – London (£30,000); Chabad Lubavitch of Bloomsbury (£14,300).
FINANCES *Year* 2015/16 *Income* £729,043 *Grants* £266,000 *Grants to organisations* £266,000 *Assets* £4,342,985
TRUSTEES Stephen Goldberg, David Cohen; Patrice Klein.
HOW TO APPLY Apply in writing to the correspondent.
WHO TO APPLY TO Stephen Goldberg, Trustee, Sutherland House, 70–78 West Hendon Broadway, London NW9 7BT *Tel.* 020 8457 3258

■ The Derek and Eileen Dodgson Foundation

CC NO 1018776 **ESTABLISHED** 1993
WHERE FUNDING CAN BE GIVEN In practice, Brighton and Hove.
WHO CAN BENEFIT Individuals and organisations.
WHAT IS FUNDED Welfare of older people.
SAMPLE GRANTS Age Concern; Grace Eyre Foundation; Brighton, Hove and Adur Social Services; Hove YMCA; Sussex Probation Services.
FINANCES *Year* 2015/16 *Income* £108,568 *Grants* £64,235 *Grants to organisations* £64,235 *Assets* £2,325,261
TRUSTEES Christopher Butler; Peter Goldsmith; Roy Prater; Ed Squires; Natasha Glover; Georgina Reed.
HOW TO APPLY Apply in writing to the correspondent. The trustees meet quarterly, or more frequently if necessary to assess grant applications.
WHO TO APPLY TO Gerry Wicks, Flat 5, 61 Wilbury Road, Hove, BN33PB *Tel.* 01273 749576 *Email* gerald.wicks@btinternet.com

■ The Dollond Charitable Trust

CC NO 293459 **ESTABLISHED** 1986
WHERE FUNDING CAN BE GIVEN UK and Israel.
WHO CAN BENEFIT Jewish organisations.
WHAT IS FUNDED Education and training; religious education; medical causes, health and sickness; disability; social welfare; religious activities.
SAMPLE GRANTS A list of beneficiaries was not available.
FINANCES *Year* 2015/16 *Income* £3,180,926 *Grants* £1,437,000 *Grants to organisations* £1,437,000 *Assets* £41,874,725
TRUSTEES Adrian Dollond; Jeffrey Milston; Melissa Dollond; Brian Dollond; Rina Dollond.
OTHER INFORMATION The latest accounts note: 'Although the constitution of the charity is broadly based, the trustees have adopted a policy of principally assisting the Jewish communities in Britain and Israel. The trustees aim to maximise the grants that it pays taking into account the return on its investments and likely infrastructure projects.' Grants were distributed as follows: religious education (£397,000); social welfare (£386,000); education and training (£280,000); health (£165,000); disability (£125,000); religious activities (£84,000).
HOW TO APPLY Apply in writing to the correspondent.
WHO TO APPLY TO Brian Dollond, Trustee, 3rd Floor, Hathaway House, Popes drive, Finchley, London N3 1QF

■ The Dorcas Trust

CC NO 275494 **ESTABLISHED** 1978
WHERE FUNDING CAN BE GIVEN UK and overseas.
WHO CAN BENEFIT Registered charities; missionaries.
WHAT IS FUNDED Christian mission work; health; community development; humanitarian aid; sports and the arts; education and training.
TYPE OF GRANT The trustees will also consider making loans to organisations and individuals.
RANGE OF GRANTS £100 to £32,500.
SAMPLE GRANTS Navigators (£32,500); Tear Fund (£5,000); Chippenham Cricket Club (£3,500); World Vision (£2,500); Christian Heritage (£1,000); Deafblind UK and Salvation Army (£500 each); Amnesty International (£250); Leukaemia Research and RNIB (£100 each).
FINANCES *Year* 2015/16 *Income* £45,572 *Grants* £56,113 *Grants to organisations* £48,934 *Assets* £1,778,096
TRUSTEES Jan Broad; Peter Butler; James Broad.
HOW TO APPLY Apply in writing to the correspondent.
WHO TO APPLY TO James Broad, Trustee, 8 Badlingham Farm, Badlingham, Chippenham, Ely CB7 5QQ *Email* JamesBroad@cygnet.org.uk

■ The Dorfman Foundation

CC NO 1120714 **ESTABLISHED** 2007
WHERE FUNDING CAN BE GIVEN Worldwide with a preference for the UK.
WHO CAN BENEFIT Registered charities.
WHAT IS FUNDED General charitable causes; Jewish causes.
RANGE OF GRANTS Up to £1 million.
SAMPLE GRANTS The Prince's Trust (£1 million); Westminster Abbey Foundation (£500,000); Community Security Trust (£77,500); West London Synagogue (£50,000); Jewish Care (£36,000); New Entrepreneurs Foundation (£20,000); Chickenshed Theatre Trust (£5,000); Beit Halochem (£1,000).
FINANCES *Year* 2015/16 *Income* £93,585 *Grants* £2,114,839 *Grants to organisations* £2,114,839 *Assets* £22,549,235
TRUSTEES Lloyd Dorfman; Sarah Dorfman; Amy Lux; Sophie Dorfman; Charles Dorfman; Anthony Wagerman; Peter Leach.
HOW TO APPLY Apply in writing to the correspondent.
WHO TO APPLY TO The Trustees, 22 Manchester Square, London W1U 3PT *Email* charity.correspondence@bdo.co.uk

■ Dorset Community Foundation

CC NO 1122113 **ESTABLISHED** 2007
WHERE FUNDING CAN BE GIVEN The county of Dorset, including the unitary authorities of Bournemouth and Poole.
WHO CAN BENEFIT Voluntary and community organisations; charities; individuals.
WHAT IS FUNDED Community; social welfare; education; health.
WHAT IS NOT FUNDED Organisations operating outside Dorset, Bournemouth and Poole; previously funded organisations with overdue end of grant form; local branches of national organisations unless they are locally managed and are

financially independent; public bodies to carry out their statutory obligations; the promotion of religion or political causes; retrospective funding – grants for a project that has started or been already completed; organisations with more than 12 months' unrestricted reserves; animal welfare organisations. Medical research and equipment; general large appeals, sponsored and fundraising events; consultancy fees (including professional bid writers fees); projects duplicating an existing service; one-off events without limited longer-term benefit; building works including access adaptations; capital purchases of more than £1,000.

RANGE OF GRANTS Mostly £1,000 to £5,000.

SAMPLE GRANTS Bridport Citizens Advice (£12,500); Future Roots (£11,100); Dorset Community Action (£10,000); Weymouth Community Volunteers (£9,500); St Andrews Community Hall (£9,000); Woodlands Hotel (£7,000); Age Concern North Dorset and Mosaic (£5,000 each).

FINANCES *Year* 2015/16 *Income* £970,604 *Grants* £341,144 *Grants to organisations* £341,144 *Assets* £1,972,617

TRUSTEES Geoffrey Trobridge; Christopher Morle; Jeffrey Hart; Sir Martin Davidson; Peter Eales; Jennifer Gould; Jeremy Mills; Frank Guinn; Nick Fernyhough; Jonathan Greenwood; Michelle Scanlon-Sanson.

HOW TO APPLY Applications can be made online through the foundation's website. Hard copies of the forms are also available. The foundation encourages applicants to discuss their project request prior to applying.

WHO TO APPLY TO Jon Yates, The Spire, High Street, Poole BH15 1DF *Tel.* 01202 670815 *Email* grants@dorsetcf.org *Website* www.dorsetcommunityfoundation.org

■ Dorset Historic Churches Trust

CC NO 282790 **ESTABLISHED** 1960

WHERE FUNDING CAN BE GIVEN Dorset.

WHO CAN BENEFIT Christian churches and chapels in Dorset.

WHAT IS FUNDED Restoration of Dorset church buildings, other items of significant historical and architectural interest.

WHAT IS NOT FUNDED According to the trust's website it will not consider: routine maintenance and decoration; works in the churchyard; heating and electrical maintenance; new buildings or extensions; new furniture or fittings; new bells or new bell frames; replacement or repair of organs; and clocks or sound-systems.

TYPE OF GRANT One-off grants.

RANGE OF GRANTS Up to £10,000.

SAMPLE GRANTS Warmwell (£10,000); Sturminster Newton (£8,000); St Edward's Corfe Castle – Cattistock (£7,000); Marshwood (£6,000); Winterbourne Whitechurch (£4,000); Toller Porcorum (£3,000); West Stafford – Hinton St Mary (£2,000); Leigh (£1,500).

FINANCES *Year* 2015 *Income* £179,350 *Grants* £85,750 *Grants to organisations* £85,750 *Assets* £470,520

TRUSTEES Elizabeth Ashmead; Col. Michael John Rose; Simon Pomeroy; Susan Bruce-Payne; Cpt Nigel Thimbeley; Barry De Morgan; Andrew Boggis; Revd Canon Eric Woods; Col. Jeremy Selfe; Robert Fox; Timothy Connor; Mike Crossley; Susan Smith; Philippa Francis; Michael Warren; James Timothy Smith.

OTHER INFORMATION In addition to the £85,750 paid in grants, a further £118,750 of grant funding was approved in 2015 to be delivered in the future.

HOW TO APPLY Applications can be made to the Deanery Representative of the trust in the area in which the church is located, on a form available to download, together with criteria and guidelines, from the website.

WHO TO APPLY TO Elizabeth Ashmead, Trustee, The Old Forge, Frome St Quintin, Dorchester DT2 0HG *Tel.* 01935 83548 *Email* grantssecretary@dhct.org.uk *Website* www.dorsethistoricchurchestrust.co.uk

■ The Dorus Trust

CC NO 328724 **ESTABLISHED** 1990

WHERE FUNDING CAN BE GIVEN England and Wales.

WHO CAN BENEFIT Registered UK charities.

WHAT IS FUNDED General charitable purposes.

WHAT IS NOT FUNDED Individuals.

TYPE OF GRANT Projects and one-off grants. Funding for one year or less.

RANGE OF GRANTS £5,000 to £8,000.

SAMPLE GRANTS DEBRA, St Raphael's Hospice (£8,000); Home-Start Merton, Practical Action (£7,000); Crisis UK (£6,000); Action for ME, Switchblade (£5,000); Landmark Trust (£4,000); Game and Wildlife Conservation Trust (£2,500).

FINANCES *Year* 2015 *Income* £31,827 *Grants* £52,500 *Grants to organisations* £52,500 *Assets* £3,708,087

TRUSTEES Bettine Bond; Charles Peacock; Sarah Peacock.

OTHER INFORMATION The trust made grants to nine organisations in 2015.

HOW TO APPLY This trust no longer accepts applications.

WHO TO APPLY TO Charles Peacock, Trustee, c/o Charities Aid Foundation, 25 Kings Hill Avenue, Kings Hill, West Malling ME19 4TA *Tel.* 01732 520028

■ The Double 'O' Charity Ltd

CC NO 271681 **ESTABLISHED** 1976

WHERE FUNDING CAN BE GIVEN UK and overseas.

WHO CAN BENEFIT Registered charities and individuals.

WHAT IS FUNDED Primarily, grants towards the relief of poverty, preservation of health and the advancement of education. However, the charity considers all requests for aid.

WHAT IS NOT FUNDED Grants to individuals towards education or for their involvement in overseas charity work.

TYPE OF GRANT Preferably one-off.

RANGE OF GRANTS Up to £75,000.

SAMPLE GRANTS NAPAC (£100,000); Refuge (£75,000); Shriners Hospital for Children (£43,000); Spirit of Recovery (£20,000); Robert George Foundation, The Vineyard Project (£5,000) Ashbury Village Hall (£3,000); Liddington Parochial Church Council, Norwood (£500).

FINANCES *Year* 2016 *Income* £524,628 *Grants* £465,005 *Grants to organisations* £311,267 *Assets* £156,158

TRUSTEES Peter Townshend; Rachel Fuller.

OTHER INFORMATION Grants were made to 12 organisations in 2015/16.

HOW TO APPLY Apply in writing to the correspondent.

WHO TO APPLY TO The Trustees, c/o 4 Friars Lane, Richmond, Surrey TW9 1NL *Tel.* 020 8940 8171

■ The Doughty Charity Trust

CC NO 274977 **ESTABLISHED** 1977
WHERE FUNDING CAN BE GIVEN England, Israel.
WHO CAN BENEFIT Jewish organisations benefitting people who are disadvantaged by poverty or who are ill.
WHAT IS FUNDED Orthodox Jewish, religious education, relief of poverty.
TYPE OF GRANT One-off grants.
RANGE OF GRANTS Up to £50,000.
SAMPLE GRANTS A list of beneficiaries is not available.
FINANCES *Year* 2015 *Income* £549,939 *Grants* £478,268 *Grants to organisations* £478,268 *Assets* £93,931
TRUSTEES G. Halibard; M. Halibard.
HOW TO APPLY Apply in writing to the correspondent.
WHO TO APPLY TO Gerald Halibard, Trustee, 22 Ravenscroft Avenue, London NW11 0WY *Tel.* 020 8209 0500

■ Douglas Arter Foundation

CC NO 201794 **ESTABLISHED** 1960
WHERE FUNDING CAN BE GIVEN UK, with preference for Bristol, Somerset and Gloucestershire.
WHO CAN BENEFIT Registered charities whose principal activity is to assist people with physical or mental disabilities.
WHAT IS FUNDED People with mental or physical disabilities.
WHAT IS NOT FUNDED Support is not given for: overseas projects; general community projects*; individuals; general education projects*; religious and ethnic projects*; projects for unemployment and related training schemes*; projects on behalf of people who have offended; projects concerned with the abuse of drugs and/or alcohol; wildlife and conservation schemes*; and general restoration and preservation of buildings, purely for historical and/or architectural. (* If these projects are mainly or wholly for the benefit of people who have disabilities then they may be considered.) Ongoing support is not given, and grants are not usually given for running costs, salaries, research and items requiring major funding. Loans are not given.
TYPE OF GRANT One-off for specific projects. Ongoing, research, core funding and major funding appeals are not supported.
RANGE OF GRANTS £250 to £2000.
SAMPLE GRANTS Jessie May Trust – Bristol (£2000); Deafblind UK – London, Little Heart's Matter, Macmillan Cancer Support – Bristol, The Rainbow Centre – Fareham (£1000 each); BAND – Bristol, Interact Stroke Support – London, Mencap – Essex (£500 each); Dressability – Swindon, Clothing Solutions – Bradford (£250 each).
FINANCES *Year* 2015 *Income* £117,876 *Grants* £82,500 *Grants to organisations* £80,500 *Assets* £2,861,459
TRUSTEES Geoffrey Arter; John Gurney; Peter Broderick; John Hudd; Peter Yardley.
OTHER INFORMATION The foundation made grants to 134 organisations and one individual in 2015.
HOW TO APPLY The foundation does not have an official application form. Appeals should be made in writing to the secretary. Telephone calls are not welcome. The foundation asks that the following is carefully considered before submitting an application – appeals must: be from registered charities; include a copy of the latest audited accounts available (for newly registered charities a copy of provisional accounts showing estimated income and expenditure for the current financial year); show that the project is 'both feasible and viable' and, if relevant, give the starting date of the project and the anticipated date of completion; include the estimated cost of the project, together with the appeal's target-figure and details of what funds have already been raised and any fundraising schemes for the project. The trustees state that 'where applicable, due consideration will be given to evidence of voluntary and self-help (both in practical and fundraising terms) and to the number of people expected to benefit from the project'. They also comment that their decision is final and 'no reason for a decision, whether favourable or otherwise, need be given' and that 'the award and acceptance of a grant will not involve the trustees in any other commitment'. While appeals are dealt with on an ongoing basis, to cut down costs appeals will not be acknowledged unless they are successful in being awarded a grant. The trustees meet four times a year in the first weeks of March, June, September and December, and successful applicants only will be notified and sent cheques for grants by the second weekend of the relevant month.
WHO TO APPLY TO Belinda Arter, Secretary, Fern Villa, Melksham Road, Patterdown, Chippenham, Wiltshire SN15 2NR *Tel.* 01249 448252

■ The Drapers' Charitable Fund

CC NO 251403 **ESTABLISHED** 1959
WHERE FUNDING CAN BE GIVEN UK, with a special interest in the City and adjacent parts of London and Moneymore and Draperstown in Northern Ireland.
WHO CAN BENEFIT Registered or exempt charities.
WHAT IS FUNDED General charitable purposes including social welfare, education, heritage, the arts, prisoner support, Northern Ireland and textile conservation.
WHAT IS NOT FUNDED Grants are not usually made for: individuals (except in certain circumstances); churches; almshouses; animal welfare; medical research/relief, hospitals or medical centres; children's disabilities, physical disabilities or medical conditions; holidays or general respite care; organisations that are not registered charities, unless exempt from registration; funds that replace or subsidise statutory funding; local branches of national charities, associations or movements; work that has already taken place; general appeals or circulars; loans or business finance.
TYPE OF GRANT Most grants are one-off payments but occasionally multi-year grants are awarded.
RANGE OF GRANTS Up to £100,000.
SAMPLE GRANTS School Home Support (£100,000); Bancroft School (£75,000); Drapers Academy (£51,000); Into University (£35,000); Cambridge House, St Anne's College Oxford (£20,000); Bounce Back, Reach Out (£15,000); Lost Chord (£11,000).
FINANCES *Year* 2016 *Income* £8,276,721 *Grants* £1,591,582 *Grants to organisations* £1,583,882 *Assets* £60,270,458
TRUSTEE The Drapers' Company.
HOW TO APPLY Applications can be submitted by post. In order to apply you will need to send a detailed proposal document explaining what your organisation does, how you intend to spend the money, and your most recent financial accounts and trustees' report, together with a completed application summary sheet, which

can be found on the charity's website alongside guidelines on how to apply.

WHO TO APPLY TO Andy Mellows, Head of Charities, The Drapers' Company, Drapers' Hall, Throgmorton Avenue, London EC2N 2DQ *Tel.* 020 7588 5001 *Fax* 020 7628 1988 *Email* charities@thedrapers.co.uk *Website* www.thedrapers.co.uk

■ Dromintee Trust

CC NO 1053956 **ESTABLISHED** 1996

WHERE FUNDING CAN BE GIVEN Worldwide.

WHO CAN BENEFIT Charitable organisations.

WHAT IS FUNDED People in need by reason of age, illness, disability or socio-economic circumstances; charitable purposes connected with children's welfare; the advancement of health and education; research into rare diseases and disorders, in particular metabolic disorders; general charitable purposes.

TYPE OF GRANT One-off and recurrent.

RANGE OF GRANTS £1,000 to £50,000.

SAMPLE GRANTS Don Bosco Hostel Boys School (£50,000); Consulata Fathers Tanzania (£30,000); Intercare; Light for the Blind (£20,000); Marie Curie Cancer Care (£19,000); Jesuit Missions; Rainbows Hospice, Leicester Hospitals Charity (£10,000); Thurnby Memorial Hall (£5,000); Tree of Hope (£1,000).

FINANCES *Year* 2016 *Income* £380,582 *Grants* £276,502 *Grants to organisations* £276,502 *Assets* £2,794,748

TRUSTEES Hugh Murphy; Margaret Murphy; Mary Murphy; Patrick Hugh Middleton; Robert Smith; Paul Tiernan; Joseph Murphy.

OTHER INFORMATION The trust gave grants to 17 organisations in 2015/16.

HOW TO APPLY Apply in writing to the correspondent.

WHO TO APPLY TO Hugh Murphy, Trustee, 1 Westmoreland Avenue, Thurmaston, Leicester LE4 8PH *Tel.* 0116 260 3877 *Email* drominteetrust@gmail.com

■ Duchy Health Charity Ltd

CC NO 271957 **ESTABLISHED** 1976

WHERE FUNDING CAN BE GIVEN Cornwall.

WHO CAN BENEFIT Registered charities; other health care organisations.

WHAT IS FUNDED Health care; relief of sickness; medical research; projects and schemes that improve health, well-being, the provision of health care and help people with health issues.

WHAT IS NOT FUNDED Individuals; applications that duplicate an existing provision.

TYPE OF GRANT Project costs; capital and revenue expenditure; equipment and services.

RANGE OF GRANTS £5,000 to £28,000.

SAMPLE GRANTS Cosgarne Hall (£28,000); Rosmellyn Surgery (£20,000); RCHT Research Work (£18,900); Merlin MS Clinic (£16,200); Hope for Tomorrow (£12,000); Cornwall Mobility Centre, iSight Cornwall, Young People Cornwall (£10,000); Cascade Theatre, Sea Sanctuary (£5,000).

FINANCES *Year* 2016 *Income* £210,614 *Grants* £143,771 *Grants to organisations* £143,771 *Assets* £4,704,572

TRUSTEES Barbara Vann; Carol O'Brien; Mary Grigg; Sally-Jane Coode; Mary Vyvyan; Tim Guy; Scott Bennett; Graham Murdoch; Mark Williams; Jonathan Croggon; Tracie North; Aldyth Hambly-Staite; James Robinson.

OTHER INFORMATION There were 14 grants awarded in 2015/16.

HOW TO APPLY Application forms can be downloaded from the charity's website. They can be submitted online (preferably) or via post. Applicants should provide a business plan (if possible), details of any other funding partners and an up-to-date set of accounts. The Grant Committee meets quarterly. Applications need to be submitted at least three weeks before a meeting (for information on when the meetings are held see the charity's website – 'Events' section).

WHO TO APPLY TO Mark Williams, Secretary, Robinson Reed Layton, Peat House, Newham Road, Truro, Cornwall TR1 2DP *Tel.* 01872 276116 *Email* mark.williams@rrlcornwall.co.uk *Website* www.duchyhealthcharity.org

■ The Royal Foundation of the Duke and Duchess of Cambridge and Prince Harry

CC NO 1132048 **ESTABLISHED** 2009

WHERE FUNDING CAN BE GIVEN UK and overseas.

WHO CAN BENEFIT Registered charities.

WHAT IS FUNDED Mental health; veterans and military families; disadvantaged children and young people; conservation and sustainable development.

RANGE OF GRANTS Up to £280,000.

SAMPLE GRANTS Glasgow Life (£280,000); EPIC Partners (£229,000); Southern African Wildlife Fund (£125,000); SkillForce (£90,000); Zoological Society of London (£87,000); Place 2 Be (£74,000); Business in the Community (£30,000); 65 Degrees North (£15,000); Armed Forces Para-Snowsport Team (£10,000).

FINANCES *Year* 2015 *Income* £4,258,880 *Grants* £1,758,884 *Grants to organisations* £1,758,884 *Assets* £5,002,835

TRUSTEES Teresa Green; Anthony James Lowther-Pinkerton; Guy Monson; Edward Harley; Charles Stuart Mindehall; Sir Keith Edward Mills; Simon Ian Patterson; Lady Demetra Aikaterini Pinsent.

OTHER INFORMATION Grants were awarded to 24 organisations in 2015.

HOW TO APPLY Currently the foundation is unable to accept unsolicited requests for support.

WHO TO APPLY TO Susan Stafford, Director of Grants and Evaluation, Kensington Palace, Palace Green, London W8 4PU *Tel.* 020 7101 2963 *Email* sue.stafford@royalfoundation.com *Website* www.royalfoundation.com

■ The Dulverton Trust

CC NO 1146484 **ESTABLISHED** 1949

WHERE FUNDING CAN BE GIVEN England, Scotland and Wales. Limited support to parts of Africa.

WHO CAN BENEFIT Registered charities.

WHAT IS FUNDED Youth opportunities; general welfare; preservation; Africa (usually Kenya and Uganda); peace and humanitarian support.

WHAT IS NOT FUNDED The following are not funded: individuals; museums, galleries, libraries, exhibition centres and heritage attractions; individual churches and other historic buildings; individual schools, colleges, universities or other educational establishments; hospices, hospitals, nursing or residential care homes; activities outside the stated geographical scope; charities whose main beneficiaries live within Greater London or in Northern Ireland. The following are rarely funded: regional charities that are affiliated with a national body; health, medicine and medical conditions including drug and alcohol addiction; therapy and counselling; specific support for people with disabilities; the arts and sport (except where used as a means of achieving a funding priority); animal welfare; expeditions; research; conferences; salaries; major building projects; endowments.

TYPE OF GRANT Project and one-off funding. Also capital and core costs. Funding is rarely given for more than one year.

RANGE OF GRANTS Up to £345,000.

SAMPLE GRANTS Cumbria Community Foundation (£345,000); Core Funding (£105,000); Prisoners' Education Trust (£90,000); Map Action (£60,000); Core Costs (£50,000); Innovation for Agriculture (£30,000); Tusk Trust (£15,000); Rescue Wooden Boats (£5,000); Waterbeach and Landbeach Action for Youth (£300).

FINANCES *Year* 2015 *Income* £3,780,713 *Grants* £2,647,803 *Grants to organisations* £2,647,803 *Assets* £88,723,951

TRUSTEES Christopher Willis; Sir John Kemp-Welch; Dr Catherine Willis; The Lord Dulverton; Tara Douglas-Home; Dame Mary Richardson; Richard Howard; The Rt Hon. Earl of Grey Gowrie; Sir Malcolm Rifkind; The Lord Hemphill.

HOW TO APPLY Read the guidelines carefully and then complete the eligibility quiz on the trust's website. If your organisation passes the eligibility quiz you will be provided with a link to the e-application form. The trustees meet in February, June and October to discuss proposals. There are no deadlines or dates and the selection process can taken between three and six months. All rejected applications will receive notification and an outline explanation for the rejection will usually be given. Applications under consideration for a grant will normally receive a visit from one of the trust's staff who will subsequently report to the trustees. Following the trustees' meeting successful applicants will be notified by email. If you wish to make initial enquiries, establish eligibility, discuss time scales or need to seek further guidance about an application, telephone the trust's office on 020 7495 7852. **Note:** The trust has asked us to emphasise that they do not accept applications via post. You should apply only through the trust's website.

WHO TO APPLY TO Andrew Stafford, Director, 5 St James's Place, London SW1A 1NP *Tel.* 020 7495 7852 *Fax* 020 7629 6501 *Email* grants@dulverton.org *Website* www.dulverton.org

■ The Dumbreck Charity

CC NO 273070 **ESTABLISHED** 1976

WHERE FUNDING CAN BE GIVEN Worldwide, especially West Midlands.

WHO CAN BENEFIT Charitable organisations. New applications are restricted to Midlands organisations.

WHAT IS FUNDED Animal welfare and conservation; children's welfare; older people; people with mental or physical disabilities; medical causes; and general charitable purposes.

WHAT IS NOT FUNDED Individuals.

TYPE OF GRANT Recurring and one-off grants.

RANGE OF GRANTS £500 to £10,000, but mainly for amounts under £1,000.

SAMPLE GRANTS St Edburgha's Church Roof Appeal (£10,000); Disasters Emergency Committee – Nepal Earthquake Appeal (£5,000); St Mary's Hospice, The British Horse Society (£2,000 each); Dogs for Good, SSAFA, Countryside Restoration Trust (£1000 each); Elephant Family, 1st Solihull Scout Group (£500 each).

FINANCES *Year* 2016 *Income* £150,573 *Grants* £158,150 *Grants to organisations* £158,150 *Assets* £4,026,844

TRUSTEES Chris Hordern; Hugh Carslake; Jane Uloth; Judith Melling.

OTHER INFORMATION Grants were made to 165 organisations in 2015/16.

HOW TO APPLY Apply in writing to the correspondent. The trustees meet annually in April/May. Unsuccessful applications will not be acknowledged. In general, priority is given to applications from the Midlands counties.

WHO TO APPLY TO Mrs P. M. Spragg, Administrator, c/o PS Accounting, 41 Sycamore Drive, Hollywood, Birmingham B47 5QX *Email* psaccounting@hotmail.co.uk

■ Dunard Fund 2016

SC NO SC046889 **ESTABLISHED** 2016

WHERE FUNDING CAN BE GIVEN In practice UK with a particular interest in Scotland.

WHO CAN BENEFIT Registered charities.

WHAT IS FUNDED Classical music; architecture; visual arts; and, to a lesser extent, environmental and humanitarian projects.

TYPE OF GRANT The trustees prefer to engage with recipients to enable long-term development of projects and initiatives which have major and lasting significance; they are therefore less inclined to provide one-off donations.

RANGE OF GRANTS £500 to £500,000.

SAMPLE GRANTS A list of beneficiaries was not available.

TRUSTEES Carol Colburn Grigor; Dr Catherine Colburn Høgel; Erik Colburn Høgel; Colin Liddell; Peter Thierfeldt.

OTHER INFORMATION In 2016 the Dunard Fund (SC039685) re-registered with the Scottish Charity Register as a Scottish CIO. In the past the grant total has been around £2 million and has mainly gone to classical music organisations, with humanitarian, environmental and architectural causes also being supported. As this SCIO is newly registered there are no accounts available on Companies House or the charity's OSCR record. We have assumed that the grant-making strategy will remain largely the same.

HOW TO APPLY No grants are given to unsolicited applications.

WHO TO APPLY TO Carol Colburn Grigor, Trustee, c/o J. & H. Mitchell W.S., 51 Atholl Road, Pitlochry, Perthshire, Scotland PH16 5BU

■ The Dunhill Medical Trust

CC NO 1140372 **ESTABLISHED** 1951

WHERE FUNDING CAN BE GIVEN UK.

WHO CAN BENEFIT Registered charities particularly those benefitting older people and academic institutions undertaking medical research.

WHAT IS FUNDED Care of older people, including rehabilitation and palliative care; research into the causes and treatments of disease, disability and frailty related to ageing.

WHAT IS NOT FUNDED Organisations based outside the United Kingdom or whose work primarily benefits people outside the United Kingdom; research staff based outside the UK; sponsorship of individuals; sponsorship of charitable events; providing clinical services or equipment that, in the opinion of the trust, would more appropriately be provided by the

National Health Service or other statutory bodies; hospices (revenue or capital costs); travel or conference fees (except where these items are an integral part of a project); new or replacement vehicles (unless an integral part of a community-based development); general maintenance; continuation/replacement funding where a project or post has previously been supported from statutory sources (or similar).

TYPE OF GRANT Project grants to research groups, as well as some grants for salaries and building or equipment costs for specific projects.

RANGE OF GRANTS Up to £674,000.

SAMPLE GRANTS University of Nottingham (£674,000); Royal College of Surgeons England (£550,000); Queen's University Belfast (£145,000); Tower Hamlets Friends and Neighbours (£93,500): Age UK Bromley and Greenwich (£90,000); University of Leeds (£86,500); Brain and Spinal Injury Centre (£30,500); Cornwall Heritage (£17,800); Relate Brighton (£9000); Arts Depot Trust (£5000).

FINANCES *Year* 2016 *Income* £3,406,882 *Grants* £4,324,312 *Grants to organisations* £4,324,312 *Assets* £1,492,835

TRUSTEES Prof. Sir Roger Boyle; The Right Revd Christopher Chessun; Helen Davies; Kay Glendinning Prof. Roderick Hay; Prof. Peter Lansley; Prof. James McEwen; John Ransford; Prof. Martin Severs.

OTHER INFORMATION In 2015/16 a total of 69% of total grants were awarded to universities for research purposes. The remaining grants consisted of core/small grants (18%); fellowship grants (12%); building and equipment grants (1%).

HOW TO APPLY Applicants for Research Grants programme should complete the appropriate online application form on the trust's website. Applicants to the General Grants programme are asked to provide an initial outline (approximately two sides of A4) by post or email, including the following information: a brief description of the organisation and its status (e.g. whether it is a registered charity); who you are and what you do within the organisation; a description of the project for which funding is being sought, where it will take place and who it will involve; an outline of who will benefit from the work and why; the key outcomes and timescales; the total cost of the project/work and the specific amount being applied for from the trust. Outline applications for all programmes can be submitted at any time and those which are eligible will be invited to submit a formal application. The formal application requirements differ depending upon the type of grant being applied for and applicants are strongly advised to visit the trust's website before making an application to ensure that they have all the relevant information. Full applications are considered by the Grants and Research Committee which meets quarterly (normally in February, May, July and November). The committee makes recommendations on whether applications should be supported and decisions are then referred to the board of trustees for approval at their quarterly meetings (normally held in March, June, September and December). Successful applicants are normally notified within two weeks of the meeting. Generally, decisions are made within three to four months.

WHO TO APPLY TO Sarah Allport, Director of Grants and Research, 6 New Bridge Street, London EC4V 6AB *Tel.* 020 7403 3299 *Email* info@dunhillmedical.org.uk *Website* www.dunhillmedical.org.uk

■ The Dunn Family Charitable Trust

CC NO 297389 **ESTABLISHED** 1987

WHERE FUNDING CAN BE GIVEN UK, with a strong preference for Nottinghamshire.

WHO CAN BENEFIT General charitable purposes including organisations benefitting people with multiple sclerosis; environmental charities; medical charities.

WHAT IS FUNDED Charities working in the fields of health facilities and buildings; support to voluntary and community organisations; MS research; conservation; bird sanctuaries and ecology.

WHAT IS NOT FUNDED Individuals. Only organisations known to the trustees are supported.

TYPE OF GRANT Core costs and one-off awards; funding for one year or less will be considered.

RANGE OF GRANTS £500 to £5,000.

SAMPLE GRANTS Christ Church Endcliffe (£5,000); Oakes Trust (£4,500); St Luke's Hospice, Support Dogs (£3,000); Peter Le Marchant Trust (£2,500); Trent Bridge Rotary Club (£2,000); Rainbow Children's Hospice (£1,500); Seafarers UK, Tearfund (£1,000 each); Haywood House (£500).

FINANCES *Year* 2016 *Income* £71,227 *Grants* £59,000 *Grants to organisations* £59,000 *Assets* £1,856

TRUSTEES Graham R. Dunn; Jacky R. Dunn; Lisa J. Dunn; Nigel A. Dunn; Peter M. Dunn; Richard M. Dunn.

OTHER INFORMATION Grants were awarded to 33 organisations in 2015/16.

HOW TO APPLY Apply in writing to the correspondent.

WHO TO APPLY TO Jacky Chester, Rushcliffe Estates Ltd, Tudor House, 13–15 Rectory Road, West Bridgford, Nottingham NG2 6BE *Tel.* 0115 945 5300 *Email* jrc@rushcliffe.co.uk

■ The Charles Dunstone Charitable Trust

CC NO 1085955 **ESTABLISHED** 2001

WHERE FUNDING CAN BE GIVEN UK and overseas.

WHO CAN BENEFIT Registered charities.

WHAT IS FUNDED General charitable purposes including education; health; social welfare; children and youth; community care; arts and culture.

WHAT IS NOT FUNDED The trustees do not normally make grants to individuals.

RANGE OF GRANTS Up to £903,000.

SAMPLE GRANTS Fullwood Academy (£903,000); The Prince's Trust (£270,000); Community Links (£100,000); Working Chance (£40,000); Greenhouse (£35,000); Blue Marine Foundation (£25,000); Ambitious About Autism (£10,000); Cancer Research (£3,500); Family Action (£500); Childhood First (£100).

FINANCES *Year* 2016 *Income* £246,641 *Grants* £2,160,867 *Grants to organisations* £2,160,867 *Assets* £3,845,270

OTHER INFORMATION Grants were awarded to 43 organisations in 2015/16.

HOW TO APPLY Proposals are generally invited by the trustees or initiated at their request. Unsolicited applications are not encouraged and are unlikely to be successful. The trustees prefer to support innovative schemes that can be successfully replicated or become self-sustaining.

WHO TO APPLY TO The Trustees, H. W. Fisher and Company, 11–15 William Road, London NW1 3ER *Tel.* 020 7388 7000 *Email* jtrent@hwfisher.co.uk

■ County Durham Community Foundation

CC NO 1047625 **ESTABLISHED** 1995

WHERE FUNDING CAN BE GIVEN County Durham, Darlington and surrounding areas.

WHO CAN BENEFIT Community and voluntary organisations that are of a charitable, educational, philanthropic or benevolent nature.

WHAT IS FUNDED Projects working to create opportunity and to combat the issues of social disadvantage and exclusion in communities. Grants are made under five main themes: Aspiring; Healthier; Greener; Safer; and Inclusive. The foundation typically supports projects working in the following areas: children and young people; vulnerable people; older people; self-help groups; community regeneration; environmental improvement; health and well-being; educational projects; and capacity and skills development.

WHAT IS NOT FUNDED Regional or local offices of national organisations (unless it can be demonstrated that they operate independently); arms-length public sector organisations; party political activity; commercial ventures; organisations that have the sole purpose of benefitting or relieving animals or plants; the advancement of religion/faith; feasibility or other investigative studies; general contributions to large appeals (specific stand-alone items, however, can be funded); groups that hold more than one year's running costs as unrestricted free reserves (unless this can be justified); improvements to land or buildings not open or accessible for the general public; groups restricted by membership other than that associated with the objects of the group itself where this is necessary for the safety/well-being of disadvantaged users and undertaken for charitable purposes; deficit or retrospective funding; sponsored events; prizes or incentives; contingency amounts. The foundation will not normally fund the following: statutory bodies (unless it can be proven that the project is community-led, will benefit the whole community and is not a statutory responsibility; medical research and equipment; multi-year grants; school projects (unless the project involves the wider community); the construction or purchase of premises and freehold or leasehold land rights; the purchase of minibuses and other vehicles; multiple IT equipment; salaries (unless it is for a few hours which will make a large contribution to the project); overseas travel. If your project falls under the 'not normally' funded criteria, contact the foundation before submitting your application. Individual funds may have their own exclusions to consider.

TYPE OF GRANT Various awards depending on funding criteria.

RANGE OF GRANTS Up to £5,000.

SAMPLE GRANTS Information on beneficiaries was not available.

FINANCES *Year* 2016 *Income* £4,937,583 *Grants* £1,292,445 *Grants to organisations* £1,292,445 *Assets* £16,761,561

TRUSTEES David Martin; Brian Manning; Colin Fyfe; Paul Chandler; Mark I'Anson; Ada Burns; Michele Armstrong; Duncan Barrie; Ray Huson; James Fenwick; Lesley Anne Fairclough; Terry Collins; Peter Cook; Stephen Hall.

HOW TO APPLY Detailed guidelines on the grant application process can be found on the foundation's website. Applications can be completed via an online form.

WHO TO APPLY TO Barbara Gubbins, Victoria House, Whitfield Court, St John's Road, Meadowfield Industrial Estate, Durham DH7 8XL *Tel.* 0191 378 6340 *Email* info@cdcf.org.uk *Website* www.cdcf.org.uk

■ Dushinsky Trust Ltd

CC NO 1020301 **ESTABLISHED** 1992

WHERE FUNDING CAN BE GIVEN Mainly Israel.

WHO CAN BENEFIT Jewish and Israeli charities.

WHAT IS FUNDED Alleviation of poverty; furtherance of Orthodox Jewish education abroad.

SAMPLE GRANTS United Institutes of Dushinsky, Minchas Yitzchok Institutions and Ish Lerehu Fund.

FINANCES *Year* 2016 *Income* £668,010 *Grants* £652,471 *Grants to organisations* £652,471 *Assets* £25,586

TRUSTEES S. Reisner; Z. Levine; M. Schischa.

HOW TO APPLY The trust does not accept unsolicited applications. Preference is given to Dishinsky and Minchas Yitzchok institutions based in Israel.

WHO TO APPLY TO Simon Reisner, Secretary, 23 Braydon Road, London N16 6QL *Tel.* 020 8802 7144

■ The Mildred Duveen Trust

CC NO 1059355 **ESTABLISHED** 1996

WHERE FUNDING CAN BE GIVEN Worldwide.

WHO CAN BENEFIT Charitable organisations.

WHAT IS FUNDED General charitable purposes.

WHAT IS NOT FUNDED Individuals.

RANGE OF GRANTS £500 to £10,000.

SAMPLE GRANTS Missing People (£10,000); Charlie Waller Memorial Trust, Masterclass Trust (£5000 each); Helping Older People, The Back Up Trust (£2,500 each); Gateway, Tree of Hope (£2000 each); Happy Days (£1000); Pump Aid (£500).

FINANCES *Year* 2016 *Income* £32,717 *Grants* £80,000 *Grants to organisations* £80,000 *Assets* £966,023

TRUSTEES Peter Holgate; Adrian Houstoun; Peter Loose; John Shelford.

OTHER INFORMATION Grants were made to 82 organisations in 2015/16.

HOW TO APPLY Apply in writing to the correspondent.

WHO TO APPLY TO Peter Holgate, Trustee, Devonshire House, 60 Goswell Road, London EC1M 7AD *Tel.* 020 7566 4000 *Email* pholgate@kingstonsmith.co.uk

■ The Dyers' Company Charitable Trust

CC NO 289547 **ESTABLISHED** 1984

WHERE FUNDING CAN BE GIVEN UK.

WHO CAN BENEFIT Hospices; churches; registered charities; schools; universities.

WHAT IS FUNDED General charitable purposes.

WHAT IS NOT FUNDED Individuals; international charities.

TYPE OF GRANT One-off and long-standing.

RANGE OF GRANTS Up to £45,000.

SAMPLE GRANTS Archbishop Tenison's School (£45,000); ABF The Soldiers' Charity (£15,000); Heriot Watt (£8,000); Textile Conservation Foundation (£7,500); Clean Up UK, Dyslexia Action, SSAFA (£2,000 each); Age Exchange, Friends of St Paul's Cathedral (£1000 each); The Scargill Movement (£150).

FINANCES *Year* 2016 *Income* £1,435,731 *Grants* £473,282 *Grants to organisations* £473,282 *Assets* £16,130,033

TRUSTEE The Dyers Company.

OTHER INFORMATION The trust also funds a bursary for a school in Norwich.

HOW TO APPLY The company's website states: 'Note that as a matter of policy, the company does not accept unsolicited applications.'

WHO TO APPLY TO The Clerk of the Dyers, Dyers Hall, Dowgate Hill, London EC4R 2ST *Tel.* 020 7236 7197 *Email* office@dyerscompany.com *Website* www.dyerscompany.co.uk

■ The James Dyson Foundation

CC NO 1099709 **ESTABLISHED** 2003

WHERE FUNDING CAN BE GIVEN UK, local community around the Dyson company's UK headquarters, in Malmesbury, Wiltshire.

WHO CAN BENEFIT Registered charities and educational institutions.

WHAT IS FUNDED Educational institutions working in the field of design, technology and engineering; charities carrying out medical or scientific research; and projects which aid the local community around Dyson, in Malmesbury, Wiltshire.

WHAT IS NOT FUNDED Individual grants were not issued in 2015.

TYPE OF GRANT One-off and recurrent.

RANGE OF GRANTS £5,000 to £1.4 million.

SAMPLE GRANTS Cambridge University (£1.4 million); Bath Schools Design Education Programme (£93,000); Royal College of Art (£50,000); Malmesbury School Project (£42,000); Alzheimer's and Sparks (£26,500); The Unicorn Press (£7,150); The Blue Surf Trust, The Mimosa Trust, The Star and Storm Foundation (£5,000 each); Imperial College London (£200).

FINANCES *Year* 2015 *Income* £5,503,345 *Grants* £2,355,380 *Grants to organisations* £2,355,380 *Assets* £7,514,283

TRUSTEES Sir James Dyson; Lady Deirdre Dyson; Valerie West; Fenella Dyson.

HOW TO APPLY Apply in writing on headed paper to the correspondent. Organisations can also apply through the 'Get in touch' section of the foundation's website.

WHO TO APPLY TO Kevin Walker, Administrator, Dyson Group PLC, Tetbury Hill, Malmesbury, Wiltshire SN16 0RP *Tel.* 01666 828416 *Email* jamesdysonfoundation@dyson.com *Website* www.jamesdysonfoundation.com

■ Eaga Charitable Trust

CC NO 1088361 **ESTABLISHED** 2001

WHERE FUNDING CAN BE GIVEN UK and European Union.

WHO CAN BENEFIT Organisations and institutions benefitting research workers, academics and medical professionals.

WHAT IS FUNDED The trust provides grants for work that helps towards the understanding of fuel poverty and helps to address its causes and effects.

WHAT IS NOT FUNDED Personal support of individuals in need; general fundraising appeals; capital works; retrospective funding; energy advice provision materials; maintenance of websites; local energy efficiency/warm-homes initiatives.

TYPE OF GRANT One-off for projects and research, including reasonable overhead costs. Funding is available for up three years.

RANGE OF GRANTS Up to £20,000.

SAMPLE GRANTS NatCen Social Research (£29,000); Future Climate (£22,800); The Children's Society (£21,000); Richard Moore and Energy Audit Company (£16,000); Changeworks (£14,700); EBX Ltd (£10,000); University of York (£4,700); University of Leicester (£800).

FINANCES *Year* 2015/16 *Income* £13,783 *Grants* £110,000 *Grants to organisations* £110,000

TRUSTEES Lord Whitty; Elizabeth Gore; William Baker; Anne Toms; Dr Eldin Fahmy; Prof. Stefan Bouzarovski; Prof. Angela Tod.

OTHER INFORMATION This charity's latest accounts were not available to view on the Charity Commission's website due to its low income. We have therefore estimated the grant total.

HOW TO APPLY Application forms and detailed guidance on the application process are available on the trust's website.

WHO TO APPLY TO Dr Naomi Brown, Trust Manager, PO Box 225, Kendal LA9 9DR *Tel.* 01539 736477 *Email* eagact@aol.com *Website* www.eagacharitabletrust.org

■ The Audrey Earle Charity

CC NO 290028 **ESTABLISHED** 1984

WHERE FUNDING CAN BE GIVEN UK.

WHO CAN BENEFIT Registered charities.

WHAT IS FUNDED General charitable purposes, with some preference for animal welfare and conservation charities.

WHAT IS NOT FUNDED Individuals.

TYPE OF GRANT Mostly recurrent.

SAMPLE GRANTS Age UK, Animal Health Trust, British Red Cross Society, World Horse Welfare, Oxfam, People's Dispensary for Sick Animals (PDSA), Sense and The Salvation Army (£2,100 each).

FINANCES *Year* 2016 *Income* -£295 *Grants* £45,650 *Grants to organisations* £45,650 *Assets* £7,141,109

TRUSTEES Paul Andrew Sheils; Richard Fleetwood Fuller.

OTHER INFORMATION Grants were made to 22 organisations during the year.

HOW TO APPLY Apply in writing to the correspondent; however, the trust tends to support the same beneficiaries year after year and, therefore, it appears unlikely that new applications will receive support.

WHO TO APPLY TO Paul Sheils, Trustee, Bedford House, 21A John Street, London WC1N 2BF *Tel.* 020 7400 7770 *Email* info@moonbeever.com

■ The Earley Charity

CC NO 244823 **ESTABLISHED** 1820

WHERE FUNDING CAN BE GIVEN The Ancient Liberty of Earley (i.e. the central eastern and southern part of Reading, Earley and Lower Earley, northern Shinfield, Winnersh, Sonning and Lower Caversham).

WHO CAN BENEFIT Individuals in need and charitable and community organisations.

WHAT IS FUNDED Health; social welfare; older people; people with disabilities; facilities for recreation and leisure; the provision and support of educational facilities; general charitable purposes.

WHAT IS NOT FUNDED The charity does not fund the following: postgraduate education; general running/living costs; core costs; open-ended salaries; general appeals; religious activities, national organisations operating in the area of benefit without a local office; general public sector appeals (apart from in a few very exceptional cases); applications from outside the area of benefit; individuals who are planning to move out of the area of benefit; individuals who have been awarded a grant within the last two years; and individuals who have received three grants in the past.

TYPE OF GRANT One-off, project and start-up costs. Funding is available for up to one year.

RANGE OF GRANTS Up to £47,500.

SAMPLE GRANTS Age UK Reading (£43,500); The Conservation Volunteers (£22,000); Readipop (£14,000); CSL Berkshire Ltd, Hillside Community Allotment Association (£10,000 each); Adviza, Progress Thyetre (£4,000 each), San Francisco Libre Association (£1,000); Xn Media (£1,500); Outrider Anthems (£300).

FINANCES *Year* 2015 *Income* £1,211,704 *Grants* £657,437 *Grants to organisations* £480,747 *Assets* £12,546,442

TRUSTEES Robert Ames; Dr Christopher Sutton; Dr Deborah Jenkins; Miryam Eastwell; Philip Hooper; Lesley Owen; Bobbie Richardson; Richard Rodway.

OTHER INFORMATION Grants were awarded to 48 organisations in 2015.

HOW TO APPLY Application forms are available from the correspondent or to download, together with criteria and guidelines, on the website; applications are considered at any time. No response is given to applicants from outside the beneficial area. Telephone calls or emails are welcome from applicants who wish to check their eligibility.

WHO TO APPLY TO Jane Wittig, Clerk to the Trustees, The Liberty of Earley House, Strand Way, Lower Earley, Reading, Berkshire RG6 4EA *Tel.* 0118 975 5663 *Email* ec@earleycharity.org.uk *Website* www.earleycharity.org.uk

■ Earls Colne and Halstead Educational Charity

CC NO 310859 **ESTABLISHED** 1975

WHERE FUNDING CAN BE GIVEN The catchment area of the former Earls Colne and Halstead grammar schools.

WHO CAN BENEFIT Organisations for the furtherance of education; individuals; local schools.
WHAT IS FUNDED Education for local children and young adults.
WHAT IS NOT FUNDED Individuals.
TYPE OF GRANT Capital; revenue.
RANGE OF GRANTS Up to £5,000.
SAMPLE GRANTS De Vere School and St Giles School (£5,000 each); Belchamp St Paul Primary School (£4,500); Ramsey School (£2,300); Honeywood School (£2,000); Earls Colne School (£1,300).
FINANCES *Year* 2015/16 *Income* £51,842 *Grants* £41,164 *Grants to organisations* £41,164 *Assets* £1,269,555
TRUSTEES Angela Paramor; Patricia Taylor; Susan Thurgate; Anthony Shelton; Chris Siddal; Frank Williams; David Hume; Julie Sarti; Helena Carter; Jeremy Evans; Rob James; James Munro.
OTHER INFORMATION During the year, 16 organisations received grants of over £1,000.
HOW TO APPLY Apply in writing to the correspondent.
WHO TO APPLY TO Victoria Brummit, St Andrew's House, 2 Mallows Field, Halstead, Essex C09 2LN *Tel.* 01787 479960 *Email* earlscolnehalstead.edcharity@yahoo.co.uk *Website* www.echec.org.uk

■ East End Community Foundation

CC NO 1147789 **ESTABLISHED** 1990
WHERE FUNDING CAN BE GIVEN The London boroughs of Tower Hamlets, Hackney, Newham and The City of London.
WHO CAN BENEFIT Voluntary and community organisations. Some grants may be made to statutory organisations such as schools.
WHAT IS FUNDED Community development; education; employment and training.
WHAT IS NOT FUNDED Individuals.
TYPE OF GRANT Capital, revenue and full project funding.
RANGE OF GRANTS Up to £20,000.
SAMPLE GRANTS Bethnal Green Spear Trust (£20,000); Saving Faces, Ladies who L-EARN (£10,000 each); Half Moon Young People's Theatre (£6,000); St Nicholas' Church and Greatfields Resident Association (£5,000 each); ecoACTIVE Education (£3,000); Wapping High School (£2,000); Well Street Community Project (£500); Hackney Wick Festival (£200).
FINANCES *Year* 2016 *Income* £2,447,272 *Grants* £953,796 *Grants to organisations* £953,796 *Assets* £19,794,455
TRUSTEES Sister Christine Frost; Gabrielle Harrington; Howard Dawber; Forhad Hussain; Sophie Fernandes; Manali Trivedi; Katherine Webster; Zena Cooke; Guy Nicholson.
OTHER INFORMATION During the year 205 grants were awarded.
HOW TO APPLY See the foundation's website for up-to-date details for each scheme.
WHO TO APPLY TO Tracey Walsh, Jack Dash House, 2 Lawn House Close, London E14 9YQ *Tel.* 020 7345 4444 *Email* grants@eastendcf.org *Website* www.eastendcf.org

■ Eastern Counties Educational Trust Ltd

CC NO 310038 **ESTABLISHED** 1922
WHERE FUNDING CAN BE GIVEN Preference for Essex, Suffolk, Norfolk, Cambridgeshire and Hertfordshire.
WHO CAN BENEFIT Those with special educational needs, particularly those under 25 who have emotional and behavioural difficulties.
WHAT IS FUNDED Education; training; welfare provision.
WHAT IS NOT FUNDED Individuals. Normally no grants are given for recurring costs.
TYPE OF GRANT One-off grants.
RANGE OF GRANTS Up to £30,000.
SAMPLE GRANTS The Albany – Bury St Edmunds (£29,200); North Cambridge Academy (£22,800); Marriotts School – Stevenage (£14,600); Thomas Wolsey school (£6,500); University of Hertfordshire (£5,000); PARC (£4,100); Basildon Mind (£3,500); Hamlet Centre Trust (£2,500), KIDS (£2,000); Excelsior Trust (£1,500).
FINANCES *Year* 2016 *Income* £128,668 *Grants* £110,353 *Grants to organisations* £110,353 *Assets* £3,694,148
TRUSTEES Lady Singleton; Deborah Reed; Harry Anderson; David Boyle; Ben Salmon; Diana Forrow; Robert Cowlin.
OTHER INFORMATION Grants were made to 16 educational institutions in 2015/16.
HOW TO APPLY Apply in writing to the correspondent.
WHO TO APPLY TO Verity Barclay, Brook Farm, Wet Lane, Boxted, Colchester C04 5TN *Tel.* 01206 273295 *Email* ahcorin@aol.com

■ The Sir John Eastwood Foundation

CC NO 235389 **ESTABLISHED** 1964
WHERE FUNDING CAN BE GIVEN UK, but mainly Nottinghamshire in practice.
WHO CAN BENEFIT Local organisations.
WHAT IS FUNDED General charitable purposes including children with special needs; older people, people with disabilities.
WHAT IS NOT FUNDED Individuals.
TYPE OF GRANT One-off projects and longer-term funding.
RANGE OF GRANTS Up to £260,000.
SAMPLE GRANTS Newark and Nottinghamshire Agricultural Society (£260,000); Nottinghamshire Hospice (£24,000); John Eastwood Hospice Trust (£10,000); Air Ambulance, Disasters Emergency Committee – Nepal Earthquake Appeal, Disabilities Living Centre, Mansfield Street Preachers, NSPCC, Rumbles Catering Project, Walesby Forest (£5,000 each).
FINANCES *Year* 2016 *Income* £291,602 *Grants* £517,050 *Grants to organisations* £517,050 *Assets* £8,165,314
TRUSTEES Diana Cottingham; Constance Mudford; Valerie Hardingham; David Marriott.
OTHER INFORMATION During the year, 12 organisations received grants of over £5,000 and a further £178,000 was distributed in smaller grants. Beneficiaries of these smaller grants were not listed.
HOW TO APPLY Apply in writing to the correspondent.
WHO TO APPLY TO David Marriott, Trustee, PO Box 9803, Mansfield NG18 9FT *Email* sirjohneastwoodfoundation@talktalk.net

■ The EBM Charitable Trust

CC NO 326186 **ESTABLISHED** 1982

WHERE FUNDING CAN BE GIVEN UK.

WHO CAN BENEFIT Charitable organisations.

WHAT IS FUNDED General charitable purposes; animal welfare; research; youth development; social welfare.

WHAT IS NOT FUNDED Individuals.

TYPE OF GRANT Recurring and one-off.

RANGE OF GRANTS £5,000 to £200,000.

SAMPLE GRANTS Lewis Manning Hospice (£200,000); The Prince's Trust (£100,000); Battersea Dogs and Cats Home, The Injured Jockeys Fund (£50,000 each); Community Links (£40,000); Austistica (£35,000); Islington Boat Club, The Cure Parkinson's Trust (£20,000 each); Missing People (£10,000); Orchid (£5,000).

FINANCES *Year* 2015 *Income* £1,238,570 *Grants* £1,190,357 *Grants to organisations* £1,190,357 *Assets* £49,269,606

TRUSTEES Richard Moore; Michael Macfadyen; Stephen Hogg; Francis Moore; Lucy Forsyth.

OTHER INFORMATION The trust manages two funds, the main fund and the Fitz' fund. The Fitz' fund is a designated fund for animal charities. In 2015/16 a total of £25,500 was distributed through the Fitz' fund.

HOW TO APPLY The trustees have previously stated: 'Unsolicited applications are not requested as the trustees prefer to support donations to charities whose work they have researched and which is in accordance with the wishes of the settlor. The trustees do not tend to support research projects as research is not a core priority but there are exceptions. The trustees' funds are fully committed. The trustees receive a very high number of grant applications which are mostly unsuccessful.'

WHO TO APPLY TO Martin Pollock, Secretary, The EBM Charitable Trust, c/o Moore Stephens, 150 Aldersgate Street, London EC1A 4AB *Tel.* 020 7334 9191

■ The ECHO Trust

CC NO 1096255 **ESTABLISHED** 2003

WHERE FUNDING CAN BE GIVEN England and Wales.

WHO CAN BENEFIT Charities that support sick children and young people.

WHAT IS FUNDED Health care; provision of medical equipment.

WHAT IS NOT FUNDED Individuals.

RANGE OF GRANTS Up to £5,000.

SAMPLE GRANTS Margaret Wix PTA (£6,000); Above and Beyond, Momentum (£5,000 each); Zoe Palace Trust (£4,700); The Daisy Garland (£4,400); Hampshire Hospital Charity, The Paediatric Trust Fund (£3,400); LATCH (£1,400); MS Society (£80); Save the Children and Breast Cancer NOW (£70 each).

FINANCES *Year* 2016 *Income* £72,266 *Grants* £124,939 *Grants to organisations* £124,939 *Assets* £109,512

TRUSTEES Maxine Bamber; Peter Marks; Kelly Young.

OTHER INFORMATION Grants were made to 31 organisations in 2015/16.

HOW TO APPLY Apply in writing to the correspondent.

WHO TO APPLY TO Maxine Bamber, Trust Manager, Aurora House, Deltic Avenue, Rooksley MK13 8LW *Tel.* 01908 544275 *Email* contact@echotrust.org *Website* www.echotrust.org

■ Echoes of Service

CC NO 234556 **ESTABLISHED** 1965

WHERE FUNDING CAN BE GIVEN Worldwide.

WHO CAN BENEFIT Children and young people; older people; people with disabilities.

WHAT IS FUNDED Religious activities, specifically Christian missionary projects; advancement of health; the prevention or relief of poverty; overseas aid.

TYPE OF GRANT Full project funding.

RANGE OF GRANTS Up to £142,000.

SAMPLE GRANTS Manara Ministries (£142,000); Chitokoloki Hospital (72,000); Operation Mobilisation (£52,000); Harvest Ministries International (£51,000); Bethesda Hospital (£47,000).

FINANCES *Year* 2015 *Income* £5,384,325 *Grants* £4,294,182 *Grants to organisations* £1,549,732 *Assets* £10,789,541

TRUSTEES John Aitken; Dr John Burness; James Crooks; Eric Noble; Paul Young.

OTHER INFORMATION In addition to the beneficiaries noted above, 182 organisations received grants of under £50,000 in 2015.

HOW TO APPLY Apply in writing to the correspondent.

WHO TO APPLY TO Echoes of Service, 124 Wells Road, Bath BA2 3AH *Tel.* 01225 310893 *Email* echoes@echoes.org.uk *Website* www.echoes.org.uk

■ The Ecology Trust

CC NO 1099222 **ESTABLISHED** 2003

WHERE FUNDING CAN BE GIVEN Worldwide. Particularly in the UK, Canada, Indonesia, the Philippines and Spain.

WHO CAN BENEFIT Registered charities working on ecological and environmental initiatives, particularly in the areas of agriculture, energy, and climate change.

WHAT IS FUNDED Sustainable development; environmental conservation; environmental education; relief of poverty; social welfare, economic regeneration.

WHAT IS NOT FUNDED The trust is unlikely to make grants to the following kinds of projects: work that has already taken place; part of general appeals or circulars; outward-bound courses, expeditions and overseas travel; capital projects (i.e. buildings and refurbishment costs); conservation of already well-supported species or of non-native species; and furniture, white goods, computer, paint, timber and scrap recycling projects.

TYPE OF GRANT One-off and recurring grants for project and core costs.

RANGE OF GRANTS Up to £40,000.

SAMPLE GRANTS Environmental Investigation Agency, Canopy (£40,000 each); The UK Without Incineration Network (£30,000 in two grants); The Rainforest Action Network (£25,000); GEN-GOB Eivissa (£29,000 in two grants); APAEEF (Associació de productors d'agricultura ecològica d'Eivissa i Formentera) (£7,600); Public Interest Research Centre (£3,000).

FINANCES *Year* 2016 *Income* £334,799 *Grants* £174,049 *Grants to organisations* £174,049 *Assets* £334,538

TRUSTEES Benjamin Goldsmith; Charles Filmer; Alexander Goldsmith.

OTHER INFORMATION Grants were made to nine organisations in 2015/16.

HOW TO APPLY Apply in writing to the correspondent.

WHO TO APPLY TO Jon Cracknell, Hon. Secretary, 48 Kidmore Road, Caversham, Reading RG4 7LU *Email* info@jmgfoundation.org

The Economist Charitable Trust

CC NO 293709 **ESTABLISHED** 1986
WHERE FUNDING CAN BE GIVEN UK and Overseas.
WHO CAN BENEFIT Charitable organisations; children and young people; older people; people with disabilities.
WHAT IS FUNDED General charitable purposes; education and training; economic and community development.
WHAT IS NOT FUNDED Individuals.
TYPE OF GRANT Full project funding; service delivery; strategic funding.
RANGE OF GRANTS The average grant size was £610 in 2015/16.
SAMPLE GRANTS Friends of the Children Myanmar; Minds Matter; Room to Read.
FINANCES *Year* 2016 *Income* £104,164 *Grants* £84,932 *Grants to organisations* £84,932 *Assets* £19,219
TRUSTEES Ada Simkins; Kiran Malik; Daniel Franklin; Cecelia Block.
OTHER INFORMATION The trust is the corporate charity of The Economist Newspaper Ltd, a multinational media company specialising in international business and world affairs.
HOW TO APPLY The trust does not accept unsolicited applications.
WHO TO APPLY TO The Economist Group, The Economist Group, 25 St James's Street, London SW1A 1HG *Tel.* 020 7576 8546 *Website* www.economist.com

EDF Energy Trust (EDFET)

CC NO 1099446 **ESTABLISHED** 1996
WHERE FUNDING CAN BE GIVEN UK; Plymouth.
WHO CAN BENEFIT Registered charities; individuals who are customers of EDF energy; people who are socially or economically disadvantaged.
WHAT IS FUNDED Social welfare; relief from poverty; money advice; debt counselling.
WHAT IS NOT FUNDED Fines for criminal offences; educational or training needs; debts to central government departments; medical equipment, aids and adaptations; holidays; business debts; catalogues; credit cards; personal loans; deposits for secure accommodation; or overpayment of benefits.
TYPE OF GRANT Core costs; capital costs; full project funding for up to three years; recurring.
RANGE OF GRANTS Up to £106,000.
SAMPLE GRANTS Plymouth Citizens Advice (£106,000); Talking Money (£88,000); Citizens Advice Thanet (£82,000).
FINANCES *Year* 2015 *Income* £7,761,654 *Grants* £2,971,073 *Grants to organisations* £276,039 *Assets* £4,954,986
TRUSTEES Denice Fennell; Vic Szewczyk; Tim Cole; Brian Cole; Bob Richardson; Richard Sykes; David Hawkes.
OTHER INFORMATION The Charity funds three organisations based in the south of England – Plymouth Citizens Advice, Citizens Advice Thanet and Talking Money (Bristol). All three organisations have received funding for a number of years to pay for specialist debt advisers.
HOW TO APPLY **Organisational grants:** it is advisable to contact the foundation for further information on future grant programmes and deadlines. **Individual grants:** applications can be submitted throughout the year. Applications must be made on a standard application form, which can be downloaded from the website, obtained from local advice centres such as Citizens Advice or by writing to the trust. The trust also has an online application form, accessible via the website.
WHO TO APPLY TO The Trustees, Freepost EDF ENERGY TRUST *Tel.* 01733 421060 *Email* edfet@charisgrants.com *Website* www.edfenergytrust.org.uk

The Gilbert and Eileen Edgar Foundation

CC NO 241736 **ESTABLISHED** 1965
WHERE FUNDING CAN BE GIVEN Worldwide with a preference for the UK.
WHO CAN BENEFIT Charitable organisations.
WHAT IS FUNDED General charitable purposes with preference towards medical research; social welfare; fine arts education.
WHAT IS NOT FUNDED Individuals.
TYPE OF GRANT Full project funding.
RANGE OF GRANTS £500 to £10,000.
SAMPLE GRANTS Royal Academy of Dramatic Art (£10,000); Royal academy of arts (£6,000); English National Ballet (£2,000); Action for Addiction, Alzheimer's Research UK, The Trinity Sailing Trust (£1,000 each); Fight for Sight, Meningitis Research Foundation, NSPCC and Wells for India (£500 each).
FINANCES *Year* 2016 *Income* £81,851 *Grants* £78,500 *Grants to organisations* £78,500 *Assets* £1,746,700
TRUSTEES Simon Gentilli; Adam Gentilli.
OTHER INFORMATION Grants were awarded to 90 organisations in 2015/16.
HOW TO APPLY Apply in writing to the correspondent.
WHO TO APPLY TO Adam Gentilli, Trustee, Greville Mount, Milcote, Stratford-upon-Avon, Warwickshire CV37 8AB *Email* trustee@milcote.uk

Edge Foundation

CC NO 286621 **ESTABLISHED** 2003
WHERE FUNDING CAN BE GIVEN UK.
WHO CAN BENEFIT Charites; educational institutions.
WHAT IS FUNDED The promotion of technical and professional learning.
SAMPLE GRANTS Baker Dearing Educational Trust (£1 million); Studio Schools Trust (£90,000); Career Colleges Trust (£25,000); Bulwell Academy (£17,000); Creative and Cultural Skills (£14,000); Working Futures (£9,000); Peter Jones Foundation (£2,000).
FINANCES *Year* 2015 *Income* £715,000 *Grants* £1,191,000 *Grants to organisations* £1,191,000 *Assets* £21,520,000
TRUSTEES Sir Kevin Satchwell; Lord Baker of Dorking; Prof. Colin Riordan; Neil Bates; Lord Adonis; Pauline Daniyan; Tobias Peyton.
HOW TO APPLY The foundation's website states: 'Edge has three grant funding rounds planned. These will take place in the autumn of 2016, 2018 and 2020. Funding rounds and funding criteria will be published on the website as the rounds open. Outside of these advertised funding rounds, Edge does not fund unsolicited approaches.'
WHO TO APPLY TO Alice Barnard, Edge Foundation, 4 Millbank, Westminster, London SW1P 3JA *Tel.* 020 7960 1540 *Fax* 020 7960 1557 *Email* enquiry@edge.co.uk *Website* www.edge.co.uk

■ Edinburgh Children's Holiday Fund

SC NO SC010312 **ESTABLISHED** 1912
WHERE FUNDING CAN BE GIVEN Edinburgh and the Lothians.
WHO CAN BENEFIT Charitable organisations; schools.
WHAT IS FUNDED Children's welfare and holidays for children who are disadvantaged.
WHAT IS NOT FUNDED Grants directly to individuals.
TYPE OF GRANT One-off grants.
RANGE OF GRANTS Mainly £1,000 to £3,000.
SAMPLE GRANTS Children 1st (£14,000); Epilepsy Scotland and The Roses Charitable Trust (£3,000); The Yard Adventure Centre (£2,500); Edinburgh Young Carers Project (£2,000); Hopscotch (£1,500); Edinburgh University Children's Holiday Venture, Scottish Spina Bifida Association, Prestonfield Primary School and Waverley Care (£1,000 each).
FINANCES *Year* 2015/16 *Income* £55,313 *Grants* £63,500 *Grants to organisations* £41,500 *Assets* £50,439
OTHER INFORMATION Grants were awarded to 19 charitable organisations during the year. There was also £22,000 awarded in grants to individuals through four local authorities.
HOW TO APPLY Application forms are available from the correspondent. The trustees meet to consider grants in January and May. Applications should be sent in mid-December and mid-April respectively.
WHO TO APPLY TO The Trustees, c/o Bryce Wilson and Co., Hill Street Business Centre, 13 Hill Street, Edinburgh EH2 3JP

■ Edinburgh Trust No 2 Account

CC NO 227897 **ESTABLISHED** 1959
WHERE FUNDING CAN BE GIVEN UK and worldwide.
WHO CAN BENEFIT Registered charities.
WHAT IS FUNDED General charitable preferences with a preference for education; armed services; scientific expeditions.
WHAT IS NOT FUNDED Individuals; non-registered charities.
TYPE OF GRANT One-off and recurrent; research.
RANGE OF GRANTS £1,000 to £3,000.
SAMPLE GRANTS Edwina Mountbatten Trust (£3,000); Game and Wildlife Conservancy Trust, Outward Bound Trust, Romsey Abbey and The Federation of London Youth Clubs (£2,200 each); Catch22 (£1,600); British Heart Foundation, Plan UK and British Heart Foundation (£1,100 each).
FINANCES *Year* 2015/16 *Income* £130,963 *Grants* £95,972 *Grants to organisations* £95,972 *Assets* £2,910,517
TRUSTEES Charles Woodhouse; George Hewson; Brigadier Archie Miller-Bakewell.
OTHER INFORMATION Grants were made to 80 organisations in 2015/16.
HOW TO APPLY Apply in writing to the correspondent.
WHO TO APPLY TO The Secretary, The Duke of Edinburgh's Household, Buckingham Palace, London SW1A 1AA *Tel.* 020 7024 4107 *Email* paul.hughes@royal.gsx.gov.uk

■ Edupoor Ltd

CC NO 1113785 **ESTABLISHED** 2006
WHERE FUNDING CAN BE GIVEN Worldwide.
WHO CAN BENEFIT Registered charities.
WHAT IS FUNDED The advancement in education and training through the world; the relief of poverty; old age; illness both mental and physical and the relief of persons suffering from any disability, general charitable purposes.
SAMPLE GRANTS A list of beneficiaries was not available.
FINANCES *Year* 2015/16 *Income* £944,145 *Grants* £936,708 *Grants to organisations* £936,708 *Assets* £17,495
TRUSTEES Alan Shelton; Michael Shelton.
HOW TO APPLY Apply in writing to the correspondent.
WHO TO APPLY TO Michael Shelton, Trustee, Flat 10, 125 Clapton Common, Stamford Hill, London E5 9AB *Tel.* 020 8800 0088

■ Dr Edwards Bishop King's Fulham Charity

CC NO 1113490 **ESTABLISHED** 1981
WHERE FUNDING CAN BE GIVEN London Boroughs of Fulham and Hammersmith: specifically the post code areas of SW6, part of W14 and part of W6.
WHO CAN BENEFIT Registered charities; people who are economically or socially disadvantaged; residents of Fulham and Hammersmith; children and young people; older people; people with disabilities.
WHAT IS FUNDED General charitable purposes; education and training; relief from poverty.
WHAT IS NOT FUNDED Application guidelines note that the charity 'does not respond to general funding appeals or give grants for trips outside the United Kingdom'. It is further noted: 'You can ask the Charity to match funding raised from other sources but not for any purpose for which funding is available from central or local government.'
TYPE OF GRANT Project funding either for a one-off grant or for a grant towards running costs.
RANGE OF GRANTS Generally up to £5,000 but higher awards would be considered.
SAMPLE GRANTS Furnish Community Furniture Store (£16,500); Sobus (£15,000); St John's Church (£13,100); Hammersmith and Fulham Action on Disability (£10,300); Hammersmith and Fulham Legal Centre (£7,300); Hammersmith and Fulham Caring for Carers (£6,000); Shepherd's Bush Families Project (£5,000); The Food Bank (£4,000); Lunch Club 4 the Blind (£3,000); Contact the Elderly (£1,400).
FINANCES *Year* 2016 *Income* £442,945 *Grants* £130,492 *Grants to organisations* £130,492 *Assets* £9,225,106
TRUSTEES Michael Clein; Charles Treloggan; Allen Smith; Ronald Lawrence; Susan O'Neill; Carol Bailey; Adronie Alford; Revd Mark Osborne; Helen Fagan; Sheila Thomas; Zahra Beg.
OTHER INFORMATION Grants were given to 21 organisations in 2015/16.
HOW TO APPLY Application forms are available, together with criteria and guidelines, from the correspondent or the trust's website. The committee meets twice a year and applications must be received at least ten working days ahead of these dates. Details of scheduled committee meetings can be found on the fund's website.
WHO TO APPLY TO Jonathan Martin, Clerk to the Trustees, Percy Barton House, 33–35 Dawes Road, Fulham, London SW6 7DT *Tel.* 020 7386 9387 *Fax* 020 7610 2856 *Email* clerk@debk.org.uk *Website* www.debk.org.uk

■ The W. G. Edwards Charitable Foundation

CC NO 293312 **ESTABLISHED** 1985
WHERE FUNDING CAN BE GIVEN UK.
WHO CAN BENEFIT Registered charities that assist in the care of older people.
WHAT IS FUNDED Social welfare; provision of care; health.
WHAT IS NOT FUNDED Individuals.
TYPE OF GRANT Principally one-off capital projects; full project funding.
RANGE OF GRANTS Up to £4,400.
SAMPLE GRANTS Toynbee Hall (£4,400); St Andrew's Hospice (£3,000); Guideposts (£2,800); Kent Association of the Blind (£2,400); Friends of the Elderly, Nightingale House Hospice (£2,000 each); The Fed (£1,500); RNIB East Sussex (£1,000); Relate (£750); Mercia MS Therapy Centre (£720).
FINANCES *Year* 2016 *Income* £129,677 *Grants* £122,930 *Grants to organisations* £122,930 *Assets* £121,631
TRUSTEES Gillian Shepherd Coates; Wendy Savage; Yewande Savage; William Mackie.
OTHER INFORMATION Grants were made to 65 organisations in 2015/16.
HOW TO APPLY Apply in writing to the correspondent.
WHO TO APPLY TO Mrs T. C. Mackie, 14 Windsor Terrace, South Gosforth, Newcastle upon Tyne NE3 1YL *Email* wgedwardscharity@icloud.com *Website* www.wgedwardscharitablefoundation.org.uk

■ The Eighty Eight Foundation

CC NO 1149797 **ESTABLISHED** 2012
WHERE FUNDING CAN BE GIVEN UK; Republic of Ireland.
WHO CAN BENEFIT Charities; individuals.
WHAT IS FUNDED Cancer and dementia research and care; disadvantaged and older people in Republic of Ireland; artists and photographers.
SAMPLE GRANTS The Astra Foundation (£475,500); The Sutton Trust (£230,000); Shine (£100,000); The LINK South Africa (£100,000); Sarah Groves Foundation (£10,000); NSPCC (£1,000).
FINANCES *Year* 2015/16 *Income* £886,743 *Grants* £908,451 *Grants to organisations* £908,451 *Assets* £12,181,890
TRUSTEES John Walker; Ann Fitzmaurice; Edward Fitzmaurice; Claude Slatner; Neelish Heredia.
HOW TO APPLY Apply in writing to the correspondent.
WHO TO APPLY TO The Trustees, Rawlinson and Hunter, 6 New Street Square, London EC4A 3AQ *Tel.* 020 7842 2000 *Email* eighty.eight@rawlinson-hunter.com

■ Elanore Ltd

CC NO 281047 **ESTABLISHED** 1980
WHERE FUNDING CAN BE GIVEN UK.
WHO CAN BENEFIT Jewish people; registered charities.
WHAT IS FUNDED Religious activities; relief from poverty.
SAMPLE GRANTS Information on beneficiaries not provided.
FINANCES *Year* 2016 *Income* £86,000 *Grants* £82,600 *Grants to organisations* £82,600 *Assets* £651,001
TRUSTEES Joachim Beck; Danielle Beck; Yael Tesler; Michal Beck.
HOW TO APPLY Apply in writing to the correspondent.
WHO TO APPLY TO J. Beck, Trustee, 25 Highfield Gardens, London NW11 9HD *Tel.* 020 8455 7173

■ The Elephant Trust

CC NO 269615 **ESTABLISHED** 1975
WHERE FUNDING CAN BE GIVEN England and Wales.
WHO CAN BENEFIT Artists, arts organisations; publications concerned with the visual arts.
WHAT IS FUNDED Education in fine arts.
WHAT IS NOT FUNDED The following categories are not supported: arts festivals; group exhibitions; charities organising community projects; students; educational or other studies; residencies or research; symposia or conferences; publications or catalogues and projects taking place outside the UK.
TYPE OF GRANT One-off contributions to specific projects by individuals or organisations.
SAMPLE GRANTS A list of beneficiaries was not available.
FINANCES *Year* 2016 *Income* £108,983 *Grants* £111,126 *Grants to organisations* £46,000 *Assets* £2,978,429
TRUSTEES Prof. Dawn Ades; Antony Forwood; Benjamin Cook; Elizabeth Carey-Thomas; Melissa Gronlund; Elizabeth Price; Antony Penrose; Oliver Basciano; Janice Kerbel.
HOW TO APPLY Only postal applications will be are accepted. Application guidelines and deadlines can be found on the website. Applications must consist of the following: cover sheet; synopsis of the project; budget; brief CV; visual material. Enquires can be submitted by telephone or email, contact details can be found on the website.
WHO TO APPLY TO Ruth Rattenbury, Administrator, Bridge House, 4 Borough High Street, London SE1 9QR *Tel.* 020 7403 1877 *Email* ruth@elephanttrust.org.uk *Website* www.elephanttrust.org.uk

■ The George Elias Charitable Trust

CC NO 273993 **ESTABLISHED** 1977
WHERE FUNDING CAN BE GIVEN UK; preference for Manchester.
WHO CAN BENEFIT Jewish organisations; registered charities.
WHAT IS FUNDED Mainly religious activities. Some smaller donations to more general charitable causes, including educational needs; health care; relief from poverty.
TYPE OF GRANT Project funding; core costs.
SAMPLE GRANTS UK Friends of Nadar Deiah (£50,000); Ahavat Shalom (£45,000); United Jewish Israel Appeal (UJIA) (£30,000); Hale and District Hebrew Congregation (£24,000); JEM (£5,000); South Manchester Mikva Trust (£4,000); British Friends of Rinat Aharon (£2,500); Moracha Ltd (£1,000); Chai Lifeline Cancer Trust (£300); Friends of the Sick (£100).
FINANCES *Year* 2016 *Income* £523,688 *Grants* £297,577 *Grants to organisations* £297,577 *Assets* £957,647
TRUSTEES Ernest Elias; Stephen Elias.
OTHER INFORMATION A list of beneficiaries was not provided.
HOW TO APPLY Apply in writing to the correspondent. The trustees meet monthly.

WHO TO APPLY TO Stephen Elias, Trustee, Shaws Fabrics Ltd, 1 Ashley Road, Altrincham, Cheshire WA14 2DT *Tel.* 0161 928 7171 *Email* textiles@kshaw.com

■ The Gerald Palmer Eling Trust Company

CC NO 1100869 **ESTABLISHED** 2003
WHERE FUNDING CAN BE GIVEN Berkshire.
WHO CAN BENEFIT Charitable organisations.
WHAT IS FUNDED Christian religion, particularly the Orthodox Church; medical research and the study of medicine; and relief of sickness and poverty.
WHAT IS NOT FUNDED Individuals.
TYPE OF GRANT One-off.
RANGE OF GRANTS Up to £15,000.
SAMPLE GRANTS Organisations which received grants over £5,000 included: Institute of Christian Orthodox Studies (£15,000); Brendon Care, Convent of the Annunciation, West Berkshire Mencap (£10,000 each); University of Liverpool (£6,000).
FINANCES *Year* 2016 *Income* £1,597,690 *Grants* £274,741 *Grants to organisations* £274,741 *Assets* £78,407,852
TRUSTEES Desmond Harrison; Robin Broadhurst; James Gardiner; Kenneth McDiarmid.
OTHER INFORMATION The grant sample listed include all organisations who received a grant over £5,000. This made up 22% of the total donations made by the charity in 2015/16.
HOW TO APPLY Apply in writing to the correspondent.
WHO TO APPLY TO Jevan Booth, Company Secretary, Englefield Estate Office, Wellhouse, Hermitage, Thatcham, Berkshire RG19 9UF *Tel.* 01635 200268 *Email* charities@elingestate.co.uk

■ The Wilfred and Elsie Elkes Charity Fund

CC NO 326573 **ESTABLISHED** 1984
WHERE FUNDING CAN BE GIVEN Staffordshire and especially Uttoxeter, including UK-wide charities benefitting the area.
WHO CAN BENEFIT Registered charities and organisations; children; older people; people with disabilities.
WHAT IS FUNDED General charitable purposes.
WHAT IS NOT FUNDED Individuals.
TYPE OF GRANT Full project funding; core costs; capital funding.
SAMPLE GRANTS Art and Soul; Child Action Northwest; Douglas Macmillan Hospice; St Mark's Church Foxt; Teenage Cancer Trust.
FINANCES *Year* 2016 *Income* £87,731 *Grants* £79,000 *Grants to organisations* £79,000
TRUSTEE Royal Bank of Scotland PLC.
OTHER INFORMATION Grants were made to 37 organisations in 2015/16.
HOW TO APPLY Apply in writing to the correspondent.
WHO TO APPLY TO The Royal Bank of Scotland, RBS Trust and Estate Services, Eden Building, Lakeside, Chester Business Park, Wrexham Road, Chester CH4 9QT *Tel.* 01244 625810 *Email* rbscharities@rbs.com

■ The Maud Elkington Charitable Trust

CC NO 263929 **ESTABLISHED** 1972
WHERE FUNDING CAN BE GIVEN Northamptonshire; Leicestershire; Rutland.
WHO CAN BENEFIT Registered charities, health care organisations; children and young people; older people; people with disabilities.
WHAT IS FUNDED General charitable purposes.
WHAT IS NOT FUNDED Individuals.
TYPE OF GRANT Full project funding, recurring funding.
SAMPLE GRANTS A list of beneficiaries was not available.
FINANCES *Year* 2016 *Income* £614,309 *Grants* £505,820 *Grants to organisations* £505,820 *Assets* £25,407,285
TRUSTEES Roger Bowder, Chair; Michael Jones; Katherine Hall.
OTHER INFORMATION The trust is committed to funding one pupil at Leicester Grammar School and two pupils at Leicester High School for Girls for the period of their education. The commitments commenced in the autumn term of 2014. The annual fees for the academic year 2016/17 are estimated to be £36,000. The trustees have also committed to pay Charity Link (Northampton) £60,000. One other conditional grant of £1,500 was outstanding at 31 March 2016.
HOW TO APPLY Apply in writing to the correspondent. There is no application form or guidelines. The trustees meet every seven or eight weeks.
WHO TO APPLY TO Emily Izzo, Administrator, c/o Shakespeare Martineau, Two Colton Square, Leicester LE1 1QH *Tel.* 0116 257 4645 *Email* emily.izzo@shma.co.uk

■ Ellador Ltd

CC NO 283202 **ESTABLISHED** 1981
WHERE FUNDING CAN BE GIVEN UK and overseas.
WHO CAN BENEFIT Registered charities; Jewish organisations.
WHAT IS FUNDED Religious activities; health care; relief from poverty.
WHAT IS NOT FUNDED Individuals.
RANGE OF GRANTS £10,300 to £26,000.
SAMPLE GRANTS Friends of Mercaz Hatorah Belz Macnivka (£26,000); Kehal Yisroel LvChassidei Gur (£15,000); Ichud Mosdos Gur Ltd (£10,300).
FINANCES *Year* 2016 *Income* £60,000 *Grants* £50,850 *Grants to organisations* £50,850 *Assets* £578,650
TRUSTEES Joel Schreiber; Helen Schreiber; Rivka Schreiber; Mr J. Schreiber; Mr Y. Schreiber; Mrs S. Reisner; Mrs C. Hamburger; Mrs R. Benedikt.
OTHER INFORMATION Grants were made to three organisations in 2015/16.
HOW TO APPLY Apply in writing to the correspondent.
WHO TO APPLY TO Joel Schreiber, Trustee, 20 Ashtead Road, London E5 9BH *Tel.* 020 7242 3580 *Email* mail@cohenarnold.com

■ The John Ellerman Foundation

CC NO 263207 **ESTABLISHED** 1971
WHERE FUNDING CAN BE GIVEN Mainly UK; East and Southern Africa.
WHO CAN BENEFIT National registered charities.
WHAT IS FUNDED Social welfare; environment; arts.
WHAT IS NOT FUNDED Individuals; round-robin appeals; capital developments; religious activities; replacement statutory funding; one-off

events; sports and leisure; education; medical research; drug and alcohol abuse; prisons and people who have offended; counselling and psychotherapy.

TYPE OF GRANT One-off and multi-year. Core costs, project funding. Funding may be given for up to three years.

RANGE OF GRANTS Up to £150,000.

SAMPLE GRANTS The Rivers Trust (£150,000); PAC-UK (£120,000); Northern Stage (£105,000); National Museum Wales (£93,000); Sky badger (£80,000); The Rachel Stewart Fund (£75,000); WellChild (£54,000); Ballet Black (£40,000); Tara Arts (£30,000); ZANE: Zimbabwe A National Emergency (£3,000).

FINANCES *Year* 2016 *Income* £3,931,000 *Grants* £4,750,000 *Grants to organisations* £4,750,000 *Assets* £128,809,000

TRUSTEES Sarah Riddle; Peter Kyle; Brian Hurwitz; Hugh Raven; Timothy Glass; Gary Steinberg; Geraldine Blake.

OTHER INFORMATION During 2015/16 the foundation made 62 grants worth £4.75 million. 50% of grants were awarded to welfare organisations; 29% to arts organisations and 21% to environmental organisations.

HOW TO APPLY Application guidelines and eligibility criteria can be found on the foundation's website.

WHO TO APPLY TO John Ellerman Foundation, Suite 10, Aria House, 23 Craven Street, London WC2N 5NS *Tel.* 020 7930 8566 *Email* enquiries@ellerman.org.uk *Website* www.ellerman.org.uk

■ The Ellinson Trust

CC NO 252018 **ESTABLISHED** 1967

WHERE FUNDING CAN BE GIVEN UK and overseas.

WHO CAN BENEFIT Jewish organisations.

WHAT IS FUNDED Jewish causes.

WHAT IS NOT FUNDED Individuals.

TYPE OF GRANT Capital and recurring grants.

RANGE OF GRANTS Up to £150,000, but mostly up to £20,000.

SAMPLE GRANTS Kesser Yeshua RP – Israel (£150,000); Three Pillars (£20,000); Kneset Yitzchak Kiryat (£17,300); Kollel Ohel Torah – Jerusalem (£12,000); Friends of Yeshivas Brisk (£8,000); Vaad Harobinim Tzeduka (£3,000).

FINANCES *Year* 2015/16 *Income* £335,697 *Grants* £231,495 *Grants to organisations* £231,495 *Assets* £3,844,226

TRUSTEES Alexander Ellinson; Aviezer Ellinson; Uri Ellinson.

OTHER INFORMATION Donations of less than £5,000 each totalled £21,000.

HOW TO APPLY Our research indicates that the foundation generally supports the same organisations each year and unsolicited applications are not welcome.

WHO TO APPLY TO Uri Ellinson, Trustee, Robson Laidler LLP, Fernwood House, Fernwood Road, Jesmond, Newcastle upon Tyne NE2 1TJ *Tel.* 0191 281 8191 *Email* u.ellinson@gmail.com

■ The Edith Maud Ellis 1985 Charitable Trust

CC NO 292835 **ESTABLISHED** 1985

WHERE FUNDING CAN BE GIVEN UK and overseas.

WHO CAN BENEFIT UK-registered charities; overseas charities; non-governmental organisations; small social enterprises; small charities; Quaker charities.

WHAT IS FUNDED Quaker work and witness; peace-building; conflict resolution; interfaith; ecumenical understanding; community development; migrants; sustainable development.

TYPE OF GRANT One-off grants; time limited support; seed money for start-up projects.

RANGE OF GRANTS £500 to £3000.

SAMPLE GRANTS Our Own Future (£2,300); Ekklesia, Quaker Action on Domestic Violence, War Resisters International (£2,000); Anbar Initiative (£1,500); Congénies, Dorothy Peace Centre, Inga Foundation, The Fostering Network (£1,000); Scholarships for Street Kids – Burma (£750); Loughborough Town of Sanctuary (£200).

FINANCES *Year* 2015/16 *Income* £37,711 *Grants* £45,800 *Grants to organisations* £45,800 *Assets* £1,193,188

TRUSTEES Michael Phipps; Jane Dawson; Elizabeth Cave; Nicholas Sims.

OTHER INFORMATION During 2015/16 grants were awarded to over 40 bodies totalling £45,800.

HOW TO APPLY Applications must be made through the website. The website states that: 'Applications should be received by the end of December and end of June in order to be considered at one of the Trustee Meetings. It is sensible to get applications in well ahead of these dates. Late applicants will be considered in the next funding round. Successful applicants will be informed as soon as possible of the Trustees' decision. If you have not heard within two calendar months of the relevant closing date you should assume you have been unsuccessful. Successful applicants will be encouraged to contribute to our website in a variety of ways and may be approached to showcase the work of the Trust. Successful applicants will not be considered for a future award within a three year period. Unsuccessful applicants will not be reconsidered within a 12 month period.'

WHO TO APPLY TO Jacqueline Baily, Virtuosity Executive Support, 6 Westgate, Thirsk, North Yorkshire YO7 1QS *Tel.* 01845 574882 *Email* jackie@virtuosity-uk.com *Website* www.theedithmellischaritabletrust.org

■ The Elmley Foundation

CC NO 1004043 **ESTABLISHED** 1991

WHERE FUNDING CAN BE GIVEN Herefordshire and Worcestershire.

WHO CAN BENEFIT Constituted organisations and groups; individual artists from Herefordshire and Worcestershire; other individual artists whose proposals have been planned in conjunction with an organisation or body in Herefordshire or Worcestershire; students born and schooled in the two counties who are enrolled on nationally-recognised specialist arts courses.

WHAT IS FUNDED The arts.

WHAT IS NOT FUNDED Non-arts projects; projects not involving professional artists; arts events outside the beneficial area; arts events intended to raise funds for non-arts causes; general appeals; applications for retrospective funding.

TYPE OF GRANT Capital, core costs, contracts and full project funding. Funding of up to, and over, three years will be considered.

RANGE OF GRANTS £250 to £25,000; rarely more than £2,000 for unsolicited applications.

SAMPLE GRANTS The Three Choirs Festival (£25,000); Ledbury Poetry Festival (£16,000);

Worcester Live Ltd (£10,000); Borderlines Film Festival (£5,000); Dancefest (£4,500); Kidderminster Chorale (£1,000); Herefordshire College of Arts (£750); University of Worcester and Wye Valley Music (£250 each).

FINANCES *Year* 2015/16 *Income* £334,353 *Grants* £227,310 *Grants to organisations* £209,460 *Assets* £3,696,265

TRUSTEES Diana Johnson; Sam Driver White; Sally Luton.

OTHER INFORMATION There are two funding schemes: the Main Programme supports proposals which fall within the foundation's objects ('to promote the appreciation, knowledge and study of the arts and of artistic achievement in all their forms in Herefordshire and Worcestershire'); and the Small Grants Scheme has two funds – one for arts events and activities and the other for arts equipment. During the year, 50 grants were paid through the Main Programme and 22 through the Small Grants Scheme.

HOW TO APPLY Applicants to the Main Programme are strongly advised to contact the foundation before making a formal application. There is an application form available to download from the website or, alternatively, applicants can send a letter including details of: what the money is needed for; an estimate of the income and expenditure for the project/programme being planned; and, in particular, who will be benefitting from the project/programme. Applications can be made at any time. Application forms and guidance notes for the Small Grants Scheme are available from the website. Deadlines are detailed on the website. Questions regarding eligibility for the scheme can be directed to Gail Mattocks at Community First on 01684 312730, or email grants@comfirst.org.uk.

WHO TO APPLY TO John de la Cour, Director, West Aish, Morchard Bishop, Crediton, Devon EX17 6RX *Tel.* 01363 877433 *Email* foundation@elmley.org.uk *Website* www.elmley.org.uk

■ The Vernon N. Ely Charitable Trust

CC NO 230033 **ESTABLISHED** 1962

WHERE FUNDING CAN BE GIVEN Not defined; there is a preference for the London Borough of Merton.

WHO CAN BENEFIT Charitable organisations.

WHAT IS FUNDED General charitable purposes, with a preference for charities in the London Borough of Merton as well as sports (particularly tennis-related) charities with which the settlor, Vernon Ely, had a long-standing personal connection.

WHAT IS NOT FUNDED Individuals.

RANGE OF GRANTS Usually up to £4,000.

SAMPLE GRANTS Age Concern, Cardiac Risk in the Young, Christchurch URC, Community Housing Therapy, London Sports Forum for Disabled People, Polka Children's Theatre, and Samaritans (£4,000 each); British Tennis Foundation (£1,750); Sobell Hospice and West Barnes Singers (£500 each).

FINANCES *Year* 2015/16 *Income* £69,596 *Grants* £327,750 *Grants to organisations* £327,750 *Assets* £1,692,531

TRUSTEES Derek Howorth; John Moyle; Richard Main.

OTHER INFORMATION The grant total includes distributions of £25,000 each made to ten charities of the trust's restricted fund.

HOW TO APPLY Apply in writing to the correspondent.

WHO TO APPLY TO Derek Howorth, Trustee, 13/15 Carteret Street, Westminster, London SW1H 9DG *Tel.* 020 7828 3156 *Email* dph@helmores.co.uk

■ The Emerald Foundation

CC NO 1127093 **ESTABLISHED** 2008

WHERE FUNDING CAN BE GIVEN West Riding of Yorkshire.

WHO CAN BENEFIT Registered charities.

WHAT IS FUNDED The performing arts; sport; animal welfare.

SAMPLE GRANTS Opera North (£580,000); Yorkshire Cricket Foundation (£150,000); Whitehall Dog Rescue (£120,000); West Yorkshire Animals in Need (£10,000); Far Place Animal Rescue and Left Bank (£5,000 each); Bradford Festival Choral Society (£3,000).

FINANCES *Year* 2015 *Income* £1,500,000 *Grants* £1,599,583 *Grants to organisations* £1,599,583 *Assets* -£107,864

TRUSTEES Peter Meredith; Karen Fojt; Dr Keith Howard; Timothy Ratcliffe.

OTHER INFORMATION Grants were broken down as follows: performing arts (£1.1 million); sport (£305,000); animals (£195,000).

HOW TO APPLY Apply in writing to the correspondent.

WHO TO APPLY TO Sylvia Hall, The Emerald Foundation, Howard House, Wagon Lane, Bingley BD16 1WA *Tel.* 01274 777700 *Email* shall@emeraldinsight.com *Website* emeraldfoundation.org.uk

■ The Emerton-Christie Charity

CC NO 262837 **ESTABLISHED** 1971

WHERE FUNDING CAN BE GIVEN UK.

WHO CAN BENEFIT Registered charities only.

WHAT IS FUNDED Health, including mental health; people with disabilities; older people; young people; the arts; education.

WHAT IS NOT FUNDED Our research suggests that no grants are given for: individuals; religious organisations; restoration or extension of buildings; start-up costs; animal welfare and research; cultural heritage; or environmental projects.

TYPE OF GRANT Donations for capital projects and/or income requirements.

RANGE OF GRANTS Usually up to £3,000.

SAMPLE GRANTS Alan Niekirk Scholarship (£10,000); Daft as a Brush, Deptford Action Group for Elderly, Hotline Meal Service, Music in Detention, Positive East and Prisoners' Education Trust (£3,000 each); Blesma (£2,000); Mental Health Foundation (£1,000).

FINANCES *Year* 2015/16 *Income* £74,778 *Grants* £86,400 *Grants to organisations* £86,400 *Assets* £2,862,594

TRUSTEES Lt Col. William Niekirk; Dr Claire Mera-Nelson; Dr Sally Walker.

OTHER INFORMATION Beneficiaries have included organisations working with disadvantaged groups such as refugees and asylum seekers, victims of human trafficking and prisoners.

HOW TO APPLY Apply in writing to the correspondent. A demonstration of need based on budgetary principles is required and applications will not be acknowledged unless accompanied by an sae. Trustees normally meet once a year in the autumn to select charities to benefit.

WHO TO APPLY TO The Trustees, c/o Cartmell Shepherd Solicitors, Viaduct House, Victoria Viaduct, Carlisle CA3 8EZ *Tel.* 01228 516666 *Email* claire.wilson@cartmells.co.uk

EMI Music Sound Foundation

CC NO 1104027 **ESTABLISHED** 1997
WHERE FUNDING CAN BE GIVEN UK and Ireland.
WHO CAN BENEFIT Schools and individuals.
WHAT IS FUNDED The improvement of young people's access to music education. Support is given to: individuals, preferably under the age of 25, who are in full-time education, for musical instrument/equipment purchase; schools, to fund music education; and music teachers working within schools, to fund courses and training. Bursaries are also awarded to students at one of eight recognised UK and Ireland music colleges/organisations.
WHAT IS NOT FUNDED Applicants based outside the United Kingdom and Ireland; non-school-based community groups; applications for tuition fees and living expenses other than as described under the Bursary Awards section on the foundation's website; applications over £2,000; funding for private instrumental lessons; the payment of staffing costs to cover the teaching of the national curriculum or peripatetic teaching costs; retrospective costs.
TYPE OF GRANT Equipment and training costs; bursaries.
RANGE OF GRANTS Up to £2,000.
SAMPLE GRANTS A list of beneficiaries was not available.
FINANCES *Year* 2015/16 *Income* £306,689 *Grants* £499,160 *Grants to organisations* £354,608 *Assets* £7,506,699
TRUSTEES Rupert Perry; David Hughes; Leslie Hill; Tony Wadsworth; James Beach; Paul Gambaccini; The Hon. Richard Lyttelton; Charles Ashcroft; Jo Hibbitt; Keith Harris; Ruth Katz; Adam Barker.
OTHER INFORMATION In 2015/16 a total of 554 individual and school applications were approved. The amount of grants given to individuals totalled £144,500.
HOW TO APPLY Application forms for instruments and equipment grants can be downloaded from the website, along with guidance notes.
WHO TO APPLY TO Janie Orr, Chief Executive, EMI Music Sound Foundation, Beaumont House, Avonmore Road, Kensington Village, London W14 8TS *Tel.* 020 7550 7898 *Email* emimusicsoundfoundation@umusic.com. *Website* www.emimusicsoundfoundation.com

The Englefield Charitable Trust

CC NO 258123 **ESTABLISHED** 1968
WHERE FUNDING CAN BE GIVEN Not defined; in practice, the Berkshire area.
WHO CAN BENEFIT Mainly registered charities; some local schools and churches are supported.
WHAT IS FUNDED General charitable purposes, including: churches and religion; conservation, heritage and arts; young people, education and community; social welfare; overseas projects; medical research; and armed forces charities.
WHAT IS NOT FUNDED Applications from individuals for study or travel are not considered.
TYPE OF GRANT Buildings, capital, interest-free loans, research, running costs, salaries and start-up costs. Funding for one year or less will be considered.
RANGE OF GRANTS £100 to £100,000.
SAMPLE GRANTS Ufton Court Educational Trust (£100,000); Englefield Parochial Church Council (£36,500); Thames Valley Chiltern Air Ambulance (£5,500); Trooper Potts VC Memorial Trust and Watermill Theatre (£5,000 each); Corn Exchange Newbury and Thrive (£3,000 each); 14–21 Time to Talk, Children's Trust and Church Housing Trust (£2,000 each); Andover Mind, The British Horseracing Education and Standards Trust and Christians Against Poverty (£1,000 each); Aldermaston Parish Hall (£500); Volunteer Centre West Berkshire (£350).
FINANCES *Year* 2015/16 *Income* £445,850 *Grants* £358,181 *Grants to organisations* £358,181 *Assets* £14,344,540
TRUSTEES Catherine Haig; Lady Elizabeth Benyon; Richard Benyon; Zoe Benyon; Melissa Owston; Richard Bampfylde; Richard Griffiths.
OTHER INFORMATION In 2015/16 the trust received 659 applications and made 151 grants.
HOW TO APPLY Apply in writing to the correspondent enclosing your organisation's latest set of accounts, and stating your charity's registration number and the purpose for which the money is to be used. Applications are considered in March and September. Only applications going before the trustees will be acknowledged.
WHO TO APPLY TO Alexander Reid, Secretary, Englefield Estate Office, Englefield Road, Theale, Reading RG7 5DU *Tel.* 01920 832205 *Email* charity@englefield.co.uk

The Enkalon Foundation

CC NO 103528 **ESTABLISHED** 1985
WHERE FUNDING CAN BE GIVEN Northern Ireland.
WHO CAN BENEFIT Community groups and organisations working to improve the quality of life for people in Northern Ireland.
WHAT IS FUNDED The foundation supports a wide range of activities, with the following interests outlined on the website: cross community groups; self-help groups; assistance for unemployed people; and groups helping disadvantaged people. It is noted that the priorities of the foundation 'may vary from year to year'.
WHAT IS NOT FUNDED Normally, grants are not made to/for: playgroups, PTAs or sporting groups outside the Antrim borough area; to individuals (other than former British Enkalon employees); medical research; travel outside Northern Ireland.
TYPE OF GRANT Mainly for starter finance, single projects or capital projects.
RANGE OF GRANTS Up to £6,000 maximum, with the average grant between £500 and £1,000.
SAMPLE GRANTS Leonard Cheshire Disability NI (£3,000); Conservation Volunteers NI Antrim, Lighthouse Trust Donaghadee and React NI (£2,000 each); Antrim Hockey Club and Dream Holidays (£1,500 each); Antrim Choral Society, Independence at Home NI and Tools for Solidarity (£1,000 each); Autism NI Antrim (£970); Little Orchids Children Centre Derry and North Belfast Food Bank (£500 each); First Antrim Presbyterian Church Friendship Group (£250).
FINANCES *Year* 2014/15 *Income* £314,925 *Grants* £235,670 *Grants to organisations* £200,002 *Assets* £7,183,992
TRUSTEES Raymond Milnes; Peter Dalton; Mark Patterson; Stephen Montgomery; John Wallace.
OTHER INFORMATION The foundation is registered with The Charity Commission for Northern Ireland. At the time of writing (June 2017) the 2014/15 accounts were the most recent available. Grants to individual ex-employees of British Enkalon and/or their families totalled £35,500.
HOW TO APPLY Applications can be made online via the website, where guidance notes are also

available. Queries regarding the applications process can be directed to the Administrator, Claire Cawley, by telephone (07740 641166) or email (claire@enkalonfoundation.org). The trustees meet quarterly (in March, June, September and December) and closing dates for applications fall one month before the meeting. Exact dates are available from the Administrator.

WHO TO APPLY TO Claire Cawley, Administrator, Antrim Civic Centre, 50 Stiles Way, Antrim BT41 2UB *Tel.* 028 9447 7131 *Email* info@enkelonfoundation.org *Website* www.enkalonfoundation.org

■ Entindale Ltd

CC NO 277052 **ESTABLISHED** 1978

WHERE FUNDING CAN BE GIVEN UK and Israel.

WHO CAN BENEFIT Orthodox Jewish organisations.

WHAT IS FUNDED The advancement of the Orthodox Jewish religion; education; the relief of poverty.

RANGE OF GRANTS Up to £500,000; typically less than £10,000.

SAMPLE GRANTS TTMH Building Fund (£500,000); Ezer Bekovoid Ltd (£132,000); Achisomoch Aid Co. Ltd (£100,000); Knesset Yechezke Synagogue (£42,000); Menorah High School for Girls (£23,000); Kahal Imrey Chaim (£10,500); Law of Truth Talmudical College (£3,000); The Cost Shop (£2,300); Academy for Rabbinical Research (£1,300); Committee for Preservation of Jewish Cemeteries, Rosecare Foundation and Yeshiva L'Zeirim Manchester (£1,000 each); Kids Care (£500).

FINANCES *Year* 2015/16 *Income* £1,993,793 *Grants* £2,139,258 *Grants to organisations* £2,139,258 *Assets* £18,377,296

TRUSTEES Allan Becker; Barbara Bridgeman; Jonathan Hager.

OTHER INFORMATION In 2015/16 grants were made to 124 organisations.

HOW TO APPLY Apply in writing to the correspondent.

WHO TO APPLY TO Joseph Pearlman, Trustee, 8 Highfield Gardens, London NW11 9HB *Tel.* 020 8458 9266

■ The Epigoni Trust

CC NO 328700 **ESTABLISHED** 1990

WHERE FUNDING CAN BE GIVEN UK.

WHO CAN BENEFIT Registered UK charities.

WHAT IS FUNDED General charitable purposes.

WHAT IS NOT FUNDED Individuals.

TYPE OF GRANT Project and one-off grants, for one year or less.

RANGE OF GRANTS £1,000 to £17,500.

SAMPLE GRANTS Pallant House Gallery (£17,500); Mondo Challenge Foundation (£15,000); Progressive Supranuclear Palsy Association (£10,000); Chichester Festival Theatre – Education Department (£7,500); St Richard of Chichester Christian Care Association, Sussex Snowdrop Trust and Switchback (£5,000 each); Crisis (£1,000).

FINANCES *Year* 2015 *Income* £32,194 *Grants* £66,000 *Grants to organisations* £66,000 *Assets* £3,810,161

TRUSTEES Bettine Bond; Charles Peacock; Andrew Bond.

OTHER INFORMATION In 2015 eight charities received grants from the trust. Generally, the same small group of charities are supported.

HOW TO APPLY Our research indicates that this trust no longer accepts applications.

WHO TO APPLY TO Charles Peacock, Trustee, c/o Michael Theodorou, Charities Aid Foundation, 25 Kings Hill Avenue, Kings Hill, West Malling ME19 4TA *Tel.* 01732 520028

■ Epilepsy Research UK

CC NO 1100394 **ESTABLISHED** 1985

WHERE FUNDING CAN BE GIVEN UK.

WHO CAN BENEFIT Researchers conducting studies that will benefit people with epilepsy.

WHAT IS FUNDED According to the website, the charity 'invests in research into all areas of epilepsy – giving priority to those areas which have the potential to produce results in immediate problem areas, including: research leading to improvements in the accuracy of diagnosis; and research into improving the treatment and quality of life of the patient. Epilepsy Research UK also supports basic scientific research and operates a fellowship programme to encourage scientists to pursue a career in epilepsy research.'

TYPE OF GRANT Projects, fellowship, research and equipment. Funding is for up to three years.

RANGE OF GRANTS Up to £250,000.

SAMPLE GRANTS University of Edinburgh (£250,000); Birmingham Children's Hospital (£211,000); Cardiff University and King's College London (£30,000 each); University College London (£29,000).

FINANCES *Year* 2015/16 *Income* £1,236,209 *Grants* £687,179 *Grants to organisations* £687,179 *Assets* £720,391

TRUSTEES Barrie Akin; David Cameron; Dr Yvonne Hart; John Hirst; Simon Lanyon; Prof. Mark Rees; Prof. Mark Richardson; Harry Salmon; Dr Graeme Sills; Judith Spencer-Gregson; Prof. Matthew Walker; Mary Gavigan.

OTHER INFORMATION In 2015/16 a total of six research grants were awarded.

HOW TO APPLY Application forms, together with criteria, guidelines and application deadlines, are available to download on the charity's website.

WHO TO APPLY TO Judith Spencer-Gregson, Trustee, PO Box 3004, London W4 4XT *Tel.* 020 8747 5024 *Email* info@eruk.org.uk *Website* www.epilepsyresearch.org.uk

■ The Eranda Rothschild Foundation

CC NO 255650 **ESTABLISHED** 1967

WHERE FUNDING CAN BE GIVEN UK and overseas; for charities working locally, preference is given to those in Buckinghamshire and Bedfordshire.

WHO CAN BENEFIT Registered charities.

WHAT IS FUNDED Medical research; education; the arts; social welfare (especially work known to the trustees).

WHAT IS NOT FUNDED Individuals; organisations which are not registered charities; capital appeals (unless of personal significance to the trustees).

TYPE OF GRANT Project, running costs and recurring costs for up to three years.

RANGE OF GRANTS Up to around £100,000.

SAMPLE GRANTS King's College London (£500,000); Dyslexia Scotland (£175,000); Caritas Anchor House and Norwood (£100,000 each); Prince's Foundation for Children and the Arts (£63,000); Alzheimer's Drug Discovery Foundation (£33,500); Liberal Jewish Synagogue (£30,000); Chopin Society UK (£25,000); Institute for Policy Research (£15,000); Guy

Mascolo Football Charity (£12,500); Bucks Association for the Care of Offenders (£10,000); Films Without Borders (£5,000); Injured Jockey Fund (£1,000); Action Medical Research (£250).

FINANCES *Year* 2015/16 *Income* £4,091,601 *Grants* £3,211,084 *Grants to organisations* £3,211,084 *Assets* £107,145,633

TRUSTEES Sir Evelyn de Rothschild; Lady Lynn Forester de Rothschild; Anthony de Rothschild; Jessica de Rothschild; Sir Graham Hearne; Sir John Peace; Ben Elliot.

OTHER INFORMATION In 2015/16, 109 grants were made across the following categories: education (£1.44 million in 42 grants); health/welfare/ medical research (£1 million in 37 grants); the arts (£769,000 in 30 grants).

HOW TO APPLY The foundation prefers applications to be made using its online form. Applications are considered at meetings held three times a year, usually in February/March, June/July and October/November. Charities should make only one application per year.

WHO TO APPLY TO Gail Devlin-Jones, Secretary, PO Box 6226, Leighton Buzzard, Bedfordshire LU7 0XF *Tel.* 01296 689157 *Email* secretary@erandarothschild.org *Website* www.erandarothschild.org

The Ericson Trust

CC NO 219762 **ESTABLISHED** 1962

WHERE FUNDING CAN BE GIVEN UK and overseas.

WHO CAN BENEFIT Registered charities.

WHAT IS FUNDED The Charity Commission record states that the trust supports 'charities concerned with UK citizens or with international development'. Our previous research suggests this may include: older people; community projects/local interest groups, including arts; prisons, prison reform, mentoring projects, and research in this area; refugees; mental health; environmental projects and research; aid to lower- and middle-income countries only if supported and represented or initiated and administered by a UK-registered charity.

WHAT IS NOT FUNDED Applications from the following areas are generally not considered unless closely connected with one of the above: children's and young people's clubs, centres and so on; schools; charities dealing with illness or disability (except psychiatric); or religious institutions, except in their social projects.

TYPE OF GRANT Project grants.

SAMPLE GRANTS Action on Elder Abuse; Anti-Slavery International; Ashram International; Bhopal Medical Appeal; Headway East London; Howard League for Penal Reform; The Koestler Trust; Minority Rights Group; Psychiatric Rehabilitation Association; Quaker Social Action; The Rainforest Foundation; The Relatives and Residents Association; Tools for Self Reliance.

FINANCES *Year* 2015/16 *Income* £20,421 *Grants* £40,000 *Grants to organisations* £40,000

TRUSTEES Valerie Barrow; Rebecca Cotton; Claudia Cotton.

OTHER INFORMATION The trust's latest accounts were not available to view on the Charity Commission's website due to its low income. We have therefore estimated the grant total based on previous years' information.

HOW TO APPLY The trust has previously stated that it supports a number of charities on a regular basis and is unable to consider new appeals.

WHO TO APPLY TO Claudia Cotton, Trustee, Flat 2, 53 Carleton Road, London N7 0ET *Email* claudia.cotton@googlemail.com

The Erskine Cunningham Hill Trust

SC NO SC001853 **ESTABLISHED** 1955

WHERE FUNDING CAN BE GIVEN Scotland.

WHO CAN BENEFIT Organisations registered in Scotland benefitting older people, young people, ex-service men and women, seamen, and the Church of Scotland.

WHAT IS FUNDED Other grants are restricted to charitable work in Scotland with older people; young people; ex-servicemen and women; seafarers; Scottish heritage and culture.

WHAT IS NOT FUNDED Individuals; charities outside Scotland.

TYPE OF GRANT Recurring grants to the Church of Scotland; one-off grants to individual Scottish charities.

RANGE OF GRANTS Approximately £1,000 each to individual charities.

SAMPLE GRANTS Age Concern Dundee, Apostleship of the Sea, Baillieston Community Care, Befriending Network Scotland, Fischy Music, Helenslea Community Hall, Royal Navy and Marines Children's Fund and Scottish Adoption (£1,000 each); Edinburgh Headway Group, MacRoberts Art Centre and Yorkhill Children's Charity (£500 each).

FINANCES *Year* 2015 *Income* £53,829 *Grants* £51,500 *Grants to organisations* £51,500 *Assets* £404

TRUSTEES R. M. Maiden; Very Revd Dr A. McDonald; I. W. Grimmond; Very Revd J. Cairns; Very Revd A. McLellan; Dr A. Elliot; The Church of Scotland Trust.

OTHER INFORMATION The Church of Scotland is the largest single focus of the trust's interest (50% of annual income), receiving a grant for £25,000 during the year.

HOW TO APPLY Apply in writing to the correspondent at the above address. An application form is available via email from the correspondent. There is a two-year time bar on repeat grants. The trustees do not consider applications from outside Scotland.

WHO TO APPLY TO Nicola Laing, Secretary, Stewardship and Finance Department, Church of Scotland Offices, 121 George Street, Edinburgh EH2 4YN *Tel.* 0131 225 5722 *Email* nlaing@cofscotland.org.uk

The Esfandi Foundation

CC NO 1103095 **ESTABLISHED** 2004

WHERE FUNDING CAN BE GIVEN UK and overseas.

WHO CAN BENEFIT Mainly Jewish organisations.

WHAT IS FUNDED General charitable purposes.

RANGE OF GRANTS Up to £65,000.

SAMPLE GRANTS Kollel Chabad (£65,000); Hand to Hand (£35,000); British Friends of Migdal Ohr, Chazek Ltd, Chozok, Community Security Trust, Jewish Care and United Jewish Israel Appeal (UJIA) (£25,000 each); The Covenant and Conversation Trust (£15,000).

FINANCES *Year* 2015/16 *Income* £568,146 *Grants* £301,498 *Grants to organisations* £301,498 *Assets* £330,504

TRUSTEES Joseph Esfandi; Denise Esfandi.

HOW TO APPLY Apply in writing to the correspondent.

WHO TO APPLY TO Joseph Esfandi, Trustee, 36 Park Street, London W1K 2JE *Tel.* 020 7629 6666

■ Esh Foundation

CC NO 1112040 **ESTABLISHED** 2005

WHERE FUNDING CAN BE GIVEN Cumbria; Durham; North Yorkshire; Northumberland.

WHO CAN BENEFIT Registered charities; community groups.

WHAT IS FUNDED General charitable purposes; children and young people; vulnerable people; environmental community regeneration; education capacity and skills development; health.

RANGE OF GRANTS Up to £20,000.

SAMPLE GRANTS Eagles Community Foundation (£20,000); SAFC Foundation (£8,000); British Transplant Games (£6,000); Butterwick Hospice, Northumberland Wildlife Trust, Durham Cricket Club, St Oswald's Hospice (£5,000 each); Child Deaf Youth Project, Hartlepool Gymnastic Club, Radio Lonsdale, Teesdale Search and Rescue (£500); 50+ Tuesday Lunch Club and Social Club (£280).

FINANCES *Year* 2015 *Income* £135,611 *Grants* £87,277 *Grants to organisations* £87,277 *Assets* £63,461

OTHER INFORMATION This is the charitable foundation of the Esh Group, a civil engineering, construction and house building company based in County Durham. The company has committed to provide the foundation with £1 million over five years until 2017, subject to profits.

HOW TO APPLY Apply in writing to the correspondent. The trustees meet regularly to review applications and further support with the process is provided by the County Durham Community Foundation.

WHO TO APPLY TO Andrew Radcliffe, Secretary, Esh Holdings Ltd, Esh House, Bowburn North Industrial Estate, Bowburn, Durham DH6 5PF *Tel.* 07976 077621 *Email* enquiries@esh.uk.com *Website* www.eshgroup.co.uk/added-value/community/esh-communities

■ Esher House Charitable Trust

CC NO 276183 **ESTABLISHED** 1978

WHERE FUNDING CAN BE GIVEN England and Wales.

WHO CAN BENEFIT Registered charities, mainly Jewish charities.

WHAT IS FUNDED Health, medical causes and sickness; Jewish causes.

WHAT IS NOT FUNDED Individuals.

RANGE OF GRANTS Mostly less than £1,000.

SAMPLE GRANTS The beneficiaries of grants exceeding £1,000 were: Magen David Adom UK (£67,500); British Emunah (£6,500); Nightingale Hammerson (£5,000); Jewish Music Institute (£1,400); Chana Charitable Trust (£1,200).

FINANCES *Year* 2015/16 *Income* £161,242 *Grants* £98,981 *Grants to organisations* £98,981 *Assets* £2,535,867

TRUSTEES Michael Conn; Hadassa Conn; Douglas Conn.

OTHER INFORMATION Grants were made to 89 charities in 2015/16, with the vast majority receiving amounts of less than £1,000.

HOW TO APPLY Apply in writing to the correspondent.

WHO TO APPLY TO Michael Conn, Trustee, 845 Finchley Road, London NW11 8NA *Tel.* 020 8455 1111

■ The Essex and Southend Sports Trust

CC NO 1092238 **ESTABLISHED** 2002

WHERE FUNDING CAN BE GIVEN Essex, Southend-on-Sea.

WHO CAN BENEFIT Charitable organisations; registered charities; community groups; sports clubs; organisations.

WHAT IS FUNDED Sports; sports equipment; sports facilities; individuals; sports projects; coaching; training; education; children and young people; community projects; disability; older people.

WHAT IS NOT FUNDED Anything outside Southend-on-Sea and the county of Essex; anything not related to sports.

RANGE OF GRANTS Up to £50,000.

SAMPLE GRANTS Southend United Community and Educational Trust (£25,000); Hadleigh and Thundersley Cricket Club (£8,000); Essex County Cricket Board, Harlow Cricket Club (£5,000 each); The Prince's Trust, Southend Rugby Club (£3,000 each); South East Essex District Cricket Board (£2,500); Giffards Primary School (£2,000); Richardson-Trek Cycling team (£1,500); RSPB (£1,200).

FINANCES *Year* 2015/16 *Income* £408,796 *Grants* £128,764 *Grants to organisations* £128,764 *Assets* £5,265,958

TRUSTEES Joseph Sims; Linley Butler; Peter Butler.

OTHER INFORMATION The trust's joint venture with Essex Community Foundation (ECF) – the Essex and Southend Sports Charitable Fund (ESSCF) – supports sporting activities for individuals. The trustees approved 15 grants in the year totalling almost £129,000. The trustees and ECF jointly agreed to make 16 grants from the ESSCF with a total value of £57,000 of which £21,000 was taken from trust's contribution and £36,000 was raised by ECF as matched funding from seven other Essex-based charitable funds.

HOW TO APPLY Contact the correspondent to enquire about making an application.

WHO TO APPLY TO Peter Butler, Trustee, Red House, Larks Lane, Great Waltham, Chelmsford CM3 1AD *Tel.* 01245 360385 *Email* mail@easst.org.uk *Website* www.easst.org.uk

■ Essex Community Foundation

CC NO 1052061 **ESTABLISHED** 1995

WHERE FUNDING CAN BE GIVEN Essex, Southend and Thurrock.

WHO CAN BENEFIT Voluntary and community organisations and other not-for-profit organisations, with an interest in small grassroots organisations. Individuals can also be supported.

WHAT IS FUNDED General charitable purposes; social welfare; community development.

WHAT IS NOT FUNDED Projects outside the beneficial area (including Romford, Ilford, Barking, Dagenham, etc.); political campaigning; religious activities which are not for the wider public benefit; statutory agencies, including parish councils and schools for their statutory obligations; general appeals; activities which solely support animal welfare; retrospective funding; organisations which fund other organisations and individuals.

TYPE OF GRANT Core costs/revenue costs, new or continuing projects, one-off initiatives and capital costs.

RANGE OF GRANTS From £250 to £10,000, with the average grant being between £3,500 and £4,000.

SAMPLE GRANTS A list of beneficiaries was not available.
FINANCES *Year* 2015/16 *Income* £4,567,715 *Grants* £2,347,002 *Grants to organisations* £2,347,002 *Assets* £33,283,757
TRUSTEES Jonny Minter; Clare Ball; Dame Kate Barker; Peter Blanc; Lee Blissett; Charles Cryer; Russell Edey; Etholle George; Peter Martin; Dr Tom Nutt; Owen Richards; Jackie Sully; Rosemary Turner; Claire Read.
OTHER INFORMATION In 2015/16 grants, including commitments from prior years, were paid out to 312 organisations and 47 individuals.
HOW TO APPLY Application forms are available from the foundation's website, along with full guidelines and other helpful information. The foundation matches applications to the most appropriate fund, so only one application form needs to be submitted. Applicants who are unsure about their eligibility or who have any general questions can read the website's helpful FAQs section or get in touch with the grants team, which welcomes the opportunity to discuss proposals with applicants before they are submitted.
WHO TO APPLY TO Grants team, 121 New London Road, Chelmsford, Essex CM2 0QT *Tel.* 01245 356018 *Email* grants@essexcf.org.uk *Website* www.essexcommunityfoundation.org.uk

■ The Essex Heritage Trust

CC NO 802317 **ESTABLISHED** 1989
WHERE FUNDING CAN BE GIVEN Essex.
WHO CAN BENEFIT Charitable organisations; individuals.
WHAT IS FUNDED Publications about or the preservation of Essex history and restoration of monuments, significant structures, artefacts and church decorations and equipment.
WHAT IS NOT FUNDED Grants involving private property.
TYPE OF GRANT Mostly one-off grants for revenue and capital costs.
RANGE OF GRANTS £500 to £10,000.
SAMPLE GRANTS St Thomas' the Apostle Church – Bradwell-on-Sea (£10,000); Epping Forest District Museum (£5,000); Bocking Public Gardens, Essex Journal and VCH Essex Trust (£3,000 each); Colchester Art Society (£2,500); St Mary the Virgin Little Baddow (£2,000); Little Baddow Village Hall (£1,100); Great Baddow Women's Institute (£500).
FINANCES *Year* 2015/16 *Income* £64,527 *Grants* £55,080 *Grants to organisations* £54,080 *Assets* £1,503,644
TRUSTEES Lord John Petre; Richard Wollaston; Mark Pertwee; Peter Mamelok; Dr James Bettley; Brian Moody; Susan Brice; Cllr Kay Twitchen; Jonathan Douglas-Hughes; Cllr John Aldridge.
OTHER INFORMATION During the year, 23 applications for grants were received of which 18 were successful. One individual received a grant of £1,000 towards the publication of a book.
HOW TO APPLY To apply for funding, complete the expression of interest form on the trust's website. The trust will then contact you with further instructions. The trustees meet three times a year to assess applications, in March, July and November and the dates of the meetings are posted on the website.
WHO TO APPLY TO Sharon Hill, Administrator, Cressing Temple, Witham Road, Braintree, Essex CM77 8PD *Tel.* 01376 585794 *Email* mail@essexheritagetrust.co.uk *Website* www.essexheritagetrust.co.uk

■ The Essex Youth Trust

CC NO 225768 **ESTABLISHED** 1963
WHERE FUNDING CAN BE GIVEN Essex.
WHO CAN BENEFIT Organisations, including youth clubs.
WHAT IS FUNDED The education and advancement of people under the age of 25, particularly those who are 'deprived of normal parental care' or disadvantaged. The annual report explains that grants are awarded 'which favour beneficiaries that develop young people's physical, mental and spiritual capacities through active participation in sports and indoor and outdoor activities. As a result they are particularly supportive of youth clubs and other organisations which provide facilities for young people to take active part in an assortment of activities as well as single activity organisations.'
WHAT IS NOT FUNDED Individuals.
TYPE OF GRANT Core costs; running costs; capital expenditure; project funding; salaries.
RANGE OF GRANTS Up to £63,500; the majority of grants were of less then £10,000.
SAMPLE GRANTS Essex Boys and Girls Clubs (£63,500); Cirdan Sailing Trust (£50,000); Stubbers Adventure Centre (£45,000); North Avenue Youth Centre (£17,300); Sea Change Sailing Trust (£14,500); Chain Reaction Theatre Company (£13,000); Signpost Colchester (£12,000). Of these beneficiaries, six had relations to the trust through its trustees.
FINANCES *Year* 2015/16 *Income* £396,452 *Grants* £350,518 *Grants to organisations* £350,518 *Assets* £8,020,357
TRUSTEES Julien Courtauld; Revd Canon Duncan Green; Claire Cottrell; William Robson; Lady Julia Denison-Smith; Michael Dyer; Richard Wenley; Michael Biegel; Julie Rogers.
OTHER INFORMATION In 2015/16 of 54 one-off applications received: 41 were successful; 11 were declined; 2 were deferred. In addition there were eight annual grants awarded.
HOW TO APPLY Apply using a form available from the correspondent. The trustees meet on a quarterly basis.
WHO TO APPLY TO Jonathan Douglas-Hughes, Clerk, Gepp and Sons, 58 New London Road, Chelmsford, Essex CM2 0PA *Tel.* 01245 493939 *Email* douglas-hughesj@gepp.co.uk

■ The Estelle Trust

CC NO 1101299 **ESTABLISHED** 2003
WHERE FUNDING CAN BE GIVEN UK and Zambia.
WHO CAN BENEFIT Charitable organisations.
WHAT IS FUNDED The trust supports community and educational projects in Zambia, as well as making smaller grants to arts, educational and social development charities in the UK.
RANGE OF GRANTS Mostly up to £2,000.
SAMPLE GRANTS Baynards Zambia Trust (£25,000); University for the Creative Arts (UCA) (£5,000); British Red Cross and Save the Children (£2,000 each); In and Out Ghetto (£1,800); Nova International (£1,200); Shelter (£1,000); Macmillan Cancer Support and Sightsavers (£500 each).
FINANCES *Year* 2015/16 *Income* £1,553,310 *Grants* £49,651 *Grants to organisations* £49,651 *Assets* £2,652,310
TRUSTEES Nigel Farrow; Gerald Ornstein; Darren Wise; Rachel Lynch; Katherine Farrow; Imogen Abed; Sarah Davies.
OTHER INFORMATION During the year, 18 organisations were supported.

HOW TO APPLY Apply in writing to the correspondent.
WHO TO APPLY TO Will Ham, Fundraising and Projects Manager (UK), 20 Padwick Avenue, Portsmouth PO6 2JL *Email* will@estelletrust.org *Website* www.estelletrust.org

■ Joseph Ettedgui Charitable Foundation

CC NO 1139615 **ESTABLISHED** 2010
WHERE FUNDING CAN BE GIVEN UK and overseas.
WHO CAN BENEFIT Registered charities; hospitals; universities.
WHAT IS FUNDED General charitable purposes, including children and young people (including in the areas of education and art), older people and homelessness.
RANGE OF GRANTS £5,000 to £40,000.
SAMPLE GRANTS Imperial College London (£40,000); The Klevis Kola Foundation (£25,000); Sistema England (£15,000 in two grants); Friends of the Elderly and Great Ormond Street Hospital (£10,000 each); International Friends of the International Lyric Art Festival (£7,100); Salvation Army and Young Urban Arts Foundation (£5,000 each).
FINANCES *Year* 2015/16 *Income* £686,479 *Grants* £172,086 *Grants to organisations* £172,086 *Assets* £3,499,474
TRUSTEES Isabel Ettedgui; Peter Ettedgui; Paul Ettedgui; Genevieve Ettedgui; Matilda Ettedgui; Coutts & Co.
OTHER INFORMATION In 2015/16, 15 grants were made to 16 organisations.
HOW TO APPLY Apply in writing to the correspondent.
WHO TO APPLY TO Coutts & Co., c/o Trustee Department, 6th Floor, Trinity Quay 2, Avon Street, Bristol BS2 0PT *Tel.* 020 7663 6825 *Email* couttscharities@coutts.com

■ Euro Charity Trust

CC NO 1058460 **ESTABLISHED** 1996
WHERE FUNDING CAN BE GIVEN Worldwide, mainly India, UK and Malawi.
WHO CAN BENEFIT Registered charities and students.
WHAT IS FUNDED Education; construction of education/training and religious establishments; welfare, including the provision of food, water, clothing and health care; medical provision. A large part of the trust's activities has been focused on projects with partner organisations in India.
TYPE OF GRANT Building costs; running costs; scholarships.
RANGE OF GRANTS Up to £2 million.
SAMPLE GRANTS Nathani Charitable Trust (£2 million); Maulana Hussain Ahmed Madani Charitable Society and Charitable Trust (£420,000); Mehboob Memorial Centre (£405,000); Imdadul Muslimeen (£300,000).
FINANCES *Year* 2015 *Income* £5,816,625 *Grants* £3,101,170 *Grants to organisations* £3,076,343 *Assets* £4,603,687
TRUSTEES Nasir Awan; Abdul Malik; Abdul Alimahomed.
OTHER INFORMATION The trust receives the majority of its income from Euro Packaging Holdings Ltd. In 2015/16 grants to individuals totalled £25,000.
HOW TO APPLY Apply in writing to the correspondent.
WHO TO APPLY TO Nasir Awan, Trustee, 20 Brickfield Road, Yardley, Birmingham B25 8HE *Email* info@eurocharity.org.uk

■ The Alan Evans Memorial Trust

CC NO 326263 **ESTABLISHED** 1979
WHERE FUNDING CAN BE GIVEN UK.
WHO CAN BENEFIT Registered charities only.
WHAT IS FUNDED According to its Charity Commission record, the trust's objective is: 'To promote the permanent preservation for the benefit of the nation of land and tenements (including buildings) of beauty or historic interest and with regards to land the preservation (so far as practicable) with their natural aspect features and animal and plant life.'
WHAT IS NOT FUNDED Non-registered charities; general appeals.
RANGE OF GRANTS £1,000 to £20,000.
SAMPLE GRANTS Cathedral Church of the Holy Spirit – Guildford; English Hedgerow Trust; Landmark Trust; Lincoln Cathedral; Peterborough Cathedral Development and Preservation Trust; Selby Abbey – the Church of Our Lord, St Mary and St Germaine; St Wilfrid's Church – Leeds; Thatcham Charity; Wells Cathedral – Somerset; Zoological Society of London.
FINANCES *Year* 2015/16 *Income* £46,305 *Grants* £194,000 *Grants to organisations* £194,000 *Assets* £1,067,344
TRUSTEES David Halfhead; Deirdre Moss.
OTHER INFORMATION In 2015/16, 100 grants were awarded, the vast majority of which were of £1,000 (60 grants) or £1,500 (25 grants).
HOW TO APPLY Appeals should be made in writing to the correspondent, stating why the funds are required, what funds have been promised from other sources (for example, English Heritage) and the amount outstanding. The trust has also previously stated that it would be helpful when making applications to provide a photograph of the project. The trustees normally meet four times a year, although in urgent cases decisions can be made between meetings. The trustees may wish to see the work undertaken with the grant money. Grant recipients may be asked to provide copies of receipts for expenditure.
WHO TO APPLY TO The Trustees, Royds Withy King LLP, 34 Regent Circus, Swindon SN1 1PY *Tel.* 01793 847777 *Email* aevans@withyking.co.uk

■ The Eventhall Charitable Trust

CC NO 803178 **ESTABLISHED** 1989
WHERE FUNDING CAN BE GIVEN UK, with a preference for the north west of England.
WHO CAN BENEFIT Charitable organisations and individuals.
WHAT IS FUNDED General charitable purposes; Jewish causes.
SAMPLE GRANTS The Federation of Jewish Services (£379,000). Previous beneficiaries have included: Aish Hatorah; ChildLine; Clitheroe Wolves Football Club; Community Security Trust; Guide Dogs for the Blind; International Wildlife Coalition; Only Foals and Horses Sanctuary; Royal National Lifeboat Institution; Sale Ladies Society; Shelter; South Manchester Synagogue.
FINANCES *Year* 2015/16 *Income* £105,369 *Grants* £557,468 *Grants to organisations* £557,468 *Assets* £3,406,237
TRUSTEES Julia Eventhall; David Eventhall.
OTHER INFORMATION A total of 71 grants were made during the year.
HOW TO APPLY Apply in writing to the correspondent. Note, however, that the trust has previously stated it only has a very limited amount of funds available.

WHO TO APPLY TO The Eventhall Family, PO Box 490, Altrincham WA14 2ZT *Email* efct@rectella.com

■ The Everard Foundation

CC NO 272248 **ESTABLISHED** 1976

WHERE FUNDING CAN BE GIVEN Leicestershire.

WHO CAN BENEFIT Registered local charities of all sizes. Grants to UK-wide organisations must be for something tangibly local.

WHAT IS FUNDED General charitable purposes, mainly citizenship/community development, social welfare, health, armed forces and education.

WHAT IS NOT FUNDED Individuals.

TYPE OF GRANT Capital costs.

RANGE OF GRANTS £100 to £16,500.

SAMPLE GRANTS Warning Zone – Leicester and Rutland Crimebeat (£16,500); Age UK Leicester and Rutland (£10,400); Home Start South Leicestershire (£6,000); National Army Museum Foundation and Tennis Leicester Charitable Trust (£5,000 each); PROSTaid (£4,300); Medical Detection Dogs (£2,000); Scout Association (£1,500); Rotary Club of Oadby and University of Leicester (£500 each); Children's Society (£300); The Bridge – Homelessness to Hope and Coping With Cancer in Leicestershire and Rutland (£250 each).

FINANCES *Year* 2015/16 *Income* £209,796 *Grants* £83,085 *Grants to organisations* £83,085 *Assets* £3,309,481

TRUSTEES Richard Everard; Serena Richards; Simon Atkinson; Charlotte Everard.

OTHER INFORMATION During the year, 42 grants were made.

HOW TO APPLY Apply in writing to the correspondent.

WHO TO APPLY TO Richard Everard, Trustee, Everards Brewery Ltd, Castle Acres, Everard Way, Enderby, Leicester LE19 1BY *Tel.* 0116 201 4307

■ The Eveson Charitable Trust

CC NO 1032204 **ESTABLISHED** 1993

WHERE FUNDING CAN BE GIVEN Herefordshire, Worcestershire and the county of West Midlands (covering Birmingham, Coventry, Dudley, Sandwell, Solihull, Walsall and Wolverhampton).

WHO CAN BENEFIT Mainly registered charities; however, some support is given, directly or indirectly, to statutory bodies for projects for which no statutory funding is available.

WHAT IS FUNDED People with disabilities; mental health; children in need; older people; homeless people; hospitals; hospices; medical research (being carried out wholly or mainly in the geographic area of benefit and into conditions associated with any of the foregoing groups). For statutory bodies, the trustees prefer to give support for the enhancement of services rather than the provision of what they consider to be basic needs.

WHAT IS NOT FUNDED Individuals, even if such a request is submitted by a charitable organisation; retrospective applications; applications for funding towards the installation of special facilities in existing community buildings and churches for people with disabilities; applications which fall outside the existing objects and policies of the trust.

TYPE OF GRANT Capital and running costs; recurring and one-off.

RANGE OF GRANTS Up to £200,000, but mostly of £5,000 or less.

SAMPLE GRANTS St Michael's Hospice – Hereford (£200,000); Megan Baker House – Leominster (£60,000); Breast Cancer Haven and Herefordshire Mind (£50,000 each); Deaf Direct – Worcester (£30,000); St Basil's Centre – Birmingham (£20,000); Bloodwise (£15,000); The Haven Refuge Wolverhampton (£12,000); Action Medical Research and ECHO for Extra Choices Across North Herefordshire (£10,000 each); AbilityNet and Perdiswell Young People's Leisure Club (£8,000 each); Revitalise (£6,000).

FINANCES *Year* 2015/16 *Income* £1,425,441 *Grants* £2,540,873 *Grants to organisations* £2,540,873 *Assets* £74,699,524

TRUSTEES David Pearson; Martin Davies; Louise Woodhead; Bill Wiggin; Richard Mainwaring; Judith Millward; The Bishop of Hereford; Vivien Cockerill.

OTHER INFORMATION In 2015/16 a total of 331 grants were made. 214 grants were of £5,000 or less.

HOW TO APPLY Applications can only be considered if they are made using the trust's standard Application for Support form, which is available from the Administrator. The form must be completed and returned along with a copy of your organisation's most recent annual report and accounts. The trustees meet quarterly, usually at the end of March and the beginning of July, October and January. Applications must be submitted at least six weeks before the meeting at which it is to be considered.

WHO TO APPLY TO Alex Gay, Administrator, 45 Park Road, Gloucester GL1 1LP *Tel.* 01452 501352 *Fax* 01452 302195 *Email* admin@eveson.plus.com *Website* www.eveson.org.uk

■ The Beryl Evetts and Robert Luff Animal Welfare Trust Ltd

CC NO 283944 **ESTABLISHED** 1981

WHERE FUNDING CAN BE GIVEN UK.

WHO CAN BENEFIT Registered animal charities.

WHAT IS FUNDED Veterinary research and the care and welfare of animals.

RANGE OF GRANTS Up to £75,000 but typically from £500 to £3,000.

SAMPLE GRANTS Animal Health Trust (£75,000); Royal Veterinary College (£60,000); Brooke Hospital for Animals (£17,000); Animal Samaritans Midland Trust (£3,000); Bulldog Rescue and Rehoming Trust (£2,500); Wellcat (£1,000); Eden Animal Rescue and National Fox Welfare Society (£500).

FINANCES *Year* 2014/15 *Income* £170,746 *Grants* £205,000 *Grants to organisations* £205,000 *Assets* £4,431,260

TRUSTEES Jean Tomlinson; Sir Robert Johnson; Brian Nicholson; Revd Matthew Tomlinson; Richard Price; Melanie Condon; Lady Ruth Bodey.

OTHER INFORMATION At the time of writing (May 2017) the 2014/15 accounts were the most recent available.

HOW TO APPLY Apply in writing to the correspondent. Our research suggests that applications from organisations that the trust has never previously funded are accepted; however, the trust has stated that it is very unlikely that grants of any higher than £5,000 would be considered. Grants are made annually and are usually administered in June.

WHO TO APPLY TO Richard Price, Trustee, Waters Edge, Ferry Lane, Moulsford, Wallingford OX10 9JF *Email* rpjprice@gmail.com

■ The Exilarch's Foundation

CC NO 275919 **ESTABLISHED** 1978

WHERE FUNDING CAN BE GIVEN Worldwide (mainly UK, Israel and Iraq).

WHO CAN BENEFIT Charitable organisations, including Jewish organisations; hospitals; universities; schools.

WHAT IS FUNDED General charitable purposes including: social welfare; education; community development; interfaith activities; hospitals, medical education and research; ethics.

RANGE OF GRANTS Up to £1.37 million.

SAMPLE GRANTS Cancer Research UK (£1.37 million); Jerusalem Foundation (£310,000); Imperial College London (£264,000); The Outward Bound Trust (£195,000); Duke of Edinburgh's Award (£91,500); Society for the Preservation of Israel Heritage Sites (£67,500); The Jewish Museum – London (£50,000); British Exploring Society (£45,000); Westminster Academy (£24,000); University Jewish Chaplaincy (£20,000); Cornell University (£13,300); Action on Hearing Loss (£6,700); Council of Christians and Jews (£5,000).

FINANCES *Year* 2015 *Income* £6,421,632 *Grants* £3,669,779 *Grants to organisations* £3,669,779 *Assets* £81,420,837

TRUSTEES David Dangoor; Elie Dangoor; Robert Dangoor; Michael Dangoor.

OTHER INFORMATION The foundation's income included a donation of £500,000 given towards its expendable endowment fund. The foundation is the sponsor of Westminster Academy.

HOW TO APPLY Apply in writing to the correspondent.

WHO TO APPLY TO David Dangoor, Trustee, 4 Carlos Place, Mayfair, London W1K 3AW *Tel.* 020 7399 0850

■ The Expat Foundation

CC NO 1094041 **ESTABLISHED** 2002

WHERE FUNDING CAN BE GIVEN UK and Africa.

WHO CAN BENEFIT Registered charities and community groups.

WHAT IS FUNDED According to the foundation's Charity Commission record, in the UK the foundation focuses on 'improving the lives of disadvantaged children and young people and improving the quality of life of elderly people, particularly providing opportunities for mental and social engagement'. In Africa there is a focus on supporting 'long term initiatives in areas such as education and social improvement'.

WHAT IS NOT FUNDED Individuals; animal welfare charities; activities outside the foundation's stated areas of support.

TYPE OF GRANT Capital, core and start-up costs. One-off and up to four years.

RANGE OF GRANTS £2,500 to £50,000.

SAMPLE GRANTS School-Home Support and Leap Confronting Conflict (£50,000 each); Build It International (£20,000); Fix It UK Ltd (£13,000); Read International (£8,000); Microloan Foundation (£6,000); Zambia Orphan Aid UK (£5,900); Choir With No Name (£5,000); Family Holiday Association (£2,500).

FINANCES *Year* 2015/16 *Income* £327,373 *Grants* £316,246 *Grants to organisations* £316,246 *Assets* £1,041,342

TRUSTEES Patricia Wolfston; Paul Tuckwell; Janet Cummins; Gill Weavers; Caroline Coombs; Dirk van Dijl.

OTHER INFORMATION In 2015/16 a total of 17 organisations received grants.

HOW TO APPLY The foundation's Charity Commission record at the time of writing (April 2017) states that it is a proactive grant-maker.

WHO TO APPLY TO Janet Cummins, Trustee, 127 Ellesmere Road, London NW10 1LG *Tel.* 020 3609 2105

■ Extonglen Ltd

CC NO 286230 **ESTABLISHED** 1982

WHERE FUNDING CAN BE GIVEN UK and Israel.

WHO CAN BENEFIT Orthodox Jewish charities.

WHAT IS FUNDED The advancement of the Orthodox Jewish religion; education; the relief of poverty.

RANGE OF GRANTS Usually from £3,000 to £500,000.

SAMPLE GRANTS Kol Halashon Education Programme (£470,000); Ahavas Chesed (£95,000); Pikuach Nefesh (£50,000); Kupath Gemach Chaim Bechesed Viznitz Trust (£40,000); British Friends of Nishmat Yisrael (£12,000); Children's Town Charity (£3,600).

FINANCES *Year* 2015 *Income* £1,145,316 *Grants* £876,067 *Grants to organisations* £876,067 *Assets* £10,884,408

TRUSTEES Meir Levine; C. Levine; Isaac Katzenberg.

HOW TO APPLY Apply in writing to the correspondent.

WHO TO APPLY TO The Trustees of Extonglen Ltd, New Burlington House, 1075 Finchley Road, London NW11 0PU *Tel.* 020 8731 0777 *Email* ml@rowdeal.com

■ The William and Christine Eynon Charity

CC NO 1134334 **ESTABLISHED** 2010

WHERE FUNDING CAN BE GIVEN UK.

WHO CAN BENEFIT Registered charities.

WHAT IS FUNDED General charitable purposes.

SAMPLE GRANTS A list of beneficiaries was not available.

FINANCES *Year* 2015/16 *Income* £11,858 *Grants* £43,000 *Grants to organisations* £43,000

TRUSTEES William Eynon; Christine Eynon; Sophie Eynon; James Eynon.

OTHER INFORMATION This charity's latest accounts were not available to view on the Charity Commission's website due to its low income. We have therefore estimated the grant total based on previous years' information.

HOW TO APPLY Apply in writing to the correspondent.

WHO TO APPLY TO William Eynon, Trustee, Tusker House, Newton, Porthcawl CF36 5ST *Tel.* 01656 782312

■ G. F. Eyre Charitable Trust

CC NO 216040 **ESTABLISHED** 1960

WHERE FUNDING CAN BE GIVEN UK, with a focus on the South West.

WHO CAN BENEFIT National charities; local charities in the South West.

WHAT IS FUNDED General charitable purposes; human medical research; health; religion; heritage.

WHAT IS NOT FUNDED Individuals.

RANGE OF GRANTS £500 to £9,000.

SAMPLE GRANTS The Melplash Agricultural Society Ltd (£7,500 in two grants); Bridport Literary and Scientific Institute (£4,500); Bridport Art Centre (£2,000); The Gurkha Welfare Trust (£1,000 in two grants); Blind Children UK, Meningitis Research Foundation and The Injured Jockeys'

Fund (£1,000 each); Royal Signals Association, St Michael's Church and St Peter's Hospice (£500 each).

FINANCES *Year* 2015/16 *Income* £78,997 *Grants* £73,500 *Grants to organisations* £73,500 *Assets* £357,409

TRUSTEES Carol Eyre; Rachel Eyre; George Eyre.

OTHER INFORMATION The trust made 53 separate grants in 2015/16. Causes are nominated to receive grants by the trustees individually. The trust's annual report lists beneficiaries under the name of the trustee who nominated them.

HOW TO APPLY Apply in writing to the correspondent. The trustees meet annually to consider applications. The annual report explains that 'In the interim, payments to good causes are nominated by individual Trustees'.

WHO TO APPLY TO c/o Andrew Richards, Managing Partner, Francis Clark Chartered Accountants, Vantage Point, Woodwater Park, Pynes Hill, Exeter, Devon EX2 5FD *Tel.* 01392 667000 *Email* andrew.richards@pkf-francisclark.co.uk

■ Matthew Eyton Animal Welfare Trust

CC NO 1003575 **ESTABLISHED** 1991

WHERE FUNDING CAN BE GIVEN England and Wales.

WHO CAN BENEFIT Animal charities.

WHAT IS FUNDED Animal welfare with a preference for farm animals; vegetarianism and veganism.

RANGE OF GRANTS £50 to £35,000.

SAMPLE GRANTS PETA's Research and Educations Foundation (£35,000); Compassion in World Farming (£6,000); Viva! (£1,100); Lord Whiskey Animal Sanctuary (£700); Animal Aid Campaign Group (£600); Sustainable Food Trust (£500); CARAT Greek Animals, Gambia Haru Donkey Trust and WDC Whale Conservation (£100 each); The Greek Cat Society (£50).

FINANCES *Year* 2015/16 *Income* £53,858 *Grants* £47,866 *Grants to organisations* £47,866 *Assets* £31,597

TRUSTEES Audrey Eyton; Paul Flood.

OTHER INFORMATION Grants were made to 23 organisations.

HOW TO APPLY Apply in writing to the correspondent.

WHO TO APPLY TO Paul Flood, Westgate House, 87 St Dunstan's Street, Canterbury, Kent CT2 8AE *Tel.* 01227 769321

The F. P. Ltd Charitable Trust

CC NO 328737 **ESTABLISHED** 1990

WHERE FUNDING CAN BE GIVEN UK, with a possible preference for Greater Manchester.

WHO CAN BENEFIT Organisations.

WHAT IS FUNDED Grants are made to a variety of causes, including schools, religious institutions and medical appeals.

SAMPLE GRANTS A list of beneficiaries was not available.

FINANCES *Year* 2015/16 *Income* £20,000 *Grants* £74,500 *Grants to organisations* £74,500

TRUSTEES Joshua Pine; Eli Pine.

OTHER INFORMATION This trust's latest accounts were not available to view on the Charity Commission's website due to its low income. We have therefore estimated the grant total based on previous years' information.

HOW TO APPLY Apply in writing to the correspondent.

WHO TO APPLY TO Joshua Pine, Trustee, 14 Westfield Street, Salford M7 4NG *Tel.* 0161 834 0456 *Email* ABURNETT@RPG.CO.UK

Esmée Fairbairn Foundation

CC NO 200051 **ESTABLISHED** 1961

WHERE FUNDING CAN BE GIVEN UK.

WHO CAN BENEFIT Organisations with charitable purposes.

WHAT IS FUNDED Funding is given across four sectors: arts; children and young people; environment; and social change. The funding priorities within each sector are as follows: **Arts**: arts with a social impact; supporting emerging talent; organisations at a pivotal point. **Children and young people**: improving support for disadvantaged children and young people; the rights of vulnerable children and young people; addressing the root causes of low educational attainment and challenging behaviour; empowering young leaders; young people leaving care (a focused funding stream). **Environment**: connecting people with nature and environmental issues; countering the effects of damaging activity; nature conservation on land and at sea; lesser known plants, animals and organisms. **Social change**: participation – marginalised and excluded individuals and groups; place – revitalising community life; injustice – systemic change around injustice and inequality. The foundation also has a **Food** funding strand which has the following priorities: innovation in alternative approaches; food and well-being; working towards a more coherent food sector.

WHAT IS NOT FUNDED Organisations with a regular annual turnover of less than £50,000; organisations without at least three non-executive trustees or directors; *work that is not legally charitable; work that does not have a direct benefit in the UK; grants to individuals, including student grants or bursaries; *capital costs including building work, renovations, and equipment; *work that is common to many parts of the UK (there are examples of the work this can apply to provided on the website); work that does not set out to have a wider impact beyond the lives of the direct beneficiaries. It must have plans to change the way professionals like social workers or artists work in future; or changes attitudes to an issue, or affect policy; research (unless the applicant can demonstrate real potential for practical outcomes); health care which has a clinical basis or related work such as medical research, complementary medicine, hospices, counselling and therapy, arts therapy, education about and treatment for drug and alcohol misuse; *work that is primarily the responsibility of statutory authorities (including residential, respite and day care, housing provision, individual schools, nurseries and colleges or a consortium of any of these, and vocational training) *the replacement or subsidisation of statutory income (although the foundation will make rare exceptions where the level of performance has been exceptional and where the potential impact of the work is substantial; the promotion of religion.*These exclusions do not apply for social investments. The food funding stream has additional exclusions. More information can be found on the website.

TYPE OF GRANT Core and project grants, including staff salaries and overheads. Funding can be given for one to five years. Social investment is also available. Through the Grants Plus scheme, recipients of grants and social investment are provided with a range of non-financial additional support.

RANGE OF GRANTS In 2015 grants ranged from £5,000 to £1.5 million; the average grant was £100,000.

SAMPLE GRANTS UK Youth and Women's Resource Centre (£500,000 each); Leap Confronting Conflict (£375,000); Girlguiding – The Guide Association (£250,000); Detention Action (£225,000); Cardiff University Otter Project, Coventry Rape and Sexual Abuse Centre and Oh Yeah Music Centre Ltd (£150,000 each); National Botanic Garden of Wales (£105,000); Edinburgh Women's Aid (£98,500); Belfast Community Circus School (£91,000); Migrant Voice (£86,500); Media Trust (£75,000); Campaign Bootcamp (£60,000); People's Trust for Endangered Species (£40,000); Phoenix Detached Youth Project (£30,000); Manchester Veg People (£25,000); Indepen-dance and Southbank Centre (£15,000 each); The School for Social Entrepreneurs (£5,000).

FINANCES *Year* 2015 *Income* £4,954,000 *Grants* £34,600,000 *Grants to organisations* £34,600,000 *Assets* £876,198,000

TRUSTEES James Hughes-Hallett; Edward Bonham Carter; Tom Chandos; Joe Docherty; Prof. David Hill; John Fairbairn; Beatrice Hollond; Sir Thomas Hughes-Hallett; Kate Lampard; Stella Manzie; Sir Jonathan Phillips; Eleanor Updale.

OTHER INFORMATION The foundation has a very informative website where further information, guidelines and examples of giving can be found.

HOW TO APPLY Applications can be made at any time. Before applying, the information on the website – what the foundation funds and what it doesn't fund – should be read carefully, and the helpful online 'Eligibility Quiz' can also be taken. The foundation operates a two stage application process, which is outlined on the website. In order to make an application, an organisation must set-up an account with the foundation's online grants system. Applicants can check the FAQs section of the website, or contact the foundation, should they have any questions.

WHO TO APPLY TO James Wragg, Director of Operations, Kings Place, 90 York Way, London N1 9AG *Tel.* 020 7812 3700 *Fax* 020 7812 3701 *Email* info@esmeefairbairn.org.uk *Website* www.esmeefairbairn.org.uk

■ The Fairstead Trust

CC NO 1096359 **ESTABLISHED** 2003

WHERE FUNDING CAN BE GIVEN Worldwide.

WHO CAN BENEFIT UK-registered charities.

WHAT IS FUNDED General charitable purposes.

RANGE OF GRANTS Usually from around £1,000 to £30,000.

SAMPLE GRANTS East Anglian Children's Hospices (£30,000); Grove House (£20,000); Paul's Cancer Centre and Family Links (£15,000 each); St Albans Cathedral Education Centre (£14,000); Afghan Connection, Castlehaven Community Association, Disasters Emergency Committee – East Africa Appeal and Hertfordshire Community Foundation (£10,000 each); Chance to Shine, Cley Memorial Hall Fund and Hillside Animal Sanctuary (£5,000 each); Hopefield Animal Sanctuary (£3,000); Smile Train (£1,500); NNDRA (£1,000).

FINANCES *Year* 2015/16 *Income* £3,963 *Grants* £153,000 *Grants to organisations* £153,000

TRUSTEES Edward Cox; Wendy Cox; Lucinda Cox; Claire Mitchell.

OTHER INFORMATION Due to its low income, this trust's latest accounts were not available to view on the Charity Commission's website. We have therefore estimated the grant total based on previous years' information.

HOW TO APPLY Apply in writing to the correspondent including the following: the aims and objectives of your charity; the nature of your appeal; the total target (if for a specific project); contributions received against the target; your organisation's registered charity number; any other relevant factors. Applications should be accompanied by your organisation's full financial statements and latest annual report.

WHO TO APPLY TO Charlotte Jackson, 22 Chancery Lane, London WC2A 1LS *Tel.* 020 7430 7159 *Email* charities@nqpltd.com

■ The Famos Foundation Trust

CC NO 271211 **ESTABLISHED** 1976

WHERE FUNDING CAN BE GIVEN UK and Israel.

WHO CAN BENEFIT Orthodox Jewish organisations.

WHAT IS FUNDED Orthodox Jewish religious education; the relief of poverty in the Jewish community; the maintenance of Orthodox Jewish synagogues, schools and colleges; medical causes.

TYPE OF GRANT One-off grants. Funding is given for one year or less.

RANGE OF GRANTS Usually up to £5,000.

SAMPLE GRANTS A list of beneficiaries was not available.

FINANCES *Year* 2015/16 *Income* £138,744 *Grants* £91,658 *Grants to organisations* £91,658 *Assets* £1,607,895

TRUSTEES Rabbi Kupetz; Fay Kupetz; Isaac Kupetz; Joseph Kupetz.

OTHER INFORMATION Grants were awarded in four categories: relief of poverty (£33,500); education (£24,500); places of worship (£17,700); medical (£15,900).

HOW TO APPLY Apply in writing to the correspondent, at any time. Previous research suggests that the trust does not accept telephone enquiries.

WHO TO APPLY TO Rabbi Kupetz, Trustee, 4 Hanover Gardens, Salford M7 4FQ *Tel.* 0161 740 5735

■ The Faringdon Charitable Trust

CC NO 1084690 **ESTABLISHED** 2000

WHERE FUNDING CAN BE GIVEN UK, with a focus on Oxfordshire.

WHO CAN BENEFIT UK-registered national and local charities and 'other recognised bodies'. Support for local causes appears to be focused on Oxfordshire.

WHAT IS FUNDED General charitable purposes, specifically: educational scholarship grants; hospitals and the provision of medical treatment for people who are sick; the purchase of antiques and artistic objects for museums and collections to which the public has access; care and assistance of people who are older or vulnerable; the development and assistance of the arts and sciences, physical recreation and drama; research into matters of public interest; the relief of poverty; and the support of matters of public interest.

WHAT IS NOT FUNDED Individuals.

RANGE OF GRANTS Generally between £1,000 and £5,000.

SAMPLE GRANTS University of West London (£50,000); The Faringdon Collection Trust (£26,500); Young Musicians Symphony Orchestra (£7,500); Alzheimer's Society and Greyhound Rescue (£5,000 each); Buscot Cricket Club (£2,700); Oxford Playhouse and Thames Valley and Chilterns Air Ambulance (£2,500 each); Anti-Slavery International, Crimestoppers Trust, Dogs for the Disabled, Future Trees Trust and Oxfordshire Youth Trust (£1,000 each); The Chelsea Physic Garden (£1,500); The Prison Phoenix Trust (£500).

FINANCES *Year* 2015/16 *Income* £231,679 *Grants* £187,035 *Grants to organisations* £187,035 *Assets* £8,461,566

TRUSTEES The Hon. James Henderson; Bernard Cazenove, Chair; The Hon. Susannah Maitland Robinson; Edward Cottrell.

OTHER INFORMATION During 2015/16, grants were given to 48 organisations. The trust regularly supports The Faringdon Collection Trust (Charity Commission no. 203770).

HOW TO APPLY Apply in writing to the correspondent. The trustees meet formally once a year. The annual report for 2015/16 explains: 'Grant applications are accepted from registered charities and other recognised bodies. All grant applications are required to provide information on the specific purpose and expected beneficiaries of the grant. This information helps the charity assess how its programme of discretionary grant-making achieves a spread of benefit.'

WHO TO APPLY TO Sharon Lander, Secretary, The Estate Office, Buscot Park, Faringdon SN7 8BU *Tel.* 01367 240786 *Email* estbuscot@aol.com

■ Samuel William Farmer Trust

CC NO 258459 **ESTABLISHED** 1929

WHERE FUNDING CAN BE GIVEN Primarily Wiltshire.

WHO CAN BENEFIT Registered charities.

WHAT IS FUNDED According to the trust's Charity Commission record at the time of writing (April 2017) grants are made 'for the benefit of poor people who through ill health, disability or old age are unable to earn their own livelihood; for educational and training purposes; and for the benefit of hospitals, nursing and convalescent homes or similar objects for the advancement of health or saving of lives.' Wildlife/conservation projects which benefit the local community are also supported.

TYPE OF GRANT One-off and recurrent.

RANGE OF GRANTS Generally between £1,000 and £2,500.

SAMPLE GRANTS Independent Age and The Royal Agricultural Benevolent Institution (£7,500 each – annual grants); Prospect Hospice (£5,000); Larkrise Special School and The Oundle School Mencap Holiday (£2,500 each); Brighter Futures and Great Western Hospital (£2,000 each); Deafblind UK, Rare Breeds Survival Trust and Swindon Therapy Centre for Multiple Sclerosis (£1,000 each).

FINANCES *Year* 2015 *Income* £59,112 *Grants* £66,402 *Grants to organisations* £64,903 *Assets* £2,550,868

TRUSTEES Bruce Waight; Jennifer Liddiard; Peter Fox-Andrews, Chair; Charles Brockis; Jean Simpson.

OTHER INFORMATION 28 organisations were awarded funding, two of which benefitted from annual grants.

HOW TO APPLY Apply in writing to the correspondent. The 2015 annual report explains: 'In addition to applications for grants made by various individuals and organisations directly to the Secretary, Trustees bring suggestions and applications for grants to their half yearly meetings.'

WHO TO APPLY TO Melanie Linden-Fermor, Secretary, 71 High Street, Market Lavington, Devizes SN10 4AG *Tel.* 01380 813299

The Thomas Farr Charity

CC NO 328394 **ESTABLISHED** 1989

WHERE FUNDING CAN BE GIVEN Nottinghamshire.

WHO CAN BENEFIT Registered charities only.

WHAT IS FUNDED General charitable purposes.

WHAT IS NOT FUNDED Individuals.

RANGE OF GRANTS Up to £60,000 but generally £1,000 to £5,000.

SAMPLE GRANTS Nottinghamshire Community Foundation (£2,000). Details of other beneficiaries were not available; however, we do know that grants were allocated within the following categories: community projects (£175,500); religious organisations (£11,000); education (£10,400); relief of poverty (£7,500); armed forces (£6,000).

FINANCES *Year* 2015/16 *Income* £341,145 *Grants* £210,300 *Grants to organisations* £210,300 *Assets* £8,085,418

TRUSTEES Rathbone Trust Company Ltd; Henry Farr; Amanda Farr; Barry Davys; Mrs P. K. Myles.

HOW TO APPLY Apply in writing to the correspondent. Applications are considered in March and September/November

WHO TO APPLY TO John Thompson, Administrator, 6A The Almshouses, Mansfield Road, Daybrook, Nottingham NG5 6BW *Tel.* 0115 966 1222 *Email* thomasfarrch@btconnect.com

The Farthing Trust

CC NO 268066 **ESTABLISHED** 1974

WHERE FUNDING CAN BE GIVEN UK and overseas.

WHO CAN BENEFIT Individuals and charitable organisations, many of which are personally known to the trustees.

WHAT IS FUNDED General charitable purposes, with a focus on the advancement of religion, education, health, human rights and the reconciliation and promotion of religious and racial harmony, equality and diversity, and the relief of people in need.

TYPE OF GRANT One-off and recurring grants.

SAMPLE GRANTS A list of beneficiaries was not available. Grants were awarded to organisations in the following categories: Christ's Servants (£42,000); UK Christian causes (£31,000); UK church (£23,500); overseas Christian causes (£22,000); local (£8,250); overseas general charities (£7,900); education – overseas (£6,000); UK general charities (£2,400).

FINANCES *Year* 2015/16 *Income* £82,314 *Grants* £144,300 *Grants to organisations* £142,800 *Assets* £2,248,208

TRUSTEES C. H. Martin; Joy Martin; A. White.

OTHER INFORMATION More than 100 grant payments were made during the year. The amount of grants given to individuals totalled £1,500.

HOW TO APPLY Applications and enquiries should be made in writing to the correspondent. Applicants, and any others requesting information, will only receive a response if an sae is enclosed. Many beneficiaries are known to the trustees personally or through their acquaintances, although applications from other organisations are considered.

WHO TO APPLY TO Joy Martin, Trustee, PO Box 277, Cambridge CB7 9DE

The February Foundation

CC NO 1113064 **ESTABLISHED** 2006

WHERE FUNDING CAN BE GIVEN UK.

WHO CAN BENEFIT Registered charities.

WHAT IS FUNDED According to the annual report 2015/16, the trustees will consider grants for charities which: are for the benefit of people who are making an effort to improve their lives; are for the benefit of people who are no longer physically or mentally able to help themselves; have a long-term beneficial impact on the future of individuals, groups of individuals, or organisations; or protect the environment. Grants are also given to 'small or minority charities where small grants will have a significant impact' and 'companies where the acquisition of equity would be in line with the foundation's charitable objectives'.

WHAT IS NOT FUNDED Childcare; Citizens Advice; community centres; higher education; housing associations; individuals; medical research; minibuses; NHS trusts; non-departmental government bodies; overseas projects; primary education; scouts, guides, brownies, cubs, and similar organisations; secondary education; single-faith organisations; sports clubs, unless for people who have mental or physical disabilities; village halls; youth clubs and centres; charities which are party politically driven, with a commercial bias for a particular product or company, or with 'an aggressive religious bias'.

RANGE OF GRANTS Usually up to £5,000.

SAMPLE GRANTS A list of beneficiaries was not available. Grants were awarded in the following categories: other (£488,000); health care and patient support (£273,500); end-of-life care (£273,000); education (£208,500); heritage (£41,000).

FINANCES *Year* 2015/16 *Income* £9,380,964 *Grants* £1,284,070 *Grants to organisations* £1,284,070 *Assets* £51,685,946

TRUSTEES James Carleton; Mark Clarke.

OTHER INFORMATION In 2015/16, 128 grants were made to 125 organisations.

HOW TO APPLY The foundation's website notes that it is 'focused on managing its current commitments, although applications from some charities are still being accepted'. Email applications are preferred and should be sent to the correspondent. They should include: details and budget of the proposed project; how many people would benefit and how those benefits might be measured (not just financially); and what the estimated cost of raising funds for the project is. The website explains that 'it is important to include in your email application full accounts for your most recent completed financial year, and, if your accounts do not contain it, what your total fundraising costs annually are'. It is noted that 'hardcopy applications take significantly longer to process than email applications'. Additional information, including DVDS, CDs, and glossy brochures should not be sent to the foundation. The website further explains: 'It normally takes 12 weeks from application to applicants being informed of the trustees' decision. There are no application deadlines as trustees make grant decisions on a monthly basis.' **Note:** Less than 5% of all applications are successful.

WHO TO APPLY TO Richard Pierce-Saunderson, Chief Executive, Spring Cottage, Church Street, Stradbroke IP21 5HT *Tel.* 01379 388200 *Email* rps@thefebruaryfoundation.org *Website* www.thefebruaryfoundation.org

■ The John Feeney Charitable Bequest

CC NO 214486 **ESTABLISHED** 1906

WHERE FUNDING CAN BE GIVEN Birmingham.

WHO CAN BENEFIT Registered charities.

WHAT IS FUNDED Arts; heritage; open spaces.

WHAT IS NOT FUNDED Applications will not be accepted: from, or on behalf of, individuals; if they do not directly benefit the Birmingham area or Birmingham charitable organisations; from organisations which have political objectives, or could be considered as denominational and promoting religion.

TYPE OF GRANT One-off; project costs; capital costs.

RANGE OF GRANTS Up to £10,000.

SAMPLE GRANTS Ex Cathedra (£10,000); Birmingham Contemporary Music Group (£9,000); Flatback Productions (£3,500); Mac Birmingham (£2,500); Women and Theatre (£2,000); Big Brum Theatre in Education Company, Birmingham Botanical Gardens (£1,000 each).

FINANCES *Year* 2016 *Income* £81,377 *Grants* £63,750 *Grants to organisations* £57,150 *Assets* £1,756,305

TRUSTEES John Smith; Hugh Carslake; Charles King-Farlow; Geoffrey Oakley; Merryn Ford Lloyd; Anouk Perinpanayagam; William Southall; Sally Luton; Lucy Reid; Catherine Organ; Deirdre Figueiredo; Andrew Spittle.

OTHER INFORMATION The charity awarded £6,600 to individuals through its Feeney Fellowships programme.

HOW TO APPLY To apply you need to fill in the charity application form which is available online. The secretary will send you a form in the post if requested. When the form is completed, post or email it with a short supporting letter and any other documents to: Amanda Cadman, Secretary, John Feeney Charitable Trust, 55 Wychall Lane Kings Norton Birmingham B388TB or Email: secretary@feeneytrust.org.uk. All applications are acknowledged, and successful applicants are notified of the outcome, normally within six weeks of the meeting. Successful applicants are required to submit a brief report, ideally with photographs, within 12 months of the award of the grant, to show how the grant has advanced their project.

WHO TO APPLY TO Amanda Cadman, Secretary, 55 Wychall Lane, Birmingham B38 8TB *Tel.* 0121 624 3865 *Email* secretary@feeneytrust.org.uk *Website* www.feeneytrust.org.uk

■ The George Fentham Birmingham Charity

CC NO 214487 **ESTABLISHED** 1906

WHERE FUNDING CAN BE GIVEN City of Birmingham.

WHO CAN BENEFIT Registered charities providing services and facilities for people who are in need, hardship or distress; individuals who are long-term residents of Birmingham studying at a college or university.

WHAT IS FUNDED Organisational grants are given mainly in the following categories: children who are sick or who have disabilities; children's holidays and play schemes; young people's clubs and associations; adults who are sick or who have disabilities; social problems; community centres/neighbourhood groups; hospital charities; and care for older people. Grants are given to individuals for educational purposes.

WHAT IS NOT FUNDED Salary costs; direct hardship grants to individuals; organisations and individuals from outside the City of Birmingham.

RANGE OF GRANTS Mostly between £1,000 and £5,000.

SAMPLE GRANTS Birmingham City Mission (£6,750); Martineau Gardens (£5,250); Barnardo's (£5,000); CF (Cystic Fibrosis) Dream Holidays (£4,500); Birmingham Federation of Clubs for Young People (£4,000); St Anne's Hostel (£3,000); Birmingham Opera Company and Northfield Eco Centre (£2,000 each); Asthma Relief (£1,600); Carrs Lane Counselling Centre (£1,250).

FINANCES *Year* 2015 *Income* £200,817 *Grants* £222,297 *Grants to organisations* £201,797 *Assets* £5,836,387

TRUSTEES John Bower, Chair; Diana Duggan; Hamid Malik; Martin Holcombe; Eluned Jones; Nahid Saiyed; Margaret Martin; Margaret Flynn; Barry Earp; Derek Ridgway.

OTHER INFORMATION Of the 82 grants made in 2015, 12 were made to individuals for educational purposes, totalling £20,500.

HOW TO APPLY There is an application form available to download from the website. It should be completed and returned to the Secretary along with a copy of your organisation's annual accounts. Dates of general grants meetings and closing dates for applications can be found on the website.

WHO TO APPLY TO Anne Holmes, Secretary, c/o Veale Wasbrough Vizards LLP, Second Floor, 3 Bindley Place, Birmingham B1 2JB *Tel.* 0121 227 3705 *Email* george.fentham@vwv.co.uk *Website* www.georgefenthamcharity.org.uk

■ The A. M. Fenton Trust

CC NO 270353 **ESTABLISHED** 1975

WHERE FUNDING CAN BE GIVEN UK, with a focus on North Yorkshire.

WHO CAN BENEFIT Registered national and local charities.

WHAT IS FUNDED General charitable purposes, including health and medical causes, disability, and children and young people.
WHAT IS NOT FUNDED The trust is unlikely to support local appeals, unless they are close to where it is based.
TYPE OF GRANT Mostly one-off.
RANGE OF GRANTS Mostly £500 to £4,000.
SAMPLE GRANTS The Tweed Foundation (£8,000); Dewsbury League of Friendship, Yorkshire Air Ambulance and Yorkshire Cancer Research (£4,000 each); Churchfields Open Space Committee (£3,000); Disability Action Yorkshire, EveryChild, National Youth Orchestra and St Peter's Church (£2,000 each); Action for Children, Rawdon Community Library and St Michael's Hospice (£1,500 each); Harrogate and Knaresborough Toy Library and War Memorials Trust (£1,000 each); Citizens Advice (£500).
FINANCES *Year* 2015 *Income* £179,034 *Grants* £107,624 *Grants to organisations* £107,624 *Assets* £5,284,452
TRUSTEES James Fenton; Charles Fenton; Annalisa Fenton.
OTHER INFORMATION In 2015 grants were made to 48 organisations.
HOW TO APPLY Apply in writing to the correspondent.
WHO TO APPLY TO James Fenton, Trustee, The A. M. Fenton Trust, PO Box 788 HG1 9RX

■ Allan and Nesta Ferguson Charitable Settlement

CC NO 275487 **ESTABLISHED** 1977
WHERE FUNDING CAN BE GIVEN UK and overseas.
WHO CAN BENEFIT UK-registered charities and individuals.
WHAT IS FUNDED Educational projects, including projects encompassing the promotion of world peace, and overseas development. Grants are also made towards the fees of postgraduate PhD students who are in their final year of their course. Gap year students can also be supported.
WHAT IS NOT FUNDED Retrospective funding cannot be given.
TYPE OF GRANT Match funding.
RANGE OF GRANTS Up to £50,000.
SAMPLE GRANTS Coventry University and London School of Hygiene and Tropical Medicine (£50,000 each); Plan International UK (£30,000); British Refugee Council and Conciliation Resources (£20,000 each); Minority Rights Group International (£15,700); African Initiatives and The Royal Northern College of Music (£15,000 each); Hope for Children (£13,000); Conflict Resolution in Sheffield Schools Training (£10,000).
FINANCES *Year* 2015 *Income* £875,346 *Grants* £2,128,813 *Grants to organisations* £2,128,813 *Assets* £26,632,720
TRUSTEES Elizabeth Banister; Prof. David Banister; James Tee; Letitia Glaister; Eleanor Banister.
OTHER INFORMATION The charity's website explains that grants to organisations are given on a match funding basis 'so that if the applicant has raised 50% of their budget the Trustees will consider awarding matching funding up to a maximum of 50% ... if the applicant has raised less than 50% of their budget the Trustees will only consider awarding a maximum of 30% funding'. Furthermore, 'evidence of actively seeking funds from other sources is seen by the Trustees as being a beneficial addition to any application'.
HOW TO APPLY Applications are only accepted if they are submitted online using the correct form. Applications set by post, email or fax will not be considered. Detailed guidance is available on the website, from where the following statement is taken: 'Do not contact us for guidance prior to making an application. All the information you require is contained here. Your application will be acknowledged but no progress reports will be given and no feedback is provided in relation to unsuccessful applications.' Applications are accepted at any time and the trustees review requests for up to £50,000 on a monthly basis. Funding requests for amounts exceeding £50,000 are considered at biannual trustee meetings, which usually take place in March and September.
WHO TO APPLY TO FAO Letitia Glaister, Trustee, Tees Law, John Street, Royston, Hertfordshire SG8 9BG *Tel.* 01279 322519 *Fax* 01279 758400 *Email* letitia.glaister@teeslaw.co.uk *Website* www.fergusontrust.co.uk

■ Elizabeth Ferguson Charitable Trust Fund

SC NO SC026240 **ESTABLISHED** 1988
WHERE FUNDING CAN BE GIVEN UK, with some interest in Scotland.
WHO CAN BENEFIT Organisations benefitting children and young people, particularly those who are sick.
WHAT IS FUNDED The welfare and well-being of children and young people. Also charities involved in medical research and hospitals where special medical equipment is needed.
WHAT IS NOT FUNDED Non-registered charities; grants overseas.
RANGE OF GRANTS £2,000 to £90,000.
SAMPLE GRANTS The Seashell Trust (£30,000); Harmony Row and The Pearce Institute and Shine (£10,000); Highland Hospice (£3,000); Muscular Dystrophy UK (£2,500); University of South Manchester (£1,000).
FINANCES *Year* 2015/16 *Income* £284,831 *Grants* £115,082 *Grants to organisations* £115,082 *Assets* £193,000
TRUSTEES Sir Alex Ferguson; Cathy Ferguson; Huw Roberts; Ted Way; Les Dalgarno; Paul Hardman; Jason Ferguson.
HOW TO APPLY An application form and guidelines should be requested in writing from the correspondent. The committee meets to consider grants at the end of January and July. Applications should be received by December and June respectively.
WHO TO APPLY TO The Trustees, c/o 27 Peregrine Crescent, Droylsden, Manchester M43 7TA

■ The Fidelio Charitable Trust

CC NO 1112508 **ESTABLISHED** 1985
WHERE FUNDING CAN BE GIVEN UK.
WHO CAN BENEFIT Individuals and groups with 'exceptional ability', particularly those who are at an early stage of their careers.
WHAT IS FUNDED The arts, particularly music, including opera, lieder, composition and dance. Grants are made to enable beneficiaries, for example: to receive special tuition or coaching; to participate in external competitions; to be supported for a specially arranged performance; to receive support for a special publication, musical composition or work of art.

WHAT IS NOT FUNDED Applications from individuals or groups seeking support for themselves will not be accepted.
TYPE OF GRANT One-off and recurrent.
RANGE OF GRANTS Up to £5,000.
SAMPLE GRANTS IMS Prussia Cove (£10,000); Central School of Speech and Drama and Handel House Trust (£5,000 each); RADA (Royal Academy of Dramatic Art) (£4,000); Oxford Lieder, Southbank Sinfonia and Tête à Tête Opera (£3,500 each); Dartington Hall Trust and Academy Concert Society (£2,000 each); Spitalfields Music (£1,000); Birmingham Chamber Orchestra (£750).
FINANCES *Year* 2015/16 *Income* £9,997 *Grants* £77,000 *Grants to organisations* £77,000
TRUSTEES Jennifer Wingate; Tony Wingate; Robert Boas; Elizabeth Rantzen.
OTHER INFORMATION In 2015/16 the trust had a total expenditure of £90,500. Due to its low income, this trust's latest accounts were not available to view on the Charity Commission's website. We have therefore estimated the grant total based on previous years' information.
HOW TO APPLY Application forms are available to download from the website, where guidelines can also be found. Individuals and groups must be recommended by an appropriate person in an institution, college, arts festival or similar organisation. The trustees usually meet three times a year, in February, June and October. Provisional closing dates for applications are detailed on the website. The trustees aim to inform successful applicants within one month of the relevant closing date.
WHO TO APPLY TO Tony Wingate, Trustee, Somerset House, New Wing (S93), Strand, London WC2R 1LA *Email* fidelio@act.eu.com *Website* www.fideliocharitabletrust.org.uk

■ The Fidelity UK Foundation

CC NO 327899 **ESTABLISHED** 1988
WHERE FUNDING CAN BE GIVEN UK, primarily London, Kent and Surrey; overseas in countries where Fidelity International has business operations.
WHO CAN BENEFIT UK-registered charities; not-for-profit organisations overseas. The website states that grants are 'generally made only to organisations with an annual operating budget in excess of £250,000 (or local currency equivalent)'.
WHAT IS FUNDED Arts, culture and heritage; community; education; health; environment.
WHAT IS NOT FUNDED Grants are not made to/for: individuals; start-up organisations; political or sectarian organisations; organisations which have been running for less than three years; sponsorships; scholarships; corporate membership; advertising and promotional projects; exhibitions; general running costs; the replacement of dated IT hardware, routine system upgrades or ongoing website content. Grants are typically not made to private schools or for retrospective costs. Only exceptionally will programme costs be supported; the website notes that 'if considered, [funding] will typically be to organisations that have an outstanding track record of delivery and clear plans for future funding'.
TYPE OF GRANT One-off, for large-scale capital improvements, technology projects, organisational development, and planning initiatives.
RANGE OF GRANTS Mostly between £25,000 and £150,000.
SAMPLE GRANTS Action for Children (£250,000); The Public Catalogue Foundation (£100,000); King's College Hospital Charity (£75,000); Toynbee Hall (£69,000); The Royal Surrey County Hospital's Charitable Fund (£70,000); Northern Stage (£40,000); AHOY Centre (£30,000); Children's Discovery Centre (£25,000); New Horizon Youth Centre (£10,000).
FINANCES *Year* 2015 *Income* £12,193,261 *Grants* £6,339,533 *Grants to organisations* £6,339,533 *Assets* £194,478,143
TRUSTEES Barry Bateman; Anthony Bolton; Richard Millar; John Owen; Sally Walden; Abigail Johnson; Elizabeth Bishop Johnson.
OTHER INFORMATION Of the foundation's income, £7 million was received in endowment funds.
HOW TO APPLY In the first instance, see the foundation's website for detailed information, including guidelines. According to the website, the foundation prefers 'to learn more about your request through an initial online enquiry process'. This can be accessed through the website. Additional queries regarding the foundation's grant-making criteria or process prior to submitting an enquiry can be directed to the foundation by telephone.
WHO TO APPLY TO Sian Parry, Head of Foundations, Oakhill House, 130 Tonbridge Road, Hildenborough, Tonbridge, Kent TN11 9DZ *Tel.* 01732 777364 *Email* foundation@fil.com *Website* www.fidelityukfoundation.org

■ The Doris Field Charitable Trust

CC NO 328687 **ESTABLISHED** 1990
WHERE FUNDING CAN BE GIVEN UK (national charities) and Oxfordshire (local charities).
WHO CAN BENEFIT Large UK organisations; local organisations in Oxfordshire; individuals.
WHAT IS FUNDED General charitable purposes.
WHAT IS NOT FUNDED It is unlikely that grants would be made for salaries, training or higher education costs.
TYPE OF GRANT One-off and recurrent.
RANGE OF GRANTS Up to £30,000 but generally from £500 to £1,000.
SAMPLE GRANTS Alzheimer's Research UK and Meningitis Now (£30,000 each); Helen and Douglas House (£5,000); Oxford International Biomedical Centre (£4,000); Abingdon Gymnastics Club and Oxford Homeless Pathways (£2,500 each); Bampton Classical Opera, Combat Stress, Oxford and District Mencap, Tackley Village Hall and Wesley Memorial Methodist Church (£1,000 each); Berks, Bucks and Oxon Wildlife Trust, Christ Church – University of Oxford, Little Wild Things CIC, Oxford Hindu Temple Project and Soil Association (£500 each); Everyone's An Artist (£250).
FINANCES *Year* 2015/16 *Income* £463,531 *Grants* £327,825 *Grants to organisations* £324,645 *Assets* £11,475,047
TRUSTEES John Cole; N. Andrew Harper; Wilhelmina Church; Helen Fanyinka.
OTHER INFORMATION A total of 226 grants were made to organisations. The amount of grants given to individuals totalled £3,200.
HOW TO APPLY The trustees' report 2015/16 explains that 'each applicant is required, except in exceptional cases, to complete a standard application form and to submit information in support of that application'. The trustees meet at least three times a year. In urgent cases, applications may be considered between meetings.

WHO TO APPLY TO Emily Greig, Blake Morgan LLP, Seacourt Tower, West Way, Oxford OX2 0FB *Tel.* 01865 254286 *Email* emily.greig@blakemorgan.co.uk

■ The Fifty Fund

CC NO 214422 **ESTABLISHED** 1963
WHERE FUNDING CAN BE GIVEN Nottinghamshire.
WHO CAN BENEFIT Individuals who are resident in the area of benefit and are in need, and charities working with such individuals.
WHAT IS FUNDED The relief of poverty.
WHAT IS NOT FUNDED Education; expeditions; travel.
TYPE OF GRANT Mostly one-off grants for revenue costs and project funding.
RANGE OF GRANTS From £250 to £10,000; most grants were between £1,000 and £3,000.
SAMPLE GRANTS The Nottingham Hospice (£10,000); The University of Nottingham – Impact Charity (£5,000); Nottingham Mencap (£2,500); Radford Care Group (£2,400); SSAFA (£2,300); Henry Whipple Primary School, Nottinghamshire Advice Network and Pintsize Theatre Company (£2,000 each); Independence at Home (£1,500); Independent Age and St John the Baptist Church (£1,000 each); Open Minds (£750); Beeston Women's Group (£250).
FINANCES *Year* 2015 *Income* £300,727 *Grants* £177,456 *Grants to organisations* £140,400 *Assets* £7,989,468
TRUSTEES Edward Randall, Chair; Revd Amanda Cartwright; Richard Bonnello; Mark Jenkinson.
OTHER INFORMATION In 2015 grants were made to 73 organisations. The amount of grants given to individuals totalled £37,000.
HOW TO APPLY Apply in writing to the correspondent. The trustees meet quarterly.
WHO TO APPLY TO Craig Staten-Spencer, Associate and Trust Manager, Nelsons Solicitors, Pennine House, 8 Stanford Street, Nottingham NG1 7BQ *Tel.* 0115 989 5251 *Email* craig.staten-spencer@nelsonslaw.co.uk

■ Dixie Rose Findlay Charitable Trust

CC NO 251661 **ESTABLISHED** 1967
WHERE FUNDING CAN BE GIVEN UK.
WHO CAN BENEFIT Charitable organisations.
WHAT IS FUNDED General charitable purposes with a focus on children, illness, disability (particularly blindness) and seafarers.
TYPE OF GRANT One-off and recurrent.
RANGE OF GRANTS £1,000 to £3,300.
SAMPLE GRANTS Braishfield School Association and Hampshire and Isle of Wight Air Ambulance (£6,000 each in two grants each); Sight for Surrey (£4,000 in two grants); St John's Wood Church (£3,300); Baildon Imagination Library, Claire House Children's Hospice, The Cirdan Sailing Trust and Ulverston Inshore Rescue (£2,000 each); Dream Holidays (£1,500); Ocean Youth Trust Scotland and Together Trust (£1,000 each).
FINANCES *Year* 2015/16 *Income* £1,526,774 *Grants* £114,300 *Grants to organisations* £114,300 *Assets* £4,698,647
TRUSTEE HSBC. Trust Company (UK) Ltd.
OTHER INFORMATION In 2015/16, 61 grants were made to 57 organisations. **Note:** The income figure includes £1.4 million received from the proceeds from sales of investments.
HOW TO APPLY Apply in writing to the correspondent.
WHO TO APPLY TO S. Hill, Trust Manager, HSBC Trust Company UK Ltd, Second Floor, 1 The Forum, Parkway, Whiteley, Fareham PO15 7PA *Tel.* 023 8072 2243

■ The Sir John Fisher Foundation

CC NO 277844 **ESTABLISHED** 1979
WHERE FUNDING CAN BE GIVEN UK, with a focus on Barrow-in-Furness and the surrounding area and, occasionally, Cumbria and North Lancashire.
WHO CAN BENEFIT Local registered charities benefitting the Barrow-in-Furness area, some community causes in Cumbria and North Lancashire, and UK national charities.
WHAT IS FUNDED **Locally** (in the Barrow-in-Furness area) support is given to projects which meet the needs of the community. Priority is given to those involving: people who are sick or who have disabilities; children; education; family support; maritime causes; arts; and music. A very limited number of community causes are supported in Cumbria and North Lancashire. **Nationally**, the website explains, 'high quality maritime, music and art projects are considered together with limited medical research projects'.
WHAT IS NOT FUNDED Individuals; sponsorship; expeditions; the promotion of religion; places of worship; animal welfare; retrospective funding; pressure groups; community projects outside Barrow-in-Furness and surrounding area (except occasional projects in Cumbria or North Lancashire or if they fall within one of the other categories supported by the foundation).
TYPE OF GRANT Capital and revenue funding.
RANGE OF GRANTS Mostly under £10,000.
SAMPLE GRANTS Loughborough University Development Trust (£73,000); University of Lancaster – Alzheimer's Research (£60,500); Leeds Teaching Hospitals NHS Trust (£50,000); Royal Northern College of Music (£20,500); SS Great Britain Trust (£15,000); Client Earth (£10,000); Freshwater Biological Association (£6,800); Lakeland Rowing Club (£7,500); Shakespeare Schools Festival and The Mission to Seafarers (£5,000 each); Create (Arts) Ltd (£4,400); South Lakes Citizens Advice (£3,500); Ulverston Rangers FC (£1,200); Sidney Sussex College (£1,000); Cumbria County Council – Children's Services (£700); Barrow and District Association of Engineers (£300); Friends of Gosforth School (£200).
FINANCES *Year* 2015/16 *Income* £1,878,558 *Grants* £1,637,892 *Grants to organisations* £1,637,892 *Assets* £103,272,257
TRUSTEES Diane Meacock; Daniel Tindall, Chair; Rowland Hart Jackson; Michael Shields; Thomas Meacock.
OTHER INFORMATION A total of £1.1 million was given in 131 grants to local charities. A further £531,000 was given in 37 grants to national charities (of these, 13 grants were to support work in the local area).
HOW TO APPLY Application forms are available from the correspondent or to download from the website, where guidelines can also be found. Completed forms should be returned to the secretary, along with your organisation's most recent set of audited accounts, at least six weeks before the trustees' meetings at the beginning of May and November each year. The closing dates for applications are 1 March and 21 September, respectively. The secretary can be contacted for an informal discussion before an application for funding is submitted. Urgent applications for small grants (less than £4,000) can be considered between meetings, but the

trustees would expect an explanation why the application cannot wait to be considered at a normal meeting.

WHO TO APPLY TO Dr David Jackson, Secretary, Heaning Wood, Ulverston, Cumbria LA12 7NZ *Tel.* 01229 580349 *Email* info@sirjohnfisherfoundation.org.uk *Website* www.sirjohnfisherfoundation.org.uk

■ Fisherbeck Charitable Trust

CC NO 1107287 **ESTABLISHED** 2004

WHERE FUNDING CAN BE GIVEN Worldwide.

WHO CAN BENEFIT Registered charities worldwide.

WHAT IS FUNDED The advancement of the Christian religion; support for the provision of accommodation for people who are homeless and meeting their ongoing needs; the relief of poverty; the advancement of education; conservation of the environment and the preservation of heritage; other charitable purposes.

WHAT IS NOT FUNDED Grants are only made to individuals known to the trust or in exceptional circumstances.

TYPE OF GRANT One-off and recurrent.

RANGE OF GRANTS Up to £45,000.

SAMPLE GRANTS Church Army (£45,000); Tear Fund (£40,000); Worthing Churches Homeless Project (£30,000); Release International (£21,000); Health Communication Resources, Hope for Lugazi and St Andrew's Hove (£15,000 each); St Matthew's Church Parochial Church Council Youth (£7,500); Christian Viewpoint for Men (£6,000); Ish RevSmale and Mission Aviation Fellowship (£5,000).

FINANCES *Year* 2015/16 *Income* £534,042 *Grants* £488,410 *Grants to organisations* £482,210 *Assets* £242,152

TRUSTEES Ian Cheal; Jane Cheal; Matthew Cheal.

OTHER INFORMATION In 2015/16, 67 grants were made to organisations. A further two grants, totalling £6,200, were given to individuals.

HOW TO APPLY Apply in writing to the correspondent; however, note the following from the trust's Charity Commission record: 'Yearly the portfolio of charities within the classification are reassessed but there is limited addition allowance due to allocation of funds.'

WHO TO APPLY TO Ian Cheal, Trustee, 63 Ferringham Lane, Ferring, Worthing, West Sussex BN12 5LL *Tel.* 01903 241027 *Email* ian@roffeyhomes.com

■ Fishmongers' Company's Charitable Trust

CC NO 263690 **ESTABLISHED** 1972

WHERE FUNDING CAN BE GIVEN City of London; Camden; Hackney; Islington; Lambeth; Southwark; Tower Hamlets; and Westminster.

WHO CAN BENEFIT Registered charities and individuals. The majority of support is given to organisations with which the trust has a longstanding relationship.

WHAT IS FUNDED For grants from the main fund there is a preference for educational causes, although charities involved with the relief of hardship and disability, heritage and the environment can also be supported. The trust also administers the Billingsgate Christian Mission Fund from which support can be given to charities (including Christian charities) working to assist people involved with the UK's fish and fishing industries, as well as to medical science (particularly by way of grants for scholarships). Individuals can receive support for educational and relief-in-need purposes.

WHAT IS NOT FUNDED Applications from individuals to the Billingsgate Christian Mission Fund cannot be accepted.

TYPE OF GRANT Usually one-off, with a preference for project funding.

RANGE OF GRANTS Mostly up to around £15,000.

SAMPLE GRANTS The Gresham's Foundation (£186,000); Gresham's School (£66,000); City and Guilds of London Art School (£35,500); St Paul's Chorister Trust (£14,000 for a bursary); The Lord Mayor's Appeal (£10,000); The Treloar Trust (£8,000); The Royal National Mission to Deep Sea Fishermen (£7,000); Coastal Forces Heritage Trust (£5,000); Bermuda Institute of Ocean Sciences (£4,100); Spitalfields City Farm (£2,000); The Shipwrecked Fishermen and Mariners Royal Benevolent Society (£1,500); Mansion House Scholarship Scheme (£1,000).

FINANCES *Year* 2015 *Income* £653,325 *Grants* £521,448 *Grants to organisations* £482,006 *Assets* £26,588,812

TRUSTEES The Worshipful Company of Fishmongers; Peter Woodward.

OTHER INFORMATION In 2015 more than 37 grants were given to organisations in the following categories: educational (£422,000); hardship (£38,500); heritage and environmental (£9,400); disability and medical (£8,000); fisheries (£4,100). A further £39,500 was given in educational and hardship grants to individuals.

HOW TO APPLY In the first instance see the guidelines, which are available to view from the website. Note, however, the following information taken from the 2015 annual report: 'The Education and Grants Committee is currently reviewing its strategy and grant-giving policy and these guidelines may change.' Grants meetings take place three times a year, usually in March, June/July and November, and applications should be received a month in advance. No applications are considered within three years of a previous grant application being successful. Unsuccessful applications are not acknowledged.

WHO TO APPLY TO Peter Woodward, Assistant Clerk, The Fishmongers' Company, Fishmongers' Hall, London Bridge, London EC4R 9EL *Tel.* 020 7626 3531 *Email* ct@fishhall.org.uk *Website* www.fishhall.org.uk

■ Marc Fitch Fund

CC NO 313303 **ESTABLISHED** 1956

WHERE FUNDING CAN BE GIVEN UK and Ireland.

WHO CAN BENEFIT Organisations and individuals.

WHAT IS FUNDED The publication of 'scholarly work in the fields of British and Irish national, regional and local history, archaeology, antiquarian studies, historical geography, the history of art and architecture, heraldry, genealogy and surname studies, archival research, artefact conservation and the broad fields of the heritage, conservation and the historic environment'.

WHAT IS NOT FUNDED Topics which aren't British or Irish; works principally concerned with the recent past (post-1945); new or revised editions of work already published; scientific or technical research; fieldwork; the costs of getting to the UK/Ireland from overseas; foreign travel or research outside the UK/Ireland (apart from in very exceptional circumstances); applications associated with vocational or educational courses (including postgraduate or doctoral research); building works, mounting or attending conferences; mounting exhibitions; general appeals.

TYPE OF GRANT Mainly publication costs and incidental research expenses. Also, special project grants and support for journal digitisation.

SAMPLE GRANTS Borthwick Institute – York (£37,500); Bedford Architectural and Archaeological Society and Institute of Historical Research (£20,000 each); Dating Old Welsh Houses Group and Reaktion Books (£3,000 each); Association of Historians of Nineteenth-Century Art and Hereford Cathedral Perpetual Trust (£2,000 each); Hornsey Historical Society (£1,500); University of Hertfordshire (£700); Preserve Our Past (£400).

FINANCES *Year* 2015/16 *Income* £231,001 *Grants* £157,030 *Grants to organisations* £111,447 *Assets* £5,962,102

TRUSTEES Lindsay Allason-Jones, Chair; Prof. John Blair; Dr Helen Forde; Michael Hall; Andrew Murison; Bernard Nurse; Prof. David Palliser; Prof. Christiana Payne; David White; Roey Sweet.

OTHER INFORMATION In 2015/16 a total of 41 grants were awarded to organisations and individuals. The amount of grants given to individuals totalled £45,500. The grant total includes £13,400 which was awarded from the fund but not taken up.

HOW TO APPLY In the first instance see the website, where full guidelines are available. Prospective applicants should send a brief outline of their project to the fund by email. Applicants whose proposals fall within the criteria will be sent an application form. The Council of Management meets to consider applications in spring and autumn, and completed applications and references should be received by the fund by 1 March and 1 August, respectively. Note that the fund is described on its website as a 'last resort' for 'worthwhile projects that are at risk of failing without a grant'. For this reason, applicants are required to provide details of other funding sources from which they have tried to secure support. It is further explained: 'We place great emphasis on the reports of referees and need to be convinced that the work being funded will make a new and significant contribution to knowledge.'

WHO TO APPLY TO Christopher Catling, Director, Flat 9, 13 Tavistock Place, London WC1H 9SH *Tel.* 01285 641108 *Email* mail2017@marcfitchfund.org.uk *Website* www.marcfitchfund.org.uk

■ The Fitton Trust

CC NO 208758 **ESTABLISHED** 1928

WHERE FUNDING CAN BE GIVEN UK.

WHO CAN BENEFIT Registered charities only.

WHAT IS FUNDED General charitable purposes.

WHAT IS NOT FUNDED Individuals.

RANGE OF GRANTS Mostly between £150 and £350.

SAMPLE GRANTS King's Medical Research Trust.

FINANCES *Year* 2015/16 *Income* £79,342 *Grants* £39,350 *Grants to organisations* £39,350 *Assets* £1,608,848

TRUSTEES Dr Rodney Rivers; Duncan Brand; Emma Lumsden; Katherine Lumsden; Lincoln Rivers; Rosemary Shaw.

OTHER INFORMATION In 2015/16 grants were made to 184 recipients. The grant total for the year is unusually low.

HOW TO APPLY Apply in writing to correspondent. The secretary scrutinises and collates applications in preparation for the trustee meetings. The trustees meet three times each year, often in April, August and December and they consider all applications.

WHO TO APPLY TO The Secretary, PO Box 70088, London SE15 9FS

■ The Earl Fitzwilliam Charitable Trust

CC NO 269388 **ESTABLISHED** 1975

WHERE FUNDING CAN BE GIVEN UK, with a preference for areas with historical family connections, chiefly in Cambridgeshire, Yorkshire and Denbighshire.

WHO CAN BENEFIT According to the annual report for 2015/16: 'It is the trustees' policy to favour charitable organisations or charitable initiatives which benefit communities that are linked in some reasonably direct way to the Fitzwilliam Estates in Cambridgeshire and Yorkshire and the Naylor-Leyland Estate in Nantclywd.' However, small and medium-sized charities that fall outside this criteria can also be supported.

WHAT IS FUNDED General charitable purposes including health, education, children and young people, disability, the environment and countryside, and churches.

WHAT IS NOT FUNDED Individuals.

TYPE OF GRANT Generally one-off.

RANGE OF GRANTS Generally in the range of £100 to £10,000.

SAMPLE GRANTS Malton Amenity CIC (£59,000); Eton College and Game and Wildlife Conservation Trust (£5,000 each); East of England Agricultural Society (£4,000); Encephalitis Society and St Helen and All Saints Church – Wykeham near Scarborough (£2,500 each); Northumberland Clubs for Young People, Saint Catherine's Hospice – Scarborough and Vivacity Culture and Leisure Trust (£2,000 each); Mepal Outdoor Centre and Peterborough Area Down's Syndrome Group (£1,000 each); St Kyneburgha of Castor Summer Festival and St Michael's Pre-school (£500 each); Llanelidan Village Hall Committee (£250); Friends of Peterborough Cathedral (£50).

FINANCES *Year* 2015/16 *Income* £184,588 *Grants* £147,498 *Grants to organisations* £147,498 *Assets* £14,563,057

TRUSTEES Sir Philip Naylor-Leyland; Lady Isabella Naylor-Leyland.

OTHER INFORMATION Grants were made to 68 organisations in 2015/16. The trust shares its trustees with the Malton Amenity CIC, which benefits the local community in Malton and Norton in North Yorkshire, where the Fitzwilliam Malton Estate is located.

HOW TO APPLY Apply in writing to the correspondent. The trustees meet about every three months.

WHO TO APPLY TO R. W. Dalgliesh, Secretary, Estate Office, Milton Park, Peterborough PE3 9HD *Tel.* 01733 267740 *Email* agent@miltonestate.co.uk

■ The Joyce Fletcher Charitable Trust

CC NO 297901 **ESTABLISHED** 1987

WHERE FUNDING CAN BE GIVEN UK, with a very strong preference for the South West.

WHO CAN BENEFIT Mainly organisations, usually registered charities.

WHAT IS FUNDED Music and the arts in a social or therapeutic context; music and special needs; children and young people's welfare, preferably through arts activities. Some grants are awarded for purposes outside these areas, usually to causes which are known by the trustees and/or are in the South West.
WHAT IS NOT FUNDED Grants to individuals and students are exceptionally rare. No support is given for areas which are the responsibility of statutory funding. No support is given to purely professional music/arts promotions. No support is given for purely medical research charities.
TYPE OF GRANT Capital and revenue funding; one-off and recurring.
RANGE OF GRANTS From £500 to £5,000, but usually between £1,000 and £2,000.
SAMPLE GRANTS Bath Festivals and Welsh National Opera (£5,000 each); Bath Philharmonia and Mid-Somerset Festival (£4,000 each); English Touring Opera and Quartet Community Foundation (£3,000 each); Combat Stress, Creative Youth Network, Julian House, Mentoring Plus – Bath, and Oddments Theatre (£2,000 each); Edington Music Festival Association, Liverpool Cathedral Foundation and Magdalen Farm Strings (£1,000 each).
FINANCES *Year* 2015/16 *Income* £75,011 *Grants* £80,000 *Grants to organisations* £79,000 *Assets* £2,289,420
TRUSTEES Robert Fletcher, Chair; Stephen Fletcher; Susan Sharp; William Fletcher.
OTHER INFORMATION New beneficiaries are supported each year, but 'a good proportion' of grants are recurring. Of the 35 grants made in 2015/16, four were awarded to new applicants and 29 to beneficiaries located in the South West. One grant (of £1,000) was made to an individual.
HOW TO APPLY Apply in writing to the correspondent before 1 November each year. New applicants are advised to write in September. Applications are considered between September and November each year, with grants made in early December. Telephone enquiries are accepted. The website notes that 'applications should include purpose for grant, indication of history and viability of the organisation, and summary of accounts.' Replies are sent to applications which enclose an sae and to those applicants who are narrowly unsuccessful.
WHO TO APPLY TO Robert Fletcher, Chair, 68 Circus Mews, Bath BA1 2PW *Tel.* 01225 314355 *Website* www.joycefletchercharitabletrust.co.uk

■ The Follett Trust

CC NO 328638 **ESTABLISHED** 1990
WHERE FUNDING CAN BE GIVEN UK and overseas, with a preference for Stevenage.
WHO CAN BENEFIT Organisations and individuals.
WHAT IS FUNDED Community work; the arts; health/medical causes; the promotion of reading, including people with dyslexia; students in higher education, including scholarships.
RANGE OF GRANTS Up to £20,000.
SAMPLE GRANTS Canon Collins Trust (£20,000); Stevenage Citizens Advice (£15,700); Donald Woods Foundation (£13,500); UCL Scholarship (£13,000); Home-Start (£9,000); Stevenage Community Trust (£5,500); Detonate (£5,400); The People's History Museum (£3,000); Book Aid, Deafblind UK, Garden House Hospice, Knebworth Parochial Church Council, Labrador Rescue, Lord's Taverners, and Sports and Community Trust (£1,000 each).
FINANCES *Year* 2015/16 *Income* £170,000 *Grants* £159,477 *Grants to organisations* £145,177 *Assets* £43,431
TRUSTEES Brian Mitchell; Ken Follett; Barbara Follett.
OTHER INFORMATION More than 36 grants were made in 2015/16. The grant total includes £14,300 awarded to individuals.
HOW TO APPLY Apply in writing to the correspondent. The annual report for 2015/16 notes that: 'The majority of successful applications, however, come from persons and organisations known to the trustee or in which the trustees have a particular interest.' Replies are not sent to unsuccessful applicants unless they have provided an sae.
WHO TO APPLY TO Jamie Westcott, The Follet Office, Follett House, Primett Road, Stevenage, Hertfordshire SG1 3EE *Tel.* 01438 810400 *Email* folletttrust@thefollettoffice.com

■ The Football Association National Sports Centre Trust

CC NO 265132 **ESTABLISHED** 1972
WHERE FUNDING CAN BE GIVEN UK.
WHO CAN BENEFIT County football associations; football clubs; sports associations.
WHAT IS FUNDED The provision, maintenance and improvement of facilities for use in recreational and leisure activities.
WHAT IS NOT FUNDED Individuals.
TYPE OF GRANT One-off grants towards community-based projects.
SAMPLE GRANTS The National Football Centre Ltd (£3.8 million).
FINANCES *Year* 2015 *Income* £2,614 *Grants* £80,000 *Grants to organisations* £80,000
TRUSTEES Geoff Thompson; Barry Bright; Raymond Berridge; William Annable; Jack Perks.
OTHER INFORMATION The charity's latest accounts were not available to view on the Charity Commission's website due its low income. We have therefore estimated the grant total based on previous years' information.
HOW TO APPLY Apply in writing to the correspondent.
WHO TO APPLY TO Richard McDermott, Secretary to the Trustees, Wembley National Stadium Ltd, PO Box 1966, London SW1P 9EQ *Tel.* 0844 980 8200 ext. 6575 *Email* richard.mcdermott@thefa.com

■ The Football Foundation

CC NO 1079309 **ESTABLISHED** 1999
WHERE FUNDING CAN BE GIVEN England.
WHO CAN BENEFIT A wide range of organisations, including: football clubs (grassroots, professional and semi-professional) and their associated community charities; multi-sport clubs; local authorities; educational establishments; registered charities; not-for-profit companies limited by guarantee; industrial and provident societies; and unincorporated not-for-profit organisations.
WHAT IS FUNDED The foundation's current objectives are: 'to put into place a new generation of modern facilities in parks, local leagues and schools; to provide capital/revenue support to increase participation in grassroots football; and to strengthen the links between football and the community and to harness its potential as a force for good in society'. It meets these

objectives by making grants through a range of different funding streams.

RANGE OF GRANTS Up to £1 million.

SAMPLE GRANTS Foundation of Light (£1 million); Ealing Council (£902,000); YMCA Plymouth (£880,000); Redditch United FC (£561,500); Gateacre School and University of Bradford (£500,000 each); Dorset County FA (£467,500); St Cuthbert's Catholic High School (£416,500); London Playing Fields Foundation (£368,500); Wreake Valley Academy (£350,500); England and Wales Cricket Board (£340,000); Haverhill Community Sports Association (£321,500).

FINANCES *Year* 2015/16 *Income* £32,084,000 *Grants* £41,423,000 *Grants to organisations* £41,423,000 *Assets* £140,000

TRUSTEES Gary Hoffman; Roger Burden; Martin Glenn; Richard Scudamore; Peter McCormick; Rt Hon. Richard Caborn; Rona Chester.

OTHER INFORMATION The foundation receives income from the professional game, and from the Department of Culture, Media and Sport via Sports England. During the year, 352 new grants were made.

HOW TO APPLY See the website for full details of funding streams which are currently open for applications.

WHO TO APPLY TO Rupen Shah, Head of Finance, Whittington House, 19–30 Alfred Place, London WC1E 7EA *Tel.* 0845 345 4555 *Email* enquiries@footballfoundation.org.uk *Website* www.footballfoundation.org.uk

■ The Forbes Charitable Foundation

CC NO 326476 **ESTABLISHED** 1983

WHERE FUNDING CAN BE GIVEN UK.

WHO CAN BENEFIT Registered or exempt charities; individuals.

WHAT IS FUNDED The provision of services for people, principally adults, with mild to moderate learning difficulties. The services eligible for support are: residential care; supported living; day services; social enterprises; employment initiatives; skills training; support for informal carers; and transition services for young adults.

TYPE OF GRANT Capital costs; revenue costs; annual grants for up to three years.

RANGE OF GRANTS Mostly between £400 and £5,000.

SAMPLE GRANTS Hft – Nigel Doggett Scholarship (£50,000); The Lodge Trust (£10,000); Acorn Village, Autism Hampshire and Plymouth Highbury Trust (£5,000 each); Merseyside Tuesday Club, Northern Ireland Association for Mental Health and The Right to Work CIC (£2,500 each); Beacons Creative and People and Gardens CIC (£1,800 each); Resources for Autism (£1,750); Strides Leicester (£1,300); Open Minds (£500); Keynsham and District Mencap (£400).

FINANCES *Year* 2015/16 *Income* £303,544 *Grants* £185,557 *Grants to organisations* £179,807 *Assets* £5,907,474

TRUSTEES C. Packham, Chair; Ian Johnson; John Waite; Nicholas Townsend; Robert Bunting; Helen Johnson; Patrick Wallace.

OTHER INFORMATION In 2015/16, 48 organisations and individuals were supported. John Waite is also a trustee of Hft, which received a grant during the year.

HOW TO APPLY The foundation's main annual support is given to between six and ten specified charities with an annual turnover of between £1 million and £20 million. The trustees identify suitable charities and invite them to submit funding proposals using the application form on the website. The foundation's website states: '**Note that the Trustees have already identified the charities to be supported through to March 2019**.'

WHO TO APPLY TO John Shepherd, Secretary, PO Box 6256, Nuneaton CV11 9HT *Tel.* 01455 292881 *Email* info@theforbescharitablefoundation.org *Website* www.theforbescharitablefoundation.org

■ Ford Britain Trust

CC NO 269410 **ESTABLISHED** 1975

WHERE FUNDING CAN BE GIVEN Local to the areas in close proximity to Ford Motor Company Ltd's UK locations. These are: Essex (including East London); Bridgend; Daventry; Liverpool; Manchester; and Southampton. A list of eligible postcodes is provided on the website.

WHO CAN BENEFIT Registered charities; state schools/PTAs; non-profit organisations.

WHAT IS FUNDED Children and young people; schools/education; Special Needs education; local communities and environment; disability.

WHAT IS NOT FUNDED Major building work; sponsorship or advertising; research; overseas projects; travel; religious projects; political projects; the purchase of secondhand vehicles; third-party fundraising initiatives (exceptions may be made, however, for fundraising initiatives by Ford Motor Company Ltd employees and retirees); independent/private/fee-paying schools; activities in areas not local to Ford Motor Company's locations.

TYPE OF GRANT Contributions to capital projects (e.g. refurbishments); capital expenditure items (e.g. furniture/equipment/computers); contributions towards the purchase or leasing of new Ford vehicles (up to a maximum of £2,000); and general funds (small grants of up to £250 only).

RANGE OF GRANTS Generally up to £3,000.

SAMPLE GRANTS The Prince's Trust (£25,500); Robert Clark School (£15,000); Business in the Community – local school projects (£4,000); 1st Warley Scouts Group, Benfleet Youth Football Club, Margam Youth Centre, One World Foundation Africa and St Joseph's Hospice (£3,000 each).

FINANCES *Year* 2015/16 *Income* £205,442 *Grants* £164,595 *Grants to organisations* £164,595 *Assets* £366,331

TRUSTEES Michael Callaghan; David Russell; Michael Brophy; Dr June-Alison Sealy; Wendy James; Jane Skerry; Paul Bailey; Lara Nicoll.

OTHER INFORMATION This is the charitable trust of Ford Motor Company Ltd. In 2015/16 a total of 148 grants were made. More than half of the grant (£87,000) was given in grants of less than £3,000.

HOW TO APPLY Application forms are available to download from the website, where guidance notes are also available. There are two types of grants that can be applied for: small grants (up to £250) and large grants (over £250 and usually up to £3,000). Small grants are considered four times a year, in March, June, September and December. Large grant applications are considered twice a year, in March and September. Deadlines are detailed on the website.

WHO TO APPLY TO Deborah Chennells, Trust Director, Room 1/623, c/o Ford Motor Company Ltd, Eagle Way, Brentwood, Essex CM13 3BW *Email* fbtrust@ford.com *Website* www.ford.co.uk/fbtrust

■ The Oliver Ford Charitable Trust

CC NO 1026551 **ESTABLISHED** 1993
WHERE FUNDING CAN BE GIVEN UK.
WHO CAN BENEFIT Registered charities; students (see 'Other information').
WHAT IS FUNDED Grants are made to charities that provide housing, educational or training facilities for people who have learning disabilities or difficulties.
TYPE OF GRANT One-off.
RANGE OF GRANTS Generally between £2,000 and £10,000.
SAMPLE GRANTS Royal Mencap Society (£10,200); Style Acre (£10,000); Assist Trust, Beds Garden Carers, Plymouth Highbury Trust and SeeAbility (£5,000 each); Little Gate Farm (£4,000); Autism Plus (£3,300); Autism Initiatives (£3,100); Groundwork Luton and Bedfordshire (£2,000).
FINANCES *Year* 2015/16 *Income* £98,624 *Grants* £139,080 *Grants to organisations* £105,653 *Assets* £2,613,867
TRUSTEES Lady Alison Wakeham; Martin Levy.
OTHER INFORMATION Grants were made to 21 charities during the year. The trust also makes grants within the following areas: Oliver Ford scholarships for students attending the Victoria and Albert Museum (£24,500 in 2015/16); assistance to students of the Royal Horticultural Society (£5,000); and assistance to students of the Furniture History Society (£3,900).
HOW TO APPLY Apply in writing to the correspondent. The trustees meet in March and October.
WHO TO APPLY TO Matthew Pintus, 20 Cursitor Street, London EC4A 1LT *Tel.* 020 7831 9222

■ Fordeve Ltd

CC NO 1011612 **ESTABLISHED** 1992
WHERE FUNDING CAN BE GIVEN UK.
WHO CAN BENEFIT Orthodox Jewish organisations.
WHAT IS FUNDED The advancement of religion in accordance with the Orthodox Jewish faith; education; the relief of poverty; general charitable purposes.
SAMPLE GRANTS Beth Jacob Grammar School for Girls; The Gertner Charitable Trust; The Lolev Charitable Trust; Society of Friends of the Torah; The Yom Tov Assistance Fund.
FINANCES *Year* 2015/16 *Income* £142,343 *Grants* £123,656 *Grants to organisations* £123,656 *Assets* £660,006
TRUSTEES Jeremy Kon; Helen Kon.
OTHER INFORMATION A list of beneficiaries was not available in the 2015/16 annual report.
HOW TO APPLY Apply in writing to the correspondent.
WHO TO APPLY TO Jeremy Kon, Secretary, Hallswelle House, 1 Hallswelle Road, London NW11 0DH *Tel.* 020 8209 1535

■ The Fore Trust

CC NO 326292 **ESTABLISHED** 1983
WHERE FUNDING CAN BE GIVEN UK.
WHO CAN BENEFIT UK-registered early-stage charities, CICs and social enterprises.
WHAT IS FUNDED Development funding and strategic support to early-stage charities and social enterprises.
TYPE OF GRANT Unrestricted development grants allocated over one to three years.
RANGE OF GRANTS Up to £30,000.
SAMPLE GRANTS West London Zone (£30,000); Arts Against Knives (£27,500); Circle Sports (£26,000); Shivia (£20,000); Panathalon Challenge (£20,000); Bridge Community (£15,000); The Doorstep Library (£10,000); Recycling Unlimited (£9,000); Purple Patch Arts (£8,700); Generation Rwanda (£8,100).
FINANCES *Year* 2015/16 *Income* £1,180,761 *Grants* £503,793 *Grants to organisations* £503,793 *Assets* £8,696,317
TRUSTEES Martin Riley; Charles Hoare; Kim Hoare; Hamish McPherson; Alex Williams.
OTHER INFORMATION The Fore Trust is a grant-making initiative of the Bulldog Trust. All financial information is for the Bulldog Trust.
HOW TO APPLY Apply online through the trust's website. The trust runs three twelve-week funding rounds to coincide with the academic calendar each year. Application dates are on the trust's website. Registration is run on a first-come, first-serve basis and once the cap is reached, the round is closed; therefore, register early.
WHO TO APPLY TO Reena Gudka, 2 Temple Place, London WC2R 3BD *Tel.* 020 7240 6044 *Email* reena@thefore.org.uk *Website* www.thefore.org

■ Forest Hill Charitable Trust

CC NO 1050862 **ESTABLISHED** 1995
WHERE FUNDING CAN BE GIVEN UK and overseas.
WHO CAN BENEFIT Organisations, particularly Christian organisations.
WHAT IS FUNDED Christian causes; health and respite; disability; the relief of poverty; social welfare; education.
RANGE OF GRANTS Mostly between £500 and £2,000.
SAMPLE GRANTS LiNX (£24,000); Barnabas Fund (£3,000); Medical Missionary News (£2,000); Children's Hospice South West, Christians Against Poverty, Compass Braille, Concern Worldwide, The Karen Hill Tribes Trust, Marie Curie Cancer Care, Mental Health Foundation, Prison Fellowship, Redcliffe College, Scripture Union and World Villages for Children (£1,000 each); Evangelical Housing Association, Family Action, Friends of Factory Row and Revival Movement Association (£500 each).
FINANCES *Year* 2015/16 *Income* £152,342 *Grants* £156,100 *Grants to organisations* £156,100 *Assets* £3,259,945
TRUSTEES Dr Horace Pile, Chair; Ronald Stanley Pile; Marianne Tapper; Michael Thomas; Patricia Pile.
OTHER INFORMATION The trust supports around 140 organisations.
HOW TO APPLY The trustees have previously stated that their aim was to maintain regular and consistent support to the charities they are currently supporting. New requests for funding are therefore very unlikely to succeed and unsolicited applications are rarely considered.
WHO TO APPLY TO Dr Horace Pile, Chair, Little Bluff, Treknow, Tintagel, Cornwall PL34 0EP *Tel.* 01840 779405 *Email* horacepilefhct@yahoo.co.uk

■ The Lady Forester Trust

CC NO 241187 **ESTABLISHED** 1979
WHERE FUNDING CAN BE GIVEN Shropshire.
WHO CAN BENEFIT Medical professional bodies; charities; other organisations; individuals.
WHAT IS FUNDED The relief of sickness; convalescence; disability.
RANGE OF GRANTS Usually between £1,000 and £5,000.

SAMPLE GRANTS Blind Veterans – Llandudno and Oswestry None Cancer Appeal (£5,000 each); Help for Heroes (£4,000); Home Start – Bridgnorth (£3,000); Age UK Telford and Wrekin and County Air Ambulance (£2,000 each); Changing Faces (£1,500); Acorns Children's Hospital Trust, Dystonia Society and The Fire Fighters Charity (£1,000 each).

FINANCES *Year* 2015 *Income* £150,248 *Grants* £155,239 *Grants to organisations* £119,440 *Assets* £5,059,822

TRUSTEES Lady Catherine Forester, Chair; The Hon. Alice Stoker; Libby Collinson; John Dugdale; Henry Carpenter; Lord Forester; The Lady Forester; Janette Stewart.

OTHER INFORMATION In 2015 almost £36,000 was distributed to individuals. A recent list of beneficiaries was not available.

HOW TO APPLY Apply in writing to the correspondent. The trustees meet on a quarterly basis to consider applications and will consider unsolicited applications. Grants for individuals are usually recommended by GPs or social workers.

WHO TO APPLY TO Janet McGorman, The Estate Office, Willey, Broseley, Shropshire TF12 5JN *Tel.* 01952 884318 *Email* lft@willeyestates.co.uk

■ Forever Manchester

CC NO 1017504 **ESTABLISHED** 1993

WHERE FUNDING CAN BE GIVEN Greater Manchester.

WHO CAN BENEFIT Registered charities and small, locally run community or voluntary groups in Greater Manchester.

WHAT IS FUNDED General charitable purposes; health; welfare; education; people with disabilities; older people; young people and children; women. Improving the quality of life and helping to build stronger communities across Greater Manchester.

WHAT IS NOT FUNDED Organisations and projects outside the Greater Manchester area; large organisations including those with a track record of attracting funding or a turnover of more than £150,000 per annum.

TYPE OF GRANT One-off; project. Start-up costs will be considered.

RANGE OF GRANTS The average grant for the year was £1,713.

SAMPLE GRANTS A list of recent beneficiaries are available on the website and included; Bloco Mente; Children of Jannah; Friends of Jubilee Colliery; Friends of Stockport Cemeteries; Monton Voices Community Choir; North Manchester Ladies Jewish Drama Group; Pastures New; Reddish Vale Men in Sheds; Safety4Sisters; St Mary's Friendship Club; The Seed Project.

FINANCES *Year* 2015/16 *Income* £3,219,945 *Grants* £1,322,050 *Grants to organisations* £1,311,150 *Assets* £9,521,880

TRUSTEES Michael Warner; Philip Hogben; Sandra Lindsay; Alan Mackin; Louise Marshall; Samantha Booth.

OTHER INFORMATION Grants to organisations and individuals totalled £1.3 million, of which £10,900 was given to individuals and the rest went to 850 community projects across Greater Manchester. There are five funding programmes with their own eligibility criteria and deadlines.

HOW TO APPLY Contact the foundation's Awards Team by telephone (0161 214 0940) or email (awards@forevermanchester.com) to discuss available funds, eligibility, criteria and deadline dates, and to receive full guidelines and an application pack.

WHO TO APPLY TO Gillian Green, Forever Manchester, 2nd Floor, 8 Hewitt Street, Manchester M15 4GB *Tel.* 0161 214 0940 *Email* awards@forevermanchester.com *Website* www.forevermanchester.com

■ The Forman Hardy Charitable Trust

CC NO 1000687 **ESTABLISHED** 1990

WHERE FUNDING CAN BE GIVEN Not defined; in practice, Nottinghamshire.

WHO CAN BENEFIT Registered charities and community groups.

WHAT IS FUNDED General charitable purposes.

RANGE OF GRANTS Mostly up to £3,000.

SAMPLE GRANTS Multiple Sclerosis Society (£50,000); The University of Nottingham and The University of Sheffield (£25,000 each for MS research); Emmanuel House (£20,000); Nottingham City Parish – St Mary's Church (£10,000); Neville Holt Opera (£3,000); Aysgarth School (£2,000); Asthma UK, Scottish Game and Wildlife Conservation Trust, Southwell Cathedral Chapter and War Memorials Trust (£1,000 each).

FINANCES *Year* 2015/16 *Income* £29,982 *Grants* £159,650 *Grants to organisations* £159,650 *Assets* £2,469,453

TRUSTEES Nicholas Forman Hardy; Jane Forman Hardy; Charles Bennion; Canon James Neale.

OTHER INFORMATION In 2015/16 £18,100 was given in grants of less than £1,000.

HOW TO APPLY Apply in writing to the correspondent.

WHO TO APPLY TO Rachael Sulley, 64 St James's Street, Nottingham NG1 6FJ *Tel.* 0115 950 8580 *Email* rachaels@formanhardy.com

■ Donald Forrester Trust

CC NO 295833 **ESTABLISHED** 1986

WHERE FUNDING CAN BE GIVEN UK and overseas.

WHO CAN BENEFIT UK-registered charities. The website explains that the trustees 'look favourably on smaller organisations where we feel our funding will provide vital support to the work of volunteers' and will also 'look positively on organisations where both overheads and fundraising costs are kept to a minimum'.

WHAT IS FUNDED Animals and birds; disability; children and young people; community care and social welfare; culture, heritage and environment; hospices and hospitals; maritime; medical relief and welfare; medical research; older people's welfare; physical and mental disability; members and ex-members of the services; overseas relief.

WHAT IS NOT FUNDED Individuals.

TYPE OF GRANT One-off and recurrent.

RANGE OF GRANTS Grants are usually for £5,000.

SAMPLE GRANTS Disasters Emergency Committee – Nepal Earthquake (£20,000); Churcher's College 1722 Committee (£15,000); St Andrew's Beesands (£10,000); Alzheimer's Society, Battersea Dogs and Cats Home, Bereavement Care, Bipolar UK, Children with Cancer, Durham Cathedral, Freedom from Torture, Hampshire and Isle of Wight Air Ambulance, Humane Slaughter Association, Listening Books, Mental Health Foundation, Mind, Missing People, RAF Benevolent Fund, Royal National Lifeboat Institution, Sightsavers International; WaterAid, Whitechapel Mission

(£5,000 each); Age Concern Ravensbourne (£3,000).

FINANCES *Year* 2015/16 *Income* £500,406 *Grants* £495,000 *Grants to organisations* £495,000 *Assets* £7,778,467

TRUSTEES Wendy Forrester; Hilary Porter; Melissa Jones; Adrian Hollands; Martin West.

OTHER INFORMATION Grants were made to 90 charities in 2015/16. The trust is administered and shares its trustees with the Gwyneth Forrester Trust (Charity Commission no. 1080921).

HOW TO APPLY Historically, both the Donald Forrester Trust and the Gwyneth Forrester Trust had a policy of not accepting unsolicited grant applications. However, as explained on the website, the trustees 'have now decided to encourage applications from a wider range of charities'. Applications should be made in writing to the correspondent, stating whether you are applying to the Donald Forrester Trust or the Gwyneth Forrester Trust. Ideally, applications should not exceed four sides of A4. Applications should include details of the impact you think a grant from the trust might make to your organisation's work. A full set of accounts is not required, although the trustees find a brief indication of an applicant organisation's financial position to be helpful. The trustees meet twice yearly in February/March and August/September, and applications should be submitted no later than 15 January and 15 July, respectively. The trust is unable to enter into correspondence with applicants.

WHO TO APPLY TO Adrian Hollands, Hon. Secretary, 11 Whitecroft Way, Beckenham, Kent BR3 3AQ *Tel.* 020 8629 0089 *Email* ah@forrestertrusts.com *Website* forrestertrusts.com/donald-forrester-trust

■ Gwyneth Forrester Trust

CC NO 1080921 **ESTABLISHED** 2000

WHERE FUNDING CAN BE GIVEN England and Wales.

WHO CAN BENEFIT National and international registered charities. The trustees favour charities where overhead and fundraising costs are kept to a minimum.

WHAT IS FUNDED The trustees support a specific charitable sector each year. The theme for 2018 is 'support for older people'. Themes in previous years have included helping young individuals and people who have offended into employment (2017), hospices (2016), and mental health (2015).

WHAT IS NOT FUNDED Individuals.

TYPE OF GRANT One-off.

RANGE OF GRANTS Grants average £40,000.

SAMPLE GRANTS A list of beneficiaries was not available.

FINANCES *Year* 2015/16 *Income* £388,076 *Grants* £400,000 *Grants to organisations* £400,000 *Assets* £23,247,838

TRUSTEES Martin West; Wendy Forrester; Adrian Hollands; Hilary Porter; Melissa Jones.

OTHER INFORMATION In 2015/16 ten charities were supported, with each receiving £40,000. The trust is administered and shares its trustees with the Donald Forrester Trust (Charity Commission no. 295833).

HOW TO APPLY Historically, both the Donald Forrester Trust and the Gwyneth Forrester Trust had a policy of not accepting unsolicited grant applications. However, as explained on the website, the trustees 'have now decided to encourage applications from a wider range of charities'. Applications should be made in writing to the correspondent, stating whether you are applying to the Donald Forrester Trust or the Gwyneth Forrester Trust. Ideally, applications should not exceed four sides of A4. Applications should include details of the impact you think a grant from the trust might make to your organisation's work. A full set of accounts is not required, however the trustees find a brief indication of an applicant organisation's financial position to be helpful. The trustees meet to consider applications in February/March, and applications should be submitted no later than 15 January. The trust is unable to enter into correspondence with applicants.

WHO TO APPLY TO Adrian Hollands, Hon. Secretary, 11 Whitecroft Way, Beckenham, Kent BR3 3AQ *Tel.* 020 8629 0089 *Email* ah@forrestertrusts.com *Website* forrestertrusts.com/gwyneth-forrester-trust

■ The Forster Charitable Trust

CC NO 1090028 **ESTABLISHED** 1997

WHERE FUNDING CAN BE GIVEN UK and overseas.

WHO CAN BENEFIT Registered charities.

WHAT IS FUNDED Medical research; animal welfare; famine relief.

RANGE OF GRANTS Usually between £2,500 and £3,500.

SAMPLE GRANTS Alzheimer's Research Trust; British Red Cross; Cancer Research UK; CARE International UK; Cats Protection League; The Donkey Sanctuary; Farm Africa; International Spinal Research Trust; Motor Neurone Disease Association; People's Dispensary for Sick Animals (PDSA); RSPCA; World Medical Fund.

FINANCES *Year* 2015/16 *Income* £100,491 *Grants* £61,408 *Grants to organisations* £61,408 *Assets* £2,263,533

TRUSTEES Roger Napier; Andrew Morgan.

OTHER INFORMATION The trust divides its income equally between animal welfare, famine relief and medical research.

HOW TO APPLY Apply in writing to the correspondent.

WHO TO APPLY TO Roger Napier, Trustee, c/o R. W. Napier Solicitors, Floor E, Milburn House, Dean Street, Newcastle upon Tyne NE1 1LF *Tel.* 0191 230 1819 *Email* rogerw.napier@gmail.com

■ The Fort Foundation

CC NO 1028639 **ESTABLISHED** 1993

WHERE FUNDING CAN BE GIVEN England and Wales, with a focus on Lancashire.

WHO CAN BENEFIT Organisations and individuals.

WHAT IS FUNDED Health; amateur sport; education; art and culture; citizenship; community welfare; religion; environmental protection and improvement.

WHAT IS NOT FUNDED Education fees.

TYPE OF GRANT One–off.

RANGE OF GRANTS Mostly of £5,000 to £7,500.

SAMPLE GRANTS The Outward Bound Trust (£40,000); The 1851 Trust (£25,000); The Royal Windermere Yacht Club (£20,000); Lancaster University – Alzheimer's research (£7,500); Community Foundation for Lancashire, Grassington Festival, Pendle and Craven Croquet Club and the Special Boat Service Association (£5,000 each).

FINANCES *Year* 2015/16 *Income* £340,838 *Grants* £193,261 *Grants to organisations* £176,011 *Assets* £785,664

TRUSTEES Edward Fort; Ian Wilson; Edward Drury; John Hartley; Peter Fort.

OTHER INFORMATION In 2015/16 a total of 12 organisations received grants. £17,300 was awarded to individuals across the categories amateur sport, art and culture, education and health.
HOW TO APPLY Apply in writing to the correspondent.
WHO TO APPLY TO Edward Fort, Trustee, c/o Fort Vale Engineering Ltd, Calder Vale Park, Simonstone Lane, Simonstone, Burnley BB12 7ND *Tel.* 01282 440000 *Email* info@fortvale.com

■ The Forte Charitable Trust

CC NO 326038 **ESTABLISHED** 1982
WHERE FUNDING CAN BE GIVEN UK and overseas.
WHO CAN BENEFIT Organisations, including churches.
WHAT IS FUNDED The trust is registered with general charitable purposes, although previous research suggests that it has a particular interest in Roman Catholic causes and health issues affecting older people, such as Alzheimer's disease and senile dementia.
SAMPLE GRANTS St Peter's Italian Church (£5,000); Festival of St Anthony and Nginn Karet Foundation for Cambodia (£4,000 each); The John Paul II Foundation for Sport and On Course Foundation (£3,000 each); Abbeyfield Reading Society (£2,500); Hot Line Meals Service – London, Methodist Homes, The Respite Association and The Royal Blind Society (£2,000 each); Bedales School, Corstorphine Dementia Project Ltd, Drama Expressions for Children and Kids 'N' Action (£1,000 each); Mildmay Mission Hospital (£500).
FINANCES *Year* 2015/16 *Income* £29,226 *Grants* £73,500 *Grants to organisations* £68,500 *Assets* £1,859,263
TRUSTEES Sir Rocco Forte, Chair; Lowndes Trustee Ltd; The Hon. Olga Polizzi di Sorrentino.
OTHER INFORMATION One grant of £5,000 was awarded to an individual.
HOW TO APPLY Apply in writing to the correspondent.
WHO TO APPLY TO Judy Lewendon, Rocco Forte Hotels Ltd, 70 Jermyn Street, London SW1Y 6NY *Tel.* 020 7321 2626 *Email* jlewendon@roccofortehotels.com

■ The Lord Forte Foundation

CC NO 298100 **ESTABLISHED** 1987
WHERE FUNDING CAN BE GIVEN UK.
WHO CAN BENEFIT Educational establishments.
WHAT IS FUNDED Training courses and research within the field of hospitality, encompassing the hotel, catering, travel and tourism industries within the UK and overseas. According to its 2015/16 annual report, the foundation 'seeks to provide financial support which rewards excellence, and specifically assists in meeting the costs of study for those from poorer backgrounds'.
TYPE OF GRANT Up to three years.
RANGE OF GRANTS Between £2,000 and £40,000.
SAMPLE GRANTS University of West London (£40,000); Beyond Food Foundation, Master Innholders and Springboard Charitable Trust (£10,000); University of Portsmouth and The Wine Guild Charitable Trust (£9,000); University of Plymouth (£5,000); University of Strathclyde (£4,500); Perth College Development Fund (£2,000).
FINANCES *Year* 2015/16 *Income* £82,828 *Grants* £99,500 *Grants to organisations* £99,500 *Assets* £2,384,253
TRUSTEES Sir Rocco Forte, Chair; Nick Scade; Andrew McKenzie; Geoff Booth; The Hon. Olga di Sorrentino.
OTHER INFORMATION Grants were made to nine organisations during the year.
HOW TO APPLY Apply in writing to the correspondent.
WHO TO APPLY TO Judy Lewendon, Rocco Forte Hotels Ltd, 70 Jermyn Street, London SW1Y 6NY *Email* jlewendon@roccofortehotels.com

■ The Foyle Foundation

CC NO 1081766 **ESTABLISHED** 2000
WHERE FUNDING CAN BE GIVEN UK.
WHO CAN BENEFIT Registered charities; state schools.
WHAT IS FUNDED Small grants scheme: general charitable purposes; charities with annual turnover of less than £100,000. Main grants scheme: arts; education; registered charities in the UK. The Foyle School Library Scheme: schools, with preference to primary schools.
WHAT IS NOT FUNDED Individuals; non-registered charities; charities working overseas.
TYPE OF GRANT Capital, revenue and project funding.
RANGE OF GRANTS Up to £250,000.
SAMPLE GRANTS National Army Museum Foundation, Royal Academy of Arts (£250,000); Royal Liverpool Philharmonic Society (£150,000); Tate Gallery (£125,000); Durham Cathedral (£100,000); Poetry Society (£83,000); Somerset House Trust (£50,000); Dance Umbrella (£20,000); Belfast Exposed Photography (£10,000); Whitegate Primary and Nursery School (£8,500) Seeing Ear Hastings (£6,000); Bafron Bowling Club (£5,000) Strabane Community Unemployed Group (£3,000) Rochdale Foodbank (£3,000) Book Trade Charity (£1,000).
FINANCES *Year* 2015 *Income* £2,686,278 *Grants* £7,471,600 *Grants to organisations* £7,471,600 *Assets* £79,938,867
TRUSTEES James Korner; Michael Smith; Dr Kathryn Skoyles; Sir Peter Duffell; Roy Amlot.
OTHER INFORMATION During the year 474 grants were awarded. Of the grants paid out, 92 were arts related (£3.5 million), 43 were learning related (£2.6 million), 120 were school library grants (£680,000), and 179 were small grants (£744,000).
HOW TO APPLY All guidelines and application forms are available in Word format via the website for the Main Grants Scheme, Small Grants Scheme and Foyle School Library Scheme. Charities and schools wishing to make an application for funding should download and read the appropriate guidelines for applicants before completing and signing the appropriate application form and sending this together with the supporting information requested to the correspondent. Applications are acknowledged usually by email or by post within two weeks of receipt. If you do not receive this acknowledgement, contact the foundation to confirm safe receipt of your request. Applications are accepted all year round. Except for capital projects, it may take up to four months, occasionally longer, to receive a decision from the trustees. Apply well in advance of the date by which funding is required. Note that for capital projects seeking more than £50,000 the foundation will now only consider these twice per year in spring and autumn. Therefore, it could be six months or more before a decision on your project is made. Guidelines for applicants and the application

forms are also available in hard copy upon request.

WHO TO APPLY TO David Hall, Chief Executive, Rugby Chambers, 2 Rugby Street, London WC1N 3QU *Tel.* 020 7430 9119 *Email* info@foylefoundation.org.uk *Website* www.foylefoundation.org.uk

■ The Isaac and Freda Frankel Memorial Charitable Trust

CC NO 1003732 **ESTABLISHED** 1991

WHERE FUNDING CAN BE GIVEN UK and Israel.

WHO CAN BENEFIT Mainly organisations and institutions benefitting people of the Jewish faith.

WHAT IS FUNDED The advancement of religion in accordance with the Orthodox Jewish faith; the relief of poverty.

WHAT IS NOT FUNDED Individuals; students; expeditions; scholarships.

TYPE OF GRANT One-off and recurrent grants.

RANGE OF GRANTS Usually £1,000 or less.

SAMPLE GRANTS A list of beneficiaries was not available.

FINANCES *Year* 2015/16 *Income* £56,048 *Grants* £57,671 *Grants to organisations* £57,671 *Assets* £402,913

TRUSTEES Montague Frankel; Geraldine Frankel; J. Steinhaus; J. Silkin.

OTHER INFORMATION During the year, the trust made grants to more than 160 organisations and institutions. A list of beneficiaries was not included in the 2015/16 annual report and accounts.

HOW TO APPLY Apply in writing to the correspondent.

WHO TO APPLY TO Montague Frankel, Trustee, 33 Welbeck Street, London W1G 8LX *Tel.* 020 7872 0023

■ The Elizabeth Frankland Moore and Star Foundation

CC NO 257711 **ESTABLISHED** 1968

WHERE FUNDING CAN BE GIVEN UK.

WHO CAN BENEFIT Registered charitable organisations.

WHAT IS FUNDED General charitable purposes. In 2015/16 grants were given in the following areas: medical research; vulnerable people; hospices; homelessness; veterans; human rights; the arts; and other.

TYPE OF GRANT Generally unrestricted.

RANGE OF GRANTS From £5,000 to £20,000.

SAMPLE GRANTS Iceni Project and ORH Charitable Fund 0013 (£20,000 each); The Glasgow School of Art Development Trust (£15,000); After Adoption (£12,500); The Howard League for Penal Reform, National Star College and Royal Surrey Hospital's Charity (£10,000 each); Kingston Hospital – Dementia Care (£8,000); Glasgow City Mission (£7,500); Cancer Support Scotland and Scottish Ballet (£5,000 each); Princess Alice Hospice (£2,500); Eyes for East Africa (£2,000); People's Dispensary for Sick Animals (PDSA), ABF The Soldiers' Charity and UK Youth (£1,000 each); Merlin Theatre Trust (£500).

FINANCES *Year* 2015/16 *Income* £314,558 *Grants* £275,500 *Grants to organisations* £275,500 *Assets* £11,148,694

TRUSTEES R. Griffiths, Chair; Anne Ely; Dr David Spalton; Janine Cameron.

OTHER INFORMATION In 2015/16 the foundation received 408 applications, of which 41 were accepted.

HOW TO APPLY Apply in writing to the correspondent. The trustees meet twice a year.

WHO TO APPLY TO Marianne Neuhoff, The Elizabeth Frankland Moore and Star Foundation, c/o Neuhoff and Co., 11 Towcester Road, Whittlebury, Towcester NN12 8XU *Tel.* 01327 858171 *Email* info@neuhoffandco.com

■ Jill Franklin Trust

CC NO 1000175 **ESTABLISHED** 1988

WHERE FUNDING CAN BE GIVEN UK, particularly the north of England and Wales, but especially Teesside and Tyne and Wear.

WHO CAN BENEFIT Charitable organisations, particularly small charities; churches.

WHAT IS FUNDED Self-help groups, advice, training and employment support for people who have mental illnesses or learning difficulties; holidays for carers (this is now supported wholly by a block grant to The Princess Royal Trust for Carers); organisations working with asylum seekers and refugees coming to or in the UK; the restoration (not improvement) of churches of architectural importance (those that command at least half a page in Pevsner's architectural guides and are listed as Grade I or II buildings) which are open to visitors every day; local schemes which help prisoners to resettle or to prevent delinquency (this is mainly supported through a block grant to the Prisoners' Education Trust); bereavement counselling (supported in the form of grants to Camden City Islington and Westminster Bereavement Service).

WHAT IS NOT FUNDED The trustees do not look favourably on appeals for building work (other than church restoration) or for endowment funds. Nor will they give grants to: replace the duties of government, local authorities or the NHS; religious organisations set up for welfare, education, etc. of whatever religion, unless the service is open to and used by people from all denominations, and there is no attempt to conduct any credal propaganda or religious rituals, or require clients to attend religious services; overseas projects; environmental charities; animal charities; students, nor to any individuals nor for overseas travel; medical research.

TYPE OF GRANT Unrestricted; one to three years.

RANGE OF GRANTS Grants are typically of £1,000 (apart from church restoration which are usually £500).

SAMPLE GRANTS Siarad Da (£12,000); Carers Trust (£7,000); Heads Up, Middlesbrough Action Project, Refugee Survival Trust, Somali Advice Link, South Lakeland Mind, Teesside Hospice and Voluntary Action Broxtowe (£1,000 each); Coleby Church, St Anietus – Liskeard and St Mary the Virgin – Great Brington (£500 each).

FINANCES *Year* 2015/16 *Income* £91,359 *Grants* £93,496 *Grants to organisations* £93,496 *Assets* £1,787,439

TRUSTEES Sally Franklin; Norman Franklin; Andrew Franklin; Dr Samuel Franklin; Thomas Franklin.

HOW TO APPLY Applicants for a grant should write enclosing a budget for the project or email (jft@jill-franklin-trust.org.uk). If your accounts are not filed with the Charity Commission or OSCR, enclose them, or provide a link to them. The trustees welcome preliminary enquiries by email; however, enquiries are not always acknowledged. Churches seeking a grant for

repairs to the fabric of the church should complete the form which can be found at www.jill-franklin-trust.org.uk/churchapplication.html. The website also notes that the trustees 'tend to look more favourably on an appeal which is simply and economically prepared: glossy, "prestige" and Mailsorted brochures do not impress the trustees.' Due to the trust's limited uncommitted resources, most applications are unsuccessful.
WHO TO APPLY TO Norman Franklin, Trustee, Flat 5, 17–19 Elsworthy Road, London NW3 3DS *Tel.* 020 7722 4543 *Email* jft@jill-franklin-trust.org.uk *Website* www.jill-franklin-trust.org.uk

■ The Gordon Fraser Charitable Trust

CC NO 260869 **ESTABLISHED** 1966
WHERE FUNDING CAN BE GIVEN UK, with a preference for Scotland.
WHO CAN BENEFIT Registered charities only.
WHAT IS FUNDED General charitable purposes with a preference for: performing arts, particularly for children, young people and people with disabilities; visual arts and museums; small medical and environmental charities, including those with a focus on the built environment. The trust also supports up to six projects per year through the **Paper Conservation Fund** which, according to the website, 'aims to help accredited museums in Scotland, in particular small and medium-sized independent ones, to work with conservators to undertake projects that conserve their collections of works on paper. Projects can be treatment, surveys, training courses and skills development workshops.'
WHAT IS NOT FUNDED Individuals.
RANGE OF GRANTS Usually between £100 and £20,000.
SAMPLE GRANTS Scottish Opera (£6,500); The MacRobert Arts Centre (£5,000); British Red Cross (£3,500); Music as Therapy (£3,000); Argyll and Bute Museums and Heritage Forum (£2,500); Project Ability and The Samaritans (£2,000 each); Lothian Autistic Society, The Outward Bound Trust, Water of Leith Conservation Trust and WheelPower (£1,500 each); Logie Old Graveyard Group, The Scottish Seabird Centre and St John's Episcopal Church – Edinburgh (£1,000 each); Christians Against Poverty (£600); West Glasgow Carers Centre (£500 each).
FINANCES *Year* 2015/16 *Income* £105,084 *Grants* £144,500 *Grants to organisations* £144,500 *Assets* £3,881,722
TRUSTEES Margaret Moss; William Anderson; Sarah Moss; Susannah Rae; Alexander Moss; Alison Priestley.
OTHER INFORMATION In 2015/16 around 100 organisations were supported.
HOW TO APPLY Applications can be made online via the trust's website. Distributions are made on a quarterly basis. Application forms and guidance for the **Paper Conservation Fund** can be obtained from the correspondent by email; in the first instance, however, see the website for more information.
WHO TO APPLY TO Claire Armstrong, Gaidrew Farmhouse, Drymen, Glasgow G63 0DN *Email* enquiries@gfct.org.uk *Website* www.gfct.org.uk

■ The Hugh Fraser Foundation

SC NO SC009303 **ESTABLISHED** 1960
WHERE FUNDING CAN BE GIVEN UK, particularly Scotland.
WHO CAN BENEFIT Charitable organisations, principally hospitals, schools and universities, arts organisations and social welfare organisations.
WHAT IS FUNDED Disadvantaged people; disability; medical research facilities; education and training; older people; homelessness; hospices; musical, theatrical and visual arts; youth organisations; conservation and environment; religion; other charitable purposes.
WHAT IS NOT FUNDED Grants are only awarded to individuals in exceptional circumstances.
TYPE OF GRANT Capital and revenue grants for up to three years, sometimes longer. Start-up costs.
RANGE OF GRANTS Up to £90,000.
SAMPLE GRANTS Yorkhill Children's Foundation (£90,000); East Park and Highland Hospice (£50,000 each).
FINANCES *Year* 2015/16 *Income* £2,292,920 *Grants* £1,412,950 *Grants to organisations* £1,399,350 *Assets* £70,342,349
OTHER INFORMATION In 2015/16 the foundation made grants to 317 organisations. In addition, four grants were made to individuals, totalling £13,600. The 2015/16 annual report notes: 'The Trustees consider that grants to large, highly-publicised national appeals are not likely to be as effective a use of funds as grants to smaller, more focused charitable appeals.'
HOW TO APPLY Apply in writing to the correspondent. Applications should also include either a copy of your latest formal accounts if prepared or a copy of your most recent balance sheet, income and expenditure account or bank statement if formal accounts are not prepared. If you are not a registered charity you should also enclose a copy of your constitution or policy statement. The trustees meet quarterly to consider applications, usually in March, June, September and December. Applications should be received early in the preceding month in order to be considered.
WHO TO APPLY TO The Trustees of The Hugh Fraser Foundation, Turcan Connell, Princes Exchange, 1 Earl Grey Street, Edinburgh EH3 9EE *Tel.* 0131 228 8111

■ The Joseph Strong Frazer Trust

CC NO 235311 **ESTABLISHED** 1939
WHERE FUNDING CAN BE GIVEN Unrestricted; in practice, England and Wales.
WHO CAN BENEFIT Registered charities only.
WHAT IS FUNDED A wide range of charitable purposes, including: medical and other research; care organisations; children and young people; hospitals; deafness and blindness; maritime causes; disability, including learning disability; religious bodies; leisure activities; animals and wildlife; armed forces; schools and colleges; and older people.
WHAT IS NOT FUNDED Individuals.
TYPE OF GRANT One-off, capital and recurring costs.
RANGE OF GRANTS Generally up to £2,000.
SAMPLE GRANTS Fight for Sight (£4,000 in two grants); The Prostate Cancer Charity (£2,500); Addaction, Army Benevolent Fund, Barnet Bereavement Project, Blond McIndoe Research Centre, Children's Country Holidays Fund, Finchale Training College, Liverpool School of Tropical Medicine, North London Hospice, Prisoners' Education Trust, The Royal British

Legion, The National Brain Appeal, Welsh College of Music and Drama and Welsh National Opera (£2,000 each).

FINANCES *Year* 2014/15 *Income* £528,289 *Grants* £390,250 *Grants to organisations* £390,250 *Assets* £13,204,487

TRUSTEES David Cook; R. Read; William Waites; William Reardon Smith; Sir W. Antony Reardon Smith; Ugo Fagandini.

OTHER INFORMATION At the time of writing (May 2017) the 2014/15 accounts were the most recent available. In 2014/15 a total of 298 grants were made, of which 211 were of less than £2,000. Almost one quarter (69) of grants were given to support medical and other research.

HOW TO APPLY Apply in writing to the correspondent. The trustees meet twice a year, usually in March and September. Application forms are not necessary. It is helpful if applicants are concise in their appeal letters, which must include an sae if acknowledgement is required.

WHO TO APPLY TO The Trustees of The Joseph Strong Frazer Trust, c/o Joseph Miller and Co., Floor A, Milburn House, Dean Street, Newcastle upon Tyne NE1 1LE *Tel.* 0191 232 8065 *Email* jsf@joseph-miller.co.uk

■ The Louis and Valerie Freedman Charitable Settlement

CC NO 271067 **ESTABLISHED** 1976

WHERE FUNDING CAN BE GIVEN UK, with a particular focus on Burnham in Buckinghamshire.

WHO CAN BENEFIT Registered charities. There is a preference for those with a link to the Freedman family.

WHAT IS FUNDED Medical research, health and sickness; children and young people; education.

WHAT IS NOT FUNDED Individuals; non-registered charities.

RANGE OF GRANTS £10,000 to £70,000.

SAMPLE GRANTS Burnham Health Promotion Trust (£70,000); Sir John Bradfield Bursary Fund (£50,000); East Anglia's Children's Hospice (£10,000).

FINANCES *Year* 2015/16 *Income* £180,530 *Grants* £130,000 *Grants to organisations* £130,000 *Assets* £4,463,463

TRUSTEES Francis Hughes; Michael Ferrier.

OTHER INFORMATION In 2015/16 grants were made to three organisations. The charity makes an annual grant to the Burnham Health Promotion Trust, a charity set up by Louis Freedman to benefit the health of people in Burnham.

HOW TO APPLY Apply in writing to the correspondent. The trustees meet periodically.

WHO TO APPLY TO Francis Hughes, Trustee, c/o Bridge House, 11 Creek Road, East Molesey, Surrey KT8 9BE *Tel.* 020 8941 4455 *Email* francis@hughescollett.co.uk

■ The Michael and Clara Freeman Charitable Trust

CC NO 1125083 **ESTABLISHED** 2008

WHERE FUNDING CAN BE GIVEN UK and overseas.

WHO CAN BENEFIT Registered charities.

WHAT IS FUNDED General charitable purposes.

RANGE OF GRANTS Generally from £1,000 to £5,000.

SAMPLE GRANTS A list of beneficiaries was not available.

FINANCES *Year* 2015/16 *Income* £2,304 *Grants* £59,000 *Grants to organisations* £59,000

TRUSTEES Michael Freeman; Clara Freeman; Laura Freeman; Edward Freeman.

OTHER INFORMATION In 2015/16 the trust had a total expenditure of £61,000. Due to its low income, its latest accounts were not available to view on the Charity Commission's website. We have therefore estimated the grant total based on previous years' information.

HOW TO APPLY Apply in writing to the correspondent.

WHO TO APPLY TO Michael Freeman, Trustee, 9 Connaught Square, London W2 2HG

■ The Charles S. French Charitable Trust

CC NO 206476 **ESTABLISHED** 1959

WHERE FUNDING CAN BE GIVEN Essex and North East London.

WHO CAN BENEFIT Registered charities based in the area of benefit; charities located elsewhere that can demonstrate activities which benefit residents of Essex and North East London or the immediate surrounding areas may also be considered.

WHAT IS FUNDED General charitable purposes, including community services and facilities.

WHAT IS NOT FUNDED Only registered charities are supported.

RANGE OF GRANTS Up to £16,000, but mostly between £1,000 and £2,000.

SAMPLE GRANTS Loughton Youth Project (£16,000); St Clare Hospice Hastingwood (£5,000); J's Hospice and Royal National Children's Foundation (£3,000 each); Essex Youth Build, Hibiscus Caribbean Elderly Association, London Wheelchair Rugby Club and Tower Hamlets Friends and Neighbours (£2,000 each); Families in Focus Essex and Marie Curie (£1,500 each); Beckton Skills Centre and Waltham Forest Dyslexia Association (£1,000 each); Crossroads Counselling (£700); Colin Macmillan Boxing Training Academy (£500); Loughton Ladies Choir (£450); Loughton Voluntary Care Association (£250).

FINANCES *Year* 2015/16 *Income* £277,575 *Grants* £173,400 *Grants to organisations* £173,400 *Assets* £8,063,324

TRUSTEES William Noble, Chair; Martin Scarth; Joanna Thomas; Michael Foster; Christopher Noble; James Foster; Antonia McLeod.

OTHER INFORMATION In 2015/16, 117 charities were supported.

HOW TO APPLY Apply in writing to the correspondent, including a copy of your charity's latest accounts. The trustees meet four times a year and grants are made at their discretion.

WHO TO APPLY TO William Noble, Chair, 169 High Road, Loughton, Essex IG10 4LF *Tel.* 020 8502 3575 *Email* office@csfct.org.uk *Website* www.csfct.org.uk

■ The Anne French Memorial Trust

CC NO 254567 **ESTABLISHED** 1963

WHERE FUNDING CAN BE GIVEN Diocese of Norwich (Norfolk).

WHO CAN BENEFIT Christians, clergy and local charities.

WHAT IS FUNDED Any charitable purpose in the beneficial area, but especially church-related causes.

TYPE OF GRANT One-off; project.

SAMPLE GRANTS Norfolk Community Foundation (£5,000).

FINANCES *Year* 2015/16 *Income* £260,063 *Grants* £194,012 *Grants to organisations* £194,012 *Assets* £7,361,424

TRUSTEE Rt Revd The Lord Bishop of Norwich.

HOW TO APPLY The trust has previously stated that 'in no circumstances does the Bishop wish to encourage applications for grants'.

WHO TO APPLY TO Christopher Dicker, Hill House, The Hill, Ranworth, Norwich NR13 6AB *Tel.* 01603 270356 *Email* cdicker@hotmail.co.uk

■ The Freshfield Foundation

CC NO 1003316 **ESTABLISHED** 1991

WHERE FUNDING CAN BE GIVEN UK and overseas.

WHO CAN BENEFIT Registered charities.

WHAT IS FUNDED Sustainable development; health and general well-being; education; overseas disaster relief.

RANGE OF GRANTS From £20,000 to £500,000.

SAMPLE GRANTS Disasters Emergency Committee (£500,000); Sustrans (£100,000); Motor Neurone Disease Association and St Mungo's Community Housing Association Ltd (£20,000 each).

FINANCES *Year* 2015/16 *Income* £770,599 *Grants* £640,000 *Grants to organisations* £640,000 *Assets* £5,557,031

TRUSTEES Paul Kurthausen; Patrick Moores; Elizabeth Potter.

OTHER INFORMATION In 2015/16 grants were made to four organisations. During the year, the trustees made the decision to reduce the number of charities supported in future.

HOW TO APPLY The foundation's annual report for 2015/16 explains that: 'The process of grant-making starts with the trustees analysing an area of interest, consistent with the charity's aims and objectives, and then proactively looking for charities that they think can make the greatest contribution.'

WHO TO APPLY TO Paul Kurthausen, Trustee, BWMacfarlane LLP, Castle Chambers, 43 Castle Street, Liverpool L2 9SH *Tel.* 0151 236 1494 *Email* paul.k@bwm.co.uk

■ The Freshgate Trust Foundation

CC NO 221467 **ESTABLISHED** 1962

WHERE FUNDING CAN BE GIVEN Sheffield and South Yorkshire.

WHO CAN BENEFIT Registered charities; small local groups (i.e. sports clubs and volunteer-run community groups); holiday projects.

WHAT IS FUNDED Education (including travel and training); heritage, restoration and environment; music and the arts; recreation (including holidays and sport); welfare, health and social care.

WHAT IS NOT FUNDED Organisations which aren't registered charities (except small volunteer-run community groups); charities with large reserves; national charities (unless for a capital project based in South Yorkshire with clear evidence of local management and local control of finances); CICs and other not-for-profit businesses (unless they are also registered charities); general appeals; individuals; religious or political organisations; animal welfare; projects taking place before the date of the next funding meeting; applications primarily for salary costs; projects that do not have sufficient funding to ensure running for at least one year from the date of the grant being applied for; new projects which need to fund salary costs (unless all salary costs are secured for at least 18 months).

TYPE OF GRANT One-off grants.

RANGE OF GRANTS Typically between £100 and £2,000.

SAMPLE GRANTS Museums Sheffield (£13,000); St Wilfred's Drop In Day Centre and St Luke's Hospice (£10,000 each); Sheffield Family Holiday Fund and South Yorkshire and Hallamshire Clubs for Young People (£4,000 each); Sheffield Dial-A-Ride Club (£2,000); City of Sheffield Youth Orchestra (£1,300); Sheffield Wildlife Trust and University of Sheffield Bursary (£1,000 each); Pro Soccer Pumas JFC (£500); Dore and Totley Day Centre Luncheon Club (£150).

FINANCES *Year* 2015 *Income* £141,899 *Grants* £85,525 *Grants to organisations* £85,525 *Assets* £3,245,324

OTHER INFORMATION In 2015 a total of 56 grants were made. A list of beneficiaries was not included in the annual report and accounts.

HOW TO APPLY Applications can be made online via the foundation's website or by post. In the first instance, applicants should read the funding criteria available on the foundation's website. Trustee meetings are usually held in the first week of March, July and November; in order to be considered, applications should be submitted at least four weeks before each meeting. The trustees or secretary cannot enter into correspondence regarding grants decisions.

WHO TO APPLY TO Jonathan Robinson, Secretary, The Hart Shaw Building, Europa Link, Sheffield Business Park, Sheffield S9 1XU *Tel.* 0114 251 8850 *Website* www.freshgate.org.uk

■ The Raphael Freshwater Memorial Association

CC NO 313890 **ESTABLISHED** 1962

WHERE FUNDING CAN BE GIVEN UK and overseas.

WHO CAN BENEFIT Charitable organisations; Jewish organisations.

WHAT IS FUNDED Advancement of the Jewish faith and education; relief of poverty; general charitable purposes.

SAMPLE GRANTS A list of beneficiaries was not available.

FINANCES *Year* 2015/16 *Income* £8,372,000 *Grants* £1,314,000 *Grants to organisations* £1,314,000 *Assets* £108,819,000

TRUSTEES Benzion Freshwater; Richard Fischer; Solomon Freshwater; Mr D. Davis.

OTHER INFORMATION Grants in 2015/16 were broken down as follows: advancement of religion and education (£944,000); relief of poverty (£370,000). A list of beneficiaries was not included in the accounts.

HOW TO APPLY Apply in writing to the correspondent.

WHO TO APPLY TO Benzion Freshwater, Trustee, Freshwater Group of Companies, Freshwater House, 158–162 Shaftesbury Avenue, London WC2H 8HR *Tel.* 020 7836 1555

■ Friarsgate Trust

CC NO 220762 **ESTABLISHED** 1955

WHERE FUNDING CAN BE GIVEN UK, with a strong preference for West Sussex.

WHO CAN BENEFIT Registered charities and community groups, with priority given to local projects and those based in West Sussex.

WHAT IS FUNDED The education and welfare of children and young people; illness; disability; the welfare of older people.

WHAT IS NOT FUNDED Local organisations outside Sussex are unlikely to be supported.

RANGE OF GRANTS Up to £5,000 but generally £500 to £2,000.

SAMPLE GRANTS Lord's Taverners (£2,400); The Point (£2,000); Tall Ships Youth Trust (£1,200); Chichester Counselling, Children with Cancer Fund, Epilepsy Society, Family Support Work, Royal Air Force Benevolent Fund and St Wilfrid's Hospice (£1,000 each); Pallant House Gallery (£750); Independent Age (£500); Rotary Club Christmas Appeal (£300).

FINANCES *Year* 2015/16 *Income* £118,174 *Grants* £90,250 *Grants to organisations* £90,250 *Assets* £3,454,024

TRUSTEES Robert Newman; Sarah Bain; Gillian Livingstone; Diana Altman.

OTHER INFORMATION In 2015/16, 68 grants were made.

HOW TO APPLY Apply in writing to the correspondent. The trustees meet to consider applications quarterly. Our research suggests that applicants are welcome to telephone first to check they fit the trust's criteria.

WHO TO APPLY TO Olga Powell, Irwin Mitchell LLP, Thomas Edgar House, Friary Lane, Chichester, West Sussex PO19 1UF *Tel.* 01243 786111 *Email* friarsgate@irwinmitchell.com

■ Friends of Biala Ltd

CC NO 271377 **ESTABLISHED** 1964

WHERE FUNDING CAN BE GIVEN UK and Israel.

WHO CAN BENEFIT Mainly Jewish organisations.

WHAT IS FUNDED Orthodox Jewish religious education; the relief of poverty.

SAMPLE GRANTS Mosdos Biala Israel (£17,000); Cholmei Dalim (£15,000); Friends of Ber Avrohom Sionim (£13,000); Yetev Lev (£10,000).

FINANCES *Year* 2015/16 *Income* £197,265 *Grants* £0 *Grants to organisations* £0 *Assets* £1,909,425

TRUSTEES Yechezkel Halberstadt; Moshe Glausiusz; Michael de Jong.

OTHER INFORMATION In previous years, the charity has made grants totalling around £55,000. However, in 2015/16 the charity' made no grants and spent £72,500 on governance costs, including for legal and professional services. The annual report 2015/16 further notes that 'HMRC have been conducting an investigation into the taxation affairs of the charity and during the year the charity has reached a settlement in the sum of £460,000. This amount has been provided for in the accounts.'

HOW TO APPLY Apply in writing to the correspondent.

WHO TO APPLY TO The Trustees of Friends of Biala Ltd, Rosenthal and Co., 106 High West Street, Gateshead, Tyne and Wear NE8 1NA *Tel.* 0191 477 2814

■ Friends of Essex Churches Trust

CC NO 236033 **ESTABLISHED** 1951

WHERE FUNDING CAN BE GIVEN Essex (including Thurrock and Southend) and the boroughs of Barking and Dagenham, Havering, Newham, Redbridge and Waltham Forest.

WHO CAN BENEFIT Christian churches.

WHAT IS FUNDED The preservation, repair, maintenance and improvement of Christian places of worship in the area of benefit. The trust also supports the Diocese of Chelmsford's **Gutter Clearance Scheme**, through which small grants are made to allow churches to have their gutters cleared.

WHAT IS NOT FUNDED Electrical work (unless there is a written report by a qualified electrician stating that electrical installations are a fire hazard); general lighting; redecoration (unless needed as part of a scheme of eligible repairs); reseating; liturgical reordering; the introduction of other furnishings and fittings; routine maintenance (however, the trust does make grants to parishes as part of the Gutter Clearance Scheme). Grants are not normally made for work which has already started.

TYPE OF GRANT One-off grants to organisations. Building repairs only.

SAMPLE GRANTS A list of beneficiaries was not available.

FINANCES *Year* 2015 *Income* £148,813 *Grants* £159,000 *Grants to organisations* £159,000 *Assets* £471,742

TRUSTEES Dr James Bettley; Keith Gardner; Canon Harry Marsh; David Lodge; Dr Christopher Starr; Ralph Meloy; Martin Stuchfield; Catharine Hutley; Jill Cole; Sandra Markham; John Pickthorn; Jeremy Beale; R. Grainger.

OTHER INFORMATION A total of 24 grants were offered during the year. These included grants for maintenance totalling £114,000, and a further £45,000 given for improvements.

HOW TO APPLY Application forms can be requested by contacting the correspondent, who can also be contacted to check whether your proposal is eligible. Applications must be submitted by an officer of the church or otherwise accompanied by a letter of support from the incumbent. Further details, conditions and application requirements are outlined on the trust's website. To apply for a grant from the **Gutter Clearance Scheme**, contact the correspondent.

WHO TO APPLY TO John Bloomfield, Secretary of the Grants Committee, 39 Lake Rise, Romford RM1 4DZ *Tel.* 01708 745273 *Email* john.bloomfield@btinternet.com *Website* www.foect.org.uk

■ The Friends of Kent Churches

CC NO 207021 **ESTABLISHED** 1950

WHERE FUNDING CAN BE GIVEN Kent; Beckenham; Bromley; Sidcup; Bexley; Erith.

WHO CAN BENEFIT Churches.

WHAT IS FUNDED Churches undertaking repairs; church maintenance; churches of architectural merit; churches of historical importance.

WHAT IS NOT FUNDED Work that has already started; reordering, redecorating (except where required for other eligible work); major new facilities; bells; clocks; organs; churchyards and churchyard walls, except for monuments of particular importance.

TYPE OF GRANT Capital grants.

RANGE OF GRANTS £250 to £15,000.

SAMPLE GRANTS SS Peter and Paul-Upper Stoke (£30,000); St Werbrugh-Hoo (£25,000); St George-Wrotham (£20,000); St Bartholomew-Waltham (£5,000); Baptists-Hawkhurst (£3,000); St Nicholas-Strude (£1,5000); URC-Birchington (£500).

FINANCES *Year* 2015 *Income* £167,729 *Grants* £123,500 *Grants to organisations* £123,500 *Assets* £583,163

TRUSTEES Charles Banks; Paul Smallwood; Angela Parish; Leslie Smith; Norman Penny; Richard Latham; Jane Boucher; Mary Gibbins; Jane Bird; Margaret Williams; Lucilla Neame.

OTHER INFORMATION During 2015, 18 grants were awarded.
HOW TO APPLY The application form can be found on the website along with full guidelines. The application form must be sent to the secretary. Applications can also be made for the National Churches Trust Partnership grants, which are available for structural repair projects with a total cost of up to £100,000. Forms and guidance notes can be downloaded from the trust's website. Grants are also distributed on behalf of WREN (Waste Recycling Environmental Ltd) for the maintenance, repair and restoration of places of religious worship. More information can be found on the trust's website.
WHO TO APPLY TO Jane Bird, Trustee, Parsonage Farm House, Hampstead Lane, Yalding, Maidstone ME18 6HG *Tel.* 01622 815569 *Email* janebird01@gmail.com *Website* www.friendsofkentchurches.co.uk

■ Friends of Wiznitz Ltd

CC NO 255685 **ESTABLISHED** 1948
WHERE FUNDING CAN BE GIVEN UK and overseas.
WHO CAN BENEFIT Jewish organisations; individuals.
WHAT IS FUNDED Orthodox Jewish religious education; the advancement of the Orthodox Jewish religion; the relief of poverty; medical causes.
RANGE OF GRANTS Up to £658,000.
SAMPLE GRANTS Igud Mosdos Wiznitz (£658,000); Mosdos Viznitz (£378,000); Lehachzikom Velehachiyosom (£287,000); Congregation Tzemach Tzadik (£265,500); Zidkat Zadik (£160,000); CMZ (£100,000); Mosdos Imrey Chaim (£88,500).
FINANCES *Year* 2015/16 *Income* £2,749,964 *Grants* £2,658,340 *Grants to organisations* £2,596,590 *Assets* £2,203,135
TRUSTEES Heinrich Feldman; Shulom Feldman; Ephraim Gottesfeld; Judah Feldman.
OTHER INFORMATION Grants to individuals for the relief of poverty totalled £62,000.
HOW TO APPLY The 2015/16 annual report advises that: 'In general the trustees select the institutions to be supported according to their personal knowledge of work of the institution. While not actively inviting applications, they are always prepared to accept any application which will be carefully considered and help given according to circumstances and funds then available. Applications by individuals must be accompanied by a letter of recommendation by the applicant's minister or other known religious leader.'
WHO TO APPLY TO Ephraim Gottesfeld, Trustee, 8 Jessam Avenue, London E5 9DU

■ Friends Provident Charitable Foundation

CC NO 1087053 **ESTABLISHED** 2002
WHERE FUNDING CAN BE GIVEN UK.
WHO CAN BENEFIT Registered charities; social enterprise; organisations; community groups.
WHAT IS FUNDED Projects that contribute to a more resilient, sustainable and fairer economic system.
WHAT IS NOT FUNDED Individual or sole trader applicants; organisations applying on behalf of another; work outside the UK, unless there is a clear link to activity or benefit to people or institutions in the UK; work that is to benefit a narrow group of beneficiaries or which cannot be shared; activities to promote a specific political party; activity that has already happened; general appeals.
TYPE OF GRANT Capital funding; core costs; revenue funding; project costs.
RANGE OF GRANTS £5,000 to £170,000.
SAMPLE GRANTS Centre for Sustainable Energy (£154,000); New Economy Organisers Network (£131,500); Fairshare Educational Foundation-Share Action (£100,000); Open Trust (£60,000); The City University London (£47,500); Resilient Economies (£20,000); Transition Town Totnes and Totnes Caring (£15,000).
FINANCES *Year* 2016 *Income* £913,357 *Grants* £1,708,240 *Grants to organisations* £1,708,240 *Assets* £32,828,920
TRUSTEES Jennifer Barraclough; Joycelin Dawes; Paul Dickinson; Joanne Elson; Jim Gilbourne; Patrick Hynes; Kathleen Kelly; Rob Lake; Stephen Muers; Heten Shah; Aphra Sklair; Raj Thamotharam; Whitni Thomas.
HOW TO APPLY Applicants are directed, where possible, to the foundation's website where details of current funding programmes, criteria, guidelines and application process are posted. The foundation asks to be contacted if there is any difficulty filling out the application form. Contact details can be found on the website.
WHO TO APPLY TO Andrew Thompson, Grants Manager, Tower House, Fishergate, York YO10 4UA *Tel.* 01904 629675 *Email* foundation.enquiries@friendsprovidentfoundation.org.uk *Website* www.friendsprovidentfoundation.org

■ The Frognal Trust

CC NO 244444 **ESTABLISHED** 1964
WHERE FUNDING CAN BE GIVEN UK.
WHO CAN BENEFIT Registered charities.
WHAT IS FUNDED Older people; children; disability; blindness; medical research; environmental heritage.
WHAT IS NOT FUNDED Animal charities; the advancement of religion; charities for the benefit of people outside the UK; educational or research trips; branches of national charities; general appeals; individuals.
RANGE OF GRANTS Usually from £200 to £3,500.
SAMPLE GRANTS Action Medical Research; Aireborough Voluntary Services to the Elderly; Canniesburn Research Trust; Elderly Accommodation Counsel; Friends of the Elderly; Gloucestershire Disabled Afloat Riverboat Trust; Leeds Society for Deaf and Blind People; National Rheumatoid Arthritis Society; Royal Liverpool and Broad Green University Hospitals; Samantha Dickson Research Trust; Stubbers Adventure Centre; Wireless for the Bedridden Society; Yorkshire Dales Millennium Project.
FINANCES *Year* 2015/16 *Income* £84,548 *Grants* £48,500 *Grants to organisations* £48,500 *Assets* £2,500,153
TRUSTEES Peter Fraser; Jennifer Fraser; Caroline Philipson-Stow; Matthew Bennett.
HOW TO APPLY Apply in writing to the correspondent. Applications should be received by February, May, August and November, for consideration at the trustees' meeting the following month.
WHO TO APPLY TO Sue Hickley, Wilson Solicitors LLP, Alexandra House, St John's Street, Salisbury SP1 2SB *Tel.* 01722 427536 *Email* sue.hickley@wilsonslaw.com

The Adrian and Jane Frost Charitable Trust

CC NO 1160012 **ESTABLISHED** 2014
WHERE FUNDING CAN BE GIVEN Worldwide.
WHO CAN BENEFIT Registered charities.
WHAT IS FUNDED General charitable purposes, with a primary focus on: the prevention or relief of poverty; education; health; and arts, culture, heritage and science. There is a secondary focus on: citizenship and community development; amateur sport; environmental protection or improvement; and the relief of people in need.
RANGE OF GRANTS £20,000 to £170,000.
SAMPLE GRANTS Newnham College (£170,000); The Egmont Trust (£125,000); Addenbrooke's Charitable Trust (£75,000); Camfed International (£60,000 in two grants); London Handel Society Ltd (£50,000); Build Africa and Mary's Meals (£40,000); Access Sport and Riding for the Disabled Association (£30,000 each); Jimmy's Cambridge (£20,000).
FINANCES *Year* 2015/16 *Income* £9,279,942 *Grants* £645,000 *Grants to organisations* £645,000 *Assets* £8,319,349
TRUSTEES Brodies and Co. (Trustees) Ltd; Adrian Frost; Dr Margaret MacDougall.
OTHER INFORMATION In 2015/16 a total of 11 grants were made to ten organisations. Of the grant total, £615,000 was given to support the trust's primary charitable objectives and £30,000 to support its secondary charitable objectives.
HOW TO APPLY The annual report for 2015/16 provides the following information: 'The charity trustees consider applications every two months and will also meet at least annually to discuss and review applications to the trust. The trustees will use their own knowledge of the applicants in question, in addition to considering each application on its own merits, as to whether the funding/grant sought will further and advance the trust's charitable purposes and in turn provide public benefit. If necessary the trustees will seek additional information from the applicants, such as details of specific project funding or annual accounts/ financial statements. Initially the charity trustees do not envisage utilising a formal application form. However, applications will be reviewed on an ad hoc basis by the trustees or the charity's administrators, who will identify suitable appeals to further assist the trustees in their consideration of applications. As the administration of the trust develops, the trustees will review the need for a formal application form. When considering which potential recipients to support, the charitable purpose being advanced will preferably be one of the primary charitable purpose descriptions, and, if not, it will be one of the secondary charitable purpose descriptions. It is anticipated that when considered in aggregate on an annual basis the majority of the donations made by the trust will have advanced one or more of the primary charitable purpose descriptions.'
WHO TO APPLY TO Helen Nelson, Brodies LLP, Brodies House, 31–33 Union Grove, Aberdeen AB10 6SD *Tel.* 01224 392242 *Email* Helen.Nelson@brodies.com

The Patrick and Helena Frost Foundation

CC NO 1005505 **ESTABLISHED** 1991
WHERE FUNDING CAN BE GIVEN UK.
WHO CAN BENEFIT Registered charities.
WHAT IS FUNDED General charitable purposes, including 'the relief and welfare of people of small means and the less fortunate members of society, and assistance for small organisations where a considerable amount of self-help and voluntary effort is required'.
WHAT IS NOT FUNDED Individuals.
TYPE OF GRANT One-off.
RANGE OF GRANTS £2,500 to £25,000.
SAMPLE GRANTS Catholic Agency for Overseas Development (£25,000); Catholic Agency for Overseas Development – Nepal Earthquake Appeal and Ocean Youth Trust South (£20,000 each); Bowel and Cancer Research, Kings World Trust for Children, Prostate Cancer UK and The Yard Theatre Ltd (£15,000 each); Read Easy UK (£12,000); Action on Addiction, The Cleft Lip and Palate Association and Demand Design and Manufacture for Disability (£10,000 each); The Gurkha Welfare Trust and London Narrow Boat Project (£7,500 each); Macmillan Cancer Support and The Martlets Hospice (£5,000 each); The Fforest Uchaf Horse and Pony Rehabilitation Centre (£3,750); The Outward Bound Trust (£2,500).
FINANCES *Year* 2015/16 *Income* £733,512 *Grants* £552,250 *Grants to organisations* £552,250 *Assets* £23,066,092
TRUSTEES Luke Valner; Dominic Tayler; Neil Hendriksen.
HOW TO APPLY The trustees are proactive in their grant-making and kindly request that unsolicited applications are not submitted.
WHO TO APPLY TO Neil Hendriksen, Trustee, The Patrick and Helena Frost Foundation, c/o Trowers and Hamlins LLP, 3 Bunhill Row, London EC1Y 8YZ

Mejer and Gertrude Miriam Frydman Foundation

CC NO 262806 **ESTABLISHED** 1971
WHERE FUNDING CAN BE GIVEN UK and overseas.
WHO CAN BENEFIT Charitable organisations.
WHAT IS FUNDED General charitable purposes; Jewish causes; education.
WHAT IS NOT FUNDED Individuals.
SAMPLE GRANTS Jewish Care and Norwood Ravenswood (£3,800 each); Friends of Yeshiva OHR Elchanan and UK Toremet (£3,000 each); Chai Cancer Care (£2,500); Kesser Torah (£2,100); North West London Jewish Day School (£2,000); Ben Uri Gallery and Jewish Learning Exchange (£1,800 each); Yeshivat Meharash Engel Radomishl (£1,200); Institute for Higher Rabbinicial Studies (£900); Pe'ylim Yad Leachim and Talia Trust for Children (£500 each).
FINANCES *Year* 2015/16 *Income* £43,146 *Grants* £39,550 *Grants to organisations* £39,550 *Assets* £85,374
TRUSTEES Keith Graham; David Frydman; Gerald Frydman; Louis Frydman.
OTHER INFORMATION A list of recent beneficiaries was not provided in the 2015/16 accounts.
HOW TO APPLY Apply in writing to the correspondent.
WHO TO APPLY TO David Frydman, Trustee, Westbury, Crusader House, 145–157 St John Street, London EC1V 4PY *Tel.* 020 7253 7272 *Email* keithg@westbury.co.uk

■ The Fulmer Charitable Trust

CC NO 1070428 **ESTABLISHED** 1998

WHERE FUNDING CAN BE GIVEN Worldwide, especially financially developing countries and Wiltshire.

WHO CAN BENEFIT Registered charities.

WHAT IS FUNDED The relief of suffering and hardship; education; religion; general charitable purposes.

WHAT IS NOT FUNDED Gap year requests.

RANGE OF GRANTS £250 to £10,000.

SAMPLE GRANTS Calstone Parochial Church Council (£10,000); NSPCC and Save the Children (£5,000 each); Christ Church Brownsover (£3,000); Baynards Zambia Trust (£2,200); Christian Solidarity Worldwide (£2,000); King's College Hospital and Prison Fellowship (£1,500 each); Amnesty International, Hospices of Hope (£1,000 each); Cheshire Autism Practical Support (£750); Acid Survivors Trust International, Evangelical Alliance, Great Western NHS Foundation Trust Charity and Magdalen Environmental Trust (£500 each); Cornwall Blind Association and Pathways through Dementia (£250 each).

FINANCES *Year* 2015/16 *Income* £399,603 *Grants* £401,279 *Grants to organisations* £401,279 *Assets* £12,546,661

TRUSTEES Caroline Mytum; John Reis; Sally Reis; Revd Philip Bromiley.

OTHER INFORMATION More than 300 grants were made in 2015/16.

HOW TO APPLY Apply in writing to the correspondent. Very few unsolicited applications are accepted.

WHO TO APPLY TO John Reis, Trustee, Estate Office, Street Farm, Compton Bassett, Calne, Wiltshire SN11 8RH *Tel.* 01249 760410

■ The G. D. Charitable Trust

CC NO 1096101 **ESTABLISHED** 2002

WHERE FUNDING CAN BE GIVEN Worldwide.

WHO CAN BENEFIT Registered charities.

WHAT IS FUNDED Animal welfare; environment; equal opportunities for people with disabilities; homelessness.

WHAT IS NOT FUNDED Individuals.

RANGE OF GRANTS From £500 to £25,000.

SAMPLE GRANTS Malden Trust (£30,000 in two grants); Blue Marine Foundation (£17,000); Flora and Fauna International (£12,900); British Film Institute Appeal and Save the Children (£8,000 each); Child Bereavement UK (£5,000); South London Gallery (£3,500); Great Ormond Street Hospital Children's Charity (£2,000); Wings for Life (£1,200); Farms not Factories (£750); Wiston Estate (£500).

FINANCES *Year* 2015 *Income* £98,488 *Grants* £89,827 *Grants to organisations* £89,827 *Assets* £3,749,330

TRUSTEES George Duffield; Alexander Fitzgibbons; Natasha Duffield.

OTHER INFORMATION A total of 12 grants were made during the year. The trust makes an annual donation to Blue Marine Foundation, where George Duffield is also a trustee.

HOW TO APPLY Apply in writing to the correspondent.

WHO TO APPLY TO Jonathan Brinsden, Bircham Dyson Bell, 50 Broadway, London SW1H 0BL *Tel.* 020 7227 7000

■ G. M. C. Trust

CC NO 288418 **ESTABLISHED** 1965

WHERE FUNDING CAN BE GIVEN UK, predominantly in the West Midlands.

WHO CAN BENEFIT Charitable organisations.

WHAT IS FUNDED General charitable purposes, including mental health.

WHAT IS NOT FUNDED Individuals; local or regional appeals outside the West Midlands.

TYPE OF GRANT One-off and recurrent.

RANGE OF GRANTS Between £100 and £20,000.

SAMPLE GRANTS Hand In Hand International and ECHO – Extra Choices in Herefordshire (£20,000 each); Beat, National Trust and Rowheath Pavilion (£10,000 each); UN Women UK (£6,000); CALM – The Campaign Against Living Miserably and PAPYRUS – Prevention of Young Suicide and Tyseley Locomotive Works (£5,000 each); Breadline Africa (£4,000); Royal Birmingham Society of Artists (£3,000); British Hedgehog Preservation Society (£3,000); Arden Academy Trust (£600); Birmingham Cathedral Flower Fund (£100).

FINANCES *Year* 2015/16 *Income* £150,273 *Grants* £169,700 *Grants to organisations* £169,700 *Assets* £3,798,275

TRUSTEES Bes Cadbury; M. Cadbury; C. Fowler-Wright.

OTHER INFORMATION Grants were made to 27 organisations during the year.

HOW TO APPLY The trust largely supports projects which come to the attention of its trustees through their special interests and knowledge. General applications for grants are not encouraged.

WHO TO APPLY TO Rodney Pitts, Secretary, Flat 4 Fairways, 1240 Warwick Road, Knowle, Solihull B93 9LL *Tel.* 01564 779971 *Email* spam@rodneypitts.com *Website* www.rodneypitts.com/pages/gmc_trust.html

■ The G. R. P. Charitable Trust

CC NO 255733 **ESTABLISHED** 1968

WHERE FUNDING CAN BE GIVEN UK and Israel.

WHO CAN BENEFIT Charitable organisations already known to the trust.

WHAT IS FUNDED General charitable purposes; Jewish causes.

WHAT IS NOT FUNDED Individuals.

RANGE OF GRANTS From £200 to £30,000.

SAMPLE GRANTS Henry Jackson Society (£30,000); ORK UK, Technion UK and Weizmann Institute Foundation (£20,000 each); Friends of Hebrew University of Jerusalem (£15,000); Eton College and Social Affairs UN (£10,000 each); Institute for Policy Research (£6,000); Anglo Israel Association and The Royal British Legion (£5,000 each); Community Security Trust (£3,000); Norwood Ravenswood Child Care (£2,000); British Library, Israel Philharmonic Orchestra and Simon Marks Jewish Primary School Trust (£1,000 each); Chickenshed Theatre Company and Personal Support Unit (£500 each); Spotlight Appeal (£200).

FINANCES *Year* 2015/16 *Income* £247,713 *Grants* £183,500 *Grants to organisations* £183,500 *Assets* £4,669,738

TRUSTEE Kleinwort Benson Trustees Ltd.

OTHER INFORMATION The 'G. R. P.' in the trust's name refers to George Richard Pinto, a London banker who established the trust.

HOW TO APPLY Unsolicited applications are not considered.

WHO TO APPLY TO The Administrator, SG Kleinwort Hambros Trust Company (UK) Ltd, 8 St James's Square, London WS1Y 4JU *Tel.* 020 3207 7091

■ The Galanthus Trust

CC NO 1103538 **ESTABLISHED** 2004

WHERE FUNDING CAN BE GIVEN UK, with a strong focus on the South West, and overseas.

WHO CAN BENEFIT Charitable organisations.

WHAT IS FUNDED General charitable purposes.

SAMPLE GRANTS A list of beneficiaries was not available.

FINANCES *Year* 2015/16 *Income* £2,006 *Grants* £80,000 *Grants to organisations* £80,000

TRUSTEES Simon Rogers; Juliet Rogers.

OTHER INFORMATION Due to its low income, the trust's latest accounts were not available to view on the Charity Commission's website. We have therefore estimated the grant total.

HOW TO APPLY Apply in writing to the correspondent. All requests for grants are considered carefully by the trustees, who decide whether to donate and the amount to donate.

WHO TO APPLY TO Juliet Rogers, Trustee, Pile Oak Lodge, Donhead St Andrew, Shaftesbury, Dorset SP7 9EH *Tel.* 07478 29138 *Email* galanthustrust@yahoo.co.uk

■ The Gale Family Charity Trust

CC NO 289212 **ESTABLISHED** 1984

WHERE FUNDING CAN BE GIVEN UK, with a particular focus on Bedfordshire.

WHO CAN BENEFIT Registered charities and organisations active in Bedfordshire; national charities and organisations; churches and church ministries, specifically those of the Baptist faith.

WHAT IS FUNDED General charitable purposes; education; religion.

WHAT IS NOT FUNDED Grants are rarely given to individuals.

RANGE OF GRANTS Usually up to £20,000.

SAMPLE GRANTS Bedford Day Care Hospice (£20,000); Bunyan Meeting Free Church (£17,000); St John's Hospice – Moggerhanger (£10,000); St Paul's Church – Bedford (£7,000); Bedford Garden Carers (£5,000); ABF The Soldiers' Charity and Cople Lower School (£2,000 each); Happy Days and Relate – Bedford (£1,000 each); Pavenham Cricket Club (£500).

FINANCES *Year* 2015/16 *Income* £94,112 *Grants* £247,730 *Grants to organisations* £247,730 *Assets* £5,660,201

TRUSTEES Anthony Ormerod; John Tyley; Doreen Watson; Warwick Browning; Russell Beard; David Fletcher; Gerry Garner; Alison Phillipson.

HOW TO APPLY Apply in writing to the correspondent. The trustees meet in April and September and applications need to be received by March and August, respectively.

WHO TO APPLY TO Alistair Law, Administrator, Northwood House, 138 Bromham Road, Bedford MK40 2QW *Tel.* 01234 354508 *Email* alistair.law@garnerassociates.co.uk

■ The Gannochy Trust

SC NO SC003133 **ESTABLISHED** 1937

WHERE FUNDING CAN BE GIVEN Scotland with a preference for Tayside, specifically Perth and Kinross.

WHO CAN BENEFIT OSCR-registered charities, especially smaller, community-led groups supporting children, young people, and people who are disadvantaged or vulnerable.

WHAT IS FUNDED The trust has two priority themes for 2015–2018: Inspiring young people (Scotland-wide); and Improving the quality of life for people in Perth and Kinross (Perth and Kinross only). For full information, see the detailed 'Funding Strategy and Guidelines 2015 to 2018' document available from the trust's website.

WHAT IS NOT FUNDED General appeals; endowment funds; statutory bodies; work benefitting people outside Scotland; work that has already taken place; individuals (and organisations applying on their behalf); organisations with more than 12 months' operating costs within their free or designated reserves; grant-making charities (unless the project has been initiated by the trust); hospitals and health authorities; medical care, medical research or general medical equipment; palliative care (except within Perth and Kinross which should be about enhancing and not providing core care); universities, colleges, schools, student bodies, student unions and the independent education sector (unless the project has been initiated by the trust); academic research; pre-school groups, play schemes, after-school clubs and PTAs; individual students or support organisations for personal study, travel or for expeditions, whether in the UK or abroad; animal welfare; the promotion of religion; projects that are solely for the restoration or conservation of places of worship; general holidays; waste disposal/landfill, pollution control and renewable energy products; political or lobbying purposes; one-off events/festivals/conferences which have no element of broader community engagement; feasibility studies (unless the project has been initiated by the trust); minibuses.

TYPE OF GRANT Revenue and capital costs. Mostly up to one year, although applications for up to three years can be made.

RANGE OF GRANTS £1,500 to £400,000, but mostly of less than £40,000.

SAMPLE GRANTS Live Active Leisure (£382,500); St Fillans Community Trust (£65,000); St Madoes and Kinfauns Parish Church (£60,000); Perth and Kinross Countryside Trust (£45,000); Braidhaugh Pavilion Trust, Fet-Lor Youth Club Endowment Trust and Perth Methodist Church (£40,000 each).

FINANCES *Year* 2015/16 *Income* £6,592,272 *Grants* £3,315,026 *Grants to organisations* £3,315,026 *Assets* £168,192,434

TRUSTEES Dr James Kynaston; Ian Macmillan; Dr John Markland; Jane Mudd; David Gray; Stephen Hay; Bruce Renfrew.

OTHER INFORMATION It is unlikely that the trust will fully fund organisations, projects or activities and expects details of potential match funding to be provided. In 2015/16 the trust received 191 funding applications, of which 155 were successful.

HOW TO APPLY There are a number of documents that applicants must complete, including an application form. These are available to download from the website, where detailed guidance notes can also be found.

WHO TO APPLY TO Fiona Russell, Secretary/Assessor, Kincarrathie House Drive, Pitcullen Crescent, Perth PH2 7HX *Tel.* 01738 620653 *Fax* 01738 440827 *Email* admin@gannochytrust.org.uk *Website* www.gannochytrust.org.uk

■ The Ganzoni Charitable Trust

CC NO 263583 **ESTABLISHED** 1971

WHERE FUNDING CAN BE GIVEN Suffolk.

WHO CAN BENEFIT Registered charities; churches; hospices; schools.

WHAT IS FUNDED General charitable purposes, including Christian causes, health and education.

WHAT IS NOT FUNDED Individuals; applications from outside Suffolk are not normally considered and will not be acknowledged.

TYPE OF GRANT Mainly capital projects (rather than ongoing running costs).

RANGE OF GRANTS Up to £7,000.

SAMPLE GRANTS Macmillan Cancer Support (£7,000); Diocesan Board of Finance (£6,000); Aldeburgh Music (£5,000); Sane and St Lawrence's Church – Lackford (£2,000 each); Bildeston Baptist Church, Bridge School, East Suffolk Association for the Blind, Home-Start East Ipswich and Coastal, Mid Suffolk Citizens Advice, New Wolsey Theatre, Prostate Cancer UK and Suffolk Building Preservation Trust (£1,000 each); Colostomy Association, Hargrave Parish Council play area, Historic Chapels Trust, Rethink Mental Illness and Suffolk Owl Sanctuary (£500 each); St Luke's Hospital for the Clergy (£50); Friends of the Clergy (£20).

FINANCES *Year* 2015/16 *Income* £205,037 *Grants* £138,895 *Grants to organisations* £138,895 *Assets* £3,971,619

TRUSTEES The Hon. Mary Jill Ganzoni; The Hon. Charles Boscawen; Nicholas Ridley; John Pickering.
OTHER INFORMATION In 2015/16 grants were made to 110 organisations.
HOW TO APPLY Apply in writing to the correspondent. Telephone calls are not encouraged. There are no application forms, guidelines or deadlines. No sae is required unless material is to be returned.
WHO TO APPLY TO The Hon. Charles Boscawen, Trustee, c/o Birketts LLP, 24–26 Museum Street, Ipswich IP1 1HZ *Tel.* 01473 232300 *Email* bill-white@birketts.co.uk

■ Gardeners of London

CC NO 222079 **ESTABLISHED** 1962
WHERE FUNDING CAN BE GIVEN Mainly City of London.
WHO CAN BENEFIT Registered charities with a link to horticulture and gardening.
WHAT IS FUNDED Garden projects; horticulture.
RANGE OF GRANTS £300 to 7,000.
SAMPLE GRANTS City and Guilds of London Institution (£6,800); London in Bloom (£4,000); Metropolitan Public Gardens Association, Professional Gardeners (£3,000 each); Kelmarsh Hall Trust, Lord Mayors Appeal (£2,000 each); Foundation and Friends of the Royal, Garden Museum, Harrington Scheme (£1,000 each); Cultivate London, Farms for City Children and Norfolk Hospice (£500 each).
FINANCES *Year* 2015/16 *Income* £108,829 *Grants* £64,750 *Grants to organisations* £64,750 *Assets* £696,278
TRUSTEES Norman Chalmers; Dr Stephen Dowbiggin; Rod Petty; Brian Porter; Louise Robinson; Roger Hedgecoe; Nicholas Evans; Stephen Bernhard; Bernard Williams; John Rochford.
OTHER INFORMATION There were 50 grants awarded during 2015/16.
HOW TO APPLY Apply in writing to the correspondent.
WHO TO APPLY TO Trevor Faris, Trustee, 25 Luke Street, London EC2A 4AR *Tel.* 020 7149 6404 *Email* paclerk@gardenerscompany.org.uk *Website* www.gardenerscompany.org.uk

■ The Garrard Family Foundation

CC NO 1089152 **ESTABLISHED** 2001
WHERE FUNDING CAN BE GIVEN Worldwide.
WHO CAN BENEFIT Charitable organisations.
WHAT IS FUNDED The advancement and promotion of education; general charitable purposes.
TYPE OF GRANT Mainly one-off.
RANGE OF GRANTS From £100 to £39,500.
SAMPLE GRANTS Interdisciplinary Center – Herzlia (£39,500); Bexley Business Academy (£37,500); University College London and Volunteering Matters (£25,000 each); Russell Educational Trust (£21,500); Burn Camp and Community Security Trust (£10,000 each); City of London Police (£1,800); Rotary Club of London (£100).
FINANCES *Year* 2015/16 *Income* £236,572 *Grants* £170,551 *Grants to organisations* £170,551 *Assets* £458,599
TRUSTEES Sir David Garrard; Susan Glover; Timothy Garnham.
OTHER INFORMATION The annual report 2015/16 states that the trustees 'have applied a significant proportion of their grants towards the provision and administration of educational facilities in the form of Bexley Business Academy in Thamesmead, Kent.' Nine grants were made during the year.
HOW TO APPLY Apply in writing to the correspondent.
WHO TO APPLY TO Michael Harris, 25 Harley Street, London W1G 9BR *Tel.* 020 7299 1400

■ Garrick Charitable Trust

CC NO 1071279 **ESTABLISHED** 1998
WHERE FUNDING CAN BE GIVEN UK.
WHO CAN BENEFIT Registered charities only.
WHAT IS FUNDED Professional organisations involved in theatre, music, dance or literature.
WHAT IS NOT FUNDED Drama training or academic studies; amateur productions; projects outside the UK.
RANGE OF GRANTS Usually between £2,500 and £5,000.
SAMPLE GRANTS Theatre Investment Fund Ltd (£5,000); Birmingham Opera Company and National Centre for Circus Acts (£4,000 each); British Library, Brunel Museum, Ledbury Poetry Festival, Leeds Lieder, Scary Little Girls and Wigmore Hall Trust (£2,500 each); National Youth Jazz Collective (£2,100); New Wolsey Theatre (£1,000).
FINANCES *Year* 2015 *Income* £67,581 *Grants* £157,850 *Grants to organisations* £157,850 *Assets* £5,747,051
TRUSTEES David Sigall; Sir Stephen Waley-Cohen; John Coldstream; Roger Braban; Stephen Aris.
OTHER INFORMATION The website explains that the trustees 'prefer to support proposals which: help professionals to develop their careers; are not capital appeals; allow our modest contribution to make a real difference.'
HOW TO APPLY The trust's website gives information regarding its two-stage application process: **Step 1 – Letter requesting support**: 'First, write a short letter, preferably one but no more than two pages, perhaps with a publicity flyer. Submit your letter by email with a hard copy sent to the address below. In your letter tell us: about your organisation, including its registered charity status, and the project you want us to support; how much money you are asking for; how your organisation will benefit from a grant and what will happen if you do not receive a grant. This request will be considered at the first available Trustees' Meeting.' **Step 2 – Application form**: 'Occasionally we are able to make an immediate grant but normally we will then send you an Application Form, asking for more detailed information about your request and your organisation, which will then be considered at the next Trustees' Meeting. The Application Form also asks you for your most recent accounts and income, including earnings and support in kind. You may wish to include CVs of the people involved in the project, reviews of previous productions or publicity flyers.' There is no deadline for applications, but trustees' meetings take place on a quarterly basis in March, June, September and December. Applicants are advised to submit their applications in good time before a meeting.
WHO TO APPLY TO Sarah Charles, Administrator, Garrick Club, 15 Garrick Street, London WC2E 9AY *Tel.* 020 7395 4136 *Email* charitabletrust@garrickclub.co.uk *Website* www.garrickclub.co.uk/charitable_trust

■ The Gatsby Charitable Foundation

CC NO 251988 **ESTABLISHED** 1967

WHERE FUNDING CAN BE GIVEN Not defined; in practice, UK and East Africa.

WHO CAN BENEFIT Registered charities only. Many beneficiary organisations are specialist research institutes.

WHAT IS FUNDED Plant science; neuroscience; science and engineering education; Africa; the arts; public policy. Detailed information about each of these areas is available from the website.

WHAT IS NOT FUNDED Generally, the trustees do not make grants in response to unsolicited applications or to individuals.

TYPE OF GRANT One-off and recurring grants.

RANGE OF GRANTS Up to £11.45 million.

SAMPLE GRANTS Sainsbury Wellcome Centre for Neural Circuits and Behaviour (£11.45 million); University of Cambridge – The Sainsbury Laboratory (£8.94 million); Two Blades Foundation (£1.88 million); Sainsbury Centre of Visual Arts (£910,000); Centre for Mental Health (£379,000); Aquifer Ltd (£200,000); STEMNET (£197,000); Columbia University (£133,000); Royal College of Psychiatrists (£110,000); Gatsby Microfinance (£76,500); Engineering UK (£50,000).

FINANCES *Year* 2015/16 *Income* £56,733,000 *Grants* £41,496,000 *Grants to organisations* £41,496,000 *Assets* £345,587,000

TRUSTEES Joseph Burns; Sir Andrew Cahn; Judith Portrait.

OTHER INFORMATION The trust is one of the Sainsbury Family Charitable Trusts which share a common administration.

HOW TO APPLY The trustees take a proactive approach to grant-making; unsolicited applications are not considered. The annual report for 2015/16 explains that 'rather than awaiting proposals from third parties, Gatsby identifies areas for action and builds hypotheses for action which can then be tested in the field. Where successful these can then be scaled up and rolled-out.'

WHO TO APPLY TO Alan Bookbinder, Head of the Sainsbury Family Charitable Trusts, The Peak, 5 Wilton Road, London SW1V 1AP *Tel.* 020 7410 0330 *Email* contact@gatsby.org.uk *Website* www.gatsby.org.uk

■ Gatwick Airport Community Trust

CC NO 1089683 **ESTABLISHED** 2001

WHERE FUNDING CAN BE GIVEN Parts of East and West Sussex, Surrey and Kent but particularly communities directly affected by operations at Gatwick Airport. A map of the area of benefit can be seen on the website.

WHO CAN BENEFIT Organisations; charitable purposes.

WHAT IS FUNDED The development of young people; the arts; sporting facilities; environmental improvement; conservation; improvements to community facilities; volunteering, older people; people with disabilities.

WHAT IS NOT FUNDED Projects or beneficiaries that are completely or largely outside the area of benefit (less attention is given to applications from areas not directly affected by the airport); recurrent expenditure or running costs, ongoing maintenance or deficits; salaries or training costs, except start-up costs in relation to an additional amenity or service being established that will be self-sustaining thereafter; costs that should be funded from other sources, e.g. public bodies; applications from organisations that have statutory responsibilities such as local authorities, hospitals, schools, unless it is a project that is over and above their core activities; the purchase of land or buildings. Grants will not be made to organisations that are working to make a profit for shareholders, partners or sole owners, nor to individuals. Grants will not normally be made where it is evident that little or no effort has been made to raise funds elsewhere.

TYPE OF GRANT The trust favours applications that involve one-off capital or project costs, rather than ongoing maintenance, salaries or training costs.

RANGE OF GRANTS £1,000 to £5,000.

SAMPLE GRANTS Home-Start Crawley, Horsham and Mid-Sussex and Horley Town Council (£10,000 each).

FINANCES *Year* 2016 *Income* £206,621 *Grants* £192,552 *Grants to organisations* £192,552 *Assets* £7,872

TRUSTEES Richard Burrett; Michael Roberts; Sally Blake; Ian Revell; Michael Sydney; John Kendall; Eddie Redfern; Julie Ayres; Dorothy Ross-Tomlin.

OTHER INFORMATION Grants were made to 137 organisations in 2016 totalling £193,000.

HOW TO APPLY Application forms are available during the period each year when applications are being accepted (see below) by contacting the trust by telephone or writing to: GACT, PO Box 464, Tunbridge Wells, Kent TN2 9PU. Forms can also be downloaded from the website. Applications are invited once a year, usually between January and March. Grants are paid by the end of May. Further information can be found on the trust's website. Telephone queries are welcomed.

WHO TO APPLY TO The Trustees, Trust Secretary, c/o Spofforths LLP, Springfield House, Springfield Road, Horsham, West Sussex RH12 2RG *Tel.* 01892 826088 *Email* mail@gact.org.uk *Website* www.gact.org.uk

■ The Robert Gavron Charitable Trust

CC NO 268535 **ESTABLISHED** 1974

WHERE FUNDING CAN BE GIVEN Mainly UK.

WHO CAN BENEFIT Registered charities, including small charities.

WHAT IS FUNDED General charitable purposes, but principally the following areas: access to the arts; education; social policy and research; prison reform; human rights; disability.

WHAT IS NOT FUNDED Individuals.

TYPE OF GRANT One-off and recurrent. Funding can be given for up to three years.

RANGE OF GRANTS Mostly up to around £60,000.

SAMPLE GRANTS Morpeth School (£60,000); Arab Israel Children's Tennis Charity (£58,500); Barbados Cricket Association (£42,500); Royal Marsden Hospital (£25,000); KeepOut Crime Diversion Scheme (£20,000); Highgate International Chamber Music Festival (£10,000); The Hardman Trust and Scottish Poetry Library (£7,000 each); The Bridge Mentoring Plus Scheme, Heathrow Special Needs Farm and John Rylands Research Institute (£5,000 each); All Ears International (£3,100); Holocaust Education Trust (£3,000).

FINANCES *Year* 2015/16 *Income* £170,190 *Grants* £668,042 *Grants to organisations* £668,042 *Assets* £7,832,668

TRUSTEES Sarah Gavron; Charles Corman; Jessica Gavron; Lady Katharine Gavron.

OTHER INFORMATION There were 38 grants of over £3,000 made in 2015/16. Grants under £3,000 totalled £36,000. An exceptionally large grant of £100,000 was made to the Charles and Ruth Corman Charitable Trust, where Charles Corman is a trustee.

HOW TO APPLY Apply in writing to the correspondent. The annual report for 2015/16 explains that: 'In many cases the Trustees prefer to make grants to organisations whose work they personally know and admire. This does not, however, mean that charities unknown to the Trustees personally do not receive grants. One freelance adviser visits and reports on some applicants to the Trust and his reports are taken into account by the Trustees when they make their decisions. This leads to a number of grants to new organisations during each financial year.'

WHO TO APPLY TO Anthony Dance, c/o The Folio Society Ltd, 44 Eagle Street, London WC1R 4FS *Tel.* 020 7400 4255 *Email* office@rgct.org.uk

■ The Jacqueline and Michael Gee Charitable Trust

CC NO 1062566 **ESTABLISHED** 1997

WHERE FUNDING CAN BE GIVEN UK and overseas.

WHO CAN BENEFIT Charitable organisations.

WHAT IS FUNDED General charitable purposes including health, education and training, arts and culture and overseas aid.

RANGE OF GRANTS Up to £14,000.

SAMPLE GRANTS My Israel – Musicians of Tomorrow (£14,000); The Philip and Nicola Gee Charitable Trust (£10,000); The Purcell School (£9,400); Food for the Brain Foundation (£5,700); British Friends of the Hebrew University of Jerusalem (£5,250); United Synagogue (£4,400); Grange Park Opera (£1,200); Almedia Theatre Company Ltd and Lifelites (£1,000 each); Chai Lifeline Cancer Care (£100).

FINANCES *Year* 2015/16 *Income* £135,049 *Grants* £115,631 *Grants to organisations* £112,271 *Assets* £84,628

TRUSTEES Michael Gee; Jacqueline Gee.

OTHER INFORMATION In 2015/16 a total of 64 grants were made to organisations. One grant of £3,400 was made to an individual.

HOW TO APPLY Apply in writing to the correspondent.

WHO TO APPLY TO Michael Gee, Trustee, Flat 27, Berkeley House, 15 Hay Hill, London W1J 8NS *Tel.* 020 7493 1904

■ The General Nursing Council for England and Wales Trust

CC NO 288068 **ESTABLISHED** 1983

WHERE FUNDING CAN BE GIVEN England and Wales.

WHO CAN BENEFIT Universities and other public bodies benefitting nurses.

WHAT IS FUNDED Research into matters directly affecting nursing or the nursing profession.

WHAT IS NOT FUNDED Organisational overheads; purchase of equipment; dissemination costs such as conference attendance.

TYPE OF GRANT One-off or annually towards revenue costs.

RANGE OF GRANTS Up to £40,000.

SAMPLE GRANTS Sheffield Teaching Hospitals NHS Trust (£20,000); Trust and University of Huddersfield (£20,000); King's College London (£19,4000); University of Southampton (£16,500).

FINANCES *Year* 2015/16 *Income* £103,806 *Grants* £78,216 *Grants to organisations* £78,216 *Assets* £3,057,094

TRUSTEES Prof. Kate Gerrish; Prof. Susan Proctor; Prof. Dinah Gould; Prof. Sigsworth.

HOW TO APPLY Application forms are available to download from the website (www.gnct.org.uk), where criteria and guidelines are also posted. All applications must be submitted in an electronic format (e.g. MS Word or PDF) using the trust's research grant application form and the review process will be undertaken electronically. A call for grant applications with a specified closing date will be advertised via the website and promoted through other avenues.

WHO TO APPLY TO Alan Haddon, Secretary, 83 Victoria Road, Lower Edmonton, London N9 9SU *Tel.* 020 8345 5379 *Email* gnct@btinternet.com *Website* www.gnct.org.uk

■ The Generations Foundation

CC NO 1110565 **ESTABLISHED** 2005

WHERE FUNDING CAN BE GIVEN Worldwide, but particularly the London Borough of Merton.

WHO CAN BENEFIT Local organisations in the London Borough of Merton; UK and overseas organisations.

WHAT IS FUNDED The provision of a better quality of life for children who are disadvantaged, ill or who have disabilities; also, environmental protection and conservation projects.

TYPE OF GRANT Capital costs, full project and unrestricted funding for up to, and in some cases over, three years.

RANGE OF GRANTS Up to £40,000.

SAMPLE GRANTS Regenerate (£40,000); Linden Lodge Charitable Trust (£37,500); Hospices of Hope (£15,100); Small Steps (£13,000); Linden Lodge School (£11,000); Second Sight and Tree Aid (£10,000 each); Kids Care London (£8,300); The Honeypot Charity (£7,700); Brainwave Centre and MERU (£5,000 each).

FINANCES *Year* 2015/16 *Income* £442,274 *Grants* £270,000 *Grants to organisations* £270,000

TRUSTEES Bob Finch; Stephen Finch; Rohini Finch.

OTHER INFORMATION At the time of writing (May 2017), the foundation's 2015/16 annual return had been received by the Charity Commission; however, its accounts for the year were overdue. We have therefore estimated the grant total based on previous years' information.

HOW TO APPLY Application forms are available to download from the website. They should be returned to the foundation by email (not post), along with your organisation's latest set of accounts. The website instructs applicants to first email or telephone the foundation to ensure their request for funding is likely to be successful.

WHO TO APPLY TO Alison Bishop, 36 Marryat Road, Wimbledon, London SW19 5BD *Tel.* 020 3542 6255 *Email* pa@taliscapital.com *Website* www.generationsct.co.uk

■ The Genesis Charitable Trust

CC NO 1148643 **ESTABLISHED** 2012

WHERE FUNDING CAN BE GIVEN Financially developing countries.

WHO CAN BENEFIT Registered charities; NGOs.

WHAT IS FUNDED The trust prioritises income-generating projects in financially developing countries. It actively seeks to support: entrepreneurial initiatives; targeted improvement of economic opportunities; improvements to the efficiency of markets and the ease of doing business.
WHAT IS NOT FUNDED Activities based outside a financially developing country; individual sponsorship or personal appeals; work that is aligned to a political party or a religious or spiritual faith; animal charities; building or infrastructure projects; funding for work that has already occurred; medical research.
RANGE OF GRANTS The trust does not set a minimum or maximum grant value, although it is exceptional for grant payments to exceed £400,000 in any single year of a project.
SAMPLE GRANTS Camfed International (£238,000); Hope and Homes for Children (£127,500); Build It International (£75,000); Precious Sisters (£30,000); Mumbai Mobile Creches (£23,500); World Sight Foundation (£15,000); Deki (£11,000); New Life Mexico (£800).
FINANCES *Year* 2015 *Income* £1,418,078 *Grants* £748,502 *Grants to organisations* £748,502 *Assets* £2,944,143
TRUSTEES Martin Ryan; Karen Roydon; Chris Ellyatt; Arindam Bhattacharjee.
HOW TO APPLY Application forms can be downloaded from the website and should be submitted by email to GenesisCharitableTrust@giml.co.uk. Applicants that are felt to be potentially eligible will be invited to an interview and asked to submit a detailed financial review.
WHO TO APPLY TO Tom Hoyle, Trust Manager, 21 Grosvenor Place, London SW1X 7HU *Tel.* 020 7201 7200 *Email* genesischaritabletrust@giml.co.uk *Website* www.giml.co.uk/charitable-trust.php

■ Genetic Disorders UK

CC NO 1141583 **ESTABLISHED** 2011
WHERE FUNDING CAN BE GIVEN England and Wales.
WHO CAN BENEFIT Genetic disorder-related charities and support groups.
WHAT IS FUNDED All types of projects and services that improve the quality of life for children with genetic disorders.
TYPE OF GRANT Project costs.
RANGE OF GRANTS £500 to £25,000.
SAMPLE GRANTS The Lily Foundation, The Redway School (£12,500 each); DBA UK (£10,000); A-T Society (£7,500); Jeune Syndrome Foundation (£6,500); The Children's Trust (£4,900) Ataxia UK (£2,400).
FINANCES *Year* 2015/16 *Income* £1,361,023 *Grants* £134,253 *Grants to organisations* £134,253 *Assets* £485,222
TRUSTEES David Barlow; Michael Berry; Alina Garcia-Lapuerta; Jill Lucas.
OTHER INFORMATION The charity awarded 21 grants to disorder-specific charities and support groups.
HOW TO APPLY Full details on how to apply are available on the charity's website.
WHO TO APPLY TO Caroline Harding, Chief Executive, 199A Victoria Street, London SW1E 5NE *Tel.* 0800 987 8987 *Email* hello@geneticdisordersuk.org *Website* www.geneticdisordersuk.org

■ The Steven Gerrard Foundation

CC NO 1140813 **ESTABLISHED** 2011
WHERE FUNDING CAN BE GIVEN UK, with a preference for Liverpool, and overseas.
WHO CAN BENEFIT Registered charities.
WHAT IS FUNDED Children and young people who are in need due to illness, family breakdown, disability, 'involvement in the streets', or who are financially or educationally disadvantaged.
TYPE OF GRANT One-off and recurring.
RANGE OF GRANTS £750 to £90,000.
SAMPLE GRANTS Rare Trust (£90,000); WellChild (£14,500); Centro De Apoio a Criança (£11,500); DEBRA Charity (£10,000); Brainwave (£7,000); Claire House and The Hugh McAuely Football Academy (£5,000 each); Alder Hey Children's Hospital Christmas Gifts (£750).
FINANCES *Year* 2015 *Income* £355,113 *Grants* £197,250 *Grants to organisations* £197,250 *Assets* £768,592
TRUSTEES Steven Gerrard; Peter Sterling; Andrew Sterling.
HOW TO APPLY At the time of writing (June 2017) the website stated: 'We currently have no further information on future grants cycles, as soon as we do the website will be updated accordingly.' See the website for updates.
WHO TO APPLY TO The Trustees, c/o Black and Norman Solicitors, 67 Coronation Road, Crosby, Liverpool L23 5RE *Tel.* 0151 931 2777 *Email* info@stevengerrardfoundation.org *Website* www.stevengerrardfoundation.org

■ The Gerrick Rose Animal Trust

CC NO 1146252 **ESTABLISHED** 2012
WHERE FUNDING CAN BE GIVEN Devon and Cornwall.
WHO CAN BENEFIT Registered charities.
WHAT IS FUNDED Animal welfare.
SAMPLE GRANTS Bath Cats and Dogs Home; Blue Cross; Clay County Cat Care; People for Ponies; RSPCA; St Tiggywinkles.
FINANCES *Year* 2015/16 *Income* £228,343 *Grants* £51,437 *Grants to organisations* £51,437 *Assets* £2,577,891
TRUSTEES Anthony Cusack; Cheryl Thomas; Jean Knuckey.
HOW TO APPLY Apply in writing to the correspondent.
WHO TO APPLY TO Anthony Cusack, Gill Akaster LLP, 25 Lockyer Street, Plymouth PL1 2QW *Tel.* 01752 203500 *Email* tony.cusack@GAsolicitors.com

■ The Gertner Charitable Trust

CC NO 327380 **ESTABLISHED** 1987
WHERE FUNDING CAN BE GIVEN UK and overseas.
WHO CAN BENEFIT Jewish charities and individuals.
WHAT IS FUNDED General charitable purposes, including education, health and welfare.
SAMPLE GRANTS Friends of Bobov (£96,000); AISH UK (£45,000); NRST (£41,000); Ohr Akiva (£35,000); Mayfair charities Ltd (£30,000); Friends of Belz Machnovkas (£25,000); London Jewish Family Centre (£21,000); Friends of United Institutions of Arad (£20,000); Friends of Beer Yaakov and Jewish Education Fund (£18,000 each).
FINANCES *Year* 2015/16 *Income* £141,717 *Grants* £150,337 *Grants to organisations* £146,237 *Assets* £5,659,142
TRUSTEES Moises Gertner, Chair; Michelle Gertner; Michael Wechsler; Simon Jacobs.
OTHER INFORMATION In 2015/16 the grant total included £4,100 given to individuals. Of the

total awarded to organisations, £104,000 was given overseas and the remaining £42,000 in the UK.

HOW TO APPLY Apply in writing to the correspondent. The trustees meet quarterly.

WHO TO APPLY TO Simon Jacobs, Trustee, Fordgate House, 1 Allsop Place, London NW1 5LF *Tel.* 020 7224 1234

■ Get Kids Going

CC NO 1063471 **ESTABLISHED** 1997

WHERE FUNDING CAN BE GIVEN UK.

WHO CAN BENEFIT Registered charities; national sporting bodies; individuals.

WHAT IS FUNDED Young athletes with disabilities, up to the age of 26 in sports.

TYPE OF GRANT One-off and recurrent; equipment costs.

RANGE OF GRANTS £4,400 to £90,000.

SAMPLE GRANTS GB Disabled Ski Team (£90,000); GB Wheelchair Rugby Team (£40,000); GB Boccia Team (£23,000); GB Disabled Sailing Team (£15,300); England Boccia (£8,000); Disabled Sport Wales (£5,000); Weir Archer Academy (£4,400).

FINANCES *Year* 2015/16 *Income* £1,192,397 *Grants* £265,966 *Grants to organisations* £193,599 *Assets* £10,484,624

TRUSTEES Lesley Tadgell-Foster; Patti Fordyce; Phillip Fordham.

OTHER INFORMATION The charity awarded grants to nine organisations. A total of £72,500 was awarded to individuals.

HOW TO APPLY Apply in writing to the correspondent.

WHO TO APPLY TO Jane Emmerson, 10 King Charles Terrace, Sovereign Close, London E1W 3HL *Tel.* 020 7481 8110 *Email* info@getkidsgoing.com *Website* www.getkidsgoing.com

■ The Gibbons Family Trust

CC NO 290884 **ESTABLISHED** 1984

WHERE FUNDING CAN BE GIVEN Devon, with a preference for East Devon, and the Isle of Thanet in Kent.

WHO CAN BENEFIT Registered charities and organisations; individuals.

WHAT IS FUNDED The welfare, education, training and recreation of children and young people up to the age of 25.

WHAT IS NOT FUNDED Ongoing fees (e.g. regular payments for education); individuals for trips overseas; private schools; organisations which have had a grant in the last 12 months.

RANGE OF GRANTS Up to £6,300.

SAMPLE GRANTS Exeter Leukaemia Fund (£6,300); Oasis Domestic Abuse and WESC Foundation (£5,000 each); Turner Contemporary (£3,200); Soil Association (£2,500); Encompass Southwest, Plympton Hub, Thanet Primary School Association for School Sport, Thelma Hulbert Gallery and YMCA Exeter (£2,000 each).

FINANCES *Year* 2015/16 *Income* £91,367 *Grants* £85,885 *Grants to organisations* £73,165 *Assets* £2,151,387

TRUSTEES Roger Dawe; Dr John Frankish; Dr Miles Joyner; Kerensa Pearson; Elizabeth Lee.

OTHER INFORMATION In 2015/16 a total of 44 grants were made to organisations and a further 23 to individuals. The average grant was of £1,700 for organisations and £550 for individuals. The success rate for applications was 87%.

HOW TO APPLY Application forms are available to download from the website, where full guidelines and deadlines are also available.

WHO TO APPLY TO Roger Dawe, Trustee, The Gibbons Trusts, 14 Fore Street, Budleigh Salterton, Devon EX9 6NG *Tel.* 01395 445259 *Email* web.enquiry@gibbonstrusts.org *Website* www.gibbonstrusts.org

■ The David Gibbons Foundation

CC NO 1134727 **ESTABLISHED** 2010

WHERE FUNDING CAN BE GIVEN Devon, with a preference for East Devon.

WHO CAN BENEFIT Registered charities and community groups; individuals.

WHAT IS FUNDED The welfare and relief of: people suffering from financial hardship; older people; and people suffering from sickness.

WHAT IS NOT FUNDED Ongoing fees (e.g. regular payments for rent); individuals for trips overseas; organisations which have had a grant within the past 12 months.

RANGE OF GRANTS Up to £6,300.

SAMPLE GRANTS Exeter Leukaemia Fund (£6,300); Families for Children (£5,000); Cullompton Family Centre and South Devon College Charitable Trust (£3,000); Devon and Cornwall Food Association and Open Door Exmouth (£2,500); Calvert Trust, Dartmouth Caring, Estuary League of Friends and Ottery Help Scheme (£2,000 each).

FINANCES *Year* 2015/16 *Income* £121,168 *Grants* £109,264 *Grants to organisations* £95,050 *Assets* £2,811,319

TRUSTEES Roger Dawe; Dr Miles Joyner; Dr John Frankish; Kerensa Pearson; Elizabeth Lee.

OTHER INFORMATION In 2015/16 grants were made to 64 organisations and 31 individuals. The average grant was around £1,500 for organisations and £440 to individuals. The success rate of applications was 85%.

HOW TO APPLY Application forms are available to download from the website, where full guidelines and deadlines are also available.

WHO TO APPLY TO Roger Dawe, Trustee, The Gibbons Trusts, 14 Fore Street, Budleigh Salterton, Devon EX9 6NG *Tel.* 01395 445259 *Email* web.enquiry@gibbonstrusts.org *Website* www.gibbonstrusts.org

■ The Gibbs Charitable Trust

CC NO 207997 **ESTABLISHED** 1946

WHERE FUNDING CAN BE GIVEN UK and overseas, with a concentration on South Wales, Bristol and South London.

WHO CAN BENEFIT UK-registered charities and Methodist churches.

WHAT IS FUNDED The trust's annual report 2015/16 states its three main areas of support as: 'innovative undertakings' by Methodist churches and organisations; other Christian causes, especially of an ecumenical nature; and 'a wider category in the fields of the creative arts, education, social and international concern'. It is noted on the website that the arts causes supported by the trust 'invariably have an educational or social dimension.' Grants are normally made to projects of which the trustees have personal knowledge.

WHAT IS NOT FUNDED Animal charities; individuals; organisations that are not registered charities; the trust does not normally fund salaries or support medical research.

TYPE OF GRANT Buildings, capital and project grants will be considered. Occasionally, regular annual grants have been given over three years.

RANGE OF GRANTS The majority of grants are between £1,000 and £3,000.
SAMPLE GRANTS Save the Children – Syria (£8,000); Brecon Baroque (£5,000); Mind – Brecon (£3,000); SolarAid (£2,500); Bristol Methodist Centre, Mid Wales Music Trust and Peace Direct (£2,000 each); Bilton Area Methodist Church, Harehills English Language Centre, Penarth Pier Pavilion and Youth for Christ (£1,000 each); Allsorts Nursery Crickhowell (£500).
FINANCES *Year* 2015/16 *Income* £93,055 *Grants* £113,900 *Grants to organisations* £113,900 *Assets* £2,389,965
TRUSTEES Dr James Gibbs; Dr John Gibbs; Andrew Gibbs; Celia Gibbs; Elizabeth Gibbs; Dr Jessica Gibbs; Dr John E. Gibbs; Patience Gibbs; Rebecca Gibbs; William Gibbs; Juliet Gibbs; James Gibbs.
OTHER INFORMATION In 2015/16 the trust made 69 grants.
HOW TO APPLY Before applying, applicants are advised to look at the list of grants already made by the trust (detailed in its annual report). The trust's website provides the following guidance on making an application: 'Apply in writing to the Secretary, at 8 Victoria Square, Bristol BS8 4ET. The Secretary says he and his Trustees are "more often provided with too much information than too little". He thinks "Many applications can be made on two sides of paper." The pages should include a covering letter, a brief description of the project and a budget. He says Trustees are interested in the answer to the question: "Who else have you applied to?" Flyers, etc., may be in addition to the two sides. The Secretary says he is "not impressed by the use of first class stamps" or by the submission of full sets of audited accounts. To keep administration to a minimum, he only communicates with successful applicants. Applications should be in an easily re-cyclable form. In practice, this means no spring-coil binding. Use both sides of the page!' The trustees meet three times a year, usually around Easter, in late summer, and after Christmas. Very few new applicants are supported.
WHO TO APPLY TO Dr James Gibbs, Secretary, 8 Victoria Square, Bristol BS8 4ET *Email* jamesgibbs@btinternet.com *Website* www.gibbstrust.org.uk

■ The G. C. Gibson Charitable Trust

CC NO 258710 **ESTABLISHED** 1969
WHERE FUNDING CAN BE GIVEN Worldwide.
WHO CAN BENEFIT UK-registered charities operating anywhere in the world. Priority is given to smaller charities with annual charitable donations of less than £1 million.
WHAT IS FUNDED General charitable purposes, with grants falling within the following categories: community and other social projects; health, hospices and medical research; art, music and education; and religion. The majority of support is already committed to existing beneficiaries; however, the trust supports around eight new applications each year. New applications are focused on a particular theme, which can vary depending on the year.
WHAT IS NOT FUNDED Individuals.
TYPE OF GRANT Mainly recurring for core costs; capital and one-off project costs are also supported.
SAMPLE GRANTS A list of beneficiaries was not available.
FINANCES *Year* 2015/16 *Income* £601,885 *Grants* £618,493 *Grants to organisations* £618,493 *Assets* £14,757,228
TRUSTEES Anna Dalrymple; Martin Gibson; Jane Gibson; Lucy Kelly; Edward Gibson; Thomas Richards Homfray.
OTHER INFORMATION The trust's website explains that ideally it can be used for matched funding to unlock further funds. In 2015/16 the trust had received 450 requests and 12 grants were awarded.
HOW TO APPLY Applications can only be made using the online form on the trust's website. Applications are open from 1 August to around 20 August each year. Note that in previous years, the application round has closed earlier than planned due to huge demand. Before applying, ensure you have read the up-to-date eligibility criteria on the trust's website. Applicants are notified of the trustees' decisions in mid- to late September. The trust can be contacted by email only; it does not respond to or acknowledge letters.
WHO TO APPLY TO Martin Gibson, Trustee, Durnsford Mill House, Mildenhall, Marlborough, Wiltshire SN8 2NG *Email* enquiries@gcgct.org *Website* www.gcgct.org

■ The Simon Gibson Charitable Trust

CC NO 269501 **ESTABLISHED** 1975
WHERE FUNDING CAN BE GIVEN UK (national charities); Suffolk, Norfolk, Cambridgeshire, Hertfordshire, Glamorganshire, Gwent, Powys and Camarthenshire (local charities).
WHO CAN BENEFIT UK-registered charities and CICs. National charities are more likely to be considered if they support local causes in the areas listed above.
WHAT IS FUNDED General charitable purposes, with a preference for organisations working with young people, older people, conservation, education or religion.
WHAT IS NOT FUNDED Individuals or organisations applying on behalf of individuals; students for educational or gap year sponsorship; conferences, seminars or workshops; overseas charities (other than those working in conservation or previously known to the trustees).
TYPE OF GRANT One-off or recurring; core costs; specific project funding.
RANGE OF GRANTS From £1,000 to £20,000, with most grants in the range of £3,000 to £5,000.
SAMPLE GRANTS Tenovus (£20,000); Royal Welsh College of Music and Drama (£15,000); Coleg Elidyr and Ely Cathedral Appeal Fund (£10,000 each); Royal National Lifeboat Institution (£6,000); Harrow School Appeal, Isabel Hospice, National Children's Orchestra, Orangutan Foundation, Reach Village Centre and The Greenpeace Trust (£5,000 each); Vale of Glamorgan Agricultural Society (£4,000); Girl Guiding UK, Help the Hospices, Hertfordshire Action on Disability and Refuge (£3,000 each); Cowbridge Music Festival (£1,000).
FINANCES *Year* 2015/16 *Income* £1,074,935 *Grants* £646,100 *Grants to organisations* £646,100 *Assets* £16,881,238
TRUSTEES Bryan Marsh; George Gibson; Deborah Connor; John Homfray.

OTHER INFORMATION Usually around 140 beneficiaries are supported during the year, of which around 60 are regularly supported.

HOW TO APPLY Application forms are available to download from the website and should be returned to the trust by post. Only postal applications submitted between 1 January and 31 March are considered. The trustees meet to consider applications in spring each year.

WHO TO APPLY TO Bryan Marsh, Trustee, The Simon Gibson Charitable Trust, PO Box 203, Barry CF63 9FD *Tel.* 01446 781459 *Email* info@sgtrust.co.uk *Website* www.sgtrust.co.uk

■ Gilchrist Educational Trust

CC NO 313877 **ESTABLISHED** 1865

WHO CAN BENEFIT Registered charities; organisations; expeditions; individuals.

WHAT IS FUNDED Organisations seeking to fill up educational gaps or to make more widely available a particular aspect of education or learning. Individuals who: are within sight of the end of self-financed degree; are on a higher education course and who are facing unexpected financial difficulties which may prevent completion of it; or are required, as part of a university course, to spend a short period studying in another country. British university expeditions proposing to carry out scientific research.

WHAT IS NOT FUNDED Primary or secondary schools; organisations or groups seeking funds to be used exclusively to build or renovate buildings; organisations or groups which show evidence of party political bias; organisations or groups formed for medical purposes, unless there is a significant educational element in the proposal for which funds are sought; organisations or groups seeking funds to help meet administrative or running costs; organisations or groups seeking such a large sum that any contribution from this trust would be a mere 'drop in the ocean' part-time students; those seeking funds to enable them to take up a place on a course; students seeking help in meeting the cost of maintaining dependants; students who have, as part of a course, to spend all or most of an academic year studying in another country; those wishing to go abroad under the auspices of independent travel, exploratory or educational projects.

TYPE OF GRANT One-off.

RANGE OF GRANTS Grants to organisation range from £500 to £4,000. Grants for expeditions from £1,000 to £2,000. Adult Study Grants and Travel Study Grants to individuals both average around £530.

SAMPLE GRANTS Disability Africa, Project Pencil Case (£2,500 each); African Promise, Children in Crisis (£2,000 each); Inspire Skills Centre (£1,500) Health Prom, READ International, University of Derby (£1,000 each); University of Edinburgh, University of Leeds (£750); University of Glasgow (£500).

FINANCES *Year* 2015/16 *Income* £89,925 *Grants* £70,247 *Grants to organisations* £70,247 *Assets* £1,884,986

TRUSTEES Charles Whitbread; John Hemming; Frederick Pearce; Stuart Harrop; Shane Winser; Valerie Considine.

OTHER INFORMATION The trust also offers the biennial Gilchrist Fieldwork Award of £15,000. This competitive award is offered in even-numbered years and is open to small teams of qualified academics and researchers in established posts in university departments or research establishments, most of British nationality, wishing to undertake a field season of over six weeks. During the trust's last financial year, 53 students received either an Adult Study Grant (average £528) or a Travel Study Grant (average £531). There were 16 grants for expeditions awarded during the year totalling £11,500.

HOW TO APPLY Applications from organisations are considered by the trustees in April or May each year and must be submitted by the end of February at the latest. Applications are unlikely to be considered for funding in consecutive years. Application forms can be obtained by email from the secretary at valconsidine@btinternet.com. The forms should be returned by email to the same address and a hard signed copy, together with any required enclosures, by post to the secretary at the address below. For grants to individuals contact the Grants Officer on gilchrist.et@gmail.com or write to 4 St Michaels Gate Shrewsbury SY1 2HL all other enquiries should be addressed to the secretary at the address below. Application forms are sent on request and must be returned before the end of February in the year during which the expedition is to take place. Application forms can be obtained by email from the secretary at valconsidine@btinternet.com The forms should be returned by email to the same address and a hard signed copy, together with any required enclosures, by post to the secretary at the address below. Full details are available on the website.

WHO TO APPLY TO Val Considine, Secretary, 20 Fern Road, Storrington, Pulborough, West Sussex RH20 4LW *Tel.* 01903 746723 *Email* gilchrist.et@blueyonder.co.uk *Website* www.gilchristgrants.org.uk

■ The L. and R. Gilley Charitable Trust

CC NO 297127 **ESTABLISHED** 1987

WHERE FUNDING CAN BE GIVEN Primarily Devon and Birmingham.

WHO CAN BENEFIT Registered charities.

WHAT IS FUNDED General charitable purposes, with a strong preference for the care and support of older people, including those who have disabilities and terminal illnesses, and medical research.

WHAT IS NOT FUNDED Individuals.

RANGE OF GRANTS Up to £5,000.

SAMPLE GRANTS Cancer Research UK and Macmillan Cancer Support (£6,000 each); RNLI (£5,500); Motor Neurone Disease Association (£4,000); Arthritis Research UK (£3,000); Accessible Coach Holidays and Age UK Barnstaple and District (£1,000 each); Rowcroft House Foundation and Torbay Hospital League of Friends (£500 each).

FINANCES *Year* 2015/16 *Income* £51,512 *Grants* £45,000 *Grants to organisations* £45,000 *Assets* £1,326,938

TRUSTEES Richard Bettinson; Hayley Bettinson.

OTHER INFORMATION In accordance with its objects, the trust also supports five specific charities: The Imperial Cancer Research Fund, The League of Friends of Torbay Hospital, The Rowcroft House Foundation (The Torbay and South Devon Hospice), The Royal National Institute for the Blind, The Royal National Lifeboat Institution.

HOW TO APPLY Apply in writing to the correspondent. Applications are not acknowledged and are usually considered in July.

WHO TO APPLY TO Richard Bettinson, Trustee, Tetstill Mill, Neen Sollars, Kidderminster DY14 9AH *Email* keltontrust@gmail.com

■ The Girdlers' Company Charitable Trust

CC NO 328026 **ESTABLISHED** 1988

WHERE FUNDING CAN BE GIVEN UK or elsewhere; a preference for The City and the East End of London, and Hammersmith and Peckham.

WHO CAN BENEFIT Charitable organisations benefitting children; young adults; academics; students; teachers.

WHAT IS FUNDED Medicine and health; disadvantaged; education; community development; children and young people; older people.

WHAT IS NOT FUNDED Individuals directly.

TYPE OF GRANT The focus of the trust's grants is on its principal charities. One-off and recurrent; core, revenue, salary and capital costs.

RANGE OF GRANTS Mainly up to £10,000.

SAMPLE GRANTS Kids Club Kampala, Margaret Carey Foundation, React (£1,000 each); Churches Housing Action Team, Integrating Children and Young People, Jerimiah's Journey (£900 each).

FINANCES *Year* 2015 *Income* £251,482 *Grants* £863,911 *Grants to organisations* £863,911 *Assets* £6,562,823

TRUSTEE The Girdlers' Company.

OTHER INFORMATION The only grant open to application is a small grant which awards to 20 small charities a year that have an income of less than 1 million.

HOW TO APPLY At the time of writing (July 2017), the website states the following information: 'The Company makes regular and significant Gift Aided donations to the Trust which makes donations and grants to a range of charities with which it has long standing and close relationships. The Trustee is undertaking a review of its grant making. One of its decisions during this review has been to close its current open application process in which it made annually 20 one-off grants of around £1,000. Once the review is complete, not expected before 2017, it will announce any new open application programme on this page.'

WHO TO APPLY TO Brigadier Ian Rees, Girdlers' Hall, Basinghall Avenue, London EC2V 5DD *Tel.* 020 7638 0488 *Email* clerk@girdlers.co.uk *Website* www.girdlers.co.uk/html/charitable-giving/the-charitable-trust

■ The Glass-House Trust

CC NO 1144990 **ESTABLISHED** 2011

WHERE FUNDING CAN BE GIVEN UK.

WHO CAN BENEFIT Registered charities.

WHAT IS FUNDED Built environment; children's development; social policy; art.

SAMPLE GRANTS Glass-House Community-Led Design (£150,00); Raven Row (£350,000); Mayday Rooms (£108,000); A Space (£55,000).

FINANCES *Year* 2015/16 *Income* £282,795 *Grants* £221,480 *Grants to organisations* £221,480 *Assets* £11,788,268

TRUSTEES Alex Sainsbury; Judith Portrait; Elinor Sainsbury.

HOW TO APPLY Unsolicited applications are not accepted. Grants are made to projects initiated by the trustees, or jointly by the trustees and the beneficiary, and to other projects which the trustees proactively seek out.

WHO TO APPLY TO Alan Bookbinder, Sainsbury Family Charitable Trusts, Allington House, 150 Victoria Street, London SW1E 5AE *Tel.* 020 7410 0330 *Email* info@sfct.org.uk *Website* www.sfct.org.uk/Glass-house.html

■ The B. and P. Glasser Charitable Trust

CC NO 326571 **ESTABLISHED** 1984

WHERE FUNDING CAN BE GIVEN UK and overseas.

WHO CAN BENEFIT Registered charities and community organisations.

WHAT IS FUNDED General charitable purposes; health; disability; social welfare; Jewish causes.

WHAT IS NOT FUNDED Individuals, including students.

RANGE OF GRANTS £750 to £10,000.

SAMPLE GRANTS Nightingale House and Practical Action (£10,000 each); Jewish Care (£8,000); Friends of Lady Home Hospital and Medical Aid for Palestinians (£5,000 each); Blind Veterans UK and Unicef UK (£3,000 each); Chiltern's MS Medical Centre (£2,500); Age UK, Fair Trials International and Norwood (£2,000 each); Abbeyfield Buckinghamshire Society and Carefree Kids (£1,500 each); Gurkha Welfare Trust and Samaritans – Chiltern (£750 each).

FINANCES *Year* 2014/15 *Income* £84,483 *Grants* £106,500 *Grants to organisations* £106,500 *Assets* £2,484,876

TRUSTEES Michael Glasser; John Glasser.

OTHER INFORMATION The 2014/15 accounts were the latest available at the time of writing (May 2017).

HOW TO APPLY Apply in writing to the correspondent. In order to keep administrative costs to a minimum, the trustees are unable to reply to unsuccessful applicants.

WHO TO APPLY TO Martin Pollock, Moore Stephens LLP, 150 Aldersgate Street, London EC1A 4BD *Tel.* 020 7734 9191 *Email* martin.pollock@moorestephens.com

■ The Gloag Foundation

SC NO SC035799 **ESTABLISHED** 2004

WHERE FUNDING CAN BE GIVEN UK and overseas.

WHO CAN BENEFIT Charitable organisations and individuals.

WHAT IS FUNDED Anti-trafficking of people; the prevention or relief of poverty; education; health; Christian causes.

RANGE OF GRANTS Up to £850,000.

SAMPLE GRANTS Freedom From Fistula Foundation (£850,000); Fundatia Usa Deschisa – Romania Women's Shelter (£304,500); Young Life (£142,500); Blythswood Care – Dorchas Project (£100,000); Kenya Children's Home (£91,000); Scottish Charity Air Ambulance (£60,000); The Christian Institute (£30,000); Hope Pregnancy Crisis Centres (£10,000); Velemegna Good News Society Hospice (£7,000); St Mary's Maidenhead (£3,000); Alpha Ireland (£2,000); Church in Need, Dundee Mental Health, Independent Age and Wellspring Family Centre (£1,000 each).

FINANCES *Year* 2015 *Income* £2,232,343 *Grants* £2,588,381 *Grants to organisations* £2,045,293 *Assets* £9,182,782

OTHER INFORMATION In 2015 new grants to charities (not including support given to the foundation's associated charities in Kenya or the Freedom from Fistula Foundation) totalled £929,000. Grants to individuals amounted to £543,000.

HOW TO APPLY Apply in writing to the correspondent via email at any time. Applications should be no more than two pages of A4, and should include the following information: your organisation and an explanation of its charitable aims and objectives; the project requiring funding, why it is needed, who will benefit and in what way; the funding being requested, a breakdown of costs, details of money raised so far and how the balance will be raised. The trustees will request further information if required so there is no need to send supporting materials (such as books, brochures, DVDs or annual reports or accounts). All applications are responded to, although the trustees are unable to provide feedback for unsuccessful applications. The trustees meet quarterly.

WHO TO APPLY TO The Trustees, Robertson House, 1 Whitefriars Crescent, Perth PH2 0PA *Tel.* 01738 633264 *Email* info@gloagfoundation.com *Website* www.gloagfoundation.org.uk

■ Global Care

CC NO 1054008 **ESTABLISHED** 1996

WHERE FUNDING CAN BE GIVEN Overseas.

WHO CAN BENEFIT Registered charities.

WHAT IS FUNDED Relief, development, education and childcare programmes which benefit children and young people who are in 'great' need.

SAMPLE GRANTS A list of beneficiaries was not available.

FINANCES *Year* 2015/16 *Income* £723,335 *Grants* £465,403 *Grants to organisations* £465,403 *Assets* £606,560

TRUSTEES Raymond Neal; Mark Curran; John Scott; Sue Matejtschuk; Revd Keith Parr.

HOW TO APPLY Applications are not recommended. The trustees seek out projects to support, as appropriate, and new grants cannot be considered.

WHO TO APPLY TO John White, Chief Executive Officer, 2 Dugdale Road, Coventry CV6 1PB *Tel.* 0300 302 1030 *Email* info@globalcare.org.uk *Website* www.globalcare.org.uk

■ Global Charities

CC NO 1091657 **ESTABLISHED** 1978

WHERE FUNDING CAN BE GIVEN UK.

WHO CAN BENEFIT UK-registered charities, with an income of between £50,000 and £1.2 million.

WHAT IS FUNDED The Make Some Noise appeal supports charities working with children and young people (aged 0 to 25) who are affected by illness, disability or disadvantage.

WHAT IS NOT FUNDED Refer to the website.

TYPE OF GRANT Project costs; capital costs. The charity also provides publicity and awareness-raising support for beneficiary organisations.

RANGE OF GRANTS At least £20,000.

SAMPLE GRANTS Prince's Foundation for Children and the Arts (£100,000); Missing People (£61,000); Impact Initiatives (£25,000); Sixth Sense Theatre (£7,500); Cambourne Youth Partnership (£5,000); Havens Hospices – Essex (£3,000); Bangladeshi Parents Association (£2,100); Howbury Friends (£1,800); Centrepoint – Hammersmith and Fulham (£1,600).

FINANCES *Year* 2015/16 *Income* £3,248,064 *Grants* £1,346,402 *Grants to organisations* £1,346,402 *Assets* £1,050,839

TRUSTEES Moira Swinbank; Paul Soames; Martin George; Jonathan Norbury; Nigel Atkinson; John McGeough; Gareth Andrewartha; Annabel Sweet; Michael Connole.

OTHER INFORMATION In 2015/16 grants were made to 43 charities. The charity also runs The Big Music Project, aiming to break down barriers for young people in the creative industries, and Music Potential, which works with young people who are not in education, training or employment.

HOW TO APPLY An expression of interest can be made using a form on the charity's website when the application window is open.

WHO TO APPLY TO Hannah Lison, Grants and Programme Manager, Global Radio, 29–30 Leicester Square, London WC2H 7LA *Email* grants@makesomenoise.com *Website* www.makesomenoise.com

■ Gloucestershire Community Foundation

CC NO 900239 **ESTABLISHED** 1989

WHERE FUNDING CAN BE GIVEN Gloucestershire.

WHO CAN BENEFIT Small local groups, voluntary organisations and charities; individuals.

WHAT IS FUNDED A wide range of causes which help to combat disadvantage in Gloucestershire, including in the following areas: disadvantaged communities; people in poverty or on a low income; minority communities; families; older people; and people with disabilities and health difficulties.

WHAT IS NOT FUNDED Individuals (although they may be considered in exceptional circumstances); general appeals; statutory organisations or the replacement of statutory funding; political groups or activities promoting political beliefs; religious groups promoting religious beliefs; arts or sports projects with no community or charitable element; medical research, equipment or treatment; animal welfare; projects taking place before the application can be processed; activities intending to raise funds for other organisations. Specific funds may be subject to their own exclusions.

RANGE OF GRANTS Main Grants programme: £1,000 to £10,000, but rarely more than £5,000.

SAMPLE GRANTS Gloucestershire Bike Project (£10,000 in two grants); Discover DeCrypt (£7,000); Farming and Wildlife Advisory Group South West (£6,500); Infobuzz Ltd (£4,500); New Brewery Arts (£4,000); Hope's Children and Young People's Support Services (£3,000); Family Space in Hesters Way (£2,500); Brockworth Community Project and Survivors of Bereavement by Suicide – SOBS Gloucester (£1,000 each); Oakridge Village Hall Trust (£940); Coaley Village Playgroup (£860); Sheiling School (£500).

FINANCES *Year* 2015 *Income* £506,281 *Grants* £256,633 *Grants to organisations* £256,633 *Assets* £5,807,550

TRUSTEES Dr Roger Head; Terry Standing; The Countess Bathurst; Richard Graham; Mark Heywood; Helen Lovatt; Martin Surl; Jane Winstanley; Alison Robinson; Jamie Tabor; Jonathan Dunley; Tom Frost; Norman Gardner.

OTHER INFORMATION In 2015 a total of 98 grants were distributed. No grants were made to individuals during the year.

HOW TO APPLY In the first instance see the website, where details of programmes which are currently open can be found along with full criteria, guidelines and details of how to apply. Organisations are encouraged to contact the foundation to discuss the most appropriate grant programme for them. Staff can give general guidance on the eligibility of a project for a particular grant programme.

WHO TO APPLY TO David Triggle-Wells, Programme Manager, The Manor, Boddington, Cheltenham, Gloucestershire GL51 0TJ *Tel.* 01242 851357 *Email* grants@gloucestershirecf.org.uk *Website* www.gloucestershirecf.org.uk

■ The Gloucestershire Historic Churches Trust

CC NO 1120266 **ESTABLISHED** 1980

WHERE FUNDING CAN BE GIVEN Gloucestershire, South Gloucestershire and North Bristol.

WHO CAN BENEFIT Places of worship of all Christian denominations.

WHAT IS FUNDED Repairs and improvements to the fabric of religious buildings and their contents, as well as to their surrounding churchyards.

WHAT IS NOT FUNDED Grants are not normally given for substantial repairs unless the work has been specified by an architect or surveyor with appropriate conservation training.

TYPE OF GRANT One-off, but repeat applications may be considered.

RANGE OF GRANTS £250 to £10,000, but typically between £1,000 and £4,000.

SAMPLE GRANTS St Mary's Minster – Cheltenham (£10,000); St Margaret of Scotland – Whaddon (£8,000); St Nicholas – Prestbury (£4,000); St Cyr – Stinchcombe (£3,000); St John the Baptist – Old Sodbury (£2,000); All Saints – Cheltenham (£500); Holy Trinity – Doynton (£250).

FINANCES *Year* 2015 *Income* £195,166 *Grants* £130,000 *Grants to organisations* £130,000 *Assets* £1,551,282

TRUSTEES David Kingsmill; Philip Kendall; Helen Whitbread; Nicholas Talbot-Rice; Stephen Langton; Jonathan McKechnie-Jarvis.

OTHER INFORMATION Grants were made to 46 places of worship in 2015.

HOW TO APPLY Application forms and full guidelines can be downloaded from the trust's website. Completed applications should be returned to the correspondent. When an application is received the trust will arrange a meeting at your church to discuss your application and view the proposed work. The committee meets in June and December. Applications should be made by the end of April for the June meeting or by the end of October for the December meeting.

WHO TO APPLY TO Jonathan MacKechnie-Jarvis, Grant Committee Chair, 73 Forest View Road, Tuffley, Gloucester GL4 0BY *Email* grants@ghct.org.uk *Website* www.ghct.org.uk

■ Worshipful Company of Glovers of London Charitable Trust

CC NO 269091 **ESTABLISHED** 1975

WHERE FUNDING CAN BE GIVEN UK with a preference for the City of London.

WHO CAN BENEFIT Charitable and educational organisations.

WHAT IS FUNDED The provision of gloves; causes that are related to the City of London; education.

RANGE OF GRANTS Up to £5,000.

SAMPLE GRANTS King Edward's School – Witley (£5,200); City of London School (£4,900); London College of Music (£4,200); Meningitis Now (£2,500); Church of St Mary – Lothbury and Lord Mayor's Charities (£2,000); Christie Charitable Fund (£1,800); Crisis (£1,400); Disaster Emergencies Committee – Nepal Earthquake Appeal (£1,300); Adopted Regiment (£650).

FINANCES *Year* 2015/16 *Income* £78,095 *Grants* £50,552 *Grants to organisations* £50,552 *Assets* £743,555

TRUSTEE Worshipful Company of Glovers of London.

OTHER INFORMATION In 2015/16 grants for 'gloves and glove related projects' totalled almost £18,600 and other charitable grants totalled almost £32,000.

HOW TO APPLY Apply in writing to the correspondent.

WHO TO APPLY TO Lt Col. Mark Butler, Clerk, Seniors Farmhouse, Semley, Shaftesbury SP7 9AX *Tel.* 01747 851887 *Email* clerk@ thegloverscompany.org *Website* www. thegloverscompany.org

■ The Godinton Charitable Trust

CC NO 268321 **ESTABLISHED** 1974

WHERE FUNDING CAN BE GIVEN Kent.

WHO CAN BENEFIT The trust provides regular support for The Godinton House Preservation Trust, as well as supporting local registered charities.

WHAT IS FUNDED General charitable purposes.

WHAT IS NOT FUNDED Individuals.

TYPE OF GRANT One-off and recurrent.

RANGE OF GRANTS Generally £500 to £2,000.

SAMPLE GRANTS The Godinton House Preservation Trust (£172,500); Oasis – Domestic Abuse Service (£2,500); Ashford Family Nursery, Kent Sharp Shooters Yeomanry Museum and Salvation Army (£2,000 each); Hothfield Parochial Church Council (£1,800); The Marlowe Theatre Development Trust (£1,500); Ashford Counselling Service, Glyndebourne Arts Trust, Kent Wildlife Trust, Pilgrims Hospices in East Kent and Plant Life – Ranscombe Farm, Kent (£1,000 each); Charing Methodist Church (£500).

FINANCES *Year* 2014/15 *Income* £165,911 *Grants* £215,650 *Grants to organisations* £215,650 *Assets* £5,086,900

TRUSTEES The Hon. Wyndham Plumptre; The Hon. John Leigh-Pemberton; Michael Jennings; Terence Bennett.

OTHER INFORMATION The 2014/15 accounts were the latest available at the time of writing (May 2017).

HOW TO APPLY Apply in writing to the correspondent.

WHO TO APPLY TO N. Sandford, Godinton House, Godinton Lane, Ashford, Kent TN23 3BP *Tel.* 01233 632652 *Email* office@ godintonhouse.co.uk

■ Worshipful Company of Gold and Silver Wyre Drawers Charitable Trust Fund

CC NO 802491 **ESTABLISHED** 1969

WHERE FUNDING CAN BE GIVEN City of London.

WHO CAN BENEFIT Charitable organisations, particularly those with a turnover of less than £75,000.

WHAT IS FUNDED General charitable purposes, including education, children and young people, armed forces and health. Our research suggests that the charity is currently focusing on supporting charities which work to improve the chances for young people fully taking their place in society by means of training or other support are welcome.

RANGE OF GRANTS £50 to £12,500.

SAMPLE GRANTS Royal Trinity Hospice (£12,500); Creative Arts (£1,500); Defence Medical Welfare Services, Forces Support, RAF Northolt Queen's Colour Squadron and Band and Whizz-Kidz (£1,000 each); St John Ambulance Cadets – Bexley Heath (£500); City and Guilds of London Institute (£50).
FINANCES *Year* 2015/16 *Income* £88,752 *Grants* £74,250 *Grants to organisations* £74,250 *Assets* £992,009
TRUSTEES Paul Constantinidi; John Walsham; Malcolm Craig; Michael Gunston; Revd Gordon Warren.
OTHER INFORMATION The charity provides regular support to a number of organisations, these include: The Lord Mayor's Charity; The Royal British Legion Poppy Appeal; the Sheriffs and Recorders Fund; bursaries at the Royal School of Needlework, The Guildhall School of Music and Drama, St Paul's Cathedral choir; and prizes at the Royal Ballet School and a number of schools in the City of London. In addition to this support in 2015/16 the charity made grants to 40 other charities.
HOW TO APPLY Apply in writing to the correspondent.
WHO TO APPLY TO Cdr Mark Dickens, Clerk, Lye Green Forge, Lye Green, Crowborough, East Sussex TN6 1UU *Tel.* 07825 157866 *Email* clerk@gswd.co.uk *Website* www.gswd.co.uk

■ Sydney and Phyllis Goldberg Memorial Charitable Trust

CC NO 291835 **ESTABLISHED** 1985
WHERE FUNDING CAN BE GIVEN UK.
WHO CAN BENEFIT Organisations.
WHAT IS FUNDED Medical research; social welfare; disability.
TYPE OF GRANT One-off, some recurrent.
RANGE OF GRANTS Between £3,000 and £15,000.
SAMPLE GRANTS Alzheimer's Research UK, Children with Special Needs Foundation, Life Centre, The British Stammering Association and The Dystonia Society (£15,000 each); British Earthquake and Tsunami Support and Nepal Earthquake Appeal (£10,000 each); The Isaac Goldberg Charity Trust (£5,000); Chailey Heritage Enterprise Centre (£3,000).
FINANCES *Year* 2015/16 *Income* £134,411 *Grants* £163,000 *Grants to organisations* £163,000 *Assets* £3,730,863
TRUSTEES Christopher Pexton; Howard Vowles; Michael Church.
OTHER INFORMATION Grants were made to 13 organisations in 2014/15.
HOW TO APPLY Apply in writing to the correspondent. Telephone requests are not appreciated. Applicants are advised to apply towards the end of the calendar year.
WHO TO APPLY TO Michael Church, Trustee, Coulthard Mackenzie, 17 Park Street, Camberley, Surrey GU15 3PQ *Tel.* 01276 65470

■ The Golden Bottle Trust

CC NO 327026 **ESTABLISHED** 1985
WHERE FUNDING CAN BE GIVEN Worldwide.
WHO CAN BENEFIT Registered charities.
WHAT IS FUNDED General charitable purposes.
WHAT IS NOT FUNDED Individuals; organisations that are not registered charities.
TYPE OF GRANT One-off and recurring.
RANGE OF GRANTS Up to £10,000 with larger grants for charities that the Hoare family has a personal relationship with.
SAMPLE GRANTS The Bulldog Trust (£300,000); Future for Religious Heritage (£68,500); The Henry C Hoare Charitable Trust (£60,000); Chartered Institute for Securities and Investment (£20,000); Institute of Cancer Research (£15,000); 20 20 Education Network (£10,500); Centre for Charity Effectiveness, Foundling Museum, Nepal Earthquake Recovery Appeal, Oxford House – Bethnal Green, Trinity College Cambridge and Westcountry Rivers Trust (£10,000 each).
FINANCES *Year* 2014/15 *Income* £1,665,934 *Grants* £1,396,190 *Grants to organisations* £1,396,190 *Assets* £9,769,552
TRUSTEE Hoare Trustees.
OTHER INFORMATION The 2014/15 accounts were the latest available at the time of writing (May 2017). The grant total does not include £180,000 given by the trust to match staff fundraising.
HOW TO APPLY The trust does not normally respond to unsolicited approaches.
WHO TO APPLY TO Hoare Trustees, C. Hoare and Co., 37 Fleet Street, London EC4P 4DQ *Tel.* 020 7353 4522

■ The Goldman Sachs Charitable Gift Fund (UK)

CC NO 1120148 **ESTABLISHED** 2007
WHERE FUNDING CAN BE GIVEN USA and the UK, and well as Canada, France and Hong Kong, although in practice organisations are supported worldwide.
WHO CAN BENEFIT Registered charities, schools and universities.
WHAT IS FUNDED Education; arts and culture; humanitarian relief; medical causes; community; other charitable purposes.
SAMPLE GRANTS Trustees of Princeton University (£269,500); Australian Independent Schools USA Foundation (£155,000); Brooklyn Academy of Music, Inc. (£66,000); Room to Read (£52,000); Autism Resource Centre – Singapore (£27,000).
FINANCES *Year* 2015/16 *Income* £1,186,748 *Grants* £1,077,331 *Grants to organisations* £1,077,331 *Assets* £9,990,391
TRUSTEES Robert Katz; Mike Housden; Peter Fahey.
OTHER INFORMATION This fund was established by Goldman Sachs International in 2007 as one of the vehicles for its charitable giving. It is also connected to Goldman Sachs Gives. The amounts details were initially reported in the fund's accounts in USD. They were converted into GBP at the time this entry was written (2 June 2017). A total of 64 grants were made in the year.
HOW TO APPLY The annual report for 2015/16 explains that the fund 'operates as a donor advised fund whereby the directors establish donor accounts for individual donors to make recommendations, although the ultimate decision for the distribution of funds rests solely with the directors of the Fund'.
WHO TO APPLY TO Jenny Evans, Executive Director, Goldman Sachs, Peterborough Court, 133 Fleet Street, London EC4A 2BB *Tel.* 020 7774 1000

■ Goldman Sachs Gives (UK)

CC NO 1123956 **ESTABLISHED** 2008

WHERE FUNDING CAN BE GIVEN UK and overseas.

WHO CAN BENEFIT Registered charities; schools; universities.

WHAT IS FUNDED Education; community; humanitarian relief; medical causes; arts and culture; other charitable purposes.

RANGE OF GRANTS Up to £2 million.

SAMPLE GRANTS Charities Aid Foundation (£2 million); Greenhouse Sports Ltd (£1.23 million); Save the Children Fund (£1.22 million); St Edmund's College (£1.17 million); Room to Read UK Ltd (£584,000); Concern Worldwide – UK (£500,000).

FINANCES *Year* 2015/16 *Income* £24,560,494 *Grants* £17,841,924 *Grants to organisations* £17,841,924 *Assets* £89,684,424

TRUSTEES Jenny Evans; Robert Katz; Mike Housden; Peter Fahey.

OTHER INFORMATION This fund was established by Goldman Sachs International in 2008 as one of the vehicles for its charitable giving. It is also connected to the Goldman Sachs Charitable Gift Fund. In 2015/16 the charity made 514 grants.

HOW TO APPLY The annual report for 2015/16 explains that the fund 'operates as a donor advised fund whereby the directors establish donor accounts for individual donors to make recommendations, although the ultimate decision for the distribution of funds rests solely with the directors of the Fund'.

WHO TO APPLY TO Jenny Evans, Trustee, Goldman Sachs, Peterborough Court, 133 Fleet Street, London EC4A 2BB *Tel.* 020 7774 1000

■ The Goldsmiths' Company Charity

CC NO 1088699 **ESTABLISHED** 1961

WHERE FUNDING CAN BE GIVEN UK, with a special interest in London charities.

WHO CAN BENEFIT Registered charities with a turnover of less than £5 million. National charities or charities operating in London can be supported.

WHAT IS FUNDED **Small grants** (up to £5,000) are awarded for: culture; general welfare; and medical welfare/disability. **Large grants** (up to a maximum of £30,000) are awarded to charities working in the following areas: disadvantaged young people, specifically young people leaving care, young carers, young people with mental health issues, and youth homelessness (affiliated members of London Youth may be considered under the small grants category); and the rehabilitation/resettlement of prisoners, particularly prisoner education and training, 'through-the-gate' mentoring, employment opportunities, arts and music, women in prison, and support for prisoners' families. Under the large grants category, the charity also supports charities working to combat isolation and loneliness among older people anywhere in the UK. The charity also supports organisations working to support the goldsmiths' craft.

WHAT IS NOT FUNDED Individuals; overseas charities and projects taking place and/or benefitting people outside the UK; medical research; animal welfare; individual housing associations and tenant organisations; endowment schemes; individual churches, for maintenance of the fabric; individual hospices; individual schools or supporting associations; play schemes, nurseries or pre-school facilities; local authorities, or work usually considered a statutory responsibility; major building projects, or capital funding; one-off events (such as festivals, conferences, exhibitions and community events); overseas projects or trips; campaigning or lobbying projects, or general awareness raising work; membership organisations; CICs or social enterprises; grant-making organisations; mailshots or letters requesting donations.

TYPE OF GRANT Project funding, although core costs may also be supported.

RANGE OF GRANTS Up to £5,000 (small grants) or up to £30,000 (large grants).

SAMPLE GRANTS National Churches Trust (£40,000 – block grant); Goldsmith's Craft and Design Council (£31,000); R L Glasspool Charity Trust (£25,000); Contemporary British Silversmiths (£21,000); King's College London (£15,000); Museum of London and Refugee Council (£10,000 each); The Wimbledon Guild (£5,000); Hounslow Action for Youth Association and The Black Cultural Archives (£3,000 each); Southwark Children's Brass Band (£2,000 each); Kinship Care Northern Ireland (£1,500); Creative Future Literary Awards (£1,200).

FINANCES *Year* 2015/16 *Income* £3,812,663 *Grants* £1,215,936 *Grants to organisations* £1,215,936 *Assets* £117,840,098

TRUSTEE The Goldsmith's Company Trustee.

OTHER INFORMATION The company regularly reviews its grant-making policy and will update guidance on its website as necessary. Organisations are advised to check the website regularly for updates.

HOW TO APPLY In the first instance see the website, where full information, including detailed eligibility criteria and guidelines, is available.

WHO TO APPLY TO Ciorsdan Brown, Grants Manager, Goldsmiths' Hall, 13 Foster Lane, London EC2V 6BN *Tel.* 020 7606 7010 ext. 2012 *Email* ciorsdan.brown@thegoldsmiths.co.uk *Website* www.thegoldsmiths.co.uk/charities

■ The Golf Foundation Ltd

CC NO 285917 **ESTABLISHED** 1953

WHERE FUNDING CAN BE GIVEN UK.

WHO CAN BENEFIT Organisations benefitting children and young people.

WHAT IS FUNDED The development, promotion and support of junior golf.

WHAT IS NOT FUNDED Individuals.

SAMPLE GRANTS A list of beneficiaries was not available.

FINANCES *Year* 2014 *Income* £1,697,218 *Grants* £259,126 *Grants to organisations* £259,126 *Assets* £3,342,584

TRUSTEES Norman Fletcher; Nicholas Sladden; Sir Robin Miller; Stephen Proctor; Di Horsley; Deborah Allmey; Ian Armitage; Nigel Evans; Sally Stewart; Nick Bragg; Stephen Lewis; Kevin Barker; Nigel Freemantle.

OTHER INFORMATION At the time of writing (June 2017) the foundation's accounts for 2015 had been received by the Charity Commission but were not available to view online. We have therefore used the latest accounts that were available to view. In 2014 grants were distributed as follows: Golf Roots Centres (£176,000); Satellite Clubs (£25,000); Golf Development Wales (£24,000); Special Projects (£18,000); Discretionary Grants – Scotland (£9,000); Schools – Special Needs (£2,500); School Sport Partnerships – PESSYP (£1,500); Community Golf Coaches (£1,000); Club Golf

Scotland (£700); County and Regional Groups (£400); Schools (£200); Other Groups (£100).

HOW TO APPLY The annual report for 2014 explains that 'in order to ensure that demand for grants does not exceed the budget available the foundation each year identifies closed lists of organisations – primarily schools and golf clubs or facilities – which are advised that they will be eligible to apply for a grant during the coming year. These lists are comprised mostly by continuation from the previous year, with vacancies being filled if budgetary constraints allow.'

WHO TO APPLY TO James McAllister, Finance Manager, The Spinning Wheel, High Street, Hoddesdon, Hertfordshire EN11 8BP *Tel.* 01992 449830 *Fax* 01992 449840 *Email* admin@golf-foundation.org *Website* www.golf-foundation.org

■ The Golsoncott Foundation

CC NO 1070885 **ESTABLISHED** 1998

WHERE FUNDING CAN BE GIVEN UK.

WHO CAN BENEFIT Charitable organisations.

WHAT IS FUNDED The foundation's objective, according to its Charity Commission record, is: 'To promote, maintain, improve and advance the education of the public in the arts generally and in particular the fine arts and music.' The foundation's website explains that the trustees' 'overriding concern is to support those projects that demonstrate and deliver excellence in the arts, be it in performance, exhibition, artistic craft, or scholarly endeavour'.

WHAT IS NOT FUNDED Individuals; applications from schools are not encouraged, nor are capital appeals from museums, galleries, theatres, arts complexes, or other projects (apart from by invitation).

TYPE OF GRANT One-off and some recurring; core costs; salaries; project funding; start-up costs; bursaries.

RANGE OF GRANTS Grants vary but do not exceed £5,000.

SAMPLE GRANTS The Marian Consort (£3,000); National Children's Orchestra (£2,000); Fusilier Museum, Garforth Brass Band, Nottingham Trent University – Sit Joseph Banks Publication Project, Poetry Book Society, Shakespeare Schools' Festival and Southbank Sinfonia (£1,000 each); Lichfield Festival and Merry Opera Company (£750 each); Salisbury Cathedral (£500); Playback Youth Theatre (£400); Ditchling Museum and St Edmundsbury Organ (£250 each).

FINANCES *Year* 2015/16 *Income* £79,402 *Grants* £61,200 *Grants to organisations* £61,200 *Assets* £2,275,880

TRUSTEES Jo Lively; Penelope Lively; Steve Wick; Dr Harriet Wood; Izzy Wick.

OTHER INFORMATION In 2015/16 grants were given to 77 separate organisations or projects. The foundation sponsors the Society of Wood Engravers' Rachel Reckitt Open Prize.

HOW TO APPLY The trustees meet quarterly to consider applications, in February, May, August and November. Applications, supplied in hard copy with an email contact address, should be sent to the correspondent by the end of the month preceding the month of the trustees' meeting. The foundation's website gives the following guidance: 'Applications should include the following: a clear and concise statement of the project, whether the award sought will be for the whole project or a component part. State what the status of the applicant/organisation is: charity, CIC, registered company etc.; evidence that there is a clear benefit to the public, i.e., does the project conform with the declared object of the trust [see 'What is funded']; the amount requested should be specified, or a band indicated. Is this the only source of funding being sought? All other sources of funding should be indicated, including those that have refused the applicant; is the grant requested part of the match-funding required by the Heritage Lottery Foundation (HLF) following an award? If so state the amount of that award and the percentage of match-funding required by the HLF and the completion date; wherever possible an annual report and accounts should accompany the application, as may any other supporting information deemed relevant.'

WHO TO APPLY TO Hal Bishop, Administrator, 53 St Leonard's Road, Exeter EX2 4LS *Tel.* 01392 252855 *Email* golsoncott@btinternet.com *Website* www.golsoncott.org.uk

■ Nicholas and Judith Goodison's Charitable Settlement

CC NO 1004124 **ESTABLISHED** 1991

WHERE FUNDING CAN BE GIVEN UK.

WHO CAN BENEFIT Registered charities.

WHAT IS FUNDED Arts and arts education.

WHAT IS NOT FUNDED Individuals.

TYPE OF GRANT Recurrent capital grants. One-off grants.

RANGE OF GRANTS Up to £27,000 but generally between £200 and £4,000.

SAMPLE GRANTS Fitzwilliam Museum (£27,000); Courtauld Institute (£10,000); British Museum (£4,700); Art Fund (£4,000); Academy of Ancient Music, Crafts Council and Handel House (£2,500 each); Wigmore Hall (£2,200); Eden Project, Goldsmiths' Centre and Mayor's Fund for Young Musicians (£1,000 each); King's College (£700); National Gallery and National Youth Orchestra (£500 each); World Monuments Trust (£350); Venice in Peril (£200).

FINANCES *Year* 2015/16 *Income* £68,483 *Grants* £72,158 *Grants to organisations* £72,158 *Assets* £1,483,921

TRUSTEES Sir Nicholas Goodison; Judith Goodison; Katharine Goodison.

OTHER INFORMATION Grants were made to 26 organisations in 2014/15.

HOW TO APPLY The trustees have stated that they cannot respond to unsolicited applications.

WHO TO APPLY TO Sir Nicholas Goodison, Trustee, PO Box 2512, London W1A 5ZP *Tel.* 020 7499 8298 *Email* goodisonn2@btinternet.com

■ The Goodman Foundation

CC NO 1097231 **ESTABLISHED** 2003

WHERE FUNDING CAN BE GIVEN UK and overseas.

WHO CAN BENEFIT Registered charities.

WHAT IS FUNDED General charitable purposes; the relief of poverty; older people; illness and disability; children; overseas assistance and disaster relief.

SAMPLE GRANTS A list of beneficiaries was not available.

FINANCES *Year* 2015/16 *Income* £824,815 *Grants* £566,240 *Grants to organisations* £566,240 *Assets* £39,645,765

TRUSTEES Laurence Goodman; Catherine Goodman; Richard Cracknell; Lesley Tidd; Philip Morgan.

OTHER INFORMATION The annual report and accounts did not include a list of beneficiaries; however, it did include the following breakdown of grants made: people who are poor, older or who have disabilities (£293,000); other charitable causes (£254,000); children's charities (£14,200); overseas assistance and disasters (£5,000).

HOW TO APPLY Apply in writing to the correspondent.

WHO TO APPLY TO The Trustees, c/o ABP, Unit 6290, Bishops Court, Solihull Parkway, Birmingham Business Park, Birmingham B37 7YB

■ The Mike Gooley Trailfinders Charity

CC NO 1048993 **ESTABLISHED** 1995

WHERE FUNDING CAN BE GIVEN UK.

WHO CAN BENEFIT Charitable organisations.

WHAT IS FUNDED Medical research; youth community projects; education; armed forces.

WHAT IS NOT FUNDED Overseas charities; individuals.

RANGE OF GRANTS Up to £400,000.

SAMPLE GRANTS A list of beneficiaries was not available.

FINANCES *Year* 2015/16 *Income* £3,835,881 *Grants* £2,694,246 *Grants to organisations* £2,494,246 *Assets* £9,138,461

TRUSTEES Mark Bannister; Tristan Gooley; Michael Gooley; Bernadette Gooley; Fiona Gooley; Louise Breton.

OTHER INFORMATION A list of grants was not included in the charity's recent accounts.

HOW TO APPLY Apply in writing to the correspondent.

WHO TO APPLY TO Michael Gooley, Trustee, 9 Abingdon Road, London W8 6AH *Tel.* 020 7938 3143 *Website* www.trailfinders.com

■ The Gordon Trust

CC NO 1098290 **ESTABLISHED** 2003

WHERE FUNDING CAN BE GIVEN Leicestershire, Nottinghamshire, Derbyshire and Northamptonshire.

WHO CAN BENEFIT Charitable organisations.

WHAT IS FUNDED Disability; social deprivation; homelessness; substance and alcohol abuse; prisoner education and rehabilitation. Very occasionally, the trust can support causes outside these areas.

WHAT IS NOT FUNDED The trust does not usually support individuals and organisations without charitable status, or provide funding for every day running expenses.

TYPE OF GRANT One-off revenue costs and capital expenditure.

RANGE OF GRANTS Usually between £250 and £1,000.

SAMPLE GRANTS A list of beneficiaries was not available.

FINANCES *Year* 2015/16 *Income* £19,868 *Grants* £71,119 *Grants to organisations* £71,119

TRUSTEES Kathryn Garnett; John Gordon; Andrea Hardie.

OTHER INFORMATION Due to its low income, this trust's latest accounts were not available to view on the Charity Commission's website. Based on previous years' information, the trust's total expenditure usually consists entirely of grants. The trust used to be known as African Steps.

HOW TO APPLY Applications must be made using the trust's application form, which is available from the website and should be returned to the correspondent by email. Applicants should also send their organisation's most recent accounts (unless these are available to view on the Charity Commission's website), as well as a budget for the project in question. Applications are considered four times a year, in February, May, August and November. The deadlines for applications are: 15 January, 15 April, 15 July and 15 October respectively. Successful applicants are usually informed within two weeks of the relevant trustee meeting. The trustees are unable to contact unsuccessful applicants.

WHO TO APPLY TO Mrs Kathryn Garnett, Trustee, 4 Charnia Grove, Swithland, Loughborough LE12 8XZ *Tel.* 01509 890067 *Email* kathryngarnett@thegordontrust.co.uk *Website* www.thegordontrust.co.uk

■ The Goshen Trust

CC NO 1119064 **ESTABLISHED** 2007

WHERE FUNDING CAN BE GIVEN UK and overseas, with a preference for North East England.

WHO CAN BENEFIT Christian organisations; churches; charitable organisations.

WHAT IS FUNDED Christian causes. In particular, the trust states in its 2015/16 annual report that its aims is to 'encourage and develop Christian projects which otherwise may not be able to reach an effective operational conclusion as well as supporting those that are already well established.'

TYPE OF GRANT Project costs.

RANGE OF GRANTS £250 to £100,000.

SAMPLE GRANTS Walsall Community Church (£100,000); Newcastle Christian Life Centre (£59,000); Naharot Mayim Chaiyim (£33,000); Elim Church Hartlepool (£12,000); Portrack Baptist Church (£10,000); Sowing Seeds Ministries (£5,000); Caring for Life (£4,600); Castleton and Danby Bowling Club and Tees Valley Youth for Christ (£1,000); The Royal British Legion (£250).

FINANCES *Year* 2015/16 *Income* £539,257 *Grants* £753,963 *Grants to organisations* £753,963 *Assets* £10,028,379

TRUSTEES Alison Dicken; Albert Dicken; Jonathan Dicken; Pauline Dicken; Raymond Oliver.

OTHER INFORMATION Not included in the 2015/16 grant total were two large donations of property, worth £1 million and £300,000, made to Mercy Ministries UK and Daisy Chain Project respectively.

HOW TO APPLY Apply in writing to the correspondent. The trustees meet several times a year to consider applications. All applications are acknowledged; if applicants do not receive any further communication from the trust within three months, they should assume that they have been unsuccessful.

WHO TO APPLY TO Raymond Oliver, Trustee, The Goshen Trust, PO Box 367, Eaglescliffe, Stockton-on-Tees TS16 9YR *Email* b.goodrum@masadadevelopments.co.uk

■ The Gosling Foundation Ltd

CC NO 326840 **ESTABLISHED** 1962

WHERE FUNDING CAN BE GIVEN UK.

WHO CAN BENEFIT Registered charities.

WHAT IS FUNDED Education; relief of poverty; religion; general charitable purposes; health; heritage and maritime causes.

WHAT IS NOT FUNDED Only in exceptional circumstances are grants made to individuals.

SAMPLE GRANTS White Ensign Association (£203,000 in three grants); Bletchley Park Trust and Lionheart (£100,000 each); Care After

Combat (£54,000 in four grants); Holy Trinity Church (£30,000); St John Hospice Antigua (£25,000); Crimestoppers Trust and Portsmouth Citizens Advice (£15,000 each); Coastal Forces Heritage Trust, Royal Navy Benevolent Trust and St James's Conservation Trust (£10,000 each); Queen's Chapel of the Savoy (£6,300); Cherubim Music Trust, Children's Trust, Christ's Hospital, Landmark Arts Centre – Teddington, Prostate Cancer UK and Teddington Athletic FC (£5,000 each); Marie Curie Cancer Care (£2,500); British Red Cross and Wallasey Sea Cadets TS Astute (£2,000 each); Richmond Mencap (£1,000); Walk the Walk (£500).

FINANCES *Year* 2015/16 *Income* £4,787,719 *Grants* £6,651,890 *Grants to organisations* £6,651,890 *Assets* £110,832,313

TRUSTEES Hon. Vice Admiral Sir Donald Gosling; Hon. Capt. Adam Gosling.

OTHER INFORMATION In 2015/16, 149 grants were committed to 115 beneficiaries.

HOW TO APPLY Apply in writing to the correspondent. The trustees meet quarterly.

WHO TO APPLY TO Anne Yusof, Secretary, 21 Bryanston Street, Marble Arch, London W1H 7PR *Tel.* 020 7495 5599 *Email* Anne.Yusof@conprop.co.uk

■ The Gould Charitable Trust

CC NO 1035453 **ESTABLISHED** 1993

WHERE FUNDING CAN BE GIVEN Not defined; in practice mainly UK and Israel.

WHO CAN BENEFIT Registered charities, including Jewish organisations.

WHAT IS FUNDED General charitable purposes, particularly education and training.

WHAT IS NOT FUNDED Individuals.

TYPE OF GRANT Up to three years. Unrestricted funding.

RANGE OF GRANTS Up to £26,000, but mostly up to around £4,000.

SAMPLE GRANTS United Jewish Israel Appeal (UJIA) (£26,000); One to One (£4,300); Loewenstein Hospital (£3,700); FCED Foundation Philippines (£3,100); Beit Halachen (£2,500); Alzheimer's Research Trust and Jewish Women's Aid (£2,000); Friends of Israel Education Foundation and Jewish Care (£1,500 each); Dignity in Dying, Médecins Sans Frontières and South Hampstead Synagogue (£1,000 each); Youth Aliyah (£500); Dignitas (£340); Education Partnership Africa (£200); Orchestra of the Age of Enlightenment and Practical Action (£100 each); National Osteoporosis Society (£25).

FINANCES *Year* 2015/16 *Income* £26,104 *Grants* £59,232 *Grants to organisations* £59,232 *Assets* £1,076,299

TRUSTEES Jean Gould; Simon Gould; Sidney Gould; Lawrence Gould; Matthew Gould.

OTHER INFORMATION In 2015/16 grants were made to 37 organisations.

HOW TO APPLY Apply in writing to the correspondent.

WHO TO APPLY TO S. Gould, Trustee, Cervantes, Pinner Hill, Pinner HA5 3XU *Tel.* 020 8868 2700 *Email* sidney.gould@gmail.com

■ Gowling WLG (UK) Charitable Trust

CC NO 803009 **ESTABLISHED** 1990

WHERE FUNDING CAN BE GIVEN Mainly the West Midlands.

WHO CAN BENEFIT Local and national charities operating in the area.

WHAT IS FUNDED Grants are generally made to charities supporting young people, older people, people who are ill or who have disabilities, and disadvantaged people.

WHAT IS NOT FUNDED Individuals; organisations which are not charities; animal charities.

RANGE OF GRANTS Between £100 and £13,000.

SAMPLE GRANTS Birmingham Children's Hospital Charity (£13,000); Dogs for Good (£10,500); SIFA Fireside (£5,000); Teach First (£4,000); Mental Fight Club (£2000); The Cotteridge Church, The Outward Bound Trust, and UCanDoIT (Internet Training) (£500); Theatre Absolute and WheelPower (£250 each); Parkinson's UK (£100).

FINANCES *Year* 2015/16 *Income* £108,154 *Grants* £107,168 *Grants to organisations* £107,168 *Assets* £39,444

TRUSTEES Lee Nuttall; Andrew Witts; Philip Clissitt.

OTHER INFORMATION In 2015/16, 137 organisations were supported.

HOW TO APPLY Apply in writing to the correspondent. The day-to-day management of the trust is carried out by Gowling WLG, including co-ordinating grant applications, which are presented to the trustees for their consideration at meetings throughout the year.

WHO TO APPLY TO Lee Nuttall, Trustee, Gowling WLG (UK) LLP, Two Snowhill, Snow Hill Queensway, Birmingham B4 6WR *Tel.* 0121 233 1000

■ The Hemraj Goyal Foundation

CC NO 1136483 **ESTABLISHED** 2010

WHERE FUNDING CAN BE GIVEN UK and overseas.

WHO CAN BENEFIT Organisations.

WHAT IS FUNDED General charitable purposes, particularly disadvantaged children, women's rights, education and people with disabilities.

TYPE OF GRANT One-off grants.

RANGE OF GRANTS Up to £40,000.

SAMPLE GRANTS iPartner India (£40,000); Battle of Bollywood (£7,500); Child Action (£5,200).

FINANCES *Year* 2015 *Income* £113,890 *Grants* £71,195 *Grants to organisations* £71,195 *Assets* £6,164

TRUSTEES Mala Agarwal; Vidya Goyal; Avnish Goyal.

OTHER INFORMATION In addition to the three payments listed, ten smaller payments were made to other charities. The foundation also expended £38,000 in charitable project support.

HOW TO APPLY Apply in writing to the correspondent.

WHO TO APPLY TO Avnish Goyal, Trustee, 2 Kingfisher House, Woodbrook Crescent, Radford Way, Billericay, Essex CM12 0EQ *Tel.* 01277 844829 *Email* info@hgf.org.uk *Website* www.hgf.org.uk

■ Grace Charitable Trust

CC NO 292984 **ESTABLISHED** 1985

WHERE FUNDING CAN BE GIVEN UK and overseas.

WHO CAN BENEFIT Registered charities, including Christian organisations.

WHAT IS FUNDED Christian and church-based activities; education; social and medical causes; general charitable purposes.

RANGE OF GRANTS £1,000 to £10,000.

SAMPLE GRANTS Alpha, the International Christian College and Euroevangelism.

FINANCES *Year* 2015/16 *Income* £400,165 *Grants* £329,900 *Grants to organisations* £329,900 *Assets* £2,251,214

TRUSTEES Eric Payne; G. Snaith; Robert Quayle; Mark Mitchell; Robert Wright.

OTHER INFORMATION Grants were distributed as follows: Christian activities (£161,000); education (£140,500); social and medical (£23,500); general charitable purposes (£4,900).
HOW TO APPLY Grants are only made to charities known to the settlors.
WHO TO APPLY TO Eric Payne, Trustee, Swinford House, Nortons Lane, Great Barrow, Chester CH3 7JZ

■ Graff Foundation

CC NO 1012859 **ESTABLISHED** 1991
WHERE FUNDING CAN BE GIVEN Worldwide.
WHO CAN BENEFIT Charitable organisations.
WHAT IS FUNDED General charitable purposes.
TYPE OF GRANT One-off and recurrent.
RANGE OF GRANTS Up to £64,000.
SAMPLE GRANTS The Museum of Contemporary Art (£64,000); Tate Foundation (£7,000); NSPCC (£6,400); Cash and Rocket sponsorship tour (£2,000); New York Academy of Art (£990); Memorial Sloan-Kettering Cancer Centre (£650).
FINANCES *Year* 2015 *Income* £76,400 *Grants* £80,939 *Grants to organisations* £80,939 *Assets* £3,953,991
TRUSTEES Laurence Graff; Francois Graff; Anthony Kerman.
OTHER INFORMATION Grants were made to six organisations in 2015.
HOW TO APPLY Apply in writing to the correspondent.
WHO TO APPLY TO Anthony Kerman, Trustee, Kerman and Co. LLP, 200–203 Strand, London WC2R 1DJ *Tel.* 020 7539 7272

■ E. C. Graham Belford Charitable Settlement

CC NO 1014869 **ESTABLISHED** 1991
WHERE FUNDING CAN BE GIVEN Northumberland.
WHO CAN BENEFIT Smaller charities and branches of larger charities based in the area of benefit.
WHAT IS FUNDED General charitable purposes.
RANGE OF GRANTS Up to £10,000.
SAMPLE GRANTS A list of beneficiaries was not available.
FINANCES *Year* 2015/16 *Income* £69,508 *Grants* £64,500 *Grants to organisations* £64,500 *Assets* £8,133,099
TRUSTEES Anthony Thompson; Robert Hutchinson; Francis Parker.
HOW TO APPLY Apply in writing to the correspondent.
WHO TO APPLY TO Anthony Thompson, Trustee, 4 More London Riverside, London SE1 2AU *Tel.* 0870 903 1000

■ A. and S. Graham Charitable Trust

CC NO 288220 **ESTABLISHED** 1983
WHERE FUNDING CAN BE GIVEN UK.
WHO CAN BENEFIT Charitable organisations.
WHAT IS FUNDED Education; social welfare; the arts; health; children and young people.
SAMPLE GRANTS A list of beneficiaries was not included in the accounts.
FINANCES *Year* 2015/16 *Income* £107,528 *Grants* £71,852 *Grants to organisations* £71,852 *Assets* £260,660
TRUSTEES Andrew Graham; Sandra Graham; Natasha Boucai; Mrs E. J. Haguenauer; Laura Graham.
HOW TO APPLY Apply in writing to the correspondent.
WHO TO APPLY TO Mr K. J. Hardy, Smith Pearman, Hurst House, Ripley GU23 6AY *Email* andrew@grahamtrust.co.uk

■ The Graham Trust

SC NO SC038269 **ESTABLISHED** 2007
WHERE FUNDING CAN BE GIVEN UK.
WHO CAN BENEFIT Registered charities.
WHAT IS FUNDED Animal welfare; social welfare; arts, heritage, culture and science; saving of lives.
RANGE OF GRANTS Up to £10,000.
SAMPLE GRANTS Canine Partners (£20,000); Pancreatic Cancer Research (£15,000); Maggie's and RNLI (£10,000 each); Contact the Elderly (£5,300); Brae Riding for the Disabled – Dundee (£1,800); Parkinson's (£1,000).
FINANCES *Year* 2015/16 *Income* £32,547 *Grants* £76,336 *Grants to organisations* £76,336 *Assets* £1,228,246
OTHER INFORMATION Grants were made to nine organisations during the year.
HOW TO APPLY Apply in writing to the correspondent by email or post. The trustees meet once a year in the autumn. The website states that the following should be included: 'a description of the project that outlines what you are seeking to achieve and who you are looking to benefit; what level of funding you are requesting and what the grant will be spent on; details of how the project will be managed; details of any funds that have already been raised and what other sources of funding are being approached; describe how you propose to monitor and evaluate whether the project has been successful; details of any funds that have already been raised and what other sources of funding are being approached; if applicable, what plans you have to fund the future running costs of the project'.
WHO TO APPLY TO The Trustees, 14 Dirac Road, Ashley Down, Bristol BS7 9LP *Email* thegrahamtrust@gmail.com *Website* www.thegrahamtrust.co.uk/index.html

■ Grahame Charitable Foundation Ltd

CC NO 1102332 **ESTABLISHED** 2004
WHERE FUNDING CAN BE GIVEN UK and overseas.
WHO CAN BENEFIT Mainly Jewish charities and organisations.
WHAT IS FUNDED The advancement of education; the relief of poverty; the advancement of religion.
WHAT IS NOT FUNDED Individuals.
TYPE OF GRANT Capital, core costs, interest-free loans, one-off, recurring costs and start-up costs. Funding for up to two years may be considered.
RANGE OF GRANTS Up to £25,000.
SAMPLE GRANTS Jerusalem College of Technology and Keren Avraham Bezalel (£25,000 each); Emunah (£20,000); Partnership for Schools (£13,600); Charities Aid Foundation (£12,500); Beis Ruzhin Trust (£11,000); Yesodey Hatorah School (£10,000); Beit Almog (£6,000); Campaign Against Antisemitism and Kehilat Kadima (£5,000 each).
FINANCES *Year* 2015 *Income* £238,498 *Grants* £233,660 *Grants to organisations* £233,660 *Assets* £999,412
TRUSTEES Alan Grahame; J. Greenwood.
OTHER INFORMATION Grants of less than £5,000 each totalled £46,500.
HOW TO APPLY Apply in writing to the correspondent.

WHO TO APPLY TO Miki Shaw, 5 Spencer Walk, Hampstead, London NW3 1QZ *Tel.* 020 7794 5281

■ The Granada Foundation

CC NO 241693 **ESTABLISHED** 1965
WHERE FUNDING CAN BE GIVEN North West England.
WHO CAN BENEFIT Organisations, preferably those with charity status.
WHAT IS FUNDED The study, practice and appreciation of fine arts and science and the promotion of education. According to the website, the foundation also 'welcomes applications which aim to engage and inspire young people and adults to take an interest in science'.
WHAT IS NOT FUNDED Individuals; courses of study; expeditions or travel abroad for whatever reason; general appeals; in general, youth or community associations.
RANGE OF GRANTS Up to £60,000, but mostly £3,000 or less.
SAMPLE GRANTS Contact Theatre (£60,000 in three annual instalments); Chester Performs (£50,000); Bury Metropolitan Arts Association (£20,000); Liverpool Biennial of Contemporary Art (£15,000); Friends of the Harris Museum and Art Gallery (£5,000); University of Manchester Faculty of Engineering (£3,000); Youth Dance England (£2,500); Daniel Adamson Preservation Trust (£2,000); Chester Zoo and Forward Theatre Project (£1,000 each).
FINANCES *Year* 2015/16 *Income* £28,922 *Grants* £219,000 *Grants to organisations* £219,000 *Assets* £3,134,438
TRUSTEES Sir Robert Scott; Philip Ramsbottom; Prof. Jennifer Latto.
OTHER INFORMATION The website notes that there is 'a clear preference for new projects. Although the foundation will support festivals and other annual events, it is on the understanding that such support should not be regarded as automatically renewable.' In 2015/16 a total of 35 grants were made.
HOW TO APPLY Organisations wishing to apply, in the first instance, should complete the enquiry form available from the foundation's website and send it to the foundation by email. Projects which meet the foundation's funding criteria will then have a full application pack sent to them by email. Dates of upcoming Advisory Council meetings, as well as relevant deadlines for applications, are detailed on the website.
WHO TO APPLY TO Irene Langford, Administrator, PO Box 3430, Chester CH1 9BZ *Tel.* 01244 661867 *Email* enquiries@granadafoundation.org *Website* www.granadafoundation.org

■ Grand Charitable Trust of the Order of Women Freemasons

CC NO 1059151 **ESTABLISHED** 1996
WHERE FUNDING CAN BE GIVEN England and Wales.
WHO CAN BENEFIT Registered charities.
WHAT IS FUNDED General charitable purposes, particularly hospitals and hospital appeals benefitting children, older people and people who have disabilities.
SAMPLE GRANTS Acorn Children's Hospice; British Polio Fellowship; Hearing Dogs for the Deaf; Maidstone Special Needs Service; Manchester Royal Infirmary Hospital Charity; North Devon Animal Ambulance; Paws Animal Sanctuary; Purley and Coulsdon Club; Samaritans; Shaftsbury Theatre; SSAFA; WaterAid; Wirral Churches' ARK Project.
FINANCES *Year* 2015/16 *Income* £180,286 *Grants* £106,216 *Grants to organisations* £103,566 *Assets* £862,253
TRUSTEES Margaret Masters; Brenda Jones; Zuzanka Penn; Dr Iris Boggia-Black; Sylvia Major; Carmen Gauci.
OTHER INFORMATION The trust donates about half of its grant total to causes related to the Order of Women Freemasons, including individual members and their dependants. The remaining half is donated to external charities. In 2015/16 grants to individuals totalled £2,700.
HOW TO APPLY Apply in writing to the correspondent. The annual report for 2015/16 explains that applications are 'made through lodges and individual members. Public applications are generally received through postal applications.' Our research indicates that applications should be submitted by the end of July each year for consideration by the trustees.
WHO TO APPLY TO The Trustees, 27 Pembridge Gardens, London W2 4EF *Tel.* 020 7229 2368 *Website* www.owf.org.uk/about-us/charitable-work

■ The Grantham Yorke Trust

CC NO 228466 **ESTABLISHED** 1963
WHERE FUNDING CAN BE GIVEN Birmingham.
WHO CAN BENEFIT Individuals aged under 25 who are in need and organisations working with them.
WHAT IS FUNDED Education, physical and social training, rehabilitation and recreational pursuits.
WHAT IS NOT FUNDED Grants to benefit people aged 25 or over.
RANGE OF GRANTS Generally up to £5,000.
SAMPLE GRANTS Barnardo's and Walsall Street Teams (£5,000 each); Holy Trinity Community Project (£3,800); E. R. Mason Youth Centre (£3,500); New Testament Church of God – The Rock and Support Help and Advice for Relatives of Prisoners (£3,000 each); St Francis Youth and Community Centre (£2,500).
FINANCES *Year* 2015/16 *Income* £245,270 *Grants* £194,505 *Grants to organisations* £185,485 *Assets* £6,740,905
TRUSTEES Barbara Welford; Fred Rattley; Howard Belton; Peter Jones; Philip Smiglarski; Sue Butler; Tim Clarke; Hugh Sherriffe; Ruth Burgess.
OTHER INFORMATION Grants were made to 64 organisations in 2015/16. A further 21 grants were made to individuals, amounting to £9,100.
HOW TO APPLY Apply in writing to the correspondent. The trustees meet four times a year, usually in March, June, September and December.
WHO TO APPLY TO Chrissy Norgrove, Clerk to the Trustees, c/o Shakespeare Martineau, 1 Colmore Square, Birmingham B4 6AA *Tel.* 0121 214 0487

■ GrantScape

CC NO 1102249 **ESTABLISHED** 2003
WHERE FUNDING CAN BE GIVEN UK, check the website for details of areas in which specific funds operate.
WHO CAN BENEFIT Registered charities; community organisations, including CICs; councils.
WHAT IS FUNDED GrantScape administers community funds on behalf of developers, such as wind farms, landfill sites, solar farms and renewable energy plants.

WHAT IS NOT FUNDED Each fund is subject to its own exclusions, consult the fund listing on the website.
RANGE OF GRANTS Up to £100,000.
SAMPLE GRANTS Groundwork North East and Cumbria (£100,000); East Leeds Community Club (£50,000); Wildfowl and Wetlands Trust (£25,000); Duddington Village Hall (£17,000); Park Roots CIC (£8,600); Skelbrooke Parochial Church Council (£8,000); Crick Primary School (£4,000); Almwch Town Juniors Football Club (£1,500); Kilsby Poors Land Charity (£1,000).
FINANCES *Year* 2015/16 *Income* £1,843,158 *Grants* £1,700,866 *Grants to organisations* £1,700,866 *Assets* £1,550,750
TRUSTEES Antony Cox; Mohammed Saddiq; Michael Singh; Michael Clarke; Philippa Lyons; John Mills.
OTHER INFORMATION A total of 165 grants were contracted in 2015/16.
HOW TO APPLY See GrantScape's website for details of funds currently available. Applications should be made online via the website.
WHO TO APPLY TO Matt Young, Chief Executive, Office E, Whitsundoles, Broughton Road, Salford, Milton Keynes MK17 8BU *Tel.* 01908 247630 *Email* info@GrantScape.org.uk *Website* www.GrantScape.org.uk

■ The J. G. Graves Charitable Trust

CC NO 207481 **ESTABLISHED** 1930
WHERE FUNDING CAN BE GIVEN City of Sheffield.
WHO CAN BENEFIT Mostly local registered charities. Other constituted groups may also be assisted.
WHAT IS FUNDED Disadvantaged groups; community-based projects and facilities; activities to improve the quality of life and the heritage of Sheffield (particularly in relation to the Graves inheritance); the promotion of sport and health; community projects connected to churches; hospital or medical facilities benefitting the community; special needs schools, for non-mainstream educational expenditure and community-based projects; local and community amenities, particularly recreational and sporting facilities, affected by restrictions on Local Authority funding.
WHAT IS NOT FUNDED Grants are generally not made to or for the benefit of individuals. Grants are not made for church fabric or church activities (only community projects connected to churches are supported) or for items, facilities or services which are the responsibility of the state.
TYPE OF GRANT There is a preference for capital projects; however, seed funding and running costs can also be supported.
RANGE OF GRANTS Usually between £500 and £3,000.
SAMPLE GRANTS Showroom Cinema and St Luke's Hospice (£5,000 each); Sheffield Family Holiday Fund and Sheffield Industrial Museums Trust (£3,000 each); Friends of Concord Park and Wolley Wood and Sheffield Mencap and Gateway (£2,000 each); Boys and Girls Clubs South Yorkshire, FareShare South Yorkshire and Friends of Charnock Recreation Ground (£1,500 each).
FINANCES *Year* 2015 *Income* £167,828 *Grants* £74,640 *Grants to organisations* £74,640 *Assets* £4,775,408
TRUSTEES Dona Womack; John Bramah; Peter Clarkson; Dr Derek Cullen; Cllr Jackie Drayton; Richard Graves; Hugh Grayson; Rick Plews; Cllr Peter Price; Kim Streets.
OTHER INFORMATION The trustees prefer to support special projects, rather than supplement regular income. During the year, 56 grants were made.
HOW TO APPLY Application forms are available to download from the trust's website. They should be returned to the secretary by 31 March, 30 June, 30 September or 31 December for consideration at the trustees' quarterly meetings held, usually during the last week, in January, April, July and October. Applicants should receive notification of the trustees' decision within four weeks of the relevant meeting.
WHO TO APPLY TO Jane Marshall, Secretary, c/o BHP Chartered Accountants, 2 Rutland Park, Sheffield S10 2PD *Tel.* 0114 266 7171 *Fax* 0114 266 9486 *Email* jane.marshall@bhp.co.uk or michelle.sargent@bhp.co.uk *Website* jggravescharitabletrust.co.uk

■ Gordon Gray Trust

CC NO 213935 **ESTABLISHED** 1960
WHERE FUNDING CAN BE GIVEN England with a preference for Gloucestershire and Worcestershire.
WHO CAN BENEFIT Registered charities.
WHAT IS FUNDED General charitable purposes, particularly medical causes, the welfare of children and older people, and the environment.
WHAT IS NOT FUNDED Individuals.
RANGE OF GRANTS Between £50 and £20,000, but mostly up to £2,000.
SAMPLE GRANTS Avon Navigation Trust (£20,000); Midlands Air Ambulance (£5,000); British Heart Foundation and St Richard's Hospice (£3,000 each); Friends of the Lake District and Keswick Mountain Rescue Team (£2,500 each); NSPCC and Royal National Lifeboat Institution (£2,000 each); Gloucestershire Wildlife Trust, New College Worcester, Samaritans – Cheltenham and District and Severn Freewheelers EVS (£1,000 each); First Bredon Guides (£500); Gloucestershire Historic Churches Trust (£50).
FINANCES *Year* 2015/16 *Income* £115,061 *Grants* £113,100 *Grants to organisations* £113,100 *Assets* £3,530,472
TRUSTEES Dr B. Gray; S. Watson-Armstrong; C. Wilder; R. Holmes; E. Roberts; M. M. Gray.
OTHER INFORMATION Grants were made to 60 organisations in 2015/16.
HOW TO APPLY Apply in writing to the correspondent. The trust's Charity Commission record notes that 'if you do not receive a reply to a request for funding, your application has been unsuccessful.'
WHO TO APPLY TO Melanie Gray, Clerk to the Trustees, Grange Farm, Main Road, Bredon, Tewkesbury, Gloucestershire GL20 7EL

■ The Gray Trust

CC NO 210914 **ESTABLISHED** 1962
WHERE FUNDING CAN BE GIVEN Nottinghamshire, especially Linby and Papplewick and the surrounding area.
WHO CAN BENEFIT Charitable organisations.
WHAT IS FUNDED General charitable purposes, primarily for the benefit of older people, and charitable purposes in the parishes of Linby and Papplewick and the surrounding area.
WHAT IS NOT FUNDED Individuals; applications from outside Nottinghamshire.
TYPE OF GRANT Capital and/or revenue projects.
RANGE OF GRANTS Mostly between £500 and £1,000.

SAMPLE GRANTS Friends of the Elderly (£77,000); Age UK Ltd (£5,000); Caudwell Children, Listening Books, St John's Day Centre for the Elderly, St Paul's Strelley Parochial Church Council (£1,000 each); Carewatch in Nottingham, the Ear Foundation and Nottinghamshire Historic Churches Trust (£500 each); Action on Hearing Loss (£300).
FINANCES *Year* 2015/16 *Income* £155,687 *Grants* £111,674 *Grants to organisations* £111,674 *Assets* £5,281,546
TRUSTEES Claire Hardstaff; Bella St Clair Harlow; Richard Pannell; Revd Canon Keith Turner; Kirstin Thompson.
OTHER INFORMATION In 2015/16 the trust made grants to 36 organisations. The trust also provides sheltered accommodation for older people.
HOW TO APPLY Apply in writing to the correspondent by letter of application together with most recent accounts.
WHO TO APPLY TO Nigel Lindley, Smith Cooper Ltd, 2 Lace Market Square, Nottingham NG1 1PB *Tel.* 0115 945 4300 *Email* nigel.lindley@smithcooper.co.uk

■ The Great Britain Sasakawa Foundation

CC NO 290766 **ESTABLISHED** 1985
WHERE FUNDING CAN BE GIVEN UK and Japan.
WHO CAN BENEFIT Voluntary, educational and cultural organisations; registered charities benefitting citizens of UK and Japan. Emphasis on younger people and on projects benefitting groups of people rather than individuals.
WHAT IS FUNDED Activities which support mutual understanding between the Japanese and UK citizens in the following fields: arts and culture; humanities; social issues; Japanese language; medicine and health; science, technology and environment; sport; young people and education.
WHAT IS NOT FUNDED Individuals directly; medical, psychological or sociological research on humans or animals; consumables; salaries; purchase of materials; capital projects such as the purchase, construction or maintenance of buildings; projects designed to extend over more than one year (the foundation is prepared to consider requests for funding spread over a period of not more than three consecutive years); completed or current projects; core costs; student fees or travel for study (apart from PhD fieldwork in Japan).
TYPE OF GRANT Mainly one-off; projects; research; up to three years.
RANGE OF GRANTS Awards average £1,500 to £2,000 and do not normally exceed £5,000 to £6,000 for larger-scale projects.
SAMPLE GRANTS Bizjapan Association; Fishguard Arts Society; National Centre for Craft and Design; Noh time like the present; The Sasakawa Japanese Studies Postgraduate Studentship Programme; University of Liverpool.
FINANCES *Year* 2016 *Income* £1,177,834 *Grants* £1,117,440 *Grants to organisations* £1,117,440 *Assets* £27,502,177
TRUSTEES Michael French; Sir John Boyd; Ambassador Hiroaki Fujii; The Earl of St Andrews; Prof. David Cope; Tatsuya Tanami; Joanna Pitman; Prof. Yuichi Hosoya; Prof. Yorkio Kawaguchi; Prof. Janet Hunter; Prof. Ryuichi Teshima.
OTHER INFORMATION The foundation is rarely able to consider grants for the total cost of any project and encourages applicants to seek additional support from other donors.
HOW TO APPLY Full application details can be found on the website. Application forms to the London office can be found on the website, once completed they must be sent via email to grants@gbsf.org.uk. To apply to the Tokyo office, the applicant must email tokyo@gbsf.org.uk before making an application. The trustees make the final decisions on awards at meetings held in London three times a year (normally March, May and November) and Tokyo twice a year (normally April and October). The deadline for London applicants are as follows:
15 December for a decision in early March;
31 March for a decision by the end of May;
15 September for a decision in early November.
The deadline for Tokyo applicants are as follows: 28 February for a decision by the end of April; 30 September for a decision by the end of October. The foundation's website states that they normally receive three times as many requests as they are able to grant, and that around 75% of applicants receive funding, but may receive less than originally requested.
WHO TO APPLY TO Brendan Griggs, Dilke House, 1 Malet Street, London WC1E 7JN *Tel.* 020 7436 9042 *Email* grants@gbsf.org.uk *Website* www.gbsf.org.uk

■ The Kenneth and Susan Green Charitable Foundation

CC NO 1147248 **ESTABLISHED** 2012
WHERE FUNDING CAN BE GIVEN UK.
WHO CAN BENEFIT Charitable organisations.
WHAT IS FUNDED Education; the relief of poverty; health; arts and culture; general charitable purposes.
WHAT IS NOT FUNDED Individuals.
RANGE OF GRANTS Up to £105,000.
SAMPLE GRANTS The Royal Opera House Covent Garden Foundation (£105,000); The Royal Ballet School (£50,000); Royal National Lifeboat Institution (£25,000); The Pepper Foundation (£20,000); The Cecchetti Society Trust and Paladin (£19,000 each).
FINANCES *Year* 2016 *Income* £1,660,843 *Grants* £273,500 *Grants to organisations* £273,500 *Assets* £3,404,864
TRUSTEES Kenneth Green; Philip Stokes; Susan Green.
OTHER INFORMATION Grants of less than £10,000 each totalled £35,500.
HOW TO APPLY Previous research suggests that the foundation supports a few specific charities and does not seek new applications.
WHO TO APPLY TO Philip Stokes, Trustee, c/o Kenneth Green Associates, Hill House, Monument Hill, Weybridge KT13 8RX *Tel.* 01932 827060

■ The Green Hall Foundation

CC NO 270775 **ESTABLISHED** 1976
WHERE FUNDING CAN BE GIVEN UK and overseas.
WHO CAN BENEFIT UK-registered charities only.
WHAT IS FUNDED The foundation makes grants to 'sustainably improve' the lives of people who are sick, older, who have disabilities or are disadvantaged, particularly in the UK but also overseas.
WHAT IS NOT FUNDED Individuals; general running costs; salaries.

TYPE OF GRANT Capital costs and special project funding. One-off for one year or less.
RANGE OF GRANTS Typically between £1,000 and £10,000.
SAMPLE GRANTS Save the Children (£15,000); Great Ormond Street Hospital and The Salvation Army (£10,000 each); Livingstone Tanzania Trust (£6,000); 22nd Hillmorton Rugby Scout Group, Crisis UK, Leeds Women's Aid, Yorkshire Dance and Trinity Sailing Foundation (£5,000 each); Prisoners' Education Trust (£4,000); Friendship Works, Richard House Children's Hospice and Vauxhall City Farm (£2,500 each); Kinship Care Northern Ireland (£1,000).
FINANCES *Year* 2015/16 *Income* £371,337 *Grants* £272,100 *Grants to organisations* £272,100
TRUSTEES Margaret Hall; Sue Collinson; Nigel Hall; Peter Morgan; Charlotte Footer.
OTHER INFORMATION In 2015/16 grants were distributed as follows: disability and older people (49% of grant total); church and community projects (16%); medical and social care (16%); children and young people (11%); and homelessness (8%).
HOW TO APPLY Applications must be made online through the foundation's website. The trustees meet twice a year, in May and November. Only the first 100 applications received by the foundation will be taken forward to be considered by the trustees. The opening dates for application cycles are detailed on the website and the cycles close when the 100th application has been received.
WHO TO APPLY TO S. Hall, Centenary House, La Grande Route De St., Pierre, St Peter, Jersey JE3 7AY *Tel.* 01534 487757 *Email* greenhallfoundation@fcmtrust.com *Website* www.greenhallfoundation.org

■ Philip and Judith Green Trust

CC NO 1109933 **ESTABLISHED** 2005
WHERE FUNDING CAN BE GIVEN UK and South Africa.
WHO CAN BENEFIT Registered charities and Christian missionaries.
WHAT IS FUNDED Support for missionaries; the upkeep and provision of Christian places of worship; the provision of educational facilities to support the development of students in underprivileged communities.
RANGE OF GRANTS Up to £85,000 but generally less than £9,000.
SAMPLE GRANTS Hope Through Action (£85,000); Inherit Your Rights (£13,300); Greyfriars Church (£8,700); Rinell Carey Holmquist (£6,600); Sentebale (£5,300); Christ Church Paarl (£2,500); British and Foreign Bible Society (£2,400); African Enterprise (£2,000); Hoedspruit Endangered Species Centre (£1,500); Greyfriars Mission (£730); Bible Society (£360).
FINANCES *Year* 2015/16 *Income* £160,187 *Grants* £144,317 *Grants to organisations* £136,937 *Assets* £416,786
TRUSTEES Philip Green; Judith Green.
OTHER INFORMATION Grants were made to 13 organisations in 2015/16. Grants totalling £7,400 were given to missionaries.
HOW TO APPLY Apply in writing to the correspondent.
WHO TO APPLY TO Philip Green, Trustee, c/o Dixon Wilson, 22 Chancery Lane, London WC2A 1LS *Tel.* 0118 984 5935 *Email* philipngreen@me.com

■ Mrs H. R. Greene Charitable Settlement

CC NO 1050812 **ESTABLISHED** 1845
WHERE FUNDING CAN BE GIVEN UK, with a preference for Norfolk and Wistanstow in Shropshire.
WHO CAN BENEFIT Charitable organisations; individuals.
WHAT IS FUNDED Social welfare and general charitable purposes.
SAMPLE GRANTS A list of beneficiaries was not included in the accounts.
FINANCES *Year* 2015/16 *Income* £90,980 *Grants* £79,068 *Grants to organisations* £73,095 *Assets* £2,488,864
TRUSTEES The Revd J. B. Boston; Mr C. Boston; Mr J. Boston; Mrs A. C. Briggs.
OTHER INFORMATION The grant total includes £6,000 in Christmas gifts.
HOW TO APPLY The trust states that it does not respond to unsolicited applications.
WHO TO APPLY TO Neil Sparrow, Administrator, Birketts LLP, Kingfisher House, 1 Gilders Way, Norwich, Norfolk NR3 1UB *Tel.* 01603 232300 *Email* neil-sparrow@birketts.co.uk

■ Greenham Common Community Trust Ltd

CC NO 1062762 **ESTABLISHED** 1997
WHERE FUNDING CAN BE GIVEN Newbury and the surrounding areas, northern edges of North Hampshire, West Berkshire.
WHO CAN BENEFIT Charitable organisations and individuals.
WHAT IS FUNDED Arts; community; education; health; nature and conservation; sport; youth disability; disadvantage/equality; older people; human rights and diversity; military and emergency services.
WHAT IS NOT FUNDED Retrospective projects; projects outside West Berkshire and specified ward areas in North Hampshire; items/refurbishment which are the responsibility of the applicant's landlord; appeals by individuals rather than organisations; work considered a statutory responsibility; organisations that do not have charitable aims; projects that will bring in profit; commercial companies; payments for membership subscriptions; provision of broadband for rural villages.
TYPE OF GRANT One-off grants and specific projects, but grant delivery on a year-by-year basis can be considered. Grants to both individuals and organisations.
RANGE OF GRANTS Up to £418,000.
SAMPLE GRANTS Corn Exchange Newbury (£418,200); Alexander Devine (£230,000); NADAS (£182,500); Community Furniture Project (£129,000); Aldworth Village Hall (£108,000).
FINANCES *Year* 2015/16 *Income* £8,409,197 *Grants* £4,058,844 *Grants to organisations* £4,030,645 *Assets* £62,105,506
TRUSTEES Sir Peter Michael; David Bailey; Graham Mather; Malcolm Morris; Dr Paul Bryant; Julian Cazalet; Charles Brims; Biddy Hayward; Victoria Fishburn.
OTHER INFORMATION The Charity awarded £28,000 to grants for individuals.
HOW TO APPLY All applications for the trust's funding should be made via thegoodexchange.com. Full details on how to apply are available on the trust's website. If you are applying for funding for a major or significant project call the trust on

01635 817444 to discuss your project in person.

WHO TO APPLY TO Chris Boulton, Chief Executive, Liberty House, The Enterprise Centre, Greenham Business Park, Newbury, Berkshire RG19 6HS *Tel.* 01635 817444 *Email* enquiries@greenham-common-trust.co.uk *Website* www.greenham-common-trust.co.uk

The Greggs Foundation

CC NO 296590 **ESTABLISHED** 1987

WHERE FUNDING CAN BE GIVEN UK, with a preference for the north east of England, and in the regional divisions of Greggs PLC.

WHO CAN BENEFIT Charitable organisations; individuals.

WHAT IS FUNDED Applications from small community-led organisations and self-help groups are more likely to be successful than those from larger and well-staffed organisations and those that have greater fundraising capacity. Projects in the fields of the arts, the environment, conservation, education and health will be considered so long as they have a social welfare focus and/or are located in areas of deprivation.

WHAT IS NOT FUNDED Large Community Projects Fund: ongoing running costs; contributions towards larger projects/fundraising appeals; animal charities; friends of associations; uniformed groups such as scouts, guides and sea cadets; sports clubs and associations; overseas travel; curricular activities that take place during the school day; religious promotion; research grants; repayment of loans; purchase of vehicles; medical equipment; major capital project; sponsorship of events or activities. Environmental Grant: ongoing running costs; overseas travel; curricular activities that take place during the school day; religious promotion; major capital projects; sponsorship of events or activities. North East Core Funding: animal charities; friends of associations; branches or federations of national charities; larger organisations with a greater capacity to fundraise; uniformed groups such as scouts, guides and sea cadets; sports clubs and associations. Hardship Fund: unspecified costs; repayment of loans; bankruptcy petition fees; holidays; funeral expenses; medical equipment; computer equipment.

TYPE OF GRANT Core costs, running costs, project, start-up costs, recurring costs, salaries, one-off. Funding may be given for up to three years.

RANGE OF GRANTS Local Community Projects Fund: up to £2,000. Environmental Grant: up to £2,000. Hardship Fund: up to £150.

SAMPLE GRANTS Beacon Hill Arts (£40,500); Families in Care (£30,000); Full Circle Food Project (£20,000); Durham Area Disability Leisure Group (£15,000); Machin Trusts-Breakfast Club (£12,000); Auckland Youth and Community Centre (£10,000) Parkinson's UK-Borders Branch (£3,000); Woodland's Community Garden, Perth Autism Support (£2,000) Crossroads Care Gateshead (£1,500); Finding your Feet (£1,000).

FINANCES *Year* 2015 *Income* £2,573,659 *Grants* £2,053,441 *Grants to organisations* £1,824,326 *Assets* £17,660,990

TRUSTEES Andrew Davison; Kate Welch; Annemarie Norman; Fiona Nicholson; Richard Hutton; Tony Rowson; Nigel Murray; Roisin Currie; Karen Wilkinson-Bell.

OTHER INFORMATION The foundation offers different grant programmes which include: Local Community Projects Fund; Environmental Grant; North East Core Funding; Hardship Fund.

HOW TO APPLY Apply online via the website. Each grants programme has its own criteria, guidelines and application process, all of which are available to view on the website.

WHO TO APPLY TO Justine Massingham, Grants Manager, Greggs House, Quorum Business Park, Newcastle upon Tyne, Tyne and Wear NE12 8BU *Tel.* 0191 212 7626 or 0191 212 7813 *Email* greggsfoundation@greggs.co.uk *Website* www.greggsfoundation.org.uk

The Gretna Charitable Trust

CC NO 1020533 **ESTABLISHED** 1993

WHERE FUNDING CAN BE GIVEN UK, with a preference for Hertfordshire and London.

WHO CAN BENEFIT Registered charities.

WHAT IS FUNDED General charitable purposes.

WHAT IS NOT FUNDED Salaries; administration costs.

TYPE OF GRANT Recurring and one-off. Seed funding or grants for specific needs.

RANGE OF GRANTS Up to £20,000, but typically between £500 and £5,000.

SAMPLE GRANTS Royal Engineers Museum (£20,000); British Australia Society and Collect a Medal (£5,000 each); Garden Museum – Lambeth and The Scout Association (£2,000 each); Mensah Recovery Support Agency (£1,500); Charlie Waller Memorial Trust and The Globe Theatre (£1,000 each); Haileybury Youth Club and World Sight Foundation (£500 each).

FINANCES *Year* 2015/16 *Income* £292,150 *Grants* £84,066 *Grants to organisations* £84,066 *Assets* £2,358,156

TRUSTEES Richard Walduck; Susan Walduck; Alexander Walduck; Alison Duncan.

HOW TO APPLY The trustees discourage unsolicited applications.

WHO TO APPLY TO Richard Walduck, Trustee, Lower Woodside House, Lower Woodside, Hatfield AL9 6DJ *Email* awalduck@imperialhotels.co.uk

Greys Charitable Trust

CC NO 1103717 **ESTABLISHED** 2004

WHERE FUNDING CAN BE GIVEN UK and locally in Oxfordshire.

WHO CAN BENEFIT Charities and voluntary bodies, both national organisations and those local to Oxfordshire.

WHAT IS FUNDED Church of England preservation projects; historical preservation; the arts.

RANGE OF GRANTS £2,500 to £10,000.

SAMPLE GRANTS Brighton College (£18,000 in three grants); The National Trust (£14,900 in two grants); Trinity College – Oxford (£10,000); Notting Hill Preparatory School (£5,500); Institute of Economic Affairs (£2,500).

FINANCES *Year* 2015/16 *Income* £28,207 *Grants* £50,900 *Grants to organisations* £50,900 *Assets* £1,019,833

TRUSTEES Jacob Brunner; Timothy Brunner.

OTHER INFORMATION In 2015/16 eight grants were made to five organisations.

HOW TO APPLY Apply in writing to the correspondent. The trustees usually meet twice a year.

WHO TO APPLY TO The Trustees of the Greys Charitable Trust, Flat 4, 2 Inverness Gardens, London W8 4RN *Tel.* 020 7727 6277 *Email* p.roberts@robco.uk.com

■ The Grimmitt Trust

CC NO 801975 **ESTABLISHED** 1989

WHERE FUNDING CAN BE GIVEN The Birmingham, Dudley, Wolverhampton and Walsall postcode areas; overseas.

WHO CAN BENEFIT Charities; charitable organisations; individuals.

WHAT IS FUNDED Community; children and young people; culture; education; medical causes; older people; overseas aid.

WHAT IS NOT FUNDED The trust does not normally support national charities, CICs or social enterprises.

TYPE OF GRANT One-off, grants of up to three years.

RANGE OF GRANTS Up to £10,000, but mostly of £2,500 or less.

SAMPLE GRANTS The King Edward's School Birmingham Trust and Lench's Trust (£10,000 each); The Methodist Church Selly Oak (£7,000); Selly Oak Live at Home Scheme (£6,000); City of Birmingham Symphony Orchestra, Coventry Law Centre, Shrewsbury and Newport Canals Trust and Walsall Street Teams (£5,000 each); Wellington Methodist Church and Centre and Youth with a Mission Scotland (£2,500 each); Action Centres UK, Birmingham St Mary's Hospice, Geese Theatre Company, Walsall Carers' Centre and Way Ahead Support Services (£2,000 each).

FINANCES *Year* 2015/16 *Income* £292,354 *Grants* £270,200 *Grants to organisations* £270,200 *Assets* £8,345,132

TRUSTEES Sue Day; Leon Murray; David Owen; Tim Welch; Jenny Dickins; Sarah Wilkey; Phil Smith; Trevor Jones.

OTHER INFORMATION From 549 applications received by the trust in 2015/16, grants were made to 233 organisations and individuals. Grants of less than £2,000 totalled £131,000.

HOW TO APPLY Applicants should contact the secretary who will advise on the best way to design a grant request and to ensure that all the necessary information is included. The trustees meet three times a year to consider applications. Applicants must demonstrate that their project is in line with the trust's objectives.

WHO TO APPLY TO Vanessa Welch, Secretary, 151B All Saints Road, Kings Heath, Birmingham B14 6AT *Tel.* 0121 251 2951 *Email* admin@grimmitt-trust.org.uk

■ The Grocers' Charity

CC NO 255230 **ESTABLISHED** 1968

WHERE FUNDING CAN BE GIVEN UK.

WHO CAN BENEFIT Registered charities only.

WHAT IS FUNDED Relief of poverty for young people; help for people with disabilities; medical research; the arts and heritage, military charities; older people.

WHAT IS NOT FUNDED Support is rarely given to the following unless there is a specific or long-standing connection with the Grocers' Company: places of worship; educational establishments; hospices; charities whose beneficiaries are overseas; charities not registered in the UK; charities with a turnover of over £500,000; individuals.

RANGE OF GRANTS £1,000 to £250,000.

SAMPLE GRANTS Oundle School (£250,000); 999 Club (£32,000); Motor Neurone Disease Association (£30,000); Charlie Waller Memorial Trust (£23,500); St Stephen Walbrook (£12,000); Childhood Eye Cancer Trust and Multiple Sclerosis Trust (£10,000 each); icandance (£7,500); BRACE and Facial Palsy UK (£5,000 each); Walk the Walk (£3,000); Asthma UK and University of Leeds (£2,000 each); The Big Issue Foundation (£1,500); St Andrews at Melcombe (£1,000).

FINANCES *Year* 2015/16 *Income* £859,946 *Grants* £859,946 *Grants to organisations* £627,438 *Assets* £163,096

TRUSTEE The Grocers' Trust Company Ltd.

OTHER INFORMATION Grants were distributed as follows: education (£369,500); medicine (£127,500); relief of poverty (£126,500); the arts (£62,500); churches (£58,000); heritage (£53,000); disability (£43,500); older people and other (£19,500).

HOW TO APPLY Applications can be made via the charity's website.

WHO TO APPLY TO Michael Griffin, Finance Director, Grocers' Hall, Princes Street, London EC2R 8AD *Tel.* 020 7606 3113 *Email* enquiries@grocershall.co.uk *Website* www.grocershall.co.uk

■ M. and R. Gross Charities Ltd

CC NO 251888 **ESTABLISHED** 1967

WHERE FUNDING CAN BE GIVEN UK and overseas.

WHO CAN BENEFIT Jewish organisations.

WHAT IS FUNDED Orthodox Jewish educational and religious activities; the relief of Jewish people who are in need; general charitable purposes.

SAMPLE GRANTS Atlas Memorial Ltd; Beis Ruchel Building Fund; Beth Hamedresh Satmar Trust; Chevras Tsedokoh Ltd; Craven Walk Beis Hamedrash; Daas Sholem; Friends of Yeshivas Brisk; Gevurah Ari Torah Academy Trust; Kehal Chareidim Trust; Kollel Shomrei Hachomoth; Talmud Torah Trust; Telz Talmudical Academy; Union of Orthodox Hebrew Congregations; United Talmudical Associates Ltd; Yetev Lev Jerusalem.

FINANCES *Year* 2015/16 *Income* £4,207,751 *Grants* £8,141,000 *Grants to organisations* £8,141,000 *Assets* £58,957,280

TRUSTEES Rifka Gross; Sarah Padwa; Michael Saberski; Leonard Lerner.

OTHER INFORMATION A recent list of beneficiaries was not included in the annual report and accounts.

HOW TO APPLY Apply in writing to the correspondent. Applications are assessed regularly and many of the smaller grants are dealt with through a grant-making agency, United Talmudical Associates Ltd.

WHO TO APPLY TO The Trustees of M. and R. Gross Charities Ltd, c/o Cohen Arnold, New Burlington House, 1075 Finchley Road, London NW11 0PU *Tel.* 020 8731 0777 *Email* mail@cohenarnold.com

■ The N. and R. Grunbaum Charitable Trust

CC NO 1068524 **ESTABLISHED** 1998

WHERE FUNDING CAN BE GIVEN UK and Israel.

WHO CAN BENEFIT Registered charities and Jewish organisations.

WHAT IS FUNDED Jewish causes.

SAMPLE GRANTS A list of beneficiaries was not included in the accounts.

FINANCES *Year* 2015/16 *Income* £44,002 *Grants* £47,435 *Grants to organisations* £47,435 *Assets* £3,301

TRUSTEES Norman Grunbaum; Rosella Grunbaum; David Grunbaum.

HOW TO APPLY Apply in writing to the correspondent.

WHO TO APPLY TO Norman Grunbaum, Trustee, 7 Northdene Gardens, London N15 6LX *Tel.* 020 8800 9974 *Email* charity@thegreentrees.co.uk

■ The Bishop of Guildford's Foundation

CC NO 1017385 **ESTABLISHED** 1993

WHERE FUNDING CAN BE GIVEN Diocese of Guildford.

WHO CAN BENEFIT Voluntary and community groups who are linked with a church or faith community, or engaged in a project working in partnership with a church or faith community. Organisations don't have to be registered charities but do have to have a constitution or set of rules, and a bank account, or be supported by an organisation that has these.

WHAT IS FUNDED Community projects. The purpose of the foundation's grants programme is to support projects and partnerships through which church or faith linked groups meet local needs or get involved in community development and regeneration. Projects cover a wide range of groups, such as homelessness, poverty, children with disabilities, family support, youth work, mental health, etc. Priority will be given to projects and partnerships which build communities' own capacity to meet local needs, especially in relation to those who are excluded or vulnerable, as well as to helping projects become sustainable.

WHAT IS NOT FUNDED Individuals; capital costs; projects which have already occurred.

TYPE OF GRANT Small project grants, usually up to £2,000; larger strategic grants, usually up to £10,000. Applications for funding for more than one year can be considered, especially where this enables projects to apply for other funding. Applicants are generally expected to obtain additional funding from other sources – the foundation only occasionally funds the full cost of a project.

RANGE OF GRANTS Up to £1,000.

SAMPLE GRANTS River Church (£5,000); Trinity Trust Team (£4,800); Stoneleigh Youth Project (£3,500); St Mark's Shared Church and Westcott Youth Club (£3,000); Generation Church West Ewell and The Family Contact Centre – Camberley and District (£2,000 each); Cobham Area Food Bank and Woking Street Angels (£1,000); Camberley Youth for Christ (£500).

FINANCES *Year* 2015/16 *Income* £43,344 *Grants* £43,750 *Grants to organisations* £43,750 *Assets* £7,673

TRUSTEES Michael Bishop; Geoffrey Riggs; Hugh Bryant; Michael Gibson; Rt Revd Andrew Watson.

OTHER INFORMATION Grants were made to 19 organisations in 2015/16.

HOW TO APPLY Grants are administered through Community Foundation for Surrey. Eligibility criteria and other information is given on The Bishop of Guildford's Foundation's website. For information on how to apply, contact Community Foundation for Surrey on 01483 409230 or go to the website: www.cfsurrey.org.uk/

WHO TO APPLY TO Michael Gibson, Secretary, 11 Woodway, Guilford, Surrey GU1 2TF *Tel.* 01483 538818 *Email* info@bgf.org.uk *Website* www.bgf.org.uk

■ Guildry Incorporation of Perth

SC NO SC008072 **ESTABLISHED** 1210

WHERE FUNDING CAN BE GIVEN Perth and its surrounding areas.

WHO CAN BENEFIT Charities; community organisations; members of the Guildry; residents of Perth and its surrounding areas who are in need.

WHAT IS FUNDED The main purpose of the trust is to provide support for its members and their families. Charitable donations are also made to local causes at the discretion of the committee.

RANGE OF GRANTS Up to £15,000.

SAMPLE GRANTS Duke of Edinburgh's Award – Perth and Kinross (£15,000); Perth Access Cars (£7,500); Perth Amateur Operatic Society, Perth Festival of the Arts and Perth Hyperbaric Services (£3,000 each); Headway (£1,300); Scone Thistle Community Club (£1,000).

FINANCES *Year* 2015/16 *Income* £211,176 *Grants* £122,016 *Grants to organisations* £47,153 *Assets* £6,374,041

OTHER INFORMATION A total of £75,000 was given in grants to 91 individuals.

HOW TO APPLY Apply in writing to the correspondent. Grants are considered on the last Tuesday of every month.

WHO TO APPLY TO Carla Murray, Secretary, 42 George Street, Perth, Perthshire PH1 5JL *Tel.* 01738 623195 *Email* guildryperth@btconnect.com *Website* www.perthguildry.org.uk

■ The Walter Guinness Charitable Trust

CC NO 205375 **ESTABLISHED** 1961

WHERE FUNDING CAN BE GIVEN UK and overseas, with a strong interest in Wiltshire.

WHO CAN BENEFIT Registered charities and community groups.

WHAT IS FUNDED The trust supports a wide range of charitable purposes, including bursaries for education, medical research, and specific and general projects relating to people with disabilities, older people, veterans, prisoners, children, families and young people.

WHAT IS NOT FUNDED Individuals.

TYPE OF GRANT Normally one-off.

RANGE OF GRANTS Grants from less than £1,000 to £10,000.

SAMPLE GRANTS Marie Curie Cancer Care (£5,000); Salisbury Cathedral Choral Foundation (£4,000 for a one year bursary for a chorister); Andover Mind, Fair Shares Gloucestershire and Prospect Hospice Swindon (£3,000 each); Home-Start South Wilts (£2,700); British Red Cross (£2,200); Action on Addiction, Contact the Elderly, Friends without Borders, Great Western Hospitals NHS Foundation Trust, Mencap – Andover and District and Writers in Prison Foundation (£2,000 each); ABF The Soldiers' Charity and FareShare South West (£1,500 each).

FINANCES *Year* 2015/16 *Income* £169,197 *Grants* £150,469 *Grants to organisations* £150,469 *Assets* £7,716,878

TRUSTEES Finn Guinness; Rosaleen Mulji; Catriona Guinness.

OTHER INFORMATION In 2015/16, 116 grants were made: 38 were of more than £1,000 and 78 were of up to £1,000.

HOW TO APPLY Apply in writing to the correspondent. Replies are only sent when there is a positive decision. Initial telephone calls are not possible. There are no application forms, guidelines or deadlines. No sae is required.

WHO TO APPLY TO The Trustees, Biddesden House, Biddesden, Andover SP11 9DN *Email* WGuinnessCT@tmf-group.com

■ The Gunter Charitable Trust

CC NO 268346 **ESTABLISHED** 1974
WHERE FUNDING CAN BE GIVEN Worldwide, mainly UK.
WHO CAN BENEFIT Local and UK organisations.
WHAT IS FUNDED General charitable purposes.
RANGE OF GRANTS Typically up to £20,000.
SAMPLE GRANTS Freedom from Torture (£5,800); Liverpool School of Tropical Medicine (£5,000); MS Society (£3,000); Friends of Dr Pearey Lal Charitable Hospital – UK and Gurkha Welfare Trust (£2,000 each); Bumblebee Conservation Trust, Nordoff Robbins and Partnership for Children (£1,300 each); Amnesty International (£1,000); Positive Action in Housing (£950); Plantlife International (£500); Council for Music in Hospitals (£370).
FINANCES *Year* 2015/16 *Income* £118,404 *Grants* £83,554 *Grants to organisations* £83,554 *Assets* £2,492,354
TRUSTEES James de Cardonnel Findlay; Richard Worrall.
OTHER INFORMATION In 2013/14 grants were made to 54 organisations.
HOW TO APPLY Unsolicited applications are not accepted.
WHO TO APPLY TO The Trustees of The Gunter Charitable Trust, c/o Forsters LLP, 31 Hill Street, London W1J 5LS *Tel.* 020 7863 8333

■ The Gur Trust

CC NO 283423 **ESTABLISHED** 1981
WHERE FUNDING CAN BE GIVEN Worldwide.
WHO CAN BENEFIT Talmudical colleges; other organisations; individuals.
WHAT IS FUNDED The advancement of education in and the religion of the Orthodox Jewish faith.
SAMPLE GRANTS Beis Yaacov Casidic Seminary, Beth Yaacov Town, Bnei Emes Institutions, Central Charity Fund, Gur Talmudical College, Kollel Arad, Yeshiva Lezeirim, Pri Gidulim, Maala and Mifal Gevura Shecehessed.
FINANCES *Year* 2014/15 *Income* £43,521 *Grants* £42,839 *Grants to organisations* £42,839 *Assets* £1,368,379
TRUSTEES Sheldon Morgenstern; David Cymerman; Shaye Traube.
HOW TO APPLY Apply in writing to the correspondent.
WHO TO APPLY TO Sheldon Morgenstern, Trustee, 206 High Road, London N15 4NP *Tel.* 020 8801 6038

■ Dr Guthrie's Association

SC NO SC009302 **ESTABLISHED** 1986
WHERE FUNDING CAN BE GIVEN Scotland, with a preference for Edinburgh.
WHO CAN BENEFIT Not-for-profit organisations benefitting disadvantaged children and young people under 22 years of age.
WHAT IS FUNDED The care and welfare of young people. Priority will be given to: organisations supporting economically and socially disadvantaged children and young people aged 10–21; small local organisations as opposed to national organisations; creative and outdoor pursuits for disadvantaged children and young people; organisations supporting young unemployed people.
WHAT IS NOT FUNDED Individuals – including students, gap year experience, etc.; environment – projects entirely of an environmental nature, e.g. geographic and scenic, conservation and protection of flora and fauna; people who are disadvantaged primarily because of physical or health-related disadvantage rather than social or economic need; mainstream activities and statutory requirements of schools, universities and colleges; mainstream activities and statutory requirements of hospitals and medical centres; activities which collect funds for subsequent redistribution to other organisations; the establishment/preservation of endowment funds; large scale building projects; historic restoration; retrospective funding.
TYPE OF GRANT One-off.
RANGE OF GRANTS £250 to £2,000.
SAMPLE GRANTS Abernethy Trust, Citylife Ministries Ltd, City Youth Café, Glasgow City Mission, Happy Days Children's Charity, Reality Adventure Works in Scotland, Riptide Music Studios, Tall Ships Youth Trust, Turning Point Scotland and Visibility (£1,000 each); ChildLine Scotland (£750); Red School Youth Centre (£700); Bibles for Children (£500).
FINANCES *Year* 2015/16 *Income* £44,063 *Grants* £83,610 *Grants to organisations* £83,610 *Assets* £1,153
HOW TO APPLY Application forms can be downloaded from the website and should be returned to the grant administrator.
WHO TO APPLY TO Grant Administrator, PO Box 28838, Edinburgh EH15 2XZ *Email* drguthrie@tiscali.co.uk *Website* www.scott-moncrieff.com/services/charities/charitable-trusts/dr-guthries-association

H. and T. Clients Charitable Trust

CC NO 1104345 **ESTABLISHED** 2004
WHERE FUNDING CAN BE GIVEN England and Wales.
WHO CAN BENEFIT Charities and community groups.
WHAT IS FUNDED General charitable purposes.
SAMPLE GRANTS A list of beneficiaries was not available.
FINANCES *Year* 2015/16 *Income* £487,984 *Grants* £312,542 *Grants to organisations* £312,542 *Assets* £748,261
TRUSTEES Hugh Lask; Ronnie Harris; Neville Newman; Charlotte Harris.
OTHER INFORMATION A list of beneficiaries was not available in the annual report and accounts.
HOW TO APPLY Apply in writing to the correspondent.
WHO TO APPLY TO Hugh Lask, Trustee, 64 New Cavendish Street, London W1G 8TB *Tel.* 020 7467 6300

H. C. D. Memorial Fund

CC NO 1044956 **ESTABLISHED** 1995
WHERE FUNDING CAN BE GIVEN Worldwide.
WHO CAN BENEFIT Charitable organisations, with a preference for small or medium-sized projects.
WHAT IS FUNDED Environmental work, particularly in relation to climate change; in the UK and Ireland, environmental and community projects, including for refugees, prisoners and people who are unemployed; in Africa, the Middle East, Central America, Palestine, Pakistan, Myanmar, Romania, Peru and Nepal, work in the fields of development, health, education, peacekeeping and prison welfare.
WHAT IS NOT FUNDED Evangelism or missionary work; individuals; nationwide emergency appeals; animal, cancer and children's charities; gap year funding.
TYPE OF GRANT Can be one-off or recurring, including core costs, buildings and start-up costs. Funding may be given for up to three years.
RANGE OF GRANTS From £10,000 to £50,000.
SAMPLE GRANTS Feedback Global (£25,000); Borderlands, Coalition Against Crime, North of England Refugees and Unseen UK (£20,000 each); Soil Association (£15,000); Blue Apple Theatre, The Centre at St Mary's, FareShare Sussex and National Energy Fund (£10,000 each).
FINANCES *Year* 2015/16 *Income* £860,766 *Grants* £833,000 *Grants to organisations* £833,000 *Assets* £582,816
TRUSTEES Nicholas Debenham; Bill Flinn; Harriet Lear; Joanna Lear; Jeremy Debenham; Susannah Drummond.
OTHER INFORMATION Grants were made to 16 organisations in the UK and to 26 organisations overseas.
HOW TO APPLY Apply in writing to the correspondent, although note that the trustees seek out their own projects and rarely respond to unsolicited applications.
WHO TO APPLY TO Suky Drummond, Secretary, 24 Fern Avenue, Jesmond, Newcastle upon Tyne NE2 2QT *Email* hcdmemorialfund@gmail.com

H. P. Charitable Trust

CC NO 278006 **ESTABLISHED** 1979
WHERE FUNDING CAN BE GIVEN UK and overseas.
WHO CAN BENEFIT Orthodox Jewish charities.
WHAT IS FUNDED General charitable purposes, including the advancement of the Orthodox Jewish religion, the advancement of Orthodox Jewish religious education, the relief of poverty, and the relief of people who are in need due to ill health or disability.
RANGE OF GRANTS Up to £16,400.
SAMPLE GRANTS Emuno Educational Centre Ltd (£16,400); Kehal Yisroel D'Chasidei Gur (£13,000); Macnivka (£12,500); The Lolev Charitable Trust (£7,800); Ezer V' Hatzalah Ltd (£5,000); Ichud Mosdos Gur Ltd (£3,300); Talmud Torah D'Chasidei Gur Ltd and Yad Shlomo Trust (£3,000 each).
FINANCES *Year* 2015/16 *Income* £329,833 *Grants* £98,470 *Grants to organisations* £98,470 *Assets* £2,129,555
TRUSTEES Arthur Zonszajn; Aron Piller; Hannah Piller.
OTHER INFORMATION Grants of less than £3,000 totalled £22,500.
HOW TO APPLY Apply in writing to the correspondent.
WHO TO APPLY TO Aron Piller, 26 Lingwood Road, London E5 9BN *Tel.* 020 8806 2432 *Email* apiller26@gmail.com

Hackney Parochial Charities

CC NO 219876 **ESTABLISHED** 1904
WHERE FUNDING CAN BE GIVEN The London Borough of Hackney.
WHO CAN BENEFIT Registered charities; schools and colleges; youth groups; pensioner groups; religious groups; community support groups; nursing organisations; individuals.
WHAT IS FUNDED Social welfare; education; organisations supporting residents of Hackney; organisations providing breaks for families and children; projects for advancement in life.
WHAT IS NOT FUNDED General appeals or letters requesting donations (Hackney Parochial Charities application forms must be used); local authorities or work usually considered a statutory responsibility; schools, colleges or universities, including schools for pupils with disabilities (the trustees will, however, consider hardship applications made by individuals); organisations that do not provide direct services to clients (such as umbrella, second tier or grant-making organisations); running costs of hospices, except for project applications; feasibility studies; professional associations, or training for professionals; organisations that do not have charitable aims (such as companies limited by shares and commercial companies); overseas trips; family holidays (apart from project applications for group trips); heritage projects, unless they may be considered as educational in the broadest sense; environmental conservation projects; social research; campaigning or lobbying projects, or general awareness raising work; projects where the main focus is website development or maintenance; IT equipment (the trustees, will, however, consider hardship applications made by individuals for this purpose); debt of any kind.
TYPE OF GRANT One-off and recurrent.
RANGE OF GRANTS Up to £20,000; however, the majority of grants are for £4,000 or less.
SAMPLE GRANTS Hackney Community Law Centre and The Hackney Food Bank (£20,000 each);

Hackney Migrant Centre (£18,900); Hackney Doorways (£15,000); Hoxton Health (£7,500); North London Action for the Homeless (£6,800); Arts for All and Woman's Trust (£6,000 each); Frampton Park Baptist Church (£4,500); Teen Action (£3,100); Happy Days Children's Charity and The Salvation Army (£3,000 each); Apollo Music Projects and Spitalfields Crypt Trust (£2,500 each).

FINANCES *Year* 2015/16 *Income* £307,501 *Grants* £223,603 *Grants to organisations* £197,881 *Assets* £6,000,298

TRUSTEES Mary Cannon; Cllr. Geoff Taylor; Nicola Baboneau; Cllr Chris Kennedy; Allan Hilton; Irfan Malik; Tracy Browne; Jayne Bailey; Rob Chapman; Revd Alexander Gordon.

OTHER INFORMATION In 2015/16 the charity made 51 hardship grants to individuals, totalling £25,500.

HOW TO APPLY Application forms are available to download from the charity's website. Applications can be submitted at any time. The trustees meet bi-annually to consider project applications.

WHO TO APPLY TO Hackney Parochial Charities, 6 Trull Farm Buildings, Tetbury, Gloucestershire GL8 8SQ *Tel.* 020 3397 7805 *Email* hackney@thetrustpartnership.com *Website* www.hackneyparochialcharities.org.uk

■ The Hadfield Trust

CC NO 1067491 **ESTABLISHED** 1998

WHERE FUNDING CAN BE GIVEN Cumbria.

WHO CAN BENEFIT Registered charities; community groups.

WHAT IS FUNDED Youth and employment; social needs; older people; arts; environment.

WHAT IS NOT FUNDED See the website for a list of exclusions.

TYPE OF GRANT Mainly one-off; capital costs; multi-year awards (when considered necessary); project funding.

RANGE OF GRANTS £250 to £20,000.

SAMPLE GRANTS Sunbeams Music Trust (£20,000); Sandylands Methodist Church Flood Relief (£10,000); Carlisle Cathedral Trust (£7,000); Carlisle Mencap, 1st St Bees Scout Group (£5,000 each); Samaritans (£4,400); Lake District National Park, Thursby Sports and Recreational Committee, Sight Advice South Lakes (£3,000 each) Active Recovery Community, Friends of the 597 (£2,000 each); British Library, Kendal Amateur Bell Ringing Society (£1,000); Embleton Community Rural Safety Group (£250).

FINANCES *Year* 2015/16 *Income* £294,964 *Grants* £440,699 *Grants to organisations* £440,699 *Assets* £8,367,285

TRUSTEES Roy Morris; William Rathbone; Alan Forsyth; Andrew Morris; Andrew Forsyth; Caroline Addison; Michael Hope.

OTHER INFORMATION The charity made a total of 153 awards totalling £440,700. Grants awarded were categorised as follows: £148,200 to social needs; £122,200 to youth and employment; £4,300 to older people; £62,800 to the arts; £19,000 to environment.

HOW TO APPLY A completed application form is always required and is available from the trust's website or offices.

WHO TO APPLY TO Caroline Addison, Trustee, Greystone House, King's Meaburn, Penrith CA10 3BU *Tel.* 01931 589029 *Email* admin@hadfieldtrust.org.uk *Website* www.hadfieldtrust.org.uk

■ The Hadley Trust

CC NO 1064823 **ESTABLISHED** 1997

WHERE FUNDING CAN BE GIVEN UK, especially London.

WHO CAN BENEFIT Registered charities.

WHAT IS FUNDED The trust's objects allow it to assist in creating opportunities for people who are disadvantaged as a result of environmental, educational or economic circumstances or physical or other disability, to improve their situation, either by direct financial assistance, involvement in project and support work, or research into the causes of and means to alleviate hardship. Grants are made in the following areas: crime and justice; young people; disabilities; social investment; local causes; medical causes; welfare reform; international; and hospices.

SAMPLE GRANTS London Centre for Children with Cerebral Palsy (£300,000); Coram Voice and Hadley Centre; Prison Reform Trust; The Project for Modern Democracy.

FINANCES *Year* 2015/16 *Income* £6,213,370 *Grants* £3,242,894 *Grants to organisations* £3,242,894 *Assets* £147,656,954

TRUSTEES Janet Hulme; Philip Hulme; Janet Love; Thomas Hulme; Katherine Prideaux; Sophie Hulme.

OTHER INFORMATION In 2015/16 the trust made grants to 79 organisations. The trustees prefer to work with small to medium-sized charities and establish the trust as a reliable, long-term funding partner.

HOW TO APPLY The annual report for 2015/16 explains that in recent years the trust has become 'increasingly focused on some core areas of activity where the trustees feel the trust is able to have the greatest impact. Consequently the trust has tended to establish more in-depth relationships with a smaller number of selected partners. The result of this policy is that the trust does not take on many new funding commitments. Nevertheless the trustees will always consider and respond to proposals which might enhance the effectiveness of the trust.'

WHO TO APPLY TO Carol Biggs, Gladsmuir, Hadley Common, Barnet EN5 5QE *Tel.* 020 8447 4577 *Email* carol@hadleytrust.org

■ Hadras Kodesh Trust

CC NO 1105885 **ESTABLISHED** 2004

WHERE FUNDING CAN BE GIVEN UK and overseas.

WHO CAN BENEFIT Jewish charitable organisations and individuals.

WHAT IS FUNDED The advancement of Orthodox Jewish religious education and the Orthodox Jewish faith, particularly through supporting the activities of religious publishers.

SAMPLE GRANTS A list of beneficiaries was not available.

FINANCES *Year* 2015/16 *Income* £5,281,839 *Grants* £5,454,779 *Grants to organisations* £4,429,476 *Assets* £13,428

TRUSTEES Pincus Mann; Yoel Fisher Y.

OTHER INFORMATION A list of beneficiaries was not included in the annual report and accounts.

HOW TO APPLY Apply in writing to the correspondent. The annual report for 2015/16 explains: 'The trustees are approached for donations by a wide variety of charitable institutions and individuals. The trustees consider all requests which they receive and make donations based on the level of funds available.'

WHO TO APPLY TO Pincus Mann, Trustee, 52 East Bank, London N16 5PZ *Tel.* 020 8880 8941 *Email* pincus@hktrust.org

■ The Hadrian Trust

CC NO 272161 **ESTABLISHED** 1976
WHERE FUNDING CAN BE GIVEN Within the boundaries of the old counties of Northumberland and Durham, including Tyne and Wear and the former county of Cleveland (north of the Tees).
WHO CAN BENEFIT Social welfare and charitable organisations working for/with people living in the area of benefit.
WHAT IS FUNDED Grants are mainly made in the following fields: social welfare; young people; disability; older people; women; ethnic minorities; education; arts; and the environment. There is a detailed list of areas of interest within each category on the website.
WHAT IS NOT FUNDED Capital projects for major building improvements; repair of buildings used solely for worship; animal protection charities; charities based outside the geographic area of benefit; national charities making general appeals; national charities without a base in the North East. Individuals are not supported, although the trust does contribute to the Greggs Foundation's hardship fund.
TYPE OF GRANT Running costs; project costs; part salaries; basic equipment costs.
RANGE OF GRANTS Usually between £500 and £2,000.
SAMPLE GRANTS A list of beneficiaries was not available.
FINANCES *Year* 2015/16 *Income* £198,735 *Grants* £198,500 *Grants to organisations* £198,500 *Assets* £6,389,018
TRUSTEES Pauline Dodgson; Kathryn Winskell; Jim Dias; Ian Brown; Colin Fitzpatrick; Catherine Wood; Dorothy Parker.
OTHER INFORMATION A total of 186 grants were made during 2015/16.
HOW TO APPLY Apply in writing to the correspondent. Detailed guidance on what the application letter must include can be found on the website. Organisations which are not registered charities must include the name of a registered charity or CVS (and its charity number) which is prepared to administer funds on their behalf. The trustees meet four times a year, usually in January, April, July and October, and applications should be received by the trust at least three weeks before the relevant meeting (see the website for upcoming important dates). Eligible applications will be acknowledged and given a date when the application will be considered. Successful applicants will hear within two weeks of the meeting; no further correspondence is sent to unsuccessful applicants. Applications for individuals should be sent to: Greggs Foundation, Greggs House, Quorum Business Park, Newcastle upon Tyne, NE12 8BU.
WHO TO APPLY TO Pauline Dodgson, Trustee, PO Box 785, Whitley Bay, Tyne and Wear NE26 9DW *Tel.* 07815 785074 *Email* enquiries@hadriantrust.co.uk *Website* www.hadriantrust.co.uk

■ The Alfred Haines Charitable Trust

CC NO 327166 **ESTABLISHED** 1986
WHERE FUNDING CAN BE GIVEN Birmingham and the immediate surrounding area.
WHO CAN BENEFIT Local organisations helping people to improve their quality of life.
WHAT IS FUNDED Grants are distributed in the following categories: family support and counselling; youth and children's work, workers and support activities; support for people who are homeless, unemployed or in debt; humanitarian and Christian overseas aid (see 'What is not funded' for more information); support for people who are medically disadvantaged; care for people who are older or who have disabilities; and holidays for disadvantaged children and teenagers.
WHAT IS NOT FUNDED Activities which are primarily a statutory responsibility; animal welfare; church buildings – restorations, improvements, renovations or new builds; environmental – conservation and protection of wildlife and landscape; expeditions and overseas trips; hospitals and health centres; loans and business finance; medical research projects; purely evangelistic projects; the promotion of any religion other than Christianity; schools, universities and colleges; projects that have unsuccessfully applied for a grant from the trust before. The trust does not normally support individuals (including students) – when it does, the individual must be recommended by somebody known to the trustees and the funding must have a long-term benefit to others. The trust does not usually support large national charities, even where there is a local project in the area of benefit. Projects outside the West Midlands, including overseas, are only considered where the applicant is known to a trustee or is recommended by somebody who is known to a trustee and has first-hand knowledge of the work. Organisations that have received support from Quothquan Trust should not apply.
TYPE OF GRANT Generally one-off. Specific projects rather than general running costs.
RANGE OF GRANTS Usually between £250 and £2,000.
SAMPLE GRANTS A list of beneficiaries was not available.
FINANCES *Year* 2015/16 *Income* £25,620 *Grants* £92,865 *Grants to organisations* £92,865 *Assets* £1,084,845
TRUSTEES Gregor Moss; Paul Gilmour.
OTHER INFORMATION In 2015/16 the trust made 90 grants. The trust shares support staff with Quothquan Trust (Charity Commission no. 1110647).
HOW TO APPLY Apply in writing to the trustees, quoting your charity's Charity Commission number. Applications should include: a brief description of the activities of your organisation; details of the project and its overall cost; what funds have already been raised and how the remaining funds are to be raised; a copy of the latest accounts including any associated or parent organisation; and any other leaflets or supporting documentation. Applicants are advised to consider the exclusion list prior to application. Applications are not acknowledged and unsuccessful applicants are not notified.
WHO TO APPLY TO The Trustees, Dale Farm, Worcester Lane, Sutton Coldfield B75 5PR *Tel.* 0121 323 3236 *Website* www.ahct.org.uk

■ The Haley Family Charitable Trust

CC NO 1146603 **ESTABLISHED** 2012

WHERE FUNDING CAN BE GIVEN England and Wales.

WHO CAN BENEFIT Registered charities.

WHAT IS FUNDED General charitable purposes.

SAMPLE GRANTS Public Memorial Appeal (£150,000); Breast Cancer Campaign (£114,000).

FINANCES *Year* 2015/16 *Income* £112,700 *Grants* £269,993 *Grants to organisations* £269,993 *Assets* £2,363,507

TRUSTEES C. Lumsden; H. Lumsden; I. Pattison; Tabitha Barker.

OTHER INFORMATION There were two beneficiaries during the year.

HOW TO APPLY Apply in writing to the correspondent.

WHO TO APPLY TO The Trustees, Hollybank, 81 Bramley Lane, Lightcliffe, Halifax, West Yorkshire HX3 8NS *Tel.* 01422 201212 *Email* ifpattison@btinternet.com

■ Halifax Foundation for Northern Ireland (previously known as Lloyds Bank Foundation for Northern Ireland)

CC NO 101763 **ESTABLISHED** 1986

WHERE FUNDING CAN BE GIVEN Northern Ireland.

WHO CAN BENEFIT Registered charities.

WHAT IS FUNDED Underfunded voluntary organisations which enable people with disabilities and people who are disadvantaged through social and economic circumstances, to make a contribution to the community. The trustees regret that, as the funds available are limited, they cannot support all fields of voluntary and charitable activity. The two main objectives to which funds are allocated are: social and community needs; education and training. For full details of the foundation's funding objectives go to the website.

WHAT IS NOT FUNDED Organisations which have an income of more than £1 million in the previous year's accounts; organisations which are insolvent; organisations which have over 12 months' reserves would not be seen as a priority; individuals, including students; animal welfare; the environment; hospitals and medical centres; schools, universities and colleges (except for projects specifically to benefit pupils with special needs); sponsorship or fundraising events either for your own organisation or another; promotion of religion; endowment funds; activities that are normally the responsibility of central or local government; loans and business finance; travel or activities outside Northern Ireland; capital build (except in the case of disability access).

TYPE OF GRANT Core costs; materials and equipment; salary costs; volunteer expenses; project costs; refurbishment; activities; training; disability access; transport costs.

SAMPLE GRANTS Aisling Centre (£5,000); Arts for All (£4,500); Age Concern Causeway (£4,000); Belfast Interface Project (£3,000); Hillstown Rural Community Group (£2,500); Newtown Butler Playgroup, the Oxygen Therapy Centre (£1,500 each); Meigh Community Pre-School (£1,000); the Open Door Centre (£600); Green Elves Playgroup (£500).

FINANCES *Year* 2016 *Income* £1,024,612 *Grants* £972,353 *Grants to organisations* £972,353 *Assets* £702,599

TRUSTEES Janet Leckey; Dr Brian Scott; Hugh Donnelly; Janine Donnelly; James McCoe; Imelda Macmillan; Paula Leathem; Aine McCoy; Mary Keightley.

HOW TO APPLY Applications can be made using the online application form.

WHO TO APPLY TO Brenda McMullan, Grants Manager, 11–15 Donegall Square North, Belfast BT1 5GB *Tel.* 028 9032 3000 *Email* grants@halifaxfoundationni.org *Website* www.lloydstsbfoundationni.org

■ Hamamelis Trust

CC NO 280938 **ESTABLISHED** 1980

WHERE FUNDING CAN BE GIVEN UK, but with a special interest in the Godalming and Surrey areas.

WHO CAN BENEFIT Registered charities.

WHAT IS FUNDED Medical research and ecological conservation.

WHAT IS NOT FUNDED Projects outside the UK; individuals.

RANGE OF GRANTS From £2,000 to £11,100.

SAMPLE GRANTS Neuroblastoma (£11,100); Deaf Plus (£10,000); Surrey Wildlife Trust (£8,100); Friends of St Mary's Church Roof Appeal (£5,800); Bowel and Cancer Research, European Squirrel Initiative and Nature Foundation (£3,000 each); Forest of Avon Trust (£2,300); Bowel Disease Research Foundation and Motability (£2,000 each).

FINANCES *Year* 2015/16 *Income* £137,296 *Grants* £133,495 *Grants to organisations* £133,495 *Assets* £3,867,122

TRUSTEES Laura Dadswell; Dr Adam Stone; Lucy Mirouze.

HOW TO APPLY Apply in writing to the correspondent. All applicants are asked to include a short summary of the application with estimated costings of the project for which the grant is requested. Unsuccessful applications are not acknowledged. Medical applications are assessed by Dr Adam Stone, who is a medically-qualified trustee.

WHO TO APPLY TO Laura Dadswell, Trustee, c/o Penningtons Manches LLP, 31 Chertsey Street, Guildford GU1 4HD *Tel.* 01483 791800

■ Paul Hamlyn Foundation

CC NO 1102927 **ESTABLISHED** 1987

WHERE FUNDING CAN BE GIVEN UK and India.

WHO CAN BENEFIT Registered charities and organisations.

WHAT IS FUNDED The foundation's mission is 'to help people overcome disadvantage and lack of opportunity, so that they can realise their potential and enjoy fulfilling and creative lives.' It is particularly interested in supporting young people and has a strong belief in the importance of the arts. In the UK the foundation currently has six strategic priorities: nurturing ideas and people; arts access and participation; education and learning through the arts; arts evidence; investing in young people; and migration and integration. In India the foundation supports work in development fields including health, education, women's rights, children's rights and political representation.

WHAT IS NOT FUNDED Proposals that are for the benefit of only one individual; website, publications or seminars, unless part of a wider proposal; funding for work that has already been delivered; general fundraising appeals, letters requesting donations and other non-specific fundraising requests; proposals that the foundation has previously considered in the past 12 months and turned down, unless it has explicitly invited the applicant to resubmit; proposals about property or which are mainly about equipment or other capital items, including the restoration of buildings or habitats; overseas travel (including expeditions, adventure and residential courses); promotion of religion; animal welfare; medical/health/residential or day care; proposals that benefit people living outside the UK (apart from the India programme); organisations that are not formally constituted; activity that is not legally charitable; more than one proposal from an individual, team or organisation at any one time; academic research, scholarships, bursaries or any kind of student fees; loan and/or debt repayments. The foundation is unlikely to support: endowments; organisations that would use the funding to make grants; proposals from organisations outside the UK (apart from the India programme); organisations that are for profit; organisations that already have an active grant with the foundation, unless the foundation has invited the additional bid. Organisations wishing to apply for any of these things are advised to talk to the foundation before submitting an application.

TYPE OF GRANT Grants are usually one-off, for a specific project or for a specific part of a project, and funding is normally given for one year only.

SAMPLE GRANTS Kids' Own Publishing Partnership CLG (£388,000); Hull UK City of Culture Ltd (£350,000); Central England Law Centre (£330,000); PRS Foundation (£255,000); HOPE not Hate Educational Ltd (£60,000); University of Sunderland (£54,000); Zahid Mubarek Trust (£50,000); Sahyogi (£27,500); Luxi Ltd (£23,500); Belfast Exposed and Glasgow Museums (£20,000 each); Restoke (£11,400); Fuse Art Space CIC (£8,700); Institute for Voluntary Action Research (£5,000).

FINANCES *Year* 2015/16 *Income* £19,776,000 *Grants* £12,783,000 *Grants to organisations* £12,353,000 *Assets* £654,036,000

TRUSTEES Jane Hamlyn; Tim Bunting; Tony Hall; Michael Hamlyn; Charles Leadbeater; James Lingwood; Jan McKenley-Simpson; Anthony Salz; Claire Whitaker; Tom Wylie.

OTHER INFORMATION In 2015/16 a total of 157 grants were made to organisations. A further nine grants, amounting to £430,000, were awarded to individuals. The foundation awarded £2 million to The Helen Hamlyn Trust.

HOW TO APPLY Applications can only be submitted via the online application process. Information about available funds and grants can be found on the website.

WHO TO APPLY TO Grants team, 5–11 Leeke Street, London WC1X 9HY *Tel.* 020 7812 3300 *Email* information@phf.org.uk *Website* www.phf.org.uk

■ The Helen Hamlyn Trust

CC NO 1084839 **ESTABLISHED** 2000

WHERE FUNDING CAN BE GIVEN Worldwide.

WHO CAN BENEFIT Charitable organisations; the trust's web page states that its 'focus is on the initiation of medium- and long-term projects linked to the shared interests of Lady Hamlyn and her late husband Lord Hamlyn. The Trust's core ethos is to develop innovative projects, which aim to effect lasting change, improve quality of life and create opportunity for the benefit of the public.' Small local and regional charities are also supported.

WHAT IS FUNDED Grants are made in the following areas set out in the annual report 2015/16: 'innovation in the medical arena' increasing access to the arts and supporting 'the professional development of artists from the fields of music and the performing arts' increasing intercultural understanding; providing 'opportunities for young people to develop new interests and practical skills which will contribute to their education and their future lives and to create opportunities for young offenders to acquire practical skills which will support their personal development for their future lives' conserving heritage in India for public access and cultural activities; supporting 'examples of good practice in the humanitarian sector' and providing practical support to enable older people to maintain their independence for as long as possible.

RANGE OF GRANTS Up to £1 million; however, small grants range up to £10,000.

SAMPLE GRANTS Imperial College (£1 million); Moorfields Eye Charity (£498,000); Institute of International Humanitarian Affairs (£330,000); The Helen Hamlyn Centre for Design at the Royal College of Art (£250,000); Royal Opera House and Design Museum (£100,000 each); V&A Museum – V&A's India Festival (£39,000); Mehrangarh Museum Trust (£20,000); International National Trusts Organisation (£10,000); Crafts Council, The Stroke Association and UCanDoIT (£5,000 each).

FINANCES *Year* 2015/16 *Income* £2,688,568 *Grants* £2,488,205 *Grants to organisations* £2,488,205 *Assets* £3,866,341

TRUSTEES Lady Hamlyn; Dr Kate Gavron; Dr Shobita Punja; Brendan Cahill; Margaret O'Rorke; Dr Deborah Swallow; Stephen Lewin.

OTHER INFORMATION Grants of £3,000 or less totalled £25,000.

HOW TO APPLY The trustees have previously noted that 'their energies are focused on the initiation of projects and they do not accept unsolicited applications for major grants'. Appeals from local and regional charities for small awards (up to £10,000) may be directed to the correspondent.

WHO TO APPLY TO John Roche-Kuroda, Director of Finance and Administration, The Helen Hamlyn Trust, 129 Old Church Street, London SW3 6EB *Tel.* 020 7351 5057 *Email* john.rochekuroda@helenhamlyntrust.org *Website* www.phf.org.uk/our-work-in-the-uk/helen-hamlyn-trust

■ Hammersmith United Charities

CC NO 205856 **ESTABLISHED** 1992

WHERE FUNDING CAN BE GIVEN Hammersmith and Fulham (area of benefit map on website).

WHO CAN BENEFIT Registered charities.

WHAT IS FUNDED Social welfare. Current funding criteria are: meeting basic needs (food, shelter, etc.); work with families and children; countering isolation; building confident individuals and communities.

SAMPLE GRANTS Action on Disability (£14,000); Projection Approaches (£10,000); Lido Foundation (£8,000); Lyric and Team Up (£6,000 each); City Mission (£5,000); Dance West (£3,800); Bush Theatre (£1,500).

FINANCES *Year* 2015/16 *Income* £1,393,253 *Grants* £343,426 *Grants to organisations* £217,840 *Assets* £32,577,667

TRUSTEE Hammersmith United Trustee Company.

HOW TO APPLY Application forms are available to download from the charity's website.

WHO TO APPLY TO Tim Hughes, Sycamore House, Sycamore Gardens, London W6 0AS *Tel.* 020 8741 4326 *Email* info@hamunitedcharities.com *Website* www.hamunitedcharities.org.uk

■ The Hampshire and Islands Historic Churches Trust

CC NO 299633 **ESTABLISHED** 1988

WHERE FUNDING CAN BE GIVEN Hampshire, Isle of Wight and the Channel Islands.

WHO CAN BENEFIT Churches of all denominations in Hampshire, the Isle of Wight and the Channel Islands.

WHAT IS FUNDED The restoration, preservation, repair, maintenance and improvement of churches, including monuments, fittings and furniture, in the area specified above.

WHAT IS NOT FUNDED No grants are paid in respect of work which has already started before approval is given.

TYPE OF GRANT One-off grants and loans. Emergency help can be given.

RANGE OF GRANTS Up to £5,000.

SAMPLE GRANTS Fyfield, St Nicholas (£10,000); Niton (Isle of Wight), St John the Baptist (£7,500); Alton, St Lawrence and Houghton, All Saints and Winchester, Hospital of St Cross (£5,000 each); Gatcombe (Isle of Wight), St Olave (£3,000); Alton, St Lawrence and Niton, St John the Baptist (£2,500); Titchfield, St Peter (£1,500); East Cowes (Isle of Wight), St James (£500).

FINANCES *Year* 2015 *Income* £92,530 *Grants* £46,500 *Grants to organisations* £46,500 *Assets* £126,835

TRUSTEES John Steel; Ven. Adrian Harbridge; The Revd Canon Dr Roland Riem; Lady Appleyard; Caroline Edwards.

OTHER INFORMATION Grants were given to 15 churches in 2015.

HOW TO APPLY Application forms are available to download, together with guidelines and criteria, from the website. The grants committee usually meets in February, June and October.

WHO TO APPLY TO Rosemary Walker, Hon. Secretary Grants, c/o Hampshire Record Office, Sussex Street, Winchester, Hampshire SO23 8TH *Tel.* 01962 760230 *Email* grants@hihct.org.uk *Website* www.hihct.org.uk

■ Hampshire and Isle of Wight Community Foundation

CC NO 1100417 **ESTABLISHED** 2002

WHERE FUNDING CAN BE GIVEN Hampshire and Isle of Wight.

WHO CAN BENEFIT Community groups; voluntary organisations; individuals; social enterprises; CICs. The trustees seek to address the needs of vulnerable and disadvantaged individuals, those suffering from discrimination, social exclusion or poverty, including homeless people.

WHAT IS FUNDED Community projects for: people of all ages; those with disabilities; families in crisis; people who are homeless; those in poor health; people looking to get back into work; those seeking protection; individuals looking to get healthier through sport, drama and singing; people who want to learn about the arts and local culture; those that are isolated or lonely; and local people struggling to cope with their lives.

WHAT IS NOT FUNDED Groups not based *and* active in Hampshire, Southampton, Portsmouth or Isle of Wight; organisations whose objects are for the sole benefit or relief of plants or animals; overseas travel/expeditions; proselytising activities, i.e. active promotion of a religion or belief system; statutory work or replacing statutory funding; projects benefitting those outside the county/unitary authority; retrospective funding; public bodies, local authorities and statutory organisations; national charities (unless locally run and led); commercial ventures; schools (except out of school hours activities); buses, minibuses or other community transport schemes (except transport costs forming part of a project); generally organisations with unrestricted reserves of over 12 months' running costs; capital building projects, building improvements/ adaptions or repair costs; any party political activity.

TYPE OF GRANT One-off and up to two years; capital and core expenditure; project costs; salaries; unrestricted funding.

RANGE OF GRANTS Up to £130,000.

SAMPLE GRANTS A list of beneficiaries was not available.

FINANCES *Year* 2015 *Income* £2,001,961 *Grants* £888,768 *Grants to organisations* £888,768 *Assets* £10,758,478

TRUSTEES Hugh Mason; Richard Prest; Jane Sandars; Dan Putty; Jo Ash; Jonathan Cheshire; Rebecca Kennelly; Tom Floyd; Revd Jonathan Frost; Richard Hibbert; Jonathan Moseley; Virginia Lovell; Adrian Rutter; James Kennedy.

HOW TO APPLY Potential applicants should see the foundation's website for details of funds currently available, or contact the foundation directly. Application criteria, procedures and deadlines may vary for each of the funds. Full details and separate application forms for each fund which can found on the foundation's website.

WHO TO APPLY TO Debbie Charlton, Grants Manager, Dame Mary Fagan House, Chineham Court, Lutyens Close, Basingstoke, Hampshire RG24 8AG *Tel.* 01256 776101 *Email* hiwcfadmin@hantscf.org.uk *Website* www.hantscf.org.uk

■ The Hampstead Wells and Campden Trust

CC NO 1094611 **ESTABLISHED** 1971

WHERE FUNDING CAN BE GIVEN The former metropolitan borough of Hampstead; organisations covering a wider area but whose activities benefit Hampstead residents among others may also apply.

WHO CAN BENEFIT Charitable organisations; voluntary groups; community projects; individuals (assisted via an agency); pensioners in need.

WHAT IS FUNDED The trust provides for grants to be made: to help persons who are sick or have disabilities; to help either generally or individually, persons who are in need and who suffer hardship or distress; to assist organisations or institutions providing services or facilities which help relieve need or distress.

WHAT IS NOT FUNDED General fundraising appeals; work which does not directly benefit people within the specific area; the payment of rates or taxes, fines, school or course fees, or in principle where statutory bodies have the responsibility to help; individuals directly (appeals must be made via a constituted local group). Multi-year grants are not currently given.

TYPE OF GRANT Running costs and occasionally capital.

RANGE OF GRANTS Up to £20,000; mainly smaller grants of up to £1,000.

SAMPLE GRANTS Caris Camden C4WS Homeless Project (£30,000 in two grants); Quaker Social Action (£25,000); Camden Community Law Centre (£20,000); Emmanuel Church West Hampstead and Home-Start Camden (£15,000); West Hampstead Women's Centre (£12,000); Beanstalk (£6,000); Hampstead Counselling Services (£5,000); The Brandon Centre (£4,000); Henna Asian Women's Group (£1,600).

FINANCES *Year* 2015/16 *Income* £479,047 *Grants* £432,560 *Grants to organisations* £261,565 *Assets* £16,967,361

TRUSTEES Ms Chung; Geoffrey Berridge; Gaynor Bassey; Revd Jeremy Fletcher; Alistair Voaden; Dr Christina Williams; Francoise Findlay; Gaynor Humphreys; Mike Bieber; Angela Mason; Charles Perrin; Christopher Knight; Stephen Bobasch; Tibor Gold; Jennifer Stevens; Alison Rankin; Christian Percy.

OTHER INFORMATION Grants were made to 51 organisations and 3,202 individuals during the year.

HOW TO APPLY Applications for up to £1,000 can be fast-tracked to provide an answer within one month of the application. Use either the application form or send a letter detailing: the work to be supported, how much it will cost what you have raised already (and your sources); the type and number of people who will benefit; your links to the trust's area of benefit; information about your group; your suitability to run and manage the work. Applications for grants of £1,000 or more must be requested on the application form. Applications can be made at any time. The trustees meet quarterly.

WHO TO APPLY TO Sheila Taylor, Director and Clerk to the Trustees, 62 Rosslyn Hill, London NW3 1ND *Tel.* 020 7435 1570 *Email* grant@hwct.co.uk *Website* www.hwct.org.uk

■ Hampton Fuel Allotment Charity

CC NO 211756 **ESTABLISHED** 1811

WHERE FUNDING CAN BE GIVEN Richmond upon Thames (Hampton, Hampton Hill, Hampton Wick, Teddington, Twickenham, Whitton).

WHO CAN BENEFIT Charities; voluntary sector organisations; community groups; individuals.

WHAT IS FUNDED Primarily grants towards fuel costs and essential equipment to individuals; assistance to not-for-profit organisations which provide services and activities for people in need. A wide range of charitable causes are assisted.

WHAT IS NOT FUNDED The charity is unlikely to support: grants to individuals for private and post-compulsory education; adaptations or building alterations for individuals; holidays, except in cases of severe need; decoration, carpeting or central heating; anything which is the responsibility of a statutory body; national general charitable appeals; animal welfare; the advancement of religion and religious groups, unless they offer a non-religious service to the community; commercial and business activities; endowment appeals; projects of a political nature; retrospective funding, both capital and revenue; organisations whose free reserves exceed 12 months' running costs; non-charitable social enterprises.

TYPE OF GRANT One-off grants; interest-free loans.

RANGE OF GRANTS Up to £55,000.

SAMPLE GRANTS Age UK Richmond upon Thames (£70,000 in two grants); Spear Housing Association Ltd (£35,000); The Mulberry Centre (£24,000); Princess Alice Hospital (£20,000); Richmond Advice and Information on Disability (£15,000); Richmond Mencap (£14,100); Addiction Support and Care Agency (£12,000); River Thames Boat Project (£9,300); Achieving for Children (£7,000); Connaught Opera (£3,500); Pod Charitable Trust (£2,400); Churches Together in Teddington (£700).

FINANCES *Year* 2015/16 *Income* £1,882,081 *Grants* £1,850,485 *Grants to organisations* £1,037,292 *Assets* £54,592,390

TRUSTEES Clive Beaumont; Dr Jim Brockbank; Jonathan Cardy; Martin Duffy; Hilary Hart; Richard Montgomery; Victoria Reid; Martin Seymour; Derek Terrington; Paula Williams.

OTHER INFORMATION A total of £813,000 was given to support individuals in need.

HOW TO APPLY Applicants are strongly advised to first read the guidance notes, which are available to download from the charity's website. Candidates who match the funding criteria should then contact the correspondent to further discuss their needs.

WHO TO APPLY TO David White, Clerk to the Trustees, 15 High Street, Hampton, Middlesex TW12 2SA *Tel.* 020 8941 7866 *Email* david@hfac.co.uk *Website* www.hfac.co.uk

■ The W. A. Handley Charity Trust

CC NO 230435 **ESTABLISHED** 1963

WHERE FUNDING CAN BE GIVEN The north east of England and Cumbria.

WHO CAN BENEFIT Registered charities.

WHAT IS FUNDED General charitable purposes, with grants commonly made for: the welfare of people who are disadvantaged, young, older or who have disabilities; maritime and armed forces causes; education, training and employment; community; historic and religious buildings; the environment; music; the arts.

WHAT IS NOT FUNDED Individuals; awards are not normally made outside the area of benefit; organisations which are not registered charities.

TYPE OF GRANT Regular payments and one-off grants.

RANGE OF GRANTS Generally between £500 and £10,000.

SAMPLE GRANTS Newcastle Cathedral (£100,000); Hospitality and Hope and Minsteracres Retreat Centre (£10,000 each); SSAFA – Battle of the Somme (£7,500); Holy Island Festival (£5,000); Citizens Advice Alnwick (£2,400); North Northumberland Hospice (£2,300); Northern Sinfonia Trust, Northumbria Coalition Against Crime and Tyne Housing Association (£1,800 each); Depression Alliance, Heartbeat, Northumberland Schools' Athletic Association, Northumberland Wildlife Trust and Tynemouth Volunteer Life Brigade (£1,000 each); Breakthrough Breast Cancer (£500).

FINANCES *Year* 2015/16 *Income* £450,230 *Grants* £392,300 *Grants to organisations* £392,300 *Assets* £8,932,464

TRUSTEES Bill Dryden; Tony Glenton; David Irvin; David Milligan.

OTHER INFORMATION Of 139 grants made, 105 were regular and 34 were one-off.

HOW TO APPLY Applications must be made in writing to the correspondent, quoting the applicant's official charity number and providing full back-up information. Our research suggests that grants

are made quarterly – in March, June, September and December.
WHO TO APPLY TO The Secretary, Ryecroft Glenton, 32 Portland Terrace, Newcastle upon Tyne NE2 1QP *Tel.* 0191 281 1292 *Email* davidmilligan@ryecroft-glenton.co.uk

■ The Kathleen Hannay Memorial Charity

CC NO 299600 **ESTABLISHED** 1988
WHERE FUNDING CAN BE GIVEN UK and overseas.
WHO CAN BENEFIT Registered charities.
WHAT IS FUNDED General charitable purposes, including health, social welfare, religious causes, education, arts and culture and environmental protection or improvement.
WHAT IS NOT FUNDED Individuals; non-registered charities.
TYPE OF GRANT One-off and recurrent grants for capital and revenue costs; unrestricted funding.
RANGE OF GRANTS Up to £50,000.
SAMPLE GRANTS A list of beneficiaries was not available.
FINANCES *Year* 2015/16 *Income* £203,243 *Grants* £225,500 *Grants to organisations* £225,500 *Assets* £12,007,018
TRUSTEES Simon Weil; Christian Ward; Jonathan Weil; Laura Watkins.
OTHER INFORMATION Awards were made to 29 charities.
HOW TO APPLY Unsolicited applications are not accepted.
WHO TO APPLY TO The Trustees, Bircham Dyson Bell, FAO: H. D'Monte, 50 Broadway, London SW1H 0BL *Tel.* 020 7783 3685

■ The Happold Foundation

CC NO 1050814 **ESTABLISHED** 1995
WHERE FUNDING CAN BE GIVEN Worldwide.
WHO CAN BENEFIT Organisations, students and engineers.
WHAT IS FUNDED Engineering and the built environment.
TYPE OF GRANT Research funding; scholarships; one-off grants.
SAMPLE GRANTS A list of beneficiaries was not available.
FINANCES *Year* 2015/16 *Income* £100,141 *Grants* £107,830 *Grants to organisations* £107,830 *Assets* £150,951
TRUSTEES Gavin Thompson; Lorraine Milne; Sean Mulligan; Ian Liddell; Michael Dickson; Michael Cook; Robert Okpala; Sarah Sachs; Emily McDonald; Tom Newby; Anna Bruni; Matthew Happold; Andrew Daubney.
OTHER INFORMATION A list of beneficiaries was not included in the accounts.
HOW TO APPLY In the first instance, see the foundation's website for information on funding currently available as well as how to apply.
WHO TO APPLY TO Sean Mulligan, Trustee, The Happold Foundation, 17 Newman Street, London W1T 1PD *Email* info@happoldfoundation.org

■ The Haramead Trust

CC NO 1047416 **ESTABLISHED** 1995
WHERE FUNDING CAN BE GIVEN Worldwide, in practice, financially developing countries, UK and Ireland, and locally in the East Midlands.
WHO CAN BENEFIT Registered charities; individuals and families in need of direct assistance.
WHAT IS FUNDED Relief in need; children's welfare; education; health. Grants are distributed across the following categories: children's charities; social and medical assistance; homelessness; and education.
TYPE OF GRANT Capital and core support, building/renovation, equipment, vehicles and project support for up to three years.
RANGE OF GRANTS Up to £215,000.
SAMPLE GRANTS Action Aid (£215,000); CAFOD (Catholic Agency for Overseas Development) (£200,000); NSPCC (£150,000); Ireland Fund of Great Britain and Leicestershire, Leicester and Rutland Community Foundation (£100,000 each); Mind and Rainbows (£50,000 each); Faith in Families and Worldwide Education Project (£25,000 each); De Montfort University (£20,000); De Paul International and St Luke's Church (£10,000 each). Donations of less than £10,000 totalled £230,500.
FINANCES *Year* 2015/16 *Income* £2,626,763 *Grants* £2,020,325 *Grants to organisations* £2,020,325 *Assets* £1,564,381
TRUSTEES David Tams; Michael Linnett; Robert Smith; Winifred Linnett; Simon Astil; Victoria Duddles; Dr Mary Hanlon.
OTHER INFORMATION From 955 requests for assistance, the trustees made 87 donations. Geographically, grants were distributed as follows: financially developing countries (£718,000); UK and Ireland (£656,500); East Midlands (£646,000).
HOW TO APPLY Apply in writing to the correspondent, providing relevant financial details of your organisation. The trustees meet every couple of months and may visit funded projects for monitoring purposes or to assess for future grants. All appeals are acknowledged.
WHO TO APPLY TO Michael Linnett, Trustee, Park House, Park Hill, Gaddesby, Leicestershire LE7 4WH *Email* harameadtrust@aol.com

■ Harbinson Charitable Trust

SC NO SC015248 **ESTABLISHED** 1984
WHERE FUNDING CAN BE GIVEN UK and financially developing countries.
WHO CAN BENEFIT Charitable organisations, particularly those working in the area of international development.
WHAT IS FUNDED Relief of poverty; education; religion; other charitable purposes, including natural environment and conservation.
TYPE OF GRANT Capital and core costs; project funding.
RANGE OF GRANTS £1,000 to £9,000.
SAMPLE GRANTS Orcadia Creative Learning Centre (£29,000); Path Foundation Centre (£13,500); Médecins Sans Frontières (£7,100); Practical Action (£6,800); Greenpeace (£4,600); Mvule Trust – Uganda (£3,000); Freedom from Torture (£2,400); Rainforest Concern (£1,700); Sightsavers (£1,200); Womankind Worldwide (£700); Marine Conservation Society (£500).
FINANCES *Year* 2015/16 *Income* £165,154 *Grants* £130,877 *Grants to organisations* £130,877 *Assets* £5,465,269
HOW TO APPLY Apply in writing to the correspondent.
WHO TO APPLY TO The Trustees of Harbinson Charitable Trust, c/o Miller, Becket and Jackson, 190 St Vincent Street, Glasgow G2 5SP *Tel.* 0141 204 2833 *Fax* 0141 248 7185

■ Harbo Charities Ltd

CC NO 282262 **ESTABLISHED** 1981

WHERE FUNDING CAN BE GIVEN UK and overseas.

WHO CAN BENEFIT Orthodox Jewish charitable organisations.

WHAT IS FUNDED The provision of financial support or basic necessities to people who are poor; the relief of sickness and disability; Jewish education; places of worship for the Jewish community.

SAMPLE GRANTS Beis Chinuch Lebonos Girls School; Beth Rochel d'Satmar; Bobov Trust; Chevras Maoz Ladol; Craven Walk Charitable Trust; Edgware Yeshiva Trust; Keren Yesomim; Kollel Shomrei HaChomoth; Tevini Ltd; Tomchei Shabbos; Yad Eliezer; Yeshiva Chachmay Tsorpha.

FINANCES *Year* 2015/16 *Income* £76,716 *Grants* £38,400 *Grants to organisations* £38,400 *Assets* £1,470,800

TRUSTEES Harold Gluck; Benjamin Stern.

OTHER INFORMATION A list of beneficiaries was not included within the latest set of accounts.

HOW TO APPLY Apply in writing to the correspondent. All requests are considered.

WHO TO APPLY TO The Trustees of Harbo Charities Ltd, Cohen Arnold, New Burlington House, 1075 Finchley Road, London NW11 0PU

■ The Harbour Charitable Trust

CC NO 234268 **ESTABLISHED** 1962

WHERE FUNDING CAN BE GIVEN UK and Israel.

WHO CAN BENEFIT Registered charities; Jewish organisations.

WHAT IS FUNDED General charitable purposes; Jewish causes; religious and inter-faith activities; education and training; the arts; children and young people; older people.

RANGE OF GRANTS £24 to £30,500.

SAMPLE GRANTS British Friends of United Hatzalah (£30,500); SAR Academy (£6,800); Designer Crafts Foundation (£5,000); Community Service Trust (£3,000); Marble Arch Synagogue and World Jewish Relief (£1,000 each); Magan David Adom (£100); Save the Children and Sightsavers (£24 each).

FINANCES *Year* 2015/16 *Income* £728,914 *Grants* £77,678 *Grants to organisations* £77,678 *Assets* £4,452,106

TRUSTEES Zena Blackman; Tamar Eisenstat; Barbara Green; Elaine Knobil.

HOW TO APPLY Apply in writing to the correspondent.

WHO TO APPLY TO Ali Alidina, 11 Leadenhall Street, London EC3V 1LP *Email* ali.a@acuityprofessional.com

■ The Harbour Foundation

CC NO 264927 **ESTABLISHED** 1970

WHERE FUNDING CAN BE GIVEN Worldwide.

WHO CAN BENEFIT Organisations and individuals.

WHAT IS FUNDED The relief of poverty, distress and suffering among refugees and other homeless people; education, learning and research, and the dissemination of the results of such research; general charitable purposes.

RANGE OF GRANTS Up to £200,000.

SAMPLE GRANTS Ben Gurion University Foundation and British Friends of the Hebrew University of Jerusalem (£200,000 each); One Voice Europe (£50,000); Israel Opera Trust (£20,000); Bread and Butter and Self Realisation Fellowship (£15,000 each); Wigmore Hall (£14,000); DKMS Bone Marrow Donor Centre (£10,000); East London Business Alliance (£6,000); Laniado Hospital (£5,000).

FINANCES *Year* 2015/16 *Income* £1,723,150 *Grants* £634,260 *Grants to organisations* £634,260 *Assets* £23,053,141

TRUSTEES Susan Harbour; Dr Daniel Harbour; Edmond Harbour; Gideon Harbour; Harry Rich; Richard Hermer.

OTHER INFORMATION In 2015/16 a total of 42 grants were made. About £603,500 was awarded to charities registered in England and Wales. Grants were made in the following categories: education (£421,500); the arts (£94,500); social organisations (£72,000); medical (£19,000); religious bodies (£18,800); relief organisations (£9,000).

HOW TO APPLY Applications can be made in writing to the correspondent. Our research suggests they need to be received by February, as the trustees normally meet in March.

WHO TO APPLY TO The Trustees, 1 Red Place, London W1K 6PL *Tel.* 020 7456 8180

■ The Harding Trust

CC NO 328182 **ESTABLISHED** 1989

WHERE FUNDING CAN BE GIVEN Mainly, but not exclusively, Staffordshire and surrounding areas.

WHO CAN BENEFIT Charitable organisations.

WHAT IS FUNDED The trust supports public education in and the appreciation of the art and science of music, mainly by providing sponsorship or other support for public concerts, recitals and performances by both amateur and professional organisations. Local hospices and medical charities also receive support.

TYPE OF GRANT One-off and recurrent.

RANGE OF GRANTS From £200 to £65,000, but mostly between £1,000 and £5,000.

SAMPLE GRANTS Stoke-on-Trent Festival Ltd (£65,000); Malvern Theatre Trust (£10,000); Royal Philharmonic Orchestra (£7,000); Clonter Farm Music Festival (£5,000); National Youth Orchestra and the Victoria Hall Organ (£3,000 each); Midlands Air Ambulance (£2,000); Katharine House Hospice (£1,500); Birmingham Royal Ballet and British Red Cross (£1,000 each); English Music Festival (£500); Abbotsholme Arts Society (£200).

FINANCES *Year* 2015/16 *Income* £154,763 *Grants* £135,700 *Grants to organisations* £135,700 *Assets* £4,384,566

TRUSTEES Geoffrey Snow; Geoffrey Wall; John Fowell; Michael Lloyd.

OTHER INFORMATION Grants were made to 26 organisations.

HOW TO APPLY Apply in writing to the correspondent. Our research suggests that the trustees meet annually in spring/early summer.

WHO TO APPLY TO Peter O'Rourke, Horton House, Exchange Flags, Liverpool L2 3YL *Tel.* 0151 600 3000 *Email* peter.o'rourke@brabners.com

■ William Harding's Charity

CC NO 310619 **ESTABLISHED** 1978

WHERE FUNDING CAN BE GIVEN Aylesbury in Buckinghamshire.

WHO CAN BENEFIT Individuals and organisations residing and benefitting the population of Aylesbury.

WHAT IS FUNDED To assist young people in education, including at an individual level, by providing scholarships, maintenance allowances, travel awards and grants for equipment. At a wider level, support is given to educational establishments for benefits or facilities not normally provided by the local education authority. The charity also provides relief in need and for the general benefit of Aylesbury residents.

WHAT IS NOT FUNDED People and organisations not based in Aylesbury Town.

TYPE OF GRANT One-off and capital costs.

RANGE OF GRANTS Up to £190,000.

SAMPLE GRANTS Aspire Project (£190,000); Aylesbury Grammar School (£101,000); Aylesbury Learning Partnership (£31,500); Broughton Infant School (£26,500); Aylesbury District Guide Hall Fund (£20,000); Queens Park Art Centre (£14,000); Aylesbury Bowls Club (£12,200); Youth Concern (£12,000); Home-Start Aylesbury and The Strategy Bucks CIC (£10,000 each); Healthy Living Centre and Islamic Education Trust (£5,000 each); Bucks County Museum Trust (£2,600); Aylesbury Visually Impaired (£1,500); Fairford Leys WI (£1,200); HM Prison Service (£1,000).

FINANCES *Year* 2015 *Income* £1,005,542 *Grants* £983,740 *Grants to organisations* £741,093 *Assets* £31,400,363

TRUSTEES Les Sheldon; Anne Brooker; Freda Roberts; Penni Thorne; Roger Evans; William Chapple; Ranjula Takodra; Lennard Wakelam; Susan Hewitt.

OTHER INFORMATION In 2015, £242,500 was given in grants to individuals. In addition, the charity owns almshouses in Aylesbury. Grants are normally given in the following categories: schools and other educational establishments; general benefits/relief in need; travel for clubs/ societies/groups; youth groups; equipment and tools for young people.

HOW TO APPLY Apply in writing to the correspondent. The trustees meet on a regular basis to consider and determine applications for charitable assistance. The charity's record on the Charity Commission's links to the charity's website; however, it did not seem to function at the time of writing.

WHO TO APPLY TO John Leggett, Clerk, 14 Bourbon Street, Aylesbury, Buckinghamshire HP20 2RS *Tel.* 01296 318501 *Email* doudjag@pandclip.co.uk

■ The Harebell Centenary Fund

CC NO 1003552 **ESTABLISHED** 1991

WHERE FUNDING CAN BE GIVEN UK.

WHO CAN BENEFIT Registered charities.

WHAT IS FUNDED General charitable purposes, including the education of young people, neurological and neurosurgical research, and the relief of sickness and suffering among animals.

WHAT IS NOT FUNDED Individuals.

TYPE OF GRANT One-off awards for core costs, research, recurring expenditure and running costs. Funding is given for one year or less.

RANGE OF GRANTS From £3,000 to £16,000, although the majority of grants were for £8,000.

SAMPLE GRANTS Blue Sky Thinking (£16,000); Changing Faces, Dog A.I.D., Foley House Trust, Helen House Hospice, Living Paintings, Success After Stroke and Talitha Arts (£8,000); Crathie School (£4,500); Foley House Trust (£3,000).

FINANCES *Year* 2015 *Income* £194,591 *Grants* £208,000 *Grants to organisations* £208,000 *Assets* £6,526,989

TRUSTEES Michael Goodbody; Penelope Chapman; Angela Fossick.

OTHER INFORMATION In 2015 a total of 26 charities were supported.

HOW TO APPLY Unsolicited applications are not requested: the trustees prefer to make donations to charities whose work they have come across through their own research.

WHO TO APPLY TO Penelope Chapman, Trustee, 50 Broadway, Westminster, London SW1H 0BL *Tel.* 020 7227 7000 *Email* pennychapman@bdb-law.co.uk

■ The Harpur Trust

CC NO 1066861 **ESTABLISHED** 1566

WHERE FUNDING CAN BE GIVEN Borough of Bedford and the surrounding area. There is a helpful facility on the website to check your postcode eligibility.

WHO CAN BENEFIT Charities; community organisations; schools.

WHAT IS FUNDED The charitable objects of the charity are: education; relief of poverty, sickness or distress and recreation with a social welfare purpose. The three priority areas are: **Transitions** – this programme is for projects which provide preparation, bridges and support for people undergoing difficult life transitions in Bedford; **Resilience or Psychological Fitness** – this programme is for projects which will help Bedford residents manage and cope with traumatic changes positively, learning to adapt and prosper despite setbacks; **Isolation** – a programme for projects which reduce loneliness and lack of social networks among Bedford's most vulnerable residents.

WHAT IS NOT FUNDED Businesses; projects that promote a particular religion, although faith groups may be funded for completely secular work; projects which are considered to be the responsibility of the local authority or national government; projects that do not benefit the residents of the Borough of Bedford; costs already incurred; trips, except in very limited circumstances.

TYPE OF GRANT Staffing; running and capital costs for projects; core services.

RANGE OF GRANTS £1,000 to £125,000; usually up to £5,000 or between £10,000 and £20,000 (often split over several years).

SAMPLE GRANTS Philharmonia Orchestra (£125,000); Mind BLMK (£80,500); The Cranfield Trust (£70,000); Community and Voluntary Service, Mid and North Bedfordshire (£50,000); Chums Child Bereavement Service (£40,000); Royal Mencap Society (£30,000); Bedford Creative Arts (£21,000); Tibbs Dementia Services (£15,500); The Bedfordshire Orchestral Society (£10,000); Putnoe Woods Preschool and SchoolReaders (£5,000 each); Arkwright Scholarships Trust (£2,000); Bedpop and Mastroe (£1,000 each).

FINANCES *Year* 2015/16 *Income* £53,185,000 *Grants* £887,288 *Grants to organisations* £770,064 *Assets* £159,263,000

TRUSTEES Murray Stewart; Anthony Nutt; Phil Wallace; David Palfreyman; Prof. Stephen Mayson; Michael Womack; Rhian Castell; Sally Peck; David Wilson; Dr Anne Egan; Randolph Charles; Justin Phillimore; Ian McEwen; David Dixon; Dr Jennifer Sauboorah Till; Sue Clark; Shirley Jackson; Tina Beddoes; David Wilson; Rae Levene; Hugh Stewart; Prof. Kate Jacques; Linbert Spencer; Prof. Seamus Higson.

OTHER INFORMATION Grants were made to 61 organisations and 29 individuals. The trust also supported 231 pupils with school fees.

HOW TO APPLY Applications can be made via the trust's website. The trust's application guidance states: 'Contact us to discuss your request well before you intend to submit an application. We are happy to provide assistance at any stage during the application process.'

WHO TO APPLY TO Lucy Bardner, Grants Manager, Princeton Court, The Pilgrim Centre, Brickhill Drive, Bedford MK41 7PZ *Tel.* 01234 369503 *Email* grants@harpurtrust.org.uk *Website* www.harpurtrust.org.uk

■ The Peter and Teresa Harris Charitable Trust

CC NO 1161183 **ESTABLISHED** 2010
WHERE FUNDING CAN BE GIVEN England and Wales.
WHO CAN BENEFIT Registered charities.
WHAT IS FUNDED General charitable purposes.
RANGE OF GRANTS Up to £25,000.
SAMPLE GRANTS Superkidz Community Trust (£25,000); Blackheath Conservative (£20,000); Greenwich Cricket and Yehudi Menuhin School (£15,000 each); 999 Club, Heritage of London Trust Operations, Samaritans and University of Greenwich (£10,000 each); Greenwich Society (£7,500); Christ Church West Wimbledon and Handicap International UK (£5,000 each); Budiriro Trust, Faith in Action and Unitarian Chapel Billinghurst (£2,500 each); Greenwich Society – Ireland-Albrecht (£2,400).
FINANCES *Year* 2015/16 *Income* £3,006,385 *Grants* £166,500 *Grants to organisations* £166,500 *Assets* £2,801,770
TRUSTEES Tim Barnes; Duncan Rabagliati.
HOW TO APPLY Applications can be made in writing or via email and are considered on a case-by-case basis. According to the annual report for 2015/16 the trust 'will consider applications by charitable organisations that it has not previously supported'. Grants are considered by all trustees on a regular basis throughout the year.
WHO TO APPLY TO The Trustees, The Peter and Teresa Harris Charitable Trust, c/o Gregsons Solicitors, 19 Tabor Grove, London SW19 4EX *Tel.* 020 8946 1173 *Email* duncan@gregsons.co.uk

■ The Harris Charity

CC NO 526206 **ESTABLISHED** 1883
WHERE FUNDING CAN BE GIVEN Lancashire, with a preference for the City of Preston (formally the borough of Preston).
WHO CAN BENEFIT Charities benefitting individuals, children and young people under 25, in the Lancashire area; individuals.
WHAT IS FUNDED Children and young people.
WHAT IS NOT FUNDED Course fees; supplement living expenses; salary costs; general grants to groups travelling overseas.
TYPE OF GRANT Capital projects and provision of equipment are preferred.
SAMPLE GRANTS A list of beneficiaries was not available.
FINANCES *Year* 2015/16 *Income* £127,049 *Grants* £50,371 *Grants to organisations* £50,371 *Assets* £3,563,832
TRUSTEES Timothy Scott; Keith Mellalieu; Audrey Scott; Edwin Booth; Simon Huck; Stanley Smith; William Huck; Peter Metcalf; Nicola Fielden; Dr Anthony Andrews; Revd Peter Hamborg; Jennifer Coulston-Herrmann.
OTHER INFORMATION Grants were split into the following categories: recreational (£40,500); charitable organisations (£9,500); educational (£500). The amount of grants given to individuals totalled about £1,700.
HOW TO APPLY Application forms can be downloaded from the charity's website and should be returned by post to the secretary. The deadline for submissions are 31 March and 30 September each year.
WHO TO APPLY TO David Ingram, Secretary, c/o Moore and Smalley, Richard House, 9 Winckley Square, Preston, Lancashire PR1 3HP *Tel.* 01772 821021 *Email* harrischarity@mooreandsmalley.co.uk *Website* www.theharrischarity.co.uk

■ The Harris Family Charitable Trust

CC NO 1064394 **ESTABLISHED** 1997
WHERE FUNDING CAN BE GIVEN UK.
WHO CAN BENEFIT Charitable organisations.
WHAT IS FUNDED Health issues and the alleviation of sickness.
SAMPLE GRANTS A list of beneficiaries was not available.
FINANCES *Year* 2015/16 *Income* £508,859 *Grants* £146,564 *Grants to organisations* £146,564 *Assets* £2,225,314
TRUSTEES Ronnie Harris; Loretta Harris; Charlotte Harris; Sophie Harris; Toby Harris.
HOW TO APPLY According to the annual report for 2013/14, the trust 'invites applications for funding of projects through various sources' and 'the applications are reviewed by the trustees that they are in accordance with the charity's objectives'.
WHO TO APPLY TO Ronnie Harris, Trustee, 64 New Cavendish Street, London W1G 8TB *Tel.* 020 7467 6300

■ The Edith Lilian Harrison 2000 Foundation

CC NO 1085651 **ESTABLISHED** 2000
WHERE FUNDING CAN BE GIVEN UK.
WHO CAN BENEFIT Registered charities.
WHAT IS FUNDED General charitable purposes, particularly health, disability and social welfare.
TYPE OF GRANT One-off grants for three years or more.
RANGE OF GRANTS £2,000 to £50,000; the majority of grants were for £5,000.
SAMPLE GRANTS Salisbury Hospice (£50,000); Listening Books (£20,000); Macmillan Cancer Care and The Salvation Army Therapy Centre (£10,000 each); Action for Blind People, Bourne Valley Good Neighbour Scheme, Dogs for the Disabled, Hot Lines Meal Service, Little Sister of the Poor, National Autistic Society, St John's Church – Redhill and The Mission for Seafarers (£5,000 each); Salisbury Rotary Club (£2,000).
FINANCES *Year* 2015/16 *Income* £77,665 *Grants* £252,000 *Grants to organisations* £252,000 *Assets* £2,140,659
TRUSTEES Geoffrey Peyer; Clive Andrews; Paul Bradley.
OTHER INFORMATION In 2015/16, 36 organisations were supported.
HOW TO APPLY Apply in writing to the correspondent. Applications for grants are normally considered and dealt with in November.
WHO TO APPLY TO Geoffrey Peyer, Trustee, TWM Solicitors LLP, 40 West Street, Reigate RH2 9BT *Tel.* 01737 221212 *Email* paul.bradley@twmsolicitors.com

■ The Peter Harrison Foundation

CC NO 1076579 **ESTABLISHED** 1999

WHERE FUNDING CAN BE GIVEN UK; South East England.

WHO CAN BENEFIT Registered charities; community amateur sports clubs.

WHAT IS FUNDED The foundation has two main grant programmes: **Opportunities through Sport** – sporting activity or projects which provide opportunities for people who have disabilities or are otherwise disadvantaged to fulfil their potential and to develop other personal and life skills; **Special Needs and Care for Children and Young People** – this programme is exclusively for the south east of England and applications are only accepted from charities meeting the needs of children and young people in the following counties: Berkshire; Buckinghamshire; Hampshire; Isle of Wight; Kent; Oxfordshire; Surrey; East Sussex; and West Sussex. Applications are welcomed for the following types of project: projects that work with or benefit children who have disabilities or are chronically or terminally ill, and provide support for their parents and carers; projects that help to engage children or young people at risk of crime, truancy or addiction; projects organised for young people at risk of homelessness or that provide new opportunities for homeless young people.

WHAT IS NOT FUNDED Requests for retrospective funding; activities that are primarily the responsibility of central or local government; individuals; overseas projects; adventure challenges or expeditions in the UK or abroad; projects that are solely for the promotion of religion.

TYPE OF GRANT Capital and core costs; salaries; project expenditure; one-off and up to three years.

RANGE OF GRANTS Up to £333,000.

SAMPLE GRANTS Young Epilepsy (£334,000); Loughborough University (£200,000); Reigate Grammar School and British Paralympic Association (£100,000); Exeter Royal Academy for Deaf Education and YMCA East Surrey (£50,000 each); Cranleigh Riding for the Disabled and The Panathlon Foundation Ltd (£30,000 each); The Rose Road Association (£25,000); Addaction and Harbour Challenge (£20,000 each).

FINANCES *Year* 2015/16 *Income* £2,463,713 *Grants* £1,874,650 *Grants to organisations* £1,874,650 *Assets* £47,781,517

TRUSTEES Peter Harrison; Julia Harrison-Lee; Peter Lee; Nicholas Harrison.

HOW TO APPLY There is a two stage application process – initial enquiry (form available online) to determine whether your project would interest the foundation, and full application (applicants successful in the first stage will be sent one). There is no application deadline but you may only apply to one of the programmes at any time. The trustees meet three times a year in spring, summer and autumn.

WHO TO APPLY TO Andrew Ross, Director, Foundation House, 42–48 London Road, Reigate, Surrey RH2 9QQ *Tel.* 01737 228013 *Email* enquiries@peterharrisonfoundation.org *Website* www.peterharrisonfoundation.org

■ The Harrison-Frank Family Foundation (UK) Ltd

CC NO 1155149 **ESTABLISHED** 2013

WHERE FUNDING CAN BE GIVEN UK and Israel.

WHO CAN BENEFIT Registered charities.

WHAT IS FUNDED General charitable purposes.

RANGE OF GRANTS From £2,000 to £164,000. The majority of grants were of £5,000 or less.

SAMPLE GRANTS New Israel Fund (£164,000); Médecins Sans Frontières, UK (£22,000); Macmillan Caring Locally and Royal Marsden Hospital Charity (£10,000 each); Age Concern, Beanstalk and Crisis UK (£5,000 each); RSPB (£3,000); St Christopher's Hospice and The Spires Centre (£2,000 each).

FINANCES *Year* 2015 *Income* £327,454 *Grants* £316,500 *Grants to organisations* £316,500 *Assets* £5,411,724

TRUSTEES Barbara Frank Harrison; Fredrik Ulfsater; Richard Harrison; David Harrison; Marc Hackney; Michele Harrison.

HOW TO APPLY Apply in writing to the correspondent.

WHO TO APPLY TO Richard Harrison, Trustee, Flat 17, 34 Seymour Place, London W1H 7NS *Tel.* 020 7724 1154 *Email* marc.hackney@vobiset.com

■ The Hartley Charitable Trust

CC NO 800968 **ESTABLISHED** 1989

WHERE FUNDING CAN BE GIVEN UK and overseas.

WHO CAN BENEFIT Charitable organisations.

WHAT IS FUNDED General charitable purposes.

WHAT IS NOT FUNDED Individuals.

TYPE OF GRANT One-off and recurrent grants for core costs, capital expenditure, projects, research and salaries. Awards can be made for one year or less.

RANGE OF GRANTS £1,000 to £30,000.

SAMPLE GRANTS Alzheimer's Society (£30,000); Open Arms Malawi (£7,500); Senior Volunteer Network (£5,000); Prostate Cancer UK (£3,000); Lowmill Outdoor Centre (£1,000).

FINANCES *Year* 2015/16 *Income* £52,307 *Grants* £46,500 *Grants to organisations* £46,500 *Assets* £1,860,564

TRUSTEES Richard Hartley; Jane Hartley; Peta Hyland.

OTHER INFORMATION Grants were made to five organisations during the year, most of which had previously been supported by the trust.

HOW TO APPLY The trust has previously stated that its funds are fully committed.

WHO TO APPLY TO Richard Hartley, Trustee, 6 Throstle Nest Drive, Harrogate, Yorkshire HG2 9PB *Tel.* 01423 525100 *Email* hartleycharitabletrust@hotmail.com

■ The Alfred and Peggy Harvey Charitable Trust

CC NO 1095855 **ESTABLISHED** 2003

WHERE FUNDING CAN BE GIVEN Kent, Surrey and South East London.

WHO CAN BENEFIT Charitable organisations.

WHAT IS FUNDED The care of and provision of accommodation for older people; the care and provision of financial support for children and young people who have disabilities and those who are socially or educationally disadvantaged; the care of people who are blind or deaf; medical and surgical studies and research.

WHAT IS NOT FUNDED Organisations outside the area of benefit.

RANGE OF GRANTS £1,000 to £350,000.

SAMPLE GRANTS St John Baptist School – Candlelight Trust (£350,000); London Reclaimed (£200,000); Ahoy Centre Sailing Project (£66,000); The Alzheimer's Society, NSPCC and The Royal Marsden Cancer Charity (£1,000 each).
FINANCES *Year* 2015/16 *Income* £179,339 *Grants* £619,000 *Grants to organisations* £619,000 *Assets* £571,246
TRUSTEES Kevin Custis; Colin Russell; John Duncan.
OTHER INFORMATION In 2015/16 six organisations were supported.
HOW TO APPLY Apply in writing to the correspondent.
WHO TO APPLY TO Colin Russell, Trustee, c/o Manches LLP, Aldwych House, 81 Aldwych, London WC2B 4RP *Tel.* 020 7404 4433

■ The Hasluck Charitable Trust

CC NO 1115323 **ESTABLISHED** 2006
WHERE FUNDING CAN BE GIVEN UK.
WHO CAN BENEFIT Charitable organisations.
WHAT IS FUNDED General charitable purposes.
WHAT IS NOT FUNDED Individuals.
TYPE OF GRANT One-off; funding is unrestricted.
RANGE OF GRANTS Usually £1,000.
SAMPLE GRANTS Barnardo's, International Fund for Animal Welfare and Macmillan Cancer Support (£5,000 each); Teenage Cancer Trust (£1,250); British Tinnitus Association, Crackerjacks, Dementia UK, Edinburgh Garden Partners, Microloan Foundation, Redditch Nightstop, St John International, Theatre Peckham, Tower Hamlets Friends and Neighbours, West London Mission and World Vision – Nepal Appeal (£1,000 each).
FINANCES *Year* 2015/16 *Income* £128,364 *Grants* £90,750 *Grants to organisations* £90,750 *Assets* £1,524,309
TRUSTEES Matthew Wakefield; John Billing; Mark Wheeler.
OTHER INFORMATION The trust makes regular payments to eight charities (Barnardo's, International Fund for Animal Welfare, Macmillan Cancer Relief, Mrs R. H. Hotblacks Michelham Priory Endowment Fund, the Riding for the Disabled Association, RNLI, RSPB and Scope), which are of particular interest to the settlor. During the year 68 awards were made to 46 charities.
HOW TO APPLY Apply in writing to the correspondent. Grants are generally distributed in January and July, although consideration is given to appeals received at other times of the year. The trustees have previously stated that it 'asks applicants not to send copies of their accounts as these can be viewed online'. Only successful applicants are acknowledged.
WHO TO APPLY TO John Billing, Trustee, Rathbone Trust Legal Services Ltd, 8 Finsbury Circus, London EC2M 7AZ *Tel.* 020 7399 0447 *Email* john.billing@rathbones.com

■ The Hathaway Trust

CC NO 1064086 **ESTABLISHED** 1997
WHERE FUNDING CAN BE GIVEN UK and overseas, with a preference for Manchester.
WHO CAN BENEFIT Registered charities; Jewish institutions; individuals.
WHAT IS FUNDED General charitable purposes, including the relief of poverty, particularly among older individuals, the advancement of education, medical assistance, the provision of interest-free loans, the advancement of religion and general community benefit. Support is mainly given to Jewish organisations and causes.
TYPE OF GRANT One-off and recurrent grants; interest-free loans.
RANGE OF GRANTS Previously up to £13,500.
SAMPLE GRANTS Toimchei Shabbos Manchester (£13,350); Sayser (£3,000); Purim Fund (£2,500); Ahavas Tzedoko Vochessed (£1,750); Meleches Machsheves (£1,500); Manchester Hacnosas Kallah (£1,000).
FINANCES *Year* 2015/16 *Income* £121,456 *Grants* £118,256 *Grants to organisations* £118,256 *Assets* £49,531
TRUSTEES Norman Younger; Miriam Younger; Rabbi Stuart Schwalbe; Jonathan Roitenbarg.
HOW TO APPLY The trustees have previously stated that they have adopted a proactive approach to funding and now only fund projects with which they have a personal connection; therefore, unsolicited requests will not be considered.
WHO TO APPLY TO The Trustees, 12 Hereford Drive, Prestwich, Manchester M25 0JA *Email* nsy@btconnect.com

■ The Maurice Hatter Foundation

CC NO 298119 **ESTABLISHED** 1987
WHERE FUNDING CAN BE GIVEN UK and overseas.
WHO CAN BENEFIT Registered charities and educational bodies, particularly those with links to the Jewish community.
WHAT IS FUNDED General charitable purposes, particularly education and social welfare. Support is also given for international policy research, Jewish religious causes, medical research, and cultural and environmental causes.
TYPE OF GRANT Grants, often recurring; loans.
RANGE OF GRANTS Up to £335,000, with the majority of grants being for £7,500 or less.
SAMPLE GRANTS World ORT (£335,000); British Friends of Haifa University (£154,500); University College Hospital Charity Fund – Hatter Cardiovascular Institute (£122,000); UCL Development Fund (£50,000); Norwood Ravenswood (£12,500); Henry Jackson Society (£7,500); Duke of Edinburgh International Award, Prostate Cancer UK, Royal Marines Charitable Trust Fund and United Synagogue (£5,000 each); Chai Cancer Care (£3,800); World Jewish Congress (£3,300); Movement for Reform Judaism (£3,000); Holocaust Survivors Initiative (£2,500).
FINANCES *Year* 2015/16 *Income* £2,884,440 *Grants* £928,665 *Grants to organisations* £928,665 *Assets* £9,700,405
TRUSTEES Piers Barclay; Richard Hatter; Sir Maurice Hatter; Fausto Furlotti.
HOW TO APPLY Unsolicited applications will not be considered.
WHO TO APPLY TO The Trustees of The Maurice Hatter Foundation, The Maurice Hatter Foundation, c/o Smith and Williamson, 1 Bishops Wharf, Walnut Tree Close, Guildford, Surrey GU1 4RA *Tel.* 01483 407100

■ The Hawthorne Charitable Trust

CC NO 233921 **ESTABLISHED** 1964
WHERE FUNDING CAN BE GIVEN UK, especially Hereford and Worcester.
WHO CAN BENEFIT Registered charities.
WHAT IS FUNDED General charitable purposes; medical causes, health and sickness; environment, conservation and heritage; disability; animal care; the relief of poverty.

WHAT IS NOT FUNDED Organisations which are not registered charities; individuals.
TYPE OF GRANT Mostly recurring.
RANGE OF GRANTS Between £100 and £5,000.
SAMPLE GRANTS Malvern Festival Theatre Trust Ltd and Nepal Earthquake Appeal (£5,000 each); St Michael's Hospice – Hereford and Stisted Parish Council (£3,000 each); Hearing Dogs for Deaf People, The Global Natural Healthcare Trust (£2,500 each); Animal Health Trust, Arthritis Research Campaign, National Council for the Conservation of Plants and Gardens, The Pace Centre and The Passage (£2,000 each); Addington Fund and Birmingham Royal Ballet (£1,000); Friends of the Public Gardens (£500); Great Malvern Priory (£100).
FINANCES *Year* 2015/16 *Income* £197,024 *Grants* £135,600 *Grants to organisations* £135,600 *Assets* £8,449,691
TRUSTEES Alexandra Berington; Richard White; Roger Clark; Thomas Berington.
OTHER INFORMATION There were 69 grants made during the year.
HOW TO APPLY Apply in writing to the correspondent. Our research indicates that up-to-date accounts should be included and applications should be received by October for consideration in November.
WHO TO APPLY TO David Boswell, c/o RSM UK Tax And Accounting Ltd, Marlborough House, Victoria Road South, Chelmsford CM11 1LN *Tel.* 01245 354402 *Email* dave.boswell@rsmuk.com

■ The Charles Hayward Foundation

CC NO 1078969 **ESTABLISHED** 1961
WHERE FUNDING CAN BE GIVEN British Isles, with some funding awarded to charities in the Commonwealth countries of Africa.
WHO CAN BENEFIT UK-registered charities.
WHAT IS FUNDED **Main grant programme**: charities with an income of more than £350,000 working in the areas of social and criminal justice, and heritage and conservation. The overseas category is for charities with an income of between £150,000 and £5 million working in the areas of: clean water and sanitation; basic health programmes; and self-sustainability through training in farming skills and income generation activities. **Small grant programme**: charities with an income of less than £350,000 working in the areas of social and criminal justice, and older people.
WHAT IS NOT FUNDED **General exclusions**: endowments; general appeals; grant-making charities; individuals; loans and deficits; retrospective funding; core costs. **Social and criminal justice**: policy and research; uniformed organisations; short-term interventions; trips and youth volunteering. Also, under the small grant programme, generic youth programmes. **Heritage and conservation**: community arts troupes; community arts centres; conservation of gardens; environmental conservation and endangered species; animal rescue; art and history workshops; academic institutions; churches; opera, ballet and theatre, including artistic productions; heritage railways; building repairs. **Older people**: purchase of minibuses; disability access; older people's projects that are restricted to one section of society; community transport; community development organisations. **Overseas**: overseas disability awareness; disaster appeals; education; gap years, electives and project visits overseas.
TYPE OF GRANT Capital and project funding.
RANGE OF GRANTS Up to £25,000.
SAMPLE GRANTS Why Me? (£25,000); City Gateway (£20,000); Village Aid Africa (£16,000); Multi-Cultural Family Base and National Army Museum (£15,000 each); Age Concern North Dorset and Children on the Edge (£5,000 each); Al-Hasaniya Moroccan Women's Project and Community Resettlement Support – HMP Bedford (£3,000 each); Spinal Injuries Association (£1,000).
FINANCES *Year* 2015 *Income* £1,349,248 *Grants* £1,274,366 *Grants to organisations* £1,274,366 *Assets* £60,337,897
TRUSTEES Sue Heath; Julia Chamberlain; Caroline Donald; Richard Griffith; Alexander Heath; Brian Insch; Nikolas van Leuven.
OTHER INFORMATION In 2015 the foundation received around 700 formal applications. Grants were paid to 141 organisations.
HOW TO APPLY Full information, including eligibility criteria and how to apply for a grant, is available on the foundation's highly informative website. Note that the foundation does not currently accept applications by email. Applications to the small grant programme are accepted on a rolling basis and are considered every two to three months. The main grant programme has a two-stage application process. Firstly, applications are considered by the grants committee, which recommends applications to be considered by the trustees at the second stage of the process. Trustee meetings usually take place in February, April, July and November.
WHO TO APPLY TO Dorothy Napierala, Administrator, Hayward House, 45 Harrington Gardens, London SW7 4JU *Tel.* 020 7370 7063 or 020 7370 7067 *Email* dorothy@charleshaywardfoundation.org.uk *Website* www.charleshaywardfoundation.org.uk

■ HC Foundation

CC NO 1148306 **ESTABLISHED** 2012
WHERE FUNDING CAN BE GIVEN England.
WHO CAN BENEFIT Charities.
WHAT IS FUNDED The relief of financial hardship, poverty and sickness; education.
SAMPLE GRANTS A list of beneficiaries was not available.
FINANCES *Year* 2015/16 *Income* £273,975 *Grants* £177,222 *Grants to organisations* £177,222 *Assets* £443,951
TRUSTEES Mrs S. Grossman; Mr B. Grossman; Mrs S. March.
HOW TO APPLY Apply in writing to the correspondent.
WHO TO APPLY TO John Hamer, 1 Bridge Lane, Suite 1A First Floor, London NW11 0EA *Tel.* 020 8458 8900

■ The Headley Trust

CC NO 266620 **ESTABLISHED** 1973
WHERE FUNDING CAN BE GIVEN UK and overseas.
WHO CAN BENEFIT 'Registered charities or activities with clearly defined charitable purposes'. The trust prefers to support innovative schemes that can be successfully replicated or become self-sustaining.
WHAT IS FUNDED Arts and heritage UK; cathedrals and major churches; parish churches; arts and heritage overseas; development projects in sub-Saharan Anglophone Africa; education; health and social welfare.
WHAT IS NOT FUNDED None of the trusts directly support individuals, education fees or expeditions.

TYPE OF GRANT One-off; capital, core and project costs; over three years or less.
RANGE OF GRANTS £5,000 to £225,000.
SAMPLE GRANTS Fitzwilliam College Cambridge (£225,000); British Museum Development Trust and IntoUniversity (£80,000 each); Tate St Ives (£75,000); Canterbury Cathedral (£50,000); King Edward Mine Museum and Plan International UK (£40,000 each); Initiative for Heritage Conservation (£30,000); Exeter Cathedral (£29,000); North Devon Maritime Museum (£20,000); National Lobster Hatchery (£10,000); York Museums Trust (£5,500).
FINANCES *Year* 2015/16 *Income* £2,292,000 *Grants* £5,556,000 *Grants to organisations* £5,556,000 *Assets* £66,055,000
TRUSTEES Lady Susan Sainsbury; Judith Portrait; Timothy Sainsbury; Sir Timothy Sainsbury; Camilla Sainsbury; Amanda McCrystal.
OTHER INFORMATION The trust is one of the Sainsbury Family Charitable Trusts, which share a common administration – application to one is considered as an application to all and directed to the most appropriate. In 2015/16, 229 grants were awarded. The grant total refers to the figure stated as 'total grants payable' in the accounts.
HOW TO APPLY Apply in writing to the correspondent. Applications should be no more than two pages and include the following information: a brief description of your charity; an outline of the project requiring funding – why it is needed, who will benefit and in what way; the budget for the project; the timescale for the project – when it will start and finish; how you plan to measure the success and impact of the project; the name and contact details of the person responsible for the application. The trust's website notes: '**It should be understood that the great majority of proposals are unsuccessful. The trustees wish to discourage charities from wasting time and resources on applications that fall outside the trusts' remit.**' One application will be considered by all the trusts.
WHO TO APPLY TO Alan Bookbinder, Director, The Sainsbury Family Charitable Trusts, The Peak, 5 Wilton Road, London SW1V 1AP *Tel.* 020 7410 0330 *Email* info@sfct.org.uk *Website* www.sfct.org.uk

■ The Health Foundation

CC NO 286967 **ESTABLISHED** 1983
WHERE FUNDING CAN BE GIVEN Unrestricted.
WHO CAN BENEFIT Research organisations; educational institutions; NHS bodies; charities; individuals.
WHAT IS FUNDED Improving the quality of health care.
WHAT IS NOT FUNDED Overheads; clinical trials and research focused on the development of new treatments. Refer to the specific exclusions for each programme on the foundation's website.
TYPE OF GRANT Typically project grants for up to three years.
RANGE OF GRANTS Up to £486,000.
SAMPLE GRANTS London Ambulance Service (£486,000); The Royal College of Anaesthetists (£400,000); East Midlands Improvement Science Development Network (£280,000); Royal Surrey County Hospital NHS Trust (£181,000); University of Hull (£96,000); Peninsula Community Health (£75,000); The Social Care Institute for Excellence (£52,000); Office of Health Economics (£30,000); The British Association for Parenteral and Enteral Nutrition (£28,000); International Futures Forum (£5,000).
FINANCES *Year* 2015 *Income* £15,512,000 *Grants* £15,797,000 *Grants to organisations* £15,649,000 *Assets* £827,855,000
TRUSTEES Prof. Andrew Morris; Sir Alan Langlands; Bridget McIntyre; David Zahn; Sir Hugh Taylor; Martyn Hole; Rosalind Smyth; Melloney Poole; Sir David Dalton; Branwen Jeffreys; Eric Gregory; Loraine Hawkins.
OTHER INFORMATION During the year 355 grants were made to both individuals and organisations.
HOW TO APPLY The foundation does not consider unprompted requests or proposals for funding. Programmes open for applications are advertised on the foundation's website. These are likely to change frequently and candidates are advised to visit the website for the most up-to-date information. You may sign up to receive alerts when new funding opportunities go live. Application forms are available online together with full guidelines and specific requirements and deadlines for each of the programme. There is also a helpful FAQ document which should be consulted by potential applicants.
WHO TO APPLY TO Programmes Team, 90 Long Acre, London WC2E 9RA *Tel.* 020 7257 8000 *Fax* 020 7257 8001 *Email* info@health.org.uk *Website* www.health.org.uk

■ May Hearnshaw Charitable Trust (May Hearnshaw's Charity)

CC NO 1008638 **ESTABLISHED** 1992
WHERE FUNDING CAN BE GIVEN UK (national charities); South Yorkshire, North Nottinghamshire, Derbyshire, East Lancashire and Cheshire (local charities).
WHO CAN BENEFIT Nationwide charities and local charities in the South Yorkshire, North Nottinghamshire, Derbyshire, East Lancashire or Cheshire areas.
WHAT IS FUNDED General charitable purposes, with a focus on education and the relief of poverty and sickness.
WHAT IS NOT FUNDED Individuals.
TYPE OF GRANT Our research suggests that one-off grants can be given for up to three years. Support for buildings, core costs, research, recurring costs, running costs and salaries can be considered.
RANGE OF GRANTS Up to £12,000, but usually between £500 and £3,000.
SAMPLE GRANTS Weston Park Hospital Cancer Charity (£12,000); Meadowhead Community Learning Trust (£7,800); Macmillan Chesterfield Appeal and Dronfield District Scouts (£5,000 each); Autism Plus, Bowel Disease Research and Tall Ships Youth Trust (£2,000 each); Nottinghamshire YMCA and Readathon (£1,000 each); National Search and Dog Rescue Association (£920); Investec Ashes Cycle Challenge and Samaritans (£500 each); Sense and Walk the Walk Worldwide (£200 each).
FINANCES *Year* 2015/16 *Income* £84,301 *Grants* £69,477 *Grants to organisations* £69,477 *Assets* £2,173,070
TRUSTEES Marjorie West; Michael Ferreday; Richard Law; William Munro.
OTHER INFORMATION A total of 36 organisations received support.
HOW TO APPLY Apply in writing to the correspondent. According to our research, the trustees usually meet three times a year when they decide on and make major grants to charitable

organisations but may decide to make grants at any time.

WHO TO APPLY TO Michael Ferreday, Trustee, BHP Chartered Accountants, 2 Rutland Park, Sheffield S10 2PD *Tel.* 0114 266 7171 *Email* paul.randall@bhp.co.uk

■ Heart of England Community Foundation

CC NO 1117345 **ESTABLISHED** 1995

WHERE FUNDING CAN BE GIVEN Coventry, Solihull and Warwickshire.

WHO CAN BENEFIT Community-based groups and charities; unregistered but charitable organisations.

WHAT IS FUNDED A wide range of general charitable purposes, including education, employment, disadvantaged and socially excluded individuals, health causes, volunteering, arts and culture, sport and recreation, crime prevention, relief of poverty and a range of other local community causes. The fund administers a range of grants programmes – refer to the website for information on what is currently available.

WHAT IS NOT FUNDED Statutory organisations; individuals (although a scheme is being developed to assist people with learning difficulties or disabilities); projects which have already started (although new, distinct elements of existing project may be assisted); statutory provision; activities that promote religious activity; activities that are not socially inclusive; organisations with a turnover of over £100,000 excluding restricted funding; grant-making bodies; mainstream activities of schools and colleges; medical research; animal welfare; political activities; organisations with substantial reserves; general and major fundraising appeals; continuation funding. The foundation does not usually provide part-funding, preferring to be the majority funder. Only one grant will be given to an organisation in any one year from the foundation.

TYPE OF GRANT Project costs, events, materials and equipment.

RANGE OF GRANTS £100 to £11,500.

SAMPLE GRANTS Coventry Somali Women's Network (£11,500); Hub @ Blackwell (£10,700); Positive Youth Foundation (£10,000); Friendship Project (£6,000 in two grants); The Open Theatre Company Ltd (£5,000); Write Here Write Now CIC (£3,000); The Friends of Kingsbury Water Park and Pop Up Communities CIC (£2,000 each); Kingshurst Arts Space (£1,500); Lower Ford Street Baptist Church (£1,000); Asperger's United and Welford Junior Football Club (£700 each); Pinley Over 60s Group (£900); Whitley Junior FC (£600).

FINANCES *Year* 2015/16 *Income* £3,602,774 *Grants* £854,251 *Grants to organisations* £854,251 *Assets* £10,063,216

TRUSTEES Sir Nicholas Cadbury; Amrik Bhabra; Sally Carrick; Christopher West; John Taylor; Paul Belfield; Phillip Ewing; Lucie Byron; Philip Pemble; Michelle Vincent.

OTHER INFORMATION During the year there were 863 awards made. A detailed breakdown is given in the Annual Grant-Making Report on the foundation's website.

HOW TO APPLY Before making a formal application you should contact the Grants Team for an informal chat at 02476 883262. Applications should be made by completing an online form. All applicants will hear the outcome of their application within 12 weeks.

WHO TO APPLY TO Tina Costello, c/o PSA Peugeot Citroën, Torrington Avenue, Tile Hill, Coventry CV4 9AP *Tel.* 024 7688 3260 *Email* info@heartofenglandcf.co.uk *Website* www.heartofenglandcf.co.uk/applying-for-grants

■ Heart Research UK

CC NO 1044821 **ESTABLISHED** 1967

WHERE FUNDING CAN BE GIVEN UK.

WHO CAN BENEFIT Community groups; voluntary organisations; research and medical institutions; CICs.

WHAT IS FUNDED Medical research and promotion of healthy lifestyles focusing on heart disease in the UK.

WHAT IS NOT FUNDED Government organisations; local authority groups.

TYPE OF GRANT One-off and recurrent (medical research grants usually of up to three years).

RANGE OF GRANTS Up to £250,000 for research and up to £10,000 for local projects.

SAMPLE GRANTS University of Leicester (£183,000); Liverpool Heart and Chest Hospital (£100,000); William Harvey Research Institute (£88,500); Glasgow Caledonian University (£76,500); Aortic Masterclass Liverpool 2015 (£25,000); Leeds Rhinos Foundation (£10,000); Access Ability CIC (£8,500); Healthy Living Centre Dartford (£5,000); Higham Ferrers Gateway Club (£1,500).

FINANCES *Year* 2015 *Income* £1,674,148 *Grants* £1,155,616 *Grants to organisations* £1,155,616 *Assets* £2,772,297

TRUSTEES Paul Rogerson; Keith Loudon; Richard Colwyn; Christine Mortimer; Dr David Dickinson; Kevin Watterson; Anthony Knight; Antony Oxley; Dr Catherine Dickinson; Anthony Kilner; Paul Smith; Richard Brown; Peter Braidley; Julie Fenwick; Pierre Bouvet; Christopher Newman.

OTHER INFORMATION The charity made grants through three programmes during the year: medical research grants (£814,500); Heart Research UK and SUBWAY* Healthy Heart Grants (£104,000); Heart Research UK Healthy Heart Grants (£87,000).

HOW TO APPLY Application forms, full guidelines and up to date deadlines for each programme can be found on the charity's website or requested from the correspondent.

WHO TO APPLY TO Barbara Harpham, National Director, Suite 12D, Joseph's Well, Hanover Walk, Leeds LS3 1AB *Tel.* 0113 234 7474 *Email* grants@heartresearch.org.uk *Website* www.heartresearch.org.uk

■ The Heathcoat Trust

CC NO 203367 **ESTABLISHED** 1945

WHERE FUNDING CAN BE GIVEN Local causes in and around Tiverton, Devon.

WHO CAN BENEFIT Local organisations to Tiverton and national charities working on projects in that area; individual grants to employees and pensioners (and their dependants) of the Heathcoat group of companies.

WHAT IS FUNDED Relief of poverty; social welfare; education and training; health causes; children and young people; older people; local causes.

TYPE OF GRANT Recurring and one-off.

RANGE OF GRANTS £1,000 to £10,000.

SAMPLE GRANTS Tiverton Market Centre (£10,000); Heathcoat Social Club (£5,000); Mid Devon Indoor Bowls Club (£2,700); Chevithorne Village Hall and Tiverton and Mid Devon Museum Trust (£2,300 each); Tiverton Junior Operatics Club

(£2,000 in two grants); Exeter Leukaemia Fund (£1,800); Force Cancer Charity (£1,500); Exmoor Search and Rescue Fund (£1,000).

FINANCES *Year* 2015/16 *Income* £773,066 *Grants* £86,568 *Grants to organisations* £86,568 *Assets* £21,692,900

TRUSTEES Mark Drysdale; Ian Heathcoat-Amory; John Stanley Smith; Susan Westlake; Stephen Butt; Julian Morgan.

HOW TO APPLY Applications should be made in writing to the correspondent giving as much relevant information as possible. The trustees meet regularly to consider applications for grants. There are application forms for certain education grants.

WHO TO APPLY TO C. J. Twose, Secretary, The Factory, Tiverton, Devon EX16 5LL *Tel.* 01884 254949 *Email* heathcoattrust@heathcoat.co.uk

■ Heathrow Community Fund (LHR Airport Communities Trust)

CC NO 1058617 **ESTABLISHED** 1996

WHERE FUNDING CAN BE GIVEN Communities local to Heathrow Airport Holdings Group's UK airports; Aberdeen, Glasgow and Heathrow.

WHO CAN BENEFIT Charities; community groups; CICs; schools or colleges (for work with the wider community or beyond the curriculum and statutory requirements).

WHAT IS FUNDED The trust makes grants in three categories: communities for youth – projects working with young people; communities for tomorrow – environment and sustainability; communities together – projects supporting community cohesion.

WHAT IS NOT FUNDED General running costs; individuals; commercial sponsorship; private companies; third party advertising; political campaigning. Refer to the website for guidance on what is/isn't eligible under each of the areas of focus.

TYPE OF GRANT Project costs.

RANGE OF GRANTS £2,500 to £25,000.

SAMPLE GRANTS London Wildlife Trust (£25,000); Cultivate London (£23,500); Volunteering Matters (£23,000); Peer Productions (£20,500); A2 Northolt Residents Association (£14,900); Venture Trust (£7,000); 6th Staines Scout Group and Hanwell Carnival (£2,500 each); Hillingdon Asian Women's Group (£1,000); Stardust Arts (£500).

FINANCES *Year* 2015 *Income* £831,000 *Grants* £851,739 *Grants to organisations* £851,739 *Assets* £201,000

TRUSTEES Alison Moore; Jason Holmes; Ian Nichol; Dr Prabhjot Basra; Michael Murphy; Andrew Kerswill; Richard de Belder; Carol Hui; Chris Johnston.

OTHER INFORMATION Grants were awarded in the following categories in 2015: communities for tomorrow (£247,500 in 21 grants); communities for youth (£240,000 in 19 grants); communities together (£49,500 in 87 grants); staff matched funding (£35,500 in 54 grants). There was also a grant of £250,000 awarded to BITC and The Challenge to jointly deliver phase two of the Inspiring Youth project.

HOW TO APPLY Each airport runs its own community fund. Application forms, criteria and guidelines, are available to download on the website., where upcoming deadlines are also posted.

WHO TO APPLY TO Dr Rebecca Bowden, Trust Director, c/o Groundwork South, Colne Valley Park Centre, Denham Court Drive, Uxbridge, Middlesex UB9 5PG *Tel.* 01895 839662 *Email* community_fund@heathrow.com *Website* www.heathrowcommunityfund.com

■ The Heathside Charitable Trust

CC NO 326959 **ESTABLISHED** 1985

WHERE FUNDING CAN BE GIVEN UK and Israel.

WHO CAN BENEFIT Charitable organisations, especially Jewish organisations.

WHAT IS FUNDED General charitable purposes.

SAMPLE GRANTS Babes in Arms; British Friends of Jaffa Institute; CancerKin; Community Security Trust; Holocaust Educational Trust; First Cheque 2000; Jewish Care; Jewish Education Defence Trust; Jewish Museum; Joint Jewish Charitable Trust; King Solomon High School; Marie Curie Cancer Care; Motivation; Royal London Institute; Royal National Theatre; Weizmann Institute.

FINANCES *Year* 2015 *Income* £126,750 *Grants* £320,982 *Grants to organisations* £320,982 *Assets* £3,420,331

TRUSTEES Sir Harry Solomon; Lady Judith Solomon; Geoffrey Jayson; Louise Jacobs; Daniel Solomon; Juliet Solomon; Sam Jacobs.

OTHER INFORMATION A total of 72 grants were made.

HOW TO APPLY Applications can be made in writing to the correspondent at any time; however, the annual report for 2015 notes: 'The trustees identify organisations and projects it wishes to support and this generally arises from direct contacts rather than speculative applications.' The trustees generally meet four times a year.

WHO TO APPLY TO Sir Harry Solomon, Trustee, 32 Hampstead High Street, London NW3 1QD *Tel.* 020 7431 7739

■ Heb Ffin (Without Frontier)

CC NO 1157947 **ESTABLISHED** 2014

WHERE FUNDING CAN BE GIVEN Rural Wales and Uganda.

WHO CAN BENEFIT Small charities; individuals.

WHAT IS FUNDED The advancement of the Christian religion, particularly evangelistic activities in South Wales and rural districts, as well as the promotion of theological, ministerial and lay training for Welsh ministers and African students; the relief of poverty with a particular emphasis on Welsh projects that practically address helping homeless people, people who have offended, those suffering from drug dependency, and trafficked or sexually exploited people; the relief of poverty in Africa, particularly Christian initiatives that address health issues, education, and support for micro-businesses.

WHAT IS NOT FUNDED General appeals or circulars; campaigning or lobbying activity; political donations; animal welfare; grant-making organisations; uniformed groups such as scouts and guides; disaster relief funds.

RANGE OF GRANTS Mostly between £1,000 and £5,000.

SAMPLE GRANTS Learna (£6,000); Build It, Christians Against Poverty, PONT, and Y GRWP (£5,000 each); Emerge Poverty Free (£3,000); Mission Aviation Fellowship, Mercy Ships, Transform Burkina, Time for Change (£2,000 each); Latin American Foundation (£500).

FINANCES *Year* 2015/16 *Income* £599 *Grants* £52,272 *Grants to organisations* £52,272 *Assets* £967,355

HOW TO APPLY Apply in writing to the correspondent by post or email. Applications must include details of the organisation and contact details, as well as a clear overview of the aims and objectives of the project. They must also include the following information detailed on the charity's website: 'contact details including (if applicable) website addresses and charitable registration; key elements and activities; anticipated timing; overall budget and an indication as to how this is to be met; the proportion of the funding received that will be used for administration of the project (must be less than 10%); indication of how any funding received from Heb Ffin will be specifically used; analysis of how the benefits secured by the project will be sustained; details of how the project will be monitored and evaluated and what feedback Heb Ffin will receive'. Full guidelines are available to download from the website.

WHO TO APPLY TO Nick Davis, Trustee, 33 Ty Draw Road, Penylan, Caerdydd CF23 5HB *Tel.* 029 2048 5063 *Email* NJSDavis@aol.com *Website* www.hebffin.com

■ The Charlotte Heber-Percy Charitable Trust

CC NO 284387 **ESTABLISHED** 1981

WHERE FUNDING CAN BE GIVEN Worldwide.

WHO CAN BENEFIT Charitable organisations.

WHAT IS FUNDED General charitable purposes; education and children; animal welfare; local environment; medical causes, cancer charities and hospices; the arts and museums; local causes; international causes.

WHAT IS NOT FUNDED Individuals.

TYPE OF GRANT Small, one-off grants.

RANGE OF GRANTS Up to £20,000, but mostly between £1,000 and £10,000.

SAMPLE GRANTS WheelPower (£20,000); Royal Shakespeare Company, Seafarers UK and SkillForce (£10,000 each); The Eloise and Katie Memorial Trust (£8,000 in two grants); The Family Survival Trust (£7,000); Brooke Hospital for Animals, Farms for City Children and Songbird Survival Trust (£5,000 each); Gloucestershire Arthritis Trust and The Chipping Norton Theatre (£4,000 each); Chipping Camden Music Festival, Spinal Research and The Norfolk Churches Trust Ltd (£3,000 each); Garsington Opera, St Antony's College – Oxford and The Guard's Company (£1,000 each).

FINANCES *Year* 2015/16 *Income* £292,790 *Grants* £218,000 *Grants to organisations* £218,000 *Assets* £6,817,467

TRUSTEES Joanna Prest; Charlotte Heber-Percy.

OTHER INFORMATION In 2015/16, 43 organisations received support.

HOW TO APPLY Applications should be made in writing to the correspondent. The trustees meet on an ad hoc basis to consider applications.

WHO TO APPLY TO The Administrator, Rathbone Trust Company Ltd, 8 Finsbury Circus, London EC2M 7AZ *Tel.* 020 7399 0820 *Email* linda.cousins@rathbones.com

■ Ernest Hecht Charitable Foundation

CC NO 1095850 **ESTABLISHED** 2002

WHERE FUNDING CAN BE GIVEN UK; in practice, England and Wales.

WHO CAN BENEFIT Registered charities.

WHAT IS FUNDED A wide range of charities working to support or improve the lives of UK nationals – particularly those who are disadvantaged, young or older – through art, health care, literature, music and theatre.

WHAT IS NOT FUNDED Individuals and charities that primarily benefit areas outside the UK.

RANGE OF GRANTS Mostly between £500 and £6,000; however, there is no maximum or minimum limit.

SAMPLE GRANTS Lucy Cavendish College (£20,000); Musiko Musika (£17,000); Coram Voice (£15,000); Liberal Jewish Synagogue (£6,800); St Michael's Hospice (£5,750); Redburn School (£4,800); Macmillan Cancer Care (£2,000); Zoë's Place (£1,900); Personal Support Unit (£1,000); North East Autism Society (£850); Age UK and RAF Benevolent Fund (£500 each).

FINANCES *Year* 2015 *Income* £103,380 *Grants* £161,391 *Grants to organisations* £161,391 *Assets* £415,650

TRUSTEES Ernest Hecht; Barb Jungr.

OTHER INFORMATION 54 grants were made during the year.

HOW TO APPLY Apply using the application form available to download from the foundation's website. The form should be returned along with copies of your organisation's two most recent sets of audited accounts. Only completed forms returned via email are accepted. There are no deadlines for applications, which are reviewed at regular intervals.

WHO TO APPLY TO Toni Zekaria, 843 Finchley Road, London NW11 8NA *Email* info@ernesthechtcharitablefoundation.org *Website* ernesthechtcharitablefoundation.org

■ The Percy Hedley 1990 Charitable Trust

CC NO 1000033 **ESTABLISHED** 1990

WHERE FUNDING CAN BE GIVEN UK with a preference for Northumberland and Tyne and Wear.

WHO CAN BENEFIT Charitable organisations and educational establishments.

WHAT IS FUNDED General charitable purposes.

TYPE OF GRANT One-off and ongoing.

RANGE OF GRANTS £250 to £3,000; most grants are for £500.

SAMPLE GRANTS The Percy Hedley Foundation (£3,000 each); Dame Allan's School (£1,500); Anaphylaxis Campaign, Northumberland Association of Clubs for Young People and Samaritans (£1,000 each); Northumberland Wildlife Trust (£750); Disability North, Jesmond Library Friends and People's Theatre Arts Trust (£500 each); Bamburgh Church – St Aidan's (£250).

FINANCES *Year* 2015/16 *Income* £54,932 *Grants* £40,000 *Grants to organisations* £40,000 *Assets* £1,481,904

TRUSTEES John Armstrong; Bill Meikle; Fiona Ruffman.

OTHER INFORMATION Grants were given to 58 organisations in 2015/16.

HOW TO APPLY Applications may be made in writing to the correspondent. The trustees normally meet twice a year. The trust has previously stated: 'We are happy to receive succinct applications. A financial statement can be welcome, but full annual report accounts are too much.'

WHO TO APPLY TO John Armstrong, Trustee, 10 Castleton Close, Newcastle upon Tyne NE2 2HF *Tel.* 0191 281 5953 *Email* contact.phct@gmail.com

Hedley Foundation Ltd (The Hedley Foundation)

CC NO 262933 **ESTABLISHED** 1971
WHERE FUNDING CAN BE GIVEN UK.
WHO CAN BENEFIT Registered charities, with a preference for smaller charities.
WHAT IS FUNDED The website states that the foundation primary objective is to support young people, through the areas of: recreation; sport; training; health; welfare; outdoor education and adventure activities. There is particular interest in charities 'persuading and deterring at-risk young people from proceeding further down the pathway to custody'. The second aim is supporting young people who have disabilities or terminal illness, through funding specialist equipment and respite breaks. Young carers are also supported.
WHAT IS NOT FUNDED Organisations which are not UK-registered charities; individuals directly; churches and cathedrals; exclusive charities (which only help people from specific groupings); appeals for general funding, salaries, deficit, core revenue costs, transport funding; appeals for building or refurbishment projects; national or very large appeals.
TYPE OF GRANT Project costs; one-off.
RANGE OF GRANTS Mostly less than £10,000. The website states that the average grant is £3,000.
SAMPLE GRANTS Map Action (£18,000); British Exploring Society and Young Musicians Symphony Orchestra (£15,000 each); English National Ballet School (£14,500); Canine Partners for Independence, Challenge 4 Change, Hertford River Children's Sailing Trust Raleigh International, The Bendrigg Trust and Wanstead Playground Association (£10,000 each).
FINANCES *Year* 2015/16 *Income* £1,278,343 *Grants* £847,705 *Grants to organisations* £847,705 *Assets* £32,260,040
TRUSTEES George Broke; Maj. John Rodwell; Lorna Stuttaford; Patrick Holcroft; Lt Col. Peter Chamberlin; Angus Fanshawe; Lt Col. Andrew Ford; David Byam-Cook.
OTHER INFORMATION The foundation made grants to 320 charities in 2015/16. Grants of less than £10,000 during the year totalled £680,000.
HOW TO APPLY Applications must be made using the application form available from the foundation's website and should include a copy of the most recent set of accounts. The trustees usually meet in February, March, May, July, September and November (for exact and most up-to-date deadlines see the website). The applicants are asked to submit the forms (completed in typescript) via post (emailed applications are not considered) at least three weeks before the date of the meeting. Note that the foundation is unable to return any enclosures that are sent in with applications. All applications will be acknowledged, but, in the case of those short-listed, not until after they have been considered by the trustees. The foundation receives many more applications than it can fund and urges that applicants should not be surprised, or too disappointed, if they are unsuccessful.
WHO TO APPLY TO Pauline Barker, Appeals Manager, Victoria House, 1–3 College Hill, London EC4R 2RA *Tel.* 020 7489 8076 *Email* pbarker@hedleyfoundation.org.uk *Website* www.hedleyfoundation.org.uk

The Michael Heller Charitable Foundation

CC NO 327832 **ESTABLISHED** 1988
WHERE FUNDING CAN BE GIVEN Worldwide.
WHO CAN BENEFIT Charitable organisations; research institutions; universities.
WHAT IS FUNDED Medical, scientific and educational research as well as humanitarian support.
WHAT IS NOT FUNDED Individuals.
TYPE OF GRANT Funding for specific projects.
SAMPLE GRANTS A list of beneficiaries was not available.
FINANCES *Year* 2015/16 *Income* £253,923 *Grants* £215,778 *Grants to organisations* £215,778 *Assets* £3,907,952
TRUSTEES Morven Heller; Michael Heller; W. S. Trustee Company Ltd.
OTHER INFORMATION Grants were distributed as follows: education (£106,000); humanitarian (£85,000); research (£24,500). The foundation has trustees in common with The Simon Heller Charitable Settlement (Charity Commission no. 265405).
HOW TO APPLY Apply in writing to the correspondent.
WHO TO APPLY TO Sir Michael Heller, Trustee, 24 Bruton Place, London W1J 6NE *Tel.* 020 7415 5000

The Simon Heller Charitable Settlement

CC NO 265405 **ESTABLISHED** 1972
WHERE FUNDING CAN BE GIVEN Worldwide.
WHO CAN BENEFIT Charitable organisations; research institutions; universities.
WHAT IS FUNDED Medical, scientific and educational research, as well as humanitarian support. Jewish causes have also been supported in the past.
WHAT IS NOT FUNDED Individuals.
TYPE OF GRANT Funding for specific projects.
SAMPLE GRANTS Aish Hatora; Chief Rabbinate Charitable Trust; Institute for Jewish Policy Research; Jewish Care; Scopus; Spiro Institute.
FINANCES *Year* 2015/16 *Income* £446,212 *Grants* £175,842 *Grants to organisations* £175,842 *Assets* £7,604,925
TRUSTEES Sir Michael Heller; Lady Morven Heller; W. S. Trustee Company Ltd.
OTHER INFORMATION Grants were distributed as follows: humanitarian (£77,500); education (£58,000); research (£40,500). The charity has trustees in common with The Michael Heller Charitable Foundation (Charity Commission no. 327832).
HOW TO APPLY Apply in writing to the correspondent.
WHO TO APPLY TO Sir Michael Heller, Trustee, 24 Bruton Place, London W1J 6NE *Tel.* 020 7415 5000

Help for Health

CC NO 1091814 **ESTABLISHED** 2002
WHERE FUNDING CAN BE GIVEN Within the boundaries of East Yorkshire, City of Kingston upon Hull, and both North and North East Lincolnshire.
WHO CAN BENEFIT Registered charities; medical and research bodies; universities.
WHAT IS FUNDED Health care provision (including facilities and equipment); medical research; medical education.
WHAT IS NOT FUNDED Individuals.
RANGE OF GRANTS Up to £12,500.

SAMPLE GRANTS HEY Mind (£12,500); Yorkshire Air Ambulance (£12,000); Autism Plus (£10,000); Crisis Pregnancy Centre (£8,000); 5 Senses, Royal Philharmonic Orchestra 'Strokestra' and Whizz-Kidz (£5,000 each); Smile Foundation (£3,800); University of Hull (£1,000).
FINANCES *Year* 2015/16 *Income* £685,228 *Grants* £73,915 *Grants to organisations* £73,915 *Assets* £4,829,557
TRUSTEES Andrew Milner; Prof. Peter Lee; Stuart Smith; Andrew Mould; Dawn Mitchell; Richard Field; Victoria Winterton.
OTHER INFORMATION Grants for less than £3,500 totalled £11,600.
HOW TO APPLY Application forms and full guidelines are available to download from the charity's website. They should be submitted through the online application form or via email. If you need to send it via email, download and save the form in a PDF format and email it to a.milner@helphealth.org.uk. Meeting dates are posted on the website and applications should be submitted at least 14 days in advance. Organisations should not re-apply until two years has passed since the receipt of a grant. Further guidance is available on the charity's website.
WHO TO APPLY TO Andrew Mould, Trustee, c/o RSM, 2 Humber Quays, Wellington Street West, Hull HU1 2BN *Tel.* 01482 607200 *Email* info@helphealth.org.uk *Website* www.helphealth.org.uk

■ Help the Homeless Ltd

CC NO 271988 **ESTABLISHED** 1975
WHERE FUNDING CAN BE GIVEN UK.
WHO CAN BENEFIT Small/medium-sized or new registered charities with a turnover of less than £1 million a year.
WHAT IS FUNDED Homelessness – all projects which assist individuals in their return to mainstream society, rather than simply offer shelter or other forms of sustenance.
WHAT IS NOT FUNDED Charities with substantial funds; individuals; funding for computers and IT equipment.
TYPE OF GRANT One-off grants for capital costs.
RANGE OF GRANTS Normally up to £5,000. Trustees will also consider applications for larger pump-priming grants for major and innovative projects.
SAMPLE GRANTS House of St Barnabas – London (£25,000); Calderdale SmartMove – Halifax (£5,000); Barnabas – Manchester (£4,500); Maggs Day Centre – Worcester (£3,000); St Cuthbert's Centre – London (£2,500); Derby City Mission (£2,000); The Furniture Station – Stockport (£1,500); Gap-Thanet Community Project – Broadstairs (£920); The Hope Centre – St Helens (£350).
FINANCES *Year* 2015/16 *Income* £69,108 *Grants* £88,944 *Grants to organisations* £88,944 *Assets* £1,209,509
TRUSTEES Terry Rogers; Peter Fullerton; Francis Bergin; Stuart Holmes; Susan Conrad; Eamon McGoldrick.
OTHER INFORMATION Grants were made to 34 organisations during the year.
HOW TO APPLY Application forms can be downloaded from the charity's website. Applicants should 'clearly describe the aims and structure of their organisation, their future plans and specific details of how any grant money will be spent' as well as provide the latest available audited accounts. The quarterly deadlines for applications each year are: 15 March, 15 June, 15 September and 15 December. Repeat applications can be made no earlier than two years after the receipt of a decision of the previous application.
WHO TO APPLY TO Terry Kenny, Secretary, 6th Floor, 248 Tottenham Court Road, London W1T 7QZ *Email* hth@help-the-homeless.org.uk *Website* www.help-the-homeless.org.uk

■ The Helping Foundation

CC NO 1104484 **ESTABLISHED** 2004
WHERE FUNDING CAN BE GIVEN Mainly Greater Manchester, also Greater London.
WHO CAN BENEFIT Jewish religious and educational institutions; registered charities.
WHAT IS FUNDED The advancement of education according to the tenets of the Orthodox Jewish Faith; the advancement of the Orthodox Jewish religion and social welfare.
TYPE OF GRANT Recurrent grants; interest-free loans.
RANGE OF GRANTS Usually up to around £50,000.
SAMPLE GRANTS Asser Bishvil Foundation (£2 million); British Friends of Ezrat Yisrael (£670,000); Notzar Chesed (£236,500); New Rachmistrivka Synagogue Trust (£201,000); Teshuvoh Tefilloh Tzedokoh (£198,500); Emuno Educational Centre (£163,000); Friends for the Centre for Torah Education Centre (£57,000); Toimchei Shabbos Manchester (£30,000); Gateshead Kollel (£20,000); Beis Naduorna (£10,000); Law of Truth (£5,500).
FINANCES *Year* 2015 *Income* £36,726,742 *Grants* £9,574,541 *Grants to organisations* £9,574,541 *Assets* £138,631,747
TRUSTEES Rachel Weis; Rabbi Aubrey Weis; David Neuwirth; Benny Stone; Sir Weis.
HOW TO APPLY Apply in writing to the correspondent.
WHO TO APPLY TO Benny Stone, Trustee, Flat 1, Allanadale Court, Waterpark Road, Salford M7 4JN *Tel.* 01617 40116

■ The Hemby Charitable Trust

CC NO 1073028 **ESTABLISHED** 1998
WHERE FUNDING CAN BE GIVEN Merseyside and Wirral.
WHO CAN BENEFIT Ideally, registered charities or those applying organisations to become one; however, any properly constituted body with charitable objectives can apply.
WHAT IS FUNDED The trust has general charitable purposes but prioritises the following areas: help for older people; the arts; social needs; youth and employment; the environment.
WHAT IS NOT FUNDED Grants are not normally given for/to: applicants from outside the area of benefit; sponsorship in any form; individuals; religious bodies; places of worship (unless there is significant non-worship community use); political organisations; pressure groups; feasibility studies; schools seeking specialist status; any form of memorial; return applicants within two years of a successful application.
TYPE OF GRANT Capital funding is strongly preferred, although revenue requests may occasionally be considered.
RANGE OF GRANTS £340 to £5,000.
SAMPLE GRANTS Zoë's Place Baby Hospice (£5,000); Child and Family Connect and West Coast Crash Wheelchair Rugby Club (£2,500 each); Arkwright Scholarships Trust, Haven Project Liverpool and Women's Enterprising Breakthrough (£2,000 each); Sefton Carers Centre and Willowbrook Hospice (£1,500 each); Anfield Boxing Club, Drake Music, National Youth Advocacy and Tate Gallery No3 (£1,000 each); Formby Council Voluntary Services (£750); Action for Sick Children and North City Adventure Playground

(£500 each); Tuebrook Community Centre (£400).

FINANCES *Year* 2015/16 *Income* £93,032 *Grants* £76,206 *Grants to organisations* £156,916 *Assets* £2,639,085

TRUSTEES Andrew Morris; Roy Morris; Caroline Tod; David Fairclough; Stuart Keppie.

OTHER INFORMATION In 2015/16, from 100 applications received, the trust made 60 grants. Grants were distributed in the following categories: social needs (£48,500); young people and employment (£17,500); the arts (£6,100); help for older people (£2,600); the environment (£1,500).

HOW TO APPLY Applications can be made using the form available from the trust's website or the correspondent. Completed application forms should be returned to the correspondent together with a copy of the applicant organisation's most recent accounts. The deadlines for submission of applications are normally on the 1st of February, June and October, for consideration in the following month. The website notes that if the 1st of the month falls on a weekend or bank holiday then the deadline date for applications would be the last working day before. Check the trust's website for the most up-to-date deadline dates. Applications are not acknowledged, although applicants are welcome to contact the administrator to ensure their application has been received. Applicants who have any doubt about the best way to complete their application form, including the amount to apply for, are strongly advised to telephone the administrator for advice. An alternative contact is Mrs Val Hewitt at 17 Foxdale Close, Oxton, Prenton, Wirral, CH43 1XW (tel: 0151 652 1714; email: val.hewitti@ntlworld.com).

WHO TO APPLY TO Tom Evans, Secretary, c/o Rathbone Investment Management Ltd, Port of Liverpool Building, Pier Head, Liverpool L3 1NW *Tel.* 07503 319182 *Email* adminathembytrust@talktalk.net *Website* hembytrust.org.uk

■ Henderson Firstfruits

CC NO 1157218 **ESTABLISHED** 2013

WHERE FUNDING CAN BE GIVEN England and Wales, overseas.

WHO CAN BENEFIT Registered charities; Christian organisations; individuals.

WHAT IS FUNDED General charitable purposes; Christianity; social welfare; children and young people; and older people.

RANGE OF GRANTS £390 to £22,500.

SAMPLE GRANTS Caring for Life (£24,00 in two grants); Christian Life Centre (£1,950); The Lighthouse Group (£1,200 per calendar month for one year); Barnardo's (£1,200); Hope for Justice (£1,000 per calendar month indefinitely); Wyke Foodbank (£1890 in three grants); Shared Life Trust and Kidz Klub Leeds (£2,000 each); Huddersfield Town Foundation (£600 per calendar month indefinitely).

FINANCES *Year* 2014/15 *Income* £134,819 *Grants* £77,994 *Grants to organisations* £77,994 *Assets* £68,017

TRUSTEES Rachel Henderson; Gareth Henderson; Elaine Elcock; Barbara Heal; Richard Gage.

OTHER INFORMATION The charity made grants to 14 organisations during the year. At the time of writing (July 2017), the 2014/15 accounts were the latest available on the Charity Commission's website.

HOW TO APPLY Application forms are available to download from the charity's website. Completed application forms should be uploaded via a link on the website, or sent by email or post, along with the organisation's latest set of accounts. If the latest set of accounts cannot be submitted applicants should explain why this is the case. The trustees meet on a quarterly basis in March, June, September and December to consider grant applications. The closing date for each quarter is the 15th day of the month prior to the meeting. Successful applicants will be informed shortly after the meeting and the grant will be paid.

WHO TO APPLY TO Rachel Henderson, Trustee, Orchard House, 1 Park Road, Elland, Halifax HX5 9HP *Tel.* 01484 880170 *Email* applications@first-fruits.org.uk *Website* first-fruits.org.uk

■ The Christina Mary Hendrie Trust for Scottish and Canadian Charities

SC NO SC014514 **ESTABLISHED** 1975

WHERE FUNDING CAN BE GIVEN Scotland and Canada.

WHO CAN BENEFIT Registered charities; hospices.

WHAT IS FUNDED Charities connected with young people (up to 21 years of age) and older people (over the age of 65). There is a particular interest in hospices and war veterans.

WHAT IS NOT FUNDED Individuals.

TYPE OF GRANT Up to one year.

RANGE OF GRANTS Average award of £7,500.

SAMPLE GRANTS Alzheimer's Research; Capability Scotland; Combat Stress; Houses for Heroes Scotland; The Prince's Trust; St Andrew's Hospice; The Yard; Veterans Scotland; Young Carers.

FINANCES *Year* 2015/16 *Income* £134,938 *Grants* £307,494 *Grants to organisations* £307,494 *Assets* £6,654,907

TRUSTEES Charles Cox; John Scott-Moncrieff; Anthony Cox; Mary-Rose Grieve; Andrew Desson; Laura Cox; Laura Irwin; Alan Sharp.

HOW TO APPLY Application forms can be downloaded from the trust's website and once completed should be returned by post or email (preferably). The trustees meet in March and October and applications should be made no later than 15 February and 15 September, respectively. Applications are acknowledged via email.

WHO TO APPLY TO Audrey Souness, Trust Secretary, 1 Rutland Court, Edinburgh EH3 8EY *Tel.* 0131 270 7700 *Website* www.christinamaryhendrietrust.com

■ Henley Educational Trust

CC NO 309237 **ESTABLISHED** 1604

WHERE FUNDING CAN BE GIVEN Henley-on-Thames and the parishes of Bix and Rotherfield Greys in Oxfordshire and Remenham in Berkshire only.

WHO CAN BENEFIT State-maintained schools and colleges; youth and sports clubs, playgroups and other organisations; individuals under the age of 25.

WHAT IS FUNDED Education of children and young people (up to the age of 25), including related purposes such as extra-curricular activities, sports, music, training, events, etc. Grants are also awarded to individuals.

WHAT IS NOT FUNDED Individual applicants must be under 25 years of age, and must either be resident in the area defined above or have attended a state-maintained school in the area for at least two years.

TYPE OF GRANT Core costs; capital costs; project costs.

SAMPLE GRANTS Henley Schools Partnership (£40,000); Gillotts Academy (£18,000); Nomad (£18,000 in two grants); Badgemore School (£7,700); Henley Youth Festival (£4,000); Music on the Meadow (£700); Chiltern Centre Music Project (£400); Nettlebed School (£300).

FINANCES *Year* 2015/16 *Income* £148,652 *Grants* £126,288 *Grants to organisations* £114,492 *Assets* £3,387,147

TRUSTEES William Parrish; Colin Homent; Elizabeth Hodgkin; Revd Canon Martyn Griffiths; Amanda Heath; Simon Smith; Kellie Hinton; Isobel Morrow; Frank Brookes.

OTHER INFORMATION Grants were made to 16 organisations during the year. There were also grants made to 55 individuals, as well as two prizes/awards.

HOW TO APPLY Apply on a form available to download from the website, where criteria and guidelines are also posted. Completed applications should be returned to the correspondent by post. The trustees meet six times a year – in January, March, May, June, September and November.

WHO TO APPLY TO Claire Brown, Clerk to the Trustees, Syringa Cottage, Horsepond Road, Gallowstree Common, Reading, Berkshire RG4 9BP *Tel.* 0118 972 4575 *Email* henleyeducationalcharity@hotmail.co.uk *Website* www.henleyeducationaltrust.com

■ Philip Henman Trust

CC NO 1054707 **ESTABLISHED** 1986

WHERE FUNDING CAN BE GIVEN Worldwide.

WHO CAN BENEFIT UK-registered charities with an expenditure of over £100,000 per annum.

WHAT IS FUNDED Children and vulnerable adults; overseas aid.

WHAT IS NOT FUNDED Ongoing concerns; one-off grants or projects attending to urgent medical need or other types of emergency.

TYPE OF GRANT Partnership grants for three to five years (projects must start and finish within five years). One-off grants are not available.

RANGE OF GRANTS Up to around £5,000 per year; a maximum of 25,000 over the course of the project.

SAMPLE GRANTS Phase Worldwide (£9,700); Build It International, Cool Earth Ltd, Global Giving UK and The National Deaf Children's Society (£5,000 each); International Children's Trust (£4,500); The United Kingdom Committee for Unicef (£1,800).

FINANCES *Year* 2015/16 *Income* £73,616 *Grants* £63,773 *Grants to organisations* £63,751 *Assets* £2,150,984

TRUSTEES David Clark; Jason Duffey; Andrew Clark.

OTHER INFORMATION Donations to institutions were made for the following purposes: overseas aid (£53,000); other (£10,800).

HOW TO APPLY Applications are only considered once a year – the deadline is always 10 September. Applications are no longer accepted by post. Use the online form available on the trust's website.

WHO TO APPLY TO Andrew Clark, Trustee, 71 High Street, Linton, Cambridge CB21 4HS *Tel.* 07713 160306 *Email* info@pht.org.uk *Website* www.pht.org.uk

■ The G. D. Herbert Charitable Trust

CC NO 295998 **ESTABLISHED** 1986

WHERE FUNDING CAN BE GIVEN UK.

WHO CAN BENEFIT Registered charities.

WHAT IS FUNDED General charitable purposes, but particularly medicine, health, social welfare and environmental resources. It mainly gives regular grants to a set list of charities, with very few one-off grants given each year (in the areas of health and welfare only).

TYPE OF GRANT Mainly recurrent, also some one-off awards.

RANGE OF GRANTS Between £600 and £2,800.

SAMPLE GRANTS Catch 22, Disability Rights UK, Friends of the Elderly, People's Dispensary for Sick Animals (PDSA), Royal College of Surgeons of England, Shelter, St Christopher's Hospice, Prostate Cancer UK, Tavistock Centre for Couple Relationships – TCCR and The Woodland Trust (£2,800 each); The National Autistic Society (£1,500); Ogbourne St George Parochial Church Council and Wiltshire Wildlife Trust (£600 each).

FINANCES *Year* 2015/16 *Income* £53,465 *Grants* £64,900 *Grants to organisations* £64,900 *Assets* £2,018,001

TRUSTEES Michael Beaumont; Judith Cuxson.

OTHER INFORMATION There were 25 regular donations and one 'special' donation made.

HOW TO APPLY The annual report for 2015/16 states that the trustees 'review donations at their annual general meeting in February/March of each year and may make some adjustments but for the most part continue the donations to the beneficiaries listed year on year.'

WHO TO APPLY TO M. Byrne, Veale Wasbrough Vizards LLP, Barnards Inn, 86 Fetter Lane, London EC4A 1AD *Tel.* 020 7405 1234 *Email* mbyrne@vwv.co.uk

■ Herefordshire Community Foundation

CC NO 1094935 **ESTABLISHED** 2002

WHERE FUNDING CAN BE GIVEN Herefordshire.

WHO CAN BENEFIT Registered charities; community and voluntary groups; individuals.

WHAT IS FUNDED General charitable purposes.

RANGE OF GRANTS £180 to £16,900.

SAMPLE GRANTS Walking With The Wounded (£16,900); Herefordshire Cider Museum (£14,500); NeuroMuscular Centre (£7,400); Telford Sea Cadets (£3,500); Presteigne Festival of Music (£2,500); Age Concern Forest of Dean (£1,500); Wheeled Sports for Hereford (£800); Rural Media (£500); Yarkhill Field to Fork (£250); Hereford in Bloom (£180).

FINANCES *Year* 2015/16 *Income* £306,554 *Grants* £206,779 *Grants to organisations* £198,276 *Assets* £3,455,088

TRUSTEES Nat Hone; Will Lindesay; Raymond Hunter; Wilma Gilmour; David Snow; Sally Pettipher; Shelagh Wynn; Oliver Cooke.

OTHER INFORMATION There were 179 grants made during the year to organisations and individuals (£8,500).

HOW TO APPLY The charity administers a number of different funds which all have specific application processes and criteria. Forms are available to download from the website. To ensure your application is directed at the correct fund complete the enquiry form on the grants page as a first step and the foundation will reply with an initial response, generally within five working days.

WHO TO APPLY TO Jayne Porchester, Director, The Fred Bulmer Centre, Wall Street, Hereford HR4 9HP *Tel.* 01432 272550 *Email* mail@herefordshirefoundation.org *Website* www.herefordshirecf.org

■ The Herefordshire Historic Churches Trust

CC NO 511181 **ESTABLISHED** 1954

WHERE FUNDING CAN BE GIVEN Old county of Herefordshire.

WHO CAN BENEFIT Parish churches of all denominations.

WHAT IS FUNDED The restoration, preservation, repair, maintenance and improvement of churches, their contents and their churchyards in Herefordshire.

WHAT IS NOT FUNDED General maintenance of lighting, heating, decoration or furnishings.

TYPE OF GRANT One-off awards for capital and core costs, project funding; loans of up to £10,000 are also available.

RANGE OF GRANTS £500 to £15,000.

SAMPLE GRANTS Sellack (£15,000); Upper Sapey (£10,000); King's Pyon (£8,000); Dewsall (£3,000); Eyton (£2,000); Aylton (£1,500); Goodrich (£1,000); Felton (£500).

FINANCES *Year* 2016 *Income* £86,297 *Grants* £51,000 *Grants to organisations* £51,000 *Assets* £915,546

TRUSTEES David Furnival; Robin Peers; Ali Jones; Jill Gallimore; The Ven. Canon Patrick Benson; James Devereux; Lady Susanna McFarlane; Sarah de Rohan; Robyn Lee.

OTHER INFORMATION There are three types of grant available: investigative grants for up to £1,000 to help with the costs of looking at a structural or building problem; project grants for up to £10,000 to cover the costs of repairs, renovations and re-ordering; cornerstone grants are made at the trustees discretion to churches that are of great historical merit or that provide a community hub.

HOW TO APPLY Application forms can be downloaded from the trust's website, where there is useful guidance. Informal contact can also be made via email. Deadlines for applications are normally 15 March and 15 September.

WHO TO APPLY TO Sarah de Rohan, Trustee, Wood House, Staplow, Ledbury, Herefordshire HR8 1NP *Tel.* 01531 641955 *Email* derohans@btinternet.com *Website* www.hhct.co.uk

■ Heritage Lottery Fund

ESTABLISHED 1994

WHERE FUNDING CAN BE GIVEN UK.

WHO CAN BENEFIT Organisations and individuals.

WHAT IS FUNDED Heritage. The fund supports projects through six main programmes: buildings and monuments; community heritage; cultures and memories; industrial, maritime and transport; land and natural heritage; and museums, libraries and archives.

WHAT IS NOT FUNDED Individual programmes are subject to their own exclusions.

RANGE OF GRANTS £3,000 to over £5 million.

SAMPLE GRANTS A list of beneficiaries was not available.

FINANCES *Year* 2015/16 *Income* £387,555,000 *Grants* £356,539,000 *Grants to organisations* £356,539,000

TRUSTEES Sir Peter Luff; Baroness Kay Andrews; Anna Carragher; Sir Neil Cossons; Sandie Dawe; Dr Angela Dean; Jim Dixon; Perdita Hunt; Steve Miller; Richard Morris; Atul Patel; Dame Seona Reid; Dr Tom Tew.

OTHER INFORMATION The grant total comprises new grant awards less grant de-commitments. The fund distributes the share of National Lottery funding apportioned to heritage.

HOW TO APPLY All applications must be submitted via the online application portal. Contact the Grant Enquiries line if you need assistance to do this: 020 7591 6042/6044. You can make a grant request under £100,000 at any time. There are deadlines for all other applications. These deadlines will vary, depending on how much you are asking for, the grant programme, and where your project is based. Check the relevant grant programme page on the website for details of deadlines and funding decision dates. The deadlines for Heritage Grants and Heritage Enterprise grant requests under £2 million are specific to your area. These are also listed on the website.

WHO TO APPLY TO Grant Enquiries Team – see 'How to apply', Heritage Lottery Fund, 7 Holbein Place, London SW1W 8NR *Tel.* 020 7591 6042/6044 *Email* enquire@hlf.org.uk

■ Hertfordshire Community Foundation

CC NO 1156082 **ESTABLISHED** 1988

WHERE FUNDING CAN BE GIVEN Hertfordshire.

WHO CAN BENEFIT Formally constituted community groups; individuals.

WHAT IS FUNDED The foundation manages more than 70 funds which each have the aim of tackling deprivation and improving social welfare in Hertfordshire. Some funds are tailored so that they specifically reflect the interests of their donors.

WHAT IS NOT FUNDED See the foundation's website for details of exclusions for specific funding programmes.

SAMPLE GRANTS Age Concern Hertfordshire; Alzheimer's Society; Broxbourne and East Hertfordshire Credit Union; Citizens Advice – Hertfordshire; Dacorum Indian Society; Grandparents' Association; Hertfordshire Area Rape Crisis and Sexual Abuse Centre; Hertfordshire PASS; Neomari Beadcraft Training Services; Satsang Manda; Hitchin Town Bowls Club.

FINANCES *Year* 2015/16 *Income* £1,034,120 *Grants* £374,738 *Grants to organisations* £332,322 *Assets* £9,144,030

TRUSTEES Jill Burridge; Jo Connell; Cllr Teresa Heritage; Henry Holland Hibbert; Brig. John Palmer; John Saner; Simon Tilley; Maggie Turner; James Williams; Penny Williams.

OTHER INFORMATION In 2015/16 grants to individuals totalled £42,500.

HOW TO APPLY In the first instance, see the website for details of funds currently available. If you are not sure about which fund is most suitable for you, then an expression of interest form can be submitted online and the foundation can advise further.

WHO TO APPLY TO Caroline Langdell, Fund Manager, Foundation House, 2–4 Forum Place, Fiddlebridge Lane, Hatfield, Hertfordshire AL10 0RN *Tel.* 01707 251351 *Email* office@hertscf.org.uk *Website* www.hertscf.org.uk

■ The Hesslewood Children's Trust (Hull Seamen's and General Orphanage)

CC NO 529804 **ESTABLISHED** 1982

WHERE FUNDING CAN BE GIVEN East Yorkshire and Gainsborough and Caistor in in Lincolnshire.

WHO CAN BENEFIT Young people aged 24 or under who are resident, or have parent(s) resident, in the area of benefit and organisations working with them.

WHAT IS FUNDED Education; relief in need; holidays for young people.

WHAT IS NOT FUNDED People over the age of 24; building work; salaries.

TYPE OF GRANT One-off grants for up to one year.

RANGE OF GRANTS Mostly between £500 and £1,500.

SAMPLE GRANTS Hull University (£10,000); Church Lads' and Girls' Brigade (£1,500); Caudwell Children, Family Holiday Association, Kids Yorkshire and Humber, Parkstone Primary and Wheeler Street Primary (£1,000 each); Go Kids Go, Life Education Bradford and St Cuthbert's Scout Group (£500 each).

FINANCES *Year* 2015/16 *Income* £92,298 *Grants* £67,729 *Grants to organisations* £31,000 *Assets* £2,718,519

TRUSTEES Gaynel Munn; Dr David Nicholas; Ross Allenby; David Turner; Capt. Philip Watts; Revd Timothy Boyns; Philip Evans; Christopher Woodyatt; Dudley Moore; Ray Mann; Denise Knox.

OTHER INFORMATION Grants to or on behalf of specific individuals totalled £36,500. There were 22 grants made for organisations.

HOW TO APPLY Our research suggests that application forms are available from the correspondent. The trustees meet to consider applications at least three times a year. No replies are given to ineligible organisations. This trust has previously stated that it promotes its work through its own avenues, receiving more applications than it can support.

WHO TO APPLY TO Lynn Bullock, Secretary, 62 The Meadows, Cherry Burton, East Yorkshire HU17 7RQ *Tel.* 01964 550882 *Email* misslynneb@aol.com

■ P. and C. Hickinbotham Charitable Trust

CC NO 216432 **ESTABLISHED** 1947

WHERE FUNDING CAN BE GIVEN UK, with a preference for Leicestershire and Rutland and a small number of applicants from North Wales and Northern Ireland.

WHO CAN BENEFIT Registered charities only; universities; wide range of projects; preference to groups working in Leicestershire and Rutland along with a small number of applicants from North Wales and Northern Ireland.

WHAT IS FUNDED General charitable purposes; disability; social deprivation; homelessness; substance and alcohol abuse, prisoner education and rehabilitation; asylum and immigration issues; rehabilitation of prostitutes; the arts; cultural projects; historical projects; youth; community development; environmental.

WHAT IS NOT FUNDED Individuals; large national charities (unless for a specific project); general running costs.

TYPE OF GRANT Usually one-off grants for equipment, premises, renovation and start-up costs.

RANGE OF GRANTS Tend to range from £250 to £1000, although there is no set upper limit.

SAMPLE GRANTS Ann McGeeney Charitable Trust (£25,000); Leicester Charity Link (£5,000); Conflict Resolution Service – Northern Ireland (£3,000); Wygglesden and Queen Elizabeth I College, The Carers Centre, The New Futures Project (£1,000 each).

FINANCES *Year* 2015/16 *Income* £83,966 *Grants* £66,420 *Grants to organisations* £66,420 *Assets* £4,054,029

TRUSTEES Catherine Hickinbotham; Roger Hickinbotham; Anna Steiger; Rachel Hickinbotham; Charlotte Palmer; Frances Hickinbotham; Alice Hickinbotham.

OTHER INFORMATION Donations under £1,000 totalled £30,000.

HOW TO APPLY Applications can be made in writing to the correspondent, giving the following details: a full postal address, a contact email address, details of any applicable website, a contact telephone number, charity registration number and instructions as to who any cheque should be made payable to as well as a brief outline of the purpose of the grant. Replies are not sent to unsuccessful applicants. Successful applicants are usually contacted within 12 weeks.

WHO TO APPLY TO Roger Hickinbotham, Trustee, 9 Windmill Way, Lyddington, Oakham, Leicestershire LE15 9LY *Tel.* 01572 821236 *Email* roger@hickinbothamtrust.org.uk or rogerhick@gmail.com *Website* www.hickinbothamtrust.org.uk

■ The Alan Edward Higgs Charity

CC NO 509367 **ESTABLISHED** 1979

WHERE FUNDING CAN BE GIVEN Within 25 miles of the centre of Coventry only.

WHO CAN BENEFIT Registered local bodies and national organisations which benefit people resident in the beneficial area.

WHAT IS FUNDED General charitable purposes; children's welfare, particularly the welfare of underprivileged children.

WHAT IS NOT FUNDED Individuals; activities outside the beneficial area; the funding of services usually provided by statutory services; medical research; travel outside the UK; evangelical or worship-related activities; organisations which are not a registered charity.

TYPE OF GRANT One-off; general; core costs; strategic funding; project funding.

RANGE OF GRANTS Mostly between £400 and £20,000.

SAMPLE GRANTS Alan Edward Higgs Centre Trust (£258,000); Drapers' Hall (£243,000); Warwick Arts Centre (£20,000); Family Holiday Association (£12,000); The Arts Exchange – Coventry Artspace Ltd (£10,000); Coventry Carers Centre (£7,500); Music Coventry (£6,600); Bradbury Club for Young People (£5,000); Vitalise (£3,400); Kairos WWT (£3,000); Coundon Care Centre Charity (£1,500); International Children's Games (£1,000); The Collection of Printed Popular Music (£410).

FINANCES *Year* 2014/15 *Income* £1,257,515 *Grants* £571,786 *Grants to organisations* £571,786 *Assets* £17,714,393

TRUSTEES Marilyn Knatchbull-Hugessen; Paul Harris; Rowley Higgs; Emily Barlow.

OTHER INFORMATION At the time of writing (May 2017) the charity's 2015/16 accounts were overdue at the Charity Commission. In 2014/15 a total of 13 organisations received support, of which 11 had not been assisted in the previous year.

HOW TO APPLY Applications should be made in writing to the clerk or using the online form on the charity's website. Detailed guidance on what to include in the application is provided on the charity's website – applicants should ensure that they address every point on the checklist provided. The charity asks to avoid sending paper where online copies can be provided. The trustees meet regularly throughout the year. The website notes that they receive 'a large number of applications for support and do not respond unless they have decided to give support'.

WHO TO APPLY TO Peter Knatchbull-Hugessen, Clerk, The Ricoh Arena, Phoenix Way, Coventry CV6 6GE *Tel.* 024 7622 1311 *Email* clerk@higgscharity.org.uk *Website* www.higgscharity.org.uk

■ Highcroft Charitable Trust

CC NO 272684 **ESTABLISHED** 1975

WHERE FUNDING CAN BE GIVEN UK and overseas.

WHO CAN BENEFIT Charitable organisations benefitting Jewish people.

WHAT IS FUNDED The advancement and study of the Jewish faith and the study of the Torah. The relief of poverty and advancement of education among people of the Jewish faith.

RANGE OF GRANTS Up to £20,000.

SAMPLE GRANTS SOFT (Support Organisation for Trisomy) (£20,000); Academy for Talmudical Research – Kollel Harabonim and Mesifta Talmudical College (£10,000 each); Chazon Avrohom Yitzchok (£7,500); Chesed Leyisruel Trust (£5,100); Friends of Be'er Miriam (£2,500); London Friends of Kamenitzer Yeshiva Jerusalem (£1,500); Keren Lehachzaka (£1,200).

FINANCES *Year* 2015/16 *Income* £97,471 *Grants* £80,579 *Grants to organisations* £80,579 *Assets* £198,962

TRUSTEES Richard Fischer; Sarah Fischer.

OTHER INFORMATION Grants of less than £1,000 totalled £4,100.

HOW TO APPLY Apply in writing to the correspondent.

WHO TO APPLY TO Richard Fischer, Trustee, 15 Highcroft Gardens, London NW11 0LY

■ The Hilden Charitable Fund

CC NO 232591 **ESTABLISHED** 1963

WHERE FUNDING CAN BE GIVEN UK and financially developing countries.

WHO CAN BENEFIT Community causes; CICs; charities; voluntary organisations; NGOs; social enterprises; educational establishments (schools – for project but not core funding). In the UK most grant aid is directed to registered charities and overseas projects will normally work with a UK charity partner or show relevant local legal status. Charities based overseas applying must have a history of working for at least five years; have an income of over £25,000 in their last two financial years but no more than £100,000. Preference is given to 'unpopular causes' and smaller organisations rather than large national charities. Scottish charities are only funded through a block grant to the Foundation Scotland (formerly known as Scottish Community Foundation) which is then distributed to the sector.

WHAT IS FUNDED In the UK: homelessness; asylum seekers and refugees; penal affairs; community initiatives for disadvantaged young people (aged 16 to 25) – 'programmes that are helping these young people in the job market, with advice, training, volunteering and work placement schemes'. Overseas: development aid.

WHAT IS NOT FUNDED Individuals; well-established causes.

TYPE OF GRANT Capital and core costs; salaries; recurring funding; project and general running costs; unrestricted expenditure; funding for over one year.

RANGE OF GRANTS Up to £22,500. The average grant is of £5,000.

SAMPLE GRANTS Tanzania Development Trust (£22,500) Joint Council for the Welfare of Immigrants (£20,000); Save the Needy, Sierra Leone (£10,000) Barts Health NHS Trust (£8,000); Guild of Psychotherapists, London (£7,000); Action in Africa (£6,500) Assist Sheffield, Haringey Migrant Support Centre, North London Action for the Homeless, Rosa London, Sussex Children and Family of Prisoners Brighton (£5,000 each) Geese Theatre Company, Birmingham (£4,000) Riley Orton Foundation Kenya (£3,000); Metropolitan Church Manchester (£2,000).

FINANCES *Year* 2015/16 *Income* £386,263 *Grants* £495,290 *Grants to organisations* £495,290 *Assets* £12,418,202

TRUSTEES C. Rampton; A. M. Rampton; Prof. D. S. Rampton; Prof. C. H. Rodeck; J. A. Rampton; Prof. M. H. Rampton; Maggie Baxter; Elizabeth Rodeck; E. Rampton; E. J. Rodeck; Samia Khatun; Jonathan Branch; Patrick Rampton.

OTHER INFORMATION In 2015/16 priorities were asylum seekers and refugees; community based initiatives for disadvantaged young people aged 16 to 25; homelessness; penal affairs; overseas development. The fund has allocated a small budget to help community groups run summer play schemes for disadvantaged communities. During the year a total of 101 grants were awarded.

HOW TO APPLY Applications have to be made using an application form available from the website outlining their request for funds, and their legal and financial status. Without this accompanying form all applications are regarded as enquiries. The applicant's case for funds must be concise (no more than two A4 pages), and supporting documentation is essential. Applications must include the applicant's most recent independently inspected accounts as well as their recent annual report and their projected income and expenditure for the current financial year.

WHO TO APPLY TO Rodney Hedley, Secretary, 34 North End Road, London W14 0SH *Tel.* 020 7603 1525 *Fax* 020 7603 1525 *Email* hildencharity@hotmail.com *Website* www.hildencharitablefund.org.uk

■ The Derek Hill Foundation

CC NO 801590 **ESTABLISHED** 1989

WHERE FUNDING CAN BE GIVEN UK.

WHO CAN BENEFIT Organisations and individuals.

WHAT IS FUNDED Arts and education.

RANGE OF GRANTS £120 to £12,000, but mostly £3,000 or less.

SAMPLE GRANTS Redfern Gallery and Exhibition (£12,300); British School at Rome (£11,900 in two grants); The London Magazine (£5,000); SSAFA London Central (£3,500); Llanfyllin Music Festival (£3,000); Darling International Summer School (£2,500); Institute of Contemporary Arts, Royal Northern College of Music and St Martin-in-the-Fields (£1,500 each); De Morgan Foundation (£500); Kinvara Visual Arts (£120).

FINANCES *Year* 2015/16 *Income* £47,125 *Grants* £112,118 *Grants to organisations* £95,094 *Assets* £1,513,391

TRUSTEES Lord Armstrong of Ilminster; Josephine Batterham; Earl of Gowrie; Ian Paterson; Rathbone Trust Company Ltd.

OTHER INFORMATION Grants to 17 individuals totalled about £17,000. There were 36 awards made to organisations.

HOW TO APPLY Apply in writing to the correspondent.

WHO TO APPLY TO Trevor Harris, Rathbone Trust Company Ltd, 8 Finsbury Circus, London EC2M 7AZ

■ M. V. Hillhouse Trust

SC NO SC012904 **ESTABLISHED** 1996

WHERE FUNDING CAN BE GIVEN UK, with an interest in Scotland and Gloucestershire.

WHO CAN BENEFIT Charitable organisations. Our research suggests that the trustees prefer to support local causes known to them.

WHAT IS FUNDED A wide range of charitable purposes, with special consideration given to: the advancement of religion, education, training, instruction and culture; the promotion of spiritual, moral, intellectual, social and physical well-being; and the relief or prevention of poverty or need.

RANGE OF GRANTS Up to £3,000.

SAMPLE GRANTS The Prince's Trust (£5,000 in two grants); The Nelson Trust (£2,000); Age Scotland, Arran Theatre, Ayrshire Hospice and Fort Augustus Church (£1,000 each); Dyslexia Scotland and Meningitis Research Foundation – Scotland (£600 each); ABF – The Soldiers' Charity, Animal Health Trust, Friends of Dundonald Castle, Glasgow Women's Aid and Positive Action in Housing (£500 each); Kilchuimen Academy (£400); Cruse Bereavement Care and Disfigurement Guidance Centre (£300 each); Gloucestershire Wildlife Trust (£250).

FINANCES *Year* 2015/16 *Income* £130,064 *Grants* £126,565 *Grants to organisations* £126,565 *Assets* £904,127

HOW TO APPLY The annual report for 2015/16 explains that 'applications for donations are sent down to Bowldown Farm, Tetbury and are approved by the Trustees at regular meetings subject to funding being available'.

WHO TO APPLY TO Ms E. Thomson, Bowldown Farm, Tetbury, Gloucestershire GL8 8UD

■ The Hillier Trust

CC NO 1147629 **ESTABLISHED** 2012

WHERE FUNDING CAN BE GIVEN Worldwide.

WHO CAN BENEFIT Registered charities, mainly those which have a Christian ethos; individuals.

WHAT IS FUNDED Development and support work for disadvantaged groups; Christian causes.

RANGE OF GRANTS Generally between £500 and £4,000.

SAMPLE GRANTS The Family Trust (£285,000); Embrace and Open Doors (£3,000 each); Hands of Compassion and Philippine Community Fund (£2,000 each); Children Change Colombia (£1,500); Age UK and Maidstone Christian Care (£1,100 each); Salvation Army and Sidmouth Parish Church (£1,000 each); Swale Youth Fund (£500).

FINANCES *Year* 2015/16 *Income* £97,658 *Grants* £317,646 *Grants to organisations* £317,646 *Assets* £3,708,509

TRUSTEES Anthony Hillier; Susan Hillier; Elizabeth Jordan.

OTHER INFORMATION Grants were made to 18 organisations during the year.

HOW TO APPLY Apply in writing to the correspondent.

WHO TO APPLY TO Anthony Hillier, Trustee, Loose Court Farmhouse, Old Drive, Maidstone, Kent ME15 9SE *Email* tonyhillier@zen.co.uk

■ The Hillingdon Community Trust

CC NO 1098235 **ESTABLISHED** 2003

WHERE FUNDING CAN BE GIVEN The London Borough of Hillingdon: Botwell; Pinkwell; Heathrow Villages; Townfield; West Drayton; Yiewsley.

WHO CAN BENEFIT 'Properly constituted voluntary bodies' community organisations; for larger awards preference may be given to registered charities. It is less likely that a grant will be made to a corporate body other than on a matched funding basis.

WHAT IS FUNDED Community projects; social welfare; relief of poverty; economic development; conservation of environment and heritage; unemployment; adult education and training; safety and crime prevention; economic development; public amenities.

WHAT IS NOT FUNDED Individuals; public bodies or projects that should be funded by public funds (projects by voluntary bodies that will be partially financed by public bodies are considered); religious bodies except for ancillary activities which meet one of the priorities); organisations that have already received funding in respect of a completed project; work that has already started; political parties or lobbying; non-charitable activities.

TYPE OF GRANT One-off or recurrent; capital funding; project costs; development or strategic funding; volunteer expenses; reasonable overheads relating to a project. Preference to fund projects rather than core costs.

RANGE OF GRANTS Grants range from £100 to £43,500. Small Grants: £100 to £7,500; Main Grants: over £7,500.

SAMPLE GRANTS Mayors Fund for London (£65,000); Bell Farm (£48,000); Hillingdon Mind (£42,000); Hillingdon Law Centre (£39,000); Hillingdon Autistic Care and Support (£29,000) Rosedale Park's Bowls Club (£25,000); Stockley Academy (£20,000); West London YMCA (£18,600) Catholic Children's Society (£16,500); Hillingdon Asian Women's Centre (£7,000) Hillingdon Table Tennis Club (£5,600) Walking Basketball UK (£3,000); Austin Sewing Club (£1,500); 1st Hayes End Girls' Brigade (£600); Harlington Locomotive (£510).

FINANCES *Year* 2015/16 *Income* £1,022,600 *Grants* £682,348 *Grants to organisations* £682,348 *Assets* £2,177,108

TRUSTEES Isabel King; Prof. Ian Campbell; Keith Wallis; Carole Jones; Matthew Gorman; Jasvir Jassal; Clive Gee; Christopher Geake; Jack Taylor; Peter Money; David Brough; Shane Ryan; Freda Ritchie; Paul Lewis; Balwinder Sokhi; Kathleen Healey; Steve Coventry.

OTHER INFORMATION A requirement of the grants is that grants shall be made for the benefit of the community in the southern part of the Borough (These are the wards of Botwell, Townfield and Pinkwell in Hayes, West Drayton, Yiewsley, and the Heathrow Villages south of the M4).

HOW TO APPLY Application forms and detailed guidelines for both schemes are provided on the trust's website. The main grants programme has a two-stage application process and organisations successful in the initial consideration will be invited to complete a full application form. Applicants are welcome to approach the trust prior to submitting a formal application. Awards are considered every second month – see the website for up-to-date deadlines.

WHO TO APPLY TO Kathleen Healy, Company Secretary and Trust Director, Barra Hall, Wood End, Green Road, Hayes, Middlesex UB3 2SA *Tel.* 020 8581 1676 *Email* info@hillingdoncommunitytrust.org.uk *Website* www.hillingdoncommunitytrust.org.uk

■ R. G. Hills Charitable Trust

CC NO 1008914 **ESTABLISHED** 1982

WHERE FUNDING CAN BE GIVEN UK, with some interest in Kent, and overseas.

WHO CAN BENEFIT Local and national registered charities.

WHAT IS FUNDED General charitable purposes.

RANGE OF GRANTS £1,000 to £10,200.

SAMPLE GRANTS Save the Children (£10,200); Canterbury Festival Foundation and KeepOut (£3,000 each); Indian Rural Health Trust (£2,800); Seeds for Africa (£2,500); Emmaus Medway (£2,300); Young Carers Together (£2,000); Kent Woodland Employment Scheme (£1,800); Young Kent (£1,600); Wellbeing of Women (£1,500); Right to Play UK Ltd (£1,100); Child Aid to Russia and the Republics, Daylight Christian Prison Trust, London Wheelchair Rugby Club, Sea Sanctuary and Sevenoaks Community First Responders (£1,000 each).

FINANCES *Year* 2015/16 *Income* £121,406 *Grants* £108,750 *Grants to organisations* £108,750 *Assets* £3,444,177

TRUSTEES David Pentin; Harvey Barrett.

OTHER INFORMATION A total of 56 organisations received grants.

HOW TO APPLY Apply in writing to the correspondent.

WHO TO APPLY TO Harvey Barrett, Trustee, Furley Page, 39–40 St Margaret's Street, Canterbury CT1 2TX *Tel.* 01227 763939

■ Hinchley Charitable Trust

CC NO 1108412 **ESTABLISHED** 1973

WHERE FUNDING CAN BE GIVEN UK and overseas.

WHO CAN BENEFIT Registered or recognised charities; mainly evangelical Christian organisations, including Christian youth organisations and Christian organisations in local communities.

WHAT IS FUNDED General charitable purposes, with particular reference to evangelical Christian work. Grants are made in the following five main categories: Christian and other charitable work in local communities (25%); Christian bodies engaged in holistic mission (20%); Christian bodies at work in the public sphere (15%); Christian leadership training (20%); Christian work among young people (20%). The charity states that 'the trustees are particularly keen to support smaller charities where a grant can make a significant difference to the work of charity'.

TYPE OF GRANT One-off or recurring; usually for projects, but capital and core costs are considered.

RANGE OF GRANTS £2,000 to £15,000.

SAMPLE GRANTS London Institute for Contemporary Christianity (£15,000); Karis Neighbourhood Scheme, Langham Partnership, SAT-7 Trust, Theos, Willowfield Parish Community Association – Belfast (£10,000 each); Youthscape (£9,000); Clean Sheet (£7,000); Panahpur Trust (£5,000).

FINANCES *Year* 2015/16 *Income* £157,878 *Grants* £134,500 *Grants to organisations* £134,500 *Assets* £3,459,145

TRUSTEES Prof. Brian Stanley; John Levick; Mark Hobbs; Roger Northcott; Rebecca Stanley.

OTHER INFORMATION The charity awarded a total of 19 grants during 2015/16. Six of these grants ranged from £10,000 to £15,000. The remaining 13 grants were all between £2,000 to £10,000.

HOW TO APPLY The trust states that 'the trustees adopt a proactive approach to grant-making meaning unsolicited applications are usually unable to be supported'.

WHO TO APPLY TO Emma Northcott, Company Secretary, 10 Coplow Terrace, Coplow Street, Birmingham B16 0DQ *Tel.* 0121 455 6632 *Email* info@hinchleycharitabletrust.org.uk *Website* www.hinchleycharitabletrust.org.uk

■ The Hinduja Foundation

CC NO 802756 **ESTABLISHED** 1989

WHERE FUNDING CAN BE GIVEN Worldwide.

WHO CAN BENEFIT Registered charities.

WHAT IS FUNDED Health; education; relief of poverty, hunger and sickness; medicine; arts and culture; social; economic and international development-related research; interfaith understanding.

TYPE OF GRANT Grants mainly to organisations although individuals are not excluded.

RANGE OF GRANTS £100 to £250,000.

SAMPLE GRANTS King's College School (£250,000); Amas Investment and Project Services Ltd (£100,000); Sangam Ltd (£65,000); King's College London (£15,000); NRI Foundation (£12,000); Hinduja Foundation Europe (£10,400); Trekstock Ltd for Young Adults (£8,000); The Elephant Family (£5,000); BAPS Swaminarayan Sanstha (£2,500); Siri Guru Singh Sabha (£2,200); Fight For Life (£2,000); Academi (£1,000); Magic Bus (£500); Help the Aged (£140) Institute for Cancer Research (£100).

FINANCES *Year* 2015 *Income* £179,360 *Grants* £386,597 *Grants to organisations* £386,597 *Assets* -£202,020

TRUSTEES Srichand Hinduja; Gopichand Hinduja; Prakash Hinduja; Shanu Hinduja.

OTHER INFORMATION In the donation to King's College School, £50,000 was made in 2015. The remaining £200,000 is to be made in four annual instalments of £50,000 payable between 2016 and 2019.

HOW TO APPLY Apply in writing to the correspondent.

WHO TO APPLY TO Michael Urwick, New Zealand House, 80 Haymarket, London SW1Y 4TE *Email* foundation@hindujagroup.com

■ The Hinrichsen Foundation

CC NO 272389 **ESTABLISHED** 1976

WHERE FUNDING CAN BE GIVEN UK.

WHO CAN BENEFIT Organisations and individuals.

WHAT IS FUNDED The performance of contemporary music, including the commissioning of new work, non-commercial recording or publication. The website explains that the trustees will occasionally fund musicological research projects 'not being conducted under the aegis of an academic institution.'

WHAT IS NOT FUNDED The purchase of musical instruments or equipment including the electronic or computer variety; retrospective funding; or, as a general rule, degree course funding. According to the website, the trustees 'do not wish to consider applications for which there are existing official schemes of help' and will not usually support 'projects with a very large over-arching budget or where the budgeting is unclear or largely speculative'.

TYPE OF GRANT Usually one-off project funding.

RANGE OF GRANTS Mostly £1,000 to £5,000, occasionally larger.

SAMPLE GRANTS Huddersfield Contemporary Music Festival and National Music Centre (£10,000 each); Tête-à-Tête (£5,000); Performances Birmingham Ltd (£4,000); Mishmash Productions (£2,000); Carducci Music Trust (£750); Clapton Ensemble (£650).

FINANCES *Year* 2015 *Income* £5,905,622 *Grants* £101,687 *Grants to organisations* £96,537 *Assets* £1,919,534

TRUSTEES Tim Berg; Mark Bromley; Tabby Estell; Eleanor Gussman; Dr Linda Hurst; Ed McKeon; Keith Potter; Prof. Stephen Walsh.

OTHER INFORMATION The grant total refers to those approved during the year. In 2015 grants were made to 44 organisations. A further six grants made to individuals totalled £5,100.

HOW TO APPLY An online form is available on the website and includes details of upcoming application deadlines. There is also a helpful page on further guidance, which sets out the supporting information required from applicants.

WHO TO APPLY TO The Secretary, 2–6 Bache's Street, London N1 6DN *Email* hinrichsen.foundation@editionpeters.com *Website* www.hinrichsenfoundation.org.uk

■ The Hintze Family Charity Foundation

CC NO 1101842 **ESTABLISHED** 2003

WHERE FUNDING CAN BE GIVEN England and Wales, particularly the Diocese of Southwark; overseas.

WHO CAN BENEFIT Registered charities; churches; museums, galleries; libraries and other cultural bodies; educational establishments.

WHAT IS FUNDED Museums, libraries and art galleries, particularly to promote access to the general public; support for schools, colleges and universities; the Christian faith; projects benefitting people who are sick or terminally ill; other charitable purposes.

TYPE OF GRANT One-off and multi-year; capital and revenue funding; salaries; core costs; projects; start-up costs; unrestricted funding.

RANGE OF GRANTS Up to about £1.2 million.

SAMPLE GRANTS Advance Charitable Fund UK; British Film Institute; Canterbury Cathedral Trust; International Theological Institute; National Portrait Gallery; New York University; Oxford Centre for Astrophysical Surveys; Southwark Diocese Clergy Support Fund Campaign; The Black Stork Charity; The Garden Bridge Trust; The Outward Bound Trust; The Prince of Wales's Charitable Foundation.

FINANCES *Year* 2015 *Income* £4,883,611 *Grants* £4,017,912 *Grants to organisations* £4,017,912 *Assets* £1,965,518

TRUSTEES Sir Michael Hintze; Sir Michael Peat; Duncan Baxter.

OTHER INFORMATION A total of 39 organisations were supported across the following categories: educational (£1.77 million); social/environment (£780,000); cultural/arts (£652,500); religious (£531,000); armed services (£254,000); health (£30,000).

HOW TO APPLY The annual report 2015 explains that the foundation 'invites applications for grants from charities which further the objectives of the foundation. No specific format is required for applications. Applications and potential donations identified by the Chief Executive and the trustees are considered at trustees' meetings.'

WHO TO APPLY TO Kate Rees-Doherty, Secretary, 4th Floor, One Strand, London WC2N 5HR *Tel.* 020 7201 2444 *Email* enquiries@hfcf.org.uk

■ The Hiscox Foundation

CC NO 327635 **ESTABLISHED** 1987

WHERE FUNDING CAN BE GIVEN Worldwide.

WHO CAN BENEFIT Registered charities or individuals, mainly those with which a member of staff of the Hiscox Group is involved.

WHAT IS FUNDED General charitable purposes; education; medical science; the arts; independent living for older people; disadvantaged or vulnerable members of society.

TYPE OF GRANT Usually one-off.

RANGE OF GRANTS £49 to £40,000.

SAMPLE GRANTS HART (£40,000); Richard House Children's Hospital (£33,000); Art Fund (£10,000); Teenage Cancer Trust (£8,000); Kennet Community Transport (£6,000); NSPCC (£3,000); St Helena's Hospital (£3,000); York Mind (£2,500); Spear, Wiltshire Bobby Van Trust, World's End Under Fives Centre, Young Enterprise, Zimbabwe a National Emergency (£1,000 each); The Ahoy Centre, Anna Plowden Trust, Excellent Development Ltd, Kids N Action, Orchid, RP Fighting Blindness (£500 each); Atlas, Aware, Heart Children Ireland, Hospice UK, Little Princess Trust (£250 each); Text Santa (£120); Friends of A (£110); Sightsavers (£49).

FINANCES *Year* 2015/16 *Income* £704,504 *Grants* £167,856 *Grants to organisations* £167,856 *Assets* £6,577,779

TRUSTEES Alexander Foster; Robert Hiscox; Rory Barker; Andrew Nix; Amanda Brown.

OTHER INFORMATION There were donations made to 80 charities.

HOW TO APPLY Our research suggests that the foundation does not accept unsolicited applications.

WHO TO APPLY TO c/o Peresha McKenzie, PA to the Chair, Hiscox Underwriting Ltd, 1 Great St Helen's, London EC3A 6HX *Tel.* 020 7448 6011

■ The Henry C. Hoare Charitable Trust

CC NO 1088669 **ESTABLISHED** 2001

WHERE FUNDING CAN BE GIVEN UK.

WHO CAN BENEFIT Charitable organisations.

WHAT IS FUNDED A range of charitable purposes. Grants have been awarded in the following categories: environmental protection and improvement; health; education; citizenship and community development; animal welfare; youth, age, ill health, disability and financial hardship; religion; public policy; and the arts.

TYPE OF GRANT One-off and annual awards.

RANGE OF GRANTS Up to £30,000.

SAMPLE GRANTS Royal Forestry Society Future Foresters Programme (£30,000); Trinity College Cambridge and Woodland Heritage (£25,000 each); Burma Campaign UK and Milton Abbey

School (£20,000 each); Zeal's Youth Trust (£13,000); Contact a Family, Cure Parkinson's Trust, Masanga UK, Vincent Wildlife Trust and Worldwide Volunteering (£10,000 each).

FINANCES *Year* 2014/15 *Income* £199,826 *Grants* £414,650 *Grants to organisations* £414,650 *Assets* £4,227,379

TRUSTEES Henry C. Hoare; Hoare Trustees.

OTHER INFORMATION At the time of writing (May 2017) the 2014/15 were the latest available. The annual report for 2014/15 explains that generally, the trust 'supports those causes where the grant made is meaningful to the recipient'.

HOW TO APPLY Apply in writing to the correspondent.

WHO TO APPLY TO Hoare Trustees, C. Hoare and Co., 37 Fleet Street, London EC4P 4DQ *Tel.* 020 7353 4522

■ The Hobson Charity Ltd

CC NO 326839 **ESTABLISHED** 1985

WHERE FUNDING CAN BE GIVEN UK.

WHO CAN BENEFIT Registered charities only.

WHAT IS FUNDED A wide range of charitable purposes, including social welfare, education, religious activities, relief of poverty, armed forces, arts, culture and heritage, animal welfare, environment and conservation, and community causes.

WHAT IS NOT FUNDED Individuals (except in exceptional circumstances).

TYPE OF GRANT One-off and recurrent.

RANGE OF GRANTS £500 to £250,000.

SAMPLE GRANTS Cancer Research UK – Crick campaign (£250,000); Bletchley Park Trust (£100,000); Royal Ballet School, University of Hertfordshire and Winchester Cathedral Trust (£10,000 each); Disability Snowsport UK (£8,000); Eastbourne Foodbank, Krazykat Theatre Company and St Raphael's Hospice (£5,000 each); Anorexia and Bulimia Care and Gloucestershire Bike Project (£2,000 each); Warrington Youth Club (£1,500); Coldharbour Mill Museum and Retired Greyhound Trust (£1,000 each); St Barnabas Church Go and Grow (£500).

FINANCES *Year* 2015/16 *Income* £1,977,161 *Grants* £1,086,726 *Grants to organisations* £1,086,726 *Assets* £51,465,702

TRUSTEES Hon. Vice Admiral Sir Donald Gosling; Deborah Hobson; Lady Hobson; Jennifer Richardson.

OTHER INFORMATION There were a total of 132 awards made. Of the total grant commitment, £25,000 falls due for payment in future.

HOW TO APPLY Apply in writing to the correspondent. The trustees meet quarterly.

WHO TO APPLY TO Deborah Hobson, Secretary, 21 Bryanston Street, Marble Arch, London W1H 7AB *Tel.* 020 7495 5599 *Email* Charity@LewisGolden.com

■ Hockerill Educational Foundation

CC NO 311018 **ESTABLISHED** 1977

WHERE FUNDING CAN BE GIVEN UK, with a preference for the dioceses of Chelmsford and St Albans.

WHO CAN BENEFIT Individuals; religious educational bodies; churches; teachers; organisations; corporate bodies; teacher training.

WHAT IS FUNDED The foundation makes grants in the field of education in three main areas: individual grants to support the education and training of teachers; research, development and support grants to organisations in the field of religious education; grants to develop the church's educational work, especially in the dioceses of Chelmsford and St Albans.

WHAT IS NOT FUNDED General appeals; bricks and mortar building projects; purposes that are the clear responsibility of another body; teachers who intend leaving the profession; those training for ordination or mission, or clergy who wish to improve their own qualifications, unless they are also involved in teaching in schools; those taking courses in counselling, therapy, or social work; training for other professions, such as accountancy, business, law, or medicine; courses or visits abroad, including gap year courses; the education of children at primary or secondary school; those training to teach English as an additional language; overseas students.

TYPE OF GRANT Recurrent for up to three years (occasionally a maximum of five years), subject to satisfactory progress reports.

RANGE OF GRANTS £50 to £50,000.

SAMPLE GRANTS In the Diocese of St Albans: Diocesan Religious Education Advisor (£50,000); Science and Religion Course for Sixth Formers (£4,500); RE Resources (£1,000). In Diocese of Chlemsford: School Governance Support (£25,000); Children's Work Advisor (£10,000); Mission in Schools (£5,000). Corporate Grants for Research and Development in Education: Religious Education Council for England and Wales (£12,000); Religious Education Quality Mark (£5,000); Sir Roberts Geoffrey's Primary School (£1,000).

FINANCES *Year* 2015/16 *Income* £298,185 *Grants* £271,920 *Grants to organisations* £213,860 *Assets* £6,676,968

TRUSTEES Hannah Potter; Jonathan Reynolds; Elwin Cockett; Lesley Barlow; Richard Atkinson; Colin Bird; Harry Marsh; John Wraw; Janet Scott; Tim Elbourne; Jonathan Longstaff; Raymond Slade; Alan Smith; Stephen Cottrell.

OTHER INFORMATION During the year grants totalling £58,000 were paid to 80 individuals. There were 26 grants awarded to institutions totalling at £214,000.

HOW TO APPLY Application forms for organisations/individuals/dioceses can be found on the website. Completed application forms should be returned by 31 March as these stand a better chance of success, but applications received during April and May will be considered as long as funds are available (final deadline 31 May 2017). Application forms may be sent by post or email.

WHO TO APPLY TO Derek Humphrey, Secretary, 3 The Swallows, Harlow, Essex CM17 0AR *Tel.* 01279 420855 *Email* info@hockerillfoundation.org.uk *Website* www.hockerillfoundation.org.uk

■ The Jane Hodge Foundation

CC NO 216053 **ESTABLISHED** 1962

WHERE FUNDING CAN BE GIVEN UK and overseas, with a preference for Wales.

WHO CAN BENEFIT Registered charities or exempt organisations with charitable objectives.

WHAT IS FUNDED General charitable purposes, with special regard given to: medical and surgical studies and research, particularly in connection with the cause, diagnosis, treatment and cure of cancer, poliomyelitis and tuberculosis, and diseases affecting children; the general advancement of medical and surgical science; education; religion.

WHAT IS NOT FUNDED Individuals.
TYPE OF GRANT One-off and up to three years; our research suggests that loans may also be available.
RANGE OF GRANTS Up to £139,000.
SAMPLE GRANTS Cardiff University – Julian Hodge Institute of Applied Macroeconomics (£140,000); Cardiff University – European Cancer Stem Cell Research Institute (£104,500); Welsh National Opera – Youth and Communities Programme (£100,000); The Prince's Trust Cymru (£60,000); Institute of Welsh Affairs (£22,000); Adoption UK, Age Connects, Macmillan Cancer Support and The Duke of Edinburgh's Award (£10,000 each); Race Equality First (£7,000); Dyslexia Action, Great Ormond Street and Mercy Ships UK Ltd (£5,000 each).
FINANCES *Year* 2014/15 *Income* £4,304,656 *Grants* £2,021,817 *Grants to organisations* £2,021,817 *Assets* £35,117,215
TRUSTEES Ian Davies; Jonathan Hodge; Adrian Piper; Karen Hodge; Keith James; Alun Bowen.
OTHER INFORMATION At the time of writing (June 2017) the 2014/15 accounts were the latest available. A total of 91 grants were made during the year.
HOW TO APPLY Apply in writing to the correspondent. The latest annual report explains that the trustees 'invite applications for grants from charitable institutions who submit a summary of their proposals'. Appeals are considered at regular meetings of the trustees.
WHO TO APPLY TO Jonathan Hodge, Trustee, One Central Square, Cardiff CF10 1FS *Tel.* 029 2078 7693 *Email* contact@hodgefoundation.org.uk

■ The Holden Charitable Trust

CC NO 264185 **ESTABLISHED** 1972
WHERE FUNDING CAN BE GIVEN UK, with a preference for the Manchester area.
WHO CAN BENEFIT Charitable organisations, primarily within the Jewish community.
WHAT IS FUNDED Orthodox Jewish education; the advancement of the Orthodox Jewish religion; the relief of poverty.
SAMPLE GRANTS Broom Foundation; Friends of Beis Eliyahu Trust; King David's School; Ohel Bnei Yaakob; Ohr Yerushalayim Synagogue; The Fed.
FINANCES *Year* 2015/16 *Income* £366,828 *Grants* £380,492 *Grants to organisations* £380,492 *Assets* £933,687
TRUSTEES David Lopian; Marian Lopian; Michael Lopian.
OTHER INFORMATION A list of beneficiaries was not included in the latest annual report and accounts.
HOW TO APPLY Apply in writing to the correspondent.
WHO TO APPLY TO The Trustees, c/o Lopian Gross Barnett and Co., 6th Floor, Cardinal House, 20 St Marys Parsonage, Manchester M3 2LG *Tel.* 0161 832 8721 *Email* david.lopian@lopiangb.co.uk

■ The Hollands-Warren Fund

CC NO 279747 **ESTABLISHED** 1977
WHERE FUNDING CAN BE GIVEN Maidstone, Kent.
WHO CAN BENEFIT Individuals; organisations providing medical and nursing care.
WHAT IS FUNDED Temporary medical and nursing services and/or domestic help for residents in the Borough of Maidstone.
RANGE OF GRANTS Up to £43,000.
SAMPLE GRANTS Rapid Response (£42,900); The Heart of Kent Hospice (£12,650).
FINANCES *Year* 2015/16 *Income* £66,677 *Grants* £55,500 *Grants to organisations* £55,500 *Assets* £2,554,177
TRUSTEES Anthony Palmer; Kim Harrington; Daniel Bell.
OTHER INFORMATION There were two grants made.
HOW TO APPLY Apply in writing to the correspondent.
WHO TO APPLY TO Kim Harrington, Trustee, c/o Brachers Solicitors, Somerfield House, 57–59 London Road, Maidstone, Kent ME16 8JH *Tel.* 01622 690691 *Email* kimharrington@brachers.co.uk

■ The Hollick Family Charitable Trust

CC NO 1060228 **ESTABLISHED** 1997
WHERE FUNDING CAN BE GIVEN UK and overseas.
WHO CAN BENEFIT Registered charities.
WHAT IS FUNDED General charitable purposes. According to the annual report 2015/16, the trustees 'make a number of relatively small but significant donations to a range of charities each year and also to identify at least one cause to which they are able to provide more substantial funding'.
TYPE OF GRANT One-off and recurrent.
SAMPLE GRANTS A list of beneficiaries was not available.
FINANCES *Year* 2015/16 *Income* £1,331,671 *Grants* £156,162 *Grants to organisations* £156,162 *Assets* £4,606,347
TRUSTEES Caroline Kemp; The Hon. Georgina Hollick; David Beech; The Hon. Abigail Benoliel; Lady Sue Hollick; Lord Clive Hollick.
OTHER INFORMATION There were 54 awards made. A list of beneficiaries was not included in the annual report and accounts.
HOW TO APPLY Apply in writing to the correspondent. The trustees meet at least twice a year.
WHO TO APPLY TO David Beech, Trustee, Prager Metis LLP, 5A Bear Lane, Southwark, London SE1 0UH *Tel.* 020 7632 1400 *Email* dbeech@pragermetis.com

■ The Holliday Foundation

CC NO 1089931 **ESTABLISHED** 2001
WHERE FUNDING CAN BE GIVEN Mainly UK.
WHO CAN BENEFIT Organisations and individuals.
WHAT IS FUNDED General charitable purposes, with particular interest in children and young people and in assisting individuals to better themselves.
RANGE OF GRANTS Usually between £1,000 and £10,000.
SAMPLE GRANTS National Centre for Young People with Epilepsy and Training for Life (£10,000 each); Charsfield Recreation Ground and Help the Hospices (£5,000 each); Sparkes Homes Sri Lanka (£2,500); The East Anglian Academy (£1,200); The Newbury Spring Festival (£1,000).
FINANCES *Year* 2015/16 *Income* £23,859 *Grants* £61,500 *Grants to organisations* £61,500
TRUSTEES David William; James Cave; Antony Wilson; Jane Garrett; Huw Llewellyn.
OTHER INFORMATION Due to its low income, this foundation's latest accounts were not available to view on the Charity Commission's website. We have therefore estimated the grant total. Our research suggests that the trustees review requests for grants and may request further

information or visit applicants before deciding whether to make a payment. The trustees will follow up the use of grants where relevant.

HOW TO APPLY Apply in writing to the correspondent. The trustees normally meet at least four times a year.

WHO TO APPLY TO Linda Wasfi, Salisbury Partners LLP, 9 Clifford Street, London W1S 2FT *Tel.* 020 7016 6700 *Email* linda.wasfi@salisburypartners.co.uk

■ The Dorothy Holmes Charitable Trust

CC NO 237213 **ESTABLISHED** 1964

WHERE FUNDING CAN BE GIVEN UK, with a preference for Dorset.

WHO CAN BENEFIT UK-registered charities.

WHAT IS FUNDED General charitable purposes.

WHAT IS NOT FUNDED Only applications from registered charities will be considered.

TYPE OF GRANT Generally one-off grants for unrestricted purposes.

RANGE OF GRANTS Normally up to £6,000.

SAMPLE GRANTS Wallingford School (£6,000); Children in Touch, Crisis and Christmas and RNLI (£5,000 each); Hyman Cen Foundation (£4,000); Army Benevolent Fund (£3,000); Action on Elder Abuse and CLIC Sargent Cancer Fund (£2,000 each); National Autistic Society and Raleigh International (£1,000 each); Royal Free Hospital Retirement Fellowship (£300).

FINANCES *Year* 2015/16 *Income* £8,542 *Grants* £83,000 *Grants to organisations* £83,000

TRUSTEES Dr Susan Roberts; Margaret Cody; James Roberts.

OTHER INFORMATION Due to its low income, this trust's latest accounts were not available to view on the Charity Commission's website. We have therefore estimated the grant total based on previous years' information.

HOW TO APPLY Apply in writing to the correspondent. Our research suggests that they should be submitted preferably from January to March each year.

WHO TO APPLY TO Michael Kennedy, Smallfield Cody and Co., 5 Harley Place, Harley Street, London W1G 8QD *Tel.* 020 7631 4574 *Email* meac@smallfieldcody.co.uk

■ P. H. Holt Foundation

CC NO 1113708 **ESTABLISHED** 1955

WHERE FUNDING CAN BE GIVEN UK, principally Merseyside.

WHO CAN BENEFIT Registered charities; small charities; preference for Merseyside; individuals.

WHAT IS FUNDED General charitable purposes; community development; environment; arts; poverty. The annual report (2015/16) states; 'The Foundation gives grants which help communities and charitable organisations create a better future for the people of Merseyside according to five priority themes: Creating opportunities for people to contribute to their local community; enabling people to overcome barriers and take control of their lives; widening access to education for people of all ages; increasing engagement in the arts for marginalised or excluded groups; encouraging care of the natural and built environment'. The trust's sister charity (Holt Education Trust) provides grants to individual students seeking to study a degree in science in Merseyside.

WHAT IS NOT FUNDED CICs; social enterprise; local branches of national charities; everyday running costs and core salaries; recurrent funding; general fundraising appeals; statutory or retrospective funding; academic or medical research; sponsorship, including sports events; holidays, holiday centres or outings and overseas travel; religious and political causes; national charities; vehicles and minibuses.

TYPE OF GRANT Generally one-off or part of a recurrent relationship. Holt Education Trust awards grants to individual students.

RANGE OF GRANTS Up to £10,000; mostly under £5,000.

SAMPLE GRANTS Emmaus Merseyside (£15,000); Imagine If Trust (£14,000); Ariel Trust (£13,000); Old Roan Baptist Church (£10,000); Malvern Primary School (£6,000); English National Ballet, Hearing Dogs for Deaf People, Mencap (£5,000 each); Hope Street Ltd (£4,250); Centre 63 (£4,200); Church Housing Trust (£1,500) Tall Ships Youth Trust (£200).

FINANCES *Year* 2015/16 *Income* £251,670 *Grants* £302,698 *Grants to organisations* £302,698 *Assets* £16,781,294

TRUSTEES Elspeth Christie; Martin Cooke; Paige Earlam; Nicola Eastwood; Anthony Hannay; Amy De Joia; Neil Kemsley; Ian Matthews; Kenneth Ravenscroft.

OTHER INFORMATION During the year 2015/16, the P. H. Holt Foundation and Holt Education Trust made grants to 73 registered charities and individual students across Merseyside dispensing £303,000.

HOW TO APPLY Application forms can be accessed on the foundation's website and should be returned by email together with a copy of your latest annual report and accounts. The website notes: 'If you wish to discuss your proposal with us before submitting, you are welcome to contact the office for an initial conversation.' The trustees meet four times a year to discuss applications and the deadlines are the first of February, May, August and November. Charities outside Merseyside are only supported occasionally. As a rule, allow three or four months from closing date for a funding decision to be reached by the trustees. Complex applications can sometimes take longer.

WHO TO APPLY TO Anne Edwards, Trust Administrator, 151 Dale Street, Liverpool L2 2AH *Tel.* 0151 237 2663 *Email* administrator@phholtfoundation.org.uk *Website* www.phholtfoundation.org.uk

■ The Edward Holt Trust

CC NO 224741 **ESTABLISHED** 1955

WHERE FUNDING CAN BE GIVEN Preference for Greater Manchester.

WHO CAN BENEFIT Registered charities; hospitals.

WHAT IS FUNDED General charitable purposes; older people; homelessness; people who are disadvantaged. The annual report states that's its principal activities are; the maintenance of flats in Manchester for the benefit of older people; 'the maintenance of Edward Holt House which is a property acquired by the trust for the use of a local charity "The Booths Centre"'.

TYPE OF GRANT Project funding, core costs, salaries, research. Funding is available for up to three years.

SAMPLE GRANTS Holt House (£124,000); Edward Holt House (£16,800); Institutional Grants (£460).

FINANCES *Year* 2015/16 *Income* £248,714 *Grants* £145,187 *Grants to organisations* £145,187 *Assets* £7,968,710

TRUSTEES David Tully; Angela Roden; Richard Kershaw; Mike Fry; Anne Williams; Michael Prior.

OTHER INFORMATION The charity undertakes its charitable activities through the running of Holt House and awarded grants in furtherance of its charitable activities.

HOW TO APPLY Applications should be made in writing to the correspondent. Note that in the past the trust has stated that unsolicited appeals are not accepted.

WHO TO APPLY TO Bryan Peak, Secretary, 22 Ashworth Park, Knutsford, Cheshire WA16 9DE *Tel.* 01565 651086 *Email* edwardholt@btinternet.com *Website* www.edwardholttrust.btck.co.uk

■ The Holywood Trust

SC NO SC009942 **ESTABLISHED** 1981

WHERE FUNDING CAN BE GIVEN Dumfries and Galloway.

WHO CAN BENEFIT Individuals; organisations that work with young people; disadvantaged, vulnerable young people.

WHAT IS FUNDED Young people primarily aged 15 to 25; personal development; sports; arts; group development activities; education; health; social welfare; residential activities. The website states that the trust 'is particularly interested in helping to fill gaps in provision, and to support innovative ideas. Your organisation should be appropriately constituted and demonstrate a commitment to equal opportunities.'

WHAT IS NOT FUNDED Organisations and individuals outside Dumfries and Galloway.

TYPE OF GRANT One-off; capital and core costs; recurring funding (usually limited to three years); salaries; project costs.

RANGE OF GRANTS £10 to £50,000. Individual grants: £50–500.

SAMPLE GRANTS Guild of Players (£212,000); Maggie's Centres (£75,000); Inspired Community Enterprise Trust (£60,500); LGBT Youth Scotland (£50,000); Independent Living Support (£35,000); Big Burns Supper (£25,000); Let's Get Sporty (£19,000); Environmental Arts Festival Scotland CIC (£14,800); Solway Sharks Ice Hockey Team (£10,000).

FINANCES *Year* 2015/16 *Income* £2,496,554 *Grants* £1,584,600 *Grants to organisations* £1,384,061 *Assets* £97,157,784

TRUSTEES Valerie McElroy; Charles Jencks; Clara Weatherall; Ben Weatherall; John Jencks.

OTHER INFORMATION During the year 111 grant awards were made to organisations totalling £1,380,000. Overall 314 individual grants awards were offered totalling £93,000, with an average award of £296.

HOW TO APPLY Applications and full guidelines are available on the website. When you have completed your application check that all information required is enclosed, sign, date and post it to the trust at Hestan House, Crichton, Bankend Road, Dumfries DG1 4TA. Also attach a copy of the Word Document and email it to funds@holywood-trust.org.uk. Organisations must contact the trust five to six months before their funding is needed to give time for consideration. Individuals should allow at least four weeks for their application to be processed.

WHO TO APPLY TO Richard Lye, Trust Administrator, Hestan House, Crichton Business Park, Bankend Road, Dumfries DG1 4TA *Tel.* 01387 269176 *Fax* 01387 269175 *Email* funds@holywood-trust.org.uk *Website* www.holywood-trust.org.uk

■ The Homelands Charitable Trust

CC NO 214322 **ESTABLISHED** 1962

WHERE FUNDING CAN BE GIVEN UK.

WHO CAN BENEFIT Registered charities benefitting children, particularly people in risk groups or those who are victims of abuse or domestic violence. Support may also be given to clergy; medical professionals; medical research work.

WHAT IS FUNDED General charitable purposes; general conference of the New Church; medical research; care and protection of children; hospices.

RANGE OF GRANTS £1,000 to £5,000.

SAMPLE GRANTS General Conference of New Church (£73,000); Broadfield memorial Fund (£16,000); New Church College (£11,000); Bournemouth Society of the New Church (£10,000); Philippines New Church (£5,000); RNLI (£3,000); Guide Dogs for the Blind, SOS Children's Villages (£2,800 each); Housing the Homeless, Morning Star Trust, Mountain Rescue, Pestalozzi, Riding for the Disabled, Simon Says, Sparks, Tall Ships Youth Trust, University of Surrey – Prostate Research (£1,800 each); Richard House Hospice (£1,500); Mind (£1,000).

FINANCES *Year* 2015/16 *Income* £315,346 *Grants* £273,000 *Grants to organisations* £273,000 *Assets* £7,781,315

TRUSTEES Nigel Armstrong; Revd Clifford Curry; Robert Curry.

OTHER INFORMATION 102 awards were made during the year.

HOW TO APPLY Apply in writing to the correspondent.

WHO TO APPLY TO Nigel Armstrong, Trustee, 4th Floor, Imperial House, 15 Kingsway, London WC2B 6UN *Tel.* 020 7240 9971

■ The Homestead Charitable Trust

CC NO 293979 **ESTABLISHED** 1986

WHERE FUNDING CAN BE GIVEN UK.

WHO CAN BENEFIT Individuals; organisations.

WHAT IS FUNDED General charitable purposes; medical causes; health; social welfare; animal welfare; environment; Christianity; the arts.

TYPE OF GRANT Usually one-off grants.

RANGE OF GRANTS £100 to £10,000.

SAMPLE GRANTS Ramakrishna Mission (£10,000); Nitti Mehra Cancer, Sankara Netralaya, Sri Ramakrishna, Agastya Indian Foundation (£5,000 each); St James RC Church (£1,000); Carmelite Missionaries (£500); WaterAid (£100).

FINANCES *Year* 2015/16 *Income* £77,597 *Grants* £71,320 *Grants to organisations* £71,320 *Assets* £5,354,051

TRUSTEES Nina Bracewell-Smith; Charles Bracewell-Smith.

OTHER INFORMATION There were 12 awards made which totalled to £51,000. The rest fell under 'other donations'.

HOW TO APPLY Apply in writing to the correspondent.

WHO TO APPLY TO Nina Bracewell-Smith, Trustee, Flat 7, Clarence Gate Gardens, Glentworth Street, London NW1 6AY

■ The Mary Homfray Charitable Trust

CC NO 273564 **ESTABLISHED** 1977
WHERE FUNDING CAN BE GIVEN Mainly Wales.
WHO CAN BENEFIT Registered charities.
WHAT IS FUNDED General charitable purposes.
WHAT IS NOT FUNDED Individuals; charities outside the beneficial area.
TYPE OF GRANT One-off and recurrent.
RANGE OF GRANTS £2,000 to £5,000.
SAMPLE GRANTS Alzheimer's Society, Hop Skip and Jump Foundation and Royal Veterinary College (£5,000 each); Cardiac Risk in the Young, Medical Detention Dogs and National Botanic Garden of Wales (£4,000 each); Glasallt Fawr, Welsh Sinfonia and Wildfowl and Wetland Trust (£3,000 each); Carers Wales and Rectorial Benefice of Cowbridge Penllyn Church (£2,000 each).
FINANCES *Year* 2015/16 *Income* £634,461 *Assets* £3,502,192
TRUSTEES Matthew Homfray; Mary Homfray; Josephine Homfray; Dr Tessa Pemberton.
OTHER INFORMATION Grants were made to 20 organisations and totalled £71,000 in 2014/15 but no grants were made in 2015/16. The trust noted in its annual report for 2015/16 that it intended to resume its grant-making next year.
HOW TO APPLY Apply in writing to the correspondent. Applications should be made towards the end of the year, for consideration at the trustees' annual meeting in February or March each year.
WHO TO APPLY TO Josephine Homfray, Trustee, c/o Deloitte PCS Ltd, 5 Callaghan Square, Cardiff CF10 5BT *Tel.* 029 2046 0000 *Email* jdeacy@deloitte.co.uk

■ Sir Harold Hood's Charitable Trust

CC NO 225870 **ESTABLISHED** 1962
WHERE FUNDING CAN BE GIVEN Worldwide.
WHO CAN BENEFIT Roman Catholic registered charities and churches.
WHAT IS FUNDED Roman Catholic charitable purposes.
WHAT IS NOT FUNDED Individuals.
TYPE OF GRANT One-off core and capital costs; project expenditure; salaries; unrestricted funding.
RANGE OF GRANTS £1,000 to £60,000.
SAMPLE GRANTS Downside Abbey (£60,000); PACT – Prison Advice and Care Trust (£36,500); Royal Navy RC Chaplaincy Trust – Portsmouth (£20,000); Diocese of Nottingham (£30,000); Youth 2000 (£10,000); St John's Hospice – Hospital of St John and St Elizabeth and Walsingham Development Fund (£5,000 each); Margaret Beaufort Institute of Theology (£3,000); Women@thewell – Institute of Our Lady of Mercy (£2,000); Oxford Youth Works and Vellore Social Service Society (£1,000 each).
FINANCES *Year* 2015/16 *Income* £685,919 *Grants* £777,142 *Grants to organisations* £777,142 *Assets* £31,663,893
TRUSTEES Dom Hood; Lord Nicholas True; Lady True; Margaret Hood; Christian Elwes.
OTHER INFORMATION In 2015/16 a total of 97 awards were given.
HOW TO APPLY Apply in writing to the correspondent, including your organisation's latest set of accounts. The trustees meet once a year to consider applications, usually in November.
WHO TO APPLY TO Margaret Hood, Trustee, haysmacintyre, 26 Red Lion Square, London WC1R 4AG *Email* nlandsman@haysmacintyre.com

■ The Hoover Foundation

CC NO 200274 **ESTABLISHED** 1961
WHERE FUNDING CAN BE GIVEN UK; special interest in South Wales, Glasgow and Bolton.
WHO CAN BENEFIT UK-registered charities; universities; small local charities working in South Wales, Glasgow and Bolton.
WHAT IS FUNDED General charitable purposes; education; religion; environmental; community development.
WHAT IS NOT FUNDED Individuals.
TYPE OF GRANT One-off donations to smaller charities; larger donations to enable charities to be self-funded.
RANGE OF GRANTS Up to £10,000.
SAMPLE GRANTS Bloodwise, Brain Tumour Research, Cancer Research UK, The Prostate Cancer (£25,000); Claire House Children's Hospice (£5,000); Bolton Lads and Girls Club (£3,000); Bolton Brass Fund (£2,750).
FINANCES *Year* 2015/16 *Income* £72,800 *Grants* £192,890 *Grants to organisations* £192,890 *Assets* £3,089,839
TRUSTEES David Lunt; Alberto Bertali; Robert Mudie; Matthew Given.
OTHER INFORMATION There were 11 grants awarded which totalled at £186,000. The rest of their donations went to grants less than £1,000. Grants are not awarded to individuals.
HOW TO APPLY Apply in writing to the correspondent.
WHO TO APPLY TO S. Herbert, Hoover Candy Group, Pentrebach, Merthyr Tydfil, Mid Glamorgan CF48 4TU *Tel.* 01685 725530 *Email* sherbert@hoovercandy.com

■ The Hope Trust

SC NO SC000987 **ESTABLISHED** 1912
WHERE FUNDING CAN BE GIVEN Worldwide, with a preference for Scotland.
WHO CAN BENEFIT Christian individuals and organisations; Church of England; evangelists; Methodists; Quakers; Unitarians; people with a substance addiction or organisations helping such individuals.
WHAT IS FUNDED The provision of education and the distribution of literature to combat the misuse and effects of drink and drugs and to promote the principles of Reformed Churches; the advancement of the Christian religion, Anglican bodies, Free Church, rehabilitation centres and health education.
WHAT IS NOT FUNDED Grants are not made to gap year students, scholarship schemes or the refurbishment of property. Awards to individuals are not made with the exception of PhD students of theology studying at Scottish universities.
TYPE OF GRANT One-off grants, largely for unrestricted purposes.
SAMPLE GRANTS Church of Scotland Priority Areas Fund; Feed the Minds; National Bible Society for Scotland; Waldensian Mission Aid; World Alliance of Reformed Churches.
FINANCES *Year* 2015 *Income* £252,759 *Grants* £280,000 *Grants to organisations* £280,000
OTHER INFORMATION The accounts were not available; therefore, we have estimated the

amount the trust spends on grants based on their expenditure.

HOW TO APPLY Applications can be made in writing to the correspondent. Our research indicates that the trustees normally meet to consider applications in June and December; therefore, applications should be submitted by mid-May or mid-November each year. Informal contact is welcomed by phone.

WHO TO APPLY TO The Secretary, Drummond Miller LLP, Glenorchy House, 20 Union Street, Edinburgh EH1 3LR *Tel.* 0131 226 5151 *Fax* 0131 225 2608 *Email* reception@drummond-miller.co.uk

■ Hopmarket Charity

CC NO 244569 **ESTABLISHED** 1964

WHERE FUNDING CAN BE GIVEN The city of Worcester.

WHO CAN BENEFIT Organisations.

WHAT IS FUNDED The relief of people who are in need by reason of age, social or financial circumstances.

WHAT IS NOT FUNDED Grants are not made to, or on behalf of, individuals.

TYPE OF GRANT Core/running costs; project funding; salaries.

RANGE OF GRANTS From £1,000 to £20,000.

SAMPLE GRANTS Worcester Housing and Benefits Advice (£20,500); Worcester Community Trust (£20,000); Maggs Day Centre (£11,300); The Asha Centre (£9,500); Disability Sport Worcester (£6,100); Sight Concern Worcestershire (£2,600); Worcestershire Lifestyles (£2,200); Arts in Minds Foundation (£1,200); Worcester Action for Youth (£1,100); Worcester Leg Club (£1,000).

FINANCES *Year* 2015/16 *Income* £200,529 *Grants* £95,000 *Grants to organisations* £95,000 *Assets* £1,016,839

TRUSTEES Allah Ditta; Dr Adrian Gregson; Roger Knight; George Squires; Steve Mackay; Revd Canon Dr Georgina Byrne; Bill Simpson; Jo Hodges.

OTHER INFORMATION There were 17 grants made.

HOW TO APPLY Applications should be made to the treasurer using a standard application form, available from the correspondent. Applicants are required to provide information about the project to be assisted, along with financial information about their organisation. Our research suggests that submissions should be made by the beginning of January or August for consideration in March or September respectively.

WHO TO APPLY TO Claire Chaplin, Democratic and Electoral Services Manager, Guildhall, Worcester WR1 2EY *Tel.* 01905 722005 *Email* claire.chaplin@worcester.gov.uk

■ The Horizon Foundation

CC NO 1118455 **ESTABLISHED** 2007

WHERE FUNDING CAN BE GIVEN Worldwide.

WHO CAN BENEFIT Registered charities; educational establishments; individuals.

WHAT IS FUNDED General charitable purposes; education; women; children and young people.

TYPE OF GRANT One-off or recurrent.

RANGE OF GRANTS £650 to £109,000.

SAMPLE GRANTS Eton College (£109,000); Armand Hammer United (£102,000); UWC Atlantic College (£68,000); Stichting UWC Nederland (£53,000); Rugby (£40,000) Maastricht University (£17,400); AOK Events (£3,300); Atlantic College (£1,500).

FINANCES *Year* 2015/16 *Income* £489,217 *Grants* £458,214 *Grants to organisations* £449,985 *Assets* £201,834

TRUSTEES Kirkland Smulders; Patrick Smulders; Coutts & Co.

OTHER INFORMATION There were 14 awards made to both individuals and organisations.

HOW TO APPLY Applications should be made in writing to the correspondent and are considered regularly.

WHO TO APPLY TO The Trustees, c/o Coutts & Co., Trustee Department, 6th Floor, Trinity Quay 2, Avon Street, Bristol BS2 0PT *Tel.* 020 7663 6825 *Email* couttscharities@coutts.com

■ The Antony Hornby Charitable Trust

CC NO 263285 **ESTABLISHED** 1971

WHERE FUNDING CAN BE GIVEN UK.

WHO CAN BENEFIT Registered charities.

WHAT IS FUNDED General charitable purposes, in particular supporting charities involved in: medicine; education; social welfare; the arts.

WHAT IS NOT FUNDED Individuals.

RANGE OF GRANTS £100 to £5,000.

SAMPLE GRANTS University of Hertfordshire (£5,000); Ataxia UK (£2,000); Keech Hospice Care for Children (£1,500); Countryside Foundation for Education, Disability Snowsport UK, Institute for Cancer Research, London Catalyst and The Art Fund (£1,000 each); Ashmolean Museum (£500); ROH Foundation (£400).

FINANCES *Year* 2015/16 *Income* £43,082 *Grants* £43,395 *Grants to organisations* £43,395 *Assets* £1,363,084

TRUSTEES Marie Antoinette Hall; Mark Loveday; Michael Wentworth-Stanley; Jane Wentworth-Stanley.

OTHER INFORMATION Grants were awarded to 35 organisations in 2015/16, as well as £25,000 that was distributed via Charities Aid Foundation.

HOW TO APPLY The trust has previously stated that it is fully committed and does not usually add new names to its list of beneficiaries unless it is a charity known to the trustees, or a very special appeal.

WHO TO APPLY TO Allan Holmes, Saffery Champness, Lion House, 72–75 Red Lion Street, London WC1R 4GB *Tel.* 020 7841 4000

■ The Thomas J. Horne Memorial Trust

CC NO 1010625 **ESTABLISHED** 1992

WHERE FUNDING CAN BE GIVEN UK and overseas, especially the financially developing countries.

WHO CAN BENEFIT Charitable organisations, particularly hospices and related charities.

WHAT IS FUNDED The vast majority of support is given to hospices, particularly children's hospices, and related charities. Support is also given to other organisations such as those working with people with disabilities or who are homeless, as well as self-help groups in the financially developing countries.

RANGE OF GRANTS From £1,000 to £25,000.

SAMPLE GRANTS Disasters Emergency Committee – Nepal Earthquake Appeal (£25,000); World Medical Fund (£20,000); Demelza House Children's Hospice and Practical Action (£10,000 each); Woodlands Hospice – Liverpool (£6,000); Acorns Children's Hospice – Worcester, Heart of Kent Hospice – Aylesford and Lakelands Daycare Hospice – Corby (£7,500 each); Down's Syndrome Association and Humberstone Hydrotherapy Pool (£5,000 each); Soundabout and Voluntary Action Maidstone (£2,500 each); Whitby Dog Rescue (£1,000).

FINANCES *Year* 2015/16 *Income* £565,503 *Grants* £744,816 *Grants to organisations* £744,816 *Assets* £6,649,349

TRUSTEES Jeff Horne; Jon Horne; Emma Horne.

HOW TO APPLY Unsolicited applications are not accepted.

WHO TO APPLY TO Jeff Horne, Trustee, Kingsdown, Warmlake Road, Chart Sutton, Maidstone, Kent ME17 3RP *Email* cc@horne-trust.org.uk

■ The Worshipful Company of Horners' Charitable Trusts

CC NO 292204 **ESTABLISHED** 1985

WHERE FUNDING CAN BE GIVEN Mainly in London.

WHO CAN BENEFIT Registered charities; educational establishments and individuals.

WHAT IS FUNDED General charitable purposes; education; the provision of scholarships and bursaries; health; disability causes; heritage.

TYPE OF GRANT One-off and recurrent. Both educational and general grants can be awarded.

RANGE OF GRANTS Up to £31,500. Usually around £2,000.

SAMPLE GRANTS Mudchute (£31,500); Polymer Study Tours (£10,000); Ralph Anderson Lecture (£6,000); Serious Trust (£5,000); Salters Horners AP (£4,000); Lord Mayor's Appeal (£3,000); IOM3 (£1,500); Plastiquarian (£1,000).

FINANCES *Year* 2015/16 *Income* £240,929 *Grants* £104,309 *Grants to organisations* £104,309 *Assets* £3,366,634

TRUSTEES Newton Grant; Colin Richards; Keith Pinker; Jack Bunyer; Brian Ridgewell; Anthony Layard; Martin Muirhead; David Giachardi; Alison Gill.

HOW TO APPLY Applications and enquiries should be addressed to the correspondent, specifying what the funding is needed for.

WHO TO APPLY TO Jonathan Mead, Clerk, c/o The Worshipful Company of Horners, 12 Coltsfoot Close, Ixworth, Suffolk IP31 2NJ *Email* clerk@horners.org.uk *Website* www.horners.org.uk

■ Horwich Shotter Charitable Trust

CC NO 1068651 **ESTABLISHED** 1998

WHO CAN BENEFIT Charities; voluntary bodies; individuals.

WHAT IS FUNDED Religion; education; general charitable purposes.

SAMPLE GRANTS A list of beneficiaries was not available.

FINANCES *Year* 2015 *Income* £91,636 *Grants* £61,965 *Grants to organisations* £61,965 *Assets* £269,090

TRUSTEES Jeffrey Horwich; Howard Horwich; Maurice Horwich.

HOW TO APPLY Apply in writing to the correspondent.

WHO TO APPLY TO Jeffrey Horwich, Trustee, 13 Singleton Road, Salford M7 4NN *Tel.* 0161 792 2441

■ Hospice UK

CC NO 1014851/SC041112 **ESTABLISHED** 1984

WHERE FUNDING CAN BE GIVEN Throughout the UK and overseas.

WHO CAN BENEFIT Hospices and other institutions (individuals or organisations) involved with hospice care in the UK.

WHAT IS FUNDED Health; hospice care; staff costs; education; refurbishment; projects; equipment; home care; resource-poor countries; individuals providing hospice care.

WHAT IS NOT FUNDED Anything not related to hospice care.

TYPE OF GRANT One-off and recurrent.

RANGE OF GRANTS Generally under £1,000.

SAMPLE GRANTS Hospiscare Exeter (£31,000); St Joseph's Hospice-Hackney (£29,000); St Catherine's Hospice-Preston (£9,000) Bluebell Wood Children's Hospice (£7,000); St Anne's Hospice-Manchester (£3,000); Oakhaven Hospice (£2,000).

FINANCES *Year* 2015/16 *Income* £3,559,000 *Grants* £785,000 *Grants to organisations* £785,000 *Assets* £4,584,000

TRUSTEES Lord Howard of Lympne; Peter Holliday; Paul Dyer; Bay Green; Andrew Ryde; Patrick Beasley; Christine Heginbotham; Francis Bourne; Christine Gibbons; Stephen Greenhalgh; Julia Delaney.

OTHER INFORMATION All 392 grants were made to organisations.

HOW TO APPLY The website provides guidelines for each programme and clear information on application procedures and deadlines. Depending on the programme, application forms can be downloaded or completed through the online application system.

WHO TO APPLY TO Grants Team, 34–44 Britannia Street, London WC1X 9JG *Tel.* 020 7520 8200 *Email* grants@hospiceuk.org *Website* www.hospiceuk.org

■ The Hospital of God at Greatham

CC NO 1123540 **ESTABLISHED** 1973

WHERE FUNDING CAN BE GIVEN The ancient diocese of Durham (Hartlepool, Stockton, Darlington, County Durham, Sunderland, Gateshead, South Tyneside, North Tyneside, Newcastle upon Tyne and Northumberland).

WHO CAN BENEFIT Large charities; local charities; the North East region. The charity's website states that it aims 'to support charities working in lower profile areas of work that reach people who are on the edges of society'.

WHAT IS FUNDED Disadvantaged/vulnerable people; older people; health; medical causes; residential care; general charitable purposes.

WHAT IS NOT FUNDED Capital works or appeals; education, travel and adventure projects; training and conferences; feasibility studies; medical equipment and related projects; organisations that do not have a base in the North East.

TYPE OF GRANT One-off and up to three years; core funding; running costs; salaries.

RANGE OF GRANTS Up to £5,000.

SAMPLE GRANTS Durham Diocese Clergy Counselling Service (£5,000); Lydia's House (£3,000); Heel and Toe Children's Charity, Hospital Care North Northumberland, Keep the Dream Alive (£2,000 each); Bell Vue Belford (£1,500); Action Foundation, Breathing Space, Full Circle Food Project (£1,000 each); Cramlington United FC, Hartlepool Men's Shed (£500 each).

FINANCES *Year* 2014/15 *Income* £4,308,687 *Grants* £16,950 *Grants to organisations* £94,000 *Assets* £40,760,537

TRUSTEES Peter Shields; Ian Jagger; John De Martino; John Allen; Stephen Croft; Geoffrey Miller; Michael Poole; Philippa Sinclair; Chris Dickinson; Mike Taylerson; Annette Nylund; Barry Winter.

OTHER INFORMATION The charity's most recent accounts were 2014/16. The charity awarded 77 grants to organisations during 2014/15 and 11 grants to individuals.

HOW TO APPLY Apply in writing to the correspondent. The application must be sent by post to The Estate Office at Greatham. Email applications will not be accepted. Applications should not be more than two sides of an A4 page and should contain: a description of the organisation; description of project; how it is to be delivered; evidence of need for the project; amount requested and how it is to be sent. Along with the application the latest set of audited accounts and/or an annual report must be sent. The name of the payee must be made clear so that the charity can issue any grants cheque correctly should you be successful in your application. Potential applicants are welcome to contact the Director at the Hospital of God for an informal discussion before applying.

WHO TO APPLY TO David Granath, Director, The Estate Office, Greatham, Hartlepool TS25 2HS *Tel.* 01429 870247 *Fax* 01429 871469 *Email* david.granath@hospitalofgod.org.uk *Website* www.hospitalofgod.org.uk

■ The Hospital Saturday Fund

CC NO 1123381 **ESTABLISHED** 1873

WHERE FUNDING CAN BE GIVEN UK, the Republic of Ireland, the Channel Islands and the Isle of Man.

WHO CAN BENEFIT Registered health charities; hospitals; hospices; clinics, medically-associated charities; welfare organisations providing health services; individuals. Organisations must be registered with the Charity Commission or regionally appropriate body (outside England and Wales).

WHAT IS FUNDED Medical causes; health care; research; specialist equipment, welfare needs; scholarships to individuals.

WHAT IS NOT FUNDED Projects outside the UK, Isle of Man, Channel Islands and the Republic of Ireland; organisations that are not registered with Charity Commission for England and Wales, HM Revenue and Customs, the Office of the Scottish Charity Regulator, the Charity Commission for Northern Ireland, the Isle of Man General Registry, the appropriate regulatory body in the Channel Islands or the Revenue Commissioners in Ireland; activities that are not medicine related; fundraising appeals.

TYPE OF GRANT Medical capital projects; medical care; research; support of medical training; grants for running costs are also considered; awards are mainly one-off.

RANGE OF GRANTS Up to £10,000; mostly £2,000.

SAMPLE GRANTS Cardiac Risk in the Young Ireland; Cerebra; Epilepsy Research; Fight for Sight; Livability; British Stammering Association; Hope House Hospice; Chronic Pain Ireland; MS North West Therapy Centre; Rainbows Hospice; Irish Community Rapid Response.

FINANCES *Year* 2015 *Income* £353,856 *Grants* £831,526 *Grants to organisations* £785,907 *Assets* £25,921,138

TRUSTEES John Greenwood; Jane Laidlaw Dalton; Michael Boyle; John Randel; David Thomas; Christopher Bottomley; Pauline Lee.

OTHER INFORMATION During the year, 78 grants were awarded to individuals. A further 273 grants totalling £786,000 was awarded to medical charities, hospices and hospitals including the special medical school grant.

HOW TO APPLY Applications for grants should be made online at www.hospitalsaturdayfund.org. Full guidelines on how to fill the application form out are available on the website. The Hospital Saturday Fund does not accept paper or letter applications. Current annual accounts/financial statements must be attached to ensure your application is considered.

WHO TO APPLY TO Paul Jackson, Chief Executive, 24 Upper Ground, London SE1 9PD *Tel.* 020 7202 1365 (charity enquiries only) *Fax* 020 7928 0446 *Email* charity@hsf.eu.com *Website* www.hospitalsaturdayfund.org

■ The Sir Joseph Hotung Charitable Settlement

CC NO 1082710 **ESTABLISHED** 2000

WHERE FUNDING CAN BE GIVEN Worldwide.

WHO CAN BENEFIT Charitable organisations.

WHAT IS FUNDED Mainly the medical, educational and cultural sectors.

TYPE OF GRANT Usually recurrent.

RANGE OF GRANTS From £1,200 to £4.27 million.

SAMPLE GRANTS British Museum (£4.27 million in two grants); Mansfield College, Oxford University – Institute of Human Rights (£2.48 million in three grants); St George's, University of London (£158,500); Chatham House (£5,000); Spinal Research (£1,200 in 12 grants).

FINANCES *Year* 2015/16 *Income* £1,568,233 *Grants* £6,919,503 *Grants to organisations* £6,919,503 *Assets* -£3,931,016

TRUSTEES Sir Joseph Hotung; Sir Robert Boyd; Peter Painton; Prof. Dame Jessica Rawson.

OTHER INFORMATION The trust tends to support a small number of organisations, often on a regular basis. During 2015/16, five organisations were supported.

HOW TO APPLY The trust has previously stated that 'the trustees have their own areas of interest and do not respond to unsolicited applications'.

WHO TO APPLY TO Sir Joseph Hotung, Trustee, Penningtons Manches LLP, 125 Wood Street, London EC2V 7AW *Email* henry.painton@blueyonder.co.uk

■ House of Industry Estate

CC NO 257079 **ESTABLISHED** 1968

WHERE FUNDING CAN BE GIVEN The borough of North Bedfordshire.

WHO CAN BENEFIT People who are in need and local voluntary, community and charitable organisations helping such individuals.

WHAT IS FUNDED General charitable purposes; the relief of poverty; education; health/medical causes; disability.

WHAT IS NOT FUNDED Funds are not given in relief of taxes or other public funds. Capital expenditure cannot include works to land or property. Neither recurrent nor retrospective funding is given.

TYPE OF GRANT Grants will normally only be awarded for capital items or one-off emergency revenue funding.

RANGE OF GRANTS Up to £25,000.

SAMPLE GRANTS A list of beneficiaries was not available.
FINANCES *Year* 2015/16 *Income* £214,013 *Grants* £178,313 *Grants to organisations* £178,313 *Assets* £4,311,274
TRUSTEES Cllr Tim Hill; Cllr Sue Oliver; Cllr David Sawyer; Cllr Tom Wootton; Cllr Stephen Moon; Cllr Mohammad Yasin; Cllr Martin Towler.
OTHER INFORMATION The grant total includes £35,000 awarded to organisations for the purposes of making grants to individuals in need. In exceptional cases, people otherwise eligible but resident immediately outside the borough or living within it temporarily may be supported.
HOW TO APPLY An application form, along with guidelines, is available from the Bedford Borough Council website. Hard copy application forms or further information can be obtained from the correspondent.
WHO TO APPLY TO The Community Welfare Team, Bedford Borough Council, Borough Hall, Cauldwell Street, Bedford MK42 9AP *Tel.* 01234 718074 or 718078 *Email* Community.Welfare@bedford.gov.uk *Website* www.bedford.gov.uk/advice_and_benefits/advice_and_benefits_-_grants/grants_for_financial_assist.aspx

■ The Reta Lila Howard Foundation

CC NO 1041634 **ESTABLISHED** 1994
WHERE FUNDING CAN BE GIVEN UK and the Republic of Ireland.
WHO CAN BENEFIT Selected registered charities.
WHAT IS FUNDED Innovative projects which are concerned with the education of or which ameliorate the physical and emotional environment of children and young people (up to the age of 16).
WHAT IS NOT FUNDED Individuals; organisations which are not registered charities; operating expenses; budget deficits; (sole) capital projects; annual charitable appeals; general endowment funds; fundraising drives or events; conferences; student aid.
RANGE OF GRANTS £5,000 to £60,000.
SAMPLE GRANTS Adam Smith Institute (£60,000); Kids Run Free (£55,000); Sense About Science (£50,000); The Tree Council (£40,000); Camden Music Trust, Kent Refugee Action Network and London Wildlife Trust (£20,000 each); Global Generation (£19,300); The Bike Project and Manchester International Festival (£10,000 each); Islay and Jura Community Enterprises (£5,000).
FINANCES *Year* 2015/16 *Income* £91,894 *Grants* £489,263 *Grants to organisations* £489,263 *Assets* £18,335,630
TRUSTEES Alannah Weston; Charles Burnett; Garfield Mitchell; Christian Bauta; Melissa Murdoch; Claudia Hepburn; Mark Mitchell; Gregg Weston.
OTHER INFORMATION In 2015/16 a total of 20 grants were made.
HOW TO APPLY The foundation has previously stated that it does not accept unsolicited applications as the trustees seek out and support projects they are interested in.
WHO TO APPLY TO The Trustees of The Reta Lila Howard Foundation, The Reta Lila Howard Foundation, Horsmonden Business Centre, The Business Centre, Green Road, Horsmonden, Tonbridge TN12 8JS *Tel.* 01892 723394 *Email* retalilahoward@gmail.com

■ The Daniel Howard Trust

CC NO 267173 **ESTABLISHED** 1974
WHERE FUNDING CAN BE GIVEN UK and Israel.
WHO CAN BENEFIT Registered charities, primarily those benefitting Jewish people.
WHAT IS FUNDED Culture; education; environment; social welfare.
WHAT IS NOT FUNDED Non-registered charities; individuals.
TYPE OF GRANT One-off and recurrent.
SAMPLE GRANTS Friends of Daniel for Rowing Association (£40,500); Spero Foundation Switzerland (£35,500); Daniel Howard Foundation Switzerland (£35,000); Tel Aviv Foundation (£21,500); Israel Family Therapy Advancement Fund (£12,500); Natan Foundation, IPO and The Wharton Fund (£6,000 each); International Scholarship Foundation (£5,000); Israeli Opera Friends Association (£1,900).
FINANCES *Year* 2013/14 *Income* £25,842 *Grants* £105,051 *Grants to organisations* £105,051 *Assets* £5,058,592
TRUSTEES Shirley Porter; Linda Streit; Steven Porter; Brian Padgett; Andrew Peggie.
OTHER INFORMATION At the time of writing (May 2017) the 2013/14 accounts were the most recent available; the trust's accounts for 2014/15 and 2015/16 are overdue. Ongoing support is given to the Daniel Amichai Education Centre and the Israel Philharmonic Orchestra, both in Israel.
HOW TO APPLY Apply in writing to the correspondent. All appeals are considered at the trustees' regular meetings.
WHO TO APPLY TO The Trustees of The Daniel Howard Trust, c/o Principle Capital, 63 Grosvenor Street, London W1K 3JG *Tel.* 020 7499 1957

■ Howman Charitable Trust

SC NO SC001387 **ESTABLISHED** 1977
WHERE FUNDING CAN BE GIVEN UK and overseas.
WHO CAN BENEFIT Charitable organisations.
WHAT IS FUNDED General charitable purposes; in practice, nature conservation.
SAMPLE GRANTS World Pheasant Association (£36,500); Countryside Learning (£7,000); Hindu Kush Conservation Association (£5,400); North Atlantic Salmon Fund (£1,000); The Heather Trust (£510); University of St Andrews (£500); The Game and Wildlife Charitable Trust (£480); Sausage Tree (£350); Mary's Meals and Second Chance (£250 each).
FINANCES *Year* 2015/16 *Income* £59,868 *Grants* £54,081 *Grants to organisations* £54,081 *Assets* £1,247,093
HOW TO APPLY The 2015/16 annual report states: 'unsolicited applications for donations are not encouraged and will not normally be acknowledged'.
WHO TO APPLY TO The Trustees, c/o William Thomson and Sons, 22 Meadowside, Dundee DD1 1LN

■ The Hudson Foundation

CC NO 280332 **ESTABLISHED** 1979
WHERE FUNDING CAN BE GIVEN Wisbech and district.
WHO CAN BENEFIT Charitable organisations.
WHAT IS FUNDED General charitable purposes, especially the relief of people who are older or in need of care.
TYPE OF GRANT Capital projects are preferred over revenue expenditure.

RANGE OF GRANTS £2,000 to £26,000.
SAMPLE GRANTS Wisbech Grammar School (£26,000); Wisbech Swimming Club (£20,000); Methodist Homes for the Aged (£7,700); Mavericks Gymnastics (£5,000); Guide Dogs for the Blind and Wisbech Sea Cadets (£2,000 each).
FINANCES *Year* 2015/16 *Income* £843,406 *Grants* £64,601 *Grants to organisations* £64,601 *Assets* £2,106,913
TRUSTEES David Ball; Stephen Layton; Edward Newling; Stephen Hutchinson.
OTHER INFORMATION There were six awards made in 2015/16.
HOW TO APPLY Apply in writing to the correspondent. The trustees meet quarterly.
WHO TO APPLY TO David Ball, Trustee, 1–3 York Row, Wisbech, Cambridgeshire PE13 1EA *Tel.* 01945 461456

■ The Hull and East Riding Charitable Trust

CC NO 516866 **ESTABLISHED** 1985
WHERE FUNDING CAN BE GIVEN Hull and the East Riding of Yorkshire.
WHO CAN BENEFIT National and local organisations benefitting people resident in Hull and the East Riding of Yorkshire.
WHAT IS FUNDED General charitable purposes.
WHAT IS NOT FUNDED Education; political causes; religion.
TYPE OF GRANT Capital and revenue costs.
RANGE OF GRANTS Mostly up to £5,000.
SAMPLE GRANTS Holy Trinity Church and Hull City of Culture (£20,000 each); CASE (£10,000); 5 Senses (£5,000); Age UK East Riding and University of Hull (£2,500 each); Recycling Unlimited (£1,500); Alcohol and Drug Service and Parkstone Primary School (£1,000 each); Meningitis Now (£500).
FINANCES *Year* 2015/16 *Income* £279,839 *Grants* £286,090 *Grants to organisations* £285,190 *Assets* £6,888,149
TRUSTEES Kate Field; Mary Barker; Adrian Horsley.
OTHER INFORMATION The trust made more than 100 grants in 2015/16. The amount of grants given to individuals totalled around £900, although grants are usually not made to individuals.
HOW TO APPLY Apply in writing to the correspondent. The website states that each request should include: a brief history of the applicant/organisation and the relevant development strategy; where relevant, both company and charity registration numbers; a copy of the most recent financial accounts of the applicant; a detailed description of the project or activity; provision of a detailed cost breakdown/budget for the use of funds; where the applicant is a national organisation, details of historic activity providing specific benefit for Hull and/or East Riding residents; strategy for fundraising and other potential sources of support being pursued; contribution from own fundraising activities; description of the benefit being provided for local people and the numbers who are projected to enjoy the benefit; future viability of the activity or project; full postal address and postcode; email address; organisation, or home, telephone number and mobile number of person writing the letter; bank sort code and account number; and name of the bank account holder.
WHO TO APPLY TO John Barnes, Secretary, Greenmeades, Kemp Road, Swanland, North Ferriby, East Yorkshire HU14 3LY *Tel.* 01482 634664 *Email* john.barnes@herct.org.uk *Website* www.herct.org.uk

■ Hulme Trust Estates (Educational)

CC NO 532297 **ESTABLISHED** 1964
WHERE FUNDING CAN BE GIVEN Greater Manchester.
WHO CAN BENEFIT Educational establishments. According to previous accounts, 'all beneficiaries are higher educational establishments, all of which are registered charities'.
WHAT IS FUNDED This charity supports educational establishments in the Greater Manchester area. There are named beneficiaries which receive fixed, non-discretionary percentages of income, while a small percentage is distributed by the schools committee on a discretionary basis.
TYPE OF GRANT Set percentage to named beneficiaries and discretionary awards.
SAMPLE GRANTS Brasenose College (£88,000); Manchester University (£44,000); Schools Committee (£29,500); William Hulme's Grammar School (£25,000); Bury Grammar School and Hulme Grammar School Oldham (£5,500 each); Manchester High School for Girls (£4,600); Manchester Grammar School (£900).
FINANCES *Year* 2015 *Income* £237,558 *Grants* £284,000 *Grants to organisations* £284,000 *Assets* £12,138,266
TRUSTEES David Claxton; Thomas Hoyle; Ian Thompson; Peter Sidwell; Philip Parker; Ian Rankin; Sarah Newman; John Bowers.
OTHER INFORMATION The annual report 2015/16 explains that the trustees have made an 'interim distribution of £105,000 (2014 £100,000), and propose a second distribution of £145,000 (2014 £145,000) to maintain their principle of distributing 2.5% of the average value of the endowment fund over the last five years'. These values are included in the grant total. William Hulme's Grammar School receives 12% of the charity's income (after expenses).
HOW TO APPLY Apply in writing to the correspondent.
WHO TO APPLY TO Jonathan Aldersley, Secretary, Butcher and Barlow LLP, 3 Royal Mews, Gadbrook Park, Northwich, Cheshire CW9 7UD *Tel.* 01606 334309

■ Human Relief Foundation

CC NO 1126281 **ESTABLISHED** 1995
WHERE FUNDING CAN BE GIVEN Conflict and disaster areas worldwide, including Somalia, Ethiopia, Chechnya, Bosnia, Kosovo, Kashmir, Pakistan, India, Bangladesh, Afghanistan and Palestine; emergency relief anywhere in the world.
WHO CAN BENEFIT Organisations; individuals; communities; groups; charities; schools; hospitals; conflict and disaster areas worldwide.
WHAT IS FUNDED Humanitarian help; emergency aid; relief of poverty; education; health; infrastructure support and development; individuals; sponsorship schemes.
WHAT IS NOT FUNDED Medical expenses; tutors or examination fees.
TYPE OF GRANT Usually one-off.
SAMPLE GRANTS A list of beneficiaries was not available.

FINANCES *Year* 2014/15 *Income* £4,089,641 *Grants* £577,206 *Grants to organisations* £577,206 *Assets* £1,901,305

TRUSTEES Haytham Al-Khaffaf; Wael Musabbeh; Nooh Al-Kaddo; Haitham Al-Rawi; Mohanned Rahman.

OTHER INFORMATION The majority of the foundation's charitable expenditure consists of direct activities with only a part of it being grant-making.

HOW TO APPLY Apply in writing to the correspondent.

WHO TO APPLY TO Mohanned Rahman, Trustee, PO Box 194, Bradford, West Yorkshire BD7 1YW *Tel.* 01274 392727 *Fax* 01274 739992 *Email* donate@hrf.org.uk *Website* www.hrf.org.uk

■ The Humanitarian Trust

CC NO 208575 **ESTABLISHED** 1946

WHERE FUNDING CAN BE GIVEN UK and Israel.

WHO CAN BENEFIT Mostly, Jewish charitable organisations and educational institutions; individual students.

WHAT IS FUNDED General charitable purposes; academia and education; social welfare; medical causes. British citizens under the age of 30 can receive student grants of £200 each.

TYPE OF GRANT One-off student grants and long-term awards to organisations.

RANGE OF GRANTS Usually from £1,000 to £5,000.

SAMPLE GRANTS Friendship Village, Institute for Jewish Policy Research, Patterns of Prejudice, The Woolf Institute of Abrahamic Faiths and World Jewish Relief (£5,000 each); Oxford University – Isaiah Berlin Visiting Professorship (£4,500); One Voice Europe and Shaare Zedek (£3,000 each); Anne Frank Trust UK (£2,500); Cosgrove Care, Jerusalem Foundation and Neve Shalom (£2,000 each).

FINANCES *Year* 2015/16 *Income* £160,868 *Grants* £64,809 *Grants to organisations* £44,000 *Assets* £4,919,944

TRUSTEES Jacques Gunsbourg; Pierre Halban; Emmanuelle Gunsbourg-Kasavi; Alexander Halban.

OTHER INFORMATION In 2015/16 a total of 12 grants were made to organisations. £20,800 was expended in 'studentships' we have taken this as the figure for grants made to individuals.

HOW TO APPLY The annual report 2015/16 explains that 'the Trustees do not accept any unsolicited applications from Charities due to the ongoing relationship that it has with a number of organisations which fulfil its charitable objectives. However, the Trust occasionally invited charities to send in applications for consideration at Board meetings.'

WHO TO APPLY TO The Trustees, 20 Gloucester Place, London W1U 8HA *Tel.* 020 7486 7760

■ The Michael and Shirley Hunt Charitable Trust

CC NO 1063418 **ESTABLISHED** 1997

WHERE FUNDING CAN BE GIVEN UK and overseas.

WHO CAN BENEFIT Charitable organisations and individuals.

WHAT IS FUNDED The relief of hardship faced by prisoners and their families; the rehabilitation of prisoners; animal welfare; general charitable purposes.

WHAT IS NOT FUNDED Capital projects; overhead costs; support costs; fines; bail; legal costs; rent deposits.

TYPE OF GRANT One-off. The trustees prefer to assist with emergency operational funding rather than with capital projects.

RANGE OF GRANTS Up to £10,000.

SAMPLE GRANTS Disasters Emergency Committee – Nepal Earthquake Appeal (£10,000); St Barnabas Hospice (£6,000); Prisoners Abroad (£3,000); Keep Out and SOFA Project (£2,500 each); Cetacean Research and Rescue Unit (£1,300); Remus Memorial Horse Sanctuary and The Dog You Need (£1,000 each).

FINANCES *Year* 2015/16 *Income* £272,469 *Grants* £69,847 *Grants to organisations* £69,847 *Assets* £6,555,174

TRUSTEES Wanda Baker; Chester Hunt; Shirley Hunt; Deborah Jenkins; Kathy Mayberry.

OTHER INFORMATION During the year, 36 organisations received support. Grants to 56 individuals (under the 'prisoners' category) totalled £7,500.

HOW TO APPLY All applications have to be made in writing. Applications are considered upon receipt and formal meetings are held as necessary, at least once a year.

WHO TO APPLY TO Deborah Jenkins, Trustee, Ansty House, Henfield Road, Small Dole, Henfield, West Sussex BN5 9XH *Tel.* 01903 817116

■ The Albert Hunt Trust

CC NO 277318 **ESTABLISHED** 1979

WHERE FUNDING CAN BE GIVEN UK.

WHO CAN BENEFIT Registered charities that 'are actively engaged in [their] field of work' which fits the trust's funding criteria.

WHAT IS FUNDED The promotion and enhancement of physical and mental welfare. Grants are made in three categories: health and well-being; hospice appeals; and homeless appeals.

WHAT IS NOT FUNDED Research or the diagnosis and treatment of specific medical conditions; overseas work.

TYPE OF GRANT One-off; capital and core costs; projects; unrestricted funding.

RANGE OF GRANTS From £500 to £50,000, with most grants of between £1,000 and £3,000.

SAMPLE GRANTS Beats on Cancer (£50,000; Alexander Devine Children's Hospice (£25,000); Blesma and Nottinghamshire Hospice (£10,000 each); Hospice UK and Winter Comfort for the Homeless (£3,000 each); Cancer Support Scotland and Community Resources Network Scotland (£2,000 each); Action on Elder Abuse, Black Country Foodbank, Colchester Furniture Project, Cruse Bereavement Care – Hertfordshire, Disability Powys, Norfolk Deaf Association, Perth Autism Support, Rape Crisis – Wycombe, Chiltern and South Buckinghamshire); Single Homeless Project, St George's Hospital Charity and Young Asian Voices (£1,000 each).

FINANCES *Year* 2015/16 *Income* £1,666,114 *Grants* £1,775,750 *Grants to organisations* £1,775,750 *Assets* £53,809,833

TRUSTEES Breda McGuire; Stephen Harvey; Coutts & Co.; Ian Fleming.

HOW TO APPLY Applications should be made in writing to the correspondent by letter containing the following: the aims and objectives of your charity; the nature of your appeal; the total target if for a specific project; contributions received against the target; your organisation's registered charity number; and any other relevant factors. Appeals are considered on a monthly basis. The trust has previously stated that no unsolicited correspondence will be acknowledged unless an application receives favourable consideration.

WHO TO APPLY TO Wealth Advisory Services, The Albert Hunt Trust, Wealth Advisory Services, Coutts & Co., 440 Strand, London WC2R 0QS *Tel.* 020 7663 6825

■ The Hunter Foundation

SC NO SC027532 **ESTABLISHED** 1998

WHERE FUNDING CAN BE GIVEN UK; Sub-Saharan Africa, primarily Rwanda.

WHO CAN BENEFIT Charitable organisations, schools and universities, social enterprises.

WHAT IS FUNDED The foundation's objectives are to support economic opportunity for all by investing in three critical pillars of enablement – poverty alleviation, education and entrepreneurship.

TYPE OF GRANT Strategic partnership; programmes.

RANGE OF GRANTS £5,000 to £200,000.

SAMPLE GRANTS New Cumnock Regeneration and Scottish Edge (£200,000 each); Coach Core (£190,000); STV Appeal (£150,000); Great Ormond Street Hospital (£100,000); Scottish Business Awards (£90,000); Cash for Kids (£55,000); Pancreatic Cancer UK (£50,000); David Hume Institute (£40,000); Ben View Resource Centre and Livingstone Volunteers (£10,000 each); Glasgow Bin Lorry Crash Donation (£5,000).

FINANCES *Year* 2015/16 *Income* £4,170,165 *Grants* £1,724,385 *Grants to organisations* £1,724,385 *Assets* £4,491,331

TRUSTEES Sir Tom Hunter; Lady Marion Hunter; Jim McMahon.

HOW TO APPLY The foundation has previously stated that it is proactive and does not seek applications.

WHO TO APPLY TO Tom Hunter, Chair, Marathon House, Olympic Business Park, Drybridge Road, Dundonald, Ayrshire KA2 9AE *Email* info@thehunterfoundation.co.uk *Website* www.thehunterfoundation.co.uk

■ Miss Agnes H. Hunter's Trust

SC NO SC004843 **ESTABLISHED** 1954

WHERE FUNDING CAN BE GIVEN Projects operating in Scotland.

WHO CAN BENEFIT Registered charities.

WHAT IS FUNDED Support for people suffering from arthritis and cancer; support for people with disabilities including physical disability, visual impairment or illness, people with mental health problems or learning disabilities; education and training of disadvantaged people.

WHAT IS NOT FUNDED Organisations that are not formally recognised as charities; organisations under the control of the UK or Scottish government; projects which are primarily intended to promote political or religious beliefs; individuals (including students); expeditions, overseas travel or international projects; projects outside Scotland; general appeals or circulars (including contributions to endowment funds); statutory requirements of local authorities, hospitals, schools, universities and colleges; clinical work within hospitals; animal welfare; the breeding and training of assistance/guide dogs for the blind/people with disabilities; the bricks and mortar aspect of capital projects; initiatives focused on sports, arts or the environment, except where the subject is being used as a vehicle to engage with one of the trust's core policy groups; normal youth club activities. According to the website, medical research and hospices will **no longer** be funded.

TYPE OF GRANT One-off and recurrent; capital and core costs; project funding; salaries.

RANGE OF GRANTS £4,000 to £20,000; main grants start at £4,000; small grants are up to £4,000 (the programme is very limited).

SAMPLE GRANTS RNIB (£20,000); Islay and Jura Community Enterprises Ltd and Waverly Care (£12,000 each); Citizens Theatre and FAIR (£10,000 each); John Muir Trust and Netherthird Community Action Training (£8,000 each); Scottish Business in the Community and Whiteinich Centre (£7,000 each); Glasgow Women's Library (£5,000); Edinburgh Headway Group (£4,000).

FINANCES *Year* 2015/16 *Income* £642,696 *Grants* £349,085 *Grants to organisations* £349,085 *Assets* £535,847

TRUSTEES Walter Thompson; Keith Burdon; Alison Campbell; Elaine Crichton; Norman Dunning; John Hume; Neil Paterson.

HOW TO APPLY At the time of writing (June 2017) both the main grant programme and the small grant programme were closed pending a move to a new online application system. Check the trust's website for information on the new application process.

WHO TO APPLY TO Sarah Wright, Trust Manager, Davidson House, 57 Queen Charlotte Street, Edinburgh EH6 7EY *Tel.* 0131 538 5496 *Email* s.wright@agneshunter.org.uk *Website* www.agneshunter.org.uk

■ The Hunting Horn General Charitable Trust

CC NO 1149358 **ESTABLISHED** 2012

WHERE FUNDING CAN BE GIVEN UK and overseas.

WHO CAN BENEFIT Registered charities.

WHAT IS FUNDED General charitable purposes, including Christian causes.

RANGE OF GRANTS Up to £50,000.

SAMPLE GRANTS Campaign for Female Education (CAMFED) (£50,000); Eden Baptist Church (£45,500); Trinity Church (£20,000); Sightsavers and SSAFA (£10,000 each); Evangelical Theological College (£7,200); OM UK (£6,700).

FINANCES *Year* 2015/16 *Income* £61,429 *Grants* £156,112 *Grants to organisations* £156,112 *Assets* £4,684,354

TRUSTEES Martin Oldfield; Sean Dubrovnik Jackson.

OTHER INFORMATION The trust also donated goods, valued at £1,700, to Eden Baptist Church.

HOW TO APPLY Apply in writing to the correspondent.

WHO TO APPLY TO Sean Dubrovnik Jackson, Trustee, 3 Adams Road, Cambridge CB3 9AD *Tel.* 01223 476769 *Email* huntinghorn@fastmail.com

■ The Huntingdon Foundation Ltd

CC NO 286504 **ESTABLISHED** 1984

WHERE FUNDING CAN BE GIVEN UK, mainly London; Israel.

WHO CAN BENEFIT Organisations benefitting Jewish people; Jewish schools.

WHAT IS FUNDED Jewish causes; education and training.

WHAT IS NOT FUNDED Our research indicates that grants are not normally made to individuals.

RANGE OF GRANTS About £1,000 to £60,000.

SAMPLE GRANTS A list of beneficiaries was not included in the most recent accounts. It does,

however, state that grants were paid to institutions, mainly in support of Jewish schools.
FINANCES *Year* 2015/16 *Income* £955,180 *Grants* £312,730 *Grants to organisations* £312,730 *Assets* £14,533,586
TRUSTEES Benjamin Perl; Dr Shoshanna Perl; Jonathan Perl; Joseph Perl; Rachel Jeidel; Naomi Tsorotzkin.
HOW TO APPLY Apply in writing to the correspondent. The trustees meet several times a year.
WHO TO APPLY TO Benjamin Perl, Trustee, 8 Goodyers Gardens, London NW4 2HD *Tel.* 020 8202 2282

■ Huntingdon Freemen's Trust

CC NO 1044573 **ESTABLISHED** 1993
WHERE FUNDING CAN BE GIVEN Huntingdon, including Oxmoor, Hartford, Sapley, Stukeley Meadows and Hinchingbrooke Park.
WHO CAN BENEFIT Local groups and organisations; individuals who are in need; students.
WHAT IS FUNDED Relief in need (including sickness and health care provision); provision of pensions; educational needs; recreation and leisure.
WHAT IS NOT FUNDED Applications from outside the boundaries of Huntingdon (the adjoining parishes, such as The Stukeleys, Godmanchester, Houghton and Wyton, Kings Ripton, Brampton and so on) are not supported. The trust cannot cover services that the government or local councils are supposed to provide, but can supplement them.
SAMPLE GRANTS A list of beneficiaries was not available.
FINANCES *Year* 2015/16 *Income* £425,204 *Grants* £442,847 *Grants to organisations* £442,847 *Assets* £15,775,489
TRUSTEES Ann Beevor; Brian Bradshaw; Jonathan Hampstead; Richard Hough; Kate Parker; Michael Shellens.
OTHER INFORMATION We were unable to determine the amount given to individuals for relief-in-need and educational purposes. The trust can also provide specialised equipment on long-term loan.
HOW TO APPLY Application forms for organisations and students can be downloaded from the trust's website. Individual applications can be made in writing to the correspondent. Applications are considered at monthly meetings.
WHO TO APPLY TO Ruth Black, Chief Executive, 37 High Street, Huntingdon, Cambridgeshire PE29 3AQ *Tel.* 01480 414909 *Email* info@huntingdonfreemen.org.uk *Website* www.huntingdonfreemen.org.uk

■ Hurdale Charity Ltd

CC NO 276997 **ESTABLISHED** 1978
WHERE FUNDING CAN BE GIVEN UK and overseas.
WHO CAN BENEFIT Charitable organisations benefitting Jewish people and promoting the Orthodox Jewish way of life.
WHAT IS FUNDED The advancement of the Orthodox Jewish religion; education; medical/health causes.
TYPE OF GRANT One-off and recurring.
RANGE OF GRANTS Up to £260,000.
SAMPLE GRANTS Moundfield Charities Ltd (£260,000); Harofeh Donations Ltd (£259,000); Fountain of Chessed Ltd (£208,000); Springfield Trust Ltd (£108,000).
FINANCES *Year* 2015/16 *Income* £1,511,461 *Grants* £1,175,800 *Grants to organisations* £1,175,800 *Assets* £21,925,783
TRUSTEES David Oestreicher; Abraham Oestreicher; Jacob Oestreicher; Benjamin Oestreicher.
OTHER INFORMATION A full list of beneficiaries was not included in the accounts; we have included the beneficiaries named under the 'Related party transactions' section of the accounts.
HOW TO APPLY Apply in writing to the correspondent.
WHO TO APPLY TO Abraham Oestreicher, Trustee, 162 Osbaldeston Road, London N16 6NJ

■ The Hutchinson Charitable Trust

CC NO 1155643 **ESTABLISHED** 2012
WHERE FUNDING CAN BE GIVEN Worldwide, with a special interest in Fenland (especially Wisbech).
WHO CAN BENEFIT Charitable organisations.
WHAT IS FUNDED General charitable purposes, but mainly agriculture, disadvantaged people and education, as well as local causes in Fenland (especially Wisbech).
SAMPLE GRANTS A list of beneficiaries was not available.
FINANCES *Year* 2015 *Income* £2,444,260 *Grants* £79,100 *Grants to organisations* £79,100 *Assets* £3,299,471
TRUSTEES Colin Hutchinson; David Hutchinson; Jean Hutchinson; Michael Hutchinson.
OTHER INFORMATION A list of beneficiaries was not included in the annual report and accounts.
HOW TO APPLY Apply in writing to the correspondent. The trustees meet at least twice a year.
WHO TO APPLY TO Clive Harrod, 10 Victory Road, Wisbech PE13 2PU *Tel.* 01945 586409

■ The Hutton Foundation

CC NO 1106521 **ESTABLISHED** 2004
WHERE FUNDING CAN BE GIVEN UK and overseas.
WHO CAN BENEFIT Charitable organisations.
WHAT IS FUNDED General charitable purposes, particularly Christian causes; health.
TYPE OF GRANT Recurring; one-off.
SAMPLE GRANTS International Theological Institute (£66,500); Emmanuel College (£2,400). Other donations totalled £36,000.
FINANCES *Year* 2015 *Income* £16,001 *Grants* £60,000 *Grants to organisations* £60,000
TRUSTEES Graham Hutton; Amanda Hutton; Richard Hutton; James Hutton; Helen Hutton.
OTHER INFORMATION This charity's latest accounts were not available to view on the Charity Commission's website due to its low income. We have therefore estimated the grant total.
HOW TO APPLY Unsolicited applications are not supported. Those interested in learning more about the foundation are encouraged to contact the correspondent.
WHO TO APPLY TO Jackie Hart, Hutton Collins Partners LLP, 50 Pall Mall, London SW1Y 5JH *Tel.* 07786 921033 *Email* jackie.hart@huttoncollins.com *Website* www.huttoncollins.com/about-us/hutton-collins-foundation

■ The Nani Huyu Charitable Trust

CC NO 1082868 **ESTABLISHED** 2000
WHERE FUNDING CAN BE GIVEN UK, but there is a strong preference for causes within 50 miles of Bristol (the old Avon area).
WHO CAN BENEFIT Charitable organisations, with a strong preference for small local charities.

WHAT IS FUNDED The annual report for 2014/15 states that the objects of the charity are 'to assist people who are underprivileged, disadvantaged or ill, young people in matters of health, accommodation and training and those requiring assistance or medical care at the end of their lives, principally within Bristol and its surroundings'.
WHAT IS NOT FUNDED National charities.
TYPE OF GRANT Capital and revenue costs; one-off and up to one year.
RANGE OF GRANTS £1,000 to £15,000.
SAMPLE GRANTS Cross Roads Care (£15,000); Rainbow Centre for Children, Southside Family Project and Womankind (£14,000 each); Young Bristol (£12,000); Brain Tumour Support (£10,000); Fairbridge (£8,000); Bristol Meditation (£7,000); Somerset Community Foundation, The Harbour and Wellspring Counselling (£6,000 each); Bristol Children's Help Society (£5,000); Blenheim Scouts (£2,000); Relate (£1,000).
FINANCES *Year* 2014/15 *Income* £216,432 *Grants* £162,000 *Grants to organisations* £162,000 *Assets* £5,054,986
TRUSTEES Ben Whitmore; Charles Thatcher; Maureen Whitmore; Susan Webb.
OTHER INFORMATION The 2014/15 accounts were the latest available at the time of writing (May 2017). In 2014/15 grants were made to 20 organisations.
HOW TO APPLY Apply in writing to the correspondent.
WHO TO APPLY TO Maureen Whitmore, Trustee, Rusling House, Butcombe, Bristol BS40 7XQ *Tel.* 01275 474433 *Email* maureensimonwhitmore@btinternet.com

■ The P. Y. N. and B. Hyams Trust

CC NO 268129 **ESTABLISHED** 1974
WHERE FUNDING CAN BE GIVEN Worldwide.
WHO CAN BENEFIT Charitable organisations.
WHAT IS FUNDED General charitable purposes.
WHAT IS NOT FUNDED Individuals.
SAMPLE GRANTS A list of beneficiaries was not available in the accounts.
FINANCES *Year* 2015/16 *Income* £77,601 *Grants* £62,710 *Grants to organisations* £62,710 *Assets* £1,027,720
TRUSTEES Miriam Hyams; Naresh Shah.
HOW TO APPLY Applications may be made in writing to the correspondent, but note that the trust has previously stated that funds are fully committed and unsolicited applications are not welcome.
WHO TO APPLY TO Naresh Shah, Trustee, Lubbock Fine, Paternoster House, 3rd Floor, 65 St Paul's Churchyard, London EC4M 8AB *Tel.* 020 7490 7766

■ Hyde Charitable Trust (Youth Plus)

CC NO 289888 **ESTABLISHED** 1984
WHERE FUNDING CAN BE GIVEN Priority areas are: Brighton and Hove Borough Council; London Borough of Brent; Chichester District Council; London Borough of Croydon; London Borough of Islington; London Borough of Lewisham; London borough of Lambeth; London Borough of Southwark; Medway Towns; Thanet District Council; London Borough of Greenwich; West Sussex District Council.
WHO CAN BENEFIT Organisations working in Hyde Housing communities; social entrepreneurs.
WHAT IS FUNDED The Successful Places Fund supports the development and implementation of activities or services designed to mitigate or prevent social challenges that negatively impact local communities and those which create a barrier to Hyde fulfilling its social purpose. Grants are also available to social entrepreneurs for projects benefitting older people in priority areas.
WHAT IS NOT FUNDED Successful Places Fund Grants cannot be spent on: activities or expenditure that happens or starts before a grant is confirmed and payment dates are set; funds reimbursed or set to be reimbursed by other grants; gifts to individuals (other than promotional items) with a value of no more than £10 a year to any one individual; entertainment (entertaining for this purpose means anything that would be a taxable benefit to the person being entertained, according to current UK tax regulations); loan repayments, endowments, statutory fines, criminal fines or penalties; any other activity which Hyde in their absolute discretion consider is not directly associated with developing the programme; fundraising activities for your organisation or others; land or building projects where the ownership or lease is not yet in place; activities that promote political or religious beliefs; projects that only support people who do not live in Hyde areas; projects that you cannot maintain because of high ongoing costs or the need for costly specialist skills; purchase of alcohol or tobacco; any unlawful/illegal/fraudulent activity.
RANGE OF GRANTS Organisations can apply for a maximum of £20,000 per 12-month period.
SAMPLE GRANTS Digital Inclusion (£79,000); Be Secure (£38,000); Cash4Communities (£34,000); Helping Hands (£25,000); Pitch2Enrich (£16,000).
FINANCES *Year* 2015/16 *Income* £389,000 *Grants* £374,000 *Grants to organisations* £287,000 *Assets* £201,000
TRUSTEES Geron Walker; Jonathan Prichard; Michelle Walcott; Andrew Moncreiff; Christopher Carlisle; Paul Cook.
OTHER INFORMATION The amount of grants given to individuals totalled £87,000.
HOW TO APPLY The trust has informed us that 'because the funding available is limited and targeted at Hyde residents the trust does not encourage unsolicited applications'. Applications to the Successful Places fund can be made through the online application portal. Applications to the Successful Places Fund are assessed by a panel four times a year between April and February. Check the website for details of application deadlines.
WHO TO APPLY TO John Edwards, Secretary, Grants Administration Team, Hyde Plus, Hollingsworth House, PO BOX 51182, London SE13 9BU *Tel.* 020 3207 2762 *Email* grantsadministration@hyde-housing.co.uk *Website* hydehousing.flexigrant.com

■ Hyde Park Place Estate Charity

CC NO 212439 **ESTABLISHED** 1914
WHERE FUNDING CAN BE GIVEN City of Westminster.
WHO CAN BENEFIT Charities and community organisations.
WHAT IS FUNDED Social welfare; education; ecclesiastical purposes.
WHAT IS NOT FUNDED Educational grants to foreign students. Grants will not be given in aid of campaigning activities, academic research,

animal charities, or the furtherance of religious causes.

TYPE OF GRANT One-off or recurring. The trust will consider capital costs, core costs, start-up costs, running costs, salaries or project costs.

RANGE OF GRANTS Up to £12,000 but mostly £1,000 to £5,000.

SAMPLE GRANTS St George's Hanover Square Parochial Church Council (£15,000, in two grants); The House of St Barnabas and The Marylebone Project and Westminster Boating Base (£5,000 each); St John's Wood Adventure Playground and Wigmore Hall Trust (£4,000 each); Westbourne Park Family Centre (£3,000); The Food Chain and Whizz-Kidz (£2,000); St Augustine's Church of England Primary School (£900).

FINANCES *Year* 2015/16 *Income* £485,014 *Grants* £182,117 *Grants to organisations* £167,618 *Assets* £14,014,087

TRUSTEES Revd Roderick Leece; Mark Hewitt; Michael Beckett.

OTHER INFORMATION Grants were made to approximately 103 individuals totalling £167,500.

HOW TO APPLY Apply in writing to the correspondent. The trustees meet four times a year.

WHO TO APPLY TO Shirley Vaughan, St George's Church, The Vestry, 2A Mill Street, London W1S 1FX *Tel.* 020 7629 0874 *Fax* 020 7629 0874 *Website* www.stgeorgeshanoversquare.org

■ Ibbett Trust

CC NO 234329 **ESTABLISHED** 1964

WHERE FUNDING CAN BE GIVEN Unrestricted, in practice UK with a preference for local organisations in Bedford and overseas.

WHO CAN BENEFIT Local charitable organisations.

WHAT IS FUNDED The trust's main objective is to accumulate funds to provide a home in the Bedford area with care facilities for older people, thereafter grants are for general charitable purposes, especially health and the relief of need for older people and children.

RANGE OF GRANTS Up to £10,000.

SAMPLE GRANTS Bechar (£10,000); Bedford Guild House and Families United Network (£5,000 each); Christian Aid (£3,000); Keech Cottage Children's Hospice and Marie Curie Cancer Care (£2,500 each).

FINANCES *Year* 2015/16 *Income* £299,162 *Grants* £65,100 *Grants to organisations* £65,100 *Assets* £16,092,485

TRUSTEES Clifton Ibbett; John Ibbett; Mrs B. Plumbly; Mr K. Borneo.

OTHER INFORMATION Grants were made to 51 organisations during the year, with donations for less than £2,000 totalling £37,100. The trust also provides a care home and associated extra-care flats.

HOW TO APPLY Apply in writing to the correspondent.

WHO TO APPLY TO Mrs B. Plumbly, Trustee, c/o Estate Office, Milton Parc, Milton Ernest, Bedford MK44 1YU *Tel.* 01234 827244

■ IBM United Kingdom Trust

CC NO 290462 **ESTABLISHED** 1984

WHERE FUNDING CAN BE GIVEN UK, Europe, Middle East and Africa.

WHO CAN BENEFIT The trust gives preference to organisations concerned with people disadvantaged by poverty and/or at risk of digital exclusion.

WHAT IS FUNDED The focus areas for IBM's community investment are: increasing the scope, usage and understanding of information technology through education; providing information technology and services to enable charities and disadvantaged people to acquire skills; research into information technology; the promotion of volunteering by IBM employees. The vast majority of IBM's community investment is delivered through specific programmes initiated and developed by IBM in partnership with organisations with appropriate professional expertise.

WHAT IS NOT FUNDED The trust does not provide core funding or contribute to appeals for building projects, religious or sectarian organisations, animal charities, individuals (including students), overseas activities or expeditions, recreational and sports clubs, appeals by third parties on behalf of charities or individuals. The company does not currently offer full-time secondments of employees to voluntary organisations.

TYPE OF GRANT Equipment and programme costs.

RANGE OF GRANTS £21,000 to £65,000.

SAMPLE GRANTS Lagos State Universal Education Board (£64,000); Vlaamse Dienst voor Arbeidsvoorziening (£49,000); Malindi Constituency (£42,000); Emmaus Connect (£34,000); City of Groningen (£32,000); Egyptian Ministry of Social Solidarity (£30,000); University of Swansea (£27,000); National College for Digital Skills (£21,000).

FINANCES *Year* 2015 *Income* £938,000 *Grants* £1,021,000 *Grants to organisations* £1,021,000 *Assets* £4,574,000

TRUSTEES Brendan Dineen; Prof. Derek Bell; Jonathan Batty; Anne Wolfe; Naomi Hill.

OTHER INFORMATION Beneficiaries were split into four different categories: increasing the use of technology in education; provision of IT and other services; promoting volunteering; and support for research.

HOW TO APPLY Very few unsolicited requests are considered. If requests are submitted then these should be by email or in writing and include a brief résumé of the aims of the organisation and a detail of what assistance is required. Those considering making an application are advised to telephone first for advice.

WHO TO APPLY TO Mark Wakefield, Trust Manager, IBM United Kingdom Ltd, 1PG1, 76–78 Upper Ground, London SE1 9PZ *Tel.* 020 7202 3608 *Email* wakefim@uk.ibm.com

■ Ibrahim Foundation Ltd

CC NO 1149438/SC043491 **ESTABLISHED** 2012

WHERE FUNDING CAN BE GIVEN UK and overseas.

WHO CAN BENEFIT Registered charities; educational institutions; community projects.

WHAT IS FUNDED General charitable purposes; social welfare; health; education. The foundation likes to fund work which others may find hard to fund, such as new ideas or core costs. There is particular interest in: community building; environment; strengthening non-profits; supporting families. Specific current projects concern development projects overseas, children and young people and the Scotland Institute, a think tank also founded by Dr Azeem Ibrahim in 2012.

WHAT IS NOT FUNDED Applications from the same organisation in successive grant cycles.

TYPE OF GRANT Capital, core and project costs.

RANGE OF GRANTS £5,000 to £55,000.

SAMPLE GRANTS A detailed breakdown of grants was not featured in the accounts. In 2015 the foundation gave grants within three main areas: Building Community (£210,500); Strengthening Not-For-Profits (£61,500); Supporting Families (£3,500).

FINANCES *Year* 2015/16 *Income* £363,429 *Grants* £275,461 *Grants to organisations* £275,461 *Assets* £24,107

TRUSTEES Dr Azeem Ibrahim; Adeel Ibrahim; Aadil Butt.

OTHER INFORMATION It would appear that currently support is given to projects already assisted and chosen by Dr Ibrahim.

HOW TO APPLY Initial contact can be made via the foundation's website, although potential applicants should note that most funding is likely to go to projects and organisations with which the foundation and Dr Ibrahim already have an involvement.

WHO TO APPLY TO Dr Azeem Ibrahim, Trustee, 18 Little Street, Glasgow G3 8DQ *Tel.* 0141 416 1991 *Email* info@ibrahimfoundation.com *Website* www.ibrahimfoundation.com

■ ICE Futures Charitable Trust

CC NO 1048724 **ESTABLISHED** 1995

WHERE FUNDING CAN BE GIVEN UK, with some preference for London.

WHO CAN BENEFIT Charitable organisations.

WHAT IS FUNDED General charitable purposes, with the specific aims of relieving poverty and advancing education, particularly the welfare and education of children and people with special needs.

WHAT IS NOT FUNDED Grants are not made to overseas causes.

TYPE OF GRANT One-off with some recurring.

RANGE OF GRANTS £200 to £6,000.

SAMPLE GRANTS Action Medical Research and The Sick Children's Trust (£6,000 each); Vimba (£5,300); Ahoy Centre and St Joseph's Hospice (£4,000 each); Aidis Trust (£3,100); React and Taylor Made Dreams (£2,500 each); Friends of Castledon School and Learning Through Landscapes (£1,500 each); The Kevin Harte Golf Day (£200).

FINANCES *Year* 2015/16 *Income* £51,692 *Grants* £60,979 *Grants to organisations* £60,979 *Assets* £272,963

TRUSTEES A. Lewis; Jonathan Maidman; Peter Ottino; Sir Bob Reid; David Peniket.

OTHER INFORMATION The total amount of the grants made in 2015 (£67,000) was significantly lower than in 2014 (£230,000).

HOW TO APPLY Apply in writing to the correspondent, although the funds available for unsolicited applications are minimal.

WHO TO APPLY TO Lisa Hood, Secretary, c/o ICE Futures Europe, Milton Gate, 60 Chiswell Street, London EC1Y 4SA *Tel.* 020 7012 8793

■ The Idlewild Trust

CC NO 268124 **ESTABLISHED** 1974

WHERE FUNDING CAN BE GIVEN UK.

WHO CAN BENEFIT Registered charities only; museums, galleries and other venues concerned with the visual arts and crafts; educational institutions.

WHAT IS FUNDED Performing and fine arts; culture; restoration and conservation; education; preservation of buildings and items of historical interest or national importance.

WHAT IS NOT FUNDED General exclusions: individuals; projects based outside the UK; charities and projects in the Channel Islands or the Isle of Man; organisations in receipt of any category of grant from Idlewild Trust within 24 months of the last award (24 months is measured between decision dates); projects that have been completed; any organisation with income of less than £5,000 per annum; CICs; social enterprises unless they are also UK-registered charities; organisations that are applying for a UK-registered charitable status but do not yet have a registered charity number; UK-registered charities that have not submitted their most recent annual return and accounts within the required time to the Charity Commission or OSCR; organisations whose sole or main purpose is to make grants from funds collected; general national or local appeals; endowment or deficit funding; primary and secondary schools, sixth form and further education colleges; universities and further education institutions in receipt of annual government grants or whose primary source of income is student fees (although the trust will consider applications from museums and galleries of national importance within universities that are UK publicly exempt charities and have their own management and budgets). For specific exclusions from particular schemes, refer to the website.

TYPE OF GRANT Projects; buildings; refurbishment; capital work; exhibition costs; event and performance expenditure; research.

RANGE OF GRANTS Up to £5,000.

SAMPLE GRANTS Black Country Living Museum and Castle Acre (£5,000 each); Birmingham Royal Ballet and St Albans Cathedral (£4,000 each); St Mary's Church Parish Pastoral Council and St Peter's Church (£3,000 each); The Poetry Trust (£2,700); Northern Ballet (£2,300); Foundling Museum (£1,500); Soho Theatre (£1,000); Eastbourne Symphony Orchestra (£500).

FINANCES *Year* 2015 *Income* £191,343 *Grants* £180,200 *Grants to organisations* £180,200 *Assets* £5,157,099

TRUSTEES Jonathan Ouvry; Tony Ford; Dr Tessa Murdoch; Helen McCabe; John Gittens; Tessa Mayhew.

OTHER INFORMATION Funding is given no more frequently than once every two years to the same applicant.

HOW TO APPLY The trust now uses an online application process. Potential applicants are welcome to telephone the trust to discuss their application and confirm eligibility. The trustees meet twice a year usually in May and November – exact dates and deadlines are published on the website. The outcome of the application is communicated within a fortnight of the trustees' meeting. Grants will not be awarded to any one charity more frequently than every two years. Unsuccessful applicants can re-apply immediately.

WHO TO APPLY TO Rachel Oglethorpe, Director, Unit 1A, Taylors Yard, 67 Alderbrook Street, London SW12 8AD *Tel.* 020 8772 3155 *Email* info@idlewildtrust.org.uk *Website* www.idlewildtrust.org.uk/apply-grant

■ IGO Foundation Ltd

CC NO 1148316 **ESTABLISHED** 2012

WHERE FUNDING CAN BE GIVEN Worldwide; in practice UK, Israel and the USA.

WHO CAN BENEFIT Charitable organisations.

WHAT IS FUNDED The relief of poverty; the advancement of the Jewish religion; the advancement of public education in the knowledge of Jewish history and culture; general charitable purposes.

SAMPLE GRANTS A list of beneficiaries was not available.

FINANCES *Year* 2015/16 *Income* £97,343 *Grants* £92,106 *Grants to organisations* £92,106 *Assets* £867,813

TRUSTEES Abraham Lipschitz; Bernard Ost; Gita Ost.

OTHER INFORMATION In 2015/16 the foundation also expended £2,800 on food parcels.

HOW TO APPLY Apply in writing to the correspondent.

WHO TO APPLY TO Bernard Ost, Trustee, 29 Grosvenor Gardens, London NW11 0HE

■ The Iliffe Family Charitable Trust

CC NO 273437 **ESTABLISHED** 1977

WHERE FUNDING CAN BE GIVEN UK, with some preference for West Berkshire.

WHO CAN BENEFIT Registered charities. The majority of donations are made to charities already known to the trustees. Thereafter, preference is given to charities in which the trust has a special interest.

WHAT IS FUNDED General charitable purposes; social welfare; education; Christianity; conservation; medical causes.
WHAT IS NOT FUNDED Grants are not made to individuals and rarely to non-registered charities.
RANGE OF GRANTS £500 to £25,000.
SAMPLE GRANTS Newbury and District Agricultural Society – new livestock building (£25,000); Afghan Connection (£10,500); Jubilee Sailing Trust and Royal National Lifeboat Institution (£10,000 each); Berkshire Community Foundation (£5,000); Yattendon and Frilsham Christian Stewardship (£3,000); Red Squirrel Survival Trust (£2,500); Southampton General Hospital – Oncology Unit (£1,000); Falkland Islands Memorial Chapel Trust, Macmillan Cancer Care and West Berkshire Citizens Advice (£500 each).
FINANCES *Year* 2015/16 *Income* £37,560 *Grants* £86,150 *Grants to organisations* £86,150 *Assets* £1,305,703
TRUSTEES Lord Iliffe; The Hon. Edward Iliffe; Catherine Fleming.
OTHER INFORMATION In 2015/16 a total of 17 grants were made.
HOW TO APPLY Apply in writing to the correspondent. Only successful applications will be acknowledged. Grants are considered at ad hoc meetings of the trustees, held throughout the year.
WHO TO APPLY TO Catherine Fleming, Trustee, Barn Close, Burnt Hill, Yattendon, Berkshire RG18 0UX *Email* ifct@yattendon.co.uk

■ Imagine Foundation

CC NO 1152864 **ESTABLISHED** 2013
WHERE FUNDING CAN BE GIVEN UK.
WHO CAN BENEFIT Registered charities and other voluntary organisations.
WHAT IS FUNDED Small scale projects and young charities with a focus on disadvantaged communities, empowering individuals and increasing community cohesion.
WHAT IS NOT FUNDED Individuals.
TYPE OF GRANT Ongoing partnerships; occasional new grants.
RANGE OF GRANTS £1,000 to £35,000.
SAMPLE GRANTS School of Hard Knocks (£35,500 in two grants); Thrive (£11,100); Bike Back and Community Cafe (£10,000 each); Vox Liminus (£8,300); Orts and Roots and Community Coffee (£5,000 each); AFRIL and Paradise Coop (£3,000 each); Oxfordshire My Life Choice Association (£1,400).
FINANCES *Year* 2015 *Income* £316,574 *Grants* £144,530 *Grants to organisations* £144,530 *Assets* £369,060
TRUSTEES Phil Stratton; Steve Eyre; Diane Eyre; Kerry McLeish; Kerry Maloney.
OTHER INFORMATION The foundation mainly provides grants to charities with which it has ongoing partnerships but has a limited capacity to take on new projects. They are primarily focusing small-scale newer charitable projects and organisations that are less than four years old with an annual income of less than £200,000.
HOW TO APPLY The foundation accepts applications by email only and operates three application windows in March, June and October. Applications received outside these windows will not be considered. The foundation does not have an application form and requests the broad framework of a project rather than lots of detail at the first stage.
WHO TO APPLY TO Steve Eyre, Trustee, Lower Farm, Oakley Road, Chinnor, Oxfordshire OX39 4HR *Email* funding@if-trust.org *Website* www.if-trust.org

■ Impetus – The Private Equity Foundation (Impetus – PEF)

CC NO 1152262 **ESTABLISHED** 2013
WHERE FUNDING CAN BE GIVEN UK.
WHO CAN BENEFIT Registered charities and social enterprises.
WHAT IS FUNDED Funding, management support from the investment team and specialist expertise from pro bono professionals for organisations supporting disadvantaged people aged 11–24.
TYPE OF GRANT Development and strategic funding along with management and pro bono support.
RANGE OF GRANTS £6,000 to £750,000.
SAMPLE GRANTS Tomorrow's People (£762,000); Street League (£384,000); Place2Be (£435,500); IntoUniversity (£200,000); Family Links (£119,000); TwentyTwenty (£46,000); Dartington Social Research Unit (£27,000); Centre of Economic and Social Inclusion (£10,400); Prisoner's Education Trust (£6,200).
FINANCES *Year* 2015 *Income* £11,464,569 *Grants* £4,302,957 *Grants to organisations* £4,302,957 *Assets* £13,439,108
TRUSTEES Louis Elson; Craig Dearden-Phillips; Johannes Huth; Prof. Becky Francis; Lionel Assant; Marc Boughton; Nathaniel Sloane; Stephen Dawson; Hanneke Smits; Nikos Stathopoulos; Caroline Mason; Lisa Stone; Patrick Healy; Simon Turner.
OTHER INFORMATION The foundation was formed from the merger of the Impetus Trust and Private Equity Foundation.
HOW TO APPLY The foundation's website states that it does not accept unsolicited applications and instead work through referrals from trusted partners who know its investment model. Once a potential charity has been identified, it will undergo a screening process to determine eligibility for the portfolio.
WHO TO APPLY TO The Trustees, 138 Eversholt Street, London NW1 1BU *Tel.* 020 3474 1000 *Email* info@impetus-pef.org.uk *Website* www.impetus-pef.org.uk/how-we-work/supporting-charities

■ Incommunities Foundation

CC NO 1152959 **ESTABLISHED** 2013
WHERE FUNDING CAN BE GIVEN Focus on Bradford.
WHO CAN BENEFIT Local organisations and projects.
WHAT IS FUNDED Community development, with a focus on: employment and training; and young people.
RANGE OF GRANTS Around £50,000.
SAMPLE GRANTS Sporting Chance (£62,000); All Things Playful (£47,000).
FINANCES *Year* 2015/16 *Income* £219,000 *Grants* £276,000 *Grants to organisations* £276,000 *Assets* £30,000
TRUSTEES Alison Herbert; David Kennedy; Elizabeth Weatherill.
OTHER INFORMATION Funding is given to both internally operated activities and external requests. A detailed list of beneficiaries was not included within the annual report and accounts for 2015/16. However, the grant expenditure was broken down into the following three categories: young people (£129,000); sports coaching (£74,000); employment and training (£73,000).
HOW TO APPLY Apply in writing to the correspondent.

WHO TO APPLY TO The Trustees, c/o Robert Ward, Incommunities Group Ltd, The Quays, Victoria Street, Shipley, West Yorkshire BD17 7BN *Tel.* 01274 254000 *Email* enquiry@incommunities.co.uk *Website* www.incommunities.co.uk

■ The Indigo Trust

CC NO 1075920 **ESTABLISHED** 1999

WHERE FUNDING CAN BE GIVEN Primarily sub-Saharan Africa.

WHO CAN BENEFIT Charitable organisations.

WHAT IS FUNDED Technology-driven projects for social change in Sub-Saharan Africa which focus on transparency, accountability or public service delivery and which use mobile and/or web technologies as a core part of the project.

WHAT IS NOT FUNDED Sponsorship requests from individuals (e.g. expeditions, scholarships, etc.); ICT training or skills; ICT equipment costs (e.g. purchasing computers or tablets); large, international NGOs; costs for events, such as workshops, conferences or meetings.

TYPE OF GRANT Core costs; project costs.

RANGE OF GRANTS £10,000 to £15,000.

SAMPLE GRANTS Publish What You Fund (£30,000); FunDza Literacy Trust (£22,200); Toro Development Network (£21,300); Open Mind (£20,400); Totohealth (£12,500); AfriLabs and myAGRO (£10,600 each); First Give (£11,700); Children's Radio Foundation (£5,000); Handicap International UK (£2,800).

FINANCES *Year* 2015/16 *Income* £203,339 *Grants* £717,502 *Grants to organisations* £717,502 *Assets* £10,396,186

TRUSTEES Dominic Flynn; Francesca Perrin; William Perrin.

OTHER INFORMATION There were a total of 46 awards made. Six of these were UK grants, totalling £43,800. 36 grants were categorised under Information Technology.

HOW TO APPLY Applications can be sent via email (indigo@sfct.org.uk). Applications should: be between two and four pages of A4; provide a brief background to your organisation and its history; offer an overview of the project for which you are seeking funding; include a rough budget for the project; give details of how you will monitor and evaluate your project. No additional documents should be submitted. There is an optional application template available to download from the trust's website. There are no deadlines. Further information about how applications are assessed is given on the website.

WHO TO APPLY TO Alan Bookbinder, Director, The Peak, 5 Wilton Road, London SW1V 1AP *Tel.* 020 7410 0330 *Email* indigo@sfct.org.uk *Website* indigotrust.org.uk

■ The Worshipful Company of Information Technologists Charity

CC NO 1113488 **ESTABLISHED** 2006

WHERE FUNDING CAN BE GIVEN UK.

WHO CAN BENEFIT Registered charities; educational establishments; organisations with a formal not-for-profit constitution.

WHAT IS FUNDED Information technology, particularly: enhancing opportunity for young people through more effective education; improving quality of life for people who are disadvantaged, who have disabilities or who are socially excluded; helping charities and not-for-profit organisations get the best out of IT; improving understanding of IT and its capabilities among the wider public. Some support may also be given for general charitable purposes.

WHAT IS NOT FUNDED Individuals.

TYPE OF GRANT Individual grants; pro bono support.

RANGE OF GRANTS £1,000 to £18,000.

SAMPLE GRANTS Thames Reach (£18,200); Gresham College (£16,000); AbilityNet (£9,500); Manor Green School (£9,300); Bristol Braille Technology CIC and LifeLites (£5,000 each); Lilian Baylis Tech School (£3,400); Panels (£200).

FINANCES *Year* 2015/16 *Income* £385,421 *Grants* £107,181 *Grants to organisations* £107,181 *Assets* £6,844,589

TRUSTEES Jo Connell; David Morriss; Mark Holford; Dr Elizabeth Sparrow; Bill Kennair; Kerri Mansfield; Anthony Buxton; Gary Moore.

OTHER INFORMATION In 2015/16, £41,000 was given in small grants under £5,000.

HOW TO APPLY Organisations interested in developing projects should complete a charity proposal form provided on the website and send it by email. Applications for funding and/or provision of pro bono IT advice may be submitted at any time and are considered by the Charities Committee at its four meetings each year. These are usually held in February, May, September and November. If the project is potentially suitable, more detailed information from you will be requested.

WHO TO APPLY TO Eleanor MacGregor, Charity Co-ordinator, 39A Bartholomew Close, London EC1A 7JN *Tel.* 020 3871 0255 *Email* eleanor@wcit.org.ok *Website* www.wcit.org.uk/apply_for_a_grant.html

■ The Ingram Trust

CC NO 1040194 **ESTABLISHED** 1994

WHERE FUNDING CAN BE GIVEN UK and overseas, with a local preference for Surrey.

WHO CAN BENEFIT Registered national charities and some local charities in the Surrey area.

WHAT IS FUNDED General charitable purposes, including children and young people, and health and disability.

WHAT IS NOT FUNDED Non-registered charities; individuals; charities specialising in overseas aid (except those dedicated to encouraging self-help and providing more permanent solutions to problems); animal charities (except those concerned with wildlife conservation).

TYPE OF GRANT Support for specific projects, including the costs of special services or projects or equipment. The majority of grants are made over periods of three to four years.

RANGE OF GRANTS £2,000 to £60,000.

SAMPLE GRANTS WWF – UK (£60,000); The Royal National Theatre (£40,000); NSPCC (£32,000); The Prince's Trust and Young Epilepsy (£30,000 each); Alzheimer's Society and Unicef UK (£25,000 each); Farm Africa and St Mungo's (£20,000 each); St Giles Trust (£15,000); Disability Challengers (£12,500); Pimlico Opera (£12,000); Clean Break, The Princess Alice Hospice and Sightsavers (£10,000 each); Cherry Trees – Respite Care (£5,000); Deaf Plus (£2,000).

FINANCES *Year* 2015/16 *Income* £247,538 *Grants* £617,500 *Grants to organisations* £617,500 *Assets* £10,274,623

TRUSTEES Christopher Ingram; Clare Maurice; Janet Ingram; Jonathan Ingram; Sally Ingram.

OTHER INFORMATION Normally the trustees' policy is to support a limited number of charities, but with a longer-term commitment to each. During the year 30 charities were supported.
HOW TO APPLY Applications may be made in writing to the correspondent, although the trust states that it receives far more worthy applications than it is able to support.
WHO TO APPLY TO Joan Major, The Ingram Trust, Ground Floor, 22 Chancery Lane, London WC2A 1LS *Email* theingramtrust@nqpltd.com

■ The Inlight Trust

CC NO 236782 **ESTABLISHED** 1957
WHERE FUNDING CAN BE GIVEN UK.
WHO CAN BENEFIT Registered charities of any religious denomination.
WHAT IS FUNDED Religious and spiritual development, healing and growth.
WHAT IS NOT FUNDED Individuals, including students; organisations which are not registered charities; general appeals from large national organisations; grants are seldom available for church buildings.
TYPE OF GRANT Usually one-off for a specific project or part of a project. Bursary schemes eligible. Core funding and/or salaries are rarely considered.
RANGE OF GRANTS £2,500 to £50,000.
SAMPLE GRANTS The Rokpa Trust (£87,000 in four grants); The White Eagle Lodge (£41,000 in two grants); West Somerset Area Quaker Meeting (£40,000); The Lendrick Trust (£20,000); The Meditation Centre and West Midlands Quaker Peace Education Project (£7,500 each); Brighton and Hove City Mission (£5,000); Inclusive Church (£2,500).
FINANCES *Year* 2015/16 *Income* £317,979 *Grants* £243,000 *Grants to organisations* £243,000 *Assets* £6,936,910
TRUSTEES Wendy Collett; Judy Hayward; Sharon Knight; Sir Thomas Lucas; Roger Ross, Jane Dunham; Dr David Panton.
OTHER INFORMATION There were 17 grants made to 13 organisations. The average grant was about £14,600.
HOW TO APPLY Applications should be made in writing to the correspondent, including details of the need, the intended project to meet it, an outline of budget, the most recent available annual accounts of the organisation, and a copy of your trust deed or your entry on the Charity Commission register. The trustees meet quarterly – in the two most recent financial years available at the time of writing (May 2017), meetings took place in June, September, November and March. Only applications from eligible bodies are acknowledged and only successful applicants are informed.
WHO TO APPLY TO Clare Pegden, Administrator, PO Box 2, Liss, Hampshire GU33 6YP *Tel.* 07970 540015 *Email* inlight.trust01@ntlworld.com

■ The Inman Charity

CC NO 261366 **ESTABLISHED** 1970
WHERE FUNDING CAN BE GIVEN UK.
WHO CAN BENEFIT A wide range of UK-registered charities; hospices. The charity also makes a regular payment (£20,000 per annum) to the Victor Inman Bursary Fund at Uppingham School of which the settlor had been a lifelong supporter.
WHAT IS FUNDED General charitable purposes; medical causes; social welfare; disability; older people; hospices; armed forces.
WHAT IS NOT FUNDED Individuals; young children and infants; maintenance of local buildings (such as churches and village halls); animal welfare; wildlife and environmental conservation; religious charities.
TYPE OF GRANT Recurring; one-off.
RANGE OF GRANTS Most grants are for £5,000 or less.
SAMPLE GRANTS Victoria Inman Bursary Fund (£20,000); Disaster Emergency Committee – Nepal Earthquake Appeal and Hospice UK (£10,200 each); British Heart Foundation and Roy Castle Lung Cancer Foundation (£6,000 each); Deafblind UK and Signature (£5,000 each); Lewis Manning Hospice and The Bolton Hospice (£3,000 each); The Dystonia Society (£2,500).
FINANCES *Year* 2015/16 *Income* £352,290 *Grants* £287,700 *Grants to organisations* £287,700 *Assets* £5,441,425
TRUSTEES A. L. Walker; Belinda Strother; Neil Wingerath; Prof. John Langdon; Michael Mathews; Inman Charity Trustees Ltd.
OTHER INFORMATION The charity also makes a regular payment (£20,000 per annum) to the Victor Inman Bursary Fund.
HOW TO APPLY All applications should be made in writing to the correspondent. They should include: a copy of your latest annual report and audited accounts; registered number, aims and objectives of your charity; nature of the appeal and the amount required; total target, contributions received against it and the timing for completion; any other relevant factors. The directors meet in April and October each year and applications should be received by the end of February and August, respectively. Only successful applicants will be contacted.
WHO TO APPLY TO Neil Wingerath, Trustee, BM Box 2831, London WC1N 3XX *Website* www.inmancharity.org

■ The Innocent Foundation

CC NO 1104289 **ESTABLISHED** 2004
WHERE FUNDING CAN BE GIVEN Worldwide.
WHO CAN BENEFIT Community-based projects and non-government organisations in financially developing countries where the Innocent Drinks company sources fruit. Generally, organisations must be UK-registered or have UK representation to receive funds.
WHAT IS FUNDED The foundation works with partner charities working to address world hunger and enable people dependent on subsistence agriculture to build sustainable futures. Support is available through the following funding streams: **Seed funding** – grants of up to £30,000 per year for three years are given to help get new sustainable agriculture projects off the ground. Funding can only be given to support work in countries categorised as 'serious', 'alarming' or 'extremely alarming' on the Global Hunger Index. **Local food poverty** – grants to charities working on projects to combat food poverty in the UK. At the time of writing (May 2017) the criteria for funding under this category was being reviewed. **Breakthrough development** – funding is given to support innovative, untested ideas to find new models that 'over time will become the gold standard to address hunger issues'. **Emergency hunger relief** – the foundation helps to get food to people affected by humanitarian crises, working

with Oxfam to support its emergency relief work around the world.

WHAT IS NOT FUNDED **Seed funding** – individuals; religious or political causes; general appeals or circulars; events or conferences; seed funding is not given for core costs alone (but these can be included as overheads pro-rated to the project); major capital costs, such as buildings or machinery.

TYPE OF GRANT Most funds are allocated in three-year partnerships; some one-off projects.

RANGE OF GRANTS £13,300 to £326,000, but mostly less than £40,000.

SAMPLE GRANTS Action Against Hunger (£326,000); Oxfam (£100,000); Kew (£40,500); Find Your Feet (£30,000); The Matthew Tree Project (£25,000); PHASE Worldwide (£21,500); Trussell Trust (£21,000); Send a Cow (£20,500); Inga Foundation (£13,300); Jeevika Trust (£11,000).

FINANCES *Year* 2015/16 *Income* £1,018,459 *Grants* £780,948 *Grants to organisations* £780,948 *Assets* £2,835,899

TRUSTEES Adam Balon; Jon Wright; Richard Reed; Christina Archer; Douglas Lamont; Sarah-Jane Norman.

OTHER INFORMATION The Innocent Foundation was set up by Innocent Drinks in 2004. Each year the company gives at least 10% of its profits to charity, the majority to the foundation. During the year grants were distributed to 19 projects (including four emergency relief donations).

HOW TO APPLY In the first instance, see the website for full information of the foundation's work. Applications are accepted for two types of funding: seed funding and local food poverty. At the time of writing (May 2017) detailed criteria for seed funding was available from the website. Criteria for local food poverty funding was under review but was due to be provided on the website in the near future. There is detailed information on how to contact the foundation regarding a project on the website.

WHO TO APPLY TO Kate Franks, Manager, The Innocent Foundation, 342 Ladbroke Grove, London W10 5BU *Tel.* 020 3235 0352 *Email* hello@innocentfoundation.org *Website* www.innocentfoundation.org

■ The Worshipful Company of Insurers Charitable Trust Fund

CC NO 279959 **ESTABLISHED** 1980

WHERE FUNDING CAN BE GIVEN London.

WHO CAN BENEFIT Individuals; charities; not-for-profit organisations.

WHAT IS FUNDED The relief of poverty of members; the advancement of insurance or financial services education.

TYPE OF GRANT Recurring; pro bono support; scholarships.

RANGE OF GRANTS £250 to £50,000.

SAMPLE GRANTS Brokerage Citylink (£50,000); The Mansion House Scholarship Scheme (£6,000); Chartered Institute of Insurance Prizes (£2,500); London Links and Maritime London Officer Cadet Scholarship (£2,000 each); Artichoke and Guildhall School of Music and Drama (£1,000 each); Livery Schools Link (£400); Insurance Institute of London Prize (£250).

FINANCES *Year* 2015/16 *Income* £156,019 *Grants* £65,445 *Grants to organisations* £65,445 *Assets* £2,328,949

TRUSTEES Andrew Hubbard; James Peace; Angela Darling; Nicholas Michaelides; John Young; Simon Byrne; Philip Grant; Jane Evans.

OTHER INFORMATION One recurring annual grant of £50,000 is given to Brokerage Citylink.

HOW TO APPLY Applications should be made by email to the secretary of the charitable trusts.

WHO TO APPLY TO Sarah Virginia, Secretary to the Charitable Trusts, The Insurance Hall, 20 Aldermanbury, London EC2V 7HY *Tel.* 020 7600 4006 *Email* clerk@wci.org.uk *Website* www.wci.org.uk

■ Integrated Education Fund

CC NO 104886 **ESTABLISHED** 1992

WHERE FUNDING CAN BE GIVEN Northern Ireland.

WHO CAN BENEFIT Schools undergoing or exploring transformation with pupils from both the Catholic and Protestant communities during their first few years of integrated education before they have had the chance to prove their worth for full Department of Education funding, as well as during the initial years of funding; community groups exploring integrated education for their area.

WHAT IS FUNDED Grants for schools and community groups exploring transformation – e.g. research, information sessions, awareness campaigns, training, etc.; grants for schools during the first two years of transformation; support grants for transformed schools – e.g. school development, marketing projects, training and growth, accommodation needs or pre-school start-up costs; The Trust Programme – supporting integration in practice. Full eligibility criteria and further details for each category are given on the website.

TYPE OF GRANT Research; evaluation; start-up costs; projects; development costs; training; salaries; capital costs. Refer to the website for further information.

RANGE OF GRANTS Exploring transformation: up to £2,500 for up to two years; schools beginning transformation: up to £15,000 for two years; transformed schools: up to £15,000 or up to £75,000.

SAMPLE GRANTS A list of beneficiaries was not available.

TRUSTEES Dr Andrew Biggart; Kenneth Cathcart; David Cooke; Marie Cowan; Barry Gilligan; Errol Lemon; Paddy McIntyre; Grainne Clarke; David Thompson; Dorothee Wagner; Roderick Downer; Michael McKernan; Ellen McVea; Richard Lemon.

OTHER INFORMATION There were no accounts available to view on the Charity Commission for Northern Ireland website at the time of writing (June 2017).

HOW TO APPLY Application forms are available to download from the website, where further guidance is also provided.

WHO TO APPLY TO Tina Merron, Chief Executive, Forestview, Purdy's Lane, Belfast BT8 7AR *Tel.* 028 9069 4099 *Email* info@ief.org.uk *Website* www.ief.org.uk

■ The International Bankers Charitable Trust (The Worshipful Company of International Bankers)

CC NO 1087630 **ESTABLISHED** 2001

WHERE FUNDING CAN BE GIVEN UK, with preference for inner London.

WHO CAN BENEFIT Registered charities only.

WHAT IS FUNDED Supporting disadvantaged young people and promoting careers in the financial services for those who 'would not normally be able to aspire to a city job'. There are four areas of focus: increasing financial literacy; supporting education; raising aspirations for education and employment; improving the likelihood of employment.

WHAT IS NOT FUNDED Large projects towards which any contribution from the company would have limited impact; general appeals or circulars; replacement of statutory funds; salaries; counselling; course fees for professionals; medical research; fundraising events and sponsorship; responses to requests for charitable aid.

TYPE OF GRANT Specific projects to cover either a significant proportion of the cost or an identified element of it; long-term funding of scholarships and/or bursaries.

RANGE OF GRANTS Typically up to £1,000; 'larger awards considered where funding can make a clear difference in accordance with Company aims'.

SAMPLE GRANTS The Brokerage Citylink Grant (£45,000); Air Cadets (£15,000); Livery Companies Apprenticeship (£10,000); Mansion House Scholarship Scheme (£5,000); University Academic Prizes (£4,000); Lord Mayors Appeal (£3,500); Guildhall School of Music and Drama (£2,500).

FINANCES *Year* 2015 *Income* £234,771 *Grants* £151,530 *Grants to organisations* £151,530 *Assets* £911,278

TRUSTEE The Worshipful Company of International Bankers.

OTHER INFORMATION £6,500 was given in small grants of £1,000 and below.

HOW TO APPLY Application forms can be downloaded from the trust's website. Previous grant recipients must wait at least two years (from the date the original grant was awarded) before re-applying.

WHO TO APPLY TO Nicholas Westgarth, Clerk, 3rd Floor, 12 Austin Friars, London EC2N 2HE *Tel.* 020 7374 0212 *Fax* 020 7374 0207 *Email* clerk@internationalbankers.co.uk *Website* internationalbankers.org.uk/charity-education/charity-applications

■ International Bible Students Association

CC NO 216647 **ESTABLISHED** 1964

WHERE FUNDING CAN BE GIVEN Worldwide.

WHO CAN BENEFIT Christian (Jehovah's Witnesses) organisations and individuals.

WHAT IS FUNDED Promotion of the Christian religion as practiced by Jehovah's Witnesses; purchase and distribution of religious literature; arranging of conventions for Bible education; financially assisting legal entities of Jehovah's Witnesses, both foreign and domestic.

TYPE OF GRANT Cash grants and in-kind support.

SAMPLE GRANTS A detailed breakdown of beneficiaries was not given in the accounts. However, the grant total was categorised by location: Europe (£2.4 million); Asia (£230,000); Africa (£48,000); North America (£34,000); Oceania (£9,000); South America (£750).

FINANCES *Year* 2015/16 *Income* £43,009,677 *Grants* £2,758,345 *Grants to organisations* £2,758,345 *Assets* £115,503,130

TRUSTEES Paul Gillies; Stephen Papps; Philip Buttner; Karl Snaith; Ivor Darby.

OTHER INFORMATION As well as cash grants totalling £2.75 million, the charity also gave in-kind grants totalling £57,000 during the year.

HOW TO APPLY Applications should be made in writing to the association.

WHO TO APPLY TO The Trustees, International Bible Students, Association, IBSA House, The Ridgeway, London NW7 1RN *Tel.* 020 8906 2211

■ International Fund for Animal Welfare (IFAW)

CC NO 1024806 **ESTABLISHED** 1992

WHERE FUNDING CAN BE GIVEN Worldwide.

WHO CAN BENEFIT Animal welfare and conservation organisations.

WHAT IS FUNDED The trust's mission is to: conserve and protect animals including wildlife and its habitats and the natural environment; to prevent cruelty to and the suffering of animals, including wildlife.

WHAT IS NOT FUNDED Individual undergraduate courses.

RANGE OF GRANTS £500 to £5 million.

SAMPLE GRANTS International Fund for Animal Welfare (US) (£5.5 million); IFAW in Action (£700,000); Wildlife Trust of India (£595,000); Game Rangers International – Zambia (£239,500); CERU (Conservation Ecology Research Unit – University of Pretoria) (£136,500); Orphan Bears Rehabilitation Centre (£61,000); Bali Animal Welfare Association (£54,000); Paws For Kids (£15,000); Wild Animal Rescue Centre (£3,200); The Fox Project and Cuan Wildlife Rescue (£750 each); Badger Trust (£350).

FINANCES *Year* 2015/16 *Income* £19,776,361 *Grants* £8,104,602 *Grants to organisations* £8,104,602 *Assets* £15,420,366

TRUSTEES Brian Hutchinson; Margaret Kennedy; David Metzler; Alexandra Denman; Kathleen Buckley; Graeme Cottam; Debobrata Mukherjee; Thomas O'Neill; Barbara Birdsey; Joyce Doria; Susan Wallace; Mark Beaudouin; James Costa; Catherine Lilly; Gregory Mertz; Margo Fitzpatrick.

OTHER INFORMATION £6.45 million of the total grants were given to IFAW organisations. £1.65 million went to non-IFAW organisations.

HOW TO APPLY Apply in writing to the correspondent. Although applications can be submitted at any time, it is best to apply between July and September.

WHO TO APPLY TO Aarti Bajrangee, UK Director of Finance and Operations, Camelford House, 87–90 Albert Embankment, London SE1 7UD *Tel.* 020 7587 6707 *Fax* 020 7587 6720 *Email* info-uk@ifaw.org *Website* www.ifaw.org

■ Interserve Employee Foundation

CC NO 1145338 **ESTABLISHED** 2011

WHERE FUNDING CAN BE GIVEN UK; worldwide.

WHO CAN BENEFIT Registered charities.

WHAT IS FUNDED General charitable purposes; disaster relief; education/training; social welfare.

RANGE OF GRANTS Up to £26,000.

SAMPLE GRANTS Nepal Disaster Recovery (£26,000); Providence Row (£2,000); Oasis Playspace (£450).

FINANCES *Year* 2015 *Income* £213,740 *Grants* £123,131 *Grants to organisations* £123,131 *Assets* £54,060

TRUSTEES Jeremy Mead; Stephen Harland; Isa Buencamino; Mark Judge; Lianne Lawson; Scott Hill; Stuart Mee; Laura Spiers; Emma Phillips; Stephanie Pound; Kim Pattison.

HOW TO APPLY The foundation supports charities nominated by Interserve employees.

WHO TO APPLY TO The Trustees, Interserve PLC, Interserve house, Ruscombe park, Ruscombe, Reading RG10 9JU *Tel.* 0118 932 0123 *Email* info.foundation@interserve.com *Website* www.interserve.com/about-us/interserve-employee-foundation

■ The Inverforth Charitable Trust

CC NO 274132 **ESTABLISHED** 1977

WHERE FUNDING CAN BE GIVEN UK.

WHO CAN BENEFIT Registered charities.

WHAT IS FUNDED General charitable purposes; health causes; heritage; education of young people; arts; military and international support.

RANGE OF GRANTS £5,000 to £10,000.

SAMPLE GRANTS Allegra's Ambition (£10,000); Art Fund, Asthma UK, Childhood First, Cornwall Hospice Care, Help for Heroes, Help for Hospices, MS Society, Save the Children, St Mungo's and Trinity Hospital (£5,000 each).

FINANCES *Year* 2015 *Income* £31,435 *Grants* £60,000 *Grants to organisations* £60,000 *Assets* £5,569,915

TRUSTEES Lord Inverforth; Jonathan Kane; Elizabeth Inverforth.

OTHER INFORMATION Each year 11 core charities are supported.

HOW TO APPLY Applications should be made in writing to the trustees. The trust asks applicants to provide concise applications. The trustees normally meet in March, June, September and November/early December.

WHO TO APPLY TO The Hon. Clarinda Kane, Secretary and Treasurer, PO Box 6, 47–49 Chelsea Manor Street, London SW3 5RZ

■ Investream Charitable Trust

CC NO 1097052 **ESTABLISHED** 2003

WHERE FUNDING CAN BE GIVEN Worldwide; in practice the UK and Israel.

WHO CAN BENEFIT Registered charities; educational establishments.

WHAT IS FUNDED General charitable purposes, with a focus on education, community, care for older people, and medical causes.

RANGE OF GRANTS Up to £103,000.

SAMPLE GRANTS Shemen Ltd (£103,000); Cosmon (Belz) Ltd (£95,000); Dover Sholem Community Trust (£81,500); Moreshet Hatorah Ltd (£72,000).

FINANCES *Year* 2015/16 *Income* £343,763 *Grants* £697,258 *Grants to organisations* £697,258 *Assets* -£92,921

TRUSTEES Mark Morris; Graham Morris.

OTHER INFORMATION Grants were distributed in the following categories: education (£580,000); community and care for older people (£106,000); and medical causes (£11,100).

HOW TO APPLY Apply in writing to the correspondent.

WHO TO APPLY TO The Trustees of Investream Charitable Trust, Investream Ltd, 38 Wigmore Street, London W1U 2RU *Tel.* 020 7486 2800

■ The Ireland Fund of Great Britain

CC NO 327889 **ESTABLISHED** 1988

WHERE FUNDING CAN BE GIVEN The Republic of Ireland; throughout Great Britain.

WHO CAN BENEFIT Charitable organisations.

WHAT IS FUNDED Supporting Irish communities through four key areas: education; community development; arts and culture; peace and reconciliation. There are two grant programmes: small grants and flagship grants. Full details are available on the website when the grant programmes are open.

WHAT IS NOT FUNDED Organisations based outside England, Scotland or Wales (although there are worldwide branches of The Ireland Funds); general appeals – assistance must be sought for clearly specified purposes; individuals; tuition or student fees; medical costs; purchase of buildings or land; construction or refurbishment projects; events; debt; retrospective costs or salary costs. CICs cannot be assisted until they have three years' audited accounts available for inspection.

RANGE OF GRANTS £1,000 to £58,000.

SAMPLE GRANTS University of Limerick Foundation (£58,000); UL Foundation and Munster Rugby Academy (£44,000); Iris O'Brien Foundation (£25,000); Lismore Music Festival (£22,000); Crumlin Medical Research Foundation and Michael Flatley Fund (£10,000 each); BeLonGTo (£9,300); Irish Elderly Advice Network (£4,500); London Irish Women's Survivors Support Network (£3,300); Luton Irish Forum and W2 Foundation (£1,000 each); St Mary's Abbey (£600).

FINANCES *Year* 2015/16 *Income* £678,207 *Grants* £307,501 *Grants to organisations* £307,501 *Assets* £401,662

TRUSTEES Seamus McGarry; Michael Casey; Ruairi Conneely; Zach Webb; Rory Godson; Garrett Hayes; Kieran McLoughlin.

OTHER INFORMATION Grants were made to 47 organisations and were split into three general categories: community development (£86,000); sharing and developing Irish arts and culture (£59,000) and education (£162,500).

HOW TO APPLY Application forms are available on the charity's website. Applicants must also attach a copy of their audited accounts and can only submit one application per organisation per year. The trustees meet quarterly. For current deadlines for each of the rounds see the website.

WHO TO APPLY TO Grants Team, Can Mezzanine, 7–14 Great Dover Street, London SE1 4YR *Tel.* 020 3096 7897 *Email* grantsinfo@irlfunds.org *Website* www.theirelandfunds.org/great-britain

■ Irish Youth Foundation (UK) Ltd (incorporating The Lawlor Foundation)

CC NO 328265 **ESTABLISHED** 1989

WHERE FUNDING CAN BE GIVEN UK.

WHO CAN BENEFIT Charities and community organisations.

WHAT IS FUNDED Projects benefitting young Irish people or enhancing their personal and social development, especially if they are disadvantaged or in need. A wide range of projects are supported which include: training/ counselling; drug rehabilitation; advice/ advocacy; youth work; family support; homelessness; educational, cultural and social activities; cross-community initiatives; travellers and disability.

WHAT IS NOT FUNDED Projects for people over 25 (in Northern Ireland) and over 30 (in England, Scotland and Wales); general appeals; large/ national charities; academic research; alleviating deficits already incurred; individuals (except for university students applying under Lawlor Foundation Education programme); capital bids; overseas travel; multiple applications from a single organisation.

TYPE OF GRANT Programme development grants; seed funding; core costs and salaries; awards to upgrade premises and/or equipment; small grants. One year only.

RANGE OF GRANTS In Northern Ireland: up to £5,000. In England, Scotland and Wales: small grants of up to £2,500; standard grants from £2,500 to £10,000.

SAMPLE GRANTS Irish Community Care Liverpool (£9,500); Artillery Youth Centre and Youth Link Belfast and Brent Centre For Young People (£4,000 each); The Brandon Centre (£3,000); Birmingham TradFest (£2,500); Bristol Playbus and Construction Youth Trust0 (£2,000 each); Irish Arts Foundation Leeds (£1,000); Irish Film London (£500).

FINANCES *Year* 2015 *Income* £213,761 *Grants* £178,150 *Grants to organisations* £178,150 *Assets* £2,424,205

TRUSTEES John Dwyer; Virginia Lawlor; June Trimble; Richard Corrigan; Ciara Brett; Cecilia Gallagher; Alan Byrne; Jacqueline O'Donovan.

OTHER INFORMATION Irish Youth Foundation (UK) Ltd merged with the Lawlor Foundation in 2005. The work of the Lawlor Foundation towards the advancement of education in Northern Ireland continues with support for Irish students and educational organisations. The latest annual report and accounts for 2015 did not provide a list of beneficiaries; however, 2016 grant recipients were listed online.

HOW TO APPLY Applications are considered on an annual basis and application forms are only available during the annual round either on the website or by request. Application forms are available in December to be submitted by the end of January for grants awarded in May/June. Unsolicited applications are not accepted outside these times.

WHO TO APPLY TO Linda Tanner, Head of Operations, 26–28 Hammersmith Grove, Hammersmith, London W6 7HA *Tel.* 020 8748 9640 *Email* linda@iyf.org.uk *Website* www.iyf.org.uk

■ The Ironmongers' Company

CC NO 219153

WHERE FUNDING CAN BE GIVEN UK, with some preference for London.

WHO CAN BENEFIT Registered charities; schools and other educational establishments; churches; iron and steel projects.

WHAT IS FUNDED There are three categories: organisations (relief in need); iron work; schools. Organisations (relief in need): supporting disadvantaged children and young people (under 25) to achieve their potential through 'educational activities that develop learning, motivation and skills'. The website states: 'The Company is particularly interested in enabling primary age children to develop a strong foundation for the future. Projects could, for example, support special educational needs, address behavioural problems or promote citizenship, parenting or life skills. Preference will be given to projects piloting new approaches where the outcomes will be disseminated to a wider audience.' Iron work: the conservation of historic ironwork or creation of new decorative iron or steel work. Schools: support for Church of England primary schools in areas with high levels of deprivation.

WHAT IS NOT FUNDED Exclusions from the organisations (relief in need) scheme: large projects towards which a contribution from the company would have limited impact; general appeals or circulars; replacement of statutory funding; general running costs (a reasonable proportion of overheads will be accepted as part of project costs); medical treatment, health care, counselling and therapy; course fees for professionals; research projects; bursaries; schools, unless a registered charity for children/ young people with disabilities; fundraising events and sponsorship; projects that begin before the date of the relevant committee meeting; building work; holidays; individuals.

TYPE OF GRANT Projects; capital costs; one-off or longer-term grants.

RANGE OF GRANTS £300 to £40,000.

SAMPLE GRANTS Make Believe Arts (£38,500); St Vincent's Family Project (£20,000); QPR in the Community Trust (£14,600); Blue Elephant Theatre (£6,900); Dawn Sailing Barge Trust (£5,000); Cambridge University (£4,000); Salisbury and South Wiltshire Museum (£1,900); Fort Amherst Heritage Trust (£1,100); Holy Trinity Church (£530); City of London Police Widows and Orphans Fund (£300).

FINANCES *Year* 2015/16 *Income* £1,897,112 *Grants* £509,125 *Grants to organisations* £509,125 *Assets* £26,826,120

TRUSTEE The Ironmongers' Trust Company.

OTHER INFORMATION The company has a number of linked charities under the Charity Commission no. 219153, namely: Sir Robert Geffrey's Almshouse Trust; Sir Robert Geffrey's School Charity; Mr Thomas Betton's Charity (Educational); Thomas Betton's Estate Charity; Thomas Betton's Charity for Pensions and Relief in Need; The Ironmongers' Foundation.

HOW TO APPLY Organisations (relief in need): Complete an application summary sheet, available to download on the website, to be returned together with a description of the project (no more than three A4 pages on both sides). The appeals committee meets twice a year in March and October with deadlines 15 December and 31 July respectively. Applications are not accepted by email. The company asks to enclose a copy of your most recent audited accounts if they are not available from the

Charity Commission's website. Iron projects: Applications should be made in writing, preferably by email to helen@ironmongers.org, including full details of the project – guidance on what should be included is given on the website. The website states that it is expected that 'any conservation of historic ironwork to follow the National Heritage Ironwork Group's Conservation Principles (see www.nhig.org.uk)' – applications should confirm that your project will meet these standards. The iron committee meets at the end of April, with deadline for applications 31 March. Schools: At the time of writing (June 2017), the website states: 'Funds are currently committed to existing partnerships. All Diocesan Directors of Education will be notified when the Company is actively seeking new partner schools. Appeals are not accepted directly from individual schools.'

WHO TO APPLY TO Helen Sant, Charities Manager, Ironmongers Hall, Barbican, London EC2Y 8AA *Tel.* 020 7776 2311 *Email* helen@ironmongers.org *Website* www.ironmongers.org

■ The Charles Irving Charitable Trust

CC NO 297712 **ESTABLISHED** 1987

WHERE FUNDING CAN BE GIVEN Mainly Gloucestershire, in particular, Cheltenham.

WHO CAN BENEFIT Charitable organisations; individuals.

WHAT IS FUNDED Priority is given to projects benefitting people who are disadvantaged by poverty, or by physical or mental disability. However, the annual report for 2014/15 states that grants will also be made in support of people who are older or homeless, young people, local community projects, victim support, the resettlement of people who have offended and 'other causes with which the settlor, Sir Charles Irving DL, was associated during his lifetime. The Trustees also appreciate projects with which the settlor's name may be linked.'

WHAT IS NOT FUNDED Ongoing grants; research; expeditions; computers or other equipment (unless benefitting people with disabilities); causes outside the county of Gloucester except for the few organisations with which Sir Charles was associated and which are already known to the trustees.

TYPE OF GRANT One-off; mainly capital projects, although the trustees 'may look for evidence that consideration has been given to onward revenue funding' project costs.

RANGE OF GRANTS Mostly in the range of £50 to £500; larger grants are sometimes made.

SAMPLE GRANTS Sue Ryder (£11,000); Gloucestershire Arthritis Trust and Willow Trust (£2,000 each); Prisoners' Advice Service (£1,800); Dogs for the Disabled, Frith Youth Centre, Lilian Faithful Homes and Samaritans – Cheltenham and District (£1,500 each); British Red Cross (£1,300); Ruskin Mill (£1,100).

FINANCES *Year* 2014/15 *Income* £76,333 *Grants* £79,523 *Grants to organisations* £79,523 *Assets* £2,021,258

TRUSTEES Tony Hilder; J. Lane; D. Oldham; Peter Shephard.

OTHER INFORMATION At the time of writing (May 2017) the 2014/15 accounts were the most recent available. In 2014/15 a total of 107 grants were made.

HOW TO APPLY The 2014/15 annual report explains that the trustees 'welcome applications by letter, giving details of the proposed project, its total cost and the amount if any already raised or promised from other sources. Other information such as a budget and details of the number of people expected to benefit will also be helpful.'

WHO TO APPLY TO Mrs J. Lane, Secretary, PO Box 868, Cheltenham GL53 9WZ *Tel.* 01242 234848

■ The J. Isaacs Charitable Trust

CC NO 1059865 **ESTABLISHED** 1996

WHERE FUNDING CAN BE GIVEN England and Wales.

WHO CAN BENEFIT Charitable organisations, including those supporting Jewish people.

WHAT IS FUNDED General charitable purposes, particularly care for children, education, the well-being of older people, tolerance in the community, and health care.

RANGE OF GRANTS Up to £77,500.

SAMPLE GRANTS Beneficiaries of larger grants, listed in the annual report were: Community Security Trust (£77,500); Norwood (£75,500); Tate Gallery and United Jewish Appeal (£70,000 each); Imperial College Healthcare (£33,000); The Prince's Trust (£20,000).

FINANCES *Year* 2015/16 *Income* £123,490 *Grants* £648,739 *Grants to organisations* £648,739 *Assets* £15,027,459

TRUSTEES Jeremy Isaacs: Joanne Isaacs; Helen Eastick; Vincent Isaacs.

OTHER INFORMATION Grants were given in the following categories: education (£282,500); care for children (£114,500); ad hoc/other (£84,500); health care (£80,500); tolerance in our community (£77,500); and well-being for older people (£9,500).

HOW TO APPLY Apply in writing to the correspondent.

WHO TO APPLY TO The Trustees, JRJ Group, 61 Conduit Street, London W1S 2GB *Tel.* 020 7220 2305

■ The Isle of Anglesey Charitable Trust

CC NO 1000818 **ESTABLISHED** 1990

WHERE FUNDING CAN BE GIVEN The Isle of Anglesey only.

WHO CAN BENEFIT Charitable and community organisations; village halls; sports facilities.

WHAT IS FUNDED General charitable purposes; community causes; sports; village halls; projects benefitting local people.

WHAT IS NOT FUNDED Individuals; projects based outside Anglesey.

TYPE OF GRANT One-off and recurring.

RANGE OF GRANTS £1,000 to £215,000; normally up to £6,000.

SAMPLE GRANTS Oriel Ynys Mon (£215,000); Menter Mon (£110,000); Anglesey Agricultural Show (£60,000); Menter Laith (£50,000); Island Games (£40,000); Eisteddfod Genedlaethol Cymru (£37,500); Young Farmers Club (£30,000); Neuadd Gymuned Coffau Rhyfel Porthaethwy (£5,900); Age Well Mon (£2,500); Cymdeithas MS (£1,400).

FINANCES *Year* 2015/16 *Income* £585,981 *Grants* £737,766 *Grants to organisations* £737,766 *Assets* £19,069,611

TRUSTEE Isle of Anglesey County Council.

OTHER INFORMATION There were 68 awards made to 66 organisations and were listed under three categories: Oriel Ynys Mon (£215,000); village halls (£80,000); and community facilities

(£125,000). Only awards above £1,000 were listed. The trust's accounts provide information as to the distribution of its income to various organisations in Anglesey; however, it is not possible to ascertain from the accounts whether any of the grants awarded are used to subsidise the county council by providing facilities and/or services which should be provided by the local authority.

HOW TO APPLY Application forms can be requested from the correspondent, following advertisements in the local press in February. The trust considers applications once a year and 'will take details of any prospective applicants during the year, but application forms are sent out annually in February'.

WHO TO APPLY TO The Secretary, Head of Function (Resources), Isle of Anglesey County Council, County Offices, Llangefni, Anglesey LL77 7TW *Tel.* 01248 752610 *Email* garethjroberts@anglesey.gov.uk

■ The ITF Seafarers' Trust

CC NO 281936 **ESTABLISHED** 1981

WHERE FUNDING CAN BE GIVEN Worldwide.

WHO CAN BENEFIT Registered charities; educational institutions; trade unions. Applicants should have a proven record of dealing with seafarers' welfare.

WHAT IS FUNDED Welfare of seafarers of all nations, their families and dependants.

WHAT IS NOT FUNDED Retrospective funding for completed projects; deficits which have already been incurred; projects which promote particular religious beliefs; recurring costs; individuals.

TYPE OF GRANT Capital costs; core costs; one-off expenditure; project grants; training and education support; feasibility studies; research.

RANGE OF GRANTS Smaller grants of £500 to £75,000; large grants of over £75,000.

SAMPLE GRANTS International Seafarers' Welfare and Assistance Network (ISWAN) (£638,000); World Maritime Museum (£196,000); International Zeeman's House (£145,000); Maritime Piracy Humanitarian Response (£92,000); Apostleship of the Sea (£74,000); Maritime Academy (£70,000); Merchant Navy Welfare Board (£40,000); Sailors Children's Society (£30,000); Mission To Seafarers (£25,000); Public World Ltd (£15,000); Amis Des Marins (£8,600); Stella Maris International Seamen's Club (£1,400).

FINANCES *Year* 2015 *Income* £1,861,147 *Grants* £1,332,696 *Grants to organisations* £1,332,696 *Assets* £40,137,524

TRUSTEES Paddy Crumlin; Dave Heindel; Stephen Cotton; Lars Lindgren; Brian Orrell; Abdulgani Serang; Jacqueline Smith.

OTHER INFORMATION Organisations which have already received a number of grants over a short time period may find it more difficult to apply successfully for further support. Note that 'the decrease in grant expenditure was largely due to the restrictions placed on grant-giving during 2013 as part of the ongoing strategic review'. Normally awards total over £1 million each year.

HOW TO APPLY Applications have to be made online on the trust's website, where full criteria and guidelines are also available. Applications must be supported by an ITF affiliated seafarers' or dockers' trade union. The trustees meet at least twice a year. Requests for small grants (up to £75,000) may take about two to six months to proceed and for large grants (over £75,000) the process can last 3–12 months.

WHO TO APPLY TO Kimberly Karlshoej, Head of Trust, ITF House, 49–60 Borough Road, London SE1 1DR *Tel.* 020 7403 2229 *Email* trust@seafarerstrust.org *Website* www.seafarerstrust.org

The J. A. R. Charitable Trust

CC NO 248418 **ESTABLISHED** 1966
WHERE FUNDING CAN BE GIVEN Worldwide.
WHO CAN BENEFIT Organisations.
WHAT IS FUNDED The advancement of religion in connection with the Roman Catholic Church; the provision of education for people under 30; relief in need (the provision of food, clothing and accommodation) for people over 55.
WHAT IS NOT FUNDED Individuals. The trust does not normally support a charity unless it is known to the trustees.
TYPE OF GRANT One-off and recurring.
RANGE OF GRANTS £1,000 to £5,000.
SAMPLE GRANTS St Joseph's Pastoral Centre (£5,000); The Passage (£4,000); Catholic Children's Society – Westminster and Liverpool Archdiocesan Youth Pilgrimage (£3,000 each); Cardinal Hume Centre, Church of St James, Friends of Tumaini – Kenya, Little Sisters of the Poor and Youth 2000 (£2,000 each); Evangelium, JMB Educational Trust, Marriage Care and St Joseph's Hospice (£1,000 each).
FINANCES *Year* 2015/16 *Income* £89,067 *Grants* £65,000 *Grants to organisations* £65,000 *Assets* £2,898,462
TRUSTEES Philip Noble; Revd William Young; Revd Paschal Ryan.
OTHER INFORMATION In 2015/16, 27 organisations were supported.
HOW TO APPLY The annual report for 2015/16 states that the trustees 'identify projects and organizations they wish to support and so the charity does not make grants to people or organizations who apply speculatively'. It is further noted that the trustees have 'a policy of not responding to any correspondence unless it relates to grants it has agreed to make or to the general management of the charity'.
WHO TO APPLY TO Philip Noble, Trustee, Hunters, 9 New Square, London WC2A 3QN *Tel.* 020 7412 0050 *Email* gt@hunters-solicitors.co.uk

The J. and J. Benevolent Foundation

CC NO 1146602 **ESTABLISHED** 2012
WHERE FUNDING CAN BE GIVEN England.
WHO CAN BENEFIT Charitable organisations; individuals.
WHAT IS FUNDED Orthodox Jewish religious causes; education; the relief of poverty; general charitable purposes.
SAMPLE GRANTS A list of beneficiaries was not available.
FINANCES *Year* 2015/16 *Income* £150,000 *Grants* £151,756 *Grants to organisations* £151,756 *Assets* £158,294
TRUSTEES Joseph Adler; Judi Adler.
OTHER INFORMATION A list of beneficiaries was not included in the annual report and accounts.
HOW TO APPLY Apply in writing to the correspondent.
WHO TO APPLY TO Joseph Adler, Trustee, Farley Court, Allsop Place, London NW11 9AB *Tel.* 020 8731 0777 *Email* mail@cohenarnold.com

The J. J. Charitable Trust

CC NO 1015792 **ESTABLISHED** 1992
WHERE FUNDING CAN BE GIVEN UK and overseas.
WHO CAN BENEFIT Registered charities or activities with clearly defined charitable purposes.
WHAT IS FUNDED Literacy; sustainable lifestyles; environmental projects in Africa.
WHAT IS NOT FUNDED Individuals; educational fees; expeditions.
TYPE OF GRANT Seed funding; project grants.
RANGE OF GRANTS Up to £285,000.
SAMPLE GRANTS National Literacy Trust (£286,000); International Broadcasting Trust (£151,000); BAFTA (£64,000); Carbon Tracker (£49,000); Share Action (£37,000); ClientEarth (£33,000); Operation Noah (£30,000); Madact (£22,000); National Union of Students (£21,000); Salisbury Festival Ltd and TEMWA (£20,000); Development Institute (£15,400).
FINANCES *Year* 2015/16 *Income* £1,401,202 *Grants* £886,036 *Grants to organisations* £886,036 *Assets* £37,566,352
TRUSTEES John Sainsbury; Mark Sainsbury; Judith Portrait; Lucy Guard.
OTHER INFORMATION The trust is one of the Sainsbury Family Charitable Trusts, all of which share a joint administration but work autonomously as an independent legal entity. An application to one is taken as an application to all.
HOW TO APPLY The 2015/16 annual report states: 'Proposals are generally invited by the Trustees or initiated at their request. Unsolicited applications are discouraged and are unlikely to be successful, unless they are closely aligned to the Trust's areas of interest. The Trustees' objective is to support innovative schemes with seedfunding, leading projects to achieve sustainability and successful replication.'
WHO TO APPLY TO Alan Bookbinder, Director, The Peak, 5 Wilton Road, London SW1V 1AP *Tel.* 020 7410 0330 *Fax* 020 7410 0332 *Email* info@sfct.org.uk *Website* www.sfct.org.uk

The JRSST Charitable Trust

CC NO 247498 **ESTABLISHED** 1955
WHERE FUNDING CAN BE GIVEN UK.
WHO CAN BENEFIT Organisations or individuals undertaking research or action in fields which relate directly to the non-charitable work of the Joseph Rowntree Reform Trust Ltd. Academics and research workers may benefit.
WHAT IS FUNDED The trust works in close association with the Joseph Rowntree Reform Trust Ltd, which is a non-charitable trust of which all the trustees of The JRSST Charitable Trust are directors, in supporting the development of an increasingly democratic and socially just UK.
WHAT IS NOT FUNDED Student grants are not funded.
TYPE OF GRANT Specific finance in particular fields of interest to the trust; progressive campaigns; one-off awards and grants of up to one year.
RANGE OF GRANTS Up to £30,000.
SAMPLE GRANTS Democratic Audit UK (£29,000); English PEN (£28,000); The Rainbow Project (£22,000); Democracy Club (£21,000); FPA in Northern Ireland (£20,000); Demos (£5,000); Liberal Democrat History Group and Social Change Agency (£1,100).
FINANCES *Year* 2015 *Income* £127,126 *Grants* £182,766 *Grants to organisations* £182,766 *Assets* £3,538,092
TRUSTEES Dr Christopher Greenfield; Baroness Sal Brinton; Julian Huppert; Lisa Smart; Andrew

Neal; Susan Mendus; Alison Goldsworthy; Sir Nick Harvey; Amy Dalrymple.

OTHER INFORMATION There were 14 grants of £1,000 or less totalling £6,575. The trust was endowed by The Joseph Rowntree Reform Trust Ltd (JRRT) and **only** gives charitable grants in areas closely related to the work of the main trust. All directors of The Joseph Rowntree Reform Trust Ltd are also trustees of The JRSST Charitable Trust. JRRT differs from the other Rowntree charities, and from almost every other charity in the UK, in that it is not a charity. Charities must not have political objectives and while they may engage in political activity in pursuit of their charitable aims, those aims must not in themselves be political. By contrast, JRRT is a limited company which pays tax on its income. It is, therefore, free to give grants for political purposes; to promote political and democratic reform and defend civil liberties. JRRT does not accept unsolicited applications from charities.

HOW TO APPLY Applications for large grants of over £7,500 are accepted on a quarterly basis in March, June, September and November. Applicants will need to submit an outline proposal followed by a full application. Applications for smaller grants of under £7,500 can be submitted at any time except for the weeks in which the trust is accepting applications for larger grants. See the trust's website for specific deadline dates.

WHO TO APPLY TO Jim Wallace, The Garden House, Water End, York YO30 6WQ *Tel.* 01904 625744 *Fax* 01904 651502 *Email* info@jrrt.org.uk *Website* www.jrrt.org.uk/apply

■ The Jabbs Foundation

CC NO 1128402 **ESTABLISHED** 2009

WHERE FUNDING CAN BE GIVEN UK, with a focus on the West Midlands.

WHO CAN BENEFIT Registered charities; universities; educational and research institutions; projects lead by medics of international reputation and standing; major university hospitals.

WHAT IS FUNDED General charitable purposes; however, the trustees have focused their grant-making on the following areas: medical research; education (including educational activities by arts organisations); enhancing personal, family and community relationships in the West Midlands; the provision of support to vulnerable members of society and the prevention of people entering the criminal justice system; and research into the health of trees and forests.

SAMPLE GRANTS A list of beneficiaries was not included in the annual report and accounts. However, the annual report does note that £137,500 was given to support medical research, including into kidney disease and brain function, and £27,000 was given to support educational activities run by major arts organisations at local schools in deprived areas of Birmingham.

FINANCES *Year* 2015/16 *Income* £476,337 *Grants* £1,730,188 *Grants to organisations* £1,730,188 *Assets* £602,729

TRUSTEES Robin Daniels; Dr Alexander Wright; Ruth Keighley.

HOW TO APPLY Apply in writing to the correspondent.

WHO TO APPLY TO The Trustees, The Jabbs Foundation, PO Box 16067, Birmingham, West Midlands B32 9GP *Tel.* 0121 428 2593

■ C. Richard Jackson Charitable Trust

CC NO 1073442 **ESTABLISHED** 1998

WHERE FUNDING CAN BE GIVEN UK.

WHO CAN BENEFIT Registered charities.

WHAT IS FUNDED General charitable purposes, particularly disadvantaged children and young people, and individuals with life-limiting disorders.

RANGE OF GRANTS Typically up to £1,000.

SAMPLE GRANTS The Prince's Trust (£56,500); St Michael's Hospice (£17,000); Christian Aid (£9,000); Prince of Wales Hospice (£1,000); Harrogate International Festival and Harrogate Spa Tennis Centre (£500 each); Motor Neurone Disease Association (£100); Martin House (£50).

FINANCES *Year* 2015/16 *Income* £127,971 *Grants* £84,495 *Grants to organisations* £84,495 *Assets* £53,168

TRUSTEES Charles Jackson; Jeremy Jackson; Lucy Crack.

OTHER INFORMATION Eight organisations were supported during the year.

HOW TO APPLY Apply in writing to the correspondent.

WHO TO APPLY TO Charles Jackson, Trustee, Loftus Hill, Ferrensby, Knaresborough, North Yorkshire HG5 9JT *Tel.* 01423 520232 *Email* agk@crjholdings.co.uk

■ The Sir Barry Jackson County Fund (incorporating the Hornton Fund)

CC NO 517306 **ESTABLISHED** 1985

WHERE FUNDING CAN BE GIVEN The West Midlands (Birmingham, Coventry, Dudley, Sandwell, Solihull, Walsall and Wolverhampton).

WHO CAN BENEFIT Organisations working in theatre and the dramatic arts.

WHAT IS FUNDED According to information available from the website, the **County Fund** supports 'the presentation of high-standard productions of plays'. There are full eligibility criteria available to download from the website. In addition, the fund may also support: the development of young people's abilities and understanding in the art of drama through educational work in schools and colleges located in the area of benefit; and the expansion of the awareness and appreciation of live theatre. Through the **Hornton Fund**, grants are made to support the development of talented children and young people, particularly in regard to the arts, who are living in the area of benefit.

WHAT IS NOT FUNDED Individuals; support is only given to established touring companies.

TYPE OF GRANT One-off.

RANGE OF GRANTS Grants from the County Fund and the Horton Fund rarely exceed £3,000 and £2,000, respectively.

SAMPLE GRANTS Birmingham Repertory Theatre Ltd – Community Tour (£60,000); Birmingham Repertory Theatre Writers' Commission (£5,000); Cloud Cuckoo Land and Vamos Theatre (£2,700 each); The Bone Ensemble (£2,500); The Old Rep and Sampad (£2,000 each); BE Next (£1,000); Tea and Tenacity (£500).

FINANCES *Year* 2015/16 *Income* £92,331 *Grants* £86,220 *Grants to organisations* £86,220 *Assets* £2,034,638

TRUSTEES David Burman Edgar; Roger Burman; Anthony Chorley; Graham Winteringham; Ian

Ayliffe King; Deborah Shaw; Barry Bowles; Claire Cochrane; Dr Angela Maxwell; Gavin Orton; Linda Morgan; Graham Saunders.

OTHER INFORMATION The majority of expenditure from the **County Fund** is received by the Birmingham Repertory Theatre. Around £6,000 is distributed from the **Hornton Fund** each year.

HOW TO APPLY In the first instance, see the website for full information, including criteria and application guidelines. Application and contact details forms are available from the Hon. Secretary or to download from the website. Applications are usually considered twice a year, in January and June, and should be submitted no later than 1 December and 1 May, respectively. The guidelines further note: 'Where possible you are advised to inform the Hon. Secretary well in advance of your intention to submit an application, using the email address.'

WHO TO APPLY TO Stephen Gill, Hon. Secretary, c/o Birmingham Repertory Theatre Ltd, Centenary Square, Broad Street, Birmingham B1 2EP *Tel.* 01983 617842 *Email* sbjt@outlook.com *Website* www.birmingham-rep.co.uk/we-are-the-rep/the-sir-barry-jackson-trust.html

The Ruth and Lionel Jacobson Trust (Second Fund) No. 2

CC NO 326665 **ESTABLISHED** 1984

WHERE FUNDING CAN BE GIVEN UK, with a preference for North East England.

WHO CAN BENEFIT Registered charities.

WHAT IS FUNDED General charitable purposes; Jewish causes; education, health and disability; medical research; relief in need.

WHAT IS NOT FUNDED Individuals.

TYPE OF GRANT One-off and regular grants; project support; research. Funding is available for one year or less.

RANGE OF GRANTS £500 to £50,000.

SAMPLE GRANTS Newcastle University – North of England Children's Cancer Research (£50,000); Newcastle University – molecular research (£20,000); United Jewish Israel Appeal (UJIA) (£15,000); WIZO UK (£6,000); Arthritis Research, Conquer and Learn (£2,000 each); Association of Jewish Ex-Servicemen, (£1,000); NE Jewish Community Services (£500); Newcastle Reform Synagogue (£330).

FINANCES *Year* 2015/16 *Income* £64,940 *Grants* £99,925 *Grants to organisations* £99,925 *Assets* £1,482,723

TRUSTEES Anne Jacobson; Malcolm Jacobson.

OTHER INFORMATION During the year the trust awarded 18 grants.

HOW TO APPLY Apply in writing to the correspondent.

WHO TO APPLY TO Malcolm Jacobson, Trustee, 14 The Grainger Suite, Dobson House, Regent Centre, Gosforth, Newcastle upon Tyne NE3 3PF *Email* mjacobson2006@gmail.com

John James Bristol Foundation

CC NO 288417 **ESTABLISHED** 1983

WHERE FUNDING CAN BE GIVEN Bristol.

WHO CAN BENEFIT Charitable bodies and schools benefitting Bristol residents.

WHAT IS FUNDED Education; health; older people; general charitable purposes.

WHAT IS NOT FUNDED Individuals.

TYPE OF GRANT Capital and core costs; unrestricted funding.

RANGE OF GRANTS Up to £200,000.

SAMPLE GRANTS Bristol Aero Collection Trust (£200,000); Hawkspring (£100,000); Redland Parish Church (£50,000); Badminton School and Bristol Grammar School and Queen Elizabeth Hospital (£30,000 each); Bristol Refugee Rights (£25,000); Farms For City Children (£15,600); Dance Voice and Open Up Music CIC (£10,100); W.E. Care and Repair (£8,100); National Osteoporosis Society (£6,000); Independent Age (£4,000); The Honeypot Children's Charity (£1,100).

FINANCES *Year* 2015/16 *Income* £2,169,019 *Grants* £1,673,032 *Grants to organisations* £1,673,032 *Assets* £72,754,993

TRUSTEES Joan Johnson; David Johnson; Elizabeth Chambers; John Evans; Andrew Jardine; Andrew Webley; Dr John Haworth; Peter Goodwin; Nicola Parker.

HOW TO APPLY The trustees meet quarterly in February, May, August and November to consider appeals received by the 15th of January, April, July and October, respectively. There is no formal application form and appeals **must be submitted by post**, to the chief executive of the foundation. Appeals should be no more than two sides of A4. All appeal applications are acknowledged, stating the month in which the appeal will be considered by the trustees.

WHO TO APPLY TO Julia Norton, Chief Executive, 7 Clyde Road, Redland, Bristol BS6 6RG *Tel.* 0117 923 9444 *Fax* 0117 923 9470 *Email* info@johnjames.org.uk *Website* johnjames.org.uk/how_to_apply

The Susan and Stephen James Charitable Settlement

CC NO 801622 **ESTABLISHED** 1988

WHERE FUNDING CAN BE GIVEN UK.

WHO CAN BENEFIT Charitable organisations.

WHAT IS FUNDED General charitable purposes, mainly Jewish and health causes.

TYPE OF GRANT Capital and other costs; generally unrestricted funding.

RANGE OF GRANTS From £50 to £50,000, but mostly of £1,000 or less.

SAMPLE GRANTS Chai Cancer Care (£50,000); Community Security Trust and Norwood (£20,000 each); Jewish Blind and Disabled and World Jewish Relief (£7,500 each); Heart Cells Foundation (£5,400); Jewish Care (£5,250); Breakaway (£780); Grief Encounter (£600); British Friends of Art Museums of Israel (£350); Breast Cancer Care, Great Ormond Street Hospital and Jewish Deaf Association (£250); North London Hospice (£100); Friends of the Sick (£50).

FINANCES *Year* 2015 *Income* £96,375 *Grants* £143,947 *Grants to organisations* £143,947 *Assets* £61,299

TRUSTEES Stephen James; Susan James.

OTHER INFORMATION In 2015 grants were given to 32 organisations.

HOW TO APPLY Applications can be made in writing to the correspondent, although the charity has previously stated that unsolicited applications are not generally considered.

WHO TO APPLY TO Stephen James, Trustee, 4 Turner Drive, London NW11 6TX *Tel.* 020 7486 5838

■ Lady Eda Jardine Charitable Trust

SC NO SC011599 **ESTABLISHED** 1960

WHERE FUNDING CAN BE GIVEN Scotland.

WHO CAN BENEFIT Charitable organisations.

WHAT IS FUNDED In addition to meeting the trust's objects in relation to support for a number of specific organisations (The Heriot-Watt College, University of Edinburgh, The Edinburgh Festival of Music and Drama and related organisations, and The National Trust in Scotland), the trustees select a different charitable sector to support each year. Chosen sectors are: children and youth (2017); heritage, conservation, the environment, gardens and the arts (2018); health and disability (2019).

RANGE OF GRANTS Between £1,000 and £7,500, mostly £1,000 to £1,500.

SAMPLE GRANTS University of Edinburgh Development Trust (£7,500); National Trust for Scotland (£6,000); Canine Partners (£4,000); Scottish Opera (£3,000); Nordoff-Robbins Music Therapy in Scotland (£2,500); Breast Cancer Care Scotland, Dream Holidays, St David's Bradbury Day Centre and Support in Mind Scotland (£1,500 each); British Wireless for the Blind Fund, Headway, National Autistic Society and Women's Rape and Sexual Abuse Centre (£1,000 each).

FINANCES *Year* 2015/16 *Income* £73,962 *Grants* £56,000 *Grants to organisations* £56,000 *Assets* £1,765,507

OTHER INFORMATION In 2015/16, 29 organisations were supported.

HOW TO APPLY Apply in writing to the correspondent. In 2015/16 the trustees agreed donations at their annual meeting, which was held in September.

WHO TO APPLY TO The Trustees of Lady Eda Jardine Charitable Trust, Anderson Strathern, 1 Rutland Court, Edinburgh EH3 8EY *Tel.* 0131 270 7700

■ The Jarman Charitable Trust

CC NO 239198 **ESTABLISHED** 1964

WHERE FUNDING CAN BE GIVEN Birmingham and the surrounding areas.

WHO CAN BENEFIT Charitable organisations.

WHAT IS FUNDED General charitable purposes, particularly social welfare.

SAMPLE GRANTS Coventry Day Centre for the Homeless; Friendship Project for Children; St Anne's Hostel for Men; St Paul's Church; Samaritans – Birmingham; Shakespeare Hospice and Victim Support – East Birmingham.

FINANCES *Year* 2015/16 *Income* £47,756 *Grants* £41,050 *Grants to organisations* £41,050 *Assets* £1,087,174

TRUSTEES Dr Geoffrey Jarman; Susan Chilton; Ilfra Jarman.

OTHER INFORMATION Grants were awarded to 169 organisations in 2015/16.

HOW TO APPLY The trustees meet in spring and autumn. Our previous research suggests that applications should be made in writing to the correspondent by the first week in February or the first week in September. The trust does not invite telephone calls and will not acknowledge applications even if an sae is enclosed. Accounts and/or budgets should be included.

WHO TO APPLY TO Susan Chilton, Trustee, 52 Lee Crescent, Edgbaston, Birmingham, West Midlands B15 2BJ *Tel.* 0121 247 2622 *Email* jarmanct@hotmail.com

■ John Jarrold Trust Ltd

CC NO 242029 **ESTABLISHED** 1965

WHERE FUNDING CAN BE GIVEN Norfolk, with a current focus on the Norwich, Wymondham and Cromer areas; and financially developing countries.

WHO CAN BENEFIT Organisations.

WHAT IS FUNDED Social welfare and community; the arts; education; medical and health; churches and historic buildings; the environment; support in financially developing countries. Special attention is given to education and research in natural sciences.

WHAT IS NOT FUNDED Individual education programmes or needs; gap year type projects are not currently assisted; applications from new charities, unless there is some specific connection to Norwich and Norfolk; individual churches.

RANGE OF GRANTS Up to £7,000, but generally up to £2,000.

SAMPLE GRANTS Norfolk Churches Trust (£7,000); Childhood First (£4,000); Concern Worldwide and Norwich Theatre Royal (£2,000 each); Cinema City Ltd (£1,700); Norfolk Mathematics Masterclasses and Prisoners' Education Trust (£1,000 each); Deafblind UK, Norfolk Carers Support, Songbird Survival and The Leprosy Mission (£500 each); The Friends of Norwich Museums (£300); Norfolk County Council, Norfolk Family Mediation Service, Norfolk Rivers Trust and St Nicholas Hospice Care (£250 each); Notre Dame High School (£25).

FINANCES *Year* 2015/16 *Income* £111,346 *Grants* £84,500 *Grants to organisations* £84,500 *Assets* £2,477,246

TRUSTEES Caroline Jarrold; Peter Jarrold; Richard Jarrold; Antony Jarrold; Waltraud Jarrold; Charles Jarrold; Susan Jarrold.

OTHER INFORMATION The trust supports historic churches in Norfolk through the Norfolk Churches Trust to which it gives regular donations.

HOW TO APPLY There is no formal application form. Applications should be made in writing to the correspondent detailing information about the project including financial information and a set of your organisation's most recent accounts (where available), as well as an email address for responses and details of the bank account name to which any cheques should be made payable if the application is successful. Preferably, applications should be submitted by post. Large packs of information should not be sent in the first instance. The trustees meet in January and June; applications should be submitted by the end of November and April respectively. Applications which do not fit the categories considered by the trustees will not be acknowledged.

WHO TO APPLY TO Caroline Jarrold, Secretary, The John Jarrold Trust, Jarrold and Sons Ltd, St James Works, 12–20 Whitefriars, Norwich NR3 1SH *Tel.* 01603 677360 *Email* caroline.jarrold@jarrold.com *Website* www.johnjarroldtrust.org.uk

■ Rees Jeffreys Road Fund

CC NO 217771 **ESTABLISHED** 1950

WHERE FUNDING CAN BE GIVEN UK.

WHO CAN BENEFIT Universities; research bodies; academic staff and students.

WHAT IS FUNDED Education and research in transport; projects that improve the roadside environment for motorists and other road users.

WHAT IS NOT FUNDED Environmental projects not related to roads and transport; individual works for cycle tracks; works of only local application; operational and administrative staff costs are rarely considered.
TYPE OF GRANT One-off; projects; bursaries; research; lectureships.
RANGE OF GRANTS £2,400 to £32,000.
SAMPLE GRANTS Rees Jeffreys Major Roads Project (£32,000); EDT Headstart (£7,800); In 2 Change (£7,000); Surrey Fire and Rescue (£5,500); Cycle Smart Foundation (£4,500); West Midland Fire Service (£4,000); SATRO (£2,400).
FINANCES *Year* 2016 *Income* £100,473 *Grants* £167,550 *Grants to organisations* £68,550 *Assets* £7,032,932
TRUSTEES Martin Shaw; Prof. Stephen Glaister; Anthony Depledge; David Hutchinson; Mary Lewis; David Tarrant; Ginny Clarke; Prof. Glenn Lyons; Steve Gooding.
HOW TO APPLY Apply in writing to the correspondent (no more than three A4 pages) stating the purpose for which funding is sought, outlining the objects, relevance and the proposed methodology of the project including the names of the principal participants. Applications can be made at any time and should be sent to the secretary. Informal contact prior to submitting a formal application is welcomed. The charity's website has further guidance for potential applicants as well as deadlines for upcoming trustee meetings.
WHO TO APPLY TO Brian Murrell, Secretary, 7 The Grove, Uxbridge, Middlesex UB10 8QH *Tel.* 05603 849370 *Email* brianmurrell@reesjeffreys.org *Website* www.reesjeffreys.co.uk

■ Nick Jenkins Foundation

CC NO 1135565 **ESTABLISHED** 2010
WHERE FUNDING CAN BE GIVEN UK and overseas.
WHO CAN BENEFIT Charitable organisations.
WHAT IS FUNDED General charitable purposes.
RANGE OF GRANTS £500 to £52,500.
SAMPLE GRANTS Operation Fistula UK (£52,500); Absolute Return for Kids (£50,000); New Philanthropy Capital and Shivia Microfinance (£10,000 each); Wings for Life (£2,000); Anna Trust, Weldmar Hospice and Wessex MS Centre (£500 each).
FINANCES *Year* 2015/16 *Income* £1,202,333 *Grants* £126,050 *Grants to organisations* £126,050 *Assets* £1,582,190
TRUSTEES Rosemary Rafferty; Alison Jenkins; Nick Jenkins.
OTHER INFORMATION In 2015/16 eight grants were made.
HOW TO APPLY The foundation 'actively seeks projects to fund and does not accept unsolicited applications for grants'.
WHO TO APPLY TO Nick Jenkins, Trustee, Bapton Manor, Bapton, Warminster BA12 0SB *Email* mail@nickjenkins.org

■ The Jenour Foundation

CC NO 256637 **ESTABLISHED** 1968
WHERE FUNDING CAN BE GIVEN UK, with a preference for Wales.
WHO CAN BENEFIT Registered charities only. Both UK charities and local charities in Wales are supported.
WHAT IS FUNDED General charitable purposes, including health causes, medical research, young people, arts and culture and animal welfare.
WHAT IS NOT FUNDED Organisations which are not registered charities.
TYPE OF GRANT Capital projects.
RANGE OF GRANTS Between £500 and £10,000.
SAMPLE GRANTS Army Benevolent Fund (£10,000); Cancer Research Wales (£9,000); Atlantic College (£8,000); Macmillan Cancer Care and Welsh National Opera (£6,000 each); Marie Curie Hospice – Penarth (£4,000); St John Ambulance in Wales (£3,000); Bath Institute of Medical Engineering, Llandovery College and Wales Millennium Centre (£2,500 each); British Scoliosis Research Foundation and Independent Age (£2,000 each); Coeliac UK and Society for the Welfare of Horses and Ponies (£500 each).
FINANCES *Year* 2015/16 *Income* £143,496 *Grants* £110,500 *Grants to organisations* £110,500 *Assets* £3,511,370
TRUSTEES David Jones; Sir Peter Phillips; James Zorab; Christopher Davies.
OTHER INFORMATION Donations were made to 41 organisations in 2015/16; all but four of these had previously received support from the foundation.
HOW TO APPLY Applications should be made in writing to the correspondent. The annual report for 2015/16 explains that: 'The majority of donations are made annually in February, but correspondence is not entered into unless it relates to donations that the Foundation has agreed to make.'
WHO TO APPLY TO Claire Thompson, The Jenour Foundation, c/o Broomfield and Alexander, 1–3 Waters Lane, Newport NP20 1LA *Tel.* 029 2026 4391 *Fax* 029 2026 4444

■ The Jephcott Charitable Trust

CC NO 240915 **ESTABLISHED** 1965
WHERE FUNDING CAN BE GIVEN Worldwide.
WHO CAN BENEFIT Charitable organisations worldwide struggling to get started or raise funds from other sources.
WHAT IS FUNDED Population control; natural environment; education; health.
WHAT IS NOT FUNDED Organisations whose administrative expenses form more than 15% of their annual income; individuals; animal welfare; heritage and buildings; retrospective expenditure. Projects which require long-term funding are not normally considered.
TYPE OF GRANT Start-up costs; seed funding; project costs.
RANGE OF GRANTS £1,000 to £13,500.
SAMPLE GRANTS John Layall Foundation (£13,500); Children of Choba, Hands, Lotus Flower Trust and Makhad Trust (£10,000 each); Supporting Dalit Children (£8,000); Vision Africa (£4,000); Enlighten Trust (£3,000); Friends of Midnapore (£2,500); Asthma International (£1,000).
FINANCES *Year* 2015/16 *Income* £76,500 *Grants* £70,756 *Grants to organisations* £70,756 *Assets* £6,032,464
TRUSTEES Anthony North; Keith Morgan; Lady Mary Jephcott; Mark Jephcott; Dr David Thomas; James Parker.
OTHER INFORMATION Grants were made to 11 organisations during the year.
HOW TO APPLY Full and detailed guidelines and application forms can be downloaded from the trust's website. The trustees meet in April and October each year. If your application is ineligible you will be notified within a few weeks of your application. Successful applicants will hear from the trust shortly after the meeting.

The website notes: 'Each year we receive many more applications than we can fund. We have to reject many applications which are eligible under our guidelines but are of a lower priority.'

WHO TO APPLY TO Dr Felicity Gibling, Secretary, The Threshing Barn, Ford, Kingsbridge, Devon TQ7 2LN *Website* www.jephcottcharitabletrust.org.uk

■ The Jerusalem Trust

CC NO 285696 **ESTABLISHED** 1982

WHERE FUNDING CAN BE GIVEN Worldwide.

WHO CAN BENEFIT Christian organisations; charitable organisations.

WHAT IS FUNDED Christian Evangelism and relief work overseas; Christian media and education; Evangelism and Christian mission in the UK.

WHAT IS NOT FUNDED Building or repair work for churches; individuals; educational fees; expeditions.

RANGE OF GRANTS Up to £666,500 typically less than £50,000.

SAMPLE GRANTS Auckland Castle Trust (£666,500); Jerusalem Production Ltd (£300,000); Tear Fund (£199,000); Safe Families For Children (£175,000); Bible Reading Fellowship and Catholic Agency For Overseas Development (£110,000); Hope Into Action (£80,000); World Vision UK (£63,000); Theos (£60,000).

FINANCES *Year* 2015/16 *Income* £2,822,000 *Grants* £4,103,071 *Grants to organisations* £4,103,071 *Assets* £86,600,000

TRUSTEES The Rt Hon. Sir Timothy Sainsbury; Lady Susan Sainsbury; Dr Hartley Booth; Phillida Goad; Dr Peter Frankopan; Melanie Townsend.

OTHER INFORMATION This trust is one of the Sainsbury Family Charitable Trusts, all of which share a joint administration but work autonomously as an independent legal entity yet have a common approach to grant-making. The trust only funds registered charities. During the year, 131 organisations were supported.

HOW TO APPLY Unsolicited applications are generally discouraged and the 2015/16 annual report states that 'proposals are generally invited by the trustees or initiated at their request'. Applications should be made in writing via post including a description (strictly no more than two pages) of the proposed project. Do not include any accounts or additional brochures. A single application will be considered for support by all the trusts in the group. If you are successful you should hear from the trust within eight weeks of the acknowledgement. Unsuccessful appeals are not notified.

WHO TO APPLY TO Alan Bookbinder, Director, The Peak, 5 Wilton Road, London SW1V 1AP *Tel.* 020 7410 0330 *Email* info@sfct.org.uk *Website* www.sfct.org.uk

■ The Jerwood Charitable Foundation

CC NO 1074036 **ESTABLISHED** 1999

WHERE FUNDING CAN BE GIVEN UK.

WHO CAN BENEFIT Arts organisations; charitable organisations.

WHAT IS FUNDED The arts and culture.

WHAT IS NOT FUNDED Non-arts projects; building or capital costs; projects involving those who have not yet left formal education; academic study or course fees, or any associated costs; formal or informal education or community participation work; projects which support artists who are not resident in the UK; general rehearsal, touring, production or staging costs for performances or exhibitions; retrospective awards or funding for retrospective activity; grants towards the purchase of musical instruments projects in the fields of religion or sport; animal rights or welfare appeals; social welfare; general fundraising appeals; appeals to establish endowment funds for other charities; medical research; environmental or conservation projects; medical or mental health projects.

TYPE OF GRANT Project support; principally one-off for a project cycle but can be recurrent as a part of a partnership.

RANGE OF GRANTS Small grants for up to £10,000. Large grants over £10,000.

SAMPLE GRANTS Royal Court (£75,000); Arvon Foundation (£56,000); Gate Theatre (£30,000); Yorkshire Dance (£27,000); Resonance FM (£25,000); Home for Waifs and Strays and Southbank Sinfonia (£10,000 each); Camden People's Theatre: Home Run (£9,500).

FINANCES *Year* 2016 *Income* £1,319,418 *Grants* £1,146,247 *Grants to organisations* £1,042,801 *Assets* £28,973,381

TRUSTEES Katharine Goodison; Rupert Tyler; Juliane Wharton; Timothy Eyles; Thomas Grieve; Phyllida Earle; Anthony Palmer; Lucy Ash; Philippa Hogan-Hern.

OTHER INFORMATION During the year a total of 51 project grants were given and the foundation worked with 91 arts organisations. The amount of grants given to individuals totalled £103,500. The foundation host an open grants programme as well as proactively funding the Jerwood Visual Arts series of events.

HOW TO APPLY In all instances, potential applicants should consult the detailed guidance on the website and contact the foundation. If the foundation thinks your project might be suitable then it will invite you to submit a two page summary of your project and budget. The foundation stresses that you must not submit an application without first contacting its office.

WHO TO APPLY TO Shonagh Manson, Director, 171 Union Street, Bankside, London SE1 0LN *Tel.* 020 7261 0279 *Email* info@jerwood.org *Website* www.jerwoodcharitablefoundation.org

■ Jewish Childs Day (JCD)

CC NO 209266 **ESTABLISHED** 1947

WHERE FUNDING CAN BE GIVEN Worldwide. In practice, mainly Israel, UK, Argentina and Eastern Europe.

WHO CAN BENEFIT Registered charities providing equipment or services of direct benefit to Jewish children (up to the age of 18).

WHAT IS FUNDED Charitable purposes of direct benefit to Jewish children who are disadvantaged, suffering or in need of special care.

WHAT IS NOT FUNDED Individuals; capital expenditure; general services and running costs; building or maintenance of property; staff salaries.

TYPE OF GRANT One-off and recurring for specific projects only.

RANGE OF GRANTS Generally £1,000 to £5,000. Occasional larger grants of up to £75,000.

SAMPLE GRANTS Biet Uri (£75,000); Arugot (£33,500); Amit (£28,000); Haifa Learning Enhancement (£20,000); Little Steps (£10,000); Women for Women (£5,000); Shaare Zadeck Medical (£4,600); Youth Space (£3,000); Shema (£2,500); SOS Children's Villages (£1,200).

FINANCES *Year* 2015/16 *Income* £1,099,795 *Grants* £784,599 *Grants to organisations* £784,599 *Assets* £457,469

TRUSTEES June Jacobs; Joy Moss; Stephen Moss; Virginia Campus; Frankie Epstein; Susie Olins; David Collins; Amanda Ingram; Gaby Lazarus; Dee Lahane; Charles Spungin.

OTHER INFORMATION The charity's website notes that, although in the main Jewish children are the beneficiaries, this should not exclude non-Jewish children.

HOW TO APPLY There is an online application portal and detailed guidance available on the website. Potential applicants should contact the correspondent first to discuss their proposal. Applications must be supported by audited accounts in English or with the main heading translated into English. and provide a breakdown of items and related costs that are being applied for. Applications should be submitted by 31 December, 30 April and 31 August for consideration in March, June and October, respectively. Organisations with dedicated UK fundraising operations must disclose this in the application.

WHO TO APPLY TO Melanie Klass, 707 High Road, North Finchley, London N12 0BT *Tel.* 020 8446 8804 *Email* natasha.brookner@jcd.uk.com *Website* jcd.uk.com/projects-grants

■ The Jewish Youth Fund (JYF)

CC NO 251902 **ESTABLISHED** 1937

WHERE FUNDING CAN BE GIVEN UK.

WHO CAN BENEFIT Jewish organisations.

WHAT IS FUNDED Jewish youth work projects, equipment and premises.

WHAT IS NOT FUNDED General appeals; individuals; formal education costs; running costs; individuals.

TYPE OF GRANT Grants for projects and equipment. Loans may be offered towards the cost of building. The charity can provide start-up costs as well as subsequent funding.

RANGE OF GRANTS £1,000 to £16,000.

SAMPLE GRANTS UJC Bristol (£16,000); Limmud (£10,000); Maccabi GB and Noam (£9,000); Chaverim and Kisharon (£5,000 each); Kidscare (£2,500); TAL – Torah Action Life (£1,000).

FINANCES *Year* 2015/16 *Income* £71,062 *Grants* £118,190 *Grants to organisations* £118,190 *Assets* £3,522,345

TRUSTEES Philippa Strauss; Adam Rose; Lady Ruth Morris of Kenwood; Lord Jonathan Morris; David Goldberg; Elliot Simberg; Stephen Spitz; David Brown; Joshua Marks.

OTHER INFORMATION Grants were given to 17 organisations – ten for education, five for recreation and leisure and two for the relief of poverty.

HOW TO APPLY Applications can be made on a form available from the correspondent. Applicants should enclose a copy of the latest accounts and an annual report. For the most up-to-date submission deadline consult the charity's website.

WHO TO APPLY TO Julia Samuel, Secretary, 35 Ballards Lane, London N3 1XW *Email* info@jyf.org.uk *Website* www.jyf.org.uk

■ Joffe Charitable Trust

CC NO 270299 **ESTABLISHED** 1968

WHERE FUNDING CAN BE GIVEN The Gambia; Kenya; Malawi; Mozambique; South Africa; Tanzania; Uganda; Zambia; and Zimbabwe.

WHO CAN BENEFIT Registered charities.

WHAT IS FUNDED Alleviation of poverty; community and economic development; human rights.

WHAT IS NOT FUNDED One-off projects (unless they show a very clear strategic purpose); work that primarily delivers basic services to poor people; emergency relief; individuals; the arts; micro credit; work primarily in the field of HIV/AIDS; physical infrastructure; large charities with income of over £5 million per year.

TYPE OF GRANT Grants and loans for up to three years; core costs; salaries.

RANGE OF GRANTS Up to £100,000.

SAMPLE GRANTS Control Arms Secretariat (£100,000); University of the Free State (£51,500); Mango (£50,000); African Prisons Project (£40,000); Tax Justice Network (£37,500); Charities Aid Foundation (£25,000); Global Alliance for Tax Justice (£20,000); Corruption Watch (£16,000).

FINANCES *Year* 2015/16 *Income* £283,296 *Grants* £581,513 *Grants to organisations* £581,513 *Assets* £10,304,660

TRUSTEES Lady Vanetta Joffe; Deborah Joffe; Myles Wickstead; Barbara Frost; Mark Poston; Alex Jacobs.

OTHER INFORMATION Grants below £10,000 totalled £112,000.

HOW TO APPLY Apply in writing to the correspondent. There is a funding policy available to download on the website which you should consult before sending a brief email (up to four paragraphs) outlining your proposal. The trust will then contact successful applicants and invite them to submit a full application.

WHO TO APPLY TO Carin Lake, Trust Manager, c/o Liddington Manor, Liddington, Swindon SN4 0HD *Tel.* 0117 973 2917 *Email* joffetrust@lidmanor.co.uk *Website* www.joffecharitabletrust.org/how_to_apply.aspx

■ The Elton John AIDS Foundation (EJAF)

CC NO 1017336 **ESTABLISHED** 1993

WHERE FUNDING CAN BE GIVEN Europe, Asia and Africa. There is a New York-based sister organisation which supports causes in Americas and the Caribbean. For a full list of specific eligible countries for each grant programme see the foundation's website.

WHO CAN BENEFIT Registered charities.

WHAT IS FUNDED The provision of focused and sustainable funding to frontline programmes that help alleviate the physical, emotional and financial hardship of those living with, affected by or at risk of HIV/AIDS, and their families.

WHAT IS NOT FUNDED Individuals; academic or pure medical research; conferences; repatriation costs; retrospective funding.

TYPE OF GRANT Specific projects; one-off and running costs; salaries; operational research; up to five years; unrestricted funding.

RANGE OF GRANTS Up to £1.2 million.

SAMPLE GRANTS Elizabeth Glaser Pediatric AIDS Foundation (£1.2 million); Y. R. Gaitonde Centre For AIDS Research and Education (£993,500); UHAI EASHRI (£987,000); APCOM (£790,000); Infectious Disease Institute and Jhpiego (£745,000 each).

FINANCES *Year* 2015 *Income* £5,069,132 *Grants* £9,205,850 *Grants to organisations* £9,205,850 *Assets* £15,104,875

TRUSTEES Anne Aslett; David Furnish; Sir Elton John; Johnny Bergius; Rafi Manoukian; Scott

Campbell; Iain Abrahams; Graham Norton; Dr Mark Dybul.
OTHER INFORMATION Total grants were broken down into five separate categories – Pioneer (£5.7 million); Support (£330,000); Advocacy (£340,000); Flagship (£3.2 million) and Robert Key Memorial Fund (£121,000).
HOW TO APPLY See the foundation's website for more information on its open funding programmes, their eligibility criteria and details of how to make an application.
WHO TO APPLY TO The Grants Team, 1 Blythe Road, London W14 0HG *Tel.* 020 7603 9996 *Email* grants@ejaf.com *Website* london.ejaf.org/grants

■ Lillie Johnson Charitable Trust

CC NO 326761 **ESTABLISHED** 1984
WHERE FUNDING CAN BE GIVEN UK, with a preference for the West Midlands.
WHO CAN BENEFIT Charitable organisations.
WHAT IS FUNDED General charitable purposes, particularly health, people who are blind or deaf, and children and young people.
WHAT IS NOT FUNDED In practice, individuals are not supported.
RANGE OF GRANTS Up to £71,000; the vast majority of grants are of £1,000 or less.
SAMPLE GRANTS Cameron Grant Foundation (£71,000); LEC Worcester (£35,000); West House School (£10,000); Birmingham Youth Theatre and Family Care Trust (£6,000 each); The Prince's Trust and Samaritans – Solihull (£4,000 each); Birmingham Women's Hospital and Harborne Carnival (£2,000 each); Acorns Hospice, Age UK, Brain Tumour Research, British Forces Foundation, City of Birmingham Symphony Orchestra, Living Hope Belfast, Nuneaton Equestrian Centre, St Richard's Hospice, Sight Concern, Warwickshire Junior Tennis Foundation, YMCA – Worcester and Zoë's Place (£1,000 each).
FINANCES *Year* 2015/16 *Income* £297,794 *Grants* £319,175 *Grants to organisations* £319,175 *Assets* £6,147,021
TRUSTEES Victor Lyttle; Peter Adams; John Desmond; Verena Adams.
OTHER INFORMATION There were 265 awards made, including 176 grants under £1,000.
HOW TO APPLY Our research suggests that applications are only considered from charities which are traditionally supported by the trust. The trustees have previously stated that they are inundated with applications they cannot support and feel obliged to respond to all of these.
WHO TO APPLY TO John Desmond, Trustee, Heathcote House, 39 Rodbourne Road, Harborne, Birmingham B17 0PN *Tel.* 0121 472 1279 *Email* john.w.desmond@googlemail.com

■ The Johnson Foundation

CC NO 518660 **ESTABLISHED** 1987
WHERE FUNDING CAN BE GIVEN City of Liverpool and the Merseyside area.
WHO CAN BENEFIT Registered charities; community care organisations; educational bodies. The annual report 2015/16 notes: 'While the Foundation is always prepared to help large charities, it tends to specialise in helping the smaller charities unable to afford professional fund raisers.'
WHAT IS FUNDED General charitable purposes, particularly education, health, and the relief of poverty and sickness.
WHAT IS NOT FUNDED Individuals.
TYPE OF GRANT One-off or up to two years. Recurrent cost, project and research grants can be covered.
RANGE OF GRANTS Up to £500,000; the majority of grants were of less than £5,000.
SAMPLE GRANTS Onside Youth Zones – The Hive (£500,000); University of Liverpool – Alder Hey Research Project (£90,000); Wirral Hospice St John's (£16,000 in two grants); Birkenhead School (£10,000); Anthony Nolan – Liverpool Marrow (£5,700); Helplink Community Support and New Brighton FC – Youth Section (£5,000 each); Upton Hall School Sixth Form Development (£2,500); YMCA – Wirral (£2,300); Arthritis Research UK and British Heart Foundation (£2,000 each); Merseyside Police Charitable Trust (£1,800); Claire House Children's Hospice, Henshaw Society for the Blind and West Wirral Scout and Guides Gang Show (£1,000 each).
FINANCES *Year* 2015/16 *Income* £314,268 *Grants* £692,334 *Grants to organisations* £692,334 *Assets* £3,617,533
TRUSTEES Christopher Johnson; Peter Johnson.
OTHER INFORMATION Grants of less than £1,000 totalled £6,200.
HOW TO APPLY Apply in writing to the correspondent. The trustees meet monthly.
WHO TO APPLY TO Margaret Johnstone, The Johnson Foundation, c/o Park Group PLC, 1 Valley Road, Birkenhead, Wirral CH41 7ED *Tel.* 0151 653 1700 *Email* margaret.johnstone@parkgroup.co.uk

■ Johnnie Johnson Trust

CC NO 200351 **ESTABLISHED** 1961
WHERE FUNDING CAN BE GIVEN UK, with a preference for the Midlands.
WHO CAN BENEFIT Charitable organisations which provide activities for children and young people, particularly those who are disadvantaged or who have disabilities.
WHAT IS FUNDED The trust normally supports activities which promote the development of individuals by being either physically and/or mentally challenging. Sailing and water sports in the Midlands are a priority.
WHAT IS NOT FUNDED Individuals.
TYPE OF GRANT Usually one-off, for equipment or for specific purposes.
SAMPLE GRANTS Docklands Sailing and Watersports Centre (£30,500); Boys2Men and Tall Ships Youth Trust (£8,000 each); Birmingham Children's Hospital (£6,500); Stubbers Adventure Centre (£6,200); Douglas Bader Foundation (£6,000); Kids'N'Action (£5,000); Fight for Peace (£3,000); Triple 'H' Trust (£2,500); Ro-Ro Sailing (£2,200); Happy Days (£2,000); Knitbury Youth Club (£1,500); Kingswood Trust (£1,200); Clooney Soccer School (£1,000); Choysez (£425).
FINANCES *Year* 2015 *Income* £119,024 *Grants* £132,000 *Grants to organisations* £132,000
TRUSTEES Jane Fordham; Peter Johnson; Victor Johnson; Katherine Cross; Christopher Johnson; Alice Johnson; Elizabeth Shurdom.
OTHER INFORMATION The trust's latest accounts were not available to view on the Charity Commission's website although they had been received. We have therefore estimated the grant total based on previous years' information.

HOW TO APPLY Apply in writing to the correspondent.
WHO TO APPLY TO Christopher Jackson, Trustee, 49 Mason Road, Redditch, Worcestershire B97 5DT *Tel.* 01527 544722

■ Johnson Wax Ltd Charitable Trust

CC NO 200332 **ESTABLISHED** 1961
WHERE FUNDING CAN BE GIVEN Areas surrounding S. C. Johnson's sites; local neighbourhood in Frimley Green, Surrey.
WHO CAN BENEFIT Local charities; not-for-profit organisations; educational establishments.
WHAT IS FUNDED General charitable purposes; social welfare; disadvantaged individuals; older people; children; education and training; employment; the environment; health and disability; the arts; local community needs.
WHAT IS NOT FUNDED Individuals.
SAMPLE GRANTS A list of beneficiaries was not included in the latest accounts.
FINANCES *Year* 2015/16 *Income* £372,525 *Grants* £219,450 *Grants to organisations* £219,450 *Assets* £250,371
TRUSTEES Faye Gilbert; Trevor Jessett; Margaret Shukla; Martina Leahy; Alan Davies; Rodrigo Dias Bueno.
OTHER INFORMATION Grants were made for the following purposes: health and wellness (£82,500); social services (£45,700); education (£44,500); community and economic development (£17,200); arts, culture and humanities (£1,000); environment and sustainability (£180).
HOW TO APPLY Apply in writing to the correspondent, specifying the amount requested and what it is needed for, details of how the grant will benefit a broad cross-section of the Frimley Green community and how a clear social need will be met within it.
WHO TO APPLY TO Faye Gilbert, Trustee, S. C. Johnson Ltd, Frimley Green Road, Frimley, Camberley, Surrey GU16 7AJ *Email* givinguk@scj.com

■ The Christopher and Kirsty Johnston Charitable Trust

CC NO 1159433 **ESTABLISHED** 2014
WHERE FUNDING CAN BE GIVEN Worldwide.
WHO CAN BENEFIT Registered charities and non-charitable organisations that exist for charitable purposes.
WHAT IS FUNDED General charitable purposes.
RANGE OF GRANTS £1,000 to £25,000.
SAMPLE GRANTS The Mission to Seafarers, The Royal Opera House Foundation and Willen Hospice (£25,000); Buckingham Almshouses and Welfare Charity, International Nepal Fellowship and Winter Night Shelter Milton Keynes (£5,000 each); Child Brain Injury Trust, The Sick Children's Trust and Support Dogs (£1,000 each).
FINANCES *Year* 2015/16 *Income* £100,000 *Grants* £93,000 *Grants to organisations* £93,000 *Assets* £36,725
TRUSTEES John Barber; Christopher Johnston; Kirsty Johnston.
OTHER INFORMATION Nine organisations were supported during the year. In its first two years of operation, the trust has received its income in the form of donations from the settlors.
HOW TO APPLY Apply in writing to the correspondent. Note that the trust has limited sources of income.
WHO TO APPLY TO Christopher Johnston, Trustee, 24 Tudor Gardens, Stony Stratford, Milton Keynes MK11 1HX *Tel.* 01908 562113 *Email* candkjct@gmail.com

■ The Joicey Trust

CC NO 244679 **ESTABLISHED** 1965
WHERE FUNDING CAN BE GIVEN Unrestricted, but in practice the county of Northumberland, the old metropolitan county of Tyne and Wear and eastern Scottish Borders.
WHO CAN BENEFIT Registered charities.
WHAT IS FUNDED General charitable purposes; community development.
WHAT IS NOT FUNDED Medical research; charities registered outside the beneficial area and whose gross incoming resources exceed £1 million are not assisted either. Grants are not generally made to individuals, except under specific circumstances where local residents are sponsored by a charity for an international development project (see more details on the charity's website).
TYPE OF GRANT One-off for capital and revenue projects, with some preference for discrete projects over running costs. Start-up costs, buildings, core costs and salaries can be covered.
RANGE OF GRANTS £300 to £10,000.
SAMPLE GRANTS The Greggs Foundation (£10,000); Holy Island Village Hall (£5,000); North East Prison After Care Society and The Chillingham Wild Cattle Association Ltd (£3,000 each); Northumberland Domestic Abuse Service (£2,000); Apna Ghar Minority Ethnic Women's Centre (£1,500); PBC Foundation (£1,200); Samaritans of Northumbria (£1,000); Dunston Community Centre and Respite Foundation (£400 each); Church of the Ascension – Kenton (£300).
FINANCES *Year* 2015/16 *Income* £281,616 *Grants* £345,050 *Grants to organisations* £345,050 *Assets* £7,922,260
TRUSTEES R. H. Dickinson; Lord Joicey; The Rt Hon. Lady Joicey; Hon. Andrew Joicey; The Hon. Mrs K. J. Crosbie Dawson.
OTHER INFORMATION In 2015/16 grants were given to 173 organisations.
HOW TO APPLY A formal application should preferably be obtained in writing to the correspondent; however, written submissions will be accepted via post or email as well. Applications will need to include supporting documents, such as annual report and accounts and details and budget of project requiring support. The trust welcomes email enquiries before submitting a full application.
WHO TO APPLY TO Andrew Bassett, Appeals Secretary, One Trinity, Broad Chare, Newcastle upon Tyne NE1 2HF *Tel.* 0191 279 9677 *Email* appeals@thejoiceytrust.org.uk *Website* www.thejoiceytrust.org.uk

■ The Jones 1986 Charitable Trust

CC NO 327176 **ESTABLISHED** 1986
WHERE FUNDING CAN BE GIVEN Primarily Nottinghamshire.
WHO CAN BENEFIT Charitable organisations.
WHAT IS FUNDED Relief of sickness; disability; welfare of older people and of young people;

to the community.

WHAT IS NOT FUNDED Individuals.

TYPE OF GRANT Awards are considered for both capital and/or revenue projects as long as each project appears viable.

RANGE OF GRANTS Up to £60,000, but mostly between £1,000 and £10,000.

SAMPLE GRANTS Rutland House School for Parents (£60,000); Barnardo's (£20,000); Dove Cottage Day Hospice and Framework Housing (£10,000 each); Pintsize Theatre Company (£6,500); Care and Community Services and Literacy Volunteers (£5,000 each); Think Children (£4,000); Southwell, District Live at Home Scheme and Newark and Sherwood Play Support Group (£2,000 each); Focus on Young People in Bassetlaw (£1,500); Meningitis Trust (£1,000).

FINANCES *Year* 2015/16 *Income* £752,123 *Grants* £312,610 *Grants to organisations* £312,610 *Assets* £20,976,827

TRUSTEES Robert Heason; John Pears; Nigel Lindley; Richard Stanley.

OTHER INFORMATION A total of 50 organisations were supported during the year.

HOW TO APPLY Applications may be made in writing to the correspondent. The trustees invite applications for grants by advertising in specialist press.

WHO TO APPLY TO Nigel Lindley, Trustee, The Jones 1986 Charitable Trust, c/o Smith Cooper LLP, 2 Lace Market Square, Nottingham NG1 1PB *Tel.* 0115 945 4300

■ The Dezna Robins Jones Charitable Foundation

CC NO 1104252 **ESTABLISHED** 2004

WHERE FUNDING CAN BE GIVEN Preference for South Wales, particularly the Rhondda Valley.

WHO CAN BENEFIT Local charitable organisations, hospitals, hospices and educational institutions.

WHAT IS FUNDED Mainly medical and educational causes, with some support given to other local charitable causes.

RANGE OF GRANTS Mostly up to £15,000.

SAMPLE GRANTS Neil Boobyer Rugby Solutions Ltd (£62,500); Mid Rhondda Band (£27,500); Sporting Marvels (£15,000); Action Aid (£10,000); Kids Cancer Charity and Velindre Hospital (£5,000 each); Bobath Cymru (£2,900); Hospice of the Valleys and Ty Hafan (£2,500 each); Lupus UK (£500); Action Medical Research, Shalom Habbakuk Trust and World Cancer Research (£250 each).

FINANCES *Year* 2015/16 *Income* £52,760 *Grants* £162,156 *Grants to organisations* £162,156 *Assets* £1,991,273

TRUSTEES Bernard Jones; Louise Boobyer; Alexia Cooke.

OTHER INFORMATION The 2015/16 annual report notes: 'The Trustees are continuing to move their focus to support more Rhondda Valley based causes.'

HOW TO APPLY Applications can be made in writing to the correspondent. The trustees meet at least twice a year.

WHO TO APPLY TO Bernard Jones, Trustee, Greenacres, Laleston, Bridgend CF32 0HN *Tel.* 01656 768584 *Email* bernard-jones@btconnect.com

■ The Marjorie and Geoffrey Jones Charitable Trust

CC NO 1051031 **ESTABLISHED** 1995

WHERE FUNDING CAN BE GIVEN Principally Torbay, Devon and the South West.

WHO CAN BENEFIT Registered charities.

WHAT IS FUNDED General charitable purposes, including health and disability, children and families, arts and culture, sport, and the environment.

WHAT IS NOT FUNDED Individuals.

RANGE OF GRANTS £250 to £4,000.

SAMPLE GRANTS Torbay Coast and Countryside Trust and Trinity Sailing Foundation (£4,000 each); Children's Hospice Southwest, Derriford Hospital – Neo-natal Intensive Care Unit, Friends of South Devon College and Teenage Cancer Trust (£3,000 each); Barton Acorn Youth Community and Sports Centre, Devon Safer Communities Trust, Headway, Torbay Advice Network and Storybook Dads (£2,000 each); The Children's Trust (£1,000); Exeter Leukaemia Fund (£250).

FINANCES *Year* 2015/16 *Income* £27,798 *Grants* £60,250 *Grants to organisations* £60,250 *Assets* £1,367,019

TRUSTEES Nigel Wollen; William Boughey; Philip Kay; Katrina Vollentine.

OTHER INFORMATION In 2015/16 a total of 26 grants were made.

HOW TO APPLY Apply in writing to the correspondent. The trustees usually meet to consider awards between two and four times a year.

WHO TO APPLY TO Lynn Young, Wollen Michelmore Solicitors, Carlton House, 30 The Terrace, Torquay, Devon TQ1 1BS *Tel.* 01803 213251 *Email* lynn.young@wollenmichelmore.co.uk

■ The Muriel Jones Foundation

CC NO 1135107 **ESTABLISHED** 2010

WHERE FUNDING CAN BE GIVEN UK and overseas.

WHO CAN BENEFIT Registered charities.

WHAT IS FUNDED General charitable purposes.

RANGE OF GRANTS £200 to £170,000.

SAMPLE GRANTS Save Open Spaces Frome (£170,000); Anti-Slavery International and Hope Not Hate Educational Ltd (£150,000 each); World Land Trust (£100,000); Reprieve (£75,000); Epatoma Foundation (£61,500 in three grants); Crossflow (£58,000 in two grants); Animals Asia Foundation (£50,000); Serenje Orphans Appeal (£1,000); American Foundation for Suicide Prevention (£200).

FINANCES *Year* 2015/16 *Income* £166,309 *Grants* £835,666 *Grants to organisations* £835,666 *Assets* £7,808,226

TRUSTEES Richard Brindle; Katie Brindle; Coutts & Co.

OTHER INFORMATION In 2015/16 a total of 14 grants were given to 11 organisations.

HOW TO APPLY Apply in writing to the correspondent.

WHO TO APPLY TO The Trustees of The Muriel Jones Foundation, Coutts & Co., Trustee Department, 6th Floor, Trinity Quay 2, Avon Street, Bristol BS2 0PT *Tel.* 020 7663 6825 *Email* couttscharities@coutts.com

■ The Jordan Charitable Foundation

CC NO 1051507 **ESTABLISHED** 1995

WHERE FUNDING CAN BE GIVEN UK (national charities); Herefordshire, particularly Hereford, and Sutherland in Scotland (local charities).

WHO CAN BENEFIT UK national charities; local charities in Herefordshire, particularly Hereford, and Sutherland in Scotland.

WHAT IS FUNDED General charitable purposes, especially medical equipment, medical research, older people, people with disabilities (including children), animal welfare and the maintenance of Hereford Cathedral.

TYPE OF GRANT One-off and recurrent; capital and core costs; unrestricted funding.

RANGE OF GRANTS Mostly between £1,000 and £5,000.

SAMPLE GRANTS Canine Partners for Independence and Herefordshire Headway (£15,000 each); Alzheimer's Research Trust, The Samaritans and The Special Air Service Regimental Association (£10,000 each); Sutherland Schools Pipe Band (£8,000); British Diabetic Association, National Trust for Scotland, Woodlands Trust and World Horse Welfare (£5,000 each); International Animal Rescue and Loth Helmsdale Flower Show Society (£2,000 each); Queen Elizabeth Castle of May Trust (£1,000).

FINANCES *Year* 2015 *Income* £1,205,786 *Grants* £827,073 *Grants to organisations* £827,073 *Assets* £51,488,339

TRUSTEES Sir George Russell; Ralph Stockwell; Christopher Bliss; Anthony Brierley; Snowport Ltd; Parkdove Ltd.

OTHER INFORMATION In 2015 a total of 49 awards were made. An exceptionally large grant of £500,000 was made to the Institute of Cancer Research to support the building of a centre.

HOW TO APPLY Apply in writing to the correspondent. The trustees meet four times a year.

WHO TO APPLY TO Ralph Stockwell, Trustee, The Jordan Charitable Foundation, c/o Rawlinson and Hunter, 8th Floor, 6 New Street Square, New Fetter Lane, London EC4A 3AQ *Tel.* 020 7842 2000 *Email* jordan@rawlinson-hunter.com

■ The Joron Charitable Trust

CC NO 1062547 **ESTABLISHED** 1997

WHERE FUNDING CAN BE GIVEN UK and overseas.

WHO CAN BENEFIT Registered charities.

WHAT IS FUNDED General charitable purposes, including education (particularly the teaching of social and communication skills) and medical research.

TYPE OF GRANT Generally one-off.

RANGE OF GRANTS £10,000 to £250,000.

SAMPLE GRANTS The Wilderness Foundation (£250,000); Child's Dream Association (£100,000); Urology Foundation (£10,000).

FINANCES *Year* 2015/16 *Income* £852,417 *Grants* £360,000 *Grants to organisations* £360,000 *Assets* £526,458

TRUSTEES Bruce Jarvis; Joseph Jarvis; Sandra Jarvis; Juliet Jarvis.

OTHER INFORMATION In 2015/16 three grants were made.

HOW TO APPLY Apply in writing to the correspondent. There is no formal application procedure.

WHO TO APPLY TO Bruce Jarvis, Trustee, Ravensale Ltd, 115 Wembley Commercial Centre, East Lane, North Wembley, Middlesex HA9 7UR *Tel.* 020 8908 4655 *Email* ravensale100@btconnect.com

■ J. E. Joseph Charitable Fund

CC NO 209058 **ESTABLISHED** 1946

WHERE FUNDING CAN BE GIVEN London; Manchester; Israel; India.

WHO CAN BENEFIT Jewish charities.

WHAT IS FUNDED The relief of poverty and suffering; education; advancement of the Jewish religion; other charitable purposes beneficial to the Jewish community.

WHAT IS NOT FUNDED Individuals (in exceptional circumstances support may be provided where there is potential for benefit for the whole community); large national charities with significant income; capital projects are generally not supported.

RANGE OF GRANTS £2,000 to £8,000.

SAMPLE GRANTS Edinburgh House – Home for the Elderly and University Jewish Chaplaincy Board (£8,000 each); Morasha Primary School and Spanish and Portuguese Synagogue Welfare Board (£5,000 each); TAL – Torah Action Life (£4,000); Alma Primary School and Hospital Kosher Meals (£3,000 each); Ilford Synagogue (£2,500); Jewish Deaf Association and Raphael Jewish Counselling Services (£2,000 each).

FINANCES *Year* 2015/16 *Income* £164,020 *Grants* £132,000 *Grants to organisations* £132,000 *Assets* £4,993,981

TRUSTEES Susan Kendal; John Corre; Abe Simon; Edward Mocatta; Robert Shemtob; Mark Sabah; Stephen Pack.

OTHER INFORMATION The annual report for 2015/16 states: 'It was agreed in 1996 to regularise the distribution of grants by the adoption of broad guidelines whereby the Trust's distributable annual income would be allocated as 55% to Home charities, 35% to Israeli charities, 5% to Eastern (India) charities and 5% to sundry charities.'

HOW TO APPLY Apply in writing to the correspondent, including a copy of the latest accounts. The trustees respond to all applications which are first vetted by the secretary. The annual report for 2015/16 explains: 'As in previous years, the Trust received far more applications than it can support from its limited funds. However, the Trust does try, if possible, to respond favourably to some new applications each year.'

WHO TO APPLY TO Roger Leon, Secretary, 10 Compass Close, Edgware, Middlesex HA8 8HU *Tel.* 020 8958 0126 *Email* roger.leon@btinternet.com

■ The Cyril and Eve Jumbo Charitable Trust

CC NO 1097209 **ESTABLISHED** 2003

WHERE FUNDING CAN BE GIVEN UK and overseas.

WHO CAN BENEFIT Charitable organisations.

WHAT IS FUNDED General charitable purposes; overseas aid. The trust's website states that its core interests are 'creating future opportunities, human interaction, the transfer of knowledge and creating a little bit of hope'.

RANGE OF GRANTS £100 to £15,000.

SAMPLE GRANTS Tzedeck and Find Your Feet (£15,000); Action For Kids (£8,000); SLH Centre and Wherever The Need (£5,000 each); Promise Works (£2,500); Teenage Cancer Trust (£1,000); National Autistic Society (£700); Leatherhead Drama Festival (£500); Marie Curie (£150).

FINANCES *Year* 2015/16 *Income* £148,540 *Grants* £107,778 *Grants to organisations* £107,778 *Assets* £2,069,471

TRUSTEES Geoffrey Margolis; Rafiq Hayat; Kayla Justice.
OTHER INFORMATION The trust made 31 awards during the year. The trust allocates 50% of funds to the UK and 50% overseas.
HOW TO APPLY Initial submissions should be made by email (charity@mjw13.com). The trustees meet on a regular basis to consider applications. Unsuccessful applications are generally acknowledged.
WHO TO APPLY TO The Trustees, Mumbo Jumbo World, 48 Great Marlborough Street, London W1F 7BB *Tel.* 020 7437 0879 *Email* charity@mjw13.com *Website* www.cejct.com

■ Anton Jurgens Charitable Trust

CC NO 259885 **ESTABLISHED** 1969
WHERE FUNDING CAN BE GIVEN UK, with a preference for the south east of England.
WHO CAN BENEFIT UK-registered charities.
WHAT IS FUNDED General charitable purposes; social welfare; health; children and young people; education; vulnerable people.
TYPE OF GRANT Generally one-off; project funding.
RANGE OF GRANTS £500 to £20,000.
SAMPLE GRANTS Bemerton Community Ltd (£20,000); Wyverne School Foundation (£5,400); Children's Hospice South West and Scottish Spina Bifida (£5,000 each); British Refugee Council, Friends of Cathedral Music and Housing the Homeless Central Fund (£4,000 each); Haringey Shed Theatre Company and The National Tremor Foundation (£3,000 each); Performing Arts Children's Charity (£2,500); Life Education Wessex and Southampton Hospital Charity (£2,000 each); Young and Free (£1,500); Nightline (£1,300); Wessex Chalk (£500).
FINANCES *Year* 2015/16 *Income* £253,034 *Grants* £246,250 *Grants to organisations* £246,250 *Assets* £8,181,979
TRUSTEES Eric Deckers; Maria Edge-Jurgens; Frans Jurgens; Steven Jurgens; Paul Beek; Frans Tilman; Hans Veraart.
OTHER INFORMATION In 2015/16 more than 70 grants were made.
HOW TO APPLY Apply in writing to the correspondent. The trustees generally meet twice a year, in June and October. Note that they do not enter into correspondence concerning grant applications beyond notifying successful applicants.
WHO TO APPLY TO Maria Edge-Jurgens, Trustee, c/o Saffery Champness, 71 Queen Victoria Street, London EC4V 4BE *Tel.* 020 7841 4000

■ The Jusaca Charitable Trust

CC NO 1012966 **ESTABLISHED** 1992
WHERE FUNDING CAN BE GIVEN UK and overseas, particularly Israel.
WHO CAN BENEFIT Charitable organisations; the annual report for 2015/16 states: 'The objective is to distribute at least 50% of donations to Jewish charities (in the UK, overseas and in Israel), of the remainder about 40% to be donated to charities operating in the UK and about 60% outside the UK.'
WHAT IS FUNDED General charitable purposes; Jewish causes; the relief of poverty; health; education; the arts; research; housing.
TYPE OF GRANT Mainly recurring.
RANGE OF GRANTS Usually, mostly up to £5,000.
SAMPLE GRANTS World Jewish Relief (£33,500); Jewish Care (£20,000); Selah Foundation (£16,200).
FINANCES *Year* 2015/16 *Income* £536,847 *Grants* £264,858 *Grants to organisations* £264,858 *Assets* £3,577,837
TRUSTEES Donald Franklin; Sara Emanuel; Diana Franklin; Carolyn Emanuel; Maurice Emanuel; Rachel Paul; Ralph Emanuel.
OTHER INFORMATION In 2015/16 a total of 93 grants were made, of which 51 exceeded £1,000.
HOW TO APPLY Grants are made at the discretion of the trustees. Unsolicited applications are not encouraged.
WHO TO APPLY TO Sara Emanuel, Trustee, 17 Ashburnham Grove, London SE10 8UH

■ Kahal Chassidim Bobov

CC NO 278823 **ESTABLISHED** 1978
WHERE FUNDING CAN BE GIVEN Worldwide.
WHO CAN BENEFIT Jewish organisations, schools and charities.
WHAT IS FUNDED General charitable purposes, including education, medical causes and the relief of poverty.
RANGE OF GRANTS From about £35,000 to £531,000.
SAMPLE GRANTS Friends of LBS Inc. (£531,000); Yesamach Levav (£367,000); Friends of Sheba Medical Centre (£135,000); Give N'Earn (£118,500); Lolev Charitable Trust (£114,500); Keren Chochmas Shlomo (£71,500); United Talmudical Associates (£51,500); Meir Hatorah (£42,000); Collel Chibath Yrushalayim (£35,000).
FINANCES *Year* 2015/16 *Income* £3,065,990 *Grants* £2,935,585 *Grants to organisations* £2,935,585 *Assets* £473,835
TRUSTEES Abraham Schlaff; L. Stempel; Zushia Hochhauser; Moshe Brinner.
OTHER INFORMATION In 2015/16 a total of 13 organisations were supported.
HOW TO APPLY This charity is a donor-advised fund, with grants made to organisations according to the wishes of donors. The trustees may also make grants from the charity's unrestricted funds at their own discretion, based on their knowledge of organisations.
WHO TO APPLY TO Kahal Chassidim Bobov, 87 Egerton Road, London N16 6UE *Tel.* 020 8880 8910

■ The Bernard Kahn Charitable Trust

CC NO 249130 **ESTABLISHED** 1965
WHERE FUNDING CAN BE GIVEN UK and Israel.
WHO CAN BENEFIT Jewish organisations and individuals.
WHAT IS FUNDED The relief of poverty and the advancement of education and religion within the Jewish community.
RANGE OF GRANTS £10,000 to £100,000.
SAMPLE GRANTS Dov Bernard and Cynthia Kahn Charitable Trust (£100,000); Achisomoch Aid Company Ltd (£80,000); Friends of Be'er Miriam (£75,000); Orthodox Council of Jerusalem Ltd (£20,000); Chazon Avraham Yitzchok (£10,000).
FINANCES *Year* 2015/16 *Income* £27,154 *Grants* £285,000 *Grants to organisations* £285,000 *Assets* £1,083,706
TRUSTEES Mirjam Kahn; Yaacov Zvi Kahn.
OTHER INFORMATION In 2015/16 grants were made to five organisations.
HOW TO APPLY Apply in writing to the correspondent.
WHO TO APPLY TO Yaacov Zvi Kahn, Trustee, 24 Elmcroft Avenue, London NW11 0RR

■ The Stanley Kalms Foundation

CC NO 328368 **ESTABLISHED** 1989
WHERE FUNDING CAN BE GIVEN UK and Israel.
WHO CAN BENEFIT Organisations and individuals.
WHAT IS FUNDED The encouragement of Orthodox Jewish education in the UK and Israel, particularly by providing scholarships, fellowships and research grants; arts; medicine; other programmes, both secular and religious.
TYPE OF GRANT One-off; research; project grants; bursaries and scholarships.
RANGE OF GRANTS Up to £20,000.
SAMPLE GRANTS Chai Cancer Care (£20,000); Social Affairs Unit (£12,500); Legatum Institute Foundation (£10,000); King's College London (£7,500); British Friends of Haifa University, Jewish Leadership Council, Lifelites, Nightingale Hammerson, ORT UK and World Jewish Relief (£5,000 each).
FINANCES *Year* 2015/16 *Income* £70,974 *Grants* £116,020 *Grants to organisations* £116,020 *Assets* £309,516
TRUSTEES Lord Kalms of Edgware; Lady Pamela Kalms; Stephen Kalms.
OTHER INFORMATION In 2015/16 a total of 32 organisations were supported. Grants of less than £5,000 totalled £36,000.
HOW TO APPLY Apply in writing to the correspondent, but note that most of the trust's funds are committed to projects supported for a number of years.
WHO TO APPLY TO The Trustees of The Stanley Kalms Foundation, c/o Steve Russell And Associates, Paddock Hill House, Sacombe Green, Sacombe, Ware SG12 0JH *Tel.* 01438 365804

■ Karaviotis Foundation

CC NO 274576 **ESTABLISHED** 1977
WHERE FUNDING CAN BE GIVEN Worldwide.
WHO CAN BENEFIT Registered charities.
WHAT IS FUNDED General charitable purposes; arts and music (particularly); Jewish causes; education; health and medical research.
RANGE OF GRANTS Mostly £100 to £5,500.
SAMPLE GRANTS Royal Academy of Music (£32,500); The Gurkha Welfare Trust (£10,000); English Touring Opera (£5,500); Salzburg Festival (£3,800); Philharmonia Orchestra Trust (£3,300); Pharos Arts Foundation (£3,100); Central British Fund for World Jewish Relief (£1,200); Friends of Yad Sarah (£1,000); British Friends of ZAKIA and United Jewish Israel Appeal (UJIA) (£500 each); Friends of the V&A Museum (£300); Stoke Association (£250); Friends of the Royal Academy (£140).
FINANCES *Year* 2015/16 *Income* £70,306 *Grants* £71,631 *Grants to organisations* £71,631 *Assets* £2,240,119
TRUSTEES Jill Karaviotis; Joseph Karaviotis.
OTHER INFORMATION In 2015/16, 21 charities were supported. The foundation's working name is J. M. K. Charitable Trust.
HOW TO APPLY Unsolicited applications will not be considered.
WHO TO APPLY TO The Trustees of Karaviotis Foundation, Saffery Champness, 71 Queen Victoria Street, London EC4V 4BE *Tel.* 020 7841 4000

■ The Boris Karloff Charitable Foundation

CC NO 326898 **ESTABLISHED** 1985
WHERE FUNDING CAN BE GIVEN Not defined; in practice UK.
WHO CAN BENEFIT Charitable organisations.
WHAT IS FUNDED The performing arts; young cricketers.
WHAT IS NOT FUNDED Individuals; charities with large resources.
TYPE OF GRANT One-off and recurring.
RANGE OF GRANTS Mostly £500 to £5,000.
SAMPLE GRANTS Young Vic (£12,600); Arundel Castle Cricket Foundation and The London Academy of Music and Dramatic Art – LAMDA (£5,000 each); Shakespeare Schools Festival (£3,000); Discover Drama and Royal Theatrical Fund (£2,500 each); British Youth Opera and Oval House (£2,000 each); Split Moon (£1,000); Papatango Theatre Company (£500).
FINANCES *Year* 2015/16 *Income* £62,065 *Grants* £63,100 *Grants to organisations* £63,100 *Assets* £2,441,860
TRUSTEES James Fairclough; Carole Fairclough; Bernard Coleman; Owen Lewis.
OTHER INFORMATION In 2015/16 a total of 21 organisations received grants.
HOW TO APPLY Apply in writing to the correspondent.
WHO TO APPLY TO Andrew Studd, Russell Cooke Solicitors, 2 Putney Hill, London SW15 6AB *Tel.* 020 8789 9111 *Fax* 020 8780 1194

■ The Kasner Charitable Trust

CC NO 267510 **ESTABLISHED** 1973
WHERE FUNDING CAN BE GIVEN UK and Israel.
WHO CAN BENEFIT Charitable organisations.
WHAT IS FUNDED General charitable purposes, with some focus on Jewish causes.
TYPE OF GRANT Small awards to a few hundred organisations each year.
RANGE OF GRANTS Up to £30,000; mainly small grants of up to £500.
SAMPLE GRANTS Yesodey Hatorah School (£30,000); United Jewish Israel Appeal (UJIA) (£10,000); Trumos (£6,000); Simon Marks Jewish Primary School Trust (£5,000); Yeshiva Horomo Talmudical Collel (£950); Gateshead Jewish Boarding School and World Jewish Relief (£500 each); University Jewish Chaplaincy (£250); The Queen Alexandra Hospital Home (£50); Spinal Research (£35); Gandhi World Hunger Fund (£22); International Fund for Animal Welfare and WaterAid (£10 each).
FINANCES *Year* 2014/15 *Income* £192,422 *Grants* £130,151 *Grants to organisations* £130,151 *Assets* £1,168,653
TRUSTEES Judith Erlich; Baruch Erlich.
OTHER INFORMATION At the time of writing (May 2017) the trust's accounts for 2015/16 were overdue at the Charity Commission; the 2014/15 accounts were the latest available. In that year grants were made to over 300 organisations.
HOW TO APPLY Apply in writing to the correspondent. The annual report for 2014/15 states that grant applications are received from 'a number of client organisations, and every application is considered by the board of trustees in relation to pre agreed parameters. The board may accept or reject the application or accept the application subject to conditions.'
WHO TO APPLY TO Baruch Erlich, Trustee, 1A Gresham Gardens, London NW11 8NX *Tel.* 020 8455 7830

■ The Michael and Ilse Katz Foundation

CC NO 263726 **ESTABLISHED** 1971
WHERE FUNDING CAN BE GIVEN UK and overseas.
WHO CAN BENEFIT International and UK schemes and organisations benefitting Jewish people, at risk groups or people who are disadvantaged by poverty or socially isolated.
WHAT IS FUNDED General charitable purposes, particularly Jewish causes and health/disability and social welfare causes.
TYPE OF GRANT One-off and recurring.
RANGE OF GRANTS Up to £15,000.
SAMPLE GRANTS University College London Institute of Ophthalmology (£15,000; Jewish Care (£12,000); Bournemouth Symphony Orchestra (£8,000); Community Security Trust and Norwood Children and Families First (£6,000 each); CLIC Sargent and The Worshipful Company of Butchers (£2,000 each); Magen David Adom UK (£1,500); Age UK, Blesma, Federation of Jewish Relief Organisations, Save a Child's Heart and Whizz-Kidz (£1,000 each).
FINANCES *Year* 2015/16 *Income* £113,506 *Grants* £86,600 *Grants to organisations* £86,600 *Assets* £2,553,571
TRUSTEES Norris Gilbert; Osman Azis.
OTHER INFORMATION At least 30 organisations benefitted and no grants were made to individuals during the year. Sundry grants under £1,000 totalled £4,100.
HOW TO APPLY Apply in writing to the correspondent.
WHO TO APPLY TO Osman Azis, Trustee, Counting House, Trelill, Bodmin PL30 3HZ *Tel.* 01208 851814 *Email* osmanazis@btconnect.com

■ C. S. Kaufman Charitable Trust

CC NO 253194 **ESTABLISHED** 1967
WHERE FUNDING CAN BE GIVEN UK.
WHO CAN BENEFIT Organisations benefitting Jewish people.
WHAT IS FUNDED Jewish causes; the promotion of Jewish faith and education.
TYPE OF GRANT One-off or recurrent.
RANGE OF GRANTS Up to £25,000.
SAMPLE GRANTS Keren Gemillas Chesed (£35,500 in three grants); Mifal Hachesed Vehatzedokoh (£25,000); The Shaarei (£6,500 in seven grants); The Maerdy Archive (£3,000); Torah Trust Gateshead Jewish Boarding School and Institute for Higher Rabbinical Studies (£100 each).
FINANCES *Year* 2015/16 *Income* £104,989 *Grants* £93,183 *Grants to organisations* £93,183 *Assets* £949,271
TRUSTEES Israel Kaufman; Simon Kaufman; J. Kaufman; L. Kaufman.
OTHER INFORMATION There were 28 awards made, with some organisations receiving more than one grant during the year.
HOW TO APPLY Apply in writing to the correspondent.
WHO TO APPLY TO The Trustees of C. S. Kaufman Charitable Trust, Ernst & Young LLP, Citygate, St James Boulevard, Newcastle upon Tyne NE1 4JD *Tel.* 0191 247 2500

■ The Caron Keating Foundation

CC NO 1106160 **ESTABLISHED** 2004
WHERE FUNDING CAN BE GIVEN UK.
WHO CAN BENEFIT Charities, support groups and hospices.
WHAT IS FUNDED Cancer – support services; research; awareness-raising and information.

Further examples of what has been funded previously are given on the website.

WHAT IS NOT FUNDED Individuals.

TYPE OF GRANT Core costs; capital; projects; research; salaries.

SAMPLE GRANTS Action Cancer Belfast (£20,000); Beating Bowel Cancer and Haven's Hospices (£10,000 each); Children's Eye Cancer Trust and Frimley Health Charity (£5,000 each); St Helena Hospice (£4,000); Keech Hospice Care, Northern Ireland Cancer Fund for Children and Prostate Cancer UK (£3,000 each); Relate Manchester South (£300).

FINANCES *Year* 2015/16 *Income* £121,766 *Grants* £263,592 *Grants to organisations* £263,592 *Assets* £806,316

TRUSTEES Michael Keating; Gloria Hunniford.

OTHER INFORMATION The Foundation assisted 66 charities in varying amounts over the course of the financial year. The total amount paid out to the charities was £263,592.

HOW TO APPLY Apply in writing to the correspondent.

WHO TO APPLY TO Mary Clifford Day, Secretary, PO Box 122, Sevenoaks, Kent TN13 1UM *Tel.* 01732 455005 *Email* info@caronkeating.org *Website* www.caronkeating.org

■ The Kelly Family Charitable Trust

CC NO 1102440 **ESTABLISHED** 2004

WHERE FUNDING CAN BE GIVEN UK, there may be some preference for Scotland.

WHO CAN BENEFIT Registered charities. Preference is given to small, local charities with an income of less than £500,000 but larger charities with pioneering pilot projects will also be considered.

WHAT IS FUNDED The trust's website states: 'The Trust has decided to prioritise its funding in favour of charities whose activities involve all or most family members in initiatives that support and encourage the family to work as a cohesive unit in tackling problems that face one or more of its members.' In particular, the trust focuses on three areas: 'interventions and support that help families to manage better and prevent the fracture of the family unit, e.g. relationship counselling, mediation; families where sexual abuse, physical abuse, domestic violence, alcohol abuse and drugs abuse threaten the integrity of the family unit; prisoners and in particular their families, during and after the period of imprisonment'.

WHAT IS NOT FUNDED Non-registered charities; grants directly to individuals; national charities (only regional projects will be considered); general appeals; organisations with specific religious or political agendas.

TYPE OF GRANT Capital and revenue grants; core funding; start-up costs; projects; salaries.

RANGE OF GRANTS Generally £1,000 to £5,000, although higher amounts may be considered.

SAMPLE GRANTS Clear; Women's Work Derby; The Lighthouse Ayr; Ormiston Child and Farm Trust; East Cumbria Family Support; Geezabreak; Hall Green Contact Centre; Hastings Rothermere Mediation; Home Start Barnet; Home Start Bridgwater; Longmead Community Farm; Made of Money; Relate North West Sussex; Donnington Doorstep; Home-Start Bristol; Fun in Action Brighton.

FINANCES *Year* 2015/16 *Income* £134,352 *Grants* £141,545 *Grants to organisations* £141,545 *Assets* £2,891,026

TRUSTEES Annie Kelly; Brian Mattingley; Jenny Kelly; Sheldon Cordell; Michael Field; Kayleigh Wiggins.

OTHER INFORMATION Grants were awarded to 17 organisations during the year.

HOW TO APPLY Application forms can be downloaded from the trust's website. They should be returned by email along with a copy of the latest annual accounts (where available). Grants are awarded twice a year and appeals must be submitted by 1 March and 1 September. The trustees will ask for more detail for those applications that pass the initial screening and may visit the projects they wish to support.

WHO TO APPLY TO Stuart Armstrong, Administrator, 8 Mansfield Place, Edinburgh EH3 6NB *Tel.* 0131 315 4879 *Email* s.armstrong@kfct.org *Website* www.kfct.org.uk/apply.html

■ Kelsick's Educational Foundation

CC NO 526956 **ESTABLISHED** 1723

WHERE FUNDING CAN BE GIVEN Lakes parish (Ambleside, Grasmere, Langdale and part of Troutbeck); any surplus income may be applied in Patterdale Ward and former county of Westmoreland.

WHO CAN BENEFIT Individuals under 25 years of age; voluntary organisations; schools; local groups and clubs for young people.

WHAT IS FUNDED Educational needs of individuals under the age of 25; school activities such as educational visits, field trips, music lessons., reading resources and items of necessary equipment; support for academic courses and apprenticeships, including equipment costs.

WHAT IS NOT FUNDED Holidays; course items without receipts.

TYPE OF GRANT Capital and project support; one-off or for longer than three years.

RANGE OF GRANTS £2,00 to £55,000.

SAMPLE GRANTS Ambleside Primary School (£55,000); Grasmere Primary School (£51,000); Langdale Primary School (£34,500); Ambleside Toddlers and Playgroup (£2,000).

FINANCES *Year* 2015/16 *Income* £393,983 *Grants* £216,444 *Grants to organisations* £141,280 *Assets* £7,200,281

TRUSTEES Peter Jackson; Linda Dixon; Leslie Johnson; Nigel Hutchinson; John Halstead; Angela Renouf; Norman Tyson; Reginald Curphey; Nicholas Martin; Margaret Weaver; Mark Blackburn.

OTHER INFORMATION A total of £66,500 was given to individuals.

HOW TO APPLY Application forms for individuals are available from the foundation's website. Grants are considered in February, May, August and November, and should be submitted by 31 January, 30 April, 31 July, 31 October respectively.

WHO TO APPLY TO Peter Frost, Clerk to the Trustees, The Kelsick Centre, St Mary's Lane, Ambleside, Cumbria LA22 9DG *Tel.* 01539 431289 *Fax* 01539 431292 *Email* john@kelsick.plus.com *Website* www.kelsick.org.uk

■ The Kay Kendall Leukaemia Fund

CC NO 290772 **ESTABLISHED** 1984

WHERE FUNDING CAN BE GIVEN UK.

WHO CAN BENEFIT UK and non-UK organisations (for work based primarily in the UK); institutions conducting research into leukaemia or related diseases; patient care and support centres. There is a preference for 'centres of excellence or those with an established international reputation in the field'.

WHAT IS FUNDED Medical research into and treatment of leukaemia or related diseases. The fund particularly welcomes proposals relating to the prevention, diagnosis or therapy of leukaemia and related diseases.

WHAT IS NOT FUNDED Circular appeals for general support; project grant applications submitted simultaneously to other funding bodies; clinical trials.

TYPE OF GRANT Research funding; capital costs; equipment; clinical support; fellowships; project grants for up to three years.

RANGE OF GRANTS £50,000 to £1 million. Some smaller grants of around £1,000.

SAMPLE GRANTS University of Cambridge (£1 million); University of Oxford (£600,000); University of Edinburgh (£198,000); Guys St Thomas' Charity (£150,000); UCL Cancer Institute (£120,000); CRUK Manchester Research Institute (£94,000); University of Leeds (£82,000); Nottingham Hospitals Charity (£52,000); Genome Research Ltd (£1,000).

FINANCES *Year* 2015/16 *Income* £624,929 *Grants* £3,356,000 *Grants to organisations* £3,354,398 *Assets* £25,040,000

TRUSTEES Judith Portrait; Timothy Sainsbury; Charles Metcalfe.

OTHER INFORMATION The charity is one of the Sainsbury Family Charitable Trusts which share a common administration. During 2015/16, the fund made small grants to individuals totalling £1,600.

HOW TO APPLY Application forms are available from the correspondent. They should include a research proposal for project grants (aims, background, plan of investigation and justification for budget) which should be three to five single-spaced pages (excluding references, costings, and CVs). Applications should be submitted by email in addition to providing a hard copy with original signatures. Guidance on what to include is given on the fund's website. Awards are normally considered in May and November and applications should be received by the end of February and mid-July, respectively. The fund welcomes preliminary phone calls, letters or emails to discuss whether a project is likely to be eligible.

WHO TO APPLY TO Alan Bookbinder, Director, The Peak, 5 Wilton Road, London SW1V 1AP *Tel.* 020 7410 0330 *Email* info@kklf.org.uk *Website* www.kklf.org.uk

■ William Kendall's Charity (Wax Chandlers' Company)

CC NO 228361 **ESTABLISHED** 1559

WHERE FUNDING CAN BE GIVEN Greater London and the London borough of Bexley.

WHO CAN BENEFIT Charitable organisations in Greater London working for relief of need and any charitable organisations in Bexley.

WHAT IS FUNDED General charitable purposes; communities; social welfare in London.

WHAT IS NOT FUNDED Grants are not made to: individuals; replace cuts in funding made by local authorities or others; schemes or activities which would be regarded as relieving central or local government of their statutory responsibilities; cover deficits already incurred. Grants are not normally made to: large charities; charities whose accounts disclose substantial reserves; non-registered charities.

TYPE OF GRANT One-off or recurring.

RANGE OF GRANTS £500 to £30,000, typical grant £2,000.

SAMPLE GRANTS Spitalfields Farm and Jus B (£30,000 each); City of London School (£5,000); Wax Chandlers In Need (£3,500); Carers Support Bexley, Insight Bexley and Cribs Charitable Trust (£2,000 each); Bexley Moorings (£1,600); Horbury Tumblers (£700); Erith School (£500).

FINANCES *Year* 2015/16 *Income* £797,111 *Grants* £104,728 *Grants to organisations* £104,728 *Assets* £3,955,695

TRUSTEES Peter Thompkins; Heather Hawker; Dr Johnathan Munday; Hon. Dr Colin Kolbert; Graeme Marrs; John Chambers; John Sleeman; Dr Andrew Mair; Quentin Truscott; Arthur Davey; Joan Beavington; Susan Green; Michael Badger; Anthony Bicmore; Lydia Marston-Weston; Ian Appleton; The Worshipful Company of Wax Chandlers.

OTHER INFORMATION A total of 21 institutions received grants during the year.

HOW TO APPLY The charity undertakes its own research and does not respond to unsolicited applications to Greater London fund or Persons in need fund. The Bexley Smalle Grants scheme is administered by Bexley Voluntary Services Council – call 020 8304 0911 for more information.

WHO TO APPLY TO Georgina Brown, Clerk, Wax Chandlers' Hall, 6 Gresham Street, London EC2V 7AD *Tel.* 020 7606 3591 *Fax* 020 7600 5462 *Email* info@waxchandlers.org.uk *Website* www.waxchandlers.org.uk/charity/index.php

■ The Kennel Club Charitable Trust

CC NO 327802 **ESTABLISHED** 1988

WHERE FUNDING CAN BE GIVEN UK.

WHO CAN BENEFIT Charitable organisations; rehoming organisations; universities and other research bodies.

WHAT IS FUNDED Rehoming and welfare of dogs in need of care and attention; research into canine diseases; training of support dogs to improve the quality of life of humans.

WHAT IS NOT FUNDED Individuals; political organisations. The fund does not generally fund: applications purely for building costs; requests from individuals; requests from organisations which are not primarily focused on dogs (e.g. general animal shelters).

TYPE OF GRANT One-off and recurring for set periods (subject to a satisfactory annual review and report of progress); capital, core and project costs.

RANGE OF GRANTS £250 to £290,000.

SAMPLE GRANTS Animal Health Trust (£290,500 given in two grants); University of Cambridge (£82,000); Royal Veterinary College (£45,000); Battersea Cats and Dogs Home (£37,000); Canine Partners (£21,000); University of Glasgow (£10,000); GSD Rescue Elite (£5,000); GSD Rescue South (£3,000); PUP Lancashire (£2,000); University of Nottingham (£800).

FINANCES *Year* 2015 *Income* £753,308 *Grants* £820,836 *Grants to organisations* £820,836 *Assets* £2,909,886

TRUSTEES Michael Townsend; Michael Herrtage; Bill King; Dr Andrew Higgins; Steven Dean; Jennifer Millard.

OTHER INFORMATION Grants were divided into: scientific and research project grants –

£545,000; educational and other grants – £276,000. Animal Health Trust remains the main grant recipient.

HOW TO APPLY Applications should be made in writing to the correspondent providing the latest accounts (and registered charity number, if applicable) and clearly stating the details of the costs for which you are requesting funding, for what purpose and over what period of time. The trustees meet four times a year. Further guidance is given on the trust's website.

WHO TO APPLY TO Richard Fairlamb, Administrator, 1–5 Clarges Street, Piccadilly, London W1J 8AB *Tel.* 020 7518 1061 *Fax* 020 7518 1014 *Email* kcct@thekennelclub.org.uk or richard.fairlamb@thekennelclub.org.uk *Website* www.thekennelclub.org.uk/charitabletrust

■ Kent Community Foundation

CC NO 1084361 **ESTABLISHED** 2001

WHERE FUNDING CAN BE GIVEN Principally the County of Kent and the Borough of Medway; UK and elsewhere.

WHO CAN BENEFIT Local charities, community groups and voluntary organisations; individuals.

WHAT IS FUNDED A wide range of general charitable needs and community projects aimed at improving the quality of life for people in Kent, focusing on the following four priority areas: enabling young people to overcome disadvantage and achieve their potential; supporting vulnerable and older adults to stay well, independent and fulfilled, playing a full and active role in their community; creating opportunities for employment, skills and enterprise for those furthest from the labour market, including young people with poverty of opportunity; strengthening disadvantaged communities and closing the inequality gap between those living in the poorest communities and those living in well-off areas. The foundation administers a number of funds established by individuals, families and organisations. In addition it has its own general fund which enables the trustees to support voluntary groups which fall outside the stated criteria of these funds. Refer to the website for information on what is currently available.

TYPE OF GRANT Core, capital and project expenditure; one-off and recurrent.

SAMPLE GRANTS Sparks (£500,000); The J's Hospice (£75,000); Romney Marsh Day Centre (£34,000); Gap (£21,600); Carers FIRST (£17,400); Ellenor (£15,200); Blackthorn Trust (£13,000); Age Concern Sandwich Centre and Kent Cricket Development Trust (£10,500 each); Friends of Holcot (£10,100).

FINANCES *Year* 2015/16 *Income* £3,571,999 *Grants* £2,120,321 *Grants to organisations* £2,077,675 *Assets* £15,128,169

TRUSTEES Blair Gulland; Sarah Hohler; Peter Williams; Ann West; Tim Bull; Vicki Jessel; Georgie Warner; Hugo Fenwick; Robert Sackville.

OTHER INFORMATION As with all community foundations, there are a number of donor advised funds managed on behalf of individuals, families and charitable trusts. Grant schemes tend to change frequently; therefore, consult the foundation's website for details of current programmes and their up-to-date deadlines.

HOW TO APPLY Further information on applications to each of the funds currently available can be found online or obtained from the Grants Team via the contact details given.

WHO TO APPLY TO Grants Team, Office 23, Evegate Park Barn, Evegate, Ashford, Kent TN25 6SX *Tel.* 01303 814500 *Email* admin@kentcf.org.uk *Website* www.kentcf.org.uk/apply

■ The Nancy Kenyon Charitable Trust

CC NO 265359 **ESTABLISHED** 1972

WHERE FUNDING CAN BE GIVEN Throughout the UK.

WHO CAN BENEFIT Registered small charities; individuals.

WHAT IS FUNDED General charitable purposes; disadvantaged individuals.

TYPE OF GRANT One-off and recurrent.

RANGE OF GRANTS £100 to £10,500.

SAMPLE GRANTS Nancy Oldfield Trust (£10,500); One More Child (£5,000); Rise Africa UK (£3,000); Hope Now, The Good Shepherd Project, The Nehemiah Project (£2,000); Cheltenham Youth for Christ, Dean Close School, The Family Haven (£1,000).

FINANCES *Year* 2015/16 *Income* £66,563 *Grants* £49,850 *Grants to organisations* £41,000 *Assets* £1,738,621

TRUSTEES Lucy Phipps; Maureen Kenyon; Christopher Kenyon; Sally Kenyon; Peter Kenyon; Kieron Kenyon.

OTHER INFORMATION The trust awarded £8,900 worth of grants to individuals.

HOW TO APPLY Applications can be made in writing to the correspondent at any time. Our research notes that applications for causes not known to the trustees are considered annually in December.

WHO TO APPLY TO Alison Smith, Correspondent, c/o Brook Financial Management Ltd, Meads Barn, Ashwell Business Park, Ilminster, Somerset TA19 9DX *Tel.* 01460 259852

■ Keren Association Ltd

CC NO 313119 **ESTABLISHED** 1961

WHERE FUNDING CAN BE GIVEN UK and overseas.

WHO CAN BENEFIT Charitable organisations, mainly those benefitting Jewish people.

WHAT IS FUNDED General charitable purposes, including the advancement of education, the provision of religious instruction and training in traditional Judaism and the relief of need.

SAMPLE GRANTS Beis Aharon Trust; British Heart Foundation; Clwk Yaakov; Friends of Arad; Friends of Beis Yaakov; Kupat Gmach Vezer NIsui; Lomdei Tom h Belz Machnovke; Yeshiva Belz Machnovke; Yeshivat Lomdei; Yetev Lev Jerusalem.

FINANCES *Year* 2015/16 *Income* £11,179,660 *Grants* £11,523,372 *Grants to organisations* £11,523,372 *Assets* £38,745,310

TRUSTEES Mrs S. Englander; Mr S. Englander; E. Englander; H. Weiss; N. Weiss; Jacob Englander; Pinkus Englander.

OTHER INFORMATION A list of grant recipients was not included in the accounts.

HOW TO APPLY Apply in writing to the correspondent. The annual report for 2015/16 states that 'the trustees consider all requests which they receive and make donations based on the level of funds available'.

WHO TO APPLY TO Mrs S. Englander, Trustee, 136 Clapton Common, London E5 9AG *Email* mail@cohenarnold.com

■ E. and E. Kernkraut Charities Ltd

CC NO 275636 **ESTABLISHED** 1973

WHERE FUNDING CAN BE GIVEN UK and overseas.

WHO CAN BENEFIT Charitable organisations.

WHAT IS FUNDED The advancement of religion in accordance with the Orthodox Jewish faith; education; general charitable purposes.

SAMPLE GRANTS A list of beneficiaries was not available.

FINANCES *Year* 2015/16 *Income* £1,096,629 *Grants* £943,555 *Grants to organisations* £943,555 *Assets* £6,361,262

TRUSTEES Eli Kernkraut; Esther Kernkraut; Joseph Kernkraut; Jacob Kernkraut.

OTHER INFORMATION A list of beneficiaries was not available in the annual report and accounts.

HOW TO APPLY Apply in writing to the correspondent.

WHO TO APPLY TO Eli Kernkraut, Trustee, The Knoll, Fountayne Road, London N16 7EA *Tel.* 020 8806 7947 *Email* mail@cohenarnold.com

■ The Peter Kershaw Trust

CC NO 268934 **ESTABLISHED** 1974

WHERE FUNDING CAN BE GIVEN Greater Manchester and and the north of Cheshire area.

WHO CAN BENEFIT Registered charities; educational establishments; medical research organisations.

WHAT IS FUNDED Social welfare; medical research, especially in the field of oncology; educational bursaries.

WHAT IS NOT FUNDED Individuals; loans; new building work (but payments for fitting out of specialist premises may be made); long-term commitments (awards may be paid for up to three years).

TYPE OF GRANT Projects; new work; pump-priming research; bursaries.

RANGE OF GRANTS Up to £25,000.

SAMPLE GRANTS M13 Youth Centre (£25,000); Mosses Centre (£18,600); St Bedes (£8,000); Manchester High School For Girls (£6,300); Cheadle Hulme School (£4,500); Emmaus Salford and Farms For City Children (£2,000 each); Beacon Counselling and Willow Wood Hospice (£1,500 each); Riverside The Beeches (£250).

FINANCES *Year* 2015/16 *Income* £206,250 *Grants* £133,589 *Grants to organisations* £133,589 *Assets* £6,158,254

TRUSTEES David Tully; Margaret Rushbrooke; Richard Kershaw; Rosemary Adams; Tim Page.

OTHER INFORMATION The support was allocated between: memorial bursary (£63,000); social welfare institutions (£30,000); school bursaries (£40,500).

HOW TO APPLY Applications should be made in writing to the correspondent by post (email applications are not accepted) and should be accompanied by the latest financial statements. However, note that the trust is always oversubscribed. The website states: 'All applications will be acknowledged – avoid the use of "Signed for" delivery as there is not always someone available to accept the delivery.' Meeting dates and deadlines are posted on the trust's website.

WHO TO APPLY TO Sarah Baron, Secretary, 1 St Peter's Avenue, Knutsford WA16 0DN *Tel.* 01565 651086 *Email* pkershawtrust@btinternet.com *Website* www.peterkershawtrust.org/Grantsavailable

■ The Ursula Keyes Trust

CC NO 517200 **ESTABLISHED** 1985

WHERE FUNDING CAN BE GIVEN The Chester area.

WHO CAN BENEFIT Charitable organisations (including national charities if there is a link to a local beneficiary); medical and social care institutions; schools; individuals.

WHAT IS FUNDED General charitable purposes, particularly health and medical causes and social care. The website further explains: 'A wide range of causes are supported, including cultural and leisure projects, particularly when matched by other fundraising efforts.'

WHAT IS NOT FUNDED Students; political groups.

TYPE OF GRANT Capital and project costs.

RANGE OF GRANTS Mostly up to £10,000.

SAMPLE GRANTS Hospice of the Good Shepherd (£200,000); R Charity (£10,900); Bishop Heber High School and Clatterbridge Cancer Clinic (£10,000 each); Queens Park High Rowing Club (£6,000); British Community Farms CIC (£5,000); Bird and Samaritans (£2,200 each); Barnardo's (£2,000); Cystic Fibrosis Dream Holidays and Roy Castle Lung Foundation (£1,800 each); Chester Gang Show and New Scene Youth Club (£1,000 each).

FINANCES *Year* 2015 *Income* £275,388 *Grants* £279,032 *Grants to organisations* £262,567 *Assets* £4,443,454

TRUSTEES Euan Elliott; J. Kane; J. Leaman; John Brimelow; Dr Ian Russell; Dr Peter Reid; John McLintock.

OTHER INFORMATION In 2015 grants of less than £1,000 totalled £3,700. An amount of £16,500 was awarded to 22 individuals.

HOW TO APPLY Applications should be made in writing to the correspondent, including a copy of the form available to download from the website. Appeals are considered at the trustees' quarterly meetings, which take place on Fridays at the end of January, April, July and October (see the website for exact dates); they should reach the trustees at least two weeks before any particular meeting.

WHO TO APPLY TO Dorothy Lawless, c/o RSM, One City Place, Queens Road, Chester CH1 3BQ *Tel.* 01244 505100 *Fax* 01244 505101 *Website* www.ursula-keyes-trust.org.uk

■ Kidney Research UK

CC NO 252892 **ESTABLISHED** 1967

WHERE FUNDING CAN BE GIVEN UK.

WHO CAN BENEFIT Recognised renal research establishments supporting medical professionals, research workers and students, and for the benefit of people with kidney and renal diseases.

WHAT IS FUNDED The fund provides grants for medical research into: kidney and renal disease generally; the acute failure of the kidneys and chronic renal failure, including the causes, effects and prevention of such disease and failure; and the congenital malformations of the kidneys and the bladder. Grants are also provided for: postdoctoral studentships and fellowships for the training of individuals, and thereby the advancement and promotion of kidney and renal research; patient welfare and care; and awareness and education. The fund also promotes and distributes the Donor Card.

TYPE OF GRANT Research grants may be awarded for between one and five years. Patient grants are mostly one-off. Loans are not made.

RANGE OF GRANTS Project grants of up to £100,000 are awarded for a maximum of three years;

start-up grants of up to £30,000 are awarded for up to two years; Career Development Fellowships are awarded for up to three years; Training Fellowships are awarded for up to three years; PHD Studentships are awarded for three years and Patient Support Grants are awarded on an ongoing basis.

SAMPLE GRANTS University College, London (£773,500) (in four separate grants); Imperial College London (£651,000) (in two separate grants); PIVOTAL sites (£396,500); University of Bristol (£234,500); King's College Hospital (£224,00); Leicester General Hospital (£219,500); University of Leicester (£201,000); King's College, London (£200,000); University of Manchester (£198,500); University of Cardiff (£191,000).

FINANCES *Year* 2016 *Income* £8,989,170 *Grants* £11,173,128 *Grants to organisations* £11,173,128 *Assets* £9,051,447

TRUSTEES Prof. John Feehally; Prof. Fiona Karet; Lorna Marson; Prof. Adrian Wolf; Iain Pearson; David Prosser; Anna-Maria Steel; Federica Pizzasegola; Charles Tomson; Tom Kelly.

HOW TO APPLY Applications are now accepted only via an online grant application management system. Hard-copy paper application forms will no longer be accepted.

WHO TO APPLY TO Research Operations Team, Nene Hall, Peterborough Business Park, Lynch Wood, Peterborough PE2 6FZ *Tel.* 0300 303 1100 *Email* grants@kidneyresearchuk.org *Website* www.kidneyresearchuk.org

■ The Kildare Trust

CC NO 1148325 **ESTABLISHED** 2012

WHERE FUNDING CAN BE GIVEN Worcestershire.

WHO CAN BENEFIT Registered charities.

WHAT IS FUNDED General charitable purposes.

SAMPLE GRANTS St Michael's Hospice (£40,000); St Richard's Hospice and The Stroke Association (£20,000 each); Guide Dogs (£15,000); Megan Baker House and Three Choirs Festival (£10,000 each); Holy Trinity Church (£7,500); Whizz-Kidz (£5,500); Orchestra of the Swan (£5,000).

FINANCES *Year* 2015/16 *Income* £213,156 *Grants* £336,462 *Grants to organisations* £336,462 *Assets* £811,186

TRUSTEES Anthony Champion; Samuel White; Dawn Oliver; Martin Needham.

HOW TO APPLY Apply in writing to the correspondent.

WHO TO APPLY TO Dawn Emma Oliver, Harrison Clark Solicitors, 5 Deansway, Worcester WR1 2JG *Tel.* 01905 744871

■ The Robert Kiln Charitable Trust

CC NO 262756 **ESTABLISHED** 1970

WHERE FUNDING CAN BE GIVEN UK, with a special interest in Hertfordshire and Bedfordshire; occasionally overseas.

WHO CAN BENEFIT Universities; small charitable organisations; museums.

WHAT IS FUNDED General charitable purposes with a particular focus on archaeology, history, heritage, environment and conservation.

WHAT IS NOT FUNDED Individuals; large national appeals; churches; schools; artistic projects (for example, theatre groups).

TYPE OF GRANT Usually one-off grants or instalments for particular projects.

RANGE OF GRANTS Up to £3,500; typically for less than £1,000.

SAMPLE GRANTS Hertford Symphony Orchestra (£3,500); University of Oxford (£2,800); Meon Valley Archaeology and Heritage Group (£2,500); The British Museum (£2,000); Friends of Pendle Heritage and University of Birmingham (£1,500 each); Ingleborough Archaeology Group (£1,400); British Institute at Ankara (£1,200); Jovik Group and The Salisbury Museum (£1,000 each).

FINANCES *Year* 2015/16 *Income* £52,326 *Grants* £45,410 *Grants to organisations* £45,410 *Assets* £968,405

TRUSTEES Dr Nicholas Akers; Janet Akers; Barbara Kiln; Stephen Kiln.

OTHER INFORMATION Grants were made to 72 organisations during the year.

HOW TO APPLY Applications can be made in writing to the correspondent, providing as much information as seems relevant and, if possible, including the costings and details of any other support available. Funds are normally distributed within one month of receiving applications, subject to funds being available. The trust does not acknowledge receipt of applications unless an sae is enclosed.

WHO TO APPLY TO Sarah Howell, Secretary to the Trustees, 15A Bull Plain, Hertford SG14 1DX *Tel.* 01992 554962 *Email* robertkilntrust@btconnect.com

■ The King Henry VIII Endowed Trust – Warwick

CC NO 232862 **ESTABLISHED** 1964

WHERE FUNDING CAN BE GIVEN The former borough of Warwick only.

WHO CAN BENEFIT Churches; educational establishments; charitable organisations; hospitals; social enterprises; individuals.

WHAT IS FUNDED General charitable purposes. Note that charitable expenditure is allocated in following proportions: 50% to the historic Anglican churches in Warwick; 30% to King's schools in Warwick; 20% to the town (including organisations for general charitable causes).

WHAT IS NOT FUNDED Projects outside the beneficial area; retrospective grants. The website notes that 'the trustees have only limited powers to make grants for projects for which central or local government has a financial responsibility'.

RANGE OF GRANTS Up to £50,000.

SAMPLE GRANTS Aylesford School (£50,000); Warwick Apprenticing Charities (£30,000); St Mary's Immaculate Catholic Primary School (£26,000); Myton School (£24,000); New Life Church (£21,000); All Saints Church of England Junior and Emscote Infant School (£18,000); Newburgh Primary School (£17,000); Budbrooke Primer School, Chase Meadow Community Centre and Citizens Advice – Warwick District (£15,000 each).

FINANCES *Year* 2015 *Income* £1,361,222 *Grants* £325,550 *Grants to organisations* £324,837 *Assets* £29,502,677

TRUSTEES Neil Thurley; Gerry Guest; Stephen Copley; Rupert Griffiths; Kathryn Parr; John Edwards; Ian Furlong; Revd David Brown; Michael Peachey; Marie Ashe; Stephen John Jobburn; Susan Grinnell.

HOW TO APPLY Application forms are available to download from the trust's website or can be requested from the correspondent. They should be returned by post or email. There are detailed guidelines and criteria, available from the trust's website. The trustees consider grants quarterly, in March and June (appeals should be received at the beginning of the month) and September and December (requests should be received by mid-August and November, respectively). The outcome of your application is normally communicated within a week following a meeting. In the case of an emergency, applications may be fast-tracked (provided such urgency is made clear on the application).

WHO TO APPLY TO Jonathan Wassall, Clerk and Receiver, 12 High Street, Warwick CV34 4AP *Tel.* 01926 495533 *Email* jwassall@kinghenryviii.org.uk *Website* www.kinghenryviii.org.uk

■ The King/Cullimore Charitable Trust

CC NO 1074928 **ESTABLISHED** 1999

WHERE FUNDING CAN BE GIVEN Worldwide.

WHO CAN BENEFIT Charitable organisations.

WHAT IS FUNDED General charitable purposes.

TYPE OF GRANT Capital, core and start-up costs; unrestricted funding; generally one-off.

RANGE OF GRANTS £5,000 to £2,000.

SAMPLE GRANTS Buckinghamshire Community Foundation (£200,000); Alexander Devine (£100,000); Green Finger (£50,000); Chilterns MS Centre (£30,000); Blond McIndoe Research (£15,000); Plat Kenya (£11,100); Duke of Edinburgh Award (£10,000); Sussex Snowdrop Trust (£5,000).

FINANCES *Year* 2016 *Income* £5,549,499 *Grants* £387,173 *Grants to organisations* £387,173 *Assets* £7,700,768

TRUSTEES Peter Cullimore; Alastair McKechnie; Christopher Gardner; Richard Davies; Jill Pye.

HOW TO APPLY Apply in writing to the correspondent.

WHO TO APPLY TO Peter Cullimore, Trustee, Cullimore, 52 Ledborough Lane, Beaconsfield, Buckinghamshire HP9 2DF *Tel.* 01494 678811 *Email* mail@petercullimore.co.uk

■ The Mary Kinross Charitable Trust

CC NO 212206 **ESTABLISHED** 1957

WHERE FUNDING CAN BE GIVEN UK.

WHO CAN BENEFIT Registered charities benefitting research workers, people in prison or leaving prison, young people and people disadvantaged by poverty.

WHAT IS FUNDED General charitable purposes. Donations confined to projects which the trust promotes and manages, particularly in the areas of medical research, to benefit the communities of which trustees have direct knowledge: youth, mental health and penal affairs. Grants made under the heading of youth are often made with crime prevention in mind.

WHAT IS NOT FUNDED Individuals.

TYPE OF GRANT Capital projects; core costs; one-off or recurring; unrestricted funding.

RANGE OF GRANTS Up to £100,000.

SAMPLE GRANTS Juvenile Diabetes Research Foundation (£100,000); Medical School, University of Exeter (£78,000); Department of Oncology, University of Oxford (£76,000); Max Planck UCL Centre, University College London (£75,000); Royal College of Surgeons of England (£50,000); Spectrum Centre, University of Lancaster (£50,000); Bendrigg Trust (£44,000); Prospex and Bipolar UK (£35,000 Each); Greenhouse Sports, Barry and Martin's Trust and Hepatitis C Trust (£30,000 each).

FINANCES *Year* 2016 *Income* £818,884 *Grants* £881,102 *Grants to organisations* £881,102 *Assets* £38,394,932

TRUSTEES Elizabeth Shields; Fiona Adams; Dr Neil Cross; Gordon Hague; Elizabeth Barber, David Milne.

OTHER INFORMATION Grants were awarded in the following areas: medical research (£498,000), youth (£202,000), penal affairs (£92,000), health (£60,000), mental health (£45,000) and miscellaneous (£24,500).

HOW TO APPLY The latest annual report notes: 'Because the Trustees have no office staff and work from home, they prefer dealing with written correspondence rather than telephone calls from applicants soliciting funds.' **Note:** Unsolicited applications to this trust are very unlikely to be successful. The majority of new grants are recommended by the chair and the secretary who can authorise small grants of up to £25,000. Other grants are discussed and agreed at trustee meetings.

WHO TO APPLY TO Fiona Adams, Trustee, 36 Grove Avenue, Moseley, Birmingham B13 9RY *Email* marykinrossct@gmail.com

■ Laura Kinsella Foundation

CC NO 1145325 **ESTABLISHED** 2012

WHERE FUNDING CAN BE GIVEN Worldwide.

WHO CAN BENEFIT Charitable organisations; individuals.

WHAT IS FUNDED General charitable purposes, particularly the arts, human rights and social welfare.

RANGE OF GRANTS £34 to £40,000.

SAMPLE GRANTS REPRIVE (£40,000); Rainmaker Foundation (£28,000); Centre for Criminal Appeals (£10,000); Centre for European Reform, Everyman Theatre and The Wrong Crowd (£5,000 each); Open Democracy (£2,500); Royal Society of Literature (£1,000); London Air Ambulance (£50); The Friends of Westonbirt Arboretum (£34).

FINANCES *Year* 2015/16 *Income* £140,548 *Grants* £122,699 *Grants to organisations* £122,699 *Assets* £3,037,215

TRUSTEES Stephen Kinsella; Alison Jolly; Michael Dickson.

OTHER INFORMATION Grants were made to 25 organisations during the year.

HOW TO APPLY Apply in writing to the correspondent, only successful applications are notified in writing.

WHO TO APPLY TO Stephen Kinsella, Trustee, c/o Bates Wells and Braithwaite, 10 Queen Street Place, London EC4R 1BE

■ The Graham Kirkham Foundation

CC NO 1002390 **ESTABLISHED** 1991

WHERE FUNDING CAN BE GIVEN England and Wales.

WHO CAN BENEFIT Charities; voluntary organisations; individuals.

WHAT IS FUNDED General charitable purposes, including: education; relief of illness, relief of poverty; relief of suffering in animals; protection and preservation of buildings and sites of historical and natural beauty.

RANGE OF GRANTS Up to £150,000.

SAMPLE GRANTS Royal Foundation (£150,000); Prostate Cancer Research (£25,000); Duke of Edinburgh (£20,000); Friendly Band (£10,000); Black Heath Bromley Harriers and Walk for Peace (£5,000 each); Saints and Sinners Charitable Trust (£4,000); Lord Dobbs (£2,000);

R.A.B.I. and Yorkshire and Humbershire Brass Band Association (£1,000 each).

FINANCES *Year* 2015 *Income* £215,560 *Grants* £233,250 *Grants to organisations* £233,250 *Assets* £74,815

TRUSTEES Lord Kirkham; The Hon. Michael Kirkham; Lady Pauline Kirkham.

OTHER INFORMATION A total number of 12 organisations were awarded grants, varying from £250 to £150,000.

HOW TO APPLY Apply in writing to the correspondent.

WHO TO APPLY TO Andrew Varnham, Administrator, 8 Ebor Court, Redhouse Interchange, Adwick-Le-Street, Doncaster, South Yorkshire DN6 7FE *Tel.* 01302 573301

■ Kirkley Poor's Land Estate

CC NO 210177 **ESTABLISHED** 1976

WHERE FUNDING CAN BE GIVEN The parish of Kirkley and the former borough of Lowestoft.

WHO CAN BENEFIT Individuals and organisations.

WHAT IS FUNDED Social welfare; health and disability. The trust administers a grocery voucher scheme enabling people of pensionable age in Kirkley to receive a grant each winter to purchase groceries. Grants are also made to support local residents undertaking their first university degree.

WHAT IS NOT FUNDED The annual report and accounts for 2015/16 state: 'It is a general policy of the Trustees not to make grants to well-known charities but to limit its assistance to small local charities and organisations who find raising funds more difficult.'

TYPE OF GRANT Generally one-off.

RANGE OF GRANTS Up to around £5,000.

SAMPLE GRANTS The Louise Hamilton Trust (£10,000); DIAL (£5,000); Salvation Army (£3,500); 4 C's Counselling Service, Lowestoft Sixth Form College, Lowestoft College and Old Warren House (£3,000 each); Lowestoft Club for Elderly People (£2,800); Shopmobility (£2,500); Catch22 (£1,800).

FINANCES *Year* 2015/16 *Income* £91,432 *Grants* £73,802 *Grants to organisations* £50,965 *Assets* £2,204,944

TRUSTEES Yvonne Cherry; Jennifer Van Pelt; Michael Cook; Ralph Castleton; Elaine High; Revd Eoin Buchanan; June Ford; Andrew Shepherd; Malcolm Pitchers.

OTHER INFORMATION £4,850 was awarded in grants to individuals towards university expenses, with a further £18,400 being granted towards the grocery voucher scheme.

HOW TO APPLY Appy in writing to the correspondent. The trustees normally meet two to three times a year. The boundaries of the beneficial area are outlined on the charity's website.

WHO TO APPLY TO Lucy Walker, Clerk, 4 Station Road, Lowestoft NR32 4QF *Tel.* 01502 514964 *Email* kirkleypoors@gmail.com *Website* kirkleypoorslandestate.co.uk

■ The Richard Kirkman Trust

CC NO 327972 **ESTABLISHED** 1988

WHERE FUNDING CAN BE GIVEN UK, with a preference for Hampshire.

WHO CAN BENEFIT Registered charities and individuals.

WHAT IS FUNDED General charitable purposes.

TYPE OF GRANT Capital; core costs; project costs; recurrent; one-off.

RANGE OF GRANTS Up to £5,000.

SAMPLE GRANTS Southampton Churches Rent Deposit Scheme (£5,000); Blesma (£4,000); Rotary Club of Southampton Trust Fund (£3,000); Countess Mountbatten Hospice Charity, Entham Trust, Stroke Association (£2,000 each); Haemophilia Society (£1,500).

FINANCES *Year* 2015/16 *Income* £75,269 *Grants* £45,300 *Grants to organisations* £45,300 *Assets* £1,883,511

TRUSTEES David Hoare; Michael Howson-Green; Brian Baxendale; M. A. Howson-Green.

OTHER INFORMATION During the year, 33 grants less than £1,000 were awarded to institutions and individuals totalling £19,800.

HOW TO APPLY Apply in writing to the correspondent.

WHO TO APPLY TO Michael Howson-Green, Trustee, Ashton House, 12 The Central Precinct, Winchester Road, Chandler's Ford, Eastleigh, Hampshire SO53 2GB *Tel.* 023 8027 4555 *Email* ashton.house@btconnect.com

■ The Kirschel Foundation

CC NO 1067672 **ESTABLISHED** 1998

WHERE FUNDING CAN BE GIVEN UK.

WHO CAN BENEFIT Registered charities; Jewish organisations.

WHAT IS FUNDED Jewish causes; medical, health and disability needs; disadvantaged individuals; education and training.

RANGE OF GRANTS Up to £68,000.

SAMPLE GRANTS Aharat Shalom Charity Fund (£68,000); Jewish Learning Exchange (£34,000); Gateshead Academy for Torah Studies (£22,000); Friends of Lubavitch Scotland (£18,000); UK Friends of Keren Tzlach (£15,000); Jewish Care (£6,500); Chai Cancer Care (£5,300); Cancer Research UK (£2,000).

FINANCES *Year* 2015/16 *Income* £300,043 *Grants* £272,540 *Grants to organisations* £272,540 *Assets* £12,597

TRUSTEES Laurence Kirschel; Ian Lipman; Ivona Kirschel.

HOW TO APPLY Apply in writing to the correspondent.

WHO TO APPLY TO Pritesh Patel, 26 Soho Square, London W1D 4NU *Tel.* 020 7437 4372

■ Robert Kitchin (Saddlers' Company)

CC NO 211169 **ESTABLISHED** 1891

WHERE FUNDING CAN BE GIVEN City of London and its contiguous boroughs.

WHO CAN BENEFIT Educational establishments; charitable organisations.

WHAT IS FUNDED General charitable purposes; education; rights and equality; community and economic development.

RANGE OF GRANTS £500 to £68,000.

SAMPLE GRANTS City University London (£101,000); St Ethelburga's Centre for Reconciliation and Peace (£30,500); the City of London School, the City of London School for Girls, the City of London Freemen's School and Reed's School (£750 each).

FINANCES *Year* 2015/16 *Income* £201,882 *Grants* £163,042 *Grants to organisations* £163,042 *Assets* £3,678,522

TRUSTEES Campbell Pulley; David Hardy; David Snowden; Hugh Dyson-Laurie; Iain Pulley; Jonathan Godrich; Michael Laurie; Peter Laurie; Peter Lewis; Tim Satchell; William Dyson-Laurie; Mark Farmar; Paul Farmar; Petronella Jameson; Nicholas Mason; Charles Barclay; John Robinson; Hugh Thomas; James Welsh; Lucy

Atherton; Hugh W. D. Taylor; Benjamin W. Laurie; Hon. Mark Maffey.

OTHER INFORMATION Each year the charity gives a fixed percentage to two organisations – City University receives 50% of net income, while St Ethelburga's Centre for Reconciliation and Peace receives 15%of net income. The remaining 35% is distributed at the discretion of the trustees.

HOW TO APPLY Applications can be made in writing to the correspondent; however, note that the discretionary element of the charity's income is generally fully committed each year and the trustees are unable to respond to applications. The annual report for 2015/16 notes: 'The Trustees seek, either through established contacts such as the City University London or by direct contact with the education departments of the City of London's contiguous boroughs or by appeals received direct from other relevant bodies, details of projects that fall within the objectives of the Charity and which, as such, the Trustees could consider for funding.'

WHO TO APPLY TO The Clerk to the Trustees, Saddlers' Company, Saddlers' Hall, 40 Gutter Lane, London EC2V 6BR *Tel.* 020 7726 8661 *Email* clerk@saddlersco.co.uk *Website* www.saddlersco.co.uk

■ The Ernest Kleinwort Charitable Trust

CC NO 229665 **ESTABLISHED** 1963

WHERE FUNDING CAN BE GIVEN UK, mainly Sussex; overseas.

WHO CAN BENEFIT Registered charities, preference for those operating in Sussex across a range of fields and environmental or wildlife organisations.

WHAT IS FUNDED Wildlife and environmental conservation; family planning; care of older and young people; disability, general social welfare; hospices; medical research; other charitable causes.

WHAT IS NOT FUNDED Large national charities having substantial fundraising potential, income from legacies and or endowment income; organisations not registered as charities or those that have been registered for less than a year; pre-school groups; out of school play schemes including pre-school and holiday schemes; projects which promote a particular religion; charities not funded by any other charity; very small and narrowly specialised activities; local authorities; individuals or charities applying on behalf of individuals; general requests for donations; expeditions or overseas travel; campaigning organisations; charities whose main aim is to raise funds for other charities; charities with substantial cash reserves.

TYPE OF GRANT Start-up and capital costs; ongoing expenses; conditionally renewable grants for up to three years may be agreed on occasions.

RANGE OF GRANTS £100 to £150,000; mostly for £10,000 or less.

SAMPLE GRANTS TUSK Trust (£200,000); WWF – UK (£75,000); River Trust (£70,000); Environmental Investigation Agency (£60,000); Royal Geographical Society and Women and Children First (UK) (£50,000 each); St Catherine's Hospice (£45,000); Marie Stopes International (£40,000); Off The Fence, The Prince's Trust, and St Peter and St James Hospice and Continuing Care Centre (£35,000 each).

FINANCES *Year* 2015/16 *Income* £1,774,857 *Grants* £1,689,814 *Grants to organisations* £1,689,814 *Assets* £56,525,959

TRUSTEES Alexander Kleinwort; Marina Kleinwort; Sir Richard Kleinwort; Edmund Christopher; Lord Chandos; Charlie Mayhew; Kleinwort Benson Trustees Ltd.

OTHER INFORMATION During the year a total of 160 appeals were supported.

HOW TO APPLY Apply in writing to the correspondent **via post**. Applications should be no longer than two A4 sides, incorporate a short (half page) summary, include a detailed budget for the project and provide most recent audited accounts (any significant surplus or deficit of income needs to be explained). Applicants must also complete and include an Accounts Summary form, which is available on the trust's website. Full details of what information is required for applications are given online. You can re-apply after 12 months from the date of your last application. Generally only successful applicants are notified – 'if you have not heard from [the trust] within five months, it is likely that your application has not been successful'. Appeals are considered approximately every four months (bigger grants over £10,000 are decided twice a year).

WHO TO APPLY TO Scott Rice, Trust Officer, Kleinwort Benson Trustees Ltd, 14 St George Street, London W1S 1FE *Tel.* 020 3207 7337 *Email* ekctadmin@kleinwortbenson.com *Website* www.ekct.org.uk

■ The Sir James Knott Trust

CC NO 1001363 **ESTABLISHED** 1990

WHERE FUNDING CAN BE GIVEN Tyne and Wear, Northumberland, County Durham inclusive of Hartlepool but exclusive of Darlington, Stockton-on-Tees, Middlesbrough, Redcar and Cleveland.

WHO CAN BENEFIT Registered charities only (unregistered organisations can be assisted through a local CVS); community projects in the local area.

WHAT IS FUNDED A wide range of general charitable causes, with special consideration for charitable activities known to have been of particular interest to Sir James Knott, including military and maritime organisations, youth clubs, projects to help older people and education and training. Support is given for the welfare of people who are disadvantaged, homeless people, young or older individuals, people with disabilities, to advance education and training, medical care, historic buildings, the environment, music and the arts and to seafarers' and services' charities.

WHAT IS NOT FUNDED Individuals; the replacement of funding withdrawn by local authorities; organisations that do not have an identifiable project within the beneficial area.

TYPE OF GRANT One-off; capital and core costs; salaries; start-up expenditure.

RANGE OF GRANTS Up to £100,000.

SAMPLE GRANTS Sunderland University Development Trust (£100,000); North of England Children's Cancer Research Fund (£60,000); North East Futures University Technical College (£50,000); Hospitality and Hope South Tyneside, and Single Homeless Action Initiative in Derwentside (£25,000 each); Northumbria Historic Churches Trust (£20,000); Diocese of Newcastle, Shelter, and Teach First (£15,000 each); Diocese of Durham (£12,500).

FINANCES *Year* 2015/16 *Income* £1,659,376 *Grants* £1,390,605 *Grants to organisations* £135,605 *Assets* £45,603,900

TRUSTEES Prof. Oliver James; John Cresswell; Sarah Riddel; Ben Speke.

OTHER INFORMATION In 2015/16 a total of 337 grants were made. Applications for awards below £1,000 (or in exceptional circumstances for larger amounts) can be considered between the trustees' meetings.

HOW TO APPLY Apply in writing to the correspondent, giving a description of the need and providing all the relevant supporting information regarding your organisation as well as a copy of the latest annual report and accounts (see the website for an extensive list of details which the trust expects to find in your appeal). The trustees normally meet in spring, summer and autumn. Applications need to be submitted at least three months before a grant is required (see the website for specific deadlines). Applicants may re-apply again in 18 months following a receipt of grant; unsuccessful applicants can try again in 12 months. The trust welcomes initial enquires by phone or email and 'endeavours to acknowledge all applications.'

WHO TO APPLY TO Vivien Stapley, Trust Secretary, 16–18 Hood Street, Newcastle upon Tyne NE1 6JQ *Tel.* 0191 230 4016 *Email* info@knott-trust.co.uk *Website* www.knott-trust.co.uk

■ The Kobler Trust

CC NO 275237 **ESTABLISHED** 1963

WHERE FUNDING CAN BE GIVEN UK.

WHO CAN BENEFIT Registered charities.

WHAT IS FUNDED General charitable purposes; the arts; Jewish causes; health and disability.

WHAT IS NOT FUNDED Grants to individuals are only given in exceptional circumstances.

TYPE OF GRANT Generally no restrictions. Awards vary from small grants on a one-off basis for a specific project to a continuing relationship.

RANGE OF GRANTS £250 to £25,000.

SAMPLE GRANTS Human Dignity Trust (£30,000); Pavilion Opera Educational Trust (£12,000); West London Synagogue and Wigmore Hall Trust (£10,000 each); Makor Charitable Trust (£8,000); Donmar Warehouse (£7,300); Treetops Hospice (£5,000); Arkwright Scholarship (£4,000); Leeds Jewish Welfare Board (£3,000); Weiner Library (£2,000).

FINANCES *Year* 2015/16 *Income* £107,025 *Grants* £101,800 *Grants to organisations* £101,800 *Assets* £3,044,361

TRUSTEES Andrew Stone; Antoine Xuereb; Joel Israelsohn; Joanne Evans.

OTHER INFORMATION There were 54 awards made during the financial year 2015/16.

HOW TO APPLY Apply in writing to the correspondent and incorporate full details of the charity for which funding is requested. The trustees meet two to three times a year. Acknowledgements are not generally sent out to unsuccessful applicants.

WHO TO APPLY TO The Trustees, c/o Lewis Silkin LLP, 10 Clifford's Inn Passage, London EC4A 1BL *Tel.* 020 7074 8000 *Email* info@lewissilkin.com

■ The Kohn Foundation

CC NO 1003951 **ESTABLISHED** 1991

WHERE FUNDING CAN BE GIVEN UK and overseas.

WHO CAN BENEFIT Registered charities; Jewish organisations.

WHAT IS FUNDED Scientific and medical projects; arts, particularly music; education; Jewish religion; relief of poverty; people with an illness or disability, especially mental health issues; other charitable causes.

RANGE OF GRANTS Up to £160,000.

SAMPLE GRANTS The Royal Society (£243,000); Royal Academy of Music (£107,000); Wigmore Hall/Kohn Foundation International Song Competition (£52,500); University of Manchester (£50,000); University of Durham (£20,000); Chai Cancer Care (£18,000); Academy of Medical Sciences, University of Cambridge, Trinity College Cambridge and Jewish Care (£10,000 each).

FINANCES *Year* 2015 *Income* £760,367 *Grants* £625,511 *Grants to organisations* £625,511 *Assets* £1,214,893

TRUSTEES Sir Ralph Kohn, Chair; Lady Zahava Kohn; Anthony Forwood.

OTHER INFORMATION In 2015 there were 79 grant recipients. Other unlisted awards under £1,000 totalled £11,143, for 44 recipients across all three categories.

HOW TO APPLY Apply in writing to the correspondent.

WHO TO APPLY TO Sir Ralph Kohn, Trustee, 14 Harley Street, London W1G 9PQ

■ Kollel and Co. Ltd

CC NO 1077180 **ESTABLISHED** 1999

WHERE FUNDING CAN BE GIVEN Worldwide.

WHO CAN BENEFIT Charitable organisations with Jewish focus.

WHAT IS FUNDED Jewish causes; relief of poverty; religious activities and education; medical needs; general charitable purposes.

TYPE OF GRANT Building; equipment; project costs.

RANGE OF GRANTS Up to £223,000.

SAMPLE GRANTS Hadras Kodesh Trust (£223,000); Ezer V'Hatzala (£193,000); Congregation Beth Hamadrash Vyoil Moshe D'Satmar (£138,500); Friends of Satmar Kollel Antwerpen (£108,000); Aniyel Haolam Trust (£94,000); Vishnitz Girls School Ltd, Rise and Shine, Give us a Chance, and The Telz Talmudical Academy and Talmud Torah Trust (£50,000 each).

FINANCES *Year* 2015/16 *Income* £1,752,344 *Grants* £1,363,290 *Grants to organisations* £1,363,290 *Assets* £2,683,581

TRUSTEES Simon Low; Rachel Kalish; Judith Weiss.

OTHER INFORMATION The annual report and accounts for 2015/16 only list the largest beneficiaries, with nine large grants coming to a total of £407,000.

HOW TO APPLY According to the annual report for 2015/16, 'grants are made upon application by the charity concerned ... in amounts thought appropriate by the directors/trustees'.

WHO TO APPLY TO Simon Low, Trustee, 7 Overlea Road, London E5 9BG *Tel.* 020 8806 1570

■ The KPMG Foundation

CC NO 1086518 **ESTABLISHED** 2000

WHERE FUNDING CAN BE GIVEN England, Scotland and Wales.

WHO CAN BENEFIT Registered charities.

WHAT IS FUNDED Children and young people in or leaving care; children and young people in disadvantaged families; refugees; young people who have offended; people lacking educational and employment opportunities.

WHAT IS NOT FUNDED The foundation will consider projects that support young people up to the age of 30.

TYPE OF GRANT Project grants.
RANGE OF GRANTS £10,000 to £247,000.
SAMPLE GRANTS The Fostering Network (£247,000); Teach First (£150,000); Future First (£143,500); Barnardo's (£111,500); Working Chance (£91,000 in two separate grants); Education Endowment Foundation (£70,000); Enabling Enterprise (£60,000); Aid for access (£34,000); Into University (£25,000); Shaftesbury Young People – Siblings United (£20,000).
FINANCES *Year* 2014/15 *Income* £1,921,696 *Grants* £956,591 *Grants to organisations* £956,591 *Assets* £6,984,522
TRUSTEES Lisa Harker; Sir Gerry Acher; Surinder Arora; Claire Le Masurier; Robin Cartwright; Peter Sherratt; Simon Collins; Marianne Fallon.
OTHER INFORMATION There were 12 awards made in 2014/15.
HOW TO APPLY According to the website, the director and advisor to the foundation 'actively seek projects to support and therefore do not accept any unsolicited applications'. The trustees can also make referrals to the director of the foundation.
WHO TO APPLY TO Jo Clunie, Director, KPMG LLP, 15 Canada Square, Canary Wharf, London E14 5GL *Tel.* 020 7311 4733 *Email* jo.clunie@kpmgfoundation.co.uk *Website* home.kpmg.com/uk/en/home/about/corporate-responsibility/kpmg-foundation.html

■ The Kreditor Charitable Trust

CC NO 292649 **ESTABLISHED** 1985
WHERE FUNDING CAN BE GIVEN UK and overseas, with a preference for London and North East England.
WHO CAN BENEFIT Charitable bodies; Jewish organisations; UK welfare organisations benefitting Jewish people, especially those disadvantaged by poverty or social isolation.
WHAT IS FUNDED Mainly advancement of religion in accordance with the Orthodox Jewish Faith; education; social and medical welfare; with focus on Jewish causes; other charitable causes.
SAMPLE GRANTS Academy for Rabbinical Research; British Diabetic Association; British Friends of Israel War Disabled; Fordeve Ltd, Jerusalem Ladies' Society; Jewish Care; Jewish Marriage Council; Kosher Meals on Wheels; London Academy of Jewish Studies; North West London Talmudical College; Ravenswood; Action on Hearing Loss; Unicef UK.
FINANCES *Year* 2015/16 *Income* £51,993 *Grants* £54,275 *Grants to organisations* £54,275 *Assets* £33,403
TRUSTEES Paul Kreditor; Merle Kreditor; Sharon Kreditor.
OTHER INFORMATION A copy of a list of material grants issued during the year can be obtained by letter request to the principal address of the Charity. Note that charitable expenditure varies and in the previous years has exceeded £100,000.
HOW TO APPLY Apply in writing to the correspondent.
WHO TO APPLY TO Paul Kreditor, Trustee, Hallswelle House, 1 Hallswelle Road, London NW11 0DH

■ The Kreitman Foundation

CC NO 269046 **ESTABLISHED** 1975
WHERE FUNDING CAN BE GIVEN UK.
WHO CAN BENEFIT Charitable organisations.
WHAT IS FUNDED General charitable purposes, particularly education, health and social welfare.
WHAT IS NOT FUNDED Individuals.
TYPE OF GRANT Generally specific project costs.
RANGE OF GRANTS £200 to £600,000.
SAMPLE GRANTS Wellington College (£600,000); UK Friends of AWIS (£279,000); Dedanist Foundation (£25,000); Myeloma UK (£5,000); Portsmouth Hospitals Charity (£600); Solving Kids Cancer (£200).
FINANCES *Year* 2015/16 *Income* £62,294 *Grants* £909,815 *Grants to organisations* £909,815 *Assets* £3,444,430
TRUSTEES Jill Luck-Hille; Peter Luck-Hille; Gareth Morgan.
OTHER INFORMATION During the year six grants were made.
HOW TO APPLY Apply in writing to the correspondent.
WHO TO APPLY TO Gordon Smith, Trustee, c/o Citroen Wells and Partners, Devonshire House, 1 Devonshire Street, London W1W 5DR *Email* jonathan.prevezer@citroenwells.co.uk

■ The Neil Kreitman Foundation

CC NO 267171 **ESTABLISHED** 1974
WHERE FUNDING CAN BE GIVEN Worldwide.
WHO CAN BENEFIT Registered charities or exempt organisations with charitable objectives.
WHAT IS FUNDED General charitable purposes, mainly the areas of arts and culture, education, health and social welfare.
WHAT IS NOT FUNDED Individuals.
TYPE OF GRANT Primarily general funds; some small capital grants or core costs.
RANGE OF GRANTS £1,000 to £114,500.
SAMPLE GRANTS Independent Shakespeare Co. (£93,500); Then Panchen Lama-Tashi Lhunpo Project (£58,500); Crocker Art Museum (£54,500); The Ashmolean Museum (£51,500); Santa Barbara Museum of Art, Ojai Valley Land Conservancy, and Médecins Sans Frontières (£39,000 each); Ojai Music Festival, Sierra Club Foundation and Amnesty International USA (£23,500 each).
FINANCES *Year* 2014/15 *Income* £834,555 *Grants* £577,275 *Grants to organisations* £577,275 *Assets* £29,702,100
TRUSTEES Neil Kreitman; Gordon Smith.
OTHER INFORMATION Financial figures are given in dollars in the foundation's accounts; we have used the conversion rate applicable at the time of writing. The 2014/15 accounts were the latest available at the time of writing (May 2017). A total of 30 awards were allocated as follows: arts and culture (£405,000); health and welfare (£123,398); education (£49,000).
HOW TO APPLY Apply in writing to the correspondent.
WHO TO APPLY TO The Trustees, Citroen Wells, Devonshire House, 1 Devonshire Street, London W1W 5DR *Tel.* 020 7304 2000

■ Kupath Gemach Chaim Bechesed Viznitz Trust

CC NO 1110323 **ESTABLISHED** 2005
WHERE FUNDING CAN BE GIVEN UK and overseas, including Israel.
WHO CAN BENEFIT Registered charities; individuals.
WHAT IS FUNDED Relief of people who are poor, feeble or have illnesses, throughout the world

and in particular but not exclusively among members of the Jewish faith; the advancement of the Orthodox Jewish faith; the advancement of the Orthodox Jewish religious education.

TYPE OF GRANT Grants; interest-free loans.

SAMPLE GRANTS Kupas Hachesed (£13,200); Kollel Imrei Boruch (£11,600). No further beneficiaries were given, but awards were distributed as follows: education (£51,000); relief of poverty (£28,500); religion (£18,400).

FINANCES *Year* 2015/16 *Income* £404,462 *Grants* £398,354 *Grants to organisations* £109,303 *Assets* £15,670

TRUSTEES Israel Kahan; Saul Weiss; Alexander Pifko.

OTHER INFORMATION Grants to organisations were made in the following areas: poor and needy (£38,500), advancement of religion (£35,500), and education (£35,000). During the year a further £289,000 was granted to individuals in need.

HOW TO APPLY Apply in writing to the correspondent.

WHO TO APPLY TO Saul Weiss, Trustee, 171 Kyverdale Road, London N16 6PS *Tel.* 020 8442 9604 or 07811 253203

■ Kusuma Trust UK

CC NO 1126983 **ESTABLISHED** 2008

WHERE FUNDING CAN BE GIVEN India; UK; Gibraltar.

WHO CAN BENEFIT Registered organisations.

WHAT IS FUNDED Education; research and advocacy; community projects.

RANGE OF GRANTS Up to £1.1 million.

SAMPLE GRANTS Kusuma Foundation (£1.04 million); Centre for Internet and Society (£155,000); Sutton Trust (£143,000); The Coalfields Regeneration Trust (£55,000); Royal Parks Foundation (£25,000); Midfield Research Services (£17,200); New Concept Information Systems (£13,200); Pratham Education Foundation (£10,700).

FINANCES *Year* 2015/16 *Income* £2,530,666 *Grants* £1,465,295 *Grants to organisations* £1,465,295 *Assets* £303,782,905

TRUSTEES Dr Soma Pujari; Andrew Hutton; Anurag Dikshit.

OTHER INFORMATION Total number of grants awarded was eight, with five being awarded in India and the rest in the UK.

HOW TO APPLY If you are interested in applying for funding and your proposal is aligned to the strategy and priorities of the trust, email info@kusumatrust.org with brief information about your organisation, proposed project and the amount of funding you are seeking. If your project meets the criteria a concept note will be asked for. The trust endeavours to respond within four weeks.

WHO TO APPLY TO Andrew Vivian, Head of Programmes, Kusuma Trust UK, 90 Long Acre, London WC2E 9RZ *Tel.* 020 7717 8998 *Fax* 020 7569 1925 *Email* info@kusumatrust.org *Website* www.kusumatrust.org

■ The Kyte Charitable Trust

CC NO 1035886 **ESTABLISHED** 1994

WHERE FUNDING CAN BE GIVEN UK and overseas.

WHO CAN BENEFIT Primarily organisations that benefit the Jewish community.

WHAT IS FUNDED General charitable purposes with Jewish focus; education; health; sports; community causes; children and young people.

RANGE OF GRANTS Up to £74,000.

SAMPLE GRANTS Maccabi London Brady Recreational Trust (£73,500); Jewish Care and United Jewish Israel Appeal (UJIA) (£25,000 each); Jewish Community Secondary School Trust (£22,500); Community Security Trust (£20,000); Presidents Club (£15,000); Chai Cancer Care (£7,200).

FINANCES *Year* 2015/16 *Income* £125,734 *Grants* £203,218 *Grants to organisations* £203,218 *Assets* £150,625

TRUSTEES David Kyte; Tracey Kyte; James Kyte; Ilana Kyte, Max Kyte.

OTHER INFORMATION A further £14,500 was awarded to organisations which received grants of under £5,000.

HOW TO APPLY Apply in writing to the correspondent.

WHO TO APPLY TO David Kyte, Trustee, First Floor, Nations House, 103 Wigmore Street, London W1U 1QS *Tel.* 020 7486 7700

■ Ladbrokes in the Community Charitable Trust

CC NO 1101804 **ESTABLISHED** 2003

WHERE FUNDING CAN BE GIVEN UK (communities in which the shops and businesses of Ladbrokes Betting and Gaming Ltd or Ladbrokes eGaming Ltd operate).

WHO CAN BENEFIT Registered charities and community groups.

WHAT IS FUNDED General charitable purposes; health; education; community projects.

SAMPLE GRANTS Barnardo's; Bobby Moore Fund; Cancer Research UK; Child Victims of Crime; Haven House Children's Hospice; NSPCC, Prostate Cancer UK and the Responsible Gambling Trust.

FINANCES *Year* 2015 *Income* £481,398 *Grants* £465,725 *Grants to organisations* £421,806 *Assets* £151,833

TRUSTEES Michael O'Kane; Susan Harley; Jan Kunicki; Elaine Moran.

OTHER INFORMATION In 2015 grants totalling £25,000 were grant to medical causes, with hospices and hospitals being granted £440,500.

HOW TO APPLY In the first instance, the support of a local shop should be secured in raising funds on behalf of a cause. The grants committee meets monthly to consider applications.

WHO TO APPLY TO Michael O'Kane, Trustee, Ladbrokes Ltd, Imperial House, Imperial Drive, Harrow, Middlesex HA2 7JW *Tel.* 020 8515 5611 *Email* charity@ladbrokes.co.uk *Website* www.ladbrokesplc.com/corporate-responsibility/communities.aspx

■ The K. P. Ladd Charitable Trust

CC NO 1091493 **ESTABLISHED** 2002

WHERE FUNDING CAN BE GIVEN UK and overseas.

WHO CAN BENEFIT Churches; charitable organisations involved in religious activities; missionary work.

WHAT IS FUNDED Christian causes; missionaries; overseas aid.

TYPE OF GRANT One-off unrestricted funding, including core costs, capital costs, project funding and salaries.

RANGE OF GRANTS £1,000 to £75,000.

SAMPLE GRANTS London Institute for Contemporary Christianity (£75,000); Kepplewray Trust (£6,000); Storehouse Church and Volunteers Outreach Working Calverton (£5,000 each); Hope in Tottenham (£4,000); Amnos Ministries, Salvation Army, and Bromley Christian Workers Trust (£3,000); Wycliffe Bible Translators, SOS Bosnia, Church Army, Liveability, and Mercy Ships (£2,000 each).

FINANCES *Year* 2015/16 *Income* £152,145 *Grants* £87,250 *Grants to organisations* £87,250 *Assets* £2,466,542

TRUSTEES Rosemary Anne-Ladd; Brian Ladd; Kenneth Ladd; Ian Creswick.

OTHER INFORMATION Grants were given to 18 organisations.

HOW TO APPLY The trust has stated that it 'is fully committed and does not reply to unsolicited requests'. The trustees select charities known to them personally.

WHO TO APPLY TO Brian Ladd, Trustee, 34 St Mary's Avenue, Northwood, Middlesex HA6 3AZ *Email* brian.ladd@licc.org.uk

■ John Laing Charitable Trust

CC NO 236852 **ESTABLISHED** 1962

WHERE FUNDING CAN BE GIVEN UK.

WHO CAN BENEFIT Existing and former employees of John Laing PLC who are in need; registered charities; in exceptional circumstances not-for-profit organisations.

WHAT IS FUNDED Education; community regeneration; disadvantaged young people; homelessness with a particular emphasis on day centres.

WHAT IS NOT FUNDED Individuals (other than to Laing employees and/or their dependants); animal charities; organisations based outside the UK.

TYPE OF GRANT Donations range from £250 to £25,000 with up to 12 charities receiving more than £10,000. Usually, charities receive one-off donations, but a small number are supported for an agreed period, often up to three years.

SAMPLE GRANTS NWG Network (£79,000); Leap (£50,000); Coram (£40,000); Hertfordshire Groundwork (£37,500); The Prince's Trust (£34,500); Business in the Community (£33,000); Young Enterprise (£30,000); Atlantic College (£26,000); Manchester Settlement (£25,500); Cumbria Community Foundation, Mosaic, The Silver line and Alzheimer's Research UK (£25,000 each).

FINANCES *Year* 2015 *Income* £1,996,000 *Grants* £1,317,000 *Grants to organisations* £671,000 *Assets* £56,293,000

TRUSTEES Christopher Laing; Sir Martin Laing; Lynette Krige; Christopher Waples; Daniel Partridge.

OTHER INFORMATION During the year about £1.4 million was awarded, to both organisations and individuals, with £646,000 being distributed to about 415 individuals who were either current or former employees of John Laing PLC. There are also other four charities set up by the Laing family and administered at the same address – for more information see www.laingfamilytrusts.org.uk.

HOW TO APPLY The trust's website states: 'The John Laing Charitable Trust is no longer processing uninvited applications.'

WHO TO APPLY TO Jenny Impey, Trust Director, 33 Bunns Lane, Mill Hill, London NW7 2DX *Tel.* 020 7901 3307 *Email* jenny.impey@laing.com *Website* www.laing.com/top/corporate_responsibility/john_laing_charitable_trust.html

■ Maurice and Hilda Laing Charitable Trust

CC NO 1058109 **ESTABLISHED** 1996

WHERE FUNDING CAN BE GIVEN UK and overseas.

WHO CAN BENEFIT UK-registered charities.

WHAT IS FUNDED Advancement of the Christian religion; relief of poverty in the UK; relief of poverty overseas.

WHAT IS NOT FUNDED General appeals or circulars; campaigning or lobbying activities; umbrella, second tier or grant-making organisations; professional associations or projects for the training of professionals; feasibility studies and social research; individual sponsorship requirements; grants to individuals for educational, medical or travel purposes including gap year projects and overseas exchange programmes; summer activities for children/young people or after-school clubs; state maintained or independent schools other than those for pupils with special educational needs; uniformed groups such as Scouts and Guides; costs of staging one-off events, festivals or conferences; animal welfare; core running costs of hospices, counselling projects and other local organisations; church restoration or repair (including organs and bells). While ongoing cost of sustaining core activities is not funded, reasonable level of management costs to cover project overheads, including some employment costs, can be covered.

TYPE OF GRANT Usually one-off for capital project funding; project costs; some project related core expenditure.

RANGE OF GRANTS £5,000 to £1.4 million.

SAMPLE GRANTS Cambridge Theological Federation (£1.3 million in four separate grants); Fegans Child and Family Care (£1.1 million in 13 separate payments); Youthscape (£250,000); SAT-7 Trust Ltd (in two separate grants) and Bombay Teen Challenge (£200,000 each); Mission Aviation Fellowship (£150,000); Moorlands College (in two separate grants) and Community of St Anselm (£110,000 each); Adventure Plus, Leicester Cathedral, The Lambeth Trust and The Woolf Institute (£100,000 each).

FINANCES *Year* 2015 *Income* £1,005,682 *Grants* £5,593,797 *Grants to organisations* £5,593,797 *Assets* £26,347,677

TRUSTEES Andrea Currie; Simon Martle; Paul van den Bosch; Ewan Harper; Charles Laing; Stephen Ludlow.

OTHER INFORMATION This is one of the Laing Family Trusts. During the year a total of 131 awards were made. Our research indicates that in 2006 the trustees made the decision to work towards winding up the trust by 2020. As such, there will be a controlled increase in the level of future grant expenditure. The trustees are making a number of significant investments to a small number of organisations that they will proactively invite to apply. Charities can still apply for the small grants programme.

HOW TO APPLY An application to any of the four charities is considered by all and directed to the most appropriate one. Appeals should be made **by post** (three to four pages) providing the following: contact details; confirmation of charitable status; charitable aims and objectives; details of the project (including costs, fundraising strategy, timing and monitoring arrangements); a copy of most recent accounts and annual report; an sae; covering letter on the charity's headed paper; any other supporting information, if appropriate. The trustees meet four times a year to consider the award of grants of over £10,000. Decisions on smaller grants are made on an ongoing basis. Bear in mind that 'fewer than 50% of unsolicited applications to the trusts are successful'. Applicants should wait at least 12–18 months before re-applying following an unsuccessful application.

WHO TO APPLY TO Elizabeth Harley, Trusts Director, 33 Bunns Lane, Mill Hill, London NW7 2DX *Tel.* 020 8238 8890 *Email* info@laingfamilytrusts.org.uk *Website* www.laingfamilytrusts.org.uk/maurice_hilda_laing.html

■ Christopher Laing Foundation

CC NO 278460 **ESTABLISHED** 1979

WHERE FUNDING CAN BE GIVEN UK with a preference for Hertfordshire and Oxfordshire.

WHO CAN BENEFIT Registered charities.

WHAT IS FUNDED General charitable purposes; arts and culture; sports; environment; health and disability causes. Particular preference for organisations supporting adults with disabilities.

WHAT IS NOT FUNDED Donations are only made to registered charities.

TYPE OF GRANT Our research indicates that grants may be recurrent and one-off, given for capital and core costs, projects, seed and feasibility funding. Loans may be given.

RANGE OF GRANTS £1,000 to £75,000.

SAMPLE GRANTS The Duke of Edinburgh's Award (£60,000); The Lord's Taverners and Fields in Trust (National Playing Fields Association) (£40,000 each); RNLI (£30,500); Swings and Smiles (£30,000); Sue Ryder (£25,000); Hertfordshire Groundwork Trust, Friends of the Princess of Wales's Royal Regiment and YMCA Henley (£10,000 each); Royal Parks Foundation and Hertfordshire Action on Disability (£5,000 each).

FINANCES *Year* 2015/16 *Income* £496,595 *Grants* £343,100 *Grants to organisations* £343,100 *Assets* £10,242,410

TRUSTEES Christopher Laing; Diana Laing; John Keeble; Michael Laing; Richard Haines.

OTHER INFORMATION There were 14 grants made during the year 2015/16 which saw £70,000 going towards the Charities Aid Foundation.

HOW TO APPLY Apply in writing to the correspondent.

WHO TO APPLY TO Vince Cheshire, Director of UK Private Client Services, TMF Management (UK) Ltd, 400 Capability Green, Luton, Bedfordshire LU1 3AE *Tel.* 01582 439200 *Email* claing_charity@tmf-group.com

■ The David Laing Foundation

CC NO 278462 **ESTABLISHED** 1979

WHERE FUNDING CAN BE GIVEN Worldwide, with a preference for the East Midlands and the south of England.

WHO CAN BENEFIT Organisations benefitting children, including those who are in care, fostered or adopted; one-parent families; people with disabilities.

WHAT IS FUNDED General charitable purposes, with a focus on young people, disability and the arts.

WHAT IS NOT FUNDED Individuals.

TYPE OF GRANT One-off; capital costs; some charities are closely associated with the foundation and would benefit more frequently.

RANGE OF GRANTS Up to £20,000.

SAMPLE GRANTS Adrenaline Alley (£20,000); The Living Room (£15,000); Campaign to Protect Rural England and Crusader Community Boating (£13,000 each); The Prince's Trust and The Duke of Edinburgh's Award (£10,000 each); Royal and Derngate (£9,000); Garsington Opera (£8,100); Northamptonshire Community Foundation (£7,000) and Northamptonshire Association of Youth Clubs (£5,000).

FINANCES *Year* 2015/16 *Income* £245,152 *Grants* £203,090 *Grants to organisations* £203,090 *Assets* £6,105,255

TRUSTEES David Laing; Stuart Lewis; Frances Laing; Francis Barlow.

OTHER INFORMATION The latest accounts for 2015/16 only list beneficiaries receiving over £5,000. Previous information has shown the foundation to make large grants to a wide and varied number of organisations as well as donating smaller grants through Charities Aid Foundation. The latest annual report for 2015/16 notes that the trustees 'propose to maintain the breadth and diversity of giving, and to concentrate spending resources to meet local demands and needs'.

HOW TO APPLY Apply in writing to the correspondent.

WHO TO APPLY TO David Laing, Trustee, The Manor House, Grafton Underwood, Kettering, Northamptonshire NN14 3AA *Email* david@david-laing.co.uk

■ The Kirby Laing Foundation

CC NO 264299 **ESTABLISHED** 1972

WHERE FUNDING CAN BE GIVEN Unrestricted, but mainly UK.

WHO CAN BENEFIT Registered charities.

WHAT IS FUNDED General charitable purposes including: promotion of the evangelical Christian faith; education, with a particular interest in the promotion of science and engineering, and youth development; medical research, with a particular emphasis on dementia and stroke; social/medical welfare projects, particularly those benefitting older people and people with disabilities; preservation of cultural/ environmental heritage and improving access to the arts for young people and people with disabilities (projects of national importance only); overseas development projects.

WHAT IS NOT FUNDED General appeals or circulars; campaigning or lobbying activities; umbrella, second tier or grant-making organisations; professional associations or projects for the training of professionals; feasibility studies and social research; individual sponsorship requirements; grants to individuals for educational, medical or travel purposes including gap year projects and overseas exchange programmes; summer activities for children/young people or after-school clubs; state maintained or independent schools other than those for pupils with special educational needs; uniformed groups such as Scouts and Guides; costs of staging one-off events, festivals or conferences; animal welfare; core running costs of hospices, counselling projects and other local organisations; church restoration or repair (including organs and bells).

TYPE OF GRANT A significant percentage of the grants awarded are made on a one-off basis for capital purposes. Most other grants are directed towards specific projects. Such grants may be made on a one-off basis or phased, often on a tapering basis, over a three-year period.

RANGE OF GRANTS Up to £1.2 million.

SAMPLE GRANTS University of Cambridge and University of Oxford (£1.2 million each); University of Edinburgh (£800,000); Oriel College (£250,000); Leprosy Mission (£130,000); Royal Academy of Arts, Leicester Cathedral and London Institute for Contemporary Christianity (£100,000 each); Peterborough Cathedral (£90,000) and University of Bristol (£75,000).

FINANCES *Year* 2015 *Income* £2,085,960 *Grants* £5,216,279 *Grants to organisations* £5,216,279 *Assets* £54,844,074

TRUSTEES David Laing; Simon Webley; Revd Charles Burch; Dr Frederick Lewis.

OTHER INFORMATION Our research indicates that charities can apply for grants of up to £5,000 while anything over this amount is by invitation only. According to the latest annual report for 2013, the trustees 'have indicated that they expect to wind up the foundation over a period of five to seven years and are in the process of implementing a strategy to achieve this'. During the year awards were given to 102 organisations (including 26 awards through Charities Aid Foundation totalling £50,000).

HOW TO APPLY An application to any of the four charities is considered by all and directed to the most appropriate one. Appeals should be made **by post** (three to four pages) providing the following: contact details; confirmation of charitable status; charitable aims and objectives; details of the project (including costs, fundraising strategy, timing and monitoring arrangements); a copy of most recent accounts and annual report; an sae; covering letter on the charity's headed paper; any other supporting information, if appropriate. The trustees meet four times a year to consider the award of grants of over £10,000. Decisions on smaller grants are made on an ongoing basis. Bear in mind that 'fewer than 50% of unsolicited applications to the trusts are successful'. Applicants should wait at least 12–18 months before re-applying following an unsuccessful application.

WHO TO APPLY TO Elizabeth Harley, Trusts Director, 33 Bunns Lane, Mill Hill, London NW7 2DX *Tel.* 020 8238 8890 *Email* info@laingfamilytrusts.org.uk *Website* www.laingfamilytrusts.org.uk

■ The Martin Laing Foundation

CC NO 278461 **ESTABLISHED** 1979

WHERE FUNDING CAN BE GIVEN UK and worldwide, particularly Malta and Thailand, and Norfolk-based projects.

WHO CAN BENEFIT Registered charities.

WHAT IS FUNDED General charitable purposes; environment and conservation; young and older people.

WHAT IS NOT FUNDED General appeals or circulars; campaigning or lobbying activities; umbrella, second tier or grant-making organisations; professional associations or projects for the training of professionals; feasibility studies and social research; individual sponsorship requirements; grants to individuals for educational, medical or travel purposes including gap year projects and overseas exchange programmes; summer activities for children/young people or after-school clubs; state maintained or independent schools other than those for pupils with special educational needs; uniformed groups such as scouts and guides; costs of staging one-off events, festivals or conferences; animal welfare; core running costs of hospices, counselling projects and other local organisations; church restoration or repair (including organs and bells).

TYPE OF GRANT One-off awards for capital costs or one-off/recurrent project grants.

RANGE OF GRANTS £250 to £15,000.

SAMPLE GRANTS Welsh National Opera (£10,500); East Anglian Air Ambulance, Macmillan Cancer Support, John Laing Charitable Trust, and WWF-UK (£10,000 each); Flimkien ghal Ambjent Ahjar and Fondazzjoni Patrimonju Malti (£8,600 each); Diabetes UK (£7,500); ABF The Soldiers' Charity and The Pushkin Trust (£5,000 each).

FINANCES *Year* 2015/16 *Income* £386,971 *Grants* £182,549 *Grants to organisations* £182,549 *Assets* £9,892,119

TRUSTEES Edward Laing; Sir Martin Laing; Lady Laing; Nicholas Gregory; Colin Fletcher; Alexandra Gregory; Graham Sillett.

OTHER INFORMATION This is one of the Laing Family Trusts. Detailed information on this and other charities can be found on the website. There were 46 awards made (including 22 through Charities Aid Foundation).

HOW TO APPLY The Laing Family Trusts are administered and co-ordinated centrally; therefore, an application to one is considered for all funds. Applications should be made **by post** providing a concise proposal (three to four pages) giving your contact details, confirmation of charitable status, overview of charity's objectives and aims, information and costings of the project to be supported and a copy of most recent accounts, an sae and covering letter on the charity's headed paper (any other supporting information can also be provided). Applications can be submitted at any time (they are not acknowledged) and the trustees normally meet at quarterly intervals. You should here the outcome within four months. If you were unsuccessful you should wait about 12–18 months before re-applying. The website states: 'Potential applicants should note that very few unsolicited approaches to this Foundation are successful.'

WHO TO APPLY TO Elizabeth Harley, Trusts Director, 33 Bunns Lane, London NW7 2DX *Tel.* 020 8238 8890 *Email* info@laingfamilytrusts.org.uk *Website* www.laingfamilytrusts.org.uk

The Beatrice Laing Trust

CC NO 211884 **ESTABLISHED** 1952

WHERE FUNDING CAN BE GIVEN UK and overseas.

WHO CAN BENEFIT Mainly registered charities. Grants to overseas projects are normally made through a registered UK charity.

WHAT IS FUNDED Relief of poverty; advancement of the evangelical Christian faith; social welfare; disadvantaged individuals; education, training and development of young people; employment; older people; homeless individuals; those with physical, mental or learning difficulties; former armed forces personnel; people who have offended; small-scale development projects overseas; direct health services (rather than medical research). A very small number of individuals are supported, mostly for retired missionaries who were known to the founders and who receive an annual grant.

WHAT IS NOT FUNDED General appeals or circulars; campaigning or lobbying activities; umbrella, second tier or grant-making organisations; professional associations or projects for the training of professionals; feasibility studies and social research; individual sponsorship requirements; grants to individuals for educational, medical or travel purposes including gap year projects and overseas exchange programmes; summer activities for children/young people or after-school clubs; state maintained or independent schools other than those for pupils with special educational needs; uniformed groups such as Scouts and Guides; costs of staging one-off events, festivals or conferences; animal welfare; core running costs of hospices, counselling projects and other local organisations; church restoration or repair (including organs and bells).

TYPE OF GRANT Mainly one-off, capital costs; one-off or recurrent project expenditure.

RANGE OF GRANTS Mostly £500 to £5,000.

SAMPLE GRANTS Home Farm Trust Ltd and Cumbria Community Foundation (£50,000 each); Castlemilk Parish Church Glasgow, IMPACT Foundation (in two separate grants) and Housing Justice (£40,000 each); Echoes of Service (£30,000); East Park School, Greenhouse Sports, Treloar Trust, The Meath Epilepsy Trust, Christchurch Baptist Church, Welwyn Garden City, Cirencester Baptist Church, Redland Parish Church, Emmaus UK, and St Wilfrid's Centre (£25,000 each).

FINANCES *Year* 2015/16 *Income* £2,611,620 *Grants* £1,527,370 *Grants to organisations* £1,527,370 *Assets* £55,456,252

TRUSTEES Christopher Laing; Sir Martin Laing; David Laing; Charles Laing; Paula Blacker; Alex Gregory.

OTHER INFORMATION This is one of the Laing Family Trusts. During the year grants were made to 235 organisations.

HOW TO APPLY An application to any of the four charities is considered by all and directed to the most appropriate one. Appeals should be made **by post** (three to four pages) providing the following: contact details; confirmation of charitable status; charitable aims and objectives; details of the project (including costs, fundraising strategy, timing and monitoring arrangements); a copy of most recent accounts and annual report; an sae; covering letter on the charity's headed paper; any other supporting information, if appropriate. The trustees meet four times a year to consider the award of grants of over £10,000. Decisions on smaller grants are made on an ongoing basis. Bear in mind that 'fewer than 50% of unsolicited applications to the trusts are successful'. Applicants should wait at least 12–18 months before re-applying following an unsuccessful application.

WHO TO APPLY TO Elizabeth Harley, Trusts Director, c/o Laing Family Trusts, 33 Bunns Lane, Mill Hill, London NW7 2DX *Tel.* 020 8238 8890 *Email* info@laingfamilytrusts.org.uk *Website* www.laingfamilytrusts.org.uk

The Leonard Laity Stoate Charitable Trust

CC NO 221325 **ESTABLISHED** 1950

WHERE FUNDING CAN BE GIVEN England and Wales – in practice, the south west of England – Bristol, Somerset (especially West Somerset), Cornwall, Devon and Dorset.

WHO CAN BENEFIT UK-registered or exempt charities; churches.

WHAT IS FUNDED Methodism; general charitable purposes, including: social welfare; medical causes; disability; children and young people; churches; community projects; the arts; overseas aid; the environment.

WHAT IS NOT FUNDED Individuals unless supported by a registered charity; institutions that are not registered charities or established churches that pay wages or other remuneration (including CICs); large projects (over £500,000 and/or with more than £250,000 still to raise); general appeals by national charities. Grants are not normally given for running expenses of a charity.

TYPE OF GRANT Usually one-off for a specific project or part of a project.

RANGE OF GRANTS £100 to £2,000.

SAMPLE GRANTS EDP Drug and Alcohol Services, Hele Lane Methodist Church and Sidmouth Parish Church (£1,000 each); Julia's House Hospice, Knappe Cross Community Association and Victim Support (£500 each); Oddments Theatre Company (£300); Parkinson's UK (£200); Bristol Playbus and World Land Trust (£100 each).

FINANCES *Year* 2015/16 *Income* £76,509 *Grants* £93,700 *Grants to organisations* £93,700 *Assets* £1,963,743

TRUSTEES Stephen Duckworth; Philip Stoate; Dr Christopher Stoate; Dr Pam Stoate; Susan Hamden; Revd Dr Jonathan Pye.

OTHER INFORMATION Due to the large number of applications it receives, applications from outside the trust's geographic area of focus are unlikely to be successful.

HOW TO APPLY Apply in writing to the correspondent (not by email or telephone), and should include the information specified on the trust's website. The majority of grants are awarded at half-yearly meetings in April and October, so the best time to submit applications are December–February or June–August.

WHO TO APPLY TO Philip Stoate, Trustee, 41 Tower Hill, Williton, Taunton TA4 4JR *Email* charity@erminea.org.uk *Website* www.stoate-charity.org.uk

■ The Lambert Charitable Trust

CC NO 257803 **ESTABLISHED** 1969

WHERE FUNDING CAN BE GIVEN UK and Israel.

WHO CAN BENEFIT Charitable organisations. Preference can be given to the Greater London area and organisations helping people of Jewish faith.

WHAT IS FUNDED Health; social welfare; education and training; children and young people; homes for older people; health and disability; Jewish causes.

TYPE OF GRANT One-off and recurrent.

RANGE OF GRANTS £250 to £15,000.

SAMPLE GRANTS Jewish Care (£11,000); Action on Addiction (£4,000); Medical Engineering Resource Unit, New Horizon Youth Centre, Quaker Social Action, Ro-Ro Sailing Project and The Brandon Centre (£3,000 each); Dreamstore, Integrated Neurological Services, London Symphony Orchestra, Freedom from Torture, Meningitis Research Foundation, Nightingale House, PALS and Vitalise (£2,000 each).

FINANCES *Year* 2015/16 *Income* £77,859 *Grants* £53,250 *Grants to organisations* £53,250 *Assets* £3,340,743

TRUSTEES Maurice Lambert; Prof. Harold Lambert; Jane Lambert; Oliver Lambert; David Wells.

OTHER INFORMATION There were a total of 23 awards made.

HOW TO APPLY Apply in writing to the correspondent.

WHO TO APPLY TO George Georghiou, Mercer and Hole, 72 London Road, St Albans, Hertfordshire AL1 1NS *Tel.* 01727 869141

■ Community Foundations for Lancashire and Merseyside

CC NO 1068887 **ESTABLISHED** 1998

WHERE FUNDING CAN BE GIVEN Merseyside and Lancashire.

WHO CAN BENEFIT Charitable organisations.

WHAT IS FUNDED A wide range of general charitable purposes; community causes; development and regeneration. The foundation manages funds on behalf of parent donors. Funding priorities will vary considerably depending on the requirements of these donors.

WHAT IS NOT FUNDED Each fund administered by the trust has separate guidelines and exclusionary criteria which are available directly from the trust's website. According to its website, the foundation will generally not fund: 'public sector organisations or those controlled wholly or in part, such as local authority or primary care trust; commercial ventures; purchase/ maintenance of vehicles; activities that will have already taken place before the grant is offered; politically connected or exclusively religious activities; projects for personal profit; organisations that are set up for the benefit of animals or plants environmental groups that work with animals or environment such as city farms are acceptable; groups comprising just one family; statutory organisations or work that is their responsibility; debts and other liabilities; reclaimable VAT'. Note that if you are applying to more than one fund at the same time it should be for either a different project or different costs of the same project.

TYPE OF GRANT Core costs; salaries; capital expenditure and project funding; start-up or development funding.

RANGE OF GRANTS £250 to £10,000.

SAMPLE GRANTS dot-art Schools; Fire Support Network; Halton Voluntary Action; Jo Jo Mind and Body; Liverpool Academy of Art; Liverpool Greenbank Wheelchair Basketball Club; The Zero Centre; Twin Vision.

FINANCES *Year* 2015/16 *Income* £2,932,789 *Grants* £2,211,065 *Grants to organisations* £2,211,065 *Assets* £12,460,529

TRUSTEES Abi Pointing; Arthur Roberts; William Bowley; David McDonnell; Andrew Myers; Wendy Swift; Chris Bliss.

OTHER INFORMATION The funds may open and close regularly; therefore, it would not be practicable to list these here and applicants are advised to visit the website to see the most up-to-date information.

HOW TO APPLY Most of the foundation's funds can now be applied for online using a standard form (supporting documents will need to be provided within seven days, preferably electronically). Forms for the other funds are also available online. Once you have submitted the form the foundation will determine which fund the proposal meets. The foundation has a membership scheme available which keeps members up to date on the latest grant schemes. The deadlines will vary according to the programmes. Applications must include the following documents: constitution of the organisation; latest accounts or income and expenditure sheet; bank statement; relevant safeguarding policies (where applicable). Unless your organisation has received a grant from the foundation in the last 12 months you *must* submit these documents, otherwise your application will not be considered. Full guidelines and application forms for individual funds are available from the foundation's website. General enquiries can be directed to info@cflm.email.

WHO TO APPLY TO Sue Langfeld, Operations Director, Third Floor, Stanley Building, 43 Hanover Street, Liverpool L1 3DN *Tel.* 0151 232 2444 *Email* info@cflm.email *Website* www.cfmerseyside.org.uk

■ Lancashire Environmental Fund Ltd

CC NO 1074983 **ESTABLISHED** 1998

WHERE FUNDING CAN BE GIVEN Lancashire (excluding unitary authority, district of Blackpool and Blackburn).

WHO CAN BENEFIT Not-for-profit organisations; registered charities; voluntary groups; parish councils; community groups. Applications for the main grant scheme will only be accepted from organisations registered with Entrust as an environmental body.
WHAT IS FUNDED Providing and maintaining public amenities and parks, within ten miles of a landfill site, when the work benefits the natural social or built environment; the provision, conservation, restoration or enhancement of a natural habitat, maintenance or recovery of a species within ten miles of a landfill site; restoring and repairing buildings which are for religious worship, or architectural or historical interest within ten miles of a landfill site.
WHAT IS NOT FUNDED Core cost of an organisation; retrospective funding; projects in school grounds; allotment or food growing projects; car parks and public conveniences; recycling projects; projects within the unitary authority districts of Blackpool and Blackburn.
TYPE OF GRANT One-off and recurrent capital costs.
RANGE OF GRANTS Up to £30,000.
SAMPLE GRANTS Proffitts CIC (£85,000 in three separate grants); Preston Little Theatre Co. Ltd, Longton Community Church, Community Solutions North West Ltd, Brierfield Methodist Church, St Mary's Church Goosnargh, (£30,000 each); Newground and Crawford Village Playing Fields (£26,500 each); Mid Pennine Arts (£25,000); Playground Upgrade at Bedford Park (£24,000).
FINANCES *Year* 2016 *Income* £1,055,487 *Grants* £1,055,487 *Grants to organisations* £992,312 *Assets* £1,681,808
TRUSTEES Cllr Janice Hanson; Francis McGinty; John Drury; John Wilkinson.
OTHER INFORMATION A total of 71 grants were awarded during the year. Note that 'the fund does not normally consider applications for 100% funding therefore, support from other grant sources is welcome'.
HOW TO APPLY Detailed and helpful guidance notes and application forms for each funding strand are available from the correspondent or may be downloaded from the fund's website. Institutional applications are invited to submit a summary of their proposals in a specified format – the 'Expression of Interest' form. The applications are reviewed against specific criteria. The trustees meet quarterly in January, May, July and October (specific dates are given on the website). All applicants will be notified of the outcome and successful request will receive a formal grant offer letter outlining the terms and conditions of the award. Staff are willing to have informal discussions before an application is made. Potential applicants are strongly advised to visit the website and view the guidelines before contacting the trust. Further guidance on the Landfill Communities Fund can be received from the regulatory body Entrust at www.entrust.org.uk or 01926 488 300.
WHO TO APPLY TO Andy Rowett, Fund Manager, The Barn, Berkeley Drive, Bamber Bridge, Preston PR5 6BY *Tel.* 01772 317247 *Fax* 01772 628849 *Email* general@lancsenvfund.org.uk *Website* www.lancsenvfund.org.uk

■ The Lancashire Foundation

CC NO 1149184 **ESTABLISHED** 2012
WHERE FUNDING CAN BE GIVEN Bermuda; Philippines; USA.
WHO CAN BENEFIT Charitable organisations.
WHAT IS FUNDED General charitable purposes.
SAMPLE GRANTS The ten largest donations were granted to: Médecins Sans Frontières, International Care Ministries, Kiva Microloans, St Giles Trust, The Family Centre, Tomorrow's Voices, Vauxhall City Farm, Operations Smile, Anti-Slavery and Find A Better Way.
FINANCES *Year* 2015 *Income* £2,131,336 *Grants* £1,515,251 *Grants to organisations* £1,515,251 *Assets* £3,658,304
TRUSTEES Michael Connor; Derek Stapley; Richard Williams.
OTHER INFORMATION During the year, the foundation matched its individual employee fundraising limit to £2,000.
HOW TO APPLY Apply in writing to the correspondent.
WHO TO APPLY TO Donations Committee, Lancashire Insurance Company (UK), Level 29, 20 Fenchurch Street, London EC3M 3BY *Tel.* 020 7264 4056 *Website* www.lancashiregroup.com/en/responsibility/lancashire-foundation.html

■ Duchy of Lancaster Benevolent Fund

CC NO 1026752 **ESTABLISHED** 1993
WHERE FUNDING CAN BE GIVEN The county palatine of Lancaster (Lancashire, Greater Manchester and Merseyside), and elsewhere in the country where the Duchy of Lancaster has historical links, such as land interests and church livings.
WHO CAN BENEFIT Individuals and a wide range of organisations.
WHAT IS FUNDED General charitable causes; young people; education; health and disability; older people; community help; religion.
TYPE OF GRANT Mainly one-off grants for specific projects. Recurrent grants occasionally given.
RANGE OF GRANTS Up to £25,000; generally under £5,000.
SAMPLE GRANTS Seashell Trust (£25,000); Walking with the Wounded (£15,000); Blackburn Cathedral and Independance at Home (£10,000 each); Lancaster Royal Grammar School bursary fund (£6,400); Little Sisters of the poor (£5,600); Barnardo's, BArton Athletic Club, Children Action North West, and Crossroads Care North West (£5,000 each).
FINANCES *Year* 2015/16 *Income* £363,659 *Grants* £401,639 *Grants to organisations* £398,085 *Assets* £12,732,388
TRUSTEES Warren Smith; Charles Shuttleworth; Alan Reid; Lorna Muirhead; Chris Adcock; David Borrow; Alastair Norris; Robert Miles.
OTHER INFORMATION In 2015/16 a total of 354 grants were made, including eight grants to individuals totalling £3554.
HOW TO APPLY Apply in writing to the appropriate lieutenancy office (see below), at any time. Applications should be by letter, including as much information as possible. All applications are acknowledged. **Lancashire lieutenancy**: County Hall, Preston, Lancashire LPRI 8XJ. **Greater Manchester lieutenancy**: Gaddum House, 6 Great Jackson Street, Manchester M15 4AX. **Merseyside lieutenancy**: PO Box 144, Royal & Sun Alliance Building, New Hall Place, Old Hall Street, Liverpool L69 3EN. Other grants are administered at the general office in London.
WHO TO APPLY TO Timothy Crow, Secretary, 1 Lancaster Place, Strand, London WC2E 7ED *Tel.* 020 7269 1700 *Email* info@duchyoflancaster.co.uk *Website* www.duchyoflancaster.co.uk

■ Lancaster Foundation

CC NO 1066850 **ESTABLISHED** 1997

WHERE FUNDING CAN BE GIVEN UK and Africa, with a local interest in Clitheroe.

WHO CAN BENEFIT Christian-based registered charities only. In practice support is given to charities personally known to the trustees.

WHAT IS FUNDED Christian causes; missionary work; activities for young people and community engagement; disadvantaged people. Practical projects addressing poverty and social issues, with underlying a Christian ethos.

TYPE OF GRANT One-off or recurrent.

RANGE OF GRANTS Up to £500,000.

SAMPLE GRANTS Re:Source Blackburn (£500,000); Message Trust (£268,500); The Grand at Clitheroe (£219,500); Mary's Meals (£159,000); Message Trust (£148,500 in two separate grants); New Generation Music and Mission (£140,000); Mission Aviation Fellowship (£127,000); Open Arms International (£103,500); Saltmine Trust (£96,000); Sparrow Ministries (£90,500).

FINANCES *Year* 215/16 *Income* £3,075,176 *Grants* £2,324,592 *Grants to organisations* £2,324,592 *Assets* £54,796,305

TRUSTEES Rosemary Lancaster; Dr John Lancaster; Steven Lancaster; Julie Broadhurst.

OTHER INFORMATION There were 52 awards made over £1,000.

HOW TO APPLY The foundation's annual report for 2015/16 states: 'Although many applications are received, the administrative structure of the charity does not allow for the consideration of unsolicited requests for grant funding.'

WHO TO APPLY TO Rosemary Lancaster, Trustee, c/o Text House, 152 Bawdlands, Clitheroe, Lancashire BB7 2LA *Tel.* 01200 444404

■ LandAid Charitable Trust (Land Aid)

CC NO 295157 **ESTABLISHED** 1986

WHERE FUNDING CAN BE GIVEN UK.

WHO CAN BENEFIT Registered charitable organisations working in the UK.

WHAT IS FUNDED Disadvantaged children and young people; homelessness; relief of need; education; employment and training. Pro bono support is also available.

WHAT IS NOT FUNDED Individuals; projects benefitting people over the age of 25; organisations whose primary purpose is a museum, gallery, library, exhibition centre or heritage attraction; individual churches, cathedrals (unless being used for purposes other than religious) and other historic buildings; individual schools, colleges, universities or other educational establishments. The following are not normally funded: rent for a premises; the purchase of property or buildings; work on premises where the lease is less than seven years; retrospective funding; work to provide office space for charity staff; the purchase/lease of vehicles; purchase/lease of IT equipment; projects outside the UK; health, medicine and medical conditions, including drug and alcohol addiction; specific projects for people with disabilities; animal welfare or projects concerning the protection of single species; expeditions and research projects; individuals volunteering overseas; conferences, cultural festivals, exhibitions and events; endowments.

TYPE OF GRANT One-off; project funding; capital costs; salaries; full or part-funding.

RANGE OF GRANTS Up to £150,000.

SAMPLE GRANTS Action (£150,000); YMCA North Tyneside (£117,00); 42nd Street (Redevco) (£100,000); Alt Valley Community Trust (£97,000); Keyhouse (£83,500); Canopy Housing (£80,000); Community Campus and Groundwork South (£75,000 each); Hope into Action (£72,000); Fencehouses and District YMCA (£70,000).

FINANCES *Year* 2015/16 *Income* £1,794,820 *Grants* £1,226,819 *Grants to organisations* £1,226,819 *Assets* £452,644

TRUSTEES Robert Bould; Michael Slade; Suzanne Avery; Elizabeth Peace; David Taylor; Lynette Lackey; Timothy Roberts; Scott Parsons; Alistair Elliott; Jenny Buck; David Erwin; Mark Reynolds; Craig McWilliam.

OTHER INFORMATION A total of 20 charities were awarded in 2015/16.

HOW TO APPLY Organisations should apply online through the charity's website. The charity announces funding opportunities via its website, newsletter and social media account. Clear guidance on who can apply for funding and how to apply will be issued with each opportunity. The charity states: 'Because of the large number of applications we expect to receive, we are sorry that we are not able to provide individual feedback on unsuccessful applications.'

WHO TO APPLY TO Grants team, St Albans House, 5th Floor, 57–59 Haymarket, London SW1Y 4QX *Tel.* 020 3102 7192 *Email* grants@landaid.org *Website* www.landaid.org

■ The Jack Lane Charitable Trust

CC NO 1091675 **ESTABLISHED** 2002

WHERE FUNDING CAN BE GIVEN Gloucestershire (south) and Wiltshire (north).

WHO CAN BENEFIT Registered charities and individuals.

WHAT IS FUNDED General charitable purposes, particularly children and young people and individuals with disabilities.

WHAT IS NOT FUNDED Large national appeals are not funded.

TYPE OF GRANT Grants for specific projects rather than general running expenses. Small awards can be made in urgent cases through the Chair's Discretionary Fund.

RANGE OF GRANTS Up to £2,000; occasionally larger awards over two years.

SAMPLE GRANTS Wroughton Youth Adventure Trust (£2,000); The PBC Foundation (£1,600); Connect AT, CLIC Sargent, and Dressability (£1,500 each); Wiltshire Air Ambulance (£1,300).

FINANCES *Year* 2015/16 *Income* £56,169 *Grants* £55,910 *Grants to organisations* £55,870 *Assets* £2,236,071

TRUSTEES Jim Toogood; David Crampton; Martin Wright; Richard White; Christine MacLachlan; Sarah Priday; Nicola Spicer.

OTHER INFORMATION There were a total of 71 grants made, with 64 institutions being awarded £1,000 or below at a total of £46,500.

HOW TO APPLY Application forms are available to download from the trust's website and can be returned via email or post. The trustees meet quarterly to consider requests. It will help to briefly explain how the grant will be used and what steps have been taken so far to raise funds. The latest set of accounts is also requested.

WHO TO APPLY TO Emma Walker, Clerk to the Trustees, Agriculture House, 12 High Street, Wotton-under-Edge, Gloucestershire GL12 7DB

Email admin@jacklane.co.uk *Website* www.jacklane.co.uk

■ The Allen Lane Foundation

CC NO 248031 **ESTABLISHED** 1966

WHERE FUNDING CAN BE GIVEN UK, except projects where the beneficiaries of the work all live in London.

WHO CAN BENEFIT Organisations (not necessarily registered charities) whose work is with groups who may be perceived as unpopular. Beneficiaries of your work should include a significant proportion of, for example, asylum seekers and refugees, LGBT communities, Roma and travellers, people who have offended, older people, people experiencing mental health problems and people experiencing violence or abuse.

WHAT IS FUNDED Work aimed at making a lasting difference, reducing isolation, stigma and discrimination and encouraging and enabling unpopular groups to share in the life of the whole community. Provision of advice or information; advocacy; arts activities where the primary purpose is therapeutic or social; befriending or mentoring; mediation or conflict resolution; practical work, such as gardening or recycling, which benefits both the provider and the recipient; self-help groups; social activities or drop in centres; strengthening the rights of particular groups and enabling their views and experiences to be heard by policy-makers; research and education aimed at changing public attitudes or policy; work aimed at combatting stigma or discrimination; work developing practical alternatives to violence.

WHAT IS NOT FUNDED Academic research; addiction, alcohol or drug abuse; animal welfare or animal rights; arts or cultural or language projects or festivals; children and young people or families; endowments or contributions to other grant-making bodies; health and health care; holidays or holiday play schemes, day trips or outings; housing; hospices and medical research; individuals; museums or galleries; overseas travel; particular medical conditions or disorders; physical or learning disabilities; private and/or mainstream education; promotion of sectarian religion; publications; property purchase, building or refurbishment; refugee community groups working with single nationalities; restoration or conservation of historic buildings or sites; sports and recreation; therapy, e.g. counselling; vehicle purchase; work the trustees believe is rightly the responsibility of the state; work outside the UK; work which will already have taken place before a grant is agreed; work by local organisations with an income of more than £100,000 per annum; those working over a wider area with an income of more than £250,000; organisations which receive funding (directly or indirectly) from commercial sources where conflicts of interest for the organisation and its work are likely to arise.

TYPE OF GRANT One-off and for up to three years; start-up costs; core or project expenditure; volunteers or participants expenses; venue hire; part-time or sessional staffing costs; training and development expenses.

RANGE OF GRANTS Usually £500 to £15,000.

SAMPLE GRANTS Why Me? UK (£15,000); Restored (£14,600); Right to Remain (£13,000); Community Chaplaincy Association, Merseyside Refugee and Asylum Seekers Pre and Post Natal, and Swansea Bay Asylum Seeker Support Group (£12,000); House of Genesis (£10,400); Borrowbrook Home Link, Derby Refugee Forum, Derbyshire Gypsy Liason Group, Footprints project, Greater Manchester Community Chaplaincy Ltd, PAFRAS, and Space4U (£10,000 each).

FINANCES *Year* 2015/16 *Income* £703,484 *Grants* £749,786 *Grants to organisations* £749,786 *Assets* £18,336,337

TRUSTEES Zoe Teale; Juliet Walker; Fredrica Teale; Margaret Hyde; Philip Walsh; Maurice Frankel.

OTHER INFORMATION According to the website, 'the foundation is particularly interested in unusual, imaginative or pioneering projects which have perhaps not yet caught the public imagination'. It receives about nine applications for every one that is successful. In 2015/16 a total of 145 grants were committed.

HOW TO APPLY There are no formal application forms, but there is a short Registration Form, available from the website, which should accompany the application. Your appeal should give basic information and be no more than four sides of A4 (the project budget may be on extra pages). You will need to include the latest annual report and accounts (if applicable) and the budget for the whole organisation (as well as the project) for the current year. Full details of what information is required for application are listed online. There are no closing dates. You will hear back from the foundation in about two weeks to be asked for more information or hear whether your appeal will be considered. Processing an application and making a grant usually takes between two and six months. The foundation reminds that 'you can always contact its office for advice' and asks that 'all applications should be made to the foundation's office and **not** sent to individual trustees'. If you have received an award or were refused you should wait a year before re-applying.

WHO TO APPLY TO Gill Aconley, Grants Officer, 90 The Mount, York YO24 1AR *Tel.* 01904 613223 *Email* info@allenlane.org.uk *Website* www.allenlane.org.uk

■ Langdale Trust

CC NO 215317 **ESTABLISHED** 1960

WHERE FUNDING CAN BE GIVEN UK, with some preference towards Birmingham.

WHO CAN BENEFIT Registered charities.

WHAT IS FUNDED General charitable purposes, including health causes, environment and conservation, young people, older individuals and social welfare, especially work with Christian ethos.

WHAT IS NOT FUNDED Individuals.

TYPE OF GRANT Capital projects are preferred over ongoing running costs; one-off.

RANGE OF GRANTS £1,000 to £6,000.

SAMPLE GRANTS Oxfam, Prisoners Abroad, Rainforest Foundation, Save the Children Fund, and Unicef (Nepal) (£6,000 each); Birmingham Federation of Clubs for Young People, 1st Maidenhead Sea Scout Group, Surfers Against Sewage, and The Civil Liberties Trust (£5,000); Barnardo's and YMCA Birmingham (£4,000).

FINANCES *Year* 2014/15 *Income* £153,636 *Grants* £145,000 *Grants to organisations* £145,000 *Assets* £4,574,599

TRUSTEES Timothy Wilson; Theresa Wilson; Jethro Elvin.

OTHER INFORMATION Grants were made to 47 organisations.

HOW TO APPLY Apply in writing to the correspondent. Applications are considered in or around June with successful applicants being notified in November.

WHO TO APPLY TO Jaime Parkes, c/o Veale Wasbrough Vizards LLP, Second Floor, 3 Brindley Place, Birmingham B1 2JB *Tel.* 0121 227 3705 *Email* poneill@vwv.co.uk

■ The Langtree Trust

CC NO 232924 **ESTABLISHED** 1963

WHERE FUNDING CAN BE GIVEN Gloucestershire.

WHO CAN BENEFIT Registered charities and community organisations.

WHAT IS FUNDED General charitable purposes. Priority is given to organisations involved in the historical and religious heritage of the county and its cultural development. Assistance is also given to children and young people to engage in character building adventures.

TYPE OF GRANT Usually one-off for a specific project.

SAMPLE GRANTS A list of beneficiaries was not available.

FINANCES *Year* 2015/16 *Income* £247,265 *Grants* £53,635 *Grants to organisations* £53,635 *Assets* £1,551,239

TRUSTEES Ann Shepherd; Katherine Bertram; Paul Haslam; Dr Richard Way; Sally Birch; Mike Page; Will Conway.

HOW TO APPLY Apply in writing to the correspondent.

WHO TO APPLY TO The Trustees, GCSD, Unit 701, Stonehouse Park, Spetty Way, Stonehouse GL10 3UT

■ The LankellyChase Foundation

CC NO 1107583 **ESTABLISHED** 2005

WHERE FUNDING CAN BE GIVEN UK.

WHO CAN BENEFIT Charities; non-charitable organisations, provided the work itself has charitable purposes and there is no private benefit to non-charitable interests; individual consultants; private companies.

WHAT IS FUNDED 'Change that will transform the quality of life of people who face severe and multiple disadvantage'. Homelessness; substance misuse; mental and physical illness; extreme poverty; violence and abuse.

WHAT IS NOT FUNDED Work that is focused **exclusively** on a particular health condition, disability issues, imprisonment and/or prisoner resettlement or issues affecting asylum seekers. The website states: 'Our focus is always on people who are experiencing a combination of severe social harms, and we are therefore very unlikely to fund work that is about a single issue, such as mental illness alone.' Note that previous exclusion of London-based projects has been dropped.

TYPE OF GRANT Core costs; revenue; project expenditure; up to three years; research; campaigning; unrestricted funding.

RANGE OF GRANTS £5,000 to £500,000.

SAMPLE GRANTS Homeless Link (£580,500 in four separate grants); Unlimted Potential (£358,916 in two separate grants); Revolving Doors Agency (£302,129); Family Action (£292,000); London Pathway (£291,000); Centre for Criminal Appeals (£262,000); Wandsworth Community Empowerment Network (£250,000); Mayday Trust (£200,000); Camerados CIC (£184,000); Cumbria Partnership Foundation Trust (£154,000).

FINANCES *Year* 2015/16 *Income* £3,393,268 *Grants* £4,450,261 *Grants to organisations* £3,446,201 *Assets* £129,962,696

TRUSTEES Suzi Leather, Chair; Hilary Berg; Morag Burnett; Paul Cheng; Martin Clarke; Robert Duffy; Jacob Hayman; Marion Janner; Peter Latchford; Jane Millar; Simon Tucker.

OTHER INFORMATION The LankellyChase Foundation is the amalgamation of two grant-making trusts, the Lankelly Foundation and the Chase Charity.

HOW TO APPLY The foundation is no longer accepting applications and on its website states: 'We are not accepting or considering proposals for the foreseeable future so that we can spend our time investing properly in the relationships we have with our existing partners. We want to focus on helping them to make wider societal change and realise that continually developing new initiatives means that we have little time to do this.'

WHO TO APPLY TO Sara Longmuir, Company Secretary, First Floor Greenworks, Dog and Duck Yard, Princeton Street, London WC1R 4BH *Tel.* 020 3747 9930 *Email* grants@lankellychase.org.uk or enquiries@lankellychase.org.uk *Website* www.lankellychase.org.uk

■ The R. J. Larg Family Charitable Trust

SC NO SC004946 **ESTABLISHED** 1970

WHERE FUNDING CAN BE GIVEN Scotland, particularly Dundee, County of Angus, occasionally Tayside and North East Fife areas.

WHO CAN BENEFIT Charitable organisations benefitting children, young adults, students, people with disabilities or those with medical condition. Funding may also be given to churches, conservation, respite care, hospices, MS and neurological research, also youth organisations, including university students associations.

WHAT IS FUNDED Grants are made for cancer research, other medical and disability causes, arts and culture, amateur music, care in the community and other community facilities, relief of poverty, religious causes and community or citizenship development. Other charitable purposes can also be considered.

WHAT IS NOT FUNDED Individuals.

TYPE OF GRANT Generally one-off, some recurring. Our research suggests that buildings, core costs, running costs, salaries and start-up costs may be considered. Funding can normally be given for up to two years.

RANGE OF GRANTS £250 to £5,000; typically around £1,000 to £2,000.

SAMPLE GRANTS Cruse Bereavement Care Scotland; Dundee City Council; High School Dundee; Home Start – Dundee; Macmillan Cancer Relief Dundee; Sense Scotland Children's Hospice; University of Dundee; V&A Museum of Design – Dundee; Whitehall Theatre Trust.

FINANCES *Year* 2015/16 *Income* £156,877 *Grants* £127,750 *Grants to organisations* £127,750 *Assets* £3,516,393

TRUSTEES R. Gibson; D. Brand; S. Stewart.

OTHER INFORMATION Preference is given to local charities without a high public profile.

HOW TO APPLY Apply in writing to the correspondent. The trustees normally meet in February and August to consider grants.

WHO TO APPLY TO The Trustees, The Trustees of The R. J. Larg Family Charitable Trust, c/o Thorntons Law LLP, Whitehall House, Yeaman Shore, Dundee DD1 4BJ *Tel.* 01382 229111 *Email* dundee@thorntons-law.co.uk

■ Largsmount Ltd

CC NO 280509 **ESTABLISHED** 1979

WHERE FUNDING CAN BE GIVEN UK and overseas, including Israel.

WHO CAN BENEFIT Educational and religious institutions; organisations set up to provide for the people in need. Mainly Orthodox Jewish charities.

WHAT IS FUNDED Jewish causes; advancement of Orthodox Jewish religion and education.

SAMPLE GRANTS A list of beneficiaries was not available.

FINANCES *Year* 2015 *Income* £677,650 *Grants* £281,291 *Grants to organisations* £281,291 *Assets* £4,702,501

TRUSTEES Simon Kaufman; Naomi Kaufman.

OTHER INFORMATION A list of grants was not included in the accounts, although previously the M. Y. A. Charitable Trust, a connected charity, has been the largest beneficiary every year.

HOW TO APPLY Apply in writing to the correspondent.

WHO TO APPLY TO Simon Kaufman, Trustee, 50 Keswick Street, Gateshead NE8 1TQ *Tel.* 0191 490 0140

■ Lasletts (Hinton) Charity

CC NO 233696 **ESTABLISHED** 1879

WHERE FUNDING CAN BE GIVEN Worcestershire and the surrounding area.

WHO CAN BENEFIT Charitable organisations; churches.

WHAT IS FUNDED Church repairs and restoration (Church of England churches and chapels); social welfare; children and young people; skills development for people who have been in prison or who have had an addiction; welfare advice; older people; homelessness.

WHAT IS NOT FUNDED Individuals (except through an eligible organisation); overseas charities; for-profit organisations. The charity is unlikely to fund: national appeals; activities outside the beneficial area; major building projects involving the acquisition of land or property.

SAMPLE GRANTS A list of beneficiaries was not available.

FINANCES *Year* 2015 *Income* £470,391 *Grants* £75,508 *Grants to organisations* £75,508 *Assets* £16,579,060

TRUSTEES Timothy Bridges; Margaret Jones; Mrs E. A. Pugh-Cook; Mr J. V. Panter; Douglas Dale; Mr A. P. Baxter; Peter Hughes; Mrs G. T. Newman; Michael Tarver; Colin Anstey.

OTHER INFORMATION A list of beneficiaries was not provided in the 2015 accounts.

HOW TO APPLY Applications can be made on a form available to download from the charity's website, which can be submitted by post or email, along with accounts and any other relevant documentation. Guidance notes are also provided on the charity's website. Applications are considered on a quarterly basis, in January, April, July and October, with the main meetings taking place on the last Tuesday of the respective month. Upcoming deadlines are given on the charity's website.

WHO TO APPLY TO Stephen Inman, Clerk to the Trustees, Kateryn Heywood House, Berkeley Court, The Foregate, Worcester WR1 3QG *Tel.* 01905 317117 *Email* admin@lasletts.org.uk *Website* wmcharities.org.uk/laslettswebsite

■ The Lauffer Family Charitable Foundation

CC NO 251115 **ESTABLISHED** 1965

WHERE FUNDING CAN BE GIVEN Commonwealth countries; Israel; USA.

WHO CAN BENEFIT Charitable organisations; Jewish charities.

WHAT IS FUNDED General charitable purposes, including education, religious activities, environment, medical health care, social welfare, children and families and recreation and culture; focus on Jewish causes.

WHAT IS NOT FUNDED Individuals.

TYPE OF GRANT Start-up costs; recurrent funding for up to five years.

RANGE OF GRANTS Up to £19,500.

SAMPLE GRANTS Kaleshwar Charitable Trust (£47,000 in three separate grants); Tesamach Leva Trust (£44,500 in four separate grants); Kehal Charedim Trust (£24,000 in two separate grants); Mesila UK (£13,500 in five separate grants); Jewish Learning Exchange (£12,000 in three separate grants); Central Sqaure Minyan (£9,500 in six separate grants); Friends of Tifereth Shlomo (£9,000 in two separate grants); Chickenshed Theatre Trust (in two separate grants) and Shirat Devora IkChochmat Shlomo Trust (£7,500 each); Hasmonean High School (£6,400 in two separate grants).

FINANCES *Year* 2015/16 *Income* £179,994 *Grants* £356,440 *Grants to organisations* £356,440 *Assets* £5,096,295

TRUSTEES Jonathan Lauffer; Robin Lauffer; Gideon Lauffer.

OTHER INFORMATION During 2015/16 a total of 179 grants were made. 75 grants awarded were below £1,000 and totalled £20,500.

HOW TO APPLY Applications may be made in writing to the correspondent and are generally considered once a year.

WHO TO APPLY TO The Trustees, c/o Clayton Stark and Co., 5th Floor, Charles House, 108–110 Finchley Road, London NW3 5JJ *Tel.* 020 7431 4200 *Email* jonathanlauffer13@gmail.com

■ Mrs F. B. Laurence Charitable Trust

CC NO 296548 **ESTABLISHED** 1976

WHERE FUNDING CAN BE GIVEN UK and overseas.

WHO CAN BENEFIT UK-registered charities, particularly organisations benefitting ex-service and service people, retired people, unemployed people and disadvantaged members of society within the UK or overseas to whom the UK owes a duty of care.

WHAT IS FUNDED General charitable purposes; social welfare; accommodation and housing; community facilities and activities; protection of environment and wildlife; health and disability; older people; vulnerable and disadvantaged individuals; justice and human rights; service and ex-service men and women; special schools and special needs education and literacy.

WHAT IS NOT FUNDED Individuals. Our research indicates that the following applications are unlikely to be considered: appeals for endowment or sponsorship; overseas projects, unless overseen by the charity's own fieldworkers; maintenance of buildings or landscape; provision of work or materials that are the responsibility of the state; where administration expenses, in all their guises, are considered by the trustees to be excessive; or where the fundraising costs in the preceding year have not resulted in an increase in the succeeding years donations in excess of these costs.

TYPE OF GRANT Generally one-off awards for core costs, project expenses and start-up costs. Funding is for one year or less.

RANGE OF GRANTS Up to £6,000.

SAMPLE GRANTS Andrew Clark Trust and Halow Project (£6,000 each); Friends of St Nicholas School, Institute of Cancer Research and St Francis de Sales and Gertrude Church (£4,000 each); Cherry Trees (£3,500); Coeliac Society and WaterAid (£3,000); Nasio Trust (£2,800); Brain Tumour Charity, Macmillan Nurses and Royal Marsden Cancer Charity (£2,500 each).

FINANCES *Year* 2015/16 *Income* £86,234 *Grants* £116,000 *Grants to organisations* £116,000 *Assets* £2,583,123

TRUSTEES Caroline Fry; William Hamilton; Payne Hicks Beach Trust Corporation.

OTHER INFORMATION There were at least 47 awards made with further smaller grants of £1,000 or less totalling £8,500.

HOW TO APPLY Apply in writing to the correspondent, including the latest set of accounts. Only registered charities will be considered. According to our research, applications should be no more than two sides of A4 and should include the following information: who you are; what you do; what distinguishes your work from others in your field; where applicable describe the project that the money you are asking for is going towards and include a business plan/ budget; what funds have already been raised and how; how much you are seeking from the trust; and how you intend to measure the potential benefits of your project or work as a whole. The trustees meet twice a year.

WHO TO APPLY TO The Trustees, BM Box 2082, London WC1N 3XX

■ The Kathleen Laurence Trust

CC NO 296461 **ESTABLISHED** 1987

WHERE FUNDING CAN BE GIVEN UK.

WHO CAN BENEFIT Charitable organisations with specific projects and events.

WHAT IS FUNDED General charitable purposes, especially health causes. The trust particularly favours smaller organisations and those raising funds for specific requirements, such as medical research, associations connected with disability and learning difficulties, organisations helping people who are sick, older people and children.

WHAT IS NOT FUNDED Running costs; management expenses; individuals.

TYPE OF GRANT One-off and recurrent; project funding.

RANGE OF GRANTS £750-£40,000.

SAMPLE GRANTS Most recent beneficiaries have included: Anthony Nolan; Arthritis Research UK; British Heart Foundation; Prostate Cancer UK; Queen Elizabeth's Foundation for Disabled People; Opening Doors; R Charity (Royal Liverpool University Hospitals); Stepping Stones; The Who Cares Trust; UCARE.

FINANCES *Year* 2015/16 *Income* £224,888 *Grants* £190,750 *Grants to organisations* £190,750

TRUSTEE Coutts & Co.

OTHER INFORMATION During 2015/16 a total of 66 grants were awarded.

HOW TO APPLY Apply in writing to the correspondent. The trustees usually meet in January and June.

WHO TO APPLY TO The Trust Manager, c/o Coutts & Co., Trustee Department, 6th Floor, Trinity Quay 2, Avon Street, Bristol BS2 0PT *Tel.* 020 7663 6825 *Email* couttscharities@coutts.com

■ The Law Society Charity

CC NO 268736 **ESTABLISHED** 1974

WHERE FUNDING CAN BE GIVEN Worldwide.

WHO CAN BENEFIT Organisations protecting people's legal rights and lawyers' welfare as well as law related projects from charities without an identifiable legal connection.

WHAT IS FUNDED Law, legal education and access to justice. This includes: charitable educational purposes for lawyers and would-be lawyers; legal research; promotion of an increased understanding of the law; promotion of human rights and charities concerned with the provision of advice, counselling, mediation services connected with the law; welfare directly/ indirectly of solicitors, trainee solicitors and other legal and Law Society staff and their families.

WHAT IS NOT FUNDED Support is not provided to: charities falling outside the fields of human rights, legal education and access to justice, such as medical charities; individual students seeking help with their studies; and locally based bodies, such as law centres or Citizens Advice.

TYPE OF GRANT One-off or spread over two-three years.

RANGE OF GRANTS £5,000 to £20,000.

SAMPLE GRANTS Uganda Legal Action Centre for Minors (£20,000); Cape Town University (£12,000); Peace Brigades International and Personal Support Unit (£7,500 each); African Prisons Project, Book Aid International and Fair Trials (£5,000 each).

FINANCES *Year* 2015/16 *Income* £41,489 *Grants* £166,530 *Grants to organisations* £166,530 *Assets* £398,698

TRUSTEE The Law Society Trustees Ltd.

OTHER INFORMATION The charity's website states: 'We may regard your asking for a very large amount as an indication that the project and your hopes for funding it are unrealistic, and reject it on that basis.'

HOW TO APPLY Application forms are available from the website. Requests are considered at quarterly trustees' meetings, usually held in April, July, September and December with precise dates available on the website. Note that applications should be received four weeks before the date of the meeting. Feedback on unsuccessful applications may be available on request.

WHO TO APPLY TO The Trustees, 110–113 Chancery Lane, London WC2A 1PL *Tel.* 020 7316 5597 *Email* lawsocietycharity@lawsociety.org.uk *Website* www.lawsociety.org.uk

■ The Edgar E. Lawley Foundation

CC NO 201589 **ESTABLISHED** 1961

WHERE FUNDING CAN BE GIVEN UK, with a preference for the West Midlands.

WHO CAN BENEFIT Registered charities; charitable organisations; hospitals and hospices; schools and universities.

WHAT IS FUNDED General charitable purposes; education in arts, commerce and industry; health and disability; medical care and research; older people; children and young people; community causes.

WHAT IS NOT FUNDED Appeals from and on behalf of individuals are not considered.
TYPE OF GRANT One-off and generally unrestricted funding.
RANGE OF GRANTS About £1,500 on average.
SAMPLE GRANTS Acorns Children's Hospice; Bag Books; Breast Cancer Campaign; Chris Westwood Charity; Focus Birmingham; Helen and Douglas House; Mildmay Mission Hospital; Shakespeare Hospice; Research Institute for Older People; Redditch Association for the Blind; Scope; WheelPower; Working Class Movement Library. Exact amounts given were not listed in the accounts.
FINANCES *Year* 2015/16 *Income* £191,654 *Grants* £223,500 *Grants to organisations* £223,500 *Assets* £4,292,761
TRUSTEES John Cooke; Gillian Hilton; Philip Cooke; Frank Jackson.
OTHER INFORMATION There were 149 awards made during the year.
HOW TO APPLY Summary grant application forms can be downloaded from the foundation's website and should be returned to the correspondent between 1 August and 31 October, preferably by email. Applicants should outline the reasons for the grant request and the amount of grant being sought. Any supporting information that adds to the strength of the application can be included. The trustees make grant decisions in January. The trustees regret that it is not possible, unless a stamped addressed envelope has been provided, to communicate with unsuccessful applicants and the fact that a grant has not been received by the end of January indicates that it has not been possible to fund it. The foundation receives about 800 requests per year but can only address about 130 of them.
WHO TO APPLY TO Frank Jackson, Trustee, PO Box 456, Esher KT10 1DP *Tel.* 01372 805760 *Email* edgarelawley@gmail.com *Website* www.edgarelawleyfoundation.org.uk

■ The Herd Lawson and Muriel Lawson Charitable Trust

CC NO 1113220 **ESTABLISHED** 1975
WHERE FUNDING CAN BE GIVEN Mainly Cumbria.
WHO CAN BENEFIT Charitable organisations.
WHAT IS FUNDED This trust supports a number of named organisations receiving grants each year and also organisations benefitting older people in need, particularly those who are members of evangelical or Christian Brethren churches.
RANGE OF GRANTS £500 to £21,000.
SAMPLE GRANTS British Red Cross Society and WWF – UK (£21,000 each); Christian Workers Relief Fund (£15,500); Hospice at Home West Cumbria (£9,000); Hospice of St Mary of Furness (£6,500); Spring Mount Fellowship (£3,000); Ambleside Welfare Charity (£2,500); Cross Roads Care Cumbria (£2,000); Sandhills Lane Christian Brethren Church (£1,000).
FINANCES *Year* 2015/16 *Income* £224,963 *Grants* £84,000 *Grants to organisations* £84,000 *Assets* £1,850,352
TRUSTEES John Scott; Peter Matthews; Robert Barker; Brian Herd; Dr Jenny Barker; William Corin.
OTHER INFORMATION There were 11 awards made during the year.
HOW TO APPLY The trust receives more applications than it can deal with and does not seek further unsolicited appeals. The trust has previously informed us that 'the trustees have established a number of charities to whom they make grants each year and they very rarely make any donations to other charities'.
WHO TO APPLY TO John Scott, Trustee, The Estate Office, 14 Church Street, Ambleside, Cumbria LA22 0BT *Tel.* 01539 434758 *Email* derekscott@ignetics.co.uk

■ Lawson Beckman Charitable Trust

CC NO 261378 **ESTABLISHED** 1970
WHERE FUNDING CAN BE GIVEN UK.
WHO CAN BENEFIT Charitable organisations.
WHAT IS FUNDED Relief of poverty; the arts; health; education; Jewish causes; general charitable purposes.
WHAT IS NOT FUNDED Individuals.
RANGE OF GRANTS £250 to £15,000.
SAMPLE GRANTS Jewish Care (£16,800); Nightingale Hammerson (£15,000); Devonshire Street Charitable Foundation (£10,000); Norwood Ravenswood, Project SEED and United Synagogue (£5,000 each); Community Security Trust (£3,000); Mental Health Foundation (£2,500); Holocaust Educational Trust (£2,000); The Henry Van Straubenzee Memorial Fund (£250).
FINANCES *Year* 2015/16 *Income* £123,551 *Grants* £77,000 *Grants to organisations* £77,000 *Assets* £2,844,309
TRUSTEES Melvin Lawson; Lynton Stock; Francis Katz.
OTHER INFORMATION Grants were made to 16 organisations in 2015/16.
HOW TO APPLY Apply in writing to the correspondent.
WHO TO APPLY TO Melvin Lawson, Trustee, AB Group Ltd, 2nd Floor, 25 Old Burlington Street, London W1S 3AN *Tel.* 020 7734 8111 *Email* martine@abplc.co.uk

■ The Raymond and Blanche Lawson Charitable Trust

CC NO 281269 **ESTABLISHED** 1980
WHERE FUNDING CAN BE GIVEN UK, with an interest in Kent and East Sussex and West Sussex.
WHO CAN BENEFIT Charitable organisations benefitting children, young adults, older people, people with disabilities and those within the armed forces. Preference is given to local organisations.
WHAT IS FUNDED According to the annual report for 2015/16: 'In considering applications which are carefully reviewed, the trustees give preference to local organisations. The trustees have adopted a policy, in the main, of giving support to organisations that fall within the following categories: arts and heritage; education; environment; health; social and economic disadvantage.'
WHAT IS NOT FUNDED Individuals.
TYPE OF GRANT One-of and up to one year; projects; research.
RANGE OF GRANTS £500 to £6,000; typically £1,000 to £2,000.
SAMPLE GRANTS The Caldecott Foundation (£6,000); Payment to Flood Victims (£5,000); Crisis, Canine Partners and Young Lives Foundation (£2,500 each); the Trinity Hospice, Kenward Trust and the Teenage Cancer charity (£2,000 each); Marie Curie Cancer Care, Ambitious about Autism, Create Arts, Jubilee Sailing Trust, Footsteps International, Abbeyfield Kent Society and Meningitis Now (£1,000 each); the British

Trust for Ornithology, Lets Face It and Great Ormond Street Hospital Charity (£500).

FINANCES *Year* 2015/16 *Income* £263,300 *Grants* £139,658 *Grants to organisations* £139,658 *Assets* £23,080,924

TRUSTEES Philip Thomas; Sarah Hill; Michael Norrie; Jennifer Thomas.

OTHER INFORMATION The Trustees have created The Lawson Endowment Fund for Kent with the Kent Community Foundation by donating a capital sum of £5 million from the trust in this financial year.

HOW TO APPLY Apply in writing to the correspondent.

WHO TO APPLY TO Raymond and Blanche Lawson, Trustees, Riverside Business Centre, River Lawn Road, Tonbridge, Kent TN9 1EP *Email* enquiries@lawsontrust.co.uk

■ The David Lean Foundation

CC NO 1067074 **ESTABLISHED** 1997

WHERE FUNDING CAN BE GIVEN UK.

WHO CAN BENEFIT Charitable organisations; educational establishments; other charitable institutions whose aims include those similar to those of the foundation.

WHAT IS FUNDED Promotion and advancement of education and to cultivate and improve public taste in the visual arts, particularly in the field of film production, including screenplay writing, film direction and editing.

WHAT IS NOT FUNDED Individual scholarship or other grants.

TYPE OF GRANT One-off and recurrent grants.

RANGE OF GRANTS £7,000 to £89,500.

SAMPLE GRANTS National Film and Television School (£89,500); British Film Institute (£68,000); British Academy of Film and Television (£56,500); Royal Academy of Arts (£42,000); Film Club UK (£9,500); British Kinematograph S and T Society (£7,000).

FINANCES *Year* 2016 *Income* £301,187 *Grants* £287,522 *Grants to organisations* £287,522 *Assets* £318,499

TRUSTEES Anthony Reeves; Stefan Breitenstein.

OTHER INFORMATION The trustees charities similar in objects to those of the foundation, principally the National Film and Television School, the British Academy of Film and Television Arts, the British Film Institute and the Royal Academy of Arts.

HOW TO APPLY Scholarship grants for students attending the National Film and Television School, Royal Holloway or Leighton Park School, are normally only awarded on the recommendation of the course provider with the trustees. Other applications for grants that would meet the aims of the foundation are invited in writing, enclosing full details of the project and including financial information and two references. Progress reports should be provided when required. The foundation has a website; however, it did not seem to be functioning at the time of writing.

WHO TO APPLY TO The Trustees, The Bradshaws, Codsall, Staffordshire WV8 2HU *Tel.* 01902 754024 *Email* aareeves@davidleanfoundation.com

■ The Leathersellers' Company Charitable Fund

CC NO 278072 **ESTABLISHED** 1979

WHERE FUNDING CAN BE GIVEN UK, particularly Greater London.

WHO CAN BENEFIT UK-registered charities; educational establishments; individuals.

WHAT IS FUNDED Charities associated with the Leather sellers' Company, the leather and hide trades, education in leather technology and caring for the welfare of poor and sick former workers in the industry and their dependants. General chartable purposes focusing on education; disability; children and young people; relief of need; arts; criminal justice and rehabilitation; advice and support.

TYPE OF GRANT One-off and multi-year grants of up to four years; core costs including salaries, rent and utilities; project expenditure; development; capital costs.

RANGE OF GRANTS Up to £75,000; typically under £20,000.

SAMPLE GRANTS Leathersellers' Federation of Schools (£75,000); St Mary the Virgin Parish Church (£40,000); Leather Conservation Centre (£30,000); Action Against Abduction, FareShare and Museum of Leathercraft (£20,000 each); Guildhall School Trust (£18,000); Blue Sky Development and Regeneration, Derby Women's Centre, Disability Challengers and Prison Advice and Care Trust (£15,000 each).

FINANCES *Year* 2015/16 *Income* £1,714,000 *Grants* £1,959,000 *Grants to organisations* £837,000 *Assets* £57,867,000

TRUSTEES The Leathersellers' Company; David Santa-Olalla.

OTHER INFORMATION Grants to 82 individuals under the Leathersellers' University Exhibitions Scheme totalled £178,000.

HOW TO APPLY Applications can be made using the online form on the Company's website. Applications to the small grants programme can usually expect a decision to have been made within six weeks. Successful applicants to the main grants programme will typically have to pass through a four stage process, which can take up to nine months, see the website for further details. Only one application can be made in a year. If a charity is in receipt of multi-year grants or a large single-year grant, the charity cannot apply for another award until four years have passed.

WHO TO APPLY TO Geoffrey Russell-Jones, Charities and Education Officer, 7 St Helen's Place, London EC3A 6AB *Tel.* 020 7330 1451 or 020 7330 1444 *Email* dmsantao@leathersellers.co.uk *Website* www.leathersellers.co.uk

■ The Leche Trust

CC NO 225659 **ESTABLISHED** 1963

WHERE FUNDING CAN BE GIVEN UK.

WHO CAN BENEFIT Individuals and charitable organisations; historical buildings and objects; museums and galleries; churches; schools, colleges and universities; concerts and festivals.

WHAT IS FUNDED Preservation and conservation of art and architecture, churches and historic collections, preference is given to objects of the Georgian period or earlier; performing arts, particularly music, dance and drama; education. There is also a programme supporting overseas PhD students.

WHAT IS NOT FUNDED General education projects; community and outreach projects; domestic or overseas social welfare; schools or school buildings; individual students (except overseas PhD students); projects promoting religion; natural environment or wildlife projects; medicine; expeditions. The trust is not likely to support the same organisation in two consecutive financial years. The website also notes that 'applications in respect of projects that are the subject of major Heritage Lottery Fund bids must have secured Stage 2 funding before consideration by the trustees'.

TYPE OF GRANT One-off projects and capital costs, not recurring expenditure.

RANGE OF GRANTS £1,000 to £5,000.

SAMPLE GRANTS City and Guilds of London Art School and West Dean College (£7,500 each); ATMA Dance, Birmingham Royal Ballet and Spitalfields Music (£3,000 each); Historic Royal Palaces and St Mary's Church, Arlingham (£2,500 each); Jermyn Street Theatre and The British Institute at Ankara (£2,000 each).

FINANCES *Year* 2015/16 *Income* £81,522 *Grants* £245,646 *Grants to organisations* £198,954 *Assets* £6,630,305

TRUSTEES Andrew Cameron; Dr Helen Jacobsen; Lady Anne Greenstock; Ariane Bankes; Caroline Laing; Thomas Howard; Robin Dhar.

OTHER INFORMATION £42,500 was awarded to individuals.

HOW TO APPLY There is no formal application form and requests should be addressed in writing to the correspondent via post only. They should include relevant supporting documents and budgets for the project. The trustees meet three times a year, in February, June and October; applications need to be received the month before. Unsuccessful applications will be notified within two weeks; however, those eligible for further consideration will not be contacted until the final selection is forwarded for the trustees' consideration. **Overseas PhD Student Programme**: Applicants can receive an application from the correspondent. It should be completed by both the student and their tutor.

WHO TO APPLY TO Rosemary Ewles, Grants Director, 105 Greenway Avenue, London E17 3QL *Tel.* 020 3233 0023 *Email* info@lechetrust.org *Website* www.lechetrust.org

■ The Arnold Lee Charitable Trust

CC NO 264437 **ESTABLISHED** 1972

WHERE FUNDING CAN BE GIVEN UK.

WHO CAN BENEFIT Established charities of high repute; mainly organisations linked to the Jewish community.

WHAT IS FUNDED General charitable purposes; Jewish causes; education; health.

WHAT IS NOT FUNDED Grants are rarely made to individuals.

RANGE OF GRANTS Up to £75,000.

SAMPLE GRANTS Aish Hatorah (£42,000); Devonshire Street Charitable Foundation (£10,000); Western Marble Arch Synagogue (£4,200); The Institute of Jewish Studies (£4,000).

FINANCES *Year* 2015/16 *Income* £300,371 *Grants* £261,659 *Grants to organisations* £261,659 *Assets* £2,142,647

TRUSTEES Edward Lee; Alan Lee.

OTHER INFORMATION A list of beneficiaries was not available; however, the trust listed the six largest recipients and another two charities.

HOW TO APPLY Apply in writing to the correspondent.

WHO TO APPLY TO The Trustees, Hazlems Fenton LLP, Palladium House, 1–4 Argyll Street, London W1F 7LD *Tel.* 020 7437 7666 *Email* PetronellaEvans@princetonplc.com

■ The William Leech Charity

CC NO 265491 **ESTABLISHED** 1972

WHERE FUNDING CAN BE GIVEN Northumberland, Tyne and Wear, Durham and overseas.

WHO CAN BENEFIT Registered charities. Preference for organisations which have: a high proportion of the work undertaken by voluntary, unpaid workers; a close connection to the Settlor, or with districts in which William Leech (Builders) Ltd, built houses during the time when the Settlor was active in business; an active Christian involvement; projects in deprived areas for the benefit of local people, especially those which encourage people to help themselves; been doing practical, new work and putting new ideas into action.

WHAT IS FUNDED **The Main Fund:** General charitable purposes, including: community welfare, medical research and health care; projects for young people; sports; homelessness and unemployment; education and training; historic buildings and churches; maritime, armed forces charities; disability. **The Lady Leech Fund:** Overseas projects focusing primarily on the medical, educational and environmental needs of children in underdeveloped countries, which usually have links with the north east of England; also emergency aid in response to natural disasters. **Volunteer Support:** Grants of £500–£1,000 to assist volunteers in small registered charities, where at least two thirds of the charitable work (excluding administration and fundraising) is done by volunteers.

WHAT IS NOT FUNDED Community care centres and similar (exceptionally, those in remote country areas may be supported); running expenses of youth clubs (as opposed to capital projects); running expenses of churches (this includes normal repairs, but churches engaged in social work, or using their buildings largely for 'outside' purposes, may be supported); sport; the arts; individuals; organisations which have been supported in the last 12 months (it would be exceptional to support an organisation in two successive years, unless support had been confirmed in advance); holidays, travel, outings; minibuses (unless over 10,000 miles a year is expected); schools; housing associations.

TYPE OF GRANT One-off and recurring grants; interest-free loans (often to churches to allow them to get on with the building work, avoiding inflation costs); running costs; capital costs.

RANGE OF GRANTS £100 to £200,500; most grants are for £1,000 or less; the maximum loan is usually £10,000 or 10% of the project cost.

SAMPLE GRANTS St John's College Durham (£200,000); Together Newcastle (£20,000); Building Futures East (£10,000); FoodCycle (£3,000); Footlight Youth Theatre (£2,000); Changing Faces (£1,000).

FINANCES *Year* 2015/16 *Income* £488,374 *Grants* £424,475 *Grants to organisations* £424,475 *Assets* £16,258,267

TRUSTEES Adrian Gifford; Roy Leech; Richard Leech; Sir N. Sherlock; David Stabler; Barry Wallace; Revd Prof. David Wilkinson.

OTHER INFORMATION The trustees allocate approximately one third of the Main Fund's income to medical research undertaken by the University of Newcastle upon Tyne. During the year 77 grants were awarded (mostly in Northumberland).

HOW TO APPLY The website notes that the trustees 'accept applications in the short form of a letter, rather than expecting the completion of a complicated application form, which may seem daunting to some applicants'. Appeals must include: registered charity address; a description of the project, who it will help, and any evidence which will support the need for this particular project; how much the project will cost, capital and revenue, with an indication of the amounts involved; how much the charity has raised so far, and where it expects to find the balance; the type of support sought; i.e. small grant, multiple grant, loan, etc.; how much does it cost to run the charity each year, including how much of the revenue is spent on salaries and employees, where the revenue came from, how many paid workers and volunteers there are. Low priority applications can be submitted using an online form, while grant requests for up to £1,000 and loan requests for up to £10,000 should signed and submitted in writing to the correspondent (if your charity has a letterhead, printing the letter onto this will aid the application). Applications to the Lady Leech Fund should also detail the connection between the project overseas and the North East England. To request volunteer support applicants should send a one page letter detailing: the organisation's name and charity registration number; name and address of a correspondent; project aims, progress, funds raised to date, how much is needed and for what; number of paid workers, total annual salary cost, total annual administration overheads and how many unpaid volunteers there are.

WHO TO APPLY TO Kathleen Smith, Secretary, Diocese of Hexham and Newcastle, St Cuthbert's House, West Road, Newcastle upon Tyne NE15 7PY *Tel.* 0191 243 3300 *Email* enquiries@williamleechcharity.org.uk *Website* www.williamleechcharity.org.uk

■ Leeds Building Society Charitable Foundation

CC NO 1074429 **ESTABLISHED** 1999

WHERE FUNDING CAN BE GIVEN Areas where one of the 67 society's branches are located.

WHO CAN BENEFIT Registered charities or groups affiliated to registered charities.

WHAT IS FUNDED General charitable purposes; community projects focusing on social welfare and relief in need; vulnerable people and disadvantaged individuals.

WHAT IS NOT FUNDED The foundation is unlikely to support: the restoration or upgrading of building, including churches; environmental charities (unless there is a benefit to a disadvantaged community); administration equipment, such as IT equipment for charity's own use. Support cannot be given for: running costs; projects with religious, political or military purposes; overseas charities or projects; individuals, including sponsorship of individuals; animal welfare projects; and medical research. Church projects will be considered only where they involve community outreach and benefit (such as supporting homeless people or disadvantaged families).

TYPE OF GRANT One-off awards for capital projects.

RANGE OF GRANTS £250 to £1,000.

SAMPLE GRANTS Opal and Sense (£10,000 each); Mencap (£3,300).

FINANCES *Year* 2016 *Income* £123,798 *Grants* £142,848 *Grants to organisations* £142,848 *Assets* £15,873

TRUSTEES Peter Chadwick; Ann Shelton; Robert Wade; Gary Brook; Martin Richardson; Michael Garnett; Gary Hetherington.

OTHER INFORMATION During the year 143 grants were made. A list of beneficiaries was not included within the annual report and accounts for 2016.

HOW TO APPLY Apply in writing to the correspondent, including the following information: the name of your organisation; the name of the project and brief information about its work; a contact name, address and phone number; the registered charity number; details of what the donation would be used for; who would benefit from the donation; your nearest Leeds Building Society branch (the branch can also forward the application for you). All applications are acknowledged, following the trustees' meetings, which are held quarterly, in March, June, September and November. The foundation is unable to consider applications if support has been provided in the last two years. The foundation operates independently of Leeds Building Society and so local branch staff are unable to answer questions about the foundation. Contact the foundation directly for further information.

WHO TO APPLY TO Luke Wellock, CSR Manager, Leeds Building Society, 105 Albion Street, Leeds, West Yorkshire LS1 5AS *Tel.* 0113 225 7518 *Email* lwellock@leedsbuildingsociety.co.uk *Website* www.leedsbuildingsociety.co.uk/your-society/about-us/charitable-foundation

■ Leeds Community Foundation (LCF)

CC NO 1096892 **ESTABLISHED** 2005

WHERE FUNDING CAN BE GIVEN Leeds.

WHO CAN BENEFIT Community and voluntary groups; registered charities; not-for-profit organisations; social enterprises.

WHAT IS FUNDED General charitable purposes; social welfare; community work. Priority is given to groups and projects that benefit people living in economically or socially deprived areas of Leeds, and/or those supporting vulnerable groups.

WHAT IS NOT FUNDED General and major fundraising appeals; overseas travel or expeditions; projects that would normally be funded from statutory sources such as the city council, local education authority or health authority; promotion of purely religious or political causes; large national charities except for independent local branches working for local people; expenditure which has already been committed before the application has been submitted; sponsorship, fundraising events or advertising. See the website for details about each programme's specific funding criteria.

TYPE OF GRANT Capital and core costs.

SAMPLE GRANTS A full list of grants recipients is available to download from the foundation's website.

FINANCES *Year* 2015/16 *Income* £4,811,000 *Grants* £4,111,000 *Grants to organisations* £4,111,000 *Assets* £21,658,000

TRUSTEES Rachel Hannan; Mike Jackson; Helen Thomson; Jonathan Morgan; Nick Lane-Fox; Nathan Lane; Roohi Collins; Mark Emerton; Pat McGeever.

OTHER INFORMATION The foundation runs a number of grant schemes that change frequently. Consult the foundation's website for details of current programmes and their deadlines. Each scheme tends to have a different criteria and size of award. The exclusions listed are given as general areas where the foundation cannot provide help. A total of 511 grants were made to approximately 393 community groups and charities.

HOW TO APPLY See the foundation's website for information on the various grants programmes. The website states that the foundation is moving towards digital applications for the majority of its grants programmes. The Grants Team can be contacted for support by emailing grants@leedscf.org.uk or by calling 0113 242 2426.

WHO TO APPLY TO Carlos Chavez, Grants and Community Manager, 1st Floor, 51A St Paul's Street, Leeds LS1 2TE *Tel.* 0113 242 2426 *Email* grants@leedscf.org.uk *Website* www.leedscf.org.uk

■ The Legal Education Foundation

CC NO 271297 **ESTABLISHED** 1975

WHERE FUNDING CAN BE GIVEN UK.

WHO CAN BENEFIT Charitable organisations; research institutions.

WHAT IS FUNDED Legal education; access to employment in the legal profession; public understanding of the law; the use of technology in legal education; research into the above objectives.

WHAT IS NOT FUNDED Funding of existing mainstream academic activities or facilities in schools, universities or other educational institutions, unless it is innovative in terms of delivery or access; provision of bursaries which do not bring the possibility of structural or cultural change on the part of the institutions involved; small scale interventions which are not subsequently scalable; funding which is likely to be viewed as a substitute for government or legal profession funding; initiatives covered by other organisations; individuals; work outside the UK.

TYPE OF GRANT Project funding; research.

RANGE OF GRANTS £6,000 to £998,000.

SAMPLE GRANTS Justice First Fellowship (£998,000); Youth Access (£195,000); Refugee Action (£149,000); Citizenship Foundation (£135,000); Asylum Aid (£97,000); Relate (£78,000); Maternity Action (£57,000); Advocates for International Development (£41,000); Public Law Project (£30,000); National Pro Bono Centre (£25,000); National Council for Voluntary Organisations (£13,000).

FINANCES *Year* 2015/16 *Income* £3,849,000 *Grants* £4,165,000 *Grants to organisations* £4,165,000 *Assets* £218,663,000

TRUSTEES Jane Reeves; Mark Harding; Edward Nally; Guy Beringer; Roger Finbow; Sally James; Timothy Dutton; Ailsa Beaton; Rupert Baron.

OTHER INFORMATION Grants were made to 79 organisations during the year. The foundation has an excellent website with detailed information about its grant-making.

HOW TO APPLY Apply on a form available from the foundation's website. A grant timetable is posted on the foundation's website, with up-to-date application deadlines.

WHO TO APPLY TO Alan Humphreys, Deputy Chief Executive and Secretary, Suite 2, Ground Floor, River House, Broadford Park, Shalford, Guildford, Surrey GU4 8EP *Tel.* 020 3005 5692 *Email* alan.humphreys@thelef.org *Website* thelegaleducationfoundation.org

■ Leicester and Leicestershire Historic Churches Preservation Trust (Leicestershire Historic Churches Trust)

CC NO 233476 **ESTABLISHED** 1964

WHERE FUNDING CAN BE GIVEN Leicester and Leicestershire.

WHO CAN BENEFIT Churches and chapels which are used for public worship, belong to the Church of England or any other Christian religious body and which were built before or around 100 years ago.

WHAT IS FUNDED The preservation, repair, maintenance, improvement, upkeep, beautification and reconstruction of churches in the United Kingdom and of monuments, fittings, fixtures, stained glass, furniture, ornaments and chattels in such churches, and of the churchyard belonging to such churches.

TYPE OF GRANT One-off awards for building, renovation and associated expenses.

SAMPLE GRANTS A list of beneficiaries was not available.

FINANCES *Year* 2015/16 *Income* £50,701 *Grants* £45,500 *Grants to organisations* £45,500 *Assets* £287,744

TRUSTEES Mark Dunkley; David Knowles; Barrie Byford; Janet Arthur; John Hemes; Revd Fabian Radcliffe; James Ireland; Revd Timothy Stevens; Michael Taylor.

OTHER INFORMATION A list of beneficiaries was not available.

HOW TO APPLY Full details on how to apply can be found on the trust's website. Grant Meetings in 2017 will be on Wednesday 3 May and Wednesday 20 September. Churches/chapels should aim to submit applications four weeks in advance of these meetings.

WHO TO APPLY TO Janet Arthur, Trustee, 20 Gumley Road, Smeeton Westerby, Leicester LE8 0LT *Tel.* 0116 279 3995 *Email* chair@lhct.org.uk *Website* www.lhct.org.uk

■ Leicestershire and Rutland Masonic Charity Association

CC NO 234054 **ESTABLISHED** 1964

WHERE FUNDING CAN BE GIVEN Rutland and Leicestershire.

WHO CAN BENEFIT Registered charities; dependants of masons or former masons.

WHAT IS FUNDED General charitable purposes.

SAMPLE GRANTS University of Leicester (£50,000); Country Holidays for Inner City Kids and St Bartholomew's Church Kirby Muxloe (£2,000 each); The Enderby Band Organisation and Wishes for Kids (£1,500 each); Asthma Relief Charity, Melton Community First Responders and Toys on the Table (£1,000 each); Tree of Hope (£500).

FINANCES *Year* 2015/16 *Income* £116,169 *Grants* £132,924 *Grants to organisations* £132,924 *Assets* £288,864

TRUSTEES John Peberdy; David Hagger; Brent Goodwin; Michael Molyneux; Anthony Sibson.

HOW TO APPLY Apply in writing to the correspondent.

WHO TO APPLY TO John Peberdy, Trustee, 38 Park Lane, Sutton Bonington, Loughborough, Leicestershire LE12 5NH *Email* lrmca@pglleics.co.uk

■ Leicestershire, Leicester and Rutland Community Foundation

CC NO 1135322 **ESTABLISHED** 2002

WHERE FUNDING CAN BE GIVEN Leicestershire, Leicester and Rutland.

WHO CAN BENEFIT Charities and community groups with some preference for smaller groups.

WHAT IS FUNDED A wide range of charitable purposes; community development; local projects.

WHAT IS NOT FUNDED Individuals are not supported, but groups can be helped.

TYPE OF GRANT One-off, running and project costs.

RANGE OF GRANTS Mostly around and under £1,000 but can be up to £30,000.

SAMPLE GRANTS SDSA Foundation (£28,000); Forward Thinking Movement and Dance and New Parks Play Association (£15,000 each); Youth Shelter (£8,000); Home-Start Leicester (£7,000); Women's Aid Leicestershire (£4,600); Voluntary Action South Leicestershire (£3,800); Belvoir Castle Cricket Trust and Leicester Karate Club (£2,000 each); Aspire Lifeskills (£1,000); Community Action Hinckley and Bosworth (£600); The Kibworth Band (£270).

FINANCES *Year* 2015/16 *Income* £631,387 *Grants* £328,517 *Grants to organisations* £328,517 *Assets* £2,397,075

TRUSTEES Steven White; John Strange; James Kirkpatrick; Rick Moore; Ivan Trevor; Nicola Philbin; Nisha Chandarana; Justine Flack; Stuart Dawkins; Sean Tizzard; Trevor Shaw; Stephanie Morgan.

HOW TO APPLY Details of funds open for applications are available online. The foundation welcomes enquiries prior to the submission of formal applications either via phone or email. The application process differs depending on the scheme applied for with some schemes using online application forms and others using more traditional paper-based forms. The annual report states that 'grants are given on a monthly basis, to enable prompt response'.

WHO TO APPLY TO Hannah Stevens, Funds Co-ordinator, 3 Wycliffe Street, Leicester LE1 5LR *Tel.* 0116 262 4916 *Email* hannah.stevens@llrcommunityfoundation.org.uk *Website* www.llrcommunityfoundation.org.uk

■ P Leigh-Bramwell Trust E

CC NO 267333 **ESTABLISHED** 1973

WHERE FUNDING CAN BE GIVEN UK, with a preference for Bolton.

WHO CAN BENEFIT Registered charities and charitable organisations; schools and universities; hospices; churches. The trust has specific regular allocations, including the RNLI, with limited opportunity to add further charities.

WHAT IS FUNDED General charitable purposes. Support is particularly given to Methodist causes and Bolton-based organisations.

WHAT IS NOT FUNDED Individuals.

TYPE OF GRANT Mainly recurrent grants are awarded to established beneficiaries.

RANGE OF GRANTS £500 to £30,000; most awards are of £1,000 to £2,000.

SAMPLE GRANTS North Bolton Methodist Mission (£30,000); The Methodist Church – Bolton Circuit (£11,000); Rivington Parish Church (£6,200); Disasters Emergency Committee – Philippines Typhoon Appeal and Fet-Lor Youth Club (£5,000 each); Barnes Methodist Church and Octagon Theatre Trust (£2,500 each); Ulverston Inshore Rescue, Save the Children and Trinity Hospice (£2,000 each); Institute of Cancer Research, The Salvation Army and The Samaritans (£1,000 each); ChildLine North West and Bolton YMCA (£500 each).

FINANCES *Year* 2015/16 *Income* £151,164 *Grants* £194,900 *Grants to organisations* £194,900

TRUSTEES Jennifer Mitchell; Brian Leigh-Bramwell.

OTHER INFORMATION The trust made 48 awards, including six charities additional to the list of regular beneficiaries.

HOW TO APPLY Apply in writing to the correspondent; however, our research suggests that there is only a small amount of funding available for unsolicited applications and therefore success is unlikely.

WHO TO APPLY TO L. Cooper, Secretary, Suite 2E, Atria, Spa Road, Bolton BL1 4AG *Tel.* 01204 364656

■ The Kennedy Leigh Charitable Trust

CC NO 288293 **ESTABLISHED** 1983

WHERE FUNDING CAN BE GIVEN UK and overseas, including Israel.

WHO CAN BENEFIT Registered charities only.

WHAT IS FUNDED According to its Charity Commission record, the trust supports 'projects and causes which will improve and enrich the lives of all parts of society, not least those of the young, the needy, the disadvantaged and the underprivileged'. The trust's objects require three-quarters of its grant-making funds to be distributed to charitable institutions within Israel, with the remainder being distributed in the UK and elsewhere.

WHAT IS NOT FUNDED Individuals.

TYPE OF GRANT Capital and core costs; usually up to three years, with the possibility of renewal.

RANGE OF GRANTS Usually up to £30,000.

SAMPLE GRANTS Shaare Zedek (£328,000); Yemin Orde (£85,000); British Friends of the Hebrew University (£31,000); Chai-Lifeline (£22,500); Jewish Care (£10,000); Magen David Adom (£5,000); other awards totalled £2,700.

FINANCES *Year* 2015/16 *Income* £527,875 *Grants* £595,978 *Grants to organisations* £595,978 *Assets* £21,775,483

TRUSTEES Anthony Foux; Geoffrey Goldkorn; Angela Sorkin; Alexander Sorkin; Carole Berman; Benjamin Goldkorn.

OTHER INFORMATION In 2015/16 there were 17 grants made over £1,000. The grant to Shaare Zedek was unusually large.

HOW TO APPLY The annual report for 2015/16 notes: 'The funds available for distribution outside of Israel are all but committed for the foreseeable future to several UK charities. The Trustees are therefore unable to consider applications for funding from charitable organisations outside of Israel at this time.'

WHO TO APPLY TO Naomi Shoffman, Administrator, ORT House, 126 Albert Street, London NW1 7NE *Tel.* 020 7267 6500

■ The Leigh Trust

CC NO 275372 **ESTABLISHED** 1976

WHERE FUNDING CAN BE GIVEN UK and overseas.

WHO CAN BENEFIT Charitable organisations benefitting disadvantaged and vulnerable people of any age, including children and young adults, older people, individuals out of work, volunteers, people in care, fostered or adopted individuals, ethnic groups, individuals at risk groups, people who have offended or are at risk of offending, refugees, asylum seekers, socially isolated people, victims of abuse and crime and people with substance abuse problems.

WHAT IS FUNDED The current priority of the trust is helping drug and alcohol rehabilitation, criminal justice, asylum seekers, racial equality and education. Awards can be made to support legal services, voluntary and community activities, volunteering, health counselling, support and self-help groups, social counselling, crime prevention and rehabilitation schemes, international rights of the individual, advice and information on social issues and similar causes.

WHAT IS NOT FUNDED Individuals.

TYPE OF GRANT Our research suggests that one-off or recurrent grants can be given for buildings, capital and core costs, projects, salaries and start-up costs. Funding is available for up to three years.

RANGE OF GRANTS £200 to £10,000.

SAMPLE GRANTS Steps 2 Recovery (£10,000); Keepout (£4,000); Arts for All, Addiction NI, Refugee and Migrant Centre and NEPACS Caravan Holidays (£2,000 each); Community Settlement Support and Sunderland Women's Centre (£1,500 each); Halow Project, Prisoners Advice Centre, Refugee Support Devon (£1,000 each).

FINANCES *Year* 2015/16 *Income* £91,442 *Grants* £98,005 *Grants to organisations* £98,005 *Assets* £3,174,586

TRUSTEES David Bernstein; Caroline Moorehead.

HOW TO APPLY Organisations applying for grants must provide their most recent audited accounts, a registered charity number, a cash flow statement for the next 12 months, and a stamped addressed envelope. Applicants should state clearly on one side of A4 what their charity does and what they are requesting funding for. They should also provide a detailed budget and show other sources of funding for the project.

WHO TO APPLY TO The Trustees, Begbies Chartered Accountants, Epworth House, 25 City Road, London EC1Y 1AR *Tel.* 020 7628 5801 *Fax* 020 7628 0390 *Email* admin@begbiesaccountants.co.uk

■ Leng Charitable Trust

SC NO SC009285 **ESTABLISHED** 1989

WHERE FUNDING CAN BE GIVEN Tayside, but primarily Dundee and to major national Scottish charities.

WHO CAN BENEFIT Registered charities.

WHAT IS FUNDED General charitable purposes; arts; education; health; social welfare; environment.

WHAT IS NOT FUNDED Individuals; overseas projects; political or religious appeals; sports or recreation.

RANGE OF GRANTS Typically £500 to £2,500.

SAMPLE GRANTS A list of beneficiaries was not available.

FINANCES *Year* 2015 *Income* £283,574 *Grants* £209,322 *Grants to organisations* £209,322

TRUSTEES A. F. McDonald; J. S. Fair; Dr J. Wood; Thorntons Trustees Ltd.

OTHER INFORMATION No information was available for current beneficiaries and trustees.

HOW TO APPLY Apply in writing to the correspondent.

WHO TO APPLY TO The Trustees, Whitehall House, 33 Yeaman Shore, Dundee DD1 4BJ *Tel.* 01382 229111 *Fax* 01382 202288 *Email* afmcdonald@thorntons-law.co.uk

■ The Lennox Hannay Charitable Trust

CC NO 1080198 **ESTABLISHED** 2000

WHERE FUNDING CAN BE GIVEN UK.

WHO CAN BENEFIT Registered charities.

WHAT IS FUNDED General charitable purposes; young people; ill health; disability; social welfare; education; health.

TYPE OF GRANT Unrestricted funding, including core and capital costs and project expenditure.

RANGE OF GRANTS Up to £30,000.

SAMPLE GRANTS The Sutton Trust (£30,000); Hampshire Hospitals and Injured Jockeys Fund (£25,000 each).

FINANCES *Year* 2015/16 *Income* £791,666 *Grants* £840,500 *Grants to organisations* £840,500 *Assets* £28,742,619

TRUSTEES Christopher Fleming; Caroline Wilmot-Sitwell; Tara Douglas-Home.

OTHER INFORMATION During the year the foundation made 123 grants to UK-registered charities only. Donations under £20,000 totalled £760,500.

HOW TO APPLY Apply in writing to the correspondent. The trustees meet twice a year to discuss applications each of which is reviewed on its own personal merit.

WHO TO APPLY TO Mrs C. Scott, Secretary, RF Trustee Co. Ltd, 15 Suffolk Street, London SW1Y 4HG *Tel.* 020 3696 6715 *Email* charities@rftrustee.com

■ The Mark Leonard Trust

CC NO 1040323 **ESTABLISHED** 1994

WHERE FUNDING CAN BE GIVEN Worldwide, but mainly UK.

WHO CAN BENEFIT Registered charities; charitable organisations; educational establishments.

WHAT IS FUNDED Environmental causes, particularly sustainable agriculture, food, climate change and renewable energy; young people, particularly socially excluded and those at risk of offending.

WHAT IS NOT FUNDED Individuals; educational fees; expeditions.

TYPE OF GRANT One-off and multi-year grants; capital costs.

RANGE OF GRANTS £2,500 to £273,500.

SAMPLE GRANTS Sustainable Restaurant Association (£273,500); Carbon Tracker (£49,000); Brockwell Park Community Greenhouses Trust (£45,000); Small Woods Association (£30,000); Only Connect (£25,000); National Union of Students (£21,500); Manchester Veg People (£12,500); Institute for Public Policy Research (£10,000); Plan International UK (£5,000); Lympne Church of England Primary School (£2,500).

FINANCES *Year* 2015/16 *Income* £1,184,477 *Grants* £1,141,356 *Grants to organisations* £1,141,356 *Assets* £17,109,423

TRUSTEES Zivi Sainsbury; Judith Portrait; John Sainsbury; Mark Sainsbury.

OTHER INFORMATION This is one of The Sainsbury Family Trusts, which share administration. A single application will be considered for support by all the charities in the group. During the year a total of 34 grants were approved (some payable over more than one year) totalling over £904,500. The figure we used refers to grants paid in the year. Awards were paid as follows: environment (£526,500); climate change collaboration (£315,500); youth work (£33,500); general (£29,000).

HOW TO APPLY Unsolicited applications are not accepted.

WHO TO APPLY TO Alan Bookbinder, Director, The Peak, 5 Wilton Road, London SW1V 1AP *Tel.* 020 7410 0330 *Email* info@sfct.org.uk *Website* www.sfct.org.uk

■ Lethendy Charitable Trust

SC NO SC003428 **ESTABLISHED** 1979

WHERE FUNDING CAN BE GIVEN Scotland, predominantly Tayside and north of Fife.

WHO CAN BENEFIT Priority is given to children and young adults in Tayside.

WHAT IS FUNDED The chief interests of the trustees are in the development of young people and supporting worthwhile causes in Tayside.

WHAT IS NOT FUNDED No grants are given to individuals for purely academic purposes such as school, university or college fees.

TYPE OF GRANT One-off.

RANGE OF GRANTS £50 to £10,000.

SAMPLE GRANTS A list of beneficiaries was not available.

FINANCES *Year* 2015/16 *Income* £83,068 *Grants* £77,550 *Grants to organisations* £71,600 *Assets* £2,582,006

TRUSTEES N. M. Sharp; W. R. Alexander; D. L. Laird; I. B. Rae; A. Thomson.

OTHER INFORMATION Grants were made to 15 individuals and totalled £5950.

HOW TO APPLY Apply in writing to the correspondent. The trustees meet once a year in July to consider grants.

WHO TO APPLY TO George Hay, Secretary, Henderson Loggie, Chartered Accountants, The Vision Building, 20 Greenmarket, Dundee DD1 4QB *Tel.* 01382 200055 *Fax* 01382 221240 *Email* ghay@hendersonloggie.co.uk

■ The Leverhulme Trade Charities Trust

CC NO 1159171 **ESTABLISHED** 1983

WHERE FUNDING CAN BE GIVEN UK.

WHO CAN BENEFIT Registered UK charities that are established specifically to provide welfare; Royal Pharmaceutical Society; UK universities.

WHAT IS FUNDED Social welfare, education and research for chemists, grocers and commercial travellers, or their families.

WHAT IS NOT FUNDED Capital grants; general appeals; individual grants are only made through charitable organisations.

SAMPLE GRANTS GroceryAid (£600,000); Royal Pinner Educational Trust (£540,000); The Salespeople's Charity (£400,000).

FINANCES *Year* 2016 *Income* £2,468,000 *Grants* £3,216,000 *Grants to organisations* £1,540,000 *Assets* £76,900,000

TRUSTEES Niall Fitzgerald; Patrick Cescau; Steve Williams; Paul Polman; Prof. Keith Gull; Clive Butler; Rudy Markham; Christopher Saul; Doug Baillie; Amanda Sourry.

OTHER INFORMATION Grants were made to three institutions for benevolence and social welfare. A further £1.4 million was given to institutions for undergraduate bursaries and £345,000 for postgraduate bursaries.

HOW TO APPLY Applications for bursaries need to be made using an online application system on the trust's website (deadlines are in November and March for undergraduate and October for postgraduate funding). Applications from eligible institutions on behalf of qualifying individuals need to be made in writing to the correspondent.

WHO TO APPLY TO Paul Read, Secretary, 1 Pemberton Row, London EC4A 3BG *Tel.* 020 7042 9881 *Fax* 020 7042 9889 *Email* pdread@leverhulme.ac.uk *Website* www.leverhulme-trade.org.uk

■ The Leverhulme Trust

CC NO 1159154 **ESTABLISHED** 1925

WHERE FUNDING CAN BE GIVEN Generally unrestricted, excluding USA.

WHO CAN BENEFIT Educational establishments; research bodies; individuals.

WHAT IS FUNDED Scholarships, fellowships and prizes for education and research.

WHAT IS NOT FUNDED Core funding or overheads for institutions; individual items of equipment over £1,000; sites, buildings or other capital expenditure; support for the organisation of conferences or workshops, which are not directly associated with International Networks, Early Career Fellowships; Visiting Fellowships or Philip Leverhulme Prizes; contributions to appeals; endowments; a shortfall resulting from a withdrawal of or deficiency in public finance; UK student fees where these are not associated with a Research Project Grant bid or Arts Scholarships; research into the following: medicine and related clinical activities in humans or animals; policy-driven research where the principal objective is to assemble an evidence base for immediate policy initiatives; projects where advocacy is an explicit component.

TYPE OF GRANT One-off; projects; research; running costs; salaries.

SAMPLE GRANTS University of Cambridge (£4.7 million in 40 grants); Royal Society/British Academy/Royal Academy of Engineering (£2.5 million in four grants); University of Liverpool (£1.9 million in 13 grants); Loughborough University (£1.1 million in three grants); Natural History Museum (£621,000 in two grants); The Mandela Rhodes Foundation (£600,000); Open University (£530,000).

FINANCES *Year* 2015/16 *Income* £86,707,000 *Grants* £80,124,000 *Grants to organisations* £80,124,000 *Assets* £2,638,976

TRUSTEES Niall Fitzgerald; Patrick Cescau; Steve Williams; Paul Polman; Keith Gull; Clive Butler; Rudy Markham; Christopher Saul; Doug Baillie; Amanda Sourry.

OTHER INFORMATION During the year a total of 619 grants were awarded to individuals and institutions. The grant total includes both organisations and individuals.

HOW TO APPLY Each programme, scholarship and award has its own individual application deadlines and procedures. Full details and guidelines for each scheme are available from the trust directly or via its website. Consult the full contact details on the trust's website to determine which person is the most suitable to approach. In assessing appeals the trustees evaluate the project's originality, importance, significance and merit. Cross-disciplinary projects may be favoured.

WHO TO APPLY TO Paul Read, Director of Finance, 1 Pemberton Row, London EC4A 3BG *Tel.* 020 7042 9888 *Email* pread@leverhulme.ac.uk *Website* www.leverhulme.ac.uk

■ Lord Leverhulme's Charitable Trust

CC NO 212431 **ESTABLISHED** 1957

WHERE FUNDING CAN BE GIVEN UK, especially Cheshire, Merseyside and Lancashire.

WHO CAN BENEFIT Registered and exempt charities.

WHAT IS FUNDED General charitable purposes; environment and animal welfare; education; the arts; health and disability; young people; religious causes; community purposes.

TYPE OF GRANT Recurrent, one-off and capital expenditure.

RANGE OF GRANTS Up to £250,000.

SAMPLE GRANTS Harper Adams (£250,000); Medical Detection Dogs (£150,000); Royal College of Surgeons (£50,000); Cavalier Centre (£25,000); Blind Veterans UK (£24,000); Princes Youth Trust (£21,500); Canine Partners and Royal Academy of Arts (£20,000 each).

FINANCES *Year* 2015/16 *Income* £701,897 *Grants* £857,424 *Grants to organisations* £857,424 *Assets* £32,597,659

TRUSTEES Sir Algernon Heber-Percy; Anthony Hannay; Henry Wilson.

OTHER INFORMATION Grants were made for the following purposes: Education (£308,500); Health (£303,500); Community (£160,500); Arts (£41,500); Animal welfare (£22,500); Religious establishments (£18,000); Environmental (£1,000).

HOW TO APPLY The trust states in its 2015/16 annual report: 'Priority is given ... to applications from Cheshire, Merseyside and South Lancashire and the charities supported by the settlor in his lifetime. Others who do not meet those criteria should not apply without prior invitation but should, on a single sheet, state briefly their aims and apply fully only on being asked to do so. A handful of charities have heeded this warning and telephoned our administrator but the continuing volume of applications from charities which plainly do not meet the stated criteria suggests that many applicants do not concern themselves with their target's policies.'

WHO TO APPLY TO Lynne Loxley, Leverhulme Estate Office, Hesketh Grange, Manor Road, Thornton Hough, Wirral CH63 1JD *Tel.* 0151 336 4828 *Email* lynne.loxley@leverhulmeestates.co.uk

■ The Maisie and Raphael Lewis Charitable Trust

CC NO 1041848 **ESTABLISHED** 1993

WHERE FUNDING CAN BE GIVEN UK.

WHO CAN BENEFIT Older people; Jewish people; medical charities.

WHAT IS FUNDED Provision and maintenance of housing/almshouses; grants for medical charities.

SAMPLE GRANTS Jewish Care and Norwood (£12,500 each); Chai Cancer Care (£10,500); British ORT (£5,000); Community Security Trust (£3,500); World Jewish Relief (£2,000); London Jewish Cultural Centre (£1,000); Great Ormond Street Hospital, Cystic Fibrosis Trust and Breast Cancer Campaign (£100).

FINANCES *Year* 2015/16 *Income* £28,165 *Grants* £57,000 *Grants to organisations* £57,000 *Assets* £546,638

TRUSTEES Jeffery Zamet; Barry Slavin.

OTHER INFORMATION No list of beneficiaries was given for 2015/16.

HOW TO APPLY Apply in writing to the correspondent.

WHO TO APPLY TO Paul Berlyn, Accountant, Arram Berlyn Gardner (AH) Ltd, 30 City Road, London EC1Y 2AB *Tel.* 020 7330 0000 *Email* HREUBEN@ABGGROUP.CO.UK

■ Bernard Lewis Family Charitable Trust

CC NO 1125035 **ESTABLISHED** 2008

WHERE FUNDING CAN BE GIVEN England and Wales.

WHO CAN BENEFIT Registered charities.

WHAT IS FUNDED Children's welfare; medical causes; general charitable purposes; medical research; older people; education; Jewish religious support.

SAMPLE GRANTS Newlife Foundation for Disabled Children (£273,000); Compassion in Dying (£213,000); Magic Bus (£152,500); Jewish Care (£53,000); Sight Savers (£50,000); Jewish Leadership Council (£30,000); Brain Research Trust and Demand (£5,000 each); Sense (£1,000).

FINANCES *Year* 2015 *Income* £2,064,180 *Grants* £1,339,400 *Grants to organisations* £1,339,400 *Assets* £5,775,050

TRUSTEES Clive Lewis; Bernard Lewis; Caroline Grange; Leonard Lewis.

HOW TO APPLY Apply in writing to the correspondent.

WHO TO APPLY TO Mark Woodruff, c/o The Giving Department, Sky Light City Tower, 50 Basinghall Street EC2V 5DE

■ David and Ruth Lewis Family Charitable Trust

CC NO 259892 **ESTABLISHED** 1962

WHERE FUNDING CAN BE GIVEN UK and Israel.

WHO CAN BENEFIT Charitable bodies and research institutions.

WHAT IS FUNDED 'Virtually every generally accepted charitable object'; health causes; medical research, particularly into possible treatments for cancer; Jewish community work; educational funding, support for older people; children and social care; poverty and disaster relief.

WHAT IS NOT FUNDED Grants are not made to individuals (unless in exceptional circumstances).

TYPE OF GRANT Potentially up to three years but mostly one-off.

RANGE OF GRANTS Up to £250,000.

SAMPLE GRANTS Sarah Hertzog Hospital Institute of Cancer Research (£300,000); The Peres Centre for Peace (£120,000); Community Security Trust (£52,500); United Jewish Israel Appeal (UJIA) (£30,000); Jewish Leadership Council (£30,000); The Jaffa Institute (£20,000).

FINANCES *Year* 2015/16 *Income* £2,271,148 *Grants* £1,107,313 *Grants to organisations* £1,107,313 *Assets* £13,259,752

TRUSTEES Julian Lewis; Deborah Lewis; Benjamin Lewis; Simon Lewis; Rachel Lewis.

HOW TO APPLY Apply in writing to the correspondent.

WHO TO APPLY TO The Secretary, Chelsea House, West Gate, Ealing, London W5 1DR *Tel.* 020 8991 4502

■ The John Spedan Lewis Foundation

CC NO 240473 **ESTABLISHED** 1964

WHERE FUNDING CAN BE GIVEN UK.

WHO CAN BENEFIT Charitable organisations; educational institutions. The focus is on applications for small projects connected with the natural sciences and of educational nature, particularly benefitting, children, young adults and research workers.

WHAT IS FUNDED Natural sciences, particularly horticulture, ornithology, entomology, environmental education, conservation and associated educational and research projects – areas of particular interests to John Spedan Lewis, the founder of John Lewis Partnership. The trustees will also consider applications from organisations for imaginative and original educational projects aimed at developing serious interest and evident talent, particularly among young people. Funding is also given to a small number of PhD research projects on specific topics chosen by the trustees and to selected universities and research institutes.

WHAT IS NOT FUNDED Support is not normally made to local branches of national organisations, to cover salaries, medical research, welfare projects, building works or overseas expeditions. Unsolicited applications for PhD funding from individuals, universities or research institutes are not considered.

TYPE OF GRANT Mostly one-off donations for project and capital expenditure. Salaries are not normally funded.

RANGE OF GRANTS £500 to £7,000.

SAMPLE GRANTS Rare Breeds Survival Trust (£5,100); Colwall Orchard Trust (£4,400); Bumblebee Conservation Trust (£2,600); Nottinghamshire Wildlife Trust (£2,300); Children's Hospice South West, The Royal Botanic Garden Edinburgh, The Swanage Pier Trust and Trees For Cities (£2,000 each); Devon Bird Watching and Preservation Society (£1,000); Manx Wildlife Trust (£500).

FINANCES *Year* 2015/16 *Income* £83,948 *Grants* £66,380 *Grants to organisations* £36,380 *Assets* £2,563,315

TRUSTEES Charlie Mayfield; David Jones; Dr Vaughan Southgate; Dr John David; Gerrard Keogh-Peters.

OTHER INFORMATION The foundation made 15 awards to organisations and two individual grants (multi-year awards for research purposes at the Durrell Institute of Conservation and Ecology at the University of Kent totalling £30,000).

HOW TO APPLY Apply in writing to the correspondent providing the latest annual report and set of accounts and a budget for the proposed project.

WHO TO APPLY TO Ruth Bone, Secretary, Partnership House, Carlisle Place, London SW1P 1BX *Tel.* 020 7592 6284 *Email* jslf@johnlewis.co.uk *Website* johnspedanlewisfoundation.wordpress.com

■ The Sir Edward Lewis Foundation

CC NO 264475 **ESTABLISHED** 1972

WHERE FUNDING CAN BE GIVEN UK and overseas, with a preference for Surrey.

WHO CAN BENEFIT Registered charities.

WHAT IS FUNDED General charitable purposes. According to the annual report for 2015/16, 'the trustees have adopted a practice to make donations to a number of charities who receive payments from the foundation on a regular annual basis; however new appeals are still regularly reviewed and donations are allocated accordingly'.

WHAT IS NOT FUNDED Individuals. Grants are generally only given to charities, projects or people known to the trustees.

TYPE OF GRANT Unrestricted, including core and capital costs, salaries and project funding.

RANGE OF GRANTS £500 to £35,000; mostly under £2,000.

SAMPLE GRANTS The Arnold Foundation for Rugby School (£30,000); Arthritis Research UK (£10,000); Children's Trust Tadworth, FareShare, Gurkha Welfare Trust, Ridgegate Home for Old People and St Bartholomew's Church – Leigh (£5,000 each).

FINANCES *Year* 2015/16 *Income* £306,334 *Grants* £225,500 *Grants to organisations* £225,500 *Assets* £8,560,888

TRUSTEES Richard Lewis; Mark Harris; Christine Lewis; Sarah Dorin.

OTHER INFORMATION The trustees prefer to support charities known personally to them and those favoured by the settlor. During the year a total of 102 awards were made. Small awards (under £5,000) totalled £140,500.

HOW TO APPLY Apply in writing to the correspondent. The trustees meet every six months, in May and December.

WHO TO APPLY TO Darren Wing, Rawlinson and Hunter, Eighth Floor, New Street Square, New Fetter Lane, London EC4A 3AQ *Tel.* 020 7842 2000 *Email* lewis.foundation@rawlinson-hunter.com

■ John Lewis Partnership General Community Fund

CC NO 209128 **ESTABLISHED** 1961

WHERE FUNDING CAN BE GIVEN UK.

WHO CAN BENEFIT UK and local registered charities, benefitting children and young adults, at risk groups, people who are sick or who have disabilities, people disadvantaged by poverty and those who are socially isolated; medical professionals and research workers may be considered.

WHAT IS FUNDED Welfare; music; arts; education; environment; community causes; young people; relief of poverty.

WHAT IS NOT FUNDED Loans; sponsorship; religious, ethnic or political groups; advertising; individuals; third-party fundraising.

TYPE OF GRANT One-off and recurring.

RANGE OF GRANTS £400 to £100,000.

SAMPLE GRANTS The British Red Cross Society (£100,000); Retail Trust (£50,000); Royal College of Music and The Voices Foundation (£20,000 each); The Trust for Sing for Pleasure (£17,500); Royal Academy of Music (£10,500); Pro Corda Trust (£10,000); Cardiff Council (£7,200); Just Enough UK and The Guide Dogs for the Blind Association (£5,000 each); Wiltshire Music Centre Trust Ltd (£4,000); Apollo Music Projects (£2,000); The Papworth Trust (£1,000); Friends of Barnwell Country Park (£400).

FINANCES *Year* 2015 *Income* £643,076 *Grants* £643,076 *Grants to organisations* £643,076 *Assets* £0

TRUSTEE John Lewis Partnership Trust Ltd.

OTHER INFORMATION The foundation made 161 grants during the year.

HOW TO APPLY The trust provided the following information: 'If you have a cause you think we could support, contact the Waitrose champion for community giving at your local branch (www.waitrose.com) or the John Lewis Community Liaison Co-ordinator at your local branch (www.johnlewis.com). As we are contacted by so many organisations throughout the year, we cannot always give you a swift reply, but we will reply as soon as possible if we can help.'

WHO TO APPLY TO The Directors, Partnership House, Carlisle Place, London SW1P 1BX *Tel.* 020 7592 5957 *Website* www.johnlewispartnership.co.uk

Liberum Foundation

CC NO 1137475 **ESTABLISHED** 2010

WHERE FUNDING CAN BE GIVEN UK, with preference for London.

WHO CAN BENEFIT Organisations; individuals.

WHAT IS FUNDED General charitable purposes, including education and training, relief of poverty, sports, recreation and well-being and community and economic development; all with a focus on disadvantaged young people.

WHAT IS NOT FUNDED Adult health; hospitals; animals; older people; the armed services; housing; heritage; environment; and religion.

RANGE OF GRANTS £400 to £50,000.

SAMPLE GRANTS School Home Support (£30,000); St Giles Trust (£25,000); Just Different (£20,400).

FINANCES *Year* 2015 *Income* £76,826 *Grants* £75,365 *Grants to organisations* £75,365 *Assets* £65,042

TRUSTEES Carolyn Doherty; Antony Scawthorn; Timothy Mayo; Nina Dixon; Mary-Jane Clarke; Anastasia Mikhailova; Joanne Kelly.

HOW TO APPLY Apply in writing to the correspondent.

WHO TO APPLY TO Justine Rumens, Company Secretary, Ropemaker Place, Level 12, 25 Ropemaker Street, London EC2Y 9LY *Tel.* 020 3100 2000 *Email* info@liberumfoundation.com *Website* www.liberum.com/about-liberum/the-liberum-foundation

The Lidbury Charitable Trust

CC NO 1078511 **ESTABLISHED** 1999

WHERE FUNDING CAN BE GIVEN Unrestricted, in practice UK.

WHO CAN BENEFIT Registered charities.

WHAT IS FUNDED General charitable purposes with consideration given to various named charities.

WHAT IS NOT FUNDED None known.

SAMPLE GRANTS Gloucester Cathedral; Yatton Parish Church; Tewkesbury Abbey; Edington Parochial Church Council Fabric Fund; Salisbury Cathedral; Wells Cathedral; Ely Cathedral; Middlewich Church; Arthritis Care; Cancer Research UK; British Heart Foundation; RNLI; National Trust; Diabetes UK; Guide Dogs for the Blind.

FINANCES *Year* 2014/15 *Income* £144,469 *Grants* £100,000 *Grants to organisations* £100,000

TRUSTEE NatWest Trust Services.

OTHER INFORMATION This was the latest information available at the time of writing (June 2017). The accounts for the year 2015/16 were overdue for submission at the Charity Commission.

HOW TO APPLY Apply in writing to the correspondent.

WHO TO APPLY TO NatWest Trust Services, NatWest Trust Services, Ground Floor, Eastwood House, Glebe Road, Chelmsford CM1 1RS *Tel.* 01245 292401 *Email* nwb.charities@natwest.com

Life Changes Trust

SC NO SC043816 **ESTABLISHED** 2013

WHERE FUNDING CAN BE GIVEN Scotland.

WHO CAN BENEFIT Registered charities; community groups; councils; individuals.

WHAT IS FUNDED Care experienced young people; people with dementia.

RANGE OF GRANTS Up to £1 million.

SAMPLE GRANTS Care and Repair Scotland (£1 million); East Renfrewshire Council (£406,500); North West Carers Centre (£105,000); Outside the Box (£94,000); Haven Centre (£93,000); The Eric Liddle Centre (£84,000); Aberdeen Council of Voluntary Organisations (£20,000); Studio LR (£17,500).

FINANCES *Year* 2015/16 *Income* £759,656 *Grants* £3,500,000 *Grants to organisations* £3,500,000

TRUSTEES Alexis Jay; Harriet Dempster; Isobel Grigor; Shona Munro; Claire Lightower; Gillian Brown; Nigel Fairhead; Eona Craig; Mike Connor; Shona Hill.

OTHER INFORMATION The trust's full accounts were not available to view on the OSCR website. We have therefore had to estimate the grant total.

HOW TO APPLY Refer to the trust's website for details of grant programmes and application deadlines.

WHO TO APPLY TO The Trustees, Edward House, 2nd Floor, 283 West Campbell Street, Glasgow G2 4TT *Tel.* 0141 212 9600 *Email* enquiries@lifechangestrust.org.uk *Website* www.lifechangestrust.org.uk

Lifeline 4 Kids

CC NO 200050 **ESTABLISHED** 1961

WHERE FUNDING CAN BE GIVEN Worldwide.

WHO CAN BENEFIT Organisations and bodies supporting children with disabilities (up to the age of 18), including hospitals, hospices, respite care homes, support centres, special schools, social workers and so on; individuals and their families.

WHAT IS FUNDED Promotion of the welfare of children with disabilities and special needs; the provision of equipment and services.

WHAT IS NOT FUNDED Building projects; garden works; research grants; fridges or washing machines (unless for medical needs); ovens or cookers; salaries; carpets or floor covering; clothing and shoes (unless specialist); childcare costs; transport costs; tuition/school lessons or fees; driving lessons; recreational activities; holidays. Requests for iPads can be awarded only if they satisfy very specific requirements (see the website) – the charity notes that they are inundated with applications for these.

TYPE OF GRANT Money for the purchase of equipment. Note that cash grants are **not** given and the purchase is undertaken on behalf of beneficiaries.

SAMPLE GRANTS The latest accounts do not give details of specific beneficiaries; however, the website gives some examples of grant recipients. Beneficiaries have included: Mapledown School – Cricklewood; Maplewood School – High Wycombe Buckinghamshire; Orcadia Creative Learning Centre – Edinburgh; Save a Child's Heart; South West Scorpions; St Michael's Hospital Bristol; Swiss Cottage SEN School – London; Tartan Army Sunshine Appeal; The Living Paintings; The Seashell Trust; Vernon House School – London.

FINANCES *Year* 2015 *Income* £161,599 *Grants* £91,308 *Grants to organisations* £91,308 *Assets* £358,269

TRUSTEES Roger Adelman; Paul Maurice; Beverley Emden; Roberta Harris; Irving Millman; Jeffrey Bonn.

OTHER INFORMATION **Note**: This charity does not give cash grants. The website states: 'We have in the past helped equip hospital neonatal units with the latest incubators, infusion pumps and ultrasonic monitors amongst other life saving equipment although today our main activity is to help the individual child.' The grant total includes both organisations and individuals.

HOW TO APPLY Refer to the website for full details. To receive an application form (specify whether via email or post is preferred) you should send an email to appeals@lifeline4kids.org outlining: a specific requirement and its cost; brief factual information about the child (name, DOB, health condition and contact details). Applications from organisations need to give their name and contact details as well as specify the number of children that are likely to benefit, their age group and details of specific requirements together with costs. Full applications are discussed and decided upon at monthly meetings; however, emergency and welfare appeals can be dealt with as soon as possible after they are received. The charity asks not to be phoned unless you are in an emergency, as this is a volunteer-led charity with insufficient people attending to answer calls.

WHO TO APPLY TO Roger Adelman, Trustee, 215 West End Lane, West Hampstead, London NW6 1XJ *Tel.* 020 7794 1661 *Fax* 020 8459 8826 *Email* appeals@lifeline4kids.org *Website* www.lifeline4kids.org

■ The Light Fund Company

CC NO 1145596 **ESTABLISHED** 2012

WHERE FUNDING CAN BE GIVEN Worldwide.

WHO CAN BENEFIT Registered charities.

WHAT IS FUNDED The Light Fund welcomes applications for funding from any charitable organisation whose beneficiaries are children, women or men.

TYPE OF GRANT The charity applications for funding should be for specific projects rather than for general funds.

SAMPLE GRANTS The Children's Trust (£7,000); Brain Tumour Charity and Challenge Africa (£5,000 each); Catholic Blind Institute and Medical Detection Dogs (£4,700 each); Epilepsy Lifestyle (£4,400); Children on the Edge (£4,300); Sparks (£4,100); Bungoma Calling (£3,800); CCHF All About Kids (£2,400).

FINANCES *Year* 2015/16 *Income* £174,951 *Grants* £148,532 *Grants to organisations* £148,532 *Assets* £12,560

TRUSTEES Trevor Charles Jones; Ashley Arun Sidney Holman; Robyn Cowling; Caroline High; Jacqueline Ann Brown; Ian David Hyder; Alicia Sophy Davenport; Hannah Mungo; Ian Michael Downes; Kelvyn Gardner; David William Scott; Martin Lowe; Alison Mary Downie; Max Arguile.

HOW TO APPLY Applications can be made through the charity's website.

WHO TO APPLY TO David William Scott, Rainbow Productions Ltd, Unit 3, Greenlea Park, Prince Georges Road, London SW19 2JD *Tel.* 020 8254 5301 *Email* info@lightfund.org *Website* www.lightfund.org

■ The Limbourne Trust

CC NO 1113796 **ESTABLISHED** 2006

WHERE FUNDING CAN BE GIVEN UK and overseas.

WHO CAN BENEFIT Charitable organisations; community projects.

WHAT IS FUNDED The trust has broad charitable objectives and supports charities around the world and including support in environment and sustainability; conservation; community projects; disadvantaged people; advancement of education; protection of health; relief of poverty and distress; research; the arts; other charitable causes.

RANGE OF GRANTS £3,000 to £17,000.

SAMPLE GRANTS English Pen (£16,500); Stepping Stones and Whirlow Hall Farm Trust (£10,000 each); Young People Take Action (£9,000); Ellen MacArthur Cancer Trust (£8,000).

FINANCES *Year* 2015/16 *Income* £464,091 *Grants* £105,627 *Grants to organisations* £105,627 *Assets* £3,394,659

TRUSTEES Elisabeth Thistlethwayte; Katharine Thistlethwayte; Jocelyn Magnus; Dr Andrew Eastaugh.

OTHER INFORMATION Grants were made to 16 organisations.

HOW TO APPLY Apply in writing to the correspondent.

WHO TO APPLY TO Elisabeth Thistlethwayte, Trustee, Downs Farm, Homersfield, Harleston IP20 0NS *Email* lizzie_wayte@hotmail.com

■ Limoges Charitable Trust

CC NO 1016178 **ESTABLISHED** 1991

WHERE FUNDING CAN BE GIVEN UK, with a preference for Birmingham.

WHO CAN BENEFIT Registered charities.

WHAT IS FUNDED General charitable purposes, including health, heritage and community purposes, animals, young people and nautical causes.

RANGE OF GRANTS Up to £10,000; most grants under £1,500.

SAMPLE GRANTS Birmingham Museum and Art Gallery (£9,300); City of Birmingham Symphony Orchestra, Edward's Trust, Moseley Community Development Trust and Town Hall Symphony Hall (£5,000 each); Hollytrees Animal Rescue Trust (£3,700); Pershore Abbey Parochial Church Council (£2,300); Birmingham St Mary's Hospice and Elgar Birthplace Trust (£2,000 each); Lansallos Parochial Church Council (£1,600).

FINANCES *Year* 2015/16 *Income* £34,616 *Grants* £70,300 *Grants to organisations* £70,300 *Assets* £1,221,026

TRUSTEES Mike Dyer; Judy Dyke; Andrew Milner.

OTHER INFORMATION The annual report and accounts on the Charity Commission's website were for the most part not legible. The grant total is based on an estimate looking at previous years.

HOW TO APPLY Apply in writing to the correspondent. The trustees usually meet four times a year to consider applications.

WHO TO APPLY TO Judy Dyke, Trustee, Judy Ann Dyke, 29 Woodbourne Road, Edgbaston, Birmingham B17 8BY *Tel.* 0121 693 2222 *Fax* 0121 693 0844 *Email* jdyke@tyndallwoods.co.uk

■ The Linbury Trust

CC NO 287077 **ESTABLISHED** 1973

WHERE FUNDING CAN BE GIVEN Worldwide.

WHO CAN BENEFIT Charitable organisations; museums and galleries; educational institutions.

WHAT IS FUNDED The arts; museums and heritage; social welfare; education; the environment; medical causes; humanitarian aid.

WHAT IS NOT FUNDED Individuals; educational fees; expeditions.

TYPE OF GRANT Running and capital costs; project expenditure.

RANGE OF GRANTS Up to £2.1 million.

SAMPLE GRANTS Royal Opera House Foundation (£2.1 million); British School at Rome (£1.25 million); Westminster Abbey (£350,000); British School at Rome (£270,500); National Theatre of Scotland (£100,000); Shoreditch Town Hall Trust (£75,000); Innovation for Agriculture (£60,000); Bodleian Library, Gurkha Welfare Trust and Marine Society and Sea Cadets (£50,000 each).

FINANCES *Year* 2015/16 *Income* £6,242,000 *Grants* £7,519,000 *Grants to organisations* £7,519,000 *Assets* £142,367,000

TRUSTEES Sir James Spooner; Richard Butler Adams; James Barnard; Lady Anya Sainsbury; Sir Martin Jacomb; Lord Sainsbury of Preston Candover.

OTHER INFORMATION The trust is one of the Sainsbury Family Charitable Trusts which share a joint administration but work autonomously as independent legal entities. A single application to The Sainsbury Family Charitable Trust is considered for support by all the trusts in the group. A total of 68 organisations were supported during the year.

HOW TO APPLY The Linbury trust, as a rule, does not consider unsolicited appeals. The annual report for 2015/16 states: 'The Trustees take a proactive approach towards grant-making; accordingly, unsolicited applications are not usually successful.' Note that a single application to The Sainsbury Family Charitable Trust is considered for support by all the trusts in the group. See further details on The Sainsbury Family Charitable Trusts website.

WHO TO APPLY TO Alan Bookbinder, Director, The Peak, 5 Wilton Road, London SW1V 1AP *Tel.* 020 7410 0330 *Email* info@sfct.org.uk *Website* www.linburytrust.org.uk

■ Lincolnshire Community Foundation

CC NO 1092328 **ESTABLISHED** 2002

WHERE FUNDING CAN BE GIVEN Lincolnshire.

WHO CAN BENEFIT Charitable organisations.

WHAT IS FUNDED General charitable purposes; education; social welfare; health; community.

TYPE OF GRANT One-off funding and grants of up to three years.

SAMPLE GRANTS Citizens Advice Mid Lincolnshire; Crosby Community Association; Fusion Creative; Heart of Sleaford; Holbeach Hospital; Lincolnshire Action Trust; Responders to Warmth; St Giles Community Garden; St Luke's Community Choir.

FINANCES *Year* 2015/16 *Income* £721,543 *Grants* £764,134 *Grants to organisations* £764,134 *Assets* £5,456,139

TRUSTEES Richard Ferens; Stephen Cousins; Jean Shaftoe; David Close; Jane Hiles; Andrew Clark; Paul Scott; Lizzie Milligan-Manby; Lesley Chester; Lynda Phillips; Paula Baumber; Sarah Banner.

OTHER INFORMATION During the year, around 250 grants were made to individuals, groups and projects. A complete list of beneficiaries was not provided in the accounts.

HOW TO APPLY Visit the foundation's website for details of current grant schemes. Application forms can be downloaded from the foundation's website or requested by phone.

WHO TO APPLY TO Sue Fortune, Grants Director, 4 Mill House, Moneys Yard, Carre Street, Sleaford, Lincolnshire NG34 7TW *Tel.* 01529 305825 *Email* sue.lincolnshire@btconnect.com *Website* www.lincolnshirecf.co.uk

■ The Lind Trust

CC NO 803174 **ESTABLISHED** 1990

WHERE FUNDING CAN BE GIVEN UK, particularly Norwich and Norfolk.

WHO CAN BENEFIT Churches; charities and charitable organisations; individuals. Generally, beneficiaries should be based in Norfolk.

WHAT IS FUNDED Development of young people; social action; community and Christian service. Christian causes and youth work are a priority.

SAMPLE GRANTS The Open Youth Trust (£200,500); Today's Lifestyle Church (£90,000).

FINANCES *Year* 2015/16 *Income* £1,507,834 *Grants* £1,250,609 *Grants to organisations* £1,250,609 *Assets* £22,754,936

TRUSTEES Leslie Brown; Dr Graham Dacre; Gavin Wilcock; Julia Dacre; Samuel Dacre.

OTHER INFORMATION Only two beneficiaries were listed in the accounts.

HOW TO APPLY Apply in writing to the correspondent at any time. However, the trust commits most of its funds in advance, giving the remainder to eligible applicants as received.

WHO TO APPLY TO Gavin Wilcock, Trustee, Drayton Hall, Hall Lane, Drayton, Norwich, Norfolk NR8 6DP *Tel.* 01603 262626 *Email* accounts@dacrepropertyholdings.com

■ Lindale Educational Foundation

CC NO 282758 **ESTABLISHED** 1981

WHERE FUNDING CAN BE GIVEN UK.

WHO CAN BENEFIT Roman Catholic institutions; charitable organisations benefitting children, young adults and students.

WHAT IS FUNDED The promotion of Roman Catholic religion; the advancement of education in accordance with Christian principles and ideals within the Roman Catholic tradition. This includes: training priests; improvement and maintenance of places of worship; improvement and maintenance of university halls or halls of residence; courses camps, study centres, meetings, conferences and seminars; the provision of grants, scholarships, loans or donations the pursuit of education or research by individuals or groups of students. Most grants are already allocated to specific charities.

WHAT IS NOT FUNDED Individuals.

TYPE OF GRANT One-off and recurrent; capital and revenue costs.

RANGE OF GRANTS £1,000 to £31,000.

SAMPLE GRANTS Netherhall Educational Association Centre (£20,500 in five grants); Thornycroft Hall (£31,000 in six grants); Hazelwood House (£4,500 in two grants).

FINANCES *Year* 2014/15 *Income* £56,900 *Grants* £56,210 *Grants to organisations* £56,210 *Assets* £39,888

TRUSTEES Dawliffe Hall Educational Foundation; Greygarth Association; Netherhall Educational Association.

OTHER INFORMATION A total of three organisations received thirteen grants.

HOW TO APPLY Apply in writing to the correspondent, but note that most funds are already committed.

WHO TO APPLY TO Jack Valero, 6 Orme Court, London W2 4RL *Tel.* 020 7243 9417

■ The Linden Charitable trust

CC NO 326788 **ESTABLISHED** 1985

WHERE FUNDING CAN BE GIVEN UK, with a preference for West Yorkshire.

WHO CAN BENEFIT Registered charities; arts organisations.

WHAT IS FUNDED The trust's current policy according to its latest annual report is to benefit 'charities specialising in cancer relief and research, those particularly involved with hospices, those involved in arts and also a wider range of charities based in and around Leeds, West Yorkshire'. The trustees have agreed to make a regular donation to Leeds International Pianoforte Competition of £10,000 per year.

WHAT IS NOT FUNDED Individuals.

RANGE OF GRANTS £500 to £10,000.

SAMPLE GRANTS Leeds International Pianoforte Competition and Yorkshire Air Ambulance (£10,000 each); Martin House and St Chads (£5,000 each); Sylvia Wright Trust and St George's Crypt (£3,000 each); Guide Dogs for the Blind, Help for Heroes, Little Sisters for the Poor, Mission to Seafarers and Yorkshire Sculpture Park (£2,000 each); St John's Catholic School for the Deaf and St Michael's Hospice (£1,000 each); Yorkshire Eye Research (£500).

FINANCES *Year* 2015/16 *Income* £66,698 *Grants* £123,500 *Grants to organisations* £123,500 *Assets* £2,483,458

TRUSTEES Gerald Holbrook; John Swales; Robert Swales; Margaret Swales; Kathryn Swales.

OTHER INFORMATION The trust made 46 awards during the year.

HOW TO APPLY Apply in writing to the correspondent. The trustees meet two or three times a year to discuss the awards. Decisions can in some circumstances also be made in between the meetings.

WHO TO APPLY TO Robert Swales, Trustee, 121 Leeds Road, Harrogate HG2 8EZ

■ The Enid Linder Foundation

CC NO 267509 **ESTABLISHED** 1974

WHERE FUNDING CAN BE GIVEN UK.

WHO CAN BENEFIT UK-registered charities or organisations with exempt status; universities and teaching hospitals; schools and other educational establishments.

WHAT IS FUNDED Medicine – to fund research, education and capital projects related to all areas of medicine through grants to selected medical universities, institutions and charities; arts – to fund projects which aim to develop and encourage individual and group talent in musical, theatre and illustrative art; general charitable purposes – to make donations to projects benefitting children, older people and people with disabilities.

WHAT IS NOT FUNDED Projects outside the UK; individuals or individual research or study.

TYPE OF GRANT Mainly one-off.

RANGE OF GRANTS £1,000 to £188,000; generally less than £30,000.

SAMPLE GRANTS National Children's Orchestra (£219,000 in three grants); Royal College of Surgeons (£110,000 in two grants); Médecins Sans Frontières and Victoria and Albert Museum (£30,000 each); Bath University and Juvenile Diabetic Research Foundation (£20,000 each); NeuroMuscular Centre (£15,000); WaterAid (£10,000); Beatrix Potter Society (£7,500); ABF The Soldiers' Charity (£6,000); The Hands Up Foundation (£1,000).

FINANCES *Year* 2015/16 *Income* £564,370 *Grants* £813,950 *Grants to organisations* £811,950 *Assets* £14,828,598

TRUSTEES Jack Ladeveze; Audrey Ladeveze; Michael Butler; Carole Cook; Jonathan Fountain.

OTHER INFORMATION The grant total includes about £112,000 in elective and hardship grants to university medical schools. During the year 35 awards were made to organisations and one made to an individual (£2,000).

HOW TO APPLY Apply using the online form on the foundation's website. The deadline is 1 January for the March trustee meeting and 1 September for the December meeting. Grants are be made in April and January. Note that the 2015/16 annual report states that unsolicited applications are largely unsuccessful.

WHO TO APPLY TO Martin Pollock, Secretary, c/o Moore Stephens LLP, 150 Aldersgate Street, London EC1A 4AB *Tel.* 020 7334 9191 *Email* enidlinderfoundation@moorestephens.com *Website* www.enidlinderfoundation.com

■ The Lindley Foundation

CC NO 1152760 **ESTABLISHED** 2013

WHERE FUNDING CAN BE GIVEN UK and overseas.

WHO CAN BENEFIT Registered charities; charitable organisations.

WHAT IS FUNDED General charitable purposes.

RANGE OF GRANTS £200 to £50,000.

SAMPLE GRANTS I Morechild; African Prisons Project; Ashoka UK; Chickenshed; Children's Hospice Charity; Gua Africa; Key is E; No Panic; Performing Arts Children's Charity; Robert F Kennedy Centre for Human Rights; The Caldecott Foundation.

FINANCES *Year* 2015/16 *Income* £393,745 *Grants* £96,777 *Grants to organisations* £96,777 *Assets* £723,474

TRUSTEES Alison Lindley; Paul Lindley; Coutts & Co.

OTHER INFORMATION There were no award amounts given in the independent examiner's review for 2015/16.

HOW TO APPLY Apply in writing to the correspondent.

WHO TO APPLY TO Coutts & Co., Trustees, 440 Strand, London WC2R 0QS *Tel.* 020 7663 6825

■ The Ruth and Stuart Lipton Charitable Trust

CC NO 266741 **ESTABLISHED** 1973

WHERE FUNDING CAN BE GIVEN UK and overseas, with some preference for London.

WHO CAN BENEFIT Charitable organisations. Preference can be given to those benefitting Jewish people and organisations in London.

WHAT IS FUNDED General charitable purposes, including health, education and arts; Jewish causes.

WHAT IS NOT FUNDED Individuals.

RANGE OF GRANTS £50 to £12,500.

SAMPLE GRANTS United Jewish Israel Appeal (UJIA) (£12,500); The Royal Opera House Foundation (£8,700); Nightingale (£5,800); Prostate Cancer UK (£5,400); Western Marble Arch Synagogue (£4,400); Barbican Centre Trust (£3,500); Schools Around The World (£2,500); Jewish Bereavement Counselling Service and St John's Hospice (£200 each); Land Aid Charitable Trust (£100); The Kensington and Chelsea Foundation (£75); Jewish Women's Aid (£50).

FINANCES *Year* 2015/16 *Income* £1,075 *Grants* £100,000 *Grants to organisations* £100,000

TRUSTEES Stuart Lipton; Ruth Lipton; Neil Benson.

OTHER INFORMATION This charity's latest accounts were not available to view on the Charity Commission's website due to its unusually low income. The grant total is an estimate based on previous years.

HOW TO APPLY Apply in writing to the correspondent. There is no minimum limit for any grant and all grants must be approved unanimously by the trustees.

WHO TO APPLY TO Neil Benson, Trustee, c/o Lewis Golden and Co., 40 Queen Ann Street, London W1G 9EL *Tel.* 020 7580 7313 *Email* charity@lewisgolden.com

The Lister Charitable Trust

CC NO 288730 **ESTABLISHED** 1981

WHERE FUNDING CAN BE GIVEN UK and overseas.

WHO CAN BENEFIT Registered charities which work with young people.

WHAT IS FUNDED General charitable purposes; children and young people; environment conservation; health.

WHAT IS NOT FUNDED Individuals, including students; general appeals from large UK organisations; smaller bodies working in areas outside the trust's criteria.

TYPE OF GRANT Usually one-off for specific project or part of a project given for up to one year. Core funding and/or salaries rarely considered.

SAMPLE GRANTS UKSA (£75,000); Wildlife Media (£66,000); Fundatia Inocenti (£23,000); Romanian Children's Relief (£16,500); Brenda Phillips Photography (£13,000); Home-Start Ashford (£10,000); Light Dragons and Mount Carmel Hotel (£5,000 each); The Royal Marsden Cancer Charity (£4,400).

FINANCES *Year* 2015/16 *Income* £77,001 *Grants* £284,502 *Grants to organisations* £284,502 *Assets* £5,317,917

TRUSTEES Penny Horne; Sylvia Lister.

OTHER INFORMATION Grants were made to 16 organisations.

HOW TO APPLY Apply in writing to the correspondent. They should include clear details of the need the intended project is designed to meet and an outline budget. Only applications from eligible bodies are acknowledged, when further information may be requested. The trustees meet quarterly to consider appeals.

WHO TO APPLY TO Penelope Horne, Trustee, 44 Welbeck Street, London W1G 8DY *Tel.* 020 7486 0800 *Email* info@apperleylimited.co.uk

The Frank Litchfield Charitable Trust

CC NO 1038943 **ESTABLISHED** 1994

WHERE FUNDING CAN BE GIVEN Mostly in and around Cambridge.

WHO CAN BENEFIT Charitable organisations and projects. The trust aims to assist 'direct good'.

WHAT IS FUNDED General charitable purposes, particularly health and disability causes, helping disadvantaged and vulnerable people, older people and children and young people. Our research also suggests that support can be given to relieve distress of those involved in agriculture.

WHAT IS NOT FUNDED Campaigning and similar expenditure is not considered of direct benefit and therefore is unlikely to be funded.

TYPE OF GRANT Capital and core cost, projects delivering 'direct good'.

RANGE OF GRANTS £500 to £5,000.

SAMPLE GRANTS Cambridge Community Foundation (£10,000); Headway and Parkinson UK (£5,000 each); Tom's Trust (£4,000); Blind Veterans UK, Carers Trust and Maggies (£3,000 each); Camtrust and Hearing Dogs for the Deaf (£2,500 each); Autism Anglia and British Red Cross (£2,000 each); Centre 33 and SkillForce (£1,000 each); Willow (£500).

FINANCES *Year* 2015/16 *Income* £69,525 *Grants* £106,500 *Grants to organisations* £106,500 *Assets* £2,143,265

TRUSTEES Michael Womack; David Chater; Michael Hamilton.

OTHER INFORMATION The trust made 35 awards in 2015/16.

HOW TO APPLY Apply in writing to the correspondent. Note that the trust receives more applications each year than it is able to fund.

WHO TO APPLY TO Michael Womack, Trustee, 12 De Freville Avenue, Cambridge CB4 1HR *Tel.* 01223 358012 *Email* womack@btinternet.com

Littlefield Foundation (UK) Ltd

CC NO 1148909 **ESTABLISHED** 2012

WHERE FUNDING CAN BE GIVEN UK and the USA.

WHO CAN BENEFIT Charities and community groups.

WHAT IS FUNDED General charitable purposes.

SAMPLE GRANTS A list of beneficiaries was not available.

FINANCES *Year* 2015 *Income* £13,568 *Grants* £125,000 *Grants to organisations* £125,000

TRUSTEES Horace Joseph Leitch; Cathey Leitch; Jeffrey Brummette.

OTHER INFORMATION Registered in September 2012, the charity's objects are general charitable purposes. The trustees are American-born. Further research suggests that Cathey and Horace Leitch have previously supported the arts, particularly music, and have an interest in sailing. Due to the low income in 2015, there were no accounts to view on the Charity Commission's website.

HOW TO APPLY Apply in writing to the correspondent.

WHO TO APPLY TO The Trustees, c/o Withers LLP, 16 Old Bailey, London EC4M 7EG *Tel.* 020 7597 6257 *Fax* 020 7597 6543

The Charles Littlewood Hill Trust

CC NO 286350 **ESTABLISHED** 1978

WHERE FUNDING CAN BE GIVEN UK, with a preference for Nottinghamshire and Norfolk.

WHO CAN BENEFIT Charitable organisations; educational establishments; churches; community organisations.

WHAT IS FUNDED General charitable causes; social welfare; health and disability; armed forces; environment; education; religious activities; arts and culture.

WHAT IS NOT FUNDED Individuals; grants are seldom made for repairs of parish churches outside Nottinghamshire.

TYPE OF GRANT In practice unrestricted funding, including capital and core costs. Applications for starter finance are encouraged but grants are seldom made to endowment or capital funds.

RANGE OF GRANTS £1,000 to £10,000; usually £5,000 or less.
SAMPLE GRANTS Norwich Cathedral (£25,500); The Norfolk Churches Trust (£7,500); The Churches Conservation Trust (£6,500); Beaumond House Community Hospice, Nottingham Hospitals Charity, Nottinghamshire Wildlife Trust and The Base Community Trust (£5,000 each); Eating Matters and The Soldiers Charity – Nottinghamshire (£3,000 each); Cinema City Ltd and Literacy Volunteers in Nottinghamshire Schools (£2,500 each); How Hill Trust and Wild Things Ecological Education Collective (£2,000 each); Asthma UK, Broxtowe Women's Project, Carewatch in Nottingham, Childhood First, Cleft Lip and Palate Association, Dogs for the Disabled, Sense and YESU The People's Place (£1,000 each).
FINANCES *Year* 2015 *Income* £217,874 *Grants* £208,031 *Grants to organisations* £208,031 *Assets* £4,478,093
TRUSTEES Charles Barratt; Tim Farr; Nigel Savory; John Pears.
OTHER INFORMATION Grants of under £1,000 totalled £13,500 and are included in the grant total given here.
HOW TO APPLY Apply in writing to the correspondent, including the latest set of audited accounts, at least one month before trustees' meetings in March, July and November. Unsuccessful applications will not be notified.
WHO TO APPLY TO John Thompson, Trust Administrator, PO Box 10454, Nottingham NG5 0HQ *Tel.* 01476 552429 *Email* charles.hill@btinternet.com *Website* www.charleshill.org.uk

■ The Second Joseph Aaron Littman Foundation

CC NO 201892 **ESTABLISHED** 1961
WHERE FUNDING CAN BE GIVEN UK.
WHO CAN BENEFIT Registered charities only; educational, medical and religious bodies.
WHAT IS FUNDED General charitable purposes, with a special focus on Jewish causes, as well as academic and medical research and relief of poverty.
WHAT IS NOT FUNDED Individuals.
TYPE OF GRANT One-off and recurrent; core costs.
RANGE OF GRANTS Usually below £10,000.
SAMPLE GRANTS The Littman Library of Jewish Civilisation (£167,000); The Jerusalem Expressive Therapy Centre – Misholim (£7,500); Leo Baeck College UK (£5,000); Holocaust Educational Trust and University College London (£2,000 each); Fight for Sight and Institute of Polish Jewish Studies (£1,000 each). Awards below £1,000 totalled £4,600.
FINANCES *Year* 2014/15 *Income* £318,096 *Grants* £216,500 *Grants to organisations* £216,500 *Assets* £5,517,209
TRUSTEES Glenn Hurstfield; Colette Littman.
OTHER INFORMATION At the time of writing (June 2017) this was the latest information available – 2015/16 accounts were overdue at the Charity Commission. The foundation provides continuing substantial support to the Littman Library and distributed smaller grants to other charities.
HOW TO APPLY Apply in writing to the correspondent.
WHO TO APPLY TO Glenn Hurstfield, Trustee, Manor Farm, Mill Lane, Charlton Mackrell, Somerton, Somerset TA11 7BQ

■ The George John and Sheilah Livanos Charitable Trust

CC NO 1002279 **ESTABLISHED** 1985
WHERE FUNDING CAN BE GIVEN UK.
WHO CAN BENEFIT Registered charities; hospitals; hospices.
WHAT IS FUNDED General charitable purposes; health; disability; medical charities; maritime charities.
WHAT IS NOT FUNDED Individuals; non-registered charities.
TYPE OF GRANT One-off and recurring; capital grants.
RANGE OF GRANTS £500 to £52,000.
SAMPLE GRANTS Bletchley Park (£52,000); Burrswood and Gainsborough House (£50,000 each); Ekklesia Project Fakenham (£24,000); Bowel Disease Research Foundation, Breakthrough Breast Cancer, Diabetes UK, Disasters Emergency Committee, London Youth, One in a Million and Paul's Cancer Support Centre (£5,000 each); Whoopsadaisy (£3,300); Barnardo's and St Mungo's (£2,500 each); South East Cancer Help Centre and The Kiloran Trust (£2,000 each).
FINANCES *Year* 2015 *Income* £50,005 *Grants* £249,209 *Grants to organisations* £249,209 *Assets* £1,420,140
TRUSTEES Philip Harris; Timothy Cripps; Anthony Holmes.
OTHER INFORMATION There were 23 grants made.
HOW TO APPLY The annual report for 2015 states: 'Unsolicited applications are accepted, but the Trustees do receive a very high number of grant applications which, in line with the Trustees' grant making policy, are mostly unsuccessful. The Trustees prefer to make donations to charities whose work they have researched and which is in accordance with the aims and objectives of the charity for the year.'
WHO TO APPLY TO The Trustees, Gordon Dadds LLP, 6 Agar Street, London WC2N 4HN *Tel.* 020 7759 1682

■ Liverpool Charity and Voluntary Services (LCVS)

CC NO 223485 **ESTABLISHED** 1970
WHERE FUNDING CAN BE GIVEN Merseyside only.
WHO CAN BENEFIT Registered charities.
WHAT IS FUNDED General charitable purposes.
WHAT IS NOT FUNDED Non-registered charities; individuals. Applications from charities in successive years are not viewed favourably as are large building appeals or revenue expenditure. Specific exclusions may apply for different funds.
TYPE OF GRANT Capital costs; equipment funding.
SAMPLE GRANTS A list of beneficiaries was not available.
FINANCES *Year* 2015/16 *Income* £3,536,470 *Grants* £1,943,033 *Grants to organisations* £1,840,780 *Assets* £7,285,883
TRUSTEES Charles Feeny; Roger Morris; Prof. Hilary Russell; Christine Reeves; Heather Akehurst; Adeyinka Olushonde; Deborah Shackleton; Andrew Whitehead.
OTHER INFORMATION The charity acts in a similar manner to a community foundation, administrating the giving of much smaller charitable trusts. Comprehensive details of all of the grants programmes are available from the charity's website and details of new programmes or new funding rounds are posted as they come up. A total of £102,500 was given to individuals in 537 grants during the year.

HOW TO APPLY Application forms are available to download from the charity's website, together with criteria, guidelines and deadlines for each programme.
WHO TO APPLY TO Grants Team, 151 Dale Street, Liverpool L2 2AH *Tel.* 0151 227 5177 *Email* info@lcvs.org.uk *Website* www.lcvs.org.uk

■ Jack Livingstone Charitable Trust

CC NO 263473 **ESTABLISHED** 1971
WHERE FUNDING CAN BE GIVEN UK and worldwide, with a preference for Manchester area.
WHO CAN BENEFIT Registered charities. Preference is given to organisations benefitting Jewish people, at risk groups, and people who are ill, disadvantaged by poverty or socially isolated.
WHAT IS FUNDED General charitable purposes; Jewish causes.
TYPE OF GRANT One-off and recurrent.
RANGE OF GRANTS Up to £50,000; generally under £10,000.
SAMPLE GRANTS The Jerusalem Foundation and Manchester Jewish Museum (£50,000 each); Federation of Jewish Services (£25,000); Langdon FDN Patrons (£7,000); Community Security Trust and North Manchester Jewish Cemeteries (£6,000 each); J Roots Ltd (£5,000); Stockdales, Room to Rent, British Friends of Darche Noam and Bet Yishai, Daniel Shuv (£1,000 each).
FINANCES *Year* 2015/16 *Income* £146,319 *Grants* £189,197 *Grants to organisations* £189,197 *Assets* £1,994,952
TRUSTEES Janice Livingstone; Terence Livingstone; Brian White.
OTHER INFORMATION Grants of less than £1,000 totalled £13,302.
HOW TO APPLY Our research indicates that the trust does not respond to unsolicited applications.
WHO TO APPLY TO Janice Livingstone, Trustee, Westholme, The Springs, Bowdon, Altrincham, Cheshire WA14 3JH *Tel.* 0161 928 3232 *Email* jackandjan@btinternet.com

■ The Ian and Natalie Livingstone Charitable Trust

CC NO 1149025 **ESTABLISHED** 2012
WHERE FUNDING CAN BE GIVEN UK.
WHO CAN BENEFIT Registered charities.
WHAT IS FUNDED General charitable purposes, with a focus on organisations working with children and young people.
WHAT IS NOT FUNDED Individuals.
TYPE OF GRANT Revenue, capital or project expenditure.
RANGE OF GRANTS Up to £250,000.
SAMPLE GRANTS Great Ormond Street Hospital Children's Charity and The Mayor's Fund for London (£200,000 each); Norwood Ravenswood (£100,000); The Centre for Vision in the Developing World Charitable Foundation (£50,000).
FINANCES *Year* 2015/16 *Income* £566,124 *Grants* £600,000 *Grants to organisations* £600,000 *Assets* £106,396
TRUSTEES Ian Livingstone; Natalie Livingstone; Mark Levitt.
HOW TO APPLY Apply in writing to the correspondent.
WHO TO APPLY TO The Trustees, c/o Hazlems Fenton LLP, Palladium House, 1–4 Argyll Street, London W1F 7LD *Tel.* 020 7437 7666 *Email* info@hazlemsfenton.com

■ The Elaine and Angus Lloyd Charitable Trust

CC NO 237250 **ESTABLISHED** 1964
WHERE FUNDING CAN BE GIVEN UK, with a preference for Surrey, Kent and the south of England.
WHO CAN BENEFIT Individuals; local, regional and UK-wide organisations.
WHAT IS FUNDED A range of general charitable purposes; health and disability; individuals' education; children and young adults; at risk groups; people disadvantaged by poverty; socially isolated people.
TYPE OF GRANT Recurrent and one-off, some may be paid quarterly.
RANGE OF GRANTS Up to £20,000. Mostly around £1,000 to £2,000.
SAMPLE GRANTS What on Earth Foundation (£12,000); EHAS (£6,000); Rhema New Bible College (£4,000); Kingdom First Church (£3,000); Diabetes UK and Martha Trust (£2,000 each); 1st Glasgow The Boys' Brigade, Charlie Waller Memorial Trust and Wokingham Vineyard (£1,000 each). Grants of less than £1,000 totalled over £19,000.
FINANCES *Year* 2015/16 *Income* £106,537 *Grants* £102,000 *Grants to organisations* £96,950 *Assets* £2,907,298
TRUSTEES Angus Lloyd; John Gordon; James Lloyd; Philippa Smith; Virginia Best; Christopher Lloyd; Michael Craig-Cooper; Revd Richard Lloyd.
OTHER INFORMATION Three grants were given to individuals totalling £5,050 and 70 grants were awarded to organisations. Grants under £1,000 totalled over £19,000.
HOW TO APPLY Apply in writing to the correspondent. The trustees meet regularly to consider grants.
WHO TO APPLY TO Ross Badger, Hillier Hopkins LLP, Ground Floor, 45 Pall Mall, London SW1Y 5JG *Tel.* 020 7930 7797 *Email* ross.badger@hhllp.co.uk

■ The W. M. and B. W. Lloyd Trust

CC NO 503384 **ESTABLISHED** 1974
WHERE FUNDING CAN BE GIVEN The old borough of Darwin in Lancashire.
WHO CAN BENEFIT Individuals and organisations.
WHAT IS FUNDED A range of support is given for: individual emergencies and disasters; equipment for schools welfare; the advancement of education, medical science and provision of medical equipment and facilities; and the provision and improvement of public amenities.
TYPE OF GRANT One-off grants.
SAMPLE GRANTS Darwen Old People's Welfare, schools, churches, museums, Scouts, Guides and Brownies.
FINANCES *Year* 2015/16 *Income* £79,070 *Grants* £77,208 *Grants to organisations* £77,208 *Assets* £2,068,840
TRUSTEES John Nicholas Jacklin; Jason Slack; Dorothy Elizabeth Parsons; Felicity Watson.
OTHER INFORMATION The trust has five committees: emergency, education, social amenities, medical and T. P. Davies. Each committee considers requests specific to its areas of remit.
HOW TO APPLY Apply in writing to the correspondent. The trustees meet in March, June, July and December.
WHO TO APPLY TO John Nicholas Jacklin, Secretary and Trustee, Gorse Barn, Rock Lane, Tockholes, Darwen BB3 0LX *Tel.* 01254 771367 *Email* johnjacklin@homecall.co.uk

■ The Andrew Lloyd Webber Foundation

CC NO 1015648 **ESTABLISHED** 1992

WHERE FUNDING CAN BE GIVEN UK.

WHO CAN BENEFIT Registered charities; theatres; schools.

WHAT IS FUNDED Arts; culture; heritage.

WHAT IS NOT FUNDED The trustees are unlikely to support projects that: are for a pilot project; are for a one-off event, such as an arts festival or production of a play; ultimately profit a commercial organisation; are for the building of a new venue where other funding has not been obtained; are for the funding of a theatrical tour; are from an individual.

TYPE OF GRANT One-off and recurring.

RANGE OF GRANTS £5,000 to £50,000.

SAMPLE GRANTS Eton College (£78,000); The Brit School (£65,000); Historic England Angel Awards and Little Kids Rock (£50,000 each); Arts Educational Schools (£43,000); Royal Conservatoire of Scotland (£27,000); Wilton's Music Hall (£15,000); Scottish Opera (£10,000); Guilford School of Acting (£9,000); RADA (Royal Academy of Dramatic Art) (£8,100); Children's Hospice South West (£5,000).

FINANCES *Year* 2015 *Grants* £1,112,670 *Grants to organisations* £1,112,670 *Assets* £39,922,782

TRUSTEES Lady Madeleine Lloyd Webber; Dr Simon Thurley; Mark Wordsworth; Philip Freedman; Louise Fennell.

HOW TO APPLY Apply online through the foundation's website.

WHO TO APPLY TO Sarah Miller, Sydmonton Court Estate, Burghclere, Newbury, Berkshire RG20 9NJ *Tel.* 01635 278594 *Email* sarah@andrewlloydwebberfoundation.com *Website* www.andrewlloydwebberfoundation.com

■ Lloyds Bank Foundation for England and Wales

CC NO 327114 **ESTABLISHED** 1986

WHERE FUNDING CAN BE GIVEN England and Wales.

WHO CAN BENEFIT Small and medium-sized registered charities.

WHAT IS FUNDED Education and training; homelessness; domestic violence; refugees; people who have offended; carers; substance misusers; young people; people with disabilities; community development.

WHAT IS NOT FUNDED Organisations not registered with the Charity Commission; CICs; second- or third-tier organisations (unless there is evidence of direct services to individuals with multiple disadvantage) also known as infrastructure or umbrella organisations; hospitals, health authorities or hospices; rescue services; nurseries, pre-schools or playgroups; schools, colleges or universities; animal charities; charities working outside England and Wales. Grants are not given for: medical care or medical research; on-line or telephone advice services; events and short-term interventions including holidays, expeditions and trips; activities for which a statutory body is responsible; capital purchases or building work. This includes IT, building work, purchase of vehicles/equipment, etc.; environmental, arts based or sports activities; the promotion of religion; loan repayments; sponsorship or funding towards an appeal; retrospective work; evaluation work; professional qualifications such as ACCA; professional fundraisers or bid writers; redundancy payments. Further examples and clarifications of what will and will not be funded can be found on the foundation's website.

TYPE OF GRANT One-off for a specific project, core funding, two- or three-year funding. Also capital, recurring costs, running costs and salaries.

RANGE OF GRANTS Up to £1 million.

SAMPLE GRANTS SafeLives (£1 million); Women's Aid Federation of England (£674,000); Harrow Carers (£183,000); Bristol Refugee Rights, IDEAL Community Action Group and Synergy Theatre Project (£75,000 each); Mind in Furness (£70,000); NCVO (£49,000); Doncaster Housing for Young People (£39,000); Grange Day Centre, Open Doors International Language School and Ryedale Carers Support (£15,000 each).

FINANCES *Year* 2015 *Income* £13,826,000 *Grants* £18,077,000 *Grants to organisations* £18,077,000 *Assets* £26,409,000

TRUSTEES Paul Farmer; Dr Neil Wooding; James Garvey; Hilary Armstrong; Prof. Patricia Broadfoot; Helen Edwards; Baroness Rennie Fritchie; Philip Cliff; Catharine Cheetham; Joanna Harris; Lesley King Lewis; Dame Gillian Morgan.

OTHER INFORMATION During the year, 1,765 small and medium-sized charities were supported.

HOW TO APPLY Refer to the foundation's website for current information for details of the application procedure and upcoming deadlines.

WHO TO APPLY TO Paul Streets, Chief Executive, Pentagon House, 52–54 Southwark Street, London SE1 1UN *Tel.* 0370 411 1223 *Email* enquiries@lloydsbankfoundation.org.uk *Website* www.lloydsbankfoundation.org.uk

■ Lloyds Bank Foundation for the Channel Islands

CC NO 327113 **ESTABLISHED** 1986

WHERE FUNDING CAN BE GIVEN The Channel Islands.

WHO CAN BENEFIT Registered charities.

WHAT IS FUNDED The main aims of the foundation are to assist disadvantaged and people with disabilities and to promote social and community welfare within the Channel Islands. The foundation's current priorities are: creating positive opportunities for people with disabilities; family support; homelessness; prevention of substance misuse; the needs of carers challenging disadvantage and discrimination. Further detail is given on the website.

WHAT IS NOT FUNDED Organisations which are not registered charities; activities which are primarily the responsibility of the Insular authorities in the Islands or some other responsible body; activities which collect funds to give to other charities, individuals or other organisations; animal welfare; corporate subscription or membership of a charity; endowment funds; environment – conserving and protecting plants and animals, geography and scenery; expeditions or overseas travel; fabric appeals for places of worship; fundraising events or activities; hospitals and medical centres (except for projects which are clearly additional to statutory responsibilities); individuals, including students; loans or business finance; promotion of religion; schools and colleges (except for projects that will benefit students with disabilities and are clearly additional to statutory responsibilities); sponsorship or marketing appeals; international appeals – trustees may from time to time

consider a limited number of applications from UK-registered charities working abroad.
TYPE OF GRANT Projects; core costs; salaries for up to three years; staff training and development.
RANGE OF GRANTS £500 to £90,000.
SAMPLE GRANTS Brighter Futures (£90,000); Families in Recovery Trust (£70,000) Jersey Mencap (£50,000); SAFER (£45,000); Autism Guernsey (£37,000); Guernsey Employment Trust (£29,000); Caesarea Association (£25,000); Jersey Citizens Advice (£20,000); Jersey Scout Association (£15,000); Offenders Deposit Assistance Scheme (£12,000); Guernsey Disability Alliance (£2,000); Creative Learning in Prison (£1,000); Wigwam (£500).
FINANCES *Year* 2015/16 *Income* £545,700 *Grants* £758,900 *Grants to organisations* £758,900 *Assets* £1,117,912
TRUSTEES Kathryn Le Quesne; Simon Howitt; Sarah Bamford; Timothy Cooke; Andrew Dann; David Hodgetts; Michael Starkey; Alison Le Feuvre; Philip Henwood.
OTHER INFORMATION The foundation also provides matched funding for the fundraising efforts of employees of Lloyds Banking Group in the Channel Islands. The grants were divided into three categories – Jersey (£355,500); Guernsey (£348,500); matched giving (£55,000).
HOW TO APPLY Application forms and guidelines are provided on the foundation's website. Applicants must contact the Executive Director to discuss an application prior to submitting it. The trustees meet three times a year to consider applications; dates are posted on the website.
WHO TO APPLY TO Jo Le Poidevin, Executive Director, Sarnia House, Le Truchot, St Peter Port, Guernsey GY1 4EF *Tel.* 01481 706360 *Email* jlepoidevin@lloydsbankfoundation.org.uk *Website* www.lloydsbankfoundationci.org.uk/HowToApply

■ Lloyd's Charities Trust

CC NO 207232 **ESTABLISHED** 1953
WHERE FUNDING CAN BE GIVEN UK, with particular interest in East London.
WHO CAN BENEFIT Charitable organisations.
WHAT IS FUNDED Disasters and emergencies and humanitarian work; disadvantaged communities in London; education, training, employment and enterprise; general charitable purposes.
TYPE OF GRANT One-off; recurrent; project costs; bursaries.
RANGE OF GRANTS Up to £100,000.
SAMPLE GRANTS A list of beneficiaries was not available.
FINANCES *Year* 2015 *Income* £534,808 *Grants* £624,108 *Grants to organisations* £624,108 *Assets* £2,921,789
TRUSTEES Graham Clarke; Chris Harman; Vicky Mirfin; Neil Smith; Victoria Carter; David Ibeson; Simon Beale; David Harris; Karen Green; Andrew Brooks.
OTHER INFORMATION Grants during the year were distributed in the following categories: Lloyd's Community Programmes (£167,000); Lloyd's Education Fund (£101,000); Ready to Respond (£100,000); Bromley By Bow Centre and The Mayors Fund for London (£80,000 each); Lloyd's Market Charity Awards (£64,000 given in a series of £2,000 donations to nominated charities).
HOW TO APPLY Lloyd's Charities Trust makes ad hoc donations; however, the majority of funds are committed to supporting the partnership charities the trust works with. Details of how to apply for the Lloyd's Market Charity Awards will be posted on the website at the relevant time – for further details contact the correspondent.
WHO TO APPLY TO Suzanna Nagle, Secretary, Lloyd's of London, Lloyd's Building, 1 Lime Street, London EC3M 7HA *Tel.* 020 7327 6144 *Email* suzanna.nagle@lloyds.com or communityaffairs@lloyds.com *Website* www.lloyds.com/lct

■ Lloyd's Register Foundation

CC NO 1145988 **ESTABLISHED** 2012
WHERE FUNDING CAN BE GIVEN Worldwide.
WHO CAN BENEFIT Universities and research institutes.
WHAT IS FUNDED Engineering-related education, research, science and technology.
WHAT IS NOT FUNDED Individuals; capital works; infrastructure.
TYPE OF GRANT Research funding including tuition costs and employment costs.
RANGE OF GRANTS £3,000 to £10 million.
SAMPLE GRANTS The Alan Turing Institute (£10 million); RNLI (£1 million); University of Birmingham (£702,000); Royal Academy of Engineering (£499,000); Educational Volunteers Foundation of Turkey (£132,000); Imperial College London (£75,000); Royal College of Art (£50,000); Blue Marine Foundation (£20,000); Children's Radio UK (£15,000); Global Young Scientists Summit (£3,000).
FINANCES *Year* 2015/16 *Income* £29,170,000 *Grants* £31,931,000 *Grants to organisations* £31,931,000 *Assets* £247,180,000
TRUSTEES Carol Sergeant; Ron Henderson; Sir Brian Bender; Lambros Varnavides; Thomas Thune Andersen; Rosemary Martin.
OTHER INFORMATION The foundation made grants to 35 institutions during the year.
HOW TO APPLY Applicants should read the guidance notes and complete a proposal form which are both available on the foundation's website. The website also details the latest calls for research funding proposals and application deadline dates. Applications for over £250,000 are considered at quarterly board meetings; all other applications are considered monthly.
WHO TO APPLY TO Michelle Davies, Company Secretary, 71 Fenchurch Street, London EC3M 4BS *Tel.* 020 7709 9166 *Email* michelle.davies@lr.org *Website* www.lrfoundation.org.uk

■ Lloyds TSB Foundation for Scotland

SC NO SC009481 **ESTABLISHED** 1986
WHERE FUNDING CAN BE GIVEN Scotland and overseas.
WHO CAN BENEFIT Charities registered in Scotland **only**; grassroots organisations providing support to the Scottish community and enabling people, primarily those disadvantaged and in need, to become active members of society and improve their quality of life.
WHAT IS FUNDED Disadvantaged individuals; families; social isolation; marginalised people; substance abuse; disability and health; older people; homelessness; equality and rights; development of young people.
WHAT IS NOT FUNDED Each programme has its own criteria. Refer to the foundation's website for more information.
TYPE OF GRANT One-off; up to one year under Henry Duncan Awards and up to three years under the

Partnership Drugs Initiative; revenue and capital funding; core activities; running costs; projects; salaries; start-up expenditure; feasibility studies, research.

SAMPLE GRANTS Clued Up Project (£396,000); Bellshill and Mossend YMCA (£108,500); Stable Life (£34,000); Voluntary Action Orkney (£13,000); Town Break SCIO (£7,000); Reidvale Adventure Play Association Ltd (£6,00); The Well Multi-Cultural Advice Centre (£5,500); Headway Highland (£5,000); Hidden Gardens Trust and Stillbirth and Neonatal Death Society Lothians (£4,500 each); Sheddocksley Baptist Church (£2,000); Relationships Scotland (£1,800); Edinburgh Chinese Elderly Support Association (£1,000); Scottish Huntington's Association – Glasgow South Branch (£700).

FINANCES *Year* 2015 *Income* £2,391,000 *Grants* £2,703,000 *Grants to organisations* £2,703,000 *Assets* £5,180,000

TRUSTEES Tim Hall; Prof. Sandy Cameron; Charles Abram; Prof. Sir John Arbuthnott; Joy Barlow; Trevor Civval; Tom Halpin; Jacqui Low; Jane Mackie; David Urch.

OTHER INFORMATION The foundation is one of four Lloyds Banking Group charities, covering England and Wales, Scotland, Northern Ireland and the Channel Islands.

HOW TO APPLY Application forms for all programmes, complete with comprehensive guidance notes and application deadlines, are available from the foundation. These can be requested by telephone, by email, or online through its website. Foundation staff are always willing to provide additional help.

WHO TO APPLY TO Connie Williamson, Grants Manager, Riverside House, 502 Gorgie Road, Edinburgh EH11 3AF *Tel.* 0131 444 4020 *Email* enquiries@ltsbfoundationforscotland.org.uk *Website* www.ltsbfoundationforscotland.org.uk

■ Localtrent Ltd

CC NO 326329 **ESTABLISHED** 1982

WHERE FUNDING CAN BE GIVEN UK, with some preference for Manchester.

WHO CAN BENEFIT Charities and educational or religious institutions.

WHAT IS FUNDED Advancement of the Orthodox Jewish faith. The trustees will consider applications from organisations concerned with Orthodox Jewish faith education and also the relief of poverty.

SAMPLE GRANTS Asser Bishvil (£138,100); Congregation Beth Medrash Chemed (£42,000); Chasdei Yoel Charitable Trust (£41,500); Zoreia Zedokos (£26,500); Teshuvoh Tefilloh Tzedokoh (£26,000); Beis Rochel School (£4,000).

FINANCES *Year* 2015/16 *Income* £470,811 *Grants* £376,864 *Grants to organisations* £376,864 *Assets* £1,391,790

TRUSTEES Hyman Weiss; Mina Weiss; Philip Weiss; Zisel Weiss; Bernardin Weiss; Yocheved Weiss.

HOW TO APPLY Apply in writing to the correspondent.

WHO TO APPLY TO Alex Kahan, Independent Examiner, Lopian Gross Barnett and Co., 6th Floor, Cardinal House, 20 St Mary's Parsonage, Manchester M3 2LG *Tel.* 0161 832 8721

■ The Locker Foundation

CC NO 264180 **ESTABLISHED** 1966

WHERE FUNDING CAN BE GIVEN UK and Israel.

WHO CAN BENEFIT Jewish charities; synagogues; educational establishments.

WHAT IS FUNDED General charitable purposes with preference for the welfare of people who are ill and those with disabilities and the teaching of the Jewish religion.

RANGE OF GRANTS £200 to £76,000.

SAMPLE GRANTS Kahal Chassidim Bobov (£76,000); St John's Wood Synagogue (£62,000); Association for the Wellbeing of Israel's Soldiers (£51,000); Tikva Children's Home (£45,000); Chai Cancer Care (£25,000); Community Security Trust (£17,000); World Jewish Relief (£12,200); Jewish Lads' and Girls' Brigade (£5,000); The Shalom Foundation of the Zionist Federation (£1,500); Chickenshed Theatre (£200).

FINANCES *Year* 2015/16 *Income* £1,189,535 *Grants* £627,917 *Grants to organisations* £627,917 *Assets* £7,382,930

TRUSTEES Susanna Segal; Irving Carter; Malcolm Carter.

OTHER INFORMATION Grants were made to 29 organisations during the year.

HOW TO APPLY Apply in writing to the correspondent. Decisions must be made by a unanimous agreement by the trustees.

WHO TO APPLY TO Irving Carter, Trustee, 9 Neville Drive, London N2 0QS *Tel.* 020 8455 9280 *Email* brian@levyscharteredaccountants.co.uk

■ The Lockwood Charitable Foundation

CC NO 1123272 **ESTABLISHED** 2008

WHERE FUNDING CAN BE GIVEN England and Wales.

WHO CAN BENEFIT Registered charities.

WHAT IS FUNDED General charitable purposes.

SAMPLE GRANTS Missing People (£86,000); Willow (£75,000); Carers UK (£65,000); Sense (£52,000); North London Cares (£50,000); Brixton Soup Kitchen (£39,000); Cherry Trees (£35,000); Build It International (£25,000); The October Club (£20,000).

FINANCES *Year* 2015/16 *Income* £461,097 *Grants* £628,402 *Grants to organisations* £628,402 *Assets* £5,607,720

TRUSTEES Richard Lockwood; Lesley Lockwood; Dr Rebecca Lockwood.

HOW TO APPLY Apply in writing to the correspondent.

WHO TO APPLY TO Richard Lockwood, The Tithe Barn, The Avenue, Compton, Guildford, Surrey GU3 1JW

■ Loftus Charitable Trust

CC NO 297664 **ESTABLISHED** 1987

WHERE FUNDING CAN BE GIVEN UK and overseas.

WHO CAN BENEFIT Jewish organisations; religious and educational institutions.

WHAT IS FUNDED Jewish causes, primarily social welfare, Jewish education and the advancement of Judaism.

RANGE OF GRANTS Typically less than £5,000.

SAMPLE GRANTS Jewish Care (£1.5 million in three grants); South Hampstead Charitable Trust (£150,000); Chai Cancer (£5,000); Carers Trust and The Jewish Leadership Council (£2,500 each); Laniado Hospital Israel (£1,250); British Friends of Hebrew University, Jewish Learning Exchange and Western Marble Arch Synagogue (£1,000 each).

FINANCES *Year* 2015/16 *Income* £1,837,850 *Grants* £1,904,152 *Grants to organisations* £1,904,152 *Assets* £130,382

TRUSTEES Andrew Loftus; Anthony Loftus; Richard Loftus.

OTHER INFORMATION There were 94 grants made to organisations during the year.

HOW TO APPLY The trustees prefer to invite applications rather than considering unsolicited applications. The annual report for 2015/16 states: 'The trustees meet regularly to consider what grants they will make and to review any feedback they have received. Nominations for grants are elicited by formal and informal means. The trustees travel widely in the UK and abroad and use knowledge gained to support the objects of the Trust and to inform grant-making. Though the trustees make some grants with no formal application, they normally ask invited organisations to submit a formal application saying how the funds would be used and what would be achieved. The trustees have a policy, which is communicated to all beneficiaries, that they make grants with no guarantees of future funding.'

WHO TO APPLY TO Anthony Loftus, Trustee, 55 Blandford Street, Marylebone, London W1U 7HW *Tel.* 020 7604 5900 *Email* post@rhodesandrhodes.com

■ The Lolev Charitable Trust

CC NO 326249 **ESTABLISHED** 1982

WHERE FUNDING CAN BE GIVEN UK; Hackney and the surrounding area.

WHO CAN BENEFIT Charitable organisations; individuals.

WHAT IS FUNDED Orthodox Jewish causes; education; religion; health.

TYPE OF GRANT General running costs.

SAMPLE GRANTS A list of beneficiaries was not included in the accounts.

FINANCES *Year* 2015 *Income* £7,100,229 *Grants* £7,002,509 *Grants to organisations* £413,275 *Assets* £90,632

TRUSTEES Abraham Tager; Eve Tager; Michael Tager.

OTHER INFORMATION Awards to organisations were made in the following categories: religious education (£132,000); poor and needy (£129,000); schools – including repairs (£99,000); medical (£53,000). The majority of awards were given to individuals (£6.6 million).

HOW TO APPLY Apply in writing to the correspondent. The annual report for 2015/16 states: 'Applications by individuals must be accompanied by a letter of recommendation by the applicant's minister or other known religious leader. In the case of applications by charities the collecting agent's references are verified by special agency, unless known to the trustees. Assistance is given according to circumstances and available finance.'

WHO TO APPLY TO Abraham Tager, Trustee, 14A Gilda Crescent, London N16 6JP *Tel.* 020 8806 3457

■ The Joyce Lomax Bullock Charitable Trust

CC NO 1109911 **ESTABLISHED** 2005

WHERE FUNDING CAN BE GIVEN Worldwide.

WHO CAN BENEFIT Registered charities.

WHAT IS FUNDED General charitable purposes.

SAMPLE GRANTS Age UK; Cancer Research UK; Guide Dogs For The Blind; IWK Health Centre Foundation; Perennial; RAF Benevolent Fund; Royal Commonwealth Society; The National Trust; The Royal British Legion; Sightsavers International. Each organisation received £8,050 in two grants.

FINANCES *Year* 2015/16 *Income* £1,018,471 *Grants* £72,450 *Grants to organisations* £72,450 *Assets* £3,151,061

TRUSTEE HSBC. Trust Company (UK) Ltd.

OTHER INFORMATION There were a total of 20 awards made to ten organisations.

HOW TO APPLY Apply in writing to the correspondent; however, note that 'grants are awarded at the discretion of the Trustee but are generally in accordance with a letter of wishes provided by the late Joyce Lomax Bullock'. This seems to dictate that a set list of charities are awarded grants each year.

WHO TO APPLY TO Trust Manager, HSBC Trust Company UK Ltd, Second Floor, 1 The Forum, Parkway, Whiteley, FAREHAM PO15 7PA *Tel.* 023 8072 3344

■ Trust for London

CC NO 205629 **ESTABLISHED** 2004

WHERE FUNDING CAN BE GIVEN The Metropolitan Police District of London and the City of London.

WHO CAN BENEFIT Voluntary, community and other not-for-profit organisations; registered charities; bodies providing advice, information and advocacy; educational and training institutions; new initiatives; shelters and re-settlement homes; CICs and social enterprises. While most recipients are registered charities this is not a requirement. Priority is given to smaller and medium-sized organisations with an income of under £1 million.

WHAT IS FUNDED Community development and social welfare. Current priorities are: employment; advice; social justice; violence; supporting small groups.

WHAT IS NOT FUNDED Proposals which do not benefit Londoners; direct replacement or subsidising of statutory funding (including contracts); work that is the primary responsibility of statutory funders, such as local and central government and health authorities; individuals; appeals on behalf of individuals; mainstream educational activity, including schools; medical purposes, including hospitals and hospices; the promotion of religion; umbrella bodies seeking to distribute grants on behalf of the charity; work that has already taken place; general appeals; large capital appeals (including buildings and minibuses); from applicants who have been rejected by the charity in the last six months; large national charities which enjoy widespread support; work that takes place in schools during school hours; where organisations have significant unrestricted reserves, including those that are designated (generally up to six months expenditure is normally acceptable); where organisations are in serious financial deficit.

TYPE OF GRANT Core and management costs; capital expenditure; work that aims to change policy; one-off and multi-year funding; unrestricted; contracts.

RANGE OF GRANTS £5,000 to £300,000.

SAMPLE GRANTS ClientEarth (£300,000); Anti-Trafficking and Labour Exploitation Unit (£102,000); ECPAT UK (End Child Prostitution, Child Pornography and Child Trafficking) (£90,000); Kurdish and Middle Eastern Women's Organisation in Britain (£72,000); Focus on Labour Exploitation and UK Lesbian and Gay Immigration Group (£50,000 each); Institute for Public Policy Research (£43,000); Justice for Domestic Workers (£30,000); Barnet Lone Parent Centre (£25,000); Forest Gate Community Garden (£15,000); Act Up Newham Theatre Group CIC (£5,000).

FINANCES *Year* 2015 *Income* £9,023,725 *Grants* £11,590,126 *Grants to organisations* £11,590,126 *Assets* £294,770,618

TRUSTEE Trust for London Trustee Board.

OTHER INFORMATION The charity is made up of three funds: Central Fund 'which aims to tackle poverty and inequality'; City Church Fund 'for the advancement of religion'; and Trust for London Common Investment Fund 'to pool the investments of the other two funds'. The grant total consists of almost £7 million given through The Central Fund and £4.6 million through The City Churches Fund. Grants were allocated as follows: social justice (31%); advice (27%); employment (11%); small groups (13%); special initiatives (6%); violence (5%); exceptional cases (4%); Strategic Legal Fund (3%). About 130 groups are funded each year.

HOW TO APPLY Applications must be made using an online form. The charity's website gives full details and extensive guidelines. These should cover all possible areas but if you are unclear about something do not hesitate to get in touch with the charity via phone. The consideration process can take approximately four and a half months from the closing date for successful applicants. Unsuccessful applicants can re-apply after 12 months following the rejection.

WHO TO APPLY TO Mubin Haq, Director of Policy and Grants, 6–9 Middle Street, London EC1A 7PH *Tel.* 020 7606 6145 *Email* info@trustforlondon.org.uk *Website* www.trustforlondon.org.uk

■ London Catalyst

CC NO 1066739 **ESTABLISHED** 1872

WHERE FUNDING CAN BE GIVEN Greater London, within the boundaries of the M25.

WHO CAN BENEFIT Charities and non-profit organisations; hospitals, homes and medical charities outside the NHS who are also registered charities; NHS hospitals throughout London; social work teams; individuals in need.

WHAT IS FUNDED Health inequalities and community projects in areas of social deprivation; relief of poverty; improvement of health and well-being of local people; raising awareness of the needs of people who are in poverty and suffer from illnesses.

WHAT IS NOT FUNDED General appeals; charities with an income over £1 million; hospitals and homes within the NHS (except Samaritan Grants); hospital league of friends for NHS and independent hospitals; government departments; profitable organisations.

TYPE OF GRANT Small awards; 'any reasonable and appropriate project cost, including salaries, training, volunteer expenses, management, supervision and evaluation costs; limited 'catalytic' project-related grants are favoured.

RANGE OF GRANTS £200 to £15,000.

SAMPLE GRANTS Lift People (£15,000); Passage 2000 (£10,000); Housing Justice (£7,000); Kingston Churches Action for Housing and Women's Therapy Centre (£5,000 each); Lasa and Young Roots (£3,000 each); Mildmay Hospital (£2,000); The Manna (£1,500); Alternatives Trust East London, Pecan and Westminster Abbey (£1,000 each); Alone in London (£500).

FINANCES *Year* 2015 *Income* £344,327 *Grants* £367,808 *Grants to organisations* £367,808 *Assets* £11,828,159

TRUSTEES Mark Palframan; Philippe Granger; Zoe Camp; Revd Adrian McKenna-Whyte; Margaret Elliott; Dr Muhammad Bari; Dr Ruth Kosmin; Andrew Davidson; Duncan McLaggan; Dr Sarah Divall.

OTHER INFORMATION There were 138 awards to organisations and projects.

HOW TO APPLY Application forms and helpful guidance can be downloaded from the charity's website or requested by phone or letter. Applications and other grant enquiries are acceptable via email. All applications are reviewed against eligibility criteria and then considered by the grants scrutiny committee before presenting to the trustees for approval. The trustees meet every three months, normally in February, June, September and December. Application should be received six weeks in advance to a meeting. The Grants Administrator of the charity is Mr Ian Baker.

WHO TO APPLY TO Victor Wilmott, Director and Company Secretary, 45 Westminster Bridge Road, London SE1 7JB *Tel.* 020 3828 4204 *Email* london.catalyst@peabody.org.uk *Website* www.londoncatalyst.org.uk

■ The London Community Foundation (LCF)

CC NO 1091263 **ESTABLISHED** 2002

WHERE FUNDING CAN BE GIVEN The London boroughs including the City of London.

WHO CAN BENEFIT Charities and community groups; small and medium-sized organisations; registered charities; social enterprises; CICs; companies limited by guarantee without share capital; faith groups; tenants and residents organisations; Friends of Schools; PTAs.

WHAT IS FUNDED Community projects including environmental groups, employment schemes, mentoring for young people, homeless shelters, day centres for older people, activities supporting particularly disadvantaged and marginalised communities, tackling challenging issues, such as domestic violence, honour killing or gang violence, relief of poverty, homelessness and social isolation.

WHAT IS NOT FUNDED Political groups; activities which promote religion (faith groups may be assisted). Specific criteria may apply for different funds, check the foundation's website for further information.

TYPE OF GRANT Unrestricted funding, including capital and core costs, feasibility studies, project, running costs, salaries and start-up costs; one-off or up to two years.

RANGE OF GRANTS £500 to £85,000.

SAMPLE GRANTS Upper Norwood Library Trust (£85,000); Faith Matters (£58,500); Young Lambeth Co-op Ltd (£32,000); Carers Bromley (£15,000); Liberty Credit Union (£10,000); Barbara Melunsky Refugee Youth Agency (£8,000); Bermondsey Community Kitchen (£4,800); Iranian and Kurdish Women's Right Organisation (£4,000); Orpington Football Club (£3,000); Westmeria Counselling Services (£2,500); Doorstep Homeless Families Project (£680).

FINANCES *Year* 2015/16 *Income* £7,761,000 *Grants* £5,929,000 *Grants to organisations* £5,808,000 *Assets* £21,456,000

TRUSTEES Gaynor Humphreys; William Moore; Sanjay Mazumder; Martin Richards; Francis Salway; Nicholas Reid; Paul Cattermull; Christopher Samuel; Rosanna Machado.

OTHER INFORMATION The foundation manages and distributes funds on behalf of several donors, including companies, individuals and government programmes and is able to offer a number of grant programmes which cover different areas and types of activity, refer to the website for more details. During the year a total of 1,033 awards were made, including 784 to organisations and 249 to individuals (£121,000).

HOW TO APPLY As the foundation offers funds on behalf of different donors, you may apply to each and every programme for which your group is eligible. The criteria will vary for each grant programme, so be sure to read the guidance carefully. The foundation looks for the following in an application: demonstration of need; sound governance; sound financial management; sound project planning; good partnership working; strong capacity and ability to deliver. Application forms, guidance notes and deadlines specific to each programme are available from the foundation and/or its website. The foundation encourages you to contact them to discuss your application before you apply.

WHO TO APPLY TO Megan Chidlow, Finance and Operations Director, Unit 7, Piano House, 9 Brighton Terrace, London SW9 8DJ *Tel.* 020 7582 5117 *Email* info@londoncf.org.uk *Website* www.londoncf.org.uk

■ London Housing Foundation Ltd (LHF)

CC NO 270178 **ESTABLISHED** 1975

WHERE FUNDING CAN BE GIVEN Principally, albeit not exclusively, Greater London.

WHO CAN BENEFIT Voluntary bodies; charities; housing and social care organisations. Projects 'must help people who are, have been, or are at risk of becoming homeless'.

WHAT IS FUNDED Housing and homelessness, particularly among single people. Aside from its core projects, the foundation's grant strategy includes the following categories: responsive grants towards 'sector collaboration and consolidation' or 'proof of concept and early stage development' homelessness in other countries, and sharing knowledge and practice with agencies in London and the UK, with a particular focus on the impacts of migration on homelessness in Europe; very occasionally, the foundation funds research, on a proactive basis.

TYPE OF GRANT Capital and revenue costs; project funding; research.

RANGE OF GRANTS £4,000 to £150,000.

SAMPLE GRANTS PACT (£146,000); De Paul International (£100,000); Housing For Women (£35,000); London Councils (£33,000); Hestia (£30,000); Safer London (£25,000); Union Chapel (£22,500); Lambeth Law Centre (£15,000); Providence Row (£12,400); Evolve (£10,900); London Network of Midwives (£5,000); Romania Homeless Agencies (£4,200).

FINANCES *Year* 2015/16 *Income* £707,693 *Grants* £463,963 *Grants to organisations* £463,963 *Assets* £15,438,470

TRUSTEES Simon Dow; Ian Brady; Donald Wood; John Stebbing; Jeremy Swain; Derek Joseph; Clare Miller; Eleanor Stringer; Victoria Rayner.

OTHER INFORMATION Grants in 2015/16 were categorised as follows: agency support (£248,000); criminal justice system interface (£146,000); organisational strengthening (£55,500); research and special grants (£14,200).

HOW TO APPLY Applicants are asked to complete a short form on the foundation's website detailing their project idea. The foundation will then follow this up with the applicant.

WHO TO APPLY TO Derek Joseph, 57A Great Suffolk Street, London SE1 0BB *Tel.* 020 7934 0177 *Fax* 020 7934 0179 *Email* jane.woolley@lhf.org.uk *Website* lhf.org.uk/programmes-and-grants

■ London Legal Support Trust (LLST)

CC NO 1101906 **ESTABLISHED** 2004

WHERE FUNDING CAN BE GIVEN London and the Home Counties.

WHO CAN BENEFIT Voluntary sector legal agencies in London and the Home Counties that employ solicitors or retain the services of solicitors as volunteers to provide free legal advice to poor or disadvantaged members the public and network organisations that support such agencies.

WHAT IS FUNDED Organisations providing free legal services. There are two grant programmes: Centres of Excellence, which provides funding and support for legal advice organisations; and Small Grants scheme, which assists charities that provide free legal advice (including pro bono help). Through the Small Grants scheme awards can be made towards: supporting new pro bono surgeries; 'keeping the doors open' for surgeries needing time to become sustainable; capital costs and capacity building to improve sustainability; development of new legal advice agencies where none exist.

WHAT IS NOT FUNDED Organisations providing general or welfare/debt advice only as opposed to specialist legal advice.

TYPE OF GRANT Small, one-off grants; core grant and support through Centres of Excellence scheme; facilities to raise funds at LLST events; pro bono support.

RANGE OF GRANTS £25 to £32,000.

SAMPLE GRANTS Anti Trafficking and Labour Exploitation Unit (ATLEU) (£32,000); Greenwich Housing Rights (£29,000); Freedom from Torture (£25,500); Hackney Law Centre (£23,000); Asylum Support Appeals Project (£21,000); Barnet Citizens Advice (£17,000); North Kensington Law Centre (£16,300); Help4Lips (£13,000); Public Concern at Work (£7,900); Toynbee Hall (£4,100); Rights of Women (£1,000); Pro Bono Community (£25).

FINANCES *Year* 2015 *Income* £1,128,912 *Grants* £1,029,379 *Grants to organisations* £1,029,379 *Assets* £252,412

TRUSTEES Richard Dyton; Marc Sosnow; Peter Gardner; Graham Huntley; Steve Hynes; Joy Julien; Jeremy Thomas; Emma Turnbull; Amanda Illing; Jessica Clark; Katherine Pasfield; Rodger Pressland; Alistair Woodland.

HOW TO APPLY Application forms for Small Grants can be downloaded from the trust's website together with criteria and guidelines. The deadline for 2017 is 15 October. If you would like to participate in the Centres of Excellence scheme get in touch with the trust and ask to be added to the waiting list. The process is explained in detail on the website.

WHO TO APPLY TO Natalia Rymaszewska, National Pro Bono Centre, 48 Chancery Lane, London WC2A 1JF *Tel.* 020 3088 3656 *Email* grants@llst.org.uk *Website* www.londonlegalsupporttrust.org.uk/grants

■ Inner London Magistrates Court's Poor Box and Feeder Charity

CC NO 1046214 **ESTABLISHED** 1995
WHERE FUNDING CAN BE GIVEN Inner London.
WHO CAN BENEFIT Individuals and organisations.
WHAT IS FUNDED Social welfare; relief of need, hardship or distress.
WHAT IS NOT FUNDED Direct relief of rates, taxes or other public funds.
RANGE OF GRANTS £3,000 to £10,000.
SAMPLE GRANTS Centrepoint (£10,000); The Passage and West London Day Centre (£6,000 each); Clean Break, Inside Out and The Salvation Army (£5,000 each); Refuge and Spitalfields Crypt Trust (£4,000 each); 999 Club (£3,000).
FINANCES *Year* 2015/16 *Income* £167,191 *Grants* £75,000 *Grants to organisations* £75,000 *Assets* £4,054,033
TRUSTEES Jane Richardson; Kevin Griffiths; Quentin Purdy; Howard Riddle; Richard Kozak; Nicholas Evans.
OTHER INFORMATION Grants were made to 14 organisations during the year.
HOW TO APPLY Apply in writing to the correspondent. The following was taken from the annual report for 2015/16: 'The trustees invite applications for grants from the courts themselves, the probation services and organisations involved in identifying and relieving need and hardship suffered in prison. The trustees are also aware that the needs and hardship of those who come into contact with the courts are often associated with homelessness, substance misuse, domestic violence and poverty and applications are invited from organisations which provide relief in those areas specifically to beneficiaries in the London region. The trustees do not commit to repeat or renew a relief grant on any occasion.'
WHO TO APPLY TO Paula Carter, City of Westminster Court, 7th Floor 65 Romney Street, London SW1P 3RD *Tel.* 020 7805 1132 *Email* ilmcpbf@btinternet.com

■ The London Marathon Charitable Trust Ltd

CC NO 283813 **ESTABLISHED** 1981
WHERE FUNDING CAN BE GIVEN London and any area where London Marathon stages an event (South Northamptonshire, Aylesbury Vale and Surrey).
WHO CAN BENEFIT Charitable organisations involved with sports, recreation and leisure; educational establishments; local groups; clubs; charities.
WHAT IS FUNDED Sports; recreation and leisure activities.
WHAT IS NOT FUNDED Exclusive clubs, unless the facility is available for regular public use; recurring or revenue costs; individuals.
TYPE OF GRANT One-off; project costs; equipment; service delivery.
RANGE OF GRANTS £5,800 to £500,000.
SAMPLE GRANTS Greenhouse Sports Ltd (£500,000); City YMCA London (£250,000); Girlguiding Surrey East and Lea Rowing Club (£100,000 each); The Botany Bay Cricket Club (£50,000); The Peabody trust (£45,000); Wheels for Wellbeing (£20,500); Mickleham Children's Playground Association (£20,000); North Dulwich Lawn Tennis Club (£19,500); Guildford Archery Club (£14,500); London Borough of Southwark (£5,800).
FINANCES *Year* 2015/16 *Income* £7,150,184 *Grants* £3,248,445 *Grants to organisations* £3,248,445 *Assets* £8,638,198
TRUSTEES John Austin; John Disley; Sir Rodney Walker; John Bryant; Simon Cooper; John Spurlin; Ruth Dombey; Peter King; Charles Johnston; Edmond Warner; Charles Reed; Alan Pascoe.
OTHER INFORMATION The trust has no connection to the fundraising efforts of the individuals involved in the race, who raise over £40 million each year for their chosen good causes. During the year, one interest-free loan was made to a charity for £200,000; and a further 45 grants were made to organisations.
HOW TO APPLY Applications can be made online through the trust's website. Full details of application process can be found on the 'How to apply' page of the website. Applications can now be submitted regularly throughout the year and the trustees meet quarterly to make funding decisions. Check the website for the latest deadline dates for the Major Capital Grants programme. Note that this is a two-stage application process and applicants invited to stage two will have 12 months in which to complete their detailed application. The trust has a very helpful FAQs page on its website and welcomes queries from potential applicants.
WHO TO APPLY TO Sarah Ridley, Chief Grants Officer/ Secretary, Marathon House, 115 Southwark Street, London SE1 0JF *Tel.* 020 7902 0200 (option 6) *Email* info@lmct.org.uk *Website* www.lmct.org.uk

■ The William and Katherine Longman Trust

CC NO 800785 **ESTABLISHED** 1988
WHERE FUNDING CAN BE GIVEN UK.
WHO CAN BENEFIT Registered charities.
WHAT IS FUNDED General charitable purposes.
WHAT IS NOT FUNDED Grants are only made to registered charities.
TYPE OF GRANT One-off and recurrent.
RANGE OF GRANTS £1,000 to £30,000.
SAMPLE GRANTS Vanessa Grant Trust (£30,000); Chelsea Festival and World Child Cancer Fund (£20,000 each); Care (£12,000); Hope Education Trust and RADA (Royal Academy of Dramatic Art) (£10,000 each); Action for ME (£5,000); The Children's Society (£4,500); Age Concern – Kensington and Chelsea (£3,500); RSPCA – Harmsworth Hospital (£3,000); St Mungo's (£2,500); Prisoners Abroad (£1,000).
FINANCES *Year* 2015/16 *Income* £60,292 *Grants* £465,000 *Grants to organisations* £465,000 *Assets* £2,407,666
TRUSTEES William Harriman; Alan Bell.
HOW TO APPLY The 2015/16 annual report states: 'The trustees' current policy is to consider all written appeals received but only successful applicants are notified of the trustees' decision. The trustees' current policy is to fully distribute the annual income of the Trust to certain selected Charities although no commitment is given to the recipients. The trustees review the selected charities and consider new appeals received at their annual meeting. It is unusual for the trustees to respond favourably to unsolicited appeals.'
WHO TO APPLY TO Karen Wall, Correspondent, 28 Julian Road, Orpington, Kent BR6 6HU *Email* karen@walltrustsupport.co.uk

■ The Lord's Taverners

CC NO 306054 **ESTABLISHED** 1950

WHERE FUNDING CAN BE GIVEN Unrestricted; in practice, UK.

WHO CAN BENEFIT Cricket clubs affiliated to a National Governing Body; individual schools; groups; other organisations directly involved in the organisation of youth cricket and other sports, including rugby, tennis, squash, basketball and boccia, and which have a genuine need for assistance.

WHAT IS FUNDED Disability and disadvantaged cricket programmes; disability programmes and Play Spaces for young people with disabilities and special needs; Fun Days for pupils with disabilities and their carers at venues across the UK; for socially deprived communities; support to Fields in Trust; pathways for young people into employment, education and training and other positive activities including mainstream cricket.

WHAT IS NOT FUNDED See specific details for each of the programmes.

TYPE OF GRANT Equipment, trips and facilities including minibuses, specially adapted sporting equipment, sports wheelchairs, sensory and soft play and outdoor play equipment and high-quality sports kits; project funding.

SAMPLE GRANTS A list of beneficiaries was not included in the annual report and accounts.

FINANCES *Year* 2015/16 *Income* £5,932,907 *Grants* £2,307,443 *Grants to organisations* £2,032,275 *Assets* £9,344,808

TRUSTEES Roger Smith; David Collier; Christine Colbeck; Richard White; Bob Bevan; Ruth Fitzsimons; John Taylor; Samantha Gladwell; Tim Graveney; Ian Martin.

OTHER INFORMATION Grants were made for the following purposes: Minibuses (£987,000); Cricket (£394,000); Disability and Special Needs (£272,500); Kit Recycling (£31,500).

HOW TO APPLY The trustees meet at least quarterly. All applications must be presented on the appropriate application forms – see the 'Applications' section on the charity's website for further information on separate programmes. Application forms with detailed application instructions are available from the charity's website or the correspondent.

WHO TO APPLY TO Zoe Stevens, Grants and Monitoring and Evaluation Team Assistant, 90 Chancery Lane, London WC2A 1EU *Tel.* 020 7025 0016 *Email* contact@lordstaverners.org *Website* www.lordstaverners.org

■ The Loseley and Guildway Charitable Trust

CC NO 267178 **ESTABLISHED** 1973

WHERE FUNDING CAN BE GIVEN UK and overseas, particularly Guildford and surrounding area.

WHO CAN BENEFIT Registered charities, charitable associations, trusts, societies and corporations benefitting people with various disabilities and terminal illness, children and victims of natural disasters.

WHAT IS FUNDED Compassionate causes, mainly local or causes with which various members of the More-Molineux family and trustees are associated. General charitable purposes, including health and disability.

WHAT IS NOT FUNDED Grants are not made to non-registered charities.

RANGE OF GRANTS Up to £7,500.

SAMPLE GRANTS Disability Challengers (£5,000); Jigsaw and Young Epilepsy (£3,000 each); Oakleaf and Transform Housing (£2,000 each); Age Concern, Canine Partners, Freedom from Torment, GUTS, Queen Elizabeth's Foundation for Disabled People and Seafarers (£1,000 each); Guildford Samaritans (£750); Combat Stress and Parkinson's UK (£500 each); Imperial College (£50); Bells Piece (£25).

FINANCES *Year* 2015/16 *Income* £67,213 *Grants* £48,785 *Grants to organisations* £48,785 *Assets* £1,272,069

TRUSTEES Michael More-Molyneux; Susan More-Molyneux; Alexander More-Molyneux; Sophia More-Molyneux.

OTHER INFORMATION The trust states that 'the major part of the available funds tend to be distributed locally to charitable institutions which the trustees consider to be particularly worthy of support'.

HOW TO APPLY Apply in writing to the correspondent. The trustees meet in February, May and September to consider applications; however, due to commitments, new applications for any causes are unlikely to be successful.

WHO TO APPLY TO Helen O'Dwyer, Secretary, Estate Offices, Loseley Park, Guildford, Surrey GU3 1HS *Email* charities@loseleypark.co.uk *Website* www.loseleypark.co.uk/charities

■ P. and M. Lovell Charitable Settlement

CC NO 274846 **ESTABLISHED** 1977

WHERE FUNDING CAN BE GIVEN UK and overseas.

WHO CAN BENEFIT Quaker organisations; registered charities; individuals.

WHAT IS FUNDED Quaker causes; medical research; social welfare; arts and heritage; humanitarian aid.

TYPE OF GRANT Unrestricted.

RANGE OF GRANTS £100 to £8,000, typically less than £500.

SAMPLE GRANTS Britain Yearly Meeting (£8,000); North of England Refugee Service (£5,000); Oxfam (£2,000); Freedom from Torture (£1,000); The Landmark Trust, Opera North Fund and Quaker Tapestry Ltd (£400 each); Arthritis Research UK, Friends of Museum of Bath at Work and Music in Prisons (£200); Send a Cow (£100).

FINANCES *Year* 2015/16 *Income* £129,273 *Grants* £48,400 *Grants to organisations* £42,400 *Assets* £2,028,762

TRUSTEES Benjamin Lovell; Martin Lovell; Jonathan Lovell.

OTHER INFORMATION During the year, there were 20 grants made to individuals totalling £6,000 and 82 grants made to institutions.

HOW TO APPLY Apply in writing to the correspondent.

WHO TO APPLY TO The Trustees, KPMG LLP, 66 Queen Square, Bristol BS1 4BE *Tel.* 0117 905 4000

■ Michael Lowe's and Associated Charities

CC NO 214785 **ESTABLISHED** 1593

WHERE FUNDING CAN BE GIVEN Lichfield.

WHO CAN BENEFIT Primarily individuals in need; increasingly awarded to organisations providing services to Lichfield City residents.

WHAT IS FUNDED Relief of need, hardship or distress; charities providing assistance, service or advice to those in need.

RANGE OF GRANTS £270 to £20,000.

SAMPLE GRANTS South East Staffordshire Citizens Advice (£21,500); South East Staffordshire Citizens Advice – fuel poverty (£1,000).

FINANCES *Year* 2015/16 *Income* £95,720 *Grants* £56,670 *Grants to organisations* £22,500 *Assets* £1,724,631

TRUSTEES Peter Boggis; N. Sedgwick; Tony Wilkins; Jeanette Allsopp; Roger Hartley; Janet Eagland; Norma Bacon; Revd Peter Clark; Terry Finn; Donald Male; Revd Ian Hayter; Mr Hitchman; C. S. Green; Revd Canon B. Maguire; Mr Warfield.

OTHER INFORMATION Fuel grants to 183 individuals totalled £13,725. Other grants to 60 individuals totalled £20,445. Grants awarded to organisations totalled £22,500.

HOW TO APPLY Apply in writing to the correspondent.

WHO TO APPLY TO Simon Roderick James, Solicitor, c/o Ansons LLP, St Mary's Chambers, 5/7 Breadmarket Street, Lichfield, Staffordshire WS13 6LQ *Tel.* 01543 267995 *Email* sjames@ansonssolicitors.com

■ The Lower Green Foundation

CC NO 1137862 **ESTABLISHED** 2010

WHERE FUNDING CAN BE GIVEN Worldwide.

WHO CAN BENEFIT Organisations and individuals.

WHAT IS FUNDED General charitable purposes. Future priorities include: education for young people; youth apprenticeship schemes; and medical research. The annual report for 2013/14 states: 'Grant requests from charities that focus on students, and particularly those that provide apprenticeship opportunities, are expected to be prioritised in the coming year.'

RANGE OF GRANTS £1,000 to £60,000.

SAMPLE GRANTS Youth and Philanthropy Initiative (£60,000); First Give and The Prince's Trust (£25,000 each); Motivation (£20,000); Tick Tock Club (£15,000); Bumley Breakfast Clubs (£12,000); Free The Children and The Pelican Trust (£10,000 each); The Lullaby Trust (£3,000); Pret Foundation (£1,300).

FINANCES *Year* 2015/16 *Income* £2,262 *Grants* £130,000 *Grants to organisations* £130,000

TRUSTEES Laurence Billett; Marina Sajitz; Sinclair Beecham.

OTHER INFORMATION Due to the low income in 2015/16 accounts were not available to view at the Charity Commission's website.

HOW TO APPLY Apply in writing to the correspondent.

WHO TO APPLY TO Pam Henness, Correspondent, 10–14 Old Church Street, London SW3 5DQ *Email* info@lowergreen.com

■ The C. L. Loyd Charitable Trust

CC NO 265076 **ESTABLISHED** 1973

WHERE FUNDING CAN BE GIVEN UK, there may be some preference for local causes in Oxfordshire.

WHO CAN BENEFIT National charities and local organisations known or associated to the trustees, benefitting at risk groups, people with disabilities, those disadvantaged by poverty or who are socially isolated.

WHAT IS FUNDED General charitable purposes; local causes; health and disability; welfare charities; animal welfare; education; arts and culture.

WHAT IS NOT FUNDED Support is not available to individuals or for medical research.

TYPE OF GRANT One-off and recurrent.

RANGE OF GRANTS Up to £55,000; mostly under £1,000.

SAMPLE GRANTS Country Buildings Protection Trust (£41,000); Affect Real Change, The Letcombe Regis Recreation Ground and Wessex Children's Hospice (£5,000 each); Canine Partners and Sue Ryder Nettlebed Hospice (£2,000 each); International Spinal Research Trust and The Theatre Chipping Norton (£1,000 each); The Earth Trust (£300).

FINANCES *Year* 2015/16 *Income* £158,154 *Grants* £88,936 *Grants to organisations* £88,936 *Assets* £2,758,044

TRUSTEES Thomas Loyd; Alexandra Loyd.

HOW TO APPLY Apply in writing to the correspondent.

WHO TO APPLY TO Thomas Loyd, Trustee, The Lockinge Estate Office, Ardington, Wantage OX12 8PP

■ LPW Ltd

CC NO 1148784 **ESTABLISHED** 2012

WHERE FUNDING CAN BE GIVEN UK.

WHO CAN BENEFIT Charities and community groups.

WHAT IS FUNDED General, relief of poverty, Jewish causes.

SAMPLE GRANTS A list of beneficiaries was not available.

FINANCES *Year* 2014/15 *Income* £829,457 *Grants* £364,925 *Grants to organisations* £364,925 *Assets* £10,440,906

TRUSTEES Irwin Weiler; Paula Weiler; Riki Greenberg; Alexander Weiler; Daniela Rosenthal; Monica Rosenthal; Nicholas Rosenthal; Talia Cohen.

HOW TO APPLY Apply in writing to the correspondent.

WHO TO APPLY TO The Trustees of LPW Ltd, c/o Cohen Arnold, New Burlington House, 1075 Finchley Road, London NW11 0PU *Tel.* 020 8731 0777

■ Robert Luff Foundation Ltd

CC NO 273810 **ESTABLISHED** 1977

WHERE FUNDING CAN BE GIVEN UK.

WHO CAN BENEFIT Medical research charities and institutions.

WHAT IS FUNDED Medical research.

TYPE OF GRANT Support to selected organisations; one-off where funds left; research.

RANGE OF GRANTS Up to £154,000.

SAMPLE GRANTS Cystic Fibrosis Trust (£154,000); Rosetrees Trust (£150,000); ESPA Research (£100,000); Bowel Disease Research Foundation (£80,000); Asthma UK and Sheffield Teaching Hospital (£50,000 each); Royal Brompton Hospital (£40,000); International Spinal Research Trust (£30,000); Myotubular Trust (£20,000); St Augustine's Church (£5,000); Trinity Hospice (£4,000).

FINANCES *Year* 2015/16 *Income* £431,022 *Grants* £877,859 *Grants to organisations* £877,859 *Assets* £32,990,387

TRUSTEES Jean Tomlinson; Richard Price; Sir Robert Johnson; Revd Matthew Tomlinson; Melanie Condon; Brian Nicholson; Lady Ruth Bodey.

OTHER INFORMATION Grants under £5,000 totalled £25,000.

HOW TO APPLY The foundation makes its own decisions about what causes to support. It has previously stated that 'outside applications are not considered, or replied to'.

WHO TO APPLY TO Richard Price, Secretary, Waters Edge, Ferry Lane, Moulsford, Wallingford, Oxfordshire OX10 9JF *Tel.* 01491 652204 *Email* rpjprice@gmail.com

■ The Henry Lumley Charitable Trust

CC NO 1079480 **ESTABLISHED** 2000
WHERE FUNDING CAN BE GIVEN UK and overseas.
WHO CAN BENEFIT Registered charities and individuals.
WHAT IS FUNDED General charitable purposes, with a preference towards medicine, education and the relief of poverty.
TYPE OF GRANT Grants of up to three years for capital and core expenditure or project costs.
RANGE OF GRANTS £2,000 to £15,000.
SAMPLE GRANTS Royal College of Surgeons (£15,000); Stroke Association and Well Being of Women (£5,000 each); Blond McLndoe Laboratories – University of Manchester and Spinal Research Trust (£4,000 each); Arthritis UK, Dystonia Society, Headway, Juvenile Diabetes Research Foundation and Multiple Sclerosis Society (£2,500 each).
FINANCES *Year* 2015 *Income* £101,836 *Grants* £121,500 *Grants to organisations* £121,500 *Assets* £3,211,077
TRUSTEES Henry Lumley; Peter Lumley; Robert Lumley; James Porter.
HOW TO APPLY Apply in writing to the correspondent.
WHO TO APPLY TO Peter Lumley, Trustee, c/o Lutine Leisure Ltd, Windlesham Golf Club, Bagshot, Surrey GU19 5HY *Tel.* 01276 458141

■ Paul Lunn-Rockliffe Charitable Trust

CC NO 264119 **ESTABLISHED** 1972
WHERE FUNDING CAN BE GIVEN UK, with some preference for Winchester; overseas.
WHO CAN BENEFIT Charitable organisations. Preference is given to smaller and locally based charities and those which may be known to the trustees, or members of their family.
WHAT IS FUNDED The trust has a Christian ethos and supports communities in poverty. Grants have been given for: overseas aid; Christian causes; children and young people; people with disabilities; families; prisoners; older people; people who are disadvantaged or vulnerable.
TYPE OF GRANT Project costs; small capital grants (up to three years). The trustees allocate a proportion of funding each year to charities not previously supported and special one-off causes.
RANGE OF GRANTS Most grants are for £1,000.
SAMPLE GRANTS Muhabura View (£87,000); British Red Cross (£2,000); Bible Society, Carroll Youth Centre, Combat Stress, Happy Child International, Koestler Awards, Winchester Live at Home Scheme and Young Carers Winchester and District (£1,000 each); Winchester Gateway Club (£500).
FINANCES *Year* 2015/16 *Income* £61,131 *Grants* £122,782 *Grants to organisations* £122,782 *Assets* £1,710,557
TRUSTEES Lucy Lunn-Rockliffe; James Lunn-Rockliffe; Bryan Boult.
OTHER INFORMATION Grants were made to 37 organisations in 2015/16.
HOW TO APPLY The 2015/16 annual report states the following: 'Following an increasing number of applications and requests for support we have found that our limited administrative resources are unable respond appropriately. Furthermore our limited financial resources mean that the vast majority of those applications for support are unlikely to be successful. However we are acutely aware that every request for support represents a need, and the very act of approaching us represents a cost to the applicant. In consequence we are moving to pro-actively sourcing charities we wish to support ourselves and therefore we will not respond to unsolicited requests for funds.'
WHO TO APPLY TO James Lunn-Rockliffe, Trustee, 6 Barnes Close, Winchester, Hampshire SO23 9QX *Tel.* 01962 625972 *Email* plrcharitabletrust@gmail.com

■ C. F. Lunoe Trust Fund

CC NO 214850 **ESTABLISHED** 1960
WHERE FUNDING CAN BE GIVEN UK.
WHO CAN BENEFIT Universities; charities; ex-employees (and their dependants) of Norwest Holst Group Ltd.
WHAT IS FUNDED Relief in need; education, training and research in the construction industry.
RANGE OF GRANTS £4,000 to £40500.
SAMPLE GRANTS I.C.E QUEST Fund (£40,500); The Danish Church in London (£15,000); University of Leeds (£12,000).
FINANCES *Year* 2015/16 *Income* £83,916 *Grants* £92,067 *Grants to organisations* £67,500
TRUSTEES Peter Lunoe; John Henke; Alexandra Coghill; John Jefkins; John Dodson; Trevor Parks.
OTHER INFORMATION There were eight grants made to individuals.
HOW TO APPLY Apply in writing to the correspondent. However, the majority of the charity's funds go to organisations already known to the trustees and as a result new applications are unlikely to be successful.
WHO TO APPLY TO Peter Lunoe, Trustee, 29 Box Lane, Hemel Hempstead HP3 0DH *Tel.* 01442 252236

■ Lord and Lady Lurgan Trust

CC NO 297046 **ESTABLISHED** 1987
WHERE FUNDING CAN BE GIVEN England (largely London), Northern Ireland and South Africa.
WHO CAN BENEFIT Registered charities; educational establishments; hospices.
WHAT IS FUNDED The trust's Charity Commission record specifies the following: 'Music and the encouragement of young musicians is a key activity. Other grants in England and Northern Ireland are mainly to medical causes with an emphasis on research and medical conditions affecting older people the care of people suffering from cancer, including support for hospices and disability, particularly deafness.'
WHAT IS NOT FUNDED Support is not given for organisations in Scotland. Grants to individuals or for expeditions are not made either. It is unlikely that the trust will be able to help with core costs and it is unable to respond to emergency appeals.
TYPE OF GRANT One-off and recurrent awards for specific projects, up to one year.
RANGE OF GRANTS £1,000 to £11,000.
SAMPLE GRANTS London Philharmonic Orchestra (£2,000); Help Musicians UK (£3,000); English National Ballet and Royal Northern College of Music (£5,000 each); Royal College of Music (£11,000).
FINANCES *Year* 2015 *Income* £20,874 *Grants* £81,970 *Grants to organisations* £81,970 *Assets* £783,764
TRUSTEES Simon Ladd; Andrew Stebbings; Diana Graves; Brendan Beder.

OTHER INFORMATION Accounts available on the trust's website. About three quarters of the overall grant total is given in the UK with the reminder awarded in South Africa.

HOW TO APPLY Application forms can be downloaded from the trust's website and should be returned preferably by email. Read the grant policy on the website before completing the form. The trustees meet twice a year, in December and July. The deadline for the December meeting is 31 October and for the July meeting – 31 May. Applications must also include: the latest signed and audited accounts; a budget for the financial year in which the project falls, separating income which relates to the project; the budget for the project; and details about any other funding received or pending.

WHO TO APPLY TO Andrew Stebbings, Trustee, 45 Cadogan Gardens, London SW3 2TB *Tel.* 020 7591 3333 *Fax* 020 7591 3412 *Email* charitymanager@pglaw.co.uk *Website* www.lurgantrust.org

■ The Lyndhurst Trust

CC NO 235252 **ESTABLISHED** 1964

WHERE FUNDING CAN BE GIVEN UK and overseas, with preferences for disadvantaged areas in North East England.

WHO CAN BENEFIT Christian organisations.

WHAT IS FUNDED Bodies connected with the propagation of the gospel or the promotion of the Christian religion; distribution of bibles and other Christian religious works; support for Christian missions in the UK and abroad; support to the clergy; maintenance of churches and chapels of any Christian denomination; work with disadvantaged people in society applying the Christian ethos; promoting awareness of the Christian gospel in those areas of the world where people are prevented from hearing it through the normal channels of communication. The accounts note: 'Agencies operating in difficult circumstances are given special consideration. The trustees have continued their policy of making funds available to the disadvantaged in the United Kingdom. In addition, the trustees have given special consideration to charities involved in supporting the members of the persecuted church around the world. Churches in the North East of England have been given continued support due to the particular needs of the communities where they are operating.'

WHAT IS NOT FUNDED Individuals; buildings.

RANGE OF GRANTS £500 to £13,000.

SAMPLE GRANTS Sowing Seeds (£13,000); Tent of Nations and The Wayfarer Trust (£10,000 each); St Luke's Church – North East England (£8,000); Junction 42 (£5,500); Guildford Baptist Church (£5,000); Starfish Asia Fund (£3,000); Friends International – Guildford; Hagar UK and Latin Link (£2,000 each); Lukas-Kirken – Norway, Newcastle CLC, St Barnabus – Linthorpe; Sports Chaplaincy UK and Together in Christ (£1,000 each); Barnabus Fund, MECO, St Andrew's Evangelical Mission – Peru, St Andrew's Church – Puerto Pollensa, Tyneside Leaders Forum and Uhuru Ministries (£500 each).

FINANCES *Year* 2015 *Income* £41,149 *Grants* £65,500 *Grants to organisations* £65,500 *Assets* £1,303,233

TRUSTEES Revd Dr Robert Ward; David Hinton; Ben Hinton; Sally Tan; Elisabeth Whiteway.

OTHER INFORMATION Support was allocated as follows: North East England (£27,500); overseas relief (£22,000); the rest of the UK (£21,000); overseas mission (£16,000).

HOW TO APPLY The trust's record on the Charity Commission's website notes that 'the trustees initiate most of the proposals and tend not to accept unsolicited applications'. The annual report also states: 'The trustees, in the course of the year, receive innumerable requests for the consideration of funding. It is not possible to respond to all these many requests; consideration is given on merit.'

WHO TO APPLY TO The Trustees, PO Box 615, North Shields NE29 1AP

■ The Lynn Foundation

CC NO 326944 **ESTABLISHED** 1985

WHERE FUNDING CAN BE GIVEN UK and overseas.

WHO CAN BENEFIT Registered charities; institutions benefitting musicians, textile workers and designers, and other artists, organisations benefitting older people and people with disabilities; hospices.

WHAT IS FUNDED General charitable causes, particularly people with disabilities, music and other arts, sponsorship of young people, medical research and hospices. Our research suggests that Masonic charities are also assisted.

TYPE OF GRANT One-off grants for core, capital and project support. Loans are also made. In practice unrestricted funding.

RANGE OF GRANTS In 2015/16 the average grant was £546.

SAMPLE GRANTS Grants were given in the following areas: children with disabilities; adults with disabilities; arts; hospices; young people's sponsorship; medical research; music; and sundry.

FINANCES *Year* 2015/16 *Income* £288,280 *Grants* £280,892 *Grants to organisations* £280,892 *Assets* £6,204,421

TRUSTEES Guy Parsons; Ian Fair; John Emmott; Philip Parsons; John Sykes.

OTHER INFORMATION A total of 514 awards were made during the year. The foundation's Charity Commission record notes that it awards about 500 grants to individuals and organisations.

HOW TO APPLY Apply in writing to the correspondent.

WHO TO APPLY TO Guy Parsons, Trustee, 17 Lewes Road, Haywards Heath, West Sussex RH17 7SP *Tel.* 01444 454773 *Email* thelynnfoundation@yahoo.com

■ The Sir Jack Lyons Charitable Trust

CC NO 212148 **ESTABLISHED** 1960

WHERE FUNDING CAN BE GIVEN UK and Israel.

WHO CAN BENEFIT Charitable organisations benefitting children and young people, people in performing arts, particularly musicians, students, at risk groups, people disadvantaged by poverty and those who are socially isolated; Jewish charities; educational establishments; projects for young people.

WHAT IS FUNDED Jewish causes; performing arts, especially music; education; humanitarian causes, particularly in Israel.

WHAT IS NOT FUNDED Individuals.

TYPE OF GRANT Mainly recurrent.

RANGE OF GRANTS £1,500 to £65,000.

SAMPLE GRANTS Banff Centre (£37,500); United Jewish Israel Appeal (UJIA) (£25,000); Wigmore Hall Trust (£18,000); Cal Performances

(£14,000); York University Celebration Award (£11,000); Calgary Jewish Federation (£5,500); Beit Halochem (£4,000).

FINANCES *Year* 2015/16 *Income* £141,344 *Grants* £188,157 *Grants to organisations* £188,157 *Assets* £3,363,582

TRUSTEES Mortimer Friedman; Paul Mitchell; David Lyons; Belinda Lyons-Newman.

OTHER INFORMATION The trust made seven grants in 2013/14.

HOW TO APPLY Apply in writing to the correspondent; however, note that in the past the trust has stated that 'in the light of increased pressure for funds, unsolicited appeals are less welcome and would waste much time and money for applicants who were looking for funds which were not available'.

WHO TO APPLY TO Paul Mitchell, Trustee, Gresham House, 5–7 St Paul's Street, Leeds LS1 2JG *Tel.* 01332 976789 *Email* paul.mitchell@sagars.co.uk

■ John Lyons Charity

CC NO 237725 **ESTABLISHED** 1572

WHERE FUNDING CAN BE GIVEN The London boroughs of Barnet, Brent, Camden, City of London, City of Westminster, Ealing, Hammersmith and Fulham, Harrow and Kensington and Chelsea.

WHO CAN BENEFIT Registered charities; state schools; organisations with automatic charitable status; youth clubs.

WHAT IS FUNDED The education of children and young people up to the age of 25.

WHAT IS NOT FUNDED Emergency appeals; retrospective funding; individuals; companies limited by guarantee; research-based projects; projects outside the beneficial area. Consult the detailed guidelines on the website for a full list of exclusions.

TYPE OF GRANT Core costs; capital and revenue costs, salaries, buildings and refurbishments, equipment and project expenditure for up to three years. One award per organisation at a time.

RANGE OF GRANTS Up to £200,000.

SAMPLE GRANTS Barnet and Southgate College (£200,000); Young Barnet Foundation (£100,000); Friends of Mapledown School (£70,000); National Resource Centre for Supplementary Education (£60,000); Lyric Theatre Hammersmith (£50,000); Paddington Arts, Prisoners' Education Trust, Refugee Youth and Samuel Lithgow Youth Centre (£40,000 each).

FINANCES *Year* 2015/16 *Income* £8,427,000 *Grants* £9,626,000 *Grants to organisations* £9,626,000 *Assets* £342,985,000

TRUSTEE The Governors of the John Lyon School, Harrow.

OTHER INFORMATION Grants were awarded in the following programme areas: arts and science (£1.4 million); youth clubs and youth activities (£1.4 million); education and learning (£1.2 million); children and families (£1.1 million); bursaries (£999,000); special needs and disability (£954,000); youth issues (£894,000); emotional wellbeing (£676,000); sport (£547,000); training (£475,000); other (£8,000).

HOW TO APPLY In the first instance, potential applicants should visit the charity's website where they will find extensive details of the charity's programme areas and grant funds, as well as full application guidelines.

WHO TO APPLY TO Cathryn Pender, Grants Director, The Grants Office, 45 Cadogan Gardens, London SW3 2TB *Tel.* 020 7591 3330 *Fax* 020 7591 3412 *Email* info@jlc.london *Website* www.jlc.london

■ Sylvanus Lysons Charity

CC NO 202939 **ESTABLISHED** 1980

WHERE FUNDING CAN BE GIVEN Diocese of Gloucester.

WHO CAN BENEFIT Individuals; organisations; religious bodies; widows of clergy; Church of England.

WHAT IS FUNDED Religious and charitable work in the areas of young people, families, community causes, music, disadvantaged individuals, relief in need for widows, clergy and other people. According to the annual report, 'the trustees have pursued a policy of giving assistance to establish projects within the charity's purposes and to support them through the initial years before they can become self-funding'.

WHAT IS NOT FUNDED The latest accounts state: 'The Trustees' policy at present is not to make grants towards the cost of repairs of churches or other buildings, other than in exceptional circumstances.'

TYPE OF GRANT One-off and recurrent.

RANGE OF GRANTS £300 to £30,000.

SAMPLE GRANTS Gloucester Cathedral Project Pilgrim and Gloucester Cathedral Stone Masons (£25,000 each); Viney Hill Christian Adventure Centre (£12,000); Teens in Crisis (£8,750); Cheltenham Street Pastors (£6,000); St Michael's Cornerstone and St Moreton in the Marsh (£5,000 each); The Door (£3,000).

FINANCES *Year* 2014/15 *Income* £341,206 *Grants* £240,478 *Grants to organisations* £214,151 *Assets* £10,956,754

TRUSTEES Graham Doswell; Revd Anne Spargo; The Ven. Robert Springett; Revd Canon Stephen Bowen; Ian Templeton.

OTHER INFORMATION At the time of writing (June 2016) this was the latest information available. During the year a total of 35 grants were made to organisations and 66 to individuals. The amount of grants given to individuals totalled £27,300. Support was classified as follows: youth work (£54,200); courses and training (£44,650); children and family work (£39,600); choirs and music (£20,000); work with disadvantaged children and individuals (£17,000); street pastors (£10,500).

HOW TO APPLY Apply in writing to the correspondent.

WHO TO APPLY TO Mr A. Holloway, 8–12 Clarence Street, Gloucester GL1 1DZ *Tel.* 01452 522047

■ M. and C. Trust

CC NO 265391 **ESTABLISHED** 1973
WHERE FUNDING CAN BE GIVEN UK.
WHO CAN BENEFIT Mainly Jewish organisations; educational establishments; health institutions.
WHAT IS FUNDED General charitable purposes; Jewish causes; social welfare; health and disability; disadvantaged people. The trust's primary objects are people of the Jewish faith and social welfare needs.
WHAT IS NOT FUNDED Individuals.
TYPE OF GRANT One-off and recurrent grants.
RANGE OF GRANTS £2,500 to £30,000.
SAMPLE GRANTS Jerusalem Foundation (£22,000); Jewish Care (£20,000); Oasis of Peace and One Voice Europe (£15,000 each); London Jewish Cultural Centre (£10,000); Nightingale Hammerson (£8,000); Ambitious About Autism, Deafblind UK, Jewish Women's Aid and WaveLength (£5,000 each); Friendship Works (£3,000).
FINANCES *Year* 2015/16 *Income* £131,384 *Grants* £227,000 *Grants to organisations* £227,000 *Assets* £4,225,070
TRUSTEES Rachel Lebus; Kate Bernstein; Elizabeth Marks; Victoria Fairley.
HOW TO APPLY Apply in writing to the correspondent.
WHO TO APPLY TO Helen Price, Correspondent, c/o Mercer and Hole Trustees Ltd, Gloucester House, 72 London Road, St Albans, Hertfordshire AL1 1NS *Tel.* 01727 869141 *Email* helenprice@mercerhole.co.uk

■ M. B. Foundation

CC NO 222104 **ESTABLISHED** 1965
WHERE FUNDING CAN BE GIVEN Some preference for Greater Manchester.
WHO CAN BENEFIT Jewish organisations; individuals.
WHAT IS FUNDED Jewish causes, particularly the advancement of the Jewish faith, Jewish education and the relief of poverty among the Jewish community.
SAMPLE GRANTS A list of beneficiaries was not included in the accounts.
FINANCES *Year* 2015/16 *Income* £1,586,513 *Grants* £637,008 *Grants to organisations* £637,008 *Assets* £6,111,167
TRUSTEES Rabbi Wolf Kaufman; Rabbi Mordechai Bamberger.
HOW TO APPLY Apply in writing to the correspondent, although the foundation states in its 2015/16 annual report that it prefers to choose which institutions it supports.
WHO TO APPLY TO Isaac Dov Bamberger, Fairways House, George Street, Prestwich, Manchester M25 9WS *Tel.* 0161 787 7898

■ The M. K. Charitable Trust

CC NO 260439 **ESTABLISHED** 1966
WHERE FUNDING CAN BE GIVEN Unrestricted, in practice mainly UK.
WHO CAN BENEFIT Orthodox Jewish organisations.
WHAT IS FUNDED General charitable purposes; Jewish causes; education; religion; health and disability; relief of poverty.
SAMPLE GRANTS In 2015/16 grants were made for: 'financial support to the poor; provision of basic necessities to the poor; relief of sickness and disabilities; Jewish education and places of worship for the Jewish community'. The annual report and accounts did not list any further details of grant recipients.
FINANCES *Year* 2015/16 *Income* £987,838 *Grants* £897,458 *Grants to organisations* £897,458 *Assets* £12,045,920
TRUSTEES A. Piller; D. Katz; Simon Kaufman; Z. Kaufman.
HOW TO APPLY Apply in writing to the correspondent. The trust accepts applications for grants from representatives of Orthodox Jewish charities, which are reviewed by the trustees on a regular basis.
WHO TO APPLY TO Simon Kaufman, Trustee, 50 Keswick Street, Gateshead, Tyne and Wear NE8 1TQ *Tel.* 0191 490 0140

■ The M. Y. A. Charitable Trust

CC NO 299642 **ESTABLISHED** 1987
WHERE FUNDING CAN BE GIVEN Worldwide.
WHO CAN BENEFIT Organisations and individuals.
WHAT IS FUNDED Orthodox Jewish causes, including religious education and the relief of poverty.
TYPE OF GRANT One-off and recurrent; short-term interest-free loans.
SAMPLE GRANTS A list of beneficiaries was not available.
FINANCES *Year* 2015/16 *Income* £620,638 *Grants* £243,380 *Grants to organisations* £233,660 *Assets* £1,759,388
TRUSTEES Myer Rothfeld; Eve Rothfeld; Hannah Schraiber; Joseph Pfeffer.
OTHER INFORMATION During the year, individuals received £9,700 in six grants. A full list of beneficiaries was not included in the accounts.
HOW TO APPLY Apply in writing to the correspondent.
WHO TO APPLY TO Myer Rothfield, Trustee, Medcar House, 149A Stamford Hill, London N16 5LL *Tel.* 020 8800 3582

■ The Madeline Mabey Trust

CC NO 326450 **ESTABLISHED** 1983
WHERE FUNDING CAN BE GIVEN UK and overseas.
WHO CAN BENEFIT Registered charities, including UK and international bodies.
WHAT IS FUNDED Children's welfare and education; medical research; humanitarian aid worldwide.
WHAT IS NOT FUNDED Individuals.
SAMPLE GRANTS A list of beneficiaries was not available.
FINANCES *Year* 2015/16 *Income* £276,997 *Grants* £287,150 *Grants to organisations* £232,730 *Assets* £123,848
TRUSTEES Alan Daliday; Bridget Nelson; Joanna Singeisen.
OTHER INFORMATION In 2015/16 grants were made to 139 organisations. A list of beneficiaries was unavailable.
HOW TO APPLY Apply in writing to the correspondent. The annual report for 2015/16 notes: 'The Trust favours identifying organisations itself, although it is willing to consider applications for grants.' Only successful appeals are acknowledged.
WHO TO APPLY TO Joanna Singeisen, Trustee, Woodview, Tolcarne Road, Beacon, Camborne, Cornwall TR14 9AB *Tel.* 01209 710304 *Email* J.Singeisen@Mabey.co.uk *Website* www.mabeygroup.co.uk/about/heritage/the-madeline-mabey-trust

■ The E. M. MacAndrew Trust

CC NO 290736 **ESTABLISHED** 1984

WHERE FUNDING CAN BE GIVEN UK.

WHO CAN BENEFIT Charitable organisations; medical and welfare charities.

WHAT IS FUNDED General charitable purposes; medical and social welfare causes; education; arts and culture; community causes.

RANGE OF GRANTS £300 to £2,000.

SAMPLE GRANTS British Red Cross Disaster Appeal (£15,000 in four grants); Buckinghamshire Community Foundation, Epilepsy Society and The Stroke Association (£2,000 each); Buckingham Almshouse, Florence Nightingale Hospice, St John Ambulance Bedfordshire and Tring Park School (£1,000 each); Willen Hospice (£300).

FINANCES *Year* 2015/16 *Income* £56,621 *Grants* £49,600 *Grants to organisations* £49,600 *Assets* £1,248,323

TRUSTEES Amanda Nicholson; John Nicholson; Sally Grant; Verity Nicholson.

OTHER INFORMATION Grants were made to 41 organisations during the year.

HOW TO APPLY The trust has informed us that they do not respond to any unsolicited applications under any circumstances, as they prefer to make their own decisions as to which charities to support.

WHO TO APPLY TO James Thornton, J. P. Thornton and Co., The Old Dairy, Adstockfields, Adstock, Buckingham MK18 2JE *Tel.* 01296 714886 *Email* jpt@jptco.co.uk

■ The Macdonald-Buchanan Charitable Trust

CC NO 209994 **ESTABLISHED** 1952

WHERE FUNDING CAN BE GIVEN Worldwide with a preference for Northamptonshire.

WHO CAN BENEFIT Registered charities, with a small preference for those benefitting Northamptonshire.

WHAT IS FUNDED A wide range of general charitable purposes including health and disability, animal welfare, children and young people and older people.

WHAT IS NOT FUNDED Grants are not made to individuals or for campaigning purposes.

RANGE OF GRANTS £2,500 to £54,500.

SAMPLE GRANTS AMB Charitable Trust (£54,500); Carriejo Charitable Trust and Orrin Charitable Trust (£30,000 each); National Horseracing Museum (£20,000); Oracle Cancer Trust (£15,000); All Saints Parish Church, Cottesbrooke (£4,500); The Haven (£3,000); Tudor Hall School (£2,500).

FINANCES *Year* 2015 *Income* £144,582 *Grants* £159,506 *Grants to organisations* £159,506 *Assets* £3,613,820

TRUSTEES Alastair Macdonald-Buchanan; Mary Philipson; Joanna Lascelles; Hugh Macdonald-Buchanan.

OTHER INFORMATION The trust reviewed its grant-making policy in 2015. It will now focus on a smaller number of more substantial projects researched by the trustees. Smaller donations will now be made by the charitable trust of each branch of the family.

HOW TO APPLY The annual report for 2015 states that the trustees will 'no longer consider appeals which are directed to the charity preferring to consider appeals that have been received by them individually'.

WHO TO APPLY TO Linda Cousins, Rathbone Trust Co. Ltd, 8 Finsbury Circus, London EC2M 7AZ *Tel.* 020 7399 0820 *Email* linda.cousins@rathbones.com

■ The R. S. Macdonald Charitable Trust

SC NO SC012710 **ESTABLISHED** 1978

WHERE FUNDING CAN BE GIVEN Scotland.

WHO CAN BENEFIT Registered charities operating in Scotland and universities.

WHAT IS FUNDED Neurological conditions; visual impairment; children's welfare; animal welfare; medical research; RNLI lifeboats.

WHAT IS NOT FUNDED Non-registered charities; individuals; projects that do not deliver a benefit in Scotland.

TYPE OF GRANT Revenue or capital costs; project funding or core funding; One-off awards; multi-year awards for up to three years; salaries, rent and other core costs; medical research grants: universities – seedcorn or unrestricted funding; charities – specific projects that have completed a peer review process.

RANGE OF GRANTS £5,000 to £74,500.

SAMPLE GRANTS Bobath Scotland (£74,500); Alzheimer's Research UK (£60,000 in two grants); University of Edinburgh Development Trust and Visibility (£50,000 each); Edinburgh Women's Aid (£36,000); Children 1st (£30,000); Aberlour Child Care Trust and Drake Music Scotland (£15,000 each); Dundee and Angus ADHA Support Group, Reidvale Adventure Play Association Ltd and South of Scotland Wildlife Hospital (£5,000 each).

FINANCES *Year* 2015/16 *Income* £1,775,867 *Grants* £2,216,251 *Grants to organisations* £2,216,251 *Assets* £68,983,037

TRUSTEES Bruce Rigby; Moira McCaig; Kenny McBrearty; Patricia Donald; Fiona Patrick; John Paterson.

OTHER INFORMATION The website states: 'We aim to distribute up to £2 million annually through our grants programmes and are also keen to assist beneficiary charities with non-financial support.'

HOW TO APPLY Applications should be made using an online system on the trust's website. Appeals must also include details of the proposed project and a copy of the latest accounts. There are different deadlines (or no deadline for small grants), depending on the purpose of the grant and the type of organisation applying, but they all fall in March or September (see the website for details). The trust asks to contact the director (Douglas Hamilton) for an early discussion before making an application for a medical research grant. Decisions on main grants are made at the trustee meetings at the end of May and November.

WHO TO APPLY TO Katie Winwick, Grants Administrator, 21 Rutland Square, Edinburgh EH1 2BB *Tel.* 0131 228 4681 *Email* office@rsmacdonald.com *Website* www.rsmacdonald.com

■ Mace Foundation

CC NO 1150134 **ESTABLISHED** 2012

WHERE FUNDING CAN BE GIVEN UK.

WHO CAN BENEFIT Registered charities, social enterprises and community groups.

WHAT IS FUNDED Education, social welfare, health and culture, heritage and sport.

WHAT IS NOT FUNDED Political parties.

RANGE OF GRANTS Strategic partner charities received between £10,000 and £48,000.

SAMPLE GRANTS WheelPower (£48,000); Teenage Cancer Trust (£30,000); The Prince's Trust and Tate (£25,000); Coram and RedR (£20,000 each); Institution of Civil Engineers and LandAid (£10,000).

FINANCES *Year* 2015 *Income* £622,914 *Grants* £478,709 *Grants to organisations* £478,709 *Assets* £80,997

TRUSTEES Amy Chapman; Deborah Reynolds; Isabel McAllister; Mark Reynolds; Shaun Tate; Simon Healey; Clare Lewis; Barbara Welch; Hannah Livesey.

OTHER INFORMATION The foundation is the charitable hand of the Mace Group, a construction and consultancy firm based in London. The foundation makes grants to its strategic partner charities as well as matching employees' fundraising.

HOW TO APPLY The foundation does not accept unsolicited applications.

WHO TO APPLY TO Jo Drummond, Fundraising, Engagement and Communications Manager, Mace Group, 155 Moorgate, London EC2M 6XB *Tel.* 020 3522 3385 *Email* mace.foundation@macegroup.com *Website* www.macegroup.com/about-us/mace-foundation

■ The Mackay and Brewer Charitable Trust

CC NO 1072666 **ESTABLISHED** 1998

WHERE FUNDING CAN BE GIVEN UK.

WHO CAN BENEFIT Charitable organisations.

WHAT IS FUNDED General charitable purposes, including health and disability causes and animal welfare.

TYPE OF GRANT Recurrent.

RANGE OF GRANTS Each organisation received £8,500 in two grants.

SAMPLE GRANTS Hampshire Association for the Care of the Blind; Macmillan Cancer Trust; Marie Curie Cancer Care; Open Doors; People's Dispensary for Sick Animals (PDSA); St John Ambulance in Wales; The National Trust for Scotland; The Salvation Army (£8,500 each).

FINANCES *Year* 2015/16 *Income* £915,746 *Grants* £68,000 *Grants to organisations* £68,000 *Assets* £2,830,270

TRUSTEE HSBC. Trust Company UK. Ltd.

OTHER INFORMATION During 2015/16, eight organisations received two grants each. The trust makes grants to these charities each year.

HOW TO APPLY Apply in writing to the correspondent.

WHO TO APPLY TO S. Hill, Trust Manager, HSBC Trust Company UK Ltd, Forum 1, The Forum Parkway, Whiteley, Fareham, Hampshire PO15 7PA *Tel.* 023 8072 3344

■ The Mackintosh Foundation

CC NO 327751 **ESTABLISHED** 1988

WHERE FUNDING CAN BE GIVEN Worldwide; in practice mainly UK.

WHO CAN BENEFIT Registered charities; educational establishments; individuals.

WHAT IS FUNDED Priority is given to the theatre and the performing arts. Medical aid, particularly research into cancer and HIV and AIDS; homelessness; community projects; the environment; refugees; other general charitable purposes.

TYPE OF GRANT Capital costs; schools' core costs; medical research; project expenditure; recurring costs up to three years.

RANGE OF GRANTS Up to £700,000; most grants £1,000 to £5,000.

SAMPLE GRANTS The Actors Fund (£700,000); The Theatres Trust (£125,000); Royal Conservatoire of Scotland (£120,000); WaterAid (£25,000); Royal Air Force Benevolent Fund (£15,000); Disasters Emergency Committee (£10,000); War Child (£6,000); Help Refugees, Soho Theatre Company and The National Student Drama Festival Ltd (£5,000 each).

FINANCES *Year* 2015/16 *Income* £186,259 *Grants* £1,542,224 *Grants to organisations* £1,526,876 *Assets* £6,421,811

TRUSTEES Nicholas Allott; Sir Cameron MacKintosh; Nicholas MacKintosh; Robert Noble; Bart Peerless; Thomas Schonberg; Richard Pappas.

OTHER INFORMATION A total of 152 grants were made to organisations. There were three individual beneficiaries who received £15,500 between them. Donations of less than £5,000 totalled £168,500.

HOW TO APPLY Apply in writing to the correspondent, outlining details of the organisation, the project for which funding is required and a breakdown of the costs involved. Supporting documents should be kept to a minimum and an sae enclosed (if materials are to be returned). The trustees meet in May and October in plenary session, but a grants committee meets weekly to consider smaller grants. The foundation responds to all applications in writing and the process normally takes between four and six weeks.

WHO TO APPLY TO Richard Knibb, General and Company Secretary, The Mackintosh Foundation, 1 Bedford Square, London WC1B 3RB *Tel.* 020 7637 8866 *Fax* 020 7436 2683 *Email* info@camack.co.uk

■ GPS Macpherson Charitable Settlement

CC NO 261045 **ESTABLISHED** 1970

WHERE FUNDING CAN BE GIVEN UK.

WHO CAN BENEFIT Registered charitable organisations.

WHAT IS FUNDED General charitable purposes; the environment, conservation and heritage; health; people with disabilities; children and young people; education and training; the armed forces and emergency services efficiency.

SAMPLE GRANTS Queens' College, University of Cambridge (£350,000); PACE (£10,000 in two grants).

FINANCES *Year* 2014/15 *Income* £369,132 *Grants* £360,000 *Grants to organisations* £360,000 *Assets* £467,970

TRUSTEES Ewen Macpherson; Strone Macpherson; Messrs Hoare Trustees.

HOW TO APPLY Apply in writing to the correspondent. Only successful applicants are notified of the trustees' decision.

WHO TO APPLY TO Messrs Hoare Trustees, C. Hoare and Co., 37 Fleet Street, London EC4P 4DQ *Tel.* 020 7353 4522

■ The MacRobert Trust

SC NO SC031346 **ESTABLISHED** 1943

WHERE FUNDING CAN BE GIVEN UK, with a preference for Scotland.

WHO CAN BENEFIT Registered charities; universities and non-fee-paying schools; local and regional organisations in Tarland and Deeside.

WHAT IS FUNDED General charitable purposes with a preference for: armed forces services and seafarers; education and training; children and young people; science, engineering and technology; agriculture and horticulture; Tarland and Deeside.

WHAT IS NOT FUNDED Religious organisations; organisations or beneficiaries based outside the United Kingdom; individuals; general appeals or mailshots; political organisations; retrospective applications; student bodies as opposed to universities; fee-paying schools, apart from an Educational Grants Scheme for children who are at, or who need to attend, a Scottish independent secondary school and for which a grant application is made through the Head Teacher; pre-school groups, after-school clubs or school PTAs other than those in the local area; expeditions, except those made under the auspices of recognised bodies such as the British Schools Exploring Society; community and village halls other than those local to Tarland and Deeside; departments within a university, unless the appeal gains the support of, and is channelled through, the principal; organisations with multiple branches should only apply through their headquarters other than those in the local area.

TYPE OF GRANT Core costs; project expenditure; capital costs; buildings; feasibility studies; research; recurring and running costs; salaries; unrestricted funding; one-off and for up to three years.

RANGE OF GRANTS Up to £50,000 but usually less than £10,000.

SAMPLE GRANTS Charlie House (£50,000); Aberdeen ARI (£32,000); Scottish Traditional Skills Centre (£23,000); Ballater and District Flood Appeal (£20,000); Horseback UK (£10,000); Western Wildcats Hockey Club (£6,700); British Exploring Society (£3,400); Scottish Association of Young Farmers Clubs (£2,300); Aberdeen Samaritans (£2,000); North East Scotland Wing Welfare Fund (£1,000); Marie Curie Cancer Care (£500); Tarland Playgroup (£390).

FINANCES *Year* 2015/16 *Income* £2,396,107 *Grants* £257,152 *Grants to organisations* £257,152 *Assets* £82,898,347

TRUSTEES K. Davis; S. Campbell; C. D. Crole; J. D. Fowlie; Air Commodore P. J. Hughesdon; D. A. J. Noble; C. B. S. Richardson; Commodore C. B. H. Stevenson; J. H. Strickland; J. C. Swan.

OTHER INFORMATION There are three levels of monetary awards: small, medium and large. Each level has its own specific governance arrangements and internal processes, for which there is guidance on the website. Grants were made to 49 organisations in the financial year. A further £76,000 was committed to seven organisations for the following two years.

HOW TO APPLY The application form and full guidelines can be downloaded from the website. Application forms must be posted along with a cover letter and a full set of audited accounts. The trust stresses the importance of including an informative covering letter; completing all sections of the application form and asks that applicants maintain a process of dialogue with the trust. The website provides details of time bars and limits. The trustees meet to consider applications twice a year, usually in March and November. To be considered, applications must be received for the March meeting by 31 October previously and for the October meeting by 31 May previously.

WHO TO APPLY TO Rear Admiral Chris Hockley, Chief Executive Office, Cromar, Tarland, Aboyne, Aberdeenshire AB34 4UD *Tel.* 01339 881444 *Email* vicky@themacroberttrust.org.uk *Website* www.themacroberttrust.org.uk

■ The Mactaggart Third Fund

SC NO SC014285 **ESTABLISHED** 1969

WHERE FUNDING CAN BE GIVEN UK and overseas.

WHO CAN BENEFIT Registered charities.

WHAT IS FUNDED A wide range of general charitable purposes, including relief of poverty, health, education, religion, community development, citizen participation, arts and culture, sports, human rights, environment, animal welfare and disadvantaged individuals.

TYPE OF GRANT One-off and recurrent.

RANGE OF GRANTS £150 to £92,000; most grants less than £10,000.

SAMPLE GRANTS Haiti Clinic Inc. (£40,000); Man-O-War Heritage Museum (£17,500); Amazon Conservation Team (£12,000); Every Child Counts (£9,000); Islay and Jura Highland Dancers (£7,000); Civil Liberties Trust (£3,000); Insight Prison Project (£1,800); Médecins Sans Frontières (£1,300); Cyclists' Touring Club (£350); Prostate Cancer UK (£250).

FINANCES *Year* 2015/16 *Income* £730,525 *Grants* £512,933 *Grants to organisations* £512,933 *Assets* £19,157,040

TRUSTEES Alastair Mactaggart; Robert Gore; Fiona Mactaggart; Andrew Mactaggart; Sir John Mactaggart.

OTHER INFORMATION According to the website the trust aims to award about £250,000 in grants each year. In 2015/16 a total of 114 grants were made.

HOW TO APPLY The charity does not accept unsolicited applications.

WHO TO APPLY TO The Trustees, 7th Floor, 80 St Vincent Street, Glasgow G2 5UB *Website* www.mactaggartthirdfund.org

■ The Ian Mactaggart Trust (The Mactaggart Second Fund)

SC NO SC012502 **ESTABLISHED** 1984

WHERE FUNDING CAN BE GIVEN UK and overseas; there may be some preference for Scotland.

WHO CAN BENEFIT Registered charities.

WHAT IS FUNDED The trust supports a wide range of activities, including education and training, arts and culture and the relief of people who are poor, sick, in need or have disabilities.

TYPE OF GRANT One-off and recurrent.

RANGE OF GRANTS £250 to £50,000, usually under £10,000.

SAMPLE GRANTS Kulen Outreach (£50,000); Robin Hood Foundation (£48,000); Battersea Arts Centre (£20,000); Slough Immigration Aid Unit (£7,000); Women's Aid (£4,300); Centre for Alternative Technology (£3,500); RNLI (£2,000); Oxford Homeless Pathways (£1,500); Sea Shepherd Conservation Society (£1,000); The Trussell Trust (£300); Elephant Family (£250).

FINANCES *Year* 2015/16 *Income* £692,766 *Grants* £430,712 *Grants to organisations* £430,712 *Assets* £16,340,036

TRUSTEES Sir John Mactaggart; Jane Mactaggart; Fiona Mactaggart; Robert Gore.
OTHER INFORMATION The website states: 'The Trust aims to make grants of circa £200,000 each year.' During the year 151 grants were made.
HOW TO APPLY The trust does not accept unsolicited applications.
WHO TO APPLY TO The Trustees, 7th Floor, 80 St Vincent Street, Glasgow G2 5UB *Website* www.ianmactaggarttrust.org

■ The Magdalen and Lasher Charity (General Fund)

CC NO 211415 **ESTABLISHED** 1837
WHERE FUNDING CAN BE GIVEN In or around the borough of Hastings.
WHO CAN BENEFIT Individuals; pensioners; charitable organisations helping those in need; educational establishments; churches.
WHAT IS FUNDED Pensions for older people in Hastings; education; health care; facilities and buildings; community services; relief of poverty.
WHAT IS NOT FUNDED Debt repayment; minibuses.
TYPE OF GRANT One-off, specific projects.
RANGE OF GRANTS £100 to £5,000. Usually less than £1,000.
SAMPLE GRANTS Hastings Advice and Representation Centre (£5,000); Amicus Horizon (£4,000 in two grants); St Clement and All Saints, Surviving Christmas and Snowflake Trust Night Shelter (£2,000 each); Association of Carers (£1,500 in two grants); Salvation Army St Andrew's Square (£750); Broomgrove Play Scheme (£700); White Rock Theatre (£600); Counselling Plus (£500); 4th Hastings Guides (£100).
FINANCES *Year* 2015/16 *Income* £410,314 *Grants* £64,061 *Grants to organisations* £35,319 *Assets* £11,814,069
TRUSTEES Keith Donaldson; Gareth Bendon; Ian Steel; Jenny Blackburn; Michael Foster; Clive Galbraith; Susan Parsons; Sue Phillips; Dawn Poole; Ann Wing; Cllr Andrew Patmore; Cllr James Bacon; Patricia Lock.
OTHER INFORMATION The origins of the charity go back to 1294 when land was donated in support of a local leper and pest house. It merged with another benefactors charity in 1691 but the Mayor and Hastings Corporation controlled the funds. In 1837 the charity was placed under independent trusteeship and in 1877 the charity was divided into three main sections – a pensions branch, an eleemosynary (alms) branch, and an education branch. In 2015/16 grants to individuals totalled about £28,500. There were 34 organisational awards.
HOW TO APPLY Application forms are available from the correspondent. Guidelines and criteria are available to view on the charity's website.
WHO TO APPLY TO Marcia Woolf, The Magdalen and Lasher Charity, Old Hastings House, 132 High Street, Hastings, East Sussex TN34 3ET *Tel.* 01424 452646 *Email* mlc@oldhastingshouse.co.uk *Website* www.magdalenandlasher.co.uk

■ The Magen Charitable Trust

CC NO 326535 **ESTABLISHED** 1984
WHERE FUNDING CAN BE GIVEN UK.
WHO CAN BENEFIT Registered charities, especially Jewish organisations.
WHAT IS FUNDED Relief of poverty; education; religious activities; Jewish causes.
WHAT IS NOT FUNDED Grant contracts.
SAMPLE GRANTS Manchester Yeshiva Kollel; Talmud Educational Trust; Bnos Yisroel School; Mesivta Tiferes Yisroel.
FINANCES *Year* 2015/16 *Income* £167,229 *Grants* £138,615 *Grants to organisations* £138,615 *Assets* £1,544,497
TRUSTEES Jacob Halpern; Rosa Halpern.
OTHER INFORMATION A full list of beneficiaries was not included within the accounts for 2015/16.
HOW TO APPLY Apply in writing to the correspondent.
WHO TO APPLY TO The Trustees, New Riverside, 439 Lower Broughton, Salford M7 2FX *Tel.* 0161 792 2626

■ The Makers of Playing Cards Charity

CC NO 232876 **ESTABLISHED** 1943
WHERE FUNDING CAN BE GIVEN UK, particularly City of London.
WHO CAN BENEFIT Charitable organisations, focusing on smaller charities with an annual income of less than £1 million.
WHAT IS FUNDED Education; children and young people; causes related to the City of London; causes with which the charity has a connection; general charitable purposes. Further detail is given on the charity's website.
RANGE OF GRANTS £500 to £1,000.
SAMPLE GRANTS A list of beneficiaries was not available.
FINANCES *Year* 2015/16 *Income* £82,999 *Grants* £61,389 *Grants to organisations* £61,389 *Assets* £889,803
TRUSTEES Peter Cregreen; Anthony Komedra; Tony Carter; Mark Winton; Edward Copisarow; Benjamin Madden; Nicholas Prentice; Revd Canon Nigel Nicholson; Richard Wells.
OTHER INFORMATION There was no list of beneficiaries in the 2015/16 accounts, but the following breakdown of grants was given: educational purposes (£32,000); children's charities (£18,400); other charities for hardship (£10,800). The charity was previously known as The Cutler Trust. The Cutler Trust was set up on 25 October 1943 by two card manufacturers, John Waddington Ltd and De La Rue Company Ltd and named after the then Master, Lindsay Cutler, (whose grandsons have been apprenticed to the Livery and are now Liverymen). Consistent to the original Livery concept, it was initially for beneficiaries and dependants of those who were or had been employed in the manufacture of playing cards.
HOW TO APPLY Apply in writing to the Prime Almoner of the Makers of Playing Cards Charity, Edward Copisarow – applications should be sent by email only (charityalmoners@makersofplayingcards.co.uk) unless otherwise agreed. The website states that applications should be no longer than one side of A4 'setting out on what you would spend a grant if it were of £500 or of £1,000, explaining briefly how the work for which you seek funds meets the Trust's charitable objects and attaching a copy of your most recent annual report and accounts'. Applications are considered in May and October and should be submitted no later than the end of March or end of August respectively. Further information is given on the website.
WHO TO APPLY TO Edward Copisarow, Prime Almoner, 256 St Davids Square, London E14 3WE *Tel.* 020 7531 5990 *Email* charityalmoners@makersofplayingcards.co.uk *Website* www.makersofplayingcards.co.uk

The Mallinckrodt Foundation

CC NO 1058011 **ESTABLISHED** 1996
WHERE FUNDING CAN BE GIVEN Worldwide.
WHO CAN BENEFIT Registered charities; charitable organisations; universities.
WHAT IS FUNDED General charitable purposes.
RANGE OF GRANTS Usually between £2,000 and £10,000.
SAMPLE GRANTS John F. Kennedy School of Government Harvard (£1.3 million in two grants); Friends of the National Libraries (£10,000); Volcker Alliance (NIPA) Ltd (£7,000); Christian Responsibility in Public Affairs and Three Faiths Forum (£5,000 each); AMREF Deutschland (£3,900); Young Musicians Symphony Orchestra (£2,000).
FINANCES *Year* 2015/16 *Income* £1,377,879 *Grants* £1,353,052 *Grants to organisations* £1,353,052 *Assets* £3,940,844
TRUSTEES Charmaine von Mallinckrodt; Bruno Schroder; Leonie Fane; Michael May; Richard Robinson; Claire Fitzalan Howard; Edward Mallinckrodt; Philip Mallinckrodt.
OTHER INFORMATION In 2015/16 grants were given to 11 organisations.
HOW TO APPLY Note that the foundation does not welcome unsolicited appeals and 'does not make grants to people or organisations that apply speculatively'. The annual report for 2015/16 states: 'The Trustees travel widely in the UK and abroad and use the knowledge gained to support the work of the Foundation and to inform their grant-making activities.'
WHO TO APPLY TO Sally Yates, 81 Rivington Street, London EC2A 3AY

Man Group PLC Charitable Trust

CC NO 275386 **ESTABLISHED** 1978
WHERE FUNDING CAN BE GIVEN UK and overseas, with some preference for London.
WHO CAN BENEFIT Registered charities; voluntary organisations.
WHAT IS FUNDED Literacy, numeracy and programmes that support disadvantaged people to engage with education and build the necessary vital life skills to improve life chances and employment prospects.
WHAT IS NOT FUNDED Large national charities; charities which use external fundraising agencies; charities primarily devoted to promoting religious beliefs; endowment funds; requests to directly replace statutory funding; individual beneficiaries; general media campaigns or campaigning or advocacy work to influence policy debates; applicants which have been successful during the last twelve months; work which has already been completed; capital projects and appeals; sponsorship or funding towards marketing appeals or fundraising events; organisations or projects whose primary purpose is political. Furthermore, the trust will not consider charities with 'high administration costs relative to the services provided'.
TYPE OF GRANT Core costs, including salaries and overheads; project costs.
RANGE OF GRANTS £10,000 to £50,000.
SAMPLE GRANTS National Literacy Trust and Tower Hamlets Education Business Partnership (£50,000 each); NSPCC (£29,000); School-Home Support (£28,000); Children's Cancer Recovery Project (£25,000); The Boxing Academy and Westside School (£12,500 each); Longford Trust and Maths on Toast (£10,000 each).
FINANCES *Year* 2015 *Income* £754,643 *Grants* £357,000 *Grants to organisations* £357,000 *Assets* £1,938,209
TRUSTEES Keith Haydon; Colin Bettison; Carol Ward; Teun Johnston; Lydia Bosworth; Antoine Forterre.
OTHER INFORMATION Grants were made to over 13 organisations in 2015.
HOW TO APPLY In the first instance, see the foundation's page on the Man Group website, where a document detailing eligibility criteria and guidelines on how to apply is available. The document states that the trust has a two-stage application process. After reading the trust's eligibility criteria, principles and exclusions, a brief expression of interest that is no longer than one side of A4 should be sent via email. If your expression of interest is successful you will be invited to submit a Stage 2 application form for consideration by the trustees who usually meet twice a year. Successful applicants will be notified by telephone or email. All unsuccessful applicants will be notified and will usually receive an outline explanation for the rejection.
WHO TO APPLY TO Angeline Boothroyd, Trust Secretary, Man Group PLC, Riverbank House, 2 Swan Lane, London EC4R 3AD *Tel.* 020 7144 1737 *Email* charitable.trust@man.com *Website* www.man.com/GB/man-charitable-trust

The Manackerman Charitable Trust

CC NO 326147 **ESTABLISHED** 1982
WHERE FUNDING CAN BE GIVEN UK, with some preference for Manchester.
WHO CAN BENEFIT Jewish organisations; educational institutions.
WHAT IS FUNDED Education; religion; relief of poverty; Jewish causes.
RANGE OF GRANTS Up to £10,000.
SAMPLE GRANTS Camp Simcha, Federation of Jewish Services and Project S.E.E.D. Ltd (£10,000 each); The Christie Charitable Fund, Laniado Hospital UK, Friends of Lubavitch Scotland (£5,000 each); British Friends of United Hatzalah Israel (£3,600); Friends of Bnei Akiva (£3,000); Manchester Charitable Trust Ltd and British Emunah Fund (£2,000 each).
FINANCES *Year* 2015/16 *Income* £75,402 *Grants* £62,870 *Grants to organisations* £62,870 *Assets* £530,194
TRUSTEES Jonathan Marks; Vanessa Marks; Aryeh Marks.
HOW TO APPLY Apply in writing to the correspondent.
WHO TO APPLY TO Jonathan Marks, Trustee, 3 Park Lane, Salford M7 4HT *Tel.* 0161 832 3434

Manchester Airport Community Trust Fund

CC NO 1071703 **ESTABLISHED** 1997
WHERE FUNDING CAN BE GIVEN Within a ten-mile radius of Manchester airport, concentrating on the areas most exposed to aircraft noise.
WHO CAN BENEFIT Charitable organisations.
WHAT IS FUNDED Conservation projects for the natural and built environment; social welfare; facilities for recreation, sport and leisure time; education and training in all matters relating to the natural, physical environment; community cohesion and welfare.
WHAT IS NOT FUNDED Maintenance or running costs (including, for example, repair work, energy costs, salaries, coach fees, uniform or kits);

purchase of land or buildings; projects which have already taken place; individuals.

TYPE OF GRANT Projects must be open to the whole community, or a large section of it, and grants are given only for 'anything which is tangible and long lasting', such as equipment.

RANGE OF GRANTS £500 to £3,000.

SAMPLE GRANTS Cheadle Golf Club, Fairey Brass Band, and Scott Avenue Allotments (£3,000 each); Friends of Romiley Park (£2,800); Knutsford Musical Theatre (£2,700); Dunham Massey Village Hall (£2,100); Manchester Rugby Club (£1,900); Chorlton Central Church (£1,500); Venture Arts (£1,000); Re-Dish (£500).

FINANCES *Year* 2015/16 *Income* £129,287 *Grants* £118,686 *Grants to organisations* £118,686 *Assets* £28,758

TRUSTEES Cllr Paul Andrews; Cllr Don Stockton; Cllr Michael Whetton; Wendy Sinfield; John Twigg; Cllr Bill Fairfoull; Cllr Bob Rudd; Cllr John Taylor.

OTHER INFORMATION Grants were made to 64 organisations during the financial year.

HOW TO APPLY Application forms can be found on the charity's website, along with guidelines. The trustees meet four times a year, in January, April, July and October and applicants should be informed of a decision within seven to ten days of a meeting.

WHO TO APPLY TO Diane Stredder, Administrator, Manchester Airport PLC, Olympic House, Manchester Airport, Manchester M90 1QX *Tel.* 0161 489 5281 *Email* trust.fund@manairport.co.uk *Website* www.manchesterairport.co.uk/community/working-in-our-community/community-trust-fund

■ The Manchester Guardian Society Charitable Trust

CC NO 515341 **ESTABLISHED** 1984

WHERE FUNDING CAN BE GIVEN Greater Manchester.

WHO CAN BENEFIT Preference is usually shown to smaller charities and community organisations in the Greater Manchester area which have difficulty in finding funding themselves.

WHAT IS FUNDED General charitable purposes, especially children and young people, ill health and disability, older people, disadvantaged individuals, education, the arts and community causes. The emphasis is very much on support in the Greater Manchester area.

WHAT IS NOT FUNDED Individuals.

TYPE OF GRANT Primarily small, one-off awards for capital projects and core costs.

SAMPLE GRANTS A list of beneficiaries was not available.

FINANCES *Year* 2015/16 *Income* £100,444 *Grants* £103,260 *Grants to organisations* £103,260 *Assets* £4,478,363

TRUSTEES Warren Smith; Lorraine Worsley; Paul Griffiths; Vivien Carter; Diane Hawkins; P. Lochery; Sharman Birtles; Lt Col. Shauna Dixon.

OTHER INFORMATION In 2015/16 grants were given to 74 organisations, but a list of beneficiaries was not available in the annual report or accounts.

HOW TO APPLY According to the 2015/16 annual report, the trust invites applications from community groups. Applications should give details about the nature of the project, the expected beneficiaries and the amount requested. The trustees meet quarterly to assess grant applications.

WHO TO APPLY TO Joseph Swift, Clerk to the Trustees, c/o Addleshaw Goddard LLP, 100 Barbirolli Square, Manchester M2 3AB *Tel.* 0161 934 6190 *Email* joe.swift@addleshawgoddard.com

■ Lord Mayor of Manchester's Charity Appeal Trust

CC NO 1066972 **ESTABLISHED** 1997

WHERE FUNDING CAN BE GIVEN The City of Manchester.

WHO CAN BENEFIT Charities, community groups, organisations and individuals in the City of Manchester. Organisations that do not have access to a professional fundraiser and experience difficulty in attracting funding from other sources are favoured, as are those with an income of less than £100,000 per annum.

WHAT IS FUNDED Social welfare and community development for the City of Manchester. In particular, the trust favours projects that are: run by local volunteers to improve disadvantaged communities; encourage involvement of local residents in the planning and delivery of activities; and promote voluntary participation, social inclusion, community involvement and self-help. Applications for individuals must be nominated by a sponsor or third party.

WHAT IS NOT FUNDED The website has detailed guidance on what the trust will not fund, which includes: major capital requests; arts-based projects; organisations trading for profit; replacement of statutory provision; academic or medical research and equipment; religious institutions or political parties; retrospective requests; sponsorship; national charities; core costs; services for individual benefit; animal welfare charities.

TYPE OF GRANT One-off; project funding.

RANGE OF GRANTS £360 to £4,000 for organisations. Up to £1,000 for individuals.

SAMPLE GRANTS St Margaret's Centre (£4,000); Lesbian and Gay Chorus (£2,400); Clayton Luncheon Club, Manchester Trafalgar Sea Cadets; Mancunian Way, Rock of Ages Diabetes Association and St Luke's Centre (£1,000 each); Wythenshawe Community Farm (£650); Sport4Life (£590); Friendship Healthcare Women Association (£360).

FINANCES *Year* 2015/16 *Income* £113,818 *Grants* £62,029 *Grants to organisations* £16,972 *Assets* £758,339

TRUSTEES Sir Howard Bernstein; William Egerton; Chair of the Fundraising Committee; Lord Mayor; Carol Culley; Rachel Downey; Anne Unwin.

OTHER INFORMATION Around £34,000 was given to individuals in 2015/16 and grants were made to 15 organisations.

HOW TO APPLY Applications should be made by email or post using a form which is provided on the trust's website, along with guidance notes. Trustee meetings take place four times each year and the deadlines are posted on the trust's website. Applications from one group for the same project will not be considered within three years.

WHO TO APPLY TO We Love MCR Charity, Lord Mayor's Office, Room 412, Level 4, Town Hall, Manchester M60 2LA *Tel.* 0161 234 3229 *Email* welovemcrcharity@manchester.gov.uk *Website* www.welovemcrcharity.org

The Manifold Charitable Trust

CC NO 229501 **ESTABLISHED** 1962
WHERE FUNDING CAN BE GIVEN UK.
WHO CAN BENEFIT Registered charities only.
WHAT IS FUNDED General charitable purposes; education and training; historic buildings and churches.
WHAT IS NOT FUNDED Individuals.
TYPE OF GRANT One-off and recurring capital costs.
RANGE OF GRANTS £5,000 or less.
SAMPLE GRANTS Eton College (£286,500); Amber Foundation (£30,000); Shottesbrooke Church (£11,000).
FINANCES *Year* 2015 *Income* £651,807 *Grants* £330,852 *Grants to organisations* £330,852 *Assets* £10,605,540
TRUSTEE The Manifold Trustee Company Ltd.
OTHER INFORMATION Of the grant total, almost £287,000 was given to Eton College. The accounts note that the trustees 'considered that none of the remaining grants that were made were material'. There were 11 awards made.
HOW TO APPLY The latest annual report for 2015 states that the trustees will no longer consider unsolicited applications from third parties.
WHO TO APPLY TO Helen Niven, Secretary, Studio Cottage, Windsor Great Park, Windsor, Berkshire SL4 2HP *Email* themanifoldtrust@gmail.com

The W. M. Mann Foundation

SC NO SC010111 **ESTABLISHED** 1992
WHERE FUNDING CAN BE GIVEN Mainly Scotland but UK-wide organisations may be assisted.
WHO CAN BENEFIT Charitable organisations; universities.
WHAT IS FUNDED General charitable purposes, including arts, education, music, medical causes and sports, disadvantaged individuals.
WHAT IS NOT FUNDED Individuals.
TYPE OF GRANT Unrestricted funding.
RANGE OF GRANTS Usually between £500 and £5,000.
SAMPLE GRANTS University of Glasgow Trust (£100,000); Royal Scottish National Orchestra (£35,000); Willow Tearoom Trust (£4,000); British Association for Adoption and Fostering, Parkhead Citizens Advice and Stonehaven Sea Cadets (£2,000 each); Glasgow Wood Recycling (£750); North Glasgow Community Food Initiative (£650); Maryhill Heritage Choir (£500).
FINANCES *Year* 2015/16 *Income* £226,164 *Grants* £267,250 *Grants to organisations* £267,250 *Assets* £6,019,340
OTHER INFORMATION In 2015/16 awards were made to 88 organisations. In 2012 the foundation changed its structure and became a SCIO. During that financial year the former trust transferred nearly £4.4 million in assets to the foundation.
HOW TO APPLY Apply in writing to the correspondent providing the latest set of annual report and accounts.
WHO TO APPLY TO The Trustees, 201 Bath Street, Glasgow G2 4HZ *Tel.* 0141 248 4936 *Fax* 0141 221 2976 *Email* mail@wmmanngroup.co.uk

R. W. Mann Trust

CC NO 1095699 **ESTABLISHED** 1959
WHERE FUNDING CAN BE GIVEN North Tyneside and East Newcastle; occasionally in the wider Tyne and Wear, Durham and Northumberland area.
WHO CAN BENEFIT Local registered charities or exempt groups such as scouts, schools, hospitals, CICs or social enterprises.
WHAT IS FUNDED A wide range of general charitable purposes; social welfare; education; health causes; children and young people; disability; older people.
WHAT IS NOT FUNDED Large, well-established national charities; individuals; church buildings except where they are used for community groups; projects or groups which can attract public funds, or which appeal to community foundations or national charitable trusts or other sources except if there is a particular part of the project which other sources would be unlikely to fund; deficits already incurred; replacement of statutory funding.
TYPE OF GRANT Recurrent expenditure, capital or one-off costs; core costs, feasibility studies, interest-free loans, project funding and salaries up to two years will be considered. In practice, unrestricted funding.
RANGE OF GRANTS Average grant of £1,000; awards can range between £100 and £10,000.
SAMPLE GRANTS Northumberland Clubs for Young People (£6,000); Skills Bridge (£4,000); People and Drugs (£3,000); Beacon Hill Arts CIC (£2,000 each); Alnwick District Playhouse Trust Ltd, Go Wild in Nature CIC and North East Maritime Trust (£1,000 each); Disability North (£500); North Tyneside Women's Voices (£250).
FINANCES *Year* 2015/16 *Income* £62,840 *Grants* £137,157 *Grants to organisations* £137,157 *Assets* £2,266,397
TRUSTEES Judith Hamilton; Guy Javens; Monica Heath.
OTHER INFORMATION During the year the trust made awards to 123 organisations.
HOW TO APPLY Apply in writing to the correspondent. The application should include a cover letter outlining the aims of your organisation and the project's aims, outcomes, beneficiaries and details of other funding. You should include a copy of your most recent accounts if available and any other information which you think will assist the trustees. It is noted that you should include an sae. The trustees meet very regularly and applicants will usually hear if their applications have been successful within a maximum of six weeks.
WHO TO APPLY TO John Hamilton, Secretary, PO Box 119, Gosforth, Newcastle upon Tyne NE3 4WF *Tel.* 0191 284 2158 *Email* john.hamilton@onyx.octacon.co.uk *Website* www.rwmanntrust.org.uk

The Manoukian Charitable Foundation

CC NO 1084065 **ESTABLISHED** 2000
WHERE FUNDING CAN BE GIVEN Worldwide.
WHO CAN BENEFIT Registered charities, with a preference for Armenian organisations.
WHAT IS FUNDED General charitable purposes, particularly social welfare, education, medical causes and arts and culture.
RANGE OF GRANTS £8,500 to £199,500.
SAMPLE GRANTS Action Innocence (£199,500); NSPCC (£98,500); St Yeghiche Armenian Church Parish (£79,500); Holy Etchmiadzin – library (£69,500); Looys Charitable Trust (£20,000); British Lebanese Association (£8,500).
FINANCES *Year* 2015 *Income* £767,964 *Grants* £478,109 *Grants to organisations* £475,609 *Assets* £228,668

TRUSTEES Tamar Manoukian; Anthony Bunker; Steven Press; Dr Armen Sarkissian.

OTHER INFORMATION The amount of grants given to individuals totalled £2,500.

HOW TO APPLY The annual report for 2015 states that 'requests for grants are received from the general public and charitable and other organisations through their knowledge of the activities of the foundation and through personal contacts of the settlor and the trustees. The foundation will consider providing assistance to projects that may be partly funded by others if this will enable the project to proceed. The trustees have tended to give greater consideration to educational and cultural projects as well as those which are intended to relieve poverty, illness and suffering.' The trustees meet at least once per year.

WHO TO APPLY TO Anthony Bunker, Trustee, St Yeghiche Armenian Church, 13B Cranley Gardens, London SW7 3BB

■ Marbeh Torah Trust

CC NO 292491 **ESTABLISHED** 1985

WHERE FUNDING CAN BE GIVEN UK and overseas, particularly Israel.

WHO CAN BENEFIT Jewish charitable organisations, especially educational establishments; individuals.

WHAT IS FUNDED Furtherance of Orthodox Jewish religious education and relief of poverty.

TYPE OF GRANT One-off and recurrent; interest-free loans.

RANGE OF GRANTS £1,800 to £122,500.

SAMPLE GRANTS Yeshiva Marbeh Torah (£122,500); Chazon Avraham Yitzchak (£82,500); Yad Gershon (£20,000); Mishkenos Yaakov (£9,600); Kollel Shaarei Shlomo (£7,000); Beis Dovid (£2,000); Y M Alsas (£1,800).

FINANCES *Year* 2015 *Income* £262,765 *Grants* £245,895 *Grants to organisations* £245,895 *Assets* £21,167

TRUSTEES Jacob Elzas; Moishe Elzas; Simone Elzas.

OTHER INFORMATION The trust made grants to seven organisations in 2015, primarily for Jewish education.

HOW TO APPLY Apply in writing to the correspondent.

WHO TO APPLY TO Moishe Elzas, Trustee, 116 Castlewood Road, London N15 6BE

■ The Marcela Trust

CC NO 1127514 **ESTABLISHED** 2009

WHERE FUNDING CAN BE GIVEN UK.

WHO CAN BENEFIT Registered charities; research institutions.

WHAT IS FUNDED General charitable purposes; medical research; the arts; education; poverty; disadvantaged communities.

WHAT IS NOT FUNDED Individuals.

TYPE OF GRANT Research grants; capital costs; projects; recurrent expenditure.

RANGE OF GRANTS £8,000 to £4,300,000.

SAMPLE GRANTS The Nuffield Orthopaedic Centre Appeal (£4,300,000); Fauna and Flora International (£430,000); Oxford Parkinson's Disease Centre (£50,000); Leg Ulcer Charity (£20,000); Society of Portrait Sculptors (£7,500).

FINANCES *Year* 2015/16 *Income* £5,273,309 *Grants* £4,807,500 *Grants to organisations* £4,807,500 *Assets* £82,151,369

TRUSTEES Brian Groves; Dawn Rose; Dr Martin Lenz; Mark Spragg; Jeanette Franklin; Paul Hotham.

OTHER INFORMATION During the year the trust awarded five grants to institutions totalling £4.8 million.

HOW TO APPLY Apply in writing to the correspondent. Although, potential applicants should be aware that grant recipients may be predetermined by the directors of OMC Investments Ltd.

WHO TO APPLY TO Jeanette Franklin, Trustee, Woodcote House, 4 Monks Close, Dorchester on Thames, Oxon OX10 7JA *Tel.* 01865 343802

■ The Marchig Animal Welfare Trust

CC NO 802133/SC038057 **ESTABLISHED** 1989

WHERE FUNDING CAN BE GIVEN Worldwide.

WHO CAN BENEFIT Organisations and individuals that make positive contributions in protecting animals and promoting and encouraging practical work in preventing animal cruelty and suffering.

WHAT IS FUNDED Animal welfare for example: spay/neuter programmes; veterinary hospitals, ambulances and medical equipment; animal shelters and sanctuaries; animal welfare education programmes.

WHAT IS NOT FUNDED Applications failing to meet the trust's criteria; expeditions; activities that are not totally animal welfare related; educational studies or other courses; salaries; support of conferences and meetings.

TYPE OF GRANT Service delivery; buildings; equipment; vehicles.

SAMPLE GRANTS Animals Asia Foundation – Hong Kong; Bedfordshire Wildlife Rescue – UK; Blue Cross of India; Free the Bears – Australia; Friendicoes Society for the Eradication of Cruelty to Animals – India; Help in Suffering – India; Tanzania Animal Protection Organisation; University of Edinburgh; VIDAS (Veterinarios Internacionales Dedicados a Animales Sanos) – Mexico; Worldwide Veterinary Service – UK.

FINANCES *Year* 2015 *Income* £1,335,763 *Grants* £2,471,724 *Grants to organisations* £2,471,724 *Assets* £18,179,332

TRUSTEES Colin Moor; Les Ward; Dr Jerzy Mlotkiewicz; Alastair Keatinge; Janice McLoughlin.

OTHER INFORMATION The annual report and accounts did not list grant recipients; however, the most recent grantees are specified on the trust's website. In addition to making grants the trust also makes The Jeanne Marchig Awards. These awards, which take the form of a financial donation in support of the winner's animal welfare work, are given in either of the following two categories: the development of an alternative method to the use of animals in experimental procedures and the practical implementation of such an alternative resulting in a significant reduction in the number of animals used in experimental procedures; practical work in the field of animal welfare resulting in significant improvements for animals either nationally or internationally.

HOW TO APPLY Application forms are available from the trust's website or the correspondent and should be returned via post or email along with the most recent accounts and annual report. Applications are accepted throughout the year and all of them are acknowledged – the trust requests applicants to be patient and do not make contact to ascertain when a decision will be made. You can re-apply after one year following the initial application. Note that applicants are expected to also have applied to other organisation for financial support for the project.

WHO TO APPLY TO Alastair Keatinge, Trustee, Caledonian Exchange, 10A Canning Street, Edinburgh EH3 8HE *Tel.* 0131 656 5746 *Email* info@marchigtrust.org or applications@marchigtrust.org *Website* www.marchigtrust.org

■ The Stella and Alexander Margulies Charitable Trust

CC NO 220441 **ESTABLISHED** 1962

WHERE FUNDING CAN BE GIVEN UK and overseas.

WHO CAN BENEFIT Charitable organisations, particularly those benefitting Jewish people.

WHAT IS FUNDED General charitable purposes, including health, social welfare and the arts; Jewish causes.

TYPE OF GRANT One-off and recurrent.

RANGE OF GRANTS Generally £100 to £5,000; up to £250,000.

SAMPLE GRANTS Botanical Gardens of Jerusalem (£250,000); Shaare Zedek UK (£110,500); Royal Opera House Foundation (£25,000); Jerusalem Foundation (£18,500); IPO Foundation (£15,500); Barbican Centre Trust (£10,000); Jewish Community Secondary School (£2,500); Kisharon and UK Toremet Ltd (£500 each); Cancer Research UK and Macmillan Cancer Support (£100 each).

FINANCES *Year* 2015/16 *Income* £139,198 *Grants* £434,412 *Grants to organisations* £434,412 *Assets* £8,396,000

TRUSTEES Martin Paisner; Sir Stuart Lipton; Alexander Sorkin; Marcus Margulies; Leslie Michaels.

OTHER INFORMATION During the year a total of 15 awards were made.

HOW TO APPLY Apply in writing to the correspondent. The annual report for 2015/16 notes that the trustees also 'search out appropriate projects'.

WHO TO APPLY TO Leslie Michaels, Trustee, 34 Dover Street, London W1S 4NG

■ Mariapolis Ltd

CC NO 257912 **ESTABLISHED** 1968

WHERE FUNDING CAN BE GIVEN UK and overseas.

WHO CAN BENEFIT Organisations and individuals.

WHAT IS FUNDED Christian ecumenism; young people, families and older people; education; relief in need.

TYPE OF GRANT Recurrent.

RANGE OF GRANTS Up to £201,000.

SAMPLE GRANTS Pia Associazione Maschile Opera di Maria – PAMOM (£201,000); Focolare Trust (£34,500); Foyer de L'Unité (£24,000).

FINANCES *Year* 2015/16 *Income* £473,501 *Grants* £261,466 *Grants to organisations* £261,466 *Assets* £3,294,421

TRUSTEES Francis Johnson; Carlo Poggi; Paul Gateshill.

OTHER INFORMATION The charity promotes the international Focolare Movement in the UK, and grant-making is only one area of its work. It has a related interest in ecumenism and also in overseas development. Activities include organising conferences and courses, and publishing books and magazines from which it derives some of its income.

HOW TO APPLY Apply in writing to the correspondent.

WHO TO APPLY TO Rumold Van Geffen, Secretary/Treasurer, Unit 1, Polaris Centre, 41 Brownfields, Welwyn Garden City, Hertfordshire AL7 1AN *Tel.* 01707 326213 *Email* rumold1949@gmail.com *Website* www.focolare.org/gb

■ The Michael Marks Charitable Trust

CC NO 248136 **ESTABLISHED** 1966

WHERE FUNDING CAN BE GIVEN UK and overseas.

WHO CAN BENEFIT Registered charities; galleries, museums and libraries; educational institutions.

WHAT IS FUNDED Arts and culture; environment; conservation.

WHAT IS NOT FUNDED Grants are given to registered charities only. Awards are not made to individuals or profit-making organisations.

TYPE OF GRANT One-off and recurring.

RANGE OF GRANTS Generally £500 to £21,000.

SAMPLE GRANTS Wordsworth Trust (£21,000); Oxford Philomusica Orchestra and National Trust (£10,000 each); Songbird Survival (£6,000); European Squirrel Activity, Marine Conservation Society, National Library of Scotland, Species Recovery Trust and Writer Centre (£5,000 each) Autism Plus (£2,300); Surfers Against Sewage (£1,000); Greek Archaeological Society of Great Britain (£500).

FINANCES *Year* 2015/16 *Income* £196,662 *Grants* £137,996 *Grants to organisations* £137,996 *Assets* £6,433,931

TRUSTEES Lady Marina Marks; Prof. Sir Christopher White; Noel Annesley.

OTHER INFORMATION During the year, the charity provided grants totalling £93,500 to charities relating to the arts and £44,500 for environmental causes.

HOW TO APPLY Apply in writing to the correspondent. Applications must include audited accounts, information on other bodies approached and details of funding obtained. The trustees meet twice a year to consider applications, usually in July. Requests will not receive a response unless they have been successful.

WHO TO APPLY TO Lady Marina Marks, Trustee, 5 Elm Tree Road, London NW8 9JY *Tel.* 020 7286 4633 *Email* michaelmarkscharitabletrust@hotmail.co.uk

■ The Marks Family Foundation

CC NO 1137014 **ESTABLISHED** 2010

WHERE FUNDING CAN BE GIVEN UK.

WHO CAN BENEFIT Charitable organisations.

WHAT IS FUNDED General charitable purposes, especially arts and culture, health causes, Jewish causes.

TYPE OF GRANT Usually one-off, unrestricted grants; also loans.

RANGE OF GRANTS £500 to £45,000.

SAMPLE GRANTS Orchestra of the Age of Enlightenment (£45,000); Weizmann Institute (£35,000); Jewish Care (£15,000); Orange Tree Theatre (£6,000); West London Synagogue (£5,900); Royal Opera House Foundation (£2,000); Jewish Child's Day (£750); Pancreatic Cancer UK and Redbridge Foodbank (£500 each).

FINANCES *Year* 2015/16 *Income* £188,287 *Grants* £110,630 *Grants to organisations* £110,630 *Assets* £262,952

TRUSTEES David Marks; Selina Marks; James Marks; Dr Daniel Marks.

OTHER INFORMATION The settlor of the foundation, David Marks, is a partner in Apax Partners LLP, private equity investment group, and also a trustee of the Apax Foundation and the R. and S. Cohen Foundation. During the year there were nine awards made.

HOW TO APPLY The annual report for 2015/16 states the following: 'The Trustees remain concerned about the volume of unsolicited approaches from other charities and the expenditure incurred by these charities in making these submissions. Accordingly, the Trustees have adopted a policy of only considering the making of grants to charitable organisations with which the Trustees have personal contact and will not respond to these unsolicited requests in the hope that this will dissuade such charities from incurring unnecessary expenditure.'

WHO TO APPLY TO David Marks, Trustee, 10 Green Street, London W1K 6RP *Email* dmarkstax@aol.com

■ The Ann and David Marks Foundation

CC NO 326303 **ESTABLISHED** 1983

WHERE FUNDING CAN BE GIVEN Worldwide, with a preference for Manchester.

WHO CAN BENEFIT Jewish organisations; registered charities; educational institutions.

WHAT IS FUNDED General charitable purposes, including social welfare, health and education; Jewish causes; humanitarian aid.

SAMPLE GRANTS According to the latest accounts, 'it is not the policy of the trustees to disclose individual donations'. However, it is noted that major donations included an award to the Morasha Jewish Primary Trust School (£20,000).

FINANCES *Year* 2015 *Income* £75,812 *Grants* £52,669 *Grants to organisations* £52,669 *Assets* £650,974

TRUSTEES Ann Marks; Ashley Marks; G. Marks; David Marks; Marcelle Palmer.

HOW TO APPLY The annual report for 2015 states: 'The Foundation envisages continuing to support Charities known to the Trustees and feels that this will absorb its available funds for the foreseeable future. For this reason the Trustees do not welcome unsolicited applications.'

WHO TO APPLY TO David Marks, Trustee, c/o Mutley Properties Ltd, Mutley House, 1 Ambassador Place, Stockport Road, Altrincham WA15 8DB *Tel.* 0161 941 3183 *Email* davidmarks@mutleyproperties.co.uk

■ The Hilda and Samuel Marks Foundation

CC NO 245208 **ESTABLISHED** 1965

WHERE FUNDING CAN BE GIVEN Worldwide; in practice the UK and Israel.

WHO CAN BENEFIT Charitable organisations.

WHAT IS FUNDED General charitable purposes; Jewish causes; relief in need; health; education; community causes.

WHAT IS NOT FUNDED Individuals.

SAMPLE GRANTS A full list of beneficiaries was unavailable, as 'the trustees do not feel it appropriate, as a general rule, to comment on individual donations'. However, the 2015/16 annual report states that grants were broken down between the following purposes: health (£82,500); welfare (£77,000); and community/education (£44,500). Donations were also made to The Rochelle and Anthony Selby Charitable Trust (£25,000) and Ann and David Marks Foundation (£25,000) whose trustees include trustees from this foundation.

FINANCES *Year* 2015/16 *Income* £130,520 *Grants* £250,976 *Grants to organisations* £250,976 *Assets* £3,229,428

TRUSTEES David Marks; Rochelle Selby.

OTHER INFORMATION The grant total was divided between UK charities (£87,000) and Israel-based charities (£110,800). A number of organisations are regularly supported on a long-term basis.

HOW TO APPLY The foundation primarily supports projects known to the trustees and its funds are fully committed. Therefore, unsolicited applications are not being sought.

WHO TO APPLY TO David Marks, Trustee, 1 Ambassador Place, Stockport Road, Altrincham, Cheshire WA15 8DB *Tel.* 0161 941 3183 *Email* davidmarks@mutleyproperties.co.uk

■ The J. P. Marland Charitable Trust

CC NO 1049350 **ESTABLISHED** 1995

WHERE FUNDING CAN BE GIVEN UK.

WHO CAN BENEFIT Registered charities and individuals.

WHAT IS FUNDED General charitable purposes, including arts, sports, medical causes, teaching and community needs.

TYPE OF GRANT One-off and up to one year; capital costs; project funding.

RANGE OF GRANTS Up to £18,000.

SAMPLE GRANTS MCC Foundation (£18,000); The Guggenheim UK Charitable Trust (£12,500); The National Theatre (£10,000); The Churchill Centre (UK) (£9,000); Downside Abbey Trust (£8,000); The Trussell Trust (£6,000); Arts Access Foundation (£3,000).

FINANCES *Year* 2014/15 *Income* £45,146 *Grants* £57,248 *Grants to organisations* £57,248 *Assets* £637,238

TRUSTEES Lord Jonathan Marland; Carol Law; Marcus Marland; Hugo Marland.

OTHER INFORMATION A total of 19 grants were given to organisations in the following categories: arts (£33,500); sports (£17,500); medical/teaching/community (£6,500).

HOW TO APPLY Apply via email to the correspondent.

WHO TO APPLY TO Lord Jonathan Marland, Trustee, Odstock Manor, Salisbury, Wiltshire SP5 4JA *Tel.* 01722 329781 *Email* jpmarlandcharitabletrust@marland.co

■ Marmot Charitable Trust

CC NO 1106619 **ESTABLISHED** 2004

WHERE FUNDING CAN BE GIVEN Worldwide.

WHO CAN BENEFIT 'Green' organisations; educational institutions; environmental and peace projects.

WHAT IS FUNDED The trust is interested in 'funding green initiatives that are working towards a sustainable future, and peace and security that are seeking to reduce international conflict including by the eventual elimination of nuclear weapons'.

TYPE OF GRANT Project and core costs can be covered.

RANGE OF GRANTS £2,000 to £15,000.

SAMPLE GRANTS British American Security Council (BASIC) and Centre for Alternative Technology (£15,000 each); UNA UK (£8,000); Artists Project Earth, Network for Social Change Charitable Trust and Poverty and Environment Trust (£4,000 each); China Dialogue Trust,

Oxford Research Group, Road Peace and UK Friends of Khwendo Kor (£2,000 each).

FINANCES *Year* 2015/16 *Income* £157,186 *Grants* £95,992 *Grants to organisations* £95,992 *Assets* £3,408,305

TRUSTEES Martin Bevis Gillett; Jonathan Gillett; Jeanni Barlow.

OTHER INFORMATION In 2015/16 there were 20 awards made with the average grant being £4,800.

HOW TO APPLY The trust has informed us directly that they do not accept unsolicited applications.

WHO TO APPLY TO Martin Bevis Gillet, Trustee, c/o BM Marmot, London WC1N 3XX *Email* marmot.trust@gmail.com

■ The Marr-Munning Trust

CC NO 1153007 **ESTABLISHED** 1970

WHERE FUNDING CAN BE GIVEN Indian subcontinent, Southeast Asia and sub-Saharan Africa.

WHO CAN BENEFIT Registered charitable organisations and NGOs with an annual income of between £25,000 and £1 million.

WHAT IS FUNDED Overseas aid projects aimed at addressing poverty and suffering in financially developing countries, particularly those likely to provide good quality education for children and effective training for adults that will improve their ability to earn a living.

WHAT IS NOT FUNDED Individuals; work taking place outside the defined beneficial area; retrospective funding.

TYPE OF GRANT Recurrent and one-off.

RANGE OF GRANTS Up to £30,000.

SAMPLE GRANTS Children's Chance International, Educaid Sierra Leone and Street Child Africa (£30,000 each); Educate for Life (£28,500); Environmental Conservation and Agricultural Enhancement Uganda (Eco-Agric) (£20,000); African Revival (£19,500); Mango Tree Orphan Support Programme (£14,000); Livingstone Tanzania Trust (£10,000); Victory Rural Development Society (£8,300); We Yone Child Foundation (£7,800).

FINANCES *Year* 2015/16 *Income* £738,771 *Grants* £376,842 *Grants to organisations* £376,842 *Assets* £16,381,349

TRUSTEES Glen Barnham; Pierre Thomas; Dr Geetha Oommen; Hur Hassnain; Adeyemi Oyewumi; Samantha Mardell; Khaled Daair; Matthew Sampson.

OTHER INFORMATION During 2015/16 the trust made 19 new grants to organisations.

HOW TO APPLY At the time of writing (April 2017) the trust was reviewing its grant application process and the way in which it allocates funds. The website stated the following: 'As well as reviewing our funding priorities and criteria we are also reviewing whether we will continue to award grants through an open application process. We will publish an update on our grant-making review here at the beginning of August 2017. Until our review is complete we are accepting no applications for support.'

WHO TO APPLY TO James Fitzpatrick, Director, 9 Madeley Road, Ealing, London W5 2LA *Tel.* 020 8998 7747 *Fax* 020 8998 9593 *Email* info@marrmunningtrust.org.uk *Website* www.marrmunningtrust.org.uk

■ The Michael Marsh Charitable Trust

CC NO 220473 **ESTABLISHED** 1958

WHERE FUNDING CAN BE GIVEN Birmingham, Staffordshire, Worcestershire, Warwickshire, Coventry, Wolverhampton and associated towns in the Black Country.

WHO CAN BENEFIT Charitable organisations; community-based organisations.

WHAT IS FUNDED General charitable purposes; children and young people; older people; education and training; relief in need; disability; religious activities.

WHAT IS NOT FUNDED Animals; entertainment charities; replacement of statutory funding; running costs. Grants to individuals are only given through charitable institutions on their behalf.

TYPE OF GRANT Generally recurrent; grants subject to remaining project funding found by the charity.

RANGE OF GRANTS Usually between £1,000 and £5,000.

SAMPLE GRANTS Broad Street Meeting Hall (£15,000); Birmingham Children's Community Venture, Broadening Choices for Older People and Wildlife Trust for Birmingham and the Black Country (£5,000 each); Awards for Young Musicians (£3,800); Black Country Foodbank (£3,000); Resources for Autism (£2,500); West Midlands Quaker Peace Education (£2,000); Royal Air Force Association and The Asha Women's Centre (£1,000 each); Tall Ships Youth Trust (£400).

FINANCES *Year* 2015/16 *Income* £169,022 *Grants* £594,720 *Grants to organisations* £594,720 *Assets* £3,483,835

TRUSTEES Peter Barber; Susan Bennett; Lee Nuttall.

OTHER INFORMATION There were 87 awards given. The trust states that it aims 'to make a roughly equal division of funds between charities concerned with old people, children, the disabled, the poor and educational needs'. Grants to specific projects for locally based smaller charities are favoured but larger projects may be considered.

HOW TO APPLY Apply in writing to the correspondent. The trustees normally meet in June and December to consider all applications received in the preceding six months. However, they will consider on an ad hoc basis any requests that they believe should not be retained until their next scheduled meeting.

WHO TO APPLY TO The Trustees, c/o Mills and Reeve LLP, 78–84 Colmore Row, Birmingham B3 2AB *Tel.* 0870 600 0011 *Email* marsh.charity@mills-reeve.com

■ The Marsh Christian Trust

CC NO 284470 **ESTABLISHED** 1981

WHERE FUNDING CAN BE GIVEN UK.

WHO CAN BENEFIT Registered charities.

WHAT IS FUNDED General charitable purposes, with a preference towards literature, arts and heritage; social welfare; environmental causes and animal welfare; education and training; health care.

WHAT IS NOT FUNDED Individuals or individual sponsorship proposals; building work or individual restoration projects; single projects; individual churches; individual hospices or hospitals.

TYPE OF GRANT Long-term core funding; running costs; volunteer expenses; unrestricted.

RANGE OF GRANTS Usually £250 to £4,000.

SAMPLE GRANTS British Museum (£7,000); British Refugee Council (£2,000); Butterfly Conservation (£1,500); English Speaking Union (£1,200); Bible Reading Fellowship (£1,000); Quaker Social Action and Prisoners' Education Trust (£750 each); Trees for Life (£650); Reach Volunteering (£550); The Church Urban Fund (£450); The British Acoustic Neuroma Association (£300); Russian Arctic Convoy Museum Project (£250); Small Woods Association (£110); Royal Society of Literature (£50).

FINANCES *Year* 2015/16 *Income* £793,159 *Grants* £251,544 *Grants to organisations* £162,744 *Assets* £9,283,439

TRUSTEES Brian Marsh; Natalie Marsh; Lorraine Ryan; Antonia Marsh; Camilla Kenyon; Charles Micklewright; Nicholas Carter.

OTHER INFORMATION The trust also maintains the Marsh Awards Scheme – to recognise individual and group achievements in the charity sector. The scheme now consists of over 70 different programmes run across the areas of social welfare, conservation and ecology, the arts and heritage. Full details are available on the website. In 2015/16 grants consisted of £163,000 given in donations and almost £89,000 in Marsh Awards.

HOW TO APPLY Apply in writing to the correspondent. The trust requires a cover letter and a full copy of the applicant's report and accounts. Every effort is made to reply to each appeal received whether it is successful or not.

WHO TO APPLY TO Brian Marsh, Trustee, 2nd Floor, 36 Broadway, London SW1H 0BH *Tel.* 020 7233 3112 *Email* reeves@bpmarsh.co.uk *Website* www.marshchristiantrust.org

■ Charity of John Marshall

CC NO 206780 **ESTABLISHED** 1627

WHERE FUNDING CAN BE GIVEN England and Wales with preference for Kent, Surrey, Lincolnshire and Southwark.

WHO CAN BENEFIT Anglican parish churches and cathedrals only.

WHAT IS FUNDED Support for parsonage buildings throughout England and Wales; help with the upkeep of Anglican churches and cathedrals in Kent, Surrey and Lincolnshire (as the counties were defined in 1855), support for the parish of Christ Church in Southwark; awards for educational purposes to Marshall's Educational Foundation (4% of the expenditure).

WHAT IS NOT FUNDED **Churches:** Applicants who have received a grant from the charity within the past three years; churches outside the counties of Kent, Surrey and Lincolnshire, as defined in 1855; churches of denominations other than Anglican; professional fees; works outside the footprint of the church, such as church halls, external meeting rooms and facilities, church grounds and boundary walls and fences; redecoration; bells; organs; clock; monuments; brasses; stained glass. **Parsonages:** Applications from individual clergy or other denominations – appeals should be made by applications from the relevant Diocesan Parsonage Board.

TYPE OF GRANT Building and other capital works; loans.

RANGE OF GRANTS Grants to churches usually of £3,000 to £5,000; awards to parsonages usually up to £4,000.

SAMPLE GRANTS Christ Church – Camberwell (£15,000); All Saints – Saxby and St Luke – Whyteleafe (£10,000 each); St John the Evangelist – Ickham (£5,000); Holy Trinity – West End (£3,000).

FINANCES *Year* 2015 *Income* £1,195,376 *Grants* £658,877 *Grants to organisations* £560,500 *Assets* £19,172,503

TRUSTEES Anthony Guthrie; Colin Bird; Stephen Clark; Bill Eason; Anthea Nicholson; Georgina Farquhar Isaac; John Heawood; Revd Jonathan Rust; Surbhi Malhotra-Trenkel; Lesley Bosman; Charles Ledsam; Alastair Moss.

OTHER INFORMATION During the year, the charity awarded £387,000 in grants for the repair and maintenance of 115 parsonages and £13,500 to fund security systems at 45 parsonages (of these amounts, £1,400 was cancelled). Further 24 grants were made to churches totalling £166,500 (of which £5,000 was cancelled). We have taken the sum of parsonage grants and church restoration grants as our grant total for the year as we feel this makes the best indicator of the amount of funding that was available to apply for.

HOW TO APPLY Application forms for church grants can be downloaded, along with full guidelines, from the charity's website and can be returned via post or email to the correspondent at any time. The Grants Committee meets three times a year (for exact dates see the website). Applications for parsonages must be made through the relevant Diocesan Parsonage Board. The website also has a helpful page dedicated to other funding sources for church improvements.

WHO TO APPLY TO Catherine Dawkins, Clerk to the Trustees, 66 Newcomen Street, London SE1 1YT *Tel.* 020 7407 2979 *Email* grantoffice@marshalls.org.uk *Website* www.marshalls.org.uk

■ Charlotte Marshall Charitable Trust

CC NO 211941 **ESTABLISHED** 1962

WHERE FUNDING CAN BE GIVEN UK.

WHO CAN BENEFIT Registered charities; educational institutions benefitting Roman Catholics.

WHAT IS FUNDED Two thirds of the trust's income can be allocated to support educational, religious and other charitable purposes for Roman Catholics and the remainder can be distributed at the trustees' discretion.

WHAT IS NOT FUNDED Individuals.

RANGE OF GRANTS £250 to £2,500.

SAMPLE GRANTS Sacred Heart Catholic Primary School (£2,500); Catholic Children's Society Plymouth, Netherley Youth and Community Initiative, NOAH Enterprise and Women at the Well (£1,500 each); Kent Association for the Blind, Pett Level Rescue Boat Association and Raystede Centre of Animal Welfare (£820 each); Bibles For Children (£420); Adventure Plus, Medina Valley Centre and Oxford Youth Works (£250 each).

FINANCES *Year* 2015/16 *Income* £79,630 *Grants* £74,879 *Grants to organisations* £74,879 *Assets* £507,622

TRUSTEES Joseph Cosgrave; Kevin Page; John Russell; Rachel Cosgrave.

OTHER INFORMATION Of the grant total, about £50,000 went to Roman Catholic charitable institutions. There were 67 awards made.

HOW TO APPLY Applications should be made by completing the trust's application form with a formal request for funds. The trustees consider appeals at their spring meeting, usually around March. Our research suggests that completed forms should be returned in advance to the meeting – by 31 December.

WHO TO APPLY TO The Trustees, c/o C. & C. Marshall Ltd, Sidney Little Road, Churchfields Industrial Estate, St Leonards on Sea, East Sussex TN38 9PU *Tel.* 01424 856655 *Email* TeresaP@marshall-tufflex.com

■ D. G. Marshall of Cambridge Trust

CC NO 286468 **ESTABLISHED** 1982

WHERE FUNDING CAN BE GIVEN Predominantly Cambridge and Cambridgeshire.

WHO CAN BENEFIT Registered charities; community organisations.

WHAT IS FUNDED Education and training; social welfare; aviation; disability; health; children and young people; community projects.

TYPE OF GRANT Project costs; unrestricted donations.

RANGE OF GRANTS £100 to £50,000; typically less than £2,000.

SAMPLE GRANTS Jesus College Wesley House Development (£50,000); ATC 104 Squadron (£23,000); Arthur Rank Hospice (£5,000); Royal Astronomical Society (£2,500); Ely Cathedral Restoration Trust, Flying Soldier Heritage Appeal, Motability and Teversham School (£1,000 each); Institute of Economic Affairs (£500); Sea Cadets (£250); Walk the Walk (£100).

FINANCES *Year* 2015/16 *Income* £120,207 *Grants* £113,950 *Grants to organisations* £113,950 *Assets* £2,319,436

TRUSTEES Sarah Moynihan; Julie Ingham; Michael Marshall; Robert Marshall.

OTHER INFORMATION Grants were made to 42 organisations for the following purposes: education (£55,500); aviation (£30,500); local community (£8,700); hospitals and related organisations (£7,800); children's charities (£5,500); disability, health and life threatening diseases (£4,800); churches (£1,000).

HOW TO APPLY The trustees will consider all applications, providing they are consistent with the objectives of the charity.

WHO TO APPLY TO Julie Ingham, Administrator, Airport House, The Airport, Newmarket Road, Cambridge CB5 8RY

■ The Martin Charitable Trust

SC NO SC028487 **ESTABLISHED** 1998

WHERE FUNDING CAN BE GIVEN Scotland, particularly Glasgow and Strathclyde.

WHO CAN BENEFIT Registered charities.

WHAT IS FUNDED General charitable purposes; there is a preference for Christian and health charities, and those working with children and older people.

WHAT IS NOT FUNDED Individuals.

TYPE OF GRANT One-off and recurrent.

RANGE OF GRANTS £500 to £8,000.

SAMPLE GRANTS Ardgowan Hospice (£8,000); Music in Hospitals (£4,000); Glasgow Old People's Welfare Association (£3,000); Mental Health Foundation (£2,000); Seafarers UK and RSPB Scotland (£1,000 each); Special Needs Adventure Playground (£500).

FINANCES *Year* 2014/15 *Income* £122,159 *Grants* £81,500 *Grants to organisations* £81,500 *Assets* £2,487,399

HOW TO APPLY Apply in writing to the correspondent, including up-to-date accounts.

WHO TO APPLY TO The Trustees, Miller Beckett and Jackson Solicitors, 190 St Vincent Street, Glasgow G2 5SP *Tel.* 0141 204 2833

■ Sir George Martin Trust

CC NO 223554 **ESTABLISHED** 1956

WHERE FUNDING CAN BE GIVEN North and West Yorkshire.

WHO CAN BENEFIT Registered charities; churches; educational establishments; hospices; museums.

WHAT IS FUNDED Children and young people; church appeals – church outreach only; countryside, environment, green issues; hospices; mental well-being; museums and historic buildings; music and the arts; older people; physical and learning disabilities; schools, education, universities – must be outreach work; social welfare; sports for disadvantaged communities.

WHAT IS NOT FUNDED Appeals that are not focused on West and/or North Yorkshire; individuals; overseas organisations; overseas seminars or exchange visits by individuals or groups; medical appeals of a capital or revenue nature; medical research projects; restoration schemes of church roofs, spires, etc.; playgroups.

TYPE OF GRANT Grants for capital rather than revenue projects; usually one-off.

RANGE OF GRANTS £500 to £5,000.

SAMPLE GRANTS Marie Curie Cancer Care (£5,500); Antibiotic Research UK (£5,000); Henshaws Society for the Blind (£4,000).

FINANCES *Year* 2015/16 *Income* £178,716 *Grants* £187,585 *Grants to organisations* £187,585 *Assets* £7,231,945

TRUSTEES David Coates, Chair; Martin Bethel; Roger Marshall; Paul Taylor; Marjorie Martin; Morven Whyte; Sir George Martin Trust Company Ltd.

OTHER INFORMATION The trust received 215 applications in the year of which 133 were successful.

HOW TO APPLY Application forms can be requested via email or phone from the correspondent. It should be returned via post along with a statement of no more than two pages outlining your proposal and a copy of your latest set of accounts and annual report. You should also specify the amount required and whether any other funding has been secured. The trustees meet in March, July and November each year.

WHO TO APPLY TO Carla Marshall, Trust Manager, 6 Firs Avenue, Harrogate, North Yorkshire HG2 9HA *Tel.* 01423 810222 *Email* info@sirgeorgemartintrust.org.uk *Website* www.sirgeorgemartintrust.org.uk

■ John Martin's Charity

CC NO 527473 **ESTABLISHED** 1714

WHERE FUNDING CAN BE GIVEN Evesham and 'certain surrounding villages' only.

WHO CAN BENEFIT Individuals and charitable or voluntary organisations and schools benefitting the residents of Evesham.

WHAT IS FUNDED Religious support – to assist the vicars and parochial church councils within the town of Evesham; relief in need – to assist individuals and organisations within the town of Evesham who are in conditions of need, hardship and distress; promotion of education – to promote education to those residing within the town of Evesham and to provide benefits to schools within Evesham; health – to support people with chronic health problems and other related health issues.

WHAT IS NOT FUNDED Payment of rates or taxes; replacement of statutory benefits; retrospective funding. The charity cannot commit to repeat or renewal funding.
TYPE OF GRANT One-off capital costs, general expenditure and project costs.
RANGE OF GRANTS £500 to £30,000.
SAMPLE GRANTS St Andrew's Parochial Church Council Hampton (£29,700); All Saints Parochial Church Council Evesham (£17,800); St Richards Hospice (£23,000); Evesham Methodist Church (£12,000); Prince Henry's High School (£11,200); Hampton Scout and Guide Hall (£9,000); Caring Hands in the Vale (£5,000); Worcester Citizens Advice and WHABAC (£2,100); Yellow Scarf CIC (£2,000); Evesham Festival of Words (£1,000).
FINANCES *Year* 2015/16 *Income* £774,933 *Grants* £625,791 *Grants to organisations* £230,820 *Assets* £21,631,686
TRUSTEES Nigel Lamb; John Smith; Richard Emson; Cyril Scorse; Diana Raphael; Frances Smith; Julie Westlake; John Wilson; Revd Mark Binney; Catherine Evans; Gabrielle Falkiner; Stuart Allerton.
OTHER INFORMATION Grants were distributed as follows: education 46%, relief in need 37%, religious support 10%, health and other grants 7%.
HOW TO APPLY There is an application form available to download on the charity's website, where it requests that organisations provide their latest annual accounts, a bank statement, relevant literature and a breakdown of expected costs. Grant applications are considered once per quarter, approximately four weeks after the following application closing dates: 1 June, 1 September, 20 November and 1 March.
WHO TO APPLY TO John Daniels, Clerk to the Trustees, 16 Queen's Road, Evesham, Worcestershire WR11 4JN *Tel.* 01386 765440 *Email* enquiries@johnmartins.org.uk *Website* www.johnmartins.org.uk

■ The Dan Maskell Tennis Trust

CC NO 1133589 **ESTABLISHED** 2009
WHERE FUNDING CAN BE GIVEN Throughout the UK.
WHO CAN BENEFIT Individuals; disability groups and programmes; tennis clubs; associations; schools.
WHAT IS FUNDED Promotion of physical health, fitness and general well-being of people with disabilities through the sport of tennis.
TYPE OF GRANT The purchase of wheelchairs, tennis equipment and grants for coaching.
SAMPLE GRANTS A list of beneficiaries was not available.
FINANCES *Year* 2015 *Income* £100,629 *Grants* £54,974 *Grants to organisations* £54,974 *Assets* £554,234
TRUSTEES Lilas Davison; Ian Peacock; John Tucker; Sue Wolstenholme; John James; Robin Maskell-Charlton; Tony Hughes; Noel McShane; Robert McCowen.
OTHER INFORMATION During the year, 80 grant applications were approved. These awards supported the purchase of 16 individual tennis wheelchairs, 6 general tennis wheelchairs for separate groups and 13 tennis equipment bags. 45 other grants were also made for a range of purposes, including 18 awards to individuals.
HOW TO APPLY Application forms are available from the trust's website. The trustees meet at least three times a year. The dates of meetings and application submission deadlines (which usually fall in the preceding month) are listed on the website. It is requested that applicants provide as much information as possible and include details of the cost for each item or facility.
WHO TO APPLY TO Gilly English, Executive Director, c/o Sport Wins, PO Box 238, Tadworth, Surrey KT20 5WT *Tel.* 01737 831707 *Email* danmaskell@sportwins.co.uk *Website* www.danmaskelltennistrust.org.uk

■ The Mason Porter Charitable Trust

CC NO 255545 **ESTABLISHED** 1968
WHERE FUNDING CAN BE GIVEN UK.
WHO CAN BENEFIT Registered charities and churches.
WHAT IS FUNDED General charitable purposes, particularly Christian causes.
RANGE OF GRANTS Up to £20,500.
SAMPLE GRANTS International Gospel Outreach (£20,500); Kingsmead School (£20,000); Proclaim Trust (£7,000); ECG Trust, Burslem Methodist (£4,000); New Creations, St Luke's Methodist Church and Youth for Christ (£2,000 each); Messengers (£1,000).
FINANCES *Year* 2014/15 *Income* £161,008 *Grants* £67,310 *Grants to organisations* £67,310 *Assets* £1,939,601
TRUSTEES Heather Akehurst; Perminder Bal; Charles Feeny; Adeyinka Lovelady; Christine Reeves; Hilary Russell; Caroline Clark; Deborah Shackleton; Andrew Whitehead.
HOW TO APPLY The trust has informed us that, as this is a personal trust, 'grants are only made to charities already known to the settlor'. The accounts confirm that 'unsolicited applications are therefore not considered'.
WHO TO APPLY TO Liverpool Charity and Voluntary Services, 151 Dale Street, Liverpool L2 2AH *Tel.* 0151 227 5177

■ Masonic Charitable Foundation

CC NO 1164703 **ESTABLISHED** 2015
WHERE FUNDING CAN BE GIVEN England and Wales.
WHO CAN BENEFIT Registered charities; research bodies; hospices (those receiving 60% or less of their funding from the NHS).
WHAT IS FUNDED There are three categories of focus: community support; medical and social research; other charitable causes. **Community support includes:** financial hardship; health and disability; education and employability; social exclusion and disadvantage. **Medical and social research grants** fund research into a wide range of illnesses and conditions, and around issues of well-being and participation in society. **Other causes include:** hospices; air ambulances; disaster relief; Lifelines. Further information on each of the areas of focus is given on the website.
WHAT IS NOT FUNDED Community support grants are not provided for: arts and heritage projects; environmental projects; animal welfare; political or lobbying activities; civil liberties and human rights; routine delivery in schools; contributions toward new build and/or large-scale capital projects (e.g. building a new hospice wing); capital repairs and/or maintenance of existing buildings; hospital equipment, such as MRI scanners; projects solely carried out outside England and Wales. Community support grants are not provided to: current active grant holders; umbrella organisations co-ordinating fundraising on behalf of others; social enterprises or CICs; community interest groups; organisations that

are not registered charities; schools (for routine delivery activities to non-priority groups); nurseries (for routine delivery activities to non-priority groups); hospitals (for routine delivery activities to non-priority groups); individuals, including PhD students (although research grants can be awarded to fund PhD students who are part of a wider research project); organisations which have had a grant from the foundation which ended less than two years ago; organisations which applied unsuccessfully to the foundation in the last 12 months.

TYPE OF GRANT Project costs; core and running costs; research; salaries; small capital projects.

RANGE OF GRANTS Small grants: £500 to £5,000; large grants: over £5,000.

SAMPLE GRANTS Blind Veterans UK (£100,000); Bipolar UK Support Line (£60,000); CHICKS (£43,000); Groundwork London (£30,000); Young Gloucestershire (£10,000); Dyspraxia Foundation and Home-Start Sutton (£5,000 each); Norwich Foodbank and Walsall Bereavement Support Service (£2,000 each); Squirrel's Nest (£1,000).

TRUSTEES John Codd; David Watson; John Boyington; Andrew Campbell Ross; Dr Charles Akle; Christopher White; Dr Michael Woodcock; James Newman; Antony Harvey; Michael Heenan; Andrew Wauchope; John D'Olier Duckworth; Timothy Dallas-Chapman; Jean-Paul da Costa; Hon. Richard Hone; Alexander Stewart; John Hornblow; Howard Sabin; Charles Cunnington; Sir Paul Williams; Adrian Flook; Christopher Head; Nigel Vaughan.

OTHER INFORMATION The foundation was established in 2015 to bring together the previous work of four national masonic charities: The Freemasons' Grand Charity; the Royal Masonic Trust for Girls and Boys; the Masonic Samaritan Fund; and the Royal Masonic Benevolent Institution. At the time of writing (June 2017) there were no accounts available to view on the Charity Commission's website. However, the foundation's website states that during its first year since its launch in April 2016 the foundation awarded over £3.2 million in grants to charities.

HOW TO APPLY **Community support grants:** firstly, complete the eligibility quiz on the foundation's website, then complete the enquiry form or small application form. The foundation aims to acknowledge applications within seven working days. Deadline dates are posted on the website along with further guidance. **Medical and social research grants:** at the time of writing (June 2017) the programme was closed to applications. Refer to the website for guidelines and application information when the programme is open. **Hospices:** an application form is available to download from the foundation's website and should be submitted with the latest set of audited accounts. Grants are made on an annual basis and further information about eligibility is given on the website. The foundation's grants to air ambulances and towards disaster relief are not open to application.

WHO TO APPLY TO Leslie Hutchinson, Chief Operating Officer, Freemasons Hall, 60 Great Queen Street, London WC2B 5AZ *Tel.* 020 7395 9360 *Email* info@mcf.org.uk *Website* mcf.org.uk

■ The Nancie Massey Charitable Trust

SC NO SC008977 **ESTABLISHED** 1989

WHERE FUNDING CAN BE GIVEN Scotland, particularly Edinburgh and Leith.

WHO CAN BENEFIT Registered charities.

WHAT IS FUNDED Older people; children and young adults; medical research; education; science; heritage and the arts.

WHAT IS NOT FUNDED Individuals.

TYPE OF GRANT Capital and core costs; salaries; one-off or recurrent grants; unrestricted funding.

RANGE OF GRANTS Usually less than £5,000 but can be up to £60,000.

SAMPLE GRANTS Dundee Museums Foundation (£60,000); Marie Curie Hospice – Edinburgh (£15,000); British Liver Trust (£6,000); Edinburgh International Science Festival, Leith School of Art and Scottish Chamber Orchestra (£2,000 each); Action on Depression, Multi-Cultural Family Base and Scottish Historic Buildings Trust (£1,000 each); Think Pacific (£100).

FINANCES *Year* 2015/16 *Income* £282,819 *Grants* £326,416 *Grants to organisations* £326,416 *Assets* £6,379,873

OTHER INFORMATION The trust made grants to 80 organisations in 2015/16.

HOW TO APPLY Apply in writing to the correspondent.

WHO TO APPLY TO The Trustees, c/o Chiene and Tait LLP, Cairn House, 61 Dublin Street, Edinburgh EH3 6NL *Tel.* 0131 558 5800 *Email* jgm@chiene.co.uk

■ The Master Charitable Trust

CC NO 1139904 **ESTABLISHED** 2011

WHERE FUNDING CAN BE GIVEN UK and overseas.

WHO CAN BENEFIT Registered charities.

WHAT IS FUNDED Education; poverty; religion; health; community development; arts and heritage; sport; science; human rights; environment; social welfare; animal welfare; armed forces.

RANGE OF GRANTS Mostly £5,000 to £100,000.

SAMPLE GRANTS University of Toronto (£1.1 million); Christopher and Dana Reeve Foundation (£163,500); Acumen Trust (£100,000); Save the Children UK (£90,000); Canterbury Cathedral Trust Fund (£50,000); The Royal Foundation (£20,000); Crisis UK (£10,000); Balliol College (£7,300); Noah's Ark Children's Hospice (£6,500); Syria Relief (£5,300).

FINANCES *Year* 2014/15 *Income* £10,361,770 *Grants* £3,757,166 *Grants to organisations* £3,757,166 *Assets* £20,699,035

TRUSTEE Hoare Trustees.

OTHER INFORMATION The 2014/15 accounts were the latest available at the time of writing (June 2017).

HOW TO APPLY Apply in writing to the correspondent.

WHO TO APPLY TO Hoare Trustees, 37 Fleet Street, London EC4P 4DQ *Tel.* 020 7353 4522

■ The Mathew Trust

SC NO SC016284 **ESTABLISHED** 1935

WHERE FUNDING CAN BE GIVEN City of Dundee; Angus; Perth and Kinross; Fife.

WHO CAN BENEFIT Registered charities; educational establishments; social enterprises; individuals.

WHAT IS FUNDED Adult education; vocational and professional training; relief of poverty by providing assistance in the recruitment of people who are unemployed, or who are likely to become unemployed in the near future.

WHAT IS NOT FUNDED Replacement of statutory funding.

TYPE OF GRANT One-off and recurrent grants up to five years (monitored on an annual basis); capital and revenue costs; salaries; project funding.

RANGE OF GRANTS £650 to £50,000.

SAMPLE GRANTS Dundee and Angus College (£50,000); Design Dundee Ltd (£46,500 in two grants); Furniture Recycling Project (£14,000); Hot Chocolate Trust (£10,000); Dundee Heritage Trust (£7,500); The Unicorn Preservation Society (£6,000); Dundee Science Centre (£5,000); Hope Garden SCIO (£3,000); Motability (£2,000); Dundee Museum of Transport (£850); Dundee Blind and Partially Sighted Society (£650).

FINANCES *Year* 2015/16 *Income* £297,537 *Grants* £169,386 *Grants to organisations* £166,986 *Assets* £8,066,045

OTHER INFORMATION During the year 17 grants were given to organisations and six to individuals to help fund overseas placements totalling £2,400.

HOW TO APPLY Apply in writing to the correspondent. Appeals are generally considered every two months.

WHO TO APPLY TO Sheena Gibson, Administrator, c/o Henderson Loggie, The Vision Building, 20 Greenmarket, Dundee DD1 4QB *Tel.* 01382 200055 *Email* shg@hlca.co.uk

■ The Matliwala Family Charitable Trust

CC NO 1012756 **ESTABLISHED** 1992

WHERE FUNDING CAN BE GIVEN UK and overseas, especially Bharuch, India.

WHO CAN BENEFIT Charitable organisations.

WHAT IS FUNDED The advancement of education for pupils at Matliwala School of Baruch in Gujarat, India. Support can include: assisting with the provision of equipment and facilities; advancement of the Islamic religion; relief of sickness and poverty; advancement of education.

TYPE OF GRANT Recurrent and one-off.

RANGE OF GRANTS Up to £217,000.

SAMPLE GRANTS Masjid-E-Salam – Preston Muslim Society (£217,000); The Matliwala Darul Aloom Charitable Trust – UK (£20,000); The Matliwala Relief Trust and The Matliwala Education Society (£10,000 each).

FINANCES *Year* 2015/16 *Income* £646,838 *Grants* £386,404 *Grants to organisations* £386,404 *Assets* £5,716,201

TRUSTEES Ayub Bux; Yousuf Bux; Abdul Patel; Usman Salya; Fatima Ismail.

HOW TO APPLY Apply in writing to the correspondent. The trustees meet monthly to assess grant applications and approve awards. The annual report for 2015/16 states: 'The charity welcomes applications for grants from all quarters and these are assessed by the trustees on their individual merits. Awards are given according to the individual needs of the applicant, depending on the funds available.'

WHO TO APPLY TO Ayub Bux, Trustee, 9 Brookview, Fulwood, Preston PR2 8FG *Tel.* 01772 706501

■ Maudsley Charity

CC NO 1055440 **ESTABLISHED** 1996

WHERE FUNDING CAN BE GIVEN UK with a preference for projects in Croydon, Lambeth, Lewisham and Southwark.

WHO CAN BENEFIT Registered charities; hospitals; CICs.

WHAT IS FUNDED Services benefitting mental health patients (including addicts) primarily across the South London and Maudsley area; learning and development projects that support mental health practices.

WHAT IS NOT FUNDED Pure research; projects, service developments and clinical or other posts that would normally be covered by core (exchequer) service funding or which essentially replace activity that is no longer supported through the NHS; individual staff development activity unless it has a direct and explicit link to recovery and service improvement.

TYPE OF GRANT Recurrent – up to three years.

RANGE OF GRANTS Usually less than £50,000.

SAMPLE GRANTS Dance United Yorkshire (£120,000); Mindapples (£53,000); South East London Arts Network (£50,000); The Rise Project (£28,000); Black Gay Mental Health Wellbeing and L'Ospedale (£5,000 each); National Med Film Festival and New Economic Foundation (£2,000 each).

FINANCES *Year* 2015/16 *Income* £4,738,000 *Grants* £4,610,000 *Grants to organisations* £4,610,000 *Assets* £127,214,000

TRUSTEES Matthew Patrick; Robert Coomber; Prof. Shitij Kapur; Dr Martin Baggaley; Dr Neil Brimblecombe; Gus Heafield.

HOW TO APPLY According to the charity's website, all applicants are encouraged to discuss their proposals with the charity's staff at an early stage. They will provide advice and support throughout the application process. The charity has a very clear website that provides details of the application process, current funding criteria and deadlines.

WHO TO APPLY TO Rebecca Gray, Chief Executive, Maudsley Charity, Trust Headquarters, The Maudsley Hospital, Denmark Hill, London SE5 8AZ *Tel.* 07787 124647 *Email* Rebecca.Gray@slam.nhs.uk *Website* maudsleycharity.com

■ The Violet Mauray Charitable Trust

CC NO 1001716 **ESTABLISHED** 1990

WHERE FUNDING CAN BE GIVEN UK.

WHO CAN BENEFIT Registered charities; Jewish organisations.

WHAT IS FUNDED A range of general charitable purposes; Jewish causes; medical causes; human rights.

WHAT IS NOT FUNDED Individuals.

TYPE OF GRANT One-off project grants.

RANGE OF GRANTS Usually £1,000 to £5,000.

SAMPLE GRANTS Peace Hospice Care (£5,000); Support Dogs Ltd (£4,000); Wikimedia UK (£3,500); ActionAid, Amnesty International, Canine Partners, Combat Stress and Jewish Care (£2,000 each); Prostate Cancer UK and The Mayhew Animal Home (£1,000).

FINANCES *Year* 2015/16 *Income* £56,473 *Grants* £60,000 *Grants to organisations* £60,000 *Assets* £2,060,351

TRUSTEES Robert Stephany; John Stephany; Alison Karlin.

OTHER INFORMATION Grants were made to 26 organisations.

HOW TO APPLY Apply in writing to the correspondent. Grants are made on an ad hoc basis.
WHO TO APPLY TO John Stephany, Trustee, 9 Bentinck Street, London W1U 2EL *Tel.* 020 7935 0982

■ Mayfair Charities Ltd

CC NO 255281 **ESTABLISHED** 1968
WHERE FUNDING CAN BE GIVEN UK and overseas.
WHO CAN BENEFIT Registered charities benefitting Orthodox Jews, particularly children and young adults; educational institutions; religious organisations.
WHAT IS FUNDED Orthodox Jewish faith; religion; education; relief of poverty; social welfare in the Jewish community.
TYPE OF GRANT One-off awards for capital and running costs.
SAMPLE GRANTS A list of beneficiaries was not available.
FINANCES *Year* 2015/16 *Income* £4,562,000 *Grants* £5,917,000 *Grants to organisations* £5,917,000 *Assets* £109,918,000
TRUSTEES Benzion Freshwater; D. Davis; Solomon Freshwater; Richard Fischer.
OTHER INFORMATION Grants were made to over 362 organisations; however, a recent list of beneficiaries was unavailable. The grant total includes £150,000 given in non-monetary donations – the provision of facilities to Beth Jacob Grammar School for Girls Ltd. Grants were made in the following categories: the advancement of religion and education (£5 million) and the relief of poverty (£1 million).
HOW TO APPLY Apply in writing to the correspondent.
WHO TO APPLY TO Benzion Freshwater, Trustee, Freshwater Group of Companies, Freshwater House, 158–162 Shaftesbury Avenue, London WC2H 8HR *Tel.* 020 7836 1555

■ The Mayfield Valley Arts Trust

CC NO 327665 **ESTABLISHED** 1987
WHERE FUNDING CAN BE GIVEN Sheffield and South Yorkshire.
WHO CAN BENEFIT Charitable organisations; schools.
WHAT IS FUNDED Young artists; music education; the arts and music.
WHAT IS NOT FUNDED The education of individual students; grants to individual students; the provision of musical instruments for individuals, schools or organisations.
TYPE OF GRANT Recurrent.
RANGE OF GRANTS £15,000 to £30,000.
SAMPLE GRANTS Live Music Now, Wigmore Hall and York Early Music Foundation (£30,000 each); Music in the Round (£25,000); Prussia Cove (£15,000).
FINANCES *Year* 2015/16 *Income* £124,433 *Grants* £130,000 *Grants to organisations* £133,000 *Assets* £2,236,506
TRUSTEES David Brown; David Whelton; John Rider; Anthony Thornton; Sarah Derbyshire; James Thornton.
OTHER INFORMATION Grants were made to five organisations.
HOW TO APPLY The trust appears to support the same charities every year.
WHO TO APPLY TO James Thornton, Trustee, 12 Abbots Way, Abbotswood, Ballasalla, Isle of Man IM9 3EQ *Email* jthornton@mayfieldartstrust.org

■ Maypride Ltd

CC NO 289394 **ESTABLISHED** 1984
WHERE FUNDING CAN BE GIVEN UK.
WHO CAN BENEFIT Jewish organisations.
WHAT IS FUNDED The advancement of the Orthodox Jewish religion; relief of poverty.
WHAT IS NOT FUNDED Individuals.
SAMPLE GRANTS A list of beneficiaries was not included in the accounts.
FINANCES *Year* 2015/16 *Income* £67,130 *Grants* £70,721 *Grants to organisations* £70,721 *Assets* £474,871
TRUSTEES Andre Sternlicht; Esther Sternlicht.
HOW TO APPLY Apply in writing to the correspondent.
WHO TO APPLY TO Esther Sternlicht, Secretary, 5 North End Road, London NW11 7RJ

■ Mazars Charitable Trust

CC NO 1150459 **ESTABLISHED** 2012
WHERE FUNDING CAN BE GIVEN UK and Ireland.
WHO CAN BENEFIT Registered charities and voluntary organisations.
WHAT IS FUNDED General charitable purposes. Support is normally only given to projects which are nominated to the management committee by the partners and staff of Mazars (chartered accountants).
WHAT IS NOT FUNDED National grants are not generally repeated within three years and they are rarely given for core costs.
TYPE OF GRANT Single strategic projects; one-off awards; research; building and capital costs. Funding is for one year or less.
RANGE OF GRANTS £45 to £25,000.
SAMPLE GRANTS The Prince's Trust (£25,000); St Catherine's Hospice Lancashire (£16,500); Women For Women International (£15,525); Humanity First (£15,000); ADRA UK, iThemba Study Centre, and Ripple Africa (£5,000 each); Crisis (£1,600); Motor Neurone Disease Association (£1,400); Sport Relief (£1,000). Grants of between £45 and £1,000 to 179 charities totalled £73,000.
FINANCES *Year* 2015/16 *Income* £400,624 *Grants* £327,338 *Grants to organisations* £327,338 *Assets* £407,701
TRUSTEES Bob Neate; David Evans; Phil Verity; Alan Edwards.
OTHER INFORMATION Grants were made to 213 organisations during the year.
HOW TO APPLY Charities cannot apply directly for funding but, rather, are nominated by Mazars partners and employees. Unsolicited applications will receive no response.
WHO TO APPLY TO Bryan Rogers, Trust Administrator, 1 Cranleigh Gardens, South Croydon, Surrey CR2 9LD *Tel.* 020 8657 3053

■ The Robert McAlpine Foundation

CC NO 226646 **ESTABLISHED** 1963
WHERE FUNDING CAN BE GIVEN UK.
WHO CAN BENEFIT Registered charities; schools; hospices; hospitals.
WHAT IS FUNDED General charitable purposes; medical research; social welfare; children with disabilities; older people.
SAMPLE GRANTS **Previous beneficiaries have included:** Age Concern, Community Self Build Agency, DENS Action Against Homelessness, Downside Fisher Youth Club, Ewing Foundation, the Golden Oldies, Grateful Society, James Hopkins Trust, Merchants' Academy Withywood, National Benevolent Fund for the Aged, National

Eye Research Centre, Prostate UK, Royal Marsden NHS Trust, St John's Youth Centre, and the Towers School and 6th Form Centre.

FINANCES *Year* 2015/16 *Income* £652,896 *Grants* £565,208 *Grants to organisations* £565,208 *Assets* £14,805,600

TRUSTEES Adrian McAlpine; Cullum McAlpine; The Hon. David McAlpine; Kenneth McAlpine.

OTHER INFORMATION A list of beneficiaries was not included in the annual report or accounts for 2015/16.

HOW TO APPLY Apply in writing to the correspondent at any time. Applications are considered annually, normally in November.

WHO TO APPLY TO Gillian Bush, Sir Robert McAlpine Ltd, Eaton Court, Maylands Avenue, Hemel Hempstead, Hertfordshire HP2 7TR *Email* foundation@srm.com

■ McGreevy No. 5 Settlement

CC NO 280666 **ESTABLISHED** 1979

WHERE FUNDING CAN BE GIVEN UK, with some preference for Oxfordshire, Bristol and Bath.

WHO CAN BENEFIT Registered charities.

WHAT IS FUNDED General charitable purposes; children and young people; health causes.

WHAT IS NOT FUNDED Individuals.

RANGE OF GRANTS £250 to £25,000.

SAMPLE GRANTS NSPCC (£25,000); Julian House and Story Museum Oxford (£15,000 each); Parkinson's UK (£5,000); ROSY – Respite Nursing for Oxfordshire's Sick Youngsters (£250).

FINANCES *Year* 2015/16 *Income* £69,215 *Grants* £60,250 *Grants to organisations* £60,250 *Assets* £2,655,623

TRUSTEES Avon Executor and Trustee Co. Ltd; Anthony McGreevy; Elise McGreevy-Harris; Katrina Paterson.

OTHER INFORMATION The charity made five grants during the year.

HOW TO APPLY Apply in writing to the correspondent.

WHO TO APPLY TO Elise McGreevy-Harris, Trustee, Yew Court, Riverview Road, Pangbourne, Reading RG8 7AU *Tel.* 0117 905 4000 *Email* elise139@aol.com

■ D. D. McPhail Charitable Settlement

CC NO 267588 **ESTABLISHED** 1973

WHERE FUNDING CAN BE GIVEN UK.

WHO CAN BENEFIT Small and medium-sized registered charities; hospices; educational institutions and research centres.

WHAT IS FUNDED Medical research; people, especially children, with disabilities; care of older people.

TYPE OF GRANT Mainly recurrent awards for projects, services and research over three years; pilot projects; salaries.

RANGE OF GRANTS Smaller grants range from £100 to £2,000. Larger grants range from £16,000 to £97,500.

SAMPLE GRANTS Childhood First (£97,500); Pancreatic Cancer UK (£50,000); Community Foundations – Cheshire, Milton Keynes, Nottinghamshire and Somerset (£20,000 each); Guideposts (£16,000); Babies in Prison, Snowdrop for Brain Injured Children, Faith in Action – Merton Homeless Project and Prisoners' Education Trust (£2,000 each); Dandelion Time and Royal London Society (£1,000 each).

FINANCES *Year* 2015/16 *Income* £295,400 *Grants* £303,654 *Grants to organisations* £303,654 *Assets* £9,417,525

TRUSTEES Julia Noble; Catherine Charles-Jones; Michael Craig; Mary Meeks; Olivia Hancock; Christopher Yates; Tariq Kazi.

OTHER INFORMATION Grants were made to 18 organisations.

HOW TO APPLY The charity's administrator is Mrs Sheila Watson. The annual report for 2015/16 states the following: 'Trustees identify potential projects for assessment by the Executive Director. The Trust makes no commitment to respond to unsolicited applications. There have also been ongoing smaller grants to causes supported by the Trustees.'

WHO TO APPLY TO Katharine Moss, Executive Director, PO BOX 432, Bicester, Oxfordshire OX26 9JL *Tel.* 07523 440550 *Email* director.ddmcphail@gmail.com *Website* www.ddmcphailcharitablesettlement.co.uk

■ Medical Research Foundation

CC NO 1138223 **ESTABLISHED** 2011

WHERE FUNDING CAN BE GIVEN Worldwide with a preference for the UK and Africa.

WHO CAN BENEFIT Universities.

WHAT IS FUNDED Health research; training; public engagement and dissemination of research.

RANGE OF GRANTS Up to £1 million.

SAMPLE GRANTS University College London (£1 million); University of Southampton (£505,000); MRC Laboratory of Molecular Biology Cambridge (£386,000); Imperial College London (£210,000); Liverpool School of Tropical Medicine (£86,000); MRC Toxicology Unit (£65,000); MRC Institute of Genetic and Molecular Medicine Edinburgh (£18,000); MRC Institute of Hearing Research Nottingham (£10,000).

FINANCES *Year* 2015/16 *Income* £2,654,000 *Grants* £3,966,000 *Grants to organisations* £3,957,000 *Assets* £52,390,000

TRUSTEES David Zahn; Prof. Nicholas Lemoine; Stephen Visscher; Prof. Daniel Altmann; Prof. Sir Andrew Haines; Prof. Calliope Farsides; Louise Ansari.

OTHER INFORMATION Grants to individuals amounted to £9,000 and there were 19 awards given to organisations.

HOW TO APPLY The foundation releases proposal call-outs for research projects on its website where you can find guidance and an application portal.

WHO TO APPLY TO The Trustees, c/o Medical Research Council, One Kemble Street, London WC2B 4AN *Tel.* 020 7395 2268 *Email* enquiries@mrf.mrc.ac.uk *Website* www.medicalresearchfoundation.org.uk

■ Medical Research Scotland

SC NO SC014959 **ESTABLISHED** 1953

WHERE FUNDING CAN BE GIVEN Scotland.

WHO CAN BENEFIT Universities.

WHAT IS FUNDED Grants are awarded for individual or group research, scholarships and fellowships, travel and visitors, and capital costs.

TYPE OF GRANT PhD and undergraduate scholarships.

SAMPLE GRANTS **PhD Studentship awards:** University of Glasgow (£167,500); Heriot-Watt University and University of Edinburgh (£85,000 each); University of St Andrews (£57,000); University of Strathclyde (£28,500). **Daphne Jackson**

Memorial Fellowship: University of Edinburgh (£61,500); University of Strathclyde (£30,000); University of Glasgow (£29,500). **Vacational Grants:** Edinburgh Napier University, Heriot-Watt University, University of Dundee, University of Stirling and University of West of Scotland (£2,000 each).

FINANCES *Year* 2015/16 *Income* £1,893,906 *Grants* £1,098,179 *Grants to organisations* £1,098,179 *Assets* £35,198,680

TRUSTEES Philip Winn; Prof. Andrew Baker; Prof. John Brown; Prof. Bernard Conway; Brain Duffin; Scott Johnstone; Prof. Andrea Nolan; Graham Paterson; Barry Rose; Prof. Jenny Woof.

OTHER INFORMATION In 2015/16 the charity awarded 15 PhD studentships and 48 undergraduate vacation research scholarships.

HOW TO APPLY Contact the correspondent for further information. Detailed information regarding the foundation's grant programmes, guidance notes, deadlines for applications and more is available from the foundation's excellent website. Application forms can also be downloaded from the website.

WHO TO APPLY TO Trust Secretaries, Turcan Connell WS, Princes Exchange, 1 Earl Grey Street, Edinburgh EH3 9EE *Tel.* 0131 659 8800 *Email* applications@medicalresearchscotland.net *Website* www.medicalresearchscotland.org.uk

■ The Medlock Charitable Trust

CC NO 326927 **ESTABLISHED** 1985

WHERE FUNDING CAN BE GIVEN Principally, but not exclusively, City of Bath and the Borough of Boston.

WHO CAN BENEFIT Registered charities, preferably smaller organisations; educational establishments; local community groups.

WHAT IS FUNDED General charitable purposes with a preference for disaffected young people; older people; ex-service people; social welfare; education and training; health.

WHAT IS NOT FUNDED Individuals; students.

TYPE OF GRANT One-off or multi-year awards; capital and revenue costs; start-up costs; unrestricted funding.

RANGE OF GRANTS £500 to £180,000; usually under £10,000.

SAMPLE GRANTS The Boshier-Hinton Foundation (£180,000); Aspire Academy (£70,000); Bath Cancer Unit Support Group (£50,000); Benington Community Heritage Trust (£25,000); The National Trust (£11,700); Boston Food Bank, St Barnabas Church – Bath and The South Bristol Consortium for Young People (£10,000 each); Taunton and District Citizens Advice (£2,000); Endeavour Radio Ltd (£1,000); Bath Recital Artists' Trust (£500).

FINANCES *Year* 2015/16 *Income* £1,025,497 *Grants* £1,149,754 *Grants to organisations* £1,149,754 *Assets* £31,754,825

TRUSTEES Jacqueline Medlock; David Medlock; Mark Goodman.

OTHER INFORMATION During the year 130 awards were made the majority of which 110 were for under £10,000.

HOW TO APPLY Apply in writing to the correspondent. The annual report for 2015/16 states that 'the trustees have identified the City of Bath and the Borough of Boston as the principal areas of the charity's activities. However, applications for assistance from areas throughout the United Kingdom are considered sympathetically.' The trustees meet on a regular basis.

WHO TO APPLY TO David Medlock, Trustee, 7 Old Track, Limpley Stoke, Bath BA2 7GY *Tel.* 01225 723148

■ Melodor Ltd

CC NO 260972 **ESTABLISHED** 1970

WHERE FUNDING CAN BE GIVEN Salford; Bury; Brent; Hackney; Israel.

WHO CAN BENEFIT Orthodox Jewish institutions, Jewish educational institutions and charities.

WHAT IS FUNDED General charitable purposes, especially education and religion, with focus on Jewish causes; relief of poverty; health; the advancement of Orthodox Jewish faith.

RANGE OF GRANTS Up to £35,000.

SAMPLE GRANTS Asser Bishvil (£35,000); Beis Aharon Trust and SOFT (Support Organisation for Trisomy) (£30,000 each); Chaim Meirim Viznitz (£20,500); Cosmon Bels (£20,000); Yetev Lev (£13,000); Yeshiva Ohel Shimon (£4,800); Beis Rochel School (£4,000); Zorea Zedokos (£2,500); Beenstock Home (£2,000).

FINANCES *Year* 2015/16 *Income* £171,030 *Grants* £239,662 *Grants to organisations* £239,662 *Assets* £538,789

TRUSTEES Hyman Weiss; Philip Weiss; Zisel Weiss; Pinchas Neumann; Maurice Neumann; Yocheved Weiss; Eli Neumann; Esther Henry; Henry Neumann; Janet Bleier; Miriam Friedlander; Rebecca Delange; Rivka Ollech; Rivka Rabinowitz; Pesha Kohn; Yehoshua Weiss.

OTHER INFORMATION Grants of less than £2,000 totalled £45,500.

HOW TO APPLY Apply in writing to the correspondent.

WHO TO APPLY TO Bernardin Weiss, 10 Cubley Road, Salford M7 4GN *Tel.* 0161 720 6188

■ Menuchar Ltd

CC NO 262782 **ESTABLISHED** 1971

WHERE FUNDING CAN BE GIVEN UK.

WHO CAN BENEFIT Jewish organisations and religious establishments.

WHAT IS FUNDED Advancement of religion in accordance with the Orthodox Jewish faith and relief of people in need.

SAMPLE GRANTS A list of beneficiaries was not available.

FINANCES *Year* 2015/16 *Income* £900,000 *Grants* £841,616 *Grants to organisations* £841,616 *Assets* £234,640

TRUSTEES Norman Bude; Gail Bude.

OTHER INFORMATION A list of beneficiaries was not included in the accounts; however, they did state that grants went to religious organisations.

HOW TO APPLY Apply in writing to the correspondent.

WHO TO APPLY TO Helena Bude, Secretary, c/o Barry Flack and Co. Ltd, The Brentano Suite, Prospect House, 2 Athenaeum Road, London N20 9AE *Tel.* 020 8369 5170

■ Mercaz Torah Vechesed Ltd

CC NO 1109212 **ESTABLISHED** 2005

WHERE FUNDING CAN BE GIVEN Worldwide with a preference for Barnet, Hackney and Israel.

WHO CAN BENEFIT Charitable organisations and individuals.

WHAT IS FUNDED The advancement of the Orthodox Jewish faith, Orthodox Jewish religious education, and the relief of poverty and infirmity among members of the Orthodox Jewish community.

SAMPLE GRANTS A list of beneficiaries was not available.
FINANCES *Year* 2015/16 *Income* £894,325 *Grants* £868,487 *Grants to organisations* £868,487 *Assets* £11,899
TRUSTEES Joseph Ostreicher; Mordche Rand.
OTHER INFORMATION A list of beneficiaries was not included in the annual report or accounts.
HOW TO APPLY Apply in writing to the correspondent.
WHO TO APPLY TO Joseph Ostreicher, Secretary, 28 Braydon Road, London N16 6QB *Tel.* 020 8880 5366 *Email* umarpeh@gmail.com

■ The Brian Mercer Charitable Trust

CC NO 1076925 **ESTABLISHED** 1999
WHERE FUNDING CAN BE GIVEN Worldwide.
WHO CAN BENEFIT Registered charities; educational institutions.
WHAT IS FUNDED Promotion of medical and scientific research and treatment for people with visual impairment and liver diseases; visual arts, especially in the North West.
TYPE OF GRANT Mainly recurrent.
RANGE OF GRANTS £900 to £250,000.
SAMPLE GRANTS Against Malaria Foundation (£250,000); Médecins Sans Frontières and Sightsavers (£100,000 each); Moorfields Eye Clinic (£50,000); Bronze Casting Residency in Pietrasanta (£14,500); Royal British Society of Sculptors (£13,000); Burnley College, Haslingden High School and NADFAS North West Area (£2,500 each); British Wireless for the Blind Fund (£1,700); Tallships (£900).
FINANCES *Year* 2015/16 *Income* £1,065,648 *Grants* £580,402 *Grants to organisations* £580,402 *Assets* £26,584,344
TRUSTEES Christine Clancy; Kenneth Merrill; Roger Duckworth; Mary Clitheroe.
OTHER INFORMATION Within the broad objectives of the charity, grant-making is focused on the following areas: prevention and relief of human suffering (75%), the arts (15%), and causes local to Blackburn, Lancashire (10%). During the year 21 grants were made to organisations.
HOW TO APPLY The trust encourages grant applications via email. They should be received at least four weeks before the trustees' meeting, the exact dates of which are listed online. The trustees meet twice a year, currently in May and October. The trust stresses the importance of highlighting the efficacy of the project or intervention and how you plan to evaluate the impact. Further guidance is provided on the trust's website.
WHO TO APPLY TO J. M. Adams, c/o Beever and Struthers, Central Buildings, Richmond Terrace, Blackburn BB1 7AP *Tel.* 01254 686600 *Email* info@brianmercercharitabletrust.org or applications@brianmercercharitabletrust.org *Website* www.brianmercercharitabletrust.org

■ The Mercers' Charitable Foundation

CC NO 326340 **ESTABLISHED** 1982
WHERE FUNDING CAN BE GIVEN UK; strong preference for London and the West Midlands. The foundation is keen to stress that it currently has geographical restrictions on its welfare and educational grant-making. See information on individual programmes for details.
WHO CAN BENEFIT Registered charities; charities exempt from registration; maintained schools; churches; graded buildings.
WHAT IS FUNDED General welfare; education; heritage and arts; advancement of Christian religion; older and young people. Recently there has been a particular focus on excellence in education and a current focus on work to reduce offending.
WHAT IS NOT FUNDED Specific exclusions apply in each of the categories – make sure you read these before applying. Generally the following are not funded: animal welfare charities; endowment appeals; loans or business finance; sponsorship or marketing appeals and fundraising events; campaigning work and projects that are primarily political; activities that are the responsibility of the local, health or education authority or other similar body; activities that have already taken place; organisations that are themselves principally grant-makers; general or mailshot appeals.
TYPE OF GRANT Building; other capital grants (with certain restrictions); feasibility studies; one-off grants; project costs; research grants; recurring costs; start-up funding; awards for up to three years; unrestricted funding.
RANGE OF GRANTS Up to £470,000 but usually less than £10,000.
SAMPLE GRANTS St Paul's School (£470,000); The Birmingham Diocesan Board of Finance (£200,000); Federation of London Youth Clubs (£100,000); The SpringBoard Bursary Foundation (£50,000); Hexham Abbey (£22,000); Brandon Centre for Counselling and Psychotherapy (£15,000); Birth Companions (£14,500); Natural History Museum (£12,500); African and Caribbean Diversity, Almshouse Association and National Youth Jazz Orchestra (£10,000 each).
FINANCES *Year* 2015/16 *Income* £5,188,000 *Grants* £4,876,000 *Grants to organisations* £4,876,000 *Assets* £17,863,000
TRUSTEE The Mercers' Company.
OTHER INFORMATION The foundation reports the following breakdown of grants made by area: education (50%); the advancement of Christianity (20%); family and social welfare (12%); heritage and arts (12%). A total of 333 organisations received grants during the year and two thirds of grants were for less than £10,000, with 34 grants awarded for sums above £20,000 and 10 major grants valued at £100,000 or more.
HOW TO APPLY Applications can be made online via the foundation's website. In addition, applicants are required to post or email the most recent annual report and accounts (produced no later than ten months after the end of the financial year), and a copy of the organisation's bank statement, dated within the last three months. Only one application in three years can be considered from any organisation. Applications must also include a project plan for the funding proposal. **Note**: This foundation is under the trusteeship of the Mercers' Company and one application to the Company is an application to all its charities, including the Charity of Sir Richard Whittington and the Earl of Northampton's Charity. There are specific email and phone contact details for grants officers working in the areas of welfare, education, religion and heritage and arts (find these online) – enquiries should be directed to an appropriate correspondent.

WHO TO APPLY TO The Grants Officer, The Mercers' Company, Mercers' Hall, Ironmonger Lane, London EC2V 8HE *Tel.* 020 7726 4991 *Email* info@mercers.co.uk *Website* www.mercers.co.uk

■ Merchant Navy Welfare Board

CC NO 212799, SC039669 **ESTABLISHED** 1962

WHERE FUNDING CAN BE GIVEN UK and overseas.

WHO CAN BENEFIT Charitable organisations.

WHAT IS FUNDED The charity makes grants to over 40 of constituent members and maintains 15 Port Welfare Committees to support the welfare and well-being of sailors and their families. It also raises awareness of issues affecting the welfare of merchant seafarers, fishers and their dependants.

WHAT IS NOT FUNDED Funding is not available retrospectively. Although grants are not made to individuals, other than in emergency, the charity acts as a 'clearing house' for those seeking assistance from other maritime charities.

TYPE OF GRANT Capital projects, evaluation studies and start-up costs.

RANGE OF GRANTS £100 to £50,500.

SAMPLE GRANTS Sir Gabriel Woods Mariners Home, Greenock (£50,500); Centres for Seafarers, Tilbury (£25,000); Liverpool Seafarers' Centre (£16,500); Maritime Charities Group, Shipwrecked Mariners' Society, Queen Victoria's Seamen's Rest, London (£15,000 each); Bristol Seafarers' Centre (£3,500); Merchant Navy Day Annual Service (£500); Merchant Navy Medal Committee (£100).

FINANCES *Year* 2015 *Income* £645,522 *Grants* £225,996 *Grants to organisations* £225,996 *Assets* £14,492,439

TRUSTEES Anthony Dickinson; Cdre Barry Bryant; Timothy Springett; Stephen Todd; Graham Lane; Robert Jones; Deanne Thomas; Capt. Andrew Cassels; Mark Carden; David Colclough; Cdre Malcolm Williams; Alexander Campbell; Martin Foley; Alison Godfrey; Stephen Gosling.

OTHER INFORMATION There were 32 grants made which were distributed among 17 organisations.

HOW TO APPLY Application forms are available to download from the charity's website and once completed should be emailed to the trustees. It is recommended that applicants contact the Chief Executive at an early stage, outlining the purpose of the application. This will help to ensure that it meets the criteria and that all the requirements are met. Applicants seeking amounts over £5,000 should submit their latest annual report and accounts. Those applying for amounts over £25,000 may also be asked to submit a five-year business plan. The trustees meet to consider applications in March, July and November (requests for larger grants of over £10,000 must be submitted by 1 September).

WHO TO APPLY TO Capt. David Parsons, Chief Executive, 8 Cumberland Place, Southampton SO15 2BH *Tel.* 023 8033 7799 *Fax* 023 8063 4444 *Email* enquiries@mnwb.org.uk *Website* www.mnwb.org

■ The Merchant Taylors' Company Charities Fund

CC NO 1069124 **ESTABLISHED** 1941

WHERE FUNDING CAN BE GIVEN Lewisham, Southwark, Tower Hamlets, Hackney and occasionally Greater London.

WHO CAN BENEFIT Charitable organisations; educational institutions; churches.

WHAT IS FUNDED General charitable purposes, including the relief of poverty, health and disability, education and training, and religious causes.

WHAT IS NOT FUNDED Building costs; medical research; generalised appeals; very large charities; individuals; funding that will be passed on to individuals or third parties.

TYPE OF GRANT One-off grants or three-year tapering grants.

RANGE OF GRANTS Usually between £5,000 and £15,000.

SAMPLE GRANTS Cure Parkinson's (£60,000); SkillForce (£15,000); Guildhall School of Music and Drama (£6,000); Dream Arts (£5,000); Merchant Taylors' School Northwood (£4,300); Corporation of Sons of the Clergy (£2,000); Tailors' Benevolent Fund (£2,500); Sheriffs' and Recorder's Fund and St Paul's Cathedral Choir School (£1,000 each); Royal School of Needlework (£500).

FINANCES *Year* 2015 *Income* £315,988 *Grants* £167,698 *Grants to organisations* £167,698 *Assets* £864,821

TRUSTEES Duncan MacDonald Eggar; Peter Magill; Rupert Bull; Simon Bass; Christopher Hare.

OTHER INFORMATION Part of the grant total is restricted to awarding prizes and grants to schools and churches associated with Merchant Taylors' Company. In 2015 this represented £22,000 of the grant total.

HOW TO APPLY According to the website, at present awards are restricted to charities nominated by the Livery Committee. Applications may only be made with the support of a member of the Merchant Taylors' Company or by invitation.

WHO TO APPLY TO Giles Hutchinson, Charities Officer, Merchant Taylors' Hall, 30 Threadneedle Street, London EC2R 8JB *Tel.* 020 7450 4440 *Email* charities@merchant-taylors.co.uk *Website* www.merchant-taylors.co.uk/charities

■ Merchant Taylors' Consolidated Charities for the Infirm

CC NO 214266 **ESTABLISHED** 1960

WHERE FUNDING CAN BE GIVEN Lewisham, Southwark, Tower Hamlets, Hackney and occasionally Greater London. National grants may be made in exceptional cases.

WHO CAN BENEFIT Small and medium-sized registered charities.

WHAT IS FUNDED Relief of ill health, especially for older people and people with disabilities; sheltered housing and residential care homes; improving well-being through the arts. Exceptionally, work which is national in scope may receive funding when it benefits members or ex-members of the armed forces or has some connection to tailoring and clothing.

WHAT IS NOT FUNDED Building costs; medical research; generalised appeals; very large charities; individuals; funding that will be passed on to individuals or third parties.

TYPE OF GRANT Seed-funding; core, revenue and project costs; up to three consecutive years.

RANGE OF GRANTS Usually between £5,000 and £15,000.

SAMPLE GRANTS Age Exchange (£30,000); Body and Soul (£14,8000); London Centre for Children with Cerebral Palsy (£12,000); Blind in Business (£10,000); British School of Osteopathy (£8,000); Ability Bow (£6,500); London Wildlife Trust and Prisoners Abroad

(£5,000 each); Connaught Opera (£1,000); Combat Stress (£500).

FINANCES *Year* 2015 *Income* £423,432 *Grants* £231,433 *Grants to organisations* £231,433 *Assets* £12,330,433

TRUSTEES Duncan MacDonald Eggar; Peter Magill; Rupert Bull; Simon Bass; Christopher Hare.

OTHER INFORMATION Grants to 28 organisations were made during the year.

HOW TO APPLY Applicants should complete the online application form available on the website, where further information about the application process is given. Potential recipients must demonstrate that they will not be wholly dependent on funding from the charity and are positively encouraged to reference the Company's support insofar as it may help you to acquire matched funding or other additional financial support.

WHO TO APPLY TO Giles Hutchinson, Charities Officer, Merchant Taylors' Hall, 30 Threadneedle Street, London EC2R 8JB *Tel.* 020 7450 4447 *Fax* 020 7588 2776 *Email* charities@merchant-taylors.co.uk *Website* www.merchant-taylors.co.uk/charities

■ The Merchant Venturers' Charity

CC NO 264302 **ESTABLISHED** 1972

WHERE FUNDING CAN BE GIVEN Greater Bristol area.

WHO CAN BENEFIT Local and regional organisations; local branches of national organisations; some individuals.

WHAT IS FUNDED Social needs (care of older people, homelessness, poverty or the prevention of crime); young people (training outside educational establishments, character development and employment prospects); education; social enterprise; health care; culture and arts; projects in Bristol, preferably associated with the Merchant Venturers' Society's spheres of interest and benefitting Bristol and its economic development.

WHAT IS NOT FUNDED Statutory organisations or the direct replacement of statutory funding; projects that take place before an application can be considered; activities that are intended to raise funds for other organisations. Grants are unlikely to be made towards the cost of an existing salaried position.

TYPE OF GRANT Grants can be for capital, equipment or ongoing revenue costs.

RANGE OF GRANTS Generally up to £5,000.

SAMPLE GRANTS The Bristol Old Vic (£50,000); University of Bristol Research Grant (£18,500); Great Western Regional Capital CIC (£15,000); Bristol Cultural Development, Windmill Hill City Farm and Unseen (£5,000 each).

FINANCES *Year* 2015 *Income* £325,930 *Grants* £285,717 *Grants to organisations* £285,717 *Assets* £7,190,027

TRUSTEES Anthony Brown; Christopher Pople; Christopher Curling; Cullum McAlpine; Anthony Kenny; Nicholas Bacon; Peter Rilett; Dr Jacqueline Cornish; Charles Griffiths; Timothy Ross; Peter McCarthy; Alastair Currie; Gillian Camm; James Ancell; Prof. Joseph McGeehan; Caroline Duckworth.

OTHER INFORMATION Grants were made in the following areas: community and social (£232,500); education (£38,500); social business (£15,000).

HOW TO APPLY Application forms and detailed guidelines are accessible on the charity's website. Once completed they can be returned via email. Re-applications may be made in three years following the award of a previous grant. Grant Giving Committees meet a number of times each year, generally in January, April, July and October. The outcome will be known within six weeks following the meeting.

WHO TO APPLY TO Richard Morris, Treasurer, c/o The Society of Merchant Venturers, Merchants' Hall, The Promenade, Clifton, Bristol BS8 3NH *Tel.* 0117 973 8058 *Email* enquiries@merchantventurers.com *Website* www.merchantventurers.com

■ Mercury Phoenix Trust

CC NO 1013768 **ESTABLISHED** 1992

WHERE FUNDING CAN BE GIVEN Worldwide.

WHO CAN BENEFIT Registered charities; NGOs.

WHAT IS FUNDED Relief of poverty, sickness and distress of people affected by AIDS and HIV and the raising of awareness of the illness throughout the world.

WHAT IS NOT FUNDED Individuals; travel costs.

TYPE OF GRANT One-off, capital, project and running costs.

RANGE OF GRANTS £500 to £25,000.

SAMPLE GRANTS Snehalaya (£25,000); Prerana (£13,500 in two grants); Restless Development and Zamuxolo Orphanage (£8,000 each); Bible Society UK, International Children's Trust, Skillshare International and Theatre for a Change (£5,000 each); Global Action (£3,000); Society for Education and Rural Development (£1,500); Dhiverse (£500).

FINANCES *Year* 2015/16 *Income* £435,228 *Grants* £153,973 *Grants to organisations* £153,973 *Assets* £1,891,416

TRUSTEES Brian May; Henry Beach; Mary Austin; Roger Taylor.

OTHER INFORMATION Over 28 grants were made in the financial year, with several organisations receiving funding for multiple projects in different countries.

HOW TO APPLY Application forms and further information are available by contacting the trust via email. In addition to a completed application form, the trust requires a budget and the following documents: a registration certificate, audited accounts for the last financial year, a copy of your charity's constitution or similar document, and the latest annual report.

WHO TO APPLY TO Peter Chant, The River Wing, Latimer Park, Latimer, Chesham, Buckinghamshire HP5 1TU *Tel.* 01494 766799 *Email* funding@mercuryphoenixtrust.com or jan@idrec.com *Website* www.mercuryphoenixtrust.com

■ The Metropolitan Masonic Charity

CC NO 1081205 **ESTABLISHED** 2000

WHERE FUNDING CAN BE GIVEN Primarily London.

WHO CAN BENEFIT Individuals and organisations (non-masonic charities), mainly within the area of London.

WHAT IS FUNDED General charitable purposes, with particular, albeit not exclusive, focus on the relief of need, poverty or distress, and health care or medical support.

TYPE OF GRANT One-off and recurrent.

RANGE OF GRANTS Usually £500 to £5,000.

SAMPLE GRANTS Air Ambulance (£1.37 million); City Music Foundation (£20,000); The London Centre for Children with Cerebral Palsy (£7,500); Royal Hospital for Neuro-disability (£6,000); Lambeth Summer Projects Trust

(£5,000); Masonic Trout and Salmon Fly Fishing Association (£3,500); Contact the Elderly (£2,500); Drop-in Bereavement Centre (£2,000); Action for Sick Children (£1,000); Delete Blood Cancer (£500).

FINANCES *Year* 2015/16 *Income* £1,793,475 *Grants* £1,518,391 *Grants to organisations* £1,518,391 *Assets* £2,038,341

TRUSTEES Rex Thorne; Robert Corp-Reader; Brian de Neut; Quentin Humberstone; Augustus Ullstein.

OTHER INFORMATION In previous years the charity has provided particular support to a major project each year. In 2015/16, the beneficiary in question was Air Ambulance. During the year there were 38 awards made.

HOW TO APPLY Apply in writing to the correspondent.

WHO TO APPLY TO 60 Great Queen Street, PO Box 29055, London WC2B 5AZ *Tel.* 020 7539 2930 *Email* c.hunt@metgl.com

■ T. and J. Meyer Family Foundation Ltd

CC NO 1087507 **ESTABLISHED** 2001

WHERE FUNDING CAN BE GIVEN UK and overseas.

WHO CAN BENEFIT Charitable organisations.

WHAT IS FUNDED The primary focus of the foundation is on education, health care and the environment.

TYPE OF GRANT One-off and recurrent.

RANGE OF GRANTS Typically under £40,000.

SAMPLE GRANTS Amani Global Works; Angkor Hospital for Children; Bahamas National Trust; Educatel; Hope and Homes for Children; Hope Through Health; Mae Tao Clinic; Street Child; University of Glasgow.

FINANCES *Year* 2015 *Income* £477,231 *Grants* £588,666 *Grants to organisations* £588,666 *Assets* £18,732,573

TRUSTEES Jane Meyer; Annabelle Ahouiyek; Quinn Meyer; Ian Meyer; Miranda Spackman.

OTHER INFORMATION During the year the foundation made 18 grants. All figures have been converted from $US at the rate of 1$ = £0.78 and were correct at the time of writing (April 2017).

HOW TO APPLY The foundation does not accept unsolicited applications.

WHO TO APPLY TO Timothy Meyer, Company Secretary, 3 Kendrick Mews, London SW7 3HG *Tel.* 020 7581 9900 *Email* info@tjmff.org

■ The Mickel Fund

SC NO SC003266 **ESTABLISHED** 1970

WHERE FUNDING CAN BE GIVEN UK, with a preference for Scotland.

WHO CAN BENEFIT Voluntary organisations and charitable groups. The trust prefers local charities but does give to organisations throughout the UK.

WHAT IS FUNDED Education; relief of poverty; health and disability; arts, culture and heritage; sports. The following categories are funded: older people; animal welfare; cancer care; cancer research; children and young people; education/ outreach; hospices; housing and homelessness; injuries; medical assistance; music/culture; medical research; veterans; 'world wide appeal based projects'. Major grants are available to Scottish charities or homelessness charities for large-scale local projects; annual grants are made to one charity per each of the above categories.

WHAT IS NOT FUNDED Events such as conferences, seminars and exhibitions; fee-charging residential home, nurseries and care facilities; fundraising events; individuals – other than through the hardship fund; loans or the repayments of loans – other than through the hardship fund; organisations promoting religion; the replacement of statutory funds; schools other than pre-school and after-school clubs and activities promoting parental and community involvement.

TYPE OF GRANT One-off and recurrent; risky and new projects; ongoing work; core funding; salaries; general running costs; capital grants; building or equipment expenditure.

RANGE OF GRANTS Major grants – £5,000 to £10,000; annual grants – £500 to £2,000; hardship grants – £50 to £500.

SAMPLE GRANTS Addaction and Hearts and Minds (£10,000 each); National Library of Scotland (£8,000); Scottish Opera (£5,400); Children 1st, Children with Cancer UK, Médecins Sans Frontières UK and Safe Strong and Free (£5,000 each).

FINANCES *Year* 2015/16 *Income* £147,074 *Grants* £126,668 *Grants to organisations* £126,668 *Assets* £3,494,772

TRUSTEES Mairi Mickel; Bruce Mickel; Findlay Mickel; Alan Hartley; Oliver Bassi.

OTHER INFORMATION Grants ranging from £50 to £3,000 totalled £73,000.

HOW TO APPLY Application forms are available from the charity's website and should be returned to the charity upon completion. A helpful check-list of requirements and eligibility criteria is also given online. Remember to include a copy of your most recent audited accounts and annual report and a budget for the year as well as the project. The outcome of your application is communicated within two months of the trustees' meeting (they are held in March and September) and awards are paid in March and/ or December. The deadline for appeals is normally mid-February and mid-August. Phone and email enquiries are welcome prior to application.

WHO TO APPLY TO Lindsay McColl, Trust Administrator, 1 Atlantic Quay, 1 Robertson Avenue, Glasgow G2 8JB *Tel.* 0141 242 7528 *Email* admin@mickelfund.org.uk *Website* www.mickelfund.org.uk

■ The Mickleham Trust

CC NO 1048337 **ESTABLISHED** 1995

WHERE FUNDING CAN BE GIVEN UK, with a preference for Norfolk.

WHO CAN BENEFIT Registered charities.

WHAT IS FUNDED Relief for abused and disadvantaged people, particularly children and young people and blind individuals.

TYPE OF GRANT Mainly recurrent.

RANGE OF GRANTS Usually between £1,000 and £5,000.

SAMPLE GRANTS NNUH Dementia Support Workers (£85,500); Motability (£5,000); The Children's Centre and The National Institute for Conducive Education (£2,000 each); Asthma Relief, Birmingham Royal Ballet, Blind Veterans, East Anglian Children's Hospice, Guide Dogs for the Blind and St Barnabas Counselling Centre (£1,000 each).

FINANCES *Year* 2015/16 *Income* £259,491 *Grants* £195,415 *Grants to organisations* £195,415 *Assets* £5,637,306

TRUSTEES Philip Norton; Revd Sheila Nunney; Anne Richardson.

OTHER INFORMATION Grants were made to 78 organisations.

HOW TO APPLY Apply in writing to the correspondent.
WHO TO APPLY TO Philip Norton, Trustee, c/o Hansells Solicitors and Financial Advisers, 13–14 The Close, Norwich NR1 4DS *Tel.* 01603 615731 *Email* philipnorton@hansells.co.uk

■ The Gerald Micklem Charitable Trust

CC NO 802583 **ESTABLISHED** 1988
WHERE FUNDING CAN BE GIVEN UK; Hampshire and West Sussex.
WHO CAN BENEFIT UK-registered charities 'working either on a national basis, or specifically in Hampshire or West Sussex' in the preferred fields; hospices.
WHAT IS FUNDED Adults and children with physical and learning disabilities; carers for older people and individuals with disabilities, especially young carers; the environment and wildlife; medical conditions affecting both adults and children; support for older people, including those with Alzheimer's or dementia.
WHAT IS NOT FUNDED Individuals; charities that are not registered in the UK; churches; drug/alcohol abuse and counselling; disadvantaged children and young people; education/schools (except those for children with disabilities); homelessness and housing; local community groups; medical research; mental health; museums, galleries and heritage; overseas aid; performing arts and cultural organisations.
TYPE OF GRANT One-off and recurrent grants for capital expenditure; core and project costs.
RANGE OF GRANTS Usually between £3,000 and £10,000.
SAMPLE GRANTS Home Farm Trust (£70,000); The Rowans Hospice (£17,000); FitzRoy Support, SeeAbility (£10,000 each); Action on Hearing Loss, Contact the Elderly, Friends of Butser Ancient Farm, Marine Conservation Society and Target Ovarian Cancer (£5,000 each); Coram Campus (£3,000).
FINANCES *Year* 2015 *Income* £323,708 *Grants* £327,140 *Grants to organisations* £327,140 *Assets* £2,366,269
TRUSTEES Susan Shone; Joanna Scott-Dalgleish; Helen Ratcliffe.
OTHER INFORMATION During the year a total of 36 awards were made.
HOW TO APPLY There is no formal application form and applications should be made in writing to the correspondent by letter – *not by email.* Applicants also have to provide a copy of their latest annual report and accounts. Enquiries prior to any application may be made by email. The trustees usually consider awards in January/February; therefore, they ask to submit your requests 'towards the end of a calendar year so that the information they contain is most up to date when considered', preferably as late as possible. Be careful though, as the appeals are not carried forward and should be with the trustees by 31 December.
WHO TO APPLY TO Susan Shone, Trustee, Bolinge Hill Farm, Buriton, Petersfield, Hampshire GU31 4NN *Tel.* 01730 264207 *Email* mail@geraldmicklemct.org.uk *Website* www.geraldmicklemct.org.uk

■ The Masonic Province of Middlesex Charitable Trust (Middlesex Masonic Charity)

CC NO 1064406 **ESTABLISHED** 1997
WHERE FUNDING CAN BE GIVEN Middlesex.
WHO CAN BENEFIT Generally only registered charities; both masonic charities and non-masonic charities are assisted; causes and charities in Middlesex, or with strong Middlesex connections.
WHAT IS FUNDED General charitable purposes and non-masonic charities; relief of poverty and assistance towards the education of Freemasons and their families.
TYPE OF GRANT One-off; capital costs; project funding.
RANGE OF GRANTS £850 to £25,000.
SAMPLE GRANTS The Royal Marsden Cancer Charity (£25,000); Royal Masonic Trust for Girls and Boys 2020 Festival (£17,000); The Disability Foundation (£8,500); Friends of the RMBI (£5,000); London Air Ambulance (£4,000); Hillingdon Autistic Care and Support (£3,800); Richmond on Thames Crossroads Care (£3,000); Happy Days Children's Charity and The Greeno Centre (£1,900 each); Skelton Explorer Scouts (£1,000); Harrow Age Concern (£850).
FINANCES *Year* 2014/15 *Income* £76,212 *Grants* £72,009 *Grants to organisations* £72,009 *Assets* £1,941,563
TRUSTEES David Yeaman; Stephen Ramsay; Jonathan Markham Gollow; Adrian Howorth; Peter Gledhill.
OTHER INFORMATION In 2014/15 grants were given to 11 organisations. About 70% of grants went to non-masonic charities.
HOW TO APPLY Applications must be submitted via a form, which is available from the correspondent. The trust will also accept applications made on the Universal Application Form, available from the Provincial Grand Lodge of Middlesex website (pglm.org.uk/charity/charities) and submitted to the Provincial Charity Awareness Committee (see details within the form). All submissions must include two years' audited accounts, supporting quotations or invoices for proposed expenditure and relevant literature to help the trustees reach a decision. The trust will also consider applications for assistance from Freemasons in distress or their families or dependants. However, these requests should be submitted in the first instance to the Provincial Grand Almoner who will report with recommendations directly to the trustees.
WHO TO APPLY TO Peter Gledhill, Secretary of the Trustees, 85 Fakenham Way, Owlsmoor, Sandhurst, Berkshire GU47 0YS *Tel.* 01344 777077 *Email* peter.gledhill@btinternet.com *Website* pglm.org.uk/charity/charities-middlesex-charities

■ The Middlesex Sports Foundation

CC NO 1119091 **ESTABLISHED** 2007
WHERE FUNDING CAN BE GIVEN UK.
WHO CAN BENEFIT Organisations benefitting children and young people, people with disabilities, injured sportsmen and sportswomen and other disadvantaged individuals.
WHAT IS FUNDED Social welfare of children and young people; people with disabilities; disadvantaged individuals; community participation; all with focus on sports and recreation.

RANGE OF GRANTS Up to £12,500; mostly from £1,500 to £2,000.
SAMPLE GRANTS GB Wheelchair Rugby (£12,500); Caudwell Children, Bolton Lads and Girls Club, Mary Hare Foundation, Inspirations, Morning Star, National Deaf Children's Society (£1,500 each); Childhood First (£500).
FINANCES *Year* 2015/16 *Income* £54,728 *Grants* £55,500 *Grants to organisations* £55,500 *Assets* £1,737,413
TRUSTEES Howard Walters; Rhidian Jones; Julian Tregoning; Gareth Rees; Dr Colin Crosby; Robert Udwin; Paul Astbury.
OTHER INFORMATION No grants were made to individuals during 2015/16.
HOW TO APPLY Apply in writing to the correspondent.
WHO TO APPLY TO Paul Astbury, Trustee, 32 Kneller Gardens, Isleworth, Middlesex TW7 7NW *Tel.* 020 8898 5372 *Email* paulastbury@uk2.net

■ Millennium Stadium Charitable Trust (Ymddiriedolaeth Elusennol Stadiwm Y Mileniwm)

CC NO 1086596 **ESTABLISHED** 2001
WHERE FUNDING CAN BE GIVEN Wales.
WHO CAN BENEFIT Charitable organisations; properly constituted voluntary organisations; not-for-profit organisations; voluntary groups working with local authorities.
WHAT IS FUNDED The arts, especially performing and visual arts; community cohesion; people with disabilities; the environment and sustainability; sport.
WHAT IS NOT FUNDED Projects outside Wales; day-to-day running costs; projects that seek to redistribute grant funds for the benefit of third-party organisations; payments of debts/overdrafts; retrospective requests; requests from individuals; payment to profit-making organisations; applications made solely in the name of a local authority.
TYPE OF GRANT Project costs; capital expenditure.
RANGE OF GRANTS Regional grants can be up to £7,500; local grants can be up to £2,500.
SAMPLE GRANTS Bangor Rugby Football Club; Cardiff Metropolitan Forest Classroom; Cardiff Metropolitan Outdoor Learning Centre; Codi'r To; Kim Inspire Social Enterprise Ltd; Porth Harlequins Sport and Social Club; Treffgarne Village Hall; Welsh Deaf Rugby Union; Wheelchair Basketball North Wales.
FINANCES *Year* 2015/16 *Income* £526,474 *Grants* £198,373 *Grants to organisations* £198,373 *Assets* £297,614
TRUSTEES Ian Davies; Martin Davies; John Lloyd-Jones; Gerallt Hughes; Russell Goodway; Linda Pepper; Andrew Walker; John Hardy Rawlins; William Jones; Cllr Peter Bradbury; David Hammond.
HOW TO APPLY The trust holds three rounds a year; one for each type of application – national, regional and local. Deadline dates can be found on the trust's website, along with full guidelines and application forms. Unsuccessful applicants may re-apply after one year. The trust welcomes applicants to get in touch for advice on how to improve an application.
WHO TO APPLY TO Sarah Fox, Trust Administrator, c/o Foxse Consultancy, Suite 1, 4 Bessemer Road, Cardiff CF11 8BA *Tel.* 029 2002 2143 *Email* info@millenniumstadiumtrust.org.uk or applications@millenniumstadiumtrust.org.uk *Website* www.millenniumstadiumtrust.co.uk

■ Hugh and Mary Miller Bequest Trust

SC NO SC014950 **ESTABLISHED** 1976
WHERE FUNDING CAN BE GIVEN Scotland.
WHO CAN BENEFIT Registered charities.
WHAT IS FUNDED General charitable purposes; disability; health.
WHAT IS NOT FUNDED Non-registered charities; individuals.
TYPE OF GRANT One-off and recurrent.
RANGE OF GRANTS Usually between £1,000 and £7,000.
SAMPLE GRANTS Haven Products Ltd (£14,800); Action Medical Research, Music in Hospitals Scotland and Spina Bifida Hydrocephalus Scotland (£7,000 each); Crossroads Caring Scotland (£5,800); The Boys' Brigade (£1,600); Alzheimer Scotland, Carers Trust in Scotland and Dyslexia Scotwest (£1,200 each).
FINANCES *Year* 2015/16 *Income* £123,797 *Grants* £108,800 *Grants to organisations* £108,800 *Assets* £2,670,593
OTHER INFORMATION The trust made 25 grants during the year.
HOW TO APPLY Apply in writing to the secretaries to the trust who administer the charity and pass on applications to the trustees for consideration at the annual meeting.
WHO TO APPLY TO Charities and Third Sector Team, c/o Maclay Murray and Spens LLP, 1 George Square, Glasgow G2 1AL *Tel.* 0330 222 1661 *Email* andrew.biggart@mms.co.uk

■ The Ronald Miller Foundation

SC NO SC008798 **ESTABLISHED** 1979
WHERE FUNDING CAN BE GIVEN UK with a preference for Scotland.
WHO CAN BENEFIT Registered charities.
WHAT IS FUNDED Animals and the environment; medical causes; education; children; general charitable purposes.
WHAT IS NOT FUNDED Individuals.
SAMPLE GRANTS A list of beneficiaries was not available.
FINANCES *Year* 2015/16 *Income* £190,151 *Grants* £169,900 *Grants to organisations* £169,900 *Assets* £5,252,519
OTHER INFORMATION The foundation made grants to 78 organisations for the following purposes: medical (£50,000); general (£37,500); education (£36,500); animals, birds, etc. (£23,500); children (£18,500); and special appeals (£4,000).
HOW TO APPLY Apply in writing to the correspondent.
WHO TO APPLY TO Charities and Third Sector Team, Maclay Murray and Spens LLP, 151 St Vincent Street, Glasgow G2 5NJ *Tel.* 0330 222 0050 *Fax* 0330 222 0053

■ The Millfield House Foundation (MHF)

CC NO 1158914 **ESTABLISHED** 1976
WHERE FUNDING CAN BE GIVEN North East England (Northumberland, Tyne and Wear, Durham and Tees Valley).
WHO CAN BENEFIT Voluntary agencies; charitable organisations; bodies undertaking policy research and advocacy that have close links with or voluntary or community organisations in the region.
WHAT IS FUNDED Social and economic inequality; research on policy.

TYPE OF GRANT Project funding; advocacy; campaigning; project-related core costs; for over three years.

SAMPLE GRANTS Institute for Public Policy Research North (£134,500); Regional Refugee Forum North East (£120,000); North East Child Poverty Commission (£72,500); Newcastle Citizens Advice (£60,000).

FINANCES *Year* 2015/16 *Income* £167,932 *Grants* £386,445 *Grants to organisations* £386,445 *Assets* £5,614,161

TRUSTEES Stephen McClelland; Jane Streather; Sheila Spencer; Rhiannon Bearne; Toby Lowe; Peter Deans; David Handyside.

OTHER INFORMATION About five to ten awards are made each year. This foundation was removed from the Charity Commission register on 17/07/2015 and has been replaced with The Millfield House Foundation (1), Charity Commission no. 1158914. The information in this directory still applies.

HOW TO APPLY The foundation does not accept unsolicited applications.

WHO TO APPLY TO Fiona Ellis, Trust Manager, Minstrel's House, West Marlish, Hartburn, Morpeth, Northumberland NE61 4ER *Tel.* 07500 057825 *Email* fiona.ellis@mhfdn.org.uk *Website* www.mhfdn.org.uk

■ The Millfield Trust

CC NO 262406 **ESTABLISHED** 1971

WHERE FUNDING CAN BE GIVEN UK and overseas.

WHO CAN BENEFIT Charitable and religious organisations; individuals; missionary societies.

WHAT IS FUNDED Religious or other charitable work; missionary work; relief in need. Preference is given where the trust has special interest in, knowledge of, or association with the applicants. Funds are normally fully allocated or committed.

TYPE OF GRANT Unrestricted support but primarily eligible expenditure and project funding.

RANGE OF GRANTS Up to £22,500.

SAMPLE GRANTS Gideons International (£22,500); Gospel Mission to South America (£10,000); Mark Gillingham Charitable Trust (£6,300); Ashbury Evangelical Free Church (£6,000); Crosslinks (£4,000); Revival Christian Radio (£2,000); Billy Graham Evangelical Association, Christian Mission Fellowship and Tear Fund (£1,500 each).

FINANCES *Year* 2015/16 *Income* £49,220 *Grants* £101,600 *Grants to organisations* £98,250 *Assets* £243,025

TRUSTEES Andrew Bunce; Philip Bunce; Stephen Bunce; Rita Bunce.

OTHER INFORMATION The awards were given as follows: charitable and religious institutions (£98,500); individual evangelist and missionaries (£3,300); and pensioners and widows (£100). Awards under £1,000 totalled about £31,000.

HOW TO APPLY Unsolicited applications are not replied to. The trust has stated: 'Most of the organisations and individuals we support are ones in which we have a personal interest and have supported for many years.'

WHO TO APPLY TO Rita Bunce, Trustee, Millfield House, Bell Lane, Liddington, Swindon, Wiltshire SN4 0HE *Tel.* 01793 790181 *Email* millfield@liddington.myzen.co.uk

■ The Millichope Foundation

CC NO 282357 **ESTABLISHED** 1981

WHERE FUNDING CAN BE GIVEN UK, especially the West Midlands and Shropshire; occasionally worldwide.

WHO CAN BENEFIT Registered charities; international organisations.

WHAT IS FUNDED Arts and culture; conservation projects worldwide; environment; heritage and conservation; disaster relief; general charitable purposes.

WHAT IS NOT FUNDED Individuals; non-registered charities.

TYPE OF GRANT Recurrent and one-off.

RANGE OF GRANTS Up to £40,000, usually between £100 and £5,000.

SAMPLE GRANTS Flora and Fauna International and Ludlow and District Community Association Ltd (£40,000 each); Brazilian Atlantic Rainforest Trust (£20,000); University of Cambridge (£5,000); Telford Christian Council (£2,500); Gurkha Welfare Fund (£2,000); Corvedale Centre for Children, Juvenile Diabetes Research Foundation and Shropshire Victim Support (£1,000 each); Music in Hospitals (£750); Wenlock Poetry Festival (£500); Isle of Jura Development Trust (£100).

FINANCES *Year* 2015/16 *Income* £386,328 *Grants* £303,300 *Grants to organisations* £303,300 *Assets* £7,511,320

TRUSTEES Bridget Marshall; Sarah Bury; Lindsay Bury; Frank Bury; H. M. Horne.

OTHER INFORMATION Grants were made to 117 organisations during the year.

HOW TO APPLY Apply in writing to the correspondent. The trustees meet several times a year to consider grants.

WHO TO APPLY TO Sarah Bury, Trustee, The Old Rectory, Tugford, Craven Arms, Shropshire SY7 9HS *Tel.* 01584 841234 *Email* sarah@millichope.com

■ Mills and Reeve Charitable Trust

CC NO 326271 **ESTABLISHED** 1982

WHERE FUNDING CAN BE GIVEN UK with a preference for charities located near the offices of Mills and Reeve LLP.

WHO CAN BENEFIT Charitable organisations.

WHAT IS FUNDED General charitable purposes with a preference for medical research and social welfare.

WHAT IS NOT FUNDED Individuals.

TYPE OF GRANT One-off and recurrent grants for research; eligible expenditure; project funding.

RANGE OF GRANTS Up to £7,000.

SAMPLE GRANTS Leukaemia Lymphoma Research (£7,000); IntoUniversity and Save the Children (£5,000 each); Anthony Nolan Trust (£4,000); Norwich Writers' Circle (£3,500); Royal Marsden Cancer Charity (£2,000); Birmingham Cathedral, Church Housing Trust, Fenland Association for Community Transport and London's Air Ambulance (£1,000 each).

FINANCES *Year* 2015/16 *Income* £93,085 *Grants* £87,314 *Grants to organisations* £87,314 *Assets* £236,386

TRUSTEES Chris Townsend; Greg Gibson; Guy Hinchley; Tom Pickthorn; Dawn Brathwaite; Justin Ripman; Sarah Seed; Alison Bull.

OTHER INFORMATION The trust is the corporate charity of Mills and Reeve LLP. The firm provides a substantial proportion of the charity's income, and each trustee is a member or a former member of the company. Grants made under £1,000 totalled £31,000.

HOW TO APPLY Apply in writing to the correspondent. According to the annual report for 2015/16, the trust makes smaller grants on an ad hoc basis and favours charities nominated by employees at Mills and Reeve LLP or based near one of their offices.

WHO TO APPLY TO Michelle Wells, Administrator, Botanic House, 100 Hills Road, Cambridge CB2 1PH *Tel.* 01223 222273 *Website* www.mills-reeve.com/charitablegiving

■ The Mills Charity

CC NO 207259 **ESTABLISHED** 1981

WHERE FUNDING CAN BE GIVEN Framlingham and the surrounding district.

WHO CAN BENEFIT Charitable organisations and local individuals.

WHAT IS FUNDED General charitable purposes; health and disability; activities for children and young people; social welfare. Separate funds also operate for the benefit of the residents of the almshouses and the upkeep of the facilities.

TYPE OF GRANT One-off and recurrent.

RANGE OF GRANTS £200 to £50,000.

SAMPLE GRANTS The Mills Educational Foundation (£50,000); Framlingham Town Council Skate Park (£40,000); Framlingham Hour Community Project (£5,500); Disability Advice Service (£2,500); Kettleburgh Village Green (£2,000); Fresh Aspirations (£1,400); Debenham Guides (£500); Meadow Children's Centre (£200).

FINANCES *Year* 2015/16 *Income* £173,903 *Grants* £106,681 *Grants to organisations* £101,818 *Assets* £7,745,991

TRUSTEES Howard Wright; Martin Kelleway; Dr Charles Wright; Persephone Booth; Revd Mike Vipond; Nick Corke; Nicola Warner.

OTHER INFORMATION Eight organisations received grants and a total of about £4,900 was also given to individuals.

HOW TO APPLY Apply in writing to the correspondent. The charity appears to have a website (www.themillscharity.co.uk); however, at the time of writing (April 2017) it was not functioning.

WHO TO APPLY TO Bob Snell, PO Box No. 1703, Framlingham, Woodbridge, Suffolk IP13 9WW *Tel.* 01728 621476 *Email* themillscharity@btconnect.com *Website* www.themillscharity.co.uk

■ The Millward Charitable Trust

CC NO 328564 **ESTABLISHED** 1990

WHERE FUNDING CAN BE GIVEN UK and overseas.

WHO CAN BENEFIT Charitable organisations.

WHAT IS FUNDED General charitable purposes; social welfare; performing arts; religious causes; education.

TYPE OF GRANT One-off or recurrent grants.

RANGE OF GRANTS Up to £25,000.

SAMPLE GRANTS City of Birmingham Symphony Orchestra (£25,000); Music in the Round (£17,000 in two grants); Dale Street Methodist Church (£10,000); Birmingham Contemporary Music (£9,500 in two grants); All Saints Church, CALM (Campaign Against Living Miserably), Coventry Youth Orchestra and Leamington Music (£5,000 each).

FINANCES *Year* 2015/16 *Income* £52,268 *Grants* £93,550 *Grants to organisations* £93,550 *Assets* £2,041,740

TRUSTEES Maurice Millward; Sheila Millward; John Hulse.

HOW TO APPLY Apply in writing to the correspondent. The trustees meet regularly to consider applications.

WHO TO APPLY TO John Hulse, Trustee, c/o Burgis and Bullock, 2 Chapel Court, Holly Walk, Leamington Spa, Warwickshire CV32 4YS *Tel.* 01926 451000 *Email* johnhulse121@btinternet.com

■ The Clare Milne Trust

CC NO 1084733 **ESTABLISHED** 1999

WHERE FUNDING CAN BE GIVEN The south west of England; in practice Devon and Cornwall.

WHO CAN BENEFIT Local and regional charities.

WHAT IS FUNDED Disability projects, especially those for adults.

WHAT IS NOT FUNDED Individuals. National charities are not normally supported.

TYPE OF GRANT Generally a partial contribution towards total cost of a project; one-off awards towards capital or core funding; salaries.

RANGE OF GRANTS Usually between £1,000 and £25,000.

SAMPLE GRANTS Calvert Trust (£25,000); Devon County Association for the Blind and Mobility Trust (£20,000 each); Merlin MS Centre (£10,000); A Brighter Tomorrow (£8,000); Community Music in Cornwall (£6,500); Children with Cystic Fibrosis (£5,000); People and Gardens (£4,000); Wheelchair Dance Association (£2,000); Parkinson UK (£1,000).

FINANCES *Year* 2015/16 *Income* £1,454,197 *Grants* £530,999 *Grants to organisations* £530,999 *Assets* £31,330,088

TRUSTEES Margaret Rogers; Nigel Urwin; Robert Spencer; Christine Channing.

OTHER INFORMATION Grants were made to 79 organisations during the year.

HOW TO APPLY Application forms can be downloaded from the trust's website. They should be returned to the secretary along with covering letter (on your letterhead), details regarding your proposal (up to two sides of A4) and a budget for the project. Detailed guidelines are available online. The trustees usually meet four times a year and to save unnecessary administration only applications which fit the trust's criteria will be responded to.

WHO TO APPLY TO Karen Colborne, Secretary (Tuesdays, Wednesdays and Thursdays), c/o Lee Bolton Monier-Williams Solicitors, 1 The Sanctuary, Westminster, London SW1P 3JT *Tel.* 020 7222 5381 *Email* milnetrust@hotmail.co.uk *Website* www.claremilnetrust.com

■ The James Milner Foundation

CC NO 1146768 **ESTABLISHED** 2012

WHERE FUNDING CAN BE GIVEN UK.

WHO CAN BENEFIT Charitable organisations working with children and young people.

WHAT IS FUNDED Education; health; sport and recreation.

TYPE OF GRANT Recurrent, to nominated charity partners.

RANGE OF GRANTS Three grants of £50,000 each.

SAMPLE GRANTS Help for Heroes, Leukaemia Research and NSPCC (£50,000 each).

FINANCES *Year* 2014/15 *Income* £327,331 *Grants* £150,000 *Grants to organisations* £150,000 *Assets* £46,469

TRUSTEES Matthew Buck; Christopher Hudson; Dylan Williams; Mark Hovell; Damaris Treasure.

OTHER INFORMATION The latest accounts available from the Charity Commission were for 2014/15.

HOW TO APPLY Apply in writing to the correspondent.
WHO TO APPLY TO The Trustees, PFA Player Management, 11 Oxford Court, Bishopsgate, Manchester M2 3WQ *Tel.* 0161 484 0876 *Email* contact@thejamesmilnerfoundation.co.uk *Website* www.thejamesmilnerfoundation.com

■ Milton Keynes Community Foundation Ltd

CC NO 295107 **ESTABLISHED** 1987
WHERE FUNDING CAN BE GIVEN Milton Keynes Unitary Authority.
WHO CAN BENEFIT Registered charities; not-for-profit community groups; CIOs; social enterprises; sports clubs; faith groups; CICs; voluntary sector organisations.
WHAT IS FUNDED Poverty, ill health, disability or disadvantage; the arts and leisure.
WHAT IS NOT FUNDED For-profit companies; political parties or groups affiliated to a political party; individuals; groups which do not have a constitution, a management committee, and relevant policies; statutory bodies; animal welfare; projects promoting religious beliefs; medical research or treatment; repayment of loans; unspecified expenditure.
TYPE OF GRANT Start-up costs; project extension or development core costs; pilot projects; equipment and resources.
RANGE OF GRANTS Micro grants of up to £200 to £300; small grants of up to £1,500; community grants of up to £5,000; extraordinary grants may also be provided.
SAMPLE GRANTS Arts For Health (£51,000 in two grants); Citizens Advice (£25,000); PACE Centre (£13,500); Winter Night Shelter Milton Keynes (£5,000); Milton Keynes BMX Racing Club (£3,600); Milton Keynes Five Star Somali Community (£3,000 in two grants); Men in Sheds Milton Keynes (£2,500); The Conservation Volunteers (£1,500); Local Media Initiatives CIC (£1,400); Breastfeeding Café Milton Keynes (£950); West Bletchley District Guides (£25).
FINANCES *Year* 2015/16 *Income* £4,961,185 *Grants* £1,070,141 *Grants to organisations* £1,055,641 *Assets* £45,342,879
TRUSTEES Michael Murray; Francesca Skelton; Peter Selvey; Peter Kara; Richard Brown; Steven Norrish; Fola Komolafe; John Moffoot; Keith Silverthorne; Stephen Harris; Lawrence Revill; Melanie Beck; Ben Stoneman; Stephen Norrish; Shaun Lee; Jill Heaton.
OTHER INFORMATION There are three main grant programmes that run throughout the year: micro grants (up to £200, no deadline); small grants (up to £1,500, deadline on the last working Friday of each month); and community grants (up to £5,000, one deadline each quarter, see website for exact dates). Grants over £5,000 may be made in exceptional circumstances, contact the foundation to find out more. As with all community foundations grant schemes can change frequently – for full details of the foundation's current grant programmes and their deadlines consult the website. Grants made to individuals during the year totalled £14,500.
HOW TO APPLY Full guidance on how to make an application is provided on the foundation's website, along with deadlines and application forms. New applicants are encouraged to contact the Programmes Team to check their eligibility before making an application.
WHO TO APPLY TO The Programmes Team, Acorn House, 381 Midsummer Boulevard, Central Milton Keynes MK9 3HP *Tel.* 01908 690276 *Email* applications@mkcommunityfoundation.co.uk *Website* www.mkcommunityfoundation.co.uk

■ The Edgar Milward Charity

CC NO 281018 **ESTABLISHED** 1980
WHERE FUNDING CAN BE GIVEN UK and overseas; with a particular interest in Reading.
WHO CAN BENEFIT Charitable organisations; registered charities; educational establishments; religious institutions; individuals.
WHAT IS FUNDED Support is distributed as follows: one-half for the furtherance of the Christian religion within the United Kingdom and throughout the world; four-tenths for such charitable purposes as the trustees may see fit; one-tenth for educational purposes within a radius of 15 miles from the Civic Centre, Reading.
TYPE OF GRANT One-off or up to three years; capital and core costs; salaries.
RANGE OF GRANTS Up to £5,000.
SAMPLE GRANTS Connect4Life (£5,000); Bible Society (£1,500); Africa Inland Mission (£1,250); The Barnabas Fund, Grace Church Dulwich, London School of Theology and Urban Saints (£1,000 each).
FINANCES *Year* 2015/16 *Income* £49,297 *Grants* £42,987 *Grants to organisations* £42,987 *Assets* £1,426,638
TRUSTEES J. C. Austin; J. S. Milward; Alec Fogwill; S. M. W. Fogwill; M. V. Roberts; Fiona Palethorpe.
OTHER INFORMATION During the year, 3 grants totalling £3,000 were paid directly to individuals. 11 grants, each under £1,000 amounting in total to £5,340, were made at the trustees' discretion to a variety of charitable causes. Grants totalling £10,000 were awarded for the furtherance of Christian religion and £2,000 was awarded for educational purposes.
HOW TO APPLY Applications can be made in writing to the correspondent, although unsolicited applications are not normally considered.
WHO TO APPLY TO Fiona Palethorpe, Secretary and Treasurer, 19A Cotterstock Road, Oundle, Peterborough PE8 5HA *Tel.* 01832 270055 *Email* edgarmilwardcharity@btinternet.com

■ The Peter Minet Trust

CC NO 259963 **ESTABLISHED** 1969
WHERE FUNDING CAN BE GIVEN Mainly South East London boroughs, particularly Lambeth and Southwark.
WHO CAN BENEFIT UK-registered charities and UK publicly exempt charities.
WHAT IS FUNDED General charitable causes, including social welfare, health, cultural and community projects; young people; people with disabilities.
WHAT IS NOT FUNDED Individuals; national appeals by large charities; appeals outside the inner boroughs of South East London; appeals whose sole purpose is to make grants from collected funds; research.
TYPE OF GRANT Main grants of up to £5,000 or small grants of up to £500.
RANGE OF GRANTS £500 to £5,000.
SAMPLE GRANTS Black Cultural Archives and Lambeth Summer Camps (£5,000 each); Communities Welfare Network (£4,700); Prisoners' Advice Service (£4,000); Camberwell After School Project (£3,500); Friends of

Windmill Gardens (£2,500); Indoamerican Refugee and Migrant Organisation, Lambeth Elderly Association from Vietnam and People Care at Christmas (£500 each).

FINANCES *Year* 2015/16 *Income* £213,657 *Grants* £155,497 *Grants to organisations* £155,497 *Assets* £5,441,567

TRUSTEES John South; Paula Jones; Rodney Luff; Linda Cleverly; Simon Hebditch.

OTHER INFORMATION During the year the trust awarded 47 grants (following 196 appeals), which included 6 small grants.

HOW TO APPLY Applications should be made using an online application process on the trust's website. There are also application guidelines which should be read carefully prior to applying, as they contain terms and conditions introduced in February 2017.

WHO TO APPLY TO Rachel Oglethorpe, Director, 1A Taylors Yard, 67 Alderbrook Road, London SW12 8AD *Tel.* 020 8772 3155 *Email* info@peterminet.org.uk *Website* www.peterminet.org.uk

■ The Mirianog Trust

CC NO 1091397 **ESTABLISHED** 2002

WHERE FUNDING CAN BE GIVEN UK and overseas.

WHO CAN BENEFIT Charitable organisations.

WHAT IS FUNDED General charitable purposes, with a preference for overseas aid, famine relief and social welfare.

TYPE OF GRANT One-off and recurrent.

RANGE OF GRANTS Usually between £500 and £2,000, but with a few larger grants of over £20,000.

SAMPLE GRANTS Cirdan Sailing Trust (£35,000); Sea-Change Sailing Trust (£20,000); Butterwick Hospice Care, Freedom of Torture and Medical Aid for Palestinians (£2,000 each); Middlesbrough Foodbank, Safe Child Africa and Survivors of Bereavement by Suicide (£1,000 each); AIDS Orphans of Myanmar, Birmingham Royal Ballet and Fish Aid (£500 each).

FINANCES *Year* 2015/16 *Income* £79,544 *Grants* £84,450 *Grants to organisations* £84,450 *Assets* £665,712

TRUSTEES Canon William Broad; Daphne Broad; Elizabeth Jeary.

OTHER INFORMATION Grants were made to 26 organisations.

HOW TO APPLY Apply in writing to the correspondent. The trustees consider awards twice each year.

WHO TO APPLY TO Canon William Broad, Trustee, Moorcote, Thornley, Tow Law, Bishop Auckland DL13 4NU *Tel.* 01388 731350 *Email* bill@billbroad.wanadoo.co.uk

■ The Laurence Misener Charitable Trust

CC NO 283460 **ESTABLISHED** 1981

WHERE FUNDING CAN BE GIVEN UK and overseas.

WHO CAN BENEFIT Registered charities; hospitals; hospices.

WHAT IS FUNDED General charitable purposes, including health, education, armed forces charities, organisations working with people with disabilities and Jewish causes.

TYPE OF GRANT One-off and recurrent.

RANGE OF GRANTS £7,000 to £40,000.

SAMPLE GRANTS Multiple Sclerosis Society, Royal Marsden Hospital and Seafarers UK (£40,000 each); Fight for Sight and RNLI (£25,000 each); Imperial War Museum Development Trust (£15,000); Disasters Emergency Committee – Ebola Crisis Appeal, St Peter and St James Home and Hospice, and Sussex Stroke and Circulation Fund (£10,000 each); World Jewish Relief (£7,000).

FINANCES *Year* 2015/16 *Income* £119,594 *Grants* £297,000 *Grants to organisations* £297,000 *Assets* £2,582,686

TRUSTEES Jillian Legane; Capt. George Swaine.

OTHER INFORMATION Grants were made to 14 organisations during the year.

HOW TO APPLY Apply in writing to the correspondent. Note the following taken from the annual report for 2015/16: 'The Trustees receive a considerable number of requests for donations and grants each year but have a policy to restrict donations approved to those charities which in their view would have been approved by the Settlor himself, or fall under the heading of approved charitable purposes.'

WHO TO APPLY TO David Lyons, c/o Leonard Jones and Co., 1 Printing Yard House, London E2 7PR *Tel.* 020 7739 8790 *Email* enquiries@leonardjones.co.uk

■ The Mishcon Family Charitable Trust

CC NO 213165 **ESTABLISHED** 1961

WHERE FUNDING CAN BE GIVEN UK.

WHO CAN BENEFIT Registered charities, particularly Jewish organisations.

WHAT IS FUNDED General charitable purposes; Jewish causes; social welfare; health and disability; children and young people.

TYPE OF GRANT One-off project and other, generally unrestricted, awards.

RANGE OF GRANTS £50 to £33,500.

SAMPLE GRANTS United Jewish Israel Appeal (UJIA) (£32,500); One to One Children's Fund (£4,000); Art Fund, Barts and the London Charity, and Crisis UK (£1,000 each); British Refugee Council (£300); Architects Benevolent Society, The Guardian and Observer Charity Appeal 2015 and Jewish Women's Aid (£250 each); Alzheimer's Research UK, Mercy Ships and Prostate Cancer UK (£50 each).

FINANCES *Year* 2015/16 *Income* £63,075 *Grants* £77,207 *Grants to organisations* £77,207 *Assets* £1,883,818

TRUSTEES Jane Landau; Peter Mishcon; Russell Mishcon.

OTHER INFORMATION Grants were made to 80 organisations.

HOW TO APPLY Apply in writing to the correspondent. Within the limited funds available each application is considered on its merits with preference given to applications for the relief of poverty from recognised organisations.

WHO TO APPLY TO George Georghiou, c/o Mercer and Hole, 72 London Road, St Albans AL1 1NS *Tel.* 01727 869141

■ The Brian Mitchell Charitable Settlement

CC NO 1003817 **ESTABLISHED** 1989

WHERE FUNDING CAN BE GIVEN UK.

WHO CAN BENEFIT Charitable organisations.

WHAT IS FUNDED General charitable purposes, especially arts and education; medical care and research; social welfare; international support.

TYPE OF GRANT One-off and recurrent.

RANGE OF GRANTS Up to £25,000.

SAMPLE GRANTS Glyndebourne Festival Society (£25,000); British Red Cross and Shakespeare's Globe Theatre (£15,000 each); Myeloma UK (£10,000); Hospice on the Weald, Macmillan Nurses and Orchestra of the Age of Enlightenment (£7,500 each); Temple Music Foundation (£7,000); Canterbury Cathedral, Child Hope and The Rose Theatre Trust (£5,000). Other awards totalled over £86,500 but were not listed.
FINANCES *Year* 2015/16 *Income* £290,487 *Grants* £226,150 *Grants to organisations* £226,150 *Assets* £2,404,849
TRUSTEES Brian Mitchell; Andy Buss; John Andrews; Michael Conlon; Fraser Reavell.
OTHER INFORMATION In 2015/16 around 60% of all grants went to supporting arts and education. There were 51 grants made to organisations.
HOW TO APPLY Apply in writing to the correspondent, although note that the charity has identified several regular beneficiaries.
WHO TO APPLY TO Brian Mitchell, Trustee, Round Oak, Old Station Road, Wadhurst, East Sussex TN5 6TZ *Tel.* 01892 782072 *Email* brnmitchell3@googlemail.com

■ The MITIE Foundation

CC NO 1148858 **ESTABLISHED** 2012
WHERE FUNDING CAN BE GIVEN UK and the Republic of Ireland.
WHO CAN BENEFIT Charities and community groups.
WHAT IS FUNDED General charitable purposes, education and training and economic and community development. There is a particular interest in supporting organisations working with young people, older people and people with disabilities.
SAMPLE GRANTS Macmillan Cancer Support and The Mary Leishman Foundation (£11,000 each). Other beneficiaries included: Catch 22; Chewton Mendip School (Schools Energy Winner); Springboard; Working Chance; Working Knowledge.
FINANCES *Year* 2015/16 *Income* £434,000 *Grants* £350,000 *Grants to organisations* £350,000 *Assets* £52,000
TRUSTEES Ruby McGregor-Smith; Suzanne Baxter; Paul Cooper.
HOW TO APPLY Unsolicited applications are not accepted.
WHO TO APPLY TO Paddy Stanley, MITIE Group PLC, Unit 1 Harlequin Office Park, Fieldfare, Emersons Green, Bristol BS16 7FN *Tel.* 07917 521268 *Email* Foundation@mitie.com *Website* www.mitie.com/sustainability/the-mitie-foundation

■ Mitsubishi Corporation Fund for Europe and Africa

CC NO 1014621 **ESTABLISHED** 1992
WHERE FUNDING CAN BE GIVEN UK, Africa and Europe.
WHO CAN BENEFIT Registered charities; non-profit organisations; academic institutions.
WHAT IS FUNDED Conservation and the environment; environmental research; poverty alleviation through the economic and social development of local communities in an environmentally sustainable manner.
WHAT IS NOT FUNDED Individuals; religious, political or lobbying groups.
TYPE OF GRANT One-off and recurrent; research.
RANGE OF GRANTS £15,000 to £65,000.
SAMPLE GRANTS BirdLife International (£65,000); WaterAid (£50,000); SolarAid (£40,000); Earthwatch Institute (£39,500); Farm Africa, Renewable World and Sustainable Fisheries Partnership (£30,000); Springboard Entrepreneurship (£15,000).
FINANCES *Year* 2015/16 *Income* £300,000 *Grants* £299,594 *Grants to organisations* £299,594 *Assets* £241,989
TRUSTEES Julie Rogers; Haruki Hayashi; Yasuyuki Sugiura; Sachio Kaneki; Yoshiyuki Nojima; Akihiro Kurosawa.
OTHER INFORMATION Grants were made to eight organisations during the year.
HOW TO APPLY Apply in writing to the correspondent. Detailed guidance and deadlines are provided on the charity's website.
WHO TO APPLY TO Emily Minton, Programme Officer, Mitsubishi Corporation International PLC, Mid City Place, 71 High Holborn, London WC1V 6BA *Tel.* 020 7025 3043 *Email* emily.a.minton@mitsubishicorp.com *Website* www.mitsubishicorp.com/gb/en/csr/mcfea

■ The Mittal Foundation

CC NO 1146604 **ESTABLISHED** 2012
WHERE FUNDING CAN BE GIVEN UK and India.
WHO CAN BENEFIT Registered charities and individuals.
WHAT IS FUNDED General charitable purposes, especially education and training; arts; prevention of poverty and malnutrition; children and young people.
TYPE OF GRANT One-off and recurrent.
SAMPLE GRANTS Unicef (£2 million).
FINANCES *Year* 2015 *Income* £11,000,000 *Grants* £2,386,150 *Grants to organisations* £2,386,150 *Assets* £9,852,220
TRUSTEES Usha Mittal; Megha Mittal; Vanisha Mittal Bhatia.
HOW TO APPLY The foundation does not accept unsolicited applications.
WHO TO APPLY TO The Trustees, c/o Mittal Investments Ltd, Floor 3, Berkeley Square House, Berkeley Square, London W1J 6BU *Tel.* 020 7659 1033

■ The Keren Mitzvah Trust

CC NO 1041948 **ESTABLISHED** 1994
WHERE FUNDING CAN BE GIVEN UK.
WHO CAN BENEFIT Registered charities, particularly Jewish organisations. The trust can also make grants to individuals.
WHAT IS FUNDED General charitable purposes; Jewish causes; relief of poverty; religious activities; education; health.
TYPE OF GRANT One-off and recurrent, generally unrestricted.
RANGE OF GRANTS Up to £27,000.
SAMPLE GRANTS KKL Charity (£27,000); Camp Simcha (£12,500); The Sunderland Kollel (£10,000); The Good Deed Foundation and UK Friends of Awis (£8,000 each); Keren Shlomo Trust, One Family UK and The European Beth Din Ltd (£5,000 each).
FINANCES *Year* 2015 *Income* £190,750 *Grants* £185,160 *Grants to organisations* £185,160 *Assets* £43,524
TRUSTEES Manny Weiss; Alan McCormack; Neil Bradley.
OTHER INFORMATION Grants under £5,000 totalled just under £48,000.

HOW TO APPLY Apply in writing to the correspondent. The trust has previously stated that the trustees generally support their own personal charities.

WHO TO APPLY TO Camilla Campbell, 1 Manchester Square, London W1U 3AB

The Mizpah

CC NO 287231 **ESTABLISHED** 1983

WHERE FUNDING CAN BE GIVEN UK and overseas.

WHO CAN BENEFIT Registered charities and individuals.

WHAT IS FUNDED Relief of poverty; education; Christian causes; medical research.

TYPE OF GRANT One-off and recurrent.

SAMPLE GRANTS A list of beneficiaries was not provided in the annual report and accounts for 2015/16; however, grants were made in the following areas: education (£131,500); promotion of Christianity (£52,000); relief of poverty (£5,500); medical research (£2,000).

FINANCES *Year* 2015/16 *Income* £140,855 *Grants* £190,964 *Grants to organisations* £190,964 *Assets* £85,667

TRUSTEES Alan Bell; Julia Bell.

HOW TO APPLY Unsolicited applications are not invited. The trust proactively distributes funds and does not responded to enquiries and requests for funding.

WHO TO APPLY TO Alan Bell, Trustee, Foresters House, Humbly Grove, South Warnborough, Hook, Hampshire RG29 1RY *Email* Alancobell@gmail.com

Mobbs Memorial Trust Ltd

CC NO 202478 **ESTABLISHED** 1963

WHERE FUNDING CAN BE GIVEN Stoke Poges and district within a 35-mile radius of St Giles' Church.

WHO CAN BENEFIT Charitable organisations.

WHAT IS FUNDED St Giles' Church and other charitable purposes including: support to voluntary and community organisations; sports and recreation; health causes; conservation and environment; schools and colleges; and community facilities and services.

WHAT IS NOT FUNDED The following applications are not normally supported: from or for individuals or private companies; from national charitable organisations, unless a specific need arises in connection with the local area; those that should be funded by national or local government; and for running costs, apart from exceptional cases within a four-mile radius of Stoke Poges.

TYPE OF GRANT Grants for buildings, equipment and projects. Funding is given for up to three years.

RANGE OF GRANTS £500 to £10,000.

SAMPLE GRANTS Alexander Devine Children's Hospice (£7,600); Stoke Poges 1st Air Scouts and Windsor Sea Cadets (£7,500 each); Reading Association for the Blind, Rennie Grove Hospice and Wheel Power (£5,000 each); Action4Youth and Windsor Horse Rangers (£3,500 each); Stoke Poges Old People's Christmas Fund (£2,500); Come Play Pre-School (£1,500); Stoke Poges Horticultural Society (£250).

FINANCES *Year* 2015/16 *Income* £85,195 *Grants* £81,160 *Grants to organisations* £80,296 *Assets* £2,720,598

TRUSTEES Sandra Greenslade; Chris Mobbs; Dr Charles Mobbs; Alexandra Mobbs.

OTHER INFORMATION Grants were made to 24 organisations and one grant of around £860 was awarded to an individual.

HOW TO APPLY Applications can either be posted or emailed to the correspondent. The trustees meet quarterly, normally in March, June, September and December. The trust prefers to support projects that benefit the general public and that obtain funding from other sources as well as Mobbs Memorial Trust.

WHO TO APPLY TO Dr Charles Mobbs, Cypress Cottage, 89 St John's Road, Newport, Isle of Wight PO30 1LS *Email* applications@mobbsmemorialtrust.com or charlesmobbs@mobbsmemorialtrust.com *Website* www.mobbsmemorialtrust.com

Mole Charitable Trust

CC NO 281452 **ESTABLISHED** 1980

WHERE FUNDING CAN BE GIVEN UK, with a preference for Manchester.

WHO CAN BENEFIT Registered charities and individuals.

WHAT IS FUNDED Jewish causes; educational purposes; the relief of poverty; organisations working with children.

SAMPLE GRANTS Three Pillars Charity (£30,000); The Shaarei Torah Trust (£19,500); Manchester Charitable Trust Ltd (£10,000).

FINANCES *Year* 2015/16 *Income* £53,368 *Grants* £80,550 *Grants to organisations* £80,550 *Assets* £2,313,057

TRUSTEES Martin Gross; Leah Gross.

OTHER INFORMATION A list of beneficiaries was not available in the 2015/16 accounts.

HOW TO APPLY Apply in writing to the correspondent. The annual report and accounts for 2015/16 state: 'The trustees receive many applications for grants, mainly personal contact, but also verbally. Each application is considered against the criteria established by the Charity. Although the Charity does not advertise, it is well known within its community and there are many requests received for grants.'

WHO TO APPLY TO Martin Gross, Trustee, 2 Okeover Road, Salford M7 4JX *Tel.* 0161 832 8721 *Email* martin.gross@lopiangb.co.uk

The Monatrea Charitable Trust

CC NO 1131897 **ESTABLISHED** 2009

WHERE FUNDING CAN BE GIVEN UK.

WHO CAN BENEFIT Registered charities.

WHAT IS FUNDED General charitable purposes; arts; health; social welfare.

TYPE OF GRANT One-off and recurrent.

RANGE OF GRANTS £1,200 to £74,500.

SAMPLE GRANTS Docubox East African Documentary Film Fund; Dr Ambrosoli Memorial Health; Family Action; Orbis; Pregnancy Sickness; Samata Hospital; Virunga Foundation.

FINANCES *Year* 2015/16 *Income* £136,836 *Grants* £156,580 *Grants to organisations* £156,580 *Assets* £303,628

TRUSTEES Patrick Vernon; Mary Vernon; Coutts & Co.

OTHER INFORMATION Grants to eight organisations were made during 2015/16.

HOW TO APPLY Apply in writing to the correspondent.

WHO TO APPLY TO The Trustees, c/o Coutts & Co. Trustee Department, 6th Floor, Trinity Quay 2, Avon Street, Bristol BS2 0PT *Tel.* 020 7663 6825 *Email* couttscharities@coutts.com

■ The Monmouthshire County Council Welsh Church Act Fund

CC NO 507094 **ESTABLISHED** 1996

WHERE FUNDING CAN BE GIVEN Blaenau Gwent, Caerphilly, Monmouthshire, the City of Newport and Torfaen.

WHO CAN BENEFIT Charitable organisations and individuals.

WHAT IS FUNDED People who are disadvantaged by poverty, social isolation or ill health and disaster victims; education; health and disability causes; relief of poverty; medical and social research; social and recreational causes; libraries, museums and art galleries; protection of historic buildings relating to Wales; places of worship and burial grounds.

TYPE OF GRANT Capital or revenue purposes, also provision, upkeep and repair of religious buildings and community halls.

SAMPLE GRANTS A list of beneficiary organisations was not available but previous beneficiaries have included: Bridges Community Centre; North Wales Society for the Blind; Parish Church Llandogo; Parish Church Llangybi; and St David's Foundation Hospice Care.

FINANCES *Year* 2015/16 *Income* £225,935 *Grants* £122,604 *Grants to organisations* £122,604 *Assets* £5,216,589

TRUSTEE Monmouthshire County Council.

OTHER INFORMATION Grants totalling £8,600 were also made to individuals for educational purposes and the relief of poverty.

HOW TO APPLY Our research suggests that applications should be made on a form available from the correspondent which must be signed by a county/city councillor. They are normally considered in March, June, September and December.

WHO TO APPLY TO Joy Robson, Head of Finance, Monmouthshire County Council, PO Box 106, Caldicot NP26 9AN *Tel.* 01633 644657 *Email* davejarrett@monmouthshire.gov.uk *Website* www.monmouthshire.gov.uk

■ The Monument Trust

CC NO 242575 **ESTABLISHED** 1965

WHERE FUNDING CAN BE GIVEN Unrestricted; in practice the UK, South Africa and the USA.

WHO CAN BENEFIT Registered charities.

WHAT IS FUNDED General charitable purposes with a preference for arts and heritage; health and community care; social development; criminal justice – including prisoners' resettlement and alternatives to custody; homelessness.

WHAT IS NOT FUNDED Individuals; educational fees; expeditions.

TYPE OF GRANT Core, capital and project costs. One-off and recurrent grants.

RANGE OF GRANTS Up to £4 million; mostly under £500,000.

SAMPLE GRANTS British Museum Development Trust (£4 million); Royal Opera House Covent Garden Foundation (£3 million); Cambridge Judge Business School (£2.5 million); Royal Academy of Arts (£2 million); Parkinson's UK (£1.5 million); UK Centre for Justice Innovation and Effectiveness (£300,000); CLINKS Prisons Community Links and HIV I-Base (£200,000 each); Woodland Heritage (£170,000); Stonewall (£150,000); Changing Tunes and Scottish Ballet (£100,000 each).

FINANCES *Year* 2015/16 *Income* £3,210,000 *Grants* £28,665,471 *Grants to organisations* £28,665,471 *Assets* £70,242,000

TRUSTEES Stewart Grimshaw; Linda Heathcoat-Amory; Charles Cator; Dominic Flynn.

OTHER INFORMATION This is one of the Sainsbury Family Charitable Trusts, which share a joint administration but work autonomously as independent legal entities. The website states that 'the trustees have almost completed their plan to spend the trust's endowment and close down, so in their final period of operation they will only be considering new grants to charities with which they already have a close association.' Grants were made to 129 organisations throughout the year and awards of less than £100,000 totalled £1.3 million.

HOW TO APPLY The trust will consider suitable proposals so long as they closely match the areas in which the trustees are interested. Generally, the trustees tend to invite or initiate proposals from organisations themselves so a large number of unsolicited applications will be unsuccessful. Eligible proposals can be sent via post to the correspondent including the following: details of your organisation (do not send a full set of accounts); information on the project requiring funding; breakdown of costs. Refrain from sending any other supporting materials. Further details can be found on the foundation's website.

WHO TO APPLY TO Alan Bookbinder, Director, The Peak, 5 Wilton Road, London SW1V 1AP *Tel.* 020 7410 0330 *Fax* 020 7410 0332 *Email* info@sfct.org.uk *Website* www.sfct.org.uk

■ Moondance Foundation

CC NO 1139224 **ESTABLISHED** 2010

WHERE FUNDING CAN BE GIVEN UK and overseas.

WHO CAN BENEFIT Charitable organisations; individuals.

WHAT IS FUNDED General charitable purposes. The foundation focuses its support on the following categories: causes in Wales; children; education; poverty; care and research for serious illness; arts and humanities.

RANGE OF GRANTS Up to £625,000; many grants are for less than £20,000.

SAMPLE GRANTS Plan UK (£625,000); NSPCC (£500,000); Safer Wales (£125,000); Teach First (£100,000); Ty Hapus (£80,000); Caerphilly Miners Centre (£55,000); Elton John AIDS Foundation (£50,000); College Bound (£34,000); Surfers Against Sewage (£30,000); Chapter Cardiff (£25,000); Tenovus Cancer (£20,000).

FINANCES *Year* 2014/15 *Income* £29,888,497 *Grants* £7,316,129 *Grants to organisations* £7,316,129 *Assets* £151,793,847

TRUSTEES Louisa Scadden; Henry Engelhardt; Diane Briere De L'Isle Engelhardt; Damien Engelhardt; Adrian Engelhardt; Shanna Briere De L'Isle Engelhardt.

OTHER INFORMATION The 2014/15 accounts were the most recent available to view on the Charity Commission's website at the time of writing (June 2017). Grants of less than £20,000 totalled £214,500 during the year.

HOW TO APPLY Apply in writing to the correspondent. The trust only replies to successful applicants. The trustees meet regularly to review applications, as well as investigating eligible causes themselves.

WHO TO APPLY TO The Trustees, c/o KPMG LLP, 3 Assembly Square, Britannia Quay, Cardiff Bay CF10 4AX *Tel.* 029 2046 8000 *Email* moondancefoundation@gmail.com

■ The George A. Moore Foundation

CC NO 262107 **ESTABLISHED** 1970

WHERE FUNDING CAN BE GIVEN Yorkshire and the Isle of Man.

WHO CAN BENEFIT Charitable and voluntary organisations.

WHAT IS FUNDED General charitable purposes.

WHAT IS NOT FUNDED Assistance is not given to/for: individuals; courses of study; expeditions and overseas travel; holidays; purposes outside the UK.

TYPE OF GRANT Grants are generally non-recurrent and the foundation is reluctant to contribute to revenue appeals.

RANGE OF GRANTS £150 to £55,000.

SAMPLE GRANTS St John's Parish Church Knaresborough (£55,000); The Carers' Resource (£30,000); OPAL Older People's Action in the Locality (£10,000); Clatterbridge Cancer Charity and Pocklington Canal Amenity Society (£5,000 each); Aberford Village Hall, Fire Fighters Charity and Marine Conservation Society (£1,000 each); St John Ambulance (£500); Sulby Horticultural Show (£250); Sulby and District Rifle Club (£150).

FINANCES *Year* 2015/16 *Income* £264,826 *Grants* £323,527 *Grants to organisations* £323,527 *Assets* £6,432,057

TRUSTEES Elizabeth Moore; Jonathan Moore; Paul Turner.

OTHER INFORMATION There were 155 awards made to organisations. The charity consists of one general fund (unrestricted) and one expendable endowment fund.

HOW TO APPLY Apply in writing to the correspondent – note that trustees *do not* favour applications via email and appreciate formal style of requests. There are no formal guidelines or application forms issued. Applications should be received by the middle of the month prior to the meeting. The meetings are held four times a year, in March, June, September and December and all applicants are notified of the outcome following the meeting.

WHO TO APPLY TO Angela James, Chief Administrator, The George A. Moore Foundation, 4th Floor, 10 South Parade, Leeds LS1 5QS *Tel.* 0113 386 3393 *Email* info@gamf.org.uk *Website* www.gamf.org.uk

■ The Henry Moore Foundation

CC NO 271370 **ESTABLISHED** 1977

WHERE FUNDING CAN BE GIVEN UK and overseas.

WHO CAN BENEFIT Not-for-profit institutions; arts organisations; educational bodies.

WHAT IS FUNDED Fine arts, in particular sculpture; research and development; projects and exhibitions which expand the definition of sculpture, such as film, photography and performance; collections and acquisitions; conferences and lectures.

WHAT IS NOT FUNDED Revenue expenditure; individuals (except fellowships); retrospective funding. No grant (or part of any grant) may be used to pay any fee or to provide any other benefit to any individual who is a trustee of the foundation.

TYPE OF GRANT One-off and longer-term funding; publication; research; development; collections; exhibitions; fellowships; conferences and lectures.

RANGE OF GRANTS Up to £20,000, depending on grant category.

SAMPLE GRANTS The Public Catalogue Foundation, London (£20,000 per annum over four years); Bodleian Weston Library University of Oxford, Lady Lever Art Gallery and Worcestershire County Council Archive and Archaeology Service (WAAS) (£10,000 each); GI (Glasgow International) (£7,000); Museum of Modern Art Warsaw, Northern Gallery for Contemporary Art and University of Winchester (conference) (£2,000 each); Frontier Publishing Norwich (£1,000).

FINANCES *Year* 2015/16 *Income* £6,197,219 *Grants* £507,211 *Grants to organisations* £507,211 *Assets* £107,574,922

TRUSTEES Nigel Carrington; David Wilson; Charles Asprey; Henry Channon; Celia Clear; William Edgerley; Laure Genillard; Antony Griffiths; Anne Wagner; Peter Wienand.

OTHER INFORMATION There were 93 grants paid in the following categories: exhibitions and new projects (58 awards totalling £196,000); conferences, publications and workshops (13 awards totalling £24,000); fellowships (4 awards totalling £64,500); research (10 awards totalling £163,000); collections (8 awards totalling £60,000). The most recent projects supported are listed on the foundation's website.

HOW TO APPLY Applicants should complete an application form which is available on the foundation's website. Applications must be posted to the grants administrator. Applications will be acknowledged by letter. The grants committee meets quarterly; consult the foundation's website for exact dates as the foundation advises that applications received late will not be considered until the next meeting. It is advised to leave six months between the grants committee meeting and the project start date as funds cannot be paid for retrospective projects. Applicants should also advise the foundation whether it is envisaged that any trustee will have an interest in the project for which a grant is sought.

WHO TO APPLY TO Lesley Wake, Chief Operating Officer, Dane Tree House, Perry Green, Much Hadham, Hertfordshire SG10 6EE *Tel.* 01279 843333 *Email* admin@henry-moore.org *Website* www.henry-moore.org

■ John Moores Foundation (JMF)

CC NO 253481 **ESTABLISHED** 1963

WHERE FUNDING CAN BE GIVEN Merseyside (including Ellesmere Port, Halton and Skelmersdale) and Northern Ireland.

WHO CAN BENEFIT Voluntary organisations; community groups; charities; social enterprises; CICs; other charitable organisations; black and minority ethnic organisations. Preference is given for small, grassroots and volunteer-driven organisations and new rather than long-established groups.

WHAT IS FUNDED Women and girls; second-chance learning; advice and information to alleviate poverty; support and training for voluntary organisations; support projects which aim to counter racism, sexism or discrimination of any kind; community cohesion and development. **In Merseyside only:** people with disabilities; carers; refugees; homeless people; family support; young people. **In Northern Ireland only:** promotion of Equal Opportunities.

WHAT IS NOT FUNDED Individuals; projects that are not substantially influenced by their target beneficiaries; national organisations or groups based outside the Merseyside region even where some of the service users come from the area; statutory bodies or work previously done by them; education (schools, colleges, universities, supplementary schools); faith-based projects exclusively for members of that faith, or for the promotion of religion; capital building costs; festivals, carnivals and fêtes; medicine or medical equipment; holidays and expeditions; gifts, parties, etc.; organising conferences; sport; vehicles; animal charities; the creative industries; heritage or local history projects; employability and enterprise schemes; academic or medical research; Credit Unions – **except** for the training of management committee members or the development of a new business plan; veterans; uniformed groups (e.g. scouts, cadets, majorettes); sponsorship, advertising or fundraising events; counsellors not registered with the BACP or IACP. The foundation states that 'applications may be refused where [it feels] that the organisation concerned is already well funded or has excessive reserves'.

TYPE OF GRANT One-off and up to three years; projects; salaries; service delivery; running costs; volunteers' expenses; equipment.

RANGE OF GRANTS £600 to £10,000.

SAMPLE GRANTS Family Tree (Wirral), Homebaked Co-operative Anfield Ltd, Sahir House, and Vauxhall Community Law and Information Centre (£10,000 each); Asylum Link Merseyside (£7,000 each); Pakistan Association Liverpool (£5,000); Jigsaw Community Counselling Centre (£4,500); Polish Saturday School Ballymena and Strabane Community Unemployed Group (£3,000 each); Merseyside Welfare Rights (£2,000); Banbridge Arthritis Care (£1,200); Tullygarley and District Residents' Association (£750); HALDS – Halton Adults with Learning Disabilities Support (£600).

FINANCES *Year* 2015/16 *Income* £931,723 *Grants* £732,658 *Grants to organisations* £732,658 *Assets* £25,311,937

TRUSTEES Barnaby Moores; Kevin Moores; Nicola Eastwood; Christina Mee.

OTHER INFORMATION During the year a total of 201 applications were received (106 in Merseyside, 83 in Northern Ireland and 12 from other areas) and 146 grants paid. Overseas and one-off exceptional grants are not open to unsolicited applications. Merseyside is the first concern of the trustees' with about 60–75% of grants given there. Furthermore, the foundation prefers to give smaller grants to a larger number of projects.

HOW TO APPLY There are slight differences between the application procedures and criteria for Merseyside and Northern Ireland (see the website for full details and eligibility criteria). Applications should be made by letter (no more than four A4 sides) accompanied by a completed application form, which is available from the foundation's Merseyside and Northern Ireland offices and can be requested via email or phone. All appeals are acknowledged. Applicants are welcome to contact the office to find out at which meeting their application will be considered. Unsuccessful applicants are advised to wait at least four months before re-applying.

WHO TO APPLY TO Phil Godfrey, Grants Director, John Moores Foundation, 7th Floor, Gostins Building, 32–36 Hanover Street, Liverpool L1 4LN *Tel.* 0151 707 6077 *Email* info@johnmooresfoundation.com *Website* www.jmf.org.uk

■ The Morel Charitable Trust (The Morel Trust)

CC NO 268943 **ESTABLISHED** 1972

WHERE FUNDING CAN BE GIVEN UK and financially developing countries. Projects supported are usually connected with places that the trustees have lived and worked in, including the cities of Bristol, Leeds, Brecon and London and the countries of Ghana, Zambia, Malawi and the Solomon Islands.

WHO CAN BENEFIT Charitable organisations.

WHAT IS FUNDED The arts, particularly drama; organisations working for improved race relations; inner-city projects and those in financially developing countries. More recently the trust has supported organisations dealing with book famine, education and agricultural development in Africa, as well as health education in Asia and South America.

WHAT IS NOT FUNDED Individuals.

TYPE OF GRANT Projects grants.

RANGE OF GRANTS £200 to £10,000.

SAMPLE GRANTS Brecknock Museum/Art Trust (£10,000); Christian Aid (£6,000); WaterAid (£4,000); University of the West of England (£3,000); Nigerian Health Care Project, Renewable World and Shakespeare at the Tobacco Factory (£2,000 each); Hodgkin House (£700); Absolute Theatre and Ghana School Aid (£500 each); Contemporary Art Society for Wales.

FINANCES *Year* 2015/16 *Income* £56,355 *Grants* £93,900 *Grants to organisations* £93,900 *Assets* £1,476,685

TRUSTEES Benjamin Gibbs; Dr James Gibbs; Dr Emily Parry; Simon Gibbs; Dr Thomas Gibbs; William Gibbs; Abigail Keane; Susanna Coan.

OTHER INFORMATION During the year 50 grants were awarded to organisations.

HOW TO APPLY Apply in writing to the correspondent. The trustees usually meet twice a year in April and December to make grants. The annual report for 2015/16 states that the trust 'normally grant aid projects of which the trustees have personal knowledge'.

WHO TO APPLY TO Simon Gibbs, Trustee, 34 Durand Gardens, London SW9 0PP *Tel.* 020 7582 6901 *Email* simoned.gibbs@yahoo.co.uk

■ The Morgan Charitable Foundation

CC NO 283128 **ESTABLISHED** 1981

WHERE FUNDING CAN BE GIVEN UK.

WHO CAN BENEFIT Registered charities and institutions. The trustees maintain a list of charitable organisations which they regularly support and the list is reviewed half yearly at the trustees' meeting.

WHAT IS FUNDED General charitable purposes; social welfare; health; Jewish causes; disadvantaged and socially isolated individuals. The trustees are primarily interested in social welfare causes.

WHAT IS NOT FUNDED Individuals.

TYPE OF GRANT Capital and core costs; projects; unrestricted funding.

RANGE OF GRANTS £1,000 to £8,000 (2014).

SAMPLE GRANTS Chai Cancer Care and Duke of Edinburgh Award (£8,000 each); Magen David Adom (£7,000); In Kind Direct Charity (£6,000); World Jewish Relief (£5,000); Asthma UK and Norwood (£2,000); Blind in Business, Pro Arte Choir, Royal National Lifeboat Institution and University of Bournemouth Student Centre (£1,000 each).

FINANCES *Year* 2015 *Income* £125,059 *Grants* £75,200 *Grants to organisations* £75,200 *Assets* £4,430,047

TRUSTEES Carmen Gleen; Leslie Morgan; Nelly Morgan; Molly Morgan.

OTHER INFORMATION A list of beneficiaries was not made available in the 2015 accounts and annual report, the sample is from 2014.

HOW TO APPLY Apply in writing to the correspondent, providing a copy of the latest annual report and accounts. The trustees meet twice a year, usually in April and October. The foundation requests not to receive telephone enquiries.

WHO TO APPLY TO The Trustees, PO Box 57749, London NW11 1FD *Tel.* 07968 827709

■ The Steve Morgan Foundation

CC NO 1087056 **ESTABLISHED** 2000

WHERE FUNDING CAN BE GIVEN North Wales, Merseyside, West Cheshire and North Shropshire.

WHO CAN BENEFIT Small to medium-sized organisations; registered charities; organisations 'which are pursuing charitable causes and where aims and objectives are not-for-profit'. Preference is given to hands-on organisations with a high volunteer input. Generally an organisation must have been in existence for a minimum of two years.

WHAT IS FUNDED General charitable causes, with preference for health and disability, social welfare, children and young people, families and older or socially isolated individuals.

WHAT IS NOT FUNDED Animal welfare; arts/heritage; conservation/environment; expeditions and overseas travel; general fundraising appeals; individual and sports sponsorship; large national charities or organisations; mainstream education/sport; promotion of specific religions; retrospective funding. Local branches of national charities which are based within the remit area, or programmes delivered locally by organisations working on a national basis are not generally supported.

TYPE OF GRANT One-off awards; capital grants; start-up project costs; ongoing running expenses; projects; multi-year revenue grants for core funding; equipment; minibuses.

RANGE OF GRANTS £100 to £100,000.

SAMPLE GRANTS Newlife Foundation (£100,000); North Perk (Ykids) (£90,000); Wirral Society of the Blind (£60,000); Chester Sexual Abuse Support Services (£45,000); Liverpool Homeless Football (£22,500); NeuroMuscular Centre (£15,400); Wolves Aid (£10,000); Burtonwood Sewing Group (£5,000); Whitechapel (£500); Down's Syndrome Association (£100).

FINANCES *Year* 2015/16 *Income* £936,013 *Grants* £2,348,893 *Grants to organisations* £2,348,893 *Assets* £12,961,327

TRUSTEES Vincent Fairclough; Ashley Lewis; Sally Morgan; Jonathan Masters; Steve Morgan; Rhiannon Walker.

OTHER INFORMATION During the year a total of 93 awards were made. The foundation also makes Morgan Foundation Entrepreneur Awards 'to recognise and support entrepreneurial spirit in fledgling businesses, young entrepreneurs, in the third sector and in individuals who have achieved against all odds'. Through Smiley Bus Awards minibuses are provided to eligible organisations to be shared with other supported groups in the community.

HOW TO APPLY Prior to making a formal appeal you should call the foundation for an informal chat. Once your eligibility has been discussed and approved you will be provided a form and asked to give some details about your organisation and your funding needs (including details and costings of a project, if you already have one), and provide a copy of the most recent annual report and accounts. All applications are acknowledged and all charities and projects visited before a grant is approved. The trustees meet regularly throughout the year but it may take up to six months for the process to be completed. It is suggested that unsuccessful applicants wait a year before re-applying.

WHO TO APPLY TO Jane Harris, Foundation Administrator, PO Box 3517, Chester CH1 9ET *Tel.* 01829 782800 *Fax* 01829 782223 *Email* contact@morganfoundation.co.uk *Website* www.morganfoundation.co.uk

■ Morgan Stanley International Foundation

CC NO 1042671 **ESTABLISHED** 1994

WHERE FUNDING CAN BE GIVEN Tower Hamlets; Glasgow; Europe; Middle East; Africa.

WHO CAN BENEFIT Registered charities and state-funded schools.

WHAT IS FUNDED Children's health, education and welfare in disadvantaged communities across Europe, the Middle East and Africa (EMEA).

WHAT IS NOT FUNDED Organisations which are not registered as a non-profit organisation with the appropriate regulatory agencies in their country (unless a state-funded school); national or international charities which do not operate in the regions the foundation is located; political or religious organisations, pressure groups or individuals outside Morgan Stanley and Co. International PLC who are seeking sponsorship either for themselves (e.g. to help pay for education) or for onward transmission to a charitable organisation; programmes that do not include opportunities for employee volunteer engagement.

TYPE OF GRANT One-off and recurrent; project funding.

RANGE OF GRANTS Up to £72,000.

SAMPLE GRANTS Magic Breakfast (£72,000); Bromley by Bow Centre and Great Ormond Street Hospital (£70,000 each); Play Association Tower Hamlets (£67,500); Glasgow Children's Hospital Charity (£64,000); Community Links (£53,500); Career Ready and Glasgow Caledonian University (£30,000 each); Comin and Die Arche (£20,500 each).

FINANCES *Year* 2015 *Income* £1,662,580 *Grants* £1,794,266 *Grants to organisations* £1,794,266 *Assets* £1,388,463

TRUSTEES Clare Woodman; Hanns Seibold; Maryann McMahon; Stephen Mavin; Fergus O'Sullivan; Sue Watts; Oliver Stuart; Jon Bendall; Simon Evenson.

OTHER INFORMATION The foundation is the corporate charity of Morgan Stanley and Co. International PLC, the financial services corporation. The foundation matches any contribution, either monetary or through volunteering, by employees to a maximum of £500 per employee in one given year. Employees are encouraged to take on up to ten weeks of pro bono work for NGOs and charities. The foundation's charity partner, Great Ormond Street Hospital, received over £1 million of the grant total. Grants to organisations from the unrestricted fund totalled £800,000.

HOW TO APPLY The foundation gives the following details on making an initial approach for funding: 'Morgan Stanley International Foundation takes a proactive approach to grant-making and therefore does not accept unsolicited proposals. If you think your organisation is a match for the criteria ... send an email to: communityaffairslondon@morganstanley.com. You will then be sent the guidelines and if your organisation is successful in the first stage of application, you will be invited to complete a full proposal. Grant applications are considered quarterly and the trustees are senior representatives from across the firm's divisions.'

WHO TO APPLY TO Anish Shah, Morgan Stanley and Co. International PLC, 20 Bank Street, London E14 4AD *Tel.* 020 7425 1302 *Email* communityaffairslondon@morganstanley.com *Website* www.morganstanley.com/globalcitizen/msif_guidelines.html

■ The Diana and Allan Morgenthau Charitable Trust

CC NO 1062180 **ESTABLISHED** 1997

WHERE FUNDING CAN BE GIVEN Worldwide.

WHO CAN BENEFIT Charitable organisations, with a particular interest in Jewish groups.

WHAT IS FUNDED General charitable purposes; Jewish causes; education; the arts; relief of poverty; health; overseas aid.

TYPE OF GRANT One-off and recurrent.

RANGE OF GRANTS Up to £33,000.

SAMPLE GRANTS Jaffa Institute (£33,000); World Jewish Relief (£20,000); Tel Aviv Foundation (£14,000); Belsize Square Synagogue (£13,000); New Israel Fund (£12,500).

FINANCES *Year* 2015/16 *Income* £180,021 *Grants* £152,460 *Grants to organisations* £152,460 *Assets* £29,157

TRUSTEES Allan Morgenthau; Diana Morgenthau.

OTHER INFORMATION In 2015/16 the breakdown of grants was as follows: education and training (£63,500); general donations and overseas aid (£40,500); arts and culture (£33,000); medical, health and sickness (£15,500).

HOW TO APPLY Apply in writing to the correspondent.

WHO TO APPLY TO Allan Morgenthau, Trustee, 272A Kentish Town Road, London NW5 2AA *Tel.* 020 7493 1904 *Email* allan.m@btinternet.com

■ The Miles Morland Foundation

CC NO 1150755 **ESTABLISHED** 2012

WHERE FUNDING CAN BE GIVEN UK and Africa.

WHO CAN BENEFIT Charitable organisations; individuals; theatres; universities.

WHAT IS FUNDED African writing and African literature; arts and heritage; human rights.

WHAT IS NOT FUNDED Mass appeals; education; literacy initiatives; health care; periodicals.

TYPE OF GRANT One-off and recurrent.

RANGE OF GRANTS Up to £50,000.

SAMPLE GRANTS The Royal African Society (£40,000); New Horizon Youth Centre (£20,000); Friends of Guy's Marsh Prison (£14,000); Donmar Warehouse (£12,000); Book Aid International, The British Museum and The Marrakech Biennale (£10,000 each); African Writers Trust (£8,500); Doctors of the World (£5,000); Ocean Somali Community Association (£2,500).

FINANCES *Year* 2015/16 *Income* £1,252,072 *Grants* £788,857 *Grants to organisations* £643,857 *Assets* £307,137

TRUSTEES The Hon. Alice Bragg; Cornelie Ferguson; Kate Gozzi; Miles Morland.

OTHER INFORMATION Grants were made to 31 UK organisations totalling £380,000 and to 25 African organisations totalling £264,000. During the year eight scholarships were made to individuals totalling £145,000.

HOW TO APPLY The foundation's website has detailed guidance for potential applicants and an application form that should be sent via email to the correspondent.

WHO TO APPLY TO Miles Morland, Trustee, 2nd Floor, Jubilee House, 2 Jubilee Place, London SW3 3TQ *Tel.* 020 7349 1245 *Email* MMF@milesmorlandfoundation.com *Website* www.milesmorlandfoundation.com

■ The Morris Charitable Trust

CC NO 802290 **ESTABLISHED** 1989

WHERE FUNDING CAN BE GIVEN UK, with a preference for Islington; overseas.

WHO CAN BENEFIT Registered charities; local Islington community projects. The trustees select national and international charities to support on an ad hoc basis.

WHAT IS FUNDED General charitable purposes, including education, community support and development, health and disability, placing particular emphasis on alleviating social hardship and deprivation.

WHAT IS NOT FUNDED Individuals; annual core costs.

TYPE OF GRANT One-off project and capital grants for one year or less are priorities.

RANGE OF GRANTS Usually between £1,000 and £5,000.

SAMPLE GRANTS Ben Kinsella Trust; City University London; Culpeper Community Garden; Islington Outlook; Park Theatre; Raleigh Expedition; Soul in the City Festival; St Marks Church of England Primary School; The Anne Frank Trust UK; The Sam Morris Nursery.

FINANCES *Year* 2015/16 *Income* £100,326 *Grants* £144,710 *Grants to organisations* £144,710 *Assets* £197,105

TRUSTEES Paul Morris; Jack Morris; Alan Stenning; Dominic Jones; Gerald Morris; Linda Morris.

OTHER INFORMATION Grants were made to 48 organisations during the year.

HOW TO APPLY Applications should be made on a form available from the trust or downloadable from its website. The completed form should be returned together with any supporting documentation and a copy of your latest annual report and accounts.

WHO TO APPLY TO Linda Morris, Trustee, c/o Management Office, The Business Design Centre, 52 Upper Street, Islington Green, London N1 0QH *Tel.* 020 7359 3535 *Email* info@morrischaritabletrust.com *Website* www.morrischaritabletrust.com

■ The Willie and Mabel Morris Charitable Trust

CC NO 280554 **ESTABLISHED** 1980

WHERE FUNDING CAN BE GIVEN UK.

WHO CAN BENEFIT Registered charities, particularly those related to health care causes.

WHAT IS FUNDED General charitable purposes, particularly medical causes in the areas of cancer, heart trouble, arthritis and rheumatism.

WHAT IS NOT FUNDED Individuals; non-registered charities.
TYPE OF GRANT One-off and recurrent.
RANGE OF GRANTS £100 to £10,000.
SAMPLE GRANTS St Thomas' Lupus Trust (£10,000); Kidney Research UK (£7,500); Motor Neurone Disease Association, Teenage Cancer Trust and Young Epilepsy (£5,000 each); Prostate Cancer UK (£2,500); St Wilfred's Hospice (£1,000); Stonewall (£750); Historic Royal Palaces (£500); Daughters of Cambodia (£250); East Anglian Air Ambulance (£150).
FINANCES *Year* 2015/16 *Income* £125,159 *Grants* £94,996 *Grants to organisations* £94,996 *Assets* £4,221,796
TRUSTEES Suzanne Marriott; Michael Macfadyen; Angela Tether; Andrew Tether; Alan Bryant; Verity Tether; Phoebe Tether.
OTHER INFORMATION Grants to 82 organisations were made during the year.
HOW TO APPLY Apply in writing to the correspondent.
WHO TO APPLY TO Angela Tether, 41 Field Lane, Letchworth Garden City, Hertfordshire SG6 3LD *Tel.* 01462 480583

■ G. M. Morrison Charitable Trust

CC NO 261380 **ESTABLISHED** 1970
WHERE FUNDING CAN BE GIVEN UK and overseas.
WHO CAN BENEFIT Registered charities.
WHAT IS FUNDED General charitable purposes; medicine and health; social welfare; education and training.
WHAT IS NOT FUNDED Individuals; charities not registered in the UK; retrospective applications; schemes or activities which are generally regarded as the responsibility of statutory authorities; commercial or business activities; short-term projects; one-off capital grants (except for emergency appeals).
TYPE OF GRANT Mostly recurrent annual awards for core costs.
RANGE OF GRANTS £750 to £4,000.
SAMPLE GRANTS **One-off grants:** Disasters Emergency Committee Nepal Earthquake Appeal (£4,000); Oxfam Refugee Crisis, Save The Children and Plan UK (£2,000 each). **Recurring grants:** International Medical Corps UK and Royal Society of Arts Endowment Fund (£2,500 each); Bowel and Cancer Research, Royal Academy of Music and YMCA England (£1,300 each); Tools for Self Reliance (£1,000); Prisoners Abroad (£830); Canine Partners for Independence, Migraine Trust and Royal National Mission to Deep Sea Fishermen (£750).
FINANCES *Year* 2015/16 *Income* £401,007 *Grants* £229,500 *Grants to organisations* £229,500 *Assets* £11,899,097
TRUSTEES N. W. Smith; Anthony Cornick; Jane Hunt; Elizabeth Morrison.
OTHER INFORMATION In 2015/16 the trust made 224 grants to organisations.
HOW TO APPLY The trust's annual report for 2015/16 states: 'Beneficiaries of grants are normally selected on the basis of the personal knowledge and recommendation of a trustee. The Trust's grant-making policy is however to support the recipient of grants on a long term recurring basis. The trustees have decided that for the present, new applications for grants will only be considered in the most exceptional circumstances, any spare income will be allocated to increasing the grants made to charities currently receiving support. In the future this policy will of course be subject to periodic review. Applicants understanding this policy who nevertheless wish to apply for a grant should write to the [correspondent].'
WHO TO APPLY TO Anthony Cornick, Trustee, c/o Currey and Co. LLP, 33 Queen Anne Street, London W1G 9HY *Tel.* 020 7802 2700 *Email* gen@curreyandco.co.uk

■ The Morrisons Foundation

CC NO 1160224 **ESTABLISHED** 2014
WHERE FUNDING CAN BE GIVEN Areas of company presence in the UK.
WHO CAN BENEFIT Registered charities.
WHAT IS FUNDED General charitable purposes; children; older people; people with disabilities.
WHAT IS NOT FUNDED Individuals; CICs; social enterprises; unregistered charitable organisations.
TYPE OF GRANT Eligible expenditure and project grants.
RANGE OF GRANTS £500 to £16,500.
SAMPLE GRANTS W.O.T.S. Project (£16,500); Willow Wood Hospice (£10,000); Hey Smile Foundation (£9,300); MedEquip4Kids (£6,900); Carers' Support Bexley (£6,600); Couple Counselling Lothian (£5,900); Theodora Children's Charity (£5,000); Mansfield Play Forum (£4,700); The Comedy Trust (£2,000); Deaf Children North West (£500).
FINANCES *Year* 2015/16 *Income* £4,097,241 *Grants* £1,691,077 *Grants to organisations* £1,691,077 *Assets* £3,308,062
TRUSTEES Jonathan Burke; Andrew Clappen; John Holden; Martyn Jones; Guy Mason; Sharon Mawhinney; David Scott; Kathryn Tunstall.
OTHER INFORMATION Information about successful projects can be found on the foundation's website.
HOW TO APPLY An application form is available to download from the website and applicants will be notified of a decision within three months of submitting an application, even if the application is unsuccessful. The website states that charities 'that have previously received a grant donation can submit an application after completing a post-grant report. We don't limit the timeframe in which charities can apply for a grant following an unsuccessful application.'
WHO TO APPLY TO Sam Burden, Hilmore House, 71 Gain Lane, Bradford, West Yorkshire BD3 7DL *Tel.* 0845 611 5364 *Email* foundation.enquiries@morrisonsplc.co.uk *Website* www.morrisonsfoundation.com

■ The Morton Charitable Trust

SC NO SC004507 **ESTABLISHED** 1987
WHERE FUNDING CAN BE GIVEN UK, with a preference for Scotland.
WHO CAN BENEFIT Registered charities.
WHAT IS FUNDED General charitable purposes.
SAMPLE GRANTS A list of beneficiaries was not available.
FINANCES *Year* 2015/16 *Income* £45,625 *Grants* £225,299 *Grants to organisations* £225,299 *Assets* £1,276,705
HOW TO APPLY Apply in writing to the correspondent.
WHO TO APPLY TO The Trustees, c/o Michael A. Brown, 17 South Tay Street, Dundee DD1 1NR *Tel.* 01382 204242

■ The Moshal Charitable Trust

CC NO 284448 **ESTABLISHED** 1981
WHERE FUNDING CAN BE GIVEN UK.
WHO CAN BENEFIT Charitable organisations and educational establishments.
WHAT IS FUNDED General charitable purposes, particularly Jewish causes.
SAMPLE GRANTS A list of beneficiaries for 2015/16 was not included in the accounts.
FINANCES *Year* 2015/16 *Income* £120,747 *Grants* £88,100 *Grants to organisations* £88,100 *Assets* £447,025
TRUSTEES David Halpern; Lea Halpern.
HOW TO APPLY Apply in writing to the correspondent.
WHO TO APPLY TO The Trustees, New Riverside House, 439 Lower Broughton Road, Salford M7 2FX

■ Vyoel Moshe Charitable Trust

CC NO 327054 **ESTABLISHED** 1986
WHERE FUNDING CAN BE GIVEN UK and overseas, including Israel, USA and Europe.
WHO CAN BENEFIT Registered charities; religious bodies; individuals.
WHAT IS FUNDED Education; religion; relief of poverty; with a focus on Jewish causes. Awards to individuals are given 'to financially deprived families, at Jewish holiday times and other special occasions' and awards to religious bodies are given to synagogues for the preservation of cemeteries, Jewish culture and heritage.
RANGE OF GRANTS £500 to £20,000 to organisations; £4,500 to £15,000 to religious bodies.
SAMPLE GRANTS Tov V'Chesed (£60,000); Toldos Aharon (£25,000); Chesed L'Avraham, Chinuch Jerusalem Mishkanos Haroyim, Rabbinical Kollel Nachlas Moshe, Toldos Aharon Beis Shemesh and UTA of Monsey (£20,000 each).
FINANCES *Year* 2015/16 *Income* £959,625 *Grants* £960,417 *Grants to organisations* £909,417 *Assets* £22,646
OTHER INFORMATION Grants were made to over 70 institutions and £51,000 was given to individuals.
HOW TO APPLY Apply in writing to the correspondent. The 2015/16 annual report states that 'the trustees select the institutions to be supported according to their personal knowledge of work of the institution. Individuals are referred to the charity by local rabbis. Any application is carefully considered and help given according to circumstances and funds then available.'
WHO TO APPLY TO Sholem Cik, Trustee, 2–4 Chardmore Road, London N16 6HX

■ The Moss Family Charitable Trust

CC NO 327529 **ESTABLISHED** 1987
WHERE FUNDING CAN BE GIVEN England and Wales.
WHO CAN BENEFIT Registered charities, Jewish organisations.
WHAT IS FUNDED General charitable purposes; health; disability; social welfare, with preference given to Jewish causes.
SAMPLE GRANTS A list of beneficiaries was not included in the 2015/16 accounts; however, previous beneficiaries have included: The Children's Charity; Hammerson House; Jewish Child's Day; Norwood; Presidents Club; West London Synagogue.
FINANCES *Year* 2015/16 *Income* £125,010 *Grants* £126,305 *Grants to organisations* £126,305 *Assets* £3,789
TRUSTEES Stephen Moss; Roger Moss; Virginia Campus.
HOW TO APPLY Apply in writing to the correspondent. Our research indicates that the trust is unlikely to respond to unsolicited applications.
WHO TO APPLY TO Kevin Sage, Administrator, 28 Bolton Street, Mayfair, London W1J 8BP *Tel.* 020 7491 5108 *Email* kevinsage@grosvenorsecurities.com

■ The Mosselson Charitable Trust

CC NO 266517 **ESTABLISHED** 1974
WHERE FUNDING CAN BE GIVEN UK.
WHO CAN BENEFIT Charitable organisations.
WHAT IS FUNDED Education; medicine and medical research; women and children's support and welfare; religion; social welfare.
SAMPLE GRANTS A list of beneficiaries was not available in the 2014/15 accounts but the trust has previously supported: ChildLine; Holocaust Education Trust; Jewish Women's Week; Family Housing Association; Nightingale House; Shaare Zedek Medical Centre.
FINANCES *Year* 2014/15 *Income* £468,122 *Grants* £118,106 *Grants to organisations* £118,106 *Assets* £3,305,789
TRUSTEES Dennis Mosselson; Marian Mosselson.
OTHER INFORMATION The trust's 2014/15 annual report states that its long-term goal is to establish a student scholarship programme at graduate level to provide financial assistance in various fields of study, with an emphasis on higher education.
HOW TO APPLY Apply in writing to the correspondent.
WHO TO APPLY TO Dennis Mosselson, Trustee, Denmoss House, 10 Greenland Street, London NW1 0ND *Tel.* 020 7428 1929

■ Moto in the Community

CC NO 1111147 **ESTABLISHED** 2005
WHERE FUNDING CAN BE GIVEN Communities local to the Moto 57 service areas around the UK (details of stations can be found on the website).
WHO CAN BENEFIT Community groups; registered charities; individuals working for Moto; schools.
WHAT IS FUNDED Road safety; conservation; community development.
WHAT IS NOT FUNDED The promotion of religion or politics; overseas applications.
RANGE OF GRANTS Usually up to £1,000.
SAMPLE GRANTS Brain Tumour Charity (£2,700); Toddington Scouts (£2,500); St Sebastian School (£1,000); The Youth Association (£930); The Children's Farm Trust (£900); Darton College (£680); Prostate Cancer and The Stroke Association (£500 each); Walton Hall Special School (£490); Moon Walk (£100).
FINANCES *Year* 2015 *Income* £602,201 *Grants* £350,922 *Grants to organisations* £338,947 *Assets* £693,494
TRUSTEES Brian Lotts; Christopher Rogers; Brian Larkin; Helen Budd; Malcolm Plowes; Ashleigh Lewis; Ian Kernighan; Jon Shore; Nicholas Brokes; Gene MacDonald; Julie Sturgess; Coral Brodie; Guy Latchem; Gavin Sanders; Brynn Hewitt.
OTHER INFORMATION Grants were made to 28 community organisations during the year, including one major grant to Moto's Charity of the Year, Help for Heroes (£300,000). A further

£12,000 was paid in 11 benevolent grants in support of Moto employees and their dependants facing hardship.

HOW TO APPLY Applications can be made online throughout the year. Grant applications can be made using a form on the charity's website where guidance notes are also available to download. Charities or schools interested in becoming a local community partner should email motocharity@moto-way.co.uk, stating: which Moto site you wish to apply to; the charity's long- and short-term objectives; ideas about how the Moto staff could work with you.

WHO TO APPLY TO Caroline Campbell, Trust Administrator, Moto Hospitality Ltd, Toddington Service Area, Junction 12 M1 Southbound, Toddington, Bedfordshire LU5 6HR *Tel.* 01525 878500 *Email* motocharity@moto-way.co.uk *Website* www.motointhecommunity.co.uk

■ Motor Neurone Disease Association

CC NO 294354 **ESTABLISHED** 1986

WHERE FUNDING CAN BE GIVEN Primarily in the UK, but also worldwide.

WHO CAN BENEFIT Universities; individuals; care centres; hospitals.

WHAT IS FUNDED Research (PhD studentships and fellowships) into motor neurone disease; care centres.

TYPE OF GRANT Research; project funding.

RANGE OF GRANTS Up to £1.5 million.

SAMPLE GRANTS University of Oxford (£1.5 million); Institute of Psychiatry (£912,000); Institute of Neurology (£455,000); Sheffield Institute for Translational Neurosciences (£277,000); Queen Elizabeth Hospital Birmingham (£207,000); University of Bradford (£175,000); Plymouth Hospitals NHS Trust (£74,000); Southampton General Hospital (£54,000); The Babraham Institute (£10,000).

FINANCES *Year* 2015/16 *Income* £16,683,000 *Grants* £12,600,000 *Grants to organisations* £11,660,000 *Assets* £10,141,000

TRUSTEES Alan Graham; Wendy Balmain; Alun Owen; Richard Coleman; Dr Heather Smith; Michael Ranson; Shane Dickson; Janis Parks; Susan Edwards; Charlotte Layton; Steven Parry-Hearn; Dr Nikhil Sharma; Janet Warren; Timothy Kidd; Lyndsay Lonsborough.

OTHER INFORMATION The amount of grants given to individuals totalled £940,000.

HOW TO APPLY In the first instance, we recommend visiting the website where full information on research funding, including how to make an application and deadline dates, is available.

WHO TO APPLY TO Research Grants Team, 10–15 Notre Dame Mews, Northampton NN1 2BG *Tel.* 01604 611873 *Email* research.grants@mndassociation.org *Website* www.mndassociation.org/research

■ British Motor Sports Training Trust

CC NO 273828 **ESTABLISHED** 1977

WHERE FUNDING CAN BE GIVEN UK.

WHO CAN BENEFIT Organisations involved with motor sports.

WHAT IS FUNDED Education and training in techniques to prevent and reduce the incidence and severity of accidents in motor sports.

TYPE OF GRANT Training and equipment; staff development.

RANGE OF GRANTS From around £1,000 to £16,000.

SAMPLE GRANTS British Motorsport Marshals Club (£15,900); ATLS Lister (£11,500); Association of Motorsport Recovery Operators (£10,100); British Automobile Racing Club (£8,700); Solway Car Club and West of Scotland Kart Club (£5,000 each); Association of Motorsport Recovery Operators (£3,800); Bo'ness Hill Climb Revival (£3,000); Sarnia Rescue (£2,400); Association of Eastern Motor Clubs (£2,100); Kirby Lonsdale Motor Club (£1,300); Trent Valley Cart Club (£1,100).

FINANCES *Year* 2015 *Income* £241,476 *Grants* £206,093 *Grants to organisations* £206,093 *Assets* £1,108,392

TRUSTEES Alan Gow; Nicky Moffitt; Rob Jones; Anthony Andrews; Rt Hon. the Lord Rooker; Nick Bunting.

HOW TO APPLY The annual report for 2015 states: 'Details on how to apply for grants, together with the relevant forms are available from the Trust Secretary.'

WHO TO APPLY TO Allan Dean-Lewis, Secretary, Motor Sport House, Riverside Park, Colnbrook, Berkshire SL3 0HG *Tel.* 01492 440754 *Website* www.msauk.org

■ J. P. Moulton Charitable Foundation

CC NO 1109891 **ESTABLISHED** 2005

WHERE FUNDING CAN BE GIVEN UK.

WHO CAN BENEFIT Registered charities; research institutions; universities; hospitals and hospices.

WHAT IS FUNDED Medical research and care; education and training; counselling; community service projects.

TYPE OF GRANT One-off and recurrent.

RANGE OF GRANTS Up to £400,000.

SAMPLE GRANTS Lancaster University (£400,000); King's College London (£379,000); Great Ormond Street Hospital and University of Manchester (£178,000 each); Guernsey Community Foundation (£40,000); Muscular Dystrophy Campaign (£37,500); Guy's and St Thomas Charity (£16,500); Salisbury Cathedral (£10,000); Caudwell Children and Humanity First (£1,000 each).

FINANCES *Year* 2015 *Income* £1,088,821 *Grants* £1,801,773 *Grants to organisations* £1,801,773 *Assets* £42,992

TRUSTEES Jon Moulton; Spencer Moulton; Sara Everett.

HOW TO APPLY Apply in writing to the correspondent.

WHO TO APPLY TO Jon Moulton, Trustee, c/o Better Capital LLP, Third Floor, 39–41 Charing Cross Road, London WC2H 0AR *Tel.* 020 7440 0860 *Email* Jon.Moulton@jonmoulton.gg

■ The Edwina Mountbatten and Leonora Children's Foundation

CC NO 228166 **ESTABLISHED** 1960

WHERE FUNDING CAN BE GIVEN UK and overseas.

WHO CAN BENEFIT Registered charities; hospitals; hospices.

WHAT IS FUNDED Expansion of the work of the Order of St John; nursing; paediatric cancer; the support of nurses caring for children with cancer.

WHAT IS NOT FUNDED Research; individual nurses working in the UK for further professional training.

TYPE OF GRANT Project grants.

RANGE OF GRANTS £3,000 to £40,000.
SAMPLE GRANTS Brecknock Hospice (£50,000); St John Jerusalem Eye Hospital (£35,000); Teenage Cancer Trust (£25,000); Gift of Sight and Ripple Africa (£10,000); InterCare Medical Aid for Africa (£5,000); World Child Cancer (£3,000).
FINANCES *Year* 2015 *Income* £180,104 *Grants* £138,000 *Grants to organisations* £138,000 *Assets* £5,713,260
TRUSTEES Countess Mountbatten of Burma; The Hon. Alexandra Knatchbull; Peter Mimpriss; Dame Mary Fagan; Lady Brabourne; Myrddin Rees; Sir Evelyn de Rothschild.
OTHER INFORMATION Grants were made to seven organisations during the year.
HOW TO APPLY Details of how to apply for grants can be obtained from the foundation's secretary.
WHO TO APPLY TO Richard Jordan-Baker, Secretary, The Estate Office, Broadlands, Romsey, Hampshire SO51 9ZE *Tel.* 01794 529750

■ The MSE Charity

CC NO 1121320 **ESTABLISHED** 2007
WHERE FUNDING CAN BE GIVEN UK.
WHO CAN BENEFIT Registered charities; CICs; credit unions; not-for-profit companies limited by guarantee; social enterprises. Small and medium-sized organisations with an income of under £500,000 are preferred.
WHAT IS FUNDED Financial literacy; money management education; debt avoidance.
WHAT IS NOT FUNDED Projects which only provide debt advice/management; core funding for an organisation. Capital equipment such as laptops, projectors or other electronics is not normally funded.
TYPE OF GRANT Activity costs, some awards to fund salaries and running costs.
RANGE OF GRANTS Up to £10,000 but usually under £5,000.
SAMPLE GRANTS Family Action; Jireh Community Project; Stevenage Solutions CIC; Malt Cross Trust; The Debt Advice Network; South Cheshire CLASP; North Tyneside District Disability Forum; The Parent House; Stroud and District Citizens Advice; Croxteth and Gillmoss Community Association; The Bus Stop Club; 4Youth; Dial South Worcestershire; Bestwood Advice Centre Ltd; Pembrokeshire People First – The Tudor Project; The Bridge Renewal Trust; Stroud Beresford Group; South Gloucestershire Deaf Association.
FINANCES *Year* 2015/16 *Income* £63,752 *Grants* £84,855 *Grants to organisations* £84,855 *Assets* £97,538
TRUSTEES Tony Tesciuba; John Hewison; Katie Birkett; Vanessa Bissessur; Teej Dew.
OTHER INFORMATION The charity made grants to 23 organisations in the financial year but a list of current beneficiaries was unavailable at the time of writing (April 2017).
HOW TO APPLY The website provides deadlines – usually in February and September – for specific funding rounds with detailed guidance and application forms. The application must be submitted electronically and the charity limits each grant round to the first 40 applications.
WHO TO APPLY TO Katie Birkett, Operations Manager, 38 Elm Grove, Norwich NR3 3LF *Email* info@msecharity.com *Website* www.msecharity.com

■ The Mugdock Children's Trust

SC NO SC006001 **ESTABLISHED** 1920
WHERE FUNDING CAN BE GIVEN Scotland.
WHO CAN BENEFIT Charitable organisations.
WHAT IS FUNDED Children up to the age of 14 who are ill, have disabilities or are disadvantaged in some manner.
RANGE OF GRANTS £500 to £10,000.
SAMPLE GRANTS Riding for the Disabled Association Ltd (£10,000); Lilias Graham Trust (£9,000); The Glasgow Care Foundation (£3,000); Children's Classic Concerts and Ochil Tower School (£2,000 each); Befriend a Child, Scottish Spina Bifida and Visibility (£1,000 each); Elgin Youth Development Group, Isla and Jura Community and Special Needs Adventure Playground (£500 each).
FINANCES *Year* 2016/17 *Income* £63,549 *Grants* £55,500 *Grants to organisations* £55,500 *Assets* £1,448,466
OTHER INFORMATION Grants were made to 38 organisations during the year.
HOW TO APPLY Apply in writing to the correspondent.
WHO TO APPLY TO The Trustees, Wylie and Bisset LLP, 168 Bath Street, Glasgow G2 4TP *Tel.* 0141 566 7000

■ The Mulberry Trust

CC NO 263296 **ESTABLISHED** 1971
WHERE FUNDING CAN BE GIVEN UK, with an interest in Essex.
WHO CAN BENEFIT Charitable organisations; hospices.
WHAT IS FUNDED General charitable purposes, particularly: parenting and family welfare; children; older people; homelessness; community development; the environment; Christian causes; education and research; health; the arts.
WHAT IS NOT FUNDED Individuals.
RANGE OF GRANTS Up to £30,000. The majority of grants are of around £5,000 or less.
SAMPLE GRANTS Pioneer Sailing Trust and Prison Dialogue (£30,000 each); Harlow Parochial Church Council – St Mary's Church (£29,000); Essex Community Foundation and Shelter – Essex (£20,000 each); Ice and Fire Theatre Company (£9,000); Suffolk Artlink (£7,000); St Clare Hospice (£5,000); Aid Africa (£2,000); The Fan Museum (£1,000).
FINANCES *Year* 2015/16 *Income* £501,648 *Grants* £473,746 *Grants to organisations* £473,746 *Assets* £3,979,162
TRUSTEES Ann Marks; Charles Woodhouse; Timothy Marks; Chris Marks; Rupert Marks; William Marks; Susan Gow.
OTHER INFORMATION During the year, grants were made to 71 organisations.
HOW TO APPLY The trust does not accept unsolicited applications.
WHO TO APPLY TO The Trustees, c/o Farrer and Co., 65–66 Lincoln's Inn Fields, London WC2A 3LH *Tel.* 020 3375 7000 *Email* secretarialservices@farrer.co.uk

■ The Frederick Mulder Foundation (the Prairie Trust)

CC NO 296019 **ESTABLISHED** 1986
WHERE FUNDING CAN BE GIVEN Worldwide.
WHO CAN BENEFIT Charitable organisations.
WHAT IS FUNDED Social change philanthropy; climate change; global poverty.
TYPE OF GRANT One-off and recurrent.

RANGE OF GRANTS Generally £2,500 to £30,000.
SAMPLE GRANTS The Funding Network (£108,500); Climate Bonds Initiative (£58,000); Center for Citizen Empowerment (£25,000); The Glacier Trust (£22,000) Carbon Tracker, Greenpeace Environmental Trust and War on Want (£20,000 each); National Health and Education Society (£7,000); Playback Theatre Southwest (£5,000); Sheila McKechnie Foundation (£2,500).
FINANCES *Year* 2015/16 *Income* £181,011 *Grants* £545,757 *Grants to organisations* £545,757 *Assets* £6,281,759
TRUSTEES Dr Frederick Mulder; Hannah Mulder; Robin Bowman.
OTHER INFORMATION The trust supports many small social change organisations around the world through The Funding Network, which was founded by Frederick Mulder.
HOW TO APPLY The trust does not accept unsolicited applications or enquiries, but rather is proactive in identifying organisations and individuals within its areas of interest.
WHO TO APPLY TO Eugenie Harvey, Director, 83 Belsize Park Gardens, London NW3 4NJ *Tel.* 020 7722 9628 *Email* eugenie@frederickmulderfoundation.org.uk *Website* www.frederickmulderfoundation.org.uk

■ Multiple Sclerosis Society

CC NO 1139257 **ESTABLISHED** 2010
WHERE FUNDING CAN BE GIVEN UK.
WHO CAN BENEFIT Recognised NHS bodies and UK academic institutions.
WHAT IS FUNDED Research into multiple sclerosis, including new treatments, prevention and the dissemination and promotion of results; support for individuals with multiple sclerosis and their carers.
TYPE OF GRANT Postgraduate research projects.
RANGE OF GRANTS Typically between £20,000 and £80,000.
SAMPLE GRANTS University of Cambridge (£807,000 in six grants); University College London (£794,000 in nine grants); Swansea University (£297,000); University of Edinburgh (£222,000 in five grants); International Progressive MS Alliance (£107,000); Plymouth University (£106,000); North Bristol NHS Trust (£105,000); Neuroscience Foundation (£72,000).
FINANCES *Year* 2015 *Income* £27,743,000 *Grants* £5,530,000 *Grants to organisations* £4,173,000 *Assets* £16,158,000
TRUSTEES Stuart Secker; Christine Gibbons; Esther Foreman; Ruth Hasnip; Nicholas Winser; Charles Bland; Dr Anna Shinkwin; Jason Atkinson; John Grosvenor; Ceri Smith; Karen Penhorwood Jones.
OTHER INFORMATION There is a separate grants programme to support individuals with multiple sclerosis and their carers. Grants made to individuals totalled nearly £1.36 million.
HOW TO APPLY Refer to the society's website for full details. There is a grants team that are happy to assist with the application process.
WHO TO APPLY TO Grants Team – Research Grants, MS Society, 372 Edgware Road, London NW2 6ND *Tel.* 0300 500 8084 *Email* grants@mssociety.org.uk *Website* www.mssociety.org.uk

■ The Edith Murphy Foundation

CC NO 1026062 **ESTABLISHED** 1993
WHERE FUNDING CAN BE GIVEN UK, with a preference for Leicestershire and the East Midlands.
WHO CAN BENEFIT National registered charities and organisations based in Leicestershire and the East Midlands.
WHAT IS FUNDED Education and research; social welfare; animal welfare; heritage; people with disabilities; young people.
WHAT IS NOT FUNDED Individuals.
TYPE OF GRANT One-off and recurrent.
RANGE OF GRANTS Most grants are under £20,000.
SAMPLE GRANTS University of Leicester (£337,000); St Mark's Hospital Foundation (£117,500); Age UK (£90,000); SAID Business School Oxford University (£55,000); Build IT International (£40,000); Target Ovarian Cancer (£37,500); Motor Neurone Disease Association and The Islamic Foundation (£15,000 each); London Air Ambulance, Scropton Riding for the Disabled and Whizz-Kidz (£10,000 each).
FINANCES *Year* 2015/16 *Income* £674,733 *Grants* £1,484,317 *Grants to organisations* £1,484,317 *Assets* £31,697,319
TRUSTEES David Tams; Christopher Blakesley; Richard Adkinson; Charlotte Blakesley; Julian Tams.
OTHER INFORMATION During the year, 204 grants were made to organisations. Grants of less than £10,000 each totalled £529,000.
HOW TO APPLY Apply in writing to the correspondent. Email applications are not accepted and enquiries by email are discouraged. Further guidance can be found on the foundation's website.
WHO TO APPLY TO Richard Adkinson, Trustee, c/o Crane and Walton, 113–117 London Road, Leicester LE2 0RG *Tel.* 0116 255 1901 *Email* richard.adkinson@btinternet.com *Website* www.edithmurphy.co.uk

■ Murphy-Neumann Charity Company Ltd

CC NO 229555 **ESTABLISHED** 1963
WHERE FUNDING CAN BE GIVEN UK.
WHO CAN BENEFIT Registered charities.
WHAT IS FUNDED The relief of economic or social disadvantage; the alleviation of chronic illnesses and disabilities; medical research into diseases that affect the very young and older people.
WHAT IS NOT FUNDED Individuals; non-registered charities.
TYPE OF GRANT One-off and recurrent grants for general costs (large charities) and specific projects (smaller organisations).
RANGE OF GRANTS £500 to £1,500.
SAMPLE GRANTS Action on Elder Abuse and Independence at Home Trust (£1,500 each); The Prostate Cancer Charity and Youth Talk (£1,300 each); Colchester Carers Centre and Deafblind UK (£1,000 each); National Literacy Trust and St Nicholas Hospice Care (£750 each); Lymphoma Association and The Research Institute for the Care of Older People (£500 each).
FINANCES *Year* 2015/16 *Income* £82,501 *Grants* £54,000 *Grants to organisations* £54,000 *Assets* £1,644,951
TRUSTEES Mark Lockett; Paula Christopher; Marcus Richman; Supamon Holmes.
OTHER INFORMATION Grants were made to 57 organisations during the year.
HOW TO APPLY Apply in writing to the correspondent, in a letter outlining the purpose of the required

charitable donation. Telephone calls are not welcome. There are no application forms, guidelines or deadlines. No sae is required. Grants are usually given in November and December. Printed grant criteria is available on request.

WHO TO APPLY TO Mark Lockett, Trustee, Hayling Cottage, Upper Street, Stratford St Mary, Colchester, Essex CO7 6JW *Tel.* 01206 323685 *Email* mnccltd@keme.co.uk

■ The John R. Murray Charitable Trust

CC NO 1100199 **ESTABLISHED** 2003

WHERE FUNDING CAN BE GIVEN UK.

WHO CAN BENEFIT Registered charities.

WHAT IS FUNDED Arts and literature (although not strictly limited to such areas) and where the award of a grant will have an immediate and tangible benefit to the recipient in question.

RANGE OF GRANTS Usually between £250 and £40,000.

SAMPLE GRANTS National Library of Scotland (£88,500); National Youth Orchestra of Great Britain (£80,000); Bodleian Library (£50,000); University of Cambridge (£33,000); Art Workers' Guild Centenary Project, Chelsea Physic Garden and Royal Institute of Architects (£10,000 each); Historic Chapels Trust and Médecins Sans Frontières (£5,000 each); Chewton House Library (£500).

FINANCES *Year* 2015 *Income* £818,160 *Grants* £836,850 *Grants to organisations* £836,850 *Assets* £26,161,821

TRUSTEES John Murray; Virginia Murray; Hallam Murray; John Grey Murray; Charles Grey Murray.

OTHER INFORMATION A total of 55 grants were made during the year.

HOW TO APPLY The trustees will not consider unsolicited applications for grants.

WHO TO APPLY TO John Murray, Trustee, 50 Albemarle Street, London W1S 4BD *Tel.* 020 7493 4361

■ The Music Sales Charitable Trust

CC NO 1014942 **ESTABLISHED** 1992

WHERE FUNDING CAN BE GIVEN UK with a preference for Bury St Edmunds and London.

WHO CAN BENEFIT Registered charities.

WHAT IS FUNDED General charitable purposes, including: health; arts and culture; education and training; religion; overseas and famine relief; disability.

WHAT IS NOT FUNDED Individuals.

RANGE OF GRANTS Mostly under £5,000.

SAMPLE GRANTS Bury Bach Society, St Edmundsbury Borough Council, Disasters Emergency Committee Nepal Earthquake Appeal, East Anglican Children's Hospices, St Nicholas Hospice Care and Westminster Synagogue (£5,000 each).

FINANCES *Year* 2015 *Income* £100,000 *Grants* £106,151 *Grants to organisations* £106,151 *Assets* £252,018

TRUSTEES Christopher Butler; Ian Morgan; Robert Wise; David Rockberger; Mildred Wise; A. Latham; M. Wise; Jane Richardson.

OTHER INFORMATION Grants were made to 107 organisations during the year.

HOW TO APPLY Apply in writing to the correspondent. The trustees meet quarterly, usually in March, June, September and December.

WHO TO APPLY TO Neville Wignall, Clerk to the Trustees, Music Sales Ltd, Dettingen Way, Bury St Edmunds, Suffolk IP33 3YB *Tel.* 01284 702600 *Email* neville.wignall@musicsales.co.uk

■ Muslim Hands

CC NO 1105056 **ESTABLISHED** 1993

WHERE FUNDING CAN BE GIVEN Overseas.

WHO CAN BENEFIT Registered charities.

WHAT IS FUNDED The relief of poverty through: education; emergency relief; environment; health; the relief of hunger; livelihoods; care of orphans; and the provision of clean drinking water.

SAMPLE GRANTS A list of beneficiaries was not available.

FINANCES *Year* 2015 *Income* £14,442,632 *Grants* £9,901,727 *Grants to organisations* £9,901,727 *Assets* £9,793,551

TRUSTEES Dr Musharaf Hussain; Syed Lakhte Hassanain; Mohammad Amin-Ul Hasanat Shah; Saffi Ullah; Sahibzada Ghulam Jeelani; Muhammad Arshad Jamil.

OTHER INFORMATION Grants were given to Muslim Hands' partner organisations in countries including the following: Pakistan; Palestine; Sudan; Bangladesh; Niger; Afghanistan; Iraq; Somalia; Mali; Malawi; Kenya; Nigeria. Grants were given for the following purposes: general charitable purposes (£3 million); orphans (£2.9 million); emergency aid (£1.4 million); food (£1.1 million); safe water (£718,500); education (£352,500); health (£139,500); Masjid (£110,500); shelter (£4,400).

HOW TO APPLY Apply in writing to the correspondent.

WHO TO APPLY TO Asad Minhas, 148–164 Gregory Boulevard, Nottingham NG7 5JE *Tel.* 0115 911 7222 *Email* contact@muslimhands.org.uk *Website* www.muslimhands.org.uk

■ The Mutual Trust Group

CC NO 1039300 **ESTABLISHED** 1994

WHERE FUNDING CAN BE GIVEN UK; USA and Israel.

WHO CAN BENEFIT Jewish organisations.

WHAT IS FUNDED Orthodox Jewish education and the relief of poverty.

TYPE OF GRANT One-off and recurrent.

RANGE OF GRANTS Up to £116,000.

SAMPLE GRANTS Yeshivas Shaar Hashamayim (£116,000); Yeshivas Kesser Hatalmud (£39,000); Bilava Academy (£27,000); The ABC Trust (£22,000); Beis Chinuch and Zichron Shlome (£8,000 each).

FINANCES *Year* 2015 *Income* £149,609 *Grants* £221,820 *Grants to organisations* £221,820 *Assets* £109,662

TRUSTEES Rabbi Benzion Weitz; Michael Weitz; Adrian Weisz.

HOW TO APPLY Apply in writing to the correspondent.

WHO TO APPLY TO Rabbi Benzion Weitz, Trustee, 12 Dunstan Road, London NW11 8AA *Tel.* 020 8458 7549

■ MW (CL) Foundation

CC NO 1134917 **ESTABLISHED** 2010

WHERE FUNDING CAN BE GIVEN Worldwide, with preference for the UK.

WHO CAN BENEFIT Charitable organisations and education providers.

WHAT IS FUNDED Projects which promote education; the relief of poverty; the advancement of the Orthodox Jewish faith.

RANGE OF GRANTS £1,000 to £103,000.
SAMPLE GRANTS Zichron Mordechai and Devorah Weisz Foundation (£103,000); Achisomoch (£65,000); Beis Medrash Elyon (£13,000); Heichal Hatorah Foundation (£11,000); Friends of Galanta (£5,500); Hasmonean High School (£4,000); Jewish Teachers Training College (£3,000); Bayis Sheli, Beis Minchas Yitzchok Trust and SOFT (Support Organisation for Trisomy) (£1,000 each).
FINANCES *Year* 2014/15 *Income* £318,548 *Grants* £233,600 *Grants to organisations* £233,600 *Assets* £2,767,836
TRUSTEES Hilary Olsberg; Vivienne Lewin.
OTHER INFORMATION The foundation is closely linked with the MW (RH) Foundation, MW (GK) Foundation and MW (HO) Foundation and shares the same charitable objectives. Grants to 21 organisations were made during the year. At the time of writing (June 2017), these were the latest accounts available from the Charity Commission.
HOW TO APPLY Apply in writing to the correspondent.
WHO TO APPLY TO Vivienne Lewin, Trustee, 38 Princes Park Avenue, London NW11 0JT

■ MW (GK) Foundation

CC NO 1134916 **ESTABLISHED** 2010
WHERE FUNDING CAN BE GIVEN Worldwide, with preference for the UK.
WHO CAN BENEFIT Charitable organisations and education providers.
WHAT IS FUNDED Projects which promote education; the relief of poverty; the advancement of the Orthodox Jewish faith.
RANGE OF GRANTS £1,000 to £81,000.
SAMPLE GRANTS Mercaz Hatorah Belz Machnovka (£81,000); Mifal Hachesed Vehatzedokoh (£73,000); Friends of Beis Chinuch Lebonos (£52,000); Friends of Beis Soroh Schneirer (£39,000); Friends of Dorog (£9,000); Chasdei Devorah (£8,000); Talmud Torah Chinuch Norim (£3,500); The Hershel Weiss Centre and The New Rachmistrivke Synagogue Trust (£1,500 each).
FINANCES *Year* 2014/15 *Income* £402,172 *Grants* £274,875 *Grants to organisations* £274,875 *Assets* £2,767,962
TRUSTEES Shlomo Klein; Gella Klein.
OTHER INFORMATION The foundation was initially known as the Weisz Children Foundation and is closely linked with the MW (CL) Foundation, MW (RH) Foundation and MW (HO) Foundation. At the time of writing (June 2017) these were the latest accounts available for the foundation.
HOW TO APPLY Apply in writing to the correspondent.
WHO TO APPLY TO Gella Klein, Trustee, 15 Brantwood Road, Salford M7 4EN

■ MW (HO) Foundation

CC NO 1134919 **ESTABLISHED** 2010
WHERE FUNDING CAN BE GIVEN Worldwide, with a preference for the UK.
WHO CAN BENEFIT Charitable organisations and education providers.
WHAT IS FUNDED Projects which promote education; the relief of poverty; the advancement of the Orthodox Jewish faith.
SAMPLE GRANTS A list of beneficiaries was not available.
FINANCES *Year* 2014/15 *Income* £269,734 *Grants* £451,082 *Grants to organisations* £451,082 *Assets* £2,810,013
TRUSTEES Hilary Olsberg; David Olsberg.
OTHER INFORMATION The foundation was initially known as the Meir Weisz Foundation and is closely linked with the MW (CL) Foundation, MW (GK) Foundation and MW (RH) Foundation. A list of beneficiaries was not provided in the accounts or annual report. At the time of writing (June 2017), these were the latest accounts available for the foundation.
HOW TO APPLY Apply in writing to the correspondent.
WHO TO APPLY TO David Olsberg, Trustee, 2B Mather Avenue, Prestwich, Manchester M25 0LA

■ MW (RH) Foundation

CC NO 1134918 **ESTABLISHED** 2010
WHERE FUNDING CAN BE GIVEN Worldwide, with a preference for the UK.
WHO CAN BENEFIT Charitable organisations and education providers.
WHAT IS FUNDED Projects which promote education; the relief of poverty; the advancement of the Orthodox Jewish faith.
SAMPLE GRANTS A list of beneficiaries was not available.
FINANCES *Year* 2014/15 *Income* £435,091 *Grants* £349,150 *Grants to organisations* £349,150 *Assets* £2,663,046
TRUSTEES Rosalind Halpern; Jacob Halpern.
OTHER INFORMATION This foundation was initially known as the Deborah Weisz Foundation and is closely linked with the MW (CL) Foundation, MW (GK) Foundation and MW (HO) Foundation. A list of beneficiaries was not included in the accounts. At the time of writing (June 2017), these were the latest accounts available for the foundation.
HOW TO APPLY Apply in writing to the correspondent.
WHO TO APPLY TO Jacob Halpern, Trustee, 29 Waterpark Road, Salford M7 4FT

■ The Janet Nash Charitable Settlement

CC NO 326880 **ESTABLISHED** 1985

WHERE FUNDING CAN BE GIVEN UK.

WHO CAN BENEFIT Charitable organisations and individuals.

WHAT IS FUNDED Medical causes; health; social welfare.

RANGE OF GRANTS Usually between £1,000 and £10,000.

SAMPLE GRANTS Eversfield School (£134,000); The Get A-Head Charitable Trust (£39,500); NSPCC (£10,000); Dyslexia Charity (£4,000); KidsAid (£2,500); County Air Ambulance Trust (£1,500); Birmingham Children's Hospital, Children in Need, Walkabout Foundation and Women for Women International (£1,000 each).

FINANCES *Year* 2015/16 *Income* £610,178 *Grants* £623,290 *Grants to organisations* £212,452 *Assets* £83,192

TRUSTEES Ronald Gulliver; Mark Jacobs; Charlotte Westall.

OTHER INFORMATION Grants were made to 16 institutions and 25 individuals in support of medical causes and hardship relief.

HOW TO APPLY The charity has previously stated that it does not accept unsolicited applications.

WHO TO APPLY TO Ronald Gulliver, Trustee, Valentine Barn, Shutford Road, North Newington, Oxfordshire OX15 6AN *Tel.* 01295 738897 *Email* JanetNashCharitableSettlement@hotmail.com

■ National Arts Collections Fund

CC NO 209174 **ESTABLISHED** 1903

WHERE FUNDING CAN BE GIVEN UK.

WHO CAN BENEFIT Public museums, galleries, historic houses, libraries and archives that are: open for at least half the week for at least six months a year; are fully or provisionally accredited under the Arts Council Scheme.

WHAT IS FUNDED For the purchase of works of art and other objects of artistic interest, dating from antiquity to the present day.

WHAT IS NOT FUNDED Objects primarily of social-historical interest, scientific or technological material, or letters, manuscripts or archival material with limited aesthetic inscription; objects which are unavailable for viewing by an Art Fund trustee or appointed representative; valuation costs, framing and display, the conservation and restoration of works, transport and storage costs, temporary or permanent exhibitions and digitisation projects; applications from individuals, artists' groups, commercial organisations, hospitals, places of worship, schools or higher educational institutions; touring costs; education or community projects; salary costs; support for those studying art or art history at any level; capital projects.

TYPE OF GRANT Collections and acquisitions.

RANGE OF GRANTS There is no fixed upper or lower limit to the size of grant the committee may offer. There are main grants and small grants schemes.

SAMPLE GRANTS Stoke City Archives – Minton (£1.5 million); Victoria and Albert Museum (£600,000); Auckland Castle (£377,500); Dyrham Park – National Trust (£100,000); Christchurch Mansion (£70,000); Wolverhampton Art Gallery (£28,000); The Royal Institute of British Architects – British Architectural Library (£20,000); Newstead Abbey – Nottingham (£7,500); Stained Glass Museum (£3,000); North Hertfordshire Museum Service (£900); Crafts Study Centre (£750).

FINANCES *Year* 2015 *Income* £14,802,000 *Grants* £4,581,256 *Grants to organisations* £4,581,256 *Assets* £49,653,000

TRUSTEES Prof. Antony Griffiths; Jeremy Palmer; Michael Wilson; Richard Calvocoressi; Sally Osman; James Lingwood; Philippa Glanville; Chris Smith; Prof. Chris Gosden; Caroline Butler; Prof. Lisa Tickner; Dame Liz Forgan; Alastair Laing; Prof. Richard Deacon; Axel Rüger; Prof. Marcia Pointon; Isaac Julien.

HOW TO APPLY Firstly discuss the application with a member of the programmes office then register on the website to access the online application form. There are extensive guidelines available to download from the website where you can also find application forms and deadlines.

WHO TO APPLY TO Eleanor McGrath, Programmes Manager (Acquisitions), 2 Granary Square, King's Cross, London N1C 4BH *Tel.* 020 7225 4815 *Email* emcgrath@artfund.org *Website* www.artfund.org

■ The National Churches Trust

CC NO 1119845 **ESTABLISHED** 1953

WHERE FUNDING CAN BE GIVEN UK; Isle of Man; Channel Islands; Scilly Isles.

WHO CAN BENEFIT Listed and unlisted churches, chapels and meeting houses of any age as long as they are open for regular public worship.

WHAT IS FUNDED Urgent structural repair works; new facilities such as kitchens and toilets.

WHAT IS NOT FUNDED Ancillary buildings and structures; bells, clocks and organs (repairs and new); internal furnishings, fixtures and fittings; monument restoration; heating or lighting; re-orderings; the construction of new places of worship; applications concerning buildings that have been converted into places of worship or from chapels within hospitals, hospices, schools or prisons. The trust does not fund work that has already begun.

TYPE OF GRANT Capital costs for building and renovation.

RANGE OF GRANTS £2,000 to £70,000.

SAMPLE GRANTS Old Christ Church – Liverpool and Merseyside (£75,000); St James – Lincolnshire (£60,000); All Saints – Norfolk (£50,000); St Joseph's Catholic Church – Staffordshire (£40,000); St Dominica – Cornwall (£30,000); St Cadoc – Monmouthshire (£20,000); Bethel Community Church – Pembrokeshire (£10,000); St Mary the Virgin – Suffolk (£9,500); Wicken Methodist Church – Cambridgeshire (£5,000); Southill – All Saints (£2,000).

FINANCES *Year* 2015 *Income* £3,900,326 *Grants* £1,798,312 *Grants to organisations* £1,798,312 *Assets* £6,052,823

TRUSTEES Luke March; Alastair Hunter; Richard Carr-Archer; Dr Julie Banham; Andrew Day; Revd Lucy Winkett; John Drew; Jennifer Page; Sir Paul Britton; Catherine Cobain; Anthony Cowell.

HOW TO APPLY Applicants are advised that each fund has different application procedures all of which are available on the trust's website. Grant programmes are usually open for applications

between January and September, check the website for the latest deadline dates.
WHO TO APPLY TO Catherine Townsend, Grants Manager, 7 Tufton Street, London SW1P 3QB *Tel.* 020 7222 0605 *Fax* 020 7796 2442 *Email* grants@nationalchurchestrust.org *Website* www.nationalchurchestrust.org/our-grants

■ The National Committee of the Women's World Day of Prayer for England and Wales and Northern Ireland

CC NO 233242 **ESTABLISHED** 1932
WHERE FUNDING CAN BE GIVEN UK and worldwide.
WHO CAN BENEFIT Christian UK-based charities.
WHAT IS FUNDED Promotion of the Christian faith; women and children.
WHAT IS NOT FUNDED Individuals.
TYPE OF GRANT Mostly one-off, project grants.
RANGE OF GRANTS £1,000 to £10,000.
SAMPLE GRANTS Bible Society Northern Ireland and Cumbrian Flood Fund (£10,000 each); Feed the Minds, Toxteth Women's Centre and Traidcraft Exchange (£5,000 each); RNIB and The Leprosy Mission (£4,000 each); Bible Reading Fellowship and Global Care (£2,000 each); Methodist Church House and Torch Trust for the Blind (£1,000 each).
FINANCES *Year* 2016 *Income* £498,221 *Grants* £264,291 *Grants to organisations* £264,291 *Assets* £408,666
TRUSTEES Dr Elizabeth Burroughs; Kathleen Skinner; Margaret Pickford.
OTHER INFORMATION Priority is given to project proposals from UK-based charities – which may operate anywhere in the world – for work with women and children. Project grants are made to charities that support only one project and they would not be expected to re-apply for at least three years. Larger organisations, which fund many projects or which operate in different countries, may apply and be awarded grants in consecutive years so long as each grant is for a different project or country.
HOW TO APPLY Application forms can be obtained by contacting the charity's office and completed applications should be received by 1 August each year.
WHO TO APPLY TO Mary Judd, Administrator, Commercial Road, Tunbridge Wells TN1 2RR *Tel.* 01892 541411 *Email* office@wwdp.org.uk *Website* www.wwdp.org.uk/grants

■ The National Express Foundation

CC NO 1148231 **ESTABLISHED** 2012
WHERE FUNDING CAN BE GIVEN West Midlands and South Essex or East London within five miles of the c2c rail line.
WHO CAN BENEFIT Community groups and educational institutions.
WHAT IS FUNDED General charitable purposes; social welfare; education, especially bursaries for disadvantaged students; sport; children and young people.
RANGE OF GRANTS Up to £30,000.
SAMPLE GRANTS Newman University (£20,000); Coventry University and South Essex College (£10,000 each); Dagenham Bangladeshi Women and Children's Association, Disability Resource Centre and Handsworth Carers Group (£2,500 each).
FINANCES *Year* 2015 *Income* £100,086 *Grants* £105,000 *Grants to organisations* £105,000
TRUSTEES Anthony Vigor; Ian Austin; Denise Rossiter; Lesley Dorrington; John Fraser; Magdalena Pilgrim.
HOW TO APPLY Apply in writing to the correspondent. The website provides further information on deadlines and successful projects.
WHO TO APPLY TO The Trustees, National Express Group PLC, National Express House, Digbeth, Birmingham B5 6DD *Tel.* 0121 460 8423 *Email* foundation@nationalexpress.com *Website* www.nationalexpressgroup.com/our-way/national-express-foundation

■ The National Gardens Scheme

CC NO 1112664 **ESTABLISHED** 2006
WHERE FUNDING CAN BE GIVEN UK.
WHO CAN BENEFIT Registered charities.
WHAT IS FUNDED Care, nursing and health charities. The Elspeth Thompson Bursaries support community gardening projects aimed at bringing the community together by the sharing and acquiring of horticultural knowledge and skills, and by inspiring a love of gardening across all age groups.
SAMPLE GRANTS Hospice UK, Macmillan Cancer Support and Marie Curie (£500,000 each); Carers Trust (£375,000); The Queen's Nursing Institute (£250,000); Horatio's Garden and Perennial (£130,000 each); Parkinson's UK (£100,000); MS Society (£100,000); National Trust Gardening Careership (£30,000).
FINANCES *Year* 2015 *Income* £3,882,661 *Grants* £2,637,000 *Grants to organisations* £2,637,000 *Assets* £936,815
TRUSTEES Martin Macmillan; Heather Skinner; Miranda Allhusen; Rosamund Davies; Susan Phipps; Peter Clay; Bridget Marshall; Patrick Ramsay; Colin Olle; Richard Thompson; Susan Copeland; Rupert Tyler; Andrew Ratcliffe.
OTHER INFORMATION The scheme helps garden owners open their gardens to the public and raises money through entry fees.
HOW TO APPLY Apply in writing to the correspondent. Beneficiary charities are nominated by the trustees each year. A guest charity is also nominated annually. For the Elspeth Thompson Bursary, an application form and guidance notes are provided on the website, along with deadlines. Queries should be submitted to: ngsbursary@rhs.org.uk or 01483479719.
WHO TO APPLY TO George Plumptre, The National Gardens Scheme, 1 Courtyard Cottage, Hatchlands, East Clandon, Guildford GU4 7RT *Tel.* 01483 211535 *Email* gplumptre@ngs.org.uk *Website* www.ngs.org.uk

■ The National Manuscripts Conservation Trust

CC NO 802796 **ESTABLISHED** 1990
WHERE FUNDING CAN BE GIVEN UK.
WHO CAN BENEFIT Record offices; libraries; other publicly funded institutions; owners of manuscript material conditionally exempt from capital taxation or owned by a charitable trust.
WHAT IS FUNDED Conservation of manuscripts, documents and archives.
WHAT IS NOT FUNDED Public records; photographic, audio-visual and printed material; capital costs;

equipment; arranging and listing manuscripts; digitisation to increase access as opposed to digitisation for preservation purposes.

TYPE OF GRANT Grants cover the cost of repair, binding and other preservation measures including reprography; the costs of conservation by commercial conservation studios or the salaries and related expenses of staff specially employed, and expendable materials required for the project.

RANGE OF GRANTS £2,000 to £25,000.

SAMPLE GRANTS Staffordshire and Stoke-on-Trent Archives (£24,000); Worcestershire Archives (£20,500); West Glamorgan Archive Service (£16,600); Woodhorn Museum and Northumberland Archives (£14,900); Sheffield Archives (£11,000); Winchester Cathedral (£10,000); Newcastle University Library (£9,700); Yorkshire Archaeological Society (£7,200); Oxford Bodleian Library (£5,000); Wrexham Archives and Local Studies (£3,800); Denbighshire Archives (£1,600).

FINANCES *Year* 2015 *Income* £192,890 *Grants* £164,497 *Grants to organisations* £164,497 *Assets* £2,131,298

TRUSTEES Lord Egremont; Dr Bernard Naylor; Charles Sebag-Montefiore; Dr Norman James; Dr Caroline Checkley-Scott.

HOW TO APPLY Application forms are available to download from the website, along with guidance notes. The trust advices you to contact the secretary for further advice and to check the website for the deadlines and further details of how to apply.

WHO TO APPLY TO Nell Hoare, Secretary, PO Box 4291, Reading, Berkshire RG8 9JA *Tel.* 01491 598083 *Email* info@nmct.org.uk *Website* www.nmct.co.uk

■ The Nationwide Foundation

CC NO 1065552 **ESTABLISHED** 1997

WHERE FUNDING CAN BE GIVEN UK.

WHO CAN BENEFIT Charitable organisations.

WHAT IS FUNDED Community development; housing; legal assistance; and social welfare.

WHAT IS NOT FUNDED Charities with unrestricted reserves which exceed 50% of annual expenditure, as shown in their accounts; charities which are in significant debt as shown in their accounts; promotion of religion or politics; charities which have been declined by the foundation within the last 12 months; applications which do not comply with the foundation's funding criteria/guidelines.

TYPE OF GRANT Project, capital and revenue costs, research and idea testing.

RANGE OF GRANTS £14,500 to £160,500.

SAMPLE GRANTS Locality (£160,500); Canopy Housing (£160,000); YMCA Glenrothes (£159,000); Action Homeless Leicester (£140,000); Grimsby Doorstep (£130,000); Generation Rent (£107,500); Community Campus 87 (£75,000); Rural Action Yorkshire (£34,000); Community Land Trust Fund (£22,000); DAH Added Value (£14,500).

FINANCES *Year* 2015/16 *Income* £1,672,512 *Grants* £1,530,525 *Grants to organisations* £1,530,525 *Assets* £1,275,502

TRUSTEES Michael Coppack; Benedict Stimson; Fiona Ellis; Graeme Hughes; Juliet Cockram; Sarah Mitchell; Bryce Glover; John Taylor; Antonia Bance; Clara Govier; Tony Prestedge.

OTHER INFORMATION The foundation made 16 grants to organisations in the financial year. Nationwide Building Society also donated services to the foundation totalling £92,000, which represented the provision of office space, technology, legal and accountancy support.

HOW TO APPLY At the time of writing (April 2017) the foundation was accepting applications for two programmes: Nurturing Ideas to Change the Housing System and Backing Community-Led Housing. Further guidance and details of both programmes can be found on the website. Proposals should be no more than 500 words and should be sent to applications@nationwidefoundation.org.uk. Your proposal should tell the foundation the following: your organisation and the work you already do; the idea you want to be funded and why it will contribute to the foundation's strategy; the estimated amount of funding you are looking for and proposed timescales. Nurturing Ideas enquiries should be directed to Samantha Stewart by email: Samantha.stewart@nationwidefoundation.org.uk or phone: 01793 657 181; and Community-Led Housing enquiries should be directed to Gary Hartin, Programme Manager, by email: Gary.hartin@nationwidefoundation.org.uk or phone: 01793 656651. There are no application deadlines.

WHO TO APPLY TO Samantha Stewart, Head of Programmes, Nationwide Building Society, Nationwide House, Pipers Way, Swindon SN38 2SN *Tel.* 01793 655113 *Email* enquiries@nationwidefoundation.org.uk *Website* www.nationwidefoundation.org.uk

■ The NDL Foundation

CC NO 1133508 **ESTABLISHED** 2010

WHERE FUNDING CAN BE GIVEN Worldwide.

WHO CAN BENEFIT UK-registered charities.

WHAT IS FUNDED General charitable purposes; education; medicine; the arts; women and children in financially developing countries.

TYPE OF GRANT One-off and recurrent.

RANGE OF GRANTS Up to £40,000.

SAMPLE GRANTS Women for Women International UK (£40,000); Myschoolpulse (£30,000); Pepo La Tumaini (£28,000); The National Gallery Trust (£27,500); Imagine Institut des Maladies Génétiques (£25,500); Don Bosco Bangalore Girls' School Maintenance (£19,000); Child Bereavement UK (£9,500); Tate Foundation (£4,500); Opportunity International (£2,500); Cultura Europa (£1,100).

FINANCES *Year* 2015/16 *Income* £374,235 *Grants* £188,066 *Grants to organisations* £188,066 *Assets* £215,633

TRUSTEES Sylviane Destribats; Laura Destribats; Frank Destribats; Diane Destribats; Nicolas Destribats.

HOW TO APPLY Apply in writing to the correspondent.

WHO TO APPLY TO Sylviane Destribats, Trustee, 8 Bolton Gardens Mews, London SW10 9LW *Tel.* 020 7835 2950 *Email* mai.brown@blickrothenberg.com

■ The Worshipful Company of Needlemakers' Charitable Fund

CC NO 288646 **ESTABLISHED** 1952

WHERE FUNDING CAN BE GIVEN London.

WHO CAN BENEFIT Charitable organisations, including those associated with the needle-making industry, the City of London, and the Lord Mayor's, the Master's and the Chaplain's chosen charities.

WHAT IS FUNDED Education; religion; social welfare; general charitable purposes.
RANGE OF GRANTS £100 to £5,000.
SAMPLE GRANTS Royal School of Needlework (£5,000); Old Palace School (£3,000); Fine Cell Work (£1,500); Needle Museum (£1,000); St Paul's Cathedral Trust and Victoria and Albert Museum (£500); Quilt and Stitch Village (£250); The Royal Masonic School for Girls, Rickmansworth (£100).
FINANCES *Year* 2014/15 *Income* £104,636 *Grants* £50,180 *Grants to organisations* £47,500 *Assets* £1,969,787
TRUSTEES Dame Elizabeth Fradd; Colin Tiffin; Douglas Chase.
OTHER INFORMATION At the time of writing (June 2017) the charity's 2014/15 accounts were the latest available.
HOW TO APPLY Apply in writing to the correspondent.
WHO TO APPLY TO Philip Grant, Clerk, PO Box 3682, Windsor SL4 3WR *Tel.* 01753 860690 *Email* needlemakers.clerk@yahoo.com *Website* www.needlemakers.org.uk

■ The James Neill Trust Fund

CC NO 503203 **ESTABLISHED** 1974
WHERE FUNDING CAN BE GIVEN Sheffield and its immediate surroundings.
WHO CAN BENEFIT Registered charities; individuals.
WHAT IS FUNDED General charitable purposes; people residing within 20 miles from Sheffield Cathedral.
TYPE OF GRANT One-off; start-up costs; capital costs; long-term support; recurrent.
RANGE OF GRANTS Up to £5,000.
SAMPLE GRANTS St Wilfrid's Centre – Residential Unit (£5,000); Boys and Girls Clubs South Yorkshire, Sheffield Sea Cadets (£2,000 each); Dyslexia Action (£1,000); The Ethel Trust Community Badge, The Prince's Trust, The Sick Children's Trust (£750); Engineering Development Trust, Listening Books, Spinal Injuries Association (£500 each); Ramsden Primary School (£250).
FINANCES *Year* 2015/16 *Income* £50,122 *Grants* £43,786 *Grants to organisations* £43,786 *Assets* £1,289,130
TRUSTEES Sir Hugh Neill; G. Peel; Lady Neill; N. Peel; A. Staniforth; J. Neill.
OTHER INFORMATION During the year, the trustees provided ongoing financial support totalling £22,500 to 18 organisations and made 17 one-off grants totalling £21,500.
HOW TO APPLY Apply in writing to the correspondent.
WHO TO APPLY TO Lady Neill, Trustee, Barn Cottage, Lindrick Common, Worksop, Nottinghamshire S81 8BA *Tel.* 01909 562806 *Email* neillcharities@me.com

■ Nemoral Ltd

CC NO 262270 **ESTABLISHED** 1971
WHERE FUNDING CAN BE GIVEN Worldwide.
WHO CAN BENEFIT Jewish organisations.
WHAT IS FUNDED Jewish religion; Jewish religious education; the relief of poverty in the Jewish community.
SAMPLE GRANTS A list of beneficiaries was not available.
FINANCES *Year* 2015 *Income* £367,259 *Grants* £136,000 *Grants to organisations* £136,000 *Assets* £1,381,492
TRUSTEES Ellis Moore; Rivka Gross; Michael Saberski.
OTHER INFORMATION A list of grant beneficiaries was not included in the charity's accounts.
HOW TO APPLY Apply in writing to the correspondent.
WHO TO APPLY TO The Trustees, c/o Cohen Arnold and Co., New Burlington House, 1075 Finchley Road, London NW11 0PU *Tel.* 020 8731 0777

■ Ner Foundation

CC NO 1104866 **ESTABLISHED** 2004
WHERE FUNDING CAN BE GIVEN UK and Israel.
WHO CAN BENEFIT Orthodox Jewish organisations, community projects, schools, yeshivos and seminaries.
WHAT IS FUNDED Advancement of the Orthodox Jewish religion and education and the relief of poverty among Jewish people.
SAMPLE GRANTS A list of beneficiaries was not available.
FINANCES *Year* 2015/16 *Income* £291,269 *Grants* £191,953 *Grants to organisations* £191,953 *Assets* £539,044
TRUSTEES Arnold Henry; Henry Neumann; Esther Henry.
OTHER INFORMATION A list of beneficiaries was not included in the accounts but grants were distributed as follows: relief of poverty (£86,000); yeshivos and seminaries (£43,500); schools (£28,000); advancement of religion (£11,500); community projects (£8,500). Grants under £1,000 totalled £14,500.
HOW TO APPLY Apply in writing to the correspondent.
WHO TO APPLY TO Arnold Henry, Trustee, 309 Bury New Road, Salford, Manchester M7 2YN

■ Nesswall Ltd

CC NO 283600 **ESTABLISHED** 1981
WHERE FUNDING CAN BE GIVEN UK and overseas.
WHO CAN BENEFIT Orthodox Jewish organisations.
WHAT IS FUNDED Orthodox Jewish causes, including education and relief in need.
SAMPLE GRANTS Friends of Horim Establishments, Torah Vochesed L'Ezra Vesaad and Emunah Education Centre.
FINANCES *Year* 2015/16 *Income* £75,400 *Grants* £58,540 *Grants to organisations* £58,540 *Assets* £657,774
TRUSTEES R. Teitelbaum; H. Wahrhaftig.
HOW TO APPLY Apply in writing to the correspondent.
WHO TO APPLY TO R. Teitelbaum, Secretary, 28 Overlea Road, London E5 9BG

■ Nesta

CC NO 1144091 **ESTABLISHED** 2011
WHERE FUNDING CAN BE GIVEN UK.
WHO CAN BENEFIT Registered charities; charitable organisations; individuals; social enterprises; universities.
WHAT IS FUNDED Social innovations, areas of work include: health and ageing; young people; digital arts and media; citizen engagement in public services; innovation policy; government innovation; new models for inclusive growth; impact investment; future thinking.
WHAT IS NOT FUNDED Schools; hospices; CIOs; churches; each funding programme has its own exclusions.
TYPE OF GRANT Project grants; research.
RANGE OF GRANTS Up to £167,000.
SAMPLE GRANTS Open University (£167,000); Newcastle University (£130,000); Stockport Metropolitan Borough Council (£100,000); Development Bank of Latin America (£60,000);

Community Music Wales (£55,000); European School of Management and Technology, University Hospital Southampton NHS Trust; WikiHouse Foundation and The Better with Data Society (£50,000 each).

FINANCES *Year* 2015/16 *Income* £14,492,000 *Grants* £2,132,000 *Grants to organisations* £2,126,000 *Assets* £384,885,000

TRUSTEES Simon Linnett; Sir John Gieve; Natalie Tydeman; David Pitt-Watson; Dame Julie Mellor; Prof. Madeleine Atkins; Kim Shillinglaw; Kersten England; Edward Wray; Piers Linney.

OTHER INFORMATION There were a total of 11 grants made to individuals in the year totalling £6,000. Grants were made to over 120 institutions.

HOW TO APPLY Information on current funding programmes is provided on the Nesta website, including details of how to apply.

WHO TO APPLY TO Corinna Theuma, Company Secretary, Nesta, 1 Plough Place, London EC4A 1DE *Tel.* 020 7438 2500 *Email* info@nesta.org.uk *Website* www.nesta.org.uk

■ Network for Social Change Charitable Trust

CC NO 295237 **ESTABLISHED** 1986

WHERE FUNDING CAN BE GIVEN UK and overseas.

WHO CAN BENEFIT Registered charities and charitable organisations.

WHAT IS FUNDED Human rights and dignity; civil society; the environment and sustainability; the promotion of peace and non-violence; asylum seekers and refugees; economic justice; health; arts and education.

WHAT IS NOT FUNDED Disaster appeals; most types of building; direct contributions to political parties.

TYPE OF GRANT Core costs; research; one-off and recurrent for up to five years.

RANGE OF GRANTS Up to £200,000.

SAMPLE GRANTS New Economics Foundation (£180,000); Student Action for Refugees (£157,000); Peace Direct (£27,000); Campaign for Better Transport Charitable Trust (£23,000); Arts 4 Dementia, First Steps Nutrition Trust and The Climate Movement (£15,000 each); The Centre for Crime and Justice Studies and The Institute of Race Relations (£14,500 each); Economic Social and Cultural Rights in the UK, Fairshare Educational Foundation and Medical Aid for Palestinians (£14,000 each).

FINANCES *Year* 2015/16 *Income* £1,558,000 *Grants* £1,471,545 *Grants to organisations* £1,471,545 *Assets* £256,730

TRUSTEES Chris Marks; Imran Tyabji; Giles Wright; Carolyn Hayman; Marian Tucker; Jessica Paget.

HOW TO APPLY The network chooses the projects it wishes to support and does not solicit applications. Unsolicited applications cannot expect to receive a reply. However, the network is conscious that the policy of only accepting applications brought by its members could limit the range of worthwhile projects it could fund. To address this, the network has set up a 'Project Noticeboard' to allow outside organisations to post a summary of a project for which they are seeking funding. Members of the network can then access the noticeboard and, if interested, contact the organisation for further information to explore the potential for future sponsorship. Projects are deleted from the noticeboard after about six months. Note only 1–2% of noticeboard entries result in sponsorship and funding. The annual report states that the trustees usually meet two or three times each year, between the biannual conferences to review the projects that have been submitted. Two pool members are appointed as assessors to examine each project in details, and obtain written references from external referees. Where possible, all projects are visited by the assessors.

WHO TO APPLY TO BM 2063, London WC1N 3XX *Tel.* 01647 61106 *Email* thenetwork@gn.apc.org *Website* thenetworkforsocialchange.org.uk

■ Newby Trust Ltd

CC NO 227151 **ESTABLISHED** 1938

WHERE FUNDING CAN BE GIVEN UK.

WHO CAN BENEFIT Registered charities; individuals.

WHAT IS FUNDED Education; health; social welfare.

WHAT IS NOT FUNDED Statutory bodies; large national charities enjoying widespread support; organisations not registered with the Charity Commission; exhibitions, conferences or events; individuals volunteering overseas; promotion of religion; work outside the UK; large capital appeals; endowment appeals.

TYPE OF GRANT Usually one-off awards for a part of a project; scholarships; equipment and activities. Occasionally core costs are considered.

RANGE OF GRANTS Up to £30,000.

SAMPLE GRANTS Durham University and Lancaster University (£30,000 each); Street Doctors (£13,000); International Boatbuilding Training College (£8,400); Doctors of the World Refugee Appeal, Freedom from Torture, Sebastian's Action Trust and Winchester College (£5,000 each); White City Theatre Company (£3,000); Hope in the Valley Riding for the Disabled (£1,000).

FINANCES *Year* 2015/16 *Income* £454,941 *Grants* £311,684 *Grants to organisations* £311,684 *Assets* £17,532,356

TRUSTEES Susan Charlton; David Charlton; Duncan Reed; Ben Gooder; Anna Foxell; Evelyn Bentley; Nigel Callaghan; Dr Stephen Gooder.

OTHER INFORMATION There is one 'special category' supported each year; in 2015/16 it was homelessness and in 2017/18 it will be dance or sport projects for disadvantaged young people. Further information is provided on the trust's website.

HOW TO APPLY In general, unsolicited applications are not accepted. Charities that fall within the 'special category', however, may send an introductory email to the Company Secretary (info@newby-trust.org.uk).

WHO TO APPLY TO Annabel Grout, Company Secretary, Hill Farm, Froxfield, Petersfield, Hampshire GU32 1BQ *Email* info@newby-trust.org.uk *Website* www.newby-trust.org.uk

■ The Newcomen Collett Foundation

CC NO 312804 **ESTABLISHED** 1988

WHERE FUNDING CAN BE GIVEN London Borough of Southwark.

WHO CAN BENEFIT Schools; colleges; organisations; individuals.

WHAT IS FUNDED Education of young people under 25 years of age including: equipment; extra-curricular activities; organisations providing educational opportunities to schools and colleges (visiting theatre groups or musicians, for example); children with learning difficulties; school uniforms.

WHAT IS NOT FUNDED Capital expenditure; rent, alterations and repairs; salaries; administration costs; retrospective grants.
TYPE OF GRANT One-off.
RANGE OF GRANTS Usually up to £1,000, occasionally more.
SAMPLE GRANTS Brunswick Park Primary School (£2,500); Heber Primary School (£2,200); Phoenix Explorer Scout Unit (£2,000); St Joseph's Camberwell Catholic Schools' Federation (£1,700); KIDS (£1,300); Pembroke Academy of Music (£1,200); Camberwell After School Project (£1,100).
FINANCES *Year* 2015/16 *Income* £182,324 *Grants* £64,328 *Grants to organisations* £64,328 *Assets* £3,347,947
OTHER INFORMATION The grant total includes the figure for individuals and organisations. During the year, 24 grants were awarded for the purchase of school uniforms; 29 grants were awarded to individuals' living costs; and 55 grants were awarded to organisations for a range of projects covering the arts, drama, sports, school trips and holiday clubs.
HOW TO APPLY Application forms are available to download, together with criteria and guidelines, from the website. The governors consider requests four times a year. The closing dates for applications are listed on the website.
WHO TO APPLY TO Catherine de Cintra, Clerk, Marshall's House, 66 Newcomen Street, London Bridge, London SE1 1YT *Tel.* 020 7939 0720 *Fax* 020 7403 3969 *Email* grantoffice@newcomencollett.org.uk *Website* www.newcomencollett.org.uk

■ The Frances and Augustus Newman Foundation

CC NO 277964 **ESTABLISHED** 1978
WHERE FUNDING CAN BE GIVEN UK.
WHO CAN BENEFIT Medical professionals; academic institutions; major research centres.
WHAT IS FUNDED Mainly, but not exclusively, funding for medical research projects and equipment including fellowships of the Royal College of Surgeons.
WHAT IS NOT FUNDED Applications are not normally accepted from overseas. Requests from other charities seeking funds to supplement their own general funds to support medical research in a particular field are seldom supported.
TYPE OF GRANT Mainly one-off. Research core costs and salaries will also be considered. Grants made can be for one to three years.
RANGE OF GRANTS £1,000 to £110,000.
SAMPLE GRANTS Royal College of Surgeons (£110,000); University College London (£55,000); Diabetes UK (£35,000); University of Oxford (£25,000); Bloodwise and Restoration of Appearance and Function Trust (£10,000 each); Najda Now International (£6,100); Progressive Supranuclear Palsy Association (£5,000); War Memorials Trust (£2,000); Delete Blood Cancer (£1,000).
FINANCES *Year* 2015/16 *Income* £583,037 *Grants* £341,829 *Grants to organisations* £341,829 *Assets* £13,859,613
TRUSTEES David Sweetnam; Lord Hugh Rathcavan; John Williams; Stephen Cannon.
OTHER INFORMATION There were 13 grants awarded in 2016.
HOW TO APPLY The annual report for 2015/16 states that the trustees 'invite applications for research grants from individuals. Applicants submit a summary of their proposals to the Trustees in a specific format; applications made in the correct format are reviewed against the research criteria established by the Trustees and the research objectives. Research posts are funded on an annual basis to undertake an agreed programme of research and continuation of the grants is subject to the annual assessment by the Trustees. The Trustees give substantial support to peer reviewed submissions from academic institutions. In respect of the limited number of other grants made, they favour projects submitted from major research centres.'
WHO TO APPLY TO Hazel Palfreyman, Administrator, c/o Baker Tilly Chartered Accountants, Hartwell House, 55–61 Victoria Street, Bristol BS1 6AD *Tel.* 0117 945 2000 *Email* hazel.palfreyman@rsmuk.com

■ Newpier Charity Ltd

CC NO 293686 **ESTABLISHED** 1985
WHERE FUNDING CAN BE GIVEN UK and Israel.
WHO CAN BENEFIT Jewish organisations.
WHAT IS FUNDED Advancement of the Orthodox Jewish faith; the relief of poverty; general charitable purposes.
SAMPLE GRANTS BML Benityashvut; Friends of Biala; Gateshead Yeshiva; Mosdos Viznitz; SOFT (Support Organisation for Trisomy) (for redistribution to other charities).
FINANCES *Year* 2014/15 *Income* £277,395 *Grants* £386,745 *Grants to organisations* £386,745 *Assets* £3,287,767
TRUSTEES Charles Margulies; Helen Knopfler; Rachel Margulies.
OTHER INFORMATION At the time of writing (April 2017) the latest accounts available were those from the 2014/15 financial year.
HOW TO APPLY Apply in writing to the correspondent. The trustees meet on a regular basis to consider applications.
WHO TO APPLY TO Charles Margulies, Trustee, 186 Lordship Road, London N16 5ES *Tel.* 020 8802 4449

■ Alderman Newton's Educational Foundation

CC NO 527881 **ESTABLISHED** 1983
WHERE FUNDING CAN BE GIVEN Diocese of Leicester.
WHO CAN BENEFIT Maintained Church of England or other maintained schools within the City of Leicester, or any other Church of England school within the Diocese of Leicester.
WHAT IS FUNDED Projects that would not normally be funded by the local education authority.
WHAT IS NOT FUNDED Equipment or costs that would normally be met from the school budget set by the local education authority.
TYPE OF GRANT One-off and recurrent. Project funding.
SAMPLE GRANTS A list of beneficiaries was not available.
FINANCES *Year* 2015/16 *Income* £168,137 *Grants* £162,210 *Grants to organisations* £162,210 *Assets* £4,208,579
TRUSTEES Suzanna Uprichard; Madan Kallow; Revd Richard Curtis; Cllr Malcolm Unsworth; Cheryl Pharoah; Dr Richard Harries; Charles Franks; Keith Jones; Wendy Martin; The Revd Canon Philip O'Reilly; Guy Newbury; John Standish; Doreen Horton.

HOW TO APPLY An application form and guidelines are available from the correspondent or to download from the charity's website.
WHO TO APPLY TO The Clerk to the Governors, Leicester Charity Link, 20A Millstone Lane, Leicester LE1 5JN *Tel.* 0116 222 2200 *Email* info@charity-link.org *Website* anef.org.uk

■ The NFU Mutual Charitable Trust

CC NO 1073064 **ESTABLISHED** 1998
WHERE FUNDING CAN BE GIVEN UK, particularly rural areas.
WHO CAN BENEFIT Charitable organisations and individuals.
WHAT IS FUNDED Community development; education; the relief of poverty; social welfare; and research focusing on initiatives that will have a significant impact on rural communities.
TYPE OF GRANT One-off and recurrent.
RANGE OF GRANTS £1,000 to £60,000.
SAMPLE GRANTS Farming and Countryside Education (£60,000); The National Federation of Young Farmers Clubs (£30,000); Addington Fund, Royal Agricultural Benevolent Institution, Rural Support (£15,000 each); Nuffield Farming Scholarships Trust (£11,000); Scottish Association of Young Farmers Clubs (£6,000); Open Farm Weekend, Northern Islands (£5,000); Farms for City Children (£4,000); Children's County Hospital Fund (£1,200).
FINANCES *Year* 2015 *Income* £258,235 *Grants* £223,798 *Grants to organisations* £223,798 *Assets* £246,407
TRUSTEES Allan Bowie; Lindsay Sinclair; Lord Curry of Kirkharle; Meurig Raymond; Richard Butler; Richard Percy; Stephen James; Stephen James; Stanley Barclay Bell; Dr Harriet Kennedy.
OTHER INFORMATION Grants were made to 17 organisations during the year.
HOW TO APPLY Apply in writing to the correspondent either via post or email. The application form is available from the trust's website.
WHO TO APPLY TO James Creechan, Secretary to the Trustees, The National Farmers Union Mutual Insurance Society Ltd, Tiddington Road, Stratford-upon-Avon, Warwickshire CV37 7BJ *Tel.* 01789 204211 *Email* nfu_mutual_charitable_trust@nfumutual.co.uk *Website* www.nfumutual.co.uk/company-information/charitable-trust

■ NJD Charitable Trust

CC NO 1109146 **ESTABLISHED** 2005
WHERE FUNDING CAN BE GIVEN UK and Israel.
WHO CAN BENEFIT Jewish organisations and individuals.
WHAT IS FUNDED The relief of poverty and hardship of members of the Jewish faith; the advancement of Jewish religion through Jewish education.
TYPE OF GRANT One-off and recurrent.
RANGE OF GRANTS Up to £30,000.
SAMPLE GRANTS Jewish Care (£30,000); United Jewish Israel Appeal (UJIA) (£20,000); Jewish Leadership Council (£7,000); Community Security Trust (£6,600); Holocaust Educational Trust (£5,000); Spanish and Portuguese Jews' Congregation (£1,400); Jerusalem Foundation and World Jewish Relief (£1,000 each).
FINANCES *Year* 2014/15 *Income* £100,046 *Grants* £77,746 *Grants to organisations* £77,746 *Assets* £151,547
TRUSTEES Nathalie Dwek; Jean Glaskie; Jacob Wolf; Alexander Dwek.
OTHER INFORMATION Other donations of £600 and below totalled £5,700.
HOW TO APPLY Apply in writing to the correspondent.
WHO TO APPLY TO Alan Dawson, Trust Administrator, St Bride's House, 10 Salisbury Square, London EC4Y 8EH *Tel.* 020 7842 7306

■ Alice Noakes Memorial Charitable Trust

CC NO 1039663 **ESTABLISHED** 1994
WHERE FUNDING CAN BE GIVEN UK and overseas.
WHO CAN BENEFIT Registered charities; universities; individuals.
WHAT IS FUNDED Research, teaching, treatment and care relating to animal welfare.
RANGE OF GRANTS £500 to £20,000.
SAMPLE GRANTS University of Cambridge (£25,000 in two grants); Animal Health Trust (£12,500); Elephant Family (£1,000); Anglo-Italian Society for the Protection of Animals, Costa Blanca Feral Cat Trust, The Gambia Horse and Donkey Trust, Prickles Hedgehog Rescue and Scottish Seabird Centre (£500 each); International Otter Survival Fund (£350).
FINANCES *Year* 2015/16 *Income* £75,540 *Grants* £54,050 *Grants to organisations* £52,050 *Assets* £2,468,879
TRUSTEES David Whipps; J. H. Simpson; Nigel Oldacre; Spencer Bayer; Jeremy Hulme; Robert Ferdinando; Stefaan Van Poucke.
OTHER INFORMATION Grants were made to 30 organisations during the year and there was one grant awarded to an individual for £2,000. The trustees set no minimum or maximum level of grant, although the majority appear to be of £500.
HOW TO APPLY Apply in writing to the correspondent. The trustees meet twice a year.
WHO TO APPLY TO David Whipps, Trustee, Bocking End, Braintree, Essex CM7 9AJ *Tel.* 01376 320456

■ Nominet Charitable Foundation

CC NO 1125735 **ESTABLISHED** 2008
WHERE FUNDING CAN BE GIVEN UK and overseas.
WHO CAN BENEFIT Mainly UK-based initiatives.
WHAT IS FUNDED Digital technology to address social issues in the UK, with a preference for: health; young people; education about digital technology, for example how to stay safe online; older people.
WHAT IS NOT FUNDED Hardware infrastructure projects, e.g. a project to equip a school with PCs, or to install Wi-Fi for a community; website improvements where no new functional or service delivery innovations are delivered; website development unless the project and organisation delivers against one of the foundation's areas of focus and meets its funding guidelines; organisational running costs; political parties or lobbying groups.
TYPE OF GRANT Usually one-off project costs; research; development initiatives.
RANGE OF GRANTS Up to £600,000.
SAMPLE GRANTS Inspiring Digital Enterprise (£600,000); Shift (£500,000); My Time to Care Ltd (£100,000); Edukit Solutions Ltd (£84,500); Enabling Play (£80,000); British Academy of Film and Television Arts (£79,000); Games for Life CIC, Limitless Travel Ltd, Maker Club, and Vision Technologies Ltd (£50,000 each).

FINANCES *Year* 2015/16 *Income* £4,061,908 *Grants* £2,710,671 *Grants to organisations* £2,710,671 *Assets* £6,488,297

TRUSTEES Bill Liao; Sebastien Lahtinen; Nora Nanayakkara; Natalie Campbell; Elizabeth Murray; Jemima Rellie.

OTHER INFORMATION Grants of less than £50,000 totalled almost £242,500 during the year.

HOW TO APPLY Regular updates and upcoming funding calls are published on the charity's website. The details of current programmes can be found on the website, along with extensive guidelines and common mistakes applicants make.

WHO TO APPLY TO Vicki Hearn, Director, Nominet, Minerva House, Edmund Halley Road, Oxford OX4 4DQ *Tel.* 01865 334000 *Email* enquiries@nominettrust.org.uk *Website* www.nominettrust.org.uk

■ The Norfolk Churches Trust Ltd

CC NO 271176 **ESTABLISHED** 1976

WHERE FUNDING CAN BE GIVEN The Diocese of Norwich and the county of Norfolk.

WHO CAN BENEFIT Churches.

WHAT IS FUNDED Church renovation and repair including, according to the trust's website: 'structural repairs to fabric of building; repair and restructuring of rain water goods and drainage; window repairs – glazing and tracery; repairs to fixtures and fittings including pews, monuments, organs and ledger stones; conservation of wall paintings and stonework; renewal of interior plaster; repairs to floors and pew platforms; repairs and refurbishment of bell frames; roof alarm systems; renewal of switchgear for electrics'.

WHAT IS NOT FUNDED Reordering projects, extensions or the installation of new facilities; rewiring or lighting works; bells. Interior decoration will only be funded as part of wall repairs.

TYPE OF GRANT Buildings and feasibility studies.

RANGE OF GRANTS £240 to £10,000.

SAMPLE GRANTS Brettenham – St Andrew (£10,000); Rushford – St John (£7,000); Griston – Sts Peter and Paul (£4,000); Alburgh – All Saints (£3,000); Beachamwell – St Mary (£2,000); Morley – St Botolph (£1,500); Upwell Methodists (£1,000); Brandon Parva – All Saints (£530) Cockley Cley – All Saints (£240).

FINANCES *Year* 2015/16 *Income* £711,233 *Grants* £106,011 *Grants to organisations* £106,011 *Assets* £1,517,060

TRUSTEES Michael Sayer; Lady Egerton; Sarah, Countess of Leicester; Lady Fraser; Peter De Bunsen; Ian Lonsdale; Lady Agnew; Sara Foster; Henrietta Lindsell; Holly Rawkins; Jonathan Ellis.

OTHER INFORMATION The trust made grants to 83 churches during the year.

HOW TO APPLY Apply in writing to the correspondent. The trust can also advise applicants on further sources of funding.

WHO TO APPLY TO Priscilla Latham, Company Secretary, Latham, Manor Farm House, Diss Road, Tibenham, Norwich NR16 1QF *Tel.* 01379 677272 *Email* secretary@norfolkchurchestrust.org.uk *Website* norfolkchurchestrust.org.uk

■ Norfolk Community Foundation

CC NO 1110817 **ESTABLISHED** 2004

WHERE FUNDING CAN BE GIVEN Norfolk.

WHO CAN BENEFIT Local community groups; town and parish councils; CICs; social enterprises; individuals.

WHAT IS FUNDED General charitable purposes with a preference for social welfare; community development.

WHAT IS NOT FUNDED Projects benefitting people outside the stated area of benefit; individuals for their personal needs; retrospective grants; direct replacement of statutory funding; organisations controlled by public sector bodies; the purchase of equipment that will become the property of a statutory body; improvements to land or buildings owned by a statutory body (except parish/town councils); improvements to land or buildings where the grant applicant does not have a legal interest in the land/building; projects where the grant award cannot be spent within the stated grant term (typically 12 months); medical research and equipment; sports projects; groups wanting to attend sporting events; arts projects; professional performance fees; environmental projects; religious or political causes or political lobbying; commercial ventures; general appeals; sponsorship; animal welfare; travel or expeditions abroad for individuals and groups; organisations raising funds to redistribute to other causes; projects that do not directly contribute to community activity (for example, street decorations, displays or furniture, war memorials or renovations to historic buildings or monuments).

TYPE OF GRANT One-off and one-year-long projects.

RANGE OF GRANTS Up to £60,000. The average grant size is £2,500.

SAMPLE GRANTS Eaton Park Nursery (£60,000); St Martins Housing Trust (£30,500); Friends of Billingford Windmill, Victim Support and YMCA Norfolk (£30,000 each); Break Charity (£28,500); Equal Lives (£24,000); North Norfolk Community Transport (£22,500); Wells Community Hospital (£20,500); Ormiston Children and Families Trust (£20,000).

FINANCES *Year* 2015 *Income* £4,308,000 *Grants* £2,232,161 *Grants to organisations* £2,149,087 *Assets* £18,445,000

TRUSTEES Lady Kay Fisher; Henry Cator; Bolton Agnew; Mary Rudd; Peter Franzen; Frank Eliel; Virginia Edgecombe; Jo Pearson; Jackie Higham; Charles Barratt; Charles Mawson; Timothy Seeley; Caroline McKenzie Money; Michael Gurney; Nick Pratt.

OTHER INFORMATION Grants were made to 453 community organisations and to 106 individuals (£83,000).

HOW TO APPLY Each fund has details of how to apply on the foundation's web page. Application processes usually take place online, consist of two parts and require submission of appropriate supporting documents.

WHO TO APPLY TO Grants Team, St James Mill, Whitefriars, Norwich NR3 1TN *Tel.* 01603 623958 *Fax* 01603 230036 *Email* info@norfolkfoundation.com *Website* www.norfolkfoundation.com

Educational Foundation of Alderman John Norman

CC NO 313105 **ESTABLISHED** 1962

WHERE FUNDING CAN BE GIVEN Norwich and Old Catton.

WHO CAN BENEFIT Individuals who are descendants of Alderman Norman; organisations benefitting children, young adults and students.

WHAT IS FUNDED The education of the descendants of Alderman Norman; general charitable purposes with a preference for education and training and services for young people.

WHAT IS NOT FUNDED No applications from outside Norwich and Old Catton will be considered.

RANGE OF GRANTS £300 to £15,000.

SAMPLE GRANTS Leeway Domestic Violence and Abuse Services (£15,000); Asperger East Anglia and Norfolk Carers Support (£10,000 each); Jubilee Sailing Trust and Ormiston Children and Families Trust (£5,000 each); Cinema City Ltd (£3,500); Angel Road Junior School and Total Ensemble Theatre Company (£2,000 each); Norfolk Fire and Rescue Service (£1,000); Sprowston Youth Engagement Project (£400).

FINANCES *Year* 2015/16 *Income* £278,382 *Grants* £263,670 *Grants to organisations* £114,535 *Assets* £7,519,565

TRUSTEES Revd Jonathan Boston; Roger Sandall; Dr Julia Leach; Revd Canon Martin Smith; Derek Armes; Tracey Hughes; Stephen Slack; Christopher Brown; Francis Whymark; James Hawkins; Roy Hughes.

OTHER INFORMATION Grants were made to 364 individuals descended from Alderman John Norman and totalled £110,000.

HOW TO APPLY Apply in writing to the correspondent.

WHO TO APPLY TO Nick Saffell, Clerk, The Atrium, St George's Street, Norwich NR3 1AB *Tel.* 01603 629871 *Email* nick.saffell@brown-co.com *Website* wp.normanfoundation.org.uk

The Norman Family Charitable Trust

CC NO 277616 **ESTABLISHED** 1979

WHERE FUNDING CAN BE GIVEN Primarily Cornwall, Devon and southern and western Somerset.

WHO CAN BENEFIT Registered charities only, preferably smaller, local organisations. National charities are only supported for projects helping the area of benefit.

WHAT IS FUNDED General charitable purposes, including: medical causes and medical research; sport and leisure; community projects; young people; individuals who are blind, deaf or have other physical disabilities; children's welfare; animals, environment and conservation; homelessness and social welfare; forces, ex-forces and emergency services; older people; mental health and learning disabilities; crime prevention, rehabilitation and addictions; employment and skills training.

WHAT IS NOT FUNDED Organisations which use live animals for experimental or research purposes; the maintenance or repair of religious buildings; projects outside the UK. Individuals are not supported directly.

TYPE OF GRANT One-off, project, research and start-up costs will be considered.

RANGE OF GRANTS Up to £30,000. Most grants are of £5,000 or less.

SAMPLE GRANTS Exeter Leukaemia Fund (£30,000); Exmouth Sea Scouts (£25,000); Devon Wildlife Trust (£15,000); St Peter's Church – Budleigh Salterton (£10,000); Resthaven (£7,000); Bristol Hospital for Sick Children, Exmouth Community College, Otterton Village Hall and Sports Aid South West (£5,000 each); Adventure Trust for Girls (£2,500).

FINANCES *Year* 2015/16 *Income* £433,678 *Grants* £378,695 *Grants to organisations* £376,695 *Assets* £8,987,523

TRUSTEES Roger Dawe; Margaret Evans; Michael Saunders; Margaret Webb; Catherine Houghton; Sarah Gillingham.

OTHER INFORMATION Grants were made to 321 organisations during the year and to one individual (£2,000).

HOW TO APPLY Full details of the application process and upcoming deadlines are available on the trust's website.

WHO TO APPLY TO Emma Le Poidevin, Grants Administrator, 14 Fore Street, Budleigh Salterton, Devon EX9 6NG *Tel.* 01395 446699 *Email* info@nfct.org *Website* www.nfct.org

The Normanby Charitable Trust

CC NO 252102 **ESTABLISHED** 1966

WHERE FUNDING CAN BE GIVEN UK, with a special interest in North Yorkshire and North East England.

WHO CAN BENEFIT Registered charities.

WHAT IS FUNDED General charitable purposes, particularly arts, culture, heritage and social welfare.

WHAT IS NOT FUNDED No grants are made to non-UK charities. Grants to individuals are only made exceptionally.

RANGE OF GRANTS £500 to £25,000.

SAMPLE GRANTS Blind Veterans UK (£25,000); The Royal Anthropological Institute (£20,000); Captain Cook Memorial Museum (£10,000); Coast and Vale Community Action (£8,000) Sunderland Women's Centre (£7,000); Yorkshire Air Ambulance (£5,000); The Runswick Bay Fisherman's Institute (£3,000); Butterfly School (£2,000); Crisis UK (£1,000); Tall Ships Youth Trust (£600).

FINANCES *Year* 2015/16 *Income* £330,438 *Grants* £238,622 *Grants to organisations* £238,622 *Assets* £11,127,690

TRUSTEES The Marquis of Normanby; The Dowager Marchioness of Normanby; Lady Lepel Kornicki; Lady Evelyn Buchan; Lady Peronel Cruz; Lady Henrietta Burridge.

OTHER INFORMATION Grants were made to 46 charitable organisations during the year.

HOW TO APPLY Apply in writing to the correspondent.

WHO TO APPLY TO The Marquis of Normanby, Trustee, 52 Tite Street, London SW3 4JA *Email* nct@normanby.org

North East Area Miners' Social Welfare Trust Fund

CC NO 504178 **ESTABLISHED** 1977

WHERE FUNDING CAN BE GIVEN North East England.

WHO CAN BENEFIT Miners' charities and miners.

WHAT IS FUNDED Social welfare; trips and outings; health of miners.

TYPE OF GRANT Equipment; refurbishment and building costs; events sponsorship.

SAMPLE GRANTS Ashington Rugby and Cricket Club; Dawdon Miners Welfare; Stobswood Miners Welfare; Harton and Westoe Miners Welfare; Seaham Sea Angling; Ellington Social Welfare Centre.

FINANCES *Year* 2015/16 *Income* £109,761 *Grants* £142,481 *Grants to organisations* £138,926 *Assets* £2,967,795

TRUSTEES Ian Lavery; William Etherington; Gerrard Huitson; Alan Cummings.

OTHER INFORMATION Grants made to individuals totalled £3,600 during the year. A full list of beneficiaries and grant amounts was not available.

HOW TO APPLY Apply in writing to the correspondent.

WHO TO APPLY TO Michael Lally, CISWO, 6 Bewick Road, Gateshead, Tyne and Wear NE8 4DP *Tel.* 01977 703384 *Email* ian.lally@ciswo.org.uk *Website* www.ciswo.org.uk

■ North London Charities Ltd

CC NO 312740 **ESTABLISHED** 1964

WHERE FUNDING CAN BE GIVEN North London.

WHO CAN BENEFIT Registered charities.

WHAT IS FUNDED Advancement of the Jewish Orthodox faith; general charitable purposes.

SAMPLE GRANTS Friends of Wiznitz; Lolev Trust; Wlodowa Trust; Viznitz Institutions; Belz Day Nursery; CMZ Trust; Achdut Ilford Torah Centre; Tchabe Kollel; Gateshead Academy.

FINANCES *Year* 2015/16 *Income* £155,406 *Grants* £822,405 *Grants to organisations* £822,405 *Assets* £837,159

TRUSTEES Heinrich Feldman; Shulom Feldman; Dvora Feldman; Israel Feldman.

HOW TO APPLY Apply in writing to the correspondent.

WHO TO APPLY TO Heinrich Feldman, Trustee, 23 Overlea Road, Springfield Park, London E5 9BG *Tel.* 020 8557 9557

■ North West Cancer Research (incorporating Clatterbridge Cancer Research)

CC NO 519357 **ESTABLISHED** 1987

WHERE FUNDING CAN BE GIVEN North West England and North Wales.

WHO CAN BENEFIT Universities.

WHAT IS FUNDED Cancer research in North West England and North Wales.

TYPE OF GRANT Project grants and equipment grants; studentships and fellowships.

SAMPLE GRANTS Bangor University; Lancaster University; University of Liverpool.

FINANCES *Year* 2015/16 *Income* £1,562,386 *Grants* £2,058,240 *Grants to organisations* £2,058,240 *Assets* £8,111,935

TRUSTEES Catherine Jones; Nigel Lanceley; Peter Somerfield; Francis Street; Moira Owen; Mark Haig; Catherine Bond; Hilary Atherton; Philip Robertshaw; Prof. David Sibson; Steven Smith.

OTHER INFORMATION Known as Clatterbridge Cancer Research (CCR), the charity in its current set-up was formed on 1 November 2012 when CCR merged with the North West Cancer Research Fund. The charity finances research at the University of Liverpool, Lancaster University and Bangor University.

HOW TO APPLY Application forms are available online along with full guidelines and deadlines.

WHO TO APPLY TO North West Cancer Research Centre, 200 London Road, Liverpool L3 9TA *Tel.* 0151 709 2919 *Fax* 0151 708 7997 *Email* info@nwcr.org *Website* www.nwcr.org

■ Provincial Grand Charity of Northamptonshire and Huntingdonshire

CC NO 1028243 **ESTABLISHED** 1993

WHERE FUNDING CAN BE GIVEN Northamptonshire and Huntingdonshire.

WHO CAN BENEFIT Registered charities; community groups; Masons.

WHAT IS FUNDED Masons and their dependants; general charitable purposes.

RANGE OF GRANTS £100 to £11,300.

SAMPLE GRANTS Sue Ryder Hospice (£25,000); Lifelites (£10,000); Peterborough Cathedral (£5,000); Leamington Rehab Hospice (£3,000); Voicability (£2,500); Peterborough Sea Scouts (£1,500); Colitis and Crohn's Disease Association (£1,000); Lincolnshire and Nottinghamshire Air Ambulance (£750); 49th Northampton Scouts (£500); Phoebe Research (£250).

FINANCES *Year* 2015 *Income* £146,271 *Grants* £91,203 *Grants to organisations* £91,203 *Assets* £618,998

TRUSTEES David Watson; David Burton; Jenny Higgins; Bill Wright; Allan Nicholls; Trevor Boswell; Gerry Crawford; Mark Constant; Mike Caseman-Jones; Charles Bennett; John Rivett.

OTHER INFORMATION Grants were made to 40 non-Masonic charities during the year.

HOW TO APPLY Apply in writing to the correspondent.

WHO TO APPLY TO William Wright, Secretary, 5 Spring Gardens, Burton Latimer, Kettering NN15 5NS *Tel.* 01536 420294 *Email* pgalmoner@northants-huntsmasons.org.uk

■ Northamptonshire Community Foundation

CC NO 1094646 **ESTABLISHED** 2001

WHERE FUNDING CAN BE GIVEN Northamptonshire.

WHO CAN BENEFIT Registered charities; local organisations; CICs.

WHAT IS FUNDED Community-based action benefitting Northamptonshire's most disadvantaged residents. Children's poverty, unemployment, homelessness, domestic violence and social exclusion are just some of the areas where the foundation looks to make a difference.

WHAT IS NOT FUNDED General and major fundraising appeals; direct replacement of statutory and public funding; work that is a statutory responsibility; schools (except 'Friends of' organisations) and parish councils; organisations aiming to convert people to any kind of religious or political belief; medical research and equipment; projects operating outside Northamptonshire; animal welfare; large national charities (except for local branches serving local people); work already completed; non-charitable work; projects that will redistribute the funding (with the exception of Surviving Winter grants). Each individual fund is subject to its own criteria and exclusions.

TYPE OF GRANT Project costs; salaries; equipment; building and renovation.

RANGE OF GRANTS Up to £10,000.

SAMPLE GRANTS Indian Hindu Welfare Organisation – Northampton (£10,000); Phoenix Community Cinema (£9,500); Free 2 Talk CIC (£8,500); Liberty Drum Corps, The Film Lab and The Salvation Army – Rushden (£5,000 each); Multiple Sclerosis Therapy Centre (£3,400); Northamptonshire Rape Crisis (£3,000); Heyford Athletic Football Club (£1,600); LGBT Partnership (£1,300); Deafconnect (£800).

FINANCES *Year* 2015/16 *Income* £1,299,468 *Grants* £1,050,645 *Grants to organisations* £987,795 *Assets* £262,066
TRUSTEES Paul Southworth; Guy Schanschieff; Anne Burnett; Sally Robinson; David Knight; Deirdre Newham; John Griffiths-Elsden; Paul Parsons; Dawn Thomas; Hassan Shah; Joanna Gordon.
OTHER INFORMATION The amount of grants given to individuals totalled £63,000.
HOW TO APPLY Application forms for each funding programme can be downloaded from the foundation's website, where criteria and guidelines are also posted. If you require support choosing the best fund for you or any support relating to the applications process, contact the grants team.
WHO TO APPLY TO Rachel McGrath, Grants Director, 18 Albion Place, Northampton NN1 1UD *Tel.* 01604 230033 *Email* enquiries@ncf.uk.com *Website* www.ncf.uk.com

■ The Community Foundation for Northern Ireland

IR NO XN45242 **ESTABLISHED** 1979
WHERE FUNDING CAN BE GIVEN Northern Ireland and the six border counties of the Republic of Ireland.
WHO CAN BENEFIT Community groups; voluntary organisations.
WHAT IS FUNDED Community development in Northern Ireland; peace building; social exclusion; poverty and social injustice.
TYPE OF GRANT One-off and recurrent.
RANGE OF GRANTS Generally between £1,000 and £5,000.
SAMPLE GRANTS Conflict Resolution Services and Ballymena Inter-Ethnic Forum (£5,000 each); Roe Valley Residents Association (£3,000); Foyle Down Syndrome Trust (£2,800); Feeny Community Association and British Red Cross (£2,000 each); Crafts With Love (£1,800); Fall Women's Centre and Newington Day Centre (£1,500 each); Lisburn Sea Cadets (£1,000); Burnfoot Seniors Group (£920); Scotch Youth Group (£450); Citizens Advice Fermanagh (£280).
FINANCES *Year* 2014/15 *Income* £10,000,000 *Grants* £3,600,000 *Grants to organisations* £3,600,000
TRUSTEES Maeve Monaghan; Joe McKnight; Fred Bass; John Healy; Niamh Goggin; Dawn Purvis; Les Allamby; Brian Dougherty; Shelley Martin; Grainne Browne; Michelle Canning; Dave Wall; Claire McGonigle.
OTHER INFORMATION As with any community foundation, funds open and close periodically. See the website for details of currently open funds. At the time of writing (June 2017) the latest accounts available were from 2014/15.
HOW TO APPLY General applications are not accepted. See the website for open funds, which each have their own criteria and exclusions.
WHO TO APPLY TO Grants Team, Community House, Citylink Business Park, 6A Albert Street, Belfast BT12 4HQ *Tel.* 028 9024 5927 *Email* info@communityfoundationni.org *Website* www.communityfoundationni.org

■ The Northmoor Trust

CC NO 256818 **ESTABLISHED** 1968
WHERE FUNDING CAN BE GIVEN UK.
WHO CAN BENEFIT Registered charities.
WHAT IS FUNDED The direct or indirect relief of poverty, hardship or distress.
WHAT IS NOT FUNDED Individuals; religion; medicine; the arts; general appeals. Grants are only made to organisations of which one or more of the trustees has direct personal knowledge.
TYPE OF GRANT One-off and recurrent.
RANGE OF GRANTS £5,000 to £20,000.
SAMPLE GRANTS Z2K (£20,000); Release (£15,000); 3 Acres Community Play Project and National AIDS Trust (£10,000 each); Blackbird Leys (£5,000).
FINANCES *Year* 2015/16 *Income* £63,552 *Grants* £55,000 *Grants to organisations* £55,000 *Assets* £1,492,775
TRUSTEES Viscount Runciman; Dame Ruth Runciman; Frances Bennett; Cathy Eastburn.
OTHER INFORMATION During the year four grants were awarded to charitable organisations.
HOW TO APPLY Apply in writing to the correspondent.
WHO TO APPLY TO Hilary Edwards, Secretary, 44 Clifton Hill, London NW8 0QG *Tel.* 020 7372 0698

■ Northumberland Village Homes Trust

CC NO 225429 **ESTABLISHED** 1988
WHERE FUNDING CAN BE GIVEN Tyne and Wear, Durham, Cleveland and Northumberland.
WHO CAN BENEFIT Charitable organisations.
WHAT IS FUNDED Social welfare; health; children and young people under the age of 21; education and training.
WHAT IS NOT FUNDED Gap year projects; medical purposes.
RANGE OF GRANTS £500 to £5,000.
SAMPLE GRANTS Barnardo's (£5,000); Newsham and New Delaval Youth Forum (£4,500); After Adoption and Cramlington Voluntary Youth Project Ltd (£3,000 each); CLIC Sargent, Engineering Development Trust and National Autistic Society (£2,000 each); Family Action (£1,200); Northumberland Clubs For Young People (£1,000); Birtley East Primary School (£500).
FINANCES *Year* 2015/16 *Income* £58,159 *Grants* £60,700 *Grants to organisations* £60,700 *Assets* £1,546,712
TRUSTEES Claire Macalpine; Lord Gisborough; Eileen Savage; Diana Barkes; Richard Savage.
OTHER INFORMATION Grants were made to 27 organisations during the year.
HOW TO APPLY Apply in writing to the correspondent.
WHO TO APPLY TO The Trustees, c/o Lambert Taylor and Gregory Solicitors, Robson House, 4 Middle Street, Corbridge NE45 5AT *Tel.* 01434 632505 *Email* corbridge@lambert-taylor-gregory.co.uk

■ The Northumbria Historic Churches Trust

CC NO 511314 **ESTABLISHED** 1980
WHERE FUNDING CAN BE GIVEN The dioceses of Durham and Newcastle.
WHO CAN BENEFIT Christian churches in the Church of England diocese of Durham or Newcastle which are either listed buildings or of historic interest.

WHAT IS FUNDED Repairs to the building.
WHAT IS NOT FUNDED New works; improvements; reinstatement of features; repair of furniture and fittings; repair or replacement of heating; lighting; bells; clocks; organs; stone cleaning; routine maintenance; clearing of gutters; replacement of slipped roof tiles; redecoration.
TYPE OF GRANT One-off awards, feasibility studies and buildings. Funding is for one year or less.
RANGE OF GRANTS £500 to £5,000.
SAMPLE GRANTS St Helen's Church – Auckland (£5,000); St Andrew's Church – Roker (£4,000); St Peter's Church – Craster (£3,000); St George's Church – Lower Middleton (£2,000); St Wilfred's Church – Kirkharle (£1,000).
FINANCES *Year* 2015/16 *Income* £47,680 *Grants* £34,000 *Grants to organisations* £34,000 *Assets* £230,653
TRUSTEES Lt Gen. Robin Brimms; Elizabeth Conran; Christopher Downs; Philip Scrope; Jeremy Kendall; Gillian Walker; Alyson Smith; Roger Norris; Revd Terence Hurst, Peter Ryder; Revd Canon Robert McTeer; Revd Canon John Ruscoe; Sir Josslyn Gore-Booth.
OTHER INFORMATION No grants are given to individuals.
HOW TO APPLY Application forms are available on the website and must be submitted online. Full guidelines on how to apply are available on the website.
WHO TO APPLY TO Peter De Lange, Secretary, 27 Devonshire Road, Sheffield S17 3NT *Tel.* 0114 236 7594 *Email* Secretary@NorthumbriaHCT.org.uk *Website* www.northumbriahct.org.uk

■ The Northwick Trust

CC NO 285197 **ESTABLISHED** 1982
WHERE FUNDING CAN BE GIVEN England and Wales.
WHO CAN BENEFIT Registered charities.
WHAT IS FUNDED Conservation and environment; social welfare; disability; young people.
SAMPLE GRANTS WaterAid (£35,000); Practical Action (£30,000); Flora and Fauna (£26,000); Alzheimer's Society (£15,000); The Children's Trust (£10,000); Mercy Ships (£7,000); Daylight Centre Fellowship (£5,000); Access All Areas (£2,000); Rainbow Development (£1,000).
FINANCES *Year* 2015/16 *Income* £342,198 *Grants* £365,000 *Grants to organisations* £365,000 *Assets* £10,389,014
TRUSTEES Lady Rachel Willcocks; Anne Wilcocks; Mary Morgan; Kate Willcocks; Xanthe Williams; Peter McCarthy; Andrew Laurie.
HOW TO APPLY Apply in writing to the correspondent.
WHO TO APPLY TO Anne Willcocks, 13 Queensway, Wellingborough NN8 3RA *Tel.* 01933 222986 *Email* petermc1711@btinternet.com

■ Northwood Charitable Trust

SC NO SC014487 **ESTABLISHED** 1972
WHERE FUNDING CAN BE GIVEN Scotland, especially Dundee and Tayside.
WHO CAN BENEFIT Registered charities; universities.
WHAT IS FUNDED General charitable purposes with a preference for health; medical research; the arts; heritage; social welfare.
TYPE OF GRANT One-off and recurring grants.
RANGE OF GRANTS Up to £200,000.
SAMPLE GRANTS University of Dundee Appeals (£200,000); Tayside Orthopaedic and Rehabilitation Technology Centre (£60,000); D. C. Thomson Charitable Trust (£75,000); Craigie Community Sports Hub (£50,000); Howe of Fife Rugby Club (£35,000); Dundee Women's Aid (£15,000); Brittle Bone Society (£14,000); Dundee Heritage Trust (£10,000); RNLI (£8,500).
FINANCES *Year* 2015/16 *Income* £2,842,930 *Grants* £2,540,576 *Grants to organisations* £2,540,576 *Assets* £80,783,872
OTHER INFORMATION Grants were made to 118 organisations throughout the year.
HOW TO APPLY The trust has previously stated that funds are fully committed and that no applications will be considered or acknowledged.
WHO TO APPLY TO The Trustees, c/o William Thomson and Sons, 22 Meadowside, Dundee DD1 1LN *Tel.* 01382 201534

■ The Norton Foundation

CC NO 702638 **ESTABLISHED** 1990
WHERE FUNDING CAN BE GIVEN Mainly Birmingham, Coventry and Warwickshire.
WHO CAN BENEFIT Registered and unregistered charitable organisations; schools; community groups.
WHAT IS FUNDED Children and young people under the age of 25 who require any help with the following: disability, drink/drug rehabilitation, medical issues, education and training; or who would benefit from counselling, holidays and social activities.
TYPE OF GRANT One-off capital grants and smaller recurring grants. Unrestricted funding.
RANGE OF GRANTS Up to £5,000.
SAMPLE GRANTS Skill Force Development (£5,000); Coventry Boys and Girls Club (£3,000); The Warwickshire Wheelchair Basketball Academy (£2,500); Birmingham Royal Ballet, Prisoners' Education Trust and Sport 4 Life UK (£2,000 each); Children with Cystic Fibrosis Dream Holidays (£1,500); Action 4 Bullying, Carers Forward Ltd and Sandwell Asian Development Association (£1,000 each).
FINANCES *Year* 2015/16 *Income* £143,369 *Grants* £511,643 *Grants to organisations* £466,363 *Assets* £4,523,337
TRUSTEES Jane Gaynor; Parminder Singh Birdi; Alan Bailey; Graham Suggett; Brian Lewis; Michael Bailey; Sarah Henderson; Richard Perkins; Richard Hurley; Bob Meacham; Louise Sewell; Wendy Carrington; William Pusey.
OTHER INFORMATION During the year, a total of 61 grants were made to organisations and 121 grants were made to individuals. Once every five years the trustees award a grant of circa £250,000 to an organisation for a capital project. In 2015/16, the grant was made to Birmingham and Solihull Women's Aid for the renovation and refurbishment of a refuge for young women and their children. A further exceptional grant of £125,000 was made to Leamington District Scout Council for replacement of their scout hut. Grants to other institutions throughout the year totalled £91,500.
HOW TO APPLY Applicants should send a completed application form to the correspondent. Guidance notes are available from the foundation's website. Applications from organisations are normally processed by the trustees at their quarterly meetings.
WHO TO APPLY TO The Trustees, c/o 50 Brookfield Close, Hunt End, Redditch, Worcestershire B97 9ZA *Tel.* 01527 544446 *Email* correspondent@nortonfoundation.org *Website* www.nortonfoundation.org

■ The Norton Rose Fulbright Charitable Foundation

CC NO 1102142 **ESTABLISHED** 2004

WHERE FUNDING CAN BE GIVEN Worldwide. The foundation also supports charities close to its London office in Southwark.

WHO CAN BENEFIT Registered charities; charitable organisations.

WHAT IS FUNDED Social welfare; medical causes; education; disaster relief.

RANGE OF GRANTS Up to £100,000, but typically under £15,000.

SAMPLE GRANTS Barretstown (£100,000); Action for Children (£40,000); South West London Law Centres (£25,000); MS Society (£20,500); Special Olympics (£35,000).

FINANCES *Year* 2015/16 *Income* £558,902 *Grants* £644,577 *Grants to organisations* £644,577 *Assets* £248,938

TRUSTEES Simon Cox; Patrick Farrell; Ffion Flockhart.

OTHER INFORMATION Grants were made to 74 organisations in the following categories: social welfare (£332,000); medical (£229,000); educational (£83,000). Grants of £15,000 or less totalled £396,000.

HOW TO APPLY Apply in writing to the correspondent. The foundation tends to support the same charities each year, but new charities are considered at trustee meetings. The trustees also meet on an ad hoc basis to consider specific urgent requests such as the support of major disaster relief appeals.

WHO TO APPLY TO Patrick Farrell, Trustee, 3 More London Riverside, London SE1 2AQ *Tel.* 020 7283 6000 *Website* www.nortonrosefulbright.com/uk

■ Norwich Town Close Estate Charity

CC NO 235678 **ESTABLISHED** 1892

WHERE FUNDING CAN BE GIVEN Within a 20-mile radius of the Guildhall of the City of Norwich.

WHO CAN BENEFIT Charitable organisations.

WHAT IS FUNDED Education.

WHAT IS NOT FUNDED Individuals who are not Freemen (or dependants of Freemen) of the City of Norwich; charities more than 20 miles from Norwich; charities which are not educational; revenue funding for educational charities; retrospective funding; salaries or running costs.

TYPE OF GRANT Buildings, capital, one-off and project costs. Matched funding is also available.

RANGE OF GRANTS £500 to £85,000.

SAMPLE GRANTS Cinema City Ltd (£85,000); Norwich Eagle Canoe Club Ltd and Norwich Hebrew Congregation (£50,000 each); Norwich Cathedral (£17,000); Moorlands Primary Academy (£10,000); Norfolk Wildlife Trust (£6,500); Norwich Playhouse (£5,500); University of East Anglia – Festival of Literature (£5,000); Norfolk Windmills Trust (£2,500); Royal Norfolk Agricultural Association (£2,000).

FINANCES *Year* 2015/16 *Income* £924,476 *Grants* £702,537 *Grants to organisations* £470,333 *Assets* £23,679,927

TRUSTEES John Rushmer; David Fullman; Brenda Ferris; Geoffrey Loades; Pamela Scutter; Philip Blanchflower; Nigel Back; Jeanne Southgate; Brenda Arthur; Robert Wellesley Self; Heather Tyrrell; Michael Quinton; James Symonds; David Barber; Stuart Lamb; Owen Gibbs.

OTHER INFORMATION There are close links with Norwich Consolidated Charities and Anguish's Educational Foundation. They share their administration processes and collaborate on grant-making. During the year 100 grants were made to individuals and 52 were made to organisations.

HOW TO APPLY Apply in writing to the correspondent. When submitting a request make sure to keep your application concise and provide details of any other financial support secured.

WHO TO APPLY TO Vanessa Soer, Grants Officer, 1 Woolgate Court, St Benedict's Street, Norwich NR2 4AP *Tel.* 01603 621023 *Email* info@norwichcharitabletrusts.org.uk *Website* www.norwichtowncloseestatecharity.org.uk

■ The Norwood and Newton Settlement

CC NO 234964 **ESTABLISHED** 1952

WHERE FUNDING CAN BE GIVEN England and Wales.

WHO CAN BENEFIT Methodist and other Free Churches. Occasionally, small charities in the London Borough of Havering.

WHAT IS FUNDED The promotion of Christianity.

WHAT IS NOT FUNDED The charity's website lists the following exclusions: 'Repairs and maintenance; salaries and running costs; equipment; lottery funded or application being processed; churches operating a policy of closed communion table; individuals; small schemes where the cost could be covered by the church or charity; small schemes made up of individual elements that could be undertaken as and when funding is available; small schemes that are purely to comply with Equalities Acts (e.g. ramps and WCs); schemes where building work has already been completed.'

TYPE OF GRANT One-off capital building projects.

RANGE OF GRANTS £2,000 to £20,000.

SAMPLE GRANTS Bridge Street Pentecostal Church – Leeds (£20,000); Lansdowne Baptist Church – Bournemouth (£15,000); Wicken Methodist Church – Ely (£10,000); St John's Methodist Church – Settle (£7,500); Tabor Baptist Church – Pontypridd (£5,000); Welling Methodist Church – Kent (£2,000).

FINANCES *Year* 2015/16 *Income* £364,290 *Grants* £305,500 *Grants to organisations* £305,500 *Assets* £9,042,403

TRUSTEES David Holland; Alan Gray; Stella Holland; Susan Newsom; Roger Lynch.

OTHER INFORMATION There were 27 grants made during the year. Of these grants, 14 were given to Methodist churches building new premises or making improvements to their existing premises.

HOW TO APPLY Apply in writing to the correspondent. In normal circumstances, an applicant is sent either a refusal or an application form inviting further information within a few days. Once satisfactory information is received, applications are considered by the trustees at quarterly meetings. Applicants are kept informed of the trustees' timescale at all times.

WHO TO APPLY TO David Holland, Trustee, 126 Beauly Way, Romford, Essex RM1 4XL *Tel.* 01708 723670 *Email* norwoodandnewton@btinternet.com *Website* norwoodandnewton.co.uk

■ The Notgrove Trust

CC NO 278692 **ESTABLISHED** 1979

WHERE FUNDING CAN BE GIVEN Gloucestershire.

WHO CAN BENEFIT Registered charities and charitable organisations.

WHAT IS FUNDED General charitable purposes.

WHAT IS NOT FUNDED Individuals; medical research; major national charities.

RANGE OF GRANTS £1,000 to £10,000.

SAMPLE GRANTS Cumbria Community Foundation (£10,000); Friends of Corinium Museum (£5,000); Brockworth Community Project (£3,000); Cleeve School, Greenwoods Therapeutic Horticulture, Stroud Sea Cadets and The Guiting Festival (£2,000 each); Birdlip Village Hall and Canterbury Association Music Trust (£1,000 each).

FINANCES *Year* 2015/16 *Income* £181,436 *Grants* £120,934 *Grants to organisations* £120,934 *Assets* £7,617,834

TRUSTEES David Acland; Elizabeth Acland; Harry Acland; Diana Acland.

OTHER INFORMATION Grants were made to 51 organisations during the year.

HOW TO APPLY Apply in writing to the correspondent, including a full copy of last year's accounts. Applications are not acknowledged and if the applicant has heard nothing within a month their application was unsuccessful. Applications by email are not accepted or acknowledged.

WHO TO APPLY TO Diana Acland, Trustee, The Manor, Notgrove, Cheltenham, Gloucestershire GL54 3BT *Tel.* 01451 850239 *Email* diana@notgrove.com *Website* notgroveholidays.com/notgrove-estate/#trust

■ Nottinghamshire Community Foundation

CC NO 1069538 **ESTABLISHED** 1998

WHERE FUNDING CAN BE GIVEN Nottinghamshire.

WHO CAN BENEFIT Voluntary and community groups.

WHAT IS FUNDED Mental health; children's poverty; community cohesion; older people.

WHAT IS NOT FUNDED Each fund has specific exclusions listed on the website.

RANGE OF GRANTS Up to £10,000.

SAMPLE GRANTS A list of beneficiaries was not available.

FINANCES *Year* 2015/16 *Income* £843,265 *Grants* £447,262 *Grants to organisations* £447,262 *Assets* £2,304,724

TRUSTEES Kevin Price; Lady Diana Meale; Amanda Farr; Simon Tipping; David Sneath; Veronica Pickering; Nikki Weston; Lynn Betts; Trevor Palmer; Thomas Gray; Mark Goldby; Alison Swan Parente.

OTHER INFORMATION A list of beneficiaries was not provided in the accounts.

HOW TO APPLY Refer to the website for full details on the criteria and application processes of the various funds currently being administered by the foundation.

WHO TO APPLY TO Nina Dauban, Chief Executive, Pine House B, Southwell Road West, Rainworth, Mansfield, Nottinghamshire NG21 0HJ *Tel.* 01623 620202 *Email* enquiries@nottscf.org.uk *Website* www.nottscf.org.uk

■ Nottinghamshire Historic Churches Trust

CC NO 518335 **ESTABLISHED** 1986

WHERE FUNDING CAN BE GIVEN Nottinghamshire and the Diocese of Sandwell and Nottingham.

WHO CAN BENEFIT Churches and chapels that are older than 30 years.

WHAT IS FUNDED The maintenance of churches and chapels including re-wiring; specialist cleaning of masonry and memorial; re-hanging of bells with new fittings; the restoration of a roof with sand case lead; the replacement of a wooden sanctuary floor; general repairs and drainage.

WHAT IS NOT FUNDED Modernisations, alterations or improvements, this includes: works of routine maintenance (repainting doors, non-specialist cleaning); new buildings, extensions, meeting rooms; disability access projects; coffee areas, sinks, new furniture; routine decoration (unless it requires some specialist materials); routine electrical work (new switches, lights, cables for new installations); repair of modern furniture, fittings, fixtures; overhead projector screens, sound systems, etc.; new bells; new bell frames entirely for new bells.

SAMPLE GRANTS A list of beneficiaries was not available.

FINANCES *Year* 2015/16 *Income* £48,686 *Grants* £115,450 *Grants to organisations* £115,450 *Assets* £107,704

TRUSTEES David Atkins; Anthony Marriott; Dr Christopher Brooke; Jennifer Mellors; Dr Jennifer Alexander; Prof. John Beckett; Richard Brackenbury; Richard Assheton Craven-Smith-Milnes; Revd Canon Keith Turner; Graeme Renton; Keith Goodman; Andrew Paris; Prof. Michael Jones; Malcolm Stacey.

OTHER INFORMATION A list of beneficiaries was not included in the most recent accounts.

HOW TO APPLY Grant application forms along with guidance notes and details of deadlines are available to download from the trust's website. Alternatively, a paper application form can be obtained from the correspondent.

WHO TO APPLY TO Margaret Lowe, Grants Administrator, 1 Gayhurst Green, Park Lane, Old Basford, Nottingham NG6 0LZ *Tel.* 0115 972 6590 *Email* info.nhct@gmail.com *Website* nottshistoricchurchtrust.org.uk

■ The Nuffield Foundation

CC NO 206601 **ESTABLISHED** 1943

WHERE FUNDING CAN BE GIVEN UK; southern and eastern Africa.

WHO CAN BENEFIT Universities; independent research institutions; voluntary sector organisations.

WHAT IS FUNDED Science and social science research into children and families; early years education; economics; education; 'finances of ageing' (financial and economic aspects of individual and population ageing); law in society.

WHAT IS NOT FUNDED Running costs of voluntary bodies, the continuing provision of a service, or any general appeal for pooled funding; capital or building costs; grants solely for purchase of equipment (including computers); grants simply to support or attend conferences or seminars; projects that could be considered by a government department, a research council or a more appropriate charity; the establishment of chairs or other permanent academic posts; projects led by individuals unaffiliated with an organisation; the production of films or videos; exhibitions; school fees, higher education/university fees, or a gap year projects; requests for funding for financial help from or on behalf of individuals in distress; projects led by schools, undergraduates, master's degree students or work towards a PhD; animal rights or welfare; the arts; conservation, heritage or environmental projects; housing; medical, health or health services research; museums, buildings or capital costs; religion; sports and recreation.

TYPE OF GRANT One-off grants for projects.

RANGE OF GRANTS Up to £245,000.

SAMPLE GRANTS University College London (£1.58 million in six grants); University of Exeter (£634,000 in two grants); Brunel University (£460,000 in two grants); London School of Economics (£410,000 in five grants); Institute for Fiscal Studies (£338,000 in two grants); University of Nottingham (£245,000); University of Oxford (£230,000 in two grants); Royal Geographical Society (£193,500); Food Foundation (£173,500); King's College London (£136,000 in two grants); National Centre for Social Research (£99,000); Prison Reform Trust (£48,500); National Institute of Economic and Social Research (£32,000); Think Global Development Education Association (£28,500); Freud Centre (£26,000); Michael Sieff Foundation (£25,000); University of York (£8,800).

FINANCES *Year* 2015 *Income* £6,637,000 *Grants* £4,405,000 *Grants to organisations* £4,405,000 *Assets* £307,511,000

TRUSTEES Lord Krebs; Prof. Sir David Rhind; Dame Colette Bowe; Prof. James Banks; Prof. Terrie Moffitt; Rt Hon. Lord Justice Ernest Ryder; Prof. Anna Vignoles.

OTHER INFORMATION The foundation received 455 initial applications, considered 89 full applications and made grants to 34 organisations. Of the grants awarded, 24 went to universities (worth £4 million); 6 went to voluntary organisations (worth £500,000); and 4 went to research institutes (worth £500,000). Many of the funding programmes have individual funding criteria and guidelines which are not listed here. Consult the foundation's excellent website before applying.

HOW TO APPLY The application process is the same for all of the research and innovation grant programmes. The foundation publishes an extensive 'Grants for Research and Innovation – Guide for Applicants' brochure available to download from the website, which should be read by any potential applicant. The first stage is to submit an outline application which will be considered and then the proposal may be shortlisted for consideration by trustees. In this case applicants will be asked to submit a full application. The trustees meet three times a year to consider applications, in March, July and November. Deadlines for these meetings are four months before for outline applications then two months before for full applications; exact deadlines are available on the website.

WHO TO APPLY TO James Turner, Finance Director, 28 Bedford Square, London WC1B 3JS *Tel.* 020 7631 0566 *Email* info@nuffieldfoundation.org *Website* www.nuffieldfoundation.org

■ The Father O'Mahoney Memorial Trust

CC NO 1039288 **ESTABLISHED** 1993

WHERE FUNDING CAN BE GIVEN Worldwide.

WHO CAN BENEFIT Charitable organisations; individuals.

WHAT IS FUNDED Missionary work; medical and educational projects in lower- and middle-income countries.

WHAT IS NOT FUNDED Gap year projects; causes benefitting the UK.

RANGE OF GRANTS Up to £6,000.

SAMPLE GRANTS International Refugee trust (£6,000); St Mary's Charitable Trust (£4,000 in two grants); Africa Mission and Catholic Agency for Overseas Development (£3,000 each); Concern Worldwide, Microloan, Pump Aid, Special Projects in Catholic Missionary Areas and Uganda Development (£2,000 each); Azadi Trust Birmingham (£1,200); St John's of Jerusalem (£500).

FINANCES *Year* 2015/16 *Income* £52,382 *Grants* £51,860 *Grants to organisations* £51,860 *Assets* £71,668

TRUSTEES Christopher Carney-Smith; Creina Hearn; Don Maclean; Michael Moran; Revd Gerard Murray; Maureen Jennings; Brenda Carney; Hugh Smith.

OTHER INFORMATION The trust made grants to at least two individuals totalling £3,500 but a full list of beneficiaries was not included in the accounts.

HOW TO APPLY Apply in writing to the correspondent. The trustees meet every two months to consider applications.

WHO TO APPLY TO Hugh Smith, Trustee, Our Lady of the Wayside Church and Presbytery, 566 Stratford Road, Shirley, Solihull, West Midlands B90 4AY *Email* trust@olwayside.fsnet.co.uk

■ The Sir Peter O'Sullevan Charitable Trust

CC NO 1078889 **ESTABLISHED** 2000

WHERE FUNDING CAN BE GIVEN Worldwide.

WHO CAN BENEFIT Charitable organisations.

WHAT IS FUNDED Animal welfare; horses.

TYPE OF GRANT One-off and recurrent.

RANGE OF GRANTS £5,000 to £50,000.

SAMPLE GRANTS Blue Cross, Compassion in World Farming, Racing Welfare Charities, The Brooke, The Thoroughbred Rehabilitation Centre and World Horse Welfare (£50,000 each); Demelza (£7,500) Philip Mitchell Smokey and Prince Fluffy Kareem (£5,000 each).

FINANCES *Year* 2015/16 *Income* £8,657,537 *Grants* £317,500 *Grants to organisations* £317,500 *Assets* £8,218,258

TRUSTEES Nigel Payne; Geoffrey Hughes; Michael Dillon; John McManus; Michael Kerr-Dineen; Sir Anthony McCoy.

OTHER INFORMATION The trust has committed grants of £50,000 each to six charities which it awards on a yearly basis.

HOW TO APPLY Apply in writing to the correspondent. Further guidance is available on the trust's website.

WHO TO APPLY TO Nigel Payne, Trustee, The Old School, Bolventor, Launceston, Cornwall PL15 7TS *Tel.* 01566 880292 *Email* nigel@earthsummit.demon.co.uk *Website* www.thevoiceofracing.com

■ The Oakdale Trust

CC NO 218827 **ESTABLISHED** 1950

WHERE FUNDING CAN BE GIVEN UK (mainly Wales) and overseas.

WHO CAN BENEFIT UK-based and registered charities; exempt charities; voluntary/community groups.

WHAT IS FUNDED Social and community projects based in Wales; medical support groups in Wales; UK-based medical research projects; environmental conservation projects; the arts (where there is a Welsh connection); UK-based and registered charities working in financially developing countries; penal reform.

WHAT IS NOT FUNDED Individuals; holiday schemes; sport activities; expeditions.

TYPE OF GRANT Project and core funding.

RANGE OF GRANTS Between £250 and £2,000. The average grant is £750.

SAMPLE GRANTS SwimNarberth (£14,000); Radnorshire Wildlife Trust (£5,000); Cwm Community Action Group (£3,000); CARE Pakistan, International Spinal Research Trust and The University of Sheffield (£1,000 each); Ebbw Valley Brass (£750); Prison Fellowship England and Wales and Volcano Theatre (£500 each); Coychurch Primary School and The Firing Line Museum (£250 each).

FINANCES *Year* 2015/16 *Income* £1,887,043 *Grants* £229,100 *Grants to organisations* £229,100 *Assets* £12,146,725

TRUSTEES Rupert Cadbury; Bruce Cadbury; Olivia Tatton-Brown; Dr Rebecca Cadbury.

OTHER INFORMATION Repeat applications are not normally accepted within a two-year period.

HOW TO APPLY Apply in writing via the website or post. Full guidelines, including closing dates for applications, are published on the website. The trust states that it will accept telephone calls; however, messages should not be left on the answerphone as this is for private use only.

WHO TO APPLY TO Rupert Cadbury, Trustee, Tansor House, Main Street, Tansor, Peterborough PE8 5HS *Tel.* 01832 226386 *Email* oakdale@tanh.co.uk *Website* www.oakdaletrust.org.uk

■ The Oakley Charitable Trust

CC NO 233041 **ESTABLISHED** 1963

WHERE FUNDING CAN BE GIVEN UK, but predominantly the West Midlands and Channel Isles.

WHO CAN BENEFIT Registered charities.

WHAT IS FUNDED Arts; heritage; welfare; education.

WHAT IS NOT FUNDED Individuals; overseas charities; non-registered charities; retrospective projects.

TYPE OF GRANT One-off awards, core costs, project funding, research, recurring costs and buildings. Funding is available for one year or less.

RANGE OF GRANTS £250 to £3,000.

SAMPLE GRANTS Birmingham Royal Ballet and RNLI (£3,000 each); Acorns Children's Hospice (£2,500); Birmingham Botanical Gardens (£2,000); Durrell Wildlife Conservation Trust (£1,500); Jersey Animal Shelter (£1,000); Asthma Relief, Firefighters Charity and Pen Museum (£500 each); Riding for the Disabled – Jersey (£250).

FINANCES *Year* 2015/16 *Income* £76,506 *Grants* £59,195 *Grants to organisations* £59,195 *Assets* £2,244,585

TRUSTEES Christine Airey; Geoffrey Oakley; Simon Sharp.
OTHER INFORMATION Grants were made to 48 organisations during the year.
HOW TO APPLY Apply in writing to the correspondent; including the details of the project and the amount you need. You cannot apply by email. The trustees meet in March, July and November.
WHO TO APPLY TO Geoffrey Oakley, Trustee, 10 St Mary's Road, Harborne, Birmingham B17 0HA *Tel.* 0121 427 7150 *Website* www.oakleycharitabletrust.org.uk

■ Odin Charitable Trust

CC NO 1027521 **ESTABLISHED** 1993
WHERE FUNDING CAN BE GIVEN UK.
WHO CAN BENEFIT UK-registered charities.
WHAT IS FUNDED General charitable purposes with preference for: the arts; care for people with disabilities; disadvantaged people; hospices; homeless people; prisoners' families; refugees; Roma and tribal groups; research into false memories and dyslexia.
WHAT IS NOT FUNDED Individuals.
TYPE OF GRANT One-off and recurrent.
RANGE OF GRANTS Usually between £1,000 and £5,000.
SAMPLE GRANTS British False Memory Society (£30,000); Shelter (£5,000); Bag Books, Roma Support Group, Survival International, Wessex Children's Hospice Naomi House and Wiltshire Music Centre (£3,000 each); Edinburgh Young Carers Project (£2,500); Contact the Elderly, Refugee Support Devon and The Big Issue Foundation (£2,000 each); Brighton and Hove Unwaged (£1,000).
FINANCES *Year* 2015/16 *Income* £467,569 *Grants* £316,000 *Grants to organisations* £316,000 *Assets* £6,795,470
TRUSTEES Susan Scotford; Mrs A. H. Palmer; Donna Kelly; Pia Cherry.
HOW TO APPLY Applications should be submitted in the form of a letter or email and contain the following information: aims and objectives of the charity, nature of the appeal, total target, if for a specific project, registered charity number, any other relevant factors. Letters should be accompanied by a set of the charitable organisation's latest report and full accounts and should be addressed to the correspondent.
WHO TO APPLY TO Susan Scotford, Trustee, PO Box 1898, Bradford-on-Avon, Wiltshire BA15 1YS *Tel.* 020 7465 4300

■ The Ofenheim Charitable Trust

CC NO 286525 **ESTABLISHED** 1983
WHERE FUNDING CAN BE GIVEN Worldwide, in practice the UK with some preference for East Sussex.
WHO CAN BENEFIT Registered charities.
WHAT IS FUNDED General charitable purposes, particularly: health; welfare; the arts, animals; the environment.
WHAT IS NOT FUNDED Individuals.
TYPE OF GRANT One-off and recurrent.
RANGE OF GRANTS Between £2,500 and £12,000; however, the vast majority of grants were of £5,500 or less.
SAMPLE GRANTS Royal Trinity Hospice (£12,000); Friends of the Elderly, Help Musicians UK and Saint Mungo's (£10,000 each); Glyndebourne Arts Trust, Motor Neurone Disease Association and National Trust (£5,500); Game and Wildlife Conservation Trust (£3,500); British Wheelchair Sports Foundation, Red Squirrel Survival Trust and Sir John Soane's Museum (£2,500).
FINANCES *Year* 2015/16 *Income* £450,709 *Grants* £369,000 *Grants to organisations* £369,000 *Assets* £13,793,604
TRUSTEES Roger Clark; Rory McLeod; Alexander Clark; Fiona Byrd.
OTHER INFORMATION Grants were made to 70 organisations during the year.
HOW TO APPLY Apply in writing to the correspondent.
WHO TO APPLY TO The Trustees, c/o RSM UK Tax and Accounting Ltd, The Pinnacle, 170 Midsummer Boulevard, Milton Keynes MK9 1BP *Tel.* 01908 687800

■ The Ogle Christian Trust

CC NO 1061458 **ESTABLISHED** 1938
WHERE FUNDING CAN BE GIVEN Worldwide.
WHO CAN BENEFIT Registered charities.
WHAT IS FUNDED The advancement of the Christian faith; evangelism worldwide; support of missionary enterprises; Bible student training; help to retired missionary workers and to famine and relief organisations.
WHAT IS NOT FUNDED Individuals; building projects; general appeals from large national organisations; salaries.
RANGE OF GRANTS £2,000 to £35,000. Usually under £5,000.
SAMPLE GRANTS Operation Mobilisation (£35,000); Tearfund (£13,000); The Balkan Protestant Research Trust (£7,500); Uganda River of Life (£5,000); Community Health Global Network, ELAM Ministries and Solomon Academic Trust (£3,000 each); Make Jesus Known (£2,500); 3P Ministries (£2,000).
FINANCES *Year* 2015/16 *Income* £114,710 *Grants* £162,150 *Grants to organisations* £162,150 *Assets* £2,270,364
OTHER INFORMATION During the year, 49 grants were made to individuals totalling £26,000.
HOW TO APPLY Apply in writing to the correspondent. Appeals should be accompanied by relevant documents and an sae. Our research suggests that trustees meet in May and November, but applications can be made at any time.
WHO TO APPLY TO Fiona Putley, Secretary, 43 Woolstone Road, Forest Hill, London SE23 2TR *Tel.* 020 8699 1036

■ Oglesby Charitable Trust

CC NO 1026669 **ESTABLISHED** 1993
WHERE FUNDING CAN BE GIVEN The north west of England.
WHO CAN BENEFIT Registered charities.
WHAT IS FUNDED Artistic development; educational grants and building projects; environmental projects; social inequality; medical aid and research.
WHAT IS NOT FUNDED Non-registered charities; activities with the purpose of redistributing collected funds to other charities; animal charities; charities mainly operating outside the UK; church and all building fabric materials; conferences; continuing running costs of an organisation; costs of employing fundraisers; expeditions; general sports, unless there is an association with a disadvantaged group; holidays; individuals; loans or business finance; charities promoting religion; routine staff training; sponsorship and marketing appeals.
TYPE OF GRANT Capital projects; research; collection and acquisition of art.
RANGE OF GRANTS Typically less than £50,000.

SAMPLE GRANTS Seashell Trust (£500,000); Manchester Cancer Research Centre (£112,500); Leukaemia and Lymphoma Research (£100,000); Community Forest Trust (£87,000); Manchester Cathedral (£50,000); Centre for Social Justice Families (£33,500); After Adoption (£30,000); Ancoats Dispensary Trust (£28,000); Manchester Carers Forum and The Clink Charity (£25,000 each).
FINANCES *Year* 2014/15 *Income* £5,676,539 *Grants* £2,258,162 *Grants to organisations* £2,258,162 *Assets* £10,166,489
TRUSTEES Jean Oglesby; Michael Oglesby; Bob Kitson; Kate Vokes; Jane Oglesby; Chris Oglesby; Peter Renshaw.
OTHER INFORMATION The latest accounts available at the time of writing (May 2017) were for 2014/15.
HOW TO APPLY The trust does not accept unsolicited applications.
WHO TO APPLY TO PO Box 336, Altrincham, Cheshire WA14 3XD *Email* welcome@oglesbycharitabletrust.org.uk *Website* www.oglesbycharitabletrust.co.uk

■ Oizer Charitable Trust

CC NO 1014399 **ESTABLISHED** 1992
WHERE FUNDING CAN BE GIVEN UK with a preference to Greater Manchester.
WHO CAN BENEFIT Jewish organisations.
WHAT IS FUNDED Causes within the Jewish community, particularly the provision of Orthodox Jewish education and the advancement of the Jewish religion according to the Orthodox Jewish faith.
TYPE OF GRANT Typically recurrent.
SAMPLE GRANTS The Bersam Trust (£12,500); B'nos Yisroel (£2,000).
FINANCES *Year* 2015/16 *Income* £664,404 *Grants* £438,350 *Grants to organisations* £438,350 *Assets* £2,676,191
TRUSTEES Joshua Halpern; Cindy Halpern.
HOW TO APPLY Apply in writing to the correspondent.
WHO TO APPLY TO Joshua Halpern, Trustee, c/o Lopian Gross Barnett and Co., 6th Floor, Cardinal House, 20 St Mary's Parsonage, Manchester M3 2LG *Tel.* 0161 832 8721

■ Old Possum's Practical Trust

CC NO 328558 **ESTABLISHED** 1990
WHERE FUNDING CAN BE GIVEN UK.
WHO CAN BENEFIT Registered charities; individuals.
WHAT IS FUNDED Literary, artistic, musical and theatrical projects; people who have a disability; people who are disadvantaged.
WHAT IS NOT FUNDED Activities or projects already completed; capital building projects; personal training and education (e.g. tuition or living costs for college or university); projects outside the UK; medical care or resources; feasibility studies; national charities that are likely to receive substantial amounts from other sources.
TYPE OF GRANT Typically recurrent.
RANGE OF GRANTS £1,500 to £110,000. Most grants fall between £500 and £5,000.
SAMPLE GRANTS Beckett Festival (£110,000); Shoreditch Town Hall (£50,000); St Stephen's Church (£25,000); The National Portrait Gallery (£15,000); Chickenshed Theatre Company, Eton College and The Book Trade Charity (£10,000 each); Garsington Opera Education (£6,000); Action for Youth (£2,000); The Little Angel Theatre (£1,500).
FINANCES *Year* 2015/16 *Income* £218,947 *Grants* £6,703,910 *Grants to organisations* £6,703,910 *Assets* £9,568,496
TRUSTEES Judith Hooper; Deidre Simpson; Clare Reihill.
OTHER INFORMATION Grants were made to 18 institutions during the year. The T. S. Eliot Foundation received three grants during the year totalling almost £6.4 million.
HOW TO APPLY Applications can only be made online through the trust's website. The trustees meet regularly to consider applications but state in the latest accounts that: 'The emphasis will be on continued support of those institutions and individuals who have received support in the past. Unfortunately we have to disappoint the great majority of applicants who nevertheless continue to send appeal letters. The Trustees do not welcome telephone calls or emails from applicants soliciting funds.' To keep administration costs to a minimum the trust does not give reasons for unsuccessful applications or allow applicants to appeal a decision.
WHO TO APPLY TO The Trustees, PO Box 5701, Milton Keynes MK9 2WZ *Tel.* 01908 687800 *Email* generalenquiry@old-possums-practical-trust.org.uk *Website* www.old-possums-practical-trust.org.uk

■ The John Oldacre Foundation

CC NO 284960 **ESTABLISHED** 1981
WHERE FUNDING CAN BE GIVEN UK.
WHO CAN BENEFIT Universities, agricultural colleges.
WHAT IS FUNDED Research and education in agricultural sciences.
WHAT IS NOT FUNDED Tuition fees.
TYPE OF GRANT One-off, recurrent, feasibility, project and research grants, and funding up to three years will be considered.
RANGE OF GRANTS Up to £52,000.
SAMPLE GRANTS Harper Adams (£65,000 in three grants); University of Bristol (£52,000); Royal Agricultural College (£40,000 in two grants); Oxford University (£25,000); Nuffield Farming Trust (£22,000); University of Exeter (£21,500); National Institute of Agricultural Botany (NIAB) (£14,900).
FINANCES *Year* 2015/16 *Income* £157,509 *Grants* £201,392 *Grants to organisations* £201,392 *Assets* £10,983,552
TRUSTEES Henry Bonner Shouler; Harvey Grove; Jill Sinnott.
HOW TO APPLY Apply in writing to the correspondent.
WHO TO APPLY TO Henry Bonner Shouler, Trustee, Hazleton House, Hazleton, Cheltenham, Gloucestershire GL54 4EB *Tel.* 01451 860752 *Email* h.shouler@btinternet.com

■ The Oldham Foundation

CC NO 269263 **ESTABLISHED** 1974
WHERE FUNDING CAN BE GIVEN UK and overseas.
WHO CAN BENEFIT Small registered charities; former employees of Oldham International Ltd.
WHAT IS FUNDED Arts, culture and recreation; conservation and environment; animal welfare and churches; relief of former employees of Oldham International Ltd.
WHAT IS NOT FUNDED General appeals; individuals.
RANGE OF GRANTS £200 to £22,000. Most grants are for less than £2,000.
SAMPLE GRANTS Cheltenham Festivals (£22,000); Classic FM (£7,500); Burton Bradstock Music Festival (£1,500); Bath Mozartfest and Dogs

Trust (£1,000 each); Bath Philharmonia, Batheaston Youth Club and Wilton Music Centre Trust Ltd (£500 each); Friends of the Strays of Greece (£350); Churches Conservation Trust (£250); CLIC Sargent and Vale Wildlife Hospital and Rehabilitation Centre (£200 each).

FINANCES *Year* 2015/16 *Income* £61,054 *Grants* £70,685 *Grants to organisations* £58,125 *Assets* £1,263,035

TRUSTEES John Wetherherd Sharpe; John Oldham; Dinah Oldham; Stephen Roberts; Michael Davies.

OTHER INFORMATION Although the foundation does not award grants to individuals, it does make a fixed annual distribution to Oldham pensioners. In 2015/16 the foundation granted £12,500 to Oldham pensioners as well as awarding grants to 26 organisations.

HOW TO APPLY Apply in writing to the correspondent. Telephone calls are not welcomed. The trustees meet annually but applications can be considered between meetings. Inappropriate appeals are not acknowledged.

WHO TO APPLY TO John Wetherherd Sharpe, Trustee, c/o Michelmores LLP, Broad Quay House, Broad Quay, Bristol BS1 4DJ *Tel.* 0117 906 9313

■ The Olga Charitable Trust

CC NO 277925 **ESTABLISHED** 1979

WHERE FUNDING CAN BE GIVEN UK and overseas.

WHO CAN BENEFIT Registered charities.

WHAT IS FUNDED General charitable purposes, particularly: children and young people; health; social welfare.

RANGE OF GRANTS £100 to £10,000.

SAMPLE GRANTS Merchiston Castle School (£10,000); Miracles (£5,000); Cornerstone (£2,000); Crisis UK, Chestnut Tree House Children's Hospice and Greenfingers (£1,000 each); Reprieve (£500); Quintessentially Foundation (£200); Royal Society of Arts (£170); Cure Parkinson's Trust (£100).

FINANCES *Year* 2015/16 *Income* £49,265 *Grants* £40,168 *Grants to organisations* £40,168 *Assets* £966,674

TRUSTEES HRH Princess Alexandra; James Ogilvy.

HOW TO APPLY Grants are only made to charities of which the trustees have direct knowledge or with which they are personally involved.

WHO TO APPLY TO Adam Broke, Fleet Place House, 2 Fleet Place, London EC4M 7RF *Tel.* 020 7236 2601 *Email* simoncoggins@mercerhole.co.uk

■ The Onaway Trust

CC NO 268448 **ESTABLISHED** 1974

WHERE FUNDING CAN BE GIVEN USA and worldwide.

WHO CAN BENEFIT Registered charities.

WHAT IS FUNDED The preservation of tribal and indigenous cultures, languages and lifestyles; the conservation of tribal and indigenous lands; research and dissemination of information about tribal and indigenous communities.

WHAT IS NOT FUNDED Administration costs; travel expenses; projects considered unethical or detrimental to the struggle of indigenous people; individuals; political organisations; religious centres; organisations without charitable status or with an income greater than £250,000 per annum.

TYPE OF GRANT Seed funding.

RANGE OF GRANTS £330 to £12,000.

SAMPLE GRANTS Disasters Emergency Committee Nepal Earthquake Appeal (£12,000); Cloud Horse Art Institute (£10,100); Friends of Hope India (£9,700 in two grants); Fundacion Tradiciones (£8,500); Plenty (£8,000 in three grants); Acaté Amazon Conservation (£7,400); Thunder Valley (£6,700); Maya Maya First (£5,000); Paramedical Educational (£2,900); Owe Aku International (£970); Help Tsieboos (£330).

FINANCES *Year* 2015 *Income* £159,162 *Grants* £85,422 *Grants to organisations* £85,422 *Assets* £4,783,591

TRUSTEES Andy Breslin; Andrew Macnaughton; David Watters; Valerie Worwood.

OTHER INFORMATION Grants were made to 18 organisations during the year, including a one-off donation to the Disasters Emergency Committee in response to an appeal following the earthquake in Nepal.

HOW TO APPLY The 2015 annual report stated that: 'In 2015 the board agreed to remove its online application form from its website as ninety per cent were unsuccessful and consideration of these had proved onerous and unproductive. All future applications were to be generated from the new social media efforts being adopted and would solicit new projects from existing contacts and personal recommendations.'

WHO TO APPLY TO David Watters, Trust Director, Donavourd Farmhouse, Donavourd, Pitlochry PH16 5JS *Tel.* 07789 743236 *Email* andrew.macnaughton@onaway.org *Website* www.onaway.org

■ One Community Foundation Ltd

CC NO 1135258 **ESTABLISHED** 2009

WHERE FUNDING CAN BE GIVEN Kirklees.

WHO CAN BENEFIT Voluntary and community groups; not-for-profit organisations; charities.

WHAT IS FUNDED General charitable purposes including: environment; older people; sport; children and young people.

WHAT IS NOT FUNDED Party political activity; promotion of religion; replacement of statutory funding; projects that have already started; groups which have not complied with previous monitoring requirements.

SAMPLE GRANTS A list of beneficiaries was not available.

FINANCES *Year* 2015/16 *Income* £268,442 *Grants* £117,068 *Grants to organisations* £117,068 *Assets* £1,520,396

TRUSTEES Judith Charlesworth; Jeremy Garside; Sir John Harman; Addul Aslam; Ian Brierley; Julie Stewart-Turner; Eric Firth; Jonathan Thornton.

HOW TO APPLY Applications can be made via the foundation's website.

WHO TO APPLY TO Beverley Couldwell, c/o Chadwick Lawrence Solicitors, 13 Railway Street, Huddersfield HD1 1JS *Tel.* 01484 468397 *Email* info@one-community.org.uk *Website* www.one-community.org.uk

■ OneFamily Foundation (known as Engage Foundation)

ESTABLISHED 2014

WHERE FUNDING CAN BE GIVEN UK.

WHO CAN BENEFIT Local community organisations and projects.

WHAT IS FUNDED A wide range of general charitable purposes and community causes. The foundation offers Community Awards of up to £5,000, £10,000 or £25,000 for community projects nominated by OneFamily customers.

There are four categories: active living; community groups; health, disability and social care; lifelong learning. Further detail is given on the website. The foundation also awards Personal Grants of up to £1,000 to help individual OneFamily customers in need.

WHAT IS NOT FUNDED Support for commercial or profit-making ventures; funding toward property bills (rent/mortgage payments, utility bills, maintenance costs, etc.), although funding towards room/facility hire may be considered; financial contribution directly towards salaries (staffing costs on an hourly basis may be considered if a necessary part of a project); funding for paid for advertising; general contributions towards large appeals or fundraising (although stand-alone items may be considered); promotion of political parties/ groups/factions; advancement of religion/faith, including projects that promote religious advocacy, attempt to convert people to another religion, or attempt to expand membership; projects involving any form of mandatory religious study or discriminate against any faith or group (although groups may be eligible for secular and inclusive community-based activities, e.g. a food bank run by a local church); refreshments for attendees of a project; groups where membership or other participation costs are considered by the foundation to be prohibitive; overseas travel or activities outside the UK; transport or entry fees for sites or attractions; regional or local offices of a national organisation (local community groups affiliated to a national organisation are only considered if they are not eligible for, or receiving, funding for the project from the parent organisation); improvements to land or buildings that are generally not open or accessible for use by members of the community; contingency amounts provided for in any project budget; deficit or retrospective funding; organisations that are for the sole relief or benefit of animals and plants; projects that have received substantial funding from another grant provider within 12 months prior to the date of the nomination; projects that are connected to for-profit business ventures or that financially compensate an idea creator beyond fair wage; use of the award amount as or part of a raffle, chance or lottery prize.

TYPE OF GRANT Project costs.

RANGE OF GRANTS Up to £5,000; up to £10,000; up to £25,000.

SAMPLE GRANTS 2nd Cuddington Scouts, Cornwall Athletic Club and Playskill (£25,000 each); Alverstoke Junior School Library, Kilsyth Woodland Music Project, Ripon Walled Garden Sensory Garden, Plymstock Cricket Club, She Sanctuary Girls' Group and Total Recall Memories Choir (£5,000 each).

FINANCES *Year* 2016 *Grants* £505,000 *Grants to organisations* £505,000

OTHER INFORMATION Engage Mutual and Family Investments merged in 2015 to become OneFamily. The foundation is not a registered charity and so there were no accounts or annual report to view. The website lists the Community Grants awarded in 2016, which totalled £505,000 altogether and were made to 65 projects across two rounds of funding.

HOW TO APPLY Nominations for a project to support can be made by OneFamily customers on the foundation's website. Once your project suggestion has been accepted you will receive a confirmation. There is at least one round of awards during the year – check the website for upcoming deadlines. Community projects are voted for by members of the public and those with the most votes are awarded grants.

WHO TO APPLY TO Foundation Team, 16–17 West Street, Brighton BN1 2RL *Tel.* 0800 373010 *Email* foundation@onefamily.com *Website* foundation.onefamily.com

■ Open Gate

CC NO 1081701 **ESTABLISHED** 2000

WHERE FUNDING CAN BE GIVEN UK; Africa; Asia; South and Central America. In the UK, support is concentrated on the North Midlands area.

WHO CAN BENEFIT UK-registered charities.

WHAT IS FUNDED Grassroots environmental, technological and educational projects to benefit small communities; social welfare; disadvantage; disability.

WHAT IS NOT FUNDED Individuals; overseas-based charities; purely medical causes.

TYPE OF GRANT Project grants for up to three years; capital grants; core costs; full project grants; unrestricted funding.

RANGE OF GRANTS £500 to £5,000.

SAMPLE GRANTS WaterAid (£5,000); Children of the Andes and Traidcraft (£3,000 each); Clean Rivers Trust, Plant Aid UK and Tools for Self Reliance (£2,500 each); Fish Aid, Wells for India and Youth Hostel Association (£2,000 each); Seeds for Africa (£1,800); Clifton Scout Group (£1,400); Derbyshire Association of the Blind (£1,300); Caring for Life (£500).

FINANCES *Year* 2015/16 *Income* £43,646 *Grants* £216,310 *Grants to organisations* £216,310 *Assets* £1,090,227

TRUSTEES Mary Wiltshire; Ned Wiltshire; John Wiltshire; Jane Methuen; Tom Wiltshire; Alice Taylor; Lesley Williamson.

OTHER INFORMATION During the year, 104 organisations received support.

HOW TO APPLY Apply in writing to the correspondent via post or email. The trustees usually meet in January, April, July and October. Applications need to be received six weeks in advance of the meetings.

WHO TO APPLY TO Mary Wiltshire, Trustee, Brownhouse Farm, Ashleyhay, Wirksworth, Matlock, Derbyshire DE4 4AH *Tel.* 01629 822018 *Email* opengate@w3z.co.uk *Website* www.opengatetrust.org.uk

■ The Ormsby Charitable Trust

CC NO 1000599 **ESTABLISHED** 1990

WHERE FUNDING CAN BE GIVEN UK.

WHO CAN BENEFIT Registered charities.

WHAT IS FUNDED General charitable purposes.

WHAT IS NOT FUNDED The trust does not generally support charities providing overseas aid or animal welfare charities.

RANGE OF GRANTS £1,000 to £4,000.

SAMPLE GRANTS In Kind Direct (£4,000); Children – 1st West Berkshire (£3,000); The Haven (£2,900); Marie Curie Cancer Care and The Hardman Trust (£2,000 each); Parkinson's UK (£1,500); RSPB, The Hardman Trust and The Woodland Trust (£1,000 each).

FINANCES *Year* 2015/16 *Income* £58,219 *Grants* £56,500 *Grants to organisations* £56,500 *Assets* £1,891,457

TRUSTEES Angela Chiswell; Katrina McCrossan; Rosemary David.

HOW TO APPLY Apply in writing to the correspondent. Grants are made to organisations known to the trustees.

WHO TO APPLY TO Katrina McCrossan, Trustee, The Red House, The Street, Aldermaston, Reading RG7 4LN *Tel.* 0118 971 0343

■ The O'Sullivan Family Charitable Trust

CC NO 1123757 **ESTABLISHED** 2008

WHERE FUNDING CAN BE GIVEN UK.

WHO CAN BENEFIT Registered charities.

WHAT IS FUNDED The care of people who have disabilities, especially children and young people; genetic research.

RANGE OF GRANTS £1,000 to £114,000. Typically less than £40,000.

SAMPLE GRANTS UBS UK Donor Advised Foundation (£114,000); The Playhouse Foundation (£89,000): University of Southampton (£30,500); Enham Trust (£20,000); Juvenile Diabetes Research Foundation (£10,000); CLIC Sargent (£9,000); Royal Navy Submarine Museum (£5,000); Hampshire Cultural Trust (£2,500); The Wheatsheaf Trust (£1,000).

FINANCES *Year* 2015/16 *Income* £169,680 *Grants* £325,918 *Grants to organisations* £325,918 *Assets* £5,591,235

TRUSTEES Diana O'Sullivan; Finian O'Sullivan; Emily O'Sullivan; Sophie O'Sullivan; Tessa O'Sullivan.

OTHER INFORMATION Grants were made to 17 organisations during the year.

HOW TO APPLY Apply in writing to the correspondent.

WHO TO APPLY TO Diana O'Sullivan, Trustee, 36 Edge Street, London W8 7PN

■ The Ouseley Church Music Trust

CC NO 527519 **ESTABLISHED** 1989

WHERE FUNDING CAN BE GIVEN England, Wales and Ireland.

WHO CAN BENEFIT Cathedrals; choirs; parish churches; choir schools; individuals.

WHAT IS FUNDED Projects that promote and maintain to a high standard the choral services of the Church of England, the Church in Wales or the Church of Ireland, for example: courses for individuals or groups; endowment grants; choir school fees; purchase of liturgical music.

WHAT IS NOT FUNDED Building projects; the making of recordings; the purchase of furniture or liturgical objects; the repair of organs; the purchase of pianos and other instruments; the design or acquisition of robes; tours or visits.

RANGE OF GRANTS Up to £50,000. For fees, £5,000 maximum.

SAMPLE GRANTS Hereford Cathedral Perpetual Trust (£10,000); Carlisle Cathedral Development Trust (£7,000); Blackburn Cathedral (£5,000); Lincoln Minster School (£4,000); East Wickham Singers (£1,000); The Wessex Festival (£600).

FINANCES *Year* 2015 *Income* £263,470 *Grants* £126,992 *Grants to organisations* £126,992 *Assets* £4,715,141

TRUSTEES Dr Christopher Robinson; Canon Richard White; Adam Ridley; Dr Stephen Darlington; The Very Revd Mark Boyling; Dr John Rutter; Gillian Perkins; Canon Paul Mason; Timothy Byram-Wigfield; Adrian Barlow; Dr Jo Spreadbury.

OTHER INFORMATION Grants were awarded for the following purposes: endowments (£66,500); fees (£57,500); music (£2,000); other (£490).

HOW TO APPLY Applications must be submitted on the trust's official application form, which is available from the correspondent, by an institution (not an individual). The trust advises potential applicants to read and consider the 'Questions' and 'Guidelines' sections on its website before a form is requested. Applications by fax or email will not be accepted.

WHO TO APPLY TO Martin Williams, Clerk to the Trustees, PO Box 281, Stamford, Lincolnshire PE9 9BU *Tel.* 01780 752266 *Email* ouseleytrust@btinternet.com *Website* www.ouseleytrust.org.uk

■ The Owen Family Trust

CC NO 251975 **ESTABLISHED** 1967

WHERE FUNDING CAN BE GIVEN UK, with a preference for the West Midlands.

WHO CAN BENEFIT Registered charities; schools (independent and church); Christian youth centres; churches; museums; community associations.

WHAT IS FUNDED Christian outreach projects; the arts; conservation; cancer research; Christian education; church and related community buildings.

WHAT IS NOT FUNDED Individuals.

TYPE OF GRANT Buildings, capital expenditure and recurring costs will be considered. Funding may be given for more than three years.

RANGE OF GRANTS Up to £5,000.

SAMPLE GRANTS Aston University, Black Country Living Museum, Library of Birmingham Development Trust, Lichfield Cathedral and Walsall Voluntary Action (£5,000 each); Premier Christian Media Trust and The Ironbridge Gorge Museum (£3,000 each); Birmingham Royal Ballet (£2,000) Elmhurst School of Dance and Friends of Warwick County Records Office (£1,500 each).

FINANCES *Year* 2015/16 *Income* £62,404 *Grants* £77,450 *Grants to organisations* £77,450 *Assets* £1,193,353

TRUSTEES Grace Jenkins; David Owen.

OTHER INFORMATION During the year, 16 grants of £1,000 or less totalled £11,300.

HOW TO APPLY Apply in writing to the correspondent including annual report, budget for the project and general information regarding the application. Organisations need to be a registered charity; however, an umbrella body which would hold funds would be acceptable. Only a small number of grants can be given each year and unsuccessful applications are not acknowledged unless an sae is enclosed. The trustees meet quarterly.

WHO TO APPLY TO David Owen, Trustee, c/o Rubery Owen Holdings Ltd, PO Box 10, Wednesbury WS10 8JD *Tel.* 0121 526 3131 *Email* david.owen@ruberyowen.com

■ Oxfam (GB)

CC NO 202918 **ESTABLISHED** 1958

WHERE FUNDING CAN BE GIVEN Worldwide.

WHO CAN BENEFIT Local, national and international partner organisations which share Oxfam's goals.

WHAT IS FUNDED Civil and political rights; women's rights; disaster relief; food supplies; better access to natural resources; better funding for basic services, such as health or education.

WHAT IS NOT FUNDED Work that falls outside Oxfam's charitable or geographical remit; work through governments or government agencies; projects that include the teaching of religion in their proposal; individuals; requests submitted by a second party on behalf of another; requests from UK-based organisations for projects overseas.

RANGE OF GRANTS The average grant per project was £67,000.

SAMPLE GRANTS Legal and Human Rights Centre (£1.2 million); Action Against Hunger USA (£950,000); Hydraulique Sans Frontières (£711,000); Bangladesh Rural Advancement Committee (£463,000); Jordanian Women's Union (£418,000); Women for Human Rights (£277,000); Islamic Relief UK (£273,000); Action for Integrated Sustainable Development Association and Afghan Women's Educational Centre (£251,000 each).

FINANCES *Year* 2015/16 *Income* £414,700,000 *Grants* £78,000,000 *Grants to organisations* £78,000,000 *Assets* £72,500,000

TRUSTEES Caroline Thomson; Katy Steward; Karen Brown; David Pitt-Watson; Nkoyo Toyo; Gavin MacNeill Stewart; Stephen Walton; Ruth Ruderham; Kul Gautam; Mohammed Khan; Lois Jacobs; Lydinyda Nacpil; Kenneth Mathieson Caldwell.

OTHER INFORMATION In 2015/16 there were 1,168 grants made to 737 organisations in the following areas: development (£57.2 million); humanitarian (£18.5 million); campaigning and advocacy (£2.3 million).

HOW TO APPLY A brief project proposal should be sent to the Oxfam team in the appropriate country, the details of which are noted on the website.

WHO TO APPLY TO Joss Saunders, 2700 John Smith Drive, Oxford Business Park South, Oxford OX4 2JY *Tel.* 0870 333 2444 *Email* enquiries@oxfam.org.uk *Website* www.oxfam.org.uk

■ Oxfordshire Community Foundation

CC NO 1151621 **ESTABLISHED** 1995

WHERE FUNDING CAN BE GIVEN Oxfordshire.

WHO CAN BENEFIT Community-based non-profit organisations constituted in Oxfordshire.

WHAT IS FUNDED Local community initiatives benefitting residents of Oxfordshire of all 'ages, ethnicities and abilities'.

TYPE OF GRANT One-off expenditure; capital and core costs; salaries; one-year start-up costs for projects, training and equipment; unrestricted funding.

RANGE OF GRANTS Refer to the foundation's website for grant ranges specific to each fund.

SAMPLE GRANTS FAI Farms (£298,500); Oxfordshire Youth (£69,000); Oxford Homeless Pathways (£32,500); Story Museum (£21,000); Streets Revolution CIC (£12,000); Refugee Resource (£10,700); Workers Educational Association (£7,800); Shotover Wildlife (£3,000); Oxford Muslim Youth Project (£2,000); Redbridge Travellers Women's Support Group (£970); Oxford Lesbian and Gay Families Group (£500); Dovecote Carer and Toddler Group (£200).

FINANCES *Year* 2015/16 *Income* £1,212,751 *Grants* £639,615 *Grants to organisations* £639,615 *Assets* £5,257,440

TRUSTEES Glyn Benson; Jane Wates; Anne Davies; Amanda Phillips; Nicholas Case; John Taylor; Laura Chapma; Neil Preddy.

OTHER INFORMATION As with all community foundations, funding rounds frequently open and close, or change their criteria. Refer to the website for more information on rounds that are currently open.

HOW TO APPLY Refer to the foundation's website for full details of how to apply to the various programmes currently being administered.

WHO TO APPLY TO Grants Manager, 3 Woodin's Way, Oxford OX1 1HD *Tel.* 01865 798666 *Email* ocf@oxfordshire.org *Website* www.oxfordshire.org

■ Oxfordshire Historic Churches Trust

CC NO 235644 **ESTABLISHED** 1964

WHERE FUNDING CAN BE GIVEN Oxfordshire.

WHO CAN BENEFIT Churches and chapels of all Christian denominations which are open for public worship.

WHAT IS FUNDED Repairs to the fixtures, fittings and structure of churches, chapels or meeting houses that are used as a place of public worship; new work, such as the installation of toilets and kitchens, disability access, security systems and electrics.

WHAT IS NOT FUNDED Routine maintenance; removal or replacement of pews; liturgical re-ordering (e.g. nave altars and platforms or re-orientation); church or parish halls on separate sites; car parks; buildings completed after 1950 (unless there are special circumstances); architects' fees.

TYPE OF GRANT One-off grants.

RANGE OF GRANTS £500 to £15,000.

SAMPLE GRANTS St Michael and All Angels – Oxford (£15,000); Bladon Methodists (£10,000); St Denys – Northmoor (£6,000); St Agatha's – Brightwell-cum-Sotwell (£5,500); St Joseph's – Carterton (£4,000); All Saints – Marcham (£1,000); St Mary – Hardwick (£500).

FINANCES *Year* 2015/16 *Income* £737,290 *Grants* £197,000 *Grants to organisations* £197,000 *Assets* £1,634,291

TRUSTEES Malcolm Airs; Jonathan Scheele; Basil Eastwood; Gillian Argyle; Giles Dessain; Cynthia Robinson; Hilary Cakebread Hall; Michael Sibly; Stephen Goss.

OTHER INFORMATION Grants were awarded to 39 places of worship during the year.

HOW TO APPLY Applications can be made by downloading an application form from the trust's website and returning it to the grants officer. The trust advises that you contact the area representative before applying. There is detailed and clear guidance provided on the website, where you can also find the contact information for parish representatives.

WHO TO APPLY TO Cynthia Robinson, Grants Officer/ Trustee, 20 Portland Street, Oxford OX2 7EY *Tel.* 01865 435076 *Email* secretary@ohct.org.uk *Website* ohct.org.uk

■ P. F. Charitable Trust

CC NO 220124 **ESTABLISHED** 1951

WHERE FUNDING CAN BE GIVEN Unrestricted. In practice the UK with local interests in Oxfordshire and Scotland.

WHO CAN BENEFIT Charitable organisations.

WHAT IS FUNDED General charitable purposes with a preference for: health; the arts; education; social welfare.

WHAT IS NOT FUNDED Individuals; non-registered charities.

TYPE OF GRANT One-off and recurring; buildings; core costs; project expenditure; research; running costs. Funding may be given for up to three years.

RANGE OF GRANTS Mainly up to £50,000.

SAMPLE GRANTS Foundation Scotland (£110,000); University of Oxford (£100,000); Alzheimer's Research UK (£75,000); Design Dundee Ltd – V&A Museum, Healing Foundation, Hop Skip and Jump Foundation, Institute of Cancer Research, Milton Abbey School and Moghissi Laser Trust (£50,000 each).

FINANCES *Year* 2015/16 *Income* £2,953,968 *Grants* £2,951,645 *Grants to organisations* £2,951,645 *Assets* £108,901,339

TRUSTEES Robert Fleming; Philip Fleming; Rory Fleming.

OTHER INFORMATION Grants of less than £50,000 each totalled £2.36 million. During the year, grants were made to 454 organisations.

HOW TO APPLY Apply in writing to the correspondent. The trustees usually meet monthly to consider applications and approve grants.

WHO TO APPLY TO The Secretary, P. F. Charitable Trust, c/o RF Trustee Co. Ltd, 15 Suffolk Street, London SW1Y 4HG *Tel.* 020 3696 6721 *Email* charities@rftrustee.com

■ The Doris Pacey Charitable Foundation

CC NO 1101724 **ESTABLISHED** 2003

WHERE FUNDING CAN BE GIVEN UK and Israel.

WHO CAN BENEFIT Charitable organisations.

WHAT IS FUNDED General charitable purposes with a preference for Jewish organisations working with ill or disadvantaged children and young people; the arts; education.

RANGE OF GRANTS £5,000 to £175,500.

SAMPLE GRANTS World Jewish Relief (£175,500); Magen David Adom (£90,000); ALEH (£53,000); Croydon Youth Theatre (£39,500); Carers Trust (£30,000); Side by Side Children (£26,000); Institute of Pre-Hospital Care (£20,000); Literacy Volunteers (£8,100); The Honeypot Children's Charity (£5,000).

FINANCES *Year* 2015/16 *Income* £123,653 *Grants* £696,176 *Grants to organisations* £696,176 *Assets* £4,861,743

TRUSTEES Ray Locke; Leslie Powell; Linda Courtney.

OTHER INFORMATION Grants were made to 16 organisations during the year.

HOW TO APPLY Apply in writing to the correspondent.

WHO TO APPLY TO Michael Theodorou, Charities Aid Foundation, 25 Kings Hill Avenue, Kings Hill, West Mailing, Kent ME19 4TA *Tel.* 0300 012 3187 *Email* paceyandbrynbergfoundations@cafonline.org

■ The Paddington Charitable Estate Educational Fund

CC NO 312347 **ESTABLISHED** 1934

WHO CAN BENEFIT Schools; organisations; charities; individuals.

WHAT IS FUNDED Education; welfare; school building repairs; children and young people; pensions.

TYPE OF GRANT Buildings; capital costs; awards to relieve hardship.

SAMPLE GRANTS A list of beneficiaries was not available.

FINANCES *Year* 2015 *Income* £125,168 *Grants* £131,637 *Grants to organisations* £105,037 *Assets* £3,193,519

TRUSTEES Michael Brahams; Revd Gary Bradley; Revd Alistair Thom; Jan Prendergast; Cllr Barrie Taylor; Revd David Ackerman.

OTHER INFORMATION The charity has two branches: Paddington Charitable Estates Educational Fund and the Paddington Relief in Need Charity. The two organisations are distinct in terms of their beneficiaries. Together, The Paddington Charitable Estates have two separate funds: Education Fund and Relief in Need. Throughout the year The Education Fund awarded £104,000 and Relief in Need awarded £27,600 in grants. Grants awarded to individuals totalled £28,600.

HOW TO APPLY Apply in writing to the correspondent.

WHO TO APPLY TO Nick Maxwell, 17th Floor, Westminster City Hall, 64 Victoria Street, London SW1E 6QP *Tel.* 020 7641 2135

■ The Paget Charitable Trust

CC NO 327402 **ESTABLISHED** 1986

WHERE FUNDING CAN BE GIVEN Worldwide, with an interest in Loughborough.

WHO CAN BENEFIT UK-registered charities.

WHAT IS FUNDED General charitable purposes; international aid and development; disadvantaged children; education; older people; animal welfare; environmental projects.

WHAT IS NOT FUNDED Individuals; people with mental disabilities; medical research; AIDS/HIV projects.

TYPE OF GRANT Typically recurrent.

RANGE OF GRANTS £500 to £15,000.

SAMPLE GRANTS Second Chance (£15,000); Tibet Relief Fund of UK (£7,300); Animals Asia Foundation and Farming Community Network (£5,000 each); Childhood First and Freedom from Torture (£4,000 each); Butterfly Hospice, Oxfam, Quaker Social Action and Southwark Community Education Council (£2,000 each); Contact the Elderly and Students' Education Trust (£1,000 each); Hospice of Hope Romania and St Andrew's Evangelical Mission (£500 each).

FINANCES *Year* 2015/16 *Income* £379,075 *Grants* £163,075 *Grants to organisations* £163,075 *Assets* £12,186,183

TRUSTEES Joanna Herbert-Stepney; Vivienne Matravers; Laura Woodhead.

OTHER INFORMATION The full registered name of the trust is The Joanna Herbert-Stepney Charitable Settlement. During the year, 112 charities were supported.

HOW TO APPLY Apply in writing to the correspondent; there is no application form. The trustees request that you state what you need in plain language. The trustees meet in spring and autumn. The trust regrets that it cannot respond to all applications.
WHO TO APPLY TO Joanna Herbert-Stepney, Trustee, Old Village Stores, Dippenhall Street, Crondall, Farnham, Surrey GU10 5NZ *Tel.* 01252 850253

■ Palmtree Memorial Trust

CC NO 1080997 **ESTABLISHED** 2000
WHERE FUNDING CAN BE GIVEN Worldwide.
WHO CAN BENEFIT Registered charities.
WHAT IS FUNDED General charitable purposes; social welfare; education; health.
SAMPLE GRANTS A list of beneficiaries was not available.
FINANCES *Year* 2015 *Income* £300,000 *Grants* £219,821 *Grants to organisations* £219,821 *Assets* £84,315
TRUSTEES Dr Asher Gratt; Dina Gratt; Pinchas Lebrecht.
OTHER INFORMATION A list of beneficiaries was not provided in the annual report or accounts for 2015. Previous research suggests that there is a preference for Jewish organisations and causes; however, we can find no indication of this in the accounts from the last four years or on the trust's Charity Commission record.
HOW TO APPLY Apply in writing to the correspondent.
WHO TO APPLY TO Dr Asher Gratt, Trustee, 24 Gilda Crescent, London N16 6JP *Email* asher@gratt.co.uk

■ The Panacea Charitable Trust

CC NO 227530 **ESTABLISHED** 1926
WHERE FUNDING CAN BE GIVEN UK, with a strong preference for Bedford and its immediate region.
WHO CAN BENEFIT Christian organisations; universities; registered charities.
WHAT IS FUNDED Research, scholarships and conferences in the field of historical theology. The trust's website states: 'The charity's grant awards have been mainly in the area of historical theology, and in particular work in the following areas: Prophecy, the Book of Revelation, The Second Coming of Christ, Jewish apocalyptic literature and Christian theology, Millennialism and Christian millenarian movements. This also includes grants in relation to book publication.' Social welfare grants are made through the Bedfordshire and Luton Community Foundation and Community and Voluntary Services Bedfordshire.
RANGE OF GRANTS Up to £50,000.
SAMPLE GRANTS Bristol University (£46,500); Salisbury Cathedral (£24,500); Bunyan Meeting Museum (£5,000); IB Tauris Publishing Ltd (£1,500); Cambridge University (£1,000).
FINANCES *Year* 2015 *Income* £631,275 *Grants* £151,520 *Grants to organisations* £151,520 *Assets* £29,192,120
TRUSTEES Prof. Christopher Rowland; Charles Monsell; Gordon Allan; Dr Justin Meggitt; Dr Naomi Hilton; Evan Jones.
OTHER INFORMATION Through its partnership with the Bedfordshire and Luton Community Foundation, the trust supported the following 15 groups: Bedford Open Door group, Fun 4 Young People, Goldington Green Academy Parents' Association, Tibbs Dementia Foundation, Friends of Chums, Bedfordshire Pilgrims Housing Association (BPHA), Reactive8, Beds Garden Carers, Bedfordshire Refugee and Asylum Seeker Support, Bedford Guild House, Agency for Culture and Change Management (ACCM), Headway UK, Road Victims Trust, Amicus Trust and Community Resettlement Support Project (CRSP).
HOW TO APPLY Apply in writing to the correspondent for grants towards funding research, publications or academic work on historical theology. Consult the Bedfordshire and Luton Community Foundation page for social welfare grants.
WHO TO APPLY TO David McLynn, Executive Officer, 14 Albany Road, Bedford MK40 3PH *Tel.* 01234 359737 *Email* admin@panaceatrust.org *Website* panaceatrust.org

■ The James Pantyfedwen Foundation

CC NO 1069598 **ESTABLISHED** 1998
WHERE FUNDING CAN BE GIVEN Wales.
WHO CAN BENEFIT Churches; Sunday schools; religious charities; other registered charities; registered eisteddfodau; postgraduate students.
WHAT IS FUNDED For the benefit of Welsh people, the advancement of religion, education, Welsh language, the arts, agriculture and other charitable purposes. Support is given in three main areas: to individual churches for the improvement and repair of fabric; to local and national eisteddfodau; and to postgraduate students.
WHAT IS NOT FUNDED Salaries; general revenue costs. Exclusions vary according to the type of grant being applied for. See the appropriate guideline document on the website for details.
TYPE OF GRANT One-off, capital costs.
RANGE OF GRANTS £40 to £18,000.
SAMPLE GRANTS National Eisteddfodau (£21,000 in two grants); Lampeter Eisteddfodau (£9,500); Bethel Community Church – Newport (£8,000); St Jerome – Llangwm (£7,000); Morlan Centre Aberystwyth (£5,000); Farms for City Children (£2,000); Emmaus – South Wales (£990); Christian Council for the Schools in Wales (£390); Babel Llandovery Eisteddfodau (£40).
FINANCES *Year* 2015/16 *Income* £589,379 *Grants* £430,998 *Grants to organisations* £178,148 *Assets* £14,737,622
TRUSTEES Gwerfyl Pierce Jones; William Phillips; Ken Richards; Roy Sharp; Dr Rhidian Griffiths; Geraint Jones; Revd Alun Evans; Prof. Derec Morgan; David Lewis; Dr Eryn White; Wyn Jones; Gwenan Creunant; Enid Lewis; Prof. Jane Aaron.
OTHER INFORMATION Grants were awarded to several types of organisation during the year: religious buildings (£82,000); eisteddfodau (£74,000); Urdd Gobaith Cymru (£13,200); registered charities (£8,400); Morlan-Pantyfedwen lecture (£540). Grants were paid to 50 postgraduate students totalling £253,000.
HOW TO APPLY Guidelines for student, local eisteddfodau and churches can be found on the website and should be carefully considered before an application is made. Application forms for grants to local eisteddfodau and students may be downloaded from the website; however, churches wishing to make an application must contact the foundation to obtain a form.
WHO TO APPLY TO Gwenan Creunant, Executive Secretary, Pantyfedwen, 9 Market Street, Aberystwyth, Ceredigion SY23 1DL *Tel.* 01970

612806 *Fax* 01970 612806
Email pantyfedwen@btinternet.com
Website www.jamespantyfedwenfoundation.org.uk

■ The Paphitis Charitable Trust

CC NO 1112721 **ESTABLISHED** 2005
WHERE FUNDING CAN BE GIVEN UK and overseas.
WHO CAN BENEFIT Registered charities.
WHAT IS FUNDED Education and sport; relief of poverty; care in the community; general charitable purposes. There appears to be a particular interest in children's and medical charities.
RANGE OF GRANTS £100 to £2,500.
SAMPLE GRANTS Nikki's Wishes (£2,500); Arts for All, Cyclists Fighting Cancer and Royal Trinity Hospice (£1,000 each); Whizz-Kidz (£750); Alder Hey Children's Charity and Lothian Autistic Society (£500 each); Institute of Cancer Research (£250); Deafblind UK (£120); The Hall Homeless Shelter(£100).
FINANCES *Year* 2015/16 *Income* £31,292 *Grants* £53,660 *Grants to organisations* £53,660 *Assets* £30,253
TRUSTEES Malcolm Cooke; Richard Towner; Kypros Kyprianou; Ann Mantz; Ian Childs.
OTHER INFORMATION Grants were made to 77 organisations during the year.
HOW TO APPLY Apply in writing to the correspondent.
WHO TO APPLY TO Ann Mantz, Trustee, 2nd Floor, 22–24 Worple Road, London SW19 4DD *Tel.* 020 8971 9890

■ Parabola Foundation

CC NO 1156008 **ESTABLISHED** 2013
WHERE FUNDING CAN BE GIVEN England.
WHO CAN BENEFIT Registered charities.
WHAT IS FUNDED General charitable purposes with a preference for: poverty relief; the arts, culture and music.
TYPE OF GRANT One-off and recurrent project costs; up to five years.
RANGE OF GRANTS Up to £391,000, but typically under £50,000.
SAMPLE GRANTS Kings Place Music Foundation (£391,000); Aurora Orchestra (£305,000); Poverty Relief Foundation (£56,500); Bowes Museum (£50,000).
FINANCES *Year* 2015/16 *Income* £1,418,056 *Grants* £879,244 *Grants to organisations* £879,244 *Assets* £575,979
TRUSTEES Deborah Jude; Anne Millican; Peter Millican.
HOW TO APPLY Apply in writing to the correspondent.
WHO TO APPLY TO Deborah Jude, Trustee, Broadgate Tower, 20 Primrose Street, London EC2A 2EW *Tel.* 07980 769561

■ Paradigm Foundation

CC NO 1156204 **ESTABLISHED** 2013
WHERE FUNDING CAN BE GIVEN The South East and East Midlands.
WHO CAN BENEFIT Registered charities; residents of Paradigm Housing Group; voluntary, community or not-for-profit groups; parish and local authorities; faith-based groups (project must meet the wider economic and social needs of the local community).
WHAT IS FUNDED Community development and cohesion, especially through projects that encourage education, training and employment, or personal financial resilience projects.
WHAT IS NOT FUNDED Organisations and projects operating solely outside the foundation's specified geographical area; organisations and projects which do not benefit Paradigm residents; projects for party political, religious or lobbying activity; relief of statutory responsibilities.
TYPE OF GRANT Project costs; up to three years.
RANGE OF GRANTS Typically under £5,000.
SAMPLE GRANTS Citizens Advice Buckinghamshire (£55,000); Small Steps (£36,000 annually, for three years); New Meaning Centre Buckinghamshire (£33,500); Families United Network (£12,000); Amersham Band (£11,000); Watford Women's Centre (£10,200); Botley Playing Fields Association, Chiltern Dial-a-Ride and Home-Start Slough (£10,000 each); Straight Talking Peer Education (£9,900 annually, for two years).
FINANCES *Year* 2015/16 *Income* £418,183 *Grants* £369,156 *Grants to organisations* £355,598 *Assets* £111,342
TRUSTEES Bob Marshall; Pat Buckland; Alfred Dench; Jane Harrison; Michael Barclay Gahagan; Trevor Stone.
OTHER INFORMATION The foundation has two grant streams: small-scale community projects up to £3,000 and larger projects over £3,000. For grants of over £5,000 applicants should not submit a form. Instead they may submit an expression of interest to the trustees. Individual grants are also made to Paradigm residents for up to £1,500. The Paradigm Housing website has a map which shows where Paradigm manages housing stock. The amount of grants given to individuals totalled £13,600.
HOW TO APPLY Applicants to the small and large community project schemes can apply online or download application forms available from the foundation's website. Those applying for £5,000 or more should not complete an application form but sent the trustees an expression of interest form. This should outline the purpose of your bid and how you consider it will support one or more of the foundation's priorities. The foundation will let you know if a full application is then required. Applications can be submitted by post or via email.
WHO TO APPLY TO Manjit Nanglu, Executive Facilitator, Paradigm Housing Group, Glory Park Avenue, Wooburn Green, High Wycombe, Buckinghamshire HP10 0DF *Tel.* 01628 811835 *Email* enquiries@paradigmfoundation.org.uk *Website* www.paradigmfoundation.org.uk

■ The Paragon Trust

CC NO 278348 **ESTABLISHED** 1979
WHERE FUNDING CAN BE GIVEN UK and overseas.
WHO CAN BENEFIT Registered charities; individuals.
WHAT IS FUNDED General charitable purposes.
RANGE OF GRANTS £250 to £3,000.
SAMPLE GRANTS Combat Stress, Freedom from Torture; Mines Advisory Group and St Michael's Hospice Hastings (£1,000 each); Church Housing Trust, Cystic Fibrosis Trust and The Society for Protection of Ancient Buildings (£750 each); GOSH (Great Ormond Street Hospital), Leonard Cheshire Disability, Sussex Housing and Care (£500 each).
FINANCES *Year* 2015/16 *Income* £93,516 *Grants* £70,750 *Grants to organisations* £63,750 *Assets* £2,328,749

TRUSTEES The Revd Canon Ronald Coppin; Lucy Whistler; Philip Cunningham; Dr Fiona Cornish; Patricia Russell; Kathleen Larter.

OTHER INFORMATION The trustees only make grants to charities and individuals that they personally know. The majority of donations are standing orders, although one individual received a grant for £4,000.

HOW TO APPLY The trust does not accept unsolicited applications. The 2015/16 annual report states the following: 'All the organisations and individuals that benefit from the Trust are known to the Trustees and no attention is paid to appeal literature, which is discarded on receipt. Fund-raisers are therefore urged to save resources by not sending appeal literature.'

WHO TO APPLY TO Stuart Goodbody, Head of Trust Management, c/o Thomson Snell and Passmore Solicitors, 3 Lonsdale Gardens, Tunbridge Wells, Kent TN1 1NX *Tel.* 01892 510000

■ The Pargiter Trust

CC NO 1157779 **ESTABLISHED** 2014

WHERE FUNDING CAN BE GIVEN England and Guernsey.

WHO CAN BENEFIT Registered charities.

WHAT IS FUNDED Projects that help older people be independent, healthy and socially included.

SAMPLE GRANTS Community Foundation for Surrey (£50,000); Kissing it Better (£9,900); Wet Wheels Solent (£5,000); Golden Years Festival (£4,700); Radio Club (£2,500); Les Bourgs Hospice (£1,000).

FINANCES *Year* 2015 *Income* £566,289 *Grants* £138,598 *Grants to organisations* £138,598 *Assets* £12,509,896

TRUSTEES Mrs C. Gardiner; Mr M. P. Cash; Victoria Westhorp; Martyn Mogford; Mr J. M. K. Goodacre.

HOW TO APPLY Apply in writing to the correspondent.

WHO TO APPLY TO The Secretary, 3 Mansion Close, Burgess Hill RH15 0NT *Tel.* 01444 246552 *Email* dbm.1958@tiscali.co.uk

■ Parish Estate of the Church of St Michael Spurriergate York

CC NO 250552 **ESTABLISHED** 1986

WHERE FUNDING CAN BE GIVEN York.

WHO CAN BENEFIT Churches and charitable organisations.

WHAT IS FUNDED The upkeep of St Michael's Church, Spurriergate; upkeep and maintenance of any Church of England in York; general charitable purposes for the benefit of the inhabitants of York.

WHAT IS NOT FUNDED Individuals.

RANGE OF GRANTS £5,000 to £23,000.

SAMPLE GRANTS York Minster Fund (£23,000); York Theatre Royal (£20,000); Bystander Children Project (£10,000); St Chad on the Knavesmire (£7,000); All Saints North Street and York City Charities (£5,000 each).

FINANCES *Year* 2015 *Income* £106,004 *Grants* £954,992 *Grants to organisations* £95,492 *Assets* £2,818,493

HOW TO APPLY Apply in writing to the correspondent. The trustees meet four times a year.

WHO TO APPLY TO Lyn Rickatson, Clerk, c/o Grays Solicitors, Duncombe Place, York YO1 7DY *Tel.* 01904 634771

■ The Park House Charitable Trust

CC NO 1077677 **ESTABLISHED** 1999

WHERE FUNDING CAN BE GIVEN UK and overseas, with a preference for the Midlands, particularly Coventry and Warwickshire.

WHO CAN BENEFIT Charitable organisations.

WHAT IS FUNDED Education; social welfare; ecclesiastical purposes; medical causes.

WHAT IS NOT FUNDED Individuals.

TYPE OF GRANT Normally one-off for general funds.

RANGE OF GRANTS £5,000 to £150,000.

SAMPLE GRANTS Scottish International Relief (£150,000); Friends of the Holy Land (£100,000); The St Barnabas Society (£50,000); Conventus of Our Lady of Consolation (£25,000); African Child Trust, Heart of Community Foundation and Médecins Sans Frontières (£10,000 each); Bibles for Children, Farm Africa, Mercy Ships and Tiny Tim's Children's Centre (£5,000 each).

FINANCES *Year* 2015 *Income* £906,573 *Grants* £935,000 *Grants to organisations* £935,000 *Assets* £1,761,728

TRUSTEES Margaret Bailey; Niall Bailey; Paul Bailey.

OTHER INFORMATION Grants were distributed between 60 organisations for the following purposes: social welfare (£721,000); ecclesiastical (£144,000); education (£40,000); medical (£30,000).

HOW TO APPLY Apply in writing to the correspondent. The trust has previously stated that it does not expect to have surplus funds available to meet the majority of applications.

WHO TO APPLY TO Paul Varney, Dafferns LLP, 1 Eastwood Business Village, Harry Weston Road, Binley, Coventry CV3 2UB *Tel.* 024 7622 1046

■ Parkinson's Disease Society of the United Kingdom

CC NO 258197 **ESTABLISHED** 1969

WHERE FUNDING CAN BE GIVEN UK and overseas.

WHO CAN BENEFIT Research institutions.

WHAT IS FUNDED Research into Parkinson's disease.

TYPE OF GRANT Research.

RANGE OF GRANTS Up to £1.4 million.

SAMPLE GRANTS University of Oxford (£1.4 million in three grants); Critical Path Institute USA (£1.4 million); University of Glasgow (£461,000); University of Cambridge (£200,000); King's College London (£141,000); Lincolnshire East Clinical Commissioning Group (£102,000); University of Manchester (£50,000).

FINANCES *Year* 2015 *Income* £31,451,000 *Grants* £5,766,000 *Grants to organisations* £5,766,000 *Assets* £14,673,000

TRUSTEES Nadra Ahmed; Richard Raine; Mary Whyham; Tim Tamblyn; Mark Goodridge; Dr Doug MacMahon; Hilary Ackland; Margaret Chamberlain; Freda Lewis; Lucie Austin; Anne MacColl Turpin.

OTHER INFORMATION Grants for less than £100,000 totalled £634,000.

HOW TO APPLY Details of how to apply can be found on the 'Research Grants' section of the charity's website.

WHO TO APPLY TO Sarah Day, 215 Vauxhall Bridge Road, London SW1V 1EJ *Tel.* 020 7932 1327 *Email* enquiries@parkinson's.org.uk *Website* www.parkinson's.org.uk

■ The Patrick Trust

CC NO 213849 **ESTABLISHED** 1962
WHERE FUNDING CAN BE GIVEN Birmingham; Coventry; Warwickshire; Worcestershire; Cornwall.
WHO CAN BENEFIT Registered charities.
WHAT IS FUNDED General charitable purposes, especially medical care and research and performing arts.
WHAT IS NOT FUNDED Individuals; projects based outside the trust's geographical area of benefit.
TYPE OF GRANT One-off or recurrent; project and equipment costs; service delivery; up to eight years.
RANGE OF GRANTS £250 to £25,000. Usually below £10,000.
SAMPLE GRANTS Birmingham Royal Ballet (£25,000); Royal Shakespeare Company (£10,000); The Peck Wood Centre (£8,000); National Trust (£6,000); Birmingham Hippodrome Theatre Trust (£5,000); Cornwall International Male Voice Choral Festival (£2,500); Primrose Hospice (£1,000); Holy Trinity Parish Church – Sutton Coalfield (£500); Resources for Autism (£250).
FINANCES *Year* 2015/16 *Income* £150,928 *Grants* £135,450 *Grants to organisations* £135,450 *Assets* £7,954,049
TRUSTEES Joseph Patrick; Mary Patrick; Heather Cole; William Bond-Williams; Graham Wem.
HOW TO APPLY Apply in writing to the correspondent.
WHO TO APPLY TO Joseph Patrick, Trustee, The Lakeside Centre, 180 Lifford Lane, Birmingham B30 3NU *Tel.* 0121 486 3399 *Email* thepatricktrust@aol.com

■ The Jack Patston Charitable Trust

CC NO 701658 **ESTABLISHED** 1989
WHERE FUNDING CAN BE GIVEN Preferably Leicestershire and Cambridgeshire.
WHO CAN BENEFIT Registered charities; rural churches; hospices.
WHAT IS FUNDED Preservation of wildlife and the environment, advancement of religion and preservation of rural churches.
WHAT IS NOT FUNDED Individuals.
RANGE OF GRANTS £1,000 to £5,000.
SAMPLE GRANTS Leicestershire Historic Churches Trust (£5,000); Friends of Launde Abbey and Train a Priest Fund (£3,000 each); Lakelands Day Care Hospice (£2,500); Bumblebee Conservation Trust, Deafblind UK and Trees for Cities (£2,000 each); Bat Conservation Trust, Plantlife and St Peter's Church – Leire (£1,500 each); The Countryside Restoration Trust (£1,000).
FINANCES *Year* 2015/16 *Income* £112,532 *Grants* £100,000 *Grants to organisations* £100,000 *Assets* £5,091,478
TRUSTEES Allan Veasey; Charles Applegate; Stephen Knipe.
OTHER INFORMATION Grants were made to 47 organisations during the year.
HOW TO APPLY Apply in writing to the correspondent.
WHO TO APPLY TO Charles Applegate, Trustee, Buckles Solicitors LLP, Grant House, 101 Bourges Boulevard, Peterborough PE1 1NG *Tel.* 01733 888888 *Email* charles.applegate@buckles-law.co.uk

■ The JGW Patterson Foundation

CC NO 1094086 **ESTABLISHED** 2002
WHERE FUNDING CAN BE GIVEN North East England.
WHO CAN BENEFIT Universities; medical research institutions; hospices.
WHAT IS FUNDED Rheumatology and arthritis research; cancer research; hospice care.
SAMPLE GRANTS Newcastle University (£1.07 million in 26 grants); Marie Curie Hospice (£30,000); St Oswald's Hospice (£22,500); National Rheumatoid Arthritis Society (£10,000); HospiceCare North Northumberland (£5,000).
FINANCES *Year* 2015/16 *Income* £1,029,034 *Grants* £1,144,947 *Grants to organisations* £1,144,947 *Assets* £18,984,247
TRUSTEES Mr D. R. Gold; Prof. Sir Alan Craft; Stephen Gilroy; James Dias; Prof. Timothy Cawston.
HOW TO APPLY Applications can be made through the foundation's website. The trustees meet quarterly on the first Tuesday in February, May, September and November. Completed applications for funding must be received at least one month prior to a quarterly meeting. Applications are usually then sent out for peer review and discussed again at the subsequent quarterly meeting of the trustees.
WHO TO APPLY TO Pippa Aitken, Sintons, The Cube, Arngrove Court, Barrack Road, Newcastle upon Tyne NE4 6DB *Tel.* 0191 226 7878 *Website* jgwpattersonfoundation.co.uk

■ Peacock Charitable Trust

CC NO 257655 **ESTABLISHED** 1968
WHERE FUNDING CAN BE GIVEN UK with a possible preference for London and the south of England.
WHO CAN BENEFIT Registered charities which are known to the trustees.
WHAT IS FUNDED General charitable purposes with a preference for medical research, disability, education, young people and social welfare.
WHAT IS NOT FUNDED Individuals. Only in rare cases are additions made to the list of charities already being supported.
TYPE OF GRANT Core costs; capital and project costs; mainly recurring.
RANGE OF GRANTS £4,000 to £103,000.
SAMPLE GRANTS The Prince's Youth Business Trust (£103,000); The Jubilee Sailing Trust (£50,000); British Heart Foundation (£36,000); The Mental Health Foundation (£27,000); Addaction (£18,000); Volunteering Matters (£13,000); Book Aid International (£10,000); Prisoners' Education Trust (£6,000); Campaign to Protect Rural England (£5,000).
FINANCES *Year* 2015/16 *Income* £429,107 *Grants* £1,444,500 *Grants to organisations* £1,444,500 *Assets* £46,242,207
TRUSTEES Charles Peacock; Bettine Bond; Dr Clare Sellors.
HOW TO APPLY Apply in writing to the correspondent. The trustees meet three times a year with representatives from the Charities Aid Foundation to decide on the grants to be made. The trust makes a lot of recurring grants therefore new applications are unlikely to be successful.
WHO TO APPLY TO The Trustees, c/o Charities Aid Foundation, Kings Hill, West Malling, Kent ME19 4TA *Tel.* 01732 520081 *Email* mtheodorou@cafonline.org

Susanna Peake Charitable Trust

CC NO 283462 **ESTABLISHED** 1981

WHERE FUNDING CAN BE GIVEN Worldwide with a preference for the south west of England, particularly Gloucestershire.

WHO CAN BENEFIT Registered charities.

WHAT IS FUNDED General charitable purposes with a preference for: education and children; local causes; medical causes, cancer charities and hospices; older people; international and overseas projects; animal welfare.

WHAT IS NOT FUNDED Individuals.

RANGE OF GRANTS £250 to £5,000.

SAMPLE GRANTS Longborough and Sezincote Cricket Club (£10,000); Bourton-on-the-Hill Retreat for Aged (£8,000); The Rugby Football Foundation (£6,000); All Ears Cambodia (£5,000); Action on Poverty, British Tinnitus Association and Cornwall Hospice Care (£3,000 each); Listening Books, Playing Fields Recreation Ground and The North London Food Bank (£2,000 each); Prostate Cancer Research (£500).

FINANCES *Year* 2015/16 *Income* £180,183 *Grants* £165,500 *Grants to organisations* £165,500 *Assets* £6,709,292

TRUSTEES Susanna Peake; Katharine Loyd.

HOW TO APPLY Apply in writing to the correspondent.

WHO TO APPLY TO Rathbone Trust Company Ltd, Rathbone Trust Company Ltd, 8 Finsbury Circus, London EC2M 7AZ *Tel.* 020 7399 0820 *Email* linda.cousins@rathbones.com

The Pears Family Charitable Foundation

CC NO 1009195 **ESTABLISHED** 1991

WHERE FUNDING CAN BE GIVEN Worldwide.

WHO CAN BENEFIT Charitable organisations.

WHAT IS FUNDED Jewish causes; community and young people; genocide education; philanthropy; international development; youth social action; special educational needs and disability; palliative care; research.

TYPE OF GRANT Core, project and capital costs.

RANGE OF GRANTS Up to £2.5 million.

SAMPLE GRANTS Anna Freud Centre (£2.5 million); Sense (£700,000); Birkbeck University of London (£450,000); Carers Trust (£400,000); National Holocaust Centre and Museum (£300,000); Havens Hospices (£250,000); RNIB Pears Centre for Specialist Learning (£190,000); Jewish Care (£150,000); The Federation of Jewish Services (£100,000); National Federation of Young Farmers' Clubs (£81,000).

FINANCES *Year* 2015/16 *Income* £14,925,559 *Grants* £16,324,065 *Grants to organisations* £16,324,065 *Assets* £17,318,784

TRUSTEES Trevor Pears; Mark Pears; David Pears.

HOW TO APPLY Unsolicited applications are not accepted.

WHO TO APPLY TO Ian Shaw, Finance Director, Clive House, 2 Old Brewery Mews, London NW3 1PZ *Tel.* 020 7433 3333 *Email* contact@pearsfoundation.org.uk *Website* www.pearsfoundation.org.uk

The Dowager Countess Eleanor Peel Trust

CC NO 214684 **ESTABLISHED** 1951

WHERE FUNDING CAN BE GIVEN Worldwide, in practice UK, with a preference for Lancashire (especially Lancaster and the surrounding district), Cumbria, Greater Manchester, Cheshire and Merseyside.

WHO CAN BENEFIT Small and medium-sized UK-registered charities; universities.

WHAT IS FUNDED Older people; disadvantaged people; medical care and research; various charities specified in the trust deed; occasionally disaster appeals are supported.

WHAT IS NOT FUNDED Individuals; children's charities; unregistered organisations; charities under the control of central or local government; projects outside the preferred geographical location (unless for a medical grant). Charities with an income above £2.5 million need to consult the guidelines on the website.

TYPE OF GRANT Projects rather than running costs.

RANGE OF GRANTS £600 to £15,000.

SAMPLE GRANTS Designability (£15,000); British Red Cross and East Coast Hospice (£10,000 each); Staffordshire Women's Aid (£9,300); Liverpool School of Tropical Medicine (£5,900); Birkenhead Young Men's Christian Association and Deafblind Scotland (£5,000); Ambleside Parish Centre (£3,000); Lancashire Flood Appeal (£2,500); Tall Ships Youth Trust (£600).

FINANCES *Year* 2015/16 *Income* £622,200 *Grants* £352,807 *Grants to organisations* £293,807 *Assets* £16,265,844

TRUSTEES Michael Parkinson; John Parkinson; Prof. Richard Ramsden; Prof. Sir Robert Boyd; Prof. Margaret Pearson; Julius Manduell.

OTHER INFORMATION During the year, grants were made to 51 organisations. Grants to individuals through The Peel and Rothwell Jackson Postgraduate Travelling Scholarship amounted to £59,000.

HOW TO APPLY Application forms can be completed online via the trust's website, where you can also find detailed guidance. The trustees usually meet three times a year (March, July and November).

WHO TO APPLY TO Michelle Bertenshaw, Hill Dickson, 50 Fountain Street, Manchester M2 2AS *Tel.* 0161 838 4977 *Email* secretary@peeltrust.com *Website* www.peeltrust.com

The Pell Charitable Trust

CC NO 1135398 **ESTABLISHED** 2010

WHERE FUNDING CAN BE GIVEN UK.

WHO CAN BENEFIT Registered charities.

WHAT IS FUNDED General charitable purposes, with a preference for the arts, particularly music.

WHAT IS NOT FUNDED Individuals.

RANGE OF GRANTS £500 to £15,000.

SAMPLE GRANTS Almeida Theatre; The Duke of Edinburgh's Award; Royal Opera House; Welsh National Opera; Garsington Opera; University of Southampton; Donmar Warehouse; Glyndebourne; Longborough Festival Opera; Amersham Festival; Oxfam; Mayor's Music Fund; Royal National Theatre.

FINANCES *Year* 2015/16 *Income* £51,565 *Grants* £79,140 *Grants to organisations* £79,140 *Assets* £82,096

TRUSTEES Marian Pell; Gordon Pell; Nicholas Pell; Victoria Pell; Coutts & Co.

OTHER INFORMATION Grants were made to 18 organisations during the year.

HOW TO APPLY Apply in writing to the correspondent.

WHO TO APPLY TO Coutts & Co., Trustee Department, 6th Floor, Trinity Quay 2, Avon Street, Bristol BS2 0PT *Tel.* 0345 304 2424 *Email* couttscharities@coutts.com

■ The Pen Shell Project

CC NO 1147958 **ESTABLISHED** 2012
WHERE FUNDING CAN BE GIVEN UK.
WHO CAN BENEFIT Registered charities; research bodies; hospitals.
WHAT IS FUNDED Alternative therapies in medicine and research; primarily homeopathy.
WHAT IS NOT FUNDED Individuals.
SAMPLE GRANTS A list of beneficiaries was not available.
FINANCES *Year* 2015/16 *Income* £235,007 *Grants* £120,000 *Grants to organisations* £120,000 *Assets* £163,492
TRUSTEES Charles Wansbrough; Amelia Heighington; Digby Leighton-Squires; Elaine Heighington.
HOW TO APPLY The charity has previously stated that it does not encourage unsolicited applications.
WHO TO APPLY TO Digby Leighton-Squires, Administrator, 52 Berkeley Square, London W1J 5BT *Tel.* 020 7495 8126 *Email* info@penshellproject.org

■ The Pennycress Trust

CC NO 261536 **ESTABLISHED** 1970
WHERE FUNDING CAN BE GIVEN UK and worldwide, with a preference for Cheshire and Norfolk.
WHO CAN BENEFIT Smaller charities, and especially those based in Cheshire and Norfolk.
WHAT IS FUNDED General charitable purposes with a preference for: arts and cultural heritage; education; infrastructure, support and development; science and technology; community facilities; campaigning on health and social issues; health care and advocacy; medical studies and research; animal welfare.
WHAT IS NOT FUNDED Individuals.
TYPE OF GRANT Recurrent and one-off.
RANGE OF GRANTS Typically £100 to £500.
SAMPLE GRANTS All Saints' Church – Beeston Regis, Brain Research Trust, Brighton and Hove Parents and Children's Group, British Red Cross, Depaul Trust, Elimination of Leukaemia Fund, Eyeless Trust, Genesis Appeal, Help the Aged, Matthew Project, Royal United Kingdom Beneficent Association (RUKBA), St Peter's – Eaton Square Appeal, Salvation Army, Tibet Relief Fund, West Suffolk Headway, Women's Link and Youth Federation.
FINANCES *Year* 2015/16 *Income* £88,890 *Grants* £79,500 *Grants to organisations* £79,500 *Assets* £2,174,362
TRUSTEES Lady Rose Cholmondeley; Anthony Baker; Charles Cholmondeley; Lady Margot Huston.
OTHER INFORMATION There were 239 grants made to organisations.
HOW TO APPLY Apply in writing to the correspondent. The trust does not have an application form and a simple letter is sufficient. Telephone applications are not accepted.
WHO TO APPLY TO Doreen Howells, Secretary to the Trustees, Flat D, 15 Millman Street, London WC1N 3EP *Tel.* 020 7404 0145 *Email* howellsdoreen@gmail.com

■ People's Health Trust

CC NO 1125537 **ESTABLISHED** 2008
WHERE FUNDING CAN BE GIVEN England, Scotland and Wales.
WHO CAN BENEFIT Charitable organisations; community groups.
WHAT IS FUNDED Health and well-being; communities; social welfare.
WHAT IS NOT FUNDED Refer to the website for the restrictions on each funding programme.
SAMPLE GRANTS West Itchen Community Trust (£369,500); Penparcau Community Forum (£300,500); Community Action Milton Keynes (£242,000); Cymunedau'n Gyntaf Mon Communities (£235,000); Home on the Range (£50,000); Hart Gables (£37,000); Asha Neighbourhood Project and Lightburn Elderly Association Project (£35,000 each); The Buzz Project (£30,500); Stockport Progress and Recovery Centre (SPARC) (£28,000); Bristol Reggae Orchestra (£25,500); Greenhill Tenants Association (£14,000).
FINANCES *Year* 2015/16 *Income* £12,141,883 *Grants* £14,915,340 *Grants to organisations* £14,915,340 *Assets* £7,215,514
TRUSTEES Barbara Simmonds; Sue Hawkett; Nigel Turner; Dr Eva Elliott; Alan Francis; Sue Cohen; Paul Ballantyne; Prof. Elizabeth Dowler; Duncan Stephenson.
HOW TO APPLY Applications can be submitted online. The trust funds nationwide in areas in which the Health Lottery operates. However, grant rounds are divided into regional schemes. Check the website to see if a grant scheme is open in your area. Note that schemes open and close throughout the year.
WHO TO APPLY TO David Jones, Director of Grant Programmes, 3rd Floor, 64 Great Eastern Street, London EC2A 3QR *Tel.* 020 7749 9100 *Email* enquiries@peopleshealthtrust.org.uk or apply@peopleshealthtrust.org.uk *Website* www.peopleshealthtrust.org.uk

■ People's Postcode Trust

SC NO SC040387 **ESTABLISHED** 2009
WHERE FUNDING CAN BE GIVEN Scotland, Wales and England.
WHO CAN BENEFIT Registered charities; constituted community organisations such as CICs or CIOs; social enterprises; not-for-profit organisations.
WHAT IS FUNDED Community development; citizenship; sports, environment, health, human rights, poverty or other causes where linked to community development.
WHAT IS NOT FUNDED Organisations that are not based in or do not bring a benefit to Scotland, England or Wales; individuals; hospices or end-of-life care; statutory bodies that the state has an obligation to fund (including schools/PTAs, councils and local authorities); parish councils; colleges or universities; medical equipment or research; any type of feasibility or research studies; building renovations that are purely for cosmetic purposes; groups with exclusive membership policies. Further exclusions can be found within the eligibility criteria on the charity's website.
TYPE OF GRANT Project funding; capital items and equipment.
RANGE OF GRANTS £500 to £20,000 (£10,000 in Wales) for small grants programme.
SAMPLE GRANTS Barnardo's and NSPCC (£100,000 each); Equal Scotland (£20,000); FareShare (£19,100); Cancer United (£15,000); Inverurie and District Men's Shed (£10,900); Bristol Avon Rivers Trust (£6,000); Bangor Gymnastics Club (£1,900).
FINANCES *Year* 2015 *Income* £8,026,963 *Grants* £1,706,214 *Grants to organisations* £1,706,214 *Assets* £306,164
TRUSTEES Lawson Muncaster; Michael Pratt; Judith Hills; Robert Flett.
OTHER INFORMATION During the year, 170 projects received funding from the trust, with 168

(£1.5 million) of these being made through the small grants programme. Organisations wishing to apply for funding of more than £2,000 must be a registered charity.

HOW TO APPLY Apply via the appropriate online application form. More details, including guidance notes and deadlines, are available from the website.

WHO TO APPLY TO Clara Govier, Executive Manager, 76 George Street, Edinburgh EH2 3BU *Tel.* 0131 555 7287 *Email* info@postcodetrust.org.uk *Website* www.postcodetrust.org.uk

■ The Performing Right Society Foundation

CC NO 1080837 **ESTABLISHED** 2000

WHERE FUNDING CAN BE GIVEN UK.

WHO CAN BENEFIT Not-for-profit organisations; individuals.

WHAT IS FUNDED The creation and performance of outstanding new music in any genre; the development of artists; inspiring audiences. This may include funding towards: touring; recording; PR and marketing; commissions of new music by creators in the UK; exciting community projects; music creator residencies; live programmes featuring UK music.

WHAT IS NOT FUNDED Companies limited by shares; technological development if it does not contain a significant aspect of new music creation; projects that contain no element of live performance (unless applying for recording costs only); the purchase of vans and cars; bursaries, tuition/education costs, or scholarships; capital projects (e.g. building work); any project raising funds for another charity; buying equipment/ building a studio; organisations or projects that have been running for less than 18 months and musicians that have not been active for 18 months; retrospective activity; activity that falls before the foundation's decision date; organisations based outside the UK; artists and music creators based outside the UK; British artists no longer permanently resident in the UK; international tours/recording internationally (see the foundation's International Showcase Fund scheme); radio stations/broadcasting costs; start-up companies or labels; a roster of artists on a record label; editing, mastering or distribution of work; salary and living costs; core organisational costs; individuals in full-time education or who are under 18 unless represented by an adult with a valid DBS check.

TYPE OF GRANT Usually one year.

SAMPLE GRANTS Birmingham Contemporary Music Group; Birmingham Royal Ballet; FACT; Halle; London Sinfonietta; Merseyside Arts Foundation; Parr Street Studios; Small Green Shoots; Unity Theatre Liverpool.

FINANCES *Year* 2015 *Income* £3,227,741 *Grants* £2,029,127 *Grants to organisations* £964,272 *Assets* £801,332

TRUSTEES Prof. Edward Gregson; Simon Platz; Royce Bell; Ameet Shah; Vanessa Swann; John Reid; Richard King; Julian Nott; Mark Poole; Caroline Norbury; Hannah Kendall.

OTHER INFORMATION The information in this entry for the grant total for organisations refers to the foundation's Open Fund for organisations and the Beyond Borders programme. The rest of the grants were made to individuals. Details of other funds operated by the foundation can be found on the website.

HOW TO APPLY Apply via the foundation's website. The application is a two-stage process. At Stage 1, you are asked to provide two examples of music and a brief description of your project. The foundation stresses that the most common reason applications are unsuccessful at this stage is because of eligibility and competition. Applicants must, therefore, refer to the guideline documents, which are available from the website, before an application is started. Those applicants who are successful at Stage 1 will be invited to continue with the second part of the application process. Returning applicants should contact the foundation before making an application.

WHO TO APPLY TO Fiona Harvey, Operations Director, 2 Pancras Square, London N1C 4AG *Tel.* 020 3741 4233 *Email* info@prsformusicfoundation.com *Website* www.prsformusicfoundation.com

■ B. E. Perl Charitable Trust

CC NO 282847 **ESTABLISHED** 1981

WHERE FUNDING CAN BE GIVEN Barnet; Brent; Hackney; Hertfordshire.

WHO CAN BENEFIT Orthodox Jewish organisations, particularly schools and higher education institutions.

WHAT IS FUNDED Orthodox Jewish faith and education; general charitable purposes.

SAMPLE GRANTS Hasmonean High School; Jewish National Fund; Society of Friends of the Torah; Yavneh College.

FINANCES *Year* 2015/16 *Income* £2,818,186 *Grants* £287,750 *Grants to organisations* £287,750 *Assets* £21,108,424

TRUSTEES Benjamin Perl; Dr Shoshanna Perl; Jonathan Perl; Joseph Perl; Naomi Sorotzkin; Rachel Jeidal.

OTHER INFORMATION Grants were made for the following purposes: advancement of religion (£121,000); education (£109,5000); relief of poverty and illness (£38,000); general charitable purposes (£19,000).

HOW TO APPLY Apply in writing to the correspondent.

WHO TO APPLY TO Benjamin Perl, Trustee, Foframe House, 35–37 Brent Street, Hendon, London NW4 2EF

■ Personal Assurance Charitable Trust

CC NO 1023274 **ESTABLISHED** 1993

WHERE FUNDING CAN BE GIVEN Mainly UK with some preference for Milton Keynes; Kenya.

WHO CAN BENEFIT Registered charities and non-registered charitable organisations.

WHAT IS FUNDED General charitable purposes, social welfare, health; education.

WHAT IS NOT FUNDED Grants are rarely made to individuals.

RANGE OF GRANTS Typically between £1,000 and £5,000. Occasionally larger.

SAMPLE GRANTS Memusi Foundation (£120,700); Alzheimer's Society (£5,900); The Outwood Bound Trust (£5,000); Cancer Research UK (£2,550); Ashgate Hospice (£1,100); Mind, Sandy Lane Nursery and Forest School, and The Sabre Trust (£1,000 each).

FINANCES *Year* 2015 *Income* £100,354 *Grants* £197,134 *Grants to organisations* £197,134 *Assets* £85,109

TRUSTEES Michael Dugdale; Philip Yates; Sarah Mace.

OTHER INFORMATION The trust made a large grant to the Memusi Foundation during the year which represents over 60% of the grant total.

Donations under £1,000 totalled nearly £20,000.

HOW TO APPLY Apply in writing to the correspondent.

WHO TO APPLY TO Sarah Mace, Trustee, Personal Group Holdings PLC, John Ormond House, 899 Silbury Boulevard, Milton Keynes MK9 3XL *Email* sarah.mace@personal-group.com

■ The Persson Charitable Trust (Highmoore Hall Charitable Trust)

CC NO 289027 **ESTABLISHED** 1984

WHERE FUNDING CAN BE GIVEN UK and overseas.

WHO CAN BENEFIT Registered Christian mission societies and relief agencies.

WHAT IS FUNDED Missionary activities; overseas aid.

WHAT IS NOT FUNDED Non-registered charities.

TYPE OF GRANT Mainly recurrent.

SAMPLE GRANTS Bible Reading Fellowship (£111,000); Tearfund – Christian Relief (£55,000); All Nations Christian College (£12,000); Christian Solidarity Worldwide (£10,000).

FINANCES *Year* 2015/16 *Income* £1,013,422 *Grants* £578,556 *Grants to organisations* £578,556 *Assets* £1,603,218

TRUSTEES Paul Persson; Andrew Persson; John Persson; Ann Persson.

HOW TO APPLY The trust states that it does not respond to unsolicited applications. Telephone calls are not welcome.

WHO TO APPLY TO Paul Persson, Trustee, Long Meadow, Dark Lane, Chearsley, Aylesbury, Buckinghamshire HP18 0DA *Email* Paul@paulpersson.co.uk

■ The Persula Foundation

CC NO 1044174 **ESTABLISHED** 1994

WHERE FUNDING CAN BE GIVEN Predominantly UK; overseas grants are given, but this is rare.

WHO CAN BENEFIT Registered charities.

WHAT IS FUNDED Homelessness; disability; human rights; animal welfare.

WHAT IS NOT FUNDED Grants cannot be given for buildings, individuals or core funding.

TYPE OF GRANT Up to two years.

RANGE OF GRANTS Up to £65,000.

SAMPLE GRANTS Amnesty International (£65,000); Compassion in World Farming (£48,000); Civil Liberties Trust (£44,000); Prison Reform Trust (£32,000); PETA (£27,000); ACTS435 (£25,000); Humane Society International (£23,000); Animal Aid (£20,000).

FINANCES *Year* 2015/16 *Income* £1,313,969 *Grants* £1,269,289 *Grants to organisations* £1,269,289 *Assets* £29,832

TRUSTEES Hanna Oppenheim; Julian Richer; David Robinson; Rosie Richer; Robert Rosenthal; Jonathan Levy.

OTHER INFORMATION The foundation made 415 grants throughout the year for the following purposes: human welfare (£557,500); human rights (£264,000); animal welfare (£270,500); disabilities (£128,500); homelessness (£49,000).

HOW TO APPLY Apply in writing to the correspondent. Applications are reviewed and levels of grants payable are decided upon by the trustees.

WHO TO APPLY TO Teresa Chapman, Secretary to the Trustees, Gallery Court, Hankey Place, London SE1 4BB *Tel.* 020 7551 5343 *Email* info@persula.org

■ The Jack Petchey Foundation

CC NO 1076886 **ESTABLISHED** 1999

WHERE FUNDING CAN BE GIVEN Greater London and Essex.

WHO CAN BENEFIT Registered charities; state schools and colleges; local authority youth clubs; other charitable organisations; individuals.

WHAT IS FUNDED Support for young people aged between 11 and 25 through various programmes.

WHAT IS NOT FUNDED Private schools; profit-making companies; grants that directly replace statutory funding; individuals (unless under the Individual Grants for Volunteering); work that has already taken place; projects outside the UK; medical research; animal welfare; endowment funds; general appeals or circulars; building or major refurbishment projects; conferences and seminars; projects where the main purpose is to promote religious beliefs.

RANGE OF GRANTS £200 to £589,000.

SAMPLE GRANTS Speakers Trust (£589,000); Table Tennis England (£171,000); Media Trust (£142,000); London Youth (£50,000); Essex Boys and Girls Clubs (£41,500); City YMCA (£26,000); Army Cadet Force (£22,000); Stepney City Farm (£15,000); St Christopher's Hospice (£6,000); Archway Project (£4,000).

FINANCES *Year* 2015 *Income* £7,155,239 *Grants* £5,841,223 *Grants to organisations* £5,693,493 *Assets* £370,926

TRUSTEE Jack Petchey Foundation Company.

OTHER INFORMATION Grants to individuals for volunteering totalled £147,500.

HOW TO APPLY Application forms for each of the grant schemes can be downloaded from the foundation's website. A typical application process takes six to eight weeks and applicants may be visited by a grants officer.

WHO TO APPLY TO Gemma Dunbar, Head of Grants, Dockmaster's House, 1 Hertsmere Road, London E14 8JJ *Tel.* 020 8252 8000 *Email* mail@jackpetcheyfoundation.org.uk *Website* www.jackpetcheyfoundation.org.uk

■ Petplan Charitable Trust

CC NO 1032907 **ESTABLISHED** 1994

WHERE FUNDING CAN BE GIVEN UK.

WHO CAN BENEFIT Animal charities and organisations benefitting students, research workers and veterinarians.

WHAT IS FUNDED Veterinary research; veterinary studies; animal welfare; education in animal welfare. Help is limited to dogs, cats, rabbits and horses only, those being the animals insured by Petplan.

WHAT IS NOT FUNDED Individuals; non-registered charities; studies involving invasive procedures or experimental animals.

TYPE OF GRANT Project funding (excluding overheads); capital costs; research.

SAMPLE GRANTS Royal Veterinary College (£156,500 in five grants); Brooke Hospital for Animals (£25,000); Blue Cross (£20,000); University of Bristol (£19,500); University of Northumbria (£10,000); Gables Farm Dogs and Cats Home (£6,400); Retired Greyhound Trust (£4,000); Rotherham Rescue Rangers (£1,500); Camp Nibble (£1,000); Abandoned Animal Association (£100).

FINANCES *Year* 2015 *Income* £863,671 *Grants* £607,087 *Grants to organisations* £607,087 *Assets* £503,556

TRUSTEES John Bower; Clarissa Baldwin; David Simpson; Patsy Bloom; Ted Chandler; Peter

Laurie; Kathryn Willis; Jamie Crittall; Gary Davess.

OTHER INFORMATION The trust made grants for the following purposes: scientific (£306,500); welfare and education (£206,500); Pedigree Adoption Scheme (£94,000).

HOW TO APPLY The dates of application rounds vary depending on the type of grant being applied for. See the website for more details.

WHO TO APPLY TO Catherine Bourg, Trust Administrator, Great West House (GW2), Great West Road, Brentford, Middlesex TW8 9EG *Tel.* 020 8580 8013 *Email* catherine.bourg@allianz.co.uk *Website* www.petplantrust.org

■ The Pharsalia Charitable Trust

CC NO 1120402 **ESTABLISHED** 2007

WHERE FUNDING CAN BE GIVEN UK with a preference for Oxford.

WHO CAN BENEFIT Registered charities.

WHAT IS FUNDED General charitable purposes, particularly the relief of sickness.

RANGE OF GRANTS Generally between £150 and £15,000.

SAMPLE GRANTS Oxford Radcliffe Hospitals Charitable Funds (£15,000); Macmillan Cancer Support (£12,000); Abingdon Bridge (£10,000); Bowel Disease UK (£5,000); The Glacier Trust (£4,500); Canine Partners (£750); Wiltshire Music Centre Trust Ltd (£500); Help for Heroes (£250); Battle of Britain Memorial Trust (£150).

FINANCES *Year* 2015/16 *Income* £93,997 *Grants* £85,210 *Grants to organisations* £85,210 *Assets* £2,621,329

TRUSTEES Nigel Stirling Blackwell; Christina Blackwell; Trudy Sainsbury.

OTHER INFORMATION The trust made grants to 43 organisations during the year.

HOW TO APPLY Apply in writing to the correspondent.

WHO TO APPLY TO Trudy Sainsbury, Trustee, The Ham, Ickleton Road, Wantage, Oxfordshire OX12 9JA *Tel.* 01235 426524

■ The Phillips and Rubens Charitable Trust

CC NO 260378 **ESTABLISHED** 2005

WHERE FUNDING CAN BE GIVEN UK.

WHO CAN BENEFIT Registered charities, mostly Jewish organisations.

WHAT IS FUNDED Jewish causes; medical and ancillary services (including medical research); education; disability; older people; poverty; sheltered accommodation; development of the arts.

WHAT IS NOT FUNDED Individuals.

TYPE OF GRANT Recurrent and one-off.

RANGE OF GRANTS Up to £80,000, although the vast majority of grants were of less than £10,000.

SAMPLE GRANTS The Phillips Family Charitable Trust (£80,000); Charities Aid Foundation (£30,000); United Jewish Israel Appeal (UJIA) (£25,000); Friends of Hebrew University of Jerusalem (£11,000); Western Marble Arch Synagogue (£6,700); Community Security Trust, Henry Jackson Society and Weizmann UK (£5,000 each); World Jewish Relief (£3,000); Jewish Community Secondary School (£2,500).

FINANCES *Year* 2015/16 *Income* £447,120 *Grants* £248,145 *Grants to organisations* £248,145 *Assets* £10,303,510

TRUSTEES Michael Phillips; Ruth Phillips; Martin Paisner; Paul Phillips; Gary Phillips; Carolyn Mishon.

OTHER INFORMATION Donations of less than £2,500 amounted to £11,000. The Phillips and Rubens Charitable Trust is connected to The Phillips Family Charitable Trust (Charity Commission no. 279120) through common trustees.

HOW TO APPLY Apply in writing to the correspondent at any time, although the trust has stated that the majority of grants are to beneficiaries they already support.

WHO TO APPLY TO Michael Phillips, Trustee, 67–69 George Street, London W1U 8LT *Email* psphillips@aol.com

■ The Phillips Charitable Trust

CC NO 1057019 **ESTABLISHED** 1995

WHERE FUNDING CAN BE GIVEN UK, with a preference for the Midlands, and particularly Northamptonshire.

WHO CAN BENEFIT Registered charities.

WHAT IS FUNDED Seafarers, animal husbandry and welfare, and smaller one-off national or local projects.

TYPE OF GRANT One-off and recurrent.

RANGE OF GRANTS Most grants were in the range of £1,000 to £5,000.

SAMPLE GRANTS Peterborough 900 (£15,000); Sportsaid Eastern (£10,000); Northamptonshire Association of Youth Clubs (£5,000); Autism Concern and Lakelands Hospice (£3,000 each); Dogs for Good, Pitsford Scout Group and RNIB (£2,000 each); Sailors' Children's Society (£1,000); Vine Community Trust (£600).

FINANCES *Year* 2015/16 *Income* £78,108 *Grants* £57,803 *Grants to organisations* £57,803 *Assets* £2,259,649

TRUSTEES John Ford; Michael Percival; Philip Saunderson; S. G. Schanschieff; Anne Marrum.

OTHER INFORMATION In 2015/16 a total of 17 organisations received grants.

HOW TO APPLY Apply in writing to the correspondent.

WHO TO APPLY TO Anne Henman, Clerk to the Trustees, 1 Church Lane, Brafield On The Green, Northampton NN7 1BA *Tel.* 01604 890748 *Email* anne@rydalchurchlane.plus.com

■ The Phillips Family Charitable Trust

CC NO 279120 **ESTABLISHED** 1979

WHERE FUNDING CAN BE GIVEN UK.

WHO CAN BENEFIT Registered charities; Jewish organisations.

WHAT IS FUNDED General charitable purposes, mainly Jewish organisations and those concerned with education, the care of people who have disabilities or are older, poverty, or the development of the arts.

RANGE OF GRANTS Up to £6,000.

SAMPLE GRANTS UK Friends of the Association for the Wellbeing of Israel's Soldiers (£6,500 in two grants); Jewish Learning Exchange (£6,000); Community Security Trust and London School of Jewish Studies (£5,000 each); British Friends of Sarah Herzog Memorial Hospital (£4,000); Royal Marines Charitable Trust Fund (£2,000); '45 Aid Society for Holocaust Survivors (£1,500); The British Friends of Haifa University (£1,000).

FINANCES *Year* 2015/16 *Income* £80,000 *Grants* £82,434 *Grants to organisations* £82,434 *Assets* £16,172

TRUSTEES Michael Phillips; Ruth Phillips; Martin Paisner; Paul Phillips; Gary Phillips.

OTHER INFORMATION During the year, 67 grants were made in total and 30 of those were for less than £1,000.
HOW TO APPLY Apply in writing to the correspondent.
WHO TO APPLY TO Paul Phillips, Trustee, 67–69 George Street, London W1U 8LT *Tel.* 020 7487 5757 *Email* psphillipsbsh@aol.com

■ The Bernard Piggott Charitable Trust

CC NO 1154724 **ESTABLISHED** 1970
WHERE FUNDING CAN BE GIVEN North Wales and Birmingham.
WHO CAN BENEFIT Registered charities mainly in the City of Birmingham and North Wales, also some national charities with projects in these areas.
WHAT IS FUNDED General charitable purposes.
WHAT IS NOT FUNDED Individuals.
TYPE OF GRANT Usually one-off capital funding.
RANGE OF GRANTS Mostly £750 to £1,500.
SAMPLE GRANTS St Mary's Church – Caerhun (£2,000); St Mary's Hospice (£1,500); Birmingham Big Art Project and Birmingham Royal Ballet (£1,000 each); Resources for Autism (£900); Athac CIC and PBC Foundation (£750 each); Montgomeryshire Youth Theatre (£250).
FINANCES *Year* 2015/16 *Income* £115,094 *Grants* £68,900 *Grants to organisations* £68,900 *Assets* £1,581,676
TRUSTEES Mark Painter; Derek Lea; Nigel Lea; Richard Easton; Ven. Paul Davies.
HOW TO APPLY Apply in writing to the correspondent.
WHO TO APPLY TO Jenny Whitworth, 4 Streetsbrook Road, Shirley, Solihull, West Midlands B90 3PL *Email* jenny@whitworth4.plus.com

■ The Pilgrim Trust

CC NO 206602 **ESTABLISHED** 1930
WHERE FUNDING CAN BE GIVEN UK (this does not include the Channel Islands or the Isle of Man).
WHO CAN BENEFIT UK-registered charities; organisations exempt from registration; recognised public bodies; registered friendly societies.
WHAT IS FUNDED Social welfare, especially preventative schemes; women and girls; heritage.
WHAT IS NOT FUNDED Individuals; charities not registered in the UK or charities registered in the Channel Islands or the Isle of Man; CICs or social enterprises; projects where the work has already been completed or where contracts have already been awarded; projects with a capital cost exceeding £5 million; projects seeking to replace statutory funding; general appeals or circulars; projects for the commissioning of new art works; publishing production costs; new facilities within a church or the re-ordering of church's or places of worship for wider community use; social welfare projects falling outside the trustees' current priorities; arts and drama projects; one-off short-term interventions; youth or sports clubs; travel or adventure projects; community centres; children's playgroups; organisations seeking funding for trips overseas or outward bound courses; organisations seeking funding for educational purposes; one-off events such as exhibitions, festivals, seminars, conferences, or theatrical or musical productions.
TYPE OF GRANT Revenue costs, such as salaries and overheads; project costs; the costs of initial 'exploratory work' for organisations wishing to preserve important buildings/monuments, etc.; capital costs where the total cost does not exceed £5 million.
RANGE OF GRANTS Small grants of less than £5,000 and main grants of over £5,000.
SAMPLE GRANTS National Churches Trust (£200,000); Working Chance Ltd (£120,000); Release Legal Emergency and Drugs Services (£92,000); New Hall Kidz Ltd Wakefield (£53,500); Labour History and Archive Study Centre – People's History Museum (£35,250); The National Art Collections Fund and Yarl's Wood Befrienders (£20,000 each); British Universities Film and Video Council (£8,400); East Worlington Parish Hall (£5,000); East Somerset Railway (£2,800).
FINANCES *Year* 2015 *Income* £1,773,254 *Grants* £2,809,267 *Grants to organisations* £2,809,267 *Assets* £60,301,083
TRUSTEES David Barrie; Lady Sarah Riddell; Prof. Sir Colin Blakemore; Sir Mark Jones; Prof. John Podmore; Michael Baughan; James Fergusson; Caroline Butler; Sarah Staniforth; Kevin Pakenham.
OTHER INFORMATION In 2015 grants were made to 89 organisations. Of the amount payable in grants committed during the year, £1.1 million was for historic buildings; £859,000 was for social welfare; £325,000 was for cataloguing grants; £198,000 was for the care of collections and acquisitions; and £105,000 was for training, research and miscellaneous purposes. The trust makes annual block grants for the repair of fabric in historic churches and towards the conservations of churches' historic contents. For details on where to apply for this funding, see the website.
HOW TO APPLY Applications for both the small grants fund and the main grants can be made using the trust's online form. Applicants should read the application guidelines available on the website in full before applying. There are no deadlines; applications are considered at quarterly trustee meetings. The trust welcomes informal contact prior to application via phone or email.
WHO TO APPLY TO Jenny Oppenheimer, Grants Manager, Alexandra House, 55A Catherine Place, London SW1E 6DY *Tel.* 020 7834 6510 *Email* info@thepilgrimtrust.org.uk or jenny@thepilgrimtrust.org.uk *Website* www.thepilgrimtrust.org.uk

■ Pilkington Charities Fund

CC NO 225911 **ESTABLISHED** 1964
WHERE FUNDING CAN BE GIVEN Worldwide, in practice mainly UK with a preference for Merseyside.
WHO CAN BENEFIT Registered charities.
WHAT IS FUNDED General charitable purposes including health, older people and people affected by poverty.
WHAT IS NOT FUNDED Non-registered charities; individuals.
TYPE OF GRANT Capital (including buildings) and core costs, one-off funding, project expenditure, research, recurring costs. Funding for more than three years will be considered.
RANGE OF GRANTS Typically between £1,000 and £6,000.
SAMPLE GRANTS C. and A. Pilkington Trust Fund (£70,000); Children with Cancer UK and Shelter (£10,000 each); Bowel Disease Research Fund (£8,000); Medical Aid for Palestinians (£7,000);

After Adoption, SOLA Arts and Toxteth Town Hall Community Resource Centre (£4,000 each); British Wireless for the Blind Fund (£3,000); Fire Fighters Charity (£1,200).

FINANCES *Year* 2015/16 *Income* £702,105 *Grants* £203,600 *Grants to organisations* £203,600 *Assets* £22,989,213

TRUSTEES Neil Pilkington Jones; Arnold Pilkington; Eleanor Jones.

OTHER INFORMATION Grants were made to 119 organisations during the year.

HOW TO APPLY Apply in writing to the correspondent. Applications can be sent by post or email and there are clear guidelines available on the website. Telephone calls are not welcome. Only send documents that relate to, or support, your application, for example: relevant budget or cost details; annual report and accounts; case studies; details of funding received from other organisations.

WHO TO APPLY TO Sarah Nicklin, Rathbones, Port of Liverpool Building, Pier Head, Liverpool L3 1NW *Tel.* 0151 236 6666 *Email* sarah.nicklin@rathbones.com *Website* pilkingtoncharitiesfund.org.uk

■ The Austin and Hope Pilkington Trust

CC NO 255274 **ESTABLISHED** 1967

WHERE FUNDING CAN BE GIVEN Unrestricted, but see 'What is not funded' section.

WHO CAN BENEFIT Registered charities only. National projects are preferred to those with a local remit.

WHAT IS FUNDED The trust has a three-year cycle of funding priorities: 2017 – music and the arts, older people; 2018 – medical causes and community; 2019 – children and young people. These categories are then repeated in a three-year rotation. In all cases, priority is given to projects focusing on: homelessness; domestic abuse; prisoners/people who have offended; training and education; counselling and support; better access to the arts for those who have limited opportunities; refugees and asylum seekers.

WHAT IS NOT FUNDED Overseas projects; capital appeals; schools; village halls; minibuses; shopmobility; charities involved with religion (including the repair of church fabric); churches, even those used by community groups; charities involved with animals; individuals (including individuals going overseas for a charitable organisation); students; scouts, guides, cubs, brownies; sea cadets; holidays; individual hospices (although national organisations may apply).

TYPE OF GRANT Grants are usually awarded for one year only.

RANGE OF GRANTS Grants are usually between £1,000 and £3,000, with the majority being of £1,000. Exceptionally, grants of up to £10,000 are made, but these are usually for medical research projects.

SAMPLE GRANTS Mental Health Research UK (£10,000); Adults Supporting Adults, Bipolar UK Ltd, London's Air Ambulance, Refugee Council, The Maytree Respite Centre and Young Vic Company (£3,000 each); British Tinnitus Association, LGBT Healthy Living Centre, The Debt Advice Network, Rehabilitation for Addicted Prisoners Trust and West Mercia Women's Aid (£1,000 each).

FINANCES *Year* 2015 *Income* £307,198 *Grants* £239,957 *Grants to organisations* £239,957 *Assets* £10,487,271

TRUSTEES Debbie Nelson; Penny Badowska; Eleanor Stride.

OTHER INFORMATION The trust has categories of funding that are repeated on a three-year cycle. The funding priorities for 2015 were medical and community causes with a focus on mental health for medical research projects. The trust has an ongoing commitment of one annual music scholarship (£32,000) at the Purcell School, a specialist music school.

HOW TO APPLY The trust prefers to receive applications via the online form on its website; however, hard copies of the application form are available for anyone who is unable to complete it online. Postal applications are not accepted. Grants are made twice a year and applications are subject to closing dates, the details of which can be seen on the website.

WHO TO APPLY TO Karen Frank, Administrator, Rathbone Trust Company, Port of Liverpool Building, Pier Head, Liverpool L3 1NW *Tel.* 0151 236 6666 *Email* admin@austin-hope-pilkington.org.uk *Website* www.austin-hope-pilkington.org.uk

■ Miss A. M. Pilkington's Charitable Trust

SC NO SC000282 **ESTABLISHED** 1972

WHERE FUNDING CAN BE GIVEN UK, with a preference for Scotland.

WHO CAN BENEFIT Registered charities.

WHAT IS FUNDED General charitable purposes.

SAMPLE GRANTS A list of beneficiaries was not available.

FINANCES *Year* 2015/16 *Income* £114,184 *Grants* £126,000 *Grants to organisations* £126,000 *Assets* £3,285,685

OTHER INFORMATION Grants were made to 115 organisations during the year.

HOW TO APPLY The trustees have previously stated that, regrettably, they are unable to make grants to new applicants since they already have 'more than enough causes to support'.

WHO TO APPLY TO The Trustees, EQ Chartered Accountants, Pentland House, Saltire Centre, Glenrothes, Fife KY6 2AH *Tel.* 01592 630055

■ Pink Ribbon Foundation

CC NO 1080839 **ESTABLISHED** 2000

WHERE FUNDING CAN BE GIVEN UK.

WHO CAN BENEFIT UK-registered charities.

WHAT IS FUNDED People affected by breast cancer.

WHAT IS NOT FUNDED Individuals.

TYPE OF GRANT One-off and recurrent.

RANGE OF GRANTS £500 to £10,000.

SAMPLE GRANTS Cancer Active (£10,000); Bosom Buddies (£8,000); Primrose Centre (£7,000); Cransley Hospice, Doncaster Ethnic Minority Partnership, Macmillan Cancer Relief and Relate Cymru (£5,000 each); Big Picture (£3,000); South Gwent Breast Cancer Support Group (£2,000); Fishing for Life (£500).

FINANCES *Year* 2015/16 *Income* £374,367 *Grants* £268,785 *Grants to organisations* £268,785 *Assets* £333,128

TRUSTEES Angela Brignall; Errol McBean; Jonathan Prince.

HOW TO APPLY Application forms can be downloaded from the foundation's website or requested by email. If applying from a general cancer charity, the grant must be specifically for those with or affected by breast cancer.

WHO TO APPLY TO Jonathan Prince, Trustee, Crofton House, 5 Morley Close, Orpington, Kent BR6 8JR *Tel.* 01689 858877 *Email* enquiries@pinkribbonfoundation.org.uk *Website* www.pinkribbonfoundation.org.uk

■ The DLA Piper Charitable Trust

CC NO 327280 **ESTABLISHED** 1986

WHERE FUNDING CAN BE GIVEN UK.

WHO CAN BENEFIT Registered charities.

WHAT IS FUNDED General charitable purposes; medical research; social welfare.

WHAT IS NOT FUNDED Individuals.

RANGE OF GRANTS Typically less than £1,000.

SAMPLE GRANTS Unicef (£10,500 in two grants); Net4Kids, The Save the Children Fund and United Way Romania (£5,000 each); Bloodwise (£7,500 in two grants); Leeds Teaching Hospitals Charitable Foundation (£2,100 in three grants); Refugee Action, Scottish Association for Mental Health and Walthew House (£1,000 each).

FINANCES *Year* 2015/16 *Income* £160,164 *Grants* £58,218 *Grants to organisations* £58,218 *Assets* £147,314

TRUSTEES Nigel Knowles; Philip Rooney; Sean Mahon.

OTHER INFORMATION During the year, 46 grants were made. Of these, 30 were of less than £1,000.

HOW TO APPLY Apply in writing to the correspondent, for consideration four times a year. Applications from members, partners and employees of DLA Piper for grants in support of charities are encouraged.

WHO TO APPLY TO Godfrey Smallman, Secretary, Wrigleys Solicitors LLP, Fountain Precinct, Balm Green, Sheffield S1 2JA *Email* godfrey.smallman@wrigleys.co.uk

■ Polden-Puckham Charitable Foundation

CC NO 1003024 **ESTABLISHED** 1991

WHERE FUNDING CAN BE GIVEN UK and overseas.

WHO CAN BENEFIT Registered charities, with a preference for new and small organisations.

WHAT IS FUNDED Peacebuilding; sustainable security; gender equality; corporate social responsibility; environmental sustainability. The foundation states on its website: 'We only support practical projects when they are clearly of a pioneering nature, with potential for influencing UK national policy.'

WHAT IS NOT FUNDED Large organisations; organisations based outside the UK (unless they are linked with a UK-registered charity and doing work of international focus); work outside the UK (unless it is of international focus); individuals; travel bursaries (including overseas placements and expeditions); study; academic research; capital projects; community or local practical projects (except innovative projects with a broad scope); environmental/ecological conservation; international agencies and overseas appeals; general appeals; human rights work (unless it relates to peace and environmental sustainability); community mediation and crime-related work.

TYPE OF GRANT Project funding for up to three years, including core costs and salaries.

RANGE OF GRANTS Normally between £5,000 and £15,000.

SAMPLE GRANTS Our Voices (£30,000); Centre for Alternative Technology (£20,000); All Party Parliamentary Group on Agroecology (£15,000); Campaign Against the Arms Trade, International Peace Bureau, Pesticide Action Network Europe and United Nations Association UK (£10,000 each); 10:10 Foundation (£5,000); Environmental Funders Network (£2,000).

FINANCES *Year* 2015/16 *Income* £740,233 *Grants* £562,800 *Grants to organisations* £562,800 *Assets* £16,422,949

TRUSTEES Martin Bevis Gillett; Stephen Pittam; Angela Seay; Jonathan Gillett; Dorothy Ball; Simon Fisher.

OTHER INFORMATION During the year 51 grants were made, with 18 (£170,000) given to peacebuilding and security projects and 33 (£393,000) given to environmental sustainability projects.

HOW TO APPLY Application forms and guidance notes can be downloaded from the foundation's website and must be submitted via email. Applicants are also asked to submit their latest set of audited accounts and an annual report, preferably via email. Application deadlines are posted on the website.

WHO TO APPLY TO The Trustees, BMPPCF, London WC1N 3XX *Tel.* 020 7193 7364 *Email* ppcf@polden-puckham.org.uk *Website* www.polden-puckham.org.uk

■ The Polehampton Charity

CC NO 1072631 **ESTABLISHED** 1957

WHERE FUNDING CAN BE GIVEN Twyford and Ruscombe.

WHO CAN BENEFIT Registered charities; educational establishments; organisations; individuals.

WHAT IS FUNDED General charitable purposes; education; hardship; community development.

WHAT IS NOT FUNDED Anyone outside Twyford and Ruscombe.

TYPE OF GRANT One-off or recurring. Limited interest-free loans to local organisations.

RANGE OF GRANTS £200 to £16,000.

SAMPLE GRANTS The Piggott School (£15,600); Polehampton Infant School (£9,600); St James Church (£6,500); Polehampton Swimming Association (£4,500); 1st Twyford Scouts (£3,000) Twyford and Ruscombe Community Association (£2,400); Ladybirds Pre-School (£1,300) Chattabox Holiday Club (£600) Bumps and Babies Group (£230).

FINANCES *Year* 2015 *Income* £97,388 *Grants* £67,908 *Grants to organisations* £64,211 *Assets* £2,942,260

TRUSTEES R. J. Fort; R. Pratt; Dr R. W. Collett; P. Derry; N. Downes; Revd S. Howard; D. A. Norris; J. Potter; W. T. Treadwell; D. Turner; J. G. Weaver.

OTHER INFORMATION The charity made ten educational, books and equipment grants to individuals totalling £3,700. Grants to schools for equipment and resources totalled £36,800 and grants to groups and organisations totalled £27,400.

HOW TO APPLY Apply in writing to the correspondent.

WHO TO APPLY TO Caroline Jane White, 65 The Hawthorns, Charvil, Reading RG10 9TS *Tel.* 0118 934 0852 *Fax* 0118 950 2704 *Email* thepolehamptoncharity@gmail.com *Website* www.thepolehamptoncharity.com

The Institute for Policy Research

CC NO 285143 **ESTABLISHED** 1982

WHERE FUNDING CAN BE GIVEN England and Wales.

WHO CAN BENEFIT Charities; research organisations; universities.

WHAT IS FUNDED Research studies, conferences and seminars which promote the education of the public concerning major social science, management studies and economic policy issues.

SAMPLE GRANTS Centre for Policy Studies (£295,500); Tax Payers' Alliance (£135,000); News-Watch (£65,000); Politeia (£25,000); Migration Watch (£11,000); Global Britain (£8,000); The Burgess Group (£5,000).

FINANCES *Year* 2015/16 *Income* £682,495 *Grants* £780,925 *Grants to organisations* £780,925 *Assets* £364,842

TRUSTEES Simon Webley; Nicholas Finney; Eric Koops; Richard Hamilton.

OTHER INFORMATION Grants were broken down as follows: research projects (£735,000); conferences/seminars (£38,000); publications (£8,000).

HOW TO APPLY Apply in writing to the correspondent.

WHO TO APPLY TO Peter Richard Orbell-Jones, Flat 38, Charleston Court, 61 West Cliff Road, Broadstairs, Kent CT10 1RY *Tel.* 01843 866423 *Email* peter.orbelljones@yahoo.com

The George and Esme Pollitzer Charitable Settlement

CC NO 212631 **ESTABLISHED** 1960

WHERE FUNDING CAN BE GIVEN UK.

WHO CAN BENEFIT Registered charities.

WHAT IS FUNDED General charitable purposes. The charity's accounts separate giving into the following categories: parenting, families and children; armed forces; homelessness; people with disabilities and older people; education; the arts; the community and environment; Jewish faith; health and medical research; and other material grants.

TYPE OF GRANT One-off and recurrent.

RANGE OF GRANTS Typically £5,000 each.

SAMPLE GRANTS The Silver Line (£7,000); The Royal Hospital for Neuro-disability (£5,000 each); The Fishermen's Mission (£3,000); Calibre Audio Library, Guide Dogs, Seafarers UK, St Mungo's, The Foundation and Friends of the Royal Botanical Gardens Kew and The National Holocaust Centre and Museum (£2,500 each); Teesside Hospice (£2,000).

FINANCES *Year* 2015/16 *Income* £140,923 *Grants* £139,000 *Grants to organisations* £139,000 *Assets* £3,631,038

TRUSTEES Richard Pollitzer; Catherine Charles; Joseph Pollitzer; Frances Pollitzer.

OTHER INFORMATION During the year, 84 grants were made. All except four of these were of £2,000.

HOW TO APPLY Apply in writing to the correspondent.

WHO TO APPLY TO Lucy Parrock, Manager – Tax and Trust, Saffery Champness, St Catherine's Court, Berkeley Place, Clifton, Bristol BS8 1BQ *Tel.* 0117 915 1617

Pollywally Charitable Trust

CC NO 1107513 **ESTABLISHED** 2005

WHERE FUNDING CAN BE GIVEN UK.

WHO CAN BENEFIT Charitable organisations.

WHAT IS FUNDED General charitable purposes, particularly education, social welfare and religious causes.

SAMPLE GRANTS The BSD Charitable Trust (£47,500); The Edgware Foundation (£5,900).

FINANCES *Year* 2015/16 *Income* £76,433 *Grants* £67,750 *Grants to organisations* £67,750 *Assets* £22,391

TRUSTEES Jeremy Waller; Jeremy Pollins; Sarah Waller; Stephany Pollins.

OTHER INFORMATION Grants were made for the following purposes: general charitable purposes (£50,500); education (£8,500); welfare (£6,500); religious organisations (£1,100); relief of poverty (£980). A full list of beneficiaries was not included in the accounts.

HOW TO APPLY Apply in writing to the correspondent.

WHO TO APPLY TO Jeremy Waller, Trustee, Berkeley House, 18–24 High Street, Edgware HA8 7RP *Tel.* 020 8238 5858 *Email* jwaller@wallerpollins.com

The Polonsky Foundation

CC NO 291143 **ESTABLISHED** 1985

WHERE FUNDING CAN BE GIVEN UK, Israel and the USA.

WHO CAN BENEFIT Universities; arts or educational institutions.

WHAT IS FUNDED Higher education (humanities and social sciences); medical research; the arts; the study and resolution of human conflict.

RANGE OF GRANTS Up to £756,000.

SAMPLE GRANTS Theatre for a New Audience (£756,000); The Van Leer Jerusalem Institute (£466,000); New York Public Library (£211,500); British Library (£192,000); The Yetzirah 7 Foundation (£84,500); Oxford Centre of Hebrew and Jewish Studies (£70,000); New York University (£60,000); Library of Congress (£58,500); British friends of Haifa University (£46,000).

FINANCES *Year* 2015/16 *Income* £833,822 *Grants* £2,503,556 *Grants to organisations* £2,503,556 *Assets* £30,267,449

TRUSTEES Dr Georgette Bennett; Dr Leonard Polonsky; Marc Polonsky; Hannah Polonsky.

OTHER INFORMATION During the year, grants of less than £45,000 totalled £229,500.

HOW TO APPLY Apply in writing to the correspondent.

WHO TO APPLY TO The Trustees, 8 Park Crescent, London W1B 1PG *Tel.* 07785 246923

The Ponton House Trust

SC NO SC021716 **ESTABLISHED** 1993

WHERE FUNDING CAN BE GIVEN Edinburgh and Lothians area.

WHO CAN BENEFIT Charitable organisations.

WHAT IS FUNDED Vulnerable and disadvantaged young people; citizenship and community development.

WHAT IS NOT FUNDED Ongoing services.

TYPE OF GRANT One-off project funding.

RANGE OF GRANTS Usually between £1,000 and £2,000.

SAMPLE GRANTS Edinburgh and Lothian Trust Fund (£9,600); Children with Cancer and Leukaemia Advice and Support for Parents, Leith School of Art and Scottish Chamber Orchestra (£2,000 each); Epilepsy Scotland (£1,600); Buckstone

Youth Project, CLIC Sargent, Edinburgh Development Group, Multi-Cultural Family Base and Scottish Association for Mental Health (£1,000 each).

FINANCES *Year* 2015/16 *Income* £56,113 *Grants* £45,858 *Grants to organisations* £45,858 *Assets* £2,192,124

TRUSTEES Revd John Munro; Shulah Allan; Patrick Edwardson; Ian Boardman; Jim Verth; David Jack; Penny Richardson; Sandra Blake.

OTHER INFORMATION Grants were made to 28 organisations during the year. The trust's website states that the pattern of aid has been as follows: 25–30% on disability, health and terminal-illness projects; 45–50% on youth work, diversionary projects for young people, anti-poverty initiatives, and support of young carers; and 25% to Edinburgh and Lothian Trust Fund (www.eltf.org.uk), a trust making grants to individual young people in need.

HOW TO APPLY Application forms are available from the trust's website, where full guidelines are also available.

WHO TO APPLY TO David Reith, Secretary, 11 Muirfield Apartments, Muirfield Station, Gullane, East Lothian EH31 2HZ *Email* pontonhousetrust@outlook.com *Website* www.pontonhouse.org.uk

■ Edith and Ferdinand Porjes Charitable Trust

CC NO 274012 **ESTABLISHED** 1973

WHERE FUNDING CAN BE GIVEN UK and overseas.

WHO CAN BENEFIT Jewish organisations; registered charities.

WHAT IS FUNDED General charitable purposes, particularly Jewish causes.

TYPE OF GRANT Typically recurrent.

RANGE OF GRANTS £5,000 to £30,000.

SAMPLE GRANTS The London School of Jewish Studies (£30,000); Jewish Book Council (£22,000); Royal Academy of Arts (£16,500); British Library (£6,500); British Emunah Fund and Ohel Sarah (£5,000 each).

FINANCES *Year* 2015/16 *Income* £45,190 *Grants* £85,000 *Grants to organisations* £85,000 *Assets* £1,374,932

TRUSTEES Martin Paisner; Anthony Rosenfelder; Howard Stanton.

OTHER INFORMATION Grants were made to six organisations during the year, many of which had been supported in the past.

HOW TO APPLY Apply in writing to the correspondent.

WHO TO APPLY TO Martin Paisner, Trustee, Berwin Leighton Paisner, Adelaide House, London Bridge, London EC4R 9HA *Tel.* 020 7760 1000

■ The Porta Pia 2012 Foundation

CC NO 1152582 **ESTABLISHED** 2013

WHERE FUNDING CAN BE GIVEN Worldwide; with a preference for the UK.

WHO CAN BENEFIT Registered charities.

WHAT IS FUNDED General charitable purposes; social welfare; community development; young people; older people.

RANGE OF GRANTS £500 to £30,000.

SAMPLE GRANTS Lewy Body Society (£30,000); Depaul UK (£15,000); Shelter and Street Child (£5,000 each); Disasters Emergency Committee Nepal Appeal (£2,000); British Association for Adoption and Fostering, Carers UK, Macular Society, Restless Development and The Archway Project (£500 each).

FINANCES *Year* 2015 *Income* £88,569 *Grants* £61,500 *Grants to organisations* £61,500 *Assets* £2,848,675

TRUSTEES Helen O'Shea; James O'Shea; Joanne Sennitt.

OTHER INFORMATION Grants were made to 14 organisations during the year.

HOW TO APPLY Apply in writing to the correspondent. The trust has stated in its 2015 annual report that most grants are made 'to a variety of charities of which the trustees have prior or personal knowledge'. All applications are 'considered with regard to need, impact and sustainability'.

WHO TO APPLY TO Petronella West, Administrator, Investment Quorum Ltd, Guildhall House, 85 Gresham Street, London EC2V 4NQ *Tel.* 020 7337 1390

■ The Portishead Nautical Trust

CC NO 228876 **ESTABLISHED** 2009

WHERE FUNDING CAN BE GIVEN Portishead, Bristol and North Somerset.

WHO CAN BENEFIT Organisations and young people.

WHAT IS FUNDED Specific projects helping young people under the age of 25 who are disadvantaged.

TYPE OF GRANT One-off, project, recurring and running costs will be considered.

RANGE OF GRANTS £500 to £20,000.

SAMPLE GRANTS Dyslexia Action (£20,000); Portishead Youth Centre (£10,000); Off the Record (£2,000); Addiction Recovery Agency, Springboard Opportunity Group and Wellspring Counselling (£1,500 each); Life Education Centre and Whizz-Kidz (£1,000 each); Tall Ships Youth Trust (£900); 1st Nailsea Scouts (£500).

FINANCES *Year* 2015/16 *Income* £100,421 *Grants* £69,216 *Grants to organisations* £60,206 *Assets* £2,057,118

TRUSTEES Tean Kirby; Stephen Gillingham; Mr M. Cruse; Mrs S. Haysom; Colin Crossman; Iris Perry; Dr Gerwyn Owen; Peter Dingley-Brown; Miss A. McPherson.

OTHER INFORMATION Most grants to organisations were between £1,000 and £2,000. In 2013/14 grants to individuals totalled £9,000.

HOW TO APPLY Apply in writing to the correspondent. The trustees meet four times a year to consider applications.

WHO TO APPLY TO Liz Knight, Secretary, 108 High Street, Portishead, Bristol BS20 6AJ *Tel.* 01275 847463 *Email* portisheadnauticaltrust@gmail.com

■ The Portrack Charitable Trust

CC NO 266120 **ESTABLISHED** 1973

WHERE FUNDING CAN BE GIVEN UK, with some preference for Scotland.

WHO CAN BENEFIT Registered charitable organisations.

WHAT IS FUNDED General charitable purposes with a preference for art and culture; the environment; overseas aid; humanitarian causes; children and young people; older people; people with disabilities; refugees.

WHAT IS NOT FUNDED Individuals.

RANGE OF GRANTS £500 to £30,000.

SAMPLE GRANTS Buccleuch Living Heritage Trust (£30,000); Medical Aid for Palestine (£15,000); Human Rights Watch (£13,000); Garden Museum (£10,000); Blue Marine Foundation, Community Law Advice Network and Disasters Emergency Committee Nepal Earthquake Appeal

(£5,000 each); Help Musicians UK (£3,000); Alternative Theatre Company Ltd (£2,000); Women for Refugee Women (£1,000); Archaeology Scotland (£1,500); Countryside Learning Scotland (£500).

FINANCES *Year* 2015/16 *Income* £129,866 *Grants* £288,400 *Grants to organisations* £288,400 *Assets* £70,747,578

TRUSTEES Charles Jencks; Lily Jencks; John Jencks.

OTHER INFORMATION Grants were made to 47 organisations during the year.

HOW TO APPLY Apply in writing to the correspondent. The trust notes on its Charity Commission record that it is not currently accepting applications and is reviewing its application process, and advises potential applicants to check the record again in December 2017.

WHO TO APPLY TO Lucy Dare, Administrator, The Old Stable, 15A Huntingdon Street, London N1 1BU *Email* portrackcharitabletrust@gmail.com

■ J. E. Posnansky Charitable Trust

CC NO 210416 **ESTABLISHED** 1962

WHERE FUNDING CAN BE GIVEN Worldwide, in practice mainly UK.

WHO CAN BENEFIT Charitable organisations.

WHAT IS FUNDED General charitable purposes with a preference for: Jewish causes; health; social welfare; humanitarian aid; the arts.

WHAT IS NOT FUNDED Individuals.

RANGE OF GRANTS £250 to £20,000.

SAMPLE GRANTS Magen David Adom UK and United Jewish Israel Appeal (UJIA) (£20,000 each); Jewish Care (£7,500); Lullaby Trust (£5,000); WaterAid (£2,500); Lyric Theatre Hammersmith Ltd (£2,000); Blesma (£1,000); Anne Frank Educational Trust and Amnesty International (£500 each); The Dystonia Society and The Sue Ryder Foundation (£250 each).

FINANCES *Year* 2015/16 *Income* £132,735 *Grants* £121,250 *Grants to organisations* £121,250 *Assets* £3,635,154

TRUSTEES Mr N. S. Posnansky; Peter Mishcon; Emma Feather; Gillian Raffles.

OTHER INFORMATION Grants were made to 35 organisations during the year.

HOW TO APPLY Apply in writing to the correspondent.

WHO TO APPLY TO Mr N. S. Posnansky, Trustee, c/o Sobell Rhodes LLP, Ground Floor, 501 Centennial Park, Centennial Avenue, Elstree, Hertfordshire WD6 3FG *Tel.* 020 8429 8800

■ Postcode Community Trust

SC NO SC044772 **ESTABLISHED** 2014

WHERE FUNDING CAN BE GIVEN England; Scotland; Wales.

WHO CAN BENEFIT Constituted voluntary and community organisations; registered charities; CICs; CIOs; co-operatives; not-for-profit companies; social enterprises.

WHAT IS FUNDED Community cohesion; sports and recreation; community arts projects; relief of isolation for older people or people with disabilities; first aid courses; mental health awareness or counselling; first responders.

WHAT IS NOT FUNDED Local Wildlife Trusts; Riding for the Disabled Association branches; general renovation work; lunch clubs; mother and toddler groups; after-school teen activities; healthy eating programmes not delivered in 'an innovative manner'; programmes that make claims that cannot be substantiated (e.g. 'boosting confidence'); community garden projects; skills-based educational training; projects that promote the human rights/ citizenship of marginalized groups.

TYPE OF GRANT Pilot and project funding; equipment; volunteer costs.

RANGE OF GRANTS £500 to £1 million. During the year an exceptionally large award was made of £750,000.

SAMPLE GRANTS Taming the Floods Somerset Levels (£750,000); Amnesty International, Jamie Oliver Foundation and Music in Hospitals (£100,000 each); St John Ambulance (£20,000); Glasgow East Women's Aid (£17,700); South Birmingham Young Homeless Project (£17,300); Bumblebee Conservation Trust (£14,000); Blantyre Soccer Academy (£13,100); Llety Shenkin Tenants Association (£1,400).

FINANCES *Year* 2015 *Income* £9,113,925 *Grants* £3,679,052 *Grants to organisations* £3,679,052 *Assets* £390,287

TRUSTEES Lawson Muncaster; Robert Flett; Judith Hills; Michael Pratt.

OTHER INFORMATION The trust has three funding streams: **Community Grants Programme** – allows charities to apply for 12-month project funding ranging from £500 to £20,000 undertaken in the UK. Decisions are made on a semi-annual basis. Registered charities can apply for up to £20,000. Community groups not formally registered as a charity can apply for up to £2,000. **Community Partnership Programme** – charities can apply for up to £100,000 to deliver a year-long project anywhere in the UK. Charities are selected by invitation only. **Special Awards Programme** – for projects that fall outside the aforementioned funding programmes and that require more than can be funded through the Community Partnership Programme. During the year, 264 organisations received grants, the majority through the Community Grants Programme.

HOW TO APPLY Application forms can be downloaded from the website where there is detailed eligibility criteria and guidance.

WHO TO APPLY TO Clara Govier, Executive Manager, 76 George Street, Edinburgh EH2 3BU *Tel.* 0131 555 7287 *Email* info@postcodecommunitytrust.org.uk *Website* www.postcodecommunitytrust.org.uk

■ Postcode Dream Trust

SC NO SC044911 **ESTABLISHED** 2014

WHERE FUNDING CAN BE GIVEN England; Scotland; Wales.

WHO CAN BENEFIT Registered charities; non-registered charitable organisations; universities; CICs.

WHAT IS FUNDED Early children's development; support for refugees; marine conservation; conservation of the environment; arts, heritage and culture.

WHAT IS NOT FUNDED Councils; local authorities; government or statutory bodies. Also note that restrictions apply regarding the income level of applicants: 'The lead partner in any application must have an annual income that is at least three times the amount being applied for.'

TYPE OF GRANT Project funding.

RANGE OF GRANTS Up to £1 million.

SAMPLE GRANTS Groundwork London – Energy Gardens (£750,000); Prince of Wales's Charitable Foundation (£600,000); Trees for Cities – Edible Playgrounds (£249,000); Not On Our Watch (£175,000).

FINANCES *Year* 2015 *Income* £9,904,735 *Grants* £1,774,180 *Grants to organisations* £1,774,180 *Assets* £2,266,359

TRUSTEES Lawson Muncaster; Michael Pratt; Judith Hills; Robert Flett.

HOW TO APPLY There is an application form and detailed guidance available to download from the website, where you can also find upcoming deadlines. It is further noted on the website: 'If you have an idea for the Dream Fund it is always worth calling the Dream Fund helpdesk and seeing if your project is suitable before applying.'

WHO TO APPLY TO Joe Ray, Trusts Manager, People's Postcode Lottery, 76 George Street, Edinburgh EH2 3BU *Tel.* 0131 603 8611 *Email* info@postcodedreamtrust.org.uk *Website* www.postcodedreamtrust.org.uk/dream-fund.htm

■ The Mary Potter Convent Hospital Trust

CC NO 1078525 **ESTABLISHED** 1999

WHERE FUNDING CAN BE GIVEN Nottinghamshire.

WHO CAN BENEFIT Charitable organisations; individuals.

WHAT IS FUNDED Relief of medical and health problems.

WHAT IS NOT FUNDED Non-registered charities; capital/building costs.

TYPE OF GRANT Mainly one-off grants, but payments over two or three years may be considered.

RANGE OF GRANTS Typically £3,000.

SAMPLE GRANTS Nottingham Hospice (£5,000); The Friary (£4,000); Age UK Nottingham and Nottinghamshire, Alzheimer's Society, Cornwater Clubs, Headway, Mary Magdalene Foundation and Radford Visiting Centre (£3,000 each).

FINANCES *Year* 2015/16 *Income* £119,408 *Grants* £95,301 *Grants to organisations* £81,624 *Assets* £3,185,551

TRUSTEES Dr J. P. Curran; Chris Bain; Jo Stevenson; Sister Jeanette Connell; Sister Anne Haugh; Mervyn Jones; Martin Witherspoon; Shaun Finn; Aidan Goulding; Godfrey Archer.

OTHER INFORMATION During the year the trust made 51 grants: 15 to organisations and 36 to individuals.

HOW TO APPLY Apply in writing to the correspondent. Unsuccessful applicants will not be notified.

WHO TO APPLY TO Martin Witherspoon, Secretary to the Trustees, c/o Massers Solicitors, Rossell House, Tudor Square, West Bridgford, Nottingham NG2 6BT *Tel.* 0115 851 1603 *Email* martinw@massers.co.uk

■ David and Elaine Potter Foundation

CC NO 1078217 **ESTABLISHED** 1999

WHERE FUNDING CAN BE GIVEN UK and overseas, particularly sub-Saharan Africa.

WHAT IS FUNDED Education, particularly projects supporting economic and social well-being in sub-Saharan Africa; civil society, including human rights, governance, anti-corruption, investigative journalism, law and legal assistance; social research. More details can be found on the foundation's website.

WHAT IS NOT FUNDED Individuals; CICs; retrospective costs; full economic costs for universities; political organisations; clinical trials; religious organisations that only work for the benefit of members of their own religion; building costs.

TYPE OF GRANT Project funding up to a maximum of three years. Joint funding with other grant-makers.

RANGE OF GRANTS Up to £200,000.

SAMPLE GRANTS Institute of Human Rights University of Oxford (£200,000); Numeric (£128,000); Amnesty International (£50,000); Philharmonia Orchestra Trust Ltd (£45,000 in two grants); Transparency International UK (£30,000); LIFEbeat (£20,000); International Press Institute (£10,900); Royal Court Theatre (£5,000); Almeida Theatre (£3,000).

FINANCES *Year* 2015 *Income* £327,616 *Grants* £1,089,301 *Grants to organisations* £1,089,301 *Assets* £17,801,367

TRUSTEES Michael Polonsky; Michael Langley; Dr David Potter; Elaine Potter; Samuel Potter; Daniel Potter.

OTHER INFORMATION Grants were distributed for the following purposes: education (£480,500); human rights (£340,000); governance (£126,000); arts (£88,000); other (£55,000).

HOW TO APPLY Applications are by invitation only, unsolicited applications are not accepted. The website states: 'If you think your work may fit our remit you should email us to discuss your potential eligibility and whether it is something that we may potentially fund. Please do not send written correspondence.'

WHO TO APPLY TO Ben Stewart, Director, 6 Hamilton Close, London NW8 8QY *Tel.* 020 7289 3911 *Email* info@potterfoundation.com *Website* www.potterfoundation.com

■ Power to Change Trust

CC NO 1159982 **ESTABLISHED** 2015

WHERE FUNDING CAN BE GIVEN England.

WHO CAN BENEFIT Community organisations and groups; local businesses.

WHAT IS FUNDED Community businesses.

WHAT IS NOT FUNDED Local authorities or statutory organisations or services which are regarded as statutory or government provision; organisations that have already received a grant; reimbursement of money already spent; payment for costs which someone else is paying for, whether in cash or in kind; existing day-to-day running costs.

TYPE OF GRANT Capital costs including building, vehicles, equipment of significant value or refurbishment costs; project-specific revenue costs like staff costs, professional fees or volunteer costs; seed funding; community shares; 'blended' funding (a mixture of loans and grants).

RANGE OF GRANTS £1,000 to £300,000, but can also be for more.

SAMPLE GRANTS Adrenaline Alley (£525,000); Granby Four Streets Community Land Trust Ltd (£391,000); Alt Valley Community Trust (£220,000); East Lancashire Football Development Association (£200,000); Bamford Community Society (£120,000); Greenslate Community Farm Ltd (£103,000); Bootstrap Company Ltd (£87,000); Kirkgate Arts (£57,000); Riverside Stewardship Company Ltd (£25,000).

FINANCES *Year* 2015 *Income* £150,695,000 *Grants* £8,185,000 *Grants to organisations* £8,185,000 *Assets* £138,043,000

TRUSTEE Power to Change Trustee Ltd.

OTHER INFORMATION Grants were made to 43 organisations during the year. The size of the grant offered will depend on the stage of development of the community business. Ideas Stage: £1,000–£10,000; Pre-venture Stage (i.e.

development and testing): £1,000–£15,000; Established Stage (i.e. diversifying income streams): £5,000–£20,000. Other funding options are available, such as blended funding, see the website for more details.

HOW TO APPLY Applications can be made through the trust's website. Some grants programmes are administered through third-party groups, and the trust recommends that you get in contact with the relevant administrator before submitting an application. Deadlines, guidance and eligibility criteria can all be found on the trust's website.

WHO TO APPLY TO Grants Team, The Clarence Centre, 6 St George's Circus, London SE1 6FE *Tel.* 020 3857 7270 *Email* info@thepowertochange.org.uk *Website* www.thepowertochange.org.uk

■ Powys Welsh Church Fund

CC NO 507967 **ESTABLISHED** 1978

WHERE FUNDING CAN BE GIVEN Powys.

WHO CAN BENEFIT Charitable organisations, churches, chapels, students and apprentices within or having some connection with the county of Powys.

WHAT IS FUNDED General charitable purposes with a preference for community development, children and young people.

WHAT IS NOT FUNDED Projects outside the beneficial area; church running costs, interior work, including redecoration and repair/installation of heating systems or for the construction of new church buildings; salaries.

TYPE OF GRANT Project costs; equipment.

SAMPLE GRANTS A list of beneficiaries was not available.

FINANCES *Year* 2015/16 *Income* £90,844 *Grants* £129,802 *Grants to organisations* £129,802 *Assets* £2,353,872

TRUSTEE Powys County Council Board.

OTHER INFORMATION The trustees will not make grants of over £100 to organisations which are not registered as a charity with the Charity Commission.

HOW TO APPLY Application forms are available from the correspondent. Applicant organisations must be able to demonstrate that they are properly constituted and keep proper accounts and financial records. All projects or facilities for which a grant is requested must be open to inspection by appropriate officers. The trustees meet to consider grants throughout the year. Applications should be received one month prior to being considered by the trustees.

WHO TO APPLY TO The Chief Financial Officer, Powys County Council, Llandrindod Wells, Powys LD1 5LG *Tel.* 01597 826337

■ The W. L. Pratt Charitable Trust

CC NO 256907 **ESTABLISHED** 1968

WHERE FUNDING CAN BE GIVEN UK, with a particular focus on York, and overseas.

WHO CAN BENEFIT Charitable organisations.

WHAT IS FUNDED Overseas aid, in particular food production; famine; religious and social causes in the UK.

WHAT IS NOT FUNDED Individuals. Grants for the upkeep and preservation of buildings are restricted.

TYPE OF GRANT Typically recurrent.

RANGE OF GRANTS £500 to £5,000.

SAMPLE GRANTS York Diocesan Board of Finance and York Minster Fund (£5,000 each); Wilberforce Trust (£3,000); Christian Aid (£2,200); Sound Seekers (£1,200); Martin House Hospice, Nepal Earthquake and RNLI (£1,000 each); Karen Hilltribes Trust, Riding for the Disabled York Group, Shelter and York Sea Cadets (£500 each).

FINANCES *Year* 2015/16 *Income* £59,511 *Grants* £56,210 *Grants to organisations* £56,210 *Assets* £1,844,117

TRUSTEES Christopher Goodway; Christopher Tetley; John Pratt.

OTHER INFORMATION In 2013/14 the trust made 52 grants, 27 of which were of £500 or less. Grants were made in the following categories: York and district (£28,500); UK national charities (£11,200); overseas aid (£10,900).

HOW TO APPLY Apply in writing to the correspondent. Applications will not be acknowledged unless an sae is supplied. Telephone applications are not accepted.

WHO TO APPLY TO Christopher Goodway, Trustee, c/o Grays, Duncombe Place, York YO1 7DY *Tel.* 01904 634771 *Email* christophergoodway@grayssolicitors.co.uk

■ Premishlaner Charitable Trust

CC NO 1046945 **ESTABLISHED** 1995

WHERE FUNDING CAN BE GIVEN UK and overseas.

WHO CAN BENEFIT Jewish organisations.

WHAT IS FUNDED The advancement of Orthodox Jewish education and the advancement of Jewish faith.

RANGE OF GRANTS Up to £20,000.

SAMPLE GRANTS Chen V'chesed V'rachamim (£20,000); Chochmas Shlomo Chasidi (£18,000); J. and R. Charitable Trust (£15,000); Kollel Welfare Fund (£10,000); Mercaz Torah Vechesed Ltd (£7,700); Ahavas Yisroel Synagogue (£6,000); Society of Friends of the Torah (£5,000).

FINANCES *Year* 2015/16 *Income* £157,310 *Grants* £192,184 *Grants to organisations* £192,184 *Assets* £359,981

TRUSTEES C. Freudenberger; Mr C. M. Margulies.

OTHER INFORMATION Donations of less than £5,000 totalled £41,500.

HOW TO APPLY Apply in writing to the correspondent.

WHO TO APPLY TO Mr C. M. Margulies, Trustee, 186 Lordship Road, London N16 5ES *Tel.* 020 8802 4449

■ Sir John Priestman Charity Trust

CC NO 209397 **ESTABLISHED** 1931

WHERE FUNDING CAN BE GIVEN Durham county, Sunderland and Yorkshire. In relation to Church of England grants, the County of York is also eligible.

WHO CAN BENEFIT Charitable organisations; churches; schools.

WHAT IS FUNDED Social welfare; older people; education; hospitals and convalescent homes; nurses; upkeep of Church of England institutions including the purchase of organs.

WHAT IS NOT FUNDED Organisations operating outside the charity's beneficial area.

TYPE OF GRANT Project costs; unrestricted funding; equipment and building costs.

RANGE OF GRANTS £1,000 to £15,500.

SAMPLE GRANTS Outward Bound Trust (£15,500); Wolsingham Parish Church (£10,000); Tudhoe Fabric Fund (£8,000); Selby Abbey Organ Appeal (£4,000); Listening Books (£3,500); Marie Curie Memorial Foundation (£3,000); Sunderland Victims Support Scheme (£2,500); Durham Choristers School (£2,000); Wildfowl and Wetlands Trust Washington (£1,900); The Weardale Museum (£1,000).

FINANCES *Year* 2015 *Income* £427,662 *Grants* £362,874 *Grants to organisations* £362,874 *Assets* £12,146,724

TRUSTEES Peter Taylor; Timothy Norton; Anthony Coates; Thomas Greenwell; Jean Majer.

OTHER INFORMATION Only in special circumstances grants are awarded outside the specified geographical area or to individuals. A number of charities are supported by way of annual grants.

HOW TO APPLY Apply in writing to the correspondent.

WHO TO APPLY TO The Trustees, c/o McKenzie Bell, 19 John Street, Sunderland, Tyne and Wear SR1 1JG *Tel.* 0191 567 4857

■ The Primrose Trust

CC NO 800049 **ESTABLISHED** 1986

WHERE FUNDING CAN BE GIVEN UK.

WHO CAN BENEFIT Registered charities.

WHAT IS FUNDED General charitable purposes with a preference for animal welfare.

TYPE OF GRANT Capital projects; core costs; unrestricted funding.

RANGE OF GRANTS £5,000 to £50,000.

SAMPLE GRANTS Free the Bears (£50,000); Animal Health Trust (£30,000); Animals Asia (£25,000); Dauntsey's School and Langford Trust (£15,000 each); Badger Trust and Scottish Badgers (£10,000 each); Bowland Pennine Mountain Rescue (£5,000).

FINANCES *Year* 2015/16 *Income* £154,868 *Grants* £122,000 *Grants to organisations* £122,000 *Assets* £4,082,241

TRUSTEES Malcolm Clark; Susan Boyes-Korkis.

HOW TO APPLY Apply in writing to the correspondent and include a copy of your organisation's most recent accounts. The trust does not wish to receive telephone calls.

WHO TO APPLY TO Jacqueline Deacy, Deloitte LLP, 5 Callaghan Square, Cardiff CF10 5BT *Tel.* 029 2026 4388 *Email* jdeacy@deloitte.co.uk

■ The Prince of Wales's Charitable Foundation

CC NO 1127255 **ESTABLISHED** 1979

WHERE FUNDING CAN BE GIVEN UK and overseas.

WHO CAN BENEFIT UK-registered not-for-profit organisations that have been active for two years.

WHAT IS FUNDED Arts and culture; education and young people; conservation and heritage; environmental sustainability; community support; health and hospices; religion; emergency relief; the welfare of service personnel.

WHAT IS NOT FUNDED Individuals; public bodies; organisations whose main activity is to distribute grants to other organisations; organisations wishing to deliver projects similar to those of any of The Prince's Charities; organisations whose annual income exceeds £1 million; organisations with political interests or affiliations; capital expenditure (with the exception of community-based, religion-related and heritage restoration projects); sponsorship.

TYPE OF GRANT One-off grants for capital or core expenditure.

RANGE OF GRANTS Typically up to £5,000, although larger grants are also made.

SAMPLE GRANTS The Great Steward of Scotland's Dumfries House Trust (£3.1 million); Prince's Foundation for Building Community (£1.6 million); The Soil Association (£500,000); Royal Drawing School (£439,000); Prince's Regeneration Trust (£250,000); The Prince's Trust International (£150,000); Turquoise Mountain (£80,000); The Tusk Trust (£49,000); The College of Medicine and Norfolk Churches Trust (£10,000 each).

FINANCES *Income* £13,454,000 *Grants* £7,699,000 *Grants to organisations* £7,699,000 *Assets* £8,986,000

TRUSTEES Clive Alderton; Dame Amelia Fawcett; Dame Julie Moore; Dr Kenneth Brockington Wilson; John Varley; Sir Ian Cheshire.

OTHER INFORMATION The foundation operates two grants programmes: Major Grants and Small Grants. The Major Grants programme does not accept unsolicited applications. Grants were made to 142 organisations during the year.

HOW TO APPLY Fill out the online eligibility form in the first instance which will give you access to the full online application form, should you be eligible. The Major Grants programme is not open to unsolicited applications.

WHO TO APPLY TO Yvonne Abba-Opoku, Company Secretary, The Prince of Wales's Office, Clarence House, St James's, London SW1A 1BA *Email* yvonne.abbaopoku@royal.gsx.gov.uk *Website* www.princeofwalescharitablefoundation.org.uk

■ The Prince Philip Trust Fund

CC NO 272927 **ESTABLISHED** 1977

WHERE FUNDING CAN BE GIVEN The Royal Borough of Windsor and Maidenhead.

WHO CAN BENEFIT Charitable organisations; individuals.

WHAT IS FUNDED The arts, literature and culture; the training of young people through undertaking voluntary work; recreation; science.

WHAT IS NOT FUNDED Grants to replace statutory funding, or for projects that are the responsibility of the local authority, unless they are also used by local voluntary organisations.

RANGE OF GRANTS £500 to £5,000.

SAMPLE GRANTS Windsor Festival (£5,000); Sports Able (£3,200); 19th Maidenhead Scout Group, Norden Farm Centre for the Arts and St John Ambulance (£2,000 each); Combat Stress and Windsor Orchestra (£1,500 each); Tall Ships Youth Trust (£1,200); Alexander Devine Children's Hospice Services (£1,000); Maidenhead Heritage Trust (£800); Maidenhead Choral Society (£500).

FINANCES *Year* 2015/16 *Income* £107,161 *Grants* £59,160 *Grants to organisations* £55,730 *Assets* £1,750,131

TRUSTEES Dame Marcia Twelftree; Governor and Constable of Windsor Castle; HRH The Earl of Wessex; Allan Wilson; Andrew Panter; Chris Aitkin; Deputy Ranger; Her Majesty's Lord Lieutenant for Berkshire; Mayor of the Royal Borough of Windsor and Maidenhead; Samantha Rayner; Diane Marshall Yarrow.

OTHER INFORMATION Grants were made to 41 organisations and 4 individuals (£3,500) during the year.

HOW TO APPLY Apply in writing to the correspondent. The trustees meet twice a year. Further information is available on the charity's website.

WHO TO APPLY TO Chris Aitken, Trust Secretary, 53 Kings Road, Windsor, Berkshire SL4 2AD *Tel.* 01753 859668 *Email* chris_aitken@btinternet.com *Website* www3.rbwm.gov.uk/info/200156/community_grants/727/the_prince_philip_trust_fund

Princes Gate Trust

CC NO 1157279 **ESTABLISHED** 2014

WHERE FUNDING CAN BE GIVEN England and Wales.

WHO CAN BENEFIT Registered charities; organisations; individuals.

WHAT IS FUNDED Children and young people who are disadvantaged; disability.

SAMPLE GRANTS Noah's Ark Children's Hospital (£35,500); FAW Trust (£10,000); Variety (£1,000); Tenby RNLI (£600); Drop for Drop Charity (£580); Caerphilly Children's Home (£300); Foodbank (£210); Help for Heroes (£40).

FINANCES *Year* 2015 *Income* £147,336 *Grants* £63,083 *Grants to organisations* £63,083 *Assets* £80,345

TRUSTEES David Jones; Sam Atkinson; Ryan Jones; Rachel McKay; Jackie Jones; Maria Young; Carrie McIntosh; Rebecca McKay; Tim Plumb.

OTHER INFORMATION The trust donated £7,400 worth of medical equipment to individuals. During the year the trust made eight grants to organisations.

HOW TO APPLY Apply in writing to the correspondent.

WHO TO APPLY TO Samantha Atkinson, Trustee, Princes Gate Spring Water, Ludchurch, Princes Gate, Narberth, Pembrokeshire SA67 8JD *Tel.* 01834 831225 *Email* info@princesgatetrust.com *Website* www.princesgatetrust.com

The Princess Anne's Charities

CC NO 277814 **ESTABLISHED** 1979

WHERE FUNDING CAN BE GIVEN UK.

WHO CAN BENEFIT Registered charities.

WHAT IS FUNDED Social welfare; medical research; children and young people; environment and wildlife; armed forces; general charitable purposes.

WHAT IS NOT FUNDED Individuals.

SAMPLE GRANTS Butler Trust, the Canal Museum Trust, Cranfield Trust, Dogs Trust, Dorothy House Foundation, Durrell Wildlife Conservation Trust, the Evelina Children's Hospital Appeal, Farms for City Children, Farrer and Co. Charitable Trust, Fire Services National Benevolent Fund, the Home Farm Trust, Intensive Care Society, and International League for the Protection of Horses.

FINANCES *Year* 2015/16 *Income* £147,803 *Grants* £120,250 *Grants to organisations* £120,250 *Assets* £5,877,615

TRUSTEES The Hon. Mark Bridges; Vice Admiral Sir Tim Laurence; Christopher Morgan; Sally Tennant.

OTHER INFORMATION Grants were made to 30 charities in the following categories: social welfare (£51,000); children and young people (£23,000); medical (£21,500); armed forces (£18,000); environment and wildlife (£6,000); other (£1,000).

HOW TO APPLY The charity has previously stated that the trustees generally make awards only to those charities of which the Princess is patron. Other appeals are considered on a case-by-case basis, but only very few are successful.

WHO TO APPLY TO Capt. Nick Wright, Buckingham Palace, London SW1A 1AA *Tel.* 020 7024 4199 *Email* nick.wright@royal.gsx.gov.uk

Prison Service Charity Fund

CC NO 801678 **ESTABLISHED** 1989

WHERE FUNDING CAN BE GIVEN England and Wales.

WHO CAN BENEFIT Charitable organisations; individuals.

WHAT IS FUNDED The fund supports the efforts of prison service staff who are fundraising to provide organisations and individuals with medical treatment or equipment.

TYPE OF GRANT One-off donations.

RANGE OF GRANTS £50 to £2,000.

SAMPLE GRANTS Charlie's Happy Fund (£2,000); Stick and Step (£1,200); Zoë's Place (£1,150 in two donations); St Bede's Palliative Care Unit (£1,000); Demelza Hospice Care for Children (£800); Myeloma UK (£500); Lincolnshire Air Ambulance (£400); National Autistic Society (£250); Blind Veterans Association (£120); Make-A-Wish Foundation (£50).

FINANCES *Year* 2016 *Income* £109,409 *Grants* £89,570 *Grants to organisations* £89,570 *Assets* £853,046

TRUSTEES Bob Howard; Nevill Joseph; Kenneth Wingfield; Peter McFall; John White; Michael Flynn.

HOW TO APPLY Applications are only accepted from members of prison service staff. Outside applications are not accepted.

WHO TO APPLY TO Bob Howard, Secretary, The Lodge, 8 Derby Road, Garstang, Preston PR3 1EU *Tel.* 01995 604997 *Email* bob@pscf.co.uk *Website* www.prisonservicecharityfund.co.uk

The Privy Purse Charitable Trust

CC NO 296079 **ESTABLISHED** 1987

WHERE FUNDING CAN BE GIVEN UK and overseas.

WHO CAN BENEFIT Charities of which The Queen is patron; ecclesiastical establishments associated with The Queen.

WHAT IS FUNDED General charitable purposes; disaster relief.

SAMPLE GRANTS Chapel Royal – St James's Palace (£71,500); Sandringham group of parishes (£62,500); Chapel Royal – Hampton Court Palace (£53,500); Chapel Royal – Windsor Great Park (£23,000); British Red Cross – Nepal Earthquake, Tapping House Hospice and The Choral Foundation (£10,000 each).

FINANCES *Year* 2015/16 *Income* £620,283 *Grants* £397,539 *Grants to organisations* £397,539 *Assets* £3,437,650

TRUSTEES Michael Stevens; Sir Alan Reid; The Right Hon. Sir Christopher Geidt.

OTHER INFORMATION Grants were made to 341 organisations throughout the year for the following purposes: ecclesiastical (£241,000); general charitable purposes (£133,500); education (£26,000).

HOW TO APPLY The fund makes donations to a wide variety of charities, but does not respond to unsolicited applications.

WHO TO APPLY TO Michael Stevens, Trustee, Buckingham Palace, London SW1A 1AA *Tel.* 020 7930 4832 *Email* mike.stevens@royal.gsx.gov.uk

The Professional Footballers' Association Charity

CC NO 1150458 **ESTABLISHED** 2013

WHERE FUNDING CAN BE GIVEN England and Wales.

WHO CAN BENEFIT Registered charities; football organisations; individuals.

WHAT IS FUNDED Community participation; community relations; recreation; education; general charitable purposes; professional footballers or those training to become professional footballers.
TYPE OF GRANT Large grants are typically recurrent.
RANGE OF GRANTS Up to £3 million.
SAMPLE GRANTS Football League Youth Development Programme (£3 million); Football Scholarship Funding (£1.4 million); Equality Development – Anti Racism (£822,500); The Prince's Trust (£500,000); Network of Councillors (£165,500); Osteoarthritis Risk Study (£17,600); Fair Play Awards (£15,000); People's History Museum (£6,000).
FINANCES *Year* 2015/16 *Income* £20,552,554 *Grants* £12,500,212 *Grants to organisations* £11,610,672 *Assets* £46,297,914
TRUSTEES David Weir; Garth Crooks; Gordon Taylor; Darren Wilson; Gareth Griffiths; Christopher Powell; Brendon Batson; Paul Elliot.
HOW TO APPLY Apply in writing to the correspondent.
WHO TO APPLY TO Darren Wilson, Trustee, 20 Oxford Court, Bishopsgate, Manchester M2 3WQ *Tel.* 0161 236 0575 *Email* info@thepfa.co.uk

■ Prostate Cancer UK

CC NO 1005541 **ESTABLISHED** 1991
WHERE FUNDING CAN BE GIVEN England and Wales.
WHO CAN BENEFIT Registered charities; research bodies; individuals.
WHAT IS FUNDED Prostate cancer research and treatment.
TYPE OF GRANT Research project funding; PhD scholarships.
RANGE OF GRANTS Up to £1.6 million.
SAMPLE GRANTS The Institute of Cancer Research (£1.6 million); Queen's University Belfast (£506,000); University College London (£393,000); Newcastle University (£210,000); University of Manchester (£140,000); Imperial College London (£126,000); University of East Anglia (£84,000).
FINANCES *Year* 2015/16 *Income* £20,027,000 *Grants* £12,768,000 *Grants to organisations* £8,050,000 *Assets* £19,577,000
TRUSTEES Prof. Jonathan Waxman; Steve Ford; Andrew Mitchell; Ray Kelly; Martin Roland; Robert Humphreys; Charles Packshaw; Michael Tye; Jacky Wright; Tom Shropshire; Prof. Sara Faithful; Simon Hammett; Marion Leslie.
OTHER INFORMATION In the accounts for 2015/16 the charity notes that it gave in three broad areas: research, support and influencing, and awareness.
HOW TO APPLY Calls for applications are advertised through the charity's website, researcher newsletter and appropriate specialist media. Each grant-making programme has its own guidelines and deadline dates, check the website for further information.
WHO TO APPLY TO The Research Team, Fourth Floor, The Counting House, 53 Tooley Street, London SE1 2QN *Tel.* 020 3310 7000 *Email* research@prostatecanceruk.org or info@prostatecanceruk.org *Website* www.prostatecanceruk.org

■ The Puebla Charitable Trust

CC NO 290055 **ESTABLISHED** 1984
WHERE FUNDING CAN BE GIVEN Worldwide.
WHO CAN BENEFIT Charitable organisations.
WHAT IS FUNDED Community development initiatives; relief of poverty.
WHAT IS NOT FUNDED Capital projects; religious institutions; research; institutions for people with disabilities; individuals; scholarships.
TYPE OF GRANT Up to three years.
RANGE OF GRANTS Up to £60,000.
SAMPLE GRANTS Action on Disability and Development, SOS Sahel International UK, South West London Law Centres and Survivors Fund (£60,000 each); Hamlin Fistula (£6,800).
FINANCES *Year* 2015/16 *Income* £95,563 *Grants* £246,750 *Grants to organisations* £256,750 *Assets* £2,516,574
TRUSTEES Justin Phipps; Martin Strutt.
HOW TO APPLY Apply in writing to the correspondent. The trustees usually meet in July. The trust is unable to acknowledge applications.
WHO TO APPLY TO The Secretary, c/o Ensors, Cardinal House, 46 St Nicholas Street, Ipswich IP1 1TT *Tel.* 01473 220022 *Email* mail@ensors.co.uk

■ The Puri Foundation

CC NO 327854 **ESTABLISHED** 1988
WHERE FUNDING CAN BE GIVEN UK (mainly the Nottingham area), India and Nepal.
WHO CAN BENEFIT Registered charities; individuals.
WHAT IS FUNDED Young people; social welfare; education; recreation.
WHAT IS NOT FUNDED Holidays.
SAMPLE GRANTS The Puri Foundation for Education in India (£415,000); Street Child (£100,000); Indian Gymkhana (£33,000); Hindu Forum of Europe (£4,700) Southwell Minister (£1,000).
FINANCES *Year* 2015/16 *Income* £733,036 *Grants* £553,771 *Grants to organisations* £553,771 *Assets* £3,291,907
TRUSTEES Nathu Puri; Anil Puri; Mary McGowan.
OTHER INFORMATION Grants were distributed for the following purposes: education (£452,500); human rights (£100,000); general support (£1,200). One major grant was made to The Puri Foundation for Education in India, which was also founded by Nathu Puri.
HOW TO APPLY Apply in writing to the correspondent.
WHO TO APPLY TO The Trustees, Environment House, 6 Union Road, Nottingham NG3 1FH *Tel.* 0115 901 3000 *Website* www.purico.co.uk/charities/puri-foundation

■ The PwC Foundation

CC NO 1144124 **ESTABLISHED** 2011
WHERE FUNDING CAN BE GIVEN UK.
WHO CAN BENEFIT Charitable organisations.
WHAT IS FUNDED Sustainable development, social inclusion, education and training, health care, the environment.
WHAT IS NOT FUNDED Political organisations; lobbying groups; animal rights groups; religious bodies.
RANGE OF GRANTS £10,000 to £45,000.
SAMPLE GRANTS Wellbeing of Women (£181,000 in 24 grants); Teach First (£113,000 in three grants); Business in the Community (£51,000 in four grants) The Shakespeare Globe Trust (£45,000); Great Ormond Street Hospital Children's Charity (£28,000); Step Up To Serve and The Connection at St Martin's (£15,000 each); Royal Exchange Theatre and School for Social Entrepreneurs Scotland (£10,000 each).
FINANCES *Year* 2015/16 *Income* £1,601,327 *Grants* £1,517,605 *Grants to organisations* £1,517,605 *Assets* £365,132
TRUSTEES Neil Sherlock; Gaenor Bagley; Kevin Ellis; David Adair.

OTHER INFORMATION The PwC Foundation is the corporate charity of PricewaterhouseCoopers LLP (PwC).

HOW TO APPLY The annual report states the following: 'Currently there is no formal open grant application process. The steering group and trustees can independently identify recipients for funding who meet the charitable objectives of the Foundation. Recipients are approved by the Trustees. All donations made are unconditional.'

WHO TO APPLY TO Sean Good, PricewaterhouseCoopers LLP, 1 Embankment Place, London WC2N 6RH *Tel.* 07764 902846 *Email* sean.good@uk.pwc.com *Website* www.pwc.co.uk/corporate-sustainability/the-pwc-foundation.jhtml

■ The Pye Foundation

CC NO 267851 **ESTABLISHED** 1974

WHERE FUNDING CAN BE GIVEN Cambridgeshire.

WHO CAN BENEFIT Registered charities; retired employees of the former Pye group of companies.

WHAT IS FUNDED General charitable purposes.

RANGE OF GRANTS Mostly £1,000 to £5,000.

SAMPLE GRANTS Alzheimer's Society Cambridgeshire (£5,000); Dial-a-Ride (£4,000); Headway Cambridgeshire (£3,000); Lifecraft (£2,500); Home-Start, Refuge and The Cogwheel Trust (£2,000 each); Bag Books (£1,700); Happy Days (£1,500); Cambridge Deaf Association, Emmaus and FoodCycle (£1,000 each).

FINANCES *Year* 2015/16 *Income* £111,825 *Grants* £141,744 *Grants to organisations* £128,244 *Assets* £3,387,672

TRUSTEES David Ball; Ashish Dasgupta; John Hemming; Roger Crabtree; Richcard McMullan; Joy Childs; Bob Bates; Rick Mitchell; Douglas Irish; Dr Anil Chhabra; Dr Michael Wassall.

OTHER INFORMATION The amount of grants given to individuals totalled £13,500.

HOW TO APPLY Apply in writing to the correspondent. The trustees meet regularly to consider applications.

WHO TO APPLY TO Roger Hall, 54 Woodcock Close, Impington, Cambridge CB24 9LD *Tel.* 01223 233441

■ Mr and Mrs J. A. Pyes Charitable Settlement

CC NO 242677 **ESTABLISHED** 1965

WHERE FUNDING CAN BE GIVEN Mainly Oxfordshire and the surrounding areas.

WHO CAN BENEFIT Small or under-funded registered charities.

WHAT IS FUNDED General charitable purposes; environment; adult health and care; children's health and care; youth organisations; education; heritage and the arts; music.

WHAT IS NOT FUNDED Individuals; non-registered organisations; animal welfare; the promotion of religion.

TYPE OF GRANT One-off awards, core costs, projects, research, recurring, running and start-up costs, and salaries. Capital costs may be considered. Funding may be given for up to or more than three years. Interest-free loans are also available.

RANGE OF GRANTS Up to £75,000.

SAMPLE GRANTS Organic Research Centre (£75,000); Association for Post-Natal Illness (£20,000); Dorset County Hospital (£10,000); Adventure Plus and The Oxford Victoria County History Trust (£5,000 each); Relate Oxfordshire (£2,500); Bumblebee Conservation Trust (£2,000); Ashmolean Museum, Beckley and Stowood Village Hall, Oxfordshire Homeless Pathways and Stadhampton Community Building Project (£1,000 each); Music Therapy at Katharine House Hospice (£750).

FINANCES *Year* 2015 *Income* £746,794 *Grants* £426,304 *Grants to organisations* £426,304 *Assets* £12,438,508

TRUSTEES Simon Stubbings; David Tallon; Patrick Mulcare.

OTHER INFORMATION Grants were made to 178 organisations during the year, with those for less than £501 totalling £43,000.

HOW TO APPLY All applications should be sent to the administrative office (and not to individual trustees). They are reviewed on a continual basis and are considered at quarterly trustees' meetings; therefore, it may be four months before a decision is made. All applications are acknowledged and all candidates are notified of the outcome. The charity notes that telephone calls are usually counter-productive. Applicants are invited to apply via email.

WHO TO APPLY TO The Trustees, Mercer and Hole, 72 London Road, St Albans AL1 1NS *Tel.* 01727 869141 *Email* pyecharitablesettlement@mercerhole.co.uk *Website* www.pyecharitablesettlement.org

■ QBE European Operations Foundation

CC NO 1143828 **ESTABLISHED** 2011

WHERE FUNDING CAN BE GIVEN UK.

WHO CAN BENEFIT Registered charities.

WHAT IS FUNDED The foundation's charitable objective, as stated on the Charity Commission's record, is: 'The relief of financial hardship in the UK by providing grants, items and services to individuals in need and/or charities in the UK and Europe whose aims include advancing education, training, skills development and healthcare projects and all the necessary support designed to enable individuals to generate sustainable income and be self-sufficient; to assist charities in such ways as the charity trustees see fit, whose focus is on providing educational opportunities, work ready initiatives and healthcare support for those in need in the UK and Europe.'

WHAT IS NOT FUNDED Political, local authority, union-affiliated and religious organisations; schools and associated PTAs; animal welfare charities (not including those whose objectives are to support people); environmental charities; aid projects and charities whose beneficiaries are predominately outside the foundation's operating areas and organisations which incur administration fees exceeding 15% of donations received.

RANGE OF GRANTS Mostly up to £10,000.

SAMPLE GRANTS The Sick Children's Trust (£56,000); Find a Better Way (£50,000); Duchenne Children's Trust (£15,000); Fundacion Balia por la Infancia (£12,300).

FINANCES *Year* 2015 *Income* £712,252 *Grants* £440,105 *Grants to organisations* £440,105 *Assets* £375,312

TRUSTEES Jonathan Parry; Robert Nias; Grant Clemence; Beth McLeod.

OTHER INFORMATION Donations under £10,000 totalled £214,500.

HOW TO APPLY Application forms can be downloaded from the foundation's website and should be returned to the correspondent by post or email.

WHO TO APPLY TO Sophie Wraith, QBE European Operations, One Coval Wells, Chelmsford, Essex CM1 1WZ *Tel.* 01245 343253 *Email* sophie.wraith@uk.qbe.com *Website* qbeeurope.com/community/the-qbe-foundation

■ Quartet Community Foundation

CC NO 1080418 **ESTABLISHED** 1987

WHERE FUNDING CAN BE GIVEN Bristol, North Somerset, South Gloucestershire, Bath and North East Somerset.

WHO CAN BENEFIT Small, local charities and voluntary groups, although national charities with a significant local presence may apply if funding will benefit local people.

WHAT IS FUNDED General charitable purposes; social welfare; community cohesion.

WHAT IS NOT FUNDED Animal welfare; arts projects with no community or charitable element; direct replacement of statutory funding; medical research; political groups or activities promoting political beliefs; promotion of religion; sports projects with no community or charitable element.

RANGE OF GRANTS Up to £50,000.

SAMPLE GRANTS Bristol Refugee Rights (£76,000 in two grants); Arnos Vale Cemetery Trust (£63,500 in three grants); Southside Family Project (£35,000); St Werburghs City Farm (£25,000); Bristol Old Vic (£12,000); Demand Energy Equality and Enfield Women's Centre (£10,000 each); Katherine House Hospice (£7,300); Bristol Drugs Project and National Council for the Training of Journalists (£5,000 each).

FINANCES *Year* 2015/16 *Income* £3,427,259 *Grants* £2,537,535 *Grants to organisations* £2,537,535 *Assets* £25,170,359

TRUSTEES Bina Shah; John Cullum; Hilary Neal; Ben Silvey; Christopher Sharp; Lesley Freed; William Lee; Julian Telling; Trevor Leonard; Merlyn Ipinson-Fleming; Robert Bourns; Annie Kilvington; Nick Baker; Pat Meehan; Helen Wilde; Christopher Johnson.

OTHER INFORMATION The foundation manages a range of funds each with their own priorities, criteria and closing dates as well as its own programmes. During the year, 911 grants were made through 47 programmes. Grants for less than £5,000 totalled £844,500.

HOW TO APPLY Applicants should refer to the fund's website for details on how to apply to each grants programme. The funding team can be contacted for any help or advice concerning grants applications.

WHO TO APPLY TO Grants Team, Royal Oak House, Royal Oak Avenue, Bristol BS1 4GB *Tel.* 0117 989 7700 *Fax* 0117 989 7701 *Email* applications@quartetcf.org.uk *Website* www.quartetcf.org.uk

■ The Queen Anne's Gate Foundation

CC NO 1108903 **ESTABLISHED** 2005

WHERE FUNDING CAN BE GIVEN UK and overseas, mainly Asia.

WHO CAN BENEFIT Charitable organisations.

WHAT IS FUNDED Education; medicine; rehabilitation.

RANGE OF GRANTS Between £5,000 and £25,000.

SAMPLE GRANTS English National Opera, Families for Children and The Citizens Foundation (£25,000); The Hong Kong Polytechnic University (£19,800); Christian Friends of Korea (£13,900); Aanchal Women's Aid, City of Exeter YMCA Community Projects and Syria Relief (£10,000 each); St Andrew's Church Cullompton (£5,000).

FINANCES *Year* 2015/16 *Income* £41,010 *Grants* £238,654 *Grants to organisations* £238,654 *Assets* £1,627,898

TRUSTEES Nicholas Allan; Jonathan Boyer; Roger Wortley.

OTHER INFORMATION Grants were given in the following areas: education (£109,500); general welfare (£68,900); children's welfare (£50,000); emergency relief (£10,000).

HOW TO APPLY Apply in writing to the correspondent. The trustees meet twice a year.

WHO TO APPLY TO Jonathan Wortley, Willcox Lewis LLP, The Old Coach House, Sunnyside, Bergh Apton, Norwich NR15 1DD *Tel.* 01508 480100 *Email* info@fisherlegal.co.uk

■ Queen Mary's Roehampton Trust

CC NO 211715 **ESTABLISHED** 1928

WHERE FUNDING CAN BE GIVEN UK.

WHO CAN BENEFIT Charitable organisations.

WHAT IS FUNDED The reception, accommodation, treatment or aftercare of ex-service people with disabilities during their service, and their dependants; medical or surgical research associated with this group.

WHAT IS NOT FUNDED Individuals.

TYPE OF GRANT Annual recurring and one-off awards. Also capital and project costs. Funding may be given for up to two years.

RANGE OF GRANTS £2,000 to £95,000.

SAMPLE GRANTS Holidays for Heroes Jersey (£95,000); Gurkha Welfare Trust (£45,000); SSAFA (£35,000); Blesma (£30,000); Combat Stress (£25,000); The Not Forgotten Association (£22,000); Bournemouth War Memorial Homes (£15,000); Canine Partners (£10,000); National Gulf Veterans and Families Association (£5,000); Association of Jewish Ex-Service Men and Women (£3,000); Deafblind UK (£2,000).

FINANCES *Year* 2015/16 *Income* £670,975 *Grants* £666,000 *Grants to organisations* £666,000 *Assets* £13,530,168

TRUSTEES James Macnamara; Col. Paul Cummings; Cdr Stephen Farringdon; Colin Green; Beverley Davies; Debbie Bowles; Stephen Coltman; Sir Barry Thornton; Anne Child; Ed Tytherleigh; Dr Rakesh Bhabutta.

HOW TO APPLY Apply on a standard application form available from the correspondent. Representatives of the trust may visit beneficiary organisations.

WHO TO APPLY TO Col. Stephen Rowland-Jones, Clerk to the Trustees, 2 Sovereign Close, Quidhampton, Salisbury, Wiltshire SP2 9ES *Tel.* 01722 501413 *Email* qmrt@hotmail.co.uk

■ The Queen's Trust

CC NO 272373 **ESTABLISHED** 1977

WHERE FUNDING CAN BE GIVEN UK.

WHO CAN BENEFIT Registered charities.

WHAT IS FUNDED Young people, particularly in the areas of their education, employment, collaboration and the development of their confidence, mental health and well-being.

WHAT IS NOT FUNDED Non-registered charities; individuals.

TYPE OF GRANT Recurrent.

RANGE OF GRANTS £45,000 to £1.5 million.

SAMPLE GRANTS The Prince's Trust (£1.5 million); IntoUniversity (£1.2 million); Teach First (£766,000); City Year (£500,000); Duke of Edinburgh's Award (£399,000); Coram (£300,000); Carers Trust (£273,000); National Youth Orchestra (£250,000); The Orpheus Centre (£60,000); Royal Commonwealth Society (£45,000).

FINANCES *Year* 2015 *Income* £310,000 *Grants* £6,186,000 *Grants to organisations* £6,186,000 *Assets* £24,550,000

TRUSTEES The Rt Hon. Christopher Geidt; Sir Alan Reid; Peter Mimpriss; Michael Marks; Sir Trevor McDonald; Sandra Robertson; Christopher Coombe.

OTHER INFORMATION The trust is aiming to spend out its funds by 2019 and is not accepting applications for funding.

HOW TO APPLY The trust states the following on its website: 'As a rule, we do not accept unsolicited applications. We seek out ambitious, well-managed charities, with proven results, that put our core purpose at the heart of what they do: to help young people help others.'

WHO TO APPLY TO Anne Threlkeld, Administrator, Buckingham Palace, London SW1A 1AA *Tel.* 020 7930 4832 *Email* anne.threlkeld@royal.gsx.gov.uk *Website* www.queenstrust.org.uk

■ Quercus Foundation

CC NO 1160720 **ESTABLISHED** 2014

WHERE FUNDING CAN BE GIVEN Worldwide.

WHO CAN BENEFIT Registered charities.

WHAT IS FUNDED Improving the lives of children and young people living in extreme poverty. The foundation has a focus on health, education and infrastructure.

SAMPLE GRANTS ICU Building – Red Cross War Memorial Children's Hospital (£302,000); Breathe Easy Programme – Cape Town (£29,500).

FINANCES *Year* 2015 *Income* £595,225 *Grants* £331,476 *Grants to organisations* £331,476 *Assets* £22,060

TRUSTEES Diego Biasi; Kristiana Carlet; Robert Fidgen; Giuliano Gregorio.

HOW TO APPLY The foundation's 2015 annual report states: 'The trustees have updated the Foundation's formal grant-making policy and when appropriate, plan to advertise the opportunity to apply for grants through appropriate methods, including the use of the charity's website and advertising in specialist press.'

WHO TO APPLY TO Diego Biasi, Quercus Investments, 11 Albemarle Street, London W1S 4HH *Tel.* 020 7871 4533

■ Quothquan Trust

CC NO 1110647 **ESTABLISHED** 2004

WHERE FUNDING CAN BE GIVEN Birmingham and surrounding area, West Midlands.

WHO CAN BENEFIT Christian organisations and individuals.

WHAT IS FUNDED Promotion of Christian faith through specific projects and initiatives aimed at relieving the poverty and sickness, assisting older people, ill individuals and those who are socially and economically disadvantaged; advancement of religious education.

WHAT IS NOT FUNDED Causes that do not promote Christianity as part of their ethos; activities which are generally the responsibility of the state; animal welfare; church buildings; environmental causes; expeditions and overseas trips; hospitals and health centres; large national charities; loans and business finance; medical research projects; overseas appeals; religions other than Christianity; schools, universities and colleges; individuals.

TYPE OF GRANT Grants are generally made on a one-off basis with an exception of the regular monthly grants.

SAMPLE GRANTS A list of specific beneficiaries was not included in the annual accounts.

FINANCES *Year* 2015 *Income* £459,014 *Grants* £226,300 *Grants to organisations* £166,950 *Assets* £2,497,123

TRUSTEES Susan Robinson; Janet Gilmour.

OTHER INFORMATION Grants totalling £59,500 were made to 35 individuals, with the rest of the grant total going to 26 organisations.

HOW TO APPLY Apply in writing to the correspondent. See the website for guidelines and criteria. Applications by email are not accepted.

Unsuccessful applicants are not notified and do not receive feedback or details.

WHO TO APPLY TO Susan Robinson, Trust Administrator, Dale Farm, Worcester Lane, Four Oaks, Sutton Coldfield B75 5PR *Tel.* 0121 323 3236 *Website* www.quothquantrust.org.uk

R. S. Charitable Trust

CC NO 1053660 **ESTABLISHED** 1996

WHERE FUNDING CAN BE GIVEN UK.

WHO CAN BENEFIT Registered charities.

WHAT IS FUNDED Jewish causes; social welfare.

SAMPLE GRANTS British Friends of Tshernobil, Forty Ltd, NRST, Society of Friends of the Torah, Talmud Hochschule, Viznitz, Yeshiva Horomo and Yeshivas Luzern.

FINANCES *Year* 2015/16 *Income* £322,627 *Grants* £60,416 *Grants to organisations* £60,416 *Assets* £2,755,797

TRUSTEES Harvey Freudenberger; Michelle Freudenberger; Stuart Freudenberger; Max Freudenberger; Charles Margulies.

HOW TO APPLY Apply in writing to the correspondent.

WHO TO APPLY TO Max Freudenberger, Trustee, 138 Stamford Hill, London N16 6QT

The Monica Rabagliati Charitable Trust

CC NO 1086368 **ESTABLISHED** 2001

WHERE FUNDING CAN BE GIVEN UK.

WHO CAN BENEFIT Charitable organisations.

WHAT IS FUNDED While keeping a general scope, the trust primarily supports 'organisations that focus on the alleviation of child suffering and deprivation'.

RANGE OF GRANTS £1,000 to £10,000.

SAMPLE GRANTS Inner Temple Scholarships (£10,000); Abelour Child Care Trust (£3,000); Balloons and Beanstalk (£2,000 each); British Exploring Society (£1,500); Special Needs Adventure Playground (£1,500); Endeavour and The Garage Trust (£1,000 each); Human Relief and Tall Ships Youth Trust (£500 each).

FINANCES *Year* 2015/16 *Income* £81,354 *Grants* £85,691 *Grants to organisations* £85,691 *Assets* £1,836,589

TRUSTEES S. G. Hambros Trust Company Ltd; Robert McLean.

HOW TO APPLY Application forms can be downloaded from the trust's website and should be returned to the correspondent. The trustees consider grants twice a year.

WHO TO APPLY TO Rachel Iles, Norfolk House, 8 St James's Square, London SW1Y 4JU *Tel.* 020 7597 3065 *Website* www.rabagliati.org.uk

Rachel Charitable Trust

CC NO 276441 **ESTABLISHED** 1978

WHERE FUNDING CAN BE GIVEN UK.

WHO CAN BENEFIT Charitable organisations; Jewish organisations.

WHAT IS FUNDED General charitable purposes; in practice, mainly Jewish charities for advancement of religion and religious education, and the relief of poverty.

TYPE OF GRANT One-off and recurrent.

SAMPLE GRANTS British Friends of Shvut Ami, Children's Hospital Trust Fund, Cometville Ltd, Encounter – Jewish Outreach Network, Choshen Mishpat Centre, Gertner Charitable Trust, Hertsmere Jewish Primary School, Jewish Learning Exchange, London Millennium Bikeathon, Manchester Jewish Grammar School, Project Seed, Shaare Zedek Hospital, Shomrei Hachomot Jerusalem, Yeshiva Ohel Shimon Trust and Yeshiva Shaarei Torah Manchester.

FINANCES *Year* 2015/16 *Income* £8,492,083 *Grants* £5,453,634 *Grants to organisations* £5,453,634 *Assets* £6,981,351

TRUSTEES Leopold Noe; Susan Noe; Simon Kanter.

OTHER INFORMATION A list of beneficiary organisations was not included in the annual report and accounts, although this information can be purchased from the correspondent.

HOW TO APPLY Apply in writing to the correspondent.

WHO TO APPLY TO Mr A. M. Jacobs, Secretary, F. & C. Reit Asset Management, 5 Wigmore Street, London W1U 1PB *Tel.* 020 7016 3549

The Racing Foundation

CC NO 1145297 **ESTABLISHED** 2011

WHERE FUNDING CAN BE GIVEN UK.

WHO CAN BENEFIT Charities associated with the UK horse racing and thoroughbred breeding industry. Organisations that do not work exclusively within the horse racing and thoroughbred breeding industry may be supported if their work is 'of exceptional quality and can be shown to directly impact industry participants'.

WHAT IS FUNDED General charitable purposes associated with horse racing, the thoroughbred breeding industry and equine welfare; social welfare of current or former members of the horse racing industry; heritage and culture of horse racing; equine science research.

WHAT IS NOT FUNDED Work that does not benefit the horse racing and thoroughbred breeding industry in the UK; individuals or causes which will benefit one person; gambling addiction work (unless it specifically focuses on participants within the horse racing and thoroughbred industry); retrospective funding; work that is not legally charitable.

TYPE OF GRANT Project costs; core costs; capital projects. This may include funding for overheads and salaries. Multi-year grants, usually up to three years, are considered.

RANGE OF GRANTS £5,000 to £500,000.

SAMPLE GRANTS Home of Horseracing Trust (£500,000); University of Oxford (£223,000); Northern Racing College (£208,000); Homing Ex-Racehorses Organisation Scheme (£160,000); National Horseracing Museum (£70,000); Racing Welfare (£42,000); Injured Jockeys Fund (£20,000); Retraining of Racehorses (£19,000); Thoroughbred Breeders Association (£10,000); Racehorse Rescue Centre (£5,000).

FINANCES *Year* 2015 *Income* £1,876,000 *Grants* £2,237,000 *Grants to organisations* £2,237,000 *Assets* £80,939,000

TRUSTEES Ian Barlow; Sir Ian Good; William Rucker; Katherine Keir; Mark Johnston.

OTHER INFORMATION During the year, 42 applications were received and 31 were successful. A further six were made to support the education and welfare of horse racing industry professionals.

HOW TO APPLY For **all grants applications apart from those for equine science research** there is a two-stage process. Applicants should submit a first stage application using the online form, providing basic details about their organisation. Guidelines, along with dates of application deadlines, are available from the website. For **equine science research applications**, the website requests you register as a user of the Horserace Betting Levy Board's equine grants system. Once registered you will be able to build and submit a grant application form. To ensure that your application is considered for Racing Foundation funding you will need to mark the relevant box on the application summary. A link for the online application system along with application deadline dates and further guidance can be found on the website. For further information, contact Annie Dodd, Grants Manager at the Levy Board on 020 7333 0043 ext. 73 or email equine.grants@hblb.org.uk.

WHO TO APPLY TO Tansy Challis, Grants Manager, 161 Blackpool Road, Lytham St Annes FY8 4AA *Tel.* 0300 321 1873 *Email* tansy.challis@racingfoundation.co.uk *Website* www.racingfoundation.co.uk

■ Racing Welfare

CC NO 1084042 **ESTABLISHED** 2000

WHERE FUNDING CAN BE GIVEN UK.

WHO CAN BENEFIT Organisations that offer services to people who work in, or are retired from, the horse racing industry.

WHAT IS FUNDED The welfare of people who work/have worked in the horse racing industry.

TYPE OF GRANT Recurrent.

RANGE OF GRANTS Up to £68,000.

SAMPLE GRANTS Sports Chaplaincy Offering Resources and Encouragement (£68,000); Racing Centre (£30,000).

FINANCES *Year* 2015 *Income* £2,520,000 *Grants* £222,000 *Grants to organisations* £98,000 *Assets* £28,361,000

TRUSTEES Joey Newton; Baroness Anne Mallalieu; Gary Middlebrook; Gavin MacEchern; Nicky Lyon; Simon Clarke; Patrick Russell; Morag Gray; William Barlow; Rod Street; Richard Farquhar; Venetia Wrigley.

OTHER INFORMATION During the year, grants were awarded to individuals totalling £124,000. The two beneficiary organisations appear to have had a long-standing relationship with the charity.

HOW TO APPLY Apply in writing to the correspondent.

WHO TO APPLY TO Jan Byrd, Management Accountant, Robin McAlpine House, 20B Park Lane, Newmarket, Suffolk CB8 8QD *Tel.* 01638 560763 *Email* info@racingwelfare.co.uk *Website* www.racingwelfare.co.uk

■ Richard Radcliffe Trust

CC NO 1068930 **ESTABLISHED** 1998

WHERE FUNDING CAN BE GIVEN UK.

WHO CAN BENEFIT Local and national charitable organisations.

WHAT IS FUNDED People with disabilities; young people; hospice care for the terminally ill; people who are deaf and/or blind; nature conservancy.

TYPE OF GRANT Mainly recurrent.

RANGE OF GRANTS £2,000 to £8,000.

SAMPLE GRANTS Sense (£8,000); Wildlife Trust (£6,000); Carers Trust (£5,000); Buckingham Youth Centre, Metal Detection Dogs and Royal Court Theatre (£4,000 each); British Tinnitus Association (£3,000); Buglife, Suffolk Owl Sanctuary and The Hospice of St Francis (£2,000 each).

FINANCES *Year* 2015/16 *Income* £58,810 *Grants* £100,300 *Grants to organisations* £100,300 *Assets* £2,173,904

TRUSTEES Adrian Bell; Penelope Radcliffe; Dr Paul Radcliffe.

OTHER INFORMATION Grants were made to 26 organisations during the year.

HOW TO APPLY Apply in writing to the correspondent.

WHO TO APPLY TO Dr Paul Radcliffe, Trustee, 77 Moreton Road, Buckingham MK18 1JZ *Tel.* 01280 813352

■ The Radcliffe Trust

CC NO 209212 **ESTABLISHED** 1714

WHERE FUNDING CAN BE GIVEN UK.

WHO CAN BENEFIT Registered or exempt charities; organisations and projects benefitting musicians and those involved in the cultural heritage and craft sectors.

WHAT IS FUNDED Classical music performance and training, especially chamber music, composition and music education. Particular interests within music education are music for children and adults with special needs, youth orchestras and projects at secondary and higher levels, including academic research. Heritage and crafts especially the development of the skills, knowledge and experience that underpin the UK's traditional cultural heritage and crafts sectors.

WHAT IS NOT FUNDED Individuals; retrospective grants; general appeals; endowment funds. Music scheme: operating costs; competitions; capital projects. Heritage and crafts scheme: conference fees or associated costs; projects whose sole or primary aim is about nature conservation; projects that are primarily social or therapeutic in nature.

TYPE OF GRANT Project funding, for up to three years.

RANGE OF GRANTS £600 to £20,000.

SAMPLE GRANTS Church Building Council (£15,000); University of Edinburgh (£8,000); Birmingham Opera Company (£4,000); British Film Institute (£3,500); Lettering and Commemorative Arts Trust (£3,000); City and Guilds of London Art School, Cowbridge Music Festival and National Heritage Ironwork Group (£2,000 each); Reach Inclusive Arts (£1,200); St Bartholomew's Hospital (£600).

FINANCES *Year* 2015/16 *Income* £499,983 *Grants* £318,919 *Grants to organisations* £318,919 *Assets* £18,870,111

TRUSTEES Felix Warnock; Sir Henry Aubrey-Fletcher; Christopher Butcher; Margaret Casely-Hayford; Timothy Wilson; Ellen Schroder; Richard Morrison.

OTHER INFORMATION Grants were distributed for the following purposes: music (£144,500); heritage and crafts (£142,500); tercentenary (£30,000); miscellaneous (£2,100).

HOW TO APPLY Applications may now only be submitted via the online application form. Visit the trust's website for further details of its schemes. The trustees meet twice yearly to oversee the charity's activities and to make decisions on grants. The trust works with specialist advisers in each of its main sectors of activity: Sally Carter, Music Adviser and Carole Milner, Heritage and Crafts Adviser. There is also a Music Panel and a Heritage and Crafts Committee which each meet twice a year to consider applications. It is advisable to submit an application well in advance of the deadline: Music deadline – 31 January for the June trustee meeting; 31 August for the December trustee meeting; Heritage and Crafts deadline – 31 January for the June trustee meeting; 31 July for the December trustee meeting.

WHO TO APPLY TO Louise Langford, The Trust Partnership LLP, 6 Trull Farm Buildings, Tetbury, Gloucestershire GL8 8SQ *Tel.* 01285 841900 *Email* radcliffe@thetrustpartnership.com *Website* www.theradcliffetrust.org

■ The Bishop Radford Trust

CC NO 1113562 **ESTABLISHED** 2006
WHERE FUNDING CAN BE GIVEN UK.
WHO CAN BENEFIT Church of England organisations, institutions and churches.
WHAT IS FUNDED Church-related projects; the education of priests, future priests and church workers; support of church ministry.
RANGE OF GRANTS £500 to £130,000. Most grants were of £15,000 or less.
SAMPLE GRANTS Anglican Communion Fund (£130,000); Bible Reading Fellowship and World Vision (£50,000 each); Interhealth Worldwide Burma (£15,100); Care for Children (£10,000); Church and Media Network, Indochina Starfish Foundation and St Barnabas Church – Bath (£5,000 each); Chester Cathedral (£500).
FINANCES *Year* 2015/16 *Income* £160,675 *Grants* £499,838 *Grants to organisations* £499,838 *Assets* £10,812,878
TRUSTEES Stephen Green; Janian Green; Suzannah O'Brien; Ruth Dare.
OTHER INFORMATION Grants were given for the following purposes: church-related projects (£378,500 in 26 grants); support of church ministry (£121,500 in 11 grants); education of priests and other church workers (£21,000 in two grants).
HOW TO APPLY Apply in writing to the correspondent.
WHO TO APPLY TO Mr D. Marks, Devonshire House, 1 Devonshire Street, London W1W 5DR *Tel.* 020 7304 2000 *Email* thebishopradfordtrust@ntlworld.com

■ The Rainford Trust

CC NO 266157 **ESTABLISHED** 1973
WHERE FUNDING CAN BE GIVEN Worldwide, with a preference for areas in which Pilkington PLC has works and offices, especially St Helens and Merseyside.
WHO CAN BENEFIT Charitable and voluntary organisations; individuals.
WHAT IS FUNDED General charitable purposes including social welfare; older people; people who are sick, people who have a disability; people who are unemployed; education including the arts; environmental and conservation projects.
WHAT IS NOT FUNDED Funding for the arts is restricted to St Helens only. Applications from individuals for grants for educational purposes will be considered only from applicants who are normally resident in St Helens.
RANGE OF GRANTS £100 to £20,000. Typically under £3,000.
SAMPLE GRANTS Citadel Arts Centre (£20,000); Willowbrook Hospice (£7,000); Tibet Relief Fund (£2,500); St Helens Youth Brass Band and The Howard League for Penal Reform (£2,000 each); Rainforest Foundation UK (£1,500); Blind Veterans UK (£1,000); Haydock Women's Club (£750); Surfers Against Sewage (£500); Tots and Toys Toddler Group (£300).
FINANCES *Year* 2015/16 *Income* £251,870 *Grants* £145,314 *Grants to organisations* £145,314 *Assets* £10,062,933
TRUSTEES Lady Kirsty Pilkington; Dr Frances Graham; Annabel Moseley; Hector Pilkington; David Pilkington; Simon Pilkington; Louisa Walker; Dr Clarissa Pilkington; John Pilkington; Andrew Pilkington; Revd David Eastwood.
OTHER INFORMATION During the year, 84 grants were made to organisations and two grants made to individuals.
HOW TO APPLY Application forms are available from the correspondent. Applications should be accompanied by a copy of the latest accounts and cost data on projects for which funding is sought. Applicants may apply at any time. Trustees normally meet in November, March and July. A sub-appeals committee meets about ten times a year and it can refuse, grant or pass on an application to the trustees.
WHO TO APPLY TO William Simm, Executive Officer, c/o Pilkington Group Ltd, Prescot Road, St Helens, Merseyside WA10 3TT *Tel.* 01744 20574 *Email* rainfordtrust@btconnect.com

■ The Rambourg Foundation

CC NO 1140347 **ESTABLISHED** 2010
WHERE FUNDING CAN BE GIVEN Worldwide, with a preference for the UK, France and Tunisia.
WHO CAN BENEFIT Established charitable partners.
WHAT IS FUNDED Education; health; human rights; arts and culture; children; general charitable purposes.
TYPE OF GRANT Funding is available for up to three years.
RANGE OF GRANTS Up to £148,000.
SAMPLE GRANTS Olfa Rambourg Prize for Art and Culture (£148,000); Champ'Seed Foundation (£124,500); Association 'Les Amis du Cinéma Vog' (£70,000); Human Rights Watch (£29,000); Forum Tunisien pour les Droits Économiques et Sociaux (£20,000); SchoolMe (£10,000); Fondation Rambourg – Tunisia (£6,000); Demelza Hospice (£370); Great Ormond Street Hospital (£260).
FINANCES *Year* 2015 *Income* £32,549 *Grants* £459,466 *Grants to organisations* £459,466 *Assets* £8,541,559
TRUSTEES Guillaume Rambourg; Olfa Rambourg; Chris Shepard.
HOW TO APPLY Apply in writing to the correspondent. The foundation has previously stated that it prefers to fund organisations with which it already has strategic partnerships.
WHO TO APPLY TO Guillaume Rambourg, Trustee, 30 Queen's Gate Gardens, London SW7 5RP *Email* rambourgfoundation@hotmail.com or contact@fondationrambourg.tn *Website* rambourgfoundation.org

■ The Edward Ramsden Charitable Trust

CC NO 502611 **ESTABLISHED** 1973
WHERE FUNDING CAN BE GIVEN North and West Yorkshire; elsewhere with family associations.
WHO CAN BENEFIT Charitable organisations; individuals.
WHAT IS FUNDED General charitable purposes.
RANGE OF GRANTS £50 to £40,000, typically less than £1,200.
SAMPLE GRANTS Holyrood (£40,000); Leith School of Art (£21,000); Henry VI Charity (£4,000); Beacon Church Ministries (£1,200); Cancer Research, Great Ormond Street Charity and Yorkshire Air Ambulance (£750 each); Noel Riley Book Fund (£500); Ethiopia Aid (£400); Royal Forestry Society (£250); Ripon Mayors Charity Appeal (£100).

FINANCES *Year* 2015/16 *Income* £107,526 *Grants* £75,350 *Grants to organisations* £75,350 *Assets* £273,488

TRUSTEES T. J. P. Ramsden; G. E. Ramsden.

OTHER INFORMATION Grants were made to 23 organisations during the year.

HOW TO APPLY Apply in writing to the correspondent.

WHO TO APPLY TO Mr J. C. Osbaldeston, Cardale Asset Management Ltd, 2 Greengate, Cardale Park, Harrogate HG3 1GY *Email* john.osbaldeston@cardale-am.co.uk

■ The Joseph and Lena Randall Charitable Trust

CC NO 255035 **ESTABLISHED** 1967

WHERE FUNDING CAN BE GIVEN Worldwide.

WHO CAN BENEFIT Registered charities.

WHAT IS FUNDED The relief of poverty and hardship, particularly among minorities; initiatives providing medical, educational and cultural faculties.

RANGE OF GRANTS Up to £11,000.

SAMPLE GRANTS RNIB (£10,000); LSE Foundation (£7,500); Croix Rouge (£4,300); Diabetes UK (£3,000); Jewish Deaf Association (£2,000); Brain and Spine Foundation (£1,500); Action of Hearing Loss, Bournemouth War Memorial Homes, and Save the Children Fund (£1,000 each).

FINANCES *Year* 2015/16 *Income* £89,157 *Grants* £87,275 *Grants to organisations* £87,275 *Assets* £2,167,363

TRUSTEE Rofrano Trustee Services Ltd.

OTHER INFORMATION Grants for less than £750 totalled £17,500 during the year.

HOW TO APPLY Apply in writing to the correspondent. The annual report for 2015/16 states that the trustees think 'it inappropriate to respond in the case of circular letters, or where we receive appeals from individuals that are not accredited and where letters are sent insufficiently franked.'

WHO TO APPLY TO David Randall, Europa Residence, Place des Moulins, Monte-Carlo, Monaco MC98 000 *Tel.* 00377 9350 0382 *Email* rofrano.jlrct@hotmail.fr

■ The Rank Foundation Ltd

CC NO 276976 **ESTABLISHED** 1953

WHERE FUNDING CAN BE GIVEN UK.

WHO CAN BENEFIT Registered charities. Applications for grants from the Small Appeals programme are only accepted from those charities with an annual income of less than £500,000.

WHAT IS FUNDED Christian communication; young people; education; older people; general charitable purposes.

WHAT IS NOT FUNDED Appeals from individuals or appeals from registered charities on behalf of named individuals; agriculture or farming projects; cathedrals; churches; cultural projects; university and school building; bursary funds; medical research; salaries; general running costs; major capital projects; hospices.

TYPE OF GRANT Small grants are largely one-off.

RANGE OF GRANTS Grants from the Small Appeals programme do not exceed £7,500.

SAMPLE GRANTS Help the Hospices (£100,000); Winston Churchill Memorial Trust (£82,000); Youth Work in Sport (£66,000); CLINK (£50,000); St Hilda's East Community Centre (£30,000); Wellingborough Youth Project (£28,000); Deaf Hill Ward, Greenbank Community Church and Prisoners Abroad (£25,000 each); Mary Hare School (£1,500).

FINANCES *Year* 2015 *Income* £3,258,000 *Grants* £7,198,000 *Grants to organisations* £7,189,000 *Assets* £214,372,000

TRUSTEES Joey Newton; Mark Davies; Andrew Cowen; The Hon. Caroline Twiston Davies; Lucinda Onslow; Lord St Aldwyn; Johanna Ropner; Rose Fitzpatrick; Daniel Simon; Nicholas Buxton; Jason Chaffer; William Wyatt; Andrew Fleming; Lindsey Clay.

HOW TO APPLY Unsolicited applications are only accepted for grants from the Small Appeals funding stream. Two online application forms are available: the Small Appeals Capital Grant Application and the Small Appeals Short Breaks Application. Further criteria and guidelines are available from on the foundation's website.

WHO TO APPLY TO Andrew Richardson, Secretary/Finance Director, 12 Warwick Square, London SW1V 2AA *Email* andrew.richardson@rankfoundation.co.uk *Website* www.rankfoundation.com

■ The Joseph Rank Trust

CC NO 1093844 **ESTABLISHED** 1929

WHERE FUNDING CAN BE GIVEN Unrestricted. In practice, UK.

WHO CAN BENEFIT Registered charities; Methodist churches.

WHAT IS FUNDED The adaptation of Methodist church properties with a view to providing improved facilities for use both by the church itself and in its work in the community in which it is based.

WHAT IS NOT FUNDED Delayed church maintenance (e.g. roof repairs); purchase of or restoration of stained glass or church bells; overseas projects; organ appeals; completed capital projects; the repayment of loans; individuals; educational bursaries; medical research; gap years; book publishing; intern placements; audio and sound equipment; hospices; social enterprises that have no charitable status; the provision of musical instruments; CICs; organisations registered under the Industrial and Provident Societies Act 1965; IT projects.

TYPE OF GRANT One-off and recurring; project funding; salaries; core and revenue costs.

RANGE OF GRANTS £10,000 to £50,000.

SAMPLE GRANTS Adventure Plus (£50,000); Counselling and Pastoral Trust, Housing Justice and London HIV/AIDS Chaplaincy (£45,000 each); The Lambeth Trust (£40,000); Cleansheet (£30,000); St Goran Church Community Project (£25,000); University of Gloucestershire (£22,000); Horbury Methodist Church (£15,000); The Exhale Foundation (£10,000).

FINANCES *Year* 2015 *Income* £485,000 *Grants* £2,552,500 *Grants to organisations* £2,552,500 *Assets* £86,457,000

TRUSTEES Revd David Cruise; Revd Darren Holland; Revd Carole Holmes; The Very Revd John Irvine; Gay Moon; James Rank; Tony Reddall; Mike Shortt; Sue Warner; Colin Rank.

HOW TO APPLY The website states: 'Ongoing commitments, combined with the fact that the trustees are taking an increasingly active role in identifying projects to support, means that uncommitted funds are limited and it is seldom possible to make grants in response to unsolicited appeals.' Applicants should endeavour to set out the essential details of a project on no more than two sides of A4 paper, with more detailed information being presented in the form of appendices. **There is no**

application form; applications must be sent in hard copy and not by email. Further information about application requirements can be found on the trust's website. If a Methodist church is applying for funding they should read the further information on the trust's website.

WHO TO APPLY TO Dr John Higgs, Secretary, Worth Corner, Turners Hill Road, Crawley RH10 7SL *Tel.* 01293 873947 *Email* secretary@ranktrust.org *Website* www.ranktrust.org

The Ranworth Trust

CC NO 292633 **ESTABLISHED** 1985

WHERE FUNDING CAN BE GIVEN UK, with a preference for East Norfolk, and lower- and middle-income countries.

WHO CAN BENEFIT Registered charities.

WHAT IS FUNDED Social welfare; overseas aid; health, including medical research; education; environment; churches and historic buildings; the arts.

WHAT IS NOT FUNDED Non-registered charities.

TYPE OF GRANT Loans and grants.

RANGE OF GRANTS £1,000 to £20,000.

SAMPLE GRANTS Sightsavers (£20,000); Acle High School (£10,800); Cancer Research UK, Jubilee Sailing Trust and Médecins Sans Frontières (£10,000 each); Norfolk Wildlife Trust (£5,000); Coeliac Society (£2,000); Canine Partners for Independence, East Anglian Arts Foundation and Rhino Rescue (£1,000 each).

FINANCES *Year* 2015/16 *Income* £195,303 *Grants* £144,800 *Grants to organisations* £144,800 *Assets* £4,509,297

TRUSTEES The Hon. Jacquetta Cator; Jane Cator; Mark Cator.

OTHER INFORMATION In 2010 a grant of £350,000 was given to Norfolk Community Foundation to establish The Ranworth Grassroots Fund. The aim of the fund is to support a wide range of charitable, voluntary and community activities across Norfolk. Applications can be made through the community foundation's website (www.norfolkfoundation.com).

HOW TO APPLY At the time of writing (June 2017), the trust's website states: 'The trustees are not considering any new applications until 2017'. Refer to the website for updates.

WHO TO APPLY TO Isabel Cator, Clerk, Reedside, Farm Lane, Ranworth, Norwich NR13 6HY *Website* www.ranworthtrust.org.uk

Rashbass Family Trust

CC NO 1135961 **ESTABLISHED** 2010

WHERE FUNDING CAN BE GIVEN Undefined. In practice, the UK with a preference for the Barnet district of London.

WHO CAN BENEFIT Charitable organisations.

WHAT IS FUNDED General charitable purposes; education/training; advancement of health or saving of lives; disability; prevention or relief of poverty; religious activities.

SAMPLE GRANTS A list of specific beneficiaries was not included in the trust's annual report and accounts.

FINANCES *Year* 2015/16 *Income* £304,515 *Grants* £353,203 *Grants to organisations* £353,203 *Assets* £8,511

TRUSTEES Jacqueline Rashbass; Andrew Rashbass.

OTHER INFORMATION All grants in 2015/16 were made to organisations for the following causes: education (£270,500); religion (£60,000); health (£15,000); relief of those in need (£4,500); relief of poverty (£3,000); other (£490).

HOW TO APPLY Apply in writing to the correspondent.

WHO TO APPLY TO Jacqueline Rashbass, Trustee, 17 Wykeham Road, London NW4 2TB *Tel.* 07974 151494 *Email* jacqueline@rashbass.com

The Ratcliff Foundation

CC NO 222441 **ESTABLISHED** 1959

WHERE FUNDING CAN BE GIVEN UK, with a preference for local charities in the Midlands and North Wales.

WHO CAN BENEFIT Any organisation that has charitable status for tax purposes.

WHAT IS FUNDED General charitable purposes.

WHAT IS NOT FUNDED Individuals.

RANGE OF GRANTS Up to £10,000, although most are for £2,000 or less.

SAMPLE GRANTS Cancer Research UK – Kemerton Branch (£10,000); Multiple Births Foundation (£6,000); National Trust – Corfe Castle, Royal National Lifeboat Institution and St David's Hospice (£5,000 each); Vetlife (£4,000); Warwickshire Wildlife Trust (£3,500); Prison Me No Way and Uffington Church (£3,000 each); Soil Association (£2,500).

FINANCES *Year* 2015/16 *Income* £235,809 *Grants* £215,000 *Grants to organisations* £215,000 *Assets* £3,566,923

TRUSTEES David Ratcliff; Edward Ratcliff; Carolyn Ratcliff; Gillian Thorpe; Michael Fea; Christopher Gupwell.

OTHER INFORMATION Grants were made to 91 organisations during the year, of which 56 were for less than £2,000.

HOW TO APPLY Apply in writing to the correspondent.

WHO TO APPLY TO Christopher Gupwell, Secretary and Trustee, Woodlands, Earls Common Road, Stock Green, Redditch B96 6TB *Tel.* 01386 792116 *Email* chris.gupwell@btinternet.com

The Eleanor Rathbone Charitable Trust

CC NO 233241 **ESTABLISHED** 1947

WHERE FUNDING CAN BE GIVEN UK, with the major allocation for Merseyside; also international projects (Africa, the Indian subcontinent, Afghanistan and Palestine).

WHO CAN BENEFIT Small and medium-sized registered charities.

WHAT IS FUNDED Women and girls; orphaned children; young people and families who are economically deprived and/or socially excluded; unpopular and neglected causes; holidays and outings provided by charities helping disadvantaged children and adults from Merseyside.

WHAT IS NOT FUNDED Activities which are the responsibility of a statutory body; individuals; medical research; gap year projects; lobbying or campaigning organisations; organisations that primarily exist to promote a religion, churches or sects; local charities based outside Merseyside.

TYPE OF GRANT Most donations are on a one-off basis, although requests for commitments over two or more years are considered.

RANGE OF GRANTS £500 to £8,000, although most grants given have been between £1,000 and £3,000.

SAMPLE GRANTS Remembering Eleanor Rathbone (£8,000); Merseyside Holiday Service (£5,000 annual donation); Bail for Immigration Detainees

(£3,000); Medical Foundation for Freedom from Torture (£2,500); Merseyside Somali and Community Association, Prison Radio Association and Women's Enterprising Breakthrough (£2,000 each); Congo Children Trust, Streets Ahead Rwanda and Wells for India (£1,000 each); Little Woods of Stockbridge Association (£500).

FINANCES *Year* 2015/16 *Income* £321,433 *Grants* £304,231 *Grants to organisations* £304,231 *Assets* £8,943,195

TRUSTEES William Rathbone; Lady Angela Morgan; Jenny Rathbone; Mark Rathbone; Andrew Rathbone.

OTHER INFORMATION During the year, 53% of the trust's total grants was awarded to Merseyside-based charities. Projects in Sub-Saharan Africa, the Indian subcontinent and Afghanistan and Palestine must be sponsored and monitored by a UK-registered charity.

HOW TO APPLY Apply using the online form; additional supporting documents are listed on the website and should be sent by post. Applications are accepted at any time and are considered at trustees' meetings held three times a year.

WHO TO APPLY TO Liese van Alwon, Administrator, 546 Warrington Road, Rainhill, Prescot, Merseyside L35 4LZ *Tel.* 0151 430 7914 or 07837 656314 *Email* eleanorrathbonetrust@gmail.com *Website* www.eleanorrathbonetrust.org.uk

■ Elizabeth Rathbone Charity

CC NO 233240 **ESTABLISHED** 1921

WHERE FUNDING CAN BE GIVEN UK, with a strong preference for Merseyside.

WHO CAN BENEFIT Registered charities. Preference is given to charities that the trust has special interest in, knowledge of, or association with.

WHAT IS FUNDED Disadvantaged women, young people and communities; asylum seekers; health; social welfare; education.

RANGE OF GRANTS £750 to £3,000.

SAMPLE GRANTS Birkenhead Youth Club, Swan Women's Centre and Wirral Narrowboat (£3,000 each); Campus Children's Holidays, Historic Chapels and Merseyside Employment Law (£2,000 each); FoodCycle and Merseyside Refugee and Asylum Seekers (£1,500 each); Child Bereavement and Somali Welfare (£1,000 each).

FINANCES *Year* 2015/16 *Income* £81,250 *Grants* £68,404 *Grants to organisations* £68,404 *Assets* £2,302,665

TRUSTEES Susan Rathbone; Caroline Rathbone; Richard Rathbone; Megan Rathbone.

OTHER INFORMATION Grants were made to 39 organisations during the year.

HOW TO APPLY Apply in writing to the correspondent.

WHO TO APPLY TO Liese van Alwon, Secretary, 546 Warrington Road, Rainhill, Prescot, Merseyside L35 4LZ *Tel.* 0151 430 7914 *Email* elrathbonetrust@gmail.com

■ The Sigrid Rausing Trust

CC NO 1046769 **ESTABLISHED** 1995

WHERE FUNDING CAN BE GIVEN UK and overseas.

WHO CAN BENEFIT Charitable or voluntary organisations.

WHAT IS FUNDED Advocacy, research and litigation; causes with the aim of stopping detention, torture and the death penalty; human rights defenders; free expression; transitional justice; women's rights; LGBTI rights; causes with the aim of stopping xenophobia and intolerance; transparency and accountability.

WHAT IS NOT FUNDED Individuals; faith-based groups; building projects.

TYPE OF GRANT One-year grants; multi-year grants.

RANGE OF GRANTS Up to £200,000.

SAMPLE GRANTS Arab Human Rights Fund (£200,000); International Federation of Human Rights (£160,000); Center for Legal and Social Studies (£125,000); Zimbabwe Lawyers for Human Rights (£100,000); International Consortium of Investigative Journalists (£80,000); Mesoamerican Initiative of Women Human Rights Defenders (£75,000); Greek Council for Refugees (£70,000); World Organisation Against Torture (£60,000); Civil Society Prison Reform Initiative (£50,000); Crude Accountability (£45,000); GENDERDOC Moldova Information Centre (£40,000).

FINANCES *Year* 2015 *Income* £24,643,169 *Grants* £26,674,099 *Grants to organisations* £26,674,099 *Assets* £3,969,494

TRUSTEES Sigrid Rausing; Andrew Puddephatt; Geoff Budlender; Jonathan Cooper; Margo Picken.

OTHER INFORMATION In 2015, 153 organisations were awarded grants, 52 were awarded for the first time and 89 were awarded as part of a multi-year commitment.

HOW TO APPLY The trust does not accept unsolicited applications for funding, but rather invites applications from organisations that it has proactively identified.

WHO TO APPLY TO Sheetal Patel, 12 Penzance Place, London W11 4PA *Tel.* 020 7313 7727 *Email* info@srtrust.org *Website* www.sigrid-rausing-trust.org

■ The Ravensdale Trust

CC NO 265165 **ESTABLISHED** 1973

WHERE FUNDING CAN BE GIVEN Merseyside, particularly St Helens.

WHO CAN BENEFIT Registered charities.

WHAT IS FUNDED General charitable purposes, particularly young people, older people and disadvantaged groups.

WHAT IS NOT FUNDED Individuals.

TYPE OF GRANT One-off and recurrent; core costs and project funding.

RANGE OF GRANTS £500 to £3,000. Occasionally larger grants are made.

SAMPLE GRANTS United Reform Church St Helens (£3,000); Liverpool Hope University (£2,500); St Helens Girl Guide Association and Willowbrook Hospice (£2,000 each); Alderhey Children's Charity, Disability Snow Sports UK, National Museums Liverpool, Tate Liverpool and Venture Arts (£1,000 each); Eccleston Lane Ends PTA (£500).

FINANCES *Year* 2015/16 *Income* £31,641 *Grants* £142,805 *Grants to organisations* £142,805 *Assets* £974,473

TRUSTEES Jane Fagan; Mark Feeny; Karen Toseland.

HOW TO APPLY Apply in writing to the correspondent.

WHO TO APPLY TO Jane Fagan, Trustee, c/o Brabners Chaffe Street, Horton House, Exchange Flags, Liverpool L2 3YL *Tel.* 0151 600 3000 *Email* jane.fagan@brabners.com

The Roger Raymond Charitable Trust

CC NO 262217 **ESTABLISHED** 1971

WHERE FUNDING CAN BE GIVEN UK (and very occasionally large, well-known overseas organisations).

WHO CAN BENEFIT Registered charities.

WHAT IS FUNDED General charitable purposes.

WHAT IS NOT FUNDED Individuals.

TYPE OF GRANT One-off and recurrent.

RANGE OF GRANTS Typically less than £4,000.

SAMPLE GRANTS Bloxham School (£176,000); Tring Park School (£4,300); Swanage Disability (£3,000); Sightsavers (£1,500); African Child Trust (£1,000).

FINANCES *Year* 2015/16 *Income* £586,516 *Grants* £227,998 *Grants to organisations* £227,998 *Assets* £14,296,393

TRUSTEES Russell Pullen; Michael Raymond; Alisdair Kruger Thomson.

OTHER INFORMATION The majority of support given each year by the trust is to Bloxham School. During the year, grants of less than £1,200 totalled £42,000.

HOW TO APPLY The trust has stated that applications are considered throughout the year, although funds are not always available.

WHO TO APPLY TO Russell Pullen, Trustee, Suttondene, 17 The South Border, Purley, Surrey CR8 3LL *Tel.* 020 8660 9133 *Email* russell@pullen.cix.co.uk

The Rayne Foundation

CC NO 216291 **ESTABLISHED** 1962

WHERE FUNDING CAN BE GIVEN UK.

WHO CAN BENEFIT Small and medium-sized registered charities; not-for-profit organisations.

WHAT IS FUNDED Health and medicine; education; social welfare; the arts; mental health, specifically for young people; carers; older people; social change.

WHAT IS NOT FUNDED Medical research, including cancer research; retrospective funding; capital appeals; campaigning and lobbying work; endowments; one-off events (including performances, festivals, conferences, holidays, respite breaks and residential trips); community transport schemes and vehicle purchases; church halls and community centres; running costs of local organisations; feasibility studies or scoping work; individuals; organisations working or based outside the UK; brand new organisations; organisations which have applied and been rejected within the last 12 months; charities supporting ex-service personnel.

TYPE OF GRANT Salaries and all types of project costs plus a reasonable contribution to overheads (there is no fixed percentage); general running or core costs (normally for a maximum of three years); capital costs of buildings and equipment (unless specifically stated in certain sectors); seedcorn projects which are likely to attract other funding, if successful.

RANGE OF GRANTS Up to £150,000. Typically less than £30,000.

SAMPLE GRANTS West London Synagogue of British Jews (£150,000); Families Outside (£60,000); Off The Record Bristol (£45,000); LGBT Centre for Health and Wellbeing (£40,000); Aldeburgh Music and Royal Exchange Theatre Company (£30,000 each); Enabling Enterprise (£22,500); The Carers' Support Centre (£20,000); OCD Action (£13,500); Vauxhall City Farm (£5,000); The Rotherham Hospice Trust (£2,000).

FINANCES *Year* 2014/15 *Income* £1,473,360 *Grants* £1,419,120 *Grants to organisations* £1,419,120 *Assets* £110,352,776

TRUSTEES Lady Jane Rayne; Rabbi Baroness Julia Neuberger; The Hon. Robert Rayne; Lady Browne-Wilkinson; Prof. Sir Anthony Newman Taylor; The Hon. Natasha Rayne; Nicholas Rayne; Sir Emyr Jones Parry.

HOW TO APPLY The foundation has a two-stage application process which is designed to minimise the time and effort spent by applicants. Stage one involves a short outline application which the foundation uses to assess the quality of your proposal and whether it fits with their objectives. Stage two provides an opportunity to provide a more fully developed and formal proposal. Stage one application forms and guidance can be downloaded from the foundation's website. Completed applications should be sent to applications@raynefoundation.org.uk.

WHO TO APPLY TO Morin Carew, Grants Administrator, 100 George Street, London W1U 8NU *Tel.* 020 7487 9656 *Email* info@raynefoundation.org.uk or applications@raynefoundation.org.uk *Website* www.raynefoundation.org.uk

The Rayne Trust

CC NO 207392 **ESTABLISHED** 1958

WHERE FUNDING CAN BE GIVEN UK and Israel.

WHO CAN BENEFIT Registered charities.

WHAT IS FUNDED Jewish organisations; older and young people and people disadvantaged by poverty or social isolation; understanding between cultures, particularly between Jews and Arabs; social welfare.

WHAT IS NOT FUNDED Individuals.

TYPE OF GRANT Salaries and all types of project costs plus a reasonable contribution to overheads (there is no fixed percentage); general running or core costs (normally for a maximum of three years); capital costs of buildings and equipment (unless specifically stated in certain sectors); seedcorn projects which are likely to attract other funding, if successful.

RANGE OF GRANTS Up to £80,000.

SAMPLE GRANTS The Old Vic Theatre Trust 2000 (£80,000); Central School of Ballet (£50,000); Hand in Hand Center for Jewish and Arab Education in Israel (£44,000); Desert Stars Association, International Health Partners UK and Israel Trauma Coalition (£30,000 each); Kav Mashve – Employers' Coalition for Equality for Arab Graduates (£25,000); Zaka (£12,500); Natal – Israel Trauma Center for Victims of Terror and War (£10,000); Jaffa Theatre (£2,000).

FINANCES *Year* 2015/16 *Income* £419,078 *Grants* £682,703 *Grants to organisations* £682,703 *Assets* £33,781,116

TRUSTEES Lady Jane Rayne; Robert Rayne; Damian Rayne.

OTHER INFORMATION Grants were made to 71 organisations in the year, 14 (£298,500) to Israel and 57 (£384,000) to UK organisations.

HOW TO APPLY Stage one application forms can be downloaded from the trust's website and should be returned to israelapplications@raynetrust.org.

WHO TO APPLY TO Nurit Gordon, Israel Grants Manager, 100 George Street, London W1U 8NU *Email* info@raynefoundation.org.uk *Website* www.raynefoundation.org.uk/grants/isr/apply/guidelines

■ The John Rayner Charitable Trust

CC NO 802363 **ESTABLISHED** 1989

WHERE FUNDING CAN BE GIVEN England, with some preference for Merseyside and Wiltshire.

WHO CAN BENEFIT UK-registered charities. There is a preference for 'smaller charities with a lower public profile' rather than larger, well-known charities. National or local (Merseyside and Wiltshire) charities can be supported.

WHAT IS FUNDED General charitable purposes, including health and medical research; disability; children and young people; older people; community projects; carers; medical research; the arts.

WHAT IS NOT FUNDED Individuals; non-registered charities.

TYPE OF GRANT Project costs; core costs.

RANGE OF GRANTS £2,000 to £4,000.

SAMPLE GRANTS Brighter Futures (£4,000); Canine Partners, Prospect Hospice and Safe Families for Children (£3,000 each); Clothing Solutions, FareShare, Trauma Recovery Centre, West Coast Crash Wheelchair Rugby and Wicked Fish (£2,000 each).

FINANCES *Year* 2015/16 *Income* £27,097 *Grants* £43,000 *Grants to organisations* £43,000 *Assets* £808,771

TRUSTEES Juliet Wilkinson; Dr Jonathan Rayner; Louise McNeilage.

OTHER INFORMATION Grants were made to 17 organisations in 2015/16 and were broken down as follows: children (£11,000); general (£10,000); disability (£9,000); medical (£9,000); arts (£4,000).

HOW TO APPLY Apply in writing to the correspondent. The trustees meet at intervals through the year to consider grant applications. Only successful applicants will be contacted. Email applications are not accepted.

WHO TO APPLY TO Juliet Wilkinson, Trustee, Manor Farmhouse, Church Street, Great Bedwyn, Marlborough, Wiltshire SN8 3PE *Tel.* 01672 870362 *Email* raynertrust@hotmail.co.uk

■ The Sir James Reckitt Charity

CC NO 225356 **ESTABLISHED** 1921

WHERE FUNDING CAN BE GIVEN Hull and the East Riding of Yorkshire, UK and, occasionally, Red Cross or Quaker work overseas.

WHO CAN BENEFIT Community organisations; Quaker organisations; national and regional charities.

WHAT IS FUNDED General charitable purposes, focusing on: children and young people; education; older people; environment; medical causes; social work; Quaker causes.

WHAT IS NOT FUNDED Local organisations outside the Hull area are not supported, unless their work has regional implications; political causes or those that conflict with Quakerism; replacement of statutory funding or activities which collect funds to be passed on to other organisations, charities or individuals.

TYPE OF GRANT Start-up and core costs; purchase of equipment and materials; building improvements; training costs; project development costs.

RANGE OF GRANTS The majority of grants are between £500 and £5,000 although larger applications may be considered, especially for organisations with which the foundation already has links.

SAMPLE GRANTS Friends School Saffron Walden (£25,000); Antibiotic Research UK (£20,000); Woodbrooke Quaker Study Centre (£15,000); Hull Rape Crisis and Sexual Abuse Service (£7,000); Farm Africa and Peace Direct (£5,000 each); Independent Age (£4,400); Scholarships for Street Kids (£3,000) Prison Reform Trust (£2,500); Hull Animal Welfare Trust, Hull Children's Adventure Society and Porch Project (£2,000 each).

FINANCES *Year* 2015 *Income* £1,306,889 *Grants* £1,185,744 *Grants to organisations* £1,091,713 *Assets* £39,858,338

TRUSTEES William Upton; James Holt; Robert Gibson; Caroline Jennings; Philip Holt; Robin Upton; Sarah Craven; Charles Maxted; Simon James Upton; Simon Edward Upton; James Marshall; Edward Upton; Rebecca Holt; Andrew Palfreman; James Atherton.

OTHER INFORMATION Each year, more than 50% of the charity's grant-making is distributed for the benefit of Kingston upon Hull, the East Riding of Yorkshire and their inhabitants. In 2013/14 289 grants were made to individuals totalling £82,000 for social welfare purposes. During the year, 91 grants of less than £2,000 were made amounting to £84,500.

HOW TO APPLY Apply in writing to the correspondent. The application should include the following key points: the name and address of your organisation; telephone number and email address; the nature of your organisation; its structure, aims, who it serves, and its links with other agencies and networks; the project or funding need – what the grant is to be used for and who will benefit from it; when the funding is required – the date of the project or event; the bank account payee name of your organisation; any links to the Hull and East Yorkshire region, or the Quakers (which together are the charity's funding priorities); a copy of your latest annual report and accounts or equivalent. Applications are measured against the charity's guidelines and decisions are taken at a twice-yearly meeting of trustees in May and October. Applications should be submitted by 31 March and 30 September respectively.

WHO TO APPLY TO James McGlashan, Administrator, 7 Derrymore Road, Willerby, Hull, East Yorkshire HU10 6ES *Tel.* 01482 655861 *Email* jim@derrymore.karoo.co.uk or charity@thesirjamesreckittcharity.org.uk *Website* www.thesirjamesreckittcharity.org.uk

■ Red Hill Charitable Trust

CC NO 307891 **ESTABLISHED** 1997

WHERE FUNDING CAN BE GIVEN South East England is defined as East Anglia, London and Home Counties west to Hampshire.

WHO CAN BENEFIT Charitable organisations.

WHAT IS FUNDED The education and training/access to education and training of children and young people under the age of 25 who have emotional and behavioural problems.

WHAT IS NOT FUNDED Individuals; research projects (generally); causes relating to medical need or social deprivation.

TYPE OF GRANT The trustees can only commit to making grants for a year at a time.

RANGE OF GRANTS £1,000 to £5,000.

SAMPLE GRANTS Goldwyn School (£5,000); Reading Repertory Theatre (£4,800); Hampshire and Isle of Wight Wildlife (£4,000); Youth and Families Matter (£3,500); Greenwich Dance (£3,000); The Prince's Trust (£2,800); University of Hertfordshire (£2,500); Richmond Crossroads Centre (£1,900); Tall Ships Youth Trust (£1,500).

FINANCES *Year* 2015/16 *Income* £52,612 *Grants* £71,875 *Grants to organisations* £71,875 *Assets* £2,991,240

TRUSTEES Antony Bunting; Will Mather; Michael Startup; Roger Barton; Bob Law; John Moore; Jenny Whittle; Kevin Moule; Allan Adams.

HOW TO APPLY An application form is available from the trust's website, which should be completed and emailed to the trust. The trustees hold meetings twice yearly, in early March and early October. Applications for these meetings must be received by 15 February or 15 September respectively. Consideration of late applications will automatically be deferred to the following meeting. The application form itself must be emailed as a word-processed document and supporting material including photographs may be sent electronically or as hard copy, but unless the material is in small e-files or compressed, it cannot be distributed to trustees in advance of the decision meeting.

WHO TO APPLY TO The Clerk to the Trustees, c/o Day Smith and Hunter, Globe House, Eclipse Park, Sittingbourne Road, Maidstone, Kent ME14 3EN *Tel.* 01622 213707 *Email* clerk@redhilltrust.org *Website* www.redhilltrust.org

■ C. A. Redfern Charitable Foundation

CC NO 299918 **ESTABLISHED** 1989

WHERE FUNDING CAN BE GIVEN UK.

WHO CAN BENEFIT Registered UK charities.

WHAT IS FUNDED General charitable purposes, with some preference for those concerned with health and welfare.

WHAT IS NOT FUNDED Building works; individuals.

TYPE OF GRANT Core costs, one-off, project and research. Funding is available for one year or less.

RANGE OF GRANTS £1,000 to £30,000, typically between the £1,000 and £5,000.

SAMPLE GRANTS South Buckinghamshire Riding for the Disabled (£30,000); Saints and Sinners (£10,000); Aspire, Canine Partners for Independence and London Air Ambulance (£5,000 each); Blesma (£4,000); Vauxhall City Farm (£3,000); Hope House Hospice (£2,000); Breast Cancer Haven, Turtle Key Arts and Woodland Trust (£1,000 each).

FINANCES *Year* 2015/16 *Income* £181,112 *Grants* £200,000 *Grants to organisations* £200,000 *Assets* £4,774,894

TRUSTEES William Maclaren; David Redfern; Simon Ward; Julian Heslop.

OTHER INFORMATION Grants were made to 53 organisations during the year.

HOW TO APPLY Unsolicited applications are not accepted.

WHO TO APPLY TO The Administrator, PricewaterhouseCoopers, One Reading Central, 23 Forbury Road, Reading RG1 3JH *Tel.* 0118 938 3128

■ Reed Family Foundation

CC NO 1154027 **ESTABLISHED** 2013

WHERE FUNDING CAN BE GIVEN Unrestricted.

WHO CAN BENEFIT Charitable organisations; individuals.

WHAT IS FUNDED General charitable purposes.

TYPE OF GRANT Project funding.

RANGE OF GRANTS Up to £900,000.

SAMPLE GRANTS Octavia Housing (£900,000); African Prisons Project (£35,000 in two grants); The Royal Foundation of the Duke and Duchess of Cambridge and Prince Harry (£25,000); Keeping Kids Company (£15,000); Ballet Black and Quintessentially Foundation (£10,000 each).

FINANCES *Year* 2015 *Income* £5,646,584 *Grants* £995,000 *Grants to organisations* £995,000 *Assets* £4,681,937

TRUSTEES Richard Reed; Charlotte Reed; Kate May.

OTHER INFORMATION Grants were made to six organisations during the year, of which £900,000 was awarded to one organisation, Octavia Housing, to fund the development of a new community centre in Portobello, London, with the purpose of providing a day facility for older people.

HOW TO APPLY Apply in writing to the correspondent.

WHO TO APPLY TO Emma Moody, Bond Dickinson LLP, 112 Quayside, St Ann's Wharf, Newcastle upon Tyne NE1 3DX *Tel.* 0191 230 8823

■ Richard Reeve's Foundation

CC NO 1136337 **ESTABLISHED** 1928

WHERE FUNDING CAN BE GIVEN Camden, City of London and Islington.

WHO CAN BENEFIT Local organisations; charities; schools.

WHAT IS FUNDED Education and training for children and young people under the age of 25 who or whose parents live or work, or lived or worked, in the area of benefit. Projects focused on: raising literacy and numeracy; progression into work; music education.

WHAT IS NOT FUNDED Building costs; independent school fees; furniture/household goods; school meals; holidays; school outings; to replace statutory funding. No grants are made directly to individuals.

TYPE OF GRANT Up to three years. Capital costs, full project funding and core costs.

RANGE OF GRANTS £1,000 to £94,000.

SAMPLE GRANTS Partners in Learning (£154,000 in two grants); Islington Giving (£43,000); Christ's Hospital (£21,000); Camden Centre for Learning (£20,500); SHINE (£1,000).

FINANCES *Year* 2015/16 *Income* £805,820 *Grants* £246,808 *Grants to organisations* £221,803 *Assets* £37,037,125

TRUSTEES John Tickle; Michael Bennett; Michael Hudson; Cllr Charlynne Pullen; Mark Jessett; Shannon Farrington; Gerald Rothwell; Revd David Ingall; Lorna Russell; Jo Emmerson.

OTHER INFORMATION During the year, grants to individuals totalled £25,000.

HOW TO APPLY An application form is available on the website, where you can check that your project meets the funding priorities. Applications are acknowledged within five working days.

WHO TO APPLY TO Andrew Fuller, Clerk and Company Secretary, 13 Elliott's Place, London N1 8HX *Tel.* 020 7726 4230 *Email* enquiries@richardreevesfoundation.org.uk or clerk@richardreevesfoundation.org.uk *Website* www.richardreevesfoundation.org.uk

■ Responsible Gambling Trust (GambleAware)

CC NO 1093910 **ESTABLISHED** 2002

WHERE FUNDING CAN BE GIVEN UK.

WHO CAN BENEFIT Registered charities; research institutions.

WHAT IS FUNDED Education, prevention and treatment services and research aimed at minimising the impact of gambling.
TYPE OF GRANT Research.
RANGE OF GRANTS Up to £3.8 million.
SAMPLE GRANTS Gamcare (£3.8 million); The Gordon Moody Association (£632,000); Central and North West London NHS Foundation Trust – Problem Gambling (£350,000).
FINANCES *Year* 2015/16 *Income* £7,632,371 *Grants* £5,668,098 *Grants to organisations* £5,668,098 *Assets* £5,576,185
TRUSTEES Alan Jamieson; Nick Harding; Christopher Pond; Annette Dale-Perera; Prof. Jonathan Wolff; Patrick Sturgis; Prof. Sian Griffiths; Brigid Simmonds; Henry Birch; Katheryn Lampard; James Mullen; Prof. Anthony Kessel.
OTHER INFORMATION The trust spent £769,000 on research during the year, but the exact breakdown was not provided in the accounts.
HOW TO APPLY The trust does not make grants, nor enter into contracts in response to unsolicited applications received. However, it does annually invite tenders for funding in relation to innovative applied research, intended to support original and creative projects that help deliver or extend the National Responsible Gambling Strategy, within the bounds of the trust's charitable objectives. See the website for more details.
WHO TO APPLY TO Natalie Simpson, Operations Manager, 7 Henrietta St, London WC2E 8PS *Tel.* 020 7287 1994 *Email* info@gambleaware.org *Website* about.gambleaware.org

■ The Rest Harrow Trust

CC NO 238042 **ESTABLISHED** 1964
WHERE FUNDING CAN BE GIVEN UK.
WHO CAN BENEFIT Registered charities.
WHAT IS FUNDED General charitable purposes.
WHAT IS NOT FUNDED Non-registered charities; individuals.
TYPE OF GRANT Occasionally one-off for part or all of a particular project.
RANGE OF GRANTS £100 to £2,000. The majority of grants were under £500 each.
SAMPLE GRANTS Nightingale Hammerson (£2,000); World Jewish Relief (£1,000); Age UK, Breast Cancer Now, Great Ormond Street Hospital Charity, Norwood, Wiener Library (£500 each); Children's Trust (£300); Action for Sick Children, Amend, Barnardo's; Changing Faces; Lifelites (£200 each); Addaction, African Promise, CHICKS, Family Haven, Housing for Women, Music Alive (£100 each).
FINANCES *Year* 2015/16 *Income* £98,470 *Grants* £51,200 *Grants to organisations* £51,200 *Assets* £1,034,182
TRUSTEES Janet Bloch; Dominic Flynn; Judith Portrait.
OTHER INFORMATION Grants are usually made to national bodies rather than local branches, or to local groups.
HOW TO APPLY Apply in writing to the correspondent. Applications are considered quarterly. Only submissions from eligible bodies are acknowledged.
WHO TO APPLY TO Judith Portrait, c/o Portrait Solicitors, 21 Whitefriars Street, London EC4Y 8JJ *Email* sarah.hovil@portraitsolicitors.com

■ Reuben Foundation

CC NO 1094130 **ESTABLISHED** 2002
WHERE FUNDING CAN BE GIVEN UK and overseas, with a focus on Israel and the United States.
WHO CAN BENEFIT Charitable organisations, including universities and Jewish organisations; individuals.
WHAT IS FUNDED Health care; education; general charitable purposes.
RANGE OF GRANTS Up to £479,000.
SAMPLE GRANTS Lyric Theatre Hammersmith (£479,000); Oxford University (£330,000); Cambridge University (£105,000); British Film Institute (£77,500); Community Security Trust (£25,000); CLIC Sargent (£22,000); Elton John AIDS Foundation (£17,000); Britain Israel Communications and Research Centre, Jewish Care and NSPCC (£10,000 each); Great Ormond Street Hospital (£6,800); Royal Marsden (£1,000).
FINANCES *Income* £4,597,288 *Grants* £1,891,706 *Grants to organisations* £1,852,156 *Assets* £85,803,218
TRUSTEES Richard Stone; Simon Reuben; Malcolm Turner; Annie Benjamin; Patrick O'Driscoll; James Reuben; Dana Reuben.
OTHER INFORMATION The amount of grants given to individuals totalled £39,500 during the year. The foundation supports a number of scholarship initiatives including the Reuben Scholarship programme alongside the University of Oxford, University College London, ARK Schools and the University of Cambridge.
HOW TO APPLY The foundation's website states that applications for grants are made by invitation only.
WHO TO APPLY TO Patrick O'Driscoll, Trustee, 4th Floor, Millbank Tower, 21–24 Millbank, London SW1P 4PQ *Tel.* 020 7802 5000 *Email* contact@reubenfoundation.com *Website* www.reubenfoundation.com

■ Rhodi Charitable Trust

CC NO 1082915 **ESTABLISHED** 2000
WHERE FUNDING CAN BE GIVEN Preston, the UK and the India.
WHO CAN BENEFIT Charitable organisations; individuals.
WHAT IS FUNDED Social welfare.
SAMPLE GRANTS Masjid e Salaam – Preston (£158,500); Matiwala Darul Uloom Charitable Trust and Preston Muslim Girls High School (£10,000 each).
FINANCES *Year* 2015 *Income* £322,254 *Grants* £327,383 *Grants to organisations* £327,383 *Assets* £1,307,987
TRUSTEES Asif Bux; Hamida Bux; Ibrahim Bux.
HOW TO APPLY Apply in writing to the correspondent.
WHO TO APPLY TO Asif Bux, Trustee, 1 Fishwick Park, Mercer Street, Preston PR1 4LZ

■ The Rhododendron Trust

CC NO 267192 **ESTABLISHED** 1974
WHERE FUNDING CAN BE GIVEN UK and overseas.
WHO CAN BENEFIT Registered charities.
WHAT IS FUNDED Arts, social welfare and the environment in the UK; humanitarian aid.
WHAT IS NOT FUNDED Individuals, for example on gap year projects with another charity; local branches of national societies; medical or academic research; missionary charities.
TYPE OF GRANT Preferably project-based.
RANGE OF GRANTS £500 or £1,000 each.

SAMPLE GRANTS Alone in London, Mines Advisory Group, Peace Direct, Sightsavers and Womankind Worldwide (£1,000 each); Build IT International, Contact the Elderly, English Touring Opera, Performing Arts Children's Charity and Tree Aid (£500 each).
FINANCES *Year* 2015/16 *Income* £69,679 *Grants* £55,000 *Grants to organisations* £55,000 *Assets* £1,707,952
TRUSTEES Sarah Ray; Sarah Oliver; Elizabeth Baldwin; Wendy Anderson.
OTHER INFORMATION Grants to 75 organisations were made during the year.
HOW TO APPLY Apply in writing to the correspondent at any time. Guidelines are noted on the website. Applicants will be informed within about a month if they have been unsuccessful. If you receive no response within this time frame, then your application has been added to a long list of possible grants. This list will be considered by Grants Officers and trustees in February or March. Following this, you will either receive a cheque or will be notified that you have been unsuccessful.
WHO TO APPLY TO The Grants Officer, 6 Bridge Street, Richmond, North Yorkshire DL10 4RW *Email* mail@rhododendron-trust.org.uk *Website* www.rhododendron-trust.org.uk

■ Rhondda Cynon Taff Welsh Church Acts Fund

CC NO 506658 **ESTABLISHED** 1977
WHERE FUNDING CAN BE GIVEN Rhondda Cynon Taff, Bridgend and Merthyr Tydfil County Borough Councils.
WHO CAN BENEFIT Church-based and other charitable organisations.
WHAT IS FUNDED Church-based organisations, young people and medical, cultural, recreational and general causes.
WHAT IS NOT FUNDED Students; individuals; clubs with a liquor licence; projects operating outside the area of benefit; normal running expenses.
TYPE OF GRANT Project funding (excluding normal running expenses).
RANGE OF GRANTS Up to £10,000.
SAMPLE GRANTS Ton Pentre and District Recreation Association CIO (£10,000); Maerdy Boxing Club (£9,900); Carmel Congregational Chapel (£8,400); Treorchy Senior Citizens Club (£7,100); Merthyr Tydfil and District Model Engineering Society (£4,700); Merthyr Tydfil Institute for the Blind (£4,300); St John Ambulance Merthyr Vale Aberfan (£3,800); Avon Street Gardening and Allotment Society, Beddau Community Church and Porthcawl Harbourside CIC (£2,000 each).
FINANCES *Year* 2015/16 *Income* £334,000 *Grants* £352,661 *Grants to organisations* £352,661 *Assets* £11,746,000
TRUSTEE Rhondda Cynon Taff County Borough Council.
OTHER INFORMATION Grants of more than £2,000 require a minimum of 50% match funding from non-Welsh Church Fund sources. Those grants which are structural in nature are only considered where a professional assessment for the necessary works has been made. Organisations received 97 grants during the year, of which 58 were of £2,000 or more totalling £289,500, and 39 grants, totalling £63,500, were of less than £2,000.
HOW TO APPLY Apply in writing to the correspondent, submitting your application together with estimates, accounts and constitutions. The 2015/16 annual report states: 'Recommendations for grant awards are made by officers in an Assessment Round Report, which is considered at special meetings regularly throughout the year on approximately a monthly basis.'
WHO TO APPLY TO The Trustees, Rhondda Cynon Taff County Borough Council, Council Offices, Bronwydd, Porth CF39 9DL *Tel.* 01443 680734 *Email* treasurymanagement@rctcbc.gov.uk

■ Riada Trust

SC NO SC028314 **ESTABLISHED** 1998
WHERE FUNDING CAN BE GIVEN UK.
WHO CAN BENEFIT Registered charities.
WHAT IS FUNDED General charitable purposes.
SAMPLE GRANTS Children's Hospice Association Scotland (£15,000); Maggie's Centre Edinburgh (£10,000); Gurkha Welfare Trust (£2,000); Alzheimer Scotland, Beating Bowel Cancer, Brain Research Trust and Carers Trust (£1,000 each); Waverley Care (£500).
FINANCES *Year* 2015 *Income* £140,491 *Grants* £80,500 *Grants to organisations* £80,500 *Assets* £1,193,963
HOW TO APPLY Apply in writing to the correspondent.
WHO TO APPLY TO The Trustees, Jeffrey Crawford and Co., 25 Castle Terrace, Edinburgh EH1 2ER

■ Daisie Rich Trust

CC NO 236706 **ESTABLISHED** 1964
WHERE FUNDING CAN BE GIVEN UK, with a strong preference for the Isle of Wight.
WHO CAN BENEFIT Charitable and community organisations and individuals (particularly former employees, or their spouses, of Upward and Rich Ltd).
WHAT IS FUNDED General charitable purposes with a preference for health, social welfare, the environment; arts and culture; young people; community services.
TYPE OF GRANT Mostly recurrent; core costs; project funding.
RANGE OF GRANTS £200 to £5,000.
SAMPLE GRANTS YMCA Young Carers Project (£5,000); Earl Mountbatten Hospice (£3,000); Carisbrooke Castle Museum (£2,000); British Red Cross, Isle of Wight Semi-Colon Group and National Rheumatoid Arthritis Society Isle of Wight (£1,000 each); People's Trust for Endangered Species (£750); Medina Marching Band (£500); St George's School (£400); Royal Victoria Yacht Club (£200).
FINANCES *Year* 2015/16 *Income* £166,671 *Grants* £127,580 *Grants to organisations* £99,100 *Assets* £3,304,211
TRUSTEES Adrian Medley; Ann Medley; Maurice Flux; David Longford; James Attrill; Claire Locke.
OTHER INFORMATION The amount of grants given to individuals totalled £28,500, of which £26,500 was given to former employees of Upward and Rich Ltd.
HOW TO APPLY Contact the correspondent for an application form. The trustees hold regular meetings to decide on grant applications and are assisted by information gathered by the administrator.
WHO TO APPLY TO Lyn Mitchell, Administrator, The Hawthorns, Main Road, Arreton, Newport, Isle of Wight PO30 3AD *Tel.* 07866 449855 *Email* daisierich@yahoo.co.uk

■ The Clive and Sylvia Richards Charity

CC NO 327155 **ESTABLISHED** 1986
WHERE FUNDING CAN BE GIVEN UK, with a preference for Herefordshire.
WHO CAN BENEFIT Charitable organisations; religious and educational institutions; individuals.
WHAT IS FUNDED General charitable purposes, although there is a preference for education, health care, heritage, and the arts.
TYPE OF GRANT One-off, project and buildings. Interest-free loans are considered. Grants may be for up to two years.
RANGE OF GRANTS The majority were of £5,000 or less. A number of larger grants were also made.
SAMPLE GRANTS Huntingdon Disease Association (£121,500); Bishop Vesey's Grammar School (£100,000); Diabetes UK (£55,000); Seafarers UK (£40,000); Welsh National Opera (£20,500); Target Ovarian Cancer (£10,500); British Library (£5,000); Phoenix Bereavement Support (£3,000); Herefordshire MS Therapy Centre (£2,500); Birmingham Museums Trust (£1,800); St Michael's Hospice (£430).
FINANCES *Year* 2015/16 *Income* £1,371,739 *Grants* £545,028 *Grants to organisations* £545,028 *Assets* £1,281,479
TRUSTEES Peter Henry; Clive Richards; Sylvia Richards; Peter Dines; David Iddon; Peregrine Banbury.
OTHER INFORMATION Grants of less than £2,500 totalled £45,500.
HOW TO APPLY The website stresses that it is 'very important' to ensure that your organisation is eligible to apply for funding before making an application. Around half of applications received by the charity are ineligible. In the first instance, we would recommend that applicants visit the charity's website for full information, including the prescriptive 'Guidance for Applicants' document.
WHO TO APPLY TO Rob Woolf, Lower Hope Farm, Ullingswick, Hereford, Herefordshire HR1 3JF *Tel.* 01432 820557 *Email* admin@csrcharity.com *Website* csrcharity.com

■ Richmond Parish Lands Charity

CC NO 200069 **ESTABLISHED** 1786
WHERE FUNDING CAN BE GIVEN Richmond, Kew, Ham, North Sheen, East Sheen, Petersham and Mortlake (the TW9, TW10 and SW14 postcode areas).
WHO CAN BENEFIT Local charities; voluntary organisations; social enterprises; individuals.
WHAT IS FUNDED Older people; the care of people who are ill or facing hardship; the provision of recreational facilities and support for leisure activities; the promotion of education and assisting people to take up courses and training; general charitable purposes.
WHAT IS NOT FUNDED Projects and organisations located outside the benefit area, unless it can be demonstrated that a substantial number of residents from the benefit area will gain from their work; UK charities (even if based in the benefit area), except for that part of their work which caters specifically for the benefit area.
TYPE OF GRANT One-off and recurring; core costs; project funding; strategic funding.
RANGE OF GRANTS £290 to £32,000.
SAMPLE GRANTS Kew Community Trust (£62,500 in three grants); Age UK – Richmond (£32,000); Marble Hill Playcentres (£24,500); Mortlake Community Association (£11,000); Care Leavers Support, Learning English at Home and London Wildlife Trust (£10,000 each); Ethnic Minority Advisory Group (£7,500); Museum of Richmond (£5,000); Queen's Road Hostel (£400).
FINANCES *Year* 2015/16 *Income* £2,172,640 *Grants* £1,483,968 *Grants to organisations* £1,157,234 *Assets* £94,000,705
TRUSTEES Paul Velluet; Ian Durant; Paul Cole; Ros Sweeting; Rosie Dalzell; Tim Sketchley; Ashley Casson; Kate Ellis; Lisa Blakemore; Gill Moffett; Roger Clark; Peter Buckwell; Owen Carew-Jones; Rachel Holmes; Paul Lawrence.
OTHER INFORMATION The figure for organisational grants includes £57,000 given to schools in children support grants. During the year, welfare grants were made to individuals totalling £279,500. At the time of writing (June 2017), 39 local charities receive regular funding from the charity, amounting annually to more than £400,000 in support of core operational activities. The Mayor of Richmond upon Thames is an ex officio trustee of the charity.
HOW TO APPLY There are separate application forms and guidelines available on the website for the various types of grants. Be sure to complete each section and to provide the required documents. Regularly funded organisations must apply by specific deadlines which are available on the website.
WHO TO APPLY TO Sharon La Ronde, Grants Director, The Vestry House, 21 Paradise Road, Richmond, Surrey TW9 1SA *Tel.* 020 8948 5701 *Email* grants@rplc.org.uk *Website* www.rplc.org.uk

■ Ridgesave Ltd

CC NO 288020 **ESTABLISHED** 1983
WHERE FUNDING CAN BE GIVEN UK and overseas.
WHO CAN BENEFIT Jewish organisations.
WHAT IS FUNDED The advancement of the Jewish religion; Jewish education and poverty relief.
RANGE OF GRANTS Up to £350,000.
SAMPLE GRANTS Keren Association Ltd (£350,000); Friends of Mercaz Hatorah Belz Macnivka (£253,500); Mifal Hachesed Vehatzedokoh (£199,000); New Bels Synagogue (£80,000); Congregation of Aden Jews in the United Kingdom (£55,500); Friends of Beis Chinuch Lebonos Trust (£33,500); Higher Talmudical Education Ltd (£19,500); Ezer Viznitz Foundation (£13,000); Side By Side School Ltd (£11,000); Kehal Charedim Trust (£10,000).
FINANCES *Year* 2015/16 *Income* £2,271,015 *Grants* £2,228,192 *Grants to organisations* £2,228,192 *Assets* £469,810
TRUSTEES Zelda Weiss; Joseph Weiss; Eliasz Englander.
HOW TO APPLY Apply in writing to the correspondent.
WHO TO APPLY TO Zelda Weiss, 141B Upper Clapton Road, London E5 9DB *Email* mail@cohenarnold.com

■ Rigby Foundation

CC NO 1011259 **ESTABLISHED** 1982
WHERE FUNDING CAN BE GIVEN England with a preference for Warwickshire.
WHO CAN BENEFIT Registered charities.
WHAT IS FUNDED Health and saving lives; education; the arts, culture and heritage; social welfare.
SAMPLE GRANTS Marie Curie Cancer Care (£50,000); Coventry City of Culture and Shakespeare Hospice Trust (£10,000 each); The C Group (£5,000); War Child (£1,500); HMS Heron Central Fund (£1,000); Fight for Sight (£360); St Peter's Church Devon (£100).

FINANCES *Year* 2015/16 *Income* £1,135,144 *Grants* £140,454 *Grants to organisations* £140,454 *Assets* £2,504,985

TRUSTEES Sir Peter Rigby; Patricia Rigby; James Rigby; Steven Rigby.

HOW TO APPLY Apply in writing to the correspondent.

WHO TO APPLY TO Manny Dos Santos, James House, Warwick Road, Birmingham B11 2LE *Tel.* 0121 766 7000

■ The Sir John Ritblat Family Foundation

CC NO 262463 **ESTABLISHED** 1971

WHERE FUNDING CAN BE GIVEN UK.

WHO CAN BENEFIT Charitable organisations.

WHAT IS FUNDED General charitable purposes.

WHAT IS NOT FUNDED Individuals.

RANGE OF GRANTS £20 to £154,000.

SAMPLE GRANTS National Trust (£154,000); British Ski and Snowboard National Foundation (£32,000); The Henry Jackson Society (£20,000); Tate Foundation (£7,900); Liberal Judaism (£4,000); ABF The Soldiers' Charity, Alder Hey Children's Charity and Winston Churchill Memorial Trust (£2,000 each); Royal Institute of British Architects (£1,000); The Royal Horticultural Society (£50).

FINANCES *Year* 2015/16 *Income* £425,282 *Grants* £243,873 *Grants to organisations* £243,873 *Assets* -£59,952

TRUSTEES Sir John Ritblat; Mr N. S. J. Ritblat; Mr C. B. Wagman; Mr J. W. J. Ritblat.

OTHER INFORMATION Grants were made to 29 organisations during the year.

HOW TO APPLY Apply in writing to the correspondent.

WHO TO APPLY TO The Trustees, RSM, The Pinnacle, 170 Midsummer Boulevard, Milton Keynes, Buckinghamshire MK9 1BP *Tel.* 01908 687800

■ The River Farm Foundation

CC NO 1113109 **ESTABLISHED** 2006

WHERE FUNDING CAN BE GIVEN Worldwide; in practice, the UK.

WHO CAN BENEFIT Charitable organisations.

WHAT IS FUNDED Health; social welfare; children's welfare; education; environment; homelessness.

TYPE OF GRANT Typically recurrent.

RANGE OF GRANTS £3,000 to £50,000. All but two grants were of £10,000 or less.

SAMPLE GRANTS The Busoga Trust (£69,000); Centrepoint Soho (£20,500); Helen and Douglas House and NSPCC (£13,800 each); The Children's Museum at Saratoga and Universal Preservation Hall (£12,900 each); Shelter (£12,700); The Woodland Trust (£11,500); Renaissance Foundation (£5,000); The Royal British Legion (£4,600).

FINANCES *Year* 2015/16 *Income* £124,959 *Grants* £1,295,709 *Grants to organisations* £1,295,709 *Assets* £38,312,033

TRUSTEES Mark Haworth; Nigel Langstaff; Deborah Fisher.

OTHER INFORMATION Grants were made to 11 organisations during the year, with £1.1 million of the grant total going to St Edmund Hall Development.

HOW TO APPLY Apply in writing to the correspondent.

WHO TO APPLY TO Deborah Fisher, Trustee, The Old Coach House, Bergh Apton, Norwich, Norfolk NR15 1DD *Tel.* 01508 480100 *Email* info@fisherlegal.co.uk

■ The River Trust

CC NO 275843 **ESTABLISHED** 1977

WHERE FUNDING CAN BE GIVEN UK, with a preference for Sussex.

WHO CAN BENEFIT Charitable organisations; missionaries.

WHAT IS FUNDED The advancement of the Evangelical Christian faith.

WHAT IS NOT FUNDED Individuals; repairs of church fabric; funding towards capital expenditure.

TYPE OF GRANT Certain charities are supported for more than one year.

RANGE OF GRANTS £500 to £19,300.

SAMPLE GRANTS Youth With A Mission (£20,500 in two grants); Barcombe Parochial Church Council (£10,000); Armed Forces Christian Union and St Stephen's Society (£2,000 each); African Enterprise, Marine Reach and Penny Trust (£1,500 each); Christ Church Turnham Green, Marriage Foundation and St Peter and St James Hospice (£1,000 each); Christians Against Poverty (£500).

FINANCES *Year* 2014/15 *Income* £88,850 *Grants* £109,675 *Grants to organisations* £109,675 *Assets* £640,927

TRUSTEES SG. Kleinwort Hambros Trust Company (UK) Ltd; Davina Irwin-Clark.

OTHER INFORMATION At the time of writing (June 2017) these were the latest accounts available for the trust.

HOW TO APPLY Apply in writing to the correspondent. It is unusual for unsolicited appeals to be successful. Only successful applicants are notified of the trustees' decision. Some charities are supported for more than one year, although no commitment is usually given to the recipients.

WHO TO APPLY TO The Trustees, SG Kleinwort Hambros Trust Company (UK) Ltd, 8 St James's Square, London SW1Y 4JU *Tel.* 020 3207 7041 *Email* katie.styles@kleinwortbenson.com

■ Rivers Foundation

CC NO 1078545 **ESTABLISHED** 1999

WHERE FUNDING CAN BE GIVEN UK and overseas.

WHO CAN BENEFIT Charitable organisations, particularly small charities.

WHAT IS FUNDED General charitable purposes, especially educational projects; social welfare; the arts; community causes.

TYPE OF GRANT One-off and recurring grants; running costs.

RANGE OF GRANTS £90 to £18,000.

SAMPLE GRANTS Rona Sailing Project (£18,000); Fly Navy Heritage Trust (£11,500); Mathari – Kenya (£10,400); Operation Smile (£10,000); Grants to Nepal and Single Homeless Project (£7,500 each); Scientific Exploration Society (£5,800); Wiener Library (£4,000); ABF The Soldiers' Charity (£100); Royal Academy (£90).

FINANCES *Year* 2015/16 *Income* £80,373 *Grants* £98,807 *Grants to organisations* £98,807 *Assets* £686,058

TRUSTEES Alan Rivers; Keith Constable; Christine Bolton; Cass Chapman; Susan Rivers.

OTHER INFORMATION Grants were made to 19 organisations during the year.

HOW TO APPLY Apply in writing to the correspondent, including details of the project, your latest audited accounts and as much background information as possible on the work of your charity. The trustees meet twice yearly.

WHO TO APPLY TO Keri Jenkin, Unit 1, Berham Mews, Blythe Road, London W14 0HN *Email* ajrultra@btinternet.com *Website* riversfoundation.co.uk

■ Riverside Charitable Trust Ltd

CC NO 264015 **ESTABLISHED** 1972

WHERE FUNDING CAN BE GIVEN Mainly Rossendale, Lancashire.

WHO CAN BENEFIT Charitable organisations; individuals.

WHAT IS FUNDED Social welfare, education, health care, older people; people employed or formerly employed in the shoe trade; general charitable purposes.

WHAT IS NOT FUNDED Political causes.

TYPE OF GRANT Recurring costs.

SAMPLE GRANTS A list of beneficiaries was not included in the accounts.

FINANCES *Year* 2015/16 *Income* £61,879 *Grants* £143,890 *Grants to organisations* £138,215 *Assets* £1,909,537

TRUSTEES Annie Higginson; Barry John Lynch; Frederick Drew; Gilbert Maden; Harry Francis; Ian Barrie Dearing; Jacqueline Davidson; Brian Terry; Angela O'Gorman; Mark Butterworth.

OTHER INFORMATION During the year, 161 grants were made for the following purposes: general charitable purposes (£85,000 in 118 grants); social welfare (£49,500 in 25 grants); death grants (£2,800 in 17 grants); educational support (£1,000 in one grant). Retired employees received £5,500.

HOW TO APPLY Apply in writing to the correspondent.

WHO TO APPLY TO Brian Terry, Trustee, E. Sutton and Sons Ltd, PO Box 2, Bacup, Lancashire OL13 0DT *Tel.* 01706 874961 *Email* ajepson@esutton.co.uk

■ The Rix-Thompson-Rothenberg Foundation

CC NO 285368 **ESTABLISHED** 1982

WHERE FUNDING CAN BE GIVEN UK.

WHO CAN BENEFIT Registered charities.

WHAT IS FUNDED The care, education, training, development and leisure activities of people with learning disabilities. A special emphasis is given to grants that will enhance opportunity and lifestyle.

WHAT IS NOT FUNDED Applications for specific learning details are not supported.

RANGE OF GRANTS £2,000 to £6,000.

SAMPLE GRANTS Llandovery Theatre Co. (£6,000); Down Syndrome Medical Interest Group, PAMIS and Step By Step Kids (£5,000 each); Museum of London and Northern Ballet (£4,000 each); Openstorytellers (£3,500); East Berkshire Down Syndrome Groups (£2,500); Reading Mencap (£2,000).

FINANCES *Year* 2015 *Income* £116,901 *Grants* £95,610 *Grants to organisations* £94,110 *Assets* £1,508,726

TRUSTEES David Rothenberg; Fred Heddell; Barrie Davis; Jonathan Rix; Suzanne Marriott; Chris Thompson; Andy Minnion.

OTHER INFORMATION During the year, grants were made to 25 organisations, and grants to individuals totalled £1,500.

HOW TO APPLY In the first instance the applicant should discuss the proposed work by telephone, or send an email or letter to the correspondent a minimum of four months in advance of a board meeting. Grants are considered in June and December. The application process is ongoing and interested applicants may apply at any time. An application form must be accompanied with a copy of the organisation's latest audited accounts.

WHO TO APPLY TO The Administrator, R. T. R. Foundation, c/o Pamis, University of Dundee, 15/16 Springfield DD1 4JE *Tel.* 07532 320138 *Email* rtrfoundation@gmail.com

■ RJM Charity Trust

CC NO 288336 **ESTABLISHED** 1983

WHERE FUNDING CAN BE GIVEN UK and worldwide.

WHO CAN BENEFIT Registered charities; Jewish organisations and institutions.

WHAT IS FUNDED General charitable purposes with a preference for Jewish causes.

SAMPLE GRANTS A list of beneficiaries was not included in the accounts.

FINANCES *Year* 2015/16 *Income* £182,508 *Grants* £217,535 *Grants to organisations* £217,535 *Assets* £218,794

TRUSTEES Joshua Rowe; Michelle Rowe.

HOW TO APPLY Apply in writing to the correspondent.

WHO TO APPLY TO Joshua Rowe, Trustee, 84 Upper Park Road, Salford M7 4JA *Tel.* 0161 720 8787 *Email* JR@broomwell.com

■ Thomas Roberts Trust

CC NO 1067235 **ESTABLISHED** 1997

WHERE FUNDING CAN BE GIVEN UK, with particular focus on Winchester.

WHO CAN BENEFIT Charitable organisations; employees and former employees of the Thomas Roberts Group Companies.

WHAT IS FUNDED Medical research and care; social welfare; older people; people who are ill, disadvantaged or who have a disability.

RANGE OF GRANTS Most grants are of between £500 and £2,500.

SAMPLE GRANTS Cancer Research UK (£10,00); Marie Curie Cancer Care (£5,000); Carers Trust and Hospice of the Valleys (£2,000 each); Canine Partners for Independence and Winchester Churches Nightshelter (£1,500 each); Parkinson's UK and The Stroke Association (£1,000 each); Anthony Nolan Trust and Winchester Gateway Club (£500 each).

FINANCES *Year* 2015/16 *Income* £35,985 *Grants* £46,212 *Grants to organisations* £45,500 *Assets* £1,203,003

TRUSTEES Gillian Hemmings; Richard Gammage; James Roberts.

OTHER INFORMATION Grants to ex-employees of Thomas Roberts Group during the year totalled £700.

HOW TO APPLY Apply in writing to the correspondent. The 2015/16 annual report states that applicants should 'submit a summary of their proposals to the trustees detailing how the funds would be used and what would be achieved'.

WHO TO APPLY TO James Roberts, Trustee, Sheridan House, 40–43 Jewry Street, Winchester, Hampshire SO23 8RY *Tel.* 01962 843211 *Email* trtust@thomasroberts.co.uk

■ Robertson Hall Trust

CC NO 1073473 **ESTABLISHED** 1999

WHERE FUNDING CAN BE GIVEN The ecclesiastical parish of Brighton.

WHO CAN BENEFIT Anglican organisations.

WHAT IS FUNDED Anglican churches; Anglican causes.

WHAT IS NOT FUNDED Individuals.

RANGE OF GRANTS £1,500 to £44,000.

SAMPLE GRANTS Brighton Parish Chapel Royal (£44,000); Chichester Diocese for Christ Church Brighton and St Luke's Advice Service

(£10,000); Brighton Evangelical Alliance (£7,500); St Paul – Brighton (£5,000); Chemin Neuf (£2,000); Books Alive (£1,500).

FINANCES *Year* 2015 *Income* £104,000 *Grants* £98,000 *Grants to organisations* £98,000 *Assets* £1,607,549

TRUSTEES Gerald Milner; John Head; Revd David Biggs; Revd Julie Newson; Revd Martin Lloyd-Williams.

HOW TO APPLY Apply in writing to the correspondent.

WHO TO APPLY TO John Head, Trustee, 15 Meadow Close, Hove BN3 6QQ *Tel.* 01273 554464

■ The Robertson Trust

SC NO SC002970 **ESTABLISHED** 1961

WHERE FUNDING CAN BE GIVEN Scotland.

WHO CAN BENEFIT Registered charities; CICs Ltd by guarantee.

WHAT IS FUNDED General charitable purposes. The trust has seven main priority areas: alcohol misuse; care; community arts; community sports; criminal justice; education and training; and health. Applications are also considered for: preservation of the environment; strengthening local communities; heritage, culture and science; animal welfare; and saving lives.

WHAT IS NOT FUNDED Individuals; political or religious bodies; projects based outside Scotland; research or feasibility studies; replacement of statutory revenue; capital costs of memorials/statues; one-off events/festivals which have no associated educational activities; one-off purchase of buildings and/or land; capital work on buildings or land not owned by the applicant or which they do not have a long-term lease; housing associations; arm's-length external organisations; charities which seek funding for onward distribution to third parties; umbrella groups which do not provide direct services; CICs limited by shares.

TYPE OF GRANT One-off grants; grants of up to three years; revenue costs; capital costs; core costs; project costs. **Note:** The trust is a match funder and does not fully fund projects.

RANGE OF GRANTS £500 to £1 million. There is no maximum or minimum amount, although grants for revenue costs are rarely awarded outside the range of £500 to £15,000. Capital donations are usually to a maximum of 10% of total capital costs.

SAMPLE GRANTS Eyemouth and District Community Trust (£250,000); Fraserburgh South Links Sports Development Trust (£111,000); Scottish Drugs Forum (£60,000); Medical Foundation for the Care of Victims of Torture (£40,000); Upper Nithsdale Art and Crafts Community Initiative (£36,000); Cruse Bereavement Scotland (£30,000); LGBT Healthy Living Centre (£22,000); Carers UK (£10,000); Hope Kitchen SCIO (£6,000); Pet Care Network (£2,500).

FINANCES *Year* 2015/16 *Income* £22,136,000 *Grants* £17,078,000 *Grants to organisations* £17,078,000 *Assets* £271,089,000

TRUSTEES Dame Barbara Kelly; Shonaig Macpherson; Judy Cromarty; Mark Laing; Heather Lamont; Andrew Walls; Lorne Crerar; Mark Batho; Garry Coutts.

OTHER INFORMATION Applicants should refer to the trust's excellent website. The trust aims to be a flexible funder that builds relationships with the organisations it funds and is happy to provide as much advice and support as possible in the application process and subsequent evaluation of projects funded. Grants were made to 704 charities during the year; 308 of those charities received grants for the first time.

HOW TO APPLY Applications can be made through the trust's website. Guidelines regarding the trust's new strategy are also available on the website.

WHO TO APPLY TO Lesley Macdonald, Head of Giving, 152 Bath Street, Glasgow G2 4TB *Tel.* 0141 353 7300 *Email* funding@therobertsontrust.org.uk *Website* www.therobertsontrust.org.uk

■ Robyn Charitable Trust

CC NO 327745 **ESTABLISHED** 1988

WHERE FUNDING CAN BE GIVEN UK and overseas.

WHO CAN BENEFIT Charitable organisations.

WHAT IS FUNDED The welfare of children, particularly the relief of need and education.

WHAT IS NOT FUNDED Individuals.

SAMPLE GRANTS All Hallows Cranmore Hall School Trust Ltd (£28,500); Friends of Home-Start Camden and Médecins Sans Frontières (£20,000); The H. and T. Clients' Charitable Trust (£2,000); Garrick Christmas Fund (£500); Cancer Research (£100).

FINANCES *Year* 2015/16 *Income* £85,214 *Grants* £71,120 *Grants to organisations* £71,120 *Assets* £1,119,956

TRUSTEES Malcolm Webber; Mark Knopfler; Ronnie Harris.

OTHER INFORMATION During the year, six grants were awarded.

HOW TO APPLY Apply in writing to the correspondent.

WHO TO APPLY TO Malcolm Webber, Trustee, c/o Harris and Trotter, 64 New Cavendish Street, London W1G 8TB *Tel.* 020 7467 6300

■ The Roddick Foundation

CC NO 1061372 **ESTABLISHED** 1997

WHERE FUNDING CAN BE GIVEN Worldwide.

WHO CAN BENEFIT Charitable organisations.

WHAT IS FUNDED Human rights; poverty; social justice; environmental; humanitarian; medical causes/health; education; media; arts and culture.

WHAT IS NOT FUNDED Sport; fundraising events or conferences; sponsorship of any kind.

RANGE OF GRANTS £5,000 to £100,500.

SAMPLE GRANTS Angola 3 (£100,500); Hepatitis C Trust (£75,000); Institute for Global Labour and Human Rights (£66,500); Actor's Gang (£48,500); Baobab Centre for Young Survivors in Exile (£30,000); Farms Not Factories (£25,000); Centre for Criminal Appeals (£20,000); Bognor Regis Foodbank (£10,000); Freedom Theatre (£5,000).

FINANCES *Year* 2015/16 *Income* £386,834 *Grants* £1,398,102 *Grants to organisations* £1,398,102 *Assets* £17,405,472

TRUSTEES Justine Roddick; Samantha Roddick; Gordon Roddick; Tina Schlieske.

OTHER INFORMATION Grants were made to 39 organisations during the year.

HOW TO APPLY The foundation does not accept unsolicited applications.

WHO TO APPLY TO Karen Smith, Unit H, The Old Bakery, Golden Square, Petworth, West Sussex GU28 0AP *Tel.* 01798 344362 *Email* karen@theroddickfoundation.org *Website* www.theroddickfoundation.org

■ The Rofeh Trust

CC NO 1077682 **ESTABLISHED** 1999
WHERE FUNDING CAN BE GIVEN Worldwide.
WHO CAN BENEFIT Charitable organisations.
WHAT IS FUNDED General charitable purposes; religious activities, with a possible preference for Jewish causes.
SAMPLE GRANTS A list of beneficiaries was not provided.
FINANCES *Year* 2015/16 *Income* £70,495 *Grants* £70,996 *Grants to organisations* £70,996 *Assets* £1,153,809
TRUSTEES Martin Dunitz; Ruth Dunitz; Vivian Wineman; Henry Eder.
HOW TO APPLY Apply in writing to the correspondent.
WHO TO APPLY TO Martin Dunitz, 44 Southway, London NW11 6SA

■ The Richard Rogers Charitable Settlement

CC NO 283252 **ESTABLISHED** 1981
WHERE FUNDING CAN BE GIVEN UK.
WHO CAN BENEFIT Charitable organisations.
WHAT IS FUNDED General charitable purposes; with a preference for overseas aid; human rights; health and the arts.
RANGE OF GRANTS £25 to £25,000.
SAMPLE GRANTS Centre for London (£25,000); Reprieve (£20,000); Save The Children Fund (£5,000); The Climate Reality Project (£3,000); Doctors of the World (£2,500); Women for Refugee Women (£2,000); Crisis, Freedom from Torture and Chickenshed Theatre Trust (£1,000 each); The Royal Marsden Cancer Charity (£500); Architects Benevolent Fund (£300); The London Society (£25).
FINANCES *Year* 2015/16 *Income* £1,565,567 *Grants* £77,513 *Grants to organisations* £77,513 *Assets* £3,540,549
TRUSTEES Lord Richard Rogers; Lady Ruth Rogers.
OTHER INFORMATION Grants were made to 29 organisations during the year.
HOW TO APPLY Apply in writing to the correspondent.
WHO TO APPLY TO Kenneth Hawkins, New Derwent House, 69/73 Theobalds Road, London WC1X 8TA *Tel.* 020 7025 4600 *Email* KHawkins@hwca.com

■ Rokach Family Charitable Trust

CC NO 284007 **ESTABLISHED** 1981
WHERE FUNDING CAN BE GIVEN Israel and UK.
WHO CAN BENEFIT Jewish organisations.
WHAT IS FUNDED Advancement of the Jewish religion; education and training; medical purposes; health; general charitable purposes.
TYPE OF GRANT Generally recurrent.
RANGE OF GRANTS Up to £38,000.
SAMPLE GRANTS MH Ltd (£38,000); Before Trust (£19,000); Cosmon Belz (£8,000); Beis Yaakov School and Torah 5759 Ltd (£6,000 each); Service to Aged Ltd (£5,000); AV Trust (£4,000).
FINANCES *Year* 2014/15 *Income* £118,003 *Grants* £109,666 *Grants to organisations* £109,666 *Assets* £362,179
TRUSTEES Norman Rokach; Helen Rokach; Esther Hoffman; Miriam Feingold; Anita Gefilhaus; Mrs N. Brenig.
OTHER INFORMATION At the time of writing (June 2017) the accounts for 2015/16 were overdue. The latest accounts available were those for the 2014/15 financial year.
HOW TO APPLY Apply in writing to the correspondent.
WHO TO APPLY TO The Trustees, c/o Purcells Chartered Accountants, 4 Quex Road, London NW6 4PJ *Tel.* 020 7328 3272

■ The Sir James Roll Charitable Trust

CC NO 1064963 **ESTABLISHED** 1997
WHERE FUNDING CAN BE GIVEN UK, with a slight preference for Kent; overseas.
WHO CAN BENEFIT Registered charities; individuals.
WHAT IS FUNDED General charitable purposes; interfaith understanding; IT education; research into specific learning disorders.
TYPE OF GRANT Unrestricted.
RANGE OF GRANTS All grants were for £1,000.
SAMPLE GRANTS Action on Elder Abuse, Basildon Community Resource Centre, Big Issue Foundation, Carers UK, Computers for the Disabled, Disasters Emergency Committee Nepal Earthquake Appeal, Family Holiday Association, Howard League for Penal Reform, IT Schools Africa, Medical Engineering Resource Unit, Tools for Self Reliance and Woman's Aid Federation England (£1,000 each).
FINANCES *Year* 2015/16 *Income* £228,604 *Grants* £171,000 *Grants to organisations* £140,500 *Assets* £4,745,609
TRUSTEES Nicholas Wharton; Brian Elvy; Jonathan Liddiard.
HOW TO APPLY Applications should be made in writing to the correspondent as a hard copy letter. The trustees usually meet around four times a year to assess grant applications.
WHO TO APPLY TO Nicholas Wharton, Trustee, 5 New Road Avenue, Chatham, Kent ME4 6AR *Tel.* 01634 830111 *Email* sirjamesroll@winch-winch.co.uk

■ The Helen Roll Charity

CC NO 299108 **ESTABLISHED** 1988
WHERE FUNDING CAN BE GIVEN UK.
WHO CAN BENEFIT Registered (or exempt) charities.
WHAT IS FUNDED General charitable purposes, particularly: education, especially higher education; libraries and museums; the arts; health and animal welfare.
WHAT IS NOT FUNDED Individuals.
TYPE OF GRANT One-off for specific projects; most charities are supported on a long-term basis.
RANGE OF GRANTS £1,000 to £10,000.
SAMPLE GRANTS Home Farm Trust (£10,000); West Oxfordshire's Citizens Advice (£8,000); Pembroke College Oxford (£6,000); Trinity Laban Conservatoire of Music and Dance (£5,000); Carers UK, Medical Detection Dogs, Oxfordshire Association for the Blind and WheelPower (£2,000 each); Nordic Health Walking (£1,500); Gerald Moore Award (£1,000).
FINANCES *Year* 2015/16 *Income* £39,034 *Grants* £109,500 *Grants to organisations* £109,500 *Assets* £1,640,973
TRUSTEES Christine Chapman; Christine Reid; Patrick Stopford; Paul Strang; Frank Williamson; Jennifer Williamson; Stephen Williamson.
OTHER INFORMATION The charity aims to distribute about £120,000 each year between around 30 charities. The trustees work with the charities and often continue to make grants over a longer period of time. Because of this, there is only capacity for one or two new grants recipients each year.

HOW TO APPLY Apply in writing to the correspondent during the first fortnight in February. Applications should be kept short, ideally on one sheet of A4. Further material will then be requested from those who are short-listed. The trustees normally make their distributions in March. Applications by email are welcomed.
WHO TO APPLY TO The Trustees, c/o Wenn Townsend Accountants, 30 St Giles, Oxford OX1 3LE *Tel.* 01865 559900 *Email* helen.roll@aol.co.uk

■ The Gerald Ronson Family Foundation

CC NO 1111728 **ESTABLISHED** 2005
WHERE FUNDING CAN BE GIVEN UK and overseas.
WHO CAN BENEFIT Registered charities.
WHAT IS FUNDED General charitable purposes with a preference for Jewish causes; children and young people; health and disability; arts and culture.
TYPE OF GRANT Preferably one-off.
RANGE OF GRANTS Generally up to £20,000 although occasionally larger grants are made.
SAMPLE GRANTS JCoSS (£200,000); Community Security Trust (£83,000); Race Against Dementia (£50,000); Royal Opera House Covent Garden Foundation (£40,000); Police Arboretum Memorial Trust (£20,000); Refugee Council (£3,000); Jewish Women's Aid (£2,000); Chiltern Centre for Disabled Children (£1,000); British Friends of Israeli War Disabled (£500); Jewish Music Institute (£260).
FINANCES *Year* 2016 *Income* £602,666 *Grants* £1,538,242 *Grants to organisations* £1,538,242 *Assets* £91,668,801
TRUSTEES Gerald Ronson; Dame Gail Ronson; Alan Goldman; Jonathan Goldstein; Lisa Althasen; Nicole Ronson Allalouf; Hayley Ronson; Jeffrey Shear; Marc Zilkha.
HOW TO APPLY Apply in writing to the correspondent. The trustees meet quarterly to discuss applications and grants are made on a monthly basis.
WHO TO APPLY TO Jeremy Trent, Secretary, H. W. Fisher and Company, Acre House, 11–15 William Road, London NW1 3ER *Tel.* 020 7388 7000 *Email* jtrent@hwfisher.co.uk

■ Mrs L. D. Rope's Second Charitable Settlement

CC NO 275810 **ESTABLISHED** 1978
WHERE FUNDING CAN BE GIVEN UK with a preference for East Suffolk.
WHO CAN BENEFIT Charitable organisations.
WHAT IS FUNDED General charitable purposes; Roman Catholic faith and ecumenical work; relief of poverty; people with disabilities; children and young people; older people.
RANGE OF GRANTS Typically less than £20,000.
SAMPLE GRANTS The Samaritans (£16,000); St Thomas Catholic Church, Woodbridge (£12,000); Royal Agricultural Benevolent Institution (£10,000); Royal Scottish Agricultural Benevolent Institution, St Mungo's Community Housing Association, Shrewsbury Cathedral, SPRED and The Joe Homan Charity (£5,000 each); Brooke Hospital and FoodCycle (£2,500 each).
FINANCES *Year* 2015/16 *Income* £145,244 *Grants* £108,030 *Grants to organisations* £108,030 *Assets* £735,725
TRUSTEES Crispin Rope; Philip Jolly; Anne Folan; Anne Ruffell.
OTHER INFORMATION During the year, 50 grants were made of which 15 were to individuals.
HOW TO APPLY It is very seldom that grants are made to organisations making unsolicited requests.
WHO TO APPLY TO Crispin Rope, Trustee, Crag Farm, Boyton, Woodbridge, Suffolk IP12 3LH *Tel.* 01473 333288

■ Mrs L. D. Rope's Third Charitable Settlement

CC NO 290533 **ESTABLISHED** 1984
WHERE FUNDING CAN BE GIVEN UK and overseas, with a particular interest in East Suffolk.
WHO CAN BENEFIT Small registered charities that have a large volunteer force.
WHAT IS FUNDED Relief of poverty; homelessness; families; people with disabilities; education for young people; the Roman Catholic religion and ecumenical work; general charitable purposes.
WHAT IS NOT FUNDED Overseas projects; national charities; requests for core funding; buildings; medical research/health care (outside the beneficial area); schools (outside the beneficial area); environmental charities and animal welfare; the arts; matched funding; repayment of debts for individuals.
TYPE OF GRANT For unsolicited requests, grants are usually one-off and small scale. Funding is given for one year or less.
RANGE OF GRANTS Up to £50,000.
SAMPLE GRANTS International Refugee Trust (£50,000); Felixstowe and District Citizens Advice (£32,000); Anglia Care Trust (£24,000); Society of St Vincent de Paul (£20,000); Ipswich Citizens Advice (£15,000); Moldova Not Forgotten, Suffolk Refugee Support and Traidcraft (£10,000 each); Ipswich Locality Homelessness Partnership (£7,000); Apostleship of the Sea (£6,000).
FINANCES *Year* 2015/16 *Income* £1,471,124 *Grants* £991,441 *Grants to organisations* £613,040 *Assets* £56,098,639
TRUSTEES Crispin Rope; Jeremy Winteringham Heal; Ellen Jolly; Catherine Scott; Paul Jolly.
OTHER INFORMATION The charity has a very informative annual report and accounts providing detailed guidance on what it will fund. Grants were made to 1,968 individuals and totalled £378,500. Grants awarded to organisations totalled £613,000 and were made for the following purposes: general charitable purposes (£363,000); relief of poverty (£169,500); advancement of religion (£43,500); advancement of education (£37,000).
HOW TO APPLY Send a concise letter (preferably one side of A4) explaining the main details of your request. Always send your most recent accounts and a budgeted breakdown of the sum you are looking to raise. The charity will also need to know whether you have applied to other funding sources and whether you have been successful elsewhere. Your application should say who your trustees are and include a daytime telephone number.
WHO TO APPLY TO Crispin Rope, Trustee, Crag Farm, Boyton, Woodbridge, Suffolk IP12 3LH *Tel.* 01473 333288 *Email* ropetrust@lucyhouse.org.uk

■ Rosca Trust

CC NO 259907 **ESTABLISHED** 1966

WHERE FUNDING CAN BE GIVEN The boroughs of Southend-on-Sea, Castle Point and Rochford District Council only.

WHO CAN BENEFIT Registered charities; CICs; community groups; churches.

WHAT IS FUNDED Young people, older people and people with disabilities in the area of benefit.

WHAT IS NOT FUNDED Organisations outside the beneficial area; individuals.

RANGE OF GRANTS £500 to £5,000.

SAMPLE GRANTS Wesley Methodist Church Leigh (£5,000); The Art Ministry (£3,000); SOS Domestic Abuse Project (£2,500); Southend Citizens Advice (£2,400); Brentwood Catholic Children's Society, Drugline Education CIC Ltd and National Coastwatch (£2,000 each); Southend Night Shelter for the Homeless (£1,100); Carers Choices (£1,000); Bipolar UK (£500).

FINANCES *Year* 2015/16 *Income* £133,230 *Grants* £84,190 *Grants to organisations* £84,190 *Assets* £677,632

TRUSTEES Nigel Gayner; Gary Hodson; Maureen Sarling; Chris Sternshine; Christopher Bailey; Alison Semmence.

OTHER INFORMATION Grants were made to 43 organisations during the year.

HOW TO APPLY Apply in writing to the correspondent. Applications are reviewed three times a year, usually in January, April and September. An sae is appreciated. Preliminary telephone calls are considered unnecessary.

WHO TO APPLY TO Nigel Gayner, Trustee, 1 Moat End, Southend-on-Sea SS1 3QA *Tel.* 01702 305064 *Email* kenbarcrowe@blueyonder.co.uk

■ The Rose Foundation

CC NO 274875 **ESTABLISHED** 1977

WHERE FUNDING CAN BE GIVEN London area.

WHO CAN BENEFIT Registered charities and exempt bodies.

WHAT IS FUNDED Building projects where the cost is of less than £200,000 in the London area. This could be a general refurbishment or a specific project. With extensive experience with projects of this size, the trustees are often able to contribute advice and recommendations, in both the design and construction phases, in addition to their donation.

WHAT IS NOT FUNDED The purchase of equipment; the purchase of a building or site; seed money required to draw up plans; fees in general. The trustees do not like to support projects already completed or give funds which will be banked indefinitely, so require projects to either commence within the first eight months of the year following approval or to have been started and still be ongoing during this period.

TYPE OF GRANT Part-funding building projects.

RANGE OF GRANTS Typically between £5,000 and £10,000.

SAMPLE GRANTS St John Ambulance (£459,000); Fred Hollows Foundation UK (£50,000); West London Synagogue (£22,000); Al-Huda Marble Arch Association (£10,000); Zoological Society of London (£8,000); Breast Cancer Haven, Paddington Arts and Royal National Theatre (£5,000 each); Mayhew Animal Home and St John Fisher Roman Catholic Church (£2,500 each).

FINANCES *Year* 2015/16 *Income* £977,660 *Grants* £842,039 *Grants to organisations* £842,039 *Assets* £26,673,632

TRUSTEES Martin Rose; Alan Rose; John Rose; Paul Rose.

OTHER INFORMATION At the time of writing (June 2017) the foundation's 2014/15 accounts were the latest available.

HOW TO APPLY Apply in writing to the correspondent including details of the organisation and the registered charity number, together with the nature and probable approximate cost of the scheme and its anticipated start and completion dates. The trustees commit to projects for the following year at their annual June meeting. Applications can be submitted anytime between 1 July and 31 March for projects taking place the year after (e.g. between July 2017 and March 2018 for projects in 2019). There are detailed guidelines on the website.

WHO TO APPLY TO Martin Rose, Trustee, 28 Crawford Street, London W1H 1LN *Tel.* 020 7262 1155 *Email* martin@rosefoundation.co.uk *Website* www.rosefoundation.co.uk

■ The Cissie Rosefield Charitable Trust

CC NO 293177 **ESTABLISHED** 1985

WHO CAN BENEFIT Registered charities.

WHAT IS FUNDED General charitable purposes, particularly Jewish causes.

SAMPLE GRANTS £3,300 to World Jewish Relief; £3,000 to Richard House Trust; £1,200 to LEVKA 2000; £500 to British Emunah; £450 to Friends of the Jerusalem Rubin Academy; £300 to The Lord Mayor's Appeal.

FINANCES *Year* 2015/16 *Grants* £62,000 *Grants to organisations* £62,000

TRUSTEES Martin Paisner; Stephen Rosefield; John Rosefield.

OTHER INFORMATION The charities accounts were not available; therefore, we have estimated the amount the charity gave in grants based on their expenditure.

HOW TO APPLY Apply in writing to the correspondent.

WHO TO APPLY TO Kenneth Martin, 33 Ely Place, London EC1N 6TD *Tel.* 020 7269 7500

■ The Cecil Rosen Foundation

CC NO 247425 **ESTABLISHED** 1966

WHERE FUNDING CAN BE GIVEN UK and Israel.

WHO CAN BENEFIT Charitable organisations.

WHAT IS FUNDED Jewish causes; people with disabilities; including people who are blind; health; education; medical research; social welfare; international disaster appeals.

WHAT IS NOT FUNDED Individuals.

TYPE OF GRANT Up to ten years.

SAMPLE GRANTS The Jewish Blind and Physically Handicapped Society (£126,500).

FINANCES *Year* 2015/16 *Income* £502,409 *Grants* £355,300 *Grants to organisations* £355,300 *Assets* £8,014,960

TRUSTEES Malcolm Ozin; John Hart; Peter Silverman.

OTHER INFORMATION Grants were made for the following purposes: welfare (£190,000); health (£52,500); medical research (£35,500); education (£34,500); religion (£21,000). A number of Israeli charities benefitted by about 9% of the total distribution spread out over the range of donations made. Only one beneficiary was listed in the accounts.

HOW TO APPLY The annual report for 2015/16 states that 'the trustees consider all applications received and give special attention to those which were originally chosen by the Settlor, Cecil Rosen'.

WHO TO APPLY TO Malcolm Ozin, Trustee, 35 Langstone Way, Mill Hill East, London NW7 1GT *Tel.* 020 8346 8940 *Email* contact@cecilrosenfoundation.org

■ Rosetrees Trust

CC NO 298582 **ESTABLISHED** 1987

WHERE FUNDING CAN BE GIVEN England, Scotland, and Wales.

WHO CAN BENEFIT Universities and medical schools.

WHAT IS FUNDED Independently vetted medical research projects, especially if departmentally backed and peer reviewed.

WHAT IS NOT FUNDED Overheads; equipment or capital; conferences; travel and accommodation; technology transfer; tuition fees; projects outside England, Scotland and Wales; researchers at pre-PhD level; PhD studentships that have already started; research into illnesses that only affect a small number of people in the UK; basic research with no translation vision; psychology or social research.

TYPE OF GRANT Project and research funding for up to three years will be considered. Seed funding for a preliminary or pilot report is also available.

RANGE OF GRANTS Usually between £5,000 and £20,000.

SAMPLE GRANTS UCL and Royal Free (£953,500); Imperial College London (£397,000); The Royal College of Surgeons (£202,000); University of Cambridge (£175,000); Hebrew University Jerusalem (£140,500) Institute of Cancer Research (£94,500); University of Liverpool (£41,000).

FINANCES *Year* 2015/16 *Income* £2,868,821 *Grants* £3,177,675 *Grants to organisations* £3,177,675 *Assets* £34,438,447

TRUSTEES Richard Ross; Clive Winkler; Sam Howard; Lee Mesnick.

OTHER INFORMATION During the year, 'other centres' received £385,500 and 'other' medical research grants totalled £90,000.

HOW TO APPLY Application forms and guidelines are available to download from the website. There is a separate application form and set of criteria for PhD applications. The trust states the following on its website: 'We ask you to complete the form as concisely as possible but with enough detail for us to understand what your research is about, this is best achieved by answering in simple lay terms.'

WHO TO APPLY TO Richard Miller, Operations Manager, Russell House, 140 High Street, Edgware, Middlesex HA8 7LW *Tel.* 020 8952 1414 *Email* rmiller@rosetreestrust.co.uk *Website* www.rosetreestrust.co.uk

■ The David Ross Foundation

CC NO 1121871 **ESTABLISHED** 2007

WHERE FUNDING CAN BE GIVEN UK.

WHO CAN BENEFIT Registered charities.

WHAT IS FUNDED The foundation's main focus is young people. Areas of work include: the arts, community, education, music and sport and enabling disadvantaged people to participate fully in society.

TYPE OF GRANT One-off.

SAMPLE GRANTS Leicester Sports Council (£25,000); Army Benevolent Fund (£10,000); Lord's Taverners (£5,100); GOSH (Great Ormond Street Hospital) (£5,000); Salvation Army (£1,000); Lincoln Castle (£830); Africa Foundation (£500); Nordoff Robbins (£200); WaterAid (£150).

FINANCES *Year* 2015/15 *Income* £327,026 *Grants* £1,665,947 *Grants to organisations* £1,665,947 *Assets* £5,608,631

TRUSTEES Mark Bolland; David Ross; Anita Bott; Christine Homer; Marcia Mercier; Lady Caroline Ryder.

OTHER INFORMATION Grants were distributed as follows: partner organisations (£589,000); David Ross Educational Trust (£690,000); one-off donations (£379,500); academies (£1,000).

HOW TO APPLY Apply in writing to the correspondent. Applications should include: an outline of your project – its purpose and activities; financials – total budget, fundraising strategy and the level of funding you are seeking from the foundation; who will benefit; community support; sustainability and legacy of your project.

WHO TO APPLY TO Joanne Hoareau, 10 St James's Place, London SW1A 1NP *Tel.* 020 7534 1551 *Email* joanne@davidrossfoundation.com *Website* www.davidrossfoundation.co.uk

■ The Rothermere Foundation

CC NO 314125 **ESTABLISHED** 1964

WHERE FUNDING CAN BE GIVEN UK.

WHO CAN BENEFIT Registered charities; individual graduates of the Memorial University of Newfoundland.

WHAT IS FUNDED General charitable purposes including education; children's charities; the arts; sport; medical research; religious organisations.

TYPE OF GRANT One-off and recurrent.

RANGE OF GRANTS Mostly up to £10,000.

SAMPLE GRANTS The Black Stork Charity (£50,000); Rothermere American Institute – Northcliffe First World War Project (£45,000); Alzheimer Society and Dorset and Somerset Air Ambulance (£25,000 each); NSPCC Digital Taskforce and Royal Horticultural Society Learning Centre (£10,000 each); Canine Partners (£5,000); Chalke Valley History Festival (£2,800); Wye Village Hall (£2,000); Daylesford Church (£300).

FINANCES *Year* 2015/16 *Income* £1,089,915 *Grants* £604,494 *Grants to organisations* £498,359 *Assets* £39,571,713

TRUSTEES Rt Hon. Viscount Jonathan Rothermere; The Viscountess Claudia Rothermere; Vyvyan Harmsworth.

OTHER INFORMATION Payments made during the year included three grants to individuals totalling £106,000. The foundation also provides accommodation for the Oxford Professor Scholarship, to a cost of £35,500 in 2015/16.

HOW TO APPLY Apply in writing to the correspondent. The trustees meet twice a year to consider grant applications.

WHO TO APPLY TO Vyvyan Harmsworth, Trustee and Secretary, Beech Court, Canterbury Road, Challock, Ashford, Kent TN25 4DJ *Tel.* 01233 740641

■ The Rothley Trust

CC NO 219849 **ESTABLISHED** 1959

WHERE FUNDING CAN BE GIVEN Northumberland; Tyne and Wear; Durham; Cleveland.

WHO CAN BENEFIT Registered charities; CICs; voluntary groups (these must be properly constituted and must find a registered charity to act as a cheque handler).

WHAT IS FUNDED Children and young people; disability; community; education; energy saving projects; ex-services people.
WHAT IS NOT FUNDED Further education; the repair of buildings solely used for worship; religious purposes; arts, heritage or science; amateur sport; human rights, conflict resolution or reconciliation (except family mediation); environmental protection or improvement; animal welfare; residents associations; parish councils; University of the Third Age.
TYPE OF GRANT Mainly one-off donations towards specific projects and not running costs. Start-up costs, buildings, equipment, resources and capital grants will be considered.
RANGE OF GRANTS Typically under £2,000 but can be up to £5,500.
SAMPLE GRANTS Durham Association of Boys and Girls Clubs (£5,500); Citizens Advice Northumbrian and The People's Theatre (£5,000 each); Combat Stress (£3,800); Community Action Northumberland and Consett Churches Detached Youth Project (£3,500 each); St Oswald's Hospice (£3,000); Brathay Hall Trust, Sedgefield Out of School Fun Club and Whizz-Kidz (£2,000 each).
FINANCES *Year* 2015/16 *Income* £294,470 *Grants* £262,675 *Grants to organisations* £224,625 *Assets* £7,311,544
TRUSTEES Alice Brunton; Julia Brown; Anne Galbraith; Mark Bridgeman; Gerard Salvin; David Holborn.
OTHER INFORMATION Grants were made to 240 organisations during the year. Grants of less than £2,000 totalled £224,500 and a further £38,000 was given in grants to individuals.
HOW TO APPLY Apply in writing to the correspondent including a copy of latest accounts/annual reports and an sae. Full details can be found at the trust's website where criteria, guidelines and closing dates for applications are posted.
WHO TO APPLY TO Gillian Allsopp, Trust Secretary, Mea House, Ellison Place, Newcastle upon Tyne NE1 8XS *Tel.* 0191 232 7783 *Email* mail@rothleytrust.co.uk *Website* www.rothleytrust.org.uk

■ Rothschild Foundation (Hanadiv) Europe

CC NO 1083262 **ESTABLISHED** 2000
WHERE FUNDING CAN BE GIVEN Europe.
WHO CAN BENEFIT Universities; libraries; museums; research institutions; National Library of Israel; registered charities.
WHAT IS FUNDED Academic Jewish studies; Jewish heritage; Jewish education.
WHAT IS NOT FUNDED Individuals; the ongoing costs of schools, synagogues or welfare organisations; the building of new museums or communal institutions; artistic projects in the fine arts, the performing arts, film production, creative writing or for book publication institutions based outside Europe. Refer to the website for specific exclusions from each programme.
TYPE OF GRANT Grants for professional development; research; archival or conservation projects.
RANGE OF GRANTS Up to £291,500.
SAMPLE GRANTS Central European University (£291,500); Association of European Jewish Museums (£200,000); Jewish Care (£150,000); John Rylands Research Institute (£120,000); Union of Jewish Students in the UK and Ireland (£90,000); Centre for Urban History of East Central Europe (£60,000); Jewish Museum in Prague (£57,000); London Jewish Cultural Centre (£50,000).
FINANCES *Year* 2015 *Income* £201,856 *Grants* £3,537,696 *Grants to organisations* £3,537,696 *Assets* £115,890,699
TRUSTEES Dr David Landau; Sir Victor Blank; Michael Kay; Lord Rothschild; Beatrice Rosenberg; Adam Cohen.
OTHER INFORMATION Grants for less than £50,000 totalled £1.26 million.
HOW TO APPLY Applications can only be submitted via the online application process. Unless specifically requested, the foundation does not accept applications by mail or email. Refer to the website for application forms, deadlines and guidance for each programme. Information on which specific staff member to contact for each programme is provided on the website.
WHO TO APPLY TO Sally Berkovic, Chief Executive, Spencer House, 27 St James's Place, London SW1A 1NR *Tel.* 01296 658778 *Email* info@rothschildfoundation.eu *Website* www.rothschildfoundation.eu

■ The Roughley Charitable Trust

CC NO 264037 **ESTABLISHED** 1972
WHERE FUNDING CAN BE GIVEN Birmingham city (excluding Wolverhampton, Coventry, Worcester and the Black Country towns).
WHO CAN BENEFIT Registered local charities with an annual turnover of less than £1 million.
WHAT IS FUNDED Community work (including church-based projects); social welfare for children and young people, older people, people with disabilities, people who have offended, people with addiction problems, other marginalised groups; homelessness; health and well-being; education; arts and leisure; heritage; and environment (particularly environmental improvement and green projects).
WHAT IS NOT FUNDED Birmingham-based medical charities; church fabric appeals; CICs; social enterprises; church-based projects which are essentially about the teaching of religion; animal charities; projects outside the city boundary of Birmingham.
TYPE OF GRANT Project funding; capital costs.
RANGE OF GRANTS Mostly £500 to £3,000. Larger grants to projects where trustees have special knowledge.
SAMPLE GRANTS Hope Projects West Midlands (£40,000); Appropriate Technology Asia (£22,000); The Wildlife Trust for Birmingham and the Black Country (£15,000); Midlands Arts Centre (£7,000); Birmingham Children's Community Venture, Freedom From Torture and Restore Birmingham Churches Together (£5,000 each); Women and Theatre (£2,000); Birmingham Bachelor Choir, Birmingham Churches Night Shelter and South Sudanese East Bank Community Association (£1,000 each); Home-Start Castle Vale and Pype Hayes (£500).
FINANCES *Year* 2015/16 *Income* £294,047 *Grants* £229,150 *Grants to organisations* £229,150 *Assets* £6,277,343
TRUSTEES John Smith; Martin Smith; Verity Owen; Victor Thomas; Rebecca McIntyre; Rachel Richards; Benjamin Newton.
OTHER INFORMATION Grants were made to 55 organisations during the year. Priority is given to small and medium-sized organisations in the city of Birmingham. The trust gives larger grants to overseas charities and national charities but only if the trustees are personally involved with them. Unsolicited applications from overseas

and national charities are not accepted and not responded to.

HOW TO APPLY Applications should be made online via the trust's website, where the trust's criteria and guidelines are also available. Applications are accepted between 1 April and 1 October each year, for a grants meeting which takes place in November.

WHO TO APPLY TO John Smith, Trustee, 90 Somerset Road, Edgbaston, Birmingham B15 2PP *Email* correspondent@roughleytrust.org.uk *Website* www.roughleytrust.org.uk

■ Mrs Gladys Row Fogo Charitable Trust

SC NO SC009685 **ESTABLISHED** 1970

WHERE FUNDING CAN BE GIVEN Edinburgh, Lothians and Dunblane.

WHO CAN BENEFIT Registered charities; local charitable groups.

WHAT IS FUNDED Medical research projects; local projects; care of older people.

WHAT IS NOT FUNDED Individuals.

RANGE OF GRANTS £1,000 to £8,000.

SAMPLE GRANTS RNLI (£8,000); Alzheimer Scotland Action on Dementia (£6,000); Age Scotland and Drum Riding for the Disabled Trust (£5,000 each); Scottish Autism and Scottish Council on Deafness (£3,000 each); Deafblind Scotland (£2,000); British Wireless for the Blind Fund, Corstorphine Dementia Project and Hearing Dogs for Deaf People (£1,000 each).

FINANCES *Year* 2015/16 *Income* £163,244 *Grants* £78,000 *Grants to organisations* £78,000 *Assets* £4,193,646

HOW TO APPLY Apply in writing to the trustees. The trustees meet once a year to consider applications, usually in September.

WHO TO APPLY TO The Trustees, c/o Brodies LLP Solicitors, 15 Atholl Crescent, Edinburgh EH3 8HA *Tel.* 0131 228 3777 *Email* Mailbox@brodies.co.uk

■ Rowanville Ltd

CC NO 267278 **ESTABLISHED** 1973

WHERE FUNDING CAN BE GIVEN UK and Israel.

WHO CAN BENEFIT Charitable organisations; Jewish organisations.

WHAT IS FUNDED The advancement of the Orthodox Jewish faith.

TYPE OF GRANT Typically recurrent.

RANGE OF GRANTS £400 to £61,000.

SAMPLE GRANTS Chevras Mo'oz Ladol (£61,000); Friends of Beis Yisrael Trust (£30,000); Beis Hamedrash Chovevei Torah (£25,000); Kollel Beis Aharon (£18,000); Achisomoch Aid Company (£13,600); The Society of Friends of the Torah Ltd (£9,100); Tashbar of Edgware Primary School (£6,000); Bnos Yisroel School (£5,000); Jewish Rescue and Relief Committee (£1,100); Mechina Manchester and Phone and Learn (£1,000 each); Jerusalem Foundation (£400).

FINANCES *Year* 2015/16 *Income* £3,188,729 *Grants* £850,012 *Grants to organisations* £850,012 *Assets* £9,294,128

TRUSTEES Joseph Pearlman; Ruth Pearlman; Montague Frankel.

HOW TO APPLY The charity has previously stated that applications are unlikely to be successful unless one of the trustees has prior personal knowledge of the cause, as this charity's funds are already very heavily committed.

WHO TO APPLY TO Ruth Pearlman, Trustee and Secretary, 8 Highfield Gardens, London NW11 9HB *Tel.* 020 8458 9266

■ The Rowlands Trust

CC NO 1062148 **ESTABLISHED** 1992

WHERE FUNDING CAN BE GIVEN West and South Midlands, including Hereford and Worcester, Gloucester, South Shropshire and Birmingham.

WHO CAN BENEFIT Charitable organisations, including schools, churches and hospices.

WHAT IS FUNDED Medical and scientific research; people who are sick, poor or who have a disability; older people; music; the arts; the environment; the maintenance and restoration of Anglican church buildings.

WHAT IS NOT FUNDED Individuals; animal charities; annual running costs.

TYPE OF GRANT One-off, capital expenditure including buildings, project and research.

RANGE OF GRANTS Mostly between £300 and £10,000, occasionally larger.

SAMPLE GRANTS Young Enterprise (£25,000); Elmhurst School for Dance (£15,000); Alzheimer's Research UK (£10,000); Friends of Westonbirt Arboretum (£5,000); Castle Bromwich Bell Restoration Project (£4,000); Canal and River Trust (£2,000); Friends of Pershore Abbey (£1,800); Wychavon Festival of Brass (£1,000); Cruse Bereavement Care (£750); The Asha Women's Centre (£300).

FINANCES *Year* 2015 *Income* £189,635 *Grants* £611,195 *Grants to organisations* £611,195 *Assets* £4,400,264

TRUSTEES Felicity Burman; Gary Barber; Timothy Jessop; Diana Crabtree; Ian Crockatt Smith.

HOW TO APPLY Application forms are available from the correspondent and are the preferred means by which to apply. Completed forms should be returned with a copy of your most recent accounts. The trustees meet to consider grants four times a year.

WHO TO APPLY TO Louise Ruane, Clerk, Bishop Fleming Rabjohns LLP, 1–4 College Yard, Worcester WR1 2LB *Tel.* 07812 743485 *Email* louise.ruane@therowlandstrust.org.uk

■ The Joseph Rowntree Charitable Trust

CC NO 210037 **ESTABLISHED** 1904

WHERE FUNDING CAN BE GIVEN Unrestricted, in practice mainly UK.

WHO CAN BENEFIT Registered charities; voluntary organisations; charitable groups; individuals.

WHAT IS FUNDED The trust's current funding priorities are: peace and security; power and accountability; rights and justice; sustainable future; and Northern Ireland. Guidelines for each of the funding areas can be found on the website.

WHAT IS NOT FUNDED Larger, older national charities with an established base of supporters and substantial levels of reserves; statutory bodies; for-profit organisations; medical research; academic research, unless this is an integral part of policy and campaigning work that is central to JRCT's funding priority areas; building, buying or repairing buildings; business development or job creation schemes; service provision, including the provision of care, training or support services; housing and homelessness; the arts, except where the project is specifically linked to the trust's issues of interest; individuals who are seeking funding for relief-in-need purposes, travel or adventure projects, or for educational bursaries; general appeals; work which is, or in the recent past has been, funded by statutory sources; work that has been already undertaken; local or national work outside the UK. Further specific exclusions are included for individual programmes and information on these can be found on the trust's website. Within its areas of interest, the trust makes grants to a range of organisations and to individuals.

TYPE OF GRANT Single and multi-year funding for core and project costs.

RANGE OF GRANTS £4,000 to £318,000.

SAMPLE GRANTS Woodbrooke Quaker Studies Centre (£318,000); Oxford Research Group (£150,000); Women's Resource and Development Agency (£116,500); Child Soldiers International (£70,000); Asylum Aid (£66,500); Demand Energy Equality CIC (£60,000); Centre for Cross Border Studies (£30,000); International Broadcasting Trust (£20,000); International Coalition to Ban Uranium Weapons (£15,000); SPEAK Network (£8,400); Society of Black Lawyers (£4,000).

FINANCES *Year* 2015 *Income* £2,348,000 *Grants* £5,622,000 *Grants to organisations* £5,622,000 *Assets* £193,374,000

TRUSTEES Linda Batten; Emily Miles; Margaret Bryan; Susan Seymour; Helen Carmichael; Imran Tyabi; John Fitzgerald; Stan Lee; Michael Eccles; Hannah Torkington; Jenny Amery; Huw Davies; David Newton.

OTHER INFORMATION The Joseph Rowntree Charitable Trust is a Quaker trust and the value base of the trustees, as of the founder Joseph Rowntree (1836–1925), reflects the religious convictions of the Society of Friends. From 419 applications received during the year, the trust made 96 grants. The 11 largest grants accounted for 26% of the total.

HOW TO APPLY Only online applications are accepted. Those sent by post, email or fax are not considered. The online form must be submitted and you should have the following information ready: a narrative proposal; budgets; accounts; (for non-registered charities) your organisation's governing document; information on your organisation's policies (equal opportunities and sustainability), should you have any. The closing dates of funding rounds are listed on the website.

WHO TO APPLY TO Nick Perks, Trust Secretary, The Garden House, Water End, York YO30 6WQ *Tel.* 01904 627810 *Email* enquiries@jrct.org.uk *Website* www.jrct.org.uk

■ The Joseph Rowntree Foundation

CC NO 210169 **ESTABLISHED** 1904

WHERE FUNDING CAN BE GIVEN UK.

WHO CAN BENEFIT Organisations carrying out social science research.

WHAT IS FUNDED This is not a conventional grant-making foundation. Working together with Joseph Rowntree Housing Trust, JRF researches the root causes of social problems and developing solutions, with the aim of achieving social change in the UK. The *JRF and JRHT Strategic Plan 2015–2017* focuses on the themes of partnerships, diversity, power and digital, and on the following strategic aims: individuals and relationships; the places where people live; and work and worth. A strategic plan for beyond 2017 was not available at the time of writing (July 2017) so we advise checking the JRF website for further details on the foundation's current areas of funding.

WHAT IS NOT FUNDED Unsolicited proposals; educational bursaries or sponsorship for individuals for research or further education and training courses; proposals that do not have the potential to make a difference to policy or practice in the UK; projects outside the topics within the current priorities; development projects that are not innovative; development projects from which no general lessons can be drawn; general appeals (e.g. from national charities); core or revenue funding, including grants for buildings or equipment; conferences and other events, websites or publications unless they are linked with work that the foundation is already supporting; grants to replace withdrawn or expired statutory funding, or to make up deficits already incurred; grants or sponsorship for individuals.

TYPE OF GRANT Project and research. Funding can be given for up to two years.

RANGE OF GRANTS Up to £565,000.

SAMPLE GRANTS London School of Economics (£565,000); Lloyds TSB Foundation (£300,000); National Centre for Social Research (£259,000); Black Training and Enterprise Group (£109,000); King's College London (£100,000); Alzheimer's Society (£60,000); Equality and Diversity Forum (£51,000); Cambridge Centre for Housing and Planning Research (£45,000); Fabian Society (£30,000); IPPR North (£25,000).

FINANCES *Year* 2015 *Income* £5,749,000 *Grants* £6,965,000 *Grants to organisations* £6,965,000 *Assets* £316,083

TRUSTEES Maureen Lloffil; Graham Millar; Prof. Dianne Willcocks; Steven Burkeman; Tony Stoller; Deborah Cadman; Saphieh Ashtiany; Gillian Ashmore; William Haire; Carol Tannahill.

HOW TO APPLY The foundation does not respond to unsolicited applications. Instead, it issues 'calls for proposals' and invites submissions to them. Detailed information on all current funding areas and how to make an application is available from the foundation's website. The York Committee has its own application guidelines and form, which are also available from the foundation's website.

WHO TO APPLY TO Campbell Robb, Chief Executive, The Homestead, 40 Water End, York YO30 6WP *Tel.* 01904 629241 *Email* info@jrf.org.uk *Website* www.jrf.org.uk

■ The Royal Artillery Charitable Fund

CC NO 210202 **ESTABLISHED** 1964

WHERE FUNDING CAN BE GIVEN UK and overseas.

WHO CAN BENEFIT Service charities.

WHAT IS FUNDED The welfare of all ranks of the Royal Artillery and the relief and assistance of any past or present members, living or deceased, their dependants and families who are in need of such assistance by way of poverty, illness or disability.

RANGE OF GRANTS £300 to £70,500.

SAMPLE GRANTS Regiments and Batteries (£70,500); Royal Artillery Sports (£65,000); Army Benevolent Fund (£60,000); Gunner Magazine (£18,000); Royal Artillery Memorials (£11,000); King Edward VII Hospital and Veterans Aid (£3,000 each); Not Forgotten

Association (£500); Army Widows' Association (£300).

FINANCES *Year* 2015 *Income* £1,826,958 *Grants* £1,177,764 *Grants to organisations* £566,388 *Assets* £27,179,436

TRUSTEES Col. Clive Fletcher-Wood; Maj. Andrew Dines; Col. Christopher Comport; Brig. David Radcliffe; Maj. General David Cullen; Maj. James Leighton; Col. William Prior; Col. Michael Kelly; Col. Nicholas Sawyer; Col. John Musgrave.

OTHER INFORMATION A further £611,500 was given in welfare grants to individuals.

HOW TO APPLY Apply in writing to the correspondent.

WHO TO APPLY TO Lt. Col. Ian Vere Nicoll, General Secretary, Artillery House, Royal Artillery House, Larkhill, Salisbury, Wiltshire SP4 8QT *Tel.* 01980 634309 *Email* rarhq-racf-welfaremailbox@mod.uk *Website* www.theraa.co.uk/about/ra-charitable-fund

■ The Royal British Legion

CC NO 219279 **ESTABLISHED** 1921

WHERE FUNDING CAN BE GIVEN UK, excluding Scotland. Grants in Scotland are made by Poppyscotland.

WHO CAN BENEFIT Charitable organisations that have been operating as a charity for at least two years.

WHAT IS FUNDED Projects and services benefitting serving and ex-service personnel and/or their families who are not already provided for by The Royal British Legion. These projects and services must be in line with the charity's funding priorities, which are: employment and training; support for families; homelessness and outreach.

WHAT IS NOT FUNDED Commercial ventures (social clubs, for example); statutory services; service units and military wives choirs; commemoration, memorials, monuments or war cemeteries; projects that duplicate services provided by the Legion. Applications for funding exceeding £20,000 for any form of building work are not normally considered unless there are exceptional circumstances.

TYPE OF GRANT One-off and recurring costs.

RANGE OF GRANTS The maximum amount for any single award is £20,000; applications for smaller amounts are encouraged.

SAMPLE GRANTS The Defence and National Rehabilitation Centre (£5 million); The Royal British Legion Centre for Blast Studies at Imperial College London (£4.6 million); The Officer's Association (£2.1 million); Combat Stress (£1.5 million); Royal Commonwealth Ex-Service League (£240,000); The Royal British Legion Industries (£120,000).

FINANCES *Year* 2014/15 *Income* £161,317,000 *Grants* £106,661,000 *Grants to organisations* £15,429,000 *Assets* £320,673,000

TRUSTEES Terry Whittles; Catherine Quinn; Adrian Burn; Una Cleminson; Denise Edgar; Martyn Tighe; Anthony Macaulay; Maj. General David Jolliffe; LtCol Joe Falzon; Jason Coward; Colin Kemp; Philip Moore; Marilyn Humphrey; Lt Col. David Whimpenny; Roger Garratt; Anny Reid.

OTHER INFORMATION Grant-making is only a small part of The Royal British Legion's work. During the year, it had a direct charitable expenditure of £76.5 million, of which almost half was spent on the provision of community welfare services. As part of its support for service and ex-service personnel, the Legion also makes welfare grants to individuals. In 2014/15 these totalled more than £9.5 million. Grants of less than £100,000 were made to 53 other charities and voluntary organisations during the year, totalling £1.2 million. Additionally, Poppyscotland awarded £127,000 in grants of less than £100,000 to ten organisations. At the time of writing (June 2017), the latest available accounts were for 2014/15.

HOW TO APPLY The application process has two stages. Stage One involves the completion of a brief 'expression of interest' form, which should be returned to the External Grants Officer (externalgrants@britishlegion.org.uk). Applicants that are successful at the first stage will be invited to complete a Stage Two application form to be considered by the Grants Panel. The Stage One application form is available to download from the website along with guidelines.

WHO TO APPLY TO External Grants Officer, Haig House, 199 Borough High Street, London SE1 1AA *Tel.* 020 3207 2138 *Email* info@britishlegion.org.uk *Website* www.britishlegion.org.uk

■ Royal Docks Trust (London)

CC NO 1045057 **ESTABLISHED** 1995

WHERE FUNDING CAN BE GIVEN Part of the London Borough of Newham.

WHO CAN BENEFIT The trust supports the community in the part of the London borough of Newham that lies to the south of the London – Tilbury Trunk Road (A13) known as Newham Way.

WHAT IS FUNDED General charitable purposes. Areas of specific interest are: educational and vocational training; recreational and leisure-time activities; the advancement of public education in the arts; general improvement of the physical and social environment; relief of poverty and sickness; housing for people with disabilities or who are otherwise in need; and preservation of buildings of historical or architectural significance.

WHAT IS NOT FUNDED Individuals; general appeals; revenue, top-up or retrospective funding is not given through the minor grants programme.

RANGE OF GRANTS Up to £30,000.

SAMPLE GRANTS Ascension Eagles Talent Central and Royal Docks Learning and Activity Centre (£30,000 each); Newham All Star Sports Academy (£23,500); West Silvertown Village Community Foundation (£20,000); Community Links Harnessing Power (£16,000); Care in Mind and Revolution Farm (£5,000).

FINANCES *Year* 2015/16 *Income* £257,832 *Grants* £167,570 *Grants to organisations* £167,570 *Assets* £7,177,618

TRUSTEES Eric Sorensen; Stephen Nicholas; Sid Keys; Amanda Williams; Robert Heaton; Kayar Raghavan; Cllr Forhad Hussain; Katie Carter; Ken Clark; James Kenworth; Belinda Vecchio; Gary Quashie; Giovanna Grandoni; Shani Thomas; Sandra Erskine.

OTHER INFORMATION Smaller grants of less than £1,000 each were also made to local groups.

HOW TO APPLY There is a broad timetable of deadlines on the website for the annual grants programmes along with detailed guidance on how to apply. Application forms for the minor grants programme, which is subject to its own criteria, may be downloaded from the trust's website.

WHO TO APPLY TO John Parker, Trust Administrator, Olive Cottage, Station Road, St Margaret's at Cliffe, Dover CT15 6AY *Tel.* 01304 853465 *Email* john.parker@royaldockstrust.org *Website* www.royaldockstrust.org.uk

The Royal Navy and Royal Marines Charity

CC NO 1117794 **ESTABLISHED** 2007

WHERE FUNDING CAN BE GIVEN England, Wales and Scotland.

WHO CAN BENEFIT Organisations and individuals.

WHAT IS FUNDED Organisations supporting serving or ex-serving personnel from the Royal Navy and the Royal Marines, and their dependants.

TYPE OF GRANT One-off and recurring.

RANGE OF GRANTS Usually from £10,000 to £150,000.

SAMPLE GRANTS Royal Naval Benevolent Trust (£1.08 million); Royal Navy and Royal Marines Children's Fund (£720,000); Royal Marines Association (£193,000); Sailors' Children's Society (£160,000); Poppy Factory (£82,000); KIDS (£50,000); Royal Marines Poole (£28,500); Royal Navy, Royal Marines Widows' Association (£25,000); HMS Neptune (£20,000); HCPT The Pilgrimage Trust (£20,000); Royal Navy Royal Marines Equestrian (£19,000); Royal Navy Ice Hockey (£15,500); Blind Veterans, Not Forgotten Association and Royal Naval Sailing Association Sailing (£10,000 each).

FINANCES *Year* 2015 *Income* £16,097,507 *Grants* £8,098,603 *Grants to organisations* £6,165,080 *Assets* £53,940,317

TRUSTEES William Stocks; Jennifer Rowe; Cdr K. L. Armstrong; Cmde Annette Picton; WO1 Gary Nicholson; The Hon. Stephen Watson; James Parkin; James Pitt; Oona Muirhead; William Thomas; Roderic Birkett; Michael Tanner; Alexander Burton; Mark Lewthwaite; Jamie Webb.

OTHER INFORMATION The charity also made grants to individuals totalling £1.9 million.

HOW TO APPLY Application forms are available to download from the website, where further guidance and deadlines are also provided.

WHO TO APPLY TO Daniel Jagger, Building 29, HMS Excellent, Whale Island, Portsmouth, Hampshire PO2 8ER *Tel.* 023 9387 1520 *Email* mygrant@rnrmc.org.uk *Website* www.rnrmc.org.uk

Royal Society of Wildlife Trusts

CC NO 207238 **ESTABLISHED** 1916

WHERE FUNDING CAN BE GIVEN UK.

WHO CAN BENEFIT Charitable organisations.

WHAT IS FUNDED The conservation and study of nature.

TYPE OF GRANT One-off and recurring.

SAMPLE GRANTS Avon Wildlife Trust (£109,000); Cumbria Wildlife Trust (£75,000); Down to Earth Project (£59,000); Out Loud Music CIC (£50,000); Friends of Dunvant Park (£30,000); Devon Wildlife Trust (£23,000).

FINANCES *Year* 2015/16 *Income* £11,818,000 *Grants* £7,158,000 *Grants to organisations* £7,158,000 *Assets* £9,018,000

TRUSTEES Harry Barton; Caroline Stewart; Ian Brown; Michael Power; Bill Stow; Ruth Sutherland; Rene Olivieri; Tony Whitbread; Roy Ramsay; Rod Aspinwall; Peter Young; Robin Harper; Anne Selby.

OTHER INFORMATION The charity is an umbrella organisation for several wildlife trusts across the country.

HOW TO APPLY Apply in writing to the correspondent.

WHO TO APPLY TO RSWT, The Wildlife Trusts, The Kiln, Waterside, Mather Road, Newark, Nottinghamshire NG24 1WT *Tel.* 01636 677711 *Email* info@wildlifetrusts.org *Website* www.wildlifetrusts.org

The Royal Victoria Hall Foundation

CC NO 211246 **ESTABLISHED** 1891

WHERE FUNDING CAN BE GIVEN Greater London.

WHO CAN BENEFIT Professional theatre groups (including youth and children's theatre).

WHAT IS FUNDED Encouragement of organisations devoted to the development of and education in theatrical pursuits, infrastructure and technical support, opera and theatre.

WHAT IS NOT FUNDED Projects that relate exclusively to music (e.g. a song or a musical recital); dance which is not within a theatrical context; projects that are wholly concerned with drama training or education or the academic study of dramatic performance; amateur dramatic projects; administrative running costs of an organisation; individuals seeking funds for personal tuition; projects outside Greater London.

TYPE OF GRANT Funding of theatre equipment, feasibility studies, production costs, disability and educational access.

RANGE OF GRANTS £750 to £2,000.

SAMPLE GRANTS Offstage Theatre (£2,000); Southwark Playhouse (£1,600); End of Moving Walkway, Little Angel Theatre and Raising Silver Theatre (£1,500 each); Camden People's Theatre, Polka Theatre and Tricycle Theatre (£1,000 each); The Actors Centre (£750).

FINANCES *Year* 2015/16 *Income* £78,224 *Grants* £72,075 *Grants to organisations* £72,075 *Assets* £1,514,889

TRUSTEES David Collier; Margaret Colgan; Gerald Lidstone; Vivienne Rochester; Brian Daniels; Katie Lancaster; Peader Kirk; Paul Gane; Patricia Myers.

HOW TO APPLY Apply in writing to the correspondent detailing what you are applying for, how much you require and the date and venue of the project. Further specifications are available on the foundation's website. Do not apply for projects planned beyond six months from the application deadline as the foundation makes its grants within the correct accounting period. This means that all projects applied for in April must be delivered by the following October, and all projects applied for in October must be delivered by the following April. Applications should be sent by post or via email to the correspondent.

WHO TO APPLY TO Carol Cooper, Clerk to the Trustees, 111 Green Street, Sunbury-on-Thames TW16 6QX *Tel.* 01932 782341 *Email* contact@rvhf.org *Website* www.rvhf.org

Rozelle Trust

SC NO SC040965 **ESTABLISHED** 2003

WHERE FUNDING CAN BE GIVEN Financially developing countries and Scotland.

WHO CAN BENEFIT Registered charities; a preference for smaller charities.

WHAT IS FUNDED Children and young people; people living in poverty; people with disabilities.

WHAT IS NOT FUNDED Animal charities; charities which collect funds for redistribution to other charities; conferences; costs of employing fundraisers; expeditions; general sports, unless strongly associated with a disadvantaged group; holidays; individuals; large national charities; medical aid and research; religion; routine staff training; sponsorship and marketing appeals.

RANGE OF GRANTS There is no minimum or maximum grant.

SAMPLE GRANTS A list of beneficiaries was not available.
FINANCES *Year* 2015/16 *Income* £8,739 *Grants* £75,000 *Grants to organisations* £75,000
OTHER INFORMATION There are no annual reports or accounts for the trust so we have estimated the grant total based on the trust's expenditure.
HOW TO APPLY Initial contact with the trust should be made using an enquiry form. This can be done directly through the trust's website or a form can be downloaded and returned by post. If your enquiry is of interest to the trustees, you will then be asked for further information on including a copy of your most recent accounts.
WHO TO APPLY TO D. Lamont, Unit 100 Embroidery Mill, Abbeymill Business Centre, Paisley PA1 1JS *Email* info@rozelletrust.org *Website* www.rozelletrust.org

■ The Rubin Foundation

CC NO 327062 **ESTABLISHED** 1986
WHERE FUNDING CAN BE GIVEN UK and overseas.
WHO CAN BENEFIT Registered charities and organisations.
WHAT IS FUNDED Jewish organisations; general charitable purposes.
RANGE OF GRANTS Up to around £200,000.
SAMPLE GRANTS Lancaster University (£200,000); United Jewish Israel Appeal (UJIA) (£100,000); UCL Development Fund (£52,500); Jewish Care and The Prince's Trust (£50,000 each); Chai Lifeline Cancer Care (£34,000); Parliamentary Committee against Anti-Semitism Foundation and Community Security Trust (£30,000 each).
FINANCES *Year* 2015/16 *Income* £1,008,727 *Grants* £705,297 *Grants to organisations* £705,297 *Assets* £1,235,380
TRUSTEES Alison Mosheim; Angela Rubin; Robert Rubin; Andrew Rubin; Carolyn Rubin.
OTHER INFORMATION In 2015/16 other grants under £20,000 totalled £159,000.
HOW TO APPLY The foundation has previously stated that 'grants are only given to people related to our business', such as charities known to members of the Rubin family and those associated with Pentland Group Ltd. **Unsolicited applications are very unlikely to succeed.**
WHO TO APPLY TO The Trustees, The Pentland Centre, Lakeside House, Squires Lane, Finchley, London N3 2QL *Tel.* 020 8346 2600 *Email* amcmillan@pentland.com

■ The Rufford Foundation

CC NO 1117270 **ESTABLISHED** 2006
WHERE FUNDING CAN BE GIVEN Worldwide.
WHO CAN BENEFIT Individuals and small to medium-sized organisations.
WHAT IS FUNDED Nature/biodiversity conservation projects and pilot programmes; wildlife trade issues; research into conservation and protection of the natural environment.
WHAT IS NOT FUNDED Projects in 'developed countries'; pure research with no obvious conservation benefit; expeditions; attending conferences or seminars.
TYPE OF GRANT Small-scale and pilot project funding.
RANGE OF GRANTS £2,000 to £184,000. Rufford Small Grants are for up to £5,000.
SAMPLE GRANTS Environmental Investigation Agency (£184,000); Zoological Society of London (£80,000); Environmental Justice Foundation, Born Free Foundation, RSPB and Wildlife Trust of India (£50,000 each); Botanic Gardens Conservation International (£20,000); AfricanBats, Painted Dog and Conservation Phoenix Fund (£10,000 each). See the foundation's annual report and accounts for a detailed list of beneficiaries, broken down by the stage of grant received.
FINANCES *Year* 2015/16 *Income* £4,564,505 *Grants* £3,843,950 *Grants to organisations* £3,843,950 *Assets* £101,827,422
TRUSTEES Robert Reilly; John Laing; Elizabeth Brunwin; Hugo Edwards; Sarah Barbour; Iain Smailes.
OTHER INFORMATION There are five different stages of grants, which may be given in sequence, beginning with a Rufford Small Grant. The grant figure displayed also includes funding awarded to individuals.
HOW TO APPLY Applications should be completed online on the foundation's website, where criteria and guidelines are also posted. Applications are considered on a rolling basis, there is no deadline.
WHO TO APPLY TO Terry Kenny, Trust Director, 6th Floor, 250 Tottenham Court Road, London W1T 7QZ *Tel.* 020 7436 8604 *Email* terry@rufford.org *Website* www.rufford.org

■ Rugby Football Foundation

CC NO 1100277 **ESTABLISHED** 2003
WHERE FUNDING CAN BE GIVEN England.
WHO CAN BENEFIT Community sports clubs, with a particular interest in rugby.
WHAT IS FUNDED Community participation in amateur rugby.
RANGE OF GRANTS Up to £5,000.
SAMPLE GRANTS A list of beneficiaries was not available.
FINANCES *Year* 2015/16 *Income* £28,630,185 *Grants* £327,120 *Grants to organisations* £327,120 *Assets* £1,876,060
TRUSTEES Malcolm Wharton; Philip Johnson; Peter Grace; Sheila Pancholi; Neil Hagerty; Richard Daniel.
HOW TO APPLY Application forms, guidance notes and criteria for all schemes are available to download on the website. Application forms for the grant schemes should be completed online at the foundation's website, printed and signed and then posted with the necessary supporting documents. Applicants can click on the email button to send an electronic copy to the foundation ahead of the printed and signed copy which will speed up the application. For any further support or information, applicants can contact their local Area Facilities Manager. Contact details for different regions are listed on the foundation's website.
WHO TO APPLY TO Stephanie Tucker, Rugby House, Twickenham Stadium, 200 Whitton Road, Twickenham TW2 7BA *Tel.* 020 8892 2000 *Email* foundation@therfu.com *Website* rugbyfootballfoundation.org

■ The Rugby Group Benevolent Fund Ltd

CC NO 265669 **ESTABLISHED** 1973
WHERE FUNDING CAN BE GIVEN Barrington (Cambridgeshire); Chinnor (Oxfordshire); Kensworth (Bedfordshire); Lewes (Sussex); Rochester (Kent); Rugby and Southam (Warwickshire); South Ferriby (North Lincolnshire); and Tilbury (Essex).

WHO CAN BENEFIT Organisations with charitable objectives.
WHAT IS FUNDED Charitable causes in communities where employees and ex-employees of Rugby Group Ltd and their dependants live.
WHAT IS NOT FUNDED Organisations operating outside the areas of benefit; support is not normally given for day-to-day revenue costs.
TYPE OF GRANT Capital costs for specific projects.
RANGE OF GRANTS Up to £50,000.
SAMPLE GRANTS Thomley Activity Centre (£50,000); Napton School (£25,000); Dogs for the Disabled (£14,000); Warwickshire and Northamptonshire Air Ambulance (£13,000); Arthur Rank Hospice (£10,000); Haslingfield Lawn Tennis Club (£8,000) Saxby Parish Church (£5,000) Rugby Hospital Radio (£2,500); Beating Bowel Cancer and Marie Curie Hospice (£1,000 each).
FINANCES *Year* 2015 *Income* £61,409 *Grants* £256,601 *Grants to organisations* £229,188 *Assets* £2,527,560
TRUSTEES Graeme Fuller; Ian Southcott; Norman Jones; Nigel Appleyard; Jim Wootten; Geoff Thomas.
OTHER INFORMATION This fund was established in 1955 with the aim of supporting employees and former employees of Rugby Group Ltd, and their dependants. The Rugby Group is now a part of CEMEX UK, a global cement manufacturer but the fund has kept its independence and is managed by a group of employees and former employees. During 2015, 47 grants were made to organisations, of which 20 grants, amounting to £7,000, were of less than £1,000. The amount of grants given to individuals totalled £27,500.
HOW TO APPLY At the time of writing (April 2017), the 'Applying' page on the fund's website stated that an initial expression of interest form and a full application form would soon be available. The page also lists guidelines.
WHO TO APPLY TO Daphne Murray, Secretary, Cemex House, Coldharbour Lane, Thorpe, Egham, Surrey TW20 8TD *Tel.* 01932 583181 *Email* info@rugbygroupbenevolentfund.org.uk *Website* www.rugbygroupbenevolentfund.org.uk

■ The RVW Trust

CC NO 1066977 **ESTABLISHED** 1958
WHERE FUNDING CAN BE GIVEN UK.
WHO CAN BENEFIT Organisations and individuals, particularly composers, musicians and music students.
WHAT IS FUNDED British composers who have not yet achieved a broad national or international reputation; assistance towards the performance and recording of music by neglected or currently unfashionable 20th and 21st century British composers; public performance of music; postgraduate students of composition taking first master's degrees at British institutions.
WHAT IS NOT FUNDED Concerts, concert series or concert tours which do not include music by 20th and 21st century British composers; concerts for which income from box office receipts, together with support from other organisations, is forecast to amount to less than half of the estimated expenditure; commissions purely for youth or children's ensembles; grants for musicals, rock or pop music, ethnic music, jazz or dance music or multi-media and theatrical events in which music is not the primary art form; workshops with no planned public performance; grants to organisations directly administered by local or other public authorities; grants to managing agents and commercial promoters; vocal or instrumental tuition; the making, purchase or repair of musical instruments, computer or multi-media equipment; the construction or restoration of buildings; projects relating to the work of Ralph Vaughan Williams.
RANGE OF GRANTS Up to £10,000.
SAMPLE GRANTS Park Lane Group (£10,000); Huddersfield Contemporary Music Festival (£9,000); Cheltenham Music Festival (£5,000); Ikon Arts (£3,500); Scottish Opera (£3,000); Scottish Chamber Orchestra (£2,500); London Ear and Spitalfields Festival (£2,000 each); City of Cambridge Brass Band and London Chorus (£1,500 each); Nash Ensemble (£1,000).
FINANCES *Year* 2015 *Income* £325,209 *Grants* £252,467 *Grants to organisations* £232,467 *Assets* £1,977,935
TRUSTEES Hugh Cobbe; Lord Armstrong; Anthony Burton; Jeremy Roberts; Andrew Hunter Johnston; Helen Faulkner; Prof. Nicola LeFanu; Sally Groves; Musicians Benevolent Fund.
OTHER INFORMATION The grant total includes those made to individuals.
HOW TO APPLY Apply in writing to the correspondent. Extensive guidelines are available from the website and should be read before an application is started. If you have any doubts as to the eligibility of your application, contact the trust in the first instance.
WHO TO APPLY TO Hannah Vlček, Secretary and Administrator, 13 Calico Row, Plantation Wharf, London SW11 3YH *Tel.* 020 7223 3385 *Email* info@rvwtrust.org.uk *Website* www.rvwtrust.org.uk

■ The J. S. and E. C. Rymer Charitable Trust

CC NO 267493 **ESTABLISHED** 1974
WHERE FUNDING CAN BE GIVEN East Yorkshire.
WHO CAN BENEFIT Organisations; individuals.
WHAT IS FUNDED General charitable purposes in East Yorkshire.
SAMPLE GRANTS Previous recipients have included local churches, community health care and a regional branch of the NSPCC.
FINANCES *Year* 2015/16 *Income* £90,045 *Grants* £67,881 *Grants to organisations* £67,881
TRUSTEES Carol Rymer; Timothy Rymer; Giles Brand.
OTHER INFORMATION The annual reports and accounts dating back to 2012 on the Charity Commission's website do not provide details of beneficiary names.
HOW TO APPLY Apply in writing to the correspondent.
WHO TO APPLY TO Beverley Gibson, Southburn Offices, Southburn, Driffield, East Yorkshire YO25 9ED *Tel.* 01377 227785

S. and R. Charitable Trust

CC NO 1098326 **ESTABLISHED** 2003
WHERE FUNDING CAN BE GIVEN London.
WHO CAN BENEFIT Registered charities and individuals in London.
WHAT IS FUNDED General charitable purposes with a preference for social welfare, health and disability.
SAMPLE GRANTS A list of beneficiaries was not available.
FINANCES *Year* 2015/16 *Income* £418,396 *Grants* £104,720 *Grants to organisations* £104,720 *Assets* £327,387
TRUSTEES Rochelle Davis; Stephen Davis; Lee Rhodes.
OTHER INFORMATION The annual reports and accounts dating back to 2012 on the Charity Commission's website do not provide details of beneficiary names. They do state, however, that the trust 'concentrates on helping poor or distressed persons, or donating directly to registered charities'. The grant total includes grants made to organisations and individuals.
HOW TO APPLY Apply in writing to the correspondent.
WHO TO APPLY TO Rochelle Davis, Trustee, 14 Deacons Hill Road, Elstree, Borehamwood WD6 3LH *Tel.* 020 8953 5226

S. F. Foundation

CC NO 1105843 **ESTABLISHED** 2004
WHERE FUNDING CAN BE GIVEN Worldwide.
WHO CAN BENEFIT Jewish organisations.
WHAT IS FUNDED The foundation supports Jewish religious education makes grants to alleviate poverty among the Jewish community throughout the world.
SAMPLE GRANTS A list of beneficiaries was not available.
FINANCES *Year* 2015/16 *Income* £9,536,204 *Grants* £3,368,857 *Grants to organisations* £3,368,857 *Assets* £33,701,023
TRUSTEES Hannah Lipschitz; Rivka Niederman; Miriam Schrieber.
OTHER INFORMATION The annual reports and accounts dating back to 2012 on the Charity Commission's website do not provide details of beneficiary names.
HOW TO APPLY The foundation's annual report states: 'The charity accepts applications for grants from representatives of various charities, which are reviewed by the trustees on a regular basis.'
WHO TO APPLY TO Rivka Niederman, Secretary, 143 Upper Clapton Road, London E5 9DB *Tel.* 020 8802 5492 *Email* sffoundation143@gmail.com

Michael Sacher Charitable Trust

CC NO 206321 **ESTABLISHED** 1957
WHERE FUNDING CAN BE GIVEN UK and Israel.
WHO CAN BENEFIT Registered charities.
WHAT IS FUNDED General charitable purposes with a preference for: arts and culture; education, science and technology; community and welfare; children and youth; health and disability; Jewish organisations and causes.
WHAT IS NOT FUNDED Individuals.
TYPE OF GRANT Recurring and one-off.
RANGE OF GRANTS £100 to £28,000.
SAMPLE GRANTS House of Illustration (£28,000); The International Centre for the Study of Radicalisation (£20,000); British Friends of the Hebrew University of Jerusalem (£16,750); The Royal Opera House Foundation (£5,000); The Honeypot Children's Charity (£2,000); Cancer Research, Dorset Opera and Jewish Care (£500 each); Glyndebourne Festival Society (£180); Welmare Hospicecare Trust (£100).
FINANCES *Year* 2015/16 *Income* £146,518 *Grants* £105,288 *Grants to organisations* £105,288 *Assets* £5,783,927
TRUSTEES Jeremy Sacher; Hon. Rosalind Sacher; Elisabeth Sacher.
OTHER INFORMATION During 2015/16, 22 grants were made to organisations.
HOW TO APPLY Apply in writing to the correspondent.
WHO TO APPLY TO The Trustees, c/o H. W. Fisher and Co., Acre House, 11–15 William Road, London NW1 3ER *Tel.* 020 7388 7000 *Email* info@hwfisher.co.uk

The Michael and Nicola Sacher Trust

CC NO 288973 **ESTABLISHED** 1984
WHERE FUNDING CAN BE GIVEN UK and overseas.
WHO CAN BENEFIT Registered charities.
WHAT IS FUNDED General charitable purposes with a preference for organisations working in the areas of arts and culture, health, community and welfare, children and young people, overseas aid, and Jewish religious organisations.
WHAT IS NOT FUNDED Individuals; organisations which are not registered charities.
TYPE OF GRANT Recurring.
RANGE OF GRANTS £350 to £20,000.
SAMPLE GRANTS British Friends of the Hebrew University of Jerusalem and Royal Opera House Foundation (£20,000 each); The Zoological Society of London (£15,500 in two grants); Random Dance Company (£10,000); National Railway Museum Opera Australia Capital Fund UK (£5,000); British Museum (£2,600); MS Society, Rays of Sunshine and United Synagogue (£500 each); Greek Animal Rescue (£350).
FINANCES *Year* 2015/16 *Income* £71,066 *Grants* £92,086 *Grants to organisations* £92,086 *Assets* £2,413,485
TRUSTEES Nicola Sacher; Michael Sacher.
HOW TO APPLY Apply in writing to the correspondent.
WHO TO APPLY TO The Trustees, c/o H. W. Fisher and Co., Acre House, 11–15 William Road, London NW1 3ER *Tel.* 020 7388 7000 *Email* info@hwfisher.co.uk

The Dr Mortimer and Theresa Sackler Foundation

CC NO 1128926 **ESTABLISHED** 2009
WHERE FUNDING CAN BE GIVEN UK and USA.
WHO CAN BENEFIT Registered charities and universities.
WHAT IS FUNDED Education; the arts; science and medical research.
TYPE OF GRANT One-off and recurrent.
RANGE OF GRANTS Mainly less than £200,000.

SAMPLE GRANTS New York Presbyterian Hospital (£4 million); Central Park Conservancy (£670,000); Chelsea and Westminster Health Charity (£300,000); Bletchley Park Trust Ltd and Expert Impact (£250,000).
FINANCES *Year* 2015 *Income* £6,536,754 *Grants* £6,545,602 *Grants to organisations* £6,545,602 *Assets* £26,638,940
TRUSTEES Dame Theresa Sackler; Peter Stormonth Darling; Mr C. B. Mitchell; Mr R. M. Smith; Mrs I. Sackler Lefcourt; Marissa Sackler; Sophia Sackler Dalrymple; Mortimer Sackler; Dr Kathe Sackler; Samantha Sackler Hunt; Michael Sackler.
OTHER INFORMATION Grants were made to 63 organisations during the year, with 58 grants made under £200,000.
HOW TO APPLY Apply in writing to the correspondent.
WHO TO APPLY TO Christopher Mitchell, Trustee, 9th Floor, New Zealand House, 80 Haymarket, London SW1Y 4TQ *Tel.* 020 7930 4944

■ The Sackler Trust

CC NO 1132097 **ESTABLISHED** 1988
WHERE FUNDING CAN BE GIVEN England, Wales and Scotland.
WHO CAN BENEFIT Larger institutions.
WHAT IS FUNDED Arts and culture; science; medical research.
TYPE OF GRANT Recurring and one-off.
RANGE OF GRANTS Up to £2.5 million, although most grants were of less than £500,000.
SAMPLE GRANTS Royal Opera House (£2.5 million); University College London (£1.4 million); The National Gallery, The Defence and National Rehabilitation Centre, MK Gallery, Royal Botanic Gardens Kew and Tate Modern (£1 million each); The Garden Museum (£750,000); Natural History Museum, Old Royal Naval College, V&A Museum of Design Dundee, Westminster Abbey (£500,000 each).
FINANCES *Year* 2015 *Income* £7,825,616 *Grants* £16,779,274 *Grants to organisations* £16,779,274 *Assets* £47,520,235
TRUSTEES Dame Theresa Sackler; Peter Stormonth Darling; Christopher Mitchell; Marissa Sackler; Sophia Sackler Dalrymple; Michael Sackler; Marianne Mitchell; Anthony Collins.
OTHER INFORMATION In 2015, 61 'miscellaneous' grants of less than £500,000 accounted for £3.1 million of the grant total; 77 grants were made overall.
HOW TO APPLY Apply in writing to the correspondent.
WHO TO APPLY TO Christopher Mitchell, Trustee, 9th Floor, New Zealand House, 80 Haymarket, London SW1Y 4TQ *Tel.* 020 7930 4944

■ The Ruzin Sadagora Trust

CC NO 285475 **ESTABLISHED** 1982
WHERE FUNDING CAN BE GIVEN UK and Israel.
WHO CAN BENEFIT Jewish organisations.
WHAT IS FUNDED The upkeep and activities of the Ruzin Sadagora Synagogue in London; other associated Sadagora institutions; and other Jewish causes.
SAMPLE GRANTS The annual reports and accounts dating back to 2012 on the Charity Commission's website do not provide details of beneficiary names. Previous beneficiaries have included: Beth Israel Ruzin Sadagora (£196,000); Friends of Ruzin Sadagora (£180,000); Beth Kaknesset Ohr Yisroel (£91,600); Mosdos Sadigur (£40,000); Yeshivas Torah Temimah (£9,000); Chevras Moaz Lodol (£6,500); Pardes House (£2,000).
FINANCES *Year* 2014/15 *Income* £402,183 *Grants* £306,556 *Grants to organisations* £306,556 *Assets* £492,495
TRUSTEES Rabbi Israel Friedman; Sara Friedman.
HOW TO APPLY Apply in writing to the correspondent.
WHO TO APPLY TO Rabbi Israel Friedman, Trustee, 269 Golders Green Road, London NW11 9JJ *Tel.* 020 8806 9514

■ The Saddlers' Company Charitable Fund

CC NO 261962 **ESTABLISHED** 1970
WHERE FUNDING CAN BE GIVEN UK.
WHO CAN BENEFIT Registered charities and other institutions.
WHAT IS FUNDED Grants are made by the company in the following categories: education; support for people with disabilities and young people who are disadvantaged; charities benefitting people who are in need, hardship or distress; armed and uniformed services; equestrian charities; the church; British saddlery and leathercraft trades; City of London; general charitable activities.
TYPE OF GRANT Usually one-off for one year.
SAMPLE GRANTS A list of beneficiaries was not included in the 2015/16 annual report and accounts.
FINANCES *Year* 2015/16 *Income* £553,051 *Grants* £412,444 *Grants to organisations* £412,444 *Assets* £11,538,340
TRUSTEES Campbell Pulley; David Hardy; David Snowden; Hugh Dyson-Laurie; Iain Pulley; Jonathan Godrich; Michael Laurie; Peter Laurie; Peter Lewis; Tim Satchell; Mark Farmar; Paul Farmar; Petronella Jameson; Nicholas Mason; Charles Barclay; John Robinson; Hugh Thomas; James Welch; William Dyson-Laurie; The Hon. Mark Maffey; Lucy Atherton; Benjamin Laurie; Hugh Medley Taylor.
OTHER INFORMATION While the majority of grants were made from general funds, within The Saddlers' Company Charitable Fund are the R. M. Sturdy Trust and the M. E. Priestly Fund. Criteria and application processes for all of the funds managed by the company are available from the website.
HOW TO APPLY The company now operates an online application form, which is accessible from the website.
WHO TO APPLY TO Clerk to the Saddlers' Company, Saddlers' Company, Saddlers' Hall, 40 Gutter Lane, London EC2V 6BR *Tel.* 020 7726 8661 *Email* clerk@saddlers.co.uk *Website* www.saddlersco.co.uk

■ Erach and Roshan Sadri Foundation

CC NO 1110736 **ESTABLISHED** 2005
WHERE FUNDING CAN BE GIVEN Worldwide.
WHO CAN BENEFIT Registered charities; community groups; religious institutions; individuals.
WHAT IS FUNDED The main objects of the foundation are: providing financial assistance for education and welfare purposes; relieving poverty by alleviating homelessness; and assisting members of the Zoroastrian religious faith.
WHAT IS NOT FUNDED Applications are unlikely to be successful if they: involve animal welfare or heritage; or are a general appeal from large UK organisations.

TYPE OF GRANT One-off grants for project costs.
RANGE OF GRANTS £750 to £35,000.
SAMPLE GRANTS Freedom To Learn (£35,000); Gurkha Welfare Trust and Zoroastrian Trust Funds of Europe (£30,000); The Abandoned and Destitute Children's Appeal Fund and British Forces Foundation (£25,000 each); Friends of Armenia (£10,800); Jessie May (£6,500) Teens Unite (£5,000); PACT (£4,000); The Passage (£2,000); The JMK Trust (£1,500); Foodbank (£750). The foundation has previously made grants to individuals (£3,500 in 2012) but we were unable to ascertain the total in the latest available accounts.
FINANCES *Year* 2015/16 *Income* £16,424 *Grants* £380,000 *Grants to organisations* £380,000
TRUSTEES Margaret Lynch; Darius Sarosh; Sammy Bhiwandiwalla; Peter Dudgeon.
OTHER INFORMATION This charity's latest accounts were not available to view on the Charity Commission's website due to its low income. We have therefore estimated the grant total based on previous years' information.
HOW TO APPLY **Unsolicited applications are not accepted.** However, if you are invited by a trustee to make an application, there are detailed guidelines on the website.
WHO TO APPLY TO Mark Cann, Administrator, 10A, The High Street, Pewsey, Wiltshire SN9 5AQ *Tel.* 01672 569131 *Email* markcann@ersf.org.uk *Website* www.ersf.org.uk

■ The Saga Charitable Trust

CC NO 291991 **ESTABLISHED** 1985
WHERE FUNDING CAN BE GIVEN 'Developing countries' – refer to the trust's website for a full list of where it works.
WHO CAN BENEFIT Charitable organisations and projects.
WHAT IS FUNDED Community projects in 'developing countries' that provide education, training, health care and income generation.
WHAT IS NOT FUNDED Individuals.
TYPE OF GRANT Capital costs; full project funding; core costs. One-off, up to three years.
RANGE OF GRANTS £1,000 to £22,000.
SAMPLE GRANTS St Jude Childcare Centre India (£22,000); International Development Enterprises Nepal (£21,000); Haller Foundation Kenya (£20,000); EMMS International India, Friends of Seva Mandir India and Gurkha Welfare Trust Nepal (£15,000 each); Agounsane Education Centre Morocco (£12,700); Centre for Early Childhood Development South Africa (£10,000); Mikoroshoni Primary School Kenya (£6,000); Education for the Children Guatemala (£5,600); Ekari Foundation Malawi (£1,700); Rope Charitable Trust India (£1,000).
FINANCES *Year* 2015/16 *Income* £449,836 *Grants* £145,183 *Grants to organisations* £145,183 *Assets* £447,982
TRUSTEES Makala Thomas; James Duguid; Andrew Stringer; Helen Adamson; Timothy Pethick; Martin Broom; Maria Whiteman.
OTHER INFORMATION Grants were made to 12 organisations in 2015/16. The majority of the trust's income came from Saga customer and staff donations.
HOW TO APPLY Applications should be made in writing to the correspondent. Note that only projects sited in or close to destinations within certain countries currently visited by Saga holidaymakers (listed on the website) will be considered for funding. The trust welcomes contact from organisations to discuss their proposals prior to application. Applications are accepted at any time throughout the year and application guidelines are available from the trust's website. Funding proposals must include the following information: outline and objectives of the project; who will benefit and how; resources required and time frame; management and sustainability of the project; how funds will be managed and accounted for; and the last three years of the organisation's audited financial accounts.
WHO TO APPLY TO Sarah Jenner, Trust Executive, Saga Group Ltd, Enbrook Park, Sandgate High Street, Sandgate, Folkestone CT20 3SE *Tel.* 01303 774069 *Email* sarah.jenner@saga.co.uk *Website* www.sagacharitabletrust.org

■ The Jean Sainsbury Animal Welfare Trust

CC NO 326358 **ESTABLISHED** 1982
WHERE FUNDING CAN BE GIVEN UK and overseas.
WHO CAN BENEFIT UK-registered national and international animal welfare charities.
WHAT IS FUNDED Animal welfare and wildlife.
WHAT IS NOT FUNDED The trust's website states that it will not normally support the following: applications from individuals; charities registered outside the UK; charities offering sanctuary to animals, with no effort to re-home, foster or rehabilitate unless endangered species; charities that do not have a realistic destruction policy for animals that cannot be given a reasonable quality of life; charities with available reserves equal to more than one year's expenditure will not qualify for consideration unless it can be demonstrated that reserves are being held for a designated project; charities that spend more than a reasonable proportion of their annual income on administration or cannot justify their costs per animal helped; veterinary schools, unless the money can be seen to be directly benefitting the type of animals the trust would want to support (e.g. welfare-related or low-cost first opinion vet treatment projects).
TYPE OF GRANT Capital, buildings, campaigning, core costs, project, running costs and recurring costs. Funding for up to one year is available.
RANGE OF GRANTS £500 to £35,000.
SAMPLE GRANTS Chiltern Dog Rescue Society (£35,000); Pennine Pen Animal Rescue (£25,000); RSPCA South Cotswolds (£20,000); Himalayan Animal Treatment Centre UK (£10,000); Greek Cat Welfare Society and Lluest Horse and Pony Trust (£5,000 each); The Fox Project (£4,000); Bunny Burrows (£3,000); April Lodge Guinea Pig Rescue, Chinese Crested Club of GB Rescue and Prickles Hedgehog Rescue (£1,000 each); Barn Owl Centre (£500).
FINANCES *Year* 2015 *Income* £565,936 *Grants* £440,957 *Grants to organisations* £440,957 *Assets* £20,872,662
TRUSTEES Colin Russell; Gillian Tarlington; James Keliher; Mark Spurdens; Valerie Pike; Michelle Allen; Adele Sparrow.
OTHER INFORMATION In 2015 grants were made to 82 organisations, split between 69 charities working in the UK and 13 UK-based charities working overseas.
HOW TO APPLY Apply in writing to the correspondent. Submit nine copies of a completed application form, which is available from the website, nine copies of the latest audited accounts and nine copies of any other information that might be relevant to the application. Do not send

originals. There are three trustees' meetings every year, usually in March, July and November and applications should be submitted by 15 January, 1 May and 1 September respectively. Further application information and policy guidelines are available by visiting the website.

WHO TO APPLY TO Madeleine Orchard, Administrator, PO Box 469, London W14 8PJ *Tel.* 020 7602 7948 *Email* orchardjswelfare@gmail.com *Website* jeansainsburyanimalwelfare.org.uk

■ The Alan and Babette Sainsbury Charitable Fund

CC NO 292930 **ESTABLISHED** 1953

WHERE FUNDING CAN BE GIVEN UK and overseas.

WHO CAN BENEFIT Registered charities and research institutes.

WHAT IS FUNDED Arts and education projects for young people in Southwark, London; civil liberties and human rights charities in the UK; educational and employment opportunities for young people in the financially developing countries, especially Africa; scientific and medical research on type 1 diabetes.

WHAT IS NOT FUNDED Individuals.

TYPE OF GRANT One-off and ongoing; research; core costs.

RANGE OF GRANTS £7,500 to £30,000, with a one-off donation of £110,000.

SAMPLE GRANTS Juvenile Diabetes Research Foundation (£110,000); Wiener Library (£30,000); Baobab Centre for Young Survivors in Exile (£25,000); Build Africa and Refugee Council (£20,000 each); CoolTan Arts and Training for Life Tanzania (£15,000 each); Forum for Discussion of Israel and Palestine and Foundation for Young Musicians (£10,000 each); Cambridge House and Talbot (£7,500).

FINANCES *Year* 2015/16 *Income* £492,156 *Grants* £468,085 *Grants to organisations* £468,085 *Assets* £14,586,687

TRUSTEES Judith Portrait; The Rt Hon. Sir Timothy Sainsbury; John Sainsbury; Lindsey Anderson.

OTHER INFORMATION In 2015/16 the charity made 23 grants to organisations, primarily to support overseas work and community development.

HOW TO APPLY The trust's website states that it 'will consider proposals, so long as they demonstrably and closely fit their specific areas of interest. However, it should be understood that the majority of unsolicited proposals are unsuccessful.' Applications should be sent via post with a description of the proposed project covering the organisation, the project requiring funding and a breakdown of costs. Supplementary documentation such as books, brochures, DVDs, annual reports or accounts are not needed.

WHO TO APPLY TO Alan Bookbinder, Head of the Sainsbury Family Charitable Trusts, The Peak, 5 Wilton Road, London SW1V 1AP *Tel.* 020 7410 0330 *Email* info@sfct.org.uk *Website* www.sfct.org.uk/the-alan-and-babette-sainsbury-charitable-fund

■ The Sainsbury Family Charitable Trusts

WHO CAN BENEFIT Registered charities and institutions.

WHAT IS FUNDED See the entries for the individual trusts – their names are listed in the 'Other information' section below.

WHAT IS NOT FUNDED Grants are not normally given to individuals by many of the trusts (although a number of them fund bursary schemes and the like operated by other organisations). Grants are not made for educational fees or expeditions.

SAMPLE GRANTS A list of beneficiaries was not available.

OTHER INFORMATION The Sainsbury Family Trusts is a group of 18 grant-making charities established by the Sainsbury family. Each charity listed below has its own entry in the guide. However, they are administered together and only one application should be sent for consideration by all relevant funds. The trusts are: The Ashden Trust; The Gatsby Charitable Foundation; The Kay Kendall Leukaemia Fund; The Linbury Trust; The True Colours Trust; The Woodward Charitable Trust; The Indigo Trust; The Alan and Babette Sainsbury Charitable Fund; The Glass-House Trust; The Headley Trust; The Jerusalem Trust; The J. J. Charitable Trust; The Mark Leonard Trust; The Monument Trust; The Staples Trust; The Tedworth Charitable Trust; The Three Guineas Trust. See the individual trust for grant totals.

HOW TO APPLY The following information has been taken from the trust's website: 'The trustees take an active role in their grant-making, employing a range of specialist staff and advisers to research their areas of interest and bring forward suitable proposals. Many of the trusts work closely with their chosen beneficiaries over a long period to achieve particular objectives.' The trusts differ in their attitude to unsolicited proposals. As a rule Gatsby, Glass-House, Linbury, Mark Leonard, Staples, Tedworth and True Colours do not consider them, although several trusts have application forms for specific grant programmes in clearly defined areas; consult the website for further information on this for The Woodward Charitable Trust; The Kay Kendall Leukaemia Fund; The Headley Museums Archaeological Acquisition Fund; The True Colours Trust. The Alan and Babette, Ashden, Headley, Indigo, Jerusalem, J. J., Monument and Three Guineas trusts will consider proposals, so long as they demonstrably and closely fit their specific areas of interest. However, it should be understood that the majority of unsolicited proposals are unsuccessful. Suitable applications to these trusts should be sent by post to The Sainsbury Family Charitable Trusts, The Peak, 5 Wilton Road, London SW1V 1AP, with a description (strictly no more than two pages please, as any more is unlikely to be read) of the proposed project, including: information about your organisation (charitable aims and objectives, most recent annual income and expenditure, and current financial situation); details about the project requiring funding (why it is need, who will benefit and in what way); details about the funding required (breakdown of costs, how much money has been raised so far and how the balance will be obtained). Do not include annual report and accounts, and do not send more than one application. One request will be considered by all relevant trusts. There is no need to send supporting material (books, brochures, DVDs, etc.).

WHO TO APPLY TO Alan Bookbinder, Director, The Peak, 5 Wilton Road, London SW1V 1AP *Tel.* 020 7410 0330 *Fax* 020 7410 0332 *Website* www.sfct.org.uk

The St Hilda's Trust

CC NO 500962 **ESTABLISHED** 1904

WHERE FUNDING CAN BE GIVEN The diocese of Newcastle (Newcastle upon Tyne, North Tyneside and Northumberland).

WHO CAN BENEFIT Organisations with charitable purposes (not exclusively registered charities); churches; community projects.

WHAT IS FUNDED The main focus is on children and young people who are disadvantaged. Particular consideration is given to projects with a degree of church involvement.

SAMPLE GRANTS A list of beneficiaries was not available.

FINANCES *Year* 2015 *Income* £72,754 *Grants* £75,630 *Grants to organisations* £75,630 *Assets* £1,878,401

TRUSTEES Revd Canon Alan Craig; Dr Margaret Wilkinson; Neil Brockbank; Rt Revd Christine Hardman; David Welsh; Revd Christine Brown.

OTHER INFORMATION A list of beneficiaries was not included in the latest set of accounts.

HOW TO APPLY Application forms can be obtained from the secretary at the address shown (or j.pinnegar@newcastle.anglican.org), and should be submitted with a budget and annual report and accounts. Any necessary additional information should not exceed one side of A4 paper. A leaflet with further information on the trust is available to download on the website. The trustees meet three times a year.

WHO TO APPLY TO Josie Pinnegar, Secretary, Church House, St John's Terrace, North Shields, Tyne and Wear NE29 6HS *Tel.* 0191 270 4100 *Email* j.pinnegar@newcastle.anglican.org *Website* www.newcastle.anglican.org/youth/st-hildas-trust.aspx

The St James's Trust Settlement

CC NO 280455 **ESTABLISHED** 1980

WHERE FUNDING CAN BE GIVEN UK and USA.

WHO CAN BENEFIT Registered charities.

WHAT IS FUNDED In the UK, the trust's areas of support are: health; education; social justice. In the USA: education; community arts; raising awareness of crimes against humanity.

WHAT IS NOT FUNDED Individuals.

SAMPLE GRANTS Homeopathy Action Trust (£40,000); CARIS and Highbury Vale Blackstock Trust (£20,000 each).

FINANCES *Year* 2014/15 *Income* £109,195 *Grants* £287,322 *Grants to organisations* £287,322 *Assets* £3,149,495

TRUSTEES Jane Wells; Cathy Ingram.

OTHER INFORMATION The 2014/15 accounts were the most recent available on the Charity Commission's website at the time of writing (June 2017). During the year, grants were made to two organisations in the UK, totalling £11,000, and to 32 organisations in the USA, totalling £276,500. A list of recent beneficiaries was not provided in the accounts.

HOW TO APPLY The trust states in its 2014/15 annual report that it 'does not seek unsolicited applications for grants and, without paid staff, are unable to respond to such applications'. The trustees identify potential beneficiaries proactively.

WHO TO APPLY TO The Trustees, c/o Begbies Accountants, Epworth House, 25 City Road, London EC1Y 1AR *Email* admin@begbiesaccountants.co.uk

St James's Place Foundation

CC NO 1144606 **ESTABLISHED** 1994

WHERE FUNDING CAN BE GIVEN UK and overseas (through UK-registered charities).

WHO CAN BENEFIT UK-registered charities and special needs schools. The small grants programme targets charities with an annual income of less than £1 million.

WHAT IS FUNDED The foundation's main themes are: cherishing children (focusing on young people who are disadvantaged or who have a disability); combating cancer; supporting hospices.

WHAT IS NOT FUNDED Administrative costs; activities which are the responsibility of statutory providers or replacement of statutory funding; research; events; advertising; holidays; sponsorship; contributions to large capital appeals; single faith charities; charities that are fundraising on behalf of another charity; charities operating outside the UK; CICs; charities with reserves of over 50% of income.

TYPE OF GRANT Capital items; revenue grants.

RANGE OF GRANTS Small grants: under £10,000.

SAMPLE GRANTS CCLASP (£227,500); Cardboard Citizens (£140,500); Brain Tumour Charity (£94,000); The Art Room (£77,000); Amantani (£8,400); Global Child Dental Fund (£10,000); Vauxhall City Farm Riding Therapy Centre (£9,900); Education for Change and See Beyond Borders (£2,500 each); Charlotte's Tandems (£420).

FINANCES *Year* 2015 *Income* £7,846,924 *Grants* £4,631,268 *Grants to organisations* £4,631,268 *Assets* £3,179,856

TRUSTEES David Bellamy; Ian Gascoigne; Malcolm Cooper-Smith; Andrew Croft; David Lamb; Michael Wilson.

OTHER INFORMATION The foundation also supports projects chosen by local offices of St James's Place, or with which employees are closely involved.

HOW TO APPLY Applications for the small grants scheme should be made using the form on the foundation's website. Guidelines for each of the foundation's themes are also available to download on the website. There are no deadlines for the small grants scheme and applications are considered throughout the year, although the process can take between four and six months. At the time of writing (April 2017), the foundation's Major Grants scheme is under review – refer to the website for current information. The foundation is working with Hospice UK to distribute funds under the 'supporting hospices' theme, so is not accepting applications from individual hospices.

WHO TO APPLY TO Mark Longbottom, Foundation Manager, St James's Place PLC, St James's Place House, 1 Tetbury Road, Cirencester GL7 1FP *Tel.* 01285 878037 *Email* sjp.foundation@sjp.co.uk *Website* www.sjpfoundation.co.uk

Sir Walter St John's Educational Charity

CC NO 312690 **ESTABLISHED** 1992

WHERE FUNDING CAN BE GIVEN The boroughs of Wandsworth and Lambeth.

WHO CAN BENEFIT Children and young people who are under the age of 25, residing in the London boroughs of Wandsworth or Lambeth and in need of financial assistance. Particular preference is given to those residing in the former Metropolitan Borough of Battersea. Grants are awarded both to individuals and local schools, colleges, youth clubs, and voluntary and community organisations. Priority is given to activities benefitting disadvantaged children.

WHAT IS FUNDED Education and training. The Small Education Grants scheme focuses on the following groups of local children and young people: living in areas of particular social disadvantage; young refugees and asylum seekers; young carers; children and young people with disabilities; looked after children and care leavers. The Strategic Grants scheme focuses on: refugees of secondary school age, particularly unaccompanied minors and those with little previous formal education; young carers; young people who are low-achieving or at risk of dropping out of education.

TYPE OF GRANT One-off and up to three year strategic grants to organisations; individual grants.

RANGE OF GRANTS Up to £1,000 for educational grants. Up to £30,000 per year for strategic grants.

SAMPLE GRANTS STORM (£90,000); Katherine Low Settlement (£15,900); South Thames College (£13,600); Providence House Community Centre (£2,000); Ethelburga Early Years (£1,900); Islamic Culture and Education Centre Battersea (£1,600); Falconbrook Primary School, South Island Children's Workshop, Transition Town Tooting and Triangle Adventure Playground Association (£1,000 each).

FINANCES *Year* 2015/16 *Income* £156,074 *Grants* £137,605 *Grants to organisations* £131,326 *Assets* £3,937,695

TRUSTEES Daphne Daytes; Col. Martin Stratton; Sarah Rackham; Col. Julian Radcliffe; Barry Fairbank; John O'Malley; Sheldon Wilkie; Godfrey Allen; Michael Bates; Canon Simon Butler; Wendy Speck; Rosemary Summerfield; Linda Bray; Christopher Wellbelove; Dave Wagner.

OTHER INFORMATION Grants to individuals during the year totalled £6,300. Small Education Grants awarded to organisations totalled £11,900 and Strategic Grants totalled £119,500.

HOW TO APPLY Application forms and further information about the charity's grants schemes can be obtained by contacting Susan Perry, the charity's Manager: manager@swsjcharity.org.uk or 202 7498 8878. Deadlines for the Small Education Grants scheme are posted on the website. Information on how individuals can apply for grants is also provided on the charity's website.

WHO TO APPLY TO Susan Perry, Manager, Office 1A, Culvert House, Culvert Road, London SW11 5DH *Tel.* 020 7498 8878 *Email* manager@swsjcharity.org.uk *Website* www.swsjcharity.org.uk

■ St Luke's College Foundation

CC NO 306606 **ESTABLISHED** 1977

WHERE FUNDING CAN BE GIVEN UK, with some preference for Exeter and Truro.

WHO CAN BENEFIT Individuals and universities, colleges and other institutions operating at university level.

WHAT IS FUNDED Theology and religious education. **Corporate awards** are made to universities and similar institutions to enable them to develop or enhance their provision in these fields, with priority given to pump-priming initiatives. **Personal awards** are made to support individuals following university-level studies or research in theology and religious education, or who are undertaking research which will lead to a master's degree or PHD. **Major awards** are occasionally made to a small number of larger corporate awards to enhance the capacity of universities and other institutions working in the fields of theology and religious education.

WHAT IS NOT FUNDED Funding is not available for building work or to provide bursaries for institutions to administer. Schools are not supported directly (although support is given to teachers who are taking eligible studies). At the time of writing (April 2017), the foundation's website stated that it would not make direct awards to PGCE religious education students in 2017.

TYPE OF GRANT Grants can be made for periods of up to three years.

RANGE OF GRANTS £1,000 to £10,000.

SAMPLE GRANTS Religious education Council for England and Wales (£10,000); University of Exeter – School of Education (£2,300); University of Exeter – Department of Theology and Religion (£1,300).

FINANCES *Year* 2015/16 *Income* £219,156 *Grants* £165,440 *Grants to organisations* £134,588 *Assets* £5,617,288

TRUSTEES Giles Frampton; The Very Revd Dr Jonathan Draper; Prof. Grace Davie; Canon Alan Bashforth; Dr Michael Wykes; Alice Hutchings; Dick Powell; Revd Dr David Rake; John Searson; Dr Karen Stockham; Rt Revd Robert Atwell; Prof. Mark Goodwin.

OTHER INFORMATION Grants were made totalling £165,500, which were broken down as £97,000 for major awards and £68,500 in personal and corporate awards.

HOW TO APPLY From 1 January each year, applicants can request an application pack from the correspondent. Applications are considered once a year and should be received by 1 May for grants starting in September.

WHO TO APPLY TO Dr David Benzie, Director, 15 St Maryhaye, Tavistock, Devon PL19 8LR *Tel.* 01822 613143 *Email* director@st-lukes-foundation.org.uk *Website* www.st-lukes-foundation.org.uk

■ St Marylebone Educational Foundation

CC NO 312378 **ESTABLISHED** 1750

WHERE FUNDING CAN BE GIVEN City of Westminster.

WHO CAN BENEFIT Educational institutions.

WHAT IS FUNDED The education of young people in the City of Westminster (i.e. people between the ages of 8 and 25 who are resident, or educated, in the St Marylebone/Westminster area).

TYPE OF GRANT Recurring grants to specific schools in the St Marylebone area.

RANGE OF GRANTS £6,000 to £46,000.

SAMPLE GRANTS St Marylebone School (£46,000); St Marylebone School Building Works (£25,000); St Marylebone Bridge School (£15,000); Royal College of Music and Westminster St Margaret's Deanery Synod (£12,000 each); Royal Academy of Music (£6,000).

FINANCES *Year* 2015/16 *Income* £178,769 *Grants* £165,566 *Grants to organisations* £116,267 *Assets* £816,531

TRUSTEES Sarah Woolman; Reverend Ralph Williamson; Lucy Dennett; Reverend Canon Stephen Evans; Michael Wrottesley; Helen Wells.

OTHER INFORMATION In 2015/16 seven grants were made totalling £49,500 to individual students to help them continue studying.

HOW TO APPLY Apply in writing to the correspondent.
WHO TO APPLY TO St Marylebone Educational Foundation, Marylebone Station, 12 Melcombe Place, Marylebone, London NW1 6JJ *Email* stmaryedf@gmail.com *Website* www.stmarylebone.org/images/stories/Publicity/Posters/Educational_Foundation.pdf

■ St Monica Trust

CC NO 202151 **ESTABLISHED** 1962
WHERE FUNDING CAN BE GIVEN Bristol and the surrounding areas.
WHO CAN BENEFIT Organisations; individuals and families.
WHAT IS FUNDED Support for people who have physical disabilities or long-term physical health problems; support for older people.
TYPE OF GRANT Capital items; running costs.
SAMPLE GRANTS Citizens Advice (£9,800); St Peter's Hospice, Headway Bristol and Motor Neurone Disease Association (£7,500 each); IT Help@Home (£5,000); the New Place (£3,900); Bristol and Avon Chinese Women's Group (£2,000); Bath Institute of Medical Engineering (£1,500); Western Active Stroke Group (£1,000).
FINANCES *Year* 2015 *Income* £28,569,000 *Grants* £482,237 *Grants to organisations* £124,337 *Assets* £246,175,000
TRUSTEE St Monica Trustee Company Ltd.
OTHER INFORMATION The trust runs retirement villages in Bristol and North Somerset which offer sheltered accommodation, nursing homes and dementia care homes to older people. It makes grants in support of the local community through the Community Fund. Grants are made to individuals in the form of one-off grants for emergency items as well as short-term monthly payments. It also funds LinkAge, an initiative helping to provide services and support to improve the well-being of older people in the community. During the year, 23 organisations were supported. 567 gifts, short-term grants and annuities were made to individuals, totalling £260,500 and expenditure on LinkAge amounted to a further £97,000.
HOW TO APPLY For more information, contact the Community Fund Team on 0117 949 4003 or by email community.fund@stmonicatrust.org.uk.
WHO TO APPLY TO Community Fund Team, Cote Lane, Bristol BS9 3UN *Tel.* 0117 949 4003 *Email* community.fund@stmonicatrust.org.uk *Website* www.stmonicatrust.org.uk

■ St Olave's and St Saviour's Schools Foundation – Foundation Fund

CC NO 312987 **ESTABLISHED** 1964
WHERE FUNDING CAN BE GIVEN London Borough of Southwark.
WHO CAN BENEFIT Schools, youth groups and other organisations working with young people under the age of 25 in Southwark.
WHAT IS FUNDED Educational and extra-curricular activities for children and young people, such as school trips; youth projects; uniformed organisations; educational workshops.
WHAT IS NOT FUNDED Salaries and administration costs; retrospective funding. The foundation is unlikely to support the full costs of a project.
TYPE OF GRANT Project funding.
SAMPLE GRANTS Camberwell After School Project (£4,800); Foundation for Young Musicians (£3,000); Brunel Museum (£2,500); London Bubble Theatre Company (£2,400); Southwark Cathedral Education Centre (£2,000); Friars Primary School (£1,800); Southwark District Explorer Scouts (£1,700); Southwark Aquatics Swimming Club (£1,600); Surrey Docks Farm (£1,400); Beanstalk (£1,000).
FINANCES *Year* 2015/16 *Income* £1,378,070 *Grants* £717,417 *Grants to organisations* £693,043 *Assets* £28,779,712
TRUSTEES Revd Neil McKinnon; Michael Lovett; Philip Mock; Roy Wisdom; Revd Jane Steen; Russel Vaizey; Cllr Neil Reddin; Malcolm Edwards; Ian Rankine; Lady Patricia Harding; Edwin Langdown; Cllr Robert Evans; Laurence Johnstone; Revd Peter Galloway; Debra Reiss; Elizabeth Edwards; Stephen Parry.
OTHER INFORMATION Grants to organisations included two exceptionally large, recurrent grants totalling £610,500 to the two schools, St Olave's and St Saviour's Grammar School and St Saviour's and St Olave's School. Foundation Fund grants awarded to organisations totalled £82,000. The amount of grants given to individuals totalled £19,500.
HOW TO APPLY Applications should be made on a form available to download from the fund's website. Deadlines and dates of the fund's meetings are provided on the website. Applications should include reference to other sources of funding.
WHO TO APPLY TO Cathy Matthews, Administration Manager, Europoint Centre, 5–11 Lavington Street, London SE1 0NZ *Tel.* 020 7401 2871 *Email* grants@stolavesfoundation.co.uk *Website* www.stolavesfoundationfund.org.uk

■ St Peter's Saltley Trust

CC NO 528915 **ESTABLISHED** 1980
WHERE FUNDING CAN BE GIVEN The dioceses of Worcester, Hereford, Lichfield, Birmingham and Coventry.
WHO CAN BENEFIT Charitable organisations, schools, colleges, individuals.
WHAT IS FUNDED Christianity; theological and religious education. Further details on the trust's areas of priority are provided on the website.
WHAT IS NOT FUNDED Fees and maintenance for personal study or research; core costs and salaries (although salaries for specific project work may be funded); capital projects; grants to 'prop up' existing work of schools, churches and other organisations.
SAMPLE GRANTS Saltley Trust Project Researcher (£27,000); Student Christian Movement (£10,300); Church of England Birmingham (£9,200); Arthur Rank Centre (£6,900); National Council of Faiths and Beliefs in Further Education (£5,800); Oswestry Schools Christian Worker Project (£6,000); Urban Devotion Birmingham (£700).
FINANCES *Year* 2015/16 *Income* £115,178 *Grants* £66,101 *Grants to organisations* £66,101 *Assets* £3,249,848
TRUSTEES David Urquhart; The Ven. Hayward Osborne; Gordon Thornhill; Dr Peter Kent; Colin Hopkins; Rt Revd Dr John Inge; Philip Hereford; Dr Paula Gooder; Rt Revd Christopher Cocksworth; Michael Hastilow; Jill Stolberg; Revd Naomi Nixon; Rt Revd Richard Frith; Revd Canon Dr Jonathan Kimber; Rt Revd Michael Ipgrave.
HOW TO APPLY Further details on the priorities the trust supports, as well as application guidelines, are available on the trust's website. After

reading the guidelines, potential applicants should get in touch with the trust and may be encouraged to make a formal application.

WHO TO APPLY TO Lin Brown, Bursar and Clerk to Trustees, Gray's Court, 3 Nursery Road, Edgbaston, Birmingham B15 3JX *Tel.* 0121 427 6800 *Email* director@saltleytrust.org.uk *Website* www.saltleytrust.org.uk

■ Saint Sarkis Charity Trust

CC NO 215352 **ESTABLISHED** 1954

WHERE FUNDING CAN BE GIVEN UK and overseas.

WHO CAN BENEFIT Smaller registered charities benefitting Armenians in the UK and/or overseas.

WHAT IS FUNDED Primarily charitable objectives with an Armenian connection including Armenian religious buildings. Support is also given to other small charities developing innovative projects to support prisoners in the UK. The trust funds the Armenian Church of Saint Sarkis in London and the Gulbenkian Library at the Armenian Patriarchate in Jerusalem on an annual basis.

WHAT IS NOT FUNDED The trust does not give grants to: individual applicants; organisations that are not registered charities; and registered charities outside the UK, unless the project benefits the Armenian community in the UK and/or overseas. In addition, the trust does not fund: general appeals; core costs or salaries; projects concerning substance abuse; or medical research.

TYPE OF GRANT Mainly confined to one-off project grants.

RANGE OF GRANTS £1,500 to £37,500.

SAMPLE GRANTS Armenian Church of St Sarkis (£37,500); Barrow Cadbury Trust (£30,000); Friends of Armenia (£25,000); Yedikule Surp Pırgiç Hospital (£17,500); British Council Armenia (£10,000); London Armenian Poor Relief (£9,000); Armenia Church website (£8,400); Centre for Armenian Information and Advice and Tsapik Music Friends of Armenia (£8,000); London Armenian Opera (£5,000); Lullaby Project (£4,100); Le Sion Festival (£3,700); Tekeyan Trust (£1,500).

FINANCES *Year* 2015/16 *Income* £247,968 *Grants* £175,895 *Grants to organisations* £175,895 *Assets* £8,874,415

TRUSTEES Martin Sarkis Essayan; Boghos (Paul) Gulbenkian; Rita Vartoukian; Robert Todd; Alexander D'Janoeff.

OTHER INFORMATION The trust made 14 grants to organisations, including £30,000 to the Barrow Cadbury Trust to recommend and administer on behalf of the trust, a small number of projects connected with reducing prisoner reoffending.

HOW TO APPLY Apply in writing to the correspondent. There is no standard application form so applicants should write a covering letter including: an explanation of the exact purpose of the grant; how much is needed, with details of how the budget has been arrived at; details of any other sources of income (firm commitments and those still being explored); the charity registration number; the latest annual report and audited accounts; and any plans for monitoring and evaluating the work. **Note that the trust is no longer accepting unsolicited applications for prisoner support projects.** Refer to the trust's website for current information.

WHO TO APPLY TO Chris Holmes, c/o Calouste Gulbenian Foundation, 50 Hoxton Square, London N1 6PB *Tel.* 020 7012 1400 *Email* info@saintsarkis.org.uk *Website* www.saintsarkis.org.uk

■ The Saintbury Trust

CC NO 326790 **ESTABLISHED** 1985

WHERE FUNDING CAN BE GIVEN West Midlands and Warwickshire (which the trust considers to be post code areas B, CV, DY, WS and WV), Worcestershire, Herefordshire and Gloucestershire (post code areas WR, HR and GL).

WHO CAN BENEFIT Registered charities.

WHAT IS FUNDED General charitable purposes; social welfare; older people; the environment; arts and culture; the promotion of health; education and training.

WHAT IS NOT FUNDED Individuals; sponsorship; scouts, guides, sea cadets and similar organisations; village halls; local churches; religious charities; cold-calling national charities or local branches of national charities; animal charities; grants rarely given for start-up or general running costs. **Note:** We have been informed that Herefordshire area (HR postcodes) is not eligible.

RANGE OF GRANTS £1,000 to £50,000.

SAMPLE GRANTS Enham Trust (£50,000); Alzheimer's Research Trust, Gloucester Cathedral and The Foundation for Conductive Education (£25,000 each); Disability Challengers, Rehabilitation for Addicted Prisoners Trust, and The Wildlife Trust for Birmingham and the Black Country (£10,000 each); Birmingham and Solihull Women's Aid, Cotswold Care and Warwickshire Association of Youth Clubs (£2,000 each); Friends of Willersey School, National Youth Orchestra of Great Britain and Sandwell Asian Development Association (£1,000 each).

FINANCES *Year* 2015 *Income* £1,102,709 *Grants* £389,000 *Grants to organisations* £389,000 *Assets* £11,870,637

TRUSTEES Victoria Houghton; Anita Bhalla; Anne Thomas; Harry Forrester; Amanda Atkinson-Willes; Jane Lewis; Cerian Brogan.

OTHER INFORMATION In 2015 the trust made 83 grants to organisations, totalling £389,000.

HOW TO APPLY Application forms are available to download on the trust's website. Completed applications should be returned via post to the correspondent accompanied by a short letter and latest set of accounts.

WHO TO APPLY TO Jane Lewis, Trustee, PO Box 464, Dorking, Surrey RH4 9AF *Email* saintburytrust@btinternet.com *Website* www.thesaintburytrust.co.uk

■ The Saints and Sinners Trust

CC NO 200536 **ESTABLISHED** 1961

WHERE FUNDING CAN BE GIVEN Mostly UK.

WHO CAN BENEFIT Registered charities.

WHAT IS FUNDED General charitable purposes, mainly welfare and medical causes. Priority is given to requests for grants sponsored by members of Saints and Sinners.

WHAT IS NOT FUNDED Individuals or non-registered charities.

RANGE OF GRANTS £600 to £6,000.

SAMPLE GRANTS RADA (Royal Academy of Dramatic Art) (£6,000); Reform Foundation Trust (£5,000); South Buckinghamshire Riding for the

Disabled (£4,000); Foundation for Liver Research (£3,000); Police Rehabilitation Trust (£2,500); Fight for Sight (£2,000); Children with Special Needs (£1,500); Docklands Settlement (£1,000); LAMDA (£600).

FINANCES *Year* 2014/15 *Income* £100,024 *Grants* £67,600 *Grants to organisations* £67,600 *Assets* £96,114

TRUSTEES Hon. Vice Admiral Sir Donald Gosling; Neil Benson; Anthony Jolliffe; David Edwards.

OTHER INFORMATION In 2014/15 the trust made grants to 27 organisations totalling £67,600.

HOW TO APPLY Applications are not considered unless nominated by members of the club.

WHO TO APPLY TO David Edwards, Trustee, 162 Eden Way, Beckenham BR3 3DU *Tel.* 020 7580 7313 *Email* Charity@LewisGolden.com

■ The Salamander Charitable Trust

CC NO 273657 **ESTABLISHED** 1977

WHERE FUNDING CAN BE GIVEN UK.

WHO CAN BENEFIT Registered charities.

WHAT IS FUNDED General charitable purposes; education and training; the promotion of health; people with disabilities; social welfare; overseas aid; accommodation and housing; Christianity; arts and culture; the environment and animals; children and young people; older people.

RANGE OF GRANTS £500 to £5,000.

SAMPLE GRANTS SAT-7 Trust, All Nations Christian College, All Saints in Branksome Park, Birmingham Christian College, Christian Aid, Churches Commission on overseas students, FEBA Radio, International Christian College, London Bible College, Middle East Media, Moorland College, St Jame's Parochial Church Council in Poole, SAMS, Trinity College and Wycliffe Bible Translators.

FINANCES *Year* 2015/16 *Income* £133,007 *Grants* £125,000 *Grants to organisations* £125,000 *Assets* £3,210,873

TRUSTEES S. Douglas; Alison Hardwick; Philip Douglas.

OTHER INFORMATION Grants were made to 112 organisations.

HOW TO APPLY The trust's income is fully allocated each year, mainly to regular beneficiaries. The trustees do not wish to receive any further new requests.

WHO TO APPLY TO Catharine Douglas, The Old Rectory, 5 Stamford Road, South Luffenham, Oakham, Leicestershire LE15 8NT *Email* info@geens.co.uk

■ The Salisbury New Pool Settlement

CC NO 272626 **ESTABLISHED** 1977

WHERE FUNDING CAN BE GIVEN Hertfordshire and Dorset.

WHO CAN BENEFIT Registered charities; churches; schools; museums; libraries; local organisations.

WHAT IS FUNDED The charity supports general charitable purposes, with a preference for heritage and conservation, social welfare and education.

RANGE OF GRANTS Up to £18,000.

SAMPLE GRANTS Comparative Clinical Science Foundation (£18,000); Shine (£12,000); Westminster Abbey (£5,000); Woodlands Heritage (£4,000); Pushkin Museum (£2,500); Alderholt Church (£1,500); Art Against Knives, Dorset Wildlife Trust and Families Unite Network (£500 each); Church of England School, Cranbourne (£250); King Edward VII Hospital (£200).

FINANCES *Year* 2015/16 *Income* £56,215 *Grants* £75,250 *Grants to organisations* £74,550 *Assets* £884,590

TRUSTEES The Most Honorable the Marquess of Salisbury; Viscount Cranborne.

OTHER INFORMATION In 2015/16 the charity made grants to over 36 organisations, including £700 to sponsor individuals.

HOW TO APPLY Apply in writing to the correspondent.

WHO TO APPLY TO Sarah Rutt, The Estate Office, Hatfield Park, Hatfield, Hertfordshire AL9 5NB *Tel.* 01707 287000 *Email* s.rutt@gascoyneholdings.co.uk

■ Salters' Charitable Foundation

CC NO 328258 **ESTABLISHED** 1989

WHERE FUNDING CAN BE GIVEN Greater London or UK.

WHO CAN BENEFIT Priority is given to funding small nationwide charities and organisations connected with the City of London, where the trust's contribution would make a 'real difference'. As a matter of general policy, the company supports those charities where Salters' are involved.

WHAT IS FUNDED The trust makes donations for a wide range of charitable purposes including children and young people, health, education and members of the armed forces.

TYPE OF GRANT Smaller one-off grants or longer-term support is available.

RANGE OF GRANTS £50 to £5,000.

SAMPLE GRANTS The Guildhall School Trust (£5,000); Arkwright Scholarships Trust, City and Guilds, Mansion House Scholarship Scheme (£2,000 each) The King's Royal Hussars Regimental Association, The Royal Naval Benevolent Trust (£1,000 each); St Paul's Cathedral Foundation (£500); St Mary's Grammar School (£50).

FINANCES *Year* 2015/16 *Income* £220,660 *Grants* £77,834 *Grants to organisations* £77,834 *Assets* £1,252,896

TRUSTEE The Salters' Company.

OTHER INFORMATION The foundation made 31 grants in 2015/16.

HOW TO APPLY The foundation does not accept unsolicited applications. However, the 2015 annual report states that should organisations or individuals have a specific project or cause they feel might be of interest to the foundation, they should contact the foundation using the details on the Salters' website.

WHO TO APPLY TO Capt. D. S. Morris, Clerk, The Salters' Company, Salters' Hall, 4 Fore Street, London EC2Y 5DE *Tel.* 020 7588 5216 ext. 235 *Email* charities@salters.co.uk *Website* www.salters.co.uk

■ The Andrew Salvesen Charitable Trust

SC NO SC008000 **ESTABLISHED** 1989

WHERE FUNDING CAN BE GIVEN Scotland.

WHO CAN BENEFIT Organisations.

WHAT IS FUNDED Education; disability; health, including medical research; social welfare; the arts and heritage.

WHAT IS NOT FUNDED Individuals.

RANGE OF GRANTS Up to £50,000.

SAMPLE GRANTS Winchester College Fund – Duncan Stewart NHS fund (£50,000); Sistema Scotland (£25,000).

FINANCES *Year* 2015/16 *Income* £218,277 *Grants* £76,200 *Grants to organisations* £76,200 *Assets* £5,605,957

OTHER INFORMATION In 2015/16 the trust made grants totalling £76,000.

HOW TO APPLY The trustees only support organisations known to them through their personal contacts. The trust has previously stated that all applications sent to them are 'thrown in the bin'.

WHO TO APPLY TO The Trustees, c/o Mr Mark Brown, Meston Reid and Co., Chartered Accountants, 12 Carden Place, Aberdeen AB10 1UR *Tel.* 01224 625554 *Fax* 01224 634666 *Email* brownm@mestonreid.com

■ Samjo Ltd

CC NO 1094397 **ESTABLISHED** 2002

WHERE FUNDING CAN BE GIVEN Greater Manchester.

WHO CAN BENEFIT Jewish organisations and individuals.

WHAT IS FUNDED The charity favours Orthodox Jewish charitable causes.

TYPE OF GRANT One-off or recurring.

SAMPLE GRANTS Oizer Charitable Trust (£402,500) and Shemtov Charitable Trust (£687,500).

FINANCES *Year* 2015/16 *Income* £1,286,469 *Grants* £1,464,900 *Grants to organisations* £1,464,900 *Assets* £16,291,898

TRUSTEES Rabbi Yisroel Friedman; Joshua Halpern; Samuel Halpern.

OTHER INFORMATION In 2015/16 the charity made grants to organisations totalling £1,464,900.

HOW TO APPLY Apply in writing to the correspondent.

WHO TO APPLY TO The Trustees, Lopian Gross Barnett and Co., 6th Floor, Cardinal House, 20 St Mary's Parsonage, Manchester M3 2LG *Tel.* 0161 832 8721 *Email* D.Stewart@prestburymanagement.co.uk

■ Coral Samuel Charitable Trust

CC NO 239677 **ESTABLISHED** 1962

WHERE FUNDING CAN BE GIVEN UK.

WHO CAN BENEFIT Registered charities only.

WHAT IS FUNDED General charitable purposes, with a preference for educational, cultural and socially supportive charities. Grants are made in the following categories: medical/socially supportive; cultural; educational; animal welfare.

WHAT IS NOT FUNDED Grants are only made to registered charities.

RANGE OF GRANTS £1,000 to £25,000.

SAMPLE GRANTS The National Gallery Trust (£25,000); The Jewish Deaf Association (£10,000); Crohn's and Colitis UK, National Children's Orchestra, RNLI and The National Autistic Society (£5,000 each); Computers for the Disabled, Foundation for Social and Economic Thinking and The Jubilee Sailing Trust (£3,000 each); Cumbria Cerebral Palsy (£2,000); Maccabi GB (£1,000).

FINANCES *Year* 2015/16 *Income* £30,062 *Grants* £182,300 *Grants to organisations* £182,300 *Assets* £4,739,426

TRUSTEES Coral Samuel; Peter Fineman; Sarah Fineman.

OTHER INFORMATION Grants were made to 42 organisations in 2015/16.

HOW TO APPLY Apply in writing to the correspondent.

WHO TO APPLY TO Coral Samuel, Trustee, Smith and Williamson, 25 Moorgate, London EC2R 6AY *Tel.* 020 7131 4376

■ The Basil Samuel Charitable Trust

CC NO 206579 **ESTABLISHED** 1959

WHERE FUNDING CAN BE GIVEN UK and worldwide.

WHO CAN BENEFIT Registered charities.

WHAT IS FUNDED General charitable purposes; education and training; the promotion of health; people with disabilities; arts and culture; the environment and animals; children and young people; older people.

WHAT IS NOT FUNDED Registered charities only.

TYPE OF GRANT One-off and recurring.

RANGE OF GRANTS £1,000 to £50,000.

SAMPLE GRANTS The Old Vic Theatre (£50,000); Teach First and The National Gallery (£25,000 each); Anaphylaxis Campaign, Dulwich Picture Gallery and Tameside and Glossop Hospice Ltd (£10,000 each); Action on Addiction, Countryside Learning, Dundonnell Mountain Rescue Team and The Attingham Trust for the Study of Country Houses (£5,000 each); Commonwealth Jewish Trust, East Anglian Air Ambulance and Surfers Against Sewage (£1,000 each).

FINANCES *Year* 2015/16 *Income* £54,515 *Grants* £396,000 *Grants to organisations* £396,000 *Assets* £8,759,585

TRUSTEES Coral Samuel; Richard Peskin.

OTHER INFORMATION In 2015/16 the trust made 62 grants to organisations.

HOW TO APPLY Apply in writing to the correspondent.

WHO TO APPLY TO The Trustees, Smith and Williamson, 25 Moorgate, London EC2R 6AY *Tel.* 020 7131 4376

■ The M. J. Samuel Charitable Trust

CC NO 327013 **ESTABLISHED** 1985

WHERE FUNDING CAN BE GIVEN UK and overseas.

WHO CAN BENEFIT Charitable organisations.

WHAT IS FUNDED The trust supports general charitable purposes in the UK and overseas, with a preference for health, environmental causes, the arts and overseas aid.

WHAT IS NOT FUNDED Individuals.

TYPE OF GRANT Funding of up to two years will be considered.

RANGE OF GRANTS Up to £30,000.

SAMPLE GRANTS Full Fact and LAMDA (£30,000 each); Jonathan Robinson (£27,500); Game and Wildlife Conservation Trust (£21,000); Child Bereavement Trust (£10,000) Somerset Community Foundation (£5,500); Cancer Research UK, Syria Relief, The Mary Hare Foundation (£1,000 each).

FINANCES *Year* 2015/16 *Income* £98,896 *Grants* £207,204 *Grants to organisations* £207,204 *Assets* £3,678,831

TRUSTEES Hon. Michael Samuel; Hon. Julia Samuel; Viscount Bearsted.

OTHER INFORMATION In 2015/16 the trust made 34 grants to organisations with 14 donations of less than £1,000 each totalling £4,650.

HOW TO APPLY Apply in writing to the correspondent.

WHO TO APPLY TO Lindsay Sutton, Secretary, Mells Park, Mells, Frome, Somerset BA11 3QB *Tel.* 020 7402 0602 *Email* lindsay@mellspark.com

The Samworth Foundation

CC NO 265647 **ESTABLISHED** 1973
WHERE FUNDING CAN BE GIVEN UK and overseas.
WHO CAN BENEFIT UK-registered charities.
WHAT IS FUNDED The social and educational needs of children and young people, particularly 'those most neglected and vulnerable'. There has been a focus on child trafficking, anti-slavery and exploitation in the UK and Africa. The trustees have also expanded their core strategy to introduce different targeted areas, notably environmental and conservation issues.
WHAT IS NOT FUNDED Individuals.
RANGE OF GRANTS £13,000 to £180,000.
SAMPLE GRANTS Firbeck Academy (£180,000); Anti-Slavery International (£40,000); Housing for Women (£32,000); Mangrove Action Project and Rainforest Foundation UK (£30,000 each); Children on the Edge (£27,000); Médecins Sans Frontières (£25,000); Client Earth (£20,000 each); Leicestershire and Rutland Community Foundation (£16,600); Chicks (£13,800).
FINANCES *Year* 2015/16 *Income* £45,688,866 *Grants* £1,227,395 *Grants to organisations* £1,227,395 *Assets* £61,507,010
TRUSTEES Clare Price; Susie Culloty; Prof. Neil Gorman; Stephen Hale; Gemma Juma.
OTHER INFORMATION 92 grants were made during the year. Of these, 55 were grants of less than £10,000.
HOW TO APPLY The foundation's grant-making policy is to support a limited number of causes known to the trustees. Unsolicited applications are not normally considered.
WHO TO APPLY TO Wendy Bateman, c/o Samworth Brothers (Holdings) Ltd, Chetwode House, 1 Samworth Way, Melton Mowbray, Leicestershire LE13 1GA *Tel.* 01664 414500 *Email* wendy.bateman@chetwodehouse.com

The Sandhu Charitable Foundation

CC NO 1114236 **ESTABLISHED** 2006
WHERE FUNDING CAN BE GIVEN Worldwide.
WHO CAN BENEFIT UK-registered charities.
WHAT IS FUNDED General charitable purposes; education and training; the promotion of health; social welfare; overseas aid; arts and culture; religious activities; economic and community development; armed forces; human rights; children and young people; older people; people with disabilities.
TYPE OF GRANT One-off, with a few multi-year.
RANGE OF GRANTS £1,000 to £200,000. Average grant: £23,500.
SAMPLE GRANTS Variety – The Children's Charity (£35,000); The Anne Frank Trust UK (£25,000); CASS Business School – City University (£15,000); Kew Foundation (£12,500); Dasru UK (£12,000); Helena Kennedy Foundation (£10,000); Prostate Cancer UK (£8,000); Amy May Trust (£3,000); MS Society (£1,000).
FINANCES *Year* 2015/16 *Income* £241,650 *Grants* £194,500 *Grants to organisations* £194,500 *Assets* £4,271,901
TRUSTEES Bim Sandhu; Pardeep Sandhu.
OTHER INFORMATION In 2015/16 grants were made to 16 organisations.
HOW TO APPLY The charity supports individual charities or charitable causes, mainly on a single donation basis, which the trustees identify.
WHO TO APPLY TO The Trustees, The Trustees of The Sandhu Charitable Foundation, First Floor, Santon House, 53–55 Uxbridge Road, Ealing, London W5 5SA *Tel.* 020 3478 3900 *Email* nsteele@thesantongroup.com *Website* thesantongroup.com/charity

The Sandra Charitable Trust

CC NO 327492 **ESTABLISHED** 1987
WHERE FUNDING CAN BE GIVEN UK.
WHO CAN BENEFIT Charitable organisations; nurses.
WHAT IS FUNDED Animal welfare and research; environmental protection; relief of poverty; youth development. Grants are also made to nurses and those studying to be nurses.
TYPE OF GRANT One-off and recurring.
RANGE OF GRANTS Up to £50,000; mostly up to £5,000.
SAMPLE GRANTS The Brooke (£51,000); British Heart Foundation (£40,000); The Florence Nightingale Foundation (£29,500); Worplesdon Primary School (£12,500); Health Poverty Action and RNIB (£5,000 each); Cardboard Citizens and Crohn's and Colitis UK (£3,000 each); Garsington Opera (£2,000); Mary's Meals (£1,000).
FINANCES *Year* 2015/16 *Income* £725,934 *Grants* £710,508 *Grants to organisations* £637,058 *Assets* £20,471,298
TRUSTEES Richard Moore; Michael Macfadyen; Lucy Forsyth; Francis Moore.
OTHER INFORMATION Grants were made to 125 organisations in 2015/16. Grants to 94 individuals during the year totalled £73,500.
HOW TO APPLY The 2015 annual report states: 'Unsolicited applications are not requested as the Trustees prefer to support charities whose work they have researched and which is in accordance with the wishes of the Settlor. The Trustees receive a very high number of grant applications which are mostly unsuccessful.' Applications may be considered from nurses and those training as nurses.
WHO TO APPLY TO Martin Pollock, c/o Moore Stephens, 150 Aldersgate Street, London EC1A 4AB *Tel.* 020 7334 9191

The Sands Family Trust

CC NO 1136909 **ESTABLISHED** 2010
WHERE FUNDING CAN BE GIVEN UK and overseas.
WHO CAN BENEFIT Organisations and individuals.
WHAT IS FUNDED General charitable purposes. Support is given particularly for the advancement of education, the relief of poverty and the encouragement of performing arts.
RANGE OF GRANTS £600 to £50,000.
SAMPLE GRANTS United World Colleges (£50,500); Kay Mason Foundation (£15,000); Chicken Town and The Girls' Day School Trust (£5,000 each); First Story and Women for Refugee Women (£3,000 each); Big House Theatre Company (£680).
FINANCES *Year* 2015/16 *Income* £4,035 *Grants* £82,225 *Grants to organisations* £82,225 *Assets* £981,933
TRUSTEES Cripps Trust Corporation Ltd; Betsy Tobin; Peter Sands.
OTHER INFORMATION Grants were made to seven organisations during the year.
HOW TO APPLY Apply in writing to the correspondent.
WHO TO APPLY TO The Trustees, Heartwood Wealth Management, 77 Mount Ephraim, Tunbridge Wells TN4 8BS *Tel.* 01892 701801 *Email* charities@heartwoodgroup.co.uk

■ Santander UK Foundation Ltd

CC NO 803655 **ESTABLISHED** 1990

WHERE FUNDING CAN BE GIVEN UK.

WHO CAN BENEFIT UK-registered charities, CICs and credit unions, focusing on small, local organisations helping disadvantaged people.

WHAT IS FUNDED The foundation provides grants 'to support knowledge, skills and innovation to give disadvantaged people the confidence to discover and create a new world of opportunities'. In 2016 the foundation amalgamated its previous three grants programmes to form one grants scheme – Discovery Grants. The website states that grants can be used to support three priorities: Explorer – 'improving people's knowledge' Transformer – 'improving skills and experience' Changemaker – 'innovative solutions to social challenges'.

WHAT IS NOT FUNDED Individuals; multi-year funding; fundraising activities; unregistered charities or groups, sports clubs or exempt or excepted charities; other funders and grant-makers; organisations which restrict their beneficiaries to one religious or ethnic group; events, conferences or sponsorship; shortfalls in funding; party political activity; beneficiaries outside UK, Channel Islands or Isle of Man; organisations without one full year of accounts.

TYPE OF GRANT One-off grants are given for complete projects and can cover equipment, materials or part-time salaries that are specific to the project.

RANGE OF GRANTS Up to £5,000.

SAMPLE GRANTS British Heart Foundation (£256,500); Anglia Care Trust, Headway, Perth Community Centre, Sight Cymru, Small Charities Coalition, Solway Credit Union, South Gloucestershire Citizens Advice, Tees Valley Women's Centre, Young Lives Foundation (£10,000 each).

FINANCES *Year* 2015 *Income* £5,550,838 *Grants* £598,690 *Grants to organisations* £598,690 *Assets* £13,356,870

TRUSTEES Jennifer Scardino; Sue Willis; Keith Moor; Christopher Fallis; Rachel MacFarlane.

HOW TO APPLY Application forms can be obtained from a local Santander branch and returned via the Discovery Grants post box in any branch. Successful applicants will be notified within six weeks.

WHO TO APPLY TO Amy Slack, Foundation Secretary, Santander Foundation, Santander House, 201 Grafton Gate East, Milton Keynes MK9 1AN *Email* grants@santander.co.uk *Website* www.santanderfoundation.org.uk

■ The Sants Charitable Trust

CC NO 1078555 **ESTABLISHED** 1999

WHERE FUNDING CAN BE GIVEN Oxfordshire.

WHO CAN BENEFIT Small charitable organisations.

WHAT IS FUNDED Children and young people; Christianity; education and training; health; social welfare; community development; arts.

RANGE OF GRANTS £100 to £15,000.

SAMPLE GRANTS Hope Corner Community Church (£15,000); Oxfordshire Historic Churches Trust (£10,000); Christians Against Poverty (£5,000); Worminghall Parish Council (£1,200); Garsington Opera (£1,000); Trinity College (£300); Harry Mahon Cancer Research Trust (£250); Buckinghamshire Foundation (£100).

FINANCES *Year* 2015/16 *Income* £37,694 *Grants* £50,850 *Grants to organisations* £50,850 *Assets* £1,137,692

TRUSTEES Caroline Sants; Hector Hepburn Sants; John Ovens; Alexander Sants; Edward Sants; Arthur Sants.

OTHER INFORMATION The trust gave grants to 13 organisations during the year.

HOW TO APPLY Apply in writing to the correspondent.

WHO TO APPLY TO The Trustees, 17 Bradmore Road, Oxford OX2 6QP *Tel.* 01865 310813 *Email* santscharitabletrust@gmail.com

■ Sarum St Michael Educational Charity

CC NO 309456 **ESTABLISHED** 1980

WHERE FUNDING CAN BE GIVEN The Diocese of Salisbury and its surrounding area.

WHO CAN BENEFIT Parishes, schools and other organisations; individuals (over the age of 16).

WHAT IS FUNDED Advancement of religious education in accordance with the principles and doctrines of the Church of England. This includes funding for: schools; parishes and associated groups; individuals in further, higher and postgraduate education; training of teachers.

WHAT IS NOT FUNDED Maintenance costs, unless an integral part of a residential course; grants for buildings, fixtures or fittings; retrospective grants; contributions to the general funds of any organisation.

TYPE OF GRANT One-off, project and research will be considered. Funding may be given for up to three years.

RANGE OF GRANTS £100 to £2,000 (except some larger corporate grants).

SAMPLE GRANTS Salisbury Diocesan Board of Education (£40,000); Sarum College (£18,700); Weymouth College (£5,400); Bridge Youth Project (£5,000).

FINANCES *Year* 2015 *Income* £206,291 *Grants* £128,348 *Grants to organisations* £72,676 *Assets* £5,299,229

TRUSTEES The Very Revd June Osborne; Canon Dr Bill Merrington; The Very Revd Alec Knight; Jennifer Pitcher; Lucinda Herklots; Rt Revd Nicholas Holtam; John Cox; Revd Jane Dunlop; Joy Tubbs; Susan de Candole; Revd Ann Keating; J. Molnar.

OTHER INFORMATION A total of 68 grants were awarded to individuals and organisations during the year.

HOW TO APPLY Only on a form available from the correspondent. Applications are considered at four or five meetings per year – deadlines are posted on the website.

WHO TO APPLY TO The Trustees, First Floor, 27A Castle Street, Salisbury, Wiltshire SP1 1TT *Tel.* 01722 422296 *Email* clerk@sarumstmichael.org *Website* www.sarumstmichael.org

■ The Save the Children Fund

CC NO 213890 **ESTABLISHED** 1921

WHERE FUNDING CAN BE GIVEN Worldwide.

WHO CAN BENEFIT Charitable organisations and occasionally individuals.

WHAT IS FUNDED The charity works internationally on the following issues affecting children: emergencies; education; children's poverty; health; hunger; children protection; children's rights. For information on current programmes, refer to the website.

TYPE OF GRANT Grants (sometimes in partnership with other funders); partnerships with organisations.

SAMPLE GRANTS Action Against Hunger (£3.9 million); Plan International UK (£1.5 million); Mercy Corps Scotland (£1.2 million); CAFOD (Catholic Agency for Overseas Development) (£928,000); HelpAge International (£823,000); Doctors of the World UK (£545,000); The Beanstalk Group (£506,000); Durham University (£240,000); Fundació Bosch Gimpera – University of Barcelona (£110,000).
FINANCES *Year* 2015 *Income* £389,717,000 *Grants* £35,129,000 *Grants to organisations* £35,129,000 *Assets* £59,561,000
TRUSTEES Sir Alan Parker; Peter Bennett-Jones; Adele Anderson; Tamara Ingram; Mark Esiri; Naomi Eisenstadt; Sophia McCormick; Sebastian James; Jamie Cooper; Diana Carney; Gareth Davies; Mark Swallow; Fiona McBain; Lisa Rosen; Anne Fahy; Arabella Duffield.
OTHER INFORMATION The grant total does not include grants made to partner organisations, Save the Children International, and other members of Save the Children, which amounted to £224,600.
HOW TO APPLY The charity does not accept unsolicited applications.
WHO TO APPLY TO Andrew Willis, Company Secretary, Save The Children, 1 St John's Lane, London EC1M 4AR *Tel.* 020 7012 6400 *Email* supporter.care@savethechildren.org.uk *Website* www.savethechildren.org.uk

■ The Savoy Educational Trust

CC NO 1161014 **ESTABLISHED** 2015
WHERE FUNDING CAN BE GIVEN England and Wales.
WHO CAN BENEFIT Educational establishments to enhance training and education facilities for their hospitality departments; associations to support those initiatives that will make a real difference to the hospitality industry; charitable organisations/social enterprises with specific hospitality-related projects; individuals studying hospitality.
WHAT IS FUNDED Hospitality training and education.
SAMPLE GRANTS University of West London (£100,000); University College Birmingham (£60,000); South Devon College (£38,500); Northbrook College (£22,000); Reeseheath College (£10,700); Mid Cheshire College (£4,000).
FINANCES *Year* 2015/16 *Income* £54,182,515 *Grants* £1,097,574 *Grants to organisations* £1,097,574
TRUSTEES Ramon Pajares; Cllr Robert Davies; Sir David Walker; Howard Field; Dr Sally Messenger.
OTHER INFORMATION Grants were made to 29 organisations during the year.
HOW TO APPLY Applications can be via the trust's website.
WHO TO APPLY TO Margaret Georgiou, Room 160, 90 Long Acre, London WC2E 9RZ *Tel.* 020 7849 3001 *Email* info@savoyeducationaltrust.org.uk *Website* www.savoyeducationaltrust.org.uk

■ The Scarfe Charitable Trust

CC NO 275535 **ESTABLISHED** 1978
WHERE FUNDING CAN BE GIVEN UK, with an emphasis on Suffolk.
WHO CAN BENEFIT Individuals (students); churches; charitable organisations.
WHAT IS FUNDED The trust supports churches and students, as well as a wide range of general charitable purposes, such as social welfare; arts and music; children and young people; disability; environment.
TYPE OF GRANT Projects; capital costs; core costs. Funding is normally for one year or less.
RANGE OF GRANTS £50 to £10,000. Many grants are under £1,000.
SAMPLE GRANTS Aldeburgh Music (£8,500); St Ethelbert's Falkenham (£2,000); St Mary's Parochial Church Council Benhall (£1,500); Shakespeare Schools Festival and Suffolk Refugee Support (£1,000 each); Hearing Dogs, Scope and New Wolsey Theatre (£750 each); Woodbridge Choral Society (£350); Ipswich Chamber Music (£180).
FINANCES *Year* 2015/16 *Income* £81,832 *Grants* £66,654 *Grants to organisations* £64,904 *Assets* £2,049,207
TRUSTEES Sean McTernan; Eric Maule; John McCarthy; Fraser Thomas; Jonathan Fuller.
OTHER INFORMATION Grants were made to 69 organisations during the year.
HOW TO APPLY Apply in writing to the correspondent by post or email. The trustees meet quarterly to consider applications.
WHO TO APPLY TO Sean McTernan, Trustee, 2 The Clubhouse, St Audrys Park Road, Melton, Woodbridge IP12 1SY *Tel.* 01394 386192 *Email* scarfetrust@gmail.com

■ The Schapira Charitable Trust

CC NO 328435 **ESTABLISHED** 1989
WHERE FUNDING CAN BE GIVEN UK.
WHO CAN BENEFIT Jewish organisations; other organisations.
WHAT IS FUNDED Jewish charitable purposes; health and education generally.
RANGE OF GRANTS £500 to £400,000.
SAMPLE GRANTS KSH (£388,000); Emuno Educational Centre (£76,500); Friends of MIR Charitable Trust (£57,500); Gateshead Talmudical College (£25,000); Friends of Tashbar Chazon ISH (£12,000); Kollal Rainbow (£1,000); Before Trust (£1,200); The Talmud Centre Trust (£700); Achisomoch Aid Co. Ltd (£500).
FINANCES *Year* 2015 *Income* £280,993 *Grants* £844,740 *Grants to organisations* £844,740 *Assets* £3,995,372
TRUSTEES Isaac Schapira; Suzanne Schapira; Alan Rose.
OTHER INFORMATION Grants were made to 31 organisations during the year.
HOW TO APPLY Apply in writing to the correspondent.
WHO TO APPLY TO Isaac Schapira, Trustee, 2 Dancastle Court, 14 Arcadia Avenue, Finchley, London N3 2JU *Tel.* 020 8371 0381 *Email* londonoffice@istrad.com

■ The Annie Schiff Charitable Trust

CC NO 265401 **ESTABLISHED** 1973
WHERE FUNDING CAN BE GIVEN UK; overseas.
WHO CAN BENEFIT Charitable organisations.
WHAT IS FUNDED Relief of poverty, particularly among the Jewish community; advancement of Jewish religion, places of worship and education.
RANGE OF GRANTS £400 to £22,000.
SAMPLE GRANTS Friends of Beis Yisrael Trust and Menorah Grammar School Trust (£15,000 each); Elanore Ltd (£10,000); WST Charity Ltd (£8,000); Friends of Ohel Moshe (£6,000); Tiferes High School, EMET and Yesamech Levav Trust (£5,000 each); North West Separdish

Synagogue (£3,000); British Friends of Nadvorne (£1,500); Golders Charitable Trust (£1,100); Beth Jacob Grammar School for Girls Ltd (£1,000); Ezra U'Marpeh (£500).

FINANCES *Year* 2015/16 *Income* £119,149 *Grants* £106,189 *Grants to organisations* £106,189 *Assets* £105,525

TRUSTEES Joseph Pearlman; Ruth Pearlman.

OTHER INFORMATION A list of recent beneficiaries was not included in the 2015/16 accounts.

HOW TO APPLY Apply in writing to the correspondent. Grants are generally made only to registered charities.

WHO TO APPLY TO Joseph Pearlman, Trustee, 8 Highfield Gardens, London NW11 9HB *Tel.* 020 8458 9266

■ The Schmidt-Bodner Charitable Trust

CC NO 283014 **ESTABLISHED** 1981

WHERE FUNDING CAN BE GIVEN UK and overseas.

WHO CAN BENEFIT Jewish organisations and other registered charities.

WHAT IS FUNDED General charitable purposes; Jewish causes.

RANGE OF GRANTS £2,500 to £21,000.

SAMPLE GRANTS World Jewish Relief (£21,000); Jewish Care, The Prince's Trust and Prostate Cancer UK (£10,000 each); Holocaust Educational Trust (£7,500); British ORT (£5,000); Maccabi GB (£2,500).

FINANCES *Year* 2015/16 *Income* £23,941 *Grants* £60,000 *Grants to organisations* £60,000

TRUSTEES Martin Paisner; Daniel Dover; Harvey Rosenblatt.

OTHER INFORMATION The trust's latest accounts were not available to view on the Charity Commission's website due to its low income. We have estimated the grant total based on the previous years' information.

HOW TO APPLY Apply in writing to the correspondent. The trustees have previously stated in their annual report that 'all applications received are considered by the trustees on their own merit for suitability of funding.'

WHO TO APPLY TO Harvey Rosenblatt, Trustee, 16 Caenwood Court, Hampstead Lane, London N6 4RU *Tel.* 07711 005151 *Email* charity.correspondence@bdo.co.uk

■ The Schreib Trust

CC NO 275240 **ESTABLISHED** 1977

WHERE FUNDING CAN BE GIVEN UK.

WHO CAN BENEFIT Charitable organisations, mainly Jewish organisations.

WHAT IS FUNDED General charitable purposes, particularly the relief of poverty and the advancement of the Jewish religion and religious education.

SAMPLE GRANTS Lolev, Yad Eliezer, Ponovitz, Craven Walk Charity Trust, Shaar Hatalmud, Beis Rochel, Beth Jacob Building Fund, Toras Chesed and Oneg Shabbos.

FINANCES *Year* 2015/16 *Income* £263,441 *Grants* £352,127 *Grants to organisations* £352,127 *Assets* £226,225

TRUSTEES Abraham Green; Jacob Schreiber; Irene Schreiber; Rivka Niederman.

OTHER INFORMATION A list of recent beneficiaries was not provided in the trust's annual report.

HOW TO APPLY Apply in writing to the correspondent.

WHO TO APPLY TO Rivka Niederman, Trustee, 147 Stamford Hill, London N16 5LG *Tel.* 020 8802 5492

■ O. and G. Schreiber Charitable Trust

CC NO 1073263 **ESTABLISHED** 1998

WHERE FUNDING CAN BE GIVEN UK.

WHO CAN BENEFIT Orthodox Jewish charities.

WHAT IS FUNDED The promotion of Orthodox Judaism; relief of poverty among the Jewish community.

SAMPLE GRANTS A list of beneficiaries was not available.

FINANCES *Year* 2015 *Income* £288,864 *Grants* £119,773 *Grants to organisations* £119,773 *Assets* £1,036,747

TRUSTEES Osias Schreiber; Gyta Schreiber.

OTHER INFORMATION A list of beneficiaries was not included in the accounts.

HOW TO APPLY Apply in writing to the correspondent. The annual report for 2015 states that the 'charity accepts applications for grants from representatives of Orthodox Jewish charities, which are reviewed by the trustees on a regular basis'.

WHO TO APPLY TO Osias Schreiber, Trustee, 34 Jessam Avenue, London E5 9DU *Tel.* 020 8806 1842

■ The Schreiber Charitable Trust

CC NO 264735 **ESTABLISHED** 1972

WHERE FUNDING CAN BE GIVEN UK.

WHO CAN BENEFIT Registered charities.

WHAT IS FUNDED Jewish causes; education and training; social welfare.

RANGE OF GRANTS £100 to £50,000.

SAMPLE GRANTS Friends of Rabbinical College Kol Torah; Gateshead Talmudical College; Mizrachi (UK) Israel Support Trust; British Friends of Gesher; SOFT (Support Organisation for Trisomy); Aish Hatorah UK Ltd.

FINANCES *Year* 2015/16 *Income* £315,484 *Grants* £253,391 *Grants to organisations* £253,391 *Assets* £4,285,541

TRUSTEES Graham Morris; David Schreiber; Sara Schreiber.

HOW TO APPLY Apply in writing to the correspondent.

WHO TO APPLY TO Graham Morris, Trustee, Schreiber Holdings Ltd, 3 Brent Cross Gardens, London NW4 3RJ *Tel.* 020 8457 6500 *Email* graham@schreibers.com

■ Schroder Charity Trust

CC NO 214050 **ESTABLISHED** 1944

WHERE FUNDING CAN BE GIVEN Worldwide, in practice mainly UK.

WHO CAN BENEFIT Registered charities.

WHAT IS FUNDED General charitable purposes; the promotion of health; social welfare; children and young people; education and training; community and economic development; overseas aid; arts and culture; heritage; the environment.

WHAT IS NOT FUNDED Individuals.

TYPE OF GRANT One-off and recurring.

RANGE OF GRANTS Up to £5,000.

SAMPLE GRANTS The Wallace Collection (£5,000); Place2Be (£4,000); Cornwall Women's Refuge Trust (£2,500); Cotswold Care Hospice, London Philharmonic Orchestra and Phab (£2,000

each); Citizens Theatre, Opportunity International UK and The Rainforest Foundation UK (£1,500 each); Royal Chapel – Windsor (£400).

FINANCES *Year* 2015/16 *Income* £407,455 *Grants* £268,450 *Grants to organisations* £268,450 *Assets* £12,094,615

TRUSTEES Bruno Schroder; Timothy Schroder; Charmaine von Mallinckrodt; Claire Fitzalan Howard; Leonie Fane; John Schroder.

OTHER INFORMATION Grants were made to 119 organisations during the year, out of 534 applications received. All grants were for £5,000 or less.

HOW TO APPLY Apply in writing to the correspondent. Applicants should briefly state their case and enclose a copy of their latest accounts or annual review.

WHO TO APPLY TO Sally Yates, 81 Rivington Street, London EC2A 3AY

The Schroder Foundation

CC NO 1107479 **ESTABLISHED** 2005

WHERE FUNDING CAN BE GIVEN Worldwide, in practice mainly UK. There is also a specific committee which awards grants for charitable causes in Islay and Jura.

WHO CAN BENEFIT Charitable causes with a previous track record and organisations in which the foundation has a special interest.

WHAT IS FUNDED General charitable purposes, mainly within the areas of the environment; education; arts, culture and heritage; social welfare; community; international relief and development.

TYPE OF GRANT One-off and repeat donations.

RANGE OF GRANTS £400 to £150,000.

SAMPLE GRANTS Hampshire and Isle of Wight Air Ambulance (£150,000); Child Bereavement UK (£100,000); Alzheimer's Research UK (£50,000); Clean Break Theatre Company and One Break Europe (£30,000 each); The Gurkha Welfare Trust (£25,000); The Ecology Trust (£10,000); Islay Museum Trust (£4,000); Cantilena Festival on Islay (£750); Friends of the Courtauld Institute (£400).

FINANCES *Year* 2015/16 *Income* £2,020,596 *Grants* £1,952,225 *Grants to organisations* £1,952,225 *Assets* £11,030,746

TRUSTEES Bruno Schroder; Edward Mallinckrodt; Charmaine Mallinckrodt; Leonie Fane; Claire Howard; Richard Robinson; Philip Mallinckrodt; Michael May.

OTHER INFORMATION The foundation shares a common administration with Schroder Charity Trust. The grant total includes £1.9 million for general causes and £36,500 for causes in Islay and Jura.

HOW TO APPLY This trust **does not** respond to unsolicited applications. The annual report states: 'The trustees identify projects and organisations they wish to support and the foundation does not make grants to people or organisations who apply speculatively.'

WHO TO APPLY TO Sally Yates, Secretary, 81 Rivington Street, London EC2A 3AY

Foundation Scotland

SC NO SC022910 **ESTABLISHED** 1995

WHERE FUNDING CAN BE GIVEN Scotland.

WHO CAN BENEFIT Small organisations helping to build and sustain local communities.

WHAT IS FUNDED There are three broad programmes, under which there are a range of different funds. Express Grants: grants of between £500 to £2,000 are made to groups across a wide spectrum of social welfare and community development activities. Guidelines are available on the foundation's website. **Community Benefit Funds:** there are a variety of programmes which benefit people in specific areas of Scotland. Each has different criteria, grant sizes and deadline dates. A list of local programmes is available on the website. **Large Grants:** the foundation manages funds for donors, most of which are administered through the foundation's other grants programmes, but some of which may consider applications for capital projects or start-up costs – refer to the website for further information.

WHAT IS NOT FUNDED The following are not normally funded under express grants: individuals; groups which do not have a constitution; groups other than not-for-profit groups; the advancement of religion or a political party (including the core activities of religious or political groups); the purchase of second-hand vehicles; trips abroad; the repayment of loans, payment of debts, or other retrospective funding; payments towards areas generally understood to be the responsibility of statutory authorities; groups which will then distribute the funds as grants or bursaries; applications that are for the sole benefit to flora and fauna, unless applications demonstrate a direct benefit to the local community and/or service users; projects which do not benefit people in Scotland.

TYPE OF GRANT Capital, revenue and project funding.

RANGE OF GRANTS Usually between £250 and £5,000 – occasionally larger grants are made.

SAMPLE GRANTS Home-Start Glasgow North (£107,500); Valley Renewables Group (£22,000); Aberlour Child Care Trust (£15,000); Forth Valley Disability Sports and Rainbow Muslim Women's Group (£2,000 each); Family Addiction Support Services (£1,300); Cowdenbeath Civic Week Committee (£1,000); Artifact Dance Company Ltd (£900); Scottish Association of Sign Language Interpreters (£500); Aberuthven Village Hall Trust (£250).

FINANCES *Year* 2015/16 *Income* £14,765,000 *Grants* £4,721,000 *Grants to organisations* £4,721,000 *Assets* £32,588,000

TRUSTEES Tom Ward, Chair; Alex Barr; Robert Benson; Gillian Donald; Ian Marr; Jimmy McCulloch; John Naylor; Ella Simpson; Lady Emily Stair.

OTHER INFORMATION In 2015/16 the foundation made 2,811 grants on behalf of its clients and dealt with 2,987 applications.

HOW TO APPLY The foundation has a comprehensive website with details of the grant schemes currently being administered. Organisations are welcome to contact the grants team to discuss their funding needs before making any application. The trustees meet at least four times a year.

WHO TO APPLY TO Grants Team, 131 West Nile Street, Glasgow G1 2RX *Tel.* 0141 341 4960 *Email* grants@foundationscotland.org.uk *Website* www.foundationscotland.org.uk

The Scotshill Trust

CC NO 1113071 **ESTABLISHED** 2006

WHERE FUNDING CAN BE GIVEN UK and overseas.

WHO CAN BENEFIT Registered charities.

WHAT IS FUNDED General charitable purposes, particularly education; arts; animal welfare;

relief of poverty and disadvantage; environment; health; social welfare.
WHAT IS NOT FUNDED Individuals.
RANGE OF GRANTS £250 to £50,000.
SAMPLE GRANTS Crisis and Queens Park Arts Centre (£25,000 each); WaterAid (£20,000).
FINANCES *Year* 2015/16 *Income* £41,885 *Grants* £70,000 *Grants to organisations* £70,000 *Assets* £1,676,935
TRUSTEES Amanda Claire Burton; Paul Howard Burton; Deborah Maureen Hazan; Jeremy John Burton.
HOW TO APPLY Applications should be made in writing only to the trust's managers. The annual report states that 'at present appeals will not be considered from charities not previously supported'. Unsuccessful appeals will not necessarily be acknowledged.
WHO TO APPLY TO Keith Pailing, Trustee Management Ltd, 19 Cookridge Street, Leeds LS2 3AG *Tel.* 0113 243 6466

■ Scott (Eredine) Charitable Trust

CC NO 1002267 **ESTABLISHED** 1990
WHERE FUNDING CAN BE GIVEN UK.
WHO CAN BENEFIT Charitable organisations.
WHAT IS FUNDED Service and ex-service charities; medical and welfare causes; environment; international development.
RANGE OF GRANTS £1,000 to £40,000. Most grants are under £5,000.
SAMPLE GRANTS Fieldrose Charitable Trust (£40,500); Spinal Research (£20,000); Maggie's Centre (£10,000); Tall Ships Trust (£7,000); The Charlie Waller Memorial Trust (£5,000); Action for Blind People, Salmon and Trout Association and World Vision (£2,800 each); Send a Cow and War Memorial Trust (£2,200 each); Royal Hospital Chelsea (£1,000).
FINANCES *Year* 2015 *Income* £472,704 *Grants* £476,479 *Grants to organisations* £476,479 *Assets* £13,792,069
TRUSTEES Keith Bruce-Smith; Amanda Scott; Col. Nick Wills; Lucy Gibson.
OTHER INFORMATION Grants were made to 79 organisations during the year.
HOW TO APPLY Apply in writing to the correspondent.
WHO TO APPLY TO Col. Nick Wills, Trustee, Bitcombe Farm, Witham Friary, Frome BA11 5HD *Tel.* 01749 850064 *Email* nick.wills431@gmail.com

■ The Francis C. Scott Charitable Trust

CC NO 232131 **ESTABLISHED** 1963
WHERE FUNDING CAN BE GIVEN Cumbria and North Lancashire (comprising the towns of Lancaster, Morecambe, Heysham and Carnforth).
WHO CAN BENEFIT Mostly registered charities addressing the needs of children and young people (up to 24 years old) in the most deprived communities of Cumbria and North Lancashire. Organisations which are pursuing charitable objectives and have not-for-profit aims/constitution may be considered. Applications from national organisations will only be considered if the beneficiaries and project workers are based within the beneficial area.
WHAT IS FUNDED The trust has a focus on working with children and young people (up to 24 years old) the following areas: victims/survivors of abuse and exploitation; homelessness and its causes; those suffering from mental health problems; those leaving care or the criminal justice system; isolation in rural areas; enterprising solutions to job creation; targeted, issue-based youth work; those living in poverty.
WHAT IS NOT FUNDED Individuals; statutory organisations; national charities without a local branch or project; charities with substantial unrestricted reserves; medical or health establishments; schools or educational establishments; infrastructure organisations or second-tier bodies; projects principally benefitting people outside Cumbria or North Lancashire; retrospective funding; expeditions or overseas travel; the promotion of religion; animal welfare. Organisations with a turnover greater than £1 million are unlikely to be supported.
TYPE OF GRANT Most grants are multi-year revenue grants for core costs (salaries and running costs); capital projects are also considered if they will 'make a tangible difference to a local community'.
RANGE OF GRANTS Most up to £20,000.
SAMPLE GRANTS Cumbria Community Foundation – Flood Recovery Fund (£100,000); North Allerdale Development Trust (£20,000); Brathay Trust (£17,000); Cumbria Youth Alliance (£16,000); Shackles Off Youth Project, Strawberry Fields Training and Women's Community Matters – Barrow (£10,000 each); Furness Multicultural Community Forum (£5,000); Silloth Rugby Club (£4,000); Soundwave (£3,500); 1st Morecambe and Heysham Boys Brigade (£400).
FINANCES *Year* 2015 *Income* £728,827 *Grants* £345,400 *Grants to organisations* £345,400 *Assets* £30,897,002
TRUSTEES Madeleine Scott; Susan Bagot; Alexander Scott; Joanna Plumptre; Melanie Wotherspoon; Malcolm Tillyer; Revd John Bannister; Carol Ostermeyer; Steven Swallow; Christine Knipe; John McGovern.
OTHER INFORMATION Grants were made to 37 organisations during the year. Applicants should refer to the trust's website which is very comprehensive and covers all aspects of the grant-making process.
HOW TO APPLY Application forms can be downloaded from the trust's website, or obtained by writing to the trust. Grants of over £4,000 are awarded at one of three trustee meetings held in March, July and November – contact the trust for exact dates. Smaller grants are considered every three to four weeks. Unsuccessful applicants should wait a year before re-applying. Charities should not apply to this trust and the Frieda Scott Charitable Trust at the same time.
WHO TO APPLY TO Chris Batten, Director, Stricklandgate House, 92 Stricklandgate, Kendal, Cumbria LA9 4PU *Tel.* 01539 742608 *Email* info@fcsct.org.uk *Website* www.fcsct.org.uk

■ The Frieda Scott Charitable Trust

CC NO 221593 **ESTABLISHED** 1962
WHERE FUNDING CAN BE GIVEN Old county of Westmorland and the area covered by South Lakeland District Council.
WHO CAN BENEFIT Small local charities, parish halls, youth groups and occasionally locally based work of larger charities.
WHAT IS FUNDED A very wide range of registered charities concerned with supporting

disadvantaged and vulnerable people, particularly: older people; people with disabilities; people with mental health problems; people with learning difficulties; children and young people; family support work; victims or survivors of abuse and substance misuse; carers; community projects and facilities; access to services for rural communities; community arts and music; amateur sports clubs; uniformed youth groups.

WHAT IS NOT FUNDED Retrospective funding; statutory bodies (including health and education); promotion of religion or places of worship; individuals; animal welfare, environment or heritage causes; museums and art galleries; national charities (apart from local branches).

TYPE OF GRANT Multi-year grants; one-off grants; revenue or capital costs; occasional larger grants.

RANGE OF GRANTS £200 to £20,000. Most grants are below £10,000.

SAMPLE GRANTS Cumbria Flood Recovery Fund – Cumbria Community Foundation (£50,000); The Birchall Trust (£18,500); Sight Advice South Lakes (£12,000); Dignity with Dementia (£10,300); Life Education Centres for Cumbria (£7,000); South Cumbria Musical Festival (£4,200); Newbiggin Recreation Committee and Temple Sowerby Village Hall (£3,500 each); Eden Carers (£3,000); 1st Windermere Sea Scout Group (£2,500); Cumbria DeafVision (£1,000).

FINANCES *Year* 2015/16 *Income* £298,919 *Grants* £354,049 *Grants to organisations* £354,049 *Assets* £8,981,307

TRUSTEES Stuart Fairclough; Philip Hoyle; Richard Brownson; Vanda Lambton; Peter Smith; Samantha Scott; Hugo Pring; Laura Southern; Samuel Rayner.

OTHER INFORMATION 41 organisations were awarded grants in 2015/16.

HOW TO APPLY Application forms can be downloaded from the trust's website or requested in writing or by phone. Applications are considered at meetings in March, June, September and December and should be sent at least a month in advance. Grants of less than £3,500 are considered by the Small Grants Committee, which meets between the main trustee meetings. Applicants are welcomed to contact the Trust Secretary for an informal discussion before application. Unsuccessful applicants must wait a year before re-applying. Charities should not apply to this trust and the Francis C. Scott Charitable Trust at the same time.

WHO TO APPLY TO Naomi Brown, Trust Secretary, Stricklandgate House, 92 Stricklandgate, Kendal, Cumbria LA9 4PU *Tel.* 01539 742608 *Email* info@fcsct.org.uk *Website* www.friedascott.org.uk

■ Sir Samuel Scott of Yews Trust

CC NO 220878 **ESTABLISHED** 1951

WHERE FUNDING CAN BE GIVEN UK.

WHO CAN BENEFIT Medical research bodies.

WHAT IS FUNDED Medical research.

WHAT IS NOT FUNDED Core funding; purely clinical work; individuals (although research by an individual may be funded if sponsored by a registered charity through which the application is made); research leading to higher degrees (unless the departmental head concerned certifies that the work is of real scientific importance); medical students' elective periods; or expeditions (unless involving an element of genuine medical research).

TYPE OF GRANT One-off and project costs.

RANGE OF GRANTS Usually £1,000 to £10,000.

SAMPLE GRANTS Cystic Fibrosis Trust and Epilepsy Society (£10,000 each); Bowel Disease Research Foundation, Meningitis Now, National Osteoporosis Society and Wellbeing of Women (£5,000 each); Islet Research Laboratory (£3,000); Blond McIndoe Research Foundation (£2,000); Clatterbridge Cancer Charity and Crohn's in Childhood Research Association (£1,000 each).

FINANCES *Year* 2015/16 *Income* £133,012 *Grants* £120,000 *Grants to organisations* £120,000 *Assets* £6,761,763

TRUSTEES Edward Haslewood Perks; Hermione Stanford; Lady Phoebe Scott.

OTHER INFORMATION Grants were made to 32 organisations during the year.

HOW TO APPLY Apply in writing to the correspondent. The trustees hold their half-yearly meetings in April and October.

WHO TO APPLY TO The Trustees, c/o Currey and Co., 33 Queen Anne Street, London W1G 9HY *Tel.* 020 7802 2700

■ John Scott Trust Fund

SC NO SC003297 **ESTABLISHED** 1984

WHERE FUNDING CAN BE GIVEN Scotland, with some preference for Ayrshire.

WHO CAN BENEFIT Registered charities only.

WHAT IS FUNDED General charitable purposes, including causes such as health; social welfare; disability; children and young people.

WHAT IS NOT FUNDED Individuals.

RANGE OF GRANTS £1,000 to £40,000.

SAMPLE GRANTS Ayrshire Hospice (£40,000); Salvation Army (£30,000); The Ark (£15,000); Combat Stress, Macmillan Cancer Support and National Trust for Scotland (£10,000 each); Save the Children (£8,000); Ayrshire Fiddle Orchestra (£5,000); Parkinson's Disease Society (£4,000); Ayrshire Society for the Deaf (£1,000).

FINANCES *Year* 2015/16 *Income* £95,368 *Grants* £228,000 *Grants to organisations* £228,000 *Assets* £2,468,027

OTHER INFORMATION Grants were made to 24 organisations during the year.

HOW TO APPLY Applications are not invited.

WHO TO APPLY TO The Trustees, Kilpatrick and Walker Solicitors, 4 Wellington Square, Ayr KA7 1EN

■ The ScottishPower Energy People Trust

SC NO SC036980 **ESTABLISHED** 2005

WHERE FUNDING CAN BE GIVEN UK.

WHO CAN BENEFIT Charitable organisations.

WHAT IS FUNDED Projects aimed at alleviating fuel poverty, particularly those working with children, young people and families. Eligible projects include: energy efficiency advice; energy efficiency measures; income maximisation; fuel debt assistance.

WHAT IS NOT FUNDED Individuals; commercial organisations; fines, loans or outstanding balances on credit cards or catalogues. Overheads or administration costs should not generally exceed 12.5% of the total funding requested for a project.

TYPE OF GRANT Project costs for up to a year.

RANGE OF GRANTS Up to £50,000.

SAMPLE GRANTS Suffolk Community Foundation (£45,000); Health Energy Advice Team (£44,500); Peterborough Environment City Trust (£44,000); Disability Resource Centre (£41,500); Greener Kirkcaldy (£40,500); East Ayrshire Carers Centre (£36,000); South Liverpool Homes (£31,000); Dartford Citizens Advice (£27,500); East Durham Community Development Trust Ltd (£20,500).

FINANCES *Year* 2015 *Income* £3,301,180 *Grants* £1,091,706 *Grants to organisations* £1,091,706 *Assets* £3,149,626

TRUSTEES Douglas McLaren; Joan Fraser; Neil Hartwell; Norman Kerr; Dr Bill Sheldrick; Alan Hughes; Peter Sumby.

OTHER INFORMATION Established by ScottishPower in 2005, the trust has distributed over £12.6 million to projects run by grassroots organisations that help people who are on low incomes, live in poor housing or suffer ill health.

HOW TO APPLY Applications should be made using the form on the trust's website. Deadlines are posted on the website and a maximum of 30 applications are considered at each meeting of the trustees. Applicants will be notified whether their application was successful within two weeks of a meeting.

WHO TO APPLY TO Irene Murdoch, Environmental and Social Policy Support Assistant, ScottishPower Energy Retail Ltd, Cathcart Business Park, 144 Spean Street, Glasgow G44 4BE *Tel.* 0141 614 4480 *Email* SPEnergyPeopleTrust@ScottishPower.com *Website* www.energypeopletrust.com

■ The ScottishPower Foundation

SC NO SC043862 **ESTABLISHED** 2013

WHERE FUNDING CAN BE GIVEN UK.

WHO CAN BENEFIT Registered charities and non-profit organisations.

WHAT IS FUNDED Education; environment; arts, heritage, culture or science; prevention or relief of poverty; relief of those in need by disability or disadvantage; citizenship or community development.

WHAT IS NOT FUNDED Projects outside the UK; general appeals and circulars, including contributions to endowment funds; marketing appeals or fundraising activities; medical research; travel or expeditions; projects intended to promote political or religious beliefs.

TYPE OF GRANT Project funding for up to one year.

RANGE OF GRANTS £5,000 to £50,000.

SAMPLE GRANTS Children's University (£50,000); RSPB Scotland (£32,500); National Library of Wales (£27,000); Prince and Princess of Wales Hospice (£25,000); Outward Bound Trust (£22,000); The Aloud Charity (£16,000); Music in Hospitals Scotland (£12,300); Shine (£10,000).

FINANCES *Year* 2015 *Income* £800,790 *Grants* £764,947 *Grants to organisations* £764,947 *Assets* £126,162

TRUSTEES Mike Thornton; Elaine Bowker; Sarah Mistry; Keith Anderson; Ann McKechin.

OTHER INFORMATION Grants were made to 30 organisations during the year.

HOW TO APPLY Applications should be made on the form on the foundation's website, where deadlines are posted and guidance notes are available to download. Applications usually open in the summer for projects in the subsequent year.

WHO TO APPLY TO María Elena Sanz Arcas, Company Secretary, 1 Atlantic Quay, Robertson Street, Glasgow G2 8SP *Tel.* 0800 027 0072 *Email* scottishpowerfoundation@scottishpower.com *Website* www.scottishpower.com/pages/about_the_scottishpower_foundation

■ The Scouloudi Foundation

CC NO 205685 **ESTABLISHED** 1962

WHERE FUNDING CAN BE GIVEN UK or overseas.

WHO CAN BENEFIT UK-registered charities supporting a range of charitable purposes. The foundation also supports the Institute of Historical Research, University of London, for publications, research and fellowships.

WHAT IS FUNDED Education; children and young people; environment; humanities; overseas aid; disability; medicine, health and hospices; social welfare; armed forces and sailors.

TYPE OF GRANT There are three categories of grant: an annual donation for historical research and fellowships to the Institute of Historical Research at the University of London; recurring grants to a regular list of charities; and 'special donations' which are one-off grants, usually in connection with capital projects.

RANGE OF GRANTS Typically £1,000 to £5,000.

SAMPLE GRANTS Institute of Historical Research – University of London (£77,000); Greater London Fund for the Blind, Help the Hospices, Oxfam and Shooting Star Chase (£5,000 each); Campaign to Protect Rural England, Mental Health Foundation, Royal Sailors Rest and Turtle Key Arts (£3,000 each); Fine Cell Work and Tree Council (£1,300 each).

FINANCES *Year* 2015/16 *Income* £210,649 *Grants* £204,697 *Grants to organisations* £204,697 *Assets* £6,507,339

TRUSTEES Sarah Baxter; David Marnham; James Sewell.

OTHER INFORMATION Grants were made to 40 organisations during the year.

HOW TO APPLY Only Historical Grants are open for applications. Copies of the regulations and application forms for the foundation's Historical Awards can be obtained from: The Secretary, The Scouloudi Foundation Historical Awards Committee, c/o Institute of Historical Research, University of London, Senate House, Malet Street, London WC1E 7HU.

WHO TO APPLY TO The Trustees of the Scouloudi Foundation, c/o Haysmacintyre, 26 Red Lion Square, London WC1R 4AG *Tel.* 020 7969 5500 *Email* pholden@haysmacintyre.com

■ The SDL Foundation

CC NO 1127138 **ESTABLISHED** 2008

WHERE FUNDING CAN BE GIVEN Worldwide.

WHO CAN BENEFIT Charitable organisations.

WHAT IS FUNDED Disadvantaged communities; relief of poverty and social welfare; sustainable economic growth and regeneration.

WHAT IS NOT FUNDED No grants will be given to causes where trustees or SDL employees would directly benefit. The foundation will also not support political or discriminatory activities; or those appeals that are recognised as being large or well known.

TYPE OF GRANT Mostly multi-year grants.

RANGE OF GRANTS £1,000 to £100,000.

SAMPLE GRANTS The Prince's Trust (£100,000); Habitat for Humanity – Romania (£55,000); Hatua Likoni – Kenya (£20,000); Bead For Life – Uganda (£16,200); Santa Maria Education Fund – Paraguay and St Wilfrid's (£15,000 each);

Microloan Foundation – Malawi (£5,000); Translators Without Borders (£3,400).

FINANCES *Year* 2015 *Income* £180,038 *Grants* £281,010 *Grants to organisations* £281,010 *Assets* £148,827

TRUSTEES Mark Lancaster; Alastair Gordon; Michelle Wilson; Roddy Temperley.

OTHER INFORMATION The SDL Foundation is the corporate charity of SDL PLC, which provides software for language translation and interpretation services. The foundation prefers to support projects where SDL employees can complement support with their own fundraising initiatives.

HOW TO APPLY Only causes supported and sponsored by SDL employees will be considered by the SDL Foundation. Contact the foundation by email for further information on how to request the support of staff and application procedures.

WHO TO APPLY TO Alastair Gordon, Trustee, SDL PLC, 64 Castelnau, London SW13 9EX *Email* agordon@sdl.com *Website* www.sdl.com/about/corporate-citizenship/foundation

■ Seafarers Hospital Society

CC NO 231724 **ESTABLISHED** 1999

WHERE FUNDING CAN BE GIVEN UK.

WHO CAN BENEFIT Medical, care and welfare organisations.

WHAT IS FUNDED Welfare of seafarers and their dependants.

SAMPLE GRANTS Seafarers Advice and Information Line (£240,500); Maritime Charities Group – Development Programme (£5,000); Annual National Service for Seafarers (£150).

FINANCES *Year* 2015 *Income* £514,455 *Grants* £245,693 *Grants to organisations* £245,693 *Assets* £9,024,037

TRUSTEES Peter McEwen; Jeffrey Jenkinson; Mark Carden; Alexander Nairne; Capt. Colin Stewart; Cdr Frank Leonard; Rupert Chichester; Dr Charlotte Mendes da Costa; Graham Lane; Dr John Carter; Mike Jess.

OTHER INFORMATION 320 grants totalling £127,500 were also awarded to individuals, mainly for medical assistance and physiotherapy.

HOW TO APPLY Application forms are available from the correspondent. Applicants are encouraged to contact the correspondent before making application.

WHO TO APPLY TO Peter Coulson, General Secretary, 29 King William Walk, Greenwich, London SE10 9HX *Tel.* 020 8858 3696 *Fax* 020 8293 9630 *Email* admin@seahospital.org.uk *Website* www.seahospital.org.uk

■ Seafarers UK (King George's Fund for Sailors)

CC NO 226446 **ESTABLISHED** 1917

WHERE FUNDING CAN BE GIVEN UK and Commonwealth countries.

WHO CAN BENEFIT Registered charities – specialist maritime charities and organisations, often small and local.

WHAT IS FUNDED Projects, services or activities that support seafarers, ex-seafarers and their dependants who are facing hardship. Also, activities run by maritime youth organisations with the aim of promoting careers at sea. The charity has four broad programme priorities: older seafarers over the usual age of retirement and their dependants; working age seafarers who are working at sea, former seafarers under the age of retirement and Merchant Navy cadets and trainees; families and dependants of current or former seafarers who are of working age; young people in maritime youth groups with a focus on those considering or pursuing a career at sea. Grants are made for purposes such as: social welfare; health and care services; maritime education and training; advice and information; accommodation and supported housing.

WHAT IS NOT FUNDED The fund does not make grants directly to individuals but rather helps other organisations which do this. Grant requests for the following are generally not considered: sailing or youth clubs (funding for youth organisations is directed at those that can demonstrate a clear link between their activities and young people choosing or beginning a career at sea); marine societies and sea cadets – individual units (the promotion of sailing or youth work are, by themselves, activities not currently supported by the charity); the promotion of religious beliefs; political/campaigning organisations; activities which are the legal obligation of the state; endowments; loans or interest payments.

TYPE OF GRANT Project costs; core costs, such as staff salaries or general running costs; some capital costs (although substantial capital funding is unlikely).

RANGE OF GRANTS From £1,000 to £180,000. Average grant during the year was £28,000.

SAMPLE GRANTS Nautilus Welfare Fund (£1.17 million); Fishermen's Mission (£176,000); Royal Navy and Royal Marines Children's Fund (£100,000); Human Rights at Sea (£98,000); Carlton Education and Enterprise (£35,000); Plymouth Communities Befriending Consortium CIC (£10,800); Somme Nursing Home (£10,000); British Ex-Services Wheelchair Sports Association (£9,500); Scottish Shipping Benevolent Association (£2,200); Ahoy Centre (£1,000).

FINANCES *Year* 2015 *Income* £2,735,000 *Grants* £3,579,000 *Grants to organisations* £3,579,000 *Assets* £37,738,000

TRUSTEES Mark Carden; Capt. David Parsons; Michael Acland; Nadeem Azhar; Christine Gould; Christian Marr; Simon Rivett-Carnac; Hon. Geffrey Evans; Mark Dickinson; Vice Adm. Peter Wilkinson; Capt. Roger Barker; Dyan Sterling; Cdre Peter Buxton; Jeremy Monroe; Evelyn Strouts; Duncan Bain; Natalie Shaw.

OTHER INFORMATION The 2015 grant total included a Centenary Grant, marking the charity's 100th anniversary, of £1.17 million (the largest grant ever made by Seafarers UK) to Nautilus Welfare Fund for the building of a Seafarers UK Centenary Wing in their supported accommodation facilities in Wallasey. Grants were made to 67 organisations during the year, including 14 which had not previously received funding from the charity.

HOW TO APPLY Applications for the Seafarers UK Grants Programme can be made on the charity's website, where guidelines are also available to download. Applications for the Merchant Navy Fund, aimed at helping UK Merchant Navy seafarers and their dependants, can be made using the same form. Only one application for funding of a particular project or service may be submitted per calendar year, but an organisation can apply for funding for different services or projects during the same year. Applications can be made at any time; decisions are made around six times a year. Applications of up to £10,000 can take at least six weeks for a decision; applications for more than £10,000 can take at least three months to assess.

WHO TO APPLY TO Deborah Layde, Grants Director, 8 Hatherley Street, London SW1P 2YY *Tel.* 020 7932 0000 *Fax* 020 7932 0095 *Email* grants@seafarers.uk *Website* www.seafarers-uk.org

■ The Searchlight Electric Charitable Trust

CC NO 801644 **ESTABLISHED** 1988

WHERE FUNDING CAN BE GIVEN UK with a preference for Manchester and the surrounding areas.

WHO CAN BENEFIT Registered charities.

WHAT IS FUNDED Teaching and understanding of the Jewish faith; social welfare and care of older people and those in ill health, and their dependants.

WHAT IS NOT FUNDED Individuals.

SAMPLE GRANTS Bnei Akiva Sefer Torah; Chabad Vilna; Community Security Trust; Guide Dogs for the Blind; Heathlands; Langdon College; Lubavitch Manchester; Manchester Eruv Committee; Nightingales; Reshet and the Purim Fund; Sense; The Federation; United Jewish Israel Appeal (UJIA); Young Israel Synagogue.

FINANCES *Year* 2015/16 *Income* £1,390 *Grants* £113,155 *Grants to organisations* £113,155 *Assets* £1,240,216

TRUSTEES Morris Hamburger; David Hamburger; Herzl Hamburger; Daniel Hamburger.

HOW TO APPLY Apply in writing to the correspondent.

WHO TO APPLY TO David Hamburger, Trustee, 21 Brantwood Road, Salford M7 4EN *Tel.* 0161 203 3300

■ Sam and Bella Sebba Charitable Trust

CC NO 253351 **ESTABLISHED** 1967

WHERE FUNDING CAN BE GIVEN UK and Israel.

WHO CAN BENEFIT Charitable bodies with a preference for Jewish organisations.

WHAT IS FUNDED The trust looks to improve the quality of life of people across a broad range of activities. Key areas in the UK are palliative care, refugees, Jewish education and welfare. In Israel there is a focus on environment, human rights and social justice, disability and at-risk youth.

WHAT IS NOT FUNDED Individuals.

TYPE OF GRANT One-off and recurring.

RANGE OF GRANTS Up to £100,000.

SAMPLE GRANTS London School of Jewish Studies (£108,000); Bliss – the National Charity for the Newborn (£70,000); Association for Civil Rights in Israel (£59,500); Jewish Deaf Foundation, Liverpool Law Clinic and Movement for Freedom of Information (£25,000 each); New Israel Fund (£15,000); Physicians for Human Rights – Israel, Medical Justice and S. Pinter Youth Project (£10,000 each).

FINANCES *Year* 2015 *Income* £1,159,823 *Grants* £2,792,237 *Grants to organisations* £2,792,237 *Assets* £59,216,369

TRUSTEES Leigh Sebba; Victor Klein; Yoav Tangir; Odelia Sebba; Tamsin Doyle; Leah Hurst; Varda Shiffer.

OTHER INFORMATION In 2015 the trust made 115 grants.

HOW TO APPLY The trust is no longer accepting unsolicited applications. The annual report for 2015 states: 'The trustees expect to limit the number of new grantees during the next two years.' It appears that due to ongoing support to organisations already known to the trust, new applications are unlikely to be successful.

WHO TO APPLY TO David Lerner, Chief Executive, Office 19, 5th Floor, 63–66 Hatton Garden, London EC1N 8LE *Tel.* 020 7723 6028

■ The Seedfield Trust

CC NO 283463 **ESTABLISHED** 1981

WHERE FUNDING CAN BE GIVEN Worldwide.

WHO CAN BENEFIT Registered charities.

WHAT IS FUNDED Advancement of the Christian faith; relief of poverty; overseas aid.

WHAT IS NOT FUNDED The trustees tend to avoid core funding or activities that may require funding over a number of years.

TYPE OF GRANT One-off project grants, mostly for projects which are also receiving support from other sources; recurrent grants to charities which were supported by the founders of the trust.

RANGE OF GRANTS Up to £10,000; typically £500 to £1,000.

SAMPLE GRANTS Overseas Missionary Fellowship (£10,000); Keswick Ministries (£5,000 each); Mission Aviation Fellowship (£2,500); Christians Against Poverty, Manchester City Mission and Street Child (£1,000 each); Global Action UK, Messianic Testimony and Sports Chaplaincy UK (£500 each); St Thomas's Community Connection (£200).

FINANCES *Year* 2015 *Income* £423,704 *Grants* £103,050 *Grants to organisations* £103,050 *Assets* £8,174

TRUSTEES David Ryan; Paul Vipond; Valerie James; Eric Proudfoot; Charlotte Bampton; Mervyn Hull.

OTHER INFORMATION Grants were made to 65 organisations during the year.

HOW TO APPLY Apply in writing to the correspondent.

WHO TO APPLY TO Janet Buckler, Trustee, PO Box 94, Workington CA14 1BP *Email* seedfieldtrust@yahoo.co.uk

■ Leslie Sell Charitable Trust

CC NO 258699 **ESTABLISHED** 1969

WHERE FUNDING CAN BE GIVEN UK.

WHO CAN BENEFIT Scout and Guide associations and individuals.

WHAT IS FUNDED Assistance for projects, equipment, activities and trips within the Scout or Guide movements. There is also the Peter Sell Annual Award, which supports initiatives to widen engagement with the Scout and Guide movements.

WHAT IS NOT FUNDED The project or trip must be part of the Scouting or Guiding movement. The trust cannot award grants within three months of an event date or the date of departure for a trip.

TYPE OF GRANT Usually one-off payments towards a small project, such as building repair works, transport, trips (in the UK or overseas), events or equipment.

RANGE OF GRANTS Up to £5,000.

SAMPLE GRANTS A list of beneficiaries was not available.

FINANCES *Year* 2015/16 *Income* £148,229 *Grants* £121,232 *Grants to organisations* £121,232 *Assets* £21,519

TRUSTEES Mary Wiltshire; Adrian Sell; Nicola Coggins.

HOW TO APPLY Applications should be made with an application form (available from the trust's website) accompanied by a letter on official notepaper. The trust provides guidance for applicants on its website. Applications should include clear details of the project or purpose for which funds are required, together with an estimate of total costs and details of any funds raised by the group or individual for the project. The trustees meet to review applications once per month throughout the year. The trustees are unable to consider applications for a trip or event date within three months of submission date. Applications to the Peter Sell Annual Award usually have to be submitted by the end of September. See the trust's website for full guidelines and future deadlines.

WHO TO APPLY TO Sharon Long, Secretary, 1st Floor, 8–10 Upper Marlborough Road, St Albans, Hertfordshire AL1 3UR *Tel.* 01727 843603 *Email* admin@iplltd.co.uk *Website* www.leslieselIct.org.uk

■ The Sellafield Charity Trust Fund

CC NO 517829 **ESTABLISHED** 1978

WHERE FUNDING CAN BE GIVEN Communities local to Sellafield sites – particularly Copeland, Allerdale and Warrington.

WHO CAN BENEFIT Charities and voluntary organisations. There is a preference for local rather than national charities.

WHAT IS FUNDED According to its website, the charity focuses on the following areas: young people's education and skills; small community-focused projects; improving the life chances of individuals; making a difference in disadvantaged areas of local communities; contributing to cultural vibrancy in local communities; improving health and well-being in local communities.

WHAT IS NOT FUNDED General running costs, including staff costs; ongoing project costs (apart from in exceptional cases); commercial sponsorship; individuals; third party advertising; political campaigning.

TYPE OF GRANT Full project funding; part-funding for projects. One-off.

RANGE OF GRANTS Up to £5,000.

SAMPLE GRANTS Citizens Advice; Creative Wellbeing; Egremont RUFC; Fit for Life; Healthy Hopes; Mirehouse Resident Group; Nurture Lakeland; Rosehill Arts Trust; Watchtree Wheelers; West Cumbria Domestic Violence; Wigton Baths Trust.

FINANCES *Year* 2016 *Income* £107,966 *Grants* £52,217 *Grants to organisations* £52,217 *Assets* £119,144

TRUSTEES Christine Lofthouse; Willie Reid; Ian Withycombe.

HOW TO APPLY Applications can be made using the form provided on the charity's website.

WHO TO APPLY TO Willie Reid, Trustee, MOC Office, B906, Sellafield Ltd, Sellafield, Cumbria CA20 1PG *Tel.* 01946 771742 *Email* willie.reid@sellafieldsites.com *Website* sustainability.sellafieldsites.com/community/charitable-donations

■ Sellata Ltd

CC NO 285429 **ESTABLISHED** 1980

WHERE FUNDING CAN BE GIVEN UK and Israel.

WHO CAN BENEFIT Charitable organisations.

WHAT IS FUNDED Advancement of the Orthodox Jewish faith; relief of poverty.

SAMPLE GRANTS A list of beneficiaries was not available.

FINANCES *Year* 2015/16 *Income* £405,846 *Grants* £325,810 *Grants to organisations* £325,810 *Assets* £432,987

TRUSTEES Eliezer Benedikt; Nechy Benedikt; Pinchas Benedikt.

OTHER INFORMATION A list of beneficiaries was not available.

HOW TO APPLY Apply in writing to the correspondent.

WHO TO APPLY TO Eliezer Benedikt, Trustee, 29 Fountayne Road, London N16 7EA *Email* management@abarisltd.co.uk

■ SEM Charitable Trust

CC NO 265831 **ESTABLISHED** 1973

WHERE FUNDING CAN BE GIVEN UK and USA.

WHO CAN BENEFIT Environmental organisations.

WHAT IS FUNDED The trust makes grants to specialist organisations working on climate change. The trust previously supported special educational needs and community development, but changed its focus in 2015.

SAMPLE GRANTS Sierra Club (£41,500); World Resource Institute (£41,000); Carbon Tracker (£30,000); EDF Action Fund and NRDC Action Fund (£20,900 each); Rainforest Alliance (£19,000); Friends of the Earth (£12,500).

FINANCES *Year* 2015/16 *Income* £90,436 *Grants* £185,906 *Grants to organisations* £185,906 *Assets* £769,235

TRUSTEES Michael Radomir; Craig Sams; Christopher Hunter.

HOW TO APPLY The trustees advise against making an application for a grant unless invited to do so by the trust.

WHO TO APPLY TO Michael Radomir, Trustee, 25 Blackstone Road, London NW2 6DA *Tel.* 07771 756065

■ The Seven Fifty Trust

CC NO 298886 **ESTABLISHED** 1988

WHERE FUNDING CAN BE GIVEN UK and worldwide.

WHO CAN BENEFIT Registered charities.

WHAT IS FUNDED General charitable purposes and advancement of the Christian religion. The trustees mainly give to causes they have supported for many years.

WHAT IS NOT FUNDED Unsolicited requests are not supported.

RANGE OF GRANTS Up to £20,000.

SAMPLE GRANTS All Saints Church (£23,500); Langham Partnership (£5,900); Sussex Gospel Partnership and Tearfund (£4,400 each); Open Doors (£3,000); Christian Solidarity Worldwide (£2,800); The Diocese of York (£1,000); Iwerne Holidays (£800); Church Mission Society (£400).

FINANCES *Year* 2015/16 *Income* £131,963 *Grants* £86,625 *Grants to organisations* £86,375 *Assets* £2,661,418

TRUSTEES Revd Andrew Cornes; Katherine Cornes; Cannon Jonathan Clark; Mary Clark.

OTHER INFORMATION Grants were made to 34 organisations during the year. There was one grant of £250 made to an individual.

HOW TO APPLY Unsolicited applications will not be considered.

WHO TO APPLY TO Revd Andrew Cornes, Trustee, 12 Cavendish Road, Eastbourne BN22 8EN *Tel.* 01323 655502

■ The Severn Trent Water Charitable Trust Fund

CC NO 1108278 **ESTABLISHED** 1997

WHERE FUNDING CAN BE GIVEN The area covered by Severn Trent Water Ltd, which stretches from Wales to the east of Leicestershire and from the Humber estuary down to the Bristol Channel.

WHO CAN BENEFIT Organisations that provide money advice and debt counselling services. Individuals in hardship and/or financial difficulties.

WHAT IS FUNDED Relief of poverty, money advice and debt counselling. There are two grants programmes: Small Grants, for developing or enhancing an organisation's activities around money or debt advice and financial literacy; and Revenue Project Funding, for projects lasting up to three years, with particular preference for organisations delivering services in the rural parts of the trust's area of benefit.

WHAT IS NOT FUNDED Only applications from organisations within the Severn Trent Trust Fund area will be considered. A map of this area can be found on the trust's website.

TYPE OF GRANT Small, one-off grants for project costs, capital expenditure, staff training or promotional work; multi-year revenue project funding.

SAMPLE GRANTS Birmingham Disability Resource Centre; CARES Sandwell; Castle Vale Tenants and Residents Alliance; Citizens Advice Leicester; Community Focus; Coventry Citizens Advice; Ladywood Project; Life Matters; Sherwood Forest Community Church; South Birmingham Young Homeless Project; Wood End Advice and Information Centre.

FINANCES *Year* 2015/16 *Income* £4,816,596 *Grants* £2,901,091 *Grants to organisations* £166,194 *Assets* £1,949,281

TRUSTEES Elizabeth Pusey; David Vaughan; Alexandra Gribbin; Lowri Williams; Clive Mottram; Andrew Phelps; Stuart Braley.

OTHER INFORMATION The amount of grants given to individuals totalled £2.7 million. Grants awarded to organisations totalled £166,000.

HOW TO APPLY Organisations interested in applying for a grant should contact the trust on 0121 321 1324 or email office@sttf.org.uk to discuss current funding criteria and future funding opportunities. Application forms for individuals are provided on the website.

WHO TO APPLY TO The Trustees, Severn Trent Trust Fund, FREEPOST RLZE – EABT – SHSA, Sutton Coldfield B72 1TJ *Tel.* 0121 355 7766 *Email* office@sttf.org.uk *Website* www.sttf.org.uk

■ The Cyril Shack Trust

CC NO 264270 **ESTABLISHED** 1972

WHERE FUNDING CAN BE GIVEN UK.

WHO CAN BENEFIT Charitable organisations.

WHAT IS FUNDED General charitable purposes.

SAMPLE GRANTS Finchley Road Synagogue; Nightingale House; St John's Wood Synagogue.

FINANCES *Year* 2015/16 *Income* £108,113 *Grants* £119,914 *Grants to organisations* £119,914 *Assets* £694,144

TRUSTEES Jonathan Shack; Cyril Shack.

OTHER INFORMATION A list of recent beneficiaries was not provided in the 2015/16 accounts.

HOW TO APPLY Apply in writing to the correspondent.

WHO TO APPLY TO The Trustees, c/o Lubbock Fine Chartered Accountants, Paternoster House, 65 St Paul's Churchyard, London EC4M 8AB *Tel.* 020 7490 7766

■ The Jean Shanks Foundation

CC NO 293108 **ESTABLISHED** 1985

WHERE FUNDING CAN BE GIVEN UK.

WHO CAN BENEFIT Medical research institutions, i.e. medical schools, medical royal colleges and similar bodies. Also medical students.

WHAT IS FUNDED Medical research, education and training; grants for medical students (made to medical schools), particularly intercalated year awards to allow an extra year of research during training.

WHAT IS NOT FUNDED Projects of a kind already supported by bodies such as the Medical Research Council or the Wellcome Trust; capital items, although the trustees will occasionally consider applications for the creation or expansion of libraries for medical education or research institutions; building projects will only be supported in exceptional circumstances; research not relating to pathology; financial hardship.

TYPE OF GRANT Research; scholarships; up to three years.

RANGE OF GRANTS £7,000 to £50,000.

SAMPLE GRANTS Pathological Society of Great Britain and Ireland (£46,000); Academy of Medical Sciences (£40,000); University of Nottingham (£21,000); Brighton and Sussex Medical School, University of Bristol and University of Manchester (£15,000 each); University of Exeter (£10,100); University of Glasgow (£7,800).

FINANCES *Year* 2015/16 *Income* £400,139 *Grants* £337,897 *Grants to organisations* £337,897 *Assets* £20,771,093

TRUSTEES Alistair Jones; Prof. Sir Nicholas Wright; Prof. Andrew Carr; Prof. Sir James Underwood; Eric Rothbarth; Dr Julian Axe; Prof. Adrienne Flanagan.

OTHER INFORMATION Grants were made to 20 organisations during the year totalling £338,000.

HOW TO APPLY Application forms can be requested from the correspondent. Full grant guidelines are available on the foundation's website.

WHO TO APPLY TO Paula Price-Davies, Foundation Administrator, Peppard Cottage, Peppard Common, Henley-on-Thames, Oxfordshire RG9 5LB *Tel.* 01491 628232 *Email* administrator@jeanshanksfoundation.org *Website* www.jeanshanksfoundation.org

■ The Shanley Charitable Trust

CC NO 1103323 **ESTABLISHED** 2003

WHERE FUNDING CAN BE GIVEN Worldwide.

WHO CAN BENEFIT Recognised international charities.

WHAT IS FUNDED Relief of poverty and hardship.

TYPE OF GRANT Recurring; one-off.

RANGE OF GRANTS £10,000 to £100,000.

SAMPLE GRANTS WaterAid (£110,000); SOS Children (£60,000); Disasters Emergency Committee – Ebola Appeal, Disasters Emergency Committee – Gaza Appeal, Disasters Emergency Committee – Nepal Appeal; Unicef Vanuatu Appeal (£10,000 each).

FINANCES *Year* 2015/16 *Income* £117,859 *Grants* £170,000 *Grants to organisations* £170,000 *Assets* £3,247,697

TRUSTEES Roger Lander; Steve Atkins; C. Shanley.

HOW TO APPLY Apply in writing to the correspondent.

WHO TO APPLY TO Steve Atkins, Trustee, Knowles Benning Solicitors, 32 High Street, Shefford SG17 5DG *Tel.* 01462 814824

The Shanly Foundation

CC NO 1065044 **ESTABLISHED** 1997

WHERE FUNDING CAN BE GIVEN Mainly Berkshire and Buckinghamshire; also: London; Hampshire; Hertfordshire; Oxfordshire; Surrey.

WHO CAN BENEFIT Registered charities; sports and social groups; community organisations; scout and guide groups.

WHAT IS FUNDED General charitable purposes.

WHAT IS NOT FUNDED Grants are only made to individuals in exceptional circumstances.

RANGE OF GRANTS Average grant: £3,000.

SAMPLE GRANTS Beech Lodge School Ltd (£293,000); Scouting Association (£200,000); Thornley Activity Centre (£30,000); Thames Valley Adventure Playground (£20,000); ShelterBox Trust (£15,000); Purple Patch Running (£11,000); Adoption UK (£8,500); Lions Club of Windsor (£1,600).

FINANCES *Year* 2015 *Income* £1,529,082 *Grants* £1,438,737 *Grants to organisations* £1,438,737 *Assets* £2,162,879

TRUSTEES Michael James Shanly; Tamra Booth; Tim Potter; Donald Tucker.

OTHER INFORMATION According to the website, over 360 grants were made in 2015.

HOW TO APPLY Apply in writing to the correspondent.

WHO TO APPLY TO Allan Davies, Sorbon, 24–26 Aylesbury End, Beaconsfield HP9 1LW *Tel.* 01494 671331 *Email* shanly.foundation@shanlygroup.com *Website* www.shanlyfoundation.com

The Shanti Charitable Trust

CC NO 1064813 **ESTABLISHED** 1997

WHERE FUNDING CAN BE GIVEN UK, with preference for West Yorkshire, and overseas.

WHO CAN BENEFIT Charitable organisations.

WHAT IS FUNDED General charitable purposes; Christian causes; health; international development.

WHAT IS NOT FUNDED Gap year students; political or animal welfare causes.

TYPE OF GRANT One-off and up to three years; capital and revenue funding.

RANGE OF GRANTS £500 to £12,500.

SAMPLE GRANTS Ear Aid – Nepal (£12,500); INF Camps (£10,500); St John's Church (£9,500); Prabhav (£8,000); Development Associates International (£5,500); Church Mission Society and World Outreach (£500 each).

FINANCES *Year* 2015/16 *Income* £19,309 *Grants* £54,000 *Grants to organisations* £54,000

TRUSTEES Barbara Gill; Andrew Gill; Ross Hyett.

OTHER INFORMATION This charity's latest accounts were not available to view on the Charity Commission's website due to its low income. We have therefore estimated the grant total based on previous years' information.

HOW TO APPLY Applications may be made in writing to the correspondent; however, note that the trust's Charity Commission record states: 'most funding/grants are made to needs and contacts personally known to the trustees'.

WHO TO APPLY TO Barbara Gill, Trustee, Parkside, Littlemoor, Queensbury, Bradford, West Yorkshire BD13 1DB

ShareGift (The Orr Mackintosh Foundation)

CC NO 1052686 **ESTABLISHED** 1995

WHERE FUNDING CAN BE GIVEN UK.

WHO CAN BENEFIT UK-registered charities.

WHAT IS FUNDED General charitable purposes, guided by the wishes of the donors of shares, from where the charity's income derives.

WHAT IS NOT FUNDED Charities not registered in the UK.

RANGE OF GRANTS £500 to £250,000.

SAMPLE GRANTS The Royal Foundation (£500,000 in two grants); WaterAid (£150,000 in six grants); Combat Stress (£45,000 in two grants); Islington Centre for Refugees and Migrants (£30,000); NCVO (£25,000); Children with Cancer UK (£22,500 in two grants); Battersea Cats and Dogs Home (£20,000); St Mary's Church – Crawley (£15,000); Freedom from Torture (£12,500 in two grants); Place2Be (£10,000).

FINANCES *Year* 2015/16 *Income* £4,167,905 *Grants* £4,019,500 *Grants to organisations* £4,019,500 *Assets* £2,448,342

TRUSTEES Stephen Scott, Chair; Paul Killik; John Roundhill; Susan Swabey.

OTHER INFORMATION ShareGift made 628 grants to 491 charities during the year. In 2016 ShareGift made its first donations to charities in Republic of Ireland – refer to the website for more information.

HOW TO APPLY Applications for funding are not accepted and no response will be made to charities that send inappropriate applications. ShareGift supports a wide range of charities based on the value of shares donated and the number of suggestions it receives for a charity. Charities wishing to receive funding should encourage their supporters to donate unwanted shares to ShareGift. The website states that ShareGift is 'happy to talk to charities about the best way to promote ShareGift to their supporters and can provide template wording for websites and printed materials upon request' (contact Julian Roberts: Julian.Roberts@sharegift.org). Further information is available on the website.

WHO TO APPLY TO Julian Roberts, Chief Executive, PO Box 72253, London SW1P 9LQ *Tel.* 020 7930 3737 *Email* help@sharegift.org.uk *Website* www.sharegift.org

The Linley Shaw Foundation

CC NO 1034051 **ESTABLISHED** 1993

WHERE FUNDING CAN BE GIVEN UK.

WHO CAN BENEFIT Registered charities in rural locations.

WHAT IS FUNDED The conservation, preservation and restoration of the natural beauty of the countryside of the UK for the public benefit. In particular, charities that organise voluntary workers to achieve these objectives.

WHAT IS NOT FUNDED Individuals; non-charitable organisations; organisations whose aims or objects do not include conservation, preservation or restoration of the natural beauty of the UK countryside, even if the purpose of the grant would be eligible.

RANGE OF GRANTS £1,000 to £5,000.

SAMPLE GRANTS CAT Charity Ltd; Derbyshire Wildlife Trust; Future Trees; Nature Foundation; London Wildlife Trust; Plantlife; Surfers Against Sewage; The Campaign for National Parks; Whale and Dolphin Conservation Trust; Woodland Trust.

FINANCES *Year* 2015/16 *Income* £797,837 *Grants* £67,850 *Grants to organisations* £67,850 *Assets* £64,065

TRUSTEE NatWest Trust Services.

OTHER INFORMATION Grants were made to 25 organisations during the year.

HOW TO APPLY Apply in writing to the correspondent. The trustees meet regularly to review applications.

WHO TO APPLY TO Trust Services, NatWest Trust Services, Ground Floor Eastwood House, Glebe Road, Chelmsford CM1 1RS *Tel.* 01245 292492

■ The Shears Foundation

CC NO 1049907 **ESTABLISHED** 1994

WHERE FUNDING CAN BE GIVEN Mainly the north east of England, with some funding for the rest of the UK or national organisations.

WHO CAN BENEFIT Registered charities only.

WHAT IS FUNDED The foundation supports community development; environment; sustainable development;, health; social welfare; culture – all with a focus on education and raising awareness.

RANGE OF GRANTS Up to £100,000.

SAMPLE GRANTS Community Foundation Tyne and Wear and Northumberland – Linden Fund (£100,000); Bradford Grammar School, St Oswald's Hospice Children's Service and Whitley Fund for Nature (£50,000 each); Alnwick Garden (£47,500); Samling Foundation (£45,000); English National Opera (£30,000); Emmaus North (£25,000).

FINANCES *Year* 2015/16 *Income* £453,471 *Grants* £842,500 *Grants to organisations* £842,500 *Assets* £16,368,743

TRUSTEES G. Lyall; L. G. Shears; P. J. R. Shears; Patricia Shears; Bruce Warnes; Mark Horner; Richard Shears.

OTHER INFORMATION Grants were made to 48 organisations during the year.

HOW TO APPLY Apply in writing to the correspondent.

WHO TO APPLY TO Lyn Shears, Trustee, c/o The Community Foundation, Philanthropy House, Woodbine Road, Gosforth, Newcastle upon Tyne NE3 1DD *Email* lyn@shears.onyxnet.co.uk

■ The Sheepdrove Trust

CC NO 328369 **ESTABLISHED** 1989

WHERE FUNDING CAN BE GIVEN UK; some overseas.

WHO CAN BENEFIT Registered charities only.

WHAT IS FUNDED General charitable purposes, particularly sustainability; biodiversity; organic farming and nutrition; health and medical research; education and research; spiritual care; arts and culture.

RANGE OF GRANTS £250 to £100,000.

SAMPLE GRANTS Newcastle University – Professorial Fellowship (£500,000); University of the Arts London Scholarships (£75,000); Fundación para la Conservación de Ibiza y Formentera (£28,500); Vauxhall City Farm (£15,000); UNHCR – Relief in Syria (£10,000); Alzheimer's Society (£5,000); Greencuisine Trust (£4,300); Newbury Spring Festival (£4,000); Royal Opera House (£350); Oxfordshire Fungus Survey (£250).

FINANCES *Year* 2015 *Income* £28,104 *Grants* £999,613 *Grants to organisations* £927,021 *Assets* £19,116,984

TRUSTEES Barnabas Kindersley; Juliet Kindersley; Peter Kindersley; Harriet Treuille; Anabel Kindersley.

OTHER INFORMATION Apply in writing to the correspondent.

HOW TO APPLY Apply in writing to the correspondent.

WHO TO APPLY TO Juliet Kindersley, Trustee, Sheepdrove Farmhouse, Sheepdrove Organic Farm, Lambourn, Hungerford RG17 7UN *Tel.* 01488 674726 *Email* lynn.long@sheepdrove.com

■ The Sheffield Town Trust

CC NO 223760 **ESTABLISHED** 1297

WHERE FUNDING CAN BE GIVEN Sheffield.

WHO CAN BENEFIT Mainly local charities; national organisations will be supported if it can be demonstrated that the grants will be used exclusively for the benefit of Sheffield or its inhabitants; organisations which are not charities can also apply if they have charitable purposes.

WHAT IS FUNDED General charitable purposes in the Sheffield area.

WHAT IS NOT FUNDED Individuals; organisations that do not benefit Sheffield or its inhabitants; animal charities; political organisations; religious groups.

TYPE OF GRANT Mainly one-off; a few recurrent.

RANGE OF GRANTS Mainly under £5,000.

SAMPLE GRANTS St Luke's Hospice (£50,000); Sheffield Chines Culture Exchange Community (£10,000); 59th Sheffield Scout Group (£4,000); St Chad's Church (£3,500); Sheffield ME Group (£2,000); British Dyslexia Association and Target Housing (£1,500 each); Osbourne House Community Nursery (£1,000); Sheffield Poetry Festival (£500); Magistrates in the Community (£300).

FINANCES *Year* 2015 *Income* £542,130 *Grants* £396,405 *Grants to organisations* £396,405 *Assets* £8,015,090

TRUSTEES Nicholas Hutton; Kim Staniforth; Jonathan Brayshaw; Penny Jewitt; Jason Heath; Jane Ferretti; Jim Fulton; Marian Rae; Sarah Thomas; Oliver Stephenson; Zahid Hamid; Julie MacDonald; Mark Swales.

OTHER INFORMATION Grants were made to 164 organisations during the year.

HOW TO APPLY Apply in writing to the correspondent for consideration in February, May, August and November. Further information is on the website.

WHO TO APPLY TO George Connell, HLW Keeble Hawson, Commercial House, 14 Commercial Street, Sheffield S1 2AT *Tel.* 0114 272 2061 *Email* sheffieldtowntrust@hlwkeeblehawson.co.uk *Website* www.sheffieldtowntrust.org.uk

■ The Sheldon Trust

CC NO 242328 **ESTABLISHED** 1965

WHERE FUNDING CAN BE GIVEN West Midlands, with particular emphasis on Birmingham, Coventry, Dudley, Sandwell; Solihull; Wolverhampton; Warwickshire; also Greater London for holiday schemes; national charities for youth development.

WHO CAN BENEFIT UK-registered charities.

WHAT IS FUNDED Relief of poverty, particularly in disadvantaged areas. The following four areas are supported: community projects – usually local (West Midlands), mainly volunteer-led; special needs groups – supporting people (in the West Midlands) who are disadvantaged through disability, age or health; youth development – supporting 16- to 25-year-olds nationally, especially those not in education, employment or training; holidays for people who are disadvantaged – in the West Midlands or Greater London.

WHAT IS NOT FUNDED Purchase of buildings or vehicles; charities with an annual income of over £1 million and/or free unrestricted reserves to the value of more than six months of their annual expenditure.

TYPE OF GRANT Project costs; salaries; core costs; equipment; furnishings and refurbishments. Multi-year grants (up to three years) are considered where appropriate.

RANGE OF GRANTS Generally up to £10,000. Average grant for holiday schemes is £600.

SAMPLE GRANTS Safeline (£16,400); Regenerate (£15,000); Warwickshire Vision Support (£9,000); Sport 4 Life UK (£7,500); The Kenilworth Centre (£6,000); Piers Road New Communities Centre Association and Young Lewisham Project (£5,000 each); Peeblesshire Youth Trust (£1,000); Birmingham Phab Camps and Children with Cystic Fibrosis Dream Holidays (£600 each).

FINANCES *Year* 2015/16 *Income* £265,828 *Grants* £212,425 *Grants to organisations* £212,425 *Assets* £5,122,328

TRUSTEES Revd Roger Bidnell; Andrew Bidnell; John England; Rachel Beatton; Ruth Gibbins; Paul England.

OTHER INFORMATION Grants were made to 38 organisations totalling £212,500.

HOW TO APPLY Applications should be submitted online, via the website, where further information and guidance is also provided. Holiday applications differ from the other schemes. The trustees usually meet to consider applications in April and October. Any queries can be directed to the Trust Administrator via the contact form on the website.

WHO TO APPLY TO Alessandra Magri, Pothecary Witham Weld, 70 St George's Square, London SW1V 3RD *Tel.* 020 7821 8211 *Email* charities@pwwsolicitors.co.uk *Website* www.pwwsolicitors.co.uk/charity-grants/8-the-sheldon-trust

■ The Patricia and Donald Shepherd Charitable Trust

CC NO 272948 **ESTABLISHED** 1973

WHERE FUNDING CAN BE GIVEN Worldwide but particularly the north of England.

WHO CAN BENEFIT Charitable organisations.

WHAT IS FUNDED General charitable purposes; young people.

WHAT IS NOT FUNDED Individuals; local authorities.

SAMPLE GRANTS A list of beneficiaries was not available.

FINANCES *Year* 2015/16 *Income* £266,796 *Grants* £485,500 *Grants to organisations* £485,500 *Assets* £561,506

TRUSTEES Patricia Shepherd; Iain Robertson; Jane Robertson; Michael Shepherd; Christine Shepherd; Patrick Shepherd; Joseph Shepherd; Rory Robertson; Annabel Robertson.

OTHER INFORMATION Grants were made to 105 charitable organisations.

HOW TO APPLY Apply in writing to the correspondent. The trustees review and respond to all applications.

WHO TO APPLY TO The Trustees, 5 Cherry Lane, Dringhouses, York YO24 1QH

■ The Sylvia and Colin Shepherd Charitable Trust

CC NO 272788 **ESTABLISHED** 1973

WHERE FUNDING CAN BE GIVEN UK, with strong preference for York and North Yorkshire.

WHO CAN BENEFIT Charitable organisations.

WHAT IS FUNDED A wide range of general charitable purposes, such as social welfare; health; arts; young people, disability; education; older people. The accounts state that the trust has 'established a policy of making a large number of regular small grants over a wide range of organisations'.

WHAT IS NOT FUNDED Applications from individuals.

RANGE OF GRANTS Generally up to £5,000; many under £1,000.

SAMPLE GRANTS Accessible Arts and Media (£5,500); Two Ridings Community Foundation (£8,000); York Mind (£3,000); Carers UK (£2,500); Kyra Women's Project (£2,000); Shelter (£600); Late Music Concerts, Science Museum Group, St Wilfrid's Church and The Donkey Sanctuary (£500 each); The British Stammering Association (£300).

FINANCES *Year* 2015/16 *Income* £262,261 *Grants* £235,123 *Grants to organisations* £235,123 *Assets* £2,788,336

TRUSTEES Sara Dickson; David Dickson; Sylvia Shepherd; Lucy Dickson; Sophie Dickson.

OTHER INFORMATION Grants were made to 186 organisations during the year.

HOW TO APPLY Apply in writing to the correspondent.

WHO TO APPLY TO Sara Dickson, Trustee, 3 Kings Cloisters, Driffield Terrace, York YO24 1EF

■ Sherburn House Charity

CC NO 217652 **ESTABLISHED** 1181

WHERE FUNDING CAN BE GIVEN The ancient Diocese of Durham (the north east of England between the rivers Tweed and Tees).

WHO CAN BENEFIT Registered charities; voluntary organisations with charitable aims; social enterprises; CICs.

WHAT IS FUNDED Relief of need and disadvantage – in particular: debt advice; crisis help; health and disability; social isolation; problems of long-term unemployment; community needs.

WHAT IS NOT FUNDED Fabric appeals for large capital projects; fundraising costs associated with fundraising events or activities; general appeals; sponsorships of activities; overseas travel or expeditions; medical research; retrospective funding; national groups that do not have a strong presence in the area of benefit; groups which have already received a grant from the charity in the previous 24 months; groups with outstanding monitoring due to County Durham Community Foundation.

TYPE OF GRANT Project costs (including new projects); core costs; capital items and equipment; capacity building; coaching or training; hire of venues; transport costs; trips; IT equipment up to £1,500.

RANGE OF GRANTS Up to £5,000.

SAMPLE GRANTS A list of beneficiaries was not available.

FINANCES *Year* 2015/16 *Income* -£704,446 *Grants* £345,607 *Grants to organisations* £252,563 *Assets* -£1,627,620

TRUSTEES Ray Pye; Margaret Bozic; William Brooks; Cllr Susan Davey; Michael Laing; Susan Martin; Dr Gillian Willmore; Cllr David Stoker; Revd Alun Ford; Kevin Cummings; James Imrie.

OTHER INFORMATION During the year, 82 grants were made to organisations. The charity also has a fund for individual hardship, which is also administered by County Durham Community Foundation. There were 568 grants made to individuals in 2015/16 which totalled £93,000.

HOW TO APPLY As of January 2017, the charity now makes grants through County Durham Community Foundation. Information on the grants programme, guidelines (including deadlines) and the online application form can be found here: www.cdcf.org.uk

WHO TO APPLY TO Grants Team, c/o County Durham Community Foundation, Victoria House, Whifield Court, St John's Road, Meadowfield Industrial Estate, Durham DH7 8XL *Tel.* 0191 378 6340 *Email* info@cdcf.org.uk *Website* www.sherburnhouse.org

■ The Sherling Charitable Trust

CC NO 1079651 **ESTABLISHED** 1999

WHO CAN BENEFIT Charitable organisations.

WHAT IS FUNDED General charitable purposes, particularly education; sport; arts; health.

RANGE OF GRANTS £800 to £20,000.

SAMPLE GRANTS Chiltern MS Centre and Junior Tennis Coaching Foundation (£20,000 each); Canine Partners (£10,000); Dorset Air Ambulance (£5,000); 1st Winlow Scouts, Hospice of St Francis and Motability (£2,000 each); Marie Curie (£1,500); Independent Age (£1,000); Deafblind UK (£800).

FINANCES *Year* 2015/16 *Income* £426,299 *Grants* £76,300 *Grants to organisations* £76,300 *Assets* £1,776,175

OTHER INFORMATION Grants were made to 13 organisations during the year.

HOW TO APPLY Apply in writing to the correspondent.

WHO TO APPLY TO Clive Sherling, Trustee, Lincoln House, Woodside Hill, Chalfont St Peter, Buckinghamshire SL9 9TF *Tel.* 01753 887454

■ The Archie Sherman Cardiff Foundation

CC NO 272225 **ESTABLISHED** 1976

WHERE FUNDING CAN BE GIVEN UK; Israel.

WHO CAN BENEFIT Charitable organisations.

WHAT IS FUNDED Health; overseas aid; community; education and training; with a preference for Jewish causes.

WHAT IS NOT FUNDED Individuals.

RANGE OF GRANTS Up to £25,000.

SAMPLE GRANTS UK Toremet Ltd (£23,500); My Israel (£9,100); Israel Tennis Centre (£6,900); New Israel Fund (£5,000); The Merephdi Foundation – Rabin Medical Centre (£2,300).

FINANCES *Year* 2015/16 *Income* £133,271 *Grants* £46,884 *Grants to organisations* £46,884 *Assets* £2,105,805

TRUSTEE Rothschild Trust Corporation Ltd.

HOW TO APPLY Apply in writing to the correspondent.

WHO TO APPLY TO The Trustees, Rothschild Trust Corp Ltd, New Court, St Swithin's Lane, London EC4P 4DU *Tel.* 020 7280 5000

■ The Archie Sherman Charitable Trust

CC NO 256893 **ESTABLISHED** 1967

WHERE FUNDING CAN BE GIVEN UK and overseas.

WHO CAN BENEFIT Charitable organisations.

WHAT IS FUNDED Education and training; overseas aid; arts and culture; health; Jewish organisations; general charitable purposes.

TYPE OF GRANT Capital and buildings; project costs.

RANGE OF GRANTS Up to £300,000.

SAMPLE GRANTS Yad Vashem – UK Foundation (£314,000); Jewish Child's Day (£167,500); UJIA (United Jewish Israel Appeal) (£77,000); The Royal National Theatre and Norwood Ravenswood (£25,000 each); Community Security Trust (£15,000); Rays of Sunshine (£2,500); Shaare Zedek UK (£2,100); The Royal Academy of Arts (£1,500); Marie Curie (£500); My Israel – Project Fund (£470).

FINANCES *Year* 2015/16 *Income* £1,402,722 *Grants* £1,307,674 *Grants to organisations* £1,307,674 *Assets* £21,225,998

TRUSTEES Michael Gee; Allan Morgenthau; Eric Charles; Rhona Freedman.

OTHER INFORMATION Grants were made to 27 organisations during the year.

HOW TO APPLY Apply in writing to the correspondent.

WHO TO APPLY TO Michael Gee, Trustee, 274A Kentish Town Road, London NW5 2AA *Tel.* 020 7493 1904 *Email* trust@sherman.co.uk

■ The Shetland Charitable Trust

SC NO SC027025 **ESTABLISHED** 1976

WHERE FUNDING CAN BE GIVEN Shetland only.

WHO CAN BENEFIT Charitable and voluntary organisations benefitting the community in Shetland.

WHAT IS FUNDED Social care and welfare; arts, culture, sport and recreation; community and economic development; the environment and heritage.

WHAT IS NOT FUNDED Funds can only be used to benefit the inhabitants of Shetland.

TYPE OF GRANT Project costs; capital and building maintenance costs; running and recurring costs.

RANGE OF GRANTS Up to £2.5 million.

SAMPLE GRANTS Shetland Recreational Trust (£2.5 million); Shetland Amenity Trust (£1 million); Shetland Arts Development Agency (£696,000); Shetland Citizens Advice (£132,000); Voluntary Action Shetland (£126,500); Shetland Befriending Scheme and Shetland Churches Council Trust (£54,000); The Swan Trust (£44,500); Disability Shetland Recreation Club (£12,600); Festival Grants (£30,000).

FINANCES *Year* 2015/16 *Income* £9,988,000 *Grants* £8,746,000 *Grants to organisations* £8,746,000 *Assets* £237,948,000

TRUSTEES Bobby Hunter; Malcolm Bell; Andrew Cooper; Allison Duncan; Robert Henderson; Tom Macintyre; Peter Malcolmson; Andrew Manson; Keith Massey; Ian Napier; Drew Ratter; James Smith; Amanda Westlake.

HOW TO APPLY Applications are only accepted from Shetland-based charities. For more information, refer to the trust's website.

WHO TO APPLY TO Michael Duncan, 22–24 North Road, Lerwick, Shetland ZE1 0NQ *Tel.* 01595 744994 *Email* mail@shetlandcharitabletrust.co.uk *Website* www.shetlandcharitabletrust.co.uk

■ SHINE (Support and Help in Education)

CC NO 1082777 **ESTABLISHED** 1999

WHERE FUNDING CAN BE GIVEN England; some programmes are focused on Great Manchester and London.

WHO CAN BENEFIT Schools and other educational organisations.

WHAT IS FUNDED Educational projects helping children and young people aged between 4 and 18 who are disadvantaged to fulfil their academic potential. Programmes fall under the following categories: teacher-led innovation competitions; SHINE Saturday programmes; school-based partnerships.

WHAT IS NOT FUNDED Programmes that take place outside England; individuals (apart from the teacher-led innovation competitions); short-term or one-off projects; bursaries or student fees; replacement of statutory funding; projects focusing on personal development of young people rather than raising academic achievement levels; capital building projects for schools or other educational institutions; projects targeted at specific beneficiary groups.

TYPE OF GRANT Project costs; long-term programmes; seed funding and start-up costs; staff costs, resources, trips.

RANGE OF GRANTS Average grant ranges from £15,000 to £35,000 depending on the grant category.

SAMPLE GRANTS Hegarty Maths (£200,000); New North Academy (£135,000); Lyric Theatre (£39,000); Sebright Primary School (£34,500); St Paul's Peel Primary School (£30,000); St Teresa's Primary School (£25,000); National Literacy Trust (£25,000); Withington Girls' School (£6,000).

FINANCES *Year* 2015/16 *Income* £2,280,830 *Grants* £1,743,972 *Grants to organisations* £1,743,972 *Assets* £5,622,164

TRUSTEES Gavin Boyle; Dr Caroline Whalley; David Blood; Cameron Ogden; Richard Rothwell; Henry Bedford; Natasha Pope; Stephen Shields; Bridget Walsh; Ann Mroz; Hassim Dhoda.

OTHER INFORMATION The grant total above refers to grants awarded during the year. The charity funded 96 projects in its portfolio in the 2016/17 academic year, benefitting 25,000 children.

HOW TO APPLY Potential applicants must first check the charity's website for current information of the programmes available. There is also a helpful list of funding FAQs. Following this, the grants team can be contacted by email (info@shinetrust.org.uk) or by telephone (0208 393 1880).

WHO TO APPLY TO Grants Team, 1 Cheam Road, Ewell Village, Surrey KT17 1SP *Tel.* 020 8393 1880 *Email* info@shinetrust.org.uk *Website* www.shinetrust.org.uk

■ The Bassil Shippam and Alsford Trust

CC NO 256996 **ESTABLISHED** 1967

WHERE FUNDING CAN BE GIVEN UK, with a preference for West Sussex.

WHO CAN BENEFIT Charitable organisations.

WHAT IS FUNDED Social welfare; young people; older people; health and medical research; education; Christian causes; arts.

RANGE OF GRANTS Mostly under £1,000.

SAMPLE GRANTS Chichester Dementia Group (£25,000); South Downs Planetarium (£15,200); South Bersted Church Hall and West Sussex Youth Music Awards (£3,000 each); Cobnor Activities Centre (£1,000); Eastergate Cricket Club and Winston's Wish (£500 each); Crohn's and Colitis UK (£300); Brighton and Hove Parents' and Children's Group (£250); British and Foreign Bible Society (£100).

FINANCES *Year* 2015/16 *Income* £156,861 *Grants* £142,107 *Grants to organisations* £135,630 *Assets* £4,356,081

TRUSTEES Christopher Doman; John Shippam; Molly Hanwell; Susan Trayler; Richard Tayler; Stanley Young; Janet Bailey; Simon MacFarlane.

OTHER INFORMATION Grants to individuals during the year totalled £6,500.

HOW TO APPLY The accounts for 2015/16 state that the trust 'invites applications for funding to be made to the trustees in writing together with a summary of their proposals; applications made by organisations should submit a copy of any reports, accounts or forecasts. Applications are reviewed by a panel of Trustees.'

WHO TO APPLY TO The Trustees, Thomas Eggar House, Friary Lane, Chichester, West Sussex PO19 1UF *Tel.* 01243 786111 *Email* shippam@thomaseggar.com

■ The Shipwrights' Company Charitable Fund

CC NO 262043 **ESTABLISHED** 1971

WHERE FUNDING CAN BE GIVEN UK.

WHO CAN BENEFIT Individuals and organisations with a maritime connection.

WHAT IS FUNDED Maritime training and education, sailors' welfare and maritime heritage; young people; City organisations.

WHAT IS NOT FUNDED Any application without a clear maritime connection.

TYPE OF GRANT Annual donations; one-off donations; educational bursaries.

RANGE OF GRANTS Mainly £500 to £5,000.

SAMPLE GRANTS Marine Society and Sea Cadets (£12,000); International Boatbuilding Training College (£6,500); University of Southampton (£5,000); Atlantic Challenge GB (£1,500); Ro-Ro Sailing Project, Sherborne Learning Centre and The Royal Alfred Seafarers Society (£1,000 each); Sea Change Sailing Trust (£750); Corporation of Sons of the Clergy (£200).

FINANCES *Year* 2015/16 *Income* £2,637,465 *Grants* £287,705 *Grants to organisations* £260,616 *Assets* £6,212,885

TRUSTEES Archibald Smith; Rear Adm. Sir Jeremy Halpert; Anthony Vlasto; John Denholm; Simon Kverndal; Laura Bugden; Worshipful Company of Shipwrights.

OTHER INFORMATION Grants to individuals for educational purposes totalled £27,000. Grants to organisations were made up of general charitable donations, including both regular beneficiaries and 'responsive' grants and restricted donations.

HOW TO APPLY Applications to be made by post or email to the correspondent. Applications from organisations should if possible be accompanied by the latest accounts and report. Application forms and further guidelines are available from the trust's website. Applications are considered in February, June and November.

WHO TO APPLY TO The Clerk, Ironmongers' Hall, Shaftesbury Place, Barbican, London EC2Y 8AA *Tel.* 020 7606 2376 *Email* clerk@shipwrights.co.uk *Website* www.shipwrights.co.uk

■ The Shirley Foundation

CC NO 1097135 **ESTABLISHED** 1996

WHERE FUNDING CAN BE GIVEN UK.

WHO CAN BENEFIT Registered charities and research institutions.

WHAT IS FUNDED The main areas of interest are information technology and autism (not excluding Asperger's Syndrome) which occasionally extend to learning disabilities in general. The foundation's mission is 'the facilitation and support of pioneering projects with strategic impact in the field of autism spectrum disorders, with particular emphasis on medical research'. The website states that there is a preference for projects which are 'innovative in nature with potential to have a strategic impact in the field of Autism Spectrum Disorders'. Research proposals should be aimed at determining the causes of autism. There is further guidance on the website.
WHAT IS NOT FUNDED Individuals; political donations.
TYPE OF GRANT Project funding; revenue; research.
SAMPLE GRANTS Research Autism (£63,500); Global Health Network (£50,000); St Thomas' Hospital (£20,000).
FINANCES *Year* 2015/16 *Income* £21,588 *Grants* £174,597 *Grants to organisations* £133,684 *Assets* £924,090
TRUSTEES Michael MacFadyen; Anne Menzies; Prof. Eve Johnstone; Dame Stephanie Shirley.
OTHER INFORMATION The 2015/16 accounts state that over the two decades of the foundation's existence, 75% of grants have been given to projects relating to autism, 22% to information technology, and 3% to other causes (mainly other learning disabilities). The foundation's 2015/16 accounts were not available to view on the Charity Commission's website, due to its low income during the year; however, they were available to view on Companies House records. The grant total included a grant for a project consultant and for a book on the employment of people on the autism spectrum.
HOW TO APPLY Apply in writing to the correspondent, initially with a simple letter and outline proposal, which can be sent by post or via the contact form on the foundation's website. The trustees meet annually but applications can be submitted at any time.
WHO TO APPLY TO The Trustees, Videcom House, Newtown Road, Henley-on-Thames, Oxon RG9 1HG *Tel.* 01491 579004 *Email* steve@steveshirley.com *Website* www.steveshirley.com/tsf

■ Shlomo Memorial Fund Ltd

CC NO 278973 **ESTABLISHED** 1980
WHERE FUNDING CAN BE GIVEN Unrestricted.
WHO CAN BENEFIT Charities; Jewish organisations.
WHAT IS FUNDED Jewish education and places of worship; social welfare; general charitable purposes.
SAMPLE GRANTS Amud Haolam, Nachlat Halevi'im, Torah Umesorah, Beit Hillel, ZSV Charities, La'yesharim Tehilla, British Friends of Tashbar Chazon Ish, Chazon Ish, Mei Menuchos, Mor Uketsio, Shoshanat HaAmakim, Millennium Trust, and Talmud Torah Zichron Meir.
FINANCES *Year* 2014/15 *Income* £8,857,389 *Grants* £1,569,984 *Grants to organisations* £1,569,984 *Assets* £53,545,865
TRUSTEES Amichai Toporowitz; Hezkel Toporowitz; Eliyah Kleineman; Channe Lopian; Chaim Kaufman; Meir Sullam; Esther Hoffner.
OTHER INFORMATION The 2014/15 accounts were the most recent available at the time of writing (June 2017). A list of recent beneficiaries was not provided in the accounts.
HOW TO APPLY Apply in writing to the correspondent.
WHO TO APPLY TO Channe Lopian, Secretary, Cohen Arnold and Co., New Burlington House, 1075 Finchley Road, London NW11 0PU *Tel.* 020 8731 0777 *Email* info@olnato.com

■ The Shoe Zone Trust

CC NO 1112972 **ESTABLISHED** 2005
WHERE FUNDING CAN BE GIVEN Preference for Leicestershire and Rutland and for certain charities operating in the Philippines and other countries.
WHO CAN BENEFIT Children and young people.
WHAT IS FUNDED Relief of poverty; education; children and young people.
RANGE OF GRANTS Up to £54,000.
SAMPLE GRANTS Shepherd of the Hills – Philippines (£54,500); Ministries Without Borders (£15,800); 500 Miles (£5,000); James 1v27 Foundation and Rotary Club of Kibworth and Fleckney (£2,000 each).
FINANCES *Year* 2015 *Income* £43,371 *Grants* £79,919 *Grants to organisations* £79,919 *Assets* £94,712
TRUSTEES Michael Smith; John Smith; Anthony Smith.
OTHER INFORMATION Donations of £250 and under totalled £550.
HOW TO APPLY Apply in writing to the correspondent.
WHO TO APPLY TO Michael Smith, Trustee, Shoe Zone Retail Ltd, Haramead Business Centre, Humberstone Road, Leicester LE1 2LH *Tel.* 0116 222 3007 *Website* www.shoezone.com/ShoeZoneTrust

■ The Shropshire Historic Churches Trust

CC NO 1010690 **ESTABLISHED** 1991
WHERE FUNDING CAN BE GIVEN Shropshire.
WHO CAN BENEFIT Churches in Shropshire.
WHAT IS FUNDED Preservation, repair and renovation, maintenance and improvement, upkeep, beautification and reconstruction of churches in Shropshire (which are listed buildings or of architectural interest) and of monuments, fittings, fixtures, stained glass, furniture, ornaments, bells, clocks and chimes, goods and chattels in such churches and of the churchyard belonging to any such for the benefit of the public.
WHAT IS NOT FUNDED Reordering; new extensions; toilets; kitchens; work that has already started; churches which are not members of the trust.
TYPE OF GRANT Buildings costs.
RANGE OF GRANTS £500 to £10,000.
SAMPLE GRANTS Tugford – Ludlow (£10,000); Ludlow – Ludlow (£7,500); Bedstone – Clun Forest (£7,000); Kinnerley – Oswestry, Stokesay – Candover (£4,000 each); Hanwood – Pontesbury (£1,100); Onibury – Ludlow (£465).
FINANCES *Year* 2016 *Income* £91,648 *Grants* £45,400 *Grants to organisations* £45,400 *Assets* £601,648
TRUSTEES Archdeacon John Hall; Dr David Harding; Marian Haslam; Bishop Michael Hooper; Andrew Ewart Harvey James; Dr John Leonard; David Taylor; Ruth Taylor.
HOW TO APPLY Application forms can be found on the website. Applicants must also send a copy of the latest accounts including balance sheet and the accounts of any Friends organisation and trusts which have the upkeep of the church as their main objective. Applications should be sent before the 15th of March, June, September or December to the Trust's Grants Administrator: Mr John Whiteside, Bryn Awel,

Pool Bank, Pontesbury Hill Road, Shrewsbury SY5 0YJ.
WHO TO APPLY TO Erica Watson-Todd, Secretary, 20 Alford Gardens, Myddle, Shrewsbury SY4 3RG *Tel.* 01939 290820 *Email* archdeacon.salop@lichfield.anglican.org *Website* www.shropshirehct.org.uk

■ Shulem B. Association Ltd

CC NO 313654 **ESTABLISHED** 1962
WHERE FUNDING CAN BE GIVEN England.
WHO CAN BENEFIT Jewish organisations; schools; charitable organisations.
WHAT IS FUNDED Jewish religion; education; general charitable purposes.
TYPE OF GRANT Capital and revenue costs.
SAMPLE GRANTS Siva Charitable Fund (£1.3 million); Aldentower Ltd (£225,000); Shaarei Rachamim Ltd (£138,500); Gerson Berger Association Ltd (£35,000).
FINANCES *Year* 2014/15 *Income* £20,553,657 *Grants* £6,401,800 *Grants to organisations* £6,401,800 *Assets* £66,690,660
TRUSTEES Samuel Berger; Sarah Klein; Zelda Sternlicht.
OTHER INFORMATION The 2014/15 accounts were the most recent available on the Charity Commission's website at the time of writing (June 2017). A list of recent beneficiaries was not provided in the accounts.
HOW TO APPLY Apply in writing to the correspondent.
WHO TO APPLY TO The Trustees, New Burlington House, 1075 Finchley Road, London NW11 0PU *Tel.* 020 8731 0777

■ The Florence Shute Millennium Trust

CC NO 1085358 **ESTABLISHED** 2001
WHERE FUNDING CAN BE GIVEN UK, with a preference for Chepstow, Monmouthshire and Forest of Dean.
WHO CAN BENEFIT Charitable organisations.
WHAT IS FUNDED Health; medical research; disability.
RANGE OF GRANTS Mostly £1,000 to £5,000.
SAMPLE GRANTS British Scoliosis Research (£70,000); Great Oaks Hospice (£5,000); The Royal Blind Society (£3,000); Brain Tumour Support, CoppaFeel, National Osteoporosis Society and Stroke Association (£2,000 each); Autism Puzzles Ltd, Riding for the Disabled and Starlight (£1,000 each).
FINANCES *Year* 2015/16 *Income* £75,091 *Grants* £137,770 *Grants to organisations* £137,770 *Assets* £2,066,459
TRUSTEES Ursula Williams; James Zorab; Richard O'Sullivan; Dr Alexander Davies.
OTHER INFORMATION Grants were made to 29 organisations during the year.
HOW TO APPLY Apply in writing to the correspondent.
WHO TO APPLY TO Judith Burke, Francis and Co., 17 Welsh Street, Chepstow, Gwent NP16 5YH *Tel.* 01291 622237 *Email* judithb@francisandco.co.uk

■ The David and Jennifer Sieff Charitable Trust

CC NO 206329 **ESTABLISHED** 1970
WHERE FUNDING CAN BE GIVEN UK.
WHO CAN BENEFIT Registered charities.
WHAT IS FUNDED General charitable purposes; community care services; arts and culture; children and young people; people with disabilities; the promotion of health; education and training; science and technology; Jewish causes; animal welfare.
WHAT IS NOT FUNDED Individuals.
RANGE OF GRANTS £50 to £27,000.
SAMPLE GRANTS Community Security Trust (£27,000); The Southbank Centre (£12,500); The Tavistock Trust for Aphasia (£10,000); Windsor Greys Jubilee Appeal and British ORT (£5,000 each); Refugee and The Koestler Trust (£2,000 each); Moorcroft Racehorse Welfare Centre (£1,200); Jewish Care, Royal College of Music, Royal National Theatre and Royal Opera House Foundation (£1,000 each); Trinity Hospice and Wiltshire Air Ambulance (£250 each); British Heart Foundation and British Red Cross (£100 each); The Royal British Legion (£50).
FINANCES *Year* 2015/16 *Income* £22,025 *Grants* £114,000 *Grants to organisations* £114,000
TRUSTEES Sir David Sieff; Lady Jennifer Sieff; Lord Wolfson of Sunningdale; Jonathan Sieff.
OTHER INFORMATION The trust's latest accounts were not available to view on the Charity Commission's website due to its low income. We have therefore estimated the grant total based on previous years' information.
HOW TO APPLY Apply in writing to the correspondent.
WHO TO APPLY TO The Trustees, H. W. Fisher and Company, Acre House, 11–15 William Road, London NW1 3ER *Tel.* 020 7388 7000 *Email* info@hwfisher.co.uk

■ Silver Family Charitable Trust

CC NO 1152141 **ESTABLISHED** 2013
WHERE FUNDING CAN BE GIVEN UK.
WHO CAN BENEFIT Charitable organisations and individuals.
WHAT IS FUNDED General charitable purposes.
SAMPLE GRANTS A list of beneficiaries was not available.
FINANCES *Year* 2015/16 *Income* £89,482 *Grants* £85,206 *Grants to organisations* £85,206 *Assets* £31,823
TRUSTEES Rebecca Silver; Simon Silver.
HOW TO APPLY Apply in writing to the correspondent.
WHO TO APPLY TO Simon Silver, Trustee, 49 Hamilton Terrace, London NW8 9RG *Tel.* 020 7467 6300

■ The Simmons & Simmons Charitable Foundation

CC NO 1129643 **ESTABLISHED** 2009
WHERE FUNDING CAN BE GIVEN Worldwide, with a preference for London and areas local to Simmons & Simmons offices.
WHO CAN BENEFIT Registered charities – with a preference for smaller charities.
WHAT IS FUNDED Social inclusion; access to justice; opportunities for those who are disadvantaged.
RANGE OF GRANTS Up to £36,000.
SAMPLE GRANTS Battersea Legal Advice Centre (£36,000); Bingham Centre for the Rule of Law and The Big Issue Foundation (£15,000); Spitalfields Music and Working Families (£10,000 each); Moreland Primary School (£6,000); Colombia Caravana, London's Air Ambulance and Prisoners' Advice Service (£5,000 each).
FINANCES *Year* 2015/16 *Income* £254,935 *Grants* £179,983 *Grants to organisations* £179,983 *Assets* £235,856

TRUSTEES Richard Dyton; Fiona Loughrey; Colin Passmore; Michele Anahory.
OTHER INFORMATION This is the corporate charity of Simmons & Simmons LLP. The foundation prioritises charities where the firm's employees can have some involvement.
HOW TO APPLY Applications can be made using a form available to download from the firm's website.
WHO TO APPLY TO The Trustees, Simmons & Simmons LLP, Citypoint, 1 Ropemaker Street, London EC2Y 9SS *Tel.* 020 7628 2020 *Email* corporate.responsibility@simmons-simmons.com *Website* www.simmons-simmons.com

■ The Huntly and Margery Sinclair Charitable Trust

CC NO 235939 **ESTABLISHED** 1964
WHERE FUNDING CAN BE GIVEN UK.
WHO CAN BENEFIT Registered charities.
WHAT IS FUNDED General charitable purposes.
WHAT IS NOT FUNDED Individuals.
TYPE OF GRANT Recurrent.
RANGE OF GRANTS Up to £10,000.
SAMPLE GRANTS Myeloma UK (£6,000); Rendcomb College, Walking with the Wounded (£5,000 each); Injured Jockeys Fund (£3,000); National Osteoporosis Society, Spelsbury Parochial Church Council (£2,000); Children with Cancer, Medical Detection Dogs (£1,000 each); County Air Ambulance Trust, Macmillan Cancer Support (£500).
FINANCES *Year* 2015/16 *Income* £49,528 *Grants* £55,200 *Grants to organisations* £55,200 *Assets* £1,408,784
TRUSTEES John Floyd; Hugh Sherbrooke; Linda Hamilton Singer.
HOW TO APPLY Apply in writing to the correspondent. Unsolicited applications are rarely accepted.
WHO TO APPLY TO Wilfrid Vernor-Miles, Administrator, Hunters, 9 New Square, Lincoln's Inn, London WC2A 3QN *Tel.* 020 7412 0050 *Email* wvm@hunters-solicitors.co.uk

■ The Sino-British Fellowship Trust

CC NO 313669 **ESTABLISHED** 1948
WHERE FUNDING CAN BE GIVEN UK and China.
WHO CAN BENEFIT Universities, researchers and educational institutions.
WHAT IS FUNDED Education of teachers and researchers in China; grants to enable Chinese academics or students to carry out research or study in the UK; grants to enable UK academics to undertake research with Chinese colleagues; funding for UK GP trainers to provide training in primary health care in China; funding for academics to enhance their knowledge of Chinese languages.
TYPE OF GRANT Scholarships and grants for research and training.
RANGE OF GRANTS Up to around £25,000.
SAMPLE GRANTS Universities China Committee London (£26,500); British Academy (£23,000); School of Oriental and African Studies (£10,600); Needham Research Institute (£3,500); Vocational Training Council (£2,400); Lingnan University (£2,300); Great Britain China Educational Trust (£1,000).
FINANCES *Year* 2015 *Income* £486,737 *Grants* £73,188 *Grants to organisations* £69,188 *Assets* £15,250,032
TRUSTEES Lady Pamela Youde; Anne Ely; Prof. Hugh Baker; Peter Ely; Ling Thompson; Prof. Wayne Luk; Dr Frances Wood; Prof. George Smith; Prof. Rosemary Foot.
OTHER INFORMATION Grants were made to seven organisations during the year. The amount of grants given to individuals totalled £4,000.
HOW TO APPLY Apply on a form available by writing to the correspondence address. The trustees meet at least twice a year to discuss grant awards.
WHO TO APPLY TO Anne Ely, Trustee, Flat 23, Bede House, Manor Fields, London SW15 3LT *Tel.* 020 8788 6252

■ SITA Cornwall Trust Ltd

CC NO 1127288 **ESTABLISHED** 2008
WHERE FUNDING CAN BE GIVEN Cornwall, within a ten-mile radius of a landfill site – a map and a distance calculator are provided on the trust's website.
WHO CAN BENEFIT Community organisations; churches.
WHAT IS FUNDED Projects that provide social and environmental benefits to communities in Cornwall. In particular, projects that fulfil one of the following objectives: bringing land back into use; reducing or preventing pollution; public parks and amenities; buildings and structures; promoting biodiversity. Priority is given to projects benefitting communities local to landfill sites and projects that are community driven. According to the 2015/16 accounts, the trust has allocated £150,000 specifically for church fabric projects – heating projects will only be considered if they include an element of sustainable energy.
WHAT IS NOT FUNDED Grants are not given to applicants that have received a grant within the last three years. Funding applications for solar panels will only be considered 'where there is a clear need for replacement of an existing heating system which is no longer serviceable or if it is part of a wider amenity project in which it makes sense to make such improvements while other work is being undertaken'. See the trust's website for full criteria.
TYPE OF GRANT Project costs; capital costs; one-off.
RANGE OF GRANTS Up to £35,000. Larger projects will only be considered in exceptional cases.
SAMPLE GRANTS Devoran Village Hall (£247,000); Boscawen Park (£100,000); Camelford Leisure Centre (£30,000); Redannick Theatre (£28,000); Murley Hall (£24,000); Wendron Football Club (£23,000); Ladock Church (£20,000); Saltash Guides (£14,800); Chyan Community Field (£9,200); St Stephen's Bowling Club (£1,500).
FINANCES *Year* 2015/16 *Income* £1,078,879 *Grants* £1,084,969 *Grants to organisations* £1,084,969 *Assets* £1,247,540
TRUSTEES George Hocking; Richard Thomas; Lee Rouse; Paul Brinsley; Betty Hale; Philip Rudin; David Attwell; Anthony Earl.
OTHER INFORMATION Grants were made to 41 projects during the year. The trust makes a larger grant to one 'flagship' project every year, which in 2015/16 was Devoran Village Hall.
HOW TO APPLY Application forms are available to download on the trust's website, along with a detailed list of criteria and application guidelines, which applicants should use to check that their project is eligible. The trust states: 'If you require further information, clarification or have any questions contact the office, and we will be able to answer all your queries.'

WHO TO APPLY TO Wendy Reading, Fund Manager, Spring Cottage, 3 Holmbush Hill, Kelly Bray, Cornwall PL17 8EP *Tel.* 01579 346816 *Email* wendyreading@btconnect.com *Website* www.sitacornwalltrust.co.uk

■ The Skelton Bounty

CC NO 219370 **ESTABLISHED** 1934

WHERE FUNDING CAN BE GIVEN Lancashire, as it existed in 1934.

WHO CAN BENEFIT Registered charities.

WHAT IS FUNDED Charities benefitting the residents of Lancashire, with an emphasis on: older people; people with disabilities; young people; and holidays for disadvantaged children and carers.

WHAT IS NOT FUNDED Grants are not usually given to large building appeals or revenue expenditure. Applications from charities in successive years are not viewed favourably. Grants are not awarded to individuals.

TYPE OF GRANT Preference for small specific capital projects (particularly equipment) rather than general expenditure.

RANGE OF GRANTS Up to £5,000, mostly in the range of £50 to £3,000.

SAMPLE GRANTS Greater Manchester Crimestoppers (£5,000); Norris Green Youth Centre Ltd (£3,000); Preston Explorer Scouts (£2,200); Rethink Mental Illness – East Lancashire Activities Group (£2,000); Age UK Wigan Borough (£1,800); The Florrie (£1,500); Salford Heart Care (£1,400); Tate Liverpool (£1,000); Chorley and South Ribble Crossroads Care North West (£900); Rossendale and Pendle Mountain Rescue Team (£600).

FINANCES *Year* 2015/16 *Income* £113,600 *Grants* £95,604 *Grants to organisations* £95,604 *Assets* £2,592,854

TRUSTEES Hon. Sir Mark Hedley; Roger Morris; Dame Lorna Muirhead; Kamruddin Kothia; Edith Conn; Christian Weaver; Robert Hough; Almana Carruthers; Gail Stanley.

OTHER INFORMATION Grants were awarded to 50 organisations during the year.

HOW TO APPLY Application forms are available from the correspondent or may be found on the LCVS website when the fund is open to applications (usually around spring time). Applications are considered at the trustees' meeting in July. For more information, contact grants@lcvs.org.uk.

WHO TO APPLY TO The Trustees, c/o Liverpool Charity and Voluntary Services, 151 Dale street, Liverpool L2 2AH *Tel.* 0151 227 5177 *Email* grants@lcvs.org.uk *Website* www.lcvs.org.uk

■ The Skerritt Trust

CC NO 1016701 **ESTABLISHED** 1992

WHERE FUNDING CAN BE GIVEN Benefitting older people living within a ten-mile radius of Nottingham Market Square.

WHO CAN BENEFIT Charitable organisations and housing bodies.

WHAT IS FUNDED Older people, particularly housing and accommodation needs.

TYPE OF GRANT Capital costs.

RANGE OF GRANTS Up to £50,000.

SAMPLE GRANTS Age UK (£48,000); Joint Homes Committee (£24,000); Radcliffe Manor House Care Home (£18,600).

FINANCES *Year* 2015/16 *Income* £93,795 *Grants* £90,609 *Grants to organisations* £90,609 *Assets* £2,162,870

TRUSTEES Roy Taylor; Roy Costa; Sandra Warzynska; David Lowe; Pamela Wilson; David Robinson; Alma Davies.

HOW TO APPLY Apply in writing to the correspondent, including annual accounts and the details of the costs of items or facilities required. The trustees consider applications at their quarterly meetings.

WHO TO APPLY TO Nigel Cullen, Cumberland Court, 80 Mount Street, Nottingham NG1 6HH *Tel.* 0115 901 5558 *Email* anna.chandler@freeths.co.uk

■ The Charles Skey Charitable Trust

CC NO 277697 **ESTABLISHED** 1979

WHERE FUNDING CAN BE GIVEN UK.

WHO CAN BENEFIT Organisations which the trustees have come across from their own research.

WHAT IS FUNDED General charitable purposes.

TYPE OF GRANT Grants are given on a one-off basis in response to requests; or on an annual or periodic basis, reviewed by the trustees.

RANGE OF GRANTS £250 to £75,000.

SAMPLE GRANTS National Maritime Museum (£75,000); French Hospital (£50,000); Samaritans (£15,000); Almeida Projects, Cleft Lip and Palate Association and Sherborne School Foundation (£5,000 each); Sportability (£3,000); Gurkha Welfare Trust, Hill City Church and WaterAid (£2,500 each); Scotty's Little Soldiers (£250).

FINANCES *Year* 2015/16 *Income* £442,586 *Grants* £447,250 *Grants to organisations* £447,250 *Assets* £12,332,546

TRUSTEES Revd James Leggett; John Leggett; David Berkeley; Christopher Berkeley; Edward Berkeley.

OTHER INFORMATION Grants were made to 42 organisations during the year.

HOW TO APPLY Apply in writing to the correspondent. The trustees meet several times a year to review grants.

WHO TO APPLY TO John Leggett, Trustee, Flint House, Park Homer Road, Colehill, Wimborne, Dorset BH21 2SP *Tel.* 01202 882180

■ Skipton Building Society Charitable Foundation

CC NO 1079538 **ESTABLISHED** 2000

WHERE FUNDING CAN BE GIVEN UK, particularly in areas near branches of the Skipton Building Society.

WHO CAN BENEFIT Registered charities, with a focus on smaller, local organisations.

WHAT IS FUNDED General charitable purposes, particularly: education, welfare, youth schemes and projects benefitting children; older people and their care.

WHAT IS NOT FUNDED Non-registered charities; individuals; activities which are the responsibility of government or statutory bodies; mainstream schools, sports clubs, scouts or guides groups; running costs, including rent or salaries; administration equipment; restoration or upkeep of buildings; holidays, residential trips, overseas travel or activities outside the UK; fundraising events, sponsorship or marketing appeals; costs or maintenance of vehicles; research; causes limited only to a specific sector of the community based on religion, ethnicity or political grounds; large national charities; charities which have received funding from the foundation within the last five years; charities which have applied to the foundation within the last two years; charities without at least one year of financial accounts.

TYPE OF GRANT Specific items or activities.

RANGE OF GRANTS Mostly up to £3,000, although requests for up to £10,000 will be considered in certain cases.

SAMPLE GRANTS Hollybank Trust (£4,800); Caudwell Children (£2,500); Ryedale Carers Support (£2,000); The Society for Mucopolysaccharide Diseases (£1,700); Brighton and Hove Unwaged Advice and Rights Centre (£1,600); Shopmobility Sheffield (£1,400); Ilkley and District Good Neighbours Community Transport (£1,000); Friends of Lea School (£900); Reading Mencap (£500); The Nottinghamshire Hospice (£300).

FINANCES *Year* 2015/16 *Income* £301,100 *Grants* £150,196 *Grants to organisations* £150,196 *Assets* £216,778

TRUSTEES Rt Revd and Rt Hon. Lord Hope of Thornes; Richard Robinson; Amelia Vyvyan; Alison Davies; Kitty North; John Dawson; Debra Ewing.

OTHER INFORMATION Grants were made to 98 organisations during the year.

HOW TO APPLY Applications can be made using a form available to download on the foundation's website, which should be sent with two years' financial accounts. The trustees usually meet in March, June, September and December to award grants.

WHO TO APPLY TO John Gibson, Secretary, The Bailey, Skipton, North Yorkshire BD23 1DN *Tel.* 01756 705000 *Email* charitablefoundation@skipton.co.uk *Website* www.skiptoncharitablefoundation.co.uk

■ The John Slater Foundation

CC NO 231145 **ESTABLISHED** 1963

WHERE FUNDING CAN BE GIVEN UK, with a strong preference for the north west of England especially West Lancashire.

WHO CAN BENEFIT Registered charities.

WHAT IS FUNDED General charitable purposes, with a preference for: animal welfare; education; social welfare.

RANGE OF GRANTS £500 to £50,000.

SAMPLE GRANTS Veterans Aid (£50,000 in two grants); Dogs Trust (£21,000); Manchester High School for Girls (£12,000 in two grants); West Cumbria Society for the Blind (£5,400 in two grants); Legacy Rainbow House (£2,500); Red Squirrel Survival Trust (£2,000 in two grants); Respite Association (£1,700); Trinity Baptist Church (£500).

FINANCES *Year* 2015/16 *Income* £2,252,485 *Grants* £112,636 *Grants to organisations* £112,636 *Assets* £97,590

TRUSTEE HSBC. Trust Company (UK) Ltd.

OTHER INFORMATION During the year, 43 grants were made to 26 organisations.

HOW TO APPLY The foundation's website states: 'The foundation is presently fully committed to its programme of giving and unfortunately is not able to receive any further new requests of any nature at this time. Should this situation change an appropriate announcement will be made on [the foundation's] website.'

WHO TO APPLY TO The Trustees, c/o HSBC Trust Company UK Ltd, Second Floor, 1 The Forum, Parkway, Whiteley, Fareham PO15 7PA *Tel.* 023 8072 2225 *Website* johnslaterfoundation.org.uk

■ The Slaughter and May Charitable Trust

CC NO 1082765 **ESTABLISHED** 2000

WHERE FUNDING CAN BE GIVEN Mainly local to the Slaughter and May offices in Islington.

WHO CAN BENEFIT Charitable organisations.

WHAT IS FUNDED Legal, educational and community projects.

SAMPLE GRANTS National Literacy Trust and The Access Project (£40,000 each); Islington Law Centre (£35,000); Action for Kids (£30,000); St Luke's Community Centre (£25,000); Teach First (£10,800); London Symphony Orchestra and Union Chapel Margins Project (£10,000 each); Moreland School (£7,500); National Youth Advocacy Service (£5,000).

FINANCES *Year* 2015/16 *Income* £333,022 *Grants* £263,097 *Grants to organisations* £263,097 *Assets* £59,990

TRUSTEE Slaughter and May Trust Ltd.

HOW TO APPLY Unsolicited applications are not accepted.

WHO TO APPLY TO Kate Hursthouse, Corporate Responsibility Manager, Slaughter and May (Trust Ltd), 1 Bunhill Row, London EC1Y 8YY *Tel.* 020 7090 3433 *Email* corporateresponsibility@slaughterandmay.com *Website* www.slaughterandmay.com

■ Sloane Robinson Foundation

CC NO 1068286 **ESTABLISHED** 1998

WHERE FUNDING CAN BE GIVEN England and Wales.

WHO CAN BENEFIT Universities; individuals.

WHAT IS FUNDED Advancement of education, particularly scholarships and bursaries to enable overseas students to study in the UK, or to enable UK students to study abroad, as well as to 'generally provide opportunities for education which would not otherwise be possible' (according to the 2015/16 annual report).

TYPE OF GRANT Grants to institutions on an ongoing relationship basis and grants to private individuals.

RANGE OF GRANTS £10,000 to £168,000.

SAMPLE GRANTS Rugby School (£177,500); Keble College, Oxford (£64,500); Lincoln College, Oxford (£54,000); St Laurence Parochial Church Council (£10,400); Syria Relief (£10,000).

FINANCES *Year* 2015/16 *Income* £491,523 *Grants* £440,732 *Grants to organisations* £316,720 *Assets* £14,495,757

TRUSTEES Deborah Fisher; Hugh Sloane; George Robinson.

OTHER INFORMATION Grants to individuals (pupils at Latymer School) totalled £124,000 during the year.

HOW TO APPLY The 2015/16 annual report states that applications are processed by WillcoxLewis LLP before consideration by the trustees, but that 'the trustees have decided to concentrate on making grants to current recipients and develop stronger relationships with those particular educational establishments without derogating from their overall discretion.'

WHO TO APPLY TO Deborah Fisher, Trustee, The Old Coach House, Sunnyside, Bergh Apton, Norwich NR15 1DD *Tel.* 01508 480100 *Email* info@fisherlegal.co.uk

Rita and David Slowe Charitable Trust

CC NO 1048209 **ESTABLISHED** 1995
WHERE FUNDING CAN BE GIVEN UK and overseas.
WHO CAN BENEFIT Registered charities.
WHAT IS FUNDED General charitable purposes, with a focus on homelessness; human trafficking; people who are disadvantaged overseas (with a focus on Africa), particularly the distribution of books and computers.
RANGE OF GRANTS £10,000 to £15,000.
SAMPLE GRANTS HERA, Magdalene Group and Shelter (£15,000 each); Big Issue Foundation, Books Abroad, Computer Aid International, Crisis, Excellent Development and Re-cycle (£10,000 each).
FINANCES *Year* 2015/16 *Income* £536,401 *Grants* £120,000 *Grants to organisations* £120,000 *Assets* £1,999,605
TRUSTEES Elizabeth Slowe; Graham Weinberg; Jonathan Slowe; Lilian Slowe; Robert Slowe.
HOW TO APPLY Apply in writing to the correspondent.
WHO TO APPLY TO Robert Slowe, Trustee, 32 Hampstead High Street, London NW3 1JQ *Tel.* 020 7435 7800

Ruth Smart Foundation

CC NO 1080021 **ESTABLISHED** 2000
WHERE FUNDING CAN BE GIVEN Worldwide, with a focus on UK and USA.
WHO CAN BENEFIT Registered charities and charitable organisations.
WHAT IS FUNDED Animal welfare.
TYPE OF GRANT One-off.
RANGE OF GRANTS £1,000 to £17,000.
SAMPLE GRANTS Monterey County SPCA (£16,800); Fauna and Flora International (£13,000); Ventana (£12,800); Mauritian Wildlife Foundation (£10,000); Animal Health Trust and Durrell Wildlife Conservation (£3,000 each); Blue Cross (£2,000); Freshfields Animal Rescue and Worldwide Veterinary Service (£1,000).
FINANCES *Year* 2015 *Income* £160,780 *Grants* £98,956 *Grants to organisations* £98,956 *Assets* £4,799,996
TRUSTEES Wilfrid Vernor-Miles; John Crosfield Vernor-Miles; Paul Williams.
OTHER INFORMATION Many of the beneficiaries are supported year after year, particularly where trustees are informed of the benefits of foundation funds from previous grants.
HOW TO APPLY Applications should be made in writing to the correspondent. The trustees respond to every application; however, the 2015 annual report states, 'The trustees support a number of charities on a regular basis and in practice finds that their income is fully committed and there is little, if any, surplus income available for distribution in response to unsolicited appeals.'
WHO TO APPLY TO Wilfrid Vernor-Miles, Trustee, c/o Hunters Solicitors, 9 New Square, Lincoln's Inn, London WC2A 3QN

The SMB Trust

CC NO 263814 **ESTABLISHED** 1962
WHERE FUNDING CAN BE GIVEN UK and overseas.
WHO CAN BENEFIT Charitable organisations.
WHAT IS FUNDED The annual report states that the trust supporting the following causes: Christian faith; social care in the UK and abroad; famine relief/emergency aid; environment and wildlife; education and medical research.
WHAT IS NOT FUNDED Individuals.
RANGE OF GRANTS £50 to £6,000; generally around £1,200.
SAMPLE GRANTS Disasters Emergency Committee/ Concern (£6,000); Pilgrim Friends Society (£4,000); Oasis UK (£2,500); Zimbabwe Educational Trust (£1,200); Save the Children (£2,000); Designability, Toxteth Women's Centre and Woodland Christian Trust (£1,000 each); Rye Street Pastors (£500); Freedom from Torture (£50).
FINANCES *Year* 2014/15 *Income* £412,426 *Grants* £263,545 *Grants to organisations* £263,545 *Assets* £10,160,806
TRUSTEES Philip Stanford; Jeremy Anstead; Barbara O'Driscoll; Ian Wilson.
HOW TO APPLY Apply in writing to the correspondent, including the aims and principal activities of the applicant, the current financial position and details of any special projects for which funding is sought. There are no application forms. Trustees normally meet four times a year to consider applications. Because of the volume of appeals received, unsuccessful applicants will only receive a reply if they enclose an sae. However, unsuccessful applicants are welcome to re-apply.
WHO TO APPLY TO Barbara O'Driscoll, Trustee, 15 Wilman Road, Tunbridge Wells TN4 9AJ *Tel.* 01892 537301 *Email* smbcharitabletrust@googlemail.com

The Mrs Smith and Mount Trust

CC NO 1009718 **ESTABLISHED** 1992
WHERE FUNDING CAN BE GIVEN Norfolk, Suffolk, Cambridgeshire, Hertfordshire, Essex, Kent, Surrey and London.
WHO CAN BENEFIT Registered charities.
WHAT IS FUNDED The main grants scheme, The Mount Fund, focuses on the following four priority areas: mental health; learning disability; homelessness; health in the community. The Mrs Smith Fund also awards block grants to registered charities to distribute in small hardship grants for individuals in need, focusing on: young people leaving care; individuals returning to the community after living in care or long-stay hospital accommodation; or those who have had to give up their home. The Spanoghe Grants Programme focuses on improving the mental health and resilience of young people in London, but applications for this scheme are by invitation only. Further information on each of the grants schemes is given on the website.
WHAT IS NOT FUNDED National organisations (apart from individual branches which are responsible for their own finances and can provide separate accounts); individuals; general counselling; charities with an income of over £1 million or unrestricted reserves representing the value of more than six months of annual expenditure.
TYPE OF GRANT Mainly project funding, but general running costs may also be considered, particularly for charities which have previously received support.
RANGE OF GRANTS £1,000 to £7,000.
SAMPLE GRANTS The Spires Centre (£10,000); Opening Doors and Tilehouse Counselling (£8,000 each); Buttle UK, Haringey Migrant Support Centre and Stand By Me Bereavement Support Service for Children (£5,000 each); Essex Dementia Care (£4,000); Nourish Community Foodbank (£3,800); Maidstone Churches Winter Shelter (£3,200); BCU Life Skills Centre (£2,000).

FINANCES *Year* 2015/16 *Income* £294,897 *Grants* £244,278 *Grants to organisations* £244,278 *Assets* £7,539,947

TRUSTEES Richard Fowler; Timothy Warren; Gillian Barnes; Lisa Weaks; Mike Wariebi.

OTHER INFORMATION Grants during the year were made to: 46 organisations through the Mount Fund and five organisations through the Mrs Smith Fund. Grants were committed for future years to six organisations through the Spanoghe Grants Programme.

HOW TO APPLY All applications must be submitted using the online application form which can be downloaded from the website, where full guidelines and criteria are also available to view. The trustees meet three times per year in March, July and November and application forms and supporting documentation must be submitted at least six weeks in advance of a meeting, or by the date specified on the website.

WHO TO APPLY TO Trust Administrator, 6 Trull Farm Buildings, Tetbury, Gloucestershire GL8 8SQ *Tel.* 020 3325 2590 *Email* admin@mrssmithandmounttrust.org *Website* mrssmithandmounttrust.org

■ The DS Smith Charitable Foundation

CC NO 1142817 **ESTABLISHED** 2011

WHERE FUNDING CAN BE GIVEN England and Wales.

WHO CAN BENEFIT Registered charities and voluntary organisations.

WHAT IS FUNDED Education and training; environmental conservation.

TYPE OF GRANT Long-term partnerships combining financial support and practical support from employees; small, one-off grants.

RANGE OF GRANTS Small grants under £1,000; larger donations up to £100,000.

SAMPLE GRANTS Keep Britain Tidy (£100,000); Zoological Society of London (£50,000); Museum of Brands (£40,000); International Red Cross (£37,500); Unicef (£36,000); Royal Institution (£30,000); Global Action Plan (£7,200).

FINANCES *Year* 2015/16 *Income* £43,458 *Grants* £319,331 *Grants to organisations* £319,331 *Assets* £2,293,817

TRUSTEES Anne Steele; Rachel Stevens; Nicholas Feaviour; Mark Greenwood; Mark Reeve; Catriona O'Grady.

OTHER INFORMATION Grants were made to 36 organisations during the year.

HOW TO APPLY Applications can be made using the form on the foundation's website. The small donations committee meets to review applications on a quarterly basis.

WHO TO APPLY TO Rachel Stevens, Trustee, 7th Floor, 350 Euston Road, London NW1 3AX *Tel.* 020 7756 1823 *Email* charitablefoundation@dssmith.com *Website* www.dssmith.com/company/sustainability/our-people/community-involvement/charitable-foundation

■ The N. Smith Charitable Settlement

CC NO 276660 **ESTABLISHED** 1978

WHERE FUNDING CAN BE GIVEN Worldwide.

WHO CAN BENEFIT Registered charities.

WHAT IS FUNDED General charitable purposes, including social welfare; health and medical research; environment; overseas aid.

RANGE OF GRANTS £400 to £2,500. Mostly £1,000 or less.

SAMPLE GRANTS Voluntary Service Overseas (£2,500); Action on Hearing Loss (£2,300); Autistica (£2,000); Brain Research Trust and Solar Aid (£1,000 each); Edinburgh Young Carers Trust and Northampton Volunteering Centre (£750 each); Treetops Hospice Trust (£640); Jura Music Festival and Young Dementia UK (£500 each); Flora and Fauna International (£400).

FINANCES *Year* 2014/15 *Income* £191,849 *Grants* £207,610 *Grants to organisations* £207,610 *Assets* £4,857,441

TRUSTEES Anne Merricks; Graham Wardle; Janet Adam; Susan Darlington.

OTHER INFORMATION The 2014/15 accounts were the most recent available to view on the Charity Commission's website at the time of writing (June 2017).

HOW TO APPLY Apply in writing to the correspondent. In 2014/15 the trustees met three times, in July, November and March.

WHO TO APPLY TO The Trustees, c/o Linder Myers, Phoenix House, 45 Cross Street, Manchester M2 4JF *Tel.* 0161 832 6972 *Email* charlotte.ashworth@lindermyers.co.uk

■ The Smith Charitable Trust

CC NO 288570 **ESTABLISHED** 1983

WHERE FUNDING CAN BE GIVEN UK.

WHO CAN BENEFIT Registered charities, usually large, well-known UK organisations, which are on a list of regular beneficiaries.

WHAT IS FUNDED General charitable purposes, particularly health.

RANGE OF GRANTS £4,000 to £10,000.

SAMPLE GRANTS RNIB, Royal National Lifeboat Institution and Research Institute for the Care of the Elderly (£9,500 each); Action for Children, Help for Heroes and St Nicholas' Hospice (£7,100 each); Artists' General Benevolent Institution, British Heart Foundation, Cancer Research UK and Scope (£4,700 each).

FINANCES *Year* 2015/16 *Income* £159,336 *Grants* £153,855 *Grants to organisations* £153,855 *Assets* £9,792,796

TRUSTEES Robert Turner; Paul Shiels; Richard Fuller.

OTHER INFORMATION Grants were awarded to 24 organisations during the year.

HOW TO APPLY Unsolicited applications are not considered.

WHO TO APPLY TO Paul Shiels, Trustee, Moon Beever Solicitors, Bedford House, 21A John Street, London WC1N 2BF *Tel.* 020 7400 7770 *Email* psheils@moonbeever.com

■ The Henry Smith Charity

CC NO 230102 **ESTABLISHED** 1628

WHERE FUNDING CAN BE GIVEN UK. Specific local programmes in the north east of England, and in Gloucestershire, Hampshire, Kent, Leicestershire, Suffolk, Surrey, and East and West Sussex.

WHO CAN BENEFIT Charitable organisations.

WHAT IS FUNDED Social welfare and disadvantage. There are a number of grants programmes: Main Grants Programme – revenue grants for up to three years, to cover running costs or project costs; County Grants Programme – small grants in the counties with which the charity has a connection; Small Grants in the north east of England – made through Community Foundation for Tyne and Wear and Northumberland; Holiday Grants for Children – for organisations to provide holidays for children who are disadvantaged or who have disabilities; Christian Projects – to promote the Christian faith, in a Church of England context; Kindred Grants – for those connected to Henry Smith.

WHAT IS NOT FUNDED Each of the charity's grants programmes has specific exclusions – refer to the website for this information.

TYPE OF GRANT Capital and revenue; one-off grants and recurrent grants for up to three years.

RANGE OF GRANTS Varies with each grants programme.

SAMPLE GRANTS Alive Activities Ltd (£176,000); Iranian and Kurdish Women's Rights Organisation (£153,000); East Belfast Independent Advice Centre (£80,000); Proud Trust (£72,500); Newhall Kidz Ltd (£64,500); West Essex Alcohol and Drugs Service (£60,000); Reaching Families (£18,000); Dramatize Theatre Charity (£6,100); Friends of Osborne School (£5,000); 6th East Paddington Brownies (£300).

FINANCES *Year* 2015 *Income* £11,700,000 *Grants* £28,090,000 *Grants to organisations* £27,377,000 *Assets* £841,754,000

TRUSTEES Gracia McGrath; Anna McNair Scott; Merlyn Lowther; Noel Manns; Diana Barran; Patrick Maxwell; Miko Giedroyc; Bridget Biddell; David Allam; Revd Canon Paul Hackwood; Vivian Hunt; James Hordern; Vivienne Dews; Piers Feilden; Emir Feisal; Lady Bella Colgrain.

OTHER INFORMATION The charity made 462 grants to organisations during the year. The amount of grants given to individuals totalled £1,100.

HOW TO APPLY Refer to the website for information on how to apply to each of the charity's grants programmes, as well as guidance and application forms. The charity states that it does not, under any circumstances, make grants in response to 'general appeals or mail shots'.

WHO TO APPLY TO The Grants Team, The Henry Smith Charity – Applications, 6th Floor, 65 Leadenhall Street, London EC3A 2AD *Tel.* 020 7264 4970 *Website* www.henrysmithcharity.org.uk

■ The Leslie Smith Foundation

CC NO 250030 **ESTABLISHED** 1964

WHERE FUNDING CAN BE GIVEN UK with a preference for Wiltshire, Norfolk, Middlesex, London and Dorset.

WHO CAN BENEFIT Registered charities, with a preference for those benefitting children with illnesses, both terminal and non-terminal, in the UK (excluding respite care and research); orphans; and schools, specifically special needs schools based in the UK.

WHAT IS FUNDED General charitable purposes, particularly: children in the UK with life-changing illnesses; orphans; education and special needs schools.

WHAT IS NOT FUNDED Individuals. Grants are given to registered charities only.

RANGE OF GRANTS £500 to £10,000.

SAMPLE GRANTS Children's Hospice South West, Dorothy House Hospice, Heaton Ellis Trust, Help for Heroes, Hop Skip Jump, Shooting Stars Children's Hospice and Wessex Children's Hospice (£10,000 each); Shakespeare Globe Education Trust (£5,000).

FINANCES *Year* 2015/16 *Income* £73,122 *Grants* £75,000 *Grants to organisations* £75,000 *Assets* £3,120,825

TRUSTEES Deborah Fisher; Alice Rutherford Prall; Curtis Rutherford Hayles; Emma Rutherford Hayles; Matthew Rutherford Hayles.

HOW TO APPLY Apply in writing to the correspondent, including a summary of the project and a copy of the latest accounts. Only successful applications are acknowledged. The trustees meet at least twice a year.

WHO TO APPLY TO The Trustees, c/o Willcoxlewis LLP, The Old Coach House, Sunnyside, Bergh Apton, Norwich NR15 1DD *Tel.* 01508 480100 *Email* info@fisherlegal.co.uk

■ The Martin Smith Foundation

CC NO 1550753 **ESTABLISHED** 2012

WHERE FUNDING CAN BE GIVEN UK with a preference for Oxfordshire.

WHO CAN BENEFIT Registered charities.

WHAT IS FUNDED The performing arts; education; ecology and the environment; recreational sport; the relief of poverty; and religion.

SAMPLE GRANTS The Smith Family Educational Foundation (£407,000); Orchestra of the Age of Enlightenment (£73,000); Glyndebourne (£15,000); National Orchestras for All (£10,000); Orchestra of St John's (£8,000); Oxford Lieder (£4,000); Music for Autism (£1,000).

FINANCES *Year* 2015 *Income* £60,772 *Grants* £583,985 *Grants to organisations* £583,985 *Assets* £2,764,488

TRUSTEES Lady Smith; Sir Martin Smith; Katherine Wake; Elizabeth Buchannan; Bartholomew Peerles.

HOW TO APPLY Apply in writing to the correspondent.

WHO TO APPLY TO Sir Martin Smith, Trustee, 5 Park Town, Oxford OX2 6SN *Tel.* 01865 554554

■ The WH Smith Group Charitable Trust

CC NO 1013782 **ESTABLISHED** 1992

WHERE FUNDING CAN BE GIVEN UK.

WHO CAN BENEFIT Charitable organisations and schools. There is a preference for organisations in which WHSmith employees are involved.

WHAT IS FUNDED General charitable purposes; education, reading and literacy. The Community Grants programme offers small grants to any charitable organisation 'supporting the community'. The trust also works with schools to promote reading.

WHAT IS NOT FUNDED Party political organisations; religious organisations; military organisations; individuals; expeditions or overseas travel.

RANGE OF GRANTS Community grants: up to £500.

SAMPLE GRANTS National Literacy Trust (£61,500); Macmillan Cancer Support (£3,200); Regain Sports Charity (£2,000); Cancer Research UK (£1,400); Wroughton Infants School (£1,300); Alzheimer's Research UK, Friends of Dorchester School, MS Society, RSPCA and The Arts Circus (£1,000 each).

FINANCES *Year* 2015 *Income* £141,204 *Grants* £128,589 *Grants to organisations* £128,589 *Assets* £88,449

TRUSTEES Anthony Lawrence; Faye Sherman; Sarah Heath; Adrian Mansfield; Natalie Davidson; Paul Green; Sue Poynton; Sharon Appleton.

OTHER INFORMATION During the year grants of £1,000 or more were made to 22 organisations. Smaller awards totalled about £14,500.

HOW TO APPLY Applications for a community grant can be made online: blog.whsmith.co.uk/community-grants-application. There are two application rounds each year: 1 October to 31 March; 1 April to 30 September. Grants are reviewed and decided by the trustees at the end of each six-month period.

WHO TO APPLY TO The Secretary, W. H. Smith Ltd, Greenbridge Road, Swindon SN3 3JE *Tel.* 01793 616161 *Email* communitygrants@whsmith.co.uk *Website* www.whsmithplc.co.uk/corporate_responsibility/whsmith_trust

■ The Stanley Smith UK Horticultural Trust

CC NO 261925 **ESTABLISHED** 1970

WHERE FUNDING CAN BE GIVEN UK and overseas.

WHO CAN BENEFIT Horticultural organisations; individuals.

WHAT IS FUNDED Horticulture, gardening and botany; promotion of biodiversity; creation, development and maintenance of gardens accessible to the public; horticultural education, training, research and publications.

WHAT IS NOT FUNDED Projects relating to commercial agriculture initiatives, commercial crop production or forestry; salaries; students taking academic or diploma courses; gap year travel; projects focused on social welfare, health or well-being, with the exception of horticultural therapy projects. The trust will only consider funding repair or conservation of physical structures relating to historic landscapes (e.g. pergolas or conservatories) if part of a wider garden restoration project. It will not consider grants for 'modern slabbing', construction materials or equipment, but may consider certain historic 'hard landscaping' projects. The trust will not support individuals for training or traineeships, instead providing a block grant to a training provider.

RANGE OF GRANTS Grants range £250 to £5,000, typically £2,000 to £4,000.

SAMPLE GRANTS Chelsea Physic Garden (£4,900); Eden Project – Bright Sparks Project (£4,000); Nairobi Botanic Garden (£3,500); St Cuthbert's College (£3,000); Shakespeare Birthplace Trust (£2,500); Chawton House Library Herb Garden (£2,000); Plant Heritage Threatened Plants Project (£1,000); Bidston Hill (£500); Biddulph Grange Dahlia Walk (£200).

FINANCES *Year* 2015/16 *Income* £77,747 *Grants* £105,376 *Grants to organisations* £105,376 *Assets* £3,754,760

TRUSTEES Alexander De Byre; Christopher Brickell; Lady Jane Renfrew; John Simmons; Phillip Sykes; Edward Reed; Dr John David.

HOW TO APPLY Guidance notes, detailing how to apply and what should be included in an application, are available to download from the trust's website. Grants are usually made in April and October.

WHO TO APPLY TO Dr David Rae, Director, c/o Dr David Rae, Royal Botanic Garden, 20A Inverleith Row, Edinburgh EH3 5LR *Tel.* 0131 248 2905 *Email* d.rae@rbge.org.uk *Website* www.grantsforhorticulturists.org.uk/Smith.html

■ Philip Smith's Charitable Trust

CC NO 1003751 **ESTABLISHED** 1991

WHERE FUNDING CAN BE GIVEN UK with a preference for Gloucestershire.

WHO CAN BENEFIT Registered charities.

WHAT IS FUNDED The trust makes grants mainly in the fields of the environment and education.

WHAT IS NOT FUNDED Individuals.

SAMPLE GRANTS Save the Children (£10,000); League of Friends of Moreton-in-Marsh Hospital and the Gamekeepers Welfare Charitable Trust (£5,000 each); St James' Parochial Church Council Chipping Campden (£4,000); The Salvation Army (£2,500); the Army Benevolent Fund and Church Urban Fund (£1,000 each).

FINANCES *Year* 2015/16 *Income* £22,050 *Grants* £130,000 *Grants to organisations* £130,000

TRUSTEES Hon. Philip R. Smith; Mary Smith.

OTHER INFORMATION The trust's latest accounts were not available to view on the Charity Commission's website due to its low income. We have therefore estimated the grant total based on previous years' information.

HOW TO APPLY Apply in writing to the correspondent. The trust states that only successful applicants will receive a response to their application.

WHO TO APPLY TO Helen D'Monte, Bircham Dyson Bell, 50 Broadway, London SW1H 0BL *Tel.* 020 7783 3685 *Email* helendmonte@bdb-law.co.uk

■ The R. C. Snelling Charitable Trust

CC NO 1074776 **ESTABLISHED** 1999

WHERE FUNDING CAN BE GIVEN Within a 30-mile radius of the village of Blofield in Norfolk.

WHO CAN BENEFIT Registered charities; charitable organisations; individuals.

WHAT IS FUNDED General charitable purposes; education and training; the promotion of health; people with disabilities; social welfare; accommodation and housing; Christianity; the environment and animals.

WHAT IS NOT FUNDED Salaries; sponsorship for more than one year; general appeals where the need could be met several times over by grantors; national appeals; continued assistance with running costs.

TYPE OF GRANT Equipment; capital appeals; specific local projects; running costs; seed funding; fundraising events.

RANGE OF GRANTS £150 to £5,000.

SAMPLE GRANTS Norwich Credit Union (£5,000); Kings Community Initiative (£2,500); Norfolk and Norwich Association for the Blind (£2,000); East Anglian Air Ambulance (£1,900); Whitlingham Boathouses (£1,500); Stepping Stones (£1,200); Great Witchingham Village Hall (£1,000); The Jubilee Family Centre (£750); Norwich Vineyard Christian Fellowship (£500); Reedham Pre School Playgroup (£150).

FINANCES *Year* 2014/15 *Income* £18,279,508 *Grants* £66,768 *Grants to organisations* £66,768 *Assets* £11,435,854

TRUSTEES Philip Buttinger; Rowland Cogman; Toby Wise; Nigel Savory; Stephan Phillips; Colin Jacobs; Samuel Barratt.

OTHER INFORMATION Grants were made to 56 organisations during the year. At the time of writing (June 2017) the 2014/15 accounts were the latest available on the Charity Commission's website.

HOW TO APPLY An online application form can be completed from the company's website. The trust is happy to receive queries via email.

WHO TO APPLY TO Rowland Cogman, Trustee, R. C. Snelling Ltd, Laundry Lane, Blofield Heath, Norwich NR13 4SQ *Tel.* 01603 712202 *Email* trustee@rcsnellingcharitabletrust.org *Website* www.rcsnellingcharitabletrust.org

■ The Sobell Foundation

CC NO 274369 **ESTABLISHED** 1977

WHERE FUNDING CAN BE GIVEN England and Wales, Israel and the Commonwealth of Independent States.

WHO CAN BENEFIT Small national or local registered or exempt charities. Overseas charities must be able to provide the details of a UK-registered charity through which funding can be channelled on their behalf.

WHAT IS FUNDED The foundation's website states that the trustees aim 'to achieve a reasonable spread' between Jewish and non-Jewish charities working in the following areas: medical care and treatment, including respite care and hospices; care and education and training for adults and children who have physical or learning disabilities; care and support of older people and of children; homelessness.

WHAT IS NOT FUNDED Individuals; organisations that have applied to the foundation within the past year. Applications from large national charities which have wide support are unlikely to be considered.

TYPE OF GRANT One-off; multi-year.

SAMPLE GRANTS A list of beneficiaries was not available.

FINANCES *Year* 2015/16 *Income* £1,971,805 *Grants* £5,292,592 *Grants to organisations* £5,292,592 *Assets* £67,093,669

TRUSTEES Susan Lacroix; Roger Lewis; Andrea Scouller.

OTHER INFORMATION 509 grants were made during the year, of which 379 were in the UK.

HOW TO APPLY Application forms are available to download from the website and should be completed and returned to the foundation by post. The foundation notes that it will write with the result of your application as soon as possible, although this may take several months. Applicants, successful or otherwise, may only re-apply to the foundation after 12 months.

WHO TO APPLY TO Penny Newton, Administrator, PO Box 2137, Shepton Mallet, Somerset BA4 6YA *Tel.* 01749 813135 *Email* enquiries@sobellfoundation.org.uk *Website* www.sobellfoundation.org.uk

■ Social Business Trust

CC NO 1136151 **ESTABLISHED** 2010

WHERE FUNDING CAN BE GIVEN UK.

WHO CAN BENEFIT Social enterprises. Must be registered charities or have a clear charitable purposes (e.g. CICs), and have an annual revenue of more than £1 million.

WHAT IS FUNDED Social enterprise. The trust outlines its unique approach on its website: 'We believe there are a number of social enterprises capable of scaling up their operations on a regional and national level and we have a clear and ambitious goal: to help transform the impact of social enterprises and thereby improve the lives of over a million of the UK's most disadvantaged people.' See the website for more information of the trust's work.

TYPE OF GRANT A package of cash grants and in-kind services. Support usually provided instalments each being conditional upon achievement of certain milestones.

SAMPLE GRANTS London Early Years Foundation (£765,000); The Challenge Network (£583,000); Hertfordshire Independent Living Service (£366,500); Brightside (£112,000); User Voice (£83,500); The Reader Organisation (£83,000); Moneyline (£58,000); Enabling Enterprise (£26,500); Bikeworks (£8,900); Inspiring Futures Foundation (£6,800).

FINANCES *Year* 2015/16 *Income* £3,448,628 *Grants* £389,384 *Grants to organisations* £389,384 *Assets* £910,661

TRUSTEES Paul Armstrong; Simon Milton; Jonathan Myers; Tim Curry; Guy Davies.

OTHER INFORMATION The grant total above accounts for cash grants only. In total during the year, the trust contributed over £2.8 million to organisations, £2.5 million of which was through the provision of in-kind services.

HOW TO APPLY The website states that eligible organisations should contact the trust about getting involved: info@socialbusinesstrust.org.

WHO TO APPLY TO Adele Blakebrough, Chief Executive, First Floor, 13 St Swithin's Lane, London EC4N 8AL *Tel.* 020 3011 0770 *Email* info@socialbusinesstrust.org *Website* www.socialbusinesstrust.org

■ Social Investment Business Foundation

CC NO 1117185 **ESTABLISHED** 2006

WHERE FUNDING CAN BE GIVEN UK.

WHO CAN BENEFIT Registered charities and social enterprises.

WHAT IS FUNDED The charity has a number of different funds; refer to the website for information on what is currently available. Funds often focus on enabling organisations to prepare for social investment or competing for contracts, or grow their scale or social impact.

WHAT IS NOT FUNDED Refer to the website for exclusions from each specific fund.

TYPE OF GRANT Grants, loans and other forms of social investment, as well as support and advice.

SAMPLE GRANTS Beyond Autism (£2 million loan); Hastings Pier Charity (£150,000 loan and £100,000 grant); Bootstrap Company (£198,500 loan and £132,500 grant); The Rare Trust (£168,500 – loan); Ashley Community Housing (£75,000); Ecological Land Co-operative (£49,000); Moving on Durham (£23,500); North East Dance (£15,000); The Fox and Hounds Community Co-operative (£8,500).

FINANCES *Year* 2015/16 *Income* £4,986,000 *Grants* £3,311,000 *Grants to organisations* £3,311,000 *Assets* £81,951,000

TRUSTEES Hugh Rolo; James Rice; Anand Shukla; Edward Lord; Jeremy Newman; Richard Pelly; Rt Hon. Hazel Blears; Jenny North.

OTHER INFORMATION Grants were made to 32 organisations during 2015/16. The foundation also made loans totalling £154 million. Sample beneficiaries were taken from the website and were not awarded in the same financial year.

HOW TO APPLY Information about how to apply for each fund is given on the website.

WHO TO APPLY TO Caroline Forster, Interim Chief Executive, Social Investment Business, 2nd Floor, Can Mezzanine, 7–14 Great Dover Street, London SE1 4YR *Tel.* 020 3096 7900 *Email* enquiries@sibgroup.org.uk *Website* www.sibgroup.org.uk

■ Sodexo Stop Hunger Foundation

CC NO 1110266 **ESTABLISHED** 2005

WHERE FUNDING CAN BE GIVEN UK and Ireland.

WHO CAN BENEFIT Charitable organisations.

WHAT IS FUNDED Health, nutrition and well-being; food poverty; disadvantaged communities. According to the 2014/16 annual report, the Stop Hunger campaign aims to 'tackle poor nutrition in local communities, promote good nutrition and healthy lifestyles, promote basic life skills such as cooking'.

RANGE OF GRANTS £2,000 to £135,000.

SAMPLE GRANTS Outward Bound Trust (£135,500); Coram Life (£24,000); Centrepoint (£23,000); Community Foundation of Ireland (£13,000); Body and Soul (£13,000); Scouts Association (£8,900); The Prince's Trust (£5,800); Osmondthorpe Resource Centre (£3,500); Aberlour Child Care Trust (£3,400); Brendoncare (£2,900).

FINANCES *Year* 2014/15 *Income* £500,691 *Grants* £243,505 *Grants to organisations* £243,505 *Assets* £154,799

TRUSTEES Phil Hooper; Harbhajan Singh Brar; Rebecca Symon; David Mulcahy; Gareth John; Margot Slattery; Neil Murray; Lee Brittain; Patrick Forbes.

OTHER INFORMATION The 2014/16 accounts were the most recent available on the Charity Commission's website at the time of writing (June 2017). Grants were made to 13 organisations during the year. The Sodexo Foundation is the corporate charity of the food services and facilities management company, Sodexo Ltd.

HOW TO APPLY Contact the foundation using the contact form on its website.

WHO TO APPLY TO Edwina Hughes, Corporate Responsibility Manager, Sodexo, 1 Southampton Row, London WC1B 5HA *Email* stophunger@sodexo.com *Website* uk.sodexo.com/home/corporate-responsibility.html

■ Sofronie Foundation

CC NO 1118621 **ESTABLISHED** 2007

WHERE FUNDING CAN BE GIVEN UK; France; Netherlands.

WHO CAN BENEFIT Registered charities; non-profit organisations.

WHAT IS FUNDED Projects that offer young people from disadvantaged backgrounds opportunities to acquire skills for higher education or training for work.

SAMPLE GRANTS Child.org (£200,000); The Prince's Trust (£100,000); The Sutton Trust (£80,000); Into University (£50,000); Royal National Children's Foundation (£35,000); Stichting Move Foundation (£14,000).

FINANCES *Year* 2015 *Income* £1,810,127 *Grants* £1,169,956 *Grants to organisations* £1,169,956 *Assets* £2,090,133

TRUSTEES Harold Goddijn; Corrin Goddijn-Vigreux; Robert Wilne; Ajay Soni.

HOW TO APPLY Applications can be made through the foundation's website.

WHO TO APPLY TO Jacqueline Higgin, 16 Great Queen Street, London WC2B 5DH *Tel.* 020 7421 3330 *Email* enquiries@sofronie.org *Website* www.sofronie.org

■ Solev Co. Ltd

CC NO 254623 **ESTABLISHED** 1967

WHERE FUNDING CAN BE GIVEN UK and Israel.

WHO CAN BENEFIT Charitable organisations; Jewish organisations.

WHAT IS FUNDED General charitable purposes, particularly Jewish education and religious activities; medical causes; relief of poverty.

SAMPLE GRANTS Dina Perelman Trust Ltd (£100,000); Songdale Ltd (£40,000); Society of Friends of the Torah (£3,900); Finchley Road Synagogue (£2,300); North West London Talmudical College (£1,500); Yesodey Hatorah School (£700); Gateshead Talmudical College (£400).

FINANCES *Year* 2015/16 *Income* £380,992 *Grants* £367,822 *Grants to organisations* £367,822 *Assets* £5,946,010

TRUSTEES Romie Tager; Chaim Frommer; Joseph Tager Simon Tager.

OTHER INFORMATION No information on grant beneficiaries has been included in the charity's accounts in recent years.

HOW TO APPLY Apply in writing to the correspondent.

WHO TO APPLY TO Romie Tager, Trustee, 1 Spaniards Park, Columbas Drive, London NW3 7JD *Tel.* 020 7420 9500

■ The Solo Charitable Settlement

CC NO 326444 **ESTABLISHED** 1983

WHERE FUNDING CAN BE GIVEN UK and overseas, particularly Israel.

WHO CAN BENEFIT Registered charities.

WHAT IS FUNDED General charitable purposes, particularly focusing on education; the relief of poverty; older people; Jewish causes.

RANGE OF GRANTS Between £250 and £25,000.

SAMPLE GRANTS United Jewish Israel Appeal (UJIA) (£25,000); Community Security Trust (£10,000); The Central British Fund for World Jewish Relief (£7,500); Chai Cancer Care and Nightingale House (£5,200 each); Dulwich College and Heart Cells Foundation (£5,000 each); Kol Nidre Appeal (£1,300); Future Dreams (£500); Jewish Care (£250).

FINANCES *Year* 2015/16 *Income* £191,463 *Grants* £87,675 *Grants to organisations* £87,675 *Assets* £6,080,708

TRUSTEES Edna Goldstein; Peter Goldstein; Dean Goldstein; Jamie Goldstein; Paul Goldstein; Tammy Ward.

HOW TO APPLY Apply in writing to the correspondent. The trustees consider applications on a quarterly basis.

WHO TO APPLY TO The Trustees, c/o Harris and Trotter LLP, 64 New Cavendish Street, London W1G 8TB *Tel.* 020 7467 6300

■ David Solomons Charitable Trust

CC NO 297275 **ESTABLISHED** 1986

WHERE FUNDING CAN BE GIVEN UK.

WHO CAN BENEFIT Registered charities.

WHAT IS FUNDED Support for people with learning disabilities.

WHAT IS NOT FUNDED Individuals.

RANGE OF GRANTS Generally up to £2,000.

SAMPLE GRANTS Down's Syndrome Association (£8,000); Claire House Children's Hospice and Friends of Castledon School (£2,000 each); My Life My Choice and Theatre Royal Bath (£1,500 each); Mudlarks Community Garden, The National Autistic Society and Toucan

Employment (£1,000 each); Stopgap Dance Company Ltd (£500); Hereward College (£400).

FINANCES *Year* 2015/16 *Income* £96,924 *Grants* £96,400 *Grants to organisations* £96,400 *Assets* £2,455,100

TRUSTEES John Drewitt; Jeremy Rutter; Dr Richard Solomons; Diana Huntingford; Michael Chamberlayne; Dr Leila Cooke.

OTHER INFORMATION Down's Syndrome Association is funded every year.

HOW TO APPLY The trustees have stated that they conduct their own research into potential applicants.

WHO TO APPLY TO Elizabeth Prior, 2 Highfield Road, Collier Row, Romford RM5 3RA *Tel.* 01708 502488 *Email* davidsolomonscharitabletrust@gmail.com

■ Somerset Community Foundation

CC NO 1094446 **ESTABLISHED** 2002

WHERE FUNDING CAN BE GIVEN Somerset only.

WHO CAN BENEFIT Local charitable organisations.

WHAT IS FUNDED The foundation's programmes aim to achieve the following objectives: tackle disadvantage; transform lives; strengthen local communities. The foundation manages a number of different grants programmes, as well as making its own grants; refer to the website for current information.

WHAT IS NOT FUNDED Refer to the website for exclusions from specific grants programmes. For the foundation's own grants, the following will not be supported: individuals; national charities and appeals; sponsorship and fundraising events; animal welfare; promotion of religion (or repair of buildings used for worship); activities which are statutory responsibilities or are not charitable; retrospective funding; funds distributed to a third party; projects taking place outside Somerset; activities taking place during school time.

SAMPLE GRANTS Community Council for Somerset (£29,500 in nine grants); Neroche Woodlanders Ltd (£7,900); Timberscombe Village Hall (£4,200); Cruse Bereavement Care (£2,700); Wincanton Men's Shed (£1,700); St Francis Youth Club (£1,000); Queen Camel Cricket Club (£500); Frome Breastfeeding Group (£400); Taunton Foodbank (£350); 1st Bridgwater Wembdon Scout Group (£50).

FINANCES *Year* 2015/16 *Income* £1,443,641 *Grants* £711,461 *Grants to organisations* £536,428 *Assets* £6,411,141

TRUSTEES Timothy Walker; Janice Ross; Kathleen Lock; Jane Barrie; Paul Hake; Martin Kitchen; Andrew Palmer; Sarah Wakefield; Karen Pearson; Lucilla Nelson; Barry O'Leary; Judith North; Richard Lloyd; Chris Bishop; John Macdonald Lyon.

OTHER INFORMATION Grants to individuals during the year totalled £175,000.

HOW TO APPLY Applications should be made using the online form. Refer to each specific grants scheme for deadlines.

WHO TO APPLY TO Programmes Team, Somerset Community Foundation, Yeoman House, The Bath and West Showground, Shepton Mallet BA4 6QN *Tel.* 01749 344949 *Email* info@somersetcf.org.uk *Website* www.somersetcf.org.uk

■ Songdale Ltd

CC NO 286075 **ESTABLISHED** 1961

WHERE FUNDING CAN BE GIVEN UK and Israel.

WHO CAN BENEFIT Charitable organisations.

WHAT IS FUNDED Jewish causes; social welfare; education and training.

SAMPLE GRANTS Moreshet Hatorah Ltd (£132,000); Belz Avreichim Synagogue (£6,000); London Rabbincal and Yeshiva Horomoh (£5,000 each); The Union of Hebrew Congregations (£4,500); Kahal Imrei Chaim Ltd (£4,300); Chinnah Vechsida and Mifal Tzedoko V'chesed Ltd (£4,000 each).

FINANCES *Year* 2015/16 *Income* £239,666 *Grants* £232,483 *Grants to organisations* £232,483 *Assets* £2,362,395

TRUSTEES Yechiel Grosskopf; Malka Grosskopf.

HOW TO APPLY Apply in writing to the correspondent.

WHO TO APPLY TO Yechiel Grosskopf, Trustee, New Burlington House, 1075 Finchley Road, London NW11 0PU *Tel.* 020 8806 5010

■ The E. C. Sosnow Charitable Trust

CC NO 273578 **ESTABLISHED** 1977

WHERE FUNDING CAN BE GIVEN UK and overseas.

WHO CAN BENEFIT Charitable organisations.

WHAT IS FUNDED Education; the arts; social welfare; health and emergency relief; Jewish causes.

WHAT IS NOT FUNDED Individuals.

RANGE OF GRANTS £1,500 to £18,000.

SAMPLE GRANTS Weizmann UK (£18,000); Africa Education Trust, British Friends of the Israel Philharmonic Orchestra and Holocaust Educational Trust (£5,000 each); Christ's College Cambridge (£3,000); Mental Health Foundation and Prostate Cancer UK (£2,000 each); British Friends of Zichron Menachem (£1,500).

FINANCES *Year* 2015/16 *Income* £59,678 *Grants* £59,600 *Grants to organisations* £59,600 *Assets* £2,130,952

TRUSTEES Elias Fattal; Fiona Fattal; Alexandra Fattal; Richard Fattal.

OTHER INFORMATION Grants were made to 13 organisations during the year.

HOW TO APPLY Apply in writing to the correspondent.

WHO TO APPLY TO The Trustees, c/o Bourner Bullock, Sovereign House, 212–224 Shaftesbury Avenue, London WC2H 8HQ *Tel.* 020 7240 5821

■ The Souter Charitable Trust

SC NO SC029998 **ESTABLISHED** 1991

WHERE FUNDING CAN BE GIVEN UK, but with a preference for Scotland; overseas.

WHO CAN BENEFIT Registered charities.

WHAT IS FUNDED Relief of human suffering, particularly projects with a Christian emphasis.

WHAT IS NOT FUNDED Capital projects and renovation works; individuals.

TYPE OF GRANT Revenue costs; mainly one-off grants, a small number of multi-year grants (up to three years).

RANGE OF GRANTS £4,000 to £500,000.

SAMPLE GRANTS The Message Trust (£508,500); Christians Against Poverty (£383,500); Hope for Justice (£263,500); Alpha International (£150,000); Scotland's Charity Air Ambulance (£60,000); Watoto Children's Choir (£48,000); Blythswood Care (£35,000); Mary's Meals (£30,000); Prison Fellowship (£18,000); Factory Skate Park (£15,000); Medair (£4,000).

FINANCES *Year* 2015/16 *Income* £2,674,554 *Grants* £8,759,756 *Grants to organisations* £8,759,756 *Assets* £27,036,411

TRUSTEES Brian Souter; Betty Souter; Ann Allen.

HOW TO APPLY Apply in writing to the correspondent or by email to application@soutercharitabletrust.org.uk. Applications should be no more than two sides of A4 and should include audited accounts. The trustees meet once a month and dates are posted on the website. All applications are acknowledged in due course. Charities can only re-apply for a grant after one calendar year.

WHO TO APPLY TO Dion Judd, Trust Administrator, PO Box 7412, Perth PH1 5YX *Tel.* 01738 450408 *Email* enquiries@soutercharitabletrust.org.uk *Website* www.soutercharitabletrust.org.uk

■ The South Square Trust

CC NO 278960 **ESTABLISHED** 1979

WHERE FUNDING CAN BE GIVEN UK.

WHO CAN BENEFIT Registered charities; educational institutions; individuals.

WHAT IS FUNDED Grants are made to individuals for educational purposes, or to schools and colleges for the provision of bursaries and scholarships, mainly around the arts (see full criteria on the trust's website). Funding is also given to registered charities for general charitable purposes.

WHAT IS NOT FUNDED Building projects; salaries; individuals wishing to start up a business; individuals under 18; expeditions; travel; courses outside the UK; short courses; courses not connected with fine and applied arts.

TYPE OF GRANT Bursaries and scholarships for schools or colleges; one-off grants to charities.

RANGE OF GRANTS Individuals: £500 to £1,500; charities: mainly under £1,000.

SAMPLE GRANTS St Paul's School (£22,000); Byam Shaw School of Art (£6,000); Royal College of Music (£5,000); Bristol Old Vic Theatre School and RADA (Royal Academy of Dramatic Art) (£5,000 each); School of Jewellery – Birmingham (£2,700); Cystic Fibrosis Trust and Scotty's Little Soldiers (£1,500 each).

FINANCES *Year* 2015/16 *Income* £177,878 *Grants* £184,050 *Grants to organisations* £151,150 *Assets* £4,404,453

TRUSTEES Stephen Baldock; Christopher Grimwade; Paul Harriman; Andrew Blessley; Richard Inglis.

OTHER INFORMATION Grants were made to 33 charities during the year, totalling £25,500, of which 31 grants were for less than £1,000. Grants were made to 17 educational organisations for bursaries and scholarships. There were also 27 grants made to individuals, totalling £33,000.

HOW TO APPLY At the time of writing (April 2017), the trust's website states the following information: 'for the current year, August 2016 to July 2017, the Trustees are not accepting any applications from charities'. For current information, refer to the trust's website or contact the trust's clerk using the form on the website.

WHO TO APPLY TO Nicola Chrimes, Clerk to the Trustees, PO Box 69, Wadebridge, Cornwall PL27 9BZ *Tel.* 01825 872264 *Website* www.southsquaretrust.org.uk

■ The W. F. Southall Trust

CC NO 218371 **ESTABLISHED** 1937

WHERE FUNDING CAN BE GIVEN UK and overseas.

WHO CAN BENEFIT Registered charities, especially imaginative new grassroots initiatives and smaller charities.

WHAT IS FUNDED Work of the Society of Friends (Quakers); peacemaking and conflict resolution; organisations tackling alcohol, drug abuse, addiction and penal affairs; environmental action and sustainability; community action; overseas development.

WHAT IS NOT FUNDED Individuals; travel or study grants; organisations that do not have charitable status. The trust tends not to support major national charities.

TYPE OF GRANT Project costs; capital costs; revenue funding.

RANGE OF GRANTS Mainly £1,000 to £3,000.

SAMPLE GRANTS Society of Friends – Yearly Meeting (£50,000); Friends World Committee for Consultation (£11,000); Seeds for Change Network – through JRCT (£6,000); FareShare (£5,000); Action on Disability and Development, Campaign Against Arms Trade, Noah's Ark Children's Venture, Oasis of Peace UK, Quaker Homeless Action and Refugee Council (£3,000 each).

FINANCES *Year* 2015/16 *Income* £334,281 *Grants* £294,411 *Grants to organisations* £294,411 *Assets* £9,709,652

TRUSTEES Annette Wallis; Donald Southall; Joanna Engelkamp; Mark Holtom; Claire Greaves; Richard Maw; Hannah Engelkamp; Andrew Southall; Philip Coventry.

OTHER INFORMATION Grants were made to 109 organisations totalling £294,500.

HOW TO APPLY Applications should be made on a form available to download from the trust's website, where guidance notes are also provided.

WHO TO APPLY TO Margaret Rowntree, Secretary, c/o Rutters Solicitors, 2 Bimport, Shaftesbury, Dorset SP7 8AY *Tel.* 01747 852377 *Fax* 01747 851989 *Email* southall@rutterslaw.co.uk *Website* wfsouthalltrust.org.uk

■ R. H. Southern Trust

CC NO 1077509 **ESTABLISHED** 1999

WHERE FUNDING CAN BE GIVEN England; Wales; Scotland; Belgium; India.

WHO CAN BENEFIT Charitable organisations.

WHAT IS FUNDED Education and training, particularly medical and scientific research; people with disabilities; social welfare; the environment. The trustees favour projects where: the work is innovative, connected to other disciplines/bodies and has diverse application; activities which have potential user involvement; projects which have difficulty attracting funding from larger sources, but could attract matched funding or lever other sources of funding; and projects on an urgent or limited timescale.

TYPE OF GRANT Research and development; projects.

RANGE OF GRANTS £3,000 to £160,000.

SAMPLE GRANTS New Economics Foundation (£160,000 in three grants); Médecins Sans Frontières and Tax Justice Network (£50,000 each); Equal Adventure (£30,000 in two grants); Oxford Research Group (£20,000 in two grants); Action Village India (£15,000 in two grants); Bristol Pound (£10,000); Global Justice Now (£5,000); Salt of the Earth (£3,200).

FINANCES *Year* 2015/16 *Income* £891,655 *Grants* £757,293 *Grants to organisations* £700,293 *Assets* £220,665

TRUSTEES James Bruges; Susan Tuckwell; Rachel Ayres; Rathbone Trust Company Ltd.

OTHER INFORMATION 26 grants were made to organisations during the year. A further seven grants, totalling £57,000, were made to individuals and businesses, for a soil fertility project.

HOW TO APPLY The trust's website states that it is not accepting any funding applications as its funds are fully committed for the foreseeable future.

WHO TO APPLY TO James Bruges, Trustee, 23 Sydenham Road, Cotham, Bristol BS6 5SJ *Tel.* 0117 942 5834 *Email* cjamesbruges@gmail.com *Website* www.rhsoutherntrust.org.uk

■ The Southover Manor General Education Trust

CC NO 299593 **ESTABLISHED** 1988

WHERE FUNDING CAN BE GIVEN East Sussex; West Sussex; Brighton and Hove.

WHO CAN BENEFIT Schools, colleges, nurseries, play groups, youth groups and any other educational organisations working with individuals under the age of 25; occasionally individuals are supported.

WHAT IS FUNDED Education of young people under the age of 25, for purposes such as the development of buildings or facilities, new learning resources, outdoor equipment, etc. Priority is given to projects which 'widen educational access and opportunity and enhance achievement'.

WHAT IS NOT FUNDED Grants are not awarded for: salaries; transport costs; educational visits or attendance at conferences, expeditions or overseas travel; tuition fees, subsistence expenses, endowments or scholarships; retrospective funding; projects with the sole purpose of promoting a particular religion or faith (although applications from faith-based organisations are accepted where there is no faith restriction in the project or the educational objectives). The website also states that the trust will not normally consider 'organisations whose sole purpose is to raise funds and who are not themselves involved in the provision of educational services'. Grants are made to individuals only occasionally in special circumstances.

TYPE OF GRANT Capital and projects. The trust particularly welcomes applicants which can demonstrate that significant resources from their own budget or their supporter's budgets are contributed towards the project.

RANGE OF GRANTS Up to £25,000.

SAMPLE GRANTS Willingdon Community School (£25,000); Mile Oak Primary School and Ringmer Community College (£16,000 each).

FINANCES *Year* 2015/16 *Income* £111,217 *Grants* £121,280 *Grants to organisations* £121,280 *Assets* £2,776,864

TRUSTEES Chloe Teacher; Clare Duffield; John Wakely; John Farmer; Wenda Bradley; Jennie Peel; Ian Jungius; Claire Pool; Charles Davies-Gilbert; Marcus Hanbury; Susan Winn; Dr Caroline Brand.

OTHER INFORMATION Grants were made to 13 organisations during the year. There were also two grants made to individuals.

HOW TO APPLY Application forms are available to download from the trust's website, where further guidance is also given. The trustees meet in May and November, and applications should be received by 31 March and 30 September respectively. Any queries should be directed to appn@southovermanortrust.org.uk

WHO TO APPLY TO J. Foot, Secretary, Old Vicarage Cottage, Newhaven Road, Iford, Lewes, East Sussex BN7 3PL *Email* info@southovermanortrust.org.uk *Website* southovermanortrust.org.uk

■ The Spalding Trust

CC NO 209066 **ESTABLISHED** 1923

WHERE FUNDING CAN BE GIVEN Worldwide.

WHO CAN BENEFIT Academic or educational institutions, libraries, colleges; individuals.

WHAT IS FUNDED Religion and inter-faith understanding. The trust makes grants 'to encourage the comparative study of the great religions of the world'. The trustees are particularly interested in 'research projects which are backed by a professional ability to raise the standard of knowledge of religious principles and practices, and to interpret their relation to contemporary society'. Non-academic projects are also considered if they have a 'practical and beneficial effect on inter-religious understanding'. The website states that grants have been given for purposes such as costs of a visiting lecturer, for travel to a conference or to study a religion where it is practiced, for the purchase of books in libraries or, in exceptional circumstances, for the establishment of an academic post.

WHAT IS NOT FUNDED First degree courses; applications where other adequate sources of finance are available; any project based on the applicant's own religion, unless there will be a significant impact on inter-religious understanding; retrospective funding.

TYPE OF GRANT Usually one-off; occasionally recurrent grants that extend over a year.

SAMPLE GRANTS A list of beneficiaries was not available.

FINANCES *Year* 2015 *Income* £83,607 *Grants* £66,270 *Grants to organisations* £66,270 *Assets* £52,231

TRUSTEES Dr Kevin Ward; Dr Edward Kessler; Dr Anne Spalding; Prof. Robert Gordon; Prof. Julius Lipner; Prof. Tim Barrett; Dr Tony Street.

OTHER INFORMATION The trust also administers the Ellen Rebe Spalding Memorial Fund, which makes grants to individuals, specifically disadvantaged women and children in Oxfordshire – for further information, refer to the website or contact the Secretary. A list of beneficiaries was not included in the accounts, so the grant total includes both organisations and individuals.

HOW TO APPLY Apply in writing to the correspondent, including the information specified in the guidelines on the trust's website. Applications are considered on a monthly basis, but it make take three months before a decision is made.

WHO TO APPLY TO Tessa Rodgers, Secretary, PO Box 85, Stowmarket IP14 3NY *Website* www.spaldingtrust.org.uk

■ Spar Charitable Fund

CC NO 236252 **ESTABLISHED** 1964

WHERE FUNDING CAN BE GIVEN UK.

WHO CAN BENEFIT Registered charities, mostly well-known national organisations.

WHAT IS FUNDED General charitable purposes; emergency appeals. Support is also given to support individuals in need in the retail sector, through the company's benevolent fund and other retail-focused organisations.
RANGE OF GRANTS £150 to £25,000.
SAMPLE GRANTS SPAR Benevolent Fund (£25,000); Oxfam Nepal Earthquake (£10,000); Retail Trust (£6,600); Cumbria Flood Foundation (£5,000); NSPCC (£300); Grocery Aid (£160).
FINANCES *Year* 2015/16 *Income* £33,883 *Grants* £47,065 *Grants to organisations* £47,065 *Assets* £859,868
TRUSTEE The National Guild of Spar Ltd.
OTHER INFORMATION The fund has provided long-term support to the group's charity partner, NSPCC, but the 2015/16 accounts state that, in future, this support will be given directly by the company.
HOW TO APPLY Apply in writing to the correspondent.
WHO TO APPLY TO Philip Marchant, Administration Committee Member, Spar (UK) Ltd, Hygeia Building, 66–68 College Road, Harrow HA1 1BE *Tel.* 020 8426 3700 *Email* philip.marchant@spar.co.uk

■ Sparks Charity (Sport Aiding Medical Research for Kids) – a subsidiary of Great Ormond Street Hospital Children's Charity

CC NO 1003825 **ESTABLISHED** 1991
WHERE FUNDING CAN BE GIVEN UK.
WHO CAN BENEFIT Those conducting research at UK hospitals and universities. The charity encourages proposals with a clear route to clinical application which can demonstrate a strong partnership between clinical and laboratory-based research.
WHAT IS FUNDED Research across the UK that aims to improve understanding of and/or outcomes in child health. Research should have the potential to lead to the development of new diagnostic tools and novel interventions.
WHAT IS NOT FUNDED See individual funding calls on the charity's website for details of exclusions applicable to research projects.
TYPE OF GRANT Project grants; Dr Simon Newell Early Career Investigator Award.
SAMPLE GRANTS University of Bristol (£399,000); Queen Mary University of London (£149,000); University of Birmingham and University of Bath (£147,000 each); University of Strathclyde (£141,000).
FINANCES *Year* 2016/17 *Income* £2,858,161 *Grants* £759,690
TRUSTEES Margaret Ewing; Mark Sartori; Dr Diana Dunston.
OTHER INFORMATION The grant total above refers to new awards made during the 2016/17 financial year.
HOW TO APPLY Guidelines and applications information for the charity's annual funding call and grant programmes can be found on the website (www.sparks.org.uk/researchers).
WHO TO APPLY TO Grants Team, Great Ormond Street Hospital Children's Charity, 40 Bernard Street, London WC1N 1LE *Tel.* 020 3841 3750 *Email* info@sparks.org.uk *Website* www.sparks.org.uk

■ Sparquote Ltd

CC NO 286232 **ESTABLISHED** 1982
WHERE FUNDING CAN BE GIVEN England and Wales.
WHO CAN BENEFIT Charitable organisations, with a preference for Jewish organisations.
WHAT IS FUNDED General charitable purposes; Jewish causes, particularly education and support for places of worship; social welfare.
TYPE OF GRANT Grants to organisations.
SAMPLE GRANTS The Wlodowa Charity and Rehabilitation Trust (£41,000); the Telz Academy Trust (£30,000); British Friends of Mosdos Chernobyl (£20,000); the Society of Friends of the Torah (£19,000); the Gevurath Ari Torah Trust (£15,000); Beis Nadvorne Charitable Trust (£10,000); the Edgware Foundation and Penshurst Corporation Ltd (£5,000 each); Gateshead Institute for Rabbinical Studies (£3,500); Dina Perelman Trust Ltd (£1,800); American Friends (£1,000).
FINANCES *Year* 2015/16 *Income* £821,032 *Grants* £694,343 *Grants to organisations* £694,343 *Assets* £8,601,981
TRUSTEES David Reichmann; Dov Reichmann; Anne-Mette Reichmann.
HOW TO APPLY Apply in writing to the correspondent.
WHO TO APPLY TO The Trustees, Sparquote Ltd, Cohen Arnold, New Burlington House, 1075 Finchley Road, London NW11 0PU *Tel.* 020 8731 0777

■ The Spear Charitable Trust

CC NO 1041568 **ESTABLISHED** 1962
WHERE FUNDING CAN BE GIVEN UK.
WHO CAN BENEFIT Individuals and organisations, particularly employees and former employees of J. W. Spear and Sons PLC, their families and dependants.
WHAT IS FUNDED Welfare of employees and former employees of J. W. Spear and Sons PLC, their families and dependants; also general charitable purposes, with some preference for animal welfare, the environment, disability and health.
SAMPLE GRANTS Fauna and Flora International and Research Autism (£5,000 each); Mobility Trust (£3,000 each); Demelza House Children's Hospice and Kidney Research UK (£2,500 each); British Hedgehog Preservation Society, Farm Africa and Target Ovarian Cancer (£2,000 each); Amnesty International UK and Suffolk Owl Sanctuary (£1,000).
FINANCES *Year* 2015 *Income* £195,134 *Grants* £204,326 *Grants to organisations* £182,777 *Assets* £4,313,904
TRUSTEES Philip Harris; Francis Spear; Hazel Spear; Nigel Gooch.
OTHER INFORMATION Grants to individuals (former employees of J. W. Spear and Sons PLC and their families and dependants) totalled £21,500 during 2015.
HOW TO APPLY Apply in writing to the correspondent. The trustees state in their annual report that they will make grants without a formal application, but they encourage organisations to provide feedback on how grants are used. Feedback will be used for monitoring the quality of grants and will form the basis of assessment for any further applications.
WHO TO APPLY TO Hazel Spear, Trustee, Roughground House, Beggarman's Lane, Old Hall Green, Ware, Hertfordshire SG11 1HB *Tel.* 01920 823071

■ Spears-Stutz Charitable Trust

CC NO 225491 **ESTABLISHED** 1964

WHERE FUNDING CAN BE GIVEN Worldwide; in practice, mainly UK.

WHO CAN BENEFIT Registered charities.

WHAT IS FUNDED General charitable purposes; relief of poverty.

RANGE OF GRANTS £650 to £75,000.

SAMPLE GRANTS West Green Opera House Ltd (£75,000); Plan UK (£35,000); Doctors Without Borders (£25,000); Bhopal Medical Appeal (£10,000); MicroLoan Foundation and Peace Direct (£5,000 each); Mayor's Fund for London (£3,000); The Children's Trust (£1,000); American Cancer Society (£650).

FINANCES *Year* 2014/15 *Income* £112,689 *Grants* £220,735 *Grants to organisations* £220,735 *Assets* £4,754,153

TRUSTEES Glenn Hurstfield; Jonathan Spears.

OTHER INFORMATION The 2014/15 accounts were the most recent available to view on the Charity Commission's website at the time of writing (June 2017). The trust made 20 grants during the year.

HOW TO APPLY Apply in writing to the correspondent.

WHO TO APPLY TO The Trustees, c/o Berkeley Law, 4th Floor, 19 Berkeley Street, London W1J 8ED *Tel.* 020 7399 0930

■ The Worshipful Company of Spectacle Makers' Charity

CC NO 1072172 **ESTABLISHED** 1998

WHERE FUNDING CAN BE GIVEN Worldwide.

WHO CAN BENEFIT Registered charities, with a preference for national or international organisations.

WHAT IS FUNDED Projects to reduce vision impairment; the development of eye health training and education internationally; projects to improve the quality of life of people with a visual impairment; research projects within vision science by organisations with established peer review processes.

WHAT IS NOT FUNDED Local causes; causes which only reach a small number of beneficiaries; individual research studies (e.g. part of a doctorate or academic causes); general fundraising; causes which are not connected to eye health, sight loss, the City of London or the Spectacle Makers' Company.

TYPE OF GRANT Specific projects, not general funds.

SAMPLE GRANTS Blond McIndoe Research Foundation; Blind in Business; The Andean Medical Mission; The British Council for the Prevention of Blindness; The British Wireless for the Blind Fund; National Eye Research Centre; Northern Ballet; The Treloar Trust; Vision Care for Homeless People; Vision Aid Overseas; World Jewish Relief; World Sight Foundation.

FINANCES *Year* 2015/16 *Income* £90,827 *Grants* £93,201 *Grants to organisations* £93,201 *Assets* £729,939

TRUSTEES John Breeze; Anita Lightstone; Felicity Harding; Dr Mary Briggs; Dr Nigel Andrew; Rosalind Kirk.

OTHER INFORMATION Grants were made to 30 organisations during the year.

HOW TO APPLY Applications should be sent by email (clerk@spectaclemakers.com); guidance on what to include is provided on the charity's website. The trustees meet on a quarterly basis, in February, May, September and November; deadlines are posted on the website. Applications for research can be submitted at any time by are only awarded once a year, in February.

WHO TO APPLY TO Helen Perkins, Clerk, Apothecaries Hall, Blackfriars Lane, London EC4V 6EL *Tel.* 020 7236 2932 *Email* clerk@spectaclemakers.com *Website* www.spectaclemakers.com

■ The Jessie Spencer Trust

CC NO 219289 **ESTABLISHED** 1962

WHERE FUNDING CAN BE GIVEN UK, with a preference for East Midlands.

WHO CAN BENEFIT Registered charities or CICs, with a preference for organisations that have significant volunteer support.

WHAT IS FUNDED General charitable purposes.

WHAT IS NOT FUNDED Grants are rarely made for: individuals; organisations that are not registered charities or CICs; endowment appeals; loans or business finance; sponsorship, marketing appeals or fundraising events; campaigning or projects that are primarily political; activities that are the responsibility or a statutory body (e.g. local health or education authority); retrospective funding; general or mail shot appeals.

TYPE OF GRANT Grants are made towards both capital and revenue expenditure. They can be recurrent for up to ten years.

RANGE OF GRANTS Generally £500 to £5,000.

SAMPLE GRANTS Nottinghamshire Historic Churches Trust (£10,000); Friary Drop-in (£5,000); Bag Books, National Youth Choirs of Great Britain and SSAFA (£1,000 each); National Rheumatoid Arthritis Society, Nottinghamshire Search and Rescue Team, Prisoners' Advice Service, The Living Paintings Trust and Trees for Cities (£500 each).

FINANCES *Year* 2015/16 *Income* £151,587 *Grants* £96,725 *Grants to organisations* £96,000 *Assets* £3,327

TRUSTEES Victor Semmens; Andrew Tiplady; David Wild; Bethan Mitchell; Helen Lee.

OTHER INFORMATION Grants were made to 68 organisations during the year. One grant totalling £725 was given to an individual.

HOW TO APPLY Apply in writing to the correspondent. Guidance on what to include is provided on the trust's website. Applications should be received by 20 January, 20 April, 20 July or 20 October each year for consideration at trustee meetings in March, June, September and December respectively. To limit costs, only successful applicants are notified.

WHO TO APPLY TO John Thompson, Trust Administrator, 4 Walsingham Drive, Corby Glen, Grantham, Lincolnshire NG33 4TA *Tel.* 01476 552429 *Email* jessiespencer@btinternet.com *Website* www.jessiespencertrust.org.uk

■ The Spielman Charitable Trust

CC NO 278306 **ESTABLISHED** 1979

WHERE FUNDING CAN BE GIVEN Bristol and the surrounding area.

WHO CAN BENEFIT Charitable organisations.

WHAT IS FUNDED General charitable purposes; social welfare; disadvantaged children and young people; health; disability; education; the arts; older people; communities.

TYPE OF GRANT Recurrent; some one-off.

RANGE OF GRANTS Up to £25,000.

SAMPLE GRANTS Royal Welsh College of Music and Drama (£25,000); Bristol Children's Help Society, The Wheels Project and Unseen

(£15,000 each); NSPCC (£10,000); The Colston Society and Friends of Bristol Oncology (£5,000 each).

FINANCES *Year* 2015/16 *Income* £253,784 *Grants* £261,110 *Grants to organisations* £261,110 *Assets* £5,437,949

TRUSTEES C. Moorsom; Karen Hann; Paul Cooper.

HOW TO APPLY Apply in writing to the correspondent.

WHO TO APPLY TO June Moody, Suite F11B, Kestrel Court Buisness Centre, Harbour Road, Portishead, Bristol BS20 7AN *Tel.* 0117 929 1929 *Email* g-s.moody@btconnect.com

■ The Spoore, Merry and Rixman Foundation

CC NO 309040 **ESTABLISHED** 1958

WHERE FUNDING CAN BE GIVEN The (pre-1974) borough of Maidenhead and the ancient parish of Bray, covering the postcode area SL6 1–9 (see the map on the website).

WHO CAN BENEFIT Charitable organisations; schools; youth clubs and community organisations; individuals.

WHAT IS FUNDED Education and training; children and young people. Grants are also made to individuals for educational purposes (e.g. schools uniforms, trips, extra-curricular activities).

WHAT IS NOT FUNDED Schools can only receive a grant for items not funded by budgets (for the development of school grounds, specialised equipment, musical instruments, etc.).

TYPE OF GRANT Capital (e.g. equipment); project costs.

SAMPLE GRANTS Alexander Devine Hospice (£100,000); Desborough College (£46,500); Norden Farm Centre for the Arts (£40,000).

FINANCES *Year* 2015 *Income* £363,436 *Grants* £304,413 *Grants to organisations* £304,413 *Assets* £11,198,736

TRUSTEES Graham Fisher; Ann Redgrave; Cllr Dorothy Kemp; Tony Hill; Ian Thomas; Cllr David Coppinger; Barbara Wielechowski; Cllr Philip Love; The Mayor of the Royal Borough; Cllr Gerry Clark; Cllr Judith Diment.

OTHER INFORMATION Grants were made to 61 organisations in 2015; only three were listed in the accounts. Grants were also made to 114 individuals, totalling £122,000.

HOW TO APPLY Applications can be made on a form available to download, together with guidelines and criteria, from the foundation's website. Applications are considered in January, April, July and October – dates of upcoming meetings are listed on the website. Applications should be received at least two weeks prior to a meeting or they will be considered at the next meeting.

WHO TO APPLY TO Helen MacDiarmid, Clerk to the Trustees, PO Box 4787, Maidenhead SL60 1JA *Tel.* 020 3286 8300 *Email* clerk@smrfmaidenhead.org *Website* www.smrfmaidenhead.org.uk

■ Rosalyn and Nicholas Springer Charitable Trust

CC NO 1062239 **ESTABLISHED** 1997

WHERE FUNDING CAN BE GIVEN UK and Israel.

WHO CAN BENEFIT Charitable organisations; individuals.

WHAT IS FUNDED Grants are made in the following categories: medical causes, health and sickness; education and training; arts and culture; religious activities; relief of poverty; general charitable purposes. There is a preference for Jewish causes.

RANGE OF GRANTS Up to £15,000, but mostly £1,000 or less.

SAMPLE GRANTS Magen David Adom UK (£14,800); United Jewish Israel Appeal (UJIA) (£9,000); Marie Curie Cancer Care (£7,800); The Ear Foundation (£5,000); Regent's Park Open Air Theatre (£1,100); Alzheimer's Research UK (£1,000); Maccabi GB (£500); Family Holiday Association (£250); Music Works (£150); Jewish Film Festival (£50).

FINANCES *Year* 2015/16 *Income* £125,014 *Grants* £120,902 *Grants to organisations* £120,902 *Assets* £38,019

TRUSTEES Rosalyn Springer; Nicholas Springer.

OTHER INFORMATION Grants were made to 68 organisations during the year.

HOW TO APPLY The trust has previously stated that it only supports organisations it is already in contact with. Of the unsolicited applications received, 99% are unsuccessful and because of the volume it receives, the trust is unable to reply to such letters. It would therefore be unadvisable to apply.

WHO TO APPLY TO Nicholas Springer, Trustee, 274A Kentish Town Road, London NW5 2AA *Tel.* 020 7253 7272

■ Springrule Ltd

CC NO 802561 **ESTABLISHED** 1992

WHERE FUNDING CAN BE GIVEN England and Wales.

WHO CAN BENEFIT Jewish organisations.

WHAT IS FUNDED Advancement of the Orthodox Jewish faith and the relief of poverty.

SAMPLE GRANTS Beis Yaakov Institutions, Friends of Horim and Mercaz Torah Vechesed Ltd (£25,000 each); Yad Eliezer (£5,000).

FINANCES *Year* 2015/16 *Income* £0 *Grants* £350,000 *Grants to organisations* £350,000

TRUSTEES Robert Nevies; Jacque Monderer; Rivka Nevies.

OTHER INFORMATION The charity's latest accounts were not available to view on the Charity Commission's website due to its low income. We have therefore estimated the grant total based on previous years' information.

HOW TO APPLY Apply in writing to the correspondent.

WHO TO APPLY TO Robert Nevies, Trustee, 45 Cheyne Walk, London NW4 3QH

■ The Spurrell Charitable Trust

CC NO 267287 **ESTABLISHED** 1960

WHERE FUNDING CAN BE GIVEN UK, with some preference for Norfolk.

WHO CAN BENEFIT Registered charities.

WHAT IS FUNDED General charitable purposes, particularly disability; health; social welfare.

WHAT IS NOT FUNDED Individuals.

RANGE OF GRANTS Up to £7,500, on average around £1,000.

SAMPLE GRANTS East Anglian Air Ambulance (£7,500); Breathing Matters (£3,000); Blind Veterans UK (£2,400); Anthony Nolan Bone Marrow Trust and Metton Parochial Church Council (£1,200 each); The Connection at St Martin-in-the-Fields (£900); Norfolk Wildlife Trust and Samaritans (£600 each); Sheringham and Cromer Choral Society (£600); Winslow Scouts (£300).

FINANCES *Year* 2015/16 *Income* £62,421 *Grants* £72,300 *Grants to organisations* £72,300 *Assets* £2,526,687

TRUSTEES Ingeburg Spurrell; Martyn Spurrell; Christopher Spurrell.

OTHER INFORMATION Grants were made to 58 organisations during the year.

HOW TO APPLY Apply in writing to the correspondent. Trustees consider applications in September of each year.

WHO TO APPLY TO Martyn Spurrell, Trustee, Harefields, Winslow Road, Little Horwood, Buckinghamshire MK17 0PD *Tel.* 01296 420113 *Email* spurrelltrust@icloud.com

■ The Geoff and Fiona Squire Foundation

CC NO 1085553 **ESTABLISHED** 2001

WHERE FUNDING CAN BE GIVEN UK.

WHO CAN BENEFIT Registered charities.

WHAT IS FUNDED General charitable purposes, particularly medicine; education; disability; welfare and health care of children.

WHAT IS NOT FUNDED The foundation does not normally consider applications from large national charities (with an income of over £10 million or assets of more than £100 million), or from causes which the trustees deem to be already well funded in the UK.

TYPE OF GRANT One-off donations.

RANGE OF GRANTS £500 to £150,000.

SAMPLE GRANTS Horatio's Garden (£150,000); Seeing Ear (£100,000); Special Olympics Great Britain (£74,500); Children's Trust (£40,000); Variety – The Children's Charity (£21,000); Changing Faces (£13,000); Music for Youth (£7,500); Jubilee Sailing Trust and Winchester Cathedral Trust (£5,000 each); Dressability (£500).

FINANCES *Year* 2015/16 *Income* £188,212 *Grants* £1,049,442 *Grants to organisations* £1,049,442 *Assets* £9,158,569

TRUSTEES Geoff Squire; Fiona Squire; B. Peerless.

OTHER INFORMATION Grants were made to 33 charities during the year. The 2015/16 annual report states that the foundation The foundation 'will willingly work in partnership with other organisations to fund initiatives beyond the scope of a single organisation'.

HOW TO APPLY Apply in writing to the correspondent.

WHO TO APPLY TO Fiona Squire, Trustee, The Walton Canonry, 69 The Close, Salisbury, Wiltshire SP1 2EN

■ The Squires Foundation

CC NO 328149 **ESTABLISHED** 1989

WHERE FUNDING CAN BE GIVEN Worldwide with preferences for North East England, Cumbria and Leeds.

WHO CAN BENEFIT Charitable organisations.

WHAT IS FUNDED Grants are given in the areas of social welfare; community development; children and young people; older people; local hospitals and hospices; Christian activities.

TYPE OF GRANT One-off or recurrent.

SAMPLE GRANTS Traidcraft (£15,000); Live Theatre (£20,000); Metro Kids Africa (£16,000); Keyfund (£10,000); Newcastle Royal Grammar School (£9,000); Newcastle Cathedral Trust (£6,000); British Red Cross and Happy Days (£2,000 each); Dyslexia North East (£550).

FINANCES *Year* 2015/16 *Income* £252 *Grants* £240,000 *Grants to organisations* £240,000

TRUSTEES John Squires; Malcolm Squires; Stephen Squires; Lynn Squires.

OTHER INFORMATION The foundation's latest accounts were not available to view on the Charity Commission's website due to its low income. We have therefore estimated the grant total based on previous years' information.

HOW TO APPLY Apply in writing to the correspondent. The trustees meet twice a year, this is usually in May and November with applications needing to be received by the beginning of April or October respectively.

WHO TO APPLY TO Lynn Squires, Trustee, c/o Muckle LLP, Time Central, 32 Gallowgate, Newcastle upon Tyne NE1 4BF *Tel.* 0191 226 1700 *Email* charitabletrust@benfieldmotorgroup.com

■ The Stafford Trust

SC NO SC018079 **ESTABLISHED** 1991

WHERE FUNDING CAN BE GIVEN UK, with a preference for Scotland.

WHO CAN BENEFIT UK-registered charities.

WHAT IS FUNDED General charitable purposes, including social welfare; health and medical research; animal welfare; children and young people; community; welfare of armed services personnel; overseas aid; sea rescue.

WHAT IS NOT FUNDED Religious organisations; political organisations; retrospective grants; student travel or expeditions; general appeals or mail shots.

RANGE OF GRANTS Mostly £500 to £10,000.

SAMPLE GRANTS Animal Health Trust (£15,000); Barrwood Trust (£10,000); World Wide Volunteering (£8,000); Highland Hospice (£7,500); Brain Tumour Charity, Edinburgh Young Carers Group, L'Arche Inverness and Oban Mountain Rescue (£5,000 each); Throsk Community Enterprises (£3,000); Polbeth United Community Football Club (£600).

FINANCES *Year* 2015/16 *Income* £463,819 *Grants* £315,525 *Grants to organisations* £315,525 *Assets* £16,595,125

TRUSTEES Hamish Buchan; Gordon Wylie; Ian Fergusson; Robert Hogg.

HOW TO APPLY An application form can be downloaded from the trust's website and should include the information specified on the website. The trustees usually meet twice a year, in spring and autumn, to review applications, and deadlines are posted on the website. Unsuccessful applicants should wait at least one year before re-applying.

WHO TO APPLY TO Margaret Kane, Trust Administrator, c/o Dickson Middleton CA, PO Box 14, 20 Barnton Street, Stirling FK8 1NE *Tel.* 01786 474718 *Email* staffordtrust@dicksonmiddleton.co.uk *Website* www.staffordtrust.org.uk

■ Staffordshire Community Foundation

CC NO 1091628 **ESTABLISHED** 2001

WHERE FUNDING CAN BE GIVEN Staffordshire.

WHO CAN BENEFIT Registered charities, community groups, CICs, individuals.

WHAT IS FUNDED General charitable purposes; social welfare; education and training; health.

WHAT IS NOT FUNDED Each funding stream has its own set of exclusions; refer to the website for details.
TYPE OF GRANT Preference for project funding but some streams also give for core costs.
RANGE OF GRANTS £100 to £10,000.
SAMPLE GRANTS Grocott Centre (£25,000); Saltbox (£17,500); Headway North Staffordshire (£10,500); Red Door Community Centre (£4,000); Aspire Boxing CIC, Cannock Cricket Club, Chase View Primary School, Staffordshire Housing Association and Queen Street Neighbourhood Resource Centre (£3,000 each).
FINANCES *Year* 2015/16 *Income* £1,824,894 *Grants* £437,848 *Grants to organisations* £420,893 *Assets* £4,961,357
TRUSTEES Sarah Elsom; Terry Walsh; Mark Wilton; Roger Lewis; Helen Dart; Charlotte Almond; Christopher Spruce; Dr Teeranlall Ramgopal; Jean Gibson; Simon Price; Lee Bates; Jonathan Andrew; Adele Cope.
OTHER INFORMATION The foundation has built up an endowment portfolio that it uses to make grants to local charities and voluntary services, as well as distributing grants on behalf of the government, businesses and national charities.
HOW TO APPLY There are separate application criteria and forms for each funding programme on the website.
WHO TO APPLY TO Lisa Healings, Dudson Centre, Hope Street, Hanley, Stoke-on-Trent ST1 5DD *Tel.* 01785 339540 *Email* office@staffsfoundation.org.uk *Website* www.staffsfoundation.org.uk

■ Standard Life Foundation

SC NO SC040877 **ESTABLISHED** 2009
WHERE FUNDING CAN BE GIVEN UK and overseas.
WHO CAN BENEFIT Organisations.
WHAT IS FUNDED The annual report states that the foundation is 'a research-led charity focused on helping to close the savings gap that exists in our society'. The foundation will continue to 'equip people from all backgrounds to aspire to a better future, and to find ways to deliver sustainable change that builds stronger communities ... our focus will be on providing opportunities through the transformative impact of being enabled to save'.
SAMPLE GRANTS The Prince's Trust (£400,000); Tomorrow's People (£205,000); The Royal British Legion (£53,500).
FINANCES *Year* 2015 *Income* £48,402 *Grants* £658,609 *Grants to organisations* £658,609 *Assets* £1,816,987
TRUSTEES Frances Horsburgh; Colin Clark; Alistair Darling; James Daunt; Naomi Eisenstadt; Sir Gerald Grimstone; David Hall; Lucy Heller; Helen Kempson; Graeme McEwan; Norman Skeoch.
OTHER INFORMATION Previously known as the Standard Life Charitable Trust, the foundation was renamed in 2016, and the company announced that it would receive the funds of the assets derived from the closure of its Unclaimed Asset Trust. Note that during 2015, the charity's focus was helping people develop skills and breaking down barriers to employment, so the beneficiary organisations during the year reflect this aim. At the time of writing (June 2017), little information about the foundation's future work was yet available.
HOW TO APPLY It is unclear at the time of writing whether the foundation will be accepting unsolicited applications; refer to the website for up-to-date information.
WHO TO APPLY TO Frances Horsburgh, Secretary, Group Secretariat, 30 Lothian Road, Edinburgh EH1 2DH *Website* www.standardlife.com/sustainability

■ The Stanley Charitable Trust

CC NO 326220 **ESTABLISHED** 1982
WHERE FUNDING CAN BE GIVEN UK.
WHO CAN BENEFIT Charitable organisations; Jewish organisations.
WHAT IS FUNDED Jewish religion and education; relief of poverty.
WHAT IS NOT FUNDED Only registered charities are supported.
SAMPLE GRANTS Teshuvoh Tefilloh Tzedokoh (£7,000); Bikur Cholim and Gemiluth Chesed Trust, and Sharei Chesed (£5,000 each); Heichal HaTorah and Keren Shlomo Trust (£4,000 each); Chasdei Shlomo, Choimel Dalim and Talmud Torah Tiferes Shlome Trust (£3,000 each).
FINANCES *Year* 2015/16 *Income* £87,296 *Grants* £467,504 *Grants to organisations* £46,750 *Assets* £851,856
TRUSTEES David Adler; Isabella Adler; Jacob Adler.
HOW TO APPLY The trust has previously said that it gives regular donations and does not consider new applications.
WHO TO APPLY TO David Adler, Trustee, 32 Waterpark Road, Salford M7 4ET *Tel.* 0161 708 8090 *Email* charities@haffhoff.co.uk

■ The Stanley Foundation Ltd

CC NO 206866 **ESTABLISHED** 1962
WHERE FUNDING CAN BE GIVEN UK.
WHO CAN BENEFIT Registered charities.
WHAT IS FUNDED General charitable purposes, including: medical care and research; education; cultural advancement; community support.
WHAT IS NOT FUNDED Organisations with political affiliations or objectives.
TYPE OF GRANT Mainly one-off; occasionally larger, multi-year projects.
RANGE OF GRANTS £250 to £15,000.
SAMPLE GRANTS North Hampshire Medical Fund (£15,000); Puzzle Centre (£10,000); Royal Horticultural Society and Prison Reform Trust (£5,000 each); Pituitary Foundation (£2,500); Courtauld Institute of Art (£2,000); Chieveley Parish Council and Salisbury Samaritans (£1,000 each); British Red Cross (£500); St Gregory's Church (£250).
FINANCES *Year* 2015/16 *Income* £70,532 *Grants* £137,474 *Grants to organisations* £137,474 *Assets* £2,352,462
TRUSTEES Elodie Stanley; Nicholas Stanley; Shaun Stanley; John Raymond; Patrick Hall; Georgina Stanley; Stephen Hall; Charles Stanley.
OTHER INFORMATION Grants were made to 41 organisations during the year.
HOW TO APPLY Apply in writing to the correspondent. The annual report states that applications are prioritised according to the following criteria: 'The foundation's ability to "make a difference" previous successful involvement with a charity; further support to past recipients of donations; requests for charitable donations from bodies directly connected with the founder's original charitable interests.'
WHO TO APPLY TO Nicholas Stanley, Trustee, N. C. Morris and Co., 1 Montpelier Street, London SW7 1EX *Email* nick@meristan.com

The Staples Trust

CC NO 1010656 **ESTABLISHED** 1992

WHERE FUNDING CAN BE GIVEN UK and overseas.

WHO CAN BENEFIT Charitable organisations.

WHAT IS FUNDED Gender issues (domestic violence, women's rights and gender studies); overseas projects which support the rights of indigenous people; charities defending human rights and civil liberties; The Frankopan Fund – small grants to allow gifted Croatian students to further their studies (there are specific priorities and guidelines for this fund, which are available from the website). The trustees also have an interest in supporting local charities in Oxfordshire.

WHAT IS NOT FUNDED Grants are not normally made to individuals.

SAMPLE GRANTS University of Cambridge – Jesus College (£250,000); University of Oxford – Ashmolean Museum (£25,000); Oxford Philomusica (£20,000); Refuge Media Productions CIC (£10,000); Clinton Foundation (£6,500); Ashden Sustainable Solutions (£5,000); Royal College of Art (£2,500); Nordoff Robbins (£1,000); Juvenile Diabetes Research Foundation (£600); Central European University (£500 each).

FINANCES *Year* 2015/16 *Income* £512,759 *Grants* £120,241 *Grants to organisations* £120,241 *Assets* £13,140,480

TRUSTEES Judith Portrait; Timothy Sainsbury; Jessica Sainsbury; Peter Frankopan.

OTHER INFORMATION The trust is one of the Sainsbury Family Charitable Trusts which share a common administration.

HOW TO APPLY See the 'How to apply' section in the entry for the Sainsbury Family Charitable Trusts. A single application will be considered for support by all the trusts in the group. However, the 2015/16 annual report states that for this, as for many of the family trusts, 'proposals are generally invited by the trustees or initiated at their request. Unsolicited applications are discouraged and are unlikely to be successful, even if they fall within an area in which the trustees are interested.'

WHO TO APPLY TO Alan Bookbinder, Director, The Peak, 5 Wilton Road, London SW1V 1AP *Tel.* 020 7410 0330 *Email* info@sfct.org.uk *Website* www.sfct.org.uk

The Peter Stebbings Memorial Charity

CC NO 274862 **ESTABLISHED** 1977

WHERE FUNDING CAN BE GIVEN UK, with a preference for London, and low-income countries.

WHO CAN BENEFIT Registered charities, focusing on small to medium-sized charities with an annual income of up to £5 million.

WHAT IS FUNDED UK charities are supported in the areas of: medical research and care; social welfare; homelessness; hospices; mental health/counselling; drug and alcohol therapeutic support; support for people who have offended; community regeneration; vulnerable families, women and children. Overseas charities are supported in the areas of: education; basic skills and tools; health; sanitation, irrigation, hygiene and access to clean water; women; help for marginalised communities.

WHAT IS NOT FUNDED Individuals; large national or international charities; animal welfare; publications and journals (unless as part of a supported project); general appeals; any charity whose beneficiaries are restricted to particular faiths; educational institutions, unless for a particular project the trustees wish to support; arts organisations, unless there is a strong social welfare focus to the work (e.g. community arts projects).

TYPE OF GRANT Project costs, although core costs will be considered for charities known to the trustees.

RANGE OF GRANTS Up to £40,000.

SAMPLE GRANTS The Generation Trust (£40,000); Superkidz Community Trust (£20,000); Redbridge Concern for Men (£12,000); Kasiisi Porridge Project (£10,300); Savannah Education Trust (£10,000); Wigmore Hall Trust (£8,400); Hackney City Farm (£7,500); Women's Therapy Centre (£6,000); Tall Ships Trust (£5,000); COCO (£2,000).

FINANCES *Year* 2015/16 *Income* £195,821 *Grants* £464,678 *Grants to organisations* £464,678 *Assets* £8,433,675

TRUSTEES Andrew Stebbings; Nicholas Cosin; Jennifer Clifford.

OTHER INFORMATION Grants were made to 50 organisations during the year.

HOW TO APPLY An application form is available to download on the charity's website. The trustees meet twice a year to allocate grants – dates and deadlines are provided on the website.

WHO TO APPLY TO Andrew Stebbings, Trustee, 45 Cadogan Gardens, London SW3 2AQ *Tel.* 020 7591 3349 *Email* charitymanager@pglaw.co.uk *Website* peterstebbingsmemorialcharity.org

The Steel Charitable Trust

CC NO 272384 **ESTABLISHED** 1976

WHERE FUNDING CAN BE GIVEN Mainly UK, with a particular focus on Luton and Bedfordshire.

WHO CAN BENEFIT Registered charities.

WHAT IS FUNDED General charitable purposes. In practice, the trust focuses on the following five areas: arts and heritage; education; environment; health; social or economic disadvantage.

WHAT IS NOT FUNDED Charities not registered in the UK; expeditions; individuals; political parties; promotion of religion.

TYPE OF GRANT Capital costs; project costs; core costs.

RANGE OF GRANTS Mostly £1,000 to £5,000, occasionally larger.

SAMPLE GRANTS University of Bedfordshire (£75,000 in two grants); Youthscape (£46,000); National Osteoporosis Society (£20,000); Greenpower Education Trust (£19,400); The Silver Line (£15,000); The Three Choirs Festival Association Ltd (£10,000); North Devon Theatres Trust (£5,500); Bowel Disease Research Foundation and The Donkey Sanctuary (£5,000); Motor Neurone Disease Association (£1,000).

FINANCES *Year* 2015/16 *Income* £2,251,298 *Grants* £1,141,990 *Grants to organisations* £1,141,990 *Assets* £27,117,551

TRUSTEES John Maddox; Anthony Hawkins; Nicholas Wright; Wendy Bailey; Dr Mary Briggs; Philip Lawford.

OTHER INFORMATION Grants were made to 122 organisations during the year, of which 113 were charities registered in England and Wales; two were charities registered in Scotland; and seven were other charitable organisations (e.g. educational or religious organisations) in the UK.

HOW TO APPLY Applications should be made using the form on the trust's website. The trustees meet to consider applications in March, June, September and November. Further information is given on the website.

WHO TO APPLY TO Sarah Kilcoyne, Trust Manager, Suite 411, Jansel Business Centre, Hitchin Road, Stopsley, Luton LU2 7XH *Tel.* 01582 240601 *Email* administrator@steelcharitabletrust.org.uk *Website* www.steelcharitabletrust.org.uk

■ The Steinberg Family Charitable Trust

CC NO 1045231 **ESTABLISHED** 1995

WHERE FUNDING CAN BE GIVEN UK, with a preference for North West England; Israel.

WHO CAN BENEFIT Charitable organisations.

WHAT IS FUNDED General charitable purposes; education; social welfare; particularly (although not exclusively) Jewish causes.

RANGE OF GRANTS Up to £150,000. Average grant in 2015/16: £11,678.

SAMPLE GRANTS Aish (£75,000); World Jewish Relief (£50,000) and Integrated Education Fund (£25,000); Hale Adult Hebrew Education Trust (£20,000); Centre for Social Justice and Policy Exchange (£15,000); Ascent, Imperial War Museum, Magen David Adom Israel and Yeshiva Bais Yisroel (£10,000 each); Chai Cancer Care and Holocaust Centre (£7,500 each); Henshaw's Society, Jewish Education in Manchester and Rainbow Trust (£2,500 each); Prostate Cancer Charity (£1,000).

FINANCES *Year* 2015/16 *Income* £3,027,220 *Grants* £1,440,017 *Grants to organisations* £1,440,017 *Assets* £32,257,837

TRUSTEES Beryl Steinberg; Jonathan Steinberg; Lynne Attias.

OTHER INFORMATION In 2015/16 grants were made to 118 organisations. A list of beneficiaries was not provided in the accounts, but the following breakdown was given: Torah (£654,500); education (£290,500); social services (£149,000); special needs (£132,000); miscellaneous (£83,500); health care (£68,000).

HOW TO APPLY Apply in writing to the correspondent on letter-headed paper, including evidence of charitable status, the purpose to which the funds are to be put, evidence of other action taken to fund the project concerned, and the outcome of that action.

WHO TO APPLY TO The Trustees, 16 Bollinway, Hale, Altrincham, Cheshire WA15 0NZ *Tel.* 0161 903 8854 *Email* admin@sfct.co.uk

■ The Hugh Stenhouse Foundation

SC NO SC015074 **ESTABLISHED** 1968

WHERE FUNDING CAN BE GIVEN Mainly Scotland.

WHO CAN BENEFIT Charitable organisations, with a preference for smaller, local initiatives.

WHAT IS FUNDED General charitable purposes, particularly relief of poverty; young people; medical causes.

WHAT IS NOT FUNDED Grants are not given for political appeals or to individuals.

SAMPLE GRANTS Maxwelton Chapel Trust (£27,000); Boys and Girls Clubs of Scotland, Glasgow City Mission, H/C Children's Action, Lintel Trust, Quality Dwelling, The Yard and Trellis (£4,000 each).

FINANCES *Year* 2015/16 *Income* £72,825 *Grants* £55,000 *Grants to organisations* £55,000 *Assets* £1,902,027

OTHER INFORMATION Grants were made to eight organisations during the year.

HOW TO APPLY Apply in writing to the correspondent.

WHO TO APPLY TO The Trustees, c/o Bell Ingram Ltd, Durn, Isla Road, Perth PH2 7HF

■ C. E. K. Stern Charitable Trust

CC NO 1049157 **ESTABLISHED** 1992

WHERE FUNDING CAN BE GIVEN UK and overseas, particularly Israel.

WHO CAN BENEFIT Orthodox Jewish charities and religious organisations.

WHAT IS FUNDED Orthodox Jewish religion and education; relief of poverty.

SAMPLE GRANTS A list of beneficiaries was not available.

FINANCES *Year* 2015/16 *Income* £285,470 *Grants* £154,226 *Grants to organisations* £154,226 *Assets* £891,184

TRUSTEES Chaya Stern; Zvi Stern.

HOW TO APPLY Applications may be made in writing to the correspondent. The latest accounts note: 'The Charity accepts applications for grants from representatives of Orthodox Jewish Charities, which are reviewed by the trustees on a regular basis. The trustees consider requests received and make donations based on level of funds available.'

WHO TO APPLY TO Zvi Stern, Trustee, 50 Keswick Street, Gateshead NE8 1TQ

■ The Sigmund Sternberg Charitable Foundation

CC NO 257950 **ESTABLISHED** 1968

WHERE FUNDING CAN BE GIVEN Worldwide.

WHO CAN BENEFIT Registered charities.

WHAT IS FUNDED The foundation supports 'interfaith activities to promote racial and religious harmony'. There is a particular focus on Christian, Jewish and Muslim faiths, and the education in, and understanding of, their fundamental tenets and beliefs.

RANGE OF GRANTS Most grants are of £1,000 or less.

SAMPLE GRANTS Three Faiths Forum (£243,500 in 15 grants); The Movement for Reform Judaism (£50,000); Culham St Gabriel (£10,000); JW3 Development (£5,000); World Congress of Faiths (£3,500); Liberal Jewish Synagogue (£3,000 in four grants); International Council of Christians and Jews and Royal College of Speech and Language Therapists (£2,000 each); British Friends of the Hebrew University of Jerusalem (£1,100).

FINANCES *Year* 2015/16 *Income* £815,173 *Grants* £345,500 *Grants to organisations* £345,500 *Assets* £4,789,691

TRUSTEES Martin Paisner; Michael Sternberg; Martin Slowe; Revd Dr Marcus Braybrooke; Noam Tamir.

OTHER INFORMATION The foundation made 103 grants during the year, of which 69 were for less than £1,000.

HOW TO APPLY Apply in writing to the correspondent.

WHO TO APPLY TO Jan Kariya, Clayton Stark and Co., Charles House, 108–110 Finchley Road, London NW3 5JJ *Tel.* 020 7431 4200 *Email* csco@claytonstark.co.uk

■ Stervon Ltd

CC NO 280958 **ESTABLISHED** 1980

WHERE FUNDING CAN BE GIVEN UK.

WHO CAN BENEFIT Charitable organisations, particularly Jewish organisations.

WHAT IS FUNDED Advancement of the Orthodox Jewish faith; relief of poverty.

SAMPLE GRANTS Machzikei Hadass Communities (£27,500); British Friends of Zichron Menachem (£25,000); Keren Hatzolas Doros Alei Siach and SOFT (Support Organisation for Trisomy) (£15,000 each); Yesamach Levav (£10,500); The Lolev Charitable Trust (£8,000); Choimel Dalim (£7,000); Chaya Reizel Hirsch Memorial Fund and New Light Trust (£5,000 each).

FINANCES *Year* 2015 *Income* £181,939 *Grants* £217,296 *Grants to organisations* £217,296 *Assets* £162,443

TRUSTEES A. Reich; Gabriel Rothbart.

HOW TO APPLY Apply in writing to the correspondent.

WHO TO APPLY TO The Trustees, 109 St Ann's Road, Prestwich, Manchester M25 9GE *Tel.* 0161 737 5000 *Email* charities@haffhoff.co.uk

■ The Stevenage Community Trust

CC NO 1000762 **ESTABLISHED** 1990

WHERE FUNDING CAN BE GIVEN The borough of Stevenage and the surrounding villages of Aston, Benington, Cromer, Datchworth, Graveley, Knebworth, Little Wymondley, Old Knebworth, Walkern, Watton-at-Stone, Weston, and Woolmer Green.

WHO CAN BENEFIT Charitable organisations and community groups; individuals in need.

WHAT IS FUNDED General charitable purposes, with an focus on disadvantage and quality of life in the local community, including: prevention or relief of poverty; health; citizenship or community development; arts, culture, heritage or science; sport; environment; relief of need or disadvantage. Grants are also given to individuals in need for purposes such as essential household items or heating during the winter.

WHAT IS NOT FUNDED Grants are not given for: political or religious objectives; trade union objectives (except for welfare functions); animal welfare; retrospective grants. The trust prefers not to fund: replacement of statutory funding; general appeals; large national charities; educational projects that should be covered by the national curriculum; medical treatment costs; general running costs.

TYPE OF GRANT Capital costs; project costs.

RANGE OF GRANTS £150 to £9,000.

SAMPLE GRANTS Age Concern; Corey's Mill Lions Club; Great Ashby Youth Club; Headway Hertfordshire; Hertfordshire Area Rape Crisis Centre; Link Up Lunch Club; Phoenix Group for Deaf Children; Shaftesbury Court Sheltered Housing; St Nicholas' School; Stevenage Arts Guild; The Breastfeeding Network; Track Autism.

FINANCES *Year* 2015/16 *Income* £158,897 *Grants* £103,395 *Grants to organisations* £103,395 *Assets* £458,720

TRUSTEES Ken Follett; Robert Stewart; Martin Addrison; Rob Case; Paul Beasley; Jeannette Thomas; Janis Daniel; Darren Isted; Bhavna Joshi; Alex Lang; Robin Macmillan; Ian Morton; Mike Phoenix; Sharon Brown.

OTHER INFORMATION The grant total includes grants given to both individuals and organisations; no breakdown was given in the 2015/16 accounts, but the annual report on the trust's website states that during the year the trust supported 62 organisations and 334 individuals. The 2015/16 accounts were not available to view on the Charity Commission's website but were available to view on Companies House.

HOW TO APPLY Applications should be made on a form available to download from the trust's website. Grants applications are considered quarterly and deadlines are posted on the website. However, the trust states that it can respond to requests from individuals in need more urgently. Applications from individuals should be submitted via a third party agency (e.g. Citizens Advice, social services or a support worker).

WHO TO APPLY TO Caroline Haskins, Manager, Follett House, Primmett Road, Stevenage, Hertfordshire SG1 3EE *Tel.* 01438 525390 *Email* enquiries@stevenagecommunitytrust.org or caroline@stevenagecommunitytrust.org *Website* www.stevenagecommunitytrust.org

■ Stevenson Family's Charitable Trust

CC NO 327148 **ESTABLISHED** 1986

WHERE FUNDING CAN BE GIVEN UK.

WHO CAN BENEFIT Registered charities.

WHAT IS FUNDED Arts and culture; conservation and heritage; education; general charitable purposes.

RANGE OF GRANTS £100 to £50,000.

SAMPLE GRANTS The Sick Children's Trust (£45,000); Southwark Cathedral Development (£10,000); National Gardens Scheme (£4,800); Newbury Spring Festival (£3,500); National Portrait Gallery (£1,300); Old Vic Theatre Trust (£1,500); Dingley Early Years Centre (£1,000); Ethiopiaid (£500); The Eye Appeal (£250); Macmillan Cancer Support (£100).

FINANCES *Year* 2015/16 *Income* £94,145 *Grants* £316,372 *Grants to organisations* £316,372 *Assets* £2,600,515

TRUSTEES Lady Catherine Stevenson; Sir Hugh Stevenson; Joseph Stevenson.

OTHER INFORMATION Grants were made to 54 organisations during the year.

HOW TO APPLY The trust has previously stated that no unsolicited applications are accepted and that causes are chosen by the trustees for support.

WHO TO APPLY TO Sir Hugh Stevenson, Trustee, Old Waterfield, Winkfield Road, Ascot SL5 7LJ *Email* hugh.stevenson@oldwaterfield.com

■ The Stewards' Charitable Trust

CC NO 299597 **ESTABLISHED** 1988

WHERE FUNDING CAN BE GIVEN UK.

WHO CAN BENEFIT Sports clubs and related organisations; individuals through scholarships at academic institutions.

WHAT IS FUNDED Support of rowing at all levels, from grassroots upwards, with a focus on young people.

WHAT IS NOT FUNDED Building or capital costs.

RANGE OF GRANTS £500 to £150,000.

SAMPLE GRANTS British Rowing Scholarships (£149,500); London Youth Rowing (£50,000); Rowing Foundation (£35,000); Molesey Rowing Ltd (£20,000); Ball Cup Regatta (£3,000); Henley Disabled Regatta (£500).

FINANCES *Year* 2014/15 *Income* £158,054 *Grants* £258,202 *Grants to organisations* £258,202 *Assets* £7,620,543

TRUSTEES Sir Steve Redgrave; Christopher Baillieu; Richard Stanhope; Richard Lester.

HOW TO APPLY Apply in writing to the correspondent.

WHO TO APPLY TO Daniel Grist, Secretary, Regatta Headquarters, Henley Bridge, Henley-on-Thames, Oxfordshire RG9 2LY *Tel.* 01491 572153 *Email* dgrist@regattahq.co.uk *Website* www.hrr.co.uk

■ Stewards' Company Ltd

CC NO 234558 **ESTABLISHED** 1947

WHERE FUNDING CAN BE GIVEN UK and overseas.

WHO CAN BENEFIT Organisations involved with training people in religious education. About half the trust's funds are given for work overseas.

WHAT IS FUNDED Christian evangelism, especially but not exclusively that of Christian Brethren assemblies. Grants given overseas are made under the following categories: church buildings; scriptures and literature; education and orphanages; education of missionaries' children; national evangelists and missionaries' vehicles. Grants given in the UK are categorised under: church buildings; evangelistic associations; scriptures and literature; teachers and evangelists; and young people and children. Substantial funds are also transferred to the Beatrice Laing Trust (see a separate entry).

TYPE OF GRANT Usually one-off.

RANGE OF GRANTS The majority of grants are for less than £25,000.

SAMPLE GRANTS Counties (£467,500); UCCF (£424,500); Beatrice Laing Trust (£265,500); Christian Workers' Relief Fund (£250,000); Retired Missionary Aid Fund (£225,000); International Fellowship of Evangelical Students (£147,500); Gospel Literature Outreach (£100,000).

FINANCES *Year* 2016 *Income* £2,298,239 *Grants* £6,170,486 *Grants to organisations* £6,127,698 *Assets* £145,132,377

TRUSTEES Alexander McIlhinney; Philip Symons; Dr John Burness; Paul Young; William Adams; William Wood; David Roberts; Denis Cooper; Alan Paterson; Glyn Davies; Andrew Griffiths; Ian Childs; John Gamble; Andrew Mayo; Simon Tomlinson; John Aitken; Keith Bintley; Dr Jonathan Loose; David Crawford Bingham; Joshua Fitzhugh.

OTHER INFORMATION Grants were made to 40 individuals and totalled £42,500. A further 426 grants were made to institutions during the year.

HOW TO APPLY Apply in writing to the correspondent.

WHO TO APPLY TO Andrew Griffiths, Trustee and Secretary, 124 Wells Road, Bath BA2 3AH *Tel.* 01225 427236 *Email* stewardsco@stewards.co.uk

■ The Andy Stewart Charitable Foundation

CC NO 1114802 **ESTABLISHED** 2006

WHERE FUNDING CAN BE GIVEN Worldwide.

WHO CAN BENEFIT Charitable organisations.

WHAT IS FUNDED Support for people with spinal injuries; health; animal welfare; young people; general charitable purposes.

SAMPLE GRANTS Spinal Injuries (£39,000); Sir Peter O'Sullevan Charitable Trust (£24,000); Best Beginnings and The Haven (£5,000 each); Children's Heart Fund (£3,600); Bob Champion Cancer Trust (£2,000); Cancer Research and Jackson Memorial Hospital (£1,000 each).

FINANCES *Year* 2015 *Income* £17,191 *Grants* £70,000 *Grants to organisations* £70,000

TRUSTEES Andy Stewart; Mark Stewart; Paul Stewart.

OTHER INFORMATION The foundation's latest accounts were not available to view on the Charity Commission's website due to its low income. We have therefore estimated the grant total based on previous years' information.

HOW TO APPLY Apply in writing to the correspondent.

WHO TO APPLY TO The Trustees, Bridger, 14 Glategny Esplanade, St Peter Port, Guernsey GY1 1WN *Tel.* 01483 407100

■ Sir Halley Stewart Trust

CC NO 208491 **ESTABLISHED** 1924

WHERE FUNDING CAN BE GIVEN UK and some overseas through UK organisations.

WHO CAN BENEFIT UK charitable organisations and researchers.

WHAT IS FUNDED Projects that focus on the prevention of human suffering – in medical, social or religious categories. In particular, the trust supports 'innovative research projects' and 'pioneering/ground-breaking development projects'. There are two grants programmes: Main Grants of between £5,000 and £60,000, over one to three years, in the form of salary contributions (or occasionally project costs); and Small Grants, one-off grants of up to £5,000 for project costs. Further detail is provided on the trust's website.

WHAT IS NOT FUNDED Grants are not usually made for the following: running costs of established organisations; conferences; projects proposed indirectly through other umbrella or large, well-funded charities; personal education fees or fees for taught courses – unless the proposal comes from a senior researcher who is seeking funds for research which could be undertaken by postgraduate student; completion of a project or PhD initiated by other bodies; educational or gap year projects for young people; completion funding for a project where the trust would not be a major supporter; contributions towards the overall costs of a project (the trust normally focuses on salaries). Grants are never made for the following: donations to general appeals of any kind; the purchase, erection or conversion of buildings; capital costs; university overhead charges; grants directly made to individuals.

TYPE OF GRANT One-off; project grants; feasibility studies; research; salaries; development costs. Funding may be given for up to three years.

RANGE OF GRANTS Up to £60,000.

SAMPLE GRANTS Durham University (£60,000); Liverpool School of Tropical Medicine (£55,000); St Albans Cathedral (£52,000); Cicely Saunders Institute (£37,000); University of Oxford – Department of Education (£30,000); Plymouth University (£25,000); PACT (£21,000); Tyndale House (£20,000); Community Chaplaincy Association (£16,000); Womankind Worldwide (£15,000).

FINANCES *Year* 2015/16 *Income* £1,028,000 *Grants* £773,000 *Grants to organisations* £773,000 *Assets* £26,606,000

TRUSTEES Prof. Phyllida Parsloe; Joanna Womack; Prof. John Wyatt; Dr Duncan Stewart; Lord Stewartby; Prof. John Lennard-Jones; Prof. Philip Whitfield; Bill Kirkman; Prof. Gordon Wilcock; Theresa Bartlett; Dr James Bunn; Louisa Elder; Amy Holcroft; Jane Gillard; Celia Atherton; Revd Prof. David Wilkinson; Andrew Graystone; Paul Harrod.

OTHER INFORMATION Grants of less than £10,000 totalled £64,000 during the year.
HOW TO APPLY Applications can be made on the trust's website, but the trust recommends contacting the secretary first to discuss the suitability of a project before applying. Further guidelines are provided on the trust's website, where the dates of the next trustee meetings and deadlines are also provided.
WHO TO APPLY TO Vicky Chant, Secretary to the Trustees, BM Sir Halley Stewart Trust, London WC1N 3XX *Tel.* 020 8144 0375 *Email* email@sirhalleystewart.org.uk *Website* www.sirhalleystewart.org.uk

■ The Stewarts Law Foundation

CC NO 1136714 **ESTABLISHED** 2010
WHERE FUNDING CAN BE GIVEN UK and overseas.
WHO CAN BENEFIT Charitable organisations.
WHAT IS FUNDED The foundation focuses on the following four areas: alleviating poverty; access to justice; supporting disability; providing educational opportunity.
RANGE OF GRANTS £2,000 to £25,000.
SAMPLE GRANTS Access to Justice Foundation (£100,000); Backup Trust (£25,500); Plan UK, SOS Children's Villages and St Mungo's (£20,000 each); Horatio's Garden (£6,500); Child Brain Injury Trust and LawWorks (£5,000 each); City Solicitors Horizons (£4,000).
FINANCES *Year* 2015/16 *Income* £545,893 *Grants* £578,445 *Grants to organisations* £578,445 *Assets* £22,051
TRUSTEES John Cahill; Bennett Townsend; Stuart Dench; Paul Paxton; James Healy-Pratt; Stephen Foster; Julian Chamberlayne; Daniel Herman; Andrew Dinsmore; Kevin Grealis; Keith Thomas; Clive Zietman; Sean Upson; Muiris Lyons; Debbie Chism; Helen Ward; Jonathan Sinclair.
OTHER INFORMATION Grants of £3,000 or less totalled £69,500.
HOW TO APPLY The website states that 'it is not the policy of the trustees to accept direct applications for funds'.
WHO TO APPLY TO John Cahill, Trustee, 5 New Street Square, London EC4A 3BF *Email* info@stewartslaw.com *Website* www.stewartslaw.com/the-stewarts-law-foundation.aspx

■ The Stobart Newlands Charitable Trust

CC NO 328464 **ESTABLISHED** 1989
WHERE FUNDING CAN BE GIVEN UK.
WHO CAN BENEFIT Registered charities.
WHAT IS FUNDED Christian religion and missionary causes.
TYPE OF GRANT Mainly recurrent.
RANGE OF GRANTS Up to £360,000.
SAMPLE GRANTS World Vision (£310,000); Mission Aviation Fellowship (£250,000); Operation Mobilisation (£175,000); Moorlands (£80,000); Tearfund (£35,000); London City Mission (£28,000); Community Reach (£22,000); Christian Aid, Torch Trust and Transworld Radio (£10,000 each).
FINANCES *Year* 2015 *Income* £1,087,299 *Grants* £1,287,491 *Grants to organisations* £1,287,491 *Assets* £201,448
TRUSTEES Ronnie Stobart; Linda Rigg; Peter Stobart; Richard Stobart.
OTHER INFORMATION Grants of less than £10,000 totalled £149,500 during the year.
HOW TO APPLY Unsolicited applications are unlikely to be successful.
WHO TO APPLY TO Ronnie Stobart, Trustee, J. Stobart and Sons Ltd, Millcroft, Newlands, Hesket Newmarket, Wigton CA7 8HP *Tel.* 01697 478631

■ The Stoller Charitable Trust

CC NO 285415 **ESTABLISHED** 1982
WHERE FUNDING CAN BE GIVEN UK, with a preference for the Greater Manchester area.
WHO CAN BENEFIT Charitable organisations.
WHAT IS FUNDED General charitable purposes, particularly: children and young people; medical research; cancer relief.
WHAT IS NOT FUNDED Individuals.
TYPE OF GRANT Some recurrent; some one-off.
RANGE OF GRANTS The 2015/16 annual report states that the trustees aim to maintain a balance between larger and smaller grants.
SAMPLE GRANTS Bauern Helfen Bauern; Onside North West; Broughton House; Central Manchester Children's Hospitals; Live Music Now; Christie Hospital, Greater Manchester Appeal; Imperial War Museum North; National Memorial Arboretum; Cancer Research UK; Oldham Liaison of Ex-Services Associations; Church Housing Trust; Commandery of John of Gaunt; Mines Advisory Group; Salvation Army; Windermere Air Show.
FINANCES *Year* 2015/16 *Income* £1,878,104 *Grants* £16,551,817 *Grants to organisations* £16,551,817 *Assets* £31,117,315
TRUSTEES Roger Gould; Sir Norman Stoller; Lady Stoller; Andrew Dixon; KSL. Trustees Ltd.
OTHER INFORMATION The trust made 116 grants during 2015/16. A list of recent beneficiaries was not provided in the accounts.
HOW TO APPLY Apply in writing to the correspondent. The trustees meet regularly to review applications.
WHO TO APPLY TO Stephen Lowe, 24 Low Crompton Road, Royton, Oldham OL2 6YR *Email* enquiries@stollercharitabletrust.co.uk

■ M. J. C. Stone Charitable Trust

CC NO 283920 **ESTABLISHED** 1981
WHERE FUNDING CAN BE GIVEN Gloucestershire.
WHO CAN BENEFIT Charitable organisations.
WHAT IS FUNDED General charitable purposes; education and training; the promotion of health; social welfare; religious causes; environment.
TYPE OF GRANT Recurrent; one-off.
RANGE OF GRANTS £20 to £2,500.
SAMPLE GRANTS InterAct Stroke Support and Sudbury Neighbourhood Centre (£2,500 each); Child Bereavement UK (£1,300); Gloucester Cathedral (£1,200); Alzheimer's Research, Brain Tumour Support and Frith Youth Centre (£1,000 each); Arundel Castle Cricket Foundation (£500); MS Society (£250); SongBird Survival (£20).
FINANCES *Year* 2015/16 *Income* £401,075 *Grants* £109,115 *Grants to organisations* £109,115 *Assets* £572,160
TRUSTEES Louisa Stone; Nicola Farquhar; Michael Stone; Andrew Stone; Charles Stone.
HOW TO APPLY Apply in writing to the correspondent. The annual report states: 'The charitable trust makes grants to core charities on an annual basis. Grants to other charities are made on receipt of applications and after discussions between the trustees.'

WHO TO APPLY TO Andrew Stone, Trustee, 8 St Albans Grove, London W8 5PN *Tel.* 020 7096 6356

■ The Stone Family Foundation

CC NO 1164682 **ESTABLISHED** 2005
WHERE FUNDING CAN BE GIVEN Worldwide.
WHO CAN BENEFIT Charities; international aid organisations.
WHAT IS FUNDED Water and sanitation (around 80% of the foundation's funding is committed to this area); mental health; disadvantaged young people. Further information about each of the foundation's areas of focus is given on the website.
TYPE OF GRANT Core costs; development funding; multi-year and recurrent grants.
RANGE OF GRANTS Up to £1 million.
SAMPLE GRANTS Water and Sanitation for the Urban Poor (£1 million); IDE Cambodia (£706,500); Acumen Fund (£435,000); WaterAid (£398,500); Watershed (£197,500); Rethink (£137,000); Mosaic Clubhouse (£70,000); The Samaritans (£60,000); Into University (£50,000); Star Wards (£10,000). *Grants to organisations* £4,176,197
TRUSTEES John Stone; Charles Edwards; David Steinegger.
OTHER INFORMATION The charity was previously registered under the Charity Commission number 1108207; in 2017, it incorporated as a CIO and the funds were transferred. Consequently, there was no financial information available on the Charity Commission record at the time of writing (June 2017). Under its previous registration, the foundation gave around £4 million per year in grants. The website states: 'The Foundation currently makes grants and investments to support water and sanitation projects of over £6 million per year. We are committed to increase this to £10 million per year.'
HOW TO APPLY The foundation's website states the following information: 'We are a small, family foundation with limited resources and as a result we do not accept unsolicited proposals. We like to foster long term partnerships with organisations aligned to our vision, beliefs and strategy focus. This proactive approach helps us maximise effectiveness and impact. If you have any questions, please feel free to email: SFF@thinkNPC.org. Please note, this email inbox is only monitored periodically.'
WHO TO APPLY TO Paul Gunstensen, 22 Upper Ground, London SE1 9PD *Tel.* 020 7663 6825 *Email* SFF@thinkNPC.org *Website* www.thesff.com

■ The Stoneygate Trust

CC NO 1119976 **ESTABLISHED** 2007
WHERE FUNDING CAN BE GIVEN England and Wales.
WHO CAN BENEFIT Charities; universities; medical research institutions.
WHAT IS FUNDED Medical research; health; social welfare; education.
SAMPLE GRANTS University College London (£250,500); University of Cambridge (£31,000); Imperial College London (£130,500); Boys Town National Research (£30,000); St Mark's Hospital Foundation (£16,500); Addenbrooke's Charitable Trust (£4,000); Cancer Research UK (£1,000).
FINANCES *Year* 2015/16 *Income* £649,257 *Grants* £1,211,198 *Grants to organisations* £1,211,198 *Assets* £13,288,514
TRUSTEES William Adderley; Nadine Adderley; Andrew Walden.
HOW TO APPLY Apply in writing to the correspondent.
WHO TO APPLY TO Deborah Fisher, The Old Coach House, Sunnyside, Bergh Apton, Norwich NR15 1DD *Tel.* 01508 480100 *Email* info@fisherlegal.co.uk

■ The Samuel Storey Family Charitable Trust

CC NO 267684 **ESTABLISHED** 1974
WHERE FUNDING CAN BE GIVEN UK.
WHO CAN BENEFIT Registered charities.
WHAT IS FUNDED General charitable purposes.
WHAT IS NOT FUNDED Individuals.
RANGE OF GRANTS £25 to £6,000, typically less than £1,000.
SAMPLE GRANTS St John the Evangelist Edinburgh (£6,000); Antibiotic Research UK (£4,000); Scarborough Theatre Trust (£1,500); Jump Ahead (£1,000); Friends of the British Museum (£600); Mary's Meals (£500); Centrepoint (£200); Blind Veterans UK (£100); Songbird Survival (£45); Foot and Mouth Painting Artists (£25).
FINANCES *Year* 2015/16 *Income* £210,544 *Grants* £113,512 *Grants to organisations* £113,512 *Assets* £5,603,207
TRUSTEES Hon. Sir Richard Storey; Wren Hoskyns Abrahall; Kenelm Storey; Elisabeth Critchley.
OTHER INFORMATION Grants were made to 208 organisations during the year.
HOW TO APPLY Apply in writing to the correspondent.
WHO TO APPLY TO Kenelm Storey, Trustee, c/o 33 Queen Anne Street, London W1G 9HY *Tel.* 020 7802 2700

■ Peter Stormonth Darling Charitable Trust

CC NO 1049946 **ESTABLISHED** 1995
WHERE FUNDING CAN BE GIVEN UK.
WHO CAN BENEFIT Charitable organisations.
WHAT IS FUNDED Heritage; education; health; sports facilities.
WHAT IS NOT FUNDED Individuals.
RANGE OF GRANTS Up to £17,000.
SAMPLE GRANTS Imperial College Research (£17,000); Royal Hospital for Neuro-disability and Westminster Abbey (£10,000 each); National Trust Scotland, Sussex Community Foundation and Walking with the Wounded (£5,000 each); Cheltenham Festivals (£4,000); National Churches Trust (£2,500); Bath Rugby Foundation (£1,000); Holburne Museum Trust (£500).
FINANCES *Year* 2015 *Income* £91,850 *Grants* £152,870 *Grants to organisations* £152,870 *Assets* £4,028,261
TRUSTEES John Rodwell; Peter Stormonth Darling; Elizabeth Cobb; Christa Taylor.
OTHER INFORMATION The trust made 34 grants to organisations during the year.
HOW TO APPLY The trustees have stated that they do not respond to unsolicited applications.
WHO TO APPLY TO Peter Stormonth Darling, Trustee, Soditic Ltd, 12 Charles II Street, London SW1Y 4QU

■ Peter Storrs Trust

CC NO 313804 **ESTABLISHED** 1970

WHERE FUNDING CAN BE GIVEN UK and overseas.

WHO CAN BENEFIT Registered charities.

WHAT IS FUNDED General charitable purposes and the advancement of education.

WHAT IS NOT FUNDED Individuals.

RANGE OF GRANTS £1,000 to £10,500.

SAMPLE GRANTS ACE UK – Africa (£10,500); Disasters Emergency Committee Philippines Typhoon Appeal (£5,000); Aids Orphans of Myanmar (£2,500); RNIB (£3,000); Afghan Connection, Age Concern, Big Brum Theatre, Mind, Sight Savers, St Martin-in-the-Fields Christmas Appeal (£2,000 each); Finsbury and Clerkenwell Volunteers (£1,000).

FINANCES *Year* 2015/16 *Income* £130,299 *Grants* £131,000 *Grants to organisations* £131,000 *Assets* £2,941,672

TRUSTEES Geoffrey Adams; Arthur Curtis; Julie Easton.

HOW TO APPLY Apply in writing to the correspondent.

WHO TO APPLY TO The Trustees, c/o Smithfield Accountants, 117 Charterhouse Street, London EC1M 6AA *Tel.* 020 7253 3757 *Email* postmaster@smithfield-accountants.co.uk

■ The Strangward Trust

CC NO 1036494 **ESTABLISHED** 1993

WHERE FUNDING CAN BE GIVEN Mainly Bedfordshire, Cambridgeshire and Northamptonshire.

WHO CAN BENEFIT Organisations concerned with people with mental and physical disabilities.

WHAT IS FUNDED Funding for care and treatment of people with physical or mental disabilities.

TYPE OF GRANT One-off, capital, core costs. Funding is for one year or less.

RANGE OF GRANTS Mostly under £5,000.

SAMPLE GRANTS Fenland Association for Community Transport (£11,500); Grafham Water Sailability (£5,000); Bedford and District Cerebral Palsy Society (£3,600); Peterborough Citizens Advice (£3,000); Mental Health Foundation (£2,500); The Norfolk Hospice (£2,000); MS Therapy Centre Bedford (£1,300); Huntingdon Nursery School (£1,100); The Nancy Oldfield Trust (£1,000); Cardea First Responders (£500).

FINANCES *Year* 2015/16 *Income* £224,177 *Grants* £104,258 *Grants to organisations* £112,050 *Assets* £10,304,775

TRUSTEES Anne Allured; Ross Jones; Paul Goakes; Clare O'Callaghan.

OTHER INFORMATION Grants were made to 40 organisations during the year.

HOW TO APPLY Application forms are available from the correspondent. Attach a copy of your latest accounts (if relevant) and any other supporting documentation (e.g. copy estimates or medical reports, when applying). The trustees meet twice a year (March and September) to decide upon donations. Applications should be submitted by the end of February and August. The trustees will consider every application submitted to them that meets the criteria of the trust. It is important that applications on behalf of national charities identify a specific need for funding in the geographic area referred to above to be considered. The trustees will consider projects where there is an annual ongoing requirement for funds for period of up to five years. Successful applicants will be expected to keep the trust informed on their projects. Only successful applicants will be notified of the outcome of their application.

WHO TO APPLY TO Ross Jones, Trustee, Glebe House, Catworth, Huntingdon, Cambridgeshire PE28 0PA *Tel.* 01832 710171 *Email* strangwardtrust@aol.com

■ Stratford-upon-Avon Town Trust

CC NO 1088521 **ESTABLISHED** 2001

WHERE FUNDING CAN BE GIVEN Stratford-upon-Avon.

WHO CAN BENEFIT Organisations benefitting people living in the Stratford-upon-Avon council area. Schools can also apply. The trust also makes grants to individuals through local organisations, for small, one-off items such as white goods or clothing.

WHAT IS FUNDED Welfare and well-being; strengthening communities; young people; poverty; older people.

WHAT IS NOT FUNDED Organisations outside Stratford-upon-Avon.

TYPE OF GRANT Capital and revenue grants for up to three years.

RANGE OF GRANTS Up to £50,000.

SAMPLE GRANTS Stratford ArtsHouse (£230,500); Citizens Advice (£70,000); Shakespeare Hospice (£57,000); Domestic Abuse Counselling Service (£40,000); Stratford-upon-Avon Boat Club (£30,000); 1289 Squadron Stratford Air Training Corps (£26,000); Orchestra of the Swan (£25,000); Voluntary Action Stratford-on-Avon District (£23,000); Lifespace Trust (£21,500).

FINANCES *Year* 2015 *Income* £3,211,713 *Grants* £1,790,487 *Grants to organisations* £1,783,487 *Assets* £54,913,941

TRUSTEES Carole Taylor; Charles Bates; Julia Lucas; Clarissa Roberts; Alan Haigh; Richard Lane; Clive Snowdon; Quentin Wilson; Eden Lee; Tessa Bates; Tony Jackson.

OTHER INFORMATION Non-discretionary grants were made during the year to King Edward VI School, for the maintenance of almshouses and to the vicar of Holy Trinity Church. Discretionary grants awarded to organisations totalled £1.13 million in 2015. Only beneficiaries of grants above £20,000 were listed in the accounts.

HOW TO APPLY Application forms can be completed via the trust's website. Awards for the Main Grants programme are made three times each year; application deadlines are listed on the trust's website. Applications for Programme Grants (for major projects for up to three years) should be made three months in advance and require additional information in the application – refer to the guidance provided on the trust's website. There is also a Fast-Track Grants scheme (grants of up to £1,000), for which decisions can be made within ten days of an application being submitted.

WHO TO APPLY TO Claire Bowry, Grants Manager, 14 Rother Street, Stratford-upon-Avon, Warwickshire CV32 6LU *Tel.* 01789 207111 *Email* admin@stratfordtowntrust.co.uk *Website* www.stratfordtowntrust.co.uk

■ The Strawberry Charitable Trust

CC NO 1090173 **ESTABLISHED** 2000

WHERE FUNDING CAN BE GIVEN UK, with a preference for Manchester.

WHO CAN BENEFIT Registered charities.

WHAT IS FUNDED The relief of poverty and hardship mainly among Jewish people and the advancement of the Jewish religion.

SAMPLE GRANTS Community Security Trust (£15,000); Magen David Adom (£5,000);

Manchester Jewish Primary School, The Fed and United Jewish Israel Appeal (UJIA) (£4,000 each); Friendship Circle (£2,100); Chai Cancer (£2,000).

FINANCES *Year* 2015/16 *Income* £38,616 *Grants* £44,186 *Grants to organisations* £44,186 *Assets* £71,316

TRUSTEES Emma Myers; Laura Avigdori; Anthony Leon.

OTHER INFORMATION Grants of less than £1,000 totalled £6,600 during the year.

HOW TO APPLY Apply in writing to the correspondent.

WHO TO APPLY TO Anthony Leon, Trustee, 4 Westfields, Hale, Altrincham WA15 0LL *Tel.* 0161 980 8484 *Email* anthonysula@hotmail.com

■ The W. O. Street Charitable Foundation

CC NO 267127 **ESTABLISHED** 1973

WHERE FUNDING CAN BE GIVEN Worldwide. There is a preference for the north west of England (the county of Lancashire before 1974), and Jersey.

WHO CAN BENEFIT Registered charities.

WHAT IS FUNDED General charitable purposes; education and training; social welfare; health.

WHAT IS NOT FUNDED Individuals.

TYPE OF GRANT One-off and recurring grants.

RANGE OF GRANTS Mainly £500 to £5,000.

SAMPLE GRANTS W. O. Street Charitable Foundation – Jersey (£40,000); Emmott Foundation (£30,000); Mothers Against Violence (£5,000); Barnsley Beacon Support Services (£4,000); St Peter's Hospice (£2,900); Cumbria Deaf Vision, Epilepsy Lifestyle and Family Tree Wirral (£2,500 each); Child Brain Injury Trust (£1,000); Anaphylaxis Campaign (£500).

FINANCES *Year* 2015 *Income* £577,874 *Grants* £548,532 *Grants to organisations* £488,732 *Assets* £16,949,575

TRUSTEES Barclays Bank Trust Co. Ltd; Clive Cutbill.

OTHER INFORMATION Grants were made to 138 organisations in 2015, which included a grant of £40,000 to the W. O. Street Charitable Foundation – Jersey, to support the foundation's objectives in this area, and a grant of £30,000 to the Emmott Foundation, which makes educational grants. There were also 37 educational bursaries directly awarded during the year, which totalled £60,000. The foundation also works with the Community Foundations for Merseyside and Lancashire to distribute grants through the W. O. Street Transformation Funds.

HOW TO APPLY Apply in writing to the correspondent. Applications are considered on a quarterly basis.

WHO TO APPLY TO The Trustees, Zedra Trust Company UK Ltd, Zedra UK Trusts, Osborne Court, Gadbrook Park, Rudheath, Northwich CW9 7UE *Tel.* 01606 313327 *Email* charities@zedra.com

■ The Street Foundation

CC NO 1045229 **ESTABLISHED** 1995

WHERE FUNDING CAN BE GIVEN England and Wales.

WHO CAN BENEFIT Registered charities.

WHAT IS FUNDED Disability; poverty; education; community; human rights; sport.

SAMPLE GRANTS A list of beneficiaries was not available.

FINANCES *Year* 2015/16 *Income* £255,323 *Grants* £582,168 *Grants to organisations* £582,168 *Assets* £481,493

TRUSTEES Richard Smith; Susan Smith; Sarah Smith; Lucinda Sharp-Smith.

HOW TO APPLY Apply in writing to the correspondent.

WHO TO APPLY TO Richard Smith, Kingsland House, Kingsland, Leominster HR6 9SG *Tel.* 01568 708744

■ The Sudborough Foundation

CC NO 272323 **ESTABLISHED** 1976

WHERE FUNDING CAN BE GIVEN Mainly Northamptonshire.

WHO CAN BENEFIT Registered charities and educational establishments.

WHAT IS FUNDED Education and training; general charitable purposes. The trustees 'particularly like to assist those who are helping themselves (e.g. by raising funds from other sources) and with a high level of voluntary work'.

WHAT IS NOT FUNDED Individuals; non-registered charities; political or pressure groups; individual fundraising, including expeditions or overseas travel; religious groups (although applications will be considered from faith-based charities running projects focusing on social welfare or other projects open to the wider community); activities which are considered the responsibility or local or national government; national charities (with the exception of local branches for local projects). While the foundation does make some grants more broadly, applications from outside Northamptonshire are unlikely to be considered apart from in exceptional circumstances.

RANGE OF GRANTS £100 to £5,000; mainly £500 to £1,000.

SAMPLE GRANTS British Psychotherapy Foundation (£25,000 in two grants); Northampton Hope Centre (£15,000); Home-Start Northampton (£10,000); Community Integrated Care (£6,200); FareShare Leicester (£2,000); Northampton College (£1,500); Oxford Radcliffe Hospitals Charitable Fund and Relate Northamptonshire (£1,000 each); Greenfields School (£690); Jewish Women's Aid (£150).

FINANCES *Year* 2015/16 *Income* £184,887 *Grants* £109,553 *Grants to organisations* £109,553 *Assets* £1,568,811

TRUSTEES William Reason; Elisabeth Engel; Richard Engel; Simon Powis; Susan Leathem; Rachel Engel; Lady Lowther; Lucy Watson; Marilyn Woolfson; Tim Parker.

OTHER INFORMATION There were 39 grants made to organisations during the year.

HOW TO APPLY An application form can be downloaded from the foundation's website and should be submitted by post or email. The trustees meet annually in October but grants may be considered during the rest of the year in some circumstances.

WHO TO APPLY TO Richard Engel, Chair of Trustees, 8 Hazelwood Road, Northampton NN1 1LP *Email* applications@sudborough.org *Website* sites.google.com/site/sudborough2/home

■ Sueberry Ltd

CC NO 256566 **ESTABLISHED** 1968

WHERE FUNDING CAN BE GIVEN UK and overseas.

WHO CAN BENEFIT Charitable organisations.

WHAT IS FUNDED Jewish causes; social welfare; education; general charitable purposes.

SAMPLE GRANTS A list of beneficiaries was not available.
FINANCES *Year* 2015/16 *Income* £80,904 *Grants* £157,521 *Grants to organisations* £157,521 *Assets* £48,297
TRUSTEES D. S. Davis; Chaim Davis; Hanna Davis; Aharon Davis; A. D. Davis; S. M. Davis; Y. Davis.
OTHER INFORMATION Details of grant beneficiaries were not provided in the trust's accounts.
HOW TO APPLY Apply in writing to the correspondent.
WHO TO APPLY TO D. S. Davis, Trustee, 15 East Meade, Prestwich, Manchester M25 0JJ *Tel.* 020 8731 0777

■ Suffolk Community Foundation

CC NO 1109453 **ESTABLISHED** 2005
WHERE FUNDING CAN BE GIVEN Suffolk.
WHO CAN BENEFIT Registered charities; voluntary and community groups.
WHAT IS FUNDED The foundation's aims are to: promote health and well-being; tackle disadvantage; support local solutions to meet local needs; promote community cohesion; develop sustainable and supportive communities. It has a range of different funds designed for small community and voluntary groups working to help local people across Suffolk. Each scheme tends to have a different application procedure and size of award. **Note:** Grant schemes can change frequently. Potential applicants are advised to consult the foundation's website for details of current programmes and their deadlines.
WHAT IS NOT FUNDED Projects not benefitting people living in Suffolk; grants to individuals or families for personal needs (with the exception of Suffolk Disability Care Fund); direct replacement of statutory obligation and public funding; promotion of religious or political causes; groups with significant financial free reserves; retrospective grants; contribution to endowment fund, payment of deficit funding or repayment of loans; national charities that are not providing clear local benefits; overseas travel or expeditions; sponsored or fundraising events or groups raising funds to redistribute to other causes; medical research and equipment for statutory or private health care; start-up funding for a project that is unable to start within nine months; commercial ventures, unless the group is a registered not-for-profit organisation; general appeals; animal welfare, unless the project benefits people (e.g. riding schemes for people with disabilities); statutory work in educational institutions; fees for professional fundraisers.
TYPE OF GRANT Core costs; project costs; one-off; capital costs.
RANGE OF GRANTS Mostly smaller grants, around £2,000.
SAMPLE GRANTS Museum of East Anglian Life (£24,000); Ipswich Community Media (£17,000); Gatehouse Caring in West Suffolk (£10,000); Artheads (£4,500); Suffolk Refugee Support (£2,000); Rural Coffee Caravan Information Project (£1,800); Ipswich Morning Stroke Club (£1,400); Suffolk Rape Crisis (£1,000); St Genevieve's Church (£500); Creeting Community Pre-School (£200).
FINANCES *Year* 2015/16 *Income* £4,608,145 *Grants* £2,436,300 *Grants to organisations* £2,436,300 *Assets* £11,288,993
TRUSTEES James Buckle; Very Revd Dr Frances Ward; Gulshan Kayembe; Nigel Smith; Iain Jamie; Terrry Ward; Jonathan Agar; Neil Walmsley; Hon. Selina Hopkins; Peter Newnham.
OTHER INFORMATION In 2015/16 the foundation awarded 608 grants to organisations.
HOW TO APPLY The foundation's website has details of the grant schemes currently being administered and how to apply.
WHO TO APPLY TO Grants Team, The Old Barn, Peninsula Business Centre, Wherstead, Ipswich, Suffolk IP9 2BB *Tel.* 01473 602602 *Email* info@suffolkcf.org.uk *Website* suffolkcf.org.uk

■ The Suffolk Historic Churches Trust

CC NO 267047 **ESTABLISHED** 1973
WHERE FUNDING CAN BE GIVEN Suffolk.
WHO CAN BENEFIT Churches and chapels which are in regular use as a place of worship.
WHAT IS FUNDED Preservation, repair, maintenance, restoration and improvement of churches. Grants are given for essential repairs and maintenance, as well as toilets, kitchens and other facilities. Priority is given to work concerning the fabric of a building.
WHAT IS NOT FUNDED Furnishings and fittings; churchyard walls; brasses and bells; monuments; organs; redecoration, unless needed as part of an eligible project; new buildings or extensions to existing buildings; work which has already taken place.
TYPE OF GRANT Grants towards capital projects.
RANGE OF GRANTS £300 to £10,000.
SAMPLE GRANTS Great Bricett (£10,000); Worlingworth St Mary (£8,000); Halesworth United Reformed Church (£6,000); Creeting St Mary (£5,000); Ampton St Peter (£4,000); Bury St Edmunds Cathedral (£2,500); Newmarket All Saints (£2,000); Walpole Old Chapel (£750); Sylham (£300).
FINANCES *Year* 2015/16 *Income* £362,062 *Grants* £264,914 *Grants to organisations* £264,914 *Assets* £759,922
TRUSTEES Patrick Grieve; Martin Favell; Hon. Charles Boscawen; Christopher Spicer; Robert Williams; Clive Paine; Simon Tennet; Celia Stephens; Nicholas Pearson; Edward Bland; Tim Allen; Geoffrey Probert; David King; John Devaux; Frances Torrington.
OTHER INFORMATION The trust also recommends some projects for partnership funding with the National Churches Trust. It also makes an annual grant to the Elix Church Maintenance Scheme, which provides annual assistance with small problems and advice for churches in the area. In 2015/16 the trust made 95 grants.
HOW TO APPLY Application forms can be downloaded from the trust's website, or can be requested from the trust by telephone, email or post. Grants Committee Meetings are held four times a year and deadlines for applications are posted on the trust's website.
WHO TO APPLY TO The Grants Secretary, Brinkleys, Hall Street, Long Melford, Suffolk CO10 9JR *Tel.* 01787 883884 *Email* shct@btconnect.com *Website* www.shct.org.uk

■ The Alan Sugar Foundation

CC NO 294880 **ESTABLISHED** 1986
WHERE FUNDING CAN BE GIVEN UK, focusing on the South East.
WHO CAN BENEFIT Registered charities.

WHAT IS FUNDED General charitable purposes; social welfare; education; health; children; older people; people who are disadvantaged.
WHAT IS NOT FUNDED Individuals; non-registered charities.
TYPE OF GRANT One-off and recurring, capital and project.
SAMPLE GRANTS Jewish Care (£100,000); Great Ormond Street Hospital (£2,500).
FINANCES *Year* 2015/16 *Income* £50,336 *Grants* £102,500 *Grants to organisations* £102,500 *Assets* £30,329
TRUSTEES Simon Sugar; Lord Alan Sugar; Colin Sandy; Daniel Sugar; Louise Baron.
HOW TO APPLY This trust states that it does not respond to unsolicited applications. All projects are initiated by the trustees.
WHO TO APPLY TO Colin Sandy, Trustee, Amshold House, Goldings Hill, Loughton, Essex IG10 3RW *Tel.* 020 3225 5560 *Email* colin@amsprop.com

■ The Summerfield Charitable Trust

CC NO 802493 **ESTABLISHED** 1989
WHERE FUNDING CAN BE GIVEN Gloucestershire.
WHO CAN BENEFIT Registered charities; CICs and other community and voluntary groups are eligible but must include a letter of endorsement from a registered charity in their application.
WHAT IS FUNDED The trustees are particularly interested in helping: the arts, museums and the built heritage; the environment and natural heritage; community work; education, sport and recreation; and vulnerable or disadvantaged sectors of society.
WHAT IS NOT FUNDED Medical research; private education; animal welfare; trips abroad; projects that have already taken place; recurring staff costs (salaries or staff will only be considered as part of one-off project or for a limited period); individuals; churches (the trust awards an annual grant to Gloucestershire Historic Churches Trust); charities which have already received a grant in the last two years.
TYPE OF GRANT The trustees prefer to award one-off grants to help fund specific projects. The trust will consider funds towards building alterations to reduce running costs and improve facilities for beneficiaries or staff.
RANGE OF GRANTS £500 to £20,000.
SAMPLE GRANTS Cheltenham Festivals (£20,000); Gloucestershire Gateway Trust (£15,000); Allsorts Gloucestershire (£5,000); Active Gloucestershire and Interclimate Trust (£4,000 each); Community Roots CIC (£3,000); Lydney Cricket Club (£2,500); Blockley Toddler Group (£1,400); Tewkesbury in Bloom (£600); The Schumacher Institute (£380).
FINANCES *Year* 2015 *Income* £627,771 *Grants* £978,058 *Grants to organisations* £978,058 *Assets* £9,774,523
TRUSTEES Edward Gillespie; Katrina Beach; Vanessa Arbuthnott; David Owen; James Millar.
OTHER INFORMATION Grants were made to 102 organisations during the year, including an exceptional major grant to Gloucester Cathedral. Grants were distributed in the following categories: arts, museums and built heritage (£553,000 in 21 grants); disadvantaged and vulnerable sectors (£205,000 in 36 grants); education, sport and recreation (£97,500 in 25 grants); community work (£76,500 in 15 grants); environment and natural heritage (£46,500 in 5 grants).
HOW TO APPLY Application forms, criteria and guidelines are provided on the trust's website. The trustees meet quarterly; usually in January, April, July and October (see the trust's website for deadline dates). The trustees prefer to support projects that will take place, or start, within six months of receiving the grant. It is therefore important when applying to be clear about timescales and be confident they will fit in with the timing of the quarterly meetings.
WHO TO APPLY TO Lavinia Sidgwick, Trust Administrator, PO Box 287, Cirencester, Gloucestershire GL7 9FB *Tel.* 01285 721211 *Email* admin@summerfield.org.uk *Website* www.summerfield.org.uk

■ The Bernard Sunley Charitable Foundation

CC NO 1109099 **ESTABLISHED** 1960
WHERE FUNDING CAN BE GIVEN England and Wales.
WHO CAN BENEFIT Registered charities and or those with exempt or excepted status.
WHAT IS FUNDED Grants are given in the following categories: community; education; health; and social welfare. Further detail on each of these priorities is given on the website.
WHAT IS NOT FUNDED Parish councils, Community Amateur Sports Clubs and CICs; running costs or revenue costs (including salaries, training costs, software licenses, utility bills and rent); feasibility studies or building surveys; projects with a total budget of less than £5,000. The foundation rarely funds 'reasonably priced, non-durable equipment subject to wear and tear' such as musical instruments, camping equipment, mobility aids or furniture.
TYPE OF GRANT One-off capital grants – new buildings; major refurbishments; equipment (single, durable items costing at least £5,000); transport. Usually paid over one year, but occasionally up to three years.
RANGE OF GRANTS Generally £1,000 to £5,000, towards a larger project total (usually up to 20% of the total budget). 80% of grants are under £5,000. Larger grants are exceptional.
SAMPLE GRANTS London Youth (£150,000); Veterans Aid (£50,000); Ambitious About Autism (£20,000); Surrey Wildlife Trust (£10,000); St Andrew's Church Catford (£5,000); Eating Disorders Association (£4,000); Heart of Kent Hospice (£2,000); Polgoth Village Hall (£1,500); 1st Compton Scout Group and Academy of St Martin-in-the-Fields (£1,000 each).
FINANCES *Year* 2015/16 *Income* £3,950,000 *Grants* £2,709,270 *Grants to organisations* £2,709,270 *Assets* £98,191,000
TRUSTEES Dr Brian Martin; Joan Tice; Bella Sunley; Anabel Knight; William Tice; Inigo Paternina.
OTHER INFORMATION Grants were awarded to 516 organisations during 2015/16, of which 24 were large (£25,000 or more); 109 medium (£5,000 to £25,000); and 383 small (£5,000 or less).
HOW TO APPLY There are guidelines for each of the grant categories on the website, which should be read before an application is started. Applications can be made using the form on the foundation's website. Potential applicants are welcome to contact the foundation to discuss an application. In exceptional circumstances a paper application may be accepted – contact the foundation to discuss this. The foundation

aims to make a decision within six months of an application.

WHO TO APPLY TO Digby Nelson, Director, 20 Berkeley Square, London W1J 6LH *Tel.* 020 7408 2198 *Email* office@bernardsunley.org *Website* www.bernardsunley.org

■ Sunninghill Fuel Allotment Trust

CC NO 240061 **ESTABLISHED** 1965

WHERE FUNDING CAN BE GIVEN The civil parish of Sunninghill.

WHO CAN BENEFIT Charitable and community organisations; individuals in need.

WHAT IS FUNDED Social welfare; older people; ill health; recreational and educational facilities; community purposes. The trust also makes grants to individuals in need.

WHAT IS NOT FUNDED Activities that would otherwise be the responsibility of central or local government, health trusts or health authorities, or which are substantially funded by them; retrospective funding.

TYPE OF GRANT Capital; core costs; project costs.

SAMPLE GRANTS Ascot District Day Centre (£34,000 in two grants); Charters School (£9,000); North Ascot Community Association and Triple A Ascot Alzheimer's (£5,000 each); All Saints Church (£2,300).

FINANCES *Year* 2015/16 *Income* £281,284 *Grants* £87,768 *Grants to organisations* £70,909 *Assets* £3,799,832

TRUSTEES Revd Stephen Johnson; Karen Clements; Lauren Davies; Wayne Phelan; Terry Gorman.

OTHER INFORMATION Grants to individuals during the year totalled £16,900.

HOW TO APPLY Apply in writing to the correspondent. Applications are acknowledged by letter or email and are considered four times a year.

WHO TO APPLY TO The Clerk, PO Box 4712, Ascot SL5 9AA *Tel.* 01344 206320 *Email* help@thesunninghilltrust.org

■ Support Adoption for Pets

CC NO 1104152 **ESTABLISHED** 2004

WHERE FUNDING CAN BE GIVEN UK.

WHO CAN BENEFIT Charitable organisations; must be a registered charity if annual income is over £50,000.

WHAT IS FUNDED Activities which make a difference to the welfare of UK domestic pets in rescue or reduce the number of domestic pets in rescue.

WHAT IS NOT FUNDED Salaries, uniforms or expenses; education centres and programmes; purchase of food; cost of leasing a vehicle, road tax, insurance or petrol costs; loan or interest payments; purchase of land or buildings; costs associated with a charity shop; fundraising costs or marketing materials; retrospective funding.

TYPE OF GRANT Core costs (limited to vet bills and boarding costs); capital items; project costs (e.g. trap, neuter and release schemes for feral cats or low-cost vaccination or neutering schemes available to the public).

SAMPLE GRANTS Ark on the Edge; Battersea Dogs and Cats Home; Cats Protection Orkney Islands; Flicka Foundation Horse and Donkey Sanctuary; Folly Wildlife Rescue Trust; Forever Hounds Trust; Leicester Animal Aid; North Clwyd Animal Rescue; Pendle Dogs in Need; RSPCA Northamptonshire.

FINANCES *Year* 2015/16 *Income* £3,665,574 *Grants* £1,953,447 *Grants to organisations* £1,953,447 *Assets* £1,117,819

TRUSTEES Louise Stonier; George Linwood; Daniel Cornwell; Jill Naylor; Brian Hudspith; Dan Laurence; Rehman Minshall; Adrian Bates.

HOW TO APPLY Applications can be made via the charity's website, where eligibility criteria and further guidance are also provided. The trustees meet every three to four months to consider applications; applications for less than £20,000 may be considered more frequently. Any questions can be directed to the Grant Funding Co-ordinator: nichola@supportadoptionforpets.co.uk or 0161 486 7538.

WHO TO APPLY TO Nichola Griffiths, Grant Funding Co-ordinator, Epsom Avenue, Stanley Green Trading Estate, Handforth, Wilmslow, Cheshire SK9 3RN *Tel.* 0161 486 7538 *Email* info@supportadoptionforpets.co.uk *Website* www.supportadoptionforpets.co.uk

■ Surgo Foundation UK Ltd

CC NO 1157510 **ESTABLISHED** 2014

WHERE FUNDING CAN BE GIVEN UK and overseas.

WHO CAN BENEFIT Registered charities; universities.

WHAT IS FUNDED Innovative approaches to health and development.

SAMPLE GRANTS Clinton Health Access Health Initiative (£770,000); Harvard University (£518,500); Into University (£31,000); Chickenshed (£5,100); The Reading Agency (£5,000); American School In London (£2,000); Tate Foundation (£1,250).

FINANCES *Year* 2014/15 *Income* £3,260,735 *Grants* £1,426,675 *Grants to organisations* £1,425,675 *Assets* £1,925,126

TRUSTEES Mala Gaonkar; Oliver Haarmann; Malcolm Gladwell.

OTHER INFORMATION The 2014/15 accounts were the latest available at the time of writing.

HOW TO APPLY Apply in writing to the correspondent.

WHO TO APPLY TO The Trustees, Withers LLP, 16 Old Bailey, London EC4M 7EG *Tel.* 020 7597 6427

■ Community Foundation for Surrey

CC NO 1111600 **ESTABLISHED** 2005

WHERE FUNDING CAN BE GIVEN Surrey.

WHO CAN BENEFIT Charities; local community and voluntary groups; individuals.

WHAT IS FUNDED Communities in Surrey, particularly improving the quality of people's lives, building community capacity and empowering local communities. Preference is given to projects which are self-sustaining and, where possible, user-led.

WHAT IS NOT FUNDED For-profit businesses; national programmes which do not specifically benefit Surrey; faith groups where the project is exclusively for the benefit of members or for proselytising; projects based outside Surrey; retrospective funding; unspecified expenditure or general appeals; fundraising events or activities; funding to make grants to others; requests to build up reserves; statutory obligations; political activities. Organisations which hold a high level of free reserves are unlikely to be funded.

TYPE OF GRANT Core costs; revenue costs; capital costs; project costs; one-off.

RANGE OF GRANTS Average grant around £4,000.

SAMPLE GRANTS Voluntary Support North Surrey (£60,000); Leatherhead Youth Project Ltd (£20,000); Transform Housing and Support (£4,000); Haslemere Fringe Festival (£3,600);

RASASC Guildford (£3,500); Autism and Nature (£2,000); Swallows Trampoline Club (£1,900); Cobham Area Foodbank (£1,000); Oakwood School (£500); The Royal Marsden Cancer Charity (£100); St Mary's Church Heart and Soul Ladies Group (£80).

FINANCES *Year* 2015/16 *Income* £1,807,967 *Grants* £1,001,054 *Grants to organisations* £1,001,054 *Assets* £10,096,891

TRUSTEES Graham Williams; Bridget Biddell; David Frank; Simon Whalley; Richard Whittington; Dr Julie Llewelyn; Graham Healy; Nigel Gillott; Martin De Forest-Brown; Julia Grant; Peter Cluff.

OTHER INFORMATION The foundation also has two grants schemes for individuals – the Surrey Supported Employment Fund and the Surrey Young People's Fund. The grant total includes 339 grants made to both organisations and individuals during the year.

HOW TO APPLY The foundation has a number of grants schemes; organisations are invited to complete an expression of interest form, which the Grants Team will review against the criteria of the various grants schemes and advise applicants whether there is a fund which may support the project – if so, you can complete an online application form.

WHO TO APPLY TO Grants Team, Church House, 30 Church Street, Godalming, Surrey GU7 1EP *Tel.* 01483 478092 *Email* info@cfsurrey.org.uk *Website* www.cfsurrey.org.uk

■ The Sussex Community Foundation

CC NO 1113226 **ESTABLISHED** 2006

WHERE FUNDING CAN BE GIVEN East Sussex, West Sussex or Brighton and Hove.

WHO CAN BENEFIT Charities, voluntary organisations and community groups, particularly grassroots groups and smaller charitable organisations (with an annual income of less than £1 million).

WHAT IS FUNDED The foundations supports activities which address disadvantage and build resilience in communities in Sussex. The foundation manages a number of different grants schemes which open and close at various times and have their own eligibility criteria – refer to the website for information on what is currently available.

WHAT IS NOT FUNDED Organisations or activities not benefitting communities in Sussex; organisations that discriminate based on race, religion, national origin, disability, age or sexual orientation; promotion of religion; political activities; small contributions to major capital appeals or campaigns; grants to be distributed to a third party; animal welfare; retrospective funding; organisations which have previously not met monitoring requirements from the foundation.

TYPE OF GRANT Capital costs (equipment and materials); salaries; training and development; core costs; project costs.

RANGE OF GRANTS Mostly up to £5,000; occasionally larger grants. In 2015/16 average grant was £3,231.

SAMPLE GRANTS Hastings Voluntary Action (£34,500); Adventure Unlimited and Parents and Carers Support Organisation (£25,000 each); Brighton Women's Centre (£23,000); Eastbourne Foodbank (£20,000); Petworth Community Garden (£15,000); Age UK West Sussex (£10,000); Managing-Bipolar CIC, Hastings Furniture Service and Sussex Nightstop Plus (£10,000 each).

FINANCES *Year* 2015/16 *Income* £3,130,594 *Grants* £1,602,547 *Grants to organisations* £1,602,547 *Assets* £12,184,782

TRUSTEES Pamela Stiles; Rodney Buse; Richard Pearson; Denise Patterson; Mike Simpkin; Humphrey Price; Michael Martin; Charles Drayson; Consuelo Brooke; Colin Field; Jonica Fox; Patricia Woolgar; Margaret Burgess; Hon. Keith Hollis; Julia Carrette; Nicola Glover.

OTHER INFORMATION The grant total includes grants to both individuals and organisations. In 2015/16 the foundation awarded 495 grants to 332 organisations and 75 individuals. 178 grants were for £1,000 or less.

HOW TO APPLY Applications should be made using the online form on the foundation's website, after checking the guidelines, eligibility criteria and deadlines for the relevant fund. Alternatively, email or call the office (grants@sussexgiving.org.uk or 01273 409440) for a copy of the application form. The process of assessing applications takes around eight to ten weeks. Applicants will be contacted regarding the outcome after consideration by the Grants Committee.

WHO TO APPLY TO Grants Team, 15 Western Road, Lewes BN7 1RL *Tel.* 01273 409440 *Email* info@sussexgiving.org.uk or grants@sussexgiving.org.uk *Website* www.sussexgiving.org.uk

■ The Adrienne and Leslie Sussman Charitable Trust

CC NO 274955 **ESTABLISHED** 1977

WHERE FUNDING CAN BE GIVEN UK and Israel.

WHO CAN BENEFIT Registered charities.

WHAT IS FUNDED General charitable purposes; Jewish causes.

SAMPLE GRANTS BF Shvut Ami, Chai – Lifeline and B'nai B'rith Hillel Fund, Child Resettlement, Children and Youth Aliyah, Finchley Synagogue, Jewish Care, Nightingale House, Norwood Ravenswood and Sidney Sussex CLL.

FINANCES *Year* 2015/16 *Income* £65,822 *Grants* £59,014 *Grants to organisations* £59,014 *Assets* £2,182,203

TRUSTEES Martin Paisner; Adrienne Sussman; Debra Sussman; Adam Sussman; Neal Sussman.

OTHER INFORMATION A recent list of beneficiaries was not available.

HOW TO APPLY Apply in writing to the correspondent.

WHO TO APPLY TO Adrienne Sussman, Trustee, 25 Tillingbourne Gardens, London N3 3JJ *Tel.* 020 8346 6775

■ The Sutasoma Trust

CC NO 803301 **ESTABLISHED** 1990

WHERE FUNDING CAN BE GIVEN UK and overseas.

WHO CAN BENEFIT Charitable and educational organisations; individuals.

WHAT IS FUNDED Bursaries and support to institutions in the field of social sciences, humanities and humanitarian activities. Grants may also be made for general charitable purposes.

TYPE OF GRANT Mainly recurrent.

RANGE OF GRANTS £250 to £20,000.

SAMPLE GRANTS Lucy Cavendish College (£20,000); Helen Bamber Foundation – Mums and Babies Project (£13,600); Life Begins (£7,000); Yangjakot Day Care Centre – Nepal (£6,300); Exceed Worldwide and Royal Anthropology Society – Radcliffe Brown Fund (£3,000 each);

Amnesty International (£2,000); Lewa Wildlife Community and Medical Foundation Allotment Project (£1,000 each); Link Community Development – Kongo Primary (£250).

FINANCES *Year* 2014/15 *Income* £95,007 *Grants* £147,420 *Grants to organisations* £147,420 *Assets* £2,695,023

TRUSTEES Dr Angela Hobart; Prof. Bruce Kepferer; Dr Piers Vitebsky; Dr Sally Wolfe; Mandy Fish; David Napier.

OTHER INFORMATION The 2014/15 accounts were the most recent available to view on the Charity Commission's website at the time of writing (June 2017). The trust made 28 grants during the year. The grant total includes both individuals and organisations.

HOW TO APPLY Apply in writing to the correspondent. The trustees meet annually.

WHO TO APPLY TO Trust Administrator, PO Box 157, Haverhill, Suffolk CB9 1AH *Email* sutasoma.trust@btinternet.com or info@sutasomatrust.org *Website* www.sutasoma.org

■ Sutton Coldfield Charitable Trust

CC NO 218627 **ESTABLISHED** 1898

WHERE FUNDING CAN BE GIVEN The former borough of Sutton Coldfield, comprising four electoral wards: New Hall, Four Oaks, Trinity and almost all of Vesey ward.

WHO CAN BENEFIT Organisations benefitting local residents; individuals.

WHAT IS FUNDED General charitable purposes, including: social welfare; education; the arts, culture, heritage and science; religion; health; community development; amateur sport; environmental protection.

WHAT IS NOT FUNDED No awards are given to individuals or organisations outside the area of benefit, unless the organisations are providing essential services in the area.

SAMPLE GRANTS Sutton Coldfield Community Games and Sutton Libraries (£30,000 each); Our Place Community Hub (£24,000); Boulevard Allotments Association (£23,000); Harvest Fields Centre (£8,100); Holy Cross and St Francis (£6,000); Birmingham Talking Newspaper (£3,000); Sutton Widows (£900); Emscote Drive Residents (£450); Midlands Pensioners Convention (£150).

FINANCES *Year* 2015/16 *Income* £1,805,073 *Grants* £1,134,578 *Grants to organisations* £1,114,222 *Assets* £52,909,334

TRUSTEES Cllr Margaret Waddington; Keith Dudley; Carole Hancox; Neil Andrews; Dr Stephen Martin; Malcolm Cornish; Linda Jones; Andrew Burley; Andrew Morris; Inge Kettner; Jane Sixsmith; Sanjay Sharma.

OTHER INFORMATION The trust made 60 grants to organisations in 2015/16. The trust also makes grants to individuals for the purposes of relief in need and school uniforms. Grants to 366 individuals totalled £63,000 during the year.

HOW TO APPLY Contact the Grants Manager on 0121 351 2262 or info@suttoncharitabletrust.org to make an application or to discuss further details.

WHO TO APPLY TO John Hemming, Grants Manager, Lingard House, Fox Hollies Road, Sutton Coldfield, West Midlands B76 2RJ *Tel.* 0121 351 2262 *Email* info@suttoncharitabletrust.org *Website* www.suttoncoldfieldcharitabletrust.com

■ Swan Mountain Trust

CC NO 275594 **ESTABLISHED** 1977

WHERE FUNDING CAN BE GIVEN UK.

WHO CAN BENEFIT Charitable organisations, particularly smaller organisations (with an income of less than £500,000).

WHAT IS FUNDED Refugees and asylum seekers, with a focus on mental health among young people in these groups.

WHAT IS NOT FUNDED Individuals; grants for annual holidays or debt repayment; large appeals; causes outside the trust's two main areas of work.

RANGE OF GRANTS Up to £5,000, most around £2,000 or less.

SAMPLE GRANTS Prisoners' Education Trust (£5,000); Finding Rhythms, Mind South Somerset, Prison Radio Association and Wellspring Family Centre (£2,000); Zahid Mubarek Trust (£1,700); The Magdalene Group (£1,500); Lantern Resources Centre and Cleveland Housing Advice (£1,000 each); G11 Community Hub (£500).

FINANCES *Year* 2015/16 *Income* £49,807 *Grants* £42,100 *Grants to organisations* £42,100 *Assets* £1,154,032

TRUSTEES Peter Kilgarriff; Dodie Carter; Janet Hargreaves; Andrew Cowan.

OTHER INFORMATION The trust previously focused on the criminal justice system and mental health; it reviewed its grant-making in 2016 and decided on the current focus. Grants were made to 25 organisations during the year.

HOW TO APPLY Apply in writing to: Jan Hargreaves, 7 Mount Vernon, London, NW3 6QS. The trustees meet in February, June and October.

WHO TO APPLY TO Janet Hargreaves, Trustee, 7 Mount Vernon, London NW3 6QS *Tel.* 020 7794 2486 *Email* info@swanmountaintrust.org.uk *Website* swanmountaintrust.org.uk

■ The Swann-Morton Foundation

CC NO 271925 **ESTABLISHED** 1976

WHERE FUNDING CAN BE GIVEN UK, with some preference for Sheffield.

WHO CAN BENEFIT Charitable organisations; individuals; employees or former employees of W. R. Swann and Co. Ltd.

WHAT IS FUNDED Medical and surgical research; education; social welfare; ill health and disability; general charitable purposes.

TYPE OF GRANT Projects; research; bursaries and scholarships.

SAMPLE GRANTS Sheffield Children's Hospital (£8,000); St Luke's Hospice (£7,500); Sheffield Teaching Hospitals (£6,900); CBA Projects (£3,500); Royal College of Surgeons and Whirlow Farm Trust (£1,000 each).

FINANCES *Year* 2015/16 *Income* £60,966 *Grants* £72,275 *Grants to organisations* £58,525 *Assets* £101,285

TRUSTEES Judith Gilmour; Michael McGinley; George Rodgers.

OTHER INFORMATION In 2015/16 'student grants and electives' totalled £13,800.

HOW TO APPLY Apply in writing to the correspondent. The 2015/16 accounts state: 'The charity invites applications for funding of projects from hospitals, charities and students. Applicants are invited to submit a summary of their proposals in a specific format. The applications are reviewed against specific criteria and research objectives which are set by the trustees.'

WHO TO APPLY TO Michael Hirst, Director, Swann-Morton Ltd, Owlerton Green, Sheffield S6 2BJ *Tel.* 0114 234 4231

■ The John Swire (1989) Charitable Trust

CC NO 802142 **ESTABLISHED** 1989

WHERE FUNDING CAN BE GIVEN UK, with some preference for Kent.

WHO CAN BENEFIT Charitable organisations, universities, schools.

WHAT IS FUNDED General charitable purposes, especially social welfare, health and medical research; environment; arts.

RANGE OF GRANTS £100 to £100,000.

SAMPLE GRANTS Moorfields Eye Charity (£100,000); Gurkha Welfare Trust (£61,000); Royal Voluntary Service (£30,000); Respite Association (£2,500); Wildfowl and Wetlands Trust (£2,000); Glyndebourne Arts Trust (£1,300); Imperial Cancer Research Fund (£1,000); Selling Sports Club (£500); Kent County Organists' Association (£250); Harlow District Scouts (£100).

FINANCES *Year* 2015 *Income* £1,260,322 *Grants* £1,415,500 *Grants to organisations* £1,415,500 *Assets* £37,068,597

TRUSTEES Barnaby Swire; John Swire; Michael Cradock Robinson.

OTHER INFORMATION Grants of less than £1,000 amounted to a total of £18,500; grants of £1,000 or more totalled £1.36 million.

HOW TO APPLY Apply in writing to the correspondent, explaining 'how the funds could be used and what would be achieved'.

WHO TO APPLY TO Sarah Irving, John Swire & Sons Ltd, Swire House, 59 Buckingham Gate, London SW1E 6AJ *Tel.* 020 7834 7717 *Email* info@scts.org.uk

■ The Swire Charitable Trust

CC NO 270726 **ESTABLISHED** 1976

WHERE FUNDING CAN BE GIVEN UK.

WHO CAN BENEFIT UK-registered charities.

WHAT IS FUNDED There are three programmes: community and social welfare; education and training; heritage. For further detail on each of these areas, refer to the guidance on the website.

WHAT IS NOT FUNDED Applications received by post or email; organisations that are not UK-registered charities; charities which have applied to the trust in the last 12 months; individual applicants or proposals that will benefit only one person; activities taking place outside England, Scotland, Wales or Northern Ireland; retrospective funding; statutory bodies or work that is primarily the responsibility of statutory authorities (e.g. residential, respite and day care, housing and provision of mainstream education through individual schools, nurseries and colleges); activities of local organisations which are part of a wider network doing similar work; medicine-related charities, including those that provide residential care, equipment or fund research; animal welfare; academic research, scholarships or bursaries.

TYPE OF GRANT Project costs; core costs; capital costs; salaries. Mostly one year, occasionally up to three years.

RANGE OF GRANTS There is no minimum or maximum grant size.

SAMPLE GRANTS Moorfields Eye Charity (£350,000); University of Southampton (£100,000); Queen's Choral Foundation (£25,000); Pagoda Arts (£20,000); British Exploring Society (£10,000); Heritage of London Trust (£7,500); Beanstalk (£5,000); Urology Foundation (£2,500); Thumbs Up Club (£2,000); Aviation without Borders (£1,000).

FINANCES *Year* 2015 *Income* £2,234,993 *Grants* £3,772,490 *Grants to organisations* £1,944,760 *Assets* £11,167,468

TRUSTEES Barnaby Swire; John Swire; Sir Adrian Swire; Merlin Swire; James Hughes-Hallett; Samuel Swire.

OTHER INFORMATION Grants were made to 193 organisations in 2015. Grants of less than £1,000 totalled £1,260. There were also 38 grants to individuals, totalling £1.8 million, in the form of educational scholarships.

HOW TO APPLY Applicants should read the guidelines and FAQs on the website first, then complete the eligibility test. If eligible, applications can be made using the online form. Grants of up to £25,000 can be considered at monthly grants committee meetings; larger grants are considered at quarterly trustee meetings. Decisions are usually made within one to four months of application, but may occasionally take longer.

WHO TO APPLY TO Sarah Irving, Grants Manager, Swire House, 59 Buckingham Gate, London SW1E 6AJ *Tel.* 020 7834 7717 *Email* info@scts.org.uk *Website* www.swirecharitabletrust.org.uk

■ The Adrian Swire Charitable Trust

CC NO 800493 **ESTABLISHED** 1988

WHERE FUNDING CAN BE GIVEN UK.

WHO CAN BENEFIT Charitable organisations.

WHAT IS FUNDED General charitable purposes.

RANGE OF GRANTS Up to £50,000.

SAMPLE GRANTS Oracle Cancer Trust (£50,000); Child Bereavement UK (£25,000); Rhinology Research Fund (£20,000); Young Musicians Symphony Orchestra (£15,000); Animal Health Trust (£10,000); South Oxfordshire Food and Education Exchange (£5,000); Goal Ball UK (£2,500); Wantage Choral Society (£1,000); Essex Yeomanry Association (£500); Mouth and Foot Painting Artists (£50).

FINANCES *Year* 2015 *Income* £1,535,731 *Grants* £725,000 *Grants to organisations* £725,000 *Assets* £27,335,264

TRUSTEES Merlin Swire; Sir Martin Dunne; Lady Judith Swire; Martha Allfrey; Richard Leonard; Samuel Swire.

OTHER INFORMATION Grants of less than £1,000 each totalled £850; grants of £1,000 or more totalled £724,000.

HOW TO APPLY Apply in writing to the correspondent, explaining 'how the funds could be used and what would be achieved'.

WHO TO APPLY TO Sarah Irving, Swire House, 59 Buckingham Gate, London SW1E 6AJ *Tel.* 020 7834 7717 *Email* info@scts.org.uk

■ The Hugh and Ruby Sykes Charitable Trust

CC NO 327648 **ESTABLISHED** 1987

WHERE FUNDING CAN BE GIVEN UK, with a focus on Derbyshire.

WHO CAN BENEFIT Registered charities.

WHAT IS FUNDED General charitable purposes.
WHAT IS NOT FUNDED Individuals.
SAMPLE GRANTS A list of beneficiaries was not available.
FINANCES *Year* 2015/16 *Income* £214,920 *Grants* £144,982 *Grants to organisations* £144,982 *Assets* £2,015,028
TRUSTEES Sir Hugh Sykes; Lady Ruby Sykes; Brian Evans.
OTHER INFORMATION A list of beneficiaries was not included in the accounts.
HOW TO APPLY Apply in writing to the correspondent.
WHO TO APPLY TO Brian Evans, Trustee, Brookfield Manor, Hathersage, Hope Valley S32 1BR *Tel.* 01433 651190 *Email* info@brookfieldmanor.com

■ The Charles and Elsie Sykes Trust

CC NO 206926 **ESTABLISHED** 1954
WHERE FUNDING CAN BE GIVEN UK, mainly Yorkshire.
WHO CAN BENEFIT Registered charities only.
WHAT IS FUNDED A wide range of general charitable purposes, including: medical research; disability; education; social welfare.
WHAT IS NOT FUNDED Individuals; overseas appeals; non-registered charities. Although the trust does support some organisations in the rest of the UK, applications from outside Yorkshire are unlikely to be successful. Applications from schools, playgroups, cadet forces, scouts, guides, and churches must be for outreach programmes, and not for maintenance projects.
RANGE OF GRANTS Mainly under £5,000.
SAMPLE GRANTS Harrogate and District NHS FT Charitable Fund (£92,000); Royal Holloway University of London (£18,200); Harrogate International Festival (£10,000); Star Bereavement and Support Service Ltd (£7,500); Alzheimer's Research UK, Ryedale Citizens Advice and York Racial Equality Network (£5,000 each); Autistica, Crosspool and District Youth Sports Trust and Trees for Cities (£3,000 each).
FINANCES *Year* 2015 *Income* £427,408 *Grants* £476,675 *Grants to organisations* £476,675 *Assets* £14,795,114
TRUSTEES John Ward; Anne Brownlie; Martin Coultas; Michael Garnett; Dr Michael McEvoy; Barry Kay; Peter Rous; Dr Rosemary Livingstone; Sara Buchan.
OTHER INFORMATION During the year, 127 grants were made.
HOW TO APPLY Application forms can be downloaded from the website. The form should be completed and then be sent to the trust along with a copy of the organisation's latest accounts, annual report and any other relevant information. It is more favourable for the application if the accounts are current. If a grant is required for a particular project, full details and costings should be provided. The trustees meet at the beginning of March, June, September and December, and deadlines for applications are the last Friday in January, April, July and October respectively. Applicants will be informed of the outcome of their application at the end of the month in which the application was considered in a meeting.
WHO TO APPLY TO Judith Long, Secretary, LCF Law Ltd, 6 North Park Road, Harrogate, North Yorkshire HG1 5PA *Tel.* 01423 817238 *Website* www.charlesandelsiesykestrust.co.uk

■ Sylvia Waddilove Foundation UK

CC NO 1118097 **ESTABLISHED** 2007
WHERE FUNDING CAN BE GIVEN UK and overseas.
WHO CAN BENEFIT Registered or exempt charities (small charities are favoured, with the exception of those undertaking medical research projects). Individuals undertaking medical research may be supported.
WHAT IS FUNDED Education, particularly organic farming, animal husbandry, veterinary science, animal welfare and surgery and research into animal surgery; visual and performing arts; medical research; the relief of disability or illness; the preservation of buildings of architectural or historical significance; accommodation of those in need. The administrator's website details essential and desirable criteria for applications in each category.
WHAT IS NOT FUNDED Individuals (except medical research projects); requests made within two years of a previous application; organisations that have been running for less than two years. Check the eligibility criteria for each area of the foundation's grant-making.
TYPE OF GRANT Project costs. Awards may be spread over two or three years.
RANGE OF GRANTS £500 to £10,000.
SAMPLE GRANTS Action on Hearing Loss (£28,500); Heckington Windmill Trust (£7,000); Target Ovarian Cancer (£5,500); Kidney Research UK (£4,000); Deafblind Scotland (£3,000); The Donkey Sanctuary and West Rhyl Young People's Project (£2,000 each); Bespoke Supportive Tenancies (£1,500); DaDaFest (£600); Engineering Development Trust (£500).
FINANCES *Year* 2015 *Income* £104,227 *Grants* £324,034 *Grants to organisations* £324,034 *Assets* £3,566,971
TRUSTEES Gerald Kidd; Percy Robson; Nadeem Azhar.
OTHER INFORMATION During the year grants were made to 93 organisations. The trustees particularly seek innovative projects that are less than five years old. Alongside its regular grants, the foundation occasionally opens an exceptional Allocated Grants Programme to support one of its objectives.
HOW TO APPLY Application forms are available from the administrator's website. If successful, applicants can expect to receive their grant within three months of completing an application. The trustees meet in January, April, July and October. Applications open shortly before each meeting and close 'when a sufficient number of applications have been received'.
WHO TO APPLY TO The Trustees, c/o Pothecary Witham Weld Solicitors, 70 St George's Square, London SW1V 3RD *Tel.* 020 7821 8211 *Email* waddilove@pwwsolicitors.co.uk *Website* www.pwwsolicitors.co.uk/charity-grants/13-the-sylvia-waddilove-foundation-uk

■ T. and S. Trust Fund

CC NO 1095939 **ESTABLISHED** 2002

WHERE FUNDING CAN BE GIVEN UK, particularly London, Gateshead and Manchester.

WHO CAN BENEFIT Jewish organisations; occasionally individuals.

WHAT IS FUNDED Advancement of the Orthodox Jewish religion and education; relief of poverty.

RANGE OF GRANTS £1,000 to £28,000.

SAMPLE GRANTS BFOI Hako (£28,000); Friends of Meleche (£20,000); Kol Yom Trust Ltd (£15,300); United Hebrew Congregation of Newcastle upon Tyne (£5,000); Yeshiva L'Zeirim (£4,600); Gateshead Jewish Primary School (£2,000); Adath Yisroel Synagogue, Gateshead Talmudical College and Youth Aliyah Gala Dinner (£1,000 each).

FINANCES *Year* 2015/16 *Income* £179,800 *Grants* £234,000 *Grants to organisations* £234,000 *Assets* £9,305

TRUSTEES Shoshana Sandler; Ezriel Salomon; Aron Sandler.

OTHER INFORMATION No grants were made to individuals during 2015/16.

HOW TO APPLY Apply in writing to the correspondent.

WHO TO APPLY TO Aron Sandler, Trustee, 96 Whitehall Road, Gateshead, Tyne And Wear NE8 4ET *Tel.* 0191 482 5050

■ Tabeel Trust

CC NO 266645 **ESTABLISHED** 1974

WHERE FUNDING CAN BE GIVEN Worldwide with a preference for Clacton.

WHO CAN BENEFIT Christian organisations.

WHAT IS FUNDED Evangelical Christian charitable purposes, where the trustees have an existing interest.

WHAT IS NOT FUNDED Short-term gap year initiatives.

RANGE OF GRANTS Up to £10,000.

SAMPLE GRANTS Leeds Diocesan Board of Finance (£7,000); Samaritan's Purse (£5,000); Ambassadors in Sport and Friends of Lowton High School (£3,000 each); Christian Literature Crusade, Interserve Pakistan and Urban Outreach Bolton (£2,000 each); Brentwood Schools Christian Worker Trust (£1,500); Gulu Mission Initiative (£1,000); Stoke Green Baptist Church (£830); LCM Clacton (£500).

FINANCES *Year* 2014/15 *Income* £121,654 *Grants* £85,825 *Grants to organisations* £85,825 *Assets* £1,097,249

TRUSTEES Douglas Brown; Barbara Carter; Dr Mary Clark; Jean Richardson; James Davey; Sarah Taylor; Nigel Davey.

OTHER INFORMATION The 2014/15 accounts were the most recent available to view on the Charity Commission's website at the time of writing (June 2017). The trust made 36 grants during the year.

HOW TO APPLY Only charities with which a trustee already has contact should apply. Grants are considered at trustees' meetings, which are usually in May and October.

WHO TO APPLY TO Barbara Carter, Trustee, East Dalcove House, Kelso TD5 7PD *Tel.* 01573 460267

■ The Tajtelbaum Charitable Trust

CC NO 273184 **ESTABLISHED** 1974

WHERE FUNDING CAN BE GIVEN UK and Israel.

WHO CAN BENEFIT Orthodox Jewish synagogues and educational establishments; care homes; UK-registered charities.

WHAT IS FUNDED Advancement of the Orthodox Jewish religion; relief of poverty and ill health.

SAMPLE GRANTS United Institutions Arad, Emuno Educational Centre, Ruzin Sadiger Trust, Gur Foundation, Before Trust, Beth Hassidei Gur, Comet Charities Ltd, Delharville, Kupat Gemach Trust, Centre for Torah and Chesed, Friends of Nachlat David and Friends of Sanz Institute.

FINANCES *Year* 2015/16 *Income* £942,578 *Grants* £765,113 *Grants to organisations* £765,113 *Assets* £4,318,826

TRUSTEES Ilsa Tajtelbaum; Jacob Tajtelbaum; Emanuel Tajtelbaum; Henry Frydenson.

HOW TO APPLY Apply in writing to the correspondent.

WHO TO APPLY TO Emanuel Tajtelbaum, Trustee, PO Box 33911, London NW9 7ZX *Tel.* 020 8202 3464

■ The Gay and Keith Talbot Trust

CC NO 1102192 **ESTABLISHED** 2004

WHERE FUNDING CAN BE GIVEN Worldwide.

WHO CAN BENEFIT Registered charities.

WHAT IS FUNDED Fistula work and other medical research; humanitarian aid; asylum seekers; general charitable purposes.

TYPE OF GRANT One-off and recurring. Capital costs, revenue costs and full project funding.

SAMPLE GRANTS A full list of beneficiaries was not included in the accounts.

FINANCES *Year* 2015/16 *Income* £77,812 *Grants* £150,848 *Grants to organisations* £150,848 *Assets* £28,291

TRUSTEES Gay Talbot; Keith Talbot.

OTHER INFORMATION Grants were distributed in the following areas: fistula work (£90,500); medical purposes (£40,000); research and development (£10,000); grants for earthquake victims and grants for asylum seekers (£5,000 each); general purposes (£500).

HOW TO APPLY Apply in writing to the correspondent.

WHO TO APPLY TO Keith Talbot, Trustee, Fold Howe, Kentmere, Kendal, Cumbria LA8 9JW *Tel.* 01539 821504 *Email* gay_talbot@hotmail.com

■ The Talbot Trusts

CC NO 221356 **ESTABLISHED** 1928

WHERE FUNDING CAN BE GIVEN Sheffield and immediate surrounding areas.

WHO CAN BENEFIT Registered charities; social workers, GPs and practice nurses (see the website for further detail).

WHAT IS FUNDED Health; people with disabilities. In 2017/18 the trust is focusing particularly on: physical well-being of people with mental health issues; and nutrition and isolation issues in older people. There is also a Small Organisations Fund for small charities working on other health-related issues.

WHAT IS NOT FUNDED Research; educational projects; major fundraising and general appeals; non-registered charities or other organisations; individuals; recurrent grants.

TYPE OF GRANT One-off.

RANGE OF GRANTS Main grants: £2,000 to £5,000. Small grants: up to £1,000.

SAMPLE GRANTS ReVitalise (£4,500); Happy Days and Whizz-Kidz (£4,000); CLIC Sargent (£3,500); SHARE Psychotherapy and Steelers Wheelchair Basketball (£3,000 each); St Luke's Hospice (£2,700); Sheffield Family Holiday Fund (£1,900); No Panic Sheffield (£1,000); Deafblind UK (£500).

FINANCES *Year* 2015/16 *Income* £92,250 *Grants* £89,200 *Grants to organisations* £89,200 *Assets* £2,119,423

TRUSTEES Tim Plant; Jo Frisby; Dr Zackary McMurray; Neil Charlesworth.

OTHER INFORMATION Grants were made to 35 organisations during the year. The trust states that, as well as accepting applications from individual charities, it also welcomes joint applications between small charities working in partnership.

HOW TO APPLY Apply in writing to the correspondent. The trustees meet in June and December to consider applications.

WHO TO APPLY TO Gill Newman, Clerk, 3 Willow Tree Drive, Clowne, Chesterfield, N. Derbyshire S43 4UP *Tel.* 01246 570643 *Email* gill.newman1@nhs.net *Website* www.thetalbottrusts.com

■ The Talbot Village Trust

CC NO 249349 **ESTABLISHED** 1867

WHERE FUNDING CAN BE GIVEN The boroughs of Bournemouth, Christchurch and Poole; the districts of East Dorset and Purbeck.

WHO CAN BENEFIT Registered charities; churches; educational institutions.

WHAT IS FUNDED Capital projects benefitting the local community, young people, education and churches.

WHAT IS NOT FUNDED Running costs, such as salaries, uniforms and regular maintenance. The trust will not normally consider an application unless at least 25–33% of the total required money has been raised or committed.

TYPE OF GRANT Grants and loans, for capital costs.

RANGE OF GRANTS No minimum or maximum grant.

SAMPLE GRANTS Hillbourne and District Community Association (£50,000); Harbour Challenge Outdoor Adventure Centre (£20,000); Wessex Cancer Trust (£15,000); Winton Primary School (£10,000); Faithworks Wessex (£5,900); Christchurch District Scouts and Woodlands Village Hall (£5,000 each); Bournemouth Youth Marching Band (£3,300); Dorset Rape Crisis Support Centre (£1,500); Wimborne United Reformed Church (£950).

FINANCES *Year* 2015 *Income* £4,197,975 *Grants* £254,179 *Grants to organisations* £254,179 *Assets* £45,107,570

TRUSTEES Sir Thomas Salt; James Fleming; Christopher Lees; Russell Rowe; Earl of Shaftesbury; George Meyrick.

OTHER INFORMATION Grants were authorised and paid to 26 organisations during the year.

HOW TO APPLY Applications can be made using the online application form, or by post, including the information specified in the guidelines on the website. The trustees meet twice a year to consider applications and applicants are notified of the outcome within a couple of weeks of a meeting.

WHO TO APPLY TO Darryl Tidd, Director, Trethowans, 5 Parkstone Road, Poole BH15 2NL *Tel.* 01202 673071 *Email* darryl.tidd@talbotvillagetrust.org *Website* www.talbotvillagetrust.org

■ Tallow Chandlers Benevolent Fund No. 2

CC NO 246255 **ESTABLISHED** 1966

WHERE FUNDING CAN BE GIVEN London, mostly City of London.

WHO CAN BENEFIT Charitable organisations, schools and universities.

WHAT IS FUNDED Children and young people; education; health and medical research; people with disabilities; social welfare. There is a preference for City of London-based charities and charities where a liveryman or freeman is actively involved.

TYPE OF GRANT One-off grants; three-year grants.

RANGE OF GRANTS Up to £20,000. One-off: £250 to £1,000.

SAMPLE GRANTS London Youth (£20,000); SOAS (£17,500); IntoUniversity (£10,000); St Paul's Cathedral School (£7,500); City of London School for Girls (£5,000); Trinity Hospice (£4,200); Clean Break Theatre Company (£4,000); Southwark Sea Cadets (£2,000); Fine Cell Work, London's Air Ambulance and Toynbee Hall (£1,000 each).

FINANCES *Year* 2015/16 *Income* £544,239 *Grants* £300,875 *Grants to organisations* £248,125 *Assets* £7,336,283

TRUSTEES Sir Michael Snyder; John Kurkjian; Nicholas Bull; Ian McIntyre; Michael Bridges Webb; Christopher Tootal; Rupert Travis; Richard Fleck; Robert Nicolle; C. R. Lambourne; N. M. Wells; Brig. N. H. Thompson; Peter Purton; Philip Edwards; R. B. Yates; Timothy Piper; David Simmonds; J. N. Harrington; Michael Sutcliffe; Sir Peter Cazalet; Brig. Keith Prosser; Ian Bowden; Robert Pick; Sir Christopher Pryke; Oliver Kirby-Johnson; Ian Robertson; David Homer; John Baxter; Dr Christopher Gibson Smith; Anthony Green; James Long; Lorraine Green.

OTHER INFORMATION Grants were made to 71 organisations during 2015/16. There were also bursaries or awards made to seven individuals, totalling £14,250.

HOW TO APPLY Apply in writing to the correspondent. Applications are considered by the Clerk, the Chair and the Education and Charity Committee. All applicants are notified of the outcome of their request.

WHO TO APPLY TO Brig. David Homer, Clerk, Tallow Chandlers Hall, 4 Dowgate Hill, London EC4R 2SH *Tel.* 020 7248 4726 *Email* clerk@tallowchandlers.org *Website* www.tallowchandlers.org

■ The Talmud Torah Machzikei Hadass Trust

CC NO 270693 **ESTABLISHED** 1976

WHERE FUNDING CAN BE GIVEN Worldwide, with a focus on Hackney.

WHO CAN BENEFIT Orthodox Jewish organisations.

WHAT IS FUNDED Orthodox Jewish religion and education.

SAMPLE GRANTS A list of beneficiaries was not available.

FINANCES *Year* 2015/16 *Income* £2,662,357 *Grants* £2,481,860 *Grants to organisations* £2,481,860 *Assets* £5,470,803

TRUSTEES Jehudah Baumgarten; Yitzchok Sternlicht; Mordechaj Wind.

OTHER INFORMATION The 2015/16 annual report states that since 2013, the trust has been working on the development of a 'modern religious complex to serve the various needs of

the thriving Orthodox Jewish community', which was set to be complete by March 2017.
HOW TO APPLY Apply in writing to the correspondent.
WHO TO APPLY TO Yitzchok Sternlicht, Trustee, 28 Leadale Road, London N16 6DA

■ Talteg Ltd

CC NO 283253 **ESTABLISHED** 1981
WHERE FUNDING CAN BE GIVEN UK, with a preference for Scotland.
WHO CAN BENEFIT Registered charities; Jewish organisations.
WHAT IS FUNDED Orthodox Jewish religion; education; relief of poverty.
SAMPLE GRANTS British Friends of Laniado Hospital, Centre for Jewish Studies, Society of Friends of the Torah, Glasgow Jewish Community Trust, National Trust for Scotland, Ayrshire Hospice, Earl Haig Fund – Scotland and RSSPCC.
FINANCES *Year* 2015 *Income* £308,089 *Grants* £153,201 *Grants to organisations* £153,201 *Assets* £4,339,922
TRUSTEES Adam Berkley; Delia Berkley.
OTHER INFORMATION A list of grants was not included in the 2015 accounts.
HOW TO APPLY Apply in writing to the correspondent.
WHO TO APPLY TO Adam Berkley, Trustee, 90 Mitchell Street, Glasgow G1 3NQ *Tel.* 0141 221 3353

■ The Lady Tangye Trust Ltd

CC NO 1158139 **ESTABLISHED** 1995
WHERE FUNDING CAN BE GIVEN UK and worldwide, with some preference for the Midlands.
WHO CAN BENEFIT Charitable organisations.
WHAT IS FUNDED General charitable purposes including Christian and environmental causes.
SAMPLE GRANTS Just Earth (£20,000); New Wine Cymru (£10,000); Chaplaincy Plus and Cymru Leadership Trust (£5,000 each); Birmingham Sherbourne Sea Cadets and The Message Trust (£2,000 each).
FINANCES *Year* 2015/16 *Income* £45,715 *Grants* £44,000 *Grants to organisations* £44,000 *Assets* £1,135,620
TRUSTEES Colin Smith; Michael Plaut; Brian Gregory; Rebecca Reading.
HOW TO APPLY Apply in writing to the correspondent.
WHO TO APPLY TO Colin Smith, Trustee, 413 Bournville Gardens, 49 Bristol Road South, Birmingham B31 2FT *Tel.* 0121 227 9413

■ The David Tannen Charitable Trust

CC NO 280392 **ESTABLISHED** 1974
WHERE FUNDING CAN BE GIVEN Barnet, Hackney, Haringey; Israel.
WHO CAN BENEFIT Charitable organisations; schools.
WHAT IS FUNDED Jewish causes; social welfare; education.
SAMPLE GRANTS Moreshet Hatorah Ltd and The ABC Trust (£50,000 each); Before Trust (£40,000); The Gevurath Ari Torah Academy Trust (£36,000).
FINANCES *Year* 2015/16 *Income* £2,035,121 *Grants* £286,100 *Grants to organisations* £286,100 *Assets* £18,712,753
TRUSTEES David Tannen; Jonathan Miller; Alan Rose.
HOW TO APPLY Apply in writing to the correspondent.
WHO TO APPLY TO Jonathan Miller, Trustee, c/o Sutherland House, 70–78 West Hendon Broadway, London NW9 7BT *Tel.* 020 8202 1066

■ The Tanner Trust

CC NO 1021175 **ESTABLISHED** 1993
WHERE FUNDING CAN BE GIVEN UK, with a slight preference for the south of England; and overseas.
WHO CAN BENEFIT Charitable organisations.
WHAT IS FUNDED General charitable purposes, particularly: gardening, gardens and farming; conservation and the countryside; youth projects; health, older people and people with disabilities; culture and preservation of buildings; overseas aid.
WHAT IS NOT FUNDED Individuals.
RANGE OF GRANTS Up to £10,000.
SAMPLE GRANTS The Ways and Means Trust (£12,000); Help Tibet Trust (£10,000); Public Catalogue Foundation (£9,800); CHICKS and Huntington's Disease Association (£3,000 each); Cornwall Red Squirrel Project and Fishermen's Mission (£2,500 each); Royal Horticultural Society (£2,000); Veterans Aid (£700).
FINANCES *Year* 2015/16 *Income* £837,252 *Grants* £427,900 *Grants to organisations* £427,900 *Assets* £8,177,812
TRUSTEES Alice Williams; Lucie Nottingham.
OTHER INFORMATION In 2015/16 there were 130 grants awarded to organisations.
HOW TO APPLY The trust states that unsolicited applications are, without exception, not considered. Support is only given to charities personally known to the trustees.
WHO TO APPLY TO Celine Lecomte, Blake Morgan, Harbour Court, Compass Road, Portsmouth PO6 4ST *Tel.* 02392 221122 ext. 552 *Email* Charity.Admin@blakemorgan.co.uk

■ The Lili Tapper Charitable Foundation

CC NO 268523 **ESTABLISHED** 1974
WHERE FUNDING CAN BE GIVEN UK.
WHO CAN BENEFIT Organisations benefitting Jewish people.
WHAT IS FUNDED Jewish causes; arts and culture; education; general charitable purposes.
SAMPLE GRANTS United Jewish Israel Appeal (UJIA), Community Security Trust (CST), Manchester Jewish Foundation, Teenage Cancer Trust, Keshet Eilon, Israel Educational Foundation, Chickenshed Theatre Company and Jewish Representation Council.
FINANCES *Year* 2015/16 *Income* £36,791 *Grants* £34,250 *Grants to organisations* £34,250 *Assets* £3,201,369
TRUSTEES Michael Webber; Dr Jonathan Webber.
OTHER INFORMATION Grants in 2015/16 were broken down into the following categories: arts and culture (£10,750); others (£23,500). A list of beneficiaries for the year was not provided.
HOW TO APPLY Apply in writing to the correspondent.
WHO TO APPLY TO Michael Webber, Trustee, 31 Wilmslow Road, Cheadle, Cheshire SK8 1DR *Tel.* 0161 428 1188 *Email* tappercharitablefoundation@gmail.com

■ The Taurus Foundation

CC NO 1128441 **ESTABLISHED** 2009

WHERE FUNDING CAN BE GIVEN UK.

WHO CAN BENEFIT Registered charities.

WHAT IS FUNDED Biodiversity, environment and species conservation; disadvantaged and marginalised young people; domestic animal welfare; the arts.

SAMPLE GRANTS The Purcell School (£28,000); Concordia Foundation, Jewish Care, Just for Kids Law and Norwood Ravenswood (£10,000 each); Core Arts, Hillside Clubhouse and Magic Me (£5,000 each); Royal Opera House (£2,500).

FINANCES *Year* 2015/16 *Income* £188,861 *Grants* £289,750 *Grants to organisations* £289,750 *Assets* £1,086,370

TRUSTEES Denis Felsenstein; Michael Jacobs; Alan Fenton; Anthony Forwood; Priscilla Fenton; Wendy Pollecoff; Carole Cook; Dominic Fenton; Anthony Felsenstein.

OTHER INFORMATION Grants were made to 28 organisations.

HOW TO APPLY **Grants will not be given for unsolicited applications.** The trustees proactively identify organisations that are eligible for funding and contact them with the relevant information to make an application.

WHO TO APPLY TO Wendy Pollecoff, Trustee and Administrator, Taurus Foundation, 25 The Boltons, London SW10 9SU *Email* wendy.pollecoff@taurus-foundation.org.uk *Website* taurus-foundation.org.uk

■ The Tay Charitable Trust

SC NO SC001004 **ESTABLISHED** 1951

WHERE FUNDING CAN BE GIVEN UK, focusing on Scotland, particularly Dundee.

WHO CAN BENEFIT Registered charities.

WHAT IS FUNDED General charitable purposes.

WHAT IS NOT FUNDED Individuals.

RANGE OF GRANTS Up to £5,000.

SAMPLE GRANTS Optimistic Sound (£10,000); Dundee Heritage Trust (£5,300); Broughty Ferry YMCA (£5,000); Taymara (£3,500); National Trust for Scotland (£2,000); Dundee Choral Union and Samaritans (£1,500 each); British Stammering Association, Faith in Community Scotland and MND Association (£1,000 each).

FINANCES *Year* 2015/16 *Income* £241,439 *Grants* £232,500 *Grants to organisations* £232,500 *Assets* £6,382,743

OTHER INFORMATION There were 103 grants of over £1,000 made to organisations during the year, totalling £175,000; grants of less than £1,000 were made to 123 organisations and totalled almost £58,000.

HOW TO APPLY Apply in writing to the correspondent, including a financial statement. The trustees have said that they do not notify applicants who have not succeeded, due to the cost of postage.

WHO TO APPLY TO E. Mussen, 6 Douglas Terrace, Broughty Ferry, Dundee DD5 1EA

■ C. B. and H. H. Taylor 1984 Trust

CC NO 291363 **ESTABLISHED** 1946

WHERE FUNDING CAN BE GIVEN West Midlands, Ireland and overseas.

WHO CAN BENEFIT Approximately 60% of funds available are currently given to the work and concerns of the Religious Society of Friends. The remaining funds are allocated charities, particularly in the West Midlands, charities outside this area where the trust has well-established links, or UK charities working overseas. Applications are encouraged from minority groups and woman-led initiatives.

WHAT IS FUNDED The general areas of benefit are: The Religious Society of Friends (Quakers) and other religious denominations; health care projects; social welfare, including community groups, children and young people, older people, disadvantaged people, people with disabilities, homelessness, housing initiatives, counselling and mediation agencies; education including adult literacy schemes, employment training, youth work; penal affairs, work with people who have offended, police projects; environment and conservation; the arts, including museums and art galleries, music and drama; Ireland, including cross-community health and social welfare projects; UK charities working overseas on long-term development projects.

WHAT IS NOT FUNDED Individuals; local projects or groups outside the West Midlands; or projects concerned with travel or adventure; annual grants for revenue costs.

TYPE OF GRANT One-off and sometimes three-year-long recurrent. Specific projects.

RANGE OF GRANTS Mainly £1,000 or less.

SAMPLE GRANTS Britain Yearly Meeting (£45,000); Central England Quakers (£11,500); Money for Madagascar (£7,000); Habitat for Humanity (£6,000); Refugee Council (£2,000); Amnesty International and Evesham Festival of Music (£1,000 each); Acacia Family Support and The Gorilla Organisation (£500 each); Bonyere Library (£250).

FINANCES *Year* 2015/16 *Income* £523,050 *Grants* £368,500 *Grants to organisations* £368,500 *Assets* £13,081,676

TRUSTEES Constance Penny; Elizabeth Birmingham; Clare Norton; John Taylor; Thomas Penny; Robert Birmingham; Simon Taylor.

OTHER INFORMATION Grants were made to 212 organisations during 2015/16. Most grants were for £1,000 or less.

HOW TO APPLY Apply in writing to the correspondent.

WHO TO APPLY TO Clare Norton, Trustee, 266 Malvern Road, Worcester WR2 4PA

■ Humphrey Richardson Taylor Charitable Trust

CC NO 1062836 **ESTABLISHED** 1997

WHERE FUNDING CAN BE GIVEN Surrey and South London boroughs.

WHO CAN BENEFIT Schools; amateur music organisations; individuals.

WHAT IS FUNDED Music and music education. A list of typical purposes for which support may be given is provided on the trust's website.

WHAT IS NOT FUNDED Music therapy; professional musicians (except in the case of requests from schools to bring professionals in to support teaching and tuition).

TYPE OF GRANT Capital projects or items; one-off grants; scholarships; music tuition; concerts and events.

RANGE OF GRANTS £250 to £50,000.

SAMPLE GRANTS Barrow Hedges School (£50,000); Royal College of Music (£34,500); Croydon Music and Arts (£6,600); Guildford Chamber Choir (£4,000); Burgess Hill Symphony Orchestra (£3,000); Surrey Arts Percussion Project (£2,700); Opera Holloway (£2,000); Horsham Garden Music Festival (£1,000);

Haslemere Schools Community Orchestra (£300); Green Lane Primary (£280).

FINANCES *Year* 2015 *Income* £495,790 *Grants* £416,174 *Grants to organisations* £401,624 *Assets* £11,683,046

TRUSTEES William Malings; Rowena Cox; Colin Edgerton; Ian Catling; Michael Wood; Stephen Oliver.

OTHER INFORMATION Grants were made to organisations for the following purposes in 2015: capital projects (£62,000); concerts and sponsorship (£100,000); tuition fees and scholarships (£158,500); instrument and equipment purchase (£81,000). Grants to individuals during the year totalled £14,500.

HOW TO APPLY Apply in writing to the correspondent. Criteria and application guidelines for schools, musical societies and individuals are available to view on the website.

WHO TO APPLY TO Mr B. M. Bennett, Administrator of H. R. Taylor Charitable Trust, c/o Palmers, 28 Chipstead Station Parade, Chipstead, Coulsdon, Surrey CR5 3TF *Tel.* 01737 557546 *Fax* 01737 554093 *Email* hrtaylortrust@btconnect.com *Website* www.hrtaylortrust.org.uk

■ The Connie and Albert Taylor Charitable Trust

CC NO 1074785 **ESTABLISHED** 1998

WHERE FUNDING CAN BE GIVEN Mainly West Midlands.

WHO CAN BENEFIT Registered charities; hospices.

WHAT IS FUNDED Research into cancer, blindness and heart disease; nursing homes and older people; hospices; facilities for education and recreation for children and young people; preservation and improvement of beauty, scientific or horticultural interest, and buildings of historic, architectural, artistic or scientific interest.

WHAT IS NOT FUNDED Individuals.

TYPE OF GRANT Project costs; capital costs; salaries; one-off, sometimes up to three years.

SAMPLE GRANTS St Giles Hospice (£100,000); Birmingham Children's Hospital and Contact a Family (£50,000 each); Sunfield Children's Home (£25,000); Avoncroft Museum (£15,000); Donna Louise Children's Hospice (£12,500); Williams Syndrome Foundation (£10,000); Multiple Births Foundation (£4,000); Blind Children UK (£3,000); Lord's Taverners (£2,300).

FINANCES *Year* 2015 *Income* £56,928 *Grants* £424,750 *Grants to organisations* £424,750 *Assets* £2,148,463

TRUSTEES Alan Foster; Jennifer Grundy; Richard Long.

OTHER INFORMATION The trustees state in their 2015 annual report that 'at the beginning of 2014 the trustees decided that they would try to work towards bringing the trust to an end, within approximately a five-year time-span. This hopefully will be achieved by working mainly with certain of the charities we have supported over the previous 15 years ... There is no particular time frame in which applications may be made and we shall continue to receive them until our funds are exhausted.'

HOW TO APPLY Apply in writing to the correspondent. The trustees prefer to receive applications via email. The trust may visit applicants/beneficiaries. The trustees normally meet quarterly to consider grants. Some projects have received long-term support from the trustees, but support is rarely given for more than three years and the trustees are unlikely to enter into any long-term pledge in future.

WHO TO APPLY TO Alan Foster, Trustee, 27 The Steyne, Bognor Regis PO21 1TX *Tel.* 01243 862808 *Email* Alan.foster55@btinternet.com *Website* www.taylortrust.co.uk

■ The Taylor Family Foundation

CC NO 1118032 **ESTABLISHED** 2007

WHERE FUNDING CAN BE GIVEN UK and overseas, with a preference for London and the South East.

WHO CAN BENEFIT Registered charities and statutory bodies.

WHAT IS FUNDED Children and young people, particularly those from disadvantaged backgrounds, including: education; arts; sports, recreation and leisure.

WHAT IS NOT FUNDED Individuals.

RANGE OF GRANTS Up to £500,000 but generally £1,000 to £50,000.

SAMPLE GRANTS Royal Opera House Covent Garden Foundation (£500,000); Tate Foundation (£260,000); The Lowry Centre Trust (£50,000); Médecins Sans Frontières (£40,000); Children's Hospice Association Scotland (£20,000); Prisoners' Education Trust (£15,000); Beanstalk (£10,000); Home-Start Merton (£7,000); Mitcham Town Community Trust (£1,500).

FINANCES *Year* 2015/16 *Income* £2,520,212 *Grants* £1,947,000 *Grants to organisations* £1,947,000 *Assets* £570,306

TRUSTEES Ian Taylor; Cristina Taylor; Neville Shepherd.

OTHER INFORMATION Grants were made to 35 organisations in 2015/16.

HOW TO APPLY Applications can be made using a form available to download from the foundation's website, which should be sent along with a written application, a 'report of activities' and a copy of financial accounts.

WHO TO APPLY TO Neville Shepherd, Trustee, Hill Place House, 55A High Street, Wimbledon, London SW19 5BA *Tel.* 020 8605 2629 *Fax* 020 8605 2484 *Email* info@thetaylorfamilyfoundation *Website* www.thetaylorfamilyfoundation.co.uk

■ Tearfund

CC NO 265464 **ESTABLISHED** 1968

WHERE FUNDING CAN BE GIVEN Worldwide.

WHO CAN BENEFIT Charitable and humanitarian organisations; churches.

WHAT IS FUNDED Overseas aid; disaster relief; Christianity; community development; social justice and humanitarian work.

TYPE OF GRANT Project work and partnerships.

SAMPLE GRANTS Kale Heywet Church (£1.3 million); Association of Evangelicals of Liberia (£508,500); Farm Concern International Development Trust (£278,000); Arab Women Today (£226,500); Food for the Hungry US (£200,000); Operation Mobilisation UK (£145,500); Oasis India (£110,000); International Nepal Fellowship (£103,000).

FINANCES *Year* 2015/16 *Income* £72,162,000 *Grants* £17,839,000 *Grants to organisations* £17,839,000 *Assets* £27,656,000

TRUSTEES Deepak Mahtani; Robert Camp; Clive Mather; Craig Rowland; Jillian Mills; John Shaw; Julia Oglivy; Revd Mark Melluish; Stephanie Heald; Ian Curtis; Rt Revd Harold Miller.

OTHER INFORMATION The sample of beneficiaries was taken from a list of the charity's top 50 partners on the website.

HOW TO APPLY The trust works only with selected partner organisations and does not accept unsolicited requests or approaches.
WHO TO APPLY TO Mary Drew, 100 Church Road, Teddington, Middlesex TW11 8QE *Tel.* 020 8977 9144 *Email* info@tearfund.org *Website* www.tearfund.org

■ Khoo Teck Puat UK Foundation

CC NO 1142788 **ESTABLISHED** 2011
WHO CAN BENEFIT Registered charities.
WHAT IS FUNDED Relief of poverty; education; health; arts, culture or science.
TYPE OF GRANT One-off; multi-year.
SAMPLE GRANTS Guy's and St Thomas' Hospital (£1 million); UCL Cancer Institute Research Trust (£226,500); Lifelites (£125,000); British Red Cross (£100,000); Breast Cancer Now and The Stroke Association (£50,000 each); Sight Savers (£20,000); British Dyslexia Association (£5,000); PAWA Donation (£1,000).
FINANCES *Year* 2015/16 *Income* £3,403,164 *Grants* £997,987 *Grants to organisations* £997,987 *Assets* £68,673,167
TRUSTEES Jennifer Carmichael; Neil Carmichael; Mavis Khoo Bee Geok; Eric Khoo Kim Hai; Elizabeth Khoo.
OTHER INFORMATION Grants were made to 12 organisations during 2015/16.
HOW TO APPLY Apply in writing to the correspondent.
WHO TO APPLY TO Jennifer Carmichael, Trustee, 2–24 Kensington High Street, London W8 4PT *Tel.* 020 7937 8000

■ The Tedworth Charitable Trust

CC NO 328524 **ESTABLISHED** 1990
WHERE FUNDING CAN BE GIVEN UK.
WHO CAN BENEFIT Registered charities.
WHAT IS FUNDED Parenting, family welfare and children's development; environment and the arts; general charitable purposes.
WHAT IS NOT FUNDED Individuals.
TYPE OF GRANT One-off; multi-year; core costs.
SAMPLE GRANTS Resurgence Trust (£85,000); Schumacher College (£34,000); Sutton Trust (£30,000); New Economics Foundation (£20,000); Peterborough Environment City Trust (£15,000); Option Institute and Oxford Parent-Infant Project (£10,000 each); Victoria and Albert Museum (£3,000); Sainsbury Archive (£880).
FINANCES *Year* 2015/16 *Income* £462,685 *Grants* £346,432 *Grants to organisations* £346,432 *Assets* £11,531,903
TRUSTEES Judith Portrait; Timothy Sainsbury; Jessica Sainsbury; Margaret Sainsbury.
OTHER INFORMATION The trust is one of the Sainsbury Family Charitable Trusts which share a common administration. An application to one is taken as an application to all. Grants were made to 22 organisations during 2015/16.
HOW TO APPLY The website states that the trust 'does not accept unsolicited proposals, as its grant-making tends to be concentrated on projects initiated by the trustees'.
WHO TO APPLY TO Alan Bookbinder, Director, The Peak, 5 Wilton Road, London SW1V 1AP *Tel.* 020 7410 0330 *Email* info@sfct.org.uk *Website* www.sfct.org.uk

■ Tees Valley Community Foundation

CC NO 1111222 **ESTABLISHED** 1988
WHERE FUNDING CAN BE GIVEN The former county of Cleveland, being the local authority areas of Hartlepool, Middlesbrough, Redcar and Cleveland and Stockton-on-Tees.
WHO CAN BENEFIT Registered charities; constituted community groups; schools; CICs; individuals.
WHAT IS FUNDED General charitable purposes, benefitting communities in Tees Valley. The foundation makes grants from various different funds, each with its own criteria – refer to the website for information on current programmes.
WHAT IS NOT FUNDED Each fund has separate exclusions which are available on the foundation's website.
RANGE OF GRANTS Mostly under £5,000.
SAMPLE GRANTS Peat Rigg Training Centre Ltd (£35,000); Middlesbrough Football Club Foundation (£19,400); Coastwatch Redcar (£4,800); Hartlepool Carnival Committee (£1,000); Teesside Homeless Action Group (£910); Roseworth Residents Association (£830); Wolviston Primary School (£800); Billingham Foodbank and Earthbeat Theatre Company (£500 each); Thorpe Thewles Pop Choir Social Group (£160).
FINANCES *Year* 2015/16 *Income* £1,093,590 *Grants* £939,164 *Grants to organisations* £939,164 *Assets* £12,805,242
TRUSTEES Peter Rowley; Wendy Shepherd; Christopher Hope; Eileen Martin; Rosemary Young; Marjory Houseman; Keith Robinson; Neil Kenley; Brian Beaumont; Jeffrey Taylor; Keith Smith.
OTHER INFORMATION As with all community foundations grant schemes change frequently. Contact the foundation or check its website for details of current programmes and their deadlines. The grant total includes 385 grants made to both organisations and individuals during 2015/16.
HOW TO APPLY Application forms are available on the foundation's website.
WHO TO APPLY TO Grants Administrator, Wallace House, Fallon Court, Preston Farm Industrial Estate, Stockton-on-Tees TS18 3TX *Tel.* 01642 260860 *Email* info@teesvalleyfoundation.org *Website* www.teesvalleyfoundation.org

■ Tegham Ltd

CC NO 283066 **ESTABLISHED** 1981
WHERE FUNDING CAN BE GIVEN UK.
WHO CAN BENEFIT Registered charities.
WHAT IS FUNDED Jewish Orthodox faith and the relief of poverty.
SAMPLE GRANTS A list of beneficiaries was not available.
FINANCES *Year* 2015/16 *Income* £411,840 *Grants* £254,002 *Grants to organisations* £254,002 *Assets* £2,713,847
TRUSTEES Nizza Fluss; Daniel Fluss.
OTHER INFORMATION No details of beneficiaries were included in the accounts.
HOW TO APPLY The trustees have stated previously that the charity has enough causes to support and they do not welcome other applications.
WHO TO APPLY TO Sylvia Fluss, Trustee, 22 Park Way, London NW11 0EX *Email* admin@geraldkreditor.co.uk

■ The Templeton Goodwill Trust

SC NO SC004177 **ESTABLISHED** 1938

WHERE FUNDING CAN BE GIVEN Mainly Glasgow; also a few national charities.

WHO CAN BENEFIT Scottish registered charities.

WHAT IS FUNDED General charitable purposes, particularly social welfare; health; community development; support of people in need or disadvantage.

SAMPLE GRANTS Girl Guides Association (£10,400); City of Glasgow Society of Social Services (£8,100); Scottish Furniture Trades Benevolent Association (£5,000); Church of Scotland Lodging House Mission (£3,700); Alzheimer's Scotland – Action for Dementia (£3,600); Muscular Dystrophy Group (£3,200); Scottish Autistic Society (£1,800); The Urban Fox Programme (£1,500); Glasgow Hospital Broadcasting Service (£1,000).

FINANCES *Year* 2015/16 *Income* £278,373 *Grants* £248,100 *Grants to organisations* £248,100 *Assets* £4,019,110

HOW TO APPLY Apply in writing to the correspondent, preferably including a copy of accounts. The trustees have previously stated applications should be received by April as the trustees meet once a year, at the end of April or in May. An sae is required from applicants to receive a reply.

WHO TO APPLY TO Mr P. Ferguson, 5 Park View, Kilbarchan, Johnstone, Renfrewshire PA10 2LW

■ The Tennis Foundation

CC NO 298175 **ESTABLISHED** 1987

WHERE FUNDING CAN BE GIVEN UK.

WHO CAN BENEFIT Tennis clubs, schools and other organisations; individuals.

WHAT IS FUNDED The foundation promotes participation in tennis. According to its website, the foundation's core areas of work are: people with disabilities – empowering and enabling; young people in education – building futures; young people in disadvantaged communities – transforming lives; supporting wider participation. Activities include: competitions; education projects; community projects and outreach; tennis development projects; coaching.

TYPE OF GRANT Capital grants; revenue costs; project costs.

SAMPLE GRANTS Arete Leisure Ltd (£500,000); Loughborough University (£153,000); Tennis Scotland (£36,000). Previous beneficiaries have included: Advanced Apprenticeship in Sporting Excellence (£443,000); Win Tennis – High performance centre funding (£300,000); Give it Your Max (£36,000) and Clissold Park Development Fund (£10,000).

FINANCES *Year* 2015/16 *Income* £11,300,000 *Grants* £2,193,000 *Grants to organisations* £2,081,000 *Assets* £5,915,000

TRUSTEES Funke Awoderu; Matthew Stocks; Barry Horne; Ian Hewitt; Karen Keohane; Dame Tessa Jowell; Baroness Margaret Ford; Baroness Tanni-Grey Thompson; Martin Corrie; Nick Fuller; Cynthia Muller.

OTHER INFORMATION In 2015/16 grants awarded to organisations totalled £2 million while grants to individuals amounted to £112,000. Grants to organisations were distributed in the following categories: education (£1.1 million); disability tennis (£283,000); coaching (£258,000); tennis development (£228,000); community (£213,000).

HOW TO APPLY Initial enquiries should be made by telephone.

WHO TO APPLY TO Joanna Farquharson, Secretary, National Tennis Centre, 100 Priory Lane, London SW15 5JQ *Tel.* 0845 872 0522 *Email* info@tennisfoundation.org.uk *Website* www.tennisfoundation.org.uk

■ Tenovus Scotland

SC NO SC009675 **ESTABLISHED** 1967

WHERE FUNDING CAN BE GIVEN Scotland.

WHO CAN BENEFIT Universities, health bodies and research institutions; researchers and students.

WHAT IS FUNDED Research in the fields of: medicine; dentistry; nursing; the medical sciences; and allied professions. According to the website, grants are given in the following categories: small pilot grants; large grants (Tayside only); scholarships and awards through universities and medical schools. There is a preference for pump-priming studies, innovative patient-related projects; early career investigators; early stages of a new project; recent recruits; new collaborations. Further detail is given on the website.

WHAT IS NOT FUNDED Applications which are not properly certificated; work outside the beneficial area; partial funding for projects; applications that fail to provide evidence of appropriate ethical permission, or statistical justification for sample/cohort sizes (where appropriate); equipment for routine patient care or for assessment of new products, which the manufacturer might be expected to finance. The following are not usually funded: applications from established investigators for work within their usual field of expertise; applications from PhD students; applications for follow-on work previously funded by Tenovus Scotland, except in exceptional circumstances.

TYPE OF GRANT Research projects – equipment, consumables, running costs, salaries, studentships; evaluations or start-up costs.

RANGE OF GRANTS Small grants of up to £15,000; large grants of up to £100,000.

SAMPLE GRANTS A list of beneficiaries was not available.

FINANCES *Year* 2015/16 *Income* £875,758 *Grants* £1,061,704 *Grants to organisations* £1,061,704 *Assets* £1,702,307

TRUSTEES Prof. Andrew Calder; Colin Black; Prof. John Connell; Prof. James Grieve; Mary Marquis; Francis McCrossin; Malcolm McIver; Prof. Kenneth Paterson; Graham Philips; Dr Heather Reid; James Watson.

OTHER INFORMATION The grant total includes the total expenditure on 'research projects and awards' during the year.

HOW TO APPLY An application form can be requested from the relevant regional correspondent – refer to the website for contact details. Application deadlines are also posted on the website.

WHO TO APPLY TO Iain McFadzean, General Secretary, The Royal College of Physicians and Surgeons of Glasgow, 232–242 St Vincent Street, Glasgow G2 5RJ *Tel.* 0141 221 6268 *Email* gen.sec@talk21.com *Website* www.tenovus-scotland.org.uk

■ The C. Paul Thackray General Charitable Trust

CC NO 328650 **ESTABLISHED** 1990

WHERE FUNDING CAN BE GIVEN UK, with a preference for Yorkshire particularly within a ten-mile radius of Harrogate; also some overseas.

WHO CAN BENEFIT Registered charities.

WHAT IS FUNDED The trust states that it supports the following areas: people with disabilities; rehabilitation of people who have offended; patients and families suffering serious illness; addiction; victims of domestic violence; 'Christian family values' the environment. It also supports UK-registered charities working overseas in the following categories: technical and medical equipment; teams from the UK providing basic surgery; homes and education for children living on the street.

SAMPLE GRANTS The Paul Thackray Heritage Foundation (£12,100); Checkpoint Christian Youth Trust (£5,000); Macmillan Cancer Support (£2,000); Headway (£1,200); St Michael's Hospice (£1,000); Fauna and Flora International (£750); Mental Health Foundation (£600); RNLI (£500); Contact the Elderly and Harrogate Homeless Project (£300 each).

FINANCES *Year* 2015/16 *Income* £44,403 *Grants* £61,100 *Grants to organisations* £61,100 *Assets* £1,081,160

TRUSTEES Matthew Wrigley; Paul Thackray; Louise Thackray.

OTHER INFORMATION Grants were made to 51 organisations during 2015/16.

HOW TO APPLY The trustees meet on an annual basis to consider applications; however, the 2015/16 accounts states that the trustees rarely consider unsolicited applications for funding.

WHO TO APPLY TO Matthew Wrigley, Trustee, 19 Cookridge Street, Leeds LS2 3AG *Tel.* 0113 244 6100 *Email* philip.nelson@wrigleys.co.uk

■ The Thales Charitable Trust

CC NO 1000162 **ESTABLISHED** 1990

WHERE FUNDING CAN BE GIVEN UK.

WHO CAN BENEFIT Young people, people with disabilities.

WHAT IS FUNDED General charitable purposes; education and training; technology; health; young people.

SAMPLE GRANTS Arkwright Scholars; Blind Children UK; Combat Stress; Happy Days Children's Charity; National Museum of Computing; Railway Children; Scottish Veterans Residences; Together for Short Lives; Young Dementia UK; Unicef.

FINANCES *Year* 2015 *Income* £175,000 *Grants* £148,986 *Grants to organisations* £148,986 *Assets* £71,207

TRUSTEES John Howe; Michael Seabrook; Marion Broughton; Craig Stevenson.

OTHER INFORMATION Grants were made to 47 organisations during 2015.

HOW TO APPLY The trust states that it 'does not generally solicit requests other than for major donations'. The trustees meet on a quarterly basis.

WHO TO APPLY TO Michael Seabrook, Trustee, Thales Corporate Services Ltd, 2 Dashwood Lang Road, Bourne Business Park, Addlestone KT15 2NX *Tel.* 01932 824800 *Email* mike.seabrook@uk.thalesgroup.com

■ The Thistle Trust

CC NO 1091327 **ESTABLISHED** 2002

WHERE FUNDING CAN BE GIVEN UK.

WHO CAN BENEFIT Charitable organisations.

WHAT IS FUNDED The arts; research, education and study in the arts.

RANGE OF GRANTS Up to £8,000.

SAMPLE GRANTS Juventus Lyrica Association (£8,000); Sing for Pleasure (£2,500); Cahoots NI, Craft Scotland and National Centre for Circus Arts (£2,000 each); Montiverdi Choir and Orchestra Ltd (£1,500); Theatre503 (£1,200); Royal Welsh College of Music and Drama (£1,000); The Faction (£600).

FINANCES *Year* 2015/16 *Income* £38,315 *Grants* £43,995 *Grants to organisations* £43,995 *Assets* £1,227,121

TRUSTEES Catherine Trevelyan; Lady Madeleine Kleinwort; Neil Morris; Donald McGilvray; Selina Kleinwort Dabbas; Dame Sue Street.

OTHER INFORMATION Grants were made to 34 organisations totalling £51,000 during the year.

HOW TO APPLY Apply in writing to the correspondent including most recent report and financial accounts. The trustees meet at least once a year with only successful applicants notified of the trustees' decision.

WHO TO APPLY TO Trust Administrator, SG Kleinwort Hambros Trust Company UK Ltd, 8 St James Square, London W1S 1FE *Tel.* 020 3207 7041 *Email* katie.styles@kleinwortbenson.com

■ The David Thomas Charitable Trust

CC NO 1083257 **ESTABLISHED** 2000

WHERE FUNDING CAN BE GIVEN UK, in particular Gloucester and surrounding districts.

WHO CAN BENEFIT Registered charities.

WHAT IS FUNDED General charitable purposes.

SAMPLE GRANTS Home-Start Stroud (£15,000); Cotswold Care (£10,000); Southern Spinal Injuries and Winston's Wish (£5,000 each); The Door Youth Project (£4,000); Sapperton Frampton Mansell Church (£3,000); Minchinhampton Sport Association (£2,500); Brain Research Trust (£1,000).

FINANCES *Year* 2015/16 *Income* £45,319 *Grants* £120,500 *Grants to organisations* £120,500 *Assets* £1,163,689

TRUSTEES Charles Clark; James Davidson; Mary-Jane Clark; Jane Davidson.

OTHER INFORMATION In 2015/16 grants were given to 25 organisations.

HOW TO APPLY Apply in writing to the correspondent.

WHO TO APPLY TO R. F. Trustee Co. Ltd, 15 Suffolk Street, London SW1Y 4HG *Tel.* 020 3696 6721 *Email* charities@rftrustee.com

■ DM Thomas Foundation for Young People

CC NO 1084220 **ESTABLISHED** 2000

WHERE FUNDING CAN BE GIVEN UK and Ireland.

WHO CAN BENEFIT Registered charities, with a preference for smaller charities (generally those with an income of less than £2 million); hospices.

WHAT IS FUNDED The Central Grants scheme provides support for education and health of children and young people who have disabilities, are ill in hospital or who have life-limiting conditions. In addition, the foundation runs regional 'Giveaways' to support smaller, local charities, and also administers donor-advised funds; refer to the website for more information. The foundation favours charities which demonstrate community involvement and volunteering.

WHAT IS NOT FUNDED Funding will not be given from the Central Grants scheme for: core costs or general donations; salaries or sessional worker fees; new capital construction projects; organisations that are not registered charities; charities which have been registered for less than 12 months, provide incomplete or out-of-date financial information, or spend more than 30% of their annual expenditure on administration or management costs; projects or organisations outside the UK or Ireland; individuals; fundraising costs or events; medical research; work with adults over 25; medical research or individual medical treatment; overseas expeditions or exchange programmes; training or conferences for staff or professionals; loans; work which excludes some faith groups; work with only boys or girls.

TYPE OF GRANT Specific project costs; equipment or refurbishment; one-off or medium-term projects (1–2 years).

RANGE OF GRANTS Central grants: from less than £5,000 up to £30,000.

SAMPLE GRANTS Northern Ireland Children's Hospice (£101,000 in two grants); Variety – The Children's Charity (£40,500 in two grants); Radio Clyde Cash for Kids (£22,500); MediCinema (£20,000); Claire House Children's Hospice (£15,200); Open Up Music (£15,000); Oasis Children's Venture (£12,300); University College Hospital Cancer Fund (£11,600); Over the Wall (£10,300).

FINANCES *Year* 2015 *Income* £1,505,168 *Grants* £1,201,735 *Grants to organisations* £1,201,735 *Assets* £1,614,987

TRUSTEES Ramesh Dewan; Dame Maureen Thomas; Christopher Ring; Simon Vincent; William Differ; Paul Farrow.

OTHER INFORMATION The foundation made 486 grants during 2015, out of a total 757 applications. There were 252 grants in the area of education and 234 in health. They were distributed among the following groups: children in hospices (35); children with disabilities (147); children in hospital (80); homelessness (26) employment and training (8); others (190).

HOW TO APPLY Applications should be made using a form available to download from the foundation's website, where guidelines are also provided.

WHO TO APPLY TO Grants Manager, 179–199 Holland Park Avenue, London W11 4UL *Tel.* 020 7605 7733 *Fax* 020 7605 7736 *Email* info@dmtfyp.org *Website* dmthomasfoundation.org

■ The Arthur and Margaret Thompson Charitable Trust

SC NO SC012103 **ESTABLISHED** 1973

WHERE FUNDING CAN BE GIVEN The towns or burghs of Kinross and Perth.

WHO CAN BENEFIT Registered charities; individuals.

WHAT IS FUNDED General charitable purposes.

SAMPLE GRANTS Milnathort Town Hall Committee (£150,000); Milnathort in Bloom (£12,600); Millbridge Hall Kinross (£7,800); Kinross Otters Amateur Swimming Club (£5,700); Light Up Kinross (£5,000); Kinross in Bloom (£3,400); La Leche League Breast Feeding Support Group (£740); Kinross Table Tennis Club (£500); British Wireless for the Blind (£360).

FINANCES *Year* 2015/16 *Income* £289,723 *Grants* £191,666 *Grants to organisations* £191,666 *Assets* £6,116,666

HOW TO APPLY Apply in writing to the correspondent. The trustees meet to consider applications three times each year.

WHO TO APPLY TO The Trustees, c/o Miller Hendry, 10 Blackfriars Street, Perth PH1 5NS

■ The Thompson Family Charitable Trust

CC NO 326801 **ESTABLISHED** 1985

WHERE FUNDING CAN BE GIVEN UK.

WHO CAN BENEFIT Registered charities.

WHAT IS FUNDED General charitable purposes.

TYPE OF GRANT The trust makes one-off grants, recurring grants and pledges.

SAMPLE GRANTS Royal National Theatre (£450,000 in two grants); Stroke Association (£355,000 in two grants); East Anglia Children's Hospices (£300,000); Ambitious About Autism (£100,000 in two grants); Sense (£75,000); Chickenshed Theatre Trust and Place2Be (£50,000 each); Opera North (£10,000); Animal Health Trust (£1,000); Worldwide Cancer Research (£500).

FINANCES *Year* 2015/16 *Income* £8,180,319 *Grants* £4,525,700 *Grants to organisations* £4,525,700 *Assets* £114,594,000

TRUSTEES David Thompson; Patricia Thompson; Katie Woodward.

OTHER INFORMATION The trust regularly builds up its reserves to enable it to make large donations in the future, for example towards the construction of new medical or educational facilities, while continuing to make grants to charities for other purposes.

HOW TO APPLY Apply in writing to the correspondent.

WHO TO APPLY TO Katie Woodward, Trustee, Hillsdown Court, 15 Totteridge Common, London N20 8LR *Tel.* 01608 676789 *Email* roy.copus@btinternet.com

■ The Sir Jules Thorn Charitable Trust

CC NO 233838 **ESTABLISHED** 1964

WHERE FUNDING CAN BE GIVEN UK.

WHO CAN BENEFIT Registered charities; universities; NHS hospitals; organisations holding exempt status.

WHAT IS FUNDED Medical research; small grants for humanitarian or social welfare causes. Medical research is only funded through universities and recognised NHS research facilities. The 2015 annual report states that the trust focuses on 'research which seeks to bring benefit to patients through improved diagnosis and/or by the development of new therapies for important clinical problems. Funding is considered for all areas of clinical research other than for cancer or AIDS, for the sole reason that such research is already well supported.' The 2015 annual report states that the Ann Rylands Small Donations scheme humanitarian grants focus on: facilities and care for the sick and disadvantaged; carers; community projects; support for people with disabilities; aid in distress.

WHAT IS NOT FUNDED Refer to the website for exclusions from each specific grant scheme.

TYPE OF GRANT Research; one-off grants; capital projects; project costs; core costs.

SAMPLE GRANTS University of Edinburgh (£1.36 million); Black Stork Charity (£340,000);

Birmingham Children's Hospital Charity (£50,000); Diverse Abilities (£25,000); Changing Faces (£1,500); High Peak Hospicecare (£1,300); Kids Cancer Charity (£1,100); Autism Hampshire and British Refugee Council (£1,000 each); Endometriosis UK (£750); Choysez (£400).

FINANCES *Year* 2015 *Income* £2,591,687 *Grants* £2,995,750 *Grants to organisations* £2,995,750 *Assets* £110,830,701

TRUSTEES John Rhodes; Prof. Sir Ravinder Maini; Prof. David Russell-Jones; Sir Bruce McPhail; Elizabeth Charal; William Sporborg; Mark Lever; Julian Ide.

OTHER INFORMATION The trust made 347 grants in 2015. Grants were distributed in the following categories: medical research grants (£1.5 million); medicine-related grants (£1.2 million); The Ann Rylands Small Donations scheme (£286,000).

HOW TO APPLY Refer to the website for detailed guidance notes for each of the grants programmes, along with details of how to apply.

WHO TO APPLY TO David Richings, Director, 24 Manchester Square, London W1U 3TH *Tel.* 020 7487 5851 *Fax* 020 7224 3976 *Email* info@julesthorntrust.org.uk *Website* www.julesthorntrust.org.uk

■ The Thornton Foundation

CC NO 326383 **ESTABLISHED** 1983

WHERE FUNDING CAN BE GIVEN UK.

WHO CAN BENEFIT Charities which are personally known to the trustees; individuals.

WHAT IS FUNDED General charitable purposes.

SAMPLE GRANTS St Paul's Church Knightsbridge Foundation (£24,500); Cirdan Sailing Trust (£10,000); Rainbow Trust (£7,500); Moorfields Eye Hospital and Prisoners of Conscience (£5,000 each); Break (£2,500); Tait Memorial Trust (£2,000); London Handel Society (£1,000).

FINANCES *Year* 2015/16 *Income* £109,664 *Grants* £106,000 *Grants to organisations* £106,000 *Assets* £3,798,860

TRUSTEES Anthony Isaacs; Henry Thornton; Susan Thornton.

HOW TO APPLY The trust does not accept unsolicited applications. The 2015/16 accounts state: 'The trustees have agreed the grants for the next 12 months and do not welcome unsolicited applications in the meantime.'

WHO TO APPLY TO Anthony Isaacs, Trustee, Jordans, Eashing, Nr Godalming, Surrey GU7 2QA *Tel.* 01580 713055 *Email* danielvalentine@begbiesaccountants.co.uk

■ Thornton Trust

CC NO 205357 **ESTABLISHED** 1962

WHERE FUNDING CAN BE GIVEN UK and overseas.

WHO CAN BENEFIT Charitable organisations.

WHAT IS FUNDED Evangelical Christian faith; education; social welfare. The 2015/16 report states that the trust's work is comprised of: 'generally a third in supporting the Christian church, training and associated societies in this country, a third in Christian missions and relief work overseas, and the balance in education, youth work, medical and other'.

SAMPLE GRANTS AIM International (£10,000); Saffron Walden Baptist Church (£9,900); Bible Society (£3,500); Mission Aviation Fellowship (£3,000); Care for the Family and Send a Cow (£2,500 each); Scripture Union and Traidcraft (£1,000 each); RAF Benevolent Fund (£500); Parasol Foundation for Contemporary Art (£250).

FINANCES *Year* 2015/16 *Income* £39,512 *Grants* £71,600 *Grants to organisations* £71,600 *Assets* £757,485

TRUSTEES Douglas Thornton; Betty Thornton; James Thornton; Vivienne Thornton.

OTHER INFORMATION Grants were made to 37 organisations during the year.

HOW TO APPLY The trustees identify organisations and projects that they wish to support and have do not respond to speculative grant applications.

WHO TO APPLY TO James Thornton, Trustee, 25 Castle Street, Hertford SG14 1HH *Tel.* 01799 526712

■ The Thousandth Man – Richard Burns Charitable Trust

CC NO 1064028 **ESTABLISHED** 1997

WHERE FUNDING CAN BE GIVEN UK, with some preference for Birmingham, London, Leeds and Manchester.

WHO CAN BENEFIT Registered charities only – national and international charities are supported, but there is also a preference for smaller charities local to Squire Patton Boggs LLP offices.

WHAT IS FUNDED General charitable purposes, particularly: children and young people; older people; people who have disabilities; health and medical research; disaster relief.

RANGE OF GRANTS Most grants are £500 or below.

SAMPLE GRANTS Barnardo's (£10,000); Cancer Research UK (£1,900); DEBRA (£1,300); Stroke Association (£450); City of Birmingham Symphony Orchestra, London Legal Support Trust and Sailors' Children's Society (£250 each); Age UK and The Science Museum Group (£200 each); Whizz-Kidz (£100); The Prince's Trust (£50).

FINANCES *Year* 2015/16 *Income* £58,510 *Grants* £73,300 *Grants to organisations* £73,300 *Assets* £156,507

TRUSTEES Simon Miller; Susan Nickson; Robert Weekes; Robert Elvin; Anne Marie O'Meara.

OTHER INFORMATION The Thousandth Man – Richard Burns Charitable Trust was formerly known as The Hammonds Charitable Trust.

HOW TO APPLY Apply in writing to the correspondent. The trustees' 2015/16 annual report states that 'The partners and staff of Squire Patton Boggs (UK) LLP are invited to make applications for which charities should be granted payment. The trustees review such requests and if deemed to be in keeping with the charity's purpose, and dependent on available funds, will at their discretion approve such requests. In addition, the trustees have reviewed and made donations in support of 50 charities which have made unsolicited applications directly to the Trust.'

WHO TO APPLY TO Linda Sylvester, Squire Patton Boggs (UK) LLP, Rutland House, 148 Edmund Street, Birmingham B3 2JR *Tel.* 0121 222 3318 *Email* linda.sylvester@squiresanders.com *Website* www.squirepattonboggs.com

■ The Three Guineas Trust

CC NO 1059652 **ESTABLISHED** 1996

WHERE FUNDING CAN BE GIVEN Worldwide, in practice mainly UK.

WHO CAN BENEFIT Registered charities or organisations with clearly defined charitable purposes.

WHAT IS FUNDED Projects in the fields of autism and Asperger Syndrome: many projects result from contact with individuals and organisations working in this field and there is a preference for schemes which can become self-sustaining and those which include service users in decision-making. Climate change and its consequences: the trust has so far only supported one project in this area. Disability, violence and access to justice: grants mainly arise from the trustees' own research.

WHAT IS NOT FUNDED Capital projects; individuals; pure research.

TYPE OF GRANT One-off and recurrent.

SAMPLE GRANTS Somerset and Avon Rape and Sexual Abuse Support (£108,000); East Thames Group – Beverley Lewis House (£100,000); Avon and Bristol Law Centre (£98,000); Autism Hampshire (£50,000); Cheshire Without Abuse (£46,500); Action for ASD (£36,500); Turning the Red Lights Green (£28,000); Cheshire Autism Practical Support Ltd (£10,000); Rethink Mental Illness (£4,000); The Sainsbury Archive (£100).

FINANCES *Year* 2015/16 *Income* £338,496 *Grants* £768,555 *Grants to organisations* £768,555 *Assets* £22,012,233

TRUSTEES Clare Sainsbury; Dominic Flynn. David Wood.

OTHER INFORMATION The trust is one of the Sainsbury Family Charitable Trusts which share a common administration. An application to one is taken as an application to all. The trust made 58 grants during the year.

HOW TO APPLY See the guidance for applicants for the Sainsbury Family Charitable Trusts. A single application will be considered for support by all the trusts in the group. The majority of grants from the Three Guineas Trust appear to be based on the trustees' own research.

WHO TO APPLY TO Alan Bookbinder, Director, The Peak, 5 Wilton Road, London SW1V 1AP *Tel.* 020 7410 0330 *Email* info@sfct.org.uk *Website* www.sfct.org.uk

■ The Three Oaks Trust

CC NO 297079 **ESTABLISHED** 1987

WHERE FUNDING CAN BE GIVEN UK, with a preference for West Sussex; overseas.

WHO CAN BENEFIT Charitable organisations; individuals, via statutory or voluntary organisations.

WHAT IS FUNDED Social welfare. The trustees tend to support the same organisations each year (see applications). Applications are accepted from individuals for relief-in-need purposes through local statutory or voluntary organisations.

WHAT IS NOT FUNDED Direct applications from individuals.

SAMPLE GRANTS Chichester Information Shop (£13,000); Crawley Open House and Freedom from Torture (£10,000 each); Basildon Community Resource Centre (£8,000); Canaan Project, Dalit Solidarity Network, Personal Support Unit, Phoenix Stroke Club and Windmills Opportunity Playgroup (£5,000 each); Macular Society (£2,500).

FINANCES *Year* 2015/16 *Income* £252,683 *Grants* £199,590 *Grants to organisations* £150,000 *Assets* £7,327,007

TRUSTEES Carol Johnson; Pamela Wilkinson; Dr Paul Kane; Sarah Kane; Carol Foreman; Polly Hobbs; Diane Ward; Giles Wilkinson; Eugina Chandy; The Three Oaks Family Trust Company Ltd.

OTHER INFORMATION Grants to individuals in 2015/16 totalled £49,500.

HOW TO APPLY The following guidelines are taken from the 2015/16 annual report: 'Grants are made to organisations that promote the welfare of individuals and families. In general, the trustees intend to continue supporting the organisations that they have supported in the past. Periodically and generally annually the trustees review the list of registered charities and institutions to which grants have been given and consider additions and deletions from the list. To save on administration, the trustees do not respond to requests unless they are considering making a donation. Requests from organisations for donations in excess of £2,000 are considered by the trustees on a quarterly basis in meetings usually held in January, April, July and September.' For the full guidelines, visit the trust's website.

WHO TO APPLY TO The Trustees, 65 Worthing Road, Horsham, West Sussex RH12 9TD *Email* contact@thethreeoakstrust.co.uk *Website* www.thethreeoakstrust.co.uk

■ The Thriplow Charitable Trust

CC NO 1025531 **ESTABLISHED** 1993

WHERE FUNDING CAN BE GIVEN UK.

WHO CAN BENEFIT Universities and other educational or research institutions.

WHAT IS FUNDED Higher and further education; research.

WHAT IS NOT FUNDED Individuals.

TYPE OF GRANT Research study funds, research fellowships, certain academic training schemes, computer facilities and building projects related to research.

SAMPLE GRANTS Cambridge University Library; Centre of South Asian Studies; Computer Aid International; Fight for Sight; Fitzwilliam Museum; Hearing Research Trust; Inspire Foundation; Loughborough University; Marie Curie Cancer Care; Royal Botanic Gardens; Royal College of Music; Transplant Trust.

FINANCES *Year* 2015/16 *Income* £612,354 *Grants* £128,195 *Grants to organisations* £128,195 *Assets* £201,742

TRUSTEES Dr Harriet Crawford; Prof. Sir Peter Swinnerton-Dyer; Prof. David McKitterick; Prof. Robert Mair; Prof. Dame Jean Thomas.

HOW TO APPLY Apply in writing to the correspondent, specifying the purpose for which funds are sought and including the costings of the project. It should be indicated whether other applications for funds are pending and, if the funds are to be channelled to an individual or a small group, what degree of supervision over the quality of the work would be exercised by the institution. Trustee meetings are held twice a year.

WHO TO APPLY TO Catharine Walston, Secretary, PO Box 225, Royston SG8 1BG *Email* catharinewalston@gmail.com

■ The John Raymond Tijou Charitable Trust

CC NO 1146260 **ESTABLISHED** 2012
WHERE FUNDING CAN BE GIVEN UK.
WHO CAN BENEFIT Registered charities.
WHAT IS FUNDED General charitable purposes, mainly health and medical research.
SAMPLE GRANTS Barnardo's (£10,000); 2 Wish Upon a Star, Cystic Fibrosis Trust, Deafblind UK, Epilepsy Research UK, Martha Trust, Meningitis Research Foundation, Mind, Spinal Research and The Moghissi Laser Trust (£5,000 each).
FINANCES *Year* 2015/16 *Income* £600,123 *Grants* £55,000 *Grants to organisations* £55,000 *Assets* £90,053
TRUSTEE HSBC. Trust Company (UK) Ltd.
OTHER INFORMATION Grants were made to ten organisations during the year.
HOW TO APPLY Apply in writing to the correspondent.
WHO TO APPLY TO The Trustees, HSBC Trust Company (UK) Ltd, Second Floor, 1 The Forum, Parkway, Whiteley, Fareham PO15 7PA *Tel.* 023 8072 2240

■ Tilney Charitable Trust

CC NO 278880 **ESTABLISHED** 1979
WHERE FUNDING CAN BE GIVEN UK.
WHO CAN BENEFIT UK-registered charities.
WHAT IS FUNDED Education and welfare of children who are disadvantaged or who have disabilities; medical research and care of older people and those who are vulnerable.
WHAT IS NOT FUNDED Individuals; politically biased organisations; promotion of religion.
SAMPLE GRANTS Age UK; Bloodwise; Devon Air Ambulance; Holly Hedge Animal Sanctuary; Live Music Now; Nakuru Children's Project; Rowcroft Hospice; Shelter; The Poppy Appeal; WaterAid; Women's Aid.
FINANCES *Year* 2015/16 *Income* £35,355 *Grants* £42,722 *Grants to organisations* £42,722 *Assets* £1,378,958
TRUSTEES David Smith; Peter Hall; Linda Payne.
OTHER INFORMATION Previously known as The Towry Law Charitable Trust, the name was changed in 2017, following the acquisition of the Towry group of companies by Tilney Group. The trust is also known as Castle Educational Trust. The trust provides matched funding for employee fundraising efforts and payroll giving.
HOW TO APPLY Unsolicited applications are not accepted; charities are recommended by trustees or group employees.
WHO TO APPLY TO Rehana Hasan, Secretary, Tilney Group Ltd, 6 New Street Square, London EC4A 3BF *Email* companysecretary@tilney.co.uk

■ Mrs R. P. Tindall's Charitable Trust

CC NO 250558 **ESTABLISHED** 1966
WHERE FUNDING CAN BE GIVEN UK, focusing on Wiltshire and Dorset; Africa.
WHO CAN BENEFIT Charitable organisations; churches; individuals; members of the clergy.
WHAT IS FUNDED Relief of poverty; the Christian Church; education; music; medical causes; social welfare. The trust also supports the welfare of Christian clergy and their dependants.
SAMPLE GRANTS The Diocese of Antsiranana (£6,300); Save the Children (£5,000); Woodford Valley Primary Academy (£4,000); Church of England Pensions Board and Salisbury-Sudan Medical Link (£2,500 each); Salisbury and District Samaritans, Students Exploring Marriage Trust, The Bridge Youth Project, The Trussell Trust and WaterAid (£1,000 each).
FINANCES *Year* 2015 *Income* £99,820 *Grants* £57,389 *Grants to organisations* £57,389 *Assets* £3,066,479
TRUSTEES Giles Fletcher; Michael Newman; Canon Ann Philp; Nicola Halls; Stephen Herbert; Claire Newman.
OTHER INFORMATION In 2015 grants to organisations were given in the following categories: social welfare (£16,600); Madagascar and Africa (£10,800); music (£10,100); Christian church (£6,700); education (£6,600); medical (£6,500). The trust also made grants to individuals totalling £2,500.
HOW TO APPLY Apply in writing to the correspondent. The trustees meet twice a year to review applications. According to the trust's annual report, the trust invites applications for funding by advertising in charitable trusts' registers.
WHO TO APPLY TO Giles Fletcher, Trustee, Appletree House, Wishford Road, Middle Woodford, Salisbury SP4 6NG *Tel.* 01722 782329

■ The Tinsley Foundation

CC NO 1076537 **ESTABLISHED** 1999
WHERE FUNDING CAN BE GIVEN UK and overseas.
WHO CAN BENEFIT Charitable organisations.
WHAT IS FUNDED According to the 2015/16 annual report, the foundation will support: 'charities which promote human rights and democratisation and/or which educate against racism, discrimination and oppression; charities which promote self-help in fighting poverty and homelessness; charities which provide reproductive health education in underdeveloped countries, but specifically excluding charities whose policy is against abortion or birth control'.
RANGE OF GRANTS £250 to £50,000.
SAMPLE GRANTS Network for Africa (£50,000); ClientEarth, Hope Not Hate Charitable Trust and Purpose Europe – More in Common Project (£25,000 each); Anti-Slavery International, Combat Stress, English National Opera, Helen Bamber Foundation, St Mary-le-Bow Young Homeless Project and Trussell Trust (£1,000 each); The Ecology Trust (£250).
FINANCES *Year* 2015/16 *Income* £526,022 *Grants* £254,550 *Grants to organisations* £254,550 *Assets* £4,830,314
TRUSTEES Henry Tinsley; Rebecca Tinsley; Tim Jones; Jane Hogarth.
OTHER INFORMATION The foundation aims to spend at least 5% of its net assets on grants each year. In 2015/16 grants were made to 27 organisations.
HOW TO APPLY Apply in writing to the correspondent. The 2015/16 annual report states that the foundation does welcome applications from eligible potential grantees, but the trustees also seek out organisations that meet their objectives.
WHO TO APPLY TO Henry Tinsley, Trustee, Office 313, 31 Southampton Row, London WC1B 5HJ *Tel.* 01780 762056 *Email* Lesleyedmunds@btconnect.com

■ The Tisbury Telegraph Trust

CC NO 328595 **ESTABLISHED** 1990

WHERE FUNDING CAN BE GIVEN UK and overseas.

WHO CAN BENEFIT Registered charities and churches.

WHAT IS FUNDED Christianity; overseas aid; the environment; social welfare.

WHAT IS NOT FUNDED Individuals.

SAMPLE GRANTS Tearfund (£74,000); Interserve (£20,500); Mission Without Borders (£20,000); All Saints Church Peckham (£13,000); Romania Care (£10,000); Christians Against Poverty (£7,000); Faith to Share (£4,000); Crisis (£2,500); Scargill Movement and World Vision (£1,000).

FINANCES *Year* 2015/16 *Income* £325,815 *Grants* £332,542 *Grants to organisations* £329,910 *Assets* £285,881

TRUSTEES Eleanor Orr; John Davidson; Roger Orr; Alison Davidson; Sonia Phippard; Michael Hartley.

OTHER INFORMATION Grants were made to 68 organisations during 2015/16. Of these, 39 were for less than £1,000.

HOW TO APPLY Apply in writing to the correspondent. However, the trust has previously stated that unsolicited applications are rarely successful and the trust does not respond to applicants unless an sae is included.

WHO TO APPLY TO Eleanor Orr, Trustee, 35 Kitto Road, Telegraph Hill, London SE14 5TW *Email* tisburytelegraphtrust@gmail.com

■ The Tobacco Pipe Makers and Tobacco Trade Benevolent Fund

CC NO 1135646 **ESTABLISHED** 1961

WHERE FUNDING CAN BE GIVEN UK, with preference for inner London.

WHO CAN BENEFIT Charities and educational establishments. There is some preference for organisations with links to the City of London.

WHAT IS FUNDED General charitable purposes, particularly supporting disadvantaged young people from inner London.

TYPE OF GRANT Ongoing scholarships, annual donations, one-off grants.

RANGE OF GRANTS £500 to £25,000.

SAMPLE GRANTS Pembroke Music and Dance Projects (£25,000); Guildhall School of Music (£15,000); S Pinter Youth Project (£10,000); Riding for the Disabled Barrow Farm (£8,000); Bobath Centre (£5,000); S3Physics (£3,000); The London Regiment Welfare Fund (£2,500); Lord Mayor's Appeal and St Paul's Cathedral Foundation (£1,000 each); The Royal British Legion (£500).

FINANCES *Year* 2015/16 *Income* £453,639 *Grants* £307,677 *Grants to organisations* £108,700 *Assets* £6,840,380

TRUSTEES Roger Merton; Stephen Preedy; David Lewis; Fiona Adler; George Lankester; David Glynn-Jones; Simon Orlik; Nigel Rich; Martine Petetin.

OTHER INFORMATION The fund provides regular funding to support students at the Guildhall School of Music and Drama. It also provides matched funding of up to £500 each for the charitable fundraising efforts of members of the company. Grants to organisations from the general fund totalled £108,700 in 2015/16. The charity's welfare fund also provides support to individuals who are related to the tobacco trade, or their dependants. In 2015/16 support from the welfare fund totalled £191,331. A further £7,600 was given from the Bernhard Baron Fund, which supports individuals who were employed at Carreras Ltd and associated companies.

HOW TO APPLY Applications should be made in writing to the secretary. The committee meets regularly during the year to review and approve grants.

WHO TO APPLY TO Ralph Edmonson, Secretary, 2 Spa Close, Brill, Aylesbury, Buckinghamshire HP18 9RZ *Tel.* 01844 238655 *Email* benevolentfund@tobaccolivery.org *Website* www.tobaccocharity.org.uk

■ The Tolkien Trust

CC NO 1150801 **ESTABLISHED** 1977

WHERE FUNDING CAN BE GIVEN UK, with some preference for Oxfordshire, and overseas.

WHO CAN BENEFIT Registered charities.

WHAT IS FUNDED General charitable purposes, including: emergency and disaster relief; overseas aid and development; homelessness and refugees; health care, especially children and older people; disadvantaged communities; medical research; religious causes promoting peace and reconciliation and work with disadvantaged communities; environment; education and the arts.

SAMPLE GRANTS Berkshire, Buckinghamshire and Oxfordshire Wildlife Trust (£90,000); Médecins du Monde (£80,000); Birdlife International (£50,000); Wiener Library (£40,000); Bodleian Library (£30,000); The Big Issue Foundation (£22,000); Peace Brigades International UK (£20,000); Oxford Playhouse Trust and Solidarités International (£10,000 each); Exeter College (£5,500).

FINANCES *Year* 2015 *Income* £2,496,161 *Grants* £1,243,500 *Grants to organisations* £1,243,500 *Assets* £27,996,551

TRUSTEES Christopher Tolkien; Priscilla Tolkien; Michael Tolkien; Baillie Tolkien.

OTHER INFORMATION In May 2013 the previous Tolkien Trust (Charity Commission no. 273615) ceased to exist, with funds being transferred to create this trust.

HOW TO APPLY Unsolicited applications are not accepted; the trustees request applications from chosen charities.

WHO TO APPLY TO Cathleen Blackburn, Secretary, Prama House, 267 Banbury Road, Oxford OX2 7HT *Tel.* 01865 339330 *Email* info@tolkientrust.org *Website* www.tolkientrust.org

■ The Tompkins Foundation

CC NO 281405 **ESTABLISHED** 1980

WHERE FUNDING CAN BE GIVEN UK, with a preference for specific parishes of Hampstead Norreys in the county of Berkshire and of West Grinstead in the county of West Sussex.

WHO CAN BENEFIT Registered charities.

WHAT IS FUNDED General charitable purposes; education and training; recreation; religious causes; the promotion of health; children and young people.

WHAT IS NOT FUNDED Individuals.

TYPE OF GRANT One-off and recurring.

SAMPLE GRANTS Royal National Orthopaedic Hospital (£100,000); The Foundation of Nursing Studies (£30,000); Chickenshed Theatre (£25,000); St John's Hospice and The Passage (£20,000); Arthritis Care (£15,000); Place2Be (£10,000); London Early Opera Co. (£7,000); CTBF Enterprises (£4,500).

FINANCES *Year* 2015/16 *Income* £369,381 *Grants* £381,500 *Grants to organisations* £381,500 *Assets* £11,948,961

TRUSTEES Peter Vaines; Elizabeth Tompkins; Victoria Brenninkmeijer.

OTHER INFORMATION Grants were made to 18 organisations in 2015/16, with 11 of the beneficiaries having received donations in the previous year.

HOW TO APPLY Apply in writing to the correspondent, although the foundation appears to support a number of chosen charities on a regular basis.

WHO TO APPLY TO The Accountant, 7 Belgrave Square, London SW1X 8PH *Tel.* 020 7235 9322

■ Toras Chesed (London) Trust

CC NO 1110653 **ESTABLISHED** 2005

WHERE FUNDING CAN BE GIVEN UK.

WHO CAN BENEFIT Jewish organisations.

WHAT IS FUNDED Orthodox Jewish faith and religious education; social welfare; children and young people.

SAMPLE GRANTS A list of beneficiaries was not available.

FINANCES *Year* 2015/16 *Income* £542,759 *Grants* £504,996 *Grants to organisations* £504,996 *Assets* £27,167

TRUSTEES Aaron Langberg; Akiva Stern; Simon Stern.

OTHER INFORMATION A list of beneficiaries was not provided within the accounts.

HOW TO APPLY Apply in writing to the correspondent. The 2015/16 accounts state: 'Applications for grants are considered by the trustees and reviewed in depth for final approval.'

WHO TO APPLY TO Aaron Langberg, Trustee, 14 Lampard Grove, London N16 6UZ *Tel.* 020 8806 9589 *Email* ari@toraschesed.co.uk

■ The Tory Family Foundation

CC NO 326584 **ESTABLISHED** 1984

WHERE FUNDING CAN BE GIVEN Worldwide, but principally East Kent.

WHO CAN BENEFIT Charitable organisations.

WHAT IS FUNDED General charitable purposes; education and training; Christian causes; social welfare; medical causes.

TYPE OF GRANT Capital costs, research. The trust does not usually fund full projects.

SAMPLE GRANTS Ashford YMCA, Bletchley Park, Canterbury Cathedral, Concern Worldwide, Deal Festival, Disability Law Service, Folk Rainbow Club, Foresight, Friends of Birzett, Gurkha Welfare, Kent Cancer Trust, The Royal British Legion, Uppingham Foundation and Youth Action Wiltshire.

FINANCES *Year* 2015/16 *Income* £120,603 *Grants* £76,122 *Grants to organisations* £76,122 *Assets* £3,514,824

TRUSTEES James Nettlam Tory; Paul Tory; S. Tory; David Callister; Jill Perkins.

OTHER INFORMATION Grants during 2015/16 were distributed in the following categories: churches (£35,500); older people (£18,300); education (£16,600); health (£3,200); local (£2,300).

HOW TO APPLY Apply in writing to the correspondent. To keep costs down, unsuccessful applicants will not be notified.

WHO TO APPLY TO Paul Tory, Trustee, Etchinghill Golf Club, Canterbury Road, Etchinghill, Folkestone CT18 8FA *Tel.* 01303 862280

■ Tottenham Grammar School Foundation

CC NO 312634 **ESTABLISHED** 1989

WHERE FUNDING CAN BE GIVEN The borough of Haringey.

WHO CAN BENEFIT Schools; youth clubs, sports organisations, arts organisations and other voluntary organisations; individuals up to the age of 25.

WHAT IS FUNDED Education of young people in Haringey. The foundation provides support for the education of individuals; however, grants are also made to local schools, voluntary organisations, arts organisations and other community groups that work with young people in the local area. Examples of purposes supported include summer activity programmes, youth sports clubs, arts initiatives and other extra-curricular activities.

WHAT IS NOT FUNDED Direct delivery of the national curriculum; the employment of staff; the construction, adaptation, repair and maintenance of buildings; the repair and maintenance of equipment; the provision of computers and other ICT equipment; vehicle purchase; staff training; resources exclusively for parents; the costs of adults attending school trips; people aged 25 or over; people who do not live in the borough of Haringey, unless they attend or have attended a school there.

TYPE OF GRANT Project costs; equipment; one-off costs.

RANGE OF GRANTS £1,000 to £100,000.

SAMPLE GRANTS Haringey Sports Development Trust (£99,500); Chaverim Youth Organisation (£35,500); Riverside Secondary Special School (£32,000); Haringey Council Music Service (£20,000); Coleridge Primary School (£9,700); Teens and Toddlers (£5,000); Pan Nation Steel Orchestra (£4,500); Haringey Sixth Form College (£3,200); London Transport Museum (£3,000); Arca Generation (£2,500).

FINANCES *Year* 2015/16 *Income* £437,995 *Grants* £868,965 *Grants to organisations* £542,812 *Assets* £24,550,752

TRUSTEES Frederick Gruncell; Keith Brown; Keith McGuinness; Paul Compton; Peter Jones; Terry Clarke; Victoria Phillips; John Fowl; Roger Knight; Andrew Krokou; Graham Kantorowicz.

OTHER INFORMATION The foundation made 87 grants to schools and other organisations in 2015/16. Grants to individuals during the year totalled £326,000.

HOW TO APPLY Apply on a form available from the foundation's website, where further guidance is also given. Meetings take place around every eight to ten weeks and applications should be submitted at least ten days in advance; dates of upcoming meetings are posted on the website. Grants of less than £1,000 may be approved by the clerk between meetings.

WHO TO APPLY TO Graham Chappell, Clerk, PO Box 34098, London N13 5XU *Tel.* 020 8882 2999 *Email* info@tgsf.info or schools@tgsf.org.uk *Website* tgsf.org.uk

■ The Tower Hill Trust

CC NO 206225 **ESTABLISHED** 1938

WHERE FUNDING CAN BE GIVEN Tower Hamlets, particularly the areas of Tower Hill, St Katharine's and Wapping.

WHO CAN BENEFIT Charities; community organisations; schools.

WHAT IS FUNDED Main grants programme objectives (in order of priority): provision and maintenance of gardens and open spaces; leisure and recreation facilities; education facilities; relief of poverty. Biodiversity Grant Programme: small grants for biodiversity enhancements by schools, charities and community groups in school grounds, around housing estates or in community gardens – further information is provided on the website.

WHAT IS NOT FUNDED Further guidelines are provided on the website.

TYPE OF GRANT Equipment or capital costs.

RANGE OF GRANTS Biodiversity grants: £100 to £2,000. Main grants: generally around £1,000 to £20,000.

SAMPLE GRANTS Shadwell Community Project (£17,000); Thames 21 (£12,000); Barbican Centre Schools and Trees for Cities (£10,000 each); Spitalfields City Farm (£7,500); Lord's Taverners (£6,000); Canal and River Trust (£5,400); Good Shepherd Mission (£5,000); Drake Music (£3,000); Friends of Mile End Park (£1,000).

FINANCES *Year* 2015/16 *Income* £215,998 *Grants* £207,500 *Grants to organisations* £207,500 *Assets* £6,057,610

TRUSTEES Susan Wood; Davina Walter; John Polk; Maj. Gen. Geoffrey Field; Ken Clunie; Jonathan Solomon; Les Chapman.

OTHER INFORMATION Some grants to organisations extend over a number of years. The trust also pays bursaries for two pupils from Tower Hamlets at the City of London School for Girls, which totalled £18,700 in 2015/16. In 2015/16 grants were made to 19 organisations, of which 70% was for the provision of gardens and open spaces; 22% for recreation and leisure facilities; and 8% for the provision of educational facilities. 79% of projects benefitted people who are disadvantaged through poverty, homelessness, ill health or disability.

HOW TO APPLY Applications for the main grants programme should be made online, using the form on the trust's website. Applications are no longer accepted by post, but if you need help with the form, contact the trust. The trustees meet on a quarterly basis to consider applications and deadlines are posted on the trust's website. If you are interested in applying for the Biodiversity Grant Programme, contact the Grant Officer to obtain an application form.

WHO TO APPLY TO Elaine Crush, Grants Officer, Oxford House, Derbyshire Street, London E2 6HG *Tel.* 020 7749 1118 *Email* enquiries@towerhilltrust.org.uk *Website* www.towerhilltrust.org.uk

■ The Toy Trust

CC NO 1001634 **ESTABLISHED** 1991

WHERE FUNDING CAN BE GIVEN UK; occasionally overseas through charities with a UK registration.

WHO CAN BENEFIT Registered charities.

WHAT IS FUNDED Children and young people up to the age of 13. In particular, the trust's website states that it provides funding to: 'alleviate suffering; support children through awful experiences; encourage achievement through adversity; purchase vital equipment; provide care; bolster existing initiatives; initiate brand new projects; satisfy basic needs'.

WHAT IS NOT FUNDED Individuals; charities which have been running for less than a year; salaries or wages; research; books or publishing; charities where administration and overheads make up more than 30% of income; charities with net assets of more than £200,000 or one year's income.

TYPE OF GRANT Equipment or services; usually one-off, occasionally longer commitments are made for special projects.

RANGE OF GRANTS Mainly under £5,000.

SAMPLE GRANTS Alexander Devine Children's Hospice (£50,000); Action for Kids and Cyclists Fighting Cancer (£30,000 each); East African Playgrounds, Ecologia Youth Trust and Wyvern School Foundation Trust (£5,000 each); Shooting Star Chase (£4,800); Family Support Link (£4,500); World Medical Fund for Children (£4,200).

FINANCES *Year* 2015 *Income* £371,200 *Grants* £282,209 *Grants to organisations* £282,209 *Assets* £157,402

TRUSTEES Kevin Jones; Jon Diver; Christine Nicholls; Foye Pascoe; British Toy and Hobby Association Ltd.

OTHER INFORMATION This trust was registered in 1991 to centralise the giving of the British Toy and Hobby Association. In 2015 grants were made to 68 organisations. Grants of less than £4,000 totalled £109,000.

HOW TO APPLY Applications can be made using a form available to download from the trust's website, where further guidance is also given. Any queries should be directed to Tracey Butcher: tracey@btha.co.uk or 020 7701 7271.

WHO TO APPLY TO Matt Jones, British Toy and Hobby Association, BTHA House, 142–144 Long Lane, London SE1 4BS *Tel.* 020 7701 7271 *Email* admin@btha.co.uk or matt@btha.co.uk *Website* www.btha.co.uk/toy-trust

■ The Toye Foundation

CC NO 1147256 **ESTABLISHED** 2012

WHERE FUNDING CAN BE GIVEN UK and overseas.

WHO CAN BENEFIT Registered charities.

WHAT IS FUNDED Christian causes; general charitable purposes. According to its website, the foundation supports 'work that actively promotes the proclamation of the gospel'.

TYPE OF GRANT One-off and recurrent.

RANGE OF GRANTS £25 to £28,000.

SAMPLE GRANTS Gangs Unite CIC (£28,000); IBA Boxing and Premier Christian Radio (£15,000 each); EG Chapel (£6,100); Goldings Church (£6,000); Euro Christian Ministries (£1,100); Evangelism Explosion (£170); United Christian Broadcasters (£120); Cancer Research (£50); Leukaemia and Lymphoma Research (£25).

FINANCES *Year* 2015/16 *Income* £42,750 *Grants* £104,255 *Grants to organisations* £104,255 *Assets* £1,938,575

TRUSTEES William Toye; Rosemarie Toye; John Worby; Jeremy Sandy.

OTHER INFORMATION The foundation made 19 grants in 2015/16, of which 13 were one-off donations (£89,000) and six were repeat donations (£15,300).

HOW TO APPLY The foundation's website states the following: 'We do not accept applications from charities requesting funds. However, if you believe that your work is something similar to the existing charities we are supporting and would like to make us aware of this send an email Kim Sandy at admin@thetoyefoundation.org.uk and very briefly (500 words or less) outline your work.'

WHO TO APPLY TO William Toye, Trustee, c/o Goldings Church, Englands Lane, Loughton,

Essex IG10 2QX *Tel.* 01763 247371 *Email* admin@thetoyefoundation.org.uk *Website* www.thetoyefoundation.org.uk/index.html

■ Toyota Manufacturing UK Charitable Trust

CC NO 1124678 **ESTABLISHED** 2008

WHERE FUNDING CAN BE GIVEN UK, with a focus on Burnaston (Derbyshire) and Deeside (North Wales).

WHO CAN BENEFIT Registered charities and local community groups.

WHAT IS FUNDED Children and young people; environment; education; health. Support may also be given to charities with which Toyota employees are involved.

SAMPLE GRANTS Bracken Hill School Fund; Comic Relief; Derbyshire Blood Bikes; Impact Derby; Macmillan Cancer Support; Miles of Smiles Chester; NSPCC; Prader-Willi Syndrome Association UK; The Burton and District Stroke Club; Welsh Air Ambulance Charitable Trust.

FINANCES *Year* 2015 *Income* £210,942 *Grants* £156,603 *Grants to organisations* £156,603 *Assets* £137,523

TRUSTEES Anthony Walker; Sarah Overson; Kevin Reader; Chris Hardie; Gary Newington; Dave Richards.

OTHER INFORMATION This is the charitable trust of Toyota Motor Manufacturing (UK) Ltd. Income is largely derived from company employees through fundraising activities. The grant total was unclear in the 2015 accounts – the figure we have used is comprised of 'end of year payments grants', 'community grants' and 'member match funding' in the accounts.

HOW TO APPLY Applications may be made in writing to the correspondent.

WHO TO APPLY TO Jean Sayers, Toyota Motor Manufacturing (UK) Ltd, Derby DE1 9TA *Tel.* 01332 283609 *Email* charitabletrust@toyotauk.com *Website* www.toyotauk.com/the-toyota-charitable-trust/charitable-trust-overview.html

■ The Trades House of Glasgow

SC NO SC012507 **ESTABLISHED** 1920

WHERE FUNDING CAN BE GIVEN Glasgow.

WHO CAN BENEFIT Charitable organisations; individuals.

WHAT IS FUNDED General charitable purposes; children and young people; social welfare; education.

WHAT IS NOT FUNDED Organisations outside Glasgow; operating costs or staff costs except for staff training to deliver a specific project; property or property-related costs, apart from fitting out a space for a designated project, purchasing equipment for disability access or where a building is used for the delivery of a charitable project or purpose; costs of hiring premises; transport or vehicle costs, including staff vehicles, maintenance and insurance – unless to transport beneficiaries, emergency equipment or medical supplies. The guidelines on the website state the following: 'Political, municipal and ecclesiastical appeals cannot be entertained. Charities duplicating rather than complementing existing services and those with national purposes and/or large running surpluses normally cannot be helped.'

TYPE OF GRANT Project costs; one-off; capital costs.

RANGE OF GRANTS Up to £25,000.

SAMPLE GRANTS STV Children's Appeal (£25,000); Sense Scotland (£19,400); East Park (£10,000); University of Glasgow (£7,900); Visibility (£4,800); Kidney Kids Scotland (£4,000); Grand Antiquity Society (£3,500); ABF The Soldiers' Charity, Bobath Scotland and Listening Books (£3,000 each).

FINANCES *Year* 2014/15 *Income* £1,860,537 *Grants* £458,369 *Grants to organisations* £221,712 *Assets* £21,737,028

OTHER INFORMATION The 2014/15 accounts were the most recent available to view on the charity's website. The charity also provides bursaries and educational grants, which totalled £40,500 in 2014/15.

HOW TO APPLY Application forms are available to download from the website, where further guidance is also provided about what to include, as well as upcoming deadlines.

WHO TO APPLY TO The Clerk, Trades Hall, 85 Glassford Street, Glasgow G1 1UH *Tel.* 0141 553 1605 *Email* katrina.tilston@tradeshouse.org.uk or info@tradeshouse.org.uk *Website* www.tradeshouse.org.uk

■ Annie Tranmer Charitable Trust

CC NO 1044231 **ESTABLISHED** 1989

WHERE FUNDING CAN BE GIVEN UK, mainly Suffolk and surrounding areas.

WHO CAN BENEFIT Charitable organisations; individuals.

WHAT IS FUNDED General charitable purposes; education and training; children and young people.

RANGE OF GRANTS £200 to £10,000; mostly £1,000 or less.

SAMPLE GRANTS East Anglian Air Ambulance (£10,000); Marie Curie Cancer Care (£5,000); St Elizabeth Hospice (£3,000); The Salvation Army (£2,000); Disability Advice Service – East Suffolk and Felixstowe Ferry Youth Sailing (£1,000 each); National Kidney Federation and Scope (£500 each); Suffolk Refugee Support (£350); Waveney Stardust Trust (£200).

FINANCES *Year* 2015/16 *Income* £120,728 *Grants* £92,214 *Grants to organisations* £75,350 *Assets* £3,694,917

TRUSTEES Valerie Lewis; Nigel Bonham-Carter; Patrick Grieve; Mary Allen.

OTHER INFORMATION Grants were made to 74 organisations in 2015/16. Grants to 22 individuals during the year totalled £16,900.

HOW TO APPLY Apply in writing to the correspondent.

WHO TO APPLY TO Anne-Marie Williams, 55 Dobbs Lane, Kesgrave, Ipswich IP5 2QA *Tel.* 07801 556002 *Email* amwilliams7903@gmail.com

■ The Transform Foundation

CC NO 1163503 **ESTABLISHED** 2015

WHERE FUNDING CAN BE GIVEN UK.

WHO CAN BENEFIT UK-registered charities; not-for-profit organisations.

WHAT IS FUNDED Digital fundraising projects. The foundation's website states that it provides 'initial funding to small and mid-size charities to help them prove the potential of online marketing as a way of recruiting donors, volunteers, campaigners, or helping beneficiaries'.

WHAT IS NOT FUNDED General software or hardware procurement projects, the development of apps or CRM projects; organisations that do not have the capacity or commitment to put internal resources behind making a project a success; organisations with very bespoke or complex technical requirements; core costs.

RANGE OF GRANTS Up to £18,000.

SAMPLE GRANTS A list of beneficiaries was not available.

FINANCES *Year* 2015/16 *Income* £462,491 *Grants* £99,152 *Grants to organisations* £99,152 *Assets* £363,339

TRUSTEES Diviya Gosrani; David Melville; Smruti Sriram.

OTHER INFORMATION Grants are to be used with the foundation's selected partners.

HOW TO APPLY Applications can be made through the foundation's website. Grants are accepted on a rolling basis.

WHO TO APPLY TO David Melville, Trustee, 10 Queen Street Place, London EC4R 1BE *Tel.* 020 7965 7132 *Email* info@transformfoundation.org.uk *Website* www.transformfoundation.org.uk

■ The Constance Travis Charitable Trust

CC NO 294540 **ESTABLISHED** 1986

WHERE FUNDING CAN BE GIVEN UK (national charities only); Northamptonshire (all sectors). The trust may also respond to international appeals.

WHO CAN BENEFIT Registered charities.

WHAT IS FUNDED General charitable purposes.

WHAT IS NOT FUNDED Individuals; non-registered charities.

TYPE OF GRANT One-off grants for core, capital and project support.

RANGE OF GRANTS Generally up to £20,000.

SAMPLE GRANTS Institute of Cancer Research (£130,000); British Red Cross (£120,000); Beanstalk (£20,000); Motor Neurone Disease Association (£18,000); Dyslexia Teaching Centre and National Trust (£15,000 each); Northamptonshire Historic Churches and Royal Shakespeare Company (£12,000 each); Royal Air Force Benevolent Fund and Unicef (£10,000 each).

FINANCES *Year* 2015 *Income* £2,120,511 *Grants* £1,158,000 *Grants to organisations* £1,158,000 *Assets* £103,739,482

TRUSTEES Ernest Travis; Peta Travis; Matthew Travis.

OTHER INFORMATION The trust has previously made small grants to local groups in Northamptonshire through the Northamptonshire Community Foundation.

HOW TO APPLY Apply in writing to the correspondent. The trustees meet at least quarterly to consider grants. The trust does not welcome contact prior to application.

WHO TO APPLY TO Ernest Travis, Trustee, 86 Drayton Gardens, London SW10 9SB *Email* travistrust86@yahoo.co.uk

■ The Treeside Trust

CC NO 1061586 **ESTABLISHED** 1997

WHERE FUNDING CAN BE GIVEN UK, but mainly in Oldham.

WHO CAN BENEFIT Mainly small local charities, as well as a few UK-wide charities which are supported on a regular basis.

WHAT IS FUNDED General charitable purposes.

RANGE OF GRANTS The trust tends to make a small number of substantial grants each year.

SAMPLE GRANTS Footprints Theatre Trust (£12,500).

FINANCES *Year* 2015/16 *Income* £19,818 *Grants* £57,000 *Grants to organisations* £57,000

TRUSTEES Catherine Gould; Diana Ives; Richard Gould; Roger Gould; Richard Ives.

OTHER INFORMATION This trust's latest accounts were not available to view on the Charity Commission's website due to its low income. We have therefore estimated the grant total based on previous years' information.

HOW TO APPLY The trust has stated that they do not welcome unsolicited applications.

WHO TO APPLY TO Roger Gould, Trustee, 4 The Park, Grasscroft, Oldham OL4 4ES *Tel.* 01457 876422

■ The Trefoil Trust

CC NO 1044101 **ESTABLISHED** 1995

WHERE FUNDING CAN BE GIVEN UK.

WHO CAN BENEFIT Charitable organisations.

WHAT IS FUNDED Health and medicine; children and young people; people with disabilities; the arts; the armed forces.

WHAT IS NOT FUNDED Individuals.

SAMPLE GRANTS Charities Aid Foundation (£22,500); WaterAid (£10,000); The Royal British Legion (£8,000); FareShare and Sussex Snowdrop Trust (£4,000 each); Chestnut Tree Hospice (£3,000); Cirencester Rugby Club and Marlowe Theatre Development Trust (£1,000 each); Witcombe and Birdlip Guides (£500).

FINANCES *Year* 2015 *Income* £52,639 *Grants* £104,500 *Grants to organisations* £104,500 *Assets* £1,060,104

TRUSTEE Trefoil Trustees Ltd.

OTHER INFORMATION Grants were made to 27 organisations during 2015.

HOW TO APPLY Applications should be made in writing to the correspondent and accompanied by the organisation's latest report and full accounts. The trustees usually meet in April and November to decide on distributions.

WHO TO APPLY TO Rupert Hughes, Brook Farm, Little Marcle, Ledbury HR8 2JY

■ The Triangle Trust (1949) Fund

CC NO 222860 **ESTABLISHED** 1949

WHERE FUNDING CAN BE GIVEN UK.

WHO CAN BENEFIT Registered charities; social enterprises; CICs. Eligible organisations should have an income of less than £2 million (priority is given to smaller organisations) and should have some volunteer input.

WHAT IS FUNDED Specialist organisations working with unpaid carers or the rehabilitation of ex-offenders. As well as those working directly with beneficiaries, organisations carrying out research, policy or campaigns one of these areas are also eligible.

WHAT IS NOT FUNDED Organisations which are not solely focused on either carers or the rehabilitation of people who have offended (organisations with a broader remit running a specific project in one of these areas are not eligible); crime prevention or restorative justice initiatives; support for people who are cared for as well as carers (e.g. patient representative groups); appointment of a trust or community fundraiser; expansion of coverage of a particular service, unless it will increase sustainability; matched funding, unless associated with developing sustainability; covering the loss of a statutory contract or grant; general running costs.

TYPE OF GRANT Development grants given over three years, covering core costs with an aim of increasing long-term sustainability.
RANGE OF GRANTS Up to £120,000 over three years.
SAMPLE GRANTS Carers Trust, Powys Carers Service and Revolving Doors Agency (£40,000); Clean Break Theatre Company (£37,000); Back on Track (£30,000); Renfrewshire Carers Centre (£27,500); Storybook Dads (£25,000); From Springhill (£10,000); Young Carers Development Trust (£5,000); Carers of Barking and Dagenham (£3,200).
FINANCES *Year* 2015/16 *Income* £656,237 *Grants* £822,700 *Grants to organisations* £799,548 *Assets* £18,388,792
TRUSTEES Andrew Pitt; Julian Weinberg; Bruce Newbigging; Kate Purcell; Karen Drury; Helen Moss; Dr James Anderson; Alison Hope.
OTHER INFORMATION There were also grants made to individuals during the year totalling £23,000.
HOW TO APPLY Application forms are provided on the website, where detailed guidance is available. Each of the two schemes has one round of funding during the year and deadlines are posted on the website. Any queries with the application process can be directed to info@triangletrust.org.uk or 01707 707078.
WHO TO APPLY TO Dr Joanne Knight, Director, Foundation House, 2–4 Forum Place, Fiddlebridge Lane, Hatfield AL10 0RN *Tel.* 01707 707078 *Email* info@triangletrust.org.uk *Website* www.triangletrust.org.uk

■ Tropical Health and Education Trust

CC NO 1113101 **ESTABLISHED** 2006
WHERE FUNDING CAN BE GIVEN Low- and middle-income countries.
WHO CAN BENEFIT Medical institutions; universities; health charities.
WHAT IS FUNDED The training of health workers in low- and middle-income countries.
SAMPLE GRANTS Selfless UK (£176,500); Royal College of Pathologists (£156,000); University of Manchester (£110,000); Association of Anaesthetists of Great Britain and Ireland (£90,000); Public Health England (£41,000); St George's Healthcare NHS Trust (£19,300); University of Liverpool (£1,500); East London NHS Foundation Trust (£360).
FINANCES *Year* 2015 *Income* £9,973,427 *Grants* £4,721,176 *Grants to organisations* £4,721,176 *Assets* £733,220
TRUSTEES Prof. Gerard Byrne; Prof. Judith Ellis; Dr Irene Leigh; James Nwabineli; Morounke Akingbola; David Alexander; Frances Day-Stirk; Andy Bacon; Vanessa Forster; Dr Gillian Thomas; Dr Simon Taylor-Robinson.
HOW TO APPLY Applicants should refer to the trust's website for information on any current funding rounds.
WHO TO APPLY TO John Beverley, Company Secretary, 1 Wimpole Street, London W1G 0AE *Tel.* 020 7290 3892 *Email* info@thet.org *Website* www.thet.org

■ The True Colours Trust

CC NO 1089893 **ESTABLISHED** 2001
WHERE FUNDING CAN BE GIVEN UK and Africa.
WHO CAN BENEFIT Registered charities; CICs; hospices; schools.
WHAT IS FUNDED Grant-making is focused on the following areas: children and young people with complex disabilities or life-limiting and life-threatening illnesses in the UK; and palliative care in Africa. The trust also makes small grants to local charities supporting children, with disabilities or life-limiting conditions, their siblings and their families. Further detail on each of the trust's areas of focus is given on the website.
WHAT IS NOT FUNDED The trust no longer makes grants to individuals. Refer to the website for specific exclusions from each scheme or area of focus.
TYPE OF GRANT One-off and recurring; projects; capital costs; salaries; pilot projects; core costs.
RANGE OF GRANTS Up to £300,000. Small grants of up to £10,000.
SAMPLE GRANTS African Palliative Care Association (£356,500); Palliative Care Association of Malawi (£310,500); Family Support Project (£208,000); Sibs (£150,000); Multiple Births Foundation (£20,000); Kenya Hospices and Palliative Care Association (£84,000); National Council for Palliative Care (£8,000); Arts Depot, Crossroads Care Isle of Man and Friends of Ysgol Pen Coch (£5,000 each); Kinship Care NI (£4,700); New Hope Worcestershire (£1,800).
FINANCES *Year* 2015/16 *Income* £1,125,979 *Grants* £1,958,552 *Grants to organisations* £1,958,552 *Assets* £8,756,014
TRUSTEES Lucy Sainsbury; Dominic Flynn; Bernard Willis; Tim Price.
OTHER INFORMATION The trust awarded 150 grants during 2015/16.
HOW TO APPLY An application form for the small grants scheme is given on the trust's website. Refer to the website for further information. In 2015/16 the trustees met four times to make grants.
WHO TO APPLY TO Alan Bookbinder, The Peak, 5 Wilton Road, London SW1V 1AP *Tel.* 020 7410 0330 *Email* truecolours@sfct.org.uk or info@sfct.org.uk *Website* www.truecolourstrust.org.uk

■ Truedene Co. Ltd

CC NO 248268 **ESTABLISHED** 1966
WHERE FUNDING CAN BE GIVEN UK and overseas.
WHO CAN BENEFIT Jewish organisations.
WHAT IS FUNDED Jewish religious education; support for Jewish people who are in need.
SAMPLE GRANTS Siva Charitable Funds (£273,500); UTRY (£50,000); Chevras Mo'oz Ladol (£48,000); Kollel Shomrei Hachomoth (£40,000); Beer Yitzchak (£36,000); Yeshiva Gedolah Torah Veyirah (£35,000); Ora Vesimcha (£30,000).
FINANCES *Year* 2015/16 *Income* £1,809,992 *Grants* £746,500 *Grants to organisations* £746,500 *Assets* £7,224,357
TRUSTEES Sarah Klein; Samuel Berger; Solomon Laufer; Sije Berger; Zelda Sternlicht.
OTHER INFORMATION Donations of less than £30,000 totalled £234,000.
HOW TO APPLY Apply in writing to the correspondent
WHO TO APPLY TO The Trustees, Truedene Co. Ltd, Cohen Arnold, New Burlington House, 1075 Finchley Road, London NW11 0PU *Tel.* 020 8731 0777

■ The Truemark Trust

CC NO 265855 **ESTABLISHED** 1973
WHERE FUNDING CAN BE GIVEN UK.
WHO CAN BENEFIT Registered charities with preference for small local charities.
WHAT IS FUNDED Social welfare and disadvantage. There is a preference for neighbourhood-based community projects and innovative work with less popular groups.
WHAT IS NOT FUNDED Individuals, including students; general appeals; large national charities; churches or church buildings; medical research projects.
TYPE OF GRANT Usually one-off for a specific project or part of a project. Core funding and/or salaries rarely considered.
RANGE OF GRANTS Average grant £1,000.
SAMPLE GRANTS Westfield Community Development Association (£6,000); Music Alive (£5,000); Second Chance (£4,000); Hibiscus Caribbean Elderly Association and Housing the Homeless Central Fund (£3,000 each); City of Sheffield Hatters Women's Basketball Club and North London Foodbank (£2,000 each); 1st Maidenhead Sea Scout Group (£1,000).
FINANCES *Year* 2015/16 *Income* £608,459 *Grants* £112,000 *Grants to organisations* £112,000 *Assets* £17,990,576
TRUSTEES Sir Thomas Lucas; Wendy Collett; Sharon Knight; Judy Hayward; Roger Ross; Jane Dunham; Dr David Panton.
HOW TO APPLY Apply in writing to the correspondent, including the most recent set of accounts, clear details of the need the project is designed to meet and an outline budget. The trustees meet four times a year. Only successful applicants receive a reply.
WHO TO APPLY TO Clare Pegden, PO Box 2, Liss, Hampshire GU33 6YP *Tel.* 07970 540015 *Email* truemark.trust01@ntlworld.com

■ Truemart Ltd

CC NO 1090586 **ESTABLISHED** 1984
WHERE FUNDING CAN BE GIVEN UK.
WHO CAN BENEFIT Charitable organisations.
WHAT IS FUNDED Orthodox Jewish faith; relief of poverty; general charitable purposes.
SAMPLE GRANTS A list of beneficiaries was not available.
FINANCES *Year* 2015/16 *Income* £472,651 *Grants* £216,590 *Grants to organisations* £216,590 *Assets* £324,995
TRUSTEES Sara Heitner; Ian Heitner.
OTHER INFORMATION Beneficiaries were not listed in the accounts.
HOW TO APPLY Apply in writing to the correspondent.
WHO TO APPLY TO Sara Heitner, Trustee, 34 The Ridgeway, London NW11 8QS *Tel.* 020 8455 4456

■ Trumros Ltd

CC NO 285533 **ESTABLISHED** 1982
WHERE FUNDING CAN BE GIVEN UK and Israel.
WHO CAN BENEFIT Charitable organisations.
WHAT IS FUNDED Jewish causes; education and training; social welfare; health.
SAMPLE GRANTS Mifal HaChessed Vehatzedoko (£87,000); Beit Midrash Abanbamel (£61,000); Asser Bishvil Foundation (£57,500); Mercaz Torah Vechesed Ltd (£44,500); Chevras Mo'os Lodol (£32,500); Ichud Mosdos Gur (£29,500); Yeshiva Chochmat Shlomo (£20,000); Beis Yosef Zvi (£19,600); Chevras Ezras Nizrochim (£13,600); Beis Chinuch LeBonos (£11,000); Gesher Charitable Trust (£10,000).
FINANCES *Year* 2015 *Income* £1,259,750 *Grants* £766,764 *Grants to organisations* £766,764 *Assets* £10,607,381
TRUSTEES Hannah Hofbauer; Ronald Hofbauer.
HOW TO APPLY Apply in writing to the correspondent.
WHO TO APPLY TO Ronald Hofbauer, Trustee, 282 Finchley Road, London NW3 7AD *Tel.* 020 7431 3282 *Email* r.hofbauer@btconnect.com

■ The Trusthouse Charitable Foundation

CC NO 1063945 **ESTABLISHED** 1997
WHERE FUNDING CAN BE GIVEN UK.
WHO CAN BENEFIT Registered charities and other not-for-profit organisations, with a preference for small to medium-sized organisations.
WHAT IS FUNDED The trust has two overarching themes – rural issues and urban deprivation. Within these themes, there are three areas of interest: community support; disability and health care; and arts, education and heritage. The trust also runs three-year grants programmes focused on a specific issue of interest to the trustees. At the time of writing (May 2017) the website stated that the next themed grants programme will open late in 2017. Grants fall into the following categories based on the type and income of the applicant organisation: small grants (revenue projects); small grants (capital projects); standard grants; large grants; village halls and community centre grants; hospices. Detailed guidance is provided on the website.
WHAT IS NOT FUNDED The foundation will not fund: individuals (including through a third party); charities or NGOs registered outside the UK; statutory services including state schools (except those specifically for pupils with disabilities), local or national authorities, prisons, NHS hospitals or services; universities, further education colleges and independent schools; organisations with an income in excess of £5 million (except for hospices); grant-making organisations; umbrella organisations. The foundation will not accept unsolicited applications for the funding of: set up costs for new organisations; projects outside the UK; animal welfare, conservation or projects with a primarily ecological aim; medical research; capital appeals for places of worship, except those primarily for community use, such as a church hall or community area in a place of worship; feasibility studies; one-off events (except in the small grants programme); PR and awareness-raising activities; fundraising salaries, events or initiatives; projects concerned with the production of DVDs or other media.
TYPE OF GRANT Core costs; salaries; project costs; capital costs (buildings or essential equipment). Grants are for one year only.
RANGE OF GRANTS Grants vary depending on category – from less than £6,000 up to £45,000.
SAMPLE GRANTS Onion Collective (£100,000); Brighton Oasis Project (£57,500); Headway Birmingham and Solihull (£30,000); Big Issue Foundation Scotland (£20,500); Titley Village Hall (£13,000); Dignity in Dementia CIC (£9,500); Syrian Community of Leeds (£3,000); Geese Theatre Company and Prison Fellowship Northern Ireland (£2,000 each); Ironbridge Brass Band Festival (£500).

FINANCES *Year* 2015/16 *Income* £2,039,000 *Grants* £2,842,000 *Grants to organisations* £2,842,000 *Assets* £74,111,000

TRUSTEES Crispian Collins; Sir Hugh Rossi; The Hon. Olga Polizzi; Lady Janet Balfour of Burleigh; Sir John Nutting; Revd Rose Hudson-Wilkin; George Hepburn; Lady Anthony Hamilton; Philippa Hamilton; Nicholas Melhuish.

OTHER INFORMATION The foundation received 971 applications and made 300 grants during 2015/16.

HOW TO APPLY Applications can be made on a form available to download from the foundation's website, accessed following the completion of a brief eligibility questionnaire, which also identifies which type of grant may be most suitable. Application forms should be completed and returned via post along with a budget for the work for which you are applying for support and a copy of your organisation's latest annual accounts. Applications are not currently accepted via email. Detailed guidelines are available to download from the website.

WHO TO APPLY TO Judith Leigh, Grants Manager, 6th Floor, 65 Leadenhall Street, London EC3A 2AD *Tel.* 020 7264 4990 *Website* www.trusthousecharitablefoundation.org.uk

■ The Trysil Charitable Trust

CC NO 1107309 **ESTABLISHED** 2004

WHERE FUNDING CAN BE GIVEN Worldwide.

WHO CAN BENEFIT Charitable organisations.

WHAT IS FUNDED Children and young people, particularly social welfare and health; general charitable purposes.

SAMPLE GRANTS Centre Hospitalier Universitaire Vaudois (£76,500); Universitätsklinikum Gießen und Marburg (£33,500); One to One Children's Fund (£20,000).

FINANCES *Year* 2015 *Income* £870 *Grants* £131,062 *Grants to organisations* £131,062 *Assets* £2,489,132

TRUSTEES David Lumley; Jonathan Dudman; Corinna Schumacher.

HOW TO APPLY Apply in writing to the correspondent.

WHO TO APPLY TO J. Dudman, Arena Wealth Management Ltd, Chiswick Gate 3rd Floor, 598–608 Chiswick High Road, London W4 5RT

■ The James Tudor Foundation

CC NO 1105916 **ESTABLISHED** 2004

WHERE FUNDING CAN BE GIVEN UK and overseas.

WHO CAN BENEFIT UK-registered charities; CIOs.

WHAT IS FUNDED The foundation has the principal aim of relieving sickness. Its six programme areas are: palliative care; medical research; health education; relief of sickness; overseas projects for the relief of sickness; other projects which meet the foundation's aims but do not fit easily into any of the other categories.

WHAT IS NOT FUNDED The foundation does not fund: individuals; overseas organisations; applicants who have applied within the last 12 months; capital projects; funding that directly replaces, or negatively affects, statutory funding; work that has already taken place; endowments; community development; adventure or residential courses, respite holidays and excursions, expeditions or overseas travel; sports or recreation; environmental, conservation or heritage causes; animal welfare. The foundation is unlikely to fund: large national charities with widespread support and local organisations which are part of a wider network. Items of equipment may be funded but applicants whose proposal includes a request for equipment funding should at first contact the foundation.

TYPE OF GRANT Project costs. Core costs may also be considered, but generally only for organisations with which the foundation has a longstanding relationship. Grants are usually for one year.

RANGE OF GRANTS £500 to £50,000; the average grant size in 2015/16 was between £8,000 and £10,000.

SAMPLE GRANTS University of Bristol (£40,500); St Peter's Hospice (£18,000); National Rheumatoid Arthritis Society (£17,500); Teenage Cancer Trust (£15,000); Cerebra (£10,000); World Medical Fund (£8,800); York Mind (£5,000); Asthma Relief (£4,000); Action on Pre-Eclampsia (£2,000); Bristol Area Stroke Association (£500).

FINANCES *Year* 2015/16 *Income* £1,155,921 *Grants* £811,519 *Grants to organisations* £811,519 *Assets* £28,736,465

TRUSTEES Richard Esler; Cedric Nash; Susan Evans; Anne McPherson; Stephanie Wren.

OTHER INFORMATION During the year, the foundation received 352 outline applications and 86 full applications. In total, 99 grants were made to organisations during the year, of which 74 had previously received funding from the foundation. The 2015/16 accounts state: 'The next review of programme categories is due to take place in 2017.'

HOW TO APPLY Potential applicants must at first read the foundation's guidelines and can complete an initial eligibility check, both of which can be found on the website. Organisations that are eligible at this stage can send an outline application along with a coversheet to the foundation and, following this, may be invited to submit a full application. There is a guide explaining how to apply on the website.

WHO TO APPLY TO Sarah Stewart, Foundation Director, WestPoint, 78 Queens Road, Clifton, Bristol BS8 1QU *Tel.* 0117 985 8715 *Fax* 0117 985 8716 *Email* admin@jamestudor.org.uk *Website* www.jamestudor.org.uk

■ The Tudor Trust

CC NO 1105580 **ESTABLISHED** 1955

WHERE FUNDING CAN BE GIVEN UK and sub-Saharan Africa.

WHO CAN BENEFIT Registered charities and other charitable organisations, with a focus on smaller organisations with an annual income of less than £1 million.

WHAT IS FUNDED Organisations which engage make a direct difference to the lives of marginalised people and are rooted in areas which are neglected or where funding is difficult to obtain. There are three categories of eligibility criteria through which the trust considers applications: display positive organisational characteristics; address marginalisation; make a difference. Full details of each of these categories are given on the website.

WHAT IS NOT FUNDED Individuals, or organisations applying on behalf of individuals; larger charities (both national and local) enjoying widespread support; statutory bodies; hospitals, health authorities or hospices; medical care, medical equipment or medical research; universities, colleges or schools; academic research, scholarships or bursaries; nurseries, playgroups or crèches; uniformed youth groups; one-off holidays, residentials, trips, exhibitions, conferences, events, etc.; animal charities; the promotion of religion; routine repairs or minor improvements to community buildings; landscaping or equipment for playgrounds, parks or recreation areas; sports and leisure (where there isn't a strong social welfare focus); the restoration or conservation of buildings or habitats (where there is not a strong social welfare focus); promotion of philanthropy or endowment appeals; retrospective costs; work outside the UK (the trust runs a targeted grants programme promoting sustainable agriculture in sub-Saharan Africa).

TYPE OF GRANT Core funding; unrestricted funding; project grants; capital grants (building or equipment); development or capacity-building grants.

RANGE OF GRANTS There is no minimum or maximum grant; grants are usually £10,000 or more. In 2015/16 the average grant was £50,614.

SAMPLE GRANTS Lloyds TSB Foundation for Scotland (£300,000); Anorexia and Bulimia Care (£150,000); Ditch the Label (£91,000); Full Circle Food Project (£75,000); Citizens UK (£50,000); Cartwheel Arts Led (£35,000); Granby Somali Women's Group (£40,000); Detention Action (£30,000); Somerset Level and Moors Sheds (£17,000); Tonagh Neighbourhood Initiative (£11,600); Dundee Lochee Parish Church of Scotland (£250).

FINANCES *Year* 2015/16 *Income* £6,336,000 *Grants* £18,272,000 *Grants to organisations* £18,272,000 *Assets* £218,377,000

TRUSTEES James Long; Dr Desmond Graves; Catherine Antcliff; Monica Barlow; Nell Buckler; Louise Collins; Elizabeth Cranshaw; Ben Dunwell; Matt Dunwell; Christopher Graves; Francis Runacres; Rosalind Dunwell; Amy Collins; Carey Buckler.

OTHER INFORMATION The trust's website includes comprehensive, clear guidelines for applicants. During 2015/16, the trust made 361 grants, which are broken down in detail in the annual report or on the grants list available to download from the website.

HOW TO APPLY Full guidance about eligibility and the application procedure is provided on the website. The application process is made up of two stages. A first stage proposal can be sent at any time by post or email (refer to the website for details on what should be included). The trust aims to notify applicants within a month whether their application has been taken to the second stage. The second stage usually takes around three months and involves further discussion with the trust. Applicants are encouraged to contact the Information Team with any queries (020 7727 8522).

WHO TO APPLY TO Grants Team, 7 Ladbroke Grove, London W11 3BD *Tel.* 020 7727 8522 *Email* general@tudortrust.org.uk *Website* www.tudortrust.org.uk

■ The Tufton Charitable Trust

CC NO 801479 **ESTABLISHED** 1989

WHERE FUNDING CAN BE GIVEN UK.

WHO CAN BENEFIT Charitable organisations; churches; individuals.

WHAT IS FUNDED Christian causes.

SAMPLE GRANTS Stowe School Foundation (£30,000); The Canterbury Cathedral Trust (£25,000); Holy Trinity – Hastings (£20,000); St Peter's Church – Brighton (£18,000); Glyndebourne Productions (£12,500); Luton Roma Church (£6,400); London Institute of Contemporary Christianity, Off The Fence and Solomon Academic Trust (£5,000 each).

FINANCES *Year* 2015 *Income* £924,472 *Grants* £155,326 *Grants to organisations* £155,326 *Assets* £1,114,368

TRUSTEES Lady Georgina Wates; Sir Christopher Wates; Wates Charitable Trustees Ltd.

OTHER INFORMATION The trust also provides accommodation for Christian retreats.

HOW TO APPLY Apply in writing to the correspondent, including an sae. The trustees meet regularly to review applications.

WHO TO APPLY TO The Trustees, Tufton Place, Ewhurst Place, Northiam, Rye TN31 6HL

■ The Tuixen Foundation

CC NO 1081124 **ESTABLISHED** 2000

WHERE FUNDING CAN BE GIVEN UK.

WHO CAN BENEFIT Registered charities; hospitals; schools; other charitable organisations.

WHAT IS FUNDED Children and young people; education; people with disabilities or learning disabilities; mental health; hospices; homelessness; relief of poverty.

TYPE OF GRANT Core costs and unrestricted funding.

SAMPLE GRANTS Impetus Trust (£100,000); Leap Confronting Conflict and Teens and Toddlers (£50,000 each); Street League and Whizz-Kidz (£30,000 each); New Philanthropy Capital (£25,000); Islington Youth Theatre (£21,000); Jewish Care and Storybook Dads (£20,000); Camp and Trek (£10,000).

FINANCES *Year* 2015/16 *Income* £14,691,907 *Grants* £736,000 *Grants to organisations* £736,000 *Assets* £36,523,810

TRUSTEES Stephen Rosefield; Leanda Kroll; Peter Englander; Paul Clements; Simon Englander.

HOW TO APPLY The website states that unsolicited applications are not sought and the foundation will not reply to correspondence.

WHO TO APPLY TO Paul Clements, Trustee, 440 Strand, London WC2R 0QS *Tel.* 020 7649 2903 *Email* Jandoole@tuixen.org.uk *Website* tuixen.org.uk

■ The Roger and Douglas Turner Charitable Trust

CC NO 1154467 **ESTABLISHED** 2013

WHERE FUNDING CAN BE GIVEN Birmingham; Dudley; Sandwell; Walsall; Wolverhampton; Worcestershire.

WHO CAN BENEFIT Registered charities; hospices.

WHAT IS FUNDED Older people; medical research; children and young people; environment and heritage; the arts; work in the community; social support; disability and health; international aid; hospices.

RANGE OF GRANTS Up to £30,000. The average grant is around £3,000.

SAMPLE GRANTS Birmingham St Mary's Hospice (£30,000); Acorn's Children's Hospice (£20,000); Stonehouse Gang (£15,000); Multiple Births Foundation (£10,000); Birmingham Botanical Gardens and Worcester Live (£10,000 each); Dorothy Parkes Centre Smethick, Kidderminster Disabled Club and Primrose Hospice (£6,000 each).

FINANCES *Year* 2016 *Income* £1,565,000 *Grants* £674,000 *Grants to organisations* £674,000 *Assets* £53,152,000

TRUSTEES Stephen Preedy; Ronald Middleton; Geoffrey Thomas; Peter Millward; Dawn Long; Amanda McGeever.

OTHER INFORMATION Grants were made to 196 organisations during the year. 69% of grants were made in four main areas: disability and health (27%); hospices (14%); children and youth (14%); community support work (14%).
HOW TO APPLY Contact the administrator for grant appeal guidelines and an application form.
WHO TO APPLY TO Tim Patrickson, Administrator, Arley House, Lion Lane, Upper Arley, Bewdley, Worcestershire DY12 1SQ *Tel.* 01386 792014 *Email* tim@turnercharitabletrust.co.uk

■ The Florence Turner Trust

CC NO 502721 **ESTABLISHED** 1973
WHERE FUNDING CAN BE GIVEN UK, but with a strong preference for Leicestershire and Northamptonshire.
WHO CAN BENEFIT Smaller projects are favoured where donations will make a 'quantifiable difference to the recipients rather than favouring large national charities whose income is measured in millions rather than thousands.' Grants are made for the benefit of individuals through a referring agency such as social services, NHS trusts or similar responsible bodies.
WHAT IS FUNDED The trust gives to general charitable purposes. Smaller projects are favoured where donations will make a 'quantifiable difference' to individuals.
SAMPLE GRANTS Leicester Charity Link (£12,000); Leicester Grammar School – Bursary (£10,000); Age Concern Leicester, Leicester and Leicestershire Historic Churches Preservation Trust and VISTA (£2,400 each); LOROS (£2,000); New Parks Club for Young People (£1,500); Four Twelve Ministries and Help for Heroes (£1,000 each).
FINANCES *Year* 2015/16 *Income* £230,826 *Grants* £142,316 *Grants to organisations* £142,316 *Assets* £6,238,972
TRUSTEES Roger Bowder; Katherine Hall; Michael Jones.
HOW TO APPLY Apply in writing to the correspondent. The trustees meet on a bi-monthly basis.
WHO TO APPLY TO Emily Izzo, Shakespeare Martineau, Two Colton Square, Leicester LE1 1 QH *Tel.* 0116 257 6136 *Email* emily.izzo@shma.co.uk

■ The G. J. W. Turner Trust

CC NO 258615 **ESTABLISHED** 1969
WHERE FUNDING CAN BE GIVEN Birmingham and the Midlands area.
WHO CAN BENEFIT Charitable organisations.
WHAT IS FUNDED General charitable purposes.
SAMPLE GRANTS Birmingham St Mary's Hospice (£40,000); Birmingham Rathbone Society (£30,000); Victoria School (£15,000); The Diabetic Foot Trust Fund (£10,000); Barnardo's, Birmingham Hippodrome and Queen Alexandra College (£5,000 each); Saltley Neighbourhood Pensioner's Centre (£3,000); St Margaret's Church Short Heath (£2,000) and The National Children's Orchestra of Great Britain (£1,000).
FINANCES *Year* 2015/16 *Income* £305,878 *Grants* £315,000 *Grants to organisations* £315,000 *Assets* £10,143,701
TRUSTEES David Pearson; Hugh Carslake; Kate Honeyborne.
HOW TO APPLY Apply in writing to the correspondent.
WHO TO APPLY TO Chrissy Norgrove, c/o SGH Martineau LLP, 1 Colmore Square, Birmingham B4 6AA *Tel.* 0870 763 1000

■ The Turtleton Charitable Trust

SC NO SC038018 **ESTABLISHED** 2007
WHERE FUNDING CAN BE GIVEN Scotland.
WHO CAN BENEFIT Registered charities.
WHAT IS FUNDED Arts, culture and heritage. A few grants are also made each year to charities for the purposes of education and supporting people who are disadvantaged.
WHAT IS NOT FUNDED Individuals.
TYPE OF GRANT Usually one-off; multi-year commitments may be considered.
RANGE OF GRANTS Mainly between £5,000 and £25,000.
SAMPLE GRANTS Art in Healthcare (£25,000); The Archie Foundation (£15,000); Cambo Heritage Trust, National Youth Choir of Scotland and The Yard Adventure Centre (£10,000 each); Calibre Audio Library, Edinburgh International Book Festival and Peter Pan Moat Brae Trust (£5,000 each); Contemporary Dance Trust – The Place (£4,000); Edinburgh International Festival (£1,200).
FINANCES *Year* 2015/16 *Income* £169,524 *Grants* £190,320 *Grants to organisations* £190,320 *Assets* £5,327,002
OTHER INFORMATION Grants were made to 24 organisations during 2015/16.
HOW TO APPLY Grants should be made via the application form on the trust's website, and should comprise no more than three sides of A4. Applications may also be sent by post if necessary and should be marked for the attention of Kenneth Pinkerton. First time applicants should also enclose a copy of their most recent set of accounts. Additional material (e.g. DVDs, other literature) should not be included will not be passed on to the trustees. The trustees meet once a year, in spring, and applications should be submitted before 31 January. Grants are normally paid before 30 June. Applications are not acknowledged upon receipt, but successful applicants will be contacted after the meeting, and the website will display when the trustees have met.
WHO TO APPLY TO Kenneth Pinkerton, Turcan Connell, Princes Exchange, 1 Earl Grey Street, Edinburgh EH3 9EE *Tel.* 0131 228 8111 *Website* www.turcanconnell.com/turtleton

■ TVML Foundation

CC NO 1135495 **ESTABLISHED** 2010
WHERE FUNDING CAN BE GIVEN UK, USA, Brazil and Israel.
WHO CAN BENEFIT Charitable organisations; individuals.
WHAT IS FUNDED General charitable purposes, particularly education and training and social welfare, as well as children and young people.
WHAT IS NOT FUNDED Political causes.
RANGE OF GRANTS Typically less than £70,000.
SAMPLE GRANTS Massachusetts Institute of Technology, USA (£833,860); Congregação Israelita Paulista Brazil (£70,500); Conib Brazil (£66,500); Sou da Paz Brazil (£65,600); Birthright Israel International (£52,000).
FINANCES *Year* 2015 *Income* £320,379 *Grants* £1,271,073 *Grants to organisations* £1,271,073 *Assets* £4,780,270
TRUSTEES Vivian Lederman; Marcos Lederman; Marcelo Steuer.
OTHER INFORMATION Grants were made to 17 organisations with grants under £50,000 totalling £183,000.
HOW TO APPLY Apply in writing to the correspondent.

WHO TO APPLY TO Dr Tania Lima, Company Secretary, 8 Sand Ridge, Ridgewood, Uckfield, East Sussex TN22 5ET

■ Two Ridings Community Foundation

CC NO 1084043 **ESTABLISHED** 2000

WHERE FUNDING CAN BE GIVEN North and East Yorkshire, York and Hull.

WHO CAN BENEFIT Charitable organisations and community groups. The foundation focuses mainly on smaller organisations, with an income of less than £500,000 (larger organisations should contact the foundation before applying).

WHAT IS FUNDED The foundation manages a number of grants programmes. Its website states: 'We encourage applications for activities that: support particularly disadvantaged and marginalised communities; tackle challenging issues; encourage inclusive community activity and participation; respond to their communities' needs; engage people who face discrimination or disadvantage; produce a wide range of benefits and provide good value for money.' Grant schemes change frequently. Consult the foundation's website for details of current programmes.

WHAT IS NOT FUNDED Each of the foundation's funding programmes has specific criteria which can be found on the website. In general, grants are not given to: private businesses; general appeals or sponsorship; national organisations and their affiliates (this does not include locally constituted and managed branches of national or large charities); statutory agencies, including parish councils and schools, in the discharge of their statutory obligations; organisations that have substantial unrestricted funds; previous grant recipients who have outstanding monitoring information; organisations that mainly give funds to other organisations or individuals. Grants are not given for: advancement of religion; activities solely benefitting animals; overseas holidays or trips; political campaigning; medical research, equipment or treatment; work normally undertaken or funded by statutory bodies; retrospective funding.

TYPE OF GRANT See individual grant programmes.

RANGE OF GRANTS Mainly £250 to £10,000. Average grant in 2014/15 was £1,700.

SAMPLE GRANTS Bridges Hull (£5,700); Make It Happen Mentoring (£4,100); Sight Support Ryedale (£3,500); Samaritans of Kingston upon Hull (£3,000); Eastrington Players and York Down's Syndrome Parents' Group (£2,700 each); Airmyn Parochial Church Council (£2,600); Ousefleet Village Hall (£1,500); Interactive Whitby and District (£580); Darley Christ Church Lunch Club (£350).

FINANCES *Year* 2014/15 *Income* £433,302 *Grants* £146,542 *Grants to organisations* £143,470 *Assets* £2,735,101

TRUSTEES Joe Leigh; Hannah Purkis; Tracey Smith; Alison Pearson; Harriet Reid; Marie Johnstone; Paul Downey; Andrew Wilson.

OTHER INFORMATION The 2014/15 accounts were the most recent available on the Charity Commission's website at the time of writing (June 2017). Grants were made to 76 organisations during the year. There were also six grants to individuals which totalled £3,100.

HOW TO APPLY Application forms for each of the grant programmes can be found on the foundation's website, along with eligibility criteria and guidance notes. For support with the application process, contact the grants team (01904 435277 or grants@trcf.org.uk).

WHO TO APPLY TO Grants Team, Suite 1.34 Innovation Centre, York Science Park, Innovation Way, York YO10 5DG *Tel.* 01904 435277 *Email* office@trcf.org.uk *Website* www.trcf.org.uk

■ Community Foundation serving Tyne and Wear and Northumberland

CC NO 700510 **ESTABLISHED** 1988

WHERE FUNDING CAN BE GIVEN Tyne and Wear and Northumberland.

WHO CAN BENEFIT Charitable organisations. The foundation is particularly keen to help grassroots community groups and small-to-medium-sized voluntary organisations.

WHAT IS FUNDED The foundation has a range of different grants programmes, which change frequently – refer to the website for information on grants currently available. In general, the foundation's grants programmes fall under three broad themes: supporting people to overcome disadvantage; creating stronger communities; making the area a good place to live.

WHAT IS NOT FUNDED Grants are not usually given to support: contributions to general appeals or circulars; religious activity which is not for wider public benefit; public bodies to carry out their statutory obligations; activities which solely support animal welfare; activities which have already taken place; grant-making by other organisations; privately owned and profit-distributing companies or limited partnerships. Grants are not usually made to large UK-wide charities, unless it has strong relationships in the local area and a proposal could achieve substantial local impact.

TYPE OF GRANT Running costs or core costs (including salaries; projects; equipment or capital developments; new work, continuing work or one-off work.

RANGE OF GRANTS Usually up to £5,000.

SAMPLE GRANTS Impact Family Services (£40,000); West End Refugee Service (£35,000); Byker Aspire (£5,000); Gateshead Storm Community Rugby League Club (£4,400); Throckley Community Hall Ltd (£3,000); Carers Association in South Tyneside (£2,000); Let's Get Growing (£940); Whitley Bay and District Scout Council (£700); Northumberland Wildlife Trust (£100); Blues and Royals Association (£20).

FINANCES *Year* 2015/16 *Income* £12,178,794 *Grants* £7,226,396 *Grants to organisations* £7,220,502 *Assets* £72,854,908

TRUSTEES Lucy Winskell; Anna Blackett; Alastair Conn; Jo Curry; Prof. Charles Harvey; Jane Robinson; Fiona Cruickshank; Patrick Melia; Nick Hall; Geoffrey Hodgson; Sally Young; Sharon Spurling; Neil Warwick; Andrew Haigh.

OTHER INFORMATION In total, 1,417 grants were awarded by the foundation in 2015/16, including those from programmes run in partnership with other funders. Of these, 1,279 were awarded to organisations and 138 were awarded to individuals. The amount of grants given to individuals totalled £74,000.

HOW TO APPLY There is one application form for the general Community Foundation grants and generally, separate forms or processes for the other rolling grants programmes and one-off funds. Funds that support individuals are advertised separately. All of these plus application guidelines are available on the website. Some of the programmes have deadlines and some do not; also, programmes change regularly so the trust's website should be checked for the most recent information.

WHO TO APPLY TO Programmes Team, Philanthropy House, Woodbine Road, Newcastle upon Tyne NE3 1DD *Tel.* 0191 222 0945 *Fax* 0191 284 8413 *Email* general@communityfoundation.org.uk *Website* www.communityfoundation.org.uk

■ Tzedakah

CC NO 251897 **ESTABLISHED** 1966

WHERE FUNDING CAN BE GIVEN Worldwide, mainly UK and Israel.

WHO CAN BENEFIT Charitable organisations.

WHAT IS FUNDED Jewish causes; education and training; relief of poverty.

SAMPLE GRANTS Hasmonean High School Charitable Trust; Gertner Charitable Trust; Society of Friends of the Torah; Hendon Adath Yisroel Synagogue; Medrash Shmuel Theological College; Torah Temimoh; Willow Foundation; Tiferes Girls School; Sage Home for the Aged; Wizo; Torah Movement of Great Britain.

FINANCES *Year* 2015/16 *Income* £299,711 *Grants* £277,539 *Grants to organisations* £277,539 *Assets* £287,092

TRUSTEES Leonard Finn; Michael Lebrett.

OTHER INFORMATION The annual report states that grants were made to over 300 charities during the year. A list of recent beneficiaries was not included in the accounts.

HOW TO APPLY Apply in writing to the correspondent.

WHO TO APPLY TO Michael Lebrett, Trustee, Brentmead House, Britannia Road, London N12 9RU *Tel.* 020 8446 6767 *Email* lfinnco@aol.com

■ The Udlington Trust

CC NO 1129443 **ESTABLISHED** 2009

WHERE FUNDING CAN BE GIVEN UK and overseas.

WHO CAN BENEFIT Registered charities.

WHAT IS FUNDED General charitable purposes.

SAMPLE GRANTS A list of beneficiaries was not available.

FINANCES *Year* 2015 *Income* £0 *Grants* £84,000 *Grants to organisations* £84,000

TRUSTEES Bruce Blackledge; Richard Blackledge; Robert Blackledge; Rebecca Blackledge.

OTHER INFORMATION This trust's latest accounts were not available to view on the Charity Commission's website due to its low income. We have therefore estimated the grant total based on previous years' information.

HOW TO APPLY Apply in writing to the correspondent.

WHO TO APPLY TO Richard Blackledge, Trustee, c/o Arrow County Supplies, Arrow House, Longden Road, Shrewsbury SY3 9AE *Tel.* 01743 283600 *Email* richard@arrowcounty.com

■ UKH Foundation

CC NO 1160507 **ESTABLISHED** 2014

WHERE FUNDING CAN BE GIVEN UK, primarily Bolton and the North West.

WHO CAN BENEFIT Registered charities.

WHAT IS FUNDED Health; children and young people; older people; disability.

TYPE OF GRANT Unrestricted.

RANGE OF GRANTS £150 to £10,000.

SAMPLE GRANTS David Lewis Centre (£10,000); Blind Veteran's UK, Bolton Young Persons Housing Scheme, Kids Cancer Charity and Winston's Wish (£5,000 each); Juvenile Diabetes Research Fund, Whizz-Kidz (£2,500); Bolton Lads and Girls (£600); Bolton District Referees Society (£200); Stroke Association (£150).

FINANCES *Year* 2015 *Income* £6,167,765 *Grants* £170,639 *Grants to organisations* £170,639 *Assets* £2,810,116

TRUSTEES Stephen Pugh; Andrew Redfern; David Udall; Julie Hulme; Stephen Bell.

OTHER INFORMATION Grants were made to 60 organisations during the year.

HOW TO APPLY An application is available to download from the website. It should be returned via email to charitycommittee@hospital-saturday.org.uk or printed off and returned to the correspondent.

WHO TO APPLY TO Stephen Pugh, Trustee, Regent House, Folds Point, Folds Road, Bolton BL1 2RZ *Tel.* 01204 522775 *Email* charity@ukhealth care.org.uk *Website* www.ukhealth care.org.uk/charitable-donations

■ Ulster Garden Villages Ltd

CC NO 101248 **ESTABLISHED** 1946

WHERE FUNDING CAN BE GIVEN Northern Ireland.

WHO CAN BENEFIT Registered charities.

WHAT IS FUNDED The main purposes for which funds are distributed are: health; disadvantaged sections of society; young people; culture and heritage; and environment. The website states that the charity prefers to fund projects that demonstrate active participation and self-help and work which is 'innovative and developmental, with an achievable, practical, sustainable objective'.

WHAT IS NOT FUNDED Retrospective applications; activities which are the responsibility of central or local government or any statutory body; direct replacement of statutory funding; individuals; organisations that are not charitable and with public benefit; sponsorship or marketing appeals; promotion of religion; expeditions or overseas travel; charities collecting funds to distribute to other charities. The charity does not usually fund office expenses or administrative staff salaries. Applications from umbrella organisations representing the community and voluntary sector are a low priority, as these are considered to be well supported.

TYPE OF GRANT Grants for specific projects; loans.

RANGE OF GRANTS Our research indicates that grants are usually in the region of £1,000 to £5,000, although larger grants may be considered.

SAMPLE GRANTS Royal Victoria Hospital – Institute of Vision Science; Belfast City Hospital – the Garden Village Suite; the Northern Ireland Children's Hospice; QUB Foundation Great Hall; Belmont Tower; the Lyric Theatre, Camphill Communities in Northern Ireland; Croft Community; Disability Sport NI; Clifton Nursing Home; Habitat for Humanity Northern Ireland; the Scout Association; Ulster Waterways Group; Rams Island.

FINANCES *Grants to organisations* £1,000,000

TRUSTEES Martie Boyd; Sir Desmond Lorimer; W. A. Crawford; Erskine Holmes; Kevin Baird; Dr Anthony Hopkins; Susan Crowe; Brian Garrett; William Webb.

OTHER INFORMATION No current financial information was available. Our research indicates that grants have previously totalled around £1 million.

HOW TO APPLY Applications must be made using the society's application form. Forms are available to download from the website – where guidelines can also be found – and should be posted or delivered to the office. Applications for amounts exceeding £50,000 require more detail with regards to project rationale, economic appraisal and building proposals, if applicable, should be included. Your organisation's most recent annual report and audited accounts should also be provided, along with evidence of charitable status. The office is normally attended on Tuesday, Wednesday and Thursday between 9am and 1pm.

WHO TO APPLY TO The Administration Officer, Forestview, Purdys Lane, Newtownbreda, Belfast BT8 7AR *Tel.* 028 9049 1111 *Fax* 028 9049 1007 *Email* admin@ulstergardenvillages.co.uk *Website* www.ulstergardenvillages.co.uk

■ Ulting Overseas Trust

CC NO 294397 **ESTABLISHED** 1986

WHERE FUNDING CAN BE GIVEN Some UK, mainly overseas (mostly, but not exclusively, Asia, Africa and South and Central America).

WHO CAN BENEFIT Christian training organisations; individuals.

WHAT IS FUNDED Christian theological training institutions or organisations with a training focus, for those who wish to train for the Christian ministry, or for those who wish to improve their ministry skills. It gives priority to the training of students in their home countries or continents.

WHAT IS NOT FUNDED Capital projects such as buildings or library stock; training in subjects other than Biblical, theological and missionary studies.

TYPE OF GRANT Bursaries and training costs.

RANGE OF GRANTS Up to £15,000.

SAMPLE GRANTS International Fellowship of Evangelical Students (£16,000); Langham Scholarships (£13,000); Oxford Centre for Mission Studies (£7,000); Pan African Christian College (£5,700); Asian Theological Seminary (£5,000); Latin Link (£4,700); Kirby Laing Institute of Christian Ethics (£1,600); Operation Mobilisation (£1,300); Kathmandu Institute of Theology (£1,100); Open Russian Theological Academy (£800).

FINANCES *Year* 2015/16 *Income* £89,495 *Grants* £116,150 *Grants to organisations* £110,150 *Assets* £3,959,845

TRUSTEES Tim Warren; John Heyward; Revd Joseph Kapolyo; Nicholas Durlacher; Roger Pearce; Jennifer Brown; Dr Carol Walker; John Whitfield.

OTHER INFORMATION Grants were made to 30 organisations during the year. There were also three grants to individuals, which amounted to £6,000.

HOW TO APPLY Apply in writing to the correspondent. Trustees examine each application against strict criteria. Grants are reviewed and awarded on an annual basis.

WHO TO APPLY TO Timothy Warren, Pothecary, Witham Weld, 70 St George's Square, London SW1V 3RD *Tel.* 020 7821 8211

■ The Ulverscroft Foundation

CC NO 264873 **ESTABLISHED** 1972

WHERE FUNDING CAN BE GIVEN Worldwide.

WHO CAN BENEFIT Recognised organisations helping people who are visually impaired e.g. libraries, hospitals, clinics, schools, colleges and social and welfare organisations.

WHAT IS FUNDED Projects which will have a positive effect on the quality of life of people who have visual impairments (people who are blind or partially sighted) or people who have a print disability.

WHAT IS NOT FUNDED Core costs or running costs; salaries, unless for a specific project; organisations that have already received a grant within the previous 18 months. Grants are rarely made to individuals.

TYPE OF GRANT Project costs; research.

SAMPLE GRANTS University of Leicester (£351,500); World Medical Education CIC (£16,000); Deafblind UK (£7,500); Calibre and Age International (£5,000 each); Vista (£4,500); Extant (£3,000); British Blind Support and Intercare (£2,000 each); York Blind and Partially Sighted Society (£1,000).

FINANCES *Year* 2014/15 *Income* £11,598,477 *Grants* £466,966 *Grants to organisations* £466,966 *Assets* £22,750,965

TRUSTEES John Sanford-Smith; Roger Crooks; Robert Gent; Pat Beech; John Bush; Rupert Clarke.

OTHER INFORMATION The foundation controls a trading subsidiary which republishes books in a form accessible by people with partial sight. The 2014/15 accounts were the latest available at the time of writing (June 2017).

HOW TO APPLY Applications should be made in writing to the correspondent and be as detailed as possible. Details should include those of any current services your organisation provides for visually impaired people, if any, and how your proposed project will be integrated or enhanced. If possible, an estimate of the number of people who use/will use your service should be provided, as well as information of any funding that has already been obtained and the names of other organisations to which you have applied. Organisations are also asked to submit a copy of their latest annual report and accounts. The trustees meet quarterly to consider applications, in January, April, July and October and deadlines for submissions fall on the 15th day of the previous month.

WHO TO APPLY TO Joyce Sumner, The Green, Bradgate Road, Anstey, Leicester LE7 7FU *Tel.* 0116 236 1595 *Fax* 0116 236 1594 *Email* foundation@ulverscroft.co.uk *Website* www.foundation.ulverscroft.com

■ The Underwood Trust

CC NO 266164 **ESTABLISHED** 1973

WHERE FUNDING CAN BE GIVEN UK, particularly Scotland and Wiltshire.

WHO CAN BENEFIT Charitable organisations.

WHAT IS FUNDED Medicine and health; social welfare; education; the arts; environment and wildlife.

WHAT IS NOT FUNDED Individuals; political activities; commercial ventures or publications; the purchase of vehicles including minibuses; overseas travel, holidays or expeditions; organisations that have had an application declined within the last 12 months.

SAMPLE GRANTS Greenpeace (£620,500 in two grants); Restorative Solutions PCCs (£239,500); Julia's House Wiltshire Children's Hospice (£1 million); Prisoners Abroad (£75,000); Campaign to Protect Rural England (£41,500); Stage One (£30,000); Living Paintings Trust and The Maytree Respite Centre (£16,500 each); The British Stammering Association (£16,500); Windmill Hill City Farm (£1,500).

FINANCES *Year* 2015/16 *Income* £293,000 *Grants* £1,531,684 *Grants to organisations* £1,531,684 *Assets* £21,857,336

TRUSTEES Robin Clark; Briony Wilson; Reg Harvey; Richard Bennison.

OTHER INFORMATION The trust made 28 grants during the year.

HOW TO APPLY The trust is unable to accept unsolicited applications. All available funds are allocated proactively by the trustees and organisations must not make an application unless invited to do so. Note that the trust is unable to deal with telephone or email enquiries regarding applications.

WHO TO APPLY TO Michele Judge, Manager, 4th Floor South, 35 Portman Square, London W1H 6LR *Email* michelej@taylorclark.co.uk *Website* www.theunderwoodtrust.org.uk

■ The Union of Orthodox Hebrew Congregations

CC NO 249892 **ESTABLISHED** 1966

WHERE FUNDING CAN BE GIVEN UK.

WHO CAN BENEFIT Charitable organisations; individuals.

WHAT IS FUNDED Orthodox Jewish causes.

SAMPLE GRANTS National Council of Shechita Boards of Great Britain; TAG.

FINANCES *Year* 2015 *Income* £1,631,370 *Grants* £712,219 *Grants to organisations* £664,219 *Assets* £1,990,157

TRUSTEES Rabbi Abraham Pinter; Benzion Freshwater; Chaim Konig.
OTHER INFORMATION Grants to individuals during the year totalled £48,000, and were mainly given to 'needy families to help with expenditure at Jewish Festivals', according to the 2015 accounts.
HOW TO APPLY Apply in writing to the correspondent.
WHO TO APPLY TO Mr D. Passey, Landau Morley, York House, Empire Way, Wembley HA9 0FQ *Tel.* 020 8903 5122

■ United Utilities Trust Fund

CC NO 1108296 **ESTABLISHED** 2005
WHERE FUNDING CAN BE GIVEN The area supplied by United Utilities Water PLC (predominantly the north west of England).
WHO CAN BENEFIT Mainly individuals, but also organisations.
WHAT IS FUNDED Relief of poverty; money advice; debt counselling; financial literacy.
WHAT IS NOT FUNDED Existing projects; charities which appear to the fund to have sufficient unrestricted or free reserves, or are in serious deficit; projects outside the specified geographical area; national charities that do not have the facility to accept the funding on a regional basis; grant-making bodies seeking to distribute grants on the fund's behalf; general appeals, sponsorship and marketing appeals; replacement of existing programmes or statutory funding.
SAMPLE GRANTS Centre 63 (£37,000); South Liverpool Citizens Advice (£32,500); Cheetham Hill Advice Centre (£31,000); Local Solutions (£30,000); Blackpool Citizens Advice (£29,500); Age UK South Lakeland and Salford Foundation (£15,600 each); Lan Comm Finance Trust (£1,500).
FINANCES *Year* 2015/16 *Income* £6,212,655 *Grants* £287,240 *Grants to organisations* £287,240 *Assets* £748,735
TRUSTEES Deborah Moreton; Alastair Richards; Simon Dewsnip; Allan Mackie; Kevin Appleton.
OTHER INFORMATION The amount of grants given to individuals totalled £5.3 million in 2015/16. Grants were made to 11 organisations during the year.
HOW TO APPLY At the time of writing (May 2017) the trust was closed to applications from organisations – check the trust's website for current information.
WHO TO APPLY TO Gay Hammett, Emmanuel Court, 12–14 Mill Street, Sutton Coldfield B72 1TJ *Tel.* 0121 362 3625 *Email* communitygrants@aurigaservices.co.uk *Website* www.uutf.org.uk

■ UnLtd (Foundation for Social Entrepreneurs)

CC NO 1090393 **ESTABLISHED** 2001
WHERE FUNDING CAN BE GIVEN UK.
WHO CAN BENEFIT Social entrepreneurs and those looking to start a social enterprise project. To be eligible, individuals must be: over the age of 16; resident in the UK; applying as an individual or informal group.
WHAT IS FUNDED Support for social entrepreneurs to start up, grow or develop a social enterprise initiative. Projects must: benefit the public or a community in the UK; require an UnLtd award to be successful; offer a learning opportunity for applicants; be a new initiative. There are a number of different award schemes with different criteria – refer to the website for information on what is currently available.
TYPE OF GRANT Award winners receive a complete, tailored package of funding, training and advice at for their project.
SAMPLE GRANTS A list of beneficiaries was not available.
FINANCES *Year* 2015/16 *Income* £6,069,638 *Assets* £129,335,015
TRUSTEES Dr Judith McNeill; Rajeeb Dey; Norman Cumming; Richard Tyrie; Martin Wyn Griffith; Natalie Campbell; Susan Charteris; Loic Menzies; Ruth Dobson; Nicolas Farhi; Mary Pollard; Nicholas Petford.
OTHER INFORMATION UnLtd is unique here in that it exists to make grants to individuals to undertake social initiatives. In effect it makes grants for the start-up costs of new organisations and community groups to enterprising individuals who need support to implement their ideas and projects for improving their communities. In 2015/16 support for social entrepreneurs comprised of: £3.8 million in grants; £4.3 million in direct costs; £2.3 million in support costs. This includes UnLtd Scotland, which is a subsidiary of UnLtd.
HOW TO APPLY Refer to the UnLtd website to find the relevant scheme for your initiative and complete an expression of interest form. Deadlines, eligibility criteria and further guidance are given on the website for each award scheme. The website states: '**Note:** We are only able to fund a limited amount of Awards per year. This means the application process is extremely competitive and we are not able to provide individual feedback to applicants who do not pass the initial assessment stage.'
WHO TO APPLY TO Mark Norbury, Chief Executive, 123 Whitecross Street, Islington, London EC1Y 8JJ *Tel.* 020 7566 1100 *Email* info@unltd.org.uk *Website* www.unltd.org.uk

■ The Michael Uren Foundation

CC NO 1094102 **ESTABLISHED** 2002
WHERE FUNDING CAN BE GIVEN UK and overseas.
WHO CAN BENEFIT Registered charities.
WHAT IS FUNDED General charitable purposes, particularly: armed forces; medical research and medical facilities; animal welfare; education; historic buildings. The foundation's restricted fund is designated for grants towards the relief of the blind and for education.
TYPE OF GRANT Mainly large project grants.
SAMPLE GRANTS Imperial College Trust (£4.56 million); Moorfields Eye Hospital (£600,000); Cool Earth (£300,000); Chatham Historic Dockyard Trust (£200,000); International Animal Rescue (£300,000); Marine Society and Sea Cadets (£50,000); Kent Wildlife Trust (£30,000); Victoria Cross and George Cross Benevolent Fund (£20,000); Selby Abbey Organ Appeal (£10,000).
FINANCES *Year* 2015/16 *Income* £7,721,847 *Grants* £5,840,000 *Grants to organisations* £5,840,000 *Assets* £54,494,396
TRUSTEES John Uren; Roger Gould; David Uren; Anne Gregory-Jones; Janis Bennett; Robert Uren.
OTHER INFORMATION Grants were made to 16 organisations in 2015/16. No grants were made from the restricted fund.
HOW TO APPLY Apply in writing to the correspondent.
WHO TO APPLY TO Mark Pattenden, Haysmacintyre, 26 Red Lion Square, London WC1R 4AG *Email* mpattenden@haysmacintyre.com

The David Uri Memorial Trust

CC NO 327810 **ESTABLISHED** 1988
WHERE FUNDING CAN BE GIVEN Worldwide.
WHO CAN BENEFIT Charitable organisations.
WHAT IS FUNDED General charitable purposes, particularly: Jewish causes; social welfare; education.
WHAT IS NOT FUNDED Individuals.
SAMPLE GRANTS National Jewish Chaplaincy Board, Age Concern, Crisis at Christmas, Jefferies Research Wing Trust, NSPCC and Yakar Education Foundation.
FINANCES *Year* 2015/16 *Income* £843,229 *Grants* £73,975 *Grants to organisations* £73,975 *Assets* £3,675,555
TRUSTEES Benjamin Blackman; Bianca Roden; Sandra Blackman.
HOW TO APPLY Apply in writing to the correspondent.
WHO TO APPLY TO The Trustees, 244 Vauxhall Bridge Road, London SW1V 1AU *Email* dumt@duvt.com

The Utley Family Charitable Trust

CC NO 1157399 **ESTABLISHED** 2014
WHERE FUNDING CAN BE GIVEN UK and overseas.
WHO CAN BENEFIT Charitable organisations; individuals.
WHAT IS FUNDED Children and young people; health; helping people with dementia through music; education; general charitable purposes.
RANGE OF GRANTS £50 to £120,000.
SAMPLE GRANTS Caudwell Children (£120,000); The On Course Foundation (£75,000); Medic Assist International (£40,000); Great Ormond Street Hospital (£10,000); War Child (£6,600); World Food Programme (£3,000); Sands (£1,000); Magic Breakfast (£500); Cystic Fibrosis Trust (£250); Pancreatic Cancer UK (£50).
FINANCES *Year* 2015/16 *Income* £5,019,039 *Grants* £380,307 *Grants to organisations* £380,307 *Assets* £15,054,675
TRUSTEES Raja Balasuriya; Melvyn Sims; Nicky Utley; Neil Utley.
OTHER INFORMATION Grants were made to 43 organisations in 2015/16.
HOW TO APPLY Apply in writing to the correspondent.
WHO TO APPLY TO The Trustees, c/o Rawlinson and Hunter, 6 New Street Square, London EC4A 3AQ *Tel.* 020 7842 2000

■ The Vail Foundation

CC NO 1089579 **ESTABLISHED** 2001

WHERE FUNDING CAN BE GIVEN UK and overseas.

WHO CAN BENEFIT Registered charities.

WHAT IS FUNDED General charitable purposes; there appears to be some preference for Jewish causes.

RANGE OF GRANTS Up to £100,000.

SAMPLE GRANTS London School of Jewish Studies (£100,000 in three grants); Community Security Trust (£85,000 in two grants); United Jewish Israel Appeal (UJIA) (£80,000 in three grants); JW3 Trust Ltd (£25,000); Chai Lifeline Cancer Care (£10,000); Chicken Soup Shelter (£5,000); Anne Frank Trust UK (£4,000); Mental Health Foundation (£2,500); Institute of Higher Rabbinical Studies (£1,500); Langdon Foundation (£1,000).

FINANCES *Year* 2015/16 *Income* £631,077 *Grants* £1,122,000 *Grants to organisations* £1,122,000 *Assets* £5,410,416

TRUSTEES Michael Bradfield; Paul Brett; Michael Goldstein.

OTHER INFORMATION Grants were awarded to 20 organisations in 2015/16.

HOW TO APPLY Apply in writing to the correspondent. 'The trustees consider all requests which they receive and make such donations as they feel appropriate.'

WHO TO APPLY TO Michael Bradfield, Trustee, 5 Fitzhardinge Street, London W1H 6ED *Tel.* 020 7317 3000 *Email* mai.brown@blickrothenberg.com

■ Vale of Glamorgan Welsh Church Fund

CC NO 506628 **ESTABLISHED** 1996

WHERE FUNDING CAN BE GIVEN Vale of Glamorgan and City and County of Cardiff council areas.

WHO CAN BENEFIT Churches; registered charities; community organisations.

WHAT IS FUNDED Restoration of churches and memorials; community groups and buildings.

WHAT IS NOT FUNDED Individuals.

TYPE OF GRANT One-off; building and equipment costs.

RANGE OF GRANTS £400 to £5,000.

SAMPLE GRANTS Saron Chapel – Treoes (£5,000); Valeways Ltd (£3,000); St Mary the Virgin Church Cardiff (£2,000 each); Elfed Avenue United Church and South Wales Methodist Church (£1,500 each); Bethel English Baptist Church (£1,000); Llandow Village Hall (£500); Parochial Church Council of the Parish of Marthyr Dyfan (£400).

FINANCES *Year* 2015/16 *Income* £30,000 *Grants* £42,900 *Grants to organisations* £42,900 *Assets* £4,803,000

TRUSTEE The Vale of Glamorgan County Borough Council.

OTHER INFORMATION Although the majority of grants are made to churches, grants can also be made for general charitable purposes, especially community projects.

HOW TO APPLY Contact the correspondent for further information about the application process. Applications are accepted throughout the year and meetings of the trustees convened to consider applications as and when required. The fund is administered by the Vale of Glamorgan Council, but Cardiff-based applicants need the support of the City of Cardiff Council to be put forward. For further details on the fund and the eligibility criteria contact Robert Giddings at voluntarysectorgrants@cardiff.gov.uk or on 029 2053 7484.

WHO TO APPLY TO Miss G. H. Jones, Vale of Glamorgan County Borough Council, Accountancy Section, Civic Offices, Holton Road, Barry, Vale of Glamorgan, CF634RU *Tel.* 01446 709152 *Email* ghjones@valeofglamorgan.gov.uk *Website* www.valeofglamorgan.gov.uk/en/working/Community-Grants.aspx

■ The Valentine Charitable Trust

CC NO 1001782 **ESTABLISHED** 1990

WHERE FUNDING CAN BE GIVEN Unrestricted, but with a focus on Dorset.

WHO CAN BENEFIT Registered charities.

WHAT IS FUNDED General charitable purposes, including environment; medical research and health; social welfare.

WHAT IS NOT FUNDED Individuals. The trust would not normally fund appeals for village halls or the fabric of church buildings.

TYPE OF GRANT One-off appeals; recurrent grants; core costs; capital costs; matched funding; loan finance.

RANGE OF GRANTS Up to £20,000.

SAMPLE GRANTS Colehill and Wimborne Youth and Community Centre (£20,000); Bournemouth Symphony Orchestra (£15,000); Dorset Youth Association (£10,000); Dorset ME Support Group (£8,000); Jubilee Sailing Trust, Prisoner's Abroad and Sports Forum for the Disabled (£5,000 each); Alcohol Concern (£3,000); Butterfly Conservation and Purbeck Art Weeks Festival (£1,000 each).

FINANCES *Year* 2014/15 *Income* £819,461 *Grants* £697,488 *Grants to organisations* £697,488 *Assets* £30,510,447

TRUSTEES Douglas Neville-Jones; Peter Leatherdale; Susan Patterson; Roger Gregory; Diana Tory; Wing Cdr Donald Jack; Susan Ridley.

HOW TO APPLY Apply in writing to the correspondent. Generally the trustees prefer to only consider applications from applicants with whom they have an established relationship, but they are occasionally able to make grants outside of this, particularly for local applicants. All applications will be acknowledged and decisions are made at quarterly trustees' meetings. The trust provides the following guidance about the application process in its annual report: 'The trustees look for value for money. While this concept is difficult to apply in a voluntary sector it can certainly be used on a comparative basis and subjectively. If the trustees have competing applications they will usually decide to support just one of them as they believe that to concentrate the charity's donations is more beneficial than to dilute them. Regular contact with the charities to which donations are made is considered essential. Reports and accounts are also requested from charities which are supported and the trustees consider those at their meetings. The trustees take great comfort from the fact that they employ the policy of only making donations to other charities or similar bodies. However they are not complacent about the need to review all donations made and the objects to which those have been given. The trustees are conscious that, particularly with the smaller and local charities, the community of those working for and with the charity is an important consideration. The trustees regularly review the classifications to which donations have been made so that they can obtain an overview of the charity's donations and assess whether their policies are being implemented in practice. They are conscious that when dealing with individual donations it is easy to lose sight of the overall picture.'

WHO TO APPLY TO The Trustees, Preston Redman, Hinton House, Hinton Road, Bournemouth BH1 2EN *Tel.* 01202 292424

■ The Valiant Charitable Trust

CC NO 1135810 **ESTABLISHED** 2010

WHERE FUNDING CAN BE GIVEN UK.

WHO CAN BENEFIT Registered charities; individuals.

WHAT IS FUNDED General charitable purposes.

TYPE OF GRANT Capital costs; project costs; unrestricted.

SAMPLE GRANTS Hitchin Rugby Club (£100,000); Preston Cricket Club (£25,000); The Prince's Trust (£20,000); Hertfordshire Multiple Sclerosis Therapy Centre (£18,700); Growing People (£10,000); Norman Hyde Trust Fund and The Hitchin Society (£5,000 each).

FINANCES *Year* 2015/16 *Income* £273,973 *Grants* £183,690 *Grants to organisations* £183,690 *Assets* £1,547,200

TRUSTEES Roger Woolfe; Lady Valarie Dixon; Paul Brenham.

OTHER INFORMATION Grants were made to seven organisations during the year.

HOW TO APPLY Apply in writing to the correspondent. The trustees meet annually to decide on grants for the year.

WHO TO APPLY TO Roger Woolfe, Trustee, Collyer Bristow Solicitors, 4 Bedford Row, London WC1R 4DF *Tel.* 020 7242 7363 *Email* roy.jordan@collyerbristow.com

■ The Albert Van Den Bergh Charitable Trust

CC NO 296885 **ESTABLISHED** 1987

WHERE FUNDING CAN BE GIVEN UK and overseas.

WHO CAN BENEFIT Charitable organisations.

WHAT IS FUNDED General charitable purposes, particularly medical research, health and disability, children and the care of older people. The 2015/16 accounts state that grants were distributed in the following categories: cultural charities; conservation; disadvantage; disability; help in the community; homelessness; hospices; medical research, care and support; overseas; people who have worked in the services; older people; churches; other charities.

SAMPLE GRANTS BLISS, Bishop of Guildford's Charity, British Heart Foundation, Counsel and Care for the Elderly, Leukaemia Research Trust, Multiple Sclerosis Society, Parentline Surrey, National Osteoporosis Society, RNID, Riding for the Disabled – Cranleigh Age Concern, SSAFA, St John Ambulance and United Charities Fund – Liberal Jewish Synagogue.

FINANCES *Year* 2015/16 *Income* £145,561 *Grants* £112,243 *Grants to organisations* £112,243 *Assets* £3,187,035

TRUSTEES Jane Hartley; Nicola Glover; Bruce Hopkins.

OTHER INFORMATION Grants were made to 63 organisations during 2015/16, although a list of recent beneficiaries was not provided.

HOW TO APPLY Apply in writing to the correspondent.

WHO TO APPLY TO Jane Hartley, Trustee, Trevornick Farmhouse, Holywell Bay, Newquay, Cornwall TR8 5PW *Email* trustees@albertvandenbergh.org

■ The Van Neste Foundation

CC NO 201951 **ESTABLISHED** 1959

WHERE FUNDING CAN BE GIVEN UK (especially the Bristol area) and overseas.

WHO CAN BENEFIT Registered charities.

WHAT IS FUNDED General charitable purposes, with a focus on: overseas aid; people with disabilities; older people; community projects; Christian causes.

WHAT IS NOT FUNDED Individuals; national appeals.

TYPE OF GRANT Usually one-off for a specific project or part of a project. Core funding is rarely considered.

SAMPLE GRANTS Clifton Cathedral (£100,000); CAFOD (Catholic Agency for Overseas Development) (£25,000); Crisis Centre Ministries (£15,000); Hartcliffe and Withywood Community Project (£10,000); Penny Brohn Cancer Centre (£6,000); MS Therapy Centre (£5,000); Apostleship of the Sea (£3,000); St Mary's Church – Bath (£2,000); Cardinal Hume Centre (£1,500); Friends of Mingnapor (£500).

FINANCES *Year* 2015/16 *Income* £323,112 *Grants* £336,400 *Grants to organisations* £336,400 *Assets* £8,248,228

TRUSTEES Martin Appleby; Fergus Lyons; Gerald Walker; Jeremy Lyons; Benedict Appleby; Tom Appleby; Joanna Dickens.

OTHER INFORMATION Grants were made to 34 organisations during 2015/16.

HOW TO APPLY Applications should be made in writing, in the form of a concise letter setting out: the objectives of the appeal; funding agreed from other sources; a timetable for achieving the planned objectives. Applications should be made by post and should include a copy of the latest audited accounts. The foundation will not deal with enquiries by email, telephone or fax. Applications are considered by the trustees in January, June and October. Unsuccessful applicants will not be notified, to keep administration costs down; successful applicants will be notified within two weeks of a meeting.

WHO TO APPLY TO Fergus Lyons, Secretary, 15 Alexandra Road, Clifton, Bristol BS8 2DD *Tel.* 0117 973 5167 *Email* fergus.lyons@virgin.net

■ Mrs Maud Van Norden's Charitable Foundation

CC NO 210844 **ESTABLISHED** 1962

WHERE FUNDING CAN BE GIVEN UK.

WHO CAN BENEFIT Registered UK charities only.

WHAT IS FUNDED General charitable purposes; armed forces; homelessness; medical research; people with disabilities; youth welfare and education; animal welfare.

WHAT IS NOT FUNDED Individuals; young children and infants; maintenance of buildings at a local level for example churches and village halls; wildlife and environmental conservation; religious charities.

TYPE OF GRANT One-off; project and research.

RANGE OF GRANTS £1,500 to £3,000.

SAMPLE GRANTS Combat Stress and Royal Hospital for Neuro-disability (£3,000 each); London Air Ambulance, Motor Neurone Disease Association and St Christopher's Hospice (£2,000 each); Action on Elder Abuse, Disasters Emergency Committee – Nepal Earthquake Appeal, Home Warmth for the Aged, Humane Slaughter Association, Police Community Clubs of Great Britain and Sailors' Children's Society (£1,500 each).

FINANCES *Year* 2015 *Income* £46,637 *Grants* £42,000 *Grants to organisations* £42,000 *Assets* £1,239,597

TRUSTEES Nicolas Merriman; John Gordon; Elizabeth Humphryes; Neil Wingerath.

HOW TO APPLY Apply in writing to the correspondent. Requests for support should be made by letter confirming your registered charity number, the aims and objectives of your charity, and any other relevant facts. Applications must be received by the end of March or the end of August to be sure of consideration at the summer and winter meetings. The trustees do not acknowledge applications and will only contact those to whom grants are awarded.

WHO TO APPLY TO The Trustees, BM Box 2367, London WC1N 3XX *Website* www.vannordencharity.org

■ The Vandervell Foundation

CC NO 255651 **ESTABLISHED** 1968

WHERE FUNDING CAN BE GIVEN UK.

WHO CAN BENEFIT Charitable organisations.

WHAT IS FUNDED General charitable purposes, particularly medical care and research; performing arts; social welfare; education; environment.

RANGE OF GRANTS Up to £30,000.

SAMPLE GRANTS Big Issue (£30,000); City and Guilds (£18,000); Arts Education School Tring Park, Barts and The London, British Exploring Society, King's College London School of Medicine, PMS Foundation and University of Nottingham (£15,000 each); The Outward Bound Trust (£10,000).

FINANCES *Year* 2015 *Income* £262,489 *Grants* £54,469 *Grants to organisations* £54,469 *Assets* £7,187,186

TRUSTEE The Vandervell Foundation Limited Trustee Company.

OTHER INFORMATION Grants were distributed in the following categories in 2015: medical care and research (38 grants); social welfare (34 grants); performing arts (12 grants); education (6 grants); environmental regeneration (3 grants).

HOW TO APPLY Apply in writing to the correspondent. The trustees meet every two months to consider grant applications.

WHO TO APPLY TO Valerie Kaye, Administrator, Hampstead Town Hall Centre, 213 Haverstock Hill, London NW3 4QP *Tel.* 020 7435 7546 *Email* vandervell@btconnect.com

■ The Vardy Foundation

CC NO 328415 **ESTABLISHED** 1987

WHERE FUNDING CAN BE GIVEN UK with a preference for North East England; overseas.

WHO CAN BENEFIT Registered charities and individuals.

WHAT IS FUNDED Social action and faith-based projects, particularly those focusing on early intervention in the following areas: strengthening families; relief of poverty; supporting people who have offended and those in prison; supporting people who are homeless or unemployed. Support can also be given for: education; the arts; skills enhancement; mentoring; and leadership development. Applications are assessed against three criteria: involvement of and support for young people; projects in North East England; projects with a backdrop of Christian values.

WHAT IS NOT FUNDED The foundation will not fund: applications for more than a three-year commitment; animal welfare projects; health-related charities; projects normally provided by central or local government; individuals, including requests for educational support costs (**Note:** The foundation does award grants to individuals; however, these are likely to already be connected to the foundation or one of the educational institutions that receive funding from the foundation); projects that do not demonstrate an element of self-funding or other funding; contribution to an organisation's healthy reserves or endowments.

SAMPLE GRANTS Safe Families for Children (£273,000); Christians Against Poverty (£100,000); Cinnamon Network (£73,000); BBC Children in Need and Hope for Justice (£50,000 each); National Youth Choirs (£45,000); Operation Mobilisation (£38,500); Maggie's Cancer Centre, Premier Christian Media and Sistema Charity (£25,000 each).

FINANCES *Year* 2015/16 *Income* £1,199,525 *Grants* £1,896,918 *Grants to organisations* £1,845,275 *Assets* £35,533,700

TRUSTEES Lady Margaret Vardy; Peter Vardy; Richard Vardy; Sir Peter Vardy; Victoria Vardy.

OTHER INFORMATION The foundation made 458 grants in 2015/16 (to both organisations and individuals). Grants of less than £25,000 to organisations totalled £423,500. Grants to individuals during the year totalled £51,500.

HOW TO APPLY Apply in writing to the correspondent. The trustees meet every two months to review grants. Each application is considered against the criteria outlined above.

WHO TO APPLY TO Sir Peter Vardy, Trustee, Venture House, Aykley Heads, Durham DH1 5TS *Tel.* 0191 374 4744

■ The Variety Club Children's Charity

CC NO 209259/SC038505 **ESTABLISHED** 1949

WHERE FUNDING CAN BE GIVEN UK.

WHO CAN BENEFIT Hospitals; schools; individuals; charitable organisations.

WHAT IS FUNDED The welfare of children and young people who are disadvantaged, or have disabilities or ill health. Grants are given to organisations in the following categories: equipment grants; sunshine coaches; great days out; children's hospitals; youth clubs; children's playgrounds. Grants are also given to individuals for equipment and wheelchairs.

WHAT IS NOT FUNDED Examples of grants outside the guidelines: repayment of loans; garden adaptions; cost of a family/wheelchair-adapted vehicle; administrative/salary costs; maintenance or ongoing costs; reimbursement of funds already paid out; hire, rental costs or down payments; computers; trips abroad or holiday costs; medical treatment or research; education/tuition fees.

TYPE OF GRANT Mainly equipment. Also days out.

SAMPLE GRANTS Everton in the Community (£39,500); Ysgol Ty Coch (£38,000); Vale of Evesham School (£37,500); Victoria Education

Centre and Zoë's Place Baby Hospice – Liverpool (£34,000 each); Baird Memorial Early Years (£33,000); Park Community Academy (£27,500); Linburn School and Kite Ridge House (£25,500 each); Silverdale – Leeds Children's Charity (£8,700).

FINANCES *Year* 2015 *Income* £6,729,520 *Grants* £2,117,018 *Grants to organisations* £1,756,873 *Assets* £2,716,920

TRUSTEES Stanley Salter; Anthony Leonard Harris; Anthony Hatch; Pamela Sinclair; Ronald Nathan; Trevor Green; Jonathan Shalit; Laurence Davis; Malcolm Brenner; Jason Lewis; Ronald Sinclair; Nicholas Shattock; William Sangster; Rodney Natkiel; Tushar Pradhu; Eliot Cohen; James Martin; Duncan Syers; Jonathan Gold; Dilaram Williamson.

OTHER INFORMATION In 2015 the charity made 117 grants to organisations totalling £1.8 million, and 164 grants to individuals totalling £360,000.

HOW TO APPLY Full information, application guidance and application forms for each of the charity's programmes are available on its website.

WHO TO APPLY TO Julie Thomas, Grants Programme Manager, Variety House, 93 Bayham Street, London NW1 0AG *Tel.* 020 7428 8100 *Email* info@variety.org.uk *Website* www.variety.org.uk

■ The William and Patricia Venton Charitable Trust

CC NO 1103884 **ESTABLISHED** 2004

WHERE FUNDING CAN BE GIVEN UK.

WHO CAN BENEFIT Charitable organisations.

WHAT IS FUNDED Relief in need for older people, particularly day centre provision; and the prevention of cruelty and suffering among animals.

SAMPLE GRANTS Age Concern Northamptonshire (£25,000); Age UK Solihull (£7,000); People's Dispensary for Sick Animals (PDSA) – Southampton, Sudbury Neighbourhood Centre – Middlesex and Guild Care (£5,000 each); Battersea Dogs and Cats Home (£2,500); Tyddyn Cat Rescue Centre (£1,000).

FINANCES *Year* 2015/16 *Income* £99,050 *Assets* £2,799,546

TRUSTEES George Hillman-Liggett; Christopher Saunby; Graham Cudlipp.

OTHER INFORMATION The 2015/16 accounts state that no grants were made during the year due to the ill health of the Chair of Trustees, but that £146,000 has been set aside for 24 grants to be paid to organisations in 2017, including 12 grants relating to support for older people (£83,000) and 12 grants concerned with animals (£62,000).

HOW TO APPLY Apply in writing to the correspondent. Following an initial approach, eligible applicants will be sent the relevant application forms, to be returned with the appropriate documentation and then reviewed by trustees. The trustees favour applications from charities with which the trust's founders had a connection, but all applications meeting the trust's objectives are considered.

WHO TO APPLY TO The Trustees, Broadlands Gate, Broadlands Road, Brockenhurst, Hampshire SO42 7SX *Tel.* 01590 623818 *Email* johngriffiths@wpventontrust.org.uk

■ The Veolia Environmental Trust

CC NO 1064144 **ESTABLISHED** 1997

WHERE FUNDING CAN BE GIVEN Areas in proximity of a Veolia site, in England and Wales. There is a postcode checker on the trust's website.

WHO CAN BENEFIT Constituted not-for-profit groups or charitable organisations; registered environmental bodies.

WHAT IS FUNDED Community and environmental projects. More specifically, capital projects in the following categories: community buildings and rooms; outdoor spaces; play and recreation spaces. Projects must be open for the use of the wider general public at least 104 days a year and should have secured all planning permissions. Applicants should have secured at least 20% of the total project costs already and projects should be complete within 12 months. The trust also funds biodiversity projects that meet ENTRUST requirements. Projects should be completed within 18 months.

WHAT IS NOT FUNDED Regulatory bodies; zoos, museums, theatres or arts organisations; schools or other educational institutions; organisations where members receive a financial benefit; projects where the public amenity is subject to a lease of less than six years' duration; shops or projects established to generate an income for use other than for the maintenance of the project; projects where there is accommodation on site; projects involving the purchase of land or buildings; exhibitions, sculptures, statues or memorials; restoration of buildings; allotments, graveyards or crematoria areas; CCTV and portable equipment such as sports kit, lawnmowers, furniture or white goods; renewable energy projects to access feed-in tariffs (e.g. solar panels); staff costs not relating to the physical project; projects that have already started.

TYPE OF GRANT Capital projects with a total cost of less than £250,000.

RANGE OF GRANTS £10,000 to £75,000.

SAMPLE GRANTS Wildlife Trust for Bedfordshire, Cambridgeshire and Northamptonshire (£108,00); Totton and Eling Town Council (£100,000); Groundwork London (£95,000); 8th Wakefield Scout Group – Horbury Bridge (£71,000); Cuerdon Valley Park Trust (£65,000); Bilston Pentecostal Church (£63,000); Butterfly Conservation (£60,000); Aldworth Village Hall Charitable Trust Ltd and Falkirk Community Trust Ltd (£55,000 each); Bookham Rifle Club (£50,000).

FINANCES *Year* 2015/16 *Income* £4,028,000 *Grants* £5,001,000 *Grants to organisations* £5,001,000 *Assets* £2,734,000

TRUSTEES Oswald Dodds; Tom Spaul; Caroline Schwaller; Derek Goodenough; Malcolm Marshall; Mike Smith; John Brown; Robert Hunt; Maggie Durran; Ben Slater; Donald Macphail.

OTHER INFORMATION Grants were made to 321 projects during 2015/16, of which 303 grants were for less than £50,000.

HOW TO APPLY After completing the online postcode checker and eligibility checker, a Stage 1 application can be made using the form on the trust's website, where guidelines are also provided. If your project is eligible, you will then be asked to complete a Stage 2 application, which will go to the trustees for a decision. There are four funding rounds each year; deadlines are posted on the trust's website.

WHO TO APPLY TO The Trustees, Ruthdene, Station Road, Four Ashes, Wolverhampton WV10 7DG *Tel.* 01902 794677 *Email* info@veoliatrust.org *Website* www.veoliatrust.org

■ Roger Vere Foundation

CC NO 1077559 **ESTABLISHED** 1999

WHERE FUNDING CAN BE GIVEN UK and worldwide, with a special interest in High Wycombe.

WHO CAN BENEFIT Charitable organisations; individuals.

WHAT IS FUNDED The relief of financial hardship in and around, but not restricted to, High Wycombe; advancement of education; advancement of religion; advancement of scientific and medical research; conservation and protection of the natural environment and endangered plants and animals; relief of natural and civil disasters; and general charitable purposes.

SAMPLE GRANTS Cord Blood Charity, the Leprosy Mission, Claire House Children's Hospice, Angels International, Signalong Group, Changing Faces, Women's Aid, St John Water Wing, UK Youth and Jubilee Plus.

FINANCES *Year* 2015/16 *Income* £121,956 *Grants* £199,833 *Grants to organisations* £199,833 *Assets* £841,654

TRUSTEES Rosemary Vere, Chair; Marion Lyon; Peter Allen.

HOW TO APPLY At the time of writing (May 2017), the foundation's website states the following: 'The Trustees no longer have the resources to make payments as in the past. In the current economic climate and trading conditions, we are unable to realise the large investment which appears in our accounts. The number of grant applications received each month continues to rise and we have a backlog of requests awaiting consideration. As a result the Trustees are not encouraging or accepting applications until the backlog has been cleared and the cash position improves. We are sorry to have to disappoint so many organisations.'

WHO TO APPLY TO Peter Allen, Trustee, 19 Berwick Road, Marlow, Buckinghamshire SL7 3AR *Tel.* 01628 471702 *Email* info@rogerverefoundation.org.uk *Website* www.rogerverefoundation.org.uk

■ The Nigel Vinson Charitable Trust

CC NO 265077 **ESTABLISHED** 1973

WHERE FUNDING CAN BE GIVEN UK, with a preference for North East England.

WHO CAN BENEFIT Organisations and individuals.

WHAT IS FUNDED General charitable purposes, including economic/community development and citizenship, education, environmental protection, the arts and other causes.

TYPE OF GRANT Capital (including buildings), one-off, project and research. Grants are awarded on an annual, irregular or one-off basis.

RANGE OF GRANTS Under £500 to £100,000.

SAMPLE GRANTS University of Buckingham (£5.5 million); Hampden Trust (£100,000); Civitas (£50,000); Songbird Survival (£23,000); Global Warming Policy Foundation (£15,000); Northumberland Citizens Advice (£8,000); Glendale Middle School and Newcastle Cathedral Trust (£5,000 each); Adam Smith Research Trust (£3,000); Chillingham Wild Cattle Association (£2,500).

FINANCES *Year* 2015/16 *Income* £155,591 *Grants* £6,018,325 *Grants to organisations* £6,018,325 *Assets* £3,541,136

TRUSTEES Hon. Rowena Cowan; Rt Hon. Lord Nigel Vinson; Thomas Harris; Hon. Bettina Witheridge; Hon. Antonia Bennett; Elizabeth Passey; Hoare Trustees.

HOW TO APPLY Apply in writing to the correspondent. The trustees meet periodically to consider applications for grants. Decisions on smaller grants may be approved by a single trustee, whereas larger grants require the approval of a number of trustees.

WHO TO APPLY TO The Trustees, Hoare Trustees, C. Hoare and Co., 37 Fleet Street, London EC4Y 1BT *Tel.* 020 7353 4522

■ The Vintners' Company Charitable Foundation

CC NO 1015212 **ESTABLISHED** 1992

WHERE FUNDING CAN BE GIVEN Greater London, with a focus on inner London.

WHO CAN BENEFIT Registered charities, particularly smaller, local organisations; schools and educational institutions.

WHAT IS FUNDED Grants are given for charities dealing with 'the social consequences of alcohol abuse'. The foundation also supports other general charitable purposes including health and social welfare; young people; education; armed forces; swans; causes relating to the City of London.

WHAT IS NOT FUNDED Medical research; construction, maintenance or restoration of buildings; applications covering areas outside London.

TYPE OF GRANT Up to two or three years; many recurrent.

RANGE OF GRANTS Mostly £3,000 to £5,000.

SAMPLE GRANTS Spitalfields Crypt Trust (£15,000); Chain Reaction Theatre Company, Counselling Pastoral Trust and London Air Ambulance (£10,000 each); National Association for Children of Alcoholics (£5,300); Hackney Pirates and Housing the Homeless (£5,000 each); Steps2Recovery (£3,000); Guildhall School and St Paul's Cathedral (£1,000).

FINANCES *Year* 2015/16 *Income* £433,156 *Grants* £158,874 *Grants to organisations* £158,874 *Assets* £1,940,920

TRUSTEES Dr Andrew Parmley; Simon Leschallas; Robert Rolls; Nicholas Arkell; Marcia Waters.

OTHER INFORMATION The foundation has a preference for charities where members of the Vintners' Company can assist as volunteers in some way. In 2015/16 grants were made to 43 organisations, of which 15 were for less than £1,000.

HOW TO APPLY Apply in writing to the correspondent, including a breakdown of the proposed project and the most recent audited accounts. Applications should not exceed three sides of A4 and should be sent by email to archivist@vintnershall.co.uk – further information is given on the website. The trustees meet four times a year, usually in March, June, September and December.

WHO TO APPLY TO Stephen Freeth, Charities Secretary and Archivist, Vintners' Company, Vintners' Hall, 68 Upper Thames Street, London EC4V 3BG *Tel.* 020 7236 1863 *Email* archivist@vintnershall.co.uk *Website* www.vintnershall.co.uk

■ Virgin Atlantic Foundation

CC NO 1097580 **ESTABLISHED** 2003

WHERE FUNDING CAN BE GIVEN UK and overseas (destinations served by Virgin Atlantic flights).

WHO CAN BENEFIT Registered charities.

WHAT IS FUNDED Welfare of children and young people. The foundation works primarily with WE (formerly known as Free the Children).

WHAT IS NOT FUNDED The foundation cannot: offer upgrades or excess baggage or cargo for any individual or charity; provide discounted or free of fare flights to individuals working for charities or assisting in charity work overseas; sponsor any individual, including employees; sponsor charity events; donate branded items for charitable causes; support any type of 'jail break' or 'escape and evade' events; advertise within Virgin Atlantic or externally for charity or fundraising events.

SAMPLE GRANTS Free the Children/WE (£629,500); Save the Children (£66,000); Chestnut Tree House (£2,000); Caudwell Children (£400).

FINANCES *Year* 2015/16 *Income* £887,264 *Grants* £698,087 *Grants to organisations* £698,087 *Assets* £2,769

TRUSTEES Ian de Sousa; Thomas Maher; Craig Kreeger; Mark Anderson David Molloy; Nicola Humphrey.

OTHER INFORMATION The foundation's income appears to be entirely generated by staff and customers of Virgin Atlantic. The foundation is able to offer a small number of free flights to children and young people requiring life-saving or life-changing medical assistance, and also occasionally offers auction or raffle prizes for charity fundraising. This support is focused on registered charities in the UK or one of Virgin Atlantic's destinations which are concerned with: supporting children facing extreme neglect, abuse, poverty, violence or social exclusion; preventing or alleviating the effects of life-threatening illness prevalent in children; alleviating suffering in disaster areas.

HOW TO APPLY The foundation's website states: 'Since 2010 we have worked almost exclusively with WE, an amazing partnership that has inspired Virgin Atlantic employees, partners and customers to raise millions of pounds for projects in the UK and in our worldwide destinations. We have recently committed to support WE for another five years, so are not looking for any new charity partnership opportunities at this time.' For applications for the other support offered by the foundation (raffle prizes and flights), the website states the following: 'If you have a request which you think meets our criteria, send details to community.investment@fly.virgin.com. We try our best to respond to all requests within three weeks. However, we receive thousands of requests each month and it takes time to thoroughly review and assess them, so be patient if this takes a little longer than expected.'

WHO TO APPLY TO Ian de Sousa, Trustee, Virgin Atlantic Airways Ltd, The VHQ, Fleming Way, Crawley, West Sussex RH10 9DF *Tel.* 01293 747128 *Email* community.investment@fly.virgin.com *Website* www.virginatlantic.com/gb/en/sustainability/community/general-funding.html

■ The Virgin Foundation (Virgin Unite)

CC NO 297540 **ESTABLISHED** 1987

WHERE FUNDING CAN BE GIVEN Worldwide.

WHO CAN BENEFIT Organisations; individuals; innovative and entrepreneurial projects.

WHAT IS FUNDED Entrepreneurial approaches to social and environmental issues. The foundation has four aims: changing business for good; market solutions to address climate change and conserve our natural resources; the power of entrepreneurs; human dignity. The foundation achieves this through a wide range of initiatives, which are categorised as follows: uniting leaders; uniting entrepreneurs; uniting voices; uniting communities. Many initiatives bring together different organisations in 'disruptive collaborations' to tackle global issues. Further information is given on the foundation's website.

TYPE OF GRANT Grants; loans; non-financial support.

SAMPLE GRANTS Carbon War Room (£495,000); The Elders Foundation (£440,000); Big Change (£301,000); Igniting Change (£45,000).

FINANCES *Year* 2015 *Income* £12,444,000 *Grants* £5,301,000 *Grants to organisations* £5,301,000 *Assets* £21,878,000

TRUSTEES Vanessa Branson; Jane Tewson; Holly Branson; Ajaz Ahmed; Peter Norris; Jose Maria Figueres Olson.

OTHER INFORMATION Financial details refer to consolidated accounts of the group, which includes Virgin Unite Trading Ltd, Virgin Unite USA Inc., Virgin Unite (Canada) Inc., VUC Catalyst Trust, Virgin Unite Nominees Pty Ltd, Virgin Unite Africa and The Branson Centre of Entrepreneurship – Caribbean Ltd. Grants in 2015 are broken down as follows: Collaborations Incubator (£3.4 million); Connecting a Community (£1.2 million); Empowering Entrepreneurs to Change Business for Good (£527,000); Shining a Spotlight (£105,000).

HOW TO APPLY The website states the following: 'Unlike some other charities, we do not run an open grant application process. On most of our initiatives, we either work with an already established circle of partners, or identify new partners we think are best placed to deliver in line with our strategy and with whom we can leverage initial investments for significant impact.'

WHO TO APPLY TO Roseanne Gray, Managing Director, 179 Harrow Road, London W2 6NB *Email* contact@virginunite.co.uk *Website* www.virginunite.com

■ The Virgin Money Foundation

CC NO 1161290 **ESTABLISHED** 2015

WHERE FUNDING CAN BE GIVEN UK, mainly North East England.

WHO CAN BENEFIT Registered charities; social enterprises; CICs; industrial and provident societies. Non-charitable organisations and groups may be funded for work that has charitable purposes and gives no private benefit to non-charitable interests.

WHAT IS FUNDED Disadvantaged communities. The foundation has two grants programmes. The North East fund supports organisations in the region which: help disadvantaged young people to find and keep a job; help people who are homeless or at risk of homelessness to find a new home; create and support community and social enterprise. The Ripple Fund supports community regeneration more widely, with a focus on locally led initiatives, through the following three aims: building community anchors; enabling inclusion; supporting social innovators.

WHAT IS NOT FUNDED The following are not eligible for support from the North East Fund: anything that is not defined as charitable by law; international appeals; sponsorship or marketing appeals; existing projects looking for backdated funding;

services that central or local government would normally pay for; individual appeals; animal welfare charities; day-to-day costs of schools and other educational establishments; medical treatment or research, hospices and medical centres; promotion of religious, political or advocacy-based groups; smaller projects like overseas travel, minibuses, holidays and outings, or sports equipment; requests which could be funded through any other existing Virgin Group or Virgin Money scheme. The foundation states that it is unlikely to fund organisations that are not already rooted in a deprived community in the North East. The foundation funds running costs rather than capital costs.

TYPE OF GRANT Running costs/core costs; project costs.

RANGE OF GRANTS £10,000 to £50,000.

SAMPLE GRANTS Changing Lives (£50,000); South Tyneside Training and Enterprise Network Ltd, and Pennywell Youth Project (£48,500 each); West End Women and Girls (£47,000); Oasis Aquila Housing (£43,000); Open Door North East (£31,500); Food Nation (£28,000); Bensham Grove Community Association (£20,000); Vision Sense (£17,000); Labelled (£7,500).

FINANCES *Year* 2015 *Income* £1,985,300 *Grants* £895,600 *Grants to organisations* £895,600 *Assets* £957,000

TRUSTEES Mike Peckham; Stephen Pearson; Edward Wakefield; Jo Curry; Sir Thomas Shebbeare; Tim Davies-Pugh; Tim Arthur; Emma Morris.

OTHER INFORMATION Grants were made to 25 organisations in the foundation's first ever round of funding in 2015. Grants were distributed in the following categories: helping disadvantaged young people into employment (£328,000); supporting new or existing social enterprises (£300,500); helping homeless people find and keep a home (£267,000).

HOW TO APPLY **North East Fund:** Refer to the website for information on when the next round of funding is open. Applications can be made using a form available on the foundation's website, after completing the eligibility checklist. **Ripple Fund:** The website states the following information: 'Our intention is to survey a broad range of organisations working to regenerate local communities and to draw from these those that are the closest fit to the Foundation's ambitions generally and for the Ripple Fund specifically. Accordingly, for the time being, applications are by invitation only and the Foundation is highly unlikely to accept an unsolicited application; however, if you have a piece of work you would like us to learn more about you can email us at info@virginmoneyfoundation.org.uk. If you do plan to email us, please include as much detail as you can, including the names of other organisations that are likely to be involved in making your project a success, other areas of (non-financial) support that would make a difference to the success of your project, the reasons why you are confident that there will be secondary benefits (a ripple effect) if the Foundation were to support your project and finally, how you might, in turn, support the Foundation's wider community of interest if we're to support your project.'

WHO TO APPLY TO Amy Williams, Programme Support Assistant, Jubilee House, Gosforth, Newcastle upon Tyne NE3 4PL *Tel.* 0330 123 3624 *Email* info@virginmoneyfoundation.org.uk *Website* virginmoneyfoundation.org.uk

■ Viridor Credits Environmental Company

CC NO 1096538 **ESTABLISHED** 2003

WHERE FUNDING CAN BE GIVEN UK, in areas within ten miles of a licensed landfill site – there is a postcode checker on the charity's website.

WHO CAN BENEFIT Any not-for-profit group with a constitution.

WHAT IS FUNDED Community; heritage; biodiversity. Community projects are aimed at improving facilities; heritage projects include restoration or repair of buildings or historic or architectural interest that are accessible to the public; biodiversity projects should help protect the environment for public enjoyment or the improvement of habitats for a particular species.

WHAT IS NOT FUNDED Work that has already started; contingencies, fees and preliminaries; works to public highways; anything that may be considered the statutory or discretionary responsibility of a local authority; projects located on or in allotments, school grounds, facilities owned and managed by a local authority (except for certain parks and play areas) or facilities primarily used for services provision or not considered a general public amenity (such as hospitals, hospices or accommodation); proportional projects; salaried posts; revenue funding; core costs (e.g. rent, energy bills, supplies); purchase or lease of vehicles; purchase of land or buildings that are not at risk of closure or loss to the community; multimedia or CCTV equipment, events, CDs, websites or marketing materials.

TYPE OF GRANT Capital costs; project costs.

RANGE OF GRANTS Small grants of up to £20,000; main grants of £20,001 to £50,000; large grants from £50,001 to £100,000; and Scottish Landfill Communities grants of up to £50,000.

SAMPLE GRANTS Bristol Aerospace Centre and Oxmead Farm (£250,000 each); Kimmeridge Fossil Museum and Community Hall (£200,000); Hadleigh Cricket Club (£135,000); St Cleer Play Area (£96,500); The Bush Theatre (£67,500); King's Sutton Parish Church (£60,000); St Mary's Church – Puddletown (£50,000); Greenhills Adventure Play Park (£48,500); Camlachie Community Park (£44,500).

FINANCES *Year* 2015/16 *Income* £10,267,232 *Grants* £11,557,197 *Grants to organisations* £11,557,197 *Assets* £4,202,011

TRUSTEES David Robertson; Peter Renshaw; Simon Catford; Mary Prior.

OTHER INFORMATION For any grant made by the charity, a Contributing Third Party payment must be made, which is based on 10% of the amount awarded. Further guidance on this and who can act as a third party is given on the website.

HOW TO APPLY Applications can be made using the form on the charity's website, where guidance and deadlines are also provided.

WHO TO APPLY TO Sophie Norman, Applications and Administration Assistant, Aintree House, Blackbrook Park Avenue, Taunton TA1 2PX *Tel.* 01823 476476 *Email* enquiries@viridor-credits.co.uk *Website* www.viridor-credits.co.uk

■ Vivdale Ltd

CC NO 268505 **ESTABLISHED** 1974

WHERE FUNDING CAN BE GIVEN UK.

WHO CAN BENEFIT Jewish people.

WHAT IS FUNDED Advancement of the Orthodox Jewish faith.

SAMPLE GRANTS Achisomoch Aid Company Ltd, Beis Soroh Schneirer, Beis Yaakov Town, Beis Yisroel Tel Aviv, Comet Charities Ltd, Friends of Harim Bnei Brak, Jewish Teachers Training College Gateshead, Mosdos Bnei Brak, Torah Vechesed Ashdod and Woodstock Sinclair Trust.

FINANCES *Year* 2015/16 *Income* £180,017 *Grants* £104,017 *Grants to organisations* £104,017 *Assets* £3,419,983

TRUSTEES David Marks; Francesca Sinclair; Loretta Marks.

OTHER INFORMATION No list of recent grant beneficiaries was included in the accounts.

HOW TO APPLY Apply in writing to the correspondent.

WHO TO APPLY TO David Marks, Trustee, 133 Leeside Crescent, Golders Green, London NW11 0JN *Tel.* 020 8202 9367 *Email* aepton@goldwins.co.uk

■ The Vodafone Foundation

CC NO 1089625 **ESTABLISHED** 2002

WHERE FUNDING CAN BE GIVEN UK and overseas (where Vodafone operates).

WHO CAN BENEFIT Registered charities and charitable organisations.

WHAT IS FUNDED General charitable purposes, particularly technology; disadvantaged communities; humanitarian crises and disaster relief; education. For information on the foundation's projects and areas of work, refer to the website.

SAMPLE GRANTS Digital Scouts (£250,000); JustTextGiving (£224,000); The Prince's Trust (£151,500); Text Santa (£100,000).

FINANCES *Year* 2015/16 *Income* £20,965,562 *Grants* £7,741,896 *Grants to organisations* £7,741,896 *Assets* £7,133,248

TRUSTEES Nick Land; Margherita Della Valle; Elizabeth Filkin; Lord Hastings of Scarisbrick; Matthew Kirk; Francisco Roman; Ronald Schellekens; Helen Lamprell; Mwamvita Makamba; Rosemary Martin; Nick Jeffrey.

OTHER INFORMATION The foundation also provides matched funding to support the fundraising efforts of Vodafone employees. The grant total includes: global projects (£4.4 million); UK employee involvement (£1.17 million); international local charitable projects (£808,000); UK national projects (£725,000); other (£379,500); group disaster fund grants (£210,000); small grants fund (£41,000). Not included in the grant total is £10.9 million which was given in grants to other Vodafone foundations internationally.

HOW TO APPLY Contact the foundation or see the website for further information. The website states the following: 'The Vodafone Foundation receives an average of 12,000 requests per year for funding and support. While seeking to respond to all requests for information, it normally approaches only those charitable organisations which it believes can help in the delivery of its charitable aims.'

WHO TO APPLY TO Andrew Dunnett, Foundation Director, Vodafone Group PLC, 1 Kingdom Street, London W2 6BY *Email* groupfoundation@vodafone.com *Website* www.vodafonefoundation.org

■ Volant Charitable Trust

SC NO SC030790 **ESTABLISHED** 2000

WHERE FUNDING CAN BE GIVEN Scotland.

WHO CAN BENEFIT Registered charities, CICs, community organisations and social enterprises.

WHAT IS FUNDED The trust's open grants programme has three areas of focus: women; children and young people; poverty and deprivation. It also funds international work and research into multiple sclerosis, but these areas are not open to application.

WHAT IS NOT FUNDED Individuals; general fundraising activities or appeals; major capital projects; funds to distribute as grants or bursaries; repayment of loans or payment of debt; retrospective funding; trips abroad; purchase of second-hand vehicles. The trust's open grants programme will not fund anything outside Scotland.

TYPE OF GRANT Project costs and core costs; multi-year awards for up to three years.

RANGE OF GRANTS Up to £10,000 per year, for up to three years.

SAMPLE GRANTS Oxfam (£600,000); British Red Cross and Médecins Sans Frontières (£250,000 each); Save the Children (£100,000).

FINANCES *Year* 2015/16 *Income* £1,534,905 *Grants* £2,322,068 *Grants to organisations* £2,322,068 *Assets* £56,457,700

HOW TO APPLY Applications for the trust's open grants programme can be made through Foundation Scotland, where guidelines are also provided. An initial enquiry form can be submitted on the website; eligible applicants will then be invited to submit a full application. The trustees meet in April and October to make final decisions on grants. Any queries should be directed to Jennifer McPhail: jennifer@foundationscotland.org.uk or 0141 341 4964.

WHO TO APPLY TO Jennifer McPhail, Grants Programme Executive, Foundation Scotland, Princes Exchange, 1 Earl Grey Street, Edinburgh EH3 9EE *Tel.* 0141 341 4964 *Email* jennifer@foundationscotland.org.uk *Website* www.volanttrust.com

■ Voluntary Action Fund (VAF)

SC NO SC035037 **ESTABLISHED** 2003

WHERE FUNDING CAN BE GIVEN Scotland.

WHO CAN BENEFIT Registered charities and other constituted voluntary or charitable organisations.

WHAT IS FUNDED VAF manages a number of grants programmes which aim to tackle disadvantage, reduce inequalities and build resilient communities. The website states that grant-making currently focuses on: supporting volunteering and community action; promoting equality and tackling discrimination; tackling intra-Christian sectarianism across Scotland; tackling all forms of violence against women and girls; providing services for older people in Glasgow; tackling social isolation and loneliness. Refer to the website for information on funding currently available.

WHAT IS NOT FUNDED Refer to the VAF website for details of exclusions for each fund.

RANGE OF GRANTS Up to £400,000; mostly less than £100,000.

SAMPLE GRANTS Lothian and Borders Community Justice Authority (£375,000); South West Scotland Criminal Justice Social Work Services (£372,000); Barnardo's Scotland (£228,500); Zero Tolerance (£177,000); Sense over

Sectarianism (£169,500); South Lanarkshire Women's Aid (£158,500); Citizens Theatre (£151,000); Youthlink Scotland (£131,000); Motherwell and Districts Women's Aid (£103,500); Scottish Book Trust (£79,500).

FINANCES *Year* 2015/16 *Income* £16,715,844 *Grants* £15,422,360 *Grants to organisations* £15,422,360 *Assets* £697,860

TRUSTEES Joanna McLaughlin; Anela Anwar; Michael Cunningham; John McDonald; Sarah Kersey; Pervin Ahmed; Michael Wilson; Graham Leydon; David McNeill; Ahmed Yousaf; Marie McQuade; Rosalind McKenna; James Nicol; Claire Stevens.

OTHER INFORMATION Grants of less than £100,000 totalled £9.88 million in 2015/16.

HOW TO APPLY Application forms and guidance notes for open programmes are available on the fund's website. The fund recommends that interested parties contact them to discuss the project before making any application. Funds may open and close at various times so applicants should check the website for the most recent updates.

WHO TO APPLY TO Maureen Munro, Head of Programmes, Suite 3, Forth House, Burnside Business Court, North Road, Inverkeithing, Fife KY11 1NZ *Tel.* 01383 620780 *Email* info@vaf.org.uk *Website* www.voluntaryactionfund.org.uk

■ Wade's Charity

CC NO 224939 **ESTABLISHED** 1530

WHERE FUNDING CAN BE GIVEN Leeds, within the pre-1974 boundary of the city (approximately LS1 to LS17 postcodes).

WHO CAN BENEFIT Charitable organisations.

WHAT IS FUNDED Recreational activities; the preservation of public open spaces. The main grants programme (£300 or above) considers applications supporting all or any section of the community, including: children and young people; older people; wider community; the arts; open space. There is also a small grants programme (up to £300) for small community groups and charities, administered by Doing Good Leeds.

WHAT IS NOT FUNDED Applications from outside the area of benefit; non-charitable organisations; individuals; church repairs; circulars or general appeals from high-profile national charities; activities which fall outside the charity's criteria; activities which are the responsibility of statutory bodies or local authorities, particularly in health and education; salaries; core costs; projects which have already taken place.

RANGE OF GRANTS Around £350 to £6,000.

SAMPLE GRANTS Leeds Children's Charity (£6,000); Diocese of Leeds (£5,000); Foundation Housing (£4,500); Rodley Nature Reserve (£4,000); Getaway Girls (£3,000); Leeds Mencap (£2,600); Live Music Now and Young Minds (£1,600 each); Left Bank Leeds (£1,000); The Haven (£350).

FINANCES *Year* 2015 *Income* £657,889 *Grants* £136,110 *Grants to organisations* £136,110 *Assets* £6,917,534

TRUSTEES Bernard Atha; Susan Reddington; John Tinker; John Roberts; John Stoddart-Scott; Hilary Finnigan; Jack Dunn; John Pike; Revd Canon Sam Corley; Mark Pullan; Bruce Smith; Tim Barber; Gerald Harper; David Richardson; Nicholas Mercer; Timothy Ward.

OTHER INFORMATION Grants were made to 60 organisations during the year.

HOW TO APPLY Main grants applications should preferably be submitted by email, including all the required information given in the guidelines on the charity's website. Applicants will then be contacted by a grants adviser to arrange a meeting, after which applications are considered by the trustees at meetings in April, July and November. Early applications are encouraged as it can take four to six weeks to process an application. The charity welcomes contact to discuss ideas before submitting an application (01937 830295 or wadescharity@btinternet.com). Small grants applications should be made through Doing Good Leeds: doinggoodleeds.org.uk/wades-charity-small-grants.

WHO TO APPLY TO Kathryn Hodges, Grants Adviser and Administrator, 5 Grimston Park Mews, Grimston Park, Grimston, Tadcaster LS24 9DB *Tel.* 01937 830295 *Email* wadescharity@btinernet.com *Website* www.wadescharity.org

■ The Scurrah Wainwright Charity

CC NO 1002755 **ESTABLISHED** 1991

WHERE FUNDING CAN BE GIVEN Preference for Yorkshire, South Africa and Zimbabwe.

WHO CAN BENEFIT Charitable organisations.

WHAT IS FUNDED The charity funds 'innovative, hard-to-fund work directed at root causes in the field of social reform.' The charity favours causes which are outside of the mainstream and unlikely to receive funding elsewhere. There are three grants programmes: Yorkshire; Southern Africa (particularly Zimbabwe); projects that have applied to the Andrew Wainwright Reform Trust but have not be accepted as they are eligible for charitable funding.

WHAT IS NOT FUNDED Individuals; large and national charitable organisation unless specifically working in the Yorkshire region and providing local control and access to the grant; organisations with an annual income/expenditure that exceeds around £250,000; animal welfare; buildings; medical research or support for individual medical conditions; substitution for government funding (e.g. in education and health); unsolicited general appeal letters; activities that have already taken place; organisations without a UK bank account into which a grant can be paid.

TYPE OF GRANT Contributions to core costs. Funding is rarely given for more than one year.

RANGE OF GRANTS Typically £1,000 to £5,000, but in 'cases of exceptional merit' larger grants may be awarded.

SAMPLE GRANTS Gipton Methodist Church (£10,600); Bradford Court Chaplaincy (£5,000); Growing Works (£4,800); Doncaster Women's Aid and Share Psychotherapy (£2,500 each); Community Furniture Store (£2,000); Involve Leeds, Refugee Action York and Sidewalk Youth Project (£1,000 each).

FINANCES *Year* 2015/16 *Income* £972,512 *Grants* £116,722 *Grants to organisations* £116,722 *Assets* £2,865,297

TRUSTEES Hilary Wainwright; Hugh Scott; Martin Wainwright; Penny Wainwright; Tessa Wainwright.

OTHER INFORMATION The Wainwright family also runs the non-charitable The Andrew Wainwright Reform Trust Ltd, which also focuses on 'work for a just and democratic society and to redress political and social injustices', but funds projects which 'are ineligible for charitable funding because they are considered to political or radical to come within the Charity Commission's guidelines'. During 2015/16, the charity made grants to 42 organisations.

HOW TO APPLY Applicants should first check the eligibility criteria on the charity's website. Applications can be made using a form available to download from the website, which may be submitted by email or post, along with a copy of the most recent audited accounts and an application including the information requested in the guidance on the charity's website. The trustees meet in March, July and November and applications should be submitted by 14 January, 14 May or 14 September respectively. Applicants can contact the administrator by email with any queries.

WHO TO APPLY TO Kerry McQuade, Administrator, 19 Wadsworth Lane, Hebden Bridge, West Yorkshire HX7 8DL *Email* admin@wainwrighttrusts.org.uk *Website* www.wainwrighttrusts.org.uk

■ The Bruce Wake Charity

CC NO 1018190 **ESTABLISHED** 1993

WHERE FUNDING CAN BE GIVEN UK.

WHO CAN BENEFIT Organisations; individuals.

WHAT IS FUNDED Grants to fund leisure activities for people with disabilities, particularly activities which aim to improve access to sport or leisure activities for people who use a wheelchair.

WHAT IS NOT FUNDED For-profit organisations.

SAMPLE GRANTS Leicester Charity Link (£28,000); WheelPower (£20,000); Disability Snowsport UK (£10,000); Evening Chronicle Sunshine Fund (£6,200); Equality Together (£6,000); Jumbulance Trust, London Wheelchair Rugby Club, Ro-Ro Sailing, Shape Arts and YMCA Coventry Wheelchair Basketball Academy (£5,000 each).

FINANCES *Year* 2015/16 *Income* £219,855 *Grants* £523,227 *Grants to organisations* £467,968 *Assets* £8,533,763

TRUSTEES Peter Hems; Robert Rowley; Penny Wake; Thomas Wake.

OTHER INFORMATION Grants were made to 43 individuals during the year, totalling £55,000. Grants to organisations of less than £5,000 totalled £280,000.

HOW TO APPLY Apply in writing to the correspondent, including financial information (charitable organisations should include a copy of their latest financial statements). The trustees meet quarterly to make grants.

WHO TO APPLY TO Peter Hems, Trustee, Grant Thornton UK LLP, Regent House, 80 Regent Road, Leicester LE1 7NH *Tel.* 0116 247 1234 *Email* wake@webleicester.co.uk *Website* www.brucewaketrust.co.uk

■ The Wakefield and Tetley Trust

CC NO 1121779 **ESTABLISHED** 2008

WHERE FUNDING CAN BE GIVEN London boroughs of Tower Hamlets, Southwark and the City of London.

WHO CAN BENEFIT Community groups and charities. For the main grants programme: organisations with a turnover of less than £500,000 (unless exceptional circumstances); for fast-track grants: organisations with a turnover of less than £300,000.

WHAT IS FUNDED Grants are made for projects which benefit 'people who face significant disadvantage and have limited choices and opportunities', aiming to reduce barriers and encourage social inclusion. In 2015/16 grants were awarded in seven key service areas, although the trust recognises there is some overlap between these: children and young people; community development; disability; health; migrants and refugees; vulnerable women and families; welfare support/advice.

WHAT IS NOT FUNDED Individuals; work that has already taken place; applicants already rejected by the trust within the last 12 months; organisations with significant unrestricted reserves or in serious financial deficit; the promotion of religion; animal welfare charities; statutory bodies and work that is primarily the responsibility of central or local government; health trusts, health authorities and hospices (or any sort of medical equipment or medical research); environmental improvements; building restoration or conservation; uniformed youth groups; schools, supplementary schools or vocational training. The trust is unlikely to fund equipment or capital costs.

TYPE OF GRANT Project costs or core costs; mainly just for one year, but some up to three years.

RANGE OF GRANTS Main grants: average around £6,500; fast-track grants: less than £2,500.

SAMPLE GRANTS All Hallows by the Tower Church (£56,000); Bede House Association (£10,000); Ocean Women's Association (£6,500); London Sustainability Exchange (£5,100); Age Concern City of London (£5,000); Volunteer Centre Tower Hamlets (£4,900); London Gypsy and Travellers Unit (£4,700); Blue Elephant Theatre (£3,000); Lambeth and Southwark Mind (£2,500); SimpleGifts Unitarian Centre for Social Action (£2,100).

FINANCES *Year* 2015/16 *Income* £371,873 *Grants* £269,887 *Grants to organisations* £269,887 *Assets* £9,064,719

TRUSTEES Helal Rahman; Lady Judith Moody-Stuart; Stuart Morgenstein; Lady Sue Reardon Smith; Peter Delaney; Patrick Kelly; Clare Murphy; Lawrence Kilshaw; Dawn Plimmer; Cherry Bushell; Fozia Irfan; Tim McNally.

OTHER INFORMATION In 2015/16 the trust made 23 main grants and 20 fast-track grants. The trust supports All Hallows by the Tower church every year.

HOW TO APPLY Applications can be made online using the form on the trust's website. Applications are no longer accepted by post or email, but the trust can provide support with the online process where necessary. Application deadlines for the main grants programme are posted on the website; applications for fast-track grants can be submitted at any time and a decision will be made within six weeks of the application being received.

WHO TO APPLY TO Elaine Crush, Grant Officer, Oxford House, Derbyshire Street, London E2 6HG *Tel.* 020 7749 1118 *Email* enquiries@wakefieldtrust.org.uk *Website* www.wakefieldtrust.org.uk

■ The Wakefield Trust

CC NO 800079 **ESTABLISHED** 1988

WHERE FUNDING CAN BE GIVEN UK, with a preference for Devon.

WHO CAN BENEFIT Charitable organisations.

WHAT IS FUNDED Education; citizenship and community development; arts, culture and heritage; environment; social welfare.

SAMPLE GRANTS Canterbury Museum (£17,700); Future Hope UK and The Arts Fund (£5,000 each); Two Moors Festival (£3,000); British Museum (£2,000); Farms for City Kids, National Trust and Trinity Sailing Trust (£1,000 each); Changing Tunes (£500); The A-T Theatre (£350).

FINANCES *Year* 2014/15 *Income* £51,000 *Grants* £39,582 *Grants to organisations* £39,582 *Assets* £2,038,143

TRUSTEES Janet Mitchell; Charles Torlesse; Jack Wakefield; Dr Tom Mitchell; Edd Mitchell; John Torlesse.

OTHER INFORMATION The 2014/15 accounts were the most recent available on the Charity Commission's website at the time of writing (June 2017). The trust made 14 grants during the year.

HOW TO APPLY Apply in writing to the correspondent.

WHO TO APPLY TO Dr John Severn, Secretary, The Coach House, Station Road, South Brent, Devon TQ10 9PU *Tel.* 01392 581580 *Email* contact1@john7.co.uk

■ The Wakeham Trust

CC NO 267495 **ESTABLISHED** 1974

WHERE FUNDING CAN BE GIVEN UK.

WHO CAN BENEFIT Registered charities.

WHAT IS FUNDED Community development especially through volunteerism; disadvantaged and socially excluded people; education.

WHAT IS NOT FUNDED National appeals; medical projects, including counselling, family therapy or self-help projects; arts and performance projects; projects outside the UK; individuals; equipment; large projects that rely on paid staff – the trust prefers to build volunteer capacity.

TYPE OF GRANT Project costs.

RANGE OF GRANTS Typically £125 to £2,500, although the trust can make larger grants.

SAMPLE GRANTS Gonville and Caiuss College (£300,000); St Peter's Church Terwick (£9,000); Midhurst Rother College/United Learning (£8,500); British Red Cross (£5,000).

FINANCES *Year* 2015/16 *Income* £25,548 *Grants* £345,446 *Grants to organisations* £345,446 *Assets* £1,432,032

TRUSTEES Harold Carter; Barnaby Newbolt; Tess Silkstone.

OTHER INFORMATION Grants for less than £4,999 totalled £23,000.

HOW TO APPLY The trust prefers contact by email. Applications can be sent by email to TheWakehamTrust@icloud.com. Full guidelines are available on the trust's helpful website.

WHO TO APPLY TO The Trustees, The Garden Office, Wakeham Farm, Rogate, Petersfield GU31 5EJ *Tel.* 01730 821274 *Email* TheWakehamTrust@icloud.com *Website* thewakehamtrust.org/2015/08/05/how-to-apply

■ Walcot Educational Foundation

CC NO 312800 **ESTABLISHED** 1990

WHERE FUNDING CAN BE GIVEN London borough of Lambeth.

WHO CAN BENEFIT Schools; registered charities, social enterprises, community groups and other voluntary organisations; individuals.

WHAT IS FUNDED Social welfare and education. As well as supporting individuals in need, the foundation also makes grants to organisations that support its beneficiary group. The website states that it is interested in organisations that help those in 'entrenched financial poverty' to achieve financial independence, focusing on at least one of the following areas: removing barriers in education; maximising learning; building employability; developing money sense. Further detail is given on the foundation's website.

WHAT IS NOT FUNDED Activities that are the responsibility of central or local government, or schools; organisations that cannot show they are working with Lambeth residents in financial need; debt repayments; crisis funding to solve an organisation's financial problems; research, other than for the specific priorities outline on the website; independent schools; capital works in schools.

TYPE OF GRANT Revenue costs; project costs.

RANGE OF GRANTS £60 to £52,000. In 2015/16 average small grant: £3,500; average large grant: £23,000.

SAMPLE GRANTS Centre 70 Advice Centre (£52,000); Springboard for Children (£25,000); Evolve Housing and Support (£23,000); Working With Men (£23,000); Help for Carers (£20,000); Southside Young Leaders Academy and Streatham Drop-in Centre for Refugees and Asylum Seekers (£20,000 each); The Elmgreen School (£19,000); Timewise Foundation (£17,000); Music Therapy Lambeth (£10,000).

FINANCES *Year* 2015/16 *Income* £2,387,000 *Grants* £1,982,000 *Grants to organisations* £1,828,000 *Assets* £91,458,000

TRUSTEE The Walcot and Hayle's Trustee.

OTHER INFORMATION The Lambeth Endowed Charities, with roots dating back to the 17th century, is an 'umbrella' title for what are now three charities: the Walcot Educational Foundation, Hayle's Charity and the Walcot Non-Educational Charity. Grants are also made to individuals. In 2015/16 the foundation made 73 new grants to organisations/schools, and continued 45 multi-year payments, totalling £1.8 million altogether. Grants were broken down as follows: employment (52%); education (36%); financial sustainability (7%); other (5%). Grants were made to 208 individuals during the year totalling £153,000.

HOW TO APPLY Refer to the website to check if the organisations grants scheme is currently open. Potential applications should initially contact a member of the Grants Team (020 7735 1925) to discuss whether their proposal is eligible and obtain an application form. Deadlines are posted on the website.

WHO TO APPLY TO Grants Team, 127 Kennington Road, London SE11 6SF *Tel.* 020 7735 1925 *Email* grants@walcotfoundation.org.uk *Website* www.walcotfoundation.org.uk

■ The Community Foundation in Wales

CC NO 1074655 **ESTABLISHED** 1999

WHERE FUNDING CAN BE GIVEN Wales.

WHO CAN BENEFIT Registered charities, community groups and other voluntary organisations.

WHAT IS FUNDED Grants for projects that strengthen communities in Wales. The foundation focuses on grassroots organisations engaged in addressing local needs and strengthening communities. The foundation's grants programmes fall under five core themes: educating and young people; communities; health; culture; environment. The foundation administers a variety of different grants programmes which open and close on an ongoing basis; refer to the website for details on what is currently available.

WHAT IS NOT FUNDED Each of the grant programmes has specific criteria. However, in general, the foundation is unlikely to fund: large capital projects; national or UK-wide organisations; organisations with an income exceeding £1 million; fundraising costs; projects that promote a certain faith or are exclusively available to those of a certain faith.

RANGE OF GRANTS The majority of grants awarded are under £5,000.

SAMPLE GRANTS A list of beneficiaries was not available.

FINANCES *Year* 2015/16 *Income* £4,071,371 *Grants* £2,813,512 *Grants to organisations* £2,813,512 *Assets* £13,586,482

TRUSTEES Kathryn Morris; Lulu Burridge; Sheila Maxwell; Thomas Jones; Lloyd Fitzhugh; Alun Evans; Nigel Annett; Geraint Jewson; Tanwen Grover.

OTHER INFORMATION The foundation promotes and manages philanthropy, 'awarding grants on behalf of clients, fund holders and donors, which enable local people to achieve inspiring change in their communities'.

HOW TO APPLY The foundation manages a number of funds, many with their own individual criteria, and some which relate to specific geographical areas of Wales. Visit the grants page of the foundation's website, where information about each of the funding programmes can be found, along with guidance notes, application forms and deadlines.

WHO TO APPLY TO Grants Team, St Andrews House, 24 St Andrew's Crescent, Cardiff CF10 3DD *Tel.* 029 2037 9580 *Email* mail@cfiw.org.uk *Website* www.cfiw.org.uk

■ Wales Council for Voluntary Action

CC NO 218093 **ESTABLISHED** 1963

WHERE FUNDING CAN BE GIVEN Wales.

WHO CAN BENEFIT Registered charities and voluntary organisations only.

WHAT IS FUNDED Local community, volunteering, social welfare, environment, regeneration. WCVA represents supports and campaigns for the voluntary sector in Wales and administers a variety of grant programmes; check WCVA's website for up-to-date information on current programmes and deadlines.

WHAT IS NOT FUNDED Grants are made to constituted voluntary organisations only. Check the WCVA website for specific exclusions for individual funds.

RANGE OF GRANTS Up to and above £1 million, depending on grant programme; most grants less than £20,000.

SAMPLE GRANTS Gwent Association of Voluntary Organisations – Gwent (£650,500); Swansea Council for Voluntary Service (£222,500); Torfaen Voluntary Alliance (£172,000); Stitching Points (£66,500); New Economics Foundation (£59,500); Groundwork North Wales (£33,000); Leonard Cheshire Disability (£28,500); Neath Port Talbot Children's Rights Unit and The Wildlife Trust of South and East Wales (£25,000 each); The Bridge Mentoring Plus Scheme (£22,500).

FINANCES *Year* 2015/16 *Income* £12,803,345 *Grants* £7,066,324 *Grants to organisations* £7,066,324 *Assets* £988,317

TRUSTEES Mair Stephens; Catriona Williams; Pauline Young; Peter Davies; Fran Targett; Simon Harris; Philip Avery; Janet Walsh; Richard Edwards; Cherrie Bija; Mair Gwynant; Lindsay Cordery-Bruce; Dr Mark Llewellyn; Jonthan Evans; Richard Williams.

OTHER INFORMATION Grants were made to 541 organisations.

HOW TO APPLY There are separate application processes for each scheme. For further information, refer to the website or contact WCVA on 0800 2888 329.

WHO TO APPLY TO Tracey Lewis, Secretary, Baltic House, Mount Stuart Square, Cardiff CF10 5FH *Tel.* 0800 288 8329 *Email* help@wcva.org.uk *Website* www.wcva.org.uk

■ Robert and Felicity Waley-Cohen Charitable Trust

CC NO 272126 **ESTABLISHED** 1976

WHERE FUNDING CAN BE GIVEN England and Wales, with a focus on Warwickshire and Oxfordshire.

WHO CAN BENEFIT Charitable organisations.

WHAT IS FUNDED General charitable purposes, particularly: health; the arts; welfare of children.

WHAT IS NOT FUNDED Individuals.

RANGE OF GRANTS £75 to £40,000.

SAMPLE GRANTS Banbury Young Homelessness Project (£40,000); Serpentine Trust (£13,700); Racing Welfare (£7,200); Cancer Research (£5,000); Eton College (£2,500); The Art Fund (£1,200); Plan International (£900); Child Bereavement UK (£250); Place2Be (£100); Rainbow Trust Children's Charity (£75).

FINANCES *Year* 2015/16 *Income* £144,962 *Grants* £121,189 *Grants to organisations* £121,189 *Assets* £1,884,974

TRUSTEES The Hon. Felicity Waley-Cohen; Robert Waley-Cohen.

OTHER INFORMATION Grants were made to 42 organisations in 2015/16.

HOW TO APPLY Apply in writing to the correspondent.

WHO TO APPLY TO Robert Waley-Cohen, Trustee, 27 South Terrace, London SW7 2TB *Tel.* 020 7581 6710 *Email* jeg@Uptonviva.com

■ The Walker Trust

CC NO 215479 **ESTABLISHED** 1897

WHERE FUNDING CAN BE GIVEN Shropshire.

WHO CAN BENEFIT Charitable organisations; hospices, hospitals and educational institutions; individuals.

WHAT IS FUNDED Health; education, with a particular focus on music, arts or drama; social welfare, with a particular focus on those with low incomes, looked-after children, young people leaving care and single parents.

WHAT IS NOT FUNDED Appeals from outside Shropshire will not be considered or replied to. The trustees generally do not assist students in higher education (due to the assistance available from student finance) with the exception of medical or veterinary courses where these are taken as second degrees.

TYPE OF GRANT Project costs.

RANGE OF GRANTS Up to £100,000.

SAMPLE GRANTS University Centre Shrewsbury (£100,000); The Lyneal Trust (£50,000); Combat Stress (£15,000); Macmillan Cancer Support (£10,000); Wellington Cottage Care (£5,000); Beanstalk (£2,500); Whittington Music Festival (£2,300); Transhouse (£2,000); Tall Ships Youth Trust (£1,200); Love Lee Productions (£1,000).

FINANCES *Year* 2015/16 *Income* £340,605 *Grants* £314,015 *Grants to organisations* £261,095 *Assets* £6,112,737

TRUSTEES Sir Algernon Heber-Percy; Caroline Paton-Smith; Shirley Reynolds; Lady Lydia Forester; Ann Hartley; Brian Williams.

OTHER INFORMATION Grants to individuals during the year totalled £53,000.

HOW TO APPLY Apply in writing to the correspondent. Details of other assistance applied for must be given and, in the case of organisations, the latest annual report and accounts. The trustees meet four times a year, but arrangements can be made for urgent applications to receive consideration between meetings.

WHO TO APPLY TO Edward Hewitt, Clerk, 2 Breidden Way, Bayston Hill, Shrewsbury SY3 0LN *Tel.* 01743 873866 *Email* edward.hewitt@btinternet.com

■ Walton Foundation

SC NO SC004005 **ESTABLISHED** 1964

WHERE FUNDING CAN BE GIVEN Glasgow and the west of Scotland.

WHO CAN BENEFIT Charitable organisations.

WHAT IS FUNDED General charitable purposes, especially education, medical causes and community care. There also appears to be some preference for Jewish causes.
WHAT IS NOT FUNDED Individuals; political causes.
TYPE OF GRANT Some recurrent.
SAMPLE GRANTS United Jewish Israel Appeal (UJIA) (£25,000); Cosgrove Care (£15,700); Targu Mures Trust (£15,000); Jewish Care Scotland (£6,500); Canine Partners, Friends of Lubavitch Scotland and Kinship Care Initiative (£5,000 each).
FINANCES *Year* 2015 *Income* £167,901 *Grants* £86,823 *Grants to organisations* £86,823 *Assets* £3,450,150
OTHER INFORMATION The foundation made grants to 19 organisations during 2015.
HOW TO APPLY Apply in writing to the correspondent. Grants are considered and approved by the trustees at their annual meeting.
WHO TO APPLY TO The Trustees, Caledonia House, 89 Seaward Street, Glasgow G41 1HJ

■ Walton-on-Thames Charity

CC NO 230652 **ESTABLISHED** 1984
WHERE FUNDING CAN BE GIVEN Ancient parish of Walton-on-Thames, Surrey (in practice, Walton, Hersham and Oatlands).
WHO CAN BENEFIT Charities; social enterprises; other community organisations. There is a focus on smaller, locally based organisations – national or regional charities are unlikely to be considered unless they can demonstrate an active presence in the local area.
WHAT IS FUNDED Social welfare. The charity's Community Grants programme provides grants to organisations which provide 'front line services' to the local community. There is a particular focus on the following themes: inequality in Elmbridge; children, young people and young adults (up to age 35); housing enablement; areas of deprivation; reduction in funding from the statutory sector; grassroots community organisations; organisational capability and capacity. Further guidance is given on the charity's website.
WHAT IS NOT FUNDED Activities which take place exclusively outside the area of benefit; activities which are the responsibility of the statutory sector to provide or fund; medical research; major capital projects or items; fundraising appeals; advancement of any religion or religious group, unless the application is to provide non-religious services to the local community; animal welfare; retrospective requests; commercial or business activities (apart from social enterprise).
TYPE OF GRANT One-off grants; multi-year grants for up to three years. Revenue and core costs; projects; pilot projects; capacity building. The charity prefers to 'actively support or otherwise enable the longer term sustainability of the organisations which it funds, although it acknowledges that some projects or organisations may have a specific life span'. The website also states that in exceptional circumstances, the charity 'could provide short notice substitute or replacement funding for excursions or activities where committed funding has been withdrawn unexpectedly'.
RANGE OF GRANTS Small grants of less than £2,000; medium grants of up to £10,000; larger grants of over £10,000. For equipment, small capital costs or short notice replacement funding: up to £1,000.
SAMPLE GRANTS Elmbridge Mencap; Frost Festival; Hersham Youth Trust; Mount Felix Tapestry Project; Music in Hospitals; River House Barn; Surrey Fire and Rescue Service Youth Engagement Scheme.
FINANCES *Year* 2015/16 *Income* £2,307,033 *Grants* £87,188 *Grants to organisations* £87,188 *Assets* £1,290,642
TRUSTEES Cllr Chris Sadler; David Nash; Ben White; Eliizabeth Kennedy; Rob Douglas; Timothy Hewens; Juliet Hobbs; Nick Stuart; Steve Wood; Paul Tajasque; James Vizzini.
OTHER INFORMATION The charity also makes grants to individuals and provides sheltered housing. It also provides other support to local voluntary sector organisations, such as office space, training and advice.
HOW TO APPLY Potential applicants should, in the first instance, discuss their proposals for funding with the Community Services Manager, by phone or email. Application criteria and guidelines are available to download on the charity's website. A list of meeting dates for both the grants committee and the trustees is also provided in the guidelines.
WHO TO APPLY TO Andrea Watson, Community Services Manager, Walton-on-Thames Charity, Charities House, 2 The Quintet, Churchfield Road, Walton-on-Thames KT12 2TZ *Tel.* 01932 220242 or 020 3328 0247 *Email* admin@waltoncharity.org.uk or awatson@waltoncharity.org.uk *Website* www.waltoncharity.org.uk

■ Sir Siegmund Warburg's Voluntary Settlement

CC NO 286719 **ESTABLISHED** 1983
WHERE FUNDING CAN BE GIVEN UK, especially London.
WHO CAN BENEFIT Registered charities only.
WHAT IS FUNDED Culture and the arts; education.
WHAT IS NOT FUNDED Individuals.
TYPE OF GRANT Revenue funding and capital projects.
RANGE OF GRANTS Up to £250,000.
SAMPLE GRANTS National Portrait Gallery (£250,000); Westminster Abbey (£200,000); Royal College of Music (£100,000); Royal Central School of Speech and Drama and Yehudi Menuhin School (£50,000 each); Wordsworth Trust (£30,000); Mousetrap Theatre and Queen Elizabeth Scholarship Trust (£25,000 each); Cambridge Music Festival and Loughborough Opera (£5,000 each).
FINANCES *Year* 2015/16 *Income* £45,646 *Grants* £1,372,500 *Grants to organisations* £1,372,500 *Assets* £2,268,203
TRUSTEES Sir Hugh Stevenson; Doris Wasserman; Dr Michael Harding; Christopher Purvis.
OTHER INFORMATION Following the trustees decision to start planning for the eventual wind-down of the trust, they have begun withdrawing larger amounts from the invested portfolio and distributing this in grants.
HOW TO APPLY The 2015/16 annual report states the following: 'The Trust does not accept unsolicited applications. Potential candidates for grants, having been identified by Trustees, are invited to submit an application.'
WHO TO APPLY TO The Trustees, 4 Queensborough Studios, London W2 3SQ *Email* applications@sswvs.org

■ The Ward Blenkinsop Trust

CC NO 265449 **ESTABLISHED** 1972
WHERE FUNDING CAN BE GIVEN UK, with a special interest in Merseyside and surrounding counties.
WHO CAN BENEFIT Charitable organisations.
WHAT IS FUNDED General charitable purposes. In the past, the trust has given support for causes including medical research, social welfare, arts and education.
SAMPLE GRANTS Action on Addiction; Chase Children's Hospice; Clatterbridge Cancer Research; Comic Relief; Depaul Trust; Halton Autistic Family Support Group; Hope HIV; Infertility Network; George Martin Music Foundation; Royal Academy of Dance; St Joseph's Family Centre; Strongbones Children's Charitable Trust; Wirral Holistic Care Services.
FINANCES *Year* 2015/16 *Income* £93,301 *Grants* £91,333 *Grants to organisations* £91,333 *Assets* £1,663,895
TRUSTEES Andrew Blenkinsop; Sarah Blenkinsop; Charlotte Blenkinsop; Frances Stormer; Haidee Millin.
OTHER INFORMATION Brief accounts available at the Charity Commission. As well as grants to organisations, grants totalling £1,200 were given to ex-employees of Ward Blenkinsop and Co. in 2015/16.
HOW TO APPLY Apply in writing to the correspondent.
WHO TO APPLY TO Charlotte Blenkinsop, Trustee, PO Box 28840, London SW13 0WZ *Tel.* 020 8878 9975

■ The Barbara Ward Children's Foundation

CC NO 1089783 **ESTABLISHED** 2001
WHERE FUNDING CAN BE GIVEN Mainly UK, some overseas.
WHO CAN BENEFIT Charitable organisations, particularly smaller charities. The foundation prefers to make grants to 'financially healthy children's charities where funding is not forthcoming from statutory bodies, where incomes and fund balances are constantly put to good use and where administration overheads are kept to a minimum'.
WHAT IS FUNDED Grants are awarded to organisations serving children who are disadvantaged in some respect. Purposes that have previously been funded include: educational projects; holidays; support, care and respite; health and well-being; and sport, play and leisure. Grants may also be given to charities supporting adults with learning disabilities.
WHAT IS NOT FUNDED Grants are not given to religious charities.
TYPE OF GRANT Grants given range from one-off donations to project-related grants that run for two to five years.
RANGE OF GRANTS £500 to £30,000.
SAMPLE GRANTS WellChild (£27,500); Whoopsadaisy (£15,000); New College Worcester (£12,000); Scottish Spina Bifida Association (£10,000); Designability (£8,500); Sebastian's Action Trust (£7,500); Resources for Autism (£7,000); Forest of Dean Children's Opportunity Centre (£6,000); Bath Area Play Project (£4,000); Down's Syndrome Training and Support (£1,400); Leeds Community Trust (£500).
FINANCES *Year* 2015/16 *Income* £481,641 *Grants* £511,731 *Grants to organisations* £511,731 *Assets* £10,387,590
TRUSTEES Barbara Ward, Chair; David Bailey; John Banks; Alan Gardner; Kenneth Parker; Brian Walters; Christopher Brown.
OTHER INFORMATION Grants were made to 80 organisations in 2015/16.
HOW TO APPLY Apply in writing detailing the purpose for which the grant is requested and including your latest annual report and set of audited financial statements. Applications should be addressed to the trustees. Beneficiaries or applicants may be visited by trustees, who usually meet quarterly to review and award grants.
WHO TO APPLY TO Christopher Banks, Trustee, 85 Fleet Street, London EC4 1AE *Tel.* 020 7222 7040 *Fax* 020 7222 6208 *Email* info@bwcf.org.uk *Website* www.bwcf.org.uk

■ Mrs N. E. M. Warren's Charitable Trust

CC NO 1060652 **ESTABLISHED** 1997
WHERE FUNDING CAN BE GIVEN Focus on Minehead, Somerset and surrounding areas.
WHO CAN BENEFIT Charitable organisations.
WHAT IS FUNDED General charitable purposes.
SAMPLE GRANTS A list of beneficiaries was not available.
FINANCES *Year* 2015/16 *Income* £284,024 *Grants* £68,096 *Grants to organisations* £68,096 *Assets* £1,912,123
OTHER INFORMATION A list of beneficiaries was not included in the 2015/16 accounts. However, the following breakdown of grant-making was given: economic/community development/employment (£30,000); environment/conservation/heritage (£13,000); religious activities (£12,000); medicine/health/sickness (£9,000); overseas aid/famine relief (£4,000). The trust also provides an annual educational bursary to individuals at Brockenhurst College.
HOW TO APPLY Apply in writing to the correspondent.
WHO TO APPLY TO Sue Hickley, Alexandra House, St John's Street, Salisbury, Wiltshire SP1 2SB *Tel.* 01722 412412 *Email* sue.hickley@wilsonslaw.com

■ The Warrington Church of England Educational Trust

CC NO 511469 **ESTABLISHED** 1952
WHERE FUNDING CAN BE GIVEN Borough of Warrington.
WHO CAN BENEFIT Church of England schools.
WHAT IS FUNDED Building schools, extensions and for repair and maintenance. Schools receive a grant from the government towards buildings/repairs and so on which covers 85% of the cost, the school governors must then provide the remaining 15%. The trust's current policy is to pay half the amount the governors must raise.
RANGE OF GRANTS £1,000 to £10,000.
SAMPLE GRANTS St Wilfred's – Grappenhall (£11,700); St Elphin's – Warrington (£10,000); St Barnabas – Warrington (£8,600); Birchwood Parish (£3,300); St Helens – Hollingfare (£2,400).
FINANCES *Year* 2015 *Income* £79,817 *Grants* £36,024 *Grants to organisations* £36,024 *Assets* £54,671,314
TRUSTEES S.Harrison; S.Woodyatt; R.Bingham; S.Robinson.
OTHER INFORMATION The trust awarded five grants during the year.
HOW TO APPLY Apply in writing to the correspondent.

WHO TO APPLY TO Davis Ridgway, 21 Palmyra Square South, Warrington WA1 1BW *Tel.* 01925 230000

■ Warwick Relief in Need Charity

CC NO 256447 **ESTABLISHED** 1976

WHERE FUNDING CAN BE GIVEN Warwick.

WHO CAN BENEFIT Individuals in need and organisations assisting such people.

WHAT IS FUNDED Social welfare.

TYPE OF GRANT Projects.

SAMPLE GRANTS The Gap/Warwick Percy Estate Community Project (£64,500 in two grants); Citizens Advice (£16,000); Warwick Apprenticing Charities (£10,000); Warwick Vision Support (£6,900); The Old Bank Partnership (£3,000); Music for Life (£2,000); Safeline (£1,000); Happy Days Children's Charity (£460); New Life Church (£450); New Hope (£60).

FINANCES *Year* 2015 *Income* £165,668 *Grants* £128,408 *Grants to organisations* £104,183 *Assets* £3,660,787

TRUSTEES Anthony Atkins; Janet Honnoraty; Revd Dr Vaughan Roberts; Sheila Brown; Cllr Martyn Ashford; Revd Linda Duckers; John Atkinson; Cllr Christine Cross; Sarah Hunt; Cllr Richard Edgington.

OTHER INFORMATION The charity provided grants to 43 individuals during 2015 for relief-in-need purposes, totalling £24,000.

HOW TO APPLY Apply in writing to the correspondent.

WHO TO APPLY TO Mr C. E. R. Houghton, Clerk, 34 High Street, Warwick CV34 4BE *Tel.* 01926 491181 *Email* choughton@moore-tibbits.co.uk

■ The Warwickshire Masonic Charitable Association Ltd

CC NO 211588 **ESTABLISHED** 1945

WHERE FUNDING CAN BE GIVEN Warwickshire and the Midlands.

WHO CAN BENEFIT Masonic charities; non-Masonic charities.

WHAT IS FUNDED Masonic charities; general charitable purposes, particularly health and social welfare.

SAMPLE GRANTS Acorns Children Hospice (£16,500); Birmingham Children's Hospital (£15,000); Midlands Air Ambulance (£10,800); Myton Hospices (£5,000); Birmingham Royal Ballet Children's Appeal (£2,000); Coventry Pantomime (£1,500); 3rd Warwick Scouts, Cerebral Palsy Midlands and Cherish Dementia Care (£500 each); The Royal British Legion Poppy Appeal (£42).

FINANCES *Year* 2015/16 *Income* £208,842 *Grants* £199,543 *Grants to organisations* £199,543 *Assets* £2,264,923

TRUSTEES Francis Jephcott; Mervyn Kimberley; Christopher Grove; Anthony Wall; Eric Rymer; Peter Britton; Gordon Law; Stanley Butterworth; Michael Morris; Alan Johnson; David Macey; William Clark; Richard Barker; Christopher Rogers; Nigel Burton; John Hayward; Trevor Sturt; Peter Manning; Philip Hall; David Greenwood; Stuart Esworthy.

OTHER INFORMATION During 2015/16, grants were made to 171 non-Masonic charities and one Masonic charity.

HOW TO APPLY Apply in writing to the correspondent, including a copy of the most recent audited accounts. The annual report for 2015/16 states: 'On receipt of a request for a grant, the policy is for the Provincial Charity Steward to appraise the substance and suitability of the application, and the nature of the applicant before submitting their proposal to the grants' subcommittee for final approval.'

WHO TO APPLY TO Provincial Charity Steward, Yenton Assembly Rooms, 73–75 Gravelly Hill North, Erdington, Birmingham B23 6BJ *Tel.* 0121 454 0554 *Email* john@warwickshirepgl.org *Website* www.warwickshirepgl.org.uk

■ Mrs Waterhouse Charitable Trust

CC NO 261685 **ESTABLISHED** 1967

WHERE FUNDING CAN BE GIVEN UK, with an interest in North West England and particularly the Lancashire area.

WHO CAN BENEFIT Registered charities only.

WHAT IS FUNDED General charitable purposes, and particularly the areas of medicine, health, community welfare, environment and wildlife, and churches and heritage.

WHAT IS NOT FUNDED Individuals.

SAMPLE GRANTS Association for Multiple Endocrine Neoplasia Disorders (AMEND), Arthritis Research Campaign, Cancer BACUP, Cancer Research UK, Christie Hospital NHS Trust, East Lancashire Hospice Fund, Lancashire Wildlife Trust, Marie Curie Cancer Care, Macmillan Cancer Relief, National Eczema Society, National Trust Lake District Appeal and National Youth Orchestra.

FINANCES *Year* 2015/16 *Income* £324,325 *Grants* £308,567 *Grants to organisations* £308,567 *Assets* £7,661,580

TRUSTEES Alistair Houghton Dunn; Helen Dunn.

OTHER INFORMATION During the year, 28 organisations were supported. Of the grant total, charities based in the North West received £145,500, with a further £60,000 awarded to national charities with North West-based projects.

HOW TO APPLY Apply in writing to the correspondent.

WHO TO APPLY TO Mark Dunn, Carlton Place, 28–32 Greenwood Street, Altrincham WA14 1RZ *Email* markdunnamalg@btconnect.com

■ The Waterloo Foundation

CC NO 1117535 **ESTABLISHED** 2007

WHERE FUNDING CAN BE GIVEN UK, with a preference for Wales, and overseas.

WHO CAN BENEFIT Charitable organisations.

WHAT IS FUNDED The foundation has four grants programmes: world development; environment; children's development; Wales. Further detail about the priorities supported within each of these schemes is given on the foundation's website.

WHAT IS NOT FUNDED Individuals; the promotion of religious or political causes; general appeals or circulars. Each of the grant programmes has specific criteria and exclusions which can be found on the foundation's website.

TYPE OF GRANT Project costs, core costs, salaries; capital costs; one-off and recurrent grants; start-up, initial stages and ongoing funding.

RANGE OF GRANTS Up to £100,000.

SAMPLE GRANTS Autistic Spectrum Connections Cymru; Cardiff University – Neuroscience and Mental Health Research Institute; CHEM Trust; IntAct; International Rescue Committee; Irise; Nasio Trust; Project Seagrass; Rainforest

Foundation UK; Torfaen Carers Centre; Young Enterprise Wales.

FINANCES *Year* 2015 *Income* £8,241,929 *Grants* £6,187,144 *Grants to organisations* £6,187,144 *Assets* £128,383,763

TRUSTEES Heather Stevens; David Stevens; Janet Alexander; Caroline Oakes.

OTHER INFORMATION In 2015 the foundation made 337 grants.

HOW TO APPLY Application guidelines, criteria and deadlines for each of the grants programmes are available on the foundation's website, which potential applicants are encouraged check before making an application. Applications are welcomed from organisations with a clear charitable purpose. There is no application form and all applications should be submitted by email to applications@waterloofoundation.org.uk. Details of what should be included in the application are specific to each grant programme and can be found on the foundation's website. All applications are reviewed at a first assessment stage, after which ineligible applicants will be informed, while those which are deemed to best meet the foundation's criteria will be contacted by the relevant Fund Manager for further information.

WHO TO APPLY TO The Trustees, 46–48 Cardiff Road, Llandaff, Cardiff CF5 2DT *Tel.* 029 2083 8980 *Email* info@waterloofoundation.org.uk *Website* www.waterloofoundation.org.uk

■ G. R. Waters Charitable Trust 2000

CC NO 1091525 **ESTABLISHED** 2000

WHERE FUNDING CAN BE GIVEN UK, also North and Central America.

WHO CAN BENEFIT Registered charities.

WHAT IS FUNDED General charitable purposes, particularly adults and children with disabilities or serious illness; ex-service personnel and their dependants; human rights.

TYPE OF GRANT Core costs; project costs; capital costs.

SAMPLE GRANTS Lawyers for Palestine Human Rights (£20,000); Katrin Cartlidge Foundation (£12,600 in two grants); Special Effect Org UK (£6,400); Children With Cystic Fibrosis – Dream and Derby Toc H Children's Camp (£5,000 each); Amnesty International (£2,800).

FINANCES *Year* 2015/16 *Income* £94,497 *Grants* £51,716 *Grants to organisations* £51,716 *Assets* £1,743,445

TRUSTEES Mark Fenwick; Christopher Organ.

OTHER INFORMATION This trust was registered with the Charity Commission in 2002, replacing Roger Waters 1989 Charitable Trust (Charity Commission no. 328574), which transferred its assets to this new trust. (The 2000 in the title refers to when the declaration of trust was made.) Like the former trust, it receives a share of Pink Floyd's royalties as part of its annual income.

HOW TO APPLY The trust's Charity Commission record states: 'The funds are fully committed. The trustees do not respond to unsolicited requests.'

WHO TO APPLY TO Michael Lewis, Howard Kennedy LLP, No. 1 London Bridge, London SE1 9BG *Tel.* 020 3755 6000

■ Wates Family Enterprise Trust

CC NO 1126007 **ESTABLISHED** 2008

WHERE FUNDING CAN BE GIVEN UK.

WHO CAN BENEFIT Registered charities; schools; universities; social enterprises.

WHAT IS FUNDED Communities; education, training and employment; sustainability; social enterprise; thought leadership.

RANGE OF GRANTS £250 to £65,000.

SAMPLE GRANTS University of Surrey – Social Enterprise Fund (£65,000); Manchester HOME (£30,000); New Economics Foundation Consulting (£15,000); Young Epilepsy (£10,000); Barnet Education Arts Trust and Royal Hospital Chelsea (£5,000 each); Camden Connect and C4 (£2,500); Downside Fisher Youth Club and Leeds FORCE Ladies Basketball Team (£500 each); Breck Foundation (£250).

FINANCES *Year* 2015 *Income* £1,001,079 *Grants* £1,060,613 *Grants to organisations* £1,048,713 *Assets* -£264,405

TRUSTEES Andrew Wates; James Wates; Paul Wates; Tim Wates; Andy Wates; Michael Wates; Charles Wates; Jonathan Wates.

OTHER INFORMATION The trust runs the Wates Giving programme, which supports causes with which Wates employees or the Wates family are involved. There are a number of schemes, including; major awards; match funding; community projects; family awards; client and supply chain fund; Give As You Earn scheme; sports sponsorship. Grants to individuals in 2015 totalled £11,900.

HOW TO APPLY Unsolicited applications are not considered – the trust only supports organisations where a Wates employee has direct involvement on a regular basis.

WHO TO APPLY TO Jerry Wright, Director, Wates House, Station Approach, Leatherhead, Surrey KT22 7SW *Tel.* 01372 861251 *Email* director@watesfoundation.org.uk *Website* watesgiving.org.uk

■ The Wates Foundation

CC NO 247941 **ESTABLISHED** 1966

WHERE FUNDING CAN BE GIVEN Most of the southern half of England.

WHO CAN BENEFIT Registered charities; social enterprises; community groups.

WHAT IS FUNDED Tackling disadvantage and social exclusion, under the following themes: building social values; employment and education; community health; safer communities; life transitions; strengthening the charitable and voluntary sector.

WHAT IS NOT FUNDED Individuals; work that is not legally charitable; political parties, lobbying or campaigning; churches or other organisations where a grant will be used for promoting religion or a specific faith (although such organisations may be awarded a grant for other charitable purposes, such as health, education, young people, etc.); statutory bodies including local authorities and their agencies and including replacement of cuts in funding by statutory bodies; other grant-making bodies, except through partnerships; organisations with a total income of over £3 million, except in special circumstances; major capital projects ('light' capital costs, such as equipment purchases, are eligible up to £30,000); general appeals and fundraising; continuation funding or bids on behalf of organisations currently receiving a grant from the foundation (beneficiaries will not be considered for 24 months after the end of a funded period).

TYPE OF GRANT One-off, mainly towards core costs and salaries, although may also be given for project costs and small capital costs.

RANGE OF GRANTS Up to around £30,000.

SAMPLE GRANTS Butler Trust (£32,000); Mayday Trust (£30,000 in two grants); Moorfields Eye Charity (£12,700); Cotswold Riding for the Disabled and The Parenting Project (£10,000 each); Cutteslowe Community Association (£8,000); Reading Quest (£6,000); Inside Out – HMP Wormwood Scrubs (£5,000); Art for Youth UK (£2,000); The Genesis Trust (£500).

FINANCES *Year* 2015/16 *Income* £343,140 *Grants* £396,843 *Grants to organisations* £396,843 *Assets* £16,588,335

TRUSTEES Andy Wates; Jonathan Heynes; Claire Spotwood-Brown; Christopher Wates; Neil Wates; Nick Edward.

OTHER INFORMATION The foundation made 44 grants during 2015/16.

HOW TO APPLY The foundation's website states: 'The Trustees of the Wates Foundation have endorsed a new pro-active grant-making strategy until March 2018. Wates Family members seek out charities to support, often from within their local community. Applications are by invitation only. Unsolicited applications will be automatically rejected.'

WHO TO APPLY TO Jerry Wright, Director, 7 Langside Avenue, London SW15 5QT *Tel.* 01372 861250 *Email* director@watesfoundation.org.uk *Website* www.watesfoundation.org.uk

■ The Geoffrey Watling Charity

CC NO 1025258 **ESTABLISHED** 1993

WHERE FUNDING CAN BE GIVEN Suffolk; Norfolk.

WHO CAN BENEFIT Registered charities.

WHAT IS FUNDED Social welfare; churches and historic buildings; education; arts; medical causes; sport; environment.

SAMPLE GRANTS Norwich Hebrew Congregation (£30,000); East Anglia Children's Hospices (£25,000); Norwich Eagle Canoe Club Ltd (£15,000); Norfolk Community Foundation, Hamlet Centre Trust and Willow Tree Garden (£10,000 each).

FINANCES *Year* 2015/16 *Income* £682,675 *Grants* £470,671 *Grants to organisations* £470,671 *Assets* £13,534,296

TRUSTEES Alan Watling; Anthony Gilbert; David Walker; Susan Watling.

HOW TO APPLY Apply in writing to the correspondent.

WHO TO APPLY TO David Lundean, The Geoffrey Watling Charity, 8A Ber Street, Norwich NR1 3EJ *Email* enquiries@geoffreywatling.org.uk *Website* www.geoffreywatling.org.uk

■ Blyth Watson Charitable Trust

CC NO 1071390 **ESTABLISHED** 1997

WHERE FUNDING CAN BE GIVEN UK.

WHO CAN BENEFIT Charitable organisations.

WHAT IS FUNDED The trust states that it supports humanitarian causes based in the UK, and other general charitable purposes.

TYPE OF GRANT Mainly one-off, some recurrent.

RANGE OF GRANTS £250 to £7,000.

SAMPLE GRANTS Society for the Relief of Distress (£7,000); Cystic Fibrosis Trust, St John's Hospice and War Child (£5,000 each); Royal Academy of Music (£4,000); Old Vic Theatre Company (£2,500); Foundling Museum (£1,500); Cruse Bereavement Care (£1,000); Great Ormond Street Hospital Children's Charity (£250).

FINANCES *Year* 2015/16 *Income* £127,835 *Grants* £104,500 *Grants to organisations* £104,500 *Assets* £3,944,296

TRUSTEES Nicholas Brown; Ian McCulloch.

OTHER INFORMATION Grants were made to 31 organisations in 2015/16.

HOW TO APPLY Apply in writing to the correspondent. The trustees usually meet twice each year, usually in June and December.

WHO TO APPLY TO The Trustees, c/o Bircham Dyson Bell Solicitors, 50 Broadway, Westminster, London SW1H 0BL *Tel.* 020 7227 7000

■ The Watson Family Charitable Trust

CC NO 1159965 **ESTABLISHED** 2015

WHERE FUNDING CAN BE GIVEN England; Wales; Uganda.

WHO CAN BENEFIT Registered charities.

WHAT IS FUNDED General charitable purposes; medical research; humanitarian causes.

SAMPLE GRANTS Dry Eye Research (£20,000); Mikwano Children's' Trust Uganda (£11,000 in two grants); CRUSE and NE Counselling Services and Matt Hampson Foundation (£10,000); Jesmond Residents Association (£1,000).

FINANCES *Year* 2015/16 *Income* £1,011,537 *Grants* £61,840 *Grants to organisations* £61,840 *Assets* £940,516

TRUSTEES Ian Watson; Claire Watson; Mark Watson; Hugh Welch.

HOW TO APPLY Applications can be made in writing to the correspondent.

WHO TO APPLY TO Ian Watson, c/o Hadrian Healthcare Holdings, Hadrian Office, 3 Keel Row, The Watermark, Gateshead NE11 9SZ *Tel.* 0191 460 5219 *Email* Enquiries@WatsonCharitableTrust.co.uk

■ John Watson's Trust

SC NO SC014004 **ESTABLISHED** 1984

WHERE FUNDING CAN BE GIVEN Scotland, with a strong preference for Lothian.

WHO CAN BENEFIT Individuals; charitable organisations; schools and educational organisations.

WHAT IS FUNDED Education of children and young people under the age of 21 with a physical or learning disability or who are socially disadvantaged. Grants may be made directly to individuals for purposes such as private tuition, educational travel costs, or equipment. Funding may be given for boarding fees in some circumstances. Grants are also made to organisations to provide educational projects, outings or research benefitting eligible children and young people.

WHAT IS NOT FUNDED General appeals; recurrent running costs or salaries.

TYPE OF GRANT Equipment; small capital expenditure; tuition; student support; personal equipment (such as special wheelchairs, special typewriters); projects and activities including travel. One year only, but can be extended.

RANGE OF GRANTS Generally under £2,000.

SAMPLE GRANTS Deaf Action (£2,000); East Craigs Primary (£1,200); Forthview Primary (£1,200); Tweeddale Youth Action (£1,100); Craigmillar Literacy Trust, Family Service Unit, James Young High School, Leith Walk Primary, Upward

Mobility and Women's Aid East and Midlothian (£1,000 each).

FINANCES *Year* 2015/16 *Income* £192,889 *Grants* £158,192 *Grants to organisations* £51,344 *Assets* -£39,192

TRUSTEES Caroline Docherty; Philippa Snell; Robin Garrett; John Kerr; Fraser Falconer; John Harding-Edgar; Gordon Wyllie; Maureen Grant; Christine Brodie; Chris Sheldon WS; Cllr Paul Godzik.

OTHER INFORMATION Grants were given to 108 organisations during 2015/16. Grants of less than £1,000 to organisations during the year totalled £25,000. Grants to 108 individuals totalled £107,000.

HOW TO APPLY Applications should be made on forms available to download, together with criteria and guidelines, on the trust's website, where application deadlines are also posted. Queries about the trust can be directed to James Hamilton: jhamilton@wssociety.co.uk.

WHO TO APPLY TO Anna Bennett, Clerk and Treasurer, The Signet Library, Parliament Square, Edinburgh EH1 1RF *Tel.* 0131 225 0658 *Email* abennett@wssociety.co.uk or jhamilton@wssociety.co.uk *Website* www.wssociety.co.uk

■ Waynflete Charitable Trust

CC NO 1068892 **ESTABLISHED** 1998

WHERE FUNDING CAN BE GIVEN Focus on Lincolnshire.

WHO CAN BENEFIT Lincolnshire-based charities and organisations (including schools, churches, sports clubs and community groups); national charities and organisations benefitting Lincolnshire residents; individual initiatives.

WHAT IS FUNDED General charitable purposes in the local area; community projects; rural communities and ecology; heritage preservation.

WHAT IS NOT FUNDED Individuals.

TYPE OF GRANT Training of existing staff; training of new volunteers; core costs, running costs and special requirements; start-up initiatives and additional stages.

SAMPLE GRANTS Lincolnshire Blind Society (£6,000); Canine Partners, Lincolnshire and Nottinghamshire Air Ambulance and the Order of St John (£4,000 each); Deaf Blind (£2,500); Action for Kids, Gurkha Welfare Trust and Marine Conservation Society (£1,000); Braille Chess Association, Children's Safety Education Foundation and Royal National Lifeboat Fund (£500 each) and Mouth and Foot Painting Artists (£100).

FINANCES *Year* 2016 *Income* £645,213 *Grants* £330,219 *Grants to organisations* £330,219 *Assets* £5,333,272

TRUSTEES Michael Worth; Graham Scrimshaw.

OTHER INFORMATION Grants were made to 135 organisations in 2016. A list of recent beneficiaries was not provided. As well as its main grants, the trust tends to fund one major project every year. In 2016 the trust gave £73,000 to Lincoln Cathedral Fabric Fund for the sponsorship of a Cathedral Mason, Stonemason and a Junior Glazier.

HOW TO APPLY Applicants should contact the trust by email or in writing, or through their local Waynflete Charity Trust Volunteer, providing name, address, organisation, contact details and a brief outline of their activities. The contact details of the trust's volunteers for East Lindsey, Boston, South Kesteven and North Kesteven are given on its website.

WHO TO APPLY TO Michael Worth, Trustee, PO Box 9986, Grantham, Lincolnshire NG31 0FJ *Tel.* 01400 250210 *Email* info@waynfletecharity.com *Website* www.waynfletecharity.com

■ The Weavers' Company Benevolent Fund

CC NO 266189 **ESTABLISHED** 1973

WHERE FUNDING CAN BE GIVEN UK.

WHO CAN BENEFIT Registered charities. There is a preference for small, community-based groups, rather than larger, established charities. Local organisations such as those working in a village, estate or small town should normally have an income of less than about £100,000; organisations working across the UK or in larger cities should normally have an income of less than £250,000.

WHAT IS FUNDED People who are disadvantaged. In particular the fund focuses on: people who have offended, particularly young people; community work with disadvantaged young people. Other general charitable purposes may be supported, including causes associated with the City of London and causes nominated by members of the Weavers' Company. Grants are also awarded as educational scholarships for students in textiles-related subjects and placements.

WHAT IS NOT FUNDED Funding is not given for: long-term support; general appeals; sponsorship, marketing or other fundraising activities; endowment funds; bursaries; long-term capital projects; grant-giving charities; retrospective funding; replacement funding or work that should be covered by statutory funding; building projects (although the trust may help with the cost of equipment or furnishings); capital projects to provide disability access; personal appeals or individuals; umbrella bodies or large, established organisations; organisations outside the UK or overseas expeditions or travel. Funding is not usually given for: work with children under five years of age; universities or colleges; medical charities or those involved in medical care; organisations of and for people with disabilities; environmental projects; promotion of religious or political causes.

TYPE OF GRANT Usually one year only, but occasionally up to three years. Pump-priming; project costs (including overheads); core costs; innovative or pioneering new work; continuation funding; emergency or deficit funding (in exceptional circumstances, usually with an organisation that has previously received support).

RANGE OF GRANTS Usually up to £15,000, but applications for smaller amounts are welcomed.

SAMPLE GRANTS Royal College of Art (£16,000); Write to Freedom (£15,000); Relate Medway and North Kent (£10,000); Chisenhale Primary School (£6,700); Zero Centre (£6,500); Dream Arts (£5,500); Prison Reform Trust (£4,500); Lord Mayor's Appeal (£2,000); St Martin's Homeless Project (£500); City of London Police Widows' and Orphans' Fund (£100).

FINANCES *Year* 2015 *Income* £469,313 *Grants* £425,370 *Grants to organisations* £425,370 *Assets* £11,510,477

TRUSTEE The Worshipful Company of Weavers.

OTHER INFORMATION The grant total includes the following categories: charitable grants (major grants under the fund's main focus and casual grants which fall outside these criteria); grants from the Millennial Fund (formed from donations of members of the company); grants for primary schools (working with selected London schools); and textile-related grants (mainly educational scholarships and awards).

HOW TO APPLY Detailed guidelines for applicants are available from the Weaver's Company website. Application forms can be downloaded from the fund's website, or obtained by post or email. Where possible, applicants will be notified within two weeks whether their initial application has been accepted for further consideration. Grants are usually considered three times through the year and deadlines for each meeting are posted on the website. The charities officer is happy to provide further advice about applications.

WHO TO APPLY TO Anne Howe, Charities Officer, The Weavers Company, Saddlers' House, Gutter Lane, London EC2V 6BR *Tel.* 020 7606 1155 *Fax* 020 7606 1119 *Email* charity@weavers.org.uk *Website* www.weavers.org.uk

■ The Webb Memorial Trust

CC NO 313760 **ESTABLISHED** 1944

WHERE FUNDING CAN BE GIVEN UK.

WHO CAN BENEFIT Universities; research bodies; other similar organisations.

WHAT IS FUNDED Social policy, with a particular focus on poverty, its causes and solutions. The trust was set up to continue the intellectual work of Beatrice Webb, with the aim of 'the advancement of education and learning with respect to the history and problem of government and social policy', through research, lectures, scholarships and other educational activities.

WHAT IS NOT FUNDED Direct party political purposes; individuals, including students.

SAMPLE GRANTS Centris (£56,000); Town and Country Planning Association (£50,500); New Statesman (£26,000); Compass (£14,500); Centre for Local Economic Strategies (£12,700); Fabian Society (£2,000).

FINANCES *Year* 2015/16 *Grants* £174,935 *Grants to organisations* £174,935

TRUSTEES Richard Rawes; Mike Parker; Kate Green; Robert Lloyd-Davies; Baroness Dianne Hayter; Mike Gapes; Chris White; Lord John Shipley.

OTHER INFORMATION The Webb Memorial Trust was established as a memorial to the socialist pioneer Beatrice Webb. In 2011 the trustees decided to spend down the remaining resources using at least 85% of the budget for a co-ordinated programme leaving a legacy worthy of Beatrice Web, committing its resources to a structured programme concentrating on the issues of poverty and inequality on the UK.

HOW TO APPLY As of 2017, the trust is no longer accepting funding applications. The 2015/16 accounts state: 'The Trust now recognises that it is entering its final phase of life. In the coming year, the Trust will concentrate on completing the research to support its work on the Legacy to Beatrice Webb in accord with earlier decisions. During this period, the Trust will continue to support the APPG on Poverty.'

WHO TO APPLY TO Mike Parker, Hon. Secretary, Crane House, Unit 19 Apex Business Village, Annitsford, Newcastle NE23 7BF *Tel.* 0191 250 1969 *Email* webb@cranehouse.eu *Website* www.webbmemorialtrust.org.uk

■ The David Webster Charitable Trust

CC NO 1055111 **ESTABLISHED** 1995

WHERE FUNDING CAN BE GIVEN UK.

WHO CAN BENEFIT Charitable organisations.

WHAT IS FUNDED General charitable purposes, mainly ecological and broadly environmental projects.

RANGE OF GRANTS £500 to £100,000.

SAMPLE GRANTS Bird Life International and National Trust (£100,000 each); Future Trees Trust and Isabel Hospice (£10,000 each); National Churches Trust (£5,000); Bat Conservation Trust and Wherry Trust (£2,000 each).

FINANCES *Year* 2014/15 *Income* £433,013 *Grants* £229,000 *Grants to organisations* £229,000 *Assets* £3,726,863

TRUSTEES Thomas Webster; Nikola Thompson.

OTHER INFORMATION The 2014/15 accounts were the most recent available to view on the Charity Commission's website at the time of writing (June 2017). Grants were made to seven organisations during the year.

HOW TO APPLY Apply in writing to the correspondent.

WHO TO APPLY TO Nikola Thompson, Trustee, Marshalls, Marshalls Lane, High Cross, Ware, Hertfordshire SG11 1AJ *Tel.* 01920 462001

■ The William Webster Charitable Trust

CC NO 259848 **ESTABLISHED** 1969

WHERE FUNDING CAN BE GIVEN North East England, principally Northumberland, Tyne and Wear, Durham and Cleveland.

WHO CAN BENEFIT Registered charitable organisations.

WHAT IS FUNDED General charitable purposes.

WHAT IS NOT FUNDED Individuals; non-charitable organisations; core/running costs and salaries.

TYPE OF GRANT One-off grants for capital projects.

RANGE OF GRANTS £500 to £4,000.

SAMPLE GRANTS Hospitality and Hope (£4,000); Cramlington Voluntary Youth Project (£3,000); All Saints Gosforth Parish Church, Beanstalk, NASUWT Riverside Band and North East Dance CIC (£2,000 each); Douglas Bader Foundation (£1,500); Hartlepool and District Hospice and Veterans at Ease (£1,000 each); The Jack Charlton Disabled Anglers Association (£500).

FINANCES *Year* 2015/16 *Income* £78,492 *Grants* £88,500 *Grants to organisations* £88,500 *Assets* £2,234,224

TRUSTEE Zedra Bank Trust Company (UK) Ltd.

OTHER INFORMATION Grants were awarded to 48 organisations in 2015/16.

HOW TO APPLY Apply in writing to the correspondent. Applications should include details of the costings of capital projects, of funding already raised, a set of the latest annual accounts and details of the current charity registration. The trustees meet four times each year to approve grants.

WHO TO APPLY TO The Trustees, c/o Zedra Trust Company (UK) Ltd, Osborne Court, Gadbrook Park, Rudheath, Cheshire CW9 7UE *Tel.* 01606 313179 *Email* charities@zedra.com

The Weinstein Foundation

CC NO 277779 **ESTABLISHED** 1979
WHERE FUNDING CAN BE GIVEN Worldwide.
WHO CAN BENEFIT Charitable organisations.
WHAT IS FUNDED General charitable purposes. The trust has previously supported a number of Jewish organisations.
WHAT IS NOT FUNDED Individuals.
SAMPLE GRANTS Chevras Evas Nitzrochim Trust; Friends of Mir; SOFT (Support Organisation for Trisomy) UK; Chesed Charitable Trust; Youth Aliyah.
FINANCES *Year* 2015/16 *Income* £41,844 *Grants* £69,612 *Grants to organisations* £69,612 *Assets* £1,681,502
TRUSTEES Michael Weinstein; Philip Weinstein; Lea Newman.
HOW TO APPLY Apply in writing to the correspondent.
WHO TO APPLY TO Michael Weinstein, Trustee, 32 Fairholme Gardens, Finchley, London N3 3EB *Tel.* 020 8346 1257 *Email* charity.correspondence@bdo.co.uk

The Weinstock Fund

CC NO 1150031 **ESTABLISHED** 2012
WHERE FUNDING CAN BE GIVEN UK.
WHO CAN BENEFIT Registered charities.
WHAT IS FUNDED General charitable purposes, particularly: medical care and treatment, including respite care and hospices; care for adults and children with disabilities; educational and training for adults and children with disabilities; care and support of older people; care and support of children; social welfare; music and the arts.
WHAT IS NOT FUNDED The fund does not support individuals, and tends not to support research projects or projects based outside the UK.
SAMPLE GRANTS A list of beneficiaries was not available.
FINANCES *Year* 2015/16 *Income* £542,190 *Grants* £483,088 *Grants to organisations* £483,088 *Assets* £166,444,457
TRUSTEES Dr Susan Lacroix; Patrica Milner; The Hon. Laura Weinstock.
OTHER INFORMATION In 2015/16 the fund made 125 grants to organisations. A list of beneficiaries was not provided but the annual report gives the following breakdown of grant-making during the year: the arts (26%); medical causes (23%); education (16%); disability (12%); social welfare (12%); community (8%); cultural or environmental (3%). This fund was established by Laura Weinstock, who had another fund of the same name (Charity Commission no. 222376) which was removed from the Charity Commission register in May 2013.
HOW TO APPLY Applications should be made using the form available to download from the website, where further guidance is given on what to include. Two copies should be sent, along with the current year's summary income and expenditure budget and the most recent annual report and accounts. There are no deadlines and applications are considered on a rolling basis, with the trustees meeting three or four times each year. Applicants must wait 12 months before re-applying.
WHO TO APPLY TO Sally Barber, Administrator, PO Box 2318, Salisbury SP2 2JX *Email* enquiries@weinstockfund.org.uk *Website* www.weinstockfund.org.uk

The Weir Charitable Trust

SC NO SC043187 **ESTABLISHED** 2012
WHERE FUNDING CAN BE GIVEN Scotland.
WHO CAN BENEFIT Smaller charities and community groups.
WHAT IS FUNDED Sport and recreational activities; animal welfare; health; culture.
WHAT IS NOT FUNDED Groups or charities which have an income of over £100,000 per year; individuals; commercial activity; research; educational establishments; social enterprises; CICs; governing bodies; public sector bodies; one-off events; sport strips; large capital projects; community councils, PTAs or Active Schools Activities; pilot projects; sponsorship. Applications from outside Scotland or for activities carried out outside Scotland will not be accepted.
TYPE OF GRANT Capital projects; running costs; one-off projects; core costs; salaries. All awards are for one year or less.
RANGE OF GRANTS The average award is around £3,500 but the trust states that in exceptional circumstances it will consider applications for funds up to £25,000.
SAMPLE GRANTS Scottish Women Warriors Wheelchair Basketball (£13,900); Lochore Miners Charitable Society (£10,000); The Scottish Animal Behaviour and Rescue Centre (£9,000); Carradale Village Hall (£8,800); Pavilion Youth Cafe (£8,000); Danderhall Judo Club (£7,500).
FINANCES *Year* 2015 *Income* £212,828 *Grants* £190,239 *Grants to organisations* £190,239 *Assets* £4,565,135
TRUSTEES Jacqui Low; Martin McLellan; Colin Weir; Christine Weir; Carole Weir; James Weir.
HOW TO APPLY Applications can be made through the trust's website or on an application form available from the website. Details of application deadlines are also available on the site.
WHO TO APPLY TO The Trustees, 27 Maritime Street, Leith, Edinburgh EH6 6SE *Tel.* 0131 554 7806 *Email* enquiries@weircharitabletrust.com *Website* www.weircharitabletrust.com

The James Weir Foundation

CC NO 251764 **ESTABLISHED** 1967
WHERE FUNDING CAN BE GIVEN UK, mainly Scotland, with a preference for Ayrshire and Glasgow.
WHO CAN BENEFIT Registered charities in the UK.
WHAT IS FUNDED The foundation has general charitable purposes, giving priority to Scottish organisations, especially local charities in Ayrshire and Glasgow.
WHAT IS NOT FUNDED Individuals.
TYPE OF GRANT One-off and recurrent. Capital and core costs.
RANGE OF GRANTS Mostly £1,000 to £3,000.
SAMPLE GRANTS Alzheimer's Research UK (£6,000); Blind Veterans UK, Kilbryde Hospice, National Autistic Society, Sea Cadets and Young Action Wiltshire (£3,000 each); Clinks, Glasgow Action for Pensioners, New Caledonian Woodlands and Target Ovarian Cancer (£1,000 each).
FINANCES *Year* 2015 *Income* £300,622 *Grants* £244,000 *Grants to organisations* £244,000 *Assets* £7,474,418
TRUSTEES Simon Bonham; Elizabeth Bonham; William Ducas.
OTHER INFORMATION The following six charities are listed in the trust deed as specific beneficiaries and receive regular donations from the foundation: the Royal Society; the British

Science Association; the RAF Benevolent Fund; the Royal College of Surgeons; the Royal College of Physicians; the University of Strathclyde. Grants were made to 82 additional organisations in 2015.

HOW TO APPLY The trust's website states that 'applications should be received by letter with supporting evidence and a copy of the latest annual report. No applications can be received by email. Unsuccessful applicants will be notified by postcard after the Trustees' meeting has taken place.' The trustees meet twice a year to review applications. Successful applicants must wait two years before re-applying.

WHO TO APPLY TO Louisa Lawson, Secretary, PO Box 72361, London SW18 9NB *Email* info@jamesweirfoundation.org *Website* jamesweirfoundation.org

■ The Wellcome Trust

CC NO 210183 **ESTABLISHED** 1936

WHERE FUNDING CAN BE GIVEN UK and overseas.

WHO CAN BENEFIT Academic researchers working in health, particularly in the fields of biomedical science, innovations, public engagement, medical humanities and society and ethics.

WHAT IS FUNDED Improving health through research and activities in science, humanities, social sciences and public engagement.

WHAT IS NOT FUNDED Specific criteria and exclusions for each funding programme are detailed on the trust's website. However, in general, the trust will not make grants for: the extension of professional education or experience; the care of patients or clinical trials; overheads; office expenses; general appeals. The trust does not make grants to supplement support provided by other funding bodies, nor does it donate funds for other charities to use. Grants to individuals are usually given via a university, although small grants for travel or developing public understanding of science may be given directly.

TYPE OF GRANT All types of grant including project grants, programme grants, fellowships, research expenses, travel grants and equipment. Grants may last for more than three years. Check the trust's website for details of each funding programme.

SAMPLE GRANTS These figures represent the total amount awarded during the year, and may comprise many grants: University of Oxford (£134.5 million); University of Edinburgh (£31.1 million); King's College London (£27.6 million); University of Manchester (£18.3 million); London School of Hygiene and Tropical Medicine (£12.3 million); Science Museum (£9.5 million); Institute of Cancer Research (£8.9 million); Medical Research Council (£7.2 million).

FINANCES *Year* 2015/16 *Income* £390,300,000 *Grants* £751,700,000 *Grants to organisations* £751,700,000 *Assets* £19,606,100,000

OTHER INFORMATION The Wellcome Trust is one of the world's leading biomedical research charities and is the UK's largest non-governmental source of funds for biomedical research – it is also the UK's largest charity. The trust has a revised strategic plan for 2010–2020.

HOW TO APPLY The trust have launched a new application and grants management system. This new system is the WT Grant Tracker and has replaced the previous eGrants as the way to submit online applications. It handles all aspects of the application review process up to the point when a grant is awarded and accepted. As criteria, processes and deadlines vary according to which award fund you are applying to, you need to check both the criteria, deadline and the process for submitting an application on the trust's website. For more information about WT Grant Tracker or the implementation arrangements, contact the Grants Information Desk on +44 (0) 20 7611 8383 or email gtsupport@wellcome.ac.uk.

WHO TO APPLY TO Lorraine Shepherd, Grants Operations Manager, Gibbs Building, 215 Euston Road, London NW1 2BE *Tel.* 020 7611 5757 *Email* l.shepherd@wellcome.ac.uk *Website* www.wellcome.ac.uk

■ The Welton Foundation

CC NO 245319 **ESTABLISHED** 1965

WHERE FUNDING CAN BE GIVEN UK and overseas.

WHO CAN BENEFIT Charitable organisations.

WHAT IS FUNDED Principally supports projects in the health and medical fields. Grants for other general charitable purposes are also considered. Other causes supported in 2015/16 include community development, disability and culture and the arts.

TYPE OF GRANT Some recurrent funding and several small and large donations.

SAMPLE GRANTS HCA (£100,000); Brain Research Trust and The Royal Academy (£50,000); Sheffield Institute for Translational Neuroscience (£25,000); One to One Children's Fund (£10,000 each); Target Ovarian Cancer (£5,000); Jumbulance Trust (£3,000); The Oasis Partnership (£2,500); London Symphony Orchestra (£1,000).

FINANCES *Year* 2015/16 *Income* £74,031 *Grants* £432,500 *Grants to organisations* £432,500 *Assets* £2,007,659

TRUSTEES Sir Hugh Stevenson; D. B. Vaughan; Dr Michael Harding.

OTHER INFORMATION Grants were made to 29 organisations in 2015/16.

HOW TO APPLY Unsolicited applications are not considered.

WHO TO APPLY TO The Trustees, Old Waterfield, Winkfield Road, Ascot, Berkshire SL5 7LJ *Email* hugh.stevenson@oldwaterfield.com

■ The Wessex Youth Trust

CC NO 1076003 **ESTABLISHED** 1999

WHERE FUNDING CAN BE GIVEN Mainly UK.

WHO CAN BENEFIT Registered charities with which the Earl and Countess have a personal interest; in practice, charities working with children and young people.

WHAT IS FUNDED Grants are given to a wide range of projects providing opportunities and support for children and young people up to the age of 21. Funding is generally given for small specific projects, rather than projects for which a number of other funding sources are available. According to the website, some preference is given to applications from 'self-help organisations and to charities requiring support to "prime the pumps" for development and more extensive fundraising initiatives.'

WHAT IS NOT FUNDED Grants are not made: to organisations or groups which are not registered as charities or charitable causes; in response to applications by, or for the benefit of, individuals; by means of sponsorship for individuals undertaking fundraising activities on behalf of any charity; to organisations or groups whose main objects are to fund or support other charitable bodies; to charities with religious objectives, political, industrial or commercial appeal. Support is not generally given to charities whose accounts disclose substantial financial resources and which have well-established and ample fundraising capabilities.

TYPE OF GRANT One-off grants. Capital costs, development funding and full project funding.

SAMPLE GRANTS Angel Shed Theatre; Auditory Verbal UK; Brainwave Centre; Carmarthenshire Domestic Abuse Services; Central London Samaritans; New Horizon Youth Centre; Portobello Toddlers Hut; Siblings Together; Stirling Carers Centre; Straight Talking Peer Education; Ubunye Foundation.

FINANCES *Year* 2015/16 *Income* £103,691 *Grants* £116,664 *Grants to organisations* £116,664 *Assets* £679,849

TRUSTEES Robert Clinton; Mark Foster-Brown; Richard Parry; Kate Cavelle; Francesca Schwarzenbach; Denise Poulton.

OTHER INFORMATION Grants were made to 19 organisations in 2015/16. The accounts stated: 'The Charity Commission has been supplied with details of amounts given to each charity together with an explanation of the reason for the non-disclosure of individual amounts in the financial statements.'

HOW TO APPLY Applicants must complete an application form which can be downloaded from the trust's website, where guidance is provided. Completed forms must be submitted by 1 May or 1 November. All of the requested information must be completed on the form rather than on supplementary documents. Clarity of presentation and provision of financial details are among the qualities which the trustees favour. Successful applicants will receive a letter stating that acceptance of funding is conditional on an update report received within six months. Unsuccessful applications will receive a letter of notification following the trustees' meeting. The trust cannot enter any further communication with applicants.

WHO TO APPLY TO Jenny Cannon, Trust Administrator, Chelwood, Rectory Road, East Carleton, Norwich NR14 8HT *Tel.* 01508 571230 *Email* j.cannon@wessexyouthtrust.org.uk *Website* www.wessexyouthtrust.org.uk

■ West Derby Wastelands Charity

CC NO 223623 **ESTABLISHED** 1964

WHERE FUNDING CAN BE GIVEN The ancient township of West Derby in Liverpool (a map is available on request).

WHO CAN BENEFIT Charitable organisations; individuals.

WHAT IS FUNDED General charitable purposes; community development; social welfare; older people; children and young people.

WHAT IS NOT FUNDED The trust has previously stated that grants are not given for education or maintenance during education.

RANGE OF GRANTS £170 to £2,700.

SAMPLE GRANTS St Vincent's School (£2,700); Hare and Hounds Bowling Club (£2,500); RNIB (£2,000); Friends of Springfield Park (£1,500); Porchfield Community Association (£1,000); Tree House Liverpool CIC (£500); 7th Fairfield Scout Group (£300); Tuebrook Hope Group (£170).

FINANCES *Year* 2016 *Income* £62,602 *Grants* £52,485 *Grants to organisations* £47,335 *Assets* £1,985,569

TRUSTEES Joan Driscoll; Barry Flynn; John Kerr; Barbara Kerr; Peter North; Barbara Shacklady; Derek Corlett; Barbara Antrobus; Anthony Heath.

OTHER INFORMATION Grants were made to 35 organisations and grants to individuals totalled £5,200.

HOW TO APPLY The charity has detailed guidance for individuals and organisations on its website where you can download an application.

WHO TO APPLY TO Lawrence Downey, Secretary, Ripley House, 56 Freshfield Road, Formby, Liverpool L37 3HW *Tel.* 01704 879330 *Email* lawrence@westderbywastelands.co.uk *Website* www.westderbywastelands.co.uk

■ The West Looe Town Trust

CC NO 228167 **ESTABLISHED** 1961

WHERE FUNDING CAN BE GIVEN Looe Town, Cornwall.

WHO CAN BENEFIT Organisations; individuals.

WHAT IS FUNDED General charitable purposes; older people; poverty; education; health; community development; sports.

TYPE OF GRANT Project costs.

RANGE OF GRANTS £100 to £10,000.

SAMPLE GRANTS Looe Town FC (£11,700); Riverside Church (£10,000); Looe Primary Academy (£3,000); Looe Literary Festival (£1,500); Looe Development Trust (£1,000); Age Concern, Cornish Lugger Association, Darby and Joan (£500 each) The Royal British Legion-Wreath (£25).

FINANCES *Year* 2015 *Income* £184,553 *Grants* £37,652 *Grants to organisations* £29,565 *Assets* £5,643,362

TRUSTEES Geraldine Oliver; Colin Crabb; James Dingle; Nicholas Pope; Brian Porter; David Stevens; Keith Wilson.

OTHER INFORMATION Grants awarded to individuals during the year totalled £8,000.

HOW TO APPLY Apply in writing to the correspondent. The applicant is expected to provide details of the project requiring assistance, explaining how any grant would be used and what would be achieved.

WHO TO APPLY TO John Currah, West Looe Town Trust, West Looe Square, West Looe, Cornwall PL13 2EU *Tel.* 01503 263655 *Fax* 01503 263655 *Email* wltt2@btconnect.com

■ The Westcroft Trust

CC NO 212931 **ESTABLISHED** 1947

WHERE FUNDING CAN BE GIVEN UK and overseas, but with a special interest in Shropshire.

WHO CAN BENEFIT Registered charities only.

WHAT IS FUNDED According to the 2014/15 accounts, the trust focuses support on five main areas: Society of Friends (Quaker) activities across the UK; international understanding, peace and reconciliation and associated education and counselling; social care and community development, particularly in Shropshire; international medical relief and aid; people with disabilities and special needs, particularly in Shropshire.

WHAT IS NOT FUNDED Individuals; medical electives; sport; the arts (unless specifically for people with disabilities in Shropshire); armed forces charities; sponsorship. Annual grants are withheld if recent accounts are not available or do not satisfy the trustees as to continuing need.

TYPE OF GRANT One-off and recurrent.

RANGE OF GRANTS Up to £5,000.

SAMPLE GRANTS Britain Yearly Meeting (£10,600); Citizens Advice Shropshire (£2,500); Arthritis Research UK and Freedom from Torture (£1,500 each); BuildIT International, Survival International and The Connection at St Martin-in-the-Fields (£1,000 each); Pain Relief Foundation (£700); Chiltern Area Quaker Meeting (£600); Shropshire Play Bus (£500).
FINANCES *Year* 2015/16 *Income* £104,509 *Grants* £110,000 *Grants to organisations* £110,000
TRUSTEES Mary Cadbury; Richard Cadbury; James Cadbury; Erica Cadbury.
OTHER INFORMATION At the time of writing (June 2017), the 2015/16 accounts had been submitted to the Charity Commission but were not available to view on the Charity Commission's website. We have therefore estimated the grant total based on previous years' information. The largest grant is usually made to the Britain Yearly Meeting of The Society of Friends.
HOW TO APPLY Apply in writing to the correspondent. Applications should consist of no more than two pages of A4, clearly stating the aims of the project and how it meets the trust's objectives, as well as the time scale of the project, any funding received so far, and information about the organisation.
WHO TO APPLY TO Martin Beardwell, Clerk to the Trustees, 32 Hampton Road, Oswestry, Shropshire SY11 1SJ *Email* westcroft32@btinternet.com

■ The Westfield Health Charitable Trust

CC NO 246057 **ESTABLISHED** 1965
WHERE FUNDING CAN BE GIVEN Mostly South Yorkshire, also UK.
WHO CAN BENEFIT Registered charities and NHS Hospital Trusts.
WHAT IS FUNDED Health, well-being and medical causes.
RANGE OF GRANTS Up to £100,000; many grants under £5,000.
SAMPLE GRANTS Transplant Sport UK (£184,000); Age UK Sheffield (£90,000); Ashgate Hospice (£51,000); Support Dogs (£12,000); Sheffield Young Carers (£9,500); Nottinghamshire Hospice (£5,000); Kidney Research UK (£2,000); Radio Nightingale (£250); Action Medical Research (£200); Brain Tumour Support and Mind (£100 each); Bliss (£50).
FINANCES *Year* 2015/16 *Income* £562,301 *Grants* £684,667 *Grants to organisations* £684,667 *Assets* £82,494
TRUSTEES Graham Moore; David Whitney; Dr Catherine Ryan.
OTHER INFORMATION The trust was previously known as The Sheffield and District Hospital Services Charitable Fund. Grants were made to 168 organisations during the year.
HOW TO APPLY The website states that charities should contact the trust by email or telephone to find out more about applying for a grant. Grants are approved by the trustees at quarterly meetings.
WHO TO APPLY TO Graham Moore, Trustee, Westfield House, 60 Charter Row, Sheffield S1 3FZ *Tel.* 0114 250 2000 *Email* charity@westfieldhealth.com *Website* www.westfieldhealth.com

■ Westminster Amalgamated Charity

CC NO 207964 **ESTABLISHED** 1961
WHERE FUNDING CAN BE GIVEN City of Westminster.
WHO CAN BENEFIT Registered charities; individuals in need. Applications from national charities are only considered if they can demonstrate that their project or service will benefit a significant number of residents in need in Westminster.
WHAT IS FUNDED The charity supports organisations working in the following areas: addiction; children and young people; community; older people; health and disability; homelessness.
WHAT IS NOT FUNDED Applications from outside the City of Westminster are not supported.
TYPE OF GRANT Specific capital costs; revenue funding and core costs; specific project or service costs. One-off grants only.
RANGE OF GRANTS Organisations: £500 to £10,000. Individuals: £100 to £400.
SAMPLE GRANTS West London Day Centre (£10,000); Pimlico Toy Library (£7,500); St John's Wood Adventure Playground (£7,000); Royal Trinity Hospice (£6,000); DreamArts and South Westminster Legal Advice Centre (£5,000 each); Contact the Elderly (£4,000); Marylebone Bangladesh Society (£3,000); Beanstalk (£2,800); Cardinal Hume Centre (£1,000).
FINANCES *Year* 2015 *Income* £384,072 *Grants* £234,389 *Grants to organisations* £202,673 *Assets* £7,007,118
TRUSTEES Mark Studer; Jenny Bianco; Dr Cyril Nemeth; Paul Gardner; Eileen Terry; Jean Rymer; Linda McHugh; Graham Mordue; Simon Carruth; David Cavaye; Kate Bowyer.
OTHER INFORMATION Grants were made to 38 organisations during the year. The charity also makes grants to individuals in need who live, work or study in the City of Westminster borough. Grants were made to 154 individuals in 2015, totalling £31,500.
HOW TO APPLY Applications can be made using the online form on the charity's website, where deadlines for the five meetings of the trustees through the year are also posted. Applications from national charities are automatically deferred to the last meeting of the year. Applicants will be notified of the outcome within two weeks of a meeting. Any queries should be directed to the Grants Administrator.
WHO TO APPLY TO Julia Moorcroft, Grants Administrator, School House, Drury Lane, London WC2B 5SU *Tel.* 020 7395 9460 *Fax* 020 7595 9479 *Email* wac@3chars.org.uk *Website* www.w-a-c.org.uk

■ The Westminster Foundation

CC NO 267618 **ESTABLISHED** 1974
WHERE FUNDING CAN BE GIVEN Westminster; Cheshire West and Chester; rural North West Lancashire (near the Forest of Bowland); North West Sunderland. Outside these areas, grants are made through local Community Foundations.
WHO CAN BENEFIT Registered charities.
WHAT IS FUNDED Social welfare. The foundation is currently focusing its grant-making on issues around poverty in the UK, in the following themes: supporting communities in need; vulnerable groups; building resilience; crisis intervention. Further detail on eligibility criteria is given on the foundation's website. The foundation also makes some grants overseas, but these are not open to application.
WHAT IS NOT FUNDED General appeals or letters requesting non-specific donations; organisations

that do not have charitable aims (e.g. commercial companies and companies limited by shares); overtly political projects (including party political and campaigning projects); individuals (or organisations applying on behalf of an individual); student fees/bursaries; projects taking place or benefitting people outside the UK; projects benefitting people outside the foundation's specific geographical criteria; holidays/trips; projects where the main focus is website development or maintenance; start-up costs or organisations that do not yet have a demonstrable track record; animal charities; medical research charities; organisations that have applied unsuccessfully within the previous 12 months.

TYPE OF GRANT Small, one-off grants; major grants over more than one year; core costs and rents.

RANGE OF GRANTS Small grants of up to £5,000; major grants: over £5,000 (closed to applications at the time of writing).

SAMPLE GRANTS Ashden (£120,000); Hong Kong Cancer Fund (£85,500); The Foundation Years Trust (£75,000); Atlantic Salmon Trust (£50,000); Fine Cell Work (£56,500); Caritas Madrid (£44,500); Forgiveness Project (£35,000); Crisis UK (£32,500); Age UK Cheshire (£25,000); Small Charities Coalition (£22,000).

FINANCES *Year* 2015 *Income* £3,168,048 *Grants* £41,904,260 *Grants to organisations* £41,904,260 *Assets* £3,962,512

TRUSTEES Mark Preston; Jane Sanders.

OTHER INFORMATION At the time of writing (May 2017), the foundation's Major Grants scheme is closed to unsolicited applications. The foundation awarded 162 grants to organisations in 2015. This included an unusually large grant of £40 million to the Defence and National Rehabilitation Centre.

HOW TO APPLY The foundation advises potential applicants to check their eligibility for a grant according to the information on the website. Organisations must be registered with the Charity Commission, or have exclusively charitable objectives, and be working to benefit people in the areas funded by the foundation. Appeals must fall within the criteria of the foundation's current funding programme. Applications should be made online at the foundation's website, where application guidelines are also available. The Grants Review panel meets around every eight weeks and successful applicants will be notified within two weeks of a meeting.

WHO TO APPLY TO Jane Sandars, Director, The Grosvenor Office, 70 Grosvenor Street, London W1K 3JP *Tel.* 020 7312 6157 *Email* westminster.foundation@grosvenor.com *Website* www.westminsterfoundation.org.uk

The Garfield Weston Foundation

CC NO 230260 **ESTABLISHED** 1958

WHERE FUNDING CAN BE GIVEN UK.

WHO CAN BENEFIT UK-registered charities; educational establishments; churches; housing associations; museums and galleries.

WHAT IS FUNDED A broad variety of activities in the fields of: arts; community; education; faith; health; museums and heritage; welfare; and young people. The website states that: 'the Trustees have a preference for charities directly delivering services and activities to those in need, and are especially keen to see applications from charities in the Welfare, Youth and Community sectors and also in regions of economic disadvantage'. The foundation gives a range of smaller and larger grants, supporting many different organisations and providing helpful information on its website.

WHAT IS NOT FUNDED Individuals; CICs; social enterprises or sporting associations that are not registered charities; work that does not deliver a direct benefit in the UK, even if the organisation is a registered charity within the UK; animal welfare charities; charities that spend the majority of their income outside the UK; local authorities and councils; one-off events such as festivals or galas, including for fundraising purposes; sponsorship; grants for a particular staff position or job (although project or revenue/core cost grants may include a contribution to salaries); feasibility studies; overseas activities or trips; start-up costs or organisations that do not yet have a track record of delivery, or have not produced financial accounts; campaigning, lobbying and awareness-raising activities; endowment appeals. The foundation is also unlikely to fund organisations with liquid reserves in excess of more than 12 months' expenditure, unless they can make a convincing case that they are in financial need.

TYPE OF GRANT Capital (including buildings); revenue and core costs; project costs.

RANGE OF GRANTS £500 to £3 million.

SAMPLE GRANTS The Courtauld Institute of Art (£3 million); Mansfield College – University of Oxford (£1 million); OnSide Youth Zones (£500,000); British Lung Foundation (£100,000); Clean Break (£40,000); East Belfast Independent Advice Centre (£20,000); Willington Methodist Church (£15,000); Swansea City Opera (£10,000); Islington Bangladesh Association (£5,000); The Green Team Edinburgh and Lothians Ltd (£2,500); Ashford Family Nursery (£500).

FINANCES *Year* 2015/16 *Income* £62,150,000 *Grants* £58,745,000 *Grants to organisations* £58,745,000 *Assets* £12,750,695,000

TRUSTEES Jana Khayat; Camilla Dalglish; Kate Hobhouse; Eliza Mitchell; Galen Weston; George Weston; Sophia Mason; Melissa Murdoch; Guy Weston.

OTHER INFORMATION In 2015/16 the foundation made 1,617 grants, of which 1,210 were for £20,000 or less, and 407 were for more than £20,000. A breakdown of the amount given to each area of focus is given in the annual report.

HOW TO APPLY Applications should be submitted via the foundation's website or by post (refer to the 'Postal Application Checklist' on the website). The website provides clear and comprehensive guidelines on eligibility, applications processes and what should be included in an application. The trustees meet regularly to review applications – regular grants (under £100,000) are reviewed on a weekly basis and major grants (£100,000 or more) are reviewed eight times each year. Applicants should allow up to four months for the whole process.

WHO TO APPLY TO Philippa Charles, Director, Weston Centre, 10 Grosvenor Street, London W1K 4QY *Tel.* 020 7399 6565 *Email* gdarocha@garfieldweston.org *Website* www.garfieldweston.org

Westway Trust

CC NO 1123127 **ESTABLISHED** 2008

WHERE FUNDING CAN BE GIVEN Royal Borough of Kensington and Chelsea, with a particular focus on North Kensington, in and around the Westway.

WHO CAN BENEFIT Social enterprises, charitable, voluntary and community organisations.

WHAT IS FUNDED The main grants scheme is the Community Grants programme, which aims to: improve the health and well-being of the local community; provide economic opportunities for the local community; improve the local environment; celebrate the local talent and diversity of the community. There is also a Festivals Fund, which supports arts and cultural festivals to bring the community together; a Creative Futures scheme, supporting creative employment opportunities for young people; and a sports grants programme, providing bursaries and scholarships. For further information, refer to the trust's website.

TYPE OF GRANT Projects costs; one-off; recurrent; capital costs; core costs. As part of the Community Grants programme, the trust will also pledge up to £4,000 for larger projects and initiatives which commit to undertake a crowdfunding campaign to raise further funds – refer to the website for more information.

SAMPLE GRANTS Age UK Kensington and Chelsea (£30,500 in three grants); Migrants Organise (£24,000); The Hip-Hop Shakespeare Foundation Ltd (£20,000); Midaye Somali Development Network (£16,900 in three grants); Baraka Youth Association (£13,000); Carnival Village Trust (£7,200); Muslim Cultural Heritage Centre and Notting Hill Churches Homeless Concern (£2,500 each); Tavistock Garden Club (£500); Action Disability Kensington and Chelsea (£400).

FINANCES *Year* 2015/16 *Income* £8,078,000 *Grants* £401,446 *Grants to organisations* £383,158 *Assets* £46,403,000

TRUSTEES Mike Jones; Cllr Malcolm Spalding; Cllr Anne Cyron; Christopher Ward; Karen Bendell; Sheraine Williams; Alan Brown; Fiona Ramsay; Angela Spence; Cllr Monica Press; Howard Richards; Jeannette Davidson.

OTHER INFORMATION The trust was previously known as Westway Development Trust. In 2015/16 grants were made to 72 organisations. Grants to individuals during the year totalled £18,300.

HOW TO APPLY Firstly, refer to the website for information on what is currently available. There are two rounds of funding for the Community Grants programme, in September and January. For further information, email grants@westway.org.

WHO TO APPLY TO Phil Nichols, Head of Charity Income and Impact, Westway Trust Office, 1 Thorpe Close, London W10 5XL *Tel.* 020 8962 5720 *Email* info@westway.org or grants@westway.org *Website* www.westway.org

■ The Barbara Whatmore Charitable Trust

CC NO 283336 **ESTABLISHED** 1981

WHERE FUNDING CAN BE GIVEN UK.

WHO CAN BENEFIT Registered charities.

WHAT IS FUNDED Arts, music and relief of poverty, focusing mainly on cultural and heritage projects, particularly in East Anglia. Eligible areas of support include: classical music education; conservation and crafts training; education projects in museums, the theatre and poetry; conservation of endangered historic artefacts and of the natural heritage environment, as well as preventive projects to protect historic or natural collections.

WHAT IS NOT FUNDED Repair work to the fabric of buildings or structures; the purchase of medical equipment or works of art; choral societies; festivals; individuals; organisations without registered charitable status.

RANGE OF GRANTS Up to £5,000.

SAMPLE GRANTS London Philharmonic Orchestra (£6,000); Campaign for Drawing (£3,600); Edward Barnsley Educational Trust (£3,000); Welsh National Youth Opera (£2,500); Countryside Restoration Trust (£2,300); The Garden Museum (£2,100); Wallace Collection (£1,800); Wonderful Beast Theatre Company and Plantlife (£1,000 each); New Lanark Conservation (£250).

FINANCES *Year* 2015/16 *Income* £81,108 *Grants* £70,150 *Grants to organisations* £70,150 *Assets* £1,867,049

TRUSTEES David Eldridge; Denis Borrow; Gillian Lewis; Luke Gardiner; Patricia Cooke-Yarborough; Sally Carter; Stephen Bate.

OTHER INFORMATION Grants were awarded to 30 organisations in 2015/16.

HOW TO APPLY Apply in writing to the trust's administrator, either by post or email. Applications can be submitted at any time but no later than 15 March or 15 September to be included in either of the two meetings in April and October.

WHO TO APPLY TO Denise Gardiner, Trust Administrator, 3 Honeyhanger, Hindhead Road, Hindhead GU26 6BA *Email* denise@bwct.org

■ The Wheeler Family Charitable Trust

CC NO 1156928 **ESTABLISHED** 2014

WHERE FUNDING CAN BE GIVEN England and Wales.

WHO CAN BENEFIT Registered charities.

WHAT IS FUNDED Education.

SAMPLE GRANTS Place2Be (£154,500); Buckinghamshire Community Foundation and Eton College Charitable Trust (£100,000 each); Best Beginnings (£30,000); Child Bereavement UK (£20,000); Peter Jones Foundation (£10,000); Wellington College (£1,400).

FINANCES *Year* 2015/16 *Income* £928,792 *Grants* £415,900 *Grants to organisations* £415,900 *Assets* £1,403,791

TRUSTEES Belinda Wheeler; Nicholas Wheeler.

HOW TO APPLY Apply in writing to the correspondent.

WHO TO APPLY TO The Trustees, 2 Whitehall Quay, Leeds LS1 4HG *Tel.* 0113 285 5000

■ The Whitaker Charitable Trust

CC NO 234491 **ESTABLISHED** 1964

WHERE FUNDING CAN BE GIVEN UK, with focus on the East Midlands and Scotland.

WHO CAN BENEFIT Registered charities.

WHAT IS FUNDED General charitable purposes, with a focus on the following areas: local charities in Nottinghamshire and the East Midlands; music; agricultural and silvicultural education; countryside conservation; Scottish charities.

RANGE OF GRANTS £100 to £27,000. Most grants under £5,000.

SAMPLE GRANTS Atlantic College (£27,000); Royal Forestry Society (£15,000); Jasmine Trust (£10,000); Batteslaw Hospice (£3,000); Prisoner Education Trust (£2,000); European Squirrel Initiative, Future Trees Trust, Home-Start Nottingham, Perth Festival of Arts (£1,000 each); Literacy Volunteers (£500).

FINANCES *Year* 2015/16 *Income* £255,059 *Grants* £140,000 *Grants to organisations* £140,000 *Assets* £8,053,702

TRUSTEES Edward Perks; Lady Elizabeth Whitaker; Sir Jack Whitaker.
OTHER INFORMATION Grants were made to 29 organisations in 2015/16.
HOW TO APPLY Apply in writing to the correspondent. The trustees meet regularly to review grant applications.
WHO TO APPLY TO The Trustees, c/o Currey and Co., 21 Buckingham Gate, London SW1E 6LS *Tel.* 020 7802 2700

■ The Colonel W. H. Whitbread Charitable Trust

CC NO 210496 **ESTABLISHED** 1953
WHERE FUNDING CAN BE GIVEN UK.
WHO CAN BENEFIT Charitable organisations; educational institutions; sports organisations.
WHAT IS FUNDED The trust supports: education, particularly for those who are disadvantaged, as well as for pupils at Aldenham School and in support of Corpus Christi College, Cambridge; amateur sports, particularly those enjoyed by the settlor (ocean racing, Finn Class sailing, National Hunt racing, flying, field sports, eventing and polo); health and welfare of service personnel; conservation projects.
RANGE OF GRANTS £500 and upwards.
SAMPLE GRANTS 1st Queen's Dragon Guards Regimental Trust, Abbey School Tewkesbury, Army Benevolent Fund, CLIC Sargent, Disasters Emergency Committee Tsunami Earthquake Appeal, Friends of Alderman Knights School, Gloucestershire Historic Churches Trust, Great Ormond Street Hospital Children's Charity, Household Cavalry Museum Appeal, Hunt Servants' Fund, Queen Mary's Clothing Guild, Royal Hospital Chelsea and St Richard's Hospice.
FINANCES *Year* 2015 *Income* £190,782 *Grants* £99,600 *Grants to organisations* £99,600 *Assets* £329,791
TRUSTEES H. F. Whitbread; Jeremy Barkes; Rupert Foley.
OTHER INFORMATION Grants were awarded to 26 organisations in 2015, but no further information about beneficiaries was provided.
HOW TO APPLY Apply in writing to the correspondent.
WHO TO APPLY TO Susan Smith, Secretary, Fir Tree Cottage, World's End, Sinton Green, Worcestershire WR2 6NN *Email* whwhitbread.trust@googlemail.com

■ The Melanie White Foundation Ltd

CC NO 1077150 **ESTABLISHED** 1999
WHERE FUNDING CAN BE GIVEN UK.
WHO CAN BENEFIT Charitable organisations.
WHAT IS FUNDED General charitable purposes, particularly health, medicine and social welfare.
SAMPLE GRANTS CLIC Sargent (£76,500 in two grants); Tiger Woods Charity (£52,500); Alfred Dunhill Foundation (£20,000); Millfield Development (£10,000); Help for Heroes (£5,000); Nordoff Robbins UK (£1,100 in two grants); Lessons for Life Foundation (£1,000); Juvenile Diabetes (£500); Bowel and Cancer Research (£300); Leukaemia Foundation (£110).
FINANCES *Year* 2015/16 *Income* £350,354 *Grants* £204,410 *Grants to organisations* £204,410 *Assets* £11,599,445
TRUSTEES Melanie White; Andrew White.
OTHER INFORMATION Grants were made to 18 organisations in 2015/16. The foundation supports CLIC Sargent on a recurrent basis.
HOW TO APPLY This trust does not accept unsolicited applications as the trustees proactively identify beneficiaries themselves.
WHO TO APPLY TO Paula Doraisamy, Secretary, 61 Grosvenor Street, London W1K 3JE *Tel.* 020 3011 1041 *Email* melaniewhitefoundation@gmail.com

■ White Stuff Foundation

CC NO 1134754 **ESTABLISHED** 2010
WHERE FUNDING CAN BE GIVEN UK – areas local to a White Stuff shop, office, distribution centre or supplier.
WHO CAN BENEFIT Registered charities, particularly those that are small and local.
WHAT IS FUNDED Communities and social welfare.
WHAT IS NOT FUNDED Grants are only made to partner charities. Charities which are religious or conflict with any of the company's values will not be supported.
SAMPLE GRANTS The Rathbone Society (£111,500); ID Care Trust (£43,000); Parents Association for Seriously Ill Children (£9,200); Lothian Autistic Society (£4,900); Dog Kennel Hill Adventure Playground (£4,800); Exeter Community Initiatives (£3,500); Ability Dogs 4 Young People and Bath City Farm (£3,400 each); No Limits (£3,300); Home-Start Elmbridge (£3,000).
FINANCES *Year* 2015/16 *Income* £569,000 *Grants* £465,061 *Grants to organisations* £465,061 *Assets* £275,266
TRUSTEES Rebecca Kong; Sean Thomas; Victoria Hodges; Louise McGarr; Jeremy Selgal; Julian Baker; Helen Marshall.
OTHER INFORMATION Grants were made to 28 charities in 2015/16. Types of grant include one-off discretionary grants; Community Chest grants to promote local community engagement; matched funding for employee-supported charities; local charity partnership grants. Volunteer support from White Stuff employees may also be offered to partner charities.
HOW TO APPLY The foundation only supports partner charities, in the areas where the company works. According to the website, potential partners must be registered charities, working in the local community, with an annual income of under £3 million. There is an online newsletter which publicises when a new shop will be opening, and therefore an opportunity to become a partner charity. A list of current partners is given on the website.
WHO TO APPLY TO Foundation Manager, Canterbury Court, 1–3 Brixton Road, London SW9 6DE *Tel.* 020 7735 8133 *Email* giving@whitestufffoundation.org *Website* www.whitestuff.com

■ The Whitecourt Charitable Trust

CC NO 1000012 **ESTABLISHED** 1990
WHERE FUNDING CAN BE GIVEN UK and overseas, with a preference for South Yorkshire.
WHO CAN BENEFIT Charitable organisations.
WHAT IS FUNDED General charitable purposes, with a strong preference for Christian causes.
WHAT IS NOT FUNDED Animal or conservation organisations; campaigning on social issues.
TYPE OF GRANT Some recurrent, some one-off.
RANGE OF GRANTS £25 to £7,000; mostly under £500.

SAMPLE GRANTS Fulwood Parochial Church Council (£7,700); Monkton Combe Bursary Fund (£3,000); South Yorkshire Community Foundation (£1,100); Latin Link (£700); Uley with Owlpen and Nympsfield Parochial Church Council (£500); Daylight Christian Prison Trust and Mercy Ships (£200 each); Macmillan Cancer Support, Rotherham Foodbank and Wells for India (£100 each); All Saints Church Totley (£25).

FINANCES *Year* 2015/16 *Income* £68,562 *Grants* £56,350 *Grants to organisations* £54,955 *Assets* £22,370

TRUSTEES Peter Lee; Gillian Lee; Dr Hannah Denno.

OTHER INFORMATION Grants were awarded to 180 organisations in 2015/16.

HOW TO APPLY Apply in writing to the correspondent.

WHO TO APPLY TO Gillian Lee, Trustee, 1 Old Fulwood Road, Sheffield S10 3TG *Tel.* 0114 230 5555 *Email* pwlee@waitrose.com

■ The Norman Whiteley Trust

CC NO 226445 **ESTABLISHED** 1963

WHERE FUNDING CAN BE GIVEN Worldwide, although in practice mainly Cumbria and Austria.

WHO CAN BENEFIT Christian evangelical organisations.

WHAT IS FUNDED Evangelical Christian causes. The trust's objects are to fund activities which further the spread of the Gospel, relieving poverty and assisting with education.

TYPE OF GRANT One-off, recurrent, capital, core costs; salaries.

RANGE OF GRANTS £200 to £13,200.

SAMPLE GRANTS International Aid Trust (£13,200); Luv Preston (£7,900); Torchbearer Trust Fund (£5,000); World Prayer Centre (£4,000); Sports Reach (£3,000); YWAM (£2,500); Great Lakes Outreach (£2,000); Bibles for Children (£1,000); St Thomas' Church (£450); Sandylands Methodist Church (£200).

FINANCES *Year* 2015/16 *Income* £124,407 *Grants* £74,095 *Grants to organisations* £68,145 *Assets* £2,664,308

TRUSTEES Derek Dickson; Jeremy Ratcliff; Paul Whiteley; Pippa Whiteley.

OTHER INFORMATION The amount of grants given to individuals totalled £6,000.

HOW TO APPLY Apply in writing to the correspondent.

WHO TO APPLY TO David Foster, Fellside Cottage, Little Asby, Appleby, Cumbria CA16 6QE *Email* normanwhiteleytrust@gmail.com

■ The Whitewater Charitable Trust

CC NO 1146069 **ESTABLISHED** 2012

WHERE FUNDING CAN BE GIVEN UK and overseas.

WHO CAN BENEFIT Registered charities.

WHAT IS FUNDED General charitable purposes.

TYPE OF GRANT One-off grants and loans.

SAMPLE GRANTS Sepsis UK (£48,000).

FINANCES *Year* 2015/16 *Income* £1,139,265 *Grants* £48,000 *Grants to organisations* £48,000 *Assets* £32,317

TRUSTEES John McMonigall; Coutts & Co.

OTHER INFORMATION The trust awarded one grant in 2015/16 and made one loan of £200,000.

HOW TO APPLY Apply in writing to the correspondent, the trustees meet regularly to discuss applications.

WHO TO APPLY TO Coutts & Co., 6th Floor, Trinity Quay 2, Avon Street, Bristol BS2 0PT *Tel.* 0345 304 2424 *Email* couttscharities@coutts.com

■ The Whitley Animal Protection Trust

CC NO 236746 **ESTABLISHED** 1964

WHERE FUNDING CAN BE GIVEN UK and overseas.

WHO CAN BENEFIT Registered charities only.

WHAT IS FUNDED Animal welfare and conservation.

WHAT IS NOT FUNDED Non-registered charities.

TYPE OF GRANT Core and project grants, one-off grants, but usually recurrent grants that last for several years.

RANGE OF GRANTS Generally £250 to £20,000, although larger grants may also be given.

SAMPLE GRANTS Whitley Fund for Nature (£117,000); Oxford WildCru Wildlife Conservation Research Unit (£20,000); WWF Mountain Gorilla Project (£10,000); Marine Conservation Society (£8,000); Fauna and Flora International and Songbird Survival (£5,000 each); Orangutan Foundation (£3,500); Brooke Hospital for Animals (£1,700); The Hawk and Owl Trust (£1,000); Welsh Dee Trust (£250).

FINANCES *Year* 2015 *Income* £375,359 *Grants* £231,197 *Grants to organisations* £231,197 *Assets* £9,592,074

TRUSTEES Edward Whitley; Edward Whitley; Jeremy Whitley; Penelope Whitley.

OTHER INFORMATION The trust made 21 grants to organisations in 2015.

HOW TO APPLY The trust's 2015 annual report states: 'A majority of the grants undertaken are repeat donations, however the Trustees do provide essential core funding to these smaller charities without which they would find it hard to maintain their activities. The Charity does also make one-off grants, but a majority of the grants are in respect of longer term commitments.'

WHO TO APPLY TO Michael Gwynne, Secretary, Padmore House, Hall Court, Hall Park Way, Telford TF3 4LX *Tel.* 01952 641651

■ The Wigoder Family Foundation

CC NO 1086806 **ESTABLISHED** 2000

WHERE FUNDING CAN BE GIVEN England and Wales.

WHO CAN BENEFIT Registered charities.

WHAT IS FUNDED General charitable purposes; Jewish causes.

SAMPLE GRANTS One Family UK and The Prince's Teaching Institute (£25,000 each); Norwood (£20,000); The National Library (£17,500); World Jewish Relief (£15,000); Community Security Trust, Holocaust Educational Trust, Nightingale Hammerson and One to One Children's Fund (£10,000 each).

FINANCES *Year* 2014/15 *Income* £1,270,798 *Grants* £332,845 *Grants to organisations* £332,845 *Assets* £36,382,851

TRUSTEES Martin Rose; Charles Wigoder; Elizabeth Wigoder.

HOW TO APPLY Apply in writing to the correspondent.

WHO TO APPLY TO The Hon. Charles Francis Wigoder, 9 Hyde Park Gardens, London W2 2LT

■ The Lionel Wigram Memorial Trust

CC NO 800533 **ESTABLISHED** 1988

WHERE FUNDING CAN BE GIVEN UK, with a preference for Greater London.

WHO CAN BENEFIT Registered charities and voluntary organisations. The trust favours charities with an income of under £500,000, and those run by volunteers, although special projects by larger charities are occasionally supported.

WHAT IS FUNDED The trust mainly supports charities providing services for people who have disabilities. It particularly favours charities mainly run by volunteers, and those with new or innovative ideas.
WHAT IS NOT FUNDED Individuals; building projects; medical research; charities providing a service outside the UK; charities which do not have a record of at least three years.
TYPE OF GRANT Core costs and project costs. Small, one-off grants and larger, recurrent grants.
RANGE OF GRANTS Mostly £250 to £750.
SAMPLE GRANTS UCanDoIT (£12,000 in three grants); Newbury Spring Festival (£1,500); Music Alive and North Cornwall Talking Newspaper (£750 each); Braille Chess Association, National Migraine Centre and TRIP Community Transport Association (£500 each); Luton Shopmobility, Nightline Association and Southampton Society for the Blind (£250 each).
FINANCES *Year* 2015/16 *Income* £55,837 *Grants* £41,466 *Grants to organisations* £41,466 *Assets* £688,807
TRUSTEES Anthony Wigram; The Hon. Sally Wigram.
OTHER INFORMATION In 2015/16, 84 grants were awarded to 71 organisations. The trust gives regular support to the charity UCanDoIT.
HOW TO APPLY Applications should be made using the form on the trust's website. Grants are awarded in March. Support is often given to charities where the applicants are known by the trustees.
WHO TO APPLY TO Tracy Pernice, Highfield House, 4 Woodfall Street, London SW3 4DJ *Tel.* 020 7730 6820 *Email* info@lionelwigrammemorialtrust.org *Website* www.lionelwigrammemorialtrust.org

■ The Felicity Wilde Charitable Trust

CC NO 264404 **ESTABLISHED** 1972
WHERE FUNDING CAN BE GIVEN UK.
WHO CAN BENEFIT Registered charities only.
WHAT IS FUNDED Children's charities and medical research, particularly into asthma.
WHAT IS NOT FUNDED Individuals.
RANGE OF GRANTS Up to £10,000; most grants are for £1,000.
SAMPLE GRANTS Asthma UK (£10,000); Sparks (£4,000); Douglas Bader Foundation and The George Coller Memorial Fund (£2,000 each); Bliss, Crackerjack Children's Trust, Hearing Dogs for Deaf People, Kidney Research UK, Martin House Children's Hospice and Motability (£1,000 each).
FINANCES *Year* 2015/16 *Income* £92,194 *Grants* £68,000 *Grants to organisations* £68,000 *Assets* £1,972,928
TRUSTEE Zedra Trust Company (UK) Ltd.
OTHER INFORMATION Grants were given to 43 organisations in 2015/16.
HOW TO APPLY Apply in writing to the correspondent at any time. Applications are usually considered quarterly.
WHO TO APPLY TO The Trustees, Zedra UK Trusts, Osborne Court, Gadbrook Park, Rudheath, Cheshire CW9 7UE *Tel.* 01606 313206 *Email* charities@zedra.com

■ The Will Charitable Trust

CC NO 801682 **ESTABLISHED** 1989
WHERE FUNDING CAN BE GIVEN UK.
WHO CAN BENEFIT UK-registered or exempt charities.
WHAT IS FUNDED Care of and services for blind people, and the prevention and cure of blindness; care of people with learning disabilities, either in a residential care or supported living environment with a wide choice of activities and lifestyle, or providing long-term day/employment activities; care of and services for people suffering from cancer, and their families.
WHAT IS NOT FUNDED CICs; individuals fundraising for a charity. The trust is unlikely to fund applications relating to academic research projects.
TYPE OF GRANT One-off; recurrent (up to three years); project costs. Applications for core costs or running costs may be considered – applicants should discuss with the grants administrator before applying.
RANGE OF GRANTS £3,000 to £30,000.
SAMPLE GRANTS Eve Appeal (£91,000); Rainbow Living (£25,000); Sue Ryder (£20,000); Bradbury Fields (£15,000); Calibre Audio Library and Positive Action on Cancer (£10,000 each); St Catherine's Hospice (£9,000); Watford Mencap (£5,000); Parity for Disability (£4,500); Saint Michael's Hospice (£3,500).
FINANCES *Year* 2015/16 *Income* £752,664 *Grants* £777,300 *Grants to organisations* £777,300 *Assets* £18,850,374
TRUSTEES Alastair McDonald; Rodney Luff; Vanessa Reburn.
OTHER INFORMATION The trust awarded 58 grants in 2015/16 from its main grants programme; there was also an exceptional grant of £91,000.
HOW TO APPLY Applications should be made in writing to the correspondent and sent by post – emailed applications will not be accepted. Guidance on what to include in your application is given on the website, along with more detailed eligibility criteria. There are separate deadlines for each area of focus: blind people and learning disabilities – should be submitted between November and 31 January, for consideration in April; cancer care – should be submitted between June and 31 August, for consideration in November. The trust advises applicants not to submit their applications too early, but in plenty of time ahead of the deadlines to allow enough time for consideration. Potential applicants can discuss an application or any queries with the grants administrator (admin@willcharitabletrust.org.uk or 020 8941 0450). Applications are usually acknowledged within three weeks.
WHO TO APPLY TO Christine Dix, Grants Administrator, Bridge House, 11 Creek Road, East Molesey KT8 9BE *Tel.* 020 8941 0450 *Email* admin@willcharitabletrust.org.uk *Website* willcharitabletrust.org.uk

■ The Kay Williams Charitable Foundation

CC NO 1047947 **ESTABLISHED** 1995
WHERE FUNDING CAN BE GIVEN UK.
WHO CAN BENEFIT Registered charities.
WHAT IS FUNDED General charitable purposes including: health; arts; animal welfare.
SAMPLE GRANTS Teddington Memorial Hospital (£400); Princess Alice Hospital and Priest's Fund (£250 each); Lord's Taverners – Mickey's Appeal (£200).

FINANCES *Year* 2015/16 *Income* £24,843 *Grants* £40,000 *Grants to organisations* £40,000

TRUSTEES Richard Cantor; Margaret Williams.

OTHER INFORMATION This foundation's latest accounts were not available to view on the Charity Commission's website due to its low income. We have therefore estimated the grant total based on previous years' information.

HOW TO APPLY Apply in writing to the correspondent.

WHO TO APPLY TO Richard Cantor, Trustee, BDO LLP, Kings Wharf, 20–30 King's Road, Reading, Berkshire RG1 3EX *Tel.* 0118 925 4400

■ The Williams Charitable Trust

CC NO 1086668 **ESTABLISHED** 2001

WHERE FUNDING CAN BE GIVEN UK.

WHO CAN BENEFIT Charitable organisations.

WHAT IS FUNDED The objects of the trust are 'to support education and training, the advancement of medicine and general charitable purposes'. In practice, the trust tends to support theatre projects and local community initiatives.

SAMPLE GRANTS Montage Theatre (£11,000); Royal Shakespeare Company (£10,000); London Firebird Orchestra (£5,000); British Film Institute (£4,100); The British Museum (£2,700); Theatre Royal Bury St Edmunds and Theatre Street School of Performing Arts (£2,000 each); Julian Campbell Foundation (£1,100).

FINANCES *Year* 2015/16 *Income* £107,776 *Grants* £101,265 *Grants to organisations* £81,320 *Assets* £3,352,932

TRUSTEES Stuart Williams; Hilary Williams; Andrew Williams; Matthew Williams; Keith Eyre-Varnier.

OTHER INFORMATION Grants were awarded to 23 organisations during the year, of which eight were grants of £1,000 or less. There were also five grants awarded to individuals, which totalled £19,900.

HOW TO APPLY Apply in writing to the correspondent. The 2015/16 annual report states: 'The trustees adopt a proactive approach in seeking worthy causes requiring support.'

WHO TO APPLY TO Stuart Williams, Trustee, Flat 85 Capital Wharf, 50 Wapping High Street, London E1W 1LY *Tel.* 020 7388 1443

■ The Alfred Williams Charitable Trust

CC NO 266652 **ESTABLISHED** 1974

WHERE FUNDING CAN BE GIVEN Suffolk.

WHO CAN BENEFIT Charitable organisations.

WHAT IS FUNDED Heritage and environmental conservation; social welfare; performing arts.

SAMPLE GRANTS Parochial Church Council Needham Market (£5,000); Guildhall Project – Bury (£4,000); Wetherden Parish Council (£2,000); Mid Suffolk Light Railway (£2,500); Museum of East Anglian Life (£1,500); Mendlesham Football Club and St Elizabeth Hospice (£1,000 each); Stowmarket Chorale and Suffolk Festival of Performing Arts (£500 each); Suffolk Historic Churches Trust (£150).

FINANCES *Year* 2015/16 *Income* £66,386 *Grants* £65,150 *Grants to organisations* £65,150 *Assets* £2,307,140

TRUSTEES Jonathan Penn; Paul Dawson Clarke.

OTHER INFORMATION Grants were made to 49 organisations in 2015/16.

HOW TO APPLY Apply in writing to the correspondent.

WHO TO APPLY TO Jonathan Penn, Trustee, Firs Farmhouse, 12 Fishponds Way, Haughley, Stowmarket IP14 3PJ *Tel.* 01449 673355 *Email* robert@haughleypark.co.uk

■ The Williams Family Charitable Trust

CC NO 255452 **ESTABLISHED** 1959

WHERE FUNDING CAN BE GIVEN UK and Israel.

WHO CAN BENEFIT Charitable organisations; individuals.

WHAT IS FUNDED Jewish causes; medical causes; social welfare; general charitable purposes.

SAMPLE GRANTS But Chabad, Friends of Mifalhtorah for Shiloh, Holon Association for Absorption of Immigrants, Ingun Yedidut, Israel Concern Society, Karen Denny Pincus, Mogdal Un, Yedidut Maabeh Eliahu and Yesodrey Hetorah Schools.

FINANCES *Year* 2015/16 *Income* £44,851 *Grants* £51,300 *Grants to organisations* £51,300 *Assets* £15,891

TRUSTEES Barry Landy; Arnon Levy; Rabbi Shimon Bension.

OTHER INFORMATION A list of recent beneficiaries was not provided in the 2015/16 accounts.

HOW TO APPLY Apply in writing to the correspondent.

WHO TO APPLY TO Barry Landy, Trustee, 192 Gilbert Road, Cambridge CB4 3PB *Tel.* 01223 570417 *Email* bl10@cam.ac.uk

■ The Williams Family Foundation

CC NO 1157478 **ESTABLISHED** 2014

WHERE FUNDING CAN BE GIVEN North Wales and Cheshire.

WHO CAN BENEFIT Registered charities.

WHAT IS FUNDED Health or the saving of lives; arts, culture, heritage or science; environment; social welfare.

WHAT IS NOT FUNDED General appeals from national charities; small contributions to large appeals for vehicles or buildings; animal charities; religious organisations; individuals; CICs.

TYPE OF GRANT Project funding; equipment.

SAMPLE GRANTS A list of beneficiaries was not available.

FINANCES *Year* 2015 *Income* £250,179 *Grants* £228,742 *Grants to organisations* £228,742 *Assets* £231,851

TRUSTEES John Gregory; Amy Sheppard; Barbara Williams; Mark Williams; Thomas Williams.

HOW TO APPLY Applications can be made through the foundation's website. Application forms are also available on the website and can be completed and returned to applications@williamsfamilyfoundation.org.uk.

WHO TO APPLY TO The Trustees, PO Box 3809, Chester CH1 9ZW *Tel.* 01244 570292 *Email* applications@williamsfamilyfoundation.org.uk *Website* www.williamsfamilyfoundation.org.uk

■ Williams Serendipity Trust

CC NO 1114631 **ESTABLISHED** 2006

WHERE FUNDING CAN BE GIVEN UK and overseas, with a preference for London.

WHO CAN BENEFIT Charitable organisations.

WHAT IS FUNDED General charitable purposes. Grants have previously been given for cause including: education; social welfare; arts and culture; young people; people with disabilities; older people.

RANGE OF GRANTS £100 to £500,000.
SAMPLE GRANTS Uppingham School (£100,000); YMCA England (£25,000); Care for Children (£15,000); Cambridgeshire Community Foundation, Pembroke College – Cambridge and West Coast Crash Wheelchair Rugby (£10,000 each); Contact The Elderly Ltd, Ecologia Youth Trust and Archway Project (£5,000 each); Eden Project and The Special Yoga Centre (£2,000 each).
FINANCES *Year* 2014/15 *Income* £3,526 *Grants* £30,000 *Grants to organisations* £30,000
TRUSTEES Alexander Williams; Sophie Williams; Gerlinde Williams.
OTHER INFORMATION This trust's latest accounts were not available to view on the Charity Commission's website due to its low income. We have therefore estimated the grant total. Both the income and expenditure (£35,500) of the trust were unusually low in 2015. In previous years, both the income and the grant total have been above £100,000.
HOW TO APPLY Apply in writing to the correspondent. Trustees' meetings are held at least twice each year.
WHO TO APPLY TO The Trustees, c/o 4 The Sanctuary, Westminster, London SW1P 3JS

■ The Willmott Dixon Foundation

CC NO 326530 **ESTABLISHED** 1984
WHERE FUNDING CAN BE GIVEN UK.
WHO CAN BENEFIT Registered charities.
WHAT IS FUNDED Focus on three priority areas: youth employment and inspiring young people; community transformation; tackling social exclusion.
SAMPLE GRANTS Chestnut Tree House Hospice (£25,000); Action for Children (£14,000); Macmillan Cancer Support (£5,200); St Basil's (£3,400).
FINANCES *Year* 2014/15 *Income* £77,013 *Grants* £66,443 *Grants to organisations* £66,443 *Assets* £10,421
TRUSTEES Rick Willmott; Alison Symmers; Jonathan Porritt; Paul Smith; Mike Hart; Rob Lambe; Julia Barrett; Andy Geldard.
OTHER INFORMATION The 2014/15 accounts were the most recent available to view on the Charity Commission's website at the time of writing (June 2017). Grants of less than £2,500 during the year totalled £18,700.
HOW TO APPLY Applications can be made in writing to the correspondent. Note that the foundation tends to work with a small number of partner charities.
WHO TO APPLY TO Alison Symmers, Head of Foundation, Willmott Dixon Holdings PLC, Spirella 2, Icknield Way, Letchworth Garden City, Hertfordshire SG6 4GY *Tel.* 01462 671852 *Email* alison.symmers@willmottdixon.co.uk *Website* www.willmottdixon.co.uk/how-we-do-it/the-willmott-dixon-foundation

■ The HDH Wills 1965 Charitable Trust

CC NO 1117747 **ESTABLISHED** 1965
WHERE FUNDING CAN BE GIVEN Mainly UK, occasionally overseas.
WHO CAN BENEFIT Registered or recognised charities only.
WHAT IS FUNDED The trust makes grants from two separate funds: the General Fund and the Martin Wills Fund. The general fund is used to make grants on a monthly basis for general charitable purposes, the environment and wildlife conservation whereas the Martin Wills Fund operates on a seven-year funding priority cycle. In years one, two and five of this cycle, grants are made to specified institutions; in years three and four, favour is given to environmental and wildlife conservation; in years six and seven grants are given for general charitable purposes. 2015/16 was the third year in the cycle.
WHAT IS NOT FUNDED Individuals; organisations that have received a grant from the trust in the last 18 months.
TYPE OF GRANT Revenue, capital or project expenditure.
RANGE OF GRANTS Grants from the general fund are typically £250 to £1,000, occasionally up to £5,000. Grants from the Martin Wills Fund are typically £2,000 to £25,000.
SAMPLE GRANTS Martin Wills Wildlife Maintenance Trust (£30,000); 21st Century Trust (£19,500); Sandford St Martin Parochial Church Council (£5,000); Action for Conservation, Ashmolean Museum, British Red Cross – Nepal Earthquake Appeal, Christian Aid, Shakespeare Schools Festival and Southwell Cathedral Chapter (£1,000 each).
FINANCES *Year* 2015/16 *Income* £2,773,103 *Grants* £577,840 *Grants to organisations* £577,840 *Assets* £90,385,450
TRUSTEES John Carson; Dr Catherine Wills; Liell Francklin; Martin Fiennes; Thomas Nelson.
OTHER INFORMATION A total of 120 grants were made from the general fund in 2015/16, of which 108 were for less than £1,000. From the Martin Wills Fund, a grant of £30,000 was made to the Martin Wills Wildlife Maintenance Trust, and a further £452,500 was given in grants to organisations concerned with wildlife and conservation. The trust also has a Knockando Church Fund for the upkeep of Knockando Church in Morayshire, which received a grant of £10,700 in 2015/16.
HOW TO APPLY General fund grants are awarded on a monthly basis and can be applied for using the online form on the trust's website, or by downloading a form to send by post or email, attaching supporting documents. Details on what should be included are given on the website. Larger grants from the Martin Wills Fund can be should also be submitted using the online form on the trust's website, or by downloading a form to send by post or email, attaching supporting documents, but applicants should first refer to the website to check what grants are currently available.
WHO TO APPLY TO Sue Trafford, Trust Administrator, Henley Knapp Barn, Fulwell, Chipping Norton, Oxfordshire OX7 4EN *Tel.* 01608 678051 *Email* hdhwills@btconnect.com *Website* www.hdhwills.org

■ Dame Violet Wills Charitable Trust

CC NO 219485 **ESTABLISHED** 1955
WHERE FUNDING CAN BE GIVEN UK and overseas.
WHO CAN BENEFIT Registered charities.
WHAT IS FUNDED Evangelical Christian activities.
TYPE OF GRANT One-off and recurrent. Capital costs; core costs; salaries; project funding.
RANGE OF GRANTS Mainly £500 to £5,000.
SAMPLE GRANTS The Training Centre – Pool (£3,000); Renacer Camps (£2,800); Redcliffe

College (£1,200); Open Air Campaigners (£1,100); Bibles for Children (£1,000); Christian Surfers (£750); Crisis Centre Ministries (£700); Network Counselling Ltd (£600); Langham Partnership and Torch Trust for the Blind (£500 each).

FINANCES *Year* 2015 *Income* £132,795 *Grants* £77,950 *Grants to organisations* £77,950 *Assets* £1,799,763

TRUSTEES Julian Marsh; Revd Dr Ernest Lucas; Revd Ray Lockhart; Derek Cleave; John Dean; Rosalind Peskett; Janet Persson; Rachel Daws; Revd David Caporn; E. Street; Yme Potjewijd.

OTHER INFORMATION Grants were made to 58 organisations.

HOW TO APPLY Apply in writing to the correspondent. The trustees meet at least annually and grants are generally more likely to be made to applicants personally known to one or more of the trustees. The trust operates a system whereby each trustee sponsors a number of causes and is responsible for the support, contact with and monitoring of a number of grant beneficiaries.

WHO TO APPLY TO Julian Marsh, Trustee, 3 Cedar Way, Portishead, Bristol BS20 6TT *Tel.* 01275 848770

■ The Dame Violet Wills Will Trust

CC NO 262251 **ESTABLISHED** 1965

WHERE FUNDING CAN BE GIVEN Preference for Bristol, Gloucestershire and Somerset areas.

WHO CAN BENEFIT Registered charities.

WHAT IS FUNDED General charitable purposes, with a preference for organisations concerned with children and medical causes. Charities with which the trust's founder was concerned during her lifetime are favoured.

TYPE OF GRANT One-off grants.

SAMPLE GRANTS Amos Vale, Bristol and the Colston Society, Bristol Cathedral Trust, Church of the Good Shepherd, Clifton Gateway Club, Guide Dogs for the Blind, Lord Mamhead Homes, RNLI, Rainbow Centre, Rowcroft Hospice, Samaritans, St Loye's Foundation; WRVS.

FINANCES *Year* 2015/16 *Income* £120,539 *Grants* £103,858 *Grants to organisations* £103,858 *Assets* £3,058,080

TRUSTEES Tim Baines; Guy Biggin; Mark Naughton.

OTHER INFORMATION The trust made 66 grants in 2015/16, but no further information about beneficiaries was provided.

HOW TO APPLY Apply in writing to the correspondent. The trustees meet three or four times per year to consider applications.

WHO TO APPLY TO Tim Baines, Trustee, Red Roofs, Station Road, Flax Bourton, Bristol BS48 1UA

■ The Wilmcote Charitable Trust

CC NO 503837 **ESTABLISHED** 1974

WHERE FUNDING CAN BE GIVEN UK and occasionally overseas, with preference for Birmingham and Midlands.

WHO CAN BENEFIT Registered charities and voluntary organisations.

WHAT IS FUNDED General charitable purposes. In previous years, grants have been awarded for the following causes: ex-service personnel; medical causes; children and young people; religion; older people; general charitable purposes.

TYPE OF GRANT Many recurrent, some one-off.

RANGE OF GRANTS Mainly around £500.

SAMPLE GRANTS Carers Trust and Douglas House (£2,000 each); City of Birmingham Symphony Orchestra Education Programme and Cotswold Canals Trust (£1,000 each); Arthritis Research UK, Birmingham Royal Ballet, Coram, Dogs for the Disabled, Domestic Abuse Counselling, Dream Makers, People's Dispensary for Sick Animals (PDSA), The Royal British Legion, Mercia MS Therapy Centre, Red Cross Typhoon Haiyan Appeal, Wilmcote Church Appeal and Young Minds (£500 each); 1st Wilmcote Scout Group, Friends of the Earth Bee Cause and SSAFA (£250 each).

FINANCES *Year* 2015/16 *Income* £23,764 *Grants* £60,000 *Grants to organisations* £60,000

TRUSTEES Jean King; Anabel Murphy; Roseamond Whiteside; Graham Beach.

OTHER INFORMATION This charity's latest accounts were not available to view on the Charity Commission's website due to its low income. We have therefore estimated the grant total based on previous years' information.

HOW TO APPLY Apply in writing to the correspondent.

WHO TO APPLY TO Graham Beach, Trustee, Warren Chase, Billesley Road, Wilmcote, Stratford-upon-Avon CV37 9XG *Tel.* 01789 298472 *Email* graham@leighgraham.co.uk

■ Brian Wilson Charitable Trust

CC NO 1059736 **ESTABLISHED** 1996

WHERE FUNDING CAN BE GIVEN Cheshire.

WHO CAN BENEFIT Charitable organisations.

WHAT IS FUNDED General charitable purposes.

SAMPLE GRANTS Leonard Cheshire Disability Support (£115,000); Help for Heroes (£25,000); The Friends of Russett School (£10,000); Cross Roads Care – North Wales (£7,000) and St Luke's Cheshire Hospice (£5,000).

FINANCES *Year* 2015 *Income* £120,817 *Grants* £160,000 *Grants to organisations* £160,000 *Assets* £4,087,816

TRUSTEES John Pickup; Vivien Roberts; Ruth Downes.

OTHER INFORMATION A list of beneficiaries was not given in the 2015 accounts.

HOW TO APPLY Apply in writing to the correspondent. The trustees meet on a quarterly basis to consider requests and approve grants.

WHO TO APPLY TO N. Steinberg, Munslows, New Penderel House, 2nd Floor, 283–288 High Holborn, London WC1V 7HP *Tel.* 01606 74970 *Fax* 01606 852733

■ Sumner Wilson Charitable Trust

CC NO 1018852 **ESTABLISHED** 1992

WHERE FUNDING CAN BE GIVEN UK.

WHO CAN BENEFIT Registered charities.

WHAT IS FUNDED General charitable purposes.

SAMPLE GRANTS St James's Place Foundation (£67,500); Macmillan Cancer Support (£50,000); Lewisham Youth Theatre (£12,000); Action Against Cancer and Young Gloucestershire (£10,000 each); Global Citizen, Landmark Trust and Nepal Youth Foundation (£5,000 each); Prince of Wales Regiment Benevolent Fund (£4,500); Great Ormond Street Hospital (£2,500).

FINANCES *Year* 2015/16 *Income* £127,871 *Grants* £214,500 *Grants to organisations* £214,500 *Assets* £6,047,358

TRUSTEES Michael Wilson; Amanda Christie; Anne-Marie Challen.

OTHER INFORMATION Grants for £2,500 or less totalled £13,000.
HOW TO APPLY Apply in writing to the trustees.
WHO TO APPLY TO John Pickup, Trustee, 36 Landswood Park, Hartford, Northwich CW8 1NF *Tel.* 020 7269 7680 *Email* nathan@munslows.co.uk

■ The Wilson Foundation

CC NO 1074414 **ESTABLISHED** 1999
WHERE FUNDING CAN BE GIVEN Northamptonshire.
WHO CAN BENEFIT Organisations working with people aged 10 to 21.
WHAT IS FUNDED Young people in Northamptonshire, particularly those facing disadvantage. Grants are given to both organisations and individuals, for a range of projects and purposes, including educational scholarships, youth projects and trips that provide opportunities for character building and where individuals would otherwise not be able to participate.
WHAT IS NOT FUNDED Individuals living outside Northamptonshire.
TYPE OF GRANT Capital costs; recurrent project funding; one-off scholarships; core costs; start-up costs.
RANGE OF GRANTS £100 to £20,000.
SAMPLE GRANTS CT Wilson Longtown Bursary (£15,000 in two grants); Holcot Cricket Club (£13,600); Pacesetter Sports (£10,800); Geddington Village School Band (£7,000); The Prince's Trust (£6,000); Bunbury ESCA Festival (£5,000); Northampton School for Boys (£4,500); Boys Brigade 7th Northampton (£1,000); Northampton Young Carers (£800); Mayor's Fund for the Housebound (£250).
FINANCES *Year* 2015/16 *Income* £112,934 *Grants* £127,323 *Grants to organisations* £117,185 *Assets* £5,947,489
TRUSTEES Anthony Hewitt; Giles Wilson; Nicholas Wilson; Fiona Wilson; Adam Welch; Pollyanna Wilson.
OTHER INFORMATION In 2015/16 the foundation made 33 grants to organisations. There were also 35 grants made to individuals, which totalled £10,100.
HOW TO APPLY Application forms for individuals are available on the trust's website. Organisations should apply in writing to the trustees.
WHO TO APPLY TO The Trustees, The Maltings, Tithe Farm, Moulton Road, Holcot, Northamptonshire NN6 9SH *Tel.* 01604 782240 *Email* polly@tithefarm.com *Website* www.thewilsonfoundation.co.uk

■ J. and J. R. Wilson Trust

SC NO SC007411 **ESTABLISHED** 1989
WHERE FUNDING CAN BE GIVEN Scotland (care of animals and birds); Glasgow and the west of Scotland (care of older people).
WHO CAN BENEFIT Charitable organisations.
WHAT IS FUNDED Causes concerned with the care of older people, or the care of both domestic and wild animals and birds.
SAMPLE GRANTS Scottish Wildlife Trust (£10,000); Glasgow Old People's Welfare Association (£6,000); World Horse Welfare (£3,500); Marine Conservation Society (£3,000); Cats Protection League and Glasgow City Mission – Older Men's Lunch Club (£2,000 each); Glasgow Care Foundation, MS Society Scotland and Strathcarron Hospice (£1,000 each); Playback Recording Service for the Blind (£500).
FINANCES *Year* 2016/17 *Income* £149,747 *Grants* £107,863 *Grants to organisations* £107,863 *Assets* £4,064,158
OTHER INFORMATION Grants were made to 40 organisations for the care of older people (totalling £63,000) and to 17 organisations for the care of animals and birds (totalling £45,000).
HOW TO APPLY Apply in writing to the correspondent.
WHO TO APPLY TO The Trustees, c/o Tho and JW Barty Solicitors, 61 High Street, Dunblane, Perthshire FK15 0EH

■ Wiltshire Community Foundation

CC NO 1123126 **ESTABLISHED** 1991
WHERE FUNDING CAN BE GIVEN Wiltshire and Swindon only.
WHO CAN BENEFIT Charitable organisations, constituted voluntary and community groups; individuals.
WHAT IS FUNDED Supporting communities in Wiltshire and Swindon. The foundation manages a number of different grants schemes which open and close frequently – refer to the website for information on what is currently available. The grant schemes generally offer funding for organisations working with those who are disadvantaged in some way – economically, socially, geographically or physically.
WHAT IS NOT FUNDED Groups with more than 12 months' running costs in unrestricted reserves; projects outside the county of Wiltshire or Borough of Swindon; organisations which deliver services in Wiltshire or Swindon but do not have a local governance structure (e.g. management committee or board of trustees) for the project; projects which will not start within six months of a grant award; projects where only a minority of beneficiaries would be considered disadvantaged; one-off events or sponsored events; general large appeals; advancement of religion; medical research and equipment; animal welfare; party political activities; substitution of funding that should be provided by the statutory sector, or local authority institutions, including schools or academies (although PTAs can apply if the project concerned does not overlap with statutory responsibilities and benefits the wider community); promotion of religion or exclusion of beneficiaries based on religion; running costs for Community Area Partnerships.
TYPE OF GRANT Project costs; core costs; small capital grants (up to £5,000 for buildings and equipment); salaries; new projects; training and development; continuation funding. Up to three years, although multi-year grants are unusual.
RANGE OF GRANTS See each grant scheme.
SAMPLE GRANTS Arts Together (£35,000); Family Counselling Trust Wiltshire (£14,000); Alzheimer's Support (£10,000); Dance Six-0 (£4,000); West Wiltshire Multi Faith Forum (£3,600); The Open Door Centre (£2,900); Foggy's Invisible Illness Support (£1,600); Devizes Hospital Radio (£1,000); Kington St Michael Autumn Club (£800); Wiltshire Magistrates Association (£380).
FINANCES *Year* 2015/16 *Income* £1,533,336 *Grants* £1,026,187 *Grants to organisations* £629,831 *Assets* £18,759,530
TRUSTEES Helen Birchenough; Christopher Bromfield; Ram Thiagarajah; Dame Elizabeth Neville; John Adams; Denise Bentley; Elizabeth Webbe; Alison Radevsky; Sally Walden; Jason Dalley; Emma Gibbons; William Wyldbore-Smith; Steve Wall; Susan Webber.

OTHER INFORMATION In 2015/16 the foundation awarded grants to 119 organisations. A further £154,500 was given in grants to 212 individuals.

HOW TO APPLY Applicant should first refer to the website for details on what is currently available and deadlines. Applicants can then fill in an expression of interest form on the website.

WHO TO APPLY TO Jane Butler, Grants Manager, Sandcliff House, 21 Northgate Street, Devizes, Wiltshire SN10 1JX *Tel.* 01380 729284 *Email* info@wiltshirecf.org.uk or jane.butler@wiltshirecf.org.uk *Website* wiltshirecf.org.uk

■ The Wimbledon Foundation

CC NO 1156996 **ESTABLISHED** 2014

WHO CAN BENEFIT Registered charities; community groups; sports clubs.

WHAT IS FUNDED The three focus areas of the Wimbledon Foundation are: the London boroughs of Merton and Wandsworth; charities associated with or promoted by key groups involved in The Championships; projects and charities that use the power of sport (and particularly tennis) to provide opportunities to assist people, especially the young, with education and personal development.

SAMPLE GRANTS A list of beneficiaries was not available.

FINANCES *Year* 2015/16 *Income* £992,000 *Grants* £285,000 *Grants to organisations* £285,000 *Assets* £1,709,000

TRUSTEES Sir Nicholas Young; Nicholas Bitel; I. L. Hewitt; P. G. H. Brook; Ashley Tatum; Sir Keith Ajegbo; Henry Weatherill.

HOW TO APPLY Contact the foundation via foundation@aeltc.com.

WHO TO APPLY TO Helen Parker, The Wimbledon Foundation, Church Road, Wimbledon SW19 5AE *Tel.* 020 8971 2702 *Email* foundation@aeltc.com *Website* www.wimbledon.com/en_GB/foundation/index.html

■ The W. Wing Yip and Brothers Foundation

CC NO 326999 **ESTABLISHED** 1986

WHERE FUNDING CAN BE GIVEN UK, particularly Birmingham, Manchester, Croydon and Cricklewood.

WHO CAN BENEFIT Individuals, particularly students of Chinese origin. Charitable organisations, particularly those with a Chinese connection.

WHAT IS FUNDED Grants are also made to charitable organisations for a range of general charitable purposes, including: community welfare; education; medical research; and religious activities. Educational grants are also given to students of Chinese origin to study in the UK, as well as scholarships for Chinese students to study at Churchill College, Cambridge and for students from this college to study in China, and also scholarships for two students at Aston University, Birmingham.

TYPE OF GRANT One-off grants; recurrent grants; project costs; capital costs.

RANGE OF GRANTS Most under £6,000.

SAMPLE GRANTS Free@last (£20,000); Wickham Court School (£6,000); St Joseph's Church (£2,000); Croydon Chinese School (£1,500); Ikon Gallery (£1,000); World Cancer Research Fund (£500); London Air Ambulance (£300); ABF – The Soldiers' Charity (£250); British Heart Foundation (£200); Little Sisters of the Poor (£100).

FINANCES *Year* 2015/16 *Income* £84,880 *Grants* £127,500 *Grants to organisations* £57,500 *Assets* £1,191,945

TRUSTEES Brian Wing Yip; Hon Yuen Yap; Jenny Loynton; Robert Brittain; Woon Wing Yip; Albert Yip.

OTHER INFORMATION In 2015/16 educational bursaries to 35 students totalled £70,000. Grants were also given to 25 organisations, including seven educational organisations.

HOW TO APPLY Apply in writing to the correspondent.

WHO TO APPLY TO Robert Brittain, Trustee, W. Wing Yip PLC, The Wing Yip Centre, 375 Nechells Park Road, Birmingham B7 5NT *Tel.* 0121 327 6618 *Email* robert.brittain@wingyip.com *Website* www.wingyip.com/Supporting-our-communities/Wing-Yip-Foundation

■ The Harold Hyam Wingate Foundation

CC NO 264114 **ESTABLISHED** 1960

WHERE FUNDING CAN BE GIVEN Mainly UK; some overseas.

WHO CAN BENEFIT Registered charities.

WHAT IS FUNDED Jewish life and learning; performing arts; music; education and social exclusion; overseas aid; medical research (travel grants). Further detail on some of the areas supported is given on the foundation's website.

WHAT IS NOT FUNDED Individuals; gap years, Duke of Edinburgh awards or similar; large charities.

RANGE OF GRANTS Up to £10,000.

SAMPLE GRANTS Queen Mary and Westfield College (£59,500); Jewish Literary Trust (£12,000); Hearing Dogs for Deaf People and The Karuna Trust (£10,000 each); Wigmore Hall Trust (£6,600); Streetwise Opera (£6,500); Institute of Imagination and Little Angel Theatre (£5,000 each); National Youth Jazz Collective (£3,500); University of Ulster (£1,000).

FINANCES *Year* 2015/16 *Income* £84,798 *Grants* £491,639 *Grants to organisations* £491,639 *Assets* £6,700,162

TRUSTEES Roger Wingate; Tony Wingate; Prof. David Wingate; Jon Drori; Prof. Robert Cassen; Daphne Hyman; Emily Kasriel; Barbara Arnold.

OTHER INFORMATION In 2015/16 grants were given in the following categories: music (28%); performing arts (24%); Jewish life and learning (19%); medical research, including travel grants (12%); education and social exclusion (9%); development projects (5%); literary prizes (3%).

HOW TO APPLY Applications should be made using the application form available from the foundation's website, sent with supporting documentation and most recent accounts. Applications are only acknowledged if a stamped addressed envelope is enclosed or if the application is successful. The administrator of the foundation only deals with enquiries by post and the website states it is hoped that the guidelines and examples of previous support for successful applicants, given on the foundation's website, provides sufficient information. There is no email address for the foundation. Trustee meetings are held quarterly and further information on upcoming deadlines can be found on the foundation's website.

WHO TO APPLY TO Sarah Mitchell, Administrator, Somerset House, New Wing (S93), Strand, London WC2R 1LA *Website* www.wingatefoundation.org.uk

■ The Francis Winham Foundation

CC NO 278092 **ESTABLISHED** 1979

WHERE FUNDING CAN BE GIVEN England.

WHO CAN BENEFIT Charitable organisations.

WHAT IS FUNDED Grants for organisations working to improve the quality of life of older people.

SAMPLE GRANTS Care and Repair (£35,500 in 49 grants); Age UK (£12,000 in five grants); NPower – Health Through Warmth (£15,000); Arthur Rank Hospice Charity and RNIB (£10,000 each); The Royal British Legion (£7,300 in ten grants); Carers UK, Nottinghamshire Hospice, The Royal Star and Garter Home and UCanDoIT (£5,000).

FINANCES *Year* 2015/16 *Income* £6,468,927 *Grants* £398,685 *Grants to organisations* £398,685 *Assets* £8,979,654

TRUSTEES Elsa Peters; Josephine Winham; Desmond Corcoran; Fuschia Peters.

OTHER INFORMATION The foundation made 274 grants to organisations during 2015/16.

HOW TO APPLY Apply in writing to the correspondent. The trust regrets it cannot send replies to applications outside its specific field of help for older people.

WHO TO APPLY TO Josephine Winham, Trustee, 18 Gilston Road, London SW10 9SR *Tel.* 020 7795 1261 *Email* francinetrust@outlook.com

■ Winton Philanthropies

CC NO 1110131 **ESTABLISHED** 2005

WHERE FUNDING CAN BE GIVEN UK, particularly London and areas local to Winton offices; overseas, in areas local to Winton offices.

WHO CAN BENEFIT Charitable organisations; academic institutions.

WHAT IS FUNDED Scientific research, particularly research that is 'experimental, bold and risk-taking' communication of scientific ideas, particularly public understanding of risk and statistics; general charitable purposes in London and in the communities around the world where Winton has offices.

SAMPLE GRANTS ARK (£200,000); National Museum of Computing (£25,000); St Mungo's Broadway and The Lyric Theatre (£30,000 each).

FINANCES *Year* 2015 *Income* £821,144 *Grants* £775,188 *Grants to organisations* £775,188 *Assets* £52,208

TRUSTEES David Winton Harding; The Hon. Martin Hunt; Claudia Harding.

OTHER INFORMATION Previously known as The Winton Charitable Foundation, the charity changed its name in 2016. The foundation also provides match funding for Winton Capital employee donations of up to £10,000; in 2015, this totalled £152,500.

HOW TO APPLY The website states the following: 'Please note that grant proposals are by invitation only – we do not accept unsolicited proposals. Because of our tightly defined grant making themes many worthwhile projects fall outside the scope of our funding priorities. However if you have thoughts or enquiries related to our work that you would like to share you can contact us at philanthropies@winton.com. Please understand that due to the volume of enquiries we receive, we are only able to commit to reviewing those which are aligned to our strategic themes.'

WHO TO APPLY TO Alexandra Openshaw, DCH Office, Office 111, Michelin House, 81 Fulham Road SW3 6RD *Email* philanthropies@winton.com or philanthropies@dchoffice.com *Website* www.winton.com/en/philanthropies

■ The Witzenfeld Foundation

CC NO 1115034 **ESTABLISHED** 2006

WHERE FUNDING CAN BE GIVEN UK, with a focus on Essex; Israel.

WHO CAN BENEFIT Charitable organisations.

WHAT IS FUNDED General charitable purposes.

SAMPLE GRANTS A list of beneficiaries was not available.

FINANCES *Year* 2015/16 *Income* £36,500 *Grants* £42,757 *Grants to organisations* £42,757 *Assets* £219

TRUSTEES Alan Witzenfeld; Lyetta Witzenfeld; Emma Witzenfeld-Saigh; Mark Witzenfeld.

OTHER INFORMATION The accounts state that 11 grants were made during the 2015/16; a list of beneficiaries was not provided.

HOW TO APPLY Apply in writing to the correspondent.

WHO TO APPLY TO Alan Witzenfeld, Trustee, Porters House, Station Court, Radford Way, Billericay, Essex *Tel.* 01702 330032 *Email* alan.witzenfeld@dckconcessions.com

■ The Michael and Anna Wix Charitable Trust

CC NO 207863 **ESTABLISHED** 1955

WHERE FUNDING CAN BE GIVEN UK; some overseas.

WHO CAN BENEFIT UK-registered charities.

WHAT IS FUNDED A wide range of general charitable purposes are supported, particularly medical causes and social welfare.

WHAT IS NOT FUNDED Applications from individuals are not considered. Grants are generally made to national bodies rather than local branches or local groups.

RANGE OF GRANTS Mostly for smaller amounts in the range of £100 to £500 each.

SAMPLE GRANTS British Friends of the Hebrew University (£2,000); World Jewish Relief (£1,000); Institute of Cancer Research (£500); Action on Addiction, Book Aid International and Crohn's and Colitis UK (£200 each); Children's Adventure Farm Trust, North London Foodbank, Royal Voluntary Service and Sportability (£100 each).

FINANCES *Year* 2015/16 *Income* £86,377 *Grants* £72,000 *Grants to organisations* £72,000 *Assets* £2,027,056

TRUSTEES Janet Bloch; Dominic Flynn; Judith Portrait.

OTHER INFORMATION Grants were awarded to 330 organisations in 2015/16.

HOW TO APPLY Apply in writing to the trustees. The trustees meet to consider applications twice each year.

WHO TO APPLY TO Sarah Hovil, c/o Portrait Solicitors, 21 Whitefriars Street, London EC4Y 8JJ *Tel.* 020 7092 6985

■ The Wixamtree Trust

CC NO 210089 **ESTABLISHED** 1949

WHERE FUNDING CAN BE GIVEN UK, primarily Bedfordshire.

WHO CAN BENEFIT Registered or exempt charities; mainly local charities, with a small number of national charities supported. Churches are referred to Bedfordshire and Hertfordshire Historic Churches Trust, to which this trust makes an annual grant each year to support such applications.

WHAT IS FUNDED General charitable purposes. Grants are awarded in the following categories: social welfare; environment and conservation; medicine and health; the arts; education;

training and employment; sports and leisure; and international.

WHAT IS NOT FUNDED Individuals.

TYPE OF GRANT Core costs; project costs; capital costs. Mostly one-off, although organisations can re-apply a year after receiving a grant.

RANGE OF GRANTS Usually grants between £1,000 and £10,000 with a small number of donations outside this range.

SAMPLE GRANTS Age UK Bedfordshire; British Epilepsy Association; Crescent Summer School Project; Dyspraxia Foundation; Keech Hospice Care; NOAH Enterprise; Nyabingi Charity; Raynham Way Pre-School; Sickle Cell and Thalassaemia Care Forum; St Christopher's Fellowship; YMCA Bedfordshire; YoungMinds Trust.

FINANCES *Year* 2015/16 *Income* £1,012,624 *Grants* £879,277 *Grants to organisations* £879,277 *Assets* £30,416,172

TRUSTEES Sir Samuel Whitbread; Lady Whitbread; Charles Whitbread; Ian Pilkington; Geoff McMullen; Elizabeth Bennett; Paul Patten.

OTHER INFORMATION Grants were awarded to 162 organisations during 2015/16. The 2015/16 annual report states that 'the trustees are also sympathetic towards applications received from organisations of which the late Mr Humphrey Whitbread was a benefactor'.

HOW TO APPLY Applications can be made using the form on the trust's website, where guidelines are also provided. For assistance with the application, or to obtain the form in a different format, contact the Trust Administrator: wixamtree@thetrustpartnership.com or 0208 777 4140. The trustees meet four times each year, usually in January, April, July and November, and the dates of upcoming meetings are posted on the trust's website. Successful applicants will be notified within 14 days of a meeting and unsuccessful applicants will be notified within seven days of a meeting. There is a separate application form for churches, which can be downloaded from the trust's website and should be sent to the Bedfordshire and Hertfordshire Historic Churches Trust – refer to the website for further information.

WHO TO APPLY TO Mia Duddridge, Trust Administrator, 6 Trull Farm Buildings, Tetbury, Gloucestershire GL8 8SQ *Tel.* 020 8777 4140 *Email* wixamtree@thetrustpartnership.com *Website* www.wixamtree.org

■ The Maurice Wohl Charitable Foundation

CC NO 244519 **ESTABLISHED** 1965

WHERE FUNDING CAN BE GIVEN UK and Israel.

WHO CAN BENEFIT Jewish organisations; registered charities.

WHAT IS FUNDED Health and medical sciences; welfare within the Jewish community; Jewish education.

WHAT IS NOT FUNDED Ongoing maintenance projects; individuals; scholarships.

TYPE OF GRANT One-off and recurrent.

RANGE OF GRANTS £300 to £488,000.

SAMPLE GRANTS Partnership for Jewish Schools (£488,000); The Gesher Trust (£297,000); Norwood Ravenswood (£51,000); The Royal Academy of Arts (£42,500); Jewish Care (£37,500); Royal College of Surgeons of Edinburgh (£21,000); Jewish Women's Aid (£10,000); Jewish Book Council (£5,000); Institute of Historical Research (£2,500); Ezra U'Marpeh (£300).

FINANCES *Year* 2015 *Income* £1,941,923 *Grants* £1,930,888 *Grants to organisations* £1,930,888 *Assets* £77,500,450

TRUSTEES Ella Latchman; Martin Paisner; Prof. David Latchman; Sir Ian Gainsford; Daniel Dover.

OTHER INFORMATION The foundation is part of the Wohl Legacy, a group of three charitable foundations established by Maurice and Vivienne Wohl.

HOW TO APPLY The foundation does not accept unsolicited applications, as trustees work with full-time staff to identify suitable projects.

WHO TO APPLY TO Joseph Houri, Secretary, Fitzrovia House, 2nd Floor, 153–157 Cleveland Street, London W1T 6QW *Tel.* 020 7383 5111 *Email* jh@wohl.org.uk *Website* www.wohl.org.uk

■ The Charles Wolfson Charitable Trust

CC NO 238043 **ESTABLISHED** 1960

WHERE FUNDING CAN BE GIVEN UK.

WHO CAN BENEFIT Registered charities, hospitals and schools.

WHAT IS FUNDED Medicine; education; social welfare. The 2015/16 annual report states that 'particular, but not exclusive, regard is given to the needs of the Jewish community'.

WHAT IS NOT FUNDED Individuals.

TYPE OF GRANT Mostly capital or fixed-term projects. Grants may be made for up to three years. The trust also provides rent-free premise to charities, and occasionally loans.

SAMPLE GRANTS Addenbrookes Charitable Trust and Yavneh College Trust (£500,000 each); Jewish Care (£350,000); Cure Parkinson's Trust (£200,000); Huntingdon Foundation (£125,000); Royal Marsden Cancer Campaign (£50,000); Sir George Pinker Appeal (£30,000); Zoological Society of London (£25,000); Priors Court Foundation (£10,000); Tavistock Trust for Aphasia (£5,000); the Roundhouse Trust (£1,000).

FINANCES *Year* 2015/16 *Income* £7,533,957 *Grants* £6,872,193 *Grants to organisations* £6,872,193 *Assets* £236,483,108

TRUSTEES Lord Simon Wolfson; Dr Sara Levene; The Hon. Andrew Wolfson; Lord David Wolfson.

OTHER INFORMATION A list of beneficiaries was not provided in the 2015/16 accounts.

HOW TO APPLY Apply in writing to the correspondent.

WHO TO APPLY TO Joanne Cowan, 8/10 Hallam Street, London W1W 6NS *Tel.* 020 7079 2506

■ The Wolfson Family Charitable Trust

CC NO 228382 **ESTABLISHED** 1958

WHERE FUNDING CAN BE GIVEN Mostly Israel; some UK.

WHO CAN BENEFIT Universities and hospitals in Israel; UK organisations serving the Jewish community. Applicants should be registered charities or organisations with equivalent charitable status, and have an income of more than £50,000.

WHAT IS FUNDED In Israel, the trust supports universities and hospitals. In the UK, grants are awarded to organisations serving the UK Jewish community, with particular interest in: supporting people with physical and learning disabilities; providing high quality secondary education; improving access to important culture or heritage, particularly supporting historic synagogues and cultural organisations with 'a national reputation for excellence'.

WHAT IS NOT FUNDED Individuals (either directly or through conduit organisations); overheads, maintenance costs, VAT and professional fees; non-specific appeals, including circulars and endowment funds; costs of meetings, exhibitions, concerts, expeditions, etc.; purchase of land or existing buildings; film or promotional materials; repayment of loans; projects which have already been completed or will be by the time of award.

TYPE OF GRANT Capital projects (buildings, refurbishment or specialist equipment).

RANGE OF GRANTS £5,000 to £25,000. Applicants are expected to provide matched funding.

SAMPLE GRANTS Weizmann Institute of Science (£280,000); Tel Aviv University (£180,000); Nightingale Hammerson (£150,000); Peres Center for Peace (£50,000); Holocaust Educational Trust (£30,000); Young Israel Philharmonic Orchestra (£20,000); Mosaic Jewish Primary School (£15,000); Shalheveth (£10,000); Coexist Foundation (£5,000).

FINANCES *Year* 2015/16 *Income* £885,000 *Grants* £1,525,000 *Grants to organisations* £1,525,000 *Assets* £31,721,000

TRUSTEES Martin Paisner; Sir Ian Gainsford; Sir Bernard Rix; Sir Eric Ash; The Hon. Laura Wolfson Townsley; The Hon. Janet de Botton; Lord Turnberg; The Hon. Elizabeth Wolfson Peltz; Alexandra Wolfson Halamish.

OTHER INFORMATION Grants were awarded to 21 organisations in the UK and Israel in 2015/16. The 2015/16 annual report states: 'During 2016–17, Trustees will consider a major programme of support for equipment at Israeli hospitals.'

HOW TO APPLY There are two stages to the application process. A Stage 1 application can be submitted on the trust's website, where guidance are also provided. All requests are responded to and eligible organisations will be invited to submit a Stage 2 application. The trustees generally meet once a year and upcoming deadlines are posted on the website.

WHO TO APPLY TO Paul Ramsbottom, Chief Executive, 8 Queen Anne Street, London W1G 9LD *Tel.* 020 7323 5730 *Email* grants@wolfson.org.uk *Website* www.wolfson.org.uk/about-us/wolfson-family-charitable-trust

■ The Wolfson Foundation

CC NO 1156077 **ESTABLISHED** 1955

WHERE FUNDING CAN BE GIVEN Mainly UK, but also Israel.

WHO CAN BENEFIT Registered charities and exempt charities (such as universities and schools).

WHAT IS FUNDED Grants are generally given for capital projects 'supporting excellence' in the following areas: science and medicine; arts and humanities; health and disability; and education. The foundation's bursary, scholarship and salary programmes are generally not open to application and are run with selected organisations. Grants for university research are awarded through designated programmes. The foundation often works in partnership with other funding bodies.

WHAT IS NOT FUNDED Individuals; overheads, maintenance cost (including for software), VAT and professional fees; non-specific appeals (including circulars) and endowment funds; costs of meetings, exhibitions, concerts, expeditions, etc.; purchasing of land or existing buildings (including a building's freehold); film or promotional materials; repayment of loans; projects that have already been completed by the time of the award; projects where the total cost is below £15,000.

TYPE OF GRANT Capital infrastructure (new buildings, refurbishment and equipment).

RANGE OF GRANTS Applicants with a total project cost of more than £50,000 are expected to provide matched funding.

SAMPLE GRANTS Science Museum (£1.17 million); University of Sussex (£1.5 million); Nightingale Hammerson (£250,000); University of Edinburgh (£249,000); St Giles Hospice (£60,000); Shakespeare Birthplace Trust (£50,000); Welsh National Opera (£28,000); Wakefield City Academy (£26,000); Dance Base (£10,000); Holy Cross – Woodchurch (£5,000); British Wireless for the Blind Fund (£2,500).

FINANCES *Year* 2015/16 *Income* £19,467,000 *Grants* £27,484,290 *Grants to organisations* £27,434,290 *Assets* £674,606,000

TRUSTEES Lord McColl; Sir Eric Ash; Hon. Laura Wolfson Townley; Sir David Cannadine; Dame Janet Wolfson de Botton; Rebecca Marks; Lord Turnberg; Dame Jean Thomas; Dame Hermione Lee; Sir Michael Pepper; Hon. Deborah Wolfson Davis; Sir Peter Ratcliffe.

OTHER INFORMATION The foundation awarded 294 grants in total in 2015/16. This included two grants to individuals (Wolfson History Prizes) which totalled £50,000.

HOW TO APPLY There are two stages to the trust's application process. After checking the eligibility criteria, a Stage 1 application can be made on the foundation's website. If an applicant is then invited to submit a Stage 2 application, they will be contacted by the foundation with further details on what to include. There are two funding rounds every year, in autumn and spring – key dates are provided on the trust's website. Applicants are advised to submit their Stage 1 application well in advance of the deadline as there is a cap on the number of applications considered at each round.

WHO TO APPLY TO Paul Ramsbottom, Chief Executive, 8 Queen Anne Street, London W1G 9LD *Tel.* 020 7323 5730 *Email* grants@wolfson.org.uk *Website* www.wolfson.org.uk

■ The James Wood Bequest Fund

SC NO SC000459 **ESTABLISHED** 1932

WHERE FUNDING CAN BE GIVEN Glasgow and the 'central belt of Scotland'.

WHO CAN BENEFIT Registered charities.

WHAT IS FUNDED General charitable purposes. Church of Scotland, historic buildings and other registered charities based in Scotland.

WHAT IS NOT FUNDED Individuals.

TYPE OF GRANT Capital costs; full project funding; one-off.

RANGE OF GRANTS £500 to £4,000.

SAMPLE GRANTS Church of Scotland Fabric Fund (£4,000); Church of Scotland Missionaries Fund (£3,000); Children's Classic Concerts (£2,500); Fire Fighters Charity, Fischy Music and New Rhythms for Glasgow (£1,000 each); Cancer Support Scotland (£900); Baillieston Community Care and Scottish Spina Bifida Association (£500 each); Way to Go (£250).

FINANCES *Year* 2015/16 *Income* £78,565 *Grants* £68,150 *Grants to organisations* £68,150 *Assets* £1,933,300

OTHER INFORMATION The fund awarded 76 grants during 2015/16.

HOW TO APPLY Apply in writing to the correspondent, including if possible a copy of the latest accounts, a budget for the project, sources of funding received and other relevant financial information. The trustees meet in January, April, July and October. Applications should be received by the preceding month.

WHO TO APPLY TO The Trustees, Mitchells Roberton Solicitors, George House, 36 North Hanover Street, Glasgow G1 2AD

■ The Wood Foundation

SC NO SC037957 **ESTABLISHED** 2007

WHERE FUNDING CAN BE GIVEN UK, with a preference for Scotland; sub-Saharan Africa.

WHO CAN BENEFIT Organisations and individuals.

WHAT IS FUNDED There are three areas of focus with the following titles: making markets work for the poor; developing young people in Scotland; economic and education development. Further details on each of these areas are given on the website.

SAMPLE GRANTS Aberdeen Youth Games; Global Learning Partnerships Scotland; Opportunity North East; Robert Gordon University; The Prince's Trust; STV Children's Appeal.

FINANCES *Year* 2015/16 *Income* £19,349,000 *Grants* £42,649,000 *Grants to organisations* £1,989,000 *Assets* £107,228,000

TRUSTEES Sir Ian Wood, Chair; Lady Helen Wood; Garreth Wood; Graham Good.

OTHER INFORMATION Grants were made to 197 organisations in 2015/16. There were ten grants made to individuals, totalling £8,000. There were also 15 'miscellaneous grants', which totalled £40.7 million. The foundation was previously known as The Wood Family Trust.

HOW TO APPLY The trust proactively seeks out beneficiaries rather than inviting open applications. However, the website states the following information: 'Whilst we do not accept unsolicited applications for most of our programmes, there is an open application process for organisations and individuals looking for sources of funding for young people in the North East Scotland to volunteer overseas to undertake life changing and development experiences.' Application forms are available to download from the website. There may also be places available for the Global Learning Partnerships programme; refer to the website for current information.

WHO TO APPLY TO Ailsa McRae, Administrator, Blenheim House, Fountainhall Road, Aberdeen AB15 4DT *Tel.* 01224 619831 *Email* info@thewoodfoundation.org.uk *Website* www.thewoodfoundation.org.uk

■ Wooden Spoon Society

CC NO 326691 **ESTABLISHED** 1984

WHERE FUNDING CAN BE GIVEN UK and Ireland.

WHO CAN BENEFIT Charitable and community organisations.

WHAT IS FUNDED Projects must enhance and support the lives of children and young people under the age of 25 with physical, mental or social disadvantages. Grants are given in the following categories: health and well-being; sensory rooms and gardens; specialist equipment and gardens; specialist equipment and facilities; playgrounds and outdoor activities; education projects.

WHAT IS NOT FUNDED Refer to the website for exclusions on different types of projects.

TYPE OF GRANT Mostly capital costs and equipment; community project costs; some salaries and core costs.

RANGE OF GRANTS Grants are unlikely to be less than £5,000.

SAMPLE GRANTS Race for Life (£80,000); 999 Club (£58,500); Quarriers Epilepsy Centre (£50,000); Camphill School (£29,000); Claytons Primary School (£23,000); Greenbank Sports Academy (£15,000); Horseworld (£11,000); PACT (£10,000); Printfield Community Project (£6,500); Scottish Spina Bifida Association (£5,000); Our Lady of Walsingham School (£1,000).

FINANCES *Year* 2015/16 *Income* £3,703,841 *Grants* £1,260,107 *Grants to organisations* £1,260,107 *Assets* £994,556

TRUSTEES Nigel Timson; David Allen; Martin Sanders; Steuart Howie; Alison Lowe; Richard Smith; John Gibson; Adam Mack; Mark McCafferty; Bob Wall.

OTHER INFORMATION Grants were awarded to 73 projects in 2015/16; a list of recent beneficiaries was not included in the accounts.

HOW TO APPLY Full guidelines and criteria are available to download on the website; application forms can be obtained by emailing projects@woodenspoon.org.uk.

WHO TO APPLY TO The Trustees, Sentinel House, Ancells Business Park, Harvest Crescent, Fleet, Hampshire GU51 2UZ *Tel.* 01252 773720 *Email* projects@woodenspoon.org.uk *Website* www.woodenspoon.com

■ The F. Glenister Woodger Trust

CC NO 802642 **ESTABLISHED** 1990

WHERE FUNDING CAN BE GIVEN West Wittering and surrounding areas.

WHO CAN BENEFIT Charities and other community organisations.

WHAT IS FUNDED General charitable purposes.

WHAT IS NOT FUNDED Individuals.

SAMPLE GRANTS St Wilfrid's Hospice (£775,000); Witterings Medical Centre (£252,500); Aldingbourne Centre (£100,000); West Wittering Tennis Courts (£86,500); Weald and Downland Museum (£20,000); Brackelsham Youth FC (£3,000); Bracklesham Bay Community Association (£1,400); Calibre Audio Library (£1,000); Manhood Mobility Volunteer Service (£750); West Wittering Allotment Association (£500).

FINANCES *Year* 2015/16 *Income* £1,334,540 *Grants* £1,313,202 *Grants to organisations* £1,313,202 *Assets* £39,534,295

TRUSTEES Richard Shrubb; Rosamund Champ; William Craven; Stuart Dobbin; Maxine Pickup; Tamaris Thompson.

OTHER INFORMATION Grants were given to 16 organisations in 2015/16.

HOW TO APPLY Apply in writing to the correspondent. The trustees meet quarterly to review grant applications.

WHO TO APPLY TO Richard Shrubb, Trustee, Wicks Farm Caravan Park, Redlands Lane, West Wittering, Chichester PO20 8QE *Tel.* 01243 513116 *Email* office@wicksfarm.co.uk

■ Woodlands Green Ltd

CC NO 277299 **ESTABLISHED** 1979

WHERE FUNDING CAN BE GIVEN Worldwide.

WHO CAN BENEFIT Charitable organisations.

WHAT IS FUNDED Orthodox Jewish faith; relief of poverty.

WHAT IS NOT FUNDED Individuals.
SAMPLE GRANTS Achisomoch Aid Company Ltd, Beis Soro Schneirer, Friends of Beis Yisroel Trust, Friends of Mir, Friends of Seret Wiznitz, Friends of Toldos Avrohom Yitzchok, JET, Kahal Imrei Chaim, Oizer Dalim Trust, North West London Communal Mikvah, TYY Square and UTA.
FINANCES *Year* 2015/16 *Income* £268,488 *Grants* £108,330 *Grants to organisations* £108,330 *Assets* £1,377,355
TRUSTEES Daniel Ost; E. Ost; J. Ost; A. Hepner.
OTHER INFORMATION The 2015/16 annual report states that the charity made grants to over 40 organisations during the year; a list of recent beneficiaries was not provided.
HOW TO APPLY Apply in writing to the correspondent.
WHO TO APPLY TO Daniel Ost, Trustee, 75 Woodlands, London NW11 9QS *Tel.* 020 8209 1458

■ Woodroffe Benton Foundation

CC NO 1075272 **ESTABLISHED** 1988
WHERE FUNDING CAN BE GIVEN UK.
WHO CAN BENEFIT UK-registered charities; educational institutions (schools, universities, etc.) whether or not they have charitable status. Smaller charities are preferred, so charities with an income over £1 million are unlikely to be funded under the small grants programme.
WHAT IS FUNDED Social welfare; older people; education and youth development; environment and conservation.
WHAT IS NOT FUNDED Organisations that operate primarily outside the UK or for the benefit of non-UK residents; places of worship seeking funds for restoration or upgrade of facilities; students requesting a grant for tertiary education or a gap year; educational organisations based outside Derbyshire; museums, historical or heritage organisations; funding of palliative care; organisations without a Charity Commission registration; organisations that have not been operating for more than 12 months; animal welfare organisations whose primary purpose is not conservation of the environment; bodies affiliated to or a local branch of a national organisation, even when registered as a separate charity.
TYPE OF GRANT One-off grants; ongoing support; small grants for one year or less. The trust prefers to fund core costs and running costs but project and capital costs are also considered.
SAMPLE GRANTS Community Links (£113,000 in three grants); Ilfield Park Care Home (£22,500 in two grants); Queen Elizabeth's Grammar School (£19,000 in six grants); Action for Stammering Children, Furniture Re-Use Network and Prisoners' Families and Friends Service (£5,000 each); Beauchamp Lodge Settlement (£4,000); Theatre Peckham (£1,500).
FINANCES *Year* 2015/16 *Income* £303,891 *Grants* £262,800 *Grants to organisations* £262,800 *Assets* £1,455,972
TRUSTEES James Hope; Philip Miles; Colin Russell; Anthony Behrens; Richard Page; Jill Wesley.
OTHER INFORMATION In 2015/16 the foundation made 186 grants, of which: 139 were small grants; 26 grants to 21 charities were for ongoing support; 21 grants were made at the discretion of the trustees. A list of recent beneficiaries was not provided in the 2015/16 accounts.
HOW TO APPLY Applications are made via an online form on the foundation's website (contact the trust if an alternative format is needed). The trustees meet quarterly, in the second or third week of January, April, July and October and the deadline for the receipt of applications is approximately six weeks prior to each meeting – upcoming deadlines are posted on the website. Applications are not considered between meetings but any received after the deadline are automatically carried forward. Multiple grants are not usually awarded to the same organisation in a 12-month period.
WHO TO APPLY TO Joanna Noles, Secretary, PO Box 309, Cirencester GL7 9HA *Email* secretary@woodroffebenton.org.uk *Website* www.woodroffebenton.org.uk

■ The Woodstock Family Charitable Foundation

CC NO 1156449 **ESTABLISHED** 2014
WHERE FUNDING CAN BE GIVEN UK.
WHO CAN BENEFIT Charitable organisations.
WHAT IS FUNDED Projects to assist young people who are at risk of offending, through guidance, coaching and life skills.
SAMPLE GRANTS St Francis Hospice (£125,000); TurnAround (£30,000); St Andrew's Mission Orphanage (£15,000); Salvation Army (£12,500).
FINANCES *Year* 2015/16 *Income* £129,311 *Grants* £182,500 *Grants to organisations* £182,500 *Assets* £313,860
TRUSTEES Paul Woodstock Harris; Peter Woodstock Harris; Thomas Woodstock Harris; Alison Swinburn; Margaret West; Nevena Harris.
HOW TO APPLY Apply in writing to correspondent. The trustees meet regularly through the year.
WHO TO APPLY TO Peter Woodstock Harris, Trustee, Sallow Copse, Ringshall, Berkhamsted, Hertfordshire HP4 1LZ *Tel.* 01442 842480

■ The A. and R. Woolf Charitable Trust

CC NO 273079 **ESTABLISHED** 1977
WHERE FUNDING CAN BE GIVEN Worldwide; UK, mainly in Hertfordshire.
WHO CAN BENEFIT Registered charities or equivalent charitable organisations.
WHAT IS FUNDED Children's welfare; animal welfare and conservation; health and medical research.
WHAT IS NOT FUNDED Individuals.
RANGE OF GRANTS Mostly £100 to £5,000.
SAMPLE GRANTS Mind (£4,100); Stroke Association (£4,000); Peach Hospice Care (£1,200); Happy House and Macmillan Cancer Support (£1,000); Tusk Trust (£750); Dogs for the Disabled, Herts Inclusive Care, Primary Trauma Care Foundation and Shooting Star Chase (£500 each).
FINANCES *Year* 2015/16 *Income* £72,193 *Grants* £33,455 *Grants to organisations* £33,455 *Assets* £3,160,158
TRUSTEES Andrew Rose; Dr Gillian Edmonds; Stephen Rose.
OTHER INFORMATION Grants were made to 44 organisations during 2015/16.
HOW TO APPLY Apply in writing to the correspondent.
WHO TO APPLY TO The Trustees, c/o Haines Watts Chartered Accountants, 4 Claridge Court, Lower Kings Road, Berkhamsted HP4 2AF *Tel.* 01442 873236 *Email* berkhamsted@hwca.com

■ Worcester Municipal Charities (CIO)

CC NO 1166931 **ESTABLISHED** 1836
WHERE FUNDING CAN BE GIVEN The city of Worcester.
WHO CAN BENEFIT Charitable organisations.
WHAT IS FUNDED Social welfare and the relief of hardship. Grants are given to local individuals to fund 'essential' items or services, and grants are also awarded to local organisations that provide services to help those in need.
WHAT IS NOT FUNDED Organisations that have not recently received a grant from the charity already; health-related organisations.
TYPE OF GRANT Revenue; one-off.
SAMPLE GRANTS Tudor House Museum (£42,000); Maggs Day Centre (£26,800); Dancefest (£10,000); Headway Worcester Trust (£8,500); Worcester Community Trust (£6,000); Worcester Action for Youth (£1,500).
FINANCES *Year* 2016 *Income* £12,273,106 *Grants* £94,772 *Grants to organisations* £94,772 *Assets* £12,294,029
TRUSTEES Paul Griffith; Brenda Sheridan; Margaret Jones; Robert Peachey; Martyn Saunders; Paul Denham; Roger Berry; Ron Rust; Sue Osborne; Graham Hughes; Margaret Panter; Mel Kirk; Richard Boorn; Roger Knight; Alan Feeney; Geogg Williams; Victoria Cooper; Geraint Thomas.
OTHER INFORMATION The charity was incorporated as a CIO in 2017. Its previous Charity Commission number was 205299. The latest accounts available on the Charity Commission's website at the time of writing (June 2017) report on the period from 1 July 2016 to 31 December 2016 – not a full year. Grants to individuals during the year totalled £97,000. The financial information relates to Worcester Municipal Charities (CIO), not Worcester Consolidated Municipal Charity and Worcester Municipal Exhibitions Foundation.
HOW TO APPLY The charity's website states the following: 'In 2016 due to impending financial constraints, the trustees resolved not to consider applications from new organisations i.e. not currently, or very recently in receipt of a grant from the charities. They believe the charity already targets the main areas of poverty in the City through individual grants or by helping the organisations already in receipt of assistance.' The website lists a number of organisations to which the charity provides 'major financial assistance'. However, it states: 'If despite the advice above you still wish to apply complete the form.' An application form is available to download from the website.
WHO TO APPLY TO Maggie Inglis, Kateryn Heywood House, Berkeley Court, The Foregate, Worcester WR1 3QG *Tel.* 01905 317117 *Email* admin@wmcharities.org.uk *Website* www.wmcharities.org.uk

■ The Worwin UK Foundation

CC NO 1037981 **ESTABLISHED** 1994
WHERE FUNDING CAN BE GIVEN UK and Canada.
WHO CAN BENEFIT Registered charities.
WHAT IS FUNDED General charitable purposes, including: education; the arts (particularly focused on young people from low-income backgrounds); health.
SAMPLE GRANTS Momentum Community Economic Society (£38,500); Big Sisters and Big Brothers Society of Winnipeg and Calgary (£35,500); Children's Health Foundation and Multicultural Arts for Schools and Communities (£33,000 each); Smile Theatre (£28,000); Arts for Children and Youth and Centennial Infant 8 Child Centre Foundation (£25,500 each); Sutton Trust (£21,100); Spinal Cord Injury Alberta (£20,500); Education Foundation of Ottawa (£20,000).
FINANCES *Year* 2015/16 *Income* £827,090 *Grants* £705,668 *Grants to organisations* £705,668 *Assets* £1,640,987
TRUSTEES John Ward; Brian Moore; Anthony Graham; Oliver McGinley; Dan Hill.
OTHER INFORMATION Grants were made to 51 organisations in 2015/16. Of these, grants of £20,000 or less totalled £425,000.
HOW TO APPLY Apply in writing to the correspondent.
WHO TO APPLY TO John Ward, Trustee, 6 New Street Square, London EC4A 3LX *Tel.* 020 7427 6400

■ The Diana Edgson Wright Charitable Trust

CC NO 327737 **ESTABLISHED** 1987
WHERE FUNDING CAN BE GIVEN UK with some preference for Kent.
WHO CAN BENEFIT Registered charities.
WHAT IS FUNDED General charitable purposes, animal conservation and social welfare causes; armed forces.
RANGE OF GRANTS £500 to £3,000.
SAMPLE GRANTS Common Wealth Ex-Services (£3,000); The British Horse Society (£2,000); Cats Protection, Kent Men of Trees, Seafarers UK, The Friends of Kent Churches and The Salisbury Museum (£1,000 each); British Hen Welfare Trust and Lepra (£500 each).
FINANCES *Year* 2015/16 *Income* £63,057 *Grants* £55,500 *Grants to organisations* £55,500 *Assets* £1,378,276
TRUSTEES Henry Moorhead; Mrs G. E. Edgson Wright.
OTHER INFORMATION Grants were made to 47 organisations during the year.
HOW TO APPLY Apply in writing to the correspondent.
WHO TO APPLY TO Henry Moorhead, 2 Stade Street, Hythe, Kent CT21 6BD *Tel.* 01303 262525 *Email* henmo4@henrymoorheadandco.co.uk

■ Wychdale Ltd

CC NO 267447 **ESTABLISHED** 1974
WHERE FUNDING CAN BE GIVEN UK and overseas.
WHO CAN BENEFIT Jewish organisations; charitable organisations.
WHAT IS FUNDED Orthodox Jewish religion; general charitable purposes.
SAMPLE GRANTS ABC Trust (£111,500); Yesamach Levav (£56,000); Kahal Chassidim Bobov (£53,500).
FINANCES *Year* 2015/16 *Income* £595,205 *Grants* £508,950 *Grants to organisations* £508,950 *Assets* £1,157,397
TRUSTEES Mr C. Schlaff; Mr J. Schlaff; Mrs Z. Schlaff.
OTHER INFORMATION The following breakdown of grants was provided in the 2015/16 accounts: advancement of religion (£232,000); relief of poverty (£101,500); education (£92,500); general charitable purposes (£83,500).
HOW TO APPLY Apply in writing to the correspondent. The 2015/16 annual report states: 'In general the trustees select the institutions to be supported according to their personal knowledge of work of the institution. Whilst not actively inviting applications, they are always prepared to accept any application which will be carefully

considered and help given according to circumstances and funds then available.'

WHO TO APPLY TO The Trustees, c/o Sugarwhite Meyer Accountants Ltd, 5 Windus Road, London N16 6UT *Tel.* 020 8880 8910

■ Wychville Ltd

CC NO 267584 **ESTABLISHED** 1973

WHERE FUNDING CAN BE GIVEN UK and overseas.

WHO CAN BENEFIT Charitable organisations.

WHAT IS FUNDED The advancement of the Orthodox Jewish faith; education; general charitable purposes.

SAMPLE GRANTS Friends of Mercaz Hatorah Belz Machnivka (£102,500); Beis Aharon Trust Ltd (£52,500); Colel D'Chasidei Belz (£50,000); Mercaz Torah Vechesed Ltd.

FINANCES *Year* 2015/16 *Income* £792,041 *Grants* £253,936 *Grants to organisations* £253,936 *Assets* £329,811

TRUSTEES Mrs S. Englander; Mr E. Englander; Mrs B. R. Englander.

HOW TO APPLY Apply in writing to the correspondent. All requests are considered by the trustees.

WHO TO APPLY TO Mrs B. R. Englander, Trustee, 44 Leweston Place, London N16 6RH *Tel.* 020 8802 3948

■ The Wyfold Charitable Trust

CC NO 1157483 **ESTABLISHED** 2014

WHERE FUNDING CAN BE GIVEN UK; some overseas, through UK-registered charities.

WHO CAN BENEFIT UK-registered charities.

WHAT IS FUNDED General charitable purposes, including: social welfare; health; arts, culture, heritage or science; education; citizenship or community development; environment; sport; animal welfare; religion.

SAMPLE GRANTS Katie and Eloise Memorial Trust, Nether Worton Church Restoration Appeal and Playing Fields Legacy Fund (£10,000 each).

FINANCES *Year* 2015/16 *Income* £245,293 *Grants* £204,750 *Grants to organisations* £204,750 *Assets* £9,082,471

TRUSTEES Adam Fleming; Nicholas Powell; Roderick Fleming.

OTHER INFORMATION The trust made 56 grants in 2015/16. Of these, 53 were for less than £10,000 and were not named in the accounts.

HOW TO APPLY Applications should be made in writing on no more than two sides of A4 and sent to the correspondent along with any supporting documentation. The Wyfold Charitable Trust should be referenced in the application. Only successful applications will be responded to, and it may be several months before trustees are able to consider an application. Only one application may be made within a 12-month period. In 2015/16 the trustees met twice during the year to consider applications.

WHO TO APPLY TO The Trustees, RF Trustee Co. Ltd, 15 Suffolk Street, London SW1Y 4HG *Tel.* 020 3696 6721 *Email* charities@rftrustee.com

■ The Wyndham Charitable Trust

CC NO 259313 **ESTABLISHED** 1969

WHERE FUNDING CAN BE GIVEN UK and overseas.

WHO CAN BENEFIT Charitable organisations.

WHAT IS FUNDED General charitable purposes. There is a particular interest in the elimination of modern slavery.

WHAT IS NOT FUNDED Individuals; organisations not known to the trustees.

TYPE OF GRANT Unrestricted.

RANGE OF GRANTS Mostly under £5,000.

SAMPLE GRANTS Anti-Slavery International (£12,000); Cancer Research UK (£5,000); Christian Aid (£3,000); Dalit Solidarity Network of the UK (£1,500); International Glaucoma Association (£1,000); New Forest Citizens Advice Ltd (£600); Kidney Research Appeal, Millennium Seed Bank and Prisoners of Conscience Appeal (£500 each); Gift of Sight Appeal (£35).

FINANCES *Year* 2015/16 *Income* £161,697 *Grants* £67,267 *Grants to organisations* £67,267 *Assets* £1,759,540

TRUSTEES John Gaselee; Juliet Gaselee; David Gaselee; Sarah Gaselee.

HOW TO APPLY The trust has previously stated that unsolicited applications are unlikely to be supported and they do not encourage requests.

WHO TO APPLY TO John Gaselee, Trustee, 34A Westfield Road, Lymington, Hampshire SO41 3QA *Email* wyndham_ct@yahoo.co.uk *Website* www.wyndham-ct.org

■ The Wyseliot Rose Charitable Trust

CC NO 257219 **ESTABLISHED** 1968

WHERE FUNDING CAN BE GIVEN UK.

WHO CAN BENEFIT Registered charities only.

WHAT IS FUNDED Health and medical causes; arts; social welfare; disability.

WHAT IS NOT FUNDED Individuals.

TYPE OF GRANT Recurrent funding; core costs, capital costs, project costs.

RANGE OF GRANTS Generally up to £5,000.

SAMPLE GRANTS Alzheimer's Research UK and Time and Talents Association (£25,000 each); Royal College of Music (£5,000); Avenues Youth Project (£4,000); Mind (£3,500); Cystic Fibrosis Trust (£3,000); The Arts Fund (£2,500); Centrepoint Soho and Neurofibromatosis Association (£2,000 each); International Glaucoma Association (£1,500).

FINANCES *Year* 2015/16 *Income* £1,046,565 *Grants* £131,000 *Grants to organisations* £131,000 *Assets* £2,637,394

TRUSTEES Jonathan Rose; Adam Raphael; Quentin Williams; William Rose; Lucy Rose.

OTHER INFORMATION Grants were awarded to 30 organisations in 2015/16.

HOW TO APPLY Apply in writing to the correspondent; however, note the trust has previously stated that the many of the same charities are supported each year, with perhaps one or two changes. It is unlikely new charities sending circular appeals will be supported and large UK charities are generally not supported. Approximately one application is successful each year.

WHO TO APPLY TO Jonathan Rose, Trustee, 17 Chelsea Square, London SW3 6LF

■ Yankov Charitable Trust

CC NO 1106703 **ESTABLISHED** 2004

WHERE FUNDING CAN BE GIVEN Worldwide.

WHO CAN BENEFIT Charitable organisations, particularly Jewish organisations.

WHAT IS FUNDED Advancement of the Jewish religion and religious education; alleviation of poverty among the Jewish community.

SAMPLE GRANTS European Yarchei Kalloh (£53,000); Keren Machzikei Torah (£23,000); Kollel Tiferes Chaim (£21,000); Agudas Israel Housing Association (£12,000); Ponovez Hachnosos Kalloh (£7,600); Freiman Appeal (£7,200); Beth Jacob Grammar School (£4,000); British Friends of Tiferes Chaim (£3,000); Yeshiva Tzemach Yisroel (£2,000); British Friends of Rinat Ahsron (£1,500); Yeshivat Givat Shaul (£1,000).

FINANCES *Year* 2014/15 *Income* £118,838 *Grants* £154,330 *Grants to organisations* £154,330 *Assets* £112,764

TRUSTEES Jacob Schonberg; Bertha Schonberg; Aryeh Schonberg.

OTHER INFORMATION The 2014/15 accounts were the most recent available on the Charity Commission's website at the time of writing (June 2017). A list of beneficiaries was not provided in the accounts.

HOW TO APPLY Apply in writing to the correspondent.

WHO TO APPLY TO Jacob Schonberg, Trustee, 40 Wellington Avenue, London N15 6AS *Tel.* 020 3150 1227

■ The Yapp Charitable Trust

CC NO 1076803 **ESTABLISHED** 1999

WHERE FUNDING CAN BE GIVEN England and Wales.

WHO CAN BENEFIT Registered charities – in particular, small, local charities with a turnover of less than £40,000.

WHAT IS FUNDED Grants are given to charities supporting the following priority groups: older people; children and young people (aged 5–25); people with physical disabilities, learning disabilities or mental health challenges; social welfare, particularly people trying to overcome life-limiting problems of a social nature (such as addiction, relationship difficulties, abuse, offending); education and learning, particularly adults or children who are educationally disadvantaged. The trust gives priority to work that is unattractive to the general public or unpopular with other funders, particularly when it helps improve the lives of marginalised, disadvantaged or isolated people. Preference is also given to charities that can demonstrate the effective use of volunteers, an element of self-sustainability, if possible, and preventive work aiming to create change through raising awareness and campaigning.

WHAT IS NOT FUNDED Charities with a total annual expenditure of more than £40,000; charities that are not registered with the Charity Commission in England and Wales (must have own charity number or be excepted from registration). Industrial provident societies and CICs are not eligible); charities operating outside England and Wales; charities with unrestricted reserves equating to more than 12 months' expenditure; branches of national charities (must have own charity number, not a shared national registration); new organisations – must have been operating as a fully constituted organisation for at least three years, even if registered as a charity more recently; new work that has not been occurring for at least a year; new paid posts – even if the work is now being done by volunteers; additional activities, expansion or development plans; special events, trips or outings; capital expenditure – including equipment, buildings, renovations, furnishings, minibuses; work exclusively with children under the age of five; childcare; holidays and holiday centres; core funding of charities that benefit the wider community such as general advice services and community centres unless a significant element of their work focuses on one of the trust's priority groups; bereavement support; debt advice; community safety initiatives; charities raising money to give to another organisation, such as schools, hospitals or other voluntary groups; individuals – including charities raising funds to purchase equipment for or make grants to individuals.

TYPE OF GRANT Core costs only (including salaries), for regular services or activities that have been running for at least a year. Grants are usually made for more than one year.

RANGE OF GRANTS Grants are normally for a maximum of £3,000 per year. Most grants are for more than one year (up to three years).

SAMPLE GRANTS Blaenllechau Youth Project and Bradford Phab Club (£9,000 each); Activate Rawmarsh and Hull Street Angels Trinity (£7,500); Age Concern St Hilda's (£6,000); Norfolk SEN Network and Shopmobility Melton Mowbray (£4,500 each); Mental Health Action Group Sheffield and Somali Advice Link (£3,000 each); Wallsend Sea Cadets (£1,500).

FINANCES *Year* 2015/16 *Income* £215,199 *Grants* £208,600 *Grants to organisations* £208,600 *Assets* £6,426,470

TRUSTEES Revd Timothy Brooke; Ron Lis; Alfred Hill; Jane Fergusson; Lisa Suchet; Liz Islam.

OTHER INFORMATION The Yapp Welfare Trust (two-thirds share) and The Yapp Education and Research Trust (one-third share) merged in September 1999 to become The Yapp Charitable Trust. In 2015/16 grants were awarded to 42 organisations.

HOW TO APPLY Application forms and comprehensive guidance are available on the trust's website. Potential applicants are advised to read the guidelines on the trust's website and check their eligibility. The trust also encourages applicants to contact the trust by telephone for a preliminary discussion before making an application. Applications are usually acknowledged within two weeks. The trustees meet three times a year to review and award grants. Grant recipients are eligible to re-apply for funding from three months before their grant expires. The trust seeks feedback and progress reports from grant recipients, particularly for grants that are paid over a number of years.

WHO TO APPLY TO Joanne Anderson, Trust Secretary, 1st Floor, Mile House, Bridge End, Chester Le Street, County Durham DH3 3RA *Tel.* 0191 389 3300 *Email* info@yappcharitabletrust.org.uk *Website* www.yappcharitabletrust.org.uk

■ York Children's Trust

CC NO 222279 **ESTABLISHED** 1976

WHERE FUNDING CAN BE GIVEN Within 20 miles of York City.

WHO CAN BENEFIT Charities, schools, community organisations and other organisations benefitting children and young people under 25 years of age; individuals.

WHAT IS FUNDED Children and young people. Grants are given in the following categories: educational; social; medical causes; travel; fostering talents; children's groups.

WHAT IS NOT FUNDED Private education fees, except in unforeseen circumstances, such as the death of a parent, would prevent a child completing the last year of a critical stage of education such as A-levels.

RANGE OF GRANTS Generally under £5,000.

SAMPLE GRANTS York Carers Centre (£4,300); City of York Council (£3,800); Relate Mid-Yorkshire (£2,400); Refugee Action Group (£2,000); Carr Junior School (£1,800); Bereavement Care York and York Child Contact Centre (£1,500); Hob Moor Community Primary School and York City Knights Foundation (£1,000 each).

FINANCES *Year* 2015 *Income* £96,093 *Grants* £65,961 *Grants to organisations* £65,961 *Assets* £2,454,672

TRUSTEES Colin Stroud; Mark Sessions; Lenore Hill; Keith Hayton; Peter Watson; William Miers; Alan Ward; Dr Anne Kelly; Rosalind Fitter; Julie Simpson; Dawn Moores; Kathy Pickard; Kitty Lamb; John Corden; Gail Tams; Vicky Mulvana.

OTHER INFORMATION Grants were made to 22 organisations during 2015. Grants were also made to six individuals during the year, totalling £23,500.

HOW TO APPLY Apply in writing to the correspondent.

WHO TO APPLY TO Margaret Brien, 29 Whinney Lane, Harrogate HG2 9LS *Tel.* 01423 504765 *Email* yorkchildrenstrust@hotmail.co.uk

■ Yorkshire and Clydesdale Bank Foundation

SC NO SC039747 **ESTABLISHED** 2008

WHERE FUNDING CAN BE GIVEN Areas of England and Scotland where the bank operates.

WHO CAN BENEFIT Young people, older people, people with disabilities, disadvantaged people and communities.

WHAT IS FUNDED Health; education; social welfare; community development; sport; environment; arts, heritage and science; animal welfare; saving of lives. The foundation's Spirit of the Community Awards consider projects in the following areas: helping people have a healthy relationship with money; helping people into employment; helping people improve their local environment.

RANGE OF GRANTS Mostly under £5,000.

SAMPLE GRANTS Hospice UK (£324,500); Money Advice Trust (£50,000); Business in the Community (£32,500); UK Community Foundations (£20,000); Chartered Institute of Bankers Scotland (£12,000); National Trust for Scotland (£7,000); Alzheimer Scotland (£5,500).

FINANCES *Year* 2015/16 *Income* £711,070 *Grants* £787,891 *Grants to organisations* £787,891 *Assets* £33,596

OTHER INFORMATION Donations of £5,000 or less totalled £321,500.

HOW TO APPLY Apply in writing to the correspondent. Application forms and guidelines for the Spirit of the Community Awards are available to download from the foundation's website.

WHO TO APPLY TO Company Secretary, Ground Floor Mezzanine, 30 St Vincent Place, Glasgow G1 2HL *Website* www.cbonline.co.uk/about-clydesdale-bank/community

■ Yorkshire Building Society Charitable Foundation

CC NO 1069082 **ESTABLISHED** 1998

WHERE FUNDING CAN BE GIVEN UK, particularly areas around Yorkshire Building Society branches.

WHO CAN BENEFIT Registered charities.

WHAT IS FUNDED The foundation's priority areas are: alleviating poverty; improving health/saving lives. There is a particular focus on beneficiary groups that are vulnerable or disadvantaged, such as children, people with disabilities or serious illness, older people and people who are homeless. Grants are also occasionally given for animal welfare or other local causes.

WHAT IS NOT FUNDED General ongoing funding; running costs; contributions towards larger funding; research; individuals; sponsorship; salaries or expenses; office items or IT equipment for the charity's own use; charities supporting a specific group based on ethnicity, faith, sexual orientation or political beliefs.

RANGE OF GRANTS Mostly £250 to £2,000.

SAMPLE GRANTS Cumbria Community Foundation (£5,000); Bradford Cat Watch Rescue (£2,300); Ipswich Baby Bereavement Group, London Air Ambulance and Rowcroft Hospice (£2,100 each); Baildon Imagination Library, Hearing Dogs for Deaf People, Peterborough Sailability and York Toy Library (£2,000 each).

FINANCES *Year* 2015 *Income* £482,329 *Grants* £392,931 *Grants to organisations* £392,931 *Assets* £201,530

TRUSTEES Christopher Parrish; Richard Brown; Vanessa White; Tanya Jackson; Gordon Rogers.

OTHER INFORMATION The 2015 accounts state that 91% of the donations during the year were to causes nominated by members or employees of the building society, with the remainder in support of applications received directly from a charity.

HOW TO APPLY The foundation only supports charities recommended by members or employees of the building society, rather than responding to requests from charities directly. Recommendations can be made using a form on the foundation's website, after which the foundation will contact the nominated charity for further information. Applications are reviewed on a quarterly basis.

WHO TO APPLY TO Fiona May, Yorkshire Building Society, Yorkshire House, Yorkshire Drive, Bradford, West Yorkshire BD5 8LJ *Tel.* 01274 472877 *Email* charitablefoundation@ybs.co.uk *Website* www.ybs.co.uk/your-society/charity/charitable-foundation/apply.html

■ Yorkshire Cancer Research

CC NO 516898 **ESTABLISHED** 1985

WHERE FUNDING CAN BE GIVEN Yorkshire.

WHO CAN BENEFIT Universities; research organisations; health bodies.

WHAT IS FUNDED Cancer research – including education around lifestyle decisions; early diagnosis; research-led innovation; improvement in cancer services. The research strategy is available to view on the charity's website.

WHAT IS NOT FUNDED Refer to the guidance notes on the website for specific exclusions.

TYPE OF GRANT Research projects, programmes and facilities.

SAMPLE GRANTS Leeds University (£1.4 million in 30 grants); Bradford University (£713,500 in four grants); York University (£452,500 in six grants); Sheffield University (£421,000 in 13 grants); Leeds NHS (£16,700); Hull University (£5,800 in three grants).

FINANCES *Year* 2015/16 *Income* £22,294,353 *Grants* £3,065,418 *Grants to organisations* £3,065,418 *Assets* £25,083,682

TRUSTEES Graham Smith; Sandra Dodson; Dr Alan Suggett; Alan Sidebottom; Graham Berville; Catherine Rustomji; Zulfi Hassain; Margaret Kitching; Janet Myers; Dr Yvette Oade.

OTHER INFORMATION In 2015/16, 57 grants were awarded to six organisations.

HOW TO APPLY Refer to the website for information on current funding rounds, as well as deadlines, guidance and application forms. The website states that potential applicants must contact the charity to discuss a proposal before making an application – email research@ycr.org.uk to schedule a telephone call.

WHO TO APPLY TO Research Team, Jacob Smith House, 7 Grove Park Court, Harrogate HG1 4DP *Tel.* 01423 501269 *Email* research@ycr.org.uk *Website* www.ycr.org.uk

■ The South Yorkshire Community Foundation

CC NO 1140947 **ESTABLISHED** 1986

WHERE FUNDING CAN BE GIVEN Throughout South Yorkshire, with specific reference to Barnsley, Doncaster, Rotherham, Sheffield.

WHO CAN BENEFIT Community and voluntary organisations benefitting communities in the beneficiary area, particularly those in poverty or disadvantage.

WHAT IS FUNDED General charitable purposes, particularly social welfare. The foundation aims to meet the needs of local communities and improve the lives of local people, particularly people facing economic hardship and barriers to aspiration. A number of grants programmes are administered by the foundation, funding a wide range of organisations supporting communities in South Yorkshire.

WHAT IS NOT FUNDED Check the website or contact the foundation for exclusions and criteria relevant to each of their funding programmes.

TYPE OF GRANT Capital costs, core costs, project costs, salaries. Grants vary according to each funding programme. The main small grants programme is for amounts under £1,500.

RANGE OF GRANTS £100 to £50,000. Most grants under £10,000.

SAMPLE GRANTS Sheffield Community Media Ltd and Sheffield Cubed (£20,000 each); JJ Associates (£17,000); Inspire Sensory and Outreach Services CIC (£9,984); Jack House, Green City Action, Sheffield Renewable, Sheffield out of School Network, Barnsley Asperger's Parents Group and Austerfield Study Centre (£5,000 each); GROW (£4,300); Moorends Hornets and Stingers Junior Football Club (£3,700); The Haven House Project (£3,000); Harthill Moris (£2,000); Home-Start Doncaster (£1,750); Brayton Junior Youth Club, WOW Academy Ltd, Atherlsey Cares, Barnsley Samaritans, FareShare Yorkshire, South Yorkshire Guide Association and the Community Workshop (£1,500 each); Age UK Rotherham (£1,500 in two grants); Re Read Ltd and Area 51 (£1,400 each); Station House Community Partnership (£1,300); Kings Bowls Club (£1,200); Age Concern and Cavendish Cancer Care (£1,000 each); The Moorends Thursday Club (£900); Ms Chelsea Brown (£750); The Old School Craft Club (£650).

FINANCES *Year* 2014/15 *Income* £1,574,245 *Grants* £1,032,029 *Grants to organisations* £1,032,029

TRUSTEES John Holt; Melvyn Lunn; Alex Pettifer; James Newman; Zaidah Ahmed; Nigel Brewster; Dr Julie MacDonald; Martin Ross; Allan Jackson; Sue Scholey; Charles Warrack; Michele Todd; The Earl of Scarborough Richard Scarborough; Roderick Plews; Paul Benington; Shahida Siddique; Craig McKay; Nicholas Kitchen; Yiannis Koursis; John Pickering.

OTHER INFORMATION The 2014/15 accounts were the latest available at the time of writing (June 2017).

HOW TO APPLY Information and guidelines on each of the foundation's funding programmes are available on the website. Before making an application, potential applicants are strongly advised to contact the grants team by telephone to check the current status of funds, discuss eligibility and receive advice and support on making an application.

WHO TO APPLY TO Sue Wragg, Fund Manager, 6 Leeds Road, Sheffield S9 3TY *Tel.* 0114 242 4294 *Email* grants@sycf.org.uk *Website* www.sycf.org.uk

■ The Yorkshire Historic Churches Trust

CC NO 700639 **ESTABLISHED** 1988

WHERE FUNDING CAN BE GIVEN Yorkshire (the historic county of Yorkshire before local government reorganisation in 1974).

WHO CAN BENEFIT Christian churches. To be eligible, the building must be in use as a place of worship and accessible to the public.

WHAT IS FUNDED The repair, restoration, preservation and maintenance of churches in the area stated above. Most grants are given for repairs to the main fabric of the church. Grants are also given for the preservation of individual items such as bells, monuments and organs.

WHAT IS NOT FUNDED New work (e.g. reordering or extensions); heating and electrical installations, including upgrading; repairs which form part of an overall reordering project); work which has already started or been completed when an application is submitted; facilities for people with disabilities; repairs to associated or ancillary buildings such as church halls or parsonage houses; applications which have not been drawn up or approved by an architect or conservation accredited surveyor.

TYPE OF GRANT Capital building grants. Funding of up to three years will be considered.

RANGE OF GRANTS £250 to £15,000.

SAMPLE GRANTS St Mary – Middleton (£15,000); St Mary of the Angels – Batley (£10,000); St John the Baptist – Mossley (£8,000); Holy Trinity and St Oswald – Finningley (£7,000); St Edmund – Roundhay (£5,000); Trinity Methodist – Netherton (£3,000); Selby Abbey (£2,500); Ripon Cathedral (£2,000); St Mary – Lower Dunsford (£100).

FINANCES *Year* 2015 *Income* £129,410 *Grants* £114,721 *Grants to organisations* £114,721 *Assets* £999,114

TRUSTEES Prof. Clyde Binfield; Anthony Hesselwood; Rory Wardroper; Richard Carr-Archer; Edward Waterson; David Quick; Macolm Warburton; Peter Johnson; Roger Gilster; Jane Hedley; Tom Ramsden; Fiona Le Masurier.
OTHER INFORMATION The trust made 27 grants in 2015.
HOW TO APPLY Applications should be made using the form available to download on the trust's website. Applicants should be able to demonstrate a good fundraising effort and are expected to have applied to a number of other funding sources – see the guidance notes on the website for further detail before applying. Deadlines and further advice are also given in the guidance notes.
WHO TO APPLY TO Jonathan Stamp, Grants Secretary, 38 Bromley Road, Shipley, West Yorkshire BD18 4DT *Tel.* 07594 578665 *Email* yhctgrants@sky.com *Website* www.yhct.org.uk

■ The William Allen Young Charitable Trust

CC NO 283102 **ESTABLISHED** 1978
WHERE FUNDING CAN BE GIVEN UK.
WHO CAN BENEFIT Registered charities.
WHAT IS FUNDED General charitable purposes, with a preference for health and social welfare.
RANGE OF GRANTS £100 to £30,000.
SAMPLE GRANTS Wooden Spoon Society (£30,000); Shelter (£20,000); Sane (£10,000); Livingstone Tanzania Trust and Royal Hospital for Neuro-disability (£5,000); Arthritis Care (£3,000); Canine Partners and RNLI (£2,000 each); Leukaemia Research (£250); Lord Mayor's Appeal (£125).
FINANCES *Year* 2015/16 *Income* £552,864 *Grants* £620,009 *Grants to organisations* £620,009 *Assets* £38,717,010
TRUSTEES Torquil Sligo-Young; James Young.
HOW TO APPLY The trust has previously stated that all funds are committed and consequently unsolicited applications will not be supported.
WHO TO APPLY TO Torquil Sligo-Young, Trustee, Young and Co.'s Brewery PLC, Riverside House, 26 Osiers Road, Wandsworth, London SW18 1NH *Tel.* 020 8875 7000 *Email* claire.cooper@youngs.co.uk

■ The John Kirkhope Young Endowment Fund

SC NO SC002264 **ESTABLISHED** 1992
WHERE FUNDING CAN BE GIVEN Scotland.
WHO CAN BENEFIT Registered charities.
WHAT IS FUNDED Health; medical research; children and young people.
WHAT IS NOT FUNDED Individuals; non-registered charities. There is a preference for smaller charities.
TYPE OF GRANT One-off grants are awarded. Funding is available for up to one year. Core costs; salaries; capital costs; project funding.
RANGE OF GRANTS £500 to £2,000.
SAMPLE GRANTS Alzheimer's Research UK (£3,000); Dr Bell's Family Centre, Spinal Research (£2,000 each); Edinburg Headway Group, Nordoff Robins, Redburn School, YMCA Edinburgh (£1,000 each); Children's Liver Disease Foundation, Equibuddy, Happy Days (£500).
FINANCES *Year* 2015/16 *Income* £45,865 *Grants* £40,000 *Grants to organisations* £40,000 *Assets* £1,087,204
TRUSTEES A. J. R. Ferguson; R. J. S. Morton; S. F. J. Judson; D. J. Hamilton.
OTHER INFORMATION The charity awarded 37 grants during the year totalling £40,000.
HOW TO APPLY Apply in writing to the correspondent. The trustees meet to consider grants in the autumn.
WHO TO APPLY TO The Trust Administrator, Quartermile Two, 2 Lister Square, Edinburgh EH3 9GL

■ Youth Music

CC NO 1075032 **ESTABLISHED** 1999
WHERE FUNDING CAN BE GIVEN England.
WHO CAN BENEFIT Registered charities; CICs; constituted community groups; schools.
WHAT IS FUNDED Youth Music funds projects that provide musical opportunities and activities for children and young people (0–25), working towards greater inclusion of youth in musical activities, across all genres and styles. It funds developmental music projects for children and young people in challenging circumstances, as well as strategic work to support the workforce and organisations in the sector. Its priority groups are: early years; special educational needs and/or disabilities; not in education, employment or training; youth justice; coldspots of access to diverse music-making opportunities. Grants are awarded from Fund A, B or C, depending on the size of the grant and duration of the project.
WHAT IS NOT FUNDED Individuals and sole traders; activities that do not benefit people in England or do not take place mainly in England; activities that promote party political or religious beliefs; activities that have already taken place; costs incurred in making an application; significant capital costs (e.g. the purchase of land, buildings, vehicles or property) or refurbishment or landscaping costs; reserves, loans or interest payments; VAT costs that can be recovered; art forms not related to music (although matched funding may be given to deliver a cross-arts project); activities that other statutory bodies would be expected to fund; projects that are unable to demonstrate that they are able to achieve the 10% match funding requirement; projects proposing to use Arts Council or National Lottery funding as their minimum match funding requirement.
TYPE OF GRANT Project duration can be from one year up to three years and longer. Core costs and salaries.
RANGE OF GRANTS £2,000 to £160,000. Matched funding of 10–15% is required, depending on the fund.
SAMPLE GRANTS Sage Gateshead (£185,000); Baby People (£179,500); mac Birmingham (£145,500); Music Arts Project CIC (£100,000); 2Funky Arts Ltd (£23,500); Castlehaven Community Association (£22,500); Irene Taylor Trust Music in Prisons (£20,000); Burnley Youth Theatre (£11,700); Khyal Arts (£10,200); The People's Pod (£3,500).
FINANCES *Year* 2015/16 *Income* £10,196,103 *Grants* £8,897,744 *Grants to organisations* £8,897,744 *Assets* £1,497,076
TRUSTEES Andy Parfitt; Richard Peel; Sean Gregory; Clive Grant; Constance Agyeman; Timothy Berg; Rafi Gokay; Ademola Adeluwoye; Chris Price; Rachel Lindley.

OTHER INFORMATION This trust is funded each year by a payment of around £10 million from the National Lottery, channelled through Arts Council England. In 2015/16 grants were given to 143 organisations to support 147 projects. The charity was previously known as National Foundation for Youth Music.

HOW TO APPLY The three funds from which grants are awarded each differ in their funding criteria and application process. Potential applicants are advised to refer to the Youth Music Network website for up-to-date criteria, priorities, guidelines and deadlines. Applications are made online, via the Youth Music Network website.

WHO TO APPLY TO Grants and Learning Team, Suites 3–5, Swan Court, 9 Tanner Street, London SE1 3LE *Tel.* 020 7902 1060 *Email* grants@youthmusic.org.uk *Website* network.youthmusic.org.uk

■ The Z. Foundation

CC NO 1134913 **ESTABLISHED** 2010
WHERE FUNDING CAN BE GIVEN UK.
WHO CAN BENEFIT Registered charities.
WHAT IS FUNDED General charitable purposes.
TYPE OF GRANT One-off grants; recurrent grants.
SAMPLE GRANTS Dulwich Picture Gallery (£37,500); London Music Masters (£10,500); Mancunian Way (£8,300); Alder Hey Children's Charity (£4,800); Friendship Works (£4,000); Shooting Star Chase (£2,500); Place2Be (£1,200); Médecins Sans Frontières (£1,100); Diabetes UK and Walk the Walk (£1,000 each).
FINANCES *Year* 2015/16 *Income* £119,888 *Grants* £110,939 *Grants to organisations* £110,939 *Assets* £124,163
TRUSTEES Anne O'Keefe; Anne-Marie Laing; Ryan Grant; Alastair Beveridge; Lindsey Hornby; Ian Nelson; Liam Colley.
OTHER INFORMATION There were 152 grants made in 2015/16. Of these grants, 133 were for less than £1,000 and totalled £16,300.
HOW TO APPLY Apply in writing to the correspondent.
WHO TO APPLY TO The Trustees, c/o AlixPartners Services LLP, AlixPartners, 6 New Street Square, London EC4A 3BF *Email* ctompson@alixpartners.com

■ Elizabeth and Prince Zaiger Trust

CC NO 282096 **ESTABLISHED** 1981
WHERE FUNDING CAN BE GIVEN UK, some preference for Somerset, Dorset and the South West.
WHO CAN BENEFIT Registered charities; occasionally individuals.
WHAT IS FUNDED Social welfare; older people; people with disabilities; education of children and young people; animal welfare; general charitable purposes.
TYPE OF GRANT One-off and recurrent.
RANGE OF GRANTS £1,000 to £50,000.
SAMPLE GRANTS Salisbury Hospital – Radiotherapy Appeal (£50,000); Variety – the Children's Charity (£25,000); Teenage Cancer Trust (£14,000); St Giles Trust (£10,000); Somerset Sight (£8,000); Spinal Injuries Association and Theatre Peckham – Youth Outreach Programme (£5,000 each); Yeovil Day Centre Society (£4,000); St David's Foundation (£3,000); Yeovil Great Lyde Scout Group (£1,000).
FINANCES *Year* 2015/16 *Income* £1,136,131 *Grants* £699,000 *Grants to organisations* £698,000 *Assets* £17,159,049
TRUSTEES John Davidge; Peter Harvey; Derek Long; Edward Parry; Dr Robin Keyte.
OTHER INFORMATION Grants were made to 33 organisations during 2015/16. Grants to individuals during the year totalled £1,000.
HOW TO APPLY The trust states on its Charity Commission record: 'Note – this trust does not respond to unsolicited applications for funds. Don't apply – it wastes your time and money.'
WHO TO APPLY TO Peter Harvey, Trustee, Gatesmoor, Hawkridge, Spaxton, Bridgwater, Somerset TA5 1AL *Tel.* 01278 671353

■ Zephyr Charitable Trust

CC NO 1003234 **ESTABLISHED** 1991
WHERE FUNDING CAN BE GIVEN UK and worldwide.
WHO CAN BENEFIT UK-registered charities.
WHAT IS FUNDED The trust's grants are particularly targeted towards three areas: enabling lower income communities to be self-sustaining; the protection and improvement of the environment; providing relief and support for those in need, particularly from medical conditions or social or financial disadvantage.
WHAT IS NOT FUNDED Individuals.
TYPE OF GRANT Mainly recurrent annual grants decided by the trustees.
RANGE OF GRANTS Mostly under £5,000.
SAMPLE GRANTS Pesticide Action Network (£50,000); Survival International (£25,000); Intercare (£4,000); Freedom from Torture (£3,300); Jessie's Fund (£3,000); Womankind (£2,500); Crisis (£2,400); Missing People (£2,200); Margaret Pyke Trust (£2,000); Action Village India (£1,500).
FINANCES *Year* 2015/16 *Income* £66,511 *Grants* £110,400 *Grants to organisations* £110,400 *Assets* £1,721,801
TRUSTEES Dr Elizabeth Breeze; Marigo Harries; David Baldock; Donald Watson.
OTHER INFORMATION Grants were made to 15 organisations in 2015/16.
HOW TO APPLY The trustees state in their annual report that unsolicited applications are not accepted.
WHO TO APPLY TO The Trust Administrator, Luminary Finance LLP, PO Box 135, Longfield, Kent DA3 8WF *Tel.* 01732 822114

■ The Marjorie and Arnold Ziff Charitable Foundation

CC NO 249368 **ESTABLISHED** 1964
WHERE FUNDING CAN BE GIVEN UK, with a preference for Yorkshire, especially Leeds and Harrogate.
WHO CAN BENEFIT Charitable organisations.
WHAT IS FUNDED General charitable purposes; education; public places; social welfare; the arts.
WHAT IS NOT FUNDED Individuals.
TYPE OF GRANT Capital costs and building work are particularly favoured by the trustees.
RANGE OF GRANTS £50 to £85,000.
SAMPLE GRANTS United Jewish Israel Appeal (UJIA) (£85,000); United Hebrew Congregation (£51,000); Leeds Jewish Welfare Board (£41,500); Chief Rabbinate Trust (£15,000); Cancer Research UK (£5,200); Clifton College Development Trust (£2,500); The Urology Foundation (£350); War Child (£100); Leeds Teaching Hospital Charitable Foundation (£50).
FINANCES *Year* 2015/16 *Income* £678,461 *Grants* £443,263 *Grants to organisations* £443,263 *Assets* £11,749,688
TRUSTEES Dr Marjorie Ziff; Michael Ziff; Edward Ziff; Ann Manning.
OTHER INFORMATION Grants were awarded to 73 organisations in 2015/16.
HOW TO APPLY Apply in writing to the correspondent.
WHO TO APPLY TO Debra Evans, Secretary, Town Centre House, The Merrion Centre, Leeds LS2 8LY *Tel.* 0113 222 1234

■ Stephen Zimmerman Charitable Trust

CC NO 1038310 **ESTABLISHED** 1994
WHERE FUNDING CAN BE GIVEN UK.
WHO CAN BENEFIT Registered charities.
WHAT IS FUNDED General charitable purposes, with a preference for Jewish causes.
SAMPLE GRANTS British ORT, Cancer Research, CIS Development Fund, London Youth, Jewish Association of Business Ethics, Jewish Care, Norwood Ltd, RNIB, United Jewish Israel Appeal (UJIA) and United Synagogue.
FINANCES *Year* 2015/16 *Income* £50,000 *Grants* £67,646 *Grants to organisations* £67,646 *Assets* £35,623
TRUSTEES Laura Zimmerman; Michael Marks; Stephen Zimmerman.
OTHER INFORMATION No information about recent beneficiaries was available.
HOW TO APPLY The trust does not respond to unsolicited applications.
WHO TO APPLY TO Stephen Zimmerman, Trustee, 36 Blomfield Road, London W9 2PF *Tel.* 020 3096 2999 *Email* stephen.zimmerman@mzcapital.co.uk

■ The Zochonis Charitable Trust

CC NO 274769 **ESTABLISHED** 1978
WHERE FUNDING CAN BE GIVEN UK, particularly Greater Manchester; some overseas.
WHO CAN BENEFIT Registered charities only.
WHAT IS FUNDED General charitable purposes, particularly education and the welfare of children.
WHAT IS NOT FUNDED Individuals.
TYPE OF GRANT One-off and recurrent.
SAMPLE GRANTS Cancer Research UK, University of Manchester, Manchester High School for Girls, British Red Cross, Breakthrough Breast Cancer, Asthma Relief and National Talking Newspapers and Magazines.
FINANCES *Year* 2015/16 *Income* £4,888,902 *Grants* £4,378,870 *Grants to organisations* £4,378,870 *Assets* £167,463,749
TRUSTEES Christopher Green; Archibald Calder; Paul Milner.
OTHER INFORMATION A list of beneficiaries was not included in the 2015/16 accounts. However, the following breakdown of grant-making during the year was given: education (£1.3 million); health (£1.2 million); other sectors (£470,000); children and young people (£459,000); overseas (£438,000); community (£124,000); family (£118,000); homelessness (£110,500); armed forces (£56,500); emergency – Nepal earthquake (£50,000); older people (£31,000); rescue services (£30,000).
HOW TO APPLY Apply in writing to the correspondent.
WHO TO APPLY TO Marie Gallagher, Administrator, Manchester Business Park, 3500 Aviator Way, Manchester M22 5TG *Tel.* 0161 435 1005 *Email* enquiries@zochonischaritabletrust.com

■ Zurich Community Trust (UK) Ltd

CC NO 266983 **ESTABLISHED** 1973
WHERE FUNDING CAN BE GIVEN UK, particularly areas local to Zurich offices; overseas.
WHO CAN BENEFIT Registered charities, voluntary organisations and non-governmental organisations.
WHAT IS FUNDED Communities and people who are disadvantaged. The trust's grant-making comes under a number of programmes. The Zurich Cares programme provides grants at a national level to three partner charities chosen by employees; at a local level to charities in the communities local to Zurich offices and employees, with local and regional grant funds available (refer to the website for further information on eligibility); and overseas, through applications from UK-registered charities. The Openwork Foundation, a subsidiary fund of the trust, supports charities working with disadvantaged children and young people (0 to 18 years) in the UK. The trust's Social Transformation programmes aim to support some of the most vulnerable in society, focusing on a few 'key social issues that are often overlooked', including drug misuse, isolation in older age and young people's mental health (application by invitation only).
WHAT IS NOT FUNDED Disaster relief or emergency work (although staff have supported emergency appeals); proposals which show any racial, political or religious bias; individuals, including personal medical equipment, expeditions or study exchanges; medical research; fundraising events or appeals; statutory organisations including mainstream schools and hospitals (unless exclusively for a special needs group); animal welfare charities; conservation or environmental projects (unless involving disadvantaged people); political organisations or those supporting military action; organisations that promote religious beliefs; sports clubs, village halls, playgroups and mother and toddler groups (unless for special needs groups); scouts, girl guides, cadets and other similar organisations (unless specifically supporting disadvantaged children); fundraising events, including appeals or events for national charities; advertising or sponsorship connected with charitable activities.
TYPE OF GRANT One-off grants; long-term partnership grants; core costs; project costs; revenue cost; salaries; seed funding; capital.
SAMPLE GRANTS CLIC Sargent (£68,000); Alzheimer's Society (£59,000); Mind (£52,000); Carers Trust (£50,000); Mental Health Foundation (£37,000).
FINANCES *Year* 2015 *Income* £4,025,000 *Grants* £1,678,000 *Grants to organisations* £1,678,000 *Assets* £4,853,000
TRUSTEES Ian Lovett; Jonathan Plumtree; Tim Culling; Vinicio Cellerini; Subo Shanmuganathan; Wayne Myslik; Miranda Chalk; Georgina Farrell; Anne Torry; Andrew Jepp; Conor Brennan.
OTHER INFORMATION The following breakdown of grants was given in the 2015/16 accounts: Zurich Cares local and overseas grants (£932,000); Openwork Foundation local and overseas grants (£332,000); Zurich Cares long-term community partnerships (£191,000); transformation grants (£182,000); Openwork Foundation long-term community partnerships (£50,000). Grants of less than £30,000 totalled £1.4 million. The trust also supports Zurich employees and ex-employees to volunteer with charitable causes.
HOW TO APPLY In the first instance, visit the trust's website and follow the links to check eligibility and download the guidelines and application forms.
WHO TO APPLY TO Pam Webb, Head of Zurich Community Trust (UK) Ltd, PO Box 1288, Swindon SN1 1FL *Tel.* 01793 502450 *Email* zct@zct.org.uk *Website* www.zct.org.uk

WEST DUNBARTONSHIRE LIBRARIES